COUNTY OF CHARLESTON
PRO BONO PUBLICO
HISTORY
INDUSTRY
CULTURE
PROGRESS
SOUTH CAROLINA

Notable Black American Men

ISBN 0-7876-0763-0

Notable Black American Men

Jessie Carney Smith, Editor

Detroit
New York
San Francisco
London
Boston
Woodbridge, CT

Notable Black American Men

Jessie Carney Smith, Editor

Gale Research Inc. Staff:

Anna Sheets and Jeffrey Lehman, Developmental Editors;
Linda S. Hubbard, Managing Editor; Catherine V. Donaldson, Ashyia N. Henderson,
Allison McClintic Marion, David G. Oblender, Rebecca Parks, Associate Editors

Susan Trosky, Permissions Manager; Margaret A. Chamberlain, Permissions Specialist

Mary Beth Trimper, Production Director; Evi Seoud, Assistant Production Manager

Cynthia Baldwin, Product Design Manager; Eric Johnson, Cover Design;
Barbara Yarrow, Graphic Services Manager; Randy A. Bassett, Image Database Supervisor;
Mike Logusz, Imaging Specialist; Pamela Reed, Photography Coordinator

Library of Congress Cataloging-in-Publication Data

Notable Black American men / Jessie Carney Smith, editor.
p. cm.
Includes bibliographical references (p.) and index.
ISBN 0-7876-0763-0 (hc.)
1. Afro-American men--Biography--Dictionaries. I. Smith, Jessie Carney.
E185.86.N68 1998
920.71'08996073--dc21
[B] 98-38166
CIP

ISBN 0-7876-0763-0

10 9 8 7 6 5 4 3

Contents

Introduction vii

Entrants xi

Advisory Board xxviii

Contributors xxix

Photo Credits xxxii

Entries 1

Geographic Index 1293

Occupation Index 1313

Subject Index 1329

Introduction

"The powers of single black men flash here and there like falling stars, and die sometimes before the world has rightly gauged their brightness," wrote W. E. B. Du Bois in *The Souls of Black Folk.* Such is the case of some, but by no means all, of the entrants in *Notable Black American Men.*

Perhaps with the exception of a few shining stars in our history, such as Frederick Douglass, W. E. B. Du Bois, and Booker T. Washington, the contributions of notable black men in America may be known, then dimmed by time. All too frequently the real significance of those black stars with familiar names is recognized by too few people, and for many, these stars may fade and be replaced by popular stars of the day without remembrance of the pioneers who lay down their souls that black men and black people may flourish.

For many years, African American scholars have recorded biographical sketches of the men of the race. In the beginning these sketches came as autobiographical witnesses from early black life; for example, in Briton Hammon's *A Narrative of the Uncommon Suffering and Surprising Deliverance of Briton Hammon* (1760); in Venture Smith's *A Narrative of the Life and Adventure of Venture, a Native of Africa but Resident Above Sixty Years in the United States of America* (1798); or in Richard Allen's *The Life, Experience, and Gospel Labors of the Rt. Reverend Richard Allen, to Which is Annexed the Rise and Progress of the African Methodist Episcopal Church in the United States* (1880). These sketches also came as slave narratives written by the former slaves themselves. Solomon Northrup did it in *Twelve Years a Slave* (1853); William Wells Brown told his story in *Narrative of William Wells Brown* (1847); Frederick Douglass gave the account of his life, his escape from slavery, and his life later on in *Narrative of the Life of Frederick Douglass* (1845, with two other versions published in 1855 and 1891); and Henry Box Brown told his story in *Narrative of Henry Box Brown, Who Escaped from Slavery, Enclosed in a Box Three Feet Long and Two Feet Wide* (1859). An early effort to publish sketches of African American men and women was seen in 1852, when Martin Delany published *The Condition, Elevation, and Destiny of the Colored People of the United States Politically Considered*; in 1855 when William Cooper Nell published *Colored Patriots of the American Revolution*; and in 1863, when William Wells Brown's *The Black Man: His Antecedents, His Genius, His Achievements* was published.

In 1883 George Washington Williams published his monumental *History of the Negro Race in America.* Though not primarily a biographical work, in the two volumes that cover the period 1619 through 1880, Williams saw a problem as well as a solution: he knew that the world needed a history of the black race in America and also needed "more correct ideas" about the people of the race. "The single reason that there was no history of the Negro race would have been a sufficient reason for writing one," he wrote in the preface to volume one. Williams acknowledged the vastness of his work but lived out his compulsion to write the history. "I have mentioned such Colored men as I thought necessary," he continued. And he had insufficient time and space "to give a biographical sketch of all the worthy Colored men in the United States," yet his work is also important for the sketches that he does include.

By the latter part of the 1800s, the need for a comprehensive biographical work on African American men was recognized. William James Simmons, whose life, like that of Williams, is chronicled in the present work, helped address that need by compiling the monumental *Men of Mark: Eminent, Progressive and Rising.* Published in 1887, the work is Simmons's response to a problem that he observed during his long years as an educator: his students "were woefully ignorant of the work of our great colored men—even ignorant of their names. If they knew their names, it was some indefinable something they had done—just what, they could not tell."

The subjects in Simmons's work were to serve as role models for young people of that period and encourage them to achieve greatness similar to that of the biographees. Most of the men in the book "came from the loins of slave fathers, and were the babes of women in bondage,'' wrote Simmons. ''[They] felt the leaden hand of slavery on their own bodies; but whether slaves or not, they suffered with their brethren because of color,'' he continued. Yet, the inhumanity they suffered ''did not crush out the life and manhood of the race.'' Nor was ''the spirituality of this race . . . diminished in slavery.'' He had faith in black people: ''I wish to exalt them; I want their lives snatched from obscurity to become household matter for conversation.''

Simmons wrote about the writers, editors, ministers, lecturers, linguists, scientists, doctors, lawyers, and college presidents of his time. Simmons saw a race implanted with a ''vigorous spiritual tree'' filled with men who built numerous churches, educated millions of youth, organized societies, addressed the needs of the sick, and buried the dead. *Men of Mark* provided a convenient source of biographical information for many of the early entrants included in the present work.

Until the compilation of *Notable Black American Men,* for over a century Simmons's work stood as the primary biographical work devoted exclusively to African American men. Sometimes the information in Simmons is questionable: both Simmons and the editor of the present volume share the difficult task of furnishing ''specimens of Negro eloquence,'' as Simmons put it, and faced similar difficulties in drawing the line when making selections. ''I do not claim that a better selection might not have been made,'' Simmons wrote. He acknowledged that ''many are entitled to a place here'' and that readers may question his selections, but he asked no pardon for the names that were omitted. ''Our country makes it impossible to secure all who may be 'eminent, progressive and rising,''' he wrote. The names of those who in some way lent assistance to Simmons and his work are examples of the men included in the present volume: religious worker and educator Alexander Crummell, journalist Thomas Morris Chester, politician P. B. S. Pinchback, bicycle-rider Marshall W. ''Major'' Taylor, and religious leader Henry McNeal Turner.

Since the publication of *Men of Mark,* sketches of African American men have continued to appear as parts of works not exclusively devoted to men or to biography. They were published in specialized works such as James Monroe Trotter's *Music and Some Highly Musical People* (1878) and D. W. Culp's *Twentieth Century Negro Literature* (1902). Even though the need for biographical works continued, Culp noted in the preface to his work that readers of books of a biographical character published around the turn of the century found the books objectionable because they included too few entries of scholarly blacks and too many sketches of blacks of ordinary ability.

With numerous resources now available, including electronic access to data and a wealth of library collections on African American themes, hopefully *Notable Black American Men* has overcome many of the difficulties that earlier editors and compilers met in their research. As a result, many stories are told in *Notable Black American Men.* Incorporated in the profiles are accounts of wars; slavery; politics; the black press and its history; the Tuskegee Airmen and other blacks in the military; the founding of the NAACP, the National Urban League, and other black organizations; the Harlem Renaissance and later the Black Arts Movement; the Civil Rights Movement; black business leaders and founders; and many other lives that help round out African American biography and history.

Notable Black American Men is designed to serve as a companion volume to *Notable Black American Women* published in 1992, with a second book in 1996, in the biographical series published by Gale Research, Inc. The work also aims to fill the need for an up-to-date comprehensive biographical listing of African American men and to influence positively the image of black men in America. Following the established format, *Notable Black American Men* gives biographies of 500 men who are living or dead and covers nearly three centuries. The earliest known birthdate of the entrants is 1711, when poet and tract writer Jupiter Hammon was born, and the most recent is 1975, when professional golfer Tiger Woods was born. The varying lengths of the essays is deliberate due to space limitations and the need to ensure that such prominent figures as Frederick Douglass, W. E. B. Du Bois, Langston Hughes, Thurgood Marshall, and Colin Powell might be given lengthy entries as expected. There are more than 400 photographs included in the volume; even more might have been added but space limitations again restricted an increase in the number.

The Selection Process

Some 2,500 names comprised the original list of names drawn from various sources from which the final 500 entries were selected for this book. Names were picked from obscure as well as prominent sources, including: *Contemporary Black Biography, Black*

Writers, Men of Mark, Who's Who in Colored America, Who's Who among African Americans with its earlier title *Who's Who among Black Americans, Dictionary of American Negro Biography, Biographical Directory of Afro-American and African Musicians,* and *A History of African-American Artists.* Research for the *Notable Black American Women* books also suggested names. The selections represent diverse occupations and areas of contribution, such as the arts, business, civil rights, education, medicine and health, music, politics, religion, science, inventions, and technology. The advisory board for this book screened the original list, made additions, and guided the editor in narrowing the base; the editor is fully responsible for the final selections. Nominees for the work met one or more of the following criteria:

a pioneer in a particular area, such as first black man elected to public office in a state or first black man to edit a newspaper, or

an important entrepreneur, such as a manufacturer of cosmetics for blacks, the founder of a publishing firm, or

a leading businessman, such as president of an advertising firm, head of a construction company or vice-president of a major bank, or

a literary or creative figure of stature, such as an outstanding poet, well-known writer, author of works on a unique theme, important artist, outstanding sculptor, or

a leader for social or human justice, such as abolitionist, freedom fighter, outstanding participant in the Civil Rights Movement, or

a major governmental or organizational official, such as U.S. Secretary of Commerce, president of the National Medical Association, president of the National Urban League, or

a creative figure in the performing arts, such as the first black man to perform at the Metropolitan Opera, outstanding popular singer, actor, or composer, or

a noted orator, elocutionist, or public speaker (particularly for the nineteenth- and early twentieth-century), or

a distinguished educator, such as the first black male principal of an early high school, president or founder of a college, first black man to receive a college degree, or

a noted scholar, such as a scientist, mathematician, historian, or sociologist, or

a leader, pioneer, or contributor in other fields or areas who meets the basic criteria suggested above for selection as an outstanding black American man.

To ensure accuracy of the essays, when possible the subjects were asked to review the work and to correct factual errors arising from published sources. In other instances where reference sources gave conflicting information, the writers were asked to address the differences.

Arrangement of Entries

Entries are in alphabetical order under the name by which the subject is best known; for example, Ferdinand ''Jelly Roll'' Morton appears as ''Jelly Roll'' Morton, Malvin R. Goode as Mal Goode, and Egbert Austin Williams as Bert Williams. Some cross-references are also added.

Contributions Acknowledged

Assisting in the preparation of this work are writers from Fisk University and other academic institutions as well as other scholars from cities across the country. Their scholarship and input has been invaluable. Some Fisk library staff shared in this project by searching databases, photocopying, and in various ways retrieving essential materials. Their work was so valuable that I mention them individually: Sue Chandler, Susie Harris, Gwendolyn Hawk, Dixie Jernigan, Beth Howse, Tye Shelton, and Rick Smith. Of special significance in this group are Cynthia Davis and Peggy Smith who were especially conscientious in their work with the project. From neighboring Tennessee State University library, I am grateful to Fletcher Moon and other members of the staff who filled bibliographical requests. Helena Carney Lambeth continued to provide much-needed news articles that helped update the entries.

I am continually impressed by the dedication of my Fisk faculty colleague, Robert L. Johns, who helped compile the list of entrants, wrote over 90 essays, read and edited each of the 500 entries here, assisted in the research process, and provided consolation during the frustrating times an editor faces in the preparation of such a monumental work. To him I will always be grateful.

Editors from Gale Research, first Anna Sheets then Jeffrey Lehman, who saw the work finished, aided in selecting the illustrations and advised the editor in other processes. Furthermore, it would be wrong not to mention Krzysztof Musial, whose programming excellence saved countless hours of editorial work.

Finally, I acknowledge with deep appreciation my family, friends, and colleagues who understood my compelling need to complete this project and my continuing determination to publish, and who always provided much-needed comfort and support.

Jessie Carney Smith

Entrants

A

Aaron, Hank (1934–)
Baseball player 1

Abbott, Robert Sengstacke (1868–1940)
Newspaper publisher, editor 3

Abdul-Jabbar, Kareem (1947–)
Basketball player, author 6

Ailey, Alvin (1931–1989)
Choreographer, dancer, dance company founder 8

Alcindor, Lew
See Abdul-Jabbar, Kareem

Aldridge, Ira (1807–1867)
Actor 12

Alexander, Clifford L., Jr. (1933–)
Lawyer, politician, humanitarian 15

Ali, Muhammad (1942–)
Boxing champion, civil rights activist, humanitarian 17

Allen, Richard (1760–1831)
Religious leader 21

Anderson, Charles W., Jr. (1907–1960)
Lawyer, state legislator, United Nations delegate 24

Armstrong, Henry (1912–1988)
Boxing champion, minister 26

Armstrong, Louis ''Satchmo'' (1900–1971)
Jazz trumpeter 29

Arnett, Benjamin W. (1838–1906)
Religious leader, educator, state politician, writer, bibliophile 34

Ashe, Arthur (1943–1993)
Tennis player, activist 36

Attucks, Crispus (1723?–1770)
Slave, sailor, patriot 40

B

Bailey, DeFord (1899–1982)
Entertainer, musician 43

Baker, George
See Divine, M. J. ''Father''

Baldwin, James (1924–1987)
Novelist, essayist, short story writer, playwright 46

Banneker, Benjamin (1731–1806)
Inventor, mathematician, astronomer 49

Baraka, Amiri (1934–)
Educator, poet, writer, publisher, editor, social and political activist, dramatist, playwright, music critic 52

Barnes, Steven (1952–)
Writer, television script writer, screenplay writer, lecturer, consultant, martial arts teacher 55

Barnett, Claude A. (1889?–1967)
Journalist, publisher 58

Barrow, Joseph Louis
See Louis, Joe

Barthé, Richmond (1901–1989)
Sculptor 60

Bearden, Romare (1912–1988)
Artist, writer, art historian, mathematician, social worker 64

Belafonte, Harry (1927–)
Entertainer, civil rights activist, humanitarian 68

Bell, Derrick A., Jr. (1930–)
Lawyer, educator, activist, writer 71

Bell, James Madison (1826–1902)
Orator, poet, political activist 73

Binga, Jesse (1865–1950)
Banker, realtor, philanthropist 75

''Black Harry''
See Hosier, ''Black Harry''

''Black Sam''
See Fraunces, Samuel

Blake, Eubie (1883–1983)
Composer, performer, songwriter, musician, historian, educator 77

Bledsoe, Jules (1897–1943)
Singer, composer 79

Blockson, Charles L. (1933–)
Curator, educator, historian, bibliophile, writer 82

Blue, Thomas Fountain (1866–1935)
Librarian, organization official 84

Bluford, Guy (1942–)
Astronaut, aeronautical engineer 86

Bojangles
See Robinson, Bill ''Bojangles''

Bond, Horace Mann (1904–1972)
Educator, college dean, college president 88

Bond, Julian (1940–)
Civil rights activist, politician, organization leader 91

Bontemps, Arna W. (1902–1973)
Librarian, writer, critic, teacher 93

Bouchet, Edward A. (1852–1918)
Educator, religious worker, community activist 97

Boyd, Richard Henry (1843–1922)
religious leader, entrepreneur 99

Bradley, Ed (1941–)
Broadcast journalist 102

Bradley, Thomas (1917–)
Mayor, law enforcement officer, lawyer, athlete 104

Braithwaite, William Stanley (1878–1962)
Poet, critic, educator, writer, publisher . . 108

Branson, Herman R. (1914–1995)
Educator, physicist, college president . . . 110

Brawley, Benjamin G. (1882–1939)
Educator, minister, college administrator, bibliophile, writer 112

Brazeal, Brailsford R. (1905–1981)
Educator, economist, writer 113

Brewer, J. Mason (1896–1975)
Folklorist, writer, educator 114

Brimmer, Andrew F. (1926–)
Economist, educator, entrepreneur 116

Bristow, Lonnie R. (1930–)
Physician, organization executive 118

Brooke, Edward W. (1919–)
U.S. Senator, state attorney general, lawyer, military officer 121

Brown, Grafton Tyler (1841–1919)
Painter, lithographer, draftsman, engineer, entrepreneur 124

Brown, James (1933–)
Musician, composer 125

Brown, Morris (1770–1849)
Minister, religious leader, civil rights activist 129

Brown, Ron (1941–1996)
Politician, Cabinet member, lawyer 131

Brown, Sterling A. (1901–1989)
Poet, critic, writer, editor, educator 133

Brown, Tony (1933–)
Television executive, producer, columnist, educator, filmmaker, activist 136

Brown, William Wells (1814?–1884)
Slave, abolitionist, writer, physician 138

Brown, Willie L., Jr. (1934–)
Mayor, politician 141

Bruce, Blanche Kelso (1841–1898)
U.S. Senator, politician, educator, orator 143

Bryan, Andrew (1737?–1812)
Religious worker 146

Bullard, Eugene (1894–1961)
Fighter pilot, boxer 148

Bullins, Ed (1935–)
Playwright, theater director, teacher, editor 150

Bunche, Ralph J. (1903–1971)
Statesman, diplomat, scholar, United Nations official 152

Burgess, John M. (1909–)
Bishop 156

Burns, Isaac
See Murphy, Isaac

Burris, Roland (1937–)
Lawyer, accountant, banker, state official 158

C

Caliver, Ambrose (1894–1962)
College administrator, educator, government appointee, writer 160

Calloway, Cab (1908–1994)
Bandleader, entertainer, songwriter, writer 162

Campanella, Roy (1921–1993)
Baseball player, entrepreneur, radio host, writer, philanthropist 166

Campbell, E. Simms (1906–1971)
Cartoonist 169

Cardozo, Francis L. (1837–1903)
Educator, politician, minister 171

Carey, Lott
See Cary, Lott

Carmichael, Stokely (1941–)
Civil rights activist, organization leader, Pan Africanist 173

Carney, William H. (1840–1908)
Soldier, postal worker, messenger 176

Carver, George Washington (1861?–1943)
Agricultural chemist and researcher 177

Cary, Lott (1780?–1828)
Religious worker, missionary, colonizer . . 180

Cayton, Horace R. (1903–1970)
Researcher, writer, educator, sociologist, lecturer, journalist 182

Chamberlain, Wilt (1936–)
Basketball player 184

Charles, Ray (1930–)
Singer, composer, arranger 186

Chavis, John (1763?–1838)
Minister, missionary, educator 190

Chenault, Kenneth I. (1951–)
Corporate executive, lawyer 191

Chesnutt, Charles Waddell (1858–1932)
Writer, lawyer 193

Chester, Thomas Morris (1834–1892)
Journalist, lawyer, civil rights activist, military officer, school official, federal government official 197

Church, Robert Reed, Sr. (1839–1912)
Entrepreneur, banker, civic leader 200

Clay, Cassius
See Ali, Muhammad

Cleaver, Eldridge (1935–1998)
Militant, writer, minister 203

Clement, George Clinton (1871–1935)
Religious leader, activist 207

Clement, Rufus E. (1900–1967)
College president, educator, minister 208

Cleveland, James (1931–1991)
Musician, composer, religious worker . . . 211

Cochran, Johnnie (1937–)
Lawyer 212

Coker, Daniel (1780–1846)
Religious leader, colonizer, abolitionist . .214

Cole, Nat ''King'' (1919–1965)
Musician, singer, composer, entertainer . .215

Coleman, William T., Jr. (1920–)
Lawyer, corporate executive, federal official 217

Coltrane, John (1926–1967)
Musician, bandleader, composer 220

Cone, James H. (1938–)
Theologian, minister, educator 223

Conyers, John, Jr. (1929–)
Congressman, civil rights advocate, lawyer 225

Coppin, Levi Jenkins (1848–1924)
Bishop, editor, writer 227

Cornish, Samuel (1795–1858)
Religious worker, editor, abolitionist 229

Cosby, Bill (1937–)
Comedian, philanthropist 230

Craft, William (1824–1900)
Abolitionist, educator, farmer 234

Crockett, George W., Jr. (1909–1997)
Congressman, judge, lawyer 236

Crummell, Alexander (1819–1898)
Religious worker, educator, writer 238

Cuffe, Paul (1759–1817)
Sailor, entrepreneur, emigrationist 241

Cullen, Countee (1903–1946)
Poet, essayist, novelist, playwright, educator 243

Cuney, Norris Wright (1846–1898)
Organizer, politician, entrepreneur 246

D

Darlington, Roy Clifford (1908–1994)
Pharmacist, teacher, researcher, writer . .251

Davis, Allison (1902–1983)
Educator, social anthropologist, psychologist 252

Davis, Benjamin Jefferson (1903–1964)
Communist, lawyer, civil rights activist, city official 253

Davis, Benjamin O., Jr. (1912–)
Military officer 255

Davis, Benjamin O., Sr. (1877–1970)
Military officer, educator, government official 259

Davis, Miles (1926–1991)
Musican, bandleader, composer, arranger 262

Davis, Ossie (1917–)
Writer, producer, actor 264

Davis, Sammy, Jr. (1925–1990)
Singer, dancer, comedian, musician, humanitarian, actor 266

Dawson, William L. (1886–1970)
Political leader, congressman 269

Dawson, William Levi (1899–1990)
Composer, educator, choral director 272

Day, Thomas (1801?–1861)
Entrepreneur 275

Day, William Howard (1825–1900)
Abolitionist, lecturer, editor, printer, educator, minister 276

DeCarava, Roy (1919–)
Photographer, artist, educator 280

Delany, Hubert T. (1901–1990)
Lawyer, educator, civil rights advocate . . 281

Delany, Martin R. (1812–1885)
Editor, physician, abolitionist, explorer, army officer, black nationalist, writer 282

Delany, Samuel R. (1942–)
Writer, poet, lecturer, literary critic, folk singer, educator, gay and women's rightsactivist 286

Dellums, Ronald V. (1935–)
Congressman 289

Denby, Charles (1907–1983)
Autoworker, newspaper editor, Marxist-humanist 291

DePriest, Oscar S. (1871–1951)
Entrepreneur, politician, congressman . . 294

Dett, R. Nathaniel (1882–1943)
Musician, composer, educator 297

Diggs, Charles C., Jr. (1922–)
Congressman, broadcast journalist, entrepreneur 301

Dinkins, David N. (1927–)
Lawyer, politician, mayor, public official, educator 304

Divine, M. J. ''Father'' (1879–1965)
Religious leader 307

Dixon, Dean (1915–1976)
Symphonic conductor 310

Dodson, Howard, Jr. (1939–)
Library curator, historian, lecturer, educator, consultant 312

Dodson, Owen (1914–1983)
Poet, novelist, playwright, director, educator 315

Dorsey, Thomas Andrew (1899–1993)
Musician, composer 319

Douglas, Aaron (1899–1979)
Artist, educator 322

Douglass, Frederick (1818–1895)
Abolitionist, orator, reformer, editor, humanitarian, statesman 326

Drew, Charles R. (1904–1950)
Educator, scientist, health administrator, surgeon, physician, publisher, athlete, coach 331

Driskell, David C. (1931–)
Artist, educator, writer, curator, foundation director 333

Du Bois, W. E. B. (1868–1963)
Writer, scholar, activist, Pan Africanist . . 336

Dudley, Edward R. (1911–)
Lawyer, diplomat, politician, judge 341

Dunbar, Paul Laurence (1872–1906)
Poet, short story writer, novelist, lyricist 344

Duncanson, Robert S. (1822?–1872)
Painter 347

Du Sable, Jean Baptiste Pointe (1745–1818)
Settler, explorer, trader 349

Dykes, De Witt S., Sr. (1903–1991)
Minister, church official, architect 352

E

Eckstine, Billy (1914–1993)
Singer, bandleader 357

Edmondson, William (1870?–1951)
Sculptor, laborer 359

Edwards, Nelson J. (1917–1974)
Labor union official, civic leader 361

Elder, Lee (1934–)
Professional golfer 362

Ellington, Duke (1899–1974)
Bandleader, composer, pianist 364

Elliott, Robert Brown (1842–1884)
Politician, lawyer, editor 367

Ellison, Ralph (1914–1994)
Writer 369

Ellison, William (1790–1861)
Slave, artisan, planter 373

Erving, Julius (1950–)
Basketball player, entrepreneur, sports analyst, basketball executive 375

Espy, Mike (1953–)
Cabinet member, lawyer, congressman . . 378

Estes, Simon (1938–)
Singer 381

Europe, James Reese (1880–1919)
Musician 382

Evers, Medgar (1925–1963)
Civil rights activist 386

F

Farmer, James L., Jr. (1920–)
Civil rights activist, educator 389

Farrakhan, Louis (1933–)
Religious leader 393

Father Divine
See Divine, M. J. ''Father''

Fauntroy, Walter E. (1933–)
Minister, civil rights leader, congressman, human rights activist . . . 396

Fisher, Rudolph (1897–1934)
Writer, physician, community leader 400

Flipper, Henry O. (1856–1940)
Military officer, writer, engineer 403

Foreman, George (1949–)
Boxer, Olympic medalist, minister, youth mentor, actor 404

Forman, James (1928–)
Civil rights activist, writer 406

Forten, James (1766–1842)
Manufacturer, abolitionist, community leader 408

Fortune, T. Thomas (1856–1928)
Journalist, civil rights activist, poet 411

Foster, Henry W., Jr. (1933–)
Surgeon, medical school educator 414

Foster, Rube (1879–1930)
Baseball player, sports administrator, sports organizer, organization founder 417

Francis, Norman C. (1931–)
College president, lawyer 420

Franklin, John Hope (1915–)
Historian, writer, lecturer, educator 421

Fraunces, Samuel (1722?–1795?)
Entrepreneur, caterer, servant 427

Frazier, E. Franklin (1894–1962)
Sociologist, educator, writer, activist . . . 428

Freeman, Morgan (1937–)
Actor, dancer, singer, director 431

Fuller, S. B. (1895–1988)
Entrepreneur 433

G

Gabriel
See Prosser, Gabriel

Gardner, Newport (1746?–1826)
Musician, community leader, schoolteacher, religious leader, missionary 436

Garnet, Henry Highland (1815–1882)
Abolitionist, religious worker 437

Garvey, Marcus (1887–1940)
Organization founder, Pan Africanist, nationalist, newspaper founder, writer, entrepreneur 441

Gaston, Arthur G. (1892–1996)
Entrepreneur 445

Gates, Henry Louis, Jr. (1950–)
Educator, scholar, literary critic, writer 448

Gibbs, Mifflin Wistar (1823–1915)
Abolitionist, entrepreneur, politician, lawyer, government official 450

Gibson, Benjamin F. (1931–)
Federal judge 452

Gibson, Truman K., Jr. (1912–)
Lawyer, boxing promoter, entrepreneur . 456

Gillespie, Dizzy (1917–1993)
Musician, bandleader, composer, arranger, entertainer 458

Gilpin, Charles S. (1878–1930)
Actor, singer 460

Gloucester, John (1776?–1822)
Religious leader 462

Glover, Danny (1947–)
Actor 464

Goode, Mal (1908–1995)
Journalist, consultant 466

Gordy, Berry (1929–)
Songwriter, record producer, entrepreneur 468

Granger, Lester B. (1896–1976)
Civic leader, organization executive 472

Gravely, Samuel L., Jr. (1922–)
Military officer 473

Graves, Earl G. (1935–)
Publisher, corporate executive 475

Gray, Frizzell
See Mfume, Kweisi

Gray, William H., III (1941–)
Foundation executive, minister, congressman 478

Greaves, William "Bill" G. (1926–)
Film producer, director, writer 481

Greener, Richard T. (1844–1922)
Educator, lawyer, government official 483

Gregory, Dick (1932–)
Comedian, civil rights activist, nutrition advocate 484

Grimké, Archibald Henry (1849–1930)
Lawyer, journalist, editor, government official, civil rights activist 487

Grimké, Francis J. (1850–1937)
Minister, civil rights activist 490

Gumbel, Bryant (1948–)
Broadcast journalist 492

H

Haley, Alex (1921–1992)
Writer, genealogical researcher 496

Hall, George Cleveland (1864–1930)
Physician, surgeon, civic worker 499

Hall, Prince (1735?–1807)
Organizer, abolitionist, leather crafter 502

Hammon, Jupiter (b.1711)
Poet, tract writer 504

Hampton, Lionel (1908–)
Musician, bandleader, composer 506

Handy, W. C. (1873–1958)
Composer, musician, music publisher, bandleader, choral director, concert producer, educator 508

Harrington, Oliver W. (1912–1995)
Cartoonist, journalist, writer 511

Harrison, Richard B. (1864–1935)
Actor, teacher, dramatic reader, lecturer, elocutionist, railroad worker, bellhop 513

Harvey, William R. (1941–)
College president, educator, entrepreneur 516

Hastie, William Henry (1904–1976)
Judge, educator, civil rights advocate, governor 519

Hawkins, Augustus F. (1907–)
Congressman 522

Hayden, Robert E. (1913–1980)
Poet, educator, editor 523

Hayes, Roland (1887–1977)
Concert singer, voice instructor 526

Haynes, George Edmund (1880–1960)
Social work educator, scholar, organization founder 528

Haynes, Lemuel (1753–1833)
Patriot, minister 532

Healy, James Augustine (1830–1900)
Religious leader 533

Henderson, Fletcher (1898–1952)
Musician, bandleader 537

Henry, Warren E. (1909–)
Scientist, inventor, educator, scholar 539

Henson, Matthew A. (1866–1955)
Seaman, explorer, writer 541

Herndon, Alonzo F. (1858–1927)
Entrepreneur, philanthropist 544

Hewlett, James (fl. 1820s)
Actor, entertainer 546

Higginbotham, A. Leon, Jr. (1928–)
Judge, educator, writer 548

Hill, Jesse, Jr. (1926–)
Corporate executive, entrepreneur 549

Himes, Chester (1909–1984)
Writer 553

Holder, Eric H., Jr. (1951–)
Federal deputy attorney general 556

Holland, Jerome ''Brud'' (1916–1985)
Educator, college president, diplomat, business executive 558

Holly, James T. (1829–1911)
Religious leader, missionary, black separatist 560

Holstein, Caspar A. (1876–1944)
Entrepreneur, racketeer 563

Hooks, Benjamin L. (1925–)
Lawyer, organization leader, minister . . .565

Hope, John (1868–1936)
College president, educator 568

Horton, George Moses (1797?–1883?)
Poet, slave 571

Hosier, ''Black Harry'' (1750?–1806)
Preacher, slave, servant 573

Houston, Charles Hamilton (1895–1950)
Lawyer, educator .575

Hubbard, William DeHart (1903–1976)
Olympic track star, public housing official 579

Hughes, Langston (1902–1967)
Writer, playwright, editor, columnist, lecturer 580

Hunton, William Alphaeus (1863–1916)
Founder, organizer, administrator, orator, writer .584

I

Imes, Elmer S. (1883–1941)
Scientist, inventor, teacher, scholar 589

Ingram, Rex (1895–1969)
Actor 591

J

Jack, Hulan (1905–1986)
Politician 594

Jackman, Harold (1901–1961)
Educator, model, editor, bibliophile, theater cofounder, patron of the arts . . 596

Jackson, Jesse L. (1941–)
Human rights activist, minister, organization founder, speaker, political appointee 598

Jackson, Maynard H. (1938–)
Lawyer, mayor, entrepreneur 602

Jackson, Michael (1958–)
Entertainer, singer, dancer, composer, actor, humanitarian 605

Jacob, John E. (1934–)
Organization and corporate executive . . . 608

James, Daniel ''Chappie,'' Jr. (1920–1978)
Military officer 610

Jarrett, Vernon D. (1921–)
Journalist, radio and television producer and moderator 612

Jefferson, Blind Lemon (1897–1929)
Musician, composer 614

Johnson, Charles S. (1893–1956)
Sociologist, college president, civil rights leader 616

Johnson, Frank (1792–1844)
Composer, bandleader, orchestra leader, violinist 619

Johnson, J. Rosamond (1873–1954)
Composer, entertainer 621

Johnson, Jack (1878–1946)
Boxing champion 624

Johnson, James Weldon (1871–1938)
Writer, lyricist, diplomat, critic, educator, lawyer, editor, activist 626

Johnson, John H. (1918–)
Entrepreneur, publisher, insurance company executive 630

Johnson, Joshua (1765?–1830?)
Painter 634

Johnson, Mordecai W. (1890–1976)
College president, educator, minister 635

Johnson, Rafer (1935–)
Athlete, Olympic medalist, public service worker 638

Johnson, Robert L. (1946–)
Television executive, entrepreneur 640

Johnson, Sargent (1887–1967)
Sculptor 642

Jones, Absalom (1746–1818)
Religious leader 644

Jones, Eugene Kinckle (1885–1954)
Social welfare organizer 645

Jones, Frederick McKinley (1893?–1961)
Inventor, refrigeration engineer 647

Jones, James Earl (1931–)
Actor 648

Jones, James Francis Marion
See Jones, Prophet

Jones, Laurence Clifton (1884–1975)
School founder, school administrator 652

Jones, LeRoi
See Baraka, Amiri

Jones, Prophet (1907–1971)
Religious leader 654

Jones, Quincy (1933–)
Composer, arranger, musician, producer, entrepreneur, civil rights advocate, humanitarian 656

Jones, Scipio Africanus (1863?–1943)
Attorney, civil rights activist, politician . . 660

Joplin, Scott (1868?–1917)
Composer 661

Jordan, Michael (1963–)
Basketball player 664

Jordan, Vernon (1935–)
Lawyer, civil rights leader, presidential adviser 667

Josey, E. J. (1924–)
Librarian, writer, activist 670

Julian, Percy L. (1899–1975)
Scientist, educator, entrepreneur, inventor 672

Just, Ernest Everett (1883–1941)
Biologist, educator, writer 675

K

Kay, Ulysses S. (1917–1995)
Composer, educator 679

Kelley, William Melvin (1937–)
Novelist, essayist, short story writer 681

King, B. B. (1925–)
Musician 683

King, Martin Luther, Jr. (1929–1968)
Civil rights leader, minister 686

King, Riley
See King, B. B.

L

Lafon, Thomy (1810–1893)
Entrepreneur, philanthropist 692

Langston, John Mercer (1829–1897)
Lawyer, politician, congressman, diplomat, educator, orator 693

Latimer, Lewis Howard (1848–1928)
Inventor, writer 698

Lawless, T. K. (1892–1971)
Dermatologist, philanthropist 700

Lawrence, Jacob (1917–)
Artist, educator 702

Lee, Don L.
See Madhubuti, Haki

Lee, Spike (1957–)
Filmmaker, screenwriter, actor 705

Leevy, Carroll M. (1920–)
Medical researcher, educator, administrator, humanitarian 709

Leidesdorff, William A. (1810–1848)
Pioneer, entrepreneur, civic leader 711

Leile, George
See Liele, George

Lewis, David Levering (1936–)
Educator, writer, historian 713

Lewis, Henry (1932–1996)
Symphony orchestra conductor, opera conductor 716

Lewis, John R. (1940–)
Congressman, politician, civil rights activist 718

Lewis, Reginald F. (1942–1993)
Entrepreneur, philanthropist 720

Liele, George (1750?–1820)
Religious worker .723

Little, Malcolm
See X, Malcolm

Little Richard (1932–)
Singer, entertainer 724

Locke, Alain Leroy (1886–1954)
Philosopher, patron of the arts, writer, educator 728

Logan, Rayford W. (1897–1982)
Historian, educator, writer, civil rights activist 732

Long, Richard A. (1927–)
Educator, writer, patron of the arts 734

Looby, Z. Alexander (1899–1972)
Attorney, civil rights activist, educator, politician 737

Louis, Joe (1914–1981)
Boxing champion 740

Lowery, Joseph E. (1922–)
Minister, civil rights activist, organization official 742

Lucas, Sam (1840–1916)
Entertainer 746

Lynch, John Roy (1847–1939)
State legislator, congressman, lawyer, realtor 748

M

Madhubuti, Haki (1942–)
Poet, essayist, educator, publisher 750

Majors, Monroe A. (1864–1960)
Physician, civil rights and political activist, editor, journalist, writer 753

Malcolm X
See X, Malcolm

Marino, Eugene Antonio (1934–)
Religious leader 756

Marrs, Elijah P. (1840–1910)
Minister, educator, school cofounder, political activist 757

Marsalis, Wynton (1961–)
Jazz and classical trumpeter, composer, lecturer, promoter, educator 758

Marshall, Thurgood (1908–1993)
U.S. Supreme Court judge, U.S. solicitor general, civil rights attorney, organizationofficial 762

Martin, John Sella (1832–1876)
Minister, abolitionist, organization worker, journalist, politician 767

Marycoo, Occramer
See Gardner, Newport

Mason, Charles Harrison (1866–1961)
Religious leader 770

Massey, Walter E. (1938–)
Physicist, college president, educator . . . 773

Massie, Samuel Proctor, Jr. (1919–)
Chemist, educator, college president, writer, entrepreneur 775

Matzeliger, Jan E. (1852–1889)
Inventor 776

Maynard, Robert C. (1937–1993)
Newspaper editor and publisher, journalist, reporter, social critic 778

Mays, Benjamin E. (1894–1984)
College president, educator, scholar, minister, civic leader, public speaker . . 780

Mays, Willie (1931–)
Baseball player 784

McCoy, Elijah (1843–1929)
Inventor 787

McCree, Wade H., Jr. (1920–1987)
Solicitor-general, judge, lawyer, educator 789

McKay, Claude (1890?–1948)
Writer, poet, editor 791

McKissick, Floyd (1922–1991)
Civil rights activist, lawyer, entrepreneur, city developer 795

McMillan, Elridge W. (1934–)
Foundation executive, government official, educator 797

McNair, Ronald E. (1950–1986)
Astronaut, physicist 798

Meredith, James H. (1933–)
Civil rights pioneer, writer, entrepreneur 801

Metcalfe, Ralph H. (1910–1978)
Congressman, politician, Olympic track star, coach, educator 803

Meyzeek, Albert E. (1862–1963)
Educator, civil rights activist 806

Mfume, Kweisi (1948–)
Congressman, civil rights leader, organization executive 808

Micheaux, Oscar (1884?–1951)
Filmmaker, novelist, farmer 810

Milady, Samuel
See Lucas, Sam

Miller, Dorie (1919–1943)
Serviceman, hero 814

Miller, Kelly (1863–1939)
Mathematician, sociologist, educator, writer, journalist 815

Mitchell, Arthur (1934–)
Dancer, choreographer, educator, dance company founder 819

Mitchell, Clarence M., Jr. (1911–1984)
Administrator, civil rights activist, lawyer 822

Mitchell, Loften (1919–)
Playwright, theater historian, writer 823

Mitchell, Parren J. (1922–)
Congressman, civil rights activist, educator 824

Molineaux, Tom (1784–1818)
Boxer, athlete 826

Mollison, Irvin C. (1898–1962)
Lawyer, scholar, judge 828

Morgan, Garrett A. (1875–1963)
Inventor, entrepreneur 829

Morganfield, McKinley
See Muddy Waters

Morial, Ernest (1929–1989)
Mayor, politician, lawyer, judge 831

Morrow, E. Frederic (1909–1994)
Lawyer, television executive, White House aide 833

Morton, ''Jelly Roll'' (1885?–1941)
Composer, musician 834

Moses, Bob (1935–)
Civil rights activist, educator 837

Mosley, Walter (1952–)
Writer 839

Moss, Carlton (1910–1997)
Filmmaker, actor, writer, social critic, educator 841

Motley, Archibald J., Jr. (1891–1981)
Painter 843

Motley, Willard (1909–1965)
Writer 845

Moton, Robert Russa (1867–1940)
Educator, writer 847

Muddy Waters (1915–1983)
Musician 850

Muhammad, Elijah (1897–1975)
Religious leader, black nationalist 853

Murphy, Eddie (1961–)
Entertainer 856

Murphy, Isaac (1861?–1896)
Jockey 858

Murray, Daniel (1852–1925)
Librarian, bibliophile 860

Murray, Peter Marshall (1888–1969)
Physician 862

Muse, Clarence (1889–1979)
Actor, entertainer, composer, writer, director 864

Myers, Isaac (1835–1891)
Labor leader, entrepreneur 865

N

Napier, James C. (1845–1940)
Lawyer, entrepreneur, register of the U.S. Treasury 868

Nell, William C. (1816–1874)
Abolitionist, civil servant, community activist, writer, historian 871

Newton, Huey P. (1942–1989)
Political activist, organization cofounder 874

Nix, Robert N. C., Sr. (1898?–1987)
Congressman, lawyer, politician 876

Nixon, E. D., Sr. (1899–1987)
Union leader, civil rights activist, railroad porter 878

O

Oliver, Joseph ''King'' (1895–1938)
Bandleader, musician 883

O'Neal, Frederick D. (1905–1992)
Actor, theater organizer 885

Ottley, Roi (1906–1960)
Journalist, writer 888

Overton, Anthony (1865–1946)
Entrepreneur, banker 890

Owens, Jesse (1913–1980)
Olympic track star, entrepreneur 893

P

Pace, Harry H. (1884–1943)
Entrepreneur, insurance executive, music publisher, record producer, educator, lawyer 897

Page, Alan Cedric (1945–)
Football player, lawyer, state Supreme Court justice, patron of education 899

Paige, ''Satchel'' (1906–1982)
Baseball pitcher, coach 901

Parker, Charlie ''Yardbird'' (1920–1955)
Musician 904

Parks, Gordon (1912–)
Photographer, writer, director, composer, musician 907

Parrish, Charles H., Sr. (1859–1931)
Educator, minister, school founder, college president, activist 911

Patterson, Frederick D. (1901–1988)
Veterinarian, educator, college president, fund raiser, organization founder 914

Payne, Daniel A. (1811–1893)
Religious leader, educator, college president, historian 917

Pembroke, Jim
See Pennington, James W. C.

Penn, I. Garland (1867–1930)
Educator, journalist, religious worker . . . 921

Penniman, Richard Wayne
See Little Richard

Pennington, James W. C. (1807–1870)
Minister, abolitionist 923

Perkins, Edward J. (1928–)
Diplomat, ambassador 925

Perry, Harold R. (1916–1991)
Priest, bishop 927

Petersen, Frank, Jr. (1932–)
Military officer 930

Pickens, William (1881–1954)
Educator, college administrator, orator, writer, civil rights leader, government official 931

Pickett, Bill (1870–1932)
Wild West show performer, cowboy 935

Pierce, Samuel R., Jr. (1922–)
Lawyer, government official 936

Pinchback, P. B. S. (1837–1921)
Politician, entrepreneur, newspaper editor 938

Pippin, Horace (1888–1946)
Painter 941

Plinton, James O., Jr. (1914–1996)
Business executive, pilot, instructor 943

Poitier, Sidney (1927–)
Actor, director, producer 944

Poole, Elijah
See Muhammad, Elijah

Poor, Salem (b.1747)
Revolutionary War patriot 947

Poston, Ted (1906–1974)
Journalist, civil rights activist, writer 949

Poussaint, Alvin F. (1934–)
Psychiatrist, educator, writer 951

Powell, Adam Clayton, Jr. (1908–1972)
Minister, councilman, congressman, civil rights activist, politician 954

Powell, Colin (1937–)
Military leader 958

Pratt, Awadagin (1966–)
Concert pianist 961

Price, J. C. (1854–1893)
Minister, college president, educator, orator 963

Pride, Charley (1938?–)
Country singer, baseball player 966

Proctor, Henry Hugh (1868–1933)
Minister, writer, lecturer 968

Proctor, Samuel D. (1914–1997)
Minister, college president, educator, public servant, lecturer 971

Prosser, Gabriel (1775?–1800)
Slave, insurrectionist 973

Purvis, Robert (1810–1898)
Abolitionist 976

Q

Quarles, Benjamin A. (1904–1996)
Historian, scholar, educator, administrator, writer 979

R

Randolph, A. Philip (1889–1979)
Union organizer, labor leader 983

Rangel, Charles B. (1930–)
Congressman, lawyer 987

Ransom, Reverdy C. (1861–1959)
Religious leader, civil rights activist 990

Rapier, James T. (1837–1883)
Congressman, farmer, government official 994

Raspberry, William J. (1935–)
Journalist, television commentator, teacher, speaker 996

Reason, Charles Lewis (1818–1893)
Educator, abolitionist 998

Redding, J. Saunders (1906–1988)
Writer, critic, educator 1000

Reid, Ira De A. (1901–1968)
Sociologist, scholar, educator 1002

Remond, Charles Lenox (1810–1873)
Abolitionist 1003

Revels, Hiram Rhoades (1827–1901)
Minister, educator, college president, U.S. senator 1005

Ribbs, Willy T. (1956–)
Automobile racer 1008

Richardson, Willis (1889?–1977)
Playwright, writer, director, drama historian, educator, government worker 1010

Riles, Wilson C. (1917–)
Educational administrator 1011

Robeson, Paul (1898–1976)
Actor, singer, activist 1013

Robinson, Bill ''Bojangles'' (1878?–1949)
Dancer 1016

Robinson, Frank (1935–)
Baseball player and manager 1020

Robinson, Jackie (1919–1972)
Baseball player, civil rights activist 1022

Robinson, Luther
See Robinson, Bill ''Bojangles''

Robinson, Randall (1941–)
Civil rights activist, lawyer 1025

Robinson, Sugar Ray (1921–1989)
Boxing champion, entrepreneur, philanthropist 1027

Rogers, J. A. (1883?–1965)
Historian, writer, journalist 1029

Rowan, Carl (1925–)
Journalist, government official, writer . .1031

Ruggles, David (1810–1849)
Abolitionist, hydrotherapist, editor, entrepreneur 1034

Russell, Bill (1934–)
Basketball player, coach 1035

Russworm, John Brown (1799–1851)
Journalist, abolitionist, colonizer 1038

Rustin, Bayard (1910–1987)
Pacifist, civil and human rights activist . . 1039

S

Satcher, David (1941–)
U.S. surgeon general, physician, medical school president, educator, research center administrator 1044

Schomburg, Arthur Alfonso (1874–1938)
Bibliophile, library curator, writer 1046

Scott, Dred (1795–1858)
Slave, litigator 1049

Scott, Emmett Jay (1873–1957)
Editor, college administrator, political activist 1051

Scott, Wendell (1921–1990)
Automobile racer 1054

Seymour, William Joseph (1870–1922)
Religious leader 1056

Shaw, Bernard (1940–)
Television journalist, reporter 1059

Shirley, George I. (1934–)
Opera singer, educator 1061

Sifford, Charlie (1922–)
Professional golfer 1063

Simmons, William J. (1849–1890)
Religious worker, educator, journalist, college president, writer 1066

Slaughter, Henry Proctor (1871–1958)
Bibliophile, organization leader, journalist, publisher 1067

Sleet, Moneta J., Jr. (1926–1996)
Photojournalist 1069

Smalls, Robert (1839–1916)
Naval hero, state legislator, congressman, customs collector 1071

Smith, James McCune (1813–1865)
Physician, abolitionist, journalist 1073

Smith, Walter
See Robinson, Sugar Ray

Spaulding, Charles C. (1874–1952)
Insurance executive, entrepreneur, civic leader 1075

Steward, William Henry (1847–1935)
Editor, publisher, church leader, activist 1078

Still, William (1821–1902)
Abolitionist, reformer, writer, entrepreneur 1080

Still, William Grant (1895–1978)
Composer, arranger, conductor 1082

Stokes, Carl B. (1927–1996)
Mayor 1086

Sullivan, Leon H. (1922–)
Minister, civil rights leader, entrepreneur 1089

Sullivan, Louis (1933–)
Medical school president, physician, government official 1092

Sutton, Percy E. (1920–)
Lawyer, civil rights activist, lecturer, public official, entrepreneur 1094

T

Tanner, Benjamin Tucker (1835–1923)
Church leader, editor, journalist 1098

Tanner, Henry Ossawa (1859–1937)
Painter 1099

Taylor, Marshall W. ''Major'' (1878–1932)
Bicycle racer 1103

Temple, Edward S. (1927–)
Track coach, educator 1105

Thomas, Clarence (1948–)
U.S. Supreme Court judge, lawyer, administrator 1108

Thomas, Franklin A. (1934–)
Lawyer, foundation executive, humanitarian 1112

Thomas, Jesse O. (1883–1972)
Educator, government official, civic worker 1113

Thurman, Howard (1900–1981)
Theologian, minister, mystic, civil rights advisor 1114

Thurman, Wallace (1902–1934)
Novelist, playwright, ghostwriter, journalist 1118

Tindley, Charles Albert (1851–1933)
Minister, composer 1121

Tobias, Channing H. (1882–1961)
Organization official, minister, social worker, civic leader 1122

Toomer, Jean (1892–1967)
Writer, philosopher 1125

Trotter, Monroe (1872–1934)
Publisher, editor, civil rights activist . . . 1130

Ture, Kwame
See Carmichael, Stokely

Turner, Henry McNeal (1834–1915)
Religious worker, emigrationist, educator 1133

Turner, Nat (1800–1831)
Slave, liberation theologian, insurrectionist 1137

Tyler, Ralph (1859–1921)
Editor, journalist, government official . . 1142

U

Underwood, Edward Ellsworth (1864–1942)
Physician, minister, editor, civil rights leader, politician 1145

V

Van DerZee, James (1886–1983)
Photographer 1147

Vann, Robert L. (1887–1940)
Journalist, lawyer, politician, civil rights activist, entrepreneur 1149

Van Peebles, Melvin (1932–)
Novelist, playwright, screenwriter, director, actor, composer, stock market trader 1152

Varick, James (1750?–1827)
Religious leader 1155

Vashon, George Boyer (1824–1878?)
Teacher, lawyer, writer 1157

Vesey, Denmark (1767–1822)
Carpenter, liberation theologian, slave, insurrectionist 1158

Vincent, U. Conrad (1892–1938)
Physician, hospital founder, reformer . . . 1163

W

Walcott, Louis Eugene
See Farrakhan, Louis

Walker, David (1796?–1830)
Abolitionist, protest writer 1165

Walker, Leroy T. (1918–)
Educator, Olympic coach, Olympic administrator 1166

Walker, Moses Fleetwood (1857–1924)
Baseball player, activist, inventor, entrepreneur 1168

Waller, Fats (1904–1943)
Pianist, organist, composer, singer, bandleader 1171

Walrond, Eric (1898–1966)
Writer, journalist 1173

Ward, Douglas Turner (1930–)
Playwright, director, producer, critic, theatrical company cofounder 1176

Ward, Samuel Ringgold (1817–1866?)
Abolitionist, religious worker, journalist 1177

Warfield, William (1920–)
Concert singer, actor, educator 1179

Washington, Booker T. (1856–1915)
School founder, college president, educator, community leader, organization founder, writer 1181

Washington, Denzel (1954–)
Actor, humanitarian 1186

Washington, Harold (1922–1987)
Lawyer, politician 1189

Washington, Walter E. (1915–)
Mayor, lawyer, housing administrator . . . 1191

Waters, Muddy
See Muddy Waters

Watts, André (1946–)
Concert pianist 1193

Weaver, Robert C. (1907–1997)
Government official, scholar, labor and housing specialist 1195

Wedgeworth, Robert, Jr. (1937–)
Library administrator, educator, organization executive 1198

Wesley, Charles H. (1891–1987)
Historian, minister, educator, college president 1200

West, Cornel (1953–)
Philosopher, scholar, educator, writer . . . 1202

White, Charles (1918–1979)
Painter 1204

White, Clarence Cameron (1880–1960)
Composer, violinist 1206

White, Walter (1893–1955)
Civil rights worker, organization executive, writer 1209

Whitman, Albery (1851–1901)
Poet, minister 1213

Wideman, John Edgar (1941–)
Novelist, short fiction writer, essayist, critic, teacher 1214

Wilder, L. Douglas (1931–)
Lawyer, governor, politician, radio talk show host 1217

Wilkins, J. Ernest (1894–1959)
Government official, lawyer 1220

Wilkins, Roy (1901–1981)
Organization executive, journalist 1222

Williams, Avon Nyanza, Jr. (1921–1994)
Lawyer, civil rights leader, politician . . . 1224

Williams, Bert (1873–1922)
Entertainer 1227

Williams, Daniel Hale (1856–1931)
Physician, educator, hospital founder and administrator 1230

Williams, Edward Christopher (1871–1929)
Librarian, educator, writer 1232

Williams, Egbert Austin
See Williams, Bert

Williams, George Washington (1849–1891)
Historian, politician, minister, journalist 1233

Williams, John A. (1925–)
Writer, journalist, educator 1236

Williams, Paul R. (1894–1980)
Architect, entrepreneur 1238

Wilson, August (1945–)
Playwright, poet 1241

Wilson, William J. (b.1810s?)
Journalist, writer, educator, school administrator, activist, banker 1244

Woodruff, Hale A. (1900–1980)
Printer, printmaker, muralist, educator . . 1247

Woods, Granville T. (1856–1910)
Inventor, entrepreneur 1250

Woods, Tiger (1975–)
Professional golfer 1252

Woodson, Carter G. (1875–1950)
Historian, writer, publisher, organization cofounder 1256

Work, John Wesley, III (1901–1967)
Composer, music educator, scholar 1259

Work, Monroe Nathan (1866–1945)
Sociologist, editor, bibliographer 1262

Wright, Isaac
See Coker, Daniel

Wright, Louis Tompkins (1891–1952)
Physician, civil rights activist 1266

Wright, Richard (1906–1960)
Writer, poet, dramatist, screenwriter . . . 1268

Wright, Stephen J. (1910–1996)
Educator, college president, organization official, public servant . . 1272

X

X, Malcolm (1925–1965)
Human rights activist, lecturer, organizer 1276

Y

Young, Andrew (1932–)
Minister, civil rights activist, politician, ambassador, mayor 1280

Young, Charles (1864–1922)
Military officer, musician, educator, cartographer, congressman 1283

Young, Coleman A. (1918–1997)
Mayor, civil rights activist 1285

Young, Whitney M., Jr. (1921–1971)
Social worker, civil rights leader 1289

Advisory Board

Charles L. Blockson
Curator, Charles L. Blockson Afro-American Collection, Temple University, Philadelphia, Pennsylvania

Howard Dodson
Chief, Schomburg Center for Research in Black Culture, New York Public Library, New York, New York

David C. Driskell
Distinguished University Professor of Art, University of Maryland, College Park, Maryland

Samuel A. Floyd Jr.
Director, Center for Black Music Research, Columbia College, Chicago, Illinois

D. Antoinette Handy
Researcher, writer, Jackson, Mississippi

Vivian Davidson Hewitt
Retired librarian and consultant, New York, New York

Richard A. Long
Atticus Haygood Professor of Interdisciplinary Studies, Emory University, Atlanta, Georgia

Haki Madhubuti
Editor, Third World Press; professor of English, Chicago State University, Chicago, Illinois

Daniel T. Williams
Archivist, Tuskegee University, Tuskegee, Alabama

Contributors

Yvette Alex-Assensoh, *Indiana University*
Nkechi G. Mgboh Amadife, *Kentucky State University*
A. B. Assensoh, *Indiana University*
Alice M. Baker, *South Carolina State University*
Kathleen E. Bethel, *Northwestern University*
Rosa Bobia, *Kennesaw State College*
Leańtin LaVerne Bracks, *Fisk University*
Phiefer L. Browne, *Chicago, Illinois*
Arthur W. Buell, *California State University, Stanislaus*
Anne S. Butler, *Kentucky State University*
Leroy E. Bynum Jr., *Albany State University*
Linda M. Carter, *Morgan State University*
Mario A. Charles, *Baruch College*
Arlene Clift-Pellow, *North Carolina Central University*
Paulette Coleman, *A.M.E. Church Review*
Grace E. Collins, *Baltimore, Maryland*
De Witt S. Dykes Jr., *Oakland University*
Mary Frances Early, *Clark Atlanta University*
Floyd C. Ferebee, *North Carolina Central University*
Vivian Njeri Fisher, *Morgan State University*
Tuliza Fleming, *University of Maryland*
Marie Garrett, *University of Tennessee*
T. Anthony Gass, *Morgan State University*
Martia Graham Goodson, *Baruch College*
Sandra Y. Govan, *University of North Carolina at Charlotte*
Horace L. Griffin, *University of Missouri, Columbia*
Johnanna L. Grimes-Williams, *Tennessee State University*
Delphine Ava Gross, *Morgan State University*
Arthur C. Gunn, *Clark Atlanta University*
Debra Newman Ham, *Morgan State University*
D. Antoinette Handy, *Jackson, Mississippi*
Donna Akiba Sullivan Harper, *Spelman College*
Alicia M. Henry, *Fisk University*
Vivian D. Hewitt, *New York City*
Ruth A. Hodges, *South Carolina State University*
Helen R. Houston, *Tennessee State University*
Juanita R. Howard, *Baruch College*
Damien Bayard Ingram, *Morgan State University*

Dona L. Irvin, *Oakland, California*
Barbara Williams Jenkins, *South Carolina State University*
Robert L. Johns, *Fisk University*
Ida Jones, *Smithsonian Archives Center*
Ilene Jones-Cornwell, *Nashville, Tennessee*
Jacqueline Jones-Ford, *University of Tennessee*
Casper L. Jordan, *Atlanta, Georgia*
Amy Kirschke, *Vanderbilt University*
Kevin C. Kretschmer, *Kentucky State University*
Candis LaPrade, *Longwood College*
Gordon K. Lee, *Lee College*
Theresa Leininger-Miller, *University of Cincinnati*
Thura Mack, *University of Tennessee*
Tony Martin, *Wellesley College*
Audrey Thomas McCluskey, *Indiana University*
John McCluskey Jr., *Indiana University*
Karen Cotton McDaniel, *Kentucky State University*
Nellie Y. McKay, *University of Wisconsin, Madison*
Richard I. McKinney, *Baltimore, Maryland*
Sheila Smith McKoy, *Vanderbilt University*
Genna Rae McNeil, *University of North Carolina at Chapel Hill*
Ronald E. Mickens, *Clark Atlanta University*
Frank T. Moorer, *Alabama State University*
Lori Michelle Muha, *Kentucky State University*
Dolores Nicholson, *Metropolitan Nashville Public Schools*
Margaret D. Pagan, *Baltimore, Maryland*
Jewell B. Parham, *Tennessee State University*
Patricia A. Pearson, *Kentucky State University*
Saundra P. Peterson, *North Carolina Agricultural and Technical State University*
Kenneth Potts, *California State University, Stanislaus*
Carolyn L. Quin, *Riverside Community College*
Cortez Rainey, *Baltimore, Maryland*
David Leon Reed, *Morgan State University*
Richard Robbins, *Sharon, Massachusetts*
Houston B. Roberson, *University of the South*
Ingrid Irene Sabio, *Kentucky State University*
Theodosia T. Shields, *Dillard University*
Frederick Douglas Smith Jr., *Fisk University*
Jessie Carney Smith, *Fisk University*
Sheila A. Stuckey, *Kentucky State University*
Ann C. Sullivan, *Kentucky State University*
Claire A. Taft, *Texas Agricultural and Mechanical University, Kingsville*
Darius L. Thieme, *Fisk University*
John Mark Tucker, *Purdue University*
Lou Turner, *North Central College*
Raamesie D. Umandavi, *Kentucky State University*

Nagueyalti Warren, *Emory University*
W. Braxter Wiggins, *Hampton University*
Audrey Williams, *Baruch College*
Betty Lou Williams, *University of Hawaii at Manoa*
Gregory Williams, *Morgan State University*
Nicole L. Bailey Williams, *Elkin Park, Pennsylvania*
Raymond A. Winbush, *Fisk University*
Flossie E. Wise, *University of Tennessee*
Linda T. Wynn, *Tennessee Historical Commission*

Photo Credits

Images appearing in *Notable Black American Men* were received from the following sources:

Cover photos (clockwise from top right): **Fisk University Library; Public Domain; Fisk University Library; AP/Wide World Photos; (background) Donna A. Sullivan Harper.**

Schomburg Center for Research in Black Culture: 1; **Fisk University Library:** 3; **Fisk University Library:** 7; **AP/Wide World Photos, Inc:** 9; **Fisk University Library:** 12; **AP/Wide World Photos, Inc:** 16; **AP/Wide World Photos, Inc:** 19; **Fisk University Library:** 21; **Fisk University Library:** 25; **AP/Wide World Photos, Inc:** 27; **Schomburg Center for Research in Black Culture:** 30; **Fisk University Library:** 35; **Bettmann Archive/Newsphotos, Inc.:** 37; **Schomburg Center for Research in Black Culture:** 38; **Fisk University Library:** 41; **AP/Wide World Photos, Inc:** 43; **courtesy of Carl Van Vechten:** 46; **Fisk University Library:** 50; **unknown:** 52; **Fisk University Library:** 58; **Fisk University Library:** 61; **Fisk University Library:** 62; **courtesy of Carl Van Vechten:** 64; **Fisk University Library:** 68; **Derrick Bell:** 72; **Fisk University Library:** 74; **Fisk University Library:** 75; **Fisk University Library:** 77; **Fisk University Library:** 80; **Charles L. Blockson:** 83; **Fisk University Library:** 85; **NASA:** 86; **Charles L. Blockson Afro-American Collection, Temple University:** 88; **AP/Wide World Photos, Inc:** 91; **Fisk University Library:** 94; **Fisk University Library:** 98; **Fisk University Library:** 100; **AP/Wide World Photos, Inc:** 103; **Corbis Corporation:** 105; **Fisk University Library:** 108; **Fisk University Library:** 112; **Special Collections, Atlanta University Center, Woodruff Library:** 114; **American Medical Association:** 119; **Fisk University Library:** 122; **AP/Wide World Photos, Inc:** 126; **Fisk University Library:** 129; **AP/Wide World Photos, Inc:** 131; **Fisk University Library:** 134; **Tony Brown Productions, Inc:** 136; **Fisk University Library:** 138; **Willie L. Brown:** 141; **Fisk University Library:** 144; **Fisk University Library:** 147; **Jamie H. Cockfield:** 149; **AP/Wide World Photos, Inc:** 151; **Fisk University Library:** 153; **Fisk University Library:** 159; **Fisk University Library:** 163; **AP/Wide World Photos, Inc:** 167; **Fisk University Library:** 170; **Fisk University Library:** 172; **Archive Photos, Inc:** 174; **Fisk University Library:** 176; **Fisk University Library:** 178; **Fisk University Library:** 181; **Corbis Corporation:** 185; **AP/Wide World Photos, Inc:** 187; **courtesy Kenneth Chenault:** 192; **Fisk University Library:** 194; **Charles L. Blockson Afro-American Collection, Temple University:** 197; **Fisk University Library:** 200; **AP/Wide World Photos, Inc:** 203; **Fisk University Library:** 207; **Fisk University Library:** 211; **Archive Photos, Inc:** 213; **Fisk University Library:** 214; **AP/Wide World Photos, Inc:** 216; **Library of Congress:** 221; **AP/Wide World Photos, Inc:** 226; **Fisk University Library:** 228; **The Brokaw Company:** 231; **Fisk University Library:** 235; **Fisk University Library:** 238; **Corbis Corporation:** 244; **Fisk University Library:** 247; **Fisk University Library:** 254; **U.S. Air Force:** 256; **Fisk University Library:** 259; **AP/Wide World Photos, Inc:** 262; **The Artists Agency:** 265; **Fisk University Library:** 267; **Fisk University Library:** 269; **Fisk University Library:** 277; **Fisk University Library:** 283; **AP/Wide World Photos, Inc:** 290; **Fisk University Library:** 295; **Fisk University Library:** 298; **Fisk University Library:** 302; **AP/Wide World Photos, Inc:** 303; **Joan Vitale Strong:** 305; **AP/Wide World Photos, Inc:** 307; **unknown:** 310; **Fisk University Library:** 316; **Fisk University Library:** 319; **Gibbs Museum of Art:** 323; **public domain:** 327; **AP/Wide World Photos, Inc:** 331; **David C. Driskell Archive:** 334; **Fisk University Library:** 337; **Fisk University Library:** 345; **Fisk University Library:** 357; **Cheekwood Museum:** 359; **AP/Wide World Photos, Inc:** 362; **Corbis Corporation:** 364; **public domain:** 368; **AP/Wide World Photos, Inc:** 370; **AP/Wide World Photos, Inc:** 376; **AP/Wide World Photos, Inc:** 379; **National Archives and Records Administration, Smithsonian Institution:** 382; **AP/Wide World Photos, Inc:** 387; **Fisk University Library:** 389; **AP/Wide World Photos, Inc:** 393; **AP/Wide World Photos, Inc:** 397; **Beinecke Rare Book and Manuscript Library, Yale University:** 401; **Fisk University Library:** 403; **AP/Wide World Photos, Inc:** 405; **Fisk University Library:** 407; **Charles L. Blockson Afro-American Collection, Temple University:** 409; **Fisk University Library:** 411; **Henry W. Foster Jr.:** 414; **Fisk University Library:** 418; **Xavier University:** 420; **Fisk University Library:** 422; **Fisk University Library:** 429; **AP/Wide World Photos, Inc:** 432; **Black Enterprise Magazine:** 434; **Fisk University Library:** 438; **Fisk University Library:** 442; **AP/Wide World Photos, Inc:** 446; **Jerry Bauer:** 449; **Fisk University Library:** 451; **courtesy of Carl Van Vechten:** 458; **AP/Wide World Photos, Inc:** 459; **Fisk University Library:** 461; **Fisk University Library:** 463; **AP/Wide World Photos, Inc:** 465; **Bettmann Archive:** 467; **AP/Wide World Photos, Inc:** 469; **Samuel R. Gravely:** 474; **Black Enterprise Magazine:** 476; **AP/Wide World Photos, Inc:** 478; **Fisk University Library:** 483; **Fisk University Library:** 485; **Fisk University Library:** 488; **Fisk University Library:** 491; **AP/Wide World Photos, Inc:** 493; **Fisk University Library:** 496; **Fisk University Library:** 499; **Schomburg Center for Research in Black Culture:** 502; **Archive Photos, Inc:** 507; **Fisk University Library:** 509; **Fisk University Library:** 513; **President's Office, Hampton University:** 516; **Charles L. Blockson Afro-American Collection, Temple University:** 519; **Fisk University Library:** 524; **Fisk University Library:** 527; **Fisk University Library:** 529; **public domain:** 532; **Archive Photos, Inc:** 537; **Fisk University Library:** 542; **Fisk University**

Library: 544; **Marvin Scott:** 550; **Fisk University Library:** 553; **Fisk University Library:** 561; **Schomburg Center for Research in Black Culture:** 564; **Schomburg Center for Research in Black Culture:** 566; **Special Collections, Atlanta University Center, Woodruff Library:** 569; **Drew University:** 574; **Fisk University Library:** 575; **Fisk University Library:** 579; **Donna A. Sullivan Harper:** 581; **Fisk University Library:** 589; **Bettmann Archive/Newsphotos, Inc.:** 592; **Special Collections, Atlanta University Center, Woodruff Library:** 596; **Vando L. Rogers Jr.:** 599; **AP/Wide World Photos, Inc:** 603; **AP/Wide World Photos, Inc:** 606; **AP/Wide World Photos, Inc:** 608; **Fisk University Library:** 611; **Vernon D. Jarrett:** 613; **Archive Photos, Inc:** 615; **Fisk University Library:** 616; **Charles L. Blockson Afro-American Collection, Temple University:** 620; **AP/Wide World Photos, Inc:** 624; **Fisk University Library:** 627; **Schomburg Center for Research in Black Culture:** 631; **Charles L. Blockson Afro-American Collection, Temple University:** 636; **Black Entertainment Television:** 640; **Fisk University Library:** 644; **Fisk University Library:** 646; **courtesy of Carl Van Vechten:** 649; **Fisk University Library:** 652; **AP/Wide World Photos, Inc:** 657; **Fisk University Library:** 660; **Fisk University Library:** 662; **Bettmann Archive:** 665; **AP/Wide World Photos, Inc:** 667; **Fisk University Library:** 672; **Library of Congress:** 673; **AP/Wide World Photos, Inc:** 676; **public domain:** 682; **AP/Wide World Photos, Inc:** 684; **Fisk University Library:** 687; **Fisk University Library:** 693; **Schomburg Center for Research in Black Culture:** 698; **Dillard University:** 701; **AP/Wide World Photos, Inc:** 702; **AP/Wide World Photos, Inc:** 706; **unknown:** 709; **Fisk University Library:** 712; **public domain:** 718; **Fisk University Library:** 723; **AP/Wide World Photos, Inc:** 725; **Fisk University Library:** 729; **Richard A. Long:** 735; ***Nashville Tennessean*** **(newspaper):** 737; **UPI:** 740; **Joseph E. Lowery:** 743; **Fisk University Library:** 748; **AP/Wide World Photos, Inc:** 750; **Fisk University Library:** 753; **Bettmann Archive/Newsphotos, Inc.:** 756; **AP/Wide World Photos, Inc:** 759; **Fisk University Library:** 763; **Elsie W. Mason:** 770; **Samuel Proctor Massie Jr.:** 775; **Fisk University Library:** 777; **AP/Wide World Photos, Inc:** 779; **Schomburg Center for Research in Black Culture:** 781; **Fisk University Library:** 784; **AP/Wide World Photos, Inc:** 786; **Fisk University Library:** 788; **University of Michigan, photo by Bob Kalmbach:** 789; **Library of Congress:** 791; **Library of Congress:** 795; **Elridge W. McMillan:** 797; **AP/Wide World Photos, Inc:** 799; **AP/Wide World Photos, Inc:** 801; **AP/Wide World Photos, Inc:** 804; **Fisk University Library:** 806; **AP/Wide World Photos, Inc:** 808; **Schomburg Center for Research in Black Culture:** 814; **public domain:** 819; **Fisk University Library:** 826; **Fisk University Library:** 828; **Schomburg Center for Research in Black Culture:** 830; **Amistad Research Center:** 831; **Fisk University Library:** 833; **Bettmann Archive:** 835; **Caesar Photography:** 837; **Jerry Bauer:** 839; **Corbis Corporation:** 844; **AP/Wide World Photos, Inc:** 846; **Fisk University Library:** 848; **AP/Wide World Photos, Inc:** 851; **Archive Photos, Inc:** 853; **AP/Wide World Photos, Inc:** 857; **unknown:** 859; **Fisk University Library:** 860; **Scurlock Studios, Moorland-Spingarn:** 862; **Fisk University Library:** 868; **Newton Foundation:** 874; **Temple University:** 876; **Tennessee State University:** 879; **Van Vechten Trust:** 886; **Fisk University Library:** 889; **Fisk University Library:** 891; **Fisk University Library:** 893; **Fisk University Library:** 897; **Alan Page:** 900; **Fisk University Library:** 902; **Bettmann Archive:** 904; **Gordon Parks:** 908; **Fisk University Library:** 912; **Frederick D. Patterson Research Institute:** 914; **Fisk University Library:** 918; **Fisk University Library:** 921; **Fisk University Library:** 923; **AP/Wide World Photos, Inc:** 928; **U.S. Marine Corps:** 930; **Fisk University Library:** 932; **Sam Pierce:** 937; **Fisk University Library:** 939; **Corbis Images:** 942; **Library of Congress:** 945; **Alvin Poussaint:** 952; **unknown:** 954; **Vando L. Rogers Jr.:** 958; **IMG Artists:** 962; **Fisk University Library:** 963; **AP/Wide World Photos, Inc:** 966; **Fisk University Library:** 969; **AP/Wide World Photos, Inc:** 972; **public domain:** 976; **Fisk University Library:** 983; **Library of Congress:** 987; **AP/Wide World Photos, Inc:** 988; **Fisk University Library:** 991; **Fisk University Library:** 994; **The Washington Post Writers Group:** 997; **Fisk University Library:** 999; **Fisk University Library:** 1000; **Fisk University Library:** 1004; **Fisk University Library:** 1006; **Sirlin Photographers:** 1012; **Van Vechten Trust:** 1014; **Fisk University Library:** 1017; **AP/Wide World Photos, Inc:** 1019; **Archive Photos, Inc:** 1021; **Schomburg Center for Research in Black Culture:** 1022; **AP/Wide World Photos, Inc:** 1026; **Fisk University Library:** 1028; **Fisk University Library:** 1030; **Fisk University Library:** 1031; **AP/Wide World Photos, Inc:** 1036; **Fisk University Library:** 1039; **public domain:** 1040; **Meharry Medical College:** 1044; **Fisk University Library:** 1047; **Fisk University Library:** 1050; **Fisk University Library:** 1051; **AP/Wide World Photos, Inc:** 1054; **AP/Wide World Photos, Inc:** 1059; **Talbot Photographers:** 1061; **Fisk University Library:** 1066; **Fisk University Library:** 1071; **Fisk University Library:** 1074; **Fisk University Library:** 1076; **Fisk University Library:** 1079; **Fisk University Library:** 1081; **Fisk University Library:** 1083; **AP/Wide World Photos, Inc:** 1087; **Leon Sullivan:** 1089; **AP/Wide World Photos, Inc:** 1093; **AP/Wide World Photos, Inc:** 1095; **Fisk University Library:** 1098; **Schomburg Center for Research in Black Culture:** 1100; **Fisk University Library:** 1103; **Edward S. Temple:** 1106; **U.S. Supreme Court:** 1108; **AP/Wide World Photos, Inc:** 1115; **Charles L. Blockson Afro-American Collection, Temple University:** 1123; **Beinecke Rare Book and Manuscript Library, Yale University:** 1126; **Fisk University Library:** 1131; **Fisk University Library:** 1133; **Library of Congress:** 1139; **Fisk University Library:** 1142; **Fisk University Library:** 1145; **AP/Wide World Photos, Inc:** 1147; **Charles L. Blockson Afro-American Collection, Temple University:** 1149; **AP/Wide World Photos, Inc:** 1153; **Fisk University Library:** 1155; **Fisk University Library:** 1157; **AP/Wide World Photos, Inc:** 1169; **Corbis Images:** 1171; **Winold Reiss Collection, Fisk University Library:** 1173; **Fisk University Library:** 1178; **unknown:** 1180; **Fisk University Library:** 1182; **AP/Wide World Photos, Inc:** 1187; **Corbis Corporation:** 1189; **Scurlock Studios, Moorland-Spingarn:** 1191; **D. Antoinette Handy:** 1194; **AP/Wide World Photos, Inc:** 1196; **Fisk University Library:** 1200; **Jerry Bauer:** 1203; **Fisk University Library:** 1206; **Fisk University Library:** 1209; **Fisk University Library:** 1213; **Jerry Bauer:** 1215; **AP/Wide World Photos, Inc:** 1218; **courtesy of Carl Van Vechten:** 1222; **Fisk University Library:** 1228; **Fisk University Library:** 1230; **Fisk University Library:** 1234; **Fisk University Library:** 1239; **AP/Wide**

World Photos, Inc: 1242; **Fisk University Library:** 1251; **AP/Wide World Photos, Inc:** 1252; **AP/Wide World Photos, Inc:** 1253; **Schomburg Center for Research in Black Culture:** 1256; **Fisk University Library:** 1260; **Fisk University Library:** 1263; **Schomburg Center for Research in Black Culture:** 1267; **Fisk University Library:** 1269; **Fisk University Library:** 1273; **AP/Wide World Photos, Inc:** 1277; **unknown:** 1280; **Fisk University Library:** 1284; **AP/Wide World Photos, Inc:** 1286; **Fisk University Library:** 1289.

Hank Aaron

(1934–)

Baseball player

Hank Aaron, known to millions of baseball fans around the world as "The Hammer," holds the game's most prestigious record of most career home runs. He is a legendary baseball figure who is known for speaking out in protest of racial discrimination in baseball, particularly in the front office.

Henry Louis Aaron was born February 5, 1934, in Mobile, Alabama. The third child born to Herbert and Estella Aaron, he was affectionately nicknamed "Man" by family members when the future home run king entered the world weighing 12 pounds. He grew up poor in a family of eight children and attended Central High School but finished at the Josephine Allen Institute where he was a star high school athlete. He received many scholarship offers to play football at the collegiate level after high school, however, by then he had set his goal to play major league baseball. His first swings had been at bottle caps with broomsticks, but by his junior year in high school, Aaron played semiprofessional baseball with the Mobile Black Bears.

Hank Aaron

Rough Road to the Record

Aaron was 18–years old when he signed his first professional contract in 1952 with the Indianapolis Clowns of the Negro League. He had never left the Mobile area up to that time. The next year he became the first African American to play in the Sally League when the Jacksonville Suns signed him. During these early days of his career when teams traveled by bus, Aaron suffered the indignities of a segregated South because of the "separate but equal" policies. He was isolated from other players after games, during meals, and while traveling. In many instances he was forced to make his own arrangements while white teammates were housed and fed as a group. Nevertheless, he won the league's Most Valuable Player award. He faced the same situation during the next season with the Atlanta Crackers of the Southern League.

Aaron was spotted by Dewey Griggs, a scout for the Braves, while playing for the Indianapolis Clowns of the American Negro League. Griggs eventually signed Aaron for the Braves' Eau Claire, Wisconsin, farm team at $350 per month in June of 1952. The Milwaukee Braves called Aaron up to the majors in 1954. By 1957 he had become the most revered 23–year–old in all of baseball. He led the league in every batting department except average, where he tied for fourth. He hit a home run against the St. Louis Cardinals in the bottom of the eleventh inning with the score tied to clinch the National League pennant for the Braves. He was named Most Valuable Player of the playoffs. As if that were not good enough, in the 1957 World Series, he hit three home runs as the Braves beat the New York Yankees.

By the time the Braves moved to Atlanta in 1966, Aaron had become a baseball superstar. For more than ten years Aaron had stolen bases, won Gold Glove Awards, driven in runs, thrown out runners, and maintained a batting average above .300. He also received praise for his character and off–field activities. Ivan Allen, former mayor of Atlanta, said that Aaron was key in confirming the end of segregation in the South through his thoughtful consideration and cooperative attitude while Southerners adjusted to their first major league baseball team.

Not until 1969 did anyone realize that Aaron was on his way to breaking Babe Ruth's career home run record. When Aaron reached 500 career homers and his 3,000th hit on May 17, 1970, sports writers began to debate seriously whether or not he would pass Ruth's 714. Aaron faced very few problems as a player in Atlanta until 1973. The vast majority of the fans cheered him on and hoped that the record would be broken in the team's home ballpark. One bitter consequence, however, was the small number of fans who greeted his accomplishments with hatred, especially through the mail. Security at the Braves' stadium was tightened after some letters suggested that he would be shot down from the stands. The Federal Bureau of Investigation (FBI) was brought in and Aaron had to travel separately from the rest of the team with a bodyguard. Other letters were addressed "Dear Nigger"—and worse—and one of his daughters was threatened at college.

Aaron credited his strong Christian faith for his being able to withstand the negative attitudes he encountered while pursuing the home run title. Throughout his life, both in and outside of baseball, he was guided by the principles of working hard, treating other people right, keeping the rules, practicing self–discipline, always giving his best, and trusting that nothing would happen to him that God did not ordain. Strengthened by his faith, Aaron was able to excel on the baseball field during one of the most stressful periods of his life.

While Aaron always spoke out against racism and prejudice, he was not perceived as a civil rights spokesperson until he began to close in on the home run record. Even after he retired, he received hate mail whenever he spoke out publicly, calling for more blacks in baseball front offices or condemning racist comments made by baseball owners. Aaron kept all of the letters, hate and otherwise, with plans to donate them to a museum one day.

It was widely assumed that most of the ugliness that Aaron experienced before and after the record came from the race–haunted South. Aaron recalled, however, that most came from the North—especially New York—and that none came from Atlanta. An indication of the nastiness he encountered from hostile fans occurred outside Chicago's Wrigley Field when a woman walked up to him and threw a glass of whiskey in his face.

In addition to the hatefulness that he experienced from racist fans, Aaron became aware of the insensitivity of organized baseball when he hit home run number 700. Being only the second man in the history of the game to reach the milestone, he assumed that congratulations would come from then–commissioner Bowie Kuhn, but that was not to be. Aaron accepted Kuhn's explanation that he had planned to wait until the record was broken, but he never forgot the snub.

The End of a Brilliant Career

A near melee erupted when Aaron hit home run number 715 on April 3, 1974, in the Braves' home ballpark against Al Downing of the Los Angeles Dodgers. He had achieved a "superhuman accomplishment, as mysterious and remote as Stonehenge, and certain to stand forever," wrote Tom Buckley in the *New York Times.* It is remarkable that the record came not at the end of Aaron's extraordinary 23–year career as a professional baseball player, but two years before he retired as an active player.

When Aaron retired from baseball in 1976, he left the game with four career batting records, including those for runs batted in and total bases. In fact, he retired holding more records than any other player in the game. Aaron's record of 755 home runs in 23 years, however, placed him at the pinnacle of professional athletics. Aaron was elected to the Baseball Hall of Fame in 1982.

When Ted Turner bought the Atlanta Braves baseball team in 1976, he phoned Aaron in Milwaukee, where he was finishing his playing career with the Brewers. Turner thought that Aaron belonged with the Braves and asked him what job he wanted with the team. Aaron returned to the Braves organization to head the minor league farm system. He helped develop the talents of Tom Glavine, David Justice, and several other Braves star players. Not long after, Aaron was asked to manage the Braves. He wore several hats with the Braves organization throughout the early 1990s, serving as board member of both the Turner Broadcasting System and the Atlanta Braves, and as vice–president for business development with the *CNN Airport Network.*

Aaron made time for non–profit work throughout his professional career. An educational scholarship program bears his name, and the Hank Aaron Rookie League establishes baseball in low–income housing projects. He supports Big Brothers/Big Sisters, and is active with the Boy Scouts of America, having never forgotten how important such organizations were to him. "The Scouts put me on the right path," Aaron told the *Atlanta Journal/Constitution* for July 28, 1996. "One of my proudest memories is the day I got to blow the whistle and direct traffic in Mobile wearing my scout uniform. I still know the pledge."

Aaron's first marriage to Barbara Lucas ended in divorce in 1971. Four children, Gaile, Hank Jr., Dorinder, and Lary, were born to that union. He has been married to Billye Williams, widow of a former civil rights leader and former co–host of the *Today in Georgia* television show. He and Billye Aaron have one adopted child.

An intensely private person according to his wife, Aaron borders on reclusiveness. Nonetheless, his life outside of baseball has been as impressive as his professional athletic career. A 1976 recipient of the Spingarn Medal from the National Association for the Advancement of Colored People (NAACP), his autobiography, *I Had a Hammer,* made the *New York Times* best–seller list in 1991, and the 1995 TBS documentary, *Hank Aaron: Chasing the Dream,* was nominated for an academy award. A statue of Aaron at the Atlanta–Fulton County Stadium stands as testament to the slugger's prowess and popularity and will grace the new Turner Field when renovations to the 1996 Olympic Stadium are completed. When the decision was made not to name the Braves' new home park after the legendary batter, but instead after the team's owner, Mobile officials moved quickly to name their city's new 6,000 seat stadium—home of the minor league Mobile Bay Bears—in Aaron's honor. A 1994 poll of young people ranked Aaron the second most admired athlete in the United States behind only Michael Jordan.

Aaron spends considerable time working for improvement in Atlanta neighborhoods and communities. He is a highly respected sports figure who is often called on for comments at athletic events and who continues his push for racial parity in professional baseball.

Current address: c/o Atlanta Braves, 755 Hank Aaron Drive, Atlanta, GA 30302.

REFERENCES

''Aaron to Have Stadium Named for Him in Mobile.'' *Atlanta Journal/Constitution,* October 24, 1996.

Baldwin, Stan, and Jerry Jenkins, in collaboration with Hank Aaron. *Bad Henry.* Radnor, PA: Chilton Book Company, 1974.

''Touching All Bases: Bittersweet Memories of the Chase No Longer Trouble Henry Aaron.'' *Atlanta Journal/Constitution,* July 28, 1996.

Arthur C. Gunn

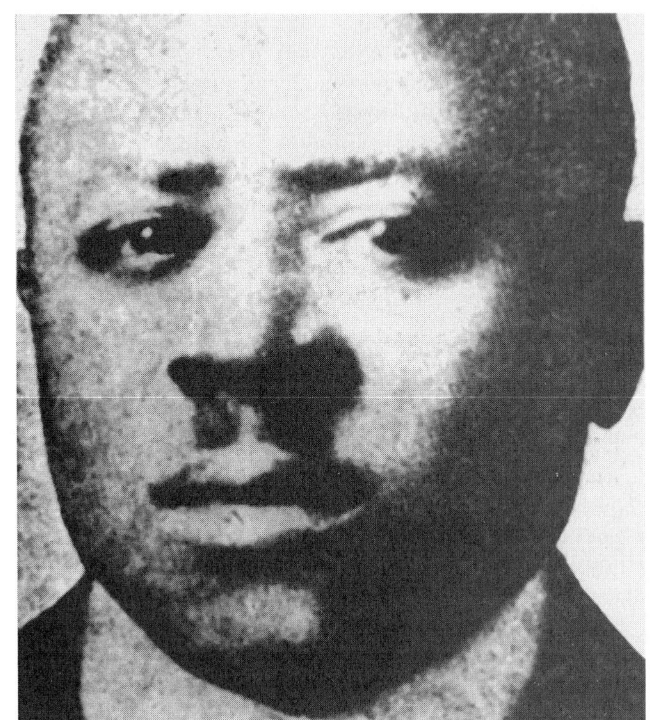

Robert Sengstacke Abbott

Robert Sengstacke Abbott
(1868–1940)
Newspaper publisher, editor

Robert Sengstacke Abbott founded one of the major black newspapers in the United States, the *Chicago Defender.* Helped by a massive migration to the North inspired by his own newspaper, he made a fortune. Although his central contribution was his newspaper, his exceptionally well–documented life throws light on many aspects of black life in the nineteenth century and the first half of the twentieth century. Through both the news and the editorial columns of the *Chicago Defender,* Abbott must be counted one of the major black spokesmen of his time.

Robert Abbott was born on November 24, 1868, in Frederica, on St. Simon's Island, Georgia, to Thomas and Flora Butler Abbott. Thomas Abbott, a man of unmixed African heritage, had been the butler on the Charles Stevens plantation. When the Stevenses fled to the mainland in the face of the imminent Union occupation of the island, Thomas Abbott successfully hid the family's property—from silver to furniture—and restored it all after the Civil War. At his death in 1869, he was one of the few African Americans to be buried in the Stevens family cemetery and therefore had a marked grave, unlike those in the slave burying ground.

At the war's end, Thomas left the island for Savannah. There he met and married Flora Butler (1847–1932), who worked as a hairdresser in the Savannah Theater. Flora Butler had been born in Savannah, on December 4, to African–born parents. Shortly after the marriage, Thomas and Flora Butler moved back to St. Simon's where Thomas ran a grocery store with little success. Shortly thereafter, Flora gave birth to Robert.

When Thomas Abbott died of tuberculosis in 1869, Flora Abbott moved back to Savannah with Robert to be close to her family because the Abbott family resented her status. They started legal proceedings to gain custody of Robert. John Hermann Henry Sengstacke (1848–1904) came to Flora's aid by hiring a white lawyer, who secured a restraining order. John Sengstacke married Flora Butler Abbott on July 26, 1874. They had seven children: John Jr., Alexander, Mary, Rebecca, Eliza, Susan, and Johnnah. The five–year–old Robert Abbott became known as Robert Sengstacke.

Eight–year–old Robert enjoyed the Woodville suburb of Savannah, where his stepfather's church and school were located. There he learned his stepfather's work ethic during an early summer job as errand boy in a grocery. As part of his training, his mother insisted he pay ten of the fifteen cents a week he earned at the grocery for his room and board. Later jobs included one as a printer's devil at a newspaper.

Learns His Trade

In the fall of 1886 Robert Sengstacke Abbott entered Beach Institute, an American Missionary School in Savannah, to prepare for college. As one of the two or three dark–skinned students, he suffered deeply from the color prejudices of his light–skinned fellows. Robert managed to persuade his stepfather to send him to Claflin University, then still a Methodist elementary school in Orangeburg, South Carolina. After six months' study there, Abbott decided to learn a trade and applied to Hampton Institute. While waiting for a place to become available, Abbott worked as an apprentice at the *Savannah Echo.* He was probably associated with his stepfather's preparations to put out a local paper, the *Woodville Times,* which began publication in November of 1889, the same month the 21–year–old Abbott entered Hampton Institute to learn the trade of printing.

At Hampton, Abbott still experienced difficulties due to color prejudice and also initially due to his own clumsy social behavior. The intervention of Hollis Burke Frissell, a white teacher and second head of Hampton, enabled Abbott to talk through some of his problems. As quoted by Ottley in *The Lonely Warrior,* Abbott later summarized Frissell as saying, "I should so prepare myself for the struggle ahead that in whatever field I should decide to dedicate my services, I should be able to point the light not only to my own people but to white people as well."

With his fine tenor voice, Abbott became the first first–year–student member of the Hampton Quartet. A classmate said that Abbott's dark skin influenced the choice since school officials preferred to send dark students on fund–raising missions. He completed his printing course in 1893 and his academic work in 1896, all at Hampton.

At the age of 28, Abbott still sought out a career. He returned to Woodville and took part–time jobs as printer and schoolteacher. After a failed romance, he left for Chicago in the fall of 1897 to enroll in the Kent College of Law (later Chicago–Kent).

Although Abbott had been known as Robert Sengstacke for more than 20 years, to his stepfather's sorrow he used the name Robert Sengstacke Abbott when he registered. On May 20, 1899, he graduated with a bachelor of law degree. He was the only African American in the class. Edward H. Morris, a prominent, fair–skinned black lawyer and politician, advised Abbott that his skin color would be a major impediment to law practice in Chicago, where black lawyers generally found law to be a part–time profession in the best of cases. After futile attempts to practice law in Gary, Indiana, and Topeka, Kansas, Abbott returned to Chicago, giving up all hope of practicing as an attorney. He never passed the Illinois bar examination.

Abbott turned to printing. Earlier he had secured a card from the printers' union, but there was a tacit understanding that he would be hired for only one day. At this point, however, black politician Louis B. Anderson forced a printing house doing city work to hire Abbott. Abbott had steady work doing the tedious job of setting railroad time tables and correcting any errors on his own time. After John H. H. Sengstacke died of nephritis on June 23, 1904, Abbott and his sister Rebecca planned to open a school on the premises of his stepfather's Pilgrim Academy. After proceeding so far as to advertise the school, Abbott suddenly changed his mind, and decided to stay in Chicago to launch a newspaper. This appeared to be an idea likely to fail since Chicago already had three marginally successful black newspapers.

Chicago Defender Appears

The first issue of the *Chicago Defender* appeared on May 5, 1905. Abbott printed, folded, and then distributed his paper himself. It was 1912 before the *Defender* acquired its first newsstand sales. Abbott canvassed every black gathering place in the community, selling his paper, soliciting advertising, and collecting news. His rounds, which he continued even after he could rely on others to distribute his papers, gave him great insight into the concerns of Chicago's black community. In spite of Abbott's hard work and personal sacrifice, the paper nearly closed down after a few months.

At this point, his landlady, Henrietta Plumer Lee, made a decisive intervention. She allowed him to use the dining room in her second–floor apartment at 3159 State Street as an office for the newspaper. The newspaper began to prosper, and eventually took over the whole building at the address that became its headquarters for 15 years.

In 1904 Lee nursed Abbott through an attack of double pneumonia. For four years, she accepted token payments on his rent and food. Lee was moved not only by maternal feelings, but she also shared Abbott's vision of a newspaper to champion black concerns. Henrietta Lee almost certainly saved the *Defender* from closing and helped it to become a major force in the black community. In 1918 Abbott bought her an eight–room brick house; when she moved in, he again followed as her lodger. Lee's daughter became a long–time employee, and her son became a stockholder in the Robert S. Abbott Publishing Company.

Robert Abbott's paper slowly grew until it had a press run of 1,000 copies. He then discovered a cause that contributed to growth. Great fires in Chicago had forced the red–light district into the unburnt black sections of town, and it stayed. In 1909 Abbott launched a campaign against vice in black neighborhoods. This proved a way of selling papers until reformers forced prostitution underground in 1912, depriving him of his best issue.

By 1908 Abbott reduced his overhead by taking the printing to a larger, white publishing house. Weekly costs ran about $13, but the paper remained essentially a one–man operation. Abbott could not even give himself a salary. Many people made unpaid contributions by reporting, collecting out–of–town news, and even writing editorials. Railroad workers collected printed materials left on the trains, which could be scanned for news of interest to blacks.

In 1910 the *Defender* experienced another lift when Abbott hired J. Hockley Smiley as managing editor. Smiley provided coherence to Abbott's racial vision and built up the paper by adopting some of the sensational tactics of yellow journalism. Under Abbott's supervision, Smiley oversaw a radical overhaul of the paper's format, which now included sensational banner headlines, often printed in red. If sensational news was lacking, Smiley was not above making up stories. He also innovated the black press by establishing theater, sports, editorial, and society departments. He followed Abbott's wishes in abolishing the use of the terms "Negro," "Afro–American," and "Black" in favor of "race," with an occasional use of "colored."

Financial irregularities would plague the *Defender*'s early history. Smiley died of pneumonia in 1915, suffering from neglect by Abbott according to a rival paper. By this time, however, Abbott attracted able associates even though most were unpaid. While he remained the paper's leader, he relied on a growing number of talented people. For example, Fay Young, long–time sports editor, began unpaid work for the paper in 1912 while also working as a dining–car waiter. In time, Abbott began paying salaries.

Defender Grows

In 1915 Abbott broke new ground for black newspapers by putting out an eight–column, eight–page, full–size paper. The format appeared in the first extra of the *Defender,* on November 14, announcing the death of Booker T. Washington. By this time, Abbott had begun to distance himself from Washington by urging blacks to leave the South to seek out better opportunities in the North. At the same time, however, Abbott moved no closer to the position of W. E. B. Du Bois, as the newspaper editor championed the hopes of the black masses rather than those of a talented tenth.

The *Defender*'s sensational, in–depth coverage of the Brownsville incident in Texas led to a nationwide, 20,000 copy increase in circulation. The *Defender* was launched on its career as a national newspaper. By 1920 the *Defender*'s circulation reached at least 230,000. More than two–thirds were sold outside of Chicago, with a tenth of the total going to New York City.

The *Defender* also drew attention from the authorities. Although Abbott was unfailingly patriotic in his editorial position, the Wilson administration disliked the paper's frank reporting of the armed forces' treatment of African Americans as second–class citizens. The *Defender* had launched its official campaign for blacks to move north—"The Great Northern Drive"—on May 15, 1917. In the South, the paper's support of migration and its frank reporting on racial conditions drew the hostility of state and local officials to the point that its distribution to eager black readers became clandestine in certain regions.

At the end of World War I the paper's circulation stabilized at approximately 180,000. Printing and costs posed major problems, especially since, unlike most newspapers, the *Defender* made most of its money from circulation rather than from advertising. On May 6, 1921, Flora Abbott Sengstacke pressed the button that put a high–speed rotary printing press in operation at 3435 Indiana Avenue, another first for black journalism. But, with the advanced technology of the press, there were no black printers able to run it. Abbott hired a union crew of whites. The arrangement worked with no problems until the Depression years, when the employment of whites and their union wages came under attack. The *Defender* replaced its white printers with blacks. The new plant also cut the printing costs by $1,000 a week. Abbott became known for the frugality of his salaries and other overhead. He also was becoming a very wealthy man.

As the paper's circulation grew, Abbott began to favor a policy of gradualism in race progress. Although coverage of lynchings and racial conflict continued, the space devoted to it declined in favor of a sharp increase in stories about crime. The coverage now included such topics as fashion, sports, arts, and blacks outside the United States. Abbott's continued push for integrating and upgrading African Americans in the workforce, eventually contributed to important gains in the police and fire departments.

Abbott himself was becoming an establishment figure. He received honorary degrees from universities such as Morris Brown and Wilberforce. He became president of the Hampton alumni association and a member of the board of trustees. On September 10, 1918, he married Helen Thornton Morrison, a fair–skinned widow some 30 years younger than himself. The Abbotts became patrons of such institutions as the Chicago Opera and began to entertain widely. The Abbotts toured Brazil in 1923, and Europe in 1929. The marriage was not happy, however, and it seems likely that Helen never loved him. Toward the end of the marriage he suddenly moved out of his house, charging her with infecting him with tuberculosis and hiring people to kill him. Helen Abbott obtained a divorce decree on June 26, 1933, which included $50,000, the house furnishings, the limousine, and lawyer's fees. On August 7, 1934, Abbott married Edna Denison, another very light–complexioned woman. She too appears not to have been moved by love.

Although his wives did not love him, Abbott had over 100 relatives to whom he was very generous. His German cousins—offspring of his father's sister—and the white descendants of the Stevens family profited from his affections. The Stevenses fell on hard times during the Depression, so Abbott provided help for several years. He paid special attention to John Herman Henry Sengstacke, the son of his half–brother Alexander. Abbott liked him so much that he educated and trained him to take over the *Defender.*

Soon after the 1923 trip to Brazil, Abbott once again had to deal with financial irregularities—this time inadequate bookkeeping. He promptly fired managing editor Phil Jones, and replaced him with Nathan K. Magill, his sister–in–law's husband. Unfortunately, Magill lacked Abbott's almost instinctive understanding of the *Defender*'s readers and supporters. Magill took an anti–union stand in the fight of railroad porters to unionize. Since the *Defender*'s distribution depended on the cooperation of porters, Abbott had to intervene to change the paper's position. In spite of his limitations, Magill was tight–fisted and aided the paper's financial success.

Defender Survives the Depression

Just one month before the stock market crash of 1929, Abbott launched the first well–financed attempt to publish a black magazine, *Abbott's Monthly.* The monthly initially succeeded, but in 1933 it fell victim to the massive black unemployment caused by the nation's dire economic situation. The *Defender* initially ran into problems, although it again showed a profit by the end of 1933. Due to more financial mishandling, Abbott fired Magill and took over running the paper himself. At this time he brought his nephew John H. H. Sengstacke into the organization. In rebuilding his staff, Abbott rehired a number of people Magill had released.

In the next three years, Abbott became very ill and was in the office for only 20 months. In 1933 he was found to have tuberculosis, the disease that had killed his birth father. In addition, he became so myopic that others had to read to him. At the end of his life he was almost permanently confined to bed. Abbott ultimately died of a combination of tuberculosis and Bright's disease on February 29, 1940. There was a large and elaborate funeral at Metropolitan Community Church followed by burial in Lincoln Cemetery.

Abbott was a shrewd businessman and a hard worker, but his success as a publisher is due in large part to his skill at discerning and expressing the needs and opinions of the black population. Abbott had the good fortune to have his beloved paper fall into the capable hands of his nephew, John H. H. Sengstacke, who was able to carry on Abbott's creation.

REFERENCES

Bontemps, Arna, and Jack Conroy. *Anyplace But Here.* New York: Hill and Wang, 1966.

"Death Comes During Sleep at Home." *Chicago Defender,* March 9, 1940.

Ingham, John N., and Lynne B. Feldman. *African–American Business Leaders.* Westport, CT: Greenwood Press, 1994.

Logan, Rayford W., and Michael R. Winston, eds. *Dictionary of American Negro Biography.* New York: Norton, 1982.

Ottley, Roi. *The Lonely Warrior.* Chicago: Henry Regnery, 1955.

Ovington, Mary White. *Portraits in Color.* New York: Viking Press, 1927.

Redding, Saunders. *The Lonesome Road.* Garden City, NY: Doubleday, 1958.

Spear, Allan H. *Black Chicago.* Chicago: University of Chicago Press, 1967.

"Thousands Mourn at Bier of Editor Abbott." *Chicago Defender,* March 9, 1940.

Who's Who in Colored America. 5th ed. Brooklyn, NY: Thomas Yenser, 1940.

COLLECTIONS

Robert S. Abbott's papers are in the *Chicago Defender* archives. The diary of his step–father, John H. H. Sengstacke, is in the possession of the Savannah Historical Society.

Robert L. Johns

Kareem Abdul–Jabbar

(1947–)

Basketball player, author

Kareem Abdul–Jabbar played basketball on championship teams at the University of California at Los Angeles and on professional teams in Milwaukee and Los Angeles from 1965 until he retired at the end of the 1984–85 season. He played in the National Basketball Association (NBA) All–Star game in 19 of his 20 seasons, received six Most Valuable Player awards, won five NBA championships, and retired as the highest scoring player of all time. Abdul–Jabbar combined exceptional athletic ability with high scholastic competence, interest in his fellow man, and devotion to his Muslim religion that sustained him on and off the basketball court.

Born Ferdinand Lewis Alcindor Jr. on April 16, 1947, in Harlem, New York, an only child, he legally adopted the name Kareem Abdul–Jabbar ("Generous Servant of Allah") after his conversion to Islam. His parents were from Trinidad. His father, Ferdinand Lewis Alcindor Sr. had a degree in classical musicology from the Juilliard School of Music but was unable to find employment in that field. He worked as a prison officer and policeman for the New York Transit Authority. Kareem's mother, Cora Alcindor, was a price checker in a department store.

Although the Alcindors were not affectionate in their relations with their son, they wanted the best for his educational, physical, and social development. Devout Catholics, they sent him to St. Jude's Elementary School for its curriculum and discipline. He learned to use his size and dexterity on the basketball court in the fourth grade, and eventually he developed the hook shot for which he became famous. He did well in his studies, and basketball became an important part of his existence. From St. Jude's, the young man went to Power Memorial Academy, an all–boys parochial high school in Manhattan in 1961.

Abdul–Jabbar was always an introspective person who enjoyed the company of school mates. He also took care to stay within the limits of conduct approved by his father. Gradually, he became more and more suspicious that people did not like him because of his size, race, politics, or religious preference. The civil rights movement escalated during his adolescence, and Abdul–Jabbar began to read about under–privileged people, especially African Americans. When a 1963 church bombing killed four African American girls, his anger over the incident caused him to withdraw further into a shell. He thought that his father and mother did not understand his grief. Luckily, at about the same time, Abdul–Jabbar discovered the value of jazz music to help release his frustrations.

Abdul–Jabbar used music, books, and basketball to fill his hours at home and at school. He was on Power's honor roll, debating team, and basketball team. Coach Donohue took

Kareem Abdul–Jabbar

him to Madison Square Garden to see Bill Russell and Wilt Chamberlain play, and groomed him for recognition on All–American and All–City teams. In one instance, Abdul–Jabbar resented Coach Donohue's use of the word ''nigger'' to goad him into performing his best. It took a lot of time and willpower for Abdul–Jabbar to put aside his hurt and questions about the coach's true feelings about him.

Abdul–Jabbar worked the summer before his senior year in the journalism workshop of the Harlem Youth Action Project. He wrote about its dance, drama, music, and community projects. He visited the Schomburg Center for Research in Black Culture and immersed himself in the music of W. C. Handy and the writings of Paul Laurence Dunbar, Langston Hughes, Countee Cullen, Richard Wright, and Ralph Ellison. This was his first exposure to a wealth of information about African Americans. It was also his first opportunity to participate in community action by writing about what the organization was doing in Harlem and about conditions of black people all over the country.

Collegiate Basketball

After high school, Abdul–Jabbar chose the University of California at Los Angeles (UCLA) with its advantages of an attractive campus in a sunny location and an apparent amiable association between black and white students. He liked the ample facilities and its winning basketball team, led by legendary coach John Wooden.

Abdul–Jabbar made few friends at UCLA since he concentrated on basketball and study. He started as an English major but changed to history when he saw that it was impossible to produce weekly papers for English classes while preparing for basketball competition. The change helped him give equal time to academics and to athletics. History turned out to be a fine choice for pursuit of the interests of his later life.

Abdul–Jabbar had to wait until his sophomore year at UCLA to play in league games and to work directly with Coach Wooden, whom he had honored for years from a distance. Abdul–Jabbar and the coach found an immediate mutual affection. With his classes going well and the basketball team defeating all opponents, Abdul–Jabbar's remaining problem was dealing with the ever–present press. He resented reporters who had no concept or feeling for his views as an African American who cared not only about basketball but also about the treatment of black people nationwide. Furthermore, he disliked the inevitability of his remarks being distorted or taken out of context for sensationalism. When he learned to completely ignore obnoxious media representatives or to respond tersely, he earned the reputation of an uncooperative, sullen, and ill–bred man.

During the summer after the 1966–67 national championship season at UCLA, Abdul–Jabbar worked for the New York City Housing Authority teaching basketball techniques to young people from housing projects all over the city. He gave the children a mixture of athletics and lessons in black pride. A year later he did the same in New York City's Bedford–Stuyvesant, Brownsville, and the East Bronx, passing on basketball skills, and instilling in young people a desire to remain in school and develop into good citizens.

Interest in Islam

Abdul–Jabbar knew that Catholicism was not the solution for him and that he needed to search for his own solutions. With the maturity of an upper–division college man, Abdul–Jabbar started to look for a more satisfying spiritual outlet. He took courses in African and black studies, read about the major religions of the world, and explored the Bible and the Qur'an. *The Autobiography of Malcolm X* prompted him to rethink his beliefs and attitudes about race, the goals of African Americans, and the role of religion in his life.

Abdul–Jabbar's in–depth analysis of Islam culminated with his acceptance of that religion in a mosque on 125th Street in New York City in the summer of 1968, and the taking of his new name. With the training of Haamas Abdul–Khaalis, a well–read Muslim, and a course in the Arabic language at Harvard University, Abdul–Jabbar refined his knowledge of Islam. Because of his friendship with Haamas, Abdul–Jabbar ultimately founded a center in New York for Haamas and other Muslims—a center that was shaken when a rival Muslim group violently took the lives of Haamas's three sons.

Abdul–Jabbar refused to participate in the 1968 Olympics in Mexico City. His vocal support of John Carlos and Tommie Smith's clenched fist ''Black power salute'' on the Olympic victory stand brought more mounds of hate mail to his door. He remained firm in his commitment, however, to voicing his opinions about the treatment of African Americans by the United States.

Before Abdul–Jabbar graduated from UCLA in 1969, his team had won three consecutive championships. Abdul–Jabbar had scored 2,325 points with an average of 26.4 points per game, and he was named All–American in each of his three years. From UCLA, Abdul–Jabbar joined the Milwaukee Bucks professional team where he was named Rookie of the Year. In six seasons with the Bucks, he averaged more than 30 points a game and won three Most Valuable Player (MVP) awards.

In 1975 Milwaukee traded him to the Los Angeles Lakers. Playing for the Lakers, Abdul–Jabbar won three more MVP awards in his first five years and more NBA championships. He retired after the 1989–90 season, having scored more points than any other player in the history of basketball. It came as no surprise, then, that in 1995 he was inducted into the Basketball Hall of Fame.

The greatest catastrophe for Abdul–Jabbar was the destruction of his home in 1983 by a fire that caused no personal injury, but consumed priceless treasures, including copies of the Qur'an and items important to his artistic, musical, and athletic loves. He turned to his religion for consolation and accepted the outpouring of gifts and good wishes from people who loved him.

Abdul–Jabbar, who married Janice (later Habiba) Brown in 1971, is the father of two sons, Kareem and Amir, and two daughters, Habiba and Sultana. He was divorced in 1973. Now free of the game he played since he was eight years old, his days are brightened by the closer relations with his parents that emerged before he left basketball, and he feels more comfortable with meeting people in social and business circumstances. As a player, he passed his knowledge of strategy to younger men on the team. In retirement, he has gone back to playgrounds in Harlem to interact with elementary and high school boys, to spur them to make the best of their mental and physical talents. In addition to his autobiography, Abdul–Jabbar has written a historical volume that was conceived during his attempt to help his son search for information to complete a black studies assignment. *Black Profiles in Courage,* stories about little–known contributors to African American history, was published in 1996 by William Morrow.

Since retiring from basketball as a professional player, Abdul–Jabbar has continued his involvement in the game by promoting an exhibition team's tour of Saudi Arabia in 1991, and by playing in a one–on–one game with another former basketball great, Julius ''Dr. J.'' Erving in 1992. Abdul–Jabbar has also been active in the motion picture industry, appearing in several movies. He had bit parts in several television shows and movies, including one about the old black baseball leagues. Through Cranbery Records, which he heads, he promotes the work of young jazz artists. President Bill Clinton honored Abdul–Jabbar in 1994 when the first National Sports Awards program was established, naming him, along with Arnold Palmer, Muhammad Ali, Wilma Rudolph, and Ted Williams, one of ''The Great Ones.''

Abdul–Jabbar's reputation as a dominant player in college and professional basketball can be balanced by his lesser–known contributions. Abdul–Jabbar is known for an awareness and concern about the history and present–day status of African Americans. As a scholar of world religions and the history of African Americans, he continues his relentless efforts to motivate African American boys and girls to excel and be proud of their heritage.

Current address: c/o Public Relations Department, Los Angeles Lakers, PO Box 10, Inglewood, CA 90306.

REFERENCES

Abdul–Jabbar, Kareem, with Peter Knobler. *Giant Steps.* Toronto: Bantam Books, 1983.

Contemporary Black Biography. Vol. 8. Detroit: Gale Research, 1995.

Dreifus, Claudia. ''Making History Off the Court.'' *New York Times Magazine* (13 October 1996): 17.

Salzman, Jack, David Lionel Smith, and Cornell West, eds. *Encyclopedia of African American Culture and History.* New York: Macmillan Reference Library USA/Simon and Schuster Macmillan, 1996.

Williams, Michael W., ed. *An African American Encyclopedia.* New York: Marshall Cavendish, 1993.

Dona L. Irvin

Alvin Ailey

(1931–1989)

Choreographer, dancer, dance company founder

A pioneer in modern dance, Alvin Ailey founded the racially–integrated and popular modern dance troupe, the Alvin Ailey Dance Theatre. His was the first black dance company sent abroad under the International Exchange Program in 1962, the first American modern dance company to perform in the Soviet Union since the 1920s, the first black modern dance company to perform at the Metropolitan Opera, and the first modern dance company sponsored by the U.S. government to tour the People's Republic of China since Sino–American relations were strengthened. *Revelations,* his signature dance piece, drew upon African American religious music he knew in his childhood. *Revelations* is also the title of his frank autobiography in which he spoke openly of his life, his search for identity, and his homosexuality.

Ailey was born in his grandfather Henry Ailey's home in Rogersville, near Waco, Texas, on January 5, 1931, the only child of Alvin, a laborer, and Lula E. Cliff Ailey. He was the

Alvin Ailey

thirteenth member of an overcrowded household where he lived with his grandfather, parents, aunt, eight cousins, and other family. Alvin Sr. left the home soon after his son was born, returned briefly when his son was about four years old, then deserted the family. Ailey admitted in *Revelations* that growing up as a fatherless child led to an inferiority complex that he never overcame. The two had no further contact until about 1975, when Ailey located his father and they had a cold, unproductive ten–minute telephone conversation.

Lula Ailey moved from town to town working as a housekeeper to support herself and her young son. Ailey was dismayed over her frequent absences. When he was seven years old he was baptized in a mudhole from which the church deacons had cleared water moccasins. Later he joined the Baptist Student Union. Sometime in his early years Ailey picked cotton. By the time he was 12–years old, the Aileys lived in Navasota, where his mother worked in a hospital. Despite the racism and poor economic conditions prevalent in Texas at the time, Ailey enjoyed the abundance of entertainment available to blacks, including Silas Green, a traveling vaudeville show from New Orleans, and such musicians as Big Boy Crudup, who often played for community gatherings. In May of 1941 his mother relocated to Los Angeles and left Ailey behind to complete the school year. He moved to Los Angeles in 1942.

Ailey graduated from George Washington Carver Junior High School and Thomas Jefferson High School, where he was practically an ''A'' student. He became an avid reader in high school, continuing into college. Having been introduced to Spanish when he lived in Texas, Ailey had an affinity for the language. By his high school years he was so fluent in the language that he was allowed to teach the class at times. Although Ailey danced around in the backyard of his house, sometimes imitating Gene Kelly and the Nicholas Brothers, and studied tap dancing from a private teacher, he had no intention of becoming a dancer. He watched Katherine Dunham perform Afro–Caribbean dances at the Biltmore in Los Angeles and was impressed with her performance, but still not inspired to become a dancer.

Carmen de Lavallade, a neighbor and schoolmate in Los Angeles, gave an extraordinary dance performance at a school assembly that impressed Ailey, and he fantasized about dancing with her. He dared not try, however, for fear of being labeled a ''sissy.'' Later, after watching Ailey perform gymnastics, de Lavallade encouraged him to study under Lester Horton, who had a studio in Hollywood. After several lessons with Horton, the instructor asked Ailey to rehearse with de Lavallade, his leading dancer. Ailey recalled in his autobiography that ''the combination was electric.'' After completing high school, Ailey studied under Horton on a regular basis, paying $12 a month for classes. De Lavallade continued to encourage, inspire, and support Ailey's development from the time of his initial study throughout his life. ''Dance, for me, would have been impossible without Carmen de Lavallade,'' he later wrote in his autobiography.

Ailey enrolled in the University of California, Los Angeles, where he was attracted to literature, especially Spanish literature, and found spiritual uplift in the works of Octavio Paz, Pablo Neruda, and other South American poets and writers. He also discovered black writers and poets John Oliver Killens, Richard Wright, Countee Cullen, and Langston Hughes. At night he continued his dance instruction at the Horton Theater with little time for study. The tug of war between Ailey's attraction to dance and his family's desire that he pursue a college education left him confused and prompted him to leave Los Angeles for San Francisco.

Becomes a Choreographer

Once there, Ailey borrowed $50 from a friend and lived in cheap hotels and later the YMCA. Hungry and jobless, he found employment as a clerk at the tax bureau. Later he enrolled at San Francisco State College, taking a job with the Greyhound Bus Company to pay the tuition, but soon found that he missed dancing. Ailey frequently attended the Halprin Lathrope Dance Studio where he met Marguerite Angelos, a tall, thin black woman, later known as Maya Angelou. They rehearsed routines on weekends while Ailey made his first attempts at choreography. After a successful dance performance at the Champagne Supper Club, Ailey and a group of dancers went to Los Angeles to do a benefit. A visit to the Horton Studio and a talk with Lester Horton convinced Ailey to give up school and become a dancer rather than a language teacher.

Returning to the Horton Company in 1953, Ailey watched his friend Carmen de Lavallade become a radiant star with the

Lester Horton Dance Theater. Horton created a *Bal Caribe,* or Caribbean Ball, that included a stylized suite of dances; *Tropic Trio,* performed on stage and in nightclubs; and an erotic suite of five dances called *Dedication to José Clemente Orozo.* In one segment of the suite, Horton made a dance for Ailey and de Lavallade, which was an instant success. Their fame spread and they were invited to dance at Circo's, a Los Angeles nightclub where big bands performed. While Ailey and de Lavallade danced on stage, Horton died of a heart attack.

Since the company was now without a choreographer and Ailey was well prepared for the job, he was appointed to the position. He choreographed a tribute to Horton, his first ballet, called *According to St. Francis,* relating Horton to St. Francis of Assisi. For his second ballet, *Mourning Morning,* Ailey said in his autobiography that he "took everything Tennessee Williams had ever written and put it onstage."

In 1954, Ailey and the Horton Company took the two ballets to the Jacob's Pillow Dance Festival in Massachusetts. After a brief return visit to Los Angeles, in December Ailey and de Lavallade accepted an invitation to join the cast for the Broadway musical *House of Flowers.* Ailey never returned to California and in 1958 the Horton organization closed permanently.

Now 24–years old, lively, athletic, and charismatic, Ailey felt that he needed more training. He studied the techniques of Louis Johnson, Pearl Reynolds, and Arthur Mitchell. He also enrolled in Martha Graham dance classes and studied ballet under Karel Shook. After *House of Flowers* Ailey danced in several musical shows, including *The Carefree Tree* (1955), and *Show Boat* (summer 1956), and Harry Belafonte asked him to choreograph *Sing, Man Sing,* in which Ailey also danced (1956). In 1957 he appeared as lead dancer in the last musical in which he would perform—*Jamaica,* starring Lena Horne. Ailey had acting parts in several plays, including *Call Me by My Rightful Name*; *Talking to You*; and *Tiger, Tiger, Burning Bright.* At the direct request of Langston Hughes, in 1963 he appeared in *Jericho Jim Crow.*

Founds Dance Company

Although there were many skilled black dancers in New York in 1958, they had no place to perform. Ailey formed a group that grew into the Alvin Ailey Dance Theatre to show the world their talent as well as his own. It became multiethnic in appearance, with 13 men and 11 women who were black, white, and Asian. Ailey and Ernest Parham decided to do a concert together and each assembled a group of extraordinary dancers, many from the cast of *Jamaica,* for Ailey's choreographed dance *Blues Suite,* based on the Dew Drop Inn from his Texas childhood. Geoffrey Holder designed the costumes. The group gave its first concert in 1958 at the Young Men's Hebrew Association (YMHA) on Ninety–second Street and Lexington Avenue. In his autobiography Ailey quoted *Dance* magazine, which called him "exceptional," adding that he "reminds one of a caged lion full of lashing power that he can contain or release at will."

Ailey then found a former hotel, later known as Clark Center for the Performing Arts, where his company could rehearse and Ailey could concentrate on his work. For a second performance he made a ballet called *Arietta Oubliée,* in which he and Carmen de Lavallade appeared; prepared a new version of *Blues Suite*; offered *Cinco Latinos*; and did one performance of *Arietta Oubliée,* in which he and de Lavallade appeared as well. *Dance News* for February 1959, quoted in *Current Biography,* commented on the enthusiastic audience and called "the stage world created by Alvin Ailey an altogether stimulating, exciting, beautiful, funny and original entertainment, meticulously presented."

Ailey's masterwork, *Revelations,* was his way of expressing the faith, hope, and joy of black choirs, congregations, and preachers he had heard singing spirituals and gospel songs in Texas, particularly "Wade in the Water" and "I've Been 'Buked, I Been Scorned." *Revelations,* a gigantic suite of spirituals, was well received at its premiere at the YMHA on January 31, 1960, but did not reach its current popularity until it was edited and performed at Jacob's Pillow in 1961. From then on *Revelations* evoked a tumultuous response from audiences wherever it was performed.

After successful performances at the Clark Center, the Boston Arts Festival, and elsewhere, in February of 1962 the Alvin Ailey company, with Carmen de Lavallade as codirector, began a 13–week tour of Australia, Southeast Asia, and Brazil sponsored by the U.S. Department of State under President John F. Kennedy's International Exchange Program. The group toured under the name de Lavallade–Ailey Dance Theater and its tour of Southeast Asia was a first for a black company. They won universal acclaim and, according to *Current Biography* they also "set the pattern for the extended international engagements that followed."

The group returned to the United States in the summer of 1962 and performed during the American Dance Festival in New London, Connecticut. Ailey and six other choreographers were invited to attend a workshop at the Watch Hill, Rhode Island, estate of Rebekah Harkness. Here he experimented with larger companies, trying out new ideas. Ailey taught workshops and dance techniques at Connecticut College in New London as well as at Watch Hill. His work at Watch Hill resulted in a ballet called *Feat of Ashes.*

Between 1962 and 1966 Ailey, his troupe, and the Clark Center continued to flourish. In 1962 the troupe gave a concert at the center to raise money for Martin Luther King and his work with civil rights. They continued to make their mark across America and Europe, moving into the ranks of established modern dance. In April of 1966 they were the only integrated company to perform at the World Festival of the Negro Arts in Dakar, Senegal. They began a 16–week tour of Europe in Spring 1967, playing at the Holland Festival in Amsterdam, the Venice Biennale of Contemporary Music, and elsewhere. They visited Europe in August 1967 and that fall made a State Department–sponsored tour of nine African nations. Ailey's choreography of a work based on the Seven Deadly Sins that he was commissioned to do for Swedish television won the Grand Prix Italia in Ravenna. The group returned home late in 1967 and began a three–month American tour. In 1970 the dancers had a triumphant Russian tour; the audience in Leningrad gave them a 23–minute standing ovation. They were the first American modern dance company to perform in the Soviet Union since the Isadore Duncan Dancers of the 1920s.

Ailey created ballets for such notable companies as the American Ballet Theatre, Royal Danish Ballet, London Festival Ballet, the Joffrey Ballet, Paris Opera Ballet, and La Scala Opera Ballet. He choreographed Samuel Barber's *Anthony and Cleopatra* for the 1966 opening of the Metropolitan Opera's inaugural season at the Lincoln Center for the Performing Arts and Leonard Bernstein's *Mass* for the 1971 opening of the Kennedy Center for the Performing Arts. He also worked with other leading artists, such as Duke Ellington, as choreographer for Ellington's show *My People,* which opened in Chicago around 1963.

In 1971 Ailey choreographed *Cry* especially for Judith Jamison, who made the 15–minute solo one of the troupe's most celebrated pieces, generally performing to sold–out houses. Created as a birthday present for Ailey's mother, the work was a hymn to celebrate the endurance, joys, victories, and sorrows of black women, especially mothers. In 1974 and 1976 he did a dance salute to Duke Ellington called *Ailey Celebrates Ellington.* In 1983 the Ailey troupe became the first black modern dance company to perform at the Metropolitan Opera, and in 1985 they were the first modern dance company sponsored by the U.S. government to tour the People's Republic of China since Sino–American relations were strengthened.

For about two decades Ailey had been a heavy drinker in addition to using drugs and diet pills. Now suffering from extreme mood swings, he turned to cocaine. The death of his good friend Joyce Trisler in October of 1979 compounded his despair, and Ailey became manic–depressive. His sexual behavior, which he kept low key earlier, was now "one many would find sordid," wrote Jennifer Dunning in *Alvin Ailey.* Altogether he led a dark and troubled life. In 1980 he was arrested for assault and later burglary. In July he was hospitalized in Westchester County's Bloomingdale Center for seven weeks; lithium was prescribed for his treatment. After his release, Ailey went back to choreography, this time producing *Phases,* with music by Max Roach. It was his last work. Ailey died in New York City on December 1, 1989, of dyscrasia, a blood disorder. His memorial service was held at the Cathedral of St. John the Divine, where thousands of friends came to honor the fallen giant. After his death in 1989, Jamison, his protégé, headed the Ailey dance troupe, which opened in 1991 under her direction.

Among the numerous awards Ailey received for his work were first prize at the International Dance Festival in Paris (1970), *Dance* Magazine Award (1975), the NAACP Spingarn Medal (1976), the Capezio Award (1979), the Samuel H. Scripps American Dance Festival Award (1987), and the Kennedy Center Award (1988). He received honorary degrees from a number of institutions, including Princeton University, Bard College, Adelphia University, and Cedar Crest College.

Reflecting on his life, Ailey admitted that he had been obsessed with dancing and his dance company. He found choreography mentally and physically draining, but discovered great joy in "creating something where before there was nothing." Ailey lamented that an overlay of racism continued in American dance companies, however, and black dancers were rarely seen in classical companies. He found European companies more open to black dancers than American companies. Considering such obstacles, Ailey's achievements are extraordinary.

Ailey, who stood 5–feet 11–inches tall, had a dancer's body that thickened later on to about 300 pounds. He also wore a small goatee and mustache. He was a sophisticated conversationalist and well read. Ailey was a world–class choreographer who combined African American soul with dance, giving modern dance mass appeal, but perhaps more importantly, Ailey used his art form to celebrate people and humanity and to give joy.

REFERENCES

Ailey, Alvin, with A. Peter Bailey. *Revelations: The Autobiography of Alvin Ailey.* New York: Carol Publishing Group, 1995.

"Alvin Ailey." *Negro Digest* 11 (October 1962): 46–47.

Contemporary Black Biography. Vol. 8. Detroit: Gale Research, 1995.

Current Biography Yearbook. New York: H. W. Wilson, 1968.

Dunning, Jennifer. *Alvin Ailey: A Life in Dance.* Reading, MA: Addison–Wesley Publishing Co., 1996.

"Obituary." *New York Times,* December 2, 1989.

Sherman, Ellen. "Bringing Dance Home Again." *Essence* 10 (February 1974): 34–35, 74.

COLLECTIONS

Alvin Ailey's collection of photographs, programs, and posters documenting the Alvin Ailey American Dance Theater are in the Schomburg Center for Research in Black Culture, New York City. The Alvin Ailey Archives are in the Dance Collection, New York Public Library for the Performing Arts at Lincoln Center.

Jessie Carney Smith

Alcindor, Lew.
See Abdul–Jabbar, Kareem.

Ira Aldridge
(1807–1867)
Actor

Ira Aldridge traveled to Europe and Russia, breaking racial barriers during a time when many of his black American contemporaries were enslaved. Defying the prevailing sentiment that the theater was the exclusive domain of white performers and patrons, Aldridge dared to claim acting as his livelihood. Known as the "African Roscius," Aldridge gained prominence as a Shakespearean tragedian in Europe, as well as Russia, and became one of the nineteenth century's most celebrated actors.

Ira Frederick Aldridge was born on July 24, 1807, in New York City, to Daniel Aldridge, who was a lay preacher and a straw vendor, and his wife, Lurona; Ira's parents were free blacks. Few additional details are known about Lurona Aldridge other than her birth in North Carolina and her death in 1818 while Ira was still a boy. Ira Aldridge attended New York City's African Free School, an institution for the education of free black American children, where he won oratory prizes. His father wanted him to become a minister. According to Ira's older brother Joshua, Ira ran away from home after his father remarried. He worked briefly on a ship that sailed South. When the ship docked in North Carolina, a slave dealer offered the captain $500 for young Aldridge. The captain, however, refused the offer and Aldridge later returned to New York.

While living in New York City, Ira Aldridge developed an intense interest in the theater. He obtained a backstage job at the Chatham Theatre, enabling him to watch actors as they performed. Aldridge gained acting experience with the African Theatre, an endeavor established by free black Americans in 1820. He made his acting debut as Rolla, a Peruvian character in the Richard Brinsley Sheridan adaptation of August von Kotzebue's *Pizarro.*

Leaves America in Pursuit of His Dream

Aldridge soon realized that his race would hinder his development as an actor in the United States because opportunities for a black American actor were rare. Marshall and Stock wrote in *Ira Aldridge* that "The only recourse for a serious, determined and aspiring young Negro actor was to emigrate," and Aldridge was determined to go to England. Two brothers, James and Henry Wallack, frequently acted in New York and they became acquainted with Aldridge. When James hired him as his personal valet, Aldridge was able to sail to Liverpool, England along with his employer. When 17–year–old Aldridge arrived in England in 1824, he distinguished himself as the first black American to establish himself as an actor in a foreign country. Henry wrote a letter of recommendation for Ira that he later presented to various Londoners.

Ira Aldridge

Aldridge attended the University of Glasgow for approximately 18 months. Fountain Peyton described his experiences there in *Glance at the Life of Frederick Aldridge*:

> The congenial surroundings, the obvious solicitude on the part of the faculty for his advancement and his eagerness to begin his life's work, encouraged him to greater endeavor. So creditable was the character of his work at this institution that Professor Sanford awarded him several premiums and a gold medal for excellence in Latin composition.

Having completed his course in Glasgow, he at once began the study of a repertoire for performance in England, Scotland, and Ireland.

Henry Wallack's letter of recommendation, along with Aldridge's talent and determination, led to his engagement at London's Royal Coburg Theatre, which was primarily a playhouse for melodrama. Aldridge debuted on October 10, 1825, in the lead role of Oroonoko in *The Revolt of Surinam, or A Slave's Revenge*; this play was an adaptation of Thomas Southerne's *Oroonoko.* The playbill for this performance described Aldridge as the "Tragedian of Colour, from the African Theatre, New York," yet his surname was listed as Keene, rather than Aldridge. In adopting the name of Keene, Aldridge observed a common theatrical practice of assuming a name that was identical or similar to that of a celebrity (in this case, Edmund Kean, who was regarded as one of the outstanding actors of his time) in order to attract attention. Aldridge resumed use of his birth name sometime between 1831 and 1833.

Aldridge continued in the role of Oroonoko for one week. Beginning the week of October 17, 1825, he performed in Thomas Morton's *The Ethiopian, or the Quadroon of the Mango Grove (The Slave)*. One week later, Aldridge appeared in *The Libertine Defeated or African Ingratitude*. During the weeks of October 31 and November 7, he was cast in H. M. Milner's *The Negro's Curse, or the Foulah Son,* which was written for him. The weeks of November 14 and 21 marked Aldridge's performance in J. H. Amherst's *The Death of Christophe, King of Hayti.*

During Aldridge's six-week engagement as a star attraction at the Royal Coburg, he earned admiration from his audiences, yet he was received less than favorably by most critics who generally attacked his lack of stage training and experience. One critic predicted that Aldridge, who was a mere lad of 18 at the time, would never find a theatrical career profitable. While it was true that Aldridge did lack training and experience, it was apparent that the London press did not welcome a black actor to the stage the way audiences did. Indeed the reaction of the press was, in general, one of indignation that Aldridge, a black man, audaciously attempted to set foot on the stage.

As a result of such hostile, negative criticism Aldridge's progress on the London stage was hindered, and he left the city in order to cultivate his craft. Aldridge retreated to the provinces where his popularity continued to grow as he toured. Aldridge's first provincial appearance was at Brighton's Theatre Royal where, in December 1825, he starred as Oroonoko and Othello, his first Shakespearean character. Aldridge's portrayal of Oroonoko was considered a strong performance while his portrayal of the Shakespearean protagonist was viewed as a weak performance. In the introduction to *Ira Aldridge,* Marshall and Stock wrote that, "The initial acceptance by provincial audiences gave Aldridge the seasoning needed before he would once again face London audiences and critics." Aldridge toured the provinces, including Halifax, Manchester, Newcastle, Edinburgh, Lancaster, Sunderland, and Liverpool, for seven years. His basic repertoire of *Oroonoko, The Slave,* and *Othello* was expanded to include Gregory Lewis's *The Castle Spectre,* Edward Young's *The Revenge,* and Issac Bickerstaff's *The Padlock.* Bickerstaff's work was a vehicle for two different types of expression for Aldridge: the role of Mungo allowed him to showcase for the first time his "fine singing voice" and to develop the character of a naive slave into a slave rebel.

Herbert and Stock called Aldridge's Liverpool appearance significant because Liverpool was:

> the greatest centre of the slave trade in the United Kingdom, where only three years before he had landed as an unknown, penniless stranger. One can imagine the feelings of the pro–slavery elements at the presumption of this Negro to appear in anti–slavery plays like *Oroonoko, The Revenge* and *The Padlock,* and furthermore to see a well–known star like Vandenhoff playing his Iago and a white woman, Miss F. H. Kelly, playing his Desdemona! Such a leap in so short a time was indeed something unparalleled in theatre history, as well as a unique challenge to racial superiority.

Indeed Aldridge, who continued to feel racism's sting throughout his career, used his talent and money to support the abolitionists. It was not uncommon for him, at the close of an evening's performance, to play a guitar and sing an anti–slavery song. In 1829, on the final nights of his engagements, Aldridge began delivering farewell addresses that focused on slavery's injustices and hope for the freedom of the enslaved. In 1832 the 25–year–old's farewell address was distributed to the audience; it was his poetic attempt entitled "William Tell, the Swiss Patriot." Cited by Marshall and Stock, among its lines are: "I risk my all upon thy power– / Life—son—yea, country, too; / To free my brethren, fetter'd slaves, / From sinking in inglorious graves." Aldridge, who reportedly asserted frequently that he could never be happy as long as one black person was enslaved, contributed significant amounts of money to the abolitionist movement and, from 1830 to 1861, to the Negro State Conventions.

One of his most memorable deeds involved the Wilson family, five slaves who escaped from Baltimore to New York; however, each family member was captured, arrested and put up for sale. When Aldridge learned of their fate, he purchased their freedom. William J. Simmons wrote in *Men of Mark*: "In all his triumphs he never lost any interest in the condition of his race."

After Liverpool, Aldridge continued to tour the provinces. He appeared in Norwich, Yarmouth, Bury, Hull, Richmond, and Belfast. In Belfast, he starred with Charles Kean, Edward's son. Aldridge was Othello to Kean's Iago; they also appeared together with Aldridge playing Aboan to Kean's Oroonoko.

Aldridge's acting style was described as realistic without ranting, exaggeration, or gimmicks. He was known for his power to captivate audiences. Having exhausted the limited number of black roles, Aldridge began playing nonblack parts. Whites had been portraying black characters; now Aldridge, donning wigs and white make–up, reversed the theatrical practice. His first white role before foreign audiences was Rolla, the same character he played years earlier at New York's African Theatre. His first white European role, performed in August 1830, was Captain Dirk Hatteraick in Daniel Terry's adaptation of Sir Walter Scott's novel, *Guy Mannering*; his second white European role, performed in May 1831, was Bertram in R. C. Maturin's *Bertram, or the Castle of St. Aldobrand.* Additional plays added to Aldridge's repertoire were *The Merchant of Venice*; *The Brigand, or Alessandro Massaroni*; *Obi, or Three–fingered Jack*; *The African's Vengeance*; *Paul and Virginia*; *The Siberian Exile*; *The Coronation Day of William IV*; *Valentine and Orson*; *Rob Roy*; *The Galley Slaves*; *Macbeth*; *The Cannibal King*; *Father and Son, or the Rock of La Charbonniere*; *Laugh While You Can*; *Banks of the Hudson, or the Congress Trooper*; *William Tell*; *The French Pirate*; and *Frankenstein, or the Man and Monster.* During this period, he enjoyed considerable success in Hull. Aldridge played at least 16 roles at the Royal

Aldelphi, and six months later in March 1832, after appearances in Dublin and Bath, he returned to Hull, where over seven weeks he appeared at the Aldelphi and the Royal Clarence.

The suave and determined Aldridge continued to battle racism. Dublin's Theatre Royal was an important house, and he was repeatedly denied the opportunity to perform there. Aldridge traveled there and met John William Calcraft, the theater's manager who had previously stated that Aldridge's acting at the Royal would be "absurd." However, after their meeting, Aldridge starred at the theater in December 1831, where Edmund Kean saw him perform. Kean praised Aldridge's "wondrous versatility" in a letter of recommendation.

Covent Garden Engagement a Career Milestone

On March 25, 1833, Kean was on stage at London's Covent Garden Theatre playing Othello to his son's Iago when he collapsed and later died. It was Aldridge's dream to appear at Covent Garden, and two weeks after Kean's death, he had the opportunity. At 26 and with only eight years acting experience, according to Marshall and Stock, he replaced England's most respected tragedian in his signature role:

> with characteristic courage, determination and dignity, Aldridge steps on to the stage of this great theatre, taking up the challenge. . . .
>
> Those two days, 10th and 12th April 1833, will for ever be red–letter days in the history of world theatre and human progress, for in those days a lone Negro from an enslaved people challenged the great white actors in the very heart of their Empire, in their own Theatre Royal, Covent Garden, in one of the greatest roles conceived by Shakespeare.

Aldridge's performance as Othello at the Covent Garden marked his return to the London stage after a seven–year tour of the provinces. After his 1833 London engagement, Aldridge continued to tour the provinces for the next 19 years. Among the additions to his repertoire were *The Black Doctor–A Romantic Drama in Four Acts,* an Aldridge adaptation of Auguste Anicet–Bourgeois and Paul Dumanoir's *Le Docteur Noir* as well as Shakespeare's *Richard III* and *Titus Andronicus,* a work that had not been staged in over a century. After his provincial tour, Aldridge appeared at London's Brittannia Theatre and the Royal Shakespeare Theatre in Stratford–upon–Avon.

Begins First Continental Tour

On July 14, 1852, Aldridge left England and began his first tour of the Continent; his travels included Cologne, Frankfurt–on–Main, Basel Leipzig, Vienna, Berlin and other cities in the German Federation, and Prague, Brunn, Budapest, Munich, and Poland. During this successful tour, the plays were frequently performed in the audiences' languages with the exception of Aldridge's roles. In *Dictionary of American Negro Biography,* it is said that "He was acclaimed for his acting in England, but especially on the continent was he accorded unqualified success."

Aldridge returned to London in the spring of 1855. For the next three years, he continued to perform in English theaters. A highlight of those years was his journey to Stockholm where he appeared at the Theatre Royal. In 1858 Aldridge again toured the Continent briefly before returning to London later that year, where he appeared at the Lyceum Theatre. Aldridge, who had performed in many English East–End theaters as well as most of Europe's royal theaters, was finally accepted at a principal West–End theater. His interpretation of Othello finally brought him critical acclaim from the London press that denigrated him more than 30 years while audiences enthusiastically applauded him. At last the entire London metropolis hailed Aldridge's talents.

Tours Russia

In November of 1858 Aldridge traveled to Russia for the first time. While it has yet to be determined if Aldridge ever starred as Hamlet, he had added King Lear, another Shakespearean character, to his repertoire by the time of his arrival. Later during 1861–66, Aldridge made several additional, extensive, and successful tours of Russia and its provinces. Indeed, during the final years of his life, Aldridge primarily toured in Russia and the Continent, adding Paris to his itinerary, with occasional returns to England. Aldridge was the first actor to perform in Serbia and Croatia and to perform Shakespeare in the Russian provinces. He arrived in Lodz, Poland, in 1867, and although in ill health, he began rehearsals only to have them discontinued and the opening performance postponed after his condition deteriorated. Aldridge died on August 7 and was buried two days later in Lodz's Evangelical Cemetery. In 1890 a tombstone with a cross was erected on his gravesite, and until at least 1958, the grave was tended by members of the Society of Polish Artists of Film and Theatre.

Aldridge was survived by his wife, the former Amanda Pauline von Brandt of Sweden and four children: Ira Daniel, Luranah, Ira Frederick, and Amanda. Aldridge married von Brandt in 1865, one year after the death of his first wife, the former Margaret Gill from England and three years after he applied for and was granted British citizenship. Among his property were Luranah Villa, the family home on Hamlet Road in Upper Norwood, as well as other homes on Hamlet Road. Aldridge considered American acting engagements as early as 1834 and in 1867, the year of his death, he was planning to travel to the United States, but he never returned to the country of his birth.

Aldridge received many honors and awards during his lifetime, including a commission in the Army of Haiti in the Seventeenth Regiment of the Grenadiers (1827); membership in the Prussian Academy of Arts and Sciences and receipt of the Prussian Gold Medal of the First Class for the Academy, (1853); receipt of Switzerland's White Cross (1854); membership in the Imperial and Archducal Institution of Hungary's Our Lady of the Manger (1856); knighthood in the Royal Saxon Ernestinischen House Order and receipt of the Verdienst Medal of the Order in Gold (1858); receipt of the Imperial

Jubilee de Tolstoy Medal (1858); and membership in the National Dramatic Conservatoire of Hungary (1858). Aldridge lectured on the drama of Shakespeare, Schiller, and Goethe at a meeting of the Conservatoire.

The Ira Aldridge Memorial Chair is located in the Shakespeare Memorial Theatre at Stratford–upon–Avon. In 1928 writer James Weldon Johnson spearheaded a successful effort by black Americans who raised $1,000 for the chair's endowment. There are additional black American tributes to Aldridge including the Ira Aldridge Theatre at Howard University, in Washington, D.C., and the Ira Aldridge Players at Morgan State University, in Baltimore, Maryland.

Ira Frederick Aldridge, a theatrical star and black American luminary, remains an inspiration to contemporary thespians.

REFERENCES

Johnson, James Weldon. *Black Manhattan.* New York: Knopf, 1940.

Kranz, Rachel C. *The Biographical Dictionary of Black Americans.* New York: Facts on File, 1992.

Logan, Rayford W., and Michael R. Winston, eds. *Dictionary of American Negro Biography.* New York: Norton, 1982.

Marshall, Herbert, and Mildred Stock. *Ira Aldridge: The Negro Tragedian.* 1958. Reprint, Washington: Howard University Press, 1993.

Peyton, Fountain. *A Glance at the Life of Ira Frederick Aldridge.* Washington, DC: R. L. Pendleton, 1917.

Simmons, William J. *Men of Mark.* 1887. Reprint, Chicago: Johnson Publishing Co., 1970.

Linda M. Carter

Clifford L. Alexander Jr.

(1933–)

Lawyer, politician, humanitarian

Clifford L. Alexander Jr. served four successive U.S. Presidents—John F. Kennedy, Lyndon B. Johnson, Richard Nixon, and Jimmy Carter—before he was 44–years old. A key African American aide in the Lyndon B. Johnson administration, Alexander influenced important decisions relative to the Civil Rights Act of 1964, the Voting Rights Act of 1965, and the appointment of blacks to strategic positions. He was the first African American to serve as Secretary of the Army. Recognized for his leadership ability as a young man, Alexander was elected the first African American student body president at Harvard University. Through many of his key administrative appointments, he played major roles in combating racial discrimination at various levels of government and provided equal access to jobs and upward mobility on jobs for minorities.

Clifford Leopold Alexander Jr. was born September 3, 1933, in New York City to Clifford Leopold Sr. and Edith McAllister Alexander. His father was a native of Jamaica and became a business manager of the Harlem Young Men's Christian Association (YMCA), apartment building manager, and bank manager. His mother was from Yonkers, New York, and began work in a real estate firm, later becoming head of the New York City welfare department. Still later she was the first black woman elected to the Democratic party's electoral college and was a staunch fighter against racial discrimination. Both parents were role models for Clifford Jr. through their successful careers. An only child, Alexander grew up in New York City, attended The Ethical Cultural School, and graduated from Fieldston School. He enrolled in Harvard University, where he later became its first African American student body president. At Harvard he met McGeorge Bundy, dean of the faculty of arts and sciences, who later became a key player in his career. After graduating cum laude from Harvard in 1955, he enrolled in the Yale University Law School and finished in 1958.

The Road to Washington

A variety of job experiences led Alexander to Washington, D.C., and to the White House. He worked for United Mutual Life Insurance Company in 1955, heading the complaints division. Serving in the army from 1958 to 1959, he later became assistant district attorney in New York County. He was executive director of Manhattanville Hamilton–Grange Neighborhood Conservation District of New York City beginning 1961 and executive director of HARYLOU (Harlem Youth Opportunities Unlimited) from 1962 to 1963. He worked with the Manhattanville Hamilton–Grange project to improve housing conditions for tenants, enforcing owner responsibilities. Landlords corrected over 3,000 violations within nine months during Alexander's administration. The Harlem youth program was designed to improve conditions and opportunities for inner city youth in the Harlem district. Politics entered into the program when Congressman Adam Clayton Powell Jr. wanted the program merged with a similar one also in Harlem. Educator Kenneth Clark, however, fought the merger; Alexander resigned his position.

Becomes Presidential Appointee

In 1963 Alexander was summoned to Washington by Louis Martin who was working for the Democratic National Committee as deputy chairman and was searching for talented African Americans to work in the John F. Kennedy administration. Alexander worked for the National Security Council from 1963 to 1964. There he reported to McGeorge Bundy, by then a presidential assistant. Alexander was appointed in 1964

Clifford L. Alexander Jr.

as deputy special assistant to President Lyndon B. Johnson. In August 1965 he moved to the position of associate special counsel to President Johnson and in 1966 became deputy special counsel.

In this position, Alexander recalled, in an article he wrote for *American Visions,* the agony and happiness over an assignment by President Johnson concerning the Voting Rights Act:

> The story had been ''leaked'' by me to a reporter with instructions that it be embargoed until that evening. But the embargo had been violated. In no uncertain terms, the president told me that the Voting Rights Act of 1965 which we had worked so hard to achieve, was probably going to be lost because that news story had appeared prematurely and Congress would therefore react negatively.

Alexander was devastated. His career was tied to the enhancement of rights for black people, and the premature release of the story might have meant there would be no Voting Rights Act at all. ''Johnson certainly knew how to make you feel fully responsible for what he perceived to be your negligence,'' he added. But all was not lost. He wrote, ''Later that evening, I made a presentation to several members of Congress with Johnson present. On that occasion, the president publicly lauded me as one of his brightest and most trusted aides.''

Alexander's influence led to the appointment of African Americans to a variety of positions, such as judges, subcabinet posts, and commissioners. During his tenure as associate special counsel, the list of a variety of African American leaders invited to attend social events at the White House was increased. In addition, the president had conferences with African Americans regarding their issues and concerns as American citizens in a democratic country.

Alexander had become successful in the civil rights arena and was appointed chairman of the Equal Employment Opportunities Commission (EEOC). During his tenure as chairman, he directed investigations for job discrimination in various industries, such as textiles, utilities, labor unions, and movies. The EEOC assisted around 70,000 people during Alexander's administration, as compared to 5,000 during the previous administration. Alexander retained that position during the Nixon administration until Senator Everett Dirksen, majority leader, accused him of harassing employers about job discrimination. Alexander resigned his position in April of 1969.

Alexander returned to the practice of law, working in the law firm of Arnold and Porter until 1976, when he joined another law firm, later known as Verner, Liipfert, Bernhard, McPherson and Alexander in Washington, D.C.

In 1977 Alexander was appointed the first African American Secretary of the Army, after the election of Jimmy Carter as president. During his tenure as secretary, he faced such problems as poorly trained minority troops and racism in the army. Alexander was responsible for 1.9 million people and a budget of $34 billion. In an interview for *Black Enterprise,* when asked about his accomplishments in this position, he commented that he wanted to increase ''the emphasis that is placed on people in the Army—recognizing their needs and stressing their importance.'' *Black Enterprise* recognized Alexander's effort to combat racism in the army in the areas of promotions, criminal justice, and social life.

After serving as Secretary of the Army, Alexander opened his corporate consulting firm, Alexander and Associates, in Washington, D.C. He married Adele Logan of New York City on July 11, 1959, and they have had two children, Elizabeth and Mark Clifford. The Alexanders had attended the Fieldston School at the same time. The tall, olive complexioned Alexander was an outstanding basketball player during his college days at Harvard University and even considered professional basketball as a career. He continues to play basketball as a pastime. Between many political appointments, he practiced law with various firms. While working for Arnold & Porter law firm, he persuaded the lawyers to hire young graduates of Howard University Law School. Between 1971 and 1974, he hosted a television program, *Cliff Alexander: Black on White,* on station WMAL–TV in Washington, D.C. Alexander made an unsuccessful bid to become mayor of the District of Columbia in 1974.

Alexander has served on numerous boards including those of Radcliffe College, Atlanta University, Harvard University, and TLC Beatrice International Holdings. He has received many awards, including: the 1955 Ames Award from Harvard University; the Kansas City Honorary Citizen Award in 1965; the Washington Bar Association Award in 1969; the Frederick Douglass Award in 1970; the Outstanding Civilian Award, Department of the Army in 1980; and the Distinguished Public Service Award, Department of the Defense in 1981.

Clifford Alexander is a humanitarian who combats racism. Alexander and Associates has been active in serving as a consultant to major league baseball to improve hiring practices of minorities. His concern for people and their conditions is reflected at each level of responsibility he assumed throughout his successful professional career.

Current address: Alexander and Associates, Inc., 400 C Street NE, Washington, DC 20002.

REFERENCES

Alexander, Clifford L. ''Black Memoir of the White House.'' *American Visions* 10 (February, 1995): 42–43.

''Board of Directors of TLC Beatrice International adds Judge William Webster, former FBI /CIA Director, and Clifford Alexander, former Army Secretary, to its number.'' *Business Wire.* (May 30, 1996).

Christmas, Walter. *Negroes In Public Affairs and Government.* New York: Educational Heritage, 1966.

Current Biography Yearbook. New York: H. W. Wilson, 1977.

Ploski, Harry A. *Reference Library of Black America.* New York: Afro–American Press, 1970.

''Secretary of the Army Man in the Hot Seat.'' *Black Enterprise* 10 (July 1980): 24.

Who's Who among African Americans, 1996–97. 9th ed. Detroit: Gale Research, 1996.

Barbara Williams Jenkins

Muhammad Ali

(1942–)

Boxer, civil rights activist, diplomat

Undoubtedly one of the most internationally known athletes of all time, Muhammad Ali serves as a role model for youth and athletes throughout the world. Ali has won the world heavyweight boxing title an unprecedented three times, 1964–67, 1974–1978, and 1978–79. ''The People's Champion,'' as he has been called, also has endeared himself to many who have seen or heard of him through his flamboyant manner and his humanitarian work. In 1964, when Ali boldly challenged the U.S. government by his refusal to serve in the military, he became a global hero to many who also opposed the Vietnam War.

Ali was born Cassius Marcellus Clay Jr. on January 17, 1942, in Louisville, Kentucky, to Cassius Marcellus and Odessa Grady Clay. He grew up in an impoverished family, with his brother Rudolph Valentino (now Rahaman Ali). By trade, Ali's father was a sign painter, who occasionally painted murals on church walls. According to Ali, the elder Clay was also a talented dancer, actor, and singer. Ali's mother, whom he affectionately calls ''Bird,'' worked as a domestic in the homes of wealthy whites.

Growing up, Ali wore ragged clothing, often with patches, and shoes with cardboard inserts that covered holes in the soles. As a youngster, Ali and his family attended the Mount Zion Baptist Church. When he was 12 years old, he received a new bicycle for Christmas, but through his carelessness, the bicycle was stolen. Ali went to a gym to report the theft of his bicycle to a police officer and was overwhelmed by the sight of boxing and the odors of the gym. The police officer, Joe Martin, happened to be the boxing trainer at the Columbia Gym. Ali enrolled in the boxing program, and Martin became his first trainer. Soon Ali discovered the talents of Fred Stoner, a black man who trained young boxers at the Grace Community Center. Stoner taught Ali the fundamentals of the game, including style and how to increase stamina. Ali trained six days a week for six hours each day, two hours with Martin and four hours with Stoner. Rather than ride the school bus, as a teenager Ali ran to school each day to work on his wind. He graduated from DuValle Junior High School and Central High School in Louisville. Ali admitted he was more interested in boxing than school and therefore did not perform at a high level as a student.

Becomes Boxing Champion

During the 1950s young Ali regularly appeared on the weekly Louisville television boxing program *Tomorrow's Champions.* He was paid four dollars for each televised match. He won six Golden Gloves tournaments in Kentucky in three weight classes—lightweight, welterweight, and heavyweight. In 1959 and again in 1960 Ali won both the Light Heavyweight National Golden Gloves and the National Amateur Athletic Union (AAU) tournaments. As the National AAU boxing champion, he was invited to the Olympic trials, and he won the position as the light heavyweight entry for the United States. In the 1960 Olympics, Ali won the gold medal by defeating "Ziggy" Pietrzykowski of Poland.

Ali predicted that he would win the heavyweight championship by the time he was 21. After the Olympics, Ali signed a lucrative contract with ten Louisville millionaires, the Louisville Sponsoring Group, who backed his budding career. The Group hired Archie Moore, a retired fighter, to serve as Ali's trainer. However, Ali hired Angelo Dundee as his trainer and manager. On October 29, 1960, in his hometown of Louisville, Ali had his first professional fight. He easily defeated Tunney Hunsaker for the $2,000 purse. Over the next four years Ali had a total of 19 professional fights, all of which he won.

In 1964 at the age of 22, Ali became the heavyweight champion by defeating Sonny Liston in Miami. During the same year, Ali announced that he had become a member of the Muslim faith and had renounced his "slave name," Cassius Clay, for the Islamic name Muhammad Ali. Muhammad means "worthy of all praises," and Ali means "most high." As the champion, Ali taunted his opponents by predicting the rounds in which he would defeat them, boasted loudly, and recited poems about his fighting abilities. Ali coined such phrases as "float like a butterfly, sting like a bee" to describe his boxing style. He also bragged about his natural good looks and abilities with statements such as "I'm pretty" and "I'm the greatest fighter of all times." Ali knew that the more publicity he achieved for each fight the higher the final box office count. His braggadocio and flippant demeanor earned him the nickname "the Louisville Lip." During the next three years, Ali defended his title nine times, including a rematch with Sonny Liston.

In 1966, when his contract with the Louisville group expired, he signed with Herbert Muhammad, the son of Elijah Muhammad, who founded the Black Muslim movement. Under Muhammad's management, Ali earned more money in six fights than he had earned in six years under the Louisville Sponsoring Group.

Defies Military Draft

In April 28, 1967, Muhammad Ali took a courageous stand against the U.S. government when he refused induction in the U.S. Army on religious grounds. Ali had earlier explained his position on the Vietnam War in a 1966 poem published in *The Greatest*:

> Keep asking me, no matter how long
> On the war in Vietnam, I sing this song
> I ain't got no quarrel with those Vietcong.

Ali's decision brought a variety of responses from people across the country. Politicians and some veterans wanted him imprisoned, and some people sent death threats. Thousands of people, however, supported his refusal to be drafted. Ali's action marked the beginning of a new era in which black athletes challenged the system and refused to be exploited. The World Boxing Association (WBA) stripped him of his boxing title, and the New York State Athletic Commission, as well as every other state boxing commission, banned him from fighting. Ali also was forbidden to travel abroad. The WBA then awarded Joe Frazier the title. Ali was later convicted, sentenced to five years in prison for draft evasion, and fined $10,000.

Although for the next three and one–half years Ali was prohibited from boxing, he stood steadfast in his religious beliefs. During the time he was barred from boxing, Ali earned a living by speaking on college campuses about civil rights and justice. Ali had a worldwide following, including college students, peace movement activists, fellow blacks, and Third World peoples.

Finally in June of 1970 the U.S. Supreme Court reversed Ali's draft–dodging conviction on a technicality. Ali said the Supreme Court decision was the biggest victory of his life. In September of that same year the NAACP also won its suit in the New York federal court against the New York State Athletic Commission, proving that the denial of his boxing license violated Ali's constitutional rights.

Ali returned to the ring. His first fight after the Supreme Court decision was against Jerry Quarry in November of 1970 in Atlanta. Ali won by knocking out Quarry in the third round. After the reinstatement of his New York license, Ali fought Joe Frazier, still the reigning heavyweight champion. In New York in March of 1971. Ali lost this fight—his first defeat as a professional—and Frazier retained the title. By the end of his career, Ali had fought Joe Frazier twice more. These three bouts have been one of the most widely discussed series in the sport because of their intensity and duration.

Muhammad Ali with the U.S. Olympic basketball team, 1996.

Regains Title

In 1974 Ali avenged his loss to Frazier with a unanimous decision victory. This retaliation did not earn Ali the title, however, since newcomer George Foreman had dethroned Frazier as the champion. Ali arranged to fight for the title against Foreman in Kinshasa, Zaire, a bout billed as the "Rumble in the Jungle." Because Foreman was younger, stronger, and larger—as well as being considered the hardest hitter in boxing—he was favored to win. As documented in the Academy Award–winning film *When We Were Kings,* Ali employed a tactic called the "rope–a–dope" in which he rested against the ropes while Foreman pummeled him with little success for almost eight rounds. Foreman expended energy while Ali bided his time. When Ali finally came off the ropes, he landed a quick succession of combinations, including a stiff right that sent the champ to the canvas where he was counted out seconds before the end of the round. Ali had regained the title.

In September of 1975, for the third time, Ali fought the unrelenting Joe Frazier. The fight was billed as the "Thrilla in Manila" and Ali won when Frazier was unable to answer the bell for the final round. Although Ali lost a title defense early in 1978 to Leon Spinks, he later defeated Spinks in a rematch to win his title for the third time. On June 26, 1979, at the age of 37, Ali retired as champion with a professional record of 59 victories and three defeats.

Because of his lavish lifestyle, Ali found himself in need of money. In 1980 he returned to the ring to fight Larry Holmes for the World Boxing Council (WBC) title and a guaranteed purse of $8 million. When Ali was unable to answer the bell for the eleventh round, Holmes won with a technical knockout. One year later Ali boxed professionally for the last time, when he fought Trevor Berbick. One month before his fortieth birthday, Ali was defeated for the fifth time in his professional career.

In 1975 Ali was co–author of his autobiography, *The Greatest: My Own Story.* Playing himself, Ali starred in the film adaptation, *The Greatest,* in 1976. He also appeared in the 1979 NBC television movie, *Freedom Road.* Muhammad Ali's life has been the subject of countless books, including many works written specifically for children and young adults. The film *When We Were Kings* was released in 1996 and chronicles the 1974 "Rumble in the Jungle."

In 1977 Ali's doctor advised him to quit boxing because of slowed reflexes. Seven years later in 1984, Ali entered the hospital to undergo tests for symptoms of neurological damage. The doctors diagnosed Ali with Parkinson's syndrome. In the 1991 Thomas Hauser book, *Muhammad Ali: His Life and Times,* Ali admitted that boxing caused his current medical condition. Ali is grateful that his condition is not contagious because he can still maintain contact with people, especially children, all over the world. Despite his impaired his speech, fatigue, and frequent tremors in his legs and hands, Ali remains involved with family, religious, political, and social activities. He travels as much as nine months a year making public appearances, and spreading the message of love and brotherhood.

Other Accomplishments

There are other sides to Ali that few people have seen. In addition to writing poetry, Ali paints. His father, a talented artist, taught Ali painting techniques as a youngster. Ali held his first one–man show of his paintings and drawings in January 1979 in New York at the Roseland Ballroom. These 24 paintings were donated to the United Nations. He also enjoys performing magic tricks, such as making items disappear or changing pennies to dimes.

President Jimmy Carter sent Ali to Africa to gain support for the U.S. boycott of the 1980 Olympic games in Moscow. Ali's second diplomatic mission came in 1985 in Lebanon, where he tried to obtain the release of four kidnapped Americans. Both of these missions were unsuccessful. Ali went to Baghdad, Iraq, in November 1990 and met with Iraqi president Saddam Hussein for several days to secure the release of American hostages. On December 4, 1990, Ali, having successfully negotiated the release of 15 American citizens, returned to the United States.

Ali has been married four times and has nine children—seven daughters and two sons. His first marriage was to Sonji Roi from 1964 to 1966. He then married Belinda Boyd (Khalilah Tolona) in 1967 but divorced in 1976. Together they had four children: Maryum, identical twins Rasheeda and Jamilla, and Muhammad Jr. His third marriage was to Veronica Porche, from 1977 to 1985; their children are daughters Laila and Hana. His fourth marriage was to Yolanda ''Lonnie'' Williams, whom he married in November of 1986 and with whom he adopted son Ahad Amin. He has two other daughters, Miya and Khalilah. Ali is a devoted father and husband, who maintains a friendly, respectful relationship with all his former wives. Ali currently resides with his wife Yolanda, also a native of Louisville, on a farm in Berrien Springs, Michigan.

Ali has received many awards and honors. In 1970 following his fight against Jerry Quarry, Coretta Scott King and Ralph Abernathy presented the Dr. Martin Luther King Memorial Award to Ali for his contributions to equality and human rights. In 1974 *Sports Illustrated* magazine named him their Sportsman of the Year and the Boxing Writers Association named him Fighter of the Year. In November of 1978 groundbreaking took place for the Muhammad Ali Youth Opportunities Unlimited Complex in Newark, New Jersey. In addition, Ali accepted an honorary Doctor of Humane Letters Degree from Texas Southern University at their commencement in Houston in 1979. He has received numerous other honorary degrees, including one from the Ortanez University in Manila. Other honors include the naming of a street after him in his hometown, Louisville, in 1979. He was recognized for his long, meritorious service to boxing by the World Boxing Association in 1985. In 1987 Ali was honored by *The Ring Magazine* when they elected him to the Boxing Hall of Fame. Ali also was inducted into the International Boxing Hall of Fame in 1990.

During the opening ceremonies for the Atlanta Centennial Olympics in 1996, Ali carried the torch the final leg of its journey and lit the Olympic caldron to mark the official beginning of the games. Athletes and people the world over cheered and choked back tears at the sight of Muhammad Ali lighting the flame with his right hand while his left arm trembled. After the ceremony, President Bill Clinton admitted to Ali that he had cried when he saw Ali light the caldron.

In February of 1997 at the fifth annual ESPY Awards—given by ESPN, the leading cable sports network—actor Sidney Poitier presented the Arthur Ashe Award for Courage to Ali. At the ceremony, when asked which moment in his life had most tested his courage, Ali responded, ''Resisting Vietnam,'' which resulted in the loss of his heavyweight title.

At the tenth annual Essence Awards in May of 1997, newsman Bryant Gumbel presented Muhammad Ali with the first Essence Living Legend Award. In making the presentation, which was aired on Fox television on May 22, Gumbel said, ''More than just a great boxer, Muhammad Ali is a great human being, an icon of black pride, a global ambassador of peace and today as he battles Parkinson's syndrome, a symbol of courage.''

In the sport of boxing, few champions have stood the test of time like Muhammad Ali. As a fighter he elevated the sport to new heights through his promotional tactics, his playful poetry, and his grandiose style. Ali displayed incredible boxing skills throughout his career, dazzling crowds with his ballet–like grace as well as his flashy ''Ali Shuffle.'' He continues to draw crowds of admirers wherever he appears. Ali, the extrovert, always has been accessible to the news media and the public alike. Since Ali's retirement, each heavyweight contender invariably has been compared to him; as yet, not one has equaled his wit, charm, personal appeal, or staying power. Muhammad Ali is truly one of the greatest boxers of all times, and for his courage and charity, a great humanitarian.

Current address: PO Box 187, Berrien Springs, MI 59103.

REFERENCES

Ali, Muhammad, with Richard Durham. *The Greatest: My Own Story.* New York: Random House, 1975.

Dunnigan, Alice A. *Fascinating Story of Black Kentuckians: Their Heritage and Tradition.* Washington, DC: Associated Publishers, 1982.
Ebony. Chicago: Johnson Publishing, March 1963–November 1989.
Essence Awards Celebration, Fox Television, May 22, 1997.
Gorn, Elliott J., ed. *Muhammad Ali: The People's Champ.* Urbana: University of Illinois Press, 1995.
Hauser, Thomas. *Muhammad Ali: His Life and Times.* New York: Simon and Schuster, 1991.
Jet. Chicago: Johnson Publishing, February 1963–June 1997.
Kleber, John E., ed. *The Kentucky Encyclopedia.* Lexington: University Press of Kentucky, 1992.
Lipsyte, Robert. *Free to Be Muhammad Ali.* New York: Harper and Row, 1977.

Karen Cotton McDaniel

Richard Allen

(1760–1831)

Religious leader

Richard Allen

Richard Allen was a remarkable man by any standard. He is revered by many as the founder of the African Methodist Episcopal Church, the first black–controlled denomination. Born a slave, Allen died bishop of a flourishing church. His role in the church enabled him to become a prominent national leader, who addressed black concerns beyond the lines of denomination. Allen was also an astute businessman.

Richard Allen was born into slavery on February 14, 1760, in Philadelphia. We do not know the names of his parents or the names, birth dates, or exact number of his brother and sisters. His father is said to have been of pure African descent while his mother was of mixed blood. As a slave Allen received no formal schooling, but became literate through his own efforts as a young adult.

A prominent Philadelphia lawyer, Samuel Chew, owned the family at the time of Richard Allen's birth. Generally poor economic conditions and increasing competition from younger lawyers weakened Chew's financial position during the decade of the 1760s, and he sold the six members of the Allen family—father, mother, and four children—as a unit, probably about 1768.

The new owner was a man named Stokeley Sturgis, who farmed in Kent County near Dover, Delaware. There Allen's mother gave birth to at least two more children. Sturgis also ran into economic difficulties and sold Allen's mother and three of his younger siblings, retaining only the three older children: Richard Allen, a brother, and a sister. Richard Allen's father may have died before the sale since his disposition goes unmentioned.

As Richard Allen was growing up, Methodism was beginning to attract a following in the middle colonies; the movement's egalitarianism, emphasis on emotionalism in worship, and antislavery position made it attractive to blacks, who joined in significant numbers from the beginning. In addition, the position of "exhorter," or unordained preacher and prayer leader, allowed blacks to have a leadership role among their fellows.

During his adolescence, a Methodist preacher converted Allen, along with his brother and sister. At some point his mother also underwent conversion. When his conversion was complete, Allen recollected in his brief autobiography *The Life Experience and Gospel Labors* . . ., "I was constrained to go from house to house, exhorting my old companions, and telling to all around what a dear Saviour I had found." Allen then joined a "class," a group of converts that met weekly in the woods at Benjamin Wells's place under the leadership of John Gray.

Buys His Freedom

Sturgis gave Allen and his brother permission to attend meetings held every two weeks on Thursday; to the neighbors this was grossly overindulging slaves. Determined to prove that religion did not ruin them as workers, the brothers voluntarily refrained from going to meetings when there was pressing work on the farm. At length Allen prevailed on Sturgis to allow Methodist preachers to preach at the farm. After preaching had been going on there for some months, Freeborn Garrettson, a celebrated white itinerant preacher, who had freed his own slaves in 1775, spoke. In his sermon, the strictures on the sinfulness of owning slaves so worked on Sturgis's conscience that he allowed the Allen brothers to purchase their freedom. In January 1780 Sturgis signed a document allowing Allen to hire out his time and buy his freedom for 60 pounds in gold or silver or $2,000 in continental money. Allen paid $150 the following year and cleared the debt after five more years.

Richard Allen claimed in his autobiography that Sturgis "was what the world called a good master. He was more like a father to his slaves than anything else. He was a very tender, humane man." Sturgis did treat the Allen brothers well in at least one respect: he did not oppose their religious development. Even before Sturgis allowed preaching at his farm, he invited them to hold family prayer in the parlor for his whole family and allowed them to go about the neighborhood exhorting and holding prayer meetings.

There is no doubt, however, about Allen's attitude toward slavery as an institution. In his autobiographical account Allen wrote, "I had it often impressed upon my mind that I should one day enjoy my freedom; for slavery is a bitter pill, notwithstanding we had a good master. . . . I have had reason to bless my dear Lord that a door was opened unexpectedly for me to buy my time and enjoy my freedom."

Freedom brought no surcease from hard labor. To support himself and earn money for his freedom, Allen worked at a variety of jobs, such as woodcutter, brickyard laborer, day laborer, and wagoner. All the while he was praying and exhorting. A job as a salt–hauler during the final years of the Revolution allowed him to develop regular stops for preaching. With the arrival of peace in 1783, he extended the range of his activities.

In the winter of 1783–84, Allen preached and worked in New Jersey. He then walked to Pennsylvania where in Radnor he had the gratifying experience of preaching for several weeks and converting many in a congregation made up mostly of whites. After acquiring a blind horse, Allen went on to Lancaster and Little York before going to Maryland where he traveled the Hartford circuit with several other exhorters.

The first General Conference, held in Baltimore in December 1784, marked the beginning of Methodism as an organized denomination in the United States. Allen was certainly aware of the meeting, although there is no evidence that he was present. Allen continued to travel on various circuits with Methodist ministers, supporting himself by working odd jobs. Francis Asbury, one of the two founding bishops of the Methodist church in the United States, invited Allen to join him as a travelling evangelist, offering food and clothing as payment. Henry Hosier, a celebrated black evangelist, had worked with Asbury in a similar role earlier but Allen declined, saying that he felt he should save something to live on in sickness and old age.

Settles in Philadelphia

In February 1786 Allen accepted an invitation to preach in Philadelphia at the request of the elder in charge of the Methodist Church in the city. He decided to settle there to evangelize a growing black population that was largely unchurched. Allen's Sunday schedule was rigorous: he regularly preached at a meeting at five in the morning at St. George's Church and on many Sundays held two or three additional meetings. In addition to the church work, Allen continued to support himself by working as a blacksmith, wagon driver, grocer, shoe merchant, chimney sweep, and landlord.

Shortly after his arrival in Philadelphia, Allen set his sights on improving the status of blacks in the church. He felt there was a need for a separate place of worship for blacks, who were marginalized at St. George's. The initial response was cool. In his biography he reported that he attracted the support of only three "respectable people of color": Absalom Jones, William White, and Dorus Ginnings.

Absalom Jones (1746–1818), a fellow Methodist and longtime resident of Philadelphia, joined Richard Allen to form a nonsectarian mutual benefit organization, the Free African Society, in 1787. Meetings were held at Allen's residence until May 1788. November 15, 1788, is the last date his name appears in the records until he became a subject for discipline in the May 1789 meeting; on June 20 Allen was expelled, but the reasons remain unknown.

In 1790, without Allen, the Free African Society began forming into a nondenominationally affiliated church. By July 28, 1791, a group named Elders and Deacons had been named and the African Church came into being. Allen claimed that he was a member of the committee set up to solicit funds. If so, he seems to have broken his ties with the new church fairly soon: his name does not appear on a fund–raising address dated August 27, 1791, and it was Absalom Jones who emerged as leader of the congregation.

Allen's presumed defection is believed to have resulted from differences of opinion regarding denomination and location of the church. Allen desired a Methodist connection while others favored the Episcopal Church. Moreover, Allen purchased a lot that was subsequently rejected in favor of one in another location. The African Church was renamed St. Thomas Episcopal Church on July 17, 1794, and soon after Absalom Jones became the first black Episcopalian priest. In May of that year, Allen persuaded his followers to rebuild a wooden blacksmith shop on the lot he owned as a place of worship. This new church was dedicated on July 28, 1794.

Allen was part of a widespread movement towards independent black churches during the early years of his church. Independent black Baptist churches had already been established in Savannah, Georgia, and Petersburg, Virginia. Black Methodists in New York, Baltimore, Wilmington, and Charleston were also seeking their own churches. The exact course of Allen's break with the white Methodists is unclear, although his participation in a walkout at St. George's Methodist Church may have contributed to his desire for independence. The walkout by Allen and his friends occurred sometime between 1787 and 1791 after blacks were asked leave their pews to alleviate overcrowding.

Bethel Church Founded

Allen won a significant victory in his campaign for an independent church when Bishop Asbury presided over the inauguration of his new church in 1794. Nonetheless, quarrels between the black Bethel Church and the white St. George's Church soon commenced. Allen and his supporters accepted the offer of the white assistant minister of St. George's help in drawing up a charter of incorporation, which was approved by the Pennsylvania Supreme Court on September 12, 1792. The members of Bethel later charged that they had been deceived since the charter assigned control of the property to the Conference as was the Methodist custom. Further, while the document specifically acknowledged that membership of the church and its board of trustees was restricted to persons of African descent, it also provided that the Methodist elder in charge of the Conference had the right to nominate Bethel's preacher. Despite these problems, however, the groups managed to scrape along without open conflict until 1805.

In that year James Smith, elder in charge of St, George's, tried to assert control over Bethel. Since there were no ordained black Methodist ministers at the time, visiting white ministers were necessary for the administration of the sacraments. For about a year Bethel acknowledged St. George's right to supply preachers, but vigorously objected to the amount of recompensation demanded and refused to relinquish control of church property. The membership at Bethel secretly met in 1807 and amended their charter to give title to the property to their board of trustees, much to the chagrin of the white Methodist leaders when they discovered the change.

In 1811 Bethel suffered from a series of aggressive elders at St. George's. One elder tried to undermine Bethel by opening another church for blacks near Bethel: the attempt failed. The next elder was physically blocked from the pulpit when he attempted to preach at Bethel. Bethel was put up for auction and repurchased by Allen for $10,125 in the summer of 1815. The elder presiding at St. George's in that year changed his plans to preach at Bethel when he learned that blacks were prepared to use force to prevent this. Finally, on January 1, 1816, Allen turned to the courts and won a decree giving Bethel its independence.

This event was a cause for celebration elsewhere as well as in Philadelphia, especially in Baltimore where Daniel Coker had been leading black Methodists in a similar battle. Allen and Coker had been in contact and agreed to withdraw from the white Methodist connection at the same time. Indeed, the break in Baltimore seems to have occurred three weeks before the one in Philadelphia.

African Methodist Episcopal Church Formed

The Baltimore and Philadelphia congregations were the largest of the five represented in a meeting held in Philadelphia on April 9, 1816. The first action of this meeting was to adopt the name African Methodist Episcopal (AME) Church and the next to adopt the Discipline order of the Methodist Episcopal Church. The delegates then elected Daniel Coker as the first bishop of the new church. For reasons that are not clear, he declined the nomination the following day. Then Richard Allen was selected. He was ordained an elder, and on the next day, April 11, 1816, bishop. From that time on Allen served as both pastor of Bethel Church and bishop of the AME Church.

Much of Allen's later life is intertwined with the history of the AME Church. The church's efforts concentrated on moral reform and growth. In fact, much time was spent in disciplining members for moral lapses—even Daniel Coker was suspended for a year on unknown charges. The church launched a vigorous campaign to induce other black Methodist congregations to join, but its efforts were not always successful. Even in Philadelphia there was a breakaway group, Wesley Church, formed by dissidents from Bethel. In New York City the AME set up a congregation, but local black Methodists remained aloof and eventually formed the denomination known as American Methodist Episcopal Church Zion. In Wilmington, Delaware, Peter Spencer maintained the Union American Methodist Episcopal Church, which has the honor of being the oldest black Methodist denomination, being founded in 1813.

After a promising beginning in the South, the AME was effectively blocked from expansion there. In Charleston, South Carolina, a flourishing AME church with some 1,500 members was suppressed in 1822 in the wake of Denmark Vesey's attempted insurrection; its pastor Morris Brown had to flee to the North. There Brown became assistant bishop and aide to Allen in 1828 and at Allen's death was elected second head of the church. In the west, Ohio's repressive Black Code also threatened the existence of fledgling AME congregations as the laws made it difficult for blacks to continue to reside in the state.

In spite of local problems, the AME under Allen's leadership grew into a stable institution, especially in the Middle Atlantic States. The denomination also expressed an early interest in foreign missionary work, although such efforts had little practical effect. The denomination's real successes came in its domestic missionary work that included the labor of evangelist Jarina Lee. Allen was an early supporter of Lee's activities at a time when most of his contemporaries, including his own congregation at Bethel, were unwilling to do the same.

Allen's prominence as a black leader enabled him to assist both blacks and whites beyond the confines of the denomination. In 1793 he provided aid during a yellow fever epidemic in Philadelphia, along with James Forten, the sail–maker, and Absalom Jones.

In 1794 Allen attempted to establish a school for blacks. He later became treasurer of the Second African Masonic Lodge, which was inaugurated in Philadelphia on June 24, 1797. Allen also took part in the founding of the Bethel Benevolent Society, a charitable women's group, which was imitated by other AME churches.

Although the white Methodist church had weakened its once adamant antislavery position, Allen remained an ardent abolitionist. Freedom was no idle word to him, and he even escaped an attempt to reenslave him in about 1810. A slavecatcher stopped Allen in the streets and accused him of being a runaway slave. Since the burden of proof of free status fell on the person accused, such occurrences were common. Allen, however, was well known in Philadelphia and respected by whites as well as by blacks. Consequently, the slavecatcher was charged with making false accusations and sentenced to jail. After the man spent three months in jail, Allen felt he had been punished long enough and asked that he be freed.

Allen also opposed the American Colonization Society, which attempted to remove free blacks to Africa. He feared that state legislatures might encourage or even force emigration through restrictive measures. Shortly after the formation of the American Colonization Society, 3,000 free blacks assembled at Bethel in mid–January 1817 to express their anticolonization sentiment. This meeting represents the first concentrated effort by blacks to defend their freedom.

The First National Negro Convention was held shortly thereafter in response to a number of anti–black activities, including repressive legislation in Ohio in 1829, which caused a black migration from that state to Canada. The minutes of the meeting do not survive, but the mere idea of a national meeting of blacks was novel enough to excite white hostility. The meeting convened in Philadelphia on September 5, 1830, and Allen was elected its president. The impetus for national meetings continued, but Allen died on March 26, 1831, three months before the second convention.

Allen had been married to a former slave named Sarah (1764–1849), since 1800. She had been brought to Philadelphia from Isle of Wight County in Virginia before she was eight. All accounts indicate that she was a very able supporter of her husband's efforts as pastor and businessman. She also was resolute and ingenious in aiding fugitive slaves. It has been suggested that she was responsible for her husband's views of women's rights, to which he was more sympathetic than most men of his era. The Allens had six children: Richard Jr., Peter, John, James, Ann, and Sarah. Both Richard Allen and Sarah Allen were originally buried in Bethel Church's cemetery in Philadelphia; in 1901 their remains were placed in a tomb under the church.

Allen stated in his will that the salaries due to him from the church from 1807 on were revoked in 1821 and that his work since that date was not compensated. His estate was valued at $60,000, and the will left the use his property to his wife if she did not remarry and contained detailed disposition of his considerable real estate holdings in case of her marriage or death. His estate also included a $10,000 bond on the Bethel Church on which the trustees were to pay interest.

As imperfect as our sources are for a full delineation of Richard Allen's life, it is certain that he was a great man. His firmness of purpose enabled him to found a black church in the face of great opposition. In so doing he foreshadowed the creation of other black institutions. He perceived that both personal and institutional freedom was necessary for blacks to work out their destiny in a hostile environment. He responded early to Methodist calls for freedom as well as for salvation and continued to seek freedom while his former church slid backward into an acceptance of slavery.

REFERENCES

Allen, Richard. *The Life Experiences and Gospel Labors of the Rt. Rev. Richard Allen.* New York: Abingdon Press, 1960.

George, Carol V. R. *Segregated Sabbaths.* New York: Oxford, 1973.

Handy, James A. *Scraps of Methodist Episcopal History.* Philadelphia: AME Book Concern, n.d.

Litwick, Leon, and August Meier, eds. *Black Leaders of the Nineteenth Century.* Urbana: University of Illinois Press, 1988.

Logan, Rayford W., and Michael R. Winston, eds. *Dictionary of American Negro Biography.* New York: Norton, 1982.

Payne, Daniel A. *History of the African Methodist Episcopal Church.* Nashville: AME Sunday School Union, 1891.

Raboteau, Albert J. *A Fire in the Bones.* Boston: Beacon Press, 1995.

Smith, David. *Biography of Rev. David Smith.* Xenia, OH: Xenia Gazette Office, 1881.

Wesley, Charles H. *Richard Allen: Apostle of Freedom.* Washington, DC: Associated Publishers, 1935. Reissue 1969.

Robert L. Johns

Charles W. Anderson Jr.

(1907–1960)

Lawyer, state legislator, United Nations delegate

In November of 1935 Charles W. Anderson Jr. became the first African American to be elected to the Kentucky Legislature and the first African American legislator in the South since Reconstruction. He was a pioneer in the civil rights movement in Kentucky, initiating numerous laws for the equality of his race.

Anderson was born on May 26, 1907, to Charles W. and Tabatha Murphy Anderson in Louisville, Kentucky. Shortly after his birth, his family moved to Frankfort. His father was a medical doctor and his mother served as the state supervisor of black schools and later became the dean of women at what is now Kentucky State University. Charles Anderson Jr. married Victoria McCall from Detroit, Michigan, and they had two children, Charles III and Victoria. Their son Charles III is currently an attorney in Detroit and their daughter, Victoria Pinderhughes, is a clinical psychologist.

Anderson's education includes a bachelor's degree from Kentucky State College (now University) in 1926 and an A.B. degree from Wilberforce University in 1927. Because of the

Charles W. Anderson Jr.

segregated education system in Kentucky, Anderson had to leave the state to pursue his studies. In 1931 he earned the LL.B. from Howard University and was admitted to the Kentucky bar in 1933. He began practicing law in Louisville with Willie C. Fleming, Harry S. McAlpin, O. B. Hinnant, and J. Earl Dearing. Anderson was an excellent trial attorney and served as a mentor and trainer to new attorneys in the firm. In 1934 representing the NAACP, he helped prosecute seven people involved in lynching a black man in Hazard, Kentucky.

Advances Rights for Blacks

After settling in his law practice, Anderson decided to enter politics and won a seat in the Kentucky House of Representatives in 1935. He was an active member of the Republican Party and remained high in that party's state political activities. He was reelected and served a total of six consecutive terms in the House of Representatives from 1936 to 1946. During his outstanding legislative career, he was instrumental in seeing that issues relative to African Americans remained before the Kentucky legislature. Anderson was a strong advocate for his race and supported better educational opportunities for blacks by introducing legislation to integrate the nursing schools and postgraduate hospital training and residency programs in the state. He was successful in obtaining the repeal of the Kentucky public lynching law. He improved the condition of blacks in Kentucky through his sponsorship of many bills.

Since Kentucky denied blacks access to professional colleges, he sponsored the Anderson–Mayer State Aid Act which was passed later and required the state to appropriate money to assist blacks to study in these professional disciplines in other states. Anderson led the fight for the integration of the state universities in Kentucky. He successfully fought and defeated a bill to segregate people by race on Kentucky buses, and in schools, libraries, trains, railroads and other public places.

Anderson also successfully sponsored bills that allowed married women to teach, and provided minimum wages and improved working conditions for domestic servants in the state. He also enhanced the rural high school educational facilities for all students through his legislative action. These pieces of legislation improved the economic and educational conditions for poor whites as well as for blacks.

Anderson resigned from the legislature to become assistant Commonwealth's attorney for Jefferson County in May 1946. This was another first for Kentucky and the South. He served in this capacity until 1952. Anderson, a long–time member of the Republican Party, received the GOP nomination for judge in the Louisville 3rd District Municipal Court in 1949 but was narrowly defeated in the election.

Anderson's political clout did not shield him or his family from the many racial injustices of the time. In fact, on one occasion when the family was in a dining room at Louisville's Standiford Field airport, they were refused service. His children were brought to tears by this painful incident. Anderson filed a discrimination suit against the airport restaurant with his children named as plaintiffs in the case. The case never went to court but the dining room became open to blacks shortly after the suit was filed.

Anderson was very actively involved in his church and other community groups. He was a devout member and leader in the Quinn Chapel African Methodist Episcopal Church. Professionally, he was a member of the national legal committee of the American Legislature Association; the American Academy of Political and Social Science; the National Association of Compensation and Claimants Attorneys; the Kentucky Trial Attorneys' Association; and the Kentucky, the Louisville, the American, and the National Bar Association, of which he served as president for two terms. Politically, he was involved in the Republican Organization and Allied Clubs and was a member of the Louisville and Jefferson County Republican Executive Committee, on which he served as a member of the policy committee from 1935 to 1958 and as a member of the executive committee.

Within the community he was a member of the Elks, the Masons, the National Home Finding Society for Colored Children, the Louisville Business League, the Board of Family, Welfare Service of the Kentucky Home Society for Children, the National Urban League, and president of the Louisville NAACP also for two terms. He also worked with other black and white leaders and the Kentucky Commission on Human Rights to push for the passage of the public accommodations law. Serving as the spokesman for the Louisville group to end segregation of restaurants, theaters and businesses, he led the group of 35 black and white leaders to the

Louisville City Hall to request an ordinance in support of their cause in January 1960.

A member of the Alpha Phi Alpha fraternity, Anderson presented the keynote address in 1956 at the national convention in Chicago on the topic of "Defensive and Offensive Struggles in Our Democracy Toward a Goal of Total Integration."

Under President Dwight D. Eisenhower's administration, Anderson was appointed alternate United States Delegate to the United Nations' 14th General Assembly in 1959. As a member of the United States delegation, Anderson helped draft documents that protected the rights of children against abuse, exploitation, and neglect. Other documents prohibited any practices that allowed discrimination based on race, religion, or other criteria.

Anderson was the first black commissioned a Kentucky Colonel by any governor. He was also the recipient of numerous awards and honors for his unparalleled achievements in government and public service. Wilberforce presented him an honorary LL.D. in 1936. In 1940 he received the Lincoln Institute Award for outstanding service to blacks. In 1945 he was awarded the Howard University Alumni Award for Distinction in Law and Government. In 1971 the Kentucky Human Rights Commission honored Anderson in their poster series of Kentucky's Outstanding African Americans. Kentucky State University's Center of Excellence for the Study of Kentucky African Americans chose Anderson as an honoree for their 1996–97 "Kentucky African–American Historical Profiles in Courage and Achievement" calendar.

On June 14, 1960, Anderson's car was struck by a train and he apparently died instantly. He was 53–years old at the time of his death. He is buried in Louisville. An historic marker honoring Anderson's distinguished career was unveiled on June 14, 1997, in Louisville in front of the Jefferson County Hall of Justice. Another tribute to Anderson is the Anderson Medal given by the Governor's Office.

Charles W. Anderson Jr. fought for justice and equality for the African American citizens of Kentucky and won many of the battles to insure the rights that were previously denied to people of African descent. He demonstrated a sense of responsibility for other people and sought measures to change the politics that restricted people because of race, religion, or economic circumstances.

REFERENCES

Dunnigan, Alice A. *Fascinating Story of Black Kentuckians: Their Heritage and Tradition.* Washington, DC: Associated Publishers, 1982.

A Gallery of Great Black Kentuckians. Frankfort: Kentucky Commission on Human Rights, 1971.

Horton, John Benjamin. *Not Without a Struggle.* New York: Vantage Press, 1979.

Kentucky's Black Heritage. Frankfort: Kentucky Commission on Human Rights, 1971.

Kleber, John E, ed. *The Kentucky Encyclopedia.* Lexington: University Press of Kentucky, 1992.

Smith, Gerald L. *A Black Educator in the Segregated South: Kentucky's Rufus B. Atwood.* Lexington: University Press of Kentucky, 1994.

Who's Who in Colored America. 5th ed. Yonkers, NY: Christian E. Burckel, 1940.

COLLECTIONS

The Charles W. Anderson Jr. papers are presently housed in Detroit, Michigan, at the home of his widow, Victoria Anderson Davenport.

Karen Cotton McDaniel

Henry Armstrong
(1912–1988)
Boxer, minister

Although Henry Armstrong's mother and grandmother wanted him to become a minister, he had a talent for fighting, a drive to become a champion, and a goal of achieving fame and fortune. In 1938 he became the first boxer in history to hold three world titles simultaneously. Later, in 1951, he became an ordained Baptist minister.

Armstrong's father, Henry Jackson Sr., a sharecropper and butcher, married America Armstrong, an Iroquois Indian (some sources say Cherokee). They lived on a plantation owned by the senior Jackson's Irish father, who had married one of his slaves. On December 12, 1912, Henry Jackson Jr., the eleventh of the couple's 15 children, was born in Columbus, Mississippi. Young Henry would later take the name Armstrong.

According to Armstrong's autobiography, *Gloves, Glory and God,* when the oldest Jackson brother, Ollus, first saw Henry, he remarked, "Gee, Mom, he looks like a little rat!" Their mother quickly defended her newest child: "He may look like a rat now, but some day he'll be the big cheese in this family. Call him a rat if you want to, but he'll win, whatever he does. And some day, he'll be a fine preacher." Henry Armstrong grew up answering to the family nickname "Rat."

When Armstrong was a child, to find employment, his father moved the family to a three–room house in St. Louis, Missouri, where he worked for the Independent Packing Company. After Henry Armstrong's mother died of consumption in 1918, his father's mother, Henrietta Chatman, raised him. According to Armstrong's autobiography, his grandmother "had one idea that was *really* firm: that Henry was to be minister, some fine day." He had no interest in the ministry

Henry Armstrong

though. His experience with preachers involved shooing the flies away from their plates while they ate his food. Armstrong thought he would rather become a doctor, having seen what big houses they owned. Grandma Chatman indicated that she could accept this occupation, but she hoped he would not become a lawyer.

At Toussaint L'Ouverture Grammar School in St. Louis, Armstrong acquired a new nickname, "Red," which, as he wrote in his autobiography, stemmed from "his curly hair [that] had a sandy, reddish glint." His small stature attracted teasing by other children. He found it necessary to defend himself and discovered that he was good at fighting. He became determined to become a boxer.

At Vashon High School Armstrong earned respect. He made good grades and later his fellow students elected him class president. At his graduation, he read a valedictory poem he had written as poet laureate of his class. Outside school, he worked to develop his athletic abilities. He often ran the eight miles to school. After school, he set pins for a local bowling alley.

By the time Armstrong had finished high school, his 60–year old father suffered from rheumatism and often missed work. His 80–year old grandmother, although almost blind, shelled pecans for a local nut factory. At the age of 17, Armstrong claimed his age as 21 to gain employment as a section hand on the Missouri Pacific Railroad. However, he did not abandon his dream of becoming a boxer. He used a sledgehammer to drive the spikes because he had read that this was how Jack Dempsey had built his strength. He would purposely miss the handcar each morning so that he could run along behind it.

In later years, Armstrong recalled "a turning point" in his life. He realized that the $35 he earned from his railroad job was committed to the support of his family and that he could not go to college on such wages. As he grappled with this problem, the wind dropped a newspaper at his feet with the headline: "Kid Chocolate Earns $75,000 for Half Hour's Work." Armstrong felt that this experience was a miracle, and he immediately quit his job, vowing to his family and friends that he would become a champion.

Armstrong bought boxing gloves and fought whomever he found willing to fight him. At the local YMCA, he met Harry Armstrong, a former boxer, who became his mentor and friend. In his first amateur fight at the St. Louis Coliseum in 1929, Henry Armstrong knocked his opponent out in the second round.

Armstrong tried professional boxing in Pittsburgh and Chicago under the name Melody Jackson. After losing his first bout and failing to become a champion, he returned to St. Louis. Then he read about boxer and hobo Jim Tully and decided to "hobo" his way to California on the railroad. Harry Armstrong accompanied him as trainer.

In August of 1934, Henry Armstrong married Willa Mae Shondy, and they had one daughter, Lanetta. The couple later divorced. In 1960 he married Velma Tartt, a girlfriend from high school days. One day after Velma Armstrong complained of chest pains, she died in his arms on the way to the hospital. He married again, although only for a brief time. Gussie Henry, a nurse's aide, became his fourth wife in 1978.

The Making of a Champion

In Los Angeles, while waiting for boxing matches, Henry Armstrong found work as a shoeshine boy. From 1931 to 1934 he maintained his own stand. When he could afford do so, he invited his father and grandmother to come to Los Angeles to live. At the local gym, he met fight manager Tom Cox, introducing himself as Harry's brother, Henry Armstrong. Cox contracted him as an amateur for three dollars. By his own count, he fought between 85 and 90 amateur bouts in 1931, winning around 66 of them by knockouts and losing none.

In 1932 Wirt Ross bought Armstrong's contract for $250, and the boxer entered professional competition in earnest. Armstrong stood only five feet five and one–half inches tall, but his style of fighting compensated for his small stature. He delivered powerful punches in rapid succession and exhibited a remarkable capacity to endure rough punishment. In *American Sports Greats,* John Robertson wrote of Armstrong's "explosive knockout power" and *The Annual Obituary* mentioned his "relentless talent for destruction."

Armstrong beat Italian Baby Arizmendi so badly that Arizmendi had to take six months off. At this bout, Armstrong first heard new nicknames for himself: "Perpetual Motion," "Homicide Hank," "The Human Buzzsaw," "Windmill," and "Hammerin' Henry." Al Jolson saw the fight and persuaded Eddie Mead to buy Armstrong's contract for $5,000, but they decided to publicize the amount as $10,000. When Ross then demanded the entire $10,000, George Raft provided the other half of the sum. Armstrong and his three new managers needed money. They also needed a plan for competing with the rising popularity of Joe Louis. The team set a goal that no other boxer had achieved—three world championships. During 1937 and the first half of 1938, Armstrong won 47 consecutive fights, 27 by knockouts. He also won three world titles.

Armstrong's first title was the Featherweight Champion of the World, Jolson offered Petey Sarron $15,000 to defend his featherweight championship title against Armstrong. On October 29, 1937, Armstrong faced Sarron at Madison Square Garden. Throughout Sarron's 12 years in the ring, no boxer had succeeded at flooring him, but the newcomer knocked Sarron out in the sixth round. In December 1938, Armstrong relinquished this title because he could not keep his weight at 126 pounds.

Armstrong's second title was Welterweight Champion of the World. On May 31, 1938, Armstrong skipped the lightweight division and defeated Barney Ross in a 15–round match on Long Island. To compete for the welterweight title, Armstrong needed to weigh in at 138. By drinking beer in the days before the match and lots of water on the day of the weigh–in, he met the weight requirement. When promoters postponed the fight for ten days because of rain, Joe Louis invited Armstrong to train at Pompton Lakes, New Jersey, and paid his expenses. Fans favored Ross to win the match at three–to–one odds, but Armstrong beat Ross so badly that Ross retired after the fight. Armstrong held this title until October 4, 1940.

Armstrong's third title was Lightweight Champion of the World. On August 17, 1938, he dropped back a weight division to take on Lou Ambers. Fans packed Madison Square Garden to see Armstrong win in another 15–round match, but the winner could not recall the victory. Quoted in *In This Corner,* he described the experience as "the bloodiest fight I ever had in my life." Ambers broke open a cut on Armstrong's lower lip. Bleeding profusely, Armstrong kept swallowing the blood so that the referee would not stop the match but blacked out at the end of the fight. He held the lightweight title until August 22, 1939.

In less than a year, this young fighter who had determined to become a champion had captured three world titles. He had also produced and starred in a movie depicting his life, *Keep Punching* by the Sports Melodrama Company, Film Art Studios, 1939. In 1940 he tried for a fourth title, but on a controversial decision he lost the middleweight division to Ceferina Garcia. In October of that year, Armstrong lost his remaining title to Fritzie Zivic in Madison Square Garden. Zivic practically blinded Armstrong, and Armstrong required eye surgery after the match. Armstrong quit fighting for a while, but in a 1970 interview with Peter Heller for *In This Corner,* he noted, "I fought Zivic three times, and the third time, in San Francisco on a comeback, I gave him a good beating." In one of his final comeback attempts, the former champ lost to a newcomer named Sugar Ray Robinson.

Armstrong retired from boxing in 1945, at age 32, having fought 174 recorded bouts, winning 145 of them, 98 by knockout. Of 26 world title fights, he won 22, drew one, and lost three. Opponents knocked him out only two times during his entire career. His thoughts then began to turn to God, to whom often he had prayed before entering the ring.

A New Goal

Armstrong had achieved fame. In addition to the world championships, he also received other honors. In 1938 *The Ring* magazine named him Fighter of the Year. He joined Joe Louis and Jack Dempsey in 1954 as the first inductees into the Boxing Hall of Fame. In addition, he was named to the Black Athletes Hall of Fame in 1975.

Armstrong had also achieved fortune. Because of his own spending habits, bad investments, and the greed of some of his managers, Armstrong retained little of his million dollar earnings. By his own account, in his autobiography, he "had a whale of a time," but he had one regret: "If I had my career to live over again," he told Peter Heller for *In This Corner,* "I would see in the boxing world that every fighter would get his own check instead of giving it all to the manager."

In the year following his retirement, Armstrong worked briefly with an orchestra and chorus. He refereed some boxing matches. Then he toured China, Burma, and India with a group George Raft had organized to entertain U.S. soldiers. According to his autobiography, while in Egypt "he thought a lot about God" and decided that he would go into the ministry. He eventually achieved that goal—the dream that his mother and grandmother had held for him—but the transition took time. When he returned to America, Armstrong managed fighters for a while. He turned to alcohol, and eventually found himself in a Los Angeles jail.

Armstrong found a new direction for his life. In 1951, he was ordained into the ministry at Morning Star Baptist Church. Crowds now assembled to hear him speak at revivals and other religious meetings. His first nine converts were youngsters. Wanting to help prevent juvenile delinquency, he established the Henry Armstrong Youth Foundation. Barney Ross agreed to become vice–president of the foundation, and a number of boxers served on the advisory board. To raise money for the project, Armstrong published a collection of poetry he had written, *Twenty Years of Poem, Moods, and Meditation* (1954). Royalties from this book and from his autobiography, *Gloves, Glory and God* (Fleming H. Revell, 1956) helped finance the foundation.

Returning to St. Louis in 1972, Armstrong became Director of the Herbert Hoover Boys Club and Assistant Pastor of First Baptist Church. He moved back to Los Angeles in 1978 after he and Gussie Armstrong were married. During the final year of his life, his health declined dramatically. He entered the hospital six times that year. Armstrong died of heart failure in Los Angeles on October 22, 1988, at the age of

75. In 1990, he was named posthumously to the International Boxing Hall of Fame.

Henry Armstrong achieved his goal of becoming a champion. In doing so he gave the boxing world what Bert Sugar in *The 100 Greatest Boxers of All Time* called "a benchmark against which all future generations will be measured." He had also honored the goal that his mother and grandmother had envisioned by becoming a minister. Quoted in *Twenty Years of Poem,* Walter Ramsey, a cofounder of the Henry Armstrong Youth Foundation, insisted Armstrong was "just as relentless in his saving of lost souls as he was in the ring."

REFERENCES

The African American Almanac, 7th ed. Detroit: Gale Research, 1997.

Armstrong, Henry. *Gloves, Glory and God: An Autobiography.* Westwood, NJ: Fleming H. Revell, 1956.

———. *Twenty Years of Poem, Moods and Meditation.* H. J. Armstrong, 1954.

Burgess, Patricia, ed. *The Annual Obituary 1988.* Chicago: St. James Press, 1990.

"Fighter for God." *Newsweek* 45 (18 April 1955): 88.

Friedman, Jack, and Lorenzo Benet. "Fifty Years After the Glory, Forgotten Legend Henry Armstrong Quietly Slips Out of the Ring." *People Weekly* 30 (21 November 1988): 79–82.

Heller, Peter. *In This Corner.* New York: Simon and Schuster, 1973.

Porter, David L., ed. *American Sports Greats: A Biographical Dictionary.* Westport, CT: Greenwood Press, 1995.

Sugar, Bert Randolph. *The 100 Greatest Boxers of All Time.* New York: Bonanza Books, 1984.

Marie Garrett

Louis "Satchmo" Armstrong

(1900–1971)

Jazz trumpeter, singer

New York Times book reviewer Terry Teachout wrote that Louis Armstrong's celebrity was "central to his place in the history of jazz," but that "He did not invent jazz, nor was he its first important figure, and it is not even quite right to call him the first great jazz soloist." Nevertheless Armstrong became "the player other players copied." Armstrong also became a much imitated song stylist due to his gravelly, raspy voice which Lawrence Bergreen in his biography, *Louis Armstrong: An Extravagant Life,* described as "the unforgettable voice that behaved like a huge instrument: growling, laughing, demented, soothing, fierce."

When Armstrong changed from the cornet to the trumpet and began to incorporate his unique manner of singing into his repertoire, he forged a distinctive style further characterized by improvisatory scat singing and catchy rhythms. As a showman he had few peers, not only because of his superior musicianship, but also because of his highly personal idiosyncrasies. He was a connoisseur of love, a renowned raconteur, and according to Bergreen, a proponent of the virtues of "marijuana for the head and laxatives for the bowels." Known in his youth as "Dipper" and "Gatemouth," Armstrong became better known as "Pops" and as "Satchmo," the latter a corruption of "Satchelmouth." He was often depicted as a grinning entertainer. His shiny teeth and infectious grin irritated many black militants in the civil rights era, and this irritation was further exacerbated by Armstrong carrying a large white handkerchief used to wipe the perspiration that beaded his forehead. Armstrong was accused of pandering to whites. This same man, however, canceled an international goodwill tour to protest the 1957 school desegregation crisis in Little Rock, Arkansas. Armstrong's innate sense of justice was also aroused by a Louisiana law prohibiting performances by racially–integrated bands. His reaction was to refuse to perform in New Orleans for some years. Both actions could have destroyed his career. Armstrong always had a disarming and seemingly simple way of speaking, singing, and playing that caused the world to underestimate his intelligence, sensitivity, and sense of fair play. Although he was often misunderstood and disrespected by his own people, Armstrong was always his own man who dealt with life and its vagaries on his own terms.

Though he claimed to have been born on the Fourth of July, Daniel Louis Armstrong was actually born on August 4, 1900, in New Orleans; some biographers claim 1898 as his birth year. When Armstrong was born, his mother, Mary Albert, and his father, Willie Armstrong, were teenagers without personal or financial resources needed to care for a baby. Known as Mayann, Armstrong's mother lived a peripatetic life that may have involved prostitution. When she and Willie Armstrong separated, her mother reared the child, and even after the couple reconciled and had a second child, Beatrice, the boy remained with his grandmother until he was of school age. Armstrong then went to live with Mayann, who was sick, and a baby sister who was a total stranger. Willie Armstrong was always a father in name only as he basically ignored the boy and his sister. Despite the paternal neglect, Armstrong always remembered seeing his father march as grand marshal with the Odd Fellows parade; Willie was dressed in the fraternal uniform and traditional high hat benefiting his position.

Armstrong was constantly exposed to music because his neighborhood had a honky–tonk joint on every corner. Ragtime, the precursor of jazz, was in vogue at the turn of the century, and the boy was also influenced by funeral bands that "cut loose" after a body was buried and the family and spectators left the cemetery in a joyful mood. Joe Oliver, one of the major influences on Armstrong, was kind to him during

Louis ''Satchmo'' Armstrong

Armstrong's adolescence and after the Onward Brass Band finished its funeral duties Oliver let the boy hold his cornet and try to play it. Boyhood memories also included annual Mardi Gras ceremonies and nightly parades. Another musical influence was the neighborhood peddlers who sang and played primitive instruments to advertise their wares. The Karnoffsky's, a Jewish immigrant family, hired Armstrong to help boy junk and sell coal, usually in the notorious ''red light'' district of Storyville where children were forbidden to go. He was also attracted to young street musicians who formed loosely knit improvisatory bands found throughout the city. The young Armstrong greatly admired the red light district drummers, who were described by Bergreen as having ''musical ability, women, and a magnificent aura of danger.''

It is likely that Armstrong's universal love of people and high tolerance for lifestyle choices stemmed from his youthful proximity to the wide variety of Storyville denizens, Mayann Armstrong's hardscrabble life, and his positive relationship with the Karnoffsky family. He respected those of questionable reputations as much as those of different ethnic backgrounds because they earned their livelihoods rather than depending on charity. The Storyville prostitutes were kind to him despite their cutthroat existences and the Karnoffskys shared their culture, their meals, and their lives with a poor, destitute boy.

When Armstrong left school, in the fifth grade, he headed for trouble although he had a job and a surrogate family. In 1912 he committed a crime that would change his life. That New Year's Eve he fired a revolver filled with blank cartridges in the air and was taken to juvenile court and sentenced to the Colored Waif's Home. Initially in a state of disgrace, Armstrong later was grateful for the experience. According to Bergreen, ''He experienced a rebirth there because he learned to thrive on discipline and finally received the attention—especially from an older man—that he craved.''

Armstrong's first musical mentor was the home's music program director, Pete Davis, who initially mistrusted the boy's checkered past. When Armstrong's attitude improved, the director invited him to join the brass band where Armstrong learned to play tambourine, bugle, and cornet. The boy already knew something of brass instruments from playing bugle on the Karnoffsky's peddler wagons, and he had learned the rudiments from Bunk Johnson, a superb trumpet player who encouraged fledgling players. From the home's musical director Armstrong learned the essential traits of real manhood: self–respect, self–discipline, moral character, a sense of equilibrium, and compassion and forgiveness. This was the boy's first real positive relationship with a male role model and, as a result, Armstrong was soon promoted to leader of the Colored Waif's Home Band, which performed on a professional level. His proudest moment was when the band paraded through his old neighborhood that he had left in disgrace. In 1914, through the efforts of Mayann Armstrong, the boy was released into the custody of his stepmother and Willie, the father who had done nothing for his son. This was not Armstrong's choice because he knew he would be treated as the hired help, not as a real family member.

Carving Out a Niche

Life after the home was precarious because relationships between Armstrong and his father were as predicted. The boy had to care for his half–brothers and cook for the family. When his stepmother had another child, Armstrong was sent back to live with Mayann. Due to his success at the home, Armstrong was invited to sit in with the band of Kid Ory, a well–known trombonist. By 1916 Armstrong's reputation was growing, but he was forced to augment his income with menial and strenuous jobs such as unloading bananas and hauling coal. He had become the recognized protégé of Joe Oliver, but still had to play in honky tonks and whorehouses owned and run by organized crime. They were so dangerous that the teenaged cornetist needed a bodyguard as escort and protector. He soon graduated from Kid Ory's band and joined an elite marching band, the Tuxedo Brass Band conducted by Oscar ''Papa'' Celestin.

As Armstrong's reputation for versatility and playing technique grew, so did his reputation for attracting the opposite sex, in particular prostitutes. One of these women, Daisy Parker, became his wife when he was only a teenager.

Leaving New Orleans

Armstrong joined the Fate Marable band in St. Louis and quickly discovered the real meaning of discipline. Marable brooked no nonsense from his charges and his boss, Captain Streckfus of the Streckfus Steamboat Line, backed him up. There was no room for improvisation, flashy showmanship, lax behavior, or for bucking Jim Crow laws. Marable's music was designed to please the white steamboat patrons' tastes, but Monday nights were "black only" affairs where alcohol was allowed and a Storyville atmosphere prevailed. This was Armstrong's introduction to the world beyond New Orleans, and the summer job took him from one end of the Mississippi River to the other. The major benefits for the young cornetist were being forced to learn to read music and the opportunity, on Monday nights, to expand his improvisatory skills.

When the season ended, Armstrong returned home and played at Tom Anderson's saloon, a notorious establishment, but he was in his element and well cared for. As quoted by his biographer, Armstrong said: "That was a swell job if there ever was one. . . . I felt real important eating all those fine meals, meals I could not have possibly paid for then." Armstrong and his drummer companion from Marable's band, Baby Dodds, returned to saloon bands and played with the Tuxedo Brass Band again. Grown wiser, Armstrong left Daisy Parker.

The Chicago Era

On August 2, 1922, Armstrong received a telegram from Joe Oliver asking him to join his band. His reaction, according to Bergreen, was automatic and immediate: "I made up my mind just that quick. Nothing could change it. Joe, my idol had sent for me—Wow." As second cornetist with King Oliver's Creole Jazz Band, Armstrong's weekly salary was $52, a phenomenal sum at the time. Not only did he broaden his travel experiences, he also made his first recordings, 35 in 1923 alone. Under Oliver's tutelage, he first gained attention by winning "cutting contests"; when Armstrong was challenged soon after being hired, Oliver made him meet any dares. Bergreen described the results of the insulting challenge issued by a well–known trumpeter: "Louis blew like the devil. Blew him out of that place. . . . So that's when Joe started to turn Louis loose by himself."

Armstrong's reputation also gained the attention of a well–known jazz pianist, Lil Hardin, a former member of Oliver's band who had featured billing at the Dreamland Café, a Chicago jazz institution. She became the most influential person in Armstrong's life. Hardin realized that Armstrong had a rare talent that was being submerged in Oliver's band. Although her first impression of him was unfavorable due to Armstrong's countrified manner, Hardin began to feel differently as Armstrong's real persona was revealed. He was dazzled by her because she was quite well educated, a rarity in the jazz world. After the two were married in 1924, Oliver was shrewd enough to lure Hardin away from her former position by paying her a $100 weekly salary. But Oliver's strategy backfired as Lil Armstrong began to bolster Armstrong's self–confidence and to dream on a scale he could not possibly imagine. According to Bergreen, Armstrong said: "I knew she was talking big, and just laughed at her. But I could see, too, that she was serious and thinking of me."

Armstrong's new wife was relentless in her efforts to dislodge Oliver as Armstrong's primary influence, especially since Oliver kept much of his protégé's earnings. Using her wifely advantage, she made her husband take control of his salary and assert his independence from Oliver. Lil Armstrong badgered her husband to leave Oliver's band and become first trumpet, a band's lead soloist. He did so in 1925, but was first rejected by Sammy Stewart, who used only Creoles and light–complected blacks in his band. Armstrong's big break came when Fletcher Henderson, a prominent Harlem band leader, offered him a first trumpet position for $50 a week. Henderson's Black Swan Troubadours played at the Roseland Ballroom, a New York landmark so famous that Armstrong turned down a higher paying position with Sam Wooding. Armstrong's New York arrival coincided with the emergence of the Harlem Renaissance, the golden era of black excellence in the arts.

Fletcher Henderson epitomized the urbane, well–educated leaders of the new black movement in the arts and he was a forerunner in establishing the jazz orchestra. But it was Armstrong who was the impetus, according to the *New York Times* for July 7, 1971: "Armstrong . . . provided the spark that made the jazz band viable. His presence in Fletcher Henderson's orchestra in 1924 changed a dance band . . . into a jazz band, the first of its kind." In that more sophisticated aggregation, Armstrong was forced to read band arrangements quickly and accurately; he was also forced to give up the cornet and become proficient on trumpet. Some of his best recordings were made with Henderson's band in 1925, particularly "Sugar Foot Stomp," one of his own compositions, and other recordings with Bessie Smith, the incomparable blues singer. Despite Armstrong's success in New York, Lil Armstrong was still not satisfied with her own lack of status in another band and she schemed to get her husband back to Chicago and under her thumb. He was not overly enthusiastic about returning to Chicago but felt loyalty to his wife. When he returned, he was shocked to learn that Lil Armstrong had secured for him star billing and a $75 weekly salary at the Dreamland Cabaret, but as a member of her own band.

In 1925 Armstrong became the leader of the Hot Five, a group originally assembled to record for the Chicago–based Okeh Record Company. All the musicians but Lil Armstrong were Louis Armstrong's New Orleans companions, and the group gained fame largely due to the recording of "Gut Bucket Blues," a funky number that featured each member as soloist; the use of multiple soloists was a device credited to Armstrong and imitated thereafter by dance bands. The group expanded to seven members and made over 50 recordings, some of which became jazz standards because of Armstrong's improvisational techniques and his "scat" singing. In 1926 the second set of Hot Five recordings became bestsellers, especially the piece "Heebie Jeebies." The title became a favorite password among professionals and after only a few weeks, the record had sold over 40,000 copies, a phenomenon in the fledgling record industry. The Hot Five series transformed jazz, and according to Kernfeld the "effect on musicians and jazz enthusiastics was instantaneous and profound; few performers, either in or outside of jazz entirely escaped [its] influence."

Despite his newfound success and rise in popularity, Armstrong's personal life was in shambles, and he and Lil

Armstrong separated. He went to live with Alpha Smith, a 19–year–old girl who would become the next Mrs. Louis Armstrong many years later after Lil Armstrong finally relinquished control.

The Effects of the Great Depression

The Chicago venues that sponsored and fostered jazz were grievously affected by the Great Depression, and Armstrong and his fellow musicians soon joined the ranks of the unemployed. Armstrong returned to New York to play in a Broadway orchestra for the popular show *Hot Chocolate*. The show's composer was Fats Waller, and Armstrong had a hit with Waller's *Ain't Misbehavin'* in the landmark show that featured black performers. This engagement led to jobs in leading Harlem nightspots, on recording dates, and in other Broadway performances. By 1932 Armstrong's reputation was such that he toured Europe and then played a command performance before England's King George V. He also headlined a show at the London Palladium where he acquired the everlasting nickname ''Satchmo.'' In 1936 Armstrong went to Hollywood and made his first important appearance on the silver screen. He had earlier wrangled a small part in a 1931 movie, *Ex–Flame,* as a member of a black jazz orchestra and another in 1932 as a leopard–skin–clad trumpeter in *Rhapsody in Black and Blue.* During this period, Armstrong was arrested on a drug possession charge after he was caught smoking marijuana in a nightclub parking lot. After six days in jail, he went to trial and received a suspended sentence.

Armstrong continued to play and make recordings in New York and Chicago throughout the 1930s while also working with a big band that toured the country; still, his financial status never changed. One major problem was Armstrong's choice of managers and the other was Lil Armstrong, who had not agreed to a divorce despite their long separation. In 1935 Joe Glaser became Armstrong's handpicked manager, a decision questioned by many in the music business. Glaser was quite notorious; nevertheless, according to Bergreen, ''Louis didn't care whether Glaser was a pimp, pedophile, rapist, bootlegger, or racketeer. He had grown up among people like Glaser and had learned long ago that they often had their uses, and even their good sides.'' When Armstrong called Glaser, he was being sued by three former managers and also by Lil Armstrong, and the legality of his recording contracts was in question. Glaser quickly straightened out Armstrong's professional and personal problems so that the musician could perform without the stresses caused by finances and romances. Armstrong soon joined the ranks of the touring elite and his earnings became commensurate with those of ranking headliners. For the first time in his life, Armstrong had a steady paycheck, a regular allowance, and the freedom to perform at top venues across the country.

In 1937 Glaser's efforts to return Armstrong to movies succeeded. When he landed a part in *Artists and Models* starring Ida Lupino and Jack Benny, it should have been a coup; instead, the scene with Armstrong and Martha Raye was deemed sexually suggestive and from then on he was forced to portray musicians with no social interaction on screen. The following year he appeared in the comedy *Going Places.* For his role as a stable hand, one that required him to serenade a racehorse, Armstrong received an Academy Award nomination. Glaser also garnered significant publicity for his client in feature articles in *Esquire* and *Vanity Fair.* Glaser engineered the publication of Armstrong's first autobiography, an outgrowth of the musician's voluminous collection of handwritten and typed letters and stories. Although Glaser's intentions and motives were questioned by many, he ensured that Armstrong never again ended up in dire poverty as did the musician's first important mentor, Joe Oliver, who was reduced to selling food from a sidewalk pushcart.

The Good Life

Louis and Lil Armstrong were finally divorced in 1938; then Armstrong married Alpha Smith—an act that sounded the death knell for their long relationship. In New York's Cotton Club, Armstrong became attracted to a chorus girl that Bergreen described as ''dark–skinned, with a round face, full figure, and large eyes.'' Lucille Wilson was the first dark–skinned dancer at the Cotton Club and she would also be the most stable of Armstrong's wives. As their courtship progressed, Armstrong's bookings grew more lucrative. During the 1940s Glaser designed a new show that paired Armstrong with tap dancer Bill ''Bojangles'' Robinson, and on the same bill were Dorothy Dandridge and her sister. The act toured from Baltimore to Minnesota, from Ohio to Florida, and points in between. Periodically, Armstrong returned to Hollywood to appear in noteworthy films such as *Pennies from Heaven* in which he played a bandleader. When in New York, he often had the opportunity to appear on Broadway and one newsworthy venture was in the musical adaptation of *A Midsummer Night's Dream* entitled *Swingin' the Dream.* Judged to be over–ambitious, the show folded after 13 performances. In 1942 Glaser advised Armstrong to sign an MGM contract to appear in *Cabin in the Sky,* a former Broadway hit. As one of five musicians, he would receive a two–week guarantee of $7,500 and an extra $2,000 should a third week be required. Accepting the job was a wise decision since, later in 1942, the American Federation of Musicians's head enacted a recording ban that negatively affected some 130,000 musicians. The movie version of *Cabin in the Sky* was notable for its lack of the racist caricatures found in most movies with black artists. It starred Rex Ingram, Ethel Waters, Eddie ''Rochester'' Anderson, Lena Horne, and Duke Ellington as well as Armstrong, who played the Trumpeter. Most of Armstrong's sequence ended up on the cutting floor.

When Armstrong returned to touring, he also divorced Alpha Smith and married Lucille Wilson, who would be his last wife. During World War II he and his bands played on military bases. At the end of this traumatic period in America's history, Armstrong had a lifelong dream come true when he was selected as Mardi Gras King of the Zulu Social Aid and Pleasure Club in New Orleans. This honor also led to his selection for the February 21, 1949 cover of *Time* magazine.

Climax of a Great Career

At the height of Armstrong's popularity, he was more notable as a performer than as a musician. In an effort to please the public, he had begun to favor swing music. However, after making the movie *New Orleans,* he began to see that a return to jazz would best meet his needs. According to Bergreen, "For any other popular performer, a decision to leave the mainstream could be suicidal, but because Louis incarnated jazz, he brought it unequaled authenticity and conviction." This move led to a new choice of performing values, one that was highly advantageous for Armstrong. Jazz gained more respectability once Armstrong had been booked into Carnegie Hall, the Metropolitan Opera House, Town Hall, and other reputable sites. A new publicist, Ernest Anderson, also assembled back–up groups that included leading jazz players of the era.

While Armstrong maintained his popularity, he faced the challenge of a new style of music that was threatening to jazz old–timers. It was faster, more innovative, more harmonically advanced, and definitely more revolutionary for trumpet players. Armstrong's main stylistic adversaries were "Dizzy" Gillespie and Miles Davis, both of whom ridiculed Armstrong for his perceived clownish behaviors. Another common but divisive perception was that be–bop was Northern urban music for the "thinking" man while Armstrong's jazz was Southern honeysuckle–scented music fraught with emotion. Armstrong disliked the modern music and castigated it and its practitioners. He told *Jazz Stars,* "Those cats play all the wrong notes." Armstrong's most formidable weapon was the All–Stars, his touring band comprised of stellar musicians such as Sid Catlet, Barney Bigard, and Jack Teagarden, and the 300–pound vocalist Velma Middleton. This aggregation, with periodic personnel changes, would be Armstrong's last basic working unit.

From the 1950s on, Armstrong also appeared in films, many featuring him and the All–Stars, and memorable only for that reason. Two examples are *The Strip,* a 1951 venture for which the band earned a weekly salary of $20,000, and *Glory Allen* for which Armstrong earned $25,000 for an appearance. In 1953 Armstrong appeared as himself in *The Glenn Miller Story,* and for two days' work earned $5,000. In 1956 he made a noteworthy contribution in the film *High Society,* a starring vehicle for Bing Crosby, Grace Kelly, and Frank Sinatra. He and the All–Stars worked for 23 days in roles that depicted them as more than token blacks. Armstrong's reviews in print were rewarding. Later that year, he and the All–Stars went to Africa and Europe on a three–month tour sponsored by the Department of State and accompanied by a CBS news crew. Glaser was shocked to see, in Africa, regular crowds in the high six figures, much larger than those in America. They played before tribal chiefs and prime ministers alike. In 1959 Armstrong was featured in *The Five Pennies,* a biographical account of the career of Red Nicholas, a white jazz trumpeter. Again he received an astronomical salary for the time, $50,000 for eleven days' work. Despite his limited time on the screen, Armstrong had a strong role, largely due to the influence of Danny Kaye, who had a starring role.

In the summer of 1959 Armstrong suffered a heart attack and he never regained his robustness. Later that year, he and the All–Stars returned to Ghana, Nigeria, Zaire, and Beirut, but were only moderately successful. In 1963 he and the band were assigned "Hello Dolly," a song to be recorded as a demo for a show that had not even opened. After the play finally opened, it became a Broadway hit and, amazingly, Armstrong's version of "Hello Dolly" displaced the Beatles as number one on the 1964 pop charts.

Throughout the 1960s Armstrong continued to perform, but as only a shell of his former self. He performed "Hello Dolly" on the *Ed Sullivan Show* and in the movie version that also featured another ballad, "What a Wonderful World," which he sang. This song only became popular in America some two decades later as part of the soundtrack of the movie *Good Morning, Vietnam.* In 1968 Armstrong was still touring, and he also recorded another album that featured Walt Disney songs. His health problems worsened as his heart and kidneys grew weaker, exacerbated by at least 40 years of smoking marijuana. In 1969 Glaser, Armstrong's longtime manager, died. In 1970 Armstrong recorded an album with some of his jazz friends and was interviewed for the *New York Times.* Both ventures were quite retrospective experiences that encapsulated Armstrong's philosophies of life and death. By then, his health was so poor that his doctor strongly advised him against ever playing the trumpet again.

At the 1970 Newport Jazz Festival, Armstrong sang an old favorite, "Mack the Knife," with surprising strength and timing, although the golden horn was stilled. The music industry was astonished when Armstrong toured later that year and in early 1971; he even sang on network television with Bing Crosby. Shortly thereafter, he suffered another heart attack and was bedridden for a few months. Armstrong believed he would tour again and even summoned the All–Stars for a rehearsal, but he died in his sleep on July 6, 1971. He still did things his way right up to the end, for he died in his own bed in his home with his wife by his side. He was survived by his sister Beatrice, foster son Clarence, and two half–brothers. Armstrong did not have the jazz funeral he had long envisioned and spoken of in a *New York Times* interview; it was a more dignified occasion that his wife planned and executed. Lil Hardin Armstrong survived her former husband by a month and died after suffering a massive heart attack while performing a Chicago Civic Center concert in his memory. Lucille Wilson Armstrong died in 1983 in Boston where she had gone to attend a concert honoring her late husband. In 1996 the New York City Department of Cultural Affairs began efforts to make a museum out of the Queens, New York, Armstrong home; it was declared a National Historic Landmark in 1977 and a City of New York Landmark in 1983.

Armstrong left a treasure trove of memories in his autobiographical writings. His life can be summed up by a description from the world–famed Duke Ellington, who labeled Armstrong as "an American original." Albert Murray, a music critic, described Armstrong's influence in a special issue of the *New York Times* for January 25, 1998: "Everyone came to hear this man who swung harder than anyone else, whose trumpet playing pushed the limits . . . and whose singing style also broke completely with convention." In the end, Armstrong had analyzed his own music in *African American Biography*: "To me, jazz has always got to be a happy music. You've got to love it to play it."

REFERENCES

African American Biography. Detroit: Gale Research, 1994.

"Armstrong Was Root Source of Jazz." *New York Times,* July 7, 1971.

Bergreen, Lawrence. *Louis Armstrong: An Extravagant Life.* New York: Broadway Books, 1997.

Bogle, Donald. *Dorothy Dandridge.* New York: Amistad Press, 1997.

"Flashbacks." *New Orleans Times–Picayune,* June 29, 1997.

"High–Stepping to an Uptown Beat." *New York Times,* January 25, 1989.

Kernfeld, Barry, ed. *New Grove Dictionary of Jazz.* New York: Macmillan, 1988.

Krantz, Rachel C. *Biographical Dictionary of Black Americans.* New York: Facts on File, 1992.

Levine, Lawrence. *Black Culture and Black Consciousness.* New York: Oxford University Press, 1977.

"Louis Armstrong, Jazz Trumpeter and Singer Dies." *New York Times,* July 7, 1971.

"Louis Armstrong on Exhibit." *New Orleans Times–Picayune,* August 10, 1997.

Lyons, Len, and Don Perlo. *Jazz Portraits: The Lives and Music of the Jazz Masters.* New York: William Morrow, 1989.

"Queens College Plans to Make Louis Armstrong's House a Public Museum." *Jet* 89 (8 April 1996): 22.

Rennert, Richard, ed. *African–American Heritage Jazz Star.* New York: Barnes and Noble Books, 1993.

Stewart, Charles, and Paul Carter Harrison. *Chuck Stewart's Jazz Files.* Boston: Little, Brown, 1985.

Teachout, Terry. "Top Brass." *New York Times Book Review,* August 3, 1997.

COLLECTIONS

Armstrong's archives are at Queens College in New York. The Armstrong Special Collections is housed at the Louisiana State Museum in New Orleans and contains photographs, newspaper and magazine articles, most of his recordings, books, letters, concert programs, and other memorabilia. A jazz exhibit in the Old U.S. Mint building in New Orleans houses Armstrong's original bugle and cornet from the Colored Waif's Home in addition to other mementos.

Dolores Nicholson

Benjamin W. Arnett
(1838–1906)

Religious leader, educator, state politician, writer, bibliophile

The seventeenth bishop of the African Methodist Episcopal (AME) Church, Benjamin W. Arnett was a noted religious leader and church historiographer who provided a sound financial system for his church. He became known also as a state politician in Ohio and as a bibliophile—his library was dispersed later to benefit other collectors and libraries and their users.

Benjamin William Arnett was born March 6, 1838, in Brownsville, Pennsylvania. Little is known of his parentage; however, Robert R. Wright stated that he was the grandson of Samuel J. and Mary Louise Arnett and was "eight parts Negro, six parts Scotch, one part Indian, and one part Irish." His father, Benjamin Sr., secured the first lot on which to erect an African Methodist Episcopal Church in Brownsville.

On May 25, 1858, Arnett married Mary Louisa Gordon and they had six children: Alonzo T. A., Benjamin W. Jr., Henry Y., Anna Louise, Alphonso Taft, and Flossa Gordon. Two sons entered the African Methodist Episcopal Church ministry: B. W. Arnett Jr., and Henry Y. Arnett. Benjamin Jr. was a chaplain in the Spanish–American War and later president of Edward Waters College in Florida and Allen University in South Carolina. Henry became a pastor and presiding elder in the Philadelphia and Delaware annual conferences.

Arnett was baptized at six months of age. He was educated near Brownsville in a one–room school taught by his uncle, Ephriam Arnett. He then worked as a wagon boy, aiding in loading and unloading wagons on steamboats, on the Ohio River, the Mississippi River, and neighboring waters. Arnett also was employed as a waiter in hotels. A tumor on his leg prompted an amputation in March 1858.

Arnett received a teacher's certificate on December 19, 1863, and was for a time the first and only black teacher in Fayette County, Pennsylvania. Arnett taught and served as a principal in Washington, D.C. for ten months (1864–1865), then returned to Brownsville and taught there until 1867. He attended Wilberforce University and took special courses in theology at Cincinnati's Lane Theological Seminary.

Arnett joined the African Methodist Episcopal (AME) Church on February 17, 1856. He was licensed to preach on March 30, 1865, at the Baltimore Annual Conference held in Washington, D.C. He joined the Ohio Conference of the African Methodist Episcopal Church on April 16, 1867, in Lexington, Kentucky, and received his first appointment at Walnut Hills in Cincinnati, Ohio. Arnett was ordained a deacon on April 30, 1868, at Columbus, and an elder by Bishop Daniel Alexander Payne on May 12, 1870, at Xenia, Ohio. He filled the following church appointments in Ohio:

Benjamin W. Arnett

Walnut Hills (1867–1869); Toledo (1870–1872); Allen Temple, Cincinnati (1873–1875); St. Paul A.M.E. Church, Urbana (1876–1877); and St. Paul A.M.E. Church, Columbus (1878–1879).

Elected AME Bishop

Arnett was a General Conference delegate from the Ohio Annual Conference of the A.M.E. Church in 1872 and elected assistant secretary of the General Conference in that year as well. He was elected secretary to the General Conferences in 1876 and 1880. In May 1880 Arnett was elected financial secretary at the General Conference held at St. Louis, Missouri, and reelected in 1884 in Baltimore. In May 1888 he was elected the seventeenth bishop of the African Methodist Episcopal Church in Indianapolis, Indiana and consecrated May 24, 1888; he was elected on the first ballot. After his elevation to the bishopric, Arnett served as presiding bishop in the Seventh Episcopal District (South Carolina and Florida), 1888–92; the Fourth Episcopal District (Indiana, Illinois, Iowa, and Michigan) 1892–1900; the Third Episcopal District (Ohio, California, and Pittsburgh), 1900–1904; and the First Episcopal District (Philadelphia, New York, New Jersey, and New England), 1904–1906.

Arnett was an active and avid Republican. In Syracuse, New York, on October 4, 1864, he joined the National Equal Rights League under Frederick Douglass's presidency. He was a member of the Equal Rights Convention held at Cleveland, of which John M. Langston served as president; in December of 1866 Arnett was secretary of the convention held at Washington, D.C. He was chaplain of the Republican State Convention of Ohio in 1880 and acting chaplain of the Ohio legislature in 1879. In 1872 he was foreman and the only black on a jury in Toledo. When the National Republican Convention met at St. Louis, Missouri, in 1896, he served as chaplain.

In 1886 Arnett was elected to the Ohio legislature by a margin of eight votes to represent Greene County, the location of Wilberforce University, and assisted in the drafting of the bill abolishing Ohio's infamous "Black Code," which had lingered after the Civil War ended. While a member of the Ohio legislature he met Major William McKinley Jr., with whom he developed a lasting friendship. He presented to President McKinley on behalf of the African Methodist Episcopal Church, the Bible upon which he took his oath as president, March 4, 1897. The *Dictionary of American Biography* said that during McKinley's administration (1897–1901) Arnett was reputed to be "the powerful individual Negro at the White House."

In 1893 Arnett was a member of the Parliament of Religions in Chicago, Illinois, and presided over deliberations on September 15. The church presented him with a gold medal for the role he played on behalf of his church.

Arnett held offices in many organizations: secretary of the Bishops' Council; historiographer of the church; trustee of the Archeological and Historical Society of Ohio; vice–president of the Anti–Saloon League of America; trustee of Wilberforce University; director of Payne Theological Seminary; trustee of the United Society of Christian Endeavor; trustee and vice–president of the Combined Normal and Industrial Board of Wilberforce University (now Central State University); statistical secretary of the Ecumenical Conference of Methodism for the Western Section (1891–1901); and chairman of the statistical committee of the Western Section (1901–1911). Arnett presided at the Ecumenical Conference held in London, England, September 7, 1901. He was a member of the Executive Committee of the National Sociological Society; chairman of the Committee on Legislation and Transportation of the National Sociological Society; life member of the Business Men's League of the United States; and president of the Publications Board of the African Methodist Episcopal Church, 1904–1906.

During Arnett's appointment to the Third Episcopal District he built a home at Wilberforce University on a beautiful property of some ten acres. This home was known as Tawawa Chimney Corner and was located near the old Indian Tawawa Springs. In this cultural center many of the intellectuals of the day gathered. Among these were Paul Laurence Dunbar, the poet; a fellow African Methodist Episcopal bishop, Henry McNeal Turner; William Sanders Scarborough, classics scholar; and Mary Church Terrell, a one–time administrator at Wilberforce. His large library was the scene of many political and religious meetings.

In 1894 W. E. B. Du Bois, one of America's greatest scholars, undertook his first teaching stint at Wilberforce.

Arnett was the chairman of the board. The bishop and his trustees came to the conclusion that Du Bois was too ''sardonic, brainy eccentric.'' Arnett and Du Bois disagreed on educational philosophy, and Arnett made life uncomfortable for the later goateed savant. According to Du Bois's biographer David Lewis, Du Bois considered the university president as the devil incarnate and the ''heavyset, one–legged . . . Arnett'' behind him ''was Moloch himself.''

In connection with his duties as statistician for several religious organizations, Arnett produced a series of annual *Budgets,* which carried valuable information concerning churches. He compiled a work entitled *Negro Literature,* a ten–volume set of sermons, addresses, and speeches of African American men.

Arnett attained note as a bibliophile and as a literary patron. In 1883 he helped found the Tawawa Sunday School Assembly, Theological, Scientific and Literary Circle and edited its *Tawawa Journal.* Additionally, as a pastor, general officer and bishop, he steadily produced books and pamphlets on African Methodist Episcopal Church history and affairs. When Bishop Daniel A. Payne died in 1893 and Arnett succeeded him as the church's second historiographer, he simply continued his role as a productive editor. He published the *Budget of the A.M.E. Church,* a comprehensive yearbook, successively from 1881, 1882, 1883, 1884, 1885–86, 1887–88, 1891, 1901, and 1904. Nearly two dozen other publications came from his busy pen. These works include the *Life of Paul Quinn* (1873), *The Wilberforce Alumnal: A Comprehensive Review of the Origin, Development and Present Status of Wilberforce University* (1885), and the *Proceedings of the Quarto–Centenary (South Carolina) Conference, 1865–1890* (1890).

Arnett collected a sizeable library of African American literature. After he died the library was sold and scattered, with Fisk University and book collector Arthur A. Schomburg acquiring a number of items. As well, W. E. B. Du Bois bought a number of his rare and out–of–print items.

Arnett died in Wilberforce, Ohio on October 9, 1906, of uremic poisoning. His funeral, attended by almost 1,300 mourners, was held in the university's Galloway Hall where the principal eulogy was delivered by Bishop Henry McNeal Turner. He was interred in a private burial plot overlooking the state highway linking Cleveland and Cincinnati. Obituaries were published in the *New York Times* and the *Cleveland Gazette.*

A man with inimitable wit, Arnett was possessed with an imperturbable optimism and warm, race love. So sweet was his nature, the *A.M.E. Church Review* stated that his opponents loved him, and so conscious was he of his own blood that white people forgot race in his presence. On the other hand, he was held in disfavor by some for firing the scholar William Scarborough and hiring several of his own sons. He materially strengthened the financial system of his church. Many charged him as historiographer of being exceedingly extravagant with means, but it must be said that he was an exceptional factor in the life and influence of African Methodism in the world, and gathered and published an abundance of information, the value of which can not be compared.

REFERENCES

Dickerson, Dennis C. *The Historiographers of African Methodist Episcopal Church.* Nashville: African Methodist Episcopal Publishing House, 1992.

Kealing, H.T. ''Bishop Arnett.'' *AME Church Review* 23 (January 1907): 282.

Lewis, David Levering. *W. E. B. Du Bois: Biography of a Race 1868–1919.* New York: Henry Holt, 1993.

Logan, Rayford W., and Michael R. Winston, eds. *Dictionary of American Negro Biography.* New York: Norton, 1982.

Wright, Robert Richard, ed. *The Bishops of the African Methodist Episcopal Church.* Philadelphia: African Methodist Episcopal Publishing House, 1963.

———. *Encyclopedia of African Methodism.* Philadelphia: African Methodist Episcopal Book Concern, 1947.

COLLECTIONS

The Arnett Papers are in the archives of the Rembert E. Stokes Library at Wilberforce University.

Casper L. Jordan

Arthur Ashe

(1943–1993)

Tennis player, activist

The dust jacket for Arthur Ashe's memoir *Days of Grace* accurately described him as the embodiment ''of courage and grace in every aspect of his life, from his triumphs as a great tennis champion and his determined social activism to his ordeal in the face of death.'' Internationally known and respected as an athlete, Ashe was the first black man on the U.S. Junior Davis Cup team, the first black man named to the American Davis Cup team, the first black man to win a major tennis title—the national men's singles in the U.S. Lawn Tennis Association—and the first black man to win a singles title at Wimbledon. He won singles titles at three of the four

Grand Slam tournaments, the pillars of international professional tennis—the U.S. Open, the Australian Open, and Wimbledon—as well as several Grand Slam doubles titles.

Born in Richmond, Virginia, on June 10, 1943, Arthur Robert Ashe Jr. had a mixed ethnic background consisting of black American, American Indian, and Mexican ancestry. His father, Arthur Robert Ashe Sr., was guardian and caretaker of a large, segregated city park for blacks in Richmond and owned a landscaping business as well. His mother, Mattie Cordell Cunningham Ashe, died when Ashe was nearly seven years old. Afterward, a housekeeper was hired to help raise Ashe and his only sibling, a younger brother, John. As he grew older, Ashe had a problem understanding himself and the loss of his mother, and briefly sought counseling.

As Ashe grew up in the caretaker's cottage in Brookfield Park where his father worked, he began to play tennis when he was only seven years old. Part–time playground instructor Ronald Charity observed his talent and arranged for him to meet Walter Johnson, a black physician in Lynchburg, Virginia, who for more than two decades had been a patron for talented black tennis players. He kept the players in his home, provided the equipment they needed, and trained them on the court that adjoined his house. Up to that time, Wimbledon champion Althea Gibson was Johnson's most celebrated student.

Ashe's first tournament championship came in 1955 with the American Tennis Association's 12–and–under singles title. He won other tournaments in 1956 and 1957. Johnson entered Ashe in the junior national tennis championship in 1958, when Ashe was 14, and he became a semifinalist in the under–15 division. In 1960 and again in 1961 he won the junior tennis indoor singles title. Then Richard Hudlin, a St. Louis tennis official, offered to coach him. Ashe accepted and left Maggie Walker High School in Richmond during his junior year to move to St. Louis. He lived with Hudlin and his family while he completed secondary school training at Sumner High School with virtually a straight–A average.

In St. Louis and under Hudlin's tutelage, Ashe's tennis game continued to improve. He became the fifth–ranked junior player in the United States in 1962. After graduation, he accepted a tennis scholarship to study at the University of California at Los Angeles (UCLA), where he received a bachelor's degree in business administration in June of 1966. The university's tennis coach, J. D. Morgan, and professional tennis player Pancho Gonzales, who lived near the campus, were his trainers. In 1963 Ashe was ranked only eighteenth in the senior men's amateur division, but he was named to the Davis Cup team. Over the next 15 years he played 32 Davis Cup matches and won 27. He also won the Eastern Grass Court matches in August of 1964 and a month later the Perth Amboy Invitational in New Jersey. He had risen to sixth in the national rankings for amateurs.

Arthur Ashe

Until 1965, Ashe had won no major titles and among amateurs was ranked third in the nation. That year, however, he played in the finals of the U.S. national tennis championship at Forest Hills, New York, against two–time champion Roy Emerson. Ashe defeated Emerson in four sets and received a 15–minute standing ovation from the 11,000 spectators in the West Side Tennis Club. In addition to a tournament tour in Australia and Davis Cup matches in 1965, Ashe led his UCLA team to a National Collegiate Athletic Association (NCAA) championship by finishing first in both men's singles and doubles.

In 1966 Ashe spent six weeks with the Reserve Officers' Training Corps as a first lieutenant. From 1967 to 1969 he was a lieutenant in the U.S. Army. His tennis game continued during this time, as did his winnings. In 1967 he won the Men's Clay Court championship; when he also won the U.S. amateur championship that year he was invited to the U.S. Open Tournament. Winning that championship as well in 1968, he became the nation's top–ranked player.

Wins Wimbledon Singles

Ashe turned professional in 1969 and played in a number of matches. In 1975 he beat Jimmie Connors and became the first black man to win the Wimbledon Singles and the first black ranked number one internationally. That year he also won the World Tennis Championship Singles over Bjorn Borg.

Arthur Ashe in action.

In 1978, his career faced a sudden change. After suffering a heart attack in mid–summer of 1979, Ashe underwent a quadruple coronary bypass operation in St. Luke's–Roosevelt Hospital in Manhattan on December 13. He was only 36–years old. Three months later, Ashe felt completely recovered, but on March 9, 1980, he learned that his life would never be the same. Angina struck while he was in Cairo. Doctors told him that he had to end his career as a competitive tennis player, becoming a professional patient instead. He underwent a double bypass heart operation at St. Luke's on June 21, 1983, but, due to tough scar tissue from his first surgery, he was in worse condition this time. Feeling weak and anemic, he decided to receive two units of blood. Ashe wrote in *Days of Grace*: "This transfusion indeed picked me up and sent me on the road to recovery from surgery; it also . . . set in motion my descent into AIDS."

Ashe retired from tennis in April of 1980. Although Ashe played his last Davis Cup Match in 1978, between 1980 and 1985 he captained the U.S. Davis Cup Team. Ashe's captaincy of the Davis Cup gave him continued public exposure in sports magazines and elsewhere. He resigned the position in October of 1985 but remained loyal to the Davis Cup competition by serving as vice–chair of its committee.

Active in Protest and Politics

Since the 1970s Ashe adamantly opposed apartheid in South Africa. He remembered the segregated Richmond, Virginia, of his childhood and the civil rights protests of the 1960s. He was aware of the different world in which he played tennis. "You never forget that you are a Negro, and you certainly can't in my case," he told Frank Deford for *Sports Illustrated,* quoted in *Current Biography.* He also resented the "whites only" signs that he saw in Johannesburg, South Africa. Although he had visited the country four times between 1973 and 1977 to participate in tournaments, he insisted that there be no segregated seating at his matches. He consciously made South Africa the focal point of his political activities within and beyond the United States. He admitted in his memoirs that he played a major role in having the country banned from Davis Cup play.

Ashe wrote in his memoirs that "My Davis Cup campaigns, my protests against apartheid in South Africa, and my skirmishes over academic requirements for athletes were doubtless the most highly publicized episodes of my life in the 1980s after my retirement.'' In the 1980s Ashe worked quietly as a lobbyist for higher academic standards for athletes in colleges as addressed by Proposition 42 and Proposition 48, implemented in 1984 by the National Collegiate Athletic Association. Clearly the 1980s were a period of protest and politics for Ashe. He protested apartheid by serving as co–chair of the TransAfrica Forum and he lobbied for African and Caribbean affairs founded by his childhood friend Randall Robinson. He also became a founding member of Artists and Athletes Against Apartheid and co–chaired the committee with Harry Belafonte. Among the group's goals were to bring pressure on South Africa and to dissuade athletes and entertainers from performing there.

On January 11, 1985, he was arrested outside the South African Embassy in Washington, D.C., for taking part in a demonstration. He wrote in his memoirs that ''the experience of being handcuffed, carted away, and booked was daunting. I also knew that, in certain circles, my arrest could cost me some influence and prestige,'' such as the loss of his Davis Cup captaincy. Later in 1985 he helped Belafonte and Jesse Jackson lead a march on the U.S. mission to the United Nations (UN). Finally, in 1989, Ashe's pleas before the board of the Association of Tennis Professionals succeeded in getting the organization to officially boycott two tournaments originally scheduled for Johannesburg. In 1991 he traveled there with a delegation of African Americans whom Nelson Mandela had invited.

After retiring from tennis, Ashe devoted his time to public speaking, teaching, writing, business affairs, and voluntary services. In his memoirs Ashe said that his work as board member of the Aetna Life and Casualty Company, which he had served for ten years, was the ''single most fascinating and satisfying involvement outside my family.'' This was due largely to the company's concern for health care—in the absence of a national health care program—and its fair treatment of minorities.

Ashe also received invitations to teach college courses. He turned down Yale for Florida Memorial College, a historically black college in Miami with an enrollment of 1,200. There he taught a seminar on ''The Black Athlete in Contemporary Society.'' He also was inspired to conduct a serious study of African Americans in sports and to publish the findings. As he prepared his course syllabus, he found the literature about blacks in sports seriously wanting even though blacks had been leading athletes in such sports as boxing, baseball, football, basketball, and track. Ashe knew that their stories needed to be told. Using his own funds—approximately $300,000—he hired a team of researchers and writers. Few primary sources existed, so the team consulted old issues of college yearbooks and black newspapers, interviewed parents, called for a search of medals and mementos to help reconstruct the past, and appealed to the public through the media for further information. From interviews with various historians, Ashe determined that the subject of the black athlete had been neglected due to ''academic snobbery and timidity,'' as he said in his autobiography. Although their interest in sports was widespread, writing about it was beneath the notice of serious historians, and publishers were unwilling to subsidize research in the field. Warner Books published the results of Ashe's study in 1988 as *A Hard Road to Glory: A History of the African American Athlete.*

Ashe's other writings included *Off the Court* (1981), which he dedicated to one of his ancestors who had been a slave. In this way he expressed pride in his roots, which were deep in the black past. His memoir *Days of Grace,* coauthored with Arnold Rampersad, was nearly completed before his death. He also wrote *Arthur Ashe on Tennis Strokes, Strategy, Traditions, Players, Psychology, and Wisdom,* with Alexander McNab—published in 1995.

''The Beast in the Jungle''

Ashe candidly discussed the last chapter of his life in his memoirs as ''The Beast in the Jungle.'' He had endured four major operations in his lifetime: a heel surgery in 1977, a quadruple bypass in December of 1979, corrective double bypass in June of 1983, and brain surgery in September of 1988. The brain surgery revealed that he did not have a brain tumor, but had an infection instead. The following day he and his wife Jeanne learned of his human immunodeficiency virus (HIV) infection and that he had full–blown acquired immune deficiency syndrome (AIDS). After searching for the roots of his infection, Ashe learned that a blood transfusion following surgery in 1983 carried the deadly virus. He wrote in his memoirs that people often committed suicide because of despair caused by HIV infection and that ''the news that I had AIDS hit me hard but did not knock me down.'' He refused to surrender to depression or to consider suicide. ''AIDS does not make me despair,'' he continued, ''but unquestionably it often makes me somber.'' The possibility of a published report in *USA Today* on his health prompted him to reveal his condition to the world in a press conference on April 8, 1992.

In time, Ashe stepped up his speaking engagements and lectured at such institutions as McGill in Canada, Duquesne, Brown, the University of Virginia, and elsewhere, answering students' questions about AIDS and his own struggle. U.N. Secretary–General Boutros Boutros–Ghali invited Ashe to address the U.N. General Assembly on World AIDS Day. Quoted in his memoirs, Ashe told the audience, ''It has been the habit of humankind to wait until the eleventh hour to spiritually commit ourselves to those problems which we knew all along to be of the greatest urgency.'' Ashe also spoke to a wide range of professional groups, such as the National Press Club, public school teachers, employees of drug companies, business people, and journalists on issues of privacy and freedom of the press.

In the face of his illness, Ashe and his wife found solace in the teachings and writings of black theologian Howard Thurman. Thurman's teachings in particular helped Ashe to keep control despite the changes that occurred in his life. Ashe said that he also remained steadfast in his Christian faith.

In retirement Ashe wrote columns for the *Washington Post* and served as a commentator for tennis matches. He worked in a variety of social programs and foundations that he either started or helped to start, including: the Ashe–Bollettieri Cities program, which used tennis to hold the attention of youth in inner cities and poor environments; Athletes Career Connection, which addressed the high attrition rate of black athletes in football and basketball at large colleges and universities; and the Safe Passage Foundation, which helped poor young people, especially blacks, to make a healthy transition to adulthood. After learning that he had AIDS, Ashe founded the Arthur Ashe Foundation for the Defeat of AIDS, to fight and help conquer the virus, and the African American Athletic Association to counsel and advise young black athletes, especially student athletes, and help to address their academic performance.

During his lifetime Ashe received wide recognition for his athletic accomplishments—including induction into the International Tennis Hall of Fame at Newport, Rhode Island, as soon as he was eligible—but he also garnered many academic honors. He received several honorary degrees, including those from such institutions as Princeton, Kalamazoo College, Loyola College of Baltimore, and Virginia Commonwealth University. He was committed to education and had a high regard for historically black colleges. Ashe demonstrated his commitment by becoming a veteran supporter of the United Negro College Fund. President Bill Clinton awarded him the Presidential Medal of Freedom posthumously in June of 1993, at the first annual National Sports Award presentation held in Washington, D.C.

Ashe wrote in his memoir that family was "the central social unit." His letter to daughter Camera, published in his memoir, spoke to her about family roots, race, languages, health, music, and art. Ashe died of pneumonia on Saturday afternoon, February 6, 1993, in New York Hospital–Cornell Medical Center in Manhattan, and was buried the following Wednesday in Woodland Cemetery in Richmond, Virginia. He was survived by his wife, Jean Moutoussamy Ashe, whom he married on February 20, 1977, and who is a professional photographer, and their daughter, Camera. A 12–foot bronze monument commemorating his life was unveiled near monuments of several Confederate leaders on Monument Avenue in his hometown of Richmond, on July 10, 1996. Inscribed on the monument is a Biblical passage that is also quoted in Ashe's autobiography: "Since we are surrounded by so great a cloud of witnesses, let us lay aside every weight, and the sin which easily ensnares us, and let us run with endurance the race that is set before us." The statue may be moved in front of the proposed African American Sports Hall of Fame when that building is completed. In his honor as well, the U.S. Tennis Association named its new stadium for the U.S. Open National Tennis Center the "Arthur Ashe Stadium."

REFERENCES

Ashe, Arthur R. Jr. *A Hard Road to Glory.* 3 vol. New York: Warner Books, 1988.

———, and Arnold Rampersad. *Days of Grace: A Memoir.* New York: Knopf, 1993.

Current Biography Yearbook. New York: H. W. Wilson, 1966.

"Seasons Change." *Nashville Tennessean,* July 11, 1996.

"Tennis Legend Arthur Ashe's Statue Unveiled in His Hometown." *Jet* 90 (29 July 1996): 46–48.

"U.S. Tennis Association Names Stadium in Honor of Arthur Ashe." *Jet* 91 (10 March 1997): 48–50.

Jessie Carney Smith

Crispus Attucks

(1723?–1770)

Slave, sailor, patriot

Historian George W. Williams in *History of the Negro Race in America* described the Boston Massacre as "the bloody drama that opened the most eventful and thrilling chapter in American history." Neither a soldier nor a leading town citizen proved the hero of that pre–Revolutionary War struggle. Instead, the first of five men to die in the massacre was a runaway slave turned sailor, Crispus Attucks. His death has forever linked his name with the cause of freedom.

Historians know little about Attucks, and they have constructed accounts of his life more from speculation than facts. Most documents described his ancestry as African and American Indian. His father, Prince Yonger, is thought to have been a slave brought to America from Africa and that his mother, Nancy Attucks, was a Natick Indian. Researcher Bill Belton identified Attucks as a direct descendent of John Attucks, an Indian executed for treason in 1676 during the King Philip War. The family, which may have included an older sister named Phebe, lived in Framingham, Massachusetts.

Crispus Attucks

Apparently, young Attucks developed a longing for freedom at an early age. According to *The Black Presence in the Era of the American Revolution,* historians believe that an advertisement placed in the *Boston Gazette* on October 2, 1750, referred to him: ''Ran away from his Master *William Brown from Framingham,* on the 30th of *Sept.* last, a Molatto Fellow, about 27 Years of age, named Crispas, 6 Feet two Inches high, short curl'd Hair, his Knees nearer together than common: had on a light colour'd Bearskin Coat.'' The owner offered a reward of ten pounds for the return of the slave and warned ship captains against giving him refuge. George Washington Williams noted that the advertisement appeared again on November 13 and November 20. Biographers surveyed that Attucks escaped to Nantucket, Massachusetts, and sailed as a harpoonist on a whaling ship.

Historians definitely place Attucks in Boston in March of 1770. While in Boston, probably awaiting passage on a ship to the Carolinas, he found a job as a dockworker. Some writers proposed that he was using the name Michael Johnson. Assuming that the *Boston Gazette* advertisement did refer to him, he would have been about 47–years old.

Boston Massacre

By 1770 Boston had become ''a storm center of brewing revolt,'' according to Benjamin Quarles in *The Negro in the American Revolution.* The British had stationed two regiments in the city following protests by the colonists against unfair taxes. Citizens welcomed neither the troops walking the streets nor the two canons aiming directly at the town hall. Describing the setting, historian John Fiske explained in *Unpublished Orations* that ''the soldiers did many things that greatly annoyed the people. They led brawling, riotous lives, and made the quiet streets hideous by night with their drunken shouts. . . . On Sundays the soldiers would race horses on the Common, or would play 'Yankee Doodle' just outside the church–doors during the services.''

As tensions mounted, the atmosphere grew ripe for confrontation. Fiske pointed out that during February of 1870, ''an unusual number of personal encounters'' had occurred, including the killing of a young boy. Regarding the evening of March 5, 1770, he explained, ''Accounts of what happened are as disorderly and conflicting as the incidents which they try to relate.'' A barber's apprentice chided a British soldier for walking away without paying for his haircut. The soldier struck the boy, and news of the offense spread quickly. Groups of angry citizens gathered in various places around town. Someone rang the church bell and such a summons usually meant that a fire had broken out. This night, however, it presaged an explosive situation between the soldiers and the townspeople.

Captain Thomas Preston called his Twenty–ninth Regiment to duty. Townspeople began pelting the troops with snowballs. From the dock area, a group of men, led by the towering figure of Attucks, entered King Street, armed with clubs. Some accounts maintained that Attucks struck soldier Hugh Montgomery. Others, for example, John Fiske, stated that he was ''leaning upon a stick'' when the soldiers opened fire. However the incident occurred, Attucks lay dead, his body pierced by two bullets. Ropemaker Samuel Gray and sailor James Caldwell also died in the incident. Samuel Maverick, a 17–year–old joiner's apprentice, died the next day. Irish leather worker Patrick Carr died nine days later, and six others were wounded. Citizens immediately demanded the withdrawal of British troops. Fiske noted in *Unpublished Orations* that the deaths of these men ''effected in a moment what 17 months of petition and discussion had failed to accomplish.''

John Adams reluctantly agreed to defend the British soldiers, two of whom were charged with manslaughter and branded. At the trial, Adams focused on Attucks, portraying him as a rabble–rouser. Because of accounts given at the trial, some historians have questioned the motives of the massacred men. Fiske evaluated that although we cannot know their motives, ''we may fairly suppose them to have been actuated by the same feelings toward the soldiery that animated Adams and Warren and the patriots of Boston in general.''

Boston Honors

The town's response to the murders expressed the significance of the sacrifices these men made. The bodies of

Attucks and Caldwell lay in state at Faneuil Hall; those of Gray and Maverick lay in their homes. For the funeral service, shops closed, bells rang, and thousands of citizens from all walks of life formed a long procession, six people deep, to the Old Granary Burial Ground where the bodies were committed to a common grave. Until the signing of the Declaration of Independence, Boston commemorated their deaths on March 5, ''Crispus Attucks Day.'' According to Ted Stewart in *Sepia,* Boston abolitionist Wendell Phillips stated on the first such occasion, ''I place. . .this Crispus Attucks in the foremost rank of the men that dared.''

Through the years, people have remembered Attucks in a variety of ways. Paul Revere created a woodcut of the incident, and the National Archives housed a painting by noted New England artist Benjamin Champney depicting the event. Negro military companies took the name Attucks Guards. Poets dedicated works to his memory, and communities named schools after him.

In 1888 Boston erected a monument to the heroes of the massacre which James Neyland in *Crispus Attucks* called ''the first ever to be paid for by public funds'' in Massachusetts. City officials had rejected earlier petitions for such a monument. Even in 1888, various Boston factions heatedly debated the appropriateness of this gesture. At the unveiling, speaker John Fiske called the Boston Massacre ''one of the most significant and impressive events in the noble struggle in which our forefathers succeeded in vindicating, for themselves and their posterity, the sacred right of self–government.''

In his 1995 biography, James Neyland wrote about Attucks: ''He is one of the most important figures in African–American history, not for what he did for his own race but for what he did for all oppressed people everywhere. He is a reminder that the African–American heritage is not only African but American and it is a heritage that begins with the beginning of America.'' Although obscure in life, Attucks played an important role in U.S. history through his death. Bill Belton in the *Negro History Bulletin* contended that the name of Crispus Attucks will stand ''forever linked to the birth of this nation and its dream of freedom, justice, and equality.''

REFERENCES

Belton, Bill. ''The Indian Heritage of Crispus Attucks.'' *Negro History Bulletin* 35 (November 1972): 149–52.

Fiske, John. *Unpublished Orations.* Boston: Bibliophile Society, 1909.

Kaplan, Sidney, and Emma Nogrady Kaplan. *The Black Presence in the Era of the American Revolution.* Revised edition. Amherst: University of Massachusetts Press, 1989.

Neyland, James. *Crispus Attucks.* Los Angeles: Melrose Square, 1995.

Quarles, Benjamin. *The Negro in the American Revolution.* Chapel Hill: University of North Carolina Press for the Institute of Early American History and Culture, 1961.

Ryan, Dennis P. ''The Crispus Attucks Monument Controversy of 1887.'' *Negro History Bulletin* 40 (January–February 1977): 656–57.

Stewart, Ted. ''Boston Blacks in the Revolution.'' *Sepia* 25 (May 1976): 58–67.

Williams, George W. *History of the Negro Race in America, 1619–1880.* 2 vols. 1882. Reprint, New York: Arno Press and the *New York Times,* 1968.

Marie Garrett

DeFord Bailey
(1899–1982)
Entertainer, musician

DeFord Bailey occupies a unique place in country music as the first and, for many years, the only black star of the Grand Ole Opry. He owed his popularity to his technical virtuosity and musicianship on the mouth harp (harmonica) although he also played other instruments and sang. He is best remembered for playing a limited number of traditional tunes to which he gave his own stamp as he explored them over the years. Bailey's abrupt dismissal from the Grand Ole Opry in 1941 virtually ended his musical career.

DeFord Bailey was born in Smith County, Tennessee, on December 14, 1899. He was the son of John Henry Bailey, a tenant farmer born on May 20, 1878, and Mary Reedy Bailey, the daughter of neighboring farmers who owned their land. Mary Bailey named her son DeFord after two of her teachers—Mr. DeBerry and Mrs. Stella Ford. DeFord Bailey's father moved away and remarried. His mother died within a year after DeFord's birth, so John Henry Bailey's younger sister, Barbara Lou Bailey, took charge of the child. This later became a permanent arrangement as Barbara Lou Bailey (d.1923) and the man she married, Chuck Odum (d.1928), eventually replaced his real parents in the daily life and affection of the youngster.

While there was musical talent in the Reedy family, the Odums and the Baileys were primarily responsible for Bailey's musical development. His paternal grandfather, Lewis Bailey (1843–1908), who lived with his daughter Barbara Lou and her family during DeFord's early years, was considered the best musician in Smith County. Moreover, Bailey's father and other family members at times formed a string band that was popular at barn dances. Bailey once claimed that, as a child, he was given a mouth harp instead of a rattle. At this time and in this part of the world blacks shared a musical tradition with the whites around them. In one of his interviews with David Morton, Bailey called it "black hillbilly music." It died out after 1920 and the coming of the blues.

Despite his precocious musical development, Bailey was expected to become a farm worker like the other men in his family. However, in 1904 he was stricken by polio and could not walk for a year. Despite medical attention and home remedies like rubbing earthworms boiled in oil on his limbs, his physical development was affected. He remained small. He was the size of a nine–year–old when he was 12. As an adult he was four feet ten inches tall, slightly crippled from the polio, and weighed less than 100 pounds. While Bailey worked hard on the farm and enjoyed working with animals, he was just too small for heavy tasks like plowing.

DeFord Bailey

Bailey began playing the harmonica and the guitar while recovering from the polio attack. His subsequent physical weakness enabled him to continue to work on his music, and his foster mother saw to it that he had ample time to practice. In addition to the harmonica, which was always his favorite, and the guitar, Bailey tried the mandolin and, to a lesser extent, the fiddle. Many of his instruments were homemade, including banjos; wash tub bass fiddles; quills (short reed pipes); and bones, a percussion instrument made from beef ribs.

In 1908, after the death of Lewis Bailey, Bailey's foster father Clark Odum took over a farm near Newsom's Station, a hamlet in Davidson County about ten miles west of Nashville. On this occasion, Bailey rode the train for the first time to visit his biological father, who was living in Nashville with his new family. After the move Bailey continued to work about the farm but still spent several hours a day practicing on his harmonica. Around 1914 the family moved to another farm, this time south of Nashville in Williamson County, and in about 1916 to yet another farm seven miles south of Franklin,

Tennessee. It was in Williamson County that Bailey first came into contact with black musicians outside of his family. There, too, he received most of his schooling. He learned enough arithmetic to handle money and also learned how to sign his name. He refused to learn to read, however. He did appreciate working with his hands and sold a set of doll's furniture he had made in manual training class for $2.75, a substantial sum at the time.

Bailey's formal schooling ended about 1917 when he was asked by a white shopkeeper, Gus Watson, to live with him and his wife. Bailey helped out in Watson's general store and also played for the customers. He was well taken care of even though he received no formal wages. Two major events occurred in 1918. In July Bailey's father died in Evansville, Illinois, and that fall Clark Odum decided to move his family to Nashville. Bailey followed the Odums to Nashville after spending several weeks nursing the Watsons through the Spanish influenza.

Clark Odum had found a job as groundskeeper for Mr. and Mrs. J. C. Bradford, one of Nashville's wealthiest and most prominent families. Bailey was hired as a houseboy but later played the harmonica to entertain the Bradfords and their guests. After leaving the Bradford family, Bailey followed Odum to work for another family. Between 1920 and 1925, he worked as an odd job person at a downtown pharmacy, a houseboy again, kitchen help at the Maxwell House Hotel, an odd job man at a motion picture theater, a shoe shine person, a delivery person, a car washer, and an elevator operator. Bailey continued to play his harmonica during breaks in work. He also discovered new kinds of music. He especially enjoyed medicine shows and haunted the main black theater, the Bijou, a stop on the Theater Owners' Booking Association (T.O.B.A.). On occasion he even played at the theater himself.

Bailey's family began to drift apart after the death of Barbara Lou Odum in 1923. Clark Odum rented a house in Nashville for the children and traveled to Detroit where he found work and was able to send money back to the family.

Begins Radio Career

In the spring of 1925, while Bailey was an elevator operator in the old Hitchcock Building, he earned five dollars by playing at a formal dinner in the new five–story National Life and Accident Insurance Company building. The year 1925 was also the year that radio came to Nashville. Bailey was persuaded to enter a contest sponsored by the first station on the air in Nashville, WDAD. Despite Bailey's obvious superiority, the promoter awarded him second prize—a decision that spared Bailey great trouble because other competitors were angered by a black being placed ahead of any white man. WSM, Nashville's second station, went on the air in the fall of 1925, and on December 26, WSM began a series of broadcasts featuring country music, programs later named *The Barn Dance.*

In early 1926 Bailey was persuaded to appear on the program and had such success that he was given two dollars and told to come back the following week. By June 19, in his first documented appearance, Bailey was doing a 15–minute set. In the fall of 1927, George D. Hay, "The Solemn Old Judge" who was the program's master of ceremonies, introduced Bailey as the first country musician on a program following a network classical music presentation from Chicago. According to Morton and Wolf, after Bailey played one of his famous train songs, "The Pan American Blues," Hays asserted, "For the past hour, we have been listening to music largely from Grand Opera, but from now on, we will present 'The Grand Ole Opry.'" The name stuck, and by December had become the official name of the Saturday night program. Between mid–1926 and April 1927 Bailey appeared on the program more than any other performer. In 1928 he appeared on 49 of the 52 programs; the next most frequent performer appeared on 29. Bailey's appearances continued through the 1930s when he often appeared first at 8:30 p.m. and then did a second segment at 10:30 or 11:00.

During 18 weeks in 1927–1928 Bailey made all of the commercial records he ever attempted—some 11 singles. Although some of the recordings had modest success, Bailey received very little money and made no further attempts to record. His success at the Opry continued. In spite of his well–received performances of other songs, audiences repeatedly demanded three songs: "The Fox Chase," "The Pan American Blues," and "Dixie Flyer." His popularity rested principally on these tunes.

Bailey was never entirely satisfied with his earnings because of a well–justified belief that other performers made more money. In 1928 Bailey tried to break away from Nashville. He worked briefly for a Knoxville station and contemplated moving to California to further his career. He was persuaded to return to WSM when his pay was raised from $7 a show to $20.

In 1929 Bailey married Ida Lee Jones, the teen–aged niece of his landlord. The marriage ended in divorce. There were three children—a son, DeFord Jr. in 1932, and two daughters, Dezoral Lee also in 1932, and Christine Lamb in 1936. Searching for ways to earn more money, Bailey opened a barbecue stand next to his house at 130 Lafayette Street about 1930. It remained in operation for eight years. In 1933 he opened a shoe shine shop with his uncle. He routinely rented out rooms in the houses in which he lived. Bailey had no expenses for automobiles since he never learned how to drive. The bicycle he got about on became famous in the city.

All Grand Ole Opry stars went on the road to cash in on their fame and earn more money. By the time WSM organized the Artists' Service Bureau in 1933, Bailey was well accustomed to touring. Many aspiring country music stars used his popularity and drawing powers to bring in audiences for their own music. After Bailey had some difficulties getting his money from several promoters, Judge Hay decreed that Bailey would get a fee of $5 a performance. This well–intentioned edict did not always work out to his advantage since Bailey often could have earned more if he had shared the normal percentage of the gate. In addition, he had trouble containing his expenses on the road and seldom came home with more than $10. Bailey did not drink and did not socialize much with his white associates or with blacks in the towns they visited so he very often stayed behind to watch over equipment. For self–protection Bailey acquired a small Smith and Wesson pistol that he always carried with him.

Bailey observed the niceties of black–white relationships in his era. Abetted by his non–threatening size, he was careful not to appear pushy and knew how to put up with the occasional verbal abuse he was subject to. Hostile happenings stood out in his memory because of their rarity. Still Bailey was burdened constantly with finding a place to eat and a place to sleep while on tour. Some performers consistently helped by threatening to boycott restaurants that would not even let him eat in the kitchen. Bailey often had to be smuggled into hotels where he would sleep on a mattress on the floor or share a bed. Morton quoted a statement made by Bailey concerning his work at the Opry: "I didn't hang around. I came to perform, then I went home." Many persons who heard Bailey on the radio did not know he was black, but this fact quickly became obvious when he was on tour, often in places where blacks were very rare indeed.

Fired from the Opry

Around 1940 a power struggle developed between the American Society of Composers, Authors, and Publishers (ASCAP) and the radio networks. ASCAP had set a deadline of January 1, 1941, for a new contract with the radio networks. The networks resisted and boycotted ASCAP–copyrighted music. This meant radio performers were forced to write new material. Although many of the tunes that Bailey used, such as "Fox Chase" and "Casey Jones," were traditional, they nonetheless had ASCAP copyrights. Bailey did not like the idea of composing music for his program; he preferred to modify and recreate the limited number of folksongs he loved. Bailey's refusal to write new material may have led to his release from the Opry in late May of 1941. Nevertheless, he remained extremely popular and, to head off criticism, WSM continued to pay him three dollars a week just to be present and visible at shows for several weeks.

Bailey then decided never to work for anyone else again. He had opened his first shoe shine shop in 1933, so he took on this line of work full time. His various shops were in the black Edgehill section of Nashville. While the majority of his clientele was black, he also attracted large numbers of whites, some of whom even mailed their footwear from out of town. To some of the tough young black men in the neighborhood sought his advice and revered him as a father figure. He also bought every gun that he was offered just to get them out of circulation.

Bailey performed occasionally during his later years but his already rocky relations with the Opry worsened when he discovered that he received only $50 for appearing in a wartime propaganda film featuring Opry performers while other performers earned $1000. In 1967 Bailey performed in two segments of a syndicated film series entitled *Grand Ole Opry,* which were included on a 1988 videotape, *Legends of the Grand Ole Opry.* In the 1950s he appeared regularly on a local television program. He also occasionally sang gospel music with his children in local churches.

Bailey was a deeply religious man whose performance of secular music occasionally troubled him. He gave up dancing at the age of 11 or 12 when his foster mother whipped him for his motions while dancing to the tango "Sally Long and Her Drop Stitch Stocking Was a Horrible Skirt." While seriously ill in the hospital in 1974, Bailey wrote a song in which he expressed his dependency on God.

In the 1960s Bailey made several appearances on Noble Blackwell's syndicated television show *Night Train* where a new generation interested in folk music rediscovered him. He performed locally, but efforts to record his music failed. In 1974 Bailey appeared for the first time in ten years when he played on the last show in the Ryman Auditorium. He could have performed more often during the period and might have had a major revival in his career, but he turned down many offers because of his suspicion that he would still be exploited. As quoted by Morton and Wolfe, Bailey once asserted:

> They say I don't like white people. They got me wrong. I'm just like white people. I just want my money. . . . I don't hate the man. I just hate his ways. . . . I just want my money from black or white. Like a union that goes on strike. I don't want more than anyone else, but I want the same as they get.

In 1970 Bailey's house was torn for an urban renewal project, and he was moved into a high–rise building for the elderly just across the street. His health was generally good until shortly before his death. Bailey's mood was greatly lifted when it was discovered around 1973 that his deafness was largely due to wax buildup in his ears. After the wax was removed he was able to resume his music. He lived very quietly, seeing mostly family and a few friends. As he told David C. Morton, whom he knew was planning to write a book about him:

> I want you to tell the world about this black man. He ain't no fool. Just let people know what I am. . . .
>
> I take the bitter with the sweet. Every day is Sunday with me. I'm happy go lucky. Amen!

DeFord Bailey died on July 2, 1982, and was buried in Greenwood Cemetery. On June 23, 1983, which had been proclaimed "DeFord Bailey Day" by Nashville's mayor, family and friends, including old–time Opry performers gathered there for a ceremony marking the unveiling of a monument at his grave. The inscription aptly summed up his achievement, "Harmonica Wizard, Musician, Composer, Entertainer, Early Star of Grand Ole Opry."

REFERENCES

The Comprehensive Country Music Encyclopedia. New York: Times Books/Random House, 1994.

"DeFord Bailey: The Legacy of the Grand Ole Opry's First Star Still Shines Brightly." *Nashville Tennessean, Weekend,* February 10, 1991.

Guralnick, Peter. *Lost Highway: Journeys & Arrivals of American Musicians.* Boston: Godine, 1979.
Morton, David C., with Charles K. Wolfe. *DeFord Bailey.* Knoxville: University of Tennessee Press, 1991.

Robert L. Johns

Baker, George.
See Divine, M. J. "Father."

James Baldwin
(1924–1987)
Novelist, essayist, short story writer, playwright

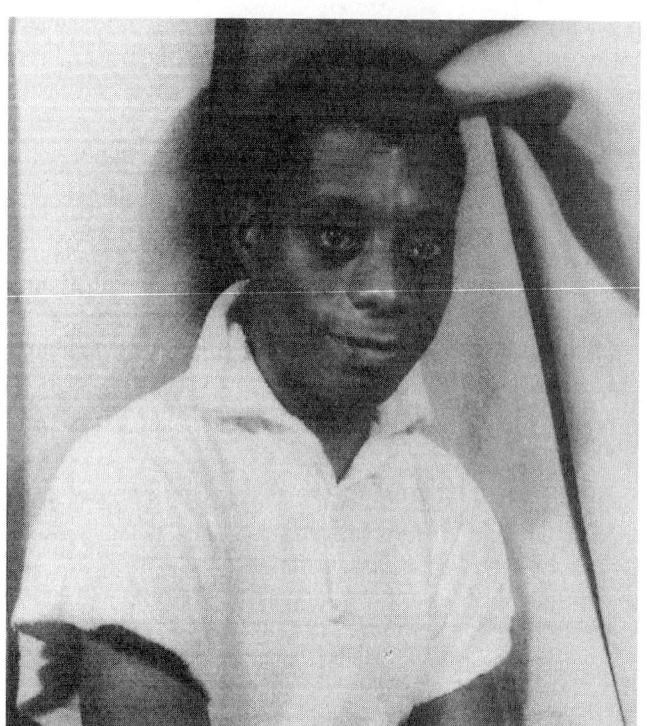

James Baldwin

Thanks in large part to the author himself, biographical information on James Baldwin abounds. One gets very detailed glimpses of Baldwin from several of his characters, such as John in *Go Tell It on the Mountain,* David in *Giovanni's Room,* or Leo in *Tell Me How Long the Train's Been Gone,* and David in *Amen Corner.* Baldwin detailed his experiences in many of his essays, including in "Equal in Paris," "Notes of a Native Son," and "Down at the Cross."

James Baldwin was born at Harlem Hospital on August 2, 1924, to Emma Berdis Jones, a quiet and gentle woman who endured a difficult existence. When Emma Jones was just a child, her mother died and she was reared first by her father, a fisherman on Maryland's Eastern Shore, and then by her older sister Beulah after her father remarried. She later traveled to Philadelphia, living with a cousin, and then to New York where she met and married David Baldwin, who David Leeming described in *James Baldwin: A Biography* as "a man several years older than she, but a respectable clergyman who seemed genuinely willing to accept her son as his son."

For a while James Baldwin felt comforted by David Baldwin and actually believed that his stepfather really loved him and his mother. Unfortunately such positive feelings did not last long. David Baldwin, a cruel and puritanical migrant to New York from New Orleans, was not only much older than his wife but also bitter, stern, abusive and tyrannical. Baldwin's stepfather labored in a bottling plant, and on weekends he served as a deacon and preached in a storefront church. The young Baldwin reminisced in "Notes of a Native Son," republished in *The Price of the Ticket,* that he did not know his stepfather very well and none of David Baldwin's children were ever happy to see him come home. There were plenty of children in the Baldwin household: George, born in 1927; Barbara in 1929; Wilmer in 1930; David in 1931; Gloria in 1933; Ruth in 1935; Elizabeth in 1937; and Paula Maria in 1943. When Samuel, David Baldwin's son from his previous marriage, left home for good at 17, eight–year–old Jimmy, according to *The Furious Passage of James Baldwin,* became "heir to a strange and unrelenting battle."

Baldwin viewed his childhood as awful. The family was poor and large, and his stepfather despised James's illegitimacy and constantly told the boy that he was ugly, too ugly, in fact, to expect anyone to love him. His stepfather never achieved any success in his churches, so the family went from church to smaller church, as David Baldwin found himself in decreasing demand as a minister. Emma Baldwin was constantly trying to appease her husband, to whom she always submitted, and she persuaded her children to do likewise.

In spite of David Baldwin's cruelties to his family and especially to James, Baldwin explained in "Notes of a Native Son" that his stepfather was undoubtedly a very sick man whose mind had been damaged by a negative society and a resulting negative self–image. On the pulpit he was powerful and chilling, but in his personal life, he was, according to James Baldwin, "certainly the most bitter man I have ever met." In retrospect, the stepson surmised that his stepfather was a very confused man who wanted to be proud of his blackness but it had caused him too much humiliation and suffering.

Relief from his father's vengeance and hate came to James Baldwin at intervals when he started school in 1929. At P.S. 24, Baldwin came in contact with people who recognized his intelligence, who encouraged him to read, write, and make use of the public library, and who did not berate him for his looks and physical features. Gertrude Ayers, the principal, made sure that Baldwin received special attention. Several teachers also worked closely with Baldwin and made him appreciate his days at P.S. 24; one of them was Orilla Miller, Baldwin's first drama teacher who nourished his love of movies and plays. At Frederick Douglass Junior High School, Baldwin was instructed and befriended by teachers who helped him develop as a writer and as an individual. Countee Cullen, a French teacher and founder of the school's literary club, and Herman W. ''Bill'' Porter, advisor to the school's magazine, were two such teachers who positively influenced Baldwin professionally and personally.

Early Experiences in the Church

During the summer when he turned 14, Baldwin underwent what he called in ''Down at the Cross,'' reprinted in *The Price of the Ticket* ''a prolonged religious crisis.'' By this time, he had become aware and afraid of the evil within and without. Many of his friends were beginning to drink, smoke, take drugs, and have sex. Baldwin decided not to follow the crowd and attended the Fireside Pentecostal Assembly Church with his friend Arthur Moore.

Shortly after joining the church, and spending a night on the church floor looking for answers, he was told that he was ''saved.'' Soon after he became a preacher, according to ''Down at the Cross,'' he knew that he ''could not remain in the church merely as another worshiper.'' Thus, the young Baldwin, in opting for the sanctuary of the church, was forced, and therefore betrayed, by the church to surrender his sexuality, to abandon many of his aspirations, and to isolate himself from worldly experiences.

At the age of 17, disillusioned with the church, and armed with an increasingly negative view of its people, its past, and its current practices, Baldwin abandoned the ministry, denounced the Christian church, and began writing his first novel. In ''Down at the Cross,'' Baldwin dated:

> the slow crumbling of my faith, the pulverization of my fortress—from the time, about a year after I had begun to preach, when I began to read again. I justified this desire by the fact that I was still in high school, and I began, fatally, with Dostoevsky. . . . I was forced, reluctantly, to realize that the Bible itself was written by men, translated by men out of languages I could not read, and I was already, without quite admitting it to myself, terribly involved with the effort of putting words on paper.

Baldwin's father's persistent mistreatment of him and his high school Jewish friends, as well as the unholy and inexplicable dreams that the young minister was having at night, also helped to drive him from the church.

The 14–year–old's discovery of God and the Christian church owed much to the boy's fear of and wish to escape the world outside the church, to his relishing the attention, excitement, safety, and relief that the church provided, and to his competition with his father. But young Bladwin soon realized that neither his motives nor the offerings of the church were sincere enough to sustain his devotion. As noted in ''Down at the Cross,'' the teenage minister would rush ''home from school, to the church, to the altar, to be alone there, to commune with Jesus, my dearest friend, who would never fail me, who knew all the secrets of my heart.'' Baldwin concluded that God did fail him, and ''that whoever wishes to become a truly moral human being . . . must first divorce himself from all the prohibitions, crimes, and hypocrisies of the Christian church.''

Of course, Baldwin's father did not revive his son's faith in Christianity or endear him to the Christian ministry when, as described in ''Down at the Cross,'' the elder Reverend Baldwin slammed him ''across the face with his great palm.'' Prior to the slapping, Reverend Baldwin had asked his son if his best friend was ''saved,'' and Jimmy responded coldly, ''No. He's Jewish.'' Baldwin realized at that time that ''all those sermons and tears and all that repentance and rejoicing had changed nothing.'' Then after telling his father that his Jewish friend was a better Christian than his Christian minister father was, he left his father's house, just as he had previously denounced, and removed himself from the other Father's house.

Professional Career Begins

The fact that Baldwin left the church and became a writer almost simultaneously is not coincidental. For 17 years Christianity had been the focal point of Baldwin's existence. For a brief while it had provided him a respite, an escape, a stage for performing. Eventually, though, when he was facing a congregation, it took all of his strength not to curse, not to tell the people to get off their knees, to throw away their Bibles, and to go home and do something far more beneficial for themselves. Rather than hurl these profanities from the pulpit, Baldwin elected to use his literary genius. Writing, then, became for him a means of personal therapy and a way for him to reach more people than just the African American members of his congregation. It is evident in Baldwin's titles, characters, settings, plots, diction, symbols, themes, and cadences, as well as in his speech making and rhetorical practices, that Baldwin the writer was greatly and somewhat positively influenced by his experiences in the church and the pulpit.

Next to the church, perhaps the second greatest influence on Baldwin as a writer was an artist, Beauford Delaney, to whom Baldwin was introduced in Greenwich Village by his high school friend, Emile Capouya, when Baldwin was 16. Baldwin stated in his introductory chapter to *The Price of the Ticket* that Beauford, without lecturing, enabled him to see, hear, think, and feel as an artist. After Beauford and Baldwin met in 1940, the two maintained a father–son relationship until Beauford died in 1979.

By the time Baldwin finished high school, he was firmly committed to becoming a writer, and he knew that he would have to achieve his goal without benefit of a higher education since he had neither the desire nor the money to attend college. So for the next four years, he worked at various jobs that he did not like to pay bills and help his family, while still concentrating on his writing. During this time his stepfather died on June 29, 1943, the same day his mother gave birth to her last child. A few months later Baldwin suffered a nervous breakdown. Between 1943 and 1944 he met Eugene Worth, whose suicide in 1946 (like Rufus, in *Another Country,* by jumping off the George Washington Bridge) further troubled Baldwin. Though they had not been lovers, Baldwin thought such a relationship may have prevented Worth's suicide. ''I remembered,'' Baldwin noted in the introduction to *The Price of the Ticket,* ''that he had, once, obliquely, suggested this possibility.'' But because Baldwin was ''unable to imagine that anyone could possibly be in love with an ugly boy like me,'' he did not act on Eugene's confession of love. Baldwin, therefore, blamed himself for Eugene's death.

Baldwin's life as a writer began in 1947 with the publication of a review of Maxim Gorki's *Best Short Stories* in *The Nation,* the first of many reviews Baldwin was to write. In 1948 the first of his essays, ''The Harlem Ghetto,'' appeared in *Commentary.* This essay which attempted to promote harmony between blacks and Jews by comparing the two groups, was no doubt inspired in part by Baldwin's close relationship with his high school Jewish friends. Also in 1948, Baldwin published his first short story, ''Previous Condition,'' a work that decries the racism Baldwin experienced in Greenwich Village. In November of that same year, Baldwin, having concluded that he needed to leave the United States in order become a novelist, left New York for Paris, where he was to spend the next three years of his life. While in Paris, Baldwin continued to write reviews, essays, and short stories, including his essay, ''Everybody's Protest Novel,'' which soured his relationship with Richard Wright due to its criticism of *Native Son* as protest literature.

Two significant events occurred while Baldwin was in Europe. He met Lucien Happersberger, a young man who was to be a part of Baldwin's life for the next 39 years. Happersberger's inability to enter into a monogamous relationship was a source of a great deal of pain for Baldwin. Also during those years in Paris, Baldwin managed to complete the novel he had begun ten years earlier, *Go Tell It on the Mountain,* allowing him to return to America as a novelist. This novel, which most critics reviewed favorably, shows the affect of Christianity and violence on the lives of the major characters, all of whom are searching for hope and answers.

Like all of Baldwin's novels, his first was autobiographical. A Harlem storefront church is the setting for almost three–fourths of the novel, the work begins in the home of the Grimes family on the fourteenth birthday of John, who, like Baldwin, is the oldest child in the family. Also, like Baldwin, John is despised and mistreated by his minister–stepfather, Gabriel, whom the children and their mother fear and dislike. The major focus of the novel is sin and retribution. The prayers of Gabriel, Elizabeth, and Florence, Gabriel's sister, reveal that a combination of circumstances and conditions, including racism, sexism, and alcoholism, as well as the church itself, has rendered the characters hopeless and denied them love and salvation. Even the novel's ending does not suggest hope. John does, indeed, undergo some type of metamorphosis on the floor of the Temple of the Fire Baptized, but its cause, nature, and consequences are certainly open to debate and analysis.

Baldwin's next two works focus on the role of the church and the minister. Sister Margaret Alexander is the pastor of the church in the play, *The Amen Corner* (1954); and on Baldwin's father David, whose death on July 29, 1943, and whose funeral on Baldwin's nineteenth birthday were the stimuli for the essay, ''Notes of a Native Son'' (1955). In his prefatory ''Notes for *The Amen Corner,*'' Baldwin recalled that his writing the play was a desperate act that he wrote out of indebtedness to his father:

> I was old enough by now, at last, to recognize the nature of the dues he had paid, old enough to wonder if I could have paid them, old enough, at last, to know that I had loved him and wanted him to love me. I could see that the nature of the battle we had fought had been that dictated by the fact that our temperaments were so fatally the same; neither of us could bend.

Baldwin also wrote that Sister Margaret's dilemma is ''how to treat her husband and her son as men and at the same time to protect them from the bloody consequences of trying to be a man in this society.''

A Successful Author and Civil Rights Advocate

When he returned to Paris in 1955, following the publication of *The Amen Corner* in 1954, Baldwin had become a noted novelist, short story writer, essayist, and playwright. For the next 25 years, he continued to write and publish at an inexhaustible rate while residing for brief periods in both America and Europe. Baldwin published *Giovanni's Room* in 1956, a novel that condemns the American David for denying his homosexual love for Gavin. The short story, ''Sonny's Blues,'' was published in 1957, promoting understanding and tolerance between two brothers. In 1961 ''Nobody Knows My Name'' was released, an essay that focuses inequality of the races and especially the inhumane treatment of black people in the North as well as in the South.

Baldwin had toured the South in 1957 in an effort to witness first–hand the struggles African American southerners were enduring in their efforts to gain civil rights. Baldwin was impressed by the work and preaching of Martin Luther King Jr. as well as by the courage of the children in Little Rock and by the participants of the Montgomery bus boycott. Baldwin, however, did not become a major figure in the civil rights battles of the 1950s and 1960s, although he returned to the South in 1960. His commitment to the struggle was displayed largely in his writing and speeches, and his advice was often sought by black leaders of the civil rights movement as well as by such government leaders as U.S. attorney general Robert Kennedy.

Just as he went South to experience the blacks' fight for civil rights, Baldwin ventured to Africa in 1962 to return to his African roots and to get an understanding of his African brethren and their ways of life. Again, Baldwin used these experiences in developing numerous essays and speeches.

Also, just as Baldwin at 17 had denounced the religion of his stepfather, he likewise rejected the Nation of Islam movement 21 years after his first trip to Africa. Baldwin could no doubt appreciate the bitterness of Elijah Muhammad and Malcolm X toward what white Christianity had done to blacks, as well as the Muslims' commitment to black economic unity and black pride. Baldwin took issue, however, with the Muslims' call for complete physical separation of the races and felt than an emphasis on vengeance, whether in the name of God or Allah, was a prescription for murder and slaughter, as Baldwin made clear in the essay, "Down at the Cross," which Baldwin first published near the close of 1962.

Baldwin also published his third novel, *Another Country,* in 1962. This work chronicles the plight of urban blacks in America through the life and death of Rufus Scott, and the effects of his suicide on others, especially on his sister, Ida, and on his white friends. Three more novels followed *Another Country. Tell Me how Long the Train's Been Gone,* which Baldwin completed in Istanbul, Turkey, in 1968, is the author's denouncement of the religion of hatred and violence through the narration of a black actor, Leo Proudhammer, who commits himself completely to Black Christopher and his Black Nationalism because they offer greater possibilities of a peaceful and loving existence than do Jesus Christ and Christianity. The love story of *If Beale Street Could Talk,* published in 1974, is also a criticism of the Christian church and hypocrisy as it pleads for family harmony and unity between the principal families, the Hunts and the Rivers, at a time when it is essential that they come together and function as a unit for the benefit and well–being of both families. Baldwin's last novel, *Just Above My Head,* published in 1979, narrates the unhappy life of a child evangelist whose liberation and happiness are achieved by forsaking her empty evangelicalism and embracing a new, non–Christian philosophy.

In addition to the novels, *Going to Meet the Man,* a collection of short stories, was published in 1965. Another play, *Blues for Mr. Charlie,* was completed in 1964. Baldwin has published over 200 essays, many of which he collected and reprinted in *The Price of the Ticket,* which he published in 1985, two years before his death.

On December 1, 1987, eight years after the publication of his last work of fiction, James Baldwin, at the age of 63, died at his home in the St. Paul de Vence in southern France. His brother, David, and his friends, Lucien Happersberger and Bernard Hassell, were at his bedside. He had been diagnosed with cancer of the esophagus eight months prior, and by the time of his death, the cancer had spread to other parts of his body. He was survived by his mother and his five younger sisters and three younger brothers whom he had helped his mother to rear.

Baldwin's funeral was held on Tuesday, December 8, 1987, at New York's Cathedral of St. John the Divine. Thousands turned out for his "Celebration of Life" service, with such notables as Toni Morrison, Maya Angelou, and Amiri Baraka praising the life of one of this country's most gifted and prolific writers of essays, novels, short stories, and plays.

For his last 40 years, Baldwin had adopted France as his permanent home, leaving the United States, to escape racism. At the time of his death, Baldwin was the United States's best–selling African American author worldwide. In many of the articles following his death, Baldwin was referred to as a noted essayist rather than as a great novelist and as a key figure in the civil rights movement during the 1960s, when he was writing extensively about race relations and participating in social protests.

REFERENCES

Baldwin, James. *The Amen Corner.* New York: Dial Press, 1968.

———. *The Price of the Ticket: Collected Nonfiction, 1948–1985.* New York: St. Martin's Press, 1985.

Campbell, James. *Talking at the Gates.* New York: Viking Penguin, 1991.

Eckman, Fern Marja. *The Furious Passage of James Baldwin.* New York: M. Evans and Co., 1966.

"James Baldwin, Eloquent Essayist in Behalf of Civil Rights, Is Dead." *New York Times,* December 2, 1987.

Leeming, David. *James Baldwin: A Biography.* New York: Knopf, 1994.

Troupe, Quincy, ed. *James Baldwin: The Legacy.* New York: Simon and Schuster, 1989.

Weatherby, W. J. *James Baldwin, Artist on Fire: A Portrait.* New York: Donald I. Fine, 1989.

COLLECTIONS

The Schomburg Center for Research in Black Culture currently houses a few of the unpublished papers and letters copyrighted by the James Baldwin estate. Most of the other materials pertaining to the life and work of James Baldwin are in the possession of his sister, Gloria Smart, 137 W. Seventy–first Street, New York, NY 10023.

Floyd C. Ferebee

Benjamin Banneker
(1731–1806)
Inventor, mathematician, astronomer

Benjamin Banneker is credited with being the first African American man of science. He was a self–taught mathematician and astronomer, and in 1791 he participated in the survey of federal territory that later became Washington, D.C. Early in life, he built a striking clock with hand–carved wooden parts from his observations of a pocket watch, and in

1792 he published the first almanac written by a black. The astronomical tables that he calculated for his almanacs were published from that year until 1797.

Born on November 9, 1731, in the Oella region of Maryland, not far from Baltimore, Benjamin Banneker was the first son of Robert and Mary Bannaky (Banneker).As the children of free parents, Banneker and his two sisters were also free. Although his ancestry was white and African, Banneker is said to have appeared African, but no definitive portrait has survived. The Banneker family began life in America in servitude. Banneker's paternal grandmother was Molly Welsh, a British maid who arrived as an indentured servant in Maryland, where she prospered. His paternal grandfather was Banna Ka, an African slave, probably of royal heritage, whom Molly Walsh purchased along with two others. Molly Walsh married Banna Ka, and they started a family which produced Robert, Benjamin Banneker's father.

Young Benjamin grew up in an agrarian setting in rural Maryland. Molly Walsh taught him to read the Bible, and this initial exposure to reading opened up a world which he continued to explore throughout his life. His formal education, however, was limited to intermittent instruction offered during the winter in a one–room school taught by a Quaker and attended by several white pupils and two or three free blacks. Banneker's innate curiosity grew, but as soon as he was old enough he had to leave school to work full–time on the farm. During this time he somehow became an accomplished musician and learned to play several musical instruments. When his father died in 1759, the 28–year–old Banneker became the family's provider and produced good crops of fruit and vegetables. There is no record of any romantic involvement in his life, and he never married.

Banneker's mechanical and scientific interests were demonstrated in 1753, when he constructed a striking clock made of wood based solely on his examination of a pocket watch. His personal character, combined with his rare ability to read and write, won him the respect of his neighbors within the limitations imposed by his social status as a free black. On January 4, 1763, he bought his first book—a Bible.

In January of 1771, John and Andrew Ellicott began building a mill on an extensive tract of land they had recently purchased. The neighbors were naturally interested in activities which led to the foundation of a new community, and Banneker, in particular, was fascinated. He met the owners and was eventually attracted to their store, where he proved an able conversationalist among those who gathered there to talk. He also fed his curiosity by reading any newspaper he could find. Banneker's associations and friendships with various members of the Ellicott family were mutually beneficial, and George Ellicott shared his own keen interest in astronomy with his older friend.

Turns to Astronomy

In the fall of 1788, George Ellicott lent Banneker four books on mathematics and astronomy and some astronomical instruments, including a pedestal telescope, as well as a sturdy drop–leaf table to work on. Banneker worked his way through the four books and began to use the instruments, but the intensity of his interests led him to neglect his work on the farm. To use his new skills, Banneker began to calculate an ephemeris, a table of astronomical data commonly contained in almanacs.

Benjamin Banneker

In 1792, Banneker published *Benjamin Banneker's Pennsylvania, Delaware, Maryland and Virginia Almanack and Ephemeris, for the Year of Our Lord, 1792; Being Bisextile, or Leap–Year, and the Sixteenth Year of American Independence, which commenced July 4, 1776.* It sold well, prompting the publishers to issue a second edition soon afterwards. Banneker appreciated the validation of his scientific skill and knew that his work provided evidence that African people could make a valuable contribution to science and humanity. The series of yearly almanacs started with the first in 1792 and continued until 1797. In all of them Banneker supplied the astronomical calculations while the various publishers supplied the literary and supplemental material commonly found in such works. Later, in 1793, Banneker published another set of astronomical tables.

James McHenry, a member of President John Adams's cabinet, wrote a sketch of Banneker for the 1792 almanac. The 1793 almanac included a letter written on August 19, 1791, from Banneker to Secretary of State Thomas Jefferson as well as Jefferson's response. Later quoted in *The Life of Benjamin Banneker,* Banneker declared that he was a proud African American who was "not under that tyrannical thraldom, and inhuman captivity to which to many of my brethren are doomed, but that I have abundantly tasted of the fruition of those blessings.'' He challenged Jefferson's views of the limitations of African intellectual ability and the inherent inferiority of blacks by using himself and his accomplishments to weaken Jefferson's position. Jefferson's response of August 30, 1791, is polite: ''No body wishes more than I do, to see such proofs as you exhibit, that nature has given to our black brethren talents equal to those of the other colors of men; and that the appearance of the want of them, is owing surely to the degraded condition of their existence, both in Africa & America.''

That edition also included ''A Plan Of a Peace Office for the United States,'' an unsigned essay which for years was attributed to Banneker until it was ultimately identified in 1947 as the work of Benjamin Rush, a Philadelphia doctor who questioned the condition and position of all people of color and of the poor. In Banneker's biography, Bedini wrote that the plan ''provided prestige that contributed largely to the almanac's impact on behalf of the antislavery movement.''

Although Banneker's achievements convinced few of those who believed in the inherent inferiority of blacks, it did provide support to antislavery whites, even if they did not embrace equality for blacks. Bedini wrote that Banneker's almanac, strengthened by the inclusion of the Jefferson correspondence and the Rush Plan, became ''one of the most important publications of its time.'' The Pennsylvania Society for the Promotion of the Abolition of Slavery used the almanac to promote its work and arranged with William Young of Philadelphia to publish another issue the following year.

Surveys Federal Area

Banneker's involvement with the survey of the federal area that had been set aside to become the nation's capital has been the subject of several legends and embellishments, including those in Shirley Graham Du Bois's fictionalized biography, *Your Most Humble Servant* (1949). Banneker worked on the survey of Washington for three months ending in April 1991 as an assistant to Andrew Ellicott, a cousin of the Maryland Ellicotts. Chronically ill at the time, he did little or no fieldwork, concentrating instead on calculation. Banneker was not, as is sometime claimed, an assistant to the notoriously secretive Pierre L'Enfant, who designed Washington, and thus would not have known his plans for the city. Nevertheless, the experience gave Banneker additional confidence in his own abilities and helped lead to the publication of his almanac the following year.

During the last years of his life, Banneker lived alone on his farm. He did his own cooking, but his two sisters, who lived within walking distance, took turns performing the other household chores. Declining health forced him to give up tobacco farming. His last years were plagued by problems with the tenants on his land, theft, and annoying raids on his orchards by neighborhood boys. He also began to drink—a trait his mother had helped to control while she was alive.

Banneker gradually sold off parcels of his land, and a sale to the Ellicotts resulted in annual payments which assured him an income for the rest of his life. He was much relieved to give up his responsibilities for the farm. He continued to devote himself to his music and now had time to lie outside, wrapped in his cloak, to observe the stars. A deeply religious man, Banneker never joined a church although he often attended the Friends Meeting House in Ellicott's Lower Mills. With advancing age, his physical infirmities worsened. As he talked to a friend on his usual morning walk on October 9, 1806, he began to feel ill. The friend helped him return home, where Banneker lay down on his couch and died.

Banneker made oral agreements about the distribution of his property but left no written will. He requested that gifts from George Ellicott be returned and that his surviving sisters, Minta Black and Molly Morton, take the family Bible. Most of his other possessions, including his clock, were destroyed in a fire that occurred either during his burial or a few days after his death. Those items designated for the Ellicotts had been returned before the fire. Banneker was buried near the family homestead, and the rediscovered site was marked in 1990. He was honored again in 1970, when a circle near L'Enfant Plaza in Washington, D.C., was named for him. The U.S. Postal Service issued a stamp in his honor in 1980, and many schools and organizations also bear his name.

Banneker was a self–educated man who was able to develop great skill in astronomy in spite of his social segregation as a free black and his physical isolation as a rural farmer. His mechanical and practical ingenuity is evident in his construction of a working clock from observation alone. He is remembered for his presence at the original survey of the nation's capital, for publishing the first almanac prepared by a black, and for promoting the equality of African people through his remarkable example.

REFERENCES

Allen, Will. *Banneker: The Afro–American Astronomer.* 1921. Reprint, Salem, NH: Ayer Company, 1971.

Baker, Henry E. ''Benjamin Banneker, the Negro Mathematician and Astronomer.'' *Journal of Negro History* 2 (April 1918): 99–118.

Bedini, Silvio. *The Life of Benjamin Banneker.* New York: Scribner, 1972.

Kyle, Robert. ''Banneker Buyer Makes Long–Term Loan to Maryland Museum.'' *Maine Antique Digest* (February 1997).

Lewis, David L. *District of Columbia.* New York: Norton, 1976.

Logan, Rayford W., and Michael R. Winston, eds. *Dictionary of American Negro Biography.* New York: Norton, 1982.

COLLECTIONS

Banneker's journal, called the Commonplace Book, and an 1862 manuscript are still in private hands. Twenty or more remaining items have been donated to the Civil War Memorial Freedom Foundation in Washington, D.C. They are on 20–

year loan to the Banneker–Douglass Museum in Annapolis, Maryland, and the Banneker Museum and Historical Park at the former homesite in Oella, Maryland, which is scheduled to open in 1998.

Robert L. Johns and Ida Jones

Amiri Baraka

(1934–)

Educator, author, publisher, editor, social and political activist, playwright

Amiri Baraka, formerly known as LeRoi Jones, has made an indelible mark on twentieth–century American and African American literature and art. In his break from tradition, he searched for rhythm, language, and a voice that would speak to the literary and artistic expression of African Americans. He is respected by his contemporaries and critics, as reflected in Arnold Rampersad's comment in *The LeRoi/ Amiri Baraka Reader,* ranking Baraka as "one of the eight figures ... who has significantly affected the course of African–American literary culture." *Contemporary Authors* called him "the primary architect of the Black Arts Movement of the 1960s."

Born in Newark, New Jersey, on October 7, 1934, as Everett Leroy Jones, Baraka is the son of Anna Lois Russ Jones and Coyette LeRoy Jones, a barber and postal worker who rose to the rank of supervisor. He has one sister, Elaine. Baraka's affinity for education and entrepreneurship were the result of his family's background. His mother came from an educated middle class family and his maternal grandparents were business owners. In 1958 Baraka married a Jewish woman, Hettie Roberta Cohen, and they had two daughters, Kellie Elizabeth and Lisa Victoria Chapman Jones. They later divorced. In 1966 Baraka married Sylvia Robinson, who later changed her name to Amina. They had five children—Obalaji Malik Ali, Ras Jua Al Aziz, Shani Isis Makeda, Amiri Seku Musa, Ahi Mwenge—whom Baraka described in his autobiography as "strong, beautiful, brilliant children who will be a match for all [the racism, deception, and inequities] their parents wrestled with [in] a more primitive world." Baraka's early years were a time of transition for his parents and grandparents. Though he was in grade school, he felt the major changes which occurred in his family. A reversal of fortune and a series of mishaps dictated several moves for the Alabama family before settling in the culturally eclectic community of Newark, New Jersey. As a youngster, he was a good student, avid reader, and prolific cartoonist. By the seventh grade Baraka had created a comic strip called "The Crime Wave" and was writing short stories. He studied at McKinley Junior High and Barringer School, a college preparatory school attended primarily by Italians.

Amiri Baraka

Baraka adopted the French spelling of his first name during his early college years. Although he was offered scholarships to several colleges, he accepted a two–year science scholarship to Rutgers University, where he remained for one year. There he studied such writers as T. S. Eliot and Ezra Pound. The overwhelming feeling of isolation he had known at Barringer was worse at Rutgers.

In 1952 Baraka transferred to Howard University where his educational experiences were enriched by exposure to the teaching of such outstanding black scholars as E. Franklin Frazier, Nathan Scott Jr., and Sterling A. Brown. In his autobiography he reflected on "the series of unofficial classes" Brown taught on African American music in the Cook Hall dormitory:

> The music classes were something intimate and wonderful to me. He was opening up to us the fact that the music could be studied and, by implication, that black people had a history. He was raising the music as an art, a thing for scholarship and research as well as deep enjoyment. Brown's music was the high point of my "formal" Howard education.

Still, Baraka became disillusioned with what he called Howard's "reeking," "bourgeois," "stiff," and "artificial" atmosphere. He lost interest in his classes and spent most of his time engaged in conversation, going to jazz clubs, and partying with friends. He eventually flunked out of school.

On October 6, 1954, one day before his nineteenth birthday, Baraka left home to begin basic training at Sampson Air Force Base in Geneva, New York. Then he was sent to

Chanute Field in Rantoul, Illinois, where he enrolled in weather training school, the only African American selected for this special training. Due to his consistently high academic standard, Baraka was elected class leader and, on one occasion, named Airman of the Month. He graduated with the highest grade point average in the class, giving him first choice to select his tour of duty. Believing that life at the base in Puerto Rico was comparable to a country club, Baraka selected Ramey Air Force Base. He read and studied widely to offset the disappointing experience there. An anonymous letter and questions concerning literature he possessed brought Baraka under suspicion of being a Communist. In 1957, following three grueling years in Puerto Rico, he was discharged from the Air Force based on the trumped–up charge of being undesirable.

Literature and Political Expression

Throughout his military career, Baraka continued reading. In 1954 or 1955 he discovered a bookstore near the University of Chicago called the Green Door. As he pursued the work of familiar and unfamiliar writers, he reached an epiphany. According to his autobiography, he realized that learning was important, and inherent in learning were "beauties" and "absolute joy."

Reading opened a whole new world of thought, ideas, and art to which Baraka responded in a journal. He also began to write poetry and submitted his work to publications such as *Accent, New Yorker,* and *Atlantic Monthly.* The 22 year old's poems were promptly rejected. Still in search of an expression, a language, and a voice that was his, Baraka was moved to tears one day in 1955 while reading an article in the *New Yorker.* He wrote in his autobiography:

> . . . I was crying because I realized that I could never write like that writer. Not that I had any real desire to, but I knew even if I had had the desire I could not do it. I realized there was something in me so "out," so unconnected with what this writer was and what that magazine was that what was in me that wanted to come out as poetry would never come out like that and be "my" poetry.

Following Baraka's dismissal from the Air Force, he lived in a bohemian community in New York City, the Lower East Side. For a time Baraka was immersed in the Bohemian lifestyle of the white–dominated countercultural community in Manhattan's East Village. There his life was consumed with reading, studying, writing, and conversing mostly with white intellectuals. He earned bachelor of arts degree in English from Howard University and studied philosophy and comparative literature at Columbia University. He also worked for the *Record Changer Magazine,* where he met his first wife, Hettie Roberta Cohen. He founded and coedited with Cohen an offbeat literary magazine called *Yugen,* which was irregularly published between 1958 and 1962. The publication featured works by such New York Beat writers as Frank O'Hara, Allen Ginsberg, and black poet A. B. Spellman. Stylistically, the Beat poets experimentalisted with poetry characterized by spontaneous thought and feeling, formless verse, and slang or vernacular.

Baraka's early poetry reflects the influence of Ezra Pound, William Carlos Williams, and T. S. Eliot, twentieth century modern writers. Baraka was also influenced by the Black Mountain School of poets, Charles Olson, Robert Creeley, and Robert Duncan. They were leading figures in the projective verse movement who taught at Black Mountain College, an experimental school in North Carolina. Baraka gained a grasp on his own voice from William Carlos Williams. In a radio interview with David Ossman in 1960, published in *Dictionary of Literary Biography,* Baraka stated that Williams taught him "how to write the way I speak rather than the way I think a poem ought to look like . . . how to get it in my own language."

Some of Baraka's work appeared in such magazines as *Naked Ear, Kulchur, Evergreen Review,* and *Big Table.* In 1959 Baraka launched his own publishing company called Totem Press, one of several publishing companies he would spearhead. In 1961 Totem Press published his first collection of poems, *Preface to a Twenty–Volume Suicide Note.* This work's poems were the result of Baraka's contact with the Beat poets. The narrative voice in *Preface* takes on three personalities: the Beat poet with his "hip" talk, the pop linguist, and the blues singer. The voice of the Beat speaker in the title poem is reminiscent of O'Hara's influence.

The poem "In Memory of Radio" was written in Baraka's pop vernacular voice. In *Black Writers,* William Harris commented that "Baraka's pop vernacular narrator mines his childhood memories of radio as sources of artistic imagery." Consequently, the poet's nostalgic references to radio personalities such as Lamont Cranston, a fictional crime fighter known as The Shadow, and others keynote one of the trademarks of the Beat poets.

"Look for You Yesterday, Here You Come Today" is the poem in *Preface* that launches Baraka's blues voice. The poem conjures up blues songs and personalities, particularly Bessie Smith. Harris wrote in *Black Writers* that "there is a 'blues feeling' throughout [the work] that is, an infusion of black culture and reference." Harris also wrote that the blues voice was not restricted to this poem.

Until 1960 Baraka's interest had been focused primarily on literature and art. After a trip to China, Baraka wrote the poem entitled "January 1, 1959: Fidel Castro." An invitation from the Fair Play for Cuba Committee to visit Cuba resulted. The following year Baraka joined a group of 12 intellectuals who traveled to Cuba. In 1984 Baraka reminiscenced in his autobiography, "The Cuba trip was a turning point in my life." It afforded him the opportunity to sightsee, meet and talk to Cuban Latin American intellectuals, and attend a discourse Fidel Castro delivered on the history of the Cuban Revolution. He also met and exchanged a few words with Castro. However, young Latino activists blasted him for not working to change the world through political involvement and his writing. Upon his return home, Baraka wrote the award–winning essay "Cuba Libre," to give an account of this event. He confessed: "One young wild–eyed Mexican poet, Jamie Shelley, almost left me in tears, stomping his foot on the floor, screaming . . ., 'In that ugliness you live in, you want to cultivate your soul? Well, we've got millions of starving people to feed, and that moves me enough to make poems out of.'''

Baraka had seen people his age involved in revolution, but after his Cuban visit he was never the same. He became a political activist and got involved with Third World artists. He formed the Organization of Young Men, who hoped to raise the political awareness of young black intellectuals, and he joined On Guard, a political action group of black intellectuals. Later he joined the Fair Play for Cuba Committee and eventually became chair and lecturer of the New York Chapter. He associated with members of the Black Liberation Movement. In later years he headed the Temple of Kawaida, an African religious institution and became a member of the Marxist organization, the League of Revolutionary Struggle.

Baraka's writing also reflected the move from Bohemian influence to black nationalism. He changed his name again, but this time more than the spelling differed. He dropped LeRoi Jones to assume the Muslim name Imamu (spiritual leader) Amiri (prince) Baraka (blessed). He delved deeply into his psyche to discover his real self, resulting in his only novel, *The System of Dante's Hell,* published in 1965. In his autobiography he admitted, "I felt . . . that I was in motion, that my writing . . . was moving to become genuinely mine."

The 1964 publication of Baraka's second book of poems, entitled *The Dead Lecturer,* addressed his feelings of separation and contradiction with his friends and peers. The same year the play *Dutchman* catapulted Baraka into fame. This, Baraka's most famous work, won the Village Voice's Obie Award for the best Off–Broadway production. *Dutchman* dissected the mythology and stereotypes inherent in the American psyche regarding race and gender. Another of Baraka's plays opened off–Broadway in 1964, *The Slave.* This play was semi–autobiographical paralleling the lives of Baraka and his wife Hettie.

Baraka's growing involvement in revolutionary thought and activities dictated that he change his lifestyle. In order to be a true black revolutionary he had to renounce the white connections in his life—wife, friends, and traditional white writing styles and techniques. Therefore, he decided to leave his white wife, partially so that his everyday life would match his rhetoric. In 1966 Baraka published *Home: Social Essays.* According to Harris in *Black Writers, Home* is "an important book of essays, in which the reader sees Baraka becoming 'blacker' and more radical in each essay." Harris also called *Home* "an invaluable compendium of Baraka's evolving nationalist ideas on race, art, politics and culture." Two works published in 1967, *Tales,* a book of short stories, and *Black Magic,* a book of poems, continue to demonstrate Baraka's move toward a black consciousness and aesthetic in his writing.

In whatever Baraka was engaged, he was never far from music. During these years of literary productivity, Baraka wrote for a number of music publications, such as *Metronome, Downbeat,* and *Jazz.* He studied the music, players, and bands from different periods as well as his contemporaries, such as John Coltrane, Charlie Parker, Thelonius Monk, Miles Davis, and Cecil Taylor. Baraka's passion for jazz led him to write seriously about music.

While employed at *The Record Trader,* a jazz magazine, he met music buffs of various persuasions and passions. What began as a clerk's job in 1965 blossomed into an opportunity to showcase his knowledge and talent for discussing jazz. Baraka's first full–length article was published in *Jazz Review* on saxophonist Buddy Tate. He also published an article in *Metronome,* "Blues, Black and White America," which gained the attention of publishers at William Morrow. After some negotiations, Baraka agreed to research further the original idea of the article; the outcome was his first publication by a major publishing company, *Blues People: Negro Music in White America* (1968). The research experience that *Blues People* demanded proved to be an excursion into the history of African American music and people. This experience fueled the great awakening that followed Baraka's trip to Cuba and his turn to drama that was steadily unfolding. Thus, Baraka turned to drama as a medium of artistic expression. He wrote in his autobiography that he wanted "some kind of action literature, where one has to put characters upon the stage and make them living metaphors."

The assassination of Malcolm X in 1965 catapulted Baraka into action. He had talked about the need for a black arts movement, originally planned as a secret organization with "paramilitary pretensions." The black arts movement was taken to the African American community of Harlem where the Black Arts Repertory Theater/School was organized. He wrote in his autobiography that the vision of revolutionary artists were to create "an art that would reach the people, that would take them higher, ready them for war and victory." Thus, the Repertory Theater/School sponsored cultural activities to achieve these ends.

The anthology *Black Fire* (1968) defined Baraka's political stance during his Black Aesthetic period. In 1969 he published *Black Magic,* a collection of poems he had written between 1961 and 1967. The 1970s found Baraka politically active, writing and speaking as a black nationalist. In 1972 he became chairman of the National Black Political Convention in Newark. His writing did not take back seat to his political activities. In 1971 he published *Raise Race Rays Raze: Essays Since 1965,* a collection of essays that addressed such topics as black nationalism, the black theater, and the black woman. As Baraka continued his search for answers to the world's social and political problems, he became interested in Marxism. A natural outgrowth of this interest was Baraka's first collection of Marxist–Leninist poetry, *Hard Facts* (1975) and a collection of Marxist plays, *The Motion of History* (1978). He eventually rejected black nationalism and became a Third World socialist. In a 1980 interview cited in *The Poetry and Poetics of Amiri Baraka,* the poet commented upon the two ideologies:

> I think fundamentally my intentions are similar to those I had when I was a Nationalist. That might seem contradictory, but they were similar in the

sense I see art as a weapon of revolution. It's just now I define revolution in Marxist terms. But I came to my Marxist view as a result of having struggled as a Nationalist and found certain dead–ends theoretically and ideologically, as far as Nationalism was concerned, and had to reach out for a communist ideology.

Baraka had more than his fair share of encounters with the law. An alleged dispute with his wife earned him a sentence of 48 consecutive weekends in a Harlem halfway house between 1972 and 1973. While there he wrote *The Autobiography of LeRoi Jones/Amiri Baraka* (1984). The work presents the soul and spirit of the ever–evolving Baraka. It is a brutally honest account of his life and his relationship to American culture.

In 1983 Baraka collaborated with his wife, Amina Baraka, on his third anthology, *Confirmation: An Anthology of African American Women. Daggers and Javelins* (1984) collected his socialist essays on art, culture, and politics. Baraka's 1987 publication, *The Music,* reflected his Marxist ideology with its poems and music criticism on such artists as Miles Davis, Chico Freeman, and Woody Shaw. The poet's enthusiasm for politics moved him to work for Jesse Jackson's 1988 presidential campaign. Amid all of this activity during the 1980s, Baraka continued to teach at Stony Brook where he is a full professor. In 1989 the American Book Awards gave him, with Edward Dorn, the Life Achievement Award.

The 1990s opened with Baraka composing "Why's/Wise," an epic poem that was compared to the efforts of Walt Whitman, Melvin Tolson, William Carlos Williams, and Charles Olson. The poem followed the tradition of the African griots, thus it is rendered in the oral tradition. As a critic, Baraka continues to voice his very strong opinions about the arts.

Harris, in *Black Writers,* summed up Baraka's contribution thus:

Baraka has created a major art, not by trying to blend into Western tradition but by trying to be true to himself and his culture. He speaks out of a web of personal and communal experience, minimizing the so–called universal features he shared with the white world and focusing on the black cultural difference—what has made the black experience unique in the West.

Current address: Department of Africana Studies, State University of New York, Long Island, NY 11794–4340. Agent: Joan Brandt, Sterling Lord Agency, 660 Madison Avenue, New York, NY 10021.

REFERENCES

Baraka, Amiri. *The Autobiography of LeRoi Jones/Amiri Baraka.* New York: Freudlich Books, 1984.

———. *Selected Plays and Prose of Amiri Baraka/LeRoi Jones.* New York: William Morrow, 1979.

Contemporary Authors. New Revision Series. Vol. 27. Detroit: Gale Research, 1989.

Donalson, Melvin, ed. *Cornerstones: An Anthology of African American Literature.* New York: St. Martin's Press, 1996.

Gaffney, Floyd. *Dictionary of Literary Biography.* Vol. 38. Detroit: Gale Research, 1985.

Harris, William J. "Amiri Baraka" [sidelights]. *Black Writers.* Detroit: Gale Research, 1989.

———., ed. "Introduction." *The LeRoi Jones/Amiri Baraka Reader.* New York: Thunder's Mouth Press, 1991.

Smith, Valerie, Lea Baechler, and A. Walton Litz, eds. *African American Writers.* New York: Macmillan, 1993.

COLLECTIONS

The largest collection of materials by and about Amiri Baraka is located in the Marvin Sukov Collection at the Beinecke Rare Book and Manuscript Library, Yale University. Additional materials are in the Lilly Library at Indiana University, the George Arents Research Library at Syracuse University, and in the Special Collections Library of the University of Connecticut.

Jewell B. Parham

Steven Barnes

(1952–)

Writer, lecturer, consultant, martial arts teacher

Although he has 15 published novels, several short stories, multiple television dramas, and several screenplays to his credit, Steven Barnes remains mysteriously cloaked, an enigma in the world of black arts and letters. Despite the advent of diversity in African American literature and its recognition through writers like Chester Himes and Walter Mosley or Octavia Butler and Samuel Delany and attention to formerly marginalized popular genres, such as detective and mystery fiction or science fiction and fantasy literature, the achievements of the versatile Steven Barnes have remained virtually unnoticed both in African American literary circles and the broader academic community. The lack of critical recognition may be a result of Barnes's rejection of mainstream realistic fiction and his choice of the forms of science fiction, fantasy, and the action adventure.

A Los Angeles native who moved to Vancouver, Washington, in the 1990s, Steven Barnes was born Stephen Emory Barnes. His parents, Eva Mae Reeves and Emory Flake Barnes had two children, Joyce Katherine, born in 1949, and Steven, born March 1, 1952. In 1972 Barnes met Toni Annelle Young; the two lived together 12 years before marrying in

1985. They have one child, Lauren Nicole, who was named for science fiction writer Larry Niven, Barnes's highly regarded mentor and co–author on seven novels.

After graduating from Los Angeles High School in 1969, Barnes attended several Los Angeles area colleges including Los Angeles City College and Pepperdine University from 1970 to 1973. Over time, he also took various courses at the University of California at Los Angeles between 1973 and 1990. He completed no university degree program, however, because he was driven to fulfill other goals. His dream was to become a financially successful published writer. Further, Barnes believed he would never find the proper guidance from college writing instructors, Barnes observed in an interview on September 27, 1995, that "while college instructors knew English and literature," they could not help him with writing for commercial publication. "I knew I wanted to be a writer and I felt I could not find any teachers there who could teach me what it was I needed to know." Noting the irony that many of his teachers had half–finished book manuscripts in desk drawers and were therefore not pursuing their own dreams, Barnes added, "I felt like I was wasting my time so I quit."

Career Accelerates

Largely a self–taught author and "schooled" by the professional writers with whom he began to associate, Barnes's career accelerated after a meeting he engineered with the commercially successful, award–winning science fiction writer Larry Niven at the Los Angeles Science Fantasy Society (LASFS) in 1979. He persuaded Niven to read several of his unpublished stories. Niven, in turn, gave Barnes one of his stories to complete. The resulting collaboration led to publication of "The Locusts," in *Analog Magazine* (June 1979), a story subsequently nominated for the Hugo Award. Later, Barnes and Niven developed what Francis Hamit in *Players,* called "A continuing personal and professional relationship that is regarded as one of the most successful in science fiction."

From 1981 through 1995, Barnes and Niven collaborated on seven novels; on two of those books, the team was joined by Jerry Pournelle as well. The novels written with Niven include *Dream Park* (1981), *The Descent of Anansi* (1982), *The Barsoom Project* (1989), *Achilles' Choice* (1991), and *The California Voodoo Game* (1991). *The Legacy of Heorot* (1987) and *Beowulf's Children* (1995) were three–way collaborations with Barnes, Niven, and Purnelle. The seven novels Barnes wrote independently are the *Kundalini Equation* (1986); the trilogy detailing the deeds of black hero Aubrey Knight, *Streetlethal* (1983), *Gorgon Child* (1989), and *FireDance* (1993); *Fusion,* a graphic novel for Eclipse Comics (1987); *Blood Brothers* (1996); and *Iron Shadows* (1998).

Along with novels and short stories in keeping with his goal of making writing pay well enough to support his family, Barnes wrote episodes for popular television programs such as *The Twilight Zone, Bay Watch, The Wizard, The Outer Limits,* and the animated *Real Ghostbusters,* among others. Barnes harbors no illusions about the relative value of one genre over another. In a letter dated March 20, 1997, he wrote that most of his writing is "just story telling" although the essential story in each format may have "a different flavor, different challenge and reward." In addition to teleplays, Barnes has written some screenplays for Hollywood, hosted a radio program and lectured on writing and the structure of creativity at the University of Southern California film school. He was also an instructor in the UCLA Creative Writing program from 1989 to 1994.

Pursues an Interest in Martial Arts

A handsome, muscular man at five feet eight inches and weighing 175 pounds, as a child Barnes was compelled to transform himself to save himself. Emory Barnes left his family when Barnes was only eight; young Steven was raised largely by his mother and sister, and although he felt his father's absence, Barnes has described his childhood as basically happy, despite bouts with loneliness. Yet towards the end of that childhood as he entered adolescence, he was small for his age. Barnes revealed in an interview that he was "not embraced" by the blacks at his school and was often physically and emotionally abused by his peers. He began to learn the martial arts as a means of self–protection, a way to help protect other weaker children, and a method to aid him in mastering his own fear of confrontation. The effects of karate as a tool for self–defense and a combined physical exercise and mental development stratagem were profound. He told Francis Hamit for *Players,* "There is no single activity that I have ever found that brings as much together of what it means to be a human being as the martial arts. I have never seen anything else that calls for as much physical, emotional, and intellectual capacity."

Barnes's avid interest in the Eastern martial arts became both a hobby and a discipline. A columnist for *Black Belt,* Barnes has contributed articles to several martial arts journals and has written books on the subject. He holds the Black Belt in Kenpo karate and Kodokan judo and a Brown Belt in jujitsu. He has studied yoga, Tae Kwon Do, and Aikdo. His interests also extend to Filipino Kali stick and knife fighting, Jun Fan kickboxing, French savate, and western self–defense pistol shooting, fencing, boxing, and wrestling techniques.

Science Fiction and Fantasy Writer

Goal–oriented and highly motivated, Barnes embarked fully on his career as a science fiction and fantasy writer in 1980, fulfilling a childhood ambition. "Before I wrote," as he related for *Players,* "I told elaborate lies and I decided that it would be more interesting to write them down than get the tar whaled out of me for lying. When I was 16, I decided I wanted to be a writer and I've been one ever since."

Science fiction and fantasy became his specialty because the form provided more latitude and freedom than other genres. Apart from his apprenticeship with Larry Niven,

Barnes credited former *Los Angeles Times* literary editor Robert Kirsch, who taught a writing class at UCLA, with lending a helping hand. While Kirsch could not teach him the technical conventions of science fiction, he did introduce Barnes to Ray Bradbury, one of the most celebrated science fiction and fantasy writers. Following his contact with Bradbury, who sent him as a novice writer two encouraging letters upon reading some of his stories, and his contact with film director, producer, and script writer John Landis, who also encouraged him, Barnes began to feel he could succeed as a writer.

Between 1978 and 1980, Barnes had a few stories published in small magazines but his only reward had come in the form of contributors' copies. He told *Players,* ''I wanted to make money as a writer and obviously I wasn't marketing myself.'' To correct the problem, Barnes set out to find a mentor. ''Obviously, if there is something you don't know how to do, then you go out and find someone who's done it and ask them what they did to break in.'' As an apprentice he maintained a specifically focused goal. He said in an interview, ''You find somebody who is already doing something; and you find out how they use their minds and how they use their emotions and how they use their body; and you imitate those things. And that's how you learn to do something.'' Through the intervention of a friend, Barnes found Niven and Jerry Pournelle at the Los Angeles Science Fantasy Society, convinced Niven to work with him and absorbed what he had to teach him.

As a child of the mid–twentieth century, Barnes absorbed the popular culture of the 1950s and 1960s as it flowed through comic books, pulp fiction, television fare, and low budget movies. Not only had he read Isaac Asimov, Arthur C. Clarke, and Robert Heinlien but he had also read Ian Fleming, Mickey Spillane, Leslie Charteris, and Robert Howard. This was the heyday of superheroes both on the big screen and the television set. As he sat mesmerized by the mythic images from the all–white action films, adventure comics, and weekly television series, Barnes pondered two questions: ''What is it to be a hero?'' and ''Why are there no, or very few, black images of heroic figures?''

Barnes felt compelled to fill the void. Since, as he commented during an interview, he could not find ''images of black people doing heroic things,'' he determined to write his own stories and make his own myths. Yet even as he penned these first stories, he too, initially created white heroes. When this irony dawned on him, he created his own mythic larger–than–life black figure—a pastiche of Robert Howard's Sword–and–Sorcery adventure tales of *Conan the Barbarian*—which featured a black thief Barnes named ''Eros the Barbarian.'' Myth, for Barnes, is ''as important as vitamin C.'' He believes that ''you develop emotional scurvy if you don't have some sense of who you are that is larger than the context of your life.''

Aubry Knight is the macho black hero at the center of Barnes's *Streetlethal* universe. This series comprises three books—*Streetlethal, Gordon Child,* and *FireDance.* Knight, a superhuman mythic figure, expert in the martial arts and futuristic ''null boxing,'' is a human fighting machine. Yet, while superior physically, Knight is also emotionally impaired. Knight grows and develops as his understanding of what it is to be a man and what it is to be a part of humanity grows. Knight learns to question his identify, question his relationship to and responsibility for others. He also learns his own history and learn about the power that comes with understanding that history. At one point in the novel a cloned figure tells Knight: ''Look at your skin. You speak the white man's language, and you think his thoughts, except that your body doesn't belong to his family. Do you now feel that there is something more?''

The series might strike some as a violence–laden science fiction action adventure story, incorporating a seemingly nihilistic, pessimistic vision of the world's future, because as the series progresses readers see a restructuring of the world order and the emergence of a newly–woven social fabric. Barnes predicts that the Aubry Knight series will be open–ended, allowing for new directions and new character development as conditions in Barnes's own life change. For in a peculiar alchemy Aubry Knight is a disturbed alter ego, a distorted refraction of Steven Barnes's mirror image.

The co–authored Dream Park novels, *Dream Park, The Barsoom Project,* and *The California Voodoo Game,* do not present a black hero at the center of the action. Characters from different ethnic backgrounds inhabit the Dream Park setting and the books are solid action–paced science fiction set in a Disneyesque futuristic theme park. *Dream Park* and its sequels build upon technological advances such as interactive video computer gaming and computerized virtual reality with the classic murder mystery.

In his life and in his books, Steven Barnes is often a man on a mission. What fascinates him is what he has dubbed ''self–directed evolution.'' In *Players,* he establishes his own pastiche of six self–help, self–motivating directives which essentially translate to: (1) have a well–defined goal; (2) be honest with yourself; (3) know your capabilities; (4) continue to learn; (5) practice effective time–management; (6) avoid the naysayers and cultivate a positive spirit.

Steven Barnes may well be his own best testimonial to his theory of self–directed evolution. His determination to reach his goal, his friendships, his frank acknowledgment of the paradoxes surrounding personal ties across racial boundaries, and his continued growth through the study of multiple martial arts forms all testify to his unceasing drive to evolve, like Aubry Knight, as a human being.

Current address: 13215 SE Mill Plain Road, #C8–243, Vancouver, WA 98684.

REFERENCES

Barnes, Steven. *FireDance.* New York: Tor Books, 1993.

———. Interview with Sandra Y. Govan, September 27, 1995.

———. Letter to Sandra Y. Govan, March 20, 1997.

Hamit, Francis. ''The Self–Evolution of Steven Barnes.'' *Players* 14 (February 1988): 36–38, 57.

''Steven Barnes' Virtual World.'' Internet Web Page. http://www.teleport.com/~djuru (accessed September 1997).

Sandra Y. Govan

Claude A. Barnett

(1889?–1967)

Journalist, publisher

Claude A. Barnett

Founder of the Associated Negro Press, Claude Albert Barnett made an important and unique contribution to journalism, the black press, and the black community by providing a vehicle for the exchange of national news releases. As he brought national news of interest to the black community, he helped to create a national black culture, increase black awareness, and heighten black self–esteem. Working also as consultant to the U.S. Department of Agriculture, he helped to address the needs of black farmers in the South by advising the federal government of their plight.

Lawrence D. Hogan, in *A Black National News Service,* explained that ''there was some confusion about Barnett's date and place of birth.'' The official records from Barnett's Department of Agriculture employment form of January 16, 1942, report the date as 1890. However, other reports say that Claude Albert Barnett was born in Sanford, Florida, on September 16, 1889, to William Barnett, a hotel worker, and Celena Anderson Barnett, a housekeeper for wealthy whites in Chicago, Illinois. During Barnett's early years, his parents divorced. He was then sent to Mattoon, Illinois, to stay with his maternal grandparents.

When Barnett began school, he was sent to stay with an aunt at Tuscola, Illinois, and attended school in Mattoon. Later, he attended Douglas Elementary School in Chicago as well as Lille Boys House of Knoxville, Tennessee. While attending Oak Park High School, he served as a houseboy in the home of Richard W. Sears, a cofounder of Sears, Roebuck and Company. Sears offered Barnett a job with his company, but Celena Barnett preferred a college education for her son. After graduating from high school, Barnett went on to Booker T. Washington's Tuskegee Institute (now University) in Alabama in 1904. In 1906 he earned what was described as the highest certificate that the institute awarded to a graduate.

Upon graduation from Tuskegee, Barnett decided to go back to his Chicago roots. He took a job working for the local post office. As a postal clerk, he came in contact with various journals, most of which he read. He chose journalism and advertising as his future vocation in 1913, when he mounted a photographic exhibition of notable black leaders at the Chicago Exposition Hall. Ill health caused Barnett to give up his postal clerk's job in 1916. Then Barnett worked at other ventures before he and other young black entrepreneurs founded the Kashmir Chemical Company, the manufacturer of Nile Queen cosmetics. He became Kashmir's advertising manager in order to promote his advertising and journalistic interests.

Founds Associated Negro Press

In 1918, to finance his visit to his mother who was remarried and living in California, Barnett sold advertisements for the *Chicago Defender.* Along the way, he sought out black editors in the Midwest and West to assess their needs. Upon his return from the cross–country trip, Barnett succeeded in persuading his partners in the Kashmir cosmetic company to invest in publishing. This work resulted in the establishment of the Associated Negro Press (ANP) in March of 1919. He directed the service for nearly half a century. The ANP used as its symbol an owl holding a scroll inscribed with the slogan ''Progress, Loyalty, Truth.''

The main objective of the new press organization—a mail service—was the exchange of national news releases to publishers and advertisers throughout the United States. For an initial fee of $25 a week, many organizations began to subscribe to the ANP's service. At its 3531 South Parkway address in Chicago, staff writers worked on the stories and news items supplied by numerous stringers, who were also paid for their contributions. Barnett wrote many of the news releases sometimes under the penname Albert Anderson and spent much of his time in routine administrative matters, recruiting reporters and columnists and persuading new publications to join the ANP. He canvassed the black community and new black enterprises for their advertising business. When Kashmir Company closed, Poro College, one of black America's first million–dollar cosmetics companies, replaced it as the ANP's major client. More than 200 newspapers, mostly black presses, subscribed to the service at its peak. Linda J. Evans wrote in *Chicago History* that "Claude Barnett was always partial to success stories — the first, best, newest, oldest, the 'most' of any respectable achievement."

There was tension between Barnett and the *Chicago Defender.* Friction arose when the ANP attracted some of its editors from the paper and the gap widened as the ANP became stronger. In the 1920s the *Defender* canceled all ties to the ANP. Barnett and a group of investors unsuccessfully attempted to buy the *Defender* in the mid–1930s.

At the height of his publishing career, Barnett married Etta Moten, a radio personality, actress, and noted singer, on June 24, 1934. They traveled widely in the Caribbean, Africa, and Europe promoting the arts and education. They also began to collect and exhibit African art.

As Lawrence D. Hogan reported in *A Black News Service,* the ANP expanded to include domestic and foreign news reports, feature reporting, sports, and theatrical reportage. Barnett tried unsuccessfully to merge the ANP with the Negro Newspaper Publishers Association (NNPA) in the early 1940s, but negotiations broke down. Lawrence Hogan claimed that Barnett's publishing efforts were undermined by an attempted hostile take–over in 1945 by a reorganized NNPA. Later, the NNPA formed its own news service to compete with the ANP. Most black newspapers continued to use ANP services and, by the early 1950s, many African newspapers were also subscribing to the service.

During its lifetime, the ANP brought aboard a number of writers who often worked without pay but gained a national forum for their ideas. These included William L. Pickens of the National Association for the Advancement of Colored People (NAACP), Frederick D. Patterson of The Tuskegee Institute, and Charles S. Johnson of Fisk University. The ANP also hired a number of editors and who became well known and who represented the association in high places. They included William L. Pickens of the NAACP; journalist Percival Prattis, who later gained access to the Periodical Gallery of both the House and Senate and in 1956 became the first black admitted to the National Press Club; poet and jazz expert Frank Marshall Davis; and fiery journalist Ida B. Wells Barnett. Alvin E. White became ANP's first full–time Washington, D.C., representative, yet Barnett was unsuccessful in obtaining Congressional press gallery credentials for the association at the time. In 1947 Alice Dunnigan, then head of the ANP's Washington office, became the first black woman journalist accredited to the White House and the State Department, and to gain access to the House and Senate press galleries. In that same year, Louis Lautier, the ANP bureau chief, became the first black since 1871 granted access to the congressional press galleries.

Successes Outside of Publishing

The ANP was never a commercial success and survived largely through Barnett's own finances and, according to Linda J. Evans, "from his ability to balance innovative ideas with tactful but persistent advocacy." Over the years he struggled for support from advertising, and finally, in the early 1950s, Liggett and Myers financed a series of short films on black achievements, thus providing the ANP another source of funds. By 1964, however, ill health took its toll on Barnett and he could no longer bear a heavy workload. He retired in July of 1964. At the time ANP went out of business in 1967 some people claim that the date was mid–1964 there were more than 112 subscribers to its news service.

In his adult life, Barnett did not forget his alma mater, Tuskegee, where he had been greatly influenced by George Washington Carver. He maintained a very close relationship with the Alabama institution and for about two decades, he served on its board of trustees, retiring in 1965. Barnett also served as advertising adviser to Poro Beauty College and as a member of Chicago–based Supreme Liberty Life Insurance Company. From 1938 to 1942, Barnett was the president of the board of directors of Chicago's Provident Hospital. He was an active member of the board of governors of the American Red Cross and worked on a Red Cross committee that fought the segregation of blood donors. He was a principal organizer of the American Negro Exhibition held in summer 1940 in Chicago. In the 1940s as well, he was adviser to the Harmon Foundation's traveling exhibit of portraits of blacks and of African art. He was also director of the Chicago Urban League, director of the National Negro Business League, and a member of the board of directors of Chicago Council of Social Agencies and of the Chicago Recreation Commission.

Barnett's national board memberships included those of the New York–based Liberia Company, the Truman Committee for the Physically Handicapped, and the Phelps–Stokes Fund which promoted black education locally and internationally. The Barnetts' travel to Africa initially was under the auspices of Phelps–Stokes. Service organizations to which he belonged were the Masons, the Pythians, and Elks Woodmen.

In the field of journalism, Barnett did much to promote minority interests. He worked with other publishers to promote black journalists as overseas and war correspondents. That subsequently led to the posting of black reporters to World War II fronts. In the 1940s he also worked through the ANP to end segregation in the armed forces. For a time, he was also involved in politics. In the 1920s, Barnett played an active role in Herbert Hoover's presidential campaign. In 1928, however, he decided to back out of politics and made that known to his friends, Robert Moton and Robert Vann, both of whom reportedly had then President Hoover's ear. As Hogan indicated in *A Black National News Service,* Barnett felt that he had done his best for his fellow blacks through the Republican Party, where he served as, in Hogan's words, the "head of publicity for Blacks for the Republican Party in presidential campaigns."

Among Barnett's meritorious national services was his position as a consultant to the U.S. Department of Agriculture, beginning in 1930 and serving such agriculture secretaries as Henry Wallace, Claude Wickard, and Charles Brannon. Barnett and his fellow consultant of Tuskegee, Frederick D. Patterson, were terminated in 1953 on the orders of new agriculture secretary E. Taft Benson.

Claude Barnett was a quiet, dignified man who was conservative in his views and actions. He began to write his autobiography after retirement, but a stroke left him partially paralyzed and confined to his home. On August 2, 1967, Barnett died of a cerebral hemorrhage at his Chicago home. His funeral was held at the African Methodist Episcopal Church's Quinn Chapel, and he was buried at Chicago's Oak Cemetery on August 5, 1967. He was survived by his wife of 33 years and her three daughters, Sue, Etta Vee, and Gladys, whom Barnett had adopted. He is remembered best for his work in strengthening the black press and for promoting racial pride in the black community.

REFERENCES

Davis, Ralph. ''The Negro Newspaper in Chicago.'' Master's thesis, University of Chicago, 1939.

Evans, Linda J. ''Claude A. Barnett and the Associated Negro Press.'' *Chicago History* 12 (Spring 1983): 44–56.

Harlan, Louis R. *Booker T. Washington, the Making of a Black Leader, 1865–1901.* New York: Oxford, 1972.

Hogan, Lawrence D. *A Black National News Service: The Associated Negro Press and Claude Barnett, 1919–1945.* Rutherford, NJ: Farleigh Dickinson University Press, 1984.

Kerlin, Robert T. *The Voice of The Negro.* New York: Dutton, 1919.

Logan, Rayford W., and Michael R. Winston, eds. *Dictionary of American Negro Biography.* New York: Norton, 1982.

Meier, August, and Elliott Rudwick, eds. ''The Claude A. Barnett Papers: The Associated Negro Press, 1918–1967.'' Part I. Microfilm.

Pride, Armistead. ''A Register and History of Black Newspapers in the United States.'' Ph.D. dissertation, Northwestern University, 1950.

Rathbun, Betty Lou K. ''The Rise of the Modern American Negro Press: 1880–1914.'' Ph.D. dissertation, State University of New York at Buffalo, 1979.

Who's Who in Colored America. 5th ed. Brooklyn: Thomas Yenser, 1940.

COLLECTIONS

The Claude Barnett Papers are located at the Chicago Historical Society, Chicago, Illinois. His collection of African art is at Tuskegee University in Alabama.

Yvette Alex–Assensoh and Jessie Carney Smith

Barrow, Joseph Louis.
See Louis, Joe.

Richmond Barthé
(1901–1989)
Sculptor

Declared ''a sculptor of unmistakable promise'' in the *New York Times,* Richmond Barthé, who was active from the 1920s through the 1970s, executed representational portrait busts and figures in bronze and marble of anonymous Africans, theatrical celebrities, and African American and Caribbean leaders. He also produced genre scenes and religious works, often in a lyric and romantic mode. Because his sculpture was easily accessible to the public yet sophisticated in style, it was frequently reproduced in the press, and won him both popularity and praise by academicians.

Barthé was born on January 28, 1901, in Bay St. Louis, Mississippi, one of the largest Catholic parishes in the South and a summer haven for prosperous New Orleans families who enjoyed its beaches. Barthé's parents, of African, French, and Native American descent, were Richmond Barthé Sr., whose occupation is unknown, and Marie Clementine Roboteau, a seamstress. Six years after Barthé's father died, his mother married William Franklin, the boy's godfather, a laborer who also played the cornet in a band. The couple had a son and daughter. Richmond Barthé was a handsome, sensitive, dark–skinned man with a trim mustache and long, slim fingers who loved fine clothing and jewelry.

Barthé began drawing as a child and first exhibited his work at a county fair in Mississippi at age twelve. He did not attend high school, but learned about his African heritage from books borrowed from a local grocer and publications given to him by a wealthy white family, the Ponds, who vacationed in Bay St. Louis. This family, which had connections to Africa through ambassadorships, hired Barthé in his teens as a butler; he moved with them to New Orleans. At age eighteen, Barthé won first prize for a drawing he sent to the Mississippi County Fair. Friend Lyle Saxon, literary critic of the *New Orleans Times Picayune,* then attempted to register Barthé in a New Orleans art school. Barthé was denied admission because of his race.

In 1924 Barthé began classes at the Art Institute of Chicago, his tuition paid by the Catholic Reverend Harry Kane, S.S.L. While living with an aunt, Barthé paid for board and art supplies by working as a porter and bus boy at a French restaurant. In his senior year, Barthé began modeling in clay at the suggestion of his anatomy teacher, Charles Schroeder. His

Richmond Barthé

busts of two classmates were shown in the "Negro in Art Week" Chicago Art League annual exhibition in 1928, the year of Barthé's graduation. At the exhibition opening, Barthé saw four of the Fisk Jubilee Singers perform. Afterward, he sculpted a small head of one of them from memory. The work appeared on the cover of the *Crisis* magazine and Barthé sold many copies of the piece. Barthé was then commissioned to produce busts of Haitian General Toussaint L'Ouverture and painter Henry O. Tanner for Lake County Children's Home in Gary, Indiana.

Within a year after his move to New York in February, 1929, Barthé had completed 35 sculptures and was offered a solo exhibition. However, Barthé believed he was not ready for it and continued his education at the Art Students League with fellowships from the Rosenwald Foundation (1929–30). Barthé received an honorary M.F.A. from Xavier University in New Orleans (1934). Later, he studied with friends Bruce Nugent and John Rhoden. His first solo exhibitions were held in 1930 at Women's City Art Club in Chicago and Grand Rapids Art Gallery in Michigan. These first exhibitions were followed by solos in New York at D. Caz–Delbo Galleries, Inc. (1934), Delphic Studios (1935), Arden Galleries (1939), DePorres Interracial Center (1945), International Print Society (1945), and Grand Central Art Galleries (1947). Barthé exhibited in numerous group shows, as well, including the Harmon Foundation shows (1929, 1931, 1933), the New York World's Fair (1939), the Whitney Museum annuals (1933, 1940, 1944, 1945), the Metropolitan Museum of Art's "Artists for Victory" (1942), and the Pennsylvania Academy of Fine Arts' annual exhibitions (1938, 1940, 1943, 1944, 1948).

Produces African Works

Many of Barthé's early works, such as *African Dancer* (1932), *Masaai* (1933), *African Woman* (ca. 1934), *Wetta* (ca. 1934), and *Shilluk Warrior* (1934) depict Africans as dignified, alert, and powerful. When asked by an interviewer about the artist's response to Alain Locke's call for racial art, Barthé told Edward Alden Jewell for the *New York Times,* "I don't think art is racial, but I feel that a Negro can portray the inner feelings of the Negro people better than a white man can." Other works, such as the elegant and sinuous *Feral Benga* and *African Man Dancing* (both 1937), are among the first sculptures of black male nudes by an African American artist. Their rhythmic grace is a result of Barthé's deep understanding of the human body; he had joined a modern dance group at Martha Graham's studio.

Numerous copies of Barthé's portrait of James Aggrey, a leading African educator (commissioned by the Phelps–Stokes Fund), were distributed in many African countries. Barthé dreamed of visiting the continent. Quoted by Samella Lewis in *Two Sculptors, Two Eras,* he said, "I'd really like to devote all my time to Negro subjects, and I plan shortly to spend a year and a half in Africa studying types, making sketches and models which I hope to finish off in Paris for a show there, and later in London and New York," but he never traveled there. However, he was able tour Europe in 1934, soon after the Whitney Museum of American Art purchased *Blackberry Woman,African Dancer,* and *The Comedian* in 1933, which prompted other museums and collectors to acquire his work. He might have seen the sculpture of Georg Kolbe abroad or in the United States. As art historian James A. Porter wrote in *Modern Negro Art,* Barthé's work is stylistically akin to the German's bronze *Somali Negro* (n.d.) in the Dresden Museum, and often has the same flowing, turning motion of a lean physique present in Kolbe's *Tänzer (Dancer)* (1914) from the Detroit Institute of Art.

Barthé's largest work is an 8' x 80' frieze of *Green Pastures: The Walls of Jericho* (1937–38) at the Harlem River Housing Project. He completed the work under the U.S. Treasury Art Project. The two bas–relief panels are based on an African American dance troupe and the Exodus scene in *The Green Pastures,* a Pulitzer Prize–winning play of the 1930s. His other public works of art include an eagle for the Social Security Board Building in Washington, D.C. (1936), an 80 foot frieze for the Kingsborough Housing Project in Brooklyn (n.d.), three Christ figures for Catholic churches and institutions, and portraits of Abraham Lincoln (1940, in New York and 1942, in India), Hearst journalist Arthur Brisbane (Central Park), George Washington Carver (1945, Nashville), and Booker T. Washington (1946, New York University).

Spiritual and Religious Pieces

A strong believer in reincarnation, the artist often called himself an "Old Soul" who had been an artist in Egypt in an earlier life. Many of Barthé's busts, such as *Birth of the Spirituals* (1941) and *The Negro Looks Ahead* (1944), are imbued with a calm spirituality. Each of these works depicts

Richmond Barthé with an example of his work.

heads which seem to be emerging from raw rock. In *Against the Odds,* Barthé described his representational work as an attempt to ''capture the beauty that I've seen in people, and abstraction wouldn't satisfy me. . . . My work is all wrapped up with my search for God. I am looking for God inside of people. I wouldn't find it in squares, triangles and circles.''

Among his Biblical and black Christian themes are *Lot's Wife* and *John the Baptist* (both heads); *Mary* (the standing young Virgin, with two long braids of hair, holds her pregnant belly); *Come Unto Me* (a six–foot figure of Jesus), and *The Mother* (1939, also known as *Supplication* and *Mother and Son*), which depicts a cowled, sorrowful woman (Mary) cradling her lynched son (the dead Christ) in her arms. Rope marks are evident on the man's neck, as they are in Barthé's *Head of a Tortured Negro.* Modeled after Michelangelo's *Pietà,* the work was exhibited at New York World's Fair in 1939. While returning from the American Negro Exposition in Chicago in 1940, the piece (one of the artist's favorites) was destroyed in a shipping accident.

Barthé produced many works of African American genre scenes, usually of a single figure in action. Art historian James A. Porter called three small bronzes (*The Harmonica Player,Shoe–shine Boy,* and *The Boxer*) ''so close to perfection . . . that their effect upon the spectator is transporting.'' *The Boxer* (1942), in the Metropolitan Museum of Art, is one of Barthé's best–known pieces. The nude athlete strides forward, head bowed, with dancerlike grace in his elongated torso and limbs. *Woman with a Scythe* (1944), also depicts a rhythmic nude; this powerful, solid worker with her feet firmly planted twists her shoulders as she wields her tool. Other works in this vein are *Blackberry Woman* (1932), *Stevedore* (1937), and *Lindy Hop* (1939).

Most Highly Publicized Black Artist in the Country

In the 1940s, Barthé received numerous awards and much publicity, beginning with Guggenheim Fellowships (1941, 1942) and the James J. Hoey Award for Inter–racial Justice (1942). He was featured in nearly every interracial organization's publication. The New York City radio station WNYC dramatized his life, and the Office of War Information filmed Barthé at work and with many of his sculptures, then distributed the film at home and abroad. In 1942, Barthé won a prize at the ''Artists for Victory'' exhibition. That year, when the U.S. entered World War II, there was a need to prove that, despite segregation and discrimination, America was democratic. The artist reflected in Bearden and Henderson's *A History of African–American Artists,* "This was the answer to Hitler and the Japanese who said that 'America talks democracy, but look at the American Negro'. . . . I think I have gotten more publicity than most white artists, much of it because I was a Negro."

In 1945 Barthé was elected to the National Sculpture Society (sponsored by Malvina Hoffman) and the American Academy of Arts and Letters. He also received the Audubon Artists Gold Medal of Honor, an honorary D.F.A. from St. Francis College, Brooklyn (1947), and election to the National Academy of Arts and Letters (1949). The sculptor was also active in several artists' organizations — the Liturgical Arts Society, the International Print Society, the New York Clay Club, and the Sculptors Guild. Additionally, he had solo exhibitions at South Side Art Center, Chicago (1942); Sayville Playhouse, Long Island (1945); Margaret Brown Gallery, Boston (1947); and Montclair Art Museum, New Jersey (1949).

In the mid–1930s, Barthé had moved from Harlem to mid–Manhattan for a larger studio and for convenient access to major theaters. He embarked on an uncommissioned series of portraits of actors, depicted in the roles they made famous. Quoted by Bearden and Henderson, critic Henry McBride thought that Barthé's portrayal of Laurence Olivier as Hotspur in Shakespeare's King Henry IV (ca. 1940) "places the theatre very much in his debt and sets a fashion to be emulated." Among Barthé's other such portrait busts are *Cyrina* (from *Porgy and Bess,* ca. 1934), *Sir John Gielgud as Hamlet* (commissioned for the Haymarket Theatre in London, 1937), *Maurice Evans as Richard II* (1938, now in Shakespeare Theatre, Stratford, Connecticut), *Katherine Cornell as Juliet* (1942), *Life Mask of Rose McClendon* (1932), and *Gypsy Rose Lee* (n.d.). Many of these works were featured in the "Theatrical Personalities" exhibition at Grand Central Galleries in New York in 1946. Unfortunately, the critical response was lackluster. Quoted by Bearden and Henderson in the *New York World–Telegram,* Emily Genauer said: "In their over–elaboration of meaningless details of costume and feature, they are made commonplace and quite empty of inner meaning." While disheartened at not capturing the force of the actors' personalities, Barthé would later produce busts of other entertainers in a similar vein, such as *Josephine Baker* (1950) and *Paul Robeson as Othello* (1975). At the time, however, Barthé was anxious, depressed, and near nervous exhaustion. His friends, actors Rose McClendon and Richard Harrison were dead, British acquaintances had returned to England, pre–war Harlem artists were scattered, and there was a critical excitement over abstract sculpture. Barthé's doctor ordered him to leave New York, so he left for Jamaica where a friend who had bought a home had invited him to come.

Caribbean Commissions

In 1950 Barthé received a commission from the Haitian government to sculpt a large monument to Toussaint L'Ouverture; it now stands in front of the Palace in Port–au–Prince. Barthé then settled in Jamaica, where he remained through the early 1960s. Some of his British friends, like Noel Coward, wintered there as well. Barthé produced many portraits and small figures as tourist commissions, and raised his own chocolate, breadfruits, bananas, and plantains on his two–acres of land which he called "Ioalus." His most notable works from this time are the General Dessalines Monument in Port–au–Prince (1952) and a portrait of Norman Manley, Prime Minister of Jamaica (1956). The Institute of Jamaica hosted Barthé's solo show in 1959. In 1964 the artist received the Key to the City from Bay St. Louis. In the later part of the decade, Barthé sculpted contemplative black male nudes, such as *Meditation* (1964), *Inner Music* (1965), and *Seeker* (1965).

Barthé left the West Indies in 1969 because of increasing violence in the islands and because his home was overrun with tourists, which prevented him from concentrating on his work. He spent five years traveling in Switzerland, Spain, and Italy, living in Florence from 1970 to 1977. He then settled in Pasadena, California, and worked on his memoirs.

In 1978 the sculptor had a solo exhibition at the William Grant Still Center in Los Angeles and was subsequently honored by the League of Allied Arts there (1981). Barthé Drive was named in his honor and a Barthé Historical Society (funded by the California Institute of Technology and the Mosley Foundation of South Pasadena) funded thirty scholarships in the arts. When friends Charles and Frances White realized that Barthé did not receive Social Security benefits because he had never been employed and had been out of the country for several decades, they aided him. Similarly, actor James Garner befriended Barthé during his last days and paid his rent and medical expenses. In gratitude, Barthé sculpted a bust of him, as well as two small heads of women. Barthé, a devout Catholic who never married or had children, died on March 6, 1989. Barthé willed his work to Garner who, in turn, gave it to art historian Samella Lewis.

The year following Barthé's death, a retrospective was held at the Museum of African American Art (1990). Barthé's work toured the country with that of Richard Hunt in the Landau Travelling Exhibition, "Two Sculptors, Two Eras" in 1992. His sculpture, in the Metropolitan and Whitney museums, the Smithsonian Institution, the Art Institute of Chicago, the Pennsylvania Academy Museum, the Theosophical Museum in Adyar, India, and numerous other collections, continues to be featured in exhibitions and survey texts on African American art.

Barthé, master of sensitive, graceful human forms, was a remarkable sculptor whose public works, spiritual and religious pieces, genre scenes, Caribbean commissions, and portraits of theatrical celebrities and anonymous Africans demonstrate many of the most compelling themes in mid–twentieth–century America.

REFERENCES

Ames, Winslow. ''Contemporary American Artists: Richmond Barthé.'' *Parnassus* 12 (March 1940): 10–17.

''Barthé's First One–man Show.'' *New York Times,* December 18, 1931.

Bearden, Romare, and Harry Henderson. *A History of African–American Artists from 1792 to the Present.* New York: Pantheon Books, 1993.

Bulliet, Clarence J. ''Art in Chicago.'' *Art Digest* 25 (1 March 1951): 9.

Lewis, Samella. *Two Sculptors, Two Eras.* Los Angeles: Landau Travelling Exhibitions and Samella Lewis, 1992.

Moore, William H. A. ''Richmond Barthé, Sculptor.'' *Opportunity* 6 (November 1928): 334.

''Painter's Paradise: Ex–Sculptor Richmond Barthé Finds Peace in Sunny Jamaica.'' *Ebony* 9 (July 1954): 95–98.

Porter, James A. *Modern Negro Art.* New York: Dryden Press, 1943.

Reynolds, Gary A., and Beryl J. Wright. *Against the Odds: African–American Artists and the Harmon Foundation.* Newark: The Newark Museum, 1989.

''Self–Taught Sculptor.'' *Newsweek* 13 (6 February 1939): 26.

''The Story of Barthé.'' *Art Digest* 13 (1 March 1939): 20.

COLLECTIONS

Barthé's works are in the Whitney Museum of American Art, the Metropolitan Museum of Art, the Schomburg Center for Research in Black Culture, Van Vechten Gallery at Fisk University, and in many private collections worldwide.

Theresa Leininger–Miller

Romare Bearden

(1912–1988)

Artist, writer, art historian, mathematician, social worker

Romare Bearden

Artist Romare Bearden achieved fame for his work with collages and photomontages, documenting the rites, rituals and ceremonies of African American culture based on his memories. His complex artistic vision drew from a wide variety of philosophical and artistic influences, including Cubism, Dadaism, Asian painting techniques, jazz, and the Bible. While his various themes—death, the family, religious rituals—were common to the human race, his depiction of distinctly African American subjects set him apart as an artist.

Romare Bearden was born in Charlotte, North Carolina, on September 2, 1912, to Howard and Bessye Bearden. Shortly thereafter, the Bearden family moved to Harlem, where Romare spent his youth and adulthood. Romare Bearden's mother worked as a New York–based editor for the *Chicago Defender,* and his father worked as a local sanitation inspector and steward for the Canadian railroad. The Bearden home, an apartment on West 131st Street, became a gathering place for such noteworthy Harlem Renaissance intellectuals, artists, and musicians as Langston Hughes, Paul Robeson, W. E. B. Du Bois, Aaron Douglas, Charles Alston (also the artist's cousin), Duke Ellington, Fats Waller and Andy Razaf. Bearden summered at the home of his paternal grandparents in Charlotte, North Carolina, during his youth. Later, Bearden spent his high school years at the home of his maternal grandmother, who owned a boarding house occupied by black steelworkers in Pittsburgh, Pennsylvania. The visual memories of the times and places where Bearden grew up and lived as an adult became the repertoire of subject matter throughout the artist's career. These subjects range from images of rural black workers from Mecklenburg County, North Carolina, to newly transplanted black Southerners laboring at the steel mills in Pittsburgh, to neighborhood scenes of Harlem, to the Island of St. Martin in the Caribbean.

Bearden received very little formal training in art during his youth. His earliest interests in art focused on drawing and an encounter with leading black cartoonist, Elmer Simms Campbell, inspired Bearden to market his political cartoons. Publications such as the *Baltimore Afro–American, Colliers* and the *Saturday Evening Post* accepted his work. Bearden attended Pittsburgh and Columbia universities and in 1935 he completed a B.S. in mathematics at New York University. While at NYU, the artist contributed his original cartoons to the humorous campus publication, the *Medley.*

Many of the visual artists from Harlem were financially supported through the Federal Arts Projects of the Works Projects Administration (FAP/WPA) during the Depression. The themes and subjects of these federally supported art projects underscored the ideals of President Franklin D. Roosevelt's New Deal. Although Bearden did not participate in the WPA–sponsored projects during his adolescence, he became an active member of the Harlem artistic community supported by this government program. Among his achievements, Bearden helped to organize the Harlem Artists Guild and wrote several articles about African American art and social topics for the Urban League's *Opportunity* magazine.

Though Bearden became heavily involved in Harlem's artistic community, he openly criticized African American art in an article entitled "The Negro Artist and Modern Art," published in *Opportunity* for December 1934. Bearden's criticisms focused on several different areas: the lack of a common aesthetic ideology, an absence of art criticism representing African American artists, and the poor quality of exhibitions representing African American artists. Furthermore, the artist defined two criteria essential to all artists: first, the ability to display inner truths, and, second, the creation of images based on personal experience and authentic cultural traditions.

In 1935 Bearden participated in a gathering of approximately 50 WPA artists at the YMCA in Harlem, on 135th Street. Bearden regularly attended gallery exhibitions at 306 West 141st Street, Harlem. Frequenters of the address became known as "the 306 Group", which attracted artists, musicians, poets, and writers from Harlem, New York, and Europe. Many of the participants of the group were also active members of the Harlem Artists Guild and were familiar with "Professor" Charles Siefert, who possessed a vast library referencing African art, culture and history. The contacts made at this time would prove to become invaluable in shaping Bearden's career.

In 1936, Bearden studied with Eastman Campbell and the German artist, George Grosz, at the Art Students League in New York City. As a result of Grosz's influence, Bearden became inspired by the sympathetic and social nature of the work of artists such as Francisco Goya, Honoré Daumier, Käthe Kollwitz, the Breughel family, Jean–Auguste–Dominique Ingres, Albrecht Dürer, Hans Holbein, Nicolas Poussin, and the Dutch Masters. After finishing his studies, Bearden took a studio at 33 West 125th Street, along with Jacob Lawrence and writer Claude McKay, where he produced works on brown paper using gouache.

An African American Translation

From 1940 to 1942, the artist painted genre pictures representing socio–cultural aspects of African American subjects. In 1940 Bearden exhibited 24 works at his first one–man show sponsored by Addison Bates. In 1941 Bearden showed two works in "Contemporary Negro Art" at the McMillen Building and contributed one work in the 1942 exhibition "American Negro Art 19th and 20th Centuries" in the Downtown Gallery. In 1944 the artist had a solo exhibition entitled, "Ten Hierographic Paintings by Sgt. Romare Bearden," and one of his works was included in the group exhibition, "New Names in American Art." Both of these exhibits were held at the G Place Gallery in Washington, D.C.

During the early phases of Bearden's career, the artist was classified as a social realist painter, along with his contemporaries Philip Evergood, Jacob Lawrence, Ben Shahn, and the noted Mexican muralists Jose Clemente Orozco, Diego Rivera, and David Siqueiros. Bearden's choice of themes at this time included the depiction of blacks living in the rural South and the great migration of blacks from the South to the North. Subjects such as the mother and child, folk musicians, a pair of women, a man serenading a woman, and women seated, seen initially in Bearden's work of this period reoccur often in his collages from the 1960s.

As the result of the end of the WPA and World War II, artists turned to private patronage and directed their attention away from social issues. In response to the changing aesthetics, Bearden shifted from social realism and genre subjects to flat geometric abstractions resembling stained glass windows consciously organized by mathematical formulas.

Bearden served in the army from 1942 to 1945. After the war, the artist was represented by Samuel Kootz Gallery in New York City, along with other noteworthy Abstract Expressionist painters such as Robert Motherwell, Adolph Gottlieb, William Baziotes, and Carl Holty. Bearden's work was featured in three exhibitions at the Kootz Gallery: "The Passion of Christ", 1945; "Bearden," 1946; and "New Paintings by Bearden," 1947. Although exhibitions showed Bearden's work alongside that of the Abstract Expressionists, he never fully acquired the attributes of the movement. While the majority of Abstract Expressionist painters produced large–scale action or color field paintings, abandoning the conventional use of stretched primed canvas and traditional methods of paint application, Bearden produced small scale Cubist–inspired transparent and opaque oil paintings based on biblical, historical, and literary themes. The artist drew inspiration from writers such as Homer, Rabelais, and Federico Garcia Lorca. Bearden gradually became opposed to the central tenets of Abstract Expressionist due to its idiosyncratic nature, and the lack of representation of social concerns. Eventually, he disassociated himself with the Abstract Expressionists and turned for advice to American artist, Stuart Davis, who encouraged Bearden to incorporate musical themes and structures borrowed from jazz in his painting.

A Mid–Life Crisis

In search of new inspiration, Bearden went to Paris to study philosophy part–time at the Sorbonne in Paris on the G.I. Bill, between 1950 and 1951. While in Paris, the artist made the acquaintance of painter Georges Braque, sculptor Constantin Brancusi, and Cubist painter Fernan Leger, among others. Despite the cosmopolitan variety of art, music, and literature Bearden witnessed in Paris, he abstained from painting altogether during his stay. Bearden utilized the opportunity to increase his knowledge of art history and awareness of contemporary trends in the arts.

Bearden was a consummate fan of American jazz music and regularly attended night clubs, cabarets, and speakeasy performances. After his return from Paris, the artist continued to abandon painting for another two–year period and turned instead to jazz composition. One of Bearden's many songs, ''Sea Breeze,'' became a hit after it was recorded by Dizzy Gillespie, Billy Eckstein, and Oscar Pettiford. In looking back over his career, the artist reflected that he had translated sound into color by listening to the music of Earl Hines.

Bearden eventually suffered a mental breakdown in the mid–1950s. By 1952 Bearden resumed employment as a social worker. In 1954 Bearden married artist and dancer Nanette Rohan. With the encouragement of his wife and companions, Bearden began to paint again. He initiated a period of self–study and rendered personal artistic interpretations of works based on paradigms of art history. Bearden was a devout scholar and life long student of art history. He manifested his expertise in this area both as a practicing artist incorporating ideas, techniques, and styles inspired by European, Western, African, and Asian traditions of art, and as a noteworthy author about African American artists. Among the artist's particular interests were the Italian Renaissance painters Cimabue, Duccio, Giotto, Titian, and Veronese. Bearden looked carefully at the subject of seventeenth–century Dutch genre paintings and interior subjects in the work of DeHooch, Vermeer, Rembrandt, and Steen. Bearden studied methods of traditional Chinese and Japanese brush painting and was familiar with Japanese block prints. He also read the writings of Wang Wei and Hokusai. The artist drew inspiration from twentieth–century modernist painters, especially Matisse, Mondrian, and Picasso. Other influences which inspired the artist's choice of subject matter were African art, the Bible, blues and jazz music, and Homer.

During the late 1950s and early 1960s, as contemporary artists headed into the Pop Art movement, Bearden engaged in a brief period of Abstract Expressionism. He painted large canvases with nonobjective subject matter in oils inspired by Zen Buddhism. Bearden's interests in Zen, and Asian brush painting and calligraphy, began in the early–1950s. In January of 1960, Bearden's work was exhibited at the Michael Warren Gallery, and in April of 1961, his work was featured at Cordier and Warren Gallery. His canvases of this period were large, unstretched and unprimed, covered with drips, splatters and stains of oil and acrylic paints. The artist was impressed with the theories of German–American painter, Hans Hofmann, who observed how composition and spatial orientation on the surface of the picture plane was achieved as the result of color harmonies. A friend of Bearden's and fellow artist, Carl Holty, who had been a student at the Hofmann School in Munich, Germany, introduced Bearden to Hofmann's aesthetic theories.

Turns to Collages

By the early 1960s, the artist departed from nearly a two–decade period of abstract subject matter. In the spirit of the Civil Rights Movement, Bearden united with a group of 12 African American artists known as ''Spiral'' to explore common concerns and pioneer African American identity through art. In 1963, Bearden suggested that the members of Spiral participate in a group collage project incorporating ripped and cut images from magazine sources. After meeting indifference from the group, Bearden proceeded alone on his suggestion. In 1964 the artist actively began making collages, composed largely of images of African Americans gathered from issues of *Ebony, Look,* and *Life* magazines from the 1950s and 1960s.

Bearden incorporated an array of unique twentieth–century collage methods including that of Picasso's Cubist period, the Surrealists, and Dadaists, and Matisse's papier colle. From the Cubists, Bearden took the geometric language of form and shape. Bearden borrowed the Surrealist use of contradictory dream–like imagery, and the emphasis upon societal issues expressed in Dadaism. Matisse's papier colle inspired Bearden to interpret his compositions in terms of flat or shallow space, and to simplify form and color. Bearden reinterpreted each of these individual periods of collage emphasizing African American events, ceremonies, rituals, culture, and history.

Acting on the advice of fellow Spiral member, Reginald Gammon, Bearden enlarged one of his photomontages using a photographic method. Dissatisfied with the results, Bearden temporarily abandoned the project. Art dealer Arne Ekstrom discovered the aborted piece in Bearden's studio and organized a forthcoming show of the artist's montages reproduced photographically. Bearden learned to utilize printing as a method of regenerating his ideas to a wider audience through mass production. In October 1964 an exhibition entitled ''Projections'' was exhibited at Cordier & Ekstrom Incorporated, which contained 27 original photomontages and corresponding photo generated prints of the same subjects consisting of a limited edition of six.

The following year, Bearden was given a second show also titled ''Projections'' at the Corcoran Gallery in Washington, D.C., which was his first exhibition at a major museum. The images contained in Bearden's exhibitions at this time stemmed from the artist's memories of ceremonies, rituals and genre subjects from Charlotte, Pittsburgh, and Harlem. During the mid–1960s, the artist returned to figurative subjects. Among the vocabulary of subjects in Bearden's work there are categories including trains, guitar players, jazz musicians, conjure women, female bathers, roosters, doves, cats, masks, the sun and moon, and scenes of neighborhoods, plantations, night clubs, eating, funerals, parades, as well as African American–inspired rituals and rites of passage.

Through exhibitions of his collages at galleries and museums, the artist achieved enormous popularity in the early 1960s among the general public, private patrons, scholars, and the art establishment. Due to the financial success derived from his exhibitions, Bearden quit his full–time job as a social worker at the New York City Department of Social Services in 1966, and devoted his attention to his career as an artist, author, and art historian of African American art.

From 1967 to 1969, Bearden initiated a series of large-scale figurative works combining collage (consisting of actual photographs, photocopies, color papers, and fabric) with painting (acrylics and oils), and drawing on a variety of two-dimensional surfaces (masonite, paperboard or canvas). The subject of these works is rural, Southern, African American culture based on ideas and images from Bearden's childhood in Mecklenburg County, North Carolina. The artist became increasingly interested in black and white photography, and the use of the color gray in conjunction with areas of vivid hue. As his work progressed throughout the late 1960s, the artist began to apply larger, more solid areas of bright color in his mixed media pieces in proportion to the areas of photographic imagery. However, the collage portions of these works are more intensely detailed and fractured due to the smaller scale and increased number of sandwiched images as compared to Bearden's earlier collages. His collages of this period typically have flat areas of color employed primarily as background. Bearden used a grid system of compositional arrangement as well as overlapping which result in both a two–dimensional as well as a three–dimensional appearance of the picture plane.

In addition to the images of the rural South, Bearden also depicted themes based on Greek mythology, and the Bible, featuring individuals with distinctly African American features. By portraying dominantly Euro–Western themes through an African American lexicon, Bearden created a bridge between African American and Euro–Western cultures, rites, rituals, and ceremonies. His handling of these themes is characterized by the dramatic set back of the subject matter and the use of mixed media collage on masonite, or watercolor on paper. These images serve as narratives, as panoramic landscapes and as epic visions seemingly inspired by live theater or wide–screen motion picture.

The Last Two Decades

Bearden focused on three subjects in his work of this period: the female nude, jazz, and St. Martin. During the early 1970s, Bearden began a new interpretation of the female not seen previously in his oveure—notably that of the female temptress or seductor. Bearden's nudes of this period were characteristically staged from the vantage point of the voyeur, with erotic overtones. Bearden also became interested in monoprinting and created a series of prints and paintings based on jazz themes. His use of color and tropical imagery became more vibrant than ever during the last two decades of the artist's life. This shift in his palette has been attributed to his exposure to tropical color, flora, and fauna witnessed on visits with his wife to St. Martin, her native country. Bearden first traveled to the island in 1960 and made several subsequent trips. The artist gained a renewed interest in watercolor at this time, in part due to the convenience of transporting light weight materials and equipment and the advantages of a full spectrum color palette which allows for spontaneous and direct documentation. In addition to landscape images depicting St. Martin, the artist also portrayed ceremonies and rituals of the Islands.

Bearden died in 1988, due to complications from cancer. His ashes were spread over the island of St. Martin in a spiritual ceremony.

Exhibitions and Honors

Romare Bearden had numerous noteworthy shows during the last three decades of his life: the Carnegie Institute, Pittsburgh, Pennsylvania, 1966; Bundy Art Gallery, Waitesfield, Vermont, 1966; Museum of Modern Art, New York City, 1971; Everson Museum, Syracuse, New York, 1975; Mint Museum, Charlotte, North Carolina, 1981; Birmington Museum of Art, Birmington, Michigan; Detroit Institute of Art, 1986; and the North Carolina Museum of Art, Raleigh, 1988.

Bearden received honorary doctorates from Pratt Institute, 1973; Carnegie–Mellon University, 1975; Maryland Institute, 1977; North Carolina Central University, 1977; and Davidson College, 1978. The artist was voted into the American Academy of Arts and Letters and the National Institute of Arts and Letters in 1966. In 1976 Bearden received the State Medal of North Carolina in Art and named Honorary Citizen of Atlanta. In 1978 Bearden received the Frederick Douglass Medal by the New York Urban League and the James Weldon Johnson Award by the NAACP. He also served as a member of the board of the New York Council on the Arts. In 1987, the artist received the National Medal of Arts.

Bearden achieved prominence as a pioneer in the history and recognition of African American artists and wrote several books on the history of African American art, including *The Painter's Mind, A Study of the Relations of Structure and Space in Painting,* with Carl Holty (1969); *Six Black Masters of American Art* (1972); and *The Caribbean Poetry of Derek Walcott and the Art of Romare Bearden* (1983). Bearden also wrote numerous articles for a variety of publications such as: *The New York Times, Essence, Leonardo, Harvard Art Review, Metropolitan Museum of Art Bulletin, Critique,* and *Opportunity.*

Although Bearden assumed legendary status among his colleagues and had mass appeal for the public, his contribution to American art of this century has been largely neglected by scholars, evidenced by an omission of information concerning the artist in text books on American Art and Western Art Historical surveys.

REFERENCES

Bunch, M., and John A. Williams. *The Art of Romare Bearden: The Prevalence of Ritual.* New York: Harry Abrams, 1973.

Campbell, Mary Schmidt, and Sharon Patton. *Memory and Metaphor: The Art of Romare Bearden, 1940–1987.* Introduction by Kinshasha Holman Conwill. New York: The Studio Museum in Harlem: Oxford University Press, 1991.

Kelly, June. Interview with Betty Lou Williams, June 6, 1997. June Kelly Gallery, New York City.

Perry, Regenia A., and Kinshasha Holman Conwill. *Free Within Ourselves: African–American Artists in the Collection of the National Museum of American Art.* Washington, DC: National Museum of American Art, Smithsonian Institution, 1992.
Schwartzman, Myron. *Romare Bearden: His Life and his Art.* New York: Harry Abrams, 1990.

COLLECTIONS

Institutions that house historical information on Bearden include the Archives of American Art, Smithsonian Institution, Washington, D.C.; Hatch–Billops Archives, New York City; Museum of Modern Art, New York City; Schomburg Center for Research in Black Culture, New York Public Library; and the Whitney Museum of American Art.
Bearden's work is featured in numerous permanent collections including the Art Institute of Chicago, Brooklyn Museum, Carnegie Museum of Art, Cleveland Museum of Art, Detroit Institute of the Arts, Hirshhorn Museum and Sculpture Garden, Honolulu Academy of Art, Metropolitan Museum of Art, Museum of Fine Arts (Boston), Museum of Modern Art in New York City, Philadelphia Museum of Art, St. Louis Art Museum, Schomburg Center for Research in Black Culture of the New York Public Library, Studio Museum in Harlem, Whitney Museum of American Art, and a number of colleges and universities throughout the United States, particularly black institutions of higher learning.

Betty Lou Williams

Harry Belafonte
(1927–)
Entertainer, civil rights activist, humanitarian

Known for his popular renditions of Calypso music, Harry Belafonte received an honorary degree from the University of the West Indies in 1996 for widening the influence of Caribbean music and for reaching the higher echelons of the performing arts. Belafonte also hit ''pay dirt'' with Robert Altman's motion picture *Kansas City,* a depression–era drama, receiving the 1996 Best Supporting Actor award from the New York Film Critics Circle. Even before his recent return to the silver screen, Belafonte was never inactive: his life always consisted of more than the glitter and glamor of the entertainment world. Belafonte has long devoted time, energy, and money to civil rights and other humanitarian activities that have benefited those in need at home and abroad.

Harold George Belafonte Jr. was born on March 1, 1927, in Harlem, New York City. His mother, Melvine Love

Harry Belafonte

Belafonte, was a Jamaican married to Harold George Belafonte Sr., a native of the island of Martinique. Belafonte's childhood years were unstable because his father was an alcoholic who worked sporadically as a merchant marine chef, and his mother, a domestic worker, was away from home for long periods of time. His mother took Belafonte and his brother to Jamaica to live for seven years in St. Anne's and Kingston with her relatives. In this setting, the young boy was immersed in a black dominant culture where high–ranking and highly respected professionals were of his race, although the island suffered colonialism. Sidney Poitier, a friend and fellow West Indian, spoke of their childhood years abroad in a 1996 *New Yorker* article:

> I firmly believe that we both had the opportunity to arrive at the formation of a sense of ourselves without having it [messed] with by racism as it existed in the United States.

When Belafonte returned to America at the age of 13, nothing had changed at home. He attended St. Thomas the Apostle School but, suffering from dyslexia, he soon became a ninth–grade dropout from George Washington High School.

In 1943 Belafonte joined the U.S. Navy as an alternative to the streets of New York. In a segregated southern setting, he was assigned the menial tasks delegated to blacks in the navy at the time, but his consciousness was being raised because of his fellow seamen. Many were older men more widely traveled and better educated; their rap sessions focused on the philosophical, historical, and sociological aspects of race and racism. When Belafonte was given a W.E.B. Du Bois article to read, he was motivated to overcome his reading deficiency and learn about himself as a black American.

Begins Entertainment Career

When Belafonte finished his tour of duty, he returned to New York and worked in maintenance at an apartment house. He was given tickets to attend a play at Harlem's American Negro Theatre and became enamored of the acting profession. Using his G.I. Bill benefits, he enrolled in Erwin Piscator's Dramatic Workshop at the New School for Social Research and joined a class whose fledgling actors included Marlon Brando and Bea Arthur. For a class assignment, Belafonte sang an original composition and was encouraged by the positive responses. Despite signs of promise, he still had to earn a living and continued with low–paying jobs while affiliating himself with the American Negro Theatre, directed by Abram Hill and housed in the basement of a public library. Belafonte worked backstage as a janitor's assistant, and there he met Sidney Poitier, the man who would become his lifelong friend and chief rival. Even at this juncture in their budding friendship, they competed for the same roles. Poitier, his understudy in *Days of Our Youth,* played the lead role on the night when prominent show backers were in the audience. This was Poitier's big break since it led to a prime role in an all–black show that led directly to Hollywood, while Belafonte was left behind in New York.

With his acting career on hold for a while, Belafonte's singing career got a boost. The owner of the Royal Roost night club remembered hearing him at the Dramatic Workshop and, after hearing him at the club's Amateur Night, hired him for what turned out to be a full–time job. As a pop singer, Belafonte was, according to his former manager in the *New Yorker,* ''a vanilla imitation of Billy Eckstine,'' but it paid bills and led to his becoming an entrepreneur. With some friends, Belafonte opened a small eatery in 1950 that lasted less than a year. It did offer the opportunity and a place for him to experiment with folk singing, the seeds of a new singing act. After the business failed, he began to study folk music seriously and even spent some time in the Library of Congress archives listening to recordings of rare and authentic music. This study increased his repertoire, which included Irish, South American, African, and Hebrew songs in addition to his beloved island music.

In 1951 Belafonte and guitarist–accompanist Millard Thomas opened at Max Gordon's Village Vanguard. The two friends then moved to Gordon's Blue Angel. As a folk singer, Belafonte was an unqualified success and soon had an RCA recording contract.

Belafonte never had a spectacular voice, but he created a persona based on sheer charisma and command of the new song genre, and his physical appearance was undeniably striking. His skin–tight mohair pants and bright silk shirts opened to expose a mocha brown chest captured the audience's attention. Despite outward appearances, all was not well with Belafonte's new–found success; as in life, racial segregation still plagued his business and personal lives. His bookings were in the swankiest and biggest venues, but like other black entertainers, he was denied the right to eat and sleep in the hotels or socialize in the night clubs where he performed. His new career continued to open doors at the best night clubs: the Coconut Grove in Los Angeles, the Copacabana in New York, and the Empire Room at Chicago's Palmer House, where he was the first black performer to appear.

In 1952 Belafonte's film career started off with a leading role in *Bright Road.* This led to a role in a Broadway revue, John Murray Anderson's *Almanac,* which earned him a Tony Award in 1954. He then appeared on the *Ed Sullivan Show* and became one of its most frequent guests. In 1954 Belafonte starred with Marge and Gower Champion in the Broadway musical *Three for the Road.* During the same year, Mike Todd's all–black version of Bizet's opera *Carmen* was adapted for film. Belafonte and Dorothy Dandridge starred in the production, which transformed the heroine from a Gypsy cigarette maker into a black parachute factory worker. Although the film received poor reviews from critics, black movie–goers were overwhelmed at the sheer physical beauty of the two stars. Belafonte subsequently starred in *The World, the Flesh and the Devil* in 1959.

Belafonte had simultaneously refined his folk–singing repertoire to concentrate on calypso songs, a genre popular in the Caribbean. Although he was severely criticized by purists and legitimate Calypsonians of Trinidad, he was crowned the ''King of Calypso'' and by 1957 was regarded as America's most popular performer. The album *Harry Belafonte—Calypso* sold 1.5 million copies, a record at the time for a single artist album. He outsold legendary singers, Elvis Presley and Frank Sinatra, and the album stayed on the charts for nearly two years. With his musical triumph, Belafonte had succeeded in modifying the dialect and rhythm to make the songs more palatable to the U.S. music–buying public. He also deleted racist and sexist connotations and emphasized positive aspects of calypso music.

Lifestyle Changes

Belafonte's professional career soared but his personal life was steadily disintegrating. His 1948 marriage to Margurite Byrd had been seriously imperiled during the filming of *Carmen Jones.* He and Byrd had met in 1944 while he was stationed in Norfolk, Virginia, and she was a student at Hampton Institute, as it was known then. They were a study in contrasts because of their disparate backgrounds and outlooks on life. Byrd, now Margurite Mazique, spoke of their early relationship in a *New Yorker* article: ''Our courtship was one long argument over racial issues. . . . He reminded me of a big kid who was about to get into trouble if somebody didn't watch and help him.'' They are the parents of two children: Adrienne, a family counselor, and Shari, an actress.

Before the marriage ended, Belafonte had met Julie Robinson, who had once performed with the Katherine Dunham Company. In 1957, while he was filming *Island in the Sun,*

Belafonte's first marriage ended and news of his subsequent marriage to Robinson became public knowledge. Perhaps fittingly, the film was about an interracial love affair. Robinson, a Russian–Jew, had an eclectic upbringing and was part of the New York Village's arty, bohemian crowd and, therefore, could fit in well with Belafonte's show business lifestyle. Black and white Americans were predictably upset at this turn of events, the former because of perceptions of racial betrayal, and the latter because of perceptions of Belafonte's "uppityness." Belafonte and his current wife are parents of David, a model and head of Belafonte's production company, and of Gina, an actress.

Belafonte's remarriage and his political leanings both affected his film career, while Poitier, his old rival, continued to gather acclaim and awards for his films, including *Porgy and Bess; To Sir, with Love;* and the film that netted him an Academy Award as the first non–honorary black recipient, *Lilies of the Field.* Belafonte turned down the two latter films in disgust at the content, and said of Poitier in the *New Yorker:* "Sidney was always more pliable, more accommodating . . . he never disturbed the white psyche in anything he did."

Television, however, continued to be a major venue for Belafonte and, in 1960, he won an Emmy for the show "Tonight with Belafonte," a Revlon Hour special. He continued to introduce African artists to U.S. audiences. In 1964 he brought Kandia Conte Fode, a Guinean tenor, and a Gueckedour Orchestra to Lincoln Center. In 1966 he became the first black American performer to produce an hour–long CBS show. "Strolling Twenties," produced by Belafonte's Harbel Company, began in 1959. The show starred Sammy Davis Jr., Diahann Carroll, Duke Ellington, Joe Williams, and Nipsey Russell; Sidney Poitier narrated the Langston Hughes script. In 1968 Belafonte guest–hosted *The Tonight Show with Johnny Carson* for a week in which he featured more prominent African Americans, including Martin Luther King Jr. Belafonte returned to the movies as a co–star with Poitier and Ruby Dee in 1971's *Buck and the Preacher* and, in 1974, *Uptown Saturday Night.* In 1984 he co–produced the hip–hop film *Beat Street.*

Shifts to Activism

Belafonte's disenchantment with Hollywood was lodged on a deeper level than personal disappointment and dissatisfaction with demeaning roles. A *New Yorker* interview described his feelings:

> Hollywood was symptomatic, and the problem was the nation. I figured unless you change the national vocabulary, the national climate, the national attitude, you're not going to be able to change Hollywood.

In the *New Yorker,* Belafonte's oldest daughter said of her father, "He wants to fix the world, and he's sad because he sees it slipping away. I believe he feels alone."

When Belafonte first met Martin Luther King Jr. in 1956, he was impressed by King's humble demeanor and sincerity, and he responded immediately when King asked for help. This was not Belafonte's first civil rights venture. As a struggling 24–year–old actor, he had walked a picket line for W. E. B. Du Bois. In 1950 Belafonte and Bayard Rustin led 1,000 students from New York to the nation's capitol to join A. Philip Randolph's March for Integrated Schools. On King's behalf, Belafonte provided two major contributions: money and intercession. He was the catalyst in persuading many famous entertainers to headline or sponsor concerts to raise funds for civil rights. In 1963 he helped found the Southern Free Theater in Jackson, Mississippi and he often used personal funds to provide bail money for workers of the Student Nonviolent Coordinating Committee (SNCC). He also put up seed money to support the group at its inception. Belafonte raised the $50,000 needed to bail King out of the Birmingham jail and promised to secure more when needed. When that time came, he was instrumental in securing $50,000 in cash from the New York Transportation Worker's Union and then $40,000 in cash from Governor Nelson Rockefeller's assistant, Hugh Morrow. At a Cleveland, Ohio, fund raiser, Belafonte's efforts netted $15,000. Realizing that King's life was always in danger, Belafonte heavily insured King's life. When King was in serious trouble over income tax matters, Belafonte and Bayard Rustin devised a fund–raising appeal through the *New York Times* in an advertisement entitled "Heed Their Rising Voices." He and Reverend Gardner Taylor devised a plan to bypass foundations for a direct appeal to black church–goers while the tax case was ongoing.

Belafonte's other asset was his ability to intercede and mediate between people and groups that were often hostile toward one another. He forged and maintained the relationship with the Kennedy establishment, one that was crucial in keeping King alive during his jail sentences. He first met Robert Kennedy in his own home when Kennedy came to solicit Belafonte's aid as a campaigner. Belafonte preferred Adlai Stevenson, however, and urged Robert Kennedy to meet King and to support civil rights causes. Surprisingly, Kennedy knew nothing of King's reputation and could not understand why he should get involved with him. After they finally met, it was Belafonte who acted as mediator and often as a bargaining agent for King. Belafonte also interceded to lessen the strife between King and SNCC leaders who strongly criticized the King family for being too bourgeois. As an unofficial liaison, Belafonte was named to the advisory board of the Peace Corps in 1961.

On a personal level, Belafonte was called on to intercede between King and his father, who insisted that his son owed Robert Kennedy loyalty. Belafonte urged that the younger King support whomever he wanted. For his efforts, Belafonte and his cohorts were vilified and attacked largely on the basis of Federal Bureau of Investigation (FBI) wiretap reports. One of the most vicious allegations Kennedy made was that Belafonte was unstable due to his mixed–race marriage. The New York FBI field office knew of every New York meeting held or attended by Belafonte. In 1960 they had reported that King and Belafonte had met with Benjamin Davis, then America's best–known black communist. Belafonte's relations with Stanley Levison—a wealthy friend and unpaid counsel to Martin Luther King Jr.—were of particular interest to Hoover, and they were hounded to the extent that Levison was finally forced to withdraw as King's counsel. The FBI never relented in its efforts to discredit King and reduce the attendance at Southern Christian Leadership Conference (SCLC) fund raisers that starred Belafonte.

The negativism never slowed Belafonte's efforts toward promoting justice and dignity for all humanity. In 1985 Belafonte conceived the idea of the concert and recording of *We Are the World,* which raised $100 million for the Ethiopian famine relief fund. Since 1986 he has traveled the globe as a United Nations International Children's Education Fund (UNICEF) goodwill ambassador. In 1990 Belafonte chaired the committee that arranged the visit of the newly–freed Nelson Mandela to the United States. Mario Cuomo appointed him to oversee the Martin Luther King Jr. Commission to Promote Knowledge of Nonviolence.

Receives Numerous Honors

Belafonte has received numerous honorary doctorates, along with a Tony Award (1953); the James J. Hoey Award for Interracial Justice from the Catholic Interracial Council (1956); the ABAA Music Award for helping African famine victims through producing the album and video *We Are the World* (1985); and a Grammy Award (1985). He began performing with an African and Third World music band, DJOLIBA.

Belafonte has a reputable catalog of recordings and songbooks. Three of his recordings of note are *Belafonte Returns to Carnegie Hall,* with Odetta, Miriam Makeba, and the Chad Mitchell Trio (1960); *My Lord What a Mornin',* with Belafonte Singers (1960); and *Paradise in Gazankulu,* an album of South African music (1988). In 1962 a collection of 40 songs, *Songs Belafonte Sings,* was published; it was illustrated by Charles White, one of America's premier black artists.

Belafonte and his wife, Julie, continue to collect Caribbean, African, and European art and to enjoy their Manhattan apartment. Belafonte bought the building where he lives as a real estate investment, sold the apartments as cooperatives, and retained one floor as living quarters. Their accumulation of artistic treasures is displayed there and stands as a record of their own struggles to survive and live in a country that still values skin color over character.

Belafonte's recent surgery for prostate cancer was deemed successful. Belafonte said in a *New Yorker* interview with Henry Louis Gates: "There wasn't all that much I would have done differently when I look back on it." Belafonte can live with that pronouncement as he forges ahead with creative projects in music and film that will continue to astound and even anger some, but never fail to entertain and educate all.

Current address: Belafonte Enterprises Inc., 830 8th Avenue, New York, NY 10019.

REFERENCES

African American Biography. Detroit: U.X.L./Gale Research, 1994.

Branch, Taylor. *Parting the Waters.* New York: Simon and Schuster, 1988.

Byrd, Rudolph P., ed. *Generations in Black and White.* Athens: University of Georgia Press, 1993.

Garrow, David J. *The FBI and Martin Luther King, Jr.* New York: Penguin Books, 1981.

Gates, Henry Louis Jr. "Belafonte's Balancing Act." *New Yorker* (26 August, 1996): 133–36; (2 September, 1996): 138–42.

"Harry Belafonte Receives Honorary Degree." *Jet* 89 (1 April 1996): 20.

Hughes, Langston, and Milton Meltzer. *Black Magic.* New York: Da Capo Press, 1967.

Lawless, Ray M. *Folksingers and Folk Songs in America.* Westport, CT: Greenwood press, 1965.

"New York Film Critic Awards." *Jet* 91 (20 January 1997): 60.

Null, Gary. *Black Hollywood: The Negro in Motion Pictures.* Secaucus, NJ: Citadel Press, 1975.

Silverman, Stephen M., and Ron Arias. "Day–O Reckoning." *People* 46 (26 August 1996): 61–64.

Southern, Eileen. *Biographical Dictionary of Afro–American and African Musicians.* Westport, CT: Greenwood Press, 1982.

Who's Who among African Americans, 1996–97. 9th ed. Detroit: Gale Research, 1996.

Dolores Nicholson

Derrick A. Bell Jr.

(1930–)

Lawyer, educator, activist, author

Best known as the first black tenured professor on Harvard University's law school faculty, Derrick A. Bell is an activist for the rights of blacks and other minorities. He was also the first black to head a non–black law school—the University of Oregon. Consistently Bell has been a mentor to law students of color and a person who refuses to compromise his principles on human rights and equality for minority faculty in law.

Born in Pittsburgh, Pennsylvania, on November 6, 1930, Derrick Albert Bell Jr. is the son of Derrick Sr. and Ada Elizabeth Childress Bell. Bell Sr. left school while a sixth–grade student and later on operated a small rubbish company. Both parents influenced the development of their son as an activist: the father by making it clear that he did not trust

Derrick A. Bell Jr.

whites; and the mother by reinforcing the importance of action rather than inaction. Young Bell delivered newspapers in a neighborhood of blacks from various socioeconomic levels.

Bell Jr. was the first in his family to enter higher education. While studying at Duquesne University, he lived at home and helped to earn money for tuition by working with his father. He graduated from Duquesne with an A.B. degree in 1952. The nation was engaged in the Korean War. In 1952 Bell joined the U.S. Air Force as a lieutenant and for a while was stationed in Louisiana. He became an activist by single handedly integrating the local Presbyterian church and sang in its choir. He had already been a choir member in his church in Pittsburgh. Bell also protested segregation that occurred on base buses outside the military installation.

Bell, who also served in Korea, left military service in 1954 and entered the University of Pittsburgh Law School hoping to become a civil rights lawyer. While there he was associate editor–in–chief of the *Pittsburgh Law Review.* He graduated in 1957 and ranked fourth in his class. On examination, Bell was admitted to three bars: the District of Columbia (1957), New York (1966), and California (1969). He was admitted to practice in both the U.S. Supreme Court and in federal courts of appeal in the Fourth, Fifth, Sixth, Eighth, and Tenth Circuits.

After law school, Bell became a staff attorney in the Civil Rights Division, U.S. Department of Justice, where he was the only black on a staff of 1,000 lawyers. The department claimed that Bell's membership in the National Association for the advancement of Colored People (NAACP) represented a conflict of interest with his work in civil rights. Rather than yield to the department's demand in 1959 that he resign membership, Bell resigned his position instead, after only two years in the department. From then until 1960 Bell was executive secretary to the Pittsburgh Branch of the NAACP. His work in civil rights continued with his appointment from 1960 to 1966 as first assistant council, NAACP Legal Defense and Educational Fund (LDEF). Under Thurgood Marshall's leadership, Bell had an assignment in Mississippi as lawyer for the fund. His experiences there included the supervision of over 300 school desegregation cases and leading James Meredith's fight to enter the University of Mississippi. Not only was Bell arrested in Jackson for refusing to leave the white waiting room at the train station, often his life was at risk as well.

Tenured on Harvard's Law Faculty

With many legal victories to his credit, Bell left the LDEF in 1967 to become executive director of the Western Center on Law and Poverty at the University of Southern California Law School, where he remained until 1969. He was named lecturer of law at Harvard University from 1969 to 1971. In 1971 he was promoted to professor and became the first black tenured professor at the Harvard Law School. Bell was well versed in the art of protest; he never compromised his views for any acts or actions that did not address equality. He promoted civil rights to his students at Harvard through a course in civil rights law which he introduced. He wrote widely on the topic in his book *Race, Racism and American Law* (1973) and in various articles that he published. He challenged Harvard to hire more minorities and also served as role model and mentor to minority students there.

On a five–year leave from Harvard from 1980 to 1986, Bell served as law professor and the first black dean at the University of Oregon Law School. With a vacancy on its law faculty, the school held an extended search that led to an Asian American woman candidate who ranked third on the list of candidates. The other top candidates, both white males, declined the position and then Bell protested a faculty directive that he deny the woman an offer. Rather than accept the Asian American woman, the faculty determined to reopen the search. Bell refused to yield and left the post in 1985. For one year, 1985–86, he was professor at Stanford University and was involved in a similar protest. Bell returned to Harvard as Weld Professor of Law from 1986 to 1992. In the mid–1980s he also co–chaired the Harvard Black Faculty and Administrators group.

Returning to Harvard in 1986, Bell's protests continued. He gained student support while dividing the faculty after his sit–in in his Harvard office to protest denial of tenure to two legal scholars. While the school questioned their scholarship and teaching, Bell accused officials of attacking the scholars' ideology. His debate over Harvard's hiring practices continued and in 1990, when the university had tenured only five women and three black professors out of sixty and refused to appoint and tenure a black woman visiting professor, Bell took a two–year leave in protest. Harvard reacted by dismissing him from his tenured position at the end of June 1992. Since 1991 Bell has been connected with the New York University Law school. He was visiting professor in 1991–93, scholar–in–residence, 1993–94, and since then has been visiting professor.

Bell's views reflect his continuing concern for the rights of blacks and minorities, including women of color. He told the *Gaither Reporter* that he is concerned about the future for blacks:

> We are undergoing a tremendous transformation in the economy, one in which jobs are disappearing and will continue disappearing. . . . The downsizing we've experienced thus far is only the beginning. As we have seen in so many inner–city communities, to take away work is to invite destructive behavior of the worse kind.

Of the Million Man March held in Washington, D.C., in 1995, he told the *Gaither Reporter* that the march reminded the world that blacks are a diverse people and that it led to a feeling of togetherness across social and economic classes. On the other hand, he was ambivalent to those black women who opposed the march, particularly when he had left Harvard's Law School in protest of its failure to hire a woman of color. ''It was black men who needed the Day of Atonement, not for all that has been done to them, but for all that we need to be doing in a society that is hostile to us all—women as well as men,'' he said. Despite contrary indications, he said that the march proved that ''black men are concerned about what's going on.'' He also addressed the permanence of racism in America. In *Faces at the Bottom of the Well: The Permanence of Racism* (1992), he wrote:

> Black people are the magical faces at the bottom of society's well. Even the poorest whites, those who must live their lives only a few levels above, gain their self–esteem by gazing down on us. Surely they must know that their deliverance depends on letting down their ropes. Only by working together is escape possible. Over time, many reach out, but most simply watch, mesmerized into maintaining their unspoken commitment to keeping us where we are, at whatever cost to them or to us.

The talented Bell has written extensively on racial injustice. His work *Race, Racism, and American Law,* first published in 1970, has appeared in three editions, the latest in 1992. He also wrote *Shades of Brown: New Perspective on School Desegregation* (1980), *And We Are Not Saved: The Elusive Quest for Racial Justice* (1987), *Confronting Authority: Reflections of an Ardent Protester* (1994), and his latest book, *Gospel Choirs, Psalms of Survival in Alien Land Called Home* (1996). His writings have been included in several books as well as in legal journals published by Harvard, Yale, Michigan, and other academic publishers. His various articles have appeared in the *New York Times Sunday Magazine,* the *Boston Globe,* the *Los Angeles Times,* and the *Christian Science Monitor.*

Cited widely for his work in law, legal education, and civil rights, Bell received the Society of American Law School's Teacher of the Year award in 1985. Named lectureships are held at several law schools, including Alabama, Case Western Reserve, Marquette, North Carolina Central, Notre Dame, Oklahoma, Clark–Atlanta, Howard University, and Baruch College. Bell received honorary degrees from Northwestern Law School (1984), Tougaloo College (1983), Mercy College (1988), and Allegheny College (1989).

Bell married Jewel Allison Hairston in 1960 and they had three children—Derrick Albert III, Douglas Dubois, and Carter Robeson. Jewel Bell died in 1990. Two years later Bell married Janet Dewart. Derrick Bell remains a compelling voice on issues of race, gender, and class. He has devoted forty years to the legal profession, legal education, and as activist and writer. A quote from ''Introductory Material'' sums up the effects of his works throughout his career and in his writings: ''he has provoked his critics and challenged his readers with his uncompromising candor and original progressive views.''

Current address: New York University School of Law, 40 Washington Square, South, New York, NY 10012.

REFERENCES

Bell, Derrick A. Jr. *Faces At the Bottom of the Well: The Permanence of Racism.* New York: Basic Books, 1992.

———. Resume, n.d.

Contemporary Black Biography. Vol. 6. Detroit: Gale Research, 1994.

Gaither, Larvester. ''Interview with an Ardent Protester (Derrick Bell).'' *Gaither Reporter* 3 (31 August 1996): 57.

''Introductory Material, Derrick Bell,'' n.d.

Jessie Carney Smith

James Madison Bell

(1826–1902)

Orator, poet, political activist

James Madison Bell was best known for his eloquently written poetry about the wrongs suffered by African Americans. Born on April 3, 1826, in Gallipolis, Ohio, Bell's first–hand experience with racial injustice inspired him to weld his passion for equal rights and his writing talent together in an effort to further the work of the early civil rights movement. The result is a body of work that celebrates the legal and moral victories of African Americans, offering hope in the midst of the struggle.

James Bell's first exposure to the radical antislavery movement was through a private night school connected to Oberlin College. In the classes he attended as part of his high school education, he learned the principles of the movement he would later vigorously support. At age 22, he married Louisiana Sanderline and to this marriage a number of children were born. He moved his family to Chatham, Canada, where he remained for six years. Chatham was a major destination of the Underground Railroad, and was a hotbed of abolitionist activity. It was in Chatham that Bell had a hands–on encounter with the abolitionist movement. The abolitionist leader John Brown stayed with Bell during Brown's Provisional Constitutional Convention which was held in Chatham in April of 1858, and the men became close friends. Bell was aware of Brown's exploits in Kansas, but had never seen him prior to the time of the convention. Brown presented himself at the Bell home with a letter of introduction from William Howard Day of Toronto, who asked Bell to help Brown in any way he could under the circumstances. In 1859 Bell helped Brown recruit men and support for the raid at Harper's Ferry.

After a congressional investigation of the raid in 1860, Bell moved to San Francisco, where he continued his brickmasonary trade and took an interest in writing poetry. During this time, Bell wrote two of his most memorable poems, "The Day and the War," and "The Progress of Liberty," both of which celebrated Abraham Lincoln's Emancipation Proclamation. Bell read "The Day and the War" at a festival to commemorate the emancipation of the slaves in the District of Columbia and in the British West Indies. This poem was dedicated to the memory of John Brown.

Bell was an active member of the African Methodist Episcopal Church and took part in their convention, held on September 3, 1868. In fact, he took part in nearly every civic and church event held by black organizations in San Francisco. In 1865 he was a member of the Fourth California Colored Convention, which fought for suffrage rights.

Upon leaving San Francisco, Bell wrote what was considered one of his best poems, "Valedictory." He rejoined his family in Toledo, Ohio, after the Civil War, and became a delegate from Lucas County to the state Republican convention, as well as a delegate–at–large from Ohio to the 1868 Republican National Convention. In 1870 Bell commemorated the Fifteenth Amendment by reading his ode "The Triumph of Liberty" at the Detroit Opera House.

Bell never truly developed his literary talent because his poetry came second to his preoccupation with civil rights. He traveled and read his poems in all of the major cities of the North and South, and instructed people on their political and civic duties. He offered a star of hope in troubled times and was well received by people everywhere. In 1884 he continued to write and give public readings, and in 1888 wrote his last political poems, dedicated to the candidacy of Republican Benjamin Harrison. In 1901 his famous works were brought together as "The Poetical Works of James Madison Bell," prefaced with a biographical sketch by Bishop Benjamin W. Arnett. After traveling for several years Bell returned to Toledo, Ohio, where his family resided. His star rested over the city on the Maumee River, and from that time he was known as the "Bard of the Maumee." Bell died in 1902, and is remembered as a strong promoter of civil rights.

James Madison Bell

REFERENCES

Bell, James Madison. *The Poetical Works of James Madison Bell.* Lansing, MI: Press of Wynkoop, Hallenbeck, Crawford Co., 1901.

Brawley, Benjamin. *The Negro Genius.* New York: Dodd, Mead, 1937.

———. *Early Negro American Writers.* Chapel Hill: University of North Carolina Press, 1935.

Kerlin, Robert T. *Negro Poets and Their Poems.* Washington, DC: Associated Publishers, 1926.

Logan, Rayford W., and Michael R. Winston, eds. *Dictionary of AmericanNegro Biography.* New York: Norton, 1982.

Loggins, Vernon. *The Negro Author: His Development in America.* New York: Columbia University Press, 1931.

Quarles, Benjamin. *Allies for Freedom: Blacks and John Brown.* New York: Oxford University Press, 1974.

Robinson, Wilhelmena S. *Historical Afro–American Biographies.* Philadelphia: Publishers Agency, 1976.

Salzman, Jack, David Lionel Smith, and Cornel West, eds. *Encyclopedia of African–American Culture and History.* New York: Macmillan Library Reference USA/Simon and Schuster Macmillan, 1996.

Sheila A. Stuckey

Jesse Binga

(1865–1950)

Banker, realtor, philanthropist

Jesse Binga

Drawing upon real estate skills developed early in life, Jesse Binga emerged from poverty and obscurity to prosperity and prominence as a Chicago realtor and owner of the first privately owned, managed, and controlled black bank in the North. By 1910 he was Chicago's leading black businessman. During the first quarter of this century, he led South Side Chicago to become a center of black business development. He was left penniless in later years due to business failures and imprisonment.

The youngest in a family of eight girls and two boys, Jesse Binga was born in Detroit on April 10, 1865, to free parents who had moved to Detroit in the 1840s. His father, Robert Binga Jr., was from Ontario, Canada, and owner of a barbershop. His mother, Adelphia Powers Binga, a native of Rochester, New York, was a strong–willed woman and a shrewd businessperson who had dealt in interstate shipping of whitefish and sweet potatoes. She was also employed in real estate, constructing tenement houses in Detroit known as Binga rows. From his father young Binga learned the barbering trade. He assisted his mother in collecting rents and repairing rental properties.

Binga dropped out of high school in his third year and worked in the office of Thomas Crispus, a young black attorney, where he also studied law. He left a potentially promising business career in Detroit in 1885 and began to roam about in Kansas City, Missouri; St. Paul, Minnesota; and Missoula, Montana, where he worked as a barber. He opened barbershops in Tacoma and later in Seattle, Washington, but soon left for Oakland, California, to work as a barber and a porter for the Southern Pacific Railroad. He left that line and became a Pullman porter on the narrow gauge line from Ogden, Utah, to Pocatello, Idaho, and Butte, Montana. Binga made a handsome profit from land investments in a former Indian reservation in Pocatello; he then settled in Chicago in the mid–1890s.

Accounts of Binga's life suggest that the land deal might have enabled Binga to reduce debts he owed, for he had very little money during his early days in Chicago. To make a living, some sources report that he ran a fruit stand at the corner of 12th and Michigan; other reports indicate that he was a wagon driver peddling coal oil and gasoline; and still others say that he shined shoes.

In 1898 Binga opened a real estate business at 3331 South State Street and rapidly became one of the wealthiest blacks in Chicago. He used half of the only money he had—ten dollars—to pay his rent and the other to purchase a desk, three rickety chairs and a worn–out stove. Drawing on his real estate experiences in Detroit, he soon rented the shabby building in which he had his office and renovated it himself, often working all night to repair boilers, plumbing, and to hang wallpaper. In 1905 he moved to more pretentious quarters at 3637 South State Street, first on a long–term lease and next as owner. He invested further, in a three–story building and in other real estate activities and practiced blockbusting to open previous white residential areas to blacks. The *Chicago Defender* for 1912, cited in *Black Metropolis,* claims that Binga also leased homes for twenty and twenty–five dollars a month, then rerented them to blacks for ten and fifteen dollars more than the original white tenants had paid—a practice followed by other real estate dealers.

Binga's marriage in 1912 to Eudora Johnson, who was the sister of John ''Mushmouth'' Johnson, gambling kingpin on Chicago's South Side who had died in 1907, is said to have led to his increased wealth. The wedding was dubbed the most elaborate and fashionable of such events for blacks anywhere in the country up to that time. Eudora Johnson's inheritance of $200,000 from her brother led some to speculate that Binga married her for her money. She also provided him with the social amenities that Binga lacked, thus giving them a favored position in social circles on the South Side. The Bingas, who had no children, were known for their elaborate annual Christmas parties held for Chicago's upper echelon of society. As the real estate market prospered, so did Binga. The black community grew rapidly after 1915 and properties he had purchased before the Great Migration increased in value. He purchased a group of storefront apartments later known as the Binga Block, located at Forty–seventh and State Streets and, according to volume one of *Black Metropolis,* ''the longest tenement row in Chicago.'' At one time he held 1,200 leases on flats and residents and by 1926, owned more frontage on State Street south of 12th Street than anyone else.

Between 1917 and 1921 Binga's properties were vandalized by whites. This was particularly true during the race riots of 1919, known as the Red Summer. His home at 5922 South Park, in an all–white area, was bombed five times. Binga hired guards, armed himself, and became a martyr in the black community for defending his empire. White opposition failed to deter him, and Binga's holdings prospered.

Opens First Bank

One of the most prosperous black realtors in Chicago at the time, Binga ventured into another enterprise. In 1908 he opened the Binga Bank at 3633 South State Street—the first owned, managed, and controlled by blacks in the North, and one of the most celebrated black businesses in the country. His small bank grew impressively during the Great Migration, between 1917 and 1921. Previously operating it as a private bank, in 1919 he took out a charter for his enterprise to become the Binga State Bank. Quoted in *Black Metropolis,* volume one, the *Chicago Defender* for December 13, 1919, called the reorganized bank ''a house of rock–ribbed foundation, which will relieve the mistable conditions brought about by kindred institutions headed by men lacking experience, credit and substantial backing.'' With the state bank Binga was to realize his dream of employing a number of young, talented blacks. He was also its largest shareholder. *Chicago Defender* editor Robert S. Abbott was a stockholder and member of the board of directors. Binga's state bank was welcomed by blacks who had experienced discrimination and discourteous treatment at the Loop banks and also served as a hedge against loan sharks. In 1924 he moved the bank to impressive larger quarters that he had built—the first bank building ever constructed by a black. Chicago alderman and later U.S. Congressman Oscar De Priest gave a dinner in his honor. Binga also opened the Binga Safe Deposit Company and organized an insurance firm.

Although the economic collapse in 1929 took its toll on the black community, about this time he built the Binga Arcade—a five–story office building with a ballroom on the roof located at 35th and State Streets. The next year the bank collapsed and his fortune of $400,000, along with the savings of thousands of blacks in Chicago, was gone. Binga was unsuccessful in his attempt to reopen his bank; thus, an important era in the history of black enterprise came to an end. First arrested on March 5, 1931, for irregularities in banking, he was acquitted. In a second trial in 1933 Binga was convicted of embezzlement and sentenced to ten years in prison. Despite their financial loss, the black community rallied behind Binga, and he was freed in 1938. Having converted to Catholicism, Binga worked as a handyman at St. Anselm's Catholic Church from 1938 on.

Black Metropolis, volume two, stated that, beyond his personal business ventures, in 1921 Binga became chairman of the board of a newly organized life insurance company, which is unnamed. That year the interracial Mid–Southside Chamber of Commerce honored him as a leading citizen. For nine years he continued to receive honors and recognition until the Great Depression set in.

A tall, handsome, and distinguished man, Binga was known for his business acumen and philanthropy. He was also called mean, arrogant, rough–hewn, and a rent–gouger. He was involved in such civic organizations as the Associated Business Club—an affiliate of the National Negro Business League. He held an important position for the league when he chaired the Grand August Carnival and Negro Exposition in 1912. He also established scholarships for many young black men and women to study at the University of Chicago. Binga contributed to the local YWCA, the Old Folks Home, and other charities and held parties for needy children and the elderly. Although a high school dropout, Binga gave liberally to Fisk, Howard, and Atlanta universities.

Binga died in St. Luke's Hospital on June 13, 1950, after suffering a stroke and falling down a staircase in his nephew's home in Chicago, where he then lived. He was buried in Oakwood Cemetery. His wife had died in 1933. A single–minded businessman, he is remembered for his pioneering work in black business development and for founding a bank that stood as a model of black business nationwide.

REFERENCES

Cantey, Inez. ''Jesse Binga.'' *Crisis* 33–34 (November 1926–December 1927): 329, 350, 352.

Drake, St. Clair, and Horace R. Cayton. *Black Metropolis.* New York: Harcourt Brace, 1945. Revised and enlarged edition. 2 vols, 1970.

Ingham, John, and Lynne B. Feldman. *African–American Business Leaders: A Biographical Dictionary.* Westport, CT: Greenwood Press, 1994.

Garraty, John A., and Edward T. James, eds. *Dictionary of American Biography.* Supplement 4, 1946–1950. New York: Scribner's, 1974.

Logan, Rayford W., and Michael R. Winston, eds. *Dictionary of American Negro Biography.* New York: Norton, 1982.

Osthaus, Carl R. ''The Rise and Fall of Jesse Binga, Black Financier.'' *Journal of Negro History* 58 (January 1973): 39–60.

Jessie Carney Smith

"Black Harry."
See Hosier, "Black Harry."

"Black Sam."
See Fraunces, Samuel.

Eubie Blake

(1883–1983)

Composer, performer, songwriter, musician, historian, educator

Eubie Blake has been considered one of America's musical treasures. During his long lifetime, he remained active through several distinguished careers as a noted stride and ragtime pianist and composer of rags, as a successful vaudevillian performer, and as a composer and songwriter. Though probably best known as a ragtime artist, Eubie Blake was one of a very few successful African American composers of Broadway musicals in the first half of the twentieth century. Most significant among such compositions was the history–making hit musical, *Shuffle Along.*

James Hubert "Eubie" Blake was born on February 7, 1883, in Baltimore, Maryland. John Sumner Blake, Eubie's father, a former slave, was a Civil War veteran and a stevedore. Eubie's mother, Emily Johnston Blake, also a former slave, was a laundress. The youngest of 11 children, Eubie was the only one of his brothers and sisters to survive infancy. The Blake home, recalled Eubie in Al Rose's *Eubie Blake,* was a very strict one. Eubie Blake's mother was a devoutly religious woman who gave much of her time to her church, and who tolerated absolutely no inappropriate behavior. Infractions of her rules, Blake remembered, resulted in corporeal punishments swift and severe.

One of the few demands of Eubie Blake's father was that his son receive an education. John Blake was taught to read as a slave a rare opportunity and, therefore, was adamant about the importance of literacy. Eubie Blake, however, did not remember his school days fondly, partially owing to general disinterest and frequent fights.

Eubie Blake's musical training began around the age of four. He first learned to play on a pump organ his mother had purchased in the hope that he would use his talents to the service of the church. Blake took his first piano lessons from Margaret Marshall, a next–door neighbor. Eubie Blake recalled being given the usual standards to play, as well as hymns, which kept his mother happy. However, he was more drawn to the music he heard drifting into his window from the many nightclubs and brothels in his neighborhood. Unable to resist the infectious rhythms and melodies of this raucous music, Eubie Blake's practice turned to perfecting this new style of playing.

Eubie Blake

Composes Rag

Blake landed his first real playing job when he was 15 years old at a neighborhood brothel, Aggie Shelton's Bawdy House. Three dollars a week plus tips was the salary, Blake recalled. He also remembered having to play in "rented long pants" on the account of having to sneak away from home each night in order to play the job. While at Aggie Shelton's, Blake composed his *Charleston Rag* in 1899. Other early jobs included brief tours with Dr. Frazier's Medicine Show as a buck and wing dancer and melodeon player in 1901 and in 1902 with the traveling show *In Old Kentucky.* Later that same year, Blake made his return to nightclub playing in Alfred Greenfeld's Saloon, where he composed his next rag, *Corner of Chestnut and Low,* the address of Greenfeld's club.

Beginning in 1905, Blake spent several summers away from Baltimore in Atlantic City, where he was pianist at the Middle Section Club. He recalled meeting and establishing lasting friendships with some of the greatest black musicians of the time, including long–time friend and competitor, pianist Hughie Wolford, and celebrated composer and performer Will Marion Cook. The older Cook took an interest in Blake's compositions, and according to Blake, became a mentor.

Blake's first big break came in 1907 when he was hired by Joe Gans, an African American prizefighter and childhood friend, who had just opened a new hotel in Baltimore called the Goldfield Hotel. The Goldfield immediately became a prominent haunt of wealthy, sophisticated businesspeople and entertainers of all races from all over the world. As a performer in this prestigious hotel, Blake became acquainted with rich and powerful people, many of whom had a profound impact on his career. While at the Goldfield, Blake continued to develop his compositional ability. He wrote rags: *The Baltimore Todolo, Kitchen Tom, Tricky Fingers, Novelty Rag,* and *Poor Katie Redd.* Blake attributed this compositional spurt to tutelage from Llewellyn Wilson, famous Baltimore conductor introduced to Blake by Will Marion Cook.

In July of 1910 Eubie Blake married Avis Lee, the daughter of a wealthy socialite from Baltimore. According to Blake, he and Avis had met in grade school. He admitted, however, that there was nothing between them until they met again as adults. Avis was not only older than he, but she was also more focused on her education and much more sophisticated, recounted Blake. In *Reminiscing with Sissle and Blake,* Blake called Avis "one of the ten most beautiful girls in Baltimore."

Avis Blake was herself a classically trained pianist, who, according to Eubie Blake, had the ability but had been too sheltered to consider having a career of her own. After they were married, she remained at home as homemaker and wife, occasionally traveling with Blake until her death from tuberculosis in 1939. They had no children.

Blake left the Goldfield in early 1911, shortly after the death of owner Joe Gans. His stay there, however, had made him famous throughout the Northeast and highly sought after. The years between 1911 and 1915 Blake described as good ones in which he played in some of the best clubs in Baltimore, New York, and Atlantic City. In 1911 Blake wrote his rags, *Chevy Chase* and *Fizz Water,* which he published later that year. Unfortunately the experience was marred by the unscrupulous dealings of his publisher. In his inexperience, Blake inadvertently gave up certain rights to his songs, causing him to lose a great deal of money in future royalties. That same year Blake also wrote *Troublesome Ivories* and *Brittwood Rag,* named after the popular Brittwood Club of Harlem.

During this period of his life, Eubie Blake was enjoying fame and privilege few musicians of his time would ever know. By most standards he was a success. Yet the events of the next years took him in an entirely different direction–into a new musical profession which eclipsed his young career as ragtime pianist for the next 40 years. Blake became a songwriter and composer of musicals.

Meets Sissle

Eubie Blake and Noble Sissle met on May 16, 1915, at Riverview Park in Baltimore. Almost immediately after their meeting they formed one of the most successful collaborative performing and songwriting teams in American musical theater history.

Noble Sissle (1889–1975) was a well–educated son of well–to–do parents from Indianapolis, Indiana. Sissle studied at DePauw and Butler Universities in Indiana. He was a naturally gifted singer and actor who had participated in plays and sung in glee clubs both in high school and college. Seeking fame as a professional performer, Sissle moved to Baltimore. Blake recalled that it was through Sissle that he met James Reese Europe, whom Rose described in *Eubie Blake* as a "monumental figure in the Negro Music World." Europe was the organizer and president of the Clef Club for black musicians. This organization was a booking agency for musicians and especially Europe's orchestras, which dominated booking in New York City. Europe hired Blake as pianist in his Long Island orchestra in 1916. The three men remained close friends until Europe's death by stabbing in 1919.

Only a few weeks after their meeting, Blake had written music to Sissle's lyrics, "Its All Your Fault," which they persuaded the legendary Sophie Tucker to sing. Two years later, in 1917, the team of Sissle and Blake was separated by World War I. Sissle enlisted, but Blake, already 34, was too old. Upon Sissle's return in 1919, they developed a vaudeville act which traveled under the name *The Dixie Duo.*

Significant about *The Dixie Duo* was the fact that this team never performed in black face as was the tradition; yet, they were still successful. "The practice of corking faces by black performers was expected for artistic survival," says Rose. And, of course white artists like Al Jolson and Eddie Cantor continued using black face. Credit must therefore be given to Sissle and Blake as pioneers among others in the rejection of the stereotypical make up. During their tour the team wrote, then favorites, *Pickaninny Shoes,* and *Oriental Blues* which was later included in their smash hit musical, *Shuffle Along.*

The hit musical *Shuffle Along,* established Eubie Blake and Noble Sissle prominently among the greats of musical theater in the twenties. *Shuffle Along* opened in 1921 and was an immediate success. Blake and Sissle financed the show themselves, along with help from Flournoy Miller and Aubrey Lyles, the Fisk educated comedy team with whom they had joined forces. Miller, Lyles, and Sissle also starred in the show. Originally titled *The Mayor of Jimtown, Shuffle Along* satirized small–town politics in a fictional black town with hilarious comedic sketches and lively musical numbers. The overwhelming success of this show made wealthy men of its creators, and stars of Miller and Lyles, as well as newcomers Florence Mills, Paul Robeson, and Josephine Baker.

Shuffle Along ran for over 500 performances on Broadway. The show also ran for an extended stay in Boston. The touring companies played to sell–out houses all over the United States. Songs from the musical included "Bandana Days," "In Honeysuckle Time," "If you've Never Been Vamped by a Brownskin, You've Never Been Vamped At All," "Love Will Find A Way," and "I'm Just Wild about Harry."

Several revivals of *Shuffle Along* were mounted years after the show had closed. Most notable were the productions of 1933 and 1952. Despite the fact that Sissle and Blake tried to rejuvenate their once hit show with new songs, neither revival was nearly as successful as the first.

Three years after *Shuffle Along,* Sissle and Blake's second successful musical came to Broadway in 1924, *The Chocolate Dandies.* Songs from *The Chocolate Dandies* included "That Charleston Dance," "There's a Million Little Cupids in the Sky," "You Ought to Know," "Dumb Luck," and "Manda."

After the break–up of Blake and Sissle in 1927, Eubie Blake teamed with several other prominent lyricists and performers of the time, including Henry Creamer, Broadway Jones, Milton Reddie, and Andy Razaf. Blake and Razaf's collaboration produced hit songs for a show called *Blackbirds of 1930,* which included tunes "Memories of You" and "You're Lucky to Me." Blake and Razaf's musical, *Tan Manhattan,* written and produced in 1940, was a great success, Eubie Blake's last big success in musical theater until the opening of the Broadway smash hit *Eubie!,* a musical review of his works, in 1978.

Returns to Ragtime

While serving as a bandleader with the United Servicemen Organizations (USO) during World War II, Eubie met and married Marion Grant Tyler, his second wife, in 1945. Tyler was also a performer and a businesswoman, who, after the couple settled in New York, became his valued manager of business and personal affairs.

From 1945 to 1950 Blake attended New York University, graduating at age 67 with a degree in music. It was certainly not uncommon for artists who had enjoyed the success that Blake had to have been considering retirement or, at least, slowing down at this age. However, Blake showed no signs of easing up. Almost prophetically, he was preparing himself for what was to become yet another upswing in his already distinguished career.

In the 1950s a revival of interest in America's ragtime music began to surface and spread throughout the country. Blake, one of the few surviving authentic artists of ragtime, found himself enticed into yet another career as ragtime artist, historian, and educator. In the years that followed, Blake signed recording deals with major companies like 20th Century Records and Columbia Records; he also lectured and gave interviews at major colleges and universities all over the world.

In the 1970s Blake's fame was once again soaring. In his late eighties and nineties, he appeared as special guest performer and clinician in all of the world's top jazz and rag festivals. He was a frequent guest of talk shows such as *The Johnny Carson Show* and *Merv Griffin.* Sold–out performances in the world's most prestigious concert halls punctuated his active schedule. Eubie Blake has also been featured under the baton of many of the world's great conductors, including Leonard Bernstein and Arthur Fiedler. Virtually every music organization in the country has honored Blake, and articles about him have appeared in *Time* and *Newsweek* as well as in all of the magazines related to his trade.

By 1975 Blake had been awarded doctorate degrees from Rutgers, the New England Conservatory, the University of Maryland, Morgan State University, Pratt Institute, Brooklyn College, and Dartmouth. In 1978 he was an invited guest and performer at the Carter White House, and in 1981 James Hubert Blake received the Presidential Medal of Honor.

Eubie Blake died five days after his 100th birthday, on February 12, 1983, in Brooklyn, New York. News of his death was carried by major newspapers and television stations internationally. That year a proliferation of concerts celebrating Blake's life and music by the music world honored his memory.

A uniquely gifted artist, Eubie Blake has left the world a rich and varied body of music and history. Blake, by his own admission, was very fortunate. Not only did this musical genius rise far above what was expected of or allowed for African American musicians of his time in mainstream musical theater, but he was also granted a life long enough to witness the world's eventual acceptance and appreciation for the music of his youth, ragtime.

REFERENCES

Carter, Lawrence T. *Eubie Blake: Keys of Memory.* Detroit: Balamp Publishing Co., 1979.

Chilton, John. *Who's Who of Jazz: Storyville to Swingstreet.* New York: DaCapo Press, 1985.

Kimball, Robert, and William Bolcom. *Reminiscing with Sissle and Blake.* New York: Viking, 1973.

Rose, Al. *Eubie Blake.* New York: Schirmer Books, 1979.

Wynn, Ron, ed. *All–Music Guide to Jazz.* San Francisco: Miller Freeman Books, 1994.

Leroy E. Bynum Jr.

Jules Bledsoe

(1897–1943)

Singer, composer

Jules Bledsoe achieved success as a singer in concert and on the stage as one of the pioneer blacks in opera. He is perhaps most famous for his creation of the role of Joe in Jerome Kerns's *Show Boat.* Nonetheless, Bledsoe's greatest achievements were in opera. Praised for his operatic talents in North America and Europe, Bledsoe was among the first African Americans to perform alongside white cast members in the United States. Although he made little mark in the field, he also had ambitions as a composer.

According to the Texas census, Julius Lorenzo Bledsoe was born in Waco, Texas, on December 27, 1897. (Bledsoe changed his first name from Julius to Jules in 1927 when he first sang in *Show Boat.*) He was the only child of Henry L. Bledsoe and Jessie Cobb Bledsoe. Two years after Bledsoe's birth his parents separated. Mother and child lived with her recently widowed mother, Feriba Cobb, a nurse and midwife. Bledsoe's maternal grandfather, Stephen Cobb, was an eminent member of the community. The first licensed Baptist preacher in Waco, he founded the New Hope Baptist Church in 1866 and was known for his fine singing voice.

Bledsoe grew up in a house filled with women: his grandmother, his mother, and his mother's younger sisters Mae Ollie and Naomi Ruth Cobb. All were apparently musical and encouraged Bledsoe's early musical development. Mae Ollie Cobb coached him in his singing debut at the age of five in church, and she was his only piano teacher until he left for college. Bledsoe was skilled enough on the piano to accompany his mother and his aunt Mae Ollie Cobb (later Stiller) when they sang in public.

Bledsoe received his primary and secondary education at Central Texas Academy, a school associated with Central Texas College, a Baptist–run institution which was in existence between 1903 and 1929. He then studied at Bishop College in Marshall, Texas, where he concentrated in liberal arts and music, graduating magna cum laude on May 14, 1918. He moved to Harpers Ferry, West Virginia, to serve in the Civilian Chaplain Service and, presumably in the fall, to join the ROTC course at Virginia Union University in Richmond, Virginia. The Armistice in November freed Bledsoe from military obligations, and the ROTC released him in December.

There are published statements that Bledsoe received a degree from the Chicago College of Music in 1919. Lynnette G. Geary's investigation of the Bledsoe papers at Baylor University found no substantiation for this. Bledsoe most likely moved to New York City after leaving Virginia Union. Geary claimed that he worked as a freelance musician before entering Columbia University to study medicine in 1920; other sources suggested that he entered Columbia in the fall of 1919. Shortly after Bledsoe's mother died during the summer of 1920, he decided to pursue music professionally. Bledsoe studied music with Claude Warford and later for two–and–a–half years with Luigi Parisotti; he also received coaching from Lazar Samoiloff.

On Easter Sunday, April 20, 1924, Bledsoe made his professional debut at Aeolian Hall in New York. He was already under contract to impresario Sol Hurok at this time. In 1929 Walter White of the NAACP would use his influence to help Bledsoe end the contract. There followed a period of intensive concert appearances. Reviewers in New York and Boston acclaimed the beauty of his voice but mentioned poor diction as a fault. In June of 1926 Bledsoe completed a concert tour of thirteen states, ending with a concert in the Dallas City Auditorium.

Bledsoe's first stage performance soon followed. He sang the role of Tizan in the opera *Deep River,* which also

Jules Bledsoe

utilized black singers Lottie Howell, Rose McClendon, and Charlotte Murray. In spite of critical praise for McClendon and Bledsoe, the show ran for only 32 performances after its opening on September 30, 1926. Nonetheless, this production was significant in that it marked the first time a racially mixed cast sang an opera.

Bledsoe continued to build his career by singing in the premiere of Louis Gruenberg's *The Creation* with the Boston Symphony Chamber Players under the direction of Serge Koussevitsky at Town Hall on November 17, 1926. The work was based on a poem by James Weldon Johnson. Beginning on December 30, he appeared briefly in Paul Green's play, *In Abraham's Bosom,* with Rose McClendon and Abbie Mitchell at the Providence Playhouse. *In Abraham's Bosom* won a Pulitzer Prize and ran for 116 performances. Frank Wilson took over Bledsoe's role when Bledsoe left the cast.

Bledsoe's next major role was that of Joe in the original Broadway production of the classic American musical, *Show Boat,* with music by Jerome Kern and the book by Oscar Hammerstein II. Paul Robeson, who sang the role in the London production, was originally chosen for the role but, due to delays in the production, he was unavailable by the time the musical opened on December 27, 1927. Paul Vodery, the black arranger and composer who directed the chorus for the show, recommended Bledsoe for the role. This musical reached 572 performances over the next two years.

Bledsoe became famous, especially in Harlem where he moved into a Sugar Hill apartment. With a keen sense of the incongruous, he bought a sky blue Packard and employed a white chauffeur to drive him around Harlem. He also became known as one of the greatest partygivers in Harlem. Heading the guest list for the party he gave when he moved into his Sugar Hill apartment was New York mayor James Walker.

At the beginning of 1929, on January 27, Bledsoe appeared in a costumed concert version of the third act of *Aida* at a New York theater. This was his first move in the direction of the operatic stage. Later that year Bledsoe sang for a movie version of *Show Boat.* Universal Film Company had made a silent version of the novel in 1925, with Stepin' Fetchit (Lincoln Perry) playing Joe. To meet the new demand for sound movies, Universal hired singers from the Ziegfeld Broadway production of *Show Boat* to supply a sound track for the film. Bledsoe spent the summer on the Radio–Keith–Orpheum (RKO) vaudeville circuit. He sang spirituals and light classic numbers alongside popular songs. That fall he joined the road company of *Show Boat,* which toured from September 21 to February of 1930.

Bledsoe then found work in radio and vaudeville. On April 10, 1931, he gave a concert at Carnegie Hall. A European tour followed. During this tour the Decca record label supplemented the few recordings he previously made in the United States. In 1932 Bledsoe returned to the United States to work in opera. On June 30 he sang in the premiere of *Tom–Tom,* an opera by Shirley Graham, who later married W. E. B. Du Bois. The opera was produced by the Cleveland Stadium Opera Company, which called on Bledsoe to take the role of Amonasro in *Aida* at the last moment. When he sang Amonasro on July 11, Bledsoe was probably the first black to sing opera in an otherwise white cast in the United States.

Bledsoe then sang on radio, toured once again in a road company of *Show Boat* in the fall, sang in an all–black variety show, *Hi–De–Ho,* in Boston in April of 1933 and the same month participated in a tribute to Flo Ziegfeld, who had died the previous year. That summer Bledsoe sang in the second cast of the Chicago Opera Company's production of *Aida* at New York's Hippodrome Theater. (The company was a commercial venture with no connection to the older Chicago Opera Company, which had gone bankrupt during the Great Depression.) Caterina Jarboro, the African American soprano, headed the first cast of *Aida.*

Bledsoe then went to Europe where he starred in the European premiere of Louis Gruenberg's one act opera—based on Eugene O'Neill's 1920 play—*The Emperor Jones* in March. A popular white baritone sang the role in performances at New York's Metropolitan Opera. Bailey's opening performances in the Netherlands were followed by successful performance in other European cities.

In April Bledsoe returned to the United States to work with the Aeolian Opera Company, an all–black company. Unfortunately, the company went broke after the three–night run of *The Emperor Jones.* Bledsoe then sang in *Aida* for the Cosmopolitan Opera Company, which appeared at the Hippodrome in the 1934–35 season. He also sang in *The Emperor Jones* for the company on November 30, 1934. Then, seeking to extend the possibilities for black singers, Bledsoe tried to arrange a production of Clarence Cameron White's opera *Ouanga.* The project was scheduled for 1941–42, but it fell through. After 1934 Bledsoe never again sang opera in the United States.

Bledsoe filled the beginning of 1935 with numerous concerts, including one at a New York rally protesting the Italian invasion of Ethiopia in September and a concert at New Hope Baptist Church on December 2. By early 1936 Bledsoe again sought work in Europe.

Bledsoe formed a short–lived vaudeville act with Clarence Johnstone, a former member of the vaudeville team [Henry Turner] Layton and Johnstone. The partnership worked from February 3 to March 28, 1936, in England and Ireland. Audiences disliked Johnstone, however, and even drove him from the stage more than once. The team broke up permanently shortly after Johnstone made a statement approving of the Italian invasion of Ethiopia. In June of 1936 Bledsoe appeared in a British productions of *Blackbirds* for a star salary of $500 a week even though he did not have a starring role. The producers subsequently tried to force him to leave the show. He sued the production in September but fulfilled his contractual obligations for the remainder of the shows. Bledsoe continued to find concert and recital work in Europe.

Bledsoe premiered his own composition for baritone and orchestra, *African Suite,* with the British Broadcasting Corporation Symphony in October of 1936. He repeated the performance with the Dutch Concertgebouw Orchestra in May of 1937. By this time, Bledsoe had begun composing songs in a folk idiom. His ambitions grew and he eventually composed an opera, *Bondage,* based on Harriet Beecher Stowe's novel *Uncle Tom's Cabin.* This opera was never produced.

The outbreak of war in Europe forced Bledsoe to return to the United States in September, where he found it difficult to arrange concerts because arrangements for the 1938–39 musical season had already been made for the most part. He mortgaged his Roxbury farm for $6,000 and arranged a successful concert at New York's Town Hall on January 28, 1940. By mid–March he also had persuaded Sol Hurok, now the leading American impresario, to take him on again. Hurok agreed on the condition that Bledsoe arrange to take vocal lessons with Samoiloff again.

In 1941 Bledsoe toured the United States, singing his composition *Ode To America* with school and choral society groups. This was a patriotic work for baritone and chorus. On May 11, 1941, he sang the work with the National Youth Administration Chorus on a NBC network broadcast hosted by Eleanor Roosevelt. Just after the United States entered the war, Bledsoe broke his leg on the set of the movie *Drums of the Congo* on December 20. It would be March of the following year before he was able to resume his concert work. Through the rest of this year and the early part of the next, Bledsoe sang frequently at concerts for charitable causes. He had just finished a tour for war bonds, when he died of cerebral hemorrhage on July 14, 1943, in Hollywood, California. His aunt Naomi Cobb had nursed him in the last week of his illness and took his body back to Waco, Texas, for burial. The funeral was held on July 21 at the New Hope Baptist Church with burial in Greenwood Cemetery.

In a review cited in "Different Appreciations of Jules Bledsoe," in Nancy Cunard's anthology *Negro,* the critic of Dutch newspaper *De Maasbode* of Rotterdam wrote:

> The Negro singer from America, Jules Bledsoe, convinces us still more than Hayes did of the excellent singing qualities of the black race. What a divine voice this singer has! It sounds like a darkly tuned cello, and especially in the mezzo voce this voice has a quality of velvet.

With this classically trained instrument, Jules Bledsoe was able to forge a musical career of true substance.

REFERENCES

Cunard, Nancy, ed. *Negro.* 1934. Reprint, New York: Negro Universities Press, 1969.

Cuney–Hare, Maud. *Negro Musicians and Their Music.* Washington, DC: Associated Publishers, 1936.

Geary, Lynnette G. "Jules Bledsoe: The Original 'Ol' Man River.'" *The Black Perspective in Music* 17 (1989): 27–54.

Johnson, James Weldon. *Black Manhattan.* New York: Knopf, 1940.

Kellner, Bruce, ed. *The Harlem Renaissance: A Historical Dictionary For the Era.* New York: Methuen, 1982.

Lewis, David Levering. *When Harlem Was In Vogue.* New York: Knopf, 1981.

Smith, Jesse Carney, ed. *Notable Black American Women.* Detroit: Gale Research, 1992.

Southern, Eileen. *Biographical Dictionary of Afro–American and African Musicians.* Westport, CT: Greenwood, 1982.

COLLECTIONS

The papers of Jules Bledsoe are located in the Texas Collection of Baylor University.

Robert L. Johns

Charles L. Blockson

(1933–)

Curator, educator, historian, bibliophile, writer

The lifework of Charles L. Blockson is the preservation of black history. He has spent more than forty years amassing one of the nation's largest private collections of items related to black history and traditions. He is a recognized authority on African American history and resources and in recent years has made other important contributions to the study and interpretation of history through his work on the Underground Railroad and black historic sites.

Born on December 16, 1933, in Norristown, a blue–collar town in Pennsylvania, Charles L. Blockson is oldest of Annie Parker Blockson and Charles E. Blockson's eight children—four sons and four daughters. While a young child, he overcame double pneumonia and scarlet fever, illnesses he was not expected to survive. The lisp that he had developed by the time he began to talk made Blockson self–conscious. He also grew fast, tall, and had a powerful build early on. As a child, Blockson helped his mother, a homemaker, with household chores. It was his mother who helped him develop a persistent faith in the human race. After school and, time permitting on weekends, he participated in athletic events. In the summer he assisted his father, who owned and operated a painting and plastering business.

At Norristown High School, Blockson was a football and track star and was rewarded for his athletic performance with offers of scholarships from 60 colleges; from 1950 to 1952 he was Pennsylvania's shot–put and discus–throwing champion. He also received honorable mention on the state scholastic football team. He played all–state football and because of his speed and strength, in the press he was dubbed "Blockbuster Blockson." He also was on the national interscholastic track and field honor roll. Blockson accepted an offer from Pennsylvania State University, where he enrolled in 1952 and majored in physical education. In college he also starred on the track team and, alternately with his roommate Rosey Grier, set records in the shot put and discus throw. He graduated in 1956 and declined a number of offers, including one from the New York Giants, for a professional career in football.

Blockson spent the next two years in the U.S. Army. After his discharge, he operated his own business in janitorial services. In 1972 he joined the Norristown Area High School as an advisor specialist for human relations and cultural affairs. He worked directly under the superintendent of schools and spent his time lecturing in the schools on African American history, recruiting black faculty, and handling matters related to race. He also pursued rigorously his long passion for collecting, preserving, and promoting the study of African American history.

Asked why and how be began collecting African Americana, Blockson told Nancy Funk Crabb for *The PennStater* that his interest in collection was spurred when he was a fifth–grade student and his teacher told the class that "Negroes were born to serve whites." From that moment, Blockson was spurred to dispel this notion and to demonstrate that he, as a black, could excel. He was determined also to show that he could succeed in whatever he wanted to do. In his childhood, Blockson visited used book stores and the used book sections of the local Salvation Army store, Goodwill industries, antique shops, flea markets, and church bazaars in search of works that bore the words "black," "Negro," or "colored." Already he had been inspired by his father's love for reading and search for antiques and he, too, developed a keen interest in reading works of history and biographies of people of African descent. He had also developed an interest in art, the writings of Colette and Chaucer, French culture, jazz, classical music, and the game of chess. He was already a loner; his

Charles L. Blockson

friends did not share his interests and left him to work in solitude. His collection was well developed by the time he reached high school.

Those disturbing and confusing words from his teacher spurred Blockson toward success in football as well; thus, while a student at Penn State he earned numerous trophies and medals that became a part of his personal collection.

Convinced that "no race of people should be deprived of the knowledge of itself," he said in the 1997 "African American Historical Calendar," over forty years had passed since Blockson embarked on his journey as a career bibliophile of Afro–Americana. Blockson became known among book dealers and antique shops throughout Pennsylvania and elsewhere. So well known and respected was Blockson among the dealers that when they knew or suspected that he had an interest in an item, they frequently held materials for him. For example, one dealer held for him a copy of Harriet Beecher Stowe's *A Key to Uncle Tom's Cabin,* an early important find.

Blockson's interest in the Underground Railroad also dated from his childhood. He never forgot the stories his grandfather told him and that he later documented. His great grandfather, James Blockson, escaped from slavery in Delaware in 1856 when he was a teenager and went to Canada. So did his grandfather's cousin, Jacob Blockson, who in 1858 escaped to St. Catharines, Ontario. "The Underground Railroad in all its abiding mystery and hope and terror took possession of my imagination," he wrote in *National Geographic.* As early as 1969 he envisioned a project to locate black slaves' route to freedom and to show the locations on a historical map of the 400 or more Underground Railroad stations. He also envisioned preserving some of the original houses used as stations whose existence had been threatened by proposed highways and other developments.

Moves Collection to Temple

Blockson was more than a packrat of items related to African Americans. Through the years, he collected rigorously and gained a reputation for his splendid private library. While his extensive collection was housed in his basement at home, he shared it generously with local students and scholars who needed information. Bowing to pressure to move his collection of Afro–Americana from his home, in 1984 he donated his materials to Temple University in Philadelphia to form the Charles L. Blockson Afro–American Collection. Unwilling to part with it entirely, however, Blockson left the Norristown schools to become curator of the collection housed in the Special Collections Department of Temple University Libraries. The collection continues to expand and now contains approximately 150,000 books, pamphlets, manuscripts, prints, drawings, pieces of sheet music, broadsides, posters, and artifacts. Using his expertise in African American history, Blockson amassed materials that span nearly four centuries and represent geographical areas from Africa through Europe and the Caribbean to the United States.

According to the 1997 "African American Historical Calendar," Blockson's determination to gather documents on African American history in a variety of formats led him to collect early on "some of the most painfully graphic moments of African–American History." For example, the original Blockson collection included a book cover made in 1933 from the skin of a black patient in a Baltimore hospital. Believed to have been commissioned by someone who hated President Abraham Lincoln and blacks as well, the cover envelopes the work *Lincoln the Unknown.*

Blockson is known internationally for his work as a bibliophile, lecturer, genealogist, expert in African American history, and scholar on the Underground Railroad, as well as for his contributions in related areas. He has lectured in the Caribbean and South America for the U.S. Information Agency, and completed a tour of Denmark. He continues to lecture, organize black studies programs in schools and colleges, and arrange exhibits. Among his exhibitions is "Of Color, Humanitas and Statehood: The Black Experience in Pennsylvania Over Three centuries, 1681–1981," which toured the state. He launched a historical marker project in 1989 designed to build 65 markers commemorating the contributions of African Americans to Philadelphia. Blockson also published a guide to the project, *Philadelphia's Guide: African–American State Historical Markers* (1993).

Among the many books Blockson has written or edited are *Black Genealogy,* written with Ron Fry and published in 1977. By 1977, Blockson had already traced his ancestors back to the eighteenth century and now wanted to share his knowledge of the genealogical search with others who shared the richness of the black heritage. The work was widely received and helped spur a national interest in black genealogical research. His other works include *Pennsylvania's Black History* (1975); *The Underground Railroad in Pennsylvania* (1981); *The Underground Railroad: First Person Narratives of Escapes to Freedom in the North* (1987); *A Commented Bibliography of One Hundred and One Influential Books by and about People of African Descent, 1556–1982 (1989)*; and *The Journey of John W. Mosley: An African–American Pictorial* (1993). In addition to the chapters he wrote for books, he has written a number of journal articles including "The Underground Railroad," the illustrated cover story for *National Geographic* for the July 1984 issue. His was one of eight articles on the Underground Railroad by various writers subsequently published in *National Geographic.* Blockson is currently writing his autobiography.

Blockson may be called an activist in African American history. He is a founder of the Afro–American Historical and Cultural Museum in Philadelphia, established in 1976. He has been president of the Pennsylvania Abolition Society. He was a member of the State Historical and Record Advisory Board for Pennsylvania and its Black History Advisory Board. His interest and expertise in the Underground Railroad led to his appointment by the Secretary of the Interior as chair of the Underground Railroad Advisory Committee. In this position, from 1990 to 1995 he directed the National Park Services' Underground Railroad Sites Study. The project resulted in the National Park Services' publications, the *Underground Railroad* (Handbook #156), and the *Official Map and Guide of the Underground Railroad.* Blockson belongs to the American Antiquarian Society, the Grolier Club, and the Author's Guild. He is also a member of the NAACP. In 1992 Blockson moderated the Black Writer's Conference in Paris. He also chaired the Valley Forge African–American Revolutionary Soldier Monument committee whose work led to the establishment of a monument commemorating the soldier's work.

Blockson's awards and honors are numerous. In 1984 he was awarded the State College Football Alumni Award. He was the first inductee in the Norristown school district's Hall of Fame and Hall of Champions, 1979–83. He received the Penn State Alumni Fellow Award for distinguished alumni in 1981 and the Before Columbus Foundation's Lifetime Achievement Award in 1987. In 1990 a bronze bust of Blockson was presented to Temple University as a gift from celebrated sculptor Antonio Salemme. In 1991 Blockson received the Philadelphia Urban League's Whitney Young Human Relations Award and in 1996 the first Lifetime Award from the African American Storytellers. He holds honorary doctorates from Villanova University (1979), Lincoln University in Pennsylvania (1987), and Holy Family College (1995).

Although now divorced, in 1958 he married Elizabeth Parker of Norristown. They have one daughter, Noelle, now in computer sales in Pennsylvania. The tall, athletic, kind, soft–spoken Blockson is an important figure in African American history who generously shares his time and expertise with others. His work as bibliophile has led to the collection and preservation of important resources on African American themes. His work as researcher, particularly on the Underground Railroad, has resulted in increased national attention to the plight of former slaves. His work on historic sites, black genealogy, and other topics has further preserved and promoted aspects of African American history and culture. He aims to continue to collect, preserve, and disseminate information on African Americans. Quoted in the *PennStater,* he said: "As long as I have my books, I have my life."

Current address: Charles L. Blockson Afro–American Collection, Sullivan Hall (007–01), Temple University, Philadelphia, PA 19122.

REFERENCES

"The African American Historical Calendar." Philadelphia: George A. Beach, 1997.

"Bio–Sketch of Charles L. Blockson," December 1993. In the personal collection of Charles L. Blockson.

Blockson, Charles L. Interview with Jessie Carney Smith, January 5, 1998.

———. "The Underground Railroad." *National Geographic* 166 (July 1984): 3–30.

Crabb, Nancy Funk. "His Books Are His Soul." *The PennStater* 84 (January/February 1997): 36–39.

Who's Who among African Americans, 1998–99. 10th ed. Detroit: Gale Research, 1997.

Jessie Carney Smith

Thomas Fountain Blue

(1866–1935)

Librarian, organization official

When the Louisville Free Public Library launched library service in 1905, the originators mapped out a plan for ten branch libraries: two of these branches were selected to give service to the blacks of that Kentucky city. The first branch was inaugurated with a librarian and two assistants—all black. The guiding light behind these library developments in Louisville was Thomas Fountain Blue, self–educated librarian, Young Men's Christian Association official, teacher, and preacher.

Thomas Blue was the second child of Noah H. and Henri Ann Blue, born March 6, 1866, near Washington, D.C. at

Thomas Fountain Blue

Farmville, Virginia. His parents were former slaves. After a preparatory school education, young Blue attended Hampton Institute from 1885 to 1888 and obtained a Bachelor of Divinity degree from the Richmond Theological Seminary (now Virginia Union University) in 1898.

Though Blue was educated as a minister, he never held an assignment as the pastor of a church. He served as a Young Men's Christian Association secretary of the Sixth Virginia Regiment Volunteers in the Spanish–American War. He carried on his association with the YMCA at the conclusion of hostilities, and was called to head the Colored Branch of the YMCA in Louisville. Blue remained as its first regular secretary from 1899 to 1903.

Blue's qualifications as a librarian were acquired through the assistance of library school graduates at the main library of Louisville Public Library and grounded upon his intuitive expertise as a planner and a community leader. The library administrators realized that it took more than mortar, bricks, and books to create a library. It was essential to have trained library personnel to manage a strong library program. Consequently, an annual library apprentice class was initiated for those interested in pursuing library work, the first instance of any venture in the South to supply library training for the prospective black librarian. These classes were so effective students from such cities as Houston, Texas, and Memphis, Tennessee, availed themselves of Louisville's project. No other means of training seemed to have been available until the inauguration of the Library School at Hampton Institute in the 1920s.

Heads Black Branch Library

In 1905, Louisville library authorities called Thomas Blue to supervise this first branch for blacks. The Western Colored Branch was joined by the Eastern Colored Branch in 1914, and Blue was given the joint direction over them.

In 1918, during World War I, Blue served as an educational secretary at a camp in Kentucky, where he helped teach thousands of new recruits to read and write. In 1919 he returned to library work and in 1920 all work for blacks was concentrated under the administration of Thomas Blue. He served with distinction in the vanguard of the evolution of branch library service. He developed a working arrangement with the schools through library stations and classroom collections, and heavy use of the buildings was evidenced by the numerous clubs and associations meeting regularly in the branches. Blue acted as director of all the Negro work in Louisville until 1935.

Blue was an active member in the American Library Association (ALA). During the Detroit meeting of 1922, he read a paper, "The Training Class at the Western Colored Branch," before the association's Work with Negroes Round Table session. It is maintained that Blue was the first black to have a place on the program of the ALA. Further, Blue is recorded as a delegate to the ALA fiftieth anniversary convention in Atlantic City in 1926.

In 1927, Blue delivered the opening address to a conference of black librarians at Hampton Institute, speaking on "Arousing Community Interest in the Library." He inspired the Negro Library Conference of 1930, held at the dedication of the Fisk University Library in Nashville, Tennessee, and he was also an outstanding speaker at the activities.

Blue was taken ill in 1935 and died on November 10 that year. In recent years, the surviving Colored Branch of the Louisville Public Library has been placed on the National Register of Historical Places as a landmark, an appropriate recognition of the work of Thomas Fountain Blue, a pacesetter librarian. His influence is much in evidence in the southeastern United States and in the American Library Association even today.

REFERENCES

Josey, E. J., and Ann Allen Shockley, eds. *Handbook of Black Librarianship.* Littleton, CO: Libraries Unlimited, 1977.

Mather, Frank Lincoln. *Who's Who of the Colored Race: A General Biographical Dictionary of Men and Women of African Descent.* Vol. 1. Chicago: Mather, 1915.

Phinazee, Annette L., ed. *The Black Librarian in the Southeast.* Durham: North Carolina Central University School of Library Science, 1980.

Wright, Lillian T. "Thomas Fountain Blue, Pioneer Librarian, 1866–1935." Master's thesis, Atlanta University, 1955.

Casper L. Jordan

Guy Bluford
(1942–)
Astronaut, aeronautical engineer

Guy Bluford, who earlier in life had been counseled to focus on safe and lesser educational and career goals, was the first black American to travel in space. He is a role model for those who must work harder and longer in pursuing their goals.

The oldest of the three sons of Guion Bluford Sr. and Lolita Bluford, Guion Stewart Bluford Jr. is a native Philadelphian, born on November 22, 1942. Both sides of his family provided positive images of success for the Bluford boys. Guion Sr. was a mechanical engineer who impressed his oldest son with his attitude toward work and his struggles with health problems that forced an early retirement. Quoted in *Contemporary Black Biography,* Bluford said of his father: ''He would charge out of the house every morning, eager to get to work. I thought if engineers enjoy their work that much, it must be a good thing to get into.''

Bluford came from a family of achievers. One of his paternal uncles was editor of the *Kansas City Call* and another was president of North Carolina Agricultural and Technical College (now A and T State University) in Greensboro. Lolita Bluford was a special education teacher in the Philadelphia public school system and a relative of Carol Brice, a noted black contralto concert artist and vocal coach.

Saddled with the nickname of ''Bunny,'' Bluford enjoyed such solitary boyhood activities as airplane model construction and working crossword puzzles. His work ethic was forged before adolescence as a paper carrier with his own route and Boy Scout activities that culminated in his earning the coveted rank of Eagle Scout. Although his parents provided love and encouragement for their three sons, Guy, as he was called later, was not the one from whom great things were expected. In *Black Biography,* his brother Kenneth described him during his high school years:

> Bunny just had to work harder than the rest of us. He put in very long hours. He was always a little behind and trying to catch up. He was not like a kid who was unusually bright, with his mind darting all over the place making discoveries here and there. In school, Bunny was always slugging it out.

When the Overbrook High School guidance counselor suggested that college might not be the best post–graduation option for Bluford, neither he nor his parents heeded the advice. He had long harbored the desire to be an aerospace engineer, and mathematics and science were his favorite academic subjects from junior high school on. At the predominantly white Overbrook High School, Bluford maintained average grades in those subjects, and, after graduation in 1960, he enrolled in Pennsylvania State University as the only black student in the School of Engineering. In 1964 he graduated, on time, with a bachelor of science degree in

Guy Bluford

aerospace engineering and an Air Force ROTC commission. Even while matriculating at Penn State, Bluford was still described as an average student earning average grades.

During his senior year in college, Bluford married Linda Tull, a native Philadelphian. When he received his commission, he completed the pilot training program at Williams Air Force Base in Arizona and received his pilot wings in January 1965. After completing F–4C combat training, he was then based at Cam Ranh Bay in the 557th Tactical Fighter Squadron and flew 144 combat missions with nearly half over North Vietnam. By the end of that tour of duty, Bluford had earned ten Air Medals, three Air Force Outstanding Unit Awards, an Air Force Commendation Medal, and the rank of lieutenant colonel.

After Bluford's Vietnam tour of duty, he returned to the United States as a seasoned, serious combat veteran of the most misunderstood and unpopular war in the nation's history. He had begun his military obligations as his patriotic duty despite strong family feelings about the country's deepening involvement in Vietnam.

Serves as Test Pilot and Trainer

The Vietnam conflict was the only war that left veterans to return home and face overt hostility rather than ticker tape parades. Bluford's military career, however, was far from over. For the next ten years he served as a test pilot and pilot trainer. His first post–combat assignment was with the 3630th Flying Training Wing, Shepard Air Force Base, Texas, as a T–38A instructor pilot. In 1971 he completed training that prepared him to return there as deputy commander of operations. Three years later, he served as chief of the Aerodynamics and Airframe Branch of the Air Force Flight Dynamics Laboratory and staff development officer at Wright–Patterson Air Force Base in Dayton, Ohio.

During these years, Bluford was recognized as distinctly above average in his military and educational accomplishments. In 1974 he received a master of science degree, with distinction, in aerospace engineering and in 1978 the Ph.D. degree in the same field with a minor in laser physics from the Air Force Institute of Technology. Bluford's doctoral dissertation was entitled ''A Numerical Solution of Supersonic and Hypersonic Viscous Flow Fields Around Thin Planar Delta Wings.''

Quoting a *Philadelphia Inquirer* writer, *Contemporary Black Biography* reported on the transformation of the once plodding, but steady student to the brilliant military academician:

> Something remarkable happened. . .school and military records suggest that he put himself though an incredible honing process—tightening up his determination and work habits until he became a perfectly disciplined and motivated specimen of an Air Force career pilot and engineer.

The year 1978 continued to be a banner year for Bluford when he was selected to be an astronaut candidate in the Space Shuttle Program by the National Aeronautics and Space Administration (NASA). This was a stellar accomplishment, because there were only 35 openings and his was one of 8,000 applications.

Although Bluford's graduate studies were of markedly high caliber as exemplified in scientific papers he wrote and presented in the area of computational fluid dynamics, this was only one aspect of his qualifications for the NASA program. During his self–described average years, Bluford consistently exhibited a strong work ethic that he developed as a paper carrier and Eagle Scout. Even his seemingly solitary boyhood hobbies had required him to refine problem–solving skills and become a highly self–disciplined and self–motivated learner. As a jet pilot, Bluford had logged nearly 5,000 hours of jet flight time in six types of jet planes and over 1,000 hours as an instructor pilot. He also had extensive administrative experience and specialized duty assignments as an aerospace engineer.

First Black American in Space

Without the intervention of fate, Bluford would possibly have been the third black American in space. Edward Dwight Jr. was the first black American candidate but he was dropped from the program in 1965. (He was the Denver–based sculptor of the proposed Black Revolutionary War Patriots Memorial.) Although President John F. Kennedy created a parallel astronaut–training program for black fliers to prepare them for space flight, after his assassination Dwight felt that the program would fail because only his white cohorts were being selected. The second black candidate, Robert Lawrence Jr., was killed in an airplane crash before participating in a mission of the Manned Orbiting Laboratory. Bluford would also have been the fourth man of color in space since a Cuban astronaut had flown with Russia's pioneer space flight.

Bluford received intensive training for five years before the August 20, 1983, STS–8 shuttle flight on its eighth mission. According to *African–American Biographies,* his preparation included ''working the remote manipulator system, Spacelab–3 experiments, Shuttle systems, Shuttle Avionics Integration Laboratory (SAIL), and the Flight Systems Laboratory (FSL).''

On his maiden voyage into space, Bluford served as a mission specialist and performed experiments on the space–medicine machine to aid in diabetes research. On a later flight, he participated in observing from space phenomena such as the Northern Lights, cloud formations, and atmospheric conditions. His inaugural flight was the first with a night launch and night landing and completed 98 earth orbits before landing on September 5, 1983. Bluford's second flight was on October 30, 1985, a joint venture with West Germany and the first Spacelab mission and the first to transfer payload to a foreign country. It landed on November 6, 1985, after completing 111 earth obits in 169 hours. In 1991 and 1992 Bluford participated in the last two flights on the orbiter *Discovery.* Earlier, in 1986, his successor, Ronald E. McNair, was killed in the explosion of the *Challenger,* a flight that also claimed the life of the first civilian observer, public school teacher Christa McAuliffe. Before resigning from NASA and the Air Force, in 1993 Bluford earned a master's of business administration degree from the University of Houston (1987). He became vice–president and general manager of the Engineering Services Division of NYMA, an engineering and computer software company located in Maryland. As a civilian, he has been able to enjoy a personal life with his wife and sons, Guion III and James.

The awards and honors earned by Bluford include: the Vietnam Cross of Gallantry with Palm and Vietnam Service Medal (1967); National Society of Black Engineers Award (1979); NASA Group Achievement Awards (1980, 1981); NAACP Image Award (1983); *Ebony* Black Achievement Award (1983); Distinguished Service Medal, State of Pennsylvania (1984); and the NASA Exceptional Service Medal (1992). Bluford also received honorary doctorates from Florida Agricultural and Mechanical, Texas Southern, Virginia State, Morgan State, Thomas Jefferson, Chicago State, and Drexel universities; Tuskegee Institute, Bowie State College, and Stevens Institute of Technology. Some representative professional affiliations are with the American Institute of Aeronautics and Astronautics (Associate Fellow); Air Force Association; Tau Beta Pi Fraternity; National Technical Association; and the Tuskegee Airmen.

Bluford has always been a reticent, retiring person in both his personal life and in professional settings, but he soon realized that his accomplishments as a first in aeronautics and space travel would place him in the limelight. He accepted the challenges and responsibilities of his accomplishments because he understood that his elevated status made him a role model for black youth and aspiring minority scientists and aviators. In *Strength for the Flight,* Nalty quoted him as advising young blacks to "get an education and be prepared as you can for any opportunities that may come your way." Bluford is a consummate professional and an extraordinary person, one who has enjoyed the rare pleasure and once–in–a–lifetime opportunity to have traveled over two million miles in space. Quoted in *Contemporary Black Biography,* he described his adventures as "a labor of love. . . . You want to stay up forever."

Current address: NYMA Inc., 2001 Aerospace Parkway, Brookpark, OH 44142–1002.

REFERENCES

Contemporary Black Biography. Vol. 2. Detroit: Gale Research, 1992.

"For Black Memorial, It's Build or Bust." *New York Times,* August 4, 1996.

Hawkins, L. *African–American Biographies: Profiles of 558 Current Men and Women.* Jefferson, NC: McFarland, 1992.

Nalty, Bernard C. *Strength for the Flight: A History of Black Americans in the Military.* New York: Free Press, 1986.

Salzman, Jack, David Lionel Smith, and Cornel West, eds. *Encyclopedia of African–American Culture and History.* New York: Simon and Schuster/Macmillan, 1996.

Who's Who among African Americans 1995–96. 9th ed. Detroit: Gale Research, 1995.

Dolores Nicholson

Bojangles.
See Robinson, Bill "Bojangles."

Horace Mann Bond

(1904–1972)

Educator, college dean, college president

Horace Mann Bond, the first African American president of Lincoln University in Pennsylvania, was an outstanding educator, scholar, and college administrator. While he wrote nearly 100 articles, he is best remembered for his classic works on black education within the social order and in the state of Alabama.

Born November 8, 1904, in Nashville, to James and Jane, Horace was first exposed to the classroom at a very early age. His mother, a graduate of Oberlin College and a teacher, took him to school with her where two cousins provided supervision. It was not long before they discovered that he had learned to read by following along with the lessons being taught to the other children. Thus, at age three, Bond's life was set on a course dedicated to academic achievement and the pursuit of educational opportunity for members of his race.

Horace Mann Bond

Bond's father James, a minister, was a graduate of Berea and Oberlin colleges. Together, he and Jane passed on their love for learning to all of their six children and were Horace Bond's greatest influence. They often told him of their desire for him to lift the Bond name to higher intellectual heights. He believed it was his parents' moral fervor, and the encouragement received from his Aunt Mamie, a physician, that were the major catalysts for his academic success and not any superior ability on his part.

Recognized as an intellectual prodigy while still very young, Bond started school at Lincoln Institute in Kentucky when he was eight years old. His reading ability at that age allowed him to begin his formal schooling at the eighth grade level. He later attended Talladega College High School in Alabama and Atlanta University High School. His parents wanted him to study at Fisk University in Nashville when he was graduated in 1919; however, officials there thought him too young at age 14 to begin college–level work. As an alternative to Fisk, he was enrolled at Lincoln University in Pennsylvania.

Bond was invited to join the Lincoln University faculty as a part–time instructor in education when he graduated in 1923. The offer called for him to serve as a dormitory prefect and allowed him to enroll in language classes to begin preparing for graduate school. In addition, Lincoln officials arranged for him to study education at the Penn State College during the summer of 1923 to prepare him for his new teaching responsibilities at the university. Much to his shame, he was forced to resign shortly after the start of the school year when he was caught gambling with the young men he was supposed to supervise, a situation that could not be tolerated at the religious–oriented university. He would not return to Lincoln until 1945 when he was named the school's first black president.

Chicago, where two older brothers lived, became home for Bond after he left Lincoln. It was there, over the next ten years at the University of Chicago, that he completed both the master's degree (1926) and the doctorate (1936) in education. Although family members helped, extreme financial difficulty throughout this period forced Bond to seek full–time employment as he pursued his graduate degrees. Relying on his father's influence, his first professional appointment came at the age of 20 when he was named director of education at the Colored Agricultural and Normal University of Oklahoma at Langston. An individual of wide ranging interests, most of Bond's intellectual effort from that time on was devoted to the history of education, educational testing, and the sociology of blacks in America and Africa.

Bond met Julia Agnes Washington, the daughter of a prominent black Nashville family, during one of several stints at Fisk University. They were married in Chicago in 1929, and their 40–year marriage produced three children, James, Julian, and Jane Marguerite. His son Julian has served as a Georgia state legislator. A long–time civil rights activist, Julian Bond is now a lecturer, television commentator, university professor, and chair of the National Board of Directors for the National Association for the Advancement of Colored People (NAACP).

Explores Mental Testing for Blacks

It was during his time of employment at Langston that Bond began to build his record of scholarly writing and became involved in research in mental testing. An example of his early work in the field involved the results of an intelligence test he gave to the children of several of Langston's black faculty and reported on in an article published in civil rights advocate and sociologist W. E. B. Du Bois's *Crisis* magazine. He used the children's exceptionally high test scores as evidence that the lack of a stimulating and positive environment was much more responsible for the low scores of blacks on intelligence tests than hereditarian explanations. The Langston children and his own life accomplishments were used as proof of the benefit that positive influences could have on the development of academic ability. Bond's work in this area was motivated, at least in part, by a University of Chicago professor who once told him that his high score on an intelligence test used to screen applicants wishing to study for the doctorate was the result of his white blood. A significant portion of Bond's academic work was aimed at refuting white psychologists who insisted that blacks were inherently inferior to the majority racial group.

Bond's first submission to the *Crisis* was the beginning of a long and respectful relationship with Du Bois. Several more articles were published in the *Crisis* over the years, and Bond once participated in a research project headed by Du Bois. He respected Du Bois's intellect but was suspicious of the northern activist's ideas about the problems faced by southern blacks. A gulf developed in their relationship during the 1950s and 1960s when Bond voiced strong opposition to Du Bois's communism and anti–Americanism.

The Education of the Negro in the American Social Order, 1934, and Bond's reworked dissertation, *Negro Education in Alabama: A Study in Cotton and Steel,* 1939, represent the most outstanding scholarly efforts of his academic career. Although he continued to publish for journals and more popular magazines and to conduct research studies for benevolent societies after 1939, he did not produce another historical work until his history of Lincoln University in Pennsylvania was published posthumously in 1976.

A noteworthy example of Bond's intellectual ability and the high esteem in which his contemporaries held him is the research he did for the NAACP as part of the group's legal campaign against school segregation, which culminated in the 1954 decision *Brown v. Board of Education.* In later years, while at Atlanta University, Bond's scholarship focused on the environmental correlates of scholastic achievement and remained his primary intellectual interest for the remainder of his academic life.

Bond received substantial support from the Julius Rosenwald Fund throughout the early years of his career. The fund also provided substantial support during this period to create Dillard, a new university, in New Orleans. It was at the urging of Rosenwald officials that Bond reluctantly agreed in 1934 to become dean at the new institution.

Because of their financial support of the school, Rosenwald officials were able to exert considerable control in developing Dillard's academic programs. In particular, they urged school officials to focus on an education plan that was committed to redesigning schools to conform to what they viewed as the realities of rural life. Bond, on the other hand, held that the focus of the plan, bound in the notions of academic excellence, should be aimed at both the large urban and rural populations throughout the southern region. Bond's idea was to initiate reform as a process of providing the proper academic experiences for students as well as a process of binding theory with practical work. The experimental school he established in New Orleans while serving as dean provided opportunities to test his theories of education for blacks.

Bond approached his work at Dillard as both a traditionalist and as an innovator. He divided the curriculum into junior and senior divisions modeled after the University of Chicago undergraduate curriculum developed by Robert Maynard Hutchins, president, adding an emphasis on the special contributions of blacks. In the social sciences his focus was on analyzing problems faced by blacks and identifying their possible solutions. In his effort to maintain the very highest academic standards at the school, he solicited help from Louisiana Governor Huey Long to build a library to support research and study. When Bond became disillusioned in his role as dean, he used his contacts within the Julius Rosenwald Fund to leave Dillard for Fisk where he served as chairman of the education department from 1937 to 1939.

Becomes College President

Urged on in 1939 by Rosenwald Fund officials, and much to his unease, Bond accepted the presidency of Fort Valley State College in Georgia. In his six years there, with considerable financial support from the fund, he took the school from the status of a junior college to that of a comprehensive, baccalaureate degree–granting institution by the time he left in 1945.

Much of Bond's time at Fort Valley was spent fund raising from the state. In his first few years he met with little success because of Governor Eugene Talmadge's belief that the Rosenwald Fund's primary objective was to promote race mixing and that Bond was their agent in this effort. Beginning in 1942, however, when Talmadge was defeated by Ellis Arnall, the new governor welcomed any money that Bond could secure and accepted support from both the Rosenwald Fund and from the General Education Board.

Bond continued to develop a reputation as both an innovator and a traditionalist at Fort Valley. The mandate of the school to do progressive work in teacher education was in keeping with Bond's desire to avoid the training of specialized teachers "in the trades and industries." Given his focus on academic excellence, Bond was pleased when the board of regents changed the school's name from Fort Valley Normal and Industrial School to Fort Valley State College.

While the top priority given to Bond at Fort Valley was to upgrade teacher education, that was not his only objective. He also wanted Fort Valley graduates to be employable in a variety of other occupational areas. According to Wayne J. Urban in *Black Scholar: Horace Mann Bond,* he believed that this could be done if the school adopted the liberal goal of producing "young people of character, balance, intelligence, and preparation." What Bond was advocating was a range of studies that would allow curricular diversification and offer students a range of non–teaching career options. Within this teacher training institution Bond was creating a liberal arts college. When he decided to leave Fort Valley, he left the school distinctly improved academically and financially, with increased enrollments and faculty size.

Because he was never fully comfortable with administrative work, Bond attempted to keep in touch with the academic side of the profession by teaching graduate courses in the social sciences at Atlanta University in Atlanta during much of his presidency. The experience allowed him to identify with the role of faculty and, as a result, he sponsored the adoption of a series of statutes modeled on those of the University of Georgia, which codified the rights, privileges, and limitations of faculty and administrators. He believed that the statutes allowed his Fort Valley tenure to be free of disputes over tenure, promotion, and salary.

First Black President of Lincoln University

Bond left Fort Valley when tensions between himself and Rosenwald officials grew. More important, however, was his desire to remove his family from the segregation of Fort Valley and to put them in a position where their opportunities for a quality education and development would be improved. He left Georgia for the presidency of Lincoln University in 1945.

At Lincoln, Bond faced opposition from many older whites who had been his instructors and were unwilling to accept him as president and from blacks who felt themselves better qualified than he for the job. Moreover, the university's growing financial difficulties were intensified by a seminary which was not cost effective but was strongly supported by the Presbyterian church, the school's primary benefactors. These concerns were not eased by the small amount of financial assistance given by the Commonwealth of Pennsylvania to support Pennsylvania students. In fact, the Pennsylvania monies were threatened because of concern over state support for a school with religious connections.

While Bond had initial success at Lincoln, raising funds from alumni and increasing enrollment as a result of World War II veterans taking advantage of their GI Bill benefits, he faced serious challenges from other alumni who felt that the school's heritage was being ignored. For example, many complained about the poor state of athletics at the university, while others became unhappy when sons and friends were denied admission because of poor academic preparation. Tensions also were raised between Bond and alumni wives when the group, accustomed to operating independently of white presidents, moved forward with plans to construct a campus guest house without the president's knowledge or approval.

Unlike his tenure at Fort Valley, Bond experienced strong disapproval from members of the Lincoln faculty. The leader of this faction was Harold Grim, his former biology professor who was dean of the university. Bond was criticized for failing to raise faculty salaries, requiring a yearly letter of appointment, even for tenured faculty, and for refusing to pay for summer teaching assignments. White faculty were especially critical because of Bond's requirement that they treat as equals the growing number of African American faculty that he recruited. Unfortunately, his position was weakened further when he attempted to reduce the salaries of librarians, most of whom were faculty wives.

Beginning in 1949, Bond made more than ten trips to Africa and, in keeping with Lincoln's missionary focus from its beginning, he used the trips to promote opportunities for Africans to study in the United States. This focus on African students and the establishment of the African Studies Institute, coupled with his reluctance to aggressively recruit white students, contributed to the board of trustees' decision to terminate him as president. Bond left Lincoln for Atlanta University in 1957.

Bond survived for 15 years after Lincoln. He served on the faculty of Atlanta University for 14 of those years, first as dean of the school of education for a period of nine years, and later, beginning in the summer of 1966, as director of the Bureau of Educational and Social Research. In his latter role, he served as grantsman for the entire university. Bond died December 1972 of natural causes and was buried in Atlanta.

Bond is remembered as a scholar and academician whose work focused on the history of education of African Americans. His academic experiences were marked by great successes as a scholar during the early stages of his career. After embracing the role of college administrator, Bond was unable to satisfy the scholarly goals of research and publication that he set for himself. He continued to publish during 20 years as president of two colleges, but he never could produce sustained scholarship after becoming a college president.

REFERENCES

Bond, Julia Washington. Interview with Arthur C. Gunn, February 25, 1997.

Urban, Wayne J. *Black Scholar: Horace Mann Bond, 1904–1972.* Athens: University of Georgia Press, 1992.

COLLECTIONS

Bond's papers are held by the University of Massachusetts.

Arthur C. Gunn

Julian Bond

(1940–)

Civil rights activist, politician, organization president

A public servant and advocate for political freedom and justice, Julian Bond moved from being cofounder of the Student Nonviolent Coordinating Committee (SNCC) in 1960 to serving in the Georgia State Senate from 1975 to 1987. Organizer of the Georgia Legislative Black Caucus and sponsor of more than 60 bills that became laws, Bond also narrated the acclaimed *Eyes on the Prize* documentary of the civil rights movement. In these and other ways he represented the quintessential African American college student struggling for freedom and equality in the Jim Crow South.

Horace Julian Bond was born in Nashville, Tennessee, on January 14, 1940. His father was the well–known educator and scholar Horace Mann Bond, president of Fort Valley State College, a historically black institution in Georgia. Though the Bonds lived in rural southern Georgia, Julia Washington Bond—a librarian—traveled to Hubbard Hospital of Meharry Medical College in Nashville to give birth to Julian, her second child. Bond has an older sister, Jane, and a younger brother, James.

Julian Bond

Because Bond's father returned to Lincoln University in Pennsylvania, his alma mater, in 1943 to become its first black president, Julian spent his childhood in the North. Horace Bond used his own children as plaintiffs in a case that successfully integrated the county schools of Pennsylvania. Thus, Julian Bond was no stranger to the struggle for civil rights. Yet, as he stated in *Up From Within,* "I never really lived the life of a Southern Negro kid."

At the age of 12, Bond enrolled in the George School in Bucks County, Pennsylvania. He was the only black in the private Quaker school. Bond excelled in everything but academics. He needed five years instead of four to graduate. Although expected by his parents to become a scholar, Bond was the goalie on the soccer team, a star swimmer, and a member of the wrestling team. At the George School, Bond encountered several racist incidents, and single–handedly integrated the Newtown movie theater by refusing to sit in the balcony section reserved for blacks.

In 1957 Bond's father accepted a position as dean of Atlanta University's School of Education. The family moved to Atlanta, where Bond enrolled as a freshman at Morehouse College. His preparatory school background enabled him to achieve higher scores on standardized tests than all of his classmates. Bond, however, had the classic symptoms of an underachiever. While his classmates scored lower in aptitude, they were ambitious and hard working. By midyear Bond found himself no longer at the head of the class.

Bond did not dislike college; he suffered the malaise affecting many second– and third–generation children of college–educated, middle–class blacks. He told John Neary in *Julian Bond,* ''It wasn't a question of being interested in something else and not being interested in college; it just wasn't that big a thing. I thought it would be enough to get through, to pass, to get a degree . . . and make a 'career choice.''' An early ''career choice'' was writer, and poetry was the genre. In pursuit of that profession, he published several poems while still in college.

From Rebel to Radical

Clearly Bond rebelled against the black elite traditions--perhaps even without a cause. Given a cause, Bond's rebellion quickly became radical political protest. The catalyst for change came in the form of Lonnie King, a Morehouse student more politically active than Bond, who enlisted Bond's assistance in organizing a meeting to discuss the black student sit–in movement. By the end of the meeting, which took place in February of 1960, they had formed COAHR, Atlanta's Committee on Appeal for Human Rights. Their first agenda item was to stage a sit–in at eating establishments that refused to serve Atlanta blacks. On March 15, 1960, Bond led a group of students to the all–white cafeteria inside City Hall. This protest resulted in his first and only arrest.

On Easter weekend in April of 1960, Bond, Lonnie King, and other COAHR members attended a mass meeting in Raleigh, North Carolina, called by Martin Luther King Jr. and the Southern Christian Leadership Conference (SCLC). Student leaders and groups throughout the South met at Shaw University to formulate strategies for obtaining civil rights. From this initial meeting the Student Nonviolent Coordinating Committee (SNCC; pronounced *snick*) was born. James Forman was the director.

The SNCC Atlanta chapter was the best organized and the best financed. Bond recalled in the book *Julian Bond,* ''We had nearly $6,000 in the bank, and we had almost 4,000 people picketing in downtown Atlanta, a masterpiece of precision. Oh, man, we had waterproof picket signs and football parkas for the girls to wear to keep the spitballs off. Martin Luther King, Jr. got arrested with us one time--and the lunch counters were integrated.'' It took 18 months to integrate the lunch counter at Rich's, the largest department store in the South.

Atlanta's black newspaper, the *Daily World,* attacked Bond's Appeal for Human Rights group, calling it ill–advised. In response, students and some faculty advisors founded another black paper, the *Atlanta Inquirer*, to voice student concerns. Bond started as a reporter for the new press and ended up as managing editor. Soon COAHR became part of SNCC. Bond led the students of the Atlanta University Center in voter–registration campaigns, and during the summer of 1960 they signed almost 10,000 new black voters.

Bond's involvement in civil rights played havoc on his academic life. He was failing at Morehouse, and he was in love with a Spelman student he wanted to marry. Deciding to forego his degree, Bond married Alice Clopton on July 28, 1961. He began working full time for SNCC as its public relations spokesman and edited its newspaper, the *Student Voice.* He earned $40 a week. By 1964, Bond was the father of two children and he and Alice were expecting a third child. SNCC's mood was changing and Bond worried over what the change would ultimately mean for him and his growing family.

Members of SNCC disagreed about the power whites should have in the organization. As more whites entered and assumed authority, black members came to believe that the organization needed black leadership. Bond agreed. By 1964 many blacks were not only disgusted with the power struggles within SNCC but were disillusioned with the treatment of the Mississippi Freedom Democratic Party (MFDP) at the 1964 Democratic National Convention. Bond recalled that when the MFDP claimed that Mississippi's regular delegation did not represent all the Democratic votes of Mississippi, especially not the black members, party leadership worked to prevent the credentials committee from supporting the MFDP minority report. Bond stated in *Julian Bond,* ''it was a sell–out, and for a lot of people that was just the last straw.''

Enters the Political Ring

The Georgia legislature reapportioned the state in 1964, and Bond decided to run for one of the newly created Atlanta seats. Campaigning on the issues of unemployment, minimum wages, and fair housing, Bond walked away with 82 percent of the votes. Assuming his legislative seat was a different matter, however. In 1966, when SNCC condemned the United States' involvement in Vietnam, Bond made a public statement in agreement, praising those who were brave enough to protest by burning their draft cards.

The Georgia legislature accused Bond of treason and, according to *Contemporary Black Biography,* of ''giving aid and comfort to the enemies of the United States and the enemies of Georgia.'' Bond refused to rescind his statement, and the controversy grew. On January 10, 1966, the Georgia House of Representatives voted 184 to 12 against seating Bond on the grounds of disorderly conduct. The controversy catapulted Bond to national prominence. The press and news media defended his right to take his seat. Bond took the issue to the federal district court, where the legislature's decision was upheld.

Refusing to give up, the next step, therefore, was the U.S. Supreme Court. On December 5, 1966, the court ruled that the Georgia House had violated Bond's right to free speech under the First Amendment. The legislature, forced to seat Bond, treated him as an outcast.

In 1968 Bond was again in the national spotlight. Despite the desire of the Democratic party to have a delegation representative of Georgia at the Democratic National Convention, Governor Lester Maddox appointed only six black delegates of 107 total members. Bond, a member of the Georgia Democratic Party Forum, challenged the official group by co–chairing a rival delegation. Bond's people won nearly half of the delegates' votes. He became the Democratic Party's first black candidate for the U.S. vice presidency, but at 28–years old he failed to meet the minimum age requirement of 35.

During the 1970s, Bond's popularity began to wane. Nevertheless he was elected to the Georgia State Senate in 1975 after nearly ten years service in the House. He may have begun to lose interest in politics, however. When Jimmy Carter's administration went to Washington, he declined their invitation to join. By 1979 he could be described as a political outsider. Bond applied for the directorship of the National Association for the Advancement of Colored People (NAACP) but was considered too radical for the job. He served instead as president of Atlanta's NAACP local branch.

Things Fall Apart

The lack of ambition that plagued Bond in his school days returned to shadow him during the 1980s. He and his wife had a family of two daughters and three sons and his wife and children were unhappy taking a backseat to politics. Trouble also loomed on the political front. Bond almost lost his Senate seat and was charged with inaccessibility, excessive absenteeism, and lack of attention to local concerns. In 1986 he gave up his Senate seat to run for U.S. Congress against his longtime friend and SNCC associate, John Lewis, but he lost. In 1987 Alice Bond accused him of using cocaine, and although she publicly rescinded her charge, Bond's alleged girlfriend received a 22–year prison sentence on drug charges. His reputation suffered.

While his political and private life deteriorated, Bond continued to write and lecture around the country. He narrated *Eyes on the Prize,* a documentary on the civil rights movement. He hosted the television program *America's Black Forum.* He wrote "Viewpoint," a nationally syndicated newspaper column. Bond was also a visiting professor at Drexel University in 1968 and at Harvard University in 1989.

On March 17, 1990, Bond married Pamela S. Horowitz, an attorney. Bond became a distinguished scholar in residence at American University and has been a member of the department of history at the University of Virginia since 1990. He received his B.A. from Morehouse College in 1971. He has honorary degrees from Dalhousie, Oregon, Syracuse, Tuskegee, Howard, and Lincoln universities. His affiliations include honorary trustee of the Institute of Applied Politics, national board member of the NAACP, and member of the New Democratic Coalition, the Southern Regional Council, and the Delta Ministry Project of the National Council of Churches. Bond was president of the Atlanta NAACP from 1974 to 1989, and in 1989 was Pappas Fellow at the University of Pennsylvania. He authored *A Time to Speak, A Time to Act* (1972) and contributed poems to three anthologies.

Julian Bond is becoming a political force again. In February of 1998, he was elected chair of the NAACP board of directors, succeeding Myrlie Evers who chose not to seek a fourth term. He also chairs the NAACP's magazine, *Crisis.* Quoted in the *New York Times,* he said, "It is a daunting responsibility. . . . I want to make sure the NAACP voice is heard wherever race is discussed." Bond continues to speak out for human justice, a trait he has not lost since becoming an important figure in the history of the civil rights movement.

Current address: NAACP, 4805 Mt. Hope Drive, Baltimore, MD 21215.

REFERENCES

Contemporary Black Biography. Vol. 2. Detroit: Gale Research, 1992.

Metcalf, George R. *Up From Within: Today's New Black Leaders.* New York: McGraw–Hill, 1971.

"NAACP Elects Julian Bond Chairman." *New York Times,* February 21, 1998.

Neary, John. *Julian Bond: Black Rebel.* New York: Morrow, 1971.

Raines, Howell. *My Soul is Rested: The Story of the Civil Rights Movement in the Deep South.* New York: Penguin, 1977.

Nagueyalti Warren

Arna W. Bontemps
(1902–1973)
Librarian, writer, critic, teacher

A prolific writer who emerged during the Harlem Renaissance, Arna Wendell Bontemps wrote, edited, and compiled numerous works in a variety of genres for nearly 60 years. In his life's work he championed freedom for all people. A librarian fond of reading, he worked to preserve African American heritage by building at Fisk University one of the nation's most outstanding repositories.

While he was named Arnaud at birth, Bontemps wrote in *Black Voices,* his maternal grandmother decided to call him Arna instead. He viewed nicknames as expressions of endearment, remarking, "I was glad my grandmother, whose love mattered so much, had found one she liked for me." Of Creole extraction, Bontemps was born on October 13, 1902, in Alexandria, Louisiana. He had one younger sister, Ruby Sarah. His father, Paul Bismark Bontemps, was a strong–willed, austere, dark–skinned man with straight hair, who, like his father and grandfather, was a brick mason. Later he became a lay minister in the Seventh Day Adventist Church. He was also a musician. Prior to her marriage, Arna Bontemps's mother, Maria Carolina Pembroke Bontemps, was a public school teacher in Louisiana. When Bontemps was three and a half years old, in 1906, the family headed for San Francisco,

Arna W. Bontemps

but settled in Los Angeles. According to *Black Voices,* their move was prompted by the elder Bontemps's refusal to act submissive to a group of drunken, racist, white men on an Alexandria street who threatened to ''walk over the big nigger.'' In Los Angeles they moved into a big house in a white neighborhood. Bontemps's maternal grandmother and a host of other relatives followed. Maria Bontemps died when Bontemps was 12 years old, after which Bontemps lived with his grandparents for a time.

The mother had stimulated in her son a love for books and reading. Bontemps and his father had a much less congenial relationship. Paul Bontemps wanted his son to continue the family tradition of brick masonry, but Arna Bontemps wanted to be a writer. The father also resented his son's relationship with Uncle Buddy (Joe Ward), the younger, mulatto brother of Arna Bontemps's maternal grandmother, who influenced the young man's aspirations of writing. In addition, the uncle's alcoholism was distasteful to the father, as were his circle of friends from the lower class. Young Bontemps, however, was influenced by his Uncle Buddy's stories in dialect. Later, Bontemps drew from these oral narrations in his writings.

To help support himself after his mother died, Bontemps worked as a newsboy and a gardener in Hollywood. He entered San Fernando Academy, located in San Fernando Valley, a white Seventh–Day Adventist boarding school, in 1917. Bontemps wrote in *Black Voices* that his father cautioned him, ''Now don't go up there acting colored,'' and ''I believe I carried out his wish,'' he continued. Reflecting on this advice, he wrote in the same source, ''How dare anyone. . .tell me not to act *colored*? White people have been enjoying the privilege of acting like Negroes for more than a hundred years.''

Bontemps finished the school in only three years, graduating in 1920 at the age of 17. He studied both at the University of California at Los Angeles and at Pacific Union College near St. Helena (Angwin), California. In college Bontemps felt that he had been miseducated at the school. Developing skill as an imaginative writer, it was while he was in a freshman English class that Bontemps received the initial stimulus that led him to New York three years later. He wrote in *The Harlem Renaissance Remembered* that he saw his teacher smile approvingly at a paper he submitted as a part of an assignment: ''I was more embarrassed than flattered by the attention it drew, but the teacher's smile lingered, and I came to regard that expression as the semaphore that flagged me toward New York City three years later.'' In college he sang in the glee club, known as the jubilee singers, and helped support himself by working as a postal clerk.

Before he graduated in 1923 from Pacific Union with a bachelor of arts degree, Bontemps had considered a career in medicine or in music, but dismissed both. He hoped to study for a doctorate in English, but pressing matters such as the hardship of the depression years, the responsibilities of employment and family, and the demands of his promising writing career interfered.

Pursues a Career as a Writer

After graduation Bontemps completed a series of postgraduate courses at UCLA, worked nights in the post office, and spent his days reading literature with a ''frenzy,'' as he acknowledged. He read novels, poems, dramas, biographies, and whatever interested him at the neighborhood library. He also began to write and send poems to several magazines, but was unsuccessful in getting published. After he noticed that the *Crisis* encouraged young blacks to contribute work, he sent one of his rejected poems, ''Hope,'' to Jessie Fauset, literary agent for the magazine, who published the work in 1924. Once Bontemps received a copy of the August issue of *Crisis* that carried his poem, he resigned and headed for New York City. As Bontemps wrote in *Black Voices,* it was impossible and unthinkable to shed his past, his ''Negro–ness,'' and he carried his culture and experiences with him to New York.

In New York, Bontemps soon met Countee Cullen, who took him to a small gathering held for Langston Hughes on Edgecombe Avenue in Regina Anderson's and Ethel Ray Nance's apartment, one of the places where Harlem Renaissance artists were likely to gather. At this gathering Bontemps met Jessie Fauset, as well as Harlem Renaissance entrepreneur Charles S. Johnson, Alain Locke, Eric Walrond, and, the honored guest and Bontemps's look–alike at the time, Hughes. He made lasting friendships and associations with the Renaissance artists, including Hughes. His relationship with Hughes was cemented in December of 1931, when according to Arnold Rampersad in *The Life of Langston Hughes,* they had ''virtually a marriage of minds, that would last without the slightest friction'' and included personal visits as well as the exchange of some 2,500 letters that continued until Hughes's death in 1967. Charles H. Nichols published their correspondences in 1980 as *Arna Bontemps–Langston Hughes Letters, 1925–1967,* noting that Bontemps told his publisher in 1969: ''All told I am convinced we have the fullest documentation of the Afro American experience in the new world, artistic, intellectual, covering the mid–20th century, one is likely to find anywhere.''

After Charles S. Johnson promoted awards dinners for the *Opportunity* magazine literary contests, Bontemps said in *The Harlem Renaissance Remembered* that he decided to enter and his life ''has never been the same since.'' Not only did he receive recognition, but he came in contact with other influential leaders of the time, including Carl Van Vechten, patron of the New Negro Movement.

Becomes a Teacher

To broaden his knowledge and prepare himself for creative writing, Bontemps studied at Columbia University, New York University, and the City College of New York. To earn a living as his writing developed, Bontemps was a teacher and later principal at the Harlem Academy, a Seventh Day Adventist high school, from 1924 until 1931. While the school's officials tolerated Bontemps's association with the Renaissance artists, when he used ''God'' in the title of his novel, *God Sends Sunday*—his first book, published in 1931, they considered it blasphemous and, according to some sources, sent him to Oakwood Junior College in Huntsville, Alabama, as a result. Kirkland Jones, however, explained in *Renaissance Man from Louisiana,* that the academy closed, leaving Bontemps unemployed. He was hired at the Oakwood school as an English teacher and librarian. Bontemps's biographical statement in the Bontemps Collection at Fisk University indicates that the Depression, the scattering elsewhere of the Harlem Renaissance artists, and Bontemps's urge ''to undertake more serious and sustained writing tasks'' compelled him to leave New York. It was in the Alabama setting, where Bontemps, his wife, and children lived in a decaying plantation mansion for a time, that he and Hughes strengthened their relationship. Bontemps also wrote for children, considering the young audience more penetrable.

Bontemps was not a disbeliever, nor a religious zealot. However, Oakwood officials considered him a Harlem radical. According to Kirkland Jones, school officials were concerned with his association with ''outside agitators;'' thus, when Langston Hughes visited him sometime in late 1932 or 1933, Bontemps nearly lost his job. He also created local suspicion by receiving many books in the mail and spending much time typing. When officials began to call writing and teaching novels sinful, the president ordered Bontemps to burn his secular books. At the end of the school year in May of 1934, Bontemps resigned. He, his wife, and three young children drove to California, then sold their car and spent a year with his father and stepmother at 10310 Wiegand Avenue in the Watts section of Los Angeles. There, conducted research in the local library, studying dialect and analyzing children's books. He also participated as a speaker at the library story hour. He invited his friend Langston Hughes, enroute from Mexico, to lecture in the library as well. Bontemps spent that summer writing his most renowned novel, *Black Thunder.* He said in the book's introduction that he ''wrote the book in longhand on the top of a folded–down sewing machine'' because his parents' extra bedroom lacked space for a typewriter. After receiving a publisher's advance for the book, the family left for Chicago.

From 1935 to 1938 Bontemps taught in Chicago at another Seventh Day Adventist school, Shiloh Academy. From 1938 to 1942 he worked as a technical assistant—in charge of black students—to the state director of the Illinois Writer's Project of the Works Progress Administration. Richard Wright, also a Seventh–Day Adventist, was hired on the project as well. The two writers developed a mutual admiration and respect for each other. In 1936 Bontemps enrolled as a graduate student in English at the University of Chicago, where he completed residency requirements for a master's degree but did not complete the degree. Instead, he studied on a Rosenwald Fellowship for creative writing and traveled to the Caribbean. Thomas Elsa Jones, president of Fisk University, invited Bontemps to become a professor of creative writing and a head librarian. Bontemps accepted, but wanted formal training in library science before he undertook duties as librarian. In 1940 Bontemps was cultural director of the American Negro Exposition held in Chicago and was primarily responsible for *The Calvacade of the American Negro* that the Work Progress Administration project issued for the celebration. In 1942 Bontemps received a second fellowship to study for his master's degree at the Graduate Library School, University of Chicago.

In September of 1943 Bontemps became head librarian and full professor at Fisk University, and six months later, in December, he received his M.A. degree in library science from Chicago. At Fisk he joined some Harlem Renaissance friends, artist Aaron Douglas and sociologist Charles S. Johnson. Bontemps became noted for building the special collections division of the library into a leading repository for research on African American themes. He gathered the papers of such black writers as Jean Toomer, Charles Waddell Chesnutt, and Langston Hughes and strengthened the book collection by adding retrospective as well as contemporary works by and about African Americans. Clearly, his main area of interest was special collections. He remained at Fisk full–time until in 1964, after which he served as acting librarian, as well as director of university relations until 1965. It was at this time that he wisely advised the library staff to enter the emerging reprint program so that black books, then becoming scarce, would be more easily available.

From 1966 to 1969 Bontemps was a professor of English at the University of Illinois, Chicago Circle. He revealed in an interview for Fisk's Black Oral History Program, ''They wanted me to introduce something in literature which is one of the things that I was promoting all of the time: that the black experience is seen better through the literature than through the history. And I think that has caught on.'' Regarding all of the literature predominating in black studies programs,

Bontemps believed that he "was the one who initiated that emphasis." In 1969, he moved to Yale University as curator of the James Weldon Johnson Memorial Collection in the Beinecke Library. Returning to Nashville in 1970, Bontemps was writer–in–residence at Fisk until 1973.

Creates Literature for Children

Bontemps wrote in a variety of genres, publishing single works as well as scholarly anthologies. In his writings he frequently drew upon his inherited Creole dialect and often used it in his letters to Langston Hughes. His fiction included his first book, *God Sends Sunday,* published in 1931, followed by *Black Thunder* (1936), *Drums at Dusk* (1939), and *The Old South: "A Summer Tragedy" and Other Stories of the Thirties* (1973). Best known for his biographies, anthologies, and novels for young people, the works that he wrote, compiled, or edited include *Sad–Faced Boy* (1937); *Golden Slippers: An Anthology of Negro Poetry for Young People* (1941); *Story of the Negro* (1948), *Chariot in the Sky; A Story of the Jubilee Singers* (1951); *Lonesome Boy* (1955); *Frederick Douglass: Slave, Fighter, Freeman* (1958), and *Young Booker: The Story of Booker T. Washington's Early Days* (1972).

Bontemps cowrote a number of other works. In 1934 he and Countee Cullen adapted the novel *God Sends Sunday* for the stage, and again they used the novel as a base for *St. Louis Woman,* a stage play that opened on Broadway in 1946. Metro–Goldwyn–Mayer bought movie rights to the play in 1952. Bontemps and Jack Conroy wrote a history of African Americans, originally titled *They Seek a City* (1945), but revised and re–published in 1966 as *Anyplace But Here.* The two men also created *Slappy Hooper, the Wonderful Sign Painter* (1946).

Bontemps described to the *Nashville Tennessean* for February 18, 1951, "My friend, Langston Hughes, indirectly started me writing. He had just returned from the West Indies and brought back loads of snapshots and toys (for my kids) from Haiti. I got interested and he and I collaborated on a book, *Popo and Fifina* published in 1932." The well–known illustrator E. Simms Campbell illustrated the book. Bontemps and Hughes also collaborated on *I Too Sing America* (1964); *The Poetry of the Negro, 1746–1949,* revised and published in 1970 as *The Poetry of the Negro, 1746–1970* and on *The Book of Negro Folklore* (1958). His other books include *We Have Tomorrow* (1945), *One Hundred Years of Negro Freedom* (1961), *Personals,* (a collection of his own poetry, 1963), and an anthology, *Hold Fast to Dreams: Poems Old and New* (1969). Among the books that Bontemps edited are *Father of the Blues: An Autobiography of W. C. Handy* (1941) and *The Harlem Renaissance Remembered: Essays with a Memoir* (1972). He also published articles in a number of journals, including *Crisis, Opportunity, New Challenge, Negro Digest, Saturday Review, American Scholar,* and *Freedomways.*

Highly honored for his work, among the awards and honors Bontemps received are, in addition to the *Crisis* award for poetry in 1926, the Alexander Pushkin poetry prizes in 1926 and 1927; *Opportunity* magazine's short story prize in 1932; a Guggenheim Fellowship for creative writing, 1949 and 1954; Jane Addams Children's Book Award for *Story of the Negro,* 1956; and with Jack Conroy the James L. Dow Award, Society of Midland Authors, for *Anyplace but Here,* 1967. He was named honorary consultant in American Cultural History at the Library of Congress in 1972 and was bestowed honorary degrees from Morgan State University in 1969 and Berea College in 1973.

Bontemps was a member of the National Association for the Advancement of Colored People (NAACP), PEN, the American Library Association, and the Dramatists Guild. He served on the Metropolitan Nashville Board of Education, and was a member of Sigma Pi Phi (the Boulé) and Omega Psi Phi fraternities.

Writing was always uppermost in Bontemps's mind, and he took pains to record his thoughts and ideas so that they might be used in his works. Quoted in the *Alexandria Louisiana Daily Town Talk,* Paul Bontemps said of his father, who always kept a note pad with him, "I thought this was the normal way that people lived, with a note pad beside the bed. In the morning there'd be scribbles all over it." Bontemps's writing began at five o'clock in the morning on a card table in the living room. "He would do two or three hours of writing before anybody else had to get up," he continued, and the mother instructed the children not to disturb their father. Bontemps told the *Nashville Tennessean* for February 18, 1951, that "I've done some of my best books at home with the children playing. . .all around me. I just pull up the card table, close the door (if that's possible) and go to work." A meticulous writer, he composed on the typewriter and rarely needed to do more than one or two drafts. He had planned to write his autobiography during his later years.

In his leisure time, Bontemps read, played bridge, and, when he could, he walked. He was also an enthusiastic sports fan. He was a lover of art and collected works by his friend, Harlem Renaissance painter Aaron Douglas, who refused to accept payment from Bontemps. Handsome, stocky, and, in his later years silver–haired, Bontemps was a kind, even–tempered man who admitted in the Black Oral History interview at Fisk that "I think I can see things as a whole a little better than some of the people I've worked with." His son, Paul, told the *Alexandria Louisiana Daily Town Talk* that Bontemps was neither a racist nor a chauvinist and "he had an amazing capacity to see the good in almost everybody and every group." He also pointed out that his father was as concerned about his French heritage as his African American.

In Bontemps's honor, the Arna Bontemps African–American Museum and Cultural Center was opened in his birthplace and childhood home in Alexandria, Louisiana, dedicated on November 12, 1992. The home, known as the Arna Wendell Bontemps House, was listed on the National Register of Historic Places on September 13, 1993. Mayor Philip Bredesen of Nashville declared October 7, 1994, as Arna Bontemps Day in Nashville, in recognition of his gifts "especially to African–American children's literature—paving the way for others to follow his courageous paths to success."

While working as his interim secretary in 1953, Jessie Carney Smith observed the reluctance of white publishers to accept his work. By the mid–1990s, however, white publishers were searching for unpublished manuscripts at Fisk.

Stricken while attending a celebration of life for a friend, Bontemps died of a heart attack on December 4, 1973, in Nashville and was buried in Greenwood Cemetery. His closest survivors were Alberta Johnson Bontemps, who had been his student at Harlem Academy and later his wife and six children: Joan Marie Bontemps Williams, Paul Bismark, Poppy Alberta Bontemps Booker, Camille Ruby Bontemps Graves, Constance Rebecca Bontemps Thomas, and Arna Alexander Bontemps. He had been deeply devoted to his family.

Bontemps was a strong voice of the Harlem Renaissance and was known for his work as poet, writer, essayist, biographer, anthologist, librarian, and an advocate for libraries. An avid reader himself, he stimulated children and adults to read as well through the works that he wrote, the numerous lectures that he gave, and the African American collection that he established at Fisk University. The *Norton Anthology of African American Literature* called Bontemps's writing ''characteristically graceful, serene, and. . .intellectually challenging and independent.'' He had a deep sense of racial pride, intellectual and emotional integrity, and sincere religious and spiritual convictions and was able to balance these characteristics and reflect them in his writings with a ''confidence matched by few other writers.''

REFERENCES

Biography File, Fisk University Library.

Bontemps, Arna W. Black Oral History interview by Ann Allen Shockley, July 14, 1972. Transcript. Fisk University Library.

———. *Black Thunder.* Boston: Beacon Press, 1938.

———. *The Harlem Renaissance Remembered.* New York: Dodd, Mead, 1972.

———. ''Why I Returned.'' Reprinted from ''The South Today. . .100 Years After Appomattox,'' Special Supplement to *Harper's,* April 1965. In *Black Voices.* Edited by Abraham Chapman. New York: New American Library, 1968.

''Bontemps' Son Recalls Life with Noted Father.'' *Alexandria Louisiana Daily Town Talk,* March 6, 1994.

Current Biography 1946. New York: H. W. Wilson Co., 1946.

Dictionary of American Library Biography. Littleton, CO: Libraries Unlimited, 1978.

Gates, Henry Louis, and Nellie Y. McKay, eds. *The Norton Anthology of African American Literature.* New York: Norton, 1997.

''A Harlem Remembrance.'' *Nashville Banner,* July 18, 1989.

Harris, Trudier, ed. *Afro-American Writers from the Harlem Renaissance to 1940.* Detroit: Gale Research, 1987.

Jones, Kirkland C. *Renaissance Man from Louisiana: A Biography of Arna Wendell Bontemps.* Westport, CT: Greenwood Press, 1992.

Nichols, Charles H., ed. *Arna Bontemps–Langston Hughes Letters, 1925–1967.* New York: Dodd, Mead, 1980.

Morrison, Ione Rider. ''Arna Bontemps.'' *The Horn Book* 15 (January 1939): 13–19.

Rampersad, Arnold. *The Life of Langston Hughes.* Volume I: 1902–1941. *I, Too, Sing America.* New York: Oxford University Press, 1986.

''Under the Green Lamp.'' *Nashville Tennessean,* February 18, 1951.

COLLECTIONS

The personal papers of Arna Bontemps are in the George Arents Research Library, Syracuse University. The James Weldon Johnson Collection in Yale University's Beinecke Library contains the Bontemps–Hughes letters. The papers of Bontemps's tenure as university librarian at Fisk University, oral history interviews, and other items are in Special Collections, Fisk University Library.

Jessie Carney Smith

Edward A. Bouchet

(1852–1918)

Educator, religious worker, community activist

Edward A. Bouchet was the first African American to attend and graduate from Yale University and the first black student to earn a Ph.D. from an American university. During the last quarter of the nineteenth century and the first two decades of the twentieth century, he taught several generations of students the fundamentals of mathematics and science and inspired them to both higher levels of knowledge and to become productive members in their communities. Many of his students became active in business and various professions; several of them achieved the rank of professor at major universities.

Edward Bouchet was born on September 15, 1852, at 42 Bradley Street in New Haven, Connecticut, to William and Susan Bouchet. His mother, a native of Connecticut, was the daughter of Asher and Jane Drake Cooley. She was born in Westport on October 1, 1817. Her death occurred in New Haven on February 11, 1920. William Francis Bouchet's birth date and place are uncertain. In some accounts his date is given as c. 1817 in New Haven; he died there in 1885. William and Susan had four surviving children of whom Edward was the youngest and only son.

For his primary education, Bouchet attended the Artisan Street Colored School. Founded in 1811, this was the oldest of four primary schools for black children in New Haven. Bouchet next attended Hopkins Grammar School for two years. How he got to Hopkins and who paid for his education

Edward A. Bouchet

there is not known. It is clear, however, that his parents could not afford the fees. He graduated first in his class and gave the valedictory address at graduation.

Entering Yale College in 1870, Bouchet became one of the outstanding students of his class. His grade average during freshman year was 3.36, with the highest grade of 3.52 in mathematics. During his undergraduate career he took courses in the sciences (astronomy, mathematics, mechanics, and physics) and also studied English, French, German, Greek, Latin, logic, and rhetoric. He also received a junior high oration and a senior philosophical oration appointment. At graduation in 1874, he ranked sixth in a class of 125. After graduation, in 1884, based on his work at Yale, he was elected to Phi Beta Kappa, the second African American to achieve this honor. (In 1877, George Washington Henderson had become the first black elected.)

In his senior year, Bouchet was approached by Alfred Cope about remaining at Yale and obtaining the doctorate in physics. Cope was on the Board of Managers of the Institute for Colored Youth (ICY), a Quaker school for black children located in Philadelphia. Cope's personal interest in science and his desire to have the students at ICY receive training in this area led him to develop a scientific department, which he hoped Bouchet would direct after finishing advanced studies at Yale.

Bouchet agreed to stay at Yale for two years of graduate study provided that he be guaranteed an initial salary of $1,500 a year at ICY. Cope agreed to this request and provided the funds necessary for Bouchet's graduate education.

In the fall of 1874, Bouchet returned to Yale as a candidate for the doctor of philosophy degree in science. At commencement in 1876, he received the Ph.D. in physics in the area of geometrical optics. The title of his dissertation was "Measuring Refractive Indices."

Makes His Mark in Philadelphia

Bouchet spent 26 years in Philadelphia teaching at the Institute for Colored Youth. In addition to his academic duties, Bouchet was actively involved in the general welfare of the black people of the city. He extensively lectured before various church, trade, and community groups. When the ICY began to give preference to industrial education over pure academics, his salary was cut. Nevertheless, he remained at the school. According to the 1919 *Biographical Record of the Class of 1874 in Yale College,* many of his pupils called him "teacher with esteem and gratitude and bear affectionate witness to his high character and blameless life."

Bouchet joined St. Thomas Church, one of the oldest black Episcopal churches in the country and a church whose congregation was composed of highly educated and wealthy blacks. He served on the vestry and was secretary of this body for many years. The bishop appointed him a lay reader, which allowed him to take part directly in the services of the church.

Bouchet also became involved in the Philadelphia Yale Alumni Association and faithfully attended its meetings and annual dinners. The *Biographical Record* for 1919 said that "he won and retained the regard and kindly interest of its other members and was always received by them with cordiality and respect."

Bouchet was a member of one of the country's oldest scientific societies, the Franklin Institute, a foundation chartered in 1824 in Philadelphia whose stated purpose was the promotion of the mechanical arts. Bouchet regularly attended its meetings, lectures, and dinners. He was also a member of the American Academy of Political and Social Science. He was on the board of directors of the Century Building and Loan Association in Philadelphia, which was organized in 1886.

In 1902 the managers, who claimed that they were "suspending" the academic department, fired Bouchet, along with all the other teachers at the ICY. This event had its genesis in the changes occurring in American society. The view was generally expressed that African Americans were not capable of responding to the various efforts being done on their behalf. In addition, the academic program at the ICY was too advanced for the practical needs of the students. The managers of the ICY began to accept this view and became very receptive to the general philosophy of Booker T. Washington, who favored industrial training in contrast to classical and academic education.

The ICY was disbanded in 1902 and moved to a rural location approximately 20 miles from Philadelphia. The new curriculum, at what became the Cheyney Training School of Teachers, was based largely on the industrial arts programs of Hampton and Tuskegee Institutes. Bouchet was not in sympathy with these changes.

The Wandering Years

In the summer of 1902, Bouchet returned to New Haven to contemplate his future and to find employment. Possibly through the efforts of Fanny Jackson Coppin, former principal of the ICY, Bouchet secured a position at Sumner High School in St. Louis, Missouri, as a teacher of mathematics and physics. He remained there until November of 1903 at which time he assumed the position of business manager at the Provident Hospital in St. Louis. Next, through the help of one of his Yale classmates, Charles F. Joy, Bouchet secured a position as U.S. Inspector of Customs at the Louisiana Purchase Exposition held in St. Louis. He remained there from June of 1904 to March of 1905.

Bouchet returned to New Haven for six months and in October of 1905 began service as the director of the Academic Department at St. Paul's Normal and Industrial School in Lawrenceville, Virginia. He also taught courses in chemistry, civics, Latin, and physics. After accidentally bumping into one of the town's prominent lawyers and then being assaulted, Bouchet left St. Paul's in June of 1908.

Following a two–month stay in New Haven, he accepted, in August of 1908, the position of principal at Lincoln High School in Gallipolis, Ohio. From 1913 to 1916, Bouchet appears to have taught at Bishop College in Marshall, Texas, and retired due to health reasons.

Returning to New Haven, Bouchet remained in the care of his mother and sisters. After nearly two years he died on October 28, 1918. The burial service was held at St. Luke's Protestant Episcopal Church of New Haven, and the interment was in the family plot in Evergreen Cemetery.

In his essay ''Edward Alexander Bouchet: America's First Black Doctoral Scientist,'' H. Kenneth Bechtel noted that although Bouchet ''was not a social activist in the mode of W. E. B. Du Bois; not known to be a creative researcher like Charles Drew or Percy Julian; nor a published scholar like Ernest Just or Charles Turner,'' he deserves a prominent place in the history of black education. Bouchet was an important, pioneering black educator in the field of science and an inspiration to his students.

REFERENCES

Allen, Lillian Mitchell. Letter to Ronald E. Mickens, February 1, 1977.

Bechtel, H. Kenneth. ''Edward Alexander Bouchet: America's First Black Doctoral Scientist.'' Unpublished. Wake Forest University, Winston–Salem, NC, 1987.

Biographical Record of the Class of 1874 in Yale College. Part 4, 1874–1909. New Haven, CT: Yale University, 1912.

Biographical Record of the Class of 1874 in Yale College. Part 5, 1909–1919. New Haven, CT: Yale University, 1919.

Dickerman, George L. *Yale College Class of 1874.* New Haven, CT: Tuttle, Morehouse and Taylor, 1879.

Lane, Roger. *William Dorsey's Philadelphia and Ours.* New York: Oxford University Press, 1991.

Logan, Rayford W., and Michael R. Winston, eds. *Dictionary of American Negro Biography.* New York: Norton, 1982.

Nelson, Richard. *Phi Beta Kappa in American Life: The First Two Hundred Years.* New York: Oxford University Press, 1990.

Obituary Record of Graduates Deceased during the Year Ending July 1, 1919. New Haven, CT: Yale University, 1920.

Perkins, Linda Marie. *Fanny Jackson Coppin and the Institute for Colored Youth, 1865–1902.* New York: Garland, 1987.

Ronald E. Mickens

Richard Henry Boyd
(1843–1922)
Religious leader, businessman

Born a slave in Mississippi, Richard Henry Boyd rose to a position of eminence in the Baptist Church. He built the National Baptist Publishing Board into a major concern, thus creating the largest black–controlled business of its era. The struggle over control of this enterprise led to a split in the National Baptist Convention, the effects of which persist today. A prominent believer in black self–help, Boyd created several businesses, including a bank that still exists. On the community level, he founded a long–lived newspaper and was a conspicuous supporter of education for African Americans.

Richard Henry Boyd was born on March 15, 1843, in Noxubee County, Mississippi. He was named Dick after his maternal grandfather. Little is known of his father except that he was a slave in Mississippi and that his son adopted the name Richard Henry Boyd around 1869 after he discovered his father's identity. His mother, Indiana (c. 1820–1915) was born to Dick and Mollie in Petersburg, Virginia, and taken to Mississippi by slavetraders when she was seven and there sold to Martha Gray.

Dick was Indiana's oldest child; two more daughters were born in Mississippi and one in Louisiana. In 1860 Indiana found religion and became a Baptist. By this time she was living in Texas, apparently in Grimes County. There in 1861 she married Sam Niblett, who later changed his name to Dickson (also Dixon). Dickson was a deacon at Midway Baptist Church in Prairie Plains, Texas. He and Indiana had six sons. Dickson died nine years after the birth of his last son. Indiana Dickson was seventy–five years old when Boyd took her into his household in Nashville where she resided until her death in 1915.

Boyd's family was separated after the death of Martha Gray in 1858. In the settlement of the estate, Benonia W. Gray

Richard Henry Boyd

purchased Boyd for $1,200. He and his mother, along with her daughters, were then taken to different counties in Texas: he went to Washington County, she and her daughters to Grimes County. At the outbreak of the Civil War, Benonia Gray's husband and their three sons enlisted in a Confederate regiment and Boyd accompanied the men as a body servant. (In 1912 Boyd supported a bill passed by the Tennessee General Assembly giving pensions to former Confederate body servants.) After serving in Virginia, the Grays traveled to Tennessee where three of the Grays were killed and the surviving son was gravely wounded at Chattanooga. Boyd nursed the son back to health and then accompanied him home to Texas sometime in 1864. Boyd worked for the Gray family after Emancipation until 1866 when the Grays decided against reestablishing their farm.

Boyd then worked at a variety of jobs. He also learned to read and write. A first marriage, to Laura Thomas in 1868, ended when she died eleven months later. Boyd was baptized at the Hopewell Baptist Church in Navasota on December 19, 1869, and changed his name from Gray to Boyd. Shortly thereafter, he decided to become a minister. In 1871 Boyd married Harriett Albertine Moore. This marriage produced six children, all of whom lived to adulthood: Henry Allen, J. Garfield Blaine, Theophilus Bartholomew, Lula, Mattie, and Annie. All the children except Annie, who married a Galveston undertaker, later moved to Nashville with their parents. Around 1875 or 1876 Boyd attended Bishop College in Marshall, Texas, where he remained for two years; but he could not complete his studies because of the financial pressures of a growing family.

In the meantime, Boyd had achieved a position of prominence and influence among Texas Baptists. He organized several churches in east Texas and, with the assistance of a white minister, worked to establish the Texas Negro Baptist Association. Between 1870 and 1874, Boyd served as a district missionary and organized a regional organization, the Lincoln District Baptist Association, in 1875. He also served as educational secretary of the Texas Negro Baptist Convention. In 1879, Boyd was moderator of the Central Baptist Association and, in 1891, he became pastor of Mount Zion Baptist Church in San Antonio.

In the 1890s a principal source of dissension among Southern black Baptists was their relationship to the northern, white American Baptist Home Mission Society, a major source of funding for schools and missionary activities in the South. Many blacks perceived the organization as paternalistic and especially wanted to assert black control over black colleges and schools. A drop in contributions to the Home Mission Society that resulted in the closing and combining of some schools exacerbated this tension. Boyd further resented the American Baptist Publication Society, which supplied material for both northern and southern Baptist churches. He believed that blacks should oversee the publication of their own printed material.

A state convention at the Mount Zion Baptist Church in 1892 brought to a head the tensions between those preachers loyal to the northern organizations and those who desired a change. In 1893 the Texas Negro Baptist Association split over this question, and Boyd and David Abner Jr. led the largest faction into a new organization, the General Missionary Baptist Convention of Texas. Boyd left Mount Zion to become superintendent of missions for the new association.

By 1895 the white Southern Baptist Convention had established its own publishing organ, the Sunday School Board, in Nashville, Tennessee. The new publishing organization did not want to directly confront the American Baptist Publication Society because the Southern Baptist Convention had recently established an alliance with the American Baptist Home Mission Society in its work among blacks. Still, Boyd contacted the Southern Baptist Convention's Sunday School Board and tried to substitute its publications for those from the north in Texas black Baptist Sunday Schools

Creates the National Baptist Publishing Board

In 1895, a meeting of various black associations in Atlanta resulted in the creation of the National Baptist Convention; the time seemed ripe for Boyd to create a black publishing company. Boyd had the cautious backing of E(lias) C(amp) Morris (1865–1922), the recently elected president of the Convention. Boyd gained the national stature necessary to support his plan when he was elected corresponding secretary of the Home Mission Board, a board of the National Baptist Convention, at the 1896 meeting, which also approved of the National Baptist Convention publishing its own Sunday School literature.

With a target date of January 1, 1897, to publish the first Sunday School lesson quarterly, Boyd had to move quickly. He had already decided to establish operations in Nashville, Tennessee, a major publishing center, where both the AME Church and the Southern Baptist Convention had publishing concerns. J. M. Frost (1848–1916) of the Southern Baptist Convention's Sunday School Board aided Boyd in making contacts with white printers in Nashville, while Boyd himself supplied the capital with $6,000 in letters of credit in his wife's name. Setting up a two–room office in the Brown Building at 408 Cedar Street, Boyd met his deadline, although the material issued was supplied by the Sunday School Board.

Success was rapid, but problems followed. Even though Boyd invested much of his own money into the National Baptist Publishing Board, many suspected the operation of being a self–serving venture. These suspicions grew as the Publishing Board branched out into subsidiary operations, including an Boyd–owned company that sold church organs and church furniture and was difficult to distinguish from the Publishing Board. In 1898 Boyd took a crucial step in securing the independence and continuity of the National Baptist Publishing Board by incorporating it under Tennessee law and giving it a self–perpetuating board of directors.

Hostility against Boyd from the American Baptist Home Missionary Board and the American Baptist Publishing Board and their supporters in the National Baptist Convention was a constant. Boyd did little to alleviate this criticism by cooperating with the Southern Baptist Convention, whose conventions he often attended as a guest. There was also a lack of convergence in the views of Boyd and his opponents in the National Baptist Convention: they viewed the Publishing Board as a denominational operation while Boyd envisioned its aim as reaching out to all black Baptists, regardless of affiliation. Bobby L. Lovett has further suggested that part of Boyd's problem with his black critics was due to the residual effects of slavery which, in Lovett's view, led to a black fear of success and fueled jealousy of successful blacks.

Boyd rapidly expanded the operations of the National Baptist Publishing Board. An economic depression enabled him to acquire printing equipment cheaply and to set up a printing plant. Although the operation brought in little real net gain, the board became highly active in book publishing; in 1902 its list of books included fifty–eight titles. A hymnal was issued in 1902, followed by many other books of music. Boyd also contracted with outside printers for cheap bibles to be issued under the board's imprint. Later, controversy was again fueled by the discovery that Boyd had registered all of the copyrights in his own name.

In addition, Boyd bolstered his position in the National Baptist Convention through his service as corresponding secretary of both the Home Mission Board and the Publishing Board. (The Publishing Board supplied funding for the Mission Board.) Boyd also received $15,000 a year from the Southern Baptist Convention for missionary activities sponsored by the National Baptist Convention's Home Mission Board. He likewise garnered support from many women's groups through his support of their concerns. Already in 1897 his first editorial board included four women among the fourteen members. Boyd was also a supporter and advisor to the Women's Convention, an influential organization of Baptist women founded in 1900. In particular, he was a close friend of the Women's Convention president, Virginia Walker Broughton. Despite tense relations with white, northern Baptists, Boyd remained on good terms with the northern Women's American Baptist Home Mission Society.

Boyd began organizing Sunday School Congresses in 1906. These meetings became immensely popular. In addition, he encouraged missionary work (through the Home Mission Board) in areas he felt had been neglected by the Foreign Mission Board, which concentrated its efforts on West Africa.

Opposition to the autonomy of the Publishing Board and to Boyd's power continued to grow. The appointment of Richard Henry Boyd's oldest son and eventual successor, Henry Allen Boyd, as assistant secretary to the National Baptist Publishing Board and secretary of the Sunday School Congresses did nothing to quiet opponents. In 1904, Baptists opposed to Boyd tried unsuccessfully to separate the management of the Home Mission Board and the Publishing Board. In 1905, they made a second attempt and also raised questions about the relationship between the Publishing Board and the National Baptist Convention. These actions began a decade long power struggle that resulted in splitting the National Baptist Convention into two factions, the National Baptist Convention of the USA, Inc., and the National Baptist Convention of America.

Problems began to escalate during the 1912 National Baptist Convention meeting in Houston, Texas. At the meeting, a commission on incorporation was formed and directed to report in 1913. It did not recommend incorporation at that meeting, held in Nashville. In 1914 in Philadelphia, the commission did recommend incorporation and changing the National Baptist Convention's charter so that the central organization could exercise control over the various boards. By a vote of 361 to 209 the convention decided to incorporate and then suspended the rules to pass a resolution to make the commission the executive board of the National Baptist Publishing Board. The sessions were described as stormy and heated.

The National Baptist Convention Splits

Boyd resigned from the Home Mission Board after the Philadelphia convention, but the executive board of the National Baptist Publishing Board did not accept his resignation. The National Baptist Publishing Board also refused to yield control of its operation to the Commission. The first meetings of National Baptist Convention in Chicago on September 8, 1915 were extremely stormy. On the first day, the president, E. C. Morris, the other officers of the Convention, and the anti–Boyd delegates adjourned the meeting in the course of a tumultuous session and left. Boyd's supporters remained behind and elected Edward Perry Jones as their president. The next day, the doors were closed to those without convention badges, thus denying admission to thousands of Boyd supporters.

The National Baptist Church was split. The successor organizations became known as the National Baptist Convention of the United States, Incorporated, (NBCUSA) and the National Baptist Convention of America, Unincorporated (NBCA). Several years later, Tennessee courts upheld the autonomy of the National Baptist Publishing Board.

After some initial problems, the National Baptist Publishing Board survived and continued to flourish. The NBCUSA formed the rival Sunday School Publishing Board in Nashville, which succeeded after an initially shaky start. Some other concerns dear to Boyd were negatively affected. Boyd had campaigned vigorously for the reopening of Nashville's Baptist Roger Williams University (1864–1907, 1909–1929), closed after a fire had destroyed its buildings in 1907, but the NBCA lost all influence there after 1915 since Roger Williams was an American Baptist Home Mission school. The NBCUSA was successful in establishing its American Baptist Seminary in Nashville in cooperation with the Southern Baptist Convention; a similar effort by the NBCA did not succeed. Moreover, support from the Southern Baptist Convention for the Home Mission Board's missionary work went to the new NBCUSA board.

In addition to leadership in the field of religious publishing, Boyd made contributions in business and journalism. He founded a Nashville chapter of Booker T. Washington's National Business League in 1902. In 1903 he was a founder of the One–Cent Savings Bank (known as the Citizens Saving and Trust Company Bank after 1920). Boyd became president of the bank and his prudent management led to its success. Some of his other companies included the National Baptist Church Supply Company, (founded in 1902), and the unsuccessful National Negro Doll Company (founded in 1908). Both were difficult for the outsider to distinguish from the National Publishing Board since they were headquartered at the same address.

In 1905 Nashville segregated seating on streetcars. Blacks protested and organized a company to supply transportation using steam–powered vehicles. (This company later failed). Boyd founded a newspaper called *The Nashville Globe* to furnish blacks with information about the boycott. Housed at and printed by the National Baptist Publishing Board, the paper first appeared on January 14, 1906, and lasted until 1960. It was Nashville's most successful black newspaper during this period.

The scope and vigor of Richard Henry Boyd's leadership is remarkable, especially when it is remembered that he was over fifty when he first came to Nashville. In 1920 he was considerably weakened by illness. In 1922 Boyd was shocked by the death of his son, J. Blaine, on April 6. He himself died at his home on August 22, 1922. The funeral was postponed. The National Baptist Convention of America, Unincorporated was scheduled to meet in December; instead it met in Nashville in September, and the funeral was held then. His body was then interred in Nashville's Greenwood Cemetery.

Boyd was a remarkable religious leader who founded the National Baptist Publishing Board, an enterprise now headed by his great–grandson. (In 1988 a dispute over the relationship between the National Baptist Publishing Board and the NBCA led Publishing Board supporters to break away and form the National Missionary Baptist Convention of America.) Boyd's position of fostering black pride and black business in an era of increasing segregation was congruent with that of Booker T. Washington. His involvement in politics was peripheral, but he was a notable community leader, called upon for leadership in tasks ranging from establishing a colored YMCA to selling war bonds during World War I. His contributions to the Baptist Church are reflected actions had consequences reflected still today among the millions of black American Baptists.

REFERENCES

"The Baptist Convention." *The Crisis* 11 (April 1916): 314–16.

Dictionary of American Biography. New York: Charles Scribner's Sons, 1943.

Freeman, Edward A. *The Epoch of Negro Baptists and the Foreign Mission Board National Baptist Convention, U.S.A., Inc.* Kansas City, KS: Central Seminary Press, 1953.

Lamon, Lester C. *Black Tennesseans, 1900–1930.* Knoxville: University of Tennessee Press, 1977.

Logan, Rayford W., and Michael R. Winston. *Dictionary of American Negro Biography.* New York: Norton, 1982.

Lovett, Bobby L. *A Black Man's Dream: The First Hundred Years, Richard Henry Boyd and the National Publishing Board.* [Jacksonville, FL?]: Mega Corp., 1993.

Melton, J. Gordon. *Religious Leaders of America.* Detroit: Gale Research, 1991.

Robert L. Johns

Ed Bradley

(1941–)

Broadcast journalist

Highly acclaimed award–winning news correspondent Ed Bradley brought a new image to television news when he joined CBS's *60 Minutes* in 1980. This was the most watched news show in television history, finishing in the top ten Nielsen ratings for 18 straight seasons. CBS picked a winner in the cool, confident, and handsome Bradley. Throughout his CBS career, Bradley's reports have garnered some of the highest accolades in broadcast journalism.

Born Edward R. Bradley on June 22, 1941, in Philadelphia, Pennsylvania, he was the only child of Edward R. and Gladys Gaston Bradley. His parents separated shortly after he was born. Reared by his mother in Philadelphia, Bradley spent summers with his father in Detroit. Recalling his childhood Bradley told *People* magazine, "I was raised by two people who worked 20–hour days at two jobs each. They had middle–class goals and values, but no middle–class money. I was told, 'You can be anything you want, kid.' When you hear that enough, you believe it."

Bradley was educated in Catholic schools in Philadelphia. In 1959 he entered Cheney State College, a historically black institution near Philadelphia. Majoring in education, he planned a career in teaching. Then he met Georgie Woods, a disc jockey at Philadelphia radio station WDAS–FM. Bradley and Woods became good friends, and he often accompanied Woods to the station and watched as Woods did the program.

Bradley graduated in January 1964, received his teacher certification and began his first job in Philadelphia, teaching the sixth grade. Still he visited Woods at the station, volunteering to work as an unpaid disc jockey on a jazz show and sometimes reading the hourly newscast. His big break came one evening when he heard news reports of a riot taking place in Philadelphia. Bradley grabbed a tape recorder, convinced an engineer to accompany him, and went to cover the riots.

Bradley's news coverage brought the offer of a paying position with the station. His starting salary was only $1.25 per hour, minimum wage in 1965. Unable to live on the paltry sum, Bradley continued to teach in the day and work at the station at night. He played jazz, read the news, and called play–by–play reports for basketball games. He continued this pattern for two years.

In 1967 Bradley applied for a position at WCBS radio, an all–news format station in New York. He was required to write some copy and submit it as part of his application, but Bradley went further and taped a story about an anti–poverty program by going on location. He got the job, which paid $45,000 a year.

The job was stressful. Bradley was forced to compete with other reporters for news and felt pretty much like he was on an assembly line. He quit. Bradley had married in 1964, but was now divorced. He had no children and a desire to see the world. He decided to move to Paris, where he planned to write "the great American novel," he told Kristin McMurran of *People* magazine.

In Paris Bradley wrote poetry, saw the countryside, relaxed, and ran out of money. In September 1971, CBS enticed Bradley to work as a stringer for the Paris Bureau, assigning him to cover the peace talks between the United States and North Vietnam. He was paid by the story. Once

Ed Bradley

when the talks were suspended for 13 weeks, Bradley got a check for $12.50, but he survived. Deciding to go back to work full–time, Bradley became a war correspondent for CBS. Assigned to Indochina, he covered Vietnam and Cambodia. In 1973 Bradley was wounded in a mortar attack on Easter morning. After the fall of Saigon, Bradley returned to the United States with the image of war fresh in his mind. U.S. involvement in South Vietnam had been he said in *Current Biography,* "another neocolonialist venture of the United States." On his return he was assigned to the Washington, D.C., bureau.

First Black White House Correspondent

Bradley's first assignment was to cover Jimmy Carter's presidential campaign. After Carter's election, CBS assigned Bradley to cover the White House. While considered a prestigious position by many, Bradley was bored in the White House pressroom. Probably because he did not enjoy his job, Bradley earned the reputation of being a difficult person to get along with.

Bradley left Washington to join *CBS Reports* and produce documentaries. Returning to Southeast Asia, Bradley produced *What's Happening in Cambodia?,* which documented the experience of the boat people fleeing Vietnam in the 1970s. He had found his forte. Bradley enjoyed interviewing and moving about with cameraman Norman Lloyd shooting on location.

In 1980 Bradley replaced Dan Rather on *60 Minutes.* His first segment of *60 Minutes* aired on October 4, 1981. *The*

Other Side of the IRA investigated the Irish Republican Army's possible connection to world terrorism. In December 1981, Bradley's interview of Lena Horne, *Lena,* garnered him his first Emmy Award. His report on the cancer–causing potential of alar created a nationwide scare among consumers, angering apple growers and the manufacturer of the chemical. Bradley's second report on alar, which aired May 14, 1989, caused Uniroyal Chemical to remove alar from the market and resulted in the EPA banning the chemical.

Sunday September 17, 1995 Bradley celebrated the beginning of his fifteenth season on *60 Minutes.* He had reported 300 stories for the show, then in its twenty–eighth season. Bradley had also traveled to 58 countries and to almost every state in the union.

For his outstanding reporting, Bradley earned 11 Emmys. His most highly acclaimed Emmy–winning segments were *Lena* (December 27, 1981); *In the Belly of the Beast* (April 18, 1982, an interview with Jack Henry Abbott, the convicted murderer; *Schizophrenia* (December 1, 1985), a report on an often misunderstood brain disorder; *Made in China* (September 15, 1991), a report on Chinese forced labor camps; and *Caitlin's Story* (November 8, 1992), an examination of the controversy between the parents of a deaf child and the deaf association.

Other awards included the Alfred I. du Pont–Columbia University Awards for *Made in China* and *Semipalatinsk* (March 27, 1994), which reported on a Soviet nuclear experiment affecting generations of people. *Is the Nuclear Nightmare Over* (October 31, 1991), and *General Sergeyev* (December 12, 1993)—two reports showing viewers top–secret military installations in Russia and the United States—earned the Overseas Press Club Award.

Bradley's most popular segments earned both an Emmy and a duPont–Columbia University Award. *Blacks in America: With All Deliberate Speed* (July 1979) was a two–hour report on the progress African Americans have made since the Supreme Court decision of 1954, outlawing the separate but equal practice. Bradley concluded that despite the legal action and media attention too much remained unchanged. Another example of Bradley's savvy reporting was *Murder—Teenage Style,* which focused on violent black Los Angeles gangs. A report on Boston Symphony's visit to China, *The Boston Symphony Goes to China* (April 1979), won both an Emmy and the George Foster Peabody Award.

Bradley was anchor for the CBS newsmagazine *Street Stories* from January 1992 to August 1993. From November 1976 to May 1981, he also anchored the *CBS Sunday Night News.*

Bradley skis for fun and works out in a local health club to keep fit. His contribution to the field of broadcast journalism will likely serve as watermark for other reporters to emulate. Because of his knowledge of the world, sensitivity to human suffering, and ability to engage in critical dialogue, Bradley has uncovered and illuminated issues that might otherwise have gone unnoticed.

Current address: *60 Minutes,* CBS News, 524 West 57th Street, New York, NY 10019–2985.

REFERENCES

Contemporary Black Biography. Vol. 2. Detroit: Gale Research, 1992.

Current Biography Yearbook. New York: H. W. Wilson, 1988.

McMurran, Kristin. "Can a Whole Life Fit into 60 Minutes? Maybe, If You're Ed Bradley." *People* 20 (November 14, 1983): 169.

Tedesco, Kevin. Press Release. CBS News, August 28, 1995.

Nagueyalti Warren

Thomas Bradley

(1917–)

Politician, lawyer

Thomas Bradley was the first African American mayor of Los Angeles, the second largest city in the United States, where he served an unprecedented five terms from 1973 until 1993. He was also one of the most respected politicians in the United States. Bradley was twice nominated as Democratic candidate for governor of California. He was also the first African American elected to the city council.

Bradley was born on December 29, 1917, on a cotton plantation in Calvert, Texas. His grandparents were slaves in the Carolinas. Bradley was second of the seven children of Lee Thomas Bradley, a sharecropper, and Crenner Hawkins Bradley. Bradley's mother had a strong influence on him, and he, in turn, was his mother's favorite child. Most of his siblings died in infancy. When Bradley was seven, his family moved to Los Angeles, where his father worked various jobs, such as waiter, porter, and crewman on a steamship. When his father moved out of their home, Bradley's mother went to work as a domestic maid. Bradley's father, however, kept in touch with the family, joining forces with Crenner Bradley in encouraging their children to strive for success. Bradley was an enterprising youngster, who worked hard at his studies and delivered newspapers while other children were out playing. To his mother's delight, Bradley always stood up for his handicapped brother Ellis when other children in the neighborhood picked on him.

Bradley attended Polytechnic High School in Los Angeles, where he was a track star in the 440–yard dash and an all–city tackle on the football team. During high school, Bradley won his first election by defeating a white student for the

Thomas Bradley

position of president of the school's Boys League. He graduated from high school in 1937 and enrolled at the University of California at Los Angeles (UCLA) on a track scholarship. He majored in education and worked to support himself as a publicity photographer for the comedian Jimmy Durante.

Bradley married Ethel Mae Arnold on May 4, 1941, after eight years of courtship. He had first met Arnold, a former beautician, at their Methodist church when they were both teenagers. They have two daughters, Lorraine and Phillis. Another daughter died on the day she was born, sadly coinciding with the Bradleys' first wedding anniversary.

In 1940, after completing his junior year at UCLA, Bradley quit college to join the Los Angeles Police Department. He advanced through the ranks for 21 years. He rose from foot patrolman to juvenile officer to vice–squad detective, and finally to lieutenant, the highest rank ever attained by an African American police officer in Los Angeles at that time. During that period, Bradley was confronted by difficult episodes of racial discrimination. Certain restaurants refused him service and he had to make special arrangements for a white couple to purchase a house for him in a white neighborhood. Bradley strived to prevail over incidents like these. While on the force, he tried to correct some blatant racist practices he encountered, such as segregated patrol cars.

In between shifts, Bradley studied law, first at Loyola University and then at Southwestern University, both schools in Los Angeles. He finally got his law degree in 1956 from Southwestern. He practiced law part–time while still working with the police department. In 1961, convinced that he would never advance above the rank of lieutenant, he retired from the police force and went into full–time law practice. He worked for Charles Matthews, a prosecutor at the district attorney's office, who was called the "dean" of black attorneys in Los Angeles because he had been practicing law since 1931. According to Matthews, Bradley handled some divorce cases but nothing truly challenging because few career–making cases were offered to an African American lawyer at the time.

Bradley's burning desire to achieve would not let him settle for this kind of legal practice and politics seemed to offer the opportunity for success. In 1963, he became the first African American to be elected to the Los Angeles City Council, representing the racially mixed Los Angeles Tenth District. In 1967, he was reelected and held the position until 1971.

Mayor of Los Angeles

In 1969, Bradley challenged the reelection of the city's conservative mayor, Sam Yorty. During the campaign Yorty exploited racial fears still fresh in the minds of the people after the 1965 Watts riots. Yorty portrayed the quiet Bradley as a tool of black militants, left–wing radicals, and communists. Bradley stands six feet, four inches tall and weighs about 215 pounds, but interviewers often described him as modest and soft–spoken. To overcome his early shyness on the campaign trail, he boarded buses and forced himself to shake hands with every passenger before the next stop. Despite such experiments, Bradley remained a mystery to the public, the press, and his employees at city hall. Bradley lost to Yorty, but immediately began to prepare for the next election.

Four years later, in a fiercely contested 1973 mayoral election, Bradley countered Yorty's racist campaign by appealing to Los Angeles voters' sense of fair play. By this time, voters were familiar with Bradley and his platform. He emphasized broader, more substantive issues. Bradley pointed out, among other things, that his opponent ran a corrupt and wasteful city hall and neglected the real problems of gangs, crime, and the need for a rapid transit system. Bradley reassured the city with his warmth, moderation, and easy accessibility, and many whites who had previously feared him joined his coalition of African American, Chicano, and white liberal supporters. Bradley won the election with a 57 percent majority, which was the largest victory in the Los Angeles mayoral contest in more than 40 years. He immediately addressed his campaign promises; one being the completion of the transit system.

According to a report in the *New York Times,* Bradley's victory in the election was attributed to a soul–searching period after the Watts riots, partly because business operators and owners were determined to prevent further racial conflict. They wanted a conciliator, someone who could stand as a symbol of goodwill to disaffected minority groups. They wanted an authority figure who enforced law and order without generating the antagonism associated with previous administrations. They found all these in Bradley, whose philosophy was to join the mainstream and not wear his race on his sleeve. In December of 1973 Bradley also took on the responsibility of presiding over the United States League of Cities.

Bradley and his wife Ethel were the first family to occupy the $700,000 Getty House, the new official mayor's residence donated to the city by the Getty Oil Company. In 1977, he was reelected with 59 percent of the vote despite facing state senator Alan Robbins and ten other white opponents. In 1981, Yorty challenged Bradley's bid for a third term, but Bradley won the election again.

California Governor Campaigns

In 1982, Bradley took advantage of his popularity and ran for governor of California against the Republican state attorney general George Deukmejian. Bradley ran a quiet campaign and was narrowly defeated in the election. The attempt in itself was remarkable as Bradley was the first African American candidate to receive the statewide support of the primarily white Democratic party. Had he been elected in 1982, he would have been the first African American elected governor in the United States.

In 1984, Bradley departed from his usual cautious attitude to bring the summer Olympic games to Los Angeles despite fears that it might be a money–losing enterprise. To make sure that the quest succeeded, according to *Current Biography,* he held prolonged negotiations with the International Olympic Committee in what he called the ''toughest, longest–running battle of his political career.'' He finally persuaded the committee to indemnify Los Angeles for any potential loss. The games offered temporary employment for the city's youth, a million newly planted trees and other civic improvements, and international publicity guaranteed to boost tourism.

In December of 1984, Bradley opened the first new shopping center in the Watts district since the riots of 1965. In that same period he employed many more young people and members of minorities at city hall. His detractors accused him of doing this because he wanted to improve his chances to be reelected for the fourth term in the coming mayoral election. On April 9, 1985, Bradley defeated his opponent, John Ferraro, a conservative city councilman, by 68 percent to 32 percent. Bradley later told his supporters, as cited in *Current Biography,* that the landslide victory ''proves that Los Angeles voters select their leaders based on content of their character and performance in office. . . . Los Angeles is the city of hope and opportunity. I am a living example of that.''

In the 1986 gubernatorial election, Bradley challenged Deukmejian again, this time with a more aggressive campaign. When he lost, some claimed he might be paying the price for not reacting sooner to the Jewish plea to denounce Louis Farrakhan, the controversial African American leader of the Nation of Islam, whose anti–Jewish statements received wide–spread publicity in the state. Bradley waited until September 15 to denounce Farrakhan's anti–Semitism. Bradley had postponed making a public statement because he had promised African American leaders to delay comments in hopes of Farrakhan redeeming himself. He had also hoped that Farrakhan would tone down his remarks. At the election, Bradley carried Los Angeles, but he lost the state of California badly, 61 percent to 37 percent. He vowed never to run for governor again.

Another Mayoral Election

Bradley announced, in an unusual way, his intention to seek a fifth term as mayor in 1989. His venue was the Joan Rivers talk show. His critics pointed out that 14 years of growth under his leadership had left Los Angeles with unhealthy air, clogged freeways, brimming landfills, overcrowded schools, rising crime, and skyrocketing housing costs intensified by a rising tide of illegal immigration. Bradley took his campaign to small shopping malls in overcrowded neighborhoods and talked about ''managed growth.'' He announced plans to plant millions of trees in vacant lots and other unshaded areas of the city over the next five years to help purify the air and called for an end to free parking to minimize auto emissions.

By early 1989, Bradley had built up a commanding lead in the polls that prompted Yaroslavsky, one of his opponents, to withdraw from the race. This event left only the freshman city councilman Nate Holder, also an African American, to challenge Bradley. Holden was supported by minorities who felt neglected by Bradley and his emphasis on the growth of the city.

Three weeks before the election, the *Los Angles Herald Examiner* broke a story that Bradley had earned tens of thousands of dollars in fees for serving as a director or a consultant for two financial institutions that did business with the city. The city attorney announced a full–scale investigation. Regardless of the bad press, Bradley won the election with 52 percent of the vote. Chastened by the first assault ever made on his integrity, he promptly returned the consulting fees, resigned from the board of directors, and appointed a special panel to draft an ethics code for city employees. According to the *New York Times,* Bradley declared ''I treasure more than anything else I know that bond of trust which has been established over forty–seven years of my service to the people of this city, and I want nothing to tarnish it, nothing to question it, nobody to doubt it.''

On September 13, 1989, the city attorney, James K. Hahn, announced that the evidence did not warrant a criminal charge, but he ruled that the mayor's conduct was unethical and filed civil charges against him. Bradley eventually paid a fine of $20,000. A concurrent investigation by federal authorities into Bradley's personal stock transactions also turned up no evidence of criminal practice.

Bradley's impeccable image was also somewhat tainted by the events surrounding the widely–publicized, videotaped beating of Rodney King, an African American motorist, by Los Angeles police officers in March of 1991. Though the city's charter limited Bradley's authority over the police, he nevertheless set up a commission to examine police brutality in the wake of the King beating. Unfortunately for Bradley, *Current Biography* reported that the commission blamed him in part for what it called his "unwillingness over the years to exert more leadership by the inherent powers of his office."

After the four white police officers charged with the beating were unexpectedly acquitted on April 29, 1992, Bradley called for calm in his television address but could not hide his own outrage over the verdict. According to *Current Biography,* he said "Today the system failed us, the jury's verdict will never blind us to what we saw on that videotape. The men who beat Rodney king do not deserve to wear the uniform of the LAPD." Bradley's remark was provocative to people who lived in parts of the city bent on venting their frustration over the verdict in five days of riot that resulted in 58 fatalities, 4,000 injuries, and 10,000 vandalized stores. John Ferraro, city council president, remarked that even if Bradley was outraged, he should have kept his composure since he was the mayor. The riot also brought to a head the long–standing antipathy between Bradley and police chief Daryl F. Gates, who subsequently resigned on June 28, 1992. On September 24, 1992, Bradley announced that he would not seek reelection when his fifth term as mayor expired in mid–1993. True to his words, he retired as mayor of Los Angeles in 1993.

During his 20 years as mayor, Bradley developed a track record of resolving major public and private sector disputes by bringing together diverse groups and facilitating negotiations. His extensive network of global business leaders and government contacts gave him the ability to assist companies interested in expanding operations domestically and overseas. Bradley was primarily responsible for the expansion of the Los Angeles International Airport and the Los Angeles Harbor. He was a leader in developing the Los Angeles Metro Rail project, the county's light rail system, a city government childcare program, and a citywide recycling program.

Bradley is a workaholic; even his wife joked about his dedication during the 1969 election campaign, saying, as quoted in the *New York Times,* "That man went to law school 18 years ago and I haven't seen him since." He has few hobbies, he rarely takes vacations, and he enjoys attending unannounced social events, sports activities, and watching games. Friendship has always been very important to Bradley; he has remained available to his friends. In a telephone interview, Chappell Connie, Bradley's administrative assistant for 27 years, praised Bradley, called him a good boss who cared about those who worked for him, and noted that he made a difference in people's lives. Bradley derives great satisfaction in influencing people's lives; this being evident in one of his speeches to a predominantly African American school in Los Angeles. Quoted in *Contemporary Black Biography,* he said: "The only thing that can stop you is you. Dream big dreams, work hard, study hard and listen to your teachers. Above all get along with each other. You can be anything your heart wants you to be."

On July 1, 1993, Bradley assumed a new position at Brobeck, Phleger, and Harrison as a senior counselor to companies in the United States and abroad. He had a heart attack in 1996 and lost his speech. When his office was contacted on November 12, 1996, he was still recuperating.

During his 50 years of public service with the city of Los Angeles, Bradley had served either as a member or chairman on several boards of directors, the League of California Cities, the World Affairs Council, the American Cancer Society of the City of Los Angeles, the United Nations Association of Los Angeles, and many more. Some of the awards he received include the Thurgood Marshall Award; the John F. Kennedy Fellowship Award from the government of New Zealand in 1978; the Magnin Award in 1984; the Spingarn Medal from the National Association for the Advancement of Colored People (NAACP) in 1984; and numerous honorary doctoral degrees. In May of 1993, Bradley received the Order of Sacred Treasure Gold and Silver Star, the highest honor awarded by the Emperor of Japan to individuals living outside the country for helping to promote international trade and improved understanding of the Japanese culture.

Bradley, with the encouragement and support of his mother, developed a resolve within himself and a belief that he could accomplish positive changes. His many contributions to the city of Los Angeles and his inspiration to those who listened resulted in a better life for many.

Current address: 550 South Hope, Suite 2100, Los Angeles, CA 90071.

REFERENCES

Bradley, Thomas. Telephone interview with Nkechi G. Mgboh Amadife, February 1997.

Chappell, Connie. Telephone interview with Nkechi G. Mgboh Amadife, November 12, 1996.

Contemporary Black Biography. Vol. 2. Detroit: Gale Research, 1992.

Current Biography Yearbook. New York: H. W. Wilson, 1992.

"Day of Rage." *U.S. News & World Report* 4 (11 May 1992): 20–26.

Estell, Kenneth. *African America Portrait of a People.* Detroit: Visible Ink Press, 1994.

Facts on File, October 11, 1985: 760.

"For Mayor Thomas Bradley and His Wife, Home is $700,000 Getty House." *Ebony* 33 (February 1978); 31–38.

"Like Los Angeles, Bradley Stands Tall." *New York Times,* April 7, 1985.

Payne, J. Gregory, and Scott C. Ratzan. *Tom Bradley: The Impossible Dream: A Biography.* Santa Monica: Round Table Publishing, 1986.

Robinson, James Lee Jr. *Tom Bradley: Los Angeles's First Black Mayor.* Ph.D. diss., University of California Los Angeles, 1976.

Who's Who among African Americans, 1996–97. 9th ed. Detroit: Gale Research, 1996.
Who's Who in American Politics, 1995–96. New York: Bowker, 1996.
Who's Who in Government. Chicago: Marquis Who's Who, 1977.

COLLECTIONS

Oral history transcripts of Thomas Bradley are in the oral history program, University of California, Los Angeles. Audiotape recordings of Bradley are in the UCLA department of special collections.

Nkechi G. Mgboh Amadife

William Stanley Braithwaite

William Stanley Braithwaite
(1878–1962)
Poet, critic, educator, writer, publisher

William Stanley Braithwaite was one of this country's most significant African American literary figures of the first half of the twentieth century. A 1918 Spingarn Medal winner, Braithwaite was an accomplished poet whose works Robert T. Kerlin described in *Negro Poets and Their Poems* as "graceful and esthetically satisfying." Braithwaite also rose to eminence as a critic of poetry. In academia, colleagues and students of Braithwaite remembered him as a consummate intellectual and an inspiring educator. However, it was in the capacity of publisher and anthologist that Braithwaite's impact was profound. Braithwaite not only managed to have his own literary works published, but he also published works of many of his contemporaries, thereby bringing recognition to and providing exposure for young writers, many of whom might otherwise have gone unpublished.

The second oldest of five children, William Stanley Braithwaite was born on December 6, 1878, in Boston, Massachusetts. His father, William Smith Braithwaite, was the son of West Indian aristocrats, and his mother, Emma DeWolfe, was the daughter of a former slave woman from North Carolina. Emma's father was unknown but presumed by young Braithwaite in *W. Stanley Braithwaite Reader* to have been the slave master of his grandmother. Braithwaite and his siblings were reared in an isolated, very strict home environment where the children were home taught by their father. William attended public schools, only briefly, beginning in 1886, just shortly after his father's death. After about four years of formal education, Braithwaite quit school to help support his family left in debt after the death of his father.

After a series of menial jobs, Braithwaite found work, first as an errand boy and eventually as a typesetter for the textbook publishing firm, Ginn and Company of Boston. Braithwaite became acquainted with and learned from great works of literature, and, at the same time, learned the business of publishing during his tenure with this company. Eager to pursue his chosen career in writing and publishing, Braithwaite moved, for a short time, to New York in 1900. However, according to Braithwaite, it was during this time in New York that he, for the first time, experienced blatant hostility and endured rejection after the literary community discriminated against him on the basis of his race. Recalling this sobering experience several years later, Braithwaite wrote in his *Reader*: "I had a taste. . .of what the difficulties and injustices were for one of color who wanted to be accepted at his worth." Unable to secure full–time employment, Braithwaite returned to Boston in 1901. Shortly afterwards, he successfully managed to have several of his poems published in prestigious Boston papers, including the *Boston Guardian,* the *Boston Journal,* and the *Evening Transcript,* where he later became literary editor. In 1902 he met Emma Kelly of Montross, Virginia, and in June of 1903 they were married. Seven children were born to the couple.

Focuses on Publishing

Braithwaite devoted the next 30 years of his life to the creation of original verse, literary criticism, and editing and publishing his poems and those of his contemporaries. His first volume of original verses, *Lyrics of Life and Love* was published at his own expense in 1904. *The House of Falling Leaves* (1908), a second book of his original poems, and several other books of poetry edited by Braithwaite followed, including *The Book of Elizabethan Verse* in 1906, *The Book of Georgian Verse* in 1909, and *The Book of Restoration Verse* in 1910.

Braithwaite made several attempts at starting and sustaining publishing companies, all of which failed. However, during the brief existence of the B. J. Brimmer Publishing Company, cofounded by Braithwaite, he published the first novel of James Gould Cozzens, *Confusion,* and a book of poetry entitled *Bronze* by Georgia Douglas Johnson.

Braithwaite's one successful publishing venture was an annual journal entitled *Anthology of Magazine Verse,* begun in 1913 and continued until 1923. It consisted of poems selected from periodicals from across the nation, presenting works that displayed a rich variety of styles by poets of diverse background and ethnic origin.

Braithwaite was awarded an honorary master's degree from Atlanta University in 1918, the same year that he was awarded the prestigious Spingarn Medal. The following year he was awarded an honorary doctorate degree from Talladega College in Talladega, Alabama. In 1936 Braithwaite accepted the position of professor of literature at Atlanta University. At Atlanta, Braithwaite was highly regarded and respected both by his colleagues and his students. Reputed to be a caring and attentive teacher, Braithwaite was, nevertheless, also considered aloof by some. He rarely involved himself in scholarly discussions with faculty members or concerned himself with the politics of academia, which fueled speculation that he was uncomfortable because of his lack of formal education or earned degrees.

Braithwaite retired from Atlanta University in 1945 and moved to Harlem, where he continued to remain active as a poet, critic and anthologist. Among his numerous projects there, *New and Selected Poems* (1948), *The Bewitched Parsonage: the Story of the Brontës* (1950), and a single revived volume of the *Anthology of Magazine Verse* (1958) were the only three that he was able to have published before his death in 1962.

A Career in Genteel Poetry

Scholars and critics of Braithwaite described his poetry as "genteel" and "refined," often mystic and displaying the obvious influence of Braithwaite's idols: Keats, Wordsworth, and Burns. No racially exclusive language, no mention of barriers of color, nor any reference to the injustices of the social environment in which he lived appear in Braithwaite's poems. In the *Braithwaite Reader,* contemporaries of Braithwaite, both black and white, criticized him for his "retreat from, and discrimination against, racial materials and interests" in his creative writing. In response, Braithwaite defended his resolve "not to treat in any phase, in any form, for any purpose, racial materials or racial experiences," thereby "acknowledging the need of a purely aesthetic voice, to express and interpret manifold interests" of himself and others like him.

Braithwaite began publishing the works of other poets as early as 1906 in his *Book of Elizabethan Verse,* which was followed by two other small volumes of Georgian and Restoration verse, respectively. In the yearly journal, *Anthology of Magazine Verse,* he chose poems previously printed in other periodicals from around the nation which he considered to be the finest works of the time. Poems by E. E. Cummings, Dubose Heyward, Robert Frost, Georgia D. Johnson, Winifred Virginia Jackson, and Wallace Stevens, among many others, appeared in Braithwaite's publications. Most significantly, poems of African Americans along with those of white artists were published together, creating unique anthologies of diverse and varied literary offerings.

Despite his personal philosophy concerning racial references or issues of race in poetry, Braithwaite included numerous poems by many writers of color which contained explicit racial content. Writers Paul Laurence Dunbar, Claude McKay, and Harriet Monroe were among the contributors. Other Braithwaite anthologies included *The Poetry Journal* (1916), the *Golden Treasury of Magazine Verse* (1918), *The Book of Modern British Verse* (1919), *Victory! Contributed by 38 American Poets* (1919), *Anthology of Massachusetts Poets* (1922), *Our Lady's Choir, a Contemporary Anthology of Verse by Catholic Sisters* (1931), and a final revived edition of the *Anthology of Magazine Verse* (1958).

Braithwaite, a scarcely remembered poet and author, deserves a more prominent place in American literary history for his creative efforts. Above all, Braithwaite should be remembered as a visionary and a pioneer in the cause of publishing culturally diverse writings.

REFERENCES

Bloom, Harold, ed. *Black American Prose Writers Before the Harlem Renaissance.* New York: Chelsea House Publishers, 1994.

Braithwaite, William Stanley, ed. *Anthology of Magazine Verse.* New York: Schulte Pub. Co., 1916–1929.

———. *The William Stanley Braithwaite Reader.* Edited by Philip Butcher. Ann Arbor: University of Michigan Press, 1972.

Brawley, Benjamin G. *The Negro in Literature and Art in the United States.* New York: Duffield and Co., 1918.

Kerlin, Robert. *Negro Poets and their Poems.* 3rd ed. Washington, DC: Associated Publishers, 1947.

Patterson, John S. *William Stanley Braithwaite: A Register of His Papers in the Syracuse University Library.* Syracuse, NY: Syracuse University Library Manuscript Collections, 1964.

Turner, Darwin T., editor. *Black American Literature.* Columbus, OH: Charles E. Merrill Pub. Co., 1969.

Who's Who among Black Americans. 5th ed. Lake Forest, IL: Educational Communications, 1988.

COLLECTIONS

The papers of William Stanley Braithwaite are in the Syracuse University Library.

Leroy E. Bynum Jr.

Herman R. Branson

(1914–1995)

Educator, physicist, college president

A scientific pioneer and an educator of international stature, Herman R. Branson was a vital force in advancing research in physics and biophysics. His work led to a greater understanding of biological systems, organic molecules, and sickle cell anemia. He discovered the alpha helix, the basic structure of proteins; made electron impact studies on small organic molecules; introduced the information theory in the study of biological molecules; examined the quantization of mass in relativistic quantum mechanics; and studied the use of radioactive and stable isotopes in transport studies in biology. For 27 years, Branson devoted his research skills to biophysics. Many of his articles have been published by national magazines and his work remains acclaimed by scientists today.

Herman Russell Branson was born on August 14, 1914, in Pocahontas, Virginia. His father, Harry P. Branson, was not well educated and supported his family by working as a coal miner. His mother, Gertrude Branson, a homemaker, instilled in her son the desire to read and question the information he learned. She read to her children frequently and encouraged their desire to achieve. In 1939 Branson married Corolynne Gray of Cincinnati, and they had two children: Corolynne Gertrude and Herman Edward.

Branson attended a segregated grade school in Pocahontas, where he was guided by many African American teachers. In 1928 he enrolled in Dunbar High School in the District of Columbia, where he came under the guidance of excellent instructors. Most inspiring were his science and mathematics teachers, who helped pave the way for much of Branson's future educational success. In 1932 Branson graduated at the top of his high school class.

Branson's climb toward higher education first began at the University of Pittsburgh, where he studied from 1932 to 1934. He then transferred to Virginia State University in Petersburg, Virginia, after his second year. Happier to be back in his home state, Branson found the tuition and living costs much lower there. His hard work and perseverance enabled him to graduate summa cum laude in 1936 with a bachelor of science degree.

Shortly thereafter, Branson was admitted to the graduate program in physics at the University of Cincinnati in Ohio, where he studied from 1936 to 1939. He received several university fellowships while there, which helped him a great deal financially. By accepting such aid as the Laws Fellowship and the Alpha Phi Alpha Fellowship, Branson was able to complete his doctoral studies in three years, graduating in 1939. He was a Rosenwald Foundation post–doctoral fellow at the University of Chicago in 1940.

A Career in Academia

Overlapping his work at the University of Chicago, from 1939 to 1941 Branson was on the faculty of Dillard University in New Orleans as an instructor in physics. Instructing at this predominantly African American institution required long hours, but Branson enjoyed being able to teach his students not only physics but chemistry and mathematics as well.

Two years later, Branson was asked to join the faculty at Howard University in Washington, D.C. There between 1941 and 1968 he served first as associate professor of physics, then professor and head of the department. In his 27 years at Howard, Branson held many other positions related to this field; for example, from 1942 to 1944, he served as director of the Engineering, Science, and Management War Training program. In 1947 he held the title of director for the office of Naval Research and Atomic Energy Commission Projects in physics. Branson was senior fellow of the National Research Council, California Institute of Technology for one year, 1948–49. He also directed the Research Corporation Project in physics from 1946 to 1950.

From Howard University Branson moved on to the presidency of Central State University in Wilberforce, Ohio, from 1968 to 1970. Then in 1970, Branson became president of Lincoln University in Pennsylvania, another historically black college. He remained at Lincoln until his retirement in 1985, when he was named president emeritus. Then he returned to Howard University as director of the Precollege Science and Mathematics Research Program from 1986 until he died. Widely recognized as an excellent administrator, Branson was nominated for the National Medal of Science by the students and faculty at Lincoln in 1980.

Work as a Researcher

When Branson first began to research biophysics, this field of science was only in its early stages. Previous studies in biology concentrated on the descriptive aspects of biology and focused on illustrating the stages a living creature went through as it developed. It was in the 1930s that biologists began to question what would happen if certain conditions for a living creature were changed. Would eating different food affect the growth rate of an animal? Would sunlight enable a plant to thrive? Questions such as these grew more widespread as physicists provided biologists with new research tools, such as X–rays.

While still a student Branson examined the effects of X–rays on small worms. He was interested in not only measuring the strength of the X–rays but in discovering how much of the radiation was absorbed by the worms as well. In doing this, Branson was forced to analyze the chemical composition of worms and whether or not these chemicals were spread evenly throughout the worms' body. Branson's study on worms was so successful that he became quickly a central figure in the field of biophysics.

Following up his original research, Branson focused on studying how the body uses raw materials such as phosphorus. He examined the chemical stages phosphorus goes through before being used by cells and devised a theory to illustrate how phosphorus is used in each of the stages. Once again, his work was respected by the scientific community so much that in 1948 he was invited to present his findings at a biophysics conference held at the Cold Spring Harbor Laboratories in Long Island, New York.

Branson's research, however, was not limited to phosphorus. In 1948 he collaborated with Linus Pauling. Pauling later won a Nobel Prize after illustrating how atoms link together to form molecules.

By 1950 Branson helped lead the way toward unlocking the mystery behind the structure of deoxyribonucleic acid (DNA). His work with hemoglobin also led to his interest in sickle cell anemia, a hereditary disease that frequently affects people of African heritage. Because of his research in this area, Branson was elected to the Institute of Medicine, a branch of the National Academy of Science in 1975.

In addition to his scholarly activities and recognition in the United States, Branson was widely respected overseas. In Europe, Branson met with experts to discuss mutual research problems. This provided an enhanced perspective on his work with radioactive and stable isotopes. He consulted with other scientists at the Max Planck Institute for Biophysics in Frankfort, Germany. As a faculty fellow of the National Science Foundation, in 1962–63 he was invited to teach his research techniques at the University of Hamburg. During this period he was consultant to the French Atomic Energy Commission in Saclay and consultant on science education to the government of India. Branson was a prolific writer. From 1938 through 1987 he published more than 100 research and analytical articles in physics, in biophysics, on black colleges, and on education and science, which were printed in such publications as the *American Journal of Physics, Bulletin of Mathematical Biophysics, Bulletin of Mathematics, Nature, Journal of Negro Education, Journal of Chemical Physics, National Academy of Science, Radiology,* and *Science.*

In honor of his achievements, Branson received many awards, including the Governor's Award for the Advancement of the Prestige of Ohio in 1969. He was also awarded honorary doctoral degrees by eight U.S. universities: Sc.D., University of Cincinnati and Virginia State University, both in 1967, and from Lincoln University in Pennsylvania, 1969; D.H.L., Brandeis University, 1972 and from Shaw College, Detroit, 1978; LL.D., Western Michigan University, 1973, and Drexel University, 1982; and another Sc.D., Northwestern University, 1985.

Branson's professional affiliations were numerous and included the National Institute of Science (national president, 1956–57); chair, Committee on Teaching Awards, the Washington Academy of Sciences, 1957–58; and member of the National Advisory Panel of the Sea Grant College Program, National Oceanic and Atmospheric Administration and chairman from 1980–95. His board memberships included those of Bank Street College of Education, New York, 1964–68; of Hartwick College, 1970–74; Woodrow Wilson National Fellowship Foundation, 1975–95 ; the Corporation of the Massachusetts Institute of Technology, 1979–84; and Carver Research Foundation, Tuskegee Institute (now Tuskegee University), 1960–95. He also held memberships in the National Academy of Sciences, American Association for the Advancement of Science, and the Sociology of Mathematics and Biology. From 1954 to 1956 he was president of Phi Beta Kappa Chi Honor Society. Socially, he was a member of the Cosmos Club in Washington, D.C.

Branson died on June 13, 1995, of heart problems, in Washington, D.C. He was survived by his wife and children. Branson, an educational leader, contributed much to the scientific community. Because of his dedication and commitment to physics and biophysics, Branson remains one of the most respected researchers in the country.

REFERENCES

"Dr. Herman Branson." *Negro History Bulletin* 15 (April 1952): 151.

"Dr. Herman R. Branson, College Prexy, Scholar Dies in D.C." *Jet* 88 (26 June 1995): 16.

Kessler, James H., J. S. Kidd, and others. *Distinguished African American Scientists of the 20th Century.* Phoenix: Oryx Press, 1996.

Resume. Herman R. Branson. n.d. Files of Jessie Carney Smith, Fisk University.

Rywell, Martin, ed. *Afro–American Encyclopedia.* North Miami, FL: Educational Book Publishers, 1974.

Salzman, Jack, David Lionel Smith, and Cornel West, eds. *Encyclopedia of African–American Culture and History.* New York: Macmillan Library Reference USA/Simon and Schuster Macmillan, 1996.

Who's Who Among Black Americans, 1992–93. 7th ed. Detroit: Gale Research, 1992.

Lori Michelle Muha

Benjamin G. Brawley
(1882–1939)
Educator, minister, college administrator, writer

Benjamin Griffith Brawley was known for his work in several areas, chiefly as a college professor, college administrator, author, and anthologist. His legacy survives in his writings on black themes, which have often been reprinted to meet continuing interest.

Brawley was born in Columbia, South Carolina, on April 22, 1882, the second son of Edward McKnight Brawley and Margaret Dickerson Brawley. His father taught at Benedict College, a small historically black, Baptist–related college, and pastored a Baptist church in Columbia. The elder Brawley, born of free parents, was also president of a number of Baptist–related colleges and earned a reputation as an effective and notable minister, as well as a dynamic speaker and writer.

The Brawley family moved several times, and young Benjamin attended schools in Nashville, Tennessee, and Petersburg, Virginia. Brawley observed that before high school his parents were his main teachers. When he was 13 years old, Brawley enrolled in the preparatory department of Atlanta Baptist College (now Morehouse College) in Atlanta, Georgia and graduated with a bachelor's degree in 1901.

After one year of teaching in a one–room country school in Georgetown, Florida, Brawley returned to his alma mater, Atlanta Baptist College, as an instructor in English and Latin. He spent his summers studying until 1907, when he received a second bachelor's degree from the University of Chicago. In 1908, after a full residential year, he earned an M.A. from Harvard University. Promoted to professor of English at Atlanta Baptist, Brawley stayed in Atlanta until 1910, when he accepted a professorship at Howard University. In 1911, he was commissioned a member of the newly appointed committee of the faculty of the Howard University College of Liberal Arts to oversee the work of candidates for the degree of master of arts.

On July 20, 1912, Brawley married Hilda Damaris Prowd. About this time, Atlanta Baptist College called Brawley back, and he returned as professor of English and dean of the college, a dual assignment he held until 1920. He then conducted a survey of educational and social conditions in the

Benjamin G. Brawley

African country of Liberia. Six months later he returned to the United States and stood for ordination by the Massachusetts Baptist Convention on June 2, 1921. He became the pastor of the Messiah Baptist congregation in Brockton, Massachusetts, in 1921.

Brawley's social and religious beliefs conflicted with those of the Baptist church; he surrendered his assignment at the Messiah Baptist Church the following year and returned to college teaching. This time he went to Shaw University, a Baptist institution in Raleigh, North Carolina, where his elderly father was a professor of theology. Brawley remained at Shaw University until 1931.

Scholar and Master Teacher

Brawley rejoined Howard University's faculty. A scholar, a master teacher, and an occasional poet, he continued there as a faculty member for the remainder of his life. Brawley carefully cultivated and guarded his reputation with some care. In 1927 he rejected the Harmon Foundation's second–place award for excellence in education. (The Harmon Foundation for a number of years had recognized distinction in many fields of intellectual, artistic and educational undertakings of people of color.) Many who had Brawley as a teacher maintained that he merited first place.

Since 1913 when he produced *A Short History of the American Negro,* Brawley had been prolifically writing historical essays, social commentaries, and book reviews which were published in *The Dial, Lippincott's Magazine,* the *Spring-*

field Republican, The Bookman, Harvard Monthly and *The Sewanee Review,* among others. Although the subject matter of most of his writings and lectures was black history, culture, or biography, he did not slight his love for English literature. He published *A Short History of the English Drama* in 1921, *A New Survey of English Literature* in 1925, and a textbook handbook for teachers entitled *Freshman Year English* in 1929. *A History of the English Hymn* was to follow in 1932. Some of the publications on English literature, and especially the *New Survey,* were adopted as texts in several institutions of higher learning and were recommended reading in others.

Brawley's principal interests, however, were the intellectual and social advancement and improvement of his people. Brawley worked hard to explain the black experience to his white audience as well as to inspire the black audience. All of his chief works contained this stress and so did his six chapbooks of poems, though to a lesser degree. His verse *The Negro in Literature and Art,* first published in 1918, was revised and republished in 1937 as *The Negro Genius.* Subsequently it has been reprinted several times. *Paul Laurence Dunbar: Poet of his People* (1936) is still an admirable biography of an eminent black poet, and *A Social History of the American Negro* (1921) was popular and definitive enough in 1971 to warrant its reprinting.

Brawley wrote 23 scholarly articles, including several in the *Dictionary of American Biography,* and 17 books. Of his books, the scholar–writer Jay Saunders Redding declared in his essay on Brawley in the *Dictionary of Negro Biography* that many reputable scholars considered about six of Brawley's works as worthy contributions to scholarship.

In addition to his collection of books on black literature and social history, Brawley acquired one of the largest collections of works, printed and in manuscript, by and about Richard Le Gallienne, poet, journalist, and critic. He possessed first and limited editions, many autographed. Brawley left this unique collection and his collection of books by and about black authors to Howard University. His legacy is now a significant part of the internationally lauded Moorland–Spingarn Research Center. Charlotte Schuster Price, a manuscript librarian in the center, compiled an annotated guide to the Le Gallienne Collection which was published by Howard University Libraries in 1973 in its Occasional Papers Series.

Brawley died on February 1, 1939, after a short sickness following a stroke at his Washington, D.C., home. He was survived by his widow, Hilda Prowd Brawley, two sisters, three brothers, two nieces, and one nephew. Funeral rites were held at the Nineteenth Street Baptist Church on February 6. Walter H. Brooks, a prominent African American Baptist divine, presided over the ceremony and delivered the eulogy. Howard University's Dean of the School of Religion, Benjamin E. Mays, also spoke. Brawley was buried in Lincoln Memorial Cemetery, Suitland, Maryland.

Brawley's commitment of service to his race extended throughout his life. As teacher, Brawley's work touched the lives of his students. Through his writings, he contributed widely to the intellectual and social progress of black people.

REFERENCES

Dyson, Walter. *Howard University, the Capstone of Negro Education: A History, 1867–1940.* Washington, DC: Graduate School of Howard University, 1941.

Logan, Rayford W. *Howard University: The First Hundred Years, 1867–1967.* New York: New York University Press, 1969.

———, and Michael R. Winston, eds. *Dictionary of Negro Biography.* New York: Norton, 1982.

Sinnette, Elinor Des Verney, W. Paul Coates, and Thomas C. Battle, eds. *Black Bibliophiles and Collectors: Preservers of Black History.* Washington, DC: Howard University Press, 1990.

Who's Who in Colored America, 1928–29. New York: Who's Who in Colored America Corp., 1929.

Casper L. Jordan

Brailsford R. Brazeal

(1905–1981)

Educator, economist, writer

While Brailsford R. Brazeal was a renowned economist and author of a classic work on the Brotherhood of Sleeping Car Porters, he achieved his greatest prominence as dean of men at Morehouse College. In that capacity, he helped shape the lives of thousands of African American men who have gone on to distinguish themselves in all walks of life.

Brailsford Reese Brazeal was born March 8, 1905, in Dublin, Georgia, the son of George and Walton Troup Brazeal. After graduating with honors from Morehouse in 1927 with a Bachelor of Arts degree, he began work at his alma mater, and continued his service there until his retirement in 1973. From 1928 to 1934, he served as instructor in economics, and from 1934 to 1946, he was chairman of the Department of Economics and dean of men. Brazeal became academic dean and professor of economics in 1946 and remained in that position until his professional career ended.

In 1934 Brazeal married Ernestine Vivian Erskine of Jackson Mississippi, a Spelman College graduate, and one-time alumnae secretary at the Atlanta University Center. They had two daughters—Ernestine Walton, born in 1941, and Aurelia Erskine, born in 1944 and now U.S. ambassador to Kenya.

Fondly remembered by former students as a demanding teacher, Brazeal's high academic standards were developed at an early age and later as an undergraduate at Morehouse. He continued his education at Columbia University in New York City, where he earned an M.A. degree in 1928 and a Ph.D. degree in 1942. In 1932, he was a Social Science Research

Brailsford R. Brazeal

Council fellow and a member of the Student Council, International House in New York. During his graduate studies, he was awarded fellowships by the Rosenwald Fund in 1938 and again in 1946. Between 1940 and 1945 he was a Hazen Foundation Associate. Brazeal was elected to honorary membership in Delta Chapter of Phi Beta Kappa at Columbia on June 2, 1959.

In addition to his teaching and administrative roles at Morehouse, Brazeal found time to be active in several professional and civic associations. At various times he was president of the National Association of Collegiate Deans and Registrars; vice–president of the Association of American Baptists Educational Institutions; a member of the executive committee of the American Conference of Academic Deans; and the chairman and president of the Commission on Colleges and Universities of the Association of Colleges and Secondary Schools.

Brazeal held membership in the American Economics Association, the Academy of Political Science, the Southern Sociological Society, the advisory council of the Academic Freedom Committee of the American Civil Liberties Union, and the NAACP. He was frequently sought out as a speaker, panelist, and consultant at various interracial, collegiate and professional conferences and meetings. He was a deacon of the Friendship Baptist Church in Atlanta, a member of the board of directors of the Mutual Federal Savings and Loan Association of Atlanta, and a member of the board of directors of the executive committee of the Southern Regional Committee. In 1956–57 Brazeal was chairman of the Council of Deans and Registrars of the Atlanta University Center, Inc. He additionally served Morehouse as chairman of the executive committee of the National Alumni Association in 1958. An early advocate of continuing education, he was a member of the advisory committee of the Center for the Study of Liberal Education for Adults, and chairman of the Committee on Adult Education of the Association of Colleges and Universities.

Brazeal's most famous work is the book *The Brotherhood of Sleeping Car Porters, Its Origin and Development,* published by Harper and Brothers in 1946. The twelfth chapter, entitled "The Present Status and Programs of Fair Employment Practices Commissions—Federal, State, Municipal," was reprinted in the yearbook number of the *Journal of Negro Education* by the Howard University Press in the summer of 1951. Brazeal wrote a number of other articles and book reviews, including an unpublished history of the wartime Fair Employment Practices Committee.

Brazeal's accomplishments as a writer and economist are noteworthy, as is his leadership in numerous influential academic organizations. As a teacher and mentor of African American college students, however, he touched the lives of countless individuals who benefited not only from his expertise in the classroom, but also from his example as a powerful African American intellectual. His impact in those roles cannot be measured.

REFERENCES

Brazeal, Brailsford Reese. *The Brotherhood of Sleeping Car Porters.* New York: Harper, 1946.

"Dr. Brazeal Elected to Phi Beta Kappa at Columbia University." Special Collections, Robert W. Woodruff Library, Atlanta University Center.

"Information about Brailsford Brazeal." Special Collections, Robert W. Woodruff Library, Atlanta University Center, November 2, 1956.

"Morehouse's Dean B. R. Brazeal Listed in *Who's Who in America.*" Special Collections, Robert W. Woodruff Library, Atlanta University Center, March 30, 1958.

Who's Who in Colored America. 7th ed. Yonkers–on–Hudson, NY: Christian E. Burckel, 1950.

Arthur C. Gunn

J. Mason Brewer

(1896–1975)

Folklorist, writer, educator

John Mason Brewer, native of Texas, was notably the best collector and publisher of black folklore of the South and Southwest. He preserved in literature the culture, history, and social conditions of the region at a time when publishing opportunities were limited. He wrote two important historical studies of blacks in Texas, five volumes of poetry and folktales, and contributed over three hundred tales to other publications. He was elected second vice–president of the American Folklore Society, the first black elected to hold office in this nationally prestigious organization. His insight into the stories he collected, his love of and talent for storytelling, and his ability to analyze the stories he collected set him apart from others of his time. His ability to remain true to the black dialect elevated his collections of tales to an art form.

Born in Goliad, Texas, on March 24, 1896, Brewer was the first of six children born to Minnie Tate Mitchell Brewer and John Henry Brewer. Brewer's mother taught in the public school system in Texas for fifty years and influenced five of her six children to become educators. Brewer's father, John Henry Brewer, worked as a wagoner, mail carrier, postmaster, grocer, and barber. He bought a home, then married Minnie Tate Mitchell and all of their children were born in a home owned by their father. He worked until he died of injuries from a fall at age ninety–two.

Located next to one of the historic battlefields of the Texas War of Independence, the home of J. Mason Brewer's Aunt Eliza, his mother's sister, was a place where history came alive during summer visits as he discovered spent shells. The Texas tales told by both of his grandfathers, Pinckney Mitchell and Joe Brewer, helped to deepen the young child's interest in hearing more stories as well as revealing the history they held.

At age 17, Brewer graduated from high school with the class of 1913. He earned his bachelor's degree from Wiley College in Marshall, Texas, in 1917. He studied folklore at the University of Indiana and earned his Master of Arts degree in 1950. He served in the United States Army from 1918 to 1919, with the American Expeditionary Forces stationed in France. When it became known to the officers of the brigade that he was fluent in Spanish, French, and Italian, Brewer was asked to serve as their interpreter. After his military service ended, he accepted a position as teacher and principal in Fort Worth.

In 1924 Brewer left the teaching profession briefly to work for an oil company in Denver, Colorado. His first published works appeared in the oil company's trade journals and in a monthly magazine entitled *The Negro American.* In 1926 Mason returned to teaching as a principle in Shreveport and eventually became a professor at Samuel Huston College (presently known as Huston–Tillotson) in Austin, Texas, and chair of the Department of Humanities in 1931. Brewer met J. Frank Dobie of the Texas Folklore Society while teaching in Austin, and in 1932 Brewer's folk tales entitled "Juneteenth" were published in the society's annual publication entitled *Tone the Bell Easy.*

Brewer left Huston–Tillotson for Livingstone College in Salisbury, North Carolina, where he was a professor of English from 1959 to 1969. He was also a visiting professor at North Carolina Agricultural and Technical State University in Greensboro from 1967 to 1969.

Collects Black Folklore

Brewer was introduced to the folklore of blacks in Texas as he listened with fascination to the stories told by his father and his grandfathers. In the dedication of his book, *The Word on the Brazos,* he acknowledged their influence. He wrote, "From them stemmed the resolution that some day I would collect and record some of the Texas Negro's folk tales."

J. Frank Dobie observed that Brewer's tales had strength in their simplicity, "literalness," and strongly written characters that needed no explanation. Influenced by his reading of the works of Paul Lawrence Dunbar and his desire to write poetry in dialect, his use of "Negro dialect" remains true to the language of the time. Brewer lived during the time of the Harlem Renaissance and his name has often been linked with folklorist and writer Zora Neale Hurston. He was considered the successor to Joel Chandler Harris, author of the Uncle Remus tales, and was influenced by Paul Laurence Dunbar.

Brewer was honored and acknowledged for his work in the state of Texas and the southwest region and the nation. He was the first black member of the Texas Institute of Letters, the only black writer to appear in the Texas Folklore Society's 1954 annual publication, the first black to deliver a lecture series for leading southwestern universities, the first black to serve on the council of the American Folklore Society, and its first black officer—vice president. He was honored as one of the 25 best authors in Texas and was awarded an honorary Doctor of Letters from Paul Quinn College in Waco, Texas in 1951.

Brewer was married to Mae Thornton Hickman, with whom he had a son, John Mason Jr. Ruth Helen Brush became his second wife on August 19, 1959. She was a kindergarten teacher as well as a collector and authority on jazz, blues, and black folk music. Early in the morning of Friday, January 24, 1975, John Mason Brewer died in Dallas, Texas, and is buried in Austin at the Evergreen Cemetery. He is important for retelling tales he had heard in childhood and for collecting and preserving others.

REFERENCES

Byrd, James W. "In Memoriam: In Memory of John Mason Brewer (1896–1975)." *CLA Journal* 18 (June 1975): 578–81.

———. *J. Mason Brewer; Negro Folklorist.* Austin: Steck–Vaughn Company, 1967.

Turner, Darwin T. "In Memoriam: J. Mason Brewer: Vignettes." *CLA Journal* 18 (June 1975): 570–77.

Who's Who in America. Chicago: Marquis, 1976.

Ann C. Sullivan

Andrew F. Brimmer
(1926–)
Economist, educator, entrepreneur

The first black named to the Federal Reserve Board, for forty years Andrew Brimmer has shared his expertise in economics with both government and business. A teacher of economics as well, he addressed such issues as monetary policies, banking, and other economic matters. He has been a firm supporter of black economic development and condemns discrimination against black–owned businesses and in hiring practices.

Andrew Felton Brimmer was born on September 13, 1926, in Newellton, Louisiana, the son of Andrew, a sharecropper and warehouseman, and Vella Davis Brimmer. Brimmer comes from a family of two older sisters, Antoinette Bland and Josie Brisca, an older brother, George W., and a younger brother, James. In 1944, when he was 17–years old, Brimmer graduated from the all–black Tensa Parish Training School in St. Joseph, Louisiana, then moved to Bremerton, Washington, where one of his sisters lived.

Brimmer served in the U.S. Army as a staff sergeant in the 645th Ordnance Ammunition Company in Hawaii from May of 1945 to November of 1946. He supplemented a federal education grant for former servicemen with his own savings and enrolled in the University of Washington in January of 1947. Since he decided to major in journalism, he worked as assistant editor of the *Dispatch,* a weekly newspaper in Seattle. His faculty adviser persuaded him to change his major at the end of his sophomore year, with the claim that the profession was unpromising for blacks. After changing to economics—a profession he felt would enable him to resolve questions he had about life in the United States, he graduated with a bachelor's degree in 1950. That summer he began a relationship with the U.S. government as he worked as a student intern with the U.S. Economic Cooperation Administration in Washington, D.C.

With a fellowship from John Hay Whitney Foundation, Brimmer was able to undertake graduate work at the University of Washington, Seattle, and received an M.A. degree in economics in 1951. He received a Fulbright fellowship to study at the University of Delhi School of Economics from July through October of 1951, and at the University of Bombay from October of 1951 through March of 1952. As a result of his study in India, in 1954 and 1955 he published papers and articles on the economy of that country.

Brimmer returned to the United States in 1952 and was an economist with the Wage Stabilization Board in Seattle from May to September of 1952. He began study toward his doctoral degree in economics, with a concentration in monetary economics and economic development, at Harvard University in 1952. From January of 1953 to September of 1954 he was research assistant in the Center of International Studies, Massachusetts Institute of Technology. He was a teaching fellow in the department of economics at Hayward in 1954–55 while he completed his doctoral dissertation on "Monetary Policy, Interest Rates, and the Investment Behavior of Life Insurance Companies." From June of 1955 to August of 1958 Brimmer was an economist for New York City's Federal Reserve Bank.

Brimmer joined a three–member team that visited the Sudan from December of 1956 to March of 1957 to determine the feasibility of organizing a central bank there. By then he had gained considerable knowledge of foreign economies and later wrote "Banking and Finance in the Sudan," published in the March of 1960 *South African Journal of Economics.*

After receiving his Ph.D. from Harvard in 1957, Brimmer accepted a position as assistant professor of economics at Michigan State University in September of 1958. This position gave him more time to write. He remained at Michigan State until June of 1961. Brimmer then moved to the Wharton School of Finance and Commerce at the University of Pennsylvania, where he taught from 1961 to 1966. In 1962 he published *Life Insurance Companies on the Capital Markets* and prepared articles for such journals as the *Banker,* the *Journal of Finance,* and the *Review of Economics and Statistics.* He took a leave of absence from the Wharton School during academic years 1963–1966.

The John F. Kennedy Administration recruited Brimmer in 1963, and he became deputy to Richard Holton, Assistant Secretary of Commerce for Economic Affairs in the U.S. Department of Commerce. When Holton retired in 1965, Brimmer took his post. One of his primary charges was to address the international balance of payments deficit. To do this, he worked with American firms encouraging them to limit voluntarily their overseas investments. He asked foreign–owned firms located in the United States to use funds from abroad for their business. Although critics in the audiences he addressed in his public speeches contended that the federal government contributed to the trade deficit significantly, Brimmer argued that private investments might not be safe if federal foreign aid programs were discontinued. By December of 1965 Brimmer's mission had met with some success.

While with the U.S. Department of Commerce, Brimmer worked in an area that provided tremendous benefits to America's poor and those whose civil rights were violated. He prepared and presented testimony to Congress demonstrating the burden of racial segregation on interstate commerce. When the U.S. Supreme Court gave its unanimous decision upholding the constitutionality of the Public Accommodations section of the 1964 Civil Rights Act, it cited Brimmer's testimony. He also helped develop the Anti–Poverty Program. His work in the area of civil rights was extended in 1965, when President Lyndon B. Johnson named Brimmer to a three–member delegation to the Watts section of Los Angeles after the 1965 riot.

Heads Federal Reserve Board

Brimmer became the first black member of the Board of Governors of the Federal Reserve System, when President Lyndon B. Johnson appointed him to a 14–year term beginning March of 1966. He held the appointment eight and one–half years, then resigned in August of 1974. Brimmer spoke out continuously on issues that affected the economy.

Brimmer also wrote to President Gerald Ford on December 20, 1974, suggesting that a ten–percent rebate of 1974 personal income taxes would stimulate the economy and help bring an end to the recession of 1973–74. Congress modified his suggestion and enacted the provision that accounted for $8.1 billion of the $22.8 billion tax reduction passed early in 1975. According to Simeon Booker of *Ebony* magazine, "[Brimmer was] the best black economist ever to invade the ranks of the government's money crowd." Rather than join the ranks of the other members of the board, he pulled away as a standout. But he also saw problems that needed to be publicized. Although many economic gains had been made in the black community as early as 1970, he saw "a deepening schism" there. According to Harry Ploski of *The Negro Almanac,* Brimmer studied the figures and concluded, "[T]he gap is widening between the able and the less able, between the more prepared and those with few skills." He saw this as the result of "the growing militancy at the bottom end of the scale, where the disparity is most keenly felt." Although financial journals published his speeches widely, he never received the level of acclaim that he deserved in the black press. According to Booker, this may be due to the fact that he attacked some of the "fat cats in our community black bankers and little business people."

Brimmer was the Thomas Henry Carroll Ford Foundation visiting professor in the Graduate School of Business Administration at Harvard University from 1974 to 1976. Since July of 1976 Brimmer has been president of his firm, Brimmer and Company, located in Washington, D.C. The firm conducts research and counsels clients on trends in economic activity and prospects, developments affecting financial institutions, and interests rates in money and capital markets. He continues to teach and was named the Wilmer D. Barrett Professor of Economics at the University of Massachusetts at Amherst.

Washington, D.C., under the leadership of Mayor Marion Barry, experienced severe financial difficulties in 1995, and the city faced cutbacks in such services as collection of trash and recycling and drastic reductions in the number of employees. President Bill Clinton selected Brimmer to head a five–member District of Columbia Financial Responsibility and Management Assistance Authority to help balance the District's budget. The first appointees, who will serve three years without pay, include, in addition to Brimmer, former Howard University interim president Joyce A. Ladner, and under secretary of the Smithsonian Institution Constance B. Newman. In the move, Congress temporarily transferred considerable authority from elected officials to appointed officials and gave the control board authority to approve the appointment of agency heads. As head of the board, Brimmer has come under extreme pressure by community advocates, who opposed the board and Brimmer's position, and by some Republicans in Congress, who claim Brimmer's progress has been too slow. He resigned from the board in 1998.

As a director of the *Black Enterprise* Board of Economists, each year Brimmer publishes a forecast of the economic conditions of black Americans. In his report in the January 1996 issue of *Black Enterprise,* Brimmer expressed a belief that the U.S. labor force will increase moderately while "the African American labor force will expand much more rapidly." He also predicted "an increase in the black share of jobs and a small decrease in the black unemployment rate." While service jobs were to increase, he predicted increases in such areas as finance and transportation as well.

In addition to the professional positions Brimmer has held, has also served as director of the following business institutions: UAL Corporation of United Airlines, 1976–94; Equitable Life Assurance; MNC Financial Corporation, 1987–93 (while also serving its American Security Bank, 1976–93, and Maryland National Bank, 1989–93); Mercedes Benz Corporation of North America, 1990–93; and BellSouth Corporation, 1984–95. Brimmer's business affiliations include the directorship of two banking and financial markets—BankAmerica Corporation and Bank of America NT&SA, and BlackRock Investment Income Trust. He serves as director of the following corporations: Carr Realty Corporation, College Retirement Equities Fund, Connecticut Mutual Life Insurance Company, and PHH Corporation. Brimmer's expertise is sought as well by industrial firms, where he is director of E. I. du Pont de Nemours, and Navistar International Corporation. He is also affiliated with media, public utilities, and transportation corporations where he is director of Airborne Express and Gannett Company.

Brimmer has been affiliated with professional organizations as a member or office holder. These include the American Academy of Arts and Sciences (fellow), Association for the Study of Afro–American Life and History (president 1970–73 and 1989–90), American Association of Collegiate Schools of Business (National Honoree), and American Economic Association (vice–president, 1989, and distinguished lecturer). His memberships also include the American Finance Association, American Statistical Association, Council on Foreign Relations, Eastern Economic Association (president, 1991–92, fellow, 1993), National Association of Business Economists (fellow), National Economists Club, North American Economics and Finance Association (vice–president, 1995), Society of Government Economists (also Distinguished Lecturer, 1988), Washington Academy of Sciences (fellow), and Western Economic Association.

During his distinguished career, Brimmer has generously contributed his service to countless volunteer groups, institutions, and agencies. These include chairman, Tuskegee University Board of Trustees; director, National Bureau of Economic Research; governor and chairman, Joint Center for Political and Economic Studies; member Visiting Committee, Economic Studies, Brookings Institution; trustee, Urban Institute; Overseer of Hayward College, 1968–74 and 1987–

93; trustee, the Ford Foundation, 1974–80; Visiting Committee, Hayward Business School, 1977–83; Trustee, National Urban League, 1975–80; director, Chamber of Commerce of the United States, 1977–83; chair, Interracial Council for Business Opportunity, 1980–84; trustee, Committee for Economic Development, 1980–92; and governor and chair, Joint Center for Political and Economic Studies, 1987–94.

In recognition of his outstanding work, Brimmer has received wide acclaim. He was named the National Business League's Government Man of the Year in 1963. In 1966 he received the Arthur S. Flemming Award from the National Jaycees, who honored him as one of the ten outstanding young men in government service. That year he was also recipient of the National Newspaper Publishers Association's Russwurm Award and the Capital Press Club's Public Affairs Award. In 1972 the University of Washington gave him the highest distinction available to an alumnus, naming him Alumnus Summa Laude Dignatus. The National Urban League gave him the Horatio Alger Award and the Equal Opportunity Award in 1974. Other citations include the Brotherhood Award, One–hundred Black Men and the New York Urban Coalition, 1975; Distinguished Service Award, Interracial Council for Business Opportunity, 1986; Samuel Z. Westerfield Jr., Distinguished Achievement Award, National Economic Association, 1990; Outstanding Achievement Award, Washington Academy of Sciences, 1991; and the Leadership Award, Benjamin Banneker Honors College, Prairie View State University, 1991. Hayward University in 1995 awarded him the Hayward Medal for faithful and distinguished service to the university. Brimmer gave the Distinguished 40th Anniversary Fulbright Lecture in Ghana and Nigeria in 1986. He is also a member of Omicron Delta Epsilon honor society in economics.

Twenty–two academic institutions have recognized Brimmer's outstanding contributions and awarded him honorary degrees. Seventeen of these degrees were the Doctor of Laws, coming from such institutions as Oberlin College (1969), Atlanta University (now Clark Atlanta) and Tufts University (1970), the University of Notre Dame (1971), Temple University (1974), University of Maryland (1976), University of Michigan (1979), University of Southern California (1980), and Indiana University (1991). Two institutions awarded him the degree Doctor of Civil Law University of Miami (1971) and the University of the South (1984). Brimmer also received an honorary Doctor of Social Science, Boston College, 1971; Doctor of Humane Letters, De Paul University, 1975; and Doctor of Public Service, North Adams State College, 1987.

Brimmer is married to the former Doris Millicent Scott of New York City, who was a graduate student at Radcliffe in 1953 when they wed. They have one daughter, Esther Diane. He is a Democrat and a member of the Unitarian church. The five–feet ten–inch tall Brimmer enjoys tennis, hiking, and writing.

The son of a sharecropper who watched his father struggle during the Great Depression of the 1930s, Brimmer has become an authority on world banking—especially the United States's foreign debt obligation to Third World countries—on economic matters relating to the black community, and on general developments in financial institutions, interest rates, and money and capital markets. Highly regarded in the financial community, in the federal government, and in the area of economics education, Brimmer is both a noted economist and entrepreneur. He is widely acclaimed for his years of service and keen, analytical insight into the nation's economic development.

Current address: Brimmer and Company, 4400 MacArthur Boulevard, NW, Suite 302, Washington, DC 20007.

REFERENCES

''Andrew Brimmer: Prideful Economist is Capital's Local Power Center.'' *New York Times,* August 20, 1997.

''Biography of Andrew E. Brimmer.'' Washington, DC: Brimmer and Company, July 1995.

''Board of Economists Report.'' *Black Enterprise* 13 (June 1983): 252.

Booker, Simeon. ''Washington Notebook.'' *Ebony* 30 (February 1975): 28.

Brimmer, Andrew F. *The World Banking System: Outlook in a Context of Crisis.* New York: New York University Press, 1985.

''Brimmer Picked to Head Panel Overseeing D.C. Budget; Ladner, Newman Also Named.'' *Jet* 88 (19 June 1995): 50.

''Brimmer Quits Fed Post to Teach at Hayward U.'' *Jet* 46 (30 May 1974): 19.

Contemporary Black Biography. Vol. 2. Detroit: Gale Research, 1992.

Current Biography Yearbook. New York: H. W. Wilson, 1968.

De Witt, Karen. ''New Washington Leader.'' *New York Times,* June 1, 1995.

Lowry, Mark. ''B. E. Board of Economist Report.'' *Black Enterprise* 26 (January 1996): 68.

''The Money Men.'' *Ebony* 22 (September 1967): 65–68.

Negro Almanac. 5th ed. Detroit: Gale Research, 1989.

Who's Who among Black Americans, 1996–97. 9th ed. Detroit: Gale Research, 1996.

Jessie Carney Smith

Lonnie R. Bristow

(1930–)

Physician, organization executive

A devoted medical practitioner who was profoundly concerned with human dignity, patient care, affordable health care for all Americans, and diversity in the nation's medical academies, Lonnie Robert Bristow has become widely known as the first African American president of the American Medical Association (AMA). Accustomed to being a pioneer in medical organizations, since 1981, when he became the first African American president of the American Society of Internal Medicine. Bristow was also the first African American member and first African American chair of the AMA's Board of Trustees.

Born on April 6, 1930, in New York City, Bristow was the son of Lonnie Harlis Bristow, a Baptist minister, and Vivian Wines Bristow, a nurse. He had one brother named Edward. Bristow grew up in Harlem where his mother often included him in her activities as a student nurse, when he was only ten years old. When he was twelve years old, he walked his mother home from the Sydenham Hospital when her shift as emergency room nurse ended at 11:00 each night. At times, she would have the doctors talk to him about their work. Bristow also glanced inside the hospital where he saw doctors and nurses who were African American, Hispanic, or Jewish engaged in the bustling of emergency room. He told Lisa C. Jones of *Ebony,* "To me, at that age [they] were real miracle workers. They were my heroes, and I wanted to be like them." This early experience stimulated Bristow to pursue a career in medicine and, later, also affected his attitude about multiculturalism and the importance of being well qualified professionally regardless of race.

After graduating from the High School of Commerce in New York City, Bristow studied at Morehouse College, in Atlanta, from 1947 to 1949, where he became acquainted with Martin Luther King Jr., who was also enrolled at the historically African American college. He was on active duty in the U.S. Navy for one year, from 1949 to 1950, and then became a Naval Reservist from 1950 to 1956. Bristow entered the City College of New York where he enjoyed local fame as a quarterback on the football team and even considered becoming a professional player. He graduated with a BS degree, in 1953, and entered New York University College of Medicine where he earned a MD degree, in 1957. From 1957 to 1958, he did a rotating internship at San Francisco City and County Hospital. From 1959 to 1960, Bristow served a residency in internal medicine at the Veteran's Administration Hospital in San Francisco. He completed his third year of residency at Francis Delafield Hospital (Columbia University Service), in New York City, and at the Veteran's Administration Hospital in Bronx, New York, in 1961. He completed an additional residency in occupational medicine at the University of California's School of Medicine in San Francisco, in 1981. Since 1964, he has been in private practice in San Pablo, California, specializing in internal medicine. He also specialized in job–related medical illnesses. In his practice, his primary concern was for improving the quality of life, for his patients. He was also on the staff of Brookside Hospital, in San Pablo.

In addition to a successful medical practice as an internist, Bristow has been highly active in medical societies which brought him wide recognition. In 1981, he was the first African American elected president of the American Society of Internal Medicine.

Bristow's affiliation with the AMA began when he joined the association, in California, after he completed his internship, in 1958. This occurred ten years before the AMA

Lonnie R. Bristow

passed a policy prohibiting any member state or county society from discriminating on the basis of race. This was as much an epoch–making event for Bristow as it was for the AMA. In 1958, the association still suffered from the after effects of discriminatory practices by some states early on, that inspired a group of African American physicians to found their own medical organization, in 1895, the National Medical Association. Moreover, state and local medical societies were so slow to change their posture on African American memberships that African American physicians picketed the AMA's annual meetings from 1963 to 1968 to force the association to bring pressure on these groups and on state and county hospitals, since a prerequisite for joining the AMA was membership in state and county medical groups. In 1968, the AMA responded by adopting bylaws banning racial discrimination, bypassing state and local membership requirements and accepting direct memberships.

For 20 years Bristow held a series of posts and served in the AMA well. He was an alternate delegate to the AMA House of Delegates, in 1978, and has been a delegate from the American Society of Internal Medicine, since 1979. He was a member of the AMA's Council of Medical Service, in 1979, and chaired the council from 1983 until 1985. He was elected to the Board of Trustees, in 1985 and served as its vice–chair from 1992 to 1993. Bristow achieved another first, in 1993, when he was elected chairman of the board.

Bristow has held a number of positions in the AMA. He was secretary–treasurer of the AMA Education and Research Foundation from 1986 to 1988 and its president from 1988 to 1990. From 1990 to 1993, he represented the AMA as a commissioner to the Joint Commission on Accreditation of Healthcare Organizations. Since 1990, he has been a member of the Executive Committee. His first post at the AMA's governing level came, in 1985, when he was the first African American elected to the Board of Trustees.

Bristow, already board chair and candidate for AMA president–elect, became a key leader pushing the AMA's position for health care reform. The policy was called Health Access America and had been developed in 1990, three years before the debate in the government had taken fire. Although the AMA's plan called for universal access, it was in marked conflict with the regulatory approach advocated by the Clinton Administration. In a three–hour interview with Dennis L. Breo for the AMA journal, Bristow said that the battle "dwarfs the fight over Medicare." He called health system reform "the most important issue that AMA has faced in the 20th century." Bristow had entered organized medicine to help establish affordable health care for all patients. "There is more to medicine than making the correct diagnosis," he continued. "Unless your patients can afford the treatment the diagnosis demands, you have accomplished nothing."

American Medical Association Elects First African American President

Bristow received widespread public acclaim in June 1995 when he was inaugurated as president of AMA. He became the first African American to take the helm in the society's 148–year history. He ran unopposed for the one–year term the previous year and became president–elect. Despite the honor, Bristow preferred to downplay the historic feat by calling it a reflection of the changes now occurring in society. As he accepted the office at the AMA's opening session, Bristow was reported as saying, the *Chicago Tribune,* "This is a day of firsts. I am not unaware that I will be the first specialty candidate, and the first African–American ever to head America's most prestigious medical organization. However, neither fact will define my term in office."

Bristow told Jones that his ability to compete in the "market for ideas" and not his race led to "his ascension through the AMA's ranks." He acknowledged, as well, that hard work and education contributed to his election. Nonetheless, Bristow aimed to continue AMA's efforts to emphasize issues of diversity and to attract more minorities to the medical academies in America. Realizing that fewer than three percent of all physicians in America are African American, Bristow called for adequate numbers of care givers who represent the demographic interests of minority communities so that competent and culturally–sensitive care will be available. He was an advocate of greater unity among the nation's physicians. Through his work he hoped to inspire the youth of all races and women.

As president and chief spokesman of the 300,000–member organization America's largest leading organization for doctors, he watched students' faces light up, in such medical schools as Meharry Medical College in Nashville and Morehouse School of Medicine, in Atlanta, when he reminded them that they may take his place one day. According to *Jet,* he told them, "I'm just keeping this seat warm for you. I want you to come and get it."

Although the task ahead for Bristow was enormous, he was firm in his views of the profession and medical care. He envisioned a time when the American people will see the AMA as their association and will understand fully its purpose and function. He wanted to know public reaction to the AMA's work and to know the public's expectations and anxieties about health care. He was opposed to the tobacco industry and, soon after his election, predicted, with accuracy, an intensified fight with the industry. The AMA would continue to oppose "Joe Camel," the big–nosed cartoon mascot for Camel cigarettes. Bristow was an advocate of health clubs for children and older Americans where they would study and learn how to derive greater benefits from medical care. He was an advocate of legislation to end "managed profiteering" by health maintenance organizations run by corporations.

Beyond his practice and AMA activities, Bristow has been active in other facets of organized medicine. From 1976 to 1977, he was a consultant to the California Department for Health Care in Prisons, in Sacramento, and, from 1976 to 1979, he was the chairman of the Sickle Cell Committee, for the California Department of Health. He has served as a member of the Genetic Disease Committee, from, 1977–79, and the Admissions Committee, of the University of California, Berkeley, from, 1972–75. Bristow has served on the National Council of Health Care Technology, Washington, DC, in 1980, and on physicians discussion group on physicians' payment, Health Care Financing Administration, in Washington, DC, from 1983–86. From 1987 to 1989, he held an appointed membership on the Institute of Medicine's Committee on the Effects of Medical Professional Liability on the Delivery of Maternal and Child Health Care. In 1988, the U.S. Surgeon General appointed Bristow to serve on the Federal Interagency Committee on Smoking and Health, and the Secretary of Human Services appointed him to serve on both the Center for Disease Control's HIV Prevention Advisory Committee and the 1989 Quadrennial Advisory Council on Social Security. He was a member of the American Society of Internal Medicine, serving as a trustee, from 1976 to 1983, and president, from 1981 to 1982. He also chaired the Section on Internal Medicine of the California Medical Association.

Bristow became a diplomat of the American Board of Internal Medicine and later a master of the American College of Physicians. Widely honored for his work, he won the annual Award of Excellence from the California Medical Political Action Committee and was elected a member of the National Academy of Science's Institute of Medicine, both, in 1977. His honors also include honorary Doctor of Science degrees from the Morehouse College School of Medicine (1994), Wayne State University School of Medicine (1995), and the City College of the City University of New York (1995).

Bristow's research interests included medical ethics, socialized medicine, as practiced in Great Britain, Canada, and China, health care financing, in America, professional liability insurance problems, sickle cell anemia, and coronary care utilization. He lectured extensively on medical science, socioeconomic, and ethical issues related to medicine, and served as reviewer for the *Journal of the American Medical Association.*

As head of the AMA, Bristow's responsibilities intensified, leaving little time for activities beyond private practice which was reduced to one day a week. There was no time for the once–avid jogger to run. Bristow spent the little free time he had collecting vintage radio tapes and reading books on African American history and the Civil War. He still spent some time in the kitchen, preparing his some of his specialties including, fiery–hot chili and champagne–soaked black–eyed peas with a wild flavor.

Described as a calm man and a skilled and compassionate physician who respected human dignity, Bristow took these traits with him into the presidency of the AMA. He married his first wife, Margaret Jeter, on June 1, 1957, and they had one daughter, Mary. They later divorced and, on October 18, 1961, he married Marilyn Hingslage, a registered nurse who managed his clinic in his absence. They had a son, Robert, and a daughter Elizabeth. The Bristows lived in Walnut Creek, California.

Bristow's elevation to head of the nation's largest medical group was in recognition of a person who had dedicated a lifetime to the health care of all his patients. Bristow was also responsible for forging a new role and image for the AMA. He left the position when his term expired, in 1997, and returned to his full–time medical practice.

Current address: c/o American Medical Association, 515 North State Street, Chicago, IL 60610.

REFERENCES

''AMA Elects 1st Black President.'' *Chicago Tribune,* June 13, 1994.

American Medical Association. Biographical fact sheet of Lonnie R. Bristow, 1995–1996.

American Men and Women of Science, 1995–96. 19th ed. New Providence, NJ: Bowker, 1995.

Breo, Dennis L. ''Choosing the Right Medicine: AMA's Lonnie Bristow, MD, Talks Reform.'' Interview. *Journal of the American Medical Association* 271 (February 16, 1994): 562–67.

Bristow, Lonnie R. Fax to Jessie Carney Smith, September 25, 1995 and October 23, 1995.

''Dr. Lonnie Bristow Takes Helm As 1st Black President of American Medical Association.'' *Jet* 88 (10 July 1995): 38–40.

Jones, Lisa C. ''New American Medical Association President.'' *Ebony* 50 (August 1995): 82, 85.

''New Leader Wants AMA to Reach Out, Be Relevant.'' *Philadelphia Inquirer,* June 22, 1994.

Who's Who in America. 46th ed. Willamette, IL: Marquis Who's Who, 1990.

Jessie Carney Smith

Edward W. Brooke

(1919–)

U.S. Senator, state attorney general, lawyer, military officer

Born into a world that invariably tried to view or describe him primarily by the color of his skin, Edward Brooke has obdurately insisted that society focus on his careers rather than his race. As a World War II officer, attorney, Massachusetts attorney general, and U.S. senator, Brooke has exerted his considerable influence in efforts to benefit all Americans.

Edward William Brooke III was born on October 26, 1919, in Washington, D.C. His father, Edward Brooke Jr., graduated from Howard University's School of Law in 1918 and for 50 years was an attorney for the Veterans Administration—a rare position for a black American at that time. His mother, Helen Seldon Brooke, would later be active in each of Brooke's campaigns; Brooke regarded his mother as an effective speaker on the campaign trail. In 1966 the National Shriners named her Mother of the Year.

Brooke lived with his parents and his older sister, Helene, in a middle–class Washington neighborhood. He attended Minor Teachers' College, a teacher–training school; William Lloyd Garrison and John F. Cooke elementary schools; Robert Gould Shaw Junior High School; and the historic Dunbar High School, considered by many the finest black high school in America. He graduated from Dunbar in 1936. Reflecting on his youth as cited in Cutler's biography, *Edward Brooke,* he remarked:

> I was a happy child. I was conscious of being a Negro, yes, but I was not conscious of being underprivileged because of that. . . . I grew up segregated, but there was not much feeling of being shut out of anything. . . . When we couldn't buy tickets for a concert or the opera in the segregated theaters of Washington, my mother simply took us to New York to Carnegie Hall or the Metropolitan.

At the age of 16, Brooke entered Howard University with plans of becoming a surgeon; however, upon finding science courses boring, he changed his major to sociology. His political science course was taught by Ralph Bunche, who later earned distinction as a diplomat, statesman, and Nobel Prize winner. Brooke was elected president of Beta Chapter of the Alpha Phi Alpha fraternity in his senior year. He later became eastern national vice president of the organization. He received his B.S. from Howard in 1941.

Distinguished Military Service

After graduating from college and the Reserve Officers Training Corps, Brooke was drafted into the army. He served as a second lieutenant in the all–black 366th Combat Infantry Regiment. At Massachusetts' Fort Devens, Brooke, in charge of discipline and recreation, also had the opportunity to

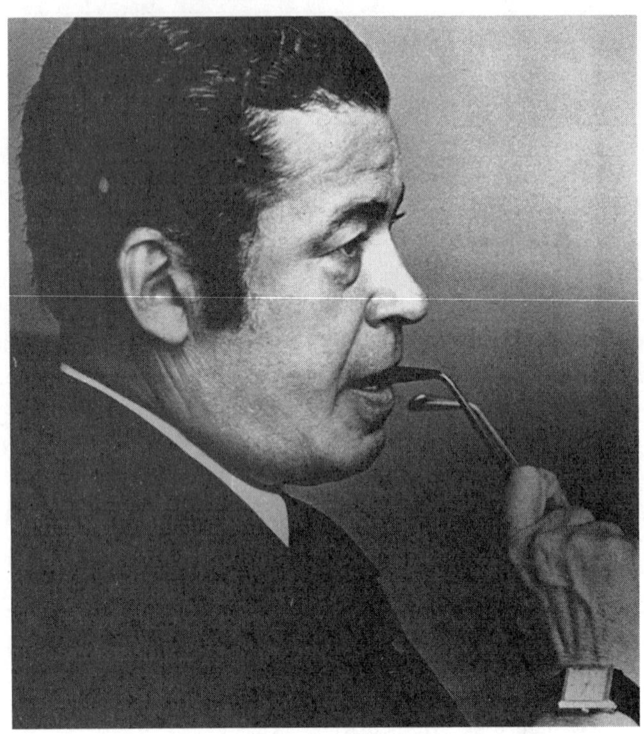

Edward W. Brooke

defend enlisted men in military court cases. The 366th's travels included North Africa and Italy. Brooke spent 195 days in combat and was promoted to captain. He received the Bronze Star for his leadership in a daylight attack on an artillery battery and observation post that was heavily fortified. In *Challenge of Change,* Brooke, who also received the Distinguished Service Award, described the situation experienced by members of the 366th. He said that the men fought hard and well, and despite heavy casualties, maintained a high morale. Because the regiment was segregated, however, there was an undercurrent of resentment in the unit. They were also "treated as second–class soldiers." He said:

> Our soldiers (first–class by any definition) asked, "Why are *we* fighting this war? It's supposed to be a war against Nazism—against racism and for democracy. Well, what about *us?* Why are black men fighting a white man's war? What's all this double–talk about democracy?" They were not easy questions to answer. I tried to explain that the first task was to defeat the common enemy. And I asked them to bear with America's racial injustices until the war was won. But I knew that this was no more than a rationalization.

Brooke continued to serve as a defense counsel in court martial cases and also assumed the identity of an Italian, Captain Carlo, in order to cross enemy lines as a liaison officer with the Italian partisans.

Before returning to the United States in 1945, Brooke met Remigia Ferrari–Scacco, the daughter of a prominent Genoan paper merchant. For two years they maintained a long–distance relationship by mail. They were married on June 7, 1947, in Roxbury, Massachusetts.

Law School and Beyond

Brooke's experience with legal proceedings motivated him to enroll in Boston University Law School in September of 1946. He served as editor of the *Boston University Law Review* and received an LL.B. in 1948 and an LL.M. in 1949. Brooke took the bar examination with 598 candidates and was among the 197 who passed.

Brooke began practicing law in Roxbury. He rejected offers to join other law firms, including a request from his father. The elder Brooke, who had never practiced private law, wanted to establish a father and son firm in Washington. When Brooke invited his father to join him in Boston, his father declined. Brooke later moved his office to downtown Boston.

Brooke's friends encouraged him to enter politics. Having decided to seek election to the Massachusetts legislature, Brooke, a man who had previously never voted (Washington, D.C., residents did not have the right to vote), ran in the 1950 Democratic and Republican Primaries in a practice known as cross–filing. He won the Republican nomination but lost the general election.

Brooke's political ambition caused domestic friction. Remigia Brooke was upset by the unkind comments about their interracial marriage during the 1950 campaign. Brooke reportedly considered abandoning his political aspirations.

In 1952 Brooke sought office a second time. In the first Massachusetts primary in which candidates were not allowed to cross–file, Brooke filed as a Republican in his bid for the state legislature. His campaign was unsuccessful. During the next eight years, Brooke focused on his law practice and increased his involvement in community affairs. He was the second vice president of the Boston branch of the NAACP, a member of the board of directors of the Greater Boston Urban League, director of the Boston Council of the Boy Scouts, state commander and national judge advocate of the American Veterans of World War II, and a member of numerous civic clubs.

In 1960 Brooke entered his third political race. In his bid to capture Massachusetts' third highest office—secretary of state—he became the first black to be nominated for a statewide office in Massachusetts. Brooke boldly sought election in a state where only 93,000 blacks resided by campaigning as an American rather than a member of a minority group. Although Brooke lost the election, he made an impressive showing with over one million votes. After the 1960 election, Brooke rejected several governmental appointments before accepting the chairmanship of the Boston Finance Commission. Until Brooke's association with the organization, it accomplished little. Under Brooke's leadership, the commission exposed corruption in the city's building, real estate, and fire departments. He benefited from the frequent publicity generated by the commission's activities; Brooke was now one of the most popular political figures in Massachusetts.

In 1962 Brooke sought the office of attorney general of Massachusetts. Although Republican leaders had endorsed Brooke's candidacy for lesser positions in previous elections, they were reluctant to offer him their support for the second highest position in the state. Thus the GOP offered him opportunities to run for lieutenant governor or to accept a judgeship, but Brooke would not be swayed. He went on to win his party's nomination and to win the primary and general election. He was the only Republican elected statewide that year, and he was the first black American to be elected to a major state office.

In 1964 Brooke ran for re–election as attorney general, although his supporters encouraged him to run for governor. During his two terms as attorney general, he continued to battle corruption in government and elsewhere. He endorsed and proposed legislation that, among other results, protected consumers, ended housing discrimination, and reduced air pollution. Brooke endured the wrath of civil rights leaders when he labeled the 1963 black student boycott to protest segregation of Boston schools illegal. Brooke told his critics that as a lawyer and attorney general, he had to serve all the people of Massachusetts; to do any less would result in his failing to do justice to his office or to advance the cause of civil rights.

Junior Senator from Massachusetts

In 1965 Brooke announced his candidacy for the U.S. Senate. Some people believe that Brooke's book published in 1966, *The Challenge of Change: Crisis in Our Two–Party System,* was an important campaign asset; in it he urged the Republican party to be more responsive to social change, and he wrote, "The conquest of space, the soaring increase in our national wealth, the flowering of our arts and sciences—our finest achievements are tarnished while more than a tenth of all Americans remain second–class citizens because of the color of their skins." Brooke won the election with a plurality of more than 400,000 votes. He became the third black American to serve in the Senate.

Upon returning to the city of his birth, Brooke received a standing ovation as he was escorted down the aisle of the Senate chamber by the senior senator from Massachusetts, Edward Kennedy, at his swearing–in ceremony. He wished his father had been in the gallery and thought about his father's frustrations about not having the opportunity to do more. His father would not have "foreseen that some day his son would sit in the U.S. Senate," Brooke wrote. He continued:

> There was one scene I shall never forget. As I left the Capitol building I noticed hundreds of high–school students crowding the steps, some from Mississippi and some from Cardozo High School in Washington. I thought of what my grandmother used to say—"Stay in your place." This advice was given to protect me from injury, because if you didn't follow this advice, you knew what would happen. But this was a statement I never could accept. Your place is anywhere you want to make it.

Brooke served two terms in Congress, where he became one of the most respected members of the Senate. During his first year, Vietnam and civil rights issues claimed much of his attention. Several months after his swearing–in ceremony, he traveled to South Vietnam and other Asian destinations on a fact–finding mission. Upon his return, Brooke demanded that the United States replace deadly napalm with tear gas, and he said that Americans continued to fundamentally support the South Vietnamese. While America, Brooke added, was ready to discuss settlement of the discord, military and economic assistance to the South Vietnamese would continue as needed.

During the summer of 1967, racial riots occurred in urban areas throughout the United States. President Johnson appointed Brooke to the President's Commission on Civil Disorders. One of the commission's recommendations was the protection of blacks and civil rights workers from harassment. Brooke and Senator Edward Mondale asked that the recommendations be broadened to include housing discrimination; it was ultimately approved by the House and Senate in the 1968 Civil Rights Act.

Brooke was also a Senate advocate of affirmative action, minority business development, school integration, improving the Social Security program, increasing the minimum wage, and increasing Medicare funds. As early as 1968, Brooke called for an end of U.S. trade with South Africa because of its oppression of blacks.

Brooke, who had endorsed President Richard M. Nixon in the 1968 and 1972 campaigns, clashed with the president on a number of issues, including Brooke's failure to vote for three Nixon nominees to the Supreme Court. Brooke became the first senator to publicly call for Nixon's resignation for his involvement in the Watergate scandal.

In 1978 Brooke was defeated in the General Election by Paul Tsongas. Brooke, the recipient of more than 30 honorary degrees and various awards, including the NAACP Spingarn Medal and the National Conference of Christians and Jews' Charles Evans Hughes Award, resumed his law practice after his senatorial career ended.

Brooke and his first wife, Remigia, were divorced in 1978; they have two daughters: Remi and Edwina. In 1979 Brooke married Anne Fleming; they have one son, Edward W. Brooke IV. The Brookes live in Virginia.

Brooke is a man who defies classification. He is a black American who demands recognition for his career accomplishments rather than his race. He is a Republican who sometimes appeared more Democratic than some of his Democratic colleagues in the Senate. Above all, Edward Brooke has endeavored to make America a better place for all Americans.

Current address: 2500 Virginia Avenue, NW, Washington, DC 20037.

REFERENCES

Brooke, Edward W. *The Challenge of Change: Crisis in Our Two–Party System.* Boston: Little, Brown, 1966.

Christian, Charles. *Black Saga: The African American Experience.* Boston: Houghton Mifflin, 1995.

Christopher, Maurine. *America's Black Congressmen.* New York: Thomas Y. Crowell, 1971.

Clay, William L. *Just Permanent Interests: Black Americans in Congress, 1870–1991.* New York: Amistad Press, 1992.

Contemporary Black Biography. Vol. 8. Detroit: Gale Research, 1995.

Cutler, John Henry. *Ed Brooke: Biography of a Senator.* Indianapolis: Bobbs–Merrill, 1972.

Kranz, Rachel C. *The Biographical Dictionary of Black Americans.* New York: Facts on File, 1992.

Salzman, Jack, David Lionel Smith, and Cornel West, eds. *Encyclopedia of African–American Culture and History.* New York: Macmillan Library Reference USA/Simon and Schuster Macmillan, 1996.

Who's Who among African Americans, 1996–97. 9th ed. Detroit: Gale Research, 1996.

Who's Who in America, 1996. 50th ed. New Providence, NJ: Reid Reference, 1995.

Linda M. Carter

Grafton Tyler Brown

(1841–1919)

Painter, lithographer, draftsman, engineer, entrepreneur

The magnificent landscapes of California, Washington, Oregon, and British Columbia were recorded in precise detail in the lithographs and oil paintings of Grafton Brown, an early black artist who worked in the Far West during the 1860s through the early 1890s.

Born in Harrisburg, Pennsylvania, on February 22, 1841, Grafton Tyler Brown was the first child of Thomas and Wilhelmina Brown. Thus far the circumstances concerning his move to San Francisco are unknown. Some sources reported that, in the 1850s he was living in a boarding house in San Francisco called What Cheer House. Other sources claimed that he had moved to San Francisco by 1861.

Regardless of the time of his relocation, he was employed as a draftsman for the firm of Kuchel and Dressel, later moving to the position of lithographer. Kuchel and Dressel specialized in capturing views of Western mining towns and California cities and printed street maps, stock certificates, diplomas, letterheads, stock certificates, and sheet music. On behalf of the firm, Brown visited new towns and cities and sketched their principal streets and buildings. The lithographs were in demand by settlers in the boomtowns of the Far West as well as by would–be settlers. Brown's designs included a number of Western towns, such as Santa Rosa, California, and Fort Churchill and Virginia City, Nevada. After Kuchel died, Brown continued to work with the firm and managed it for Kuchel's widow.

In 1867 Brown opened his own business, G. T. Brown and Company, located at 520 Clay Street in San Francisco. He became known for his fine designs of stock certificates and lithographs of California towns, and his lithographs of San Francisco were especially popular. While sources differ on the date, sometime between 1869 and 1879 Brown sold his company to one of his employees and moved to Victoria, British Columbia. He appeared to have kept an office on Clay Street. In Victoria he joined the Amos Bowman team that conducted a geological survey for the Canadian government. Brown traveled widely on the expedition and made a number of detailed pencil sketches. When he returned to Victoria in the fall of 1882, he reproduced many of his works in watercolor. His works were known for their precision, sharp detail, and fidelity to the original scenes.

The *Williams British Columbia Directory,* cited in *The Afro–American Artist,* listed Brown in an 1883 advertisement as an artist, living at the Occidental Hotel in Victoria. Beginning in June 1883, Brown held a number of exhibits of his works. His first exhibit showcased 22 paintings, including *Long Lake* and *The Gorge.* According to Samella Lewis in *Art: African American,* he drew praise from the local press as "the originator of intellectual and refined art," while critics called him "a great painter of realism." His works also appealed especially to young people in Victoria. He sold several of his paintings.

Brown continued to travel. In 1884 and 1885, he captured in paint the mountain landscapes of the state of Washington. From 1886 through 1890 he was listed in Portland, Oregon's directories as an artist and joined the Portland Art Club. He used letterhead with his mountain scenes to advertise his work: Mt. Tacoma, Mt. Hood, and Mt. Baker—as well as scenes from the Puget Sound. He visited the Grand Canyon, where in 1889 he painted the Lower Falls. The fine precision of his earlier works were still reflected in his paintings of this period. During his stay in San Francisco, his work may have been influenced by Chinese artists, although his use of an elevated vantage point is uncharacteristic of most Sung paintings.

The last 25 years of Brown's life were spent in St. Paul, Minnesota, where he lived at 646 Hague Avenue. From 1892 to 1910 he was a draftsman for the U.S. Engineers and the St. Paul Civil Engineering Department. There is no evidence that he continued to paint or to produce lithographs for sale in Minnesota. The fact that he continued to work as a draftsman suggests that the sale of his paintings did not afford a comfortable living. By 1911 he was no longer listed in local directories.

Brown suffered either seizure or a stroke about 1911 and was unconscious for a time. He recovered, but his health gradually deteriorated. By 1911 he had become and on

February 13, 1918, entered St. Peter State Hospital in Minnesota, dying there on March 2 of pneumonia and arteriosclerosis. He was 77 years old. He was survived by his wife, whom he married in 1896.

Of his work, Bearden and Henderson noted that he gave "equal emphasis to all the objects on his canvas" and was unable to "select a focal point. . .and organize a painting around it." On the other hand, artist and art critic David Driskell, in *Two Centuries of Black American Art,* commented that Brown was an itinerant artist of the late 1800s, who had a "semi–naturalistic style that records geographic locations so realistically that often they can still be identified from nature." He should be remembered as a pioneer artist of the West, who captured the picturesque scenery of that area in art.

REFERENCES

Bearden, Romare, and Harry Henderson. *A History of African–American Artists from 1792 to the Present.* New York: Pantheon Books, 1993.

Driskell, David C. *Two Centuries of Black American Art.* New York: Los Angeles County Museum of Art and Alfred A. Knopf, 1976.

Fine, Elsa Honig. *The Afro–American Artist: A Search for Identity.* New York: Hacker Books, 1982.

Lewis, Samella. *Art: African American.* New York: Harcourt Brace Jovanovich, 1978.

COLLECTIONS

The works of Grafton Tyler Brown are in the Kahn Collection of the Oakland, California, Museum.

Jessie Carney Smith

James Brown
(1933–)
Musician, composer

James Brown is a major American musician. He first gained prominence in the field of rhythm and blues, and then was instrumental in developing the fusion of R&B with gospel that became soul. His search for new sounds led the way from soul to funk, and his music remains an inspiration to the new generation of hip hop and rap musicians. Brown achieved immense popularity with frantic stage performances and a series of hit records that yielded more chart–topping songs than any other performer or band except for Elvis Presley and the Beatles. His driving belief in himself allowed him to overcome his apparently unpromising origins and made Brown an emblem of black pride for many people.

James Joe Brown Jr. was born on May 3, 1933, to Joe Brown and Susie Behlings Brown nine miles from Barnwell, South Carolina. James appeared stillborn, but his great–aunt Minnie Walker was able revive him. The child was supposed to be named for his father, with James added as a middle name, but the given names were reversed on the birth registration. The "junior" was retained nonetheless, and to his family he was known as Junior or—when living with an elder cousin also called Junior—as Little Junior.

When Brown was four his mother departed, and he did not see her again for more than 20 years. For the next two years James Brown was alone much of the time. In his solitude he learned to play the harmonica. Finally Joe Brown asked Minnie Walker to join him in caring for the child, and at the end of 1938 the family moved to Augusta, Georgia.

In Augusta James Brown and great–aunt Minnie Walker lived at 944 Twiggs Street with another aunt, Handsome (Honey) Washington, and Washington's grandson Willie Glenn Jr. (Big Junior) in a whorehouse. Both Jack Scott, who was Washington's brother and ran the house, and Joe Brown were violent men who beat the child severely on occasion.

James Brown ran into problems in school because of his background. A neglected child, he was sent home at least twice for insufficient clothing. Still, he became popular at school because of his athletic ability and his musical talents. Out of school James Brown and Jack Scott made money by dancing in the streets and soliciting business for the house. Brown also learned to play the drums, the piano, and some guitar. One of his occasional mentors on the guitar was the famous blues guitarist Tampa Red (Hudson Whittaker), although James Brown did not generally like the blues.

During World War II the federal government began a crackdown on prostitution, forcing the shutdown of redlight districts nationwide. The Twiggs Street house was closed down, and James Brown and Minnie Walker moved into a two–room house. Joe Brown was drafted into the U.S. Navy, and a monthly allotment check for $37.50 supported his son and Minnie Walker during his absence. This meager income was augmented only by what James Brown could hustle in the streets. Brown continued his interest in music. In particular, he became interested in the movie shorts of Louis Jordan and his Tympany Five. Brown began to win amateur night contests with his singing, first at the Lennox Theater and later in Harlem. He also formed a group, the Cremona Trio.

When he became a teenager, James Brown was more interested in sports than music, especially boxing and baseball. His career aims were seriously jeopardized by another of his activities—burglary. After a first arrest for which he received a warning, he was arrested again and charged with four counts of burglary. Brown turned 16 in jail and was tried as an adult. On June 13, 1949, he pled guilty and received two to four years for each of the four counts. The sentences were to be served consecutively. Brown was taken to the Georgia Juvenile Training Institute in Rome, Georgia.

James Brown

Music and sports eased Brown's adaptation to reformatory life. He formed a gospel quartet soon after his arrival, and a band using homemade instruments. Because of his music activity he was nicknamed Music Box. In 1951 the reformatory was moved from Rome to Toccoa. There he became a trustee and met a local boy with a reputation as a musician, Bobby Byrd. On June 14, 1952, Brown was paroled on the condition that he stay out of Augusta and Richmond County. He got a job at an automobile agency washing cars and cleaning up.

Brown lost his job at the car agency after taking a customer's car out for an unauthorized spin and bringing it back damaged. This stunt jeopardized his parole, but the Byrd family helped him appease his parole officer, and soon he found a job in a plastics factory. Meanwhile, Brown formed a gospel group, the Every Ready Gospel Singers, with three women, then joined Bobby Byrd's group, which was then comprised of seven musicians. Since their only instrument was a piano, the group used their voices to imitate other instruments. After flirting with gospel music, the group developed a repertory of ten rhythm and blues numbers and began to pick up a few dollars performing at area juke joints, using the name The Toccoa Band. Local bookings began to pick up, but Brown had a couple more close brushes with having his parole revoked.

On June 19, 1953, Brown married Velma Warren. This marriage produced three sons, Teddy, Terry, and Larry. The marriage broke up around 1957; Brown began a relationship with another woman. The couple officially separated in 1964 and divorced in 1969.

Helps Create the Famous Flames

Just about the time of Brown's marriage, the band ran into internal problems from jealousy over the lead positions assumed by Brown and Byrd. Since the band's success was growing, the members resolved their problems and, to mark a new start, took a new name, the Flames. Brown began to create his own material with the song ''Please, Please, Please,'' which became the regular closing number for the group. On occasion in later years, Brown would work the audience and sing this song for as long as 40 minutes until he was so exhausted that he had to be helped off the stage.

The Flames became a well–established local group. In search of greater recognition, they took over the stage uninvited during the intermission in a show by Little Richard, who would soon cut his first major hit ''Tutti Frutti.'' They made such an impression that Little Richard's manager, Clint Brantly, of Macon, signed them. Brown had to receive the permission of the parole board for his move to Macon. Brantly renamed the group the Famous Flames, and they began to find more lucrative gigs. When Little Richard suddenly left his band after his first big hits, Brantly called on Brown to appear as Little Richard in 15 appearances.

Brown received the tacit approval from his parole officer for trips out of state, but he still continued to run into problems that threatened his freedom. In one instance, Brown was arrested and held in jail after a traffic accident. A warrant for his return to prison was issued on October 28, 1955, but Clint Brantly was influential enough to smooth over the difficulty.

Soon thereafter the Famous Flames' song ''Please, Please, Please,'' became extremely popular locally when a Macon radio station aired it. The recording attracted the attention of Ralph Bass, a talent scout for Cincinnati–based King Records, a small independent label run by Syd Nathan. When the group arrived in Cincinnati to record, Syd Nathan immediately disliked ''Please, Please, Please,'' and had to be persuaded to record it. After a slow start the song reached number six on the Billboard Rhythm and Blues chart, remained on the charts for 19 weeks, and eventually sold over a million copies. As is customary with new artists, the direct financial returns were meager—the money came from touring.

The Famous Flames attracted the attention of Ben Bart of Universal Attractions in New York, who began booking the group. Eventually he became Brown's manager and business partner and one of the few persons Brown fully trusted. Even as this relationship began, King Records was beginning to lose interest in the group since the records after *Please, Please, Please* did not sell well. As part of the campaign to rebuild the group's recognition, in early 1957 Bart recommended changing the name to James Brown and the Famous Flames. The name change reignited old jealousies, and everyone but Brown left the group—an incident that would recur in Brow's relations with his future bands.

In late 1957 Brown recorded for King Records again with little success. Then Brown made a demonstration recording of ''Try Me,'' which Nathan refused to issue. Air play, however, built up such a demand for the song that it was re–

recorded on October 18, 1958, and went immediately to number one on the rhythm and blues charts and 48 on the pop charts when it was issued the following month. In January of 1959 Brown's first album, called *Please, Please, Please,* was released to great success.

After recruiting and dissolving another group of Flames in early 1959, Brown had two weeks to recruit a third group for an appearance at New York's Apollo Theater. Bobby Byrd rejoined the group for the occasion and remained with Brown for many years. At the Apollo the group's success took it from the opening spot to the next–to–last position. The day after the engagement closed, Brown saw his mother for the first time since she had left him more than 20 years earlier.

Brown continued to argue with Syd Nathan about recordings. Using an assumed name, Brown and his band issued *Mashed Potatoes, Parts One and Two* on Dade Records in February of 1959. This record made the rhythm and blues chart's top ten. Brown continued to work hard, performing as many as 350 nights a year in an act noted for its high level of energy and fast dancing. These efforts earned him the title "The Hardest Working Man in Show Business," and a growing black audience. Brown also became famous for the tight discipline of his band. Fines were imposed if musicians had unshined shoes or showed up late. Later fines would be imposed for mistakes in music and in dancing.

Launches Soul Music

The sound of Brown's music was changing by 1960, the year his career really took off. Brown takes credit for inventing soul with his combination of gospel, rhythm and blues, and jazz. The first smash hit to embody his new sound was "Think," Brown's third record to sell a million copies. Nathan and the other executives of King Records were still not in tune with the new direction, but Brown relied on the reactions of his audiences to the changes in his material. By the end of the year Brown and the Famous Flames were heading the bill at the Apollo Theater.

Brown continued the rigorous schedule of live performances. By 1962 he wanted to record a live performance and issue it as an album. Since at this time live performance albums were still a novelty, King Records would not back the project. Brown put his own money into the project and rented the Apollo Theater for a series of four performances beginning on October 19. When *Live at the Apollo* appeared in January of 1963, it was an immediate success, reaching number two on the pop charts and appearing there for 62 weeks. It opened up a new market for Brown among white teenagers, who heard of the album by word of mouth. Today, it still ranks as one of the best live albums ever made.

In 1963 Brown moved to the borough of Queens in New York City. At the end of the year he also set up his own record label, Fair Deal, which was affiliated with Mercury Records. "Out of Sight," which Brown cut for Mercury in June of 1964, reached number 24 on the pop charts. His band was called the Flames for the last time at those sessions for Mercury. "Out of Sight" also marked a new stage in Brown's music; using all musical elements, including voice and lyrics, to establish rhythms with few chord changes, the record marked the beginning of funk. Conflicts with Nathan continued and by October King Records had obtained an injunction that prevented Brown from recording vocals for another label—although Mercury did have rights to his instrumental performances.

As 1964 ended Brown taped the "T.A.M.I. (Teen Age Music International) Show," which, along with other television appearances, began to give mainstream audiences exposure to the visual aspect of his performances and build his cross–over appeal. In spite of his success, from 1964 to 1965, Brown did not record. King Records finally yielded and gave him complete artistic and marketing control of his records, as well as his own publishing company and a greatly increased share of the royalties. From this point on Brown took physical possession of the recording masters and returned them to King only when he thought the music should be issued.

In mid–1965 "Popa's Got a Brand New Bag" reached number eight on the pop charts and was Brown's first in the top ten. It topped the rhythm and blues charts for eight weeks and sold one million copies. It was also Brown's first big crossover hit and earned him a Grammy in 1966. The year closed with a similar success for "I Got You (I Feel Good)."

Brown's recording success continued in 1966 with another million–selling record, "It's a Man's, Man's, Man's World," but "Soul Brother No. 1," as he was now called, was having to respond to the political pressures surrounding the civil rights movement. Inevitably he ran into the problem of not being able to satisfy everyone. On the stage of the Apollo in the spring, he took out a life membership in the NAACP. In the summer, he visited James Meredith in the hospital after Meredith had been shot during his Freedom March in Mississippi and gave a show for the persons who had gathered in Tupelo to continue the march. He also cut a record, "Don't Be a Dropout," as part of a Stay in School campaign. In the summer of 1967, after racial violence had scarred many urban areas, James Brown turned down the request of H. Rap Brown, then secretary for the black militant Student National Coordinating Committee, that he call for blacks to stage an armed revolt.

Brown was attracted more by black capitalism than by armed revolution. By the end of 1967 he had purchased the radio station WJBE of Knoxville, Tennessee. The following year he bought WEBB of Baltimore, Maryland, and WRDW of Augusta, Georgia. Brown's touring continued unabated. The record "Cold Sweat" continued Brown's movement toward funk, and it, too, sold one million.

Martin Luther King Jr. was assassinated in Memphis on April 4, 1968. With some difficulty, arrangements were made to televise Brown's Boston concert on April 5 in the hope that keeping people off the streets would avert violence. Between songs, Brown talked of King and urged calm. The following day Brown repeated his performance in Washington, D.C., which had been hit by two nights of rioting.

Builds Bridges

Brown appeared to be building bridges to the establishment. On May 8, 1968, he attended a dinner at the White House hosted by President Lyndon B. Johnson. The patriotic record *America Is My Home* drew much criticism, especially from the black community, as did the presence of a white bass player in his band. In June, Brown went to Vietnam to entertain the troops. In October *Say It Loud—I'm Black and I'm Proud* became another million–selling record. Brown claims that this statement of black pride alienated most of his white audience.

Brown not only was becoming visible for his politics in 1968, he was also developing his music. "I Got the Feeling" became another million–selling record after it appeared in April, and "Licking Stick, Licking Stick," which appeared in June, was hailed as the definite presentation of funk. More ominous developments for Brown's personal life that year were the death of his longtime business manager, Ben "Pop" Bart, and shortly thereafter a claim from the Internal Revenue Service that Brown owed $1,879,000 in back taxes.

In 1969 Brown faced a paternity suit which he resolved by agreeing to pay child support without admitting he fathered the child. After finally divorcing his first wife, from whom he had long been separated, Brown married his second, DeeDee (Deirdre), on October 22. They had two children, both girls, and the couple divorced in 1979.

In 1969 Brown moved back to Augusta. When rioting broke out that year in the city, Brown used his influence to calm the situation. In August Brown announced his intention to stop touring after July of 1970; in fact, he did not appreciably slow down until 1975. Brown played Las Vegas for the first time in 1970 to great success.

Brown soon ran into problems with his career. Syd Nathan of King Records died, and after long negotiations Brown signed with Polydor, a multinational recording company, in August of 1972, bringing with him his entire catalog. Although Brown still had full creative control of his recording, he blamed Polydor for the decline of his record sales in the late 1970s. He accused the label of overlooking the changes in the music business, such as new play lists and formats on radio, and the decline in black venues able to bear the expense of his show.

Although Brown's success in music continued, 1973 marked a downturn in his fortunes. His oldest son died in June. Longtime colleague Bobby Byrd left for good. The IRS claimed that Brown owed $4.5 million in taxes and threatened to charge him with fraud. By 1975 Brown had cut back on his touring and faced competition from the new disco craze. In January of 1978 Brown had to sell WJBE; by 1980 the other two stations were also gone. Other ventures did not work out. Brown sustained a syndicated television dance program, *Future Shock,* from 1974 to 1976, but it did not make money. In 1978 his second marriage broke up, and he spent time in jail for contempt of court in a case involving his radio stations. One result of his difficulties was a turn to religion, which began to play an increasing part in his life.

Brown now began to work in rock and roll clubs. Although he strenuously resisted the labeling, his audiences began to view him as a musician from an earlier era and his former hits as golden oldies. A boost to his career came with his cameo appearance in the film *The Blues Brothers* in 1980, and his status as a pioneer was recognized when he was inducted into the Rock and Roll Hall of Fame at the first annual dinner in January of 1986. That same year, "Living in America," the theme from *Rocky IV,* became Brown's first million–selling record in 13 years, reaching number four on the pop charts. For the recording, Brown received a Grammy for best male rhythm and blues singer.

In the meantime, news accounts depicted a personal life that appeared to be in considerable disarray. Rumors that he beat women had circulated for years, along with rumors of drug use, in particular the use of phencyclidine, better known as PCP or angel dust. Brown's third marriage in 1982 to Adrianne, a television hair stylist and make–up artist, did not settle him down. The couple established a home on 62 acres near Beach Island, South Carolina, across the river from Augusta, and their homelife became marred by frequent run–ins with the law on drug and assault charges.

On July 21, 1988, Brown pleaded no contest to PCP possession and guilty to carrying a gun and resisting arrest. He received a two–year suspended sentence and $1,200 fine. On September 24 Brown interrupted an insurance seminar at his headquarters in Georgia by waving a rifle and demanding to know who had used his personal bathroom. The subsequent police chase through two states ended with Brown being sentenced to a six–year jail term.

Brown remained in prison until February 27, 1991. He was transferred from his initial assignment at a minimum security facility in July of 1989 after more than $40,000 in checks and cash was discovered in his possession. Then in April of 1990 he was transferred to an Aiken County work center, where he became a youth drug counselor in a work release program. His wife waited for him in the Beach Island home, which now belonged to Brown's lawyer.

On his release Brown began a five–year period of probation. Brown filed for legal separation from his wife in April of 1994, and he was charged with misdemeanor wife–beating in an incident that is alleged to have occurred on December 7, 1994. The charge was dropped. The IRS also claimed an outstanding tax liability of $11 million. The couple was still married when Adrienne Brown died in January of 1995 due to a combination of heart disease and PCP use after elective surgery.

In his statements after his release from prison, James Brown said that he faced the future with confidence. In spite of his stormy personal life, his musical achievements will endure. In 1992 he was honored with the Lifetime Achievement Award from the Rhythm and Blues Foundation. Few artists have surpassed Brown's accomplishments in the field of popular music, where his records not only sold in the millions but defined soul, created funk, and influenced rap.

Current address: c/o Brothers Management Associates, 141 Dunbar Ave., Fords, NJ 08863.

REFERENCES

''Adrienne Brown, Wife of Singer, Dead At 47.'' *Nashville Tennessean,* January 7, 1995.

Brown, James, with Bruce Tucker. *James Brown.* 1986.

Current Biography Yearbook. New York: H. G. Wilson, 1992.

''Death of James Brown's Wife Linked to Drugs.'' Reuters/ Variety, America On Line, February 11, 1996.

Guralnick, Peter. *Sweet Soul Music.* New York: HarperCollins, 1986.

Hirshey, Gerri. *Nowhere to Run.* New York: Times Books, 1984.

Johnson, Robert E. ''James Brown Talks About What's Ahead Now That He Has Been Paroled.'' *Jet* 79 (18 March 1991): 54–58.

Rees, Dafydd, and Luke Crampton. *Rock Movers and Shakers.* Santa Barbara, CA: ABC–Clio, 1991.

Rose, Cynthia. *Living in America: The Soul Saga of James Brown.* London, England: Serpent's Tail, 1990.

''Singer James Brown Arrested for Beating Wife.'' *Chicago Tribune,* America On Line, December 9, 1994.

Turner, Renée D. ''The Ordeal of James Brown.'' *Ebony* 46 (July 1991): 38–40.

Robert L. Johns

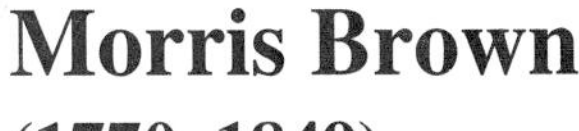

Morris Brown
(1770–1849)
Religious leader

Morris Brown

In many ways Morris Brown's life is poorly known. He performed a heroic feat in helping to build an independent African American Methodist church in Charleston, South Carolina. The massive suppression of that church in the wake of the attempted insurrection by Denmark Vesey left both Brown's church and Brown's early life poorly documented. After he fled to Philadelphia, his life is visible mostly in the documents of church conferences. Enough remains, however, to make clear the important role he played as the second bishop of the African Methodist Episcopal (AME) church and successor of Richard Allen.

Morris Brown apparently was born free on January 8, 1770. He lived in Charleston, South Carolina, where he worked as a shoemaker. He was of mixed parentage and a light–skinned, impressive man more than six–feet tall. Daniel A. Payne, the first church historian, who served on occasion as Brown's secretary, said that Brown had no schooling at all, spoke very broken English, and was illiterate. Payne added that Brown was also keenly aware of the contemporary world.

At some point during his life in Charleston, Brown joined the Methodist church, which was very successful in attracting black members. During his trips to Charleston between 1785 and 1799, pioneering Methodist bishop Francis Asbury found blacks more responsive to his preaching than whites, who often reacted violently to the early Methodist opposition to slavery. The growth of the church among white Southerners increased markedly after it modified its position about the turn of the century.

In the early 1800s there were several thousand black Methodists who had a limited autonomy within the white churches, controlling, for example, church trials of fellow blacks. The cancellation of these rights in 1815 was the occasion for a secession movement. Given the coincidence in dates of efforts by African Americans in ports like Philadelphia, Baltimore, Wilmington, and Charleston to break away from the white Methodists, it is possible though unprovable that there was coordination among the groups—certainly knowledge of what was happening must have been available through the large numbers of black sailors working in the coastal trade. In Charleston more than 4,000 blacks withdrew to form three separatist churches.

The black Methodists immediately ran into legal problems. In 1817, 469 worshippers were arrested on disorderly conduct charges, which were later dismissed. In June of 1818

140 blacks of the Hempstead church were arrested, and a bishop and four ministers were given the choice of a month in prison or leaving the state. In spite of the hostile climate, the black churches managed to stay open until 1822.

Morris Brown was involved in the struggle although we do not have details of his activities or position. He probably led the group. Brown did not attend the organizational meeting of the African Methodist Episcopal Church in Philadelphia in April of 1816, but he was present at the Philadelphia Annual Conference on May 9, 1818, where he was admitted into full connection and ordained. On more than one occasion, Brown managed to evade the obstacles imposed by South Carolina on travel by blacks so that he could attend meetings in Baltimore and Philadelphia.

In June of 1822 disaster struck the church. Rumors about a slave insurrection in Charleston had been circulating some weeks. On June 14 a black Methodist blacksmith named George Wilson discovered from a fellow Methodist that Denmark Vesey had planned a major revolt for the following Sunday, June 16, and informed white officials. Denmark Vesey was a member of the Hempstead church and had recruited many of his supporters from fellow Methodists—one investigation claimed that all except for one was a member of the African Methodist church.

Brown likely returned to Charleston from the North shortly before the moment set for the insurrection. During the subsequent trials, Billy, a conspirator who had pleaded guilty, said: "Gullah Jack [one of Vesey's lieutenants] had gone to Father Morris to ask him whether he would sanction the insurrection, and Morris Brown replied, if you can get men go on, but don't mention my name. I am going shortly to the North and I shall hear there, what you are about." This statement may not have been true but it placed Brown under suspicion. He and Henry Drayton, a fellow church leader, were arrested on the charge of violating an act of 1820 which forbade free blacks to enter the state and ordered to leave. Future governor James Hamilton and other white friends helped ensure their safe departure. The independent African church was firmly suppressed.

Becomes AME Bishop

Brown settled in Philadelphia, took up his trade of shoemaking, and continued to work to further the AME Church. In 1826 he was given charge of the Bristol Circuit in Bucks County, Pennsylvania. It appears that he was also the first to travel west to build up the church in western Pennsylvania and Ohio. Richard Allen was growing older and weaker. He was overburdened by the work involved in leading the denomination. Earlier, in 1822 while Brown still had a church to supervise in Charleston, Jacob Matthews had been selected to aid Allen, but in 1828 the church decided that the time had come to elect a second bishop to share the burden. Morris Brown was elected, and he was consecrated at Bethel Church on May 25, 1828. In 1829 Allen was ill and for the first time did not preside at the Baltimore Annual Conference; Brown took his place. Brown also undertook the strenuous journey to preside at the organization of the Ohio/Western Conference at Hillsboro, Ohio, on August 28, 1830.

Richard Allen died in 1831, and Brown became sole bishop. He was a vigorous leader who presided over a rapid and widespread development of the denomination. The development of churches as far afield as Illinois and Missouri demanded many arduous trips. For much of the period, he followed Richard Allen's example and served as pastor of Mother Bethel Church in Philadelphia as well as bishop. In one of the few references to service outside the church, Brown was a member of the board of managers of the American Moral Reform Society in 1834.

On May 8, 1836, Edward Waters of Baltimore was ordained assistant bishop of the church. Waters seems to have done little to relieve Brown's burden. In *Scraps of African Methodist Episcopal History,* James A. Handy claimed that this was due to the fact that only the presiding bishop received a $25 fee at conferences so Brown always took care to be present, leaving Waters with no financial incentive to travel from Baltimore. It has also been bruited that the election of Waters, who was dark skinned, was a sop to dissidents unhappy with a man of Brown's complexion leading the church. Both Brown and Waters were older than 70 when Paul Quinn was consecrated the third bishop of the AME church on May 19, 1844.

In 1844 Brown suffered a stroke on July 21 while attending a church conference in Toronto, Canada. He was partially paralyzed and his mental faculties were impaired. In spite of extreme feebleness he presided over a New York conference for six days until the arrival of Paul Quinn, who replaced him. In a move of doubtful legality for a single conference, the Philadelphia conference superannuated him with a pension of $200.

For the remainder of his life Brown was mostly confined to his home on Queen Street in Philadelphia where he died on May 9, 1849. He left a widow, Maria, and six children. Funeral services were held at his home.

Brown followed a founding leader and was a worthy successor who built up and expanded the work of the African Methodist Episcopal Church. In the eyes of Daniel A. Payne, later one of the denomination's most famous bishops and the man who preached the funeral sermon, Brown's greatest legacy was his support of a learned clergy. In 1843 Brown stated his opposition to the ordination of three illiterate ministerial candidates. The following year Payne's proposal for the education of ministers was first voted down in the General Convocation. Brown insisted on bringing it up again the next day and only with his vigorous backing did it pass. Brown thus was not only a continuer, he gave an original inflection to his church.

REFERENCES

George, Carol V. R. *Segregated Sabbaths.* New York: Oxford, 1973.

Handy, James A. *Scraps of African Methodist Episcopal History*. Philadelphia: AME Book Concern, 1902.
Lofton, John. *Insurrection in South Carolina*. Yellow Springs, OH: Antioch Press, 1964.
Logan, Rayford W., and Michael R. Winston, eds. *Dictionary of American Negro Biography*. New York: Norton, 1982.
An Official Report of the Trials of Sundry Negroes Charged with an Attempt to Raise and Insurrection in the State of South Carolina. 1822. Reprint, *The Trial Record of Denmark Vesey*. Boston: Beacon Press, 1970.
Payne, Daniel Alexander. *History of the African Methodist Episcopal Church*. Nashville: AME Sunday–School Union, 1891.
———. *Recollections of Seventy Years*. Nashville: AME Sunday School Union, 1883.
Wesley, Charles H. *Richard Allen, Apostle of Freedom*. 1935. Reprint, Washington, DC: Associated Publishers, 1969.

Robert L. Johns

Ron Brown
(1941–1996)
Politician, lawyer

Ron Brown

The first African American in the history of the United States to head a major political party, Ron Brown demonstrated a political savvy, traditional values, and progressive vision that accounted for much of his success. As deputy chairman of the Democratic National Committee, Brown was a highly visible power broker. His appointment as Secretary of Commerce in 1993, by President Bill Clinton, placed him at the summit of a career begun 23 years earlier. In this time, he redefined the role of the department and transformed it into a high–profile advocate for U.S. businesses everywhere.

Ronald Harmon Brown was born in Washington, D.C., August 1, 1941. His parents, William H. and Gloria Osborne Carter Brown, both graduates of Howard University, moved to New York following the birth of their only child and settled in Harlem. William Brown managed the Theresa Hotel on 125th Street, where the family resided next door to the legendary Apollo Theater. The theater and hotel were both famous for attracting celebrities of all races. *Current Biography* reported that 11–year–old Brown took a campaign photograph in 1952 with Richard M. Nixon. Young Brown acquired his social grace in the company of experts.

Brown's formal education was exclusive. In 1946 he was the only African American student at Hunter College elementary school located on the city's Upper East Side. He learned early to balance the politics of two worlds—those of Harlem and the elite white world beyond. His parents' determination for him to have the best education New York had to offer led him to travel great distances across the city. He attended the Rhodes School and the Walden School, both private prep schools on New York's West Side. In 1958 Brown entered Middlebury College in Vermont.

Brown's political philosophy was formed not in the hotbed of civil rights activism sweeping the South at the time, but rather, his isolated situation forced him to become an expert at nonconfrontational negotiations. One situation in particular tested his courage but strengthened his resolve to stand for what's right even when it meant standing alone. As the only African American freshman on campus, Brown was rushed by Sigma Phi Epsilon fraternity. But the fraternity had a clause excluding African Americans. The national organization objected to Brown's membership, but he refused their offer of house privileges without full membership. When it was clear Brown would not back down nor ignore their bigotry, fraternity members supported him, which resulted in the chapter's expulsion from national membership. This single act of bravery by 18–year–old Brown caused Middlebury to prohibit from campus all organizations with exclusionary clauses. Later, Brown became a trustee at the still predominantly white school.

Brown earned a B.A. in political science in 1962. Having helped finance his education through service in the Army ROTC, upon graduation he joined the United States Army. Stationed overseas, Brown supervised a staff of 60 German civilians where, again, he was the only African American officer at the U.S. Army post in West Germany. When transferred to Korea he attained the rank of captain, training Korean soldiers. In an interview with *Time* magazine reporter

Walter Isaacson, Brown revealed that in Korea he "learned to be comfortable taking charge."

Brown returned to New York in 1966 and accepted a job with the National Urban League as welfare caseworker and job training coordinator in the Bronx. He also enrolled in St. John's University School of Law, where he took evening classes. He received his law degree in 1970. Brown held various positions with the Urban League, including that of Washington lobbyist, until 1979.

Climbing the Political Ladder

In 1971 Brown won his first political election, becoming district leader of the Democratic party in Mount Vernon, Westchester County, New York. His popularity was based on his ability to make peace between warring factions. Brown himself credited his 1973 move from New York to Washington, D.C., for his rise to prominence. He told Thomas Edsall of the *Washington Post* for February 11, 1989, "Coming to Washington was a way for me to establish my own identity, my own base, my own group of contacts and relationships, putting me into a spokesman role . . . when the Urban League was a very important organization."

Brown's growing prominence brought him to the attention of Senator Edward Kennedy, who wanted him to become the deputy manager of his 1979 presidential campaign. Brown's acceptance thrust him onto the stage of national politics. His successful engineering of the California campaign paid off more for Brown than for Kennedy, who lost his bid for the presidency. In 1980 Brown became chief counsel to the Senate Judiciary Committee and the following year general counsel and staff director for Senator Kennedy. In 1981, he took over as chief counsel for the Democratic National Committee, the following year becoming its deputy chairman. As deputy chairman Brown enabled more low–income voters to participate in the national conventions without upsetting conservative budget watchers in the National Committee.

Brown's term as deputy chairman expired in 1985. Deciding to remain in the Washington area, he accepted a job with the prestigious law firm Patton, Boggs and Blow, where he earned a reputation as a first–rate corporate attorney.

In a 1989 *Washington Post* article, African American Harvard professor Martin Kilson dubbed Brown "the new black transethnic politician." He was referring to Brown's acceptance statement to head the Democratic National Committee. Throughout his campaign Brown had avoided the issue of race. But in his acceptance speech for the chairmanship, cited in the same article, he said: "Let me speak frankly. I did not run on the basis of race, but I will not run away from it. I am proud of who I am and I am proud of this party, for we are truly America's last best hope to bridge the divisions of race, region, religion, and ethnicity. . . . The story of my chairmanship will not be about race. It will be about the races we win in the next four years."

Despite his best intentions, Brown was not free from the race issue. His work as Jesse Jackson's top strategist in the 1988 convention made it difficult for him to raise funds for the National Committee because, in the eyes of many Jewish contributors, Brown had not sufficiently distanced himself from Jackson, whom they believed guilty of making anti–Semitic remarks. Conservative white Democrats thought that Brown's election would further tarnish the party image as being too black and too liberal, despite Brown's declaring in *Gentlemen'sQuarterly,* "I embrace the traditional values of the Democratic party, but I'm progressive."

Political Power Broker

As the first African American chairman of the Democratic National Committee, Brown successfully raised funds, and he saw the election of a black Democrat governor in Virginia and a black mayor in New York City. Brown's skills in dealing with opponents and his ability to walk a political middle road unified the party, and his expert maneuvering behind the scenes helped Bill Clinton win the 1992 nomination and the election.

When Clinton won the presidency, he appointed Ron Brown Secretary of Commerce. This came despite objections raised by many people who thought Brown's experience as a Washington insider and political lobbyist might pose ethical questions. Brown was confirmed by the U.S. Senate on January 14, 1993, becoming the first African American Secretary of Commerce.

As Commerce secretary, *Emerge* magazine reported, "he led the way on trade and economic policy." Often controversial, his role as architect of Clinton's China policy was deemed especially controversial, and enabled China to retain its Most Favored Nation trade status.

Accused of Corruption

In spite of his outstanding performance as Secretary of Commerce, Brown was attacked by Republicans who, in May of 1995, accused him of shady business dealings and influence–peddling. Brown challenged his detractors to prove their allegations. Attorney General Janet Reno in July of 1995 appointed Daniel S. Pearson independent counsel to investigate Brown's business dealings with Nolanda Hill. Investigations into business activities continued. Undaunted, Ron Brown continued to perform his duties as commerce secretary with the finesse that first won him recognition.

Brown received American Jurisprudence awards for outstanding achievement in poverty law in 1975 and for outstanding achievement in jurisprudence in 1990. He received honorary doctor of law degrees in 1989 from Hunter College and Rhode Island College. In 1980 Harvard University awarded Brown a fellowship to its Institute of Politics at the John F. Kennedy School of Government. Brown served on the boards of trustees for the United Negro College Fund, the University of the District Columbia, and the Community Foundation of Greater Washington.

Brown, who was said to have a towering ego and loved the spotlight, was also deemed a sincere person who could disarm his adversaries instantly with his trademark smile and overpowering personality. He retained the respect of people from high–powered establishments to the streets of Harlem.

Ron Brown married Alma Arrington on August 11, 1962. They lived in a town house near Rock Creek Park in Washington, D.C. Tracey Lyn and Michael Arrington, their two adult children, are both attorneys.

On April 3, 1996, an airplane carrying Brown and 36 federal officials attempted to land in bad weather at Dubrovnik off the coast of Croatia, but it crashed into a mountain instead. All aboard the plane were killed. Brown and his staff had gone to the war–torn area to assist American businesses in rebuilding the region.

Services for Brown were held April 10 at Washington Cathedral. He is buried at Arlington National Cemetery. As the nation mourned his death, flags were flown at half–staff, and he was honored with a 19–gun salute. Called the Standard Bearer, Brown was extraordinary because he recognized and remembered the best about people, which enabled him to get along with friend or foe. He opened doors previously closed to African Americans because he was adept at building bridges between races, classes, gender, and other identities that often divide Americans. *Emerge* magazine said at his death: "When the game was lobbying, Brown was rainmaker extraordinaire, hauling in high–powered clients by the dozens; when the game was politics, he was kingmaker . . . laying the groundwork for the Clinton victory in 1992; and when the game was commerce, he was a visionary leader inventing 'commercial diplomacy.'" He was highly visible both as head of the Democratic National Committee and as U.S. Secretary of Commerce. At Brown's funeral, President Clinton said that "Ron Brown. . . was a magnificent life force."

REFERENCES

Contemporary Black Biography. Vol. 5. Detroit: Gale Research, 1992.

Current Biography Yearbook. New York: H. W. Wilson, 1989.

"Ex–prosecutor to Probe Ronald Brown Finances." *Los Angeles Times,* July 7, 1995.

"FBI Seize Documents in Brown Probe." *Washington Post,* October 4, 1995.

Frisby, Michael K. "Standard Bearer." *Emerge* 7 (June 1996): 31–37.

Issacson, Walter. "Running As His Own Man." Interview. *Time* 133 (30 January 1989): 133–56.

Kelly, Michael. "Ten Steps, Then We Shoot." *Gentlemen's Quarterly* 59 (July 1989): 143.

"Ron Brown Declares Innocence as GOP Probes." *Amsterdam News,* May 27, 1995.

Who's Who among Black Americans, 1996–1997. 9th ed. Detroit: Gale Research, 1996.

"World Mourns Death of Ron Brown, First Black U.S. Secretary of Commerce." *Jet* 89 (22 April 1996): 4–18, 51–56.

Nagueyalti Warren

Sterling A. Brown
(1901–1989)
Poet, critic, editor, educator

In a distinguished and multi–faceted career spanning seven decades, Sterling A. Brown played a key role in the development and assessment of African American literature. He was an innovative poet, an astute critic, and a skilled editor. His poetry captures the beauty and depth of the African American oral tradition. His criticism, which explores a wide range of genres, includes trenchant assessments of racially–based stereotypes. As an educator, he influenced many generations of students through his warmth and clarity of vision. In all aspects of his career, Brown celebrated folk culture, even when it was not popular to do so.

Brown's father, Sterling Nelson Brown, had been born a slave in Tennessee, but through persistent effort, he was able to graduate from Fisk University in Nashville and from Oberlin Theological Seminary in Oberlin, Ohio. In 1892 he joined the faculty of the School of Religion at Howard University in Washington, D.C., where he also served as pastor of Lincoln Temple Congregational Church. His wife was fellow Tennessean and Fisk graduate Adelaide Allen. Their only son, Sterling Allen Brown, was born in Washington on May 1, 1901, the youngest of six children.

Brown's early years were shaped by his parents' commitment to education and to African American culture. The family had an extensive library that enabled him to cultivate the habit of reading. His biographer, Joanne V. Gabbin, has noted that Adelaide Brown, who was valedictorian of her college graduating class, helped instill in her son a love of poetry and a sense of the value of African American spirituals. (One of her cousins, Georgia Gordon, was a member of the original Fisk Jubilee Singers.) Gabbin has also acknowledged the strong influence of Reverend Brown, noting that "though [Sterling Allen] Brown's fun–loving personality rejected his father's penchant toward sobriety and reserve, the Reverend Brown's standards of integrity and spiritual strength made an indelible mark on his son's character."

Excels in Academics

In addition to his parents' nurturing, Brown benefited from the scholarly environment of the Howard University campus, which attracted many prominent blacks teachers and visitors. He received his own education at the Paul Laurence Dunbar High School, an institution known for its excellent academic program.

After graduating from Dunbar in 1918, Brown entered Williams College in Williamstown, Massachusetts, on a scholarship. Despite the relative isolation of the few black students enrolled there, he participated in a variety of activities, including the debate team. He was also elected to Phi Beta Kappa by the time he graduated in 1922.

Sterling A. Brown

Brown then went on to attend Harvard University, where he earned a master's degree in 1923. The courses he took at Harvard deepened his appreciation of writers such as Robert Frost and Carl Sandburg, whose attention to seemingly prosaic subjects and use of down–to–earth language reflected Brown's own interests and inclinations.

During the 1920s Brown taught at several historically black institutions: Virginia Seminary and College in Lynchburg (1923–26); Lincoln University in Jefferson City, Missouri (1926–28); and Fisk University (1928–29). In 1929, he joined the faculty of Howard University, and there he remained until his retirement in 1969.

In 1927, Brown married Daisy Turnbull. Blessed with a lively, gregarious personality much like her husband's, she was an enthusiastic supporter of his work. The couple had no children of their own but were the adoptive parents of a son, John Dennis.

Launches Writing Career

At the same time Brown was establishing his academic career, he was also making a name for himself as a writer. Some of his poems were published during the 1920s in *Opportunity,* the journal of the National Urban League, which helped disseminate the work of young writers. His work is also included in Countee Cullen's 1927 anthology *Caroling Dusk.*

Brown's emergence on the literary scene coincided with the Harlem Renaissance, a period of explosive creative activity among African Americans. The term ''Harlem Renaissance'' did not particularly appeal to Brown, however. He preferred the name ''New Negro Renaissance'' to make it clear that the movement was not limited just to Harlem.

In his pioneering anthology *The Book of American Negro Poetry* (1931), James Weldon Johnson identified Brown as one of the younger African American writers who had ''dug down into the genuine folk stuff.'' Brown, in fact, played a major role in the development of Johnson's book: in addition to the headnote that introduces Johnson's poetry in the volume, Brown also wrote the teaching guide for use with the entire anthology.

Southern Road, a collection of Brown's poetry, was published in 1932. James Weldon Johnson wrote the introduction, again praising Brown's ability to bring out the beauty and depth of folk–based materials without sentimentalizing. *Southern Road* contains almost all of his best–known works, including ''Odyssey of Big Boy,'' ''Ma Rainey,'' ''Strong Men,'' ''Sporting Beasley,'' and several ballads featuring the likable rascal Slim Greer. In addition to poems that reflect African American folk language and ethos, the collection includes sonnets and other poems that do not explicitly mention race.

Serves as Literary Critic

In addition to his poetry, Brown evaluated many works written by others about the African American experience. He served as a book review editor for *Opportunity* from 1926 into the 1930s and published essays and reviews in periodicals such as the *New Republic,* the *Journal of Negro Education,* and *Phylon.* Arthur P. Davis noted in *From the Dark Tower* that Brown's criticism ''has a refreshing common–sense quality'' and that ''[he] is at his best when he presents panoramic reviews of large segments of American writing which treat the Negro.''

Brown also wrote two books of criticism: *The Negro in American Fiction* (1938) and *Negro Poetry and Drama* (1938). In them, he devoted particular attention to stereotypical depictions of black people frequently found in the works of white authors. He focused on stereotypes in other pieces of criticism as well, especially in ''Negro Character as Seen by White Authors,'' published in the *Journal of Negro Education* in 1933, and ''A Century of Negro Portraiture in American Literature,'' published in the *Massachusetts Review* in 1966. In the latter article, he identifies eight stereotypes: the contented slave, the wretched freeman, the brute Negro, the noble savage, the comic minstrel, the submissive Christian, the tragic mulatto/octoroon, and the exotic primitive.

Although he produced mainly poetry and literary criticism during his career, Brown also wrote essays on African American music (namely blues, spirituals, and jazz) as well as several stories and sketches. Furthermore, he was a lively raconteur, describing himself in ''A Century of Negro Portraiture in American Literature'' as a ''long talker.'' His resonant baritone made him an especially effective reader of his own work.

Joins Staff of Federal Writers' Project

From 1936 to 1939, Brown was editor on Negro affairs for the Federal Writers' Project (FWP) of the Works Progress Administration (WPA). Robert O'Meally noted in *College Language Association Journal* that "Brown helped edit virtually every Project essay dealing with black life." For an assignment that involved interviewing former slaves in all of the Southern states and a few Midwestern ones, Brown developed guidelines to help FWP workers record their subjects' language appropriately. He was especially close to the Virginia ex–slave project, which culminated in the publication of *The Negro in Virginia* (1940). In all of his work for the FWP, Brown fought not only for unbiased portrayals of blacks in the materials he developed but also for fair treatment of black FWP workers themselves.

Brown's expertise as a poet was recognized in 1937 when he received a Guggenheim fellowship that enabled him to continue his writing. In 1942, he was awarded a Rosenwald Fund fellowship that made it possible for him to tour the South and write down his observations.

In 1941, Brown returned to the anthology format as editor (with Ulysses Lee and Arthur P. Davis) of *The Negro Caravan.* From the 1940s until the 1990s, it remained one of the very few comprehensive and reliable anthologies in the field. Also during the 1940s, Brown was a staff member of Gunnar Myrdal's landmark study of African Americans, the results of which were published as *An American Dilemma.* Brown's contribution was a very thorough report on black theater.

Influences Generations of Young People

As a college professor, Brown influenced many generations of students. Besides his longtime post at Howard University, he held visiting professorships at the University of Illinois, the University of Minnesota, New York University, the New School for Social Research, Sarah Lawrence College, and Vassar College.

During the 1960s, a new generation of blacks helped draw attention to Brown's achievements. Beginning in the 1970s, he received many honorary degrees, including ones from Atlanta University, Howard University, the University of Massachusetts, Northwestern University, Williams College, Boston University, Brown University, Lewis and Clark College, Harvard University, Yale University, the University of Maryland Baltimore County, the University of Massachusetts at Amherst, Lincoln University (Pennsylvania), and the University of Pennsylvania.

In 1976, Broadside Press published *The Last Ride of Wild Bill, and Eleven Narrative Poems,* Brown's first collection of poetry since *Southern Road.* The volume illustrates his continuing emphasis on storytelling in the folk tradition. Four years later, *The Collected Poems of Sterling Brown* appeared and captured the 1982 Lenore Marshall/*Saturday Review* Poetry Prize. In 1984, Brown was named poet laureate of the District of Columbia. Five years later, on January 13, 1989, the venerable writer, critic, and educator died of leukemia at the age of 87 in Tacoma Park, Maryland.

In a 1970 essay entitled "A Strong Man Called Sterling Brown," Stephen A. Henderson offered a concise and respectful assessment of Brown's many achievements, which assure him a place of honor in American literary history. Observed the author:

> In a time when many Black people were equating a superficial respectability with real dignity, this man—scholar, teacher, and poet—was demonstrating in his life and his work the profound dignity which the common man embodied in his everyday life—in his work, his struggles, his tragedies and his joys. He did it by making that life his own. . . . Moreover, he did this without condescension, without sentimentality and without fakery.

REFERENCES

Brown, Sterling A. "A Century of Negro Portraiture." *Massachusetts Review* 7 (winter 1966): 73–96. Reprinted in *Black Voices: An Anthology of Afro–American Literature,* edited by Abraham Chapman. New York: New American Library, 1968. 564–89.

———. "Negro Character as Seen by White Authors." *Journal of Negro Education* 2 (April 1933): 179–203.

Davis, Arthur P. *From the Dark Tower: Afro–American Writers 1900–1960.* Washington, DC: Howard University Press, 1981.

Gabbin, Joanne V. *Sterling A. Brown: Building the Black Aesthetic Tradition.* Westport, CT: Greenwood Press, 1985.

———. "Sterling A. Brown's Poetic Voice: A Living Legacy." *African American Review* 31 (Fall 1997): 423–31.

Gates, Henry Louis, Jr. "Songs of a Racial Self: On Sterling Brown." In *Figures in Black,* edited by Gates. New York: Oxford University Press, 1987.

Harris, Trudier. *Afro–American Writers from the Harlem Renaissance to 1940.* Detroit: Gale Research, 1987.

Henderson, Stephen A. "A Strong Man Called Sterling Brown." *Black World* (September 1970): 5–12.

O'Meally, Robert G. "An Annotated Bibliography of the Works of Sterling A. Brown." *College Language Association Journal* 19 (December 1975): 268–79.

COLLECTIONS

Brown's papers are in the Moorland–Spingarn Research Center at Howard University, Washington, D.C.

Arlene Clift–Pellow

Tony Brown
(1933–)
Television executive, producer, columnist, educator, filmmaker, activist, radio personality

Tony Brown expressed in a February 3, 1994, press release that "The color of freedom is green," an idea that is both controversial and often misunderstood. Regardless of what one thinks of his philosophy, Brown's impact on the television industry in America is far reaching. *Tony Brown's Journal,* the longest running black news program in television history, addresses crucial issues concerning black people. Brown works assiduously as an educator, political activist, syndicated columnist, filmmaker and producer to effect change in America and to achieve equal treatment for African Americans.

Tony Brown

Born April 11, 1933, in Charleston, West Virginia, William Anthony "Tony" Brown was the youngest of five children born to Royal Brown and Catherine Davis Brown. Speaking about his childhood, Brown omits references to his father or to his older brother. He acknowledges the love and encouragement he received from his sisters, Billie Brown and Jackie McCullough. From the time he was two months old until he was 12 years old, he was reared by Elizabeth Sanford and her daughter Mable Holmes, friends of the family. When these women died, within months of each other, Brown went to live with his mother in a housing project located in a section of Charleston called the Minor. His parents were divorced.

Brown learned early of poverty and segregation. He recognized the value of money and fortunately connected its acquisition to hard work and thrift rather than criminal activity. He purchased a hen and a rooster from money he earned selling soft drink bottles and started a small poultry farm and peddled eggs and chickens throughout his community. Paul H. Easley Jr., a childhood friend and Clark Atlanta University Chaplain, recalled in the January 8, 1989, *Chicago Tribune* that Brown was always "a hustler." Brown earned money for having fun too, and in segregated Charleston that meant an afternoon at Furgerson Theater with his buddies Arthur Fisher, Lewis Smoot, and Reginald Taylor. Brown also was active in the youth choir and Boy Scouts at Simpson Memorial United Methodist Church.

In 1939, Brown entered Charleston's public schools, first attending Boyd Elementary, then Boyd Jr. High, and finally Garnet High School. He joined the high school track and field team and ran the 440, 220, and relays. Brown excelled in academics, especially English and drama. His favorite teacher, Ruth Norman, affected him profoundly and contributed to his love for literature and drama. Mr. Barnes, the drama teacher, recognized Brown's talent and cast him for a leading part in the school play, *Our Town.* On May 7, 1951, shortly before his high school graduation, Brown performed segments of *Julius Caesar* on WGKV radio in Charleston. Although he was quite articulate, according to friends, he was shy and somewhat reserved. "But you couldn't tell him he wasn't good looking," Robert Easley, another childhood buddy, recalled in an interview.

Brown joined the army in 1953, rising to the rank of corporal, and in 1955, enrolled at Wayne State University in Detroit where he worked part-time in a warehouse to help finance his education. He studied sociology and psychology, earning a B.A. degree in 1959. Concerned about the plight of African Americans and wanting to alleviate the suffering caused by poverty, Brown chose to continue his studies at the university, focusing on psychiatric social work and earning a M.S.W. degree in 1961. However, dissatisfied with his role as social worker, in 1962, Brown became drama critic for the *Detroit Courier.* He worked his way up to the position of city editor at the newspaper and, in 1968, accepted a job in public affairs programming at WTVS, Detroit's public television station.

Using Media to Reach the Masses

Brown became the producer of *C.P.T. (Colored People's Time)* WTVS's first show programmed for a black audience. He also produced and hosted *Free Play,* another community-oriented program. Meanwhile in New York City another black news program, *Black Journal,* funded by the Corporation for Public Broadcasting (CPB) began airing in 1968. This nationally syndicated show was the only one of its kind. Through interviews, documentaries, commentaries, and surveys, *Black Journal* examined social and political issues of concern to African Americans. *Black Journal* received an

Emmy, a Peabody, and a Russwurm award all prior to 1970, when Tony Brown became the executive producer and host of the show.

The 1970s marked a turning point for Brown. He had found the niche for his career and found a partner in marriage. His only child, Byron Anthony, was born in 1971. Brown's marriage ended in divorce several years later.

Brown's approach at *Black Journal* stirred controversy and garnered bitter criticism from many in the broadcasting industry for his candor and his criticism of the White House. Despite the controversy the program was successful, expanding from an hour show once a month to a 30–minute weekly segment. Brown's goal was to spotlight the positive aspects of the African American experience. His approach, which emphasized self help, undercut his intent and caused some African Americans to view him as condescending, arrogant, and even uninformed regarding the struggles of black people in the United States. According to *Contemporary Black Biography,* Brown insisted that if African Americans desire respect they "must have something to be respected for. We should have learned long ago, we can't depend on anyone but ourselves."

Brown sought to bring blacks into the television industry. The majority of his staff came from the black community, and he found white production companies willing to train African Americans to enter the field. Brown's involvement in this training led to his appointment in 1971 as the founding dean of the School of Communications at Howard University, a position he held until 1974. While dean he initiated the Careers in Communications Conference, now an annual event that enables students to secure jobs in the communications industry.

When the Corporation for Public Broadcasting announced that it would not fund *Black Journal* for the 1973–74 season, James D. Williams, in *Black Enterprise,* observed "Tony Brown had become a thorn in the side of the establishment with his often bitter attacks against what he described as racism in public broadcasting." However CPB's announcement angered the national black community which responded in angry protest. As a result the show was funded but the programming was cut. By 1977, Brown, weary of the limits of public television, negotiated a contract with the Pepsi Cola Company to sponsor the show, changed its name to *Tony Brown's Journal* and moved to commercial television. The syndicated show aired in 85 cities, and his show *Tony Brown at Daybreak* on WRC–TV in Washington, D.C., was equally successful. Brown moved the *Journal* back to public television in 1982, however, because he was dissatisfied with the viewing times commercial stations offered.

In 1980, Tony Brown initiated "Black College Day," his one–man effort to save and support black colleges, and formed the Council for the Economic Development of Black Americans in 1985. CEDBA epitomizes Brown's philosophy of self–help. A major aspect of the organization is the "Buy Freedom" campaign. African American consumers are asked to patronize black businesses displaying the Freedom Seal. In order to display this seal, a business must agree to a five–point program, pledging courtesy, competitive prices, employment opportunities, discounts, and active community involvement.

In 1988 Brown's most ambitious effort to reach the black community through the media resulted in a film which he wrote, directed, produced, and distributed. According to Brown the film, entitled *The White Girl* (a street name for cocaine), dealt "with two destructive trends in society, drug addiction and self–hate." While some people credited Brown's effort, the film failed miserably. *Los Angeles Times* film critic Jack Mathews called *White Girl* "a condescending morality play." Hal Hinson, writing for the *Washington Post* concurred, "Tony Brown's well–meaning but harrowing amateurish film about the horrors of drug addiction, is a 'Just Say No' commercial, plain and simple."

Brown was less concerned with the art of the film than he was with the business aspects. In "The Marketing of 'White Girl,'" Brown admitted that he "looked at it from a business, artistic and community–development perspective." Using a community development approach to distribute the film, he circulated it in the black community for 18 months with local groups showing it to raise money for him and charity.

Education Plus Hard Work Equals Success

Brown's formula for success has garnered him numerous honors and awards, which include the 1995 Ambassador of Free Enterprise Award, presented by the Sales and Marketing Executives International Academy of Achievement. Brown is the first African American to receive this award. He also earned the 1993 Community Service Award from the Institute for American Business. In 1991, the NAACP presented Brown with its Image Award. He is also the recipient of the 1989 Solomon Carter Fuller Award for promoting self–esteem through education, broadcasting, and movie distribution. In 1977, Brown was honored with The National Urban League Public Service Award and received the Operation PUSH Communicator for Freedom Award in 1973.

Brown has maintained an active presence within the community. He has served on the board of trustees at Shaw Divinity School and as an advisor to the Harvard Foundation for Intercultural and Race Relations. In addition, Brown has served as a member of the National American Slavery Memorial Advisory Board, the National Advisory Board of the Republican Mainstream Committee, and on the board of directors for the Association for the Study of Afro–American Life and History. Despite his busy schedule, Brown finds time for horticulture, bird collecting and astrology. Recent projects included the publication of his first book, *Black Lies, White Lies: The Truth According to Tony Brown* (1995) and *Tony Brown Online,* a nationwide membership– based computer network offering full internet access beginning December 14, 1995. Tony Brown, a warrior for black equality, continues to use the media to speak out on black issues.

Current address: Tony Brown Productions, 1501 Broadway, Suite 412, New York, NY 10036; (212) 575–0876; E–mail: tbprod@ix.netcom.com.

REFERENCES

Brown, Tony. *Black Lies, White Lies: The Truth According to Tony Brown.* New York: William Morrow, 1995.

———. Press Release. February 3, 1994.

Contemporary Black Biography. Vol. 3. Detroit: Gale Research, 1992.

Easley, Paul and Robert. Telephone Interview with Nagueyalti Warren, December 8, 1995.

"GOP Goes the Weasel: Tony Brown Stands Up for Republicans." *Village Voice,* August 20, 1991.

"The Marketing of 'White Girl:' Tony Brown Targets Message." *The Washington Post,* February 10, 1990.

"Racism is Green." *Chicago Tribune,* January 8, 1989.

"A Treatise Against Drug Use." *New York Times,* February 11, 1990.

"'White Girl' a Condescending Morality Play." *Los Angeles Times,* February 23, 1990.

"'The White Girl' an Anti–drug Melodrama." *Chicago Tribune,* February 9, 1990.

"'White Girl' Message Pales." *The Washington Post,* February 10, 1990.

Williams, James D. "Blacks & Public TV." *Black Enterprise,* 4 (January 1974): 31–33.

Nagueyalti Warren

William Wells Brown

William Wells Brown
(1814?–1884)
Slave, abolitionist, writer, physician, orator

A prolific writer, powerful and persuasive speaker, crusader for freedom and justice, and healer, William Wells Brown rose from the confining ignorance and poverty of American slavery to the heights of international acclaim. He escaped from slavery, became a conductor on the Underground Railroad, lectured on the evils of the slave system, and became a practicing physician. He symbolized the ability of the human spirit to soar above all adversity. Brown, along with Frederick Douglass and Charles Lenox Remond, was among the best and most popular abolitionist leaders. In 1862, according to *They Who Would be Free,* Brown told a white audience in New York: "The nation owes the colored people a great debt," and he, ever mindful of the debt, pressed it upon the American conscience.

According to his daughter's account, William Wells Brown was born a slave on Dr. John Young's plantation near Lexington, Kentucky, on March 15, 1815. William Farrison and other biographers list the date as 1814. Brown's mother was named Elizabeth, and in his own narrative he described her as being of mixed–blood. Elizabeth had seven children; Brown was the youngest. It is possible that Brown's maternal grandfather was a slave named Simon Lee who served in the Continental Army during the American Revolution. Brown himself never mentions Lee, but Farrison deems it a likely story since the Youngs moved to Kentucky from Virginia. Brown's father was George Higgins, a half–brother to the master, John Young. Farrison reports that Higgins and Young were more likely first cousins.

John Young moved his family and slaves from Kentucky to a farm in Missouri Territory in 1816. It was on this farm near the Missouri River that Brown became aware of slavery. At eight Brown served as Young's office boy. He was also sent to the fields and then was made a house slave. During this time he served as part–time assistant to Young, who allowed him to prepare medicine and administer to sick slaves. Brown probably was ten years old when he heard his mother being beaten by Grove Cook, overseer and slave–driver. She was whipped for reporting 15 minutes late to the fields.

When Brown was 13–years old, the Youngs moved again, this time to St. Louis. A new overseer named Haskell was put in charge of the slaves, and Brown was leased to Major Freeland to work in his St. Louis tavern. His experience here contributed to his abhorrence for liquor and his desire to work for the Temperance Movement. Not long after moving to St. Louis, Doctor Young faced financial difficulties. To remedy this problem he sold some of his slaves, among them Brown's mother, sister, and two brothers. His mother was sold locally, but his two brothers and sister were sold to the deep South. Brown was hired out to a local printer named Lovejoy and worked in his printing office. At sixteen Brown was again hired out for one year to James Walker, a slave trader along the Mississippi River. Upon Brown's return, Young informed him that he was to be sold. In 1833 Brown was sold to Samuel Willi, a tailor in St. Louis. Then on October 2, 1833, Willi sold Brown to Enoch Price, a steamboat owner.

In the spring of 1833, Brown and his mother made an ill–fated attempt to escape. They were re–captured in Central Illinois and returned to their owners. As a result of this escape, Brown's mother was sent down the Mississippi River to be auctioned off in New Orleans. Because Brown was related to his master, he had escaped a similar fate. However, Brown escaped again, this time with more success, on January 1, 1834.

Freedom: A New Year's Resolution

Price made the mistake of taking Brown into Cincinnati in the free state of Ohio. Hiding in the swamps and woods by day and traveling only at night, Brown made his way from Cincinnati to Dayton. When he left Dayton, Brown was exhausted, hungry and sick. He knew that if he did not get assistance from someone he might die. Fortunately, Brown met an old Quaker named Wells Brown, who befriended him and nursed him to health.

On his road to freedom, William Wells Brown took a new name. When he was made a house slave in the home of John Young, Mrs. Young had taken the liberty of changing his name to Stanford. When he escaped from slavery, Brown assumed the name William again. But when asked by the Quaker what his full name was, he confessed that he did not have one. In gratitude for the old man's assistance, Brown gave him the privilege of naming him. The man offered his own name but Brown would not agree to part with William. Thus William Wells Brown became his new name.

Brown arrived in Cleveland in the middle of winter but could not make it across the frozen Lake Erie into Canada. Instead he found work and remained in the city until spring. When spring came, however, Brown did not go to Canada, at least not to live. Because of his experience on the steamers on the Mississippi River, he got work on a Lake Erie steamer. Working on a ship moving from place to place made it safer for Brown, who was a fugitive. He earned a good salary which enabled him to purchase books and begin his education.

In the summer of 1834 Brown met Elizabeth Schooner. He fell in love with her, and by fall they were married. Betsey, as Brown called her, was unfaithful and the marriage ended unhappily with their separation in 1847. The couple had three daughters. The oldest died an infant. In 1836 a second daughter, Clarissa, was born. The youngest one, Josephine, born in 1838, was educated in France and wrote her father's biography.

Rebel with a Cause

By 1836 Brown was active in the abolitionist movement and used his work on the steamer to help fugitive slaves escape to freedom. Around 1838, Brown moved his family from Cleveland to Buffalo, New York. Buffalo was a terminus for the steamboats which made it a more convenient place to live than Cleveland. Buffalo was three times larger than Cleveland with a larger population of blacks. It was easy to move from Buffalo into Canada should the need arise. The Browns resided at 13 Pine Street, and their home became a station on the Underground Railroad. Brown met Frederick Douglass, another famous abolitionist during this time.

Brown was drawn into temperance work and organized a temperance society in 1840. It was the first to be organized in western New York, and Brown served as president for three years. In 1843 he retired from this office. By then, the membership was holding national conventions. The temperance society held a National Convention of Colored Citizens in Buffalo August 15–19, 1843. Brown's involvement in the temperance movement did not thwart his commitment to helping fugitive slaves. In 1842 during a seven–month period, he took sixty–nine slaves to Canada. In the fall of 1843, Brown became a lecturer for the New York Anti–Slavery Society.

In 1845, Brown moved his family to Farmington, a small town near Rochester, New York. Farmington was the center of the anti–slavery activities for the western and central part of the state. Brown also wanted to move because the schools in Buffalo were segregated. He believed the educational opportunities for his daughters would be better in Farmington. The Brown family however, was not happy, and in May 1847 Brown and his wife separated. He took custody of their two daughters, moving to Boston to lecture for the Anti–Slavery Society of New England. Boston was the center of the abolitionists activities. Here he met William Lloyd Garrison, Wendell Phillips, and other famous abolitionists, and became prominent in the Massachusetts and American Anti–Slavery Societies. An avowed Garrisonian, Brown's lectures denounced the United States Constitution and pro–slavery churches, and advocated disunion with slave states.

Brown and his daughters moved to 106 Cedar Street in Boston's West End. However, since Boston's schools were segregated, he sent Clarissa and Josephine to school in New Bedford, Massachusetts, where they boarded during the week with abolitionist friends. Soon after his arrival in Boston, Brown completed his manuscript *Narrative of William W. Brown* and submitted it to Edmund Quincy. Quincy liked the manuscript; in fact, he thought it equal if not superior to Douglass' *Narrative.* Brown's autobiography was published in 1847 by the Boston Anti–slavery Office. The narrative was so popular it went through four American editions and five British editions in a nine–year period.

International Lecturer

As a lecturer Brown was praised for his logical, rhetorical, and critical ability. He received many invitations to speak abroad. Brown traveled to Europe in July 1849, as a representative of the American Peace Society at the International Peace Congress in Paris. Following the Peace Conference, he went to England where he promoted the sale of his book and lectured for the British anti–slavery cause. He arrived in London in September 1849, but was forced to remain in Europe until 1854 because the Congress passed the Fugitive Slave Act of 1850. Had Brown returned to the United States he would have risked being arrested and enslaved. In the spring of 1854, however, a group of friends in England purchased his freedom. Thus, while he left the land of his birth as a fugitive, he returned a free man. Fortunately, Brown had taken his daughters with him to Europe and was able to enroll them at the prestigious Home and Colonial School in London. In December 1853 they both passed examinations and became certified schoolmistresses. Clarissa became mistress of a school in Essex County and decided to remain in England. Josephine, who was only fourteen, traveled to France to continue her education. Brown returned to the United States in September 1854.

Brown's estranged wife, Elizabeth, died in Buffalo, New York while he was abroad. Although they were separated in 1847, they never divorced. On April 12, 1859, Brown married Annie Elizabeth Gray (d. 1902) in Boston. She was twenty–five years old, the daughter of William H. and Harriet Gray of Cambridgeport, Massachusetts. The couple moved next door to her parents on Webster Avenue in Cambridgeport where they lived for the next eighteen years. They had two children, but both died before the age of five.

"The Heroes of Insurrection"

William Wells Brown knew abolitionist John Brown well. He had no close contact with him, however, in the days before the guerrilla attack by John Brown and his followers on October 16, 1859, at Harper's Ferry, West Virginia. Brown thought violence was justified in the cause for freedom. He praised John Brown and his followers, calling them the "Heroes of Insurrection." Brown influenced the Grand Division of Massachusetts Sons of Temperance to rename themselves the John Brown Division of the Sons of Temperance.

When the Civil War began, Brown was too old to enlist, but he worked with Frederick Douglass and other abolitionists to recruit blacks for the service. While his body might have been beyond its prime for combat, his mind was as sharp as ever. Brown studied medicine privately, became an apprentice and finally a practicing physician.

When the Civil War ended, Brown was a main speaker at the emancipation ceremonies and celebrations. On January 3, 1868, at Rand Hall, Troy, New York, he spoke about the black war heroes and further advocated all black men's right to vote. After emancipation Brown again became greatly involved in the temperance movement. He continued to lecture, only now both in the North and in the South. In 1871 Brown went to Kentucky to lecture for the National Association for the Organization of Night Schools and the Spread of Temperance Among the Freed People of the South. While in the state of his birth, he was kidnapped by the Ku Klux Klan and taken to a small cottage where he was to be lynched at sunrise. Brown's knowledge of medicine apparently saved his life. It seems the Grand Dragon was not feeling well (otherwise they might have lynched him that very night) and Brown used a hypodermic to put the man to sleep and escape.

Brown continued to travel throughout the South, and spent Christmas and the winter of 1879–80 in Huntsville, Alabama. He also visited Tennessee. Even though he was diagnosed with a tumor of the bladder, he did not become inactive until just a week before he died, on November 6, 1884, in his home in Chelsea, Massachusetts. A private service was held at his home, followed by a public funeral at A.M.E. Zion Church on North Russell Street in Boston on November 9, 1884. William Wells Brown was buried at the Cambridge Cemetery, southwest of Harvard Square. According to Farrison, the grave has no headstone.

Brown was an exceptional man who led a remarkable life. He became a man of letters, distinguishing himself in several genres and writing a dozen or more books and pamphlets. Beginning in 1847 Brown wrote the following: *Narrative of William W. Brown, A Fugitive Slave, Written by Himself; Three Years in Europe* (1852), the first travel book by an African American; *The American Fugitive in Europe* (1855); a revised edition of *Three Years*; *Clotel; Or, The President's Daughter* (1853), the first novel by an African American, although published in London. (Harriet Wilson's novel, *Our Nig* (1859), was the first novel by an African American published in the United States.) The president to whom Brown refers is Thomas Jefferson, who was accused of fathering children by a slave named Sally Hemings. This 1853 edition of *Clotel* was not published in the United States until 1969.

Three other versions of the novel were: *Miralda; Or, The Beautiful Quadroon* (1860–61), serialized in New York; *Clotelle: A Tale of Southern States* (1864); *Clotelle; Or, The Colored Heroine* (1867). In Farrison's opinion, none of the versions offer any improvement.

Experience; Or, How to Give a Northern Man a Backbone (1856) was a three–act antislavery play. Brown read the drama to intrigued audiences but never published it. *The Escape; Or Leap for Freedom* (1858) was a five–act play, the first to be published by an African American. *St. Domingo: Its Revolutions and its Patriots* (1855); *The Black Man, His Antecedents, His Genius, and His Achievements* (1863); and *The Negro in the American Rebellion* (1867) were all historical, the last one making him the first to write a history of African Americans in the military. In this work he brings together the black man's contribution and role in the American Revolution, the War of 1812, and the Civil War. William Nell's *The Colored Patriots of the American Revolution,* published in 1853, is limited to blacks who served during that war alone.

Brown's best historical efforts are *The Rising Son; Or, The Antecedents and Advancement of the Colored Race* (1874) and *The Black Man,* which contains 110 biographies of black men and women who might otherwise have been forgotten. He, in fact, produced the first dictionary of black biography. *My Southern Home: Or, The South and Its People* (1880) was Brown's last work. It relates the events of his trip through the South during 1879–1880.

William Wells Brown is widely studied in schools and colleges, keeping alive his work as crusader for freedom, which he pursued through many channels. His writings contribute significantly to black scholarship.

REFERENCES

Brown, Josephine. *Biography of an American Bondman* (1856). In *Two Biographies by African-American Women*. Edited by Henry Louis Gates. New York: Oxford University Press, 1991.

Brown, William Wells. *Narrative of William W. Brown 1815–1884*. 1847. Reprint, New York: Johnson Reprint [1970].

Farrison, William Edward. *William Wells Brown: Author and Reformer*. Chicago: University of Chicago Press: 1969.

Logan, Rayford W., and Michael Winston, eds. *Dictionary of American Negro Biography*. New York: Norton, 1982.

Nagueyalti Warren

Willie L. Brown Jr.

(1934–)

Mayor

Willie L. Brown Jr.

Mayor Willie L. Brown Jr., surveying San Francisco's diverse cityscape and sweeping bay area from his seventeenth-floor apartment on Cathedral Hill, comments, "It's great to look out there and know that you are mayor of everything—as far as you can see," according to a profile of Brown by Marshall Frady in *The New Yorker* magazine of October 21–28, 1996. Brown scrambled from humble beginnings to become one of the most politically astute and powerful men in the United States.

Willie Lewis Brown Jr. was born on March 20, 1934, in the small East Texas railroad town of Mineola, about 80 miles east of Dallas. Originally called Sodom, it was "a backwater in American life. . . . Most Mineola adults—black or white—were poorly educated and few could look forward to opportunities beyond farm, cotton gin, or oil patch," wrote James Richardson in *Willie Brown: A Biography*. "Brown was born black at a time when racial segregation was whipped furiously by the economic havoc of the Great Depression. . . . Segregation was not just a system of racial separation at the lunch counter; it was a system whereby whites kept blacks on the bottom rung in everything from education to justice, jobs to health care."

Brown's mother, Minnie Collins (1909–1993), the daughter of Anna Lee Nolan and Richard Collins, and father, Willie Lewis Brown (1908–1994), the son of Ella Roberts and Lewis Brown, were among the Mineola blacks struggling on the bottom rung to earn a living and survive. Survival meant finding work outside Mineola. When Brown was about four years old, his father left his native town for Los Angeles, where he worked variously as a Pullman train porter and in a stove foundry before enlisting in the U.S. Army during World War II. He never returned to Mineola. About a year after Lewis Brown's departure from Mineola, Minnie Brown also left and accepted employment as a live-in domestic worker in various white households in Dallas. Young Willie Brown and his siblings were entrusted to his maternal grandmother, Anna Lee Nolan Collins, who supported her extended family by operating the Shack—a combination dance hall, saloon, and casino—with an adjacent shed where Willie Brown's two uncles sold moonshine that they produced in stills outside town.

The second and third generations of the family were enlisted to work in the Collins family business, and Willie Brown also began picking beans and berries on various Mineola farms during the summer by the time he was 11. In his teenage years, he took a job shining shoes in a downtown barbershop. Yet young Willie was determined and destined to outgrow the small Texas town. In school he had a marked aptitude for mathematics and was an able student in other subjects. As soon as he graduated from Mineola Colored High School in 1951, he accepted his Uncle Rembert ("Itsie") Collins's invitation to stay with him in San Francisco. There he enrolled at San Francisco State College (SFSC), supporting himself as a janitor, then youth director, for Jones Methodist Church. After graduating in 1955 from SFSC, he attended Hastings College of Law at the University of California, from which he received the J.D. degree in 1958. He passed the bar exam that summer, and on September 1 he married Blanche Vitero of Berkeley, a "petite dance major" he had met and fallen in love with at SFSC. Blanche Vitero's father, according to Richardson, was "a Filipino fisherman in Oakland and her mother was black," but their names were not given. Over the next five years, three children would be born to Willie and Blanche Brown: Susan Elizabeth (b. August 5, 1958), Robin

Elaine (b. February 20, 1960), and Michael Elliott (b. October 22, 1963).

Brown and fellow attorney Terry Francois established a law practice in the Fillmore district of San Francisco, and Brown won his first case defending a prostitute. After the word spread within the ''world's oldest profession'' that the working girls had a capable defender, the young lawyer was swamped with business. ''I made cash money every day representing whores,'' recalled Brown to writer Robert Scheer in *Los Angeles Times Magazine.* ''I became the whores' lawyer . . . until I got elected'' to the California State Assembly.

Enters State Politics

During the years leading to that fateful 1964 election, Brown supported his family through his law practice and continued his activities at Jones Methodist Church. The church was the meeting place of the local NAACP chapter and according to Richardson was ''at the forefront of the civil rights movement in San Francisco.'' Through his work with the NAACP chapter and as legal counsel for Jones Methodist Church, he was called on frequently to represent civil rights activists, and his reputation for ''courtroom panache'' grew quickly throughout the early 1960s. Building on his work with the NAACP and his growing reputation as a civil rights advocate, Brown and his allies launched a sit–in during the summer of 1961 to protest segregated housing in San Francisco after his wife was rebuffed as a possible homeowner by a white real–estate development company. Although the protest did not end housing discrimination, it brought public attention to the issue and thrust Willie Brown into the media spotlight.

The following year he undertook his first campaign for election to the California State Assembly as representative of the Eighteenth District, comprising the Haight–Ashbury area of black, Asian, Latino, and white residents. Although he fell short of being elected in 1962, he maintained momentum over the following two years until the 1964 primary for the same seat. He won the Democratic nomination on June 2, 1964, and went on to win the general election in November, becoming the first African American to represent San Francisco in the California State Assembly.

After Brown's election to the state legislature, he joined a fellow civil rights advocate and lawyer, John Dearman, in a new law practice, which would continue over the following two decades. Brown's arrival in Sacramento in early 1965 as Eighteenth Assembly District Representative marked the beginning of a 31–year career in that office, of which 15 years were spent as the first black Speaker of the House and the longest–serving Speaker in the history of California (1980–1995).

Willie Brown's early political career—when the 80–member state legislature's minority members consisted of only four blacks and one woman—reflected the upheaval of the confrontational 1960s. ''He found the boundaries of his district under legal attack [his district was finally redrawn by one man–one vote reapportionment and became the Thirteenth Assembly District], and he unwittingly stepped into a major controversy over the Vietnam War. Threatened with recall, Brown kept his cool, and won moderate success legislating,'' wrote biographer Richardson. The freshman legislator also learned to develop alliances ''outside the traditional power structure'' in the state capital, and during his first term demonstrated that he was an ''emerging force Sacramento politicians needed to take seriously.''

The wisdom of taking Representative Brown seriously was underscored as he tenaciously reviewed and drafted legislation primarily directed toward improving conditions for the poor, the elderly, and minorities. His advocacy for the powerless, as well as his continued civil rights activities in the San Francisco area, earned him the reputation among white legislators as ''a kind of undersized but over–egoed Adam Clayton Powell in their midst,'' observed Frady. For Brown's constituents during that ultraconservative Age of Reagan in California politics, his Powellesque ''in–your–face'' style was a forceful attribute which guaranteed his continuous reelection 16 times to the Thirteenth Assembly District seat.

In 1971, about the time Willie and Blanche Brown's turbulent marriage was fraying into a formal separation, the legislator added another notch to his belt of political achievements. At age 37 he became chairman of the powerful House Committee on Ways and Means—the youngest lawmaker in the Assembly's history to attain the chairmanship and the first African American to hold the post. Three years later, he made an unsuccessful attempt to become Speaker of the House, but he remained focused on attaining that goal. By 1980, he ''had become a wizard in playing the margins'' and, as he initiated a new push for the speakership, he ''quietly engineered an impasse among the other Democratic contenders for the post. At the same time, he formed a discreet coalition with Republican members [to reward them with appointive positions] . . .if they aided in delivering the gavel into his hands,'' wrote Frady. Brown's unorthodox coalition delivered the speaker's post to him with 28 votes from Republicans and 23 votes from Democrats. ''I think they were very sincere in their belief that I was such a party boy that I would never focus long enough to run a good operation,'' Brown told Frady. ''It's a perfect hide–behind position.''

The day arrived in the early 1990s, however, when there was no longer a hide–behind position for veteran representative and Speaker Willie Brown. California voters had approved a proposition to impose varying term limits on all elected state officials. The seniority death knell began in 1994 for Brown, who would now have to retire from office. In an adroit use of his legendary power brokerage, ''Brown ousted a Republican member of the Assembly on a technicality, won another Republican vote to his side and kept the speakership for six more months,'' wrote Sharon Waxman in the *Washington Post.*

San Francisco's First Black Mayor

After he stepped down as Speaker of the House on June 5, 1995, Brown devoted his considerable energy to his campaign for mayor of San Francisco, which offered him ''an opportunity to vindicate every doubt that's ever been associated with my ability, whether on the ethical side or whether on the substantive side,'' he told biographer Richardson. Willie Brown won a landslide victory in the mayoral runoff election on December 12.

Brown faced the urban infrastructure problems facing all major cities—and the problems of public transit, affordable housing, homelessness, and unwieldy government bureaucracy specific to San Francisco. The concern was addressed on February 15 by Mayor Brown in ''Moving Swiftly, Decisively: My First Six Weeks in Office,'' prepared for the San Francisco Neighborhood Newspaper Association. ''There appears to be a renewed commitment to getting things done, a citywide can–do attitude, bustling in the San Francisco breeze,'' wrote Brown. After promising to ''foster that can–do spirit,'' he noted that he had ''moved quickly to improve our Municipal Railway system, to convene a San Francisco Economic Summit, to stabilize our public housing crisis, and to fill city government with a collection of San Franciscans who reflect the City's diversity, as well as its best interests.''

On April 18, 1996, ''Mayor Willie's First 100 Days in Office at a Glance,'' the first state–of–the–city report, was issued. Brown's four–page progress report outlined several dozen items of activity, including steps taken to improve the city's Municipal Railway; results of a San Francisco Economic Summit focusing on affordable housing; revamping of the city's Housing Commission; plans to develop a new Youth Center; staging of two seminars in ethics orientation for city employees and appointees; and CalTrans receiving ''the green light on tearing down the Central Freeway, which had been declared unsafe and slated for retrofit since the 1989 Loma Prieta earthquake.''

If Brown can sustain the momentum of constructive change—making his desire for validation of his substantive qualities a self–fulfilling prophecy—''Da Mayor,'' as he refers to himself and uses as his Internet e–mail address, will have added further credence to his title ''King of the Hills.'' It would be a political coup if Mayor Willie Brown's view from Cathedral Hill were even more gratifying in the closing years of the twentieth century.

REFERENCES

''Brown Embraced by Old Hometown.'' *San Francisco Examiner,* April 28, 1996; included in online archives of *San Francisco Examiner.* http://www.sfgate.com/cgi–bin/examiner.

City and County of San Francisco Internet home page. Includes ''Welcome from Mayor Brown,'' ''Mayor Brown Says. . .,'' and ''Moving Swiftly, Decisively: My First Six Weeks in Office,'' by Willie L. Brown, Jr., February 15, 1996. http://www.ci.sf.ca.us/mayor/.

Frady, Marshall. ''An American Political Fable.'' *The New Yorker* 72 October 21–28, 1996. 200.

Kaplan, David A., and Patricia King. ''City Slickers: The 25 Most Dynamic Mayors in America.'' *Newsweek* 128 (11 November 1996). 28–35.

King, John. ''Brown's Single–Minded Goal: Creating a City of Style, Glitz.'' *San Francisco Chronicle,* February 13, 1997, and ''The New Darling of National Media: New Yorker to Esquire: They All Want Willie.'' October 14, 1996; included in online archives of *San Francisco Chronicle.* http://www.sfgate.com/cgi–bin/chronicle.

''Mayor With the Keys to the City: San Francisco's King of the Hills.'' *Washington Post,* May 15, 1996.

Morse, Rob. ''Sunrise Over a Stylish New S.F..'' *San Francisco Examiner,* January 8, 1996; ''25 ways to Suck Up to Willie Brown,'' October 27, 1996; and ''Mayor–elect Shows Class in Victory,'' December 13, 1995; included in online archives of *San Francisco Examiner.* http://www.sfgate.com/cgi–bin/examiner.

Office of the Mayor, San Francisco, California. Press packet including biographical sheet and photo of Willie L. Brown, Jr.; ''Mayor Willie's First 100 Days in Office at a Glance;'' and assorted press clippings, April 29, 1997.

Richardson, James. *Willie Brown: A Biography.* Berkeley and Los Angeles: University of California Press, 1996.

Saunders, Debra J. ''Forget Trust, This City Wants Style.'' *San Francisco Chronicle,* December 15, 1995. http://www.sfgate.com/cgi–bin/chronicle.

Scheer, Robert. ''Mr. Speaker: The Flash.'' *Los Angeles Times Magazine,* June 23, 1991.

''What Will Brown Do With His Mandate?'' editorial. *San Francisco Chronicle,* December 14, 1995. http://www.sfgate.com/cgi–bin/chronicle.

Ilene Jones–Cornwell

Blanche Kelso Bruce

(1841–1898)

U.S. Senator, politician, plantation owner, educator, orator

The life and political career of Blanche Kelso Bruce reflects the remarkable achievements as well as the disappointments and contradictions of the post–Civil–War Reconstruction era. From 1870 to 1880, Bruce moved easily within the chaotic climate of Reconstruction society and politics to become the first black Republican senator from Mississippi to serve a full term in the U.S. Senate. His entire career illustrates the high degree of public distinction that many former slaves achieved, given education, determination, and a favorable political climate. Before entering politics, Bruce was a successful educator, first in Kansas, then in Bolivar County, Mississippi. In *Black Leaders of the Nineteenth Century,* Historian Howard N. Rabinowitz considered Bruce's contributions: to the field of education as Bruce's most important social legacy in Bolivar County:

> His most impressive contribution came as superintendent of schools [in Bolivar County], taking a faltering system and turning it into one of the healthiest in the state. By the end of 1872 the county had twenty–one schools with more than a thousand students.... By helping to establish the county's first school system and by assuring blacks a place within it, Bruce had furthered his own interests as well as those of his race.

Although Bruce was not credited with forcing any landmark decisions on the Senate floor, he and his black senatorial colleagues were remembered by James G. Blaine, a contemporary politician, in *From Slavery to Freedom*: "The colored men who took seats in both Senate and House did not appear ignorant or helpless. They were as a rule studious, earnest, ambitious men, whose public conduct... would be honorable to any race." Bruce is remembered for many unpopular stands he took in the Senate, but he may be remembered best for his thorough investigation into the collapse of the Freedmen's Savings and Trust Company. Highly respected, Bruce, nevertheless, failed to win a second term when the Radical Republicans lost power in the South. After leaving the Senate in 1881, the popular and resourceful politician, plantation owner, and educator easily gained other political appointments.

Blanche Kelso Bruce

Blanche K. Bruce was born on March 1, 1841, the eleventh child of Polly, a slave, on a plantation in Farmville, Prince Edward County, Virginia. According to John W. Cromwell in *The Negro in American History,* he was named Blanche Bruce, but he added Kelso as he approached adulthood. William Gatewood in *Aristocrats of Color,* claims that Bruce probably was the son of Polly's master, Pettus Perkinson.

Various historical accounts of Bruce's childhood acknowledged that the young, mulatto slave had more advantages than many children of bondage. Although Pettus Perkinson moved his family several times within six years, Bruce learned to read and demonstrated an eagerness to learn. In one of the few references to his famous brother, Henry K. Bruce wrote in his autobiography that Blanche learned to read and write while taking care of his half–brother Willie, Perkinson's son by marriage. Henry K. Bruce credited his mother for encouraging her children to take advantage of learning opportunities:

> There was a trait of character running through my mother's family, a desire to learn, and every member could read very well when the war broke out, and some could write. The older ones would teach the younger, and while mother had no education at all, she used to make the younger study the lessons given by the older sister or brother, and in that way they all learned to read.

Bruce's friend, George C. Smith, further substantiated that Bruce was an eager learner. Smith had learned some facts about Bruce's early years from Congressman Cosgrove of Missouri. Cosgrove had worked with Bruce at a printing office in Brunswick, Missouri. "Mr. Bruce was the 'devil' on the press, and whenever he was wanted, he was always found with his head buried in a book or a newspaper, that it was a difficult job to keep him at work."

Rise in Politics

During the early years of the Civil War, Bruce fled to Laurence, Kansas, and became a fugitive slave. When he returned to Missouri in 1864, the state was forced to recognize him as a free man. At this time, Bruce taught at a school that he founded specifically for black children in Hannibal, Missouri. Different historical accounts have Bruce attending Oberlin for either a few months or one year. However, Jessie Carney Smith wrote in the biography of Bruce's wife: "Although a number of published sources state that he studied at Oberlin College, the college has never been able to establish his attendance." By 1868, Bruce began to display his entrepreneurial skills as a cotton farmer in Mississippi. Willard Gatewood, in *Aristocrats of Color,* claimed that Bruce also began his political career at this time.

In 1868, Bruce was ready to take advantage of all of the opportunities that the post–Civil War south offered an ambitious, emancipated black man. Certainly, Bruce had the gifts: he was literate, articulate, ambitious, and light–skinned. Gatewood quoted David S. Barry, a contemporary of Bruce, who said that Bruce was of "high moral, mental, and physical standards ... a handsome man, well–built, with a finely shaped head covered with curly black hair." Apparently his dress was also impeccable.

Bruce's political career truly gained momentum in January of 1870 when he was elected sergeant–at–arms of the

Mississippi Senate. In 1871, he became sheriff and tax assessor of Bolivar County. A firm Republican, he also earned the distinction in 1880 of becoming the first black man to lead the Republican National Convention, which was held in Chicago. His rise in politics was due in large part to his recognizing and seizing opportunities. When Congress began the radical reconstruction of 11 former Confederate states in 1867, opportunities for black leaders were abundant in the South. The U.S. government, demanding sweeping changes from the South's antebellum practices, established the Freedmen's Bureau. Under the bureau's jurisdiction, former rebel states were to have constitutional conventions in which black men participated and voted in order to build a more equitable South. Radical Republicanism, a nemesis to conservative "white Democrats," posed a threat to Southerners who had not only lost the Civil War, but also now faced losing an entire way of life. White Republicans needed black leaders.

Historian Howard N. Rabinowitz stated in *Black Leaders* that white planters who dominated the politics of the area considered Bruce, who had offended no local whites, "safe–a dignified and educated mulatto who did not identify himself with threatening issues." He was also a landowner, which made him even more appealing to them. He had turned 640 acres of swampy land into a plantation. He then acquired even more land and, by the 1880s, had become a wealthy man.

Nevertheless, while white planters and Republicans may have viewed Bruce as "safe," the former slave was not just a passive recipient of favors. In fact, Bruce planned his rise in politics. According to Bruce's black colleague, John R. Lynch, Bruce declined in 1873 to run for lieutenant governor under the newly elected Governor Adelbert Ames. Apparently, Bruce knew that he would have a good chance at a senatorial seat in Mississippi but revealed his intentions to no one. Most Republicans wanted Bruce in the Senate, especially James Hill, the most influential black leader in Mississippi. According to Cromwell, Hill had earlier told Bruce as they once walked through the Senate chambers, "I can and will put you there [in a Senate seat]; no one can defeat you."

Elected to U.S. Senate

In 1874, three years after Hill's promise, Bruce announced his candidacy for a Senate seat. Despite political maneuvering by his opponents, Bruce defeated two white carpetbaggers and was elected to the U.S. Senate. Bruce became the second black man from Mississippi to serve in that position. In March of 1875, at age 34, Bruce began a full term in the Senate, occupying the seat until 1881. On inauguration day, his fellow senator from Mississippi, James Lusk Alcorn, refused to escort Bruce, as was customary. Although Alcorn had extended many political favors to Bruce, he was angry that Bruce did not help him in a bitter personal struggle with Governor Ames. Cromwell quoted a record of Bruce's reaction to Alcorn's lack of respect:

> Mr. Alcorn made no motion to escort me, but was buried behind a newspaper, and I concluded I would go it alone. I had got about half–way up the aisle when a tall gentleman stepped up and said, "Excuse me, Mr. Bruce, I did not until this moment see that you were without escort, permit me. My name is Conkling," and he linked his arm in mine and we marched up to the desk together. I took the oath and then he escorted me back to my seat.

In 1878 Blanche Bruce married Josephine Beall Wilson, a teacher. They had one son, Roscoe Conkling Bruce, whose name was given in gratitude to the New York Senator who saved Bruce from humiliation.

During the next six years, Bruce maintained a secure reputation as a representative of Mississippi, often presiding over the Senate. Bruce's polished manners and integrity overshadowed any reservations his white colleagues had.

Within the Senate, Bruce was viewed as a moderate in his political views. Like Booker T. Washington, Bruce wanted civil rights for blacks, not necessarily social equality. According to Rabinowitz, Bruce argued for the desegregation of the U.S. Army. While Bruce rejected the "Back to Africa" movement, Rabinowitz stated that he, like most black leaders, wanted blacks to obtain "land, education and civil rights that included equal access to public accommodations and conveyances." In 1876 Bruce argued strongly, but unsuccessfully, for P. B. S. Pinchback when the Senate denied him the seat to which the voters of Louisiana had elected him.

Bruce's role in chairing the investigation into the Freedmen's Savings and Trust scandal constituted his most notable work. Since 1865, when the federal government authorized a bank specifically for black depositors to help former slaves become economically stable, mismanagement and corruption had plagued it. By 1874, the bank had collapsed despite Frederick Douglass's heroic efforts to preserve it. Bruce chaired a Senate investigation into the causes of the bank's failure. Among Bruce's papers located at Howard University is a newspaper report of the committee's findings. The article quoted the committee:

> If . . . the trustees who conducted this bank had been men of great discretion, great integrity, and entire devotion to the purpose of the enterprise under their control, there is no reason why either loss to the depositors [i.e., freedmen] should have followed or disaster to the institution should have come.

By 1877, several national events greatly diminished the effectiveness of the Republicans and, hence, of black leaders. Northern leaders, with their emphasis on industrialization, had lost interest in the agrarian south. Since Democrats had "redeemed" the South, Bruce had no chance to remain in the Senate after his term expired. The Reconstruction Era had ended.

Becomes Register of the Treasury

Bruce, one of the most influential men of the black middle class at the time, had formed strong alliances with white Republican leaders. Although he did not use his handsome appearance or polished manners for frivolous socializing, he did use his reputation and status as a gentleman farmer, politician, and educator to secure positions after he left office. In 1881, he became the first black Register of the Treasury under President James Garfield. In 1889, President Benjamin Harrison appointed Bruce as Recorder of Deeds of the District of Columbia. Bruce held this post until May 25, 1894. In 1895, under President William McKinley, Bruce held an appointed post of Register of the Treasury for three months until he became ill. Frequently, during the remainder of his public career, he lectured on the issue of race. In private life, Bruce operated a successful business in Washington, D.C., handling investments, claims, insurance, and real estate. He also served on the Board of Trustees of Howard University from 1894 to 1898, and received an honorary degree from the school in 1893.

Despite the confusion, contradictions, and final tragedy of Reconstruction, Bruce is remembered as a highly principled educator and politician who left a positive imprint upon the U.S. Senate. He was a polished speaker who, in J. W. Cromwell's words, ''bore himself manfully'' when the need for debate arose. He was polite, gracious, and self–confident. Although he and his wife Josephine Beall Bruce enjoyed the good life and were regarded as perhaps too removed from the ordinary black Washingtonian during his term as senator, Bruce actually was continually involved in issues concerning the larger black population. Unpretentious and serious about his work, Bruce is regarded by some historians as the most successful black politician of the Reconstruction period.

Blanche Bruce died from diabetic complications in March of 1898, in Washington, D.C., at the age of 57. He was buried in Suitland, Maryland, the final resting–place of many other early, prominent blacks.

REFERENCES

Bruce, H. C. *The New Man: Twenty–nine Years As a Slave, Twenty–nine Years a Free Man; Recollections of H. C. Bruce.* 1895. Reprint, Miami: Mnemosyne Publishing Co., 1969.

Cromwell, John W. *The Negro in American History.* Washington DC: The American Negro Academy, 1914.

Gatewood, Willard B. *Aristocrats of Color: The Black Elite 1880–1920.* Bloomington: Indiana University Press, 1990.

Johnson, Allen, ed. *Dictionary of American Biography.* New York: Charles Scribner's Sons, 1953.

Litwack, Leon, and August Meier, eds. *Black Leaders of the Nineteenth Century.* Chicago: University of Illinois Press, 1988.

Logan, Rayford W., and Michael R. Winston, eds. *Dictionary of American Negro Biography.* New York: Norton, 1982.

Lynch, John R. *The Facts of Reconstruction.* New York: Neale Pub. Co., 1913.

Smith, Jessie Carney, ed. *Notable Black American Women.* Detroit: Gale Research, 1992.

Stamp, Kenneth M. *The Era of Reconstruction, 1865–1877.* New York: Random House, 1975.

COLLECTIONS

The papers of Blanche K. Bruce are in the Moorland–Spingarn Research Center, Howard University, Washington, D.C. Records relating to his office as Register of the Treasury are in the National Archives of the Smithsonian.

Grace E. Collins

Andrew Bryan
(1737?–1812)
Religious worker

On January 20, 1788, Andrew Bryan founded First African Baptist Church, the first continuing Baptist church in Savannah, Georgia. The first Baptist church in the city (1779–1782) was also black, but it dispersed with the end of British occupation, sending future church founders George Liele to Jamaica, David George to Canada, Brother Amos to the Bahamas, and Jesse Peter (or Galphin) to Georgia's Macon area. Bryan's reestablished church preceded the first white Baptist church by twelve years. In 1802 membership in the First African Baptist Church reached 850, and two more churches were created from it: Second African Baptist Church of Savannah, with 200 members, and Ogeechee Baptist Church, with 250. At the time of Bryan's death in 1812, the membership of First African stood at about 1,000. This rapid growth in membership stems from the one man and three women baptized by black pastor and missionary George Liele shortly before Liele's ship sailed for Jamaica in 1782. These four were Andrew Bryan, his wife Hannah, Kate Hogg, and Hagar Simpson.

Andrew Bryan was born in 1737, according to his own estimation, in Goose Creek, South Carolina, near Charleston. This statement comes from a letter printed in 1800 and cited by Carter G. Woodson. This should be decisive, but two other pieces of evidence suggest an earlier birth date. James M. Simms cites a letter written by white Baptist minister Henry Holcombe of Savannah, also dated 1800, in which Bryan's age is given at eighty. However, Holcombe may have guessed the age based on Bryan's white hair and venerable appearance. Finally, the tablet placed on Bryan's grave in 1821 states that he was ninety–six when he died in 1812. Andrew C. Marshall (1755?–1856), Bryan's nephew and successor, would seem a logical source for this information.

Bryan's owner, Jonathan Bryan, brought him to Brampton, a plantation about three miles southwest of Savannah. By the time of his baptism, Bryan was the family coachman and body servant to his owner. Sometime before 1790 Bryan was allowed to purchase his freedom for a nominal price. Little of Andrew Bryan's wife is known beyond her name. She was also free by 1800. The couple had one daughter who was still a

Andrew Bryan

slave in that year. The daughter married a free black, probably named Whitfield, since a Sampson Whitfield is later identified as her son. She was a slave, so her five sons and three daughters were also legally slaves.

Begins Ministry

Bryan may have come into contact with George Liele as early as 1773 or 1774 when Liele began preaching occasionally at Brampton plantation. After his baptism in 1782, Bryan meditated and prayed for some nine months and then began to preach. About this time he learned to read. He may not have learned to write since he signed a deed with his mark.

One of Bryan's first converts was his brother, Sampson Bryan (1747–1799), who later became a deacon in the church. Jonathan Bryan was sympathetic to Andrew Bryan's religious vocation and gave him permission to use the barn on Brampton plantation for religious services. Soon thereafter, another white sympathizer, Edward Davis, allowed Bryan and his followers to construct a rough wooden building for worship on land Davis owned just west of Savannah at Yamacraw. About 1785 an elderly white Baptist minister passed through the area and baptized Sampson Bryan and 17 others. It is surmised that the number would have been higher except for the requirement that slaves have the written permission of their masters before being baptized.

In 1788 Abraham Marshall, a white minister from Kioke, Georgia, visited Savannah. He was accompanied by the black preacher Jesse (otherwise known as Peter), a former member of the Silver Bluff Church in Silver Bluff, South Carolina, the first black Baptist church in America. Marshall baptized 45 more persons, ordained Bryan, and organized a church.

The early years of the church were not easy, especially after British protection ceased in 1782. Slaves were required to have written passes from their owners to move about and were subject to curfew at night. Even so, gatherings of slaves were suspect because slave owners feared the possibility of insurrection. Many whites were also ambivalent about the conversion of slaves; established white churches were particularly shocked by a church that rejected paedobaptism—baptism of infants—and insisted on baptism by immersion.

To overcome these obstacles, Bryan and his supporters formed Christian cells on plantations: one male was appointed watchman to open and lead prayer services. These services were either open or clandestine depending on the disposition of the plantation owners. Whenever possible, members from the plantations would come to services at Brampton and later Yamacraw. Bryan held three Sunday services: morning prayer at sunrise, preaching at ten in the morning, and again at three in the afternoon. Communion services were held four times a year.

Persecution of the black Baptists was harsh throughout this period. Around 1791, news of a major slave rising in northern Haiti, known as the Night of Fire, generated fears of slave insurrections throughout the Caribbean and the slaveholding areas of the United States. Patrols became more vigilant and severe and, as a result, large numbers of Bryan's congregation were arrested and beaten for being out even though they carried passes. Both Andrew and Sampson Bryan were beaten so severely that the blood ran down their backs to the ground. The brothers, along with 50 other blacks, were then imprisoned and accused of plotting insurrection.

Jonathan Bryan intervened on their behalf and, after examination by the Justices of the Inferior Court of Chatham County, the brothers were declared innocent and released. They resumed their meetings in the barn at Brampton. Meetings were also resumed in Yamacraw in a temporary shelter on a lot between Mill Street and Indian Street Lane, which was donated by Thomas Gibbons.

To secure official permission to hold services, Bryan had a noted lawyer, Lachlan McIntosh, draw up a petition to the mayor and aldermen of Savannah. As reprinted by Simms, this document points out the church members' "orderly conduct at the place of thier [sic] meeting," "thier submission & obedient behaviour to thier Masters & Mistresses," and the "standing rule to admit none who have not only the Approbation but the recommendation of thier Masters for thier good morals & faithful behaviour." Although this plea was rejected by city officials, the Chatham County militia, in a document dated March 19, 1796, granted Bryan permission to hold services on Sundays between sunrise and sunset.

Erects a Church

In 1793 Bryan acquired a lot in Yamacraw, now within the Savannah city limits. The area was underdeveloped and mostly covered with brush. On this lot Bryan built a small house into which he moved his family in 1794, the year he began building a 42– by 49–foot church. The rough building the church had been using for worship was also moved onto the lot. The whole was surrounded by a high board fence. The plain church building was completed in 1795. The last service was held in it on September 28, 1873, and it was then torn down. By this time the congregation was meeting regularly in a new building on the site and the old one was very run down.

On July 3, 1797, Bryan witnessed a deed transferring ownership of half of the lot on which church stood to white trustees, as was required by law. The first trustee named in the deed, Thomas Pohill, had been converted in 1789, along with his wife, after Bryan had preached in the yard at Pohill's home at Newington, in Effingham County. The couple was also involved in the founding of the first white Baptist church in Savannah in 1800. That same year the First African Baptist Church was over a decade old and had some 850 members in and around Savannah.

First African Baptist became a recognized member of several Baptist associations. In 1790 it joined the Georgia Baptist Association, but it was dismissed in 1795 to join the Lower District Georgia Baptist Association after the parent body decided to divide. In 1802 First African and two small white churches at Newington and Savannah organized into the Savannah River Association. The Savannah River Association then decided to ordain new black ministers and create two new churches. Second Colored Baptist, under Henry Cunningham, was set up on the affluent east side of Savannah. Its 200 members soon included younger city dwellers—mostly domestic servants and some mechanics. Ogeechee Baptist, under Henry Francis, ministered to some 200 plantation workers.

As Bryan grew older, his nephew and eventual successor as pastor of First African Baptist, Andrew Cox Marshall, assisted his uncle by preaching and baptizing. People remembered Bryan in his old age as a moderately heavy man with white hair and his own very white teeth. He appeared to be of unmixed African descent. During baptisms, Bryan observed from a two–wheel carriage at the river bank. Songs of Zion were sung during the ceremony. One church member often improvised on an appropriate theme and was answered by a choral response such as a stanza beginning, "I am bound for the promised land." Such hymns were often sung from memory.

Bryan upheld strict standards of morality for members of his flock. Persons who wished to receive baptism had to be married, not simply living together as was common at the time. In so far as was possible, Bryan and his church also insisted on the sanctity of the marriage bond. Because slave owners often separated married slaves, the church accepted what it could not remedy and allowed remarriage when the separation was definite. Bryan was also a resolutely orthodox Baptist. On a key point of Baptist doctrine, no person was admitted to communion unless baptized by immersion.

Andrew Bryan died on October 6, 1812, after a gradual decline in health. By the time of his death his daughter was a free woman, and he left an estate valued at $3,000. After the funeral in the church Bryan erected, 5,000 persons accompanied the funeral cortege to his burial spot in the local cemetery for blacks. In 1821 Bryan's grave was bricked over and covered with an inscribed marble stone.

Andrew Bryan was a pioneer in the development of the Baptist faith among blacks. When he began his work, he could not have foreseen the end. Yet he persevered and built a large black church in the midst of a relentlessly oppressive society.

REFERENCES

Freeman, Edward A. *The Epoch of Negro Baptists and the Foreign Mission Board.* Kansas City: Central Seminary Press, 1953. Reprint, New York: Arno Press, 1980.

Logan, Rayford W., and Michael R. Winston. *Dictionary of American Negro Biography.* New York: Norton, 1982.

Love, E. K. *History of the First African Baptist Church.* Savannah: Morning News Print, 1888.

Simms, James M. *The First Colored Baptist Church in North America.* Philadelphia: Lippincott, 1888.

Woodson, Carter G. *The History of the Negro Church.* 1921. 2nd ed. Washington, DC: Associated Publishers, 1945.

Robert L. Johns

Eugene Bullard
(1894–1961)
Fighter pilot, boxer, nightclub host

Eugene Bullard was an attractive, restless, and quick–tempered man. He ran away from home very young and eventually made his way to France. He entered the French air service and became the first black combat pilot. In so doing he won a rather large bet.

Eugene Jacques Bullard was born on October 9, 1894, in Columbus, Georgia. He was the seventh of the ten children of Octave C. Bullard and Josephine "Jayakee or Yokalee" Thomas Bullard (1866–99). Three of the children died in infancy. Josephine was a Creek Indian. The Bullard line traced its descent to Martinique. Abandoned in a ditch during the chaos of the aftermath of the Civil War, three–month–old Octave Bullard was rescued by the Bullards, a white family of French extraction who farmed next to the plantation where the infant had been born. This family raised him as a Roman Catholic, saw that he learned to read and write, and gave him a small sum when he married and moved to Columbus with his bride.

Octave Bullard worked as a stevedore on the Chattahoochee River docks. Octave Bullard was a role model for Eugene,

Eugene Bullard

who delighted in hearing his father talk of France, where blacks were supposedly treated as well as whites. The young boy became aware of the racial climate in spite of the family's efforts to shield him. In 1901, when Octave Bullard was struck by his white supervisor, he fought back and injured him. A drunken mob appeared at the Bullard cabin that evening but after concluded that Octave Bullard was not there and left. Octave Bullard's employer supported him, arranging for him to go to Florida and work for the railroad; in the meantime he provided support for the family.

According to his own account, in 1902 when Eugene Bullard was eight, he sold a pet goat for $1.50 and ran away from home to make his way to France, believing that it was possible to walk there. Bullard spent the next three years wandering through the South and finally came to Newport News, Virginia, about 1905. There he stowed away on a German–registered ship bound for Hamburg.

Bullard was put off the ship in Aberdeen, Scotland. He made his way first to Glasgow and then to Liverpool, supporting himself by taking odd jobs, like dancing for street organ grinders, serving as a lookout for gamblers, and working as a stevedore. He even stuck his head through a sheet as target for a penny–a–ball throwers at an amusement park. About 1911 he became a boxer, fighting first as a bantamweight. He fought 42 times over the next 10 or 11 years without making much of a mark.

Bullard was working in London fight clubs when a fight in Paris on November 28, 1913, gave him the first chance to realize his childhood dream of traveling to France. Since he could not schedule more fights scheduled in France, he joined a vaudeville troop called Freedman's Pickaninnies, which was undertaking a tour on the continent. After it played in Paris in the spring of 1914, Bullard remained behind and found work as a prize fighter and sparring partner.

Becomes Military Aviator

A month after World War I broke out (it began in August 1914), Bullard joined the Foreign Legion. He experienced two years of trench warfare, including the brutal battles of Artois and Champagne. The legion had endured so many casualties that it appeared to be finished as a fighting force, and Bullard transferred in 1915 to a regular French regiment, the 107th Infantry, which was nicknamed "The Black Swallows of Death." He was twice wounded at Verdun in 1916, the second time very seriously in the leg. This injury prevented his return to combat.

During Bullard's convalescence, he spoke of joining the air service while talking with comrades in a Parisian cafe. Challenged by a $2,000 bet to prove that this was possible for a black man, Bullard drew on influential connections he had formed in an intermediate care hospital and was accepted as a member of the Lafayette Flying Corps. He began training on November 15, 1916, and completed it on May 5, 1917.

Bullard was not immediately assigned to fly combat. He was placed in an administrative position, running the barracks for the other American pilots. Finally, he flew his first mission on August 27. Through November, Bullard flew a number of missions, scoring one confirmed kill. On his plane he put a dagger in a bleeding heart with the motto "Tout Sang Coule Rouge" (All Blood Runs Red), and he flew with a small monkey he had bought from a Parisian prostitute. As he became a celebrity, he contacted his father for the first time since he ran away.

Rejected by U.S. Army Air Service

When the United States entered the war in April 1917, Americans flying for France were given the opportunity of taking a U.S. Army commission. Bullard, however, was greeted with incredulity when he presented himself for the physical. In spite of efforts to declare him unfit on dubious grounds, such as flat feet, Bullard was told that he had passed the physical but heard no more of a transfer or commission. On November 11, 1917, Bullard was suddenly returned to his old infantry regiment, ending his flying for France.

Bullard ascribed the transfer to racism. However, according to one interviewer, he said that the transfer was a result of an eye injury. Other accounts stressed his propensity for fighting. Bricktop (Ada Smith) spoke of him having a hair–trigger temper. Another account claimed he got into a fight when he tried to get into a truck transporting soldiers. Another possibility is that he hit an officer who insulted him. Bullard spoke of such an incident but did not mention a blow. In any case he spent the rest of the war in south–central

France, far from the fighting. Bullard's war contributions were recognized by France with 17 awards and medals. He became a *Chevalier* in the *Légion d'Honneur* in 1959.

After the war Bullard stayed in France, where he first managed Le Grand Duc night club in Paris. (Langston Hughes washed dishes there for a while, and Bricktop eventually took it over.) For a while he ran a gymnasium and trained boxers. He even faked skills as a musician to get a job, capitalizing for a while on the vogue for black musicians in Paris. Eventually, Bullard had his own night club called L'Escadrille. His ebullient and flamboyant personality served to make him a popular figure in Parisian night life during the 1920s and 30s.

In July 1923 Bullard married Marcelle Eugénie Henriette de Straumann, daughter of a French countess. After having three children—two daughters, Jacqueline (b. 1924) and Lolita Josephine (b. 1926), and a son, Eugene Jr. (b. 1926), who died—the couple separated in 1930. Bullard took complete charge of the children. His ex–wife died in 1936.

In 1940 Bullard joined up with a regiment and fought briefly during the collapse of the French army to the Nazis, then fled to the United States via Lisbon. His daughters joined him later that year in New York. He found as a stevedore, but took odd jobs again after deciding stevedore work as too difficult. At one point after the war, Bullard traveled as a factotum on a Louis Armstrong tour of Europe. The last job he held was operating an elevator in the Empire State Building, where he met David Garroway and as a result was featured on a segment of the *Today Show* in 1954. Bullard lived in a small Harlem apartment. He traveled to France several times but was unable to get much compensation for the property he had left behind. The French government remembered him, however, as a war hero. In 1954 Bullard was one of the three men to relight the Everlasting Flame over the Tomb of the Unknown Soldier under the Arc de Triomphe.

Bullard died in New York of stomach cancer on October 12, 1961. He was buried in the uniform of the Foreign Legion in the French War Veterans Cemetery in Flushing, New York. In an era of severe discrimination against African Americans, Bullard achieved a better life and impressive feats, but only after leaving his native country. A century after his birth, Georgia celebrated Eugene Bullard Day on October 9, 1994. On August 23 of that year the United States posthumously made Eugene Jacques Bullard a second lieutenant in the U.S. Air Force.

REFERENCES

Bricktop [Ada Smith], with James Haskins. *Bricktop.* New York: Atheneum, 1983.

Carisella, P. J., and James W. Ryan. *The Black Swallow of Death.* Boston: Marlborough House, 1972.

Cockfield, Jamie H. "All Blood Runs Red." *Legacy,* (February/March 1995): 7–15.

———. "The Black Icharus: Eugene Bullard in the Dawn of Military Aviation." No publication data; article supplied by author. 362–67.

———. "Personality: Eugene Bullard, America's First Black Military Aviator Flew for France During World War I." *Military History,* (10 February 1996): 74–78.

———. "To Heaven, Hell or Glory." *Georgia Journal,* (November/December 1993): 10–14.

Contemporary Black Biography. Vol. 12. Detroit: Gale Research, 1996.

Smith, Mary H. "The Incredible Life of Monsieur Bullard." *Ebony* 23 (December 1967): 120–28.

Robert L. Johns

Ed Bullins

(1935–)

Playwright, theater director, teacher, editor

Ed Bullins is one of the most prolific and influential of African American dramatists. He both nurtured and was nurtured by the Black Arts movement of the late 1960s and early 1970s, playing a central role first as playwright–in–residence and then as associate director of the most prominent black theater of the period, Harlem's New Lafayette Theater. He has written more than 50 plays, 40 of which have been professionally produced. Unapologetically for and about blacks, these plays examine the disillusionments and frustrations of black ghetto life. Yet early in his career as a dramatist, Bullins also captured the attention of white mainstream critics who, according to *Black Writers,* often praised his work for its "lyricism and depth."

Ed Bullins was born and raised in a ghetto area of North Philadelphia, the son of Edward and Bertha Marie Queen Bullins. His mother, a civil servant, managed to provide some of the accoutrements of middle–class life, including summer vacations in Maryland farming country. He attended a largely white grade school, where he was an excellent student. After transferring to an inner–city junior high school, however, he became immersed in street life, running with a gang called the Jet Cobras and selling bootleg whisky. In one fight he lost his front teeth; in another he nearly died after suffering a stab wound to the heart.

Bullins looked upon this brush with death as a defining point in his life. During this period he wrote copiously, producing a novel, short stories, poetry, and an autobiography. In 1952 he dropped out of high school and joined the U.S. Navy, becoming a lightweight boxing champion on one of the ships of the Mediterranean fleet. In 1955 Bullins was discharged and returned to Philadelphia, where he enrolled in night school and once again turned to the streets. The details of his life over the next three years are obscure, but some

Ed Bullins

information may be gleaned from his highly autobiographical novel, *The Reluctant Rapist* (1973).

Seeks a Fresh Start in California

In 1958 Bullins relocated to Los Angeles, a move that probably saved his life. He earned his GED (general equivalency diploma) and then enrolled part–time at Los Angeles City College. Although he was an erratic student, he read extensively and wrote short stories and poetry. He also created and briefly edited a black literary magazine, *Citadel*, to give voice to campus writers.

In Los Angeles, Bullins began associating with a segment of black society he had rarely encountered back in Philadelphia—politically active black intellectuals engaged in the study of black culture and history. As a member of this group he found himself in an environment amenable to his own literary interests and pursuits. Reading Bullins's writings help illuminate his mental outlook during this period.

In 1964 Bullins moved to San Francisco and enrolled in the creative writing program at San Francisco State College (now University). He then tried his hand at writing for the stage "when he realized that the black audience he was trying to reach did not read much and also that he was naturally suited to the dramatic form," according to *Black Writers*. In 1965 he wrote three plays, *How Do You Do?,Dialect Determinism,* and *Clara's Ole Man.* But no one wanted to produce Bullins's early work because of his obscene language and untraditional dramatic form. He then formed several theatrical companies and produced his plays in bars, coffeehouses, and lofts, including the Firehouse Repertory Theater in San Francisco in August 1965.

After seeing productions of *The Slave* and *Dutchman* by the black writer LeRoi Jones (now Amiri Baraka), Bullins was inspired to continue with his own work. He also teamed up with a group of fellow black writers and political activists such as Baraka, Sonia Sanchez, Huey Newton, Bobby Seale, and Eldridge Cleaver to establish Black House, an organization that served as a focal point for both political and cultural activity. It was closely associated with the Black Panther Party, for which Bullins briefly served as Minister of Culture.

Black House ultimately fell victim to a clash of ideologies. Some militant black political activists such as Cleaver viewed art as a propagandistic tool and encouraged alliances with white radicals to obtain political goals. Bullins, on the other hand, belonged to a group of cultural nationalists who rejected any alliances with whites.

During his association with Black House, Bullins produced one play, *It Has No Choice,* in 1966 at the Black Arts/West Repertory School. Its depiction of an interracial sexual relationship is notable for the dramatic debut of Steve Benson, a character modeled on Bullins himself, and for its thematic use of rape, a common element in his works. By 1967, however, a disillusioned and unfocused Bullins had left Black House.

Joins Harlem's Lafayette Theater

In 1967 Robert Macbeth, a struggling young black director who had read some of Bullins's plays, recruited him as playwright–in–residence at his newly formed Lafayette Theater in Harlem. Although this fledgling company saw its home destroyed by fire in January 1968, it quickly relocated to the American Place Theatre downtown and mounted a production of *Three Plays by Ed Bullins (The Electronic Nigger, Son, Come Home,* and *Clara's Ole Man)* in February 1968. The trio went on to win the Vernon Rice Drama Desk Award for 1968.

His reputation established, Bullins served as guest editor of an issue of *Drama Review* devoted to the New Black Theater movement that contained plays by Bullins and other black playwrights such as LeRoi Jones, Ron Milner, and Jimmy Garrett. As a result, he emerged as one of a group of young black artists who transformed African American theater, especially on the campuses of traditionally black colleges. Usually, the drama departments of these colleges played it safe with proven Broadway hits and those few works by black playwrights considered inoffensive to trustees and the white community. However, members of the New Black Theater movement, along with the students themselves, prompted black colleges to put on more plays addressing the black experience.

In 1968 the New Lafayette Theater was christened with a performance of Bullins's first full–length play, *In the Wine Time.* This work was the first of a proposed group of 20 plays Bullins has called the "Twentieth Century Cycle." A link is provided throughout the cycle by a group of young men who come of age during the 1950s in a ghetto area reminiscent of the North Philadelphia community in which the author himself grew up. Several of the cycle plays have been written and produced. But not all Bullins's plays have been part of the cycle, and several major characters in the cycle have appeared in non–cycle plays.

Sparks Controversy Within the Black Arts Movement

Besides generating controversy outside the Black Arts movement with his work, Bullins has occasionally created a stir within the movement as well. In 1969 the New Lafayette Theater produced his *We Righteous Bombers,* an adaptation of French writer Albert Camus's *The Just Assassins* (1958). This play, which Bullins denied writing, was published under the pseudonym Kingsley B. Bass Jr., described as a 24–year–old black man killed by the police during the Detroit race riots of 1967. This futuristic work questions the merit of revolutionary activity that results in blacks killing other blacks. In May 1969 the play was the subject of a lively symposium at the New Lafayette Theater involving several prominent black writers and critics. Bullins himself, who has customarily played little or no part in the critical debate about his work, did not attend.

Bullins was most productive from 1968 to 1980; during the first five years alone, 15 of his plays were produced in New York. Although he was closely associated with the New Lafayette Theater, which produced ten of his plays and named him associate director in 1971, he also saw his works produced by a variety of other community theaters in New York. His achievements brought him a number of honors, including three Rockefeller grants, two Guggenheim fellowships, a Black Arts Alliance Award, a New York Drama Critics' Circle Award, an honorary doctorate from Columbia College in Chicago, and three Obie Awards for distinguished play writing.

In addition to writing his own plays, Bullins edited the six issues of *Black Theater,* the New Lafayette Theater's biannual magazine. He edited the anthologies *New Plays from the Black Theatre* (1969) and *The New Lafayette Theater Presents* (1974), a compilation of plays by six authors, including himself. He also taught playwriting classes, wrote screenplays, and published a collection of short stories entitled *The Hungered One: Early Writings* (1971). Bullins wrote two children's plays as well, *I Am Lucy Terry* and *The Mystery of Phillis Wheatley,* both produced in 1976, and the books for two musicals, *Sepia Star* and *Storyville,* produced in 1977.

Reaches out to More Diverse Audience

When it became obvious that the New Lafayette Theater would be forced to close due to a lack of funds, Bullins accepted a position as playwright–in–residence at the American Place Theater. His works then began to address a more diverse audience, racially and otherwise. After 1977, however, his plays appeared less frequently on New York stages.

From 1975 to 1983 Bullins served on the staff of the New York Shakespeare Festival. He then relocated to the San Francisco area to teach and to write. He has lectured on and taught playwriting at a number of colleges and universities around the country, among them Hofstra University, Amherst College, Sonoma State University, and the City College of San Francisco. He also authored the book for the musical *I Think It's Gonna Work Out Fine,* which was produced in 1990, but by and large he has released little else since 1980.

Despite this long stretch of apparent inactivity in his literary career, Bullins remains one of the most influential of African American dramatists. As a prolific writer of plays on the black experience, an editor of anthologies featuring plays by fellow black authors, a reviewer of stage productions during the time of the Black Arts movement, and an associate director of a prominent black theater, he has left a lasting impression on African American drama.

Current address: 2128A Fifth Street, Berkeley, CA 94710.

REFERENCES

Black Literature Criticism. Detroit: Gale Research, 1992.

Black Writers. 2nd. ed. Detroit: Gale Research, 1994.

Davis, Thadious M., and Trudier Harris, eds. *Afro–American Writers after 1955.* Detroit: Gale Research, 1985.

Hatch, James V., ed. *Black Theater, U.S.A.* New York: Free Press, 1974.

Twentieth Century American Dramatists. Detroit: Gale Research, 1981.

COLLECTIONS

An interview with Ed Bullins is in the Hatch–Billops Oral History Collection of Black Theater Artists in New York City.

Phiefer L. Browne

Ralph J. Bunche

(1903–1971)

Statesman, diplomat, scholar, United Nations official

To see the world not as it is but as it should be, to accept people with all their foibles, and to embrace goodness characterizes the vision of Ralph Johnson Bunche, the first African American Nobel laureate. He was sometimes slandered by his own—called an "Uncle Tom" by militant blacks—and also attacked by conservative whites who, according to *Contemporary Black Biography,* called him "a UN mercenary, a man with an undistinguished mind and rather bad personal manner.'' Nevertheless, he became the highest ranking black American in the United Nations.

Bunche traces his mother's family history back to slavery. His great–grandfather, James H. Johnson, was a Baptist preacher from Virginia who married Eleanor Madden, the daughter of a house slave and an Irish Catholic planter. James and Eleanor had 11 children—six sons and five daughters. Thomas Nelson Johnson, their youngest son, was Ralph Bunche's grandfather, a teacher who graduated from Shurtleff College in Alton in 1875. One of his students was Lucy A. Taylor from Sedalia, Missouri, born March 10, 1855. The daughter of a house slave and an Irish planter, she married Thomas Nelson Johnson on September 8, 1875.

Lucy and Thomas Johnson's second child, Olive, was Ralph Bunche's mother. She was born in Kansas on April 3, 1882. In 1890 Thomas suffered an attack of malaria which killed him, and Lucy Johnson, with no job and five children, sold everything in order to have enough money to return to Alton, Illinois. In 1900 Lucy Johnson moved her family from Alton to Detroit into a white house with green shutters and a large front porch. This is the house where Ralph Bunche was born.

Olive Johnson met and married Fred Bunche, a trained barber whose family background remains something of a mystery. Fred and Olive Johnson lived with Olive's family—described as large, warm, and talented—with which he was ill at ease. In 1907 he moved the family to Cleveland, Ohio, then to Knoxville, Tennessee, then back to Toledo, Ohio. Ralph Bunche's sister, Grace, was born in Toledo in 1909. Fred Bunche was not a good provider. When Grace was born, Olive Johnson's sister visited her and found them in a one room flat, Fred had no work and Olive was sick. Ethel Johnson brought them back to Detroit where Olive was diagnosed with tuberculosis and sent to a sanitarium where she spent two years recovering.

Bunche was born on August 7, 1903, at 434 Anthony Street, in Detroit, Michigan. Confusion over his actual birth date resulted when his birth certificate was lost, and his aunt used the incorrect date registered in the family Bible. The best times of Bunche's childhood are recorded in a letter Bunche wrote in late 1959 to William T. Nobel of the *Detroit News* and cited in Brian Urguhart's work, *Ralph Bunche.* He recalled that he enjoyed:

> hitching my sled in winter onto the tailgates of horsedrawn beer trucks; swimming on Belle Isle in the summer and in the river down by the ice–house; . . . the thrill of the circus parade, and particularly the calliope at the end of it, when Barnum and Bailey came to town—and the still bigger thrill of slipping into the big tent under the canvas sides; rooting for the Tigers and especially Ty Cobb; hawking newspapers on the street—and how we yelled!—and the excitement when ''extras'' came out as they frequently did then and never do now.

Ralph J. Bunche

The Johnson family left Detroit in 1914. Charlie Johnson, who also suffered from tuberculosis, was sent to Albuquerque, New Mexico, to recover and Olive followed him. Lucy Johnson, Bunche's grandmother, brought Bunche to Albuquerque in October of 1915 on the train. Fred Bunche, without money or job, followed them by riding box cars.

In New Mexico, Bunche went on hunting trips with his uncle Charlie. The family lived in an adobe house at 621 North Street. In school Bunche was smart, but often got into trouble for talking in class. He was one of only two blacks in his class, but recalled with pleasure his teacher, Emma Belle Sweet.

In October of 1916, Fred Bunche, who had not lived with his children and wife since Ohio, left Albuquerque to look for regular work. He promised to send for his family when he found work and could support them. In February Olive's health was complicated by a rheumatic condition; she died in February of 1917. Three months later Uncle Charlie committed suicide. Bunche was 13–years old. The child suffered greatly at the loss of his mother and agonized over a terrible but unnecessary guilt. According to Urquhart, as late as 1967 Bunche wrote, ''I can never get out of my mind that on the night of her death in Albuquerque she had asked for milk and there was none in the house because I had drunk it up.''

Bunche's father did not return for him and his sister after Olive's death. Nor did Fred Bunche die as some sources report, but he remarried. In 1928 he contacted Ralph Bunche's Aunt Ethel in Los Angeles in an effort to talk to Grace, Ralph's sister, but Bunche never saw his father again. As an adult Bunche contacted his father's second wife, Helen, in an attempt to locate his father, but she did not know his whereabouts.

Lucy Johnson took Ralph and his sister and moved to Los Angeles where they settled in a house on 37th Street and Central Avenue. In 1918 the neighborhood was white and middle class. In the 1920s it began a rapid decline and today is part of the notorious South Central, in the Slauson and Watts Area of Los Angeles. Bunche enrolled at Jefferson high School just half a block from his new home.

Lucy Johnson, called Nana by Bunche, set a simple but high standard for the children to follow. Although she could have passed for white, she did not and taught her family a fierce pride in race. Recalling his grandmother's teachings, Bunche, as quoted by Urquhart, said:

> In and out of school, I have always been motivated by a spirit of completion, particularly when pitted against white people.—I suppose this was an inevitable response to Nannie's constant adamantine to let them, especially white folks know that you can do anything they can do.

Bunche graduated from Jefferson High School in 1922. The school principal, Mr. Fulton, made the mistake of saying to Bunche and his grandmother that they never had thought of Ralph as a "Negro." Lucy Johnson's reply epitomized for her grandson the dignity and self–respect she expected him to demand for himself. According to Urquhart, she told Fulton:

> You are very wrong to say that. It is an insult to Ralph, to me, to his parents and his whole race. Why haven't you thought of him as a Negro? He is a Negro and he is proud of it. So am I. What makes you think that only white is good?

In high school Bunche had played basketball and also worked as a paperboy for the *Los Angeles Times.* He was the valedictorian of his class and delivered the graduation address entitled "Our New Responsibility."

The Genesis and the Catalyst

According to Bunche, he never would have attended college had it not been for Lucy Johnson's insistence. Bunche had worked all summer laying carpet and knew that his family needed the money he had earned. At summer's end, however, Lucy Johnson made him quit his job to attend college. Bunche enrolled in the University of California in Los Angeles (UCLA) on Vermont Avenue, now the site of Los Angeles City College. Speaking at the dedication of Ralph Bunche Hall at UCLA on May 23, 1969, Bunch said that UCLA "was when it all began . . . where in a sense, I began; college for me was the genesis and the catalyst." At UCLA Bunche became an all–around scholar and athlete. He wrote for the *Daily Bruin,* the campus newspaper, became president of the Debating Society, and was a star basketball player and played football until he injured his leg.

Bunche graduated summa cum laude from UCLA in 1927 with a B.A. degree in political science and a Phi Beta Kappa Key. Again he was class valedictorian and delivered a commencement address. His speech attacked excessive materialism, urged international mindedness, and promoted the importance of being a socially valuable man. Bunche would become such a man.

A tuition fellowship enabled Bunche to enroll at Harvard University and earn a master of arts degree in June of 1928. While at Harvard Bunche supported himself by working in John Phillips's secondhand bookstore in Harvard Square for ten dollars a week. Robert Weaver, who became U.S. secretary of the Interior and later chief of Housing and Urban Development, and William H. Hastie, who became U.S. Federal Appeals Court judge, were classmates and friends of Bunche. Bunche was offered the Thayer Fellowship to continue his study for a Ph.D. at Harvard but he declined. Percy L. Julian, a Howard University professor, had recruited Bunche to come to Howard in Washington, D.C., and organize a political science department.

Bunche came to Howard under the presidency of Mordecai Wyatt Johnson, the first African American to head the historically black university. This was an exciting time at Howard, and Bunche benefitted from such colleagues as poet and critic Sterling P. Brown, philosopher and culture critic Alaine Locke, and sociologist E. Franklin Frazier. Bunche also chafed under the blatant racism and segregation in the nation's capital and felt inhibited by Mordecai Johnson's iron rule of the university.

In the fall of 1929, Bunche took a leave from Howard and started course work for his doctorate at Harvard. While he was in graduate school at Harvard, Bunche became addicted to cigarettes. His highly competitive nature had added more stress than he could handle.

On June 23, 1930, Bunche married a young woman he had met at Howard University in 1928. Ruth Ethel Harris was a teacher in Washington, D.C. She attended night classes at Howard and had taken Bunche's course in political science. Ruth was born in 1906 in Montgomery, Alabama. She graduated from Alabama State Normal school. Their marriage, which produced three children— two daughters and a son— would last 41 years. Joan Harris Bunche was born in 1931, Jane Johnson Bunche in May of 1933, and Ralph J. Bunche Jr. in 1943.

Bunche completed his dissertation in February of 1934. His thesis on decolonization in Africa won the Toppan Prize for the year's best dissertation. He was awarded the Ph.D. degree in government and international relations. Two years later he published his first book, *World View of Race.* The book examines colonial policy throughout the world and the status of non–European people in South Africa. Bunche took courses in anthropology at Northwestern University in Chicago to prepare for his research abroad. He also studied at the London School of Economics and at the University of Cape Town.

The American Dilemma

Bunche returned to Howard University after 20 months abroad. In 1938 he began working with Gunnar Myrdal, a Swedish social scientist commissioned by the Carnegie Corporation to study African Americans. This study became *An American Dilemma:The Negro Problem and Modern Democracy,* published in 1944. Bunche was one of Myrdal's six top staff members and the one closet to Myrdal. Bunche wrote four monographs for this study; the last monograph consisted of 19 chapters. It was published in 1973 as *The Political Status of the Negro in the Age of FDR.*

Conducting field work in the South—mainly North Carolina, South Carolina, Alabama, and Georgia—Bunche was away from home more than he or his wife and family wanted. In 1941 when the children were eight and ten years old, Bunche had a few months of extended time with them. During that time, the family moved into a house at 1510 Jackson Street N.E. in Washington D.C. As Bunche achieved more acclaim, however, there was a terrible price to pay. His wife's poignant letter summarizes the price of success. In 1945 she wrote:

> I know you think you are the Miracle Negro with the Whites, but I am sure you are just a novelty and whom they can get two men's work out of one from you, though it may be killing you and hurting your family. . . . Achievement is a grand thing and I am very proud of yours but we shouldn't let it blind us to the values of life. . . . I must realize that as you grow more important you will be away from us the best part of our lives and I'll always have the responsibility of rearing the three children alone.

Both partners valued the sanctity of marriage, and for them separation or divorce were inconceivable.

Bunche was rejected for military service in World War II because of an injury he had received playing football at UCLA. An injury to his left leg resulted in a permanent blood clot that would cause him increasing difficulty as he grew older. He was also deaf in his left ear as the result of a punctured eardrum. He, therefore, served his country by joining the National Defense Program Office of Information as senior analyst. He was soon advanced to chief of the African section and worked at the U.S. State Department where he became a participant in the first conferences leading to the formation of the United Nations. Bunche wrote the charter for handling the colonies of defeated countries.

As the first African American to serve on the U.S. delegation to the first General Assembly of the United Nations, by 1946 Bunche was well placed for his next promotion. In 1947 United Nations Secretary General Trygve Lie appointed him director of the Trusteeship Department. From this position he became Undersecretary General of the United Nations. He was now the highest U.S. official black or white at the United nations. He became the highly respected and valued assistant of three U.N. heads, Trygve Lie, Dag Hammarskjold, and U Thant.

A Bias for Peace

The United Nations was the perfect place for Bunche to fulfill his calling. All his years of preparation and experience stood him in good stead for his diplomatic challenges. That preparation and his clearly articulated ''biases'' proved to be a winning combination. Bunche once revealed what he called his biases to a writer for *Ebony* (1972). As quoted in *Contemporary Black Biography,* Bunche said:

> I have a deepseated bias against hate and intolerance. . . . I have a bias against racial and religious bigotry. I have a bias against war, a bias for peace. I have a bias which leads me to believe in the essential goodness of my fellow man, which leads me to believe that no problem in human relations is ever insoluble. And I have a strong bias in favor of the United Nations and its ability to maintain a peaceful world.

Bunche accompanied United Nations–appointed mediator Folke Bernadotte of Sweden to the Middle East to attempt a peaceful resolution of the Arab–Israeli conflict in 1948. The Arabs and Israelis were on the verge of war as a result of the establishment of a Jewish state. This was a perilous assignment as the conflict involved not only land issues but religious differences. Near the end of the year, Bernadotte was assassinated by an Israeli terrorist. The task of making peace thus fell to Bunche. He gained the confidence of both sides through his fairness and objectivity. In 1949 Bunche successfully negotiated a truce, an armistice, and the end of that particular conflict.

Bunche was eating in the United Nation Delegates Dining Room on September 22, 1950, when his secretary informed him that he had been awarded the Nobel Peace Prize. Though honored, Bunche felt that he should not receive an award for a job he was paid to do. Bunche drafted a letter stating that ''peacemaking at the United Nations was not done for prizes.'' But Trygve Lie was of a different opinion. He insisted that the letter not be sent. Bunche was the first black person in the history of the Nobel awards to receive the prize.

Bunche exhibited a single–minded commitment to keeping peace. In 1956 Bunche's efforts during the Suez crisis in Egypt were responsible for the creation of the 6,000 man U.N. Emergency Forces, which supervised the Egypt–Israeli border for 11 years. The 1960 assignment to keep peace in the former Belgian Congo (Zaire) was in Bunche's opinion his most difficult. He did succeed, however, after two months of intense work in enabling Zaire's survival. Zaire's treacherous transition from colonialism to independence, however, resulted in two tragic deaths. On February 13, 1956, Patrice Lumumba's death was announced. Many African Americans were outraged and one even blamed Bunche. Describing the demonstration at the United Nations, Urquhart noted that one black man carried a placard saying, ''Kill Bunche.'' Bunche was saddened by Lumumba's death. He was equally grieved when on Monday, September 18, he learned that Dag Hammarskjold had been killed in the crash of a United Nations DC–6 in route to Leopoldville. Bunche nominated Hammarskjold for the Nobel Peace Prize. On September 22 Bunche wrote: "Mr. Hammarskjold has given new meaning and dimension to dedication and effective contribution to the cause of peace through brilliant statesmanship great wisdom and rare courage." The prize was awarded to Dag Hammarskjold on October 23.

Bunche's troubles with his fellow African Americans would not end with the Congo crisis. America was facing its own revolution in the late 1950s and early 1960s and Bunche was called upon to choose sides. Some black militants called Bunche an "Uncle Tom." Bunche quickly reminded the newcomers to the civil rights struggle that he had carried his first picket for civil rights in 1937. He also demonstrated with Martin Luther King Jr. at the March on Washington and participated in the march from Selma to Montgomery.

For his work in the areas of race, international relations, and peace, in 1949 Bunche was awarded the NAACP's Spingarn Medal. In addition to the Nobel Prize, Bunche received the Theodore Roosevelt Association Medal of Honor, 1954; the Presidential Medal of Honor, 1963; the U.S. Medal of Freedom, 1963; and in 1991 he was inducted into the African American Hall of Fame.

Bunche's role in and contribution to international affairs and public life is unimpeachable, but it came at great cost and personal sacrifice. The most traumatic event of his adult life occurred October 9, 1966, following a game at Shea Stadium; when Bunche and his wife arrived home after 2:00 a.m., a police officer notified them of their daughter Jane's death. The 33–year old mother of three had committed suicide. The old guilt originating with the loss of his mother and abandonment by his father did not make his grief any easier to bear, and it may have increased the rapid decline in his physical condition. An insulin–dependent diabetic, Bunche suffered from phlebitis and failing eyesight.

In 1967 Bunche tried to resign form his post at the United Nations. However, the pressure from U Thant and from President Lyndon B. Johnson to stay was overwhelming. In the end Bunche gave in and remained on the job. Ralph Bunche remained undersecretary–general until the fall of 1971. He was relieved of his duties then because of his health. On December 9, 1971, he died in New York Hospital at 12:40 a.m. His funeral took place in New York's Riverside Church at noon on Saturday, December 11. People all over the world mourned his passing. He is buried at Woodlawn Cemetery in the Bronx.

Peace Form On, a great steel monolith was erected in 1980 in a park on First Avenue across the street from the United Nations. This memorial was created by Daniel Johnson, a young African American sculptor whose father had known Bunche in Los Angeles. The park was renamed Ralph Bunche Park. Perhaps the most meaningful memorial to Bunche took place in 1992 when Anthony Perry, a former gang member in Los Angeles, visited the University of Southern California library and researched the Rhodes Armistice of 1949 that Bunche had drafted. On the bases of that document, Perry negotiated a truce between the Bloods and the Crips, two of the largest and most violent Los Angeles street gangs. A lasting peace among young African American men would surly serve as a fitting tribute to one who gave his life in the struggle for peace.

REFERENCES

Bunche, Ralph. "The Best Advice I Ever Had." *Reader's Digest* 66 (March 1955): 133–35.

———. *Peace and the United Nations.* Leeds, England: Leeds University Press, 1952.

———. *The Political Status of the Negro in the Age of FDR.* Interview. Chicago: University of Chicago Press, 1973.

———. *A World View of Race.* Washington, DC: Associates in Negro Folk Education, 1936.

Contemporary Black Biography. Vol. 5. Detroit: Gale Research, 1994.

Cornell, Jean G. *Ralph Bunche: Champion of Peace.* New York: Garrard, 1976

Edgar, Robert R., ed. *An African American in South Africa; Travel Notes.* New York: Swallow, 1992.

Haskins, Jim. *Ralph Bunche: A Most Reluctant Hero.* New York: Hawthorn, 1974.

Jakoubek, Robert. *Ralph Bunche: Fighter for Peace.* New York: Messner, 1962.

Urquhart, Brian. *Ralph Bunche: An American Life.* New York: Norton, 1993.

Young, Margaret B. *The Picture Life of Ralph Bunche.* New York: Franklin Watts, 1968.

COLLECTIONS

Ralph Bunche's papers are housed at the University of California, Los Angeles, and in the United Nations archives in New York. Some personal papers are also available at the Schomburg Center for Research in Black Culture in New York City.

Nagueyalti Warren

John M. Burgess

(1909–)

Bishop

After serving as suffragan bishop of the Episcopal Diocese of Massachusetts, John Melville Burgess was elected bishop coadjutor and then became the twelfth diocesan bishop of the Diocese of Massachusetts. This achievement marked the inauguration of a succession of "firsts" in the life of an Episcopal priest, who had begun a life of ministry during the Depression era. Burgess was the first black priest to be elected, consecrated, and instituted as a diocesan bishop of the Episcopal church. There were other black priests consecrated as Episcopal bishops before him, but only in strictly prescribed roles as bishops for ''colored work'' in America and for overseas jurisdiction in Haiti and Liberia.

John Melville Burgess was born on March 11, 1909, in Grand Rapids, Michigan. His father, Theodore Thomas Burgess, was an Ohioan who worked as a railroad dining car waiter and a lifelong Episcopalian. John Melville Burgess's mother was the former Ethel Inez Beverly, a Grand Rapids native who was educated as kindergarten teacher at the Grand Rapids Kindergarten Training School. She, too, was an Episcopalian. Burgess had one brother, Theodore, who was an automobile mechanic.

In Grand Rapids Burgess graduated from the Henry Street Elementary School and Central High School. In an interview, he remembered two teachers who exerted much influence on him. One of his Henry Street School teachers was a Miss Hanchett, described as ''an old lady with great patience with children, one who taught them to enjoy books.'' A high school teacher, Angeline Wilson, was remembered as a great disciplinarian who demanded much of her students in a kindly, attractive, yet non–authorative manner.

Burgess attended the University of Michigan and received an A.B. degree in 1930 and an M.A. degree in sociology in 1931. During summer job as a social worker, he felt led towards the ministry. He attended the Episcopal Theological Seminary and graduated with a bachelor of divinity degree in 1934. In seminary, Burgess was greatly influenced by professor Angus Dun, who would continue to exert considerable influence on Burgess in later years.

After ordination to the priesthood, Burgess was placed at St. Philip's in Grand Rapids, the church where he was baptized as an infant, confirmed, ordained as deacon (July 1934), and as priest (January 1935) by Bishop McCormick. Burgess had been a parish priest for 11 years when he married Esther Taylor, whom he met at a conference at St. Augustine's College in Raleigh, North Carolina. She was a graduate of the school. They married on August 21, 1945, and became the parents of two children—Julia and Margaret.

Laying the Foundation

As a young priest preparing to minister to poverty–stricken communicants affected by the Great Depression, Burgess looked to David Ferguson, rector of St. Cyprian's, as a role model. Burgess described him in an interview as ''one who had patient understanding of people in poverty in a kindly way. . . . He was a great pastor.'' Ferguson's pastorate exhibited understanding and compassion in ministering to people in dire need of material as well as spiritual sustenance.

During Burgess's tenure at St. Philip's, he was active in the Conference of Church Workers among Colored People, which was organized in 1882 by the Reverend John Peterson. In 1937 Burgess attended the Cincinnati meeting of the conference held at St. Andrew's Parish. The body successfully petitioned to the church's Executive Council to establish a secretariat for ''colored'' work with black leadership. Burgess was also active in fathering black concerns in the church as an early member and past president of the Union of Black Episcopalians, incorporated in 1968.

In 1938 Burgess became vicar of the Mission of St. Simon the Cyrene in Lincoln Heights, Ohio. During that time his former seminar professor, Angus Dunn, was moving up in the church's hierarchy while continuing to serve as Burgess's mentor. In 1942 Dun was elected bishop of Washington and invited Burgess to be one of the attending presbyters at his consecration. This was the first time a black priest had served in such a position. In 1946 Dun was instrumental in Burgess's move to the nation's capitol to become the first denominational chaplain at Howard University. He was also director of the Canterbury House, an Episcopal student center. In 1951 Burgess achieved another first with his appointment as the first black canon of the Washington Cathedral.

Burgess was appointed archdeacon of Boston and superintendent of the Episcopal City Mission in 1956. In an interview, he described this position as ''social work again!'' His work assignment was not designed for him specifically to minister to members of his race, another first for a black priest. During his six–year tenure, he monitored and supervised the work of the diocese in the inner city of Boston, assisted and worked with mission churches, and worked to relate the church's mission to the city's social agencies.

Moves to the Episcopate

On December 8, 1962, Burgess was consecrated suffragan bishop of Massachusetts. This position as an assistant bishop to the Right Reverend Anson Phelps Stokes, the eleventh bishop of the diocese, had Burgess supervising the eastern part of the state. He was elected bishop coadjutor in 1969, a transition period since Bishop Stokes was retiring in a few months. As coadjutor, he could succeed Stokes. On January 12, 1970, Burgess assumed the office of diocesan bishop and thus secured his place in the history of the Episcopal church as the first black diocesan bishop.

As the twelfth bishop of the Diocese of Massachusetts, Burgess worked to bring black Episcopalians into the mainstream of the church on both the diocesan and national levels. In an interview, he discussed three areas of concern he addressed during his tenure: to make the church aware of its black membership through its mission to black people and recognizance of its prejudices and shortcomings; to make the church more willing to minister in urban communities and support ongoing work; and to effect racial conciliation among all peoples.

After retiring from the Episcopate in 1976, Burgess joined the faculty of Berkeley Divinity School of Yale University in New Haven, Connecticut. As an assistant professor, he taught pastoral care, an area in which Burgess was an acknowledged role model. He was happy at Berkeley because of the ecumenical spirit that permeated the school's atmosphere.

Burgess was active in and out of the church. In mid–March 1979 he gave an address entitled ''The Place of Preaching in Our Church Life'' and it was published in *Preaching in the Black Episcopal Tradition: Lectures and*

Addresses from Conferences Held at the College of Preachers, held in Washington, D.C., by the Office of Black Ministries of the Episcopal Church Center. Burgess also contributed to pastoral letters from the church's black bishops and UBE publications. In 1982 he edited the book *Black Gospel, White Church,* a collection of sermons delivered by black priests from the 1800s to the present.

Before his election to the Episcopate, Burgess attended the Central Committee to the World Council of Churches in Lucknow, India, in 1953. In 1961 he represented the Episcopal church as an official delegate to the Third Assembly of the World Council that met in New Delhi, India. In the church, Burgess was active in the Massachusetts Council of Churches and on the National Executive Council. Burgess made history again in 1967, when he was elected to the Church Pension Fund Board of Trustees. A life member of the NAACP, Burgess is also a member of the Massachusetts Civil Liberties Union, Omega Psi Phi Fraternity and the Sigma Pi Phi (the Boulé).

Burgess and his wife are reputed to hold a sincere graciousness and sense of concern toward all people. The focus of Esther Taylor Burgess's life has always been her family and her home, but has also been involved in church and civil rights organizations. She was an active participant in the Civil Rights Movement to the extent that she was jailed in St. Augustine, Florida, while trying to integrate a restaurant. Esther Burgess devotes her life to making the Burgess's Vineyard Haven home a permanent residence and vacation home for their children, grandchildren, and great–grandchildren. Still in service to others, Burgess serves as a hospice volunteer. Burgess received seven honorary degrees. He continues to embody the spiritual qualities that characterized his leadership in the church.

Current address: 53 Pine Street, PO Box 1641, Vinyard Haven, MA 02568.

REFERENCES

Black Ministries. New York: Episcopal Commission for Black Ministries, Executive Council of the Episcopal Church, 1981.

Burgess, John M. Interview with Dolores Nicholson. January 3, 1996.

———. Letter to Dolores Nicholson, January 13, 1996.

Directory of Black Clergy in the Episcopal Church 1990 and Annual Reports of the Episcopal Commission for Black Ministries 1988 and 1989. New York: Office of Black Ministries, Episcopal Church Center, 1990.

Episcopal Clerical Directory 1995. New York: Church Hymnal Corporation, 1994.

Hines, Deborah Harmon. "President's Report—The Union of Black Episcopalians." Nashville: June 1984.

Martin, Harold C. *Outlasting Marble and Brass:The History of the Church Pension Fund.* New York: Church Hymnal Corp., 1986.

An Opportunity for Christian Action. Union of Black Episcopalians, n.d.

Prayer Book and Hymnal Containing the Book of Common Prayer and the Hymnal 1982 According to the Use of the Episcopal Church. New York: Church Hymnal Corp., 1986.

Sumner, David E. *The Episcopal Church's History: 1945–1985.* Wilton, CT: Morehouse–Barlow, 1987.

UBE National Newsletter (December 1986): 5–6.

Who's Who among African Americans, 1996–97. 9th ed. Detroit; Gale Research, 1996.

Dolores Nicholson

Burns, Isaac.
See Murphy, Isaac.

Roland Burris

(1937–)

Lawyer, accountant, banker, state official

As a prominent lawyer in the state of Illinois, Roland W. Burris enjoyed a rapid succession of important positions in the law profession, including a four–year stint as the attorney–general of Illinois from 1991 to 1995. Upon his election to that office, Burris became the state's chief legal officer, with responsibilities which included legally representing the people of Illinois, the executive branch, the state General Assembly, and all of the state's agencies, commissions, and departments. In the pursuit of his official duties, he filed lawsuits on behalf of Illinois residents, administered laws which regulated charities and charitable funding, indefatigably prosecuted consumer fraud, recovered sums of money owed the state of Illinois, handled criminal appeals for the state, and tirelessly ensured that state laws were enforced.

From 1979 to 1991, Burris served as the elected Illinois state comptroller, the first African American to be elected to a state–wide office. Earlier in 1973, Burris's impressive legal and public service backgrounds brought him to the attention of the governor of Illinois, who appointed him to the governor's cabinet as director of general services of Illinois. Burris continues to excel as a lawyer in his current position as the managing partner of the Chicago–based law firm of Jones, Ware and Grenard.

Roland Wallace Burris was born on August 3, 1937, in Centralia, Illinois. He earned his B.A. degree, with honors, in 1959 from Southern Illinois University. In 1960 he completed post–graduate studies in international law as an exchange student at the University of Hamburg in West Germany. Upon his return to the United States he entered Howard University Law School, where he earned his J.D. degree in 1963.

Roland Burris

Upon graduation from law school, Burris accepted the position of comptroller and national bank examiner in the Office of the Comptroller of the Currency in the United States Treasury Department, a position which he held from 1963 to 1964. Between 1964 and 1971, Burris worked for the Continental Illinois National Bank and Trust Company as a tax accountant and later as the second vice–president; from 1973 to 1976 he served as director in the State of Illinois's General Services Department.

Burris's political interests prompted him in 1977 to accept the position of national executive director of Operation PUSH (People United to Serve Humanity), founded and led by Jesse Jackson. From 1979 to 1991 he was the comptroller of the state of Illinois and in 1991 he became the attorney–general of the State.

Throughout his professional life, Burris has belonged to numerous professional and socio–cultural organizations, including the American Bar Association, NAACP, Kappa Alpha Psi Fraternity, Chicago Cook County Bar Association, American Institute of Banking, and National Association of Attorneys–General, for which he served as the chairman of the Civil Rights Committee. Burris has received numerous distinguished service awards, including being listed as one of ''100 Most Influential Black Americans'' in *Ebony* for 1979 and 1980.

Politically, Burris is very active in Democratic Party politics. He served as a leader of the Illinois delegations to several National Democratic Conventions and he served as the vice–chair of the 1992 National Democratic Committee working closely with former Commerce Secretary Ron Brown. In 1997 he announced his bid for the Illinois governor's seat.

Burris is married to the former Berlean Miller, who is a scholar in her own right and holds a doctoral degree. The Chicago–based couple are the proud parents of two children, Rolanda Sue Burris and Roland Wallace Burris II.

Burris has made invaluable contributions to his native state of Illinois. His most notable contributions have included the creation in 1992 of the Women's Advocacy Division in the Illinois Attorney–General's Department, which has continued to serve women who are victims of stalking and domestic violence. His establishment in 1993 of a Children's Advocacy Division in his former position as the attorney general of Illinois was seen as a first for the victims of child abuse in Illinois. Above all, as a civil rights advocate, Burris spearheaded the creation in 1993 of the Civil Rights Division of the Illinois attorney–general's office.

Current address: S. Indiana Ave., Chicago, IL 60619.

REFERENCES

Black Americans Information Directory. 3rd ed. Detroit: Gale Research, 1995.

Burris, Roland. Vita, 1996. Office of Roland Burris.

''Newsmakers.'' *Jet* 92 (22 September 1997): 34.

''The 100 Most Influential Black Americans.'' *Ebony* 24 (May 1979): 33; 25 (May 1980): 63.

Who's Who among Black Americans, 1996–97. 9th ed. Detroit: Gale Research, 1996.

Yvette Alex–Assensoh

Ambrose Caliver

(1894–1962)

College administrator, educator, government appointee, writer

Ambrose Caliver spent a lifetime addressing the educational needs of African Americans that spanned the spectrum from manual and academic training to adult literacy. Widely known and respected as the principal official concerned with African American education in the U.S. Office of Education, from the 1930s through the early 1960s, he worked through his federal positions to identify and address special phases of African American education. Furthermore, he convened or served on various national councils and committees to act on the results of his research findings. He published his views on education in 18 or more books and bulletins and in more than 50 articles.

Born in Saltsville, Virginia, on February 25, 1894, Ambrose Caliver was the son of Ambrose and Cora Saunders Caliver. When he was 11–years old his father died. Young Caliver worked in the coal mines, to help support the family. Although he completed elementary school in Bramwell, West Virginia, he was sent to Knoxville, Tennessee, to live with his grandmother and complete high school studies at Knoxville High School. He graduated from Knoxville College, in 1915, with a B.A. degree, and, after one year at Tuskegee Institute, in Alabama, he received a diploma in industrial arts, in 1916. He took a special course at Harvard University, in the summer of 1919 for which he received a diploma in personnel management and administration. In 1920, Caliver received a M.A. in education, from the University of Wisconsin. He received a Ph.D. degree from Columbia University in 1930.

Caliver married Evelyn Rosalie Rucker on December 24, 1916. They had one daughter, Jewell Alta Mae, born October 19, 1925.

Begins His Career

Caliver spent a lifetime in education. His first appointment came in 1916 as high school principal in Rockwood, Tennessee. He was teacher and assistant principal of Douglass High School in El Paso, Texas, in 1917. He moved to Fisk University in Nashville, Tennessee, where he was assistant professor and later associate professor of manual arts and industrial arts from 1918 to 1926. He developed the manual arts program at Fisk, perhaps drawing on his training at Tuskegee. He also taught courses in education. In 1919, after World War I, he was a personnel worker, at Ohio Rolling Mill Company in Middleton, Ohio. In 1923, Caliver was the first–prize–winner of $500 award in a national essay contest, in which more than 600 people competed. The contestants represented some of the largest institutions in the United States, Canada, Puerto Rico, and Hawaii (then a territory), and held esteemed positions, in vocational education. His winning essay was called "The Educational Function of the Industrial Arts." That same year, he received a patent for an invention useful in the beauty culture industry and later incorporated his invention into his own small business.

During the 1915–16 school year, Caliver was publicity director at Fisk. He wrote and directed a movie on school's history, in 1921, and he traveled and lectured with the film. The university recognized Caliver's expertise and leadership ability and, in 1925, named him assistant dean of the university and a member of the Interim Committee that oversaw the school's operations. He was at Fisk during a crucial time. Fayette Avery McKenzie had resigned on April 16, 1925, because he was unable to quell student unrest at the school and to bring the needed financial and emotional stability. Caliver's appointment was made to soothe those who charged that all important positions at Fisk were held by whites. He was named dean of the scholastic department in the 1926–27 school year. When Thomas Elsa Jones took office as president of Fisk in September of 1926, he immediately worked to pacify the Fisk constituencies, and promoted Caliver to dean of the university, in the summer of 1927, making him the first African American to hold the position.

Caliver had a deep appreciation and respect for students and held the predominantly African American student body at Fisk in high regard. He said, in *The Greater Fisk Herald,* "I believe the average student here is solid, sane and balanced with high ideals, because of their heritage." He gained a reputation as a firm believer in scholarship and a promoter of exactness. The *Herald* quoted him on these themes:

> If there is such a quality of sternness, exactness, etc., in me . . . it is due to my early association with men in the business world as well as my early reading of books and magazines on business and efficiency. I soon learned that success in anything could not be attained through oscillating and half–hearted methods. . . . The greater need of America today in scholarship, as well as in other things, is an appreciation of exactness and precision.

Becomes Specialist in Education of African Americans

On leave from Fisk in 1930 to study for his doctorate, at Columbia University, Caliver and the president of Fisk were at odds over the conditions of his leave. Although Caliver expected to return to Fisk, the president and the board of trustees filled his vacancy and offered him the position of research professor and director of educational studies. He was to head the new department of education. Jones wrote to Caliver that, "It is quite impossible for you to act as Dean of the College and at the same time develop this Department or School of Education . . . or . . . develop this department of education into a school." Caliver refused the position. He then joined the U.S. Office of Education in 1930, as senior specialist in Negro education, a position he held until 1946. He conducted many research projects through the office, including surveys of critical problems in education. He initiated and directed the Federal Emergency Relief Administration and Works Projects Administration emergency education programs under President Franklin D. Roosevelt's New Deal. From 1935 to 1938, he directed the National Survey of Vocation and Guidance of Negroes and, in 1938, published the results of the study as *Vocational and Educational Guidance of Negroes.* During his tenure, his office published 19 leaflets, pamphlets, and circulars as well as 36 articles, all important for the study of African Americans and education, during that period. He became, perhaps, the best authority in the field. His works included *Bibliography on Education of the Negro, Comprising Publications from January, 1928 to December, 1930* (1931); *Background Study of Negro College Students* (1933); *Rural Elementary Education among Negroes under Jeanes Supervising Teachers* (1933); and *The Education of Negro Teachers* (1933). His work, *Sources on Instructional Materials for Negroes* (1946), was a useful guide to information for students and teachers from elementary schools through college and for out-of-school adults. The bibliography includes general works on African American themes as well as transcriptions, films, radio scripts, plays, and photographs and a list of agencies engaged exclusively or partially in activities relating to African Americans. He also wrote articles for *Opportunity* magazine.

Highly successful in his position and distinguished for his research and writings, Caliver was promoted to specialist for higher education of Negroes and adviser on related problems in the Office of Education in 1946. In that same year, he directed the Project for Literacy Education, resulting in an assessment of the extent of literacy; the preparation of appropriate instructional materials; and the training of teachers to work with adults with lower than fourth-grade literacy. He was promoted again in 1950, this time to the assistant to the U.S. commissioner of education. This was a position he held until 1962.

From 1955 to 1962, Caliver held a joint appointment as chief of the recently-formed Adult Education Section of the U.S. Office of Education. His responsibility was to plan and execute a program for teaching three million adults who were illiterate and ten million others, including three million African Americans who had not advanced beyond a fourth grade education. He saw himself in a limitless role as he monitored all areas of public and private adult education, including formal and informal programs. By 1956, according to *Ebony,* Caliver saw a critical need to convince the unschooled that they could become effective citizens if they increased their competence in work and their capacity to enjoy life. According to *Ebony,* he dispelled the old notion of education as "a rigid process taking place in childhood and youth." Illiteracy, in his view, was "dangerous to democracy." It also "constantly hammers at the theme that poverty, disease and personal maladjustments are most plentifully found among the least educated." He developed a national plan to accelerate the pace of adult learning that would impact all families in America. During Caliver's tenure with the federal government, he prepared for the U.S. Attorney General a lengthy feasibility report for implementing a possible Supreme Court decision on the desegregation of schools.

Fully attuned to the educational requirements of America, Caliver was as active in the formal requirements of his various positions as he was in directing projects in response to the community's needs. While living in Nashville, he became involved in numerous civic and social movements to build up the community. He was active in the Community Chest. In the winter of 1919, he was relieved of a portion of his duties at Fisk to organize the Tennessee Colored Anti-Tuberculosis Society. He directed the society for two years and spent two more years as chair of the Executive Committee. Later, he was one of the first members of the Tennessee Inter-Racial Committee. A man with a vision for business, he was associate editor for *Business Magazine* in 1922, and proprietor of a small manufacturing firm in Nashville, from 1923 to 1925. From 1928 to 1929, he was president of the National Association of College Deans and Registrars in Negro Schools. While in Nashville he was a member of the Agora Assembly and the Masons.

The National Advisory Committee on the Education of Negroes, in existence from 1930 to 1950, was the result of Caliver's recommendations on African Americans and education. He convened the National Conference on Fundamental Problems in the Education of Negroes in 1934, and, the next year, published the results as *Fundamentals in the Education of Negroes.* The National Survey of Higher Education of Negroes, which he directed from 1939 to 1942, was published in 1942, under the same title. It became a key work and one of several early studies of its type undertaken by the federal government. From 1941 to 1942, he created and directed *Freedom's People,* a nationwide radio series on African American participation in American life.

Caliver continued working in high-level and highly-visible positions of national and international prominence. He was appointed as a consultant to the U.S. Displaced Persons Commissions in 1949. In 1950, he was advisor to the United Nations Special Committee on Non-Self-Governing Territories. Also that year, he was a member of the Survey Staff of Education in the Virgin Islands. In 1951, he was a member of the committee to explore federal participation in community-college movement and the U.S. Delegation to the Inter-American Cultural Council. In 1955, he was consultant to the Adult Education Association's National Commission on Literacy Education and was elected president of the association in 1961.

Caliver held memberships in many outstanding societies and organizations, including the Committee on the White House Conference on Children in a Democracy in 1941, and the Citizen's Committee on Integration of Negroes into the National Defense Program. Other memberships included the National Association of Teachers in Colored Schools, the National Association of College Deans and Registrars in Negro Schools, where he was a vice–president, the National Education Association, and the Association for the Study of Negro Life and History.

An effective administrator and a highly recognized leader in education, especially in the fields of adult education and literacy, Caliver was in demand as workshop leader, consultant, adviser, and speaker.

Religion was a central part of Caliver's life. He became a deacon in the Congregational Church at 19, while he was a student at Knoxville College. At Fisk, he became a deacon in the Fisk Union Church. He remained a Congregationalist throughout his lifetime.

On January 29, 1962, after a long illness, Caliver died of a heart attack at his home on Lamont Street in Washington, DC. He was survived by his wife and daughter, among others. His funeral was held on February 2 at Lincoln Temple Congregational Church, followed by burial in Lincoln Memorial Cemetery in Suitland, Maryland.

Ambrose Caliver continues to hold an important place in the history of African American education. An advocate of the eradication of illiteracy and a proponent of adult education, he concentrated on these two important issues of education in America.

REFERENCES

''Ambrose Caliver.'' *Ebony* 11 (May 1956): 40–42.

Logan, Rayford W., and Michael R. Winston, eds. *Dictionary of American Negro Biography.* New York: Norton, 1982.

Morgan, C. Wesley. ''High Points in the Life of Dean Ambrose Caliver.'' *The Greater Fisk Herald* 2 (December 1927): 11–12.

Newman, Debra L., comp. *Black History: A Guide to Civilian Records in the National Archives.* Washington, DC: National Archives Trust Fund Board, General Services Administration, 1984.

Richardson, Joe M. *A History of Fisk University, 1865–1946.* University, AL: University of Alabama Press, 1980.

Robinson, Wilhelmina S. *Historical Negro Biographies.* New York: Publishers Company, 1968.

Who's Who in Colored America. New York: Who's Who in Colored America Corp., 1927.

COLLECTIONS

Fisk University Library contains the Ambrose Caliver Collection as well as the Thomas Elsa Jones Papers, where additional information on Jones from 1926 through 1930 is found. Files and documents relating to Caliver during his years with the federal government are in the Records of the Office of Education, Records of the Office of the Secretary of the Interior, Records of the Works Projects Administration, and Records of the Bureau of Employment Security all in the National Archives in Washington, DC.

Jessie Carney Smith

Cab Calloway

(1908–1994)

Band leader, entertainer, songwriter, writer

One of the most successful bandleaders of the 1930s and 1940s, Cab Calloway used night clubs, the stage, the screen, and radio to entertain the public for over six decades. Flamboyant and colorful, Calloway became known for his skat singing and the famous line ''hi–de–hi–de–hi–de–ho.'' He paved the way for many of America's great entertainers.

Cabell Calloway III was born in the family home at 18 Cypress Street in Rochester, New York, on Christmas Day 1907, the second of Cabell and Eulalia Reed Calloway's four children. His parents had moved to Rochester in 1906 and relocated to Baltimore around 1918. In Baltimore the family lived with the children's paternal grandparents, Cabell and Elizabeth Johnson Calloway, at 1017 Druid Hill Avenue, located in the black community. The grandparents moved there from Danville, Virginia, in the mid–1800s. According to Calloway's autobiography, *Of Minnie the Moocher & Me,* ''They may have been slaves.'' Later, after Cab Calloway II died, Eulalia Calloway and her children moved in with her parents, Andrew and Canna Credit Reed, who were probably Baltimore natives. Eulalia Calloway later married John Nelson Fortune and had two other children—John and Camilla.

Cabell Calloway II a graduate of Lincoln University in Pennsylvania, was a lawyer and operated a real estate business. Eulalia Calloway, who attended Morgan State College in Baltimore, was a teacher in the local public schools. Since both parents were professionals, they were well respected in the black community and lived a comfortable life.

The Calloways were a musical family. Calloway's mother was a church organist and his brother Elmer and sister Blanche were professional musicians. Determined to get into show business, Blanche Calloway (1902–1973) left home when she was about 15–years old. By the 1930s she had become one of the most successful bandleaders of the decade, as well as the first black woman to lead an all–female band.

Around age 13, Calloway spent considerable time home alone while his parents worked. ''My direction was hustling on the streets,'' he wrote in his autobiography. Concerned about his future, in 1921, Calloway's mother and stepfather sent him to a school in Downingtown, Pennsylvania, operated by his grandmother Reed's brother, Reverend William Credit,

Cab Calloway

of Philadelphia. Recalling the experience, Calloway later wrote, "I hustled just the same as I had on the street." Although two of Calloway's cousins were enrolled as well, one year later he had had enough of the school, packed his bags, and returned to Baltimore unannounced.

Calloway resumed street–hustling for two months, until the family relocated to a small suburban development called Wilson Park. He attended Laurenville junior high school and went to church because "there was nothing else to do." He studied voice and sang in the Bethlehem Methodist Church choir, where his mother was organist. Calloway soon became a serious student, graduating as valedictorian from his junior high school. Cab Calloway sold newspapers after school to earn extra money. Already musically inclined, he sang solos in the Bethlehem Methodist Church.

In the summer of 1924 the family returned to Baltimore and rented a house at 1306 Madison Avenue, near their former residence on Druid Hill Avenue. Calloway was enrolled at Frederick Douglass High School, where he became fully involved in school activities. He developed as a good basketball player with professional basketball potential and continued to hustle, making "a hell of a lot of money." By his senior year, he played with the professional basketball team, the Baltimore Athenians.

Meanwhile, Calloway's voice lessons continued. Realizing that he had the ability to entertain people, he began to play the drums, sing with a small group, and engage in vaudeville acts with some of his schoolmates. In time, Calloway learned that he "could get paid for entertaining." The money that he made went to support his mother and siblings. By then he had developed what he called "a lovely robust tenor voice." He sang whenever he had a chance—in church choirs and nightclubs around town. In one of his favorite songs, "Muddy Waters," he sang "'bout the Delta, muddy waters at my feet," that earned him the nickname "Muddy Waters." By then Baltimore had become one of the leading jazz centers in the United States, and featured such musical greats as Johnny Jones and his Arabian Tent Orchestra and Chick Webb—both became Calloway's idols.

In his senior year of high school, Calloway had a serious relationship with Zelma Proctor. Although they did not marry, they dropped out of school and Zelma gave birth to their daughter, Camay, on January 15, 1927. Calloway returned to school to complete his senior year while singing in clubs and playing basketball. Having failed chemistry, he graduated in 1927, a year behind his class.

After high school Calloway's sister Blanche paid his way to Chicago and helped him find his place as an entertainer. In his autobiography Calloway acknowledged Blanche's impact on his life in his dedication: "To my sister Blanche who introduced me to the wonderful world of entertainment." She taught him acting, and he went on the road with her in the show *Plantation Days,* in which she had the lead role. For eight weeks the show traveled from Baltimore to Pittsburgh to Detroit and to Columbus. Since the main hotels in the cities where they played refused accommodations to black players, the company rented rooms from black families.

In September of 1927, Calloway enrolled in Crane College in Chicago reportedly to study law, and played on the school's basketball team. In 1928, Abe Saperstein of the Harlem Globetrotters offered him a contract with the team, but he refused. He continued his career as an entertainer while studying at Crane, working nights and weekends in Chicago's nightspots.

Calloway's first Chicago gig was at the Dreamland Cafe on State Street. In the spring of 1928 he became a drummer at the Sunset Cafe, a popular club on Chicago's South Side, where most of the city's good jazz, called "Chicago jazz," was played. Sunset Cafe was Chicago's equivalent of New York's Cotton Club. At the Sunset, Calloway became friendly with Louis Armstrong, and performed a lead number for Adelaide Hall, who later starred in the *Blackbirds* reviews of the late 1920s and early 1930s. Calloway worked first as a drummer, then strictly as a singer. He later filled in as master of ceremonies for his friend, Ralph Cooper of the dance team Rector and Cooper, eventually acquiring the position on a permanent basis.

Calloway married Wenonah Conacher, known as Betty, on July 26, 1928; they later had one daughter named Constance. The couple was divorced in 1949. He continued at the Sunset and took saxophone lessons as well. When Louis Armstrong and Carroll Dickerson and their band left the Sunset for Connie's Inn in Harlem in 1929, Marion Hardy's band, the Alabamians, took the stage. After rehearsing with the band whenever he had a chance and improving its sound dramatically, Calloway replaced Lawrence Harrison as leader of the Alabamians. This began Calloway's career as a bandleader that was to last for 30 years. The band had a jumping, jiving style that pleased the Chicago crowd. A year later the group left the Sunset and did road tours, finally settling in New York City.

While Calloway acknowledged that the Chicago style of music differed from that of New York, his players disagreed. His band played old–time tunes and Dixieland jazz, which sounded weak when compared to the jumping jazz of New York City. When the band first opened at the Savoy Ballroom in November of 1929—Calloway dressed in a white tuxedo and using a white baton—they failed to please the audience, and the engagement was canceled. Calloway dissolved the band.

Calloway turned to show business and, with the help of Louis Armstrong, landed a singing job in the new all–black musical comedy *Connie's Hot Chocolates*—one of the biggest hits on Broadway that year. A month later the show went on the road to Philadelphia and Boston. The act included such famous singers as Edith Wilson and Margaret Simms, and comedians Eddie Green and Johnny Hudgins. Calloway also won fame for his rendition of the song ''Ain't Misbehavin'.'' When the show closed, Calloway, a bandleader at heart, returned to New York City, signed a contract with Moe Gale, and was set to open at the Plantation Club—a rival to the Cotton Club—as leader of the band, the Missourians. The club—set up like a southern plantation with slave cabins—was soon destroyed, however, perhaps by its chief competitor, the owner of the Cotton Club.

After a brief but highly successful stint at the Crazy Cat, the band moved to the Cotton Club and played with Duke Ellington's Cotton Club Orchestra. Whenever Ellington was away for any length of time, Calloway and his band played. Their first prolonged stay was in the summer of 1930, when Ellington began to travel more, and they were a big hit. By Thanksgiving of 1930, while Ellington was away, the Missourians' performance was broadcast over the radio. In time, the Missourians became Cab Calloway's Cotton Club Orchestra. Over the next decade, between 1929 and 1939, Ellington and Calloway played alternately at the Cotton Club. The club, under mob control, occupied the second floor of a two–story building in Harlem at 142nd Street and Lenox Avenue. The bandstand was a replica of a southern mansion, and the waiters, dressed in red tuxedos, looked like butlers. The club became synonymous with the greatest black entertainment of the 1920s and 1930s.

''Minnie the Moocher'' and ''Hi–de–ho''

The big bands of the day each had a theme song. Duke Ellington's band used ''Mood Indigo,'' while Cab Calloway's band, without a real theme song of its own, used ''St. James Infirmary,'' a traditional blues song that Louis Armstrong and Kid Ory had made famous in the early 1920s. In the spring of 1931 Calloway's agent, Irvin Mills, joined him in composing his theme song ''Minnie the Moocher,'' with Minnie characterized in Calloway's autobiography as ''a rough, tough character, but with a heart as big as a whale.'' Soon after the band began using its own theme song, Calloway sang during a show that was broadcast over radio nationwide and forgot the lyrics of a new song he introduced. Calloway wrote in his autobiography: ''I had to fill the space, so I just started to scat–sing the first thing that came into my mind. 'Hi–de–hi–de–hi–de–ho . . . Hi–de–ho–de–ho–de–hee.' The crowd went crazy and I went on with it—right there over live radio—like it was written that way. . . .'' From then on Calloway's fans saw ''Minnie the Moocher'' and ''hi–de–ho'' as inseparably related to Calloway and his fame.

Also in the spring of 1931, Calloway formed his own company, Cab Calloway, Incorporated, to handle his business undertakings. Around that time Calloway and his band cut their first record, *Minnie the Moocher.* All together, he either wrote or collaborated on more than 100 tunes. In 1933 Calloway wrote ''Lady with the Fan'' to honor Amy Spencer, ''the finest fan dancer the Cotton Club had ever known.''

By the fall of 1931, Calloway had returned to the Cotton Club for his third long stint. The show was aired over the radio three nights a week, providing Calloway and his band with a national following. Around this time he took his band on a tour of the South, to Virginia Beach, Raleigh, Savannah, St. Petersburg, and elsewhere. They returned to New York to the theater circuit. The Cotton Club era climaxed in 1935, about the time Calloway and his band went to Europe for a five–week stay. He returned to the United States to play at the Cotton Club and tour the American Southwest and West.

Calloway lived in Harlem during the cultural revolution known as the Harlem Renaissance. Writers and poets–including Langston Hughes, Claude McKay, James Weldon Johnson, and Countee Cullen–read their works together, but, according to Calloway in his autobiography, ''the two worlds, literature and entertainment, rarely crossed.'' But he did meet E. Simms Campbell, the first successful black cartoonist, who, like himself, was ''a hard worker, a hard drinker, and a high liver.'' They became lifelong friends.

Calloway's band of the 1930s and 1940s, known as the Cab Calloway Cotton Club Orchestra and later the Cab Calloway Band, was one of the ten most outstanding bands of the time. Others included Duke Ellington, Jimmie Lunceford, Fletcher Henderson, Earl Hines, and Count Basie. All were acknowledged worldwide.

In 1936 the Cotton Club moved downtown and closed in 1941. Calloway and his band then performed to standing–room–only audiences in theaters throughout the United States. They also appeared at such popular places as the Casa Manana in California and the Panther Room in Chicago's Hotel Sherman. They had an extended engagement at the Park Central's Coconut Grove in New York City, and a prolonged stay at the Cafe Zanzibar.

Throughout his professional life, Calloway worked with musicians who later became celebrated jazz greats. Those who served in his bands included John "Dizzy" Gillespie, Leon "Chu" Berry, Quentin Jackson, Robert "Jonah" Jones, William "Cozy" Cole, and Benny Payne. Vocalists who sang with his band in the thirties included Lena Horne and June Richmond, and by the 1940s he had discovered Pearl Bailey. The 1940s was a decade of continued success and personal growth. Calloway married Zulme "Nuffie" MacNeal on October 7, 1949. A flamboyant dresser, according to his autobiography he had "fifty suits and fifty pairs of shoes and fifty pairs of pearl–grey gloves." His zoot suits—characterized by oversized jacket, pants, hat, and chain–were both expensive and spectacular. Some writers have speculated that he owned more zoot suits than anyone in Harlem. His famous yellow zoot suit and matching hat were among the memorabilia from his collection displayed during his seventy–fifth birthday celebration at the White Plains, New York, Public Library and in 1983 at Fisk University.

In 1947, about the time the big band era ended, Calloway dismantled his band and toured with small groups, and, on occasion, as leader of a big band. By 1952 his singing career had begun, taking him to nightclubs, theaters, and resort areas.

Begins Film Career

In 1931 Calloway appeared in his first movie: he costarred with Al Jolson in the film *The Singing Kid,* in which his band also appeared. Other film appearances included *Big Broadcast* (1932), *International House* (1933), *Ali Baba Goes to Town* (1937), and *Roadshow* (1941). In 1943 he appeared with Lena Horne in *Stormy Weather,* for which the Negro Actors Guild awarded him an "Oscar." He played the leading role in Andrew Stone's *Sensations of 1944.* Younger audiences were introduced to Calloway when he played in *The Blues Brothers* (1980) and *The Cotton Club* (1984). Calloway spent some time in the theater as well, appearing in George Gershwin's folk opera *Porgy and Bess* (1953), and with Pearl Bailey in the Broadway musical *Hello, Dolly,* (1967). In 1965, he accepted Abe Saperstein's offer to join the Harlem Globetrotters, this time as an entertainer during the half–time show. In the mid–1970s he toured with a show entitled *Sounds of the Forties.* In the 1980s he began to tour with his daughter Chris, the only one of his five daughters who entered show business.

Calloway was less known as a writer. In 1938 he published the first edition of his *Hepster's Dictionary,* and in 1976, he wrote *Of Minnie the Moocher and Me.* The book also includes the 1944 edition of his dictionary and "Professor Cab Calloway's Information Bureau," originally published in 1939.

Calloway's honors and awards were numerous. He won a Grammy Award in 1976, and in 1981 the Black Business Association honored him for 50 years in show business. In 1985 he received the Ebony Lifetime Achievement Award also for his remarkable career.

Calloway, who had a long and abiding affection for horses and race tracks, spent considerable time at such tracks as the Aqueduct in Ozone Park, New York, and Belmont Park in Elmont, New York. A gambling man since his teenage years, he found horses and the race track relaxing and satisfying; he loved the racing crowd, and they loved him. Calloway also performed at race tracks and helped promote racing. According to his biography, he was the first black allowed in the grandstand at Hialeah Park, in Hialeah, Florida, where the owners and trainers often had their photographs taken with him. In 1962 he was the first entertainer to perform at the Preakness held at Pimlico Race in Baltimore, Maryland.

Calloway suffered a severe stroke at the family's White Plains, New York, home on June 12, 1992, and was left paralyzed. He was later relocated to a retirement community in Cokesbury Village near Hokessin, Delaware, where Nuffie Calloway had moved to be near him. She recalled in an interview that his smile had faded. He died on November 18, 1994, with his family by his side. In addition to his wife, Nuffie, he was survived by daughters Camay Murphy and Constance Calloway (from his earlier relationships), Chris Calloway, Lael Calloway–Tyson, and Cabella Langsam, as well as seven grandsons. A memorial mass was held at St. John the Divine church in New York City.

Cab Calloway was a legend who gave a lifetime to his profession through the songs he composed, the bands he directed, and the acts he performed on screen and stage. He is remembered as much for his talent as he is for the manner in which he danced about and shook his straight hair from his face as he sang "Hi–de–hi–de–ho," a chant he made famous.

REFERENCES

Calloway, Cab, and Bryant Rollins. *Of Minnie the Moocher & Me.* New York: Thomas Y. Crowell Company, 1976.

———, and Nuffie Calloway. "Can Marriage Survive on Love Alone?" *Ebony* 10 (January 1955): 45–50.

"Calloway Made Mark On Music." *Nashville Tennessean,* November 20, 1994: A–10.

Calloway, Zulme. Telephone interview with Jessie Carney Smith, September 10, 1994.

"Celebrates His 75th Birthday with His Wife Nuffie at The Museum Gallery of the White Plains (N.Y.) Public Library." *Jet* 63 (27 December 1982): 41.

Current Biography Yearbook. New York: H. W. Wilson Co., 1945.

Hitchcock, H. Wiley, and Stanley Sadie, eds. *The New Grove Dictionary of American Music.* New York: Macmillan, 1986.

Kernfield, Barry, ed. *The New Grove Dictionary of Jazz.* New York: Macmillan, 1988.

"Nation Mourns Passing of Music Great Cab Calloway: 1904–1994. *Jet* 87 (12 December 1994): 58–63.

"Of Minnie the Moocher and Me: An Exhibition Highlighting the Life and Career of America's Legendary Entertainer, Cab Calloway." The Learning Library Program, Fisk University, Nashville, Tennessee, February 28–March 18, 1983.

The Negro Almanac. 5th ed. Detroit: Gale Research, 1989.
"Orchestra Wives." *Ebony* 6 (May 1951): 36–42.
Southern, Eileen. *Biographical Dictionary of Afro-American and African Musicians.* Westport, CT: Greenwood Press, 1982.
Who's Who among Black Americans, 1994–95. 8th ed. Detroit: Gale Research, 1994.

COLLECTIONS

The private collection of Cab Calloway was donated to Boston University. Memorabilia from his career as a performer are also at Coppin State College.

Jessie Carney Smith

Roy Campanella

(1921–1993)

Baseball player, entrepreneur, radio host, philanthropist, writer

Roy "Campy" Campanella was a member of that small roster of black sports pioneers who, after Jackie Robinson, helped shatter racial barriers through superior baseball play on a professional level. Campanella was a first-string catcher at the age of 16 with the Baltimore Elite Giants of the Negro National League. Ten years later, he joined the Brooklyn Dodgers. Though he was stockily built, he played with a deadly swiftness that added special excitement to his game and garnered him many awards, including election to the Baseball Hall of Fame. One of the memorable games of 1950 was the contest on August 26 between Brooklyn and Cincinnati in which Roy Campanella hit three 400-foot home runs. The Dodgers lost to the Philadelphia Phillies in that year's struggle for first place, but Campanella led all other National League catchers in chances and putouts, and hit 31 home runs. In 1951, Roy made his greatest contributions and won the New York Baseball Writer's award as the "most valuable player" in the National League. A tragic automobile accident ended his career as the age of 36 and left him confined to a wheelchair for the rest of his life. Campanella nevertheless remained active in the sport and in his business, which only enhanced his status as a hero.

Roy Campanella was born on November 19, 1921, in Philadelphia, Pennsylvania, to an Italian-American father and a black mother, Ida Mercer Campanella. His siblings included Lawrence, Gladys, and Doris. His father, John, peddled fruits and vegetables, but money was always in short supply in the Campanella household. Young Roy helped out by selling newspapers and working with his brother, Lawrence, who had a big milk route that earned Campanella 50 cents a day. In his spare time, he liked to fish, and he was also a model railroader.

Plays Negro League Baseball

When Campanella was still a child, his family moved to North Philadelphia. There he attended Simon Gratz High School for three years and lettered in football, basketball, track, and baseball. In fact, he was so good in sports that during his junior year he was paid $50 by the Bacharach Giants to catch for the Philadelphia Negro team on a weekend tour of the suburbs of New York City. While on the tour, Campanella was invited by the manager of the Baltimore Elite Giants to play for his club in the Negro National League. Three days later the talented teenager caught both games of a double-header for the Elites in Baltimore. After Campanella returned to school, the coach of a rival team said he had become a professional and should no longer be permitted to play in school games. He therefore quit his high school team and continued to catch for the Elites. By the beginning of the 1937–38 school year he was so well established with the team that he decided not to return to his studies.

Campanella spent the years between 1937 and 1945 as backstop for the Elites. He supplemented his meager pay by playing winter ball in Cuba, Puerto Rico, Venezuela, and many other places. A right-hander who stood a little more than five-feet nine-inches tall and weighed about 200 pounds, he was an excellent power hitter whose skills helped the Elites win a Negro League Championship in 1939.

Excused from military service during World War II, Campanella played with the Baltimore team until the summer of 1942, when he joined the Monterey Club of the Mexican League and was paid more than he had earned with the Elites. When the owner of the Elites offered Campanella $3,000 a summer to play again for the Baltimore team, however, the catcher returned to the Negro National League. There he backstopped so well that in 1945 Effie Manley, owner of a club in Newark, New Jersey, asked him to play a post-season series between an all-star Negro team and a squad of barnstorming major leaguers.

Joins the Brooklyn Dodgers

In 1945, Campanella turned down the opportunity to become the first African American player in the major leagues when he mistakenly understood Brooklyn general manager Branch Ricky's offer as a contract with a rumored black team in Brooklyn. Ricky later gave him a contract with the Dodgers organization. Campanella was then sent to the Nashua, New

Roy Campanella (right) with Sammy Hughes, 1942.

Hampshire, team of the Class "B" New England League where, although he made 15 errors, he established a season's record with 687 putouts and 64 assists. He also drove in 96 runs with his timely hitting. In 1947 he was sent to Montreal, where he improved his fielding average to .988 (the best in the International League), batted .273, and established the season's records for putouts and assists.

In 1948 Campanella went to training camp in Florida with the Brooklyn Dodgers. But since they already had one first–rate catcher in Bruce Edwards, he was farmed out to the St. Paul, Minnesota, team of the American Association not long after the regular season had begun. In his debut appearance with St. Paul on May 22, Campanella struck out twice and made a throwing error; but thereafter, he showed his true form, hitting 11 home runs in his first 24 games.

The Dodgers, meanwhile, were not doing well. At the end of June, Campanella was recalled by manager Leo Durocher to Brooklyn, where he made his major league debut against the New York Giants. "Campy" finished his first half season with Brooklyn with a mere .258 batting average, but came decidedly into his own in the early summer of 1949, when he batted around .400 and began regularly to display that intelligence and insight in the handling of batter–mates which alone would cause him to stand out from the rank and file of catchers. By mid–season Campanella was behind the plate more frequently than Bruce Edwards, and in the All–Star game of that year was used by the National League team's manager, Billy Southworth, through most of the contest in preference to Andy Seminick of Philadelphia. He caught for the National League in several subsequent All–Star games. Campanella's fine teamwork with his pitchers, his .985 fielding average (best in the league) and his respectable all–season batting percentage of .287 were key elements in Brooklyn's successful 1949 pennant drive. In that year's World series with the New York Yankees, the Dodgers' catcher played errorless ball and made four hits, one a home run and another for a double. He was the spark responsible for Brooklyn's success in baseball in 1949, 1952, 1953, 1955, and 1956.

In 1950, the Dodgers lost to the Philadelphia Phillies in the year's battle for first place, but Campanella led all other

National League catchers in putouts and hit 31 home runs. The following season, he missed about a dozen games due to injuries that plagued him from time to time. Despite these setbacks, he continued to excel and hit 33 home runs in 1951, enough to earn him the New York Baseball Writer's award as the Most Valuable Player in the National League. In fact, Campanella was the only black baseball star to be named Most Valuable Player for three separate years, in 1951, 1953, and 1955.

Accident Ends Baseball Career

On January 28, 1958, the 36–year–old Campanella saw his baseball career came to an abrupt end. He had worked late at his wine and liquor store in Harlem and was on his way home when his car skidded off the road and crashed into a pole. The accident left him paralyzed from the chest down, and he was confined to a wheelchair for the rest of his life. It also transformed him from a sports hero into a universal symbol of courage as he became an inspiration and spokesman for the handicapped.

Doctors initially gave Campanella from 10 to 20 years to live, but he outlasted that prediction despite having to battle many illnesses. He was determined to persevere and get on with his life. As he once remarked in *Sports Illustrated,* "When they put me in that wheelchair I accepted it." He continued with his liquor store business and became the host of *Campy's Corner,* a radio interview show. After CBS bought the Yankees, however, Campanella's radio show was cancelled. Later, when New York State changed its liquor laws and removed price controls, many small liquor dealers, including Campanella, were badly hurt.

Through all the setbacks, Campanella endured. He had realized early on in his career that he could not play baseball forever, so he had gone into business to provide security for himself, his wife, and five children. He had also remained active in the game as a sports commentator and for nearly two decades served as a special instructor for young catchers during spring training.

In 1959 a benefit game in Campanella's honor was held at the Los Angeles Coliseum. According to *Time* magazine, the 93,103 fans who turned out for the event constituted perhaps the largest crowd ever to attend a baseball game up to that time. They had come to acknowledge the talents of an intelligent, strong, and natural–born leader who had often helped manage the clubs he played with whenever it became necessary for someone to step in. They also knew him as a very unassuming man. As quoted in *Sports Illustrated,* in his later years Campanella would say, "I never felt like a pioneer, just a ballplayer." The title of his autobiography, *It's Good To Be Alive,* published in 1959, indicates how much he loved and appreciated life even though he had been dealt such misfortune.

Elected to Hall of Fame

In 1969 Campanella, following in the footsteps of his friend Jackie Robinson, became the second black player to be elected to the Baseball Hall of Fame. According to the *New York Times,* he said, "This completes my baseball career, all my disappointments are behind me. There is nothing more I could ask for in baseball." In March 1975 Campanella was also inducted into the Black Athletes Hall of Fame in Las Vegas, Nevada. He continued to be active in baseball whenever his health permitted.

After the death in 1963 of his first wife, Ruthe Willis, whom he had married on January 3, 1939, and later divorced, Campanella married Roxie Doles, a former nurse. They remained virtually inseparable for the rest of his life. Together they raised five children—three sons (Roy Jr., Tony, and John) and two daughters (Joanie and Ruth).

Roy Campanella died at age 71 of an apparent heart attack at his home in Woodland Hills, California, on June 26, 1993. During his career, he had posted a .276 batting average and accumulated 1,161 hits (including 178 doubles, 18 triples, and 242 home runs) and 856 runs batted in—numbers that would have undoubtedly been higher had it not been for the color barrier that kept him out of the major leagues until he was 26. While he will be remembered for his contributions to both Negro League Baseball and Major League Baseball, he also endures as an inspiration to all for his courageous and upbeat approach to life in the face of injury and illness.

REFERENCES

Campanella, Roy Sr. *It's Good to Be Alive.* Boston: Little, Brown, 1959.

Current Biography Yearbook. New York: H.W. Wilson, 1953.

Current Biography Yearbook. [Obituary.] New York: H.W. Wilson, 1993.

Fimrite, Ron. "Baseball's Best Ambassador." *Sports Illustrated* 79 (5 July 1993): 70.

———. "Triumph of the Spirit." *Sports Illustrated* 73 (24 September 1990): 94–107.

"Hall of Fame Catcher Roy Campanella Dies at 71." *Jet* 84 (12 July 1993): 14–17.

Henderson, Edwin B., and the Editors of *Sport* Magazine. *The Black Athlete.* Cornwells Heights, PA: The Publishers Agency, 1976.

"Milestones." *Time* 142 (12 July 1993): 19.

Negro Almanac. New York: Bellwether Pub. Co., 1976.

Riley, A. James. *Biographical Encyclopedia of the Negro Baseball Leagues.* New York: Carroll & Graf, 1994.

"Roy Campanella, 71, Dies; Was Dodgers Hall of Famer." *New York Times,* June 28, 1993.

Who's Who among Black Americans, 1992–93. 7th ed. Detroit: Gale Research, 1993.

Nkechi G. Mgboh Amadife

E. Simms Campbell
(1906–1971)
Cartoonist

E. Simms Campbell was the first African American artist hired by a national publication, *Esquire* magazine, and the first black syndicated cartoonist. While he is perhaps best known for his voluptuous enchantresses and ''Esky''—the white–mustachioed, bulging–eyed connoisseur of feminine pulchritude featured in *Esquire*—Campbell produced award–winning artwork for numerous periodicals throughout his career. He was a master cartoonist of urbane humor, caricaturist, and artist.

Born in St. Louis, Missouri, on January 2, 1906, Elmer Simms Campbell was the son of Elmer Cary, a chemistry teacher and assistant principal in a high school in St. Louis. His mother, Elizabeth Simms Campbell, stimulated her son's interest in art as she frequently painted with water colors for her own amusement. Campbell's first wife, Constance, whom he married in 1936, died in 1940, and he married her younger sister, Vivian. They had one child, Elizabeth Ann.

Campbell received his early education in St. Louis. When he was ready for high school, he went to live with his aunt in Chicago, graduating from Englewood High School. Englewood students and teachers were very interested in student artwork. Some of the school's earliest graduates had already made names for themselves as cartoonists, and students whose artwork appeared in *The 'E' Weekly,* were given special notice. Campbell's drawings were soon among the most familiar ones in the school paper. In fact, his name was as well–known to classmates as were the names of Englewood's athletes. In 1923 he won a nationwide contest in a high school paper for an Armistice Day cartoon showing the debt of the nation to those who died in World War I.

After high school Campbell attended the Lewis Institute and later tried the University of Chicago for a year. Neither school seemed right for him at the time, but he stayed in Chicago and worked on the staff of the *Phoenix,* a humor magazine. Campbell registered at the Art Institute of Chicago and there he remained as a student for three years. At the institute he entered pictures in the International Water Color Exhibits, where they were accepted and commended. He financed his education through scholarships and summer jobs as a post office messenger and a dining car waiter. While in study at the Art Institute, Campbell also participated in the creation of *College Comics,* a magazine in which he did many drawings under various pseudonyms. The magazine failed and Campbell returned to St. Louis. The dates of his stay in Chicago and return to St. Louis are unavailable.

Back in St. Louis Campbell was discouraged against a career in commercial art because of his skin color, but he was dogged in his determination to break down the discrimination barrier in his area of interest. Serving as a waiter on a dining car, he drew caricatures of the train passengers. Later he succeeded in showing his work to the manager of Triad Studios, J. P. Sauerwein. Triad was one of the largest commercial art studios in the Midwest, located in St. Louis. Campbell was hired. His wages were better than those of most young men in their twenties and his job was secure. But Campbell continued to have a tenacious yearning to do magazine illustrations, covers, cartoons, and caricatures. Campbell worked for Triad for a year and a half, then went to New York City to try his luck as a freelance cartoonist.

In 1929 Campbell wrote to Elmer A. Carter, editor of *Opportunity* magazine, the prestigious black publication of the National Urban League and a staunch champion of the Harlem Renaissance. In Carter's article in *Opportunity* quoted Campbell:

> I do not like the covers on *Opportunity.* I am sending you a cover per your request and I should like to do twelve for you. You needn't pay me a cent until the end of the year and then if your news stand sales have not increased you owe me nothing; if they have, then pay me. . . .

Editor Carter was taken aback by the letter and its sharp criticism. And so he answered Campbell:

> I know that you have reached a high place in the commercial art field in St. Louis and I also know that you were awarded the St. Louis *Post Dispatch* Prize for your excellent black and white study, ''The Tornado,'' but if you are so good as you think you are, and as I think you are, you will come to New York where the competition is ''hot.'' If you can draw, you should be able to draw not only for *Opportunity,* but for *Life, Judge,* and other magazines.

Campbell accepted Carter's challenge to come to New York and acknowledged the editor's letter in person. Carter's *Opportunity* article described Campbell as being of ''medium height, of unblemished brown skin, with a frank, open countenance and a disarming smile. About him was an air of confidence.''

Campbell found a job in a New York advertising studio earning about one–eighth of his St. Louis salary. He also sold gags to other artists, sometimes 50 a week. He enrolled in the Academy of Design to increase his technical knowledge, and he studied at the Art Students League under the noted artist and printmaker George Grosz.

Soon Campbell contacted Ed Graham, a friend from Chicago who also worked on *The Phoenix.* Graham had become one of America's notable cartoonists and was a regular contributor to humorous magazines. Impressed with Campbell's work, Graham promised to help him effect his dreams. With Graham's counsel, Campbell was able to show his work to the editors and make his first sales.

Campbell's covers in *Opportunity* were eye–catching, original, lifelike, and genuine. At Christmas 1930 he had covers on both *Life* and *Judge*; during Christmas 1931, he designed the cover of *Judge.* Sometime in the early 1930s, after Campbell had become a well–established cartoonist, he and entertainer Cab Calloway met at the Dunbar Apartments

E. Simms Campbell

in Harlem. After that, the Campbell and Calloway families became friends. In *Of Minnie the Moocher and Me,* Calloway wrote about the close friendship the two men established. Calloway asserted, ''He was also, like me, a hard worker, a hard drinker, and a high liver. I used to think that I worked hard. . . . But Campbell outdid me. He drew a cartoon a day, not little line drawings, but full watercolor cartoons.'' The two men frequented the Harlem after–hours establishments like the Rhythm Club, drank, and enjoyed each other's company until the next morning. ''Somebody would get us home and pour us into bed, and we'd be back at it again the next night,'' Calloway later recalled.

Begins Work for *Esquire*

Campbell began receiving plenty of commissions and soon after published his well–known ''A Night–Club Map of Harlem,'' an engraving locating cafes and such sites as the Lafayette Theater, the Cotton Club, Connie's Inn, and Small's Paradise; Campbell placed his friend Cab Calloway in a prominent position at 142nd Street and Lenox Avenue. The original drawing became a part of Calloway's personal collection.

The editors planning the first issue of *Esquire* magazine, in October 1933, approached Campbell after having seen his work. Campbell was commissioned to do a full–page drawing in color. He was permitted to use any subject he liked as long as it had plenty of beautiful girls. For days myriad ideas dazzled him until one day he completed a design of a sultan surrounded by his harem of shapely *femmes fatales.* The editors published it. The cover was a smash hit and the public clamored for more. *Esquire* hired Campbell under a long–term contract, and the sprawling signature E. Simms Campbell soon became well–known to a vast number who avidly read America's humorous magazines.

Campbell's seraglio beauties paid his bills, built him a bank account, and bought him a beautiful sprawling estate in White Plains, New York. Campbell's splendid black and white illustrations appeared in many other magazines, indicating that Campbell's talent was not confined to caricatures and cartoons. His art appeared also in hundreds of newspapers and magazines as a syndicated feature, and commercial advertising agencies employed his talent in the composition of their ads. In his early thirties, Campbell became one of the highest paid commercial artists in his field. He was a tireless worker, producing about three hundred full page drawings a year; creating many drawings for ads, serving as cartoonist for newspaper syndicates, and producing creative drawings for special purposes.

Campbell contributed cartoons and other art work to *Cosmopolitan* magazine, *Red Book* magazine, *The New Yorker, Colliers* magazine, *The Saturday Evening Post, College Humor, Playboy,* and *Opportunity.* He contributed advertising illustrations and cartoons to *Esquire* magazine; did full pages of cartoons for the New York *Sunday Mirror*; and black and white illustrations for Jack Kofoed's *Great Dramas in Sports,* which appeared in *Life* magazine. Campbell designed the cover *Into the Light,* a brochure in honor of the fiftieth anniversary of the Young Men's Christian Association.

Because Campbell worked under a contract with King Features Syndicate, which served leading daily papers, his cartoons appeared in 145 newspapers throughout the United States. He won the $1,000 prize in the 1936 national competition offered by the Chicago Hearst newspaper for the best cartoon depicting the tax–grabber as the greedy profiteer. Campbell also won an honorable mention for water color at the American Negro Exposition, 1940. A member of the Society of Illustrators, the Society of Artists, and the National Society of Cartoonists, he held honorary degrees from Lincoln and Wilberforce Universities. For a number of years he was represented in the International Water Color Society's shows. Campbell's work was gathered in two books, *Cuties in Arms* (1942) and *More Cuties in Arms* (1943), both collections of his cartoons by David McKay.

One of Campbell's most satisfactory hobbies was functioning as a tutor and advisor to many rising young artists. A great deal of fan mail came to him, much of it from aspiring artists, often very young, or from parents who were eager to learn whether their children possessed an artistic gift. Campbell answered all of this mail and gave generously of his time to young artists by inviting them to his home for criticism and advise, making connections for them in the commercial art world, and encouraging them as once he needed encouragement.

In 1938 Campbell lost a New York Supreme Court application in White Plains that would have required mortgage trustees to sell a twelve–acre estate in Mount Pleasant to him for $18,500. His counsel, renowned civil libertarian Arthur Garfield Hays, contended that Campbell's proposal was rejected because of his color.

In 1957, after his primary employer, *Esquire,* changed its format, Campbell and his family moved to Switzerland, where they lived for fourteen years. After his wife, Vivian, died of cancer in October 1970, Campbell returned to the United States. He was diagnosed with cancer as well and died on January 27, 1971. His daughter Elizabeth Ann Parks and a granddaughter survived Campbell. His daughter had married Gordon Parks, the celebrated photographer, author, and filmmaker. Funeral services were held in the White Plains Community Unitarian Church. Campbell dedicated his life to amusing countless readers of the periodicals that published his drawings and sources claim that he found peace through achieving his goal.

REFERENCES

Bontemps, Arna W. "We Have Tomorrow: The Story of E. Simms Campbell." *Classmate* (11 February 1945): 8–11.

———. *We Have Tomorrow.* Boston: Houghton Mifflin, 1945.

Brawley, Benjamin G. *The Negro Genius.* New York: Dodd, Mead, 1937.

Calloway, Cab, with Bryant Rollins. *Of Minnie the Moocher & Me.* New York: Crowell, 1976.

"The Campbells Keep Coming." *Esquire* (November 1952): 62–65.

Carter, Elmer A. "E. Simms Campbell—Caricaturist." *Opportunity* 10 (March 1932): 82–89.

Current Biography Yearbook. New York: H. W. Wilson, 1941.

Current Biography Yearbook. [Obituary] New York: H. W. Wilson, 1971.

Downs, Karl E. *Meet the Negro.* Pasadena, CA: Login Press, 1943.

Murray, Florence. *The Negro Handbook.* New York: Wendell Malliet and Co., 1942.

National Urban League. *He Crashed the Color Line!* New York: National Urban League, 1933.

———. *They Crashed the Color Line!* New York: National Urban League, 1937.

Negro Year Book: An Annual Encyclopedia of the Negro, 1937–38. Tuskegee, AL: Negro Year Book Publishing Co., 1937.

Obituary. *New York Times,* January 29, 1971.

Robinson, Wilhelmina S. *Historical Negro Biographies.* New York: Publishers Company, 1968.

"These Are My Funniest." *Pageant* (December 1950): 78–83.

Watkins, Sylvester C. *The Pocket Book of Negro Facts.* Chicago: Bookmark Press, 1946.

Who's Who in Colored America. Supplement. Yonkers–on–Hudson, NY: Christian Burckel and Associates, 1950.

Casper L. Jordan

Francis L. Cardozo

(1837–1903)

Educator, politician, minister

Francis L. Cardozo is noted for his highly visible achievements in education and public service. He served more than honorably as an elected official in his native state of South Carolina, and he made substantial contributions to the development of two key black educational institutions: Avery Institute in Charleston, South Carolina, and Paul Laurence Dunbar High School in Washington, D.C.

Cardozo was born on February 1, 1837, in Charleston, South Carolina, to Jacob N. Cardozo, a white journalist, and a free woman of mixed African and Native American ancestry. We know of two siblings, Thomas W. Cardozo and Mrs. C. L.

Francis L. Cardozo

McKinney. All appear to have been educated in the quite illegal—but tolerated—schools for free black children. At the age of 12, Francis L. Cardozo was apprenticed to a carpenter and completed five years as apprentice and four years as a journeyman. He had joined the Second Presbyterian Church and received a letter of recommendation from the church's pastor when he left to study in Great Britain about 1848, having saved $1,000 and continuing to work to earn additional money as he attended school. He spent four years at the University of Glasgow, followed by three years in Presbyterian seminaries in Edinburgh and London.

Enters Ministry

Upon his return to the United States in 1864 Cardozo became pastor of the Temple Street Congregational Church in New Haven, Connecticut, where he spent a year. He married Catherine Romena Howell of New Haven. The couple had four sons and two daughters; at least one of the daughters died in infancy. Cardozo aimed at being an educator rather than a minister, and he asked the American Missionary Association to send him south to establish a school to train black teachers. The first task the AMA assigned him was to go to Charleston to investigate rumors about the conduct of his brother Thomas.

Thomas Cardozo had secured an education and taught school in Flushing, New York; he had married Laura J. Williams of Brooklyn. Also teaching in Flushing was the Cardozos' sister, Mrs. C. L. McKinney and her husband C. C. McKinney. The McKinneys would join Francis Cardozo as teachers in Charleston in January of 1866. Before Thomas left for Charleston to take charge of the AMA school there in April of 1865, he had either seduced one of his students or been seduced by her, and she was blackmailing him. Although Thomas confessed his wrongdoing to his brother and promised to mend his ways, the AMA instead appointed Francis head of the Charleston school in August. Francis Cardozo served as principal until April of 1868 and laid the firm foundations of Avery Institute, a very successful teacher training institute and later a bastion of Charleston's black elite for many years.

Cardozo directed an integrated staff of white teachers from the North and black teachers from both the North and South. His requests for northern teachers were sometimes mistaken as betraying a lack of confidence in the abilities of black instructors, but he countered with the assertion that he wanted northern teachers of both races because of the superior training available in the North. He also responded to charges of favoring light–skinned black students by pointing out that many of them were former free blacks who had obtained a head start on education. Despite problems with AMA superiors like Samuel Hunt, who had no difficulty in alienating teachers and principals, especially black teachers and principals, Cardozo led his school under difficult conditions.

Cardozo also had to find a place for the school as southerners reclaimed confiscated property. Matters had reached a crisis when Cardozo learned of the Charles Avery estate's plan to contribute $10,000 to establish a school in Atlanta. Cardozo could hope to receive a similar sum from the trustees of the estate if he could win the backing of the governor of the state and the mayor of the city. Cardozo called on his contacts among former free blacks and obtained the backing of the white establishment. Money from the Freedmen's Bureau was added to that from the Avery estate. In April of 1867 Cardozo and his teachers moved to Bull Street and in the fall an elegant new building rose on the lot next door. The newly renamed Avery Institute became a normal school, retaining a primary department mainly for the purpose of teacher training. In April of 1868 Cardozo handed over the reins of the school to what was envisioned as a temporary replacement.

Enters Politics

Early on Cardozo participated in politics. In the spring of 1866 he served on a board advising the military commander of South Carolina about regulations for voter registration. He was elected to the state constitutional convention held in Charleston in the spring of 1868; he attended the convention while still heading the school, but he had to give up teaching classes. While principal, Cardozo also drew up plans for state–supported public education. Realistically in the situation, the plan, which was eventually adopted in its essentials, allowed but did not require separate schools. Cardozo's leadership qualities displayed in his school and in the state convention led to his election as secretary of state. He was the only black candidate on the state–wide Republican ticket. He resigned his school position on May 1 just days before Avery Institute was formally dedicated on May 7, 1868.

Also in 1868 Cardozo served as president of the Union League, which worked to ensure a Republican victory in the elections. The supposed rituals and night meetings of the league were demonized by angry white detractors, who portrayed the league as a sort of black Ku Klux Klan, although that characterization is wildly off the mark. As secretary of state Cardozo worked hard to counter fraud in the Land Commission. He was reelected secretary of state in 1870, and there was some support in the legislature for electing him to the U.S. Senate. *Men of Mark* places him as a teacher of Latin at Howard University in Washington, D.C., in 1871–72 while he was still a state official.

In 1872 Cardozo reorganized the graft–ridden Land Commission, making it much more honest and effective. He became state treasurer, a position he held until 1876, and he supported the efforts of reform Republicans to lower taxes and do away with corruption even though one man he supported for governor in the interests of party unity tried to steal $25,000 as soon as he was inaugurated. Nonetheless, Cardozo never yielded in his attempts to enforce fiscal responsibility. In 1876 he played a key role in rallying an agitated Republican state convention—pistols were drawn on the floor of the convention—to a reform ticket. He was too late, however, as resurgent Democrats took control of the state at the elections.

Cardozo left South Carolina in 1877 to accept a post in the Treasury Department in Washington, D.C., during the Hayes administration. The South Carolina Democrats engaged in wholesale smearing of all Republicans, and Cardozo was charged on eight counts of fraud. In 1879 a political deal resulted in a pardon and dismissal of the other charges.

After serving in the Treasury Department, Cardozo became principal of the Colored Preparatory High School in Washington. The school was renamed the M Street High School in 1891 and became best known by its later name, Paul Laurence Dunbar High School. Between 1884 and 1896 he effectively built the high school into the leading black preparatory school in the United States. A commercial department was formed in 1884, and in 1887 Cardozo introduced a two–year non–college preparatory course in business. Later in 1928 the District's new business and vocational high school was named in his honor. Not all was sweetness and light however. William Calvin Chase of the *Washington Bee* led a long campaign to oust Cardozo, and it appears that Cardozo's departure was not voluntary.

Francis L. Cardozo died on July 22, 1903. He left behind a family of high achievers, including his granddaughter Eslanda Goode Robeson and his grandson William Warrick Cardozo, a physician who was a pioneer researcher of sickle cell anemia. A leader in education, in addition Cardozo gave honest and efficient service in high political office in his home state.

REFERENCES

Drago, Edmund L. *Initiative, Paternalism, and Race Relations: Charleston's Avery Normal Institute.* Athens: University of Georgia Press, 1990.

Greenwood, Willard B. *Aristocrats of Color.* Bloomington: University of Indiana Press, 1990.

Holt, Thomas. *Black over White.* Urbana: University of Illinois Press, 1977.

Logan, Rayford W., and Michael R. Winston, eds. *Dictionary of American Negro Biography.* New York: Norton, 1982.

Richardson, Joe M. *Christian Reconstruction.* Athens: University of Georgia Press, 1986.

———. "Francis L. Cardozo: Black Educator during Reconstruction." *Journal of Negro Education* 48 (Winter 1979): 73–83.

Simmons, William J. *Men of Mark.* Cleveland: Geo. M. Rewell, 1887.

Terrell, Mary Church. "History of the High School for Negroes in Washington." *Journal of Negro History* 2 (July 1917): 252–66.

Turner, Geneva C. "School Names." *Negro History Bulletin* 20 (November 1956): 45–46.

Williamson, Joel. *After Slavery.* Chapel Hill: University of North Carolina Press, 1965.

COLLECTIONS

The Francis L. Cardozo papers are in the Library of Congress, Washington, D.C. Letters concerning his educational work in Charleston are in the American Missionary Association Archives, Amistad Research Center, Tulane University.

Robert L. Johns

Carey, Lott.

See Cary, Lott.

Stokely Carmichael

(1941–)

Civil rights activist, organization official, Pan Africanist

Stokely Carmichael was a 1960s black radical who could raise his fist in the air, shout "Black Power!" and polarize white and black Americans in an instant. As a Freedom Rider, he went to Mississippi to get a firsthand view of the South's mistreatment of black Americans. As chairman of the Student Nonviolent Coordinating Committee (SNCC) and prime minister of the Black Panthers, he became a leading spokesperson for the black power movement, and a messianic leader to many young people.

Born on June 29, 1941, in Port–of–Spain, Trinidad and Tobago, Stokely Carmichael came to America in 1952. His

Stokely Carmichael

parents were Adolphus Carmichael, a carpenter, and Mabel Charles Carmichael, now a retired domestic worker. She lives in Miami, Florida, as does his sister, Nagib Malik, a psychiatric nurse. The family settled in Harlem, where Carmichael graduated from the Bronx High School of Science in 1960. Then he entered Howard University in Washington, D.C., with the intention of majoring in philosophy.

Carmichael watched the violent results of sit–in demonstrations at segregated lunch counters on television. As he watched the young integrationists being manhandled while refusing to resist, he said in a *People* interview, "Something happened to me, suddenly I was burning."

In 1961 Carmichael responded to an advertisement in the new SNCC newsletter, the *Student Voice,* for volunteers to join the Freedom Rides. Carmichael was in the group of Freedom Riders that originated in Washington, D.C., nearly three weeks after the first one that resulted in the vicious beating of John Lewis. Carmichael was arrested. This event was a catalyst for the budding Marxist, Southern Christian Leadership Conference (SCLC) scholarship student, who was an early admirer of Martin Luther King Jr. and his nonviolent demonstrations. Carmichael became a hard–core civil rights activist credited with popularizing the slogan "Black Power!"

Carmichael was transferred to the infamous Parchman Penitentiary, where he spent seven weeks stoically awaiting news of his fate. Along with other students who had not undergone the advanced and highly sophisticated training in Mahatma Gandhi–based nonviolent techniques perfected by the Nashville, Tennessee, students, he was not overly impressed by the often fanatically religious fervor and lofty discourses on fasting. The headiness of being martyrs for the cause was tempered by the news that SNCC was planning to make the voter registration drive a top priority. Under the leadership of James Forman, this campaign spread all across Mississippi, but personal violence was soon supplanted by shotguns and bombs.

SNCC was formalized in May of 1960 with the adoption of the group's formal name and statement of purpose. This Atlanta University conference had developed from April of 1960 meetings at Highlander Folk School in Tennessee and at Shaw University in North Carolina, hosted by Septima Clark and Ella Baker respectively. The SCLC emerged in 1957 from the aftermath of the Montgomery church and home bombings and as an outgrowth of the Montgomery Improvement Association (MIA), which had coordinated the Montgomery bus boycott. As it widened its focus to nonviolent mass movement and civil disobedience tactics, it also supported SNCC with financial gifts and temporary office space. By 1966 many SNCC members had become disillusioned by the political system and by black leaders they perceived as being willing to compromise the issue of full equality for black Americans. By the time Carmichael assumed leadership of SNCC, he had become disillusioned by internecine divisiveness and by the increasingly violent opposition to voter registration projects. This was the basis for his alliance with the Black Panthers, who advocated a more militant stance and outright separatism to achieve black power.

Under Carmichael's chairmanship, SNCC became more militant and known for the "Black Power" slogan that struck terror and evoked hatred in much of white America. According to Ronald Copeland, a New Jersey community activist, the term was originally a concept focusing on three issues: 1) an economic base within the black community; 2) collective efforts to halt financial exploitation of the black community; and 3) building a political base in the black community by raising political consciousness and electing black representatives to local, state, and national offices. It was meant to help end de facto segregation in a small New Jersey township by involving working–class black families in efforts to obtain better educational conditions for all the citizenry.

To Carmichael the concept of black power was far removed from community–based efforts to rectify economic inequalities. Gordon Parks traveled with Carmichael as a photojournalist after Carmichael had outgrown SNCC and became a Black Panther leader, and thus anathema to all black civil rights groups as a die–hard critic of the white man. In his 1990 autobiography, Parks quoted his remarks made at a Berkeley, California, student gathering:

> The white man says, "work hard nigger, and you will overcome!" If that were true, the black man would be the richest man in the world! [My dad] worked like a dog, day and night! But only death came to that poor black man!—and in his early forties! My grandfather had to run, run, run. I ain't running no more.

In answer to a charge of inciting violence, Parks quotes Carmichael's answer: ''I'm just telling the white man he's beat my head enough. I won't take anymore.'' Parks further relates how Carmichael witnessed a pregnant black woman flattened in the street by a burst of water from a fire hose, how he saw people trampled by police horses and left bleeding in the streets. It was too much and he was bodily carried to the airport in a state of shock. To Parks, he said: ''From that day on, I knew if I was hit, I would hit back.''

As chair of SNCC, Carmichael kept Mississippi and Alabama as operations bases through 1966. Using the symbol of a black panther as a challenge to the Alabama Democratic Party's use of a white rooster, Carmichael tried to develop black consciousness in the black county residents and in Selma as well, by stressing black power and separatism. Carmichael became the living symbol of the group that adopted a militant stance leading to its polarization from more moderate groups. With Charles V. Hamilton, he coauthored *Black Power* in 1967 before leaving his SNCC post that same year.

By summer's end, Carmichael had traveled to Hanoi to meet with leaders of the North Vietnamese National Assembly. There he said that American blacks and the Vietnamese were allies against American imperialism. On the day he pledged support of American blacks to the Vietnamese cause, Thurgood Marshall was pledging his support to the Constitution of the United States of America as the first black member of the Supreme Court.

Carmichael left SNCC and became a Black Panther in 1967, and in 1968 was the prime minister of the most militant group of young black separatists of the mid–1960s. Their symbol, as noted in *Pride and Power,* was the black panther, described as ''a sleek, cunning, black, and beautiful animal . . . that attacked only when it was attacked.'' It was a fitting symbol. The party, organized in Oakland, California, in 1966, believed in defensive violence, as described by its founder Huey Newton and cited in *The Negro in the Making of America:* ''We feel it necessary to prepare the people for the event of an actual physical rebellion.'' The Panthers and other groups of its ilk saw racial conflict as being parallel to international struggles, especially of the darker races across the world. While other groups espoused either integration or mere separatism, the Panthers declared that blacks would be free or America would be destroyed.

By 1969 Carmichael had become disenchanted with the Black Panthers and moved on to the Pan African movement. He became an organizer for Kwame Nkrumah's All–African People's Revolutionary Party. This change in allegiance was a natural outcome of Carmichael's adherence to cultural nationalism, with its focus on nation–building within the black community—a stance rejected by the Panthers, especially Eldridge Cleaver, minister of information, and those of a more revolutionary bent. In *Voices in a Mirror,* Parks described the enmity among the once notorious and feared Panthers:

> Stokely shares no enthusiasm for Newton or Seale, nor they for him. The kinship has blown apart. The affinities that once forged them into a heroic brotherhood disintegrated with the unfolding of history. All of them have changed clothes and moved to quieter landscapes, vanished without hardly a sound.

Carmichael had not vanished. He moved to Conakry, Guinea, to escape police harassment in the United States, changed his name, and married the internationally famed South African singer Miriam Makeba. They divorced in 1978. Later he married a Guinean physician, Marlyatou Barry, with whom he had a son, Boca Biro. The couple divorced in 1992.

Since 1969 Carmichael has been involved with the Marxist political party of the late Guinean president Sekou Toure. Citing lack of organization and failure to see the need for a unifying ideology, Carmichael still believes that America will undergo a revolution because Americans, especially women, are more politicized than they were in the 1960s. The ultimate goal for black people, according to Carmichael, is a unified and socialist Africa. This is the reason Carmichael makes annual visits to America, to seek out recruits who will be mesmerized by the clipped voice, still piercing eyes, and the strident, pounding, insistent message of what *People* called ''an unreconstructed rebel . . . a black separatist who proselytizes for a unified, Socialist Africa . . . [who] expects America's dispossessed to overthrow the capitalist system one day.''

The increasingly strident rhetoric that acknowledged and approved the need for violence and hatred of whites alienated the black old guard of the more moderate civil rights organizations. Now a 30–year resident of Guinea and a Pan Africanist, he is no longer Stokely Carmichael, having renamed himself Kwame Ture after two leading African Socialists—Kwame Nkrumah and Sekou Toure. As of the late 1990s, he has been suffering from the effects of prostate cancer and has undergone radiation therapy at New York's Columbia–Presbyterian Medical Center and at a Havana, Cuba, hospital. Although gray–headed, gray–bearded, and physically weakened, he cheerfully answers the telephone with the 1960s greeting of ''Ready for revolution!''

In 1971, Carmichael published his speeches and a series of essays entitled *Stokely Speaks: Black Power Back to Pan Africanism.* In 1994, he was awarded an LL.D. by Shaw University, recognizing his efforts to free black people.

Current address: c/o Random House, 201 E. 50th St., New York, NY 10022.

REFERENCES

Branch, Taylor. *Parting the Water; America in the King Years 1954–1963.* New York: Simon and Schuster, 1988.

Chestnut, J. L., Jr., and Julia Cass. *Black in Selma.* New York: Farrar, Straus, and Giroux, 1990.

Ebony Pictorial History of Black America. Vol. 3. *Civil Rights Movement to Black Revolution.* Chicago: Johnson Publishing Co., 1971.

Franklin, John Hope. *From Slavery to Freedom: A History of Negro Americans.* 5th ed. New York: Knopf, 1980.

Gates, Henry Louis Jr. ''Second Thoughts—After the Revolution.'' *New Yorker* 72 (29 April 1996; 6 May 1996): 61.
Giles, Raymond H. *Pride and Power—From Watts to Mexico City.* Middleton, CT: American Education Publications, 1971.
Goldstein, Rhodal, ed. *Black Life and Culture in the United States.* New York: Crowell, 1971.
''Hospital Visit.'' *Jet* 90 (3 June 1996): 33.
Parks, Gordon. *Voices in the Mirror: An Autobiography.* New York: Doubleday, 1990.
Quarles, Benjamin. *The Negro in the Making of America.* Rev. ed. New York: Macmillan, 1969.
Rogers, Patricia, and Ron Arias. ''Update: A Panther in Winter.'' *People* 45 (22 April 1996): 63–64.
Salzman, Jack, David Lionel Smith, and Cornel West, eds. *Encyclopedia of African–American Culture and History.* New York: Macmillan Library Reference USA/Simon and Schuster Macmillan, 1996.
Thorpe, Earl E. *Struggle for a Nation's Conscience—The Civil Rights Movement.* Middleton, CT: American Education Publications, 1971.
Who's Who among African Americans, 1995–96. 9th ed. Detroit: Gale Research, 1995.

Dolores Nicholson

William H. Carney

William H. Carney
(1840–1908)
Soldier, postal worker, messenger

William Harvey Carney was the first African American to earn the Congressional Medal of Honor, one of the 16 awarded to African Americans for service in the army during the Civil War. His medal was not authorized, however, until May 23, 1900, making him the last African American Civil War veteran to actually receive the award. (The first 11 were awarded on April 6, 1865, for gallantry in engagements near Chaffin's Farm, New Market Heights, and Fort Harrison in Virginia on September 29 and 30, 1864. Two more African Americans were later honored for their roles in these actions.) Outside of his army exploits, Carney lived a quiet life of solid but modest achievement.

Carney himself gave a brief account of his family in a letter published in the magazine, *Liberator,* on November 6, 1863, and reprinted by Aptheker. He was born in Norfolk, Virginia, in 1840 to William and Ann Dean Carney. His mother was a slave of Major Carney and freed upon his death in 1854 along with her fellow slaves. William H. Carney attended school for a time when he was 14. He experienced a religious conversion the following year, and joined his father, William Sr., as a sailor in the coasting trade. In 1856 his father decided to move the family to the North. After considering Philadelphia and New York, he settled on New Bedford, Massachusetts.

William H. Carney, along with his mother, soon joined his father in Massachusetts. He joined a local church headed by William Jackson, a black Baptist minister also born in Norfolk, and found work at odd jobs. He also contemplated preparing himself for the ministry.

When black army units finally came into existence during the Civil War, Carney was one of the 27 African Americans recruited in New Bedford for the 55th Massachusetts Infantry. Their regiment trained at Readville, Massachusetts, where William Jackson became one of the two African American New Bedford ministers to attend to its spiritual needs. On May 28, 1863, the largest crowd in Boston history at that time saw the regiment march off to war.

On July 18 the 55th Massachusetts led the attack on Fort Wagner, South Carolina, one of the defenses of Charleston Harbor. The attackers were repulsed with a heavy loss of life, including that of the regimental commander, Robert Gould Shaw. Carney carried the regimental colors in the attack; he maintained the colors on the rampart and then carried them back to the remnant of the regiment, even though he received three severe wounds. He had to creep on one knee but refused to lay down or give up the colors until he reached the regiment's only surviving officer, Louis F. Emilio. Emilio commended him for gallantry, and Congress later awarded him the Medal of Honor. His actions also inspired a patriotic song by Rosamond and James Weldon Johnson, ''Boys, the Old Flag Never Touched the Ground.''

Carney received an honorable discharge from the army because of his disabilities on June 30, 1864. In October he married Susanna Williams of New Bedford. For a year following the marriage he was superintendent of street lights for the city. In 1867 he became a shipping clerk in the office of James T. Hoyt, an assistant army quartermaster stationed in San Francisco.

Carney then returned to New Bedford, where he established residence at 128 Mill Street, the family home of his wife. He became one of the four mail carriers in the city, a position he held until 1901. Through thrift and prudence he acquired several pieces of real estate. When he left the postal service, he became a messenger at the State House in Boston. There he suffered an elevator accident which led to his death on December 9, 1908. The governor ordered the flag at the State house flown at half mast, an unprecedented act of honor formerly reserved for presidents, ex–presidents, governors, ex–governors, and senators.

Carney was survived by his wife and a daughter, Clara Heronia. His wife was the first African American woman to graduate from the New Bedford high school and one of the first black teachers in Massachusetts public schools. Carney's hobbies included collecting china and music. Possessing a fine singing voice, he passed on his musical talent to his daughter, who became a piano teacher.

Throughout his life Carney was a living memorial to the Civil War and delighted in telling schoolchildren of his exploit. He was an honored participant in Memorial Day observances. His flag was enshrined in Memorial Hall. He himself continues to stride in bronze immediately behind Robert Gould Shaw on the monument on the grounds of the Massachusetts State House. He is an outstanding example of those African Americans who showed skeptics that African Americans were willing to fight heroically for freedom.

REFERENCES

Aptheker, Herbert. *A Documentary History of the Negro People in the United States.* New York: Citadel Press, 1951.

Blanchet, Carrie Lee. ''William Harvey Carney.'' *Negro History Bulletin* 7 (February 1944): 107–08.

Duncan, Russell, ed. *Blue–eyed Child of Fortune: the Civil War Letters of Colonel Robert Gould Shaw.* Athens: University of Georgia Press, 1992.

Greene, Robert Ewell. *Black Defenders of America, 1775–1973.* Chicago: Johnson Publishing, 1974.

Lee, Irvin H. *Negro Medal of Honor Men.* 3rd ed. New York: Dodd, Mead, 1969.

Logan, Rayford W., and Michael R. Winston, eds. *Dictionary of American Negro Biography.* New York: Norton, 1982.

Moebs, Thomas Truxton. *Black Soldiers—Black Sailors—Black Ink.* Chesapeake Bay, VA: Moebs Publishing, 1994.

''Sergeant Carney.'' *Colored American Magazine* 7 (October 1904): 636–37.

''Sergeant Carney is Dead.'' *Alexander's Magazine* 7 (15 January 1909): 109.

Robert L. Johns

George Washington Carver (1861?–1943)

Chemist, researcher

Using products available from the red clay of Alabama where he conducted research for over 40 years, George Washington Carver produced more than 400 different products from the peanut, sweet potato, pecan, and other sources. His scientific work improved the quality of life for people worldwide, enhanced the agriculture of the South, and brought lasting recognition to his memory and to the reputation of Tuskegee Institute where he pioneered.

George Washington Carver's birth date has been given in separate sources as 1860, 1861, and 1864. The second son of three children, he was born to slave parents on a plantation near Diamond Grove, Missouri. His father was killed in an accident when Carver was an infant. There are conflicting accounts concerning Carver and his family. Whether Arkansas raiders carried away his mother and sister in the last year of the Civil War or the family's master, Moses Carver, sent them to Arkansas to avoid kidnapping, Carver's mother and sister were never heard from again. Moses Carver and his wife Mary told young George the story that he chose to believe, that they were actually kidnapped. When Carver was located, he was ill with whooping cough and almost died; he remained sickly throughout childhood. The Carver family raised the youngster, who assumed their name. The frail child was unable to manage physically stressful jobs around the house; instead, he learned cooking and sewing, skills which facilitated his employment later on. He developed a keen interest in plant life, collecting flowers and specimens for a small, concealed garden near his home.

Recognizing his keen ability to learn, Mary Carver encouraged his early education, giving him his first book—a blue–backed speller—and later a Bible, large portions of which he memorized. When he was about 14—some sources say ten—Carver left his adoptive family to pursue a formal education then unavailable to blacks in the Diamond Grove community. He took odd jobs to support himself while he attended grade school for two years in nearby Neosho, Missouri. He moved about in Kansas, Minnesota, Colorado, and Iowa, relying on the cooking, sewing, and other skills he

George Washington Carver

learned early to find odd jobs and support himself while he studied. Carver completed high school in Minneapolis, Kansas. In 1885 his application to Highland College in northeast Kansas was rejected because of his race. Carver was an unsuccessful homesteader and farmer for two years, living near Beeler, Kansas. He mortgaged his farm in 1888 and then moved to Winterset, Iowa, where a friendly white family encouraged him to continue his studies. He did fine laundry, knitting, tatting, embroidery, and other odd jobs to earn money for college. He worked in a laundry to support his three–year stay at Simpson College in Indianola, Iowa, where he had enrolled in 1890. Despite his interest in the arts, he was encouraged to study agriculture. Around this time Carver considered a career in art. He was encouraged when four of his paintings of flowers were shown in an Iowa art exhibition in 1892, then at the World's Columbian Exposition in Chicago.

Carver transferred to Iowa State College of Agricultural and Mechanical Arts in Ames where in academics he ranked at the top of his class. He graduated with a B.S. degree in 1894—the school's first African American graduate—and earned an M.S. in 1896. At Iowa he was in touch with three men who later became U.S. Secretary of Agriculture. Two of them—James Wilson and Henry C. Wallace—influenced Carver's thoughts on agricultural problems. The third was Henry A. Wallace. Carver was in charge of the greenhouse where he conducted experiments in plant cross–fertilization and propagation; he was also faculty assistant to eminent botanist Louis H. Pammell. After graduation, he was in charge of the bacteriological laboratories. He continued his work in the greenhouse and did research on systematic botany. By now Carver's reputation in horticulture and mycology—that aspect of botany related to fungi—had become known and his work was cited in scientific papers. He also lectured throughout Iowa.

Moves to Tuskegee

Carver's reputation also came to the attention of Booker T. Washington, founder and head of Tuskegee Institute, as it was known then. Washington wrote to Iowa State in regard to a "colored graduate." In his response to Washington, W. M. Beardshear, whose March 5, 1896, letter appeared in the *Booker T. Washington Papers* for 1895–88, suggested that Carter—who had graduated two years earlier—had made good "standings" in horticulture and with the experiment station. He called Carver a "Christian gentleman and scholar" who would receive the school's "iron–clad recommendations. Any school would be fortunate in securing his services."

Carver accepted Washington's invitation to join the Tuskegee staff as head of the Department of Agriculture which Carver would have to create. As well, he learned that he was to build his own laboratory from all sorts of discarded materials he found around the campus. Meanwhile, Washington was successful in persuading the Alabama legislature to establish and support a branch experiment station at Tuskegee which would provide information on agriculture to blacks. Legislation to that effect was approved on February 15, 1897, and Carver became the director. It was his work at the experiment station that led to Carver's international acclaim as a researcher and agricultural chemist.

Carver had anticipated a partnering between himself and Washington but, although the two men respected each other, their relationship remained stormy until Washington's death in 1915. At times they were at odds over what Carver saw as insufficient support of the experiment station. Washington asserted in a letter dated December 27, 1912, that the school had "gone some distance in the matter," certainly "as far as. . .finances would permit." Carver offered his resignation to Washington in 1910, 1912, and again in 1913. In her biography, *George Washington Carver,* Linda O. McMurray saw differences as well as similarities between the men which probably helped fuel the fire between them. Carver, who was inept at administrative duties, she wrote, was "a dreamer and idealist; Washington was preeminently a realist and pragmatist." On the other hand, "both men were exceedingly sensitive to criticism, filled with a sense of mission, and anxious to prove their own merit." Carver knew that the agricultural department and the experiment station needed his full attention, yet Washington poured on an odd assortment of responsibilities that ranged from serving as school veterinarian to maintaining the grounds.

In 1899 Carver and one of his promising students, Thomas M. Campbell, began to disseminate the work of his laboratory by taking Carver's mule–drawn "movable school" on weekend visits to impoverished farm lands in nearby areas to teach farmers how to improve and preserve foods. In 1906 Campbell designed a wagon to replace the old cart, using funds donated by philanthropist Morris K. Jesup. He outfitted the wagon, renamed it the Jesup Wagon, and took it on a regular schedule to surrounding communities. The wagon, a farmer's college on wheels, marked the beginning of the Federal Government Service in the South for Negroes. In *George Washington Carver,* Rackham Holt quotes Campbell, who described the movable school as a means to carry out the "ideas on the potentialities of art and science through creative research, to turn the ugly into the beautiful, the waste into the useful, that even the poorest of God's creatures might be healthier, his home more comfortable, his surroundings more beautiful, his life more significant."

Carver followed the Booker T. Washington mission of taking education to the people both by visiting their home sites and through training institutes held at Tuskegee. When Carver first reached the farmers, his early concentration was on crop rotation. Although Carver had already begun to make great strides in agriculture by the early 1900s, during his first ten years at the school fellow researchers and farmers in Alabama barely recognized him for his efforts. He traveled the area weekly, teaching farmers and their wives ways to better their conditions. He taught the farmers to substitute peanuts, pecans, and sweet potatoes, all money–making crops, for the cotton they were used to growing. As Tuskegee reached out more to the South with its farmers conferences, institutes, and fairs with Carver a lecturer or presenter at them, he became more widely known and respected by blacks and whites as well.

With his high–pitched voice he blended humor and drama in his lectures, producing such a magnetic quality that he became a drawing card whenever he spoke at farmers' meetings. The size of his audiences began to reach into the thousands. He brought soil and crop specimens to his lectures and spoke on the variety of research projects he had underway at Tuskegee, such as experiments with the sweet potato, the peanut, cowpeas, and products he made from clay. He also prepared exhibits to demonstrate his work.

Research Leads to Fame

In his meager laboratory, Carver concentrated his research on the peanut, the crop he had encouraged farmers to plant as a rotation crop. In time, he derived some 300 products from the peanut, including face powder, butter, cheese, milk, printer's ink, creosote, soaps, and stains. By 1924 he had become firmly established as the "Peanut Man" and was called on by peanut growers and processors for his expertise. Early on he had seen value in the clay of Macon County, where Tuskegee was located. He asserted that color from the clay could be used to stain and thus enhance the appearance of local farm houses. He later extracted from Alabama's red clay soil valuable pigments including blue, red, and purple. His secret of lasting color was equated with that known to the Egyptians. He used cotton stalks to make starch, gums, and dextrins. Using palmetto and green wood shavings, he made synthetic marble; and he made fiber and rope from the cornstalk.

Carver's research led him to explore the possibilities of numerous products. For example, he derived over 100 products from the sweet potato and 60 more from the pecan. Carver was called on during World War I to help relieve the crisis that occurred in the dye industry when dyes could no longer be imported from Germany. At that time he used 28 kinds of plants to extract some 500 dyes. In the 1930s he had become interested in developing some relief for patients with paralyses. His peanut oil therapy was effective for many paralysis victims, while the oil itself was readily available to consumers in drugstores.

Still dedicated to agricultural research, in 1940 Carver decided to establish the George Washington Carver Research Foundation at Tuskegee. He contributed most of his life savings of $60,000 to the foundation to support continued research in the field. He worked there for three years before he died.

Although Carver worked apart from mainstream scientific research, did not attend scientific meetings, and did not have papers published in scientific journals, his work still brought him local, national, and international recognition. He had published bulletins from his experiment station but these were directed to farmers and housewives rather than to scientists. Sometimes recognition came in the form of job offers; for example, he was invited for employment or to serve as consultant to the Thomas A. Edison research laboratories. In 1935 the Department of Agriculture appointed him a collaborator in the Mycology and Plant Disease Survey of the Bureau of Plant Industry. He was recognized in other ways as well. In 1916 he was elected a fellow of the Royal Society of Arts of Great Britain. The NAACP awarded him the Spingarn Medal in 1923 for distinguished work in agricultural chemistry. He received the Franklin Delano Roosevelt Medal in 1939 and in 1940 was presented with an award from the International Federation of Architects, Engineers, Chemists, and Technicians. In 1941 he became an honorary member of the American Inventors Society. His numerous other awards and honors were not widely publicized.

While Carver rose from slavery, was raised by white adoptive parents, and became prominent in the world, the segregated environment in which he lived and traveled touched him but did not seem to affect him adversely. He maintained a deep Christian faith that gave him a genuine love for humanity. Even as events awakened his consciousness of race relations in the South, he refused to express bitterness toward Southern whites for their abuse of blacks. While he had friends who were Marxists, Carver was neither political nor an activist.

Although he never married, Carver supposedly had a serious relationship with Sarah L. Hunt, the sister–in–law of Warren Logan, Tuskegee's treasurer. Friends' efforts to match him with other women apparently produced no serious results. He probably had little time for a serious relationship, given his deep immersion in church activities and his own work at Tuskegee. Mackintosh's description of Carver in "The Carver Myth" was that Carver was "considered an eccentric local character, and he played the part, knitting his own socks, living on the second floor of a girls' dormitory which he entered by the fire escape, singing in a high voice at Sunday School, and wearing various flowers and weeds in his buttonhole to advertise their properties."

Carver had a cultural side as well. He was an accomplished pianist as well as a skilled painter, having created watercolors and oils—mostly still lifes. He was charitable, giving Tuskegee several pianos and at times refusing to accept a salary increase. Although he received small honoraria and financial donations for his lectures, it appears that Carver donated such monies to the Carver Foundation. Still, his financial records were poorly kept: he often forgot to deposit checks, sometimes as many as six salary checks. Except for the small amounts he spent on medical and dental services, he spent little on himself.

Carver died at Tuskegee from anemia on January 5, 1943, and was buried on campus alongside Booker T. Washington. He received many posthumous recognitions. Carver's photograph appeared on a commemorative stamp issued January 5, 1948. Five years later, the George Washington Carver National Monument was erected in his honor near Diamond Grove, Missouri, presumably on the site where he was born. Dedicated on July 17, 1960, this was the first federal monument built to honor an African American. He was enshrined in the New York University Hall of Fame in April 23, 1977, in a ceremony held at Tuskegee. He was featured on a U.S. postage stamp again in 1998, this time in the U.S. Postal Service's "Celebrate the Century" stamp series. According to *Jet* magazine in 1998, in the stamp series Carver and W. E. B. Du Bois are heralded among "the most memorable and significant people, places, events, and trends of each decade of the twentieth century." A naval vessel and dozens of public buildings and schools have been named in his honor.

A man of modest origins, George Washington Carver has been heralded for his achievements in science and for producing numerous products from a wide range of crops common in the rural South, where he spent most of his lifetime. He work was a stimulus for agricultural and economic development worldwide.

REFERENCES

"Black History." *Jet* 93 (23 February 1998): 20.

Current Biography Yearbook. New York: H. W. Wilson, 1940.

Hines, Linda O. "White Mythology and Black Duality: George Washington Carver's Response to Racism and the Radical Left." *Journal of Negro History* 62 (April 1977): 134–46.

James, Edward T., ed. *Dictionary of American Negro Biography, 1941–1945.* Supplement Three. New York: Charles Scribner's Sons, 1973.

Logan, Rayford W., and Michael R. Winston, eds. *Dictionary of American Negro Biography.* New York: Norton, 1981.

Mackintosh. "The Carver Myth." In *The Booker T. Washington Papers.* Volume 4, 1895–98. Urbana: University of Illinois Press, 1975.

Who's Who in Colored America. Vol. 1. New York: Who's Who in Colored America Corp., 1927.

COLLECTIONS

Carver's papers, items from his research laboratory, and his paintings and handicrafts are in the George Washington Carver Museum at Tuskegee University.

Jessie Carney Smith

Lott Cary

(1780?–1828)

Religious worker, missionary, colonist

Lott Cary, along with his colleague, Colin Teague, were the first black Christian missionaries to Africa. A devoted Baptist, Cary worked in the region that eventually became the country of Liberia. There he founded a Baptist church, labored in missionary work, and tended the sick. He also proved an effective head of the colony before his untimely death caused by an accidental gunpowder explosion. The Lott Carey Baptist Foreign Mission Convention was named such in honor of his achievements.

Lott Cary was born a slave on the plantation of William A. Christian in Charles City County, Virginia, about 1780. His birthplace is about 30 miles from Richmond. He was an only child, and little is known of his parents except that his father was a member of the Baptist Church.

By 1804 Cary was hired out by his owner as a laborer in a Richmond tobacco warehouse. His life at this point has been characterized by Ralph Randolph Gurley in *Life of Jehudi Ashmun,* as "entirely regardless of religion, and much addicted to profane and vicious habits." Cary made his profession of faith in 1807 and was baptized as a member of the First Baptist Church in Richmond. Later, as he sat in the church gallery reserved for blacks, he heard a sermon on Nicodemus which inspired him to acquire a New Testament and learn to read the relevant chapter. He soon learned to both read and write.

Cary's regeneration evinced itself in his behavior: he became a model employee. His reading and writing skills

Lott Cary

enabled him to earn extra money at the tobacco warehouse, which he saved. In 1813, with the help of his employers, he bought his freedom and that of his two children; his wife had died sometime earlier. Cary continued to work at the tobacco warehouse where his wages were $700 in 1819. With his earnings, he acquired some land below Richmond.

Soon after his conversion Cary began to preach, first on plantations near Richmond and then as pastor of the African Baptist Church. As a preacher Cary was moving and expressive in spite of an unpolished manner and grammatical inaccuracies.

In 1815 two white members of First Baptist opened a triweekly night school in the gallery of the old church. Lott Cary and Colin Teague joined some fifteen others as pupils. That same year this group became the Richmond African Baptist Missionary Society. Since Virginia law required all meetings of blacks to have white sponsors, the chief officer of the society was William Crane. Out of his activity in the society, Cary became resolved to preach the gospel in Africa.

Crane recommended Cary and Teague to the American Baptist Mission Society and also to the American Colonization Society, both of which agreed to sponsor the two men. The Colonization Society's endorsement did not include funding, and it seems that the American Baptist Mission Society was mainly a conduit for funds raised by the Richmond African Mission Society, which contributed $483 of the $500 authorized by the Mission Society's board in 1820.

Before their departure on January 23, 1821, for Sierra Leone, Cary and Teague were ordained, and they and a small group of other black emigrants were organized into a church. Since the American Colonization Society had not yet completed negotiations for the purchase of a site for the settlers, the group remained in Freetown for several months. There they were placed on a farm to work to support themselves and a number of Africans rescued from slave traders. Cary's second wife soon died, leaving him with two children to raise alone. In spite of the difficulties, Cary did undertake missionary activities as his circumstances allowed.

On December 11, 1821, King Peter and other African leaders signed a treaty permitting a settlement at Cape Montserado, the nucleus of the future country of Liberia. The transfer of settlers from Sierra Leone began the following month. The American flag was raised on April 25 to mark formal possession. Initial conditions were appalling. The Africans proved hostile, and the rainy season was beginning. Early on, Cary was influential in persuading the settlers not to give up and abandon the settlement. He also proved brave and resolute in resisting heavy attacks by Africans in November and December 1822.

Cary began missionary activities in the city of Monrovia, establishing a church and securing six converts by 1823. He was soon the sole Baptist missionary there. His colleague Colin Teague returned to Sierra Leone. By 1825 membership in the church had increased to 60 or 70, and in October of that year, Cary completed and dedicated a meeting house.

In the meantime, Cary and the white governor, Jehudi Ashmun, had a serious disagreement. In September of 1823 Ashmun attempted to redistribute the lots of the earliest settlers, who resisted, asserting that they would neither take up new, undeveloped lots nor work on public improvements. In December Ashmun endeavored to cut a dozen healthy but nonworking persons from the distribution of rations. The excluded proceeded to the Agency House and seized their rations. Cary was a ringleader in this dispute. Soon after the storehouse disturbance, Cary and Ashmun were reconciled.

Cary continued to do good work both for the colony and his mission. On April 18, 1825, he opened a day school for African children with 21 pupils. In addition, he spent about half of his time caring for the sick. He had been appointed health officer at the time of the settlement, and a trained physician was present only for a brief period during Cary's life in Africa. In 1826 his church founded its own missionary society, and the following year the church counted 100 members.

In September of 1826 Cary was elected vice–agent of the colony. When health concerns convinced Ashmun to return to the United States in 1828, Cary was left in charge. He was vigorous in the discharge of his duties. Difficulties arose with Africans later that year, and Cary prepared to defend the property of the colony. He called out the militia and started to make cartridges. On November 8, the powder exploded. Six men died the following day, and Cary and another died on November 10.

In spite of his premature death, Cary accomplished much in the establishment of Liberia as a country. His efforts as a missionary and as a leader spurred the fledgling settlement to press forward in spite of the hardships. His name lives on through the Lott Carey Baptist Foreign Mission Convention.

REFERENCES

Fisher, Miles Mark, comp. ''Documents, Letters, Addresses, and the Like Throwing Light on the Career of Lott Cary.'' *Journal of Negro History* 7 (1922): 427–448.

———. ''Lott Cary, the Colonizing Missionary.'' *Journal of Negro History* 7 (1922): 380–418.

Gurley, Ralph Randolph. *Life of Jehudi Ashmun.* 1835. Reprint, New York: Negro Universities Press, 1969.

Huberich, Charles Henry. *The Political and Legislative History of Liberia.* New York: Central Book Company, 1947.

Logan, Rayford, and Michael R. Winston. *Dictionary of American Negro Biography.* New York: Norton, 1982.

Robert L. Johns

Horace R. Cayton

(1903–1970)

Researcher, writer, educator, sociologist, journalist

During the decades of the 1930s and 1940s, Horace Roscoe Cayton distinguished himself as one of America's leading sociologists and black intellectuals. He may be known best for the extensive four–year investigations into the social structure of Chicago's South Side that he undertook with St. Clair Drake. Their work resulted in the publication of *Black Metropolis.* A graduate of the University of Chicago School of Sociology, Cayton was a student of, and greatly influenced by, the world famous and eminent University of Chicago sociologist Robert E. Park.

Born in Seattle, Washington, on April 12, 1903, Cayton was the third of four children born to Horace Roscoe Cayton Sr. and Susie Revels Cayton. Horace had one brother, Revels, and two sisters, Ruth and Madge. His mother was the daughter of Hiram Revels, the first black from Mississippi to serve in the U.S. Senate, elected during the Reconstruction era of the 1870s. Following his term in the Senate, Hiram Revels was appointed president of Alcorn State College in Alcorn, Mississippi. In contrast, Cayton wrote in his autobiography *Long Old Road* that his paternal grandparents, who are unnamed, had a profound influence on him and his family. Born in slavery, his paternal grandfather was ''proud and courageous, refusing to be held down by caste or class proscription.'' His paternal grandfather valued education and provided sufficient education for his son, enabling Horace Cayton's father to become a newspaper owner, editor, and publisher.

Cayton grew up confused about and bothered by issues of identity, race, class, and place. Whether in all–black, predominantly white, or in international communities in European cities, which he visited frequently, the search for his fit in varying social environments plagued him throughout his life. He was taught to be proud of the accomplishments of the middle and upper middle class heritage and status of his family and grandparents. The Cayton children studied music, Horace the violin. Living in a well–to–do section of Seattle, however, as the only black family in the neighborhood, Cayton soon learned that the outside world, both black and white, had different perspectives of his family, and these perceptions, racial and elitist in scope, often devalued the principles that he had been taught to value.

Cayton's family experienced difficulty when his politically minded, entrepreneurial father began losing subscribers to his newspaper. As his father's political voice grew stronger in editorial columns, the family fell victim to the changing patterns of racial relations in Seattle. Against this backdrop, Cayton was perpetually engaged in inner turmoil. Symptoms of the inner conflict and his largely unsuccessful attempts to resolve them were detailed in frank disclosures in his autobiographical narrative, *Long Old Road,* published in 1965.

Coming of Age

Cayton dropped out of high school during his sophomore year. He started working longshoremen's jobs to help support his family. Eventually, he returned to complete his high school requirements, graduated, and entered the University of Washington, where he was one of only three black students; he graduated with an A.B. degree in 1931. Experimentation with alcohol and drugs turned into a perennial habit. He married and worked as a deputy for the sheriff of King County from 1929 to 1931 to help support himself and his wife, Bonnie, a white schoolmate at the university. They divorced while Cayton was in graduate school. Sociology, as a discipline, held promise for helping him to analyze and understand the complexity of social, political, and economic organization and the impact of race and class in a socially defined world. Thus, at the root of his empirical studies was a desire to find social meaning in the world of black people, his people. Although Cayton completed all the requirements for a doctoral degree in sociology at the University of Chicago between 1931 and 1935, he never finished or defended a dissertation.

Cayton's intellectual development began to blossom during graduate studies in Chicago. While in graduate school he worked as a research assistant in political science for the black educator Harold Gosnell, interviewing black policeman in 1931–33. He also spent a summer at Tuskegee Institute in Alabama, as an intern. Cayton was later research assistant in sociology, 1933–34 and in anthropology, 1936–37. After his divorce from Bonnie, he experimented with a number of intimate relationships, some of which were interracial and others that led to marriage (to Irma Jackson and Ruby Jordan) and subsequently to divorce. While his studies helped him to decipher social facts, the discipline of sociology did not involve examination of the anger, rage, and ambivalent feelings related to race relations. He also had not found insight onto his own feelings about race. Moreover, his inner struggle with his identity stimulated a search that caused him internal conflict for the rest of his life. Recognizing that he had shut down emotionally, he was treated by a psychoanalyst for four years. Several times he was at the verge of experiencing nervous breakdowns. In his autobiography, Cayton described his struggle in detail.

Cayton was a special assistant to the U.S. Secretary of the Interior in 1934–35. Later, Cayton moved to Fisk University to teach economics and labor. He worked under Charles Spurgeon Johnson who headed the Department of Sociology. He discovered early that he could not live fully in the South because of the racist atmosphere. A Rosenwald fellowship in 1937–39 allowed him the opportunity to conduct research and finish his work at the University of Chicago and to live in Europe for a year.

By 1939 Cayton had become well established in the black community of Chicago. He took a job in 1940 as director for the Chicago Parkway Community House, a large community center for blacks. This position exposed him to the culturally elite circles of Chicago, but did not offer him opportunity to develop satisfying relationships with Chicago's black communities. He joined the Council of Social Agencies and became known as well for his columns in the *Pittsburgh Courier,* which he began in 1942 and wrote for several years. He interacted with younger intellectuals including Langston Hughes, Richard Wright, and Arna Bontemps. For a while Cayton wrote articles and was book reviewer for the *Chicago Sun* and the *Chicago Tribune.* He spoke out against the Jim Crow army and other forms of racial discrimination.

Although the dates are unclear, Cayton left Chicago for New York. As his health improved, he became a *Pittsburgh Courier* representative at the United Nations. Three years later he left the UN and worked as an assistant in the research division of the National Council of Churches. By 1959 Cayton decided to leave New York to live on the West Coast. With this move, he rounded out his career by taking a teaching position at the University of California at Berkeley. He continued the role of a scholar, teaching, conducting research, and writing for the remainder of his life.

Publishes Major Works

In addition to publishing his autobiography, *Long Old Road,* in 1965, Cayton was coauthor of two major sociological texts: one was an urban study of black life; the other addressed attitudes and perceptions of the field of social work as reported by several different religious denominations. The latter book was entitled, *The Changing Scene: Current Trends and Issues* and was published in 1965 with Setsuko Matsanuga as coauthor. It was a project that Cayton completed while he was hired as a researcher by the National Council of Churches.

With George S. Mitchell, Cayton published *Black Workers and The New Unions* in 1939. This classic study was reprinted in 1970, the year Cayton died. Centered in industrial sites including a meat–packing operation, a railroad shop, and the iron and steel industries, the study examined the economic effects of racism on black workers during their movement from agricultural–based occupations to industrial–based employment. The book covered economic indicators, social stratification, and the dynamics of population shifts and movement, a subject of great relevance as millions of black workers migrated to northern cities during the 1930s, 1940s, and 1950s.

Cayton's best known work is *Black Metropolis,* a two–volume book, now considered a classic sociological study. Coauthored with St. Clair Drake, it won the coveted Anisfield–Wolf award as one of the year's best books on race relations when it was published in 1945. Cayton's colleague and friend, author Richard Wright, wrote the introduction for *Black Metropolis.* By making use of statistical measurements developed by Robert Park of the Chicago School of Sociology, Cayton and Drake collected data on the central neighborhoods of Chicago, where the majority of Chicago blacks lived. Richard Wright later made use of this data for several books, including the novel *Native Son,* the novella *Uncle Tom's Children,* and *12,000,000 Black Voices.*

In 1969 Cayton went to Paris to spend a year in search of materials to support a book he planned to write about his friend and colleague Richard Wright, who had died there in 1960. Cayton, however, died in 1970 while in Paris, and the book was never written. Much has been written, however, about the friendship between Wright and Cayton, offering varying views about the extent of their relationship. Cayton wrote in his autobiography that Wright was the person who most influenced his life during the Chicago years. Two of Wright's principal biographers suggested that the friendship, while genuine, was limited to a particular span in time when both men lived and worked in Chicago.

Cayton was important as a sociologist and researcher, particularly for his efforts to analyze black communities in Chicago. His works have become classics in sociology, as well as black literature.

REFERENCES

Cayton, Horace. *Long Old Road: An Autobiography.* New York: Trident Press, 1965.

———, and George Mitchell. *Black Workers and The New Unions.* Chapel Hill: University of North Carolina Press, 1939.

Drake, St. Clair, and Horace Cayton. *Black Metropolis: A Study of Negro Life in a Northern City.* New York: Harcourt, Brace, 1945.

Fabre, Michael. *The Unfinished Quest of Richard Wright.* Urbana: University of Illinois Press, 1993.

"Horace C. Cayton, Sociologist Dies." *New York Times,* January 25, 1970.

Salzman, Jack, David Lionel Smith, and Cornel West, eds. *Encyclopedia of African–American Culture and History.* New York: Macmillan Library Reference USA/Simon and Schuster Macmillan, 1996.

Walker, Margaret. *Richard Wright: Daemonic Genius.* New York: Wagner Communications, 1988.

Who's Who in Colored America. 7th ed. Yonkers–on–Hudson, NY: Christian E. Burckel, 1950.

COLLECTIONS

The papers of Horace R. Cayton are in the Vivian Harsh Collection of the Chicago Public Library.

Anne S. Butler and Jessie Carney Smith

Wilt Chamberlain

(1936–)

Basketball player

Wilt Chamberlain is remembered as professional basketball's greatest offensive player during the 1960s and 1970s. Not only was he the highest scorer for eight years, he holds the single game scoring record of 100 points. He dominated the league and during his career held most of basketball's records for individual achievement.

Wilton Norman Chamberlain was born on August 21, 1936, in Philadelphia, one of six sons and three daughters of William and Olivia Chamberlain. His father was first a welder in a shipyard, then for 20 years a handyman at a Sears Roebuck retail store. During most of Chamberlain's childhood, however, his father was a porter for the Curtis Publishing Company, and earned extra money by working odd jobs. His mother hired herself out several days a week as a domestic. The parents provided a comfortable living for the family in a row house in Philadelphia's west end.

Since the family was so large, the younger Chamberlain children wore clothes handed down from the older ones. When the youngsters were old enough to work, each of them found jobs and pitched in to buy items needed for the house. Wilt had his first job at age four, helping the milkman return empty bottles to his truck. At age five he delivered papers, shoveled snow, and did odd jobs. He continued to work throughout his school years; he experienced occasional misadventures that taught him the value of the dollar and the value of his own work. Chamberlain learned to negotiate, to judge people, and to know prices—valuable lessons that carried over into his professional life.

While in the fourth grade, Chamberlain ran the anchor leg on the 300–yard shuttle in the 1946 Penn Relays and also ran other races while in grade school. He wanted to pursue running and to be an Olympic Games track champion; instead, he became serious about basketball while he was a student at Shoemaker Junior High School. At six feet, three inches by the age of 12, his height gave him a natural advantage. Chamberlain said in his autobiography, *Wilt,* that he "capitalized on these opportunities" and had the capacity to concentrate on whatever he wanted to master. Whether at work, participating in his earlier sport, shot–putting, or playing basketball, he focused on the task at hand. In basketball he practiced afternoons, evenings, and weekends the year round. He entered Overbrook High School in 1952 as a six–foot eleven–inch tall freshman. By his junior year he had become a serious basketball player, scoring 2,252 points in three years. He also ran a 47–second quarter mile, hurled a 16–pound shot put 55 feet, and leaped 6–feet 10–inches in the high jump.

High School Superstar

A Philadelphia sportswriter, Jack Ryan, gave Chamberlain the nickname "Wilt the Stilt" when he first started playing basketball in high school. In *Wilt,* Chamberlain admitted that he did not like the name and said that none of his friends used it. "It makes me sound like an attraction in a carnival sideshow—and not a very good one at that," he wrote. His friends and family called him "Dip" or "Dippy," and one nephew even called him "Uncle Dip;" later on his nickname evolved into "Big Dipper." The idea was that he was so tall he had to dip under things. Chamberlain admitted that he felt strongly about the issue of height and lamented the fact that people always made "such a big deal out of it."

In high school Chamberlain had considered studying business or law, and possibly enrolling in Harvard. Then the National Basketball Association's (NBA) territorial draft rule gave professional teams first choice at players within 50 miles of their home base. Chamberlain envisioned that the Boston Celtics would then have territorial rights to him. He learned, however, that rules could be set to apply to only one person, and in his case, to Wilt Chamberlain. The NBA knew Chamberlain's game and was interested in attracting him to professional basketball. At the time NBA rules, however, prevented a player from competing in a professional league until his college class graduated. According to his book *Wilt,* he learned that more than 200 colleges and universities—79 major schools and 128 minor ones—were after him during his senior year. The pressure was unbearable for the first black high school superstar, and Chamberlain turned the matter over to his high school coach, Cecil Mosenson. Then Eddie Gottlieb, who owned the Philadelphia Warriors, obtained permission to gain territorial rights to Chamberlain, who was scheduled to graduate from college in 1959.

Chamberlain accepted a basketball and track scholarship to study at the University of Kansas at Lawrence. As soon as he announced his decision, "the roof fell in," he said in *Wilt.* The NCAA (National College Athletic Association), the Federal Bureau of Investigation, and the Internal Revenue Service thought he was being highly paid and wanted to talk with him. "I was grilled and badgered and hounded and cross–examined like I was some rapist or murderer," he wrote. Chamberlain was to receive a scholarship for tuition, room, board, and $15 a month for incidentals. Just like the

Wilt Chamberlain

other top stars, after he became a sophomore and played for the varsity squad, he had access to spending money whenever he needed it.

On his way to school in Kansas, Chamberlain learned some of the hard, cold, ugly facts of racism when he was refused table service at a restaurant in Kansas City but offered service in the kitchen. At that time, the area around Lawrence and Kansas City was segregated. He tested restaurants within a 40–mile radius and wrote in *Wilt* that after about two months he "singlehandedly integrated that whole area."

Chamberlain had a successful stay at Kansas, racking up 52 points against Northwestern in his first varsity game and generally outscoring other players in all games. He led Kansas to the NCAA basketball tournament but the team lost to the University of North Carolina. Although opposing players guarded him sometimes as much as four–to–one, he averaged 30 points per game while there. By the end of his second year, he was making paid appearances at night clubs in Kansas City and was disc jockey on the campus radio station. He also did shows on stations in Lawrence and Kansas City that provided him an income. He continued to compete in track and field throughout his years at Kansas. He won the Big Eight high jump championship in his sophomore year (1955–56) and the Big Eight indoor high jump title in his junior year (1956–57).

A Terror on the Court

Chamberlain left Kansas without graduating and for one year, 1958–59, joined the Harlem Globetrotters, a black professional basketball team run by Abe Saperstein, who was also part owner of the Philadelphia Warriors. He was paid $65,000 while he honed his skills for the NBA. Chamberlain joined the Warriors in 1959 and on October 24 that year played in the league's opener at Madison Square Garden against the New York Knicks. He became a terror on the court, to the consternation of such well–known players as Bill Russell and Johnny Kerr. At the end of the season he became the first person named Rookie of the Year and the Most Valuable Player in the same year. By March of 1960 he had set eight NBA records. He was also starting center for the NBA All Star game in Philadelphia and was named its most valuable player.

When the season ended, Chamberlain left the Warriors and the NBA and joined the Harlem Globetrotters on their summer basketball tour. He returned to the Warriors in late 1960 and continued his record–breaking performance for six seasons. He averaged 50.4 points in 1961–62. That summer the Warriors were sold to San Francisco. Chamberlain averaged 44.8 points in 1962–63. At about this time, he began to receive recognition as the greatest player in NBA history at that time. Chamberlain was traded to the newly–formed Philadelphia 76ers in 1965, and in 1967 he led the team to the world championship. He was traded to the Los Angeles Lakers in 1968, where he remained until 1973. In 1972 he assisted in winning the Lakers their first world championship.

In the NBA Chamberlain again saw rule changes that were custom designed for him, a seven–foot one–sixteenth–inch player. According to *Wilt,* "they prohibited offensive goal–tending and widened the free–throw lane from twelve to sixteen feet and adopted the 'three–second rule'—prohibiting an offensive player from remaining in the free–throw lane for more than three seconds without trying to shoot." Chamberlain's high scoring and record–breaking seasons started a leaguewide trend of dominant players who were at least seven–feet tall. He also popularized the "dunk."

Hall of Famer

When the 1973 season ended, Chamberlain left the Lakers, refused an offer to join the Houston Rockets, and became player–coach and part franchise owner of the now–defunct American Basketball Association's San Diego Conquistadors. A court ruling obtained by the Lakers kept him from playing, leaving him as coach of a team that had a 38–47 record that year. He retired from basketball at the end of the season.

For his outstanding basketball career, Chamberlain was elected to the Basketball Hall of Fame in 1979. In 1991 he received the Living Legend Award from the Philadelphia Sports Writers Association. He also was elected to the NBA's 35th Anniversary All–Time Team in 1980 and was among the NBA's 50th anniversary "50 Greatest."

A multitalented sportsman, Chamberlain pursued his interest in volleyball by becoming a professional when he was about 34–years old. He also founded the International Volleyball Association and sponsored track and field meets. For a while he had a losing business venture as a racehorse owner. He also continued his business ventures, having owned in the 1960s the Big Wilt's Small Paradise in Harlem, where Malcolm X worked for him as a waiter. Later Chamberlain owned Los Angeles's Basin Street West, a string of restaurants known as Wilt Chamberlain's Restaurants, and Wilt's Athletic Club. Pursuing a performing career as well, Chamberlain appeared in a number of television commercials, and in 1984 had a part in the film *Conan the Destroyer.* Chamberlain recorded his life in two books: *Wilt* (1973) and *The View from Above* (1991) and has in process another nonfiction work and book of fiction. He has also written two screen plays.

Chamberlain, who never married, described himself in *A View from Above,* a book of personal thoughts, as one who "owns a car he helped design and build," a millionaire in the top one percent of Americans financially, and a Republican. He was often criticized for his sexual encounters with women, which he admitted in *A View from Above* reached "20,000 different ladies," or, by then, 1.2 women daily since he was 15 years old. "I give the numbers here not to impress," he said. "I give them because it's like when I played basketball—many of my numbers were so unbelievably high that most people dismiss them as fables or found them impossible to relate to." His favorite charities are Best Buddies—involving work with mentally handicapped children—the Special Olympics, and Operation Smile, an organization that supports the correction of facial defects of children.

Chamberlain is remembered as professional basketball's greatest offensive basketball player during the 1960s and 1970s, but is often overlooked as a talented all–round athlete.

Current address: c/o Seymour Goldberg, 11111 Santa Monica Boulevard, Suite 1000, Los Angeles, CA 90025.

REFERENCES

Chamberlain, Wilt. *A View From Above.* New York: Random House, 1991.

———, and David Shaw. *Wilt: Just Like Any Other 7–Foot Black Millionaire Who Lives Next Door.* New York: Macmillan, 1973.

Current Biography Yearbook. New York: H. W. Wilson, 1960.

Hickok, Ralph. *A Who's Who of Sports Champions.* Boston: Houghton Mifflin, 1995.

Robinson, Louis. "Big Man, Big Business." *Ebony* 19 (August 1964): 57–64.

———. "The High Price of Being Wilt Chamberlain." *Ebony* 30 (January 1974): 94–101.

Sachare, Alex, ed. *The Official NBA Basketball Encyclopedia.* 2nd ed. New York: Villard Books, 1994.

Who's Who among African Americans, 1996–97. 9th ed. Detroit: Gale Research, 1996.

Who's Who in America, 1996. 50th ed. New Providence, NJ: Marquis Who's Who, 1995.

Jessie Carney Smith

Ray Charles

(1930–)

Singer, composer, arranger

Frank Sinatra in *Blues Revue* called Ray Charles "The only genius in the business," but his friends and grass-roots fans just call him Brother Ray. Both sobriquets define the breadth and diversity of the man's talents and the depth of feelings his music engenders in the hearts of his listeners, but Charles is also a walking contradiction. He has a reputation as a highly self–disciplined performer, yet he was a long time heroin addict. He refused to bow to vanity by dying his snow–white hair, but he wears the most fashionable sunglasses on the market. He has long been accused of profaning gospel music by "bluesing" it up, while music critics and theorists analyze the "Ray Charles style" as being a synthesis of gospel music's soul and rhythm. They also point out the earthy, gut–wrenching pain of the blues merged with the exuberance of pop music. Viv Broughton, a London–based gospel historian, succinctly defined Charles's place in history: "Ray Charles is the greatest gospel singer who never was."

From the time of his birth in Albany, Georgia, on September 23, 1930, life became an unending challenge for Ray Charles Robinson. He may have been the love child of Bailey Robinson and Aretha Robinson. His life was not only defined by grinding poverty, but also by death, disease, and deprivation. When Charles was only five years old, his brother George drowned as Charles helplessly watched. Within two years, glaucoma stripped him of his eyesight but Aretha Robinson never allowed him to wallow in self–pity. Two recurring maternal messages have followed him throughout life. The first was when well–meaning friends protested her decision to send her son to the State School for the Blind in St. Augustine, Florida. Charles and David Ritz wrote in *Brother Ray* that Aretha's response was: "He's blind, but he ain't stupid. He's lost his sight, but he ain't lost his mind." The second was her strict moral code: "You do not beg and you do not steal." The decision to send the young boy away was a sound one because Charles learned to read Braille, mastered workshop crafts, and learned the rudiments of car mechanics and typing. He was exposed to classical and big band music, learned to play the piano and clarinet, and expanded his knowledge of gospel, country, and blues music on his own.

While still a teenager, Charles sat in with Julian "Cannonball" Adderly, then a college student but later a leading jazz saxophonist. Adderly's college band was Charles' first real gig and, as he got older, he became more skillful at writing band arrangements by dictating the notes. It was soon apparent that he was not only musically gifted but also a quick study in many areas. All the knowledge and experience gained at the school and in fledgling bands would be needed to prepare the teenager to become an independent adult. At the age of 15, Charles' world fell apart with the unexpected death of his mother. He was at school with no one to comfort him. In his autobiography, he wrote: "Nothing had ever hit me like that. Not George drowning. Not going blind... Mama had raised me, and now she was gone . . . for a while, I went a little crazy." He had to regroup quickly and focus on surviving in a world where he was now a sightless orphan without even a high school diploma.

The Apprentice

After leaving school, Charles joined the Musician's Local Union 632 in Jacksonville, Florida. Although he was still a teenager, he was laying the foundation for a career in music. In *Brother Ray* he wrote: "Music's the only way I've ever thought about making a living. . . . I suppose I could have been a mechanic, or a carpenter, or a weaver. But I never featured those things in those early days when I first hit the streets. It was music that drove me."

Ray Charles

It was rough and he met rejection head on. In 1946, he was turned down by Lucky Millinder, a prominent black band leader of that era. Charles, while trying to find his niche in music, even played with the Florida Playboys, a white country–and–western band. By 1948, there was nothing left for him in Florida and he moved to Seattle, Washington, where he permanently adopted the name "Ray Charles" and began developing his own style. Times were still hard and, in a *Rolling Stone* interview, Charles related the severity of his plight: "I became very ill a couple of times. I suffered from malnutrition, you know. I was really messed up . . . and I wouldn't beg . . . hell, I'd starve first."

The Seattle stay was notable for three reasons. He cut his first record for the Los Angeles–based Swing Time label and had two minor R&B hits in 1949 and 1951. He also unknowingly fathered his first child, a fact that came to light years later. Lastly, Charles discovered the deceptive pleasures of hard drugs, a youthful diversion that would lead to a 20–year heroin addiction.

When Charles moved to Los Angeles, his biggest break was becoming pianist and musical director for Lowell Fulson, a big name blues artist in the 1950s. As Charles's own style began to evolve, major companies began to pay attention, especially Atlantic Records, which in 1952 bought his Swing Time contract for $2,500. He continued to travel across the country and, in New Orleans, arranged and produced Guitar Slim's million–seller single ''The Things That I Used to Do.'' Larkin called the artist an ''impassioned, almost crude blues performer.'' Guitar Slim was a strong influence on Charles's increasing use of the gospel–based style of singing. English music critic John Broven who cited this period as the time ''when Ray Charles had just started that church thing.''

That ''church thing'' would prove to be Charles' emancipation from the early dual influences of Nat ''King'' Cole and Charles Brown. All the church music he had heard in the Deep South plus the influence of gospel artists he had heard on the road were being incorporated into a new, energetic, spirit–filled music that spread like wildfire.

In 1954, Charles had his first big hit, exactly nine years after his mother's death. According to Silver, this was the time when Charles ''gave his earthy voice its freedom, hammered some gospel chords on the piano, and invented soul music.'' That hit, ''I've Got a Woman,'' was quickly followed by many more, all reflecting the same sure–fire formula that thrilled his fans and infuriated church folk. In his autobiography Charles described it as ''my first real smash. . . . This spiritual–and–blues combination of mine was starting to hit.''

Charles responded to the black church that criticized his blues/gospel songs as blasphemy. He said in *Nowhere to Run,* ''I got a lot of criticism from the churches, and from musicians, too. They said I must be crazy . . . and then . . . everybody started doing it . . . it worked, so I was a genius.'' He was not a gospel singer who defected to the pop music scene. Since spirituals were not copyrighted, he never stole that music, as claimed by critics. Charles, to his credit, steadfastly refused to perform religious and popular music at the same venue. In his autobiography he defended his stance: ''I was raised to believe that you can't serve two gods.''

Charles became successful now for other reasons as well. He put together a background group that became the archetype for ''doo–wop girls.'' The Raeletts came into existence in 1957 for a recording date and then as a permanent fixture for concerts. Charles had long admired such female gospel soloists as Albertina Walker and gospel groups, in particular the Davis Sisters of Philadelphia. He stated in his autobiography, ''I wanted the flavor of . . . my voice set against women . . . that was what I was searching for.'' After molding the group totally to his satisfaction, he changed its original name ''Cookies'' to the Raeletts and always sought to get the effect he wanted, as further stated: ''I liked that male/female friction and once I had it, I never let it go.'' The Raelett sound helped define the major hits, most notably ''Hit the Road, Jack,'' ''What'd I Say,'' ''Tell the Truth,'' and ''The Night Time is the Right Time.''

Charles was always determined not to be pigeonholed in any one musical category and after moving to ABC Records, he branched out and recorded in any musical genre he chose. According to Piazza in the *New York Times,* ''He turned out to be not merely a good interpreter of popular standard material but a great one. A series of albums in the 1960s . . . earned him a wider, whiter popular market than that of any soul singer of the time, with the possible exception of Sam Cooke.''

This was the era when the term ''cross–over'' gained a new meaning as Charles, a black soul singer, conquered and redefined the idiosyncrasies of country–and–western music, described by Piazza as ''Southern white soul music.'' The best examples of Charles's country songs are his 1959 version of Hank Snow's ''I'm Movin' On'' and the 1962 remake of Don Gibson's ''I Can't Stop Loving You;'' the latter sold 2.5 million copies and topped the R&B, pop, *and* C&W charts for 14 weeks.

The Achilles Heel

From 1961 to 1965, Charles was named the top male American vocalist by *Downbeat* magazine. Although he spent the mid–1960s touring abroad, Charles also began to exert his independence from record companies and management agencies. In 1963, he established RPM International to oversee his own recording, publishing, and management concerns and, in 1965, he began producing his own records. The control of his professional life sharply contrasted with his own personal life and the debilitating effects of his longtime drug habit. Having started with marijuana as a teenager in Seattle, he soon moved on to heroin despite the efforts of older musicians to dissuade him. Charles never blamed anyone or any circumstance for his decision to use drugs. In a *Blues Revue* article, he said: ''Every experience I've had good and bad has taught me something. I was born a poor boy in the South. I once fooled with drugs, but all of it was like going to school and I tried to be a good student. I don't regret a damn thing.''

Charles labelled himself as being a ''junkie'' but insisted that he was always in control of his money, his career, and his life. In 1958 and 1961 he was involved in drug raids. The first time, charges were dropped due to lack of evidence; the next time, he was actually in possession of heroin but charges against the officers for illegal entry and search worked in his favor. In 1964, however, he was arrested in Boston on a charge of heroin possession by federal narcotics agents. This time, prison was a possibility and Charles realized the effect this could have on his family. Vowing to kick the habit, he entered a Los Angeles clinic and went ''cold turkey'' while rejecting the clinic's regimen. During that time, he learned to play chess and eventually became an expert player. Because of positive recommendations from the clinic psychiatrist, sentencing was postponed for a year while Charles underwent random periodic checks for drug use. The next year, he received a five–year probated sentence. He was finally free of a harrowing addiction and the threat of a prison sentence, either of which could have seriously imperilled a brilliant career.

Mastering Other Musical Styles

Real ''Brother Ray'' aficionados know that Charles is also a superb jazz musician. His 1960s big bands are still considered, by music critics, to be among the premier jazz bands of all time. When Charles switched labels, he was accused of becoming too middle–of–the–road and of having lost his characteristic sharp edge. He began to cover the songs of such pop composers as Stevie Wonder, Randy Newman, and the Beatles.

As if in refutation of charges of becoming too predictable and mainstream, Charles became involved in quite diverse musical ventures. He has appeared quite often on television's *Sesame Street* with the Muppets and made "It's Not Easy Being Green" his personal song. He also did the searing vocal on the soundtrack for the movie *In the Heat of the Night.* He was a major participant on the USA for Africa release of "We Are the World," a blockbuster hit engineered by his colleague, Quincy Jones. With a Raelett–like trio, Charles cut one of the most popular television commercials ever for Pepsi Cola; he had previously done others for Coca Cola, Olympia Beer, and Scotch recording tape. In November of 1997 Charles appeared on the television show *The Nanny* as the fiancé of the main character's Jewish grandmother, Yetta. Some of his finest television appearances are on video: *An Evening with Ray Charles* (1981); *The Legends of Rock 'n' Roll* (1989); and *Ray Charles Live* (1991).

Charles has definite opinions on the current state of music and the music industry. When asked if he could begin a music career today, he told Silver for *U.S. News and World Report*: "No. When I was coming up, the record people looked at the talent. I made about four records at Atlantic [Records] before I got a hit. Ain't no way I could be with a big company today and make four records that was not hits and they'd still keep me." Commenting on rap music, he said in the same source that "You can't even print what I think. . . . Just to talk to music, I did that years ago on 'It Should've Been Me' and 'Greenbacks'."

But Charles has groomed, nurtured, and influenced many outstanding musicians in the same ways he was helped during his formative years. Quincy Jones, prolific composer and Hollywood arranger, and Hank Crawford, jazz saxophonist, arranger, and musical director, were early sidemen, arrangers, and musical directors for the Ray Charles big bands. In a *Rolling Stone* article, Wild noted that Charles has influenced singers "from Joe Cocker and Steve Winwood to Michael Bolton," to which Charles replied. "It's the ultimate compliment. When I started out, all I wanted to do was sing like Nat King Cole."

Charles has reached the half–century mark of performing, composing, and arranging his own music and that of anybody else's he chooses. The 101–song, five–CD box set that commemorated his fiftieth anniversary is testament to a life devoted to music. He told *People* magazine: "Music is my life, my bloodstream, my breathing. I'm gonna make music until the good Lord says to me, 'Ray, you've been a good horse. It's time to put you out to pasture.'"

In the summer of 1996, Charles received an honorary doctorate of music from Occidental College in Los Angeles. This was the culmination of a succession of public accolades starting at the beginning of his illustrious career. For example, he won the New Star Award, *Downbeat* Critic's Poll (1958, 1961–64). He was named Number One Male Singer in the International Jazz Critic's Poll (1968) and named to the Playboy Jazz and Pop Hall of Fame and the Songwriter's Hall of Fame. In 1975, he received the Man of Distinction Award from the National Association for Sickle Cell Disease. Charles was named honorary life chairman for the Rhythm and Blues Hall of Fame and became a member of *Ebony* Black Music Hall of Fame. B'Nai Brith named him Man of the Year. In 1983 he received the NAACP Image Award and in 1986 a Kennedy Center Honors Medal. Charles was named to the Rock and Roll Hall of Fame in 1986 and received the *Ebony* Magazine Lifetime Achievement Award in 1993. He has also won 11 Grammy awards.

Charles is twice divorced, currently unmarried, and the father of nine children. His feelings about his fame and his musical talents were best expressed to a *Rolling Stone* writer in 1993: "When people call me a genius or a legend, they're just showing the ultimate respect for my music. I know very well that I'm far from a genius. I'm just a guy who does a lot of things in music pretty well."

Current address: Ray Charles Enterprises, 2107 West Washington Boulevard, Los Angeles, CA 90018.

REFERENCES

Broughton, Viv. *Black Gospel.* Poole, Dorset, England: Blandford Press, 1985.

Broven, John. *Rhythm and Blues in New Orleans.* Gretna, LA: Pelican Publishing Co., 1974.

Charles, Ray, and David Ritz. *Brother Ray: Ray Charles' Own Story.* New York: Dial Press, 1978.

Cullen, Thomas J., III. "The Genius of Soul Talks about the Blues and Nothing But the Blues Ray Charles." *Blues Review* (August/September 1996): 24–31.

"Doctor of Music." *Jet* 90 (3 June 1996): 27.

Fong–Torres, Ben. "Ray Charles RS 126 (January 18, 1973)." *Rolling Stone* 641 (15 October 1992): 56.

Hirshey, Gerri. *Nowhere to Run: The Story of Soul Music.* New York: Penguin Books, 1984.

"An Individualist Who is Master of All Styles." *New York Times,* November 9, 1997.

Larkin, Colin, ed. *The Guinness Encyclopedia of Popular Music.* Middlesex. England: Guinness Publishing, 1992.

Paul, Alan. "A Half Century of Soul." *People* 48 (22 September 1997): 31.

"Ray Charles Celebrates 50 Years of Music with Greatest Hits Collection." *Jet* 92 (27 October 1997): 33.

Silver, Marc. "Still Soulful after All These Years." *U.S. News and World Report* 123 (22 September 1997): 76.

Sturkey, Don. *A Slice of Time A Carolina's Album 1950–1990.* Asheboro, NC: Down Home Press, 1990.

Wild, David. "Brother Ray At It Again." *Rolling Stone* 655 (29 August 1993): 23.

Who's Who among African Americans, 1998–99. 10th ed. Detroit: Gale Research, 1997.

Dolores Nicholson

John Chavis
(1763?–1838)
Minister, missionary, educator

John Chavis, the first black home missionary of the Presbyterian Church, was equally known as a preacher and a teacher during the antebellum period, ministering to the needs of both blacks and whites. Highly respected for his scholarship and citizenship, Chavis became the most prominent black in North Carolina during his time.

John Chavis's place of birth has been disputed. He was born free about 1763 either in the West Indies or near Oxford, in Granville County, North Carolina. It is known that, in Granville County, he lived in a section called Reavis Cross Roads or Reavis' Crossing. The son of Lottie Chavis and the grandson of Peggy Chavis, he had one brother, Anthony. Nothing more has been discovered about his early life. While details are missing, it is said that John Chavis owned one slave.

Both Chavis and his brother Anthony were said to have served in the Revolutionary War; Chavis enlisted at age 15 with Captain May Cunningham on December 29, 1778. The brothers also fought at Brandywine at White Plains, New York, and at Yorktown, Virginia, under the leadership of George Washington and the Marquis de Lafayette. Some sources, however, question Chavis's so–called service, saying that he made the claim without documentation.

Chavis pursued the regular course at Washington Academy, the forerunner of Washington and Lee University in Virginia. He appears to have been a student at Princeton, where president John Witherspoon tutored him privately. Sources are unclear about the order of his studies; however, he might have been at Princeton prior to 1794.

In October of 1799, Chavis became a communicant in the Presbyterian Church, and when the Presbytery of Lexington, Virginia, met on November 18–19, 1800, he was licensed to preach. The next year the General Assembly appointed him a missionary to slaves, making him the first black in the church to become a home missionary. He transferred from the Lexington to the Hanover Presbytery in southern Virginia, and was a "riding missionary."

Chavis returned to North Carolina in 1805, where he joined the Orange Presbytery. Some sources suggest that it was in that year that he was licensed. In addition to being an able and impressive speaker, he was well prepared in rhetoric, the classics, and the Bible. According to *The Free Negro in North Carolina,* George Wortham, a Granville County lawyer, remarked that "His English was remarkably pure, containing no 'Negroisms.'" Altogether for 30 years, 1802–1832, Chavis was active in the ministry intermittently, rode his horse through the countryside and preached to slaves, free blacks, and whites in North Carolina, Virginia, and Maryland. Frequently, he preached in white churches in Granville, Wake, and Orange counties in North Carolina.

Opens Day School

By 1808 Chavis had opened a Day School, perhaps in Raleigh, and began to teach black and white children in the same classroom. However, when his white patrons objected to the racial mixing, he separated the students. He then taught his black students, who were the children of free blacks, in the Evening School. He charged whites $2.50 per quarter and blacks $1.75. His white students were the children of some of the most aristocratic white families in North Carolina. Among his white students were Willie P. Mangum, who became one of his life–long correspondents and a U.S. senator for several terms; Mangum's brother, Priestly H.; Archibald and John Henderson, the sons of Chief Justice Henderson; Charles Manly, who became governor of the state; and others who entered such professions as law, medicine, the ministry, and politics. As well, his white students included those whom Chavis prepared to enter the University of North Carolina at Chapel Hill. He affectionately called his former students his "sons." It is said that Chavis was without peer as far as the teaching was concerned. Chavis appears to have maintained a school in several locations; at different times he taught in Chatham, Wake, Orange, and Granville counties. Between 1808 and about 1832, when he retired from active teaching, he had also educated countless numbers of free black children, thus changing the social status of free blacks in antebellum North Carolina.

In the 1820s Chavis took an active interest in politics. He knew well the politics of the Raleigh area and continued to express a deep interest in the political life of his best friend, Willie Mangum, a Federalist. He wrote numerous letters to Mangum, offering him advice on such issues as the judicial system, Mangum's choice for U.S. President, and items of public concern.

Chavis's career as teacher and preacher came to a close during the aftermath of Nat Turner's slave rebellion in Southampton, Virginia, in 1831. He opposed emancipation of blacks nevertheless, saying that immediate freedom of blacks would bring about a great curse on them and they should not be made more miserable than they were already. According to *Dictionary of American Negro Biography,* Chavis acknowledged that slavery was bad and added "all that can be done is to make the best of a bad bargain." He called Nat Turner's rebellion "that abominable insurrection in Southampton."

The need for financial assistance was a way of life for Chavis. His friend Mangum persuaded state treasurer John Haywood to support Chavis. Chavis's letter to Haywood dated July 3, 1822, published in the *Mangum Papers,* volume 1, shows that he wanted Haywood to pay a bank note for him. By 1827 Benjamin Rogers had given him some land located in Wake County that he and his wife were to use during their lifetime. According to *From Slavery to Freedom,* "white people had done so much for Chavis that he came to expect assistance in various forms. His pride did not prevent his making solicitations wherever he thought they could be effective.'' He also became indignant if the help did not come. Certainly by 1832, when laws silenced his teaching and preaching, his income was likely to suffer. In that year the Orange Presbytery voted to give lifetime support for Chavis and his wife.

As further reaction to Nat Turner's slave rebellion, the North Carolina General Assembly disenfranchised Chavis in 1835, and he never voted again. Agitated, he wrote ''The Extent of Atonement.'' In 1837 he wrote another document, ''Chavis Letter on the Doctrine of the Atonement of Christ,'' which was widely circulated. The booklet contained about 6,000 words and sold for 15 cents.

John Chavis, described as dark–brown and a ''full–blooded Negro,'' died on June 13, 1838, when he was about 75 years old. He had been a remarkable man whose distinguished life as preacher and teacher led officials of Raleigh to name a federal housing project and a recreation park in his honor. The North Carolina Historical Commission honored him in 1938 with the erection of a marker near the park.

REFERENCES

Bontemps, Arna. ''Even Money on John Chavis.'' *Common Ground* X (Autumn 1949): 36–38.

Brawley, Benjamin. *Negro Builders and Heroes.* Chapel Hill: University of North Carolina Press, 1937.

Franklin, John Hope. *The Free Negro in North Carolina 1790–1860.* Chapel Hill: University of North Carolina Press, 1943.

Johnson, Allen, and Dumas Malone, eds. *Dictionary of American Biography.* New York: Charles Scribner's Sons, 1943.

Kaplan, Sidney. *The Black Presence in the Era of the American Revolution.* New York: New York Graphic Society in association with the Smithsonian Press, 1973.

Logan, Rayford W., and Michael R. Winston, eds. *Dictionary of American Negro Biography.* New York: Norton, 1982.

Shanks, Henry Thomas, ed. *The Papers of Willie Mangum.* Vol. 1, 1807–1832; Vol. 2, 1833–1838. Raleigh, NC: State Department of Archives and History, 1950.

———. *References to John Chavis in the Papers of Willie Person Mangum.* Vol. 1, 1887–1832. Raleigh, NC: State Department of Archives and History, 1950.

Shaw, George C. *John Chavis: 1763–1838.* Binghamton, NY: Vail–Ballou Press, 1931.

COLLECTIONS

The original letters of John Chavis are at the Library of Congress, Duke University, and in the Willie P. Mangum Papers at the University of North Carolina at Chapel Hill.

Jessie Carney Smith

Kenneth I. Chenault

(1951–)

Business executive, lawyer

In 1997, American Express, a worldwide travel and network service provider, named Kenneth I. Chenault president and heir apparent to the position of chief executive officer, which would elevate him to be the highest ranking African American executive in corporate America. He earned this prestigious position after a rapid series of promotions and professional successes. His career at American Express since 1981 had strongly contributed to the company's steady ascent in the business world, making it one of the nation's largest in terms of annual revenues. Throughout his career, Chenault has stressed hard work, communication, and a commitment to technological progress in the world of business.

Born on June 2, 1951, in Hempstead, New York, Kenneth I. Chenault is the son of Hortenius Chenault, a dentist, and Anne N. Quick Chenault, a dental hygienist. The third born of four children, he has two brothers and one sister. His potential for becoming an achiever, strategist, and effective communicator was demonstrated early in life. He attended the Waldorf School, a private, elite high school in Garden City, New York, where he was an excellent student and president of his class throughout high school. An athlete as well, he was captain of his track, basketball, and soccer teams. He also was fascinated by other achievers and leaders, and devoured biographies of such luminaries as Frederick Douglass, W. E. B. Du Bois, and Winston Churchill. After graduation, Chenault studied at Bowdoin College in Maine and completed his studies in 1973 with a B.A. in history. Then he went to Harvard Law School where he was a moot court champion; he graduated in 1976 with the degree of juris doctor. On August 20, 1977, Chenault, a Congregationalist, married Kathryn Cassell, who later became a lawyer; they have two sons, Kenneth Jr. and Kevin A. The Chenaults live in New York State.

Chenault was an associate with Rogers & Wells, a corporate law firm in New York City, from 1977 to 1979. In 1979 he left to join Bain & Company, a business consulting firm based in Boston. This position was pivotal to his career, as it familiarized him with a number of large corporations and with the important executives who headed these companies.

Chenault's fast–track career at American Express began in 1981, when he left Bain and was named director of strategic planning for American Express Company in New York City. He was promoted to the position of vice president of Merchandise Services in 1983; to senior vice president and general manager of Merchandise Services in 1984; and then to executive vice president and general manager of the Platinum/Gold Card Division of American Express from in 1986. Under his various leadership positions, American Express became the fifth leading direct marketer in the nation. Merchandising

Kenneth I. Chenault

Services used direct mail to market such products as luggage and personal computers to card members. While in Merchandising Services, Chenault transformed a rather obscure unit into a powerhouse, persuading the company to move to a more upscale line of goods and services and to upgrade its technology to ensure better customer services. The February 1988 issue of *Black Enterprise* cited Chenault in its article on ''America's Hottest Black Managers,'' calling him one of the 25 ''most powerful black executives in corporate America.''

Chenault was named executive vice president and general manager of the Personal Card Division less than two years later, where he served from 1988 to 1990. Again, during his administration, the company saw record growth. In February 1988 he told *Black Enterprise,* ''I had experience running a complete operating unit. Now I have to create a culture in which all areas will operate jointly . . . and bring people together to understand the new objective and to see my vision of where we could take the division.'' Chenault was president of the Consumer Card and Financial Services Group from 1990 to 1993. The additional responsibility for managing all establishments that accepted the American Express card was given to Chenault in 1991. In 1993 he became president of the American Express Travel Related Services, where he was in charge of marketing and operations for all U.S. Consumer Card products. He continued to work to make American Express better by examining marketing trends, demographics, and consumer needs, and by recognizing the importance of computer–driven technology for the company's continued strength. In recognition of his achievements, Chenault was named vice chair of the American Express Company in 1995.

Heads American Express

American Express announced in February of 1997 that Chenault had been named heir apparent to the position as president and chief operating officer of the company, chosen to succeed Harvey Golub, now chairman and chief executive of American Express, seven years hence when Golub retires. At that time, Chenault may well be the first African American to take control of one of the nation's biggest companies. According to the February 28, 1997, *Nashville Tennessean,* American Express is ranked the sixty–fifth largest in the country by *Fortune* magazine. In the new position of CEO he would also be in charge of American Express Financial Advisors and American Express Bank. Quoted in the same article, Chenault, who was nominated to sit on the company's board of directors, commented on the question of whether race was a consideration in the appointment: ''It would obviously be naive and untrue to say that race is not a factor in our society [but] . . . at American Express, I have been totally judged on my performance.''

Chenault is a community servant as well as a businessman. Early on he co–sponsored fund raisers for the campaigns of Virginia governor L. Douglas Wilder and Atlanta mayor Maynard Jackson. He chaired the fiftieth anniversary gala for the NAACP Legal Defense Fund. His board memberships include the Brooklyn Union Gas Company, the Quaker Oats Company, the American Council for Drug Education, Junior Achievement of New York, the New York Medical Center, and the Bowdoin College Board of Overseers. He holds membership on the Council of Foreign Relations and is a member of the American Bar Association. Chenault has also been named Corporate Patron of the Arts by the Studio Museum of Harlem. He has been honored as well by Adelphi University, Morgan State University, Iona College, Stony Brook University, and his alma mater, Bowdoin College, with honorary degrees.

The trim, six–foot–tall Chenault has an athletic build and a Boy Scout smile. He admits to being a voracious reader and still prefers biography, particularly the works of Howard Thurman. He has been called a shrewd, articulate, even–tempered, approachable, confident, diplomatic, and quick–minded strategist who is an excellent leader as well as a supportive manager. He is a team–builder and a motivator. Much of his success may be attributed to his focus on the importance of communication early on. In the December 1985 *Black Enterprise* he said, ''You can be the greatest analyst around, but if you can't communicate your ideas to management, you won't be effective. . . . The one who'll be successful is the one who can communicate and inspire belief. Being able to write, speak and crystallize your thoughts is important.'' He communicated his ideas to American Express to become one of the leading black business executives in the country. As quoted by American Express vice president Paula DiDonato, Chenault commented on the field of technology in business:

> As we rush ''head–long'' into the 21st century, participants in the field of business and commerce will survive in the marketplace only if they fully utilize the facilities provided to them by the dramatic technological advances being made around the world, every day. These advances will enable us to understand our customers better and deliver to them vastly improved levels of service. The resulting enhanced customer satisfaction will in turn ensure the healthy, profitable growth of businesses.

Chenault has been recognized by corporate America as one who mastered business techniques, developed key business strategies, and rose through the ranks to become a top business executive.

Current address: Office of the President, American Express Consumer Card Group, USA, American Express Tower C, New York, NY 10285–0001.

REFERENCES

''American Express Appoints President, Likely CEO Successor.'' *Nashville Tennessean,* February 28, 1997.

Clarke, Caroline V. ''Meeting the Challenge of Corporate Leadership.'' *Black Enterprise* 26 (August 1995): 156.

Contemporary Black Biography. Vol. 4. Detroit: Gale Research, 1993.

DiDonato, Paula. Letter to Jessie Carney Smith, July 7, 1997.

Dingle, Derek T. ''The Manager of Tomorrow—Today.'' *Black Enterprise* 20 (March 1990): 43–50.

———. ''Return of the Top 25.'' *Black Enterprise* 19 (February 1989): 95–100.

———, Alfred Edmond Jr., and Sheryl Lee Hilliard. ''America's Hottest Black Managers.'' *Black Enterprise* 18 (February 1988): 81–116.

''Kenneth I. Chenault.'' *Michigan Chronicle,* February 22, 1994.

''Kenneth I. Chenault Appointed President and CEO of American Express Company.'' *Jet* 91 (17 March 1997): 8–9.

Pierce, Ponchetta. ''Kenneth Chenault: Blazing New Paths into Corporate America.'' *Ebony* 52 (July 1997): 58–62; 134–35.

Squires, David. ''Success in the Cards.'' *Black Enterprise* 16 (December 1985): 76–78, 96.

Who's Who in America, 1996. 50th ed. New Providence, NJ: Marquis Who's Who, 1996.

Jessie Carney Smith

Charles Waddell Chesnutt (1858–1932)

Author, lawyer

Charles W. Chesnutt's novels and short stories earned him a prominent place in American literary history. Bernard Bell noted that Chesnutt ''is generally . . . [recognized as] the first major Afro–American fiction writer.'' Sylvia Lyons Render pointed out in her biography of Chesnutt that he ''was the first Afro–American to produce an aesthetically satisfying novel of black life and the first to depict in such narratives a balanced and objectively treated array of both black and white characters.'' In *Afro–American Writers Before the Harlem Renaissance,* William L. Andrews concluded that Chesnutt ''taught white America for the first time to respect a black fiction writer as a critical realist.'' Chesnutt also wrote many essays and newspaper articles in which he spoke out strongly against serious injustices including lynching practices and disenfranchisement. Trained as a lawyer, Chesnutt supported his family at various stages of his life through his own stenography and court reporting business. Overall, Chesnutt was a respected author, civic leader, and legal professional.

Charles Waddell Chesnutt was born June 20, 1858, in Cleveland, Ohio; he died in the same city on November 15, 1932. Because he spent many of his formative years in Fayetteville, North Carolina, his experiences there also provided motivation and material for his literary career.

Chesnutt's own family roots were set deeply in North Carolina. The Fayetteville area was the home of both sets of Chesnutt's grandparents. Both of his grandfathers were white. Chesnutt's paternal grandfather, Waddle Chesnutt (sometimes spelled in other ways, including Waddell) provided property for his colored family members (Charles Chesnutt's grandmother and her children).

In the mid–1800s North Carolina enacted laws which restricted the rights of free people of color. Chesnutt's grandmothers, Ann Chesnutt and Chloe Sampson, and their children were among the free people of color who left North Carolina in 1856 in a wagon train bound for the more promising North.

Then young adults, Andrew Jackson ''Jack'' Chesnutt (Charles Chesnutt's father) and Ann Maria Sampson (Chesnutt's mother) traveled to Cleveland with their individual families as part of the migration. After a brief period in Indiana, where he had relatives, Jack Chesnutt returned to Cleveland, where Sampson was living. Jack Chesnutt and Ann Maria Sampson were married there in 1857. Charles Waddell Chesnutt was their oldest child. Two other children also lived past infancy, Lewis and Andrew Jr.

In Cleveland, Jack Chesnutt was a horse–car conductor. Chesnutt's mother, Ann Maria Chesnutt, was a ''born educa-

Charles Waddell Chesnutt

tor'' who taught slave children clandestinely in defiance of the law, according to Sylvia Lyons Render in her biography of Chesnutt. In keeping with her interest in education, Ann Maria moved the family closer to Oberlin College for a summer when Charles was just a toddler. The move reflected Chesnutt's mother's awareness of the openness at Oberlin College; she knew that it would likely assist her children's development.

Chesnutt received some of his early public schooling in Cleveland. When he was eight years old, his family moved back to North Carolina. The Civil War had ended, and Jack Chesnutt, who had been a teamster in the Union army, was able to have a home for his family and to open a grocery store. (Chesnutt's paternal grandfather provided financial backing.) In Fayetteville, Charles attended the newly founded Howard School, established through the Freedman's Bureau.

Ann Maria Chesnutt died in 1871, when Charles was 13. The next year brought other major changes in the family. First, Chesnutt's father remarried. Over the ensuing years, Jack Chesnutt and his second wife, Mary Ochiltree Chesnutt, had six children. Also, it was not very long after Ann Maria Chesnutt's death that Jack Chesnutt's grocery store failed. The family moved to the country, and Charles's schooling was jeopardized, since he was needed to assist the family financially. That problem was alleviated when Robert Harris, the principal of the Howard School, hired Chesnutt, who was only 14, as ''a salaried pupil–teacher'' at the school.

Although Chesnutt never officially graduated from the school, he was a disciplined and independent learner, and it is doubtless that he enhanced his education extensively in the process of his own teaching experience. He studied Greek and German largely on his own, and was well versed in English literature. He taught briefly in Spartanburg, South Carolina, and for two years (from 1875 until 1877), he taught in Charlotte, North Carolina. This experience included some time as a public school principal. He returned to Fayetteville in 1877 as assistant principal of the newly established State Colored Normal School, a development of the Howard School. (The State Colored Normal School was in turn the forerunner of Fayetteville State University.)

In 1878 Charles Chesnutt married Susan W. Perry, a teacher at the Howard School. A native of Fayetteville, Susan Perry was the daughter of a well–to–do barber. Between 1879 and 1890, Charles and Susan Chesnutt had four children: Ethel, Helen, Edwin, and Dorothy.

Once the Chesnutts began a new family, Charles grew even more dissatisfied with the limitations of living in Fayetteville. During his summer vacation in 1879, as noted in Render's biography of Chesnutt, he made a ''fruitless job–hunting trip'' to Washington, D.C. Even though he recognized that city's shortcomings, he also enjoyed the more lively cultural atmosphere there. In 1882, he wrote in his journal: ''I get more and more tired of the South. I pine for civilization and 'equality'. . . . And I shudder to think of exposing my children to the social and intellectual proscription to which I have been a victim. Is not my duty to them paramount?''

Chesnutt addressed his frustration and went to New York City where he worked as a stenographer and as a reporter in the summer of 1883. In November, he moved on to Cleveland, where he worked for the Nickel Plate Railroad Company, first as a clerk and then as a stenographer, and prepared for his family to join him.

Professional Career

Chesnutt's family joined him in Cleveland in 1884. In 1885 he began to study law with Judge Samuel E. Williamson, the legal counsel for Nickel Plate Railroad Company. Chesnutt had performed stenographic work for Judge Williamson at that company. Render's biography of Chesnutt noted that he passed the Ohio bar examination in 1887 ''with the highest grade in his group,'' and in 1888 he opened his ''own office as a court reporter.'' Between 1899 and 1901, he closed the office to devote full time to writing. He reopened the business following the poor success of his novel *The Marrow of Tradition* in 1901. Chesnutt's legal training thus provided a firm livelihood when needed.

Chesnutt travelled to Europe in 1896 and again in 1912. He also travelled extensively within the United States. In 1901 he gave lectures throughout the South, and he published several articles focusing on impressions. As a part of that lecture tour, he conducted research in Wilmington, North Carolina for *The Marrow of Tradition* which is based to a great extent on the riots that occurred there in 1898.

The bulk of Chesnutt's literary work was published between 1899 and 1905. In addition to short fiction and novels, he also published extensively as an essayist. His works include ''What is a White Man?,'' published in the *New York Independent* on May 4, 1889 and ''The Disenfranchisement of the Negro,'' a chapter in *The Negro Problem: A Series of Articles by Representative American Negroes of Today* published in 1903. Chesnutt's series of articles on the ''Future American'' in the *Boston Evening Transcript* in 1900 carried these subtitles: ''A Complete Race Amalgamation Likely to Occur,'' ''A Stream of Dark Blood in the Veins of Southern Whites,'' and ''What the Race is Likely to Become in the Process of Time.''

Chesnutt's professional contacts and distinctions were many. He was well acquainted with both Booker T. Washington and W. E. B. Du Bois and in 1904 was named to Booker T. Washington's group of advisors called the Committee of Twelve. At the 70th birthday party of noted author Mark Twain in 1905 Chesnutt was among the guests. In 1912, Chesnutt became a member of the Cleveland Chamber of Commerce. He was one of the founders in 1914 of the drama group Playhouse Settlement, famous later as Karamu House. In 1928 he was awarded the Spingarn Medal by the National Association of Colored People (NAACP).

Literary Career

Chesnutt's journal, kept sporadically but informatively from 1874 to 1882, reveals his ever–growing interest in writing, as well as examples of his early attempts at fiction. In a journal entry in 1880, Chesnutt capsulized his literary aim:

> The object of my writings would not be so much the elevation of the colored people as the elevation of the whites,—for I consider the unjust spirit of caste which is so insidious as to pervade a whole nation, and so powerful as to subject a whole race and all connected with it to scorn and social ostracism—I consider this a barrier to the moral progress of the American people; and I would be one of the first to head a determined, organized crusade against it. Not a fierce indiscriminate onslaught; not an appeal to force, for this is something that force can but slightly affect; but a moral revolution which must be brought about in a different manner.

That ''different manner'' included the artist's ability to entertain the development of themes of marked significance with respect to his times. Within a period of seven years, Chesnutt published two short story collections, a biography, and three novels. The short story collections were *The Conjure Woman* in 1899, and *The Wife of His Youth and Other Stories of the Color Line* in 1900. The biography, *Frederick Douglass,* was also published in 1899. In 1900 he wrote his first novel *The House Behind the Cedars,* and in 1901 *The Marrow of Tradition. The Colonel's Dream* appeared in 1905. Throughout his career, Chesnutt also published approximately 30 essays, articles, and columns. Approximately 80 selections of short fiction have been collected by Sylvia Lyons Render in *The Short Fiction of Charles Chesnutt.* Render's collection includes ten previously unpublished stories. Unpublished materials by Chesnutt are found in the Fisk University Special Collections. These include six novels, early versions of his first novel, plus a drama, and miscellaneous works of fiction.

Chesnutt's first major publication was ''The Goophered Grapevine,'' which appeared in *Atlantic* in 1887. The story features the wise and wily Uncle Julius. Uncle Julius speaks in dialect, but it is not a crude literary dialect characteristic of the plantation school of fiction of white writers such as John Pendleton Kennedy or Thomas Nelson Page; nor is Uncle Julius an Uncle Remus in the tradition of Joel Chandler Harris. Uncle Julius uses storytelling to achieve his own ends and to convey subtly but clearly the cruelty of slavery. His stories are self–contained within the frames of the overall larger narrative. The narrator of the ''outer story'' is a naive Northerner, who often misses or chooses to downplay the implications which his more empathetic wife discerns. Other stories featuring Uncle Julius were ''Po' Sandy,'' first published in the May 1888 issue of the *Atlantic,* and two stories published in 1899: ''The Conjurer's Revenge'' in *Overland Monthly,* and ''Dave's Neckliss'' in the *Atlantic Monthly.*

In 1899, Houghton Mifflin published Chesnutt's first book, *The Conjure Woman.* Along with the Uncle Julius stories this volume includes ''Mars Jeems's Nightmare,'' ''Sis Becky's Pickanniny,'' ''The Gray Wolf's Ha'nt,'' and ''Hot–Foot Hannibal.'' In *The Literary Career of Charles Chesnutt,* William Andrews notes that *The Conjure Woman* was well–received critically, and that sales were adequate. In Chesnutt's biography, Sylvia Lyons Render deems *The Conjure Woman* ''Chesnutt's most popular work.'' Render points out as well that Chesnutt's *Frederick Douglass,* also published in 1899 as part of the Beacon Biographical Series, is ''brief but excellent''.

Although he never tried to conceal his background, Chesnutt's racial identity was not widely known at the time when ''The Goophered Grapevine'' was first published. Chesnutt qualified as a ''voluntary Negro,'' meaning that he was so light–skinned that he could have passed for white had he chosen to do so. His experiences and perceptiveness made him especially well qualified to address the ''unjust spirit of caste'' resulting from racial intermarriage (miscegenation).

''The Wife of His Youth,'' picked up by *Atlantic Monthly* in July of 1898 was the first of his stories of the ''color line'' to be published in a major periodical. Chesnutt was well acquainted with the type of people he depicted in this story as members of the Blue Vein Society. Membership in this exclusive group was possible only for those so light–skinned that their veins could be easily seen. Such persons were often given more education and other benefits as a result of being the offspring or descendants of mixed race liaisons. In ''The Wife of His Youth,'' the Blue Vein Society members were not merely snobbish social climbers; they conclude that Mr. Ryder, the story's protagonist, should acknowledge the old, dark–skinned woman, the wife he had under slavery, and who comes back into his life. At the same time, the story makes clear that the old woman was a marriage partner in Mr. Ryder's youth–slavery, that the marriage was not a love relationship, and that that portion of Mr. Ryder's life is closed. In "The Sheriff's Children," published in the *New York Independent* in 1899, the white sheriff's mulatto son carries deep emotional scars. Typically, in both "The Wife of His Youth" and "The Sheriff's Children," Chesnutt captures without preaching the reality and complex effects of miscegenation.

Chesnutt's second book, published in 1900 also by Houghton Mifflin, was *The Wife of His Youth and Other Stories of the Color Line.* The volume includes "The Wife of His Youth" and "The Sheriff's Children" plus "Her Virginia Mammy," "A Matter of Principle," "Cicely's Dream," "The Passing of Grandison," "Uncle Wellington's Wives," "The Bouquet," and "The Web of Circumstance." *The Wife of His Youth* was less popular and less commercially successful than *The Conjure Woman.* However, the literary importance of the book is unmistakable. In *The Literary Career of Charles Chesnutt,* William Andrews notes, "As a literary 'pioneer of the color line,' Chesnutt made a crucial break with conventional literary sensibility in judging many ignored aspects of Afro–American life worthy of literary treatment and revelatory of profound social and moral truths." As a result of such perceptive treatment, Andrews notes further that, "[T]he stories of *The Wife of His Youth* showed . . . Chesnutt was a writer of national significance."

Chesnutt published three novels shortly after the turn of the century. *The House Behind the Cedars* in 1900, *The Marrow of Tradition* in 1901, and *The Colonel's Dream* in 1905. *The House Behind the Cedars* draws extensively on Chesnutt's knowledge of Fayetteville, called Patesville in most of Chesnutt's fiction. Like the Waldens in the novel, the Chesnutts lived in a house with cedars lining the front. Like his protagonist, Rena, Chesnutt could have passed for white, but chose not to do so. Rena has more scruples about passing than does her brother, John, who does pass. Rena has several suitors; only as she is dying does she understand that the most worthy is the faithful, brown–skinned Frank.

In The Marrow of Tradition Chesnutt draws extensively on the 1898 Wilmington, North Carolina race riot. The plot explores the interconnections of the white and mulatto branches of the Carteret families. At the novel's conclusion, the mulatto family's generosity of spirit makes possible the reconciliation of the two families. The novel presents an alternate attitude through the highly militant character, Josh Green, whose father was killed by the Ku Klux Klan in an incident long before the riot. When urged to acquiesce since whites outnumber blacks, Josh answers in *Marrow* with statements prefiguring Claude McKay's "If We Must Die": "Dey're gwine ter kill us anyhow . . . ; an' we're tired er bein' shot down like dogs, widout jedge er jury. We'd ruther die fightin' dan be stuck like pigs in a pen!" William Andrews in *Literary Career* notes that neither *The Marrow of Tradition* nor *The Colonel's Dream* was a commercial success.

The title of *The Colonel's Dream* refers to the reform efforts of a white during the Reconstruction era. The colonel's efforts are not successful, and he gives up—perhaps too readily, the novel implies. The novel did not appeal to the critics; many felt the book was too controversial.

"Chesnutt's best story . . . is 'Baxter's Procrustes'," according to Render in *Short Fiction.* The story was first published in *Atlantic Monthly* in June 1904 and is "universally considered" to be among Chesnutt's finest wherein he deftly satirizes the pretensions of exclusive clubs. The tale was based on the Rowfant Club in Cleveland which had failed to accept Chesnutt as a member in 1902. In 1910 Chesnutt was finally invited to join the club, and he did so.

Over the course of his literary career, Chesnutt interacted extensively with Albion Tourgee, George Washington Cable, and William Dean Howells. While still in North Carolina, Chesnutt had read Tourgee's *A Fool's Errand,* and Chesnutt's decision to become a writer was influenced "by the knowledge that he had an even more thorough understanding of Southern life than did Tourgee, a native of the North. Cable and Howells provided encouragement, although they did not always demonstrate complete understanding of Chesnutt's work.

Charles Chesnutt's best fiction dealt with the issues of his day in a realistic and gripping fashion. Despite the preconceptions and expectations of his intended audiences, he avoided stereotypes. He handled satire and humor deftly and entertainingly. In his nonfiction works and speeches, he spoke out with directness and insight. His achievements, especially in their historical context, are impressive indeed, and they establish his place as a major American author.

REFERENCES

Andrews, William L. *The Literary Career of Charles W. Chesnutt.* Baton Rouge: Louisiana State University Press, 1980.

———. "A Reconsideration of Charles Waddell Chesnutt: Pioneer of the Color Line." *College Language Association Journal* 19 (December 1975): 136–51.

Bell, Bernard W. *The Afro–American Novel and Its Tradition.* Amherst: University of Massachusetts Press, 1987.

Brodhead, Richard H., ed. *The Journals of Charles W. Chesnutt.* Durham, NC: Duke University Press, 1993.

Chesnutt, Charles W. *The Marrow of Tradition.* 1901. Reprint, Ann Arbor: University of Michigan Press, 1969.

Chesnutt, Helen M. *Charles Waddell Chesnutt: Pioneer of the Color Line.* Chapel Hill: University of North Carolina Press, 1952.

Ellis, Curtis W., and E. W. Metcalfe Jr. *Charles Chesnutt: A Reference Guide.* Boston: G. K. Hall, 1978.

Harris, Trudier, ed. *Afro–American Writers Before the Harlem Renaissance.* Detroit: Gale Research, 1986.

Keller, Frances Richardson. *An American Crusade: The Life of Charles Waddell Chesnutt.* Provo, UT: Brigham Young University, 1978.

Render, Sylvia Lyons. *Charles W. Chesnutt.* Boston: G. K. Hall, 1980.

———, ed. *The Short Fiction of Charles W. Chesnutt.* Washington, DC: Howard University Press, 1981.

COLLECTIONS

The Chesnutt papers are in the Special Collections of Fisk University. Other materials are in the Western Reserve Historical Society Library.

Arlene Clift–Pellow

Thomas Morris Chester

Thomas Morris Chester

(1834–1892)

Journalist, lawyer, civil rights activist, federal government official

Thomas Chester was a dedicated journalist and the only black war correspondent for a major daily newspaper during the Civil War reporting first–hand accounts of the activities of black soldiers. A multitalented man of exceptional ability, he became the first black to pass the English bar, the first black admitted to the Louisiana bar, and the first black admitted to practice before the Pennsylvania Supreme Court. He was also known as a dogged defender of human rights.

Thomas Morris Chester, a tall, muscular, articulate man, was born in Harrisburg, Pennsylvania, on May 11, 1834. He was the second son and the fourth of twelve children born to George and Jane Maria Chester. Seven of the children reached adulthood. George Chester, born 1784, may have been the son of an Indian chief in San Domingo, who was brought to the United States by slave traders and settled in Harrisburg in the early 1820s. Jane Chester was born a slave in Virginia in 1806. She moved to Baltimore with her new slave owner, then escaped in 1825 to York and moved on to Harrisburg where she worked as a maid. She soon met George Chester, whom she married in April 1926.

By that time, George Chester was an oysterman and restaurant owner on Market Street, which was a center of social and political activity, including that of abolitionists. Through their restaurant the Chesters catered many of the city's gatherings and dining at the restaurant on special holidays became fashionable. After George Chester died in the late 1850s, Jane continued the work at her home at 305 Chesnut Street and became the city's chief caterer. Although the Chesters were abolitionists, the local abolitionist groups, such as the Pennsylvania Colonization Society who had a stronghold in the community, did not necessarily appreciate their work.

The Chesters were strong proponents of education for their children. The oldest surviving daughter, Charlotte, became Harrisburg's first black teacher. Although Thomas Chester's early life is unrecorded, he had an early determination to become a lawyer that took him 40 years to realize. When he was 16 years old Chester left home and entered Allegheny Institute in Allegheny City. The school, which later became Avery College, opened in April of 1850 to educate blacks in science, literature, and ancient and modern languages. Although Chester was a serious student, he was also undoubtedly influenced by black nationalist developments in the immediate and larger communities.

Notwithstanding the work of abolitionist groups, the combination of disfranchisement, the Fugitive Slave Law, and growing discrimination against blacks prompted a black nationalist emigration movement calling for blacks to settle outside the United States. Some fugitives fled to Canada while others followed Martin R. Delany's movement to settle in Liberia. Chester decided to emigrate. With the assistance of the Pennsylvania Colonization Society, he left Avery Institute in April of 1853 to attend Alexander High School in Monrovia, Liberia. He found conditions there unsatisfactory and in September 1854, with the support of New York colonizationists, he left Liberia to attend Thetford Academy in Vermont. He enrolled in the classical department in December 1854, an older student and the only black in the school. Chester was active in a number of activities, including the debating society, where he became skilled in forensics—an expertise for which be became well known later in life. After graduating second in his class in 1856, with the support of colonizationists, he returned to Liberia where he taught in the colonizationists' school for "recaptive slaves" and emigrants. He left Liberia under a cloud of suspicion about activities at the school, which he denied, and returned to the United States in February of 1859. Late that year the Pennsylvania Abolitionist Society hired him to work with blacks in the state to promote Liberian colonization further. In September of 1860 he returned to Liberia and in 1861 resumed publication of the *Star of Liberia,* the newspaper he had founded earlier.

Chester returned to the United States at the height of the Civil War. In 1863, as the north prepared for a possible attack by Confederate forces, John Andrew, governor of Massachusetts, began to organize a black volunteer regiment. Frederick Douglass, Martin R. Delany, and Charles Lennox Remond were named to seek recruits in northern states. Chester helped recruit for the 55th Massachusetts Regiment and the state militia by heading a drive in Harrisburg.

Becomes War Correspondent

In August of 1864, while the Civil War was in full force, John Russell Young, editor of the *Philadelphia Press,* who was familiar with Chester's work on the *Star of Liberia,* hired him to report on the war. Prior to 1864, no major dailies were interested in the activities of black troops. Chester, therefore, became one of the first black war correspondents and the first and only black war correspondent for a major daily. He was sent to Virginia to report on activities around Richmond and Petersburg. Writing under the name "Rollin," he paid special attention to the black soldiers and gave repeated accounts of their bravery and dedication, dispelling the notion that blacks would not fight. He criticized the racist acts of white commanders of black troops and praised those who treated the black soldiers fairly. He had a precise eye for detail and gave extensive first–hand accounts of war activities.

According to his biographer R. J. M. Blackett, Chester was among the first reporters to enter Richmond when the Confederacy evacuated. As well, Chester confirmed in the *Philadelphia Press* for April 6, 1865, quoted by Blackett, that he "was ahead of every part of the force but the cavalry, which of necessity must lead the advance. I know whereof I affirm when I announce that General Draper's brigade [the black 55th Massachusetts Cavalry] was the first organization to enter the city limits." Chester wrote this dispatch from the desk of the Speaker of the Confederacy. He remained in Richmond until June of 1865 writing about efforts to rebuild the city and activities in the black community.

Returning to Harrisburg, Chester became active in black Pennsylvania's civil rights protests, such as segregation on public transportation and denial of the freedom to vote. Meanwhile, the October of 1864 meeting in Syracuse of the National Convention of Colored Men, which had held its landmark convention in Buffalo in 1843, had as delegates men and women of the black liberation movement. They represented eighteen states, including seven from the South. The Syracuse meeting led to the founding of the National Equal Rights League that concentrated on temperance, morality, education, and other issues. Pennsylvania established its own chapter called the Pennsylvania State Equal Rights League. Harrisburg formed a chapter in August of 1865 known as the Garnet Equal Rights League, named in honor of abolitionist and minister Henry Highland Garnet. Chester was named solicitor, literary critic, and later corresponding secretary to the league and traveled abroad, raising money in Russia and England.

When Chester completed his mission in May of 1867, he returned to England to enroll in one of the Inns of Court. He had read law earlier under a Liberian lawyer and by now had saved enough money to concentrate on his training. Chester spent three years at London's Middle Temple—one of the four Inns of Court—supplementing his income through periodic lecture tours and through his appointment as Liberia's roving ambassador in Europe. In April of 1870 he was the first black American called to the English bar. After he successfully argued his first case a few weeks later at the Old Bailey, the eloquent, sharp–tongued lawyer became a celebrity in royal courts of Europe.

Although Chester returned to the United States permanently in the summer of 1870, he always considered Liberia his home. That summer he began to address the social conditions that blacks faced. Like many black leaders of the time, Chester supported the Republican party because of his respect for former president, Abraham Lincoln. In his summer of 1871 lecture tour through Louisiana and Kentucky, where large crowds greeted him, he called for full participation of blacks in the economic, social, and political life of the country. He accepted a clerkship in the Customs House of New Orleans about the time P. B. S. Pinchback emerged as the state's leading black figure, replacing Oscar Dunn, the black lieutenant governor who had died mysteriously. During this period, Louisiana politics had degenerated into a squabble between Republicans, led by Governor Clay Warmouth, and radical Republicans, headed by Dunn. During an altercation on January 1, 1872, involving Pinchback's supporters and opponents, Chester was shot in the head and dangerously wounded. According to Blackett in *Thomas Morris Chester,* suspicions abounded "that the shooting was a botched attempt by [Pinchback's] supporters to get rid of Chester." When he recovered by the end of the month, Chester spoke at St. James Chapel before a meeting called by blacks to show black unity. He warned of possible retaliation by the radical members of the Republican party.

Chester returned to Harrisburg, perhaps out of concern for his own safety after his controversial speech, but would not remain silent about the warring Republican factions in New Orleans and elsewhere. He returned to New Orleans in May as a representative to the "Colored Convention." There were blacks at the convention—Pinchback, for example—who were determined to follow Charles Sumner, who had introduced a civil rights bill in Congress, and the principles of Lincoln, whom Frederick Douglass supported. Chester's candidate for governor, William Pitt Kellogg, won and blacks received important state offices, such as lieutenant governor and superintendent of education. Pinchback was denied a senate seat in Washington after his campaign opponent successfully contested Pinchback's election. Involvement at the polls was dangerous for blacks. Between 1865 and 1873, 5,000 Republicans, most of them black, had been killed. Chester held the federal government responsible for protecting black citizens.

Heads Public Education

In 1873, Chester became the first black admitted to the Louisiana bar where he built an impressive record of victories. In May that year, Kellogg commissioned Chester brigadier general in the Fourth Brigade, First Division, of the state militia. Prior to then Chester had filled in briefly in the First Brigade for A. E. Barber, who had been on leave. He headed the Fourth Brigade until 1876, when the Republicans went out of state office. In 1875, however, Kellogg appointed Chester superintendent of public education for the First Division, filling an unexpired term of P. M. Williams. Chester now had control over education in parishes in the southeast, north, and northeast of New Orleans, spanning the area from Baton Rouge to the Gulf of Mexico. A year later Chester was named superintendent of the Fifth Division and held the position until Kellogg left office that year.

Chester sought a federal position in New Orleans and in late 1878 was named U.S. Commissioner for New Orleans, a position he held for two years. In 1879 he was appointed special assistant to the U.S. Attorney for the Eastern District of Texas to examine serious legal offenses. He used an assumed name, given the impending violence, and was sent to Texarkana for his work. He was fired before completing the job; his superiors claimed that his report was too long and rambling and his reimbursement forms were illegible.

Many black Louisianians began to move to Kansas in 1877. It is estimated that by March of 1879, approximately 10,000 joined the exodus of southern black laborers moving to Kansas. Chester, an emigrationist at heart, was in favor of the move. The *New Orleans Picayune* of this period (April 5, 18, 19, 20, 22, and 26), cited in *Thomas Morris Chester,* condemned the exodus, denied that any prominent blacks had been killed in the state for political reasons, and accused black officials of selling public functions for money. In particular the *Picayune* made claims of sexual improprieties against Chester during his stay in Europe. While Chester denied the charges, the newspaper continued its attack.

Chester spent little time in New Orleans after 1879, having returned to his mother's home. He had married around this time, taking Florence Johnson, 21 years his junior, as his bride. Johnson, who lived with her mother–in–law, was born in Natchez, Mississippi, and after the war moved to New Orleans. In the early 1870s she enrolled in Straight University (later Dillard University) and graduated in the school's first class in 1875. She taught in Tangipahoa Parish, one of the districts Chester oversaw when he was superintendent. Later she attended Peabody Normal School and studied at Tuskegee Institute and Cheyney State College as well. After 50 years of service as teacher and school principal, she retired in 1927. In 1944 the Orleans Parish School Board dedicated a black elementary school in her honor.

In 1881 Chester became the first black admitted to practice before the Pennsylvania Supreme Court. After 1883 Chester relied on his law practice in Louisiana, Washington, D.C., and Pennsylvania, for income. Since his clients were generally black and poor, some speculate that his income suffered. In January of 1884 he became president of the Wilmington, Wrightsville and Onslow Railroad company, chartered in 1883, and the first black–owned railroad project in the country. His work primarily involved selling stock and his clients included the Board of Bishops of the African Methodist Episcopal church, the Inter–State Convention of Colored Men of the Northern States, and Frederick Douglass. However, the company failed and the railroad was out of business by the end of the year.

According to Chester's biographer R. J. M. Blackett, "the rest of his life is a complete mystery." The Chesters returned to New Orleans in 1888, where he resumed law practice and she taught at the all–black Robinson School. Chester had lost his feistiness, arrogance, and spirit and now seemed disillusioned. Conditions for blacks in the South had deteriorated, yet Chester continued to defend the South as a place of wholesome race relations. Although neither the nation, the South, nor the *Picayune* accepted him, his biographer says that he took refuge in conservatism.

Chester returned ill to his mother's home in April of 1892, suffering from disease exacerbated by dropsy and heart trouble. He died of an apparent heart attack on September 30, when he was 58 years old, and was buried three days later in the family plot in Harrisburg's segregated Lincoln Cemetery. His life had been colorful and full, while his last days were unrepresentative of the enormity of his contribution to black and American life in journalism, racial agitation, and law.

REFERENCES

Blackett, R. J. M., ed. *Thomas Morris Chester, Black Civil War Correspondent.* Baton Rouge: Louisiana State University Press, 1989.

"Civil War Reporter." *Ebony* 15 (November 1959): 131–32, 136.

Haley, James T., comp. *The Afro–American Encyclopedia.* Nashville: Haley & Florida, 1895.

Proceedings of the National Convention of Colored Men, Held in the City of Syracuse, N.Y., October 4, 5, 6, and 7, 1864, with the Bill of Wrongs and Rights and the Address to the American People. 1864. Reprint, Philadelphia: Rhistoric Publications, 1969.

Simmons, William H. *Men of Mark.* Cleveland: George M. Rewell, 1887.

Jessie Carney Smith

Robert Reed Church Sr.
(1839–1912)
Entrepreneur, banker, civic leader

In an era when American blacks had little of which to be proud and when there were few Southern black heroes, Robert Reed Church Sr. was recognized as a forceful, ingenious, and resourceful community leader. He founded a bank that encouraged black people to manage and save their earnings. This bank also came to the rescue of black organizations in times of dire need. When the city government would not provide recreational facilities for black Memphians, Church constructed a multi–use facility for blacks—one of the largest in the nation. Black Americans looked up to Church because he made whites respect him whether they wanted to or not. If friendly persuasion failed, his fists, guns, and money earned him the right to be taken seriously as an entrepreneurial peer. As the patriarch of a three–generation Memphis dynasty, Church lived by example, providing future generations with a black role model.

George Lee, in his book, *Beale Street: Where the Blues Began,* called Church one of Memphis's most notable citizens, and wrote, "Without some eulogy to him no book concerning the history of Memphis would be complete." This is a remarkable legacy for a man who was born a Mississippi slave to white riverboat captain Charles B. Church and a slave seamstress named Emmaline on June 18, 1839.

Although Church was not emancipated until New Year's Day in 1863, he did not consider himself to have ever been a slave, despite his mother's status, which he openly acknowledged. She was the legal property of Captain Church but was described in *African American Business Leaders* as "a born aristocrat . . . with exquisite manners . . . [and] never treated as a slave." Denying any black ancestry, Emmaline claimed that her mother was a woman named Lucy, a red–complexioned, long–haired, French–speaking Malaysian princess who had been taken prisoner and sold into slavery because of civil strife. Purchased by a Norfolk, Virginia, tobacco merchant, she was readily identifiable by the pendulous gold earrings and coral and gold necklace she always wore. This jewelry has been handed down through the generations of the Church family and is considered a valuable part of the family history.

Emmaline raised her son until her death in 1851, when he went to live with his father. The lessons learned as a dishwasher, cabin boy, cook, steward, and trader under the riverboat captain's tutelage greatly influenced Church's ability to manage money for the rest of his life. The captain also taught his son the value of self–defense, both with his fists and with weapons. Life on the river was hard, but it prepared Church to later enjoy his hard–won reputation as the wealthiest black man in the South.

Robert Reed Church Sr.

From Slavery to Respectability

Church might have stayed with his father on the Mississippi River indefinitely had not the Civil War intervened. Both survived an 1855 fire that sank a luxury steam boat under the captain's command. His next charge was a steamer, *The Victoria,* which was seized by Federal troops outside Memphis. Although Church was initially taken into custody, he quickly changed status from contraband to freedman. Once he decided to settle in Memphis, he realized that his riverboat experiences as a steward had prepared him to embark on a career of personal and professional services to others. An astute money manager, he resolutely saved and invested his earnings in a saloon and pool hall in the black waterfront area of the city.

His rapid ascent in the business world was nearly thwarted when Church was shot in the back of the head in his own saloon during the 1866 Memphis Riots. He was targeted not only by white rioters, but also by Irish policemen, who were openly stealing his liquor and raiding his cash box. He gained a measure of notoriety by testifying in federal court and identifying the perpetrator, a rare act for a black man. Despite this setback, Church continued to acquire prime property, including a hotel in downtown Memphis at South Second and Gayoso Streets. According to Lee, it was advertised as the "only first–class Colored hotel in the city [with]. . .large airy rooms, a dining facility, and. . .furnished with the best equipment of that day." That location was also the site of another altercation in which Church was shot by the sheriff of Lee County, Mississippi, supposedly over a black woman. Church had always had problems with the police and with underworld figures who wanted total control over liquor, gambling, prostitution, and pawnshops. Due to the nature and location of his businesses, Church was reputed to have been involved in all of these enterprises. Neither the law nor the lawless could take anything from him. He was always armed and always adhered to his father's personal creed to "never be a coward."

Church lacked formal education due to his peripatetic lifestyle on the river as an adolescent and a young man, but he was always a supremely self–contained man who communicated easily with people from all social strata. Being a ship's steward taught him how to perceive people's needs, determine how to meet them, and ensure that he got what he wanted. By the 1870s Church had amassed a small fortune and was able to engage in a business venture that would forever cement his place in the city's history.

In 1878 and 1879 Memphis was depopulated by repeated yellow fever epidemics. Accounts of early historians report that Church asserted his allegiance to the city that enabled him to become a man of prestige and wealth. As a show of faith in the city's revitalization efforts, he supposedly purchased the first $1,000 bond, Municipal Bond #1, to set up a fund to enable the city to pay its debts and regain its charter, which had been revoked by the state. Because local records often omitted factual information about black citizens, there is no record showing Church's purchase of the bond. There was much abandoned property and inexpensive real estate to be had for investors able to capitalize on the situation brought on by the epidemic. Church had the wherewithal to do just that, taking advantage of a disastrous situation. His personal fortune rose in direct proportion to his civic status in Memphis.

The Boss of Beale Street

Although he was a solitary man known to keep his own counsel, Church did not live in total isolation. His first marriage took place when he was just 18 years old. Described as a "slave marriage" by Ingham and Feldman in *African American Business Leaders,* this union was with a New Orleans native named Margaret Pico. They had one child, Laura Napier, whom Church educated. Some years later he married a Bluff City, Tennessee, woman who was a maid. It was the income from her hair salon that enabled them to purchase their first home. Louisa Ayers Church became the mother of Church's most prominent offspring, Mary Church (Terrell) (1863–1954), and his first son, Thomas Ayers Church. The couple divorced in 1870. Accounts of the financial settlements and final dissolution of real estate and property vary in biographical accounts of Church's life. Most report that Church greatly increased his financial status because the divorce decree granted him possession of many of Louisa's land holdings. Only one account reports that she received a substantial financial windfall that enabled her to continue as a successful hairdresser, first in Memphis and then in New York. She did receive custody of the two children, who continued to enjoy a luxurious lifestyle.

In 1885 Church married Anna S. Wright, former principal of the Winchester Colored School. She was the descendant of a white Kentucky colonel, an English–born Philadelphia Quaker, a wealthy Memphis plantation–owner, and a rich Chickasaw Indian brickyard owner. The new Mrs. Church was indeed the "fairest of the fair." She is listed as being the first graduate of LeMoyne College in Memphis; later she also graduated from Antioch College in Yellow Springs, Ohio. She became an accomplished pianist as well as a trained vocalist. Her education, breeding, and skin color made her quite acceptable to the black upper echelon of society, and Stephen Birmingham described her in *Certain People: America's Black Elite* as being "the unquestioned leading grande dame" of Memphis's black society. In recognition of the significance of such a promising union, the Church family moved to a 13–room mansion on Lauderdale Street in a neighborhood of upper class white families. Built at a cost of over $15,000, it was in the Queen Anne architectural style, three stories high, and included such amenities as servant's quarters, horse stables, and a full laundry.

This third marriage produced two children. The most noted was Robert Jr., who became known as the "Dictator of the Lincoln Belt" due to his founding of the Lincoln League, an organization formed to increase the number of black voters and exercise political influence in west Tennessee. His sister, Annette Elaine, was an Oberlin College graduate, a staunch Republican, and one of three female charter members of the local chapter of the NAACP. With her niece, Roberta, she was also the chief family historian and keeper of family records. Roberta, Robert Jr.'s daughter, was the first black woman elected to Tennessee's Republican State Committee. Until her 1982 retirement, she served in the cabinet departments of Labor and Health, Education and Welfare.

Although Mary Church Terrell was the most outstanding of all Church's offspring, Church provided them equally with all the privileges his immense wealth could provide. They had private tutors, northern educators, European vacations, summer retreats at the finest resorts on the Eastern Seaboard, and instant entry into black society across America.

Church eschewed the political arena. His political and professional connections, however, resulted in close relationships with such notables as Blanche Kelso Bruce of Mississippi and Washington, D.C., Robert Terrell, also of Washington, P. B. S. Pinchback of New Orleans, George L. Ruffin of Boston, Daniel Hale Williams of Chicago, and James C. Napier of Nashville. Although they differed in political and economic philosophies, Church and Booker T. Washington were personal friends.

Building an Empire

The foundation for Church's reputation as the South's first black millionaire was real estate. Although historians dispute this claim, stating that his actual worth was closer to $700,000 in 1912 currency, that was still more than almost all blacks and most whites were worth. Church owned undeveloped land, commercial buildings, and residential properties, the latter bringing in around $6,000 in monthly rents. Much of the property was in the red light district of the city and as long as vice was confined to a controlled area, the price was what the market would bear. Most of Church's conflicts with the law and the underworld centered on who would control the area: a black man with seemingly unlimited wealth and a gun, or white Memphis, lawful and lawless.

Biographers and historians have accused Church of being paternalistic, but he provided the city's black citizenry what the city would not. In 1899 he purchased land on the south side of Beale Street and created Church Park and Auditorium at a cost of $50,000. The six–acre park featured flowers and walkways, a picnic ground, a playground, a bandstand, and peacocks proudly spreading their tail feathers and strutting the grounds. The 2,000–seat auditorium contained a theater, banquet hall, bar, soda fountain, and concert hall. As the cultural center of black Memphis, most conventions, commencement exercises, and rallies were held there. Black entertainers were regular performers, including the Black Patti Troubadours, the Fisk Jubilee Singers, and W. C. Handy. President Theodore Roosevelt spoke there in 1902, and in 1909 Booker T. Washington was the honoree at a breakfast banquet and at a later public ceremony. In 1911 the city bought the park and removed the Church name, which was restored in 1956. The area was finally bulldozed by the Memphis Housing Authority and later, a sesquicentennial commission paid for a bronze plaque commemorating both Church Sr. and Jr. This plaque was finally placed in the Memphis State University—now University of Memphis—library. In 1993 the property was added to the Beale Street Historic District and listed in the National Register of Historic Places.

Church was the leader in founding the Solvent Savings Bank and Trust Company in 1906, his cleverest act took place when the Panic of 1907 threatened all banks. As president, he put sacks of money in the bank windows with a large sign stating that his bank would pay off all depositors; this prevented a run on the bank by hysterical depositors. Although Church's main interest was never politics, he did run for city offices in 1882 and 1886 but was defeated by black candidates. On the national level, he was a delegate to the Republican National Convention in 1900 as a William McKinley supporter.

Due to Church's influence, I. N. Ruttin and W. J. Yerby were appointed to the Department of State's Foreign Service. On the civic side, Church and his bank saved Beale Street Baptist Church when it was threatened with foreclosure in 1908. He saw to it that the creditors were paid and the institution, now the First Baptist Church of Beale Street, stands today thanks to the largesse of the "Boss of Beale Street."

Unfortunately, the dynasty founded by Church could not maintain the raw power and momentum of the slave boy who in 1984 was named one of Memphis's pioneer businessmen by the local Chamber of Commerce. Although *African American Business Leaders* called him the acknowledged "Kingpin of Beale Street business for over thirty years," cleaning up the red light district devalued his extensive property holdings. His son, more politician than businessman, could not maintain what his father had built. The Great Depression ultimately resulted in his inability to pay property taxes. The city finally seized the properties for back taxes, an amount far less than their actual value. In 1940, the Lauderdale Street mansion was sold for less than one third of its original cost.

When Robert Church Sr. died on August 12, 1912, he was honored by both black and white Memphis. Breaking a longstanding tradition, white newspapers ran long obituaries about the son of Captain Church. Ingham and Feldman wrote, "Robert Church never attended school, wrote a letter, or made a public speech, but he gained the respect and admiration of his community, black and white." Church was buried in Elmwood Cemetery in an $11,000 mausoleum. He may have come into the world as a pauper and slave, but he left it a rich, influential man.

REFERENCES

Birmingham, Stephen. *Certain People: America's Black Elite.* Boston: Little, Brown and Co., 77.

Coppock, Paul R. *Memphis Memoirs.* Memphis: Memphis State University Press, 1980.

Gatewood, Willard B. *Aristocrats of Color: The Black Elite, 1880–1920.* Bloomington: Indiana University Press, 1990.

Ingham, John N., and Lynne B. Feldman, eds. *African–American Business Leaders: A Biographical Dictionary.* Westport, CT: Greenwood Press, 1994.

Lee, George W. *Beale Street: Where the Blues Began.* College Park, MD: McGrath Publishing, 1934.

Logan, Rayford W., and Michael R. Winston, eds. *Dictionary of American Negro Biography.* New York: Norton, 1982.

Lovett, Bobby, and Linda T. Wynn, eds. *Profiles of African Americans in Tennessee.* Nashville: Annual Local Conference on Afro–American Culture and History, 1996.

Miller, M. Sammye. "Document—Last Will and Testament of Robert Reed Church, Senior (1839–1912)." *Journal of Negro History* 65 (Spring 1980): 156–63.

———. "Mary Church Terrell's Letters from Europe to Her Father." *Negro History Bulletin* 39 (September/October 1976): 615–18.

———. "Portrait of Black Urban Family." *Negro History Bulletin* 42 (April/May/June 1979): 50–51.

"Sara R. Church, Republican Leader, Dies." *Nashville Tennessean,* July 17, 1995.

"Sara Roberta Church, 81, Dies: Served in GOP Administrations." *Jet* 88 (7 August 1995): 53.

COLLECTIONS

The Robert R. Church Family Papers are in the library of the University of Memphis. Those of Mary Church Terrell are in the Library of Congress and the Moorland–Spingarn Research Center at Howard University, Washington, D.C. Shelby County Public Library has the papers of Sarah Roberta Church. Interviews with Roberta Church and Annette E. Church are in the Oral History Office at the University of Memphis.

Dolores Nicholson

Clay, Cassius.
See Ali, Muhammad.

Eldridge Cleaver

Eldridge Cleaver

(1935–1998)

Militant, writer, minister

Eldridge Cleaver achieved considerable notoriety in the 1960s by his best–selling collection of prison writings, *Soul on Ice* (1965), and through his leadership position in the Black Panther Party for Self–Defense. He remained a figure of great interest for the media into the 1970s when he fled into exile in Cuba, Algeria, and France, helped split the Black Panther Party, and returned to the United States a penniless, born–again Christian, anti–Communist, conservative Republican designer of sexually–explicit pants for men.

Leroy Eldridge Cleaver was born in Wabbaseka, Arkansas, on June 5, 1935, and grew up in Phoenix, Arizona, and the Watts section of Los Angeles, California. His long career in and out of reform schools and prisons began in 1947 at the age of 12, when he was arrested for stealing a bicycle. In the 1950s he served time in reform school and prison for selling marijuana. In reform school he converted to Roman Catholicism, thereby beginning a lifetime of religion–hopping that would take him into the Nation of Islam, the Unification Church of Reverend Sun Myung Moon and the Mormon Church, among others.

Less than a year after his release from prison in California during the mid–1950s, Cleaver was back in jail, charged with the rape of a white woman. He was convicted of assault with intent to kill and served nine years of a one–to–14–year sentence. He was released on parole in 1966.

This time in prison, Cleaver studied seriously and read widely. His main teacher, whom he called ''The Christ,'' was Chris Lordjieff, a white instructor in the California prison system. Cleaver read Karl Marx, Richard Wright, Jean Jacques Rousseau, Thomas Paine, Voltaire, and Bakunin, among others. He also read Elijah Muhammad, and became Eldridge X, a prison minister in Muhammad's Nation of Islam. Cleaver supported Malcolm X in Malcolm's break with the Nation of Islam in 1964.

While still incarcerated in 1965, Cleaver wrote to Beverly Axelrod, a white San Francisco lawyer. She visited him in jail and introduced his prison essays to the editors of *Ramparts* magazine, who began publishing them in 1966, even as Cleaver plied her with letters professing his love for her. Axelrod helped Cleaver obtain parole, on the strength of his *Ramparts* publications, the promise of a job at the magazine, and a book contract from McGraw–Hill.

Cleaver was paroled in December of 1966 and settled in the Bay Area to be close to his *Ramparts* job. He tried unsuccessfully to start a local branch of the Organization of Afro–American Unity (OAAU), founded by Malcolm X in 1964. He did, however, help bring Malcolm X's widow, Betty Shabazz, to town for a commemoration of her husband's life. Together with poet and playwright Ed Bullins, playwright Marvin Jackman, and singer Willie Dale, Cleaver in January of 1967 opened a ''Black House'' in San Francisco. This group affiliated with the Bay Area Grassroots Organization Planning Committee.

Through Beverly Axelrod, Cleaver met Jerry Rubin and other Jewish New Left radicals, with whom he later associated in the Peace and Freedom Party. He also wrote for *Esquire, Black Dialogue, Liberator,* and *Mademoiselle,* among other publications.

In February of 1967 Cleaver met Huey P. Newton and Bobby Seale, founders of the Black Panther Party (BPP). The BPP was organized in Oakland, California, in 1966, to protect the African American community from police brutality and provide social services, such as health care and free breakfast programs. Armed Panthers patrolling the streets with unconcealed weapons quickly came to the attention of law enforcement agencies, especially the Federal Bureau of Investigation, which considered them North America's greatest menace. The Panthers also quickly came to the attention of their own admiring constituency and their membership grew quickly.

Cleaver joined the BPP shortly after meeting Seale and Newton. According to Bobby Seale in *Seize the Time,* he and Newton saw in Cleaver a heroic figure emerging like Malcolm X from jail into revolutionary prominence. They were awed by his ability to write. He became minister of information and editor of *The Black Panther,* organ of the party. On April 15, 1967, Cleaver made his first appearance as a speaker at a major Panther event, a San Francisco anti–Vietnam War rally. His parole officers threatened to return him to jail.

A month later, in May of 1967, the Panthers staged a spectacular demonstration at the California state capitol in Sacramento. They showed up armed, with a proclamation to read to the state legislature. Cleaver was arrested and briefly imprisoned as he covered the event for *Ramparts* magazine. His parole authorities now imposed severe restrictions on Cleaver, together with a ban on public speeches.

Cleaver decided to ignore these efforts to fetter him by late 1967. Both Huey Newton and Bobby Seale were in jail and he considered himself well positioned to fill the leadership void. He resumed his public speaking. In December he married Kathleen Neal, daughter of an African American professor and diplomat and a member of the communication department of the Student Nonviolent Coordinating Committee (SNCC) in Atlanta.

Leads Black Panther Party

Cleaver's notoriety was consolidated with the February of 1968 publication of *Soul on Ice.* The Black Panther Party was by now an internationally known and widely reported phenomenon. Cleaver's leadership in the party, and his support in white and Jewish radical and liberal circles, together with his fine writing abilities and the unlikely story of his life (petty thief to dope seller to rapist to Black Panther leader to the *New York Times* best–seller list) all contributed to his success. The *New York Times* in due course proclaimed *Soul on Ice* one of the ten outstanding books of the year.

In the eclectic and haphazard way that would become more readily apparent later, Cleaver was simultaneously able to please disparate audiences. In *Soul on Ice* some African American radicals probably saw a revolutionary work. The New Left doubtless found it to its liking. There was also much in it for white liberals, and even conservatives, to love.

Cleaver sounded like a true African American radical when he denounced the United States as racist murderers of Malcolm X, destroyers of Paul Robeson and Marcus Garvey, exilers of Robert F. Williams and W. E. B. Du Bois, and bestowers of the Nobel Prize on the moderate and acceptable Martin Luther King Jr. (King was assassinated a mere two months after the book's publication). He denounced the prominence bestowed by the white world on ''Uncle Tom'' entertainers, intellectuals, and athletes.

Yet it was not difficult to see why *Soul on Ice* became a North American best–seller, for there was much in it to please a white audience. Cleaver denounced Elijah Muhammad. He dismissed Muhammad's disciple Muhammad Ali, heavyweight boxing champion, as ''a Black Muslim racist,'' though praising him as ''also a 'free' man.''

Cleaver managed to sound like a white liberal when he saw, in the young white generation, a group who had rejected the colonialism and imperialism of their ancestors. The generation gap among whites, he claimed, was wider than the racial divide in the United States. He assured his apprehensive white readers that African Americans did not want revenge for past wrongs. Although he asserted that ''the ritualistic lynchings and castrations inflicted on Southern blacks by Southern whites'' were no worse than African American ''punk–hunting'' of homosexuals, three pages later Cleaver denounced homosexuality as a ''sickness, just as are baby–rape or wanting to become the head of General Motors.''

The aspect of *Soul on Ice* most calculated to appeal to a white audience was Cleaver's obsession with the white woman question, which dominated the book. His fixation with this question went back to his childhood rejection by a white female schoolmate and a slap from a blond teacher whom he loved. This supposedly prepared him for his life of rapine. In jail, he said, a guard embarrassed him by tearing down the white pin–up from his wall. In jail too, he had a ''nervous breakdown'' after feeling attracted to a photo of the white woman who caused teenager Emmett Till to be lynched in Mississippi. He saw a psychiatrist on this occasion and was placed in a padded cell.

Soul on Ice contained several disparaging references to African American women as ''bitches,'' ''amazons,'' and the like. ''There's a softness about a white woman,'' one of his characters was made to say in a *Soul on Ice* short story. ''But a nigger bitch seems to be full of steel. . . . The white woman is like a goddess. . . . I worship her. I love a white woman's dirty drawers.''

The culmination of all of this was a self–confessed rapist who targeted white women, but only after ''practicing'' on his own kind ''I became a rapist,'' he wrote. ''To refine my technique and *modus operandi,* I started out by practicing on black girls in the ghetto.'' He sought to dignify his madness as acts of insurrection for past racial injustices.

Cleaver's preoccupation with white women led him to adopt a pseudo–scientific notion of super–sexed but mentally deficient African American men as the natural partners for ''ultrafeminine'' white women. In *Soul on Ice* he quoted Norman Podhoretz's envy, expressed in the American Jewish Committee's *Commentary* magazine, of the ''superior physical grace and beauty'' of African Americans. Cleaver seemed to conclude in the work, as Irving Louis Horowitz hinted in another Cleaver quote from *Commentary,* that African American minds "are in a general state of underdevelopment."

Maxwell Geismar, in his introduction to *Soul on Ice,* seemed to accept at face value Cleaver's contention that he was somehow speaking for the generality of African American men on the subject of white women. Cleaver's book fed every negative stereotype of the rapist African American male. One wonders whether the book or extracts published earlier may have emboldened William Styron's distortion of slave revolutionary Nat Turner as a white–woman–fixated idiot. *Soul on Ice* ended, erratically and unconvincingly, with a paean of praise for African American women. "Across the naked abyss of negated masculinity," he wrote, "of four hundred years minus my Balls, we face each other today, my Queen." This sounded like the Negritude poet of an earlier generation who wrote praise songs to naked African women, while snugly ensconced in the embrace of his white wife.

With the Black Panther Party's major leaders in jail, and with the party targeted for annihilation by the FBI, it may be that Cleaver's book escaped the immediate critical intra–party review and debate that it merited. In any event, in a party that considered itself socialist and "inter communal," and viewed African nationalism as racism, Cleaver's views probably found some space to develop unmolested. Future Panther leader Elaine Brown says she read it, loved it, wrote a poem to Cleaver, and felt compelled to entice him to a motel for a night. Bobby Seale and Huey Newton loved it. Seale interpreted it positively as a frank expression of Cleaver's long journey from destitute madness to revolutionary prominence—that is, a sort of *Autobiography of Malcolm X.*

On April 6,1968, two months after the publication of *Soul on Ice,* and two days after the murder of Martin Luther King Jr., Oakland police killed Little Bobby Hutton, Panther treasurer, and wounded Eldridge Cleaver. Cleaver was jailed and his parole rescinded. A judge freed him but the Court of Appeals overruled this decision. Finally even Supreme Court Justice Thurgood Marshall refused to stay the state's intention to return him to jail.

Meanwhile Cleaver, who took credit for steering the BPP into alliance with white radicals, became the presidential nominee for the Peace and Freedom Party. Jerry Rubin was his vice–presidential running mate. Kathleen Cleaver, Bobby Seale, and Huey Newton all ran on the Peace and Freedom Party ticket against other African American candidates. Cleaver argued that African Americans had now realized the dream of the Black Power movement in controlling their own organizations. They could therefore enter into coalitions with whites. Cleaver was less enthusiastic about the short–lived 1968 Black Panther Party–SNCC alliance, though he supported it.

Flees the United States

Unwilling to return to jail, Cleaver fled the United States on November 28, 1968. He surfaced in Cuba, where he remained until 1969. The Cuban authorities kept a wary eye on him, and he accused them of racism. His next stop was Algiers, where he had been deposited by the Cubans, who were anxious to be rid of him.

In September of 1969 Cleaver took 11 journalists—with Elaine Brown and Cleaver being the only African Americans in the group—on a trip to the Soviet Union, North Korea, Vietnam, and China. Cleaver announced to the group that he represented the left wing of the BPP, thereby setting the stage for an angry public rift with Huey Newton.

In Algeria, Cleaver officially launched an international section of the BPP (September of 1970) and was even suspected by some of committing murder. In *A Taste of Power,* Elaine Brown, who spent some time with him in Algeria, claims that he threatened to make her his third murder victim. "I'll bury your ass," Cleaver allegedly said. "I've got a burial ground [in Algiers]. I've put two niggers in the ground already. [Algerian President] Boumédienne doesn't give a fuck."

In 1971 Huey Newton expelled Cleaver from the party. He received a little unsuspected help from the FBI's Cointelpro (Counter Intelligence Program), who were actively working to foment and exacerbate tensions within the African American human rights movement. Newton and Bobby Seale accused Cleaver of pushing the Panthers away from their early emphasis on self–defense and into a posture of reckless aggressiveness. They also accused Cleaver of delivering the party into the undue influence of white hippies, thereby fatally alienating the party's African American base.

Cleaver entered France in 1972 on forged travel documents. In Paris he enlisted the support of such major political figures as François Mitterand, Jacques Chirac, and Valéry Giscard d'Estaing, who eventually helped him regularize his status there. On November 18, 1975, he returned to the United States homesick, disenchanted with the poverty he had seen in other countries, and hoping to collect the substantial royalties for *Soul on Ice,* which the government had frozen since his flight to Cuba.

There was considerable speculation as to whether Cleaver negotiated a deal with the U.S. authorities in order to ease his re–entry. Though he was arrested and briefly imprisoned on his return, he eventually escaped the possible 72–year sentence he faced for attempted murder and other charges arising out of the 1968 shoot–out. In 1980 he was sentenced to probation. Whether there was a formal deal or not, the components of a *de facto* deal are evident based on several changes in Cleaver's attitudes.

First, Cleaver proclaimed his patriotism. Cleaver let it be known that he preferred jail in the United States to freedom anywhere else. The November 19, 1975, *New York Times* reported his discomfiture at being "locked outside the gates of the paradise I once scorned, begging to be let back in."

Second, Cleaver disavowed radicalism. Cleaver now accused Fidel Castro of racism, rejected the Communism he had formerly espoused, and in time became a conservative Republican. He supported Ronald Reagan for president in 1980 and ran for congressional office as a Republican on more than one occasion. He opposed welfare and abortion, advocated capital punishment, and spoke out against Mexican immigration.

Third, Cleaver was born again a Christian while in jail in San Diego, California, in 1976. The man who had eased himself into the leadership of the Black Panther Party, who had charmed influential Jewish liberals into clearing a path for him onto the *New York Times* best–seller list, who had mingled with the leaders of Cuba, the Soviet Union, North Korea, Vietnam, China, Algeria, and France, now moved with practiced effortlessness into the highest echelons of the Christian evangelical movement. Billy Graham, Charles Colson, and Pat Boone became his new associates. The fund–raising efforts of these evangelicals helped make short shrift of his $100,000 bail. Senator Daniel Patrick Moynihan, whose academic views on African American family life have long been a cause of upset, chipped in with $500.

Cleaver, demonstrating the same gusto that had earlier characterized his career as communist sympathizer, Panther, rapist, Nation of Islam minister, and petty criminal, in 1977, formed his own Christian outfit, the Eldridge Cleaver Crusades. Christians opened the doors of their colleges and churches to his lectures. Tiring of the Crusades after two years, he opened a Christlam (fusion of Christianity and Islam) church in Oakland, California. Christlam boasted an auxiliary, ''Guardians of the Sperm,'' which venerated God's presence in this life–giving substance.

Christlam was overtaken by a stint in the Unification Church of the Reverend Sun Myung Moon. Still seeking new fields to conquer, Cleaver became a Mormon in 1982. By this time the traditional African American abhorrence for the racist doctrines of Mormonism may actually have endeared the church to Cleaver.

Fourth, Cleaver made a fool of himself by, among other things, manufacturing and promoting pants called ''cleavers.'' They sported a codpiece—sometimes akin to an athlete's protective cup, sometimes consisting of a tubular protrusion and pouch to accommodate the penis and testicles. Cleaver opened a manufacturing plant and retail outlet for this venture. He himself wore the cleavers for several years, to the possible chagrin of his Christian associates.

Fifth, Cleaver attacked the Arabs and praised the Jews. Cleaver's record on the Arab–Jewish question was erratic and as opportunistic as on every other issue. His rise to fame was greatly facilitated by the Jewish liberals and radicals at *Ramparts* magazine and in the Peace and Freedom Party.

In Algeria Cleaver became an avid supporter of the Palestinian Al Fatah and endorsed the United Nations condemnation of Zionism as racism. The BPP's effort—articulated especially by Huey P. Newton—to distinguish Zionism from Jews *per se,* was largely lost on Jewish commentators. ''The rantings of such Panther leaders as Eldridge Cleaver sound like the nightmarish ravings of Adolf Hitler,'' said one such in a 1971 publication, *The Black Panther Menace.* Cleaver and other Panthers drew Jewish fire for pointing out that Jewish judges (Friedman and Hoffman), had, in their opinion, participated in the unjust persecution of Huey P. Newton and Bobby Seale. According to the same source, the FBI's J. Edgar Hoover likewise blamed Cleaver for ''a flood of anti–Zionist and anti–Semitic propaganda.''

On his return to the United States, Cleaver quickly adopted a pro–Jewish, anti–Arab position, as showcased in his article ''Racism and the Arabs,'' published in *Dissent* in the spring of 1976, a publication edited by radical Jews.

The results were immediate. The Eldridge Cleaver Defense Fund, featuring a motley crew of Jews and pro–Jewish African Americans, sprang into existence. It helped raise his bail money, procured a lawyer, and supported his children. Among its Jewish members were Albert Shanker of the American Federation of Teachers. Shanker had successfully led the late 1960s fight of the Jewish community against African American efforts to control their own children's education in Ocean Hill–Brownsville, Brooklyn, New York. There was also Joseph L. Rauh Jr., a Jewish lawyer and civil rights activist. Bayard Rustin headed the fund. He and his fellow fund raiser A. Philip Randolph were, among other things, leaders of Black Americans to Support Israel Committee (BASIC). Jewish Nat Hentoff and African American Julian Bond were members. The American Jewish Committee's Norman Podhoretz denied allegations that they held a fund–raiser for Cleaver.

The Black Panther Party, which had expelled Cleaver in 1971, was not amused. Elaine Brown and others now accused him of being a Cointelpro double agent. They accused him of murdering Little Bobby Hutton and a couple of other Panthers, including one in Algeria.

Cleaver nevertheless continued on his erratic and seemingly charmed life into the 1980s. His marriage ended in divorce. In 1987 he was arrested for cocaine possession, his Mormonism notwithstanding, and in 1988 was placed on probation for burglary. The media forgot him for a while but in the latter 1990s he reappeared in *People* magazine working with children in Florida and caring for a mentally retarded new son, the child of Cleaver and a white woman. Eldridge Cleaver died on Friday, May 2, 1998, in a Pomona, California, hospital of undisclosed causes. He had suffered from prostate cancer and diabetes.

In retrospect Cleaver seems to have been the consummate opportunist. The Black Panthers exalted the lumpenproletarians—the most destitute of the disenfranchised—but he may have represented their worst traits. The Panthers argued, following Frantz Fanon, that lumpenproletarians, with nothing to lose, were the most revolutionary element in society. Karl Marx, from whom Fanon deviated, saw this element—the hustlers, the petty criminals, those lacking the discipline imposed on the working class by regular employment—as the scum of the earth.

Cleaver's rise to prominence also demonstrates, once again, the power of the larger society to manipulate and appoint African American leadership, even in ostensibly radical circles. There can be no doubt that the promotion of Cleaver by Beverly Axelrod, *Ramparts* magazine, and the *New York Times,* together with his own radical sounding rhetoric, were critical to his acceptance by the Black Panther Party hierarchy.

REFERENCES

Brown, Elaine. *A Taste of Power: A Black Woman's Story.* New York: Pantheon Books, 1992.

Cleaver, Eldridge. *Eldridge Cleaver: Post Prison Writings and Speeches.* Ed. by Robert Scheer. New York: Random House, 1969.

———. *Soul on Fire.* Waco, TX: Word Books, 1978.

———. *Soul on Ice.* New York: Dell, 1968.

———. "Why I Left the U.S. and Why I Am Returning." *New York Times,* November 19, 1995.

"Eldridge Cleaver, '60s Militant, Dies." *Los Angeles Times,* May 2, 1998.

Hill, Norman, ed. *The Black Panther Menace: America's Neo–Nazis.* New York: Popular Library, 1971.

Newton, Huey P. *Revolutionary Suicide.* New York: Harcourt Brace Jovanovich, 1973.

Rout, Kathleen. *Eldridge Cleaver.* Boston: Twayne, 1991.

Seale, Bobby. *Seize the Time.* New York: Random House, 1970. Reprint, Baltimore: Black Classic Press, 1991.

Tony Martin

George Clinton Clement

George Clinton Clement
(1871–1935)
Religious leader, activist

George Clinton Clement was a prominent and highly respected religious leader of the African Methodist Episcopal (AME) Zion Church. As an activist, he worked toward the elimination of racial barriers to blacks in Kentucky.

Born on December 23, 1871, in Mocksville, North Carolina, to Albert Turner and Eveleanor Carter Clement. Converted at an early age, Clement followed his father's career path and also became a Methodist minister. He was licensed to preach September 18, 1888, and ordained a minister of the African Methodist Episcopal Zion Church in 1893. His first ministry was as pastor of the AME Zion church in Cleveland, North Carolina, in 1894. He also pastored churches in other towns and cities in North Carolina, including Zebulon (1895–97), China Grove (1897–98), Charlotte (1898–99), and Salisbury (1899–1900).

Clement went to Salisbury, North Carolina, to attend Livingston College, an AME Zion institution. There he met Emma Clarissa Williams, whom he married on their college commencement day, May 25, 1898. With the exception of the time Emma Clement spent as an assistant teacher at Livingston College in 1899, her entire life was devoted to her husband's ministry, raising their family, and involvement in numerous civic, women's, and religious clubs. She became the 1947 American Mother of the Year, a first for African Americans. Their marriage produced seven children, all of whom graduated from college and became prominent figures in black communities across the country. One son, Rufus Early Clement, became president of Atlanta University.

Clement's education included a bachelor's degree in 1898, master's degree in 1904, and an honorary doctorate of divinity in 1906, all from Livingston College. In 1929 Wilberforce University in Ohio awarded him an honorary doctorate of law degree.

In 1900 Clement moved his family to Louisville, Kentucky, where he accepted the position of pastor for the Twelfth Street African American Episcopal Zion Church. He led the congregation in the purchase of another building on the corner of Thirteenth and Broadway which became known as Broadway Temple AME Zion Church. His expert leadership improved both the financial and spiritual bases of the church during the four years he was pastor. In 1904 Clement was selected to edit the *Star of Zion,* the denomination's periodical. As the editor for 12 years, he encouraged his readers to seek ways to uplift and empower blacks. Clement served as a delegate to the Methodist ecumenical conferences in Toronto, Canada, in 1911; in London, England, in 1921; and in Atlanta, Georgia, in 1931. From 1914 to 1916 he was manager of the AME Zion Publication House in Charlotte, North Carolina. At the May 1916 General Conference meeting in Louisville, Clement was consecrated Bishop of the AME Zion Church in Louisville and the Third District, which included Kentucky, Indiana, and part of North Carolina.

Through his writings in the *Star of Zion,* 1904–16, Clement became influential in the church and the community. For 13 years he served as chairman of the Committee on Church and Race Relations of the Federal Council of Churches of Christ in America. As a member of the council, he served as speaker at both national and international conventions. In *The Fascinating Story of Black Kentuckians,* Alice Dunnigan described him as "thoughtful, logical, sincere and impressive."

In 1920, when the University of Louisville refused to promise that a portion of a proposed million–dollar bond issue include funds for the education of blacks, Clement, Albert E. Meyzeek, and other black leaders in Louisville led a successful campaign to defeat the bond issue. Through the continued efforts of Clement and J. A. C. Lattimore, the University of Louisville finally included opening a college for blacks in its proposal to their board of regents, which lead to the establishment of its Louisville Municipal College in 1925.

Clement was one of the most respected clergymen in the country. He was listed in *Who's Who in Colored America,* the *National Cyclopedia of American Biography,* and *Who's Who of the Colored Race.* His professional involvement and affiliations crossed racial boundaries and included service on the executive committee of the Federal Council of Churches of Christ in America, the executive committee of the Methodist Ecumenical Council, the Historical Commission of World Methodism, and boards of trust of the A.M.E. Zion Publication House, and Livingston and Atkinson colleges. In 1925 he published *Boards for Life's Building.*

Clement was heavily involved in community affairs and served in many capacities, including president of the board of directors of the Reform and Manual Training School for Colored Youth, member of the Southern Cooperative League, vice–president and director of Louisville's First Standard Bank, member of the American Academic Political and Social Science, and member of the Association for the Study of Negro Life and History. Clement was a member of the Commission on Inter–Racial Relations which was actively engaged in civil rights issues. This commission included among its members such prominent moderate Louisville blacks as William H. Steward, James Bond, and Charles H. Parrish Sr. Socially, Clement was a member of the Masons, Order of Eastern Star, and Kappa Alpha Psi Fraternity.

Clement died in Louisville on October 23, 1935, and was buried in the Louisville Cemetery, Louisville, Kentucky. He was one of the most influential religious leaders in Kentucky's history. Deeply devoted to furthering the interests of his race, he sought ways to remedy the racial injustices of his day. His Christian approach to problems earned him the respect and admiration of white and black citizens of Louisville. In *Reminiscences of College Days,* W. H. Fonvielle described Clement as "a country man [who]. . .for a long time looked and acted the part." He reasoned well and was "an earnest and entertaining talker." Clement was described in the *Fascinating Story of Black Kentuckians* as "an outstanding churchman, a devoted husband and father, a man who was more than a friend or neighbor among those where he lived and to those whom he served. An ideal leader, an ideal churchman, and ideal citizen and an ideal friend, he was a hard worker and an uncompromising race champion."

REFERENCES

Dunnigan, Alice A. *The Fascinating Story of Black Kentuckians: Their Heritage and Tradition.* Washington, DC: Associated Publishers, 1982.

Fonvielle, W. F. *Reminiscences of College Days.* Goldsboro, NC: The Author, 1904.

The National Cyclopedia of American Biography. New York: J. T. White, 1950.

Who's Who in Colored America. 3rd ed. Brooklyn: Thomas Yenser, 1933.

COLLECTIONS

The personal papers of George Clement are maintained by his daughter Ruth Clement Bond in Washington, D.C.

Karen Cotton McDaniel

Rufus E. Clement

(1900–1967)

College president, minister

An important educator in the South, for more than 40 years Rufus Clement held various positions as college teacher and dean, then as president of Atlanta University. He developed the university into a leading educational institution that provided graduate study, strengthening its various schools and adding new ones. He successfully worked to improve race relations and eliminate all forms of segregation and discrimination. His election to the Atlanta Board of Education in 1952 made him the first black office holder in Atlanta since 1870.

Rufus Early Clement was born June 26, 1900, in Salisbury, North Carolina, the son of African Methodist Episcopal Zion (AME Zion) bishop George Clinton Clement (1871–1934) and Emma Clarissa Williams Clement (1874–1952). Both parents were graduates of Livingstone College. George Clement was born in Mocksville, North Carolina, and before his elevation to the bishopric in 1916, held ministerial assignments in North Carolina, edited his church organ, the *Star of Zion* from 1904–16, and managed the AME Zion publishing house. Emma Clement was born in Providence, Rhode Island, and in 1946 was chosen the "American Mother of the Year," the first African American woman so honored.

In 1919 Rufus Clement married Pearl Anne Johnson of Sumner, Mississippi; she was an alumna of Livingstone College in Salisbury, North Carolina. The couple had one daughter Alice Clarissa.

Clement also obtained his B.O., with honors, from Livingstone College in 1919. He earned a B.D. from Garrett Biblical Institute, in Evanston, Illinois, and an M.A. from Northwestern University, Evanston, in 1922.

Clement returned to his alma mater, Livingstone College, as an instructor of history in 1922. In 1925 he was elected dean of the college—one of America's youngest college administrators. An ordained minister, he pastored an AME Zion church in Landis, North Carolina, in addition to his duties at Livingstone. Clement, a three–letter athlete during his undergraduate student days at Livingstone, was also baseball coach at Livingstone, and he was an official of the Colored Intercollegiate Athletic Association.

Clement received his Ph.D. as a University Fellow in History at Northwestern University in Evanston in 1930, and in 1931 he was elected the first dean of Louisville Municipal College for Negroes. This was a new educational institution for blacks affiliated with the University of Louisville in Kentucky. In addition to his labors at Louisville, Clement functioned as president of the National Association of Collegiate Deans and Registrars from 1932 to 1934 and as a member of the executive committee of the same organization; and in 1936 he served as president of the National Association of Teachers in Colored Schools. Notwithstanding his administrative duties, Clement found time to contribute articles to various publications, including the *Dictionary of American Biography,* the *Journal of Negro History, Social Forces, Phylon,* and the *Journal of Higher Education for Negroes.*

Heads Atlanta University

Clement was elected president of Atlanta University in 1936. Seven years prior to his election, in 1929, a significant educational revolution in the city of Atlanta brought about the reorganization of Atlanta University as a graduate institution. Originally founded as an undergraduate institution in 1865, Atlanta University established a collaborative plan with several undergraduate institutions in the surrounding area. As a result, one of the first assignments confronting Clement was fostering greater accord among the diverse alumni groups.

Clement discerned that the alumni were divided into two groups: the old Atlanta University group, which was composed of persons who had been graduated before 1929, and those who had received master's degrees since 1931. Therefore, during his first year as president, he addressed himself to the problem by making as many communications as possible with the first group in order to inform them of the developments of Atlanta University as a graduate institution. The results were satisfactory and the Alumni Association made a contribution to the endowment fund with the Ware Professorship (the Wares had been early presidents of Atlanta University) and pledged itself to the advancement of the university in its activities. The new alumni agreed to cooperate with the old to further the university's general interests. It was during Clement's administration that the Atlanta School of Social Work became an integral part of the new university. Originally founded by Jesse O. Thomas in 1920 with a group of social workers and interested laymen, the Atlanta School of Social Work had been independent for a number of years. In 1927 the school began to grow. It became affiliated with Atlanta University in 1933 and was recognized by the American Association of Social Work. Under Clement's administration, the school became an official member of the university on September 1, 1938, at which time it was renamed the Atlanta University School of Social Work. The various colleges in Atlanta offering educational opportunities to black students were located in several sections of the city. Clark College was relocated from south Atlanta to a new campus site in close proximity to Atlanta University in 1941, near Spelman College, Morehouse College, and Morris Brown College. An Interdenominational Theological Center (ITC) was created in 1956, composed of several independent sectarian seminaries. ITC became affiliated with the university. These schools became members of the Atlanta University Center.

During Clement's administration, the School of Library Service, the School of Education, and the School of Business Administration were organized. The university's effort to establish a school of library service was realized when Hampton Institute (now University) announced that its library school would close in May of 1940. As a result of a study sponsored by the American Library Association, Atlanta University officials decided that a library school for blacks was essential. Further, educators agreed that Atlanta University was the logical place for library science training, and the Carnegie Corporation of New York expressed its willingness to give $150,000 to the university for the operation of a library school with a matching grant made by the General Education Board in 1940.

In September of 1941 the School of Library Service opened with an experienced and competent faculty. With the closure at Hampton, the Atlanta University School of Library Service became the only accredited library school in the field of black library education. The establishment of the School of Education was authorized by the Atlanta University trustees. It started on September 19, 1944. The faculty was composed of university professors and members of the departments of education in the Atlanta University Center institutions.

Clement was cognizant of the need of business training for African Americans and immediately developed plans for this. In the spring of 1944, the university, in cooperation with the National Urban League, surveyed business education at black colleges and black–owned businesses. As an outcome of the survey, the trustees sanctioned Clement's proposed organization of the Graduate School of Business Administration to begin work in September of 1946.

W. E. B. Du Bois, a longtime professor at the university, and several other members of faculty had sought funds to support a journal which would deal with race and culture. In 1939, upon Clement's recommendation, the university trustees authorized the publication of a quarterly magazine that would be under the control of an editorial staff composed of university professors, the president, and selected scholars from other institutions, under the editorship of Du Bois. The quarterly made its first appearance in January of 1940, under the title *Phylon, The Atlanta University Review of Race and*

Culture. The name was taken from the Greek word *phylon*, which means a tribe or genetically related group. The magazine launched a successful subscription campaign, and after a while, according to Clement's Report of 1949–50, quoted in *The Story of Atlanta University*, *Phylon* held a unique position in its field as "the only scholarly journal in America whose major concern is that of race and culture."

Fosters Race Relations

Clement identified with the South and was devoted to the improvement of race relations. As early as 1927, while still teaching in North Carolina, he had been elected to the board of the Commission on Inter–racial Cooperation. Clement administered to its political programs. He was identified with the struggle to abolish the poll tax and guarantee voting rights for all citizens.

On January 6, 1944, as a result of a petition signed by Clement; Ralph McGill, editor of the *Atlanta Journal–Constitution*; Arthur J. Moore, bishop in the Methodist Church; Charles S. Johnson, president of Fisk University; and Howard W. Odum of the University of North Carolina at Chapel Hill, the Southern Regional Council (SRC) was chartered by the State of Georgia. According to *The Story of Atlanta University*, the SRC was formed "for the improvement of economic, civic, and racial conditions in the South . . . to attain, through research and action programs, the ideals and practices of equal opportunity for all peoples in the region." It was organized on the campus of Atlanta University and until segregation was outlawed in the South, the university was the site of most of its deliberations.

In 1952 Clement announced his candidacy for membership on the Atlanta Board of Education. He ran as a member–at–large and won handily, receiving the largest majority of any candidate, and defeating his white opponent by a margin of 10,000 votes. He carried eight of the nine wards and became the first black officeholder in Georgia since December 1870. Clement served 14 years on the school board. In 1960, while he was a board member, he devised a plan for the integration of the Atlanta public schools under a federal court decree.

Clement's activities extended into other areas. In 1954 President Dwight D. Eisenhower designated him as one of the nine members of the United Service Organization (USO). Two years later he spent the month of July surveying USO installations in Italy and France, and spoke in England under the sponsorship of the Department of State. In 1957 he attended the World Federation of the United Nations Association in Geneva, Switzerland, as a delegate of the American association. During the following summer, Clement was one of three delegates of the National Education Association (NEA) to the World Confederation of Organizations of the Teaching Profession at Oxford University, and one of 16 from the United States.

On October 1, 1960, Clement observed the independence celebration of Nigeria as an honored guest. This trip, which was financed by the Nigerian government, permitted him to make worthwhile contacts with representatives of many African nations in behalf of the Business Fellowship Program which Atlanta University planned to set up for African students.

Many other distinctions came to Clement as president of Atlanta University. In 1945 he was selected one of the two vice–chairpersons of the American Council on Education. In June of 1948, at the annual celebration of Alumni Day at Northwestern University, Clement accepted the Merit Award "in recognition of worthy achievement which has reflected credit upon Northwestern University and each of her alumni." In the summer of 1949, he accepted an invitation to attend a meeting in Berne, Switzerland, as a delegate of the NEA. At the request of the Mutual Security Agency of the United States Department of State, he was invited in the summer of 1952 to head a mission to Indonesia for the purpose of establishing certain educational resources in that country. He was unable to accept the mission because of business pertaining to the university.

In 1957 Clement was elected an honorary member of Phi Beta Kappa at Brown University. In 1966, *Time* magazine selected Clement as one of the 14 most influential university presidents in America.

Clement was the recipient of honorary degrees from the University of Liberia, Livingstone College, Virginia Union University, Manhattanville College of the Sacred Heart, and Virginia State College.

Clement was associated with a number of important national organizations. He held membership on the boards of directors of the Southern Regional Council, United Nations Association of America, United Negro College Fund, National Science Foundation, and the Institute of International Education. He was also a member of the Advisory Council on African Affairs of the U.S. Department of State. He was chosen by President Lyndon B. Johnson to represent the United States on the occasion of the independence celebration of the African state of Malawi in 1964.

While attending a series of meetings with Atlanta University trustees, Clement died in his room in New York City's Roosevelt Hotel on November 7, 1967. Funeral services were held on the campus of Spelman College, Atlanta, and at Broadway Temple African Methodist Episcopal Zion Church, Louisville, Kentucky, with burial in Louisville Cemetery. He was survived by his widow. He left an important legacy in the field of black higher education, in the integration of the public schools, and in improving race relations.

REFERENCES

Bacote, Clarence A. *The Story of Atlanta University: A Century of Service 1865–1965*. Princeton, NJ: Princeton University Press, 1969.

"The Extracurricular Clout of Powerful College Presidents." *Time* 87 (11 February 1966): 64–65.

Logan, Rayford W., and Michael R. Winston, eds. *Dictionary of American Negro Biography*. New York: Norton, 1982.

COLLECTIONS

The Rufus Clement Papers are in the Special Collections of the Atlanta University Center, Robert W. Woodruff Library, Atlanta.

Casper L. Jordan

James Cleveland
(1931–1991)
Musician, composer, religious worker

James Cleveland

Among the first innovators of modern gospel music, James Cleveland made his mark as a composer, piano player, and arranger. Writing over 400 gospel compositions, his manifold activities forwarded the spread and growth of the genre.

James Cleveland was born on December 3, 1931, in Chicago, the only son of Ben Cleveland. He had three sisters. His grandmother, Mrs. Annie Hicks, was a devout member of Pilgrim Baptist Church, where the renowned music director, Thomas Dorsey, led the gospel choir. Cleveland first performed in public with the Pilgrim Baptist gospel choir when he was eight years old, and later joined the junior choir.

Counts Mahalia Jackson and Roberta Martin as Influences

Cleveland's musical development during adolescence was profoundly influenced by Mahalia Jackson and Roberta Martin. He took every opportunity possible to listen to Jackson and patterned his own style of piano–playing from that of Roberta Martin. He took lessons in gospel piano from the Roberta Martin Singers' organist Lucy Smith and, informally, from Martin herself.

Under Martin's influence Cleveland started composing while he was still a teenager. An early song, ''Grace Is Sufficient,'' was presented at the 1948 Baptist convention. Roberta Martin began publishing his songs for a flat fee of $40 a song. Having injured his beautiful boy soprano voice through strain, it took a number of years for his mature, raspy baritone voice to settle. He then became a lead singer.

Around 1949 Cleveland joined the Gospelaires, a group formed by former Roberta Martin singers Bessie Folk and Norsalus McKissack, as pianist and occasional third lead. His first recording with this group was ''Oh, What a Time'' with this group on the Apollo label in 1950. He also toured with Mahalia Jackson during the early 1950s. In 1954, Cleveland became prominent when he joined the Caravans, which had been formed the preceding year by Albertina Walker. Then in 1955 his singing began to attract attention as he sang on the Caravans' first big hits ''The Solid Rock'' and ''Old Time Religion.'' Cleveland continued to work with the Caravans through the late 1950s, left them for a while to join the Gospel All Stars, and then briefly rejoined the Caravans. In 1959 he formed his own group the Gospel Chimes, whose most notable member was Jessy Dixon, who would go on to establish his own group, the Jessy Dixon Singers.

In 1959 Cleveland moved to Detroit to become music director at the New Bethel Baptist Church, pastored by C. L. Franklin. In addition to his other work, Cleveland trained Franklin's daughter Aretha. Although she took a different direction in music, Cleveland and Aretha Franklin joined forces with the Southern California Community Choir in the spring of 1972 in a benefit performance that was recorded and released as the outstanding gospel double album *Amazing Grace.* This album reached number seven on the pop charts, sold half a million copies in its first year, and won a Grammy award in 1973 as the Best Gospel Soul Performance.

In Detroit, Cleveland worked as a musician and also preached as a licensed minister of the Church of God in Christ. His musical activities brought him into contact with Charles Crain and Leslie Bush of the Prayer Tabernacle. Cleveland recorded ''The Love of God'' with the Voices of Tabernacle Choir on the Hob label. This became a local hit and attracted the attention of other recording companies. The persistence of Herman Lubinsky of Savoy Records persuaded Cleveland to sign with that label in 1960.

The year 1963 brought an important breakthrough: ''Peace Be Still,'' Cleveland's third album recorded with the Angelic Choir of Nutley, New Jersey, became a major hit. It remained on the gospel charts for more than 15 years. In a field where a sale of 5,000 records constitutes a 'hit,' it sold over 750,000 in the first ten years and topped one million by 1985. The figure is even more impressive since practically all of the buyers were from the black community. Cleveland's releases now sold an average of some 70,000 copies, and Savoy gave him a guaranteed annual salary for recording four albums every year. By the late 1960s Cleveland was affluent, especially by the standards of the music field. Although he did accept engagements such as a two–week stint at the Olympia Theater in Paris, France, in 1966, he resisted the temptation to move into club performances as other gospel singers were beginning to do.

In 1963 Cleveland moved to Los Angeles to become pastor of the New Greater Harvest Baptist Church and formed the James Cleveland Singers. In 1968 he convened the Gospel Music Workshop of America, which competes directly with the older Thomas Dorsey Gospel Convention. Beginning with 3,000 people in the first year, by the mid–1980s the workshop was attracting 15,000 of 100,000 members from all over the world.

In 1969 Cleveland founded the Southern California Community Choir; his example was followed by other workshop chapters, resulting in the foundation of many other community choirs. Cleveland also founded in Los Angeles the Cornerstone Institutional Baptist Church in 1970. It grew into one of the largest congregations in the city and moved into a $2 million church with seating for 1,250 in 1983.

Cleveland lived in a house in View Park and provided houses for his grandmother and his three sisters. He and his wife were divorced, and his daughter LaShone lived with her mother, who had remarried.

James Cleveland died on February 9, 1991. Four thousand people attended his funeral at the Shrine Auditorium in Los Angeles, for which Stevie Wonder and Shirley Caesar, among others, sang. The celebratory note of the funeral was somewhat obscured by later developments, including a fight over the disposition of the church property, a dispute about his estate, and a suit alleging that Cleveland had infected a young man with HIV.

Still Cleveland's accomplishments during his lifetime must not be forgotten. He was an outstanding gospel performer and composer of his era whose albums sold millions of copies, winning him three Grammys. Moreover, he was the first gospel performer to claim a star on Hollywood's Walk of Fame. In 1975 Cleveland received the National Association of Negro Musicians Award and in 1976 the NAACP Image Award.

REFERENCES

"'Adopted' Son of Late James Cleveland Seeks Share of $6 Mil Estate." *Jet* 81 (2 March 1992): 62.

Broughton, Viv. *Black Gospel.* Poole, England: Blanford Press, 1985.

Current Biography Yearbook. New York: H. W. Wilson, 1985, 1991.

"Factions Feud Over Fate of Cornerstone Baptist in Wake of Cleveland's Death." *Jet* 80 (12 August 1991): 28–29.

Garland, Phyl. *The Sound of Soul.* Chicago: Henry Regnery, 1969.

Heilbut, Tony. *The Gospel Sound.* New York: Simon and Schuster, 1971.

"James Cleveland Infected L.A. Youth With HIV, $9 Mil. Lawsuit Claims." *Jet* 81 (2 March 1992): 62.

"James Cleveland: King of Gospel." *Ebony* 24 (November 1968): 74–82.

"Thousands Gather In L.A. to Mourn James Cleveland." *Jet* 79: (11 March 1991): 28–30.

"A Week of Gospel Happiness." *Ebony* 28 (November 1972): 86–92.

Robert L. Johns

Johnnie Cochran
(1937–)
Lawyer

Johnnie Cochran is best known for his work as a primary defense lawyer in the 1995 O.J. Simpson murder case. He is more aptly acknowledged by many as a legal hero who actively pursues justice and fair treatment in a system that often is blinded by its own prejudices. Cochran has handled cases, not only for the rich and famous, but for average citizens who found themselves powerless against injustice.

Johnnie L. Cochran Jr. was born in Shreveport, Louisiana, on October 2, 1937, to Hattie Bass and Johnnie L. Cochran Sr. He was the eldest of four siblings including Pearl, Martha Jean, and RaLonzo. In 1945, the family moved to California as Johnnie Cochran Sr. pursued his life–long career as an insurance salesman. Armed with his father's generosity and entrepreneurial spirit and his mother's strong Christian faith and belief in family, Cochran went on to earn his B.S. degree from the University of California, Los Angeles in 1959 and a J.D. in 1962 from Loyola University School of Law in Los Angeles.

In 1965, Cochran began his legal career as a prosecutor in the criminal division of the deputy city attorney's office in Los Angeles. After only two years, he left to form the legal firm of Cochran, Atkins and Evans. In 1966, Cochran successfully prosecuted the murder case against Los Angeles police officer Jerold Bova. Bova had been accused of killing Leonard Deadwyler, a black man who was shot while driving his pregnant wife to a hospital. Although the shooting of Deadwyler may have been accidental, attempts by the Los Angeles Police Department to cover up the incident were ruled as intentional misconduct.

Johnnie Cochran

In 1971 Cochran represented Elmer "Geronimo" Pratt, a former Black Panther who was charged with a robbery and murder that took place in 1968. Because the weapon used in the crime was seized at a house frequented by the Panthers and Pratt was alleged to have confessed his involvement in the crime to a party member, he was convicted.

It was the case of Geronimo Pratt that transformed Cochran's perception of the justice system and solidified his mission to represent victims of injustice. Cochran, like many others both inside and outside of law enforcement, believed that Pratt was innocent. Cochran stated in his autobiography *Journey to Justice* that "We didn't know it at the time, but Geronimo Pratt had been singled out by the FBI as the Los Angeles Panther it most wanted off the street." The case taught Cochran a valuable lesson: "Always question the official version." Pratt served over 26 years in prison, but Cochran was able to secure his release on June 10, 1997.

Cochran continued his private practice until 1978 when he was sworn in as the first African American assistant district attorney and the third ranking prosecutor in the county of Los Angeles. While in that capacity he initiated several reforms, including the Domestic Violence Council, the Sexual Assault Program, and the Rollout Unit. The Rollout Unit assigned a deputy district attorney and a district attorney's investigator to every police shooting case within Cochran's jurisdiction. In 1982, Cochran returned to his private practice.

Since 1982, Cochran's legal practice has flourished. He has represented such famous clients as Michael Jackson, who was accused of sexual molestation; Snoop Doggy Dog, the controversial rapper accused of murder; "Different Strokes" television star Todd Bridges, accused of shooting a man in a alleged drug deal; and football star Jim Brown, accused of rape. He has been a successful defense attorney in both high profile and lesser–known cases.

Cochran has held many professional and community positions within the Los Angeles area. He served as adjunct professor at the Los Angeles School of Law and at the Loyola University School of Law. In 1994, he served as chairman of the Rules Committee of the Democratic National Convention. In 1990, Cochran became the only lawyer to win both the Criminal Trial Lawyer of the Year Award and the Los Angeles Civil Trial Lawyer of the Year Award in the same year. In a humanitarian gesture, he donated funds to the Los Angeles Family Housing Corp. These funds helped to create Cochran Villa, a housing development that opened in 1991. In 1994 and 1995 he received the Man of the Year Award from the Brotherhood Crusade, a philanthropic organization devoted to funding community programs throughout Los Angeles. The Turner Broadcasting Systems also presented him with the Trumpet Award.

In 1994 Cochran served as one of the primary defense lawyers for O. J. Simpson, a former football star and celebrity accused of murdering his former wife and her friend. In his defense of Simpson, Cochran questioned the validity of the evidence presented by the prosecution and challenged the jury to strike a blow against racial intolerance within law enforcement. In 1995, the jury acquitted Simpson. The O.J. Simpson case propelled Cochran into the national spotlight.

In his autobiography *Journey to Justice,* Cochran remarked that Martin Luther King Jr.'s statement: "If you don't stand for something, you'll fall for anything," has deeply influenced both his legal career and personal life. Although he has achieved much, Cochran is most proud of his children. He has two daughters, Melodic and Tiffany, from his first marriage to Barbara Berry. He also has a son, Jonathan, from his longtime relationship with a girlfriend. In 1985, Cochran married for the second time to Sylvia Dale Cochran.

Current address: Law Office of Johnnie L. Cochran Jr., 4929 Wilshire Boulevard, Suite 1010, Los Angeles, CA 90010.

REFERENCES

The African American Almanac. Detroit: Gale Research, 1997.

Cochran, Johnnie L. Jr., with Tim Rutten. *Journey to Justice.* New York: One World Book, 1996.

Gleick, Elizabeth. "Johnnie Cochran Jr." *Time* 146 (25 December 95): 102.

Weathers, Diane. "The Other Side of Johnnie Cochran." *Essence* 26 (November 1995): 86.

Who's Who among African Americans, 1998–99. 10th ed. New York: Gale Research, 1997.

Leaŕtin LaVerne Bracks

Daniel Coker

(1780–1846)

Religious leader, colonizer, abolitionist

An important early religious leader, Daniel Coker fanned the discontent among black members of the Methodist Episcopal church in Baltimore and led many into an independent black Methodist church which became one of the major founding components of the African Methodist Episcopal (AME) Church. As with so many early notable American blacks, his life is known only in broad outline.

Daniel Coker was born Isaac Wright to a slave father, Edward Wright, and a white indentured servant Susan Coker in 1780 in Frederick or Baltimore County in Maryland. From his mother's prior marriage, he had at least one older white half–brother. According to information collected by Daniel Payne in his history of the AME church, this brother was also named Daniel Coker and refused to go to school unless Isaac Wright accompanied him. While very young, Isaac Wright ran away to New York City. There he adopted the name of his brother, became a Methodist, and was ordained a deacon by Francis Asbury, one of the founding bishops of the Methodist Episcopal church in the United States.

Around 1800 the free blacks of Baltimore received tacit permission to establish a school. Coker and George Collins were asked to be teachers. Since Coker was a runaway slave, he could not appear in public until his purchase had been arranged. Opening with 17 students in 1802, Coker's school grew to as many as 150 when he gave up teaching in 1816. He then taught in the African Bethel Church to 1820.

Coker joined the black Methodists at the Sharp Street Church. There he soon became a leader due to his position as an ordained deacon, his ability as a preacher, and his education. (Most of the early black exhorters in Baltimore were illiterate.) David Smith, a preacher and an associate, asserted that Coker became "the leading spiritual overseer of the Colored M. E. Church of Baltimore." An excellent singer, Coker established the first choir in the Sharp Street Church. A writer as well, he published in Baltimore an anti–slavery tract called *A Dialogue Between a Virginian and an African Minister* in 1810.

Black Methodists in Baltimore experienced difficulties in their relations with the parent white church similar to those faced by blacks in Philadelphia and Charleston. Between 1785 and 1787 blacks withdrew from white congregations to form Sharp Street Church, which retained an uneasy relation with the parent denomination. Early in the nineteenth century, Coker became the catalyst building black discontent in Maryland into a complete break. He first tried to get exhorters from the Eastern Shore to go along with his plans for a separatist church. When they refused, he formed a secret group of supporters in Baltimore. They continued weekly meetings and became unanimously and firmly committed to separation. On May 9, 1815, they selected the name the African Methodist

Daniel Coker

Bethel Society for their group but seemed to have delayed their open break from the Sharp Street Church until the end of the year.

Coker was in contact with Richard Allen, the leader of the black Methodists in Philadelphia, and the two men coordinated a complete separation in Baltimore and Philadelphia. In Baltimore the open split probably occurred in December 1815, some three weeks before the Philadelphia Methodists won legal recognition of their ownership of church building. When news of the event in Philadelphia reached Baltimore, Coker preached a "Sermon delivered extempore in the African Methodist Episcopal Church in the city of Baltimore, on the 21st of January, 1816, to a numerous concourse of people, on account of the colored people gaining their church (Bethel) in the Supreme Ct. of the State of Pennsylvania," which can be found in Aptheker's documentary history.

Once a large number of blacks withdrew in a body from the Sharp Street Church, Coker moved swiftly to consolidate the newly independent congregation and rented a Presbyterian church as a temporary meeting place. By the following Tuesday seven or eight study and prayer groups had been formed, and by the following Sunday Coker and his associates had agreed to buy a large church in Fish Street for $12,000.

Conference Establishes AME Church

In April 1816 representatives from Baltimore; Philadelphia; Wilmington, Delaware; Attenborough, Pennsylvania; and Salem, New Jersey, met in Philadelphia to organize a new denomination, the African Methodist Episcopal Church. On

April 9 Coker was elected the first bishop; the following day he declined the nomination. According to Coker's Baltimore associate David Smith, dissention arose because of Coker's light color. Smith wrote, "[Him] being nearly white, the people said they could not have an *African Connection* with a man as light as Daniel Coker at its head; therefore the Rev. Richard Allen was their choice." This account has been contested, but its plausibility is supported by the difficulties Coker encountered later as agent for the American Colonization Society in Africa, when he was attacked by unmixed black colonizers for being a mulatto.

On April 10, 1818, the Baltimore Conference found Coker guilty on an unknown charge. After another committee examined the work of the trial committee, the verdict was upheld and Coker was expelled from the denomination. He was restored to his position as a minister in 1819.

Coker accepted the offer of the Maryland Colonization Society to accompany the first ship of free blacks to be repatriated to Africa (efforts which would eventually result in the founding of Liberia). The expedition on the navy store ship *Elizabeth* set sail on January 31, 1820, and was paid for by U.S. government. Coker's published journal revealed that he acted alongside the two white agents of the society as a leader of the expedition.

When the colonists were transferred from the British Sierra Leone to Sherbro Island, where the nucleus of an independent settlement was to be established, dissention and disease played havoc with the poorly sited new town. Since the last white agent had died in Sierra Leone, Coker became acting agent for the society and responsible for the people and the property of the government and the society. He acquitted himself well, but the settlers on Sherbro Island had to be taken back to Sierra Leone. On March 8, 1821, Coker was replaced as agent, since the policy of the Colonization Society was to appoint only white agents. The abilities Coker demonstrated as interim agent were rewarded with a present of $150.

Coker elected to remain in the British colony with his family when the attempt to develop the settlement of the future Liberia was made. He founded a church in Freetown, where he lived until his death in 1846.

Daniel Coker exemplified two prominent themes of his era: the impulse towards creation of separate black churches and the problem of repatriation to Africa. His anti–slavery position and his quest to build black institutions were important among blacks. Few blacks followed him into the colonizing effort, however, and Richard Allen and the his church would become outspoken opponents of the colonization societies shortly after Coker's decision to leave the United States.

REFERENCES

Coker, Daniel. *Journal of Daniel Coker. . .on a Voyage for Sherbro, in Africa.* Baltimore: Edward J. Coale, 1820.

George, Carol V. R. *Segregated Sabbaths.* New York: Oxford, 1973.

Graham, Leroy. *Baltimore: The Nineteenth Century Black Capital.* Lanham, MD: University Press of America, 1982.

Huberich, Charles Henry. *The Political and Legislative History of Liberia.* Vol. 1. New York: Central Book Company, 1947.

Logan, Rayford W., and Michael R. Winston, eds. *Dictionary of American Negro Biography.* New York: Norton, 1982.

Payne, Daniel A. *History of the AME Church.* Nashville: AME Sunday School Union, 1891.

———. *Recollections of Seventy Years.* Nashville: AME Sunday School Union, 1888.

Smith, David. *Biography of Rev. David Smith.* Xenia, OH: Xenia Gazette Office, 1881.

Wesley, Charles H. *Richard Allen: Apostle of Freedom.* Washington, DC: Associated Publishers, 1935. Reprint, 1969.

Robert L. Johns

Nat "King" Cole

(1919–1965)

Musician, singer, composer, entertainer

Nat "King" Cole was one of this country's most successful, versatile, and beloved performers. He was the first black to have national radio and television shows. He began to win major recognition with the cafe–society crowd in the 1940s, primarily as a pianist. As such, he was an important figure in the transition from swing era styles to modern jazz. His career as a singer was launched in 1943 and his vocal contributions became "unforgettable." As Cole explained to *Time* magazine, "I'm an interpreter of stories, and when I perform, it's like I'm just sitting down at my piano and telling fairy stories."

Nathaniel Adams Coles, the youngest son of Reverend Edward James and Perlina Adams Coles, was born in Montgomery, Alabama, on March 17, 1919. The family consisted of four boys and one girl. In addition to Nathaniel, brothers Isaac, Eddie, and Freddie all became professional musicians. Sister Evelyn was also a musician, though nonprofessional.

In 1924 the family moved to Chicago where Edward Coles assumed the pastorate of True Light Baptist Church; Nat, meanwhile, was surrounded by the best of jazz during the 1920s and 1930s. In addition, the family lived within four blocks of the old Grand Terrace, home of the Earl "Fatha" Hines Orchestra. Earl became young Nathaniel's idol. By age 12 Coles had become the church organist and sang in the church choir, which his mother directed. All of the Coles children's first musical instruction came from their mother.

Nat Coles attended Wendell Phillips High School, where he encountered one of Chicago's finest musical pedagogues, Walter Dyett. While at Phillips, he played in various combos

Nat ''King'' Cole

and organized his first band, consisting of 12 pieces. Though the leader was only a teenager himself, according to Henry Ford as quoted in Dempsey Travis's *An Autobiography of Black Jazz:*

> He was authoritative without being dictatorial, and he was able to whip a bunch of undisciplined teenagers into a music unit in less than sixty days. His objective was to make us sound like Earl ''Fatha'' Hines's band.

The group's name was Royal Dukes and it collected one dollar and fifty cents for its one–night stands.

When his brother Eddie formed a band called the Rogues of Rhythm, Nat Coles became the pianist. Their pay was a substantial improvement—$18 a week. Maria Cole, his second wife, a singer and mother of his children, wrote:

> Eddie, Nat and the Rogues eventually joined a revue called ''Shuffle Along.'' It was while playing piano in the revue that Nat, who was then only 17–years old, met dancer Nadine Robinson, whom he later married. When ''Shuffle Along'' got ready to shuffle westward, . . . leader Eddie Coles chose to stay behind. Nat Coles chose to go.

Coles became arranger–musical director of the Broadway road company of ''Shuffle Along'' shortly following high school graduation in 1936. The show folded in Long Beach, California, in 1937. After ''giggling'' at various ''joints'' in Los Angeles for about a year, Coles formed the King Cole Trio (minus the final ''s''). Coles was pianist, Oscar Moore, guitarist, and Wesley Prince, string bassist. Originally scheduled to be a quartet, when the fourth member, drummer Lee Young, failed to show on opening night at the Swanee Inn, the trio was born.

Nat Cole Named King

The King Cole Trio was formed in California in 1938. Rumor has it that the ''King'' title was given to him when the trio appeared in Hollywood and the manager urged him to wear a gold paper crown. Another speculation is that a patron placed a crown on his head and the title ''King'' followed.

It was 1940 before the trio became fully accepted. But the jazz community never forgave Cole for moving into the commercial arena. In later years, if he had desired to return to the ''purity'' of jazz, his new lifestyle would not have permitted it. Albert McCarthy wrote:

> Cole's success as a popular singer virtually robbed jazz of a talented pianist. . . . Prior to that date Cole's vocals had occupied a chorus or so on otherwise instrumental recordings by his piano–guitar–bass trio.

By 1954 John S. Wilson of the *New York Times* wrote:

> Cole has seen fit to make his transition complete so that in place of a pianist who occasionally plays the piano. . . . Cole has developed an alarming ability to lend credence to even the most atrocious Tin Pan Alley products.

His first big hit, in 1943, was his own ''Straighten Up and Fly Right,'' based on one of his father's sermons. With his recording of ''The Christmas Song'' in 1947, his fame reached phenomenal levels. His recordings were selling a million copies each. Many believe his most sensational recording is Cole's 1948 hit ''Nature Boy.'' According to James Haskins:

> Within a week, it was the number one song in the country, and Nat King Cole became one of the first black male singers to accomplish a nearly complete crossover to the white market. . . . His recordings . . . consistently topped the white and black record charts for many years.

A succession of hits followed: ''Lush Life,'' ''Mona Lisa,'' ''Frosty the Snow Man,'' ''Unforgettable,'' ''Sweet Lorraine,'' ''Too Young,'' ''I Love You for Sentimental Reasons,'' ''Chestnuts Roasting on an Open Fire,'' ''It's Only a Paper Moon,'' ''Embraceable You,'' ''Caravan,'' ''When I Fall in Love,'' ''Mood Indigo,'' and many others. Maria Cole's complete discography in her 1971 biography listed more than 800 titles released between November of 1943 and March of 1965.

The King Cole Trio was an official unit in 1939, but attracted wide attention in 1943 with its recording of Cole's *Straighten Up and Fly Right.* Gradually, his audience began to request more vocals. By 1952, he was more of a popular singer than a jazz pianist. The King Cole Trip was a summer 1946 replacement for Bing Crosby on the *Kraft Music Hall* radio show, the same year that the trio appeared in four musical motion pictures. Cole's first European tour was in 1950. In 1955 he made ten guest appearances for CBS–TV and was the subject and featured star of the movie, *The Nat "King" Cole Musical Story,* produced by Universal Pictures. In 1958 he was honored by the Ralph Edwards television show, *This Is Your Life.* Maria Cole, Nat's second wife, following his divorce from his first wife in 1946, collaborated with writer Louie Robinson on the intimate biography *Nat King Cole,* published in 1971, six years following her husband's death.

Not all of Cole's experiences were pleasant ones. When he refused to join the NAACP in speech–making—though he attended many benefits for the organization—a press release suggested that he flatly refused to take out a membership in the NAACP. Blacks referred to him as a sort of "Uncle Tom." Cole saw this as a public insult and was infuriated. Only at the insistence of his wife and manager did he join the organization.

In the all–white neighborhood of Hancock Park in Los Angeles, where his luxurious 20–room house was located, there was extreme hostility when Cole and his wife moved in because they were black. Only his fame brought any kind of tolerance. A national sponsor could not be found to keep his extremely successful television show on the air in 1956–57. Then he was viciously attacked by six white men while he was performing in an integrated show before a segregated audience in Birmingham, Alabama. Finally, the government's claim that Cole owed taxes amounting to some $150,000 was believed to be a contributing factor to his acute ulcers in 1953, which caused him to collapse during an Easter Sunday concert at Carnegie Hall in New York City.

Cole appeared successfully in several film musicals, including *Breakfast in Hollywood* (1946), *China Gate* (1957), and *St. Louis Blues* (1958). In the latter, Cole starred as W. C. Handy. His final film was *Cat Ballou,* completed prior to his February 15, 1965, death. He died at St. John's Hospital in Santa Monica, California, on February 15, 1965, from complications following an operation for lung cancer. He was 45. More than 500,000 letters and postcards arrived during his hospitalization. Visitors included major personalities from the world of show business. Besides his wife, Nat King Cole left four daughters and a son.

Be it jazz or pop, piano or voice, Cole was a pioneer. According to Eileen Southern, the King Trio was one of the first jazz combos; the trio was "the first instrumental group to have a sponsored radio series," and Cole, along with William "Billie" Eckstine, was one of the first black entertainers to earn international attention "as a singer independent of association with an orchestra." His legendary status, in live performance and on recordings, was the result of sheer talent, hard work, good advice, and strategic planning.

On February 17, 1965, it was announced that a permanent memorial would be erected at Los Angeles's new music center in honor of Cole. Cole was selected posthumously to receive the Lifetime Achievement Award at the 32nd Grammy Awards Ceremony in 1990, and Capitol Records declared February of 1990 as Nat King Cole month.

Becomes Unforgettable

Cole's songs are almost as familiar today as they were when he was alive. He was a consistent winner of popularity polls conducted by *Down Beat, Metronome, Esquire,* and *Billboard.* His gifted singing daughter Natalie used the electronic innovations of recent years to release a duo adaptation with her father. The remixed version of the original 1961 song "Unforgettable" earned her Grammy Awards for record of the year and album of the year in 1991.

Nat King Cole, without a doubt, paved the way for future African American entertainers on the stage, in radio, movies, and television. Both the name and the music have endured.

REFERENCES

Berendt, Joachim. *The Jazz Book: From New Orleans to Rock and Free Jazz.* Rev. ed. Westport, CT: Lawrence Hill and Co., 1973.

Cole, Maria, with Louis Robinson. *Nat King Cole: An Intimate Biography.* New York: William Morrow, 1971.

Current Biography Yearbook. New York: H. W. Wilson, 1956.

Ellington, Edward Kennedy. *Music is My Mistress.* Garden City, NY: Doubleday, 1973.

Gourse, Leslie. *Unforgettable: The Life and Mystique of Nat King Cole.* New York: St. Martin's Press, 1991.

Haskins, James. *Black Music in America: A History Through Its People.* New York: Harper Collins, 1987.

Logan, Rayford W., and Michael R. Winston, eds. *Dictionary of American Negro Biography.* New York: Norton, 1982.

McCarthy, Albert, and others. *Jazz on Record: A Critical Guide to the First 50 Years, 1917–1967.* London: Hanover Books, 1968.

"Nat King Cole, 45, is Dead of Cancer." *New York Times,* February 16, 1976.

"Remember the Public." *Time* 58 (30 July 1951): 63.

Southern, Eileen. *Biographical Dictionary of Afro–American and African Musicians.* Westport, CT: Greenwood Press, 1982.

Travis, Dempsey J. *An Autobiography of Black Jazz.* Chicago: Urban Research Institute, 1983.

"Versatile Jazzman." *New York Times,* July 11, 1954.

D. Antoinette Handy

William T. Coleman Jr.

(1920–)

Lawyer, corporate officer, federal official

Born in a nation with both unwritten rules and codified laws that prevented blacks from achieving their potential, William T. Coleman broke those rules and helped tear out those laws during a life defined by the word "achievement."

Coleman's resume is sprinkled with firsts in the legal, corporate, and government sectors. Through strength of character, this man of great intellect and judgment reached his potential. His many accomplishments were acknowledged by President Bill Clinton when he awarded Coleman the Presidential Medal of Freedom in 1995.

William Thaddeus Coleman Jr. was born in the Germantown district of Philadelphia on July 7, 1920. He was the second of three children born to William Thaddeus and Laura Beatrice Mason Coleman. He married Lovida Hardin, a Boston University graduate and daughter of a New Orleans physician, on February 10, 1945. The couple had three children: William T. III, Lovida H. Jr., and Hardin L. Coleman.

Coleman was born into a middle–class family that counted six generations of teachers and Episcopal ministers on one side of the family, and numerous social workers on the other. His father, William T. Coleman Sr., was the director of the Quaker–supported Germantown boys club for 40 years. Through his father and other family members, young William met some of the country's greatest black leaders, including W. E. B. Du Bois and Thurgood Marshall. From the time he was 10– or 12–years old he dreamed of becoming a lawyer, and would spend vacation days slipping into courtrooms trying to absorb as much as he could.

Coleman attended a racially segregated elementary school before entering Germantown High School, which was all white save for a contingent of seven token black students. An incident at the high school summed up the sort of racism that was a constant in that day. When he tried joining the all–white swimming team, he was suspended from school. Later, school officials reinstated him but cut the sport until he graduated.

Though Coleman earned excellent grades in high school, they were attained in an atmosphere of bigotry in which he was not encouraged by his teachers. Racism existed in higher education as well, but did not prevent him from persevering and excelling. He received his B.A. degree summa cum laude from the University of Pennsylvania. To fulfill his childhood dream of becoming a lawyer, he entered the Harvard Law School in 1941.

World War II prevented Coleman from gaining his degree promptly, but gave him some valuable on–the–job training instead. In 1943 he dropped out of law school to join the U.S. Army Air Corps. Although he had completed but a single year of legal studies, he was assigned as defense counsel in 18 court–martial proceedings. Of those, he won 16 acquittals, with one of the two convictions later reversed.

After the war, Coleman returned to Harvard. He became the first black ever to serve on the board of editors of the *Harvard Law Review*. It was there that he first met a student named Elliot Richardson, with whom he would cross paths throughout his career. In 1946 he earned his LL.B. degree magna cum laude, graduating at the top of his class. As a Langdell Fellow, he stayed on at Harvard for an additional year of study.

Coleman was admitted to the Pennsylvania bar in 1947 and quickly garnered a position as law secretary to Judge Herbert F. Goodrich of U.S. Court of Appeals for the Third Circuit. After several months in that job, he left it for an even more prestigious position. In 1948 he became a law clerk to U.S. Supreme Court Associate Justice Felix Frankfurter, becoming the first black to serve in that capacity for the nation's highest court.

One of the other clerks in Frankfurter's office was Richardson. They soon became good friends, regularly arriving early to read poetry together for an hour (they preferred W. H. Auden and Shakespeare) before getting their official duties underway. Their friendship lasted long beyond their stay there, with Richardson becoming godfather to Coleman's daughter.

After Coleman's clerkship ended in 1949, the young attorney was made an associate at the eminent New York law firm of Paul, Weiss, Rifkind, Wharton, and Garrison. While there, he was approached by Thurgood Marshall, the founder and head of the NAACP Legal Defense and Educational Fund (NAACP–LDF). Marshall told Coleman that he was working on cases that the NAACP hoped would lead to the end of segregation and asked Coleman to volunteer his help. Coleman was up to the challenge. "I would work at Paul, Weiss from nine to six and then go to L.D.E.F. 'til 10 or 11 and then back to Paul, Weiss," he was quoted as saying later in a *New York Times* article. "On weekends, I would work with him (Marshall) again." They became good friends, with Coleman becoming the future Supreme Court justice's personal lawyer.

An opportunity for Coleman to return to Philadelphia arose three years later. District attorney and future Philadelphia mayor Richardson Dilworth offered him a spot on his staff. Sensing that he would just be the city's token black associate district attorney, Coleman turned him down. When Dilworth came back with an invitation to join his prominent Philadelphia law firm, Dilworth, Paxon, Kalish, Levy and Green, Coleman accepted. In so doing, he became the first black in the history of Philadelphia to join a white firm.

Works in Civil Rights

Coleman continued to work in civil rights on his own time. The five cases he worked for the NAACP during that period led to the historic Supreme Court decision in *Brown v. Board of Education* (1954), which ended school segregation. Coleman, in fact, was coauthor of the brief presented to the court in the case. In the coming years he would defend freedom riders and other civil rights workers in cases throughout the South. He also served as cocounsel on the landmark case, *McLaughlin v. Florida* (1964), which established the constitutionality of interracial marriages.

At Dilworth, Paxon, he specialized in corporate and antitrust litigation, gaining recognition for his expertise in transportation law. Philadelphia and Cincinnati were among the cities he represented in mass transit and labor matters. He would go on to serve as special counsel and negotiator for both the Philadelphia and the Southeastern Pennsylvania Transportation Authorities. He became a partner at the firm in

1966; soon after, his election to senior partner was reflected in the name change to Dilworth, Paxon, Kalish, Levy and Coleman.

In 1959 President Dwight D. Eisenhower asked Coleman, a longtime Republican, to serve on the President's Commission on Employment Policy, which dealt with increasing minority hiring in the government. It was the first of several presidential commissions on which Coleman would serve over the next two decades for Presidents Kennedy, Johnson, and Nixon.

Coleman's knack for high finance and his understanding of labor issues were key to his being courted to join the boards of many corporations. He accepted the invitations of Penn Mutual Life Insurance, First Pennsylvania Banking and Trust, the Philadelphia Electric Company, and the Western Savings Fund Society. As he gained prominence, his board memberships took on a more national character, including Pan American World Airways, the Rand Corporation, and the American Stock Exchange.

In 1964 Coleman was named senior consultant and assistant counsel to the Warren Commission, which was charged with investigating the assassination of John F. Kennedy. It was as a member of that body that Coleman first met Congressman Representative Gerald R. Ford, the future president.

The next year, Coleman represented the Commonwealth of Pennsylvania in litigation against Philadelphia's Girard College, a segregated institution. Similar attempts made in the mid–to–late 1950s to end the racially biased policies at the college had ended in defeat. This time, with Coleman in charge, the commonwealth won.

In 1971, four years after Thurgood Marshall had been elevated to the U.S. Supreme Court, Coleman was elected president of the NAACP–LDF. He also served on the boards of a number of educational, charitable, and service agencies, including the National Civil Service League, the Brookings Institution, the Council on Foreign Relations, Harvard University, and the Metropolitan Opera.

In the midst of the Watergate scandal in 1973, Elliot Richardson, now the U.S. attorney general, offered Coleman the opportunity to become Watergate special prosecutor. Coleman, who had been a member of President Nixon's National Commission on Productivity and the successful Phase II Price Commission (1971–72), turned his friend down. In fact, he reportedly advised the president to resign rather than face impeachment, and is on record as being in favor of allowing a president to destroy tapes and documents prior to leaving office.

Becomes Secretary of Transportation

Early in 1975, Coleman received a call from President Ford concerning the vacant secretary of transportation post. Coleman had been offered full–time government appointments several times previously, but had always declined. He enjoyed working in the private sector and felt he could be more effective there. Besides, taking a position in the federal government also meant resigning from his law partnership and corporate directorships, taking a sizeable pay cut and selling his transportation stocks. Nevertheless, he decided to do the courteous thing, which was to meet with the president and hear him out.

To Coleman's astonishment, Ford's sincerity and the challenge of the job offered were enough to sway him to accept. He became the second black ever to hold a cabinet–level position (the first was Robert C. Waver as secretary of Housing and Urban Development in 1966–68 under Lyndon B. Johnson).

As secretary of transportation, he took over the fourth–largest department in the government, with a budget exceeded only by those of the Departments of Defense and Health, Education and Welfare. Established just nine years earlier, the department was facing major problems in several of the areas over which it had jurisdiction. The nation's railroads, mass transit and federal highway systems, and international airlines all had crises that needed to be addressed.

In an interview with the magazine *Black Enterprise* for June of 1975, Coleman said that his first concern was that:

> I would like to leave Washington with the same reputation for integrity that I had when I came here. Secondly, I hope I can leave Washington with the reputation of having helped to guide and put together a very important department, of having gathered around me a lot of very good people who made tremendous gains in solving the problems in the areas you mentioned.

Coleman made it his first priority to develop a comprehensive national transportation policy, something the American government had never really attempted before. Coleman was instrumental in creating the 53–page study *A Statement of National Transportation Policy,* which he sent to Congress in September of 1975. Rather than a list of possible solutions, the document contained general principles that he felt should guide the government's decision–making process.

Coleman's ability to influence the problems facing transportation in this county, however, proved modest during his short, two–year tenure. As a fiscally responsible member of a Republican administration, Coleman tried to make the various transportation sectors less reliant on tax–supported assistance. Instead, he favored imposing user fees on those who use the majority of an industry's services. However, the Democratic Congress kept appropriations high and, in some cases, even doubled the recommendations sent down from the White House. Though no one called his integrity into question, his efforts went unappreciated, although they may have helped set the stage for the Reagan Revolution four years later.

Upon his resignation when President Carter took office, Coleman opted for a return to the private sector. He stayed in the capital to become head of a 32–lawyer Washington office of O'Melveny & Myers, a large Los Angeles–based firm. By the early 1980s, he was earning $500,000 or more a year for representing major companies including Ford, IBM, and the Insurance Company of North America. He also returned to corporate boardrooms, serving on nine boards of directors. He remained active in civil rights, arguing cases, writing an occasional editorial, and continuing his affiliation with the NAACP.

On September 29, 1995, Coleman received the highest honor given to civilians, the Presidential Medal of Freedom, awarded to individual Americans for distinguished civilian service. President Clinton said, ''I can honestly say, if you are looking for an example of constancy, consistency, disciplined devotion to the things that make this country a great place, you have no further to look than William Coleman, Jr.'' Clinton first met Coleman at Yale Law School, where he roomed for a year with Coleman's son, William T. Coleman III.

When Coleman's long–time friend and colleague Thurgood Marshall died in 1993, Coleman was one of four speakers at the funeral. Four years later, Coleman was honored with the Thurgood Marshall Lifetime Achievement Award of the NAACP–LDF. In addition to serving as the fund's president in the early 1970s, he later became chairman and long served in that capacity.

Coleman is a short, stocky man with a jowly face and high forehead. He wears rather large spectacles and dresses impeccably. He has been, or continues as, a member of numerous organizations and clubs, including the American College of Trial Lawyers, the American Academy of Appellate Lawyers, the Philadelphia Bar Association, and the Arbitration Association.

Coleman is important as a public servant and civil rights and corporate lawyer. His work to end school segregation with the landmark decision in 1954 enshrined him in the annals of U.S. history.

Current address: c/o O'Melveny and Myers, 555 12th Street, NW, Suite 500W, Washington, DC 20004–1109.

REFERENCES

''Chronicle.'' *New York Times,* November 17, 1997.

Clinton, Bill. ''Remarks on Presenting the Presidential Medal of Freedom.'' *Weekly Compilation of Presidential Documents* 31 (2 October 1995): 1734–1739.

Current Biography Yearbook. New York: H. W. Wilson, 1977.

''Ford to Nominate Black to Cabinet.'' *New York Times,* January 14, 1975.

''No Stranger to the High Court.'' *New York Times,* April 20, 1982.

''Secretary William Thaddeus Coleman.'' *Black Enterprise* 5 (June 1975): 125.

''Transportation Choice.'' *New York Times,* January 15, 1975.

Who's Who in America, 1998. New Providence, NJ: Marquis Who's Who, 1997.

Kevin C. Kretschmer

John Coltrane
(1926–1967)
Musician, band leader, composer

John Coltrane was a consummate musician and band leader; an innovator in the avant garde and free jazz era from its inception. As a saxophone player he continually sought new levels of technical expression, reaching for new sounds, tonalities, and extensions of range and dynamics. As a melodic stylist, he greatly stretched the boundaries of thematic and harmonic development, merging improvisation, tone color, dynamics, and rhythm. He expanded the range of his instrument, adding sonorous depth on the lower end and tense emotional peaks on the higher end of the tonal spectrum. In many ways, John Coltrane sought a spiritual level of communication with his audience. His music challenged the jazz public to listen deeply and seek new levels of understanding and appreciation.

Personal Life

John William Coltrane was born on September 23, 1926, in Hamlet, North Carolina, the son of John Robert and Alice Blair Coltrane. The Coltranes' home life included music: his father, a tailor, played violin and ukulele for enjoyment; his mother was a church pianist and sang in the choir. Both of his grandfathers were ministers, perhaps foreshadowing the importance of religion later in his life. His cousin, Mary Alexander, was one of his strongest supporters throughout his life, and he later dedicated a composition to her, ''Cousin Mary''. The Coltranes and the Blairs, his mother's parents, had close family ties. The family moved to High Point, North Carolina, when he was a few months old. A few years after her husband died in 1939, Alice moved to Philadelphia to seek work. His mother took a job in Atlantic City, and Mary Alexander came north later, moving in with Coltrane and John Kinzer in Philadelphia. Coltrane and two close friends, John Kinzer and Franklin Brower, also moved to Philadelphia after high school graduation in 1942.

Although Philadelphia remained a base for him, Coltrane's career drew him to New York in the 1950s. His mother, aunt, and cousin, however, kept the north Philadelphia home as a place of refuge for him. It was there that he met and married his first wife, Juanita Naima Grubb, in 1955. They moved to New York, where his career was then centered. Coltrane and Naima shared many crises, including his transformation and healing from drug dependency in 1957. Her faith as a Muslim added a new dimension to his religious search and further growth.

John and Naima Coltrane drifted apart, however, and he left her in 1963. He met Alice McLeod, a gifted jazz pianist, during an engagement at Birdland, in New York City, in July of that year, where she was playing with vibraphonist Terry Gibbs. John and Alice soon married, moved to Huntington, Long Island, and she replaced McCoy Tyner when he left the

John Coltrane

John Coltrane Quartet in 1966. Alice and John Coltrane had three sons: John Jr., born in 1965, and twins Ravi and Oranyan, born in 1967.

Serious illness struck John Coltrane in 1967, and he died in New York on July 17, 1967, of liver disease. His widow, Alice Coltrane, moved to California, continued to perform both his and her own music, and subsequently a cultural and religious society dedicated to his memory was later founded in San Francisco. To preserve Coltrane's memory, Mary Alexander, together with a group of Philadelphia women, founded the John W. Coltrane Cultural Society at the family home at 1511 North 33rd Street, Philadelphia, in 1984.

Life's Work

Coltrane's musical studies began in 1938, in the Community Band at High Point, North Carolina, directed by Warren Steele, pastor at St. Stephen's Metropolitan AME Church. Members of Steele's Boy Scout Troop, of which he was scoutmaster, formed the band's nucleus. Steele personally raised money for instruments, recruited the young musicians, taught them to read music, as well as how to play, and directed the band. Coltrane, fast becoming an outstanding band member, played alto horn and later clarinet. Coltrane also joined the band at William Penn High School, directed by Grace Yokley, where he played first played the clarinet and switched to the alto saxophone, and performed in the school's dance band.

Coltrane's musical activities continued in Philadelphia in 1943, having moved there from High Point with his two friends, Franklin Brower and James Kinzer. He found a job and studied clarinet, alto saxophone, and theory at the Ornstein School of Music with Mike Guerra. His career as a professional musician also began at this time, appearing with the Jimmy Johnson Big Band. In 1945 he was inducted into the U.S. Navy and played the clarinet with the band in Hawaii during 1945–46. Following Coltrane's release from service, he returned to his north Philadelphia home, resumed his musical studies, performed regularly, and produced his first recording.

During Coltrane's period of apprenticeship he worked mostly with bands in the Philadelphia area led by Joe Webb, King Kolax, Eddie ''Cleanhead'' Vinson, and Jimmy Heath. Vinson offered him the opportunity to play tenor saxophone, which then became his primary instrument. Later in Coltrane's career he added soprano saxophone, flute, and bass clarinet. In developing his technique and searching for tonalities as yet unheard, he freely sought ideas, listened, and accepted advice from many reed players and other musicians over the years. These included his lifetime friend Eric Dolphy, Sonny Rollins, Johnny Hedges, Lester Young, Earl Bostic, Stan Getz, Dexter Gordon, Sonny Stitt, Archie Shepp, and Coleman Hawkins. Thelonious Monk, another lifelong friend and collaborator, showed Coltrane unorthodox ways of blowing overtones, while Sun Ra saxophonist John Gilmore and Indian sitar virtuoso Ravi Shankar encouraged him to think of other sound and aesthetic dimensions. Dizzy Gillespie, Miles Davis, and the Nigerian percussionist Michael Olatunji, influenced his concepts of harmony, melody, and rhythm. Sounds he imagined and heard in meditation further influenced him.

Coltrane's sojourn as a band musician continued as he worked with more prominent groups, joining Dizzy Gillespie's large and small bands in 1949–51, as well as Earl Bostic, Johnny Hodges and Miles Davis for two periods. In 1951, he returned to Philadelphia and resumed his formal training at the Granoff Studios, recommended by Percy Heath and Dizzy Gillespie. He studied saxophone with Matthew Rastelli and theory with Dennis Sandole. Rastelli worked with him on technique, while Sandole introduced him to a thorough understanding of harmony, modes, scales, combinations, and to the literature of orchestration, especially Debussy, Ravel, Bartok, and Hindemith. Sandole found Coltrane to be an avid and inquisitive student.

Coltrane's musical career, meanwhile, developed rapidly, placing him in the forefront of the burgeoning bop and new jazz era. His contemporaries, with whom he shared many performances and recordings, included the jazz giants Charlie Parker, Dizzy Gillespie, Thelonious Monk, Cannonball Adderley, Miles Davis, Paul Chambers, Roy Haynes, Art Davis, Art Taylor, Reggie Workman, Steve Davis, Billy Higgins, Pharaoh Sanders, and Rashied Ali. After a period of working in groups led by others, Coltrane formed his own quartet in 1960 consisting of McCoy Tyner, piano; Elvin Jones, drums; Jimmy Garrison, bass; and himself, principally on tenor saxophone. The John Coltrane Quartet recorded many albums, which have since been re–released on compact disk. Many jazz critics consider this group to be among the greatest ensembles of all time.

Coltrane was a very prolific recording artist. In his biography, Bill Cole provides a list of recording dates and personnel for sessions of the various groups with which Coltrane played from 1949 to 1967. John Fraim's biography gives a complementary listing or discography of the titles of more than 110 recordings produced during this same period featuring or including Coltrane. Together, these two sources give a basic guide to his prolific recordings.

Perhaps the most significant of Coltrane's collaborators over the years, in terms of his career development, were Dizzy Gillespie, Theolonius Monk, and Miles Davis. Coltrane performed with Dizzy Gillespie on a number of occasions in 1950–51 as a member of Gillespie's Big Band and Sextet with recordings issued by Capitol and DeeGee Records: *The Dizzy Gillespie Orchestra* and *Dizzy Gillespie Sextet.* This association affected Coltrane's early development as an artist as it enabled him to experience close at hand the vibrant talent of this major figure who helped break the mold and create a new artistic form. The humor, witticism, and melodic improvisation Gillespie exhibited, as well as his innovative use of bebop speech intonations and Latin American and African–derived percussion and dance rhythms, are well known and strongly influenced the developmental process not only of young John Coltrane, but of jazz history in general.

Coltrane collaborated closely with Thelonious Monk. Coltrane discussed musical matters with him frequently. One of his last discussions about his desired goals in music was at Monk's apartment in Manhattan in April of 1967, just shortly before Coltrane's death. Early in Coltrane's career, Monk introduced him to innovative and unexpected harmonies, the proper use of "space" (or rests, in music), the superimposition, or "stacking" of chords, and use of modal scales and harmonies.

Coltrane benefited greatly from his association with friend and colleague Miles Davis. In the early 1950s Davis played with concern for straight, clean melodies and a pure sound, but with ample harmonic flexibility. Their concepts blended well for the most part, as is demonstrated by the *Milestones* duet album (Columbia Records, No. 1386 D263 M61).

In 1957 Coltrane experienced a dramatic life transformation and overcame his strong drug dependency that began in 1948. In gratitude, he composed and dedicated the album *A Love Supreme* to God in thanks for his rebirth. His expressed desire to share his gift, his belief, his joy, and his music with others became a life purpose for Coltrane. He gave a poetic dedication of his life and his music to God in the liner notes. In setting the words of the composition, Coltrane shows his indebtedness to his friend, Nigerian master drummer Michael Olatunji, and his grasp of West African musical values and techniques. Typically, in playing lyrical works such as this at concerts and club dates, Coltrane and his assisting artists took their time, playing long solo expositions, probing the possibilities of the work. These long evocations were usually not heard on longplaying records, given the time limitations. With the advent of the CD, however, lengthy solo renditions captured on tape could now be included on a disc. Such is the case, for instance, with a version of "A Love Supreme" recorded at the Juan Les Pins Jazz Festival, Antibes, July 26–27, 1965 and released in 1992 on the CD *John Coltrane; Immortal Concerts* (Giants of Jazz, Sarabandas srl, SAAR srl No. CD 53068). The solos by each quartet member are long and fully explored, extending to a total of more than 47 minutes.

John Coltrane's diversity as an expressionist in music is preserved by his recorded legacy. The legacy presents a diverse and complex artist; a singer of soulful ballads as well as a painter of new and almost bizarre, unfathomable sounds; a man who wove a fabric of whole cloth that transmitted to us a tapestry of raw emotions as well as a preacher of love and unity.

REFERENCES

Blume, A. "An Interview with John Coltrane." *Jazz Review* 2, no. 1 (1959): 25.

Carno, Zita. "The Style of John Coltrane." *Jazz Review* 2, no. 9 (1959): 16–21; 2, no. 10 (1959) 13–21.

Cole, Bill. *John Coltrane.* New York, Schirmer Books, 1976.

Davis, Brian. *John Coltrane: Discography.* 2nd ed. Staten Island, NY: B. Davis and R. Smith, 1976.

Fraim, John. *Spirit Catcher; the Life and Art of John Coltrane.* West Liberty, OH: GreatHouse Co., 1996.

Fujioka, Yasuhiro. *John Coltrane: A Discography and Musical Biography.* Metuchen: Scarecrow Press; Institute of Jazz Studies, Rutgers, State University of New Jersey, 1995.

Gitler, Ira. *Swing to Bop; an Oral History of the Tradition in Jazz in the 1940's.* New York, Oxford University Press, 1985.

———. "Trane on the Track." *Down Beat* 25, no. 21 (16 October 1958): 16–17.

Hazell, Ed. "Alice Coltrane." In *New Grove Dictionary of Jazz.* Ed. by Barry Kernfeld. New York: Macmillan, 1988.

John Coltrane Anthology (2–CD set) Text supplement (introduction and eight articles), edited by John Dorn. New York, Rhino Records, 1993. Atlantic Jazz Gallery, No. R2 71255.

"The John W. Coltrane Cultural Society." Philadelphia: John W. Coltrane Cultural Society, 1996.

Jost, Ekkehard. *Free Jazz.* New York: DaCapo Press, 1981.

Kernfeld, Barry. "John Coltrane." In *New Grove Dictionary of Jazz.* Ed. by Barry Kernfeld. New York: Macmillan, 1988.

———. "Two Coltranes." *Annual Review of Jazz Studies* 2 (1983): 7–66.

McRae, B. "John Coltrane: The Impulse Years." *Jazz Journal* 24 (1971): 2.

Nisenson, Eric. *Ascension: John Coltrane and His Quest.* New York: St. Martin's Press, 1993.

Palmer, Robert. "Exploring the Legacy of John Coltrane." *New York Times Magazine* (29 September 1974): 8, 10.

Porter, Lewis. "John Coltrane's A Love Supreme: Jazz Improvisation as Composition." *Journal of the American Musicological Society* 38 (Fall 1985): 593–621.

Priestley, Brian. *Jazz on Record; a History.* London: Hamish Hamilton, 1988. Reprint, New York: Billboard Books, 1991.

Rivelli, Pauline, and Robert Levin, eds. *Giants of Black Music.* New York: Da Capo Press, 1980.

Roach, Hildred. *Black American Music: Past and Present.* Malabar, FL: Krieger Pub. Co., 1992.

Simpkins, Cuthbert O. *Coltrane; a Biography.* New York: Herndon House, 1975.

Slonimsky, Nicholas, ed. *Baker's Biographical Dictionary of Music and Musicians.* 8th ed. New York: G. Schirmer, 1983.

Southern, Eileen. *Biographical Dictionary of Afro–American and African Musicians.* Westport, CT: Greenwood Press, 1982.

———. *Readings in Black American Music.* 2nd ed. New York: Norton, 1983.

Spellman, A. B. "John Coltrane 1926–1967." *The Nation* (14 August 1967): 119–20.

Taggart, John, ed. *Poems for John Coltrane.* Syracuse, NY: Syracuse University Press, 1969.

Terkel, Studs. *Giants of Jazz.* Revised ed. New York: Crowell, 1975.

Thomas, J. C. *Chasin' the Trane: The Music and Mystique of John Coltrane.* Garden City, NY: Doubleday, 1975.

Turner, Richard. "John W. Coltrane: A Biographical Sketch." *Black Perspective in Music* 3 (Spring 1975): 3–16.

Wild, David. *Recordings of John Coltrane: A Discography.* Ann Arbor: Wildmusic, 1979.

Darius L. Thieme

James H. Cone

(1938–)

Theologian, minister, educator

Albert Cleage Jr. described James Cone in his book, *Black Christian Nationalism,* as "undoubtedly a most interesting and meaningful Black theologian." He further portrayed Cone as "an apostle to the Gentiles" who "drags white Christians as far as they are able to go (and then some) in interpreting Black theology within the established framework which they can accept and understand."

From the time Cone entered seminary in 1958 until the 1970 publication of *A Black Theology of Liberation,* Cone had spent over a decade on the journey to articulate what he described in *Contemporary Black Biography* as "my attempt . . . to understand the meaning of faith, the meaning of God, in a world that is broken." Although his theological writings were forged in seminary settings, they did not evolve out of the milieu of the academic ivory tower, but rather from his life experiences colored by the effects of segregation. They also represent his attempt to make meaningful a vision of Christ to black Christians who live and worship God as oppressed people.

On August 5, 1938, James Hal Cone was born in Fordyce, Arkansas, to parents who were poor in material possessions, but rich in those values that sustain life. His father, Charlie Cone, cut wood for a living, but he had a vision for his son. In the segregated town of Bearden, Arkansas, where he and his wife raised James and his brother, Cecil—also a theologian—Charlie Cone realized that a dream could become a reality only through action. He could see that the all–black schools of Bearden were substandard for all black children there, not just his own. He took a bold step that put him in danger of being lynched: he filed a lawsuit against the local school board to desegregate Bearden's public schools. From that time on, in the early 1950s, he was James Cone's role model of a poor man who could be proud and stand upright in the midst of a predominantly white Southern environment. In *Contemporary Black Biography* Cone said of his father: "No person has influenced me more than my father in his courage, sense of self, and the clarity of his commitment to end racial injustice." This was indeed a courageous act because organized civil rights efforts were nearly a decade in the future, and the Ku Klux Klan and White Citizen's Councils reigned supreme in the small rural towns of Arkansas.

Cone's mother, Lucille Cone, a highly respected orator in the African Methodist Episcopal (AME) church, also wielded great influence on her son. In *Contemporary Black Biography* he said of her: "[She] gave me the gift of speech and faith [in the church] which is where I discovered my own voice." It was natural that the AME church would be another guiding light in Cone's development. His biographer Dwight N. Hopkins wrote in *Encyclopedia of African–American Culture and History*: "His intellectual, emotional, and racial identities developed out of two childhood experiences. First, the wholesome encouragement and support of the [AME church] and Bearden's black community reinforced fundamental beliefs in Cone's self–worth and Christian convictions. Second, the negative effects of segregation and white racism left an instinctive intolerance for discrimination."

Cone attended Shorter College for two years and then transferred to Philander Smith College in Little Rock, Arkansas, from which he graduated with the A.B. degree in 1958. To prepare himself for the ministry, he enrolled in the Garrett Biblical Institute in Evanston, Illinois, which later became the Garrett Evangelical Theological Seminary. As a native son of the South, Cone was certainly no stranger to racial discrimination, but the Midwest had its own special atmosphere. Evanston and the seminary proved that the South held no monopoly on racial prejudice. The school, in particular, offered an especially polarized environment, one purporting to train ministers yet systematically seldom giving grades above average to black students. Despite the obvious inequities, Cone refused to be deterred and earned the Bachelor of Divinity degree in 1961. He then earned the master of arts and doctor of philosophy degrees from Northwestern University in 1963 and 1965 respectively. While pursuing doctoral studies, Cone taught at his alma mater, Philander Smith (1964–66) and pastored the Woodlawn AME Church. He then moved to Michigan to teach at Adrian College (1966–69), the academic setting where he began the crystallization of his lifelong ideas and beliefs about Christianity from a black perspective.

A Black Theology of Liberation

As a seminarian and graduate student, the major forces of the Black Power movement; the writings of Joseph Washington, a prominent social ethicist and professor of religious studies; and Gayraud Wilmore, a leading black theologian had influenced Cone. In his book, *Speaking the Truth,* Cone described the effect of the Black Power movement on black clergy who had begun to question the validity of Martin Luther King Jr.'s philosophical beliefs: "Black power forced black clergy to raise the theological question about the relation between black faith and white religion . . . with its accent on the cultural heritage of Africa and political liberation. . . . Black power shook black clergy out of their theological complacency."

In 1966 the National Committee of Negro Churchmen published a black power statement in the *New York Times* that advocated supporting those elements of the movement that suited their needs and were congruent with their beliefs. This ad hoc group became the National Conference of Black Churchmen (NCBC) in 1967. As the religious counterpart of the Black Power movement, it directly confronted perceived and real evils in the white church. Lincoln and Mamiya described the major functions of the NCBC in the *Black Church in the African American Experience* as being the main source for interpreting black religious militancy to the white church, the place where the consciousness of black clergy is developed, and an advocate of economic development in the North.

Gayraud Wilmore was the first chairman of the NCBC Theological Commission and instigator of the organization's publications. He has been a longtime mentor of Cone's as well as a supportive critic who urged Cone and other liberation theologians to lessen their dependence on dominant culture theologians. The NCBC only lasted through the early 1980s, but its primary value was the provision of a forum out of which evolved the seeds of black theology. In 1968 Cone wrote an early manifesto entitled "Christianity and Power" that he described in *For My People* as having "initiated the development of a theological consciousness that separated radical black Christianity from the religion of white churches. It set in motion a series of events that led seminary professors and other members of the black clergy to create what has since been called black theology."

Joseph Washington's book *Black Religion* (1964) focused on the relation of an emerging black theology to African culture and history. Despite a lack of support from leading black theologians, Washington held fast to a strong belief that seemed heretical to many, as described in Cone's *Speaking the Truth*: "he claimed that black religion was a unique non–Christian folk religion derived from the African heritage and the black struggle for social and political betterment."

In a later book, *Black Sects and Cults,* Washington more cogently expressed his belief that black religious people needed a theology derivative of their life and subculture rather than attempting to develop a black theology within the framework of a white Christian theology that would allow the inclusion of the black experience. This latter point was the basis of Washington's criticism of Cone and his radical cohorts who all contributed to the emergence of a black theology. By the mid–1970s Cone had begun to depend less on mainstream theological thought and more on the rich and valid heritage of black culture in his writings.

In 1969 Cone wrote *Black Power and Black Theology,* the book that thrust him into the limelight and attracted the attention of major theologians the world over. Cain Felder, Howard University's professor of New Testament language and literature and author of *Troubling Biblical Waters,* credited Cone's first publication as being "significant ... in establishing new foci for future theological discourse about the political implications of the gospel for Blacks and the Third World." Leonard Barrett, in *Soul Force,* described Cone as "by far the most perceptive religious thinker in Black America . . . [whose] writing centers around the theological implications of Black Power."

With the publication of this first scholarly treatment of black theology that forced both white and reluctant black theologians as well as white seminaries to recognize black theological thought, Cone was offered a faculty position at Union Theological Seminary in New York City, where he is currently Briggs Professor of Systematic Theology. In 1970 he wrote *A Black Theology of Liberation,* described in *Contemporary Black Biography* as "a groundbreaking influential work that links the study of Jesus Christ's Life with the African–American experience." The work was further characterized in the *Encyclopedia of African–American Culture and History* as "the first attempt to develop a black theology by investigating major church doctrines through the eyes of the African–American poor."

Cone's subsequent publications include *The Spirituals and the Blues: An Interpretation* (1972); *God and the Oppressed* (1975); *My Soul Looks Back* (1982); *For My People: Black Theology and the Black Church* (1984); *Speaking the Truth: Ecumenism, Liberation, and Black Theology* (1986); and *Martin and Malcolm and America: A Dream or a Nightmare* (1991). In 1979 Cone and Gayraud Wilmore coedited *Black Theology: A Documentary History, 1966–79.* Cone is a contributing editor of *Christianity and Crisis, Review of Religious Research,* and *The Journal of the Interdenominational Theological Center*; he also serves as editor of the Bishop Henry McNeal Turner Studies in North American Black Religion, a series published by Orbis Books.

Cone is a member of the American Theological Society, the Society for the Study of Black Religion, the American Academy of Religion, and the Ecumenical Association of Third World Theologians. He is also affiliated with the *Union Theological Quarterly Review,* the *Journal of Religious Thought,* and the Black Theology Project of Theology in the Americas. His honors and awards include the LL.D. degree from Philander Smith and Edward Waters colleges, both in 1981, and the Black Achievement Award in the category of religion in 1992. Cone was married to Rose Hampton, now deceased, who assisted him in his research. Their sons are Michael Lawrence and Charles Pierson Cone.

Impact of Cone's Black Liberation Theology

Nearly 30 years after the publication of Cone's first book, it is perhaps difficult to understand the struggle to legitimize black theology. Nineteenth–century thinkers like Robert Young and Henry McNeal Turner led the way, but it was twentieth–century theologians who began to challenge the establishment with hope of success. Many clergy were resistant because the implications of a black theology threatened the idea of the universality of the Christian gospel of liberation. Peter Paris, author of *Black Leaders in Conflict,* criticized Cone's second book on that basis: "The outstanding weakness of this brilliant theological work . . . is his attempt to relate divine concern, and to reduce all of the great historic theological truths of the Christian religion to the historic conflict between blacks and whites."

In the 1990s prominent womanist theologians are also critical of Cone's writings. Delores S. Williams of Union Theological Seminary offers this criticism in *Sisters in the Wilderness*: "language about the struggle assumes an androcentric black history. Therefore a masculine indication of person and masculine models of victimization dominate the language and thought of black liberation theology."

To Cone's credit, each subsequent publication has reflected his sincere and systematic attention to and consideration of valid criticism. In the final analysis, Cone's brilliant and highly original scholarly literary works in black liberation theology have continually reflected and supported his own personal and professional beliefs about the place and meaning of theology in the life of all Christians as stated in *Speaking the Truth*: "Theology is the church applying a critical self–evaluation of what it says and does on behalf of the one who defines the church's identity—namely, Jesus Christ."

Current address: Union Theological Seminary, 3041 Broadway, New York, NY 10027.

REFERENCES

Cleage, Albert B. Jr. *Black Christian Nationalism: Reflections for the Black Church.* New York: Morrow Paperback Editions, 1972.

Cone, James H. *For My People: Black Theology and the Black Church.* Maryknoll, NY: Orbis Books, 1984.

———. *Speaking the Truth: Ecumenism, Liberation, and Black Theology.* Grand Rapids, MI: Wm. B. Eerdmans Publishing Co., 1986.

Contemporary Black Biography. Vol. 3. Detroit: Gale Research, 1992.

Ebony Success Library. Vol. 1. *1,000 Successful Blacks.* Nashville: Southwestern Co., 1973.

Ellis, Carl F. Jr. *Beyond Liberation: The Gospel in the Black American Experience.* Downer's Grove, CA: Intervarsity Press, 1983.

Felder, Cain Hope. *Troubling Biblical Waters: Race, Class, and Family.* Maryknoll, NY: Orbis Books, 1989.

Lincoln, C. Eric, and Lawrence H. Mamiya. *The Black Church in the African American Experience.* Durham, NC: Duke University Press, 1990.

Paris, Peter J. *Black Leaders in Conflict.* New York: Pilgrim Press, 1978.

Salzman, Jack, David Lionel Smith, and Cornel West, eds. *Encyclopedia of African–American Culture and History.* New York: Macmillan Library Reference USA/Simon and Schuster Macmillan, 1996.

"Teaching and Testifying." *Ebony* 46 (August 1991): 70–73.

Webber, Brenda L. "A Colorful Translation." *Emerge* 6 (April 1995): 26–34.

Who's Who among African Americans, 1996–97. 9th ed. Detroit: Gale Research, 1996.

Williams, Delores S. *Sisters in the Wilderness: The Challenge of Womanist God–Talk.* Maryknoll, NY: Orbis Books, 1993.

Williams, Ethel L. *Biographical Directory of Negro Ministers.* 2nd ed. Metuchen, NJ: Scarecrow Press, 1970.

Dolores Nicholson

John Conyers Jr.

(1929–)

Congressman, civil rights advocate, lawyer

For almost three decades as a U.S. congressman, John Conyers has focused on bringing about social justice and economic opportunities for his constituents. As a freshman congressman, Conyers was assigned to the House Judiciary Committee, which addresses issues of civil rights, and joined those who sponsored the Voting Rights Act of 1965.

Born in Detroit on May 16, 1929, John Conyers Jr. is the great–grandson of a former slave who fought in the Spanish–American War. He is the oldest of the four sons of John and Lucille Janice Simpson Conyers. John Conyers Sr. was born in Monroe, Georgia. He had to go to work before finishing high school to help support his family. He came north to Detroit in the 1920s and took a job with Chrysler spray–painting auto bodies. At this time black workers applied the primer coat, and white workers received an extra dime per hour to put on the colored finish. This so angered Conyers that he eventually confronted Walter P. Chrysler, who corrected the situation. Frequently fired for demonstrating union sympathies, his close ties with the workers eventually brought him back. Lucille Simpson Conyers came to Detroit from Jackson, Mississippi, as a young girl and graduated from Miller High School. Throughout her life she believed that to get ahead, one must work. John Conyers Jr.'s brother Nathan is a lawyer in Detroit, and his other two brothers, Carl and William, are no longer living.

John Conyers Jr.

The family grew up on the east side of Detroit, which was largely populated by Italian American families. While still young, Conyers's family saved enough money to make a down payment on a house on the west side of Detroit, which was, in his judgment, a nicer neighborhood because "it was all black." At 14, Conyers went to work after school in a drugstore to earn the money to buy a cornet and take lessons. He graduated from Samson Elementary School in 1943, the same year Detroit suffered a devastating race riot. Commenting on the riot, Conyers was quoted by Bruner in *Black Politicians* as saying:

> The 1943 race riot was classic. Every black man considered every white man his mortal enemy, and vice–versa. It operated on a very personal, animalistic level; they were reduced to trying to destroy each other. People were being pulled off street cars and literally beaten to death right out in public; it was a form of insanity.

Conyers was bored by high school. It seemed to him to be "a place into which they forced kids before they were grown up enough to get jobs," he commented in the same source. "I was mostly unchallenged by high school. So I began to spend a lot of time in pool rooms." When Conyers graduated it was clear that his parents could not afford to send him to college, however, his father was able to get him a job at the Lincoln Motors Company. He enrolled in night school to make up the courses he had not taken in high school—such as chemistry and physics—and worked as a spot–welder during the day. He began going to Wayne University at night, then decided to go to school full time, majoring in civil engineering.

In 1950 Conyers enlisted in the U.S. Army as a private; after attending Officer's Candidate School at Ft. Belleville, Virginia, he was commissioned a second lieutenant and assigned to the Corps of Engineers. He served a year in Korea and received several combat and merit citations. After his discharge in January of 1954, he returned to college, financing his tuition with veteran's benefits.

Conyers entered politics while still in college, inspired partly by his father's involvement in the labor movement as an international representative for the United Auto Workers and partly by a visit to the House of Representatives. He changed his major to law, joined the Young Democratic Club, and ran for Democratic Party precinct delegate, which would allow him to serve on the party's organizing committee. The precinct was about four city blocks square and contained less than 1,000 voters. He won his first election by a few votes.

Conyers received his bachelor of arts degree from Wayne State University, Detroit, in 1957 and a doctorate in jurisprudence in 1958. Admitted to the Michigan Bar in 1959, he began to practice law in the same building as the congressional district office, taking cases of criminal matters and landlord–tenant disputes, which exposed him to the social problems of the city. He was a legislative assistant to Congressman John Dingell of Detroit from 1959 to 1961, as well as senior partner of the law firm of Conyers, Bell and Townsend until 1961. He was then appointed by Governor John B. Swainson as a referee of the Michigan Workmen's Compensation Department, a position Conyers held until 1964.

Enters the Political Arena

In January of 1964 Conyers resigned from the Workmen's Compensation Department and opened a congressional campaign office. In the Democratic primary, Conyers defeated Richard H. Austin by a narrow margin of 44 votes, and in the November election he defeated his Republican opponent by a vote of 138,589 to 25,735. Conyers was reelected in 1966 with 84 percent of the votes, and he was unopposed in the 1968 campaign. Conyers continues to serve Michigan's First (now Fourteenth) District.

In January of 1967 Conyers became the only black member of a special house committee appointed to investigate charges of misconduct brought against Adam Clayton Powell Jr., whom he admired. In the spring of 1967 he spearheaded a fight against a bill aimed at delaying one–man/one–vote redistricting until 1972, an issue Conyers considered integral to civil rights: the bill would have perpetuated the present districting patterns that disperse black voting power. In an article in *Ebony* magazine for August of 1969, Conyers wrote:

> Politics is important—much too important for black people to "give up" on the political process through which today, with the heightening of black awareness, and the stirring of long dormant black voter power, black people can gain control of large cities, can exert strong influence on state govern-

ments, can pressure Capitol Hill and force quite a bit of listening at the White House.

Conyers has been persuasive legislatively. In 1969 he sponsored a full opportunity bill, which offered, among other things a two–dollars–per–hour minimum wage. He initiated and coordinated the drive for the passage of the Martin Luther King Jr. Holiday Bill, founded the Justice Department's national study on police brutality, and was the original sponsor of the Hate Crimes Statistics Act, which required the Justice Department to collect data on the instances of crime based on race and sexual prejudice.

Conyers continues to be active as a congressman and member of several organizations. He is a senior member of the Congressional Black Caucus, and Trustee of the Martin Luther King, Jr. Center for Non–Violent Social Change. He is also former chairman of the Judiciary Committee, past director of Local 900 United Auto Workers, a member of the advisory council of the Michigan Liberties Union, general counsel of the Detroit Trade Union Leadership Council, vice–chair of the national board of directors of Americans for Democratic Action, vice–chair of the advisory council of the American Civil Liberties Union, an organizer of Members of Congress for Peace Through Law, a member of the executive board of directors of the Detroit chapter of the NAACP, and member of the boards of directors of numerous other organizations, including the African–American Institute and the National Alliance Against Racist and Political Repression.

Conyers was a contributing author of *American Militarism* (1970), *War Crimes and the American Conscious* (1970), and *Anatomy of an Undeclared War* (1972). Conyers was honored with the Rosa Parks Award for civil rights activities from the Southern Christian Leadership Conference in 1967 and an honorary Doctor of Literature Degree from Wilberforce University, Ohio, in August of 1969. He also held a Lamson–McElhone labor scholarship in 1957, and is a member of Kappa Alpha Psi Fraternity.

As a congressman, Conyers has addressed many issues and causes, introducing legislation on voter rights and registration, alcohol warning labeling, social security, public housing, family farmers, foreign affairs, and many other concerns to secure the rights of all American citizens.

Current address: 2426 Rayburn House, Office B, Washington, DC 20515.

REFERENCES

Bruner, Richard. *Black Politicians.* New York: David McKay, 1971.

Conyers, John, Jr. ''Politics and the Black Revolution.'' *Ebony* 24 (August 1969): 162–66.

Current Biography Yearbook. New York: H. W. Wilson, 1970.

Who's Who in America. 50th ed. New Providence, NJ: Marquis Who's Who, 1996.

Thura Mack

Levi Jenkins Coppin (1848–1924)

Bishop, editor, writer

Levi Jenkins Coppin was a leader in the African Methodist Episcopal (AME) Church. For most persons he is known only as the husband of the celebrated educator, Fannie Jackson Coppin (1837–1913), long–time head of Philadelphia's Institute for Colored Youth. Coppin had a distinguished career of his own, during which he served as editor of the *AME Church Review* for eight years and rose to become the first AME bishop assigned to South Africa. He also left a very interesting blend of local history and autobiography, *Unwritten History,* which portrays, among other things, a rural free black community on Maryland's Eastern Shore around the time of the Civil War. In keeping with its author's interests, it is very informative about African American religion.

Coppin was born in Frederick Town, a small town in Cecil County, in northeastern Maryland, on the Sassafras River opposite Georgetown, on the night of December 24 to 25, 1848. Since there were no clocks or watches available, he could have been born on either day, but the family chose the 24th as his birthday. He was one of the seven children of John Coppin and Jane Lilly Coppin, both of whom were born free.

Little is known of John Coppin's family, but he may have been a relation of the white Coppins in the neighborhood. As a widow, his mother married Christopher Jones, a clandestine member of the African Methodist Episcopal Church who was a respected preacher and prominent local leader. Jones had a profound influence on Levi Coppin, especially since John Coppin's family moved close by to Jones's house before the child was old enough to remember.

Perry and Amelia Lilly, Levi Coppin's maternal grandparents, had a large family—all girls with one exception. Amelia Lilly chose her daughter Jane as the most promising and sent her to an aunt, Lucy Harding, in Baltimore, where Jane went to school. After her marriage to John Coppin, she carried on a very risky secret school over her husband's objections. After the outbreak of the Civil War when she could carry on the school more openly, Levi Coppin helped as her assistant. At the end of the war he would teach in a newly established school until the arrival of a more qualified teacher.

John Coppin was an upright man, who never drank or swore but was not a church member. Jane Coppin was a pillar of the Methodist church, where she was a leader in singing and had memorized a prodigious number of hymns. She saw that her children had a religious upbringing. Levi Coppin underwent conversion in the fall of 1865. As soon as his six month's probation was over, he was elected superintendent of the Sunday school, which made him become a very diligent Bible student. His church broke from the white Methodists to become African Methodist Episcopal officially in 1866.

Levi Jenkins Coppin

Leaves Home

Coppin had gone out to do farm work since he was nine. He was a hard worker and saved money, but he decided to leave for the wider world. On February 15, 1869, he and some friends went to Philadelphia. His stay there was short; he was soon living with his aunt Clara Lilly Backus and her husband, John Backus, in Wilmington, Delaware, and working at a brickyard. Violating brickyard custom and astounding old–timers, he soon became a master brickmaker. Since he could finish his daily task of producing 2,332 bricks in four hours, he was able to devote much time to study. With the money he earned, towards 1875 he and some other young men opened a flour store.

Coppin became politically active in Wilmington as an undeviating Republican. At first he often accompanied relatives to the Methodist Ezion church. He was the only AME member among the family in the city—although he maintained his membership in Wilmington's Bethel AME Church. At Ezion he sang in the choir, which gave him the chance to learn to read music in classes organized at the church. He took additional lessons on his own. In disgust at a sermon preached by a guest white minister, he left the Ezion choir to join the one at Bethel. The following year he was elected director of the choir at the death of its former leader. When Theopolis Gould Stewart became minister of Bethel, Coppin fell under the spell of Stewart's quiet way of preaching, which was radically different from the emotional style to which he was accustomed. Coppin was now teaching with the International Course of prepared Sunday school materials, a stimulus and a great help to his Bible study.

In September 1875 Coppin married Martha Grinnage of Wilmington, a schoolteacher. They had a son, Octavius Valentine, named for the teacher at Philadelphia's Institute for Colored Youth, Octavius Valentine Cato, who had recently been murdered at the election polls. The son died at the age of six months, and his mother, 18 days later.

When Coppin's business venture in the flour store collapsed because of overextending credit, he became a schoolteacher in Smyrna, Delaware. There he combined his day school work with continued involvement in church activities. He credited his intense involvement in community and church affairs at this juncture as being an important education in leadership for him.

Enters Ministry

In the spring of 1877 Coppin, 29, entered the ministry at Bethel Church in Wilmington. Delaware was part of the Philadelphia Annual Conference, and his first assignment was to the Philadelphia City Mission, where the most notable of the three stations was the Morris Brown Mission.

In 1879 Coppin became a deacon. At that moment the pastor of Mother Bethel Church in Philadelphia, George C. Whitfield, was gravely ill, and Coppin was sent to help him. Whitfield died in less than two weeks, and presiding bishop Daniel Payne put off naming a successor for 60 days because of pressing church business. During this time Coppin succeeded in healing a long–standing breach in Bethel. The congregation was so impressed by his performance that they asked for Coppin as their pastor. It was unprecedented for a newly minted deacon, who could not even administer the sacraments, to become pastor of a denomination's mother church, but Coppin received the appointment.

In 1879 Fannie Jackson, head of the Institute for Colored Youth and probably the most influential black leader in Philadelphia, organized a bazaar to raise funds for the AME Book Concern and for the *Christian Recorder,* an AME periodical established as the *Christian Herald* in the 1840s and now the oldest continually published black periodical. She was Episcopalian and had established her distance from men to the extent of hiring the school janitor to escort her in the evenings. On a bet that he would not dare ask her to let him accompany her home from the bazaar, Coppin struck up an acquaintance that ripened into a marriage performed by Daniel Payne in Washington, D.C., on December 21, 1881, in the Nineteenth Street Baptist Church, the church of Jackson's sister. Fannie Jackson Coppin became active and very effective in women's work in her new church. She did not accede, however, to her husband's wish that she give up teaching, and their marriage began with their residence in different cities.

Coppin's time at Bethel in Philadelphia came to an end in 1881 under church regulations, which limited a pastor's stay in one city to four years. At the General Conference of 1880 Daniel Payne was moved to the Baltimore Conference, and he asked Coppin to switch conferences in that year. Coppin was given charge of Bethel church in Baltimore, where he remained until 1884. In the General Conference of that year he was elected president of the Sunday School Union and was assigned at his own request to the small Allen Chapel in Philadelphia. This allowed him to be with his wife and to attend the Protestant Episcopal Seminary in West Philadelphia. The seminary's program was rigorous: students had to read the New Testament in Greek from the beginning of their studies and the Old Testament in Hebrew from the second year on. Having an English Bible at school was grounds for automatic dismissal. Coppin graduated in 1887. Then in 1888 he followed Benjamin Tucker Tanner, who was elected bishop, as editor of the *AME Church Review,* a position he held for the next eight years. In Philadelphia Coppin and his wife boarded out–of–state girl students at the Institute for Colored Youth in their home and in a rented house next door, caring for as many as 15 students at one time.

Elected Bishop

It seemed probable that Coppin would be elected bishop in 1896, but his status as a protege of Daniel Payne and outstanding exemplar of a learned clergy roused enough animosity to ensure his defeat. Not only had Coppin completed seminary studies and edited the leading intellectual publication of the AME, he also devoted considerable time and money to building his own personal library. He fell victim to a campaign denouncing him for an alleged lack of sympathy for Southern churchmen, many of whom were poorly educated. In 1900 his friends were better organized, and after some judicious campaigning on his part, he won election to the bishopric in some last–minute maneuvering at the conference. From 1896 to 1900 Coppin enjoyed a second period as pastor of Mother Bethel in Philadelphia. Unfortunately in 1896 Fannie Jackson Coppin suffered a severe attack of pleurisy and her health declined hereafter.

On his election to the bishopric in 1900, Coppin became the AME's first missionary bishop in Africa. Arriving in Africa in January 1901, he worked to regularize the situation of the AME in Cape Colony, now part of South Africa, and established a school, Bethel Institute, dedicated on December 1, 1901. Fannie Jackson Coppin was forced out of her position at the Institute for Colored Youth in 1902. She then accompanied her husband back to Africa, where they remained from December 1902 to December 1903. In the spring of 1904 the Coppins toured Europe. At the General Conference that year he was assigned responsibility for South Carolina and Alabama. Fannie Jackson Coppin accompanied him on his first trip to the district, but she became an invalid and was confined to their home after 1905. While her body became progressively weaker, her mind remained sharp until near the end.

Coppin followed the pattern for bishops of taking up the supervision of a new district every four years, often serving in the South. In addition to his duties as bishop, Coppin served as president of the Educational Board from 1908 to 1912 and of the Church Extension Board from 1912 to 1920.

Fannie Jackson Coppin died on January 21, 1913, leaving her husband distraught. After a period of mourning, he met Baltimore physician M. Evelyn Thompson. They were married on August 14, 1914. A daughter, Theodosia, was born a year and a half later. In 1919 Coppin published *Unwritten History.* This was not his only published work, but the remainder of his writing, such as *Relation of Baptized Children to the Church* and *Fifty–two Sermon Syllabi,* tends to be more narrowly focused on church concerns. He also wrote a number of hymns and gospel songs.

Coppin was senior bishop of the AME church at the time of his death at his Philadelphia home at 1913 Bainbridge Street on June 25, 1924. He had been ill for several weeks. His funeral was at Mother Bethel Church on July 1. His wife and daughter survived him.

Coppin is not only an important leader of the AME church, he is an exemplary figure for the understanding of African American religion during his era. Growing up in an isolated local church, he came to learn of the newest developments in nineteenth–century theology and biblical interpretation. Although his voice was most often deliberately quiet and nonabrasive, his message was not subservient as he moved from rural isolation to the center of a large and flourishing denomination.

REFERENCES

Chirenje, J. Mutero. *Ethiopianism and Afro–Americans in Southern Africa, 1883–1916.* Baton Rouge: Louisiana State University Press, 1987.

Coppin, L. J. *Unwritten History.* Philadelphia: AME Book Concern, 1919.

Logan, Rayford W., and Michael R. Winston, eds. *Dictionary of American Negro Biography.* New York: Norton, 1982.

''Senior Prelate of A.M.E. Church Died June 25 at Phila.'' *New York Age,* July 5, 1924.

Smith, Jessie Carney, ed. *Notable Black American Women.* Detroit: Gale Research, 1992.

Wright, R. R., ed. *Encyclopaedia of the African Methodist Episcopal Church.* 2nd ed. Philadelphia: AME Book Concern, 1947.

Robert L. Johns

Samuel Cornish
(1795–1858)
Religious worker, editor, abolitionist

Samuel Cornish was an early Presbyterian minister and a prominent abolitionist. A conservative in religious and social views, he lost influence in the early 1840s as many black leaders became more militant, although he remained a respected figure. In addition, Cornish was an important newspaper editor, a co–founder of *Freedom's Journal,* the first black newspaper, and later editor of the *Colored American.*

Samuel Eli Cornish was born in Sussex County, Delaware, in 1795. Little is known of his family background except that his parents were free. He moved to Philadelphia in 1815, and there came under the influence of John Gloucester, the minister who founded the first black Presbyterian church. Gloucester educated him and trained him for the ministry. Since Gloucester was already gravely ill with the tuberculosis which killed him in 1822, Cornish gained practical experience filling in for his mentor. Cornish was licensed to preach in 1819 and spent a year as a missionary in Maryland.

Cornish established himself in New York City in 1821 and gathered a congregation which officially became the New Demeter Street Presbyterian Church when he was ordained in 1822. In 1824 he married Jane Livingston (d. 1844). The couple had four children: Sarah Matilda (1824–1846), William (b. 1826), Samuel (1828–1838), and Jane Sophia Tappan (1833–1855). He resigned from New Demeter Street Presbyterian Church in 1828 to work as an itinerant preacher and missionary.

Cornish's reputation rests more on his work with abolitionist organizations than on his career as a minister. In 1827 and 1828 he was an agent for the New York African Free Schools, charged with visiting parents in their homes to encourage attendance. In 1831 the First Annual Convention of the People of Color appointed him agent to collect funds for a college for African Americans to be built in New Haven, Connecticut. This project came to nothing due to overwhelming local opposition.

In 1827 Cornish joined John Russworm in editing *Freedom's Journal,* which first appeared on March 16. Russworm assumed sole editorial control on September 24, 1827, but Cornish took over the paper in 1829 when Russworm was forced to resign because of his support of the colonization movement. After a two–month hiatus, Cornish continued the paper for less than a year under the name *The Rights of All.* For a few months in 1832 he served as pastor of the First African Presbyterian Church in Philadelphia, founded by John Gloucester. Cornish further devoted his energies to eradicating the stain of slavery; he joined William Lloyd Garrison in the founding of the American Anti–Slavery Society in 1833, and helped found a local branch of the New York Anti–Slavery Society. Cornish also joined the American and Foreign Anti–Slavery Society, and spent at least nine years on its executive committee. He was an active member of the American Missionary Society, which incorporated the black Union Missionary Society Cornish had helped found. He was on the AMA's executive committee for three years and served as its vice–president.

In 1837 Cornish again became a newspaper editor, this time of the *Colored American,* a paper subsidized by noted white abolitionist Arthur Tappan. His associate on the paper was Philip A. Bell, later a noted California newspaper editor. Cornish held this post until the middle of 1839. Cornish was more conservative in his views than many of his younger contemporaries. For example, in an 1837 editorial he was part of a minority opposing the use of demonstrations and force to resist enforcement of the fugitive slave laws. This controversial opinion led to his estrangement from David Ruggles and the New York Committee of Vigilance, an organization dedicated to helping fugitive slaves.

In 1838 Cornish and his family moved to Belleville, New Jersey. *The Colored American* was in financial straits, Cornish's salary was unpaid, and Cornish hoped to raise his children in an environment less prejudiced than New York City. Tragedy struck, however, when the younger son drowned and the older son faced degradation in the public school. Around 1840 Cornish moved to Newark, New Jersey, where he headed a church for a brief time. After his wife died in 1844, Cornish moved his family back to New York City where he organized Emmanuel Church which he led until 1847. His older daughter died in 1846, and his younger daughter became ill in 1851 and died insane in 1855. In this year, Cornish, in very poor health himself, moved to Brooklyn, where he died in 1858.

Cornish was an important early figure in the abolition movement although younger colleagues overshadowed him in his later years. His reputation, as well as most of the information about his life, rests on his work as a journalist.

REFERENCES

Andrews, Charles C. *The History of the New–York African Free Schools.* 1830. Reprint, New York: Negro Universities Press, 1969.

Bell, Howard Holman. *Minutes and Proceedings of the National Negro Conventions, 1830–1864.* New York: Arno Press and the *New York Times,* 1969.

Gross, Bella. "Freedom's Journal and The Rights of All." *Journal of Negro History* 17 (July 1932): 241–86.

Logan, Rayford W., and Michael R. Winston, eds. *Dictionary of American Negro Biography.* New York: Norton, 1982.

Pease, Jane H., and William H. Pease. *Bound with Them in Chains.* Westport, CT: Greenwood Press, 1972.

Sterling, Dorothy. *Speak Out in Thunder Tones.* Garden City, NY: Doubleday, 1973.

[Tappan, Lewis]. *The Life of Arthur Tappan.* London, England: Sampson Low, Son, and Marston, 1870.

Robert L. Johns

Bill Cosby

(1937–)

Comedian, philanthropist, actor

Entertainer Bill Cosby, a popular father image on television, has consistently used the entertainment industry to portray a positive image of black people. He is the first black actor to star in a nationally broadcast dramatic television series. He has long had success as a stand–up comedian in night clubs and he is a dominant comic on television and on record albums. He has demonstrated his advocacy for education by becoming highly educated himself and by contributing significantly to black academic institutions.

Born in Germantown, Pennsylvania, a predominantly poor black section of North Philadelphia, on July 12, 1937, William Henry Cosby Jr. was the eldest of William Cosby Sr. and Annie "Anna" Pearl Cosby's four sons. The Cosbys' second son, James, had rheumatic fever and died in 1945 when he was six years old. His job as a welder enabled Cosby Sr. to support his family, but after the family increased the Cosbys moved to a low–income, all–black public housing project, the Richard Allen Homes. Later the senior Cosby joined the U.S. Navy, where he became a mess steward. This took him away from the family for long periods of time. To provide for the family then, Annie Cosby worked as a domestic. She still had time to read to her family selections from the Bible and the works of Mark Twain and Charles Dickens. Bill Cosby's new role was caretaker of his brothers, Russell and Robert, as he also shined shoes and delivered groceries to help make ends meet. Still, at times the family's income was supplemented by public assistance.

Cosby attended Mary Channing Wister Elementary School, then Fitz–Simons Junior High School. The talented Bill Cosby had a high IQ and later joined a class for gifted students at Central High School. Due to his poor grades, he decided to transfer to Germantown High School. He was talented in athletics as well and was captain of the track and football teams. He also played basketball, baseball, and football and continued to practice the humor that he had started earlier in school. His athletic endeavors along with his work schedule took their toll on his studies; consequently, Cosby was asked to repeat the tenth grade at Germantown High. By now economic conditions had improved for the family, and the Cosbys moved back to Germantown to Twenty–First Street where he had his own room for the first time. Still needing money, however, he worked at several menial jobs.

Cosby dropped out of Germantown High in 1956 and worked for a while as a shoe repairman. That same year he joined the U.S. Navy. Although his buddies had joined the air force, Cosby wanted to be different and chose the navy instead. The lean 160–pound six–footer worked to keep his weight under 190 pounds, ran track, and won track awards on the navy's team. The physical therapy that he learned while in the navy led him to an assignment at Bethesda Naval Hospital where he enjoyed being able to help those with physical needs. He also had some travel experience to such places as Newfoundland and Guantanamo Bay, Cuba, and still found time to complete his high school equivalency and received a GED (General Equivalency Diploma). When his four–year term was over, he was honorably discharged in May 1960 and in September enrolled in Temple University on an athletic scholarship and majored in health, physical education, and recreation. He joined the football team and his success there led to his induction into the Temple Hall of Fame in 1984. A scout from the New York Giants thought that he might become a professional player. Cosby also excelled in track, including discus and javelin throwing, high–jump, and broad–jump; he earned a letter in track. Although sports took a considerable amount of his time, he maintained a B average.

Bill Cosby

To help support himself at Temple, Cosby worked as a bartender in a local basement bar known as The Underground, which paid him $5 a night plus tips. His humor made him a popular bartender; consequently, when the regular stand–up comedian was absent, Cosby was asked to perform instead. This increased his regular income to $25 dollars each performance. Soon he became known around Philadelphia for his comedy, and The Cellar Bar next door hired him as a comedian for $12.50 nightly. Meanwhile, his cousin, Del Sheilds, a popular local radio disc jockey who had helped him land the new job, also showed him ways to increase local bookings. Cosby became serious about comedy and prepared himself well for the jokes he would tell. He refused to tell dirty jokes but did add some racial quips. He was funny and had a natural "cool." He also borrowed material from such successful comedians as Dick Gregory, Lenny Bruce, Nipsey Russell, Flip Wilson, George Carlin, and Jonathan Winters.

By 1962 Cosby began to take his talent elsewhere—to New York City on weekends where he worked at the Gaslight Cafe in Greenwich Village starting at $60 a week but in time he earned $175 a week. His positive reviews by newspaper critics further increased his popularity, and he accepted a gig at Chicago's Gate of Horn for $200 a week. Now that he felt he was doing rather well financially, Cosby decided to ignore the advice his mother had always given him—to get an education—and left his athletic scholarship and Temple University in the middle of his junior year to go for bigger purses. In early 1963 Cosby, then only 26–years old, had bookings at popular night spots as an opening act across the country and he began to use his own material rather than comedy borrowed from others. His bookings picked up to the extent that he hired the William Morris Agency to aid in his career development.

Cosby worked hard to be a funny entertainer and he developed nonracial routines that were good, true, and real, like the Mark Twain stories his mother had read to him in his childhood. Soon Cosby landed contracts to do albums with Warner Brothers and in 1963 recorded his first live album at the Bitter End Club in Greenwich Village. Other comedy and music albums followed, reaching a total of 20 recordings over several years; he sold millions of copies and became highly successful. In August 1963 he appeared at Mr. Kelly's in Chicago as an opening act for $500 a week. In September 1963 he appeared at the Hungry I as an opening act in San Francisco for $750 a week.

In 1963 as well, Cosby met Camille Olivia Hanks. That meeting was arranged by mutual friends. At that time she was a student at the University of Maryland and attended his performance at a local club called The Shadows. Two weeks later he asked her to marry him and she said no, but three weeks later she agreed. Her parents thought the 19–year–old was too young, wanted her to complete her studies, worried about Cosby's future as a comedian, and initially opposed the marriage. Cosby and Hanks married on January 25, 1964, in Olney, Maryland.

Comedian's Career Takes Off

Beginning 1965, Bill Cosby's career blossomed and Camille Cosby left school and traveled with her husband. Cosby's performance on Johnny Carson's *The Tonight Show,* hosted by stand–in Allan Sherman, led to other offers, particularly as costar with Robert Culp in NBC's television series *I Spy.* Sheldon Leonard was the executive producer. Cosby broke television's color barrier and became the first black person in a nontraditional role and the first black star in a television series that excluded racial themes. The show was also the first since *Amos 'n' Andy* to cast a black person in a lead role. *I Spy* aired from 1965 to 1968. In summer 1968 he narrated the first of a seven–part series, *Of Black America,* on the *CBS News Hour.* The "Black History: Lost, Stolen or Strayed?" segment illustrated the negative racial themes depicted in the media and stimulated widespread concern for removing such images. A videotape of the two–part segment was frequently used as a teaching tool in academia. Cosby also produced and performed in *Prejudice.* Cosby's television appearances continued with *The Bill Cosby Show,* NBC, 1969 to 1971; and the *Electric Company,* PBS, 1971 to 1976. Cosby's friends at Wister Elementary School, where his education began, became Fat Albert, Dumb Donald, Weird Harold, Mush Mouth, Weasel, and others who were preserved in his TV cartoons, *Fat Albert and the Cosby Kids,* later called *The New Fat Albert Show,* which aired on CBS from 1972 to 1984.

As a comedian, Cosby made show business history as a stand–up comic. In 1986 his 15 shows at Radio City Music Hall grossed $2.8 million, setting a record in the hall's 54–year history.

Continuing with television, Cosby was featured in the *New Bill Cosby Show,* CBS, 1972 to 1973; and *Cos,* ABC, September–October 1976. He appeared regularly during the 1970s on such children's television programs as *Sesame Street* and *Electric Company.* His next series *The Cosby Show,* NBC, 1984 to 1992, was a family–based program reflecting elements of his own life. He helped to create the show, was a coproducer, served as executive consultant, and composed some of the theme music. So concerned was Cosby with presenting real–life situations and with making a positive impact on his audiences that he hired psychiatrist Alvin Poussaint as consultant and advisor for the show. Cosby played the character Dr. Heathcliff Huxtable, while Phylicia Rashad played his wife, an attorney. Cosby's son Ennis was the inspiration for the character Theo, the son on the show. Although the entire Huxtable family concentrated on positive images of black people, some critics claimed that the show was an unrealistic portrayal of black family life.

At its peak the show had as many as 80 million viewers. Although Cosby no longer accepts Emmy nominations, *The Cosby Show* won three Emmys in 1985, for outstanding comedy series, outstanding writing in a comedy series, and outstanding directing in a comedy series. The show also received a Golden Globe award from Hollywood's Foreign Press Association and four People's Choice awards. (Cosby no longer accepts Golden Globe awards but continues to accept People's Choice awards.) Syndicated in 1987, *The Cosby Show* earned for Cosby, who was half–owner, a handsome sum of $333 million. Its spinoff, *A Different World,* first telecast on September 24, 1987, was aired concurrently with *The Cosby Show* for a while. Again Alvin Poussaint was his script consultant. Set on a fictional black college campus, the show was an advocate for education and some critics claim it helped stimulate an enrollment increase in black colleges. Cosby stimulated curiosity and interest among his viewers by wearing sweatshirts from various black colleges; the sweatshirts became his trademark. Cosby's next shows were the short–lived *You Bet Your Life,* 1992 to 1993 and *The Cosby Mysteries,* 1994; and beginning 1996 he appeared again with Phylicia Rashad in *Cosby.* In May 1997 he hosted a special *Kids Say the Darndest Things,* a salute to the show's founder Art Linkletter. The show became a weekly.

In addition to his television shows, Cosby has appeared in a number of films, including *Hickey and Boggs* (1971). He teamed with Sidney Poitier in *Uptown Saturday Night* (1974) and *A Piece of the Action* (1977). Other films included *Man and Boy* (1972), *Let's Do It Again* (1975), *Leonard Part VI* (1987), and *Ghost Dad* (1990). In 1996 he appeared with Robin Williams in the Francis Ford Coppola comedy and drama film, *Jack.*

His writings include *Fatherhood* (1986), *Bill Cosby's Personal Guide to Power Tennis* (1986), *Time Flies,* 1987, *Love and Marriage,* 1989 and *Childhood,* 1991. Scholastic's Cartwheel Books has begun to publish his series of books for children, targeting readers aged seven to ten. His Little Bill stories use subtlety, humor, and storytelling to discuss a variety of subjects, such as honesty, kindness, courage, family, and friendships.

Education and Philanthropy

Bill and Camille Cosby are firm believers in higher education. Bill Cosby never lost sight of his mother's urging to get an education. He studied at the University of Massachusetts at Amherst and received a master's degree in education in 1972 and an Ed.D. in 1977. He said in *Bill Cosby in Words and Pictures,* "I didn't get that degree to have something to fall back on." Instead, he has used it as a teaching tool at home and elsewhere with young people. Later Camille Cosby received both a master's and a doctorate degree from the University of Massachusetts at Amherst. The Cosbys continue to advocate higher education for their children.

The Cosbys' concern for education led them to provide substantial support to black colleges as well. The Cosbys gave $1.3 million to Fisk University in 1986. In 1987 they contributed $1.3 million to be divided among Central State (Wilberforce, Ohio), Howard University, Florida Agricultural and Mechanical State University, and Shaw University. The next year they gave another $1.5 million to be divided between Meharry Medical College and Bethune–Cookman College. That same year they endowed a scholarship for African American art students at the Skowhegan School of Painting and Sculpture in Maine in the amount of $195,000. Their largest gift was to Spelman College. In 1988 they gave Spelman $20 million to erect the Camille Olivia Hanks Cosby Academic Center which houses classrooms, offices, the Women's Research and Resources Center, the college's archives, art museum, and other facilities and programs. The building was dedicated in February 1996. The Cosbys continued their philanthropy to higher education in 1994 by giving $100,000 to Morehouse College to establish a scholarship in the name of *Jet* magazine editor Robert E. Johnson Jr. In 1994 as well, the Cosbys supported the work of African American women again by assisting the National Council of Negro Women in their campaign to establish the National Center for African American Women in Washington, D.C. The Cosbys gave the organization a building located at 1218 16th Street, N.W., valued at $1.8 million. Their interest in art and in education prompted the Cosbys to give Tougaloo College $100,000 in 1976 for art, the same to Talladega College that year for science programs, and $100,000 in May 1977 for scholarships for art students at Xavier University in New Orleans and at Fisk University in Nashville.

In recognition of his contributions as an entertainer, Bill Cosby has been honored widely. He received four Emmy Awards for outstanding performance by an actor in a leading role in a dramatic series, *I Spy,* 1966 through 1968. He also received Emmys for *The Bill Cosby Special,* 1969, and for outstanding achievement in children's programming for "The Secret" episode of *The New Fat Albert Show,* 1981. Cosby won eight Grammys for his recordings from 1963 through 1976.

A star bearing Cosby's name was added to Hollywood's Walk of Fame in 1979, and in 1983 Harvard University's *Lampoon* gave Cosby its first Lifetime Achievement Award. In 1985 he won the Spingarn Medal from the NAACP. He won the NAACP Image Award and in 1996 he was awarded the College Board Medal, the highest award given by the organization. The award recognizes individuals who demonstrate a commitment to the purposes of the College Board. In 1997 Cosby won his fifteenth People's Choice Award, as favorite male in a new television series, *Cosby.* Again that year Bill and Camille Cosby won an Essence Award for philanthropy. Bill Cosby was inducted into the Academy of Television Arts and Sciences Hall of Fame in 1994. Both Bill and Camille Cosby continue to deplore negative and stereotypical images of black people on television and work to promote positive images.

Among the numerous honorary degrees awarded to Cosby are those from such institutions as Fisk, Howard, Temple, and George Washington universities and Colby, Spelman, Talladega, Morehouse, Rust, and Swarthmore colleges.

Cosby is equally well known for his television commercials, especially the Jell–O brand products commercials that he has made with children. He has promoted such products as Kodak Film, Del Monte foods, Birds' Eye frozen foods, and other products.

His memberships include the United Negro College Fund, the NAACP, and Operation PUSH (People United to Serve Humanity). He has been president of Rhythm and Blues Hall of Fame, a member of the Sickle Cell Foundation, and a board member of the Centers for Disease Control.

The Cosbys have four children: Erika Ranee, Errin Chalene, Ensa Camille, and Evin Harrah. All of his children's names begin with "E", signifying excellence. The nation joined the Cosbys in mourning the death of their fifth child and only son, Ennis William, who was fatally shot early on January 16, 1997, while changing a tire on his father's car on a California freeway near the Santa Monica Mountains. A separate issue arose two days later. Autumn Jackson, a young woman who claimed to be his daughter out of wedlock, and three other people—Jose Medina, Boris Sabas, and Antoney Williams—tried unsuccessfully to extort $40 million from Cosby. Soon after his son's death, Bill Cosby returned to stand–up comedy. *The Nashville Tennessean* for February 3, 1997, summarized his comments on his return to stand–up comedy tour just two weeks later, stating he needed to have release for himself and his audience. On July 25, 1997, Autumn Jackson and Jose Medina were convicted in New York City of extortion, conspiracy, and crossing state lines to commit a crime. Boris Sabas was convicted of conspiracy and crossing state lines; Antoney Williams was convicted of conspiracy and aiding and abetting an extortion plot. Later, Jackson was unresponsive to Cosby's efforts to explore the paternity issue further by taking a paternity test.

Bill Cosby is a devoted family man who publicly acknowledges his wife's wisdom, beauty, and business acumen. Bill Cosby is an art collector, a collector of automobiles, and a lover of show dogs. He is an avid tennis fan and also has played in celebrity tournaments for charity. Cosby remains a supporter of civil rights causes, and political, educational, and social organizations and institutions. He is one of the nation's highly successful comedians. He has quick humor, much of it based on personal experiences. He is a storyteller whose anecdotes are filled with the cold truth as well as warm remembrances of his life and family. He has a special view of life that appeals to all ages, whether in films, on television, or on the stage.

Current address: William Morris Agency, 1325 Avenue of the Americas, New York, NY 10019.

REFERENCES

"Bill Cosby Honored with College Board Medal." *New York Amsterdam News.* November 9, 1996.

Bogle, Donald. *Blacks in American Film and Television.* New York: Simon and Schuster, 1988.

Contemporary Black Biography. Vol. 7. Detroit: Gale Research, 1994.

"Cosby Endowment Will Benefit Fisk's Art Department." *Nashville Tennessean,* May 20, 1997.

"Cosby Returns to Stand–up Comedy." *The Nashville Tennessean,* February 3, 1997.

"Cosbys Donate $1.8 Million to the National Council of Negro Women." *About. . .Time Magazine* 22 (30 April 1994): 5.

Current Biography Yearbook. New York: H. W. Wilson Co., 1986.

"Jackson Guilty of Extortion." *Nashville Tennessean,* July 26, 1997.

Johnson, Robert E. "Bill and Camille Cosby: First Family of Philanthropy." *Ebony* 44 (May 1989): 25–34.

———. *Bill Cosby: In Words and Pictures.* Chicago: Johnson Publishing Company, 1986.

Norment, Lynn. "Three Great Love Stories." *Ebony* 43 (February 1988): 150–56.

Smith, Jessie Carney. *Notable Black American Women.* Detroit: Gale Research, 1992.

Smith, Ronald L. *Cosby.* New York: St. Martin's Press, 1986.

"Woman Tries to Extort $40 Million from Bill Cosby." *New York Times,* January 21, 1997.

Jessie Carney Smith

William Craft
(1824–1900)
Abolitionist, educator, farmer

William Craft and his wife Ellen made a daring and well–publicized escape from slavery, an event that tended to overshadow their achievements during the remainder of their lives. After their escape, they continued to forward the cause of black liberation. William Craft became an effective anti–slavery worker in Great Britain. After he spent time in Africa exploring the possibility of developing agriculture and trade there, the Crafts returned to the American South to work among the newly freed blacks. Their valiant efforts to develop a cooperative farming and schools ultimately failed due to low agricultural prices and white hostility.

William Craft was born in Georgia in 1824. He was brought to Macon as a child and apprenticed there as a carpenter. Members of his family—mother, father, brother, and sister—were sold, and in 1840 he was mortgaged to a bank as collateral for a loan to grow cotton. When cotton prices collapsed, the bank foreclosed, and he was sold to the bank cashier, Ira H. Taylor. Taylor sent him back to the cabinet shop where he apprenticed. He married fellow slave Ellen Smith in 1846.

Ellen Smith was born about 1826; she was the daughter of James Smith, a rich cotton–planter, and one of his slaves, Maria. Ellen Smith looked white. Smith's wife was angered by Ellen's presence and gave Ellen as a wedding present to her daughter who married Charles Collins of Macon in 1837.

The Crafts had put off their marriage for some time in hope of a change in their situation. They then asked Collins for permission to marry. Despite his disapproval of slaves marrying off the plantation, he agreed. After two years of discussion, the Crafts settled on a daring escape plan. In December of 1848 Ellen Craft assumed the role of an crippled man traveling for health care. William Craft acted as the servant. They successfully reached Philadelphia and then Boston.

Their escape attracted national attention. After a brief tour of New England with fellow fugitive slave and abolition speaker William Wells Brown and an appearance at a Massachusetts Anti–Slavery Society meeting in January 1849, the Crafts dropped from the public eye in the Boston African American community. For 18 months Ellen worked as a seamstress and William as a cabinet maker.

The Fugitive Slave Act of 1850 posed a threat to black communities in the North. The law allowed seizure of escaped slaves and required federal magistrates to assist in returning them to their owners. Many fugitives left for Canada, but the Crafts stayed in the United States. In October of 1850 two slave–catchers from Georgia appeared in Boston to reclaim them. The black community and a number of whites sprang to their defense. Ellen Craft was hidden in private homes. Craft first barricaded himself in his cabinet making shop and then moved to the home of Lewis Hayden, a black activist. Armed blacks kept a lookout, and Hayden proclaimed that he would blow up his house before surrendering Craft. The slave–catchers were presented continually with arrest warrants intended to harass them, and eventually a mob drove them out of Boston. The Crafts were safe, but it was possible that the federal government may intervene to enforce the law. A three–week clandestine journey took the Crafts to Halifax, Nova Scotia, where they boarded a ship to Great Britain. They remained there for 16 years.

William Craft

Great Britain and Abolition

Ellen Craft was in very poor health when they arrived in England, but William Craft reluctantly left her to join William Wells Brown on a British lecture circuit for six months, speaking out against slavery and for temperance. Ellen joined him as soon as she recovered. Appearing onstage at the end of the program, she caused a stir because she looked like a white woman.

After the tour, the Crafts spent the next three years attending an agricultural school in Ockham, Surrey. The Crafts' first child, Charles Estlin Phillips, was born there on October 22, 1852. (Three more children would follow: Ellen, William Jr., and Brougham.) The Crafts turned down offers for positions at the school and settled in London. Ellen Craft continued to sew, and William Craft lectured and worked as a cabinet maker. Eventually they opened a fairly successful fancy–goods export–import business. He also wrote an account of his escape, *Running a Thousand Miles for Freedom,* published in 1860.

Craft's antislavery lectures now included support for the free–produce movement, a boycott of slave–produced goods. British supporters of the free–produce movement envisioned developing another source of cotton in Africa. This led to the formation of the African Aid Society in 1860. In 1861 Craft gave his support to the society to develop contacts in Dahomey (now Benin). From the winter of 1861 through the spring of 1862, he toured to raise funds for a mission to Africa. His contacts with the king of Dahomey were encouraging, and he returned to London in the summer of 1863.

Craft attended the annual meeting of the British Association for the Advancement of Science to offer a report. He responded vigorously to two papers delivered at the meeting that implied African inferiority to Europeans. In December 1863 Craft returned to Dahomey, where he remained for the next three and a half years, leaving his family in England. His priorities there were opening a school and establishing a merchant business. His school, which opened in mid–1864, was successful. Raising funds for his school was difficult as his relations with the Company of African Merchants, an association that joined with him to develop trade in Africa, deteriorated. In 1867 Craft returned to England for health reasons. Before his departure the king sent 50 slaves to repay debts. Craft was willing to accept 50 percent of the loss for freeing these slaves, but the merchant company insisted that he was responsible for the whole amount. He was eventually forced to sell his home to pay his debts.

During her husband's absence Ellen Craft had been able to arrange for her mother, with whom she had not been in contact since 1848, to come to England in November 1865. She also continued her efforts in the abolitionist movement and supported the newly formed Women's Suffrage Society. William Craft arrived home in time for the Crafts to attend an international abolitionist meeting in Paris. The following year, they decided to return to the United States.

The Crafts Return to the American South

During a fund–raising campaign in December 1868, William Craft was able to raise a considerable amount of money to establish an agricultural cooperative in Georgia. In early 1870 the Crafts established themselves at Hickory Hill, a plantation just over the state line in South Carolina. Ellen Craft established schools, one for children and one for adults. That fall, night riders burnt their house and barn and destroyed their crops. Unhurt, the Crafts took refuge with their son, who was running a boarding house in Savannah.

Determined to remain in the South, the Crafts leased Woodville in 1871, an abandoned plantation 20 miles from Savannah in Bryan County. A poor harvest and low agricultural prices exhausted their funds, but they remained. William Craft spent most of 1873 in New England raising funds to buy the plantation. Ellen Craft ran the plantation when he was absent and opened a school. Unfortunately, the "begging" efforts of William Craft cost them the support of prominent friends like Wendell Phillips by the early 1870s. (Many prominent abolitionists did not approve of public fund–raising efforts, which they labeled "begging.") Phillips and Philadelphian William Still, of the Underground Railroad, also came to feel that Craft was neglecting his family.

By 1876 there was little real return on the Crafts' investment. Cotton prices and land values dropped, and their debts were growing. In addition, their white neighbors were becoming increasingly hostile. In June 1876 William Craft attended the Republican Convention in Cincinnati. By September he was facing accusations that he used money raised for the development of Woodville for personal gain. This was the beginning of a coordinated campaign directed against him.

The Crafts filed suit against the person who first published these accusations, but lost the case and spent a considerable amount of money in the process.

The Crafts had to try to carry on with little money, and the family was breaking up. In 1881 William Jr. returned to England, where he remained for the rest of his life. Daughter Ellen married Dr. William Crumm of Savannah. Charles and Brougham found work in the U.S. Postal Service.

Records of the Crafts after 1878 are scanty. Maintaining the plantation was a continual struggle. Ellen Craft died in 1891 and was buried under her favorite oak on the plantation. In 1899 William Craft lost the plantation to debt. He died at his daughter's home in Savannah in very early 1900, just before the plantation's title legally passed to the Southern Fertilizer Company.

William and Ellen Craft did much to advance the cause of abolition. William Craft was also a pioneer in opening Africa to trade. Although the Craft's efforts to build a new future for blacks in the South after the Civil War also foundered, probably in large part due to white intransigence, their vision deserves remembrance.

REFERENCES

Blackett, R. J. M. *Beating Against the Barriers.* Ithaca, NY: Cornell University Press, 1989.

[Craft, William]. *Running a Thousand Miles for Freedom.* London: William Tweedie, 1860.

Ripley, C. Peter, ed. *The Black Abolitionist Papers.* Vol. 1. Chapel Hill: University of North Carolina Press, 1985.

Smith, Jessie Carney, ed. *Notable Black American Women.* Detroit: Gale Research, 1992.

Still, William. *The Underground Rail Road.* Philadelphia: Wm. Still, 1883.

Robert L. Johns

George W. Crockett Jr.
(1909–1997)
Congressman, judge, lawyer

George W. Crockett Jr. compiled a long and often controversial record as a defender of civil liberties, personal rights and unpopular causes. Crockett went to Washington, D.C., in 1939 as the first African American lawyer to work for the U.S. Department of Labor. He quickly rose to become the highest ranking black lawyer in the federal government. Crockett was considered the finest expert on the Constitution to serve on the Detroit bench. He served ten years in the U.S. House of Representatives, representing Michigan's 13th Congressional District.

George William Crockett Jr. was born in Jacksonville, Florida, on August 10, 1909, the son of George William Crockett Sr., a carpenter, and Minnie A. Jenkins Crockett. He had one sister, Alzeda Crockett Hacker. His first marriage was to the Ethelene Jones Crockett, a physician in 1934. They had three children: Elizabeth Ann Crockett Hicks, George William III, and Ethelene Crockett Jones. Crockett's second marriage was to a pediatrician, Harriette Clark Chambliss, in the summer of 1980. Harriette had two sons, Cleveland Roberts Chambliss Jr., Marque Chambliss. George W. Crockett Jr. died of cancer on Sunday, September 7, 1997, at the Washington Home and Hospice in Washington, D.C.

Crockett's first job was delivering groceries when he was 12–years old. He attended public schools in Jacksonville and graduated with a Bachelor of Arts (A.B.) degree from Morehouse College in Atlanta in 1931. He received his Juris Prudence (J.D.) degree from the University of Michigan in 1934, where he was the only African American student in his class. Crockett returned to Jacksonville to begin his law practice, then moved to Fairmont, West Virginia, where he practiced from 1934 to 1939.

Crockett went to Washington, D.C., in 1940 as a protégé of West Virginia's senator Matthew M. Neely, the man who had converted him from a Lincoln Republican to a New Deal Democrat. Although he had been assured a position with the Justice Department, they shunted Crockett to the Labor Department. It was holding a series of posts that convinced him that African Americans and American workers were often fellow victims of an oppressive society.

In 1943 Crockett was the first African American examiner appointed to a government labor board. President Franklin D. Roosevelt appointed Crockett a hearing examiner of the wartime Fair Employment Practices Committee. In this position, he regularly ordered companies to adopt race–neutral hiring and promotion policies that would not become standard until the 1970s. A chance meeting with a top official of the International United Auto Workers union led to a job organizing and running a union fair–employment division. It was through his work with the union in Detroit that Crockett was asked to join the team defending 11 Communist leaders.

In 1948 the government accused those Communist leaders of teaching the overthrow of the federal government. This was a violation of the Smith Act, a law regarded by those who believed in civil liberties as contrary to the rights guaranteed by the First Amendment. Years later the U.S. Supreme Court nullified the Smith Act. Crockett defended Carl Winter of Michigan in this celebrated trial. He was such a strong advocate for his client that after the trial and conviction of the defendant Judge Harold Medina cited the attorney for contempt. Medina sentenced Crockett to a four–month stay at an Ashland, Kentucky, federal prison in 1952. While serving his sentence, he became a "jailhouse lawyer," helping inmates with appeals and suits against the prison system and advising them of their legal rights. This experience had its impact. He told the *New York Times* for April 1, 1969:

> I think I have always been a champion of the underdog in our society and, if anything, that segre-

gated prison life probably pushed me a little further along the road. I know from physical contact what it means when a judge says one year, two years, three years. I don't want to wish it on any of my associates, but I think it would do them some good if they would spend some time in jail.

In 1952 Crockett defended future State Senator and Detroit mayor Coleman Young, whom the House Un–American Activities Committee had charged with subversion. Criticism and suspicion of Crockett's alleged support of leftist causes followed him throughout his career. In 1987 the *National Review* accused Crockett and other Democratic representatives of being Communist sympathizers. The article cited Crockett's association with the Civil Rights Congress and the National Lawyers Guild; his representation of witnesses before the House Committee on Un–American Activities; a reception he sponsored in support of Julius and Ethel Rosenberg (then in prison awaiting execution for spying for the Soviet Union); a petition drive he led charging the U.S. government with genocide against African Americans; and, suggested that during the 1960s Crockett was a registered agent of Cuba. His son, George Crockett III, a judge, stated that he and his two sisters grew up with pickets, threats, tapped telephones and FBI surveillance.

As vice–president of the National Lawyers Guild, Crockett led a contingent of 65 volunteer civil rights lawyers to the South. The Mississippi Project provided free legal defense for civil rights workers jailed in the state. That summer of 1964 left George Crockett shaken after the three young people, Andrew Goodman, James Chaney and Michael Schwermer, whom he asked to investigate a church burning in Philadelphia, Mississippi, were lynched and buried in an earthen dam.

Crockett was elected Recorders Court judge in 1966. A University of Michigan Law School report praised him as perhaps the only judge who kept his head during the 1967 Detroit rioting and administered justice impartially. Crockett refused to impose what he considered excessive and unlawful bail on scores of suspects accused of participating. He was convinced that African American judges had to lead the fight for equal justice.

In March 1969 Crockett gained nationwide attention and condemnation for his action in upholding the Constitutional rights of 142 blacks, including women and children, arrested by the Detroit police. The police raided a cell of the militant organization, Republic of New Africa, at a meeting at C. L. Franklin's New Bethel Baptist Church. Shooting began and a white police officer was killed. Some 50 white officers shot their way into the church and corralled all present, holding them in the police garage. Crockett rushed to police headquarters, set up an impromptu courtroom, and began releasing prisoners on their own recognizance. Crockett freed most of the suspects because the evidence being used to hold them was inadmissible. Police had ignored their right to counsel while requiring them to submit to gunpowder tests. Two investigating commissions found Crockett's rulings within the law. Many felt that he had again kept an explosive situation from erupting into a repeat of the 1967 riot.

Elected to Congress

Following his retirement from the Recorder's Court in 1978, Crockett served briefly as a visiting judge in the Michigan Court of Appeals and later as the Acting Corporation Counsel for the City of Detroit. Crockett was a well–known leader in Detroit's African American community when he declared his candidacy for the congressional seat left vacant by the 1980 resignation of Charles Diggs. He was elected to fill that vacancy on November 4, 1980, and simultaneously was elected for the full term of the 97th Congress. He was sworn in on November 12, 1980.

One of the oldest members of Congress at 71 when he replaced Charles C. Diggs Jr., (D–Mich.), he went on to compile a voting record described as one of the most liberal in Congress. A member of the Congressional Black Caucus, Crockett served on the House Judiciary and Foreign Affairs committees. An honorary member of the Congressional Hispanic Congress, Crockett served on the Select Committee on Aging and the executive board of the Democratic Study Group. Crockett, who represented most of inner–city Detroit, became the first member of Congress to call for decriminalizing drugs. While in Congress, he was one of the first members to be arrested at the South African Embassy in protests there against white minority rule. As a member of the Africa Subcommittee on Foreign Affairs, he wrote the Mandela Freedom Resolution, which called on the government of South Africa to release Nelson Mandela and his wife, Winnie Mandela, from imprisonment and banning.

Both houses of the Congress passed the resolution in 1986. He displayed sympathy for the Palestine Liberation Organization when most political figures shunned the group as a terrorist organization.

Crockett sued the Reagan administration to keep U.S. troops out of El Salvador. He was also opposed to the U.S. invasions of Grenada and Panama. In 1987 and 1988 Crockett served as a member of the United States delegation to the 42nd General Assembly of the United Nations. He was previously a member of the U.S. congressional delegation to the International Parliamentary meeting in Havana in 1981 and the Seventh United Nations Congress on Prevention of Crime meeting in Milan, Italy, in 1984.

Crockett founded the law firm of Goodman, Crockett, Eden and Robb, in 1946. This Phi Beta Kappa and Kappa Alpha Psi Fraternity member was also a trustee of Morehouse College. Founder and first chair of the Judicial Council of the National Bar Association, Crockett belonged to the National Lawyers Guild and the Congress for Peace Through Law. Crockett's hobby was carpentry. He enjoyed photography, swimming, cycling, and was a member of Hartford Baptist Church. *Time* magazine described George Crockett as having "a thorough legal mind, limitless self–assurance, and militant sympathies."

REFERENCES

Contemporary Black Biography. Vol. 10. Detroit: Gale Research, 1996.

"Crockett and the Patriots." *National Review* 39 (14 August 1987): 18–19.

Crockett, George W. Jr. "The American People are Misinformed and Lied To." *Freedomways* 21.4 (1981): 234–241.

———. *Freedom is Everybody's Job! The Crime of the Government Against the Negro People; Summation in the Trial of the 11 Communist Leaders*. New York: National Non–Partisan Committee to Defend the Rights of the 12 Communist Leaders, [1949?].

Flint, Jerry M. "Controversial Judge George William Crockett Jr." *New York Times* April 1, 1969. 18.

"Former Michigan Congressman and Judge, George William Crockett Jr., 88, Dies of Cancer." *Jet* (22 September 1997): 56.

Heldman, Louis and Kathy Warbelow. "Crockett and New Bethel: He Stood His Ground." *Biography News* 2.2 (March/April 1975): 297–298.

"Judge in a City of Fear." *Time* (6 April 1970): 60.

Sanders, Charles L. "Detroit's Rebel Judge Crockett." *Ebony* 24 (August 1969): 114–124.

Thomas, Robert McG., Jr. "George W. Crockett Dies at 88; Was a Civil Rights Crusader." *New York Times*, September 15, 1997. B7.

Waller, J. Michael, and Joseph Sobran. "Congress's Red Army; Authors Accuse Some Democratic Congressmen of Being Communist Sympathizers." *National Review* 39 (31 July 1987): 25–28.

Kathleen E. Bethel

Alexander Crummell
(1819–1898)
Religious worker, educator, writer, colonizationist

Alexander Crummell was one the leading black nationalists of the nineteenth century. While he saw contemporary blacks in both America and Africa as degraded, he firmly believed that Christianization and education would in time civilize blacks and lead them to become the dominant world race. Before the American Civil War, Crummell was a prominent supporter of African colonization. After spending several years abroad, however, he changed his position, but his nationalist views remained constant. In fact, Crummell's conviction was so great that he had an aversion to race–mixing, which led to his mistrust of most mulattos.

Alexander Crummell was born on March 3, 1819, in New York City to Boston Crummell and Charity Hicks Crummell. Both parents were of unmixed African descent. Alexander was the oldest child. He had at least two brothers, Charles and Henry. Crummell's mother was born at Jericho on Long Island to a family long established in the United States. Boston Crummell was born in Africa and brought to America when he was 12– or 13–years old and sold into slavery. One source gives 1780 for the date of his arrival, which would make him over 50 when Alexander was born. Boston Crummell is said to have emancipated himself from Peter Shermerhorn after refusing to continue on the grounds that ten years was enough to justify his release from slavery.

Alexander Crummell

Boston Crummell, who supported his family as an oysterman, achieved recognition in the black community by joining with other prominent New York City African Americans to found a high school for blacks. According to a letter by Alexander Crummell, his father seriously considered establishing a farm in Liberia in early 1856. After Boston Crummell's death, Alexander's mother traveled with him to Liberia, where she died around 1868.

Secures an Education

Alexander Crummell attended African Free School No. 2 at 137 Mulberry Street. There he associated with many boys who would later achieve prominence. Crummell particularly admired classmate Thomas S. Sidney, who was somewhat older and notable for piety and studiousness. Another close friend was next door neighbor Henry Highland Garnet, who was three years older and member of a family that had escaped from slavery.

Crummell, Sidney, and Garnet found themselves together in the same high school Boston Crummell founded. The doors to higher education seemed barred, but in 1835 the young men learned that Noyes Academy, just established by abolitionists in Canaan, New Hampshire, was open to blacks. White hostility made the trip that summer difficult for all three, especially Garnet who had a leg infection which later led to its amputation.

The white population of Canaan was hostile to both abolitionists and blacks and did not welcome the 14 young young blacks who eventually joined the 40 whites at the academy. On August 10, a mob hitched oxen to the school building and dragged it off, warning the blacks to leave within two weeks. Crummell discouraged nightriders threatening the boarding house by firing a shotgun at them. Fearing for their lives, Crummell, Sidney, and Garnet left the academy.

Crummell, Sidney, and Garnet soon discovered that Oneida Institute in Whitboro, New York, would accept them. This time the reception was more favorable. By February of 1836, Crummell and Sidney were there as sophomores, while Garnet was in the preparatory department. With the encouragement of the faculty and fellow students, Crummell underwent a conversion experience in 1837. In 1838, while nearing satisfactory completion of his studies, Crummell declared to the Episcopal bishop of New York, Benjamin T. Onderdonk, that he intended to pursue holy orders.

The head of the General Theological Seminary, William Whittingham, was not opposed to admitting him, but Onderdonk had already forced Whittingham to dismiss Isaiah de Grasse, a very light–skinned black, who had been accepted by students and faculty with no problems. In an interview after the seminary trustees turned down Crummell's petition for admittance, Onderdonk berated the young man in terms that reduced him to tears.

At this time John Jay, who was named after his grandfather—the first chief justice of the United States Supreme Court—sought Crummell out and supported his admission to the seminary, but racism in the church made the efforts of the outnumbered white supporters nugatory. Between 1839 and 1842, Crummell continued his studies in New England, part of the time as a private student. In some capacity he also studied at Yale. In New Haven Crummell led black parishioners out of Trinity parish to form a separate black congregation, Saint Luke's, in 1840, where he served as a lay reader. Alexander Du Bois, grandfather of W. E. B. Du Bois, was the first treasurer of Saint Luke's, and his grandson was baptized there.

Crummell's friend Sidney died after a long illness in 1840. In 1841 Crummell married an eighteen–year–old woman named Sarah. The marriage was plagued by extreme poverty, especially in the early years, and the relationship between the two soon became very cold. Poverty likewise contributed to the early death of their first child. Alexander Jr., their youngest boy, also died after swallowing a button in 1851. Sidney Garnet, their surviving son, became undependable as an adult. There were at least three daughters. Frances and Sophia Elizabeth survived childhood, although Sophia died in 1879. Their third daughter, Dillwinna died as a child in Africa. At the time of Sarah Crummell's death in New York in 1878, she and Alexander were no longer living together and apparently had been separated for some time. On September 23, 1880, Alexander Crummell married Jennie Simpson. This marriage appears to have been happier than the first.

Begins Church Ministry

In the spring of 1841 Crummell answered the call of a small black congregation, Christ Church in Providence, Rhode Island, by reducing the congregation's debt and building a new church. But relations with the congregation went sour, due in large part to Crummell's apparent rigidity and coldness. He become a deacon in May of 1842, but by fall of that year the split with the church's vestry was irreparable, and with a considerable sense of humiliation, Crummell moved to Philadelphia.

There Crummell faced Bishop Henry U. Onderdonk, brother of Benjamin T., bishop of New York. Onderdonk refused to accept Crummell as a member of the church convention, a right normally held by all clergy but denied to blacks. Crummell tried to establish a church and a school in Philadelphia without great success. Bishop Alfred Lee of Delaware ordained him in 1844.

In 1845 Crummell returned to New York to take charge of the second black Episcopal church there, the Church of the Messiah. He was not generally popular in New York, although there was some talk of asking him to become rector of Saint Philip's. Crummell won some acclaim as an orator during these years and gained political visibility. For example, he was successful in securing passage of a resolution calling for the establishment of a black college at the 1847 meeting of the National Convention of Colored People and Their Friends in Troy, New York, although the project went nowhere because prominent leaders like Frederick Douglass and Henry Highland Garnet were opposed to the resolution.

Crummell left for England in 1848, ostensibly to raise funds for the Church of the Messiah. His family soon followed. There Crummell undertook an extensive schedule of speaking engagements. Ironically, one of his earliest major triumphs as an orator was an attack on the American Colonization Society. At this time Crummell decided to attend college. After some remedial work in Latin and Greek, he was admitted to Queen's College of Cambridge University. Mathematics was much stressed at Cambridge at this time, and Crummell was not especially good in the subject. In addition, he was often ill, but in early 1853 Crummell earned a degree from the university.

Moves to Africa

Despite his reputation as an anticolonizationist, Crummell decided to emigrate to Liberia. With his family, he left for Monrovia, Liberia, in May of 1853, where he became a missionary of the Protestant Episcopal Church of America. His ecclesiastical superior in Africa was white Virginian John Payne, stationed at a missionary settlement further down the

Liberian coast at Cape Palmas. Payne installed Crummell as rector of Trinity Church. There was a rival black Episcopalian priest in Monrovia, Eli Worthington Stokes, whom Payne considered reliable. In time both Stokes and Crummell developed ambitions to become bishop of an independent, black–led Liberian Episcopal Church, and Stokes, Payne, and Crummell engaged in shifting alliances of two against the remaining one. Crummell did not succeed in this pursuit largely because his style of worship was less appealing to Liberians than that of Stokes.

Crummell worked hard, however, establishing a Sunday school, assembling a catechism class, and working toward constructing a church building. He remained poor despite his salary from the missionary society. Toward the end of the first year, Crummell moved into the country, where he built a house and tried to farm. The illness of his wife, who was confined to bed for almost a whole year, worked against the success of this endeavor. Crummell then completed a small church building, established a day school, and raised funds from America to build a public library but his congregation remained small. He also began agricultural experiments aimed at developing cash crops for the colony.

In late 1856 Crummell resigned from his position with the Board of Missions in the hopes of easing the financial strain of his family through another project. Payne arranged for financial help and gave him a job at Mt. Vaughan High School in Cape Palmas. Crummell took up this position in July of 1858 and remained in Cape Palmas until January of 1861. There he was visited by Martin Delany in August of 1859, when Delany was on his expedition to Africa to find a location for colonization efforts.

In the spring of 1861 Crummell and his family returned to the United States to drum up support for African colonization. This stay was prolonged until late 1862 since in the spring of that year he discovered that he had been named a commissioner by the Liberian government and charged with encouraging emigration from the United States.

Disputes Follow Career

Crummell and a fellow commissioner, Edward W. Blyden, were named to the faculty of Liberia College shortly after its organization. The third teacher, Joseph Jenkins Roberts, was the former founding president of Liberia. Roberts was president of the college, and both Blyden and Crummell soon quarreled with him. Crummell weakened his position with the trustees of the college when he suddenly returned in 1865 to the United States to collect his two daughters whom he had left in Oberlin, Ohio, for their education. Crummell did not return for seven months and the college dispensed with his services on July 11, 1866.

Even as he was battling college authorities, Crummell continued his ecclesiastical disputes. After he was forced out of the college, Crummell established an up–country church at New Georgia in May of 1867 and undertook a steady round of mission work up and down the river. His son Sidney, whom he had earlier sent to England to be educated for two years, wrote a letter to Bishop Payne on May 15, 1869, charging his father with being a family tyrant and starving them. Crummell had the humiliation of having to clear his name before a grand jury. His daughter Frances appeared to defend her father, while his wife, Sarah, did not testify in his defense.

Crummell became increasingly disenchanted with his situation in Africa. Then in August of 1871, after arranging a disastrous loan in London, Liberian president Edward James Roye was overthrown and died while trying to flee. In the chaos that followed, Crummell was assaulted in the streets and threatened with death. In the midst of these trying times Crummell had a major quarrel with Blyden, who Crummell believed had committed adultery with Roye's wife. In the spring of 1872 Crummell left for America.

In the United States Crummell was called to take over the chapel of Saint Mary's in Washington, D.C., in the fall of 1873. Crummell was able to enlarge his congregation and build a new stone church named Saint Luke's at 1514 Fifteenth Street, N.W. His relations with the church over the years were stormy, but by the time of his retirement in 1894 he had a congregation of 135 families and 600 individuals. Typical of the troubles with his congregation was a dispute with the choir beginning in 1879 that caused much newspaper comment. It came to a head over music for Easter services and resulted in a replacement choir appearing on that occasion. In 1882 the vestry petitioned Bishop William Pinkney for Crummell's removal. Pinkney overruled the recommendation, however, and Crummell remained.

Crummell's local influence was weakened by his struggles within his church, but his national reputation as a thinker and orator grew nonetheless. Persons who came into intermittent contact with Crummell even found him pleasant. In a preface to Henry A. Phillips's memorial address, Matthew Anderson, a black clergyman in whose summer house Crummell died, said Crummell was "most congenial. . . . No man could have been more agreeable than he, humor, wit, repartee and even playfulness gushed from his exuberant spirit [and] made him a most acceptable guest." In the eulogy Phillips admitted Crummell's formidable side: "He was a born ruler and could not brook opposition. . . . Dealing with a people who have not yet learned to submit gracefully to authority, when exerted by one of their own race, this trait of character . . . often militated against his immediate usefulness."

It is uncertain whether or not Crummell's retirement from Saint Luke's in December of 1894—upon the celebration of his fiftieth anniversary being ordained—was entirely voluntary. Nonetheless, he continued to participate in groups such as the Ministers' Union of Washington, D.C., which he had founded, and the Commission on Work among Colored People, an interracial Episcopalian group he had helped to found. He seems to have been free of pressing money problems during this period, and his health was good for his age. His failing eyesight was relieved by a cataract operation in the spring of 1894 and a second in 1897.

During a speaking tour in 1895, Crummell delivered the commencement address at Wilberforce where 27 year old W. E. B. Du Bois met him. Du Bois wrote a much idealized portrait of him in *The Souls of Black Folk* and, according to David Levering Lewis, Crummell remained a major influence on Du Bois until late in the 1930s.

Crummell greatly influenced the formation of the American Negro Academy, an organization designed to foster a black intellectual elite. At the initial meeting of the academy on March 5, 1897, he was elected by acclamation. By now Crummell had become a leader, if only in spirit, among those blacks opposed to Booker T. Washington and his Tuskegee machine.

In June of 1897, Crummell, ever an Anglophile, undertook a five months' visit to England. In August of 1898, he left for a vacation in Point Pleasant, New Jersey. Toward the end of the month Crummell's physical strength began to fail and he died on September 10 with his second wife at his side. His body was taken to New York City, and his funeral services were held at Saint Philip's Episcopal Church. It appears that neither of the two surviving children, Frances and Sidney, attended the funeral, although Sidney's wife was there.

Crummell's legacy has been somewhat overlooked by posterity. Many Garveyites failed to recognize Crummell's nationalism as influential to their own. Moreover, when black nationalism came to the fore in the 1950s and 1960s, Crummell was again overlooked. Still, many contemporary thinkers contend that knowledge of Crummell and his efforts are essential to understanding black intellectual history.

REFERENCES

Crummell, Alexander. *Destiny and Race: Selected Writings, 1840–1898.* Edited by Wilson Jeremiah Moses. Amherst: University of Massachusetts Press, 1992.

Lewis, David Levering. *W. E. B. Du Bois: Biography of a Race, 1868–1919.* New York: Henry Holt, 1993.

Logan, Rayford W., and Michael P. Winston. *Dictionary of American Negro Biography.* New York: Norton, 1982.

Moses, Wilson Jeremiah. *Alexander Crummell: A Study of Civilization and Discontent.* Amherst: The University of Massachusetts Press, 1992.

Phillips, Henry L. *In Memoriam of the Late Rev. Alex. Crummell, D.D.* Philadelphia: The Coleman Printery, 1899.

Simmons, William J. *Men of Mark.* Cleveland: Geo. M. Rewell, 1887.

Robert L. Johns

Paul Cuffe
(1759–1817)
Sailor, entrepreneur, emigrationist

Paul Cuffe had a dual heritage: African and Native American. Raised in the principles of the Society of Friends, he developed habits that led him to become a successful sailor and merchant, accumulating probably the largest fortune of any black person prior to the War of 1812. His concerns for the position of blacks in the United States led him to investigate the possibilities of black return to Africa, and he conveyed colonists to Sierra Leone in early 1816, largely at his own expense.

Paul Cuffe was born on Cuttyhunk Island, Massachusetts, on January 17, 1759, the youngest son of Cuffe (Kofi) Slocum (c. 1718–72) and Ruth Moses (d. 1787). Kofi means born on Friday, and Cuffe Slocum was an Ashanti slave before he was brought to the United States in 1728 when he was about ten. His owner, Ebenezer Slocum of Dartmouth, Massachusetts, sold Cuffe Slocum to his nephew John Slocum on February 16, 1742. The Slocums were Quakers, and growth of antislavery sentiment among Friends resulted in Cuffe Slocum's unexpected emancipation three years later. On July 27, 1746, Cuffe Slocum married Ruth Moses, a Native American of the Wampanoag group.

While Cuffe and Ruth Slocum were not accepted as members of the society, they attended meetings and raised their children in the Quaker tradition. Their son Paul joined the Westport (MA) Meeting in 1808. The Slocums lived in Dartmouth for some time and then moved to a farm on Cuttyhunk Island, which is near Martha's Vineyard. Cuffe Slocum became a prosperous small–scale merchant and moved to Chilmark on Martha's Vineyard. In 1766 the family moved to a farm in Dartmouth. Cuffe Slocum died in 1772. All the children except the youngest girl took their father's first name as a surname since the white Slocums objected to the use of their family name. Cuffe Slocum's eldest son took over the farm on Cuttyhunk Island, and the second moved to the property at Chilmark. In 1773 Paul Cuffe began to work as a sailor. At the beginning of the American Revolution the British imprisoned Cuffe for three months when they seized a vessel he was on.

The rise of revolutionary conflict also meant sharp increases in taxes from which Indians were exempt but blacks were not. On February 10, 1780, John and Paul Cuffe and five other local blacks petitioned the state for relief. This relief was denied. In October John and Paul Cuffe, who now owed 154 pounds in back taxes, petitioned the Bristol County Court of Common Pleas for relief on the grounds that they were exempt from taxation as Indians. The issue of voting rights had also become involved, since it was claimed that taxpayers should have the right to vote. Finally on June 9, 1781, the tax claim against the Cuffe brothers was settled out of court for 8 p., 12 s. The town of Dartmouth seems not to have come to any decision about black and Native American voting rights.

From about 1777 Paul Cuffe had taken up maritime trade as a blockade runner, at first in an open boat. He had encounters with pirates and other misadventures before his first successful voyage to Nantucket. According to a notation by one of his brothers, Paul Cuffe also took to drink during these stressful times. Later on Cuffe did not deal in spirits at all. On February 25, 1783, Paul Cuffe married a Native American woman named Alice Pequit. Their first child was born two weeks later, and the family grew to two sons and six daughters. Two of the daughters predeceased their father.

Becomes Successful Merchant

With the coming of peace in 1783, Cuffe was able to expand his maritime endeavors. He invested money in a shoemaker's shop and in 1789 bought property on the Acoaxet River in Massachusetts. He took on his brother–in–law Michael Wainer as a business partner and began engaging in any line of endeavor that offered profit. He carried cargo, caught codfish, and whaled. Cuffe and Wainer invested in several vessels. Cuffe was even bold enough to sail to Virginia and Maryland in search of cargo in spite of the dangers faced by a crew of blacks and Indians in slave states. By 1800 Cuffe's assets amounted to nearly $10,000, including his investments in ships, a waterfront farm, and a windmill. It seems probable that he was the wealthiest African American in the United States at this time. To accommodate the 15 children in his family connection, around 1797 Cuffe started a school in Westport, which also attracted some of his white neighbors' children.

Cuffe appears to have spent much of his time ashore, keeping an eye on his family and investments. In 1802 he attracted white investment in his newly launched ship. He also began to send his ships to trade in Europe and, braving the dangers from slavers, to pursue whales in African waters. Despite his position as a wealthy member of his community, Cuffe continued to be careful in accepting business arrangements with whites and saw that the family–owned vessels had black captains and crews.

Cuffe himself captained his new ship, *Alpha,* in 1806. He was in Savannah in December when he learned of Napoleon's declaration of a blockade of Great Britain. This ruled out his plan to proceed to Liverpool, and after three months he set sail for Russia but dared not enter the eastern Baltic. After a difficult crossing of the Atlantic on his way back, he reached Philadelphia in September. Shortly after his return, in January 1808 Jefferson's Embargo Act stopped all international trade. The slowdown in business activity gave Cuffe the time to contemplate Africa and the abolition of the slave trade.

Supports Return to Africa

Cuffe's success brought him to the attention of abolitionists on both sides of the Atlantic, in particular the British African Institutes, which backed Sierra Leone as a place to settle newly liberated slaves. His stay of several weeks in Philadelphia in 1807 brought him into contact with prominent blacks like James Forten and Absalom Jones and also with white Quaker abolitionist and head of the Pennsylvania Abolition Society, James Pemberton. Soon efforts were underway to recruit Cuffe as an agent to "civilize" and Christianize Africa.

War and changing American foreign policy continued to make difficulties for New England shipowners. The temporary reopening of international trade brought new hope, and Cuffe joined a partnership with two of his sons–in–law to open a store for West Indies goods and groceries in 1809, but the renewal of the embargo in the summer of that year once again turned Cuffe's mind towards exploring trade with Africa. He also shared the deep religious concerns that were a major motivation among antislavery activists, seeing his interest in Africa as part of a divine mission. His relations with powerful Quakers also continued to develop as he became the first black to attend a New England Yearly Meeting.

On November 25, 1810, Cuffe set sail for his first trip to Africa, winding up his grocery business and appointing his brother John as guardian of his children. After a stop in Philadelphia, Cuffe arrived in Freetown, Sierra Leone, on March 1, 1811, following a stormy passage. There he explored conditions in the colony, met leading black colonists, and experienced great difficulties in trading. Nonetheless he became enthusiastic about the prospects for the colony and for trade with Africa. In July 1811 Cuffe arrived at Liverpool, England.

In England Cuffe met and talked with many influential men, as well as addressing a meeting of the directors of the African Institutes on August 27. In September Cuffe left on a return trip to Sierra Leone. There Cuffe traded and had many discussions with the black merchants of Sierra Leone about the future development of trade. His ship left for the United States on February 19, 1812. He arrived home on April 19 only to find his ship and cargo seized by customs as part of the trade war—soon to become open war—between the United States and Great Britain. Cuffe traveled to Washington, where he and his supporters were successful in appealing to President James Madison to release the ship. He roused support for emigration to Africa as he awaited the outcome of the war; African Institutions were formed in cities like New York and Philadelphia.

With the end of the war between the United States and Great Britain in December 1814, Cuffe renewed his plans to carry emigrants to Sierra Leone, but problems arose. Cuffe's only ship now was the *Traveller.* The British African Institutes were distracted by charges of mismanagement, and Cuffe did not secure his hoped for British trading license. Only one emigrant was able to pay any money for passage, and money promised by other sources was not forthcoming. Nonetheless Cuffe pushed ahead.

James Forten, the Philadelphia sail–maker, issued a statement of support for the voyage in September of 1815 as the *Traveller* was sailing north to Westport, embarking passengers and cargo along the way. Then on December 8 the first black–led return to Africa began as Cuffe set sail for Freetown taking, in addition to his crew of seven, 18 adults and 20 children. Upon the *Traveller's* arrival in February of 1816, Cuffe encountered difficulties in trading. Eventually he did receive some concessions and disposed of most of his cargo though with lower profit than expected. The settlement of the emigrants was successful, but Cuffe seems to have run up a debt of $8,000 which was not offset by his trading profits. His British supporters contributed nothing to cover the debt. Thus it was clear that Cuffe's hope of making a yearly voyage was doomed. Cuffe set sail for the United States on April 4, 1816. Landing in New York, he satisfied the members of that city's African Institution about the good reception of the emigrants and relied on their efforts to correct mistaken rumors elsewhere, especially in Philadelphia. After spending some time at home concerned with family matters, Cuffe became alarmed at an apparent deterioration of the position of blacks in the United States and sought to build support for emigration. This was answered by the creation of the American Colonization Society, founded by white Robert Finley. Unfortunately the movement attracted the support of leading white racists and aroused the hostility of many blacks. The goal of the American Colonization Society was ultimately the same as that of Cuffe, but it failed because of its racism and its refusal to work with black leaders. Cuffe, however, never openly disassociated himself from the organization.

In Philadelphia James Forten and Richard Allen both supported Cuffe's efforts but presided at a mass meeting in January of 1817 which roundly condemned the American Colonization Society. In early February Cuffe had some sort of attack which prostrated him for eight hours. He never fully recovered his health, sweating excessively, having chills, and coughing in such a way as to arouse alarm among his family and friends. On August 27 Cuffe called his family together to say farewell; he died on September 7. The funeral was held the following day at the Westport South Meeting house, and he was buried in a distant corner of the burial ground, separated even in death from the graves of white Friends.

The short description included in the *History of Prince Lee Boo* says of Cuffe: "In his person, he was large and well proportioned. His countenance was serious, but mild. His speech and dress, plain and without any shew. His manners, kind and good–natured; joining gravity with modesty and sweetness; and firmness with gentleness and humility. His whole outward appearance shewed, that he was a man of respectability and piety."

Buoyed by his religious convictions, Paul Cuffe became a successful Yankee merchant and sailor. He used his wealth and position to initiate the first attempts led by American blacks to return to Africa. He died just as the tide of black sentiment began to run strongly against emigration, especially the efforts sponsored by the American Colonization Society.

REFERENCES

Harris, Sheldon H. *Paul Cuffe.* New York: Simon and Schuster, 1972.

History of Prince Lee Boo, to Which is Added the Life of Paul Cuffe. Dublin: G. Crookes, 1820.

Logan, Rayford W., and Michael R. Winston, eds. *Dictionary of American Negro Biography.* New York: Norton, 1982.

Miller, Floyd J. *The Search for a Black Nationality.* Urbana: University of Illinois Press, 1975.

Sherwood, H. N. "Paul Cuffe." *Journal of Negro History* 8 (January 1923): 153–229.

A Short Account of the Life of Captain Paul Cuffe. Philadelphia: Thomas Kite, 1830.

Thomas, Lamont D. *Rise To Be a People.* Urbana: University of Illinois Press, 1986.

"The Will of Paul Cuffe." *Journal of Negro History* 8 (April 1923): 230–32.

COLLECTIONS

The Paul Cuffe papers are in the New Bedford, Massachusetts, Free Public Library.

Robert L. Johns

Countee Cullen
(1903–1946)
Poet, essayist, novelist, playwright, educator

One of the most prolific poets of the Harlem Renaissance, Countee Cullen's work embodied ideals espoused by W. E. B. Du Bois and Alain Locke in their quest to articulate a black aesthetic. Cullen was a man who lived a life of many contrasts. A romantic and a lover of French culture, he was also a pragmatist and enamored of the "low" musical arts. A master of conventional poetic art forms and an ardent admirer of John Keats, Cullen used conventional stylistics in a most unconventional way: to expound upon the problematic racial politics of America. Cullen left an extraordinary creative legacy which reflected the ideals of the New Negro Renaissance.

Perhaps Cullen's many childhood identities made him well–suited for a life of contrasts. Cullen himself, in the words of his widow, Ida, quoted in Alan Schucard's *Countee Cullen,* was "led... to fabricate various pasts" due to both "personal" and "social" pressures. Despite naming both Baltimore and New York as his birthplace, Cullen was actually born Countee LeRoy in Louisville, Kentucky, on May 30, 1903. He was the son of Elizabeth Lucas, about whom little is known. Lucas did not raise her son. He was reared by his grandmother, Elizabeth Porter, in New York.

Countee Cullen

Young Countee Porter remained in his grandmother's care until her death in 1918. After her death, he was "adopted" by a Harlem minister and his wife, Reverend Frederick Asbury Cullen and Carolyn Mitchell Cullen. The Cullens were the first family of the Salem Methodist Episcopal Church, a devoutly fundamentalist congregation. The household was both fundamentalist and politically engaged. Within a year after young Countee was adopted by the Cullens, Reverend Cullen led a delegation to call on President Woodrow Wilson to convince him to halt the lynchings of black servicemen in Texas. The elder Cullen was also president of the Harlem chapter of the NAACP and, in that capacity, supported W. E. B. Du Bois in his efforts to represent African Americans before the League of Nations. The combination of these different social and political experiences complemented Cullen's creative abilities. Indeed, the fact that Cullen began to write poetry in elementary school suggests that his early life experiences provided him with an unusual emotional maturity. This maturity uniquely prepared him to use his creative energy to make his readers aware of the position of the Negro in America.

Early Influences

Cullen attended De Witt Clinton High School, a predominately white school in the Bronx, where his academic excellence won him membership in the school honor society as well as awards in oratory. While at De Witt Clinton, Cullen also won the first of many awards for his poetry. His piece entitled "In Memory of Lincoln" won second place in a competition sponsored by the Inter–High School Poetry society, an organization which Cullen served as treasurer. While at De Witt, Cullen also edited *The Magpie,* the literary magazine of the school. It was in *The Magpie* that Cullen was first published; in 1921, the magazine published both his short story entitled "The Frenchman's Bath" and his poem, "I Have a Rendezvous with Life," which also won an award from the Federation of Women's Clubs. The short story provides readers with the earliest example of the life–long fascination with France and French culture which would shape Cullen's later career. The theme of "Rendezvous" reflects the hopes of the post World War I era when African Americans were demanding to participate in the American dream, and was also the focus of his most endearing and enduring writings. That the Cullen household was at the center of the social and political debates of the era is evidenced in the focus of this poem. Cullen's creative coming of age was enriched by the birth of the social movement that his poetry eventually came to reflect.

After graduating from De Witt Clinton in 1922, Cullen attended New York University at University Heights, New York. While at NYU, his writing continued to bring him accolades. In 1923, he was awarded second prize in the Witter Bynner Poetry Contest for "The Ballad of the Brown Girl." This piece is Cullen's earliest attempt to subvert Western form and social associations in order to portray the ways in which racist practices operate in the lives of African Americans. Unlike the classical portrait of the brown girl of Western poetics who is marked only by her low social status, Cullen's brown girl is literally killed by the social realities of race. Although she marries her white lover, she is strangled by her husband in defense of white womanhood. Cullen continued to win recognition in the Witter Bynner Poetry Contest, in 1924 receiving honorable mention for his entry. He finally won first prize in 1925 for "One Who Said Me Nay," a poem which was won second prize in *Opportunity*'s literary competition.

Like many of his contemporaries, including his friend Langston Hughes, Cullen increasingly became interested in spending time abroad, especially in France. He promised to go along when Hughes embarked for France in 1924, but eventually decided to remain in the States to earn money to continue his education. Remaining at home proved to be the best decision because 1925 was a pivotal year in Cullen's life. In that year, he was elected to Phi Beta Kappa and continued to win academic and literary honors. Cullen was awarded *Poetry Magazine*'s John Reed Memorial Prize for his poem, "Threnody for a Brown Girl." He also won *Crisis* magazine's Spingarn Contest for "Two Moods of Love," having won the attention of the magazine's editor, W. E. B. Du Bois.

By the time Cullen graduated from New York University in 1925, Harper and Row was in the process of publishing *Color,* his first volume of poems. The collection includes some of the poems that established Cullen as a true voice of the Harlem Renaissance. "Incident" and "Yet Do I Marvel," both poems about the difficulties of simply being black in America, are among his best known and most often anthologized poems. True to Cullen's fascination with contrasts, the volume also includes pieces on Paul Laurence Dunbar and "To John Keats, Poet." J. Saunders Redding wrote in his essay,

''The New Negro Poet in the Twenties,'' that despite the confusion that would dominate succeeding volumes of poetry, *Color* is clearly about race, ''the biggest, single most unalterable circumstance in the life of Mr. Cullen.'' *Color* sold more than 2,000 copies, establishing Cullen as a major writer of the era. It also brought him to the attention of the Harlem Renaissance literati including Alain Locke, who included Cullen's work in his anthology, *The New Negro* (1926), editor Charles Johnson, who hired him as an assistant editor for *Opportunity,* and writer James Weldon Johnson. These associations helped establish Cullen as an eminent literary figure in Harlem and enabled him to influence the movement in his capacity as an editor. By the time Cullen received his M.A. degree from Harvard University in 1926, his position in the Harlem Renaissance was about to precipitate a physical, intellectual, and social sojourn that would later characterize his life as one marked by contrasts and confusion.

Life Abroad

When Cullen finally got the opportunity to travel to France in 1926, he was at the height of his popularity in Harlem. His popularity had risen along with the sales of *Color* and, true to the ideals espoused by Du Bois's ''talented tenth,'' he had just completed his M.A. degree from Harvard. His initial visit abroad lasted only a few weeks in the summer, during which he and his father visited France, the Holy Land, and finally, Rome, where he visited the grave of John Keats. When he returned home, Paris—not an image of Africa, upon which he could continue to articulate a black aesthetic—was the focus of his creative attention. Thus began the confusion that Redding has identified in Cullen's work: a vacillation between writing about Negro experience and insisting that the Negro experience—because it is so confusing and diverse—is impossible to delineate. In 1927, Cullen published two volumes of poetry, *The Ballad of the Brown Girl: An Old Ballad Retold* and *Copper Sun*; he also edited *Caroling Dusk: An Anthology of Verse by Negro Poets.* Despite the fact that his intellectual focus remained centered on race, Cullen used ''The Dark Tower,'' his editorial column in *Opportunity* magazine to caution writers about making their art accessible and the importance of avoiding the label of *Negro* poet. Cullen's contrasting and often conflicting racial focuses support Reds contention that Cullen was forever confused in his exploration of race. It is not surprising then, that when he received a $2,500 Guggenheim grant in 1928, he chose to travel to France where he planned to write narrative poetry and a libretto for an opera.

Before Cullen could experience France again however, he was again catapulted to the apex of Harlem society. In the most publicized social event of the period, Cullen married Yolande Du Bois, daughter of his friend and mentor, W. E. B. Du Bois, on April 9, 1928. Yolande was attended by 16 bridesmaids; more than 3,000 guests attended the ceremony. The marriage, however, lasted less than a year. In fact, when Cullen left for France in June, he did not take his bride with him. Numerous difficulties ended the marriage, not the least of which was Cullen's close relationship with his long–time companion and best man, Harold Jackman. It was Jackman who accompanied Cullen to France in 1928 while Yolande remained at home. There was only what Du Bois himself would describe as an ''intellectual'' attraction between the Cullens, while his most intimate relationship was with Jackman. Although homosexuality was not a taboo subject among the Renaissance writers, Cullen never broached the subject of his sexuality in his writings. With an eye toward avoiding a scandal and maintaining his intellectual relationship with Cullen, Du Bois remained loyal to Cullen after the divorce was finalized in 1929. Indeed, Du Bois assured Cullen's continued popularity in Harlem by publishing a series of ''Letters from Paris'' in *Crisis* for the duration of his time in France.

Cullen's sojourn in France resulted in the publication of his third collection of poems, *The Black Christ and Other Poems* (1929). The title piece focuses on the narrator's struggle with his faith in a white Christ who refuses to intervene when his brother is lynched by a white mob because he loves a white woman. The poem ends with Cullen associating the narrator's brother with ''costly fruit'' grown on the tree ''where Christ himself once stood.'' There remains an ambivalence about religion in the collection which likely stems from the discomfort with the fundamentalist upbringing he experienced with the Cullens.

Other poems in *The Black Christ* focus on love, although the love is associated with death and incongruity. In *When Harlem Was in Vogue,* David Levering Lewis has linked these associations with Cullen's struggle with his sexual orientation. Whatever its roots, in *The Black Christ,* ''Nothing endures / not even love.'' This was Cullen's last volume comprised entirely of new poetry.

Following the publication of *The Black Christ,* Cullen began to focus on the study of the French language and on French poets, especially on Baudelaire. He attended the University of Paris and studied with a private language teacher. His sojourn in France lasted for two years; he would continue to return to Paris every summer. Cullen's initial experiences in France marked a turning point in his creative life. He turned to writing plays, children's literature, and a single novel, never again publishing a volume composed entirely of new verse.

New Creative Turns

Upon his return to the United States, Cullen began work on his only novel, *One Way to Heaven* (1932). The novel was a failure; its shortcomings were immediately obvious to both critics and his contemporaries. The novel is comprised of two plots: one based on the common folk whom Cullen has so assiduously avoided in his poetry, the other on a Harlem socialite whose soirees attract black literati, black nationalists, and Van Vechten–like white liberals. Unfortunately, the plot lines did not adequately intersect. After the failure of this novel, Cullen began to teach and then turned to the theater as an outlet for his creative energy.

In 1934 Cullen accepted an appointment to teach English and French at the Frederick Douglass Junior High School in

New York. He continued to write after he accepted this appointment. The first volume to appear after he began teaching was *The Medea and Some Poems,* named for his treatment of the classic poem which it contains. *The Medea* obviously has its roots in both Cullen's experiences in France and in his return to the racial polemics of America. The volume contains several translations of Baudelaire and poems written in tribute to France including two entitled, "To France." Significantly, the volume also includes "Scottsboro, Too, Is Worth Its Song," Cullen's response to the convictions of nine young African American youths known as the Scottsboro Boys, who were wrongly accused of raping two white women in Alabama in 1931. Once again, Cullen's focus was split between focusing on the world outside America and having to expose America's racial disquietude.

In 1935 Cullen also adapted *One Way to Heaven* for the stage with the assistance of a collaborator, Harry Hamilton. In the adaptation, which was entitled *Heaven's My Home,* Cullen and Hamilton attempted to address the shortcomings of the novel by including a love affair that links the two plots, but the play was never mounted commercially. Cullen continued to teach, returning to France each summer to continue his study of French language and culture. In 1939 he again began to work on a play. With his friend, Arna Bontemps, Cullen adapted Bontemps's novel, *God Sends Sunday* (1931) for the stage. The dramatization, a musical entitled *St. Louis Woman,* was highly problematic. Critics of the play charged that it was degrading to blacks. Cullen refused to abandon the project and continued to work to bring it to the stage. He stopped work on the project in 1940 to marry Ida Mae Roberson, the sister of singer Orlando Roberson. While waiting for the project to come to fruition, Cullen also published two volumes of children's stories, *The Lost Zoo* (1940) and *My Lives and How I Lost Them* (1942).

By 1945, despite the criticism of his detractors—which apparently included his long–time companion, Harold Jackman—Cullen's *St. Louis Woman* was about to be staged and filmed. The project had attracted attention from both Broadway and from Hollywood. Lena Horne had agreed to play the role of the protagonist, Della Greene. Ironically, the same mindset that made Cullen's poetry acceptable early in the Renaissance now made the play objectionable. Concerned with the way in which blacks were portrayed in the drama, the Harlem intelligentsia wanted it suppressed.

In reality, the images of blacks in the play were not highly problematic. Set around the race tracks of St. Louis, the drama focuses on the lower socioeconomic class. Unfortunately, this was the class whose image was incongruent with Du Bois's position that art, like propaganda, should focus only on racial uplift. Horne abandoned the project due to the delays caused by the controversy surrounding the play. Unable to bring the project before an audience, Cullen completed work on two final projects: *The Third Fourth of July,* a one–act play co–authored with Owen Dodson, and a compilation of his work that he wanted to serve as his memorial, *On These I Stand: An Anthology of the Best Poems of Countee Cullen.* While hospitalized at the Sydenham Hospital in New York, Cullen succumbed to uremic poisoning on January 9, 1946, at the age of 42.

Despite his effort to become a successful novelist and playwright, Countee Cullen was a man whose life is defined by his poetry. Delineated by his view of American life as a Negro from within and an artist from abroad, his poetry embodies his ambivalence toward being defined as a Negro artist. Cullen is best remembered for the poems he penned about the racial situation in American culture during the 1920s; however, these are the same poems that the Black Arts poets of the 1960s rejected because of Cullen's ambivalence toward embracing his blackness. Like the cat whose experiences form the basis for his two children's books, Countee Cullen obviously looked at the race question with two differently colored eyes. Cullen's greatness lies, perhaps, in his ability to describe both extremes.

REFERENCES

Cullen, Countee. *The Black Christ and Other Poems.* New York: Harper & Bros., 1929.

———. *On These I Stand: An Anthology of the Best Poems of Countee Cullen.* New York: Harper, 1947.

Fabre, Michel. *From Harlem to Paris: Black American Writers in France 1840–1980.* Chicago: University of Illinois Press, 1991.

Lewis, David Levering. *When Harlem Was in Vogue.* New York: Knopf, 1981.

Redding, J. Saunders. "The Negro Poet in the Twenties." In *Modern Black Poets.* Compiled by Donald N. Gibson. Englewood Cliffs, NJ: Prentice–Hall, 1973.

Shucard, Alan R. *Countee Cullen.* Boston: Twayne Publishers, 1984.

COLLECTIONS

Countee Cullen's papers are located at the Woodruff Library, Clark Atlanta University, Atlanta, Georgia, at the University of California at Berkeley Library, Berkeley, California, and in the James Weldon Johnson Collection at the Beinecke Library, Yale University, New Haven, Connecticut.

Sheila Smith McKoy

Norris Wright Cuney
(1846–1898)
Organizer, politician, entrepreneur

In Texas, during Reconstruction and for a surprisingly long time thereafter, black men stood on an equal footing with whites in the political realm. No one better exemplifies the heights of power then attainable by a black Texan than Norris

Wright Cuney, nicknamed "The Yellow Rose of Texas," the political mastermind of the state Republican Party. From 1885 until 1896, not only was Cuney the leader of the black vote in the party, but he was the acknowledged leader of the party as a whole.

Norris Wright Cuney was born on May 12, 1846, at Sunnyside Plantation in Waller County, near Hempstead, Texas. He was the fourth of eight children born to Colonel Philip N. Cuney and one of his slaves, Adeline Stuart. Norris Cuney's father was a Virginia native from an established Swiss family of planters. Cuney's mother was of mixed parentage—Potomac Indian, Caucasian, and African. In the early 1800s, the Cuney family and their slaves—including Adeline Stuart—moved to Rapides Parish, Louisiana, where they established a plantation. A planter by trade, Philip Cuney also dabbled in politics as a member of the Whig party. In 1842 Philip Cuney moved to Texas and established a plantation, named Sunnyside, on the east side of the Brazos River, in Waller County, Texas. There he fathered six of the eight children he had with Adeline Stuart, whom he eventually set free. Norris, the fourth and darkest of the eight children, favored his mother. His olive complexion, brown eyes, and straight black hair caused many to mistake him for being of Italian or Spanish ancestry. Despite the fact that it was the pre–Civil War South, Philip Cuney treated all his children as free and educated them in private schools.

In 1853 Philip Cuney moved the family to Houston. In 1859 13–year–old Norris was sent to the Wyle Street School, a black institution in Pittsburgh, Pennsylvania, where his two older brothers already were enrolled. Philip Cuney was planning to send his boys to Oberlin College in Ohio after they finished at the Pittsburgh school, but the Civil War squelched that scenario.

With the country in turmoil, 17–year–old Norris left his studies behind and found work on the great riverboats traveling between the booming cities of the mid–continent: Cincinnati, St. Louis, New Orleans. Following the end of the war, Cuney chose Galveston, Texas, as his new home. Galveston, due to its seaport, was then the wealthiest city in the state. He began a period of self–education, studying literature and law, in an effort to acquire the knowledge he had missed.

During the yellow fever epidemic of 1867, Cuney volunteered as a nurse, traveling among several Texas cities to help bring both black and white patients back to health. Eventually, he too was stricken with the illness, though he recovered rapidly. Shortly thereafter, Cuney's mother and most of his siblings moved to Galveston.

Cuney, a handsome, mustachioed man standing five feet, ten inches tall, was a confident sort who made friends easily. A heavy smoker and drinker, he comfortably mixed enterprise with entertainment. Although he was a Christian, he did not belong to a church. Instead, he chose to belong to more outwardly social organizations, such as the regional lodge of the Prince Hall Masons. He made many contacts and had a knack for ingratiating himself to people with the power to help his career. Cuney was a natural for politics and his own inclination thrust him in that direction. The timing of his entry into the political realm was perfect.

Norris Wright Cuney

The post–Civil War era of Reconstruction began a period of social mobility for Texas's population of 140,000 former slaves that almost lasted out the century. The restoration of Texas into the Union in 1870 occurred at a time of political domination by the state Republican Party, starting from its inception in 1867. It has been estimated that in the decades immediately following the Civil War, blacks accounted for as many as five of every six Republican voters in the state.

Early Political Involvement

Cuney was taken under the wing of George T. Ruby, a black New Yorker educated in Maine, who had come to Texas by way of Louisiana as an agent of the Freedmen's Bureau. He was elected to the Twelfth and Thirteenth Texas legislatures as a representative from Galveston and served in several capacities in the state Republican party before returning to Louisiana in the late 1870s. Ruby introduced Cuney to influential politicians and was instrumental in helping him land an appointment as first assistant to the sergeant–at–arms of the Twelfth Legislature in 1870. The next year Cuney was appointed to the Galveston County school board, on which he served for many years as a strong advocate of equal education for blacks.

During that time Cuney met and married Adelina Dowdie, a petite 16–year–old who had migrated to Texas in 1864. The youngest of six sisters, Dowdie was the daughter of a white planter from Woodville, Mississippi. and a mulatto slave. Strongly religious and vigorously active in charitable organizations, she proved a fine complement to her ambitious husband. They had a daughter, Maud Cuney Hare—famous in her own right as a concert pianist and music lecturer—and a son, Lloyd Garrison Cuney.

On the state level, Cuney aligned himself with the supporters of E. J. Davis, the state's radical white governor, who championed black suffrage and supported other black issues. In 1872 Cuney was selected to serve as an alternate delegate to the National Republican Convention. He also received a patronage job when he was appointed Inspector of Customs in Galveston. He was dismissed from that job a short time later, however, after accusing the white Collector of Customs of prejudice in filling lower level patronage jobs. Instead of lying down, Cuney rallied support from the white citizens of Galveston, who helped get him reinstated.

Cuney began taking the lead in public forums. He presided over a Colored Men's Convention in Brenham, Texas, on July 3–4, 1873. The convention was held to promote a civil rights bill that would guarantee equal access to public accommodations, transportation, and recreation facilities. The delegates also endorsed the administration of President Ulysses S. Grant and the national Republican Party for its efforts to protect the rights of black citizens.

By the mid–1870s, the Democrats had wrested control of most state and federal offices from the party of the emancipation, which was now derisively called "the nigger party" in Texas. E. J. Davis lost the 1874 gubernatorial race. Despite his defeat, Davis remained the de facto Republican leader. Cuney's own rise in the Republican party was swift. In 1874 he was appointed secretary of the state executive committee. In the country's centennial year, 1876, he was again selected as a delegate to the national convention.

Despite his increasing fame, Cuney was not free of political setbacks. In 1875 he was the Republican nominee in the Galveston mayoral race, but was defeated by his Democratic opponent. The next year, Cuney was nominated for state representative, but lost in the general election. In 1877 Cuney again ran afoul of the Collector of Customs. This time, despite efforts by E. J. Davis to prevent it, the Collector of Customs was successful in dismissing Cuney.

In addition to his political involvement, Cuney had various business interests over the years. One of these was a tobacco and liquor establishment that he operated in the mid–1870s. In fact, he was twice arrested by the U.S. marshal in Galveston for violating revenue laws.

From the moment that the military occupation of the South ended in 1877, terminating Reconstruction, conditions for Southern blacks gradually worsened. As civil rights increasingly were denied Southern blacks, more of their number emigrated north. A national convention of blacks held in Nashville on May 6–9, 1879, addressed the great exodus. Cuney, a member of the Texas delegation, opposed the movement. While acknowledging the right to move anywhere one might find a better life, he believed doing so would magnify the problems of those blacks forced to remain behind. He was also against the re–colonization of Africa, believing that black Americans had become too tied to the United States to make such a radical change successfully.

In 1880 Cuney was selected as a delegate to the Republican National Convention for a third time. The next year he ran for, and was elected, alderman of Galveston's twelfth ward, a predominantly white district. Also in 1881, Cuney was named Chief Inspector of Customs in Galveston as patronage from the national Republican Party. Despite prior indications from federal authorities that filling both posts would not create a conflict of interest, white adversaries within the Customs House managed some political duplicity that resulted in his having to choose between the positions. Cuney chose to remain an alderman, in the first of several elected terms. In 1882 he ran for the state legislature from the Sixty–sixth District, but lost.

No longer a federal employee, Cuney was free to go into private business again. He chose to use his knowledge of the Galveston docks to start a stevedore business. Cuney, supported by white ship owners, underbid his rivals and hired 500 black workers from as far away as New Orleans. Their four to six dollars per day pay was still a princely sum for the time, especially for blacks. White resistance to the black longshoremen was immediate. White workers feared wage cuts and stiffer competition for jobs. A strike by the white longshoremen was broken by Cuney's men on the condition that they receive equal opportunity and wage rates after the strike was settled. Subsequently, Cuney was threatened with physical harm, as were many of his white supporters. Rumors of a lynching party one night drew dozens of Cuney's friends and workers to his home to protect him, though the attack never transpired.

Heads State Political Party

In February of 1883, E. J. Davis died, leaving the state Republican Party leaderless. One of four Texas delegates–at–large at the 1884 national convention, Cuney's unwavering support of eventual presidential nominee James G. Blaine thrust Cuney into the national spotlight. At convention's end, he was chosen to be in the 50–man committee that traveled to Augusta, Maine, to notify Blaine officially of his nomination. The following year, the national committeeman for Texas, judge C. C. Binkley, died. Cuney was elected to fill the prestigious position, one that he would hold until 1896. By virtue of his long friendship with the radical white element in the party and his firm grip on the party's large black contingent, Cuney consolidated his power and became the acknowledged head of the state party.

A small minority of white Republicans refused to be led by blacks, however, and began a movement aimed at ridding the party of them. As head of a fragmented party that was numerically inferior to its Democratic rival, Cuney was forced to form coalitions and support compromise candidates, third–party candidates, and independent candidates in hopes of defeating the nominees of their major opponent. In fact, the Republicans seldom were capable of putting together viable tickets to run under the party banner, and rarely did a black candidate receive party backing.

At the 1888 national convention, Cuney's activism on Benjamin Harrison's behalf helped the Indiana senator secure the presidential nomination. After winning the election that fall, Harrison rewarded Cuney by nominating him for Collector of Customs at Galveston in 1889. When the senate confirmed Cuney's nomination, it gave him the most important federal job in Texas and put him among the highest ranking black federal officials in the South.

In 1890 the "lily–whites" took control of the party machinery at the state convention. Cuney out–maneuvered them two years later to win back control. The "lily–whites" then formed a racially segregated party, which held its own convention and selected its own national delegates. When the renegade delegation showed up at the national convention, President Benjamin Harrison saw to it that the official, Cuney–led delegation was seated.

Unfortunately for Cuney, though Harrison was re–nominated, he was not reelected. That resulted in Cuney losing the important Collector of Customs position after Grover Cleveland regained the office. Returning to private life, Cuney went back into the stevedoring business. He also entered building contracting as a member of the firm of Clark and Company.

Attempts to reunite the rival factions of the state Republican Party in 1894 met failure. Even so, enough "lily–whites" returned to the state convention to shake up the proceedings. Things started slowly for the Cuney contingent, which lost some early procedural battles. The Cuneyites rebounded quickly, however, getting most of their choices for the state ticket selected. They also filled the party's key personnel posts, including that of state party chairman, taken by Dr. John Grant, a white man handpicked by Cuney. By the end of the convention it was clear that the black and liberal white majority had successfully fought off attempts by the racist minority to steal the reins of the state party for another two years.

Adelina Cuney, Norris Cuney's loving and supportive wife, long suffered from tuberculosis. In 1895 her condition worsened considerably. Though the family moved her to the healthier climate of San Antonio, she showed only a short–term improvement before continuing her steady decline. On October 1 of that year she died, at just 39 years of age.

Ousted from Leadership

In 1896 after 11 years as head of the state party, Cuney was forced out for refusing to support popular Ohio Governor William McKinley for the presidential nomination. McKinley's campaign manager, businessman Mark Hanna, set the standard for the methodically run, well–organized, pre–convention campaign with that election. Hanna doggedly sought Cuney's endorsement. Cuney, however, remained in the camp of William B. Allison, a senator from Iowa and a minor candidate, but a longtime political ally.

At a meeting of the state convention in Austin during late March, Cuney, sensing the strength of the McKinley force, successfully sought to be made temporary chairman, over his protégé, John Grant, a McKinley supporter. The state delegates were split into groups supporting McKinley, Speaker of the House Thomas B. Reed of Maine, and Allison. With no single faction large enough to control the convention, the Reed and Allison contingents joined forces in order to remain viable.

The convention progressed according to accepted procedure with the outcome that the executive committee awarded national delegates to all three candidates. The vocal McKinley force was not satisfied with that arrangement, however, and tried to disrupt the proceedings. A riot broke out on the floor. When Cuney was unable to call the meeting back to order, he adjourned the convention without a floor vote. When order was restored by Austin police, a second convention was immediately opened by John Grant, with Richard Allen, a black delegate from Houston, as temporary chairman. They selected a new set of delegates all favoring McKinley. Then in April, the "lily–whites" held yet another convention, choosing a third group of delegates.

In between the state and national conventions, Cuney traveled to Washington, D.C., where he met with several colleagues to discuss political issues and strategies. He was also in the capital city to visit Howard University, the fledgling black institution for which he had used his influence to raise funds and elevate the school's profile. In gratitude, Cuney was given an honorary master of arts degree during the commencement ceremony.

That summer, at the national convention in St. Louis, McKinley delegates gained control of the rules committee, and of the proceedings in general. They ignored the credentials held by the Cuney–led Texas regulars and seated most of the McKinley delegates instead. McKinley easily secured the nomination in a then–rare first ballot decision. Subsequently, Grant was elected the new National Committeeman from Texas. The seating incident, later criticized by McKinley and others in the party, nevertheless damaged Cuney's credibility as state party leader.

In September, at the state convention in Fort Worth, Cuney favored fusion with the state's Populist Party, a move designed to form a voting bloc large enough to defeat Democratic candidates. Cuney supported railroad tycoon E. H. R. Green for chairman of the state executive committee, and put himself up for temporary chairman. In opposing his former mentor, Grant, chairman of the executive committee, recommended Charles Ferguson, a black politician from Fort Bend County, for temporary chairman. Grant was successful in getting Ferguson elected, but rankled so many in ousting Cuney that it necessitated his own withdrawal from the chairmanship race. Cuney's followers quickly rallied: Green was elected chairman, their former leader's fusion proposal was victorious and most of their other measures were adopted. "The Yellow Rose of Texas" was defeated, but the party remained on the course he had set. After the convention, Cuney took his defeat in good grace and made speeches supporting the Republican slate, including McKinley.

Before long, Cuney's health began a downward spiral. His grief over his wife's death and his long working hours combined with continuing insomnia, a case of grippe, and several colds wore him down. He continued to meet with his Republican colleagues, attend party conferences, make political speeches, and keep up his considerable correspondence. His doctor, however, recommended rest and a change in climate.

Like his wife, he moved to the western part of the state, spending much time in San Antonio, Austin, and the health resort of Boerne, Texas, during 1897. His daughter Maud traveled with him, serving as his secretary. He wintered in San Antonio, where by the end he was all but bedridden. Still, he received frequent visits from friends and colleagues who sought his opinions. Sensing the end was near, family members were summoned. His children, his brother Joseph, and his mother were all there to share his last hours. Norris Wright Cuney died in San Antonio on March 3, 1898.

The next day, Cuney's body was held in state at a local Methodist Episcopal Church before being placed aboard a special train draped in mourning. It was escorted back to Galveston by an honor guard made up of members of the black militia regiment the Excelsior Guards of San Antonio. In Galveston his remains were held in state at Reedy Chapel until his funeral on March 6 at Harmony Hall, followed by a Masonic service. Hundreds attended the services and hundreds more were turned away. A massive funeral procession followed his body to Lake View Cemetery, where he was buried in the family plot.

Cuney's passing was more than an individual event; it marked the end of an era in Texas politics during which black men possessed real power, if not actual equality with whites. Not long after Cuney's position within the Republican party was diminished, the ''lily–whites'' were welcomed back. Within a few years, black leadership in the Republican Party was no more.

REFERENCES

Hare, Maud Cuney. *Norris Wright Cuney: A Tribune of the Black People.* New York: Crisis Publishing Co., 1913.

Rice, Lawrence D. *The Negro in Texas 1874–1900.* Baton Rouge: Louisiana State University Press, 1971.

Kevin C. Kretschmer

Roy Clifford Darlington (1908–1994)

Pharmacist, teacher, researcher, writer

Roy Clifford Darlington was the first African American to receive a doctorate in pharmacy in the United States. As a teacher, he helped develop the careers of health professionals in the United States and in other countries. Through his research, writing, and organizational involvement, he contributed to the advancement of pharmaceutical practices all over the world.

Roy Darlington was born on February 22, 1908, in Massilon, Ohio, the son of John and Corrine Garvin Darlington. After he graduated from Washington High School in that city, he entered Ohio State University and earned the bachelor of science in pharmacy degree cum laude in 1941. He became a licensed pharmacist in the state of Ohio in 1942, and as a fellow of the American Foundation for Pharmaceutical Education, continued his studies at Ohio State for the master of science degree, awarded in 1943, and the doctor of philosophy degree, conferred in 1947. He then received a license to practice pharmacy in the District of Columbia in 1948.

In 1943 Darlington began work at Howard University in Washington, D.C., starting as an instructor in the College of Pharmacy and Pharmacal Sciences and progressing to other administrative and teaching capacities. Starting in 1947 he was an associate professor and in 1949 became a full professor. From 1955 to 1973 he was chairman of the Department of Pharmacy and from 1971 until his retirement in 1976, he was assistant dean, acting dean, and associate dean of the college. After more than 33 years at Howard, Darlington retired on June 30, 1976.

Outside the university circle, Darlington was well–known in professional and scientific organizations, notably the American Pharmaceutical Association (APhA) and the National Pharmaceutical Association, the latter an offshoot from the National Medical Association, the organization of African Americans in the field of medicine. He held the important position of historian of the Washington, D.C. section of the APhA and at one time occupied the chair of the editorial board of the *Journal of the National Pharmaceutical Association,* which was based at Howard University. Other appointments included chair and vice–chair of the Conference of Teachers of Pharmacy of the American Association of Colleges of Pharmacy. He was also a member of other scientific fraternities, including Sigma Xi, Rho Chi, Eta Sigma, and Phi Rho Alpha.

Darlington contributed to professional journals and penned articles on over–the–counter medications for the *Handbook of Non–Prescription Drugs,* APhA's reference for teachers in pharmaceutical colleges and practicing pharmacists all over the country. Some of his publications were on cinnamon oils and ointment bases. While on the faculty of Howard University, Darlington was a consultant to the Food and Drug Administration's Advisory Panel on Oral Cavity Drug Products.

Among the most prized tributes to Darlington's value to the field of health care and his service to the population at large is the Distinguished Alumni Award bestowed by Ohio State University.

Darlington married Wilmoth Greene, of Danville, Virginia, in 1946 and they had two children: Charles Ashley and Roy Clifford Jr. He died at age 86, in Fayetteville, North Carolina, on August 13, 1994, 18 years after he retired. He was survived by his wife, a son, three grandchildren, and three great–grandchildren. His son, Charles, a teacher, lives in Fayetteville.

Roy Darlington's influence remains strong in the quality of work of his former students, now practicing pharmacists in cities in the United States and abroad. Thousands of other successful practitioners are still guided by the wisdom of his writings and the utility of his practical knowledge.

REFERENCES

Low, W. Augustus, and Virgil A. Clift, eds. *Encyclopedia of Black America.* New York: McGraw–Hill, 1981.

Nnadi–Okolo, Eucharia E. Letter to College of Pharmacy and Pharmacal Sciences Faculty and Staff, Howard University. In files of the College of Pharmacy and Pharmacal Sciences, Howard University, Washington, DC.

Robinson, Ira C. Letter to Alumni and Friends, August 9, 1996. In files of the College of Pharmacy and Pharmacal Sciences, Howard University, Washington, DC.

Who's Who in Colored America. 7th ed. Yonkers–on–Hudson, NY: Christian E. Burckel, 1950.

Dona L. Irvin

Allison Davis
(1902–1983)
Educator, social anthropologist, psychologist

Allison Davis brought the nation's attention to the inadequacies of intelligence tests as reliable instruments for measuring the educational potential of children on the lower end of the socioeconomic scale, altering forever the use of IQ testing to perpetuate racial caste and class. His socio–anthropological study of caste and class on cotton plantations in Mississippi broke new ground in the use of anthropological techniques, and his appointments to government commissions influenced the field of education at the national level.

Allison Davis and Elizabeth Stubbs were married in 1929; they had two sons—Allison S., who eventually settled in Chicago, and Gordon J., who became the New York City commissioner of parks and recreation. Elizabeth Davis, died in 1966. Lois Mason became his second wife in 1969.

Allison Davis was born the only child of John Abraham Davis, a federal employee, and Gabrielle Dorothy Beale Davis, a homemaker, on October 14, 1902, in Washington, D.C. Davis had the good fortune to be brought up in a household of privilege unknown to many other black children of his time. Encouraged and supported by his parents, Davis read authors such as William Shakespeare and Charles Dickens.

Davis attended the prestigious Williams College in Massachusetts, where, in spite of the obstacles of segregation that prevented him from living in campus housing, he completed his bachelor's degree and was the valedictorian of the class of 1924. He continued his education at Harvard University, where he earned a master's degree in comparative literature in 1925.

Davis taught for two years, then became increasingly interested in the study of culture, specifically the rampart culture of racism in America. He studied anthropology at the London School of Economics then returned to Harvard to earn a second master's in anthropology in 1935.

Pursues a Career as a Scholar

After two years as codirector of field research in social anthropology at Harvard, Allison Davis became a professor of anthropology at Dillard University in New Orleans from 1935 to 1938. For the next year he was a research associate at Yale University's Institute of Human Relations.

In 1939 Davis arrived at the University of Chicago as a research associate at the Center on Child Development and earned his doctorate in 1942. Davis spent nearly 40 years at the University of Chicago, where he and his colleague Abram Lincoln became the first blacks to be granted tenure. His position as professor at the university continued the pattern of privilege which began at birth, as well as the pattern of discrimination in spite of his credentials and achievements. Allegations regarding the source of funds for Davis's salary and the fact that he was unable to buy a house in the university–affiliated neighborhood of Hyde Park are indications that his life of privilege did not exempt him from the effects of racism that was the subject of his anthropological studies and the numerous articles and books he authored.

The American Council on Education published Davis's first book, *Children of Bondage; The Personality Development of Negro Youth in the Urban South,* in 1940. This study of the life experiences of eight selected black adolescents looked at the unique experiences of a caste–like system that limited their social and economic growth as well as their societal boundaries. The study demonstrated that upward mobility in class was indeed possible.

Deep South; a Social Anthropological Study of Caste and Class, published in 1941 was, for two reasons, a ground–breaking publication. This book was the product of a collaboration between Burleigh and Mary Gardner, a white couple who interviewed the whites in the study, and Davis and his wife, Elizabeth, who interviewed the blacks in the study. Both couples took considerable risks to gather the information needed to complete the study. Davis also broke new ground by using the anthropological techniques in this study that were usually applied to indigenous people outside the United States.

Finds IQ Tests Biased

Davis was highly critical of the use of standardized tests for determining the IQ of children at the lower end of the socio–economic spectrum, especially black children. It was his voice that brought the nation's attention to the effect of culturally biased standardized tests on the future of these children, which led to the systematic elimination of a large pool of untapped talent and intelligence.

The annual Inglis Lecture at Harvard University was delivered by Davis in 1948 and published as the book, *Social–Class Influences Upon Learning.* He discussed the nature of the intelligence tests, cultural differences, and mental behavior in children, and he proposed a revised school curriculum that would teach children to use their life experiences to think through and solve problems. Davis called for intensive research to determine what curricula should be used to develop children's basic mental activities, including "the analysis and organization of observed experiences, the drawing of inferences, [and] the development of inventiveness." He found the curricula of his time to be "stereotyped and arbitrary selections from a narrow area of middle–class culture." Furthermore, the standard curriculum lacked a functional connection with real life situations. "For over a generation," he concluded, "no basically new types of mental problems have been added to intelligence tests." According to Davis, educators who continued to rely on "vocabulary–building, reading, spelling, and routine arithmetical memorizing" were failing to guide their students' basic mental development.

Davis's career included a Distinguished Service Medal from the Columbia Teachers College in 1977 and an appointment to the President's Commission on Civil Rights from 1968 to 1972. He was elected in 1967 by the American Academy of Arts and Sciences as their first fellow from the field of education.

Davis's last book, *Leadership, Love and Aggression: How the Twig is Bent,* was published in 1983. It examined the personalities and psychological profiles of Martin Luther King Jr., W. E. B. Du Bois, Richard Wright, and Frederick Douglass. Allison Davis underwent open heart surgery in October of 1983 and died in November of that year at Michael Reese Hospital in Chicago. The United States Post Office issued a postage stamp honoring Davis as part of the Black Heritage Series, on February 1, 1994, citing his work as having helped to end legalized racial segregation.

REFERENCES

''Allison Davis, Psychologist, Dies; Wrote About Blacks in America.'' *New York Times,* November 22, 1983.

Contemporary Black Biography. Vol. 12. Detroit: Gale Research, 1996.

Davis, Allison. *Children of Bondage; The Personality Development of Negro Youth in the Urban South.* Washington, DC: American Council on Education, 1940.

———. *Social–Class Influences upon Learning.* Cambridge: Harvard University Press, 1948.

———, Burleigh B. Gardner, and others. *Deep South; a Social Anthropological Study of Caste and Class.* Chicago: University of Chicago Press, 1941.

Hillis, Michael R. ''Allison Davis and the Study of Race, Social Class, and Schooling.'' *Journal of Negro Education* 64 (Winter 1995): 33–41.

Ann C. Sullivan

Benjamin Jefferson Davis
(1903–1964)
Attorney, civil rights advocate, city official

Often confused with Benjamin O. Davis Jr., the first black general in the U.S. Air Force, Benjamin J. Davis is considered one of the most influential leaders of the Communist Party in the United States. In his fight against the racism of the early 1900s, Davis emerged as a member of and advocate for the party. He devoted his early career to informing African Americans about communist and socialist philosophies that would aid in their social and political progress. Later, as a New York City councilman in the 1940s, he proposed legislation that would provide better jobs and housing for African Americans. Although his success with African Americans and the Communist Party was short–lived, he maintained the view that it was the best alternative for blacks in the United States.

Born on September 8, 1903, Benjamin Jefferson Davis Jr. was the son of Benjamin J. Sr. and Jimmie W. Porter, rural laborers of Dawson, Georgia. Davis learned early the evils of southern slavery and racial segregation. While he was a child, his grandmother shared with him the horrors that she experienced as a slave in south Georgia. She told him about the whippings that almost ended her life. Davis grew up in a world that did not differ very much from her condition. Blacks struggled to endure the hardships of dilapidated housing and inadequate food and health services. The youngest of a family of five, Davis and his sister were the only two to survive infancy. In 1909 his father moved the family from impoverished Dawson to the more affluent Atlanta.

Davis's father, an aggressive, politically active Republican, viewed education as a way out of the plight faced by the majority of African Americans. Having completed the junior and senior high school departments of Morehouse College in Atlanta, the younger Davis enrolled in the college. Davis found that blacks in this community were ambitious and polished, quite different from the negative stereotypes. While attending Morehouse, Davis also discovered his militant personality. In a disagreement with the strict control that faculty members exercised over students, Davis and others rebelled. He was outspoken against restrictions on freedom and the right to protest.

After completing a year at Morehouse, Davis transferred to Amherst College in Massachusetts. During this period, not many African Americans had the money or access to attend major white universities. The few blacks who were able to attend college in the early 1900s usually ended up at one of the black schools. For Davis, the social injustice overshadowed his ability to study at a white institution. He agonized over the fact that he lived within a society that denied him the freedom to experience life as an equal American citizen.

After completing his first year at Amherst, Davis had an experience which changed the course of his life. While riding a trolley car in Atlanta, Davis took a seat in the white section after he gave up his seat in the black section to a pregnant black woman. This was the 1920s in the South, where Jim Crow laws mandated that blacks and whites use separate public facilities. As a result of breaking this law, Davis was manhandled and arrested by a policeman, who referred to him as a ''nigger.'' The next day he appeared in court and witnessed abusive and obscene acts committed by the police toward helpless black women who had been arrested with him. It was this incident that motivated Davis to enter law school at Harvard after receiving his B.A. degree from Amherst in 1925. His father had advised him that going into law would allow him to fight injustice and defend the rights of African Americans.

A Lawyer for Justice

A very stocky and well–built man, Davis looked every bit the part of a football star. At Amherst, Davis had played on

Benjamin Jefferson Davis

the football team. However, he had no intention of pursuing the sport after college. Instead, he worked as a journalist while in law school, serving from 1929 to 1931 as a feature editor at the *Atlanta Independent,* a newspaper founded by his father.

In 1932, Davis received the J.D. degree from Harvard Law School. In the same year, he was admitted to the Georgia bar and began practicing law in Atlanta. He entered law when few blacks were attorneys. Black lawyers found themselves primarily restricted to black clients. It was virtually impossible for them to represent whites. Davis continued to struggle with the extreme racism of Georgia. He recalled in *Communist Councilman from Harlem* that newspapers constantly reminded blacks that they were living in a ''white man's country.''

Davis's father allowed him to use his old office in the Odd Fellows building. Davis operated out of this office with a few clients. He was later joined by another black attorney, John Geer, with whom he began the law firm of Davis and Geer.

A case in June of 1932 moved Davis to use his position as an attorney in the fight against injustice. Angelo Herndon, a 19–year–old black Alabama male, had joined the Communist Party in Alabama to help unemployed whites and blacks. He had demonstrated great skill in mobilizing groups and leading peaceful demonstrations. During a demonstration by the unemployed in Atlanta, Herndon was arrested and charged with leading an insurrection, which carried the death sentence. This incident had similarities to the previous year's Scottsboro case, in which nine Alabama males were accused of raping two white women. Davis became interested and made a visit to Herndon.

As in the Scottsboro case, the International Labor Defense (ILD), a legal arm of the Communist Party designed to defend communists, had been assigned to the Herndon case. Davis and Geer both agreed to be added to ILD's legal defense team. They argued on the grounds of the unconstitutionality of the Georgia law that restricted citizens from their right to assemble and the exclusionary practices of keeping blacks from jury service and participating in the political process. Davis had been impressed with the racial inclusiveness of the Communist Party, and decided to become a member.

Although Davis presented a very strong and compelling case, Herndon was found guilty by a white jury after three hours of deliberation. Davis agreed to an appeal. National and international support followed. Labor unions responded with outrage. Letters poured into Davis's office protesting the injustices of white society. The appeal went to Georgia's State Supreme Court where the justices upheld the verdict. The next step was the U.S. Supreme Court, and there Davis had to defer to the more experienced and qualified attorneys who would argue the case. In 1937, five years after Herndon's arrest, the nation's highest court, in a five–to–four decision, ruled in his favor. In the *Communist Councilman from Harlem,* David lauded it as ''a triumph for free speech, free press, free assembly—hailed everywhere by the democratic people of the country.'' A major accomplishment of this case was placement of blacks on Georgia juries for the first time in history.

Becomes Communist Councilman

Shortly after the Herndon decision, Davis moved to New York. He was now an active member of the Communist Party. In *The Communist Councilman from Harlem,* he described being black and communist as a ''double weapon against the ruling class.'' He viewed the philosophies of Marx and Lenin as tools that could aid blacks in their struggle against social and racial oppression. He connected with other famous African American communists like Paul Robeson and William Patterson. In 1943, he followed the example of Peter Cacchione, a Communist city council member from Brooklyn, and ran for New York City Council on the party's ticket.

New York City newspapers predicted that it was impossible for Davis to be elected on this ticket—a prediction that Davis proved wrong. He won election with heavy support from Harlem's labor–black people's progressive coalition and many liberal whites. The Jewish community strongly supported him. Davis perceived that his campaign had shown that conscientious and consistent work with the Communist Party could produce results. He had motivated blacks to get involved.

Davis joined the one other African American on the Council, the Reverend Adam Clayton Powell Jr.; however, Powell was elected to the U.S. House of Representatives the following year. Davis and Cacchione began to work on the issues that they felt best represented the concerns of working class people and the Communist Party. One of their early victories was rent control legislation; however, Davis discovered that most of the concerns of his black constituents centered around segregation and job and housing discrimination. As a result, Davis introduced a bill to outlaw segregation in the Stuyvesant Town Housing project. *The Communist Councilman from Harlem* noted that ''the measure provided for the withdrawal of the tax–exemption privilege from any landlord or realty owner who discriminated in the selection of tenants.'' The bill prohibited discrimination after 1945, but did nothing to remedy past practices.

In this and other issues, Davis had become a voice for black people, making sure that the city was sensitive and inclusive of African American concerns and events. For example, the Council gave its official endorsement to Carter Woodson's original Negro History Week.

A Man in Exile

Davis was reelected to the council in 1945, but his success began to wane. Communists were viewed suspiciously, and government investigation made it increasingly difficult for party members to survive. There was a significant decline in support from the blacks who had previously backed the party. In 1949 Davis lost his council seat.

On October 21, 1949, Davis and other leftist leaders were convicted of violations of the Smith Act, drafted by and named for Howard Smith, a U.S. congressman from Virginia. As described in *The Communist Councilman from Harlem,* this act ''stipulated that it is crime to conspire to teach and advocate the overthrow of the government by force and violence.'' Appeals to a higher court that their convictions violated First Amendment rights were unsuccessful. Davis was convicted of unlawfully conspiring to organize a Communist Party that advocated the overthrow and destruction of the U.S. government. In 1951, he was sentenced to a five–year prison term in the federal penitentiary at Terre Haute, Indiana. His stay in prison was extremely difficult because of the hostility directed toward black communists.

After Davis was released on April 15, 1955, he married Nina Stamler, a woman of Lithuanian descent with whom he had maintained a relationship while in prison. Davis ignored the criticism that he received from both African Americans and whites for his interracial marriage. They had one daughter, Emily.

In the last years of his life, Davis continued as an advocate for communist concerns and the civil rights of African Americans. In 1963, on his 60th birthday, the Smith Act was abolished and the charges against him under the act were dropped. But the crackdown on the Communist Party and the turbulent five–year prison term had taken a toll on his health. On August 22, 1964, after a long illness, Benjamin Davis died.

REFERENCES

Davis, Benjamin J. *Communist Councilman From Harlem: Autobiographical Notes Written in a Federal Penitentiary.* New York: International Publishers, 1969.

Horne, Gerald. *Black Liberation/Red Scare.* Newark: University of Delaware Press, 1994.

Horace L. Griffin

Benjamin O. Davis Jr.

(1912–)

Military officer

Benjamin O. Davis Jr. devoted his life to his country as a military officer and a civilian. He was the first twentieth–century black West Point graduate, the second black general in the U.S. military, and the first black U.S. Air Force officer to earn the three star rank of lieutenant general. His military fame also rests on the record set by the Tuskegee ''Red–Tails'' of which he was a charter member. Davis's command of the elite corps of black airmen who served under his command was a deciding factor in the desegregation of the U.S. Air Force.

Davis was born on December 18, 1912. His father, Benjamin O. Davis Sr., was a cavalry officer, his grandfather, Louis P. H. Davis, a government official. Davis's mother, Elnora Dickerson Davis, was a dressmaker whose father was a prominent Washington businessman. Until the age of four, Benjamin lived with his older sister Olive and his mother as they traveled to army bases where his father was stationed. His mother died after the birth of a second daughter. The grandparents took the children into their Washington home when their father was sent to the Philippines; he remarried when Benjamin was seven. When his parents returned stateside, they moved to Tuskegee Institute in Alabama where, as a lieutenant colonel, Davis Sr. was given a military science and tactics assignment. In 1924 the family moved to Cleveland, where the younger Davis was graduated in 1929 from the racially integrated Central High School. Davis attended summer school at Nashville's Fisk University to study mathematics before enrolling in Western Reserve University. His freshman year was unsettled, probably because he was only 16 years old, boarding with his older sister, and rather aimless about his future. Although he dreamed of flying, Davis knew the profession was closed to blacks; those open to blacks had no appeal to him.

Planning for the Future

In 1931 Davis began to consider a military career as a means of entering the flying profession. His father wanted him to go to West Point and had already broached the idea to

Benjamin O. Davis Jr.

Oscar DePriest of Illinois, the lone black in Congress. Davis was at first unable to accept DePriest's offer of an alternate appointment due to residency requirements. His parents sent him to Chicago to attend the University of Chicago and establish residency. He received another appointment but failed the academic part of the three–day examination. Davis then studied to make up history deficiencies and take more mathematics courses. In 1932 he finally passed the exam and was notified by the War Department to report to the U.S. Military Academy on July 1, 1932.

The reality of being the only minority in an isolated setting geared towards making everyone the same became crystal clear soon after Davis was assigned living quarters. He alone had no roommate supposedly because no white cadet could be asked to share his quarters since the request had to be voluntary. Long after Davis retired, he returned to West Point for a nostalgic visit and found a copy of the commandant's orders that his assigned room would have only one occupant. Davis's fellow cadets were not initially hostile and even the company commander encouraged him. The Basic Cadet Training, known as "Beast Detail," was the hazing meted out to all incoming cadets; it gave Davis no real problems because it was tradition. Then came the moment of truth when he was told to report to the barracks basement for a meeting. In his autobiography, Davis reported what happened when he arrived at the door and heard a voice say: "What are we going to do about the nigger?" He returned to his room with the impact of the question indelibly imprinted on his mind. From that moment, no cadet spoke to him directly, except in the line of duty, in the hope that he would be so unhappy he would resign and vanish. (Silencing was a West Point tradition that punished violators of the honor code who refused to resign; however, the Honor Committee had not formally cited Davis.) At the end of his plebe (freshman) year, Davis participated in the recognition ceremony, but when the cadets traveled to army bases, he was seated alone and assigned isolated living quarters.

Davis never told his parents about the indignity, not even when his father visited the academy during his plebe year. His only respite was family visits and meeting Agatha Scott, a Chicago Art Institute student who would become his wife. Still hoping to be a pilot, Davis formally applied for the U.S. Army Air Corps in October 1935, but was rejected because there were no black air corps units. In 1936 Davis was graduated as the fourth black and the first in the 20th century, ranking 35th in a class of 276. He was commissioned a second lieutenant and assigned to the 24th Infantry Regiment at Fort Benning, Georgia.

A Major Breakthrough

On June 20, 1936, Davis and Agatha Scott were married in the West Point Cadet Chapel. The newlyweds, from that day on, realized that they would be bound together for life, not only out of love but out of necessity for their survival. After honeymooning in Chicago, they arrived at Fort Benning. There they quickly discovered that racism would ensure another form of silencing, since white superior officers extended no social invitations. Davis could not join the Officers' Club and his wife was snubbed by neighbors. After being made officer in charge of recruits, he was sent to Infantry School, then in 1938 to Tuskegee as professor of military science and tactics, the same position his father had held. This appointment ensured that he had no chance of commanding white units. Davis described his two–year tenure in his autobiography as "[as] close to nothing as it could be and still be called a job."

In 1940 the senior Davis was promoted to the rank of brigadier general and sent to Fort Riley, Kansas, to command the Fourth Cavalry Brigade. He sent for his son to serve as his aide. Davis was there only four months when his father received a letter that would change the son's life forever.

The Tuskegee Airmen

The chief of the Army Air Corps suggested that the senior Davis release his son to begin pilot training. Davis was rejected on the basis of the flight physical examination due to an apparently deliberately false report by the flight surgeon. After being sent to another base, Davis passed the physical, and the disease from which he supposedly suffered disappeared from his health history. Davis, an officer trainee, and 12 other black aviation cadets became members of Class 42C in July 1941, the first black class accepted for air corps pilot training. They reported to Tuskegee Army Air Base, a highly controversial site due to accusations that the Army Air Corps was perpetuating Jim Crow (legally mandated segregation).

The importance of training war–time flyers was soon vindicated when Pearl Harbor was attacked in December. During pilot training, rumors started as to Davis's ability. One account is in the "Chappie" James biography, as cited by Phelps: "He had almost washed out of flying training only to be saved by the War Department as its 'hand picked' officer to lead the 99th." Nalty, in *Strength for the Fight,* also referred to the difficulty Davis had in learning to bank the biplane trainer, and noted that he was not as skillful a flier as George S. "Spanky" Roberts, a captain with proven leadership experience. In *Red Tails, Black Wings,* Holway wrote that Davis was always considered to be "commander–presumptive of the squadron to be formed." Despite problems, Davis succeeded. On March 7, 1942, he and four classmates graduated and received their pilot wings. The Tuskegee Experiment refuted claims that blacks were incapable of being trained as army air corps pilots.

Davis and other Tuskegee airmen always credited Noel Parrish, supervisor of primary instruction, for his continuous efforts to defuse racial tension on the base. He was a white cavalry sergeant and civilian training instructor (CPT) whose willingness to be fair and honorable toward blacks in the armed forces probably caused him to forfeit his own chances for advancement.

The 99th Pursuit Squadron

In response to President Franklin D. Roosevelt's directive to the War Department to create a black flying unit, the 99th Pursuit Squadron was formed. According to Davis, it was always known that he would be the commander: "Once I had satisfactorily completed pilot training, I was to command this squadron. Naturally, I was elated and my father immediately approved of the Air Corps's suggestion." After graduation, Davis continued to gain experience flying different types of pursuit aircraft. In May 1942 he was promoted to major and then to lieutenant colonel within a two–week period with orders retroactive to March 1, 1942, since all 1936 West Point graduates who were army air force officers were promoted to meet war–time needs. Although Davis and his command "chafed at the bit" to enter the war, they were forced to wait until July 1942 when the fourth class had graduated to complete the compliance requirement of a 26–man squadron roster. There were also black support personnel who entered the squadron as specialists in the areas of communications, hydraulics, electronics, and fuel systems. At the Air Corps Technical School at Chanute Field, Illinois, 275 were trained for seven months and sent to either Maxwell Field or Tuskegee in Alabama.

On August 24, 1942, Davis officially took command of the 99th, but he was absent when Secretary of War Henry Stinson visited Tuskegee. When the black press publicized the slight to Davis, someone superimposed Davis's picture on the photograph of Stinson greeting the base commander and this altered copy was used thereafter.

Davis would never be known as a natural flyer, but as a commander, he had few peers. Holway quoted Felix Kirkpatrick, Davis's poker pal and former West Point attendee, who said of him: "Davis was respected by most and hated by some, but it was because of the discipline exacted that we were able to make the record we did." Holway also cited Willie Fuller, a civilian instructor, who said "he went strictly by the book."

On April 14, 1943, the 99th joined 3,500 white servicemen on the *Mariposa,* a converted luxury liner. When it left the Brooklyn docks, Davis was officer in charge and troop commander since he commanded the only combat unit on the ship. He and his squadron decided to ignore the rope stretched across the deck to separate blacks and whites. They could not ignore the fact that most of their equipment was not on board and it arrived at their base eight months later. When they arrived in Casablanca, Morocco on the north African coast, Davis ordered the squadron members to disembark in dress uniforms. They were greeted by the mayor and the American expatriate, singer Josephine Baker, who served as their translator.

World War II

Davis immediately faced two problems: the lack of combat–experienced pilots and his inability to assign white pilots to his squadron. Fortunately, three white pilots volunteered to teach the unseasoned 99th pilots the techniques of combat flying. In June 1943 the 99th was assigned to the 332d Fighter Group whose commander was extremely prejudiced toward Davis. He later criticized the 99th for lack of aggressiveness and credited aerial victories to white fighter units. In September Davis was ordered stateside to take command of the 332d Fighter Group of three Tuskegee squadrons.

One month later, Davis was ordered to testify before the McCloy Committee of the War Department. Written charges had been filed accusing the 99th of being inferior, with a recommendation that all black squadrons be assigned non–combat roles. Davis successfully refuted the charges as both erroneous and racist. The real turning point for black flying units came when a 15th Strategic Air Force general stated the need for fighter pilots to protect bombers. Davis knew that the 332d would be fully equipped for this duty and instructed his pilots to forget their dreams of being glamorous fighter pilots. They were threatened with grounding and court–martial should his orders be disobeyed. Holway quoted Hannibal Cox of the 99th who spoke of the absolute need for control: "You had a bunch of young and well–educated blacks to control and discipline, which was not easy to do. He did it. He was the epitome of an officer and a role model for us."

The 332d moved to a new base at Ramatelli, Italy, got new P–47 Thunderjets designed for strafing, and prepared for its first mission of conducting daylight bomber raids and protecting the bombers. Davis's pilots clearly understood his orders not to veer from that mission. He was a harsh taskmaster who showed no favoritism and was even forced to relieve two of his own Tuskegee classmates of their duties due to discipline problems. The 332d became known as the "Red Tails" because of the readily identifiable design on the group's planes. They flew escort duty and never lost a bomber to enemy fighters. When Davis was awarded the Distinguished Flying Cross for mission leadership, he was pinned by his father. By that time, he had been promoted to the rank of colonel and awarded the Legion of Merit.

The Ugly Face of Prejudice

Davis was assigned command of the 477th Composite Group in July 1945 to prepare for war against Japan. While Japan's surrender in August 1945 meant that the 477th would not see combat, Davis had to deal with a difficult situation at Selfridge Field in Michigan. Extreme racist conditions caused severe and dangerous morale problems on the base. After repeated efforts to integrate the Officers' Club, 101 black officers were arrested. Although the War Department finally dismissed charges, Davis was in a bind. He had fought on every level for the right to be judged on merit, not by race, but this effort was largely overlooked when the officers faced court–martial. He had even established a training program for pilots using the latest combat techniques. Phelps quoted Chappie James, an off–and–on adversary, who still defended Davis:

> Sometimes I feel that Colonel Davis was really with us but he couldn't come out publicly and say so, naturally. . . . There are many who will damn him today for the seemingly impersonal approach he took towards us, and a really hardline approach in many things.

When the general court–martial convened at Godman Field, Davis had to serve as the board president but his presence was challenged, according to Phelps, because ''he was referred to as a 'book soldier'—meaning that he did everything 'by the book'—undeviatingly.''

Nevertheless, Davis assumed command not only of the composite group but of the entire post as well. Phelps described the formal review parade:

> It was the first time in the history of the army air force that an all–black group had paraded without the presence of one white face in its ranks . . . and, surrounded as if by an aura, stood that mustachioed and ''youthful West Pointer'' Colonel B. O. Davis, Jr. It was a day of which every black man in the entire United States Army Air Force would have been proud could they have been there.

In late 1945 the 332d was deactivated, and Tuskegee was retired as a training site after graduating the last class of pilots in 1946. In 1947 the 332d was reactivated.

In 1948 President Harry Truman issued Executive Order 9981 signaling the end of racial discrimination in the air force. Davis was a key player in drafting desegregation plans and implementing them at Lockbourne Army Air Base, Ohio, which was deactivated in 1949; its personnel were transferred to previously all–white units. He later served at the Air Force College and became deputy chief of staff operations, Headquarters U.S. Air Force. After graduating from the advanced jet fighter gunnery school, he became the commander of the 51st Fighter Interceptor Wing, Far East Air Forces, Korea. Other tours of duty included Formosa, Germany, the Philippines, and additional assignments as commander in chief of the Middle East, Southern Asia, and Africa. In 1954 Davis was promoted to the rank of brigadier general and in 1965 to lieutenant general.

An Office in Retirement

After retiring in 1970, Davis and his wife considered the many job offers available. He was only 57 years old and looked forward to a continued active life. The couple set up housekeeping in Arlington, Virginia, so Davis could begin an MBA program at George Washington University. This was put aside when Carl Stokes, first black mayor of a major American city, offered Davis the position of safety director in Cleveland. Davis was clearly forewarned as to what lay ahead. In his autobiography he cited the *Tampa Tribune* editorial: ''We were on our way to 'a new combat zone'—Cleveland had had a rising crime rate and severe racial troubles.''

For a man steeped in an environment that demanded ''going by the book,'' Cleveland politics would be confounding and unacceptable. The unrelenting deal–making and deal–cutting undermined Davis's efforts to support a mayor he respected and protect a city and its people he had loved since his high school years. Davis was ill–suited by temperament to deal with Stokes's major problems of trying to satisfy polarized groups and having to contend with police action that negatively affected local racial relations. Davis and his wife were positive elements in fostering open communications with all strata of the city's populace. As a ''by the book'' man, Davis had no qualms about the arrest of law violators in any neighborhood. He perceived that his detractors never stopped trying to drive a wedge between him and Stokes, finally coming to believe that the mayor was not supporting him but listening to input from racial extremists who had the ear of City Hall. Davis was proud of the data that showed a reduction in crime, lessening of complaints against the police, and improvement in the morale of the police force, but he would not serve in an atmosphere that reeked of tainted politics. He resigned after less than a year, and resumed working with the Campus Unrest Commission to which he had received a presidential appointment.

Davis returned to the federal government as director of civil aviation security in the Department of Transportation, a job he held for the next five years. He dealt with domestic and international hijacking, training and deploying air marshals, functioning as spokesman for the government at home and abroad, and overseeing airport security. In 1971 he became assistant secretary for safety and consumer affairs where he supervised efforts to curtail cargo thefts from airports, railroads, freight carriers, and maritime vessels; he was also responsible for oversight of Federal Aviation Administration regulations, consumer affairs, pipeline safety, and hazardous materials. Under his leadership, electronic detectors came into more prevalent use and the Cargo Data Interchange System (CARDIS) was developed. Davis also became known as ''Mr. 55'' for his efforts in implementing the 55 mile–per–hour speed limit enacted by Congress.

When Davis retired from that position, he continued on as a part–time consultant on safety matters and as personal representative of the secretary of transportation, both positions allowing him to speak publicly under the aegis of a federal agency. He then joined the corporate world as a board member of the Retired Officers Association and the Manhattan Life Insurance Company. He also affiliated with the Presidential Commission on Military Compensation and the Air Force Academy Foundation, serving on the academy's board of visitors. In 1978 Davis was appointed to the American Battle Monuments Commission administering cemetery memorials and monuments in America and abroad.

Davis's outstanding military achievements earned him several military decorations, including the Distinguished Service Medal, Silver Star, Distinguished Flying Cross, Legion of Merit, Air Medal, croix de guerre, Star of Africa, medals and clusters from the Republics of China and Korea, and many others for service as commander of the Tuskegee Airmen ''Red Tails'' and other squadrons. In the foreword to Davis's autobiography, L. Douglas Wilder, former governor of Virginia, summed up the significance of his service to his country: ''Throughout his achievements, General Davis has exemplified the West Point Motto, 'Duty, Honor, and Country'. . . . [His] life is testament that we are living to see the moral reconstruction of this country.''

Current address: 1001 Wilson Boulevard, #906, Arlington, VA 20560.

REFERENCES

Adams, Russell L. *Great Negroes: Past and Present.* 3rd ed. Chicago: Afro–Am Publishing Co., 1984.

Davis, Benjamin O., Jr. *An Autobiography—Benjamin O. Davis, Jr.—American.* Washington, DC: Smithsonian Institution Press, 1991.

''General B. O. Davis, Jr. Pens Autobiography; Holds to Longtime Race Beliefs.'' *Jet* 79 (11 February 1991): 10.

Harris, Jacqueline. *The Tuskegee Airmen: Black Heroes of World War II.* Parsippany, NJ: Dillon Press, 1996.

Holway, John B. *Red Tails, Black Wings.* Las Cruces, NM: Yucca Tree Press, 1997.

Lanning, Michael Lee. *The African American Soldier: From Crispus Attucks to Colin Powell.* Secaucus, NJ: A Birch Lane Press Book, 1997.

McKissack, Patricia, and Frederick McKissack. *Red–Tail Angels: The Story of the Tuskegee Airmen of World War II.* New York: Walker, 1995.

Means, Howard. *Colin Powell: Soldier/Statesman–Statesman/Soldier.* New York: Donald I. Fine, 1992.

Nalty, Bernard C. *Strength for the Fight: A History of Black Americans in the Military.* New York: Free Press, 1986.

O'Neill, Alexis. ''Benjamin A. Davis.'' *Cobblestone* 18 (February 1997): 16–18.

Ottley, Roi. *Black Odyssey: The Story of the Negro in America.* New York: C. Scribner's Sons, 1948.

Parks, Edwards. ''Around the Mall and Beyond. *Smithsonian* 21 (March 1991): 18.

Phelps, J. Alfred. *Chappie: America's First Black Four–Star General—The Life and Times of Daniel Chappie James, Jr.* Novato, CA: Presidio, 1991.

Salzman, Jack, David Lionel Smith, and Cornel West, eds. *Encyclopedia of African American Culture and History.* New York: Macmillan Library Reference USA/Simon and Schuster Macmillan, 1996.

''Still Flyin' High.'' *Ebony* 50 (November 1994): 62.

Who's Who among African Americans, 1997–98. 10th ed. Detroit: Gale Research, 1997.

Dolores Nicholson

Benjamin O. Davis Sr.
(1877–1970)
Military officer, educator, government official

As the first black American general in the U.S. Army, Benjamin Oliver Davis Sr. served as a role model and mentor for black military men and women in World War II. He was not only a leader but also a living lesson in coping with and overcoming adversity, especially the effects of segregation in the armed forces. His rewards came late in his life and career, but he stood erect in victory the same way as in his darkest moments, serving the country he loved.

Davis was born on May 28, 1877, the youngest of the three children of Louis Patrick Henry Davis and Henrietta Stewart Davis of Washington, D.C. Although his father was a house servant, the circumstances of that service were not those of the usual master–servant relationship. Louis Davis worked for General John A. Logan, who later served as the U.S. representative and senator from Illinois. Louis Davis was so well respected by Logan that Louis became the companion of Logan's son and was rewarded for his service with an appointment as messenger in the Department of the Interior. As a measure of his financial standing, Louis Davis became a homeowner in northwest Washington, then a prestigious neighborhood for blacks in the nation's capitol. The next two generations of the Davis family would be born at the Eleventh Street address.

Benjamin Davis was afforded opportunities not available to most black youths in Washington or elsewhere. He was a graduate of M Street High School, an institution with a sterling reputation. He was an outstanding cadet there and after graduating, Davis attended Howard University and became a member of the black unit of the District's National Guard. Louis Davis realized that his son had great potential and sought to find ways to lead him toward a military career through his connections to General Logan. Despite Logan's reputation and prestige, Davis was denied an appointment to the U.S. Military Academy; not even President William McKinley could overthrow the shackles of racial discrimina-

Benjamin O. Davis Sr.

tion that kept West Point ''lily white.'' Louis Davis was bitterly disappointed, but his son took it in stride and enlisted in the army as a means of seeking a military commission by competitive examination. Davis's mother disapproved of this course of action as well, because she wanted her son to enter the ministry. Benjamin O. Davis Jr. wrote of the effects of this decision in his autobiography: ''a breach developed between my father and grandfather that lasted almost until my grandfather's death in 1921, when I believe some sort of reconciliation occurred.''

Volunteers and Advances

In 1898 Davis enlisted as a volunteer soldier during the Spanish–American War and served in the 8th Volunteer Infantry as one of the ''black immunes,'' those supposedly immune to tropical fevers. On June 14, 1899, he reenlisted in the regular army and was assigned to the 9th Cavalry at Fort Duchesne, Utah, at a pay rate of $25 every two months. He advanced rapidly because he was highly literate. Because of his prior military experience, Davis was already familiar with army regulations and administrative procedures and soon achieved the rank of sergeant–major. By 1901 Davis had achieved his goal of receiving a regular commission by being promoted to the rank of second lieutenant in the 10th Cavalry. He was assigned to Troop M, 9th Cavalry in the Philippines and thus joined an elite group of only four black American officers other than chaplains.

Before being promoted to captain, Davis served at Fort Washakie, Wyoming; at Fort Robinson, Nebraska; in Monrovia, Liberia as a military attache; at Wilberforce University as instructor of military science; at Fort D. A. Russell, Wyoming, and its successor in Douglas, Arizona, where the 9th Cavalry patrolled the U.S.–Mexican border. In 1915 Davis was reassigned to Wilberforce as professor of military science and tactics. For 14 years as an army officer, Davis served in noncombat positions that ensured that he would not have the opportunity to either command white enlisted men or outrank white officers. His son, Benjamin Davis Jr., wrote in his biography:

> This policy remained the paramount consideration . . . [and he was] restricted to ''safe'' assignments: Junior Reserve Officer Training Corps (ROTC) units at black colleges, black national guard units, military attache to Liberia . . . [despite] his strong preference for duty with troops.

With each successive promotion, Davis became more of a problem for the War Department. Personally, he faced the dilemma of his family's welfare. In 1902 Davis had married Elnora Dickerson. Elnora Davis was trained as a dressmaker and began traveling with her husband to his assigned bases. She returned to Washington only to have their first two children, Olive in 1905 and Benjamin Jr. in 1912. During their 15–year marriage, the couple was constantly shunned by white officers' families on American army bases. Overseas duty assignments were always preferable since American blacks were treated more humanely on foreign soil than in their own homeland.

In 1906 Elnora Davis died in Wilberforce, Ohio, after bearing another daughter, Nora. Newly promoted lieutenant colonel, Davis had to deal with the ramifications of a new duty assignment and the raising of three children in addition to coping with the loss of his wife. Within a year of her death, Davis was reassigned to the Philippines as supply officer of the 9th Cavalry at Camp Stotsenburg. His parents volunteered to keep the children. During his three–year overseas assignment, Davis began a letter–writing courtship with Sadie Overton, a Wilberforce English teacher who was a member of a prestigious black Mississippi family. Her father was a state representative and a teacher whose children were college educated. In 1919 the couple married in the Philippines.

In 1920 Davis and his new wife returned stateside and she became mother to three children who adored her. Davis was assigned to Tuskegee Institute, as it was known then, as a professor of military science and tactics. Although he would return there for a six–year stint (1931–37), this was a special time because now his family was intact for the first time since Elnora Davis's death.

When the Davises moved to Cleveland, Ohio, in 1924, they became homeowners for the first time as Davis began a new assignment as instructor of the 372nd Infantry of the Ohio National Guard. This was another in a long line of noncombat long–term tours of duty. While commanding this all–black unit, Davis was at least able to travel across the state and supervise annual maneuvers at an Ohio army camp. In 1929 he went to Europe as the official army representative for a group of World War I mothers and widows of slain soldiers buried in European cemeteries. His exemplary service was rewarded with a promotion to colonel in 1930. That same year Davis was reassigned to Wilberforce, but only for a year before being reassigned to Tuskegee and back to Ohio. Every few years he was rotated to avoid being placed over a white company and over white officers.

Becomes First Black American General

After 42 years of stoical and faithful service as a career soldier in the army Davis loved, in October of 1940 he became the first black American general in the U.S. Army with a promotion to brigadier general. There was controversy over the promotion of an officer due to retire in less than one year. Many army officers complained, calling it a political move designed to appease the large number of black voters in New York and Illinois and the NAACP, an unrelenting advocate for fair treatment of blacks in the military. Until his retirement in June of 1941, Davis served as brigade commander at Fort Riley, Kansas, with the 2nd Cavalry Division. Whatever plans Davis and his wife may have made for his golden years were not realized at that time because he was recalled to active duty before the end of the month. Davis was activated as assistant to the Inspector General, a job that entailed such duties as investigating racial incidents and supporting promotions of black soldiers and officers. In conjunction with this position, Davis was also appointed to the Committee on Negro Troop Policies. From 1942 to 1945, he served in Europe as adviser on the use of black troops and to avert and deal with racial problems.

One of Davis's first tactics was to film the all–black 92nd Division in Italy. The resulting product, an unabashedly propagandistic tool, was entitled ''Teamwork'' and designed to make more palatable the plan to increase the number of black combat troops in Europe. The presence of Winston Churchill congratulating the men was an added public relations coup. Davis was also adviser to General Dwight D. Eisenhower, then commander of the European Theater and a well–documented balker at efforts to integrate black troops into white units. One of Davis's greatest achievements was his unrelenting insistence on instituting a proposal to retrain black service troops as combat soldiers. This was a critical venture because the bravery, aptitude, and morale of black soldiers had been seriously questioned, especially by some of the more highly visible army commanders. In particular, the 92nd Division had received much negative criticism about combat behavior in the Italian mountains against heavy German opposition. Lieutenant General George S. Patton Jr. was an unabashed segregationist who openly declared blacks to be inferior, especially for armored combat. Quoted in *Black America,* he gave another view: he said of the all–black 761st Tank Battalion, ''I would have never asked for you . . . if you weren't good enough.''

Davis has always been credited as being a major player in the efforts to change the military's policies of segregation and he was awarded the Distinguished Service Medal for his untiring efforts to combat segregation in the armed forces. As well, he was a role model in illustrating that blacks could effectively serve in positions of authority and leadership. At his July 20, 1948, retirement ceremony, Davis received tributes from President Harry S Truman and high ranking military officials. Thereafter, he served as a member of the American Battle Monuments Commission, a job that required overseas travel to inspect American cemeteries.

Despite his stellar accomplishments, Davis was often criticized for his rigid and unyielding adherence to the army's way of doing things. One such incident occurred earlier in his career when he served as the ROTC commanding officer at Wilberforce University. In his autobiography, Benjamin Davis Jr. wrote about the friction between his father and the college administrators over applying army regulations in a civilian setting. Davis was also criticized for his absolute insistence on firm discipline of cadets by the school's commandant, who was not strict enough for a diehard army officer. Davis, however, was highly respected by students and faculty alike and many of his programmatic suggestions and plans were implemented.

Most photographs of Davis show a stern, unsmiling visage, one guaranteed to elicit immediate attention and obedience to orders and instructions. These were reactions that were expected and taken for granted by a career soldier who realized from the beginning that the ordinary friendships and close relations enjoyed by the average citizen would have little, if any, place in the army of the first half of the twentieth century. Before his final retirement in 1948, Davis had the pleasure of seeing his son accomplish what the army had denied him. In 1944 he was privileged to pin the Distinguished Flying Cross on his son at the Ramitelli Air Force Base in Italy. He also vicariously experienced the joy and pleasure in his son's promotion to the rank of brigadier general in the U.S. Air Force by President Dwight D. Eisenhower, whom the senior Davis had advised in the European Theater during World War II. Just as he had been the first black American general in the army, now his son was the first black American general in the air force. He also saw his son become the first black American lieutenant general. Other awards and decorations presented to the senior Davis were: the Bronze Star Medal; the Grade of Commander of the Order of the Star of Africa (Liberia); and the French Crois de Guerre with Palm.

Davis died of leukemia on November 26, 1970, at Great Lakes Naval Hospital in North Chicago. His funeral was held at Fort Myers Chapel outside Washington, D.C., and he was buried in Arlington National Cemetery with full military honors. This grandson of a slave who bought his freedom in 1800 strove to end racism in the institution designed to guarantee the safety and well–being of all Americans. Still willing to serve the U.S. Army that he loved, according to *Book of Firsts,* just before he retired Davis said: ''I think I have done my share but if the War Department desires me to continue to serve in the national emergency, I will have an open mind.''

REFERENCES

"Benjamin Davis, Sr., First Negro General in the U.S., Dies at 93." *New York Times,* November 27, 1970.

Davis, Benjamin O., Jr. *Benjamin O. Davis, Jr., American: An Autobiography.* Washington, DC: Smithsonian Institution Press, 1991.

"Davis, First Black General, Buried in Arlington Rites." *New York Times,* December 1, 1970.

Haynes, George E. *The Trend of the Races.* New York: Council of Women for Home Missions and Missionary Education Movement of the United States and Canada, 1922.

Naity, Bernard C. *Strength for Fight: A History of Black Americans in the Military.* New York: Free Press, 1986.

The Negro Almanac. New York: Bellwether Publishing, 1976.

Phelps, J. Alfred. *Chappie: America's First Black Four–Star General; The Life and Times of Daniel James, Jr.* Novato, CA: Presido Press, 1991.

Ploski, Harry A., Otto J. Lindenmeyer, and Ernest Kaiser, eds. *Reference Library of Black America.* Book 4. New York: Bellwether Publishing, 1971.

Rennert, Richard, ed. *Book of Firsts: Leaders of America.* New York: Chelsea House, 1994.

Salzman, Jack, David Lionel Smith, and Cornel West, eds. *Encyclopedia of African–American Culture and History.* New York: Macmillan Library Reference USA/Simon and Schuster Macmillan, 1996.

Dolores Nicholson

Miles Davis
(1926–1991)
Musician, bandleader, composer, arranger

Miles Davis, called the Father of Cool and the Prince of Darkness, stands out as one of jazz's prime innovators. He was the catalyst for more distinct genres of jazz than any other twentieth–century musician. His lengthy career embraced bebop, cool jazz, modal jazz, fusion or jazz–rock, and electronic funk–infusion. Miles Davis pointed the way for the evolution of jazz for more than 40 years and, along the way, delighted many while confusing others.

Miles Dewey Davis III was born on May 25, 1926, in Alton, Illinois, as the second child of an upper middle-class family. His father Miles Dewey Davis II was a dentist, his mother Cleota Henry Davis was a housewife and played the violin and piano. He had an older sister Dorothy, and younger brother Vernon.

Davis's father moved his family from Alton to East St. Louis where he set up his dental practice. The Davises lived in a well–appointed, integrated neighborhood. Miles Davis's early interests were sports–related. He particularly enjoyed boxing and continued it for much of his life as a body–building activity. He observed, however, in his autobiography, *Miles,* that "by the time I was twelve, music had become the most important thing in my life." Davis had begun playing the trumpet, one a neighbor gave him when he was ten. He had taken a few lessons. He really began to progress when he went to Attucks Junior High School and joined the school band. His father bought him a new trumpet when he was 13–years old. He participated in band at Lincoln High School while continuing to study privately. Davis met Clark Terry, the famed trumpet player, while on a trip with the high school band. Terry was Davis's idol and was later to become his friend and mentor.

Miles Davis

Davis and some of his high school friends started a small band that played on weekends at church events, social affairs, and at Huff's Beer Garden. When he was 17, Davis got a job playing trumpet in Eddie Randle's Blue Devils' band. When Billy Eckstine's band, with fellow musical giants Dizzy Gillespie and Charlie Parker, came to St. Louis, the 18–year–old Davis got the chance to fill in for a sick trumpeter for two weeks.

Though musically Davis was moving ahead at a rapid pace, his home life was not very happy. His parents decided to separate and Davis had to live with his mother. Their relationship was strained, and he considered a move to New York City after high school graduation so that he could attend Juilliard. The experience of playing with Gillespie and Parker helped him to make the decision. His mother wanted him to attend Fisk University where his sister was enrolled, but

Davis's father supported his son's choice. Davis admitted in his autobiography that "Juilliard was only a smokescreen, a stopover, a pretense I used to put me close to being around Bird and Diz."

The young musician auditioned and was admitted to Juilliard after moving to New York in September of 1944. He found Dizzy Gillespie and finally located Charlie Parker with whom he roomed for a while. Davis went to school by day and with other hopeful musicians haunted local jazz clubs, particularly Minton's Uptown at night. He discovered that Juilliard's curriculum did not really meet his needs because, he wrote in his biography, "We was all trying to get our master's degrees and Ph.D.s from Minton's University of Bebop under the tutelage of Professors Bird and Diz." Davis was sharp enough to realize that some of Juilliard's courses could help him to become the quintessential jazz player. He remained in school for an entire year and went home to tell his father that he was quitting Juilliard to devote his time to playing jazz. According to Davis in his autobiography, his father, to his amazement, again supported the decision, but told him, "You want to be your own man, have your own sound . . . don't be nobody else but yourself. You know what you got to do and I trust your judgment."

Enters the World of Jazz

Davis had already played as a sideman in several bands. He played with Coleman Hawkins' band, which featured Billie Holiday as vocalist, and with Charlie Parker's group at the Three Deuces as a replacement for Dizzy Gillespie. Davis's first important recording session was in 1945 when Parker was asked to do a record for the Savoy label. Parker asked Davis to play trumpet for the session. The recording, *Charlie Parker's Reboppers,* represented a landmark because it brought Miles Davis's name before the public.

During these early days, Davis slowly developed his own style of playing. Though he admired the excitement of bebop and Dizzy Gillespie's lightning–speed, upper–register playing, he worked hard to sound different. He preferred playing in the middle register and using a sparse, lyrical tone that was resonant and intense but without vibrato. Davis preferred spaces of silence around his notes. He admired the arranging style of Gil Evans and began working with him in 1948. This was the beginning of a long and profitable relationship for both men because their first major collaboration resulted in the album *Birth of the Cool,* which launched the cool jazz era.

In 1958 Davis changed his course again with his recording of the album *Milestones.* This was the first time that Davis wrote in the modal form. He also used the pianist, Bill Evans, who was an expert in modal playing. *Milestones* was the catalyst for the album *Kind of Blue,* which firmly established Miles Davis in his new modal style.

During the early and mid–1960s, Davis's band experienced several personnel changes. He hired younger musicians like bassist Ron Carter, percussionist Tony Williams, pianist Herbie Hancock, alto saxophonist George Coleman, and tenor saxophonist Wayne Shorter. Davis began slowly, but surely changing the direction of jazz again. In his magazine article "Prince of Darkness," Gene Santoro pointed to "albums like *Filles de Kilimanjaro* (Columbia), on which Davis had Hancock play electric piano, causing major consternation among jazz purists of the time." In 1969 albums *In a Silent Way* and *Bitches Brew* marked the genesis of the fusion of jazz–rock. By this time, Davis and his producer Teo Macero were taking the studio sessions and constructing albums from selections of tape much as a film editor pieces a film. This methodology elicited much criticism from jazz critics and jazz purists alike. The youth of America, however, gave much acclaim to Miles Davis and his up–to–date music.

Davis's creativity was inhibited from 1975 to 1981 because illness and his heavy use of drugs forced him to take a six–year hiatus. When he reemerged, he forged yet another direction for jazz. At this point of his career, Davis, according to some critics, sold out to commercialism when he recorded the rock and funk album, *You're Under Arrest.* It included his interpretations of Cyndi Lauper's "Time After Time" and Michael Jackson's "Human Nature." The album, and those that followed, were heavy with electronics, but were best sellers with young audiences.

Wins Numerous Honors

When Davis was 21–years old, he received *Esquire's* New Star Award. He was voted into *Metronome Magazine's* All Star Band in 1950 and won a total of 29 *Down Beat* polls for Best Trumpet, Jazzman of the Year, and Best Combo. He was Jazz Musician of the Year in *Jazz Forum* for 1982 and the 1984 recipient of the National Endowment for the Arts' American Jazz Masters Award. In 1984 Davis was awarded Denmark's Sonning Prize for lifetime achievement in music; this was the first time that a jazz musician or a black man had received the award. He won three Grammies for *We Want Miles* in 1982, *Decoy* in 1983, and *Tutu* in 1987. New York Governor Mario Cuomo presented him the Governor's Arts Award in 1989. He was recognized by his hometown when the Miles Davis Elementary School in East St. Louis was named in his honor.

Among the many superb recordings that Davis produced, mostly under the Columbia label, over a 40–year period are: *Birth of the Cool, Walkin', Milestones, Porgy and Bess, Kind of Blue, Sketch of Spain, At Carnegie Hall, E.S.P., Nefertiti, Filles De Kilimanjaro, In a Silent Way, Bitches Brew, Live at the Fillmore, We Want Miles, Decoy,* and *Tutu.*

Davis's music was loved by many, but his personality was disliked by even more. He seemed cold, aloof, and arrogant because of his disturbing stage presence. He rarely acknowledged his audiences. He would turn his back, play to the floor, walk off the stage when he was not playing, and fail to announce his program or acknowledge applause.

Chris Albertson in *Saturday Review* provided an explanation for Davis's personality: "the forbidding mask of hostility that in many minds characterizes Miles is just that: an image fostered by his own deliberate lack of showmanship and sculptured by reporters who have failed to recognize a serious artist at work.'' Richard Harrington observed in the *Washington Post* that ''It was Duke Ellington who first compared Davis to Picasso: two men connected by constant artistic flux, oblivious to tradition and unsympathetic artistic and social climates.'' Miles Davis was, in fact, an artist himself. In his later years, Davis devoted several hours a day to his drawing and painting. He had one–man shows not only in America, but also in Germany, Spain, and Japan. Some of his original drawings were included on the covers of late albums.

Davis was small in stature but dressed stylishly throughout his life. He never compromised his own standards in terms of music or dress to garner favor with fans or with critics. He was highly critical of whites when he felt that they were racist. Despite his enigmatic disposition he represented his personification of cool to his admirers.

Plagued with frequent illnesses and drug addiction for much of his life, Miles Davis died of pneumonia, respiratory failure, and stroke on September 28, 1991. His death occurred at St. John's Hospital in Santa Monica, California. He was 65. Davis was married to and divorced from Frances Taylor, a dancer; Betty Mabry, a singer; and Cicely Tyson, an actress. He had three sons, Gregory, Miles IV, and Erin, and one daughter, Cheryl.

Following his death, the news media was filled with articles about Davis. Herb Boyd in the *New York Amsterdam News* praised him because ''right to the very end he never lost his ear for talent, how to assemble a band and to get the best from it.'' ''The first thing I learned from Miles was about being true to yourself,'' Marcus Miller explained in *Down Beat.* ''Here was a guy who was acclaimed and criticized, and nothing that was ever said to him made him change what he felt he had to do.'' This opinion perhaps best described the legacy that Miles Davis left the world. His determination to perform, write, and record in his own way resulted in a body of jazz recordings that the world can enjoy forever.

REFERENCES

Albertson, Chris. ''The Unmasking of Miles Davis. *Saturday Review* 54 (27 November 1971): 67.

Davis, Miles, and Quincy Troupe. *Miles: The Autobiography.* New York: Simon and Schuster, 1989.

''Miles Davis: Father of Cool.'' *New York Amsterdam News,* October 5, 1991.

''Miles Davis: Well–Tempered Trumpet.'' *Washington Post,* June 2, 1985.

Miller, Marcus. ''The Legacy.'' *Down Beat* 58 (December 1991): 20.

Santoro, Gene. ''Prince of Darkness.'' *Nation* (11 November 1991): 602.

Mary Frances Early

Ossie Davis

(1917–)

Writer, producer, actor

Ossie Davis, in the eighth decade of his life, can justifiably be called an elder statesman in the dramatic arts. His high visibility in commercial television public service announcements, public television, and film productions affords him instant recognition by millions of viewers at home and abroad. His sincerity and integrity transcend even the smallest television screen and most gargantuan movie screen. His believability quotient is one of his greatest assets and when one hears Davis's immediately recognizable voice and sees him, clear–eyed, focused, sincere, and more handsome in his vintage years than in the days of his youth, it is clear that his presence is not just that of an actor, playwright, or civil rights activist but of a true humanitarian.

On December 18, 1917, Ossie Davis was born in Cogdell, Georgia. His name was to have been ''R. C.'' Davis in honor of his grandfather, Rayford Chapman, but the white clerk apparently thought his parents were saying ''Ossie'' and wrote that name on his birth certificate. His father, Kince Charles Davis, was a railway construction worker and preacher, and his mother was Laura Cooper Davis. Although neither parent could read, they were both exemplars of the southern oral traditions of storytelling and preaching, both highly regarded talents in the black community.

In the Davis household it was a certainty that Davis was going to school and attending church. He completed his secondary education in Waycross, Georgia, and looked forward to going to college. Because he lacked money for living expenses, Davis was unable to accept a scholarship to Tuskegee Institute. He hitchhiked his way to Washington, D.C., to live with his aunts and to attend Howard University, where he stayed for two years. His Howard mentor was Alain Locke, professor of philosophy, author, and drama critic, who recognized Davis's raw, untapped talent and persuaded him to move to New York City and join the Harlem–based Rose McClendon Players.

In New York City Davis was forced to take on all kinds of jobs. He studied acting when finances were available and bordered on homelessness. After two years of study, he finally debuted in the 1941 McClendon Players production of *Joy Exceeding Glory.* Then World War II intervened and Davis joined the army, serving first as a surgical technician in Liberia and then being transferred to the Special Services Department. There he was able to write and produce stage works that both utilized and entertained military personnel.

Acting Career Begins

Davis was honorably discharged from the army in 1945 and returned to his home state. A call came from the McClendon Players' director Richard Campbell, and Davis returned to New York and won the lead role in Richard Ardrey's play,

Ossie Davis

Jeb, making his Broadway debut. Although the play received poor reviews and closed after only nine performances, Davis fared better. The critics loved him and so did a fellow cast member, Ruby Ann Wallace, now Ruby Dee. They joined the touring company of *Anna Lucasta* and married in 1948. The next decade was one of intense suffering as they, along with other black actors, struggled to reconcile their moral convictions with the need to work.

Although many biographical accounts cite Davis as one who steadily progressed and prospered as an actor, his perceptions differ, especially during the lean years of the 1950s. Preferences aside, Davis had a family to support and his longtime dream of being a writer had to take a back seat to being an actor.

In 1953 Davis wrote a one–act play, *Alice in Wonder,* on the topic of the McCarthy era politics. It was later reworked and renamed *The Big Deal* but received poor reviews. Not surprisingly, Davis and Dee were blacklisted for affiliating with left–wing organizations and causes. To offset the commensurate loss of jobs and income, they followed in the footsteps of numerous other black artists by going on the college circuit where they staged dramatic readings. The few parts that Davis did get were in *The Emperor Jones,* a 1955 television production, and on Broadway in *Jamaica,* and starring vehicle for Lena Horne in 1955.

During the next decade his career options improved and in 1960 Davis replaced Sidney Poitier in the highly acclaimed Lorraine Hansberry play, *A Raisin in the Sun.* In 1961 Davis finally hit pay dirt with his play *Purlie Victorious,* which satirized southern racism and provided starring roles for Davis and Dee. After a seven–month run, the play was adapted as a movie entitled *Gone Are the Days.* In 1970 it was transformed into *Purlie,* a Broadway musical. Its stars—Cleavon Little and Melba Moore—won Tony Awards.

The 1960s were productive in television and film as Davis secured roles in the movies *The Cardinal* (1963), *The Hill* (1965), *A Man Named Adam* (1966), *The Scalphunters* (1967), and *Slaves* (1969); he also played in episodes of the television series *The Defenders, The Doctors, The Fugitive, Bonanza,* and *East Side, West Side,* for which Davis wrote an episode. In 1965 he narrated *History of the Negro People,* a National Education Television (NET) production. In 1968 Davis wrote a play *Curtain Call, Mr. Aldridge, Sir,* that was produced at the University of California, Santa Barbara. He received an Emmy nomination in 1969 for his performance in the Hallmark Hall of Fame teleplay, *Teacher, Teacher.* During this time he and Dee also worked on a pet project by performing as a nightclub team at New York's Village Vanguard. Davis was again successful in 1970 with the movie adaptation of Chester Himes's novel *Cotton Comes to Harlem,* a venture that grossed more than $9 million and starred Godfrey Cambridge and Raymond St. Jacques.

Because of his strong sense of social and political responsibility, Davis complemented his professional life with such activities as testifying before Congress on racial discrimination in the theater and joining the advisory board of the Congress of Racial Equality (CORE) in 1962. In 1963 he wrote a skit for the March on Washington for which he and Dee served as official hosts. But it was the year 1965 that truly tested his mettle with the assassination of Malcolm X. Arna Bontemps and Jack Conroy described his contribution to his slain friend:

> The funeral obsequies (February 27, 1965) included a fervent panegyric by Ossie Davis, Negro playwright and actor. ''Malcolm,'' he said, ''had been one of Harlem's brightest hopes—extinguished now and gone from us forever. . . . Malcolm was our manhood, our living black manhood . . . we shall know him . . . for what he was and is—a Prince—our own black shining Prince!—who didn't hesitate to die, because he loved us so.''

During that same year Davis served as one of the 60 sponsors for Paul Robeson's sixty–fifth birthday salute staged by *Freedomways* magazine, an event excoriated and shunned by many prominent black public figures. Ten years later he and his wife attended and participated in the 75th Birthday Salute for Paul Robeson held at Carnegie Hall.

The Measure of His Success

From the 1970s on Davis began to reap success from the acting, writing, and producing efforts of the prior 20 years. Although these films were not critical successes, Davis honed his skills as producer and director with *Kongi's Harvest* (1971), *Black Girl* (1972), *Gordon's War* (1973), and *Countdown to Kusini* (1976). From 1974 to 1976 he and Dee performed in a radio series, *The Ossie Davis and Ruby Dee Hour* and in a 1981 public television series *With Ossie and Ruby,* the latter an effort coproduced by their own family company, Emmalyn II Enterprises. Davis played Martin Luther King Sr. in the 1977 Abby Mann television miniseries *King.* The year before he appeared in the film *Let's Do It Again* and in the play *Escape to Freedom.*

Instead of slowing down with the advent of the 1980s, Davis became a bona fide matinee idol courtesy of Spike Lee, who featured him in *School Daze* (1988), *Do the Right Thing* (1989), *Jungle Fever* (1991), and *Get On the Bus* (1996). Davis also starred in *I'm Not Rapaport* at Burt Reynolds's Florida–Jupiter Theater (1986) and after winning a Tony Award as a Broadway production, it became a movie production starring Davis and Walter Matthau in 1996. It is now receiving rave reviews. Davis was a semiregular cast member, Ponder Blue, in the television weekly series *Evening Shade,* a starring–vehicle for Reynolds that also provided recurring episodes for Dee as Ponder Blue's old flame. In 1996 he had a regular role in the CBS production *The Client.* In the summer of 1996, Davis, as an actor and World War II veteran, starred in a series of public service announcements to commemorate Black Patriots Week and ongoing efforts of the Black Patriots Foundation to construct a memorial to Black Revolutionary War soldiers. In that year Davis also served as one of the commentators on the PBS special, *Lena Horne: In Her One Voice.* He applauded her efforts as a World War II USO entertainer and her strong advocacy for civil rights, especially her journey to Mississippi to support Medgar Evers.

Davis, Dee, and their three children and spouses formed Emmalyn II Enterprises, a production company formed to distribute the senior Davis's dramatic reading of the New Testament. Its production credits include PBS and CBS specials as well as an album by Max Roach, Abbey Lincoln, and other prominent musicians. Nora, the eldest daughter, brings production talents and her husband, Bill Day, is an art director. Their son, Guy, is a film and television actor, musician, playwright, and producer who also conducts acting workshops; his wife, Dorothy, is a museum curator. The youngest daughter, Hasaan, is a published author whose husband, Abdul Muhammad, is an accomplished musician. Davis and Dee are also authors of published children's books and plays.

Howard University honored Davis in 1973 by awarding him an honorary doctorate. The New York Urban League honored Davis and Dee in 1970 for civil rights leadership with the Frederick Douglass Award. Dee also received the NAACP Image Award and was inducted into the NAACP Image Awards Hall of Fame in 1989. He received the Monarch Award in 1990. The Ruby Dee and Ossie Davis Collection of Black Film was established by the Afro–American Studies Program at Yale University in April 1992.

In *American Visions,* W. Calvin Anderson quoted Davis who spoke about his future goals at the age of 74: "I'm closer to being a writer now than I've ever been in my life. That is only what I've always wanted to do. To be a writer to me meant fulfilling a dream that existed before I knew who I was." About achieving the couple's goals, Davis continued, "What we try to do is tell the truth of our vision as effectively as we possibly can." Anderson wrote:

> [They are] "rare jewels" because they are unusually blessed with multiple talents. In one capacity or another, their work is always in front of us and their magnificent ability to reach us all has made them timeless.

Current address: The Artists Agency, 10000 Santa Monica Boulevard, Los Angeles, CA 90067.

REFERENCES

Anderson, W. Calvin. "One Miracle At a Time: Ossie Davis and Ruby Dee Are Still Making Dreams Come True." *American Visions* 7 (April/May, 1992): 20–24.

Bontemps, Arna, and Jack Conroy. *Anyplace But Here.* New York: Hill and Wang, 1966.

Byrd, Rudolph P., ed. *Generations in Black and White.* Athens: University of Georgia Press, 1993.

Denby, David. "Ticket to Ride." *New York Magazine* 29 (21 October 1996): 52–53.

Ebony Pictorial History of Black America. Vol. 3. Nashville: Southwestern Co., 1971.

Hughes, Langston, Milton Meltzer, and C. Eric Lincoln. *A Pictorial History of Black Americans.* 4th rev. ed. New York: Crown Publishers, 1973.

Kranz, Rachel C. *The Biographical Dictionary of Black America.* New York: Facts on File, 1992.

Salzman, Jack, David Lionel Smith, and Cornel West, eds. *Encyclopedia of African–American Culture and History.* New York: Macmillan Library Reference USA/Simon and Schuster Macmillan, 1996.

Vassell, Olive. "Black Patriots Foundation Wants Memorial to Honor Revolutionary Soldiers." *Tennessee Tribune* 7 (14–20 June 1996): 11.

White, Jack. "In the Driver's Seat." *Time* 148 (21 October 1996): 78.

Who's Who among Black Americans, 1994–95. 8th ed. Detroit: Gale Research, 1994.

Dolores Nicholson

Sammy Davis Jr.
(1925–1990)
Entertainer, humanitarian

Sammy Davis Jr. was one of the world's greatest entertainers because of his versatility. The June 4, 1990, issue of *Jet* described him as "a megastar whose career span showcased him as a dynamic drummer, talented trumpeter, brilliant bassist, sensational singer, dazzling dancer, acclaimed actor, venturesome vibraphonist, master mimic, renowned recording artist, creative cook, consummate comedian, and author of three books . . . a businessman, philanthropist, producer/director, and collector of art, cars and guns.'' Despite racism, he became popular with white audiences in a career that began in vaudeville.

Davis was born December 8, 1925, in New York City's Harlem, to Elvera Sanchez Davis, a chorus dancer, and Sammy Davis Sr., a tapdancer who toured with a troupe headed by Will Mastin. Because his parents were at the peak of their careers and constantly traveled, he and his sister Ramona were left with family to be reared, Davis with his paternal grandmother, ''Mama Rosa'' M. Davis made his stage debut at the age of one.

By the time Davis was three years old, his parents had separated, both professionally and maritally, and his father gained custody of him. At this time, he began to travel and perform with the Mastin troupe and became a full–time professional. He and the troupe continued to perform with a great deal of success until vaudeville began to be replaced by the movies. Mastin then began cutting back on the troupe membership; over a period of time, it went from twelve members to three and became known as The Will Mastin Trio, featuring Sammy Davis Jr. During his travels with the troupe, he came under the influence and tutelage of Bill ''Bojangles'' Robinson, the world's greatest tapdancer; later in his career, Davis immortalized Robinson in the song ''Mr. Bojangles.''

This lifestyle allowed little time for formal schooling and it was not until he was drafted into the U.S. Army and sent to Fort Francis E. Warren in Cheyenne, Wyoming, that this was corrected. Davis was befriended by an African American sergeant who gave him remedial reading lessons and the basics of a high school education. It was also during this period that he encountered the violent and brutal racism with which he was to contend throughout his career. While in the army, he was assigned to a Special Services unit and toured various military installations. He produced and performed in shows that were often revisions of his old vaudeville acts. At the end of his tour of duty in the army, he rejoined the Will Mastin Trio.

Appears in Clubs and Films

After the army, Davis returned to performing and appeared in small places as well as Chicago, New York, and Los Angeles. Just as his touring prior to the war led to his meeting Robinson, after the war it led to contact and work with rising stars like Mickey Rooney, Frank Sinatra, Bob Hope, and Jack Benny. He continued to appear in clubs throughout his life. In 1954 Davis was in a near fatal automobile accident in which he lost an eye. Most importantly, he began to concern himself with his spiritual life and to study Judaism. In spite of the fact that his mother was a Roman Catholic and his father a Baptist, he converted to Judaism. When he returned to performing following his 1954 accident, he rejoined the Trio and appeared at such clubs as Copa City in Miami, the Chez Paree in Chicago, and the Latin Casino in Philadelphia. Davis was a regular on the Las Vegas club circuit and as part owner of the Tropicana Hotel was a regular performer. Often appearing with him were his friends Jerry Lewis, Liza Minelli, and others. He regularly appeared at top nightclubs, supper clubs, and concert halls in the United States. In 1988 he embarked on a national tour with Frank Sinatra, Dean Martin, and Liza Minelli. Davis was known for his showmanship and integrity. At a 1977 performance at Harrod's Tahoe Club, he picked up the tab for the entire club night because he believed his performance had not met his standards.

Sammy Davis Jr.

Davis began his film career with *Rufus Jones for President,* in which he starred in the title role as a little boy who falls asleep in his mother's lap and dreams he is president. This was followed in the same year by *Season's Greetings.* Between 1931 and 1989, he appeared in more than 29 films. He played Fletcher Henderson in *The Benny Goodman Story* (1956); costarred with Eartha Kitt in *Anna Lucasta* (1958); he played Sportin' Life in the screen version of Gershwin's folk opera *Porgy and Bess* (1959), a role for which he is well known; he appeared as himself in *Pepe* (1960); he sang the title song for the soundtrack for *Of Love and Desire* (1963); as the ballad singer in *The Three Penny Opera* (1963), he sang ''Mack the Knife''; and in 1965 he played the supporting role in *Nightmare in the Sun.* In 1972 he appeared in *Save the Children,* an all–star music documentary filmed at a benefit show for Jesse Jackson's Operation PUSH (People United to Serve Humanity) in Chicago. His last screen appearance was in 1989 in *Taps,* in which he co–starred with Gregory Hines and performed his last dance routine for the camera.

Davis became a member of a group of Hollywood actors called the "Rat Pack" which included Frank Sinatra, Tony Curtis, Dean Martin, Peter Lawford, and Joey Bishop. They appeared with Davis in such films as *Oceans Eleven* (1960), *Sergeants Three* (1962), *Johnny Cool* (1963), *Robin and the Seven Hoods* (1964), *Salt and Pepper* (1968), and *One More Time* (1970). As a result of these movies, Donald Bogle in *Toms, Coons, Mulattoes, Mammies, and Bucks* wrote that "he alienated black movie patrons because he was too much the coon–pickaninny figure. On the surface the clan pictures were egalitarian affairs; underneath they rotted from white patronizing and hypocrisy." Bogle wrote in *Blacks in American Film and Television* that "Davis was frequently used as a token . . . [and] portrayed . . . mainly as a comic sidekick, with racial jokes sometimes at Davis's expense."

Recording, Television, and Stage Career

Davis began recording songs for Capitol Records in 1946. During his career, he recorded with other labels such as Decca, Reprise, and Warner Brothers. His "The Way You Look Tonight," one of his first cuts, was named *Metronome's* Record of the Year. Other songs recorded by him are "Mr. Bojangles"; "Candy Man," his all–time best–seller; "Hey There"; "The Lady is a Tramp"; "Birth of the Blues"; "Too Close for Comfort"; "Gonna Build a Mountain"; and "Who Can I Turn To." His numerous record albums include *Starring Sammy Davis, Jr.*, which contained impersonations of such artists as Dean Martin and Jerry Lewis, Jimmie Durante, Johnny Rae, and Big Crosby; *Sammy Swings; Mood to Be Wooed; I've Got a Right to Swing; As Long As She Needs Me;* and *Sammy Davis and Count Basie: Our Shining Hour.*

Contacts made by Davis during his travels following his stint in the army were instrumental in his initial appearances on television. He was provided a place on Eddie Cantor's *Colgate Comedy Hour* television program. His small troupe then was a summer replacement for an NBC regular. Davis appeared in both variety shows and series on television. These included *The Ed Sullivan Show; All in the Family,* where he was the first celebrity to appear; *Mod Squad; General Electric Theatre; The Cosby Show;* and *Dick Powell Theatre.* He revised Pigmeat Markham's vaudeville routine, "Here Come De Judge," for the *Laugh In* program and hosted *The Tonight Show* several times in place of host Johnny Carson. Davis was so well received that he was able on several occasions to have his own television shows, *The Swinging World of Sammy Davis, Jr., Sammy and His Friends,* the short–lived network series *The Sammy Davis, Jr. Show,* and *Sammy and Company.*

Davis's major Broadway appearances came after 1954. In 1956 he opened on Broadway in *Mr. Wonderful,* a musical comedy created especially for Davis, about an African American entertainer who used his talent and will to overcome racial odds and become a star. It ran for over 380 performances. In 1965 he had the lead role in Clifford Odet's *The Golden Boy,* the story of an African American boxer struggling to free himself from poverty; it ran for over 560 performances. For his performance, he was nominated for a Tony for best actor in a musical in 1965. He returned to Broadway in 1974 in *Sammy on Broadway,* a revue.

Davis was the author of three popular autobiographies. *Yes I Can, The Story of Sammy Davis, Jr.* (1965) was written with Jane and Burt Boyar. It chronicles the trials, especially the racism Davis experienced in the U.S. Army, and triumphs in the first 35 years of his life. The second autobiography, *Hollywood in a Suitcase* (1980), details not only his life in show business but also personalities with whom he came in contact during this period of his career. His final book, *Why Me* (1989), was again written in collaboration with Jane and Burt Boyar. According to *Jet* magazine, "It explores the song–and–dance man's glitzy lifestyle on America's West Coast and its effect on his health, finances, fatherhood role, civil rights stance and alienation from the Black community to name a few" of the answers to the questions posed by the title.

Davis was one of the largest donors to the United Negro College Fund (now UNCF/The College Fund). He participated in numerous fund raisers for the organization, including serving as chairman of the special events committee for the *Lou Rawls Parade of Stars* yearly fund raisers for the UNCF. In spite of the fact that he was a registered Democrat and a supporter of the Kennedy family, at the 1972 Republican Convention he came under fire when he publicly endorsed Richard Nixon. However, in 1974, he renounced his support. He was a life member of the NAACP and aided or led fund raising drives.

Davis was an avid collector of art, a highly regarded photographer, and a collector of photographs. His collection contained paintings of him by both Pablo Picasso and Charles Wright.

In Davis's entertainment career, he garnered numerous awards and recognitions. He was named the Most Outstanding Personality of 1946 by *Metronome* magazine; in 1969 Davis was awarded the NAACP Spingarn Medal for his outstanding achievements; in 1979 he was awarded *Ebony*'s first Lifetime Achievement Award for his years of joy and goodwill to all peoples; and in 1986 he received an honorary degree from Howard University. In 1974 he won the grand prize at the Cannes Film Festival for his television commercials for Japan's Suntory Whiskey and was honored by the National Academy of TV Arts and Sciences for his unique contributions to television. Additionally, he received honors from various Jewish organizations in recognition of his efforts to bring African Americans and Jewish Americans together. Before he died in Los Angeles on May 16, 1990, Davis was given a tribute that was enormous even by Hollywood standards. The event was televised and featured stars such as Eddie Murphy, Frank Sinatra, Michael Jackson, and Clint Eastwood. The proceeds from the show went to the United Negro College Fund.

The *Nashville Tennessean* called Davis "one of the first black performers to cross into the entertainment mainstream and . . . to be embraced by all audiences of all types." On the day of his passing, all of the lights in the Las Vegas Strip were extinguished for ten minutes, an American institution paying tribute to an American original.

REFERENCES

Bennett, Lerone. "Sammy Davis, Jr., 1925–1990: The Legacy of the World's Greatest Entertainer." *Ebony* 45 (July 1990): 118–20.

Bogle, Donald. *Blacks in American Films and Television: An Illustrated Encyclopedia.* New York: Simon and Schuster, 1988.

———. *Toms, Coons, Mulattos, Mammies, and Bucks: An Interpretive History of Blacks in American Films.* New enlarged edition. New York: Continuum, 1989.

Current Biography Yearbook. New York: H. W. Wilson, 1978.

Fisher, Murray, ed. *Alex Haley: The Playboy Interviews.* New York: Ballentine Books, 1993.

Jet 78 (4 June 1990): 11–23, 30, 57–63.

Salzman, Jack, David Lionel Smith, and Cornel West, eds. *Encyclopedia of African–American Culture and History.* New York: Macmillan Library Reference USA/Simon Schuster Macmillan, 1996.

"Sammy Davis Takes Final Bow at 64." *Nashville Tennessean,* May 17, 1990.

Williams, Michael W., ed. *The African American Encyclopedia.* New York: Marshall Cavendish, 1993.

Helen R. Houston

William L. Dawson

(1886–1970)

Congressman

William L. Dawson moved north from Georgia to Chicago where he became the most powerful African American politician of his era. His power was firmly based on the political organization he fashioned and controlled in Chicago's South Side black community. On the local level, he could deny a mayor of Chicago another term; on the national level, he played a pivotal role in at least two presidential elections by producing needed votes for Democratic candidates. His political style was built on organization and the ability to turn out votes: he preferred quiet negotiation and the solid coin of patronage to the rhetoric of protest. No one mounted an effective challenge to his base of power during his lifetime.

William Levi Dawson was born on April 26, 1886, in Albany, Georgia, to Levi and Rebecca Kendrick Dawson.

William L. Dawson

(The musician and composer William Levi Dawson was a cousin.) William was the second son, one of seven children. Rebecca Dawson died while William was young, but his father, who lived until about 1942, and a sister kept the family together. Levi Dawson was a barber in Albany and prosperous enough to give some financial assistance toward the education of his children.

Dawson attended Albany Normal School, an American Missionary Association (AMA) school, which charged tuition; he graduated in 1905. About 1906, he reached Chicago; there he found work as a bellhop and railroad station porter. He managed to raise enough money during the summers to attend Fisk University, another AMA school, from which he graduated magna cum laude in 1909. At Fisk he was captain of the debating team and captain of the football team, and he joined Alpha Phi Alpha Fraternity. Dawson moved permanently to Chicago in 1912. Beginning in 1915, he studied law at Chicago–Kent College of Law. While he was a student, Dawson lived in the Fourteenth Ward and was a precinct worker for Crip Woods, a blind black political leader.

Dawson married Nellie W. Brown, daughter of the rector of St. Luke's Church in Washington, D.C., on December 20, 1922. She was a follower of Christian Science later in life. Dawson himself professed the Methodist religion at Albany Normal School. (He said he was sitting on the mourners' bench during a revival meeting, as required of unconverted students by the school, while some of his classmates were outside playing ball. He leaped up to join those who said that they had received the call so that he could get out to play ball himself.) During the Depression he was baptized and joined the Progressive Baptist Church on Wentworth Avenue. He broke off active connection with the church when the minister invited a white politician to make a speech during a Sunday morning service. After this Dawson seems to have maintained no formal church connection, although his funeral was held at the Progressive Baptist Church. There were two children from Dawson's marriage: William L. Jr. and Barbara Ann (Morris), both of whom survived their father.

Serves in the Army

Dawson was 31 at the outbreak of World War I and not subject to the draft. Nonetheless, he enlisted in the army in April 1917, became a first lieutenant, and saw active service with the 365th Infantry in Europe. He suffered wounds and gassing and carried shrapnel in his body for the rest of his life and was unable to raise his left arm above shoulder level without assistance. (In later life Dawson also had a wooden leg, the result of a railroad accident.)

Upon his return to civilian life, Dawson enrolled in law classes at Northwestern University. Although he did not complete a law degree, in 1920 he was admitted to the Illinois bar and established a law practice in Chicago. About this time, he moved to the Second Ward, which offered more possibilities to an aspiring black politician than the Fourteenth. He first sought major elective office in the Republican primary of 1928, when he opposed the party leader and incumbent U.S. Representative, Martin B. Madden. Dawson stated that the First Congressional District, which had a black majority, should be represented by a black. He won only 29 percent of the votes.

Soon Dawson gravitated toward Oscar DePriest, at the time a prominent black ward leader. Dawson became a faithful lieutenant of DePriest, who was elected to Congress after Madden's sudden death in 1928. Dawson himself became a Republican state central committeeman in 1930, although he failed to win a position as Republican ward committeeman during the 1930s. In 1933, Dawson won election as Second Ward alderman, a nominally non–partisan position he held until 1939, when he was defeated by a Democrat. In 1938, Dawson was the losing Republican congressional candidate, opposing black Democrat Arthur W. Mitchell, who had defeated DePriest in 1936.

In 1939, Dawson switched parties when Mayor Edward J. Kelly picked Dawson to become the Second Ward Democratic committeeman. With the backing of Kelly, Dawson easily won formal election to the position in 1940. Dawson vindicated Kelly's choice by building a very strong organization in the ward. On this base Dawson built a smoothly run and powerful organization, which systematically extended its control. A supporter won control of the Third Ward in 1943, the Twentieth Ward in 1951, the Fourth Ward in 1955, the Sixth Ward in 1956, the Twenty–fourth Ward in 1961, and the Twenty–first Ward in 1963. These wards comprised the majority of the South Side black community and produced reliable party votes for the Democrats, usually two–thirds of the turnout, although the percentage might be higher in crucial elections. Dawson's hard work and genius for politics is shown by the lack of factionalism in his organization, and in spite of some murmuring, his solid control continued even as he aged. James Q. Wilson quoted one opponent as saying of Dawson in the midst of a vigorous controversy:

> He is a man who gets things done. If you get his word to do something, then it's as good as done. You can count on him once he makes a promise. . . . And he is intelligent. That counts a lot with me. There aren't many men these days whose word you can count on. . . . He's not afraid to work, either. I saw him working in his office on Easter Sunday once. I figure any man who will work on Easter works hard enough to deserve my vote, I don't care how many times they say he has been away from his desk in Congress.

The organization delivered crucial support in important political campaigns. In 1948, Harry S Truman carried Illinois by 33,600 votes, many of them from Chicago's South Side. In an even closer contest, John F. Kennedy's narrow victory over Richard M. Nixon, Dawson's contribution was even more vital. Christopher quoted Dawson's remark regarding this election to the *Chicago News,* "[Kennedy] carried Illinois by less than 10,000; my district gave him a margin of 30,000." Even before his pivotal role in the election, Dawson had played a vital part at the Democratic National Convention in allaying black suspicions about Kennedy's choice of running mate, Lyndon B. Johnson. After the election, Kennedy announced Dawson's appointment as Postmaster General, a position Dawson declined. Cynical observers maintained that Kennedy was quite sure that the 74–year old Dawson would not accept before the president–elect released Dawson's name to the press. Had Dawson responded affirmatively, he would have been the first black cabinet member.

In 1955, Dawson helped elect Chicago's long–term and very powerful mayor, Richard J. Daley, as the South Side organization gave Daley 40 percent of his winning margin. Dawson had turned against reform mayor Martin J. Kennelly shortly after Kennelly took office in 1949, and the new mayor sent police to arrest black policy operators. Policy operators normally ran the wide–spread but illegal numbers games free of police harassment as long as they contributed generously to the political machine. Dawson bided his time. In 1952, Dawson stunned the Democratic political leaders by announcing that he found Kennelly unacceptable. Dawson then humiliated Kennelly at a secret political meeting. Journalist Mike Royko described him as "limp[ing] back and forth on his artificial leg, cursing and shouting, blistering [Kennelly] for his coolness to the political chiefs in general, and his arrogance to Dawson in particular." Party leaders agreed that Kennelly must be dumped after one more term. The way was open for Richard Daley's selection as a candidate and his election. After 1960, when Dawson was named to the party committee to select primary candidates, his influence grew at the state level. It was claimed that he "controlled" three state representatives.

Dawson was scrupulous about not taking money for his own personal gain, but he felt that if numbers operations existed in predominantly black communities, then blacks should control the operations. The record of the congressional memorial quoted him as saying: "If anybody is to profit out of gambling in the Negro community it should be the Negro. It is purely an economic question. I want the money my people earn to stay in the community." In return for protection both from reform–minded mayors and white gangsters eager to take over the gambling, the policy makers were a fertile source of money for the organization.

Goes to Congress

Dawson's power was firmly based in the Chicago African American community, and he used it to secure election to Congress. When Arthur W. Mitchell retired from Congress in 1942, Dawson won the primary and the subsequent election. He held his seat in the House of Representatives for 28 years until his death on November 9, 1970. Dawson's style of leadership made him a very influential member of the House. In 1947, Dawson was the first black to serve as chair of a regular House committee, the Executive Department Expenditures Committee, later renamed the Government Operations Committee. Except for the two years the Republicans controlled the House—1953 to 1955—Dawson remained chair until his death.

Dawson became the first black vice–chair of the Democratic National Committee in 1950. The appointment was announced in December 1949, then apparently rescinded in deference to Southern protests, and then confirmed in March 1950, in wake of the protests about the cancellation. This position increased Dawson's influence in political appointments on the national level.

The seniority system in the House meant that Dawson accrued great power, and he astutely used House rules and procedures to accomplish his ends. For example, his detailed knowledge of the rules allowed him to stop a committee hearing he did not wish to take place. In 1956, during a congressional recess, a subcommittee was going to hold hearings designed to show that desegregation was not working in the schools of the District of Columbia. Dawson marched into the hearing room and handed out printed copies of the rule which prohibited hearings during recess without express permission of the House. The hearings immediately broke up. As president, Lyndon B. Johnson in 1967 turned to Dawson's committee to effect limited home rule for Washington, D.C., turning the roadblock presented by the regular House committee on the District of Columbia.

Illness combined with age led Dawson to announce his retirement a year before the end of his last Congress. He died just six days after the election of his hand–picked successor, Ralph H. Metcalfe, a star of the 1936 Olympics, who had become a leader in the organization. Another of Dawson's workers was the father of Chicago's first black mayor, Harold Washington, who in turn served his political apprenticeship working for Dawson.

Dawson, as leader of an organization centered on power and built on the rewards of patronage, was not a very visible leader. He avoided confrontation and sought quiet compromise, alienating him from militant leaders, who faulted Dawson for not speaking out. When the number of blacks in the House grew to the point that the Black Caucus was organized, Dawson's name was often absent from organization statements.

Dawson had contempt for persons who avoided politics and sought their ends through statements of principle and agitation. The record of the congressional memorial provided a compendium of his favorite sayings. One was, "Don't get mad. Get smart!" He also said, "If you learn to handle the men, the right ones—all men for that matter—you can get what you want." Thus, his relationship with organizations like the Chicago chapter of the NAACP was not always easy. On occasion he lent his organization's support to candidates for the presidency of the branch who were running against vocal opponents.

In line with his own experience, Dawson lent his support to efforts to secure black voting rights and increase voter registration. A constant theme was one he reiterated in a speech delivered in Richmond in 1949: "If you put yourself in a position to vote, and exercise the right to vote, you'll find that you have friends that you never knew you had—because you've got something they want." In support of this idea, he undertook a voter registration project in the South in 1953 and achieved some success in persuading white politicians to allow blacks to register.

In spite of his avoidance of occasions for public protest, Dawson did not hesitate to further what he perceived as the interests of blacks behind the scenes, and also in public on carefully chosen occasions. On April 13, 1951, he delivered one of his rare speeches in the House in support of the Price Amendment to the Universal Military Training Act which was designed to strike down a section of a bill designed to undermine President Truman's executive order establishing desegregation in the Armed Forces. He finished his appeal for racial justice to a standing ovation from fellow House members, and his position prevailed.

Dawson worked hard at politics. The record of the House memorial included his statement: "Politics with me is a full–time business. It is not a hobby to be worked on in leisure hours, but it's a job—a full–time job that pays off only if a man is willing to apply the energy, start from scratch and profit by his experience." He was bitter in his closing years about being labeled an Uncle Tom. Edward T. Clayton cited a January 27, 1957, interview from the *Afro–American* newspaper in which Dawson said:

> How is it that after fighting all my life for the rights of my people, I suddenly awaken in the September of life to find myself vilified and abused, and those who know me well and what I have stood for are accusing me of being against civil rights. . . Name calling and playing the grandstands is not the way to get things done here on Capitol Hill.

Dawson visibly showed the effects of age towards the end of his long life. He died on November 9, 1970. Services were held at the Progressive Baptist Church on South Wentworth Avenue on November 12. His body was cremated, and the ashes were placed in the Columbariun of the Griffin Funeral Home, Chicago, Illinois.

Bill Dawson was perhaps out of tune with the era in which he died, but he had a political career remarkable for longevity and the sheer accumulation of power. He was not the most visible African American leader of his time, but he did much to build black political power and advance the cause of racial justice.

REFERENCES

Biographical Sketch. Undated typescript, c. 1967. Fisk University Library Special Collections.

Christopher, Maurine. *America's Black Congressmen.* New York: Thomas Y. Crowell, 1971.

Clayton, Edward T. *The Negro Politician.* Chicago: Johnson Publishing Co., 1964.

"Cops Can Help in Politics, 2d Ward Learns." *Chicago Sunday Tribune,* January 27, 1946.

Current Biography Yearbook. New York: H. W. Wilson, 1945.

"Dawson's Power in Political Appointments Strengthened." *Louisiana Weekly,* April 1, 1950.

Drake, St. Clair, and Horace R. Cayton. *Black Metropolis.* New York: Harcourt, Brace, 1945. Revised and enlarged edition. 2 vol. 1970.

"First Negro Chairman of Committee of Congress Recalls Long Road Upward." *Washington Post,* January 2, 1949.

Granger, Bill and Lori. *Lords of the Last Machine.* New York: Random House, 1987.

"The Life of a Negro Congressman." *New York PM,* August 12, 1945.

"Meet Rep. Bill Dawson—S. Side Powerhouse." *Chicago Sun–Times,* February 9, 1955.

"Rep. Dawson Has 2d Ward in the Palm of His Hand." *Chicago Sunday Tribune,* May 1, 1960.

"Rep. Dawson In Seclusion: Hint Illness." Unidentified newspaper clipping, c. November 1, 1962.

Royko, Mike. *Boss: Richard J. Daley of Chicago.* New York: E. P. Dutton, 1971.

"Virginia Negroes Are Urged To Concentrate on Politics By Dawson in Speech Here." *Richmond Times–Dispatch,* March 21, 1949.

U.S. Ninety–First Congress, Second Session. *Memorial Services Held in the House of Representatives and Senate of the United States, Together With Tributes Presented in Eulogy of William Dawson.* Washington, DC: U.S. Government Printing Office, 1971.

Who's Who in America. 31st ed. Chicago: Marquis Who's Who, 1960.

"Why Did Jack Ring Twice for Postmaster?" *Washington Daily News,* January 6, 1961.

"William (Bill) Dawson's Rise—Democracy on the March." *Chicago Defender,* January 8, 1949.

Wilson, James Q. *Negro Politics.* New York: The Free Press, 1965.

COLLECTIONS

The William L. Dawson Papers are in the Fisk University Library, Special Collections, Nashville, Tennessee.

Robert L. Johns

William Levi Dawson (1899–1990)

Composer, educator, choral director

William Levi Dawson's life presents an excellent model of an "up by the bootstraps" success story of self–development, personal motivation, and achievement. William Levi Dawson presented an excellent model. Rising from humble beginnings in Anniston, Alabama, and inspired by Booker T. Washington, Dawson left home at the age of 13, gained admission to Tuskegee Institute, worked his way through his studies, and graduated, in 1921. He continued his music education at Washburn College, in Topeka, Kansas, the Horner Institute in Kansas City (B. Mus., 1925), the Chicago Musical College and American Conservatory of Music (M. Mus., 1927), with additional graduate work at the Eastman School of Music in Rochester, New York. He went on to a lengthy and successful career as a pioneering composer, teacher, arranger, and director of choral music. The high point of his academic career was his return to Tuskegee Institute, where he served, from 1931 to 1956, as the chair of the music program, where he directed and built an international reputation for the Tuskegee Choir, and developed a strong department, noted for the quality of its music education program.

To quote from Dawson's eulogy delivered on May 5, 1990, at the Tuskegee Chapel by James Earl Massey, "Knowledgeable, alert, courageous, determined, disciplined, earnest, as well as gifted, Dawson was a man worth knowing, a man worth following. Many did follow him, and they took pride in doing so." Perhaps more than any other individual, his love for the spiritual and his practical output, in making its interpretation accessible and readily available, lead to a surge of popularity of this genre among America's choirs and school choruses.

Dawson was born on September 26, 1899, in Anniston, Alabama, the youngest of seven children born to Eliza M. and George W. Dawson. He was a cousin of the Illinois Congressman of the same name. Dawson's father was strongly opposed to education, on the grounds that the son needed to work to help support the family. Dawson's resolve for it was firm. Seeking an education, he ran away, taking a train to Tuskegee, Alabama, to study at Tuskegee Institute. At Tuskegee, Booker T. Washington saw that Dawson found employment. He worked for the agriculture department, as music librarian, and in other capacities for the school for the next seven years.

Dawson began learning music and musical instruments, and was admitted to the institute's band, directed by Frank L. Drye. He studied piano and harmony with Alice Carter Simmons, and joined the choir as well as an elite vocal performance male quintet, the Tuskegee Singers, who traveled and played in concerts often, in support of the school's mission. His principal instruments were the trombone and euphonium. He appeared as a soloist on these instruments in concerts, with the Tuskegee Band, in neighboring southern cities, as well as on tour with the Redpath Chatauqua Circuit. The next stepping stones on his musical career path were Topeka, Kansas, and Kansas City, Missouri.

Following his graduation from Tuskegee, Dawson went to Topeka, Kansas, where he attended Washburn College, and then on to Kansas City, where he received his bachelor of music degree from the Horner Institute of Fine Arts, in Kansas City, in 1925. Roy Wilkins described the graduation, in his autobiography *Standing Fast.* He was present as Dawson was graduated from Horner Institute the first African American to receive the Bachelor of Music degree from the school. Both he and Dawson sat together in the balcony during the graduation ceremony, because Dawson could not sit with the white graduates due to the Kansas segregation laws. Dawson was not even allowed to take a bow when one of his compositions was played, in the program, despite the fact that the white musicians who played it received a rather long ovation. He experienced further insult when the school's president passed out the diplomas to the graduates. Although his name was called, he had to wait until after the ceremony, to get his diploma. Dawson probably felt some measure of vindication, in 1963, when he was formally awarded the Alumni Achievement Award from the University of Missouri, at Kansas City.

In Kansas, Dawson began his teaching career as director of music, at Kansas Vocational College at Topeka, He worked in that capacity from 1921 to 1922. In 1922, he became director of music at Lincoln High School, in Kansas City, and supervisor of music for the ''colored'' schools of that city. At Lincoln High School, his predecessor had been N. Clark Smith, a Tuskegee alumnus, and the composer of the Tuskegee Alma Mater. Following his tenure in Kansas City, he went to Chicago in 1926, where he undertook graduate studies in composition at the American Conservatory of Music. He received his master of music degree in 1927 after studying composition with Adolph Weidig. Also in 1927, he married Cornelia D. Lampton. They were married only a short time before she died in 1928. His other activities in Chicago included performing as first trombonist in the Chicago Civic Orchestra, and directing the choir at the Ebenezer African Methodist Episcopal Church. He also completed a period of further graduate studies at the Eastman School of Music in Rochester, New York.

Leads Tuskegee's Choir

In 1930 Dawson received a call to return to Tuskegee to direct the music program. He headed the program for some 24 years, from 1931 to 1955, with a proud vision and established a first rate music program while molding the Tuskegee Choir into a college choir of national stature.

During their years under Dawson, the Tuskegee Choir's performances took them to concerts throughout the United States. Perhaps their most celebrated tour occurred in December–January 1932–33, when they were invited for a month's engagement at the opening of New York's Radio City Music Hall. They became instant favorites among New York's concertgoers. Following this illustrious New York debut, they were invited to perform for President–elect Franklin D. Roosevelt's family. Concerts followed at New York's Carnegie Hall, at the Forum in Philadelphia, and at the White House for President Herbert Hoover. In New York Dawson met New York financier and entertainment mogul, S. L. ''Roxy'' Rothafel. Rothafel conveyed the manuscript of Dawson's recently completed *Negro Folk Symphony* to Leopold Stokowski. Stokowski accepted the work for performance by his Philadelphia Orchestra, and gave the work its world premiere in November of 1934.

In 1934 the *Negro Folk Symphony* became the first symphony by an African American composer to be premiered by a major U.S. symphony orchestra. Following a trip to West Africa for a study of indigenous traditional music during his sabbatical leave, Dawson revised the work by incorporating rhythms and performance values harvested during his visit to the continent. The work was subsequently recorded by Stokowski and released on Columbia Records. This composition has since become a programming favorite, having been heard on programs of most of the country's major orchestras. Dawson's pioneering effort opened a door and set a model that many African American composers have since followed.

Dawson's work as a choral conductor, adjudicator, and guest clinician continued apace. As a guest conductor, Dawson conducted All–State High School Choruses in Tulsa, Oklahoma; Rochester, New York; Durham, North Carolina; and Louisville, Kentucky. He was invited as guest conductor of the senior and junior high school choirs at the Annual Festival, ''Music for Unity,'' in Schenectady, New York, in May of 1949, and returned in succeeding years. He adjudicated and served continually as guest conductor and panelist at music educators' and choral directors' conventions and meetings, including the Kentucky Education Association, American Choral Directors Association, Music Educators National Conference, and the Maryland State Teachers' Association.

At Tuskegee Dawson remained as chairman and director of the music program until his resignation in 1955. On September 21, 1935, he married Cecile DeMae Nicholson, and they had a long and happy marriage. After 1955, Dawson remained musically prolific. He composed his own works, guest conducted, adjudicated, directed choral groups, lectured, and directed institutes on choral music throughout the United States and abroad. He received an honorary doctorate of music degree at Tuskegee University's diamond jubilee celebration in April of 1956.

Composes Black Work Songs and Spirituals

In 1940 20 composers including Dawson were invited by the Columbia Broadcasting System to compose orchestral works for the American School of the Air. Dawson wrote *A Negro Work Song* in response to this commission, and the work was subsequently broadcast by CBS numerous times over the years and was performed in concert by the Birmingham Symphony, Richmond Symphony, and Virginia Symphony orchestras. In addition to his *Negro Folk Symphony* and *A Negro Work Song,* other compositions included a *Scherzo,* a *String Trio,* a *Sonata* for violin, and many excellent arrangements of spirituals for chorus and soloists, including "King Jesus is A–Listening," "Talk About a Child That Do Love Jesus," "Jesus Walked This Lonesome Valley," "Out in the Fields," and "My Lord, What a Mourning."

Dawson became one of the country's leading authorities and a steadfast champion of this genre, leading workshops on performance and interpretation. Matters of dialect, inflection, nuance, control, tempo, emotional impact and religious centrality were pervasive concerns. As a composer, he also showed his fondness of the Negro Spiritual, arranging literally dozens of these moving songs for chorus and soloists and incorporating several in his pioneering works, the *Negro Folk Symphony* and *A Negro Work Song.*

In his compositions, particularly the *Negro Folk Symphony,* Dawson found a way to use the melody and harmony surrounding spirituals and folk songs to "sing a new song" and transform the standard symphonic form. He taught the oboe and violin to sing a song of pride, the trombone to proclaim triumph over tribulation, the French horn to express the theme of the middle passage, and the percussion selections to become the "Bond of Africa." His other instrumental works exhibit clear and effective writing and the ability to achieve coloristic balance. In the arrangements of the spirituals, he exhibited a keen awareness of the expressive capabilities of the male and female vocal registers. The settings were moving and the music always enhanced the quality of the text. No baroque composer ever made better use of the ability of the voice to model affections heard in the poetry or set the mood for a story than Dawson did in setting "King Jesus is a–Listening" or "Jesus Walked this Lonesome Valley." His approach was best defined in his own words, which were quoted in John Lovell's *Black Song*: "Every melody has a personality. . . . Every time you sing you hear something you never heard before. . . . Everything going on today, the creator of Negro song has already said it."

Dawson received many awards over the years for his contributions to music. He was awarded honorary doctorates by Tuskegee (1956), Lincoln University (1978), and Ithaca College (1982). He won the Wanamaker Contest prize twice (1930 and 1931) for vocal and orchestral compositions, the *Chicago Daily News* contest for band leader (1929), the University of Missouri at Kansas City Alumni Achievement Award (1963), and the Pennsylvania Glee Club Award (1967). In 1975 he received the American Choral Directors Association award for "pioneering leadership, inspiration and service to the choral arts," and was elected to the Alabama Music Hall of Fame. On May 12, 1989, the Tuskegee Board of Trustees awarded him its Distinguished Service Award. Tuskegee honored him again on September 24, 1989, as he celebrated his ninetieth birthday. On that occasion, he directed the University Choir, augmented by previous choir members, in one of his own choral compositions, in what was no doubt a very memorable occasion for all present. He died in Tuskegee on May 2, 1990. Massey said in his eulogy honoring Dawson that not only was Dawson an outstanding choral conductor and musical educator, he carried on and strengthened the African American musical heritage with his compositions.

REFERENCES

Abdul, Raoul. *Blacks in Classical Music.* New York: Dodd, Mead, 1977.

Bardolph, Richard. *The Negro Vanguard.* New York: Rinehart, 1959. Reprint, Westport, CT: Negro Universities Press, 1971.

Ewen, David. *American Composers Today.* New York: H. W. Wilson, 1949.

Hare, Maude Cuney. *Negro Musicians and Their Music.* Washington, DC: Associated Publishers, 1936.

Hitchcock, H. Wiley, ed. *The New Grove's Dictionary of American Music.* New York: Macmillan, 1986.

Lovell, John. *Black Song; The Forge and The Flame.* New York: Macmillan, 1972.

Malone, Mark Hugh. "William Dawson and the Tuskegee Choir." *Choral Journal* 30 (March 1990): 17–23.

Massey, James A. "He Endured; A Eulogy Honoring William Levi Dawson." Tuskegee University Chapel (Alabama), May 2, 1990.

Obituary. *American Organist* 8 (1990): 38.

Obituary. *Choral Journal* 31 (August 1990): 32.

Obituary. *New York Times,* May 4, 1990.

Roach, Hildred. *Black American Music.* Malabar, FL; Krieger Pub. Co., 1992.

Robinson, Wilhelmena. *Historical Negro Biographies.* New York: Publishers Co., 1967.

Sadie, Stanley, ed. *New Grove Dictionary of Music and Musicians.* New York, Macmillan, 1985.

Slonimsky, Nicholas, ed. *Baker's Biographical Dictionary of Musicians.* 8th ed. New York: Macmillan, 1992.

Southern, Eileen. *Biographical Dictionary of Afro–American and African Composers and Musicians.* Westport, CT: Greenwood Press, 1982.

———. *The Music of Black Americans.* 2nd ed. New York: Norton, 1983.

Spady, James G., ed. *William L. Dawson, a Umum Tribute and a Marvelous Journey.* Philadelphia: Creative Artists Workshop, 1981.

Tischler, Alice. *Fifteen Black American Composers; A Bibliography of Their Works.* Detroit: Information Coordinators, 1981.

Turner, Patricia. *Dictionary of Afro-American Performers.* New York: Garland, 1990.

Who's Who in America, 1988–89. 45th ed. Willamette, IL: Marquis Who's Who, 1988.

Who's Who in Colored America. New York: Who's Who in Colored America Corporation, 1927.

Wilkins, Roy, with Tom Mathews. *Standing Fast: The Autobiography of Roy Wilkins.* New York: Viking Press, 1982.

COLLECTIONS

The papers of William Levi Dawson are in the archives at Tuskegee University.

Darius L. Thieme

Thomas Day
(1801?–1861)
Entrepreneur

Thomas Day, a free black cabinet and furniture maker in North Carolina, built and operated one of the largest furniture-making businesses in the state. Recognized throughout the South as an exceptional craftsman and one of the finest artisans of the day, he was as impeccable in his craft as he was in his business transactions. Evidence of his work, some carved ornately, was represented throughout the community, including the homes of distinguished families in the state.

The life of Thomas Day has been recounted in many sources that drew information from one or two basic references as well as legends in Caswell County, North Carolina, where he flourished. Since much of his story begins and ends with insufficient documentation, his life has not been recorded with historical accuracy. Some sources claim that Day was born on the British West Indies island of Nevis, in Milton, North Carolina, or in the rural portion of Caswell County, North Carolina, approximately two miles from Milton. The most recent sources, Rodney Barfield's sketch of Day in *Thomas Day, Cabinetmaker,* and Lenwood Davis's *A Travel Guide to Black Historical Sites and Landmarks in North Carolina,* which give his birthplace as Halifax County, Virginia, may be the most reliable sources for information on Day. His birthdate has been reported variously—between 1785 and 1795, in 1790, and between 1794 and 1804. According to the 1850 and 1860 censuses for North Carolina, cited in the Day exhibition catalog, he was born about 1801, in Halifax County, Virginia.

Nothing is known of Day's father. Although the date of her freedom is unclear, his mother is said to have been freed in North Carolina. Day moved to Caswell County, North Carolina, about 1823 with the intention of staying four years, but, according to Day's letter to his daughter in 1851, published in the *Negro History Bulletin,* he had stayed "7 time 4."

Opens First Business

Day's beginning as owner of a cabinet-making business is questionable. Day may have been a cabinetmaker while he lived in Virginia, opening his first shop in Halifax County in 1818. When he moved to Milton, North Carolina, in 1823 he may have opened another shop. According to Rodney Barfield's sketch of Day, it was not until 1827, that he opened a shop, on Milton's mainstreet. Caswell County was in the heart of the state's tobacco industry, where prosperous white planters lived. They provided Day with a steady market for his furniture.

Although Day is said to have been a free black, the method by which he became free in the slave state of North Carolina is unclear. Except for a possible apprenticeship in Milton, there is no evidence that he received an education. Records of his business transactions and personal papers, however, indicate that he was able to read and write. On January 7, 1830, Day married Aquilla Wilson, also a free black, in Halifax County, Virginia, even though he knew that she could not legally reside in North Carolina due to the restrictions of North Carolina's immigration law of 1827. Some claim that Day threatened to move to Virginia to be with his wife. White residents, who by then had declared Day a valuable citizen and a first-rate artisan, successfully petitioned the General Assembly to waive the law and allow Aquilla Day to live in the state without fines or penalties. The law was abolished on December 31, 1830.

Thomas Day flourished in North Carolina at a time when a number of free blacks made impressive contributions to the culture of that state and the South. They were skilled artisans, tailors, tanners, and businessmen. Between 1827 and the 1850s, Day became involved in several businesses in Milton. First he paid $550 cash for his shop in 1827; in 1834 he bought stock in a local agency of the state bank; and in 1848 he bought Union Tavern, sometimes called the Yellow Brick Tavern, which had been one of the largest and finest taverns in the Milton area. Day converted the tavern into his workshop and residence, later adding a two-story brick wing in the rear of the gabled brick building with Flemish bond facade. According to Rodney Barfield, the 1850 industrial census noted that Day invested $5,800 in a business and hired 12 workers. By the standards of the time, he was clearly a man of significant financial means. Day operated the business there until 1859.

Day also owned a farm in the area and became a slaveholder. Although some sources say that he used his slaves only to work his farm and hired white workers for his furniture business, according to *The Free Negro in North Carolina,* his slaves worked in his furniture business for 30 years. He apprenticed three slaves as well as white bondservants, altogether having more apprentices than any other workshop in the state. Both Lenwood Davis's travel guide report and

Rodney Barfield's sketch agree that Day controlled about "one–fourth of the investment by all carpenters and builders in the state."

Earns the Reputation of a Skilled Craftsman

Thomas Day, an artisan in great demand, operated one of the largest furniture industries in North Carolina. Using mahogany, walnut, and oak, he crafted custom furniture, including French sofas, chairs, bedsteads, chests, benches, and tables. A talented woodcarver as well, Day added minute details to some of his pieces. He sold directly to customers and to retail merchants, eagerly accepting any return items that did not meet the customer's standard. Day also built coffins and did interior carpentry, such as stairways, rooms, and other interior trim. Throughout the 1850s he supplied large, custom orders for furniture to David S. Reid, governor of North Carolina from 1851 to 1854, and other prominent families. Day likewise built library shelving for the Philanthropic and Dialetic societies of the University of North Carolina at Chapel Hill.

Day built the pews at Milton Presbyterian Church where he and his wife worshipped in a racially–mixed congregation. According to Rodney Barfield, noted silversmith M. P. Huntington and merchant John Wilson attended at least two church meetings in Day's home. Devoutly religious, Day required his slaves to attend service and Bible study at his home each Sunday. Since the state had stringent laws dealing with education of free blacks, Day also ensured his children Mary Ann, Devereux, and Thomas Jr. an education by sending them to Wilbraham Academy in Massachusetts. In his letter to daughter Mary Ann dated November 27, 1831, and cited in the *Negro History Bulletin,* Day expressed concern that she study music: "I want you to persevere in the practice of music.... Music has a happy tendency to soothe the unregular & bad Pashions [sic] of our nature." He also encouraged her to learn "all other Branches" that she had studied and give attention to her posture, manner, and expression. He wanted her to be refined. Mary Ann also appears to have been the first black to study at Salem College.

W. A. Robinson said in the *Negro History Bulletin* that Day "was a man of fine physique and commanding appearance, but was unaffected and unassuming." Some sources suggest that he was also a mulatto. After Thomas Day died in 1861, his son, Thomas Jr., took over his father's business for a while, then sold it in 1871. While there is no further mention of Day's wife, his children survived him. Reportedly, Thomas Jr. moved to Asheville, then to Seattle, Washington, and entered the furniture business. Descendants of Thomas Day currently live in Durham, New Bern, and Henderson, North Carolina; New York City; and Maplewood, New Jersey. Union Tavern is now identified with an historical marker. Although local tradition claims that Thomas Day is buried on a farm near Milton, there is no known marker at the site. Notwithstanding the mysteries of Thomas Day's poorly documented life, he left an indisputable legacy as a fine antebellum craftsman.

REFERENCES

Barfield, Rodney. "Thomas Day." In *Thomas Day, Cabinetmaker. An Exhibition at the North Carolina Museum of History.* Raleigh: North Carolina Museum of History, Department of Cultural Resources, 1975.

Cantor, George. *Historic Landmarks of Black America.* Detroit: Gale Research Inc., 1991.

Chase, Henry H. "Thomas Day." *American Visions.* Advertising Travel Supplement, North Carolina's African–American Culture. 1995.

Davis, Lenwood. *A Travel Guide to Black Historical Sites and Landmarks in North Carolina.* Winston–Salem, NC: Bandit Books, 1991.

Franklin, John Hope. *The Free Negro in North Carolina 1790–1860.* Chapel Hill: University of North Carolina Press, 1943.

Logan, Rayford W., and Michael R. Winston, eds. *Dictionary of American Negro Biography.* New York: Norton, 1982.

Paths Toward Freedom. Raleigh: Center for Urban Affairs, North Carolina State University, 1976.

Robinson, W. A., and others. "Thomas Day and His Family." *Negro History Bulletin* 13 (March 1950): 123–26, 140.

COLLECTIONS

Documents on the life and work of Thomas Day are in scattered archival sources, including the North Carolina Division of Archives and History in Raleigh. The Manuscript Department at Duke University has the John Wilson Papers and the Wilson–Smith account book that show trade between merchants Wilson and Richard Smith. Examples of his furniture are also displayed at the North Carolina Museum of History in Raleigh, in Greensboro at North Carolina Agricultural and State University's Mattie Reed African Heritage Museum, and in the Greensboro Historical Museum. A number of private residences in the South contain works by Day as well.

Jessie Carney Smith

William Howard Day

(1825–1900)

Abolitionist, editor, educator, minister

For more than 50 years, William Howard Day labored persistently to advance black America. As an abolitionist, he became a popular orator in the United States and abroad. He eloquently denounced the evils of slavery and diligently edited and published various newspapers that promoted liberty for all. As a teacher, superintendent, and school board official, Day made invaluable classroom and administrative contributions. As an ordained minister, he worked for the advancement of the African Methodist Episcopal (AME) Zion Church's objectives. Day's prolific activities consumed his attention to the point that he had little time for a personal life, and he jeopardized his health several times. As a result of his dedicated and relentless endeavors, Day was one of the nineteenth century's most prominent and influential black leaders.

William Howard Day was born in New York City in October 16, 1825, to John and Eliza Day; he was the youngest of their four children. John Day was a sailmaker who, prior to his marriage, fought in a number of battles including the War of 1812 and Algiers in 1815. He was honorably discharged from the U.S. Navy in 1816. Thirteen years later, Day drowned after falling from a ship; William was only four years old when his father died. His mother's responsibility of providing for her children was eased somewhat when William's oldest brother found employment on a ship. Eliza Day was a founding member of the first AME Zion Church and an abolitionist. In 1833 she escaped from the Chatham Street Chapel when it was attacked by antiabolitionists. The following year, the Days and other members of their community barricaded their homes when antiabolitionists destroyed black churches and homes.

Eliza Day was determined that William would be well educated. He attended private and public grammar schools in New York. She made financial sacrifices so he could attend a private high school because there were no black public high schools in New York. A visitor to William's high school, J. P. Williston who was a Northampton, Massachusetts, ink manufacturer and advocate of the abolitionist and temperance movements, was so impressed with William, that he persuaded Mrs. Day to give him custody of her son.

According to R.J.M. Blackett in *Beating Against the Barriers,* the experience of residing with the Willistons, a white family, had a profound effect on Day:

> Northampton allowed William time and space to develop, free from the pervasive racism of a big city like New York. Although he would never forget the riots of 1834 and the continuous threats of violence from angry white mobs, Northampton did offer a needed respite, and demonstrated to the young man that there were some whites who still clung to the vaunted principles of freedom, equality, and brotherhood. He attended school and openly competed with white children, regularly sat by the side of his foster–father in the choir of the local church, worked with white apprentices and master printers at the Hampshire Herald, and no one expressed shock or protested his presence. It was an experience he would carry with him for the rest of his life.

Although Day was exposed to a new way of life and was quite busy with school and work in the *Hampshire Herald*'s print shop, he found time to teach fugitive slaves in a room Williston provided at his factory.

Eighteen–year–old Day enrolled in Oberlin College, Ohio, in 1843. He was the only black in the freshman class and the third in its collegiate course. During his successful matriculation at Oberlin where he was recognized for his strong oratorical abilities, Day paid his tuition by working in the college's print shop and teaching school in Buffalo. He taught fugitive slaves in Ontario when his college classes were not in session. Also during his undergraduate years, Day became a leader in the black community near the college. He drafted a series of resolutions condemning Maryland's government for imprisoning and refusing to pardon abolitionist Reverend Charles Turner Torrey and for not extending sympathy to Torrey's widow and children upon his death. Day and Sabran Cox, a former Virginian slave, became a duo in efforts to advance abolition as they lectured and sang antislavery songs before various groups. Day spoke at his 1847 commencement ceremony, and his speech, "The Millennium of Liberty," was published later that year.

William Howard Day

A Civil Rights Crusader

After graduating from Oberlin, Day was promoted to foreman at the college's print shop. His length of employment there is not known, however, Day spent the rest of his life campaigning for the rights of blacks. He joined the Liberty Party and later its successor, the Free–Soil Party, and was an Ohio delegate to the national convention in Buffalo in 1847.

Day became secretary of the National Negro Convention in Cleveland in September of 1848. As such, he was a committee member with Frederick Douglass and others who generated an "Address to the Colored People of America." In fact, Day was an elected representative of most, if not all, of the state or national Negro conventions from 1845 to at least 1852, and he frequently became an officer at many of the conventions.

Along with his involvement with national conventions, Day focused on the specific problems faced by blacks in Ohio. He joined with other black residents of the state to battle legalized discrimination. Ohio's Black Laws, enacted in 1802, prohibited blacks from residing in Ohio without freedom certificates and $500 bonds, attending public schools, and testifying in court cases involving whites. The Black Laws were repealed in 1849, and, according to William J. Simmons in *Men of Mark,* Day:

> held a prominent part, having been, with John L. Watson, elected by the colored citizens in convention assembled to address the members of the Legislature in the Hall of the House of Representatives. It was unheard of presumption in that early day, on the part of the colored people, to ask for the hall of the house, but Mr. Day proposed that it be done and the result was that under God the repeal was secured. The most notable benefit deprived from the repeal was the school system which was to be enjoyed by seven thousand children who, up to that time, had practically been derived of school privileges. The influence of this worthy man at this time in Ohio was so extended that members of Congress and judges of the courts admitted their indebtedness to him for their election. This, too, was fifteen years before the Fifteenth Amendment.

In addition to using the political arena to promote black concerns, Day used the power of the press to advance black life. In 1850 Day became a black community reporter for Cleveland's *True Democrat.* After moving from Oberlin to Cleveland in 1851, he was employed as a compositor and local editor of the paper. During his long career as a champion of civil rights, Day purchased a printing press and for a time published various black newspapers, yet his efforts failed to generate adequate funds to cover operating expenses.

In the shadow of the Fugitive Slave Act of 1850—which permitted slave hunters to retrieve runaway slaves anywhere in the United States—and the failure of state constitutional conventions to affirm the rights of blacks, Day attempted to remind the nation that the Constitution acknowledged that all men were equal. As reported in *Beating Against the Barriers,* he demanded "to be shown clauses in the Constitution that specifically excluded blacks from all rights and immunities of citizenship." He also attempted to awaken America to the contributions made by blacks. Inspired by the valiant military efforts of his deceased father, Day invited black veterans of the War of 1812 to Cleveland in 1852. This occasion marked the first official recognition of black military efforts, and, in command of his exceptional oratory talents, Day seized the opportunity to demand liberty for blacks. Day was also concerned with the rights of nonblacks. For example in 1852, he was chairman of a committee of Cleveland citizens that generated funds to help promote the cause of freedom in Hungary.

An important milestone for Day was his marriage in 1852 to Lucy Stanton, a schoolteacher who was the first black woman to complete Oberlin's collegiate course. She was from a prominent Cleveland family, was raised in a predominantly white community, and was enrolled in a white school until her attendance was protested. As a result, her stepfather built a school for black children.

In 1853 Day recommended to Frederick Douglass, president of a former National Negro Convention, that another national meeting be held. In July of that year, a national convention was held in Rochester, New York. For the first time in approximately 20 years, most national black leaders attended. The convention created the National Council of People, an advocate of black interests, and Day was named one of Ohio's two council representatives.

While Day was now a leading public figure in Ohio as well as the nation, his personal life was extremely stressful. The first two children Lucy bore died in infancy. Day's efforts to publish black newspapers tended to deplete his financial resources. In order to generate income, he accepted a job as a librarian at the Cleveland Library Association in 1854. The appointment of a black man, even one as well–known as Day, resulted in controversy.

Advances Black Life While Abroad

Day's demanding lifestyle adversely affected his health, and his doctor advised him to retire to a farm. In 1855 Day moved to Dresden, Ontario, where he and Lucy purchased a 40–acre farm. Day refused to abandon his crusade for the advancement of blacks, however. He sought educational opportunities for the more than 50,000 fugitive slaves residing in Canada.

Years earlier when Day was an undergraduate at Oberlin, he met John Brown whose father was a trustee of the college. As reported in *Dictionary of American Negro Biography,* "while in Canada, Day printed John Brown's constitution for a new United States that was to be established in the event of the success of the Harpers Ferry venture. Because of secrecy, just how close Day's connections were to this conspiracy is still not known."

During the late 1850s and early 1860s, Day continued to live abroad. In 1858 Day, Lucy, and their infant daughter, Florence Nightingale, moved to Chatham, Canada. Day taught at Reverend William King's fugitive slave settlement in Buxton and lectured in Ontario and Chatham on segregation in Canadian schools. His friend Martin Delany also resided in Chatham. Blackett wrote, "While Day was busy organizing John Brown's convention in April, 1858, Delany was trying to raise money for his expedition to Africa." Day was elected president of the National Board of Commissioners of the Colored People of Canada and the United States in 1858. From this position, he authorized Delany's trip to Africa. Two years later in London, England, Day, Delany, and others founded the African Aid Society.

In 1859 Day traveled with King to England, Ireland, and Scotland in order to raise funds for the building of a school and church in Buxton. Day's lectures were well–received in each country. At a music hall in Dublin, for example, he orated to an audience of 3,000. Day was offered a teaching position at an academy which he declined. His wife and child did not accompany him on his fund raising mission for the Buxton settlement. Day and Lucy remained separated until their divorce in 1872.

Day returned to New York in December of 1863 and on January 1, 1864, he delivered the featured address at the meeting commemorating President Lincoln's signing of the Emancipation Proclamation one year earlier. He then became active in the American Freedmen's Friend Society, raising funds and lecturing on its behalf. In addition, Day joined other blacks in New York in an unsuccessful effort to eliminate constitutional limits on voting rights.

In 1866 Day was appointed lay editor of the *Zion Standard and Weekly Review,* a paper published by the AME Zion Church. In either 1866 or 1867, he joined Wesley Zion Church in Washington, D.C., and was ordained a minister at the Virginia Conference. Day continued to work at the *Zion Standard* until he was appointed superintendent of the Freedmen's Bureau schools in Maryland and Delaware. He was responsible for approximately 140 schools, 150 teachers, and 7,000 students. Day's tenure ended when the bureau underwent reorganization.

Day then moved to Wilmington, Delaware, where Simmons said, "he risked his life in organizing the colored citizens as voters, and was successful at the end of a year in entirely changing the representation in the lower house of Congress, a change for the first time in twenty years." During this period, Day concentrated on the interests of blacks in Wilmington, Harrisburg, and Philadelphia.

In 1872 Day moved to Harrisburg, Pennsylvania. He married Georgia Bell whom he met at Wesley Zion Church in Washington and who was 24–years his junior. Day's impressive work for the Republican Party led to his appointment as a clerk in the corporation department of the auditor–general of Pennsylvania, where he was employed for two–and–a–half years. In 1875 Day became general secretary of the AME Zion's General Conference.

Works for School Board and AME Zion Church

In 1877 Day was reported near death. He recovered from his bout with consumption, and one year later, he was elected to Harrisburg's school board in his second campaign for the position, becoming the first black member of a Pennsylvanian school board. He was reelected in 1881 and served as the board's president from 1891 to 1893. Day, who remained on the board until poor health compelled him not to seek reelection in 1899, was, according to *Dictionary of American Negro Biography,* "perhaps the first Negro city school board president in any 'white' American community." During his tenure with the board, his accomplishments were many. Among his most significant achievements were his successful campaigns to gain black admittance to Harrisburg high schools and to establish night schools. In 1896 Day's fiftieth anniversary as an educator was celebrated with a six–day conference held in Harrisburg where admirers presented papers focusing on Day's life and educational career.

Day was an eminent member of the AME Zion Church. His services were instrumental in the growth of Sunday School programs and the establishment of the Wesley Union Christian Association, an educational organization. He helped raise funds for the creation of a Biblical Institute to train church licentiates; and upon its establishment, Day trained many of the enrollees. In 1885 he was elected presiding elder at an annual AME conference and delivered a sermon. Day arranged a visit to the White House for the conference delegation, and he was the official spokesman for the members as they met with President Grover Cleveland. In 1886 poor health forced Day to resign from the position that required traveling to Washington, D.C., Maryland, Pennsylvania, and Virginia. Yet Day, who had received an honorary doctorate of divinity from Livingstone College in 1888, remained dedicated to the church. According to Blackett, "whenever unexpected problems arose, Day volunteered his services, temporarily filling vacancies, for example, on occasions where ministers were unable to meet their commitments."

In 1895 partial paralysis after a stroke forced Day to limit his activities for approximately one year. In either 1899 or 1900, he suffered a second stroke. In October of 1900 he celebrated his seventy–fifth birthday at Wesley Union, and the bedridden honoree was later presented a gold medal from grateful Harrisburg residents.

Day died on December 2, 1900. His front–page obituary in the *Harrisburg Telegraph* marked the first time the paper acknowledged a black person's death in such a manner. Although Day was buried at the Lincoln Cemetery in Penbrook, another Pennsylvania cemetery in Steelton was named in Day's honor, and the dedicatory address was delivered by W. E. B. Du Bois. William Howard Day devoted his life working to guarantee a better day for all and especially for members of his race.

REFERENCES

Blackett, R. J. M. *Beating Against the Barriers.* Baton Rouge: Louisiana State University Press, 1986.

Logan, Rayford W., and Michael R. Winston, eds. *Dictionary of American Negro Biography.* New York: Norton, 1982.

Quarles, Benjamin. *Black Abolitionists.* New York: Oxford University Press, 1969.

Simmons, William J. *Men of Mark.* 1887. Reprint, Chicago: Johnson Publishing Co., 1970.

Linda M. Carter

Roy DeCarava

(1919–)

Photographer, artist, educator

First a printmaker and painter, Roy DeCarava is best known as a photographer whose social commitment to African American people is captured in his pictures. His work surveys black life in Harlem, and among his best known photographs are images of workers in New York's garment district, civil rights demonstrators, and jazz artists. DeCarava is also recognized as an influential promoter of the work of other African American artists.

Roy Rudolph DeCarava was born in Harlem Hospital on December 9, 1919, the only child of Elfreda, a Jamaican, and Andrew DeCarava. By age five he began to demonstrate his artistic ability: he made jewelry with his friends, chalk drawings in the streets where he played, and sketches of "cowboys and Indians." From early childhood through high school, DeCarava worked such odd jobs as shining shoes, hawking newspapers on the subway, making deliveries, or hauling ice.

DeCarava attended Textile High School's annex in Harlem, where, as he later recalled in *Roy DeCarava,* black students learned "absolutely nothing," while white students attended the main Textile High on 18th Street in New York and learned to design and manufacture textiles. After a year at the annex, he and his close friend Alfonso Merritt transferred to the main school where they were the only African Americans. Later on, Merritt became a professional sign painter and was one of the subjects DeCarava photographed.

At the main school DeCarava studied art history and was introduced to the works of Vincent Van Gogh, Michelangelo, and Leonardo da Vinci. He developed an informed sense of art: "That is when everything opened up for me. Then I knew what I was aspiring to," he said in *Roy DeCarava.* He graduated in 1938 and, on examination, was admitted to The Cooper Union School of Art, where he studied art for two years. He became frustrated with the increasing incidents of racial prejudice he encountered on the way between home and school and subsequently left Cooper Union in 1940. DeCarava continued his studies at the Harlem Community Art Center on 125th Street, where he met other young, black artists and encountered such figures as Paul Robeson and Langston Hughes. Still in school, DeCarava took a job in the poster division of the Works Progress Administration which enabled him to learn silkscreen printing.

World War II interrupted DeCarava's studies. He was drafted in 1942, sent to Virginia, and then to Fort Claiborne, Louisiana. He was unable to cope with the harsh racism that he encountered and was institutionalized for about a month in the psychiatric ward of the army hospital until he received a medical discharge. "I had nightmares about it for twenty years," he recalled in *Roy DeCarava.*

DeCarava had been too young to be an active part of the cultural renaissance in Harlem in the 1920s. As well, he left printmaking and painting and took up photography; therefore, his life is not chronicled in the art history of that period. Nonetheless, the WPA had ended, and Harlem's Community Art Center had closed; in 1944 and 1945 he studied painting and drawing with Charles White at the George Washington Carver Art School—a partial replacement for the Harlem art center's program.

None of DeCarava's paintings of the early 1940s, which included a portrait of Harriet Tubman, survive. By the mid–1940s he rarely painted and instead concentrated on printmaking, particularly serigraphy or silkscreen. He joined the National Serigraph Society in 1944, and in 1946 he won a prize at the Atlanta University Annual. His first solo exhibit was held in 1947 at New York's Serigraph Galleries. He was pleased that now he could make works that were affordable in his own community.

Turns to Photography

DeCarava bought an Argus A camera and made photographs as material for his prints, but soon his photographs gained primary significance among his works. He had labored for several years as an illustrator for Burman Studios, a small advertising firm, where he honed his technical skill. When his workday ended there, he took his camera to the street and worked as an independent artist. The subway that he rode to and from work became one of his early subjects as did vacant lots, streets, and apartment houses in Harlem. DeCarava matured quickly as a photographer and turned decisively to photography. A successful photographer in 1949, he soon began to create lasting works of photography. The first exhibition, consisting of 160 photographs, was mounted in 1950. Young photographer Homer Page's response to the exhibit had a positive influence on DeCarava's photographs and career, and DeCarava was prompted to change his style to show softer prints and to narrow the range of deep tones.

DeCarava's career was also promoted by Edward Steichen, an influential photographer who headed the Department of Photography at the Museum of Modern Art and purchased for the museum three of his prints. The museum began to include DeCarava's work in group exhibitions as well. Steichen also was instrumental in DeCarava's winning a fellowship from the John Simon Guggenheim Memorial Foundation in 1952, making him the first African American photographer to win the honor. He took a leave of absence from work and used the fellowship to survey through photography the full range of black life in Harlem.

DeCarava still was unable to find a publisher for the works from his Guggenheim project. In summer 1954 DeCarava showed his photographs to Langston Hughes, with whom he had a passing acquaintance; Hughes liked them and insisted that they should be published. Hughes selected the photographs, and in November 1955 Simon and Schuster published 140 DeCarava photographs, with text by Hughes, as *The Sweet Flypaper of Life,* a book on black life in Harlem. Peter Galassi wrote in *Roy DeCarava: A Retrospective* that DeCarava was disappointed with the book's small size, and that the book diluted the power of DeCarava's photographs, masking their eloquence. In 1955 as well, four of DeCarava's photographs were published in Steichen's *The Family of Man.*

DeCarava and his wife, whom he had married about the time he entered the army, opened A Photographer's Gallery at 48 West 84th Street in Manhattan which he operated until it closed in May 1957. Quoted by Galassi, DeCarava said that the gallery "grew out of the need of a creative photographer to find a place for himself and for others like him," to showcase works of art. He also began a photographic series on jazz artists; the series included the spiritual and rhythm and blues artists. In time he became known for extraordinary shots of jazz luminaries Billie Holiday, John Coltrane, and others. The works were shown in 1983 at the Studio Museum in Harlem under the title "The Sound I Saw."

In 1958 DeCarava left steady employment and moved to a loft on Sixth Avenue in the garment district. For nearly 20 years he worked primarily as a freelance photographer. His subjects in the early 1960s included workers in New York's garment district where he lived as well as civil rights protestors. In July 1963 he photographed a demonstration in Brooklyn by African Americans protesting the planned demolition of their homes to expand Downstate Medical Center. He attended the historic March on Washington, held on August 28, 1963, and photographed march scenes.

From 1968 to 1975 DeCarava held a contract as photographer for *Sports Illustrated.* He made photographs on the set of *Requiem for a Heavyweight,* a film released in 1962, and for a while worked for *Scientific American.* He was adjunct professor of art from 1970 to 1973 at Cooper Union. In 1975 he joined the faculty at Hunter College, where he continues as distinguished professor of art.

In addition to his work as a photographer and educator, DeCarava has been active in social issues. In the late 1940s he helped establish a union at the advertising agency where he was employed. He also joined the Committee for the Negro in the Arts, an advocacy organization for African American artists founded in 1947. In 1963 DeCarava became founding chairman of the Kamoinge Workshop, a merger of two groups of African American photographers. The new group opened a gallery on 125th Street and produced and sold portfolios of their works. During this same period he was a member of the American Society of Magazine Photographers. Among DeCarava's tributes are honorary doctorates of fine arts from the Maryland Institute (1986) and Rhode Island Institute of Fine Arts (1985). In 1991 the Friends of Photography awarded him the Distinguished Career in Photography Award, and in 1991 the American Society of Magazine Photographers gave him a Special Citation for Photographic Journalism.

On September 4, 1971, Roy DeCarava married Sherry Turner; they have three children—Susan, Wendy, and Laura. Summarizing the significance of DeCarava's work, Galassi wrote: "[He] is famous for his luxurious shadows, for the delicate interplay of tones in pictures that reside at the dark end of the photographic scale." This is illustrated in the photographs throughout the book and photographs on his life, *Roy DeCarava: A Retrospective,* and defined further by the artist who said that the photographs are "not about darkness but about light." If there were no light, nothing could be seen at all.

Current address: Division of Humanities and Arts, Hunter College of the City University of New York, 695 Park Ave., New York, NY 10021.

REFERENCES

Fax, Elton C. *Seventeen Black Artists.* New York: Dodd, Mead, 1971.

Galassi, Peter. *Roy DeCarava: A Retrospective.* New York: The Museum of Modern Art, 1996.

Who's Who among African Americans, 1996–97. 9th ed. Detroit: Gale Research, 1996.

Jessie Carney Smith

Hubert T. Delany

(1901–1990)

Lawyer, educator, civil rights advocate

An intelligent, ambitious man, Hubert T. Delany is known for having run for Congress in New York in 1929. A Republican, he won the primary for District 21, which included a large portion of Harlem and Washington Heights, but he lost the general election. Later, Delany became the fifth black jurist in New York City.

Hubert T. Delany was born in Raleigh, North Carolina, in 1901. He was one of ten children of Henry Beard Delany (1858–1928) and Nanny Logan Delany (1861–1956). Born into slavery, Henry Delany became one of the first two African Americans elected suffragan bishop of the Episcopal Church in America. He met Nanny Logan at St. Augustine's school in Raleigh, where she was valedictorian; the couple married on October 6, 1886. All of the Delany children graduated from college at a time when few Americans attended post–secondary schools. Hubert Delany spent a good deal of his childhood and adolescence on the campus of St. Augustine College, where his father was vice principal and his mother was matron of the school. Hubert Delany's sister Annie Elizabeth "Bessie" Delany (1891–1995) was the second African American woman licensed to practice dentistry in New York City, and his sister Sarah Louise "Sadie" Delany (1889–) was the first African American teacher in the New York City public schools. In 1993 the sisters published their autobiography, *Having Our Say.*

When Hubert T. Delany arrived in New York City, around 1919, he worked as a Red Cap in Pennsylvania Station. He used his wages to pay his tuition at the College of the City of New York. As a student Delany also worked on farms in Connecticut and in Harlem elementary schools as a teacher. He graduated from City College in 1923 and enrolled in New York University, where he earned a law degree in 1926. At this time (until the 1960s) African Americans were not admitted to the American Bar Association. Application to the bar required a statement of ethnic origin, and African Americans were automatically denied access. Hubert T. Delany, therefore, set up a private practice. He represented black operatic singer Marian Anderson, who received the support of the First Lady Eleanor Roosevelt, when the Daughters of the American Revolution (DAR) refused to schedule Anderson in concert in their Constitution Hall because of her race. Eleanor Roosevelt resigned from the DAR in protest. An early civil rights advocate, Delany was soon appointed to the post of Assistant United States Attorney in the criminal division by Charles H. Tuttle. He remained there for five years, from 1927 until 1933. Delany was also a member of New York City's Tax Commission for eight years.

Becomes a Jurist

In 1942, Delany became the fifth African American to sit on the bench in New York City when Fiorello H. LaGuardia appointed him to the New York City Domestic Relations Court. He served for 13 years. Delany made a conscious effort to be fair to all people when he sat on the bench. He spoke often on the topic of discrimination and race relations. According to the *New York Amsterdam News* for February 5, 1944, he was an advocate for children: ". . . it is the purpose in the Domestic Relations Court to see that our children shall not lose hope." Justice Delany continued, "The grown–ups of the community must teach their children respect for law and order. . .so that all decent and law–abiding citizens will not be classified as persons who have no respect for the law."

In 1955 Delany was not reappointed. The newly elected Democratic mayor Robert Wagner was quoted in the *New York Amsterdam News* for September 17, 1955, as saying Delany, a Republican for over 30 years, did "not see eye to eye on a number of points" with him. Edward R. Dudley, a former ambassador to Liberia, replaced him in the ten–year term position. The City Bar Association, Citizens' Committee for Children of New York and other professional and civic groups rallied to have Delany reinstated. In a letter to the *New York Age* for October 22, 1955, the Citizens Union, a civic group, stated: "In failing to reappoint justice Hubert Delany to the Court of Domestic Relations, we believe you have made a really serious error." However, the Mayor did not waver on his decision.

Delany took over as chairman of the Intergroup Committee on New York Public Schools in 1955 when his tenure as a jurist ended. The purpose of the group he chaired was to eradicate segregation in New York City schools. The committee also served as a coordinating agency for integrating the city's public school system.

Delany was active in a number of organizations, including the YMCA, the NAACP, the National Urban League, the Wiltwyck School for Boys, the USO, the National Lawyers Guild, and the Citizens City–wide Committee on Harlem.

On January 28, 1990, Delany died of heart disease in Presbyterian Hospital in New York City. He was survived by his wife Willetta, his son Mickey Delany, daughter Madelon Mickey, six grandchildren and four great–grandchildren. His survivors also included three sisters, Sadie Delany, Bessie Delany, Laura Murrell Delany, and brother, Henry Delany. Delany was admired for his humanity on the bench, having earned high praise from the Association of the Bar of the City of New York.

REFERENCES

"A Century of Being Sisters; They Saw Jim Crow Come and Go—and So Much More." *Washington Post,* November 25, 1993.

Delany, Sarah, and A. Elizabeth Delany; with Amy Hill Hearth. *Having Our Say: The Delany Sisters' First 100 Years.* New York: Kodansha International, 1993.

"Delany Case 'Shocking' to Citizens Committee." *New York Amsterdam News,* October 8, 1955.

"Dudley In, Delany Out In Court Appointment." *New York Amsterdam News,* September 17, 1955.

"Dudley Takes New Post As Judge." *New York Amsterdam News,* October 29, 1955.

Hearth, Amy Hill. "Bessie and Sadie: the Delany Sisters Relive a Century." *Smithsonian* (24 October, 1993): 144–46.

"Hubert T. Delany, 89, Ex–Judge and Civil Rights Advocate, Dies." *New York Times,* December 31, 1990.

"Justice Delany Active in and out of Court." *New York Amsterdam News,* February 5, 1944.

"Now Chairman of Intergroup Committee on New York Public Schools." *New York Amsterdam News,* December 17, 1955.

"Questions Softness in Handling of Juveniles." *New York Age,* June 4, 1965.

Rosen, Marjorie. "Free Spirits: Sadie and Bessie Delany." *People Weekly* 40 (22 November 1993): 97–98.

"Snubbing of Delany Rocks N.Y." *Pittsburgh Courier,* April 24, 1954.

Mario A. Charles

Martin R. Delany
(1812–1885)

Editor, physician, abolitionist, explorer, army officer, black nationalist, writer

Martin R. Delany was for many years a vigorous and effective black leader and thinker. His analysis of the prospects for African Americans in the United States led him to become a founder of black nationalism and advocate of emigration, eventually focusing on a return to Africa. He was always a spirited defender of the black race. Victor Ullman in *Martin R. Delany* quoted Frederick Douglass in *Douglass' Monthly* of August 1862:

> ''I speak (said [Delany]) only of the pure black uncorrupted by Caucasian blood.'' In his lectures he passed all others in silence. This feature of his discourses is so marked and decided as sometimes to make the impression on those who do not know Mr. Delany, that he has gone about the same length in favor of black, as the whites have in favor of the doctrine of white superiority. He stands up so straight that he leans back a little.

Martin Robison Delany was born on May 6, 1812, in Charles Town, then in Virginia and now in West Virginia, to Samuel Delany, a slave, and Pati Peace Delany, a free woman of color. Martin Delany's ancestry was purely African, and he believed—most probably quite correctly—that he was descended from royalty on both sides. Delany took fierce pride in his ethnic identity. Frank Rollin (Frances Rollins Whipper) wrote in her Delany biography: ''It is frequently said by those best acquainted with his character, that in order to excite envy in him would be for an individual to possess less adulterated blackness, as his great boast is, that there lives none blacker than himself.'' She also quoted the famous Douglass quip, ''I thank God for making me a man simply; but Delany always thanks him for making him a *black man.*''

Pati Delany got into legal trouble in 1822, probably in the wake of white reaction to the discovery of the Denmark Vesey conspiracy in Charleston, South Carolina, the most extensive slave revolt in U.S. history. She had violated the law by teaching her children to read. She surreptitiously moved her family to Chambersburg, Pennsylvania, in that year. Samuel Delany, in the meantime, had also proved troublesome. In 1822 he resisted being whipped by an overseer; a very strong man, Delany merely tore off the overseer's clothes nine times in a row. Either through buying his freedom or through flight, he was able to join the family in Chambersburg in 1823.

Little is known about Martin's life in Chambersburg except that he was able to continue his education until the marriage of his older brother Samuel in 1827. At that point, he was obliged to work to help support the family. Four years later, Martin set out on foot for Pittsburgh in search of more education. Although he traveled extensively during the period, Pittsburgh would be his home for the next 25 years.

Moves to Pittsburgh

Upon his arrival in Pittsburgh's small but growing black community, Delany soon established his credentials as a leader among such prominent blacks as the barber and abolitionist, John B. Vashon, the father of poet and lawyer George Boyer Vashon. He was an officer of the Pittsburgh Anti–Slavery Society, as well as other literary, temperance, and moral reform societies. Probably the most important of these

Martin R. Delany

was the Philanthropic Society, a very effective fugitive slave organization.

Delany furthered his education in a night school held by Lewis Woodson in the basement of the African Methodist Episcopal (AME) church and received further tutoring from a young black divinity student, Molliston M. Clark, a future editor of the *Christian Recorder.* In addition to this schooling, Delany received enough training from a white doctor to set himself up as a cupper, leecher, and bleeder in 1836.

By 1838 Delany was recognized by blacks and whites alike as a community leader, and the following year he was instrumental in averting mob violence directed against blacks through a plan of pairing armed blacks with whites to patrol the streets. He was also very active in the protest movements following Pennsylvania's abolition of the right of blacks to vote.

In 1843 Delany married Catherine Richards, the youngest daughter of Charles Richards, a butcher and reputedly the wealthiest black in Pittsburgh. Between 1846 and 1864 the couple had seven surviving children. It was Catherine's skill as a seamstress which later supported the family and made her husband's travels and political activities possible.

Soon after their marriage Delany began to publish *The Mystery,* the first black newspaper west of the Alleghenies. Only a very few issues of this four–page weekly survive. The paper ceased publication in 1847. The AME Church took over the paper's subscription list to establish a national organ, the *Christian Herald,* later renamed the *Christian Recorder,* published continuously to this day. Delany then joined Frederick Douglass as co–editor of his *North Star.* Delany toured the Midwest to seek out news and subscribers for the paper. He often spoke three times a day, facing great hostility, and on one occasion narrowly escaped lynching. Delany's letters to the paper became a regular feature in the weekly.

By joining Douglass in opposition to Garrisonian leadership in the antislavery movement, Delany took a firm first step toward radicalism. The followers of William Lloyd Garrison and his paper *The Liberator* called for moral suasion as the way to end slavery, while Douglass and others favored political action. Delany's travels gave him wide experience of the events leading up to the Fugitive Slave Act of 1850, and he began to despair of prospects for blacks in the United States. In June 1849 Douglass indicated that henceforth he would be sole editor of the *North Star,* although Delany's contributions to the paper continued.

After seeking more medical training unsuccessfully in Pennsylvania and New York, Delany was admitted to Harvard Medical School in November 1850. White students protested, and Delany was permitted to finish the semester but barred from further study. Nonetheless, he assumed the title of doctor (there were no licensing requirements at that time). Delany returned to Pittsburgh where he organized resistance to the Fugitive Slave Act, practiced medicine, and served for a year as the principal of the ''colored'' school. His despair at the worsening conditions faced by blacks led him to endorse emigration as a solution. In 1851 he went to Canada for the first time to attend the North American Convention held by Henry Bibb, a prominent leader of emigrants to that country.

Adopts Emigration as a Solution

Delany's position on emigration as a solution to the problems faced by black Americans came through clearly in the small book, *The Condition, Elevation, Emigration and Destiny of the Colored People of the United States, Politically Considered* (1852). Delany went beyond advocating the contemplation of emigration as a possibility to urge serious planning and exploration. In the text his suggested destination was Central or South America; in an appendix, Africa. The book met with condemnation on all sides—prominent black leaders like Douglass simply ignored it in print. Nevertheless it struck a chord in the black community strong enough to draw 100 men and women to Cleveland on August 24–26, 1854, to the National Emigration Convention organized by Delany. This convention has been cited by authors like Victor Ullman as marking the birth of a new concept of black nationalism. The convention established Delany as the head of a board charged with finding a homeland for blacks in Central or South America.

About this time Delany moved his family to Chatham, Ontario, where they were part of the more than 10,000 black emigrants to Canada in the wake of the Fugitive Slave Law. In 1858 Delany helped John Brown organize a secret gathering in Chatham, but by the time of Brown's raid on Harper's Ferry, Virginia, Delany was in Africa. A third Emigration Convention was held in Chatham in August 1858, and Delany proposed to investigate the Niger Valley in Africa as a site for a colony. The officers of the convention were opposed to Africa as a destination but did not block Delany's acting on his own. Delany and Robert Campbell, a chemist and head of the science department at the Institute for Colored Youth in Philadelphia, set out for Africa in May 1859, where they traveled in Liberia and the Niger Valley, leaving Africa in April of the following year for an extended stay in Great Britain.

Delany had begun publish a novel, *Blake,* in 1859 in the *Anglo–African Magazine* but publication broke off when he left for Africa. For many years this was the only portion known to scholars but more was discovered, though not the conclusion, in the *Weekly Anglo–African* of 1861 and 1862. Book publication of what remains did not take place until 1970. This early black separatist novel is important for African American literature. Leading literary historian Blyden Jackson wrote: ''*Blake* contains more than its share of puerile passages. . . . But *Blake* lacks art, not mind. There was, and is, nothing small about Delany's grasp of the realities which meant much to his circumstances as a Negro in America in the 1850s. And into *Blake* he carried his perception of those realities, the largeness of his vision of them.''

Leads Expedition to Africa

Delany was successful in negotiating a treaty with local authorities in Africa which gave African Americans the right to establish a colony. Interest among Londoners in Delany's explorations led to many speaking engagements and an invitation to attend the International Statistical Congress, a major scientific gathering in July 1860. There Lord Brougham called attention to his presence. Delany rose to thank him, saying according to his own account in the Rollin biography, ''I rise, your royal Highness [Prince Albert], to thank his lordship, the unflinching friend of the negro [sic], for the remarks he has made in reference to me and to assure your royal highness and his lordship *that I am a man.*'' Brougham's intervention, the reply of Delany, and the applause aroused in the audience offended the American ambassador, who was present on the platform, and caused the American delegation to walk out of the meeting. The hubbub nearly caused a diplomatic incident and took some time to die down.

Delany returned home to Canada by Christmas 1860. He published the *Official Report of the Niger Valley Exploring Party* simultaneously in London and New York in 1861. This publication launched him on a further round of speaking engagements. He firmly rejected the project of emigration to Haiti supported by fellow emigrationist and future Anglican bishop of Haiti, James T. Holly. Setting up headquarters for a while in Brooklyn, he pressed on with his efforts for colonization in Africa. They fell through when the attack on Fort Sumter in South Carolina opened the Civil War and radically changed the terms of the debate.

Lincoln's changing stances—initially he favored colonization and did not speak of abolition of slavery—caused difficulties for blacks. On July 16, 1862, a Congressional committee published Delany's 1854 pamphlet in favor of emigration, *The Political Destiny of the Colored Race On the*

American Continent as propaganda in favor of Lincoln's colonization plan. It was not until the Emancipation Proclamation of 1863 that support of Lincoln and the war effort became widespread among blacks. When Lincoln approved the acceptance of black troops in the Union army, Delany became an effective official recruiter.

In 1864 Delany moved his family to Wilberforce, Ohio, to a house which became the final family home although Delany himself was seldom there. He, his wife, and two of his children are buried there. One attraction of the location was the opportunity for the education of his children furnished by the preparatory school of the AME's Wilberforce University. Delany's papers and memorabilia were stored in the main building of the university, which was totally destroyed by fire on the night of Lincoln's assassination, April 14, 1865, days after the Civil War ended.

Becomes Army Officer

At the time he moved to Ohio, Delany was pressing a plan to recruit black troops to be commanded by black officers, with a major effort to be made in the South. On February 8, 1865, he had an interview with President Lincoln, who not only accepted the plan but arranged to have Delany commissioned as a major in the U.S. Army—the first black field officer. Delany was ordered to Charleston, South Carolina, and was present at the raising of the flag at Fort Sumter on April 14, the fourth anniversary of the surrender. Delany began to recruit vigorously but was ordered to suspend his efforts on June 7 due to the cessation of hostilities. Delany was transferred to Beaufort, South Carolina, and placed under the command of the Freedman's Bureau. His career with the army and the bureau ended in August 1868.

Delany aroused alarm in the army and among other whites by his fire–eating speeches to black audiences on the Sea Islands. Nonetheless his popularity among blacks and his efficiency at his job protected his position. He persisted in spite of President Andrew Johnson's restoration policies which returned land on the Sea Islands to the original owners—blacks were able to hold on to only about ten percent of the lands abandoned by whites fleeing the occupation of the U.S. Army earlier in the war. Delany even won the grudging admiration of white planters as his policies brought prosperity and stability to the region.

White political leadership was restored in South Carolina by Johnson's activities and lasted until First Reconstruction Act of March 2, 1867, placed the army in control of the provisional state governments. Ullman argued in the Delany biography that it was the only the efforts of the commanding general, Daniel E. Sickles, and Delany together with those of a few other moderate leaders that prevented open warfare between blacks and whites during the period.

Blacks voted for the first time in South Carolina in November 1867, almost unanimously supporting a state constitutional convention to be held in January and February 1868. Delany attended the convention as much his army duties allowed. Also during summer and fall of 1867 he worked with Frances Rollins (Whipper) on his biography, published the next year.

By the end of 1868 Delany had handed in his final accounts to the Freedmen's Bureau and left the army. He lobbied for an appointment as minister to Liberia and also undertook a lecture tour, selling his biography as a sideline. In his lectures he managed to alienate most of the black leaders by demanding a pro rata share of patronage for blacks from the Republican Party; that is, a quota system. After spending a few months in Wilberforce and then two in Washington, D.C., Delany returned to South Carolina early in 1870. During his time in Washington, he was principal speaker at the first mass meeting at the founding convention of the Negro National Labor Union on December 6.

Delany did not re–enter politics for two years. He set himself up as a real estate agent, but economic conditions undermined his chances for success as did his involvement in the successful 1872 gubernatorial campaign of Franklin J. Moses Jr., who quickly showed himself as more corrupt than his predecessor.

Disillusioned, Delany found a minor clerical job with the federal government. He now completed his alienation from much of the national black leadership by joining a revolt against the regular Republican machine. He broke rank in the governor's election of 1874 to run as a candidate for lieutenant governor of an independent Republican faction opposed to the regular Republican nominee. Delany's party lost, but the conservative Democrats who supported the independent Republicans took control of 14 of 32 counties.

Delany's influence was not destroyed by the results of the election. From August to December 1875 he was again editor of a newspaper, the *Charleston Independent.* He also began to practice medicine again. In a strange twist in South Carolina politics, Delany became a trial justice on October 8, 1875, named by his opponent in the governor's race of the year before, Daniel H. Chamberlain.

Delany was active and competent as a judge but he ran into legal problems. He was convicted in February 1876 of defrauding a church of $212. He had received the money in 1871 and placed it Charleston County Tax Anticipation Warrants, which later proved worthless. Deeply wounded by the conviction, Delany admitted owing the money but vigorously denied committing fraud and appealed his conviction to the Supreme Court. After negotiations for a pardon broke down, Chamberlain removed Delany as a trial justice; his nomination had never been officially presented to the legislature. Only on August 29, the eve of the new gubernatorial elections, and under pressure from Delany's friends, did Chamberlain issue a pardon.

Delany was not won over; he announced that he would support Democrat Wade Hampton for governor. No one knows who actually won the South Carolina election that year since fraud and violence were widespread. Hampton was declared the winner by the congressional investigating committee; thus, the state's electoral vote remained in favor of Rutherford B. Hayes. This enabled Hayes to win the presidency by one electoral vote, 185 to 184. Hayes upheld his end of the bargain by ending Reconstruction in the South.

Hampton did not break his promises to blacks even as his party was organizing to eliminate the Republican Party as a political force in the state. Delany held the position of trial justice for two years under Hampton until Hampton was elected to the U.S. Senate in 1879. By 1878 Delany was again taking up emigration as a solution for the problems of blacks. Many southern blacks shared this vision, most prominently the 20,000 who joined the millenarian attempt to emigrate to Kansas from 1878 to 1879. Delany worked to forward the colonization efforts of the Liberian Exodus Joint Steam Ship Company, which went bankrupt after carrying seven shiploads of emigrants to Liberia.

Despite the disappointment of his hopes in South Carolina by 1880, Delany did not return home to Wilberforce, turning instead to medicine to support himself. He continued to lecture and sold his *Principles of Ethnology: The Origins of the Races with an Archaeological Compendium of Ethiopian and Egyptian Civilization* (1879) to his audiences. Late in 1884 Delany returned to Wilberforce; he died there in January 1885.

After his death, Delany fell into oblivion. It took more than 100 years and the rise of modern black nationalism for second and third full–length biographies to appear almost simultaneously. The ongoing re–examination of 19th–century black history that has flourished in recent years allows him to be restored to his rightful position as one of the most important black leaders and thinkers of his era.

REFERENCES

Delany, Martin R. *Blake; or, The Huts of America.* Edited by Floyd J. Miller. Boston: Beacon Press, 1970.

Griffith, Cyril E. *The African Dream: Martin R. Delany and the Emergence of Pan–African Thought.* University Park: Pennsylvania State University Press, 1975.

Jackson, Blyden. *A History of Afro–American Literature.* Vol 1. Baton Rouge: Louisiana State University Press, 1989.

Litwack, Leon, and August Meier, eds. *Black Leaders of the Nineteenth Century.* Urbana: University of Illinois Press, 1988.

Logan, Rayford W., and Michael R. Winston, eds. *Dictionary of American Negro Biography.* New York: Norton, 1982.

Rollin, Frank A. (Frances Rollins Whipper). *Life and Public Services of Martin R. Delany.* Boston: Lee and Shepard, 1868.

Sterling, Dorothy. *The Making of An Afro–American: Martin Robinson Delany.* Garden City, NY: Doubleday, 1971.

Surkamp, Jim. *To Be More Than Equal: The Many Lives of Martin R. Delany 1812–1885.* http://www.wvu.edu/~library/delany/home.htm (last updated January 20, 1998).

Ullman, Victor. *Martin R. Delany: The Beginnings of Black Nationalism.* Boston: Beacon Press, 1971.

Robert L. Johns

Samuel R. Delany
(1942–)
Novelist, poet, lecturer, literary critic, educator, gay and women's rights activist

Samuel R. Delany, called ''Chip'' by his friends, fellow writers, and science fiction fans, is without question one of the most adroit, inventive, and productive American writers to emerge from the 1960s. From the publication of his first science fiction novel, *Jewels of Aptor* in 1962, to the appearance of the intricately patterned *Atlantis: Three Tales* in 1995, Delany has been extraordinarily energetic. A writer difficult to categorize, he has been active across a variety of genres. He also has established a reputation as a leading critical theorist of science fiction; his detailed and elaborate essays examining this ''para–literary'' genre are considered masterpieces. As John Sallis noted in *Ash of Stars: On the Writing of Samuel R. Delany,* because Delany is ''one of the field's preeminent stylists,'' many critics and fans of science fiction see him as ''a major influence on two generations of writers.'' He has even created an entirely new genre, the reflexive self–interview. *Silent Interviews* (1994) is a collection of revised and considerably extended previously published interviews.

A Harlem native, Samuel Ray Delany was born April 1, 1942, to Bronx native Margaret Delany and Samuel R. Delany Sr., a North Carolinian who migrated to New York in the early 1920s. Delany's father established himself as a significant figure in the Harlem business community. He first opened a men's clothing store in the 1930s with a man named Bell. Subsequently, he formed a partnership with a Mr. Levy to establish Levy and Delany Funeral Associates. A year later, Delany bought Levy out and operated the funeral home as a family business with the assistance of his second wife, Margaret Carey Boyd Delany. Delany Sr. died of lung cancer in 1960 when his son was 18. Nearly a year after his father's death, Delany married the Jewish poet, Marilyn Hacker, despite the fact that both of them knew he was gay. Hacker had been pregnant with what Delany called their ''second sexual experiment'' but she suffered a miscarriage. The couple later had a daughter, Iva Alyxander Hacker–Delany. Hacker and Delany divorced in 1980.

Delany's formal education began at age three when his parents placed him in kindergarten in Harlem's Horace Mann Lincoln School. From 1947 until 1956, his parents sent him out of Harlem to attend the private and progressive Dalton Elementary School in midtown Manhattan. The Dalton faculty recognized that young Sam was a precocious child, intelligent, creative, and outgoing. He was also a child who, despite difficulties with reading and spelling, enjoyed the sounds of language and verbalizing stories he created. Yet he was apparently somewhat rebellious and undisciplined. Delany's problems in these early years stemmed in part from undiagnosed dyslexia. Other problems developed because he was a black boy in a white school, daily traveling across town. Following graduation from Dalton, Delany enrolled at Bronx High School of Science, where he excelled in mathematics and science. Following graduation, he took classes at City College (now the City University of New York), in 1960 and 1962–63; he never obtained a degree.

Childhood Provides Autobiographical Elements

The story of Delany's early life and youth is a series of recursive tales, recast in various essays. These also emerge by fragments in biographical treatments prefacing studies of his works, and are frequently folded into critical essays he has written about his life. These reflections on the nature of science fiction are offered to scholars through lengthy personal correspondence, and shared with readers through the rich and compelling autobiographical voice animating *Heavenly Breakfast: Essays on the Winter of Love* (1979) and *The Motion of Light in Water: Sex and Science Fiction Writing in the East Village, 1957–1965* (1988).

As a child, the center of Delany's world was the fluid middle class enclave his parents and extended family had carved out in Harlem and the surrounding New York environs. His parents provided warmth, stability, exposure to classic books, to Greek and Roman mythology, to the legends of King Arthur, and to music and the arts. As a teen and an avid reader, Delany later discovered some of the major figures in African American literature and culture—Paul Laurence Dunbar, Langston Hughes, Countee Cullen, James Weldon Johnson, Jean Toomer, Bruce Nugent, James Baldwin, Zora Neale Hurston, Chester Himes, William Demby, and Amiri Baraka. This eclectic mix of early influences also included music lessons with folksinger Pete Seeger and reading pulp magazine science fiction stories as well as some of the foremost science fiction novels by major writers such as Theodore Sturgeon, Alfred Bester, Arthur C. Clarke, and Robert A. Heinlein.

While not always traumatic, Delany's relationship with his family during his youth was sometimes strained by the tension between himself and his father. In *Motion,* Chip Delany perceived his father as an "angry, anxious man." This anxiety often led to frustrating confrontations between father and son. Because the senior Delany believed in administering stern discipline, he unwittingly fostered rebelliousness in his son. Delany repeatedly ran away from home from the time he was five until he turned 17. An observant black child growing up in Harlem, going to school beyond the boundaries of the black community, and spending summers in largely white progressive summer camps from the time he was six years old, Delany noted the multiple intersections of human interaction which would later become texts and subtexts for his fiction.

Delany completed his education through travel, reading, a variety of work experiences, and writing. In the early 1960s, he earned a living as an itinerant folksinger and musician in Greenwich Village coffeehouses and nightclubs; he also worked as an actor, teacher, reviewer, and freelance writer. Between June of 1965 and July of 1966, he hitchhiked from New York to the Gulf coast of Texas to work on the shrimp boats. He also visited Greece, Turkey, and Europe, and worked as a traveling minstrel. And he kept journals. Portions of his adventures were transformed into the short stories and segments of novels he drafted as he traveled. In 1966 he visited England and met John Brunner and Michael Moorcock, two of the English writers then developing science fiction's New Wave. In 1967 Delany returned to New York's lower East Side to live in the Heavenly Breakfast Commune and play with the Heavenly Breakfast rock band. He moved briefly to San Francisco's Haight–Ashbury in 1969, but returned to New York City in 1970. While often associated with the New Wave writers, Delany never considered himself a part of this group; his work is allied with the group of science fiction writers included in Harlan Ellison's anthology, *Dangerous Visions* (1967).

In the mid–1960s Delany played the black Bohemian, a Negro "Flower Child." He wore one earring, dressed colorfully, and sported a full, flowing beard. Some in the science fiction community saw him as a Renaissance Man. Science fiction writer and critic Judith Merrill described him in Peplow and Brevard's *Samuel R. Delany, a Primary and Secondary Bibliography, 1962–1979* as being "where it is at: multi–mediumed, transcultural, interracial, call it multi–plicit." In 1964, because of the demands he placed on himself to produce stories and novels in rapid succession, Delany suffered a temporary nervous breakdown. According to Peplow and Brevard he was hospitalized at Mt. Sinai, preoccupied by a "fixation with subways and suicide." Elements of this brush with death—the anguish, the fear, the potential for violence or self–destruction—surfaced repeatedly in Delany's later fiction, particularly his short stories.

Career Develops

Delany began to write stories while still in grade school. His first publications were in summer camp newspapers or newsletters and school literary magazines. He attempted a number of science fiction novels and stories throughout the 1950s. He entered essay and story contests and, in 1958, he began to win awards and recognition. In 1960 he won a fellowship to the acclaimed Breadloaf Writers Conference where he received support and encouragement from the assembled writers, including poet Robert Frost. His first commercially successful novel, *The Jewels of Aptor,* came on the heels of the Breadloaf award. With this novel, Delany became the celebrated multitalented *wunderkind* of science fiction in the 1960s.

The success of *Jewels,* published as one side of an Ace Double, was rapidly followed by several hurriedly written, fast–paced novels. By the time he was 23 Delany had published five novels: *Captives of the Flame* (1963), the first book in the *Fall of the Towers* trilogy (revised and republished under Delany's original title, *Out of the Dead City* in 1968), *The Towers of Toron* (1964), the second book in the trilogy, and *City of a Thousand Suns* (1969), the third volume. *The Ballad of Beta–2* first appeared in 1965 as an Ace paperback. *Empire Star* was published in 1966. *Babel–17* also first appeared in 1966, followed by *The Einstein Intersection* in 1967. *Nova* (1968), an intergalactic adventure epic, closed out the decade for Delany and marked a shift in the kind of books he had been writing.

Many of Delany's science fiction stories and novels during the 1960s had the sweep and grandeur and many of the classic conventions of the space opera form of science fiction. Their span was enormous. There were aliens, spaceships, intergalactic warfare, far–flung galaxies, computers, shifts in time, colonization of planets, alternate universes, civilizations destroyed and rebuilt. But the tales also took a subtly subversive approach to the genre. Rather than concentrate on the typical, anticipated science fiction hero—white and male—Delany created protagonists who were out of step with their world. They were artists—musicians or poets—and outcasts; his heroes were often physically or psychologically damaged; moreover, his characters were often black, of mixed–blood, or racially diverse. Many of his protagonists were women as well. Issues of identity and language, and modes of communication further contributed to the essential subtexts of the Delany story. On yet another level, the stories were frequently saturated in myth or were about the creation of myth. Astute observers of his fiction would argue that in his novels of the 1960s, which consciously employed a far more literary language than the typical science fiction tale, Delany invested his characters with elements of his own identity and experiences.

From the 1970s into the 1990s, Delany's critical writings—he has written several non–fiction books—and his speculative fiction grew increasingly complex and dense. For example, the ornate and controversial *Dhalgren* (1976), considered by many his magnum opus, chronicles the journey of the Kid, a wandering artist, through a dystopian nightmare, what Sallis has called "a self–discrete universe–city." And Bron Helstrom, the unlikable white male "hero" of *Triton* (1976), must undergo a gender change in an attempt to find a more comfortable identity. These novels, like the pornographic *Equinox,* (first published as *Tides of Lust,* 1973), *Distant Stars* (1981), and *Stars in My Pocket Like Grains of Sand* (1984), build upon a more sophisticated narrative structure and reflect Delany's deepening interest in psychoanalysis, linguistic theory, and literary deconstruction as significant theoretical constructs. Over time, however, for readers more comfortable with standard science fiction, the challenge of reading this more densely packed and highly stylized science fiction has proven daunting. Delany contested the fundamental nature of the form. Unlike the science fiction of the past, he was not simply concerned with a problem to be solved by scientific method; he placed the emphasis in his novels on characters within communities and he drew his readers' attention to the objective world within which his characters functioned.

In the late 1970s, Delany turned his attention to an even more elaborate and marginal genre: sword–and–sorcery or fantasy fiction. For almost ten years, from 1979 to 1987, he stepped away from science fiction to compose the *Return to Nevèrÿon* series. These four interconnected "prehistorical" texts, *Tales of Nevèrÿon* (1979), *Neveryóna: or the Tale of Signs and Cities* (1983), *Flight from Nevèrÿon* (1985) and *The Bridge of Lost Desire* (1987), are possibly the most engaging, literate, and challenging fantasy fictions ever penned by an American author. For his stylistic innovations he has been compared favorably to such literary giants as Jorge Luis Borges, Thomas Pynchon, and James Joyce.

In the 1990s, Delany returned to theoretical discussions focusing on the nature of science fiction—on reading it, writing it, or critiquing its history and developments. Other topics included language, race, sex, marginality, and comic books. These discussions are wonderfully framed and fully aired in the brilliant and critically useful *Silent Interviews* (1994). In addition, Delany reclaimed and republished a very early fantasy tale, *They Fly at Çiron* (1993). *The Mad Man* (1994) has been described by reviewers as a highly disturbing pornographic crime novel; however, in a 1997 letter to the author, Delany wrote, "it was a book began in a paroxysm of perfect rage" developing as a response to an article on AIDS in a 1993 issue of *New Yorker.* By contrast, *Atlantis: Three Tales* (1995), while more structurally innovative and complex, is seen by some reviewers as a tribute to the Harlem Renaissance and by others as an accolade to the role of memory and the shaping effect it has on our lives. The first tale, "Atlantis, Model 1924," also seems to the discerning eye a fictive recreation of the journey that took Samuel R. Delany Sr. from North Carolina to New York—itself a magical, mythic city for African Americans during the 1920s.

Throughout the 1970s Delany held a number of academic appointments. He became the Butler Professor of English at the State University of New York at Buffalo in 1975. He was appointed senior fellow at the Center for Twentieth Century Studies at the University of Wisconsin–Milwaukee in 1977 and was a senior fellow at the Society for Humanities at Cornell University in 1987. In 1988 Delany was invited to become a professor of comparative literature at the University of Massachusetts at Amherst. In the course of his career he has also taught classes for budding science fiction writers at the Clarion Workshop.

Babel–17 (1966) and *The Einstein Intersection* (1967) won Nebula Awards from the Science Fiction Writers of America (SFWA). The SFWA also awarded a Nebula for his 1967 story, "Aye, and Gomorrah." In the category of best novelette, for the "Time Considered as a Helix of Semi–Precious Stones" (1969), Delany won both the Nebula and a subsequent Hugo award from the Science Fiction Convention in 1970. In 1980, for *Tales of Nevèrÿon,* he earned an American Book Award nomination; in 1984 he won the Pilgrim Award, conferred by the Science Fiction Research Association, for excellence in science fiction–related scholarship. In 1993 Delany received the William Whitehead Memorial Award for Lifetime Contribution to Lesbian and Gay Writing.

In his mid–fifties, the author of more than 30 books—novels, short story collections, critical texts, and memoirs—in the course of over 30 years, Delany is no longer the *wunderkind* of science fiction; with the passage of time he has become the genre's grand old man. He is generous and supportive of the efforts of others to study his works. He is passionate and articulate about what he believes. He has carved a unique space for his work as a result of his considerable achievements as both a writer and a theorist. Delany's life is inseparable from his finely honed artistic sensibility, his sense of himself as a writer, the homage he pays to the written word. As he steadfastly maintained in the introduction to *Silent Interviews:* "I am a writer—which is another way of saying that my thoughts and my feelings are intimately and intricately *formed* by writing."

Current address: Department of Comparative Literature, University of Massachusetts at Amherst, South College Building, Amherst, MA 01003.

REFERENCES

"A Cult Following." *The Chronicle of Higher Education,* June 28, 1996.

Delany, Samuel R. *The Jewel–Hinged Jaw.* Hastings–on–Hudson, NY: Dragon Press, 1977.

———. Letter to Sandra Y. Govan, February 13, 1997.

———. *The Motion of Light in Water: Sex and Science Fiction Writing in the East Village, 1957–1965.* Westminster, MD: Arbor House, 1988.

———. *Silent Interviews.* Hanover, NY: Wesleyan University Press of New England, 1994.

Govan, Sandra Y. "The Insistent Presence of Black Folk in the Fiction of Samuel R. Delany." *Black American Literature Forum* 18 (Summer 1984): 43–48.

Peplow, Michael, and Robert S. Brevard. *Samuel R. Delany, A Primary and Secondary Bibliography, 1962–1979.* Boston: G. K. Hall, 1980.

Sallis, John. Introduction to *Ash of Stars: On the Writing of Samuel R. Delany.* Jackson: University Press of Mississippi, 1996.

Samuelson, David. "Necessary Constraints: Samuel R. Delany on Science Fiction." In *Ash of Stars: On the Writing of Samuel R. Delany.* Edited by John Sallis. Jackson: University Press of Mississippi, 1996.

Sandra Y. Govan

Ronald V. Dellums

(1935–)

Congressman

Ronald Dellums has been one of the most influential and outspoken black leaders on Capitol Hill. As one who believes people should have the courage of their convictions, Carol Swain in *Black Faces* credited him with "bold statements that set him apart from other politicians, white and black." Quoted in *Contemporary Black Biography,* Dellums commented, "... democracy is not about being a damn spectator against the backdrop of tap–dancing politicians swinging in the winds of expediency."

Ronald Vernie Dellums was born November 24, 1935, in Oakland, California, to Vernie Dellums, a longshoreman and a former Pullman porter, and Willa Dellums, a government clerk–typist. He was politically influenced by his uncle C. L. Dellums, a leader of A. Philip Randolph's Sleeping Car Porters Union, and, according to the *New Republic* for July 1994, moved "toward a politics of class coalition rather than simply race." In "Afro–American of Black," Dellums credited his mother with "the sense of consciousness and pride to communicate to ... [him] at age 14 that ... [he] should be proud to be a Black and to be an American of African descent." From then on Dellums was proud to be an African American. He attended McClymonds High School and Oakland Technical High School. In 1954 he enlisted in the U.S. Marine Corps. Using the G.I. Bill, he enrolled in 1958 in Oakland City College where he earned an A.A. degree. He went on to earn a B.A. in 1960 from San Francisco State College and an M.S.W. in 1962 from the University of California at Berkeley. In the same year, 1962, he married Leola Roscoe Higgs, a lawyer; they have one daughter, Piper, and two sons, Erik and Brandy. He has a daughter, Pamela, from a previous marriage.

From 1962 to 1964 he was a psychiatric social worker for the California Department of Mental Hygiene; from 1964 until 1965 he was program director for the Bayview Community Center in San Francisco; and from 1965 to 1966 he was associate director and later director of the Hunters Point Youth Opportunity Council. From 1968 to 1970 he lectured at San Francisco State College and the University of California's School of Social Work. As a result of his upbringing and training as a psychiatric social worker, he became involved in community affairs and local politics. *Contemporary Black Biography* noted that "he began to realize that being a young black from the ghetto with a master's degree in psychiatric social work was not sufficient contribution on his part to solving the problems of society that he saw as the causes of human suffering he observed."

Dellums's political career, began when he was convinced to run for Berkeley City Council in 1967. He was endorsed by both Berkeley's Democratic Caucus and the Community for New Politics. Dellums was one who transcended race; he was more ideological than racial, and he was both intellectual and articulate. Additionally, he proved to be an independent thinker, denounced police brutality toward students and minorities, and served as liaison between the student groups on Berkeley's campus and the Council. He won a seat on the Berkeley City Council. Throughout Dellums's political career he has been motivated by the welfare of his constituents as well as the general public and has maintained a national agenda rather than one restricted to the local district.

Wins Congressional Seat

In 1970 Dellums challenged the incumbent Democrat, Jeffrey Cohelan, in the Oakland–Berkeley area Democratic primary election. Both Coretta Scott King and union activist Cesar Chavez endorsed his campaign. In spite of Spiro J. Agnew's attempts to detract from his candidacy by linking

Ronald V. Dellums (speaking), 1990.

him with the Black Panthers and branding him a ''radical element'' and the fact that his district had a 22 percent black population, Dellums won the election. Indicative of his military interest and his boldness, the *New Republic* reported that he ''addressed the World Conference on Vietnam, Laos, and Cambodia in Stockholm, which hosted representatives of the Khmer Rouge and the South Vietnamese National Liberation Front.''

In his first term in Congress, Dellums held ad hoc hearings on military policy in Vietnam and racism in the armed services and became the first African American to win a seat on the Armed Services Committee. In 1971 he was appointed to the committee that oversees the District of Columbia, and in 1973 he was the first legislator to call for comprehensive economic sanctions against South Africa due to its policy of apartheid. Dellums participated in demonstrations at the South African embassy in Washington, D.C., in 1974. His forward thinking was recognized when in 1986, according to *Current Biography,* the United States adopted his sanctions bill, barring most of the trade with and investment activities in South Africa and suspending commercial air travel between that country and the United States. As one of the cosponsors of the Nuclear Freeze Resolution in 1979, he was appointed by House Speaker Thomas T. ''Tip'' O'Neill as a member of a U.S. Congressional delegation to Moscow to discuss a pending arms–limitations treaty. That same year he was elected chair of the House Committee on the District of Columbia.

In 1980 Dellums was elected chair of the House Armed Services subcommittee and became the first black to head a defense–oriented group on Capitol Hill. He was the first to introduce and debate on the House floor an alternative military budget and the first to introduce legislation to end funding of the MC, Pershing II, and Minuteman missiles. His determination to aid in solving the problems of society did not go unchallenged; in 1982 drug charges, which could not be substantiated and which failed to deter him, were lodged against him but ultimately were dropped. He continued to speak out against military spending. From 1983 to 1989 he was chair of the Military Installations and Facilities subcommittee; he monitored expenditures for the operation and maintenance of overseas bases.

Dellums also served as chair of the Congressional Black Caucus from 1988 until 1991. In spite of objections, he won membership on the Intelligence Committee in 1991. In 1993 the Democrats elected him to the chairmanship of the House Armed Services Committee, the first African American in this position. Dellums has not hesitated to speak his mind. In the July 1984 *Harper's,* quoted in *Current Biography,* he alleged ''the Reagan administration has subverted Lincoln's hope for a government of the people, by the people, and for the people, creating in its stead a government of the few, by the few, and for the few.'' His views on the military were published in 1983, in the book he co–authored with R. H. Miller and H. L. Halterman, *Defense Sense: The Search for a Rational Military Policy.*

Dellums, throughout his political career, has remained a servant of the people, not of a specific race. His actions substantiate his beliefs in the evenness of peoples. According to *Contemporary Black Biography,* he reasoned, ''I'm black, I'm [an] ethnic minority, I'm a human being. . . . In all three of these categories I have been oppressed. And I live with millions of people who are oppressed.'' In November of 1997, Dellums announced that he would retire from the House of Representatives in February of 1998. He told the *New York Times* that he chose ''to make a personal decision and to empower myself to regain my life.''

Current address: 2136 Rayburn House Office Building, Washington, DC 20515.

REFERENCES

''Afro–American or Black: What's in a Name? Prominent Blacks and—or African Americans Express Their Views.'' *Ebony* 44 (July 1989): 76–80.

Alterman, Eric. ''Profiles. Ron Dellums: Radical Insider.'' *World Policy Journal* 10 (Winter 1993): 35–46.

Contemporary Black Biography. Vol. 2. Detroit: Gale Research, 1992.

Current Biography Yearbook. New York: H. W. Wilson, 1993.

Judis, John B. ''The Dellums Dilemma.'' *New Republic* 4 (July 1994): 23–25.

Mauravchik, Joshua. ''Dellums' Dilemma.'' *New Republic* 204 (11 March 1991): 14–16.

Salser, Mark R., ed. *Black Americans in Congress.* Portland, OR: National Book Co., 1991.

Swain, Carol M. *Black Faces, Black Interests: The Representation of African Americans in Congress.* Enlarged ed. Cambridge: Harvard University Press, 1995.

"Two California Representatives to Leave House." *New York Times.* November 18, 1997.

"Two High–Profile House Democrats to Step Down." *USA Today.* November 18, 1997.

Williams, Michael W., ed. *The African American Encyclopedia.* New York: Marshall Cavendish, 1993.

Helen R. Houston

Charles Denby

(1907–1983)

Autoworker, newspaper editor, Marxist–Humanist

Born in Lowndes County, Alabama, August 25, 1907, the son of independent farmers and the grandson of slaves, Charles Denby, whose real name was Simon Peter Owens, was a Detroit auto worker and labor militant who helped foster a revolutionary socialist movement in the United States called Marxist–Humanism. Associated for more than 30 years with Raya Dunayevskaya, the founder of the philosophy of Marxist–Humanism, Denby was the worker–editor of the movement's newspaper *News and Letters* from its beginning in Detroit in 1955 until his death October 10, 1983.

Charles Denby is most noted for his autobiography, *Indignant Heart: A Black Worker's Journal.* It is considered a proletarian classic among scholars of African American and labor history. *Indignant Heart* was originally published in 1952 under the pen name Matthew Ward and published in enlarged form in 1978. Likewise, the identities of many of the people and places had to be altered. The original manuscript with the real names, however, is held in the files of *The Raya Dunayevskaya Collection.*

Indignant Heart covers Denby's life from a child listening to his grandmother's stories of slavery to 1948 when he met C. L. R. James and Raya Dunayevskaya, the leaders of what was called the Johnson–Forest or State–Capitalist Tendency, at the national convention of the Socialist Workers Party (SWP) in New York City. Johnson and Forest were the pseudonyms of James and Dunayevskaya at the time.

Not long after his meeting Dunayevskaya and James, Denby became a member of the Johnson–Forest Tendency. Upon breaking with the SWP in 1951, the Tendency became the Committees of Correspondence until a further split occurred between James and Dunayevskaya in 1955. Among the majority of workers who followed Dunayevskaya, Denby and his wife Ethel Dunbar became founding members of the Marxist–Humanist organization, News and Letters Committees.

Denby began the second part of his autobiography, written in 1977–78, with his return to his birthplace in Lowndes County at the time of the 1955–56 Montgomery Bus Boycott. Subsequent chapters in part two of his autobiography continue Denby's narrative of the southern Civil Rights Movement. The second part of *Indignant Heart* climaxes Denby's experience as an autoworker militant in the same way that the first part of his narrative recounts his beginnings as a working class militant.

Though a son of the rural South, the industrial and mechanical nature of the jobs Denby worked throughout his life was not accidental. He attended Tuskegee Institute briefly in the 1920s to study mechanics in order to get factory work, he so disliked the drudgery and toil of farm labor. While at Tuskegee he took a class with the noted scientist George Washington Carver.

The Making of an *Indignant Heart*

Denby came north to Detroit in 1924 in the second great migratory wave of 1924–25 which saw Detroit's black population grow more than 600 percent in the decade between 1916 and 1926. His autobiography is one of the great narrative testaments of this historical shift in the life and labor of African Americans.

Along with the chronic housing shortage and rent gouging by unscrupulous landlords, outside the factory, the crucial issues inside the factory that black workers like Charles Denby organized around was discrimination in job classification and upgrading. Like other black industrial workers, Denby, then a young 17–year–old, was employed in the "hot, dirty and dangerous" foundry department when he got his first job in Detroit's automobile industry in 1924.

With the 1930s depression, black unemployment grew 30 to 60 percent higher than white unemployment. Denby was laid–off a number of times from the auto industry in this period and had to find work in the public sector, working for the city of Detroit as a day laborer. The Depression forced Denby to return to the South, where he worked for nearly a decade as a chauffeur for the prominent Montgomery attorney Thomas Bowen (T. B.) Hill. He returned to Detroit in 1943, just weeks before the outbreak of the Detroit riot. Charles Denby witnessed the 1943 Detroit riot and participated in the strike actions and in–plant organizing of black workers' committees that developed in its aftermath. Denby came of age as a politicized militant worker in this period.

Denby often discussed how crucial black labor was to the organization and struggles of the American working class as a whole and how racism has historically undermined both. The relation between race and class in trade union questions became more complex in Denby's dealing with radical left parties like the Stalinist Communist Party and the Trotskyist Socialist Workers Party. When he led his first wildcat strike during World War II, Denby encountered the United Auto Worker's duplicity on the race question when the UAW used a black union official to thwart black rank–and–file efforts to break down job discrimination.

From this experience Denby came into contact with Communist Party (CP) members, who eagerly pointed out the limitations of race identification in his experience with the black union official, while insisting on the importance of fighting for racial equality. Inside the plant, however, Denby found that the CP's support of the no–strike pledge, because the Soviet Union was an ally of the United States during World War II, meant that the party withheld its support of the kind of strikes Denby and other black workers organized. He describes how other black worker militants like George Harding, chief shop steward of the janitors department, fought the union and the CP to get black workers upgraded. It was the rank–and–file work actions organized by Harding and others, not the policies of the UAW or the politics of the CP, that moved black workers "from brooms to better jobs."

In the two decades after the war, the 1953–54 recession, automation, and competition with Ford for second place among the Big Three automakers led to a significant drop in employment at Chrysler, from 100,000 to 35,000. "The year 1954," he wrote, "was also when an executive at Ford first coined the word 'automation' to describe what the workers were wildcatting against." West Virginia coal miners of the United Mine Workers of America (UMW) had been the first to battle the new technology with a general strike in 1949–50. Denby recorded the worker solidarity he witnessed when the striking coal miners came to Detroit UAW Local 600 to appeal for relief. Denby would mobilize the same kind of material support and solidarity a decade and a half later, in the midst of the Civil Rights Movement when he organized the Michigan–Lowndes County Christian Movement for Human Rights to aid black sharecroppers evicted from white–owned plantations for registering to vote.

Another issue Denby often took the UAW to task over was the appalling lack of African Americans in the union's leadership. "Blacks have never gotten real power in the union itself," he charged. This lack of black power in the union leadership was one of the issues that led to the black caucuses movement at the end of the 1960s in which Denby participated.

Denby also thought that gender inequality was significant. He turned over two chapters of *Indignant Heart* to his wife Christine who wrote for *News & Letters* under the name Ethel Dunbar, and whose real name was Effie Owens (1912–1993) to speak for herself about what she faced as a working woman in the South and the North. Denby had touched on the gender question when telling of the first strike he led in Detroit's wartime industry to upgrade black women workers who were not permitted to work in the cleaner and less demanding sewing department in which white women worked.

Civil Rights Challenge to Labor

Over the 1956 Christmas holidays, Denby made a trip to Birmingham and Montgomery, Alabama, and was there for the first and second day of the court–ordered desegregation of public transportation.

Montgomery's black youth and workers, especially young black women workers, were the ones from whom Denby heard the first criticism of the Montgomery movement's leadership. It was a criticism that foreshadowed the formation of the Student Non–Violent Coordinating Committee (SNCC). Whatever Denby discussed with working people and youth in Montgomery, the conversation always rolled around to the leadership of the movement. The young and working people respected King, "but they have criticism in regard to his not going forward forcefully enough. They appreciate his looking for peaceful solutions. They don't oppose peaceful solutions. But, as many of them told me, 'If violence comes, we're not running away from it.'"

As a journalist Denby established in 1955 *News and Letters* to record the voices and struggles of common working people. The bus boycott organized by black working class Montgomery was barely two months old when Denby wrote: "There is need for a paper like *News and Letters.* The union papers and the Negro papers pretend to write about the same things, but the rank and file cannot and do not write and express themselves in those papers."

In the 1960s, United Auto Workers (UAW) president Walter Reuther was often the subject of Denby's attack on racial discrimination and its new economic basis in automation. The Chrysler Corporation's layoff of thousands of workers due to automation hit Denby's own Local 212 hard, resulting in Reuther cutting his staff. "Not one of the whites was cut off," wrote Denby in March 1963, "but the Negroes were, and came back into the shop." What most upset Denby, however, was that "For a worker to call this discrimination is considered a crime."

The UAW's silence on racial discrimination and the civil rights struggles then blanketing the country came home to affect the labor movement in another way at the end of 1963. In a series of articles he launched in the March 1963 issue of *News and Letters* entitled "Labor Must Clean Its Own House," Denby exposed the problem of discrimination in the labor movement. He held that racial discrimination constituted the real inner weakness of organized labor when it came to fighting the anti-labor assault of Congress and the corporations. So long as trade union leaders failed to clean their own house of discrimination, they were in no position to fight the anti-labor laws passed by Congress that affected all workers. In the same period, and often in the same articles, he wrote incisively of the changes in industrial production wrought by automation and black demands for civil rights.

As the social and political content of the black struggles of the 1960s deepened, Denby's call for labor and civil rights unity became a call for the movement to work out a total philosophy of liberation. By spring 1965 and the Selma–to–Montgomery march which passed through Lowndes County, Alabama, the labor movement did start to actively support the Civil Rights Movement.

Denby traveled to Lowndes County to report on the situation in the county's segregated schools and on the displacement of black sharecroppers from white–owned land because they dared to vote and had allowed civil rights marchers to camp on the land they worked. The June–July 1965 issue of *News and Letters* carried the first appeal for support of the Lowndes County movement, and announced the first meeting of former Lowndes Countians living in Detroit. The Lowndes County Christian Movement for Human Rights was begun by William Cosby and John Hulett following the Selma–to–Montgomery march in 1965.

The March 17, 1966, issue of *Jet* magazine carried an article about Charles Denby's efforts to organize support for the Lowndes County tent city entitled ''Factory Worker Helps Lowndes County Poor.'' A high point of Denby's political efforts in this period was his initiating and helping to organize a mass solidarity rally at Detroit's Cobo Hall, June 19, 1966, where Martin Luther King Jr. spoke. Part of the proceeds from the rally went to the Lowndes County tent city to buy land for displaced farmers and their families, and to provide them food, clothing, and shelter. Local unions collected 20 tons of food and clothing for the tent city residents. Through its fund raising efforts, the Lowndes County Association, headed by Denby, was able to purchase 200 acres of land in Lowndes County as a refuge for displaced farmers and their families. In 1967 there was a second fund raiser which together with a loan from the UAW completed the funds needed to purchase the land and aid the farmers.

This rich experience and social consciousness impelled Denby's entry into the ideological debates then emerging over the meaning of Black Power. Complaining that some exponents of Black Power dismissed the labor movement because it represented the solidarity of black and white workers, Denby reiterated the importance of the black and labor movements uniting.

At the Crossroads

As the vitality of the 1960s' Civil Rights Movement waned, its watershed reached with the assassination of Martin Luther King Jr. and the ensuing urban rebellions which swept the United States in 1968, a new stage of black labor militancy arose within the production process itself. New forms of organization appeared in 1968 with the spontaneous creation of black caucuses within industrial trade unions, especially within the UAW. Denby participated in these black workers' organizations, wrote about their developments in the pages of *News and Letters,* and provided space in the newspaper for workers to discuss and debate the issues the caucuses were fighting in the plants and in the union. He also edited one of the many shop newsletters generated by the black caucuses movement, the Chrysler Mack Avenue *Stinger.*

The event that began to determine a new manner of writing by Denby at this time, however, occurred in theory, not practice. The publication of Raya Dunayevskaya's work *Philosophy and Revolution,* in 1973, had a marked influence on Denby. In an August 1975 ''Worker's Journal'' column that also served as a lead article, ''Black intellectuals probe role of Marxism and American workers,'' Denby took up the debate then underway in the intellectual journal, *Black Scholar,* on nationalism, separatism, and Marxism. The black workers Denby spoke to about the debate dismissed it as remote from the new onslaught against labor that capitalism was just beginning to unleash with the decline of heavy industry and restructuring.

Denby understood, painfully, the consequences of the ideological pitfalls that led to the demise of the black caucus movement on the threshold of the most far–reaching economic restructuring of capitalist production relations in this century. He believed that the ideological and the economic were linked. The radical challenge by labor to capital spearheaded by young black workers calling themselves revolutionaries, and the potential it had to call forth the rank–and–file militancy of white labor, had so threatened industrial capitalism that it could not possibly have regained its equilibrium without the aid of the union bureaucracy. Once the ideological battle waged by the union leadership against this worker militancy succeeded with the discrediting and defeat of the black caucuses, capitalist restructuring commenced its great industrial purge of black labor in the decade of the mid–1970s to the mid–1980s.

The ensuing mass unemployment of the black work force, and the alienation of the succeeding generation of young workers from the labor market, became a major concern of Denby's from the mid–1970s onward. On the one hand, he criticized the abstract discussion about nationalism among black radical intellectuals, when black and white workers were preoccupied with the question of forging a new unity to fight back against the industrial purges of black workers and the union concessions that paved the way for economic restructuring. On the other hand, the growing problem of black unemployment, which he thought was not properly understood by black intellectuals, was producing a militant spirit among the black working class, one, however, that was deeply alienated. What also deepened was the desire for more activism and the notion that it alone would bring change. ''It isn't so,'' Denby explained at an editorial board meeting of *News and Letters,* June 15, 1975. He said: ''But we have to know that the unemployed are desperate and they want to upset the whole system, and when they can't have the revolution now, they can become disillusioned unless we make it clear that working out the philosophy is also the way to revolution. We have to find a way to work out philosophy as it relates to our daily lives.''

Denby strove tirelessly to have black working people and intellectuals engage Dunayevskaya's work. As early as 1969, four years before *Philosophy and Revolution* was published, he and News and Letters Committees convened a ''Black–Red Conference'' in Detroit of black workers, activists and intellectuals, along with Marxist–Humanists, to discuss the work–in–progress Dunayevskaya presented on the book at the conference.

At the time of the 1978 publication of the second, expanded edition of his autobiography, now entitled *Indignant Heart: A Black Worker's Journal,* after the name of his *News and Letters* column, Denby told readers of the December 1978 issue of the paper that workers' own ideas have always been weapons in the class struggle once the intellectuals recognized that ''workers think their own thoughts . . . [and] understand their type of revolt, their type of organization, and their philosophy,'' none of which is separated in the minds of the workers.

Although Denby retired from Chrysler in 1973, he continued to write his ''Worker's Journal'' column. He also continued to write on the need for international solidarity with the freedom struggles in other lands, such as the workers' Solidarity movement in Poland and the Black Consciousness movement in South Africa.

Although the proletarian scope of Charles Denby's thought reached globally to solidarize with all the liberation struggles of his times, he never abandoned his deep–rootedness in the ongoing struggles in his native South. Whether it was the struggle against exploitative conditions of labor in sweated industries like textiles, garment, meat processing, and light manufacturing, or against the unscrupulous financial practices of whites trying to appropriate black–owned land, Denby's heart and mind never left the South.

Never one for taking the latest appearances of the white backlash or retrogression on race matters as the leading characteristic of a historic period, Denby never let go of what the civil rights and labor movements had achieved, especially regarding the transformation of social relations and consciousness among working people. For Denby, anything won through arduous struggle and often in blood could not be easily rolled back. So, even as he recognized the latest expressions of racial and class oppression, or trade union concessions, he also found evidence of continuing militancy. His favorite expression for this condition of historical ambiguity was that the movement had arrived at a ''crossroads.''

If the test for white labor was to get behind the facade of Reagan's smile, the test for African Americans was to get behind the facade of black political power. Denby believed that ''No one can take away from the greatness of the Civil Rights Movement of the 1960s in Lowndes County and all across the South. . . . But what we have to see in 1982 is how much more total a revolution is needed to get to freedom. Whenever the movement is not complete, a way is left for the old oppressors to get back in. That is what the white system is doing behind black faces today. Instead of ruling by KKK terror, they are strangling black farmers and workers economically.''

Meeting the crises in the black and labor movements in what would be the last months of his life meant rising to the stature of a new level of articulating the meaning of his life and struggles. Denby died on October 10, 1983, after battling cancer for nearly a decade. The newspaper of which he had been editor since its founding in 1955 carried a full front–page in memoriam article by Raya Dunayevskaya. That same November 1983 issue of *News and Letters* published the very last column Denby wrote, it also announced the November 6th memorial meeting to honor Denby by his long time comrades, fellow workers, labor historians, as well as his life–long comrade and companion Ethel Dunbar, and Rosa Parks and Raya Dunayevskaya.

REFERENCES

Denby, Charles. ''Black Caucuses in the Unions.'' *American Civilization on Trial.* Detroit: *News and Letters,* 1983.

———. *Indignant Heart: A Black Worker's Journal.* Detroit: Wayne State University Press, 1989.

Dunayevskaya, Raya. *Marxist–Humanism: A Half–Century of ItsWorld Development.* Vols. 13 and 14 of the *Raya Dunayevskaya Collection* housed in the Wayne State University Archives of Labor and Urban Affairs, Walter P. Reuther Library. Detroit: Graphic Services, 1988–1989.

Foner, Philip S. *Organized Labor and the Black Worker, 1619–1981.* New York: International Publishers, 1982.

Grigsby, Daryl Russell. *For the People: Black Socialists in the United States, Africa and the Caribbean.* San Diego: Asante Publications, 1987.

Harris, William H. *The Harder We Run: Black Workers Since the Civil War.* New York: Oxford University Press, 1982.

Jones, Jacqueline. *The Dispossessed: America's Underclass from the Civil War to the Present.* New York: Basic Books, 1992.

Peterson, Joyce Shaw. ''Black Automobile Workers in Detroit, 1910–1930.'' *Journal of Negro History* 64 (3) (Summer 1979): 176–90.

Thomas, Richard W. ''The Black Urban Experience in Detroit: 1916–1967.'' In *Blacks and Chicanos in Urban Michigan.* Lansing: Michigan Historical Commission, 1979.

Turner, Lou. *Charles Denby, the Idea of Marxist–Humanism, and the Needed American Revolution.* Chicago: News and Letters, 1997.

Lou Turner

Oscar S. DePriest

(1871–1951)

Businessman, politician, congressman

Oscar DePriest rose from humble beginnings as the son of former slaves in Alabama to become the first black congressman from the North and the first elected in the twentieth century. His humble origins allowed him to reach out to black voters and rouse their enthusiastic support. He also applied his native intelligence to his real estate business. For many years he was a major force in local politics in Chicago.

Oscar Stanton DePriest was born in Florence, Alabama, on March 9, 1871, to Alexander R. and Mary Karsner DePriest. Alexander DePriest was a farmer and teamster who was active in the Republican party during the Reconstruction era. He was a small but fiery man. His son was six feet tall and weighed 200 pounds as an adult—a heritage from Mary DePriest, who worked as a laundress and played an important role in making decisions for the family. Oscar DePriest had sandy hair, blue eyes, and a light complexion.

A friend and supporter of black congressman James T. Rapier, Alexander DePriest forestalled an attempt to kidnap Rapier in 1968. Shortly after Rapier's narrow escape, a white Republican politician was shot by white Alabamans near the DePriest cabin. Because of the violent and repressive racial climate, the DePriest family moved to Salina, Kansas, about 1878 when Oscar was seven.

Oscar DePriest had begun his schooling in a school sponsored by the Congregational Church school before he left Alabama. As an adult he was a Presbyterian (there were close connections between the two churches in the nineteenth century, reflected in the joint American Home Missionary Society). In Salina there was only one other black family, and the DePriest children entered the all–white school. Oscar DePriest studied business and bookkeeping at the County Normal School for two years. DePriest was intelligent and shrewd but as an adult made grammatical mistakes and retained elements of a nonstandard accent. He was very good at calculation, but his limited formal education marked him off from the older and usually highly educated elites in Chicago.

Establishes Himself in Chicago

DePriest arrived in Chicago in 1889—the previous year he had run away to Dayton, Ohio, with two white companions. In Chicago, he became a painter and decorator, trades practiced by his uncles. At first he often found work as a white and then lost the job when his racial identity was discovered. Finally, he went into business for himself as a housepainter and decorator. DePriest got his start in politics around the turn of the century when he attended a meeting held to elect a precinct captain. The vote was evenly split. To break the tie, DePriest offered to vote for one of the candidates in return for a political favor. The candidate was elected, and DePriest, in turn, became secretary.

DePriest was an unimpressive orator, but he developed great organizational skills. As he devoted his time to politics, he also founded a family. He married Jessie Williams on February 23, 1898. Their only child, Oscar Stanton Jr., was born on May 24, 1906. DePriest's first political nomination came in 1904. In exchange for his support of Congressman Martin B. Madden, the Republican political boss of the First Congressional District, DePriest was nominated for a position on the county board of commissioners and won election. DePriest won a second term in 1906, but in 1908 he backed a faction opposed to Madden and was denied the nomination.

Oscar S. DePriest

He did manage to become an alternate delegate to the Republican National Convention.

At this time the pace of black migration to Chicago was increasing, and DePriest turned his attention to real estate. He built up his wealth by leasing buildings formerly occupied by whites and in turn leasing to blacks at sharply inflated rents—twice what the earlier tenants were paying. In politics DePriest maintained his organizational work and waited for black political fortunes to rise. The increase in black population, which was bringing him wealth, also increased black political power.

DePriest planned his 1914 campaign for political office carefully and won the backing of Madden and the Republican organization. After 1908 DePriest appears to have been constant in his support of Madden but opportunistic in his support of other candidates. As a result he won election as Chicago's first black alderman in 1915. He supported Mayor Bill Thompson, introduced a civil rights ordinance, and took care of his constituents, but his record did not find favor in the eyes of civic reformers. In particular, DePriest was going along with black underworld figures like Robert Motts, owner of the Pekin Theater, who was heavily involved in gambling, prostitution, and liquor violations. DePriest had to deny in 1916 that he received money to allow the Panama Cafe, another underworld haven, to open and continue to operate. In January of 1917 DePriest was indicted for conspiracy to allow gambling and prostitution and for bribery of police officers. During the trial in June, DePriest admitted he had received money from Henry "Teenan" Jones, owner of the Elite nightclub and a gambler, but claimed that it was a campaign contribution for Republican candidates. He won acquittal in that trial but faced six more indictments, which were not dropped for several years. Denied the Republican aldermanic nomination in 1918, he ran as an independent and narrowly lost the 1919 election. DePriest realigned himself with rival black political leader Edward H. Wright and his faction, which had proved too strong to oppose. DePriest's reward was to become a delegate to the 1920 Republican National Convention.

During the Chicago race riots in the summer of 1919, DePriest won a reputation for physical bravery. Accounts connected him with making repeated trips into the stockyards to rescue black workers trapped inside. Another account described him crossing through a hostile white neighborhood to bring meat to black neighborhoods.

In 1921 part of the old Second Ward became part of the Third Ward. This gradual shift of the black population eventually gave DePriest firm control of the Third Ward. Initially, however, he faced bombings of his property and had to struggle against white ward leaders. In 1923 DePriest threw his support to Democratic mayoral candidate William E. Dever. Dever won the election and gave DePriest some patronage. In that year DePriest also began to position himself as a candidate to replace Madden once he left his Congressional seat.

The following year DePriest again shifted factional alliances. He broke with Wright and announced his support for the reelection of Thompson as mayor in the race scheduled for 1923. The DePriest organization lost in the alderman election. It seemed that DePriest's political fortunes had dissipated.

DePriest was no quitter, however. He continued to work and maintain his position as a ward leader. Thus, he was able to respond when political alignments changed once again. In 1926 Thompson won reelection as mayor and aided DePriest to become informal head of the Third Ward Republican organization. In 1928 DePriest was a candidate for election as Third Ward committeeman and for selection as a delegate to the Republican National Convention. He supported Madden's renomination to Congress in the primary although William L. Dawson, later a Democratic congressman, was also running. Dawson said the heavily black first district should be represented by an African American.

Wins Election to Congress

Madden died April 27, 1928, shortly after the primary. DePriest moved fast and secured the nomination before other aspirants were aware. DePriest faced an independent candidate in the person of the white assistant state attorney general Harry Baker, who denounced him for his connections with racketeers. In addition, DePriest was indicted by a Special Grand Jury investigating election fraud on October 9. The prosecution later declined to act in the case, which was dismissed a few days before a special session of Congress convened in April of 1929. The election from a normally Republican district was close; DePriest's victorious plurality was slightly under 4,000 votes, some 10,000 less than Madden's total in the previous elections.

Skillful maneuvering by Republican politicians prevented any challenge to DePriest's swearing in on April 15, 1929, and he thus became the first black congressman since George L. White of North Carolina decided he had no chance of reelection in 1900 and left Congress after the lame duck session of 1901. DePriest was also the first black congressman elected from a Northern state. As the only African American in Congress, he naturally became a national symbol. Her husband won service for himself in the House restaurant but in 1934 discovered that a new directive denied service to any other black, even members of his own staff. Despite his vigorous efforts, he could not effect a change. Hubbub also arose about whether DePriest's wife would be invited to Mrs. Herbert Hoover's teas for congressional wives. Despite the objections of many Southerners, Jessie Williams DePriest did have tea with the president's wife.

After his election DePriest was in great demand as a speaker and showed great courage in refusing to be intimidated into giving up engagements in the South. As a freshman congressman faced with the stock market crash and the Great Depression, he busied himself in watching out for the interests of black Americans and introduced a few bills and amendments. DePriest easily won nomination for reelection in April of 1930, winning the subsequent general election by some 12,000 votes. He won publicity by threatening to hold up organization of the following Congress unless some action was taken against job discrimination in the South. DePriest's greatest single legislative achievement was probably his amendment to the 1933 bill establishing the Civilian Conservation Corps. The antidiscrimination amendment for the corps survived the legislative process and became the law of the land.

As a rock–ribbed Republican, DePriest opposed federal aid for the jobless until the dire conditions in his own district forced the reversal of his position in the winter of 1932. He was consistently opposed to President Roosevelt's emergency aid measures. DePriest was also a vocal anti–Communist who proposed a special House committee to investigate the spread of communism, but this proposed forerunner of the notorious House Un–American Activities Committee did not come into existence. Still he sprang to the defense of Howard University president Mordecai Johnson, who in 1933 was accused by detractors of being a communist on the grounds of remarks published in the *Chicago Defender.*

In 1932 DePriest prevailed over a well–organized attempt to deny him renomination to Congress. DePriest's victory enabled him to add control of the Second Ward organization to his base in the Third Ward. The following year his primary opponent left the Chicago City Council, making way for the election of William L. Dawson, one of DePriest's lieutenants.

In 1934 a factional quarrel between Dawson and another lieutenant in the organization weakened DePriest, who supported Dawson, who narrowly missed election as Second Ward committeeman. In the fall election DePriest had to face a light-skinned black Democrat for the first time. Arthur W. Mitchell, a resident of Chicago for only six years, attracted white voters and enough of the black vote to defeat DePriest in the Democratic landslide of that year. Mitchell, who ended DePriest's congressional career after three terms, was the first black Democrat elected to Congress.

DePriest resumed his real estate business in Chicago but continued his interest in politics. He tried to unseat Arthur W. Mitchell in 1936. His political fortunes had declined, however, with the massive shift of black voters from the Republican to the Democratic Party during the Great Depression. In 1943 he won election to the Chicago City Council. During his service on the council DePriest led efforts to establish fair employment standards. His defeat in the 1947 election was attributed to his support of an unpopular Democratic mayor.

DePriest was not a great orator: opponents said he sounded as if his mouth was full of pancakes. Still people listened, and his size made him stand out in crowds. As a political leader DePriest was opportunistic and not bound by principle or loyalty to party or person. He could even set aside his appeals for race representation to support a white candidate against a black. DePriest had great skill in appealing to black voters, who found it easy to believe he shared their views and their humble beginnings. DePriest's coarseness and bombast were part of his appeal to them. He also worked hard at politics. In addition, he was forceful in asserting the rights of blacks.

The *Chicago Defender* gave an example of his frank furtherance of black rights in its front-page article of May 19, 1951, on DePriest's death. A white superintendent of West Point specifically asked for a white boy to replace a black candidate who had washed out of the academy. DePriest responded, "No sir! I'll not send a white boy until a Negro is graduated. If need be, I'll send them bigger and blacker each time until you military people finally make up your minds to let one graduate." (The appointee was Benjamin O. Davis Jr.) Another article in the same edition of the *Defender* talked of his beating up a white politician who reneged on a promise. The article also summed up part of his appeal as a leader: "Perhaps more than any DePriest had the common touch. In his anger, he acted like the least restrained of his followers. In what he felt was due his people, face of need [sic], he moved with unswerving determination."

DePriest died May 12, 1951, in Provident Hospital in Chicago of a kidney ailment. He had entered the hospital after being struck by a bus. He was survived by his wife, son, grandson, and five sisters. After services in the Metropolitan Community Church, he was buried in Graceland Cemetery.

DePriest was not a pioneer in black involvement in Chicago politics, but he was very effective in building on foundations laid by others. His political fortunes were aided by the movement of blacks from the South to northern cities. His election to Congress marked the beginning of the black breakthrough in the politics of northern urban areas. A man with the common touch, he became a symbol for blacks throughout the United States when he entered an institution which had been lily-white for some 28 years. He was a ray of hope in the political gloom on the national scene caused by the failure of Reconstruction.

REFERENCES

Christopher, Maurine. *America's Black Congressmen.* New York: Thomas Y. Crowell, 1971.

Clayton, Edward T. *The Negro Politician.* Chicago: Johnson Publishing, 1964.

Day, David S. "Herbert Hoover and Racial Politics: The DePriest Incident." *Journal of Negro History* 65 (Winter 1980): 6–17.

"Death of Oscar DePriest Marks End of Era of Fighting Leaders." *Chicago Defender,* May 19, 1951.

Drake, St. Clair, and Horace C. Cayton. *Black Metropolis.* New York: Harcourt, Brace, 1945. Rev. and enlarged ed. 2 vols., New York: Harper and Row, 1962.

Gosnell, Harold F. *Negro Politicians.* Chicago: University of Chicago Press, 1935.

Logan, Rayford W., and Michael R. Winston, eds. *Dictionary of American Negro Biography.* New York: Norton, 1982.

Mann, Kenneth Eugene. "Oscar Stanton DePriest: Persuasive Agent for the Black Masses." *Negro History Bulletin* 35 (October 1972): 134–137.

"Oscar DePriest, 80, Dies in Coma." *Chicago Defender,* May 19, 1951.

Spear, Allan H. *Black Chicago.* Chicago: University of Chicago Press, 1967.

Who's Who in Colored America. New York: Who's Who in Colored America, 1940.

Robert L. Johns

R. Nathaniel Dett

(1882–1943)

Musician, composer, educator

R. Nathaniel Dett was one of the most noted and influential African American musicians of the early 1900s. Dett was Canadian born, a second-generation descendant of runaway slaves. He earned critical acclaim as an accomplished pianist and performed concerts to diverse audiences throughout the United States and Canada. Dett was a highly respected professor of music and a choral director; he left a legacy of musical excellence with each of the institutions of higher education at which he taught. Dett is best remembered today as a talented composer and arranger of piano, vocal, and choral works, many of which are based upon African American folk melodies.

Robert Nathaniel Dett was born in Drummondville, Ontario, on October 11, 1882. His parents were Robert Tue Dett and Charlotte Johnson Dett. Nathaniel was the youngest of four children, after Samuel, Arthur, and Harriet. Neither Arthur nor Harriet lived to adulthood. Arthur, at the age of nine, was accidentally shot and killed during a Halloween prank, and Harriet became ill and died at the age of only two years old. Dett's parents separated by the time he was 14.

Robert Dett, Nathaniel's father, a rather colorful character reputed to be a "man about town," was neither a guiding nor a constant figure in his son's life. Nathaniel did however continue a very close, loving relationship with his mother whom he admired and respected very much.

Both of Dett's parents were fond of music and each had some musical background, but it was Nathaniel's mother who encouraged and supported his early musical growth. Charlotte Dett recognized her son's musical ability early on and saw to Nathaniel's musical training.

Although Dett worked when he was still in high school, he also found time for his music. He spent time practicing, played the piano for social events and for church, and composed songs in addition to his job. Dett's rapid progress at piano technique was owed to his good ear and natural ability, which was also blamed for his relatively slow grasp of note reading. Dett was nonetheless fueled by a desire to play the works of the great masters, such as Bach, Beethoven, and Brahms, and he especially wished to fulfill his own compositional desires—all of which spurred him to correct this impediment early on. Dett's first published compositions were two short piano pieces, both written before he was in college: "After the Cakewalk" was published in 1900, and "Cave of the Winds March" in 1902.

After completing high school, Dett attended Oberlin University in Oberlin, Ohio, from 1903 to 1908. There he pursued a double major in piano and composition. While at Oberlin, Dett supported himself by performing around that locale as well as near his home. He also was employed as a choir director. Dett was fortunate enough to have had a wealthy benefactor—a businessman by the name of Frederick H. Goff. Goff was the first of a long list of many such patrons who helped support Dett through his college years. Upon his graduation, Dett dedicated several works to Goff and his wife.

While at Oberlin, Dett became inspired by the music of his black heritage, specifically the songs of the slaves of the South, songs that had in the past caused him embarrassment. He came to appreciate the emotionally evocative African American folksong melodies heard in works by composers like Antonin Dvorak. Dett later recalled the experience of hearing the slow movement of Dvorak's *American Quartet,* about which he wrote in *The Etude*: "Suddenly it seemed I

R. Nathaniel Dett

heard again the frail voice of my long departed grandmother calling cross the years; and in a rush of emotion which stirred my spirit to its very center, the meaning of the songs which had given her soul such peace was revealed to me."

In time Dett experienced a "spiritual renaissance," a pivotal revelation that shaped the rest of his life as a composer and musician, after which he was compelled and inspired to learn to integrate successfully African American folk melodies into the fabric of his own work. Dett graduated from Oberlin in 1908 as a Phi Beta Kappa with a bachelor of music degree in piano and composition. At graduation he received highest honors for his compositions.

In the fall of 1908, Dett accepted a faculty position at Lane College in Jackson, Tennessee. At Lane College he taught piano and voice, and was director of the choir. Dett also continued to concertize extensively throughout the state. While on the faculty at Lane, Dett made the acquaintance of E. Azalea Hackley, a well–connected and influential singer, lecturer, and voice teacher, then living in Philadelphia. Hackley, herself a performer, promoted the careers of talented young African American musicians, among them Dett, Harry T. Burleigh, and Clarence Cameron White. The professional association between Dett and Hackley was a long and mutually beneficial one.

In the fall of 1911 Dett accepted a teaching position at Lincoln Institute (now Lincoln University) in Jefferson City, Missouri, lured by a raise in salary and the promise of better conditions. At Lincoln Institute, Dett taught voice classes and gave piano lessons. According to Dett's own account, his stay at Lincoln was a pleasant one; he was well liked and respected by students and faculty. Also while at Lincoln, Dett completed his first important compositions, two suites for the piano, both of which were published by Summy–Birchard. The first suite, a set of five pieces entitled *Magnolia Suite* was published in 1912. The second suite, entitled *In the Bottoms* was published in 1913 and includes the very popular ''Juba Dance.'' Both works were performed often by Dett and other noted concert artists of all races. *In the Bottoms* which was a particular favorite of the legendary pianist and composer Percy Grainger.

At Hampton Institute

In 1913 Nathaniel Dett accepted a position as an instructor of music at Hampton Institute (later Hampton University) in Hampton, Virginia. Dett's stay at Hampton was the longest of any of his teaching positions. Moreover, this period of Dett's life was punctuated by creative productivity and milestone achievements. Dett, who was recommended for the position by his colleague E. Azalea Hackley, immersed himself in his duties of piano teacher, vocal instructor, teacher of theory and composition, and choir director, and all the while he continued to concertize.

Dett put a particularly immense amount of effort into the continued development of the choral program at Hampton Institute. Under his direction, the Hampton Institute Choir, the Hampton Quartet, the Men's Glee Club, and the Women's Chorus achieved a consistently high level of performance excellence. Their performances before capacity crowds across the United States and in Europe were repeatedly documented by rave reviews. In 1914 Dett also established a short–lived civic choral group in Hampton called the Choral Union. Concerts by the Choral Union were generally well attended and featured some of the nation's finest African American singers as soloists, including Roland Hayes and Harry T. Burleigh. Financial problems eventually forced the dissolution of that group after only six years. Dett composed his most famous choral work, ''Listen to the Lambs'' in 1914. One of only a handful of Dett choral works still performed, ''Listen to the Lambs'' is a favorite of choirs the world over.

A desire for further musical study took Dett to Columbia University and to Northwestern in 1915. In Chicago Dett met the renowned Australian pianist, Percy Grainger. Over the years Grainger remained a supporter of Dett and his work. Grainger included compositions by Dett in his own recital repertoire. In appreciation, Dett dedicated several of his works to Grainger, including a piano suite entitled *Enchantment,* published in 1922, a programmatic suite whose four movements were originally published separately.

Dett married Helen Elise Smith in December of 1916. Helen was an accomplished pianist and musician from New York who also had an impressive musical background, having graduated with honors from what is now the Juilliard School of Music. She was eventually appointed to the music faculty of Hampton as a piano teacher and accompanist. The marriage produced two daughters, Helen Charlotte Elise, born in 1918, and Josephine Elizabeth, born in 1922.

Work Wins Recognition

During his years at Hampton, Dett's service to the institution and his own musical growth are evidenced by an impressive number of accomplishments and personal honors. In 1919 Dett founded Hampton's Musical Arts Society which sponsored a yearly recital series in the campus's Ogden Hall. In the same year Dett helped to found the National Association of Negro Musicians (NANM). He became the organization's president in 1924 and served until 1926. Dett took a leave of absence from Hampton from 1919 to 1920 to study at Harvard University. While there Dett received two major honors: the Bowdoin Literary Prize for his essay, ''The Emancipation of Negro Music,'' and the Francis Boott Prize for his composition, ''Don't Be a Weary, Traveler.''

Dett returned to Hampton and was appointed the director of music in 1926. As director, Dett established scholarships for many of Hampton's deserving students. In the summer of 1929 Nathaniel traveled abroad to study composition with the internationally renowned Nadia Boulanger. However, foremost among Dett's achievements were the continued successes of the various Hampton Institute Choirs in their performances nationwide, and one history–making European concert tour in 1930 under the direction of Dett.

Under Dett's leadership, Hampton choirs developed a far–reaching reputation for the quality and versatility of their performances. Surviving concert brochures and critical reviews attest that Dett's choirs performed some of the most sophisticated art–music ever written in a choral repertory adapted from all periods of music history. Their arrangements of Negro spirituals, as adapted by Dett and other composers, were interpreted with polish and appropriate sensitivity. In 1928 the Hampton Choir made its Carnegie Hall debut. They received critical acclaim and attracted the attention of such important figures as George Foster Peabody, who remained a valued supporter of Dett and the Hampton Institute.

With the financial assistance of George Peabody, John D. Rockefeller, and other Hampton trustees and friends, Nathaniel Dett took the Hampton Institute Choir, three chaperons, and his mother on a six week European Concert tour in the spring of 1930. The tour, hailed as a critical success, covered seven countries: England, Holland, Belgium, France, Germany, Switzerland, and Austria. Reporters in the United States and Europe chronicled the warm reception received by the choir as well as the outstanding quality of the performances.

Dett himself published two insightful accounts of the choir's travels abroad. The first, entitled ''A Musical Invasion of Europe, the Hampton Choir Abroad'' was published in *Crisis* in December of 1930. The second, ''From Bell Stand to Throne Room,'' appeared in *Etude* in February of 1934. Following the European tour, the choir was in greater demand than ever. During the year that ensued, the Hampton Choir performed in leading concert halls in cities across America: Boston, New York, Chicago, Cincinnati, St. Louis, and Washington, D.C., to name only a few.

Writes Extended Works and Collections

The bulk of Dett's vocal and choral works were written during his years at Hampton. His commitment to "elevating the Negro spiritual and folksong to a high level," as noted by Ann K. Simpson in *Follow Me,* was evidenced in his many art–songs, piano pieces, and choral works which improvise on the melodies of slave songs and other musical idioms identifiable with African American culture.

Most notable among Dett's choral works, in addition to "Listen to the Lambs," are two large–scale works plus two volumes of spirituals. "Chariot Jubilee," written in 1919, uses the Negro spiritual "Swing Low Sweet Chariot" as a foundation. Best described as an extended work, *Chariot Jubilee* is scored for tenor solo, chorus, piano, organ, and orchestra. Dett's oratorio, *The Ordering of Moses,* was written between 1931 and 1932 as his final project for a master's degree at the Eastman School of Music. However, it was not published or performed publicly until several years later. The spiritual "Go Down Moses" is the main theme for the oratorio that is scored for five soloists, chorus, and orchestra.

Dett edited a collection of African American folksongs in 1926, which was published a year later as *Religious Folksongs of the Negro as Sung at Hampton Institute.* The 165 songs of this volume are predominantly a capella arrangements of familiar, and not so familiar, spirituals and other folk songs of the American slaves. Of them Dett wrote in *Religious Folksongs*: "[I]t was a religious 'urge' born of great experience which gave rise to these songs." Ten years later Dett in a four volume set entitled *The Dett Collection of Negro Spirituals* published his own arrangements of many of the spirituals found in the earlier anthology. The more recent volumes contain chorus and solo arrangements, some with accompaniment and others without. Dett also included insightful essays on the spiritual as a music form in the preface of these volumes.

In 1931 Dett took a leave of absence from Hampton to study at the Eastman School of Music in Rochester, New York. He never returned to the Hampton faculty. Dett resigned his position at the request of the institute's new president, Arthur Howe, in 1932. That same year Dett received a master of music degree from Eastman, and moved his family to Rochester where for the next several years he remained active as a composer, piano recitalist, lecturer, and teacher. During that time, Dett organized and conducted the Negro Community Chorus of Rochester, and was very active in the city's chapter of the National Association for the Advancement of Colored People (NAACP). For a short stint in 1935 he was a visiting professor of music at Sam Houston College in Austin Texas.

The year 1937 was a one of triumph and tragedy for Dett. The Cincinnati premier of his oratorio, *The Ordering of Moses,* written five years earlier while at Eastman, was a huge success, initiating a string of performances by leading choruses in major cities across the country. Also in that same year, Dett accepted the position of director of music at Bennett College in Greensboro, North Carolina. The year was marred, however, by the death of Dett's beloved mother, Charlotte.

Final Years

At Bennett College, a school for women of color, Dett was director of music and his duties included the directorship of the college choir. Under his leadership, the Bennett Women's Choir toured annually all over the United States, receiving accolades for their musical excellence. The Bennett choir also made appearances on a nationally broadcast CBS radio series in the early 1940s.

During his years at Bennett, Dett continued to compose and arrange music for piano, voice, and chorus. *Eight Bible Vignettes,* a programmatic piano suite based on texts from the Old and New Testaments, was written and each vignette was published separately during the years from 1941 to 1943. Dett also arranged a set of six concert spirituals for one of his more talented pupils from Hampton, singer Dorothy Maynor. Maynor went on to become a successful concert artist. The six solos—"Ride on King Jesus," "I'm Goin' to Thank God," "Go On Brother, I'm Trav'ling to the Grave," "Now Take This Feeble Body," "What Kind of Shoes You Going to Wear?" and "In That Morning"—were published during the years from 1940 to 1943.

Understandably, most of Dett's choral compositions during those years as well as many arrangements of his previous works were adapted for women's voices. "The Lamb," a three part a capella chorus, and Dett's very satisfying setting of the Isaac Watts text "When I Survey the Wondrous Cross" for four part women's choir (also a capella), stand out among Dett's compositions while he taught at Bennett.

Dett resigned from his position at Bennett College in 1942 and returned to Rochester where he continued to compose, perform, teach, and conduct. He toured briefly with the United Services Organizations (USO) in 1943, conducting a chorus of Women's Army Corps singers.

Dett suffered a series of heart attacks in the fall of 1943, and he died on October 2 of that year. When the news of Dett's death spread throughout the musical communities of the United States, his colleagues, mentors, students, fans, and friends paused to mourn his passage and to pay tribute to his genius. A number of memorial services were held, most notably at Hampton, Bennett, and Niagara Falls. Dett's funeral was held in Rochester, New York, and he was buried in a family plot in a Niagara Falls cemetery.

During his lifetime Dett was the recipient of honorary doctorate degrees from Howard University and Oberlin College in 1924 and 1926, respectively. In 1927 he was listed in *Who's Who in Colored America.* Also in 1927, Dett received the Harmon Award for Creative Achievement in Music.

African American music and musicians owe a great deal of gratitude to R. Nathaniel Dett. Under the tutelage of Dett there developed a number of outstanding young black musicians, many of whom went on to become leaders and innovators in music education, performance, and composition. Among these musicians are Dorothy Maynor, the famous concert singer, and Noah F. Ryder, a prominent music educator. Moreover, Dett forced the world to appreciate African American musicians in their own right, as legitimate artists of substance and sophistication. He also embraced the music of his African American ancestry, the Negro spirituals from the culture of slavery. Dett incorporated them into the foundation of his most famous compositions, thus assuring that they would be preserved. Robert Nathaniel Dett should certainly be remembered for his many contributions to African American art–music.

REFERENCES

Abdul, Raoul. *Blacks in Classical Music: A Personal History.* New York: Dodd, Mead, 1977.

Brooks, Tilford. *America's Black Music Heritage.* Englewood Cliffs, NJ: Prentice–Hall, 1984.

DeLerma, Dominique–René. *Bibliography of Black Music Reference Materials.* Vol. I. Westport, CT: Greenwood Press, 1981.

———. *Black Music in Our Culture.* Kent, OH: Kent State University Press, 1970.

———. *Reflections on Afro–American Music.* Kent, OH: Kent State University Press, 1973.

———, and Vivian F. McBrier, eds. *The Collected Piano Works of R. Nathaniel Dett.* Evanston, IL: Summy–Birchard Company, 1973.

Dett, R. Nathaniel. *The Album of the Heart.* Jackson, TN: Mocowat–Mercer, 1911.

———. "As the Negro School Sings." *The Southern Workman* 56 (July 1927): 304–305.

———. "The Emancipation of Negro Music." *The Southern Workman* 47 (1918): 176–86.

———. "From Bell Stand to Throne Room." *The Etude* 52 (February 1934): 79–80.

———. "A Musical Invasion of Europe, the Hampton Choir Abroad." *Crisis* 37 (December 1930): 405–407, 428.

———. "Negro Music of the Present." *The Southern Workman* 47 (1918): 243–47.

———, ed. *Religious Folk–songs of the Negro as Sung at Hampton Institute.* Hampton, VA: Hampton University Press, 1927.

Gray, Arlene. *Listen to the Lambs: A Source Book of the R. Nathaniel Dett Materials in the Niagara Falls Public Library.* Crystal Beach, Ontario: A. E. Gray, 1984.

McBrier, Vivian Flagg. *R. Nathaniel Dett, His Life and Works.* Washington, DC: Associated Publishers, 1977.

Simpson, Ann Key. *Follow Me: the Life and Music of R. Nathaniel Dett.* Metuchen, NJ: Scarecrow Press, 1993.

Turner, Patricia. *Afro–American Singers: An Index and Preliminary Discography of Long–Playing Recordings of Opera, Choral Music and Song.* Minneapolis, MN: Challenge Productions, 1977.

———. *Dictionary of Afro–American Performers.* New York: Garland Publishing, 1990.

White, Evelyn Davidson. *Choral Music by Afro–American Composers.* Metuchen, NJ: Scarecrow Press, 1981.

COLLECTIONS

The papers of R. Nathaniel Dett are in the Niagara Falls Public Library; Hampton University Archives, Hampton, Virginia; the Moorland–Spingarn Research Center at Howard University, Washington, D.C.; Bennett College Library, Greensboro, North Carolina; and Oberlin College Archives, Oberlin, Ohio.

Leroy E. Bynum Jr.

Charles C. Diggs Jr.

(1922–1998)

Congressman, mortician, broadcast journalist

Charles C. "Charlie" Diggs Jr. has many impressive firsts to his credit. He was the first black member of Congress from Michigan (Thirteenth District); the founder and first chairman of the Congressional Black Caucus; and the first member of Congress to resign from the U.S. delegation to the United Nations General Assembly.

Diggs comes from a family that had been prominent in public life in Michigan for quite some time. Charles Diggs Sr., one of the wealthiest businessmen in Detroit's black community, was the proprietor of the *House of Diggs,* a successful mortuary, funeral insurance company, and ambulance service. He was also an important politician in Detroit during the 1920s and 1930s, and was one of the leaders of the exodus of black voters from the Republican to the Democratic Party. In 1937 the elder Diggs became the first black member of the Michigan House of Representatives to serve more than one term.

Charles Jr., the only child of Charles Sr. and Mamie Ethel Jones Diggs, was born on December 2, 1922. He was brought up to be very aware of his family's position in the Motor City's African American community. Over the years, the Diggs political machine had built up a great deal of support among black Detroiters by keeping in close touch with them; this strategy also served to protect the family's other political and economic interests. A pivotal moment in the younger Diggs's life occurred when his father was convicted of graft and sentenced to 15 months in prison. After serving his sentence, Diggs Sr. returned home to such strong support that he was reelected in the Michigan House of Representatives, but the Senate refused to seat him. It was this refusal by the Republican–controlled Michigan legislature to readmit Diggs Sr. that inspired his son to enter politics. While

Charles C. Diggs Jr.

a student in the Detroit College of Law in 1951, Diggs Jr. was elected to his father's old seat by a three–to–one majority. Diggs Jr. served in the Michigan State legislature from 1951 to 1954.

Diggs Jr. was educated in the Detroit public school system. He graduated in 1940 from Miller High School, where he displayed his skill as a debater. He once said that his talent for communicating began to develop in grade school when he won several spelling bees. Later on he became the oratorical champion of the University of Michigan in Ann Arbor, which he attended from 1940 to 1942. In fall 1942 he enrolled at Fisk University in Nashville, Tennessee, where he stayed for three months before being drafted into the U.S. Army on February 19, 1943.

In spite of the overt racism then rampant throughout the military, especially toward black officers, Diggs moved up quickly in rank from private to sergeant and was sent by the Army Air Corps to Officer's Candidate School in Miami. He received his commission as a second lieutenant and was appointed as a processing officer at what later became Maxwell Air Base near Montgomery, Alabama.

Diggs was discharged from service on June 1, 1945, and returned to school in September 1945 to complete his education at Detroit's Wayne College of Mortuary Science. He graduated as a licensed mortician in June 1946 and subsequently went into business with his father in the House of Diggs, Inc. Later he became a licensed mortician and chair of the firm's board. Around this same time his family began sponsoring a weekly program on a black radio station in Detroit. Diggs Jr. served as the host of the show, which featured gospel music and news about activities in Detroit's black community.

Political Career Launched

Diggs took courses at the University of Detroit School of Law in 1951–52. In August 1954 he was elected as a Democrat to Congress and was seated on January 3, 1955. In Congress Diggs also became prominent in the fight against racial discrimination. In September 1955 he went to Sumner, Mississippi, to observe the trial of the two white men accused of killing Emmett Till, a 14–year–old black youth, for whistling at a white woman. The men were acquitted, but Diggs, discovering that the county did not have a single registered black voter, proposed that Mississippi's representation in Congress should be reduced accordingly. He was reelected in November 1952 to a second two–year term in Congress.

The youngest of the three black members then seated in the U.S. House of Representatives when the Eighty–fourth Congress convened in January 1955, Diggs was assigned to the Committees on Interior and Insular Affairs and Veteran's Affairs. Commenting on the U.S. Supreme Court's ruling of May 31, 1955, that directed district courts to enforce desegregation in public schools as soon as practicable, he expressed his belief in the *New York Times* for July 15, 1955, that ''nothing would come of . . . Southern threats to abolish public schools rather than submit to integration.'' When the U.S. Fourth Circuit Court of Appeals ruled six weeks later that the same principle ''should be applied in cases involving transportation,'' Diggs proposed to the House Commerce subcommittee that it ''ban segregation practices at Federally–aided airports.'' Speaking at a state–wide meeting of the National Association for the Advancement of Colored People (NAACP) in Jackson, Mississippi, on May 19, 1957, as reported in the *New York Times* for May 20, 1957, Diggs concluded that ''integration is as inevitable as the rising sun—even in Mississippi.''

Diggs took on a number of other political responsibilities during the 1950s. In 1956, for instance, he served as a member of the platform and resolutions committee of the Democratic National Convention. And in May 1957 he had the honor of being part of the U.S. delegation headed by then Vice–President Richard Nixon to the inaugural ceremonies of the African nation of Ghana. In 1959 Diggs was founder and chairman of the Congressional Black Caucus.

Diggs became involved in an international political controversy in 1968 when the United Nations Security Council, including the U.S. representatives, voted to impose complete mandatory sanctions against all forms of trade with what was then known as Southern Rhodesia. President Johnson seconded this action with executive orders. Union Carbide and Foote Mineral, both of which operated chrome–producing mines in Southern Rhodesia, opposed the embargo. This eventually led to the Byrd Amendment (March 29, 1971),

Charles C. Diggs (left) shaking hands with Adam Clayton Powell Jr.

which allowed importation of ''strategic and critical material from any free world country for so long as the importation of like material from any communist country is not prohibited by law.'' Subcommittees of both the House and Senate held hearings and rejected the amendment. Byrd responded by attaching his amendment to the Military Procurement Bill, and it was passed as part of a $21 billion defense–spending package.

Diggs tried to rally opposition to the Byrd Amendment through a campaign of letters and phone calls. Soon an effort led by Minnesota Democrat Don Fraser was started in the House to repeal the amendment. As a result of the hearings, section 14 of the Foreign Assistance Act of 1972 was drafted. It restored presidential authority to prohibit or regulate the importation into the United States strategic materials from such countries as Southern Rhodesia when the United States was obligated to control or prohibit such importation as a consequence of the conditions of membership in the United Nations. Despite the efforts of Diggs and others, section 14 was struck down on a 252–140 vote, and the United States continued to buy Rhodesian chrome. In protest to America's sale of arms and transport planes to Portuguese and South African forces and the purchase of Rhodesian chrome by the Defense Department, Diggs resigned from the UN in December 1971.

A member of the Committee on the District of Columbia since 1963, Diggs played an important role in securing partial self–government status for the District as chair in 1972. President Nixon signed the District of Columbia Self–Government and Governmental Reorganization Act on December 24, 1973, that for the first time enabled the residents to elect a mayor and a city council.

On October 7, 1978, despite cries of racially–motivated selective justice, Diggs was convicted in the federal district court of 29 counts of mail fraud and false statements concerning payroll kickbacks from his congressional staff. On July 31, the House voted 414–0 to censure Diggs, an action that amounted to little more than a public scolding since it allowed him to retain his seat. By December Representative Peter Kostmayer (D–Pa.) was leading the move within the House Democratic Caucus to expel the black congressman. The full House voted not to expel Diggs by a margin of 322–77, with five representatives, including Black Caucus members Shirley Chisolm (D–N.Y.) and Augustus Hawkins (D–Calif.)

abstaining. On November 7, 1978, Diggs was reelected to his thirteenth term in the House with 81 percent of the vote. In 1980 he resigned his post after serving as a U.S. Representative for over 25 years. He has since returned to practicing mortuary science as the operator of a funeral home in Maryland.

Diggs was awarded an honorary degree of doctor of laws by Wilberforce University, Wilberforce, Ohio, in 1955. He is a Mason and Elk, member of the Cotillion Club, American Legion, Veterans of Foreign Wars, and a past president of the Metropolitan Funeral Association. His religious affiliation is Baptist.

Diggs has been married three times. He was divorced from his first wife, Juanita Rosario, in 1960; they had three children—Charles Cole III, Denise, and Alexis. His second wife, Anna Johnston, whom he married in 1960, worked in his Detroit office until 1971. That same year Diggs married his third wife, Janet Elaine Hall. He has three other children—Douglas, Carla, and Cindy. He died of a stroke on August 25, 1998.

REFERENCES

"Charles Cole Diggs, Jr." In *United States Black On–Line* internet service. http://www.usbol.com/etjournal/cdiggsbio.html (accessed June 1998).

Christopher, Maurine. *Black Americans in Congress.* New York: Crowell, 1976.

"Diggs Released from Prison." *New York Times,* March 7, 1981.

Garrett, Romeo B. *Famous First Facts about Negroes.* New York: Arno Press, 1972.

Hornsby, Alton. *Chronology of African–American History.* Detroit: Gale Research, 1991.

Parker, Pearl T. *A Political Activist: Charles Coles Diggs Jr., Michigan's First Black Congressman.* Nashville: Tennessee State University, 1984.

Report on U.S. Business in Southern Africa: Remarks of Hon. Charles C. Diggs, Jr., of Michigan in the House of Representatives. Washington, DC: Government Printing Office, 1975.

"Representative Diggs Sees South Winning." *New York Times,* May 20, 1957.

"Segregation on Buses is Barred by Federal Appeals Court Ruling." *New York Times,* July 15, 1955.

U.S. House of Representatives. *Committee on the District of Columbia.* Washington, DC: Government Printing Office, 1978.

———. Committee on the District of Columbia. *Unveiling of a Portrait of the Honorable Charles C. Diggs, Jr.: Chairman, Committee on the District of Columbia.* Washington, DC: Government Printing Office, 1974.

Who's Who among Black Americans. 2nd ed. Detroit: Gale Research, 1977.

Thura Mack

David N. Dinkins

(1927–)

Lawyer, public official, educator

Courtly, calm, cautious, deliberate, and always polite are the terms used most often to describe David Dinkins. These characteristics are not generally recognized as selling points in winning elections in New York City's rugged, rough politics. They did, however, help to overcome white New Yorkers' suspicions that David Dinkins lacked leadership qualifications and enabled him to be elected New York's mayor in 1989, the first African American to hold that position of power.

David Norman Dinkins was born on July 10, 1927, in Trenton, New Jersey, the older of the two children of William H. Dinkins and his wife, Sally. His father, initially a barber, became a real estate agent in 1962. His sister, Joyce, lives in a Trenton, New Jersey, suburb. Dinkins was six–years old when his parents divorced. He and his sister lived briefly with their mother in Harlem where Sally Dinkins worked as a domestic and later as a manicurist. They grew up mostly in a predominantly middle–class neighborhood in Trenton with their father and stepmother, Lottie Hartgell Dinkins, a high school English teacher, who encouraged them in their studies. Dinkins and his wife have two children, David Jr. and Donna Hoggerd, and two grandchildren, Jamal and Kalila Hoggard.

In school, "Dink," as he was called by his classmates, was ambitious and responsible even as a youngster. He earned money by delivering newspapers and doing odd jobs around the neighborhood. At one time, he sold shopping bags on 125th Street in Harlem. He graduated from a segregated junior high school in Trenton. His leadership qualities surfaced when he was elected president of his high school homeroom class in 1943, winning over his white classmate. No stranger to institutional racism at the time, the predominantly white Trenton High School even barred blacks from the swimming pool. After graduation from high school in 1945, he tried to enlist in the Marine Corps but was rejected because the "Negro quota" was filled.

Dinkins was then drafted into the U.S. Army, but later he transferred to the marines, spending most of his 13–month military service at Camp Lejeune, North Carolina. Once, while on military leave and returning from Washington, D.C., he was denied one of two remaining seats on a bus, even though he was in uniform. The memory of that episode still angers him. Later on he brought to his job as mayor of New York a personal knowledge of the ravages of racism and empathy for those who suffer oppression.

Honorably discharged from the service in August of 1946 and making use of the G.I. Bill, Dinkins enrolled in Howard University, where he majored in mathematics and graduated magna cum laude in 1950. Awarded a mathematics fellowship to Rutgers University, he grew restless, dropping out after attending only one semester. He then sold insurance

David N. Dinkins

for a firm in Red Bank, New Jersey, and became one of its top salesmen. In 1953 he entered Brooklyn Law School. On August 30 of that year, he married his college sweetheart, Joyce Burrows, the daughter of Daniel Burrows, the state assemblyman from Harlem who introduced him to politics. While in law school, he worked nights in his father–in–law's liquor store in Harlem.

After receiving his law degree in 1956, Dinkins joined the firm of Dyett and Phipps, reconstituted the following year as Dyett, Alexander, and Dinkins. He remained there until 1971, when he went into law practice with Basil Paterson, then the vice–chairman of the Democratic National Committee. At the Dyett firm, Dinkins had a modest neighborhood practice involving banking, probate, and real estate matters. Meanwhile, he developed a reputation as a skilled mediator.

Public Service Career Begins

Dinkins eventually complied with the wishes of his wife's father, who introduced him to J. Raymond Jones, nicknamed the ''Harlem Fox'' and the leader of the Carver Democratic Club. The organization was the training ground for young black business and political leaders. The club was well entrenched within the city's power structure. Dinkins became a cog in a powerful political machine, doing all kinds of footwork such as hanging posters at Harlem subway stops, searching out unregistered voters, and other necessary activities that are part of every campaign. J. Raymond Jones recognized Dinkins's ambition and made Dinkins his protégé. With Jones's support, he started on his career in public service with his election to the New York State Assembly in 1966. After Dinkins's district was redrawn, he chose not to run again at the end of his two–year term. In 1967, he succeeded his mentor as district leader of the Carver Democratic Club, a position that he held for the next two decades.

Dinkins served as president of the New York City Board of Elections from 1972 to 1973, establishing guidelines that encouraged wider voter registration. He was appointed city clerk in 1975, a post he held for ten years. His responsibilities mainly involved signing marriage certificates and processing the financial disclosure forms of public officials. This plum patronage position afforded him the opportunity to establish political ties that would later prove useful. Tuxedo–clad almost every night, he attended several events, shaking hands and stopping to talk to guests. During this time, he headed the Coalition of Black Elected Democrats. Despite his reputation for caution, he took a bold position in 1984, endorsing Jesse Jackson for president when most mainstream black politicians were supporting the former vice president, Walter F. Mondale.

In 1977, when Percy Sutton resigned as Manhattan borough president to become the first African American to run for mayor of New York City, he urged Dinkins to try for the borough presidency. Defeated twice, Dinkins was elected on his third try in 1985. The primary power of a borough president derived from his ex officio seat on the Board of Estimate, New York City's governing body until 1990. The board reviewed the city's budget and major contracts. During his four–year term, Dinkins put together task forces on a range of urban issues and took a strong stance in support of community–based AIDS services. He earned a well–deserved reputation as a friend of the poor and the homeless, and as a voice of reason in a racially tense city. Because he withheld his opinions or votes until he could confer with aides, he was called a procrastinator by political enemies. To the public, however, he appeared deliberate and cool–headed.

In 1989 Dinkins came under increasing pressure from his political friends to challenge Edward I. Koch, who was making a bid for an unprecedented fourth term as mayor. Dinkins commissioned a poll to determine his chances, and bolstered by its findings, announced his candidacy. Drawing heavily on his political stronghold in Harlem, he defeated Koch in the Democratic Party primary election by about 50 to 42 percent. Dinkins's ''nice guy'' image attracted a multiethnic coalition of African American, Hispanic, and white voters, which, in his public speeches, he called a ''gorgeous mosaic.'' Ninety–one percent of the African Americans and 65 percent of the Hispanics voted for him, along with about 30 percent of the whites, including about 30 percent of the Jewish voters. His dignified reserve, cautious speech, and behind–the–scenes diplomacy were also prime factors in his defeating the popular Republican district attorney, Rudolph Giuliani, in the general election in November of 1989. Dinkins became the 106th mayor of New York City.

When Dinkins went into mayoral politics, the perception of him as a healer, coupled with his abilities as a conciliator, enabled him to reduce the racial tensions besieging the city after 12 years of combative, confrontational government under Koch. Having risen to power as a quiet champion of the poor, once in office he faced the formidable task of dealing with racial violence, drugs, and crime in addition to the city's ominous fiscal crisis.

During his tenure as mayor, Dinkins experienced first–hand the difference between a candidate who can promise the sky and an office–holder who cannot deliver all things to all people. His priorities were the construction of more housing for the poor and homeless, better health care—especially for children—and a crackdown on drugs and crime. In the eyes of many politicians, the city he inherited was looking more ungovernable with each passing day. Confronted with a budget deficit leaving few resources for programs that he cherished, Dinkins began to face attacks on his financial handling of the city. His 1991 budget included $800 million in new taxes, representing the largest tax increase in the city's history. In addition to cuts in spending in nearly all social services, he had to cut the city's work force as well. These actions, though praised as fiscally prudent, had political reverberations later on.

Besides the attacks on his financial handling of the city, Dinkins faced further shattering of his "gorgeous mosaic." In 1991 violent protests erupted after a car in the entourage of a Brooklyn Jewish leader struck and killed a black child. Dinkins brokered a fragile peace when he appealed to both sides to be reasonable rather than violent. Also in 1991, when riots erupted in many places after white officers were found not guilty in the Rodney King police brutality case in Los Angeles, Dinkins visited several New York neighborhoods urging calm. His healing powers deactivated a racial time bomb and earned for him a temporary respite from critics.

David Dinkins's sound fiscal management produced a budget surplus in 1992. The mayor added another feather in his cap by having the city become host to the lucrative Democratic National Convention. Nevertheless, as the 1993 election approached, Dinkins faced a steady stream of criticism. Forgotten were his real successes during a recession. He had kept the city's budget balanced, won new taxes in order to hire thousands more police officers, extended library hours, and had seen crime decline. As an incumbent, he did not want to be the first black mayor of a major city to lose his first reelection bid.

In New York City, Democrats normally outnumber Republicans five to one. New York voters, however, had been known to switch sides when the issues were race and liberal ideology. Dinkins won easy renomination in the Democratic primary election. He was defeated in the November general election by the Republican candidate, Rudolph Giuliani, whose prosecutor's image was softened by a media campaign portraying him as a warm family man and a good manager.

Dinkins was many things to many people, but even his political enemies would agree that he was and is always a gentleman. People were impressed by his dignified demeanor, even during chaotic and trying times. He had worked hard at being a good mayor, but New Yorkers did not fasten on Dinkins's strengths.

Since leaving office, Dinkins has enjoyed the affection shown by New Yorkers he encounters every day in his still very public life. When he stops for a red light while behind the wheel of his car, nearby drivers honk their horns and wave enthusiastically. When he walks down the street or enters a restaurant, someone will stop to shake his hand and wish him well.

Maintains High Visibility

Dinkins currently teaches at Columbia University, where he is professor in the practice of public affairs at the School of International and Public Affairs and senior fellow of the Barnard–Columbia Center for Urban Policy. He hosts, twice a week, an hour–long interview and call–in radio show, "Dialogue with Dinkins," on WLIB–AM, and continues to advocate help for children and education, a compassionate urban policy, and tolerance.

The former mayor is active as a member of several corporate boards and at least two dozen nonprofit charitable groups and other organizations. He is on the board of the Aaron Diamond Foundation, the Andrew Goodman Foundation, the Association to Benefit Children, the Federation of Protestant Welfare Agencies, Friends of the Nelson Mandela Children's Fund, Goods for Guns, Hope for Infants, the Howard Samuels Foundation, the Lenox Hill Neighborhood Association, the March of Dimes, the New York State International Partnership Program, and the New York Junior Tennis League. He was also a founding member of the Black and Puerto Rican Legislative Caucus of New York State, the Council of Black Elected Democrats of New York State, 100 Black Men, and the Black Americans in Support of Israel Committee. He is an honorary life trustee of the Community Service Society of New York, an honorary trustee of the Friends of Harlem Hospital, and a life member of the NAACP.

The former mayor also works as a consultant to Ronald O. Perelman, the financier who is chairman of the Revlon Corporation. He was the first male member of the National Women's Political Caucus, and at one time the vice president of the U.S. Conference of Mayors.

Among the many awards Dinkins has received are Pioneer of Excellence, World Institute of Black Communications, 1986; the Righteous Man Award, New York Board of Rabbis, 1986; Man of the Year Award, Corrections Guardians Association, 1986; Man of the Year Award, Association of Negro Business and Professional Women's Clubs, 1986; Distinguished Service Award, Federation of Negro Civil Service Organizations, 1986; and Father of the Year Award, Metropolitan Chapter, Jack and Jill of America, 1989.

Affable, neat, and impeccably groomed, about the only hint of extravagance Dinkins displays is his penchant for elegant custom–made pinstripe suits. He loves big band music. An avid tennis player with a strong forehand, he still plays, even after heart surgery in August of 1995. Among his peers and cronies are Basil Paterson, Percy Sutton, and Charles Rangel—all important among New York City's former or current black politicians.

While he is no longer a candidate for elected office, David Dinkins still makes the rounds, attending receptions, dinners, cocktail parties, benefits, fund raisers, and award ceremonies that are the staple of an elected official's day.

Current address: 625 Madison Avenue, New York, NY 10022.

REFERENCES

''The Best Ex–Job In the City.'' *New York Times,* February 26, 1995.

''Biography of David Norman Dinkins.'' Office of David Dinkins, July, 1996.

Cheers, D. Michael. ''Mayor of 'The Big Apple.''' *Ebony* 45 (February 1990): 28.

Contemporary Black Biography. Vol. 4. Detroit: Gale Research, 1993.

''This Time, Race Is a Murkier Issue.'' *New York Times,* September 19, 1993.

Who's Who among African Americans, 1996–97. 9th ed. Detroit: Gale Research, 1996.

Vivian D. Hewitt

M. J. ''Father'' Divine

M. J. ''Father'' Divine
(1879–1965)
Religious leader

In Brooklyn in 1917, a man who called himself the Messenger took on a new name to satisfy the demands of a society that required persons to have a name and surname. He named himself M. J. Divine. His followers knew the initials stood for Major Jealous (''for the Lord, whose name is Jealous, is a jealous god.'' Exodus, 34:14); they also believed he was God. For many years this new identity concealed his earlier life, and Father Divine was known only as the leader of a religious cult that attracted wide–spread and often hostile attention in the 1930s. Divine's Peace Mission Movement was a true cult and has been the object of study for several classic analyses, but it is also increasingly studied as a creative religious reaction to the plight of poor urban blacks.

Father Divine was born George Baker Jr. in Rockville, Maryland, in May of 1879, the oldest child of George Baker and Nancy Smith Baker. Little is known of George Baker except that he was probably a former slave and worked as a farm laborer when he moved to Rockville and married Nancy Smith. Before emancipation, Smith had two Catholic masters who required attendance at Catholic services. In Rockville Smith joined a black Methodist church controlled by the predominately white denomination. Until she became too overweight to work she continued the domestic work she had begun as a slave. The local newspaper noted her death in 1897 because this five–foot tall woman weighed 480 pounds.

Nancy Smith had three children before her marriage: Annie (b. 1860); Margaret (Maggie; b. circa 1864); and Delia (b. 1866). The girls eventually took the Baker surname. There was another Baker son, Milford, born in 1880. The census of that year gives some idea of the poverty the family endured. Fourteen people lived in Luther Snowden's Rockville cabin: Snowden's family of four, a young married couple, a bachelor, and the seven Bakers. In spite of their poverty, the Baker children received at least a rudimentary education. George Baker Jr. also acquired the skills of a yard worker and gardener.

In 1899 George Baker Jr. had moved to Baltimore where he sought work as a gardener; he was fortunate enough to find housing in the servants' quarters of a white household. As an underemployed black manual worker, Baker was not attracted by the established black churches but instead entered the world of storefront churches, where he developed his powers as a preacher and worked out his own religious ideas. Drawing on Methodist, Catholic, and popular black traditions, he was also profoundly influenced by the movement called New Thought, a forerunner of both the Christian Science of Mary Baker Eddy and the modern New Age movements. In particular, Baker was profoundly influenced by the Unity School of Christianity founded by Charles Fillmore.

In 1902 Baker set out to save souls in the South and then in 1906 went to the West Coast, where he heard William J. Seymour at the Azuza Street revival meetings in Los Angeles that sparked the Pentecostal movement among both blacks and whites. Baker himself experienced speaking in tongues. This experience led to a reshaping of his religious thought, which continued after his return to Baltimore.

In 1907 Baker met Samuel Morris, who came into a storefront church to preach. When Morris proclaimed, "I am the Father Eternal," the congregation threw him out for blasphemy, but Baker was interested. Morris joined Baker in lodgings at the house of Harriet Anna Snowden, laundress and religious worker. Morris was accepted as Father Jehovia, and Baker assumed the identity of the Messenger, the Son, and obliquely proclaimed Father Jehovia was God during the services held several times a week. Next to appear was Reverend Bishop Saint John the Vine (John A. Hickerson), who also drew on elements of New Thought but explicitly claimed affiliation to Ethiopianism, a black tradition maintaining all blacks in the country were descendants of Ethiopian Jews and that Christ was African.

For some years the three collaborated in building up a following at their Fairmont Avenue residence. The true leader in terms of teaching and organizing was the Messenger, who in the 1910 census gave his name as Anderson K. Baker and changed the year and place of his birth, foreshadowing a more profound change of identity. In 1912 the three broke: Baker denied both Father Jehovia's claim to be God and Bishop John the Vine's claim that everyone is God.

The Messenger Establishes a Sect

In the next few years, the Messenger traveled about, often in the South, spreading his message and meeting great hostility. He had already established a pattern of worship: preaching, singing, and Holy Communion banquets as lavish as resources allowed. Worshippers sang, danced, and testified in free–form services that often lasted into the night. Perhaps alone among itinerant ministers, Divine did not pass a collection plate at services and consistently rejected money from non–members. The "International Modest Code" may not yet have been formalized but its tenets were upheld: "no smoking; no drinking; no obscenity; no vulgarity; no profanity; no undue mixing of the sexes; no receiving of gifts, presents, tips or bribes." No undue mixing of the sexes also implied the celibacy Divine demanded of his followers.

There was often hostility from black ministers. In 1913 a confrontation in Savannah led to Divine's serving 60 days on the chain gang. The most fully documented case of community reaction occurred in Valdosta, Georgia. After being thrown out of a local church for proclaiming himself God, Divine built up a following among black women who found a liberation from male chauvinism in his teaching. He also alarmed the black men of the community, especially when he ordered the women to stop having sexual relations with their husbands. African American men arranged for his arrest on lunacy charges on February 16, 1914. This only increased his notoriety and the number of his followers. Improvised services held at the jail even attracted some white worshippers. J. R. Mosely, a white peach farmer and religious seeker, was impressed by Divine and obtained the free services of one of the town's leading lawyers to defend him. In spite of the defense, the jury found Divine insane but not in need of incarceration, much to the anger of the black men of the town. At their insistence Divine was rearrested on a charge of vagrancy. The uproar continued for some time until Divine agreed to leave town and not come back in exchange for his release.

Alone among black cults, the mission had the distinction of attracting a significant minority of whites, some of whom were quite affluent. The presence of an interracial membership and a political agenda explains the hostile attention given to the sect in sensation–seeking publications like the Hearst newspapers, and the sustained interest of law enforcement officials ranging from local authorities to the Federal Bureau of Investigation, which maintained extensive files on the movement. For the next few years Divine continued to travel both in the South and in the North, accompanied by a group of disciples ranging in number from six to twelve, mostly women. One woman named Peninnah, older and larger than Divine, joined him, possibly in Macon, Georgia, after he cured her of arthritis. Her origins are completely obscured and the date given for her marriage to Divine—June 6, 1882—has a spiritual rather than a literal meaning. Peninnah became known as Mother Divine and was a very able second–in–command. In 1917 Divine and his followers settled in a Brooklyn apartment, continuing the communal living tradition of the group. Some members worked outside while others maintained the living quarters.

On October 27, 1919, Divine purchased a house in Sayville on Long Island, some 70 miles from New York. He became the first black homeowner in the town. Nine followers accompanied Mother and Father Divine in the move that winter. Divine found work as domestics for many of them, and their willingness to work hard, coupled with absolute honesty, appealed to employers. Initially the growth of Divine's following was slow, and he had time to read extensively in New Thought literature borrowed from the local library. He reflected and developed his theology. Biographer Jill Watts points out that while his sermons rambled and contained neologisms, "they had a consistent and comprehensible core. Indeed, he was as intelligible as any New Thought advocate."

Divine turned to distributing New Thought literature that supported his views. This led to a growth in the number of persons he attracted. He also began to win more white supporters. The combination of self–help ideas and the promise of healing, affluence, and bodily immortality in this world was a heady mixture. By 1930 the number of people living in the house in Sayville and the number of seekers visiting on Sunday began to fray the tolerance of the white neighbors. In April of 1930, a young black police informant, Susan Hadley, infiltrated the house where 30 persons were living. She discovered that the rumors about sexual license were completely unjustified and that nothing illegal was taking place. The only thing that baffled her was the affluence of the household, which she could not believe rested on the work of the members. Her report was sensationalized in various Long Island newspapers. One result was to attract even more attention to Divine. William Lanyon, a noted New Thought lecturer, was one of the whites converted, and he spread the message in Europe. Still, after much insistence by the fearful neighboring whites, Divine was finally arrested by the local authorities on May 8, 1931 for creating his interracial denomination.

Bond was set at $1,000, and Peninnah immediately paid it in cash. Trial was set for the fall. All summer Divine tried to control the noise and the crowds, but on November 15, 1931, he deliberately prolonged the service and allowed the noise level to increase. The police arrived after midnight and arrested 78 blacks and 15 whites. Tensions in Sayville were high, and some residents went so far as to call for lynching. Divine apparently negotiated an agreement with the police that legal charges against him would be dropped in exchange for his departure—a promise that was broken.

Divine was now attracting wide support in New Thought circles, attracting new white followers, mostly middle– and upper–class, and poor, working–class blacks. He began to shift his base of operations from Long Island to New York City. In December of 1931 Divine held the first of a series of successful meetings at the Rockville Palace in Harlem, where he moved in March of 1932. On Easter Sunday of that year 1,500 people appeared for a communion banquet in a space that had seats for only 600. The overflow was housed in a neighboring church. Finally on May 24, Divine's Sayville case came to trial, and he was found guilty. On June 5 Divine was sentenced to a year's imprisonment and a fine of $500. On June 9, Lewis J. Smith, the judge in the trial, died of a heart attack at the age of 55. This supposed example of divine justice struck fear into many hearts. Divine was soon freed on appeal.

Peace Mission Grows

Restaurants were the first Peace Mission businesses. Many others soon followed and provided the mission with much of its revenue. The movement grew nationwide, and the Los Angeles missions were especially successful. Since newspapers portrayed Divine as heading a very large movement, he was courted by the communists. He formulated his own political program, the Righteous Government Platform, to further civil rights and religious reform. Ultimately, he had little impact on electoral politics. In spite of the publicity the Peace Mission generated, the number of followers and sympathizers at the peak was probably about 40,000 to 50,000 in New York with another 10,000 nationwide. Among these were a substantial number of Garveyites, who came in spite of Divine's insistence on racial integration.

After a period of spectacular growth, 1937 was a year of crisis as a string of events, which had begun the year before, reached a climax. John the Revelator (John Wuest Hunt), a wealthy and unstable white disciple, had sexual relations with 17–year–old Delight Jewett, whom he had taken across state lines. His trial for violating the Mann act was a national sensation. Sternly reprimanded by Divine, John the Revelator openly confessed at the trial and took the name of the Prodigal Son as he began his prison sentence. One of the persons testifying for the prosecution was Faithful Mary (Viola Wilson), a former tubercular alcoholic from Georgia who had risen to a prominent position as one of the leading angels in the mission. She had accepted money from a contributor in direct violation of Divine's instructions. Breaking in a spectacular fashion with Divine, she was supported by the Hearst papers and the *New York Amsterdam News* in her allegations of sexual misbehavior against Divine. She repeated these stories in a book, *God, He's Just a Natural Man* (New York: Gailliard Press, 1936). In addition, Peninnah fell sick and entered a hospital, apparently to die. This cast doubt on Divine's promises of earthly immortality. Tensions within the movement as a result of these developments reached such a level that on April 20, followers beat up a process server in New York, forcing Divine to go into hiding. And finally, Verinda Brown won a judgment for $4,000 against the movement, which Divine refused to pay.

There was a rebound in 1938. A repentant Faithful Mary, who had turned to drink and drugs after her sponsors abandoned her, returned to the fold although not to her former position of power. Peninnah recovered. The judgment in favor of Brown, however, continued to hang over Divine's head. Thus, after the final failure of appeals in 1942, Divine could appear in Harlem only on Sundays since New York law did not allow subpoenas to be served on that day.

The institutional response to these difficulties was a gradual restructuring of the Peace Mission and its eventual incorporation as a church, completed by 1942. Communion banquets were closed to non–members, and relief missions disappeared. The unemployed were no longer allowed to testify, and control of the whole movement was much more centralized. Some political activity continued. Divine managed to collect 250,000 signatures in support of an anti–lynching bill, but his influence was still slight. With the outbreak of World War II, Divine, the patriotic pacifist, had to guide the mission through the war years.

With the move to Philadelphia, the Peace Mission began a slow decline. Peninnah died in 1943, affecting Divine profoundly. On April 29, 1946, he married a young white Canadian, Sweet Angel (Edna Rose Ritchings), who became the new Mother Divine, or rather, in the movement's view, the same one reincarnated. Divine assigned a black angel to be ever at her side to show that husband and wife remained celibate. In 1953 Mother and Father Divine moved into a large house near Philadelphia. The house, Woodmont, became the center of the movement and a place of pilgrimage. It was a serene setting for an aging and increasingly frail Divine, who was rumored to be suffering from arteriosclerosis and diabetes. He ceased public appearances in 1963 and died on September 10, 1965. His earthly remains are in a "Shrine to Life" at Woodmont. His followers speak always of him in the present tense and set a place for him at Communion banquets. Mother Divine has skillfully continued to lead a movement that is dwindling as its members age and few recruits join.

In folk memory Divine is still maligned. He was caricatured in a 1980 television film on Jim Jones and the People's Temple. *The National Enquirer* reprinted old hostile stories in connection with the Jim and Tammy Bakker scandal in 1987. Divine did lead a cult that radically reshaped members' beliefs and controlled their behavior. Still, for many persons, including some who stayed only for a time, he offered stability and a chance to integrate personality denied by the outside world. Father Divine and his Peace Mission form an interesting chapter in the history of religion and throw much light on relations between the races during his era.

REFERENCES

Burkett, Randall K., and Richard Newman, eds. *Black Apostles.* Boston: G. K. Hall, 1978.

Burnham, Kenneth E. *God Comes to Harlem.* Boston: Lambeth Press, 1979.

Cantril, Hadley. *The Psychology of Social Movements.* New York: John Wiley and Sons, 1941.

Fauset, Arthur Huff. *Black Gods of the Metropolis.* New York: Octagon Books, 1974.

McKay, Claude. *Harlem: Negro Metropolis.* New York: E. P. Dutton, 1940.

Watts, Jill. *God, Harlem U.S.A.* Berkeley: University of California Press, 1992.

Weisbrot, Robert. *Father Divine and the Struggle for Racial Equality.* Urbana: University of Illinois Press, 1983.

Robert L. Johns

Dean Dixon
(1915–1976)
Symphony conductor

Dean Dixon

Dean Dixon, an outstanding black conductor, made his debut at Town Hall in New York on May 7, 1938. His performing career spanned a period of more than 40 years. In 1935 he founded the Dean Dixon Symphony, his first orchestra, when he was only 17. Following college and graduate school, he conducted opera and major symphony orchestras in the United States, and traveled abroad in 1949, taking regular conducting assignments in Goteborg, Frankfurt, Melbourne, and Sydney. He gave guest appearances in Europe, Israel, South America, Japan, and Australia.

Charles Dean Dixon was born on January 10, 1915, in New York City. His father, Henry Charles Dixon, a Jamaican trained in law in Jamaica, supported his family by working in a New York hotel. His mother, McClara Dixon, recognized that her son was a musically talented youth, and frequently took him to concerts. She purchased a violin for him when he was about three and a half, after noticing him playing with two sticks in what she perceived as a violin–playing position. She found a teacher for him and closely monitored his practice times. At one point his teacher cautioned that there was not much progress and that perhaps further study was a waste of money. Undaunted, Dixon and his mother persevered; she got him another teacher and his lessons and practice continued. Popular music was banned in the house, and the radio was ''out of order'' continuously. He was, however, told that if he practiced, he might one day play music over the radio.

Dixon was educated in the New York City public schools. He attended DeWitt Clinton High School, where Harry Jennison, the music director, took an interest in his further training. Jennison suggested Dixon enroll at the Juilliard School of Music and wrote to Walter Damrosch on his behalf. Dixon attended the Juilliard School from 1932 to 1936, studying violin and receiving his bachelor of music degree in 1936. He was awarded a conducting fellowship and studied with Albert Stoessel at the Juilliard Graduate School from 1936 to 1939. He also enrolled in the teacher education program at Columbia University's Teachers College, where he received his master of arts degree in 1939.

Dixon's conducting experiences began early. In 1932 he started the Dean Dixon Symphony Orchestra at the Harlem YMCA, with the aim of providing experience for young musicians in symphonic literature. The orchestra soon grew to 70 members and held regular public concerts. In 1939 Dixon founded the New York Chamber Orchestra and initiated a New Talent contest featuring a concert performance prize. In addition, the WPA National Youth Administration sponsored an orchestra led by Dixon. His mother's earlier prediction about broadcasting on the radio came true. This group presented many educational programs featuring talented young artists as well as a Beethoven cycle and Saturday morning music appreciation programs broadcast by New York City's radio station, WNYC.

Makes Conducting Debut

In addition to conducting, Dixon taught violin and piano privately, and this income partly supported his orchestral conducting initiatives. In 1937 community support crystallized in Harlem, leading to a musical performance of the "John Henry" legend in 1939, featuring Paul Robeson. Dixon made his professional debut as a conductor at an orchestral concert in Town Hall on May 7, 1938. About this time Eleanor Roosevelt took an interest in supporting his career. He was also engaged for a guest appearance with the New York City Symphony in 1940, at which point the musicians tested the young conductor. During a rehearsal, a strange sound emanated from somewhere in the auditorium. Stating that he heard a French horn, but none was indicated in the score, he soon spotted the impish musician, hiding beneath the stage. Having passed this test, he won the support of the musicians and conducted a very successful concert.

Eleanor Roosevelt arranged for the use of the Hecksher Theater for a concert in 1941, and asked NBC executive Samuel Chotzinoff to attend. He, too, was impressed with Dixon's command of the podium and arranged for him to conduct the NBC Symphony in the summer of 1941. Following this successful engagement, Dixon made a guest appearance with the New York Philharmonic at Lewisohn Stadium in August, 1941. He appeared with the Philadelphia Orchestra in 1943 and the Boston Symphony Orchestra in 1944; this marked the first time a black conductor had led either of these prestigious orchestras.

Dixon's career continued apace. He founded the American Youth Orchestra in 1944 and led impressive public concert seasons with it in the following years. The American Youth Orchestra was led at a professional level and admission was by blind audition, supervised by Dixon. The orchestra earned the endorsement of prominent music educators and leaders of the music community, including Leonard Bernstein, Bruno Walter, Yehudi Menuhin, Aaron Copland, and Oscar Hammerstein II, as well as the support of *New York Times* music critic Olin Downes. The orchestra's concerts stressed community performances for a wide audience, including young people and school groups, and had a demanding repertoire, including opera.

Following several successful concert seasons with this orchestra and many guest appearances with major U.S. orchestras, Dixon received a Rosenwald Fellowship for 1945–47 and the prestigious Alice M. Ditson Award in 1948 for his contribution to American music. As an indication of his interest in contemporary music, he conducted a New York Chamber Orchestra concert in May 1950 that included the works of six black composers from five countries, including Samuel Coleridge–Taylor of England, William Grant Still of the United States, and Amadeo Roldan of Cuba.

Despite these credentials, Dixon was not offered a position in a major American orchestra and decided in 1949 to move to Europe to further his career. In this endeavor, he followed a path similar to that taken by writer James Baldwin and jazz musicians Sidney Bechet and Kenny Clarke. His first engagement was as guest conductor of the French National Radio Orchestra in 1949. During the concert year 1951, Dixon conducted 32 concerts in nine countries. Dixon's hopes were further rewarded when he was appointed music director of the Goteborg Symphony Orchestra in Sweden, where he served from 1953 to 1960. He earned respect for his talents and successful leadership of the orchestra, and a warm reception from his audiences.

Dixon's next position was as principal conductor of the Hessischer Rundfunk Orchestra from 1961 to 1974, in Frankfurt, Germany, where he made his home. He also served in Australia as principal conductor of the Sydney Symphony Orchestra from 1964 to 1967. He made his London debut in 1963 with the BBC Symphony Orchestra.

During his sojourn abroad, Dixon conducted as many as 125 concerts in one year, and conducted orchestras in more than 23 countries. His repertoire was very broad, including most major classical composers; his favorites were Beethoven, Brahms, and Bruckner. Contemporary music was also featured, including, for example, the composers Hans Werner Henze and Jean Sibelius. He was also noted as a champion of American music, conducting performances of more than 50 works by major contemporary composers, including Aaron Copland, Henry Cowell, Howard Hanson, Ulysses Kay, Douglas Moore, William Schumann, Howard Swanson, and many others. His reputation for conducting works by American composers earned him the praise of noted critic and composer Virgil Thomson. According to Raoul Abdul, who cited Thomson in *Blacks in Classical Music,* Thomson called Dixon "our most assiduous ambassador of American music," certainly an ironic role considering his career. Upon his return to conduct concerts in the United States in 1970, reviewers remarked that Dixon was better known by concert audiences abroad than in his home country.

On the subject of race, Dixon was sensitive and often outspoken. To a Swedish promoter's suggestion that he consider appearing in whiteface with white gloves, he replied that he had appeared in that promoter's city a more than a dozen times in blackface. Asked upon his return to the United States if he wished to be known as a Negro conductor, he commented that he would prefer to be known as a successful international conductor. On the subject of his sojourn abroad, D. Antionette Handy quoted him in *Black Conductors* as saying, "by getting away I have helped those at home. I have shown what can be done."

A highlight of Dixon's return to performances before American audiences was a New York Philharmonic concert on July 19, 1970, in Central Park, before an audience of some 75,000 people. After a romantic and touching rendition of his program, he was given a standing ovation by the crowd.

Tours America

During his tour of American cities in 1971–72, Dixon presented concerts with seven major orchestras in seven cities, concluding with a concert by the Prague Symphony Orchestra in Philadelphia's Academy of Music. He returned to Europe for continuing engagements and settled in Switzerland in 1974. He returned to the United States for a belated regular season debut with the Philadelphia Orchestra in April 1975. Once again, he was greeted with a warm ovation by musicians and public alike.

Dixon resumed his travels, going to Australia in 1975 for a series of 24 concerts with the Melbourne and Sydney Orchestras. Illness interrupted his career in December, 1975, when he underwent open–heart surgery. He resumed conducting in 1976, but he suffered a stroke, was hospitalized, and died on November 4, 1976. Dixon was married three times, first to the late concert pianist and fellow Juilliard alumnus, Vivian Rivkin, in 1948. They divorced in 1954 and he married Mary Mandelin, of Finland. Divorced again, he married Ritha Blume in 1973. He had two daughters from his first two marriages, Nina, of Frankfurt, and Diane of Topanga, California.

Dixon leaves a recorded legacy estimated at some 20 discs. More are probably available in library record collections in various compilations from small labels, particularly those on Desto Records, and the American Recording Society. Noah A. Trudeau gave an overview of some of these in his 1985 article in *High Fidelity* reviewing the conductor's life and works. He particularly recommended Dixon's renditions of classics by Von Weber, Haydn, and Beethoven, and his recordings of some works by contemporary Americans such as Howard Hanson, Leo Sowerby, and Howard Swanson.

As a conductor, Dixon was a groundbreaker. He was the first black symphonic conductor to have an eminently successful career. In addition to the standard classics, he championed contemporary works and pioneered the introduction abroad of works by American composers. Establishing bases in Scandinavia, Germany, and Australia and finding success on four continents, Dixon paved the way for others to follow. It is ironic that history may well look upon him as a musical leader who could not find a podium in his own country.

REFERENCES

Abdul, Raoul. *Blacks in Classical Music.* New York: Dodd, Mead, 1977.

Bontemps, Arna W. *We Have Tomorrow.* Boston: Houghton Mifflin, 1945.

"Dean Dixon Dies, Conductor in Exile." *New York Times,* November 5, 1976.

"Dixon Leads Philharmonic 'Pastoral'." *New York Times,* November 27, 1970.

Ewen, David. *Dictators of the Baton.* 2nd ed., revised. Chicago: Ziff Davis, 1948.

Handy, D. Antoinette. *Black Conductors.* Metuchen, NJ: Scarecrow Press, 1995.

Hitchcock, H. Wiley, and Stanley Sadie, eds. *The New Grove Dictionary of American Music.* Vol. 1. New York: Macmillan, 1986.

Richardson, Ben Albert. *Great Black Americans* New York: Thomas Y. Crowell, 1956.

Roach, Hildred. *Black American Music: Past and Present.* Malabar, FL: Kreiger Publishing Company, 1992.

Ross, David P. *Modern Negro Contributors.* Chicago: Afro–American Publishing Company, 1966.

Sadie, Stanley, ed. *New Grove Dictionary of Music.* Vol. 5. New York:, Macmillan, 1980.

Salzman, Jack, David Lionel Smith, and Cornel West, eds. *Encyclopedia of African–American Culture and History.* New York: Macmillan Library Reference USA/Simon and Schuster Macmillan, 1996.

Slonimsky, Nicholas, ed. *Baker's Biographical Dictionary of Musicians.* 8th ed. New York: G. Schirmer Books, 1992.

Southern, Eileen. *Biographical Dictionary of Afro–American and African Musicians.* Westport, CT: Greenwood Press, 1982.

Thompson, Era Bell. "Dean Dixon: Conductor Without a Country." *Ebony* 21 (12 October 1966): 79–86.

Trudeau, Noah Andre. "When the Doors Didn't Open." *High Fidelity* 5 (May 1985): 57–58.

"World's Foremost Negro Conductor." *Ebony* 13 (December 1957): 48–56.

Darius L. Thieme

Howard Dodson Jr.

(1939–)

Library curator, historian, lecturer

A scholar and experienced manager of information on African and African American history and culture, Howard Dodson Jr. is best known for his work as curator of the Schomburg Center for Research in Black Culture of the New York Public Library. He has enhanced the center's historic role as an international library for the collection, promotion, preservation, and dissemination of information on the African and African American diaspora. He has also propelled the center into the age of technology by mounting programs and services to make its resources more easily accessible internally and on the Internet.

Howard Dodson Sr., a laborer, and Lou Birda Jones Dodson, a dry–cleaning plant worker, had four children.

Howard Jr., their first child and only son, was born in Chester, Pennsylvania, on June 1, 1939. Young Dodson's life revolved around home, church, and school. From his mother, Dodson learned to cook and, since he was the oldest child, by the time he was in junior high school he had basic responsibility for preparing meals. To earn extra money during this period, he delivered newspapers and gathered discarded cardboard, newspapers, scrap metal, and wiring, selling them at the local junkyard. From his father, Dodson learned a number of skills, including construction, electrical work, and automobile repair.

An active member of Bethany Baptist Church, Dodson sang in the male choir and the junior choir. He also belonged to the Cub Scout and Boy Scout chapters based at the church. His musical talent was demonstrated again in junior high school, where he played in the marching band. In both junior and senior high school, Dodson sang in the choir and played the trombone. He became an athlete in high school and ran track and cross–country, but he was disappointed when his basketball skills proved insufficient to land him a place on the team. The versatile young man was also sports editor for the high school paper.

Achieves Early

Both his parents and teachers were academic stimulants for Dodson, offering advice to the young scholar to live up to his potential and to achieve excellence. With such encouragement, he performed well academically from grade school through senior high, each year ranking among the top students in his class. Dodson said in an interview that he was generally viewed as ''something bordering on a nerd.'' His grades frequently set the curve for his classes. This resulted in failure for many of his peers, and he was at times pressured to stop performing so well.

The Chester public schools maintained racial segregation through the junior high level. When the junior high teachers prepared their best students to enter the integrated high school, Dodson was among them. Notwithstanding Dodson's outstanding academic achievement, his guidance counselor tried to persuade him to choose a career in shop. He was one of the nine students from his junior high class of 89 students to complete the academic program and attend college.

Dodson obtained a scholarship to help pay for books and tuition at West Chester State College, where he enrolled in 1958. He graduated in 1961 with a B.S. degree in social studies. While there, he pursued his love for geography to the fullest, taking all of the geography courses offered at the school. This love for geography led to a deep interest in history. He learned at the end of his sophomore year that he had scored off the chart in a mathematics aptitude examination, suggesting that he would do well as a mathematics major, yet Dodson did not want to change his major so late in his college career.

Upon graduating Dodson might have become a teacher, but he had been disappointed with his academic preparation, reporting in an interview that he ''didn't know enough then to teach.'' Instead, Dodson enrolled in a dual master's program in history and political science at Villanova University, receiving his degree in 1964. He spent the next two years as a Peace Corps volunteer in Ecuador, South America, where he directed the Credit Union Education Programs for the National Credit Union Federation of Ecuador. From 1966 to 1968 he was a national Peace Corps office staff member, serving as a recruiter, and training officer, as well as deputy director of recruiting and director of minority and specialized recruiting nationally.

Searches America's Soul

The assassination of Martin Luther King Jr. in 1968 left Dodson distressed and awakened in him a need to search the soul of black and white America for insight into the social ills that characterized the time. He told *Contemporary Black Biography* that he went into ''retirement'' in San Juan, Puerto Rico, where he had spent some time during his years in the Peace Corps. Now he would spend a year in Mayaguez ''reading, studying, and contemplating the convergence of various social and historical factors that had resulted in the civil rights and Black Power movements of the 1960s.'' At times he contemplated a response to the violence of King's death that would equal the violence that caused that death. But ultimately, he told *CBB,* he set out to search for ''new bases'' for evaluating the time through reading black classics. Unable to find a suitable for the upheavals of the 1960s in his reading, he decided to return to formal study and research. In 1969 Dodson entered the doctoral program in black history and race relations at the University of California at Berkeley, then the only program of its kind in the country. He left the program in 1974 while writing a dissertation entitled ''Blacks and the Political Economy of South Carolina: 1790–1830.''

After leaving the graduate program, Dodson embarked on a number of intellectual endeavors before he settled in Harlem in 1984. He spent five years (1974–79) as executive director of the Institute of the Black World in Atlanta. While in Atlanta he was part–time lecturer in Afro–American History at Emory University. He left the position in September of 1979 for a stint with the National Endowment for the Humanities (NEH). He was consultant to the chairman of the NEH in Washington, D.C., from October of 1979 to January of 1982, and from September of 1980 to June of 1982 he directed the NEH's Grantsmanship Workshop Series for Minority Scholars and Institutions. Dodson held a series of assignments—some concurrently with other positions—as administrator of the Institute of the Black World's Black Studies Curriculum Development Project and director of the institute's television project, ''The Other American Revolution.'' He worked on the research project, ''American History Textbooks and Social Justice Issues,'' for the Racism and Sexism Resource Center, CIBC in New York from 1983 to 84). From March to July of 1984 he curated an exhibition entitled ''Censorship and Black America'' held at the Schomburg Center for Research in Black Culture at the New York Public Library. This position led to a major new phase in Dodson's career.

The Schomburg Experience

In September of 1984 Dodson was tapped as chief of the Schomburg Center–the position he now holds. He has continued the legacy of the leading scholars and bibliophiles who have headed the center originating with its first curator, Arthur A. Schomburg, for whom the library was named. Schomburg's 1926 donation formed the primary collection of the 135th Street library, known previously as the Division of Negro Literature, History, and Prints. Among those who have guided the distinguished center are Ernestine Rose, Catherine Latimer, Lawrence D. Reddick, and Jean Blackwell Hutson. The library has enjoyed a rich history as a mecca for study and research on African American topics. It has served as a cultural gathering place for black artists, writers, poets, musicians, scholars, political officials, and the general public, from the Harlem Renaissance to the present time. It is that legacy that Dodson has nourished and sustained.

Dodson has secured the library's position as the leading international center for the study of the African American diaspora. Since 1986 Dodson has directed the center's Scholars–in–Residence program, which supports the study and research of African American themes with six– and twelve–month fellowships at the center. Early in his tenure at the Schomburg Center he completed a successful $15.2 capital drive and developed an $8.8 million construction and renovation project. The renovated and expanded center opened for its sixty–fifth anniversary celebration in the spring of 1991, and now featuring an new auditorium, an exhibition wing, an expanded Moving Image and Recorded Sound Division, and additional space for research materials.

As chief of the Schomburg Center, Dodson has enabled the library to maintain a pivotal position in promoting black culture at home in Harlem, throughout New York City, the country and even the world. The center often sponsors or hosts lecture series, exhibitions, and other activities that unite the library and the community. For example, as a part of its tenth annual Heritage Weekend in 1995, the center sponsored a symposium and other activities on the theme ''Traditions and Transformations.'' Heritage Weekend offers a time for spiritual renewal and celebration of black heritage. Dodson organized two other notable celebrations: ''Paul Robeson: A 90th Birthday Tribute,'' held at Schubert Theater in 1988, and ''Ella Fitzgerald: A 75th Birthday Tribute,'' held at Carnegie Hall in 1992. Through the center's research collections, Dodson has propelled the Schomburg Center into a leadership role in the maintenance, preservation, and dissemination of information on African Americans. Much of this has been done through conferences and through service to scholars internationally. Dodson has also fostered cooperation among other repositories of African and African American collections, particularly those in the historically black colleges.

On January 27–28, 1995, Dodson led the center's national symposium on the theme ''Africana Libraries in the Information Age.'' This focus grew out of his concern that during this period of rapid advances in information technology relatively little meaningful information on the African and African American diaspora was available on the Internet. ''The principle challenge posed by the symposium was to continue to explore ways of expanding the number and quality of Internet accessible resources on the African and African Diasporan experience,'' he wrote in a letter dated November 17, 1997. Still concerned about the availability of such information on the Internet, Dodson organized a round–table discussion at the Schomburg Center in 1997, with service providers from a variety of institutions who had made or were in process of making such materials available on the Internet.

Among his many talents and missions, Dodson is an educator and writer as well. In addition to his teaching experiences previously mentioned, Dodson taught African American history at California State College at Haywood (1969–70), at Shaw University (1976–77), and at Columbia University (1990–92). Among his writings are *Thinking and Rethinking U.S. History,* with Madelon Bedell (Council on Interracial Books for Children, 1988); *Black Photographers Bear Witness: 100 Years of Social Protest,* with Deborah Willis (Williams College Museum of Art, 1989), and ''The Schomburg Center for Research in Black Culture'' in *Afro–American Writers, 1940–1955* (Gale Research, 1988). Articles by Dodson have also appeared in *Library Quarterly* and *Research Libraries Notes.*

Dodson has enjoyed a wide range of consultantships with such diverse groups as the Georgia Association of Black Elected Officials, Congressional Black Caucus, National Council of Churches, Martin Luther King Jr. Center for Social Change, National Association for Equal Opportunity in Higher Education, National Urban Extension Association, World Council of Churches, the City of Atlanta, Atlanta University, Library of Congress, Smithsonian Institution, United States Department of Education, African American Museums Association, DuSable Museum, and the New York State Black and Puerto Rican Legislative Caucus.

Dodson has served on boards of overseers or trustees for Eugene Lang College at the New School for Social Research (1988–94), Bronx Botanical Garden (1989–92), Nation Institute (1991–present), Center for Cuban Studies, Institute for International Education (1993–present), and Tougaloo College (1993–96). Some of his memberships and affiliations are the African Heritage Studies Association, Southern Historical Association, National Council of Black Studies, and the Association for the Study of Afro–American Life and History. He has belonged to the New York Partnerships since 1990 and is a member of the New York City chapter of One Hundred Black Men.

In partial recognition of his achievements, Dodson received a doctorate of humane letters from Widener University in 1987. Other selected awards and honors include the Association of African American History's Service Award in 1975, the Governor's Award for African–Americans of Distinction in 1982, and the Chairman's Award of the Black and Puerto Rican Caucus.

Dodson is six feet tall, slender, and fit. His love for dancing is partially fulfilled by incorporating dance into his exercise program. In the rare moments he calls spare time, Dodson reads mysteries or watches basketball games. In 1970 he married Jualynne White, a sociologist and educational administrator from Pensacola, Florida. They have two children, Alyce Christine and David Primus Luta, and are now divorced.

An articulate and effective communicator, Dodson is impressive whether in the office, the classroom, or at the podium. As curator of the Schomburg Center, Dodson has successfully blended a well–established legacy of service to a world community and a program of cultural development in the local community with the rapid advances in technology so vital in propelling the center into the next century. He is motivated in this mission by the interests of students, scholars, writers, artists, and other contributors to black history and culture.

Current address: Schomburg Center for Research in Black Culture, 515 Malcolm X Boulevard, New York, NY 10037–1801.

REFERENCES

"Africana Libraries in the Information Age." Flyer. Schomburg Center for Research in Black Culture, New York Public Library, 1995.

Contemporary Black Biography. Vol. 7. Detroit: Gale Research, 1994.

Dodson, Howard, Jr. Letter to Jessie Carney Smith, November 17, 1997.

———. Telephone interview with Jessie Carney Smith, March 13, 1998.

"Howard Dodson: Biographical Sketch." Office of Howard Dodson, Schomburg Center for Research in Black Culture, New York Public Library, n.d.

Resume. "Howard Dodson." Office of Howard Dodson, Schomburg Center for Research in Black Culture, New York Public Library.

Who's Who among African Americans, 1998–99. 10th ed. Detroit: Gale Research, 1998.

Jessie Carney Smith

Owen Dodson

(1914–1983)

Poet, novelist, playwright, director, educator

Owen Dodson's poetry has been compared with that of Robert Frost and Carl Sandburg. His novels have been compared with those of Ishmael Reed and Toni Morrison. His theatrical heirs include playwright August Wilson and director Lloyd Richards. Dodson, who taught at four of black America's finest colleges and universities, influenced many students including playwrights Debbie Allen, Amiri Baraka, and Ted Shine. He is one of the twentieth–century's most eloquent and versatile interpreters of the human experience.

Owen Vincent Dodson was born on November 28, 1914, in Brooklyn, New York. He was the ninth child born to Nathaniel and Sarah Goode Dodson and the grandson of former slaves. Prior to Nathaniel Dodson's graduation as salutatorian from Wayland Seminary (now Virginia Union University), he taught school and was an elevator operator. Dodson was subsequently employed by the American Press Association and served as chairman of the National Negro Press Association (NNPA). He was also a syndicated columnist and press agent for black advocates Booker T. Washington and James Shepard. As a result of Dodson's association with various black American luminaries, Owen and his siblings met Washington and W. E. B. Du Bois as well as other black American leaders. Both of Dodson's parents were active in community endeavors.

Death frequently claimed members of Owen Dodson's family. Prior to his birth, a boy and a girl, who were twins, died. Before Owen's tenth birthday, meningitis claimed the life of his brother Harold, while tuberculosis took his sister Evelyn. His mother, who suffered a series of stokes, died in 1926; one year later, Nathaniel died of lumbar pneumonia. Thus at the age of 12, Owen Dodson was an orphan. His sister Lillian, 16 years his senior, a graduate of Hunter College (the only girl in her class), and an elementary school teacher, assumed the responsibility for the Dodson clan.

Education was always important to the Dodson family. Young Owen attended Brooklyn's P.S. 64 where the assistant principal, Albert Blum, served as a sartorial role model for Owen whose father used to refer to his two youngest sons, Kenneth and Owen, as his Chesterfields. The nickname, according to James Hatch in *Sorrow Is the Only Faithful One,* was in honor of Lord Chesterfield, "the epitome of a gentleman." Throughout his life, Dodson valued a gift from Blum, Charles Dickens's *The Mystery of Edwin Drood*; inside Blum had inscribed an acknowledgment of Dodson's "greatest proficiency in declamation," wrote Hatch. Dodson's talents were also recognized at Thomas Jefferson High School. Declamation and elocution contests were frequently held at the school, and Dodson and his brother Kenneth always gave outstanding performances. After winning a prize for his recital of James Weldon Johnson's inspirational poem, "Go Down Death (A Funeral Sermon)," Dodson wrote the well–known poet and enclosed clips of the most recent speech contests. Dodson was jubilant when he received Johnson's congratulatory letter.

Throughout Dodson's high school years, he continued to win medals, including one from the *New York Times* oratorical contest during his senior year. His love of the theater was nurtured by Mrs. Enoch Wells, whose brother was the president of Standard Oil. She was fond of the Dodson brothers, and they accompanied her to various plays where they were enthralled by the performances of such theatrical legends as Judith Anderson, Ethel Barrymore, Maurice Evans, Basil Rathbone, and Orson Wells.

After graduation in 1932, Dodson went to Bates College in Lewiston, Maine. As early as his freshman year, Dodson was active in extracurricular activities. He won the freshman

Owen Dodson

speech award, was elected to the editorial staff of the *Garnet,* Bates's biannual literary magazine, and joined the Spoffard Literary Club. During the remainder of Dodson's undergraduate years, he cofounded a poetry society as well as acted, wrote, and directed plays. After receiving his B.A. in 1936, Dodson enrolled in the Yale School of Fine Arts, School of Drama where he received the M.F.A. degree in 1939.

Creates Poetry

Although Dodson displayed an appreciation of poetry as early as his high school years when he recited verse during various contests, he did not begin writing poetry until his freshman year at Bates when he enrolled in Robert Berkelman's class. Decades later Dodson remembered in *Interviews with Black Writers* an important episode in his development as a writer when he was asked to evaluate John Keats's ''On First Looking into Chapman's Homer'':

> Once, at Bates College, my teacher asked me ''What do you think of this sonnet of Keats?'' I said, ''I don't think nothing of this sonnet of Keats.'' He said, ''Oh, it is considered one of the great sonnets of the world.'' I answered, ''I don't think so.'' And he said, ''All right, Owen, you will write four sonnets a week.'' (He didn't even laugh.) He meant what he said. So for four years I wrote four sonnets a week.

Berkelman's sonnet assignment led to the publication of Dodson's poetry prior to his graduation from Bates in such periodicals as the *Garnet, Opportunity,* and *New Masses.* ''Jungle Stars,'' a collection of eight sonnets dedicated to his father, appeared in the *Garnet* (1936) during his senior year. Also Dodson's ''Ode to the Class of 1936 Everywhere'' was printed in the *New York Herald Tribune.* Over the decades, numerous periodicals published Dodson's verse; among them are *Challenge*; *The Christian Century*; *Common Ground*; *Crisis*; *Harlem Quarterly*; *Negro Digest*; *Omega: An International Journal for the Psychological Study of Dying, Death, Suicide, and Other Behavior*; *Phylon*; *Theatre Arts*; *Trend*; *Voices: A Quarterly of Poetry*; and *The Yale Literary Magazine.* To date more than 50 anthologies include Dodson's poetry; his most frequently anthologized poems include ''Sorrow Is the Only Faithful One,'' about the omnipresence of sadness; ''Yardbird's Skull,'' a tribute to the jazz legend

Charlie ''Yardbird'' Parker; ''Poems for My Brother Kenneth,'' Dodson's poignant tribute to his deceased sibling; and ''Black Mother Praying,'' about the social injustice encountered by black American war veterans and their families.

Dodson's first volume of verse, *Powerful Long Ladder* (1946), included excerpts from his *Divine Comedy* verse play, *Poems for My Brother Kenneth,* as well as 36 additional poems. *Powerful Long Ladder* was praised by reviewers. Pulitzer Prize winning–poet Richard Eberhardt hailed Dodson as ''the best Negro poet in the United States.'' Dodson's second collection of verse was *The Confession Stone: Song Cycles* (1970), a collection of various monologues concerning the life of Jesus. Dodson then assembled *Cages* (1953), a small collection of verse dedicated to Berkelman, his former Bates professor. Dodson's final published verse was *The Harlem Book of the Dead* (1978), poems for a series of funeral photographs taken by the acclaimed James Van DerZee and assembled by Camille Billops. To date, Dodson's other collection of verse, ''Life on the Streets,'' remains unpublished; however, in May of 1982, the New York Public Theatre staged it as poetry in performance.

There are at least ten recordings of Dodson reading his poetry, among them two Library of Congress tapes. In December of 1960 Dodson was asked to record his verse for the Library of Congress and in May of 1973 he was invited to read there.

Writes Novels

Five years after the publication of *Powerful Long Ladder,* the poet revealed his talent in another form: the novel. *Boy at the Window* (1951) is his autobiographical novel about Coin Foreman, a nine–year–old Brooklyn boy and the guilt he experiences after his mother's death. Coin assumes that his conversion to the Baptist faith could have saved his mother's life. Excerpts were published in *The Book of Negro Folklore* (1958), edited by Langston Hughes and Arna Bontemps, and *Cavalcade: Negro American Writing from 1760 to the Present* (1971), edited by Arthur P. Davis and J. Saunders Redding. When the novel was published in paperback in 1967, the title was changed to *When Trees Were Green.* Regardless of the title, Dodson's first novel remains a sensitive, universal story of boyhood.

Dodson began writing his second novel, *Come Home Early, Child* in 1952, but it was not published until 1977. In an *Interview with Black Writers,* he blamed the delay on perception:

> Then I got a Guggenheim Fellowship and wrote the second novel which I now have in manuscript form. But I was told that the novel was not ''black enough.''. . . So the second novel is here, but it ain't ''black.'' It's about the growing up and fulfillment of a little boy, and that's why it has not been published.

In Come Home Early, Child, Coin Foreman is now an adult. He is a member of the U.S. Navy stationed in Italy who returns to Brooklyn only to experience alienation. The novel's first chapter, ''Summer Fire,'' placed second in the *Paris Review's* contest for best short story (1956), and was included in the book *Best Short Stories from the Paris Review* (1959) as well as *Come Out of the Wilderness* (1965), edited by L. N. Schielman. ''Come Home Early, Chile,'' another excerpt from Dodson's second novel, was printed in *Soon, One Morning* (1963), edited by Herbert Hill, and *The Best Short Stories by Negro Writers: An Anthology from 1899 to the Present* (1967), edited by Langston Hughes.

Makes His Mark on the Theater

Dodson's lifelong love of theater motivated him to act, write plays as well as other theatrical pieces, direct, teach, and become a theater critic. By engaging in all of these activities, he made valuable contributions to American drama.

As early as his high school days, he had displayed acting talent. At Bates and Yale, Dodson acted in various plays. Even after he assumed college faculty positions, he had opportunities to act in such plays as *Family Portrait, Hamlet, Homecoming, Our Town,* and *School for Scandal.*

Dodson wrote at least three plays while at Bates; several of these brought him recognition as a promising, young playwright. His first play during his Yale years was *Gargoyles in Florida* (1936), an adaptation of Langston Hughes's a story ''Red–Headed Baby.'' It won Tuskegee Institute's first annual play writing contest (1941). *Divine Comedy* (1938), Dodson's best–known play and a verse drama in two acts, centers around Father Divine, the self–proclaimed religious leader. It was produced at Yale University Theatre and reviewed favorably in *Variety. Garden of Time* (1939), also a verse play, was Dodson's interpretation of *Medea* with settings in Greece; Athens, Georgia; and Haiti. The music for *Garden of Time* was composed by Shirley Graham (later Du Bois) who was also enrolled in Yale's Drama School. The play won Stanford University's Maxwell Anderson verse drama award (second place) in 1942. Also during his graduate years at Yale, Dodson was commissioned by Talladega College, Alabama, to write a play, *Amistad,* commemorating the 100th anniversary of the slave ship mutiny led by Joseph Cinqué.

Several years after his graduation from Yale, Dodson's career as an educator was interrupted when he enlisted in the U.S. Navy in 1942; yet he continued writing plays. Stationed at the Great Lakes Naval Training Center in Illinois, Dodson wrote and directed a 15–minute radio show each week depicting the lives of naval heroes. His first military play, *Robert Smalls,* honors the black American naval hero of the Civil War. By the end of basic training, Dodson's plays included *John P. Jones, Lord Nelson: Naval Hero, Old Ironsides, Don't Give Up the Ship,* and *The Ballad of Dorie Miller,* the latter receiving national attention when an excerpt was published in *Theatre Arts.* After a brief furlough, Dodson would have received a new assignment to a special training school. However his lieutenant commander kept him at the base where he wrote and produced longer morale plays in addition to the shorter works. Before receiving a medical discharge in 1943, he wrote six more plays and produced five including *Everybody Join Hands, He Planted Freedom,* and

Freedom the Banner. The military and the public were pleased with Dodson's naval plays; some were performed by other military drama groups in the United States and abroad.

Additional Dodson plays include *Doomsday Tale* (n.d.), about the burning of a black southern town on Good Friday; *Bayou Legend* (1946), Dodson's adaptation of Ibsen's story of Peer Gynt; and *The Third Fourth of July* (1946), a play he co–wrote with poet Countee Cullen. Dodson collaborated with composer Mark Fax and wrote two operas: *A Christmas Miracle* (1955) and *Till Victory Is Won* (1965). Twenty–seven of Dodson's 37 plays have been produced. The largest audience for a Dodson play attended Madison Square Garden on June 26, 1944. Twenty–five thousand people saw Dodson's *New World A–Coming: An Original Pageant of Hope.*

Heads University Drama Department

That Dodson was a prolific writer and director is even more remarkable when one remembers that he had to meet the demands of an academic career. Beginning in 1939 with his appointment at Spelman College, Atlanta, Dodson concurrently taught and directed drama departments and/or summer theater at Atlanta University and its Morehouse College, and Hampton Institute (now University) in Virginia before joining the faculty of Howard University in Washington, D.C., in 1947. Ten years later, Dodson was appointed chair of the Drama Department. At Howard Dodson continued his routine of teaching and/or serving as a director or department head during the day and directing during the night. During his long career, Dodson directed more than 100 plays. Sometimes he would cast nontraditionally; for example he cast white parents with black sons in Arthur Miller's *Death of a Salesman.*

There were a number of highlights during Dodson's Howard years. In February of 1948, Dodson directed Miller's *All My Sons*; it was the first time that white drama critics attended a Howard play. Later that year Fredrik Hasliend, a Norwegian delegate to the United Nations, saw a performance of Ibsen's *The Wild Duck* at Howard; as a result Dodson, along with Anne Cooke and James Butcher, led the Howard Players on a three–month tour of northwestern Europe during the fall of 1949. The students performed *The Wild Duck* and DuBose Heyward's *Mamba's Daughters,* a play Dodson directed. The U.S. government was so pleased with the group's success that upon its return, Howard University was presented with the American Public Relations Award. A versatile director, Dodson continued to direct Greek and Shakespearean drama, but he also directed the premier performance of James Baldwin's *Amen Corner* during the 1954–55 season. In 1964 Dodson staged productions of Ted Shine's *Sho' Is Hot in the Cotton Patch* and Amiri Baraka's *Dutchman.* Shine and Baraka (then known as LeRoi Jones) were former students of Dodson's at Howard. The Howard years were a time of extreme productivity for Dodson. Hatch, Dodson's authorized biographer, reported in *Sorrow Is the Only Faithful One* that: ''From 1963 to 1965, he wrote twenty–five theater reviews of performances at Arena Stage, the Howard Theatre [not Howard University's theater], and the National Theatre. In the same period, he directed twenty–one shows, often back to back.''

In 1967 Dodson relinquished the chairmanship of the Drama Department, and in 1970 he retired but continued to direct plays as well as read at colleges and writers conferences. Dodson taped *The Gossip Book,* 60 biographical sketches of various artists including James Baldwin, Langston Hughes, and Paul Robeson. He taught creative writing at the City College of New York, and he was a visiting professor at York College in Queens.

Dodson was the recipient of a number of major writing grants including the Rosenwald, Guggenheim and Rockefeller General Education Board Fellowships. In 1951, 15 years after graduating from Bates College, the alumni membership elected him to Phi Beta Kappa. He received the Audience Development Committee award from the New York Black Theatre Alliance. An additional honor was *Owen's Song,* a collage of his plays, poetry and stories assembled by two of his former students, Glenda Dickerson and Mike Malone. It premiered at the Colony Theatre in Washington, D.C., in October of 1972, and on New Year's Eve, 1974, it opened at the Kennedy Center with Robert Hooks as producer. The *Crisis* reported:

> It was generally expressed by those who participated in or witnessed the production of *Owen's Song* that no one was more deserving of such an overwhelming display of love and appreciation and affection than was this literary and theatrical genius who had given so much of his talent and inspiration to so many of his students, colleagues, proteges, and devotees.

Dodson outlived many of his family members and friends, including W. H. Auden, Arna Bontemps, Countee Cullen, Langston Hughes, and Paul Robeson. His final years were plagued by arthritis and alcoholism. He died in June of 1983.

Owen Dodson, a man of great talent and creativity, created poetry and prose, acted, directed, and taught. American literature is richer today because of his significant contributions in three genres: poetry, novels, and dramas.

REFERENCES

Andrews, William L., Frances Smith Foster, and Trudier Harris, eds. *The Oxford Companion to African American Literature.* New York: Oxford University Press, 1997.

Hatch, James V. *Sorrow Is the Only Faithful One: The Life of Owen Dodson.* Urbana: University of Illinois Press, 1995.

———, Douglass A. M. Ward, and Joe Weixlmann. ''The Rungs of a Powerful Long Ladder: An Owen Dodson Bibliography.'' *Black American Literature Forum* 14 (Summer 1980): 60–68.

O'Brien, John, ed. *Interviews with Black Writers.* New York: Liveright, 1973.

Peterson, Bernard L. Jr. ''The Legendary Owen Dodson of Howard University: His Contributions to the American Theatre.'' *Crisis* 86 (November 1979): 373–78.

COLLECTIONS

Dodson's papers are located at the Moorland–Spingarn Research Center, Howard University; the James Weldon Johnson Collection at the Beinecke Library, Yale University; the Countee Cullen–Harold Jackman Memorial Collection, Clark Atlanta University; and the Hatch–Billops Collection, New York City.

Linda M. Carter

Thomas Andrew Dorsey
(1899–1993)
Musician, composer

Thomas Andrew Dorsey has been called the Father of Gospel Music. The title is not quite exact: gospel music and its precursors had long existed in the black church. His great achievement was reintroducing blues–based gospel music into black churches through gospel choruses. In doing this Dorsey brought congregations into more active involvement in worship by vocalization and movement. He also brought gospel soloists and groups into increased prominence and respectability by establishing the gospel music concert with paid admission. In addition, Dorsey wrote nearly a thousand pieces, 500 of which have been published. His crowning achievement is ''Precious Lord, Take My Hand,'' one of the most profound expressions of Christian faith ever written.

Thomas Andrew Dorsey was born on July 1, 1899, in Villa Rica, Georgia, the oldest child of Thomas Madison Dorsey and Etta Plant Spencer Dorsey. Thomas Madison Dorsey's parents were farmers who rented their land and, although illiterate themselves, stressed the value of education to their eight children who survived childhood. Thomas Madison Dorsey graduated from Atlanta Baptist College (now Morehouse) in 1894, but instead of seeking a permanent position, he became an itinerant preacher.

Etta Plant of Villa Rica had first married a railroad worker, Charles Spencer, with whom she traveled to various eastern cities. In addition to a solid elementary education, Etta Plant learned to read music and play keyboard instruments. She had a beautiful singing voice. Her first husband was killed in a railroad accident before her eyes. Perhaps with the insurance money, she bought two acres of land in Villa Rica and 50 acres in the country nearby. Despite her initial aversion to Dorsey, whom she found too fat, she was married to him on October 15, 1895.

For the next four years, the Dorseys traveled; he preached and she helped him with her music. After trying to live in Atlanta, the Dorseys returned to Villa Rica in 1903, where Thomas Madison Dorsey combined farming with pastoring

Thomas Andrew Dorsey

two small country churches. There were a number of specific musical influences on their young son. One was the portable reed organ his mother played, which he was eager to learn to play himself. Thomas Dorsey was also influenced by his mother's brother Phil Plant, a guitar player and a hobo who probably played country blues. The third influence on Dorsey was the schoolmaster, Corrie Hindsman, who was the son of the founder of Mt. Pleasant Baptist Church and the husband of Etta Dorsey's sister. Hindsman was a trained musician who published a collection of hymns and taught the congregation of Mt. Prospect Baptist Church to sing ''shaped note'' hymns. In addition to these individuals, Dorsey also remembered ''moaning,'' the wordless vocalization of embellishments to hymns. This kind of music rose from and could inspire profound religious fervor.

Around 1908 the Dorseys were unable to continue to work the farm and moved to Atlanta to join the urban poor. Thomas Madison Dorsey found work as a laborer and, it is believed that he stopped preaching entirely. Etta Dorsey took in washing. Thomas Andrew Dorsey suffered a particular blow to his self–esteem when he was demoted from the third grade to the first at the Carrie Steele Orphanage School, a one room school where two teachers, whose salaries totaled $45 a month, taught 112 children in the first three grades in two four–hour shifts. Dorsey left school after completing the fourth grade at the age of 13 or 14. Under the impact of city life, his attachment to religious beliefs also became much weaker.

One way in which Dorsey adapted to the urban milieu was to frequent Decatur Street, the entertainment center for

Atlanta's black community, especially the Eighty–One Theater. With access to an organ at home and to a piano in the home of James E. Dorsey, his uncle, Dorsey worked hard at developing his keyboard skills. He learned mostly by ear, receiving tuition from pianists like Ed Butler, the principal pianist of the Eighty–One Theater, where Dorsey had secured a job selling refreshments at intermission.

By the time he was 14–years old Dorsey was playing for dances at rent parties and in brothels if he was permitted to enter. He soon realized that he needed formal training to gain status in the musical community. For a brief time he took some lessons from a Mrs. Graves, a teacher associated with Morehouse College, but the formal lessons were soon discontinued. Since the skills of reading music, arranging, and sight–reading were important to his career, Dorsey sent for books and taught himself the basics of notation. He also honed skills such as improvising slow, intimate, and quiet dance music for long periods, which brought him work, especially at house parties.

Moves to Chicago

In July of 1916 Dorsey left Atlanta for Philadelphia to seek work in the naval yards. His first stop, however, was Chicago where an uncle, Joshua Dorsey, was a pharmacist. With family present to fall back on in case of need, Dorsey elected to stay in Chicago. He found work at odd jobs and played at parties, returning home to Atlanta in the winter. This pattern continued until he settled permanently in Chicago in 1919. In 1918 Dorsey had to register for the draft, but was exempted when he became an early victim of the Spanish influenza epidemic.

When Dorsey first arrived in Chicago, he was still performing ''gut bucket'' blues, a style that was being replaced by ''jass.'' While the fancier, more progressive venues were closed to him, he found work in wine rooms, house parties, and buffet flats. There his quiet playing and singing was preferable to loud music, which could attract the attention of the police. In addition, many in his audiences were recent immigrants from the South, and they were accustomed to Dorsey's kind of music. Still, this brand of music did not make him prominent enough nor did it provide him with the requisite skills to join the musician's union.

Dorsey was ambitious, however. To develop his skills Dorsey enrolled in the Chicago School of Composition and Arrangement. His ability to compose and arrange developed rapidly to the point that he had a profitable sideline to fall back on when work became scarce. In October of 1920, seven months or so after Okeh recorded Mamie Smith for the first time, Dorsey registered his first composition at the copyright office.

Dorsey had his first nervous breakdown in the late fall of 1920. He weighed only 128 pounds, and his mother had to come to Chicago to take him back to Atlanta. Dorsey recovered and was able to return to Chicago before September of 1921. On September 12 of that year, Dorsey's uncle persuaded him to pay ten cents to attend the last session of the National Baptist Convention, Inc. There he heard W. M. Nix, who would become one of the best–selling preachers of sermons on records in the second half of the decade, sing ''I Do, Don't You'' from the just published official songbook of the convention, *Gospel Pearls.* Nix undoubtedly followed the black tradition of embellishing the written music, and the result moved Dorsey to conversion.

Dorsey then became music director at Chicago's New Hope Baptist Church and began to write religious songs. He copyrighted his first religious song, ''If I Don't Get There,'' on September 11, 1922. Dorsey's religious conviction did not stand up to the temptation of earning $40 a week as a member of a band called The Whispering Syncopators. This was a step up the musical hierarchy for Dorsey, who now began to meet such prominent musicians as W. C. Handy. The band became popular around Chicago.

During 1923 Dorsey began writing and publishing a series of songs in a modified popular format. A popular singer of the day, Joe ''King'' Oliver had one of his biggest recording successes with Dorsey's ''Riverside Blues'' in 1924. Unfortunately, Dorsey had adopted his new musical sophistication just as the older ''down home'' blues, represented by the breakthrough of Bessie Smith's recordings, took over the market. In 1924 he registered only one composition. Dorsey waited until 1928 before registering more music. That year, he registered 11 blues compositions.

Dorsey now began to earn his living by arranging music. He became associated with the Chicago Music Publishing Company, which was run by J. Mayo ''Ink'' Williams, who was also a talent scout and producer for Paramount Records. In addition to arranging, Dorsey also coached singers for Paramount.

In the wake of Bessie Smith's success Paramount became interested in Ma Rainey. To publicize Rainey's recordings, in 1924 the record company arranged for her to tour with a band. Dorsey was asked to pick and train the musicians. For the next two years he would back Rainey's highly successful tours, playing the down–home blues and the popular vaudeville songs in Rainey's repertory, as well as jazz in the band's solo numbers.

Turns to Religious Music

On August 1, 1925, Dorsey married Nettie Harper, Ma Rainey's wardrobe mistress. Then in 1926 Dorsey had a second nervous breakdown. He was unable to work for two years, and his wife took a job in a laundry to support them. In 1928 he attended a church service at the urging of his sister–in–law, and he attributed the cure of his depression to the words of the minister, H. H. Haley. Dorsey's resolve to return to religion was reinforced by the sudden death of a young man from appendicitis in the apartment above his. To mark this change, Dorsey wrote his first gospel blues song, ''If You See My Savior, Tell Him That You Saw Me.''

Dorsey decided to distribute his song by publishing it at the moment when the market for sheet music had collapsed because of recording. He had a thousand copies made and hired Louise Keller to demonstrate the song to his accompaniment as he attempted to sell it from church to church. Formally trained, Keller sang the music as written; thus, it made little impression. Although Dorsey's ideas about how to sell his music would bear fruit some years later, the immediate results were unpromising. To earn money quickly Dorsey returned to secular music in less than a year. For four years Dorsey lived an uneasy compromise between his devotion to religious music and his life as a secular blues composer and performer.

In late 1928 Hudson Whitaker (the name is also given as Whittaker and Woodbridge) asked Dorsey to write the music for a lyric Whitaker had written. "It's Tight Like That," recorded with the novel instrumental accompaniment of piano (Dorsey) and guitar (Whitaker), was a runaway hit on Vocalion records, for which Mayo Williams was now working. Georgia Tom (Dorsey) and Tampa Red (Whitaker) became major stars and produced a whole series of blues songs full of double meanings, a new feature on records though already practiced in live performances. Dorsey, either as part of the team of Georgia Tom and Tampa Red or as a soloist, made more than 60 recordings between 1928 and 1932.

In the meantime, Dorsey continued to try to sell his religious songs. Again he hired a performer to demonstrate them; this time he chose Rebecca Talbot, who had been in show business. She did not produce the effect Dorsey was seeking, and he then turned to a singing preacher, E. H. Hall, who was able to move the audience to shouting and moaning with the songs. Chance further favored Dorsey's efforts to place his music with religious audiences. In the opening song session of the National Baptist Convention on August 23, 1930, Willie Mae Fisher made a great impression on the audience by singing Dorsey's "If You See My Savior." Hall introduced Dorsey at the convention where he met and made a favorable impression on major figures in Baptist musical circles like E. W. D. Isaacs, director general of the Baptist Young People's Union (BYPU), and Lucy Campbell, a famed composer of hymns and pianist of the BYPU. Dorsey set up a table at the convention and sold 4,000 copies of his music.

Shapes Gospel Choruses

Dorsey's greatest contribution to church music, however, was through gospel choruses. Gospel choruses in major established churches, which are musical groups separate from the main choir responsible for Sunday services, can be traced in Chicago as far back as the early 1920s, although much of the subsequent history of these early efforts is undocumented. In 1928 Magnolia Lewis (Butts) organized a chorus, the W. D. Cook Gospel Choir, at Metropolitan Community Church. This group sang at funerals and prayer services but not at Sunday worship. It was also rather decorous by Dorsey's standards, and he would later coach the members in how to holler, move, and shout.

The appearance of a gospel chorus during Sunday service did not occur until late 1931 when James Howard Lorenzo Smith, pastor Chicago's Ebenezer Baptist Church, decided to establish a gospel choir. A Southerner, Smith wanted to warm up the church's worship and hear hollers and cries from the congregation. He decreed that the new choir would occupy the space immediately behind his pulpit, and asked Theodore Frye, an urban evangelist, to establish it. Dorsey seconded Frye; together they put on an impressive display. Frye would "strut" while singing as Dorsey would rise to play standing up.

From the moment the chorus made its entrance by marching down the aisle on the second Sunday in January of 1932 its fame grew. The old choir still occupied its place in the balcony, but the gospel chorus claimed a place in the Sunday worship; taboo on vocal expression and movement in the congregation disappeared.

The third gospel chorus in a main line church appeared at Pilgrim Baptist Church, the church the Dorseys attended. After an enthusiastically received performance of the Ebenezer chorus at Pilgrim in February of 1932, Junius C. Austin of Pilgrim asked Dorsey to form a chorus. The director of Pilgrim's choir, Edward Boatner, a composer of great repute, was the highest–paid choir director in Chicago's black churches and resented being supplemented by a gospel chorus. He was able to relegate the gospel chorus to the balcony, but that was his only victory in the competition between the two groups. After a trial of classically trained Dorothy Austin, the pastor's daughter, Dorsey hired former jazz player Mabel Mitchell as pianist for his chorus.

Dorsey never anticipated that choruses would lead the breakthrough of gospel into established black churches. Prior to this date he had written no choral music nor did he use any of his own music with the new choirs. Nevertheless, after the first three gospel choruses in Chicago were established, the movement spread rapidly.

In August of 1932 the gospel choruses from Ebenezer, Pilgrim, and Metropolitan gave a joint concert, a musicale, to great success. After the concert Butts and Frye urged Dorsey to establish the organization that later became the National Convention of Gospel Choirs and Choruses. Dorsey reluctantly accepted the challenge, as well as his friends' suggestion that he become president of the organization.

A short time after the concert, Dorsey reluctantly traveled to St. Louis to second the efforts of Augustus Evans, former assistant director of the Pilgrim chorus, to establish choruses in that city and also to sell Dorsey's music. Nettie Dorsey was pregnant with the couple's first child and the end of her term was near. Although the pregnancy had been normal, Nettie died in childbirth on August 26. Learning of the death after a concert, Dorsey drove to Chicago where he saw a live and healthy nine–pound baby before being given a sedative and put to bed. When Dorsey awakened the following day, the child was dead.

Under the stress of these events, Dorsey wrote his most famous work, "Precious Lord, Take My Hand." When

Dorsey and Frye introduced the song the week after its composition, the congregation went wild. Dorsey continued to write gospel songs in the same vein. In addition, he began a collaboration with Sallie Martin, who joined the Pilgrim chorus in 1932. Martin, who had met Dorsey in 1929, was one of the four women in his first radio singing group, The University Radio Singers. This group appeared on Chicago radio from 1932 to 1937. Their collaboration became closer after 1932, when Martin toured with Dorsey as a soloist. In addition to her musical abilities, she was highly organized. Dorsey believed that she was partly responsible for the successful spread of the gospel movement. In 1939 Martin left Dorsey to establish a profitable music publishing company with Kenneth Morris.

Another woman singer influential in bringing Dorsey's music to wider audiences was Mahalia Jackson. In 1939 Dorsey was so moved by her singing that he proclaimed her the Empress of Gospel Singers, and from about 1940 to 1942 he toured with her as official pianist.

As the formation of gospel choruses became more and more frequent in 1933, Dorsey devoted greater attention to the National Convention of Gospel Choirs and Choruses, which was formally organized in August of that year with Dorsey as founding president. The meeting demonstrated the wide acceptance of gospel music. It was marked by addresses from old–line choir directors like J. Wesley Jones of Chicago, old–line ministers, and even a welcoming speech from William L. Dawson, a Chicago city alderman who later became a congressman. In 1934 Sallie Martin became national organizer for the convention. Dorsey remained president into the 1970s. Even with the competition later furnished by James Cleveland's popular gospel workshop, Dorsey's organization still attracted 3,000 participants to its 1970 convention in Detroit.

In 1935, the National Baptist Convention, Inc., installed a gospel choir, directed by Dorsey. By the 1937 convention, gospel music was so pervasive that it had become fully accepted in the church. Dorsey nonetheless continued to work for his music. Between 1932 and 1944, he traveled extensively, presenting "Evenings with Dorsey."

Beginning in 1940, Dorsey served as dean of evangelistic musical research and ministry of church music for the Gospel Choral Union of Chicago. He continued to write and publish extensively, as well as serving as assistant pastor of Pilgrim Baptist Church through the 1970s. In the late 1960s he became a popular after–dinner speaker and lecturer.

Dorsey's greatest hit after "Precious Lord, Take My Hand" was "We Shall Walk through the Valley in Peace," a postwar crossover hit written in 1939. Recordings by country artist Red Foley and Elvis Presley both sold over a million records.

Dorsey married Kathryn Mosley in 1940; they had two children. He died on January 23, 1993, after having long suffered from Alzheimer's disease.

Dorsey's work with gospel blues resulted in a major reorientation of worship practices in black churches. For many individuals it brought comfort and deepened religious feelings. Through the work of great singers associated with the movement, gospel music reached a larger secular audience in the post–war era.

REFERENCES

Broughton, Viv. *Black Gospel.* Poole, England: Blandford Press, 1985.

Charters, Samuel B. *The Country Blues.* 1959. Reprint. New York: Da Capo, 1975.

Cohn, Lawrence, and others. *Nothing But the Blues.* New York: Abbeville Press, 1993.

Harris, Michael W. *The Rise of Gospel Blues.* New York: Oxford, 1992.

Harris, Sheldon. *Blues Who's Who.* 1979. Reprint. New York: Da Capo, 1979

Heilbut, Tony. *The Gospel Sound.* New York: Simon and Schuster, 1971.

New Grove Dictionary of American Music. 4 vols. New York: Macmillan, 1986.

Oliver, Paul. *The Story of the Blues.* Radnor, PA: 1969.

Santelli, Robert. *The Big Book of Blues.* New York: Penguin, 1993.

Southern, Eileen. *The Music of Black Americans.* 2nd ed. New York: Norton, 1983.

Robert L. Johns

Aaron Douglas
(1899–1979)
Artist, educator

Growing up in Kansas in the early years of the twentieth century, Aaron Douglas had little understanding of the world of the arts. He knew, however, that he loved to watch his mother dabble in watercolor, and that what his mother drew was beautiful. He longed to do the same. Trained by itinerant artists who traveled through Topeka, Elizabeth Douglas did modest still lifes which inspired her son, who showed an early fascination with color and shade. From early in his life, Douglas demonstrated a refusal to accept the limits that the America of this era placed on African Americans. Optimistic, adventurous, and self–confident, he was determined to become an artist, determined to receive the best training possible, and convinced that he should play a role in the changing fortunes and fate of his race. It was this unflinching resolve and dogged faith in his own ability that would lead Douglas to become the primary illustrator of the Harlem Renaissance and one of the most significant African–American artists of the twentieth century.

Aaron Douglas was born in Topeka, Kansas, on May 26, 1899. His father, also named Aaron, had worked as a baker in Nashville, Tennessee. His mother was a native of Alabama. Douglas had several brothers and sisters. The Douglas family experienced constant financial struggle through his childhood, but his parents insisted upon an education. He was determined to continue his education after graduating from Topeka High School, and in order to achieve this, he went north to the factories, first in Detroit and then in Dunkirk, New York, to make money. After working at several factory jobs, Douglas returned to Topeka late in 1917. It had been a successful adventure, and it whetted his appetite for more.

Douglas spent a month in Topeka, then left for Lincoln and the University of Nebraska there. He wrote in "An Autobiography" in the Douglas Collection at Fisk University that he became "the fair–haired boy" of the UNL Art Department when he received first prize for drawing. Douglas's first serious painting was created the first or second year of college, as part of a rigorous course in the drawing of plaster casts. At Lincoln Douglas deepened his acquaintance with the writings of W. E. B. Du Bois and began to ponder the larger dimensions of the nation's racial situation. By 1921 Douglas had become a constant reader first of *Crisis,* then of *Opportunity* magazine. Douglas wrote in his speech, "The Harlem Renaissance," in the Douglas papers at Fisk University:

> The poems and stories, and to a lesser degree the pictures and illustrations were different. The poems and other creative works were *by* Negroes and *about* Negroes. And in the case of one poet, Langston Hughes, they seemed to have been created in a form and technique that was in some way consonant or harmonious with the ebb and flow of Negro life.

After four years of hard work, Douglas received a bachelor of fine arts degree from the University of Nebraska in 1922. He worked various jobs to obtain the diploma, including tough physical labor. He came to regard the drudgery as simply one more dimension of his artistic preparation. He wrote in "An Autobiography," "Fortunately, this experience proved to be the best possible training and orientation for the creation and interpretation of the life that I was later called on to depict." Douglas always sympathized with, and even romanticized, the role of the laborer, whose experience he had briefly shared.

In 1923 Douglas received a bachelor of arts degree from the University of Kansas. He secured a job that fall, teaching art at Lincoln High School in Kansas City, Missouri. His teaching experience in Kansas City provided more than a secure income. Douglas experienced an enlightenment of his own on a small scale when he met William L. Dawson, a black musician, with whom he developed a lifelong friendship. According to his speech, "The Harlem Renaissance," Douglas felt this was more than just a chance meeting of two young ambitious artists of "like mind and purpose." For Douglas, it was an "embryo, or first step" of a renaissance or revival.

Aaron Douglas

Finding someone of common racial and cultural background, who lived and worked "in the same milieu" made all the difference. He no longer felt isolated, which he later called "the cross the Black artist had to bear, who was often isolated physically, as well as in time, interest and outlook." This desire to overcome isolation would play a critical role in his decision to go to Harlem.

Douglas's confidante through this period was Alta Sawyer, a bright young teacher who was very unhappily married to someone else. The two fell in love and remained determined to someday be together. They wrote wonderful love letters over a period of two years, which have provided some of the very best information on Douglas's hopes and dreams. Alta Sawyer was Douglas's main support, but he also had friends who encouraged him to submit his works to new venues. While still in Kansas City Douglas received letters from a friend in Harlem, urging him to enter his work in a competition sponsored by *Survey Graphic Magazine* for a special issue it planned on "Negro life in Harlem." As it turned out, Douglas was profoundly impressed by the spectacular issue of *Survey Graphic* magazine (1925), the issue that would later be expanded into Alain Locke's *New Negro. Survey Graphic* was, Douglas explained in his "Harlem Renaissance" speech in the Douglas Collection at Fisk, "the most cogent single factor that eventually turned my face to New York," and *The New Negro* "eventually proved to be one of the most extraordinary books of the period and more clearly than any other single publication reflects the nature and extent of this unique movement." Douglas decided to make the move to New York.

Studies with Winold Reiss

Upon arriving in Harlem, Douglas almost immediately began to study with Bavarian artist Winold Reiss, who had provided the cover of *Survey Graphic,* featuring Roland Hayes. He greatly admired the forthright manner in which Reiss portrayed blacks, and Reiss encouraged him to paint his own people in a way that he felt only a black man could really accomplish.

Harlem itself also played an important role in Douglas's decision to stay. In moving to what had become the largest black city in the world, Douglas sought to end the isolation from other blacks that had hindered his artistic growth.

One can see Douglas's growth and experimentation through his magazine illustrations, where he created some of his most forceful and interesting works and evolved his artistic language, a language immersed in African art like no other American artist's. These illustrations anticipate the style of his murals, which came a few years later, yet are simpler and bolder, because of the format in which they were included. The murals have more ambitious programs, including lessons from African and African American history. The magazine illustrations, both covers and interior drawings, are usually just a few simple figures, either illustrating a basic idea or just showing images of African Americans.

In fact, a new passion for African art took hold among many of the Harlem Renaissance artists of the 1920s and 1930s, a passion that would spread across the country. This interest in African art was fueled by the architect of the Harlem Renaissance, Alain Locke, who encouraged the casual artists of the movement as well as the writers to express Africanism in their art form. Locke believed that a complete development of black art could not take place without some significant artistic reexpression of African life, and the traditions associated with it. African art was a tangible way to teach African Americans—indeed all Americans—about the connection of black America to Africa and Africa's rich culture.

In the past African American artists had no opportunity to truly explore a connection with Africa, but for the first time, during the Harlem Renaissance, several visual artists led by Douglas began to incorporate Africanisms in their work. This trend did not just occur in painting and sculpture, but in illustrations too. Illustrators had the unique ability to bring Africanisms to a large and varied audience, and Douglas was the ideal person to carry out this goal.

Becomes Harlem Renaissance Artist

Within weeks of his arrival in Harlem in 1925, Douglas was recruited by the NAACP's W. E. B. Du Bois, editor of *Crisis,* and the Urban League's *Opportunity* editor Charles S. Johnson, to create illustrations to accompany articles on lynching, segregation, theater, and political issues as well as poems and stories. Within this largely literary movement, Douglas was hired to create a visual message for a public that had grown dramatically due to the increase in black migration to the north during World War I. Du Bois had complained often in *Crisis* of a lack of both black patronage and a black audience, most notably in his ''Criteria of Negro Art'' in the October 1926 issue. It was his hope that Douglas could reach an emerging black public across the United States, starting with Harlem. This was a role that only an illustrator could carry out. *Crisis* had a wide national readership, and any illustrations Douglas made, which frequently appeared on its cover, would be seen in libraries, schools, and homes across the country. Douglas tried to reach this new black middle class public using the language of African art.

Douglas was unsure of his abilities as an artist when he first started illustrating for *Crisis.* His work was acclaimed, however, and in 1925 his work *The African Chieftain* won *Crisis* magazine's first prize for drawing. He stated in his speech, ''The Harlem Renaissance'':

> These first efforts. . .were gladly received with no questions asked. They seemed to have been in a miraculous way of heaven–sent answer to some deeply felt need for this kind of visual imagery. . . . I began to feel like the missing piece that all had been looking for to complete or round out the idea of the Renaissance.

Douglas tried to carry out Du Bois's wishes by creating a new, positive African–influenced black image for his audience. He was tired of the white man's depictions of blacks and felt his work could touch the black audience in a unique way. He wanted to change the way blacks were shown in art and to bring the language of African art to Harlem, and then across the United States. Douglas explained this desire in a 1925 letter to Alta Sawyer, part of the Douglas papers in the Schomburg Collection. He wrote:

> We are possessed, you know, with the idea that it is necessary to be white, to be beautiful. Nine times out of ten it is just the reverse. It takes lots of training or a tremendous effort to down the idea that thin lips and a straight nose is [sic] the apogee of beauty. But once free you can look back with a sigh of relief and wonder how anyone could be so deluded.

It is clear from his extensive letters that Douglas learned about African art through his own readings and studies, by studying the art collections of friends (including Alain Locke), by viewing published photographs, and by examining works in such prominent collections as those of the Barnes Foundation. He also saw African art at various exhibition spaces in Harlem, including the Countee Cullen Library at 135th Street and Lenox.

The May 1926 issue of *Crisis* provides an ideal example of Douglas's signature style. Du Bois published Douglas's ''Poster of the Krigwa Players Little Negro Theatre of Harlem'' in the issue, not representative of any particular play, but rather as a type of advertisement for Du Bois's theatre project.

This illustration was heavily influenced by Egyptian and African imagery. It is in solid black and white, very boldly executed, almost resembling a woodblock print. The poster shows a single figure sitting in a cross–legged position, with his or her face in profile. The figure is angular, a primarily rectilinear form, with exaggerated thick lips, the appearance of tribal makeup in geometric form, an afro hairstyle and a large hoop earring dangling from the only visible ear. Stylized plants, flowers, and a palm tree, resembling both African motifs and Art Deco patterning, surround the figure. The figure's left hand holds an African mask or ancestral head. Above the figure the influence of Egypt is everywhere, with pyramids on the left, a sun form above, and a sphinx on the right. Wave patterns form the bottom one–third of the composition, perhaps representing the Nile. The obvious inspiration is Africa, and no matter how closely based on actual African imagery it is, the viewer can see the connections immediately.

In the spirit of the Harlem Renaissance, Douglas often collaborated with other artists of the movement, especially his good friend, poet Langston Hughes. In his December 21, 1925, letter to Hughes, located in the James Weldon Johnson Collection at Yale University, he said of their collaboration:

> Your problem, Langston, my problem, no our problem is to conceive, develop, establish an art era. Not white art painted black. . . . Let's bare our arms and plunge them deep through disappointment, into the very depths of the souls of our people and drag forth material crude, rough, neglected. Then let's sing it, dance it, write it, paint it. Let's do the impossible. Let's create something transcendentally material, mystically objective. Earthy. Spiritually earthy. Dynamic.

Late in the summer of 1926, a group of Harlem artists, including Douglas, created the more radical publication *Fire!!,* to lash back at limits on artistic freedom. Only one issue of *Fire!!* ever appeared, but it was important because it demonstrated an effort to break from the confines of Harlem leadership, both black and white, and voiced an artistic message freely and without censorship to a younger, separatist, more militant black audience.

Douglas's book illustrations exhibit his innovative draftsmanship, a skill that impressed both authors and publishers. The book illustrations are executed in the same style as the magazine illustrations, heavily influenced by Art Deco, Art Nouveau, Synthetic Cubism, and Egyptian art. Some examples of Douglas's work have been lost, since his book jackets in the 1920s are no longer used on reprinted copies of the books. His more notable illustrations include his work for Alain Locke's *New Negro,* for James Weldon Johnson's *God's Trombones,* and for Paul Morand's *Black Magic.* One of Douglas's most striking images was that of Brutus Jones in *Plays of Negro Life,* which accompanied *The Emperor Jones.* This also appeared in the magazine *Theatre Arts Monthly.* Jones appears with a hard silhouette outline. The surrounding forest is made up of jagged edges. *Forest Fear* is a particularly successful example of the dramatic flat, hard–edge, cut–out Douglas style.

Paints Murals

Some of Douglas's most important commissions were his murals. He executed a number of important works based on African and African American history. These include his impressive series in Cravath Hall at Fisk University in Nashville, Tennessee—done with the assistance of Edwin A. Harleston—created to represent a panorama of the history of black people in the New World, beginning in Africa and culminating with freedom. He also executed a smaller series at Fisk portraying philosophy, drama, music, poetry, science, day, and night. His restoration of the murals in 1966 was captured in the film *A Thing of Beauty,* produced at Fisk.

In 1930, when he had barely begun work on the Fisk murals, Douglas agreed to paint a small–scale mural series for the College Inn Room of the Sherman Hotel in Chicago. In this series he duplicated some of the designs of the Fisk murals.

Douglas's most famous mural series was executed in 1935, the Marxist–inspired WPA murals now at the Schomburg Center in Harlem. Douglas's large murals chronicled the struggle of the black man and woman beginning in Africa, through slavery, emancipation, and their role as workers in the machine age. The murals appealed directly to a public suffering from the harsh conditions of unemployment and poverty. They show Douglas's talent as a colorist and storyteller.

Douglas spent 1928 studying at the Barnes Foundation in Merion, Pennsylvania. In 1931 he studied at L'Académie Scandinave in Paris. He also studied under Charles Despiau, Henry de Waroquier, and Othon Rieze. But the majority of his career was spent as the founding chairman of the Art Department at Fisk University. He loved teaching and hoped he could bring his unique experiences as the premier visual artist of the Harlem Renaissance to his students. While at Fisk he studied at Columbia University for four consecutive fall terms and received a master of fine arts degree in 1944. He remained in Nashville from 1937 until his death in 1979, but became professor emeritus from Fisk in 1966. The university also honored him in 1973 with a doctor of fine arts degree.

Douglas was always interested in painting the common man, the common experience, the average worker. The mural commissions for the Countee Cullen Library, executed in 1934 when Douglas was 35–years old, mark the most politically vocal point in Douglas's career. Douglas led the illustrators of the Harlem Renaissance in his quest to explore their African heritage. He was unique in his efforts because he was the first black artist in the United States to consistently create racial art and, as an illustrator, was able to reach a vast readership through black magazines. He had to confront the problem of trying to reach a geographically isolated public that was still difficult to define and locate. Despite these challenges, Douglas was successful in his efforts to address issues important to a growing black middle class. He was sought repeatedly by black leaders to illustrate their messages and received regular commissions until his departure from Harlem in 1937. Douglas brought African art to Harlem in a new, accessible, immediate way. Through his illustrations he presented African art to Americans, both black and white. In addition to his murals and other drawings, he designed bookplates and did portraits of such black luminaries as Mary McLeod Bethune, Charles S. Johnson, and John W. Work. He was the first African American artist—indeed American artist of any race—to regularly incorporate African imagery into his work. Douglas's message was one of pride in African heritage, a message which found a life beyond the white fascination with what was called ''primitivism.'' It was also a message that would find rebirth in the work of later artists and subsequent movements.

In his speech, ''Harlem Renaissance,'' Douglas spoke of the successes of that movement, reminding his students that it was a time ''fraught with hope, bitter frustration and struggle against an indifferent and frequently hostile environment.'' Knowing that they were in the midst of their own struggle to deal with contemporary America, he encouraged his students to remain optimistic and hopeful in keeping their eyes on the prize, a credo he maintained throughout his career.

Douglas died of natural causes in his Nashville home on February 2, 1979. He was 79–years old. His ashes were shipped to New York for burial beside his wife, Alta Douglas. After his death, an art and scholarship fund was established at Fisk University. In 1972 the Aaron Douglas Wing, a large art gallery, was established in his honor in the university library.

REFERENCES

Douglas, Aaron. Letter to Langston Hughes, December 21, 1925, James Weldon Johnson Collection, Beinecke Library, Yale University.

Harlem Renaissance Art of Black America. New York: The Studio Museum in Harlem and Harry N. Abrams, 1987.

Kirschke, Amy Helene. *Aaron Douglas: Art, Race, and the Harlem Renaissance.* Jackson: University of Mississippi Press, 1995.

COLLECTIONS

The papers of Aaron Douglas, including ''An Autobiography,'' his speech entitled ''The Harlem Renaissance,'' and oral history interviews with the artist are in Special Collections, Fisk University Library. Other papers are located at the Schomburg Center for Research in Black Culture, New York. Galleries and museums housing Douglas's works of art include the Brooklyn Museum, the Harmon Foundation in New York, the Carl Van Vechten Gallery at Fisk University, Hampton University in Virginia, Howard University in the District of Columbia, the Museum of Fine Arts in Dallas, and New York's Gallery of Modern Art. His works are also in private collections.

Amy Kirschke

Frederick Douglass
(1818–1895)
Abolitionist, orator, reformer, editor, humanitarian, statesman

Frederick Douglass was one of the most important and influential African American leaders of the nineteenth century. That's a lofty achievement for someone who spent the first 20 years of his life as a slave. Eventually, Douglass escaped to the North, gained his freedom, and joined the abolitionist movement. Douglass became an eloquent spokesperson and acclaimed writer in the fight to abolish slavery in the United States. Many found it hard to believe that an ex–slave could achieve such intellectual greatness. From 1841 until his death in 1895, Douglass gained national and international prominence as an abolitionist, editor, orator, reformer, and champion of human rights. Douglass rallied for civil rights for African Americans, which included the right to be free, the right to own property, and the right to vote. He was also an early supporter of women's rights. As a staunch Republican, he served as an advisor to several presidents. Because of his party loyalty, he was later appointed to three governmental positions. Douglass's greatest legacy is the saga of his extraordinary life preserved in three autobiographies that are still widely read to this day.

Douglass was born Frederick Augustus Washington Bailey in his grandmother's cabin on Holme Hill Farm along Tuckahoe Creek, Talbot County, on Maryland's Eastern Shore in February of 1818. Douglass never knew his exact birth date, but claimed February 14 as his day because his mother, Harriet Bailey, once referred to him as her ''valentine.'' Douglass was the fourth of seven children born to Harriet, a field hand living on a plantation. Douglass was around eight–years old when his mother died in 1825, a year after he was sent to live in the home of his master, Aaron Anthony. Douglass did not know much about his mother, but what he remembered of her remained with him forever. Douglass never knew the identity of his father, though he always maintained that his father was white, possibly his first master, Anthony.

Anthony was the general overseer of Colonel Edward Lloyd's plantation on the Wye River. Douglass was too young to work in the fields, so he ran errands and performed other simple chores. It was while at his master's home that Douglass experienced the hardships of slavery, mostly suffering from hunger and cold.

Frederick Douglass

In 1826, Douglass was sent to Baltimore to serve as a houseboy in the home of Hugh and Sophia Auld, the brother and sister–in–law of Thomas Auld, who was the husband of Lucretia Auld, Anthony's daughter. But it was Thomas Auld who became Douglass's owner following Anthony's death in 1826. His stay in Baltimore over the next seven years profoundly impacted Douglass. It was here that Douglass learned to read and write and received his introduction to the power of the spoken and written word, having purchased the *Columbian Orator,* speeches collected by Caleb Bingham.

In 1833, Douglass returned to the Eastern Shore to live on Thomas Auld's plantation. The next year Douglass was hired out for a year to a local farmer, Edward Covey, well known as a "Negro–Breaker" or one who had a reputation for reforming recalcitrant slaves. Covey whipped Douglass almost weekly. Douglass, who was now age 16, slave fought back. In *Narrative of the Life of Frederick Douglass,* Douglass said that the recurring battle with Covey "was the turning–point in my career as a slave. It rekindled the few expiring embers of freedom, and revived within me a sense of my own manhood. . . . It inspired me again with a determination to be free." He left Covey's service on Christmas day in 1833 and on January 1, 1834 was assigned to William Freeland. During this period, Douglass held at least two "Sabbath" schools. Of course, it was illegal to teach slaves to read and write, but that did not stop Douglass. He managed to gather some old books for his students. "They were great days to my soul," he continued. "The work of instructing my dear fellow–slaves was the sweetest engagement with which was ever blessed." Still, Douglass was restless. The life of a field hand was more restrictive and difficult than that of a city houseboy; he yearned to be free. It was not long before Douglass plotted to escape. Around the end of 1834, after forging passes for himself and four companions, he made ready to flee bondage. Unfortunately, the plot was discovered and Douglass was jailed in Easton, Maryland. Surprisingly, Douglass was not branded or sold to a slave owner in the Deep South, a fate met by others who tried to run away. Instead he was sent back to Baltimore to become a servant for Hugh and Sophia Auld, with the promise that his master Thomas Auld would emancipate him at age 25.

The Life of a Fugitive

Back in Baltimore in 1836, Hugh Auld hired out Douglass as a caulker in the Baltimore shipyards. For the next two years Douglass stayed in Baltimore, coming in contact with the large, free black community there. That made him more determined to be free. In the meantime, he and five other youths formed the East Baltimore Mental Development Society, a secret debating club where Douglass honed his debating and oratory skills. In time, he would develop a powerful and appealing oratorical style. It was at one of its social gatherings that Douglass met Anna Murray, a free black woman who worked as a domestic. They fell in love and became engaged. Murray later assisted Douglass when he impersonated a sailor while using protection papers he borrowed to facilitate his escape on September 3, 1838.

Upon reaching New York City, Douglass was assisted by David Ruggles, the fearless secretary of the New York Vigilance Committee, an organization which assisted fugitives. At Ruggles's home, Douglass was joined by Anna Murray. They were married on September 15, 1838, in a ceremony presided over by James W. C. Pennington, a minister and fugitive from Maryland. The newlyweds later settled in New Bedford, Massachusetts, where Douglass took the name by which he is popularly known. This union produced five children: Rosetta (b. June 24, 1839), Lewis Henry (b. October 9, 1840), Frederick (b. March 3, 1842), Charles Remond (b. October 21, 1844), and Annie (b. March 22, 1849). Unable to find work in the shipyards because of discrimination, Douglass worked at odd jobs to support his family.

The Beginnings of an Abolitionist Career

In New Bedford, Douglass became a subscriber to the *Liberator,* a militant anti–slavery weekly newspaper edited by William Lloyd Garrison, an uncompromising abolitionist. At an abolitionist gathering in August of 1841 in Nantucket, Massachusetts, Douglass was unexpectedly called on to speak. Speaking haltingly but passionately, Douglass related his experience as a slave, holding his audience captive. Garrison was among the listeners.

So riveting was his presentation that the officers of the Massachusetts Anti–Slavery Society asked him to become an agent. Douglass accepted and embarked on a lecture tour of the North for the next four years, often in the company of

Wendell Phillips, a member of the society and gifted orator. At first Douglass simply related his experiences as a slave but later, as he became more confident in his new role, he lectured about the evils of slavery, presenting the same abolitionist arguments as other members of the society.

In physical appearance Douglass was an imposing figure on the platform or in person. Douglass stood over six–feet tall, had a solid build, possessed deep–set eyes, a well–formed nose, and a mass of hair that was neatly combed and parted on the side. His rich, persuasive, baritone voice could hold an audience captive for hours and was tuned to the point where all could hear his words loudly and clearly. It was this voice that made Douglass one of the most effective and sought–after speakers of his day.

Douglass was an accomplished author, too. The 1845 *Narrative of the Life of Frederick Douglass, an American Slave, Written by Himself,* which revealed Douglass's true identity, was a testament to the evils of slavery, detailing its dehumanizing nature and its attempt to crush one's spirit. Most importantly, it showed how its author overcame these hardships and freed himself from physical and mental enslavement.

The book, consisting of 125 pages with introductions by Garrison and Phillips, quickly became a bestseller in reformist circles. Because the book used real names and places, Douglass was in danger of being recaptured. This was one of the reasons Douglass decided to leave the United States and tour the British Isles.

On August 28, 1845, Douglass arrived in Liverpool, England, and spent the next 21 months touring England, Scotland, and Ireland. Besides speaking for the abolition of slavery, Douglass also spoke out on temperance, the repeal of the Corn Laws, Irish home rule, and a plea to the Free Church of Scotland to return money received from pro–slavery Southern Presbyterian churches. Douglass found his audiences receptive and sympathetic. While there, British friends raised money for Douglass to purchase his freedom from Thomas Auld. They also raised money for Douglass to start a newspaper, something he planned to do when he returned to the United States. Although Douglass was given the opportunity to stay and live in England, he realized that his fight to free his people had to be waged in the United States.

The *North Star* is Born

Douglass returned to the United States in August of 1847 and announced plans to start a newspaper. Although Garrison and Phillips were opposed to the idea, Douglass proceeded with his plans. Five weeks after moving his family to Rochester, New York, the first issue of the *North Star* appeared. For a short time, Douglass served as co–editor with Martin Delany, the founder and former editor of the *Pittsburgh Mystery.*

With the publication of the *North Star,* Douglass came into closer contact with the free black community than as an agent of the Massachusetts Anti–Slavery Society, which mostly consisted of white abolitionists. He developed a deeper identification with other African Americans and used his weekly paper to champion their cause. His paper spoke against slavery and oppression, and its office in Rochester served as a station on the Underground Railroad. In a 10–year span, Douglass assisted close to 400 fugitives by providing them with food, shelter, advice, and comfort before they reached Canada. His most famous "passengers" were William Parker and two other fugitives from Christiana, Pennsylvania, who had killed a Maryland slaveholder who was pursuing his slaves.

Douglass had a close or familiar relationship with almost every known reformer in the United States. Among black abolitionists, Douglass counted as his friends or rivals, such people as Reverend Henry Highland Garnett, Reverend Jermain Loguen, Martin R. Delany, Reverend Samuel Ward, Henry Bibb, novelist William Wells Brown, noted abolitionist speaker Charles Remond and his sister, Sarah Parker Remond, and Harriet Tubman. Douglass worked with most of them, particularly in the National Negro Conventions of the 1840s and 1850s.

Douglass was a true reformer, not only as a fervent opponent of slavery, but one who abhorred all forms of oppression, particularly against women. Douglass also supported prominent persons in the woman's rights movement. He was a close friend of Elizabeth Cady Stanton, Susan B. Anthony, Lucretia Mott, and Sojourner Truth and associated with them until the end of his life. Douglass attended the first Woman's Rights Convention at Seneca Falls, New York, in July of 1848, and remained a staunch supporter of the movement, holding a lifelong commitment to woman's rights.

With the dawn of a new decade, Douglass increasingly saw a need to become more politically active in the 1850s. Douglass had become a close associate of New York abolitionist Gerrit Smith, a Garrison opponent and a political activist. Smith's influence, in part, encouraged Douglass to become a voting abolitionist in 1851. This move, however, would mean breaking politically with Garrison. A bitter feud ensued. For the next seven years Douglass supported Smith's Liberty Party and the new Republican Party, endorsing its candidate, John C. Fremont, for president in 1856.

In the meantime, Douglass changed the name of the *North Star* to *Frederick Douglass' Paper,* accepting a subsidy from Gerrit Smith. He also continued to lecture in the North, delivering one of his most famous speeches on July 4, 1852, "What to the Slave is the Fourth of July?," published in *My Bondage and My Freedom*:

> What to the American slave is your Fourth of July? I answer, a day that reveals to him, more than all other days in the year, the gross injustices and cruelty to which he is the constant victim. . . .
>
> Go where you may, search where you will, roam through all the monarchies and despotisms of the old world, travel through South America, search out every abuse, and when you have found the last, lay bare your facts by the side of the every–day practices of this nation, and you will say with me,

that, for revolting barbarity, and shameless hypocrisy, America reigns without a rival.

In 1855, Douglass published his second autobiography, *My Bondage and My Freedom,* a more complete autobiography than the first. This decade saw several events that moved the North and South closer to war, starting with the Fugitive Slave Act of 1850. Many abolitionists were particularly hostile to this act, which denied a fugitive the right to testify on his or her behalf as well a trial by jury. In the round of condemnations against the Act, none was stronger than Douglass's. He told an audience in Boston that if there was an attempt to enforce the law in that city the streets would run with blood. Later, he told an audience in Pittsburgh that the only way to make the Fugitive Slave Law a dead letter was to make a few dead kidnappers. The nation was further divided over the Dred Scott decision in 1857, which declared that blacks had no rights that whites needed to respect.

An event that made war between North and South seem inevitable was John Brown's raid on the federal arsenal at Harpers Ferry, West Virginia, in October of 1859. Douglass had known Brown since 1848, having met him in Springfield, Massachusetts, and they remained cordial friends. The two men, however, differed on strategies for abolishing slavery. Brown advocated violent actions; Douglass chose peaceful persuasion. Even still, Brown stayed in Douglass's home in February of 1858 while perfecting the plans for the raid. In August of 1859, two months before the planned attack, Douglass met Brown in Chambersburg, Pennsylvania, where he rejected Brown's invitation to join the attack. The unsuccessful raid on Harpers Ferry ended in Brown's capture; Douglass fled to Canada to escape federal charges of aiding and abetting Brown. From Quebec he sailed to England, where he stayed for six months. Douglass returned to the United States in May of 1860 after learning of the death of his youngest child, Annie.

Fighting for Emancipation

In the spring of 1860, Douglass began to campaign for Abraham Lincoln, the Republican candidate for president. Lincoln's subsequent election to the presidency caused southern states to break away from the Union, a development that Douglass welcomed. He celebrated the news of Southern forces firing upon Ft. Sumter in South Carolina, believing that a civil war was the only way that slavery could be destroyed and his people set free. He also called on Lincoln to enlist black troops in the Union armies, feeling that African Americans should have a hand in their own liberation.

Lincoln issued the Emancipation Proclamation, effective January 1, 1863, thus freeing all slaves in the rebellious states of the Confederacy. It was then that black soldiers were welcomed to join the Union forces. Douglass became an active recruiter, traveling throughout the North enlisting more than 100 black men to fight with the 54th Massachusetts Regiment, two were his own sons Lewis and Charles. Oddly, Douglass ceased recruiting in 1863 and visited President Lincoln to protest discrimination against black soldiers, particularly because they were receiving lower pay than white soldiers.

In 1863, Douglass had a conference with Lincoln and Secretary of War Edwin Stanton in hopes of receiving an army commission. In anticipation of receiving the commission, Douglass ceased publication of his paper, called the *Douglass Monthly,* ending 15 years as an editor. To Douglass's disappointment, the commission never came.

In 1864, Lincoln called Douglass to the White House and asked him to be one of his advisors to plan for his reelection. Douglass was tempted to oppose Lincoln's reelection because of the slowness of his administration in officially making African Americans U.S. citizens; finally he decided to endorse him. In 1865 he attended Lincoln's second inaugural ball and spoke at many "Jubilee meetings" in black communities across the North in support of Lincoln before his assassination.

Douglass endorsed the Republican Reconstruction plans, which included calling for black suffrage throughout the South. He was part of the black delegation that met with Lincoln's successor, Andrew Johnson. The delegation was highly critical of the new president's agenda, and they left the meeting receiving little support from Johnson. Sometime later, the Republican–controlled Congress impeached Johnson and then took over the reconstruction of the nation. Congress ratified the Fifteenth Amendment in 1870, giving black men the right to vote. Despite its limitations, Douglass celebrated the passage of the amendment, but split with the women's movement over this issue because the amendment made no provisions for woman's suffrage. Meanwhile, Douglass established the *New National Era* in Washington, D.C.

Douglass's life between 1871 and 1872 was marked by trials and tribulations. On January 12, 1871, President Ulysses S. Grant appointed Douglass assistant secretary of the commission of inquiry to Santo Domingo (now Haiti and the Dominican Republic). He toured Santo Domingo from January 18 through March 26 and defended President Grant's decision to annex the island. After the trip, Douglass was persuaded that annexation would be useful to both countries. Tragedy struck Douglass on June 2, 1872, when his Rochester home was destroyed by fire, burning important copies of Douglass's newspapers and personal letters. Suspecting arson, Douglass moved his family to Washington, D.C.

In March of 1874, Douglass was named president of the Freedmen's Bank, which was designed to help the newly–freed African Americans deposit their savings. The bank was in deep financial trouble before Douglass became its leader. When the bank failed, however, Douglass bore the brunt of the blame for its demise. Following that fiasco, Douglass closed down the *New National Era,* and threw himself into his work for the Republican Party. He was rewarded when he was appointed to public office. In March of 1877, President Rutherford B. Hayes appointed him U.S. marshal of the District of Columbia, a first for an African American. In March of 1881 he was appointed recorder of deeds for the District of Columbia by newly–elected President James A. Garfield, another African American first. He held this position for five years. In both positions Douglass took his duties and responsibilities seriously, but despite being appointed by the President himself, he never hesitated to speak his mind about issues that affected black people. He never stopped pushing the nation toward full equality. It was later, in November of 1881, that Douglass published his third and final autobiography, *The Life and Times of Frederick Douglass.*

Tragedy again befell the Douglass household when Anna, his wife of 44 years, died after a long and painful illness. Two years later, on January 24, 1884, Douglass remarried, this time to Helen Pitts, his white secretary when he was recorder of deeds. This marriage brought on a storm of controversy. His black contemporaries accused him of selling out. Douglass, though, insisted that his marriage proved that blacks and whites could live in equality under the same roof. Holding no office at this time, Douglass and his wife decided to travel, visiting England, Egypt, France, Greece, and Italy.

After returning, Douglass assisted the Republican Party in campaigning for Benjamin Harrison for the presidency in 1888. After Harrison was elected, he appointed Douglass minister–resident and counsel general to Haiti on July 1, 1889. Douglass was well received by the Haitians, as they were familiar with his career. He remained in that position until January of 1891, when he resigned in protest after American business groups and the U.S. State Department sought to acquire Mole St. Nicholas over the objections of the Haitians.

The next few years of Douglass's life were quiet. From 1892 until 1893 he served as commissioner for the Republic of Haiti at the World's Columbian Exposition in Chicago. Douglass also joined Ida B. Wells Barnett, the fiery journalist and anti–lynching activist, in forcefully speaking out against lynching. In 1893 he also introduced Wells's pamphlet, *The Reason Why the Colored American Is Not in the World Columbian Exposition* in Chicago. In January of 1894 Douglass delivered his last major speech ''Lessons of the Hour,'' in which he strongly denounced lynching in the South.

Douglass delivered a speech to a meeting of the National Council of Women, held in Washington, D.C., on February 20, 1895. Later that evening, at the age of 71, he suffered a heart attack and died at Washington home. His body was buried in Mount Hope Cemetery in Rochester, New York. In 1955 the National Park Service of the U.S. Department of the Interior declared his home, located in the Anacostia section of Washington, a national shrine.

A Lasting Legacy

At times Douglass agreed with many, particularly when it came to emphasizing race pride and economic self–reliance among African Americans. Other times, they disagreed and, sometimes, he found himself in the minority. Douglass disagreed with such influential people as Martin Delany and James T. Holly over the issue of integration or separation. Douglass believed that African Americans should become a part of American society in order to build a colorblind society. Douglass stood virtually alone on his position on the exodus of black people to the state of Kansas and other states in the Midwest to escape racial violence and economic oppression in the 1870s and 1880s. He believed that the government should protect the lives of its black residents to the point that migration for the sake of a better life would be unnecessary. In time, he realized that the protection was not there and modified his view.

Douglass was honored by many—black and white—because he was dedicated to uplifting all oppressed people. He never restricted himself to addressing one issue that affected humanity, but a variety of concerns. He recognized that America's strength depended on full participation of African Americans in society. He also declared that that America's treatment of its black citizens would be the litmus test of whether or not America was a true democracy. Because of these insights, Douglass was one of the most influential African Americans during the last two centuries, and his legacy lives on.

REFERENCES

Andrews, William, ed. *The Oxford Frederick Douglass Reader.* New York: Oxford University Press, 1996.

Blassingame, John W., ed. *The Frederick Douglass Papers.* 5 vols. New Haven: Yale University Press, 1979–.

Blight, David W. *Frederick Douglass' Civil War: Keeping Faith in Jubilee.* Baton Rouge: Louisiana State University Press, 1989.

Douglass, Frederick. *The Life and Times of Frederick Douglass.* 1881. Reprint, New York: Citadel Press, 1983.

———. *My Bondage and My Freedom.* 1855. Reprint, New York: Dover Publications, 1969.

———. *The Narrative of the Life of Frederick Douglass, An American Slave, Written by Himself.* 1845. Reprint, Boston: Bedford Books of St. Martin's Press, 1993.

Foner, Philip S. *Frederick Douglass.* New York: Citadel Press, 1964.

———, ed. *Frederick Douglass on Women's Rights.* New York: DaCapo Press, 1992.

———, ed. *The Life and Writings of Frederick Douglass.* 5 vols. New York: International Publishers, 1950–1975.

Huggins, Nathan Irvin. *Slave and Citizen: The Life of Frederick Douglass.* Boston: Little, Brown, 1980.

Logan, Rayford W., and Michael R. Winston, eds. *Dictionary of American Negro Biography.* New York: Norton, 1982.

McFeely, William. *Frederick Douglass.* New York: Norton, 1991.

Martin, Waldo E., Jr. *The Mind of Frederick Douglass.* Chapel Hill: University of North Carolina Press, 1984.

Quarles, Benjamin. *Frederick Douglass.* Washington, DC: Associated Publishers, 1948.

Preston, Dickson. *Young Frederick Douglass: The Maryland Years.* Baltimore: Johns Hopkins University Press, 1980.

COLLECTIONS

The personal papers of Frederick Douglass can be found on microfilm at the Library of Congress, Washington, D.C.,

Manuscript Division, and the Moorland–Spingarn Research Center, Howard University, Washington, D.C.

T. Anthony Gass

Charles R. Drew

(1904–1950)

Educator, scientist, health administrator, surgeon, athlete

Charles R. Drew achieved international prominence for his pioneering efforts in the preservation of blood plasma and the establishment of blood banks for emergency needs. His system for the safe storage of blood plasma saved thousands of military lives during World War II, and his work laid the foundation for the blood program of the American Red Cross, earning him the title ''Father of Blood Plasma.''

Born in Washington, D.C., on June 3, 1904, Charles Richard Drew was the eldest of five children born to Richard T. and Nora Burrell Drew. His father was a carpetlayer, and his mother was a graduate of Miner Normal School in Washington who was known for her beauty and graciousness. Drew grew up in a cultured, Christian, close–knit family. His primary education was completed at Stevens Elementary School in 1918 and Paul Laurence Dunbar High School in 1922. During these years he developed leadership skills and competitive qualities through his ability as a good student and a gifted athlete. At age eight he began to compete in swimming and gained experience by paddling around in the harbor of Washington's Foggy Bottom, a poor section of the city, and later at the 12th Street YMCA. By age nine he had won a medal for swimming. During his four years at Dunbar he participated in track, football, basketball, and baseball. For his athletic prowess he received the James E. Walker Memorial Trophy for two consecutive years and was acknowledged by his senior classmates as the best athlete, the most popular, and the student who had done the most for Dunbar.

Immediately following high school, Drew entered Amherst College in Massachusetts on an athletic scholarship. During his freshman year he was the star player on the football team and won a letter in track. He was selected for the All Little Three Elevens as the halfback in 1924 and 1925. Also during his junior year he won the Thomas W. Ashley Memorial Trophy as the most valuable player on the football team. His years on the football team were not unlike Jackie Robinson's racial experience as the first black major league baseball player for the Brooklyn Dodgers. According to his wife Lenore's account in *Reader's Digest,* Drew endured ''racial slurs both on and off the field. The insults made him flush the dangerous, dark red color that earned him the nickname 'Big Red.' He controlled his temper though, for he had decided that our people—any people—could make more real progress by doing and showing than by any amount of violent demonstration.''

Charles R. Drew

As a senior, he was elected captain of the track team, won the National Junior AAU Championship in the 120–yard hurdles, and won honorable mention for All–American Eastern halfback in football. For his outstanding athletic ability in five sports, Amherst honored him with the Pentathlon Award. At graduation in 1926, his crowning moment came when he was awarded the Howard Hill Mossman Trophy, an annual award given to the student who had contributed the most to athletics during his four years at Amherst.

Drew had decided to pursue a career in medicine. Writing in the *Negro History Bulletin* for November 1973, Anne Bittker reported that while an athlete at Amherst, Drew received a severe football injury which required surgery. This experience was his first personal encounter with surgery and perhaps encouraged him to select medicine as a career. After graduation he had hoped to attend medical school, but financial obligations delayed his plans. In order to pay off some of his debts, he worked for two years as director of athletics and instructor of biology at Morgan College in Baltimore, Maryland. Within two years he had transformed the school's football and basketball teams from ''insignificant quality to championship caliber,'' Montague W. Cobb wrote in the *Negro History Bulletin* for June 1950. Although he had earned an extraordinary reputation as a coach, his ultimate goal was still a career in medicine. To realize this dream, he first applied to Howard University Medical School but was denied admission because of what Bittker called ''a technical insufficiency of points.''

In 1928 Drew was accepted at Magill Medical College in Montreal, Canada. At Magill he won first prize in the annual neuroanatomy competition, membership in Alpha Omega Alpha, the medical honorary scholastic fraternity; a $1,000 Rosenwald Fellowship; and in his senior year the Williams prize, awarded annually on the basis of a competitive examination to the five top men in the graduating class. In reference to that award, Drew said that after taking his final examinations in his senior year, he received a call from the dean telling him that he had to take another examination. Believing that he had done quite well on his examinations, he did not understand the request. Presuming the worst, he went to the dean's office, where he learned that he would be taking a comprehensive examination for the Williams Prize. Despite stiff competition, he earned the top honors. In athletics he won the Canadian championships in hurdles, high and broad jumps, scoring in one meet an all–time record of 66 points. He served as captain of the track team in 1931.

Drew graduated from Magill with high honors in 1933 at age 29 and received the M.D. and C.M. (Master of Surgery) degrees. After graduating, he spent a year as an intern at Royal Victoria and another as a resident at Montreal General Hospital in Canada. After completing his residency, he switched from internal medicine to surgery.

In 1935 Drew accepted a faculty position at Howard University Medical School as an instructor in pathology. That year he lost his father. As the eldest son, he now became head of the family and was consulted about important family matters. The following year he became a resident in surgery at Freedmen's Hospital, a federally–operated hospital affiliated with Howard. In 1938, he was awarded simultaneously a two–year Rockefeller fellowship for graduate work at Columbia University and a residency in surgery at Presbyterian Hospital, both in New York.

Researches Blood Plasma

At Columbia, while working on his doctorate, Drew became a research assistant to John Scudded and worked with a team on blood chemistry. Their major problem was how to increase the length of time that blood could be stored.

In April 1939, while on his way to a medical convention in Tuskegee Institute in Alabama, Drew stopped in Atlanta for a dinner party, where he met Lenore Robbins, 28, a home economics teacher at Spelman College. Three nights later he returned to Atlanta. As Lenore recalled in the *Reader's Digest,* ''he roused the matron of our dormitory at one o'clock in the morning and insisted that she wake me. I went down to meet Dr. Drew on the moonlit campus. He proposed and six months later we were married.''

After they were married, Lenore Drew moved to New York. Any hopes of spending long hours with her husband were dashed. Charles Drew had three time–consuming jobs: one as a member of a research team, a second as an assistant research surgeon, and a third completing his doctor of medical science degree. Realizing that she would see little of her husband, Lenore Drew volunteered as a laboratory assistant, an arrangement that allowed her to see him. Columbia University awarded him the doctor of medical science in 1940.

A year after World War II began, Drew published his dissertation thesis, ''Banked Blood: A Study of Blood Preservation,'' which proposed the storing of plasma rather than whole blood in blood banks. With the help of the research team, he demonstrated that plasma, unlike whole blood, could be stored for months unrefrigerated without spoiling. In addition, patients could be given plasma from any blood type. Three months after Drew returned to Howard, John Beattie, a former anatomy teacher and a close friend, suggested Drew as the medical supervisor of the Blood for Britain Project. On a leave of absence from Howard, he returned to New York to serve in this capacity. In February 1941 Drew was appointed director of the American Red Cross Blood Bank at New York's Presbyterian Hospital. He also became assistant for the National Research Council's blood procurement program, where he was in charge of blood for use by the U.S. Army and Navy.

As a result of his administrative and organizational skills, the collection and shipping of blood plasma to Great Britain and the national blood bank program were a success. By 1941 Britain had taken over the blood bank operations, and the American Red Cross had set up blood donor stations to collect blood plasma for the American war effort. After three months the program was operating smoothly, but racial issues led Drew to resign as director of the American Red Cross Blood Bank: the armed forces had informed the Red Cross that they would only accept Caucasian blood for transfusion to members of the military forces. In his resignation statement, published in the *New York Times,* Drew said:

> I feel that the ruling of the United States Army and Navy regarding the refusal of colored blood donors is an indefensible one from any point of view. There is no scientific basis for the separation of the blood of different races except on the basis of the individual blood types or groups.

After his resignation, Drew returned to Howard University to become a professor of surgery and medical director of Freedmen's Hospital. He soon embarked on a third career, teaching, and turned all of his enthusiasm to training well–qualified and skilled surgeons. During Drew's nine–year tenure at Howard, more than half of the nation's black surgeons who received A.B.S. certification studied directly under him.

Many different groups recognized his research, publications, and contributions to science. Among his awards were the E. S. Jones Award for Research in Medical Science in 1942; the Spingarn Medal of the NAACP for his work on the British and American blood plasma projects in 1944; an honorary degree of D.Sc. from Virginia State College in 1945; and another honorary D.Sc. from Amherst College in 1947. He was elected a Fellow of the International College of Surgeons in 1946; and in the summer of 1949, he was the first black to serve as a surgical consultant to the surgeon general of the U.S. Army.

Drew accepted many invitations to speak to professional and lay groups. The last week of March 1950, he spent hours writing a proposal for his next research project. After a grueling day at the hospital on March 31, he was scheduled later that evening to speak at a student banquet. Early the next morning he left with three other doctors—John R. Ford, Walter R. Johnson, and Samuel Bullock—to attend the annual John A. Andrew Clinic in Tuskegee, Alabama. Near Burlington, North Carolina, Drew's car overturned, injuring his passengers, and inflicting mortal chest injuries on Drew. Observers of the accident believe that Drew may have fallen asleep at the wheel and run off the pavement onto the soft shoulder of the road. Upon realizing his predicament, he attempted to return the car to the pavement but overcorrected, causing the car to overturn several times. Accounts conflict about the hospital care he received immediately after the accident. He was taken to the Alamance County Hospital where *Crisis* magazine said that he received ''excellent care, including blood and plasma transfusions, but died about forty–five minutes after the accident.'' The *New York Times,* however, reported that he was taken to a ''segregated hospital, ironically, that had no blood plasma that might have saved his life.''

Services for Drew, who had been 45–years old, were held at the 19th Street Baptist Church in Washington, D.C., a church he had attended since his childhood. On the day of the funeral, it was reported that flags at some government buildings in Washington and Great Britain were flown at half–mast. Years later, a monument honoring Drew for his work was erected on the road near the site of his death.

Drew's surviving relatives were his wife, Lenore Drew; daughters Bebe Roberta, age nine, Charlene Rosella, age eight, and Rhea Sylvia, age six; one son, Charles Richard Jr., age four; mother, Nora Drew; two sisters, Nora Gregory and Eva Johnson; and one brother, Joseph Drew. His youngest daughter, Sylvia, attended Howard University Law School and became a civil rights attorney. His middle daughter, Charlene Drew Jarvis was a member of the Washington, D.C., city council in 1979.

Charles Drew was a public servant of the world. His research with blood and blood plasma enriched and saved the lives of many in war and peace. According to Anne Bittker, Drew once said, ''There must always be the continuing struggle to make the world bear some fruit in increasing understanding and in the production of human happiness.''

REFERENCES

Bittker, Anne S. ''Charles Richard Drew, M.D.'' *Negro History Bulletin* 36 (November 1973): 144–50.

Cobb, Montague W. ''Charles Richard Drew, 1904–1950.'' *Negro History Bulletin* 13 (June 1950): 202–206.

Drew, Lenore Robbins. ''Unforgettable Charlie Drew.'' *Reader's Digest* 112 (March 1978): 135–40.

''He Pioneered the Preservation of Blood Plasma.'' *New York Times,* June 14, 1981.

''Plasma Expert Mourned.'' *Pittsburgh Courier,* April 15, 1950.

Scott, Waldo C. ''Biography of a Surgeon.'' *Crisis* 58 (October 1951): 501–506, 555.

''Three Other Doctors Hurt in N. Carolina Automobile Crash.'' *Pittsburgh Courier,* April 8, 1950.

Patricia A. Pearson

David C. Driskell

(1931–)

Artist, educator, writer, curator, foundation director

''It is important that black people be the ones who define their art because unless we take matters in hand, do the proper research and define the field . . . we will continue to be left out,'' David C. Driskell told *Black Issues in Higher Education.* Rather than make art for art's sake, ''we make it to use it, to tell a story,'' he continued. Driskell has taken the matter of African and African American art into his own hands, identified it, defined it, and promoted the collection and appreciation of it. In doing so, he became one of the world's leading authorities on African American art and is highly regarded as an artist and scholar. He has made major contributions to scholarship in the history of African American and African art and the role of the black artist in American society. His reputation transcends international boundaries to include Europe, Africa, and the Americas.

The grandson of a slave, David Clyde Driskell was born in Eatonton, Georgia, on June 7, 1931, the only son of George W. and Mary L. Clyde Driskell. He had three older sisters—Miley Eugene, Virtie Lee, and Georgia Mae. His father, a Baptist minister, moved his family to North Carolina in search of a better life. David Driskell grew up in the mountains of western North Carolina, in the Polkville community.

Driskell began drawing at the age of six under the tutelage of Edna Freeman, a local elementary school teacher, and was educated in the public schools of Rutherford County from 1937 to 1949. After graduating from Grahamtown High School in Forest City, he entered Howard University in the winter of 1950. He studied at the Skowhegan School of Painting and Sculpture in Skowhegan, Maine, in 1953, and in 1955 he received a B.A. degree in fine arts from Howard University in Washington, D.C. Because of his Reserve Officers' Training Corps experience during college, he was commissioned a second lieutenant in the U.S. Army upon graduating from Howard. In 1957 he became a first lieutenant, and upon leaving the service continued his education at the Catholic University of America. Driskell graduated with the M.F.A. degree in 1962. He remained in the Army Reserves

David C. Driskell

until 1965. He pursued post–graduate study in art history at the Netherlands Institute for the History of Art in The Hague and received a certificate in 1964. Since then Driskell has studied independently African and African American cultures in Europe, Africa, and South America. He was also trained under such artists as James A. Porter, James L. Wells, Lois Mailou Jones, and Morris Louis at Howard University; Jack Levine and Henry Varnum Poor at Skowhegan; and Nell Sonnemann and Ken Noland at Catholic University.

Driskell's teaching career began in 1955 at Talladega College in Alabama before he received his M.F.A. degree. He remained there until 1962. From there he moved to Howard University as associate professor of art from 1962 to 1966. There he worked with James A. Porter, his former teacher who had helped him kindle his interest in art and who then headed the art department.

Promotes African and African American Art

In 1966 Driskell became professor and chairman of the department of art at Fisk University, succeeding Harlem Renaissance artist Aaron Douglas. The department flourished under Driskell's administration, and he developed the art program into an outstanding center for study, creativity, and exhibition. He established the Aaron Douglas Gallery in the Fisk library and added the Division of Cultural Resources to the art program. Of special interest was Driskell's introduction of sculpture into the Fisk art curriculum. He strengthened the faculty by hiring artists with expertise in various sculpture media, including Earl Hooks and Martin Puryear. Stephanie Pogue, a printmaker of national note, joined the faculty in 1968. Driskell brought to the campus such renowned artists as Alma Thomas, Palmer Hayden, James A. Porter, Richard Hunt, Walter Williams, Jacob Lawrence, and Romare Bearden, among others.

While at Fisk in 1970, Driskell, with the cooperation of his staff and students, arranged an exhibition of the extensive African art works in the Fisk collections for the Forty–first Annual Arts Festival at Fisk University. This marked the first time these works had been shown in a single place since they were collected as far back as the 1930s. The exhibit successfully introduced African art to the Nashville community. Driskell wrote in the foreword to the exhibition catalog *African Art*:

> History now bears witness to the fact that the art of Black Africa brought about a revolutionary change in form and content throughout western art. . . . It is important for those of us who view African art outside of its original context to remember that these objects were not made to be museum pieces but were intended to serve a particular function. . . . The tribal arts of Africa have been made according to societal needs thus touching the masses as well as the elite.

In 1977 Driskell left Fisk to become professor of art at the University of Maryland, College Park. He became chairman of the department in 1978 and served as head of a faculty of 46. He stepped down from the chairmanship in 1983 but remained on the faculty and continued his career in the arts as teacher, curator, administrator, and art consultant. Since 1995 he has been Distinguished University Professor of Art at the university. He also began to devote more time to his painting.

During his teaching career, Driskell has held a number of adjunct appointments. He was visiting professor, University of Ife, Ife–Ife, Nigeria (now Awolowo University, 1969–70); visiting professor of art at Bowdoin College and Bates College (spring 1973); adjunct professor, Vanderbilt University (1975–76); distinguished United Negro College Fund scholar, Talladega College (spring 1987); distinguished visiting scholar, Queens College of the City College of New York (spring 1989); and Distinguished Visiting Lecturer, University of Michigan (spring 1990).

Driskell's expertise also led to a number of positions with major art galleries and museums. He was associate director of the Barnett Aden Gallery (1962–66); guest curator, Smithsonian Institution (1972); guest curator, Los Angeles County Museum of Art (1975–77); visiting artist, the Haystack Mountain School of Crafts, Deer Isle, Maine (summers 1975 and 1992); and visiting artist (1976) and resident artist (summer 1978) of the Skowhegan School of Painting and Sculpture. Since 1977 Driskell has served as cultural advisor to Bill and Camille Cosby and as curator of their collection, The Cosby Collection of Fine Arts.

Drawing upon his surroundings in the mountains of his childhood in North Carolina as well as on the landscape of Maine where he has spent his summers since 1961, Driskell made pine trees the theme in many of his paintings from 1961 to 1971. Painting principally in oils, he relied on heavy brush strokes and the use of colors, especially vivid shades of blues and greens. Driskell began a series of paintings in 1980 that reflected on his religious upbringing, themes reflected in his paintings *The Archangel Gabriel, Jonah in the Whale,* and *Ezekiel Saw the Wheel.* Later his style changed to become more expressionistic, creating works that were more autobiographical in nature. Works in the 1990s often included classical themes from literature. His painting, *Daphne Hiding from Apollo* (1992), in the author's collection, is a collage and mixed media on paper, representing his style since 1990. He incorporated generous use of greens seen in his earlier works as well as collage and egg tempera mediums that aided the delivery of a personal black style. His works also showed Brazilian and African influence. He has been influenced by renowned black artist Romare Bearden and nineteenth–century French Impressionist painter Paul Cézanne. His interpretation of early landscape, particularly pine trees, showed an affinity for the landscapes of Cézanne.

Focuses on Black Art

The works of black American artists have long been an area of focus for Driskell's research and teaching. He wrote in an essay in *Harlem Renaissance Art of Black America* that Harlem in the 1920s became a mecca for blacks to explore all the arts and a likely place for black artists to call home. The time called ''for a rebirth of the artistry Black people once had in their native Africa.'' Driskell pointed out the impact of African designs in the works of such premier modernists as Picasso, Modigliani, and Brancusi. Additionally, the artists in black Harlem in the 1920s responded to the call of Alain Locke, who wished to found a ''Negro School of Art'' in Harlem, turn away from modernist trends, and draw upon African art as the source of aesthetics and iconography.

Among Driskell's various writings are catalogs to numerous exhibitions as well as books that accompanied exhibitions, including *Two Centuries of Black American Art* (the bicentennial exhibition and text for the Los Angeles County Museum of Art, published by Alfred A. Knopf, 1976), *Hidden Heritage: Afro–American Art* (Art Museum Association, 1985), *Amistad II,* (United Church of Christ, 1975), *Contemporary Visual Expressions* (Smithsonian Institution, 1987), and *African American Visual Aesthetics: A Postmodernistic View* (Smithsonian Institution Press, 1995). His numerous articles and essays on African American Art have been published in more than 20 major publications worldwide and include the *Christian Science Monitor, New Art Examiner, American Quarterly,* and *Smithsonian Magazine.* He joined David Levering Lewis and Deborah Ryan to author *Harlem Renaissance Art of Black America* (Henry Abrams, 1987). He has served on the boards of various national and international committees, organizations, and institutions including those of the Barnett Aden Gallery (1962–60), Duke Ellington School of Arts (1977–80), the Smithsonian Institution's National Museum of African Art (since 1979), American Federation of Arts (since 1968), the Skowhegan School of Painting and Sculpture (since 1988), Lincoln University (Pennsylvania, 1988–91), Amistad Research Center (1990–97), and Bowdoin College Museum of Art (1994). He was a member of the African American Museum Initiative of the Smithsonian Institution (1990–92). Driskell has served the National Endowment for the Arts as a member of its museum advisory panel (1974–77) and on its policy panel (1980–82).

Driskell has lectured widely at academic institutions and museums throughout the United States, England, Africa, and elsewhere, and has served as consultant to the United Church of Christ, Educational Testing Service, the Institute for Services to Museums, and the National Endowment for the Humanities. In 1974–75 he served on the National Humanities Faculty.

Driskell is widely respected for his work with Bill and Camille Cosby as president of their Clara Elizabeth Jackson Carter Foundation, which he has headed since 1989. He also served on the Cosby Foundation Scholarship Advisory Committee and consulted for *The Cosby Show* (1987–88). In 1995 when President Bill Clinton and Hilary Rodham Clinton sought to add a work by an African American artist to the permanent collection in the White House, they called on Driskell and Sylvia Williams to make the selection. They chose Henry O. Tanner's celebrated work, *Sand Dunes at Sunset: Atlantic City,* which was unveiled and installed in the Green Room on October 29, 1996.

Driskell has received a number of commissions for creative works and for films on art and has made many radio and television appearances. In 1990 the Peoples Congregational Church in Washington, D.C., commissioned him to design two stained glass windows, and in 1993 he designed 65 stained glass windows for DeForest Chapel at Talladega College. He wrote the script and narrated for the film *Hidden Heritage, 1750–1950,* a one–hour documentary for CBS in 1977 which won a CBS award and was aired for three consecutive years. The Arts Council of Great Britain funded a documentary in 1989 to highlight Driskell's contributions to the interpretation of African American art and history under the title *Hidden Heritage: The Roots of Black American Painting* which premiered November 8, 1990, at the British Academy of Film and Television Arts in London. He has collaborated on films about Paul Laurence Dunbar, black American art, and other productions. He appeared on the *Today Show,* CBS's *In The News,* and on stations in foreign countries.

Driskell's memberships include the Smithsonian Associates, College Art Association of America, American Federation of Art, and the National Conference of Artists.

Driskell has received numerous scholarships, fellowships and grants for research and study from such agencies as the Rockefeller, Harmon, and Danforth foundations. The funding he received led to his travel in the United States, Egypt, Saudi Arabia, Yemen, Peru, Japan, Mexico, Holland, Italy, Israel, and Brazil. He has also received numerous awards and prizes including the Distinguished Alumni Award in Art from Howard University in 1981 and the Catholic University of America in 1996. He has been recognized by nine universities with honorary doctoral degrees in art. These include Tougaloo College and Daniel Payne College (1977); State University of New York, Old Westbury and Bowdoin College (1989); Rust College (1991); Talladega College (1993); Baruch College (1994); Maine College of Art (1996); and Fisk University (1997).

An art collector, early on Driskell began to collect the works of black artists Aaron Douglas, Jacob Lawrence, and Romare Bearden, and African sculpture. He has had one–person exhibits at Midtown Payson Galleries and Collectors Gallery in New York City, Colby College Museum of Art, Carl Van Vechten Gallery at Fisk University, Bowdoin College Museum of Art, Barnett Aden Gallery, and the University of Maryland Art Gallery. Among the group shows that included Driskell's work are the American Academy of Arts and Letters, Baltimore Museum of Art, High Museum of Art in Atlanta, California Afro–American Museum, Studio Museum of Harlem, Chrysler Museum in Norfolk, Corcoran Gallery in the District of Columbia, the Whitney Museum of American Art in New York City, and the White House. Driskell's works have been exhibited also in the Santiago, Chile's National Museum. He is also the featured artist in the *International Review of African American Art* (vol. 14, no. 1, 1997), in which a number of his works are reproduced.

Of medium stature, David Driskell is polished, gracious, and moderate in temperament. His devotion to art is balanced by his devotion to family. In his spare time, Driskell enjoys gardening, playing the piano, and cooking. On January 9, 1952, David Driskell married Thelma G. DeLoatch of Henrico, North Carolina. They have two daughters—Daphne and Davrine—and five grandchildren. The Driskells maintain homes in Hyattsville, Maryland; Falmouth, Maine; and in New York City.

David Driskell's expertise as art historian and promoter of works by African and African American artists have led many cultural institutions to expand their collecting and exhibiting practices. He also has stimulated an interest in such art among many people who had not known or understood the works of African and African American artists. He has therefore helped to shape a cultural revolution in art.

Current address: Department of Art, University of Maryland, College Park, MD 20742.

REFERENCES

''African–American Art: Teaching the History.'' *Black Issues in Higher Education* 12 (15 June 1995): 18–21.

Contemporary Black Biography. Vol. 7. Detroit: Gale Research, 1994.

Curriculum Vitae. From the files of David C. Driskell.

''David C. Driskell. Career Summary Statement,'' n.d. From the files of David C. Driskell.

Dover, Cedric. *American Negro Art.* New York: New York Graphic Society, 1960.

Driskell, David C. ''The Flowering of the Harlem Renaissance: The Art of Aaron Douglas, Meta Warrick Fuller, Palmer Hayden, and William H. Johnson.'' In *Harlem Renaissance Art of Black America.* New York: The Studio Museum in Harlem and Harry N. Abrams, 1987.

———. Foreword to *African Art: The Fisk University Collection.* Exhibition catalog. Nashville: The Art Gallery, Fisk University, April 19–May 16, 1970.

———. Interview with Jessie Carney Smith, August 28, 1997.

———. Introduction to *Black Dimensions in Contemporary American Art,* compiled and edited by J. Edward Arkinson. New York: New American Library, 1971.

———. *Two Centuries of Black American Art.* New York: Los Angeles County Museum of Art/Alfred A. Knopf, 1976.

Hooks, Earl J. Interview with Jessie Carney Smith, August 28, 1997.

Who's Who among African Americans, 1996–97. 9th ed. Detroit: Gale Research, 1996.

Who's Who in American Art, 1995–96. 21st ed. New York: Bowker, 1995.

COLLECTIONS

Driskell's works are in such collections as the Corcoran Gallery (Washington, D.C.), the Portland Museum of Art (Maine), Fisk University (Nashville, Tennessee), Howard University (Washington, D.C.), and Tougaloo College (Tougaloo, Mississippi). Privately, his works are in the Cosby Collection of Fine Art, the John Payson Collection, and elsewhere.

Jessie Carney Smith

W. E. B. Du Bois

(1868–1963)

Writer, scholar, educator, activist, Pan Africanist, editor

W. E. B. Du Bois abhorred the status quo. He challenged conventional wisdom and made no apologies for his progressive ideas. He made white America look at their treatment of African Americans at a time when it preferred to ignore them. And he forced black America to look at the realities of their situation in an era of deplorable conditions. The picture was not always pretty. ''I would have been hailed with approval if I had died at fifty. At seventy–five my death was practically requested,'' wrote W. E. B. Du Bois in the *Boulé Journal* for October of 1948, cited in *W. E. B. Du Bois: A Reader.* With this statement Du Bois summarized his life, spanning nearly a century, as one of controversy and protest. A scrutiny of his life is an examination of a critical period for black people in America. He rose to become a towering twentieth–century figure in worldwide race relations. He fused a concept of Pan African socialism with his intellectual progression toward Communism as an ideal arrangement for civilized human society. Du Bois diligently sought the truth, and regularly published his ideas in books and articles.

William Edward Burghardt Du Bois was born on February 23, 1868 in Great Barrington, Massachusetts to Mary Sylvania Burghardt. Early on, Mary Burghardt nicknamed her younger son Willie. Burghardt had another son, Idelbert, fathered five years earlier by her first cousin. The boys had different fathers and the mother attempted to protect Du Bois from the rumors swirling about, regarding his mulatto father, Alfred Du Bois, a descendent of French Huguenot ancestry from Haiti and a barber by trade. In Du Bois's autobiography, he says his father was "run off by the clannishness of the Black Burghardts who disliked his father's light skin complexion." When Du Bois was born, his father moved to Milford, Connecticut, and died shortly thereafter.

Du Bois was raised by the "Burghardt clan" in a section of town that was more concerned with income and ancestry than race. Though most of the Burghardts were literate, Du Bois became the first of this poor working class black family to graduate from high school in 1884. "Ordinary farmers and laborers," he wrote in *Dusk of Dawn,* the Burghardts were to Du Bois "primarily Dutch and New England in outlook." It is this lineage that determined his life and race as a black man.

Du Bois did not know much about his father, although he was able to trace his father's ancestry to a seventeenth century white French Huguenot farmer, Critien Du Bois, residing in the West Indies. Further down the lineage was Du Bois's grandfather, the short, but stern Alexander Du Bois who was light enough to pass for white, but chose a black identity instead. He married three times; each time he married a black woman. Du Bois's father was born to Critien Du Bois's first wife in 1825 in Haiti. As a product of this mixed ancestry, Du Bois, as a mature man of 72 wrote in *Dusk of Dawn*:

> What is Africa to me? Once I should have answered this question "fatherland" or perhaps better "motherland" because I was born in the century when the walls of race were clear and straight—as I face Africa I ask myself: what is it between us that constitutes a tie that I can feel better than I can explain? Africa is of course my fatherland. Yet neither my father nor my father's father ever saw Africa or knew its meaning or cared overmuch for it. My mother's people were closer and yet their direct connection, in culture and race, became tenuous; still my tie to Africa is strong.

From Great Barrington to the University

While growing up, Du Bois added to his mother's limited income by working odd jobs after school. That included mowing lawns, selling newspapers and tea, and, as a teenager, writing for the *Springfield Republican* and T. Thomas Fortune's weekly *New York Age* (later the *New York Globe,* where he reported on Great Barrington's black community). He attended Great Barrington High School from 1881 to 1885 and excelled academically with an almost perfect attendance record from six to sixteen. His white

W. E. B. Du Bois

benefactors, Frank Hosmer—who was also his high school principal—and Edward Van Lennep, saw his early genius as editor of *The Howler,* the school's newspaper. Hosmer also recognized the young lad's intelligence and encouraged him to attend college, as did a local white Congregationalist minister named C. C. Painter. Du Bois was the only black student in his class of 13, but served as the class valedictorian. He delivered a masterful speech about the great abolitionist Wendell Phillips which received praise in a local newspaper.

Harvard University was his choice for college, but he could not meet the high admission standards, as his high school was ill–prepared to provide such a high level of education. Harvard would have to wait until he "became a Negro," he declared. The local Congregationalist church, with Painter and principal Hosmer in full support, raised money to send Du Bois south to Fisk University. His family was disappointed that he was not accepted at Harvard, and were unhappy with Fisk as his second choice.

This decision, however, was an eye–opening experience. He entered Fisk in 1885 at age 17 as a sophomore, and it was his first exposure to the variety of talent and genius of young African Americans: their beauty and brains was a pleasant surprise for him. Fisk was also his introduction to the land of the South—a region he had only read about. His southern colleagues relayed eyewitness accounts of mob violence, lynching, and consequence of Jim Crow segregation that endangered and degraded southern black communities.

Du Bois determined that these black students should become the trained educated elite that would protect and advance the race. From a liberal northern–trained white faculty that included only one black professor, Du Bois learned Greek, mathematics, philosophy, and science. He became concerned with local and national events, and quickly rose to a leadership role at Fisk. In 1885, he became editor of the school's literary journal, the *Fisk Herald*, and transformed it into a vehicle for delivering the opinions and thoughts of young African Americans.

One of the more profound experiences Du Bois encountered was teaching summer school in the rural back country of East Tennessee. In *The Souls of Black Folk,* he said the ''sorrow songs'' were the old Negro spirituals of the black church. These gripping songs moved Du Bois to tears, as they were a testament of how blacks survived slavery. The people he met during these summers were humble and poor, yet lively and expressive compared to his reserved Massachusetts background. Though he taught in dilapidated one–room schoolhouses without chalk, black board, or desks, he was impressed with the number of black students of all ages determined to get an education.

Du Bois graduated with honors from Fisk in 1888 and was accepted at Harvard University as an undergraduate. He was granted the Price Greenleaf Award of $300 to be used toward tuition, and majored in philosophy under the tutelage of the famed professor William James. He took three degrees from the institution: an additional bachelor of arts degree in 1890; a master of arts degree in 1891; and a Ph.D. in 1895. After receiving his M.A., Du Bois studied sociology and economics at the University of Berlin from 1892 to 1894. He also traveled to Switzerland, France, Austria, Italy, Hungary, and Poland and saw himself as the progenitor of a movement to overcome the racism shackling African Americans. This experience broadened his perspective on race relations abroad and would later influence his efforts to deal with race problems on a global level.

Short on money and time, Du Bois was forced to return to Harvard without completing degree requirements at Berlin. For his Harvard doctorate, which he received in 1895, he studied under the tutelage of Albert Bushnell Hart and wrote his dissertation on ''The Suppression of the African Slave Trade,'' the first scientific monograph by a black American and the first published by the prestigious Harvard Historical Series. He was the first black to receive the Ph.D. from Harvard.

Scholar and Activist

Two years after receiving his doctorate, Du Bois, along with Alexander Crummell, one of the greatest black intellects of the nineteenth century, became founding members of the American Negro Academy. In a pamphlet entitled *Conservation of the Races,* Du Bois wrote: ''We need our race organizations; we must lead our own liberation.''

Du Bois was unable to impart his philosophy immediately to a captive audience. Several institutions—including his alma mater, Fisk University—rejected his application to teach. Wilberforce University in Ohio eventually hired him, but Du Bois left after one year. The one bright spot at Wilberforce was student Nina Gomer, whom he married on May 12, 1896, the same year that he accepted the University of Pennsylvania's offer to join their faculty. While there he conducted a study of black people, appropriately titled *The Philadelphia Negro* (1899). This study pioneered what scholars now call ''urban sociology.'' His meticulous obsession for detail provided a model for future sociologists in the study of ethnic groups. From that time on until his death, Du Bois evolved to become a prolific author, editor, and writer, as well as a scholar and social activist. His writing was concentrated in the areas of history, sociology, and critical pieces about current events.

After his Philadelphia study, Du Bois took a position in history and economics at Atlanta University, where he began the famous series of monographs on black life in America. In 1898, ten years after graduating from Fisk, he delivered the Fisk commencement address and urged the graduates to engage in uplifting the black community.

The following year, tragedy struck. His first child, two–year–old Burghardt Gomer Du Bois, died of dysentery in Atlanta. While still recovering from the death of his son, Du Bois attended the Pan African Conference in London, England in 1900. A Trinidadian barrister, Henry Sylvester Williams, convened the conference, but Du Bois added clarity to Williams's revolutionary idea that all people of African decent, regardless of national origin, are tied to a common destiny in a world dominated by whites, particularly the European powers France and England. Du Bois wanted Ethiopia, Liberia, and Haiti, the only free black republics, to remain independent.

While professor of economics and history at Atlanta University (1898–1909), he produced his most popular book, *The Souls of Black Folk* (1903). These 14 passionately written essays, some previously published in other publications, sought to explain ''the meaning of being black in America at the turn of the century.'' ''Double consciousness'' of ''unreconciled ideals'' is the term Du Bois used to describe what is was like to be both black and American. The book contained Du Bois's often–cited prophesy that ''the problem of the twentieth century is the problem of the color line,—the relation of the darker to the lighter races of men in Asia and Africa, in America and the islands of the sea.''

Du Bois was not the only voice challenging racist practices, nor was he the most popular. From 1896 to 1915, Booker T. Washington was widely known as an influential leader in the struggle for civil rights. Du Bois and Washington did not agree on much, as their individual personalities clashed. Washington was willing to surrender the ballot and accept second class citizenship for blacks in exchange for white philanthropic support of industrial and manual training, an idea Du Bois disavowed. In contrast, Du Bois conceded nothing, and wanted all rights due the black race without compromise. Moreover, he argued, that there could not be black advancement unless one–tenth of the black population had access to the ballot, higher education, and all rights of citizenship. "The Talented Tenth," was discussed in an anthology titled *The Negro Problem.*

The Niagara Movement and the NAACP

In two years, the ideological split between Washington and Du Bois would be complete with the formation of the Niagara Movement (1905–1909). Started in Ontario, Canada, the movement endorsed total integration of blacks into mainstream society with all the rights, privileges, and benefits of other Americans. Nearly 60 people were invited to the 1905 Niagara meeting, and about half showed up to establish what would eventually evolve into the National Association for the Advancement of Colored People (NAACP). This movement, nonetheless, was in direct opposition to Washington's "Tuskegee machine," and, in some circles, was viewed as the "anti–Bookerite camp," which was not far off the mark. Washington worried about these meetings, as they grew in frequency and popularity. He even exercised his influence among white philanthropists discourage support of the movement, and, in 1908, Du Bois blamed Washington when funds for his famous Atlanta University Publications, reports on sociological investigations, were cutoff. Interestingly, even though the two men often collided on ideologically views involving the black race, they made several appearances together and remained in close contact until Washington's death in 1915.

It seemed that nothing could stop the rising Niagara Movement. The National Negro Committee was formed in 1909 and reorganized in 1910 as the NAACP—a multiracial civil rights organization that would aid in the advancement of black Americans. Du Bois left his teaching position at Atlanta University to join the NAACP headquarters in New York; he was the only black member of the executive board. With increased funding, better organization, and more members, the NAACP became even more of a threat to the conservative Washington. In November of 1910, Du Bois became director of publications and research, and founding editor of the *Crisis* magazine, the NAACP's official media organ. Du Bois worked hard on the *Crisis* and used the magazine almost as a private journal to relay his views on nearly every important social issue that confronted the black community, ranging from the presidential election of Woodrow Wilson in 1912 to lynchings and World War I. Thousands of subscribers to the magazine, particularly in the black community, could now keep abreast of local, state, national, and international events that were of consequence to the black community.

From the beginning, Du Bois had ideological clashes with the NAACP board. His ideas were far too radical for an organization that recognized the presence and philanthropy of whites and Jews as essential to black progress. Simply put, Du Bois felt the organization was not aggressive in pushing for black civil rights. Furthermore, Du Bois's vision of the struggle was international. His conflicting views created tension between Du Bois and the board, however, the NAACP board stopped short of dismissing Du Bois the *Crisis* editor. By 1913 its circulation had already reached 30,000, and each issue was widely anticipated. He traveled to France in 1919 to document the heroics of black soldiers to further bolster his position. His fact–finding report caused the U.S. Post Office to delay distribution of the *Crisis.* It only sparked excitement: 106,000 copies were sold, a record for the Crisis.

In 1920, Du Bois created the *Brownies Book,* an offshoot of the *Crisis,* to reach children. But this, as so many other efforts, was short–lived because of a lack of finances. Around this time he wrote *Dark Water: Voices From Within the Veil* (1921), the first of three autobiographies. This stirred controversy, as it alluded to a worldwide race war triggered by inattention of the global problem of racism.

In the book and in the *Crisis*, Du Bois was highly critical of Marcus Garvey, and the schism between the two continued to increase. In addition, the rift with the NAACP was widening. Walter White, the new executive director, made it clear that he thought Du Bois's outspokenness in editorials was intolerable. Finally Du Bois, under pressure, retired from the board in 1934 after serving as editor of the magazine for 24 years.

Du Bois was not idle for long. That same year, he accepted an invitation from John Hope, president of Atlanta University, to chair the department of sociology in 1934. Following Hope's death in 1936, Du Bois's influence in Atlanta waned, with colleagues and administrators secretly demanding his retirement, and were successful in 1943. He was offered positions at both Howard and Fisk but decided to return to the NAACP after a nine–year absence. Arthur Spingarn offered him the position of director of special research and he accepted. His activism was still unabated, and the NAACP, knowing what to expect of him by now, shrugged its shoulders and accepted Du Bois for what he was—an outspoken Pan–Africanist who viewed his people as the primary source for his inspiration.

Du Bois and Pan Africanism

With Germany's defeat at the end of World War I and the founding of the League of Nations among the European allied powers in 1918, Du Bois resurrected the concept of Pan Africanism. His call for African unity was answered and the Pan African Congress convened in Paris in February of 1919 (the congress also met in 1921, 1923, and again in 1927). This historic conference brought together black leaders from the United States, the Caribbean, Africa, and Europe. Du Bois believed that defeated Germany's colonial territory in South West Africa should be given back to the Africans it belonged to. Du Bois also advocated the participation of Africans in the European colonial governments in Africa. He visited Africa in 1923, amid the third Pan African Congress, and called Africa home for the black race.

Du Bois traveled throughout Europe and Asia for nearly a decade, returning to the states in late 1937. His alma mater, Fisk, awarded him an honorary doctorate in 1938—50 years after his graduation. He joined the multi–talented Paul Robeson, an actor, singer, lawyer, and Pan Africanist, in the Council on African Affairs to monitor developments with the colonial situation in Africa in 1939. In 1940, during his second tenure as professor at Atlanta University, Du Bois created *Phylon,* a periodical established to study race relations. That same year, he wrote his second autobiography, *Dusk of Dawn: An Essay Toward an Autobiography of a Race Concept,* which contained information about his ancestry and childhood years.

By the fifth Pan African Congress held in 1945 in Manchester, England, Du Bois was dubbed the "Father of Pan Africanism." A year later, he published *The World and Africa,* a sweeping history of Africa's role in world civilization. At home, with the NAACP, Du Bois was not so well esteemed. In 1948 White, once again, called for Du Bois's dismissal, this time for his overt support of the Soviet Union and unrelenting criticism of racist practices in America. This was to be his final separation from the organization he started. He left and became vice–chairman of the Council of African Affairs, a job that he would have until 1956.

In the 1950s, Du Bois developed more of a socialist viewpoint, and grew critical of the capitalistic system. During this period, Du Bois made an unsuccessful run on the Progressive ticket for a senate seat in New York. He was chairman of the Peace Information Agency, which took a unilateral stand against atomic weaponry.

For many years the Justice Department sought ways to silence Du Bois and told him he would have to register as an "agent of a foreign principal." He refused and was indicted; the indictment brought with it the potential of a prison term and a heavy fine. Du Bois was jailed briefly in New York; the NAACP and many prominent blacks turned their backs on the embattled Du Bois. Many felt that he had simply said too much, too often, and that the "chickens were coming home to roost." Du Bois was deeply hurt by their lack of support, and wrote about this experience in his book, *In Battle For Peace* (1952).

Du Bois's wife Nina had died in 1950; in 1951 Du Bois married long–time friend Shirley Graham, who helped raise money for his impending legal battle. He was acquitted at his trial that year. The shadows of Joe McCarthy loomed large over America and any citizen with socialist leanings, sympathy for Russian politics, or who was critical of the American government, faced harassment.

In *The Auto–Biography of W. E. B. Du Bois,* he addressed the nation saying:

> I speak with no authority of age or rank; I hold no position, I have no wealth. One thing alone I own and that is my own soul. Ownership of that I have ever while in my own country for near a century I have been nothing but a nigger.

In 1958, thousands attended Du Bois's ninetieth birthday celebration in New York. He set out on a world tour that lasted nearly a decade. And in that time, the aging warrior drew closer to the Communist Party; he joined in 1961, the same year he and his wife moved to Ghana. He worked on his long time dream, *Encyclopedia Africana.*

On his ninety–fifth birthday, Du Bois received his last honorary doctorate, this time from the University of Ghana, and became a citizen of the country. Six months later, he died on August 27, 1963, the evening before the March on Washington for Jobs and Freedom. After an elaborate state funeral at the behest of Ghana's president Kwame Nkrumah, Du Bois was buried at 22 First Circular Road. Du Bois now has one living grandchild, Du Bois Williams, born in 1932, and an adopted son, David Du Bois.

Du Bois is probably one of the greatest examples of a black intellect. A prolific writer, Du Bois wrote 20 books, two novels, a play, and numerous articles and essays. He produced numerous studies and engaged in a variety of scholarly and cultural endeavors. Though labeled "elitist," "color struck," and "arrogant," critics often failed to examine Du Bois and his work under the circumstances under which he said and did things. The Du Bois that was critical of Marcus Garvey's notion of Pan Africanism in 1923 is clearly different from the Du Bois who died a Pan Africanist in 1963. Du Bois was always changing, adjusting, and adapting his thoughts and ideas to the times in which he was living. He was flexible in adjusting his ideas about black liberation during the period when the "Negro question" was constantly being reframed in the social context of racial oppression. He remained unchanged in his early commitment to uplift his race, and this unfaltering message was consistently delivered throughout his life.

REFERENCES

Aptheker, Herbert. *Annotated Bibliography of the Published Writings of W. E. B. Du Bois.* New York: Kraus–Thompson, 1993.

———, ed. *The Correspondence of W. E. B. Du Bois.* Volume I: Selections 1877–1934. Amherst: University of Massachusetts Press, 1973.

Broderick, Francis. *Negro Leader in a Time of Crisis.* Stanford: Stanford University Press, 1959.

Christian, Charles. *Black Saga: The African American Experience.* New York: Houghton Mifflin, 1995.

Clarke, John Henrik, and others, eds. *Black Titan: W. E. B. Du Bois.* Boston: Beacon Press: 1970.

Cruse, Harold. *The Crisis of the Negro Intellectual.* New York: Morrow, 1967.

Du Bois, W. E. B. *The Auto–biography of W. E. B. Du Bois: Soliloquy on Viewing My Life From the Last Decade of Its First Century.* New York: International Publishers, 1968.

———. "Closed Ranks." Editorial. *Crisis* 16 (July 1918): 111–14.

———. *Dark Water: Voices from Within the Veil.* New York: Harcourt, Brace, 1921.

———. *Dusk of Dawn: An Essay Toward an Auto–biography of a Race Concept.* 1940. Reprint, New York: Kraus–Thompson, 1975.

———. *Writings.* New York: The Library of America, 1986.

Lewis, David Levering. *W. E. B. Du Bois: A Reader.* New York: Henry Holt, 1993.

———. *W. E. B. Du Bois: Biography of a Race, 1868–1919.* New York: Henry Holt, 1993.

———. *When Harlem Was In Vogue.* New York: Knopf, 1981.

Logan, Rayford W., ed. *W. E. B. Du Bois: A Profile.* New York: Hill and Wang, 1971.
Marable, Manning. *W. E. B. Du Bois: Black Radical Democrat.* Boston: Twayne, 1986.
Rudwick, Elliot. *W. E. B. Du Bois Propagandist of Negro Protest.* New York: Atheneum, 1968.
Walden, Daniel, ed. *W. E. B. Du Bois: The Crisis Writings.* Greenwich, CT: Faucett Publications, 1972.

COLLECTIONS

The bulk of the writings, correspondence, and other personal papers of Du Bois are in the library of the University of Massachusetts, Amherst. There are also important Du Bois materials in the Fisk University Library and in the Woodruff Library in the Atlanta University Center. In addition, the Du Bois Papers are contained on microfilm at the Library of Congress and several university libraries including Morgan State University in Baltimore and Howard University in Washington, D.C.

Raymond A. Winbush and David Leon Reed

Edward R. Dudley
(1911–)
Lawyer, statesman, judge

Edward R. Dudley has enjoyed a varied career in law and politics. Beginning with a law career, he rose in the political ranks to become the first black American to serve as an ambassador. Following a successful stint as ambassador to Liberia, Dudley returned to the United States and began a career as a judge to the New York State Supreme Court. His close ties to the Democratic Party resulted in his election to the chair of the New York County Democratic Committee, the first black to hold the position.

Dudley was born on March 11, 1911, in South Boston, Virginia, the son of Edward Richard Dudley, a dentist, and Nellie Johnson Dudley. Young Dudley grew up in Roanoke, Virginia, where he attended public schools. Upon high school graduation, he set out to follow in his father's footsteps. He left Roanoke for Charlotte, North Carolina, to enroll as a pre–dental student at Johnson C. Smith University, his father's alma mater. Dudley proved himself capable in the classroom and starred on university tennis and basketball courts. During breaks he worked in Roanoke as a waiter in a downtown hotel. After his junior year, however, he went north to manage a club for executives' families at Shoreham, Long Island. The experience proved a turning point in Dudley's life. May years later he told the *New York Times,* "For the first time I was treated like a man," he said, "and [I was] called Ed instead of just George or boy." Although he returned to Charlotte to complete his undergraduate studies, he knew he would eventually go back north, where, "[H]e breathed free air for the first time."

Dudley obtained a bachelor of science degree in 1932 and then awaited admission to a dental program. Meanwhile he accepted a teaching position for $60 per month in a one–room frame schoolhouse where he taught first through seventh grades. The job also paid an additional ten dollars for driving the school bus. Years later, as an assistant special counsel for the National Association for the Advancement of Colored People (NAACP), he would bring suits to equalize teacher salaries in tax–supported schools throughout the South.

In 1934 Dudley accepted a scholarship to the Howard University dental school. At the end of his first year, he ranked third in the class, but financial difficulties due to the Great Depression necessitated his withdrawal. He left Washington, D.C., for New York City to be near his uncle, Edward A. Johnson, a politician and real estate broker.

Initially Dudley worked at odd jobs during those years. He bellhopped and waited tables, and he also signed on with the WPA Federal Theatre project. At the theater he was the stage manager of a unit directed by a young Orson Welles. Other actors in the troupe included Canada Lee and Carlton Moss, all of whom, along with Welles, gained professional prominence after the project ended in 1938.

Dudley himself left the theater to work at his uncle's real estate agency during the day and to study law at night. He enrolled at St. John's Law School in Jamaica, New York, and earned an LL.B. degree in 1941. Dudley was admitted to the New York state bar that same year. He spent the following year in private practice.

Through the influence of his mother's brother, Edward A. Johnson and Daniel L. Burrows, a Harlem insurance broker, the young lawyer became politicized. (Johnson, a Republican, later became the first black American to serve in the state legislature when he was elected to the New York State Assembly in 1917.) Burrows, the Democratic leader of the 19th Assembly District, convinced Dudley to serve as a district captain and go door–to–door to drum up votes for the party. Meanwhile, Dudley also became a member of the Carver Democratic Club in Harlem.

Dudley's new political connections soon paid off. When Burrows became an assemblyman, he sponsored Dudley for a vacant position on the staff of the Attorney General, John J. Bennett. However, Dudley's tenure as an assistant attorney general lasted a mere ten months. When Republican candidate Thomas Dewey was elected governor in the 1942 election, Dudley was forced to resign early in 1943.

On January 31, 1942 Edward Dudley married his wife, Rae. While her husband developed a resumé for himself, Rae Dudley taught school. Years later, after a lengthy stint in Harlem, she became the head of the city's all–day neighborhood school at Public School 171, in Astoria, Queens. The Dudleys have one child, Edward Richard Dudley III, born in 1943, who is also a lawyer.

Dudley meanwhile went to work for a small, but growing company, Pepsi–Cola. Dudley, by then a tall, trim, balding lawyer, went from army camp to army camp across the country to hawk the fizzy beverage. Before long, however, Thurgood Marshall convinced Dudley to join a team of lawyers at the NAACP. As assistant special counsel under the future U.S. Supreme Court Justice, Dudley wrote briefs, prepared preliminary papers and helped manage the legal office.

A Rapid Rise in the Diplomatic Ranks

The Democratic Party, which had wooed black voters away from the "Party of Lincoln" during the Depression, was ready to reward its new constituents by placing qualified blacks in higher–level posts. In 1945, party officials began searching for prospective candidates to integrate previously white branches of the federal bureaucracy. President Truman was still three years from integrating the military, but the integration movement had already begun in other areas of the government. At the close of World War II, Dudley was selected to serve as legal aide to Virgin Islands governor Charles Harwood at the recommendation of Brigadier General William O'Dwyer, who was an acquaintance of Dudley's. Dudley took a leave of absence from the NAACP to accept the position. Responsible for writing opinions on local laws, he earned the highest salary of his career up to that point: $7,800 a year, a considerable sum for a person of color at that time.

Within a few months, Governor Harwood moved on and William Hastie, an associate of Dudley's at the NAACP, was appointed to fill the vacancy. Hastie initiated a general "housecleaning" of Harwood's staff, but Dudley was retained, and in fact became the new governor's right–hand man. Later, when Hastie was appointed to the federal judiciary by President Truman, political insiders in the Virgin Islands anticipated that Dudley would assume the governorship. There were also those who predicted that the President would name Dudley to be the ambassador to Romania, Poland, or Yugoslavia. As it was, all speculation proved incorrect. Instead, after two years as one of the governor's closest confidants, Dudley himself elected to return to work at the NAACP in 1947.

In August of 1948 Truman induced Dudley to once again join the diplomatic corps as minister to Liberia. Dudley was sworn in on August 27 in Washington, D.C., and spent several weeks in the capital city attending briefings by the State Department before departing for Monrovia. Dudley's appointment to Liberia followed those of other black diplomats who served as head of the legation, a ministerial post used by contemporary U.S. presidents to win sympathy among black voters.

Dudley accepted the appointment amid popular rumors that his predecessor, Raphael O'Hara Lanier, had quit the post to become president of Texas State University for Negroes (later Texas Southern University) in Houston, in anticipation of a landslide Republican victory for presidential candidate Thomas Dewey in the upcoming November election. That result would have forced all political appointees of the Democratic administration out of their posts, not only in the United States but throughout the world. To the surprise of nearly everyone, and in spite of heavy Republican gains in House and Senate seats, Harry Truman achieved one of the greatest upsets in U.S. political history.

Truman immediately rewarded Dudley's loyalty by upgrading the Liberian legation to an embassy, the highest diplomatic level, thus making the minister's post an ambassadorship. Truman nominated Dudley for the post of ambassador in mid–March of 1949. The nomination was unanimously approved by a Senate subcommittee before gaining ultimate approval by the full Senate. Thus, Dudley became the first black Ambassador in the history of the United States.

As ambassador, Dudley supervised a staff of 16 Americans and 4 Liberians, for which he received $15,000 annually plus living expenses and a limousine. Much of his daily routine involved cutting through red tape to solve problems between the Liberian government and American businesses that were trying to increase their presence in the country. At state functions he was routinely called upon to represent the foreign diplomatic corps as he was the only diplomat of ambassador level in the country at the time.

Dudley further distinguished himself when he helped supervise the implementation of the first Point Four Program in Africa. Truman introduced the Point Four Program in his inaugural address on January 20, 1949. In it, the president outlined the four parts of his proposed foreign–aid program. The last part would provide for technical assistance, skill training, and agricultural and industrial equipment for underdeveloped countries as a way to improve the living conditions of their people. The program also sought to prevent the spread of communism by bolstering the economies of those countries deemed most susceptible to governmental overthrow.

Dudley received first–hand knowledge of conditions in Liberia by accompanying President William V. S. Tubman on walking safaris to up–country tribes. Dudley participated in tribal ceremonies, sitting on his heels and joining in drum–pounding sessions. He remained as ambassador to Liberia until 1953.

Law and Politics

Back in the United States, Dudley rejoined the NAACP as a special assistant in charge of the "Fight for Freedom," a fund–raising project. Dudley's stay at the NAACP was brief. In October of 1955 he was named to a $19,500–a–year domestic relations court judgeship by New York Mayor Robert F. Wagner Jr. Dudley replaced Hubert T. Delany, a black judge just months short of retirement. Wagner, a Democrat, said that he removed Delany from the post for holding "left wing views," but despite the appointment of Dudley, the NAACP and the National Urban League reacted to the mayor's charges by violently protesting the dismissal of Delany, who was also supported by several bar associations.

Even as a judge, Dudley found himself unable to escape overt racism. In 1957 the Virginia State Chamber of Commerce held a banquet in Richmond to honor distinguished natives of the commonwealth who were then living in other states. Among those invited to the affair was Judge Dudley. However, when the organizers learned that the former ambassador was black, they rescinded the invitation.

Dudley served in the Domestic Relations Court post until 1961, when he resigned to become the borough president of Manhattan. Dudley completed the term of a fellow Harlemite, an African–American named Hulan E. Jack, who was convicted on conflict–of–interest charges. Dudley, Mayor Wagner's choice, was elected by a two–thirds vote of the Manhattan members of the city council on January 31. Wagner considered Dudley's election to be a personal victory in his sustained reform campaign to end widespread corruption by party regulars in the Democratically–controlled city.

As the Manhattan borough president, Dudley supported urban renewal projects on the densely populated island. He feared that affordable housing for middle–income families was disappearing as corporations claimed ever–larger portions of Manhattan. Without government–sponsored urban renewal coupled with residential housing programs, Dudley believed that the borough would be split between luxury accommodations and housing authority projects with nothing for the middle class in between.

When his term expired later that year, Dudley decided to run in the general election as a Democratic–Liberal candidate, on the same ticket as Wagner. In the November 7 election, Dudley polled 302,452 compared to 158,774 votes for his opponent, Dorothy Bell Lawrence. He won 14 out of 16 districts.

On September 18, 1962, Dudley earned yet another distinction when he became the first black to be nominated by either major political party for a high–ranking state office: attorney general of New York. Dudley ran as a Democratic–Liberal against the Republican incumbent Louis J. Lefkowitz. Lefkowitz retained the office with 3,052,218 votes to Dudley's 2,405,405. Dudley successfully edged Lefkowitz on his own home turf, but was trounced in the suburban and upstate polling.

Dudley continued in the $25,000–a–year position as borough president through January 1, 1965. During that time he was unanimously elected chairman of the New York County Democratic Committee. Though Dudley was interested in returning to the judge's bench, he accepted the largely ceremonially post anyway, and as with so many of his previous positions, he was the first black to hold it. The selection of Dudley by the Democratic Committee at the September 25, 1963 committee meeting was intended as a political ploy by party regulars who were eager to fill the office with someone of no long–term political ambition. That strategy would give them time to handpick one of their own for a face–off with a reform candidate in the ensuing election.

A vigorous career did not deter Dudley from enjoying personal and social activities. Bald, fit, and trim, Dudley is an avid golfer, swimmer, and tennis player, and he is regarded as a keen bridge player. He takes pleasure in entertaining friends with sleight–of–hand tricks. Dudley also feels at home in the kitchen, where he counts beef vegetable soup and dried lima bean with ham hocks among his specialties.

The New York State Supreme Court

In May of 1964, Dudley told friends that he would seek the Democratic nomination for the state Supreme Court later that year as a preliminary to running for judge surrogate in 1966. Dudley's decision ignited a political controversy over who would succeed him as borough president. The awkward timing of Dudley's decision did not hinder his political career because of his history of accepting political posts under difficult circumstances.

In the November 3 election, Dudley ran for one of five vacancies on the State Supreme Court, First District, Manhattan and the Bronx. Dudley, once again with the endorsement of the Democrats and Liberals, was elected easily to the court. Two of the five vacancies were filled by candidates having the endorsement of all three parties, and were uncontested. Dudley was third. He garnered over 1,155,000 votes, more votes than any of the 12 candidates who vied for the three remaining slots. He was sworn into office the following January.

In December of 1966 Dudley was designated administrative judge of the New York City criminal court in an effort to put that lower court in better working order. The change, which took effect January 1, 1967, was a step down for Dudley, though he retained his title and salary. As an administrative judge he oversaw 78 judges and 903 nonjudicial employees.

The reform effort, which was originally anticipated to be a short–term agenda, lasted five years. In May of 1970 Dudley declared that he had had enough. He had not affected significant change in the court structure due to a lack of sufficient funding. As no such funding was expected to be forthcoming, he asked for reassignment by the state Supreme Court, in the hopes of escaping the administrative routine in return for a courtroom.

Though he was reassigned in November 1970, Dudley was once again named an administrative judge, this time of the New York State Supreme Court for Manhattan and the Bronx, effective January 1, 1971.

In the October 1972 issue of *New York* magazine Jack Newfield attacked Dudley along with a number of other local justices in an article entitled, "The Ten Worst Judges in New York." Newfield alleged that Dudley was an "upward failure" who was promoted beyond his capabilities, among other charges. The article prompted an investigation into the accusations, by a committee of the Association of the Bar of the City of New York. The committee's report was not released until April 8, 1974. As reported in the *New York Times* on the following day, Dudley and two other judges were exonerated in the report which stated that Newfield's article with respect to Dudley was "materially inaccurate and unfair." However, it also said that "There is a substantial body of informed opinion to the effect that Justice Dudley simply has not been an effective administrator."

By the time the report was released, however, Dudley at his own request was relieved of his unwanted administrative duties. He was reassigned as presiding justice of the Appellate Term of the Supreme Court for the First Department. In 1978, with the full endorsement of the *New York Times* and the four leading local political parties, he was reelected to the bench with the highest vote total received by any of the 11 candidates seeking one of five openings. Dudley retired from the bench in 1985.

Dudley, a Presbyterian, is a member of Alpha Phi Alpha, the National Bar Association, and the NAACP. In the 1970s Dudley became a trustee of the Fund for the City of New York. He received honorary LL.D.s from several institutions, among them the University of Liberia, Morgan State College, and his alma mater, Johnson C. Smith University.

Edward R. Dudley's groundbreaking career was as varied as it was successful. He repeatedly took appointments at the behest of others, often putting aside his own best interests. He accepted those positions because they provided opportunities to positively affect the lives of others, not because they might serve as opportunities to advance his career. As a lawyer, diplomat, judge, and politician, he devoted himself to public service and set an example by leading the way.

Current address: 549 West 123rd Street, New York, NY 10027.

REFERENCES

''America's First Negro Ambassador.'' *Ebony* 5 (October 1950): 79–82.

''Bar Report Clears 3 on State Bench of Accusations Leveled in Magazine.'' *New York Times,* April 9, 1974.

Bennett, Charles G. ''Dudley Predicts Wider Renewal.'' *New York Times,* March 19, 1961.

''Court Elections in the City.'' *New York Times,* November 9, 1978.

''Democrats Name Dudley, a Negro, to State Ticket; Donovan to Oppose Javits.'' *New York Times,* September 19, 1962.

''Democrats Name Dudley Chairman.'' *New York Times,* September 26, 1963.

''Dudley Is Named to Succeed Streit.'' *New York Times,* November 20, 1970.

''Dudley Will Run for Court Post.'' *New York Times,* May 18, 1964.

''Edward Dudley Named to $19,500 N. Y. Court Post.'' *Jet* 8 (29 September 1955): 11.

''Edward R. Dudley: Manhattan President.'' *Jet* 19 (16 February 1961): 10.

''Election Day.'' *New York Times,* November 7, 1978.

''Gets Virgin Islands Post.'' *New York Times,* October 10, 1945.

''Impatient City Judge.'' *New York Times,* May 12, 1970.

''Justice Dudley Named to Head City's Criminal Court System.'' *New York Times,* December 7, 1966.

''Mayor's Choice Gets Jack's Job; De Sapio Balked.'' *New York Times,* February 1, 1961.

''Minister to Liberia Sworn In.'' *New York Times,* August 28, 1948.

''No. 1 Manhattanite: Edward Richard Dudley.'' *New York Times,* February 1, 1961.

''Results of the Balloting in City, Suburbs and New Jersey; Questions, Amendments.'' *New York Times,* November 9, 1961.

Robinson, Wilhelmena S., ed. *Historical Afro-American Biographies.* Cornwells Heights, PA: Publishers Agency, 1976.

''State and City Tally for President, Senator and Other Offices; Local Judiciary Vote.'' *New York Times,* November 5, 1964.

''Tally for Governor, Senator and Other Statewide Offices; Vote on the Judiciary.'' *New York Times,* November 8, 1962.

''Telesford Beats Starke Handily.'' *New York Times,* November 4, 1964.

''Truman Defies GOP, Files Nominations.'' *New York Times,* July 30, 1948.

''U.S. Names First Negro Ambassador.'' *Pittsburgh Courier,* March 26, 1949.

Who's Who among African Americans, 1998–99. 10th ed. Detroit: Gale Research, 1997.

Who's Who in American Politics, 1979–1980. 7th ed. New York: Bowker, 1979.

''Woman opposes Dudley for Post.'' *New York Times,* October 30, 1961.

COLLECTIONS

Dudley's papers are deposited in the Amistad Research Center, Dillard University, New Orleans.

Kevin C. Kretschmer

Paul Laurence Dunbar
(1872–1906)
Poet, short story writer, novelist, lyricist

Near the end of the nineteenth century, Paul Laurence Dunbar emerged as a poet of considerable merit after years of struggle in a culture that did not willingly provide outlets for African Americans–that is, unless their aspirations conformed to acceptable stereotypical occupations and roles. Despite the acknowledgment of his talent and the early acceptance of his work, Dunbar has had a rather controversial reputation, one that has waxed and waned with the politics of his readers and critics. There are those who enjoyed hearing recitations of his poems, notably those written in dialect, in their youth, only to be embarrassed later on for having enjoyed them; these poems posed somewhat of a dilemma for

Dunbar as well as for some of his readers. It was the poet's fate during his lifetime to have his standard English verses play a secondary role to those in dialect, those "jingles in a broken tongue," as he called them. It is in the dialect pieces—whether poetry or prose—that Dunbar exhibits his distinctive facility for capturing the variations in speech characteristic of southern rural African American culture in the slavery and post–slavery eras.

Paul Laurence Dunbar was born in Dayton, Ohio, on June 27, 1872. His parents, Joshua and Matilda Glass Burton Dunbar, were former slaves from Kentucky who met in Ohio. Joshua had escaped slavery by way of the Underground Railroad and fought on the Union side during the Civil War. Before her marriage to Joshua, Matilda, a house servant until the end of the Civil War, had been married to Robert Weeks Murphy and had two sons from that union. Unfortunately, the Dunbars' marriage did not last, and Joshua and Matilda were divorced when Dunbar was only 18–months old. When Dunbar's two stepbrothers moved to Chicago, he and his mother were left to survive alone. His own family consisted of Alice Moore Dunbar whom he married on March 6, 1898, much to her family's dismay. It was an unhappy match that ended in divorce four years later.

Dunbar's early education was acquired in the public schools of Dayton where his literary promise was first recognized. When he was graduated from high school in 1891, he composed and delivered the class poem. While he expressed a desire to become a lawyer, his economic circumstances and the restrictions on what an African American could choose as a profession were not hospitable to his career goals. His formal education ended with the high school diploma.

While his literary talents led him to eventually become a man of letters, his employment began as an elevator operator. In this limited world, Dunbar continued to hone his writing skills, rereading his favorite authors and producing his own poetry. His devotion to the written word led him to other jobs that called upon his talent. These included founder and editor of the Dayton *Tattler* in Dayton (1889–90), a brief stint as a clerk at the World's Columbian Exposition in Chicago—a job for which black abolitionist Frederick Douglass was responsible (1893), court messenger (1896), and assistant clerk at the Library of Congress in Washington, D.C. (1897–98). His fortunes depended upon patrons who supplied him with financial assistance. In spite of his economic straits and the illness that plagued him throughout his career, Dunbar's national and international reputation brought him into contact with a number of luminaries in addition to Douglass. These included religious leader and intellectual Alexander Crummell, poet and playwright Angelina Grimké, antilynching crusader Ida B. Wells, social activist Mary Church Terrell, poet and diplomat James Weldon Johnson, and Booker T. Washington, educator and reformer.

Works of the Early Years: 1888–1896

Dunbar's poems began appearing in the *Dayton Herald* in 1888. However, his editorials in the Dayton *Tattler* during the same period revealed Dunbar's two–sided literary personality, one masked by the primacy given his later dialect expressions. Rather than being a writer devoid of social conscience, unaware of the social and political milieu strangling the political, social, and economic aspirations of African Americans, Dunbar was well aware of the relationship between the newspaper and the possible economic development of the African American community. Further, they demonstrate his awareness of the devastation visited upon that community. In *A Singer in the Dawn,* he wrote of his objectives for the newspaper, conveying a desire "that some word . . . shall reach . . . our colored voters and snatch them from the brink of . . . paid democracy." He was later to take up the theme of political corruption and disappointment again in his short story, "Mr. Cornelius Johnson, Office Seeker," in *The Strength of Gideon.* As editor, he emphasized the importance of pride, commitment, and self–sufficiency to the economic development of the African American community. However, one can discern his tendency to dissemble at times. In addressing the issue of race, he said that the issue is "threadbare," thus seeming to suggest that writers should not address it in their newspapers. However, he admonished his fellow editors in *A Singer in the Dawn* that their cry should be "We must agitate, we must agitate."

Paul Laurence Dunbar

The poetry collections of the early period included *Oak and Ivy* (1893), *Majors and Minors,* and *Lyrics of Lowly Life* (1896). The latter is significant for its preface written by William Dean Howells. The noted author and critic praised the dialect poetry, setting the stage for the public's reception and perception of the poet. Referring to the African American characters in the verses, Howells complimented Dunbar on his depiction of his speakers' "delightful personal attempts and failures for the written and spoken language," his "ironical perception of the negro's [sic] limitations" and the "humorous quality" that Dunbar had added to the literature. While acknowledging the talent evidenced in the poems written in standard English, Howells noted that these were not distinctive; rather, it was in the dialect pieces that Dunbar distinguished himself.

While Howells undoubtedly considered his praise of Dunbar to be generous, it is clear that his perception of the dialect poems on the whole is quite limited. In "An Ante-Bellum Sermon," for example, Dunbar's mask slips just a little as he depicts an African American plantation minister who preaches to his congregation about temporal freedom in the guise of spiritual freedom. In this portrayal of the minister, Dunbar has managed to present a rather subversive character who expresses the sentiments of the poet in his inaugural editorial to the *Tattler*—"we must agitate"—albeit behind a mask of humor and irony. In other poems in the volume, some in dialect, Dunbar reveals a deeper appreciation of the characters depicted than Howells and others perceive. In the poem, "When Malindy Sings," for instance, the speaker celebrates the African American artist of the spiritual as her incomparable voice travels throughout the community.

The Middle Passage: 1897–99

While Dunbar continued to write poetry during this period, he turned increasingly to fiction. *Folks from Dixie,* a collection of short stories, appeared in 1898 along with *The Uncalled,* a novel. The "folks from Dixie" are either still living in the South or are transplanted southerners encountering the hostile forces of the North, as in "Jimsella." Ironically, it was during this time that he made his first trip to the South, at the invitation of Booker T. Washington. Contrary to the view of Dunbar as a writer who generally ignored the economic realities facing African Americans of the period, the story "At Shaft 11" focused on efforts to unionize the workers in a West Virginia mine, and the resulting strike which brought in African American workers. It highlighted the heroism of the African Americans whose leader became an assistant to the white foreman once the strike was broken. It may be troubling to some that the narrator was clearly unfriendly to the designs of the union and its drive to improve working conditions; yet the African American males, although occupying a secondary role, contrast sharply with the stereotype of the servile individuals that many associate with Dunbar's work. It is a tale that shows the seriousness that lay behind the mask of humor or servility.

Poems of Cabin and Field (1899) is illustrated with photographs taken by the Hampton Institute Camera Club. The significance of these poems written in dialect is the image that they preserve. Contrary to the stereotypical view of the African American family as fragmented or lacking in those human ties that are evident among others, "Little Brown Baby" conveys the love of a father for his son. The family setting is also depicted in "A Banjo Song," a poem that goes beyond the usual image of carefree African American characters whose only forte is entertainment. It celebrates a key survival element in African American culture that enables the characters to "forget the troubles of the world" if only for a time, offering joy and solace to the "weary slave." In "The Deserted Plantation," there are unfortunate references to "happy days gone by," i.e., the antebellum (post–Civil War) period. It is important to note that another view would credit Dunbar's focus on the survival of the speaker in the midst of devastation.

Dunbar also continued writing prose pieces, several of which contain some of his most strident language. One entitled "Recession Never" and published in the Chicago *Record* (December 1898) condemned the hypocrisy of a nation that would utilize a group of people to fight in its wars, and yet expect those same people not to agitate for full participation in the political process; even more serious was the white community's tendency to feel that it had the right to murder these same people with impunity for demanding their rights. Like more overt activists before and after him, as well as his contemporaries, he addressed the culpability of the church in the trampling of African American rights, ". . . a disgrace . . . an insult to the God they profess to serve." Additional prose pieces of this period included "The Negroes of the Tenderloin: Paul Laurence Dunbar Sees Peril for his race in Life in the City" (*Columbus Dispatch*) and "The Hapless Southern Negro" (*Denver Post*). This period also saw publication of a collection of poems, *Lyrics of the Hearthside.* Dunbar traveled to England where he did two reading tours in London in 1897. There he met the poet Samuel Coleridge–Taylor with whom he collaborated on the operetta "Dream Lovers."

The Final Years: 1900–1906

While this period brought growing critical acclaim, it was marred by continuing health problems and the demise of his marriage. He continued his work with short fiction, publishing *The Strength of Gideon* in 1900, as well as venturing into the longer novelistic form, producing *The Love of Landry* (1900), *The Fanatics* (1901), and *The Sport of the Gods* (1902). The latter is regarded as his most effective expression in this longer form. In it, the writer focuses on the economic precariousness of African American characters transplanted to the urban North, a topic he had explored earlier in *Folks from Dixie.*

Several of the fictional works that surfaced during this period explore the theme of stereotypical behavior. For example, there is the character Gideon in the title story from *The Strength of Gideon* who decides to stay with his old mistress even after freedom has been declared. There is Nelse Hatton, whose "turn–the–other–cheek" attitude prevents him from exacting revenge on the son of his former owner even though the son admits to his torment of Nelse. When the son appears in the city where Nelse and his family have settled, he has already spent some time alone, frustrated, and destitute. Much to the consternation and confusion of Nelse's wife, the former slave dresses the man in one of his finest garments and refuses to exact revenge for the past. There are also characters, like the title role in "Viney's Free Papers," for example, who initially are determined to leave their restricted status only to change their minds. However, Viney's decision may be read not merely in terms of loyalty to the slave past, but also loyalty to the familial bond that keeps her tied to her place, and ultimately to slavery. On the other hand, there is Joshua in "The Ingrate" whose thirst to gain knowledge leads him to take advantage of the opportunity to escape while he is on "loan" to another slave owner.

As in the past, Dunbar reserved his most direct statements regarding the ironies of the African American's position in American society for the newspaper. Echoing Douglass's essay "What to the Slave is Your Fourth of July," Dunbar published in the July 10, 1903, issue of the *New York Times* an article "The Fourth of July and Race Outrages: Paul L. Dunbar's Bitter Satire on Independence Day." The writer's ire is directed at his African American audience, reminding them that in the face of daily news of hangings and burnings, they celebrate and sing "My Country 'Tis of Thee." He ended the article in Martin's *A Singer* with words that foreshadow Martin Luther King many years later: "There be some who on this festal day kneel . . . and with hands upraised and bleeding hearts cry out to God . . . How long O God, How Long." The content and tone of "The Tragedy of Three Forks," a short story in *Gideon* on lynching, is totally consistent with that of the *New York Times* piece.

Although plagued by illness during his final years, Dunbar continued to produce poetry and short stories. These collections included *Lyrics of Love and Laughter* (1903), *The Heart of Happy Hollow* (short stories, 1904), and *Lyrics of Sunshine and Shadow* (1905). He received several honors, including an honorary master of arts degree from Atlanta University in 1899, and an invitation to join the Executive Council of the American Social Science Association in 1900.

In the years since Dunbar's death on February 9, 1906, his contribution to the development of African American letters has been in dispute because of the duality of his vision and voice. What is evident, however, is that he preserved in verse and prose images of survival within the culture, celebrated personages known and unknown, and challenged his readers to recognize the shortcomings of the American social and political milieu.

REFERENCES

Black Literature Criticism. Detroit: Gale Research, 1992.

Black Writers: A Selection of Sketches from Contemporary Authors. Detroit: Gale Research, 1989.

Dunbar, Paul Laurence. *Folks from Dixie.* 1898. Reprint, Freeport, NY: Books for Libraries, 1969.

———. *The Heart of Happy Hollow.* 1904. Reprint, Freeport, NY: Books for Libraries, 1970.

———. *Lyrics of Lowly Life.* 1896. Reprint, New York: Citadel Press, 1984.

———. *Poems of Cabin and Field.* 1899. Reprint, Salem, NH: Ayer Company Publishers, 1991.

———. *The Strength of Gideon and Other Stories.* 1900. Reprint, New York: Arno Press, 1969.

Harris, Trudier, and Thadious Davis, eds. *Afro-American Writers before the Harlem Renaissance.* Detroit: Gale Research, 1986.

Martin, Jay, ed. *A Singer in the Dawn.* New York: Dodd, Mead, 1975.

Wiggins, Lida Keck. *The Life and Works of Paul Laurence Dunbar.* Nashville: Winston–Derek, 1992.

COLLECTIONS

Collections of Dunbar's papers are located in the Ohio Historical Society in Columbus, the Schomburg Center for Research in Black Culture in New York, and the Houghton Library at Harvard University.

Johnanna L. Grimes–Williams

Robert S. Duncanson

(1822?–1872)

Painter

Robert S. Duncanson was a celebrated painter of the nineteenth century known for his romantic landscapes. According to Guy C. McElroy's *Artists' Notebook* for *Sharing Traditions,* newspapers of his day called him "the best landscape painter in the West." A well educated and well traveled man, he flourished during a period in U.S. history when African Americans were rarely afforded the opportunities to pursue professions in the creative arts or many other fields. Duncanson's vision and endurance moved him to create in an often hostile, racist environment. He is known for his landscapes and portraits, which have been praised for their technique, skill, and vision. His work influenced his contemporaries as well as future artists.

Robert Scott Duncanson, an only child, was born in 1821 or 1822 in upstate New York. His mother, was a black woman from Ohio and his father a white man of Scottish ancestry from Canada. Some sources claimed that the family moved to Canada to escape racial discrimination. His parents later separated, and Duncanson remained in Canada, growing up under the care of his father. He had a good public school education and developed a life–long interest and passion for art and literature. At age 19, probably after the death of his father, Duncanson joined his mother near Cincinnati, Ohio.

Soon after relocating to Ohio, Duncanson married a runaway slave, whose name is not known today. Little time passed after the birth of their only child, a son, when his wife died. The baby was mostly reared by Duncanson's mother. In 1857 Duncanson married a woman named Phoebe, and they had two children—Milton and Bertha.

The Making of an Artist

Duncanson decided to become an artist while in school in Canada. Articulate, outgoing, and sociable, Duncanson was a self–taught artist. His interaction with others, intellectually and artistically, worked to shape his artistic development.

Racial barriers he faced in Ohio did not discourage him from his artistic pursuits. On the contrary, Cincinnati was fertile ground for an aspiring artist as it had become a center for the arts. As early as 1842, exhibition catalogs of local exhibits listed his portraits, scenes from everyday life, and prints. Through contacts he made among his mother's friends (who were involved in anti–slavery efforts), he began to meet and show his drawings to members of the local art community, resulting in white patrons commissioning him to paint portraits. Among his artist acquaintances were Miner K. Kellogg, a known portrait painter; Thomas Worthington Whittredge, who would later become president of the National Academy of Design; and Thomas Buchaan Read, a painter and writer. Impressed by Duncanson's talent, these artists encouraged him to enter the annual and highly–competitive Western Art Union competition. Each year all of the works that Duncanson submitted were accepted, an unusual achievement. He became the first African American to show his work among non–African Americans in the context of competition.

Hoping to achieve artistic success in a smaller city, Duncanson relocated to Detroit in 1845. Although viewers admired his works, they did not purchase them. After a time, Duncanson was penniless and extremely depressed. His sale of a painting to Henry N. Walker, a rich merchant, allowed him to meet the travel expenses of returning to Ohio in 1846.

In Cincinnati Duncanson's work quickly began to sell, and his talent was in increasing demand. As was customary at the time, the wealthy and middle class had their walls adorned with paintings, still lifes, and scenes of popular sites. He was commissioned to paint eight murals. One he finished in 1852 entitled *Blue Hole, Little Miami River,* a depiction of a site along the route of the Underground Railroad.

During the 1840s and 1850s Duncanson worked with J. P. Ball, an African American daguerreotypist who owned his own shop. Ball was then working on a panorama that depicted the history of slavery and the life of African Americans in the United States. After Ball trained him in the daguerreotype process, Duncanson created paintings of the images Ball had made. The works were displayed in a large, lavish exhibition hall. By the end of the 1850s, his work was well–recognized, and he set up studios in Detroit and Cincinnati.

The Artist in a Larger Context

Duncanson's long–held desire to travel to Europe was finally realized in 1853, when he made his first of several trips there. He went along with fellow artist and friend William Sonntag, and for eight months they traveled throughout Europe together. Duncanson viewed works by Rembrandt, Titian, Raphael, Michelangelo, and J. M. Turner, and was profoundly impressed by the old masters, as well as some of the contemporary artists he had met. On his return to the United States, Duncanson spoke of his appreciation for artists who were more than copyists of nature but who could capture their real feelings for their environment in their paintings. Duncanson's creations from then on were based on European landscapes and the hills and lakes from his father's Scotland. He produced idyllic scenes in his works, as seen, for example, in *Lock Long*. Duncanson took a number of trips to locales he wanted to paint in order to experience the places first hand.

Perhaps to avoid the violence of the Civil War, Duncanson traveled to Europe and Canada. England's nobility and notables, such as poet Alfred Tennyson, often invited him to their homes. He returned to the United States in 1872 and continued a successful career.

Duncanson began to display strange mental and physical behavior in 1871 and was committed to Michigan State Retreat in September 1872, where he died on December 21, 1872. Because of his fairly swift death, it is now believed that he suffered from a brain tumor.

Duncanson was known for his creative spirit, talent, and drive. As an African American, he felt pressured to prove himself and constantly demonstrate his talents. Because of his perseverance, examples of his vision, dedication, and talent are extant. They are housed in museums such as the Cincinnati Art Museum, Taft Museum, Corcoran Gallery of Art, Fine Arts Collection at the University of Cincinnati, National Gallery of Canada in Ottawa, Detroit Institute of Arts, and in private collections. His more popular works are described as calm, poetic visions of America and Europe as depicted in landscapes.

REFERENCES

Ayres, William, ed. *Picturing History American Painting 1770–1930.* New York: Rizzoli International, 1993.

Bearden, Romare, and Harry Henderson. *A History of African–American Artists: From 1792 to the Present.* New York: Pantheon, 1993.

Bogle, Donald, ed. *Black Arts Annual, 1987–1988.* New York: Garland, 1989.

McElroy, Guy C. *Sharing Traditions: Five Black Artists in Nineteenth–Century America: Artists Notebook.* Washington, DC: National Museum of American Art, Smithsonian Institution, 1985.

———. *Sharing Traditions: Five Black Artists in Nineteenth–Century America: Study Guide.* Washington, DC: National Museum of American Art, Smithsonian Institution, 1985.

Wilmerding, John. *Audubon, Homer, Whistler, and Nineteenth–Century America.* New York: Lamplight Publishing, 1975.

Alicia M. Henry

Jean Baptiste Pointe Du Sable (1745–1818)

Settler, explorer, trader

Among Native American people in the Midwest, it is affectionately noted that the first ''white man'' to settle *Eschikagou* was a black man. Jean Du Sable established the first permanent residence in the area, building an estate that included one bake house, two barns, one dairy, one mill, one poultry house, large livestock holdings, and a comfortable dwelling equipped with contemporary furnishings and 23 pieces of art work. He enjoyed harmonious relations with Native American tribes of the region including the Chippewa, Illinois, Miami, Ottawa, and Potawatomi. In fact, he was regarded so highly by the Potawatomi that he was made an honorary member of their tribe and was allowed to marry one of its daughters. He also established trading posts in Michigan City, Indiana, and Peoria, Illinois, as well as in Port Huron, Michigan. His most impressive post, which measured 40 feet by 22 feet, was built near the Chicago River area that he called home.

Jean Baptiste Pointe Du Sable was born to a Congolese former slave and a wealthy mariner and merchant in St. Marc, Saint–Domingue, which became Haiti in 1804. Du Sable's mother, Suzanne, was purchased from a neighboring plantation by a Frenchman named Du Sable. Du Sable freed Suzanne and she lived with the Frenchman on his coffee and hardwood plantation, bearing one son, Jean Baptiste, in 1745.

Saint–Domingue, a French possession, was embroiled in a bitter battle with the Spanish. Around 1755 while the elder Du Sable was away from the island on business, the Spanish ravaged his plantation, burning the family's home to the ground and killing Suzanne. Learning of this tragedy on his return, Du Sable boarded a ship and sent his son to school in France. Young Jean Baptiste Du Sable and Jacques Clemorgan, the son of a wealthy planter at a nearby estate, were enrolled in St. Thomas school in Saint Cloud, situated near Paris. After settling the enrollment fees with the headmaster of the school, the elder Du Sable never returned to France.

Sails to New Orleans

Jean Baptiste Du Sable and Clemorgan returned to Haiti upon completing their schooling, and Jean Baptiste worked as a seaman on his father's ships and observed his father's business deals at his Cap Francais trading post. The two grew bored with the island, and in the spring of 1764 they decided to establish new lives for themselves. Taking with him all of his personal possessions, Jean Baptiste set sail for Louisiana, known as New France at the time. With him and Jacques on the ship named after his mother, Suzanne, were three crewmen.

After making their way to nearby New Orleans, Du Sable was worried because he had lost on the ship his papers of French citizenship. He feared that he might be mistaken for a slave because of his dark complexion. He sought asylum with a Jesuit priest by the name of Father Pierre Gilbault whom he persuaded to give him work as a groundskeeper at the Catholic mission. Clemorgan found work as a clerk in a merchandising house. Because interracial mingling was discouraged, the boyhood friends rarely saw each other. They did, however, maintain sporadic contact.

Frustrated with the type of work to which he was assigned as a black man in eighteenth–century America, Du Sable dreamed of adventure on the Mississippi River. He shared this desire with a Native American man named Choctaw whom he had befriended and with Clemorgan. The only push Du Sable needed came when he learned that Louisiana's governor D'Abbedie had surrendered the territory to the Spanish under the Treaty of Paris. Du Sable, who harbored bitter anger against the Spanish, decided to leave New Orleans in February of 1765 with the blessings of Gibault. Du Sable and Choctaw fashioned a large boat from cottonwood trees. The priest donated supplies to the men and bid them farewell as they set sail 600 hundred miles up the river.

The area along the Mississippi was still largely unexplored by non–Native Americans. Aside from the intertribal friction, Native Americans were somewhat hostile toward explorers, who consequently, turned away. Du Sable proved to have different luck. With the assistance of Choctaw, who was familiar with several Native American languages, he made the acquaintance of members of many tribal groups. Around 1766 Du Sable met the great chief Pontiac. Despite their 30–year age difference, the two developed an immediate affinity.

As the years passed, Du Sable, a trader, learned the art of hunting. He was able to identify animals by the markings they left on the ground, and he was admired for his adept use of the bow and arrow. He also learned the languages of nearby tribes.

Pontiac recognized Du Sable's strong interpersonal skills, and consequently, sent the young man on a diplomatic mission. Pontiac, who had been a fierce warrior, sought to make peace between the warring tribes of the region and form an alliance that could stand united against the British. As a result of the French and Indian War, which ended in 1763, all land east of the Mississippi became British territory. In a proclamation negotiated by the British and the Native American leaders, a vast amount of Midwestern land had been allotted to Native Americans; however, with tensions mounting between the American colonists and Great Britain, Native American leaders were growing fearful about their fate. Pontiac suspected that if the British obtained a foothold in Midwest America, Native peoples would be marginalized.

Complicating matters, during Du Sable's stay in Pontiac's village in 1769, the great chief was assassinated. A member of another tribe had entered the village in the guise of an Ottawa and stabbed to death the man known as the greatest Native American organizer. This would make Pontiac's charge to Du Sable an even more challenging task, for the warrior was loved by many.

Du Sable set out on the St. Joseph River in a pirogue to apprise nearby tribes of Pontiac's wishes. He met with tribal leaders at the council of chiefs and subchiefs meeting in the Potawatomi village. To his dismay, Du Sable found many of them making preparations for war, having learned of Pontiac's death from a foot messenger. He urged them to stop fighting among themselves. The tribes considered Du Sable's stirring plea, and consented to honor the last wishes of Pontiac.

After delivering Pontiac's message, Du Sable, Clemorgan, and Choctaw decided that it was time to move on. They moved further north on the Mississippi until they reached the lands of the Potawatomi where they were embraced by the tribe. Again, Du Sable and Choctaw resumed hunting, this time, however, with a different goal in mind.

Du Sable was 24, the owner of a barge that could be used for transporting pelts for the fur trade down the Mississippi to New Orleans where Clemorgan had established a joint business with Du Sable. He and Choctaw donated some of the profits to Gibault's mission on every trip that the barge made south.

As indicated by Clemorgan's regular deposits into the Banco de Orleans and the new store he opened in St. Louis, business was thriving. By this time, Du Sable had also established a trading post in Peoria. After losing his father in 1770, he determined to marry. He had one woman in mind. Her name was Catherine.

Catherine was a member of the Potawatomi tribe. This posed a problem for Du Sable. While he had been accepted by the tribe and felt comfortable among them, he was an outsider. The Potawatomi would not usually marry intertribally, let alone interracially. He became a member of the tribe and took his bride. The two married in a traditional Potawatomi ceremony and asked permission from tribal elders to use land not far from them in an area known as *Eschikagou,* or place of bad smells. The elders consented, and in 1772 the Du Sables moved out of the village to establish their residence at Chicago.

Settles Chicago

Du Sable built an elaborate house for his bride in the style of other French settlements in America. The house had five rooms and was well furnished. Inside the door, a sign read "Bienvenue A Des Plains" (Welcome to the Plains). Paying homage to his new extended family, the Potawatomi, Du Sable painted an elk, the symbol of the tribe, on a bark plaque. The entire structure was surrounded by a porch.

Du Sable also built the accompanying structures with the utmost care. An example of this was his guesthouse. In order to accommodate guests from different cultures, Du Sable provided beds complete with blankets and mattresses as well as comfortable bear skin rugs for those who preferred to sleep on the floor. Du Sable built birch furniture and used dried deerskin for curtains. He weatherproofed the logs with a substance called creosote. He would soon receive gifts from his friend to make the dwellings more comfortable.

Clemorgan arrived at the Chicago site bearing copper kettles, china, books, linens, pillows, oil lamps, and silk dresses for Catherine. During his brief visit, Clemorgan and Du Sable decided to dissolve their partnership. Upon parting, Clemorgan agreed to make arrangements for Du Sable's holding of 8,000 livres (former French money of account) to be transferred to the Bank of Quebec.

The Du Sable clan began to grow. In March of 1773 Catherine bore a son, naming him Jean Baptiste Pointe Du Sable Jr. One month later, seeking further stability for his growing family, Du Sable set out eastward to find a wholesaler who could supply his trading house. In Detroit, he learned that one Thomas Smith was a highly respected businessman. Du Sable paid him a visit and was favorably impressed. Smith even offered to take him to meet Colonel Arent Schuyler de Peyster, commander of the British troops at Fort Michilimackinac in northern Michigan.

After meeting Colonel de Peyster in May, Du Sable returned home to help Catherine with the planting of crops and to continue preparations for the opening of the trading post. Considering the loneliness of the family's surroundings, the Du Sables extended an open invitation to the Potawatomi tribe, asking members to move their families to the new settlement at Chicago. About 100 families responded affirmatively, and upon moving, they each took 100 acres of land for building and farming.

The trading post was opened and business began to thrive. News about the well–stocked post spread throughout the region. Du Sable produced so much corn, milk, cheese, and beef that much of it was exported to Louisiana and Quebec. This fortified the family's stability, making them feel more secure. By 1775 the Du Sable's daughter was born, the first recorded birth in the new settlement. She was named Suzanne after Du Sable's mother.

In the spring of 1777, Clemorgan visited the family again, this time bringing bad news of problems with his business in the Mississippi Valley due to the high taxes, travel restrictions, and stringent rules on buying and selling imposed by the British government. He disclosed his plans to move east to take up arms with the American settlers against the British. By 1778 Clemorgan had become an officer in the Virginia militia.

Shortly thereafter, Du Sable noticed an influx of French–speaking travelers passing through the area, many of whom stayed at the lodging house. Du Sable learned that the British had grown suspicious of people of French descent. Fearing that the French might conspire with disgruntled Americans to overthrow British forces in America, the British restricted free assembly, imposed heavy taxes, and limited travel. This group asked Du Sable's permission to build on his land. Du Sable agreed to give each man a ten–acre plot pending approval from Potawatomi elders. The elders consented, the families moved in, and soon after, 100 families followed. Most of them became dairy farmers, trappers, and lumbermen.

One man, a Québecois named Jean LeLime, arrived in Chicago and established a home for his family along the St.

Lawrence River. After Du Sable built an additional wing onto the trading post, LeLime became a full–time employee, assisting Choctaw in attending to the daily needs of the customers.

Du Sable observed the rapid growth of his settlement, and he was pleased with the number of families who had found the place suitable. However, he felt that something was missing. He wrote to Gibault, asking him to consider establishing a school at Chicago. Gibault sought the counsel of his supervising bishop, who consented; by December, he arrived ready to educate Chicago's children.

The settlement at Chicago was being closely watched by anxious British commanders and American militiamen. Both groups took note of the superb position of the site as they plotted to build a fort there. In 1779 Colonel George Rogers Clark, an American soldier who captured British forts Cahokia, Kaskaskia, and Vincennes, approached Du Sable, requesting that Americans be allowed to build a fort there. Du Sable refused, saying that the affairs of the British and Americans were none of his concern.

In the same year, Sir Henry Chilton, a British leader, ordered Colonel de Peyster to built a fort at Chicago, and to arrest Du Sable if he refused to let them build. When British troops arrived, Du Sable refused as expected and was arrested. In his official report, de Peyster described Du Sable as handsome and intelligent, but indicated that his loyalty and sympathy seemed to lie with the French. He was sent to Mackinac Island in northern Michigan.

The British governor of the region, Patrick Sinclair, was so impressed by Du Sable that he ordered the release of the prisoner, who spoke enough English to convince his captors that his loyalty lay with the British crown. Charges against him were dropped, and Du Sable was given the position of monitor of the Native American tribes of the Chicago region.

Du Sable returned to his estate where he continued to conduct business. In 1788 the Du Sables formalized their marriage in a traditional Christian ceremony. They traveled to Peoria with their 13– and 15–year–old children, where Father Paul Lusson performed the ceremony on October 27, 1788. Their daughter Suzanne married Jean Baptiste Pelletier in 1790, and six years later gave birth to their granddaughter, Eulalie.

In 1796 Du Sable ran for chief of the local tribes around Mackinac. After losing, Du Sable seemed to grow disenchanted, but he continued to conduct his business. He made the acquaintance of Daniel Boone, a pioneer who explored Kentucky. Boone and his wife Rebecca visited with the Du Sables; they felt comfortable among the Native Americans, Boone having been raised with them.

Relocates to Peoria

In 1800 Du Sable was approached by men, among them Kohn Kinzie, stating that they worked for the U.S. government. They wanted him to sell his land so they could build a fort there. Wary of them but ready to move on, Du Sable sold 400 acres to Jean LeLime on May 17, 1800, for 6,000 livres ($1,200). In 1804 Kinzie, a land commissioner and trader, bought the land from LeLime. After leaving Chicago, the Du Sables moved to Peoria, where they owned 400 acres of land. The family cultivated and farmed the land and continued to operate a trading post. He acquired another 400 acres from the federal government.

After Catherine Du Sable died during the first decade of the nineteenth century, Du Sable left the Peoria estate to his son and daughter–in–law and moved to St. Charles, Missouri, with his daughter and her family. When his granddaughter Eulalie married Michael Derais in June of 1813, Du Sable transferred a house, lot, and half of his stock of animals to the newlywed couple. In 1814 he filed for bankruptcy. Four years later, he died on August 29, 1818.

After LeLime sold the land at the Chicago settlement to Kinzie, rumors circulated surrounding the identity of the original settler of Chicago. For years, it was incorrectly assumed that Du Sable was not the founder. This fallacy was perpetuated by many including Kinzie's daughter–in–law Juliette Augusta Kinzie, who touted her father–in–law as being the builder of the Chicago settlement. In her book, *Wau Bun—the Early Days of the Continent,* she did acknowledge Du Sable's presence but intimated that his stay in Chicago was only temporary.

Finally, on October 25, 1968, Jean Baptiste Pointe Du Sable was recognized as its founder by the City of Chicago and the state of Illinois. There are numerous plaques in the city paying him homage. One marks the location of Du Sable's cabin in the business district on the northeast approach of the Michigan Avenue Bridge. This was designated a National Historic Landmark on May 11, 1986. A second is at Du Sable High School at 49th and State Streets, a third at the Chicago Historical Society. The Du Sable Museum of African–American History, which opened in 1961, houses a bust of the pioneer. In 1965 Du Sable was one of eight Illinoisans whose images were selected for the embellishment of the Illinois Centennial Building in Springfield.

REFERENCES

Cortesi, Lawrence. *Jean du Sable: Father of Chicago.* Philadelphia: Chilton Book Co., 1972

Drake, St. Clair, and Horace Cayton, eds. *Black Metropolis.* New York: Harcourt, Brace, 1945.

Franklin, John Hope. *From Slavery to Freedom.* 5th ed. New York: Knopf, 1980.

Gates, Henry Louis. *African–American Voices of Triumph: Perseverance.* Alexandria, VA: Time–Life Books, 1993.

Green, Richard L., ed. *A Gift of Heritage: Historic Black Pioneers.* Vol. 3. Chicago: Empak Enterprises, 1990.

I Have a Dream: A Collection of Black Americans on U.S. Postage Stamps. United States Postal Service, 1991.

Katz, William Loren. *Black People Who Made the Old West.* Trenton, NJ: Africa World Press, 1992.

Logan, Rayford W., and Michael W. Winston, eds. *Dictionary of American Negro Biography.* New York: Norton, 1982.

Lowe, David. *Lost Chicago.* Boston: Houghton Mifflin, 1975.
Savage, Sherman. *Blacks in the West: Contributions in Afro–American and African Studies.* Westport, CT: Greenwood Press, 1976.

Nicole L. Bailey Williams

De Witt S. Dykes Sr.

(1903–1991)

Minister, church official, architect

De Witt Sanford Dykes Sr. achieved distinction as a minister, a church official, and the first African American to become a registered architect in East Tennessee. He not only pastored local churches and served as a regional and national church official in the Methodist church, but also designed and supervised the construction of many churches in the southeastern United States.

De Witt Dykes was born August 16, 1903, in Gadsden, Alabama, the fifth of six children—three girls and three boys—of Henry Sanford Roland Dykes and Mary Anna Wade Dykes, also known as "Molly." Henry Dykes, also known as "H. S. R.," earned a living as a brick mason and building contractor and also served as a lay minister in the Methodist church. Mary Anna Dykes was a homemaker and a pianist. About 1909 the Dykes family moved to Tennessee, living for a while in Johnson City before taking up long–term residence in Newport.

H. S. R. Dykes served as a circuit riding Methodist minister with as many as three or four churches as his responsibility at one time, including Newport, White Pine, and Jefferson City. From his home base in Newport, he pastored these churches for over 30 years, from the early 1910s until his death in 1945. After a severe storm damaged the wood structure church in Newport, H. S. R. was responsible for rebuilding the Woodlawn Methodist Church with a brick exterior in the early 1910s.

De Witt Dykes received valuable inspiration and guidance from his parents. His father taught him job skills, personal discipline, and the importance of sharing his skills with others. His mother was insistent that he receive a formal education as high as his ability would take him. H. S. R. Dykes established a family construction business which spanned over three generations and lasted through most of the twentieth century. He taught brick masonry to his sons, Roland, De Witt, and Percival, as each grew into their early teens. By the age of 14, De Witt Dykes was considered a master brick mason and by age 17 was employed as a job foreman with a large construction company. After his teenage years, De Witt Dykes worked in the family business only occasionally. He resumed regular work with the company in the late 1940s and early 1950s while pastoring a church in Knoxville, Tennessee, approximately 40 miles from Newport. Even though they were employed regularly, they did not receive the recognition that should have accompanied their achievements. During the days of racial segregation, whites needed the skills of the black brick masons and employed them, but avoided listing their names on building cornerstones or building permits, maintained nominal control in numerous ways at the worksite, and placed many limitations on black workers.

Dykes's academic education was delayed because Newport did not have adequate schools accessible to blacks until the late 1920s. According to memories shared with his family, Dykes did not start school until he was nine–years old. Though his parents had only attended grade school, his mother, Mary Anna, had a strong desire for De Witt to receive a formal education and encouraged him to enroll in the lower school (pre–college) division of Morristown Normal and Industrial College, a school approximately 40 miles from Newport. For several years in the 1910s, Mary Anna Dykes was in declining health due primarily to complications from childbirth and inadequate medical care. She died in 1920, leaving De Witt Dykes emotionally upset but determined to fulfill his mother's dreams of acquiring the best education possible. Dykes enrolled in the grammar school of Morristown College, a school for black Americans supported by the Methodist church. Throughout his studies, Dykes received encouragement from his parents and siblings, but because of limited finances, they contributed little to the tuition, room, and board charges of his education. Dykes often used his brick mason's skills to earn the money to pay his expenses. At Morristown, Dykes was employed as a teacher of brick masonry and also helped build one of the brick buildings on the campus.

During his teen years and early adulthood, Dykes considered a career as either an architect or as a minister. While a student at Morristown, he pursued college preparation courses as well as industrial courses relating to brick masonry and construction. Additionally, while working in Detroit in the summer of 1925, he studied architectural drafting at Cass Technical High School. Still, in the 1920s, there were very few African American professional architects: the 1910 U.S. census counted only 59 among a national total of 16,613 architects, and, as late as 1950, there were only 135 of 23,578. As he was finishing high school, Dykes was offered an instructorship in masonry and the opportunity to study architecture at North Carolina Agricultural and Technical College in Greensboro. His father advised him that it would be extremely difficult for a black to earn a living as an architect. Dykes decided to enter the ministry instead, but never forgot his desire to become a professional architect.

Dykes graduated with a certificate from the high school division of Morristown College in 1926 and entered Clark University (Clark Atlanta University since 1987) in Atlanta, Georgia, in the fall term of 1926. At that time, two Methodist schools, Clark University and Gammon Theological Seminary, shared a campus. Several upper division students with high grades were allowed to "double enroll" and pursue degrees at both schools simultaneously. Thus, Dykes was able to finish the equivalent of seven years of academic work in five years, receiving his bachelor of arts (B.A.) degree with honors from Clark University in 1930 and his bachelor of divinity (B.D) with honors from Gammon Theological Seminary in 1931. Receiving first prize in Christology at Gammon and awarded a tuition scholarship to do additional study, Dykes entered Boston University's graduate program in theology in 1931. That year, being the height of the Depression, was a difficult one for Dykes. In later years he often told his family members that he did not know "where my next meal was coming from." He received the master of sacred theology (S.T.M.) degree in 1932.

Enters the Ministry

Dykes spent the summer of 1932 working at a mission church in New York City. At the urging of his father, he returned home and accepted a position in the same Methodist Conference the East Tennessee Annual Conference in which his father served. For the next 22 years, he was a full time pastor. His first assignment was to pastor Mt. Pleasant Methodist Church in Marion, Virginia, where he served from 1932 to 1936. He then served two of the larger churches in the East Tennessee Conference: Wiley Memorial Methodist Church in Chattanooga, Tennessee, from 1936 to 1946 and East Vine Avenue Methodist Church in Knoxville, Tennessee, from 1946 to 1954.

In Chattanooga, Dykes found a "church in debt and the people discouraged," according to the *Christian Advocate* for November 23, 1939. Within three years, using the theme "The Cooperative Spirit," Dykes had raised $14,000 to pay the debt, remodeled the church school, made repairs himself on both the church and parsonage, making both more attractive.

On November 29, 1932, in Bristol, Virginia, he married Violet Thomasine Anderson, a native of Meadowview, Virginia, who was a former schoolmate at and 1923 graduate of the high school department of Morristown College. In 1927 she received a B.A. degree from Morgan College, at that time a Methodist school (later Morgan State University), and worked for a while in Washington, D.C. Two children were born of this union: Reida B. and De Witt S. Jr. Violet, whom the *Christian Advocate* for November 23, 1939, called "a talented musician," played the piano, directed the church's junior choir in Marion, Virginia, and reared the children. Tall, stately, and very personable, she was considered an asset in her husband's work as a minister. Violet died January 19, 1943, in Chattanooga, Tennessee. He did not marry again for almost eight years. He proved himself adept at housekeeping, cooking, parenting, and many other skills, but he also had relatives and friends who assisted him in childrearing.

Dykes married Viola G. Logan, a native of Lake Lure, North Carolina, on December 14, 1950, in Asheville, North Carolina. A graduate of Shaw University, Viola Logan taught elementary school for three years before joining the Dykes household in Knoxville, Tennessee, in the summer of 1951. Viola added warmth, strength, and perspective to the Dykes family and also served as a role model in the wider community. While performing housekeeping and parenting tasks and participating fully in church activities, in 1958 Viola Dykes became one of the first blacks to receive a degree at the recently–integrated University of Tennessee.

In 1946, Dykes became pastor of East Vine Avenue Methodist Church in Knoxville, serving until 1954. The district superintendent, Reverend L. P. Whitten, stated in the *Official Journal and Yearbook,* East Tennessee Annual Conference, 1953, that "Brother Dykes is one of the great preachers and leaders of our conference. . . a pulpiteer of first rank." Shortly after his pastorate, the church moved from East Vine Avenue to Dandridge Avenue and was renamed Lennon Memorial (later Lennon–Seney) Methodist Church. The late 1940s and 1950s was a period of inflationary prices, but Dykes was pastoring a church with a predominately working class membership which paid its pastor less than $3,000 yearly. With a daughter in college and other family expenses to pay, Dykes decided to use his brick mason skills to supplement his ministerial income. First, he resumed regular work with the family construction business. Later, from 1951 to 1953, he taught brick masonry at night at the Austin Vocational School for veterans of the armed forces. Occasionally, he did masonry and construction contracting on his own. In 1953, after living over 20 years in church parsonages, Dykes planned a long–term residence for his family. He purchased land and designed plans for his own home at 2139 Dandridge Avenue in Knoxville. A ranch style house with a basement, it was constructed largely of brick with Tennessee marble prominent in the front center and Georgia marble inside the house. Dykes performed much of the masonry work himself. In later years, he designed two different additions to the house, also performing some of the work himself and making it a multi–level structure. He lived there from 1954 until his death in 1991.

Dykes was a leader in church affairs at the annual conference level, heading committees and encouraging pastors to continue developing their knowledge of theology in order to be more effective preachers and leaders. From 1939 until 1966, the Methodist Church maintained segregated churches and administrative structures, with blacks belonging to the unit known as the "Central Jurisdiction." The formal beginning of desegregation coincided with a merger with the Evangelical United Brethren Church and the adoption of a new name, The United Methodist Church. Many black pastors had only a public school education and, though some had attended college, few had finished theological seminary. The Methodist Church required those without a seminary education to enroll regularly in a "Conference Course of Study." For 16 or more years, Dykes taught philosophy and ethics in the Minister's Summer School and for several years was chairman of the Conference Board of Ministerial Training. He was also chairman of the Conference Board of Evangelism and a member of the Board of Trustees of the East Tennessee Annual Conference.

Becomes District Superintendent

In 1954 Dykes was elevated to the position of district superintendent of the Chattanooga District of the East Tennessee Annual Conference. He was responsible for more than

25 churches and pastors in this district. As district superintendent, he was a member of the Bishop's Cabinet and was consulted about a wide range of administrative between local churches and the Annual Conference, including assigning of pastors. After a year and a half, he was appointed to a position with responsibilities over a wider geographical area.

In January of 1956 Dykes became a staff member of the General Board of Missions of the Methodist Church, working in the Division of National Missions, Section of Church Extension, Department of Finance and Field Service. The national office of the Methodist Church gave financial assistance to enable ''mission'' churches to construct new sanctuaries, educational units, or parsonages or to build additions to existing facilities. Dykes's job was to consult with those seeking such assistance, give advice concerning possibilities and limitations, see that building and site plans were approved according to the standards of the Board of Missions, authorize the awarding of contracts to perform the work, inspect the construction at various stages, and to authorize payments to contractors when work had been satisfactorily completed. Most of his work involved travel in a 13–state area, but he did consulting in two additional states.

Dykes's background in the ministry in addition to his practical experience as brick mason and construction contractor gave him the skills to excel in this work. His interest in architecture was engaged when churches asked him to help them secure building plans. He began drafting them, getting them approved by the architects employed by the national office. Dykes often listed himself as the ''Designer'' on these plans since he was not a registered architect. During his years of service with the Board of Missions, Dykes supervised the construction of approximately 87 churches, educational units, and parsonages and one fire hall, frequently supplying the architectural designs and drawings for these buildings. The overwhelming majority of the congregations he worked with were African American, though a few were white. Virtually all of the construction companies were white and occasionally friction with racial overtones occurred between Dykes and the white contractors.

Most of them were unaccustomed to having their work scrutinized and evaluated by an African American authorized to withhold payment for unsatisfactory work. In a few cases, white contractors who failed to follow the specifications of the approved architectural plans resisted altering their work to meet requirements. But Dykes insisted that written agreements and specifications be followed and contractors had to make the necessary changes at their own expense. Traveling over a wide area of the southeastern United States from the mid–1950s through the late 1960s posed some risk of personal danger. This was the period of civil rights boycotts and demonstrations as well as violence aimed at ''outsiders'' who might be ''agitators'' or ''troublemakers.'' Additionally, some of the black churches Dykes worked to build in the South had been destroyed or damaged through deliberate acts of vandalism or retaliation for use as meeting places for civil rights activities.

Becomes Registered Architect

During the years of employment by the Board of Missions, Dykes resumed his study of architecture, both informally and formally. He read on his own and received tutoring and advice from the architects working in the Philadelphia office of the Board of Missions. As he made architectural drawings and had the board architects evaluate them, he learned from their comments. He also enrolled in a course of study with the International Correspondence School, receiving a Certificate in Architecture in 1965. Upon his retirement from the Board of Missions on September 1, 1968, he undertook an intensive year of reading and preparation to qualify to take the architectural licensing examinations for the state of Tennessee. He learned that part of the requirements for registration could be met by previous experience, so he submitted evidence of his architectural and construction experience. He also worked as an intern in the office of a local architect to have his experience and knowledge verified. He, therefore, was judged to have satisfied a portion of the examination based upon his past activities in the field. He then took the three–day examination, part written and part oral, in 1969. He passed the examination on his first try and became a registered architect in the state of Tennessee as of March 5, 1970, just as he approached his sixty–seventh birthday. His registration was recognized by the State of Virginia in 1973. Upon the recommendation of three practicing architects, in May of 1970, Dykes was inducted into the American Institute of Architects, the major professional organization in the field of architecture. He also joined the Guild for Religious Architecture in 1973 which later changed its name to the Interfaith Forum on Religion, Art and Architecture in 1979. Dykes was one of a few minister–architects in the nation. According to Mary Sessions in a letter to Dykes Sr. dated March 26, 1970, it was estimated that there were ''possibly 400 registered architects in the United States who are negro [sic] . . . and approximately 200 black members'' of the American Institute of Architects.

Dykes continued his architectural practice from an office in the basement of his home from 1970 to 1976, specializing in church and residential structures. Then, in 1976 at the age of 73, he formed De Witt S. Dykes & Associates, Architects, and moved into an office on McCalla Avenue in the Home Federal Building, later relocating to the Fort Hill Building on East Summit Hill, close to the original East Vine Avenue Church. At the request of the University of Tennessee School of Architecture, several students were able to satisfy school requirements to gain practical experience by working as draftsmen in his offices. Faced with declining health and a drop–off in business, he closed the Fort Hill office in 1986 and entered semi–retirement at age 83. He still provided consultant services from his home.

Even as a registered architect, Dykes still faced racial discrimination and career limitations. For example, approaching a white whose brick building he had helped construct while working with the Dykes Masonry Company and explaining his new status as architect, Dykes was told by his former employer that he would hire him to do brick work but not hire him to design his buildings. Though many white architects were outwardly cordial and shared information Dykes might specifically request, only a couple of white architects were willing to engage in joint ventures to design projects and share commissions. Lack of potential partners to collaborate in bidding on large projects limited the opportunity to design a major building which would attract attention, showcase his talent, and interest those private persons who did not use competitive bidding but merely chose their own architect. Thus, most of the structures designed by Dykes were either churches or residences in the black community or were buildings funded by a government agency. Several of the churches and Unity Mortuary were projects funded in the range of $300,000 to $500,000. The Golden Age Retirement Village was funded at $3.8 million. His projects in the black community attracted other commissions to do buildings in the black community.

The buildings Dykes designed in Knoxville, Tennessee, are distinctive for their number, style, and variety. Urban renewal practices in Knoxville displaced many African American congregations, homes, and businesses. Many church groups not only needed to relocate to a different section of the city, but chose in several cases to build a new sanctuary rather than purchase an existing building. Starting in the 1960s, Dykes designed, in Knoxville, nine churches, a mortuary, a recreation center for the handicapped, a senior citizens home, and additions to an existing recreation center and to a day care center. He also occasionally drew plans to build or to remodel residences. In addition, working as an associate architect for the 1982 World's Fair held in Knoxville, Dykes designed 11 merchandising and snack shops located throughout the grounds of the World's Fair.

Dykes's church designs are distinctive for blending traditional religious symbols and design elements with contemporary structural shapes. He often used distinctive roof patterns such as steep roofs or soaring cathedral ceilings. Shiloh Presbyterian and Calvary Baptist have a circular sanctuary design connected to low–rise rectangular shaped educational, office, and fellowship hall units. Others use marble as a central feature on the facade, or as incidental trim. Lennon–Seney United Methodist Church is the only neo–classical building Dykes designed in Knoxville. Dykes designed an addition to an older, existing structure which consisted of a totally new sanctuary on the side of and connected to the original building, blending the designs to present a unified look.

Dykes's community activities include service as national president of Clark College's Alumni Association from 1942 to 1944 and as a trustee of Morristown College in the 1970s. He was a charter member of Alpha Phi Chapter of Alpha Phi Alpha Fraternity at Clark University on January 28, 1927, and eventually became a life member. He designed a pylon, representing the ideals and principles of Alpha Phi Alpha, which was placed on permanent display on the campus of Knoxville College. Alpha Mu Lambda Chapter presented him with the Alpha Meritorious Brother Award for "Dedicated Noble Performance to the Fraternity and the Community" on May 9, 1975.

Rust College, Holly Springs, Mississippi, awarded him an honorary doctor of divinity degree in 1971 and the Minority Business Bureau extended the President's Outstanding Achievement Award to him on February 10, 1979. Over a period of years, De Witt and Viola Dykes gave residence in their home to nine young people, aged 13 to 21, at different times to allow them to attend school. Their contributions in raising their own family and to the larger community were recognized in 1989 when the Knoxville Alumnae Chapter of Delta Sigma Theta gave De Witt and Viola a Black Family Achievement Award.

Dykes enjoyed playing the piano and organ and also grew flowers and vegetables. For many years, flowers grown at the Dykes home were on display at the annual Dogwood Arts Festival in Knoxville. Dykes was not only an outstanding pastor and church official, but he also left a legacy of service that continues to touch the lives of thousands in the United States who worship in the churches or use the buildings he designed. The religious, ethical, and intellectual values which guided his life had both a spiritual and material manifestation in his service to the church and his work as the first African American to become a registered architect in east Tennessee. He died August 4, 1991, and was buried in Sherwood Memorial Gardens in Knoxville.

REFERENCES

"Architect Dykes Moves Office to Magnolia Ave." *Knoxville News–Sentinel,* February 22, 1976.

"Bids To Be Let On Center For Handicapped." *Knoxville Journal,* October 16, 1976.

"The Black Family Achievement Awards." Program, Delta Sigma Theta, Inc. Knoxville Alumnae Chapter, Saturday, June 3, 1989.

"Church Breaks Ground for Retirement Village." *Knoxville Examiner,* October 7, 1982.

Clay, Mary Ella Steele. Telephone interview with De Witt S. Dykes Jr., November 1997.

Cocke County Heritage Book Committee. *Cocke County, Tennessee and Its People.* Waynesville, NC: Don Mills, 1992.

Dozier, Richard K. "Architects." *Black Enterprise* 7 (September 1976): 16–22, 50, 58.

Dykes, De Witt S. Sr. Letters to De Witt S. Dykes Jr., July 5 1997, December 4, 1997.

Dykes, Viola Logan. "De Witt Sanford Dykes, Sr. . . . 1903–1991." Typescript, November 1996. Dykes Family Papers Detroit in the author's files.

Fulton, Faye E. "Black American Contributions to the Built Structures of Knoxville, Tennessee." Anthropology 501 Term Paper, University of Tennessee, December 1992.

Gardiner, Reida Dykes. Interview with De Witt S. Dykes Jr., December 1997.

"Here's De Witt Dykes." *Our Voice* 1 (October 1970): 12, 26–27.

"In Memoriam, De Witt Sanford Dykes, 1903–1991." Funeral Program, August 9, 1991.

Interview with De Witt S. Dykes Jr., November 1997.

Jones, Thomas J. *Negro Education.* Vol. 2. 1916. Reprint, New York: Arno Press, 1969.

Journal of the Holston Annual Conference of the United Methodist Church. Official Record of The Twenty–Sixth Session Held at Lake Junaluska, NC, June 14–17, 1993.

''Murals Unveiled at Wiley Memorial.'' *Christian Advocate* 61 (23 November 1939).

Official Journal and Year Book. Diamond Jubilee Edition, Seventy–Sixth Session, the East Tennessee Annual Conference, the Methodist Church, July 13–17, 1955.

Official Journal and Year Book. Eighty–Third Session, the East Tennessee Annual Conference, The Methodist Church, June 7–10, 1962.

''Omega Chapter.'' *The Sphinx.* Alpha Phi Alpha Fraternity Magazine, Summer 1992.

Sessions, Mary. Letter to De Witt S. Dykes Sr., March 26, 1970.

Swagerty, Nettie Sue Dykes. Telephone interview with De Witt S. Dykes Jr., October 23, 1997.

De Witt S. Dykes Jr.

Billy Eckstine

(1914–1993)

Singer, bandleader

William Clarence Eckstine (originally spelled Eckstein), better known as "Billy" or "Mr. B.," was one of America's most popular vocalists and a sex–symbol in the 1940s and early 1950s. His striking good looks and rich baritone sound captivated many night club and concert hall audiences around the world. Eckstine was also instrumental in launching the careers of many jazz greats.

Eckstine was born in Pittsburgh, Pennsylvania, the youngest of three children and the only son of William and Charlotte Eckstine. When Eckstine was a young boy, his father, a chauffeur, purchased a piano when he thought that one of his daughters was musically inclined. It turned out that his son Billy displayed a talent for singing and at age 11, gave a recital at a church bazaar. At this time, however, Eckstine's first love was football. He attended Peabody High School in Highland Park before his family relocated to Washington, D.C., where he attended Armstrong High School and then studied at St. Paul Normal and Industrial School in Lawrenceville, Virginia. He furthered his education at Howard University for one year, majoring in physical education with hopes of becoming a football coach. Some years later, he received a B.A. degree from Shaw University in Raleigh, North Carolina.

Music Career Launched

In 1933 Eckstine got his start in show business after winning first prize in an amateur–night contest at the Howard Theater in Washington. Shortly afterwards, he began singing in small nightclubs in various cities, including Pittsburgh, Washington, D.C., New York, and Chicago. He was soon discovered by Earl "Fatha" Hines and joined Hines's band in Chicago in 1939 as lead vocalist. They recorded two blues hits, "Jelly, Jelly" and "Stormy Monday." Eckstine remained with the Hines group for four years, during which time he learned to play trumpet. He introduced Hines to a young group of unknown jazz musicians who were incorporated into the band. Some of them were Charlie "Yardbird" Parker, Dizzy Gillespie, Wardell Gray, and vocalist Sarah Vaughan.

Billy Eckstine

In recalling his memories of the band in Dizzy Gillespie's book *to Be, or not. . .to Bop,* Eckstine stated:

> Well, I will say we had our fun. We were wild, but wild in a good way. I mean it wasn't wild to the point of anything detrimental. I think the guys were full of enthusiasm, everybody, and it came off. New things, learning, everything was new in concept. And it was a beautiful study. I mean, I've seen times, heck, when we were in the Booker T. Washington Hotel in St. Louis, and hell, we'd rehearse at three o'clock in the morning, right in the room. Heck, Bird would take the reed section, and, man, nobody knocked on the wall, things like that. We'd rehearse any time, all night long. Just play! It was definitely a schooling period for everybody concerned.

Eckstine left the Hines band in 1943 and worked as a soloist in New York nightclubs until a 20 percent cabaret tax discouraged many club owners from offering entertainment. In 1944 Eckstine started his own band, which included such jazz greats as Dizzy Gillespie, Fats Navarro, Kenny Dorham, Miles Davis, Freddy Webster, Charlie "Yardbird" Parker,

Gene Ammons, Lucky Thompson, Dexter Gordon, Clyde Hart, Oscar Pettiford, and Art Blakely. There were others, including the Hines band singer, Sarah Vaughan. This group of young, talented musicians started the bebop era. Eckstine's original intent was to have a band to back his vocals. He played trumpet with the band but was no match for Gillespie, so he took up the valve trombone. The band was doing well financially, grossing $100,000 in its first ten weeks of touring.

Eckstine was a real sharp dresser. He even started a fashion craze when he started rolling back his shirt collar, which became the ''Mr. B'' collar. His style, good looks, and smooth sound enabled him to attract large audiences, most of whom were women. Some of his band's more popular recordings were: ''Cottage for Sale,'' ''Blue Moon,'' and ''I Surrender Dear.''

In 1946 MGM offered Eckstine a contract to appear opposite Lena Horne in the movie *Till the Clouds Role By*. He turned down the role because the band was not included in the offer. Despite his loyalty, it became financially difficult for him to maintain the band. By this time, Eckstine had gained substantial recognition and began a very successful solo career that lasted several decades.

In 1949 and again in 1950 *Metronome* named Eckstine ''Top Male Vocalist,'' and *Down Beat* magazine called him the most popular singer for five consecutive years beginning in 1948. *Esquire* magazine chose him as ''New Star'' for 1946, and, when in 1949 three million of his records were sold, MGM named him its most popular singer. He was the first black singer to grace the cover of *Life* magazine and the first black singer signed by MGM records.

At the Oasis Club in Los Angeles in April 1950, he attracted a record–breaking attendance of 4,587 paid admissions, and his appearance at the Paramount Theater on Broadway surpassed Frank Sinatra's six–year attendance record. He made a cross–country tour with the George Shearing Quintet which grossed $262,000. Eckstine's music crossed racial barriers as both whites and blacks admired him.

Eckstine recorded many hits. His albums included: *Live At Club Plantation, Los Angeles* (1945); *Sarah Vaughan and Billy Eckstine: The Irving Berlin Songbook* (1957); *Imagination* (1958); *Basie, Eckstine Inc.* (1959); *No Cover, No Minimum* (1959); *Once More With Feeling* (1959); *Billy Eckstine and Quincy Jones at Basin Street East* (1961); *I Apologize* (c. 1960); *Feel the Warm* (c. 1971); *The Prime Of My Life* (c. 1970s); *I'm a Singer* (c. 1984); and *Billy Eckstine Sings With Benny Carter* (1986). Other compilations included: *Mr. B and the Band* (1945–47); *Together* (1945–47); and *Everything I Have Is Yours* (1949–57). He also appeared in several films including: *Skirts Ahoy* (1953), *Let's Do It Again* (1975), and *Jo Jo Dancer: Your Life is Calling* (1986).

Toward the end of his career, Eckstine recorded a new single with Ian Levine as part of Levine's Motown revival project on the Motor City Label. Whenever he got the chance, Eckstine came home to Pittsburgh. He performed in the traditional ''battle of the bands'' sponsored by the Pittsburgh Courier and sang the national anthem for the Pirates' World Series. When Eckstine was not performing, he was an avid golf player.

Eckstine enjoyed a productive career that spanned over 60 years. His style and distinctive sound influenced many singers including Joe Williams, Lou Rawls, Arthur Prysock, and Johnny Hartman.

Eckstine was married twice: first, in 1942, to June Payne (the couple adopted a son, Billy Jr.); and next in 1954 to Carolle Drake, with whom he had six children: Ed, Guy, Ronnie, Kenny, Gina, and Charlotte Carolle. Both marriages ended in divorce.

On Monday, March 8, 1993, Billy Eckstine died at Montefiore Hospital in Pittsburgh, from complications of a stroke he suffered the previous year. He was 78–years old. He was survived by his two former wives, seven children, four grandchildren, and one great–grandchild.

Eckstine's childhood home in Highland Park is marked by a plaque erected by the Pennsylvania Historical and Museum Commission. Family members and friends were present for the ceremony to unveil the marker proclaiming the home as a landmark in honor of the legendary jazz vocalist.

REFERENCES

''Billy Eckstine's Golden Voice is Silenced: Famous Vocalist Band Leader Helped Many Musicians.'' *Sacramento Observer,* March 17, 1993.

''Billy Eckstine Passes On.'' *New York Voice Inc./Harlem USA,* March 17, 1993.

Current Biography Yearbook. New York: H. W. Wilson, 1952.

Gillespie, Dizzy. *to BE or not to BOP.* New York: Doubleday, 1979.

''Jazz Balladeer Billy Eckstine Memorialized with Historic Site.'' *New Pittsburgh Courier,* March 13, 1993.

Larkin, Collin, ed. *The Guinness Encyclopedia of Popular Music.* New York: Guiness Publishing, 1992.

''Man With Cashmere Voice.'' *Negro Digest* 9 (November 1950): 22–26.

''Mr. B. Singer–bandleader Billy Eckstein.'' *Washington Afro–American,* March 13, 1993.

Salzman, Jack, ed. *Encyclopedia of African–American Culture and History.* New York: Macmillan Library Reference, 1996.

Southern, Eileen. *Biographical Dictionary of Afro–American and African Musicians.* Westport, CT: Greenwood Press, 1982.

Tapley, Mel. ''Billy Eckstine, Romantic Voice of Jazz, Dies.'' *New York Amsterdam News,* March 13, 1993.

Sheila A. Stuckey

William Edmondson
(1870?–1951)
Sculptor, laborer

An important folk artist of the twentieth century, William Edmondson began his craft by creating simple stone carvings as grave markers in response to a divine vision. He borrowed heavily from Biblical and folk symbols, such as doves, angels, and figures from Noah's ark, and added likenesses of notable figures such as Eleanor Roosevelt and Jack Johnson. The first black artist to be honored with a one–man show at New York's Modern Museum of Art, Edmondson rose from obscurity as a creative visionary artist.

Edmondson told his biographer, Edmund L. Fuller in *Visions in Stone,* ''How old I is got burnt up.'' Although the family Bible that documented William Edmondson's birth was destroyed in a fire, his death certificate gives his age at ''abt [sic] 68,'' which implies that he was born around 1883. According to *William Edmondson: A Retrospective,* however, family oral history suggests that he was much older than 68 when he died. Edmondson's chronology in the same source gives his birth year as c.1870.

Edmondson was one of six children born to parents who were slaves of Edmondson and Compton, of the Nashville, Tennessee area. His father, whose name is omitted from published sources, died while the children were young, leaving Edmondson's mother, Jane Brown, to provide for them. To sustain the family, she picked cotton, perhaps on the land of a former owner until the children reached their early teens and obtained jobs. She died in 1922.

Edmondson held various jobs in Nashville from 1882 to 1900, serving as a laborer, a porter, and a livestock trader. From 1900 to 1907, he worked for the Nashville, Chattanooga, and St. Louis Railway shops. Disabled by an accident in the local roundhouse, he left the railroad and later worked as a servant, a fireman, a janitor, and an orderly at the Women's Hospital in Nashville, subsequently known as Baptist Hospital. Mary Brown, Edmondson's stepsister, recalled in *Visions in Stone,* that ''Nobody paid no attention'' to him at work, and that ''If he didn't feel like doing nothing he just wouldn't do

William Edmondson

it.'' Edmondson would tell his coworkers, ''I am tired working too hard. I'm going home and relax. God don't intend nobody to work themselves to death. Slave time is over.'' The hospital closed in 1931, 25 years after he joined the staff. Unemployed again and now well into his fifties, Edmondson devoted his time to his extensive vegetable garden and to odd jobs in the segregated neighborhood where he lived.

By then, Edmondson owned a home on 14th Avenue in South Nashville, which he shared with his family. He decided to become a sculptor after receiving two powerful visions. *Visions in Stone* describes his first vision, which occurred when he was a boy of about 13 years. In the vision, Edmondson saw ''the flood'' that ''covered up the rocks and went over the mountains.'' By the time his stone cutting began, he had another directive from God. In describing his second vision, Edmondson claimed:

> I was out in the driveway with some old pieces of stone when I heard a voice telling me to pick up my tools and start to work on a tombstone. I looked up in the sky and right there in the noon daylight He hung a tombstone out for me to make.

Although unable to read or write and untutored in sculpturing, Edmondson began to carve in stone. His tools were those of a handyman—a short, wood–handled hammer, a flat chisel, and a file. He crafted several chisels, using large ones for roughing out surfaces and smaller ones for finishing surfaces. In time Edmondson may have used other tools as well as stone abrasives. He had a ready supply of free or inexpensive material to carve, using pieces from the Ezell Mill and Stone Company quarry located in nearby Newsom Station, Tennessee, and from demolished city buildings and curbs from rebuilt streets. According to *Visions in Stone,* these stones were generally rectangular limestone blocks and some were quite small. Their grain, color, and texture varied as Edmondson could not afford to be selective.

Visions Cut in Stone

Edmondson began by crafting crude gravestones, first for Nashville's black community. As his work evolved, Edmondson's tombstones included angels, Biblical characters, and animals or "varmints." He then began to sculpt human figures such as nurses, brides, women from the local community, and celebrities such as Eleanor Roosevelt and heavyweight boxer Jack Johnson. Edmondson also crafted birdbaths, flower pots, and garden sculptures.

Edmondson remained a sculptor of only local interest until Louise Dahl–Wolfe, a photographer for *Harper's Bazaar,* became interested in his work between 1934 and 1937. Her photographs of his garden and samples of his work led to a one–man show for Edmondson at the Museum of Modern Art in New York City from October 20 through December 12, 1937. Edmondson was the first black artist to have a one–man show at the museum. The next year Edmondson's work was included in the exhibition *Three Centuries of Art in the United States* held at the Jeu de Paume in Paris. Moreover, Edmondson's works were shown at Willard Gallery (New York), City College (the City University of New York), LaJolla Museum of Contemporary Art, Willard Gallery (New York), Montclair Art Museum, and several galleries in Nashville, including the Nashville Art Gallery, Lyzon Galleries, Peabody College, and Cheekwood Fine Arts Center.

From 1939 to 1941 Edmondson was employed under the Works Projects Administration's Federal Art Project and, unlike other WPA artists who were required to create pieces for federal buildings, Edmondson was allowed to continue with his regular work. George Ridley, who, as a boy, knew Edmondson and observed him at work, described him in an interview as short and squabby in stature, but also kind and gentle. He never married, claiming later in life that he was too old for marriage. Certainly, by then Edmondson was dedicated to his stone carving. A religious man, he attended United Primitive Baptist Church, where he developed many friendships and found customers for the tombstones that he carved. After five years of declining health, due to arteriosclerosis and malnutrition, Edmondson died in his home on February 7, 1951, of cerebral thrombosis. He was buried in Mount Ararat Cemetery in Nashville.

The value of Edmondson's sculptures and interest in his work have increased dramatically in recent years. In fact, since his death, thieves have removed several of Edmondson's tombstones and carvings from cemeteries throughout Tennessee and the South. In 1981–82 the Tennessee State Museum displayed a Will Edmondson Retrospective, published a catalog of his work, held a major symposium, and presented discussions of his work in local schools. His works were showcased in Nashville again from February 7 through April 7, 1988, in the Metro Arts Commission Gallery's exhibition.

Edmondson's home and garden, once filled with hundreds of his stone carvings, have been replaced by Carter Lawrence elementary school. A marker was erected on the site where he carved his tombstones and figures. As a perpetual memorial to Edmondson, the William Edmondson Park, located on Charlotte Avenue, was dedicated on June 1, 1979. Appropriately, it contains a limestone tombstone decorated with a peace dove and crafted from the cornerstone of a local bank that had been demolished. It gives a tribute to the unlettered sculptor who transformed his visions into stone.

REFERENCES

Driskell, David C. *Two Centuries of Black American Art.* New York: Knopf, 1976.

Fletcher, Georganne, ed. *William Edmondson: A Retrospective.* The Catalogue of an Exhibition Organized by the Tennessee State Museum. Nashville: Tennessee Arts Commission, 1981.

Fuller, Edmund L. *Visions in Stone: The Sculpture of William Edmondson.* Pittsburgh: University of Pittsburgh Press, 1973.

James, Milton M. "Art." *Negro History Bulletin* 22 (November 1958): 41–42.

Lewis, Samella. *Art: African American.* New York: Harcourt Brace Jovanovich, 1978.

Porter, James A. *Modern Negro Art.* New York: Dryden Press, 1943.

Ridley, Gregory. Interview with Jessie Carney Smith, June 12, 1995.

"Spirit & Form." *The Sculpture of William Edmondson and Puryear Mims.* Nashville: Metropolitan Arts Commission Gallery, February 4–7, 1988.

"William Edmondson, A Primitive Sculptor." *New York Times* (February 10, 1951): 13.

COLLECTIONS

Selected collections containing works by William Edmondson are located at the Abbey Alrich Rockefeller Collection of Folk Art, Williamsburg, Virginia; Cheekwood Fine Arts Center, Nashville, Tennessee; Columbus Museum of Arts and Crafts, Columbus, Ohio; Hirshhorn Museum and Sculpture Garden, Washington, D. C.; Historical Association, Cooperstown, New York; Memorial Art Gallery, University of Rochester,

Rochester, New York; Montclair Museum, Montclair, New Jersey; San Francisco Museum of Art, San Francisco, California; and Stony Point Folk Art Gallery, Stony Point, New York. He is also represented in many private collections in Tennessee and elsewhere.

Jessie Carney Smith

Nelson J. Edwards
(1917–1974)
Labor union official, civic leader

Nelson Edwards was among the first African Americans to reach high levels of responsibility within the American labor movement. He rose through the ranks from one of the most menial jobs in the assembly plants of Detroit to become vice president of the United Auto Workers (UAW) union. The upward climb began as a result of his conscientious work habits and leadership skills that came to the attention of the members and officials of the union when he was a young man in the first year of employment.

Born in Lowndes County, near Montgomery, Alabama, on August 3, 1917, Nelson Jack Edwards spent his early years on a sharecropper farm, where his father was never able to pay off the debt to his landlord with the profits from the year's harvest. With his brothers Garfield and John, Edwards plowed the fields—sometimes from dawn to dusk—walking behind a mule.

In 1934 Edwards married his long–time sweetheart, Laura Logan. They had two children, Nelson Jr., and Lorraine (Harris). Edwards and his wife moved from the rural area to Montgomery, where he found work for the Southern Oil Company. His salary for a 12–hour day, 15 cents an hour, came to a total of ten dollars and 80 cents for a week's work. Before long, his brother John, who migrated to Detroit as a hobo, returned for a visit driving a car he had purchased with wages he earned in the city. Unable to resist the promise of such improved monetary returns, Edwards went back with John in 1937, and sent for his wife and newborn son seven months later.

With John's assurance that the newly–created UAW was free of the racial prejudice associated with organized labor, Edwards went to work in the Chrysler plant. Four years later, in 1941, when the company's restructuring for war needs brought about layoffs, he went to the Ford Lincoln plant, the site of his introduction to union activity. Soon he began working on the education, citizenship, and by–laws committee of Local 900. His career from then on developed into a series of firsts for an African American in the labor movement. In 1945 he became chair of the union's bargaining committee, the top position on the most important committee of that predominantly white local organization.

The next step took Edwards from the assembly line of a manufacturing plant in 1948 and placed him in the International Union that covered 18 regions in the United States and Canada. As an international representative, he was responsible for Region 1A, which included a part of Detroit. He worked on contract negotiations for more than one local, discussing adequate benefits and security as well as increased pay scales. He became an influential part of the UAW, already noted for its interest in social issues and for its large African American membership in top positions as well as in the rank and file.

In 1962, Edwards became a member of the International Executive Board of the UAW, a post he held for eight years. In the crowning point of his career, delegates to the 1970 annual convention gave him an overwhelming majority of votes for vice president of the entire union. In this capacity he directed departments having to do with sensitive areas such as education, fair employment, working conditions, compensation of retired workers, skilled trades, and workers' appeals.

Edwards was known as a writer as well as a speaker. Most widely circulated was his article published in the *Free Labor World,* the official journal of the International Confederation of Free Trade Unions, and later translated into four other languages for distribution abroad. This work, appearing at the height of the civil rights struggle in the South, resulted from his visit to Birmingham, Alabama, in 1963, at the suggestion of Walter P. Reuther, president of the UAW. Reuther wanted to demonstrate the union's awareness of the plight of African Americans.

Edwards presented a well–received paper, "Problems of Industry in Employing the Disadvantaged," at the 22nd annual meeting of the National Academy of Arbitrators, which was then printed in *Arbitration and Social Change,* published by the Bureau of National Affairs.

Edwards's involvement in community, state, and national civic and political affairs is demonstrated by a partial list of organizations in which he participated: American Civil Liberties Union, General Advisory Committee on Vocational–Technical Education for Detroit Public Schools, NAACP, and the Detroit Labor Action Council.

Although he left school before the end of high school, Edwards was a well–educated man whose intellectual curiosity led him to continuous reading, courses at institutions of higher education, and seminars and workshops conducted by the UAW.

Edwards gave full credit for the breadth of his success in the labor movement to two sources—the support of his wife, and his own firm belief in hard work, both physical and mental. His life came to an untimely end on November 3, 1974, at a Halloween party sponsored by union members. He was fatally shot by a reveler who took umbrage when Edwards, as an official of the union, objected to the man's boisterous behavior.

REFERENCES

The African American Encyclopedia. Vol. 2. Miami: Educational Book Publishers, 1974.

"Blacks and Organized Labor." *Black Enterprise* 2 (July, 1972): 17.

"He is a Firm Believer that 'Labor Disgraces No Man'". *The Ebony Success Library.* Vol. 2. Chicago: Johnson Pub. Co., 1973.

Ploski, Harry A., and Warren Marr, eds. *The Negro Almanac.* New York: Bellwether Co., 1976.

"Trial Set in Edwards Killing." *Detroit Free Press,* November 13, 1974.

Williams, Michael W., ed. *The African American Encyclopedia.* New York: Marshall Cavendish, 1993.

Dona L. Irvin

Lee Elder

(1934–)

Professional golfer

Lee Elder

Until the second half of the twentieth century, segregation made golf a white man's sport. In 1975 Lee Elder broke a barrier by qualifying to play in the Masters Tournament in Augusta, Georgia. He made the dream of getting to the Masters a reality for young, upcoming black golfers and proved that there was nothing inherently white about the game.

Robert Lee Elder, one of eight children, was born on July 14, 1934, in Dallas, Texas, to Charles and Sadie Elder. His father, a coal truck driver, was killed in combat in World War II, and his mother soon died as well. It became necessary to separate Elder and his seven brothers and sisters. He was shunted around and then sent to Los Angeles to live with an older sister.

As with most of his black golfing contemporaries, Elder developed an interest in golf while serving as a caddy. Although he was only 12 years old, golf was becoming the most important activity in his life. He attended Manual Arts High School in Los Angeles for only two years, but he preferred caddying at the local golf courses and playing at night until the park officials chased him away. His family offered him no encouragement in his goal of being a professional golfer, but he would not be dissuaded. As a black teenager, segregation provided no avenue to a school sports team or country club facility. Elder had to follow a path taken by many black golfing aspirants: hustling. Two expert hustlers helped him develop his skills. Returning to Dallas in the early 1950s, Elder continued to hustle, perfecting his golf game.

Elder met Ted Rhodes, Joe Louis's personal golf instructor, who offered Elder valuable instruction in the game of golf. *Black America* quoted Rhodes as stating, "I owe everything to Rhodes. He taught me everything I know about golf." The two traveled the United Golf Association (UGA) golf circuit and in the early 1960s ended up in Nashville, Tennessee. According to an interview with Joe Hampton, designer of the Cumberland golf course in Nashville, most black golfers considered Nashville a golfing mecca because Cumberland was regarded as one of the best in the United States. By being black–operated, black golfers need not worry about racist bystanders or players.

At this time Elder had just been discharged from the army, where he had served a two–year stint on "golf duty" in a special services unit. As captain of the Fort Lewis, Washington, golf team, Elder won the post championship twice and took second place in the All–Service Tournament in 1960. In the Sixth Army Championship, he lost only to Orville Moody, a future U.S. Open Champion.

Turning professional at the age of 25, Elder played on the UGA tour circuit for ten years and won the national title four times, in 1963, 1964, 1966, and 1967. As a four–time titlist, Elder had prestige but not the earnings commensurate with victory; the UGA circuit was derisively named "the peanut tour." Realizing that his opportunities as a professional golfer would never reach fruition in a segregated setting, Elder raised $6,500 to qualify for the PGA Tour and, in 1967, received his PGA card. As the second black to play on the regular PGA Tour, he had no corporate sponsor but still made respectable showings in his first nine PGA events in 1968.

The year 1968 would prove to be important for Elder as the top tours were televised with large viewing audiences. In

August he was playing in the American Golf Classic at the Firestone Country Club in Akron, Ohio. Elder was facing one of the world's top golfers, the legendary Jack Nicklaus, in a five–hole, sudden–death playoff. Coming in second with a $12,000 purse, golfdom took notice of him. Elder was hardly a rookie, since he had played his first 18 holes at the age of 12 and had been a pro for about nine years. When Charlie Sifford became the first black to win a PGA Tour event in 1969 in Los Angeles, he and Elder became role models for young black golfing aspirants.

Enters the Masters

In 1971 Elder became the first black American invited to play in the South African PGA Open, and he also played an exhibition match in Swaziland against white South African golfer Gary Player. That same year Elder won the Nigerian Open. In 1975 he finally qualified to play in the Masters Tournament, having won the 1974 PGA Monsanto Open. There he had beaten England's Peter Oosterhuis in a four–hole, sudden–death playoff at the Pensacola, Florida, match. On April 10, 1975, Elder entered the record books as the first black entrant in the Masters.

In Ashe's *A Hard Road to Glory,* a definitive history of blacks in sports, Elder is reported to have said, before qualifying for the Masters. ''Why should I, who have served in the military and fought for my country, be invited to play in apartheid South Africa, and yet be denied the opportunity to play in the Masters?'' Furthermore, foreign white golfers were allowed to play in the Masters as guests without meeting qualifications. According to Ashe, Charlie Sifford had always described the Masters as ''a lily–white club. . .[and] white people seem to want to keep it that way. . .[yet] everybody must use the resident caddies and they are all black.''

By the time Elder completed his final year on the PGA Tours, in 1984, he had passed the one–million–dollar earning mark of his career. Between the 1975 Masters and 1984, he won the 1976 PGA Houston Open, 1978 PGA Greater Milwaukee Open, and the 1978 PGA Westchester Classic. In 1979 he became the first black on the American Ryder Cup team.

When Elder retired to the Senior PGA Tour circuit, he continued winning with two victories in 1984: the PGA Senior's Suntree Classic and the PGA Senior's Hilton Head Tournament. He won the Jamaica PGA Championship in Kingston in 1984, and in 1984 and 1986 the Coca–Cola Grand Slam Championship in Japan. For the first three years on the Senior's Tour, his earnings averaged $300,000. In 1987 Elder suffered a heart attack after playing in the Gus Machado Classic in Key Biscayne, Florida. When he recovered, he went back and won that same tournament in 1988. As of 1998, Elder was still a Senior PGA Tour regular.

All of these victories were hard–fought and hard–won because financial sponsorship was difficult for black golfers to secure. Elder was self–supporting for a long time before a company was willing to endorse him. Elder spoke of the pressures on him due to racism. Spectators in the galleries openly called him and other black golfing pioneers ''nigger'' and ''boy.'' He even refused to play in certain tournaments because of the difficulty in trying to concentrate in the midst of overt hostility. In April 1969, at the Greater Greensboro Open in North Carolina, four white men were so blatantly and vocally hostile to Charlie Sifford that they were arrested.

Elder's civic endeavors and affiliations included board directorships of the Metro Washington Police Boys Club and Goodwill Industries. He was founder of the Lee Elder Summer Youth Golf Development Program and the Lee Elder Scholarship Foundation. He is a life–member of the NAACP and a member of the Washington, D.C., Touchdown Club.

Elder has won a number of outstanding awards and honors. In 1974 Washington, D.C., declared May 3 Lee Elder Day and gave him the key to the city. He won the Golf Writers of America Charles Bartlett Award in 1977 and in that same year the Herman A. English Humanitarian Award, in Los Angeles. In 1978 he received the A. G. Gaston Award. He also received an honorary degree from Daniel Hale Williams University.

In 1966 Elder married Rose Harper, who became his manager and played an important role in his successful golfing career. He is president of his own public relations, marketing, and promotions firm. The ''rags to riches'' saga of Elder's life and career contains two important lessons for those who would emulate him. First, Elder always stressed that he had to work hard and delay immediate gratification as he was not gifted with natural skills. Secondly, he learned not to let his emotions rule him when confronted with racial discrimination but to maintain his personal dignity and his self–respect. Elder proved that the seemingly insurmountable obstacles of poverty and racism were not barriers for one who had a clear goal.

Current address: Lee Elder Enterprises, 1725 K Street, NW, Suite #1112, Washington, DC 20006.

REFERENCES

Ashe, Arthur R. Jr. *A Hard Road to Glory: A History of the African–American Athlete Since 1946.* Vol. 2. New York: Warner Books, 1988.

Bonner, Alice, and others. *In Black America.* Los Angeles: Presidential Publishers, 1970.

Contemporary Black Biography. Vol. 6. Detroit: Gale Research, 1994.

Ebony Pictorial History of Black America. Vol. 3. Nashville: Southwestern Company, 1971.

Hampton, Joe. Interview with Dolores Nicholson, June 26, 1996.

Ploski, Harry A., Otto J. Lindenmeyer, and Ernest Kaiser, eds. *Reference Library of Black America.* Book III. New York: Bellwether Publishing Co., 1971.

Salzman, Jack, David Lionel Smith, and Cornel West, eds. *Encyclopedia of African American Culture and History.* New York: Simon and Schuster Macmillan, 1996.

Who's Who among African Americans, 1996–97. 9th ed. Detroit: Gale Research, 1996.

Dolores Nicholson

Duke Ellington
(1899–1974)
Band leader, composer, pianist

To tell the story of Duke Ellington is to tell the story of jazz; to tell the story of his orchestra is to tell the story of his compositions. The man, the music, the life that he lived, the compositions that he wrote, and the orchestra that he fronted were one and the same. As jazz critic Ralph Gleason wrote in 1966, "the man is the music, the music is the man, and never have the two things been more true than they are for Ellington." Duke Ellington is one of the most important figures in the history and development of American music. Often referred to as the greatest single talent in the history of jazz (for many, the history of music), he was variously referred to as "The Aristocrat of Swing," "The King of Swing," and "The King of Jazz."

Edward Kennedy "Duke" Ellington was born April 29, 1899 in Washington, D.C. The youngest of two children, his parents were James Edward "J.E." Ellington and Daisy Kennedy Ellington. His mother, a Washington, D.C., native, was a housewife; his father, a North Carolina native, was a butler, caterer, and finally a blueprint worker in the Navy Yard. His mother was a high school graduate and his father had an eighth grade education. Both were well–spoken however, and sought only the best for Duke and his sister Ruth. As Ellington recalled in his autobiography, *Music is My Mistress,* he was "pampered and pampered, and spoiled rotten as a child." He was almost an adult when his sister was born.

Both parents played the piano, the mother "by note" and the father "by ear." Duke Ellington began taking piano lessons at the age of seven, studying with a local piano teacher called Miss Clinkscales. Unofficially he was guided by pianists Oliver "Doc" Perry, Louis Brown, and Louis Thomas. Piano was not his recognized talent initially; he leaned to drawing and painting. The other interest was baseball—seeing it played. As he wrote in his autobiography:

> The only way for me to do that was to get a job at the baseball park. . . I had to walk around . . . yelling, "Peanuts, popcorn, chewing gum, candy, cigars, cigarettes, and score cards!". . . By the end of the season, I had been promoted to yelling, "Cold drinks, gents! Get 'em ice cold!"

Duke Ellington

Other early employment included dishwashing at a hotel and soda jerking at the Poodle Dog Cafe. As a result of the latter employment, he wrote his first composition, "Soda Fountain Rag," which met with favorable approval. He was a student at Armstrong High School, but dropped out just three months short of graduation. Having won a poster contest sponsored by the NAACP in 1917, he was offered a scholarship by the Pratt Institute of Applied Art in Brooklyn, but turned it down in order to pursue music full time. Ellington received his diploma in 1971, long after he was the recipient of several honorary doctorates. "I needed this diploma more than anything else," he wrote in his autobiography.

One of his first professional jobs as a musician was playing for a half magic, half fortune–telling act. One individual was featured; Ellington was the backup, with the job of matching the featured artist's moods. Then he became relief pianist for the leading local pianist. According to Ellington in his autobiography:

> I was beginning to catch on around Washington, and I finally built up so much of a reputation that I had to study music seriously to protect it. Doc Perry had really taught me to read, and he showed me a lot of things on the piano. Then when I wanted to study some harmony, I went to Henry Grant.

The nickname "Duke" was given to him even before high school. It was a childhood friend who noted Ellington's impeccable taste in dress, food, and lifestyle. He carried himself like one of means. He was a natural aristocrat, tall, debonair, and urbane, with a sophisticated manner at all times.

Forms First Band

Ellington formed his first band, The Duke's Serenaders, in 1917. The band's first job was at the True Reformers Hall in Washington, D.C. For five dollars a night (total), they played at dance halls and lodges. During the day, Ellington operated a sign and poster business. He also played with other bands, led by a contractor. When the contractor sent Ellington's band out on a job, one which paid $100, the contractor instructed Ellington to take $10 and bring him the remaining $90. Discovering this aspect of the business, within a short period, Ellington had assembled several bands and was supplying the city with "a band for any occasion."

Ellington also supplied bands for the wealthy in nearby Virginia. His personal earnings increased to $10,000 a year. He married his childhood sweetheart, Edna Thompson, in 1918. By age 20, Ellington was able to buy a house for his parents and purchase an automobile. Son Mercer, who in later years joined the band as trumpeter and road manager, was born in 1919.

The Duke's Serenaders—a trio made up of Ellington on piano, Otto Hardwick on saxophone, and Sonny Greer on drums—made its first trip to New York City in 1922, working with the clarinetist and leader Wilbur Sweatman. After a short while, they returned to Washington, not quite ready for the requirements of "the Big Apple." One year later, upon the suggestion of pianist Thomas "Fats" Waller, the trio, along with trumpeter Arthur Whetsol and banjoist Elmer Snowden, returned to New York City. This move brought an end to his marriage.

The five–piece band worked under the name The Washingtonians3 , originally under the leadership of Snowden. Ellington assumed the group's leadership in 1924 and expanded the number to nine. By the time the band moved to the Cotton Club in 1927, it had grown to 11 musicians. Nightly radio broadcasts enhanced the band's popularity throughout the country. Joel Dreyfuss of the *Washington Post* for May 25, 1974, wrote:

> The Cotton Club was a perfect place for him to develop his skills as a composer. There were new stage shows frequently and Ellington was required to write fresh music to accompany the shows, dance routines and tableaux. His tenure at the Cotton club led to important recording contracts and between 1928 and 1931 he made more than one hundred and sixty recordings.

In 1929, the band played its first Broadway musical, *Show Girl,* and made the first of many films, *Check and Double Check,* in 1930. Other film appearances followed: *Murder at the Vanities, Belle of the Nineties, A Day at the Races, Cabin in the Sky,* and *Reveille with Beverly.*

Ellington began experimenting with extended compositions in 1931, with the writing of *Creole Rhapsody.* He inaugurated a series of annual concerts at Carnegie Hall in New York City in January 1943. On this occasion, the band performed Ellington's monumental work *Black, Brown and Beige.* The annual Carnegie Hall concerts continued until 1955, with Ellington writing a new work for each occasion, including *Liberian Suite, Harlem, Such Sweet Thunder, New World A–Comin',* and *Deep South Suite.* Written in 1963 for the Century of Negro Progress Exposition in Chicago was his *My People.* There were five film scores provided by Ellington: *Anatomy of a Murder, Paris Blues, Assault On a Queen, The Asphalt Jungle,* and *Change of Mind.* In 1957 he wrote the score for the television–show production *A Drum is A Woman* (CBS). In 1970 he composed the ballet, *The River,* for Alvin Ailey and the American Ballet Theater.

Goodwill Ambassador

The band's first trip to Europe took place in 1933, followed by another in 1939. Foreign tours became more and more frequent: to the USSR, Japan, and Australia, with return visits to Europe. An entire section of *Music is My Mistress* is devoted to the 1963 State Department Tour, a trip that he referred to in the book as "one of the most unusual and adventurous" the band had ever taken.

Ellington worked 20–hour days and was referred to as "the busiest man in the business." Ellington wrote in the foreword of the piano version of his *Sacred Concerts:*

> The incomparable Ellington Orchestra . . . was the only musical aggregation in the world playing 52 weeks a year and rarely with a day off. . . . Little wonder that President Nixon appointed the personable Dr. Duke Ellington official goodwill envoy for American music abroad.

Ellington rarely featured himself as a soloist, though he was an extremely capable pianist. Instead, he fed ideas to the band. Wrote musicologist Eileen Southern, "His music represented the collective achievement of his sidemen, with himself at the forefront rather than the sole originator of the creative impulse." Ellington's bands were unique. As jazz historian Dan Morgenstern indicated:

> The development of Ellington's band followed that of jazz bands in general. His originality expressed itself in what he did with this format and instrumentation, which was to imbue it with an unprecedented richness of timbre, texture and expressiveness. . . . Each member of the ensemble was an individual voice, each had a special gift, each contributed to the totality of what could be called an organism as well as an organization.
>
> Gleason in *Celebrating the Duke* reminded us that:
>
> Duke lived well. He came from a family that lived well. . . .He traveled in the 30s on his tours of the United States not on a bus, but in two railroad cars. "That was the way the President traveled."

Duke himself reminded us:

> It's a matter of whether you want to play music or make money. I guess I like to keep a band so that I can write and hear the music the next day. The way to do that is to pay the band and keep it on tap fifty–two weeks a year. . . . [B]y various little twists and

turns, we manage to stay in business and make a musical profit. And a musical profit can put you way ahead of a financial loss.

The collection of instrumentalists playing Ellingtonia for close to half a century included Harold Baker, Sidney Bechet, Louis Bellson (the band's first white member), Barney Bigard, Jimmy Blanton, Lawrence Brown, Harry Carney, Wilbur DeParis, Mercer Ellington (Duke's son), Tyree Glenn, Sonny Greer, Jimmy Hamilton, Johnny Hodges, Ray Nance, Russell Procope, Elmer Snowden, Rex Stewart, Billy Strayhorn (Ellington's collaborator, protégé, and alter ego), Clark Terry, Ben Webster, and Cootie Williams.

Three Periods of Ellingtonia

Dreyfuss in the *Washington Post* for May 25, 1974, divided Ellingtonia into three periods: (1) the 1920s and 1930s, when he established his trademark—the large orchestra with virtuoso instrumentalists, (2) the 1940s, when he reached a height of productivity and became a culture hero, and (3) the period following his appearance at the Newport Jazz Festival in 1956—Ellington's most adventurous. This was the period when he concentrated on extended works, including a satirical suite for the Shakespeare Festival at Stratford, Connecticut; *My People,* which traced the history of blacks in America on the occasion of the 100th anniversary of the Emancipation Proclamation; and his *Sacred Concerts.* The first of his sacred concerts was performed in 1965, at Grace Cathedral Church in San Francisco, California; the second, in 1968 at the Cathedral of St. John the Divine in New York City; and the third, on United Nations Day in 1973 at Westminster Abbey in London.

Ellington wrote in the introduction to the score *Sacred Concerts Complete*:

> As I travel place to place by car, bus, train, plane . . . taking rhythm to the dancers, harmony to the romantic, melody to the nostalgic, gratitude to the listener . . . receiving praise, applause and handshakes, and at the same time, doing the thing I like to do, I feel that I am most fortunate because I know that God has blessed my timing. . . . When a man feels that that which he enjoys in his life is only because of the grace of God, he rejoices, and sometimes dances.

Dreyfuss contended that Ellington's greatest contribution was perhaps ''forcing the critical world to deal seriously with jazz as an art form.'' Most Ellington historians would concur with this assessment. Jazz journalist Leonard Feather wrote, ''It is. . . Ellington . . . of concert halls, cathedrals and festival sites around the world that deserves his longest life of all.''

Ellington was deservedly honored during his lifetime. Recognition includes: the Spingarn Medal (NAACP, 1959); a gold medal from President Lyndon B. Johnson (1966); Grammy Awards (National Academy of Recording Arts and Science, 1968, 1969, 1973); National Association of Negro Musicians Award (1964); appointment to the National Council on the Arts, National Endowment for the Arts (1968); Pied Piper Award (American Society of Composers, Authors and Publishers, 1968); Presidential Medal of Freedom, President Richard M. Nixon (1969); Fellow, American Academy of Arts and Sciences (1971); *Down Beat* Awards (Duke Ellington Band)—First Place (1946, 1948, 1959, 1960, 1962–72); *Esquire* magazine (Duke Ellington Band), and the Gold Award (1945, 1946, 1947). He received honorary doctoral degrees from 16 institutions. In 1965 the Pulitzer music committee recommended Ellington for a special award, but the full Pulitzer committee turned down the recommendation.

Edward Kennedy ''Duke'' Ellington died at Columbia Presbyterian Medical Center on May 24, 1974. He had cancer of both lungs and a week prior to his death developed pneumonia. After his death, Western High School in Washington, D.C., was renamed The Duke Ellington School for the Arts. The Calvert Street Bridge, also in the nation's capitol, was named The Duke Ellington Bridge. Streets, schools, art centers, and scholarships throughout the country have been named in his honor. The first of The International Duke Ellington Conferences was held in 1983, and continue annually. The U.S. Postal Service issued a commemorative stamp on April 29, 1986.

In 1988 the National Museum of American History of the Smithsonian Institution in Washington acquired more than 200,000 pages of documents reflecting his life and career, following more than three years of negotiation with the Ellington estate. The acquisition was made possible by a special $500,000 appropriation from Congress. Included were more than 3,000 original and orchestral compositions, 500 studio tapes, scrapbooks of world tours, more than 2,000 photographs, programs, posters, awards, citations, and medals. The American Masters series, focusing on the cultural contributions of prominent American artists, included a two–part documentary on the music and influence of Ellington. ''A Duke Named Ellington'' was aired on PBS (Public Broadcasting Service) July 18 and 25, 1988. The 1943 Carnegie Hall debut of Duke Ellington and His Orchestra on January 23, 1943, was recreated in July 1989, Maurice Peres conducting, at Carnegie Hall.

Ellington excelled as a composer, pianist, and leader. He stood tall among his contemporaries and remains in that position more than two decades following his death. His instrument was his orchestra; together, they produced the epitome of sophisticated jazz for all others to emulate. The Duke is today a popular subject for conferences, dissertations, and biographies.

REFERENCES

Current Biography Yearbook. New York: H. W. Wilson Co., 1970.

Dance, Stanley, *The World of Duke Ellington,* New York: Da Capo Press, 1981.

''Duke Ellington, a Master of Music, Dies at 75.'' *New York Times,* May 25, 1974.

''Duke Ellington: Most Charming Septuagenarian.'' *Washington Post,* April 20, 1974

''Duke Ellington: Musician of Elegance,'' *Washington Post,* May 25, 1974.

''The Duke, Our Unrecognized Royalty.'' *Washington Post,* May 1, 1989.

''The Duke's Day.'' *Time* 83 (6 June 1964): 60.

Elam, Joe. ''Endless Ellington Era.'' *Dawn Magazine* (27 July 1974): 16.

Ellington, Duke. *Music is my Mistress.* Garden City, NY: Doubleday, 1973.

———. *Sacred Concerts Complete, Inspirational Music.* Miami Beach, FL: Hansen House, 1984

''Ellington Papers to Smithsonian.'' *Washington Post,* April 27, 1988.

''Ellington's Music Dominates Funeral.'' *The Evening Bulletin.* May 28, 1974.

Feather, Leonard. ''Duke Ellington: The Man and His Music.'' *Crisis* 89 (April 1982): 40–41.

Gleason, Ralph J. *Celebrating the Duke.* New York: Dell, 1975.

Handy, D. Antoinette. *Black Conductors.* Metuchen, NJ: Scarecrow Press, 1995.

Morgenstern, Dan. ''The Ellington Era.'' *Listen.* December 1963.

''Performing Arts Series Honors 'The Master.''' *New York Times,* April 20, 1986.

Southern, Eileen. *Biographical Dictionary of Afro–Americanand African Musicians.* Westport, CT: Greenwood Press, 1982.

''Undefeated Champ.'' *Time* 103 (4 June 1974): 83.

Williams, Martin. ''Duke Ellington: The Grand Old Man of Jazz.'' *Washington Post* September 20, 1987.

COLLECTIONS

Yale University is a repository for Ellington materials. Other items are in the National Museum of American History in Washington, D.C.

D. Antoinette Handy

Robert Brown Elliott
(1842–1884)
Congressman, lawyer, editor

Twice elected to the U.S. House of Representatives, Robert Brown Elliott, a nineteenth–century politician, was best known as a leader of the Republican Party and a state official in South Carolina. A forerunner in South Carolina politics for African Americans, he was delegate to the People's Convention in 1868 and was elected to the South Carolina House of Representatives in the same year. He also served as assistant adjutant general in the militia. He fought discrimination against blacks in the courts, voting practices, schools, and public accommodations, and sought federal aid for schools. His work as militant defender of rights for black people and his reputation as an eloquent orator, charismatic leader, controversial and militant lawyer, and politician led him to national acclaim.

The story of Robert Brown Elliott's early life is filled with inconsistencies. His biographer Peggy Lamson bore this out both in her full–length work, *The Glorious Failure,* and in *Dictionary of American Negro Biography.* He was born August 11, 1842 to parents who may have been West Indian or natives of South Carolina. The place of his birth may have been Boston, Massachusetts; Jamaica; or Liverpool, England.

Elliott's educational background is just as questionable. He may have enrolled in private schools in Boston and then been sent to Jamaica to stay with a rich uncle and continue his education. He may have gone to England in 1853 to attend High Holborn Academy, also known as High Hollow Academy. Although Lamson was uncertain of Elliott's exact schooling and study of law, she mentioned that reportedly he entered Eton College in 1855 and graduated with honors in 1859. He also is rumored to have read law in England with Sergeant FitzHerbert and then returned to the United States in 1861.

The inconsistencies in his biography continue. Elliott married Grace, an attractive mulatto, in Boston and reportedly the couple moved to Charleston, South Carolina, in 1867. He may have served in the British Navy at some point. Lamson also noted Elliott's claim that, when he returned to America, he joined the Union Army and cited contemporary reports that he was wounded while in the Union Navy, which accounted for the slight limp that he had the remainder of his life. It is clear that by March 23, 1867 he was associate editor, under the leadership of Richard Harvey Cain, of the *South Carolina Leader,* a weekly established in 1865 and one of the first in the South published and edited by blacks. Although short–lived, the newspaper was influential in the developing black social order. The newspaper was renamed the *Missionary Record* on April 17, 1868. Elliott became known for his eloquence and wisdom as expressed in masterly articles he wrote.

Life in Politics

By the time he arrived in South Carolina, the Colored People's Convention, held in Charleston in November 1865, was over. It was a pivotal convention that produced many of the state's leaders. Afterward, South Carolina sent six blacks to the U.S. House of Representatives the largest delegation from any Southern state. These six were Richard Harvey Cain, Robert C. De Large, Joseph H. Rainey (the first black to sit in the House of Representatives), Alonzo J. Ransier, Robert Smalls, and Elliott.

Elliott was of medium height and had dark brown skin with an oval and mustached face. Some sources claimed that he was graceful, had an easy manner, and was commanding in appearance. Others described Elliott as ''uppity'' and a ''race first man'' who aligned himself with radical Republicans. He also spoke several languages.

Robert Brown Elliott

Elliott emerged during Reconstruction and quickly became involved in the political arena. He became an important figure in the Republican Party and the state legislature, and a recognized black spokesman and leader. Elected from Edgefield County, he served as a delegate to the People's Convention or Constitutional Convention of 1868. This convention, 70 percent African American, passed key legislation on relief, education, taxes, and elections. Among its delegates were Francis L. Cardozo, William J. Whipper, Robert De Large, and Robert Smalls. Cardozo resented Elliott's vindictive aggressiveness and frequently clashed with him. Elliott, however, managed to swing the convention and thus began his political ascent. Delegates had to reorganize the state of South Carolina since it had seceded from the union prior to the Civil War. Elliott helped to formulate and gain approval for the South Carolina Constitution.

Elliott was elected to the state legislature later in 1868 and served until 1870. While serving in the House of Representatives, he read law and passed the South Carolina bar. On March 25, 1869, he was appointed assistant adjutant general, in charge of the state militia.

Elected to the U.S. Congress

Charleston, South Carolina, hosted the Colored People's Convention in November of 1865, which produced many of the state's leaders, including black U.S. Representatives Richard Harvey Cain, Robert C. De Large, Joseph H. Rainey, Alonzo J. Ransier, and Robert Smalls. Elliott reached South Carolina after the convention, but still reaped some of the benefits. He was elected to the U.S. Congress in 1870, and was seated in 1871. While in Congress, he fought for the protection of African Americans. After being defeated in the race for U.S. Senate in 1873, he handily won the U.S. House seat again, and rallied behind civil rights bills. It is evident that he was highly educated for he gave passionate and eloquent speeches on issues of his concern. He understood the new role of the African American in guarding his or her rights, yet acting wisely as free men. He knew that blacks had to shape their own future, and that the duty to do so was commensurate with their rights.

On January 6, 1874, Elliott made a celebrated speech before the House in support of the Civil Rights Bill, following speeches against the bill from representatives Alexander Stephens of Georgia and James Beck of Kentucky. *The Glorious Failure* quoted his speech:

> The results of the war, as seen on reconstruction, have settled forever the political status of my race. The passage of this bill will determine the civil status, not only of the Negro but of any other class of citizens who may feel themselves discriminated against.

Further testimony of Elliott's eloquence came a few months later, when he gave Charles Sumner's eulogy at a memorial service held in Boston's Faneuil Hall and was catapulted into national acclaim.

All was not well in the state of South Carolina and the political climate there was changing. African American legislators in South Carolina faced racists' allegations of illegal activities. Elliott resigned his seat in Congress near the end of the term in May of 1874, returned to the state, and was again elected to the South Carolina House of Representatives where he became speaker. Elliott was highly respected, but political changes showed the Democrats were gaining power through any means necessary. African American legislators, including Elliott, were accused of corruption; some fought back and lost while others did not challenge the system. White Democrats began to run political affairs.

In a highly–charged campaign in 1876, Elliott ran for attorney general, hoping it would lead to his election as governor. After a bitter campaign, both the Democrats and Republicans claimed victory. Months later the Democrats took control of the legislature and installed Wade Hampton as governor. The Republican office holders, including Elliott, were ousted, and their removal was upheld by the state Supreme Court.

After the Democrats' takeover, Elliott and many other African American politicians lost political power. He practiced law in Orangeburg with T. McCants Stewart and Daniel Augustus Straker; however, the law practice ended in about two years because of the scanty income it provided. Although Elliott was said to have been worth $100,000 in 1871 and had owned a fashionable home and other property in Columbia, South Carolina, by 1879 he was in dire financial straits.

Elliott was appointed customs inspector with the Treasury Department in Charleston, on a small salary, and later promoted to special agent with a slight pay increase. After attending the National Republican Convention in 1880, Elliott and a group of southern African Americans approached James Garfield, president–elect, about the disenfranchisement of African Americans in the south with the change of political parties. According to his biographer, on May 20, 1881, without prior notice, Elliott was ordered to move as special agent to New Orleans; however, he was terminated from his position on April 29, 1882. By now he had lost his spirit and sense of adventure and knew that the political life he had known in South Carolina was over. He opened a law office with Thomas de S. Tucker, whom he had met in Florida, but income was scarce. He also worked as an attorney in New Orleans. He eked out a bare existence which caused him to move from one residence to another until he died. During Elliott's law career he built a sizable law library said to be one of the best private libraries in the state.

Having contracted malaria in Florida when he was on assignment with the Treasury Department, Elliott continued to have bouts of the disease after moving to New Orleans. On August 9, 1884, two days before his forty–second birthday, Elliott died from malaria. Tuberculosis and alcoholism most likely hindered his health also. His wife Grace Lee Elliott survived him. At times while he was in political power, Grace often attended legislative proceedings. However, later in their marriage, she became ill and required medical attention. His funeral was held at his residence, the corner of Villere and Le Sharpe Street. He was buried at St. Louis Cemetery No. 2.

Obituaries of Elliott, quoted by Lamson in her biography, gave various accounts of his importance. The *CharlestonNews and Courier* gave considerable attention to his death and titled the abusive article "Another of the South Carolina Thieves Gone to His Account." Lamson quoted Frederick Douglass, who knew Elliott and his abilities and wrote of them to the editor of the *New York Globe*:

> To all outward he might have been an ordinary Negro, one who might have delved, as I have done, with spade and pickax or crowbar. Yet from under that dark brow there blazed an intellect and a soul that made him for high places among the ablest white men of the age.... I ... was waiting and hoping to see him emerge from the obscurity of his later years and stand in the halls of the national Congress and there lift the standard for his people with a power which no other man of his day could do.

A controversial and able lawyer and politician who practiced confrontational politics, Elliott was an important African American leader during the Reconstruction period in South Carolina. While in power, he never relented in his efforts to bring about binding legislation to promote and protect the civil rights of black people.

REFERENCES

Christopher, Maurine. *Black Americans in Congress.* New York: Thomas J. Crowell, 1971.

Davis, Marianna W. *South Carolina's Blacks and Native Americans 1776–1976.* Columbia: South Carolina Human Affairs Commission, 1976.

Holt, Thomas. *Black Over White: Negro Political Leadership in South Carolina during Reconstruction.* Urbana: University of Illinois Press, 1977.

Lamson, Peggy. *The Glorious Failure: Black Congressman Robert Brown Elliott and the Reconstruction in South Carolina.* New York: Norton, 1973.

Litwack, Leon, and August Meier, eds. *Black Leaders of the Nineteenth Century.* Urbana: University of Illinois Press, 1988.

Logan, Rayford W., and Michael R. Winston, eds. *Dictionary of American Negro Biography.* New York: Norton, 1982.

Simkins, Francis, and Robert Woody. *South Carolina During Reconstruction.* Chapel Hill: University of North Carolina Press, 1932.

Taylor, Alrurtheus Ambush. *The Negro in South Carolina During Reconstruction.* Washington, DC: Association for the Study of Negro Life and History, 1924.

Tindall, George Brown. *South Carolina Negroes 1877–1900.* Columbia. University of South Carolina Press, 1952.

Barbara Williams Jenkins

Ralph Ellison
(1914–1994)
Writer

Ralph Ellison was one of the nation's most important novelists of the twentieth–century. A writer who believed that the novel as a form was both an ethical and aesthetic instrument, Ellison was the author of one published novel, *Invisible Man,* and it has been upon that sole work that his reputation as a novelist rests. Critics have praised the novel for its near–encyclopedic use of American idioms—black and white, Northern and Southern. They have praised it, as well, for its reach for the commonalities within the American experience, both rural and urban, and his technical and conceptual abilities to identify and freight social and political rituals with uncommon resonance. In addition to the novel Ellison has published two collections of non–fiction prose, *Shadow and Act* and *Going to the Territory.* These works display the lucid and elegantly argued reviews, commentaries, interviews, and essays that mark him as an important student of American culture.

As much as the celebrated novel, the essays explore the impact of the African American experience on American character. Never viewing that experience as separate or constricting, Ellison insisted on its centrality to the modern American temperament. Richard Wright once asserted that

Ralph Ellison

the Negro was America's metaphor. Ellison demonstrated this ably in both his published novel and his essays.

Ellison's commentary has caused problems for those who have described a linear and rather simplistic theory of cultural and expressive influences. With blues as a bedrock for his aesthetic positions, he nonetheless posed no romanticized or genetic assertion of Blackness. Ralph Ellison was suspicious of all easy notions of victimhood; he was more intrigued by the reach for the heroic in the face of oppression. It was the heroic and its elegant stylization that he sought out in expressions seemingly simple and humble. This quest informed his best thought and stands as a challenge for writers and critics working now.

Ralph Waldo Ellison was born March 1, 1914 in Oklahoma City to Ida Milsap Ellison and Lewis Alfred Ellison. The father was a construction crew foreman who loved to read and pass on books to his sons. His father named his son for Ralph Waldo Emerson. Lewis Ellison died in 1917. His mother Ida was active in church and local political clubs during his years in public school. Ellison had one younger brother, Herbert. From interviews as well as autobiographical details drawn from his essays, Ellison grew up in a bustling southwestern city, a city without the deep racial tensions evident in most areas of the Deep South.

Keywords in his accounts of his childhood are ''possibility'' and ''affirmation''. The possibility was born of the capacity and encouragement to explore the diverse black, white, and Native American worlds around him. The affirmation was rooted in a sensibility that was fascinated by the complexity, humor, and courage of what he saw and heard. Such a note is sounded early in any description of Ellison's childhood, as well as in his mature notions of African American culture. To establish boundaries is to accept defeat. Definition is the end of exploration, not the random and arbitrary limitation by color.

Young Ellison took careful note of the active music scene in Oklahoma City and related not only to the various jazz and blues idioms but also the style of dress and deportment of the performers. Style was an assertion of their tastes upon the world, not a simple imposition of social class.

A fine student, Ellison graduated from Frederick Douglass High School. During a festival held in Ellison's honor at Brown in 1979, Ellison described a high school incident with the same relish for incongruity and ribaldry which marks specific scenes in his fiction and social commentary. During a march into a high school assembly, Ellison had grown impatient with the rough–housing going on around him. He had promised himself to strike back if provoked. When he was provoked, he grabbed the person closest behind him and fell to the floor on top of him. That person happened to be the principal, Page Inman, a dignified model of academic excellence. Flustered and embarrassed, Ellison fled the school. He recalled, however, that in spite of his great shame and quick struggle to disengage himself, he could hear Inman laughing a strange laugh. One need only reflect upon the Norton–Trueblood and Lucius Brockway scenes, as early examples from his novel, to recognize a similar penchant as witness, composer, and participant in the ''little eruptions of chaos.''

By the time Ellison left to study at Tuskegee Institute in 1933, his experiences had conditioned him to ambiguity, elegance, and ribald humor. Heading off to college is memorable enough for any new student, given the break with tradition and the step toward the unknown. Ellison's trip to school is instructive and informative about the rest of his adult years and to the minor characters he would recall in his fiction.

Though Ellison had won a scholarship, neither he nor his mother had enough money for fare to school after purchasing a trumpet and new clothes. He elected to hobo, to ride the rails from Oklahoma City to Tuskegee, Alabama. He was tutored by Charlie, a friend of their closest neighbors and a professional hobo. Charlie was fair–skinned and could pass for white when he needed to. This helped them through a tense moment or two during the early stages of their journey. After they reached East St. Louis, Charlie fell ill and waved on young Ellison. Alone, he reached school a week later remembering the lessons from a man whose knowledge he had to trust. It must be noted that Ellison took his journey through a state still in a furor over the Scottsboro Trial. Clearly, he took physical and legal risks to reach his goal.

Ralph Ellison majored in music while at Tuskegee, studying under composer William Levi Dawson and concert pianist Hazel Harrison. After three years he left in 1936 to study sculpture in New York City. Among the first people he met was Langston Hughes who eventually introduced him to Richard Wright. The Wright–Ellison relationship has been revisited by many discussants. Suffice it to say on this occasion that Wright encouraged Ellison to attempt reviews and short fiction for *New Challenge.* His first attempts at fiction were naturalistic and dramatically violent, much like Wright's earlier pieces. To develop his writing skills, from 1938 to 1942 Ellison also became a part of the New York City Federal Writers' Project. However, by the time his apprenticeship was ending, Ellison was working through the technical problems of the use of myth and symbol, as well as folk vernacular. He was no longer working exclusively to the call of naturalistic impulses, but reaching for resonances that he admired in the work of Mark Twain, Herman Melville, Henry James, Lev Tolstoy, and others. Around this time he was also managing editor of the short–lived publication *Negro Quarterly.* He attempted to join the U.S. Navy in 1943, was rejected, then joined the Merchant Marine as a cook until the war ended in 1945. By 1944, however, he had written part of a novel and had salvaged part of it as a distinguished short story, ''Flying Home''. This primed him to begin *Invisible Man.*

Develops *Invisible Man*

According to Ellison, he started the novel in the summer of 1945 with the words ''I am an invisible man.'' From this opening line, he proceeded to develop a work that melded his experience, his broad reading, and close study of African American expressive forms and world literature. Indeed he kept these on equal footing. *Invisible Man* is a novel that chronicles a young man's journey from south to north, from a rural to an urban sensibility. It is also, in terms Ellison claimed in *Shadow and Act* to have borrowed from friend and noted critic Kenneth Burke, an odyssey ''from purpose to passion to perception.'' From his hideaway underground, the unnamed narrator tells his story and takes us back to the beginning of his journey. Like Ellison, he is awarded a scholarship to an all–Black college. The school is located in an idyllic setting within the rural South and is presided over by a man who must offer a pleasing face to his trustees, all white, Northern, and wealthy. To his students he offers a sterner face. However, the narrator has progressed well in his chosen course of study. By his junior year he has been selected as one of the trusted drivers for visiting guests. It is on one of these drives that a trustee, on a wrong turn, hears the confession of a black sharecropper, Jim Trueblood. The shock of his story of incest and betrayal overwhelms the man and the narrator drives him to a nearby roadhouse for water and recovery. However, these two men—student and trustee—are confronted by veteran solders on leave from an insane asylum, as well as high–spirited prostitutes. Reeling from these experiences, they arrive back at the college. The president is incensed by the incident.

These early incidents signal the uses of unlikely, though not contrived, coincidences for often comic effects. These moments of chaos—of instances when order and disorder, tragedy and comedy, sanity and insanity are questioned—establish a pattern which will continue until the novel's end.

In New York, the narrator must face the unknown with his naivete still the thinnest of shields. In short order he loses a job in a paint factory, defends an old couple during their eviction from an apartment, and is drafted as the new black spokesman by the Brotherhood, an organization based on the scientific study of class and race. He soon crosses swords with representatives of another brotherhood personified by Ras and his followers. The latter brotherhood is based solely on race. Populating the scenes are wonderfully developed minor characters such as Mary Rambo, Petie Wheatstraw, and Brother Tarp, who attempt, no matter how briefly, to anchor the narrator to some historical and cultural tradition that will, at least, position him within a modern urban culture. Within explosions of sexual and social chaos, the narrator will have to salvage lessons from traditional value to guide him to survival. With no seemingly complete and affirmative models before him, improvisation becomes key. He has just begun to work through these conclusions and put them into action when a riot ensues. Caught in a racial cross fire during a riot, he is chased underground by whites. With conflicts of ethnicity boiling above him, he settles in the cellar to brood and finds out much about himself and his purpose and responsibility before he introduces us to this extraordinary novel.

Novel–in–Progress

Ellison related that he worked on as many as four novels. Two of these were attempted during the 1943–50 period, one before and the other during the writing of *Invisible Man.* A fire in his Plainfield, Massachusetts, summer home destroyed 340 text pages of an unfinished novel in 1964. Ellison's untitled work–in–progress, at his death earned curiosity of American readers for 40 years. These episodes were started after the publication of *Invisible Man.* Judging from the excerpts, a reader can gather that the work was to be an elaboration on Ellison's concerns on play and power, of willfulness and disguise, of the one American voice with many sounds, but neither chaos nor cacophony, but a chorus of ideals and emergent harmonies.

One core story emerges from the seven published episodes of the novel–in–progress. Reared by a master rhetorician and musician by the name of Daddy Hickman, a child minister with the last name of Bliss grows to maturity in the South. His mother was white and his father was black. At some point he decides to pass for white and emerges in later episodes with the last name of Sunraider. He is elected to the Senate before his secret is discovered. A man from his home state attempts to assassinate him on the floor of the Senate. He is wounded, brought to a hospital, and while moving in and out of consciousness, recalls his childhood and his travels with Hickman.

Other episodes (''Cadillac Flambe'' and ''Backwhacking'') present hilarious satire on the relationship among national politicians, the press, and the ethnic stereotypes both groups lean upon as they develop policy and ''takes'' on news stories. The writing is rich and precise. The interior states of a wounded Bliss are denser than anything we find in *Invisible Man,* outside of the prologue. It is now the daunting task of Ellison's literary executor, John Callahan, to connect the pieces and shape a whole. What is currently available to readers suggests another courageous foray into the waters of

American culture into which Ellison will beckon readers, critics, and fellow writers.

Writes Short Stories

As related above, Ellison's earliest stories were naturalistic in their colorings and actions. In ''Slick Gonna Learn,'' the lead character's wife is about to give birth in the hospital and he is out of work. After a fistfight during a crap game, he manages to hit a white policeman who arrives on the scene. He is arrested, taken to jail, humiliated by the judge and miraculously set free. Enroute to the hospital, Slick is kidnapped by a trio of policemen not happy with the verdict. Leaving the city limits in their squad car, they begin to beat him. However, their radio calls them to a fire at the plant where Slick once worked. He is thrown out of the car left to suffer outside the city. He walks back to town, is passed up by many drivers, until a white truck driver gives him a ride. The story asserts class solidarity among progressive workers. Still, the circumstances in this very early story are very much contrived.

By the time Ellison advances to the Buster and Riley pieces (''Afternoon,'' ''Mr. Toussan,'' ''That I Had the Wings,'' and ''A Coupla Scalped Indians''), the emphasis is less on violent encounters, than it is on the easy unfolding of the world through the eyes of two young boys. ''Mr. Toussan'' shows a maturing Ellison using the sermonic call–and–response method to vividly relate the heroic deeds of Touissaint L'Ouverture, who played a major role in the liberation of Haiti from France. The piece also slyly comments on history education, as well as stereotypes that Westerners, blacks and whites, hold regarding Africans. Ellison would work the sermonic form into the prologue to *Invisible Man,* as well as the impromptu speech made at the New York eviction. ''Juneteenth'' from the novel–in–progress traces the slave trade and the gradual shaping of a culture and collective voice. The short stories demonstrate Ellison's early and continual quest to integrate vernacular forms with formal narrative language.

Ellison's most distinguished short story is ''Flying Home'',a long excerpt from an early novel never completed. First published in 1944, it is a story of conflicting sensibilities related to region, age, and education. A young pilot, training at Tuskegee, crashes into a field owned by a racist farmer. He is discovered by two black men. The much older man preoccupies the pilot while the younger man goes for help. By turns ashamed for, humiliated by, and angry with the old man and his talk, the pilot eventually learns the saving power of perspective. Humor can preserve sanity in an insane world. From a filmed interview in 1968 called ''Ralph Ellison on Works in Progress,'' Ellison relates that this early novel would later place this black pilot as the highest ranking officer in a Nazi prison camp. All of the captured Americans would be white. Ellison wanted to explore the ways in which the Nazis manipulate racism among the Americans. Whether this novel was ever completed and exists as a full manuscript, we will only know after the work of Ellison's literary executor is completed.

Another fine story by Ellison was published also in 1944. ''King of the Bingo Game'' introduces a man who is down on his luck and enters a theater to join a bingo game. He eventually wins and goes to claim his prize. However, by this point in the story it is clear that there is more at stake in his triumph than the small money prize. His very identity is tied up with the small triumph and the ending reaches briefly for the surreal as did the ending for ''Flying Home''.

Essays Focus on American Culture

The essays of Ralph Ellison, spanning four decades, deal with a number of diverse issues; yet all are related to the nature of American culture—its roots and elaborations. Contrary to popular belief, Ellison's pieces did take on deeply sociological and political issues. For Ellison the essays run consistently and should always be against over–simplification. The issue here was not merely a war against the stereotypes of slavery, jazz/blues musicians and American performers. His essays insist that we continually inspect terms such as ''Black'', ''white'' and ''American''. For example in his celebrated review of Leroi Jones's *Blues People,* he can be feisty and cantankerous in the face of Jones's generalizations. To Jones's ''a slave cannot be a man'' Ellison thundered in *Ralph Ellison: A Collection of Critical Essays* with the same sense of indignation of one of his fictional orators:

> But what, one might ask, of those moments when he feels his metabolism aroused by the rising sap in spring? What of his identity among other slaves? With his wife? And isn't it closer to the truth that far from considering themselves only in terms of that abstraction, ''a slave,'' the enslaved really thought of themselves as *men* who had been unjustly enslaved?

In the ''Little Man at Chehaw Station'' from his second collection, he addresses the issue of American vernacular and the American audience with a close logic, imaginative analysis and characteristic wit over the protean nature of American character. The responsibility of the artist to take her diverse audience seriously and as equals was at issue. Indeed how do you develop a language that reflects commonalities? And what are the commonalities?

Throughout both collections Ellison's commentary on music reflects his high regard for elegance, style, and democracy. Indeed one of his central insights into the workings of a true democracy in which the collective and the individual can co–exist is the jazz performance. In such a performance the soloists are free to improvise within the constraints of the agreed–upon and collective melody. How that dynamic can work off the bandstand and within other institutions remains a question.

Ellison's positions brought him sharp disfavor from leading figures of the Black Arts Movement during the late 1960s and from members of the liberal establishment throughout his career. Indeed, as early as the publication of his novel, reviewers sympathetic to radical Left–wing causes saw his work as a critique of Leftist ideology and programs. No stranger to controversy, his ideas and carefully crafted works will be debated well into the future.

Ellison's work has received widespread acclaim in the academy, the general American literary establishment, and institutions around the world where serious attention is given to the humanities and literature. His novel was awarded the National Book Award in 1953. In 1954 he won the Prix de Rome Fellowship of the American Academy of Arts and Letters. In 1963 he received the Russwurm National Newspaper Publishers Award and in 1970 was named a Chevalier de L'Ordre des Arts and Lettres. This latter honor was particularly gratifying, for the medal was awarded by one of Ellison's favorite authors, André Malraux, then Minister of Cultural Affairs in France. Two years later *Invisible Man* was named the "most likely to endure" among two dozen novels published between 1945 and 1972, in a survey of leading American critics. This award echoed the *Book Week* poll of 1965, in which the novel was selected Best American Novel in the post–World War II era.

Ellison was elected as a member to and served as vice–president of American P.E.N. (1964). He also served as a member of the National Council of Arts (1965), the Carnegie Commission on Educational Television (1966), National Institute for Arts and Letters (1967), and the American Academy of Arts and Letters (1975). He was awarded the Medal of Freedom from President Lyndon Baines Johnson in 1969. In recognition of his teaching and writing, in 1985 Ellison won a National Medal of Arts. He received 12 honorary doctorates from colleges and universities including Tuskegee Institute (1963), Rutgers (1966), Williams College (1970), Adelphi University (1971), and Harvard (1974). He accepted a number of visiting professorships at schools as diverse as Bard College (1958–61), the University of Chicago (1961), and Rutgers University (1962–69). He was Albert Schweitzer, Professor of the Humanities at New York University from 1970 to 1980. He lectured widely in the United States, as well as in Europe. After he published *Invisible Man,* he made his living from teaching, lecturing, and book royalties. He held fellowships from a number of sources, including the Rosenwald (1945) and the Rockefeller (1955) foundations.

Ellison and his works are the subjects of numerous articles and interviews in academic and popular journals. There are also several book–length works including *The Craft of Ralph Ellison,* by Robert O'Meally.

Ralph Ellison has been described in *Current Biography* as a handsome man, above medium height with "eyes that wait for a trustful look." He filled his Washington Heights apartment in New York City with thousands of books that filled floor–to–ceiling bookcases. Aside from writing, he enjoyed birdwatching and photography. He died of pancreatic cancer on April 16, 1994, in New York City. Although he had married twice, he rarely discussed his first marriage. His survivors included his second wife, Fannie McConnell, whom he married in 1946. At a memorial service held at the American Academy of Arts and Letters one month after his death, novelist Toni Morrison described Ellison as a man of humor and generosity, of intelligence and integrity. Critic Stanley Couch spoke of Ellison's concerns that rose above race and opportunism. Clearly, in his life and work, Ralph Ellison insisted that we honor the precision and poetry of language. At the same time we continually define ourselves in the broadest of categories.

REFERENCES

Current Biography Yearbook. New York: H. W. Wilson, 1993.

Ellison, Ralph. "Blues People." In *Collected Works of Ralph Ellison.* Edited by John Callahan. New York: Modern Library, 1995.

———. *Flying Home and Other Stories.* Edited by John F. Callahan. New York: Random House, 1996.

———. "Portrait of Page Inman: A Dedicated Speech." *Carleton Miscellany* 18 (Winter 1980): 28–32.

———. *Shadow and Act.* New York: Random House, 1964.

"'Flying Home': Early Ellison, Before the Master Found His Voice." *New York Times,* December 10, 1996.

New York Times Obituaries, May 27, 1994.

O'Meally, Robert. *The Craft of Ralph Ellison.* Cambridge: Harvard University Press, 1980.

"Ralph Ellison on Works in Progress." Filmed Interview. *USA: The Novel Series,* WNET/13, Indiana University Audio–Visual Center, Bloomington.

Rule, Sheila. "Ellison Recalled As an Artist of Great Range." Obituaries. *New York Times,* May 27, 1994.

COLLECTIONS

In 1996 the Library of Congress was named the repository for the Ralph Ellison papers. They are to be deposited there over a four–year period.

John McCluskey Jr.

William Ellison

(1790–1861)

Slave, artisan, planter

Born a slave in South Carolina, William Ellison accomplished the improbable feat of becoming one of the six wealthiest free persons of color in the South and quite probably the wealthiest outside of Louisiana. Ellison's skill at building and repairing cotton gins and his tremendous self–discipline were the keys to his success in winning the tolerance and respect of the white community that he needed to survive and prosper.

William Ellison of Stateburg, South Carolina, was born in 1790, probably to one of the 17 slaves on the plantation of Robert Ellison, situated two miles from Winnsboro, South Carolina. He was named April. Nothing is known of his mother except that she died a slave in 1837 when Ellison returned to Winnsboro for the funeral, providing her with a very fine coffin. Given his exceptional treatment by his owners, it is probable that he was the son either of 48–year–old Robert Ellison or of Robert's 17–year–old son William. Before Robert Ellison's death in 1806, April's ownership had passed to William. About 1802 April was apprenticed to cotton gin–maker William McCreight. Thus April had the chance to acquire a highly skilled knowledge of a new and flourishing technology along with the business skills needed to thrive. McCreight himself was an innovative craftsman and devised an effective variation in the design of gins. It appears that by the end of his apprenticeship, April was living almost as a free black.

In January of 1811 April had a ''natural'' daughter, Eliza Ann (d. 1870), by a 16–year–old slave named Matilda (1795–1850), who was and remained his wife despite the fact that there was no legal basis for slave marriages. April had another daughter, Maria Ann, by another slave woman in 1815. Maria Ann technically remained a slave all her life. She was purchased by her father in 1830 and immediately sold for one cent to William McCreight under a trust that allowed her to live as a free person of color and required her manumission either in South Carolina or in another state on her father's death. (South Carolina law had forbidden emancipation of slaves in 1820.) Maria Ann also received a legacy of $500 from her father.

Gains Freedom

On June 8, 1816, April gained his freedom under the name April Ellison. Since the white Ellisons were firm believers in self–sufficiency, the familial sentiment that led to this step was almost surely accompanied by April Ellison's payment for his freedom. By January of 1817, Ellison must have purchased his wife and daughter and freed them since his three sons, Henry (1817–1883), William Jr. (1819–1904), and Reuben (1821–1861) were all freeborn.

In order to avoid competing against the man who had trained him, Ellison moved to Stateburg, probably in 1816. Beginning with the repair of gins, Ellison began to prosper and started to build them as well. By 1820 he had increased his labor force by purchasing two male slaves. In that same year, to underline his rise in the world, he successfully petitioned on June 2, 1820, to change his name from April, easily identified as a slave name, to William.

More milestones testify to his increasing fortune and his acceptance by whites in the district during the decade of the 1820s. In 1821 Ellison felt sure enough of his position in the community to sue a white man for debt. In 1822 he bought an acre of land for $375 at a major crossroad in Stateburg, a prime commercial location, and there established his own shop. Ellison had probably begun to attend Holy Cross Episcopal Church soon after moving to Stateburg, choosing it over High Hills Baptist Church, and in 1824 the Holy Cross vestry allowed the Ellison family to move from the gallery reserved for slaves and free persons of color to a bench at the back of the main floor under the organ. While this move hardly meant acceptance as an equal by whites, it did symbolically as well as physically separate the Ellisons from other blacks in the community. Twenty years later, in 1844, Ellison was able to rent a pew in the same church. While the pew was at the very back, it was at the center of the church and rented for $35 a year, more than any of the side pews.

The census of 1840 listed Ellison as owning 36 slaves, and Ellison now began to buy women. Previously he had bought men to work in his shop, which included general blacksmith and carpentry work along with making and repairing gins. He had also bought land and owned some 330 acres compactly grouped around his shop. Women could be sent to the fields and increase his capital by having children as well. Among the slaves listed in the following censuses, the children are almost all male and about 20 of the girls one would expect to find from natural increase are not present. It is difficult to escape the conclusion that Ellison systematically sold the girl children for whom he had no need. By 1860 Ellison held 63 slaves and owned nearly 900 acres of land.

Ellison also owned two substantial homes across the road from his shop. By 1838 he had bought the Miller house, the childhood home of the famous Civil War diarist, Mary Chesnut. This was a well–built brick house with four rooms on the ground floor and four on the first. In the 1840s he bought another house immediately to the south.

Ellison needed the space to accommodate his growing family. In true patriarchal fashion he maintained control of his business and his family until his death. His sons worked in the business for wages and had some freedom to earn money through independent work on their own account. His daughter's husbands and his sons' wives joined the family in Stateburg.

The children conformed to the pattern of new upstate elites marrying into the Charleston elite. In a second marriage Eliza Ann married James M. Johnson, son of a prominent Charleston tailor. The sons married between 1844 and 1847. Henry married Mary Thornton Mishaw, daughter of a prosperous shoemaker. William Jr. married Mary Elizabeth Bonneau, and Reuben married Harriett Ann Bonneau. Both Bonneau brides were daughters of Thomas S. Bonneau (d. 1831), a community leader and schoolteacher.

In 1850 there were 16 family members living together in the two houses, and surprisingly enough there is no indication of major family problems. There may have been some tension between Reuben and his father since Reuben appears to have fathered five unacknowledged family members by a slave woman he owned. Reuben died in April of 1861, a few months before his father, and is the only Ellison not to have a grave marker in the family burying ground.

The slave basis of the family fortune was of course threatened by the Civil War, but William Ellison did not live long enough to face the problems posed by the war and Emancipation. He died on December 5, 1861. The next day he was buried in the family cemetery next to his wife.

As Ellison's sons aged, revenues from the store, which replaced the shop, and the land, which was now rented out, dropped off. Members of the family moved away. William Jr.'s widow Gabriella, his second wife, was the last member of the family to live in the family home, where she died on December 14, 1920.

William Ellison was extraordinarily successful for a black in his time and place. Beyond luck and hard work, much of his achievement was based on friendly relations with the whites of his community. Maintaining the respect of whites involved a thoroughgoing adoption of their values, especially in his attitude toward slavery. There is no evidence of any conflict in his mind due to his ownership of slaves, and unreliable local tradition labels him a harsh master. Ellison, like many other free blacks in his situation, opted for survival in the limited space for action open to him. Only the size of his success makes him unique.

REFERENCES

Johnson, Michael P., and James L. Roark. *Black Masters: A Free Family of Color in the Old South.* New York: Norton, 1984.

———. *No Chariot Let Down: Charleston's Free People of Color on the Eve of the Civil War.* Chapel Hill: University of North Carolina Press, 1984.

Robert L. Johns

Julius Erving

(1950–)

Basketball player, analyst, and executive

To commemorate the National Basketball Association's (NBA) fiftieth anniversary, Julius Erving, better known as "Dr. J.," was recently named one of the 50 greatest basketball players in the league's history. After years of exceptional deeds on the court, he became a common fixture on NBA television broadcasts as an announcer and commentator. He was also named executive vice–president of the NBA's Orlando Magic franchise. This is the latest of many honors given to a man who was the personification of basketball as a team sport as envisioned by its inventor.

Erving's reputation as a team player began when he was a teenager. As a first–year high school varsity player, he was the best on the team, but the five senior starters had been together since junior high school. Erving, therefore, accepted the fact that he would be the "sixth man." Ray Wilson, the Roosevelt High basketball coach, was quoted by Wilker in *Julius Erving* as saying of Erving: "I knew he could come off the bench and handle it, while some of the others could not. . . . Julius is of the nature that he will do whatever is necessary to win at the expense of individual glory."

While many current players refuse to be role models for young people, this was never a problem for Erving. Despite his well–deserved reputation as a showman for his dazzling and inventive style, he is still remembered as a positive force in the sport of basketball. Outside the Philadelphia Spectrum stadium is a statue of Erving, erected in 1989, with the inscription "Athlete–Sportsman–Gentleman," a fitting description of one of the 50 greatest stars of all–times.

Julius Winfield Erving was born on February 22, 1950, to Callie Mae and Julius Winfield Erving Sr., who lived in Hempstead, Long Island, New York. Right after Erving was born, a hospital nurse suggested that it would be appropriate to name him after the "Father of the Country" since they share the same birth date. Wilker quoted Callie Erving as having replied, "Have your own baby if you want to name him George Washington. I'm naming mine Julius Winfield Erving, the Second." Erving's mother was the daughter of South Carolina sharecroppers, and she worked diligently as a housecleaner to support her three children whose father left the home when the children were quite young.

Callie Erving strived to be an effective parent, by rewarding positive behavior and punishing negative behavior. She relied on her Christian faith to sustain her in her efforts as a single parent. Callie organized her schedule to be at home to greet her children in the late afternoons so that she could monitor their behavior and activities. She refrained from displaying a negative attitude about the family's limited financial resources. Instead, she helped her children focus on learning and creating goals to prepare for the future.

Erving, a quiet, introspective child, constantly sought a means for nonverbal expression and first found it in a playground game called "Geronimo." As he soared through the air after jumping out of a swing, Erving discovered a daring, fearless side of himself that set him apart from many of his peers. Soon after, he discovered basketball and began to display skills that seemed to come naturally. Erving was fascinated by the older players who were able to score under intense pressure and he worked to imitate them. Erving began to make basketball a daily routine, sometimes practicing alone, sometimes with other students. He had an innate feeling for certain ways of handling the ball, positioning his feet, and moving his body, and he felt confident that game by game, he would improve. Erving played on a Long Island Youth League Salvation Army team for preteens and this gave him opportunities to venture out beyond the confines of his neighborhood. His first coach noticed that Erving was more mature than his peers on and off the court. He certainly needed this maturity to cope with his father's death, for it made the eleven–year–old boy realize that any hope of a family reunion was lost forever.

In 1964, Callie Erving remarried and moved the family to Roosevelt, New York. Erving easily adapted to the move by finding a playground and playing his game. At Roosevelt's Centennial Park, the players were bigger and stronger, but, according to Wilker, Erving had begun to define and analyze his own strengths: "I was always small, yet I always had big

Julius Erving

hands and could jump, so I learned to be trickier than the big guys.''

Until he went to college, Erving totally immersed himself in the Riis Park summer playground basketball programs. As a 15–year–old, he played against Kareem Abdul–Jabbar, then known as Lew Alcindor, the most heavily–recruited high school player in the nation. Even Abdul–Jabbar took notice of Erving's very large hands and amazing court moves. At that time, Abdul–Jabbar was seven feet tall but Erving soared over and around him as if Abdul–Jabbar was extremely short and slow. Abdul–Jabbar, the long–time NBA mainstay, never forgot that Riis Park experience and was quoted by Wilker as saying, ''one summer, all of a sudden, there was Julius Erving.''

By the time he was a Roosevelt High senior, Erving was the acknowledged team leader but, oddly enough, he was not the most noticeable player as college scouts were much more interested in one of his teammates. Erving's goal was to win the Nassau County Championship, but his team lost. He was undeterred in his quest to improve his ball handling skills, and after graduation, he attended a summer basketball camp where NBA stars in attendance were astounded by his prowess. It was strange, therefore, that Erving was almost an unknown entity to big–name college recruiters. He was not that concerned because he did not consider basketball as the key to his future. Erving had reassured his mother that he was laying the foundation for a successful life and the first step, for him, was a college education. His choice of the University of Massachusetts at Amherst was largely based on Coach Wilson's friendship with the university's coach. Erving also desired to be near his family, however, because his sister Alexis was getting married, and his brother Marvin had a chronic disease.

Soars as College Player

Erving worked and played hard during his time at the University of Massachusetts at Amherst. The freshman team he led to an undefeated season actually created more excitement for spectators than the varsity team. On his birthday that year, his mother and brother attended the scheduled game. After returning to New York in a severe snowstorm, Marvin suffered a serious setback and was hospitalized. Soon after being diagnosed as having lupus, an incurable illness, he rapidly declined and died. Erving had greatly admired and loved his younger brother and felt distraught. Marvin had been the extrovert of the family despite his frailties and was Erving's major supporter. The summer of his freshman year, Erving worked at the playground where he first learned to play basketball and when the summer ended, Erving had managed to work through and learn to control some of his grief. He had learned that his future was his to shape, life could be short, and he needed to go all out to achieve his goals.

As a first year varsity player, Erving led the team to the National Invitational Tournament (NIT) where they almost defeated Marquette, then a national powerhouse coached by Al McGuire. McGuire was greatly impressed when Erving almost single–handedly brought his team so close to victory. McGuire wondered how anyone of his talent could be completely unknown to him. After his sophomore year, Erving was invited to attend a Colorado–based Olympics Development Camp. Although he was a last–minute replacement, he surprised his better–known peers by setting scoring and rebounding records. As a second–year varsity player, Erving led the team to the school's best record, but he set no national scoring records because of the coach's emphasis on ball control. At that year's NIT, Erving suffered a rare off–night, but one professional coach, Al Bianchi of the American Basketball Association's (ABA) Virginia Squires, saw the raw potential and realized that Erving was a diamond in the rough. When Erving was offered a contract with the Squires, his coach was shocked because small New England colleges were so far off the beaten track of most professional scouts. Erving was shocked, too. After conferring with his mother, he signed a four–year, half–million–dollar contract to become a bona fide professional basketball player. For the first time since picking up a basketball at the age of nine, Erving realized that this game could be a way of life.

Rises to Fame and Security

Basketball analyst Bob Costas described the ABA as ''basketball's Wild West,'' in Wilker's book *Julius Erving.* The young league thrived on controversy and based its reputation on innovations that are now NBA mainstays. Wilker quoted a player–agent who succinctly stated the differences between the two leagues: ''The NBA was a symphony, it was scripted. . . . The ABA was jazz.'' The ABA appreciated former playground league players' improvisatory style of play. ABA spectators came to see fast–

paced, run–and–shoot games in which spontaneity was a valued commodity. Erving was the supreme playground veteran; he and the ABA were tailor–made for each other. The ABA had plenty of flashy players who were crowd favorites, but Erving still stood our as the player to watch. The *Lincoln Library of Sports Champions* described his style: ''. . .exciting driving moves to the basket . . . sensational shot–blocking . . . flashy passes . . . powerful rebounding. He would soon come to be regarded as the best one–on–one player ever.''

As a first year Virginia Squires player, Erving became known as ''Dr. J,'' not just ''The Doctor,'' the sobriquet given during his high school days. In his second year, he led the team to the ABA play–offs. He made the All–ABA First Team from 1972 to 1976 and the ABA All–Star Team for five consecutive years. Erving caused a lot of controversy by joining the NBA to play for the Atlanta Hawks. After playing in three exhibition games, a federal court judge ruled that he must return to play for the Squires. In 1973 Virginia traded Erving to the New Jersey Nets. Now back on home turf as a Nets' star, Erving was voted the league's Most Valuable Player the next three seasons. Erving led the Nets to the last ABA championship, in 1976, before the league folded and merged with the NBA. Erving averaged 38 points per game in the six games final series with the Nuggets. Allegedly, Raymond Boe, Nets owner, promised to renegotiate Erving's contract if the leagues merged. It was therefore a newsworthy event when the New Jersey owner traded him in 1976 to the Philadelphia 76ers in order to work out his team's financial responsibilities.

Road to the NBA

The 1976 ABA–NBA merger was really an absorption of four ABA teams. These franchises regularly lost money and seldom garnered the level of attention and respect accorded the NBA. In the *Modern Encyclopedia of Basketball,* Hollander agreed with the common belief that Erving was the catalyst for the merger. He stated that ''it was really Erving [the NBA] was after. . . . He was a crowd pleaser, a showman who could fill the house.'' The trade to Philadelphia assured Erving higher visibility and better working conditions, but two years would pass before his flashes of genius became consistent.

Erving was forced to endure some unpleasantness in adjusting to life in the NBA. With all the negatives of the ABA, at least there had been a genuine love for the game and team spirit. To Erving's dismay, playing basketball was not the top priority for some NBA players and some teammates simply did not like each other. Wilker described the situation this way: ''The millionaires' club that was the Philadelphia 76ers refused to undergo the hard introspection that had brought Erving and his Nets teammates a championship in 1974.'' He also quoted one disgruntled player as saying, ''what we got here is a bunch of babies who don't look where the real trouble is in the mirror.''

Even though he was a first–year 76er, Erving was still elected to the All–Star team and voted the Most Valuable Player in the 1977 finals. The Portland Trailblazers beat Philadelphia in the NBA finals despite Erving's average of more than 30 points per game in the series. That year, he was honored again as the 1976 Performer of the Year by *Sport* magazine. Erving was an All–NBA player in 1978 and 1979. Some basketball authorities feel his best year was the 1978–79 season when he averaged 26.9 points a game and ranked fourth among the NBA's scoring leaders and seventh in steals. In 1980 Erving led the 76ers to the championship series again and averaged 25.5 points per game in the finals. In 1983 the team won the NBA championship by beating the Los Angeles Lakers during Magic Johnson's rookie season. Porter quoted Johnson as saying of Erving's unbelievable windmill reverse lay–up: ''[his] hang time seemed like eight seconds.''

Before his retirement in 1987, Erving set standards that are still the envy of professional players. He made the NBA All–Star Team in ten consecutive years. In nearly 1,500 regular season games for both the ABA and the NBA, Erving averaged more than 24 points and 8.5 rebounds per game. Only Kareem Abdul–Jabbar and Wilt Chamberlain totaled more points in a career. He won championships in both leagues, was chosen Most Valuable Player in both leagues, and received First Team All–League honors in both leagues.

As Erving approached 40 years of age and his knees weakened, he began to look beyond the courts to fulfill a promise he made to his mother when he left college and turned professional in 1971. Callie Erving Lindsay joined her daughter–in–law, Turquoise, and grandchildren in watching Erving cross the stage to receive his diploma at the University of Massachusetts at Amherst graduation ceremony in 1986. He received the bachelor's degree in business as well as an honorary doctorate.

During his playing days, Erving became part owner of a Coca–Cola franchise owner with J. Bruce Llewellyn, a black New York entrepreneur, by purchasing the majority interest of a Philadelphia–based bottling plant. He had starred in commercials for the soft–drink company for three years. Furthermore, Erving, J. Bruce Llewellyn, and television star Bill Cosby had been shareholders in New York's Coke bottler since 1983. The three partnered to trade their stock for the minority interest of a Philadelphia–based bottling plant, which they then made a new Coca–Cola franchise. In 1984, the company had revenues exceeding $100 million.

In 1987 Erving began his journey to retirement with a farewell tour. Ashe, in *A Hard Road to Glory,* described it as ''a sentimental journey unlike any seen in modern sports. He was literally showered with gifts and affection from adoring fans.'' Also labeled a victory tour, Erving's grand finale was an opportunity for opposing teams to honor him. Callahan, a writer for *Time* magazine, described one setting: ''Home teams [introduced] their own players first in order to build a crescendo for Dr. J., the National Basketball Association's star who [played] for everyone.'' Erving maintained his characteristic cool demeanor until the 76ers played the Nets, his old team, and then suddenly it was too much. At halftime his old Nets uniform—number 32—was hoisted to the rafters. His mother, his college coach, and his former Nets teammates were there and helped him cope with the overwhelming emotions that flooded him. The city of Philadelphia honored Erving with a parade just before his final NBA game.

Helping Erving to prepare for his retirement from the game that had largely defined him was his wife, Turquoise Brown, whom he met in 1971 while playing for the Nets. She was a native of Winston–Salem, North Carolina, who worked for the New York–based IBM Company and turned many heads at the Nets' home games. They married after a whirlwind courtship. Their life together changed with Erving's trade to Philadelphia. In an *Ebony* article about the wives of sports superstars, Turquoise Erving spoke about her priority of ensuring a normal life for her family. Neal quoted her about her self–imposed responsibility to her husband and, at the time, two children:

> I just worked very hard and made up my mind that no matter what, outside influences were not going to pull us apart . . . they were only going to make us closer, and they did. . . . The role of family manager meant learning to become a very strong–willed person.

Life Beyond the NBA

Porter described Erving as ''a positive role model for youth . . . [who] helped change the negative perception of African Americans in pro basketball. . . . [and] forced people to look beyond outward appearances through his class–act behavior and eloquent speaking ability.'' For these and other achievements, Erving has received many honors and awards, including a doctor of arts degree from Temple University (1983) and the Father Flanigan Award for youth work (1984). Before his retirement, he served as Special Olympics coach, March of Dimes advisor, national chairman of the Hemophilia Foundation, and spokesman for the Lupus Foundation in honor of his brother. In 1993, in his first year of eligibility, Erving was inducted into the Naismith Memorial Basketball Hall of Fame. During that year, he was also hired as a studio analyst ''Insider'' on NBC's *Showtime.* Signed to a multiyear deal with *NBC Sports,* Erving was hired to bring diversity to the otherwise white analyst staff. According to *TV Guide*'s Jim Baker, the executive producer also hired Ewing because he was ''so well spoken and well–received by current players. Many say he was their role model when they were growing up.'' In addition to Erving's employment as executive vice–president of the Orlando Magic, he is also a vice–president for the team's parent company, RDV Sports.

In 1994 Erving was ranked fortieth on the *Sports Illustrated* ''40 for the Ages List.'' Of all the honors, however, the one that might well be the closest to his heart is the ''award'' for young players who frequent the Hempstead, Long Island, Salvation Army Youth Center where Erving played as a young boy. One player is allowed to wear number 32 and is called ''The Doctor.'' Hollander said of Erving, ''He was at his best, it seems, while in mid–air'' and quoted Erving as explaining his ability to out–dunk his peers: ''It's easy once you learn how to fly.''

Current address: Director, DJ Group, Inc., 1420 Locust Street, Suite 12K, Philadelphia, PA 19102.

REFERENCES

Ashe, Arthur R. Jr. *A Hard Road to Glory: A History of the African American Athlete Since 1946.* New York: Warner Books, 1988.

Baker, Jim. ''Dr. J. To Diagnose NBA B–Ball for NBC.'' *TV Guide* 41 (25 December 1993): 34.

Callahan, Tom. ''Dr. J is Flying Away.'' *Time* 128 (22 December 1986): 82.

''Dr. J Buys a Bottler.'' *Fortune* 113 (20 January 1986): 10.

''Dr. J. Earns a Real Degree; Fulfills Promise to Mom.'' *Jet* 70 (13 June 1986): 22.

''Dr. J.'s Statue Unveiled at Philadelphia Spectrum.'' *Jet* 75 (6 February 1989): 50.

''The 50 Greatest Ball Players Over NBA's Past 50 Years.'' *Jet* 91 (18 November 1996): 46–48.

Hollander, Zander, ed. *The Modern Encyclopedia of Basketball.* 2nd rev. ed. Garden City, NY: Doubleday, 1979.

''Hoopster, Dr. J, Wife Rated Sexy Sports Pair.'' *Jet* 70 (15 September 1986): 54.

''Julius 'Dr. J.' Erving Accepts Orlando Magic VP Post.'' *Jet* 92 (23 June 1997): 48.

The Lincoln Library of Sports Champions. 3rd ed. Columbus, OH: Frontier Press, 1984.

Noel, Pamela. ''Wives of Sports Superstars.'' *Ebony* 39 (September 1984): 114.

Porter, David, ed. *African–American Sports Greats: A Biographical Dictionary.* Westport, CT: Greenwood Press, 1995.

Wilker, Josh. *Julius Erving.* New York: Chelsea House Publishers, 1995.

Who's Who among African Americans, 1996–97. 9th ed. Detroit: Gale Research, 1996.

Dolores Nicholson

Mike Espy
(1953–)
Congressman, lawyer, cabinet member

Mike Espy's political career was marked by firsts. He was not only the first African American to be elected to the U.S. Congress from the state of Mississippi since Reconstruction, he was also the first African American secretary of the U.S. Department of Agriculture (USDA). But in spite of his remarkable ability to appeal to voters across racial and class lines, and his efforts on behalf of his district, Espy's career in the USDA came to a controversial end. He was charged with ethics violations and forced to resign.

Alphonso Michael Espy was born on November 30, 1953, in Yazoo City, Mississippi. Growing up in the impoverished Mississippi Delta, Espy experienced racism firsthand. He attended a mostly white local high school. The son of Henry, a former county agent for the USDA, and Willie Jean Huddleston Espy, he never knew poverty firsthand but saw it among his neighbors. His grandfather, T. J. Huddleston Sr., assisted in the building of Mississippi's first black hospital and founded a chain of funeral homes as well.

Espy, along with his twin sister Michelle, was the youngest of seven children. His father, a graduate of Tuskegee Institute (now University) in Alabama, joined the family funeral home business after working for the USDA in the 1930s and 1940s. While in school, young Espy often helped out his family by assembling caskets or driving a black Cadillac which doubled as a hearse or a limousine for mourners.

Espy was senior class president and after high school graduation was educated at Howard University (B.A., 1975) and the University of Santa Clara (California) School of Law (LL.B., 1978). He returned to his native state to serve as managing attorney at Central Mississippi Legal Services until 1980.

Two years later, Espy became assistant secretary of state for the Public Lands Division. He served in this capacity for four years, and during this time first entered the political arena. He became the Second Congressional District coordinator for Ed Pittman's campaign for state attorney general in 1983. One year later, he became a member of the Democratic National Committee's Rules Committee. His ambition in politics served him well. In 1984 he was awarded the Jack H. Young Sr. Award from the NAACP (National Association for Colored People). That same year he received an award from the Yazoo Hometowners Club.

Espy next served as assistant attorney general for consumer protection from 1984 to 1985. One primary responsibility Espy had in this position was the collection of fees on behalf of consumers. He netted $2.4 million, which was more money collected than in the decade before his arrival. It was during this time that Espy began speaking at various events, which increased his name recognition across the state.

Elected to U.S. Congress

District lines in Mississippi were redrawn during the early 1980s, increasing the number of black voters. In addition, both black registration and participation were up due to an unsuccessful political campaign by another black candidate. As a result, Espy's timing in running for Congress was excellent. His determination and vigorous campaigning led to victory over two white candidates in the Democratic primary.

Espy continued to draw out black voters in the general election. He crossed over racial lines and discussed important agricultural issues with conservative whites. He sought out the white Democratic establishment as well, including state officials and sheriffs. Campaigning in the poverty–stricken Mississippi Delta, Espy promised reform. By election time, the black population's support for Espy enabled him to win with only ten percent of the white vote.

Mike Espy

Espy's constituents were pleased with Espy's concern for those living in rural areas. He stressed the importance of rural economic development and sought to lessen the poverty rampant in the Delta. Such commitment enabled Espy to win three subsequent bids for re–election. In 1988 Espy's opponent, Republican attorney Jack Coleman, attempted to undermine Espy's status by claiming he was against America and against Americans. When Espy's home was vandalized with racial epithets, Coleman claimed he staged the incident for sympathy. Despite such an ugly campaign, Espy was re–elected, this time with 40 percent of the white vote.

Espy impressed supporters with both his upbeat attitude and his straightforwardness. He disagreed with the Democratic leadership when he felt strongly over issues, and established himself as somewhat conservative as well. He supported prayer in public schools and the death penalty for certain drug–related crimes. At the same time, he promoted abortion rights and opposed the buildup of defense in the Reagan Administration. In what many considered a controversial move, Espy became the first federal lawmaker to appear in an advertisement for the National Rifle Association, having been a member since 1974.

Espy continued to work toward serving the Delta and its disadvantaged farmers by becoming a member of the House Agriculture Committee. More than 17,000 people in his district were employed in the production of 90 percent of the world's supply of pond–raised catfish, and Espy used every opportunity at hand to encourage catfish consumption. He convinced the Pentagon to increase its purchase of Mississippi Delta catfish by 65 percent and persuaded the U.S. Army to serve catfish once a week at all its bases. He later helped establish June 25 as National Catfish Day.

In addition, Espy initiated a bill that established the Lower Mississippi Delta Commission to study the extent of poverty in the area and to develop worthwhile programs to fight it. He felt Mississippi as a state could not move forward without improving the Delta area first, and thus sponsored the Lower Mississippi River Valley Development Act in 1988. He also assisted in the creation of the Lower Mississippi Delta Congressional Caucus, of which he later served as chairman. His work on this caucus resulted in provisions to the 1990 Housing and Community Development Act that increased funding for several impoverished counties in the area.

Named USDA Secretary

Espy was one of the first blacks in Congress to endorse Bill Clinton's candidacy for president. He defended Clinton over criticism that ensued following the riots in Los Angeles in 1992, and was co–author of Clinton's program to reform the welfare system. When Espy was not asked to serve on the House Appropriations Committee or become secretary of Housing and Urban Development, a position Espy desperately wanted, he focused his energy on becoming Agriculture Secretary. In fact, Espy so wanted the job that he made a list of the ten reasons why Clinton should appoint him. It was written on the back of an envelope and passed to Clinton at a dinner they were both attending. Reportedly, Clinton read it and gave Espy the "thumbs–up" sign. In January 1993 Espy became the first black head of the USDA and the first secretary from the Deep South.

He wasted no time in his attempt to improve the department. On his first day in office, he issued an across–the–board job freeze and announced plans to trim staff in Washington, believing the USDA was too large and consequently does not and cannot serve the needs of consumers and farmers.

Furthermore, Espy vowed to modernize the USDA's meat inspection system after the death of four children and many illnesses due to tainted hamburger. He hired more meat inspectors, promoted safer handling of all raw meat and poultry products, and urged wider use of organic sprays to eliminate surface bacteria on carcasses.

Espy was an active participant in the Clinton administration and was frequently seen in the media, announcing such things as national disaster–aid initiatives and agricultural trade pacts with other countries. In fact, Espy was the first member of the Clinton cabinet to visit China. He met with Chinese leaders in an effort to convince them to lift their country's restrictions on importing American wheat.

Ethics Violations

Espy's contributions to both Mississippi's Delta and to the USDA are unquestioned. His achievements were numerous and farmers appreciated his concern and his genuine passion for his job. However, allegations of ethics violations and other improprieties emerged that would ultimately end his career in the USDA.

In August 1994, U.S. Attorney General Janet Reno announced that an independent counsel had been established to investigate charges that Espy had violated ethics laws. Among the many allegations were charges that Espy and Patricia Jensen, an assistant secretary responsible for meat and poultry inspection, received free travel, meals, and tickets to sporting events from Tyson Foods, including sky–box seats at a Dallas Cowboys game and tickets to a Chicago Bulls play–off game. Espy's close relationship with Tyson Foods had also aroused suspicion that Espy's intervention in delaying new stricter poultry inspection rules was for the benefit of Tyson.

Other allegations include charges that Espy asked the Environmental Protection Agency to postpone a ban on an particular insecticide used by a business that had contributed to his congressional campaigns, that for seven months in 1993 he had leased a car for personal use at government expense, and that his girlfriend received a $1,200 scholarship from a foundation affiliated with Tyson Foods.

It has been reported that Espy had partially reimbursed both Tyson and other corporations, as well as the government, but the damage had been done. The White House insisted on Espy's resignation. He left on December 31, 1994, and returned to law practice in Jackson, Mississippi, with the firm of Crosthwait Terney. He was replaced as Secretary of Agriculture by Dan Glickman. On August 27, 1997, Espy was indicted by a federal grand jury on 39 felony charges that, according to the *New York Times,* included "mail and wire fraud, violations of the Meat Inspection Act of 1907, taking illegal gratuities, making false statements and tampering with a witness." Although his brother Henry was named in the indictment, he was acquitted in March 1997 of unrelated charges of fraudulently obtaining a bank loan. An agricultural cooperative, Sun Diamond Growers of California, was indicted in 1996 for bribing Mike Espy and making illegal contributions to his brother's congressional campaign. In December of 1997, U.S. District Judge Ricardo Urbina dismissed three of the most serious charges against Mike Espy.

Espy's memberships include the National Conference of Black Leaders and the presidency of the Howard University Alumni of Mississippi in Jackson. He has served on the boards of Common Cause of Mississippi, Mississippi First, and the Jackson Urban League. Espy belongs to the American Bar Association, the Magnolia Bar Association, and the bar associations of Mississippi, and Hinds and Yazoo counties.

Espy has two children, Jamilia and Michael, from his marriage to Sheila Bell in 1978 which ended in divorce. His religious affiliation is Baptist.

Despite the unfortunate circumstances surrounding his brief tenure in the cabinet, Espy made important strides in agriculture, particularly for the small farmer. He secured a place in history both as politician and federal appointee.

Current address: Crosthwait Terney, 401 East Capitol Street, Jackson, MS 39201.

REFERENCES

Behar, Richard. "On Fresh Ground." *Time* 144 (26 December 1994): 111–12.

"Black Clout in the Clinton Administration." *Ebony* 48 (May 1993): 62.

Contemporary Black Biography. Detroit: Gale Research, 1994.

Current Biography Yearbook. New York: H. W. Wilson Company, 1993.

"Former Agriculture Secretary Mike Espy: Plowing the Fields of Patronage." At the *Republican National Committee* website. http://www.rnc.org/clinton/people/espy.htm (accessed July 9, 1997): last updated September 19, 1996.

"Former Secretary of Agriculture Indicted." *New York Times,* August 28, 1997.

"Judge Tosses Three Counts Against Espy." *New York Times,* December 16, 1997.

Lloyd, Fonda Marie. "Farmers' Champion On the Way Out." *Black Enterprise* 25 (December 1994): 19.

Mack, Kibibi Voloria, ed. *The African American Encyclopedia.* New York: Marshall Cavendish, 1997.

Searcy, Joyce Espy. Interview with Jessie Carney Smith, August 22, 1997.

Williams, Michael W., ed. *The African American Encyclopedia.* New York: Marshall Cavendish, 1993.

Lori Michelle Muha

Simon Estes

(1938–)

Singer

Born into poverty in the American Midwest, Simon Estes became a major international operatic star, enchanting audiences with the artistry he displayed in the use of his fine bass–baritone voice. His impressive physical presence added to his memorable performances.

Simon Lamont Estes was born into a poor family in Centerville, Iowa, on February 2, 1938. His father was not formally educated beyond the third grade, and the home had no running water. Nonetheless, Estes and his brother and sisters grew up in a deeply religious home, where the parents also stressed the importance of education. *Current Biography* quoted his father as saying, "Whatever else people can take away from you, they can't take away what's in your head." Simon Estes sang as a boy soprano in the choir of the Second Baptist Church but had no career goals in the field of music.

Estes, who grew to be six–feet one–inch tall, was a good athlete in high school, participating in football, basketball, track, and baseball. He focused on his academic achievement, however, and entered the University of Iowa in 1956 as a pre–med student. When his father suddenly died in 1961, Estes had to support of his family working 40–hour weeks while continuing his studies. During what would have been his senior year, he changed his major to theology, and the following year to social psychology.

About this time Estes began to sing again. He was not accepted by the university choir but joined a campus pop group called the Old Gold Singers. Charles Kellis, a music teacher at the university, noticed the strength of Estes's voice. According to Estes, as quoted in *Sepia,* "Kellis heard me singing in a group, and said, 'You've got a voice to sing opera.' I more or less replied, 'What's opera?' because I'd never seen or heard one in my life." Kellis demonstrated with recordings, and Estes decided to aim for an operatic career.

Estes studied voice with Kellis until the teacher sent him on to the Juilliard School of Music in New York in 1964. The following year Estes followed a former Juilliard student whom he had a romantic interest in to Europe.

Estes received support for his move to Germany from the Martha Baird Rockefeller Foundation, the New York Community Trust Fund, and office workers of the National Association for the Advancement of Colored People (NAACP) who passed the hat. He made his debut at the Deutsche Oper in West Berlin as Ramfis in Verdi's *Aida* in April 1965. It went well despite the fact that he had no rehearsals and never met the conductor before the performance. During the ten months he stayed with the Berlin Opera, Estes won a prize in a singers' competition in Munich. In 1966 Estes won a silver medal in the first Tchaikovsky competition in Moscow.

Estes returned to the United States to perform at the White House for President Lyndon B. Johnson and to sing all four villains in the *Tales of Hoffman* for the San Francisco Opera. Although he sang for the Chicago Lyric Opera in 1969 and performed in the American premier of Shostakovich's Fourteenth Symphony with the Philadelphia Orchestra under Eugene Ormandy in 1971, Estes's American career languished due to discrimination. In reaction, he consciously behaved as a role model for younger blacks. He was always immaculately dressed and used clear and precise language when he delivered his criticisms on racism in the operatic world.

Sings *Flying Dutchman*

Estes's career began to take off in 1977, when the Metropolitan Opera in New York finally offered him secondary roles, which he refused. A performance in the title role in Wagner's *Flying Dutchman* in Zurich led to a performance in the role at the Bayreuth Wagner Festival the following year, where he became the first black male singer. By the time he sang the role for five more consecutive years at Bayreuth and at most major European opera houses, he was recognized as one of the greatest all–time interpreters of the role.

Estes impressed critics with his solo recital debut at Carnegie Hall in New York in December 1980. He sang opposite Brigit Nilsson in a concert version of Act III of *Die Walküre* on the Metropolitan stage in 1981. His official operatic debut at the Metropolitan Opera was on January 4, 1982, in the role of the Landgrave in *Tannhaüser.* He won acclaim although the role is better suited to a bass voice than to Estes's bass–baritone voice. He was the fourth black man to sing major roles with the company since Robert McFerren first led the way in 1955, followed by George Shirley and Seth McCoy. In 1983 Estes's previously smooth career at Bayreuth suffered due to racism. Music director George Solti accepted him for the 1983 *Ring of the Nibelung* cycle, but famed British director Peter Hall turned him down because of his color. Despite this momentary setback, Estes's career continued to flourish.

In February 1985 Estes sang the role of Porgy when the Metropolitan Opera finally staged the Gershwin opera *Porgy and Bess.* Then on October 22, 1986, he sang Wotan in *Die Walküre* for the first time at the Metropolitan. In addition to Wagner roles, his repertory included roles from Strauss's *Electra* to Verdi's *Macbeth,* totaling more than 90 different roles.

Estes signed a major recording contract in 1984. Among his recorded performances are Beethoven's Ninth Symphony (1992); Stravinsky's *Oedipus Rex* (1992); Haydn masses (1993); Verdi's *Don Carlo* and *Oberto* (1994); and Goldschmidt's *Beatrice Cenci* (1996). Video performances include Strauss's *Salome* and *The Flying Dutchman,* both in 1992.

Continuing to maintain a busy performance schedule, Estes is active in giving master classes and talks in schools on subjects from music to drugs. He is involved in projects like collecting used musical instruments for the use of South African students. He has also established scholarships at a number of universities.

In 1980 Estes married Yvonne Baer of Zurich, Switzerland. They had two daughters by 1986 and were splitting their time between Zurich and suburban New Jersey.

Estes has an outstanding career in the field of opera and had devoted much time and effort to furthering social goals, including the advancement of African Americans.

Current address: Harrison/Parrot Ltd., 12 Penzance Place, London W11 4PA, England. ALSO: c/o Columbia Artists Management, 165 West 57th Street, New York, NY 10019–2201.

REFERENCES

Cheatham, Wallace McClain. ''Black Male Singers at the Metropolitan Opera.'' *Black Perspective in Music* 16 (Spring 1988): 3–19.

Current Biography 1986. New York: H. W. Wilson, 1986.

Hitchcock, H. Wiley, and Stanley Sadie, eds. *The New Grove Dictionary of American Music.* London, Macmillan, 1986.

Toms, John. ''Wagner Opera Sung by Blacks.'' *Sepia* 29 (June 1980): 69–71.

Who's Who in America 1996. New Providence, NJ: Marquis Who's Who, 1995.

Robert L. Johns

James Reese Europe
(1880–1919)
Musician

James Reese Europe was one of the most important musicians of the era leading up to and including World War I. He led the breakthrough of black groups into a near monopoly of dance music in the 1910s through his organization of the Clef Club and the Tempo Club. He also gave impetus to the development of jazz through the performance practices of his groups. Throughout his career he promoted the music of African Americans without distinguishing between the popular and the learned tradition.

Europe was born in Mobile, Alabama, on February 22, 1880, to Henry (1847–1899) and Lorraine Saxon Europe (1849–1937). Henry Europe was an ex–slave, who had become a Baptist minister and, after holding a variety of jobs, worked in Mobile for the federal government from 1872 until 1885. Lorraine Saxon was born to free parents; she acquired enough education to be employed as a teacher at the time of her marriage and to serve as her children's first music teacher.

Henry and Lorraine Europe had five children, Minnie (b. 1868), Ida (b. 1870), John (1875–1932), James (1880–1919), and Mary Lorraine (1885–1944). Minnie and Ida died in the 1920s. The three youngest children made their careers in music. John made his living as a performer primarily in bars and clubs. Mary won fame as a recitalist and accompanist and later taught music at the M Street (later Dunbar) High School in Washington, D.C., for 30 years

With the inauguration of Democrat Grover Cleveland as president in 1885, Henry Europe lost his government job. Then with the election of Republican Benjamin Harrison, Europe received an appointment in the postal service in Washington, D.C., in 1889.

James Europe continued his involvement in music after the family's move to Washington. He took violin lessons from Joseph Douglass, the grandson of abolitionist Frederick Douglass. He also practiced the piano and violin under Enrico Hurlei, the assistant conductor U.S. Marine Core Band led by John Philip Sousa. James's active involvement in his church's musical and dramatic activities honed his performance and leadership skills. His impressive physical presence aided his leadership as an adult; he grew into a 200 pound, six foot frame.

James Reese Europe

Henry Europe gave up his job in the postal service in 1894 to become involved in real estate. His sudden death on June 21, 1899, plunged the family into financial chaos. Everyone had to make adjustments and work together. Lorraine Europe had been a housewife for 30 years and did not work. The two older daughters lived in Mobile, too far away to help. In 1900 John moved to New York City to seek work as musician. James remained in Washington, D.C., and left school to work whatever jobs he could find. Mary graduated from Miner Normal School, and then found work in public schools and private teaching. Ida also returned from Mobile, allowing James to leave for New York to seek work as a musician in late 1902 or early 1903.

James Reese Europe found work after switching from the violin to mandolin and piano. He also continued his studies of noted black musicians like Harry T. Burleigh (1866–1949). While much of Europe's public career was documented, he kept his personal life out of the public eye. Around 1908 he began a liaison with entertainer Bessie Simms (1889–1931); they may have married. On January 5, 1913, he married a widow, Willie Angrom Starke (1872?–1930)–. Europe's only child, James Reese Jr., was born on February 2, 1917, to Bessie Simms.

In 1903 Europe met John H. Love, private secretary of Rodman Wanamaker, and Europe joined a string quartet formed to play at Wanamaker's three–day birthday celebration. The association between Wanamaker and Europe gave the aspiring musician valuable contacts among the elite of New York and Philadelphia, who proved to be a major source of employment for black musicians.

At this time Europe had some success as a composer of popular songs. His association with black musical theater began when he directed the orchestra and chorus for *A Trip to Africa* during the production's New York run in October and December 1904. His involvement with musical theater grew towards the end of the next year when famed entertainer black Ernest Hogan (1865–1909) formed the Memphis Students and hired Europe to play. In addition to playing, the orchestra danced and sang—this was a novelty at the time. The group was a major summer hit at Oscar Hammerstein's Roof Garden in New York.

Directs Musical Comedies

Europe remained with Hogan when Will Marion Cook enticed many members of the group, including star Abbie Mitchell, then Cook's wife, into the rival Tennessee Students. In the late winter of 1905 Europe directed the orchestra and 40–member chorus of Bob Cole and the Johnson brothers' *Shoo–Fly Regiment,* a three act musical farce. The long road tour beginning in March of 1906 was difficult in terms of bookings and finances, but after the show opened to great acclaim in New York on June 3, 1907, the following season's tour was more successful.

Europe left the show in March, before the New York opening, to become musical director for The Smart Set's 1907–1908 touring show. In April of 1908 Europe left that show and joined Cole and J. Rosamond Johnson in preparing *The Red Moon.* Ernest Hogan died of tuberculosis the following year, underlining the need for an organization to promote the welfare of black entertainers. Before Hogan's death, Europe organized a huge benefit concert. He joined such celebrated musical duos as Bert Williams and George Walker, and Bob Cole and J. Rosamond Johnson as one of the 11 original members of the Frogs, a benevolent and playful social organization.

The Red Moon opened in Wilmington, Delaware, on August 31, 1908. After extensive touring, the show opened in New York in May of 1909 for a week's run, and was extended to three. The show started a second season, but Europe and star Abbie Mitchell left abruptly in late November, probably due to financial problems. Bert Williams's show, *Mr. Lode of Koal,* hired Europe as music director and he remained its last performance in March of 1910.

From 1905 to 1910, Europe spent much of his time on the road. The closing of *Mr. Lode of Koal* marked the temporary end of the large and lavish black shows capable of attracting white audiences until *Shuffle Along* became a hit in 1920. Dancing, however, became increasingly fashionable and won social acceptance. Black musicians created new dance steps such as the turkey trot and the accompanying dance music, but often found it difficult to secure jobs. They lacked a central meeting place, and the local musicians' union excluded them.

Europe undertook the formation of the Clef Club and became its first president. The Clef Club functioned as a union and a booking agency. To raise money for premises, Europe gave a large orchestral concert. The availability of performers determined the instrumentation. An overwhelming majority of the original members of the club played plucked instruments like the banjo and mandolin; there were a fair number of players of bowed string instruments, and a few percussionists, but no woodwind or brass players. Ten upright pianos filled out the sound, not as solo instruments. Over the years woodwinds and brass slowly appeared Europe's big ensembles, beginning with two clarinets in May of 1911.

Many of the players could not read music, and limitations of rehearsal space meant that sections practiced separately and came together as a whole only for the concert. The initial performance of the Clef Club Orchestra at the Manhattan Casino in Harlem on May 27 preceded the variety acts. The orchestra, consisting of over 100 musicians, attracted a favorable response and contributed much to the success of the evening. A second program was held at the Manhattan Casino in October, inaugurating a semi–annual pattern Europe would retain for the Clef Club Orchestra and its successors. The programs grew longer but the orchestra always led, followed by a series of variety acts and dancing. The orchestra devoted many of its programs to black composers.

By the end of December the Clef Club settled into permanent quarters. The club successfully fought for better working conditions for black musicians, insisting that they be hired and not perform for tips. Musicians wore tuxedos for events booked ahead and dark suit and bow tie for pick–up engagements.

In 1911 Europe began his association with David Mannes, concertmaster of the New York Philharmonic. Growing up as a poor boy in New York, Mannes studied free of charge under John Thomas Douglass (1847–86), a noted black violinist and composer of the first opera written by a black (*Virginia's Ball,* 1868). Mannes ran a music school for poor whites and wished to establish a similar school for black children. Mannes turned to Europe for advice in opening the Music Settlement School in Harlem. The Clef Club Orchestra performed a benefit concert at Carnegie Hall on May 2, 1912, the first major concert consisting primarily of black music performed by black musicians and singers. In spite of doubters, the concert proved a popular and critical success. Europe led additional concerts to help the Music Settlement School at Carnegie Hall in 1913 and 1914.

The large number of plucked instruments gave the orchestra a distinctive sound difficult to imagine and impossible to recreate—highly proficient banjo and mandolin players, to say nothing of bandore and harp guitar players, are in short supply. The completely nonsegregated audience was distributed evenly among blacks and whites.

Fosters Dance Craze

By the end of 1913, Europe played regularly for Vernon and Irene Castle, icons of the new dance craze. The Castles demonstrated and taught new dances like the one–step and later the fox trot; the Castles' dances and the music for the dances grew from black roots. On some occasions before they met Europe, they demonstrated their new dance steps without music because white groups were unable to play the kind of music they demanded. Europe developed dance ensembles that foreshadowed the future by moving away from exclusively string–based groups. James Reese Europe's Exclusive Society Orchestra, for example, had two violins, two banjolines, cello, bass violin, piano, cornet, trombone, baritone, clarinet, and drums and traps. It soon became common to refer to the groups as bands rather than orchestras. Recordings show that Europe used the fast tempos developed by ragtime pianists with his dance ensembles, and his musicians interjected vocal shouts and laughter into the performance. Interpretation of the music took on as much importance as the music itself.

The Clef Club Orchestra undertook a short tour in the fall of 1913. It played in Philadelphia, Baltimore, Richmond, Washington, and Hampton, Virginia, to great applause. The 20 selections on the program aimed at demonstrating the progress of the race from the past to the present. The orchestra was back in New York just in time to give its fall concert in Harlem on November 13. Europe's success led to jealousy on the part of some Clef Club members who complained that the organization unduly fostered Europe's own position. Thus at the end of the year Europe suddenly resigned as president of the Clef Club and announced the formation of a new group, the Tempo Club. Both the old and the new organizations were able to coexist.

Just before the breakup of the Clef Club, Europe achieved a first when Victor Records gave the first ever recording contract to a black group. Despite primitive recording techniques and few recordings, enough survived to indicate how Europe's groups sounded. Europe continued to achieve firsts, when on January 12, just after the break, he led the first black orchestra to perform at a leading white vaudeville theater. During this performace for the Castles at the Palace Theater, the musicians appeared on the state to comply with the union's ban of black musicians in the orchestra pit.

Europe drew on musicians from both his former and his current clubs to form a large ensemble to play at Carnegie Hall on March 11, 1914, under the name National Negro Symphony Orchestra. Europe remained extremely busy as the Tempo Club continued its domination of popular dance and the twice a year programs at the Manhattan Casino. After a benefit concert given by the National Negro Orchestra in Brooklyn, Europe and his musicians joined the Castles on four–week tour of the United States. The trip gave primarily white audiences the opportunity to see black musicians supporting white stars. Europe continued to innovate by increasing the importance of percussion. Buddy Gilmore, the only musician seated on stage, performed drum solos between dances. In addition, the group was the first to include a saxophone. In the spring 1915 Tempo Club concert Europe furthered the increasing importance of percussion by holding what could be the first true public drum contest.

Another musical innovation began during the tour. During the tour Europe played W. C. Handy's "Memphis Blues" for the Castles, who worked out the steps of the fox trot to the music. The dance proved an immediate sensation when they introduced it at private parties after the tour. Not only was the fox trot a very important dance in its own right, leading to many variations, it began the introduction of blues into mainstream music as dance music six years prior to the first vocal blues recording.

In early 1914 Europe won a significant victory as the local musicians' union dropped its all–white policy. Europe promptly joined and urged other blacks to do so. The battle to enter this union soon gave way to a greater battle that would affect Europe's career.

The outbreak of World War I led to the abandonment of a projected European tour with the Castles. The Tempo Club Orchestra performed Europe's Harlem concert in the fall of 1914, 75 players short. The following spring Europe and the Tempo Club Orchestra suddenly withdrew from the planned Carnegie Hall performance. The sudden decision of J. Rosamond Johnson and the other black members of the board of the Music School Settlement for Colored Children to oust the white members of the board shortly before the concert probably caused the withdrawal. Europe was not consulted, and although he had advised Mannes to relinquish control of the school as soon as feasible, Europe also realized that suddenly severing ties to white philanthropy ensured the end of the school, which in fact closed in September 1915.

The war caused the Castle's act to break up: Vernon Castle, a British citizen, joined the Royal Air Force as an aerial photographer. He died in a non–combat crash in February of 1918. In 1915 Europe met Noble Lee Sissle and Eubie Blake, who became his closest musical associates. The dance craze continued, supporting Europe's 16 orchestras. Although it was impossible for him to lead them all, he tried to appearance with as many as he could.

Enters U.S. Army

On September 18, 1916, Europe joined the recently created 15th Infantry Regiment of the New York State National Guard as a private. William Hayward, the white commander, supervised its organization and promised to replace the initial white officers with blacks as soon as possible. By December Europe passed the officer's examination. Hayward, in an attempt to help lagging recruitment, asked Europe to build a band. Europe persuaded Hayward to bend regulations to recruit top–notch musicians.

Noble Sissle became Europe's assistant in the regiment, and Eubie Blake took charge of Tempo Club activities. When the United States entered the war in April of 1917, the band had still not come into existence. On a three–day visit to Puerto Rico in May, Europe recruited 13 talented players, mostly the reed instrument players rare among blacks. By the end of May the band was shaping up, but Europe's health deteriorated from hyperthyroidism.

After a well–received band concert on June 22, Europe collapsed and underwent the first of two operations on the 27th. The organization and training of the band proceeded during Europe's recovery. Then in October the regiment relocated to Spartanburg, South Carolina, for training. There hostility between white Southerners and black soldiers nearly reached a flash point, and the regiment was hastily ordered to France to complete training. Before it left, Sissle was involved in an incident again nearly provoking a violent confrontation. Europe intervened to stop the disturbance.

The regiment finally arrived in France on January 1, 1918. The band first startled and then pleased the French with its spirited playing. The regiment, now renamed the 369th, prepared for combat duty with French units in late March. It marched into line on April 23, with Europe as the first black officer to lead troops into combat during World War I. He was also probably the first to lead a raid on enemy lines.

A poison gas attack in June temporarily disabled Europe. During his recuperation in Paris the Army decided that all officers of a unit must be of the same race, and he was due to be reassigned to another regiment. However, the Army sent Europe back to the 369th to lead the band, and ordered a single performance in Paris on August 18. After the first two numbers inspired wild enthusiasm in the audience, the band performed in Paris for eight weeks.

What the French heard in the musicians' performance they called jazz. Badger summed up the performance practices as "slight alterations (smears, slurs, unusual tonguing techniques, rhythmic or dynamic shifts), occasional 'blue' notes, tonal coloration through the use of mutes, and improvised or paraphrased breaks." Europe may not have been producing fully developed big band jazz, but eminent jazz historian Gunther Schuller wrote that James Reese Europe and Ferdinand "Jelly Roll" Morton are the two most influential musicians in the "prehistory" of jazz.

After the November 11 armistice, the French army ordered the 369th regiment to advance towards the Rhine, making them the first American troops to reach that river. The regiment returned home on February 25, 1919, to a tumultuous welcome by New Yorkers.

The Tempo Club had not survived the war, but the Clef Club, which would function until the Depression, offered Europe the position of paid president. Europe had plans for the future, but his immediate project was to lead the band in a nationwide tour. Beginning with a major success at the Oscar Hammerstein Opera House in New York on March 16, 1919, the band traveled as far west as Chicago and then returned to appear in Boston on May 9.

The events of that evening are unclear, but drummer Herbert Wright believed that Europe unduly criticized him. During the intermission he burst into Europe's dressing room and attacked Europe with a small knife. Wright was subdued, and the small wound in Europe's throat was not believed to be serious. However, the jugular had been severed, and Europe died at 11:45 that night. (Wright eventually pleaded guilty to manslaughter and was released on parole on April 1, 1927.)

New York City held its first public funeral for Europe. After the body lay in state in a Harlem funeral home, an elaborate procession made its way to St. Mark's Episcopal Church, then on West 53rd Street. The body was then buried in the National Military Cemetery in Arlington, Virginia.

Europe was still a young and vigorous man. If he had survived to carry out his plans, the course of jazz in the 1920s would have been different. In his life he had done much to bring a black inflection into American popular music. Many years later Eubie Blake was still convinced of his importance. He told Al Rosen:

> Before Europe, Negro musicians were just like wandering minstrels. Play in a saloon and pass the hat and that's it. Before Jim, they weren't even supposed to be human beings. Jim Europe changed all that. He made a profession for us out of music. All of that we owe to Jim. If only people would realize it.

REFERENCES

Badger, Reid. *A Life in Ragtime.* New York: Oxford, 1995.

Charters, Samuel B., and Leonard Kunstadt. *Jazz: A History of the New York Scene.* Garden City, NY: Doubleday, 1962. Reprint, New York: Da Capo, 1981.

Fletcher, Tom. *100 Years of the Negro in Show Business.* New York: Burdge, 1954. Reprint, New York: Da Capo, 1984.

Kimball, Robert, and William Bolcom. *Reminiscing with Sissle and Blake.* New York: Viking, 1973.

Little, Arthur W. *From Harlem to the Rhine.* New York: Covici Friede, 1936.

Logan, Rayford W., and Michael R. Winston, eds. *Dictionary of American Negro Biography.* New York: Norton, 1982. [The entry on Europe by Gunther Schuller is reprinted in his book *Musings* (New York: Oxford, 1986).]

Rose, Al. *Eubie Blake.* New York: Schirmer, 1979.

Scott, Emmett J. *Scott's Official History of The American Negro in the World War.* Chicago: Homewood Press, 1919.

Southern, Eileen. *The Music of Black Americans.* 2nd ed. New York: Norton, 1983.

Robert L. Johns

Medgar Evers
(1925–1963)
Civil rights activist

Aware of the need to be politically conscious as he lived in Mississippi's Delta area, Medgar Evers devoted his adult life to civil rights activities. He is known for losing his life to an assassin's bullet, a tragedy that helped to prompt passage of comprehensive federal civil rights laws.

Medgar Wiley Evers, the leading civil rights leader of Jackson, Mississippi, in the 1960s, was born to James and Jessie Evers at Decatur, Mississippi, on July 2, 1925. He was the third of the Evers's four children, who were brought up on their parents' farm. While the father, James, supplemented his income with a part–time sawmill job, Jessie Evers, who was of mixed white, Indian, and black parentage, served as a domestic worker, cleaning homes for rich whites and ironing at home for others.

Young Evers's education initially began in a one–room elementary school in Decatur, Mississippi, at six years old, but he later had to join other children of his age group to walk 12 miles one way to attend another school in Newton, Mississippi. He was a serious youngster who may have had a mission. Quoted in *Ghosts of Mississippi,* Medgar's sister, Elizabeth Evers Jordan, said, "Medgar was more quietish. I used to see him go way down in himself, like he's in a deep, deep studying. He used to always carve his name on the trees and things: M. W. Evers. See, he had a dream, it was something in him that he wanted."

In 1946 Evers returned to Mississippi from service in the Army during World War II, and that same year he decided to exercise his voting rights. When he and his brother, Charles Evers, attempted to vote, white supremacists threatened their family. At the time, Charles was already enrolled at Alcorn Agricultural and Mechanical (A and M) College, the oldest statewide college for black students, located at Norman, Mississippi.

As a U.S. Army veteran, Medgar Evers could return to school on his veteran's benefits. As a result, he decided to complete his high school education, which had been interrupted by the war. To achieve his aim, Evers enrolled in the laboratory school of Alcorn A and M College, earning his high school diploma and enrolling at the college to study business administration in order to open his own business. His brother Charles majored in social sciences. At Alcorn, Charles and Medgar Evers made the football team, on which Medgar was a noted halfback. In order to earn additional money to help their family back in Decatur, Charles operated a taxi service for students of the college and, later, both brothers used their dormitory room to operate a ham sandwich business. Medgar Evers was selected to participate on the college's track team, sang in the choir, and played active roles in the debating and business clubs, sometimes volunteering to work for the local YMCA. Editor of Alcorn's 1951 yearbook, Medgar Evers did so well in college that he was selected to be included in *Who's Who Among Students in American Colleges and Universities.*

Medgar and Charles Evers were very active in the social life at Alcorn and, during the fall semester of 1950, Medgar began to date a seventeen–year–old freshman by the name of Myrlie Beasley, from Vicksburg, Mississippi, who had gradu-

Medgar Evers

ated second in her high school class. After almost a year of courtship, the couple married on December 24, 1951. They had three children—Darrell Kenyatta (b. 1953), named after the anti–British colonial rule agitator and first President of Kenya, Jomo Kenyatta; Reena Denise (b. 1954), and James Van Dyke (b. 1960). Medgar Evers wanted his brother Charles to be his best man at the wedding, but that was not possible because the outbreak of the Korean War had prompted the army to call Charles back to his reserve unit.

When Medgar Evers graduated in July of 1952, he was employed by Theodore Roosevelt Mason Howard's Magnolia Mutual Life Insurance Company of Mound Bayou, Mississippi—a sleepy town on Mississippi's Highway 61 in the heart of the Delta; he was to sell insurance policies in the Clarksdale area of Mississippi. Although Myrlie Evers had ambitions to move with her new husband to the North, possibly to Chicago, she had to stay at Mound Bayou, where she also served as a secretary in the insurance office.

Theodore Howard was to influence Medgar Evers in various ways, especially as the founder of the Regional Council of Negro Leadership in the Delta area, a serious lobby group very similar to the NAACP, which distributed bumper stickers reading "Don't Buy Gas Where You Can't Use the Restroom." It was on joining the council in 1952 and, later that same year, the Mound Bayou branch of the NAACP that Evers came into contact with other politically conscious African American men and women, including Cleveland, Mississippi, businessman Amzie Moore, local NAACP president Aaron Henry—a pharmacist by training—and Thomas Moore, also an insurance agent.

Evers's work gave him extensive first–hand knowledge of conditions faced by rural blacks in the Delta as he traveled throughout the area, selling insurance. As a member of the council, Evers used various forms of boycotts to assist in mobilizing his fellow blacks against racism and economic inequality. In 1954 he was appointed salaried field secretary of the then very inactive NAACP in Mississippi. In that position, he fearlessly insisted that the state should enforce the 1954 Supreme Court decision declaring segregation in public education unconstitutional; that insistence and other NAACP activities caused Evers to be marked by white supremacists as being too revolutionary. He became an avowed supporter of Martin Luther King, Jr. When the Atlanta native formed the Southern Christian Leadership Conference (SCLC), Evers threw his support to it, although Evers still worked for the NAACP.

Civil Activism Leads to Death

Like other civil rights stalwarts, Evers was often threatened with death, beaten by white racist thugs, arrested, and jailed. In the early hours of June 11, 1963, he was shot in the back and killed in the driveway of his Jackson, Mississippi, home. Evers's death caused blacks to riot in many major cities, and prompted President John F. Kennedy—who was himself to become the victim of an assassin's bullet—on June 19, 1963, to seek congressional action for a comprehensive civil rights law. Evers, an army veteran, was buried in Arlington National Cemetery in May of 1964. Byron De La Beckwith Jr., a white local postal employee, was tried twice by all–white juries in 1964 but was acquitted on both occasions when the juries deadlocked. On February 5, 1994, a multiracial jury re–tried him and found him guilty of the crime. He was sentenced to life in prison, to be eligible for parole in ten years.

Myrlie Evers gathered their three children and left for Pomona College in California to complete her first degree, which had been interrupted by marriage. She still pressed on to find her husband's killer and, as a result, Beckwith was arrested a third time, on this occasion in Tennessee, and charged with the murder of Evers. Beckwith's lawyers filed a motion to get the charge dismissed by the U.S. Supreme Court. On October 4, 1993, the court refused to do so, thus clearing the way for the third trial to begin. On February 5, 1994, very frail and wearing a tiny pin of the Confederate flag pinned to the lapel of his jacket, Beckwith was found guilty by a jury at his third trial, sentenced to life in prison by Judge Hilburn, to be eligible for parole in ten years.

In time, life for blacks in Mississippi changed: Charles Evers rose to become the mayor of Fayette, Mississippi, and now runs the WMPR weekly radio talk show. Myrlie Evers, who later remarried, served as chairman of the board of the NAACP. Medgar Evers gave his life for the freedom of blacks in Mississippi and wherever society oppresses them.

REFERENCES

Carter, Hodding III. *The South Strikes Back.* New York: Doubleday, 1959.

Evers, Charles, and Andrew Szanton. *Have No Fear: The Charles Evers Story.* New York: Wiley, 1997.

Evers, Charles, with Grace Halsell. *Evers.* New York: World Publishing, 1971.

Evers, Medgar. "Why I Live in Mississippi." *Ebony* 14 (November 1958): 65–70.

Evers, Mrs. Medgar (Myrlie Evers), with William Peters. *For Us the Living.* Garden City, NY: Doubleday. 1967.

Logan, Rayford W., and Michael R. Winston, eds. *Dictionary of American Negro Biography.* New York: Norton, 1992.

Lowery, Charles D., and John F. Marszalek, eds. *Encyclopedia of African–American Civil Rights: From Emancipation to the Present.* New York: Greenwood Press, 1992.

Massengill, Reed. *Portrait of a Racist: A Revelatory Biography of Byron De La Beckwith, Written by His Own Nephew.* New York: St. Martin's Press, 1994.

McMillen, Neil R. *The Citizens Councils: Organized Resistance to the Second Reconstruction.* Urbana: University of Illinois Press, 1971.

———. *Dark Journey: Black Mississippians in the Age of Jim Crow.* Urbana: University of Illinois Press, 1989.

Raines, Howell. *The Story of The Civil Rights in the Deep South.* New York: Penguin, 1983.

Salter, John R. Jr. *Jackson, Mississippi: An American Chronicle of Struggle and Schism.* Malabar, FL: Krieger Publishers, 1987.

Scott, R. W. *Glory in Conflict: A Saga of Byron De La Beckwith.* Camden, AR: Camark Press, 1991.

Sinclair, Mary Craig. *Southern Belle.* New York: Crown, 1957.

Vollers, Maryanne. *Ghosts of Mississippi: The Murder of Medgar Evers, the Trials of Byron De La Beckwith, and the Haunting of the New South.* New York: Little, Brown, 1995.

A. B. Assensoh

James L. Farmer Jr.

(1920–)

Civil rights activist, educator

James L. Farmer, Jr. stands as a living symbol of the tumultuous 1960s, an era in which the fabric of American society was rent from seam to seam. Founder of the Congress of Racial Equality (CORE), Farmer was one of the few activists whose personal background and professional training enabled him to perfect nonviolent demonstration tactics in one historical era and utilize them in another without being regarded as out of step with the times.

James Leonard Farmer Jr. was born on January 12, 1920, in Marshall, Texas, where his father served as a Methodist minister. He is the son of James L. Farmer Sr. and Pearl Houston Farmer. Before James Farmer's first birthday, the family moved to Holly Springs, Mississippi, where the senior Farmer was hired as a faculty member, academic dean, and campus minister at Rust College. The father was a magna cum laude, bachelor of arts degree graduate of Boston University, where he also earned a bachelor of sacred theology and doctor of philosophy degree. He spoke seven languages and was probably the first black in Texas to hold a Ph.D. degree.

Pearl Farmer earned a teaching degree from Bethune–Cookman Institute and taught in Jacksonville, Florida. After James Farmer Sr. completed his studies, they married and moved to Texarkana, where Farmer's sister was born, and then to Galveston, Texas. In Holly Springs, the children were burdened by being teachers' and preacher's kids and by the painful experience of Farmer's learning that being black meant denial of basic rights accorded to white children. Farmer began school before the age of five and was soon skipped to the second grade. The family moved to Austin, Texas, where the senior Farmer was hired as professor of religion and philosophy at Samuel Houston College. The fact that the senior Farmer possessed an earned doctorate made no difference to many whites who still treated him as they would any other black man. The younger farmer began to be troubled by disparities in his father's behavior when confronted by whites. Jeff Sklansky wrote of Farmer's feelings about his father in *James Farmers: Civil Right Leader,* ''James would take from his father a lifelong burning commitment to moral principles. He would also take a deep revulsion from the kind of hypocrisy he sensed in his father's varying personality.''

James L. Farmer Jr.

Outlook Changes

At the age of 12, Farmer received a four–year scholarship awarded for his superior oratorical skills. Two years later, in 1934, he entered Wiley College in Marshall, Texas. The person who wielded the greatest influence on Farmer was Melvin Tolson, Wiley's English professor and debating coach. Then an unknown writer, Tolson would shortly achieve fame with the production of his volume of poetry, *Rendezvous with America* (1944).

As Wiley's representative to the 1937 National Conference of Methodist Youth at Miami University, Farmer was one of few blacks there but made his presence known by having the body pass a motion urging U.S. Congress to pass an anti–lynching bill. He also attended the Richmond, Virginia, meeting of the National Negro Congress and Southern Negro Youth Conference, where he was exposed to Mordecai Johnson, A. Philip Randolph, and Ralph Bunche, three giants who were exemplars to him.

Although Farmer chafed under his father's strong personality and physical presence, he decided to study for the ministry at Howard University, where the senior Farmer had been hired as professor of New Testament and Greek. In

Howard's School of Religion, Farmer studied under theologians and biblical scholars. Prominent among them was Howard Thurman, described by Farmer in *Lay Bare the Heart* as "mystic, poet, philosopher, preacher." He was also professor of social ethics and dean of the chapel. As Farmer's spiritual mentor as well, Thurman guided him through the comprehensive study of the life and guiding principles of Mahatma Ghandi, whom Thurman knew personally. Thurman also encouraged and served as adviser for Farmer's thesis, "A Critical Analysis of the Historical Interrelationships Between Religion and Racism." Because Farmer was already an avowed pacifist, Thurman recommended him for an appointment as part–time student secretary at the Washington office of the Fellowship of Reconciliation (FOR), an organization that would shape Farmer's adult philosophy and life's work. At this point, he began to turn away from his original goal of the ordained ministry.

In 1941 Farmer completed his seminary studies and informed his father that he would not pursue ordination. The elder farmer loaned his son $300 to begin his projected life's work—ridding the world of segregation. Due to his part–time FOR position, Farmer was able to secure a full–time job with the organization, first in Chicago and later in New York, the city of his dreams.

FOR and CORE

In *Lay Bare the Heart,* Farmer described the Fellowship of Reconciliation as "A kind of nondenominational Quaker body, eschewing all violence and rejecting all war." Its 12,000 members were committed to pacifism and focussed on seeking new ways to resolve personal differences. In the Chicago office, Farmer's job as race relations secretary required him to present formal anti–war speeches throughout the Midwest. His first large–scale project was formulating a proposal to fight racial segregation entitled "A Provisional Plan for Brotherhood Mobilization." While awaiting a response from A. J. Muste, FOR's executive secretary, Farmer became involved in interracial housing action. He and University of Chicago students formed a racially mixed study group devoted to Gandhian principles of civil disobedience. Within a year, their sit–in tactics resulted in the integration of a local coffeehouse.

CORE was first a committee that FOR allowed Farmer to establish in lieu of his original plan for FOR "shock troops" to fight segregation overtly. The eight–member group had great success in Chicago and, as more middle–class students joined, efforts in integrating eating and recreational establishments became more successful. Sklansky quoted an Urban League official who expressed: "The Urban League is the State Department of civil rights; the NAACP is the War Department and CORE is the Marines."

CORE chapters expanded throughout the West and North and, on June 15, 1943, Farmer presided over the first national CORE conference where he helped write the charter and monitor the continuing rise of CORE chapters. CORE was becoming better known than the fellowship. A. J. Muste offered Farmer a generous salary increase and a transfer to the New York FOR national office. Despite the potential for losing sight of his grandiose ideas for CORE, Farmer accepted the additional responsibility because he had always wanted to live in New York.

After a period of rapid growth, CORE changed the "C" in its name from "committee" to "congress," becoming the Congress of Racial Equality in recognition of the organization's expansion of its efforts. At the 1944 convention, Farmer was reelected national chairman with the mandate to bar communists from membership due to their reputation of taking over organization operations. Farmer resigned his paying FOR position and after he and Winnie Christie married in 1945, he was hired as an organizer by the Upholsterer's International Union of North America (UIU), which represented furniture industry workers in Virginia and North Carolina. This new position would allow Farmer to continue integration efforts since trade unions were notorious for hiring blacks only for menial positions. He was largely unsuccessful because Southern blacks had no faith in unions and owners often reacted by firing new members. Farmer's personal life deteriorated, and he was divorced in 1946.

CORE prospered during Farmer's absence and gained worldwide attention as the first activist group to test the 1946 Supreme Court ruling that intrastate segregated bus seating was unconstitutional. On April 9, 1947, 16 CORE volunteers, including the FOR field secretary Bayard Rustin, boarded buses in North Carolina to test the ruling. Farmer always felt regret and guilt over missing the Journey of Reconciliation, a venture that netted Rustin and others a 30–day chain–gang sentence.

In 1949 Farmer remarried, this time to Lula Peterson, a white CORE worker who was fighting Hodgkin's Disease. She became the Institute of International Education's budget director, and Farmer was hired by the League for Industrial Democracy as student field secretary, a position that entailed touring college campuses and recruiting LID members. CORE was still part of the Farmers' lives as they hosted local meetings and participated on the local level.

In 1955 the Montgomery Bus Boycott became the focus of national news. Farmer had just become a successful union organizer for the New York City section of the American Federation of State, County, and Municipal Employees. He watched Martin Luther King Jr. become the spokesman for nonviolent civil rights protests, a movement he had been the leader of. In 1959, after the birth of his first child, Tami Lynn, Farmer became the program director of the NAACP, a position he thought would catapult him into the thick of civil rights battles being waged in the South. In *The Negro Revolt,* Lomax described Farmer's dilemma: "He had been chafing at the bit. . . . His suggested programs of mass action were lying in state—killed by cautious politics, embalmed by inaction, neatly tucked into coffins of conservatism."

The emergence of the Student National Coordinating Committee (SNCC) worked in Farmer's favor, because the current CORE executive secretary was neither an activist nor black. Because the focus in the South was militancy—not interracial harmony—white people were ineffective in the late 1960s. Jimmy Robinson was going to be replaced because CORE leaders could see that he was ineffectual in dealing with the turn of events in the South. King was the first choice to head CORE, but he refused since he would not be allowed to merge CORE and the Southern Christian Leadership Conference (SCLC). Roy Wilkins urged Farmer to take the position before Farmer had resigned his NAACP position. Wilkins also urged him to be ruthless and immediately confront rebellious and fractious CORE old–timers. According to Branch, he told Farmer, ''You're going to be riding a mustang pony, while I'm riding a dinosaur.''

Heads CORE

CORE officially hired Farmer as its national director on February 1, 1961, just days after the inauguration of John F. Kennedy as president of the United States. Farmer's first act was to announce the renewed attempt to test Southern segregation of interstate buses—the Freedom Rides. Tom Gaither, a CORE staffer, tested the waters between the nation's capitol and New Orleans. Gaither was promptly jailed, and his prediction of violence in Anniston, Alabama, a planned leg of the upcoming rides, would soon bear fruit. Farmer and his recruits began Freedom Ride training with John Lewis, a SNCC member who had learned of the project in the SNCC *Student Voice* publication. Despite national publicity about the sit–ins, the media largely ignored the Freedom Rides plans, but on May 4, 1961, the two groups began the journey from Washington, D.C., one on a Greyhound bus and the other on a Trailways bus. Lewis was beaten by a white mob in Rock Hill, South Carolina, but within a week the groups had covered 700 miles. During that time Farmer's father died and, according to Sklansky, Farmer's mother maintained that ''he had timed his death to interrupt their son's trip before he could reach the most dangerous part of the Freedom Ride.''

As Gaither predicted, Anniston was a hotbed of violence and was in the news after the Freedom Riders' Greyhound bus was firebombed and its passengers beaten. The Trailways bus riders were attacked in Anniston and in Birmingham. By the time they arrived in New Orleans and disbanded, Diane Nash, Fisk University student and SNCC leader, got Farmer's permission to bring in a Nashville student contingent to take over the Freedom Rides in Birmingham. Tardy federal government intervention followed a violent white reaction. Martin Luther King Jr. and those in attendance at a mass meeting at a local church were under siege by a white mob until the next morning. Farmer flew in to the meeting and was hailed as the originator of the Freedom Rides, but he disappointed the students. Farmer seemed so pompous and officious that they virtually ignored him. When the New Orleans CORE group finally arrived, the group was stunned when Farmer announced that he was not going on with them due to pressing business back in the New York office. Finally, an overwhelming sense of guilt changed his mind and he traveled on the second bus. Members of the group were all arrested and jailed. They refused to make bail and so garnered a two–month sentence at the infamous Parchman State Penitentiary in Mississippi. By then, the national media had lionized Farmer and contributions rolled into the New York office.

In 1963 the proposed March on Washington for Jobs and Freedom was on the agenda of civil rights activists: CORE, the Urban League, SCLC, SNCC, American Jewish Congress, National Council of Churches, AFL–CIO, United Auto Workers, and the NAACP sponsored the march. A. Philip Randolph and Bayard Rustin were principal organizers, and relations were fractious from the start, especially concerning Rustin and the need for civil disobedience. Powers as high as the White House wished to control the march. Farmer was absent from the march since he was serving time in Louisiana jails. When he returned to Louisiana—after the march—to fulfill another commitment, he put his life in peril. The atmosphere was so hostile that he finally escaped to New Orleans in a hearse while another was used as a decoy. He then flew to New York and later discovered from government insiders that high level state officials had issued orders that he be killed and his body well hidden.

Farmer's leadership of CORE was threatened by a proposal that a white staffer be named national chairman. He refused to consider the promotion and was assailed by whites and blacks who, according to Farmer, charged: ''This is not CORE. CORE is colorblind.'' Floyd McKissack, a black North Carolina CORE official, was elected to the position. Too much of Farmer's time was spent on defusing internecine power struggles that damaged him and CORE. Finally, there was a failed move to oust him as national director at the 1964 convention. That same year, he proposed shifting CORE's focus from the South to urban ghettos but his directive to the editor of the *CORElator,* the organization's newsletter, was disregarded. After Farmer dismissed the white editor, Jim Peck, he was accused of being a black nationalist and black racist. That summer, Farmer returned to the South to investigate the disappearance of three CORE workers in Neshoba County, Mississippi. When he returned to New York, Farmer tried to defuse the tension and anger of a black mob protesting police brutality by starting a march to get them to go to their homes; the police panicked when they thought bricks and bottles were being thrown at them and fired into the crowd. Farmer retreated, realizing that he was powerless; the Harlem Riots of 1964 had begun.

Takes New Stand

A strategy to change the future for poor and black Americans was Farmer's plan to combat functional illiteracy. When summoned to the White House, Farmer outlined his plan to President Lyndon Johnson and was told to submit a detailed proposal for a comprehensive program. The proposal was submitted to the Office of Economic Opportunity. Farmer was later placed in a damaging situation when the literacy proposal was approved by the OEO director, Sargent Shriver, but prematurely announced on December 25, 1965, in a *Washington Post* article. Farmer had not informed CORE of his intentions, and CORE officials were upset at having to face media questions for which they were unprepared. By January 1966, it was clear that Farmer's caution about leaving CORE was justified since the project had not been funded, but he was forced to resign anyway, an action effective December 1, 1966. Floyd McKissack was elected as the new CORE national director. At the age of 46, Farmer now had two daughters—Tamil Lynn and Abbey Lee—and exorbitant medical bills due to his wife's ongoing health problems. Quite unexpectedly, Congressman Adam Clayton Powell further sabotaged any hope of the literary program by his effective opposition.

Farmer turned to the lecture circuit and teaching to earn a living. He also ran for a House of Representatives seat from a new Brooklyn congressional district. His Liberal Party campaign was waged against Democratic candidate Shirley Chisholm, who easily defeated him. In 1968 Richard M. Nixon offered Farmer the post of assistant secretary for administration at Health, Education, and Welfare (HEW). Immediately after being sworn in on April 2, 1969, Farmer tackled bureaucratic problems. An initial assessment showed that one–fifth of HEW minorities had low level jobs, the intern program was nearly all–white, and there appeared to a "glass ceiling" for blacks. He had to battle long and hard over the relocation of Head Start to HEW, since Senator Russell Long, chairman of the Senate Finance Committee, vigorously opposed Farmer's CORE activities in the South. He implemented plans to require that half of the management interns be minorities and that the HEW Fellows Program include highly trained minorities with ten–month rotations through various HEW offices. Farmer also established an Office of New Careers to promote upward mobility.

Farmer tired of HEW's bureaucratic tangles. He planned to resign after the new secretary was in place long enough to prevent perceptions of a clash between them. A reporter who promised to keep off–the–record comments and complaints secret immediately released the story to the Westinghouse News Radio where the black newspapers picked it up. He was forced to resign on December 28, 1970, earlier than he had scheduled.

Farmer's financial situation became critical as Lula Farmer's health rapidly deteriorated. He returned to the lecture circuit. Farmer also developed a think tank proposal, the Council on Minority Planning and Strategy (COMPAS), that the U.S. Office of Education funded in 1973 at Howard University as the Public Policy Training Institute (PPTI). In 1974 serious allegations were lodged citing that Farmer was financially rewarded for endorsing Richard Nixon for reelection. The *New York Times* and *Washington Post* published stories accusing Farmer of being a sellout to black Americans. The project was not refunded despite its proven successes.

Farmer and a friend established the Fund for an Open Society in 1975 as a nonprofit company that would provide low–interest mortgage loans to people planning to live in integrated housing. The salary was minuscule and insufficient for Farmer's needs, and he later found a better paying job with the American Federation of State, County, and Municipal Employees as associate director of the Coalition of American Public Employees, a lobbying group. In 1976 Lula Farmer died.

In 1979 Farmer was afflicted with retinal vascular occlusion, an eye ailment that destroyed the sight in his right eye and threatened that in his left eye. He moved to Virginia to complete his autobiography, which was published in 1985. Recognized as a preeminent scholar in the history of civil rights, he has been a visiting professor at Mary Washington College in Fredericksburg, Virginia, since 1985.

Farmer's greatest achievement was founding CORE in 1942 and he has been duly honored for his civil rights achievements. He received the Omega Psi Phi Fraternity Award (1961 and 1963); First Citizen Award, Queens Region Hadassah (1969), American Humanist Award (1976), and nearly 20 honorary doctorates. In January of 1998 President Clinton presented him with the Presidential Medal of Freedom, the highest civilian honor. The president praised Farmer in *Jet,* commenting that he "never sought the limelight, and until today, I. . .think he's never gotten the credit he deserves." Farmer authored numerous articles and essays and wrote his first book, *Freedom When,* in 1976. Farmer's most enduring legacy is his work to dismantle segregation. Recognizing that current civil rights issues can be complicated, he pointed out in an interview for the *New Yorker,*

> Most of us thought that if we would wipe out Jim Crow the race problem would be solved. In the sixties, problems were simple. The front seat of a bus, a hot dog at a lunch counter. It was good against evil, right against wrong. Now, sometimes, it's right against right.

He remarked to Sklansky, "The tired among us must recharge our batteries. The uninitiated must learn to gird their loins. We have not finished the job of making our country whole." Despite total blindness and being confined to a wheelchair due to a leg amputation, Farmer continues to fight racism. He also planned to write another book, *An Old Warrior Speaks: Of Race and Nation.*

Current address: Mary Washington College, 1301 College Avenue, Fredericksburg, VA 22401.

REFERENCES

Barksdale, Richard, and Keneth Kinnamon. *Black Writers of America.* New York: Macmillan, 1972.

Branch, Taylor. *Parting the Waters: America in the King Years 1954–63.* New York: Simon and Schuster, 1988.

"Civil Rights Veteran James Farmer Awarded Medal of Freedom." *Jet* 93 (2 February 1998): 4–5.

"Denial of a Soda on a Summer Day Forges Activist." *New Orleans Times–Picayune,* March 30, 1997.

Farmer, James. *Lay Bare the Heart: An Autobiography of the Civil Rights Movement.* New York: Arbor House, 1985.

Garrow, David J. *The FBI and Martin Luther King, Jr.* New York: Penguin Books, 1981.

Gates, Henry Louis. "After the Revolution." *New Yorker,* Special Issue, 72 (29 April and 6 May, 1996): 60.

Kasher, Steven. *The Civil Rights Movement: A Photographic History, 1954–68.* New York: Abbeville Press, 1996.

Lomax, Louis E. *The Negro Revolt.* New York: Harper and Row, 1963.

Quarles, Benjamin. *The Negro in the Making of America.* Rev. ed. New York: Macmillan, 1969.

Sklansky, Jeff. *James Farmer: Civil Rights Leader.* New York: Chelsea House Publishers, 1992.
"Ticker Tape." *Jet* 91 (24 March 1997): 10.
Who's Who among Black Americans, 1996–97. 9th ed. Detroit: Gale Research, 1996.

Dolores Nicholson

Louis Farrakhan
(1933–)
Religious leader, activist

Louis Farrakhan is the head and spirit of the resurrected Nation of Islam (NOI) or Black Muslims (BM). Farrakhan is a recognized public figure in the United States and in many other countries throughout the world. The frequently provocative nature of this self–styled religious crusader for "freedom, justice and equality" for African Americans and others garners him significant attention, both positive and negative, and has affected the culture of thousands of African Americans. *Time* magazine recognized him as one of the 25 most influential Americans, and featured him on its cover as did *Newsweek, Emerge* and many other major publications. Farrakhan's appearances in recent years on television shows such as *Sixty Minutes, Nightline, 20/20,* and *C–Span,* have also kept him in the public eye.

Sarah Mae Manning Clarke, a St. Kitts immigrant and domestic worker, gave birth to Farrakhan on May 11, 1933, in the Bronx. Her estranged husband, a Jamaican immigrant taxi driver named Percival Clarke was the biological father, but was not recognized on his son's birth certificate. Farrakhan's mother originally named him Louis Eugene Walcott, for her lover, Louis Walcott, who had fathered Farrakhan's older half–brother and sole sibling, Alvan Walcott. The family subsequently moved to the Roxbury section of Boston, Massachusetts when young "Gene," as Farrakhan was then known, was approximately four years old.

Farrakhan's early life was nothing like that of his future teacher and mentor, Malcolm X. Farrakhan grew up in and benefited from Roxbury's West Indian enclave. Sarah Clarke worked diligently at various domestic jobs for whites, mainly Jewish people, but still needed some public assistance to make ends meet and provide for her boys, as Louis Walcott apparently drifted away a year after they arrived in Roxbury. She somehow managed to save small loose change to pay for Alvan's piano lessons and Gene's violin lessons.

One of young Farrakhan's violin instructors was a Jewish woman from Russia. His public violin performances began at Roxbury's St. Cyrian's Episcopal Church, where he was also in the choir and served as a cross–bearing acolyte in the early 1940s.

Louis Farrakhan

Farrakhan performed well educationally from elementary through high school, and earned a placed in Boston's top–ranked historic Latin School in 1947. He was one of a handful of African Americans at Boston Latin and in 1948 transferred to Boston's next best high school, English High, so that he could be around more of "his own." Farrakhan remained an honor student at the English school, as he had been at the Latin school. Moreover, he discovered the sport of track and field and his ability to run fast. Farrakhan ranked among the top track performers in the dashes and sprints. He also continued his violin performances. On May 15, 1949, he celebrated the month and year of his sixteenth birthday with a classical violin performance on the then popular *Ted Mack Original Amateur Hour* television program.

Farrakhan's musical performances were not limited to classical violin presentations; he had also discovered Caribbean Calypso and was known as "The Charmer" around Boston's African American nightclubs. His guitar– and ukulele–accompanied songs and gyrations earned him some much–needed money, but he was also exposed to life's seamy side. He resisted temptation except for some indulgence in marijuana and alcohol.

Though he did not give up future violin and calypso performances, Farrakhan chose to attend Winston–Salem Teacher's College—now University—in North Carolina, over New York's Juilliard School of Music. He enrolled in September 1950. Jim Crow was alive and well, and one of Farrakhan's responses to this racism was the writing and performance of "Why America is No Democracy" in 1950. He performed better musically and athletically than he did academically at Winston–Salem, and found a new love interest during his first mid–year vacation away from college. Betsy Ross, a Roman Catholic, was from Roxbury. He married her on September 12, 1953, after ending his college education—she was pregnant at the time. He continued his entertainment career as ''Calypso Gene,'' a potential rival to Harry Belafonte. It was during a 1955 eight–week Midwest tour of Gene Walcott's ''Calypso Follies'' that he encountered a man and a movement that changed his life.

Embraces Nation of Islam

Farrakhan had first heard about Elijah Muhammad and the Nation of Islam when he attended one of Malcolm X's early Roxbury meetings. This time—in 1956—Farrakhan encountered Elijah Muhammad when he and his wife attended a Nation of Islam annual convention gathering at Temple No. 2 on the South side of Chicago, Illinois. He was moved by Minister Muhammad's message, but highly conscious of Muhammad's poor grammar; the leader had no formal education beyond the third grade. According to an article in the May 1975 edition of *Sepia,* Elijah Muhammad had been informed of who Farrakhan was and where he was sitting. Speaking directly to him by name, Elijah Mohammad said, ''[B]rother, don't pay attention to how I speak. Pay attention to what I'm saying. I didn't get the chance to go to the white man's fine schools, because when I tried to go, the doors were closed. But if you take what I say and place it into the beautiful way of speaking you know, you can help me save our people.'' When new members were solicited, Farrakhan and his wife joined the Nation of Islam.

The religion Farrakhan embraced is a curious mixture of orthodox Islamic beliefs, Christianity, and invention. The ''Nation of Islam in the Wilderness of North America'' has its roots in the Moorish American Science Temple Movement of Noble Drew Ali, founded in 1913 in Newark, New Jersey, and some of the principles and philosophy of Marcus M. Garvey's Universal Negro Improvement Association and the African Communities Imperial League founded in 1914 in Jamaica. The leader of the Nation of Islam was Elijah Poole. Poole was known by many aliases, but primarily as the Messenger Elijah Muhammad. Muhammad had migrated to Detroit in 1923 in search of employment. There, in 1930, he met a man who was long identified as Allah incarnate, W. D. Fard. Fard used many names as well, among them Master Wali Farrad Muhammad, Wallace Ford, and Willie D. Ford. Fard vanished in 1934, but left Elijah Muhammad with a religious belief system claiming that the black race was created as the original chosen people by Allah, and constituted the Tribe of Shabazz. However, the Tribe of Shabazz was placed under the hegemony of corrupt ''white devils''—created by a mad black scientist named Yacub—for a period of 6,000 years. Elijah Muhammad was recognized as a prophet alongside Moses and Jesus, among others. These are some of the things Malcolm X and Farrakhan taught to all who would listen.

Dropping the name of Gene Walcott to become Louis X in 1955, Farrakhan was appointed a captain in the male police–like cadre known as the Fruit of Islam. Shortly thereafter he was promoted to minister and set out to develop and expand Temple No. 11, Malcolm X's former Temple in Boston. Minister Louis X sought converts and followers primarily among the lower socioeconomic class of African Americans. He emulated Malcolm X and Elijah Muhammad while making his own contributions to the growth, development, and popularization of the movement. One of his latter 1950s contributions was a popular song he recorded entitled, ''A White Man's Heaven is a Black Man's Hell.'' ''A White Man's Heaven'' is nearly ten and a half minutes long with a calypso beat, and was played on jukeboxes within and outside the Nation of Islam. His next recording was entitled, ''Look at My Chains.'' Minister Louis X went a step further when he wrote and performed in two plays. *The Trial* was about whites on trial and *Orgena, or A Negro Spelled Backwards,* was a satire about worldly ''Negro'' prostitutes, dope fiends, alcoholics, and other misguided non–members of the Nation. Both his and Malcolm X's stars were on the rise, until revelations about their leader surfaced in 1963.

Trouble in the Nation

News about adulterous behavior by Elijah Muhammad surfaced when two of his former young secretaries revealed he had impregnated them in 1955 and 1956 respectively. Four more former secretaries had come forward by 1960 to claim he had fathered their children as well. Minister Malcolm X confirmed the revelations after speaking with Wallace Muhammad, Elijah Muhammad's legitimate seventh child, and informing, in confidence, select Nation of Islam ministers. Louis X was one of those Malcolm X informed of the matter; Malcolm X was dismayed that Louis did not share his anguish and reprehension. Malcolm X immediately met with his leader, and much to his chagrin, the ''Messenger'' confirmed and ''biblically justified'' his misdeeds. Malcolm X, was further shaken when allegations surfaced that Louis X—his mentee—and his own Temple No. 7 Fruit of Islam captain Joseph, had sent a report to Elijah Muhammad accusing Malcolm X of spreading provocative rumors about the ''Messenger's'' liaisons. Things went from bad to worse for Malcolm X and he was ultimately removed as the Nation of Islam's national representative and minister of Temple No. 7 in Harlem. Malcolm X refused to hold his tongue and publicly rebuked Elijah Muhammad for his indiscretions. Louis X subsequently played an active role in excoriating Malcolm X after he left the Nation of Islam's Pilgrimage, made the pilgrimage (Hajj) to Mecca, changed his name to El Hajj Malik Shabazz, and formed his own non–racialist organizations.

Minister Louis X's verbal attacks on Malcolm X helped create, as he publicly admitted in 1985, the volatile conditions that led up to the February 21, 1965, assassination of El Hajj Malik Shabazz (Malcolm X) by members of the Nation of Islam as his wife and children watched. Louis X was renamed Abdul Farrakhan by Elijah Muhammad in May 1965, and stepped into Malcolm X's former position as minister of Temple No. 7 in Harlem. In 1967 he became Muhammad's Nation of Islam national representative. Perhaps Minister Farrakhan believed he would become the leader of the Nation of Islam if he outlived Elijah Muhammad, but fate was not that kind.

Revives Nation of Islam

The Nation of Islam's membership and wealth rebounded between 1965 and 1975. When Elijah Muhammad died of congestive heart failure on Savior's Day, February 26, 1975, he left behind a fortune exceeding $46 million, 76 temples throughout the United States, and a membership of between 60 and 100,000. Farrakhan's hopes to succeed Muhammad were dashed the evening of the Savior's Day celebration in honor of W. D. Fard when it was announced that Wallace D. Muhammad, who had previously left the nation and denounced his father, had been divinely chosen to be Elijah Muhammad's successor. In June 1975, Wallace moved Farrakhan from Temple No. 7 in Harlem to Nation of Islam headquarters in Chicago, and named him his special ambassador. Farrakhan's head continued to spin when Wallace Muhammad, a student of Islamic orthodoxy, precipitately demystified and dismantled the beliefs, doctrines, and eschatology of the Nation of Islam Muhammad. Wallace Muhammad claimed his father had manufactured the Black Muslim religion to recruit African Americans, but had ordered it to move out of its ''baby phase'' of existence and into the ''mature phase'' and into orthodox Islam. Wallace Muhammad also revealed, to everyone's shock, that W. D. Fard was still alive and serving as the minister of the Oakland, California, mosque (he died at the age of 87 in June 1992).

Wallace Muhammad began referring to his followers and those of Negroid ancestry as ''Bilalians,'' in recognition of Bilal, a black slave reputed to be the second convert of the prophet Mohammed and the first Muezzin. Farrakhan was shaken again when Wallace named New York's Mosque No. 7 for Malcolm X and ceased to consider whites as devils. Whites were recognized as being as respectable as Bilalians, as long as they did not display a devil mentality, and were even allowed to become members of the ''vanishing'' Nation of Islam. The Nation of Islam was formally dismantled by Wallace Muhammad on October 18, 1976, and renamed the World Community of Al–Islam in the West. Wallace's ''new orthodoxy'' spurred Farrakhan to break with him in September 1977 and to revive Elijah Muhammad's Nation of Islam.

Resurrected Nation and Troublesome Times

Minister Farrakhan resurrected the Nation of Islam in Chicago in a funeral home he purchased on 79th Street. It was there that he established and began publishing the *Final Call* in 1979, a newspaper with the same name as one previously published by Elijah Muhammad in 1934. He reestablished the entire belief system of Elijah Muhammad's Nation of Islam and elevated Elijah Muhammad, his ''risen Savior,'' to Messiah status. Interestingly, he upgraded the status, recognition, and involvement of women in the Nation of Islam. Moreover, Farrakhan cleverly placed the ''blood'' of Elijah Muhammad upon center stage in the form of the 13 children Muhammad fathered by his six former secretaries, and they, along with their mothers, became members of the ''New Nation.'' Finally, in 1986 Farrakhan purchased Elijah Muhammad's mansion in Chicago's Hyde Park for a $500,000 and in 1988 also purchased the majestic former Temple No. 2 in Chicago. These actions helped rebuild the membership of his Nation of Islam. There are more than 20,000 current members and many more sympathizers. He and his ministers have also diligently fished for converts during the late 1970s and early 1980s and capitalized upon the publicity—some positive and much negative—that has kept the Nation of Islam in the public eye.

The Nation of Islam's ''positive press'' was a result of having cleaned up many dope–ridden street corners, housing units, and neighborhoods. However, the negative press outweighed the positive and embroiled the Nation and Farrakhan in one of the ugliest public battles it ever fought with Jews and Judaism. Problems developed shortly after Jesse Jackson declared in November 1983 that he was a candidate for the Democratic Party's presidential nomination. In December Farrakhan and Jackson traveled together to Syria to negotiate the release of African American Robert O. Goodman, a U.S. Navy lieutenant airman whose plane had been shot down while on a bombing mission over Lebanon. Farrakhan publicly involved himself and the Nation of Islam in electoral politics for the first time in its history when Jackson had declared his candidacy, and later led a group of his followers to Chicago's City Hall where they all registered to vote.

Jewish leaders were quick to question the campaign relationship of Jackson and Farrakhan, and took advantage of a statement by African American journalist Milton Coleman, who reported in the *Washington Post* in 1984 that he had heard Jesse Jackson privately refer to Jews as ''Hymies'' and called New York City ''Hymietown'' or ''Hymieville.'' Jackson attempted to repudiate the allegation and publicly apologized. The situation worsened when Farrakhan vehemently attacked Milton Coleman for his statement, and the media twisted his diatribe into an outright threat against Coleman and his wife. Jackson's campaign was sorely hurt, and he quietly maneuvered away from Farrakhan. The *New York Times* reported in 1984 that Farrakhan had referred to Adolph Hitler as a ''wickedly great man'' at a rally in Chicago. Farrakhan was not adulating Hitler, but repudiating him, while admitting Hitler had achieved recognition as a wicked man. Another storm erupted in June 1984 when the *Chicago Sun–Times* reported, inaccurately and out of context, that Farrakhan had called Judaism a ''gutter religion.'' The furor was great enough to motivate a misinformed United States Senate to vote 95–0 to censure Farrakhan.

Many African Americans believed Farrakhan was being unfairly treated and continued to rally when he gave speeches. Jewish efforts to get African American leaders and politicians to condemn Farrakhan were largely unsuccessful. Nevertheless Farrakhan could not shake his problems when future Nation of Islam spokesman Khallid Abdul Muhammad uttered many inflammatory statements between 1990 and 1994.

Farrakhan refused to be silenced and sought greater exposure outside the United States beginning in the late 1980s. He visited Europe, the Mid–East, and Africa. His attention turned to economics when he secured a 5,000,000–

dollar interest–free loan from Libya's Muammar Quaddafi to fund the manufacturing of "clean and fresh" personal care products under his People Organized to Work for Economic Rebirth (POWER) organization. Farrakhan had an opportunity to secure more funds during his controversial "World Friendship Tour" in January and February 1996 but the U.S. government said he must register as a foreign agent if he accepted foreign monies.

Prior to his World Friendship Tour Farrakhan successfully dealt with an alleged assassination plot by Malcolm X's daughter Quibilah Shabazz in 1995. He made history once again with the October 16, 1995, Million Man March in Washington, D.C., attended by at least 1,000,000 African American men. Farrakhan's two and a half hour speech was not one of his best, but he and the many speakers who preceded him inspired those gathered there as they called for respect, dignity, and atonement.

Farrakhan speaks widely and can be heard on radio and seen on television. He represents himself as a voice, conscience, and world "Reconciliator." The 64–year–old minister remains married to his wife Khadijah (Betsy) after 44 years, nine children, and nearly 30 grandchildren. He and his family still reside in the mansion in Chicago's multiracial Hyde Park.

Current address: Nation of Islam, 734 W. 79th Street, Chicago, IL 60620.

REFERENCES

"Bilalians." *Bilalian News.* November 15, 1975.
"Black Muslims?" *Muhammad Speaks,* March 21, 1975.
Eure, Joseph D., and Richard M. Jerome, eds. *Back Where We Belong: Selected Speeches by Minister Louis Farrakhan.* Chicago: PC International Press, 1989.
"Farrakhan Calls Judaism a Gutter Religion." *Chicago Sun Times,* June 24, 1984.
Farrakhan, Louis. "The Price of Faith." *Essence* 27 (November 1996): 95–96.
Hobbs, Sterling X. "Miracle Man of the Muslims." *Sepia* 24 (May 1975): 26–29.
"A Holy Day." *The Final Call,* October 16, 1995.
"Jackson Criticizes Remarks Made by Farrakhan as 'Reprehensible.'" *New York Times,* June 29, 1984.
Magida, Arthur J. *Prophet of Rage: A Life of Louis Farrakhan and His Nation.* New York: Basic Books, 1996.
Mamiya, Lawrence H. "From Black Muslim to Bilalian: The Evolution of a Movement." *Journal for the Scientific Study of Religion* 21 (June 1982): 138–51.
———. "Louis Farrakhan and the Final Call: Schism in the Muslim Movement." In *The Muslim Community in North America.* Waugh, Earle H., Baha Abu–Laban and Qureshi, Regula B., eds. Alberta, Canada: University of Alberta Press, 1983.
Wiggins, W. Braxter. *X Cards.* New York: Unbeatables, 1992.

W. Braxter Wiggins

Father Divine.
See Divine, M. J. "Father."

Walter E. Fauntroy

(1933–)

Minister, civil rights leader, congressman

During his work in the Civil Rights Movement and in the U.S. Congress, Walter E. Fauntroy employed the principles of nonviolent civil disobedience to fight racial discrimination and poverty in the United States and human rights abuses in South Africa.

Fauntroy was born February 6, 1933, in the Shaw neighborhood of the District of Columbia, during the midst of the Great Depression. His mother, Ethel Vine Fauntroy, worked as a housewife, rearing young Walter and his seven other siblings. His father, William Thomas Fauntroy, supported his family as a clerk at the U.S. Patent Office. Ethel and William Fauntroy were natives of the District of Columbia.

Growing up in his parent's Westminster Street row house, Fauntroy participated in sports at the Police Boys Club at 12th and U streets and roamed the tumultuous streets beyond. But the poverty and "For Whites Only" signs he encountered soon made him aware that he was surrounded by an oppressive social evil. When a Patterson Junior High School teacher asked him to write an essay about what he wanted to become, he wrote about the ministry, explaining that a religious career would enable him to improve conditions in his community.

Fauntroy started spending time at New Bethel Baptist Church, located down the street from his house. Charles David Foster, New Bethel's pastor, encouraged the youngster and eventually allowed him to preach in the church. Fauntroy made a great impression on the congregation. When he graduated from Dunbar High School in 1950, church members sold chicken, fish, and chitterling dinners to help pay his tuition at Virginia Union University.

One evening at Virginia Union, a fellow student, Wyatt T. Walker, asked Fauntroy to provide overnight lodging for a friend who was on his way to Massachusetts to begin his doctoral studies. Fauntroy honored the request, but did not allow Martin Luther King Jr. to rest. Instead, the two young men stayed up until four o'clock in the morning talking about the philosophy of Mahatma Ghandi. They also discussed racism in the United States and resolved to do something about it.

After graduating from Virginia Union in 1955 with a degree in history, Fauntroy entered Yale University on a

Walter E. Fauntroy

scholarship. In 1958 the school awarded him a Bachelor of Divinity. When he returned to the District of Columbia with his new wife, Dorothy Sims, he wondered where he would go to minister. That issue was decided two weeks after his return, when Reverend Foster died. New Bethel's congregation installed Fauntroy as their new pastor.

Becomes Civil Rights Leader

Fauntroy had barely settled into his pastorate when he started experimenting with the concept of nonviolent civil disobedience. He organized students and began picketing Woolworth stores and businesses that refused black patronage. He also led the city's Interdenominational Ministers Alliance in protesting the removal of blacks from valuable downtown land. For Fauntroy, these experiences made clear the usefulness of nonviolent civil disobedience as a strategy for changing established policies. In an interview on November 8, 1996 for this essay, Fauntroy recalled, ''We found that by [nonviolently] attracting the public's attention to a problem and, then, heightening their consciousness of the injustice in it, we could move them to pressure their power holders into solving the problem justly.''

King, who had by this time acquired a national reputation as the leader of the fight for racial equality, took note of Fauntroy's tactics. In 1960 he asked Fauntroy to join his staff as director of the Southern Christian Leadership Conference's Washington bureau. Fauntroy helped the SCLC to develop its strategy and acted as the organization's lobbyist in Congress. In addition, at King's direction, Fauntroy met with national leaders such as President John F. Kennedy, Attorney General Robert F. Kennedy and FBI Director J. Edgar Hoover.

Fauntroy's involvement in the SCLC's strategic deliberations and high–level consultations became more frequent. This was especially true during the Freedom Rides in 1961, the Albany Movement in 1962, and the Birmingham demonstrations. King was so impressed with Fauntroy's talent for analyzing problems and developing strategy for these campaigns that he asked him to coordinate the SCLC's involvement in the 1963 March on Washington.

More than logistical problems were faced in preparing for the Washington demonstration. For instance, on the day before the march, the SCLC's top aides were told that King would have only eight minutes to address the marchers. This decision upset Fauntroy and his associates, Wyatt T. Walker, Ralph Abernathy, and Andrew Young, but they labored through the night with King in his hotel suite, advising him on how to cut down the length of his ''I Have a Dream'' speech.

The dream of which King spoke on the day of the march seemed to fade later that year when President Kennedy was assassinated. Nevertheless, Fauntroy went with King to the White House to urge the new president, Lyndon B. Johnson, to push for passage of civil rights legislation. Fauntroy then immersed himself in lobbying Congress to pass the measures.

Eventually the Civil Rights Act of 1964, which gave blacks equal access to public places, became law. It, however, lacked provisions for enforcing the right of blacks to register and vote in the South, so King began planning demonstrations for Selma, Alabama. He wanted to orchestrate a series of confrontations that would show the public that the South's racist power structure would not allow blacks to register and vote. He hoped that the public would respond by pressuring President Johnson into sending voting rights legislation to Congress. King picked Fauntroy, one of his best strategists, to coordinate the campaign.

As the crisis in Selma escalated, King dispatched Fauntroy to the District of Columbia to lead religious leaders to the White House. Sitting in the Oval Office, Fauntroy pressed the President to take action. Responding to Fauntroy's appeal and the public's outrage over the unprovoked violence that greeted Selma's peaceful black protesters, President Johnson, rushed legislation for the Voting Rights Act of 1965 to Congress. He signed it into law a few weeks later.

Following this success, Fauntroy followed the lead of the SCLC's national campaign by devoting more attention to District slums. To ensure that the Shaw neighborhood would be consulted on redevelopment in the area, he created the Model Inner City Community Organization in 1966. This, and his work on the District's varied social problems, led President Johnson to appoint Fauntroy vice–chairman of the District's first city council.

Meanwhile, King, under attack for his losing battle to eliminate Chicago's slums, summoned his aides to SCLC's headquarters in Atlanta. He directed them to begin planning for another Washington March, the object of which was to get the public to pressure Congress into doing something about the nation's urban poor. A few weeks later, while they worked on strategy at Ebenezer Baptist Church, King made a surprising announcement. He told his aides that he was postponing the Washington campaign and going first to Memphis to help protesting sanitation workers. Most of King's aides argued against the decision. But it was strongly defended by Fauntroy who, according to Stephen B. Oates in *Let the Trumpet Sound: The Life of Martin Luther King, Jr.*, Fauntroy told his associates, "We've got to go all the way with Martin."

After King's assassination in Memphis, his successor, Ralph Abernathy, decided to go ahead with plans for the Poor People's campaign. Fauntroy coordinated the demonstration, but his strategy was unsuccessful in arousing public support for the poor. After the 50,000 black, Chicano, Puerto Rican, and Native American demonstrators left the capital, Fauntroy turned his attention to the District's ghettos.

It was not long before a militant faction of a city–wide coalition, the Black United Front (BUF), called for a black vigilante force to protect blacks from the District's white police, and Fauntroy came under attack. He had helped Stokely Carmichael establish the BUF. Now, influential members of Congress denounced the BUF and demanded that Fauntroy either resign from it or the city council. Fauntroy held on to his membership in both groups, claiming that his association with the Front would help to keep it nonviolent.

In 1969, however, as frustration rose over the lack of "black power" in the District, a riot erupted. Making the most of the disturbance, Fauntroy used it to lure President Nixon to the area's rubble–strewn streets. With his personable manner, he persuaded the president to pledge millions of dollars in federal grants for housing and social programs in the District. He also got the President's support for District congressional representation.

Becomes a Politician

In 1970 President Nixon signed into law a provision for an elected nonvoting delegate to the Congress from the District. Fauntroy announced that he would be a Democratic candidate for the office. Although considered an underdog in the Democratic primary, he stunned political observers by defeating Channing Phillips in the primary and the white Republican candidate in the general election.

In 1971 Fauntroy became the first person to represent the District in the U.S. Congress in one hundred years. Civil War general Norton P. Chapman was the first, elected in 1871. He served until 1873, when the seat was abolished during an anti–home rule reaction. After his election, Fauntroy immediately launched a campaign to obtain home rule for the District—an elected municipal government chosen by the people for the District. With Senator Edward W. Brooke, Fauntroy established a national coalition to educate and mobilize blacks to pressure their U.S. representatives to vote in favor of home rule legislation. In addition, he built support by taking on leadership roles at the National Black Political Convention and in the 1972 presidential campaign of Senator George S. McGovern.

Despite these efforts, John L. McMillan, chairperson of the House District Committee, refused to send legislation for home rule to the House floor for a vote. Fauntroy responded by taking District activists to McMillan's congressional district during the next election. There, he organized McMillan's black constituents and caused the chairman's defeat at the polls. During the next term, Fauntroy skillfully guided home rule legislation through Congress, giving the District's majority black population locally elected government in 1975.

The U.S. Constitution had to be amended in 1964 to give District residents the right to vote for Presidential and Vice–Presidential electors. The District would now have to go through the same process—get the approval of Congress and 36 state legislatures—to obtain the right to be represented in the Congress by two voting representatives and senators. While working on the 1976 presidential campaign of former Georgia governor Jimmy Carter, Fauntroy urged black voters to use their influence to get the amendment proposal through Congress. In 1978 he succeeded, and Congress sent the District of Columbia Voting Rights Amendment to the States for ratification.

Fauntroy crisscrossed the country promoting the amendment. In his professorial and energetic manner, he informed audiences that although the District had more residents than any congressional district and a larger population than several states, it still did not have a floor vote in Congress. Initially the public favored the amendment. Public opinion changed when Fauntroy became ensnared in a controversy surrounding the U.S. Ambassador to the United Nations, Andrew Young.

Violating official U.S. government policy, Young had secretly met at the United Nations with Aehdi Labib Terzi, an observer for the Palestine Liberation Organization. The PLO had refused to recognize Israel's right to exist. News of the meeting angered Jewish leaders and embarrassed the Carter Administration. Young was forced to resign. Fauntroy, however, staunchly defended him, and then defiantly led an SCLC delegation to the Middle East and met with the PLO leader, Yasser Arafat.

An avalanche of criticism from Jewish and black leaders greeted Fauntroy when he returned to the United States. In the October 16, 1979 *Washington Post,* Vernon Jordan, then president of the Urban League, criticized "ill–considered flirtations with terrorist groups devoted to the extermination of Israel" if they endangered black–Jewish relations. Others, such as Bayard Rustin were more direct, claiming that the delegate had created tension between blacks and Jews, groups that had been allies in the civil rights movement. Fauntroy responded in the same article, saying, "Obviously, we have some disagreement with Mr. Jordan and Mr. Rustin if their position is that our appeal for peace through nonviolence should not be communicated directly to PLO leaders by ourselves, leaders of conscience around the world or by the United States government." Fauntroy's position regarding the PLO, which would later be embraced by the U.S. government, and his later support for Senator Edward M. Kennedy's losing campaign against President Carter during the 1980 Democratic presidential primaries, did not prevent his reelection.

As President–elect Reagan prepared to move into the White House, the eighteen blacks who had been elected to serve with Fauntroy in the 97th Congress turned to the District delegate for leadership. They elected him chairperson of the Congressional Black Caucus. As its chairperson, Fauntroy attempted to fight Reagan's agenda but was unable to get his white Democratic colleagues to go along. In 1983, he organized the 20th Anniversary March on Washington. The object of the march was to demonstrate the extent of economic and social need in the United States and to build public support for the Black Caucus's jobs and social programs legislation. An estimated 500,000 demonstrators from across the country poured into the Nation's capital. Soon after the march, President Reagan signed the Black Caucus's Martin Luther King, Jr. federal holiday legislation. The President and the Congress were slow to take action on other Black Caucus proposals, however.

Fed up with Republican and Democratic leaders, Fauntroy started talking with black leaders around the country about fielding a black Democratic presidential candidate. He told black leaders that such a candidacy would provide a forum for issues of concern to blacks and help to build support for policies that were beneficial to blacks, women, and the poor. In 1984 he urged Jesse Jackson to run. When his old SCLC associate agreed, Fauntroy joined his campaign as a strategist. But former vice–president Walter Mondale won the party's nomination and then, rejecting Fauntroy's offer to help with his campaign, lost to Reagan in the general election.

Becomes Human Rights Activist

With the reelection of President Reagan, Fauntroy began to turn his attention from domestic issues to foreign affairs. As chairperson of the House Banking Committee's Subcommittee on International Development, Finance, Trade, and Monetary Policy, he led Congress in examining the Third World debt problem. He also urged his colleagues to do something about racial discrimination and human rights abuses in South Africa. But Congress and the President, as well as the media and the public, paid little attention to these injustices. Undeterred, Fauntroy decided to use nonviolent civil disobedience, in an ingenious way, to draw public attention to these problems.

Using his influence as a member of Congress, Fauntroy arranged a meeting at the South African embassy with ambassador Bernardus G. Fourie. The meeting was scheduled for the day before Thanksgiving. Mary Frances Berry, Randall Robinson, and Eleanor Holmes Norton—veteran civil rights activists—were approved to accompany Fauntroy. After talking briefly with the ambassador about apartheid and the unfair imprisonment of blacks in his country, Fauntroy demanded the immediate release of nine South African labor leaders. Fourie became irritated and asked the party to leave. Fauntroy boldly refused to leave until his demands were met. Shocked, the ambassador summoned the police to arrest the trespassers.

National media coverage of the U.S. Representative being removed from the embassy in handcuffs and later demonstrations at the embassy fueled increased media coverage of South Africa and moved the public to pay more attention to the injustices of apartheid. With these developments, the public's empathy for black South Africans increased. An aroused electorate put pressure on the Congress and the President to change U.S. foreign policy. Congress responded by imposing economic sanctions against South Africa. The new U.S. stance forced the South African government to release Nelson Mandela and to dismantle apartheid.

When Fauntroy turned his attention to human rights abuses in Zaire and Haiti, District residents began to openly debate whether he was still interested in the local issues that had initially taken him to Congress. Responding to constituent concerns, Fauntroy dusted off the District of Columbia Voting Rights Amendment idea. In 1987 he started lobbying Congress to give the District statehood. Three years later, as momentum for statehood was building, he stunned District residents by announcing that he was giving up his safe Congressional seat to run for District mayor. Many District voters felt he could do more in Congress for the statehood effort by remaining there. Their backlash elected Sharon Pratt Kelly mayor. Eleanor Holmes Norton succeeded Fauntroy as the District's delegate.

Fauntroy returned to Shaw, the neighborhood where he had started his social ministry. In addition to spending time with his wife and children, Marvin and Melissa Alice, he actively promotes economic development in Shaw and private investment in South Africa. On Sundays, however, he puts on his pastoral robes and preaches at New Bethel Baptist Church. According to the *Washington Post,* January 25, 1992, Fauntroy told his congregation, "Religion is not something you preach from a pulpit and then lock up in a church with no relevance from Monday to Saturday." He reminds them of Jesus's ministry and urges them to continue it long after they leave the church.

Walter Fauntroy used the principles of nonviolent civil disobedience and his abilities as a master strategist to improve the conditions of life for black people. His activities helped to end racial discrimination and to bring about social and economic justice in the world. These accomplishments have been profound and lasting, and they clearly distinguish him as one of the African diaspora's most noteworthy African American men.

Current address: New Bethel Baptist Church, 1739 9th Street, NW, Washington, DC 20001.

REFERENCES

"Congressional Black Caucus Picks Fauntroy as Chairman." *Washington Post,* December 13, 1980.

"Congressman Urges Alaska To Support Special Amendment." *Anchorage Daily News,* March 11, 1984.

"D.C. Tenor's 'Dream' Wins Voters Hearts in Milwaukee." *Washington Post,* April 1, 1980.
"Del. Fauntroy Quits His Post With MICCO." *Washington Post,* January 28, 1972.
Fauntroy, Walter E. Interview with Cortez Rainey, New Bethel Baptist Church, Washington, DC, November 8, 1996.
"Fauntroy Alone in Statehood Optimism." *Washington Times,* 1989.
"Fauntroy Arrested in Embassy." *Washington Post,* November 22, 1984.
"Fauntroy Backs Resident Status For Haitians." *Washington Afro–American,* February 18, 1984.
"Fauntroy Busy Enjoying Life Away From Politics." *Washington Post,* August 31, 1992.
"Fauntroy Claims He Sees No Legal Conflict." *Washington Daily News,* February, 27, 1968.
"Fauntroy Condemns Budget." *Washington Afro–American,* January 13, 1987.
"Fauntroy Defends His PLO Moves." *Washington Post,* October 16, 1979.
"Fauntroy Doubles Roles on Sunday." *Washington Post,* July 21, 1975.
"Fauntroy Drops Bid for Post." *Washington Post,* June 17, 1971.
"Fauntroy Heads Bi–Partisan Delegation Studying Haiti." *Washington Afro–American,* April 5, 1986.
"Fauntroy Ouster Pushed." *Washington Daily News,* July 30, 1968.
"Fauntroy Says He'll Give Up Non–voting Seat in Congress to Run for D.C. Mayor." *Baltimore Sun,* March 4, 1990.
"Fauntroy Sees Caucus Budget Only Cure for Nation's Ills." *Washington Afro–American,* July 28, 1981.
"Fauntroy to Head New Task Force on Zaire." *Washington Afro–American,* May 17, 1985.
"Fauntroy Urges Black Presidential Candidacy." *Washington Times,* March 21, 1983.
"500,000 March on Washington." *Congressional Newsletter,* Fall 1983.
"A Grateful City Salutes One of Its Favorite Sons." *Washington Afro–American,* April 4, 1981.
Hawkins, Walter L. *African–American Biographies.* Jefferson, NC: McFarland, 1992.
Oates, Stephen B. *Let the Trumpet Sound: The Life of Martin Luther King, Jr.* New York: New American Library, 1982.
"Politics Yields to Religion." *Washington Post,* January 25, 1992.
"Underdog Reprising a Familiar Role." *Washington Post,* August 28, 1990.
Walter, Ronald. *Black Presidential Politics in America.* Albany: State University of New York Press, 1988.

COLLECTIONS

Walter Fauntroy's personal and Congressional papers are housed in the Gelman Library at George Washington University.

Cortez Rainey

Rudolph Fisher
(1897–1934)
Writer, physician, community leader

Rudolph Fisher was one of the leading writers during the Harlem Renaissance. He was a local colorist whose novels and short stories realistically depict Harlem speech, environments, and the diversity of Harlem's people in socioeconomic background, skin color, interests, and values systems. Fisher was innovative in his humor—spiced satire directed at this black society. He was also the first black American writer of detective fiction.

Rudolph Fisher was born on May 9, 1897, in Washington, D.C. He was one of the three children of John Wesley Fisher, a clergyman, and Glendora Williamson Fisher. In 1924 he married Jane Ryder, a Washington, D.C., teacher, and the couple had one son, Hugh.

Fisher grew up in a middle–class family and received a rigorous, liberal education at primary and secondary schools in Providence, Rhode Island, and New York City. He graduated with honors from Classical High School in Providence and then attended Brown University. At Brown, where he was a biology major, he won a number of recognitions for public speaking as well as academic achievement. He was a member of three honor societies, including Phi Beta Kappa. He was the Class Day orator and also the Commencement Day speaker, elected by the faculty. Fisher earned a B.A. from Brown in 1919 and an M.A. a year later.

In 1920 Fisher entered the Howard University Medical School. While at Howard he served as an instructor of embryology. At this time he honed his skills as an amateur musician by accompanying Paul Robeson on his concert tours and arranging some of his music. In 1924 he graduated from Howard summa cum laude and married Jane Ryder. Then he served a one–year internship at Washington's Freedmen's Hospital. During his internship Fisher published his first short story "The City of Refuge" in the *Atlantic Monthly.* This ironically titled story depicts the adventures of a black Southerner, King Solomon Gillis, who flees to Harlem after killing a white man. Instead of a "refuge" from Southern injustice, Harlem is a scene of corruption for Gillis, who is duped into a drug–selling scheme by a fellow black Southerner. This story was included in the collection *Best Short Stories of 1925.*

In 1925 Fisher continued his medical education at Columbia University's College of Physicians and Surgeons. For two years he trained in bacteriology, pathology, and roentgenology. During this period he carried on a correspondence with Carl Van Vechten, well–known white patron of black literature. In this correspondence he expressed the conflict he felt in engaging in two such disparate professions as medicine and creative writing. Van Vechten used Fisher to critique the manuscript of *Nigger Heaven* (1926), his own controversial novel of Harlem life.

Rudolph Fisher

The next year, 1927, was a particularly busy and fruitful one for Fisher. In this year he went into private practice, published five short stories in the *Atlantic Monthly* and *McClure's,* an article in the *Journal of Infectious Diseases,* and an essay in *American Mercury.* By publishing frequently in nonblack publications, Fisher was able to reach a wider audience than many other black writers during the period.

Fisher's stories "The Promise Land" and "The Backslider" use realistic details such as the storefront church and the rent party to depict Harlem life. "The Promise Land" uses the black Southern immigrant, a recurring figure in Fisher's fiction, and "Blades of Steel," the violence–prone Harlem gambler. In his essay "The Caucasian Storms Harlem," Fisher conveys the *joie de vivre* of the Harlem of the 1920s and the diverse backgrounds and interests of its inhabitants, but he deplores the exploitation of Harlem by whites drawn to the exoticism of its nightlife.

Publishes Critically Well–Received First Novel

The first of Fisher's two novels *The Walls of Jericho* was published in 1928. Van Vechten was instrumental in getting his own publisher Alfred A. Knopf to issue the work. The motivation for the writing of the novel was not only his success in shorter fiction but a bet from a friend, who, according to Eleanor Q. Tignor in *Afro–American Writers from the Harlem Renaissance to 1940,* "had challenged him to try his hand at blending all of Harlem society into a single story." Consequently the novel contains a cross–section of contemporary Harlem society: the "rats," the black lower–class, the upper–class, well–educated "dickties," represented by the mulatto lawyer Fred Merrit, and the black working class, the bridge between the upper and lower classes, represented by several characters in the novel. *The Walls of Jericho* contains even the white liberal character, Agatha Cramp, whose liberalism fades when Merrit buys a house in her neighborhood. This house is burned to the ground by Patmore, a man whom Merrit had prosecuted, but a group of the working–class blacks are instrumental in bringing about the punishment of Patmore and thus a degree of black intra–class cooperation and harmony.

The novel uses typical Harlem locales such as the pool hall and the recurring rite of the community–wide dance in its satirical depiction of black urban life of the 1920s. The pool hall is the watering hole of working–class blacks, and the Annual Costume Ball of the General Improvement Association is patronized by all elements of black society and even liberal, uplifting whites such as Miss Cramp. *Black Literature Criticism* comments: "In this dramatic comedy of manners, Fisher satirized the angry new Negro, professional uplifters, thrill seekers from downtown, and organizations like the NAACP."

The Walls of Jericho was praised by many black critics and writers such as Eric Walrond, Sterling Brown, Alice Dunbar Nelson, and Hugh M. Gloster. In *The Negro in American Fiction* Brown praises the "jaunty realism" and breadth of Fisher's portrayal of Harlem character types from poolroom patrons to race leaders. Gloster says in *Negro Voices in American Fiction,* "This novel reveals the first Negro author skilled in comic realism and able to use irony and satire not only upon whites but also upon various classes of his own people. . . . Much of Fisher's success in depicting the Negro in New York City is traceable to his mastery of Harlem speech."

W. E. B. Du Bois acknowledges that Fisher captures the speech of Negro laborers, but in his review of *The Walls of Jericho* he continues to describe the characters Jinx Jenkins and Bubber Brown, two piano movers, as a "little smutty and certainly not humanly convincing." Du Bois deplores the novel's lackluster better–class Negro characters and Fisher's timidity in depicting his own kind, "Negroes like his mother, his sister, and his wife."

After the publication of *The Walls of Jericho,* Fisher became superintendent of the International Hospital in Manhattan, holding this position from 1929 to 1932. From 1930 to 1934 he worked as a roentgenologist for the New York City Health Department, and he served as a first lieutenant in the medical division of the 369th Infantry. His community involvement is seen in his service on the literature committee of the Harlem YMCA and his lectures at the 135th Street Branch of the New York Public Library.

Produces the First Detective Novel by a Black Author

Fisher's *The Conjure–Man Dies: A Mystery Tale of Dark Harlem* published in 1932, is the first full–length black detective novel, having an all–black cast of characters. The conjure–man is N'Gana Frimbo, a Harvard–educated African prince. Jinx Jenkins and Bubber Brown are brought over from *The Walls of Jericho.* Jinx is framed for the murder of the conjure–man, to whom he had gone for advice. And in a very complex plot in which N'Gana is allegedly murdered, his body disappears, and then he reemerges alive and well, Bubber uses his newly–found detective skills to exonerate his friend. Bubber receives help in his quest from Sergeant Perry Dart, the professional detective, and his associate, Dr. John Archer, a physician and amateur detective, the more insightful of the two. In a radio interview quoted by Margaret Perry in her introduction to *The Short Fiction of Rudolph Fisher,* Fisher says, "The Negro detective, for example, is suggested by an acquaintance of mine on the force.... There are perhaps a dozen in Harlem alone... one of whom is a lieutenant.... And the physician has an actual model." Dr. Archer is a persona for his creator, serving as the mouthpiece for Fisher's musings on science and philosophy. This work shows the influence of Dashiell Hammett and S. S. Van Dine, masters of detective fiction.

In 1932 and 1933 Fisher published two children's stories, "Ezekiel," and "Ezekiel Learns." These stories chronicle a 12–year–old Georgia boy's growth in self–knowledge and adjustment to a colorful Harlem with its Garvey parades and outbreaks of riots.

In 1933 Fisher published two short stories: "Guardians of the Law" and "Miss Cynthie." In "Guardians of the Law," Grammie uses trickery to protect the interests of her grandson Sam, a rookie policeman. The story shows the growing assimilation of the Southern immigrant in Harlem in Sam's position as an authority figure in the community. "Miss Cynthie" is the best known and most anthologized of Fisher's short fiction. Miss Cynthie is a sprightly, 70–year–old woman visiting Harlem for the first time at the invitation of her prosperous grandson David. She speculates he must be an undertaker, a respectable, middle–class profession for a black man in the highly segregated Southern society from which she comes. But Miss Cynthie soon discovers David and his wife Ruth are stage performers in a vaudeville–type show. At first the conservative and deeply religious Miss Cynthie is taken aback by their performance, but the story ends in her acceptance of and even pride in David and his wife's talents and means of livelihood. This story was included in *Best Short Stories of 1934.*

The critically well–received "Miss Cynthie" testifies to Fisher's developing abilities as a writer. It was his last published work before his death. In 1934 Fisher became ill and was taken from his home in Jamaica, Long Island, to the Edgecombe Sanatorium. After a third operation for an intestinal ailment, he died in New York City in December 1934. A magazine carrying his longest his story, "John Archer's Nose," was on the newsstands at the same time as newspapers carrying accounts of his death. This sequel to *The Conjure–Man Dies* features the two detectives Perry Dart and Dr. John Archer, whom Fisher had planned to feature in a series of detective novels. "John Archer's Nose" reflects the importance of Fisher's field of roentgenology. In it a father refuses x–ray treatment for his ill baby, instead relying on a charm of human hair fried in snake oil supplied by a conjure woman. The child, who wears the charm, dies a victim of the superstitious rejection of modern medical technology.

At the time of his death from cancer on December 16, 1934, in New York City, Fisher was working on a dramatization of *The Conjure–Man Dies.* In 1936 it was produced as a folk play at the Lafayette Theater by the black unit of the Federal Theater. Several critics described this three–act play as inferior to Fisher's other works. Fisher's death precluded the necessary cutting and rewriting of the play during its rehearsal period, but, despite its flaws, it was very popular, being seen by over 80,000 people during its six–month run.

Fisher is the author of two other unpublished and unproduced plays, *The Vici Kid* and *Golden Slippers.* Brown University houses the manuscripts of four undated short stories, "Across the Airshaft," "The Lost Love Blues," "The Man Who Passed," and "The Lindy Hop."

Margaret Perry quotes Fisher's sister Pearl M. Fisher, who mentions his literary ambitions, cut short by death: "Like most writers, Dr. Fisher's ambition was to write the great Negro novel. His plan was to write a trilogy based on African backgrounds, life in a new land, and the modern social order as reflected in the lives of several generations of a Negro family."

Arna Bontemps says in *The Harlem Renaissance Remembered,* "Rudolph Fisher, who had the lightest touch of all the Renaissance writers, managed an intermingling of kindly satire and bittersweet tensions in his fiction." His characters are not the "primitives" found in the works of other writers of the period such as Jean Toomer, Claude McKay, and Carl Van Vechten. Nor are they the paragons of black middle–class respectability found in the works of other contemporary writers such as Nella Larsen and Jessie Fauset. As Bontemps says, "During his brief life, he gave us pictures of the ordinary workaday black who was largely neglected by other Renaissance writers."

Although Fisher was a radiologist, he is known best for his work as a Harlem Renaissance writer. His satirical fiction illuminates such facets of the 1920s as the plight of the Southern black immigrant in Harlem, the tensions between West Indian and native–born blacks, and the black class structure from the "dicties" to the "rats." Because of his untimely death, Fisher did not reach his full potential as a writer.

REFERENCES

Black Literature Criticism. Vol 2. Detroit: Gale Research, 1992.

Bontemps, Arna. *The Harlem Renaissance Remembered.* New York: Dodd, Mead, 1972.

Brown, Sterling. *The Negro in American Fiction.* New York: Arno Press, 1969.

Du Bois, W. E. B. *The Walls of Jericho.* Review. *Crisis* 35 (November 1928): 374.

Gloster, Hugh. *Negro Voices in American Fiction.* Chapel Hill: University of North Carolina Press, 1948.

Harris, Trudier, and Thadious M. Davis, eds. *Afro–American Writers from the Harlem Renaissance to 1940.* Vol. 51 of *Dictionary of Literary Biography.* Detroit: Gale Research, 1987.

Perry, Margaret. ''The Life and Art of Rudolph Fisher.'' *The Short Fiction of Rudolph Fisher.* New York: Greenwood Press, 1987.

Phiefer L. Browne

Henry O. Flipper
(1856–1940)
Military officer, author, engineer

Henry O. Flipper was one of the original Buffalo Soldiers and the first African American to graduate from the United States Military Academy, or West Point.. Flipper's military career was cut short when he was falsely accused of mishandling company funds and of conduct unbecoming of an officer. Acquitted of the first charge, he failed to clear his name of the second. When he was discharged from the army after serving nine years, Flipper went on as a civilian to become an author, engineer, and a notable figure in American history.

Henry Ossian Flipper was born on March 21, 1856, in Thomasville, Georgia, to Festus and Isabella Flipper. Festus Flipper, a shoemaker, later bought the freedom of his wife and children, who were slaves. Henry was the oldest of five sons, all who became men of achievement: Joseph was a bishop in the African Methodist Episcopal Church; Carl became a college professor in Georgia; E. H. was a physician in Florida; and Festus Jr. was a wealthy and respected farmer and landowner in Georgia. Henry, however, was the only one among them who earned recognition in history.

Henry Flipper received his education from several schools founded by the American Missionary Association, including Atlanta University. In 1873, while at Atlanta University, he was selected to attend the United States Military Academy. Other black Americans had attended West Point previously, but dropped out because of the isolation and abuse they experienced. After living through four years of ostracism himself, Flipper became the first black to graduate from the academy in 1877. Fiftieth out of his class of 76, he received a commission as second lieutenant. Only two other black cadets graduated from West Point during the nineteenth–century, with nearly half a century passing before another African American would graduate from this academy.

In January of 1878 Flipper was assigned to the 10th Cavalry Regiment, one of the first all–black regular army regiments. He served first at Fort Still in Indian Territory

Henry O. Flipper

(Oklahoma) and then in Texas at Fort Elliott, Fort Concho, Fort Davis, and Fort Quitman. Flipper was given the duties of surveying and supervising construction projects. He also experienced combat against Apache Indians led by Chief Victoria. The 10th Cavalry Regiment was one of four regular army regiments making up what became known as the Buffalo Soldiers, black men serving in post–Civil War military regiments.

While he was at Fort Davis, Flipper became the focus of a controversial court–martial proceeding. In August of 1881, Flipper was arrested and tried on charges of failing to mail $3,700 in checks to the Army Chief Commissary. Although the checks were later found in his quarters, he was acquitted of this charge. He was convicted, however, of misconduct. President Chester Arthur confirmed his sentence, and Flipper was dismissed from service on June 30, 1882.

Returning to civilian life, Flipper remained in the West, working over the next half century as a surveyor, civil and mining engineer, consultant and a translator and interpreter of Spanish land grants. The *Dictionary of American Negro Biography* called Flipper a ''valuable asset to the various companies which employed him'' because of his ''fluent Spanish, his skill as an engineer, and his knowledge of the law.'' He worked with private land claims between 1892 and 1903, when he served as a special agent of the Department of Justice. In 1892 he published a book on Spanish laws, which helped bring about the return of sizeable amounts of land to their rightful owners and earned him the animosity of land grabbers. Flipper also wrote other technical reports dealing with Mexican and Venezuelan laws.

When the Spanish–American War started in 1898, Flipper volunteered to serve militarily. Congress failed in efforts to restore Flipper to his former rank. Bills were introduced to restore Flipper to his former rank and to give him command of one of the four newly–proposed black regiments. Both bills died in their committees, however, and no new black regiments were recruited.

Flipper continued working for mining companies in the West. It was during this time that he befriended Albert B. Fall, who later became a U.S. senator. Fall used Flipper's reports on the Mexican political situation in his work concerning the impact of the Mexican Revolution on American economic interests, and he later brought Flipper to Washington as a translator and interpreter for his committee. Fall became Secretary of the Interior, and Flipper was hired his assistant. However, when Fall was found guilty in the infamous Teapot Dome Affair, Flipper, who was not implicated, left the government and went to work for an oil company in Venezuela from 1923 to 1930.

Vindicated of False Accusations

Flipper tried several times to vindicate himself officially from the military charges that brought him disgrace. Insisted that he had not been guilty of any wrongdoing in 1882 and should never have been dismissed from the Army, he blamed his dismissal on racial prejudice, specifically on jealousy on the part of his white colleagues of his relationship with a white woman. Flipper fought until the 1920s to clear his name, but it was not until nearly a century after he left West Point that a careful review of military records revealed that he had been framed by his fellow officers. His records were corrected, and he was posthumously exonerated and granted an honorable discharge. A bust by Helene Hemmans, an African American sculptor, was unveiled at West Point on the one hundredth anniversary of Flipper's graduation.

Flipper was living in Atlanta with his brother Joseph, a bishop of the African Methodist Episcopal Church, when he died of a heart attack on May 3, 1940. In 1978 his remains were taken from an unmarked grave on a family plot in Atlanta and moved to his hometown. Flipper was reburied in Thomasville with full military honors.

Flipper's military career in particular led to his recognition as notable figure in African American history. His autobiography, *The Colored Cadet at West Point* (1968), offers insight into his life and his character.

REFERENCES

African America: Portrait of a People. Detroit: Visible Ink Press, 1994.

Carroll, John M. *The Black Military Experience in the American West.* New York: Liveright, 1971.

Logan, Rayford W., and Michael R. Winston, eds. *Dictionary of American Negro Biography.* New York: Norton, 1982.

Low, W. Augustus and Virgil A. Clift. *Encyclopedia of Black America.* New York: McGraw–Hill, 1984.

COLLECTIONS

Original manuscripts of Henry Ossian Flipper are available at Fort Huachuca Museum in Arizona. A portrait collection of Flipper is available at the New York Public Library.

Raamesie D. Umandavi

George Foreman

(1949–)

Boxer, minister

From an early life beset with the problems of finding fulfillment in Houston, Texas, George Foreman developed into an Olympics gold medal winner, heavyweight boxing champion of the world, founder of his own church, mentor of young people in his community, and actor. He is best known inside and outside the sports world as the fighter who regained the championship title at age 45, nearly 20 years after it had passed from him to Muhammad Ali. Despite the peccadillos of his youth and his mastery in the boxing ring, Foreman is a gentleman, blessed with a captivating personality that radiates an aura of naivete, good will, and honesty.

The fifth of the seven children of J. D. Foreman and Nancy Nelson Foreman, George Edward Foreman was born on January 10, 1949, in the farming area near Marshall, Texas. With her husband absent more often than he was present, Nancy Foreman moved her family to Houston when George was a small child and supported them with the wages she earned as a cafe cook. As he increased in years and in shortness of temper, young George learned to use his size and strength to gain recognition in the streets of Houston's Fifth Ward, where confrontations and fights were frequent. Uninterested in school, a bully among his age mates, and already a heavy smoker, he played hooky from classes and dropped out before the end of junior high and entered a life of petty crime.

Foreman might have graduated from small–time robberies, theft, and muggings into more serious infractions of the law had he not heard Jim Brown and Johnny Unitas—professional football players—speak about President Lyndon Johnson's War On Poverty and its Job Corps component. He entered the Job Corps Center first in Grant's Pass, Oregon, and later transferred to Parks Center, near Pleasanton, California. All meals were provided, as were daily reading, writing, and vocational classes offered along with a monthly allowance of 30 dollars. The center withheld an additional 50 dollars each month to be paid to each worker at the end of the two–year stint. Foreman brought home 1,200 dollars in cash, a newly discovered joy in the printed word, a GED certificate, and most precious of all, an introduction to the skill of boxing.

Charles ''Doc'' Broadus, supervisor of security at Parks Center, recognized Foreman's potential and led the neophyte

George Foreman

boxer to understand that his powerful fists could be used for more than disorganized fighting provoked by anger. Before he left Parks, Foreman won the corps's Diamond Belt tournament but lost in the Golden Gloves competition. Back at home, however, he reverted to his old habits of theft, street fighting, and use of tobacco and alcohol.

Enters the Sports World

Doc Broadus arranged employment for Foreman at Parks, where he would have time for training and conditioning and motivation to foreswear all contact with cigarettes and alcohol. Broadus and a cadre of trainers helped Foreman complete 18 amateur bouts and qualify for the 1968 Olympics in Mexico City, where he won the gold medal for heavyweight boxing.

Foreman's response when he received the gold medal in Mexico City—at the height of the Civil Rights Movement at home—initiated a mixture of consternation, approval, and conjecture about his choice to carry a small U.S. flag to the victory stand. This was in direct conflict with the actions of John Carlos and Tommie Smith, African American track winners who stood during the playing of the ''Star Spangled Banner'' with clenched fists raised in a display of anger about the racial tensions in the states; the two were ejected from the Olympic Village as a result. He thought of joining the sprinters with a protest of his own by refusing to complete the round of bouts still pending in his event. However, he received a message from John Carlos asking him not to abandon the competition and decided to continue until the gold was his. Foreman concentrated on beating his Soviet opponent. Acquaintances in Houston questioned Foreman's loyalty to the crusade for racial equality in the United States.

Unable to savor the Olympics victory at home, Foreman returned to Parks Center to teach boxing and continue his training. He filled his free hours with extensive reading and avoided female companionship, cigarettes, and alcohol. He rose quickly through the ranks of fighters. In his first match, on June 23, 1969, he defeated Don Waldhelm and went on to 11 knockouts out of 13 victories without a loss. By virtue of knockouts of all but one of the 12 men he faced in 1970, *The Ring,* a magazine for boxing aficionados, listed him second of all heavyweight contenders.

Twelve more victories in 1971 and 1972 earned Foreman a date to fight heavyweight champion Joe Frazier. On January 22, 1973, Foreman entered the ring in Kingston, Jamaica, a three–to–one underdog, scoring six knockdowns before the referee ended the battle in less than two full rounds. George Foreman won the heavyweight champion title and the coveted championship, the most prestigious treasure of professional boxing.

Foreman defended his title twice, easily beating Jose ''King'' Roman on September 1, 1973, and Ken Norton on March 26, 1974. The match with Muhammad Ali in Kinshasa, Zaire, on October 30, 1974, ended with Ali taking the championship. Many months passed before Foreman recovered from the emotional toll of the defeat. He thought that he had scored well during the first seven rounds, but he knew that the 60,000 onlookers were united behind Ali and were happy with the eighth round blow that sent him to the floor, unable to answer the bell.

Foreman's most spectacular bout took place on November 6, 1994, when at age 45, he stood toe to toe with 26–year old Michael Moorer and regained the title with a tenth round knockout, making him one of the few fighters to reclaim a relinquished championship. Five months later, in April, 1995, he successfully defended his crown against Axel Schulz of Germany by a split decision. His unwillingness to approve further challengers offered to him, however, forced Foreman to surrender the title.

Becomes a Religious Figure

When Foreman acknowledged the need to end the life style of his troubled youth so that he could cope better with the trials and disappointments of a fighting career, he developed into a religious man. From preaching on the streets, he founded the Church of the Lord Jesus Christ to minister to his congregation and to people in prisons and hospitals. In response to his desire to ease the struggle for children facing problems similar to those he faced as a child, Foreman purchased a building in Houston to house the George Foreman Youth and Community Center. He offered activities here with the hope that they would fill the idle hours of children and keep them from the temptations of engaging in criminal activity. He supported the center with his fees for speaking engagements and the receipts of a fight he undertook specifically to fund the project. In addition, Foreman donated $100,000 to Texas Southern University for scholarships in its Thurgood Marshall School of Law and the Department of Communications.

The situation–comedy television show *George* was a project conceived by ABC in 1993 for Foreman to star in a nearly complete biographical role of himself—a retired boxing champion with a strong commitment to motivate neglected children. He played the part with his natural charm, but in the competition for ratings, *George* lasted only eight episodes.

Foreman used his penchant for ingesting large quantities of foods in media commercials, but discontinued this when he realized the damage this did to his public image and his physical condition. He then adjusted to a more acceptable diet. He became more selective in his menu, often choosing pasta or a large salad in place of steaks, hot dogs, and hamburgers. An opportunity to understand George Foreman more clearly came with the publication of his autobiography, *By George,* in 1995, in which he wrote frankly of his personal life—marriages, divorces, successes, failures, and embarrassments. In the book he admitted to his difficulty in accepting former champion Muhammad Ali as a superior fighter.

George Foreman was married five times. A devoted father, he has nine children: Michi, Freeda George, Georgetta, Natalie, Leola, and four sons, all named after their father, George Edward. The duplication of the name, George, resulted from his reaction to a devastating challenge that arose during his sadness about the loss to Ali in Zaire. He suddenly learned that Leroy Moorehead, a man from Texarkana, Arkansas, was his biological father, not J. D. Foreman of Houston, Texas. To protect his sons from future uncertainties about their identity, he used his name as a symbol of their heritage.

Nearing the age of 50 and knowing that his boxing career is just about finished, Foreman no longer needs the accouterments important to his former lavish way of life. He has the love of his children, the beauty of his 300–acre ranch in Texas, and his ministry. He works out regularly with a punching bag for physical fitness. He knows he will continue his evangelism and perhaps accept another acting assignment.

African Americans honor Foreman's evolution from a youth who lacked the ability to define or pursue purposeful goals into an adult with the discipline to achieve success in athletic endeavors and make meaningful contributions to people of all ages in his community. He has not lost one of his principal attributes, the warm smile that symbolizes good will and love for humankind.

Current address: c/o World Boxing Association, 412 Colorado Ave., Aurora, IL 60506.

REFERENCES

Contemporary Black Biography. Vol. 1. Detroit: Gale Research, 1992.

Foreman, George. *By George.* New York: Villard Books, 1995.

''George Foreman Makes Gift of $100,000 to Texas Southern University.'' *Jet* 81 (2 December 1991): 50.

Massaquoi, Hans J. ''Home on the Range, George Foreman.'' *Ebony* 50 (July 1995): 86–92.

''A New Television Series Becomes Foreman.'' *New York Times,* October 27, 1993.

Dona L. Irvin

James Forman

(1928–)

Civil rights activist, author

Throughout the Civil Rights Movement of the 1960s, James Forman was among the most prominent activists. Although his contributions were far greater, he was known principally as director of the Student Nonviolent Coordinating Committee (SNCC), and as the presenter of the *Black Manifesto,* which demanded financial compensation for the indignities of slavery and immediate righting of continuing wrongs against black people.

James Forman was born in Chicago on October 4, 1928. He grew up as the oldest of the two children of Octavia and James ''Pops'' Rufus, a stockyard worker and owner of a gas station. Forman was known as James Rufus until he discovered, at age 14, that Pops was his stepfather. He met his biological father, Jackson Forman, a jitney driver in Chicago, and took on his name, but never formed a bond with him.

Forman lived most of his first six years with his maternal grandmother in rural Mississippi. His first lesson in racial differences as a young boy was that African American boys could not sit at the counter of an ice cream parlor and were not permitted to drink a Coca–Cola from a glass, but had to take the bottle outside. He learned at his grandmother's table to ask for food by spelling out what he wanted on his plate: meat, bread, corn, chicken, or ice cream.

When he joined his mother and stepfather in Chicago, Forman attended an almost all–black Catholic school, St. Anselm's, although his parents were staunch members of the African Methodist Episcopal Church (AME). Told by his teachers that his fate after death was not the same as that of Catholic children, Forman took on a burden of spiritual uncertainty. He asked to leave St. Anselm's and started the sixth grade in Betsy Ross public school.

Throughout his elementary education Forman worked as a paper boy selling the *Chicago Defender,* an influential African American newspaper. He read its articles about the problems of black people in Chicago and throughout the United States. He branched out to studying the works of black

James Forman

writers, such as Booker T. Washington, W. E. B Du Bois, and Richard Wright, and attended protest meetings held by A. Philip Randolph and various churches. As he matured, he expanded his reading to Carl Sandburg's biography of Abraham Lincoln and other texts having to do with national and international conditions for underprivileged and under represented people. Joseph L. Roberts, pastor of Coppin Chapel AME Church, encouraged young Forman's budding ambitions for service.

When time came for him to go to high school, Foreman argued with his parents about pursuing general studies or vocational training. Unable to convince his parents of his choice to enter college in preparation to follow the example of educated black leaders in the fight for freedom, Forman enrolled in shop classes in Englewood High School in 1943. After failures in the vocational courses, disciplinary troubles, and finally suspension from school, Forman joined a gang of boys engaged in gambling, extortion, drugs, and idleness. However, Forman rejected this as an acceptable way of life and returned to school in the general studies program. He graduated with honors in 1947 after earning the *Chicago Tribune*'s student honors award. At this time he began defining a focus for himself and after high school enrolled in Wilson Junior College.

Not long afterward, rather than wait for the draft, Forman tried to volunteer for the army. He was considering becoming a lieutenant in ROTC. However, the recruitment corporal told him that the army's quota for black men was filled and suggested that he join the air force. He took the air force oath in 1947 and went from Lackland Air Force Base in San Antonio, Texas, to Fairfield Air Force Base in California, then to Okinawa, Japan. When he transferred into a formerly all white unit, he was infuriated to see the better quality of food and living conditions there than what was provided for the segregated units. He was discharged from the Air Force in 1951.

Develops Interest in Humanistic Problems

In the period before, during, and after World War II, Forman's concern about national and international human rights issues intensified. With the United States, the Soviet Union, and other countries fighting as allies against fascism, his interest in black issues in the United States grew. He contemplated about serious subjects, such as capital punishment, fair employment practices, anti–lynching laws, the League of Nations, and the value of Marxism.

In 1952 Forman enrolled at the University of Southern California in Los Angeles to study public administration. In Los Angeles the police falsely accused him of robbery, jailed him, beat him, and released him without charge several days later. As a result of the abuse, he required a long term of mental and physical rehabilitation. Once recuperated, he entered Roosevelt University in Chicago in 1954, where he studied with professors who helped him develop his philosophy and a plan for civil rights action. The teacher he admired most was St. Clair Drake, for his scholarship in anthropology and sociology and his knowledge about the newly freed African countries and those still aspiring for independence.

From Roosevelt, Forman registered as a graduate student in the African Research and Studies Program at Boston University, but left when he felt a calling to improve conditions for American blacks. The sight of the National Guard's bayonets at Little Rock's Central High School and the rhetoric of Alabama Governor George Wallace convinced Forman of the necessity for an immediate crusade for human rights.

Forman learned from the success of Kwame Nkruma in Ghana convinced Forman that the key to change was action, preferably nonviolent. The situation in Little Rock demonstrated the need for a strong, broadly based African American activist organization. The Congress of Racial Equality (CORE)—which had a large proportion of white participation—the Southern Christian Leadership Conference (SCLC)—led by ministers—and the NAACP—largely made up of black middle class members—failed to appeal to Forman's vision. His ideal structure was to be built upon the ideas of socialism, promoting principles of social, political, and economic equality for everyone.

While working out the outline for his organization, Forman taught in the Chicago public schools, worked on the census team in South Chicago, studied French at the University of Chicago, and went to a French Summer School at Middlebury College in Vermont. He went to Fayette and Haywood counties, Tennessee, to help sharecroppers fight for their land and civil rights and worked with CORE, SCLC, and the NAACP, arranging sit–ins, freedom rides, and other forms of protests all over the South.

Involvement with SNCC

The SNCC, impressed with Forman's administrative skills and experience, appointed him executive secretary in 1964 to oversee voter registration drives and other activities that led to legislation protecting voter rights and civil rights. As a mastermind of demonstrations, Forman was often the target for arrest and persecution by police.

The SNCC also selected Forman to lead its short–lived alliance with the Black Panthers, whose objectives paralleled its own. He took on the title Minister of International Affairs, because of his familiarity with African life and politics. When a segment of the SNCC wanting more dramatic victories resulting from stronger action became especially vocal, the leadership changed and Forman assumed a position of lesser importance. This uprising weakened the organization so that it was unable to survive the harassment wreaked upon it by the government, and Forman's failing health decreased his activities for a while.

On May 4, 1969, the date chosen by the National Black Economic Development Conference to interrupt church services around the country, Forman took the bold step of seizing the podium of New York City's interdenominational, interracial Riverside Church to give an unscheduled speech to unveil the *Black Manifesto.* The *Black Manifesto,* which Forman wrote in 1969, was a document of demands from whites, such as $500 million from white churches and synagogues as reparations for the abuses blacks endured during slavery. The manifesto was unsuccessful in raising the $500 million it sought to compensate for the damage done to black people throughout the history of the United States, but it was a dramatic way to direct attention to existing unequal conditions. The funds it generated established Black Star Publications and supported the League of Revolutionary Black Workers in Detroit.

In 1974 Forman accepted the presidency of the Unemployment and Poverty Action Committee (UPAC), a social action organization concerned with political education, voter registration, and statehood for the District of Columbia. He witnessed President Clinton's signature to the 1993 National Voter Registration Act, legislation that removed any remaining restrictions to voting. One of earliest honors bestowed upon Forman came in 1963, when he received Roosevelt University Alumni's Eleanor Roosevelt Key Award for outstanding humanitarian. Three years later the Ward I Democrats of the District of Columbia inducted him into its hall of fame. Among the many tributes to Forman's work are the National Conference of Black Mayor's Fannie Lou Hamer Freedom Award, presented in 1990, and the 1992 ceremony held at Morgan State University to recognize his achievements. Forman has written several books, notably his autobiography, *The Makings of Black Revolutionaries* (1985), and *Liberation Viendra d'une Chose Noir* (1968), published in French in Paris.

Forman earned a master's degree from Cornell University 1980 and a doctorate from the Union Institute in 1982. In spite of the ravages of cancer that initially appeared in the early 1990s, Forman continues to work from his Washington, D.C., office. He and Constancia Romily, his divorced wife, had two sons—James Jr., a public defender in Washington, D.C., and Chaka, a member of the Screen Actor's Guild.

Current address: Office—Unemployment and Poverty Action Committee, PO Box 21097, Washington, DC 20009.

REFERENCES

Forman, James. *The Making of Black Revolutionaries.* Seattle: Open Hand Publishing, 1985.

Haskins, James. *Profiles in Black Power.* Garden City, New York: Doubleday, 1972.

Levy, Mark, Karel Weissberg, and Elizabeth Sutherland Martinez. "Friends of James Forman." *Nation* 262 (6 May 1996): 67.

Salzman, Jack, David Lionel Smith, and Cornell West eds. *Encyclopedia of African American Culture and History.* New York: Macmillan Library Reference USA/Simon and Schuster Macmillan, 1996.

Williams, Michael W., ed. *An African American Encyclopedia.* New York: Marshall Cavendish, 1993.

Dona L. Irvin

James Forten
(1766–1842)
Manufacturer, abolitionist, community leader

James Forten was a man of considerable ability who became one of the richest blacks of his era. Although the luck of being in the right position at the right time had much to do with his amassing wealth, he earned his success through hard work and skill in personal relations. His business acumen and inventiveness made him a natural leader. For 40 years and more he led efforts improve conditions for blacks. His exemplification of the moral values of the American middle class and his own conviction of racial equality had a significant impact on white abolitionists as they began to organize in the 1830s. He was also fortunate in having a family capable of effectively supporting his efforts and carrying them on after his death.

Forten was born in Philadelphia on September 2, 1766, to Thomas (d. 1775) and Sarah Forten (d. 1808), free blacks. He had a sister named Abigail. Forten's great–grandfather was brought to the American continent as a slave, but his son, Thomas's father, won his freedom. Forten married twice; nothing is known of his first wife, whom he married about 1794. She died in 1804, 18 months before he married Char-

James Forten

lotte Vandine (1785–1884) in December 1805. There appear to have been no children from the first marriage, but the second produced eight, four girls and four boys: Margaretta (1808–1875), Harriet (1810–1885), Sarah (c. 1811–1898?), James Jr., Robert Bridges, Mary Isabella, Thomas Willing, and William Deas.

Forten's father, Thomas Forten, was a worker in the sail loft owned by Robert Bridges, whose labor force of 40 was about one fourth black. Forten attended the school for blacks run by Quaker Anthony Benezet until his father was killed in an accident in 1775. Forten then had to go to work to help support his family, and his formal education ended.

After a brief stint as a chimney sweep, Forten found work in a grocery. The American Revolution began the following year, and in the fall of 1776, British forces occupied Philadelphia. Friction arose between the soldiers and the inhabitants of the city. As a large and strong 11–year old, Forten was forced by older boys to fight with the drummer boys and other young men attached to the occupiers. Much to his relief, the fights were stopped by threats of severe retaliation after one drummer boy was killed. In June 1778, the British evacuated the city.

In 1781, Forten signed on the privateer *Royal Louis* as a powder boy at 4 dollars a month plus a small share of all prizes taken. The newly commissioned ship's first voyage began on July 23 and resulted in the capture of two ships. On the second voyage in October, the *Royal Louis* was captured. Fortunately, Forten impressed Captain John Beasly, who held him prisoner, and won over Beasly's son by playing marbles. Thus, Forten escaped being taken to the islands and sold as a slave, a common fate for blacks. He also turned down an offer of patronage and an education in Great Britain from the captain by stressing his own patriotism. Forten ended up as a prisoner on the hulk *Jersey* on the shore of Long Island.

The imprisonment lasted seven months. Forten had one chance to escape but allowed an ill white companion, Daniel Brewton, to escape in his stead. Forten was released in a general exchange of prisoners and made his way on foot to Philadelphia, where he delighted his family, who had given him up for dead.

With the American Revolution long over, Forten decided to visit England. His sister's husband found him a job as a sailor on a ship bound for Liverpool. He arrived there sometime in March 1785. There he came into contact with abolitionists Granville Sharp and Thomas Clarkson, who expanded his intellect. His experience working in the port of Liverpool also taught him about the slave trade. By the fall of 1786, Forten was back in America and became an apprentice to Robert Bridges, the sailmaker.

Becomes Sailmaker

Within two years, Forten had become a foreman, a skilled workman able to design, cut, and sew sails. In the spring of 1793, he met the black captain of a small ship, Paul Cuffe of Massachusetts, initiating a relationship that continued until Cuffe's death in September 1817. In 1794, Forten was elected a member of the first vestry of Saint Thomas. It was the first black Episcopal church, organized under the leadership of Absalom Jones, which opened just a few days before the black Methodist church, Bethel, led by Richard Allen.

In the summer of 1798, Forten bought out Bridges and became master of the sail loft. There were 38 workers, and only one of the 19 white employees left when a black became his employer. Forten received a loan for the buyout from Thomas Willing, a prominent Philadelphia merchant and ship owner, who was impressed both by the man and by the potential of his newly devised sail–handling device. Forten continued to prosper. By 1800, he was living in a three–story house at 92 Lombard Street. Investing in real estate, banking, and railroads, his fortune was estimated to be about $100,000 in 1832. His was a model success story of rising to riches through hard work, but, due to his race, he still experienced discrimination. For example, he could not send his children to existing schools in Philadelphia and, therefore, founded a school to secure an education for them. Part of the Forten children's education was through private tuition, but, in 1819, he organized a school with the help of Grace and Robert Douglass, who had five children of their own who needed an education.

Works Toward Abolition

In January 1800, Forten was among the first to sign a petition of Philadelphia blacks to the House of Representatives protesting the Fugitive Slave Act of 1793 and the continuing slave trade. A resolution condemning such petitions passed the House by a vote of 85 to one. Forten wrote a letter of thanks to Representative George Thatcher of Massachusetts, who cast the sole negative vote. In this letter, published by John Parrish in 1806, Forten said:

> Though our faces are black, yet we are men, and though many amongst us cannot write because our rulers have thought proper to keep us in ignorance, yet we have the feelings and passions of men. . . . Judge what must be our feelings to find ourselves treated as a species of property, and leveled with the brute creation; and think how anxious we must be to raise ourselves from this degrading state. . . . Humane people will wish our situation alleviated. Just people will attempt the task, and powerful people ought to carry it into execution.

As anti–black sentiment rose during the early part of the nineteenth century, the Pennsylvania legislature debated in 1813 a bill to bar free blacks from moving to Pennsylvania. Forten was the author of a pamphlet, *Letters From a Man of Color,* opposing the bill, which did not pass. Although he continued to fight racism in legislation over the years, but was often not successful. Black voters in Pennsylvania were disenfranchised in 1837, for example, and the threat of mob violence was ever present. The increase in racism, however, unified blacks as they responded and began to organize to defend their interests.

A major early issue was colonization—the efforts to persuade free American blacks to emigrate to Africa or some other site out of the United States. Forten at first supported his friend Paul Cuffe, who explored black resettlement in Africa and took a shipload of settlers there in 1816. In January 1817, Forten presided at a mass meeting held to protest the plans of the recently formed American Colonization Society. Although the persons attending unanimously condemned colonization, he wrote shortly afterwards, in a letter of January 25 to Paul Cuffe, that he still privately favored emigration. Cuffe died in September 1817, and, by 1819, Forten came out unreservedly against colonization, a position he stoutly maintained until his death.

Forten's emphasis on uplift caused him to found and serve as first president of the American Moral Reform Society. He did not stop his activities on the state level. As long as he was healthy, he continued to organize meetings and send petitions to the legislature. He was ably seconded by his wife and children. For example, his wife, three of his daughters, and a future daughter–in–law were among the founding members of the Philadelphia Female Anti–Slavery Society in 1833. His son William carried on the family activism into the 1870s, when he was a crucial player in Philadelphia politics through his influence on the black vote.

Forten was also important in the formation of Garrisonian abolitionism, both through his personal example and through his financial support. He was an unwavering upholder of the equality of races and an exemplar of values cherished by white abolitionists. His influence operated as he opened his home as a stopping place for abolitionists like William Lloyd Garrison and L. Maria Child. He was an agent for Garrison's paper, *The Liberator,* launched on January 1, 1831. His financial subsidies to the paper and to abolition societies in general were topped only by those of the wealthy white New York merchants and abolitionists Arthur and Lewis Tappan. When the American Anti–Slavery Society was formed in 1833, most of the planning for the sessions took place around the Forten family table.

Age did not lessen Forten's commitment to reform and abolition. He gave support to other movements such as the Temperance Movement and the Peace Movement. In addition, his service in rescuing people from drowning was recognized by the Humane Society of Philadelphia, when it presented him with a certificate on May 9, 1821, for saving four individuals on different occasions, a memento he framed and hung on a wall in his home. In 1839, he joined his son–in–law Robert Purvis as a founding member of the Philadelphia Vigilant Society, and his handwriting is found in a number of entries in the minute book.

Forten began to suffer debilitating ill health in 1841 and died in early 1842. His funeral was one of Philadelphia's largest, attracting several hundred whites and thousands of blacks. His estate was valued at 67,000 dollars, down from an estimated 300,000 dollars at its peak.

Forten occupies a unique position in black history. One of the few blacks of his era able to amass a considerable fortune, he became one of the leaders of the early abolition movement and continued anti–slavery and anti–racism efforts throughout his life. Forten left behind a family which continued to work indefatigably for his goals.

REFERENCES

Aptheker, Herbert, ed. *A Documentary History of the Negro People in the United States.* New York: The Citadel Press, 1951.

Bracey, John H. Jr., and others, eds. *Blacks in the Abolitionist Movement.* Belmont, CA: Wadsworth, 1971.

Child, L. Maria. *The Freedmen's Book.* Boston: Ticknor and Fields, 1865.

Douty, Esther M. *Forten the Sailmaker.* Chicago: Rand McNally, 1968.

Logan, Rayford W., and Michael R. Winston, eds. *Dictionary of American Negro Biography.* New York: Norton, 1982.

Nell, W[illia]m C. *The Colored Patriots of the American Revolution.* 1855. Reprint, New York: Arno Press and the *New York Times,* 1968. [The pages on Forten are an abridgment of the eulogy delivered by Robert Purvis at Bethel Church, Philadelphia, March 30, 1842.]

Parrish, John. *Remarks on the Slavery of the Black People.* Philadelphia: Printed for the Author by Kimber, Conrad, and Co., 1806.

Porter, Dorothy. *Early Negro Writing: 1760–1837.* Boston: Beacon Press, 1971.

Smith, Jessie Carney, ed. *Notable Black American Women.* Detroit: Gale Research, 1992.

Robert L. Johns

T. Thomas Fortune
(1856–1928)
Journalist, civil rights activist, poet, printer

T. Thomas Fortune was the most famous black editor of the late nineteenth–century. From the relative safety of New York, he commented on changes affecting African Americans, openly voicing sentiments that blacks living in the South could not. He might well be called the "Afro–American Agitator," the title of an editorial he published in his newspaper, the *Age,* on December 21, 1889. The reach of his voice increased as white–owned papers commented, usually unfavorably, on statements he made. In spite of personal hardship and a hostile social climate, Fortune continued to act as the voice of the dispossessed African American community.

T. Thomas Fortune

Timothy Thomas Fortune was born a slave on October 3, 1856, in Marianna, Florida, the third child and first son of Emanuel and Sarah Jane Fortune, slaves of Ely P. Moore. He grew up to become a tall, fair–complexioned, and very handsome, though slight, young man—his weight seldom reached 140 pounds. In addition to two older sisters Fortune had a younger sister and a brother, Emanuel Jr., with whom he was very close.

Union troops first visited Marianna, the county seat of Jackson County, in September of 1864, and on May 14, 1865, the Union general commanding the area issued an emancipation order. T. Thomas Fortune received his first schooling in a school run by two Union soldiers and developed a thirst for learning which remained with him throughout his life, although he had little formal education. Emanuel Fortune took his family and left Moore to establish himself as a farmer. T. Thomas Fortune retained fond memories of his rural childhood, but he discovered his true interests when he visited the office of the weekly *Marianna Courier.* He became fascinated with the workings of the newspaper business, and began to regularly spend time in the office.

T. Thomas Fortune followed in the footsteps of his political father, who served as a politician during the Reconstruction era, by acting as a page in the legislature. His experience as a page in three subsequent sessions gave him a close–up view of politics in action. In Jackson he attended two sessions at the Stanton Institute which completed his formal elementary education. His practical education continued when he served as printer's devil and typesetter on the *Tallahassee Sentinel,* the *Jacksonville Courier,* and *Jacksonville Daily Union.* He worked temporarily as a clerk in the Jacksonville Post Office in 1872. He also secured federal appointments, first as a mail route agent in the Railway Postal Service, then as a special inspector of customs in Delaware.

Fortune resigned his customs post to enroll in the preparatory department of Howard University for the winter term of 1874. He enjoyed most of his classes but deplored the heavy emphasis on religion at the school. In spite of his disparaging remarks about religion, he was a faithful member of the African Methodist Episcopal Church as an adult, even serving as a lay delegate to the 1884 General Convention.

Fortune found work in the print shop of the *People's Advocate,* a recently established black weekly run by John Wesley Cromwell. Fortune's attempts to combine work with the study of law in Howard's night school petered out. He was in charge of the printing of the paper and also wrote a column for it under the name Gustafus Bert. Fortune's time in Washington brought him into contact with leading blacks like Frederick Douglass and John Mercer Langston. He also became acquainted with John E. Bruce (Bruce Grit), who remained a life–long friend.

On February 22, 1877, the 20–year–old Fortune married Caroline (Carrie) Charlotte Smiley of Jacksonville. Fortune's prospects now took a turn for the worse. Due to financial exigencies, his salary at the *Advocate* was cut, and his political influence and thus his ability to secure federal appointments diminished sharply with the overthrow of Reconstruction in Florida in 1876. Caroline Fortune was expecting their first child, and the family returned to Jacksonville. The child, a son, died as an infant in Florida, and the second son also died as an infant soon after they moved to New York. A daughter, Jessica (Jessie), was born in 1883, and a son, Stewart, was born in 1884, who died of pneumonia in 1888. A fourth son, Frederick White, was born in 1891.

In Florida, Fortune tried but soon gave up teaching school as he found both the salary and the teaching conditions intolerable. He then worked in the office of the *Jacksonville Daily Union.* In 1879 the offer of a job on a New York weekly paper through a black printer, Walter Sampson, gave him the chance to leave the South.

Moves to New York

Fortune initially worked for a religious paper, *The Weekly Advocate,* published by a white man, John Dougall. During the year Fortune spent working for Dougall, he met a young black man named George Parker, who was publishing a weekly called *Rumor.* At night Fortune and fellow worker Walter Sampson wrote and set type for the periodical, which changed its name to the *Globe* around July of 1881; the *Globe* and its successors the *Freeman* and the *Age* would achieve an impressively–long publication history, which ended in 1960.

The editor of the *Globe* for the first few months was John F. Quarles with Fortune as managing editor. The paper strove to have a national perspective and developed unpaid local correspondents in many localities, among them 16–year–old W. E. B. Du Bois in Great Barrington, Massachusetts. In the eyes of many of the *Globe*'s readers, however, Fortune's vigorous and militant editorials were still the main attraction.

The *Globe* appeared to be flourishing by 1883, with a circulation of 6,000. However, political and financial dealings prepared the way for its demise. As the 1884 elections approached, there was a power struggle for control of the paper between Fortune and George Parker, who each owned a quarter share. Out of disgust at the Republican's betrayal of their tradition of support for black rights, Fortune joined other blacks in flirting with the Democratic Party. Parker sold his share in August to William B. Derrick, a Republican stalwart, who circumvented Fortune through impenetrable financial dealings. The last issue of the *Globe* appeared on November 8. Shortly thereafter Fortune returned to the paper's premises to find presses and office furnishings removed.

Fortune became sole proprietor and editor of the *Freeman,* whose first issue appeared two weeks after the demise of the *Globe.* It is not evident how he financed the paper, and he had continuing monetary difficulties even as he maintained the quality of the paper with such features as a humor column by Bruce Grit and, beginning in 1885, a women's section edited by Philadelphia women's rights activist and suffragist Gertrude Bustill Mossell. Still, Fortune's editorials continued to be the major attraction of the paper.

Fortune continued to veer in political alignment and even considered supporting the Prohibition Party. In October of 1887, the *Freeman* was reorganized as the *New York Age,* with Fortune retaining half–ownership with other half going to Jerome B. Peterson. Perhaps because of the financial problems of the paper in providing a living for both partners, Fortune left the paper to become a free–lance journalist working for the election of Grover Cleveland. T. Thomas Fortune also began a long–term relationship with the *New York Sun,* which paid reporters for articles published. This was a useful supplement to his income when he returned to the *Age* as editor in February of 1889, a position he held until 1907. In an editorial on August 31, 1889, he renounced his support of the Democrats.

Becomes Leading Black Spokesperson

In an attempt to counter the tide running against the rights of African Americans, Fortune added work with civil rights organizations to his editorial efforts in the 1890s. In 1890 he played a critical role in founding the National Afro–American League, of which John Charles Price became president. This prototype of twentieth–century civil rights organizations foundered by 1893 because of the refusal of prominent African Americans like Frederick Douglass to join and its inability to attract funding and mass support. A continual worsening of conditions led to a second attempt to create an organization in September 1898, the National Afro–American Council. Fortune was in ill health and had doubts about the viability of the movement so he resigned as president to be followed in that position by Booker T. Washington. Fortune felt that there was considerable overlap between the programs of these two organizations and that of the Niagara Movement in 1905.

Fortune also favored the efforts of black women activists. He was a consistent supporter of Victoria Earle Matthews and her White Rose Mission, a social center for black migrants to New York City. In the summer of 1892 he located black activist Ida B. Wells in Jersey City to tell her that a mob had destroyed the office of the *Free Press,* her Memphis paper. Warning her against returning to Memphis, he gave her work at the *Age* and in June of 1892 published a special edition containing a lengthy article by Wells on lynching. He helped her orchestrate the lecture engagements which made her into a national figure. In addition, in July of 1895 he was one of three men to participate in the Negro Women's Convention in Boston. This convention gave rise to the National Federation of Afro–American Women, one of the constituents of the National Association of Colored Women.

Allied with Booker T. Washington

Fortune was well–acquainted with many black Southern Republicans like Norris Wright Cuney of Texas and William A. Pledger of Georgia. He also met Emmett J. Scott, a protege of Cuney, who became Booker T. Washington's private secretary in 1897. Fortune, who had long known Washington, reprinted Washington's celebrated 1895 Atlanta address in full in the *Age,* and visited Tuskegee several times, spending seven weeks there in the winter of 1897–98. In 1898, he wrote an introduction to a collection of speeches by Washington, the text of which was edited by his friend Victoria Earle Matthews.

Black–Belt Diamonds was the first of many books to present Washington's views to the public. Fortune followed up this effort by heavily editing *The Future of the American Negro* published by Washington in 1899 and ghost–writing *A New Negro for a New Century* (1900) and *The Negro in Business* (1907) as well as various magazine articles.

Though Fortune's militancy would appear to be ideologically opposed to Washington's accomodationist stance, the alliance was not completely paradoxical. They shared many ideas, and Fortune had urged industrial education for the masses before Washington did. In great secrecy Washington made efforts to assert civil rights in the South. Tactically, Washington could always point to Fortune to underline his own moderation. The differences, however, were real. Nonetheless there was initially a genuine friendship between the two men.

In his efforts on behalf of Washington, Fortune in effect became his press agent, albeit a poorly–paid one. Still the occasional earnings eased Fortune's difficult finances. Until 1907 Fortune was a consistent defender of Washington, who in turn subsidized the *Age* secretly. Thus, Fortune found himself increasingly dependent on Washington and obliged to support positions with which he disagreed. Part of the strain with Washington was due to the fact that Washington reached the apogee of his political power when Theodore Roosevelt became president in 1901 while Fortune could see that, in fact, blacks continued to lose ground. Fortune had become a heavy drinker by the mid–1890s, and in the early 1900s caused scandals with his drunkenness on several very visible occasions. By 1906 Washington had become the dominant partner in the relationship. He was alarmed by Fortune's unreliable behavior, but saw no easy way of breaking with him. Fortune was in turn becoming increasingly depressed and pessimistic, and his money problems were acute. In 1901 Fortune had bought a house in Red Bank, New Jersey, which increased his financial needs. He desperately sought a federal appointment, which explains his constant, though somewhat begrudging, support of the Republican Party. Fortune did not improve his financial standing when he received a six–month federal appointment at the end of 1902 as a special agent of the U.S. Treasury Department assigned to investigate race and trade conditions in the Philippines.

Fortune's family life was also breaking up. Although he adored his two surviving children, especially Jessie who became a schoolteacher in 1902, he had little contact with his son, an honors student and outstanding athlete in high school. He and his wife spent long periods apart and they separated in 1906.

In 1907 the *Age* was incorporated: Washington held 950 shares of stock and Fortune and his partner, Jerome Peterson, each held 1250. In response to the strains he was under, Fortune suffered a mental breakdown and in October sold his share of the *Age* to Fred R. Moore, or rather to Booker T. Washington who put up the money without Fortune's knowledge.

For the next three years Fortune lived a precarious hand–to–mouth existence, unable to hold a permanent job. He recovered enough to begin writing editorials and articles in 1910. He was now living alone in various places in New Jersey. In 1911 he was hired by the *Amsterdam News* at five dollars a week, and from 1911 to 1914, he was associate editor in charge of the editorial page of the *Age* at ten dollars a week. Fortune found short–lived jobs on other papers including the *Washington Sun,* which started up in 1914 and went under in March of 1915. In 1917 he was appointed assistant director of a New Jersey Negro welfare bureau set up by the governor of that state to deal with migrants from the South. In 1919 Fortune began to write editorials and articles for the *Norfolk Journal and Guide,* a position he held until his death. In 1923 after Marcus Garvey had been sentenced to prison, he became editor of the Universal Negro Improvement Association's paper, *Negro World,* holding the position for the rest of his life. He completed most of his work from his home in New Jersey. His desire for a reconciliation with his wife was rejected although relations became cordial.

In the last year of his life Fortune became increasingly frail. He collapsed in New York City in early April of 1928. His son, Frederick White Fortune, a surgeon at Mercy Hospital in Philadelphia, took him to that city a week later. There Fortune suffered a relapse and died of heart disease on June 2, 1928. He was buried in Philadelphia's Eden Cemetery four days later.

T. Thomas Fortune lived in an era when new barriers against blacks were rising and old rights were disappearing. It is perhaps too harsh to say that his efforts to counter these developments came to nothing; given the current of the times, it is hard to see how anyone could have done better. He fought with the weapons at his command, principally the written word, and continued to struggle for freedom in adverse circumstances, both historical and personal.

REFERENCES

Harlan, Louis R. *Booker T. Washington.* 2 vols. New York: Oxford, 1983, 1986.

———, ed. *The Booker T. Washington Papers.* 14 vol. Urbana: University of Illinois Press, 1972–89.

Logan, Rayford W., and Michael R. Winston. *Dictionary of American Negro Biography.* New York: Norton, 1982.

Sherman, Joan R. *Invisible Poets.* Urbana: University of Illinois Press, 1974.

Thornbrough, Emma Lou. "T. Thomas Fortune: Militant Editor in the Age of Accommodation." In *Black Leaders of the Twentieth Century.* Edited by John Hope Franklin and August Meier. Urbana: University of Illinois Press, 1982.

———. *T. Thomas Fortune: Militant Journalist.* Chicago: University of Chicago Press, 1972.

COLLECTIONS

A scrapbook of materials in the possession of Mrs. Aubrey Bowser, Fortune's daughter, has been microfilmed by the New York Public Library.

Robert L. Johns

Henry W. Foster Jr.
(1933–)
Surgeon, medical school educator

Dr. Henry W. Foster Jr. is most well known for his broad involvement in vital programs to extend quality health care services to the poor and underserved in the United States of America. He personally developed a highly effective agenda to educate teen–agers about the far–reaching implications of sexual activity. He then implemented his plan in the residential setting of local communities where it proved most beneficial. Foster came to international prominence in 1995 when a U.S. Senate filibuster denied him the opportunity to become the surgeon general of the United States. Foster, who would have been only the second black American to hold the post was denied the appointment as a result of partisan politics. He was ultimately assigned to an influential position as an advisor to President Bill Clinton, to lead a national campaign against teen pregnancy.

Born in his parents' house on Linden Street in Pine Bluff, Arkansas, on September 8, 1933, Henry Wendell Foster Jr. is the son of Henry Wendell Foster Sr. and Ivie Foster. Both parents were strong advocates of education and taught Henry Foster and his only sibling, Doris, who was four years older, to value it highly. The senior Foster grew up in the college environment of Arkansas Agricultural, Mechanical, and Normal College and graduated from Morehouse College. Later he earned a master's degree from the University of Arkansas in Little Rock, and became a high school teacher and athletic coach. He left teaching when World War II began and headed a unit that built incendiary bombs at the Pine Bluff Arsenal. Ivie Foster came from a family of educators. She met Foster senior while she was a student at Tuskegee Institute in Alabama, and they later married and settled in Pine Bluff. Later she taught art at Arkansas A. M. and N. During the war years she took a job with the Rural Housing Authority and taught poor rural women homemaking skills, especially food preparation and preservation. Her work took her away from home all week but she returned home on weekends. About this time the Fosters sent their daughter Doris to boarding school at Palmer Memorial Institute in Sedalia, North Carolina.

The Fosters taught their children to value education highly and helped them to develop good self–esteem as well. As a result, the Foster children grew up knowing they were as good as, if not better than, anybody else. Foster wrote in his autobiography *Make a Difference* that he was nourished in his upbringing by his mother, who enhanced the emotional quality of Foster family life with her ''quiet words of encouragement.'' Foster Sr. enriched his son's life, too, with gratifying experiences that would stay with the boy into adulthood.

Among the most vivid memories of his youth Henry Foster, Jr. recalls a ride in a private airplane which was arranged by his father when the boy was only seven years old.

Henry W. Foster Jr.

The outing was a ''physics in action'' field trip for Foster Sr.'s high school students, but young Foster Jr. was allowed to accompany the class. Foster was only a tiny lad at the time, and he had to sit between the legs of a larger youth, Wiley Branton. Although Foster was destined to become a highly respected doctor and surgeon, he never forgot the thrill of that first plane ride; and Branton, Foster's ''seatmate,'' would eventually attain national prominence in his own right, as a civil rights lawyer during the 1950s and as law school dean at Howard University.

For all the fun of the airplane ride, Foster's father was nonetheless a strict taskmaster who rejected the idea of idle hands. Consequently he taught his son survival skills, enforced the work ethic, and always maintained that hard work is good for a man. By the time Foster was 12 years old, he and his father were working as partners in a poultry business called Foster and Son. They sold chickens and eggs. Young Foster was in charge of the business enterprise—He did the purchasing and made deliveries. The business thrived and the young adolescent developed a great deal of confidence in his own entrepreneurial skills. His social and communication skills also matured rapidly because of the interaction with his customers.

As Foster developed into a young man, he never lost his fascination with airplanes. As a student at the college laboratory school at Arkansas A. M. and N. he considered enrolling in an aeronautical engineering curriculum one day, in the hope of becoming an airline pilot. He was a realist, however, and he knew that the field held no promise for a black person. Instead, he studied his lessons at the school and learned to celebrate and appreciate the work of African American achievers.

In time Foster became particularly impressed by the work of his father's best friend, Clyde Lawlah, the Foster family doctor. Lawlah had graduated from Morehouse a few years before Henry Foster, Sr. Lawlah practiced his medicine in Pine Bluff, and young Foster was known to accompany the doctor on house calls and even carry his medical bag for him. Foster's fascination with medicine was further aroused when his "Aunt Odell" developed a condition of eclampsia—convulsions followed by a coma—during pregnancy. The doctors at the University of Arkansas hospital in Little Rock saved not only her own life but the lives of her twin babies. Foster knew then that he would choose a medical career.

Foster graduated high school in 1950 as valedictorian of his class. His sister Doris had just graduated from Talladega College in Alabama, and she encouraged him to spend the summer reading in preparation for his freshman year at Morehouse College. By the time school started in the fall he was a respectable storyteller, and he used this social skill to ingratiate himself with the popular men on campus and thus to make friends.

Foster was younger than most (not yet 17) at the time he started college. He was also short, slightly chubby, and had a bad case of acne. The summer after his freshman year he slimmed down considerably and grew six inches to become five feet eight inches tall. That fall when he returned to school he felt more secure in the friendships he made. He joined Kappa Alpha Psi Fraternity and the club became the pivot of his social activities.

Despite a preoccupation with social life and a devotion to extracurricular activities, Foster, in his own words, was never "academically irresponsible." He knew that academic proficiency was a prerequisite for acceptance to medical school and he was attentive to his studies.

When the time came for Foster to apply to medical school he was well aware that few blacks were admitted to mainstream institutions. For the most part they earned their medical degrees at Howard University in Washington, D.C., or Meharry Medical College in Nashville, Tennessee. He took a chance however and applied to the University of Arkansas where Edith Irby Jones attended in 1948 and where a small number of other blacks followed.

Foster was encouraged in part by the weekly addresses of the Morehouse College president, Benjamin E. Mays. Mays, a noted educator and a compelling orator spoke to the students regularly during the four years that Foster attended Morehouse. Mays encouraged the students to dream, and to aim high. As Foster grappled over his decision he was further influenced by Daisy Bates, a newspaper editor and then president of the National Association of Colored People (NAACP) in Arkansas, who recommended that he pursue his goal. Foster was only 20 years old when he graduated from Morehouse College in the spring of 1954 and went on to the University of Arkansas Medical School.

At the medical school in Arkansas, Foster was the only African American in a class of 96 students. He was subsequently nominated and elected to Alpha Omega Alpha, the honor society in medicine, despite efforts by some faculty members to block the nomination. Foster was the first African American at the university to be elected to that most prestigious honor for a medical school student.

In the fall of 1957, Foster's final year of medical school, severe racial tension arose in Arkansas. He watched as federal troops—the 101st Airborne Screaming Eagles—protected black students as they integrated Little Rock's Central High School. Interestingly the confrontation in Little Rock was instigated when Wiley Branton, Foster's first airplane ride partner, brought suit against the Little Rock Board of Education to integrate the school.

After graduating from medical school in 1958, Foster went to Detroit's Receiving General Hospital, associated with Wayne State University, to begin a rotating internship in obstetrics and gynecology (ob/gyn). In 1959 Foster, as was required of all medical doctors at that time, entered the U.S. Air Force as a captain. The air force told Foster that they had a shortage of doctors with ob/gyn training and gave him the option of taking a course in that area of specialty. He would then receive a permanent assignment to work exclusively in ob/gyn with a civilian ob/gyn consultant. He accepted. After an intensive three-month ob/gyn training program at Carswell Air Force Base located near Fort Worth, Texas, he was assigned to Larson Air Force Base at Moses Lake, Washington where he practiced with obstetrician Anson Hughes of Moses Lake. Foster delivered almost 500 babies while he was in the military.

Upon his discharge from the air force in 1961, Foster did a compulsory year of surgical training at Malden Hospital in Boston. Rather than return to Detroit to continue his residency, Foster accepted a residency at Hubbard Hospital of Meharry Medical College in Nashville. His experience at Malden and in the military was a boon to Meharry but caused some concern among his supervisors who had difficulty accepting the diagnoses of a young, upstart resident. In 1965 he left for a six-month stint in the rural South, at the John A. Andrew Memorial Hospital at Tuskegee Institute in Alabama. There he worked in a high-need environment and served seven counties in Alabama as well as patients from elsewhere in the Deep South. In 1965, a few days after completing his residency, Foster, who previously had been appointed chief of ob/gyn at the hospital, returned to Tuskegee.

Develops Rural Health Program

The longer Foster stayed in Alabama the more he saw a need to make profound changes in the area's health care system. He wrote in his biography that he wanted to avoid "applying Band-Aids to hemorrhages." He obtained a grant from the Title V Children's Bureau, Maternity and Infant Care Projects, and used Andrew Memorial Hospital as the tertiary-care facility for patients and outlying clinics as secondary-care facilities. Doctors on the Veteran's Hospital staff at Tuskegee were enlisted for support. Andrew hospital was the site for continuing medical education in the region and a research center as well.

Foster worked long hours but still needed assistance for the demanding and time–consuming work. He persuaded Meharry Medical College to begin a student rotation in ob/gyn at Tuskegee. Third–year medical students rotated for a few weeks to lend assistance and gain experience as well. So impressed with the program was the Children's Bureau director that visiting health officials from developing countries were brought in to see the model rural health care program and to witnesses the decrease in infant mortality that resulted. Foster's long time interest and previous training in flying and his hectic schedule led him to take up flying again. In 1970 he bought a new Cessna Cardinal 177B, earned his instrument rating, and flew his plane over a 21–year period. The plane provided travel opportunities for the Foster family, pleasure for Foster as a pilot, and was useful for medical emergencies as well. He still considers himself a weekend pilot.

In the 1960s little was known about sickle–cell disease and few health care centers anywhere provided screening. Foster's Maternal and Infant Care Program began to screen routinely, especially since those patients with the sickle–cell trait generally had no symptoms. Foster wanted to know whether or not parents who carried the trait learned of their risk and then risked passing the disease state to their children.

Foster remained in Alabama from 1965 to 1973. He returned to Nashville as chair of the Department of Obstetrics and Gynecology at Meharry Medical College. From 1973 to 1990 he was professor and chairman in the department, and in 1975 he joined Vanderbilt University as a clinical professor of obstetrics and gynecology.

In 1980 the Robert Wood Johnson Foundation chose Foster to head its $12 million project at Meharry, to consolidate health services for adolescents at high risk. The foundation was interested in new ways to bring health services to vulnerable populations that included infants and poor mothers. Thus, Meharry was the administrative site for the High–Risk Young People's Program. By its nature the program that Foster headed demonstrated a need to locate a multiservice program in a residential setting. Most programs aimed to address the needs of teenagers had been school–based or elsewhere. Through Meharry, Foster applied to the Carnegie Corporation for funds to support the I Have a Future project, a service program that targeted young people with a high risk for failure. The program was located in two public housing sites in Nashville, John Henry Hale and Preston Taylor homes. Participants took trips to local sites and then encouraged their friends to apply. After that, the young people traveled to Disney World, Atlanta, and Washington, D.C. The program had a tutoring component and was designed to enhance their self–esteem. The adolescents were encouraged to go on to college or to other forms of advanced training. In 1991, the program received national recognition as an innovative community service program when it was named one of President George Bush's Thousand Points of Light.

In the 1989–90 academic year, Foster was special assistant to Meharry Medical School president David Satcher. In 1990 he was named dean of the School of Medicine at Meharry. He was also a key part of the negotiating team to bring about a merger between Meharry and the city–owned General Hospital. Meharry needed a way to pay for the health care that it already provided to the uninsured poor, both black and white. About the same time, David Satcher was named head of the Centers for Disease Control in Atlanta. Foster was then named acting president of Meharry for the 1993–94 year. When a new president was appointed in 1994, Foster took his first sabbatical leave in 38 years to conduct research at the Association of Academic Health Centers in Washington, D.C. He focused on "Gender Shift in the Physician Work Force." While there, President Bill Clinton nominated him for a position on the presidential cabinet as Surgeon General of the United States.

Nominated as U.S. Surgeon General

On February 2, 1995, President Bill Clinton nominated Foster for U.S. Surgeon General to replace Foster's good friend Jocelyn Elders, the first black to hold the post. Foster had a string of vocal supporters, but he also met with a toxic atmosphere immediately from nonprofit groups who used the media to protest his association with Planned Parenthood and his I Have a Future program. The protestors were proponents of sexual abstinence as the only teen–age birth control. The group displayed little empathy for the health or life of those who disagreed. Critics latched on to the issue of abortion—abortion foes were outraged that the obstetrician–gynecologist had performed 39 abortions in his medical career. Some say that he was a pawn in the abortion battle. His record for delivering more than 10,000 babies and developing a program to deter teen pregnancy was lost in the debates. Senators Bob Dole and Phil Gramm were leaders in the assault against Foster. Clearly, Foster acquitted himself well on the issues raised, but partisan politics clouded the arena. Foster's name emerged from committee with a favorable recommendation, but two days of parliamentary delay (a Republican–led filibuster) prevented Foster's nomination from going to a full vote of the senate. Foster's nomination remained in limbo until David Satcher's name was placed in nomination for the position in 1997.

The Senate's refusal to approve Foster did not keep him from the forefront of public life. Disappointed by the rejection yet honored to have been involved in the process, Foster said in the *Nashville Tennessean* for June 23, 1995, "I intend to keep fighting for the things I believe in with all my heart." His beliefs include a woman's right to choose an abortion. Seven months after the failed confirmation hearing, President Clinton named Foster as his senior advisor on teen pregnancy reduction and youth issues. In this capacity Foster serves as the president's liaison to the recently–structured "Campaign to Prevent Teen Pregnancy." This time, Senate approval was not required.

Women's groups had lobbied the president to make teen pregnancy a prominent issue, and Clinton responded that the appointment "ought to be completely without partisan politics," as quoted in the *Nashville Tennessean.* The assignment takes Foster around the world to call attention to the issue. He speaks out at meetings with business leaders and the media. His work is coordinated through the Department of Health and Human Services, where he maintains an office.

During the course of his medical career, Foster has received numerous honors. His experiences in Alabama brought Foster to the attention of the prestigious Institute of Medicine of the National Academy of Sciences. In 1972 the institute elected him a member and he became one of the youngest doctors ever admitted. The membership gave Foster a permanent opportunity to sit on other national committees that conduct research in medicine and evaluate new, important developments. Many policy–making bodies find Foster to be "politically attractive," and his is often asked to serve on national committees that concentrate on improving maternal and perinatal care. Foster's work with such groups has been an educational experience for him in terms of learning to tap the potential of "power plays."

In 1978 U.S. Health, Education, and Welfare Secretary Joseph Califano appointed Foster to the department's Ethics Advisory Board. The board's purpose was to examine moral and ethical issues in science. He also has served on the Ob/Gyn Test Committee for the National Board of Medical Examiners. He has served on the editorial board for *Academic Medicine* (formerly the *Journal of Medical Education*) of the Association of American Medical Colleges. Foster is active in many local and national medical groups, and provides medical consultation in many foreign countries as well. In 1995 *Nashville Scene* named Foster Nashvillian of the Year which catapulted him as a high profile public speaker and health care professional. He is a professor of obstetrics and gynecology at Meharry and practices office gynecology.

While serving his internship in Detroit, Foster met St. Clair Anderson, a native of Washington, D.C., a graduate of Freedmen's Hospital School of Nursing at Howard University, and a nurse in the Dearborn Veterans Administration hospital. Later on she received her bachelor's degree from Tuskegee University. They married on February 6, 1960, in Salem Baptist Church in Washington, D.C., and are the parents of a daughter, Myrna Faye, and a son, Wendell. They have one granddaughter, Claire Elizabeth.

Current address: Professor of OB/GYN, School of Medicine, Meharry Medical College, 1005 Todd Blvd., Nashville, TN 37208.

REFERENCES

Foster, Henry W. Jr. Interview with Jessie Carney Smith, November 20, 1997.

———, with Alice Greenwood. *Make a Difference.* New York: Scribner, 1997.

"Foster Loses to Politics." *Nashville Tennessean,* June 23, 1995.

"Foster to Lead Teen Pregnancy Fight." *Nashville Tennessean,* January 30, 1996.

"Nashvillian of the Year." *Nashville Scene* (21 December 1995).

Jessie Carney Smith

Rube Foster

(1879–1930)

Baseball player, sports administrator, organization founder

For his achievements as a pitcher, manager, and founder and administrator of the first viable black baseball league, the Negro National League (NNL), Andrew "Rube" Foster became known as "The Father of Black Baseball." He made it a respectable sport, both financially and artistically. He also founded the American Giants—one of the greatest black baseball teams in history.

Biographical sources on Foster give conflicting information on his place of birth, dates of affiliation with baseball teams, and other details. When conflicts have occurred, generally information in the most recent published sources has been used in this essay. Andrew Foster was born September 17, 1879, in Calvert, Texas, a farming community near Waco. He was the son of Andrew, the presiding elder of Calvert's Methodist Episcopal Church, and Sarah Foster. As a child, Rube was asthmatic. He was as devoted to church each Sunday morning as he was to baseball each Sunday afternoon. He showed promise early as an organizer and administrator of the sport and operated a team while a grade school student. After Sarah Foster died, Andrew Sr. remarried and moved to southwest Texas. By then, baseball already drove young Andrew's life. After completing the eighth grade, he left school and ran away to Fort Worth to pursue his love of the sport.

When he was only 17–years old, Foster had already begun to play for the Fort Worth Yellow Jackets. He traveled with the Jackets in Texas and bordering states and was introduced early to the prejudice that existed then toward baseball players. Quoted in *Only the Ball was White,* Foster said that the players "were barred away from homes . . . as baseball and those who played it were considered by Colored as low and ungentlemanly." He also pitched during batting practice when big–league clubs held spring training in Texas.

In 1901, when he was 21–years old, the big, brash, six–foot four–inch tall player who weighed over 200 pounds pitched against Connie Mack's Philadelphia Athletics and

Rube Foster

caught the eye of big–city clubs. He refused an offer to pitch semiprofessional ball in Iowa and joined the black Leland Giants (also called the Chicago Union Giants) owned by Frank Leland, a veteran of black baseball in Chicago.

In 1902 Foster switched to E. B. Lamar's Union Giants, or Cuban Giants—a club from Philadelphia comprised of American blacks—earning $40 a month and 15 cents a meal for "eating money." By then he had become so self–assured about his talent that he called himself the best pitcher in the country. Sources disagree about the outcome of the first few games; however, *Blackball Stars* said that, after losing the first, Foster won 44 straight games. During this period as well, he beat the great Rube Waddell, whose record was 25–7 with the Philadelphia Athletics, and won the nickname "Rube" that was to remain with him for life. Foster led his team to victory over the Philadelphia Giants, the black baseball champions of the previous year. It has been said that the players disliked Foster, primarily because he "engaged in personalities" when he pitched. He was known also as a gunman and always carried his Texas six–shooters with him, which probably sparked the fear that many had of him.

Joins the Cuban X–Giants

Foster joined the Cuban X–Giants in 1903. Also a black American club from across town, they were rivals with the Philadelphia Giants. In the fall of 1903 Foster pitched in black baseball's first World Series, winning four games for the team. The Cuban X–Giants won the championship five games to two. According to legend, that year John McGraw of the New York Giants hired Foster to teach his screwball to Christy Mathewson, Iron Man McGinnity, and Red Ames. The Giants jumped from last place to second.

Nearly the entire Cuban X–Giants team switched to the Philadelphia Giants the next year and led them to victory in the World Series against their former club. Although Foster was sick when the three–game series opened, he won the first game 8–4, with 18 strikeouts, and the third and deciding game 4–2.

While data on Foster for 1904 are lacking, by 1905 he had remarkable power, winning 51 games and losing only five. According to *Blackball Stars,* Honus Wagner, Pittsburgh's great shortstop, called him "the smoothest pitcher I've ever seen." Foster knew how to unnerve rival players when the bases were loaded. He appeared jolly, unconcerned, and smiled generously; more often than not, he came out victorious. Foster continued a successful career, then about 1906, unable to get a salary increase, left for the Leland Giants as manager and player who would do the booking and run the team as well. He took seven teammates with him. He persuaded Frank Leland to fire his previous players and hire Foster's, resulting in a team so successful that they won the Chicago semipro league title and finished ahead of the City All Stars, who hired big league players.

In 1907 the Lelands won 48 straight games for a total of 110 that year. They lost only ten games and won the pennant in Chicago's otherwise all–white city league. The press as well as baseball managers continued to praise Foster's ability. *Blackball Stars* quotes an undated issue of the *Chicago Inter–Ocean* that commented on Foster's tricks, speed, and coolness, calling him "the greatest baseball pitcher in the country." Willie Powell remembered in *Blackball Stars* that

> Rube had a way to grip that ball, throw underhand, and he could hum it. And he was a trick pitcher, always tried to trick you into doing something wrong. If you were a big enough fool to listen to him, he'd have you looking at something else and strike you out.

In 1908 Foster changed the team's name to the American Giants to form what might have been the greatest black baseball team in history. In fact, according to *Blackball Stars,* Foster himself called it "the greatest team he ever assembled." Although there were other good black teams, the American Giants were consistently superior. In 1910 the team won 123 games out of 129. The Giants advertised their star–studded lineup and used heavyweight boxing champion Jack Johnson to hand out souvenirs to the women fans. The team's fame spread widely and rivaled that of the Chicago White Sox, who played two blocks from owner Charlie Comiskey's park. One Sunday in 1911 when the American Giants played, their attendance outdrew the Cubs and the White Sox.

There are conflicting accounts of this period in black baseball. According to *Only the Ball was White,* the American Giants were not formed until 1911, with players from the Leland Giants. Foster had entered a friendly partnership with John M. Schorling, a white tavern owner, who verbally agreed to a 50–50 split of receipts. This was a curious act for Foster, who was a shrewd businessman and should have known the importance of a signed contract.

Both in 1911 and 1912 the American Giants won the Chicago semipro crown. The Giants, who by now traveled by private Pullman, moved across the country for spring training and regular season games. They were an attraction to their fans, who watched them wear a different set of uniforms each day and use a variety of bats and balls. By 1916 when Foster was 35 years old, he had gained considerable weight and pitched less. That fall, however, the American Giants beat the Brooklyn Royal Giants to win the "colored World Series." Foster continued his tricks in the ball game and would do anything to win, including freezing baseballs before a game to spoil the opponent's ability land a good hit. Black baseball star James "Cool Papa" Bell said in *Blackball Stars*: "He built almost imperceptible ridges along the foul lines to insure that any bunted ball would stay fair while his race horses streaked across first base safely." He enticed young players to join his team by flaunting his immense prestige and bragging about the team's elaborate methods of travel.

The race riots of 1919 erupted in several cities. In Chicago alone, 38 people died. When Foster's team returned to their park, they found it occupied by tents of National Guardsmen. As well, during this period eastern black baseball teams threatened to raid Foster's team. By 1918 he paid his players $1,700 a month—more than teachers and mailcarriers earned—yet many of the players were illiterate. Still, the players were attracted by the promise of higher salaries from other owners.

Founds Negro National League

Black organizers had made unsuccessful attempts to form a viable black league in 1887 and again in 1906. In 1919, Foster called a meeting of the best black clubs in the Midwest and proposed the formation of a Negro National League and its governing body, the National Association of Colored Professional Base Ball Clubs. He used the *Chicago Defender* to launch his campaign for the new organization. Meeting on February 13–14, 1920, at the Kansas City YMCA (Young Men's Christian Association), owners of the black clubs drew up a constitution barring player raids and team–jumping, setting fines for unsportsmanlike conduct on and off the field, and other restrictions. Foster wanted an all–black enterprise that would be patterned after the major leagues but would ensure that money earned from the games would stay in black pockets. The group formed an eight–team league comprised of the American Giants, Joe Green's Chicago Giants, the Cuban Stars, the Detroit Stars, the St. Louis Stars, the Indianapolis ABCs, the Kansas City Monarchs, and the Dayton Marcos.

Foster foresaw the time when white and black teams would play each other in a World Series and wanted to be ready to integrate white teams when the time came. According to *Blackball Stars,* Foster told his colleagues, "We are the ship, all else the sea." Club owners criticized Foster, who became president of the league, for the power he had to serve as booking agent and hire umpires for the league since he owned a club himself. The players accused him of hiring umpires who favored the Giants. Foster survived the criticism in part by moving players from one team to another, apparently to effect parity among them. The colorful manager ran the league as a generous and benevolent autocrat, advancing loans to meet payrolls, sometimes from his own pocket. He helped players when they were in financial need. He believed in paying good salaries to keep good players. According to some writers, he may have saved black baseball.

The American Giants won the first three pennants in the new league, in 1920, 1921, and 1922. Foster's league prospered and prompted sports leaders in other parts of the country to form leagues. The Southern League was formed around this time, followed by the Eastern Colored League in 1923. Foster was unsuccessful in 1924 in his efforts to merge the NNL and the Eastern Colored League. Each manager wanted to retain his powerful position. When the teams met that year in a World Series, the Kansas City Monarchs of the NNL beat the Hilldale Club of the East. These games showcased some of the best black baseball players of the period.

Foster, who by then owned a barbershop as well as an automobile service shop, continued to oversee both the Negro National League and the American Giants. Throughout his baseball career he manipulated his players like robots and wholly directed his teams. According to *Total Baseball,* "Foster's teams specialized in the bunt, the steal, and the hit and run," which he advocated strongly, and characterized black baseball as well. A man with a remarkable memory who called everyone "darling," he never drank intoxicants but puffed on a big pipe. He was both feared and respected by his players and fellow baseball managers. He was often called the greatest baseball manager of any race and shared his talent with others by teaching baseball subtleties to a generation of black managers, including Dave Malarcher, Biz Mackey, and Oscar Charleston. But, according to some writers, he wore himself out.

After being exposed to gas that leaked in his room in Indianapolis in May of 1925, he became unconscious and had to be dragged from his room to safety. Although he recovered, he became prone to illness thereafter. He began to act erratically the following year. Foster was placed in the state insane asylum at Kankakee, Illinois, with baseball still on his mind. He constantly raved about wanting to get out of bed and win another pennant. After his death of a heart attack at age 51 on December 9, 1930, a mammoth funeral drew 3,000 mourners who stood outside the church in the falling snow to watch Foster's final trip to Chicago's Lincoln Cemetery. Unfortunately, Foster's wife was unfamiliar with his business arrangements and realized no benefits from his baseball ventures. Foster's partner, John Schorling, ran the club until 1928, then sold it to a white florist, William E. Trimble. Black business leaders revived the club briefly in the early 1930s, but it never reached its original level of power.

Although Foster's league died with him during the Great Depression, black baseball was reborn in the mid–thirties. By 1945 Jackie Robinson became the first black to enter major league baseball of the modern era. As well, 36 players from the old Negro leagues went to the majors during this early period. Foster's dream of an integrated baseball league was realized. The ultimate recognition for Foster came in 1981, when he was elected to the baseball Hall of Fame in Cooperstown, New York.

REFERENCES

Chalk, Ocania. *Pioneers of Black Sport.* New York: Dodd, Mead, 1975.

Holway, John B. *Blackball Stars: Negro League Pioneers.* Westport, CT: Meckler Books, 1988.

———. *Voices from the Great Black Baseball Leagues.* New York: Dodd, Mead, 1975.

Logan, Rayford W., and Michael R. Winston, eds. *Dictionary of American Negro Biography.* New York: Norton, 1982.

Peterson, Robert. *Only the Ball Was White.* Englewood Cliffs, NJ: Prentice–Hall, 1970.

Ribowsky, Mark. *A Complete History of the Negro Leagues 1884 to 1955.* New York: Carol Publishing Group, 1995.

Riley, James A. *The Biographical Encyclopedia of the Negro Baseball Leagues.* New York: Carroll & Graf Publishers, 1994.

Rogosin, Donn. *Invisible Men.* New York: Atheneum, Macmillan, 1983.

Thorn, John, and Peter Palmer, eds. *Total Baseball.* New York: Warner Books, 1989.

Young, A. S. "Doc." *Negro Firsts in Sports.* Chicago: Johnson Publishing Co., 1963.

Jessie Carney Smith

Norman C. Francis
(1931–)
College president, lawyer

Norman C. Francis, educator and lawyer, is the first layman and also the first African American male to serve as president of Xavier University of Louisiana, the only historically black Catholic college in the country. He is a leading educator who is often called on as a spokesperson on issues in black higher education.

Francis was born March 20, 1931, in Lafayette, Louisiana, of very religious parents. His father, Joseph A. Francis, was a shoeshine boy and later became a house painter. Norman Francis has three sisters and one brother. The parents taught their children the meaning of compassion, compromise, and hard work.

A graduate of St. Paul High School in Lafayette, he attended Xavier University in New Orleans and received the bachelor of arts degree in 1952. He continued his education at

Norman C. Francis

Loyola University Law School in New Orleans, where he became the first African American to receive the Doctor of Jurisprudence in 1955.

Xavier University of New Orleans opened on September 27, 1915, founded by Katherine Drexel and the Sisters of the Blessed Sacrament. The College Department was added in 1925. The school was the first and remains the only black Catholic college in the country. Francis joined the staff of Xavier in 1957 and served in various capacities. He has been dean of men, director of student personnel services, assistant to the president for student affairs, assistant to the president in charge of development, and executive to the president. He became president of Xavier University in 1968.

Under Francis's administration the school has made tremendous strides. He built the school's enrollment from about 1200 to 3400. Annually alumni contributions have soared from $15,000 to almost $300,000. The university's endowment has jumped from $2 million to more than $18 million. Francis resurrected the College of Pharmacy and built it into a program with a national reputation for excellence. He also focused on enhancing the institution's physical facility. An academic and science complex and a six–story $51 million library and resource center have been constructed with monies from two major fund–raising campaigns led by Frances.

During Francis's administration, Xavier has ranked first in the number of black graduates receiving degrees in physical sciences and second in the nation in placing African American students in medical schools. All the while, Francis has focused on achievement for the school and its students. Commenting on his vision for Xavier, Francis told *SEF News:*

> There's an African saying that goes, "It takes a whole village to raise a child." The parallel of that is that it takes an entire community to provide what we call a sound education to young people today.

Francis's entire working life has been spent working for causes such as civil rights, education, and religion. In recognition of his commitment to these causes, John J. McKeithen, former governor of Louisiana, selected Francis to participate in the special committee which recommended to the legislature in 1968 the discontinuance of separate public facilities for blacks and whites in Louisiana.

In 1972, Francis, along with 14 community leaders, founded the Liberty Bank and Trust, the first bank in New Orleans comprised predominantly of African Americans or other minorities as major stockholders. The purpose was to provide independence, power, and a strong economic development base for all citizens in the community.

In addition to serving in an advisory role to many leaders in academia, Francis often served in an advisory capacity with various political leaders in New Orleans, including former mayors Moon Landrieu and Ernest Morial. Beyond local and state activities, he served as an advisor to U.S. Presidents Richard M. Nixon, Jimmy Carter, Ronald Reagan, and Bill Clinton. Under the Ronald Reagan administration he was on the National Committee on Excellence in Education which wrote the 1983 publication *Nation at Risk.*

Francis now serves on more than 50 boards and commissions. He is chairman of the board for the Southern Education Foundation in Atlanta. His other board memberships include the National Foundation for Improvement in Education, Carnegie Foundation for the Advancement of Teachers, American Council on Education, American Academy of Arts and Sciences, Equitable Life Assurance Society of the U.S., the advisory board for the Environment Management for the Department of Energy, First National Bank of Commerce, the Greater New Orleans Board of the Louisiana Children's Museum, and the Greater New Orleans Foundation.

The numerous awards that he has received from local organizations include the Weiss Brotherhood Award from the New Orleans chapter of the National Association of Christians and Jews for distinguished service in the field of human relations in 1988; and the *New Orleans Time Picayune* Loving Cup, awarded annually to citizens of New Orleans who have worked unselfishly for the community without expectation of public recognition or material award in 1991. He has received 22 honorary degrees from various institutions throughout the country including Villanova University (1969), Tulane University (1980), Catholic University of America (1986), and Hunter College (1988).

Norman Francis is married to Blanchard Macdonald and has six children: Michael, Timothy, David, Kathleen, Patrick, and Christina.

Francis continues his work as a champion for educational reform on local, state, and national levels. Despite the widespread presence of violence and drug abuse in this country, it is his philosophy that society must not give up on its youth. He told *Black Issues in Higher Education:*

> We have to try and stop it, and I think those of us in the universities need to reach out to the parents and teachers and churches, indeed the whole community and try to harness this human capital of our young people today. We have to at least try. That's something I have committed myself to.

REFERENCES

"Board and Staff Notes." *SEF News* 9 (Winter 1994): 2.

Boulard, Gurry. "Norman Francis Continues to Chart New Course for Xavier: Educator Marks 25th Anniversary with Big Goals." *Black Issues in Higher Education* 10 (10 February 1994): 38–39.

"Francis Urges Residents to Meet Two Challenges." *New Orleans Time Picayune,* June 8, 1992.

Xavier Herald 69 (14 October 1993): 3.

"Xavier President, Norman Francis is Loving Cup Winner." *New Orleans Time Picayune,* March 29, 1992.

"Xavier's President Celebrates 25 Years." *New Orleans Time Picayune,* June 8, 1993.

COLLECTIONS

Materials on Norman Francis include his papers in the Office of the President and in the University Archives, Xavier University.

Theodosia T. Shields

John Hope Franklin

(1915–)

Historian, author, lecturer, educator

On September 29, 1995, John Hope Franklin, a scholar of U.S. history, received the nation's highest civilian award, the Presidential Medal of Freedom. According to the program, it is awarded by the President of the United States "to those persons whom he deems to have made especially meritorious contributions to . . . the United States, to world peace, or to cultural or other significant public or private endeavors." In so honoring Franklin, President Bill Clinton spoke of Franklin's outstanding contributions. The citation read in part: "His extraordinary work in the field of American History and his studies of the South have earned John Hope Franklin the respect and admiration of people throughout the world. . . . Following his maxim to 'look history straight in the face and call it like it is,' he has helped to define who we are and where we have been, and he has encouraged each of us to look forward to where we are going.''

Although it had not been his first choice of careers, when introduced to the exhilaration of exploring historical problems by Fisk University Professor Theodore Currier, Franklin chose to become an historian. He told the *Winston–Salem Journal,* that he committed himself not just to ''a life of learning,'' but to a life ''involved in *truth* and learning.'' According to *Strong Men and Women,* from his mother, Mollie Parker Franklin, who was his ''first and best teacher,'' Franklin learned early ''never to be satisfied by anything but the best.''

Franklin did not stop his formal studies until he had earned a Ph.D. at Harvard University. With the subsequent publication of *From Slavery To Freedom,* an authoritative text in African–American history, and such works as *The Militant South and Reconstruction after the Civil War,* studies that constituted intrepid assaults upon misleading or racist historiography, Franklin came to be known for his high standards, prodigious research, felicity of language, clarity of thought, and compelling revisionist interpretations in his landmark publications. His colleagues in academia have acknowledged this by electing him to the highest offices of professional and scholarly organizations, including the American Historical Association and Phi Beta Kappa National Honor Society. The recipient of more than 100 honorary doctoral degrees and scores of prestigious awards, in the last decade of the twentieth century, David Levering Lewis wrote in *John Hope Franklin: The 90th Birthday Celebration* that there is a consensus that Franklin is ''a pioneer scholar, a splendid humanist, a shining model to generations of students, scholars, and activists.''

John Hope Franklin—named after John Hope, the former president of Atlanta University who on different occasions had taught each of Franklin's parents was born on January 2, 1915, in Rentiesville, Oklahoma, an all–African American town in McIntosh County, to Buck Colbert Franklin and Mollie Parker Franklin. Mollie, a teacher who had earned her certificate at Roger Williams University, and Buck, a lawyer who had attended Roger Williams University and Atlanta Baptist College, had married in 1903. Thereafter they had lived briefly in both Ardmore and Springer, Oklahoma (then Indian Territory). According to *The Vintage Years,* they moved to Rentiesville ''to be free from the pressures and insults that they had experienced in the larger world,'' after Buck Franklin's eviction from a Shreveport courtroom by a judge who insisted that ''no 'nigger lawyer' could represent clients in his court.'' In Rentiesville, Buck Franklin farmed, practiced law, edited *The Rentiesville News,* and served as both justice of the peace and postmaster while his wife, who had taught school in Mound Bayou, Mississippi, prior to her marriage, became an elementary school teacher in the public schools.

Franklin was the youngest of four children. His sisters, Mozella and Anne Harriet were born in 1906 and 1913, respectively. His brother, Buck Colbert, Jr., was born in 1907. Franklin married Aurelia E. Whittington of Goldsboro, North Carolina, a Fisk graduate and librarian, in 1940. To that union was born one son, John Whittington Franklin, on August 24, 1952. In later years, Franklin's family came to include one foster son, Bouna N'diaye of Senegal, West Africa.

John Hope Franklin

The Formative Years

Franklin, a precocious child who sat in his mother's elementary school classroom in Rentiesville, learned to read and write before the age of five because of his mother's tutelage and exposure to the lessons of the upper elementary grades. At home and at school, his mother was a teacher with high standards. In 1921, seeking to increase his earnings and improve the quality of life for his family, Franklin's father left Rentiesville, which Franklin said in *The Vintage Years* had proven to be less than ''a bastion of racial unity,'' and moved to the city of Tulsa. The family temporarily remained in Rentiesville. There Franklin attended public school, skipping a grade ''to conform to the level of learning that most clearly identified [him] with [his] intellectual peers. . . . Thus , when [he] was nine years old [he] was in the sixth grade.''

While separated from his father, the young Franklin experienced the indignity and virulence of racism. The family had more than its share of unsettling experiences, which included anxiously awaiting word about Buck Franklin's safety following the infamous 1921 Tulsa race riot and the ejection of Mollie Franklin, John Hope, and Anne from a train when Mrs. Franklin refused to move out of the coach designated for whites. By December of 1925, however, the family reunited in Tulsa.

The adolescent Franklin completed his secondary education in Tulsa's Booker T. Washington High School. Despite hardships resulting from financial difficulties and racial segregation, Franklin's parents emphasized self–confidence, equality, and racial pride. Consistently, they continued to expose their children to the life of the mind. "I had two highly intelligent parents, [whose] . . . discussions were high level," Franklin once remarked in the *Winston–Salem Journal.* "I had a father who read and wrote every night. I grew up thinking that's what you did every night you either read or wrote." At the age of 16, Franklin graduated as valedictorian of his high school class and won a scholarship to Fisk University, an historically African American university in Nashville, Tennessee, that had been founded in the nineteenth century.

Franklin entered Fisk in 1931 when virtually all Americans were being adversely affected by the Great Depression. Since the scholarship was insufficient and family funds limited, Franklin worked in the library and the dining hall to earn money. In his first year of college, Franklin was determined to follow in his father's professional footsteps. He told the *Winston–Salem Journal*: "My father would always take me down to the courthouse and introduce me to the lawyers and judges." He remembered, in *Emerge* magazine, "When I went into the courtroom with him,. . . . if it was a jury trial, I'd sit at the table with him. . . . I admired him so. . ."

In Franklin's second year, he reached a significant turning point in his life. Theodore S. Currier, a Harvard–trained white professor of history from Maine who had joined the faculty of Fisk at age 22 and by 1932 was serving as the chairperson of the history department, introduced Franklin to history—its perplexities and problems, its issues and interpretations, its continuity and changes. Franklin later explained in *Currents* the influence of his Fisk mentor, Theodore Currier: "He raised questions that pushed [our] mind[s] right to the edge." Franklin knew that law had been the right choice for his father, but for Buck Franklin's younger son, history and teaching had irresistible appeal. Franklin abandoned his pursuit of a career in law and decided to devote himself to historical studies. An excellent student who was also a popular student leader, Franklin served as president of the campus chapter of his fraternity, Alpha Phi Alpha, and in his senior year was elected student body president. In that capacity, he gave leadership to programs as well as to student protests against racial injustices such as lynching. Franklin graduated from Fisk in 1935, earning his bachelor of arts degree magna cum laude. Although, at that time, Fisk had no Phi Beta Kappa chapter, Franklin was a founding member of Fisk's chapter, established in 1953.

Receiving financial assistance from Theodore Currier, who borrowed $500 to help Franklin attend Harvard, Franklin entered the university's graduate program in history during the fall of 1935. Franklin's first choice for his field was British history, but he knew primary research was required and he believed that he would have no opportunity to travel to England. Franklin decided his field of concentration would be U.S. history and he would subsequently focus on history of the South, then an emerging field. He took courses with professors whose rigorous requirements were met with aplomb by the young Franklin. Franklin would later recall in *Emerge,* "I admired [my father] so because he never let it out of his mind that he was as good as anybody in th[e] courtroom. I grew watching him and imbibing that. So that when I got to Harvard, I didn't think anybody there was any better than I was. . . ." Franklin earned his Master of Arts degree in 1936 at the age of 21. He worked hard and devoted almost all of his time and energy to his graduate studies. Franklin made time, however, to do some special teaching of his own. Remembering his mother's teaching and his own experiences, Franklin befriended a 50–year old neighbor and taught him how to read and write.

After a year of teaching history at Fisk University during the academic year 1936–37, Franklin returned to Harvard for the academic years 1937–38 and 1938–39 with the support of the Edwin Austin and Julius Rosenwald Fund fellowships. Franklin's time was spent completing the requirements for the Ph.D., editing his first refereed journal article on Edward Bellamy (which appeared in *New England Quarterly* in December of 1938), and taking his examinations. For Franklin's advanced studies, Arthur Schlesinger Sr. served as his advisor, and Paul H. Buck supervised Franklin's dissertation. Franklin's dissertation research required his return to the South and he taught while investigating primary sources on free African Americans in antebellum North Carolina. During these years of dissertation research and writing, Franklin was reminded how little Harvard credentials meant in the American South with its own apartheid. Among other experiences of racial discrimination as a young scholar, he was denied permission to sit with white researchers in the North Carolina State Archives and shunted off to a separate, isolated room. Such impediments to research notwithstanding, Franklin wrote an outstanding dissertation of publishable quality and, in 1941, Harvard University awarded him the Doctor of Philosophy degree in history.

Early Academic Career

Franklin had served as a history instructor with a M.A. degree at his alma mater, Fisk University, in Nashville, Tennessee. He held the first professorial appointments of his academic career, however, in North Carolina and Washington, D.C. Combining research and teaching, Franklin served as a professor of history on the faculties of St. Augustine's College of Raleigh, North Carolina, from 1939 to 1943, North Carolina College for Negroes in Durham (now North Carolina Central University), from 1943 to 1947, and Howard University of Washington, D.C., from 1947 to 1956. "With five preparations in widely disparate fields . . .," he wrote in *Race and History,* he "learned more history than he had learned [while studying] at Fisk and Harvard." At North Carolina College as well as at Fisk, St. Augustine, and Howard, Franklin taught many of the brightest and best African American undergraduate students of the 1930s, 1940s, and 1950s. In these early years, he also learned more about himself and his commitments. He wrote in the same source that, less than two years into his career, he declined an invitation to become dean of an African American liberal arts college "on the grounds that [his] work in the field of history precluded [his] moving into college administration.''

Although he never regretted the decision to remain a scholar–teacher rather than a college administrator, Franklin recognized that during these years, for an African American, any career path meant confronting racial segregation. Train conductors seating Nazi prisoners of war while forcing African American citizens to stand and staff of archival repositories and libraries discriminating against African American scholars in the most capricious ways are examples of such racial discrimination. In contrast, however, opportunities in combination with Franklin's dogged determination, perseverance, discipline, and industriousness resulted in noteworthy achievements. While teaching at historically African American institutions of higher education, mainstream publishers printed works in which Franklin disclosed history of African Americans that countered myths of inferiority and insignificant achievement. In 1943, Franklin's revised dissertation was published by the University of North Carolina Press as *The Free Negro in North Carolina, 1790–1860.* Four years later Franklin completed, and Alfred Knopf released, the first edition of *From Slavery To Freedom, A History of Negro Americans.* This work was dedicated to his supportive and encouraging wife, Aurelia, who since their marriage in 1940 had often read and critiqued manuscripts written by her husband.

During these years, Franklin's energies were given to family, teaching and research. It was a time of great accomplishments. In what would be the beginning of the establishment of an international reputation, he traveled during 1951 to Europe where he taught at the Salzburg Seminar in American Studies. In the following year, John Hope and Aurelia Franklin became the parents of John Whittington. Franklin regularly uncovered notable primary sources that would assist him in his work on the militant South during the antebellum period and the era of Reconstruction. It was an exciting time, as well, because African Americans were moving more aggressively to demand civil rights. When historical expertise was needed, Franklin responded to the calls of Thurgood Marshall, counsel for the National Association for the Advancement of Colored People (NAACP) Legal Defense and Educational Fund.

Career Varies in the Post–Brown Era

In 1956, the year of the publication of his controversial *Militant South, 1800–1860,* news of Franklin's desegregation of Brooklyn College's history department and appointment as chair of the 52–person department appeared on the front page of the *New York Times.* His becoming the first African American to head the history department at a major predominantly white academic institution was discussed at length. No mention was made of the new chairperson's encounters with racial discrimination while searching for housing to accommodate his family of three in the vicinity of Brooklyn College. During his eight years at Brooklyn College, Franklin published his pathbreaking revisionist study, *Reconstruction After the Civil War* (1961). He served as Pitt Professor of American History and Institutions at Cambridge University in England from 1962 to 1963 and in 1963, the centennial of Abraham Lincoln's Emancipation Proclamation, Doubleday published Franklin's monograph, *The Emancipation Proclamation.*

By his own admission in *Race and History,* ''There came a time in [his] own teaching career when [he] realized that . . . [he] would never be able to write on all the subjects in which [he] was deeply interested'' and he determined that he should consider a move to an institution in which he could work with graduate students. The University of Chicago provided just such an opportunity and many more. In 1964, he joined the history faculty of the University of Chicago. He immediately began teaching graduate students and undergraduates. Within three years, he was chosen to serve as departmental chairperson and headed the department from 1967 to 1970. He was appointed the John Matthews Manly Distinguished Service Professor in 1969. Continuing his research and scholarship throughout his tenure at Chicago from 1964 to 1982, Franklin not only published *A Southern Odyssey: Travelers in the Antebellum North* (1976) and *Racial Equality in America* (1976), a series of lectures given by Franklin for the bicentennial of the nation, but also began editing a series entitled ''Negro American Biographies and Autobiographies'' for the University of Chicago Press. Particularly rewarding to him during his 18 years at the University of Chicago was his supervising more than 30 dissertations of students who later published over a dozen books. During his professorship at the University of Chicago, Franklin's influence as a teacher had its most tangible results with respect to the training of young scholars aspiring to academic careers. It was Franklin's goal, as published in the *Winston–Salem Journal,* to ''instill in his students a high standard of scholarship;'' as he publicly contended, ''you can't have that without having a high standard of integrity, because the essence of scholarship is truth.''

In 1980, for reasons related to research and publication goals, his health, and the severity of the Chicago climate, Franklin took a leave of absence and moved to Durham, North Carolina, where he became the Mellon Fellow at the National Humanities Center. He later retired in 1982 from the University of Chicago, but retained his title of John Matthews Manley Professor Emeritus. Although courted by a number of academic institutions, Franklin eventually accepted an appointment as the James B. Duke Professor of History at Duke University. In this capacity, he was a member of the history department's faculty from 1982 to 1985. Thereafter, he assumed emeritus status with the history department and limited his teaching to service as professor of legal history, an interest of his earlier years.

While at Duke University Franklin published several works: *George Washington Williams: A Biography,* Franklin's personal favorite; *Race and History: Selected Essays, 1938–88,* which he dedicated to his secretary of more than 30 years, Margaret Fitzsimmons; and *The Color Line: Legacy for the Twenty–first Century.* In January of 1995, Duke University expressed appreciation to Franklin for his service in a university–wide celebration, chiefly organized by Vice–

Provost George Wright. Fellow Fiskite and prize–winning historian David Levering Lewis delivered an eloquent and brilliant keynote address that not only traced the life and work of Franklin, but also offered an assessment of his contributions to history, historiography, and social progress. The proceedings were later published by Duke in *John Hope Franklin: The 80th Birthday Celebration.*

Publications and Scholarship

Franklin is an exceptional and indefatigable researcher as well as a prolific scholar. Franklin authored 12 books. In addition to those already mentioned, his books include *Land of the Free,* which he wrote with John Caughey and Ernest May in 1963; and *Illustrated History of Black Americans* (1970). Franklin edited ten other works: *The Civil War Diary of James T. Ayers* (1947); T. W. Higginson's *Army Life in a Black Regiment* (1962); Albion Tourgee's *A Fool's Errand* (1965); *Three Negro Classics* (1965); *The Negro in the Twentieth Century,* coedited with Isadore Starr, (1967); *Color and Race* (1968); W. E. B. Du Bois's *The Suppression of the African Slave–Trade to the United States, 1638–1870* (1969); *Reminiscences of an Active Life: The Autobiography of John R. Lynch* (1970); *Black Leaders of the Twentieth Century,* co–edited with August Meier, (1982); and *African Americans and the Living Constitution,* coedited with former student Genna Rae McNeil, (1995). Franklin also has written more than 125 scholarly articles about U.S., Southern, and African American history. Kenneth B. Clark, eminent scholar, friend, and colleague of Franklin for more than 40 years, commented in *Currents*: ''[John Hope Franklin] has filled a void in probing and communicating the role of race as an integral part of American History.''

Franklin is most widely known for *From Slavery To Freedom,* now in its seventh edition and co–authored with former student Alfred Moss Jr. Since its first edition of 1947, this work has sold over three million copies, has been translated into Chinese, Japanese, German, French, and Portuguese, and has maintained its distinction as the authoritative history of African Americans.

In the post–*Brown v. Board of Education* era, Franklin's 1956 *Militant South* ''was among the earliest works heralding an interpretive shift to a political–cultural paradigm in which economic and political forces are focused through the lens of hegemonic belief systems.'' Also according to David Levering Lewis, Franklin ''elevated the South's pandemic violence into the organizing principle of its society.'' Franklin's 1961 book on Reconstruction, *Reconstruction After the Civil War,* as the distinguished historian William Leuchtenburg reminded us in the *Duke Law Journal,* ''did more than any other volume to correct the racist assumptions that, unhappily, once prevailed.'' With new evidence amassed from historical research, Franklin wrote of African American agency in political leadership and participation as well as reform during this brief period of biracial experimentation with democracy. In subsequent historical writing, Franklin continued to contribute findings from extensive research and offered analyses to illuminate not only the history of African Americans and the South but also that of the United States.

Remarkably prolific, Franklin began his career as part of a generation that began with W. E. B. Du Bois's *Black Reconstruction* in 1935, yet boasted work of Carter G. Woodson and Charles Wesley, but also included studies of his friends and professional colleagues such as Rayford Logan, Benjamin Quarles, and Helen Edmonds. Work in progress includes three collaborations: one edited biographical work with his son, John Whittington Franklin, on the life of Buck Franklin Sr., John Hope Franklin's father; another with former student Loren Schweninger, ''Dissidents on the Plantation: Runaway Slaves''; and with Alfred Moss Jr. an eighth edition of *From Slavery To Freedom.* To this list Franklin has added a fourth project, his autobiography.

Public Service, Activism, and Advocacy

Franklin published in *Race and History* that:

> historians with no governmental connections should participate in the discussion of public policy issues, . . . raise questions about the operation of a given policy that is defended on the ground that it is in line with historic public policy, . . . [and] challenge the . . . validity of a traditional policy that is followed for the sake of tradition and not necessarily for the sake of the public interest.

Accordingly, having once been barred from the University of Oklahoma's graduate school, Franklin, in 1948, was pleased to testify as an expert witness in the case of Lyman Johnson who was seeking admission to the all–white history graduate program of the University of Kentucky. Later, in 1953, Franklin provided historical research for Thurgood Marshall and the other attorneys fighting racial segregation in the consolidated cases of *Brown v. Board of Education*: ''I wrote historical essays, coordinated the work of some researchers, and participated in the seminars that the lawyers regularly held,'' wrote Franklin in *Race and History* when describing his efforts to assist Marshall with responses to the Supreme Court's questions regarding the original intent of the framers of the Fourteenth Amendment. ''One might argue,'' Franklin continued, when considering the historian's role in relation to the development of public policy, ''the historian is the conscience of [the] nation, if honesty and consistency are factors that nurture the conscience.''

Beyond this professional role, Franklin has believed that being an historian has compelled his activism as a citizen. Unabashedly, he has admitted in *Emerge,* ''I think knowing one's history leads one to act in a more enlightened fashion. I can [not] imagine how knowing one's history would not urge one to be an activist.'' So it has been throughout his life that, as he noted in *Race and History,* he believed it ''necessary, as a black historian, to have a personal agenda, that involved a type of activism.'' Franklin deems activism and advocacy appropriate responses to the nation's history, policy, and traditional practices with respect to justice. Having been in England during the 1963 March on Washington, in 1965

Franklin joined the Selma to Montgomery March led by Martin Luther King Jr. "With more than thirty historians who came from all parts of the country to register their objection to racial bigotry in the United States," Franklin wrote in *Race and History* that he "marched from the city of St. Jude, Alabama to Montgomery."

In 1987, Franklin—with his friends and colleagues Walter Dellinger and William Leuchtenburg—traveled to Washington, D.C., in order to appear before the Senate Committee on the Judiciary and oppose the appointment of Robert Bork to the Supreme Court. With other past presidents of the Organization of American Historians, including Mary Frances Berry, a younger friend and distinguished scholar–activist, Franklin enthusiastically submitted an amicus brief in the racial discrimination case of *Brenda Patterson v. McLean Credit Union.* Franklin later added his voice to other proponents of civil rights, affirmative action, and intellectual excellence who opposed the nomination of Clarence Thomas to the U.S. Supreme Court. Franklin has written and taught history, but he has also helped to make it.

Recognition, Awards, and Honors

As of 1998, Franklin remains the only person to have been elected national president of the five major national organizations of scholars: the American Studies Association (1966–67), the Southern Historical Association (1970–71), the United Chapters of Phi Beta Kappa (1973–76), the Organization of American Historians (1974–75), and the American Historical Association (1978–79). In 1986, the American Studies Association established a John Hope Franklin Publication Prize and in 1987, Adelphi University inaugurated a John Hope Franklin Distinguished Lecture. Duke University not only chose, in 1995, to establish a research center for African and African American studies in honor of Franklin, but has commissioned a portrait of its James B. Duke Emeritus Professor of History to be placed with founders of the University and other distinguished Duke scholars in the university's library. To celebrate the fiftieth anniversary of the publication of *From Slavery to Freedom,* Duke University, the Association for the Study of Negro Life and History, and North Carolina Central University sponsored a symposium held in Durham on September 19 and 20, 1997.

Franklin has received more than 105 honorary doctoral degrees from colleges and universities in the United States and abroad. In addition to the 1995 Presidential Medal of Freedom, Franklin is the recipient of scores of awards and honors from states, national publications, organizations, and institutions of higher education. Among these are induction into the Oklahoma Hall of Fame (1978), citation by *Who's Who in America* for significant contributions to society (1978), the Jefferson Medal of the Council for the Advancement and Support of Education (1984), Black History Makers Award of the Associated Black Charities (1988), the first Cleanth Brooks Medal of the Fellowship of Southern Writers for Distinguished Achievement in Southern Letters (1989), Encyclopedia Britannica's Gold Medal for the Dissemination of Knowledge (1990), the Bruce Catton Award of the Society of American Historians (1994), the Sidney Hook Award of Phi Beta Kappa (1994), the Distinguished Service Award of the Organization of American Historians (1995), the first W. E. B. Du Bois Lifetime Achievement Award from the Fisk University Alumni Association (1995), and the coveted Spingarn Medal of the NAACP (1995). In June of 1997, President Bill Clinton appointed Franklin chair of the White House Initiative on Race and Reconciliation. The panel's charge was to lead a year–long dialogue about race.

Franklin is six feet tall and thin. He has closely–cropped gray hair and a moustache. He resides in Durham, North Carolina, and there continues his historical research and writing. Franklin's hobbies include fishing, listening to classical music, collecting African American art and cultivating more than 700 orchids, which he grows in his greenhouse. "He has often been called America's greatest black historian. But that term is a misnomer on two counts," according to William Leuchtenburg in the *Duke Law Journal.* "John Hope [Franklin] is one of America's greatest historians, indeed greatest scholars, . . . irrespective of race. And though he has written extensively on the black race, he ought to be thought of as a historian of the South, a historian of America, a historian of the human condition." That is consistent with Franklin's own assessment of himself as historian and scholar, fully committed to learning, truth and the creation of a better world. He defined himself in *Currents*: "I am a historian of the American people." His philosophy is noted further in *Race and History* when Franklin wrote: "I have never regretted the decision to remain a student and teacher of history. . . . From the time that I taught at the Salzburg Seminar in American Studies . . . , I have been a student and an advocate of the view that the exchange of ideas is more healthy and constructive than the exchange of bullets. . . . When we learn that this country and the western world have no monopoly of goodness and truth or of skills and scholarship, we begin to appreciate the ingredients that are indispensable to making a better world. In a life of learning that is, perhaps, the greatest lesson of all."

REFERENCES

Applebome, Peter. "Keeping Tabs On Jim Crow: John Hope Franklin." *New York Times Magazine* (23 April 1995): 34–37.

Baker, Beth. "Forcing Americans to Keep Faith." *AARP Bulletin* 38 (September 1997): 8, 20.

Briggs, Jimmie. "Dialogue: Hope of Our Past." *Emerge* 5 (March 1994): 21–24.

Franklin, John Hope. *Race and History: Selected Essays, 1938–1988.* Baton Rogue: Louisiana State University Press, 1989.

———. *Racial Equality in America.* Chicago: University of Chicago Press, 1976.

———. *The Vintage Years: The First Decade.* Washington, DC: Cosmos Club, 1994.

"John Hope Franklin." Citation of President William Jefferson Clinton on the Occasion of the 1995 Presidential

Medal of Freedom Ceremony. Washington, DC, September 29, 1995.

"John Hope Franklin." Citation of the National Association for the Advancement of Colored People on the Occasion of the 80th Spingarn Medal Ceremony, Minneapolis, Minnesota, July 13, 1995.

John Hope Franklin: The 80th Birthday Celebration, Duke University, 1995. Program. Durham, NC: Duke University, African and Afro–American Studies Program, 1996.

"John Hope Franklin." *Winston–Salem Journal,* August 6, 1989.

Leuchtenburg, William. "Tribute John Hope Franklin." *Duke Law Journal* 42 (March 1993): 1022–27.

Matthews, Frank L. "The Genius of John Hope Franklin." *Black Issues in Higher Education* (13 January 1994): 16–22.

McRae, Shirley, and Norman McRae. *Strong Men and Women, Excellence in Leadership.* Richmond, VA, and Roanoke Rapids, NC: Virginia/North Carolina Power, 1996.

"Race Panel Head Sees Progress, Backsliding." *USA Today,* November 17, 1997.

Taylor, Karla. "The Flowering of Hope." *Currents* (October 1984): 9–11.

COLLECTIONS

Letters and papers of John Hope Franklin are at Duke University in the John Hope Franklin African and African American Research Center and in the Perkins Library.

Genna Rae McNeil

Samuel Fraunces

(1722?–1795?)

Entrepreneur, caterer, servant

One of New York's early black entrepreneurs and a patriotic servant to his country and to George Washington, Samuel Fraunces founded Fraunces Tavern and became a highly successful and well–respected businessman during the American Revolution. A caterer as well, Fraunces operated what would become one of the most historic and famous landmarks in New York City and the nation.

Samuel Fraunces, familiarly known as "Black Sam," was born a free black about 1722 on an island in the French West Indies. He was one of seven children. Nothing more is known of his early life or family background. Some of Fraunces's followers dispute his race, yet numerous scholars and printed accounts confirm that he was black. He moved to New York City in 1957. From 1759 to 1762 he became a caterer and was proprietor of the Mason's Arms, located on Broadway. In 1762 Fraunces purchased property known as the "De Lancey mansion," located at the corner of Broad and Pearl streets for two thousand pounds. The mansion was built as a residence in 1719 and in 1757 became a warehouse and store. A few months later he opened a tavern there that bore the royal title "Sign of Queen Charlotte" or the Queen's Head.

Fraunces left the tavern in 1765 and established Vauxhall, a garden and museum located on the North River in upstate New York. He charged the public four shillings to view the works in the wax museum. Apparently, the business was not successful. He returned to the inn in 1770, about the time the American Revolution began. The site of the tavern has a curious history. Although Fraunces was not at the site at the time, according to James Weldon Johnson in *Black Manhattan,* it was at Fraunces Tavern that the New York Chamber of Commerce was organized in 1768. When Fraunces returned, the business became known as Fraunces Tavern and served as a favorite meeting place for rebellious groups, such as the Sons of Liberty who met there in 1774 and later dumped East Indian tea into the river. As well, during the British occupancy of the area red–coated officers frequently drank at the tavern as they discussed upcoming maneuvers.

While his wife, Elizabeth, managed the tavern in his absence, Fraunces joined Washington's army, serving as a private. In 1776, Fraunces's daughter, Phoebe, became Washington's housekeeper at his residence, Abraham Mortier's house, located atop then–suburban Richmond Hill. Thomas Hickey, a regular visitor at the tavern and a self–professed British deserter, became one of Washington's personal bodyguards. When Phoebe Fraunces became romantically involved with Hickey, he became confident that she would support his plot to kill Washington by adding poison to his dinner. Instead, as Phoebe served Washington, she warned him of the danger and Hickey later confessed to the conspiracy, was court–marshaled, and hanged.

The New York Provincial Congress held a celebration dinner at Fraunces Tavern for the uncovered plot, where at least 31 toasts were proposed and drunk. Phoebe Fraunces became a heroine and her father prospered from her fame and his own as well.

The public knew Fraunces as a connoisseur of wines and an excellent steward. In May of 1783, when Washington and Sir Guy Carleton held a peace conference, Washington asked Fraunces to provide refreshments. The tavern was also the site of major celebration when the British evacuated the city. It is said that Washington was a frequent visitor to the Fraunces Tavern and on December 4, 1783, delivered his famous farewell speech to his officers there.

Fraunces was exceptionally well–liked and well–respected. The American Congress and the New York State Legislature rewarded him financially for his attention to American prisoners and other patriotic services. Sometime later Fraunces sold his tavern for 1,950 pounds and enjoyed a short–lived retirement in the New Jersey countryside. When Washington was inaugurated as President and then moved into the White House at 3 Cherry Street in New York City, he summoned Fraunces to become the steward of his household. Fraunces supervised the household staff at the mansion. When the nation's capital moved to Philadelphia, Fraunces and his family moved with Washington to the new site and his work as steward continued. Fraunces died about 1795 and was survived by his wife, Elizabeth, two sons, and five daughters.

The Sons of Revolution purchased Fraunces Tavern in 1905 and restored it as an historical building. Fraunces Tavern continues to stand in the Wall Street district of New York City, near the New York Stock Exchange. The oldest historic site in the city, its bicentennial was celebrated in 1976, during which the tavern offered an early American dinner at 1775 prices of three shillings and five pence, or 76 cents. Illustrations documenting the tavern's history are on display in the Long Room, where Washington held his farewell banquet. The room has been restored to its original appearance at the time of the fete. A restaurant is also operated from the site.

Samuel Fraunces is celebrated for his service during the American Revolution, both in the military and in other patriot causes. His tavern is the site of important events in the early history of this country.

REFERENCES

Cantor, George. *Historic Landmarks of Black America.* Detroit: Gale Research Inc., 1991.

Johnson, Allen, and Dumas Malone, eds. *Dictionary of American Biography.* New York: Charles Scribner's Sons, 1943.

Johnson, James Weldon. *Black Manhattan.* New York: Knopf, 1930.

O'Dwyer, Paul. "Correcting Ethnic History." *Crisis* 79 (February 1972): 59–60.

"Profiles." *Black Enterprise* 6 (June 1976): 121–27, 214.

Stewart, Ted. "George Washington and Black History: The Pros and Cons of the 'Father of Our Country.'" *Sepia* 25 (January 1976): 50–56.

Jessie Carney Smith

E. Franklin Frazier

(1894–1962)

Sociologist, educator, writer, activist

E. Franklin Frazier was a prolific writer who gained national and international recognition. He diligently studied black America's family, youth, church, and middle class in an effort to boost black self–perception and self–respect. Beginning with his doctoral dissertation, *The Negro Family in Chicago* (1932), and ending with his posthumous *The Negro Church in America* (1962), Frazier's impressive 30–year legacy of books, research articles, monographs, and other writings remain authoritative sources for subsequent generations of scholars. As an educator, Frazier combined theory with practice as he influenced several generations of college students.

Edward Franklin Frazier was born on September 24, 1894, in Baltimore, Maryland, to James and Mary (Clark) Frazier. His paternal grandfather was a slave who purchased freedom for his family and himself. Frazier's father never attended school, yet he taught himself to read and write, became a bank messenger, and bought a house for his wife, daughter, and three sons. James Frazier, a voracious reader and frequent writer of letters to the editor, stressed race consciousness and education with his offspring. James Frazier died in 1905 and every member of the household worked to maintain the family. Mary Frazier worked as a maid while ten–year–old Franklin sold newspapers before school and delivered groceries after school. He attended segregated schools in Baltimore. He graduated from the Colored High School in June 1912, with the school's annual Howard University scholarship.

Frazier entered Howard in the fall of 1912. Although he was a scholarship recipient, he worked odd jobs, such as dishwasher, boiler stoker, waiter, bellhop, and stevedore. At the same time, he pursued a rigorous liberal arts education that included courses in Latin, Greek, German, and mathematics. He was nicknamed Plato by his classmates, and his extracurricular activities centered around the drama, political science, German, and social science clubs as well as the National Association for the Advancement of Colored People (NAACP) and the Intercollegiate Socialist Society. Frazier served as class president in 1915. In 1916, he graduated cum laude with a bachelor's degree in arts and sciences. An example of Frazier's activism occurred during his freshman year. Howard planned to send a student delegation to march in Woodrow Wilson's inaugural parade. However, Frazier and other students discovered that the parade would be segregated and the Howard delegation would march at the end of the black American collegiate section. The Howard students protested that all colleges should participate alphabetically. A compromise was reached; Howard could lead the black marchers. Frazier, refusing to accept the compromise, did not march.

Begins Teaching Career

A few months after graduating from Howard, Frazier moved to Alabama where he taught mathematics at Tuskegee Institute (now University). He soon realized that he could not endorse Tuskegee's mission of emphasizing vocational education at the expense of scholarly pursuits. He was reprimanded for walking across campus with books and was advised that white visitors to the campus would assume that Tuskegee was focusing on intellect rather than vocation. Frazier left Tuskegee in 1917.

In 1917 he taught summer school at Fort Valley High and Industrial School—later Fort Valley State College, then University—in Georgia. He then took a position at St. Paul's Normal and Industrial School in Lawrenceville, Virginia, where he taught English and history from 1917 to 1918. About 1917 Frazier wrote, published, and sold *God and War,* an antiwar pamphlet. Anthony M. Platt, author of *E. Franklin*

E. Franklin Frazier

Frazier Reconsidered, cited Franklin's pamphlet as one of the first antiwar publications by a black American intellectual.

Frazier was drafted in 1918, and he worked from June to September at Camp Humphreys, Virginia, as a business secretary for the Young Men's Christian Association; his employer was the War Department's War Work Council. Frazier also taught mathematics at a Baltimore high school in 1918.

Frazier interrupted his teaching career to pursue graduate study. He was awarded a fellowship to Clark University in Worcester, Massachusetts in 1919. He completed his thesis, "New Currents of Thought among the Colored People of America," in an academic atmosphere that included sociology professors G. Stanley Hall and Frank Hankins, two proponents of Nordic superiority. Frazier received a master's degree in sociology in 1920. Later that year he received a Russell Sage Foundation fellowship to the New York School of Social Work. His investigation of 82 black New York City longshoremen was, according to Platt, one of the first empirical studies of Northern black industrial workers.

From 1921 to 1922, Frazier was an American Scandinavian Foundation (ASF) fellow at the University of Copenhagen. He was the first black American to apply for and receive an ASF fellowship, yet his name and photograph were excluded from the ASF's publication of 1921 to 1922 fellows. While in Denmark, Frazier lived with a local family. He researched Danish rural folk high schools and cooperative agriculture in an effort to improve the quality of life for poor Southern blacks. Before returning to the United States, Frazier attended the second Pan–African Congress in Paris where he supported a resolution condemning the United States' occupation of Haiti and debated Marcus Garvey's back–to–Africa plan.

Frazier arrived back in America in time to serve as director of summer school at Livingstone College in Salisbury, North Carolina. While attending a conference in Raleigh, he met Marie Brown, a member of a prominent Winton, North Carolina, family. She was also a promising poet who was encouraged by Countee Cullen to write; several of her poems were published in the 1920s. Her dream was to attend law school, but after she married Frazier in September 1922, she abandoned both her writing and her plans to attend law school.

During the fall of 1922, the couple moved to Atlanta, where Frazier assumed the dual positions of acting director of Atlanta University's School of Social Work (he would later be appointed director) and professor of sociology at Morehouse College. The Atlanta and Morehouse assignments involved career sacrifices: Frazier abandoned potential northern jobs with the NAACP and the National Urban League and postponed doctoral study.

Frazier's five–year stay in Atlanta was highly productive. He transformed the two–year–old, understaffed School of Social Work with a student body of only 14 into a professional program that attracted black students from across the nation.

Despite his demanding schedules at both Atlanta University and Morehouse, Frazier pursued other endeavors. During the summer of 1923 he began his first doctoral classes at the University of Chicago. He also wrote several short stories and one play, and took photographs that appeared in *Crisis,* the magazine of the NAACP. In 1925 a Frazier essay won first prize in the National Urban League's literary contest. Three years later he won the Carl Van Vechten prize for an essay that was published in *Opportunity.*

Publishes Sociological Research

Frazier was a prolific writer during his Atlanta years. He wrote at least 33 articles and a number of book reviews that were published in various professional and civil rights organizations' publications. His writings during this period led the *Encyclopedia of African–American Culture and History* to identify him as "part of a cadre of activists, intellectuals, and artists who after World War I formed the cutting edge of the New Negro Movement that irrevocably changed conceptions of race and the politics of race relations." In his essay, "Durham: Capital of the Black Middle Class," which appeared in Alain Locke's anthology, *The New Negro* (1925), Frazier encouraged readers to realize that the New Negro/ Harlem Renaissance as more than creative expression; black Americans were respectable workers, producers, entrepreneurs, and middle class. This theme was reiterated in his article, "La Bourgeoisie Noire," published in *Modern Quarterly* (1928), in which he asserted that black Americans were heterogeneous due to class, property, and family distinctions.

In "Racial Self–Expression," an essay published in Charles Johnson's *Ebony and Topaz* anthology in 1927, Frazier downplayed the debate over whether black Americans should develop their own unique culture or conform to American culture. He stressed the roles of history and society in shaping black American experience as opposed to a biological inheritance, and advocated black American group efficiency.

Nationally, Frazier was recognized as a prominent black American intellectual, yet Atlanta University's Board of Trustees and white faculty viewed Frazier's writings as militant and requested his resignation. When Frazier refused to resign, he was fired in 1927 although, in an attempt to avoid controversy, the board announced that Frazier had resigned anyway. Further controversy was generated with the publication of Frazier's article, "The Pathology of Race Prejudice" in *Forum* in June 1927. In this article he compared racism to abnormal behavior characterized by delusional thinking and paranoia. After the Atlanta press attacked the article, Frazier and his wife received lynching threats. They heeded their friends' advice to leave Atlanta immediately.

The couple moved to Chicago where Frazier continued his doctoral studies, supported by a grant from the Rockefeller Foundation and a part–time job as the Chicago National Urban League's research director. He received a $12,000 grant from the Social Science Research Council for a three–year study of the black family, and after Frazier completed all coursework for the degree, he and his wife moved to Nashville, Tennessee, in 1929. There Frazier was appointed research professor of sociology at Fisk University. He completed his dissertation, "The Negro Family in Chicago," and was awarded a Ph.D. in August of 1931. According to G. Franklin Edwards in *Dictionary of American Negro Biography,* Frazier's dissertation "was comparable to the classic study *The Philadelphia Negro* published by W. E. B. Du Bois in 1899." In 1933 Frazier was hailed further as one of 32 promising young black leaders and was invited by the NAACP to participate in a conference focusing on black life at Joel E. Spingarn's estate.

Frazier remained at Fisk until 1934. As he had at Atlanta University, he published many writings. In addition to his dissertation, Frazier wrote approximately 12 articles while at Fisk. He influenced the development of the Social Work Program there. Frazier's demanding schedule did not deter him from protesting racial injustice when a Fisk student was expelled for attempting to desegregate a theater near campus, when Fisk's dean of women and a student died after an automobile accident because the segregated hospital near Chattanooga refused to admit them, and when a young black man was lynched in Nashville.

Moving to Washington, D.C., in 1934, Frazier began a professional association with Howard University that lasted 28 years. He was appointed professor and head of the Department of Sociology, and from 1935 to 1943 he also served as director of the Social Work Program. He developed the program in social work, reorganized the Department of Sociology's curriculum, and masterminded its growth from a student enrollment of 200 in 1934 to approximately 2,000 by 1949. He was also extremely competent in the classroom; his students nicknamed him Forceful Frazier because he was a demanding, stimulating, and motivating professor.

Continues Sociological Research

During his years at Howard, Frazier added to his impressive body of research. Among the articles published during this period were "The Status of the Negro in the American Social Order," in *Journal of Negro Education* (July 1935), "Sociological Theory and Race Relations," in *American Sociological Review* (June 1947), "Ethnic Family Problems: The Negro Family in the United States," in *American Journal of Sociology* (May 1948), and "The Negro Middle Class and Desegregation," in *Social Problems* (April 1957).

Frazier also participated in a number of research projects funded by various organizations during this period. After the Harlem riot of 1935, New York City mayor Fiorello LaGuardia appointed a panel to investigate causes and prevention. Among the panel members were Countee Cullen and A. Philip Randolph; Frazier served as research director. For eight months, 30 researchers helped him conduct an in–depth study for the Harlem Commission. This was Frazier's first large scale research project, and *The Negro in Harlem: A Report on Social and Economic Conditions Responsible for the Outbreak of March 19, 1935* was the end result. In 1940 he published *Negro Youth at the Crossways,* a study funded by the American Youth Commission. Frazier's subjects were black adolescents in Louisville, Kentucky, and Washington, D.C., who were interviewed in an investigation of personality diversity. That same year, Frazier was awarded a Guggenheim Foundation grant to study Brazil's race relations and family life; one of the papers resulting from this understanding was "A Comparison of Negro–White Relations in Brazil and the United States." In 1942 when the Carnegie Corporation began a study of black America, Frazier evaluated the initial research prospectus and wrote an article, "Recreation and Amusement among American Negroes," which was shortened to several pages in the final report.

Frazier wrote several books during his Howard years. *The Negro Family in the United States* (1939), winner of the 1939 Anisfield Award for the most significant race relations publication, examined black American families from slavery to the mid–twentieth century and discussed problems in the black community within sociological rather than genetic contexts. A textbook, *The Negro in the United States* (1949), offered sociological and historical perspectives from a black sociologist's viewpoint. *Race and Culture Contacts in the Modern World* (1957) analyzed race relations from a global perspective and documented black American diversity. *Black Bourgeoise* (France, 1955; United States, 1957), Frazier's most controversial book, identified the emergence of a black middle class and highlighted its insecurities and weaknesses including conspicuous consumption and superficial attention to education, the arts, and other areas. Many blacks and whites alike were extremely critical of the book, and some book stores refused to sell it.

Even before the publication of *Black Bourgeoisie,* Frazier was viewed as a controversial figure by J. Edgar Hoover and others at the FBI as well as members of intelligence agencies and Congressional committees. He was harassed by the government from 1941 to 1962 for alleged Communist and subversive activities. Throughout two decades of intense governmental pressure, Frazier remained an academician and a man of dignity who would not be intimidated. When Frazier testified before a Congressional committee in 1955, Anthony Platt wrote that he boldly asserted, "If you want to hear me discuss Communism. . .then you come to my class in Sociology and hear what I have to say about Communists, all aspects of Communism." A few years later, just prior to his death, Frazier intended to write Secretary of State Dean Rusk and professional organizations protesting that scholars were harassed because they were black and/or participated in international organizations.

During the entire ordeal, Frazier earned great distinction in the academic community. In 1942 he was appointed resident fellow at the Library of Congress. He was a founding member and president (1943–44) of the District of Columbia Sociological Society, president of the Eastern Sociological Society (1943–55), vice–president of the African Studies Association, and president of the American Sociological Society. Upon assuming the ASA office, Frazier became the first black American to head a primarily white national professional organization. He was later awarded the ASA's MacIver Award.

In 1949 Frazier relinquished the chair of Howard's Department of Sociology. From 1951 to 1953 he served as chief of the Division of Applied Sciences of the United Nations Educational, Scientific, and Cultural Organizations (UNESCO). During that time he lived in Paris, traveled to Africa as well as to the Middle East, and lectured at the University of London, the University of Edinburgh, and the University of Liverpool. He retired as professor emeritus of sociology in 1959, although he continued to teach in Howard's Program of African Studies (1959–62) and at the Johns Hopkins School of Advanced International Studies (1957–62).

Terminally ill with cancer, Frazier died of a massive heart attack on May 17, 1962. He was survived by his wife, Marie. Later that year, his *The Negro Church in America,* which traced slavery's impact on the church's role in the lives of black Americans, was published posthumously.

REFERENCES

Contemporary Black Biography. Vol. 10. Detroit: Gale Research, 1996.

Logan, Rayford W., and Michael R. Winston, eds. *Dictionary of American Negro Biography.* New York: Norton, 1982.

Platt, Anthony M. *E. Franklin Frazier Reconsidered.* New Brunswick, NJ: Rutgers University Press, 1991.

Salley, Columbus. *The Black 100: A Ranking of the Most Influential African Americans, Past and Present.* New York: Citadel Press, 1993.

Salzman, Jack, David Lionel Smith, and Cornel West, eds. *Encyclopedia of African–American Culture and History.* New York: Macmillan Library Reference USA/Simon and Schuster Macmillan, 1996.

COLLECTIONS

The Frazier Papers are housed at Howard University's Moorland–Spingarn Research Center.

Linda M. Carter

Morgan Freeman

(1937–)

Actor, dancer, singer, director

Morgan Freeman, a versatile actor of stage, television, and film, has been recognized for his exceptional work through three Obie awards and nominations for Academy and Tony awards.

Freeman, the fourth child in his family, was born June 1, 1937, in Memphis, Tennessee, to Morgan Porterfield and Mayme Edna Revere Freeman. Morgan Freeman's mother sent him to live with his maternal grandmother in Charleston, Mississippi, at a very early age. Freeman's world changed at the age of six, however, when his grandmother died. He then returned to live with his mother, who traveled from Chicago to Nashville, Tennessee, and finally settled in Greenwood, Mississippi. Freeman has said little about his biological father or his early childhood but, in *New York* magazine, referred to this period as a difficult family situation.

At the age of eight Freeman began to display his acting ability in a school play in Greenwood, where he played the role of Little Boy Blue. His interest in acting became more focused when he was in the seventh grade. In hopes of gaining a girl's attention, Freeman pulled her chair away from her. His teacher took him out of class. He recounted the incident in *New York* magazine thus:

> I thought sure I was gonna be 'xpelled. But he opens this door and flings me into this room, and there's this English teacher and he asks me, "You ever done any actin'?" Well, under the circumstances, I'm quick to say yes. Turns out there's these dramatic tournaments—every school does a play—

Morgan Freeman

> and the winner goes to the state finals. Well, we do this play 'bout a family with a wounded son just home from the war—I play his kid brother. We win the district championship, and dadgummit, I'm chosen as best actor. All 'cause I pull this chair out from under Barbara.

Although acting would become Freeman's forte, in 1955 he joined the U.S. Air Force hoping to become a jet pilot. His dream was shattered when he ended up as a radar technician. In *New York* magazine, Freeman attributed this outcome to racism and the "good old boy" network in the South. After a few years, he left the military to pursue his career in acting. He moved to Los Angeles, looked up the Paramount Studio address, and then took a bus to the studio to get a job. Once there he obtained an application, which, to his chagrin, asked many questions about his knowledge of office equipment.

Determined not to give up on an acting career, Freeman took a job as a clerk at Los Angeles City College and enrolled in theater classes. He also took dance lessons because, according to *Ebony,* his stage movement teacher indicated that he had a "feel for dance" and should pursue it as a career. His first opportunity to dance professionally came when he successfully auditioned for the 1964 World's Fair in New York City. When the job ended, he sold hot dogs and orange drink at Penn Station in New York City. Freeman admitted, though, that acting classes, for him, were merely theory without practical application. In an interview with a *New York* contributor, Freeman said, "I'm not much for talking about acting. I've been called an intuitive actor . . . I go with what I feel. It doesn't do me any good to intellectualize about it."

Acting Career Begins

Feeling that his acting career was developing too slowly in Los Angeles, Freeman settled in New York during the 1960s and worked at a variety of odd jobs before landing his first feature role in an off–Broadway play in 1967. The play, *The Nigger–Lovers,* was short–lived but he had gained visibility. That same year he made his Broadway debut in the all–black version of the musical *Hello, Dolly!* starring Pearl Bailey and Cab Calloway. Freeman learned valuable lessons from both performers, but particularly from Bailey. He said in the *Philadelphia Tribune,* "She was so professional. Eight performances a week and she tore it up. I got lessons like that—mostly from women."

After the musical ended its run, Freeman worked primarily in off–Broadway plays for several lean years. He also married Jeannette Adair Bradshaw on October 22, 1967; from this union four children were born but, 12 years later, the marriage ended in divorce. The instability of his work ended in 1971, when he became a member of the Public Television Service series known as the *Electric Company,* an educational program aimed at teaching school–age children to read. Freeman appeared on the program for five years in the character of Easy Reader, a role with which he is still associated. In *Ebony* magazine, Freeman commented about a fear he has relative to this character. He quipped, "One of my nightmares is that I'm this old . . . guy and somebody about 50–years old comes up to me and says, 'Easy Reader, right?'" The monotony of the series, he said, forced him to drink heavily. After waking up one morning in 1975 from a night of boozing and finding himself on the floor, he acknowledged his problem and decided to stop drinking.

Three years later Freeman's performance as an aging wino, named Zeke, in *The Mighty Gents* earned him a Tony Award nomination and the Derwent Award for promising new actor. During the next two years, Freeman earned Obies for his off–Broadway performances in *Coriolanus,* 1979, and *Mother Courage and Her Children,* 1980. He also starred in *Gospel at Colonus,* 1983; other plays included *Othello* in 1982 and *The Taming of the Shrew* in 1990. The *Gospel at Colonus,* which *Rolling Stone* called "an ambitious musical merger of the Oedipus myth and a black Pentecostal church service, starring Freeman as the preacher," was about to resolve his bouts with unemployment. The year 1987 was a pivotal one for Freeman; major film critics recognized his stunning performance in the movie *Street Smart.* Although the movie was a box office failure, Freeman's role as the sinister Fast Black, a rough, insensitive, half–crazed pimp, earned him an Academy Award nomination.

Drives Miss Daisy

Just as the movie *Street Smart* was released, Freeman was opening in the stage version of *Driving Miss Daisy,* which earned him a third Obie for his portrayal of Hoke Coleburn, a black chauffeur for an elderly and wealthy white Southern woman. Freeman was also cast in the same role in the popular and successful film version in 1989. For his performance, Freeman won the National Board of Review Award and Golden Globe Award for Best Actor. After both events, he stated in *Ebony,* "It's like God said, I'm gon' treat this boy right, finally."

In 1989 as well, Freeman appeared in what he described as his favorite film, *Glory,* a film about the all–black Fifty–fourth Massachusetts Regiment during the Civil War. He accepted the role as sergeant major in the film because he felt an obligation to tell about the black historical legacy. The black legacy, according to Freeman in *Ebony,* "is as noble, is as heroic, is as filled with adventure and conquest and discovery as anybody else's. It's just that nobody knows it." His film credits, which totaled 29 as of 1998, include: *Who Says I Can't Ride a Rainbow?,* 1971; *Brubaker,* 1980; *Teachers,* 1984; *Clean and Sober,* 1988; *Lean on Me* and *Johnny Handsome,* 1989; *Unforgiven,* 1992; *The Shawshank Redemption,* 1994; *Outbreak* and *Seven,* 1995; *Moll Flanders,* 1996; *Kiss the Girls* and *Amistad,* 1997; and *Deep Impact* and *Hard Rain,* 1998. Freeman's career also has included directing. His debuted as a director in 1993 with the film *Bopha!,* starring Danny Glover.

When Freeman seeks relaxation, he turns to sailing, a skill he learned in 1967. Sailing is more than a passing interest, who approaches it much as he does his acting. According to Freeman, sailing is about pacing, taking and accepting risks and challenges. He usually travels in his 38–foot sailboat, the *Sojourner* (named for Sojourner Truth), with his second wife, Myrna Colley–Lee, a costume and set designer, and his eight–year–old granddaughter, E'Dena.

Freeman's versatility, patience, and perseverance have elevated him to the realm of America's greatest actors. Freeman keeps it all in perspective; he referred to himself as a character actor rather than a star, explaining in *Reunion,* "Once you become a movie star, people come to see you. You don't have to act anymore and I think that is a danger."

Current address: c/o Jeff Hunter, ATTN: Donna M. Lee, Executive Assistant, Triad Artists Inc., 888 7th Ave., Ste. 1602, New York, NY 10106.

REFERENCES

DeCurtis, Anthony. "Morgan Freeman." *Rolling Stone* (5 May 1988): 27.

"Morgan Freeman Talks About His Craft: Veteran Actor Stars in New Film, 'Moll Flanders.'" *Philadelphia Tribune,* June 11, 1996.

"Morgan Freeman to Be Interviewed on the Audio Journal in Worcester." *Reunion,* March 31, 1996.

Wetzsteon, Ross. "Morgan Freeman Takes Off." *New York* (14 March 1988): 54–66.

Whitaker, Charles. "Is Morgan Freeman America's Greatest Actor?" *Ebony* 45 (April 1990): 32–34.

Patricia A. Pearson

S. B. Fuller
(1895–1988)
Entrepreneur

Equipped with a sixth–grade education, a desire to succeed, and a talent for sales, S. B. Fuller invested $25 to build a company that reached multimillions of dollars in assets. He made door–to–door sales successful in both white and black communities and became known throughout the country as the head of Fuller Products Company. His training techniques guided others in establishing multimillion–dollar businesses of their own.

Widely known as S. B. Fuller, Samuel B. Fuller, was born in Monroe, Louisiana, in 1905, to parents who were sharecroppers. By the time he was nine years old he had learned the value of door–to–door sales, perhaps from experiences in his community. Fuller dropped out of school when he was in the sixth grade. When he was 15–years old, the Fullers moved to Memphis, Tennessee. While nothing more is known about his father, Fuller's mother died two years later and apparently the seven children provided for themselves without government assistance.

Perhaps in search of a better living than he had in Memphis, Fuller hitch hiked to Chicago in 1928 and found work as a coal hiker. Later Fuller worked as an insurance representative for Commonwealth Burial Association; after four years he was promoted to a managerial position. Assisted by his friend Lestine Thornton, whom he later married, Fuller spent $25 to buy soap that he peddled from door–to–door. Since the investment proved successful, he soon he put $1,000 in the venture; Fuller Products Company, now an infant business, was incorporated in 1929. Fuller established a line of 30 products and hired salespeople to market them door–to–door, primarily on Chicago's South Side where there was a concentration of black people. By 1939 his business had grown from a small office space above a store to a small factory, also located on the South Side. By expanding his sales force to meet the needs of the market, Fuller had become one of the city's most prominent black businessmen.

Determined to expand his business, in 1947 Fuller acquired Boyer International Laboratories, a white cosmetics manufacturer. In an effort to avoid criticism and possibly boycotts from whites who were loyal to Boyer products—Jean Nadal Cosmetics and H. A. Hair Arranger—the transaction remained secret. Fuller's customers then were primarily in the South: Atlanta, Birmingham, Montgomery, Dallas, and North Carolina.

Throughout the 1950s Fuller was known as a master salesman. His Chicago plant included such products as face creams, lotions, perfumes, and a complete line of household necessities. According to the November 1957 *Ebony,* the attractive, modest, and unbelievably energetic Fuller had a charming and magnetic quality about him. "He cajoles,

S. B. Fuller

questions, lectures, coddles and spanks his dealers with words that have come to be gospel to Fullerites.'' The formula for his success, cited in the November 1975 *Ebony,* is given in Fuller's own statements:

> The door–to–door salesman is the backbone of today's economy. . . . At Fuller Products Company, there's only one race—the human race. . . . A man doesn't have to have a lot of degrees behind his name to earn $10,000 a year.

A motivational genius, Fuller held spiritual meetings and published weekly bulletins, distributing them to independent dealers so that his sales people throughout the country always knew his doctrine on selling and living. Furthermkore, Fuller held annual meetings for his employees that allowed him an opportunity to honor them. For example, when Fuller and his staff met in Chicago's Palmer House in 1957, his top three salespeople were awarded automobiles and 24 other salespeople divided a jackpot of more than $3,000. Most of his administrative staff were college graduates. His employees, who called themselves ''Fullerites,'' included George Johnson, later owner of the well–known Johnson Products, and Joe L. Dudley, now owner of a multimillion–dollar–business in Greensboro, North Carolina.

By 1959 Fuller had built a 12–room, $250,000 dream house in Robbins, Illinois, where he and his wife lived alone. The suburban showplace was replete with maids' quarters, 14 telephones, imported Italian terrazzo tile floors, Indian wool carpeting, and Japanese raw silk draperies designed especially for the Fullers.

Business soared after the acquisition of Boyer and by the early 1960s sales peaked at $10 million. Sixty percent of his customers were white. Fuller now had a line of 300 products and employed 5,000 salespeople, 600 of whom were on direct payroll. His employees were black as well as white. According to the November 1957 issue of *Ebony,* he inspired his black employees by saying: ''Anything the white man can do, so can you. Don't ever feel the way is closed to you because you are a Negro. All you need is faith in God and faith in yourself.'' He also established 85 branches in 38 states. The astute businessman decided to diversify his investment further and bought an interest in J. C. McBrady and Company and Patricia Stevens Cosmetics. He became a major shareholder of the Pittsburgh Courier Publishing Company—the owner of the country's oldest black newspaper, the *New York Age,* and the *Pittsburgh Courier,* the largest circulated black newspaper.

Fuller also invested in real estate, farming, and cattle. He owned a real estate trust in New York City, the buildings housing branches of his business in various cities, and Chicago's Regal Theater—the city's counterpart of Harlem's Apollo Theater for black entertainment. He owned the Fuller Guaranty Corporation and Fuller–Philco Home Appliance Center.

Empire Crumbles

Fuller's business investments began to decline in the 1960s. When the White Citizen's Council learned that Boyer had been sold to a black, they proceeded to destroy the company by boycotting sales throughout the South. This was at the same time that blacks launched economic boycotts of southern white businesses. Drugstore chains owned by whites removed the Boyer line from their shelves. Since 60 percent of the company's sales came from whites, the boycott devastated Fuller Products Company. Jean Nadal products had no market at all and Fuller sold the line. Although he believed that black producers should sell to white customers just as whites sell to blacks, he attempted to move his market to northern whites and to blacks in both the North and South. When a New York liquor dealer reneged on its offer to buy the Jean Nadal line, Fuller's enterprise was devastated further. Fuller's attempt to reinvest his money in Fuller's Department Store, formerly the South Center Department Store on South Side Chicago, left him financially overextended.

In 1964 the Securities and Exchanges Commission charged Fuller with selling unregistered high interest promissory notes on his business and he was placed on probation for five years. In addition, a social service agent in Chicago campaigned against him for giving credit to clients on welfare. The agent persuaded the clients not to honor their debts with Fuller, leaving him with over $1 million in unpaid accounts. In late 1968 Fuller divested himself of his publishing concern and his retail stores. Despite his sale of the mortgages he held on real estate, in 1969 Fuller Products Company declared bankruptcy.

Many of Fuller's problems emerged from the negative attitude toward the African American community. Nonetheless, according to *African–American Business Leaders,* he rarely condemned whites. Instead, he lashed criticism out at blacks, saying that "Negroes lack initiative, courage, integrity, loyalty and wisdom." He accused the Chicago NAACP of ignoring blacks and working only to change the attitude of whites. Clearly, the views Fuller expressed around this time departed from his earlier assertion that blacks could succeed in business. He began to draw the black community's wrath and blacks boycotted his products. Fuller knew that his business suffered further by the black boycott; nevertheless, he never recanted his negative statements toward blacks in business and attributed the whole matter to a misunderstanding.

Fuller revived his business in the 1970s when he reorganized under the federal bankruptcy laws, and by 1972 the firm reported $300,000 in profits. Still based in Chicago, he had centers in Atlanta, Los Angeles, New York, Newark, Richmond, Greensboro, Washington, D.C., and Cleveland. By 1975 Fuller's company manufactured 60 products, including cosmetics and other beauty items.

In honor of Fuller's seventieth birthday, on June 4, 1975, George Johnson and Johnson Publishing Company executive John H. Johnson cosponsored a testimonial dinner. Illinois Governor Daniel Walker declared the day "S. B. Fuller Day" in his honor as well. Some 2,000 people paid $50 a plate to attend the Chicago event. John H. Johnson presented Fuller with a check for $70,000, representing funds raised at the event. According to the June 16, 1976, issue of *Jet,* George Johnson told Fuller, "If there had been no you, there would be no us." He also presented Fuller with 2,000 shares of Johnson Products stock valued at $50,000. All funds were to help Fuller rebuild his company.

Joe L. Dudley, who had worked with Fuller in the past and was already operating a booming cosmetics business in Greensboro where three years before he saw over 400 percent profit, teamed up with Fuller to develop a $100,000 business in the next ten years and to perpetuate door–to–door selling. By 1978 Dudley had become president of the Fuller Products Company.

During his lifetime Fuller divided his time between his company and other professional and civic activities. He found black businessmen in Chicago clannish and protective of each other. Sometime in the 1930s black businesses founded the Chicago Negro Chamber of Commerce and later included older, more established companies such as Park Sausage, Metropolitan Sausage, Supreme Life Insurance Company, and Baldwin Advertising. Their motto was "For your economic emancipation, patronize your own." Fuller was president of the organization until 1947 and, through parades and stickers, guided its continuous campaign for self–sufficiency. Fuller himself consistently supported black businesses. In the 1950s for example, when Johnson Products was burned out of its small cosmetics operation, Fuller enabled George Johnson and his company to use Fuller's facilities in the interim. That Johnson was a competitor was irrelevant.

In 1960 Fuller was chairman of the *Pittsburgh Courier*'s board of directors. By 1962 he also had become licensed as a Baptist minister and later became assistant pastor of St. Andrew Temple of Faith, Truth and Love Baptist Church. At some point Fuller was also head of the South Side chapter of the NAACP and the first black member of the National Association of Manufacturers. During President Eisenhower's administration he raised contributions for the Republican National Committee. He also contributed generously to various charities and scholarship funds.

Fuller died on October 24, 1988, at St. Francis Hospital in Blue Island, apparently of kidney failure. Funeral services were held at St. Andrew Temple of Faith. His survivors included his wife, five daughters, 13 grandchildren, and 18 great–grandchildren. Fuller is remembered as a trailblazing entrepreneur mentor to many of the leading black businesspeople in the country.

REFERENCES

"Blacks Pay Tribute to Businessman Fuller on His 70th Birthday." *Jet* 48 (26 June 1976): 28–32.

"Fete Planned for Founder of Fuller Products in Chicago." *Jet* 48 (29 May 1975): 9.

"Genius of Direct Selling." *Ebony* 13 (November 1957): 119–24.

Ingham, John N., and Lynne B. Feldman. *African–American Business Leaders: A Biographical Dictionary.* Westport, CT: Greenwood Press, 1994.

The Kaiser Index to Black Resources, 1948–1986. Vol. 2. Brooklyn: Carlson Publishing, 1992.

"A Man and His Products." *Black Enterprise* 6 (August 1975): 46–50.

"S. B. Fuller Dead; a Business Legend." *Chicago Defender,* October 25, 1988.

"Suburban Showplace." *Ebony* 14 (February 1959): 36–42.

"A Tribute to a Black Business." *Ebony* 30 (September 1975): 118–22.

Jessie Carney Smith

Gabriel.

See Prosser, Gabriel.

Newport Gardner
(1746?–1826)
Musician, community leader, schoolteacher, religious leader, missionary

Newport Gardner is the first African American singing master to win recognition beyond his local community. In addition, he was an effective leader in his community as he organized benevolent associations, taught black children, and worked to establish the first black church in Newport, Rhode Island. At the advanced age of 80, he returned to Africa as a missionary.

Gardner, then named Occramer Marycoo, was kidnaped from Africa in 1760 when he was about 14. He became the slave of a Newport, Rhode Island, man named Caleb Gardner, a prosperous merchant and Revolutionary War figure. A very intelligent young man, Newport Gardner thoroughly mastered English by the time he was 18 although he tried to hold on to his native African language in the hope of one day returning there. Many years later he was able to use the language to address two men he recognized as former acquaintances among a cargo of newly imported slaves and boasted of his ability to still speak it when he was nearly 80–years old. He learned to read after only a few elementary lessons and was equally adept in learning music. Sometime very early on in his life, Garner became a fervent convert to Christianity and joined the Congregational Church.

The indulgence of Caleb Gardner's wife allowed Newport Gardner to study music with an itinerant singing–master, Andrew Law, who taught in Newport in 1783. Gardner played no instrument, but he had a strong, clear voice. He soon became a singing master himself, winning a reputation as a strict disciplinarian. He and his mostly white pupils met in an upstairs room on High Street while he lived in Pope Street with his family.

Gardner is said to have begun composing music as early as 1764. It is possible that the song ''Crooked Shanks'' by a Gardner with no first name given and published in an 1803 collection is a Newport piece. His choral work ''Promise Anthem'' was performed in Newport and in Boston. Only the text is extant although tradition maintains that the piece was performed in a local Newport church as late as 1940. A January 13, 1826, advertisement in a Boston paper offered the anthem for sale. His compositions were said to be numerous and popular but no others beyond these two have been traced.

Music was at best a part–time vocation, and Gardner remained a slave until 1791. He was allowed to use his free time as he wished and keep any money he earned. He was a long–time sexton of the Congregational Church.

An account republished in *The Black Perspective in Music* describes Gardner as an adult: ''In his person he was tall, straight, and well formed; in his manners, he was dignified and unassuming.'' He early took on an important role in the black community. Gardner helped organize and became secretary of the first attested black mutual aid society, the African Union Society established November 10, 1780.

Samuel Hopkins, pastor of the Congregational Church from 1770 on, wished to send blacks back to Africa as missionaries. Gardner was a top candidate in his mind. Hopkins wrote of Gardner in a letter quoted in *Readings in Black American Music*: ''He is a discerning, judicious, steady, good man, and feels greatly interested in promoting a Christian settlement in Africa, and promoting Christianity there.'' Hopkins goes on to give the terms offered for Gardner's freedom.

Fate intervened that year. Gardner and nine other slaves won $2,000 in the Boston lottery. His share brought his own freedom nearer but not that of the members of his family. In this situation his master overheard Gardner fervently praying for their liberation and thereupon manumitted them all on very easy conditions. The plan to send black missionaries to Africa fell through at this time.

Gardner continued to be active in the church and in his community. In December of 1807 he helped organize the African Benevolent Society, which established a school for black children in 1808. Gardner became head teacher. From this society grew the first black church in Newport, the Colored Union Church, dedicated on June 23, 1825. Gardner and John Solmar Nubia were the two deacons, and an anthem by Gardner was sung at the ceremony.

Gardner was now about 80–years old, but his desire to return to Africa had not flagged. Gardner and John Solmar Nubia, who was about 70–years old, were among the 32 black emigrants to Liberia that set sail from Boston on the brig *Vine* on January 4, 1826. The two men were once again deacons together, this time of the newly formed 16–member church they were leading to Africa. At the church's organizing ceremony in Boston previous to the departure, the choir had agreeably surprised Gardner by singing his anthem. Gardner's wife had died by now, but at least one son, a man with a very fine bass voice, was in the party. Newport Gardner and John Solmar Nubia arrived in Monrovia on February 6, but both died about six months after their arrival.

While the identification cannot be entirely certain, it seems most probable that Gardner was the elderly person referred to in the description of the emigrants to Africa on the *Vine* quoted in both *Readings in Black American Music* and in *The Black Perspective in Music.* The sentiments are surely his:

> One aged black was among the number, who seemed to be filled with almost youthful enthusiasm for the cause. ''I go!'' he exclaimed, ''to set an example to the youth of my race; I go to encourage the young. They can never be elevated here; I have tried it for sixty years—it is vain.''

REFERENCES

Johnson, Allen, and Dumas Malone. *Dictionary of American Biography.* Vol. 4. New York: Scribner's, 1931.

Smith, Jessie Carney, ed. *Black Firsts.* Detroit: Gale Research, 1994.

Southern, Eileen. *Biographical Dictionary of Afro–American and African Musicians.* Westport, Conn.: Greenwood Press, 1982.

———. *The Music of Black Americans.* 2nd ed. New York: Norton, 1983.

———, ed. *Readings in Black American Music.* New York: Norton, 1971.

Wright, Josephine, and Eileen Southern, eds. ''Newport Gardner.'' *The Black Perspective in Music* 4 (July 1976): 202–07.

Robert L. Johns

Henry Highland Garnet
(1815–1882)
Abolitionist, religious worker

Henry Highland Garnet was a leading member of the generation of black Americans who led the abolition movement away from moral suasion to political action. Garnet himself did not stop with politics: he urged slaves to act and claim their own freedom. A constant theme throughout his life was the necessity for blacks to take their destiny into their own hands. Not only did he seek to build up black institutions, he became an advocate of colonization in the 1850s and after. He was also a firm Christian who devoted his life to ministry in the Presbyterian Church. His efforts were ably seconded by his oratorical skills which placed him in the front rank among his contemporaries.

Henry Highland Garnet was born into slavery near New Market, Kent County, Maryland, on December 23, 1815. His father, George Trusty, was the son of a Mandingo warrior prince, taken prisoner in combat. George and Henny (Henrietta) Trusty had one other child, a girl named Mary. George had learned the trade of shoemaking. The Trusty's owner, William Spencer died in 1824. A few weeks later 11 members of the Trusty family received permission to attend a family funeral. They never returned. Travelling first in a covered market wagon and then on foot for several days, the family group made its way to Wilmington, Delaware. There they separated; seven went to New Jersey, and Garnet's immediate family went to New Hope, Pennsylvania, where Garnet had his first schooling.

In 1825 the Garnets moved to New York City. There, after earnest prayer, George Trusty gave new names to the family. His wife Henny became Elizabeth, his daughter Mary, Eliza. Although the original first names of George and Henry are unknown, the family name became Garnet. George Garnet found work as a shoemaker and also became a class–leader and exhorter in the African Methodist Episcopal Church, Bethel, in Mott Street.

Henry Highland Garnet entered the African Free School in Mott Street in 1826. There he found an extraordinary group of school mates. They included Alexander Crummell, an Episcopal priest and a leading black intellectual, who was Garnet's neighbor and close boyhood friend; Samuel Ringgold Ward, a celebrated abolitionist and a cousin of Garnet; James McCune Smith, the first black to earn a medical degree; Ira Aldridge, the celebrated actor; and Charles Reason, the first black college professor in the United States and long–time educator in black schools. Garnet and his classmates formed their own club, Garrison Literary and Benevolent Association, and soon had occasion to demonstrate their spirit. Garrison's abolitionism had little mass support among whites at this time, and abolition meeting in New York City easily lead to mob violence. Thus, even the school authorities feared the use of his name for a club meeting at the school. The boys retained the club's name and moved their activities elsewhere.

As a boy, Garnet was high–spirited and quite different from the sober and quiet adult he later became. In 1828 he made two voyages to Cuba as a cabin boy, and in 1829 he worked as a cook and steward on a schooner from New York to Washington, D.C. On his return from this voyage, he learned that the family had been scattered by the threat of slave catchers. His father had escaped by leaping from the upper floor of the house at 137 Leonard Street—next door to the home of Alexander Crummell. His mother had been sheltered by the family of a neighboring grocer. His sister was taken but successfully maintained a claim that she had always been a resident of New York and therefore no fugitive slave. All of the family's furniture had been stolen or destroyed. Garnet bought a large clasp–knife to defend himself and wandered on Broadway with ideas of vengeance. Friends found him and sent him to hide at Jericho on Long Island.

Since Garnet had to support himself, he was bound out to Epenetus Smith of Smithtown, Long Island, as a farm worker.

Henry Highland Garnet

While he was there he was tutored by Smith's son Samuel. In the second year there, when he was 15, Garnet injured his knee playing sports so severely that his indentures were canceled. The leg never properly healed, and he used crutches for the rest of his life. (After 13 years of suffering and illness, the leg was finally amputated at the hip in December 1840.) Garnet returned to his family, which had reestablished itself in New York. He then continued his schooling, and in 1831 he entered the newly established high school for blacks, rejoining Alexander Crummell as a fellow student.

The leg injury may have sobered Garnet, who became more studious and turned his thoughts to serious consideration of religion. Sometime between 1833 and 1835 he joined the Sunday school of the First Colored Presbyterian Church, located at the corner of William and Frankfort streets. There Garnet became the protegé of minister and noted abolitionist Theodore Sedgewick Wright, the first black graduate of Princeton's Theological Seminary, who brought about Garnet's conversion and then encouraged him to enter the ministry. Wright baptized Garnet, and Garnet later preached Wright's funeral sermon.

Garnet married Julia Ward Williams (1811–1870) in 1841, the year he was ordained an elder. Julia Williams was born in Charleston, South Carolina, but came to Boston at an early age. She studied at Prudence Crandall's school in Canterbury, Connecticut, which was suppressed by law, and also at Noyes Academy. She taught school in Boston for several years. After her marriage she was head of the Female Industrial School while the family lived in Jamaica. When she was back in New York, she ran a store at 174 West Thirtieth Street, and in Washington, in the 1860s, she worked with freedmen. The couple had three children: James Crummell (1844–1851); Mary Highland (born c.1845), and a second son (born 1850). Some sources say this son died; however, a 20–year old Henry Garnet is listed as living with his father in the Pittsburgh city directory of 1870–71. There was also an adopted daughter Stella Weims, a fugitive slave. Henry Highland Garnet was noted for his ability to establish rapport with children and for his respect for his wife. In his eulogy Alexander Crummell remarked, "I was both struck and charmed with the same gallantry displayed to the wife *after marriage* that he had shown her before." Julia Garnet died in 1870, and about 1879 he married Susan Smith Thompkins (1831–1911), a noted New York teacher and school principal.

Seeks Higher Education

In 1835 Garnet, Alexander Crummell, and Thomas S. Sidney, classmates from New York, made the difficult journey to the newly–established Noyes Academy in Canaan, New Hampshire. Founded by abolitionists, Noyes was open to both blacks and whites and to men and women. (There Garnet met Julia Williams.) The students from New York were in New Hampshire by July 4, when they delivered fiery orations at an abolitionist meeting. A vocal minority of local townspeople were determined to close down the school and drive away the 14 blacks enrolled. In August they attached teams of oxen to the schoolhouse, dragged it away, and burned it.

The mob also surrounded the house where Garnet and some of the other blacks were living, and someone fired into the room he was occupying. That evening the mob gathered again but Garnet fired a shot which discouraged them. Although Garnet was ill with a fever, he and the two friends set out for New York. They crossed the mountains to Albany and came down the Hudson. On the steamboat blacks were forced to travel on the open foredeck. Garnet was now very sick, and his friends spread their coats under him and shielded him from the sun with an umbrella. On his arrival in New York, Garnet spent nearly two months in bed.

Fortunately, there was another institution which opened its doors to black students, and this time the local townspeople did not rise up physically to reject them. In early 1836 Garnet joined Crummell and Sidney at Oneida Institute in Whitesboro, New York. Garnet began in the preparatory department while his fellow students were listed as sophomores. In May 1840 Garnet attended the meeting of the American Anti–Slavery Society in New York and delivered a well–received maiden speech. In September, he graduated from Oneida with honors and settled in Troy, New York.

Establishes a Career

Even though Garnet was not yet ordained, he had been called as minister to the newly established Liberty Street Presbyterian Church at Troy, New York. Garnet studied theology with the noted minister and abolitionist, Nathaniel S. S. Beman, taught school, and worked toward the full establishment of the church whose congregation was black. In 1842 Garnet was licensed to preach and in the following year ordained a minister. He thus became the first pastor of the Liberty Street Presbyterian Church in Troy, where he remained until 1848.

Teaching and the ministry hardly filled all of Garnet's time. He assisted in editing *The National Watchman,* an abolitionist paper published in Troy during the latter part of 1842, and later edited *The Clarion,* which combined abolitionist and religious themes. Closely interwoven with Garnet's church work was his work in the Temperance Movement, in which he took a leading part. By 1843 he received a stipend of 100 dollars a year from the American Home Missionary Society for his work for abolition and temperance. When the society expressed its objections to ministers engaging in politics on Sundays, Garnet withdrew his services. His work for temperance was widely recognized. In 1848 one of the two Daughters of Temperance unions in Philadelphia was named for him.

State politics also brought Garnet into prominence. There were black state conventions from 1836 to 1850 (unfortunately only the minutes of the 1844 convention survive today). Garnet worked for the extension of black male voting rights in New York state, but a property holding qualification was imposed upon blacks. He presented several petitions to the legislature on this subject. However, the state property qualification remained the law until the adoption of the Fifteenth Amendment in 1870.

Gerrit Smith, a wealthy white abolitionist, decided to increase the number of black voters by giving some of his land to black farmers in 1846. Garnet was one of his agents in delegating land; most of his choices were still farming several years later.

Urges Rebellion

In 1839 the Liberty Party came into existence with abolition as one of its major planks. Although its vote in the 1840 elections was minuscule, the party set its sights on the 1844 election. Garnet became an early and enthusiastic supporter of this reform party. He delivered a major address at the party's 1842 meeting in Boston. He was also able to secure the endorsement of the revived National Convention of Colored Men, held in Albany in August 1843 for the party. Garnet gave a convincing demonstration of his oratorical powers soon afterwards when he turned around a New York City meeting convened to disavow the convention's action. Much to the organizers' disappointment the meeting ended by endorsing the Liberty Party. The year 1844 marked a peak for the party. Then the Free Soil Party and later the Republican Party began to attract reform–minded voters. Garnet was late and unenthusiastic in supporting the Republicans.

Garnet's turn towards activism marked his break with leading abolitionist William Lloyd Garrison, who rejected politics in favor of moral reform. Garnet's impatience with Garrison's position was expressed publicly as early as 1840 when he was one of the eight black founding members of the American and Foreign Anti–Slavery Society which formalized the split in the ranks of abolitionists. Garnet gave further proof of his disaffection in 1843. The August 1843 National Negro Convention in Albany, New York, gathered more than 70 delegates in the first such convention since the early 1830s. Garnet was a prominent member; in particular he was chairman of the nine–member business committee, which was charged with organizing the issues for discussion. He electrified the convention with a speech "An Address to the Slaves of the United States of America," in which he urged slaves to take action to gain their own freedom:

> You had far better all die—*die immediately,* than live slaves, and entail your wretchedness upon your posterity. . . . However much you and all of us may desire it, there is not much hope of redemption without the shedding of blood. If you must bleed, let it all come at once—rather *die freemen, than live to be the slaves.*

The audience was profoundly moved: some wept, others sat with clenched fists. Frederick Douglass, who was not ready to abandon Garrisonian moral suasion, joined with others in opposition to Garnet's position. Douglass spoke for more than an hour against adopting the speech. The rules were suspended to allow Garnet to reply for an hour and a half in a speech, which James McCune Smith said was Garnet's greatest. Unfortunately neither Douglass's speech nor Garnet's reply survive today. The original address was referred to the business committee for moderation and eventually failed to be adopted by one vote.

Garnet's call for action echoes that of *David Walker's Appeal* of 1829, and Garnet underlined the similarity in 1848, when he first published his speech together with the *Appeal* to support the Free Soil Party's campaign for the presidency. Part of the money for the publication is said to have come from abolitionist John Brown.

Just as Garnet was in the vanguard of the blacks who began to seek remedies in political action and even revolution, he also led the way in proposing emigration as a solution for black plight in the United States as proposed by the American Colonization Society. Since 1817 most American blacks condemned the American Colonization Society and were suspicious of the society's aims and of its creation, the nation of Liberia, which became independent in 1847. Garnet, however, was coming to favor black emigration to any area where there might be hope of being treated justly and with dignity. Bitter personal experience soon underlined his position: in the summer of that year he was choked, beaten, and thrown off a train in New York State.

Travels Abroad

Garnet moved from Troy to Geneva in 1848. Then in 1850 he went to Great Britain at the invitation of the Free Labor Movement, an organization opposing the use of products produced by slave labor. The following year he was joined by his family. There he remained for two and a half years, undertaking a very rigorous schedule of engagements. Both James McCune Smith and Frederick Douglass felt he was doing especially well because he was the first American black of completely African descent to appear there to speak in support of abolition. Douglass did not relax his general hostility to Garnet, however, and gave little attention to Garnet's activities abroad.

In the latter part of 1852, the United Presbyterian Church of Scotland sent Garnet to Jamaica as a missionary. He did effective work there until a severe prolonged illness caused his doctors to order him north. In 1855 he was called to Shiloh Church on Prince Street, where he became the successor of his mentor, Theodore S. Wright. It is reported that the church was in parlous condition, but Garnet soon had it flourishing again. His reputation as an orator and spokesperson grew, and his sermons were often printed in their entirety.

Although the support for emigration was growing in the black community, Garnet had to face sharp criticism for his position in favor of it, particularly from Frederick Douglass. Douglass commented sharply on a request for American blacks to go to Jamaica made by Garnet before his return. Criticism grew when Garnet founded the African Civilization Society in 1859. He explained the society's aims in an 1860 speech, reprinted in Ofari's book *"Let Your Motto Be Resistance,"* "We believe that Africa is to be redeemed by Christian civilization and that the great work is to be chiefly achieved by the free and voluntary emigration of enterprising colored people."

Alexander Crummell, Garnet's boyhood friend and fellow student who had established himself in Liberia after earning a degree from Cambridge University in England endorsed the goal, as did the influential West–Indian born educator Edward Wilmot Blyden. Garnet made a trip to England as president of the society in 1861. In conjunction with this trip he established a civil rights breakthrough by insisting that his passport contain the word Negro. Before this time the handful of passports issued to blacks had managed to skirt the issue of whether blacks were or were not citizens of the United States by labelling the bearer with some term such as dark. Although Garnet's and Martin Delany's efforts at colonization at this time were running in parallel and not coordinated, the pair agreed on aims. Garnet proposed a visit to Africa to follow up Delany's 1859 efforts there, but the plan fell through with the outbreak of the Civil War.

A side–effect of Garnet's support of emigration and his trip to England in 1861 was an attempt of the board of trustees of Shiloh Church to force him out as pastor. The controversy ended in 1862 when the congregation accepted the resignation of the entire board by a wide majority.

Supports Civil War Efforts

With the outbreak of the war, Garnet joined other blacks in urging the formation of black units. When this goal was realized during the beginning of 1863, he traveled to recruit blacks and served as chaplain to the black troops of New York State, who were assembled on Ryker's island for training. He led the work of charitable organizations which worked to overcome the unfavorable conditions initially facing the men due to wide–scale corruption and anti–black sentiments in the city.

Garnet's prominence made him one of the prime targets of a white working–class mob during the July 1863 draft riots in New York City when blacks and leading abolitionists were assailed. The rioters appeared on Thirtieth Street, where Garnet resided, calling for him by name. Fortunately his daughter had torn off the brass door plate with an axe, so the house escaped plundering, and several white neighbors helped conceal him and his family. In the aftermath of the insurrection, Garnet headed the distribution of charitable contributions collected by a committee of white merchants.

In March 1864 Garnet became pastor of the Fifteenth Street Presbyterian Church of Washington. D.C. There he delivered a sermon in the chamber of the House of Representatives on February 12, 1865, the first black to do so, and also one of the first blacks allowed to enter the Capitol. He moved his residence to Washington and became the editor of the Southern Department of the *Anglo–African.* As an assignment Garnet undertook a four month trip to the South at the end of the war, which included a visit to his birthplace.

Garnet accepted the presidency of Avery College in Pittsburgh in 1868, but returned to Shiloh Church in New York in 1870.

Alexander Crummell reported that Garnet went into a physical and mental decline about 1876 and that "sorrow and discouragement fell upon his soul, and at times the wounded spirit sighed for release." In this mood, in spite of the discouragement of his friends, Garnet actively lobbied for the position of minister to Liberia, which he obtained. Crummell recorded Garnet as saying:

> Please the Lord I can only safely cross the ocean, land on the coast of Africa, look around upon its green fields, tread the soil of my ancestors, live if but a few weeks; then I shall be glad to lie down and be buried beneath its sod.

Garnet's wish was granted. He preached his farewell sermon at Shiloh on November 6, 1881. He landed in Monrovia on December 28 and died on February, 12, 1882. He was given a state funeral by the Liberian government, and Edward Blyden preached the funeral sermon. When Alexander Crummell delivered his eulogy of Garnet in Washington, D.C., Frederick Douglass, his former opponent, and Henry McNeil Turner, Garnet's intellectual heir as leader of the emigration and black nationalist movement in the later nineteenth century, were platform guests.

Henry Highland Garnet was six–feet tall and a handsome man. Crummell, whose standards were high, said that he was no thorough scholar due to his constant illnesses but that he was outstanding for sheer intelligence and flair. Speaking from his own experience, James McCune Smith said that few persons who faced him in debate on the platform cared to do so a second time. His friends testified to his wit and humor, which made him popular, even among children.

Garnet was an important figure among black abolitionists. He was independent in forming his own views and bold in expressing them. At an early date he helped articulate many of the themes of black nationalism. He wished to build up black–controlled institutions, and in the early 1840s he was calling unsuccessfully for the establishment of a black printing company and a black college. He consistently supported black efforts of self–improvement, and included emigration as one of these efforts. It was his conviction that blacks must take their control of destiny that led him in 1843 to call upon slaves to take action and end slavery.

REFERENCES

Bell, Howard Holman, ed. *Minutes of the Proceedings of the National Negro Conventions: 1830–1864.* New York: Arno Press and the *New York Times,* 1969.

Brewer, W. M. "Henry Highland Garnet." *Journal of Negro History* 13 (January 1928): 36–52.

Crummell, Alexander. "Eulogium on Henry Highland Garnet, D.D." In *Africa and America.* Springfield, MA: Willey and Co., 1891.

Litwack, Leon, and August Meier, eds. *Black Leaders of the Nineteenth Century.* Urbana: University of Illinois Press, 1988.

Moses, Wilson Jeremiah. *Alexander Crummell.* Amherst: University of Massachusetts Press, 1992.

Ofari, Earl. *"Let Your Motto Be Resistance": The Life and Thought of Henry Highland Garnet.* Boston: Beacon Press, 1972.

Penn, I. Garland. *The Afro–American Press and Its Editors.* Springfield, MA: Willey and Co., 1891.

Proceedings of the National Convention of the Colored Men of America Held in Washington, D.C., on January 13, 14, 15, and 16, 1869. Washington, DC: Great Republic Book and Newspaper Printing Establishment, 1869.

Quarles, Benjamin. *Black Abolitionists.* New York: Oxford, 1969.

Ripley, C. Peter, ed. *The Black Abolitionist Papers,* Vol. 1. Chapel Hill: University of North Carolina Press, 1985.

———. *Witness for Freedom.* Chapel Hill: University of North Carolina Press, 1993.

Schor, Joel. *Henry Highland Garnet.* Westport, CT: Greenwood Press, 1977.

Simmons, William J. *Men of Mark.* Cleveland: George M. Rewell and Co., 1887.

Smith, James McCune. "Sketch of the Life and Labors of Rev. Henry Highland Garnet." Introduction to *A Memorial Discourse; Delivered in the Hall of the House of Representatives, Washington City, D.C., on Sabbath, February 12, 1865.* Philadelphia: Joseph M. Wilson, 1865.

Sterling, Dorothy, ed. *Speak Out in Thunder.* Garden City, NY: Doubleday, 1973.

Walker, David, and Henry Highland Garnet. *Walker's Appeal and Garnet's Address to the Slaves of the United States of America.* 1848. Reprint, Nashville: James C. Winston Publishing, 1994.

Willson, Helen M., Historical Society of Western Pennsylvania, letter to Robert Johns, September 21, 1995.

Robert L. Johns

Marcus Garvey

(1887–1940)

Organization founder, Pan Africanist leader, newspaper publisher, writer, entrepreneur

Marcus Garvey founded and led the Universal Negro Improvement Association and African Communities League (UNIA), the largest mass movement in African American history. The UNIA flourished from about 1919 to the mid–1920s and existed in almost 40 states domestically and more than 40 countries internationally. Estimates of its membership range as high as eleven million worldwide, making the UNIA also the largest Pan African movement of all time.

Marcus Mosiah Garvey was born on August 17, 1887, in St. Anns Bay, Jamaica, to Marcus and Sarah Garvey. He had one surviving sibling, a sister named Indiana. His father was a stonemason with a love for reading and a library in his home. His parents sometimes engaged in small–scale peasant farming.

It is difficult to surpass the eloquence of Garvey's own account of his beginnings and influences. He recalled in *The Philosophy and Opinions of Marcus Garvey,*

> My father was a man of brilliant intellect and dashing courage. He was unafraid of consequences. He took human chances in the course of life, as most bold men do, and he failed at the close of his career. He once had a fortune; he died poor. My mother was a sober and conscientious Christian, too soft and good for the time in which she lived. She was the direct opposite of my father.

Garvey received an excellent elementary education, but in lieu of secondary schooling he was apprenticed in his early teens to his godfather's printing business. At the age of 16 he moved to Kingston, Jamaica, where he became the country's youngest foreman printer. He also became active in politics, public speaking, and journalism.

In 1910 Garvey immigrated to Costa Rica, part of a large exodus of Caribbean workers seeking work in Latin America. He wandered for the next four years around Central and South America and Europe. He observed the plight of African descendants everywhere, agitated on their behalf, and worked at a variety of jobs. In England he worked for the foremost Pan

Marcus Garvey

African journal of the day, the *Africa Times and Orient Review,* published by the African Duse Mohamed Ali. In London he also attended law lectures at Birkbeck College of the University of London.

His travels and reading exposed Garvey to the universal suffering of the African race. Africa itself was in the last stages of European imperialist conquest. African Americans had largely lost the civil rights gained during Reconstruction. Disenfranchisement, Jim Crow, and lynching had become their lot. Africans in the Caribbean were mostly excluded from the political process and suffered the myriad discriminations associated with colonial status. Caribbean immigrants in Latin America were treated badly, even wantonly killed. Garvey pondered all of this as he prepared to leave England for home. He feared that a weak and prostrate African race was a standing invitation to reenslavement or even extinction. Towards the end of his European sojourn he had been reduced to penury in England and had come close to being repatriated as a pauper at public expense. But by the summer of 1914 Garvey was able to pay his own way home.

Before leaving Garvey read Booker T. Washington's autobiography, *Up from Slavery.* He admired Washington for his race pride and, above all, for his efforts to pull himself and his race up by their own bootstraps. For Garvey, Washington's book became the final key to unraveling the puzzle of his own life's work. Garvey later recalled in his *Philosophy and Opinions,* in a famous and much quoted passage:

> I asked: "Where is the black man's Government?" "Where is his King and his Kingdom?" "Where is his President, his country, and his ambassador, his army, his navy, his men of big affairs?" I could not find them, and then I declared, "I will help to make them."
>
> My young and ambitious mind led me into flights of great imagination. I saw before me then, even as I do now, a new world of black men, not peons, serfs, dogs and slaves, but a nation of sturdy men making their impression upon civilization and causing a new light to dawn upon the human race.

What Garvey lacked in money and influence he made up for in the intensity of his dream. He felt that the power of organization led to African advancement. And so within five days of arriving home on July 15, 1914, he founded the UNIA. Garvey corresponded with Booker T. Washington and led the UNIA on a round of social, charitable, and educational work throughout Jamaica. The organization's stated goals included the provision of educational facilities, upgrading the status of women, providing for the needy, building African power, and establishing a sense of "confraternity" within the race worldwide.

On March 23, 1916, Marcus Garvey arrived in New York to begin a five–month fund–raising lecture tour to finance his Jamaican operation. He would return to Jamaica to live more than 11 years later. In the interim he would become the best known, most loved, and most hated African in the world.

Soon after his arrival in New York Garvey toured the United States and Canada. Back in Harlem in 1917 he took to the streets, haranguing crowds on a regular basis. As his popularity as a street speaker grew, he hired a hall for weekly indoor meetings. By 1918, Garvey moved the UNIA from Jamaica to Harlem. The Harlem–based UNIA now took off into a period of explosive growth. Garvey's travels had yielded him valuable contacts and the movement became instantly international. By 1919 branches had been established or were in the making in Canada, the Caribbean, Central and South America, West Africa, and England.

UNIA Consolidates

Garvey moved to consolidate the new organization with great skill. A variety of subsidiaries and related ventures appeared. A Negro Factories Corporation appeared in 1918 and eventually employed over a thousand African Americans in a doll factory, a tailoring establishment, grocery stores, restaurants, a printery, and more. The *Negro World* weekly, soon to become the most widely circulated African newspaper in the world, began publication in 1918. The UNIA's most ambitious economic venture, the Black Star Line Steamship Corporation, launched its first ship in 1919. The line raised over $1,000,000 and its ships sailed to Haiti, Cuba, Jamaica, Costa Rica, and elsewhere. Its intention was to provide employment for many African seamen, dignified accommodation for African travelers, and a vehicle for Pan African trade and emigration.

The line was sabotaged by opportunists within and forces—including governmental—without, all compounded by the UNIA's lack of business experience and the rapid growth of the company, which almost overwhelmed the organizers. The Black Star Line, nevertheless, caught the imagination of African people around the world like nothing else. There were scenes of great rejoicing wherever the ships appeared. In Costa Rica, African workers stopped work for the day and inundated the Black Star Line ship with flowers and fruit. In Havana, Cuba, people rowed out to the ship in small boats and literally showered it with fruits and flowers. In Aiken, South Carolina, the African community chartered a special train to take them to Charleston to see a Black Star Line vessel.

In 1920 the UNIA held the first of several international conventions—the last being in Toronto, Canada in 1938. Twenty–five thousand people from around the African world filled New York's Madison Square Garden for the opening ceremony. There they elected Garvey president–general of the UNIA.

The conference produced one of African America's major historical documents in the Declaration of Rights of the Negro Peoples of the World. The declaration listed the major grievances of the race and put forward demands to redress them: it declared red, black, and green the colors of the race; it adopted the Universal Ethiopian Anthem as the UNIA's anthem; and it called for African history to be taught in schools attended by African children. The organization was divided into regions for better administration. A commissioner headed each region and organizers systematically traversed their regions, starting new branches, resuscitating faltering ones, adjudicating disputes, and spreading the word of Garveyism everywhere. The work of paid organizers was supplemented by many volunteers, often strangers to the organization, who spread the doctrine of Garveyism with missionary zeal.

Garvey was aided at the helm of the UNIA by a number of talented men and women, many of whom were important figures in their own right. These included John Edward Bruce, one of African America's most famous journalists; T. Thomas Fortune, the "dean" of African American newspapermen, editor of the UNIA's *Negro World,* and for many years a close confidant of Booker T. Washington; William H. Ferris, with a bachelor's degree from Yale and a master's from Harvard, who presided over the UNIA's literary activity; Lady Henrietta Vinton Davis, UNIA international organizer, Shakespearean actress, and former associate of Frederick Douglass; Hubert H. Harrison, Harlem's most popular scholar–activist; Amy Jacques Garvey, one–time personal secretary, *Negro World* associate editor, and Garvey's wife; Archbishop George Alexander McGuire, sometime chaplain–general of the UNIA and founder of the African Orthodox Church, and many others.

Up to early 1920 Garvey also benefited from the assistance of his first wife, Amy Ashwood Garvey. Ashwood claimed to be the UNIA's first recruit in Jamaica in 1914. She married Garvey in Harlem in 1919 but the marriage effectively lasted only a few months.

Ideology of UNIA Spreads

The spread of the UNIA was due to many factors. The New Negro radicalism of the war and post–war years provided a receptive milieu for Garvey's activities. Garvey's indefatigable energy, his powerful oratory, his moving writing style, and his general charisma drew people to him. Of great importance also was his ideology, for Garvey articulated a well–planned body of ideas that appealed to millions of people.

Garvey was a proponent of African nationalism. This had always been and continues to be an important influence in African American and Pan African life. Garvey's predecessors in this ideology included Paul Cuffee, John B. Russworm, Martin R. Delany, Henry McNeal Turner, Chief Alfred Sam, Henry Sylvester Williams, Edward Wilmot Blyden, and many others. Garvey succeeded like none of his predecessors of Pan Africanism, however, in channeling these ideas directly into a massive organization.

Race first, self–reliance, and nationhood were the three planks of Garvey's ideological platform. Race first meant that African people should put their self–interest first, as other races did. Garvey cheerfully allowed other groups a similar right, as long as it did not lead to the oppression of anyone else. Race first also meant that African people must see physical beauty in themselves, and African people should critique their own literature. Garvey expressed these ideas in his most famous essay, "African Fundamentalism," republished in the present author's book of the same title:

> The time has come for the Negro to forget and cast behind him his hero worship and adoration of other races, and to start out immediately to create and emulate heroes of his own. We must canonize our own saints, create our own martyrs, and elevate to positions of fame and honor black men and women who have made their distinct contributions to our racial history. . . . We must inspire a literature and promulgate a doctrine of our own without any apologies to the powers that be. The right is ours and God's. Let contrary sentiment and cross opinions go to the winds.

Race first could be seen in practically everything Garvey did, including his desire for an independent African media and his contention, in the tradition of Bishop Henry McNeal Turner, that African people should depict God in their own racial image and likeness.

Self–reliance meant simply that without the psychological benefits of doing for self, an oppressed people ran the risk of perpetual dependency and lack of independence.

Nationhood emphasized the necessity for political self–determination at all levels. Africa assumed special significance as the ancestral home of the race and a place of great natural potential. Garvey attempted in the early 1920s to move his headquarters to Liberia, the only independent country in

West Africa. He also planned to facilitate the immigration there of thousands of African American and Caribbean people, imbued with a pioneering spirit and having technical or educational skills to offer.

Opposition Towards UNIA

Garvey's phenomenal success brought with it an intense opposition from several disparate directions. Some felt eclipsed by his success; others opposed him on ideological grounds. Imperialist governments resented his radicalizing impact on their African subjects. J. Edgar Hoover, later head of the FBI, considered him a rabble rouser and a fit candidate for deportation. The Communist International was frustrated by Garvey's much greater success with the workers and peasants of the African world. The success of his "race first" idea seemed a reproach to their "class first" theories.

The African American integrationists of the National Association for the Advancement of Colored People (NAACP) and the powerful Jewish element who dominated this association waged all–out war on Garvey and the UNIA. W. E. B. Du Bois was the main spokesman for the NAACP. He maintained a constant barrage of criticism, both from the pages of the NAACP's *Crisis* and elsewhere. Garvey's Black Star Line was as much a source of annoyance to Du Bois as were his physical features, which Du Bois described as black and ugly. He described Garvey, in a famous *Crisis* editorial in 1924, as a "lunatic or a traitor."

Judge Julian Mack, an NAACP member and prominent Jewish leader, sentenced Garvey to the maximum jail term, imposed the maximum fine, ordered Garvey to pay the entire cost of the trial, and refused him bail after Garvey's conviction on a trumped–up charge of mail fraud in 1923. Early in the trial Garvey refused to rescue himself, despite his membership in the hostile NAACP, which had recently been waging a "Marcus Garvey Must Go" campaign.

The mail fraud conviction was the major reversal for which Garvey's enemies had long worked. Garvey was accused of defrauding subscribers to Black Star Line stock. After losing his appeal he entered Atlanta Federal Penitentiary on a five–year sentence in 1925. His sentence was commuted by President Calvin Coolidge in 1927 after millions of people signed petitions and otherwise clamored for his release. Commutation was accompanied by deportation, however.

It was during his trial and imprisonment that the most important of Garvey's books were published. All were compiled and edited by his wife, Amy Jacques Garvey. Amy Garvey published the seminal *Philosophy and Opinions of Marcus Garvey, or Africa for the Africans* in two volumes in 1923 and 1925. These consisted largely of Garvey's speeches and writings. Garvey hoped through these volumes to counter the misrepresentations of his work appearing in the major media. In 1927 Amy Garvey also published two volumes of Garvey's poetry, namely *The Tragedy of White Injustice* and *Selections from the Poetic Meditations of Marcus Garvey.* The title poem of the former compilation was a lengthy epic chronicling the raping, slaughter, and enslavement perpetrated by Europeans against other races. It was republished in Tony Martin's *The Poetical Works of Marcus Garvey.* It was very popular among Garveyites. Garvey's other major book, a secret course of instruction given to his top organizers in 1937, was first published 49 years later as *Message to the People: The Course of African Philosophy,* the seventh title in a series called "The New Marcus Garvey Library."

The Post–United States Years

Garvey returned to Jamaica on December 10, 1927, to the largest crowds the island had ever seen. Over the next few years he established two newspapers, *The Blackman* and the *New Jamaican.* In 1929 he held a spectacular Sixth International Convention of the Negro Peoples of the World, which attracted delegates from around the world. In the same year he founded the Peoples Political Party, one of the first modern political parties in the Anglophone Caribbean.

Garvey entered the race for the upcoming 1930 Legislative Council elections and was promptly arrested and jailed by the British authorities, at the start of a country–wide tour. The colonialists thought he committed contempt when he explained that if elected he would work to discourage judicial partiality. From his jail cell he entered the campaign for the Kingston and St. Andrew Corporation Council and won a seat. He was released shortly before the Legislative Council elections and lost. Apart from the disadvantage of a truncated campaign, most of his followers were disenfranchised in the restrictive colonial polity, where mostly white people and a few rich Africans could vote.

In the United States, meanwhile, the UNIA split into rival factions. One major faction remained loyal to Garvey and published the *Negro World* up to 1933. Another sought to supplant Garvey with a United States–based leadership. Garvey renamed the loyal faction the Universal Negro Improvement Association and African Communities League of the World. Whether loyal to Garvey or not, the UNIA remained an important presence in several North American cities, especially New York, into the 1950s.

In addition, several important new organizations rose out of the ashes of the UNIA. Most important was the Nation of Islam, whose leader, the Honorable Elijah Muhammad, is thought to have been a UNIA member in Detroit in the 1920s. Carlos Cooks's African Nationalist Pioneer Movement, an important Harlem–based organization in the 1950s and 1960s, was also an outgrowth of the UNIA. In Jamaica the founders of the Rastafarian movement came out of the UNIA and never lost their reverence for Garvey, despite differences of opinion over Haile Selassie of Ethiopia. (Garvey was critical of Selassie during the Italian aggression against Ethiopia in the 1930s. Selassie has always been the most revered figure in the Rastafarian pantheon.)

In 1934 Garvey relocated to London, England. He continued to publish *The Black Man* and toured Canada and the Caribbean. He died in London on June 10, 1940, after suffering a series of strokes. He was 52–years old. The period of his greatest glory had begun when he was barely into his thirties.

Garvey's body was returned home in 1964 amidst much pomp and splendor. The newly independent nation of Jamaica made him its first national hero. He remains one of the most popular historical figures around the African world and is frequently celebrated in poetry and song; in the naming of roads, buildings, and schools; on postage stamps and coins; and in the erection of statues bearing his likeness. Prime Minister Kwame Nkrumah of newly independent Ghana in 1957 named his country's merchant marine the Black Star Line. An imposing Black Star Square was constructed in Accra, Ghana. Adulation of Garvey peaked during his centennial year of 1987, when governments, organizations, and individuals around the world honored him in many ways. Congressman Charles Rangel introduced a bill in the U.S. Congress to have Garvey cleared of his mail fraud conviction—the bill apparently died in committee. The London borough of Haringey erected a new library named after Garvey. A statue of Garvey was erected in San Fernando, Trinidad. The University of the West Indies in Jamaica held a major conference to commemorate his work.

Garvey's eminence in history is assured. Perhaps more than any other single individual, he infused a pride in self, a confidence to struggle, and a determination to move his people forward out of the low point of imperialist conquest, disfranchisement, and lynching that threatened to suffocate the African world of the early twentieth century.

Garvey was the ultimate leader made by his own people. The establishment journalists and historians of the United States especially, vilified him, lampooned him and sought to portray him as a buffoon, and a charlatan. Between his death in 1940 and the 1970s, he came close to disappearing from the historical record, as mainstream historians pretended he had not existed. They broke their silence only for the occasional disparaging remark.

The Black Power movement of the 1960s and 1970s helped usher in a Garvey revival, first in the street and then in academia. Since the 1970s there has been a vast outpouring of scholarly works on Marcus Garvey.

REFERENCES

The Black Man, 1933–39.

Du Bois, W. E. B. "A Lunatic Or A Traitor." *Crisis* 28 (May 1924): 8–9.

Garvey, Amy Jacques. *Garvey and Garveyism.* Kingston, Jamaica: A. J. Garvey, 1963.

———, ed. *The Philosophy and Opinions of Marcus Garvey; or, Africa for the Africans.* 2 vols. 1923, 1925. Reprint, Dover, MA: The Majority Press, 1986.

Garvey, Marcus. *Message to the People: The Course of African Philosophy.* Edited by Tony Martin. Dover, MA: The Majority Press, 1986.

———. *The Poetical Works of Marcus Garvey.* Edited by Tony Martin. Dover, MA: The Majority Press, 1983.

Hill, Robert A., ed. *The Marcus Garvey and UNIA Papers.* Vol. 1. Berkeley: University of California Press, 1983.

Lewis, Rupert, and Patrick Bryan, eds. *Garvey: His Work and Impact.* Kingston, Jamaica: ISER, 1988.

Martin, Tony. *Literary Garveyism: Garvey Black Arts and the Harlem Renaissance.* Dover, MA: The Majority Press, 1983.

———. *Marcus Garvey Hero: A First Biography.* Dover, MA: The Majority Press, 1983.

———. *The Pan-African Connection.* Cambridge, MA: Schenkman Pub. Co., 1983. Reprint, Dover, MA: The Majority Press, 1984.

———. *Race First: The Ideological and Organizational Struggles of Marcus Garvey and the Universal Negro Improvement Association.* Westport, CT: Greenwood Press, 1976. Reprint, Dover, MA: The Majority Press, 1986.

———, ed. *African Fundamentalism: A Literary and Cultural Anthology of Garvey's Harlem Renaissance.* Dover, MA: The Majority Press, 1991.

The Negro World, 1918–33.

COLLECTIONS

Garvey's personal papers are spread around many locations in several countries. Among the more important repositories are the National Library of Jamaica, the Schomburg Center for Research in Black Culture in Harlem, New York, and the Fisk University Library in Nashville, Tennessee.

Tony Martin

Arthur G. Gaston
(1892–1996)
Entrepreneur

Arthur G. Gaston, who began his career with a tenth-grade education, opened his first business in 1923—a burial society for blacks, later incorporated as the Booker T. Washington Insurance Company—and developed an empire worth over $24 million. A man whose will to achieve began in childhood, Gaston lived by his philosophy: find a need in the black community and fill it.

Born on July 4, 1892, in a log cabin built by his paternal grandparents, Joe and Idella Gaston, in the rural southern Alabama town of Demopolis, Arthur George Gaston was the grandson of former slaves. His father, who had been a railroad worker, died when Gaston was a baby. As a young boy, he watched a lynching in Demopolis and, convinced then that all white men were honest and just, he thought that justice had

Arthur G. Gaston

prevailed. To support her young son, his mother Rosie Gaston moved to Birmingham in 1900 to work as a cook for A. B. and Minnie Loveman, founders of Alabama's premier department store chain. Mother and son lived in servants' quarters built over the Loveman's stables. Later, when Rosie Gaston opened her own catering business, the Lovemans were among her customers.

Rosie Gaston enrolled her son in the Carrie Tuggle Institute, a boarding school operated by Granny Tuggle, a former slave committed to the education of black children. Gaston completed the tenth grade at Tuggle—the highest grade offered at the school. He longed to attend college at Tuskegee Institute, as it was called then, having been influenced by a Booker T. Washington speech that he heard during his years at Tuggle. He was inspired by Washington's advice to seize an opportunity to grow when it came.

Gaston became an entrepreneur early in life and never lost his zeal for business. While living with his grandmother, he charged neighborhood children a fee—a button or a pin—to use the swing in their yard. Neighborhood women who sewed came to him when they needed items he had. His flair for business was further developed when he graduated from Tuggle. Gaston sold subscriptions to the black newspaper, the *Birmingham Reporter,* then went to Mobile and worked as a bellhop at the Battle House Hotel. He earned a fairly good income from the hotel and from the other businesses he operated when the saloons closed.

Gaston entered the U.S. Army in 1910, serving as a sergeant in the segregated forces in France as a member of the all–black 317th Ammunition Train of the 92nd Division. After his military service ended in 1918, he went to work as a laborer for the Tennessee Coal and Iron Company in Westfield, Alabama. Gaston wanted to make more money and "to be somebody," he said in the January 1963 issue of *Ebony.* "I was poor as a church mouse, a common laborer making 31 cents an hour in a Birmingham steel mill. I had no prospects and I had no backing. All I had was a plan." His plan led to the success that he would soon enjoy. His mother prepared box lunches that he sold to his coworkers at the steel plant, and he ran a financial lending service as well. Although he remained frugal with his own salary, Gaston lent money to his coworkers and received a return of 25 cents on the dollar on every biweekly payday. In his spare time he operated a popcorn and peanut stand.

Enterprises Take Shape

Black communities at the time were accustomed to collecting money in church to bury their dead. Gaston observed a woman who came to the coal mines to collect money for her husband's funeral expenses and had watched preachers follow the same practice. He wondered if people would support a burial society for this purpose. In 1923 he founded a small company, Brother Gaston's Burial Society, later renamed the Booker T. Washington Burial Society. About this time he married his childhood friend Creola Smith. Her father, A. L. "Dad" Smith, supported Gaston's business venture and was elected vice–president of the firm. Creola Gaston was named secretary. The society grew and in 1932 was incorporated as the Booker T. Washington Insurance Company—the cornerstone for the Gaston empire and the source of capital for all of his business ventures that followed. Through mergers and acquisitions of smaller burial societies and insurance companies in Alabama, the insurance company flourished.

The Gaston enterprises grew. Creola Smith Gaston died, and in 1939 he married Minnie Gardner, a graduate of Tuskegee Institute. Both Minnie Gaston and their son, Arthur George Gaston Jr., are now deceased. In 1939 he also founded the Booker T. Washington Business College to train clerks and stenographers for his company and funeral home. When he found that students in the school were unable to read and write, he sponsored a statewide spelling course in the public schools. Outside demand for training led to the school's expansion, and Minnie Gaston headed the institution. In 1939 Gaston founded the Brown Belle Bottling Company purely as a profit–making venture. When the business lost $60,000, he closed the company; but rather than share the financial loss with the stockholders, who were his friends, Gaston absorbed it himself. Later, the impending scarcity and advancing prices of burial plots led Smith Gaston Funeral Directors to purchase New Grace Hill Cemetery to provide moderately priced burial sites for clients.

Recognizing the need for a motel and restaurant to serve black travelers, who were barred from white–owned facilities, in 1954 he opened the A. G. Gaston Motel. It became a landmark site during the civil rights movement as the headquarters for the Southern Christian Leadership Conference and a stopping place for the leaders and demonstrators, and it was bombed by white protestors. In 1955 Gaston opened the Vulcan Realty and Investment Corporation to handle real estate purchased by his insurance company. Urged by his friends to organize a savings and loan association, in 1957 he opened the Citizens Federal Savings and Loan Association. Through the firm he made mortgage money available to blacks for their homes and churches.

In 1960 Gaston moved his headquarters into a new building. Three years later he opened the A. G. Gaston Home for senior citizens in a peaceful area called the G. G. Gaston Subdivision. He provided for the comfort and security of many old friends and former employees of his companies.

The A. G. Gaston Boys and Girls Club that began with a $50,000 donation in 1966 enabled thousands of young people to benefit from athletic training and moral guidance. Quoted in the June 1992 issue of *Black Enterprise,* Charles A. McCallum, a local college president, said: "Perhaps most important among Gaston's contributions has been his work with young people."

Continuing to expand, in 1970 Gaston moved his headquarters to the new Citizens Federal building. In 1975 he acquired WENN–FM, now a rhythm and blues radio station, and WAGG–AM, now a gospel station. He regarded both stations as his favorite business ventures for the public voice they now gave to blacks in the listening area. In 1986 he opened the A. G. Gaston Construction Company. After building a business conglomerate in Birmingham, Gaston created an employee stock option plan and sold the parent company, the Booker T. Washington Insurance Company, to his employees in 1987 for a fraction of its value. His empire also included Citizens Drugstore and Zion Memorial Gardens and Mausoleum. According to Eric L. Smith, in time Gaston either owned or controlled nine corporations with assets of more than $35 million.

Gaston figured prominently in Alabama's civil rights movement, working primarily behind the scenes. In 1957 he aided blacks involved in an economic boycott in Tuskegee, Alabama, to gain voting rights by advancing mortgage or business loans when whites brought pressure on the boycotters. Through the Gaston Motel he provided lodging to civil rights leaders such as Martin Luther King Jr., and he paid bail for arrested demonstrators. He posted the $5,000 bail to free King from jail after King was arrested for marching without a permit. While jailed, King wrote his famous "Letter from Birmingham City Jail." Although labeled an "Uncle Tom" for his seemingly passive role in the protests and for refusing to participate in the public marches, he strengthened the dialogue between black activists and white business leaders in Birmingham following the demonstrations in 1963.

Gaston knew well the reasons for his success: he always wanted to make money, he fulfilled a need, and he worked hard toward his goals. Booker T. Washington Insurance president Louis J. Willie told *Black Enterprise* for June 1992 that Gaston was "a genius of psychology, someone who knows what makes people tick, and how to get the best out of them." Early in his career, Gaston said he wanted to put some of what he had earned back into the community. Becoming rich was "accidental," he told *Black Enterprise* in June 1992. His wealth also brought unwelcome recognition, particularly in 1976 when he and his wife were assaulted in their home and Gaston was driven around handcuffed in his car until his kidnappers were apprehended.

Active in civic and community activities, Gaston served as a member of the Board of Trustees of Tuskegee University, Daniel Payne College, and the YMCA. Other board memberships included the Board of Directors of the Jefferson County Survey Committee, the Coordinating Council of the City of Birmingham, the Citizens Committee of Birmingham, the Birmingham Chamber of Commerce, Boys' Club of America, and the American Legion. He was president of the Birmingham Negro Business League and twice served as president of the National Negro Business League.

Gaston's work brought him a steady stream of recognition throughout his life. His hometown, Demopolis, gave him the Native Son Award and beginning in 1962 declared August 31 "Dr. A. G. Gaston Day." Birmingham celebrated A. G. Gaston Day on October 24, 1975. Gaston received awards of achievement from the Alabama Newspaper Association, the National Association of Colored Women's Clubs, the Boys' Club of America, the U.S. Commission on Civil Rights, the YMCA, the Courts of Calanthe, the Birmingham Jaycees, the Alabama Education Association, and various other churches, businesses, and fraternal organizations. He received the National Newspaper Publishers Association's Russwurm Award and special recognition from President Harry S. Truman. Gaston was honored by the U.S. Department of Commerce, the U.S. Small Business Administration, and the Chamber of Commerce of the United States. He received more than ten honorary doctorates from such schools as Tuskegee University, Paul Quinn College, Daniel Payne College, Pepperdine University, University of Alabama, and Monrovia College and Industrial Institute of Liberia.

Once called the richest black man in America, Gaston became a centenarian in July 1994 and received *Black Enterprise* magazine's Entrepreneur of the Century award in 1994 for "legendary contributions to the development and growth of black business." In the August 1992 issue of *Black Enterprise,* Earl Graves said Gaston was "a tireless benefactor of black institutions, a patron saint of the Civil Rights Movement and a visionary businessman . . . [who] has inspired countless entrepreneurs throughout the 1900s."

In the mid–1980s Gaston lost a leg to diabetes and was confined to a wheelchair. Although he suffered a mild stroke on January 22, 1992, four weeks later he was back at work on the top floor of Citizen's Federal Savings Bank and continued to work nearly every day. He continued to serve as chairman of the board of Citizens Federal and Booker T. Washington Insurance Company, which in 1992 ranked number six on the

Black Enterprise's BE Insurance list of one hundred top black businesses. Referred to as "not a tall man," Gaston wore a small mustache and white hair that fell back from his forehead. His voice was somewhat high–pitched.

After suffering his second stroke in four years, Gaston died on January 19, 1996, at the Medical Center East in Birmingham, leaving several grandchildren and great–grandchildren. John H. Johnson said in *Jet* magazine that "Gaston was a pioneer and a bridge builder. He blazed a trail in a wilderness of prejudice and racism. . . . He left a legacy of progress and achievement that should inspire and motivate all Blacks who want to go into business for themselves." Earl G. Graves said in *Black Enterprise* for March 1996 that "his accomplishments are especially noteworthy because they were made during the era of Jim Crow, long before the advent of affirmative action and minority set–asides, when black entrepreneurs faced seemingly unsurmountable odds." Kirkwood Balton, president and chief executive officer of Booker T. Washington Insurance Company wrote in *The Birmingham News*: "He developed businesses when the odds were against it. He developed businesses when a man of color didn't do that. And he developed people to operate his businesses, people of color, and his businesses were a success." Through his legendary business ventures, Gaston enhanced the life of countless blacks in Alabama, influenced numerous black entrepreneurs, and gained international recognition.

REFERENCES

"A. G. Gaston Dies." *The Birmingham News,* January 19, 1996.

"A. G. Gaston, Pioneer Business Leader, Dies in Birmingham." *Jet* 89 (5 February 1996): 56–58.

"Blacks, Whites Mourn Loss of 'Leader–Citizen.'" *The Birmingham News,* January 19, 1996.

Gaston, A. G. *Green Power: The Successful Way of A. G. Gaston.* Birmingham, AB: Southern University Press at Birmingham Publishing Co., 1968. Reprint, Troy, AB: Troy State University Press, 1977.

———. "How to Make a Million." *Ebony* 18 (January 1963): 110–16.

"Gaston's Work Ethic is in Executives." *The Birmingham News,* January 20, 1996.

Jackson, Harold. "True Grit." *Black Enterprise* 22 (June 1992): 230–34.

Lloyd, Foda Marie. "Footprints in Time." *Black Enterprise* 26 (August 1995): 109–120.

Marshall, David. "A. G. Gaston." *Black Enterprise* 6 (July 1976): 31–33.

Smith, Eric L. "Blazing a Path for 100 Years." *Black Enterprise* 26 (March 1996): 15–16.

Thompson, Kevin D. "The BE 100s Anniversary and Conference Celebrate for Black Business." *Black Enterprise* 23 (August 1992): 13, 16–17.

Wormley, Stanton L., and Lewis F. Fenderson, eds. *Many Shades of Black.* New York: William Morrow and Co., 1969.

Jessie Carney Smith

Henry Louis Gates Jr.

(1950–)

Educator, scholar, literary critic, writer

Literary scholar Henry Louis Gates Jr.'s critical studies have a wide–ranging impact on American oral and literary traditions, and have brought the teaching and analysis of black literature to the forefront in the American academy. In his many studies and popular essays, he argues for the inclusion and valuing of differences both in the literary canon and in American society.

Henry Louis Gates Jr. was born in Keyser, West Virginia, on September 16, 1950. Keyser is located in the Piedmont area of Mineral County, a valley surrounded by the Allegheny Mountains and their foothills. The town's principal employer was Westvaco Paper Mill. Gates's father, Henry Louis Sr., was a loader at the mill. To make ends meet Henry Sr. also worked nights as a janitor at the local telephone company.

The few blacks who lived in West Virginia formed close–knit and stable communities. In 1954 integration occurred smoothly without the hatred and violence that plagued other parts of the United States. But this is not to suggest that Gates did not encounter racism. When he was 14 years old, Gates injured his hip playing touch football. To make conversation during the examination, the white doctor attending him asked of his future plans. Gates informed the doctor that he intended to become a physician, at which point the doctor quizzed him, attempting to access his knowledge of science. Gates answered all of the doctor's questions correctly. The doctor then diagnosed Gates's hairline fracture as a psychosomatic illness. "The boy from the hills of Appalachia was an over–achiever," he informed Gates's mother. Recalling this experience years later, Gates told the *New York Times,* "Over achiever designated a sort of pathology: the overstraining of your natural capacity." The racism that prevented a correct diagnosis resulted in Gates's sustaining a permanent injury, with his right leg becoming more than two inches shorter than the left. In 1990 Gates's remarks to Maurice Berger for *Art in America* reveal the destructive potential of racism. Gates said, "The most subtle and pernicious form of racism against blacks [is] doubt over our intellectual capacities."

The Crossroad of Childhood

In 1956 Gates entered the Davis Free School, Piedmont's only elementary school, with a history dating back to 1906. He excelled in school. The 1960s ushered in a decade of growth, change, and expanding awareness. Gates was in the fifth grade when he became aware of Africa as the class

Henry Louis Gates Jr.

studied current events. Still, the political turmoil of the 1960s did not compare to the personal trauma Gates experienced as a result of his mother's illness. In 1962, at the age of 46, Pauline Gates was diagnosed with clinical depression and hospitalized. In his memoir *Colored People* Gates describes his own childhood behaviors, behaviors that parallel the symptoms of obsessive compulsive disorder:

> I had developed all sorts of rituals. I would . . . always walk around the kitchen table only from right to left, never the other way around. I would approach a chair from its left side, not the right. I got into and out of the same side of bed, slept on the same side, and I held the telephone with the same hand to the same ear. But most of all, as if my life depended on it, I crossed my legs right calf over left, and never, ever the other way around. Until one Sunday. For a reason that seemed compelling at the time, probably out of anger or spite, I decided to cross my legs in reverse.

Gates did not die as he feared for his solitary act of anger, but he believed that his act produced his mother's illness. He feared that she would die. Fortunately for his own sanity, she lived. Still, his sense of guilt was enormous. To atone for his imagined sin, Gates decided to join the church.

Gates's Uncle Harry, a minister in the Methodist Church, persuaded him to go to church camp. In the summers of 1965 and 1966, Gates spent two weeks at Peterkins Episcopal Church camp. This gave him time to reflect on his new religion and grow mentally. The camp provided two uninterrupted weeks where, Gates stated in *Colored People,* he "drank ideas and ate controversy."

In 1968 Gates graduated at the top of his class and, as valedictorian, he delivered a militant commencement address. In the fall he entered Potomac State College of West Virginia University, planning to go from there to medical school. Meeting professor Duke Anthony Whitmore changed the course of his career. Taking English and American literature from the professor opened Gates to new possibilities. Whitmore, glimpsing the spark of genius in Gates, encouraged him to apply to the Ivy League schools. Gates applied and was accepted at Yale University.

Graduating summa cum laude from Yale with a B.A. in history in 1973, Gates won a fellowship to England to study at Clare College, Cambridge University, where he received a master of arts degree in 1974. From 1973 until 1975 he worked as a London Bureau staff correspondent for *Time* magazine. Gates returned to the United States in 1975 and became a public relations representative for the American Cyanamid Company. From 1976 until he completed his Ph.D. in English language and literature in 1979, Gates held the position of lecturer at Yale University. On September 1, 1979, Gates married Sharon Lynn Adams. The couple has two daughters.

Gates's essay, "Preface to Blackness: Text and Pretext," in Robert Stepto and Dexter Fishers's *Afro-American Literature:The Reconstruction of Instruction,* marked his entry into the world of academia as an assistant professor of English at Yale University, a position he held until 1984. In 1981 the MacArthur Foundation awarded Gates a grant for $150,000. He became widely known for discovering and reissuing a 1859 novel written by a black woman, *Our Nig* (reprinted in 1983), the first novel by an African American published in the United States. Gates's research inspired the growing interest in the black woman's literary tradition.

Gates's Black Periodical Literature Project, initiated in 1980, unearthed numerous 19th century literary works that were long forgotten. Soon Gates was promoted to associate professor of English and undergraduate director for the Department of Afro-American Studies at Yale in 1984. That year his edited work *Black Literature and Literary Theory* was published and a debate erupted over a definition of black literary theory. In the fall of 1985, Gates accepted a full professorship in English and Africana Studies at Cornell University. The 1988 publication of the 31-volume *Schomburg Library of Nineteenth-Century Black Women Writers* is noted for altering the landscape of "American cultural thought, demonstrating that black men and black women have never hesitated to grasp the pen and write their own powerful story of freedom." The collection is dedicated to Gates's mother. In

1988 Gates was named the W. E. B. Du Bois Professor of Literature, becoming the first African American male to hold an endowed chair in the history of Cornell University.

His publication of *The Signifying Monkey: Towards a Theory of Afro–American Literary Criticism* (1989) earned Gates the American Book Award. He set forth a theory for judging black literature and also accused whites of intellectual racism. In 1990 Gates accepted an endowed chair at Duke University in Durham, North Carolina. Becoming a John Spenser Bassett Professor of English, Gates remained at Duke for only one year. In 1991, Harvard University recruited him for the W. E. B. Du Bois Professorship in Humanities and as chair for the Department of African American Studies.

Gates is the recipient of numerous awards, including grants from the National Endowment for the Humanities, 1980–84; Rockefeller Foundation Fellow, 1981; American Book Award, 1989; and the Anisfield–Wolfe Book Award 1989. His edited works include *Black Is the Color of the Cosmos: Charles T. Davis's Essays on Black Literature and Culture, 1942–1981* (1982); Harriet E. Wilson's *Our Nig; or, Sketches From the Life of a Free Black* (1983); *The Slave's Narrative: Texts and Contexts* (1985); *Race, Writing, and Difference* (1986); and *The Classic Slave Narratives* (1987). He also edited *The Norton Anthology of Afro–American Literature* (1990); *Reading Black, Reading Feminist: A Literary Critical Anthology* (1990); *Three Classic African–American Novels* (1990); *Bearing Witness: Selections from 150 Years of African–American Autobiography* (1991); and *Future of the Race* (1996). In 1995 Gates was awarded both the Hartland Award and the Lillian Smith Prize for his autobiography, *Colored People.*

Gates is a member of International PEN and the Modern Language Association, and president of the Afro–American Academy. In 1991 he created for the Public Broadcasting System the television series *The Image of the Black in the Western Imagination.* In 1995 Gates delivered the commencement address at Emory University in Atlanta, Georgia, where he was awarded an honorary doctorate. A prolific writer and researcher, Henry Louis Gates Jr. has advanced African American literary and critical theory to a new level of understanding.

Current address: Office of African American Studies Department, Harvard University, Cambridge, MA 02138.

REFERENCES

Berger, Maurice. *Art in America* 78 (9 September 1990): 78–85.

Contemporary Black Biography. Vol. 3. Detroit: Gale Research, 1993.

Gates, Henry Louis, Jr. *Colored People: A Memoir.* New York: Knopf, 1994.

———. "Men Were Men, and Men Were White." *New York Times,* May 29, 1988.

Nagueyalti Warren

Mifflin Wistar Gibbs
(1823–1915)
Abolitionist, entrepreneur, politician, lawyer, government official, college president

Mifflin Wistar Gibbs was an abolitionist who became a pioneer in California and in British Columbia. When he settled in Little Rock in 1871, he became a leading figure in the Arkansas Republican party. He was the first black elected a municipal judge in the United States. On the national level, he received several federal appointments, finally becoming consul in Madagascar. He was a noted entrepreneur who hoped to see the creation of a black middle class.

Mifflin Wistar Gibbs was born in Philadelphia on April 17, 1823, to Jonathan Clarkson Gibbs, a Methodist minister, and Maria Jackson Gibbs. Of six children born to the couple, three sons survived to adulthood: Jonathan Clarkson, Mifflin, and Isaiah. The youngest, Isaiah, was a California pioneer. Jonathan graduated from Dartmouth College in 1852 and after studying at Princeton Theological Seminary became a Presbyterian minister. During Reconstruction, he had a notable political career in Florida, serving as secretary of state from 1868 to 1872.

The elder Gibbs died shortly after Mifflin's eighth birthday, ending the boy's schooling. Gibbs had attended a Free School for a year under an Irishman named Kennedy, an old–fashioned teacher who believed in the liberal use of corporal punishment.

After his father's death, Gibbs was put out to work as a stableboy for three dollars a month. He worked at a series of similar jobs until he was 16 when he was apprenticed to carpenter James Gibbons, a southern slave who had bought his freedom. Gibbons built several black churches and bid on the rebuilding in brick of Richard Allen's Mother Bethel Church in the 1840s. Gibbs's older brother also seems to have been apprenticed to Gibbons; at some point both young men became Presbyterians. During his apprenticeship, Mifflin studied in his free time and also joined the Philomatheon Institute, a black literary society. This membership put him in contact with leading Philadelphia blacks like Isaiah Wear and Robert Purvis. He also became an ardent abolitionist.

After finishing his apprenticeship, Gibbs won a place for himself in Philadelphia as an abolitionist and a businessman. He was an active member of the Underground Railroad, a network which helped fugitive slaves reach safety in the North and Canada, and was a member of a committee which presented a petition for black enfranchisement to the Pennsylvania legislature. Gibbs joined with two other men in 1848 to establish a black cemetery to replace church burial grounds; however, the group ran up debts which were liquidated by selling part of the property to the Harriet Smith Home for Aged and Infirm Colored People. After the National Antislav-

Mifflin Wistar Gibbs

ery Convention held in Philadelphia in 1849, Frederick Douglass, a former slave and leading black abolitionist, invited Gibbs to accompany him on a speaking tour in western New York, Ohio, and Pennsylvania. Gibbs had just completed the tour and returned to Rochester, New York, when he decided to join the Gold Rush to California.

Joins Gold Rush

Gibbs took steerage passage to the Isthmus of Panama in 1850. After recovering from an attack of fever in Panama, he found passage on a steamship and arrived in San Francisco. After paying 50 cents to have his trunk brought to his boardinghouse, he spent his last ten cents on a cigar. For a while Gibbs found work as a carpenter until the field was closed by the refusal of white carpenters to work with him. He then turned to shining shoes and other menial jobs. He saved his money and then worked for a year in a clothing store with Nathan Pointer. In 1852 he entered a partnership with Peter Lester, a skilled bootmaker and also a fellow Philadelphian and abolitionist. Their Pioneer Boot and Shoe Emporium on Clay Street prospered until 1858 when both men left San Francisco for what later became British Columbia.

California laws were very unfavorable to blacks; in April 1850 a state law barred non–whites from testifying in court in any case involving a white. On one occasion a disgruntled customer beat up Lester in the presence of Gibbs. Immediate physical resistance would have meant death, and there was no legal redress since neither man could testify in court against the assailant. Gibbs joined other blacks in 1851 to draw up the first black protest, which was published in one of the leading papers. He was also active in a series of state conventions held in 1854, 1855, and 1857 to protest the status of blacks in California.

Gibbs was active in the San Francisco Atheneum, the intellectual center for blacks in the city, formed in July 1853. Members of this group, including Gibbs, established the black newspaper, *Mirror of the Times,* in 1856. Gibbs and Lester also refused to pay the California poll tax on the grounds that they could not vote. When no one bid on the goods that had been seized for nonpayment of the tax, the goods were returned and the law was no longer enforced against blacks.

A black community contemplating the possibilities of emigration was attracted toward what became British Columbia by two developments in 1858. A bill excluding blacks from entering California narrowly failed but demonstrated the continuing problem of bias, and gold was discovered on the Fraser River. In addition, land was available cheaply, and the governor of the Crown colony of Vancouver Island, whose West Indian mother may have been a mulatto, was sympathetic to blacks. Eventually some 400 to 800 blacks settled in the capital, Victoria. Gibbs and his partner Lester, whose daughter had been driven from California schools, soon followed.

Gibbs rapidly became a success in Victoria, putting together business enterprises which made him a small fortune. Although antiblack prejudice in British Columbia would grow as time passed, there were no legal foundations for segregation. Gibbs, along with many others in the black community, applied for British citizenship. In 1859 he returned to the eastern United States to marry Maria A. Alexander, who came from Kentucky and was educated at Oberlin College. The marriage produced five children, four of whom survived: Donald F., Ida A. Gibbs Hunt, Horace E., and Harriet (Hattie) E. Gibbs Marshall.

Gibbs was able to settle in an upscale part of town, and continued to be a community leader. In 1861 he organized a black militia, and the following year made an unsuccessful run for town council. He was elected five years later and became chair of the municipal finance committee; he was reelected in 1867. That was the same year that he undertook to build a railroad from a coal mine on Queen Charlotte Island to the harbor, overseeing the construction and the first shipment of coal. But within two years, Gibbs found that economic conditions in the colony were stagnant; while overtly supporting confederation with Canada, he was covertly urging annexation by the United States in Philip A. Bell's California newspaper, *The Elevator.* In March of that year he decided to seek wider opportunities in the States.

Returns to United States

It appears that Gibbs did not immediately join his family, which had moved to Oberlin before he did. He wrote in his autobiography that they had preceded him by four years, and his wife remained there when he moved to Arkansas. The children visited Gibbs in Little Rock. Gibbs himself did some study of law at a business college in Oberlin (not at Oberlin College as is sometimes stated) before he settled permanently in Arkansas. He already had a foundation for his legal career since he had read law with a British barrister in Victoria.

Plunges into Politics

Gibbs had determined to settle someplace in the South. He visited his brother Jonathan, who was secretary of state for Florida, but decided to look elsewhere. He first visited Arkansas in May 1871; he may not have settled there immediately but he did study in the law office of Benjamin and Barnes before opening a law office with Lloyd G. Wheeler in 1872. He immediately plunged into politics.

Gibbs attended the Republican National Convention as a spectator in 1872. In that year the Arkansas Republicans split. Gibbs canvassed for the Republicans in the elections. In 1873 he was named county attorney for Pulaski County, a post which he resigned to take the post of municipal judge, the first black elected to such a position. Gibbs's tenure was short and ended because he was on the losing side in a small–scale civil war between the factions.

Gibbs remained an influential Republican politician. In 1876 he led the party's ticket for delegates to the national convention. The disputed election resulted in the selection of Rutherford B. Hayes. Part of the compromise which led to this result was the withdrawal of federal troops and the collapse of Republican control in Southern states. Debt peonage and lawlessness in the South led to a mass emigration to Kansas and the surrounding states in 1879. Gibbs joined Alabama congressman James P. Rapier to spend 20 days in Kansas examining the conditions of black participants in the mass migration from the South. An emigrant himself, Gibbs approved of any attempt at improving one's chances in life.

In 1877 Gibbs was appointed register in the U.S. Land Office of the Little Rock district, a position he held for 12 years under successive Republican presidents. He continued his political work, faithfully attended Republican National Conventions, and became secretary of the Republican State Central Committee in 1887, a position he held until his departure for Madagascar in 1897. In 1884 he served as honorary commissioner of Arkansas for the New Orleans World Exposition of 1885. Another appointment in the Interior Department came his way in 1889 when President Harrison named him receiver of public moneys for the Little Rock land office.

Gibbs received notice of his appointment as U.S. Consul in Madagascar in October 1897. His future son–in–law and successor, William Hunt, became his clerk. Gibbs held the position from February 1898 until August 1901, when he resigned at the end of a leave of absence. That same month he was a delegate to the National Negro Business Men's League held in Chicago.

When Gibbs returned to Little Rock, he continued his business interests. He became the first president of Capital City Savings Bank in 1903, which closed in 1908 due to allegedly fraudulent mismanagement. Gibbs was indicted but reached an out–of–court settlement. A partner in the Little Rock Electric Light Company, he also owned substantial shares in other companies and considerable real estate in and around Little Rock. He traveled and lectured extensively. Gibbs died on July 11, 1915, at the age of 92. He was survived by a son, Horace Gibbs, a businessman in Aurora, Illinois, and two daughters who were distinguished in their own right, Ida Gibbs Hunt and Harriet Gibbs Marshall.

Mifflin Gibbs was an indefatigable entrepreneur and politician. He constantly strove for uplift, seeing education and accumulation of wealth as the keys to the improvement of conditions for blacks. Although he was keenly aware of the limits of politics, he nonetheless remained active in the Republican party. The title of his memoir, *Shadow and Light,* sums up his career. He was well aware of the shadow of oppression of blacks, but endeavored to be mindful of the light of evidence of black progress.

REFERENCES

Dillard, Tom W., ed. ''Introduction.'' *Shadow and Light.* By Mifflin Wistar Gibbs. Lincoln: University of Nebraska Press, 1995.

Gibbs, Mifflin Wistar. *Shadow and Light.* Washington, DC: n.p., 1902.

Lapp, Rudolph M. *Blacks in Gold Rush California.* New Haven, CT: Yale University Press, 1977.

Logan, Rayford W., and Michael R. Winston, eds. *Dictionary of American Negro Autobiography.* New York: Norton, 1982.

Simmons, William J. *Men of Mark.* Cleveland: Geo. M. Rewell, 1887.

Smith, Jessie Carney, ed. *Notable Black American Women.* Vol. 2. Detroit: Gale Research, 1996.

Winks, Robin W. *The Blacks in Canada.* New Haven, CT: Yale University Press, 1971.

Woodson, Carter G. ''The Gibbs Family.'' *Negro History Bulletin* 11 (October 1947): 3–12, 22.

Robert L. Johns

Benjamin F. Gibson

(1931–)

Federal judge, lawyer

Benjamin Franklin Gibson was the first black to be appointed a federal judge in the Western District of Michigan and the first black to become chief judge of that same court. He had a notable career as an attorney including becoming the first black assistant prosecuting attorney in Ingham County, Michigan.

Born in Saffold, Alabama, on July 13, 1931, Gibson was the middle of three children—a girl and two boys—of Eddie and Pearl Ethel Richardson Gibson. The family moved to Detroit, Michigan when Benjamin was four years old. Eddie Gibson worked in a Ford Motor Company factory in the Detroit area for many years and Pearl Gibson was a homemaker. The family lived on the east side of Detroit.

Gibson attended public schools in Detroit, graduating among the top four in his class from Miller High School in 1948. Still only 17 years old and unable to find a job, Gibson secured the permission of his parents to volunteer for the U.S. Army. For two years, he held the rank of private, serving in peacetime between major wars. Most of his time was spent on the island of Guam, where he used his spare time to read and ponder his future. His parents encouraged him to go to college but were unable to help him financially. He was the first in his family either to attend or to graduate from college. He enrolled in Wayne University (now Wayne State University) in 1950, majoring in business administration with a specialty in accounting. Believing that "business administration was key to our free enterprise economic system," he wrote in a letter to De Witt S. Dykes, Jr. in 1997, that he pursued accounting because it "dealt with numbers and was extremely logical." Financing his own education, Gibson worked full-time as a medical records clerk at Receiving Hospital in Detroit and as a temporary post office clerk while an undergraduate. He received his B.S. degree in 1955 and was inducted into Beta Gamma, the fraternity for honor graduates of the business school. After working as an accountant with the city of Detroit from 1955 to 1956, he became the first black hired for a professional position—as an accountant—by the Detroit Edison Company in 1956.

On June 23, 1951, Gibson married Lucille Nelson, a native of Memphis, Tennessee. A high school graduate, she later attended Lansing Community College for two years. The Gibsons became parents of six children: Charlotte, Linda, Gerald, Gail, Carol, and Laura.

Working for Detroit Edison, Gibson found himself in numerous situations where he felt a knowledge of law would have enhanced his ability to do his job. Quoted in *Benchmark,* he said, "I was dealing with tax matters in accounting, and working more and more with the law, and that stimulated my interest." This job "involved dealings with the SEC and with regulatory bodies," he said in *Amicus: The Magazine of the Detroit College of Law* in 1991. As a result, he decided to attend law school, choosing to enroll at the private Detroit College of Law because of its emphasis on the practical aspects of law practice. Continuing to work full time during the day, he attended night school. At first, he merely wanted a knowledge of the law in order to enhance his ability to perform his accounting duties, but law study proved so fascinating and challenging that accounting now seemed dull. He said in *Benchmark,* "When you get into constitutional and criminal law and some of those really meaty subjects, taxes become a little dry." He told *Amicus,* "at some time in the process, I became more interested in law than in accounting and decided to pursue a legal carer." He graduated "with distinction," ranking fifth in a class of 100 in 1960. Most law school graduates received an LL.B. (Bachelor of Laws) degree, but Gibson received a J.D. (Juris Doctor) degree, which at that time was reserved for those in the top five percent of the class. In later years, Gibson pursued a master's degree in labor law, taking courses at Wayne State University Law School and at Michigan State University, but did not complete the degree after being appointed a federal judge. He was awarded an honorary Doctor of Laws degree by Detroit College of Law in 1982.

Gibson had assumed that he could work as a lawyer for Detroit Edison, but found the company unwilling to risk being publicly represented by a black person. An accountant's work was largely done inside the walls of the company office where few could see. However, an attorney would interact with others outside the firm and represent the company in court. Gibson continued to work for Detroit Edison for nine months until he secured employment as an attorney. From 1961 to 1963, Gibson was an assistant attorney general for the state of Michigan with offices in Lansing. Ironically, his first assignment was to work with the Michigan Public Service Commission which regulated utilities, such as his former employer, Detroit Edison.

In 1963 he was appointed assistant prosecuting attorney for Ingham County, Michigan, becoming the first black to work in that capacity. He not only gained experience as a criminal trial lawyer, but also was appointed head of the criminal division, in charge of all criminal prosecutions in Ingham County, which includes Lansing, Michigan's capital.

From 1964 to 1978, Gibson was in private practice. He was a partner in the firm of Dunnings and Gibson from 1964 to 1974, and a principal in the firm of Dunnings, Gibson and Canady from 1974 to 1975. He went into solo practice from 1975 to 1978. In January 1979, Gibson became a full time professor at the Thomas M. Cooley Law School in Lansing, the first black teacher at that school. Gibson ended his teaching duties in September 1979 right before becoming a district judge, but continued as an adjunct professor until about 1984.

Receives Federal Judgeship

When U.S. Senator Donald Reigle (Dem—Michigan) announced in April 1979 that he was recommending Benjamin Gibson be appointed a federal district judge, several prominent attorneys in Michigan praised Gibson as an excellent choice. In the *Lansing State Journal* in 1979, former law partner Stuart Dunnings predicted that Gibson would "be dynamic as a judge" because of his "judicial temperament," calling him "very competent." Ingham County circuit judge Jack W. Warren described Gibson as "a class person. . .a gentleman" who "is thorough. . .understanding" and "considerate." In general, Lansing attorneys described Gibson as "a respected, even feared, opponent in the courtroom who is also unanimously admired by the lawyers who know him." Several commented on his constructive attitudes and positive outlook in the face of adversity. Gibson experienced racial discrimination on several occasions: inability to get a job after high school graduation, Detroit Edison's refusal to hire him as an attorney, and the refusal of real estate agents to show him homes for sale in a white Lansing neighborhood. Still, he never displayed bitterness and, rather than using these events as an excuse to do less, Gibson felt motivated to work harder and to perform at the highest level possible.

Gibson was considered a candidate with good credentials: a quiet but committed member of the Democratic party, with a very good legal background and considerable civil rights activity. He was a member of the board of directors of both the Ingham County Bar Association and the Lansing NAACP, a cofounder of the Greater Lansing Urban League, a candidate for the Lansing City Council in 1964, and an activist in opening housing for blacks in the late 1960s. Gibson was the beneficiary of two factors: the creation of several new judgeships nationwide with three to be located in the Western District of Michigan and Democratic President Jimmy Carter's announced desire to consider qualified minorities for some of the new judgeships to compensate for their underrepresentation among federal judges. Gibson's appointment to the Western District of Michigan was confirmed by the U.S. Senate in late September 1979 and he was sworn in on October 2, 1979.

Gibson remained humble in his new position: "My biggest shock was the enormous responsibility and power that I suddenly had," Gibson said in the *Lansing State Journal* in October 1981. "I sat up there on the bench and suddenly I could enjoin strikers, and declare state laws unconstitutional and send people off to prison. It really got to me at first." Gibson showed special concern in deciding cases which involved human and civil rights as well as in determining sentences in criminal cases.

Gibson believed that courts should help resolve difficult issues presented in lawsuits. In reference to the tendency of some judges to refer controversial matters back to Congress or to a state legislature, Gibson pledged in the *Lansing State Journal* in April 1979, "I will not run away from controversy." Several cases gave him the opportunity to live up to that pledge. A 13–year–old mentally impaired girl wanted an abortion, had secured her guardian's approval, and had been advised by her doctor that it must be done by a particular time and needed court approval. A Kalamazoo judge, because of his personal values, tried to avoid giving a decision in time for the abortion to be performed. When the issue came to Judge Gibson's court, he ordered the Kalamazoo judge to decide one way or the other. The Kalamazoo judge denied permission for the abortion, forcing the child to have the baby and place it in a foster home since she could not take care of it. In other decisions, Gibson ordered the reinstatement of a Muskegon, Michigan, police officer who had been fired because he left his wife to live with another woman, and prohibited the Grand Rapids Police from arresting actors because of the nude scenes in a 1982 production of the musical *Oh! Calcutta.*

Issues involving the separation of church and state were often prominent: prayer at public school commencement exercises, religious symbols in public schools, and challenges to shared–time arrangements "in which public school teachers in specialized areas go to church–related schools to teach such courses as driver education, art and music," according to the *Lansing State Journal.* Gibson was pragmatic and flexible in permitting customasectarian prayer at commencement but prohibiting displays specific to a particular religious faith. According to the *Lansing State Journal* in 1985, Gibson believed that "controversial cases aren't found in the courts. They're found in society" and "might better be resolved by the parties themselves or the Legislature. But the courts are often looked to as arbiters."

Gibson's most publicized case received attention because of news stories alleging improprieties outside the courtroom rather than actual courtroom proceedings. In 1980 Americans United for Separation of Church and State filed a lawsuit against the Grand Rapids Public Schools, objecting to their use of teachers paid with public funds to teach students in private schools leased by the Grand Rapids Public Schools. At a cost of $3 million, the program operated in 45 non–public schools and brought $6 million in state aid to the school district. In a September 1981 ruling, Gibson refused to issue an injunction prohibiting the shared time arrangements while the case was under consideration. However, in June 1982, as the issue was still pending in his court, the *Grand Rapids Press* printed an article alleging a breach of judicial conduct on Judge Gibson's part because Gibson "allowed" Grand Rapids superintendent of schools, John Dow, to spend $129.36 of public school funds to entertain Gibson, his wife, and others at a music scholarship fund–raiser. Gibson's first response was to point out that he was unaware of the source of the funds, that the event was purely social, that at no time had he discussed the time share case with Dow or anyone else, and nothing Dow had done influenced his decisions in any way. He also stated that the newspaper was maliciously attempting to malign him as it had other blacks in the past two years, writing stories he described as "hatchet jobs" done in a "sleazy manner." In his written statement in the *Press,* Gibson asserted that the newspaper "appears to have a vendetta against black public officials" and named six black public officials he thought had been the subject of "suspect journalism." Gibson stopped short of accusing the paper of racial prejudice, saying, "I can only state the facts. It appears—I don't know what the actual motivation is," he said in the June 8 issue of the *Press.*

When the story first came to public attention, Gibson met with attorneys representing all sides in the lawsuit; all believed that Gibson would be able to reach a fair and impartial verdict in the case and had no plans to appeal based on the allegations of impropriety. Thus, Gibson initially planned to continue to preside over the case. However, after several days of stories in the print and electronic media about the allegations of impropriety, Gibson voluntarily removed himself from the case, an action which, according to the *Grand Rapids Press* for June 9, 1982, "appears to be in the best interest of the community" because "any decision on the shared time lawsuit must have the confidence of the community." Gibson also announced that he would send a check to the Grand Rapids School Board for the portion of funds used to pay for the admission, food, and drink charges for Gibson and his wife. Gibson announced new personal policies of limiting his social engagements, of always paying his own expenses in all future situations and plans to review his approximately 500 pending cases with the intent to remove himself from any case where he had "more than a casual relationship" with any of the persons or attorneys involved, according to the *Grand Rapids Press* on June 11. Gibson's new code of personal ethics was considered a more restrictive standard than that required by the Code of Judicial Conduct.

Becomes Chief Judge

On February 15, 1991, Gibson became the chief judge of the district court of the Western District of Michigan. Gibson, the first black to be chief judge in this district, was chosen automatically based on seniority. His new responsibility was to administer a court with jurisdiction over a large geographic area: 49 of Michigan's 83 counties, covering all of the western part of Michigan plus the upper peninsula. Gibson especially enjoyed the administrative role of chief judge. His duties included scheduling cases and chairing meetings of the dozen judges, senior judges, and magistrates in the district. A computer buff, Gibson was responsible for automating the work of the Western District, putting important documents on computer and introducing standardized procedures to the different courtrooms in the district, and making the work of the court more businesslike and efficient. A little over four years after assuming the role of chief judge, Gibson resigned the position effective May 1, 1995, so that he could make a transition to a semi–retirement status known as senior judge in 1996.

Gibson assumed the status of senior judge on July 13, 1996, which allowed him to reduce his civil caseload by half and to take few criminal cases. He will continue to receive his full salary each year whether he retires fully or continues to hear cases. After assuming senior status, Gibson sold his Grand Rapids home and moved to Las Vegas where the warm weather was better for his health problems. He did most of his court work via computer from his new home and returned to Grand Rapids for two weeks at a time to preside over trials. Until mid–1997, the federal courts paid the air fare and a per diem fee of $94 for each trip. A change in policy not to reimburse these expenses for senior judges who live outside their judicial district prompted Gibson to reevaluate and to announce his planned retirement no later than September of 1998 or sooner, if he can finish all his cases. In 1997 The *Grand Rapids Press* called Gibson "a fine judge" whose "absence from Grand Rapids is a loss," but not only defended the new policy of non–reimbursement of travel expenses but also questioned whether federal judges should receive "full pay in the hammock" during their retirement years.

Gibson's professional, civic, and social activities over the years have been extensive. He has been a member of several bar associations, including the Ingham County, Grand Rapids, Floyd H. Skinner, Michigan State, American, and Federal bar associations. He is also a member of the Black Judges of Michigan, the Federal Judges Association, the Sixth Circuit Judicial Council, and the Committee on Automation and Technology of the United States Judicial Conference. A member of the Michigan Trial Lawyers Association, he also serves on the Board of Directors of the Cooley Law School. A long–time member of the Rotary Club, Gibson was a charter member of a Lansing chapter of Sigma Pi Phi (the Boulé, a fraternity for black professionals) and the founder and chief organizer of its Grand Rapids chapter in 1981. Gibson's efforts to improve the standing of blacks in Grand Rapids include membership on the Board of Directors of L. I. N. K., a tutoring and mentoring program for minority youngsters, and his organization of Project Blue Print, associated with the United Way, designed to prepare minority professionals to become members of the board of directors of institutions in the larger community.

Throughout his career, Gibson was involved in community improvement projects and civil rights activities. His personal character and his professional achievements made him a role model for many. For over 40 years he pioneered as a high–achieving African American professional accountant, assistant prosecutor, and law school professor before becoming the first African American federal judge and later the first African American chief federal judge in the Western District of Michigan.

Current address: Judge, Michigan Western District, 616 Federal Building, 110 Michigan St. NW, Grand Rapids, MI 49503–2363.

REFERENCES

"Benjamin Gibson Has Come a Long Way Since 1961." *Lansing State Journal,* April 22, 1979.

"Calling a Recess." *Grand Rapids Press,* October 10, 1996.

"Dow Entertained Judge Gibson While Shared Time Case Was Pending." *Grand Rapids Press,* June 6, 1982.

"Full Pay in the Hammock." *Grand Rapids Press,* October 14, 1997.

"Gibson Backs U.S. Court Here." *Lansing State Journal,* April 18, 1979.

Gibson, Benjamin F. "Hon. Benjamin F. Gibson Biography." n.d. Typescript in the chambers of Judge Gibson.

———. Letters to De Witt S. Dykes Jr., October 31, 1997; December 12, 1997.

———. Resume. N.D.

"Gibson Accuses Press of Trying to Malign Him, Other Blacks." *Grand Rapids Press,* June 7, 1982.

"Gibson: No Desire for Fight With The Press; Avoids Direct Charge of Racial Prejudice." *Grand Rapids Press,* June 8, 1982.

"Gibson Nominated for Federal Judgeship." *Lansing State Journal,* April 17, 1979.
"Gibson Quits as Chief Federal District Judge." *Grand Rapids Press,* May 2, 1995.
"Gibson Removes Self from Shared Time Suit." *Grand Rapids Press,* June 9, 1982.
"Gibson to Examine Docket for Interest Conflicts." *Grand Rapids Press,* June 11, 1982.
"Grand Rapids Bench is Home Now." *Lansing State Journal,* October 5, 1981.
"Hon. Benjamin F. Gibson." *Benchmark: The Thomas M. Cooley Law School Magazine* 19 (Hilary Term 1997): 21.
"Judge Gibson Honored for His 'Quiet' Leadership." *Grand Rapids Press,* October 20, 1991.
"Judge Gibson True to His Word." *Lansing State Journal,* June 27, 1985.
"Judges' Travel Pay Cut; Gibson to Retire." *Grand Rapids Press,* October 7, 1997.
"L.I.N.K's Tutors Assist Minority Kids." *Grand Rapids Press,* January 14, 1987.
"The Road Best Traveled." *Amicus: The Magazine of the Detroit College of Law* (Summer 1991): 19.
"Standing Tall." *Grand Rapids Press,* February 1, 1996.
"3 Named as Judges for U. S. Court Here." *Grand Rapids Press,* April 17, 1979.
Who's Who among African Americans, 1998–99. 10th ed. Detroit: Gale Research, 1998–99.
Who's Who in American Law, 1996–97. 9th ed. Chicago: A. N. Marquis, 1997.

De Witt S. Dykes Jr.

Truman K. Gibson Jr.
(1912–)
Lawyer, boxing promoter, entrepreneur

Truman K. Gibson Jr. was known for his contributions to boxing and the law profession, particularly as attorney for heavyweight boxing champion Joe Louis. He was the first black boxing promoter and secretary of the International Boxing Club. He played a vital part in moving the boxing world from New York to Chicago. He was appointed civilian aid to Secretary of War Stimson in 1940 and investigated racial problems among American soldiers in European theater during World War II.

Born in Atlanta, Georgia, on January 22, 1912, Truman K. Gibson Jr. was the son of Truman Kella Gibson Sr. and Alberta Dickerson Gibson. The Gibsons had two other children: Harry H., and Albert A. Harry and Truman Jr. would have significant business careers. The senior Gibson, a native of Macon, Georgia, graduated from Atlanta University and was a cum laude graduate of Harvard University in 1908 with a second bachelor's degree in business administration. He taught at Saint Paul School in Lawrenceville, Virginia, and then joined the staff of Atlanta Mutual Life. He left racism in the South in 1917 and moved to Columbus, Ohio, where in 1919 he organized the Supreme Life and Casualty Company of Ohio. In 1929 the company merged with Liberty Life and Northeastern Life Insurance Company of Newark to become Supreme Liberty Life Insurance Company. The senior Gibson became first president of the new company. He was also active in several businesses and civic enterprises.

Truman Kella Gibson Jr. grew up in Columbus. While in high school he was a discus thrower and a member of the track team for Columbus's East High School. He studied at the University of Chicago, where he was a second–string guard on coach Alonzo A. Stagg's mediocre basketball team. As a political science student, Gibson studied under Harold F. Gosnell and helped support himself financially by working as a political observer for Gosnell at rallies in black wards. Gibson's observations went into Gosnell's book *The Negro Politician.* During this time he also met leading Republican William L. Dawson. Gibson graduated in 1932 with a bachelor of philosophy degree. He continued his studies at the University of Chicago and received his J.D. degree in 1935. On February 9, 1939, Gibson married Isabelle Carson of Cleveland, who was a social worker. They had one child, Karen Isabelle.

Gibson began law practice in Dawson's office in Chicago from 1935 to 1940. In 1940 Gibson was appointed assistant to William H. Hastie, civilian aide of the U.S. Secretary of War Stimson. Disgusted with military racism, Hastie quit the post and Gibson replaced him as acting aide from February to September of 1943. His acting status was then removed and he became civilian aide until 1945.

The United States entered World War II with a segregated military structure. The 92nd Division, comprised of 12,000 officers and enlisted men, had 200 white officers and 600 black officers. The division was attached to General Mark W. Clark's Fifth Army in the Italian theater known as the "Forgotten Front." Rumors that the black troops made an unsatisfactory showing in Italy prompted the War Department to send Gibson to Italy to make an inspection tour of black military installations. Gibson reported in a press conference that the black troops were as courageous as whites, but 92 percent of the men were illiterate or semi–illiterate. He found them to be poorly trained and knowing little about the objectives of the war. Leaping upon Gibson's report, the press declared the black troops a failure. Since the white command of the division remained silent, some suspected collusion between Gibson and the War Department. Although negative stories abounded at home and abroad, nothing was done to reorganize the segregated infantry and blacks were no longer recruited for combat in Europe.

Gibson received recognition for his efforts. He was appointed to the President Harry S. Truman's Advisory Committee on Universal Military Training in 1946. In 1947 Truman also honored him with the Medal of Merit Award for

Civilians, making him the first African American so honored. In 1948 he was appointed to the President's Committee on Religion and Welfare in the Armed Forces.

Promotes Boxer Joe Louis

In 1945 Gibson resigned the government post and returned to Chicago to practice law with his father and his brother Harry. He also became director and secretary of Joe Louis Enterprises along with fight manager Marshall Miles and accountant Theodore Jones. Gibson and Louis had met earlier when Louis needed some legal work. They were reunited when Gibson, as civilian aide to the war secretary, arranged a traveling troupe of black boxers that Louis took to U.S. military bases in Europe and North Africa to boost the soldiers' morale. Also, in 1942, Gibson arranged the second Joe Louis–Billy Conn title fight to benefit the Army Relief Fund. Their friendship continued and Louis, in tax trouble with the government in 1949, hired Gibson to work on his tax case. Gibson helped Louis organize Joe Louis Enterprises and handled many of his boxing promotions. Gibson managed to get the two of them into the International Boxing Club when it was organized in 1949.

Gibson was highly respected in the IBC. He also told *Ebony* for November of 1951, "I'm very much interested in boxing. I always did like people and you certainly meet a lot of different kinds in the boxing business." Gibson's upper crust black friends questioned his ability to associate successfully with the "fight mob" of the rough sports world. He handled the job well, however, admitting that "we are out to make money." Gibson also promoted the Sugar Ray Robinson–Jake LaMotta world's middleweight title fight in the spring of 1950.

Faces Legal Battles

As Gibson's career in boxing continued in the 1950s, he began to face a number of legal problems. A New York federal judge declared the IBC dissolved in 1957 on the basis that, as a monopoly, it violated antitrust laws. The FBI arrested Gibson in September 22, 1959, after he and four other men were indicted in Los Angeles for extorting money from welterweight champion Don Jordan. The men were convicted on May 30, 1961, and Gibson received a five–year sentence and was fined $5,000.

In 1959 Gibson was named one of three directors of Chicago's newly–formed National Boxing Enterprises. He was one of the company's administrative heads, along with Arthur M. Wirtz, chairman and president of the Chicago Stadium Corporation, and James D. Norris, who at one time was president of IBC. The company operated nationally and presented Wednesday night fights on television. Gibson signed on boxing contenders Ezzard Charles and Jersey Joe Walcott in exclusive contracts and, hoping to seal Joe Louis's financial security, paid Louis $350,000. (It was Norris and Gibson who, in the late 1940s and early 1950s were credited with moving the boxing world from Madison Square Garden to Chicago Stadium, making Chicago the new boxing capital of the world.)

Gibson left the boxing world in the early 1960s and returned to law practice in his own firm Gibson and Gibson. He also was a director and executive committee member of Supreme Life Insurance Company.

In 1977 Gibson was indicted in a stock–swindle suit in New York City involving a Bahamas resort. In 1982 he was placed on six months' probation and ordered to pay $1,000 monthly to the federal government. He defaulted on payments, and in 1988 owed more than $200,000. He plead poverty and escaped a jail term. A federal court jury in Montana indicted Gibson in September of 1987 for bank fraud, for which he received a five–year probationary term and was ordered to make restitution. In a separate ruling concerning an Italian winery deal, he was ordered to pay $138,000 to two men.

Gibson's legal problems continued. He was involved in the nationwide healthcare firm Dental Health Care Alternatives in 1988. Early that year the federal government investigated the company to determine whether the firm paid bribes for the contracts it received. Gibson declared that adverse publicity would prevent the company from successfully negotiating the contracts. He avoided imprisonment for any of the charges brought against him.

Gibson worked with the School for Automotive Trades in Chicago, and was secretary of the Chicago Land Clearance Commission. He was on the board of directors of Chicago Community Fund and Roosevelt College. Professionally, he was a member of the Cook County Bar Association and socially, the Kappa Alpha Psi Fraternity and Sigma Pi Phi (the Boulé).

Despite his legal entanglements, Gibson had a colorful and successful career as a lawyer and boxing promoter.

Current address: 471 E. 31 Street, Chicago, IL 60616.

REFERENCES

"Boxing's New Braintruster." *Ebony* 7 (November 1951): 52–58.

"Gibson Moved into Boxing with Aid of Ex–champ Louis." *Ebony* 7 (November 1951): 54–58.

Greene, Robert Ewell. *Black Defenders of America 1775–1973.* Chicago: Johnson Publishing Company, 1964.

Ingham, John N., and Lynne B. Feldman. *African–American Business Leaders.* Westport, CT: Greenwood Press, 1994.

Mead, Chris. *Champion—Joe Louis: Black Hero in White America.* New York: Charles Scribner's Sons, 1985.

Ottley, Roi. *Black Odyssey.* New York: Charles Scribner's Sons, 1948.

"Truman Gibson Named Co–Director of Boxing Co." *Jet* 15 (5 March 1959): 53.

Who's Who in Colored America. 7th ed. Yonkers–on–Hudson, NY: Christian E. Burckel, 1950.

Jessie Carney Smith

Dizzy Gillespie
(1917–1993)
Musician, band leader, composer, arranger, entertainer

Dizzy Gillespie, one of bebop's founders and a virtuoso jazz trumpeter with a career of almost 60 years, influenced more than five generations of jazz performers. His creative genius turned the tide of jazz performance in the early 1940s and forever changed the sound of jazz.

Dizzy Gillespie was born John Birks Gillespie on October 21, 1917, in the small rural town of Cheraw, South Carolina, He was the youngest of nine children of James and Lottie Powe Gillespie. His father was a bricklayer by trade, but on weekends, he changed his role to that of amateur musician and band leader. His mother was kept busy as a housewife and mother to nine children until her husband died. She then did domestic work to support her children. Dizzy married Lorraine Willis, a dancer, who also grew up in rural South Carolina. They had no children.

Gillespie's musical experience began when he was 12 years old. He had already experimented with playing the piano and decided that when the opportunity presented itself, he wanted to play in the school band. His first instrument was the trombone, but he quickly changed to trumpet because he preferred its sound. Because his father died when Gillespie was only ten years old, his mother struggled with near poverty and could not afford the purchase of an instrument. He played a friend's trumpet and a battered cornet that belonged to his school. These circumstances did not deter him from becoming highly skilled on the trumpet, though he could play in only one key. Gillespie's talent and reputation earned him a scholarship to North Carolina's Laurinburg Technical Institute in 1933. While there, Gillespie learned to play the trumpet in all keys and studied harmony and theory. He focused his efforts on music because he had already decided that this was his future career. According to Gillespie in his autobiography, *To Be or Not to Bop,* "I started fooling around with the piano and my ideas expanded greatly. I practiced constantly, until all times of the night, and anytime I wanted. I'd practice the trumpet and then the piano for twenty–four hours straight if they didn't come around and shut me up when they checked the locks every night." He withdrew from the school before the end of his senior year to join his family in Philadelphia.

Gillespie's first job, at age 18, was with the Frankie Fairfax band in Philadelphia. He arrived at the first rehearsal carrying his trumpet in a brown paper sack because he did not own a case. During his stint with the Fairfax band, Fats Palmer, another band leader, called him "Dizzy" because of his effervescent personality and frequent pranks. The nickname stuck. Gillespie moved to New York City and made his first recording with the Teddy Hill Orchestra in 1937. His enviable trumpet skills enabled him to tour Europe with the band even though most of the older musicians rebelled against such a young player joining their group. Gillespie's performance style at that time was based on that of his idol, Roy Eldridge.

Dizzy Gillespie

Dizzy's Trumpet Sounds

As he played in several bands over the next few years, including Cab Calloway's in 1939 and Earl Hines's in 1943, Gillespie developed his own performance style. It was characterized by playing in the upper register, substitute chords, particularly the flatted fifth, and astounding dexterity. His naturally extroverted persona and comic wit on stage and off made him popular with the public and an effective spokesman for jazz.

Though he enjoyed playing and entertaining, Gillespie found that performance alone did not always earn him enough money. He began to write arrangements for various bands. His considerable piano skills helped him with his writing. As he explained in his autobiography, "Really, the way that I began writing arrangements came from the piano. Often, when I'd find myself strapped for vittles, I'd write an arrangement and fend off starvation." His procedure was to "sit down, at the piano and test out all the chords and combinations." One of his first arrangements, "Pickin' the Cabbage," was written for the Cab Calloway band and helped to solidify his fame as an arranger.

During the early 1930s Gillespie, Charlie Parker, Thelonious Monk, Kenny Clarke, and other musicians jammed after hours at Minton's Playhouse and Monroe's Uptown House on 52nd Street. The young musicians felt constrained by big band

Dizzy Gillespie performing.

swing and decided to develop a style of their own. Gillespie reminisced, in his autobiography, that he coined the word "bebop" in an attempt to explain how the ending notes of a musical phrase should sound. Acceptance of the new style came slowly because audiences were accustomed to music for dancing and the new jazz style was more suitable for listening. Music critics were particularly polarized over bebop's viability; many ridiculed the new genre by calling it "Chinese music."

After playing with many outstanding bands including those led by Ella Fitzgerald, Coleman Hawkins, Benny Carter, Charlie Barnet, Les Hite, Lucky Millinder, Earl Hines, and a short stint with Duke Ellington, and serving as musical director for Billy Eckstine's group, Gillespie founded his own big band in 1945. While playing in Earl Hines' band, which included Charlie Parker, Gillespie began to promote publicly the new bebop style. These early days of bebop were not documented because the musicians union had a rift with the record companies that resulted in a strike and a ban on recording.

In 1947 Gillespie again enriched jazz expression by synthesizing bebop with Afro–Cuban rhythms. He was the first band leader to utilize the conga drum in his instrumentation. He hired the talented Cuban conga player, Chano Pozo, as a regular in his band, and together they wrote the best–selling songs "Manteca" and "Cubana Be, Cubana Bop." Gillespie's band made its debut at Carnegie Hall in September of 1947 with not only Pozo but also Charlie Parker as performers. The band received rave reviews from the critics for its innovative Afro–Cuban style. In later years, Gillespie also used his creative genius to pioneer the fusion of Afro–Brazilian music with jazz. According to Peter Watrous in the *New York Times,* "Without the sophisticated arrangements and the conjunction of Latin rhythms and jazz harmonies that Mr. Gillespie provided, both jazz and Latin music would be radically different today."

Jazz Band Tours

During the 1950s, Gillespie continued to refine bebop which by that time had become the basic mode of jazz expression. In 1956 the U.S. Department of State asked Gillespie to represent the country and take a band on a tour of Europe, Africa, and the Middle East. This represented the first State Department subsidized tour for a jazz band. From 1962 to 1967 he fronted a series of jazz quintets that included the legendary saxophonist, James Moody. During the 1970s and 1980s Gillespie maintained a busy touring and recording schedule, sometimes playing up to 300 shows a year. In 1988 he organized another big band called the United Nations Orchestra, so named because it included musicians from Cuba, Puerto Rico, Brazil, Panama, and the Dominican Republic. In 1988 the new band recorded *Dizzy Gillespie and the United Nations Orchestra: Live at Royal Festival Hall in London,* for which he won a Grammy award in 1991.

The indefatigable Gillespie continued an exhausting schedule of performances and recording sessions almost until his death. In 1992 he was honored with a year–long diamond jubilee celebrating over 50 years of performance and his 75th birthday. He participated in a month–long recording session at the renowned Blue Note Club in New York that resulted in two live albums: *To Bird with Love* and *To Diz with Love.* This lengthy session featured many of the young trumpeters and earlier colleagues whose talents he had nurtured: Wynton Marsalis, Jon Faddis, and Doc Cheatham.

Gillespie wrote or cowrote many jazz standards, including: "A Night in Tunisia," "Salt Peanuts," "Woody 'n You," "Groovin' High," "Tin Tin Deo," "Manteca," and "Con Alma." He performed at the White House for presidents Lyndon B. Johnson, Richard Nixon, Gerald Ford, and Jimmy Carter. He received Grammy awards in 1975, 1980, and 1991, the National Medal of the Arts from the U.S. government in 1989, and in 1990, the prestigious Kennedy Center Award.

Gillespie's autobiography, *To Be Or Not to Bop Memoirs,* written with Wilmot Alfred Fraser and published in 1979, included multiple interviews with his musician friends. Most of them attest to his genius, his amiable personality, his generous spirit, and his lifelong mentoring of young musicians.

International Fame

Gillespie had many friends from the jazz world, but none as close as legendary saxophonist Charlie Parker. Gillespie recognized Parker's role in developing bebop, and said in his autobiography that Parker was "musically, the other side of my heartbeat." Gillespie's wife, Lorraine, who was married to him for 52 years, spoke of his closeness to Parker by saying that the only times Gillespie was sad were when his mother died and when Charlie Parker died in 1955 at the young age of 34.

Gillespie became an international figure through his many performances abroad. He was revered by people wherever he went. Gillespie was always recognized by his trademark ballooning cheeks and upward–bent trumpet bell. During the early days of bebop, young jazz fans copied his fashionable dress, his goatee, horn–rimmed glasses, and beret as outward symbols of their love for him and his music.

Gillespie died of pancreatic cancer on January 6, 1993, aged 76. Quoted in the *Washington Post,* a young saxophonist who was nurtured by Gillespie gave tribute saying, "I knew Dizzy Gillespie the last 16 years of his life, and I can tell you that he was one of the greatest men I have ever met. I am proud to have called him my boss, but more than that, he was my friend." This moving testimony summarized Gillespie's true legacy as a giant of jazz whose music will live on through the lives of those he inspired.

REFERENCES

Gillespie, Dizzy, and Al Fraser. *To Be or Not to Bop.* New York: Doubleday, 1979.

Gourse, Leslie. *Dizzy Gillespie and the Birth of Bebop.* New York: Atheneum Press, 1994.

"Horn of Plenty, Horn of Joy: Playing It the Dizzy Way." *Washington Post,* January 10, 1993.

Watrous, Peter. "Dizzy Gillespie, Who Sounded Some of Modern Jazz's Earliest Notes, Dies At 75." *New York Times,* January 7, 1993.

Mary Frances Early

Charles S. Gilpin

(1878–1930)

Actor, singer

Charles S. Gilpin was one of the first black dramatic actors to appear on Broadway. When he was growing up, there were practically no roles open to serious black actors—black roles in professional plays were almost without exception played by whites in blackface. Beginning as a singer and comic actor, Gilpin seized on opportunities to play in black stock companies and developed his acting abilities. He was therefore ready to meet the challenge posed by the title role of Eugene O'Neill's play *The Emperor Jones* and become the first black to star on Broadway. Not only was the role a personal triumph for Gilpin, it also opened the door for other blacks in the professional theater.

Charles Sydney Gilpin was born November 20, 1878, in Richmond, Virginia, to Peter and Caroline White Gilpin. He was the youngest of 14 children. He attended a Catholic school until he was 12 and then trained as a printer with a local black newspaper, the *Richmond Planet.*

Gilpin first tried his hand at show business by appearing locally on stage in Richmond, where he made his debut on October 24, 1890. At this time opportunities for African American actors were practically nonexistent, so he worked as a singer, using his excellent baritone voice. He left town in 1896 with a minstrel show, the Big Spectacular Log Cabin Company, which went broke two towns later. He then became

Charles S. Gilpin

affiliated with the Great Southern Minstrel Barnstorming Company, which lasted a few more months before running out of money.

Gilpin then worked at a variety of jobs in Philadelphia, including stints as a printer and as a barber. In time, he found work as a singer at events like fairs and also on the church concert circuit. He eventually discovered that he could earn better money as a janitor, which in turn led to his becoming a trainer of prize fighters. In 1903, however, he joined the Canadian Jubilee Singers and stayed with them for two years.

Lands Vaudeville Role

Gilpin's first big break came at the end of 1905 when he landed a supporting role in "The Two Real Coons," a vaudeville act starring Bert Williams and George Walker that was based on a scene from their musical *In Abyssinia.* Gilpin worked with Williams and Walker until he joined the Smart Set Company in November of 1906, playing the role of Remus Bareland. In 1907 Gilpin became associated with the Pekin Stock Company in Chicago, where he first attracted attention on April 20 in the three–act musical *The Husbands* by Flournoy Miller and Aubrey Lyles.

Besides singing, Gilpin's specialty at the Pekin was blackface comedy. His work on the programs (which changed every two weeks) gave him valuable stage experience. In 1909, for instance, there are records indicating that he performed in several plays through July. But the Pekin Stock Company seems to have closed by the end of 1909.

From 1911 to 1913 Gilpin toured with the Pan American Octette. In 1913 he appeared in *The Old Man's Boy,* which opened on May 12 in Philadelphia and moved to New York in June. Offered by the Negro Players, a stock company then headed by Alex Rogers and Henry Creamer, this play featured many songs and dances and a third act that was originally straight drama. (A musical number was added later.)

The first completely dramatic play done by black professionals, however, was *The Girl at the Fort,* presented by the Anita Bush Stock Company at the Lincoln Theatre in Harlem on November 15, 1915. (It was around this same time that Gilpin joined the troupe.) By the end of the year the Anita Bush Stock Company had transferred to the Lafayette Theatre, where it later became known as the Lafayette Players. (This group would endure until 1932 and provide an important training ground for black actors.) The new name first appeared in March of 1916 in advertisements for the play *Southern Life,* which starred Gilpin. By April of 1916, however, he had quit the troupe in a dispute over salary.

Little is known about the next few years of Gilpin's life. According to Tom Fletcher in the book *100 Years of the Negro in Show Business,* he tried to form his own stock company but failed. Gilpin then attempted to find work in vaudeville and also toiled as an elevator operator and a railroad porter.

Makes Broadway Debut

In 1919, Gilpin secured his first Broadway role in British playwright John Drinkwater's *Abraham Lincoln,* which opened on December 15. Gilpin had one scene as the Reverend William Custis, a character based on Frederick Douglass. The play was mildly successful, with Gilpin winning favorable notices despite the fact that he had to speak a kind of pidgin English that was at odds with historical reality. His appearance nevertheless marked a minor breakthrough of sorts, because typical theatrical practice at that time would have been to use a white actor in blackface to play the role.

That practice was about to change, however. Playwright Eugene O'Neill, who was then working with the Provincetown (Massachusetts) Players and had yet to make his mark on the Broadway stage, had been experimenting with black characters in his work. His one–act play, *Moon of the Caribees* (1918), had been produced with whites playing blacks. On October 31, 1919, *The Dreamy Kid,* another one–act play starring four black actors, made its debut. Then, on November 3, 1920, *The Emperor Jones* opened with Gilpin playing the title role. (According to one account, he had been hired for the part while running the elevator at Macy's department store.) A week later, the influential *New York Times* theater critic Alexander Woollcott noted in an article that was later reprinted in the book *On Stage:*

> [The play] weaves a most potent spell, thanks partly to the force and cunning of its author, thanks partly to the force and cunning of Charles S. Gilpin in a title rôle so predominant that the play is little more than a dramatic monologue. His is an uncommonly

> powerful and imaginative performance, in several respects unsurpassed this season in New York. Mr. Gilpin is a negro.

Triumphs in *The Emperor Jones*

On January 29, 1921, the play moved to a Broadway theater and ran for 204 performances before going on a two–year tour. In February of that same year the Drama League named Gilpin one of the ten persons who had contributed most to the American theater and stood firmly by the invitation it had issued to him to attend the presentation banquet in spite of some protests by whites. On June 30 the NAACP awarded Gilpin the Spingarn Medal. A side benefit of all this acclaim was the eagerness of vaudeville houses to book him and his partner Lillian Woods for shows during the summer season.

O'Neill himself had high praise for Gilpin's ability to realize the playwright's intentions but found other aspects of his performance disturbing. For one, the actor began changing lines that he found offensive to blacks. He also drank, although accounts disagree as to how much his drinking affected his performances. In any case, O'Neill hired Paul Robeson for the London production of *The Emperor Jones* and the subsequent 1924 American revival.

In March of 1924 Gilpin appeared in a revival of Nan Bagby Stephens's *Roseanne,* which had failed with a white cast. Rose McClendon won plaudits for her performance in the title role, but Gilpin fared badly with the critics. In 1926 he lost his voice and again turned to running an elevator to earn a living. It was in this same year that he made his only film, *Ten Nights in a Barroom,* a 60–minute feature for the Colored Players of Philadelphia. Gilpin played the lead role of an alcoholic father in this adaptation of a famous temperance work.

Gilpin married twice. His 1897 union with Florence Howard produced one son, Paul Wilson, in 1903. His second wife, Alma Benjamin, survived him. Gilpin died on May 6, 1930, in Eldridge Park, near Trenton, New Jersey. At first, he was buried quietly in Lambertville. Then Lillian Woods had the body exhumed and taken to New York, where a more lavish funeral was held on June 1. The subsequent reburial was in Woodlawn Cemetery.

Gilpin made a valuable contribution to the advancement of blacks in show business. He also played a part in developing a specifically black theater. For example, he once visited a little theater group in Cleveland while on tour in *The Emperor Jones.* As reported by Arna Bontemps and Jack Conroy in an essay published in *Anthology of the American Negro in the Theatre,* Gilpin took a few moments to talk to the young black actors who had gathered to meet with him:

> "Look here, you're all wrong," Gilpin said to the group sitting along the apron of the crude stage. "Why don't you take yourselves seriously and really do something? Make this a real Negro theater. You could do it. Look at the material all around you. Learn to see the drama in your own lives, and someday the world will come to see your plays. If there aren't any plays, get somebody to write them."

Gilpin's advice and $50 donation launched the Gilpin Players and the Karamu Theater, both distinguished pioneers in black theater. It was a fitting legacy for a man who had himself blazed more than a few trails in his day.

REFERENCES

Anderson, Jervis. *This Was Harlem.* New York: Farrar Straus Giroux, 1982.

Beckerman, Bernard, and Howard Siegman, eds. *On Stage.* New York: Arno Press with Quadrangle/New York Times Book Co., 1973.

Fletcher, Tom. *100 Years of the Negro in Show Business.* 1954. Reprint, New York: Da Capo, 1984.

Hill, Errol, ed. *The Theater of Black Americans.* Vol. 2. Englewood Cliffs, NJ: Prentice–Hall, 1980.

Johnson, James Weldon. *Black Manhattan.* New York: Knopf, 1930.

Kellner, Bruce. *The Harlem Renaissance.* New York: Methuen, 1984.

Klotman, Phyllis Rauch. *Frame by Frame.* Bloomington: Indiana University Press, 1979.

Logan, Rayford W., and Michael R. Winston, eds. *Dictionary of American Negro Biography.* New York: Norton, 1982.

Patterson, Lindsay, ed. *Anthology of the American Negro in the Theatre.* Publishers Company, 1970.

Riis, Thomas L. *Just Before Jazz.* Washington, DC: Smithsonian Institution Press, 1989.

Sampson, Henry T. *The Ghost Walks.* Metuchen, NJ: Scarecrow Press, 1988.

Southern, Eileen. *Biographical Dictionary of Afro–American and African Musicians.* Westport, CT: Greenwood Press, 1982.

Who's Who in Colored America. New York: Who's Who in Colored America, 1927.

Robert L. Johns

John Gloucester
(1776?–1822)
Religious leader

John Gloucester founded the first black Presbyterian church in the United States and was one of the small number of early black ministers in the denomination. Since Presbyterian churches were unsuccessful in attracting black members in large numbers, Gloucester has often been overlooked, and there are few records of his life. For the growth of his denomination among African Americans, it was a distinct disappointment that he died at the age of 46, when there were only two other black Presbyterian ministers in the North.

Little is known of John Gloucester's life before 1807 when he arrived in Philadelphia. In that year he was the slave of Gideon Blackburn (1772–1838), who was ordained a Presbyterian minister in 1792. After serving as pastor of a church, Blackburn established in 1804 a mission to the Cherokee Indians and founded a school which he continued until 1810. Blackburn converted Gloucester, who served as his body servant. Gloucester was married and had four children before he came to Philadelphia. Three sons became Presbyterian ministers. (Sons Jeremiah and Solomon worked in Philadelphia and James M. in Brooklyn, New York. James M. became relatively affluent and was a supporter of John Brown, the white abolitionist who raided Harper's Ferry.)

Blackburn gave Gloucester a religious education and sponsored him as a ministerial candidate. In Philadelphia during the early years of the nineteenth century, the growth of Presbyterianism among blacks was negligible in comparison with the rapid growth of Methodism, especially in the semi-independent church led by Richard Allen. In early 1807 Gloucester was recommended by the Presbytery of Union Synod of Tennessee to the General Assembly meeting in Lexington, Virginia, as a candidate for licensure. This brought him to the attention of Archibald Alexander (1772–1851), a prominent minister who had just recently accepted a post in Philadelphia, and the Philadelphia Evangelical Society. Blackburn and Gloucester traveled to Philadelphia at the close of the Lexington meeting. There Gloucester was hired as a missionary by the society, and Blackburn gave him his freedom. Purchasing the freedom of his wife and four children was a major concern of Gloucester over the following years.

Gloucester began his activity by preaching in private houses. In a short time his congregation grew too large to meet in a house, and he took to street preaching. Gloucester had a very good voice, and he opened his meetings at the corner of Seventh and Shippen streets as early as six o'clock in the morning by singing to attract a crowd. In case of inclement weather he obtained the use of a nearby schoolhouse. In the latter part of May 1807 or early June nine women and 14 men were organized as the First African Presbyterian Church. His success as a missionary was such that he was offered great inducements to switch denominations, but he refused on doctrinal grounds.

On July 7, 1807, the Philadelphia Presbytery rejected a request from the General Assembly to consider Gloucester's ordination, citing that his original presbytery could better judge of his character and abilities. Gloucester returned to Tennessee and the jurisdiction of the Presbytery of Union Synod, which undertook to sponsor him as a ministerial candidate. He then had to split his activities between his ministerial work in Philadelphia and his studies until he was ordained by the Tennessee presbytery on April 30, 1810. On April 16, 1811, he became a member of the Philadelphia presbytery.

John Gloucester

Gibson's church met either in a large room in Gaskill Street or in the school house on Seventh Street. By the summer of 1809 the congregation had reached the point that it needed a permanent home. On July 31, 1809, the Evangelical Society launched an appeal for support, reprinted in Catto's history, pointing out that many black Presbyterians "find it to be inconvenient and unpleasant, for reasons which need not now be stated, to attend the houses of worship frequented by white people."

The appeal resulted in the purchase of a lot at the corner of Shippen and Seventh Street. The cornerstone of the church was laid in 1810, and the structure was dedicated on May 31, 1811. It was a plain brick building capable of seating 650 people in comfort. At the time of its dedication the church had 123 members. While the church became part of the Philadelphia Presbytery, Gloucester never became its official minister. Instead he remained in the employ of the Evangelical Society for financial reasons.

Even before the church was dedicated, Gloucester was working to raise monies to purchase his wife and his four children. His efforts led to extensive travels, and he collected money in almost all major cities in the North and in the South. Unable to raise the entire sum needed in the United States, he undertook a trip to England, where he finally gathered enough money to buy and free his family.

Like most black ministers of the period, Gloucester was a community leader. He was a leader in the 1817 meeting in Philadelphia called to oppose the American Colonization Society and its desire to repatriate free blacks to Africa. He was also a founding member of the Pennsylvania Augustine Society for the Education of People of Color in 1818. As a minister he labored at moral reform and uplift. He conducted both a day school and a Sunday school. Catto provided a description of the sorts of problems he had to deal with among his congregation, appraising that Gloucester was able to hold "within bounds the turbulent dispositions of men." He added:

> His situation was trying one, particularly when we consider that his congregation was a mixed one, made up of some who had come from other churches, each holding more or less peculiar views of his own, others from a conviction of duty to God and the exceeding sinfulness of sin; these were from the world, snatched from the very jaws of the lion; still they were unacquainted with government, and had to be broken in to the rule and order of the church.

Gloucester died young of tuberculosis. By June 27, 1820, his health had deteriorated to the point that he had to ask for ministers to replace him in the pulpit. He had already produced two candidates for the ministry, Samuel Cornish and Benjamin Hughes. On April 18, 1821, he recommended his son Jeremiah as a ministerial candidate. He died on May 2, 1822.

The church lost members over the succession of Jeremiah Gloucester. Those who were not willing to wait for Jeremiah to finish his schooling called Benjamin Hughes to the church. Hughes could not support himself on the salary paid by the church and soon resigned to go into business, dying shortly afterwards in Africa. This left the church to the care of a succession of white ministers, since Cornish, the only other black Presbyterian minister, could not be lured to Philadelphia from his New York church. When Jeremiah Gloucester was ordained, he led the greater part of the congregation into the Second African Presbyterian Church.

Gloucester had substantial powers as a minister and religious worker. Founding a black Presbyterian church was an exceptional accomplishment in a city where there was already a flourishing Episcopal church that attracted many of the older black elites and a rapidly growing black Methodist church. His death at an age when he should have been reaching the height of his career was a misfortune for his church.

REFERENCES

Alexander, Archibald, and Gideon Blackburn, eds. *Dictionary of American Biography.* New York: Scribner's, 1943.

Aptheker, Herbert, ed. *A Documentary History of the Negro People in the United States.* New York: Citadel Press, 1951.

Catto, William T. *A Semi–Centenary Discourse, Delivered in the First African Presbyterian Church, Philadelphia, May, 1857.* 1857. Reprint, Freeport, NY: Books for Libraries Press, 1971.

George, Carol V. R. *Segregated Sabbaths.* New York: Oxford, 1973.

Smith, Edward D. *Climbing Jacob's Ladder.* Washington, DC: Smithsonian Institution Press, 1988.

Robert L. Johns

Danny Glover

(1947–)

Actor

Community politics and an interest in acting emerged simultaneously in the life of Danny Glover as a student studying economics at San Francisco State University in the late 1960s. The pragmatic, socially conscious family man has built a career on stage, screen, and in television by taking chances with roles that have made a statement. He took an active role in opposing apartheid in South Africa. He spends much of his time speaking at schools, working with family literacy programs, the underprivileged, and other causes. Remembering his roots, he continues to give to the Haight Ashbury community where he grew up and currently lives.

Danny Glover, the first of James and Carrie Glover's five children, was born on July 22, 1947, in San Francisco, and grew up in a strong, loving family. As a child he was gawky, tall and skinny. Other children made fun of his dark skin and his wide nose and he grew up feeling uncomfortable with himself. He spent summers with his grandparents in Louisville, Georgia. At age 11, he had a paper route. A mild case of dyslexia caused him some problems with reading but he was a good student, especially in mathematics. In high school, he played tight end on the football team until a series of epileptic episodes ended his play at age 16. (The seizures ended at 30, as quickly as they began.) At this stage in his young life, Glover enjoyed performing with his church choir but showed no interest in acting.

When Glover graduated from high school, he enrolled at San Francisco State University with a major in economics. In the late 1960s, racial, political, and social activism was sweeping college campuses across the nation. Glover's politics and community involvement evolved during these turbulent times. In an article in *Ebony* magazine, Aldore Collier quoted Glover on the start of his interest in politics and acting:

> My interest began simultaneously with my political involvement. My acting is also an extension of my involvement in community politics, working with groups like the African Liberation Support Committee, tutorial programs, etc. All of these things, at some point, drew me into acting.

Glover joined the Black Student Union where he made rousing speeches before groups of students and helped to organize a strike that eventually led to the reversal of the

Danny Glover

decision to eliminate the school's ethnic studies department. Even though his parents were postal workers, union organizers, and members of the NAACP in the 1950s, they were nonetheless upset when their son's activities resulted in his being arrested. In addition to working with the Black Student Union, Glover revealed to Gene Siskel in an interview published in the *Chicago Tribune* March 8, 1987, that he was a member of the Black Panther Party.

During Glover's college years he also worked with the African Liberation Support Committee as well as the Western Addition Community Organization, an organization involved with the problems of people displaced by urban development. He was also active in tutorial and reading programs for inner city children. He graduated from college and began work as a civil servant in the Bay Area.

In the midst of all his activities he met Asake Bomani, an English major at the university and a native of Wilmington, Delaware. She won his heart immediately and they were married in 1972. In an article for *People* magazine, Glover said of his wife, "I have always been infatuated with Sake. She has a strong sense of morality, coupled with a strong sense of herself." As of 1998, she was the owner of the Bomani Gallery, a jazz singer, and the mother of their 21–year–old daughter, Mandisa.

Politics and Acting Converge

When Amiri Baraka appeared on campus in 1967, Glover was asked to act in some of his plays. He auditioned for a play that only a few actors had chosen and got the part. He began his acting career playing activist roles and believed that he was making a statement in the plays.

Plays written by Athol Fugard first gave voice to Glover's changing view of the world, bringing together his politics and his acting. When, in the mid–1970s, he decided to become an actor, he quit his job as an evaluator for the city of Berkeley and joined the Black Actors' Workshop of the American Conservatory Theater in New York City; his wife, Asake, supported him through the trials and triumphs of that decision. One of his triumphs was his appearance in Fugard's play, *Blood Knot* in 1978.

When Fugard's play *Master Harold . . . and the Boys* premiered at the Yale Repertory Theatre, Glover appeared as Willie. His performance earned him the Theatre World Award as one of the most promising talents of 1982. This appearance attracted the attention of director and screenwriter Robert Benton, who cast him as Mose in the 1984 film, *Places in the Heart.* This Academy Award–nominated film is about a black hobo farmer who goes to work for a white southern widow and helps her save the family farm. This role was a life–changing event for Danny Glover.

Three movies followed in 1985. Glover played a small but favorably reviewed part in *Witness,* as a suave, former police officer turned murderer. In the hip western, *Silverado,* Glover played a black cowboy and a hero. This role made him aware of the responsibility he has in maintaining his image as a black actor. Lisa Belkin quoted Glover on the subject of his choice of roles in a *New York Times* article on January 26, 1986. Referring to the often quoted lines of his character, Malachi, he said: "I've run into black kids who flash their two fingers at me like guns and who say 'This ought to do' or 'I don't want to kill you and you don't want to be dead.'" Glover knows he is being watched by kids and he recognizes responsibility.

Glover's role in Steven Spielberg's film, *The Color Purple,* sparked controversy. Glover defended, but did not excuse, the character, Mister, as a mean wife abuser because he had been abused by the world and was a product of his environment as well as his inability to have that which he idealized. The *New York Times* for January 26, 1986, also addresses Glover's concern for the lack of black role models: "I have to be careful about the parts I take. Given how this industry has dealt with people like me, the parts I take have to be political choices."

Glover's other acting credits include the films *Escape from Alcatraz, Chu Chu and the Philly Flash, Iceman, Birdy,* the *Lethal Weapon* series, *Mandela, Bat 21, Predator 2, Flight of the Intruder, Bopha!,* and *Angels in the Outfield.* His television performances include *Lonesome Dove, Many Mansions,* and *A Raisin in the Sun,* plus guest appearances on other popular series. His stage credits include *The Island, Sizwe Bansi Is Dead, A Lesson from Alloes* by Athol Fugard, *Joe Turner's Come and Gone* and *The Piano Lesson* by August Wilson, and *Suicide in B Flat* by Sam Shepard.

The Heart of the Man

Glover is pragmatic about his career, recognizing that an actor is only as good as his last work and that the next good part may be a long time coming. Kevin Powell, writing in *Essence* magazine in July of 1994, quoted him on his profession:

> I want to feel that I made choices that empowered me and substantiated me as a human being. My career is going to be here and gone. But I'm always going to be a human being. And I want to look myself in the mirror and say that I was the human being I wanted to be.

Glover's family still lives in San Francisco, where he is involved in community activities in the Haight Ashbury neighborhood, not far from where he grew up. In the June 13, 1996, issue of the *San FranciscoSun Reporter,* an article by Amelia Ashley–Ward entitled "Fathers making a Difference," Glover was named one of five fathers who are "not just looking out for their own families, but they play leading roles in the community as well."

Danny Glover's community is the world. He is a humanitarian who sees in all human beings miracles waiting to happen. In the article entitled "Conversations with Danny Glover" published in the *Philadelphia Tribune* for September 16, 1994, Alexia Hudson revealed the essence of the actor and the man as she quoted him saying:

> I can only account for my belief that we have an amazing capacity to be God–like and to find the God within ourselves and the miracles within ourselves. And I'm always excited about our ability whether it's in the inner city or in school or a child's face. And I saw more angels at a church in Soweto than I've seen in my entire life. They had waged the good fight, they had transformed their lives, they had created the miracles.

Current address: Actor, c/o William Morris Agency, 151 El Camino Dr., Ste. 233, Beverly Hills, CA 90212.

REFERENCES

Chicago Tribune, March 8, 1987.

Collier, Aldore. "Danny Glover: The Reluctant Movie Star." *Ebony* 41 (March 1986): 83–84.

Contemporary Black Biography. Vol. 1. Detroit: Gale Research, 1992.

"Conversations with Danny Glover." *Philadelphia Tribune,* September 16, 1994.

Current Biography Yearbook. New York: H. W. Wilson, 1992.

"Danny Glover." *New York Times,* January 26, 1986.

"Fathers Making a Difference." *San Francisco Sun Reporter,* June 13, 1996.

Powell, Kevin. "What a Man!" *Essence* 25 (July 1994): 52–54.

Rosen, Marjorie, and Lois Armstrong. *People* 37 (10 February 1992): 91–92.

Ann C. Sullivan

Mal Goode
(1908–1995)
Journalist, consultant

Mal Goode was the first black correspondent hired by network television news. He became known for his work in civil rights during the 1960s, when his assignments included covering the assassinations of civil rights leaders, and in human rights through his work as the American Broadcasting Company's correspondent at the United Nations, particularly during the Cuban missile crisis.

Born in White Plains, Virginia, on February 13, 1908, Malvin "Mal" R. Goode was third in a family of four boys and two girls—James, William, Mary, Allan, and Ruth. His mother, the daughter of slaves from Augusta County, Virginia, had attended West Virginia Collegiate Institute (now West Virginia State University). She therefore stressed the importance of education and instilled a sense of pride in her children. According to *Many Shades of Black,* she said, "I want you children to remember two things: one, you are no better than anyone else; and two, no one else is any better than you." Goode was guided permanently by her wisdom. His father, on the other hand, had only three weeks of formal education in a rural school in Brunswick County, Virginia, where his parents had been slaves. He favored work over education for his children.

When Goode was a young child his family moved to the steel town of Homestead, Pennsylvania (a suburb of Pittsburgh), perhaps in search of better employment opportunities and education for the children. His father became a steelworker for the old Carnegie Steel Company in Homestead and later reached the top position for a black in the company—first helper in the open hearth. After World War I he also established a fish and poultry business.

Goode attended the local public schools, first at Fifth Ward elementary school, where rarely more than two black children were enrolled at any given time. His teachers were important and influential. Writing in *Many Shades of Black,* Goode said that "their teaching and training methods were fair, and equality was a watchword for them." His mother visited frequently to show her support. Later, while attending high school, Goode was a night worker in the same plant where his father had been employed for almost 30 years.

After graduating in 1926, Goode continued working in the local steel mills to pay his expenses at the University of Pennsylvania. Because his brothers James and William were already in college and the family had little money to help support him, Goode delayed his entrance into college until 1927 and received a bachelor's degree in 1931.

Goode then went to work as a porter at Richman Brothers' Clothing Company at a starting wage of eight dollars per week. He remained there until 1936, when he was appointed probation officer for Pittsburgh's juvenile court for $125 a month. After two years, he left the position and then spent five

Mal Goode

years as director of boys' work for the Centre Avenue YMCA in Pittsburgh, where he fought to eliminate discrimination in local branches of the organization.

On July 1, 1942, Goode was named manager of the Bedford Dwellings Development, one the few racially–integrated housing units in the nation at that time. Three years later he was transferred to head a larger housing project, Terrace Village. A heart attack in 1948 kept him from work for nearly six months.

Becomes a Journalist

In 1949 Goode began a career in radio journalism as commentator on station KQV in Pittsburgh and moved from there to radio station WHOD in Homestead, where his sister, Mary Dee, was a disc jockey. He and his sister became a well–known team on the station. Goode broadcast the news as well as sports and interviewed celebrities such as Jackie Robinson, Monte Irvin, and Willie Mays.

Also in 1949, Goode accepted an offer to work in the circulation department for the *Pittsburgh Courier,* thus launching his career in print journalism. To build the newspaper's circulation, he traveled to a number of cities, including Chicago, Memphis, Nashville, Roanoke and other places across the South. Along the way he met mayors, governors, and prominent black business and civic leaders.

Goode's duties with the *Pittsburgh Courier* eventually expanded to include troubleshooter, public relations representative, advertising salesman, and general utility man. Meanwhile, he continued with his radio work, and in 1952 he was named news director of WHOD. He was forced to leave the station when it was sold in 1956 and then moved to WMCK in McKeesport, Pennsylvania. Within the year, Goode sought employment at Pittsburgh's major radio and television stations but was denied a position because of racially discriminatory hiring practices.

First Black TV Correspondent

On September 10, 1962, when he was 54 years old, Goode was hired as a correspondent by ABC News on the recommendation of his friend, baseball star Jackie Robinson. With this appointment he broke a racial barrier and became the first black network television reporter. According to the *African–American Almanac,* Goode said that one reason he was chosen was because "he was considered dark enough so blacks would know he was black, but light enough so that whites wouldn't feel threatened." His wealth of experience also made him stand out among the 30 candidates for the job.

ABC swiftly moved Goode to its bureau at the United Nations, where as correspondent he had both domestic and foreign assignments. Goode received national acclaim during the Cuban missile crisis, particularly during the weekend of October 27–28, 1962, when he had the major responsibility for reporting UN activities. On October 28, for example, Goode was the lone reporter at the UN when the Russian and United States representatives and Acting Secretary–General U Thant held a series of meetings. He did 17 radio and television reports on that day alone—a crucial moment in world history.

In June of 1963 ABC selected Goode and three of his colleagues to conduct ten–week journalism seminars under the auspices of the UN for African students in Lagos, Nigeria; Addis Ababa, Ethiopia; and Dar es Salaam, Tanzania. Later, Goode worked with the network's News Election Unit, covering the 1964 and 1968 presidential primaries for both the Republican and Democratic parties. He covered many of the major events during the civil rights struggle of the 1960s as well, including a number of demonstrations, the assassinations of Malcolm X and Martin Luther King Jr., and the Poor People's March on Washington. He also worked with the news department of the ABC–affiliated station WABC–TV in New York.

Active "Retirement"

Goode spent 20 years with ABC before retiring. Even then, he continued to serve the network as a consultant and maintained an office at the United Nations Building in New York City until he was nearly 80 years old. Regarded as the dean of black professional broadcast journalism, Goode was widely sought as a speaker on topics such as civil rights and the United Nations.

Goode's numerous organizational affiliations included the Association of Radio–TV Analysts, the National Association of Radio and TV News Directors (of which he was the first black member), and the United Nations Correspondents Association (of which he served as president in 1972). Also around 1972, Goode teamed up with a number of American corporate representatives as a member of the President's Plan for Progress Committee. In addition, he was a consultant to the National Black Network as special correspondent for international affairs, a board member of the NAACP, and a trustee of the First Baptist Church of Teaneck, New Jersey. Goode was also a member of the New York Chapter of 100 Black Men.

Goode's numerous awards and citations included an honorary doctor of humanities degree from Shaw University, the Mary McLeod Bethune Award from Bethune–Cookman College, keys to 35 cities across America, and the Michelle Clark Award from Columbia University School of Journalism. Alpha Phi Alpha Fraternity named him Man of the Year in 1964 and later gave him their highest honor, the Award of Merit. He also received the Polish Government Award from the United Nations in 1972.

After suffering a stroke, Goode died at Margret's Memorial Hospital in Pittsburgh on Tuesday, September 12, 1995, at the age of 87. His life and death touched many people, particularly those at ABC where he had worked for so many years. Commenting in the *New York Times,* Peter Jennings described Goode as a mentor and said that ''Mal could have very sharp elbows. If he was on a civil rights story and anyone even appeared to give him any grief because he was black he made it more than clear that this was now a free country.''

ABC medical correspondent George Strait, a black reporter, noted in the same source that Goode ''refused to be pigeon–holed. He wouldn't let them assign him only to so–called black stories. . . . He opened the way for the next generation . . . and that's why I'm on the medical beat.''

Bernard Shaw, whom Goode also mentored, said in a special telecast reported on in *Jet* that ''Goode certified himself as a man of the universe when he answered the question: 'How do you want to be remembered.' Goode responded: 'I'd like to be remembered as somebody who tried to do something to make life better for someone, not better for Black people, not better for Afro Americans, not better for White people, but better for humanity.'''

Goode was eulogized at Pittsburgh's Lincoln Avenue Church of God by his son, Richard A. Goode, pastor of Atlanta's Fellowship of Prayer Church of God. He was survived by his wife, Mary Levelle; two daughters, Roberta Wilbur and Rosalie Parker; three other sons, Robert, Malvin Jr., and Roland; a sister, Ruth Goode White; and seven grandchildren.

A pioneer black television journalist, Goode is perhaps best remembered as a civil and human rights advocate. But to his peers, many of whom are now journalists in the forefront of network television reporting, he was an invaluable mentor.

REFERENCES

The African American Almanac. 6th ed. Detroit: Gale Research, 1994.

Bennett, Hal, and Lew Roberts. ''National Black Network: Black Radio's Big Brother.'' *Black Enterprise* 8 (June 1977): 141–47.

''Mal Goode, First Black TV Reporter, Advocate Journalist, Dies at 87.'' *Jet* 88 (2 October 1995): 17–18.

''Malvin R. Goode, 87, Reporter Who Broke a TV Color Barrier.'' *New York Times,* September 15, 1995.

Who's Who among African Americans, 1996–97. 9th ed. Detroit: Gale Research, 1996.

Wormley, Stanton L., and Lewis H. Fenderson, eds. *Many Shades of Black,* New York: William Morrow and Co., 1969.

Jessie Carney Smith

Berry Gordy
(1929–)
Songwriter, record producer, entrepreneur

Berry Gordy was the driving force in the creation of Motown Records, which became the largest black–owned business in the country at the time and changed the course of popular music. Having launched the careers of many recording stars from Mary Wells to Diana Ross, he is a man of many talents, but some of his methods leading to success have brought great bitterness on the part of former associates. He benefitted in the 1960s from changes in the music industry that made possible the success of Motown; further changes in the industry during the 1980s influenced him to sell the company.

Berry Gordy III was born in Detroit on Thanksgiving Day, November 28, 1929, to Berry Gordy II (1888–1978) and Bertha Ida Fuller (1900–1975). The Gordys had eight children: Fuller, Esther, Anna Ruby, Loucye (originally Lucy), George, Gwendolyn, Berry, and Robert. The first Berry Gordy, who was the son of Georgia Esther Johnson, a slave, and white slave owner Jim Gordy, married Lucy Hellum. They had twenty–three children, nine of whom lived to adulthood. Berry Gordy was a successful farmer in Ocoee County, Georgia, where he had acquired 388 acres of land by the time of his death on May 31, 1913, when a lightning bolt killed him.

Berry Gordy II became administrator of the estate. He married Bertha Ida Fuller, a schoolteacher, in 1918. Astute like his father, he was a successful farmer and also ran a produce and meat business, selling from a wagon on a regular round. Three children had already been born when Berry Gordy II moved his family to Detroit in 1922, to cash a check for $2600; he did not return to the South.

Berry Gordy II faced difficulties in adjusting to the new city environment. Early in the Great Depression, sometime

Berry Gordy

after the birth of Berry Gordy III, he lost a house he was in the process of buying, forcing the family to go on welfare. Berry Gordy II persevered by opening a grocery store, learning how to plaster, and securing a building contractor's permit. He soon acquired real estate, eventually opening other businesses, such as a printing shop.

Until Berry Gordy III was six and a half, he remembers living in a small house crowded by a large family on Detroit's west side, which was considered the good black neighborhood. The Gordys were and always remained an exceptionally close family. Commenting on this period, Gordy recalled in his autobiography *To Be Loved,* "We were a close family. We had to be, always bumping into each other just moving from room to room in our new home, where eight kids, four girls and four boys, had to scramble for a place to sleep. Crowding was a way of life. I loved it. I didn't know any better." Physical crowding and the presence of family, both real and figurative, were marked characteristics of the early years of Motown.

A brief period of piano instruction during childhood was Gordy's only formal music instruction, except for a week or so of instruction on the clarinet in high school. By that time his reputation for misbehaving in class was so well–established that his music teacher tossed him out of the only class he wanted to do well in, despite good behavior. Gordy would remain a musical illiterate. While he could not read or write music, his musical gift would be displayed later through his extraordinary ability to shape lyrics and melodies, to catch popular taste, and to provide meticulous attention to all details of performances and recordings.

Gordy Family Moves to Detroit's East Side

When Gordy was six–and–a–half years old, the family moved to the east side where Gordy II had purchased a two story commercial building located just a block from the infamous Hastings Street, a center for night life, gambling, and prostitution. The family lived in the two apartments on the upper story of the building and ran the Booker T. Washington Grocery in the largest of the four storefronts on the ground floor.

Growing up in an achievement–oriented family, Gordy's inability to perform as well as his siblings in school, in addition to his suffering from a bedwetting problem, proved difficult for him as a child. He turned to hustling on the streets, and at school he took to gambling—an activity which remains a favorite pastime. Endeavoring to prevent him from spending too much time on the streets, his parents taught him the value of hard work, and Gordy joined his father on weekends on contracting jobs as early as nine or ten years old. Despite conflicts that arose between father and son during adolescence, Gordy remained close to his father and credits his father's advice as a major influence on his life achievements.

As a young man, Gordy was torn between two ambitions: becoming a songwriter or becoming a boxer. Prize fighting became his principal aim for a while, and he even dropped out of high school to concentrate on the sport. He eventually fought fifteen professional fights with a record of ten wins, two draws, and three losses. On November 21, 1948, he had the thrill of appearing as a 128 pound boxer on the same ticket as his childhood hero Joe Louis, who gave a six–round exhibition bout.

In August of 1950 Gordy gave up fighting, opting to pursue his other dream of making music as his career. After spending the next few months writing songs, Gordy's only successful effort was a one–minute radio commercial for the Gordy Print Shop, which he wrote and performed. He was drafted in September of 1951 and sent to Korea, where he escaped front–line combat. While in the army he passed the high school equivalency test.

Soon after his return home Gordy opened a record shop with a friend, (Roquel) Billy Davis, also known as Tyran Carlo. Gordy used his army severance pay with additional money from the family as capital. The two young men were determined to specialize in selling jazz, unaware that customers were demanding rhythm and blues. By the time they began to change their music selection, it was too late to avoid losing the store. After a stint of selling cookware in homes, Gordy concentrated on song writing.

Gordy married Thelma Coleman in late 1953. Hazel Joy, their first child was born in August of 1954, Berry IV in 1955, and Terry James in 1956. His father owned an old apartment building and let Gordy and his wife live there rent free. Still, song writing proved inadequate as a means to support a growing family. With the help of his wife's mother, Gordy eventually found a job on the assembly line at Lincoln–

Mercury. The repetitive nature of the assembly line work allowed him to write songs in his head while he was working. With this income, he bought a house which paid for itself through the rent from two kitchenette apartments upstairs.

Enters Music Business

After a couple of years in the factory, Gordy became disenchanted with blue–collar work, and quit his factory job in early 1957 to try his luck at song writing again. His sister Gwen had the photo concession at the Flame Bar, a premier nightclub featuring black talent which enabled Gordy to make influential contacts. Thelma Gordy soon filed for divorce, although the marriage was not officially dissolved until 1959.

Some of the songs Gordy worked on began to reap success. His first hit was Etta James's recording of ''All I Could Do Was Cry,'' written with Gwen Gordy and Roquel Billy Davis. Roquel Billy Davis also collaborated with Gordy on ''Reet Petite,'' a smash hit sung by Jackie Wilson. In late 1957 Gordy met William ''Smokey'' Robinson, a member of a group called the Matadors. Gordy worked with Robinson on a song, which was issued by the Miracles, the newly–renamed group, on Robinson's nineteenth birthday, February 19, 1958. The collaboration between Gordy and Robinson over the years was one of the key elements in Motown's success.

By the late 1950s, Gordy was moving closer to forming his own recording company. First, Gwen Gordy proposed that her brother join her and Roquel Billy Davis in forming a record company. Gordy turned her down, reasoning that he would not be happy in a business in which he had partners. He had a keen sense of where the money in recording was, seeking to follow the example of Vee Jay Records, created in 1953 by Vivian Carpenter and Jimmy Braken, a husband and wife team, in Chicago. At a time when independent record companies were coming to dominate the field of pop music, Vee Jay had a tremendous success as the largest black–owned business in the country; for example, the Beatles issued their first half dozen records on the label in 1964. Infected with financial difficulties, Vee Jay also played a cautionary role for Gordy when persistent money problems closed it down in 1966.

Gordy created a music publishing company named Jobete after his children, JOy, BErry, and TErry. Publishing his music himself was the first step to gaining lucrative financial returns from his song writing. Gordy also entered into producing musical material for acts. During this time, he auditioned a singer named Raynoma Liles. Although he disliked her singing voice, he was attracted to her buoyant personality and skills in arranging and writing sheet music. Their professional relationship soon developed into a personal one, and on June 25, 1959, Kerry Gordy was born to Gordy and Ray Liles, who married about a year later. (The marriage ended with a mail–order Mexican divorce in 1962. However, this later proved invalid, and final legal separation ensued.) A vital collaborator in the early days of Motown, Raynoma Liles presents her version of the events in her autobiography, *Berry, Me, and Motown.*

Founds Motown

At the end of 1958, Gordy needed money to produce a record. After other sources turned him down, he faced a skeptical family council as he, for the first time, asked for a loan from the family investment fund. On January 12, 1959, Gordy received an eight hundred dollar loan at six percent interest, and founded Tamla Records. The company's first release was a 45 rpm recording of ''Come to Me,'' sung by Marv Johnson, which became a hit. Other records followed with varying success. Then, in order to issue the song ''Bad Girl,'' written by Smokey Robinson and Gordy, Gordy formed a new company, Motown. The new release became a hit.

Another milestone in the summer of 1959 was the company's move to 2648 West Grand Boulevard in a small house which Gordy turned into an office and studio, and named ''Hitsville.'' Motown eventually took over eight neighborhood houses. In 1988, the original ''Hitsville'' house and the one next door became the Motown Museum.

Filling the house with recording studios and offices, Gordy also prepared a space for his immediate family to live in until he could move them to a separate dwelling. In addition he began to assemble a team of talented people to operate his company. Through his business acumen he sensed that it was necessary that he distribute his music product nationwide to fully profit from Motown's activities. His choice of material for the national debut of Motown's music was a song performed by Smokey Robinson and the Miracles entitled ''Way Over There.'' The song was becoming a big hit when Gordy recut the record and added strings, thereby killing the sales. Nonetheless, he successfully launched Motown as a national music distributor.

Gordy's impulse to insist on making changes in records until he was satisfied misfired in the case of ''Way Over There.'' However, this intervention contributed to the development of the Motown sound. This sound, which was especially prominent in Motown's recordings during the first half of the 1960s, featured elaborate arrangements with large orchestras. In the course of production the elements of black music and performance style were smoothed over, without being abolished.

Motown Enters the Pop Field

When Gordy met Mary Wells, he felt he had found the singer who could break Motown out of the restricted rhythm and blues market into the more lucrative field of pop music favored by white audiences. Wells would be extremely popular until 1964, when she turned 21, making her Motown contract invalid because of her change in legal status. She had little success with other record companies after leaving Motown. To obtain the widest possible market, Gordy hired white salesman Barney Ales to distribute his records. Since Ales had to deal mostly with white owners of radio stations all over the country, including the south, he built up a sales department staffed by white salespersons. Only later, when Motown had the power and prestige necessary to insist that people treat any Motown representative with respect, did Gordy insist that Ales hire black salespersons. The preliminary hiring of whites to sell Motown products is one of the reasons underlying the mixed reaction to Motown among blacks. There was pride in Motown as the most successful black business, as well as suspicion of a sell–out against the black community due to Gordy's tapping into the white market and his use of whites in key marketing positions. In some quarters, especially in Detroit's black community, Gordy was never forgiven for Motown's move to Los Angeles in 1970. He was also criticized for his sale of the company to MCA in 1988 for $61 million, which was seen as a betrayal of the black community.

During the early 1960s, Gordy built Motown by introducing to the public new stars like Marvin Gaye, who would became both a major Motown artist and Gordy's brother–in–law. In 1961 he signed the four Supremes, who later became a trio consisting of Diana Ross, Mary Wilson, and Florence Ballard; they achieved stardom three years later. Gordy also signed the Temptations and a young boy named Stephen Hardaway Judkins, better known as Stevie Wonder. Other groups included Martha Reeves and the Vandellas and the Marvelettes.

By October of 1962, as Gordy's marriage to Raynoma Liles was ending, Motown had enough stars to staff an entire tour, and the first Motortown Revue got underway. A brief relationship with Jeana Jackson in midst of a longer, ongoing affair Margaret Norton resulted in the birth of Gordy's fifth child, Sherry.

By the early to mid–1960s, Gordy had perfected his management style. Many have noted its resemblance to the production line of an automobile factory. His creative staff, the songwriters and producers, competed in weekly meetings to develop new products. While he did hire female executives like Suzanne De Passe in addition to his sisters Esther and Loucye, who occupied key positions, his creative staff was entirely male. Artists were expected to accept Motown's control over their acts and material. Gordy even hired Maxine Powell away from her own charm school and modeling business to instruct performers in social graces and to tour with acts from 1964 to 1967. The slogan he originally ran his business by was "Create, Make and Sell," which later became "Create, Sell, and COLLECT." Gordy ran Motown as a factory for producing hits. In *The Motown Album,* Michael Jackson ably characterized the man who brought the Jackson Five to superstardom: "Berry was my teacher and a great one. He told me exactly what he wanted and how he wanted me to help him get it. Berry insisted on perfection and attention to detail. I'll never forget his persistence. This was his genius."

In March of 1964, Margaret Norton gave birth to Gordy's sixth child, Kennedy William. Motown continued to grow despite the defection of Mary Wells that year. The Supremes achieved a major breakthrough to stardom with "Where Did Our Love Go," and Gordy began to open the door to major clubs and showrooms for Motown stars by persuading the television program *Hullabaloo* to allow the Supremes to perform "You're Nobody 'Til Somebody Loves You." It was in Paris just after the conclusion of the Motortown Revue's first European tour in 1964 that Gordy became involved with Diana Ross. This relationship eventually resulted in the birth Gordy's seventh child—a daughter named Rhonda—born in August of 1971, after Ross's marriage to Robert Silberstein in late January of 1971. Ross informed Silberstein of the affair, and Rhonda was later told of her parentage.

There were also numerous setbacks along the way to Motown's success. Not all of Motown's musicians and acts were satisfied. The defection of the song writing team of Eddie Holland, Lamont Dozier, and Brian Holland, who had produced an eviable string of hits for Motown, was a major blow. Not all of Motown's labels proved successful. Yet, despite such setbacks and defections, new groups added new luster to the company, such as Gladys Knight and the Pips in 1966, and the Jacksons in 1969. In 1976 Stevie Wonder received an unprecedented $23 million for renewing his contract with Motown.

Gordy moved to Los Angeles in 1968, and Motown's operations moved there in 1970, although Los Angeles did not become the company's official headquarters until 1972. This change of location occurred as the company became increasingly involved in other entertainment fields such as film and television.

Enters Film Business

Gordy's first major involvement in the movie business was with *Lady Sings the Blues,* starring Diana Ross. His perfectionism and desire for control led to immediate conflict. Gordy insisted on the script being rewritten as shooting was getting underway and the movie went over budget. After refinancing the film, Gordy achieved control over the editing. When it opened in October of 1972, the film was a triumph for Diana Ross, who received an Oscar nomination for best actress.

Gordy seems to have been less directly involved with other Motown films like *Bingo Long Traveling All–Stars and Motor Kings, Scott Joplin,* and the megaflop *The Wiz.* He was, however, extremely active in the production of *Mahogany,* starring Diana Ross, which began production in December of 1974 and opened in October of 1975.

A brief liaison with Nancy Leiviska produced his eighth child, Stefan, in November of 1975. Yet, overall, the year 1975 was especially difficult for Gordy. There were problems on the set of *Mahogany* with Diana Ross, so Gordy fired the director and took over the movie himself. The movie was a critical and financial disaster. Gordy would not reenter the movie business again until *The Last Dragon* in 1985. His mother died in late January. In the spring the Jacksons left Motown, except for Jermaine, who had married Gordy's daughter Hazel. (She filed for divorce in 1987 after nearly fourteen years of marriage.)

During the 1970s Motown's success was beginning to slow down, and Gordy wondered if his management style was suited for running an established enterprise. By late 1979 Gordy was insolvent; however, a bank loan, which he repaid within a year, tided him over until the crisis passed. Despite Diana Ross's move to RCA in 1981, Motown still had stars like Lionel Richie, the Commodores, Smokey Robinson, and Stevie Wonder. However, because Motown was relatively small for the industry, it was in danger of being overtaken by media giants. In 1983 Gordy nearly sold Motown to MCA, but withdrew at the last moment. He did turn distribution over to MCA.

In 1988, Gordy once again entered into negotiations with MCA to sell Motown. On June 28 Motown was purchased by the entertainment conglomerate for $61 million. Gordy retained control of Motown's movie and television interests (now Gordy–De Passe Productions) as well as his publishing company Jobete, estimated to be worth $100 million. These properties were organized under the umbrella of the Gordy Company. Berry Gordy is chairman of the board, and his son, Berry Gordy IV, is president.

Gordy married once more, to Grace Eaton in 1990, but filed for divorce in 1993. In addition to overseeing his company, he has pursued his interest in horse racing as an owner. Gordy also has taken to trading on the futures market.

On January 20, 1988, Gordy was inducted into the Rock 'n' Roll Hall of Fame. His tremendous achievements in the music industry are perhaps best summed up in the *Billboard* listings for the last week of 1968, cited in his autobiography. Five of the top ten hits in the United States, including Marvin Gaye's "I Heard It Through the Grapevine," Stevie Wonder's "For Once In My Life," Diana Ross and the Supremes' "Love Child," Diana Ross and the Supremes' and the Temptation's "I'm Gonna Make You Love Me," and The Temptations' "Cloud Nine," were Motown productions. In addition, Motown had held the first three positions on the list for an entire month—a feat that has not been repeated by any company. Berry Gordy's Motown had created the music all America wanted to hear.

Current address: The Gordy Company, 6255 Sunset Boulevard, 18th Floor, Los Angeles, California 90028.

REFERENCES

Contemporary Black Biography. Vol. 1. Detroit: Gale Research, 1992.

Current Biography Yearbook. 1975. New York: H. W. Wilson, 1976.

Early, Gerald. "One Nation Under a Groove." *The New Republic* 205 (15 and 25 July 1991): 30–41.

Encyclopedia of Rock. New York: Schirmer Books, 1988.

Gordy, Berry. *To Be Loved.* New York: Time Warner, 1994.

Gordy, Berry, Sr. *Movin' Up.* New York: Harper and Row, 1979.

The New Grove Dictionary of American Music. 4 vols. New York: Macmillan, 1986.

Singleton, Raynoma Gordy. *Berry, Me, and Motown.* Chicago: Contemporary Books, 1990.

Taraborrelli, J. Randy. *Call Her Miss Ross.* New York: Ballantine, 1991.

Robert L. Johns

Lester B. Granger

(1896–1976)

Civic leader, organization executive

A pioneer in race relations and a leader in the field of social work, Lester Blackwell Granger served as executive director for the National Urban League for 20 years. He was born on September 16, 1896, in Newport News, Virginia, one of six sons born to William Randolph Granger, a physician from Barbados, West Indies, and Mary L. Turpin, a teacher from Newport News, Virginia. On August 11, 1923, Granger married Harriet Lane, a young lady he met while working at Bordentown.

Granger received a B.A. degree from Dartmouth College in 1918, a time when few blacks were going to college, and fewer to an Ivy League school. Granger had planned to attend Harvard Law School, but his plans were interrupted by World War I, during which he served overseas with the 92th Infantry. After military service, Granger changed his mind about studying law, and in 1919 he served briefly as industrial secretary of the Newark chapter of the National Urban League. In 1920 he moved to North Carolina and taught at the Slater Normal School in Winston–Salem and at St. Augustine College in Raleigh. After two years of teaching in North Carolina, he took a job as an extension worker at the Bordentown, New Jersey, Manual Training and Industrial School for Colored Youth. There he organized the New Jersey Federation of Boy's Clubs. During this time, he also took graduate classes at New York University, remaining with the school until 1934, with a year's sabbatical in 1930 to organize the Los Angeles Urban League.

In 1934 at the National Urban League office in New York, Granger served as the first business manager of the League's magazine *Opportunity* and headed the Worker's Bureau. He was given a two–year leave of absence in 1938 to serve the New York City Welfare Council in the interest of African Americans. He returned to the National Urban League in 1940 as assistant executive secretary and led the National Urban League for the next 20 years.

Granger was active in many other service organizations. He was a member of the board of directors of the American

Association of Social Workers and vice–president of that organization in 1942. He also served on the executive committee of the National Conference of Social Work and on the advisory committee on Social Service of the United States Children's Bureau. In 1954, Columbia University awarded him an honorary doctorate in humane letters.

On the onset of World War II, the National Urban League under Granger's leadership was active in the fight to eliminate racial segregation and discrimination in the military and defense employment. As a result of comments expressed by the league, the Navy adopted new policies which repudiated all theories of racial superiority and urged the fullest use of black manpower.

In 1945 the Secretary of the Navy James Forrestal selected Granger as a special adviser on race relations. With this appointment, Granger toured naval bases and spoke with high–ranking naval officials, as well as with both black and white enlisted personnel. He reported that the Navy's new policy was sound but that it needed "vigorous policing."

Granger received many awards for his service. In 1944 the Congress of Industrial Organizations presented him with an award for outstanding work in race relations. In 1943, for the same reason, he was cited by the New Jersey Organization of Teachers of Colored Children. On December 31, 1945, he received the Navy's highest civilian decoration, the Distinguished Civilian Service Award, in recognition of his counsel on Navy policy toward black personnel. According to *Current Biography Yearbook,* the citation from the Secretary of the Navy read:

> By inspection of continental and overseas naval activities during which his tactful and forthright advice won the respect of men and officers alike, Mr. Granger personally evaluated the position of the Negro in the Navy, suggesting general policies as well as solutions for specific cases. Courageous and fair in criticism, honest and temperate in praise, Mr. Granger has performed a delicate and important task in a manner deserving of the Navy's highest civilian award.

Granger was responsible for a number of significant changes within the National Urban League, including the development of a Pilot Placement Project, in which blacks were placed in significant jobs previously barred to them, and the establishment of a Commerce and Industrial Council and Trade Union Advisory Council. During his tenure in office, the number of League affiliates grew from 41 to 65, and the budget increased from $600,000 to $45 million.

Granger retired from the National Urban League in October of 1961, when he was 65 years old. The *Reference Library of Black America* quoted President Eisenhower praising him as a "man of the highest character and integrity." In the following years he taught at Dillard University in New Orleans, Louisiana, and was named Amistad Scholar in Residence. Granger died in Alexandria, Louisiana, on January 9, 1976. He is remembered for his contributions to the National Urban League and his dedicated service to American society.

REFERENCES

Brooks, Lester, and Guichard Parris. *Blacks in the City: A History of the National Urban League.* Boston: Little, Brown, 1971.

Current Biography Yearbook. New York: H.W. Wilson, 1946.

Reference Library of Black America. Vol. 1. New York: Afro–American Press, 1990.

Salzman, Jack, David Lionel Smith, and Cornel West, eds. *Encyclopedia of African–American Culture and History.* New York: Macmillan Library Reference USA/Simon and Schuster Macmillan, 1996.

Weiss, Nancy J. *The National Urban League, 1910–1940.* New York: Oxford University Press, 1974.

COLLECTIONS

Lester B. Granger's papers are housed in the Amistad Research Center at Tulane University.

Sheila A. Stuckey

Samuel L. Gravely Jr.

(1922–)

Military officer

Vice Admiral Samuel L. Gravely, the first three star African American admiral in the U.S. Navy, served 34 years with responsibilities that included management of major communications programs, operational and administrative command of a major shore activity, command of four destroyers, command of a naval surface group, and most authoritative of all, command of a navy fleet composed of from 80 to 120 ships. His experiences and contributions reflect the changes in official policy about acceptance of African American personnel and the broadened opportunities for black people in the military services of this country.

Gravely was born on June 4, 1922, in Richmond, Virginia, to Samuel Lee Gravely Sr., a post office mail handler, and Mary George Simon Gravely, a housewife. He had two sisters, Christie Ann Johnson and Mary Elizabeth White, and two brothers, Edward Chandler and Robert Welton. In the Gravely home, the father was the disciplinarian, committed to the unity of the family, and the mother was the goal setter.

Samuel L. Gravely Jr.

With the intent of keeping the family together after his wife died, Samuel Sr. thought it best for his oldest son to remain in Richmond and enter Virginia Union University after he graduated from high school in preference to his mother's expressed desire that he go to Hampton Institute and join the Army ROTC. But, wanting to serve his country in the aftermath of Pearl Harbor in a branch of the military of his choosing rather than waiting to be drafted, Gravely delayed completion of college to join the Naval Reserve on September 15, 1942, thus taking the first step toward the dual accomplishments of fulfilling his mother's goal and starting his brilliant career. He returned to Virginia Union to finish course work for a bachelor's degree in history in 1948.

Gravely reported for recruit training at the segregated Camp Robert Smalls, Great Lakes, Illinois. With swift advancement, he rose through the ranks with advanced training and further study at Hampton University, the University of California at Los Angeles, Columbia University, and the Naval War College. He progressed from Seaman to Midshipman to Ensign, and was commissioned vice admiral on June 2, 1971.

During his experience with the Navy from 1942 to 1980, Gravely observed significant differences in the ethnic composition of its officer corps. When he was commissioned as an ensign in ceremonies at St. Johns Cathedral in New York City, he was the only African American among the more than 1,000 graduates. He saw the progress from a total absence of black officers to almost 4,000; from 13 ensigns and no admirals to seven admirals on active duty, and a nominee to four star admiral, the highest peacetime rank in the U.S. Navy. Through the years, African American officers, who had been restricted from going to sea on United States warships, were assigned to command of specific ships and fleets. Gravely left a mark of commitment, perfection, and encouragement for young African American servicemen.

As a high ranking officer of the armed forces in an official capacity, or at social events in the White House or elsewhere, Gravely has met Presidents John F. Kennedy, Lyndon B. Johnson, Richard M. Nixon, Gerald R. Ford, George Bush, and Bill Clinton. He has responded, over and over again, under varied circumstances, in active duty or in retirement, whenever his government sought his council.

At age 58, satisfied with his contributions as a trailblazer in the navy and his service to his country, Gravely retired on August 1, 1980, after 34 years of military life. He had served in World War II, the Korea War, and the Vietnam War, in areas of command, joint and international communications systems, cryptology, systems engineering, automated data processing, electronics, amphibious warfare, naval warfare, antisubmarine warfare, guided missiles, and personnel management. He gives credit to the navy for helping him mature from a new recruit of 20 into a responsible man capable of making crucial decisions having widespread effects upon the lives of thousands of people in times of war and peace.

In retirement, Gravely and his wife, Alma Bernice Clark, live in peace on their 2.8 acres of land in Haymarket, Virginia. The Gravelys married on February 12, 1946; they had met as undergraduates, she at Virginia State University, and he at Virginia Union. They had two sons—Robert Michael, deceased, and David Edward—and one daughter—Tracey Ernestine. Gravely enjoys his fish pond, tends fruit trees and a vegetable garden, and cans their yield—sometimes taking top prizes in county fairs for his jellies. Gravely is one in the small number of racing pigeon fanciers in this country. He shared his knowledge of African American history by traveling to Guantanamo, Cuba, to address United States military forces during Black History Month in 1985. He did the same in London and Scotland in 1990.

Gravely was in demand as a consultant to civilian industrial management needing assistance to understand terms and concepts expressed in unfamiliar military terminology. In 1984 he joined the Educational Foundation of the Armed Forces Communications and Electronics Association and remained there as president until he chose renewed retirement in 1987.

The military awards given to Vice Admiral Gravely include: the Defense Distinguished Service Medal, Legion of Merit with gold star, Bronze Star Medal, Navy Commendation Medal with gold star, Naval Reserve Medal, American Campaign Medal, Korean Presidential Unit Citation, National Defense Medal with one bronze star, Chinese Service Medal, Korean Service Medal with two bronze stars, and the United Nations Service Medal.

Among his civic awards are the Golden Hills United Presbyterian Church Military Service Award, Alpha Phi

Alpha Fraternity Alpha Award of Merit, Distinguished Virginian, Los Angeles Chapter of the National Association of Media Women, Communications Award, and the Scottish Rite Prince Hall Masonic Bodies of Maryland, Prince Hall Founding Fathers Military Commanders Award. He has received honorary advanced degrees from Virginia Union University, the University of Richmond, and Morehouse College.

In his community, Gravely was a member of the Gainsville Ruritan Club, a men's service club, member and past chairman of the Prince William County Mental Health, Mental Retardation and Substance Abuse Board, and the Olive Branch Baptist Church. Gravely had a distinguished career in the military that secured his place in history as naval officer and the first African American to achieve the rank of three star Admiral.

Current address: 15956 Waterfall Rd., Haymarket, VA 22069.

REFERENCES

Gravely, Samuel L., Jr. Interview with Dona L. Irvin, September 9, 1996.

Haywood, Richette. "Adm. Samuel L. Gravely, Jr." *Ebony* 46 (December 1990): 92.

Potter, Joan, with Constance Claytor. *African–American Firsts.* Elizabeth, NY: Pinto Press, 1994.

Williams, Michael W., ed. *The African American Encyclopedia.* New York: Marshall Cavendish, 1993.

Dona L. Irvin

Earl G. Graves

(1935–)

Publisher, corporate executive

Earl G. Graves is considered the preeminent authority in America on black business and the locus of that authority is *Black Enterprise,* the magazine he founded in 1970 that now has a circulation of nearly 300,000 and revenues of $24 million. He is the magazine's publisher as well as its president, chief executive officer of the parent company, Earl G. Graves Limited, and co–owner with Earvin "Magic" Johnson of a Washington, D.C.–based Pepsi Cola distributorship, the largest minority–controlled Pepsi franchise in the nation. Johnson serves as chief executive officer. These two business ventures have served as the springboard that has propelled Graves into the ranks of elected board members of prestigious businesses and trustees of well–known foundations. He has become a leading spokesperson on issues that affect the well–being and economic success of black Americans. He has used his expertise to educate others on trends and opportunities in black entrepreneurship.

Earl Gilbert Graves was born on January 9, 1935, in Brooklyn, New York, to Earl Godwin Graves and Winifred Sealy Graves, long–time West Indian residents of the Bedford–Stuyvesant area. Graves's father was a role model and mentor whose economic circumstances curtailed his own plans for the future. The senior Graves was the only black in his graduating class at Erasmus High school—the second oldest school in America—and his son would be one of only two blacks when he graduated years later. Although he never earned a large salary, Graves's father stressed the value of education, and his brother and sisters and both parents preached the virtues of cleanliness and thrift. Although he died before the age of 50, *African–American Business Leaders* noted that the senior Graves had instilled in his children "the twin notions of owning a business and developing a strong economic base for the black community."

Graves took these lessons to heart and, at the age of five, was known as an annual top seller of Christmas cards. After high school graduation, he entered Morgan State University as a scholarship student. He was a high school and college track star and used his athletic skills to help with tuition and fees by working as a New York beach lifeguard during the summer months. As a college student, Graves displayed self–discipline and goal–oriented behaviors that led to his later success in the business world. While maintaining Dean's List grades, he also operated several campus businesses and joined various campus organizations.

Graves graduated in 1958 with a B.A. degree in economics and, as a ROTC member, was commissioned a second lieutenant in the U.S. Army. Before leaving active service, Graves completed the Airborne and Ranger's School and was promoted to the rank of captain as a member of the Green Berets of the 19th Special Forces Group. In 1962 he worked as a narcotics agent with the U.S. Treasury Department and returned to his old neighborhood in Brooklyn. For the next three years, Graves sold and developed real estate and then formed an alliance that would have a tremendous effect on his future.

The Will to Succeed

In 1966 Graves was hired as an administrative assistant on the staff of Senator Robert F. Kennedy. His job was to plan and supervise events. Graves considered Kennedy another mentor who would influence the course of his future. Quoted in *African–American Business Leaders,* Graves said of the senator:

> The main thing Kennedy did was to continue to foster my attitude that anything could get done once you made up your mind to get on with the work. There was no such thing in Kennedy's mindset as

Earl G. Graves

we can't do, it was just a matter of how long it would take us to get it done.

As traumatic as Kennedy's death was in 1968, it also meant that Graves no longer had a job. After a short period of grieving, restlessness, and reflection, Graves focussed on the legacies of his father and Kennedy: the constant injunctions to own his own business and to make up his mind to get on with it. In 1968 Graves formed Earl G. Graves Associates, a management consulting firm to advise corporations on urban affairs and economic development. As evidenced by the number of multinational corporations the firm had as clients, Graves was a success, but he had not addressed the second program that his late father had stressed: contributing to the economic development of black America. The impetus for formulating a strategy to address this need was Graves's journey to Fayette, Mississippi, to work on the mayoral campaign for Charles Evers, brother of slain NAACP leader Medgar Evers. After Evers was elected as the city's first black mayor in 1969, he used his money and influence to improve the lot of the town's black community. Graves carefully studied Evers's effort and then planned a strategy to tap into the Nixon Administration's effort to bring black Americans into the country's economic development programs.

Because there was a national focus on black economic development, Graves knew that the time was right to plan, develop, and produce a monthly periodical devoted to news, commentary, and articles for blacks interested in business. After receiving a Ford Foundation grant to study black–owned business in Caribbean countries, he narrowed his focus to developing a business plan and editorial prospectus for the projected magazine. In 1970 Graves borrowed $150,000 from the Manhattan Capital Corporation of Chase Manhattan Bank, which, in turn, bought 25 percent of the company as equity.

Graves presented the prospective lenders with a working draft of *Black Enterprise,* a periodical that would foster black economic development, create viable role models for blacks to emulate, and showcase successful blacks whose careers had transcended the traditional norms of thought of what black business leaders should be. A major part of the draft was a list of the endorsements of 100,000 black community leaders representative of organizations such as the National Urban League, the Organization of Industrial Centers, the NAACP, the Black Advisory Council of the Small Business Administration, and others of equal importance. Since Graves was not an experienced journalist, L. Patrick "Pat" Patterson later became editor–at–large when Graves decided to become both publisher and editor of *Black Enterprise.*

Black Enterprise Flourishes

Black Enterprise began to turn a profit by its tenth issue and at the end of the first year it reported $900,000 in advertising revenues. Its ongoing success was due to visionary thinking. Two years after the first issue came off the press, attention was turned to researching market possibilities. The publication had been given little, if any, attention by the black media. Under the aegis of other Graves corporations, BCI Marketing, a development firm, and a market research firm, attention was focused on buying patterns of potential readers and subscribers, the differences between black and nonblack buying patterns, and the effectiveness of advertising copy. This strategy has enabled *Black Enterprise* to attract general as well as black businesses in luring the black population market, whose purchasing power has been estimated as worth $100 billion. The promotions arm of Graves's business conglomerate has been the means by which *Black Enterprise* is now included in the magazine offerings on major airlines. Another promotions tactic has been an allocation from each press run to large corporations regardless of race.

In *The Black Press USA,* Roland E. Wolseley highlighted the strategies and procedures employed by Graves's publishing company and its subsidiaries to ensure the success of *Black Enterprise.* Its paid circulation is verified by the Audit Bureau of Circulations, the leading agency in this business. The magazine is highly attractive to its readership because of the high quality of materials, advertising, and editorial contributors. It has also reached beyond its original target audience of black business people to encompass large–scale entrepreneurs and the general consumer. Articles now focus on a variety of economic interests ranging from personal investments to solutions for unemployment to science, technology, health, and political issues that impinge on the business world. Finally, advertisements are mostly full–page, in color, and identical to those seen in general and specialty magazines purchased by the general population. It is quite common to have 170 pages of advertisements in a single issue including high–end consumer products such as Rolls–Royce automobiles, Godiva chocolates, and Merrill–Lynch financial services. Each year *Black Enterprise*'s top–selling issue is the one containing the "List of Top Black Businesses," a feature begun in 1972.

Included under the parent publishing umbrella are ancillary business ventures that support the entire structure. For example, the marketing and research company has developed a Minority Business Information Institute with a census tract data library, and the EGG Dallas Broadcasting Company operates AM and FM stations in Dallas, Texas. The Pepsi Cola franchise owned by Graves and Magic Johnson is headquartered in Forrestville, Maryland, and covers a 400–square–mile territory that includes Washington, D.C. and Prince Georges County, Maryland. Some of its key accounts are the White House, the United States Capitol, and Air Force One.

The Graves Dynasty

Graves provides a nurturing home environment for his family. In 1960 Graves married Barbara Kydd of Brooklyn. After teaching school for some years, she became a full partner with her husband and now serves as vice–president and general manager of Earl G. Graves Publishing Company. In the Silver Anniversary Commemorative Issue of *Black Enterprise,* Graves praised her in a letter to his grandchildren, saying, "You must know that while I get all the glory, without Gramma there would be no BE. She has been the glue of our business, she is the heart of our family and the love of my life." In an interview in the same issue, Graves further detailed his wife's contributions: "Barbara has been the most important thing in everything we have done, by being a part of it here as well as encouraging me. There were so many nights over the last 25 years when you feel that you really have gotten your butt kicked and her support was all that got me through to the next day."

The three Graves sons are all involved in the family business. The oldest, Earl Jr., is a Yale–trained economist who also earned an MBA from Harvard Business School. Despite being drafted by the Philadelphia 76ers, he chose to join *Black Enterprise* and is now vice–president of advertising and marketing. Graves's second son, John, was a Brown University history major who received his law degree from Yale. He was an associate with a prominent New York law form and now serves as vice–president of business ventures and legal affairs for the Earl G. Graves Publishing Company. Youngest son Michael was a football player at the University of Pennsylvania where he majored in communications and sociology. He joined the Pepsi Cola franchise as development manager.

Graves has long been recognized as a civic leader and authority on black business development. He is a member of the board of directors of the Rohm and Haas Corporation, the New York State Urban Development Corporation, the Chrysler Corporation, the National Supplier Development Council, and the Magazine Publishers Association. He holds membership in organizations such as the American Museum of Natural History, the NAACP, Sigma Pi Phi, the Statue of Liberty Ellis Island Centennial Commission, and the Visiting Committee of Harvard University's John F. Kennedy School of Government.

Having served as National Commissioner of Scouting for the Boy Scouts of America in the early 1960s, Graves has received the organization's highest volunteer service awards: the Silver Beaver (1969), the Silver Buffalo (1988), and the Silver Antelope (1986). He is a member of the executive committee of the Greater New York Council of the BSA and is also on the executive board of the National Boy Scouts of America. *Ebony* magazine has continuously listed Graves as one of the 100 Influential Blacks and President Richard Nixon recognized him as one of the ten most outstanding minority business leaders in the United States. In the last 25 years, Graves has been awarded more than 25 honorary doctorates from several institutions including his alma mater, Morgan State University, where in 1996 he donated $1 million to establish the Earl G. Graves School of Business and Management.

Graves has always made public service to educational institutions a priority in his professional life. The depth of that commitment was revealed early in 1996 when he was scheduled to teach two classes at Middle Tennessee State University in Murfreesboro. Despite learning of a family death the day before, he kept the appointment and even made time to talk with students at a luncheon before flying home to Scarsdale, New York.

Graves is a true entrepreneur, businessman, and corporate executive whose lifestyle is now commensurate with his stellar achievements. In the twenty–fifth Anniversary Issue of *Black Enterprise,* Graves engaged in a dialogue with the executive editor, Alfred Edmond Jr., who questioned him about the evolution of the magazine. Graves explained how he has kept his professional and personal lives in proper perspective. He stated:

> Had we not been involved in so many other causes, we might have been even more profitable and achieved even greater things. But, along the way, other values kicked in. . . . If I had been willing to spend less time with my family, I might have ended up being a couple of million dollars more ahead in terms of what this business represents. On the other hand. . .my children and grandchildren. . .want to be with us. So, I think I have achieved the best of both worlds: a solid family and a solid business. I would not trade that.

Graves gave further practical advice to black entrepreneurs in his book, *How to Succeed in Business Without Being White: Straight Talk on Making It in America* (HarperCollins, 1997). He remains one of the most influential black business leaders in the country.

Current address: Earl G. Graves Publishing Company, 130 Fifth Avenue, New York, NY 10011.

REFERENCES

"Black Enterprise Magazine's Top 100 Black Firms Hit the $13 Billion Mark." *Jet* 90 (27 May 1996): 24.

Clarke, Caroline V., ed. ''Inside View: Earl G. Graves on the Record.'' *Black Enterprise—Silver Anniversary Commemorative* 26 (August 1995): 13–14, 54–62.

Hawkins, Walter L. *African American Biographies: Profiles of 558 Current Men and Women.* Jefferson, NC: McFarland, 1992.

Ingham, John N., and Lynne B. Feldman. *African–American Business Leaders.* Westport, CT: Greenwood Press 1994.

Kidd, Florence S. Telephone interview with Dolores Nicholson, November 11, 1996.

''Publisher Visits MTSU, Stresses Goals for Success.'' *Nashville Tennessean,* February 7, 1996.

Salzman, Jack, David Lionel Smith, and Cornel West, eds. *Encyclopedia of African–American Culture and History.* New York: Macmillan Library Reference USA/Simon and Schuster Macmillan, 1996.

''The Sweet Sell of Success.'' *Washington Post,* June 17, 1997.

Who's Who among African Americans, 1995–96. 9th ed. Detroit: Gale Research, 1995.

Wolseley, Roland E. *The Black Press U.S.A.*. 2nd ed. Ames: Iowa State University Press, 1990.

Dolores Nicholson

William H. Gray III

Gray, Frizzell.
See Mfume, Kweisi.

William H. Gray III

(1941–)

Foundation executive, minister, congressman

William H. Gray's consistent efforts to improve his community and nation help black Americans continue to progress spiritually, educationally, politically, socially, and economically. Currently pastor of a 5,000–member church and administrator of the College Fund/UNCF, Gray is also a former six–term U.S. congressman whose tenure in the House of Representatives proved beneficial to America and Third World countries. Gray remains a dynamic, influential figure.

William Herbert Gray III was born August 20, 1941, in Baton Rouge, Louisiana. He was the second child of William H. Gray, Jr., and his wife, Hazel Yates Gray. After William's birth, the family moved to St. Augustine where the senior Gray served as president of Florida Normal and Industrial College—now known as Florida Memorial College—from 1941 to 1944. In 1944 he became president of Florida Agricultural and Mechanical College—now University—in Tallahassee. Five years later, the family moved to Philadelphia where the senior Gray succeeded his late father as pastor of Bright Hope Baptist Church.

The younger William Gray attended public elementary and secondary schools in Philadelphia, and in 1959 graduated from Simon Gratz High School. That year he entered Franklin and Marshall College in Lancaster, Pennsylvania. He majored in history and was urged to consider a public service career by his political science professor, Sidney Wise. During his senior year, Wise recommended him for a congressional internship in the office of Pennsylvania representative Robert Nix. Gray received his B.A. in 1963.

One year after graduating from Franklin and Marshall College, Gray was appointed assistant pastor of Union Baptist Church in Montclair, New Jersey. In 1966 he became the church's senior pastor; Martin Luther King, Jr. officiated at Gray's installation service. That same year, Gray received a master's degree in divinity from Drew Theological Seminary in Madison, New Jersey. He did postgraduate work at the University of Pennsylvania in 1965, Temple University in 1966, and Mansfield College of Oxford University in 1967 before earning a masters degree in theology from Princeton Theological Seminary in 1970.

Gray's church and graduate school responsibilities did not deter him from becoming an activist in the Montclair community. He founded the Union Housing Corporation and other nonprofit organizations that built apartments for low–

and middle–income members of the community. Gray waged a successful battle against housing discrimination in 1970 when he sued a landlord who denied him an apartment because of his racial status. The New Jersey Superior Court awarded Gray financial damages as a victim of racial discrimination and established a precedent that had national repercussions. As a result of these and other deeds on behalf of the Montclair community, Gray was hailed as a community leader.

Gray remained at Union Baptist until his father's death in 1972. He then returned to Philadelphia and assumed the pastorate of Bright Hope Baptist Church where his grandfather served from 1925 to 1949, and his father, from 1949 to 1972. Gray continues to preside there today.

In Philadelphia Gray continued his community activism, and improving housing conditions remained a major goal. As in Montclair, he established nonprofit housing corporations. Gray battled home lending discrimination by helping to create the Philadelphia Mortgage Plan, which enabled individuals in low income communities redlined by banks to obtain mortgages.

Becomes Philadelphia's Congressman

As an outgrowth of his intense concern with the community's inadequate housing, high rate of unemployment, and other problems, Gray challenged the black incumbent for the Second District congressional seat in 1976. Gray's opponent was the same man he had interned for during his senior year in college—Robert Nix. Gray now believed that Nix was unresponsive to the district's needs. Nix defeated Gray in the primary election by approximately 300 votes, but two years later, Gray ran against him again and defeated him in the primary election by capturing 58 percent of the vote to Nix's 40 percent. After his upset victory over Nix, Gray easily defeated his Republican opponent, Roland Atkins, in the general election where he received 84 percent of the vote to Atkins's 16 percent. Thus he succeeded Nix as Pennsylvania's second elected black congressman. He now had the opportunity to exercise his political talents to advance the social causes he advocated.

During his 13–year tenure in Congress, Gray served on many congressional and political committees including Foreign Affairs, Budget, Democratic Steering and Policy, Appropriations, and Foreign Operations, among others. Gray's most significant congressional contributions were his work as Black Caucus member and later chair of the Budget Committee, membership on the Subcommittee on Foreign Operations, Democratic Caucus chair, and Democratic Whip.

Gray began his congressional career two years before Ronald Reagan was sworn in as President of the United States in 1981, and he remained in the House of Representatives three years after Reagan's two terms had ended. Saving social programs from devastation from the Reagan Administration was a major objective for Gray. In 1981 and 1982, Gray and other members of the Congressional Black Caucus vehemently opposed the administration's economic plan and created alternative proposals advocating expansion of social programs. In 1983, as a member of the Budget Committee, Gray helped negotiate a budget compromise between the House and the Senate that established an $8.5 billion reserve for recession–relief programs. Two years later, Gray was elected chair of the Budget Committee by acclamation, and he immediately battled the administration's budget for fiscal 1986, which proposed increasing military expenditures by approximately $30 billion at the expense of social programs. William L. Clay, Gray's colleague from Missouri and fellow caucus member, analyzed the outcome in *Just Permanent Interests: Black Americans in Congress, 1870–1991*:

> Gray succeeded in his efforts to retain essential funding for programs designed to rebuild urban America and to meet the human needs of low–income Americans. Striving for a budget of compassion, fairness, and economic justice, Gray's committee provided an increase to offset inflation in thirty–two out of thirty–three low–income programs.

Gray successfully maneuvered through Congress fiscal budgets for 1987, 1988, and 1989.

Education was another of Gray's priorities. He cosponsored the Black College Act, which provided federal financing to enhance facilities, faculties, and programs in historically black colleges and universities (HBCUs). Gray wrote set–aside provisions that required HBCU participation in the U.S. Agency for International Development (AID) assistance program. He also wrote set–aside provisions to require participation by minority and women business owners in AID; consequently, they received $300 million in AID contracts in a three–year period. Gray's work as a public servant extends beyond American shores. He emerged as a leading spokesman on African Affairs and an advocate for increased federal aid to Africa. In 1980, as a freshman representative, Gray authored a bill to establish the African Development Foundation which channeled federal funding directly to villages in Africa. Gray, who was one of the first members of Congress to warn of famine in Africa, sponsored an emergency relief bill for Ethiopia in 1984. He wrote the House version of the Anti–Apartheid Acts of 1985 and 1986 which implemented economic sanctions against the South African government; Gray helped ensure passage of these acts, despite presidential vetoes. The Anti–Apartheid Acts of 1985 and 1986, along with the Sullivan Principles, contributed to the dismantling of South Africa's apartheid government in 1992.

Gray was able to influence national legislation and policy as well as international affairs because of his political stature. He became one of the most powerful and visible members of Congress. In 1985, the same year Gray became Budget Committee chair, he was elected chair of Congress's Democratic Caucus. In 1989 he was elected Majority Whip, the number three leadership position in the House of Representatives. Gray was then the highest ranking black American ever to serve in Congress. He was respected by Republican as well as Democratic colleagues for his legislative leadership, political acumen, fairness, personal integrity, pragmatism, and ability to build coalitions. Gray was regarded as a charismatic, dignified, and intellectual leader. He was an extraordinary politician. Political insiders speculated about Gray's future; they predicted he would be Speaker of the House, Secretary of the Treasury, or the 1988 vice–presidential nominee. However, they failed to anticipate that Gray would walk away from Congress and politics.

Heads College Fund/UNCF

In June of 1991 Gray announced his resignation from Congress, effective that September. On September 11, 1991, he became president and chief executive officer of the United Negro College Fund, now known as the College Fund/UNCF. Americans were stunned by Gray's career change, but many praised him for the move. In *The Black 100: A Ranking of the Most Influential African Americans, Past and Present,* Columbus Salley wrote that Gray's decision showed:

> courage and vision in taking his fame, visibility, and influence—at a time when his political star was rising—to seize the sociology of this particular moment in history to strengthen and expand the role of historically black colleges and universities. Gray's decision came at a critical time, when black America faced the scandalizing and sobering fact that more college age black males are in prison, jail, or on probation than in institutions of higher learning.

In assuming leadership of the UNCF, Gray followed family tradition a second time. His grandfather was a professor. His father was president of two black colleges. His mother was a dean at Southern University in Baton Rouge, Louisiana. His sister, Marion, is a professor. Prior to promoting education in Congress, Gray taught religion and history during the late 1960s and early 1970s at St. Peter's College, Jersey City State College, Montclair State College, Eastern Baptist Theological Seminary, and Temple University.

Gray told Matthew Scott for *Black Enterprise* that his work at UNCF "is just as important as being a member of the leadership of Congress." He has produced dramatic results in fund raising, administrative reorganization, and initiatives. Approximately one–third of the nearly $1 billion raised in the UNCF's history has been generated since Gray's arrival. Campaign 2000, the organization's most ambitious fund–raising project, has exceeded its $250 million goal by 12 percent. A $50 million gift from media mogul Walter Annenberg helped the campaign raise $86 million in its first year. To increase efficiency, administrative expenses have been reduced while staff was restructured and UNCF headquarters were moved to the Fairfax, Virginia, area. The Gray administration has also undertaken the development of a technology center electronically linking its offices and member colleges as well as a research institute to study issues affecting African American students from grade school through graduate school.

In the *Washington Post,* Gray stated the importance of black institutions:

> If America is to prosper in the global marketplace and maintain our economic strength, we will have to rely on the skills and productivity of that 21st–century workforce. Thus we need to support the educational institutions that know how to take not just the best and brightest, but also the talented and intelligent, and give them the skills America will need.

He added:

> Just as the religious and ethnic colleges of early immigrants—Georgetown, Yeshiva, Brigham Young—provided doorways for their rejected community, HBCUs continue to serve all of us. They have a vital role to play. From their halls have come—and will continue to come—the business persons, physicians, scientists, engineers, architects, teachers, public servants and artists we need to be strong in the 21st century.

Gray has received more than 50 honorary degrees from colleges and universities. In 1995 Haitian President Jean–Bertrand Aristide awarded Gray the Medal of Honor for his 1994 work as a special advisor to President Clinton in developing and implementing policy to restore Haitian democracy.

In taking up the UNCF post, Gray commented that he could spend more time at Bright Hope and with his family. He married Andrea Dash in 1971. They have three sons: William H. IV, Justin, and Andrew. The Grays live in Vienna, Virginia. While Gray is remembered for his service as an influential politician in both state and federal governments, he continues to serve the needs of black people through his church and his work as head of the nation's most influential fund–raising organization for black colleges. William H. Gray III remains a man of God, a man of the people, and a man of the future.

Current address: The College Fund/UNCF, 8260 Willow Oakes Corporate Drive, PO Box 10444, Fairfax, VA 22031–4511.

REFERENCES

"The Case for All–Black Colleges." *Washington Post,* July 28, 1996.

Christian, Charles M. *Black Saga: The African American Experience.* Boston: Houghton Mifflin, 1995.

Clay, William L. *Just Permanent Interests: Black Americans in Congress, 1870–1991.* New York: Amistad Press, 1992.

Contemporary Black Biography. Vol. 3. Detroit: Gale Research, 1993.

Current Biography Yearbook. New York: H. W., Wilson, 1988.

Perry, Nancy J. "The Many Shades of Gray." *Fortune* 116 (November 9, 1987): 159–60.

Ruffins, Paul. "Passing the Torch: A Look at the Leaders of the '90s." *Black Enterprise* 19 (January 1989): 46–7.

Salley, Columbus. *The Black 100: A Ranking of the Most Influential African Americans, Past and Present.* New York: Citadel Press, 1993.

Salzman, Jack, David Lionel Smith, and Cornel West, ed. *Encyclopedia of African–American Culture and History.* New York: Macmillan Library Reference USA/Simon and Schuster Macmillan, 1996.

Scott, Matthew S. ''Gray Accepts UNCF Post.'' *Black Enterprise* 22 (September 1991): 16.

———. ''A Higher Calling.'' *Black Enterprise* 22 (February 1992): 228–30.

Who's Who among African Americans, 1996–97. 9th ed. Detroit: Gale Research, Inc., 1996.

Who's Who in America, 1996. 50th ed. New Providence, NJ: Reid Reference Co., 1995.

''William H. Gray, III.'' The College Fund/UNCF, 1995.

Linda M. Carter

William ''Bill'' G. Greaves

(1926–)

Film producer, director, writer

William Garfield Greaves is the dean of African American independent filmmakers. His television work and documentaries are award winning productions. Greaves's documentaries are innovative, clearheaded, and often politically motivated. He has sought ways to present independent black perspectives on film. The multifaceted Greaves has excelled at his craft because film has been an intensely satisfying creative form within which he could use all of his creative talents.

Greaves was born October 8, 1926, in New York City and grew up in Harlem. He is one of seven children of Emily Muir Greaves and Garfield Greaves, a cab driver and sometimes a minister. At 14 William Greaves won a scholarship to the prestigious Little Red Schoolhouse in Greenwich Village. Greaves graduated from Stuyvesant High School. He was educated at the City College of New York, 1944–45, and at the Film Institute of City College, 1950–52.

A true student of the arts, Bill Greaves was an actor, amateur boxer, dancer, and freelance songwriter (of more than 100 songs) in New York City from 1944 to 1952. While enrolled as an engineering student at City College, Greaves used his skills as a social dancer to become a performer in African dance troupes. He danced with the Pearl Primus and the Sierra Leonean Asadata Dafora Dance Companies during 1944 and 1945. Greaves was a featured actor with the noted American Negro Theater, appearing in Owen Dodson's *Garden of Time* and *Henri Christophe.* As a young man, he competed with actors Sidney Poitier and Harry Belafonte for stage parts before becoming interested in film production.

Greaves's first film role was *The Fight Never Ends* with Joe Louis in 1946. Greaves also had parts in the films *Miracle in Harlem* (1947) and *Lost Boundaries* (1948). He was featured in Broadway's *Finian's Rainbow,* and *Lost in the Stars.* Greaves felt that he had a promising career, with parts in two feature films and a featured role in a stage play, all running simultaneously. In 1948 he was accepted as a full member of the Actors Studio. Marlon Brando, James Dean, Anthony Quinn, Al Pacino, and Shelley Winters were among his classmates. As a young actor, however, the roles he was asked to play troubled Greaves. He was insulted by the images of black people on the movie screens. After turning down a part in a revival of *Twentieth Century* on Broadway in 1950, Greaves decided to go behind the camera.

Greaves struggled to establish himself as a filmmaker. He enjoyed the opportunity to work with noted documentary filmmaker Louis DeRochemont; yet, Greaves found it necessary to leave the country for further work and training. For more than ten years he worked for Canada's National Film Board as writer, chief editor, assistant director, or director on nearly 80 films. *Emergency Ward* (1958) is one of his most noted films of his Canadian tenure. His last two years in Canada were spent as the public information officer for the International Civil Aviation Organization in Montreal. For this agency of the United Nations, Greaves made the film *Cleared for Takeoff* (1963) featuring Alistair Cooke. Also while in Canada, Greaves served as an acting teacher and as artistic director of the Canadian Drama Studio in Montreal and Toronto.

After returning to the United States in 1963, Greaves became a film producer and director for United Nations Television. He produced three films for UN–TV before starting his own film company. William Greaves Productions was started in 1964 with a $5,000 loan from the Small Business Administration. His Canadian work brought him to the attention of the United States Information Agency's (USIA) film division, for which he made two movies. *Wealth of a Nation* (1964), about dissent in America, and *The First World Festival of Negro Arts* (1966), which the Senegal government selected as the official film of its world festival, allowed Greaves to express African American perspectives on film. The next breakthrough film for Greaves was *Still a Brother: Inside the Negro Middle Class* (1967) for National Educational Television (NET).

Producer of *Black Journal*

William Greaves Productions leased its president to NET to produce *Black Journal* from 1968 to 1970. *Black Journal,* a one hour monthly program, was a 1970 Emmy Award winning, black oriented, network news show. The show claimed to be ''of, by, about and primarily for the Black community.'' Greaves became the first African American executive producer in network television. Greaves's short tenure with *Black Journal,* as executive producer and co–host, spawned a new breed of television programming nationwide.

Many black filmmakers credit Greaves with significant mentoring. He has said that *Black Journal* enabled him to encourage younger African American directors such as St. Clair Bourne, Stan Lathan, and Kathleen Collins. Greaves also served as an instructor at the Lee Strasberg Theatre Institute from 1968 to 1982. He lectures on film in the United States and abroad. He has conducted workshops for film directors and screen actors throughout the world.

Film Producer

Greaves developed a documentary style that uses the montage technique, which juxtaposes images, sounds, and ideas to create cinematic statements. Greaves has noted that he attempts to put into his films a zest for life often absent in documentaries. His experimental film *Symbiopsychotaxiplasm: Take One,* shot in 1968, made a strong reappearance at a 1991 Greaves retrospective at the Brooklyn Museum. This movie–about–a–movie pioneered the ''self reflective'' genre. As one who has broken many barriers, Greaves is sensitive to the issue of African American artists going uncredited for their innovations.

Greaves produced, wrote and/or directed many award winning films: *In the Company of Men* (1969, eight awards), made for *Newsweek* magazine, is a depiction of a workplace racial conflict; *Nationtime: Gary* (1972) covered the historic National Black Political Convention; and *Voice of La Raza* (1972, four awards), featuring Anthony Quinn, documented discrimination against Spanish–speaking Americans for the Equal Opportunity Commission. *The Fighters,* on the 1971 fight between Muhammad Ali and Joe Frazier, is a boxing masterpiece. *From These Roots* (1974), a winner of 22 international film festival awards, is based on the 1920s Harlem Renaissance. His 1974 black exploitation film was *The Marijuana Affair,* and *Just Doin' It* (1976) is a cinéma–vérité look at two Atlanta barbershops. *Space for Women* (1982), produced for NASA about female astronauts and women in science, won eight awards including the Cine Golden Eagle and an NAACP Image Award. Greaves was also executive producer for *Bustin Loose* (1981), starring Richard Pryor and Cicely Tyson in a Universal Pictures feature film. He finished the decade with *Black Power in America: Myth or Reality?* (1986), *The Deep North* (1988), and *That's Black Entertainment* (1989).

Many of Greaves's films explore the lives of extraordinary African Americans. This work began with profiles created on the ground breaking PBS series *Black Journal.* In its two years, Greaves produced some 80 film segments. For the National Park Service, Greaves produced the films *Frederick Douglass, An American Life* and *Booker T. Washington: The Life and the Legacy* in 1985. Greaves also directed and coproduced *A Tribute to Paul Robeson's 90th Birthday* at the Shubert Theater. *Ida B. Wells: A Passion for Justice,* (PBS, 1989) is an award–winning memoir of the crusading journalist, with readings by Toni Morrison.

Award–winning Movie–maker

In 1970 Greaves won ten major awards for film and television productions about the problems and ambitions of African Americans, including the Russworm Award from the National Newspaper Publishers Association. Already a member of the advisory board, he was inducted into the Black Filmmakers Hall of Fame in 1980. He received the Dusa Award from the Actors Studio in 1980. Special homage and a retrospective of his work were the high points of the 1980 Festival of Black Independent American Cinema in Paris (Greaves produced six of the 40 films shown). The Association of Independent Video and Filmmakers presented him its Indy Special Life Achievement Award in 1986. He is the recipient of more than 80 international film festival awards. Greaves has an honorary degree from Tougaloo College in Mississippi.

Greaves has served as a trustee of the New York Public Library's Schomburg Center for Research in Black Culture since 1981. He is also a member of many arts advisory boards, and has been the chair of the film panel of The Princess Grace Foundation. William Greaves's commitment to changing the screen image of African Americans compelled him to create a space for his particular talents in an insular community, and in the process, Greaves has created an enormous film legacy. In *Who's Who in America,* he responded to his own thoughts on life: ''Success is largely dependent on an individual's capacity to convert the most adverse and negative experience or circumstance into something constructive and productive.'' Greaves married Louise Archambault on August 23, 1959; they have three children: David, Taiyi, and Maiya.

Current address: William Greaves Productions, 80 Eighth Avenue, New York, NY 10011.

REFERENCES

''Bill Greaves' Work Gains New Following.'' *The Bay State Banner,* June 25, 1992.

''Black TV: Its Problems and Promises.'' *Ebony* 24 (September 1969): 88–94.

Greaves, William. ''Afterthoughts on the Black American Film Festival.'' *Black American Literature Forum* 25 (Summer 1991): 433–36.

———. ''Two Fighters on Film.'' *Black American Literature Forum* 12 (Winter 1978): 135–37.

Hansen, Liane. ''All Black Films to Be Shown on Turner Classic Movies.'' *National Public Radio's Weekend Edition—Sunday,* February 25, 1996. Transcript #1164–7.

Kalamu ya Salaam. ''Making the Image Real: Black Producers of Theater, Film and Television.'' *The Black Collegian* 7 (March/April 1977): 56–58.

Knee, Adam, and Charles Musser. ''William Greaves, Documentary Film–making, and the African–American Experience.'' *Film Quarterly* 45 (1992): 13–25.

Lee, Rohama. ''The Whirlwind World of William Greaves.'' *American Cinematographer* 66 (August 1985): 68–72.

Murray, James. *To Find an Image: Black Films From Uncle Tom to Super Fly.* Indianapolis: Bobbs–Merrill, 1973.

Who's Who in America. 52nd edition. New Providence, RI: Marquis Who's Who, 1998.

Kathleen E. Bethel

Richard T. Greener
(1844–1922)
Educator, lawyer, government official

Richard Theodore Greener was the first black graduate of Harvard University. In later life he pursued a commensurate success, a search which proved elusive. His close friend Francis J. Grimké, pastor of the Fifteenth Street Presbyterian Church in Washington, D.C., wrote in his *Stray Thoughts and Meditations* on the day of Greener's funeral:

> He was a generous big–hearted fellow, gifted in speech, widely read, finely educated, a man of broad culture. . .our only regret was that he did not stick to some one thing, and put his strength into it, strength of intellect and enthusiasm.

Greener was born on January 30, 1844, in Philadelphia. His paternal grandfather, Jacob Greener, was a whitewasher and teacher in Baltimore. His father, Richard Wesley Greener, was a ship steward. In 1853 Greener's father tried his hand at finding gold in California; he fell out of contact with his family soon thereafter and was presumed dead. Richard Greener's maternal grandfather was a West Indian of Spanish extraction which contributed to Richard Greener's very light complexion. His mother's maiden name was Mary Ann Le Brun or Le Brune. Much of the information about his early life is from an 1870 autobiographical sketch in the Harvard University Archives.

In 1853, when Greener was nine years old, Mary Ann Greener moved to Boston and then across the river to Cambridge so that her son could attend a racially–mixed school. Richard Greener left school about 1858 and held various jobs. He was attracted for a while to a career in art, for which he showed marked ability when he worked for a firm of wood engravers, but he quit that job soon after he was struck by his employer.

Employment at the Pavilion Hotel gave Greener contacts which he used to further his education, and his employer at a subsequent night watchman's job helped him finance study in Oberlin's precollege program. Handicapped by his lack of preparation, Greener completed one year of that program. He then set his sights on Harvard and spent a preparatory year at Andover. In the fall of 1865 he was admitted to Harvard, where, despite his preparation, he found it necessary to repeat his freshman year.

After this difficult beginning Greener enjoyed considerable success at Harvard, winning the Bowdoin Prize for elocution as a sophomore and another prize for a senior English essay. He graduated in 1870 and faced the choice of a career.

Greener first considered a career in the church, but his unorthodox religious beliefs kept him from obtaining any serious positions. He decided instead to practice law, but he first became a teacher. He taught for two years as principal of

Richard T. Greener

the Male Department of Philadelphia's Institute for Colored Youth. From 1872 to 1873 he was principal of the Preparatory High School for Colored Youth in Washington, D.C. There he met Washingtonian Genevieve Ida Fleet, whom he married in 1874. The couple had seven children before the marriage broke down in the 1890s. He also devoted efforts during this period in Washington to the ill–fated newspapers, the *National Era* and the *New National Era,* attempts to establish a national black paper.

In October 1873 Greener became a professor of metaphysics and logic at the University of South Carolina. In 1875 he became the University's librarian. He also studied law and was admitted to the South Carolina bar in 1876, the year antireconstruction whites seized political control in the state and again barred all African Americans from the university.

Greener returned to Washington and in 1877 passed the bar again and became a law instructor at Howard University. That same year he supported black emigration to western states in opposition to Frederick Douglass. From January 1879 to July 1880 Greener was dean of the Howard law school, losing the post when the board of trustees of Howard University temporarily closed the school. Greener next found work as a law clerk in the Treasury Department. When this position ended in 1882, he practiced law in the district. He also turned his considerable oratorical powers to support the Republican Party.

Political appointments soon came his way. Between 1885 and 1892 he was secretary of the Grant Monument Society of New York state and from 1885 to 1889 he became chief examiner of the municipal civil service board of New York city. Financial and family problems made the following years difficult. Finally, though, Greener was able to secure the post he had sought in the Foreign Service. He turned down a post in Bombay because of reports of an epidemic of plague there, but in July 1898 he accepted a post in Vladivostock.

Some people wondered why Greener accepted this out of the way post with small financial return. Serving over five years in such isolation certainly removed him from any possible leadership role. Nonetheless, he served capably until 1905, first as consul and then as commercial agent, remaining through the end of the war between Russia and Japan which gave Vladivostock a sudden temporary prominence in world affairs. The Chinese government gave him the Order of the Double Dragon for his help in famine relief. In 1905 he was dismissed from his post in a political decision probably turning on his race. He unfortunately had no opportunity to rebut the vaguely formulated charges of misconduct, which seemed without any real merit, and he went home.

Greener established himself in Chicago in 1906. He continued to lecture and maintained his interest in national politics. In 1912 he broke with the Republicans to support Woodrow Wilson. The full scope of his activities during these years remains as yet unknown. He suffered a cerebral hemorrhage and died May 2, 1922, at his home at 5237 Ellis Avenue in Chicago.

Richard T. Greener faced the problems of the college trained black in his era of limited possibilities—problems compounded by the prestige conferred by his Harvard degree. His inability to accept traditional Christianity ruled out a career as a minister, and a career as a lawyer was not exceptionally lucrative given the persuasive racism of the legal system. Politics and political action became less open as the Republican Party first abandoned Reconstruction and then continued its retreat from commitment to black Americans. Greener was an exceptional orator; he wrote much but produced no major sustained work. His temperament and commitment to individualism seem to have combined to bar him from filling a role as a major black leader.

REFERENCES

Blakely, Allison. "Richard T. Greener and the 'Talented Tenth's' Dilemma." *Journal of Negro History* 59 (October 1974): 305–21.

Johnson, Allen, and Dumas Malone, eds. *Dictionary of American Biography*. New York: Scribner's, 1943.

Logan, Rayford W., and Michael R. Winston, eds. *Dictionary of American Negro Biography*. New York: Norton, 1982.

Simmons, William J. *Men of Mark*. Cleveland: Geo. W. Rewell, 1887.

Sollors, Werner, and others, eds. *Blacks at Harvard*. New York: New York University Press, 1993.

Williams, George W. *History of the Negro Race in America*. 2 vol. New York: G. P. Putnam's Sons, 1883.

Woodson, Carter G., ed. *The Works of Francis J. Grimké*. 4 vol. Washington: The Associated Publishers, 1942.

Robert L. Johns

Dick Gregory

(1932–)

Comedian, civil rights activist, nutritional advocate

Dick Gregory has been characterized as one of the four trailblazers for contemporary comics. In *Billboard* magazine, Bill Holland credited Tom Lehrer, Mort Sahl, Lenny Bruce, and Gregory with modernizing social satire "by enlarging the form [and] expanding its reach from nightclub gigs to concert halls and then to the widely accessible media of albums and TV shows."

Unlike his fellow trailblazers, Gregory greatly expanded the scope of his life's activities. After reaching the pinnacle of success, he became a civil rights activist, a natural progression from integrating social issues in his comedy act. He traveled across America to speak at benefits and support voter registration efforts. After becoming interested in nutritional issues, he became an entrepreneur in the weight–loss industry. When he became aware of the benefits of fasting, he also became a marathon runner and used both as a means of focusing attention on issues he deemed crucial to the welfare of the nation and the world: world hunger, the homeless, drug proliferation, apartheid, statehood for Washington, D.C., gangsta' rap music, and war. After a 30–year hiatus, he has returned to stand–up comedy, and in 1996 began performing in a Brooklyn theater. He has settled into a highly successful off–Broadway show as well as fulfilling over 200 live dates yearly.

Richard Claxton Gregory, popularly known as "Dick" Gregory, was born on October 12, 1932, in St. Louis. The poverty that surrounded him at birth remained with Gregory as he grew up in St. Louis. His father, Presley Gregory, deserted his wife and six children during Gregory's childhood, and the cruel taunts from other children became a challenge for survival early in his life. He is quoted in *Contemporary Black Biography*:

> I got picked on a lot around the neighborhood; skinniest kid on the block, the poorest, the one without a Daddy. I guess that's when I began to learn about humor, the power of a joke. . . . They were going to laugh anyway, but if I made the jokes, they'd laugh with me instead of at me. I'd get the kids off my back, on my side.

Dick Gregory

Gregory's mother, Lucille Franklin Gregory, was forced to work long hours to feed, clothe, and house her family. As a young child, Gregory became a hustler who sold newspapers, shined shoes, scrubbed steps, and even piled sandbags on the Mississippi River. Since the water pipes in his home were often frozen, he cleaned the high school band room in exchange for the opportunity to use the school showers. He excelled as a high school track runner and won the Missouri state mile race in 1951 and 1952. Because black school track–meet records were not included, his accomplishments were omitted from the state records. He did win an athletic scholarship to Southern Illinois University where he was named Outstanding Athlete in 1953.

Gregory was drafted into the U.S. Army in 1954 and continued to run track and to compete in talent shows, a continuation of early ventures into satirical comedy begun in college. Because of a "smart–mouth" attitude largely unappreciated by his army superiors, he was ordered to win an army talent show comedy competition or face court–martial charges. After winning, Gregory was transferred to the Special Services entertainment division.

Realizing a Dream

In 1956 Gregory was discharged from the army and returned to college, but dropped out to pursue his dream of being a full–time stand–up comic. He actually paid to be allowed to perform at a Chicago South Side club and, after gaining more experience, opened his own club, the Apex, outside the city. Lillian Smith, a friend he knew from his first club gig, became a financial partner. They married in 1959 and eventually became the parents of ten children. The Apex business venture had failed by that time because there were too few patrons and too much bad weather. Until Gregory got his first big break in 1961 at Chicago's Playboy Club, he worked many menial jobs to make ends meet for his family which by then included their first child.

In January of 1961 Gregory received a call to replace a white comedian who had become ill just before the first show. Gregory arrived at the Playboy Club only to be rebuffed by the club's booking agent because the room had been booked for a convention of Southern executives who would not appreciate a black comedian. Having walked 20 blocks in freezing weather and too broke even to afford bus fare, Gregory insisted on being allowed to perform to an audience that was indeed initially hostile. Gregory treated the Playboy Club audience as he had his childhood tormentors, as described in *Contemporary Black Biography*:

> I was faster, and I was funny, and when that room broke it was like the storm was over. They stopped heckling and they listened. What was supposed to be a fifty–minute show lasted for about an hour and forty minutes.

Gregory had hit the big time. His performance earned him a three–year contract at the Playboy Club. *Time* magazine ran a feature article and photograph in the May 17, 1961, issue proclaiming him the first black comedian to break into the nightclub venue. Gregory was an acknowledged master of satirical and topical humor, joking about himself first and then about current racial issues. In *Emerge,* Mel Watson, an author of the history of black comedy said of his comedic style: "By [1962] the Civil Rights Movement was well on its way and Gregory's comedy fit perfectly. Mort Sahl started to deal with social issues in comedy. When Gregory came on, he began to do the same thing. No Black comic had done this, not publicly."

Beyond the Confines of a Stage

Gregory's rise coincided with the advent of the civil rights movement during the turbulent sixties, and he performed for the cause as well as for the applause. He entertained in nightclubs and did satires on racism. As early as 1961 Gregory got involved with the cause; that was the year he responded to Medgar Evers's request to speak at a voter registration rally in Jackson, Mississippi. He answered the call for the Congress of Racial Equality (CORE), the Student Nonviolent Coordinating Committee (SNCC), the Southern Christian Leadership Conference (SCLC), and any other organization that needed a high–profile presence to help raise funds and inspire the people to rise up against injustice. James Farmer called Gregory and asked him to come South and assist him in investigating the disappearance of three young CORE workers reported missing in Neshoba County, Mississippi. They met in Meridian during a time of great tension and paralyzing fear, when not even the state police would guarantee their safety. Farmer was absolutely terrified when Gregory confronted the county sheriff and demanded that he admit knowing more about the disappearance and whereabouts of the missing men than he was letting on.

During the voter registration marches in Greenwood, Mississippi, Gregory was the first celebrity to join the effort, and he again openly defied the authorities. One of his arrests netted front page coverage by the *New York Times* in a photograph showing him with his arms twisted behind his back by the local police. By 1964 Gregory had become so involved that his nightclub earnings had dropped nearly $250,000. Meanwhile, the escalating tension and violence of events were greatly affecting his life. Medgar Evers was assassinated two weeks after their last meeting. He was also having difficulty with the concept of nonviolence after having witnessed a Mississippi sheriff strike his wife, an act against which he did not retaliate out of fear and in keeping with the spirit of the nonviolent protests. Reflection on this event was one catalyst that led to Gregory's becoming a vegetarian. In *Emerge,* he is quoted as saying:

> How can I justify not hitting a sheriff that kicked my pregnant wife and participate in the destruction of a cow or chicken that ain't never done nothing to me? I didn't know it was gonna change my life.

In *Black in Selma,* J. L. Chestnut Jr. praised Gregory for the impact he had on Selma's black population during voter registration efforts. Lillian Gregory, pregnant at the time, even led a march of young black women, much to the dismay of the Dallas County jail warden who feared mistreatment of jailed black women by the sheriff. Chestnut credited Gregory and Bernard Lafayette, now president of Nashville's American Baptist College, as key in making the city's black adults more assertive and militant in fighting for their rights.

On occasion, Gregory took positions that were questioned by civil rights leaders. At the peak of the Birmingham movement, it was Gregory to whom Burke Marshall, assistant attorney general for the Justice Department, and Robert F. Kennedy, attorney general, turned for advice about the internecine squabbling among the movement's black leadership. He recommended that they use James Baldwin, noted black author, to assemble a group of the black intelligentsia to explain why black people were angry and why their supposed leaders could not solve the problem. This New York meeting was a fiasco, in part because those attending were not active participants in the movement and few had firsthand experience or knowledge of the South. Gregory also supported the Brooklyn chapter of CORE in opposition to Farmer and the national office over sponsoring a car stall–in on the opening day of the 1964 World's Fair, an effort that was aborted and failed.

Politics and Business

Gregory's decision to stop eating meat necessitated dietary changes to ensure proper nutrition. In 1967 he fasted for 40 days to protest the Vietnam War; he lost nearly 100 pounds. Since his weight had greatly escalated after giving up meat, health issues had become a dominant theme in his life. In addition to fasting and other lifestyle changes, Gregory stopped performing in places that permitted smoking and drinking, a decision he explained in *Contemporary Black Biography*:

> How can I get up there and tell those students that drugs and alcohol and even meat is bad for them, then afterwards say "come on down and catch my act at the club and have a drink."

Gregory also increased his political activities and went beyond the civil rights arena. He ran for mayor of Chicago in 1967, and in 1968 was the presidential candidate for the U.S. Freedom and Peace party. As a college lecturer, Gregory crisscrossed the country speaking to America's youth about the dangers inherent in the political and judicial systems, focusing especially on 1960s conspiracy theories involving the FBI (Federal Bureau of Investigation) and its controversial leader, J. Edgar Hoover.

During the 1970s Gregory continued to write, an outlet for his outspoken viewpoints begun a decade earlier with *Back of the Bus* (1962) and *Nigger: An Autobiography* (1964). New publications were *No More Lies: The Myth and Reality of American History* (1971), *Code Name Zorro: The Murder of Martin Luther King, Jr.* (1971), and *Dick Gregory's Political Primer* (1972). Having completely changed his lifestyle based on nutritionally sound eating habits, Gregory became an authority and television talk show guest. In 1974 he and Alvenia Fulton collaborated on writing *Dick Gregory's Natural Diet for Folks Who Eat: Cookin' with Mother Nature.*

In 1984 Gregory became an entrepreneur with the founding of Health Enterprises, a venture based on marketing the Slim–Safe Bahamian Diet, a powdered diet mix. This product was developed out of Gregory's concern and firm belief that being overweight was a serious form of malnutrition just as devastating as the ill effects of hunger. He also pursued other financial ventures including a 1987 health food distribution company that was ranked 74th on the *Black Enterprise* 1989 list of America's largest black–owned businesses. It all came crashing down because disagreements between Gregory and his partners led to legal warfare. Before the smoke cleared, Gregory lost to foreclosure his Massachusetts farm home, where his family resided. Eventually winning his lawsuit and regaining control of his company, he also regained ownership of his property. Gregory is currently considering the feasibility of starting up a marketing company to be called Peace Through Nutrition.

A New Day

In the midst of a successful comeback as a stand–up comic, Gregory is being taken seriously when he revives 30–year–old conspiracy theories and allegations about CIA (Central Intelligence Agency) efforts to infiltrate Los Angeles neighborhoods to ensure the proliferation of crack cocaine. Gregory was never concerned about others' perceptions of the validity of his claims. He is quoted as saying in *Emerge*: "I've always felt that truth don't have to be validated by ignorance."

Having returned to the first arena of his success, Gregory is once more a winner, but with notable differences. He is now gray–bearded and gray–headed; he carries a glass of water in one hand and a rolled up newspaper under the other arm instead of the once–omnipresent cigarette of the 1960s; he wears a kente (African fabric) cloth–trimmed tuxedo in place of the expensive Italian suits of his earlier years. But he still has the power to hold audiences in the palm of his hand just as he did three decades ago. In *Emerge,* Laura Williams, a theatre company manager, said of him: "The moment you announce Dick Gregory, there is an interest. People have always been curious to hear what he has to say."

Gregory remains a highly respected public figure in the worlds of entertainment and social justice. He is still married to Lillian Gregory who still manages his career and finances.

In 1978 Gregory received the *Ebony*–Topaz Heritage and Freedom Award. He has received numerous honorary doctorates, including those from Malcolm X College in Chicago (1970) and Southern Illinois University at Carbondale (1989). Although Gregory's forays into politics were unsuccessful, he received nearly 200,000 write–in votes for president of the United States in 1968. He was sworn in as "president in exile" by supporters and "inaugurated" in the nation's capital. As testimony to his promise to fight the racist system intent on destroying America, one writer in *Contemporary Black Biography* said that Gregory "preaches freedom; he teaches it; he satirizes over it, and no one is safe from his keen wit or common sense." In addition to the books he has written, Gregory created the comedy routines featured in recordings made during his early career through the 1970s.

Current address: Dick Gregory Health Enterprises, 39 South LaSalle, Chicago, IL 60603.

REFERENCES

Branch, Taylor. *Parting the Waters: America in the King Years 1954–1963.* New York: Simon and Schuster, 1988.

Chestnut, J. L., Jr., and Julia Cass. *Black in Selma: The Uncommon Life of J. L. Chestnut, Jr.* New York: Farrar, Strauss and Giroux, 1990.

Contemporary Black Biography. Vol. 2. Detroit: Gale Research, 1992.

Farmer, James L., Jr. *Lay Bare the Heart: An Autobiography of the Civil Rights Movement.* New York: Arbor House, 1985.

Gregory, Dick. "And I Ain't Just Whistlin' Dixie." *Ebony* 26 (August 1971): 149–51.

Holland, Bill. "50's Trailblazers Brought Social Satire to Masses." *Billboard* 108 (28 September 1996): 1–5.

Howard, Sherry L. "He's No Joke." *Emerge* 8 (December/January 1997): 46–51.

Levine, Lawrence W. *Black Culture and Black Consciousness.* New York: Oxford, 1977.

Salzman, Jack, David Lionel Smith, and Cornel West, eds. *Encyclopedia of African–American Culture and History.* New York: Macmillan Library Reference USA/Simon and Schuster Macmillan, 1996.

Who's Who among Black Americans 1996–97. 9th ed. Detroit: Gale Research, 1996.

Dolores Nicholson

Archibald Henry Grimké

(1849–1930)

Lawyer, journalist, editor, government official, civil rights activist

Archibald Henry Grimké became a leading member of the first college–educated generation of African Americans. Born a slave in Charleston, South Carolina, he rose from his humble beginnings to become a lawyer and a writer, employing his talents for the benefit of numerous causes. His command of communication through oratory and writing, together with his influence in the black communities of Boston and Washington D.C., made him a major spokesman of the Northern black elite. He was an independent thinker who gave forceful expression to his views on politics and civil rights.

Archibald Grimké was born on August 17, 1849, at Cane Acre, a plantation some 16 miles from Charleston, South Carolina. He was the oldest son of Henry Grimké, a lawyer and plantation owner, and Nancy Weston, a slave. He had two full brothers, Francis James and John. Nancy Weston was of mixed heritage and was a strong–minded woman who practically raised Henry Grimké's children by his first wife. Shortly before the birth of Archibald's brother, John, Henry Grimké died of typhoid.

Under state law, manumission was illegal, but Nancy (Weston) Grimké was allowed to live as free in Charleston, where she bought a three–room house. The Grimké family did not support her, so Nancy Grimké worked as a laundress to earn a living for herself and her children with occasional help from some of her free black relations. She was fierce in her defense of her children and made sure that they had a strict religious upbringing and attended school.

For eight years the white Grimkés did not interfere with Nancy Grimké's family. Then in 1860 Archibald's older half–brother, Montague Grimké, who was his legal owner, made Archibald and his brother Francis house servants. They continued to live with their mother and attend school. Archibald did not accept the situation easily; he feigned stupidity and was slow to learn his tasks. When Nancy Grimké protested the treatment of her child, Montague had her imprisoned for a week in the workhouse. In 1862 Archibald was sent to the workhouse where he was severely beaten.

Archibald Henry Grimké

Sent home to recover from the beating, Archibald decided to run away. After spending several weeks in hiding, he revealed his whereabouts to his mother who insured that, disguised as a girl, he reached the house of a free relative. Archibald spent the next two years there until the Union troops arrived in Charleston in February 1865.

At the end of the war Nancy Grimké found work as a housekeeper at the Morris Street Freedmen's school, headed by Frances Pillsbury. Pillsbury arranged for Archibald and Francis to go to school in the North. The boys boarded with different families and worked in exchange for room, board, and an education. Because of the exceptional progress of the young students, Frances Pillsbury soon arranged an interview for the boys with Isaac Rendall, president of Lincoln University in Chester, Pennsylvania. Support for Archibald and Francis was found—it was never generous and they were chronically short of money and had to work for additional funds—and they soon became students at Lincoln in spite of their youth.

College Years

Archibald and Francis spent a year and a half in the preparatory department of Lincoln University, entering in the fall of 1867. Archibald soon established himself as a remarkable student, and graduated in 1870.

In 1868 Archibald established contact with his aunts Angelina Grimké Weld and Sarah Grimké, both prominent abolitionists and suffragists. The sisters decided to accept him as a full family member, becoming surrogate parents and contributing as much monetary support as their limited means permitted.

After graduation in 1870, Archibald found a position at Lincoln teaching in the preparatory department so he could study law in the newly established Law Department. In addition, Archibald served as the school's first black librarian. Archibald received an M.A. in 1872.

Moves to Boston

Archibald Grimké entered Harvard Law School in 1872. He won a Bussey scholarship for his second year and was one of only half his entering class to graduate in 1874. There seems to have been few instances of overt prejudice during his time in school. An important part of his support came from the Welds, Angelina Grimké and husband, who also introduced him to white abolitionist circles in Boston. He formed long–lasting friendships with some whites at the same time he became, as his daughter Angelina Weld Grimké phrased it in her biographical sketch, "a liberal in religion, a radical in the Woman Suffrage Movement, in politics, and on the race question."

After graduation Archibald Grimké worked in a law office while he studied for the bar examination, which he passed in 1875. He lived in Hyde Park, where the Welds lived. He would later establish his own home there, with only one black family, the John Trotters, as neighbors. In 1875 Grimké formed a law partnership and concentrated on building up his practice for the next few years.

On April 19, 1879, Grimké married Sarah Stanley, crossing racial lines. Grimké's only child, Angelina Weld, was born on February 27, 1880. The marriage began happily, but by 1883 it broke down completely when Sarah did not return from a visit to her parents in Michigan. Efforts at reconciliation failed, including some by his father–in–law, who had opposed the marriage at first. Initially Angelina remained with her mother, who began an independent career as an occultist writer and lecturer. In 1888 Sarah went abroad, and Angelina went to live with her father permanently. Sarah committed suicide in San Diego, California, in 1898.

Grimké began his public career in 1883 when he became co–editor of *The Hub.* This magazine was a Republican party organ aimed at influencing the hotly–contested elections of that year and had gone through two editors and two name changes before Grimké came aboard. He undertook the task of working for the defeat of Benjamin Butler, the incumbent governor. He continued the paper after the election, managing to keep it going until 1886, by which time he had shifted his support to the Democrats. In 1884 he worked for Republican presidential nominee, James G. Blaine, in spite of massive defection from the party by leading Massachusetts Republicans.

Editorship of the paper brought Grimké into closer association with Boston's black elite at the same time that it brought him to the notice of influential white politicians. His visibility also increased due to his highly publicized public lectures. On April 9, 1884, he was principal speaker in a

Boston tribute to the recently deceased abolitionist Wendell Phillips. In the same year, he became a member of the board of trustees of the Westborough State Hospital, a homeopathic institute for the insane. Grimké was elected secretary of the board and held that position for ten years.

Grimké also actively took up the cause of women's suffrage and became increasingly radical in his criticism of capitalism and industrial concentration. Grimké was attracted by the ideas of economist Henry George and felt that there was an economic basis to the race problem in the South.

Political Appointment

In 1884 Grimké campaigned for the reelection of Grover Cleveland. Grimké also ran for state representative as a Democrat; he made a respectable showing but lost. Cleveland made a lame–duck appointment of Grimké as consul to the Dominican Republic but the Senate did not approve it.

Grimké continued his interest in politics. He was president of the Hyde Park Single Tax Club and worked for a prohibition amendment which carried Hyde Park but failed state–wide. He gave more time to his writing, producing full–length biographies of abolitionists William Lloyd Garrison (1891) and Charles Sumner (1892). After the death of the current consul in Santo Domingo, the Senate approved Grimké's nomination to the post on July 30, 1894. Afterward Grimké spent almost all of his time in the Dominican Republic until 1898. He found his position as consul in a black–controlled, multiracial society rewarding.

Between 1898 and 1905 Grimké divided his time between Boston and Washington, before permanently moving into his brother's residence in Washington with Angelina. There he resumed his political and intellectual interests. He became a member of the American Negro Academy in 1899 and served as its third president from 1903 to 1919, following Alexander Crummell and W. E. B. Du Bois. He wrote some of his most important papers for the academy, including a pioneering study of the insurrection attempt by Denmark Vesey in Charleston in 1822. He also became active in the Bethel Literary and Historical Society, a very prestigious Washington organization. Grimké's analyses of racial relations in speeches and papers demonstrated his continued militancy and his increasing skepticism about any prospects for widespread cooperation between whites and blacks, positions at variance with those of powerful black leader Booker T. Washington.

Relationship to Booker T. Washington

The rise of Booker T. Washington to national power added a new dimension to race relations. Washington's accomodationist stance often drew the criticism of more militant black leaders who felt that Booker's advice to African Americans to "cast your bucket down where you are," lacked the force and ambition needed for advancement. Grimké did not agree with Washington's philosophies and, although the two men tried to maintain cordial relations, Grimké clearly aligned with the anti–Washington camp. In Washington, D.C., the Negro Academy and the Bethel society gradually became anti–Washington, and in Boston Grimké was a close friend of William Monroe Trotter, editor of the *Guardian* and widely known as an ardent opponent of Washington.

Even after the "Boston Riot" in July of 1903–a disruption of a Boston speech by Washington fomented by Trotter and his allies– Grimké strove to keep open lines of communication. Although Washington privately listed Grimké as an enemy after 1903, both men refrained from public condemnation of the other. The accommodation with Washington was probably made easier when Grimké returned to the Republican fold to support the reelection of Theodore Roosevelt.

Grimké began to write a column for *New York Age,* a paper secretly backed by Washington, in March 1906. He refrained from direct attacks on Washington until January of 1907 in the wake of the Brownsville incident in which a group of African American soldiers in Texas were accused of rioting during the summer of 1906 and suffered dishonorable discharges, an action backed fully by Roosevelt. Washington could not speak out against the president without risking his political power, but Grimké felt no need to conceal his beliefs and began to challenge Washington's policies of accommodation openly. Grimké moved closer to Du Bois and the Niagara Movement, much to William Monroe Trotter's very vocal dismay. Grimké found a new outlet for his anti–Washington positions when he became an editor of the Booker T. Washington–controlled *Alexander's Magazine* for three issues beginning in September 1907. The final breach with Washington was due to Grimké's refusal to support Taft in the presidential election of 1908.

In 1910, Grimké attended some of the original organizational meetings and discussions that helped form the National Association for the Advancement of Colored People (NAACP). In addition to his continued interest in national affairs, he was also much involved in local Washington, D.C. concerns, especially in public school politics.

Grimké reluctantly supported Roosevelt in the 1912 elections, correctly assessing Woodrow Wilson's segregationist sympathies. Wilson's election projected Grimké into active involvement in the NAACP. J. Milton Waldron, president of the Washington, D.C. chapter, had supported Wilson and wanted a federal job, so he refrained from actively opposing the steps toward segregation taken by the new administration. In June of 1913, two months after his election as president, Waldron was removed from the post, and Grimké was called in as a replacement. Elected on January 16, 1914, he proved to be very effective as he built consensus among the membership and led the struggle against attempts to increase segregation and remove blacks from federal positions. Grimké was also elected to the national board of the NAACP. One of Grimké's first roles as a member of the national board of the NAACP was to lead the vote against W. E. B. Du Bois's 1914 attempt to make the NAACP monthly journal, *Crisis,* autonomous. Tension between Du Bois and Grimké would remain high over the years. World War I also caused problems for Grimké. He was not happy with the decision to run a segregated training school for black officers, and in 1917 he was one of the few blacks to come out openly against black men fighting for a racist country. He did not endear himself to Du Bois by opposing Du Bois's attempt to revisit Europe as an Army intelligence officer and later the NAACP's subvention to Du Bois to attend a Pan-African Congress in Paris in 1919. In 1918 Grimké came under surveillance by the federal government as a suspected subversive because of his disenchantment with the war. Grimké headed the local branch of the NAACP until 1923, when he resigned after a bitter dispute with the national organization about allocation of the funds collected locally. He was dropped from the national board of the NAACP in the same year, but Grimké's prestige was still sufficiently high to allow him to act as a transitional president of the local branch through 1924.

Grimké was indeed becoming more radical. Much to the concern of the conservative members of the NAACP, Grimké began to associate with A. Philip Randolph and sympathized with Randolph's socialist and union activities. Grimké's attempt to invite Randolph to address the American Negro Academy in 1919 led to a revolt by the members which ended Grimké's presidency of the organization. In that same year, Grimké was awarded the Spingarn medal, one of the highest honors accorded by the NAACP.

Grimké continued to be both cantankerously independent and a very effective local leader, but he scaled back his activity around 1920. He became less active and vigorous in his leadership of the NAACP branch. Beginning in 1925 he virtually ceased all public activity, although he remained in contact with old friends. In the summer of 1928 his health failed, and he spent most of his time in bed. By April of 1929 he needed constant attendance from two nurses and his daughter. He died at his brother's home, 1415 Corcoran St. NW in Washington, D.C., leaving an estate valued at over $30,000. Angelina Weld Grimké read a poem she wrote at the ceremony and named one of the District of Columbia's schools after her father in 1938.

Archibald Grimké did not have a full-length biography until 1993, and his works remain uncollected. Thus his importance as a leader and his originality as a thinker have been undervalued. Throughout a very difficult period he maintained an uncompromisingly independent stand and fought hard and effectively for civil rights.

REFERENCES

Birney, Catherine H. *The Grimké Sisters: Sarah and Angelina Grimké.* 1885. Reprint, Westport, CT: Greenwood, 1969.

Bruce, Dickson D., Jr. *Archibald Grimké.* Baton Rouge: Louisiana University Press, 1993.

Grimké, Angelina W. "A Biographical Sketch of Archibald H. Grimké." *Opportunity* 3 (February 1925): 44–47.

Grimké, Francis J. *Works.* 4 vol. Washington, DC: Associated Publishers, 1942.

Harlan, Louis R. *Booker T. Washington.* 2 vol. New York: Oxford, 1972, 1983.

Lerner, Gerda. *The Grimké Sisters from South Carolina.* Boston: Houghton Mifflin, 1967.

Logan, Rayford W., and Michael R. Winston, eds. *Dictionary of American Negro Biography.* New York: Norton, 1982.

Memoirs of Archibald H. Grimké. Typescript. Fisk University Library.

Moss, Alfred A., Jr. *The American Negro Academy.* Baton Rouge: Louisiana State University Press, 1981.

Smith, Jessie Carney, ed. *Notable Black American Women.* Detroit: Gale Research, 1992.

COLLECTIONS

The Archibald H. Grimké papers are in the Moorland–Spingarn Library at Howard University.

Robert L. Johns

Francis J. Grimké
(1850–1937)
Minister, civil rights activist

Francis J. Grimké was a Presbyterian minister of such conservative theological views that more than one author accepted the label of "Black Puritan" for him. Early on he became minister of one of the leading churches of the black elite in Washington, D.C., an association he maintained for all but four of the 55 years between 1878 and 1937. He became a leader among black Washingtonians. He fought racism in his denomination and in his society.

Francis James Grimké was born on November 4, 1852, on a plantation near Charleston, South Carolina to Henry Grimké, a lawyer and plantation owner, and Nancy Weston, a slave. He had two full brothers, Archibald Henry and John. Nancy Weston was of mixed heritage and was a strong-minded woman who practically raised Henry Grimké's children by his first wife. Shortly before the birth of Francis' brother, John, Henry Grimké died of typhoid.

Under state law, manumission was illegal, but Nancy (Weston) Grimké was allowed to live as free in Charleston, where she bought a three-room house. The Grimké family did not support her, so Nancy Grimké worked as a laundress to earn a living for herself and her children with occasional help from some of her free black relations. She was fierce in her defense of her children and made sure that they had a strict religious upbringing and attended school.

For eight years the white Grimkés did not interfere with Nancy Grimké's family. Then in 1860 Francis' older half-brother, Montague Grimké, who was his legal owner, made Francis and his brother Archibald house servants. They continued to live with their mother and attend school. When Nancy Grimké protested the treatment of her children, Montague had her imprisoned for a week in the workhouse. In

Francis J. Grimké

1862 Francis was sent to the workhouse where he was severely beaten.

Sent home to recover from the beating, Francis decided to run away. He first became a valet in the Confederate army for two years. When he was recognized on a visit to Charleston, he was imprisoned in the workhouse for several months and then sold to a Confederate officer. He finished out the war with the officer and then returned to Charleston.

At the end of the war Nancy Grimké found work as a housekeeper at the Morris Street Freedmen's school, headed by Frances Pillsbury. Pillsbury arranged for Francis and Archibald to go to school in the North. The boys boarded with different families and worked in exchange for room, board, and an education. Because of the exceptional progress of the young students, Frances Pillsbury soon arranged an interview for the boys with Isaac Rendall, president of Lincoln University in Chester, Pennsylvania. Support for Francis and Archibald was found—it was never generous and they were chronically short of money and had to work for additional funds—and they soon became students at Lincoln in spite of their youth.

College Years

Francis and Archibald spent a year and a half in the preparatory department of Lincoln University, entering in the fall of 1867. Francis soon established himself as a remarkable student, and graduated in 1870 valedictorian of his class.

In 1868 Francis established contact with his aunts Angelina Grimké Weld and Sarah Grimké, both prominent abolitionists and suffragists. The sisters decided to accept him as a full family member, becoming surrogate parents and contributing as much monetary support as their limited means permitted.

After graduation in 1870, Francis found a position at Lincoln teaching in the preparatory department so he could study law in the newly established Law Department. Francis resumed his law studies in 1872 at the Lincoln law school, which had now moved to Westchester, Pennsylvania, and spent the next year at Howard University's law school in Washington, D.C.

Francis Grimké now decided to change direction and study for the ministry. In the fall of 1875 he entered the Princeton Theological Seminary, where he won high praise from his teachers. Upon his graduation in 1878, Grimké became pastor of the Fifteenth Street Presbyterian Church in Washington, D.C. He retained this connection for the rest of his life, except for the period from October 1885 to 1889 when he took charge of the Laura Street Church in Jacksonville, Florida. Grimké says that he took that position hoping to improve his health. In 1923 Grimké tried to retire, but it was not until 1925 that an associate pastor was chosen. This system of dual leadership for the church, which lasted until Grimké's death, did not prove entirely satisfactory for the vitality of the church. Not only did Grimké set high standards for his associates, but he held firmly to a conservative orthodox theology and did not accept any hint of modernism.

Grimké married Charlotte Forten (1837–1914) on December 19, 1878. She was the granddaughter of James Forten Sr. of Philadelphia. Well–educated and well–connected, she was an educator and a writer. The Grimkés had one child born on January 1, 1880: Theodora Cornelia, who died at six months. In spite of Charlotte Grimké's bouts of ill health, the marriage was a happy one for both partners. When she died July 23, 1914, after an illness had confined her to bed for thirteen months, her husband was devastated.

Grimké Is Leading Minister

As pastor of one of the leading churches of Washington's black elite, Grimké became a leader in local affairs. His words reached more than local listeners since many of his sermons were circulated as pamphlets. As a black in a white–led denomination, Grimké found much to criticize in the willingness of the denomination's leaders to acquiesce in racism. He was a founding member in 1893 of the Afro–Presbyterian Council, an organization devoted to furthering the concerns of African American Presbyterians. Between 1898 and 1902 he was chair of the Hampton Institute Negro Conference and lectured at the institute (now university) for several summers.

Grimké's eminence led to academic offers that he did not take. In 1891 Biddle University, Charlotte, North Carolina, offered him a professorship. When the white president of Howard University, John B. Gordon, was forced to resign at the end of 1905, Grimké's name was put forward as a successor. Grimké's major long–term service to education was as a member of the board of Howard University on which he served from 1880 to 1925. He divided his extensive library between Howard and Lincoln before his death and left substantial bequests to both institutions in his will.

Grimké was a founding member of the American Negro Academy in 1905 and long served as the organization's treasurer. In that year his brother Archibald and Archibald's daughter Angelina, a teacher in the Washington schools, established residence in Francis' home. (Their mother Nancy Weston Grimké had come to live with Francis earlier; she was living in his home when she died in 1895.) There was some tension in the household since Francis came to feel that Angelina was trying to come between the brothers, and Angelina and Francis quarreled about payment for Archibald's medical expenses during his long final illness. Francis felt that payment should come from Archibald, who was well off, and from his estate not from him. Angelina moved to New York after her father's death.

Francis Grimké was much concerned with civil rights, and for many years that meant taking a position about Booker T. Washington. In 1895 he wrote Washington about the Harris incident which had been roundly condemned in a meeting Grimké had just left. Harris had been wounded by a white mob and was openly turned away by Washington. As a former Southerner, Grimké could appreciate Washington's need for dissimulation expressed in the reply—Washington had turned Harris aside to protect the school but had secretly arranged to help him. Contacts increased. For example, in January 1896 Grimké was visiting Tuskegee to preach and lecture, and they became friends. It would be many years before Grimké's uncompromising views on civil rights led to a break. Even before the break, there were differences—the only black leader Grimké ever admired without reservation was Frederick Douglass, whom Grimké married to Helen Pitts in Douglass' controversial second marriage to a white woman.

Even in the field of civil rights, most of Grimké's work was in connection with his ministry. His concern for rights was tempered by his concern for religion. He qualified, for example, his praise of W. E. B. Du Bois as a civil rights leader by condemning Du Bois's religious beliefs. Grimké served on the Afro–American Council alongside his brother and he signed in 1908 the call for the meeting which led to the formation of the NAACP, but he was not as active in politics and organizational responsibilities as his brother. His positions on civil rights were, however, as outspoken and as radical.

Francis J. Grimké died on October 11, 1937. He gave long service to his community and church. Religiously and morally conservative, he gave militant voice to his civil rights convictions.

REFERENCES

Bruce, Dickson D. Jr. *Archibald Grimké.* Baton Rouge: Louisiana University Press, 1993.

Burkett, Randall K., and Richard Newman. *Black Apostles.* Boston: G. K. Hall, 1978.

Grimké, Francis James. *Works.* 4 vol. Washington, DC: Associated Publishers, 1942.

Harlan, Louis R. *Booker T. Washington.* 2 vol. New York: Oxford, 1972, 1983.

Logan, Rayford W., and Michael R. Winston, eds. *Dictionary of American Negro Biography.* New York: Norton, 1982.

Moss, Alfred A. Jr. *The American Negro Academy.* Baton Rouge: Louisiana State University Press, 1981.

Simmons, William J. *Men of Mark.* Cleveland: Geo. M. Rewell, 1887.

Smith, Jessie Carney, ed. *Notable Black American Women.* Detroit: Gale Research, 1992.

Stevenson, Brenda, ed. *The Journal of Charlotte Forten Grimké.* New York: Oxford, 1988.

COLLECTIONS

The Francis J. Grimké papers are in the Moorland–Spingarn Library at Howard University.

Robert L. Johns

Bryant Gumbel

(1948–)

Broadcast journalist

Bryant Gumbel was the first black to cohost *Today,* a popular morning talk show on NBC which has been broadcast for more than 30 years. Until he left the show in 1997, he remained an influential and a highly visible journalist known the world over and reigned as king of early morning television. Relentless in his preparation, Gumbel consistently demonstrated a hard–driving style that produced mixed reactions among viewers to the articulate and well–read journalist. He has now become a major news star with CBS television.

The second child of Richard Dunbar Gumbel and Rhea Alice LeCesne Gumbel, Bryant Charles Gumbel was born in New Orleans, Louisiana, on September 29, 1948. He has two younger sisters, Rhonda and Renee, and an older brother, Greg, who is now a well–known sports announcer. The Gumbels moved to Chicago when Bryant and Greg were infants. There Richard Gumbel, the son of a New Orleans gambler, who had graduated from New Orleans's Xavier University and worked his way through Georgetown Law School, became a Cook County probate judge during Mayor Richard Daley's political reign. Both parents were active in Democratic party politics in Chicago.

As Bryant Gumbel grew up in the Hyde Park section of Chicago, a middle–class neighborhood near the University of Chicago, his father remained a central influence in his life and stressed the importance of reading, writing, speaking, and

Bryant Gumbel

listening. He also introduced his sons to sports, particularly baseball and the art of catching. Bryant Gumbel attended Roman Catholic elementary and high schools in Chicago, then in 1966 entered Bates College in Lewiston, Maine, where he played baseball and football. The long–haired young man stood out as one of three blacks in a student body of nine hundred. Although he was only an average student, he developed a sense of self–confidence that he has never lost. He decided also that he would devote his time to studies and not become an activist in the Civil Rights Movement of that era. After graduating in 1970 with a B.A. in history, a sports–related injury in college prevented him from being drafted for military service.

For half a year after graduation, Gumbel became a sales representative for the Westvaco Corporation, a manufacturer of paper bags and folding cartons. He quit the job and did nothing for a while, but he maintained an interest in becoming a sports writer. His article about Harvard University's first black athletic director in *Black Sports* led him to a contract with the magazine; nine months later he was its editor, earning an annual salary of eleven thousand dollars. This position enabled him to move upward as he came in contact with many people who were in a position to drop his name in the right places.

Gumbel's father died in 1972 before Gumbel's career as a journalist began. After auditioning on July 21, 1972, Gumbel was hired at age 23 as a weekly sportscaster for KNBC–TV in Los Angeles at a salary of $21,500. He became weeknight sportscaster on the 6:00 p.m. news eight months later, then in 1986 became sports director for the station.

It was Gumbel's flair for television journalism and ability to develop appealing stories on a variety of topics that made him attractive. In 1975, after he gave an off–the–cuff commentary on John Wooden, then basketball coach for the University of California at Los Angeles, he was tapped as cohost of the National Football League's pregame show *Grandstand,* televised from New York. Continuing with KNBC in Los Angeles, he kept the New York assignment from 1976 to 1980, commuting on weekends to work for NBC Sports as anchor for NFL football, major league baseball, and NCAA basketball. Beginning in 1976, his assignments with NBC Sports expanded to included three Super Bowls, one World Series, five Thanksgiving Day Parades, and several golf tournaments. On December 1, 1973, Gumbel married artist June Carlyn Baranco, and they became parents of two children—Bradley Christopher and Jillian Beth.

Signing a three–year, $1.5 million contract with NBC network in 1980, Gumbel was responsible for three sports features each week on the *Today* show. In August that year he became cohost with Cyndy Garvey on *Games People Play* and was anchor for NBC's *NFL '80.* By then, *Today*'s rival show, *Good Morning America* on ABC–TV, had climbed above *Today* in ratings.

Cohosts the *Today* Show

Today's anchor Tom Brokaw left to anchor *NBC Nightly News,* and in August of 1981 Gumbel was asked to sit in as cohost on the *Today* show with Jane Pauley. On January 4, 1982, the *Today* show was reorganized; along with regular members Jane Pauley, Gene Shalit, and Willard Scott were newcomers Gumbel and news anchor Chris Wallace. Gumbel, the show's first black cohost, was well–read, performed well, and became a young master of live television interviewing. After three years of a close race for first place in morning television viewing ratings with rivals *CBS Morning News* and *Good Morning America,* in March of 1985 *Today* finally reached first place. That fall Gumbel also hosted a late afternoon NBC news program each month, and on April 1 that year he broadcast the show from a private mass at the Vatican. The full cast gathered for an audience with the Pope.

Gumbel's success continued. In 1988 he was key anchor for the Olympic Games in Seoul, South Korea. Cohost Jane Pauley told Oprah Winfrey of her years on the show with Gumbel that "he has a challenging personality and I enjoy that. . . . [He] made me work harder. He made me be on my toes. We were a darn good team." Deborah Norville was added as news reader from January of 1990 to April of 1991, and Pauley then decided to move off the show. The show's ratings suffered during Norville's presence. Gumbel added that he had not encouraged Norville's appearance to give Pauley a jolt, although there was some speculation that he had.

Gumbel's confidential memorandum to producer Marty Ryans in 1989 concerning Willard Scott's birthday recognitions on the show generated negative publicity. It had been solicited and written six months before it was leaked to the public. Oprah Winfrey cited Gumbel's memo, which said that Scott "was holding the show hostage with his assortment of whims with his birthdays and bad taste.'' Gumbel responded that Ryans ''asked me to give him a laundry list of things to respond to. And he said 'I need your input on these,' and I gave it to him.'' He never knew who leaked the memo, and thought ''it was better that I just didn't know and just move on. . . . In retrospect, the only thing that I really regret terribly was a poor choice of words in a lot of instances. I should have been more sensitive to things, but in a business sense, it was simply an attempt to respond to a producer's request.'' After the memorandum, Gumbel and Scott talked over the phone, cried, and expressed their regrets over the matter. The press gave the affair wide publicity. After that, the Gumbel–Scott relationship was rumored to be strained, a view that Gumbel denied.

In 1992 Gumbel took the *Today* show on a week–long visit to sub–Saharan Africa, later calling it in *Jet* for January 20, 1997, his ''proudest achievement.'' During his career he took the show across the world to Europe, China, and Australia. During the Persian Gulf conflict, Gumbel covered events from Saudia Arabia.

Three years before his good friend Arthur Ashe died in 1993, Ashe confided to Gumbel that he had AIDS. Gumbel told Oprah Winfrey that in keeping the confidence, ''the world was not any worse off in not knowing what I knew. This wasn't a case of national security. And so, it was hard and even when Arthur and I had talked on the air, before his death, knowing he had AIDS, it was hard.'' Gumbel knew that journalists should share their information, but the news had come through their friendship and he was satisfied that he was not professionally negligent in keeping the secret.

Perhaps the greatest offense Gumbel endured was the denial of an opportunity in October of 1995 to join a team to interview his friend O. J. Simpson, who had been charged with murdering his wife and her friend. Gumbel told Oprah Winfrey that he was offended because his producers thought he could not be objective and that he was a ''subjective risk.'' ''I told the producers that I could not work that day. . . . I was not going to tell people, 'Hey, watch NBC tonight as Tom Brokaw and Katie Couric interview O. J. Simpson.' . . . I wasn't going to be a phoney.'' Only one day short of fifteen years as anchor, Gumbel left the *Today* show on January 3, 1997, with its highest ratings, dominating ABC's rival *Good Morning America.* On hand during his tearful departure were, in addition to his NBC colleagues, poet Maya Angelou, boxing great Muhammad Ali, and the former Prince. Gumbel was succeeded by Matt Lauer, who had joined the team in January of 1994 as news anchor.

After his retirement, Gumbel played golf and sorted through his offers, which included bids from three television networks. Then on Thursday, March 13, 1997, Gumbel and CBS News announced Gumbel's new position. Gumbel accepted an offer from CBS for a Wednesday night magazine and prime–time interview special, *Public Eye,* which began airing in the fall of 1997. He also was given the opportunity to own and develop syndicated programs with the CBS's syndication arm, Eyemark. The deal may well net him over $5 million annually, possibly more if the syndicated programs become big hits. CBS needed to boost its sagging news ratings and Gumbel liked the opportunity for creative ventures. Gumbel also announced his intention to begin an internship program and make other opportunities available for minorities. In the meantime, Gumbel remained in public view as host of the *Forty–Ninth Annual Prime–Time Emmy Awards* in September of 1997.

Gumbel has been widely recognized for his work. He has won three Emmy Awards: in 1984 for hosting the Macy's Thanksgiving Parade; in 1988 as a writer for the Olympics; and in 1991 as best interviewer for his work on *Today.* He received the Los Angeles Press Club's Golden Mike Award in 1978 and 1979. In 1985 he received a New York City Brotherhood Award. After his trip to Moscow in 1988, Gumbel won the Overseas Press Club's Edward R. Murrow Award for Outstanding Foreign Affairs Work. Twice the *Washington Journalism Review*'s Annual Readers Poll named him Best Morning Television News Interviewer, in 1986 and 1987, and the Associated Press voted him a co–winner as Broadcaster of the Year. Gumbel also received international awards for orchestrating and anchoring the *Today* show's broadcasts from Africa. In 1993 he received the TransAfrica's International Journalism Award and the U.S. Committee for UNICEF'S Africa's Future Award, and in 1984 he won the Edward Weintal Prize for diplomatic reporting. In 1993 the Association of Black Journalists named him Journalist of the Year. He also received two Image Awards from the NAACP. He received the Martin Luther King Award from the Congress of Racial Equality and the College Fund/UNCF's highest honor, the Frederick D. Patterson Award. He is a benefactor of The College Fund/UNCF, and over seven years he has raised over $3 million for UNCF scholarships through the Bryant Gumbel/Walt Disney World golf tournament. He is active in other philanthropies and has served on the boards of directors for Xavier University and the United Way.

Gumbel demonstrated a hard–driving style on the *Today* show that has been variously characterized as arrogant and tough. Some blacks claimed that he does not sound black enough. Yet from early childhood he had been taught to read widely and to speak correctly, and he did not perceive his speech as a matter of race. He told Joanne Harris in an interview that he hoped that the *Today* show did not ''define things as 'black issues.''' He wanted audiences to see a black man in a position of responsibility or intelligence whether the subject was inner–city poverty, food stamps, or welfare programs. ''We strive as much as possible when we're having a medical discussion to have a doctor who happens to be black,'' he continued. Quoted in *Current Biography,* his wife, June Gumbel, revealed another dimension: ''He has a temper the public never sees. He can't stand professional ineptness, and sometimes he'll take it out on a door or wall when he gets home.'' But the public saw him as arrogant and explosive.

Bryant Gumbel brought an appeal, skill, and precision to television interviewing that drew large audiences and made him a sought–after journalist and an image–builder for those who would enter the field. His comments to Joanne Harris in an interview addressed his interviewing skills: He considered himself a communicator and thought it was his job ''to serve as an effective conduit . . . between someone who has information to impart and someone who wants to know what that person had to say.''

Current address: CBS News, 524 West 57th Street, New York, NY 10019.

REFERENCES

African American Biography. Vol. 2. Detroit: UXL, 1994.

''CBS Gets Gumbel At $5M a Year.'' *USA Today,* March 13, 1997.

Contemporary Black Biography. Vol. 14. Detroit: Gale Research, 1997.

Current Biography Yearbook. New York: H. W. Wilson, 1986.

''Gumbel Fights Back Tears At Farewell Tribute.'' *Nashville Tennessean,* January 4, 1997.

''Gumbel Gives Back. *Jet* 90 (19 August 1996): 23.

''Gumbel Nets CBS Show.'' *Greensboro (NC) News and Record,* March 14, 1997.

''Gumble's New Gamble.'' *USA Weekend.* In the *Nashville Tennessean,* September 5–7, 1997.

Harris, Joanne. ''Questions, No Doubt: Bryant Gumbel Questions All Comers and Answers All Questions.'' Interview. *American Visions* 7 (October–November 1992): 22–25.

Oprah Winfrey Show. Interview with Bryant Gumbel. NBC Television, October 2, 1996.

''Veteran Television Anchor Bryant Gumbel Officially Says Good–Bye to NBC's 'Today'.'' *Jet* 91 (20 January 1997): 51–53.

Who's Who among African Americans, 1995–96. 9th ed. Detroit: Gale Research, 1996.

Jessie Carney Smith

Alex Haley
(1921–1992)
Writer, genealogical researcher

Alex Haley

Alex Haley achieved the stunning feat of tracing his ancestry back to his great–great–great–great–grandfather, Kunta Kinte, who was kidnapped from Africa into American slavery in 1767. Haley was able to do so in large part because of the family's preservation of Kunte Kinte's story through oral transmission from generation to generation. Haley's corroborating research resulted in *Roots: The Saga of an American Family* (1976). The book set publishing records, and two television miniseries growing out of the book set ratings records. Before he wrote *Roots,* Haley had collaborated with Malcolm X on *The Autobiography of Malcolm X* (1965), another major achievement. Although financial problems often plagued him, Haley remained committed to making his living as a writer. Down–to–earth and soft–spoken, he persevered with distinguished results in a career lasting more than 40 years.

Alexander Murray Palmer Haley was born on August 11, 1921, in Ithaca, New York to Samuel Alexander and Bertha George Palmer Haley. Simon Haley, a native of Savannah, Tennessee, graduated from North Carolina Agricultural and Technical College in Greensboro, North Carolina. After serving in France in World War I, he earned the master's degree in agricultural studies from Cornell University, and taught agriculture at several historically black colleges.

Haley's mother, Bertha George Palmer, was born in 1895 to Will and Cynthia Murray Palmer in Henning, Tennessee. She was their only child to live past infancy. Will Palmer had a thriving lumber company. Cynthia Palmer, Alex Haley's grandmother and the great–great–grandaughter of Kunta Kinte, played a major role in Alex Haley's knowledge of "the African," as Kunta Kinte was often called.

Simon Haley and Bertha Palmer met at Lane College in Jackson, Tennessee, where Simon studied before he transferred to North Carolina Agricultural and Technical College. They were married in 1920 in Ithaca, New York, where Simon was pursuing his Cornell degree and Bertha was studying at the Ithaca Conservatory of Music.

Simon and Bertha Haley had three sons. Alex was the eldest; the others were George, born in 1925, and Julius, born in 1929. The Haley family returned to Henning to live after the death of Will Palmer in 1926. Simon Haley managed the lumber company, and Bertha taught school. Bertha Haley died in 1931. In 1933, Simon Haley married Zeona Hatch. They had one child, Lois.

From an early age, Alex Haley spent much time at his grandparents' home in Henning. It was there that he began to become acquainted with the details of the life of Kunta Kinte. Haley was only 15 when he entered college. He attended Alcorn Agricultural and Mechanical College in Lorman, Mississippi. After a brief time there in 1937, he moved on to Elizabeth City State Teachers College in Elizabeth City, North Carolina, where he studied from 1937 to 1939.

Haley's apprenticeship as a writer occurred during his service in the U.S. Coast Guard, which he joined as a mess boy in 1939. Using his portable typewriter, which he identified in *Roots* as his "most precious shipboard possession," he first wrote letters to everyone he knew in an attempt to alleviate his boredom. Fellow sailors were impressed by the volume of responses he received, and he soon became in great demand as a writer of the sailors' love letters. Haley was also motivated to write after he had read all the books in the ship's library more than once; he decided to see whether he could write stories of his own. In *Contemporary Fiction Writers of the South,* Mary Kemp Davis pointed out that many rejection slips followed, but after eight years, he succeeded in having a work accepted for publication by the Sunday newspaper supplement *This Week.* Davis noted that "by the time he retired from the Coast Guard, . . . he had published perhaps one hundred sea stories and research–based articles." His official duties also eventually included writing, for he was the first person to serve as the Coast Guard's chief journalist, the position from which he retired.

Haley married Nannie Branch in 1941. After being separated for several years, they divorced in 1964. Haley then married Juliette Collins; they were divorced in 1972. Haley's third wife was Myran Lewis, from whom he was separated at the time of his death. Alex and Nannie Haley had two children, William Alexander and Lydia Ann. Alex Haley's third child, born of his marriage to Juliette Collins, was Cynthia Gertrude.

Career as a Writer

Determined to make a living as a writer, Haley settled in Greenwich Village, where he endured lean times before receiving enough acceptances to feel that he could succeed. In 1962, Haley conducted an interview with Miles Davis, the first in a series published in *Playboy* magazine. Other of Haley's *Playboy* interviews featured Quincy Jones, Johnny Carson, George Lincoln Rockwell (head of the American Nazi Party), Martin Luther King Jr., and Malcolm X.

Haley and Malcolm X subsequently collaborated on *The Autobiography of Malcolm X* (1965). After a rocky start, they worked together well. Significantly, Haley was the godfather of Malcolm X's oldest daughter, Attallah Shabazz. The manuscript was completed just two weeks before Malcolm X was assassinated. A bestseller, *The Autobiography* established Haley as a writer of national and international prominence.

Research and Writing of *Roots*

Haley then began to move into the project that would occupy him for the next 12 years—documenting his ancestry. In doing so, Haley would be filling in for his own family the "X"—the rendering of the unknown heritage in a name such as Malcolm X.

On a writing assignment in London, Haley visited the British Museum, where he saw the Rosetta Stone. The example of its deciphering spurred Haley to seek to trace the clues to the background of Kunta Kinte. These included the term "ko" for guitar, "Kamby Bolongo" for a river, and the pronunciation of the name as "Kin–tay." Another point, handed down in *Roots,* was that Kunta Kinte had said that he "was chopping wood to make a drum when he was captured."

Haley's first attempted to follow up on the clues through African diplomats, waylaying them as they completed their day's work at the United Nations—an unsuccessful approach. In *Roots,* Haley reflected that:

> [W]ithin a couple of weeks, I guess I had stopped about two dozen Africans, each of whom had given me a quick look, a quick listen, and then took off. I can't say I blame them—me trying to communicate some African sounds in a Tennessee accent.

Haley made more progress after he was referred to scholars. With their help and with confirmation from Gambian citizens, Haley ascertained that "ko" referred to the kora, a stringed instrument and that the Kamby Bolongo referred to the Gambia River. The name Kinte was recognizable as occurring among the Mandinka people in The Gambia. Haley flew to Dakar, Senegal, and made arrangements to travel to Juffure, a village in The Gambia identified as the home of one of the Kinte clans. There, the village's oral historian—its *griot*—Kebba Kanji Fofana, provided a chronology that included a reference to Kunta, the oldest of four sons of Omoro Kinte, who had gone from the village to chop wood and who was never seen again.

Haley also combed written records, including newspapers, ships' logs, and insurance files. Through them, he determined that the kidnapping took place in 1767 and that the *Lord Ligonier* was the ship that brought Kunta Kinte to Annapolis, Maryland. In the process of documenting his findings, Haley flew to Dakar and took a ship back to the United States. He spent nights in the ship's hold trying to gain some sense of what it must have been like for Kunta Kinte and his fellow Africans during the middle passage. Although Haley knew he would not come close to the conditions the Africans suffered, the experience had its significance for Haley's own trials. Discouraged by debts incurred to finance the search, he was at one point tempted to commit suicide by jumping overboard. However, after sensing his ancestors' presence encouraging him to persevere, he was revitalized. From then on too, Haley felt he had an even deeper understanding of Kunta Kinte.

Fortuitously published in the year of the United States's bicentennial celebration, *Roots* covers the entire story, tracing the generations from Juffure to Henning. In America, Kunta Kinte, who always resisted being called by a slave name—Toby, was first owned by John Waller in Spotsylvania County, Virginia. After several unsuccessful attempts to escape, Kunta was punished by having part of a foot cut off. He was then purchased by Waller's brother, William, a physician. Kunta and Bell, a slave owned by William Waller, had a daughter, Kizzy. Kizzy was sold from Virginia to North Carolina when she was sixteen. Her new owner was Tom Lea, who fathered Kizzy's son, George. George became known as "Chicken George" because of his skill in training gamecocks for fighting. Chicken George and his wife Matilda had eight children; the fourth was Tom Murray. Tom and his wife, Irene, also had eight children. Their youngest was Cynthia Murray Palmer, Alex Haley's grandmother. Haley wrote in *Roots* that Cynthia was "two years old when her father, Tom, and grandfather, Chicken George, led a wagon train of recently freed slaves westward to Henning, Tennessee."

Impact and Critique of *Roots*

Roots sold approximately 1.5 million hardback copies—setting a publishing record—and another six million in paperback. Haley characterized the book as "faction," indicating a blend of fact and fiction. Nonetheless, key aspects of the book's accuracy were challenged by Mark Ottoway, a British journalist, who charged that the *griot* in Juffure was aware of the specifics needed by Haley to confirm his lineage and that the information provided by the *griot* had been manufactured to fit Haley's search. Ottoway also asserted that archival records did not bear out 1767 as the year Kunta Kinte would have been brought to America. However, Haley stood by his genealogical research—oral and written—and scholars have supported him.

There were also two plagiarism suits brought against *Roots.* Margaret Walker Alexander charged that Haley had used materials from her novel, *Jubilee,* based on the life of Alexander's great–grandmother. The case was ultimately dismissed. A second suit, filed by Harold Courlander, was settled out of court. A passage in *Roots* was found to be from Courlander's novel *The African.* Haley indicated any unauthorized use was inadvertent, conceding that the passage had been given to him by a researcher.

In 1977 Haley was awarded a National Book Award citation, the Spingarn Medal, and a Pulitzer Prize. Haley's projects at the height of the popularity of *Roots* included the Kinte Corporation, based in Los Angeles and which, the article "Alex Haley" in *Ebony* noted, focused on "the production of films, records, and other similar ventures."

Roots: The Miniseries

In January 1977 the American Broadcasting Company presented a television miniseries based on *Roots.* According to the *New York Times* for February 11, 1992, the viewing audience over the eight nights of the program (January 23–30) "ranged from 28.8 million households to 36.3 million households" and the miniseries "still ranks among the 100 highest rated programs." The success of the first miniseries led to *Roots II: The Next Generations,* shown in seven parts in February 1979. It too was a ratings success. This series covered the family saga from 1882 to Alex Haley's completion of the search.

Also in 1979, Haley worked with Norman Lear in producing *Palmerstown, U.S.A.* (subsequently called just *Palmerstown*). This television program depicted the friendship between a black boy and a white boy in the segregated South. The program had seven episodes, shown starting in January 1980. In 1988 Haley published a novella, *A Different Kind of Christmas.* At the time of his death, Haley was writing segments of the history of Henning, Tennessee. He was also helping to develop the miniseries *Queen,* which aired in three parts in February 1993. Dedicated to Haley's memory, *Queen* centered on the life of Haley's paternal grandmother. Although he published less about it, Haley had also traced his paternal forebears back to Ireland.

At the time of his death, Haley had several homes, one in Seattle, Washington; one in Knoxville, Tennessee, and a farm of 127 acres in nearby Norris, Tennessee. He was attempting to sell the farm in order to pay debts. He died on February 10, 1992, of a heart attack in Seattle, where he had travelled to present a lecture at the nearby Bangor Naval Submarine Base. His funeral was held at the Greenwood Christian Methodist Episcopal Church in Memphis, Tennessee. He is buried in Henning, Tennessee, on the family homestead that played a central role in his upbringing and in his success in tracing his ancestry.

Alex Haley's forte was biographical and autobiographical writing. Throughout his career, he chronicled "unforgettable characters," the focus some of his early pieces which appeared in the *Reader's Digest* series of that name. The people he illuminated in the *Playboy* interviews, in the Malcolm X book, and most spectacularly in *Roots* are indeed singular. Although *Roots* lacked universal praise, the book and the dramatizations that it engulfed focused national and world attention on the pain of slavery even as the overall message was one of hope and resilience. *Roots* had special resonance for African Americans; however, it sparked enormous interest in genealogical research among people of various ethnic groups throughout the world. In 1997 the U.S. Coast Guard announced plans to name a cutter the *Alex Haley.*

REFERENCES

"Alex Haley Mourned by Family, Friends, During Rites in Memphis, Tenn." *Jet* 81 (2 March 1992): 16–18.

"Alex Haley, 70, Author of 'Roots' Dies." *New York Times,* February 11, 1992.

Baye, Betty Winston. "Alex Haley's *Roots* Revisited." *Essence* 22 (February 1992): 88–92.

"Coast Guard to Name Ship in Honor of 'Roots' Author Alex Haley." *Jet* 92 (7 July 1997): 16–17.

Current Biography Yearbook. New York: H. W. Wilson, 1992.

Davis, Thadious M., and Trudier Harris, eds. *Afro–American Writers after 1955: Dramatists and Prose Writers.* Detroit: Gale Research, 1985.

Flora, Joseph M., and Robert Bain. *Contemporary Fiction Writers of the South: A Biobibliographical Source Book.* Westport, CT: Greenwood Press, 1993.

Haley, Alex. "My Furthest–Back Person—'The African.'" *New York Times Magazine* (July 16, 1972): 12–16.

———. *Roots: The Saga of an American Family.* New York: Doubleday, 1976.

Hill, George H., and Sylvia Saverson Hill. *Blacks on Television: A Selectively Annotated Bibliography.* Metuchen, NJ: Scarecrow Press, 1985.

MacDonald, J. Fred. *Blacks and White TV: Afro–Americans in Television since 1948.* Chicago: Nelson–Hall Publishers, 1983.

Massaquoi, Hans J. "Alex Haley in Juffure." *Ebony* 32 (July 1977): 31–42.

———. "Alex Haley: The Man Behind 'Roots.'" *Ebony* 32 (April 1977): 32–40.

McFadden, Robert D. "Some Points of 'Roots' Questioned; Haley Stands By Book as a Symbol." *New York Times,* April 10, 1977.

Othow, Helen Chavis. "Roots and the Heroic Search for Identity." College Language Association Journal 26 (March 1983): 311–24.

Shenker, Israel. "Some Historians Dismiss Charge of Factual Mistakes in 'Roots.'" *New York Times* April 10, 1977.
Who's Who among Black Americans, 1992–93. Detroit: Gale Research, 1992.
X, Malcolm, with Alex Haley. *The Autobiography of Malcolm X.* New York: Grove Press, 1965.

Arlene Clift–Pellow

George Cleveland Hall
(1864–1930)
Physician, surgeon, civic worker, critic

George Cleveland Hall

George Cleveland Hall was best remembered by his contemporaries as a humanitarian who helped the masses of his race. One of the leading African American medical practitioners in the country at the turn of the century, he spent 30 years at Chicago's Provident Hospital, serving as chief of staff as well as physician and surgeon. He provided health care for countless African Americans in the South by establishing infirmaries in their local areas. He encouraged the development of young African American nurses, physicians, and surgeons, and sought to improve relationships between black and white health care professionals wherever he worked.

George Cleveland Hall was born in Ypsilanti, Michigan, on February 22, 1864, the son of John Ward Hall, a Baptist minister, and Romelia Buck Hall. The family moved to Chicago in 1869, where young George attended public elementary and high schools. He graduated from Lincoln University in Pennsylvania in 1886, with honors and first in his class. He then entered Chicago's Bennett Medical College where he attended classes only half of each day, allowing time to work to support himself. He graduated in 1888, first in a class of 54. After attending evening classes, he also completed studies at Harvey Medical College, receiving a diploma in 1896.

Meets Daniel Hale Williams

Hall opened a medical practice in Chicago immediately after receiving his medical degree. During this period he came to know Daniel Hale Williams, the eminent surgeon who founded Provident Hospital in Chicago in 1891 and in 1893 performed the world's first successful heart operation. Although Hall initially idolized Williams as a surgeon and a gentlemen, in time a lifelong feud developed between them that affected their work at Provident and spilled over to their activities in the National Medical Association. Hall sought a position on Provident's staff, but Williams would not hire him. Williams considered Hall inept because he had graduated from an unaccredited medical school, which Williams considered inferior. According to Saunders Redding in *Lonesome Road,* Hall had in fact completed one of the nation's most rigorous courses of study at Chicago Medical College. At Provident, Williams had employed only light–skinned African Americans, possibly continuing the practice seen in slavery where "a protective tribal instinct operated." In Redding's view, Hall suspected that he was "too dark for Dr. Dan Williams' taste."

Hall, however, had a number of influential friends who appealed to the hospital's governing board and to Williams on Hall's behalf. Hall was also known and respected in Chicago's ghetto. Some sources claim that Williams weakened and allowed him to join the staff of the Pediatrics Department. Redding wrote, Hall was "to look after measles and chicken pox, and such" and was required to bring in a consultant for even the simplest cases. This infuriated Hall, who wanted another position. Other sources report that Hall gained access to Provident only in Williams's absence.

From 1893 to 1897, Williams relocated to Washington, D.C., where he was on staff of Freedmen's Hospital. A hunting accident in 1893 nearly cost Williams his life and delayed his departure for Freedmen's. Hall seized the occasion to attack Williams. According to Redding, Hall still felt he had been treated unfairly and neither wanted Williams to stay at Provident nor to receive world–wide recognition for his appointment at Freedmen's. As Williams lay critically ill, Hall wrote to the black public through the Washington newspaper, the *Colored American,* claiming that "Freedmen's new chief will never assume his post there." He exhorted others to take up the attack, including the *Chicago Defender's* founder and editor Robert Sengstacke Abbott, whose mind

Redding said was "as dark and twisted as Hall's—and for the same tragic reasons."

Hall's 1896 diploma from Harvey Medical College is said to have helped to remove a stumbling block to his entry into the Provident Hospital staff. Some sources also call Hall crafty and devious. As he advanced professionally, he was said to have done so by the art of ingratiation, winning over white lay members of Provident's board of trustees. From 1894 until his death, he served the hospital in a variety of capacities. By 1898 he was an assistant in gynecology and by 1907, a surgeon. Redding claimed that he did "uncomplicated surgery on hernia [sic]." He also became chief of staff. Hall became a member of the hospital's Board of Trustees in 1900, and remained on it until he died. According to Redding, "he presented himself to the public as the medical rival of Dr. Dan [Daniel Hale Williams]," yet many blacks knew better.

During Williams's absence, Hall occupied a preeminent position at Provident and in the Chicago community. Angered over Hall's position of leadership, Williams sought on his return to embarrass him before patients in the hospital, the Board of Trustees, and the National Medical Association. Williams petitioned the hospital to remove Hall from the staff and the board, and threatened to quit the hospital and remove all of his patients unless his conditions were met. Reportedly, Williams called the left–handed surgeon a butcher. So vehement was Williams in his criticism of the hospital and the board that, when he threatened to resign in 1910, the board accepted his offer. Although he removed 80 percent of the patients from the hospital he had founded 21 years earlier, the hospital survived. The vendetta was not one–sided. Hall, who never forgave Williams for rejecting his appointment early on, missed no opportunity to put obstacles in Williams's way, and openly harassed him. He questioned William's commitment to the race.

Although he was a leading figure at Provident, Hall never directed the hospital. It was not until 1926 that the Board of Trustees named him chief of staff. He also headed the Medical Advisory Board which was responsible for the staff and medical practices, and worked with the board to set policies and determine programs. During this period white physicians dominated membership on the attending staff. As chair of the committee, Hall controlled all medical and other staff appointments, and anyone seeking an appointment had to meet his approval.

In *A Century of Black Surgeons,* historians of Provident Hospital called Hall "a man who ruled with a big stick and picked his people on a personal basis." Not only had he developed a strong reputation in Chicago, he had become widely respected throughout the country as a surgeon, diagnostician, and therapist. He performed procedures his way, whether or not the procedures conformed to newer techniques of younger surgeons, yet he was successful with some difficult operative procedures. While physicians throughout the country saw him as a complete surgeon, some of his Chicago colleagues did not. Hall's supporter, Robert S. Abbott, however, used his newspaper to plug Hall's work by noting his attendance at a doctor's meeting in Richmond. Abbott also described Hall's success as a physician and saw to it that a photograph and a biographical sketch were published in 35 newspapers.

Establishes Infirmaries in the South

Although many patients traveled long distances to Chicago to have Hall perform surgical procedures, he practiced at a time when surgeons traveled to clinics throughout the country performing operations and teaching their techniques to others. Hall visited state medical meetings in Missouri and in the South, particularly in Alabama, Tennessee, Kentucky, Virginia, and Georgia, and conducted surgical clinics for the members and local physicians. For example, when the Nashville Medical Association met in 1902, he was invited to attend; he held a clinic unlike anything the physicians had seen before.

Hall stimulated the development of African American surgeons as well as small hospitals and clinics in the South. In 1906 he conducted the first surgical clinic attempted at the Tuskegee Institute Hospital. Booker T. Washington invited him to Tuskegee to lecture. Twice a year until 1907 he travelled South to operate with his understudy, Dr. Steers, and he welcomed the white physicians who were present for each session. He helped start infirmaries in such cities as Clarksville and Memphis, Tennessee, and Birmingham, Alabama. He was quoted in the *Colored American Magazine* as saying, "My object is to encourage young Negroes along surgical lines wherever there is opportunity for successful operation of an infirmary. Wherever there are three or four Negro doctors I want to make them co–operate." Published accounts of Hall's importance give conflicting views on the extent of his success and popularity. According to Redding, Hall also set up clinics in Georgia and South Carolina, but none of them lasted a year. At a demonstration in Birmingham, a country doctor took over Hall's operation to save a patient's life.

Although as early as 1900 Daniel Hale Williams had written and lectured about the need to establish hospitals and training schools for blacks in the South, it was not until 1917, and under Hall's leadership, that Provident Hospital began to work toward such instruction. The next year Hall directed its first postgraduate course.

Civic and Humanitarian Interests

According to John W. Lawlah's profile in the *Journal of the National Medical Association,* Hall's civic and humanitarian interests outweighed his contributions to medicine and overshadowed his professional achievements. All of his work, whether professional or civic, was designed to enhance the welfare of black people, and he was most active in the enhancement of race relations in the city. In 1897 he organized the Civic League of Chicago and worked through the organization to improve housing conditions for blacks in that city. He was a member of the Governor's Commission on Race Relations, which investigated the 1919 Chicago Riots. He was responsible for bringing the National Urban League to Chicago, served briefly as its vice–president, and in 1913 participated in a meeting between the league and trade union leaders. He also founded the Cook County Physicians' Association of Chicago. He was a member of the NAACP and an organizer and chairman of the Board of Managers of the first YMCA in Chicago.

Hall was one of the founders of the Association for the Study of Negro Life and History, now the Association for the Study of Afro–American Life and History. His contact with Julius Rosenwald enabled him to persuade Rosenwald to support the organization. He became director and treasurer of Chicago's Frederick Douglass Center. He criticized blacks for their reluctance to support black businesses, newspapers, and institutions and worked on behalf of such enterprises through the Chicago branch of the National Negro Business League. First a member of the NNBL, in 1912 he became its president. He was a board member of his alma mater, Lincoln University, and belonged to the National Medical Association. Hall was a member of the Executive Committee of the Municipal Voters. A Republican, he also dabbled in politics, running for the Chicago Board of Commissions in 1914 on the Progressive slate.

As a board member of the Chicago Public library, he persuaded Julius Rosenwald to erect cultural centers for residents near the Rosenwald–funded apartment complex for middle class blacks built at Forty–seventh and Michigan avenues on Chicago's South Side. Having prevailed upon Rosenwald to donate the land, he then influenced the library board to build a branch library there. Although he died before it was completed, the building was named in his honor. Hall also belonged to the Alpha Phi Alpha Fraternity and the Presbyterian church. He delivered the principal address at Tuskegee Institute, when a monument for his friend, Booker T. Washington, was unveiled. Early on, Hall aligned himself with Washington's views on self–help and racial solidarity, but considered his accommodationist methods inappropriate in the North.

Hall actively solicited and contributed funds to Lincoln University and was an active fundraiser for Fisk University, Tuskegee and Hampton Institutes, and Meharry Medical College, garnering support from black and white contributors. His ready access to Rosenwald and other people of wealth led to substantial growth and development of many black enterprises, including the Greater Provident Hospital, established in 1933, whose development he spearheaded.

On June 7, 1894, Hall married Theodosia Brewer, a woman from Council Bluffs, Iowa, and a graduate of the Council Bluffs Seminary for Women. She became a fundraiser for the New Provident Hospital. They had two children, one of whom died in early infancy. The other, Hortense, was born in 1908, and survived both parents. The Halls lived in a palatial home at 3638 South Parkway. Chicago's black society, however, never forgot the deplorable Hall–Williams controversy involving two of its leading citizens, and had difficulty in planning social events which Hall and Williams factions were to attend. The Halls and the Booker T. Washingtons at Tuskegee were friends and visited each other on occasion.

A cheery man of boundless energy, Hall was also a good mixer and a good storyteller. He was rough, ambitious, and a spirited fighter who feared no one, black or white. He died in Chicago on June 17, 1930 following a five–month illness. He was survived by his wife, daughter Hortense, and a sister, Blanche Hancock. A controversial national figure, Hall greatly influenced black medical education through a graduate teaching program at Provident Hospital and the surgical clinics he held in various states, as well as his practice in Chicago.

REFERENCES

''Along the Color Line.'' *Crisis* 37 (September 1930): 311.

Buckler, Helen. *Doctor Dan: Pioneer in American Surgery.* Boston: Little, Brown, 1954.

''Dr. George C. Hall.'' *Journal of the National Medical Association* 22 (July–September 1930): 170–71.

Hartshorn, W. N., ed. *An Era of Progress and Promise 1863–1910.* Boston: Priscilla Publishing Co., 1910.

Lawlah, John W. ''George Cleveland Hall, 1784–1930: A Profile.'' *Journal of the National Medical Association* 46 (May 1954): 207–10.

Majors, Gerri, with Doris Saunders. *Black Society.* Chicago: Johnson Publishing Co., 1976.

Morais, Herbert M. *The History of the Negro in Medicine.* New York: Publishers Company, 1967.

Organ, Claude H., Jr., ed. *A Century of Black Surgeons.* Vol. 1. Norman, OK: Transcript Press, 1987.

Ottley, Roi. *The Lonely Warrior.* Chicago: Henry Regnery, 1955.

''A Prominent Colored Surgeon.'' *Colored American Magazine* 14 (September 1908): 480–83.

Redding, Saunders. *The Lonesome Road.* Garden City, NY: Doubleday, 1948.

Smith, Jessie Carney, ed. *Notable Black American Women.* Detroit: Gale Research, 1992.

''Some Chicagoans of Note.'' *Crisis* 10 (September 1915): 311.

Spear, Allan H. *Black Chicago: The Making of a Negro Ghetto 1890–1920.* Chicago: University of Chicago Press, 1967.

Who's Who in Colored America, 1930–1931–1932. Brooklyn, NY: Who's Who in Colored America, 1933.

Jessie Carney Smith

Prince Hall

(1735?–1807)

Organizer, abolitionist, leather crafter

Civic leader Prince Hall was the most famous black in the Boston area during the American Revolution and through the turn of the nineteenth century. He was the founder and master of the world's first black masonic lodge, African Lodge No. 459, which laid the basis for an organization that continues to this day. Though apparently self–taught, he used his eloquence to organize the black community politically on such issues as slavery, public education, and economic equality.

Prince Hall's parentage, birthplace, and date of birth are unknown, but he is believed to have been born about 1735. Little is known of his personal life. The most widely circulated version of his life, which originated in William H. Grimshaw's 1903 book *The Official History of Freemasonry among the Colored People in North America,* has been strongly discredited; but most history books draw directly or indirectly from it for their own sketches of Hall. In truth, almost nothing about Hall can be documented prior to 1770. Compounding the lack of recorded information is the existence of other blacks named Prince Hall living in the Boston area during this period.

Prince Hall

The earliest mention of Hall's name in a documented statement indicates that he was the slave of a Boston leather–dresser named William Hall in the late 1740s. Prince Hall, consequently, was taught leather crafting as a trade. During his servitude, he joined the Congregational Church, School Street, Boston, in 1762 and married fellow slave Sarah Richie on November 2, 1763. The marriage ended with her death on an unrecorded date.

William Hall gave Prince Hall his freedom on April 9, 1770, as reward for 21 years of steadfast service. A few months later, on August 22, he married Flora Gibbs of Gloucester, a small seaside town northeast of Boston. They had one son, Prince Africanus, who was baptized on November 14, 1784, at the New North Church, Boston. At some point in his life he may have fathered a second son, Primus Hall, by a woman named Delia. Shortly after his marriage to Gibbs, Prince Hall opened his own leather goods shop, The Golden Fleece, which became successful. He also worked as a caterer.

Free Black Lodge Founded

Free blacks in and around Boston had little social or political power in the Revolutionary War era. They also lacked formal organizations through which to coordinate beneficial endeavors. In early 1775, Hall petitioned to become a member of Boston's St. John's Lodge of Freemasons but was turned away, presumably because of his race.

Soon thereafter, he and 14 other free black men approached a British army lodge of Freemasons attached to the 38th Foot Regiment, stationed near Boston. Hall and the others were initiated into the lodge on March 6, 1775. The regiment withdrew from the area a short time later, and Sergeant John Batt, who had been in charge of the initiation, issued a limited permit on March 17 allowing the group certain masonic privileges as well as permission to meet as a lodge. On July 3, 1775, the group formed African Lodge No. 1, the first lodge of black Free and Accepted Masons in the world. and Hall was made master. Provincial Grand Master of North America John Rowe granted the lodge a second limited permit to continue their activities.

Meanwhile, the Revolutionary War had begun with skirmishes at Lexington and Concord on April 19, 1775. Rumors that Hall took up arms as a patriot have not been substantiated. Many blacks served in the Continental Army, and historians have claimed that as many as one in seven were men of color. It is certain, however, that Hall used his leather crafting skills to provide five leather drumheads for the Boston Regiment of Artillery, as stated in a bill of sale dated April 24, 1777, written by Hall.

Public records from the time show that Hall was both a taxpayer and regular voter. He was politically active and rallied his fellow Masons and the Boston community at large to support black causes in which he was involved.

On January 13, 1777, Hall was among eight black petitioners to the Massachusetts state legislature requesting the abolition of slavery in the state. Hall's signature was one of four belonging to Masons, whose names topped the document. The petition adopted the same terminology used by the nation's founding fathers to state their case for freedom from

Britain. It was also similar to one sent to Governor Thomas Gage on May 25, 1774, which had been rejected by the British governor. State legislators referred the 1777 petition to the Congress of the Confederation, possibly as a way to avoid the issue themselves. Slavery in Massachusetts was later ended by a state judicial decision in 1783.

Reference to African Lodge No. 1 virtually disappeared from the public record during the latter years of the war for independence, perhaps because many members were away fighting. At war's end, the lodge was still without a permanent charter. Hall wrote to his Most Worshipful Master William Moody of Brotherly Love Lodge No. 55, London, on March 2, 1784, but received no reply. A second letter on June 30, 1784, had the desired effect. On September 29, 1784, a charter was granted authorizing the organization of African Lodge No. 459 in Boston under the leadership of Prince Hall as master. After a lengthy wait, the charter arrived in Boston on April 29, 1787.

In 1786 another rebellion began brewing in the western half of Massachusetts. Named for Captain Daniel Shays, the Shays' Rebellion pitted former patriots who had returned to debt–ridden properties, mostly farms, against the moneyed classes who controlled the banks that were now foreclosing on them. Governor James Bowdoin called for troops to travel west to crush Shay's insurgents. On November 26, Hall wrote a letter to Bowdoin offering the governor the services of 700 black troops he said he could raise; but Hall's offer, which may have been made to declare the black community's loyalty to the new state, was rejected. White politicians were perhaps as afraid of the possible consequences of arming a large group of black men as they were of dealing with the already–armed white farmers of the west.

The following year, Hall reversed his loyalty to the state government and proposed that the state organize a back–to–Africa movement in a petition of January 4, 1787. Leading a committee of twelve members from the African Lodge, Hall proposed that the state secure funds for sending Massachusetts' black population to a point on the African coast. The proposal also called for a colonization effort that would result in mutual benefit to both parties, including extensive future trade between the two states. The petition, which appears to be the first major statement on African colonization by black Americans, died in committee.

Hall then turned his attention to other issues. On October 17, 1787, he petitioned the state legislature to provide education for black children. Blacks were taxed on an equal basis with whites, but only white children received state–supported education. The petition failed, and Hall was equally unsuccessful in obtaining local support for public schools.

Hall was successful, however, in helping to end the slave trade in Massachusetts. In early February 1788, three free black Bostonians, one a Mason, were lured aboard a ship by a captain promising work. Instead, the men were kidnapped, shipped to the Caribbean, and sold as slaves. In a February 27 petition attacking the slave trade, Hall and 21 other Masons stated their outrage at the seizure of their fellow citizens. The state legislature passed an act on March 26 designed to prohibit the slave trade within the state's borders and to provide recourse for the families of those abducted. Sufficient pressure was applied by Governor John Hancock and the French consul in Boston to obtain the release of the men from the French island of St. Bartholomew. The African Lodge organized a celebration to mark their return home in July of that year.

Hall pressed on for equal education. In 1796 he urged the selectmen of Boston to create a separate school for black children. His request was approved, but the selectmen claimed that no suitable building could be acquired, and the issue remained unresolved.

In an address to the African Lodge at Menotomy (now West Cambridge) on June 24, 1797, Hall focused on slavery in the United States. Reflecting on the recent slave revolt on the West Indies island of Hispaniola that resulted in the creation of Haiti, he encouraged his audience to have faith in God and to bear their burdens quietly, but to be ready for the day of deliverance. *The Voice of Black America* quotes Hall's petition:

> Now, my brethren, nothing is stable; all things are changeable. Let us seek those things which are sure and steadfast, and let us pray God that, while we remain here, he would give us the grace and patience and strength to bear up under all our troubles, which, at this day, God knows, we have our share of. Patience, I say; for were we not possessed of a great measure of it, we could not bear up under the daily insults we meet with in the streets of Boston, much more on public days of recreation. How, at such times, are we shamefully abused, and that to such a degree that we may truly be said to carry our lives in our hands, and the arrows of death are flying about our heads. Helpless women have their clothes torn from their backs, even to the exposing of their nakedness. . . .
>
> My brethren, let us not be cast down under these and many other abuses we at present are laboring under, for the darkest hour is just before the break of day. My brethren, let us remember what a dark day it was with our African brethren, six years ago, in the French West Indies. Nothing but the snap of the whip was heard, from morning to evening. Hanging, breaking on the wheel, burning, and all manner of tortures were inflicted upon those unhappy people. But, blessed be God, the scene is changed.

Hall did not hold all white men accountable for the institution of slavery; in fact, he hoped that with the support of like–minded whites, black men could help bring about abolition through persuasion. However, he was not encouraged by the fact that even white Masons did not freely accept their black counterparts, despite their claims to liberty, fraternity, and love of God.

As black masonry continued to remain separate from white masonry in the United States, Hall spread his organization to other cities. On June 24, 1797, a second black lodge was chartered in Providence, Rhode Island. A year later, a third one was started in Philadelphia, with Absalom Jones as worshipful master and Richard Allen as treasurer.

On June 28, 1798, Hall appears to have married for a third time. Sylvia (or Zilpha) Ward would remain his wife until his death a decade later.

In 1800 Hall made a second request to the selectmen of Boston to acquire a building for a black school. After another refusal, Hall offered his own home for the school. A pair of Harvard College students served as teachers until 1806. At that point, increased enrollment forced a move to larger facilities, which were provided by the African Society House on Belknap Street.

Prince Hall died in Boston on December 4, 1807. Funeral rites, in accord with masonic rites, were performed at his home in Lendell's Lane one week later. He was buried in the 59th Street Mathews Cemetery, Boston, in late March, 1808, after a large procession of blacks followed his body to the gravesite. Within a year of his death, Hall's followers renamed their order for their former, much–beloved leader.

Born in obscurity, Prince Hall literally worked himself free of his lowly beginnings. Through diligence and effort he cultivated his abilities, then used them to help others do the same. His name lives on in the title of the largest and most well–regarded black fraternal order, the Prince Hall Masons.

REFERENCES

Foner, Philip S., ed. *The Voice of Black America.* New York: Simon and Schuster, 1972.

Kaplan, Sidney. *The Black Presence in the Era of the American Revolution 1770–1800.* Greenwich: New York Graphic Society, 1973.

Logan, Rayford W., and Michael R. Winston, eds. *Dictionary of American Negro Biography.* New York: Norton, 1982.

Salzman, Jack, David Lionel Smith, and Cornel West, eds. *Encyclopedia of African–American Culture and History.* New York: Macmillan Library Reference USA/Simon and Schuster Macmillan, 1996.

Kevin C. Kretschmer

Jupiter Hammon
(b. 1711)
Poet, tract writer

Until recently, Jupiter Hammon's broadside "An Evening Thought: Salvation by Christ with Penetential [sic] Cries" (1760) was identified as the first known poem by a black writer in the North American British colonies. That distinction has since been conferred upon Lucy Terry's "Bars Fight," which commemorates a 1746 battle. Hammon remains noteworthy, however, as an eighteenth–century black author who provides, as Sondra O'Neale has established in her essay on Hammon in *Afro–American Writers Before the Harlem Renaissance,* "the first and most comprehensive statement of black theology and the earliest antislavery protests by a black writer in American literature." Notably, too, Hammon's surviving works include three prose tracts in addition to his four poems. Whatever the genre, however, Hammon's key theme was Christian redemption and his primary purpose was exhortation.

Jupiter Hammon was born October 17, 1711, most likely on the Henry Lloyd family estate (known as Queens Village) near Oyster Bay on Long Island, New York. O'Neale identifies his father as "a rather militant slave whom the Lloyds named 'Opium'" and his mother as "probably a slave named Rose, who was sold when the boy was quite young." Hammon never mentioned having a wife or children of his own.

The Lloyd family had grown wealthy as merchants (including slave trading) and landowners. A slave throughout his life, Hammon served four generations of Lloyds. A 1730 letter, apparently from a physician, indicates that he received special attention from the family. Quoted in Oscar Wegelin's "Biographical Sketches of Jupiter Hammon," which was published in Samuel Ransom's *America's First Negro Poet,* the letter details the care to be given to Jupiter—then about 19 years old—who was suffering from "a gouty Rumatick Disorder." Over the course of his life, Hammon also received encouragement from whites other than the Lloyds.

After Henry Lloyd died in 1763, Hammon's master was Henry's son Joseph. During his time with the Joseph Lloyd family, Hammon lived for a while in Connecticut, mainly in Hartford, where Joseph had relocated during the American Revolutionary War. Hammon's last owner was John Lloyd Jr., one of Joseph's grandsons. After the war, Hammon returned with the Lloyds to the family estate. O'Neale notes that in the last decades of his life, "[t]he Lloyds' ledgers indicate that . . . [Hammon] maintained a private garden, worked as a clerk in the community store, and often acted as a banker by holding funds for the younger Lloyd sons." He was also described as a minister. Hammon died sometime between 1790 and 1806. His burial site has never been located.

Produces Both Prose and Poetry

Hammon's literacy is made clear in several ways. He introduces all of his sermonic tracts as works prepared initially for dissemination through printing, not as transcribed oral presentations. All of his works contain frequent scriptural quotations and glosses that suggest more than merely memorized references. According to its printers, as noted by Ransom, Hammon's New York "Address to the Negroes in the State of New York" was written "in his own hand."

Hammon's seven surviving works—four poems and three prose tracts—span a period of approximately 25 years. The poems are "An Evening Thought: Salvation by Christ with Penetential [sic] Cries" (1760), "An Address to Miss

Phillis Wheatly [sic], Ethiopian Poetess, who came from Africa at eight years of age, and soon became acquainted with the gospel of Jesus Christ'' (1778), ''A Poem for Children with Thoughts of Death'' (1782), and ''A Dialogue Entitled the Kind Master and the Dutiful Servant,'' which is undated but contains references to the American Revolution as ''the present war,'' according to Ransom. The publication date may have been 1783.

The latter two poems were each appended to prose pieces. ''A Poem for Children with Thoughts of Death'' was printed at the conclusion of ''A Winter Piece: Being a Serious Exhortation, with a Call to the Unconverted: and a Short Contemplation on the Death of Jesus Christ.'' The second poem, ''A Dialogue Entitled the Kind Master and the Dutiful Servant'' was printed with ''An Evening's Improvement, Shewing, the Necessity of beholding the Lamb of God.''

Hammon's most widely circulated work, ''An Address to the Negroes in the State of New York,'' was completed in 1786 and published the following year and again in 1806. To date, no copy of his work ''An Essay on the Ten Virgins'' has been located. Perhaps a poem (despite its title), it was advertised in a Connecticut newspaper in 1779.

Stresses Christian Salvation

As O'Neale noted in *Afro-American Writers,* Hammon's theology consistently emphasizes the ''belief that Christ died for all people and that anyone can exercise free will to choose salvation.'' In ''An Evening's Improvement, Shewing, the Necessity of beholding the Lamb of God,'' he called attention to his acceptance of the views of the liberal Calvinist Samuel Stoddard who stressed that ''God hath promised life unto all that believe in this righteousness.'' A stanza in his first known poem, ''An Evening Thought: Salvation by Christ with Penetential [sic] Cries'' (1760), captures this sentiment: ''Lord turn our dark benighted Souls;/Give us a true Motion,/And let the Hearts of all the World,/Make Christ their Salvation.'' In such a context, ''dark benighted Souls'' does not refer to Africans, but to all people.

Hammon depicts Africa as a ''dark abode'' and ''heathen shore'' in his poem to Wheatley. Like Wheatley—who uses similar terms in her poetry—Hammon, in ''An Address to Phillis Wheatly [sic]'' (cited by Ransom), believed that being brought from Africa to America was the result of ''God's tender mercy.'' At the same time, Hammon underscores Wheatley's special mission, as in the lines: ''The humble soul that loves His word,/He chooses for His own.'' ''Humble'' status fits the enslaved rather than those in power.

''A Poem for Children with Thoughts of Death'' depicts dire consequences for children who die before they become Christians. O'Neale points out that this poem also has its elements of protest, for Hammon is rejecting the more liberal colonial religious doctrine that regarded the children of the ''elect'' as saved through their parents' status without any action from the children themselves.

In ''A Dialogue Entitled the Kind Master and the Dutiful Servant'' the servant at the outset willingly accepts the master's command: ''Come my servant, follow me,/According to thy place.'' The poem continues in a series of call and response stanzas, antiphonal exchanges between the master and servant. The final seven stanzas are spoken solely by the servant, who identifies himself at last: ''Believe me now my Christian friends/Believe your friend called Hammon.'' He stresses God's power in determining whether the war in progress can be ended. Typically for Hammon, the ending of this poem emphasizes eternal rewards: ''ev'ry soul [should] obey . . . [God's] word,/And seek the joy of heaven.'' It is also clear that this conclusion moves completely away from the sentiment expressed in the opening lines that earthly servants should obey their slave masters. The servant has moved out of his ''place'' to admonish his ''Christian friends.''

Examines Notion of Freedom

Hammon's most widely distributed work, ''An Address to the Negroes in the State of New York,'' cited by O'Neale, develops most fully the attitude toward ''temporal freedom'' that is found more briefly in each of his other prose works. Characterizing the piece as the ''dying advice, of an old man'' who is ''upwards of seventy years old,'' Hammon writes, ''I have had more experience in the world than most of you, and I have seen a great deal of the vanity and wickedness of it. . . . I have great reason to be thankful that my lot has been so much better than most slaves have had.'' He says he would be ''glad if others, especially the young Negroes, were to be free.''

Nonetheless, here as in his other works, Hammon views the assurance of eternal liberty as more urgent than obtaining earthly liberty. He stresses admonitions such as do not steal, commonly heard from slave owners. His argument is partially pragmatic; obedient, law-abiding slaves may receive better treatment from their masters. His major argument—being enslaved is no justification for immoral acts—rests on Christian morality.

Not surprisingly, in this work too, Hammon emphasizes heavenly rewards. Yet, as noted in O'Neale's essay, he treats the overall issue of justice with some equivocation: ''Now whether it is right, and lawful, in the sight of God, for them to make slaves of us or not, I am certain that while we are slaves, it is our duty to obey our masters, in all their lawful commands, and mind them unless we are bid to do that which we know to be sin, or forbidden in God's word.'' Hammon allows for questioning the ''rightness'' of slavery itself. Furthermore, he indicates that slaves should not be obedient if sinful behavior would result, and he proclaims that judgment will come to all ''rich and poor, white and black.''

In general, even the scholars who helped rescue Hammon's work from oblivion have found little artistic merit in his poetry. His major purpose was to exhort, and that purpose shaped his versifying. His poems are highly influenced by the hymn as a form (four-line stanzas, usually rhyming a-b-a-b). His phrasing is often formulaic, drawing extensively on Scripture. His form and diction are typical of other American religious poetry of the colonial period, although his work is less polished.

In any case, in both his poetry and his prose, Hammon wrote with marked confidence. As a result of his comprehensive theological perspective, he spoke directly as well as subtly on the plight of the enslaved.

REFERENCES

Baker, Houston, Jr. *The Journey Back: Issues in Black Literature and Criticism.* Chicago: University of Chicago Press, 1980.

Bell, Bernard. "African–American Writers." In *American Literature 1764–1789: The Revolutionary Years.* Ed. Everett Emerson. Madison: University of Wisconsin Press, 1977.

Davis, Arthur P., J. Saunders Redding, and Joyce Ann Joyce. *The New Cavalcade: African American Writing from 1760 to the Present.* Vol. 1. Washington, DC: Howard University Press, 1991.

Harris, Trudier, ed. *Afro–American Writers Before the Harlem Renaissance.* Detroit: Gale Research, 1986.

Jackson, Blyden. *A History of Afro–American Literature.* Vol. 1. *The Long Beginning, 1746–1895.* Baton Rouge: Louisiana State University Press, 1989.

Kaplan, Sidney, and Emma Nogrady Kaplan. *The Black Presence in the Era of the American Revolution.* Rev. ed. Amherst: University of Massachusetts Press, 1989.

Logan, Rayford W., and Michael R. Winston, eds. *Dictionary of American Negro Biography.* New York: Norton, 1982.

Ransom, Samuel A., Jr. *America's First Negro Poet: The Complete Works of Jupiter Hammon of Long Island.* Port Washington, NY: Kennikat Press, 1970. Includes Oscar Wegelin, "Biographical Sketch of Jupiter Hammon" (1915) and Vernon Loggins, "Critical Analysis of the Works of Jupiter Hammon" (1900).

Arlene Clift–Pellow

Lionel Hampton

(1908–)

Musician, bandleader, composer

In a career spanning more than 70 years, Lionel Hampton has earned a reputation as one of jazz's most exciting and enduring performers. As a featured soloist with such jazz greats as Louis Armstrong and Benny Goodman and later as the leader of his own bands, Hampton has performed around the world, appeared on countless recordings, and been the recipient of numerous awards and honors. The multitalented Hampton is an accomplished drummer and also plays piano, sings, and composes, but he is best known as a vibraphonist, an instrument he is responsible for introducing into jazz and establishing as a legitimate solo instrument. Always the consummate showman, his performances are invariably characterized by his boundless enthusiasm and energy and his unflagging rhythmic drive.

There is some disagreement about Hampton's birth date, but according to Hampton's autobiography, *Hamp,* he was born on April 20, 1908, in Louisville, Kentucky, to Charles Edward and Gertrude Morgan Hampton. Hampton's father went into the army when the United States entered World War I and was declared missing in action just weeks after being sent to France. He remained lost to the family for more than 20 years, but Hampton was finally reunited with him by chance in 1939, shortly before the elder Hampton's death. Gertrude later married Samuel Davis and they had a son, Hampton's half brother Samuel Davis Jr. On November 11, 1936, Hampton married Gladys Riddle, who had been his business manager since the early 1930s, and she remained his wife and business manager until her death in 1971.

Hampton's uncle, Richard Morgan, moved to Chicago in 1919, and Hampton and his mother soon followed. At that time Chicago was a major jazz center, and in that conducive environment Hampton's musical talents blossomed. He started playing the drums in school and then joined the newsboys' band of the *Chicago Defender* newspaper. The director of the *Chicago Defender* band was Major N. Clark Smith, who, in his autobiography Hampton calls "about the greatest musician I guess I have ever known." Smith had a major impact on the young Hampton's musical development, encouraging his talent, and providing him with a solid foundation in harmony, theory, and sight–reading. Though the drums were Hampton's main instrument at this point, he also learned to play the timpani and the xylophone.

Another major source of inspiration for Hampton during his formative years was the music he heard at his uncle Richard's parties. Richard Morgan was an avid jazz fan, and some of the greatest jazz musicians of the time attended his parties, including Jelly Roll Morton, Louis Armstrong, Bix Biederbecke and King Oliver. Meeting these musicians and listening to them play was the ideal complement to the formal musical training Hampton received from Major Smith. Given this rich musical environment and his innate talent, it is no surprise that Hampton soon began to make a name for himself. While still in high school he began playing drums professionally with the Les Hite big band in Chicago. Hite moved to Hollywood in the early 1920s, and after a year or so he invited Hampton to join him. Though Hampton had not yet graduated from high school, he made the trip to Hollywood after promising his mother he would finish high school in California. Through his appearances with Hite and other local musicians he soon earned a reputation as one of the top drummers on the West Coast.

Had Hampton concentrated exclusively on the drums he would certainly have had a successful musical career, but on October 16, 1930, an event occurred that changed his life forever. While on a break at a recording session with Louis Armstrong, the musicians noticed a vibraphone sitting in the corner. As Hampton tells it in "Lionel Hampton & Tito Puente," "I had played xylophone when I was a kid in this

Lionel Hampton

military band, the *Chicago Defender* newspaper boys' band. We used to play overtures, like *William Tell* and *Poet and Peasant,* and I used to play the flute part on the xylophone. So Louis asked me, did I know anything about the instrument, and I said, 'Sure.' I had never played the vibes before in my life, but I picked it up and played Louis' solo from his record 'Chinese Chop Suey' note for note.'' Armstrong was so impressed that he insisted Hampton include the instrument on a recording of Eubie Blake's ''Memories of You.'' This was the first recorded use of the vibraphone in an authentic jazz setting. Over the next two years Hampton began to focus more and more on the vibraphone, and the instrument eventually became his trademark. The vibraphone's limpid, bell–like tone and percussive attack proved perfectly suited to his musical style, allowing him to retain the compelling rhythmic feel that characterized his drumming while adding harmony and melody to his musical palette.

The next big step in Hampton's career came in 1936 when he joined Benny Goodman. The Benny Goodman Orchestra was already very popular, but in 1936 Goodman decided to add a small ensemble to his show, and he formed the Benny Goodman Quartet, with Hampton on vibraphone, Teddy Wilson on piano, and Gene Krupa on drums. Hampton's tenure with Goodman was significant for two reasons: it catapulted him into the national spotlight, and it marked the first time a well–known band had been racially integrated. Though Goodman took pains to ensure that Hampton and Teddy Wilson received the same first–class accommodations as the other musicians, the prevailing climate of racial intolerance made for some unpleasant moments. Looking back on the experience, Hampton noted in his autobiography, ''With Benny, touring with two black musicians was a pioneering effort. Nobody had ever traveled with an integrated band before, and even though Teddy Wilson and I were only part of the Benny Goodman Quartet, not the whole orchestra, that was still too much for some white folks.'' Nevertheless, the group was an instant success. The quartet setting allowed each musician ample space to display his talents, and Hampton excelled in this environment. In addition to his exciting soloing and tasteful ensemble playing, he contributed several compositions to the group, including the popular ''Flying Home.''

Hampton's Big Band

In the summer of 1940 Hampton left Benny Goodman to form his own big band. With Hampton as the leader and his wife Gladys as the manager, the band quickly became an artistic and commercial success, both in the United States and abroad, and it remained so for the next twenty–five years. Many future jazz stars got their start in Hampton's big band, including Quincy Jones, Dinah Washington, Howard McGhee, Joe Williams, and Dexter Gordon. As a bandleader Hampton expressed the full range of his talents and showmanship; he played the vibes, piano and drums, often juggling his sticks deftly during his drum solos, and he also sang and composed songs. Inspired by Hampton's energy, the band became famous for its bravura performances and extended solos. In the 1950s the band performed on a number of highly successful goodwill tours around the world, which greatly enhanced Hampton's international reputation.

The changing musical trends of the early 1960s finally made it economically impossible to continue the big band on a regular basis; nevertheless, Hampton's career has continued unchecked. Since that time, he has had various small groups of his own and has reunited his big band on occasion for performances at concerts and jazz festivals. He has also performed and recorded with many other jazz greats, including Earl Hines, Woody Herman, Charlie Mingus, Gerry Mulligan, and Chick Corea. Hampton has had some difficult times in recent years. In 1995 he suffered two mild strokes just months apart from each other; he recovered well from the strokes but now needs to use a cane or wheelchair to get around. On January 7, 1997, a fire at his apartment destroyed all his belongings, including such irreplaceable items as his vintage record collection, his many honorary degrees, his collected correspondences and all his musical instruments. Despite these setbacks the octogenarian Hampton continues to perform regularly and to amaze audiences with his musical energy and enthusiasm.

Hampton has been the recipient of a host of awards and honors throughout his career. In addition to being awarded a number of honorary degrees from universities around the world, he received the Papal Medal from Pope Paul VI in 1968, the Medal of the City of Paris in 1985, the keys to the cities of New York, Los Angeles, Chicago,and Detroit, the *Ebony* Magazine Lifetime Achievement Award in 1989, and the Kennedy Center Lifetime Achievement Award in 1992, a

1996 National Medal of Arts (awarded in 1997), and other honors.

Hampton has also participated in politics throughout his career. A staunch lifelong Republican, Hampton campaigned actively for many politicians, including Richard Nixon, Nelson Rockefeller, Ronald Reagan, and George Bush, and he has performed often at the White House. In 1964 he temporarily shifted his allegiance to the Democrats and campaigned for Lyndon Johnson. As Hampton explains in his autobiography:

> I may be a Republican, but I'm first of all an American, and I thought what President Johnson was doing was good for the country. So in 1964, when he ran for election as president, I jumped party lines to support him. I had nothing personally against Barry Goldwater—in fact, we were good friends—but Johnson had signed the 1964 Civil Rights Act and said, "We shall overcome," and he was the man I wanted to support.

In addition to his political campaigning, Hampton has long been involved in civic and philanthropic activities. New York City appointed him human rights commissioner from 1984 to 1986, and in 1985 he served as the United Nations ambassador of music. In the 1980s he sponsored the Lionel Hampton Houses and the Gladys Hampton Houses in Harlem, projects that provided low–income housing. Hampton has also been a strong supporter of music education, setting up music scholarships at a number of universities, creating the Lionel Hampton Jazz Endowment Fund, and raising money for the University of Idaho's performing arts center, which was named the Lionel Hampton Center for the Performing Arts in his honor. The University of Idaho also produces an annual Lionel Hampton Jazz Festival, and Hampton's performances there are always a highlight.

Lionel Hampton can truly be called a living jazz legend. His storied career has spanned nearly the entire history of jazz, from his early years in Chicago to the big band era in the 1930s and 1940s and on to the present. Through his enormous contributions to music, his continued support for education, and his indefatigable spirit, he has earned a permanent place in our country's history.

Current address: Lionel Hampton, c/o Glad–Hamp, 1995 Broadway, New York, NY 10023.

REFERENCES

Birnbaum, Larry. "That's Entertainment: Tito Puente; Lionel Hampton." *Downbeat* 62, no. 11 (1995): 16–20.

Contemporary Musicians. Vol. 6. Detroit: Gale Research, 1992.

"Hampton Better after Stroke." *Rocky Mountain News,* June 30, 1995.

Hampton, Lionel, with James Haskins. *Hamp: An Autobiography.* New York: Warner Books, 1989.

Kernfield, Barry, ed. *The New Grove Dictionary of Jazz.* London: Macmillan, 1988.

Salzman, Jack, David Lionel Smith, and Cornel West, eds. *Encyclopedia of African–American Culture and History.* New York: Library Reference USA/Simon & Schuster Macmillan, 1996.

"To Lionel Hampton, Help after Blaze is 'Amazing.'" *New York Times,* January 9, 1997.

Who's Who among African Americans: 1996–1997. 9th ed. Detroit: Gale Research, 1996.

Who's Who in America: 1997. 51st ed. New Provident, NJ: Marquis Who's Who, 1997.

Arthur W. Buell

W. C. Handy
(1873–1958)
Composer, musician, music publisher, bandleader

W. C. Handy, the most celebrated black musician of his time, is universally known as "Father of the Blues." He gave his 1941 autobiography the title *Father of the Blues,* but never claimed to have originated the musical genre. According to blues historian William Ferris, "Handy became one of the most prominent figures in the popularization of blues." His twelve–bar blues patterns influenced the development of popular music in America, making the blues a part of the American vocabulary.

William Christopher Handy was born November 16, 1873, in Florence, Alabama. At age 12, he secured work as a water boy in a rock quarry near Muscle Shoals. From this position, he graduated to apprenticeships in plastering, shoemaking, and carpentry. But music was always his primary interest. His father, Charles Bernard Handy, was an African Methodist Episcopal minister, as was his paternal grandfather. His mother, Elizabeth Brewer Handy, and his father hoped that young William would follow the tradition. There was no musical background on either side of the family except for Handy's maternal grandfather, who was known to play the fiddle for dances before he became a Christian. Since there were no instruments in the Florence District School for Negroes, all music was vocal. Handy wrote:

> We learned all the songs in *Gospel Hymns.* . . . [We] advanced to a point where we could sing excerpts from the works of Wagner, Bizet, Verdi and other masters—all without instrumental accompaniment.

Handy recalled in his 1941 autobiography, *Father of the Blues,* that though music was forbidden in the Handy household, he saved his money and purchased a guitar. Returning from the store with his purchase, he hastened to show it to his parents. The reaction was not what W. C. anticipated. Outraged, his father said:

> "A guitar! One of the devil's playthings. Take it away. Take it away, I tell you. Get it out of your

W. C. Handy

hands. Whatever possessed you to bring a sinful thing like that into our Christian home? Take it back where it came from. You hear? Get!''

W. C. suggested that the store might not take it back. His father insisted. ''For the price of a thing like that you could get a new Webster's Unabridged Dictionary—something that'll do you some good.'' The exchange was made and Handy's father enrolled him in organ lessons, monitoring his progress. But the lessons were of limited duration.

The appearance of a prominent trumpeter in Florence convinced Handy that music should become his career pursuit and the trumpet should be his instrument for personal expression. He purchased a rotary–valve cornet for $1.75. His instructor was Y. A. Wallace, a Fisk University graduate and former Jubilee Singer. Handy credited Wallace with teaching him the fundamental elements of music.

In his early teens, Handy began performing with the local band and minstrel shows. Having joined a quartet as a first tenor, he and the other members hopped a freight train and headed for Chicago and the World's Fair. Upon their arrival, they were informed that the Fair had been delayed until the next year. He returned to Alabama, but sensing that he needed broader exposure, more opportunities, and competition, he left again. He took on many jobs—singer, trumpet player, band director, choral director, and educator. At the age of 23, he became bandmaster of Mahara's Colored Minstrels. As an itinerant musician, he directed and played his trumpet in various bands. Seeking work, he traveled to St. Louis, Missouri. St. Louis would later serve as the inspiration for his classic ''St. Louis Blues.'' In 1898, Handy married Elizabeth Virginia Price.

Between 1900 and 1902, Handy taught music at Alabama's Agricultural and Mechanical College for Negroes in Huntsville. This career was short lived. He soon resumed his life as a bandmaster and, for a brief period, worked at the Bessemer Iron Works, where the salary was fairly attractive. He eventually settled in Memphis, Tennessee.

Handy became a tenant of the Solvent Savings Bank, where the cashier was Harry H. Pace. Handy wrote in his autobiography that Pace ''was a handsome young man of striking personality and definite musical leanings.'' In 1908, Handy and Pace became collaborators in writing songs, with Pace serving as lyricist. They later founded the Pace and Handy Music Company–Publishers. Pace was president, Handy's brother Charles was vice president, and W. C. was secretary–treasurer.

Writes Blues Songs

In 1909 one of Handy's bands was hired to work for one of the three mayoral candidates, Edward Crump. For the campaign, Handy wrote the successful ''Mr. Crump,'' with a blues flair. Unable to find a publisher, he prepared one thousand copies for distribution in 1912, at his own expense. With new lyrics and a new title, the song became ''Memphis Blues.''

Handy's fame as a song writer began to spread. He eventually sold the rights to ''Memphis Blues'' for $100,000. ''St. Louis Blues,'' which became one of the most popular tunes in the history of songwriting, was published in 1914. Forty years after its publication, Handy was still earning yearly royalties of $25,000 for ''St. Louis Blues.'' The publisher of both ''Memphis Blues'' and ''St. Louis Blues'' was Pace and Handy Music Company–Publishers. Other successful blues compositions by Handy were ''Beale Street Blues,'' ''Mississippi Blues,'' ''Joe Turner Blues,'' ''Yellow Dog Blues,'' ''Aunt Hagger's Children's Blues,'' and ''Harlem Blues,'' to name only a few.

The Pace and Handy Music Company–Publishers moved to New York City in 1918. Two years later, Pace and Handy dissolved their partnership. Pace moved on to form the first black–owned recording company, Black Swan, and the publishing company continued as a Handy family business. The company published works by other black composers as well as Handy's compositions. More than 150 sacred musical compositions and folk song arrangements and roughly 60 additional blues compositions were published by the Pace and Handy Music Company–Publishers.

For many years, Handy collaborated with the New York Urban League in presenting annual concerts featuring talented young black instrumentalists and singers. He also promoted the music of other black composers as well as his own. Of particular note was Handy's April 27, 1928, concert at Carnegie Hall. Handy, according to Eileen Southern, ''was the first to present the full spectrum of black music from plantation songs to orchestral works.'' Presented by W. C. Handy's

Orchestra and Jubilee Singers, the concert was an overwhelming success. The featured program included spirituals, blues, plantation songs, work songs, piano solos, a Negro rhapsody, and jazz. Works by notable black composers such as Will Marion Cook, James P. Johnson, H. T. Burleigh, J. Rosamond Johnson, and Nathaniel Dett were performed. The concert concluded with a performance of ''St. Louis Blues,'' with Thomas ''Fats'' Waller as organ soloist. Handy also produced concerts for the Chicago World's Fair (1933–34), ASCAP Silver Jubilee Festival (1939), New York's World Fair (1939–40), and the Golden Gate Exposition in San Francisco (1939–40).

A prolific writer, Handy wrote and edited five publications—*Blues: An Anthology* (also published as *A Treasury of the Blues,* 1926 and 1949); *Negro Authors and Composers of the United States* (1935); *Book of Negro Spirituals* (1938); *Father of the Blues* (autobiography, 1941); and *Unsung Americans Sung* (1944). Of special interest is a series of letters written by Handy to his very good friend, composer William Grant Still (1895–1978) and published in *Black Perspective in Music.* Their friendship began in 1915, when Still was hired as an arranger for Handy's band in Memphis, Tennessee. Still also played cello and oboe in the band. In 1919 Still joined Handy in New York City and worked at the Pace–Handy Music Publishing Company.

During World War I, Handy began to lose his eyesight. He regained some of his lost vision, but a fall from a subway platform in 1943 fractured his skull and caused total blindness. After the death of his first wife, Handy married his secretary, Irma Louise Logan, in 1954.

In 1938, to commemorate Handy's 65th birthday, a series of celebrations were held. The celebrations included a testimonial dinner at the famous Cotton Club in New York City; the playing of ''St. Louis Blues'' 15 times by 15 different bands at an American Federation of Musicians jamboree in Hollywood; and a concert at Carnegie Hall, featuring ''name bands'' performing the ''St. Louis Blues'' in a variety of arrangements. In 1940 an all–Handy program was broadcast on NBC.

W. C. Handy died March 28, 1958, at the age of 84. He was survived by his wife, two sons, Wyer Owens and William Christopher Jr., and a daughter, Katherine Handy Lewis. For his funeral, approximately 150,000 people gathered in the streets surrounding Harlem's Abyssinian Baptist Church. The presiding minister eulogized Handy as a man who ''captured the heart throbs of a forlorn and stricken people and set them to music.'' New York City Mayor Wagner remarked that Handy's life was ''an example for generations to come.'' Congressman Adam Clayton Powell Jr. extolled, ''Gabriel now has an understudy—a side man. And when the last trumpet shall sound I am sure that W. C. Handy will be there to bury this world as a side man.'' Trumpeter Charles ''Cootie'' Williams played Handy's favorite melody, ''The Holy City.'' The Brass Band of Prince Hall Masonic Temple led the funeral procession, alternating Frederic Chopin's ''Funeral March'' with Handy's immortal ''St. Louis Blues.''

In 1958, the year of his death, the movie *St. Louis Blues* was released by Paramount Pictures and featured Nat King Cole in the role of William Christopher Handy. A commemorative stamp was issued on May 17, 1969, in Memphis, Tennessee.

The centennial of Handy's birth was celebrated in the city of Florence, Alabama, with music and special tours of the restored Handy Home and Museum. The W. C. Handy Festival in Florence, Alabama, is now an annual event. In Memphis, centennial activities took place at Handy Park on Beale Street, where the Handy statue stands. Other ceremonies took place in St. Louis, at Yale University, and at the Library and Museum of Lincoln Center in New York City. Earl ''Fatha'' Hines recorded an album of Handy compositions, and Columbia Records reissued Louis Armstrong's album of Handy tunes originally recorded in 1954.

Fisk University in Nashville, Tennessee, declared November 10, 1978, as W. C. Handy Day, and Handy's younger brother Charles presented some of Handy's sheet music to the university library's special collection. Throughout the United States, the name W. C. Handy is kept alive through the dedication of schools, housing projects, streets, theaters, parks, awards, and scholarships bearing his name.

Handy earned his place in history with his composition ''St. Louis Blues,'' which is still one of the world's most popular songs. His style of the blues inspired numerous later composers. His publishing company made available to the world the music of other black composers, and Handy himself played a pioneering role in bringing the blues to the attention of the world.

REFERENCES

Adams, Russell L. *Great Negroes Past and Present.* Chicago: Afro–Am Publishing Co., 1964.

''Band Sees Handy Out of Harlem.'' *New York Times,* April 3, 1958.

Current Biography Yearbook. New York: H. W. Wilson, 1984.

Ferris, William. ''Blues Roots and Development.'' *The Black Perspective in Music* 2 (Fall 1974): 122–27.

''Fisk University to Receive W. C. Handy's Papers.'' Press Release, Fisk University, November 16, 1978.

''Half–Century with W. C. Handy at Carnegie Hall.'' *New York Amsterdam News,* March 14, 1981.

Handy, W. C. *Father of the Blues: An Autobiography.* New York: Macmillan, 1941.

Haskins, James. *Black Music in America: A History Through Its People.* New York: Harper Collins, 1987.

''In Retrospect: Letters from W. C. Handy to William Grant Still.'' *The Black Perspective in Music* 7 (Fall 1979): 199–233; 8 (Spring 1980): 65–119.

''The Man Who Made the Blues.'' *Washington Post,* November 16, 1973.

Nichols, Charles H., ed. *Arna Bontemps–Langston Hughes Letters, 1925–1967.* New York: Dodd, Mead, 1980.

Slonimsky, Nicholas, ed. *Baker's Biographical Dictionary of Musicians.* 7th rev. ed. New York: Schirmer Books, 1984.

Southern, Eileen. *Biographical Dictionary of Afro–American and African Musicians.* Westport, CT: Greenwood Press, 1982.

Toppin, Edgar A. "W. C. Handy: Father of the Blues." *Richmond Afro–American,* June 3, 1972.

Wilson, John S. "100th Anniversary of the Birth of W. C. Handy." *International Musician* (November 1973): 3, 21.

COLLECTIONS

In addition to the materials at Fisk University, there is a substantial Handy collection of memorabilia at the Watkinson Library of Trinity College, Hartford, Connecticut.

D. Antoinette Handy

Oliver W. Harrington
(1912–1995)
Cartoonist, journalist, writer

A pioneering black cartoonist, Oliver Harrington was one of the nation's most popular cartoon artists and a first–rate social satirist who used the medium to fight racial oppression. He was best known for creating the soulful cartoon character "Bootsie," featured in his panel called *Dark Laughter,* a satire of Harlem's black community in the 1930s and published in black newspapers for about 40 years. In the 1930s and 1940s Harrington contributed humorous and editorial cartoons to the black press. He also drew under the name "Ol" Harrington, then "Ollie" Harrington.

The best source of biographical information on Harrington is M. Thomas Inge's introduction to his book *Dark Laughter: The Satiric Art of Oliver W. Harrington,* which includes information from the author's interview with him on October 28, 1992, in Columbus, Ohio. Oliver Wendell Harrington, popularly known as "Ollie," one of four children, was born February 14, 1912. The Valhalla community of Westchester County north of New York City, where Harrington was born, was a settling place for recent European immigrants as well as African Americans who sought work on local dams and reservoirs. His father, whose name is not given in published sources, was a free black who came up from North Carolina. His mother, Eugenia Turat, of Budapest, Hungary, was of Jewish descent. The Harringtons moved to the South Bronx when Ollie was seven years old, settling in a neighborhood comprised of separate ghettos of Italians, Irish, Polish, and African Americans.

Ollie Harrington was introduced to the pains of racism when he was in the sixth grade. In *Why I Left America* he wrote about one of his teachers, a Miss McCoy, who sought out and ridiculed Harrington and his only African American classmate, Prince Anderson. She told the class, "these two, being Black, belong in a waste basket." Unable to defend himself against her ridicule, Harrington built up a rage against McCoy. To vent his frustration, Harrington, who until then had no interest in drawing cartoons, sketched in his notebook what he called "vicious" images of McCoy. Although she never saw the cartoons, they depicted her as a poor, dumb, sloppy woman; as a result, Harrington experienced catharsis. In drawing the cartoon, Harrington also discovered a source of pleasure that would sustain him for life.

Harrington graduated from De Witt Clinton High School in 1929 and when 17 years old, went to Harlem where he roomed at the YMCA. He arrived when the high productivity of the talented black cultural artists of the Harlem Renaissance was waning and, according to Inge, was stimulated by the "afterglow of their example." He became friends with Charles Drew, another resident at the Y, who eventually developed the medical use of blood plasma. As well, Harrington developed friendships with Rudolph Fisher, Wallace Thurman, and Arna Bontemps, all participants in the Renaissance movement. Langston Hughes became his mentor.

To support himself and develop his talent further, Harrington sought out freelance art work. He also had a small scholarship to study at the National Academy of Design. In 1940 he graduated from Yale University with a bachelor of fine arts degree and started work on an M.F.A. He admitted that El Greco and Thomas Benton Hart influenced the techniques he used while at Yale. Although Yale awarded him a European fellowship, when the Germans invaded Poland and World War II began, he lost the opportunity to complete his degree.

In 1932 Harrington published political cartoons in two black newspapers, *The National News*—which he signed O. Wendell Harrington—and the *New York State Contender.* This success led to assignments from influential major black newspapers such as the *New York Amsterdam News,* the *Baltimore Afro–American,* and the *Pittsburgh Courier.* The *Courier* remained a major venue for his cartoons for 30 years.

Comic Strips Published

Harrington's first work with the *Courier* was a comic strip called *Boop,* published on March 11, 1933 and renamed *Scoop* on March 18, when it became a regular series about the mishaps of a small child. On March 29 the gag strip became a melodrama about Scoop's stepmother. Continuing to find his way, Harrington drew about issues that were then timely. When the *New York Amsterdam News Magazine* first appeared on May 25, 1935, as the newspaper's tabloid section, 16 contributors were listed with full–page advertisements. Among them were E. Simms Campbell's *Harlem Sketches* and Ol Harrington's *Dark Laughter,* the inaugural appearance of his series, which illustrated the experiences of urban black life.

On December 28, 1935, the *Dark Laughter* panel first used the name "Bootsie," depicting two disreputable men speaking to clerks in a liquor store. From then on, Bootsie, a fat, bald, mustachioed black man who loved soul food, liquor, and women, and his thin, unnamed buddy appeared in nearly every issue of the *Amsterdam News* for several years. While racism and conflict in the white community were common topics, for the most part the series targeted blacks themselves. Langston Hughes later developed a similar character called Jesse B. Semple that appeared in weekly newspapers by 1943. Inge's *Dark Laughter* called Bootsie and Semple (or Simple) "urban everymen whose actions and comments puncture the pomposities of those trying to get ahead in a racist society through ruse and compromise."

Adam Clayton Powell Jr., a civil rights activist and pastor of the Abyssinian Baptist Church, cofounded with Harlem businessman Charles Buchanan *The People's Voice,* a weekly newspaper. Powell hired Harrington as art director, beginning with the first issue on February 14, 1942. This was Harrington's first full–time job. The paper published the Bootsie character under the title *Dark Laughter* as well as Harrington's new comic strip, *Jive Gray.* Jive was a character who was a key reporter on the race paper, *Liberator.* The strip lasted only three weeks. The *Voice* also serialized Richard Wright's *Native Son* with illustrations by Harrington. The two men had never met. Harrington continued to work for the *Voice* and his work appeared through the July 17, 1943, issue. By then, presumably the *Pittsburgh Courier* had lured him away.

On May 8, 1943, Harrington revived his comic strip *Jive Gray* in the *Pittsburgh Courier.* The character was now seen in a war setting. Readers enjoyed the cartoon but wanted Bootsie as well. *Dark Laughter* and Bootsie returned to the paper beginning with the February 16, 1945 issue.

In the fall of 1943 the *Courier* sent Harrington on a tour of certain military bases in America to study blacks' contributions to the war effort. On October 30, Harrington prepared a full–page feature sketch of his findings called "Army Air Force." Since he was not called to military duty, the *Courier* sent Harrington to North Africa and Europe as a war correspondent. At the end of the war, Walter White, whom Harrington had met in Italy and escorted to the battlefront, asked Harrington to develop a public relations department for the NAACP, the organization that White then headed. Reluctant at first, Harrington accepted after he learned about a series of lynchings in the South and the mistreatment of black veterans.

His new work pushed Harrington into the public political arena and into speech–making and debates. When he attended the *New York Herald Tribune's* forum on "The Struggle for Justice as a World Force" held on October 28, 1946, he had a confrontation with U.S. Attorney General Tom Clark, who announced federal investigations of lynchings in Monroe, Georgia, but reminded the audience that there had never been any convictions for the crimes of race hate and lynchings. Harrington criticized federal justice agencies for allowing lynchings and vicious vandalism to occur when the same agencies successfully located foreign spies. Harrington believed that the debate led Clark to label him a Communist. As the federal government rigorously investigated people and organizations considered subversive, the NAACP became a prime target. With Harrington a major spokesperson for the NAACP, he, too, was under investigation.

Harrington preferred to work as a cartoonist and continued to draw for the black press. He also taught art at the Jefferson School of Social Science in New York and in 1950 worked as art editor for the paper *Freedom.* In late 1951, acting on the warning of a friend that he was about to be investigated for alleged Communist activities, Harrington left the United States for France, where he painted and studied art in Paris. By now talented black artists and writers such as Beauford Delany, James Baldwin, and Chester Himes, were gathering in Paris in a movement stimulated by Richard Wright after his 1946 arrival. When Harrington arrived in 1951, he finally met Wright and their lifelong friendship began.

Harrington continued to submit his cartoons to the *Courier* and the *Chicago Defender,* which gave him a modest income. As suspicions about Harrington's political activities lingered, the American Embassy attempted to lift his passport. The embassy harassed Harrington, Richard Wright, and other blacks in the American community in Paris. After Wright died in 1960 under questionable circumstances, Harrington speculated that his death was the result of an arranged assassination.

With Wright gone, life in Paris was not the same for Harrington. He went to East Berlin in 1961 to illustrate a series of American literary classics that Aufbau Publishers was to translate and publish in German. East Berlin became his new home. His work as a political cartoonist for the humor magazine *Eulenspiegel* and the general interest publication *Das Magazine* made him enormously popular in East Germany—something like a cult figure. Although German authorities were irritated that he avoided the Communist Party, he was tolerated because of his wide appeal as a political cartoonist. On October 19, 1968 he contributed editorial cartoons to the *New York Daily World*—formerly *The Worker*—and his work became a mainstay of the paper. In honor of his sixtieth birthday, the *Daily World* published a portfolio of his drawings in 1972, called *Soul Shots.* Artist Elton Fax wrote the introduction. Harrington returned to the United States for the occasion, his first visit in 20 years. He returned again in 1991, when he delivered the address, "Why I Left America" at Detroit's Wayne State University on April 18. He was sponsored by Walter O. Evans, a Detroit physician and collector of African American art and culture.

Artist Becomes Illustrator and Author

In addition to his work as cartoonist for the black press, Harrington illustrated a number of black books for children. Among these were Ellen F. Tarry's *Hezekiah Horton,* published in 1942, and her 1950 children's book *The Runaway Elephant.* In 1951 the American Institute of Graphic Arts selected the cover and illustrations from the latter work for an award in its annual competition for the Fifty Best American Books. This was the first time the institute had honored a black artist. In 1958 Harrington's anthology of cartoons, *Bootsie and Others,* was published by Dodd, Mead; his friend Langston Hughes wrote the introduction. In 1993 Harrington published the address given at Wayne State along with other essays and articles under the title, *Why I Left America.* Harrington's articles and essays were published in such journals as *Freedomways, Daily World, The People's Voice,* and *Ebony.*

Harrington died in 1995, at his East Berlin home at the age of 84, leaving a wife, Helma Richter Harrington—an economist and later broadcast journalist whom he met in the early 1960s—and their son, Oliver W. Jr. Harrington found that he had to live in exile from the country he loved in order to have reasonable peace and dignity. His work as a cartoon artist transcended racial, political, and international boundaries and brought him wide acceptance as a social satirist.

REFERENCES

Harrington, Oliver W. *Why I Left America and Other Essays.* Jackson: University Press of Mississippi, 1993.

Inge, M. Thomas, ed. *Dark Laughter: The Satiric Art of Oliver W. Harrington.* Jackson: University Press of Mississippi, 1993.

Johnson, Terry. "Ollie Harrington: Artist With Vision to Transform the World." *People Weekly World,* October 31, 1992.

COLLECTIONS

The largest collection of original art by Harrington in this country is in the Walter O. Evans collection of African American art in Detroit.

Jessie Carney Smith

Richard B. Harrison
(1864–1935)
Actor, teacher, dramatic reader, lecturer, elocutionist

Richard B. Harrison dreamed of playing Shylock. Instead, he would achieve fame in a role he twice turned down. At the age of 65, Harrison "walked out on to the stage of the Mansfield Theater in New York," as the *Christian Herald* noted, "to answer the most amazing entrance cue in all stage history: 'Gangway! Gangway for de Lawd Gawd Jehovah!'" Harrison played the lead role in Marc Connelly's *The Green Pastures,* which the actor emphasized in the *Christian Herald* was "not just a show. Each time we present it we lay bare the soul of a race."

Richard Berry Harrison was born on September 28, 1864, in London, Ontario, Canada. His parents, Thomas L.

Richard B. Harrison

and Isabella Chauteau Harrison, had escaped slavery through the Underground Railroad. Richard was their fourth child, the oldest son. He married Gertrude Janet Washington on December 11, 1895. Gertrude Harrison, the first black person to graduate from the Chicago Conservatory of Music, studied under Flo Ziegfield's father and was both a music instructor and a church organist. The couple had two children, Lawrence Gilbert, who became a choir director, and Marian Ysobel. Richard Harrison died on March 14, 1935, in New York City.

A Fascination with Drama

Harrison credited his fascination with the theater to his mother, who was so moved by a performance of Shakespeare's *Richard III* that she chose to name her son Richard. As a young teenager, Richard sold newspapers to help the family survive after his father's death. Working near the theater, he found ways to get to know the actors and when possible saved his money so that he could watch performances from the gallery. Even in his early years, he was known for his skill at impersonation. Often he would gather his friends in a barn to play for them the parts he had seen portrayed on stage. He won many awards at school and church for recitations.

Young Harrison's desire to become an actor led him to Detroit, where he studied drama at the Detroit Training School of Dramatic Art. He also studied privately under British drama coach, Edward Weitzel, then drama editor of the Detroit *Free Press.* Harrison did not have the luxury, however, of devoting all his time to this pursuit. He supported himself first as a bellhop at Detroit's Russell House and then by working as a porter, waiter, and mail clerk for the railroad.

Harrison's heart was still with the theater, however, and he continued to develop his dramatic skills. From 1892 through 1896, he traveled widely, presenting readings for popular literary societies of the time, first for the L. E. Behymer Lyceum Bureau and then for the Chatauqua circuit. His repertoire included readings of Shakespeare's works and a selection from his favorite poets, including many by his friend Paul Laurence Dunbar, a popular black poet of the time. He and Dunbar spent time travelling together to promote the poet's book *Oak and Ivy,* and the two became lifelong friends. Dunbar served as best man at Harrison's wedding. The Harrisons settled in Chicago, and from that base, Richard Harrison toured the country giving recitals, working from a selection of seven plays and more than a hundred recitations he had memorized. He became well known in black communitities.

The young actor's energies found another focus as well. In his travels across the country, he saw a desire for dramatic training among the people he visited and decided to try teaching. He began to coach individuals and to offer training sessions for larger groups. Seeing schools as the appropriate place for such education, Harrison convinced James B. Dudley, president of the Agricultural and Technical College in Greensboro, North Carolina, to let him establish a drama school. He began offering courses during the summer of 1922. Still drawn to the stage itself, however, Harrison moved his family to New York for most of the year. There he read and taught in churches and played a lead role in *Pa Williams' Gal* at the Lafayette Theatre.

How Green Were His Pastures

Richard Harrison was destined for a greater role. Marc Connelly had written a play based on Roark Bradford's book *Ol' Man Adam and His Chillun,* which Connelly described in *Voices Offstage* as "a new and delightful way of retelling some of the stories of the Old Testament." From the sketches in Bradford's book, he developed a drama with its "own dimensions," one that depicted "the search of God for man, and man's search for God." Connelly visited Bradford in New Orleans to learn more about southern black customs and tested his dialogue in various settings to ensure its authenticity.

After finishing the work, the playwright's first challenge was to find funding for such a controversial play. Just when prospects of finding a producer "could not have been more dim," he wrote in *Voices,* Connelly met Roland Stebbins. He felt obliged to warn the enthusiastic benefactor that they "might go to jail for their temerity." Nevertheless, Stebbins agreed to finance the venture under the name of Lawrence Rivers Inc.

The next big hurdle was to find someone who could play the role of God. Connelly continued in *Voices,* "The actor needed to be physically big, have a bearing not only dignified but noble, and a voice rich with quiet authority and capable of thunderous wrath." Adam Clayton Powell Jr. turned down the part. None of the numerous people who tried out for the role seemed suitable. Just four days before time for rehearsals to begin, while Connelly and Stebbins sat "silently plumbing new ocean–like depths of depression," the casting agent introduced Richard B. Harrison. Both playwright and producer were impressed. Connelly remembered that first encounter: "Topping his six–foot height was a head of leonine gray hair. Below it, we saw a face that had managed to weather sixty–five years of struggle and disheartenment. It was a face maturely serene because of the dauntless inner strength of the gentle being who wore it. He spoke with a voice like a cello's."

Twice Harrison declined the playwright's urging. According to Connelly in *Voices,* Harrison was "doubtful of his qualifications to the play De Lawd," and he "questioned his ability to learn to speak in the dialect of the Deep South." More importantly, Harrison feared that in taking the role he might offend other members of his race. Herbert Shipman, bishop of the Episcopal Diocese of New York, encouraged Harrison to set aside his reservations and take the part, but he still intended to refuse. However, to his own surprise, when Connelly called, he accepted. Later Harrison wrote in the *Christian Herald,* "I haven't yet been able to fathom that answer." But he felt fate had chosen him and the other actors "to help establish better understanding between our people and white people."

Amazing Success

The play opened at Mansfield Theatre on Broadway on February 26, 1930. Harrison, then sixty–five years old, took his part very seriously. He said in the *Christian Herald,* "I do not believe anyone could play my role without feeling that he had something alive in his hands—something that transcends its mere physical boundaries. Something that shines like laughter on the face of a happy child. Something that can sear like a flame, then soothe like the still waters of the psalm from which the title of the play was taken." Harrison played the role beautifully then and more than a thousand other times. He also became a mentor and role model for the cast.

After a 16–month run on Broadway, the cast took the play on the road across the United States. After a triumphant tour, the play returned to New York after covering 40,000 miles, 203 towns, forty states, and part of Canada. One reporter observed in the *New York Times* for February 21, 1935, "Although two generations of cherubs have outgrown the Fish–Fry scene (the play is now in its third generation), the Lawd still wears his original wide–brimmed black felt hat, his original Prince Albert suit, his original shoes." Even during the Great Depression, the drama was remarkably successful. It was eventually released as a film by Warner Brothers.

The success and quality of the play were quickly recognized. In 1930, after just three months of performances, it won the Pulitzer Prize. According to *Black Manhattan,* the jurors declared, "One play—*The Green Pastures* by Marc Connelly—towers so far above the other American plays of the season and comes so near to setting a new standard of excellence for the American drama of all time that the jurors desire with unusual enthusiasm to recommend it for the Pulitzer prize. . . . On this occasion, the jurors state emphatically that they have no second choice."

Also in 1930, Harrison was awarded the seventeenth Spingarn Medal, an award given annually by the NAACP to a black American for distinguished achievement. Harrison was the second actor to receive the medal. Other honors, such as honorary degrees from a number of colleges and universities, came Harrison's way as well. But two incidents proved particularly meaningful for the aging actor. On his seventieth birthday, he received numerous telegrams, fourteen of them from college or university presidents and seven of them from governors. A reception was also given in his honor. Touched by the occasion, he was quoted in the *New York Times* on February 24, 1935: "It's a glorious thing to have lived long. It is a great satisfaction to know you have lived so people will recognize something in you that is worthwhile." Also on that day, his name appeared in lights for the first time. With characteristic humility, the *New York Sun* said that Harrison remarked, "That's mighty fine," and proceeded to prepare for the night's performance.

Harrison's life had been difficult. In the *Christian Herald,* he observed, "Some of those years were pretty lean and most of them fraught with adversity of one sort or another, but scarcely one of them passed without contributing something that has helped me in my portrayal of 'de Lawd.'" Of his role in the drama, Harrison observed in the *New York Sun,* "It's a hard part to play—hard to control, I mean. There are a lot of big moments in it, and you've got to watch yourself so you won't get to rantin'. After all, you're playing God—and he doesn't have to rant." According to the *New York Times,* he once remarked that his favorite line in the play was "'Even bein' de Lawd ain't no bed of roses." But on another occasion, reports the *Christian Herald,* he wrote, "If the truth be known, being 'de Lawd' of "The Green Pastures" has been an inspiration, the fulfillment of a life's ambition—a bed of roses!" He also noted the play's effect on his life. Quoted in the *New York Times* for March 24, 1935, he told one reporter, "My landlady says that I am more patient than I used to be before I was playing in Mr. Connelly's drama."

Remarkable Tributes

After *The Green Pastures,* Harrison planned to return to teaching at the Agricultural and Technical College in Greensboro. He still dreamed of playing Shylock, and, as quoted in the *Christian Herald,* he wanted to "have a hand in the true Negro opera that is bound to be produced one of these days." But none of these events was to take place. Just before one of the performances, Harrison collapsed. Although his physician thought Harrison was improving, the actor suffered heart failure and died on March 14, 1935.

Harrison is buried at Lincoln Cemetery in Chicago. More than fifteen thousand men and women of all races, creeds, and stations of life came to Harrison's home to pay homage the night before the funeral service at St. Edmund's Episcopal Church.

Richard Harrison had reluctantly accepted the role of De Lawd in *The Green Pastures;* but having made the commitment, he gave himself to the role. In so doing, he significantly influenced the development of the play itself. W. E. B. Du Bois observed in *Crisis:*

> *The Green Pastures* has helped our hope and it has helped not so much in form and word and authorship as in the deft and subtle marvel of its interpretation. For skillful as the written play may be, the secret of its triumph lies in its interpretation by Negro actors, and above all in the high and delicate genius of Richard Berry Harrison. . . . By the breadth of a hair and half–turn of a phrase—by a gesture and a silence, he guided a genial comedy into a great and human drama.

REFERENCES

Connelly, Marc. *Voices Offstage: A Book of Memoirs.* Chicago: Holt, Rinehart and Winston, 1968.

"'De Lawd' Returns to City Pastures." *New York Times,* February 21, 1935.

Du Bois, W. E. B. "Beside the Still Waters." *Crisis* 38 (May 1931): 169.

"Funeral Service For 'De Lawd' Fills Cathedral." *New York Herald Tribune,* March 18, 1935.

"Green Pastures Claim De Lawd." *New York Sun,* March 14, 1935.

"*The Green Pastures* Comes Home." *New York Times,* February 24, 1935.

"Harrison Funeral to be in Cathedral." *New York Times,* March 16, 1935.

Harrison, Richard B. "Jes Like a Natchel Man." *Christian Herald* 58 (March 1935): 12–13, 41–47.

Johnson, James Weldon. *Black Manhattan.* New York: Knopf, 1930. Reprint, New York: Arno Press and the *New York Times,* 1968.

"Lawds New and Old." *New York Times,* March 24, 1935.

Logan, Rayford W., and Michael R. Winston, eds. *Dictionary of American Negro Biography.* New York, Norton, 1982.

"R. B. Harrison Gets Spingarn Medal." *New York Times,* March 23, 1930.

"R. B. Harrison, 70, 'De Lawd,' is Dead." *New York Times,* March 15, 1935.

"7,000 in Cathedral at Rites for 'Lawd.'" *New York Times,* March 18, 1935.

"Simple But Impressive Funeral Rites Held for Richard Berry Harrison at Cathedral of St. John the Divine: 10,000 Mourners." *New York Age,* March 23, 1935.

"Throng in Chicago Mourns 'De Lawd.'" *New York Times,* March 19, 1935.

COLLECTIONS

Richard B. Harrison's papers are at North Carolina Agricultural and Technical State University in Greensboro, North Carolina.

Marie Garrett

William R. Harvey
(1941–)
College president, educator, entrepreneur

In his nearly 20 years of leadership as president of Hampton University, William Robert Harvey has led the school to solid financial footing, redirected and expanded the academic program, and increased the student enrollment from 2,700 to an all–time high of over 6,000. A shrewd entrepreneur, he led the school into commercial ventures in Hampton, Virginia. He is also the first African American to fully own a Pepsi Cola Bottling Company franchise.

William R. Harvey

Harvey was born to Mamie Claudis and Willie D.C. Harvey on January 29, 1941, in Brewton, Alabama. Brewton, like other typical southern Jim Crow towns, was an inhospitable place for African American residents. But not all would succumb to it. Willie Harvey beat the odds to become a prosperous construction entrepreneur, and imparted that same go–getting spirit to his son. He taught his son to strive for success and, as Harvey said in an interview, to never let anyone make him feel inferior. Harvey's father supported and encouraged him during his early childhood education and beyond. Harvey's participation as a member of Southern Normal School's honor society, choir, football and basketball teams, and business managership of the student paper, along with his development as a tennis player, made him an attractive college recruit. Moreover, his unfortunate experiences with segregation strengthened him and intensified his resolve to triumph.

Harvey elected to stay in Alabama for the first stage of his college education. Armed with an academic scholarship, he entered Talledaga College in 1957. A history major, he participated in state–wide civil rights activities, played varsity level basketball and tennis, sharpened his tongue as a member of the debating team and college council, and performed as a Little Theatre "Thespian." Harvey was popular on campus and sought out others. He graduated with a bachelor of arts degree in 1961 and served in the U.S. Army (1962–65). Subsequently, he became active in the army reserve and achieved the rank of lieutenant colonel in 1981, before joining the ranks of the inactive reserve a little more than a decade later.

Harvey's real interest rested in education and administration. To pursue this interest, he enrolled in Virginia State College in 1965 and later earned a M.A. in American history with a concentration in educational administration. He also taught U.S. history on the secondary level during this period, before serving as deputy director of the Southern Alabama Economic Opportunity Agency (1966–1968). In 1968, he was selected as a Woodrow Wilson Foundation's Martin Luther King Fellow and began attending graduate school at Harvard University. He was named a Harvard University Higher Education Administrative Fellow in 1969 and in the same year served as a Adams House, Harvard University, Summer Studies Program tutor. An intern fellowship from the Woodrow Wilson Foundation helped sustain him until he received a Harvard University doctorate of education in administration of higher education (1972). Harvey's stay at Harvard included serving as an elected member of the Student Cabinet, membership on the Faculty Committee on Academic Policy, the board of directors of Phi Delta Kappa, chairman of the Colloquium Board, and assistant to the dean for governmental affairs (1969–70). Harvey's next academic position took him to Fisk University, where he served as assistant to the university president (1970–72). He then moved to Tuskegee Institute in Alabama as vice president for student affairs (1972–74), and later as vice president for administrative services (1974–78).

Named Hampton University President

In July 1978, Harvey became president of Hampton Institute (as it was known then), succeeding Carl McClellan Hill, Hampton's 11th president. Hampton's search for a new president was protracted and competitive. This was a highly sought after position, with at least 140 candidates submitting applications for it.

Hampton's $29–$33 million endowment ranked the school first among historically black colleges and universities and 53rd nationally. Hampton, however, had some financial problems, and Harvey inherited each one. He was extremely concerned about Hampton's budget and operational deficits. Undaunted by the bleak picture, Harvey worked diligently to stop the financial hemorrage. At the end of his first year at Hampton, he eliminated the deficit and netted a $44,000 surplus. Furthermore, Hampton has not experienced a deficit during Harvey's nearly 20–year tenure.

While grappling with the financial woes, he was also unsatisfied with the academic programs. He set high academic standards for the faculty, students, administration, and staff. Harvey did not call for student–academic exclusivity, as a number of admissions slots would go to promising, academically challenged students, but they, like all students, are expected to meet specific standards before receiving Hampton's imprimatur.

In his inaugural address on March 24, 1979, published in Martha Dawson's *Hampton University,* Harvey said his administration would

> continue to strive for truth and beauty and excellence in all of the things we do. We shall emphasize dignity and decency. In curricular and extra–curricular activities, we shall promote the ideals of self–reliance, learning by doing, and the dignity of labor. . . . No man should consider himself literate until all men [sic] can read and write. None of us are free until all of us are free. Eugene Debs perhaps said it best: ''As long as there is a lower class, I am in it. As long as there is a criminal element, I am of it. As long as there is a man in jail, I am not free.''

Additionally, Harvey wanted to establish a core of required courses and stressed the importance of students doing ''some thinking about ethics and morals. It is my firm belief that decency is as important as degrees, and I want the Hampton students to not only be good doctors, lawyers, professors, engineers and nurses, but I want them to be good moral leaders who have a sense of commitment to the community and service as well,'' he said.

Fourteen years later, on April 1, 1993, during Hampton's 125th Anniversary celebration, Harvey called attention to the general deterioration of ''basic oral and written communications skills. We stopped open discussions of values, ethics, and character and their development in the classrooms, and began to insert sensational, empty and directionaless 'rap sessions',' he said. Harvey challenged African Americans and others, to reclaim their neighborhoods. At that point, he proposed establishing a four–year mandatory leadership program emphasizing ''values, decency, dignity, honesty, respect for oneself, respect for others [and] integrity.'' Also, before graduating, each student ''would be required to work one year in a school, community center, or some other community uplift program.'' Although this visionary plan has not yet been fully achieved, these attributes are included in the Hampton University Code of Conduct.

In 1986 Harvey faced some criticism when he expressed his determination to increase the percentage of white enrollment from around seven percent to 15 percent to 20 percent (it reached approximately 12 percent by the early 1990s, and was mainly concentrated in the graduate and professional schools). The president also angered a group of disgruntled students when in March, 1993 he rejected their request for a Black Studies Program at Hampton. Quoted in the *Virginia Daily Press* he said: ''At a white school you need a black studies department. Why do you need one at Hampton? We don't need to emulate a white school with a black studies department.''

Harvey faced additional protest during graduation ceremonies in 1991, when Hampton graduated 1,023, the largest class in its history. Specifically, Harvey secured President George Bush, who had vetoed the Civil Rights Act of 1990, as the commencement speaker. Some protestors, including students, held signs mocking President Bush, who frequently exercised conservative political views when addressing race relations. Their anger heightened when President Bush expressed his support for school choice.

Harvey, for his part, was undaunted by all the hoopla. The establishment and maintenance of relationships with those able to provide support, especially financial, was a sine qua non for Harvey's development and expansion of Hampton. He and his staff developed a ''Hampton University Marketing Portfolio,'' and successfully enlisted corporations, foundations, and philanthropists, among other entities, in building Hampton's endowment and stature. He continues to concentrate on fund raising, developing friendships and networks, and locating prospective board of trustee members. Harvey also expects various schools of the university, through the deans and faculty, to contribute to fund raising through grant preparation. In 1984, Harvey announced that each school's dean was required to raise external funds sufficient to finance one–third of its annual operating budget. That same year, Hampton Institute was renamed Hampton University; the undergraduate college is still known as Hampton Institute.

These fund raising efforts, combined with other financial assistance, helped Hampton reach notable objectives and goals during Harvey's tenure; among these is the 1989 Hampton Harbor Project. This project benefitted from a $2.3 million grant from the U.S. Department of Housing and Urban Development. (Some governmental officials looked at this grant with askance, since the former secretary of HUD, Samuel R. Pierce, was a member of the Hampton Board of Trustees.) The Harbor Project opened in the fall of 1990 and now boasts a modern facade with 60,000 square feet of commercial space for rent, 246 two–bedroom apartments, and many other facilities. All of Hampton Harbors profits, over $1 million a year, are primarily used for Hampton student scholarships. The City of Hampton tax base also benefits from the harbor complex, as it does from the rest of the university.

Hampton has grown and developed significantly during Harvey's tenure. The budget has been balanced—with a surplus—each year since his arrival. A successful five–year,

$30 million fund–raising campaign yielded $46.4 million in two and one–half years. Hampton's current endowment is in excess of $100 million and another fund raising campaign is planned. The student enrollment grew from 2,700 students in 1978 to more than 6,000 in 1997–98, and the faculty has increased. SAT scores have risen over 300 points and programs and buildings have burgeoned. Some 33 new academic programs were added to the academic offerings; these include airway science, graduate programs in business administration, marine science, criminal justice, chemical and electrical engineering, emergency medical assistance management, museum studies, chemistry, a Ph.D. in physics program, applied mathematics, and a School of Pharmacy. Eleven new buildings, including the state–of–the–art Convocation Center, the Harvey Library, and the Olin Engineering Building have been added to Hampton's beautiful landscape. Moreover, over $20 million has been spent on campus renovation.

Harvey's endeavors extend beyond Hampton University and the city of Hampton. He initiates and supports programs to fight juvenile delinquency, truancy, and illiteracy. He developed a 1930s–like Civilian Conservation Corps, known as the Job Education Training (JET) Corps, in 1992. Students from the Hampton, Newport News, Williamsburg, and James City County, Virginia school districts participate in sessions designed to develop and strengthen understanding of reading, communication, mathematics, and health issues. JET participants spend their afternoons working at public work areas for 40 hours a week at minimum wage. Harvey established Hampton's Opportunity Program for Enhancement (HOPE) in 1989. This program admits African American males to Hampton University upon demonstration of potential, although they are not academically prepared for regular admission; each participant is awarded a $1,000 scholarship.

Service to the Hampton Roads community is also part of Harvey's efforts. He served as the first African American to chair the Virginia Peninsula United Way Campaign (1994), and helped raise $6.6 million—a new record. Harvey also hosted a 1995 celebrity luncheon for the Hampton Roads Chapter of the American Red Cross which raised over $17,000 for Disaster and Relief and Health Safety programs.

A "First" for Pepsi Cola

Harvey's service on governmental and corporate boards is extensive. He served on President Richard Nixon's National Presidential Advisory Council on Elementary and Secondary Education; President Gerald Ford's Defense Advisory Committee on Women in the Service, and the Fund for the Improvement of Post–secondary Education; President Ronald Reagan's Commission on Presidential Scholars; and President Bush's Advisory Board on Historically Black Colleges and the Advisory Board of the U.S. Department of Commerce Minority Economic Development Advisory Board. A partial listing of other past and current board memberships includes the Alumni Council of Harvard University, the Harvard University Cooperative Society, the National Merit Scholarship Corporation, the American Council of Education, University of Virginia, U.S. Air Force's Air University, Trigon Blue Cross Blue Shield of Virginia, International Guaranty Insurance Company, Signet Banking Corporation, and Knoxville College. He was selected as a Virginia Laureate Awardee and received honorary doctorates from Salisbury State University, Medaille College, and LeMoyne–Owen College. Additionally, Harvey serves on the board as chairman and president of the Pepsi–Cola Bottling Company of Houghton, Michigan. He purchased this franchise in 1986 and became the first African American to fully own a Pepsi–Cola Bottling Company franchise.

Harvey's family life includes his wife of more than 30 years, Norma Baker Harvey, of Martinsville, Virginia. The Harveys are the parents of Kelly Renee, William Christopher, and Leslie Denise. Harvey's family have watched him and Hampton grow to its current state and know his leadership style; a style represented by these statements in the *Virginia Daily Press* for March 28, 1993, attributed to Harvey: "I don't shrink from leadership, from adversity. . . . When the game gets on the line I want the ball. I want to take the shot."

Current address: Office of the President, Hampton University, Hampton, VA 23668.

REFERENCES

Adams, Jerry. "Minorities in Beverage Bottling Big Business." *Minorities and Women in Business* (November/December 1986): n.p.

"Confident Leader Drives HU to Top." *Virginia Daily Press,* March 28, 1993.

Dawson, Martha E. *Hampton University: A National Treasure—A Documentary History from 1978 to 1992.* Silver Spring, MD: Beckham House Publishers, 1994.

"Hampton University: Celebrating 125 Years—The Legacy Continues." *Virginia Daily Press,* Special Section, April 1, 1993.

Hampton University Highlights. Commemorative Issue (Commencement 1991); 12, No. 7, (1992); Special Edition (April 1993); 13, No. 4, (1993). Hampton, VA, Office of University Relations.

"Hampton University 125th Anniversary Scrapbook: 1868–1993—The Legacy Continues." Hampton University, Office of University Relations, n.d.

Hampton University President's Annual Report, 1987–1988; 1990–91; 1978–1993. Hampton, VA: Hampton University Press.

Harvey, William R. Interview with W. Braxter Wiggins, June 24, 1997; October 14, 1997.

———. "Internationalizing Education: An Imperative for the 1990's and Beyond." *Virginia Maritimer* (December/January 1990): 18, 20.

———. "A Vision for Our Time." Hampton, VA: Secretarial Services, 1993.

"Local Minority Firms Invited to Seek Business with Pepsi." *(Detroit) Michigan Chronicle,* May 22–28, 1991.

"Longtime Financial Goal Met at Hampton University: School's Endowment Reaches $100 Million." *Virginia Daily Press,* November 4, 1995.

Wash, Scott. "Money, Power and Education." *Port Folio Magazine: The Magazine of Hampton Roads* (18 February 1986): 3–7.
"White House Dinner." *Washington Post,* June 19, 1991.

W. Braxter Wiggins

William Henry Hastie
(1904–1976)
Jurist, educator, civil rights advocate, governor

Throughout his illustrious career, William H. Hastie was a central figure in social, political, and civil rights struggles of African Americans in the middle part of this century. He was the first black appointed to a federal bench. In 1937 he became U.S. district judge in the Virgin Islands, and in 1949 he became the first black to sit on the U.S. Court of Appeals. He was also the first black governor of the Virgin Islands. He was the architect of the Organic Act that protected the rights of people in the Virgin Islands. As an educator and dean, he prepared African American students for professional careers as lawyers. Hastie aided the National Association for the Advancement of Colored People (NAACP) in its fight to eliminate discriminatory salary schemes in the educational system. He also helped prepare lawsuits that set the foundation for the end of racial segregation in public education.

The grandson of slaves and an only child, William Hastie was born in Knoxville, Tennessee, in 1904. His father, William Henry Hastie, studied mathematics at Ohio Wesleyan Academy and pharmacy at Howard University but could not find a position as an actuary or pharmacist because of bigotry. Instead, he took a job in the United States Pension Bureau in Washington, D.C., becoming the first African American clerk appointed to the position. His mother, Roberta Childs, attended Lincoln Normal Institute, Fisk University, and Talladega College and became a teacher in Chattanooga, Tennessee. It was in Chattanooga that she met the senior Hastie. Education was important to the Hasties so the family moved to Washington, D.C., to provide their son with a better education. Hastie attended the renowned Dunbar High School in Washington, D.C., and graduated in 1921 with W. Montague Cobb and Charles Drew. The three entered Amherst that fall and concentrated on sports and scholarship, becoming members of the track team; Hastie became the team's captain. In 1925 he graduated Phi Beta Kappa and magna cum laude, turning down graduate fellowships to study at Oxford University or the University of Paris to become a teacher at the New Jersey Manual Training and Industrial School for Colored Youth, known as the Bordentown Manual Training School. Two years later, in 1927, he entered Harvard's law school where he studied under Felix Frankfurter and earned his law degree in

William Henry Hastie

1930. He returned to study for a doctorate of juridical science in 1933.

When Hastie graduated in the 1930s, out of approximately 150 thousand lawyers in the United States fewer than twelve hundred, less than one percent, were black. During this period African American attorneys in many southern communities could not enter a courtroom through the front door. Black lawyers risked their lives practicing law in the South, and they were not admitted to the bar. The bar application inquired about ethnicity, and individuals of African descent were automatically denied admission to the association. It was not until the 1960s that the American Bar Association began to admit non–whites.

After graduation William Hastie joined the prestigious black law firm of Houston and Houston in Washington, D.C. Hastie worked with his old friend Charles Hamilton Houston. Houston was ten years William Hastie's senior, and Hastie admired him. Quoted by Gilbert Ware, he said:

> Indeed . . . I followed his footsteps through college and law school, into the practice of law with him and his father, and into law teaching and, under his inspiration and leadership, into the struggle to correct the appalling racism of American law.

Hastie believed that Houston was undisturbed by racism until he enlisted in the service during World War I. After the war, according to Ware, he stated that Houston was a man "with a hatred for American Racism that he never wore on his sleeve but would always retain as a motivating force." Ware notes that after his military experience Houston, in Hastie's opinion, was "the effective leader of the essential first stage of the 20th century struggle to make the concept of America as a nation 'with liberty and justice for all,' a reality rather than a hypocritical platitude."

As an attorney, Hastie represented Thomas R. Hocutt, a student who applied for admission to the University of North Carolina School of Pharmacy but was denied admission on the basis of race. Cecil A. McCoy and Conrad O. Pearson also represented Hocutt. The white bar in attendance during the trial admired the black attorneys' bravery. Hastie's carriage in the courtroom was outstanding. Judge M. W. Barnhill, the jurist in the case, said the Holcutt case was the most brilliantly argued case he had heard in his 20 years as a judge. Faculty from the University of North Carolina talked about how Hastie showed up the attorney general that had been called in to try the case. Hastie was also the attorney in a case regarding equal pay for black teachers in North Carolina. In 1933, according to *Ebony* for September 1994, the NAACP announced that:

> A legal fight on the new salary schedules for Negro teachers in North Carolina will be waged.... It is the plan of the association to attack the unequal salary scale on the basis of its being a violation of the constitution.... William H. Hastie ... will go to North Carolina to lay plans for court action.

Begins Federal Career

William Hastie began his career in the federal government in 1933 as a solicitor for the Department of the Interior. His responsibilities in the department encompassed matters of race. Hastie, quiet and dignified, was also a jurist.

William Hastie contributed to the destruction of Jim Crow laws in the United States Armed Forces. Appointed by President Franklin D. Roosevelt as a civilian aide to the secretary of war, Henry L. Stimson, Hastie resigned the post in protest over the continued separation of black and white soldiers. Many agreed that his deed, the first of its kind by such a high–ranking black official, increased the pressure to integrate the military.

While a lawyer with the Department of Interior, Hastie wrote the Organic Act of 1936 along with a staff of lawyers and legislators from the Virgin Islands. The legislation facilitated the Virgin Islands' political transition from Danish Colonial Law and gave Virgin Islanders basic American rights.

Prior to the Organic Act, the Supreme Court ruled that the U.S. Constitution did not require a grant of full citizenship rights to people of incorporated territories such as the Virgin Islands. Ware wrote in *William Hastie,* "Congress enjoyed complete command over them." The mandate Hastie and others created helped to clarify any suspicion about democracy and empire in American territories.

The Organic Act also abolished property and income requirements for voting, and extended the franchise to women and men who were able to read and write English and were citizens of the United States. This clause of the act increased the percentage of Virgin Islanders who were eligible to vote and complimented Hastie's belief that blacks had to vote to share the principal means of control over government. Quoting Hastie, Ware wrote, "Nothing ... reveals the essence of democracy as does the history of black suffrage: 'Its essence is eternal struggle.'"

In 1936 Harold Ickes, secretary of the interior, submitted Hastie's name to President Franklin D. Roosevelt. Ickes nominated Hastie for a seat on the United States District Court in the Virgin Islands. Ware notes Ickes's description of Hastie:

> He has more than made good [as an assistant solicitor].... He is not only an excellent lawyer but a man of fine character and sensibilities who, in my judgement, is qualified to be judge of any United States District Court anywhere.

Hastie, aware of the seat on the Court, had not considered himself a candidate for the position. According to Ware, Hastie had discussed the vacancy with Charles Houston asking, "Upon whom could we concentrate as a candidate to be pushed?"

Ickes also recommended Hastie to Homer S. Cummings, the attorney general, who opposed the appointment of a "colored continental" to the Virgin Islands. Cummings successfully held up the nomination for months until February 5, 1937, when the president sent the nomination to the Senate.

Hastie's appointment encountered additional opposition in the United States Senate. William H. King, a senator from Utah, opposed the nomination despite promises not to interfere with the appointment. Like Cummings, he contended that native Virgin Islanders did not want a "colored man" in that position. According to Ware, the senator doubted that Hastie could maintain "a judicial point of view" regarding interactions between black islanders and the government. King also questioned Hastie's skills in the courtroom. Millard E. Tidings, senator from Maryland, also resisted Hastie's appointment. He backed down after Ickes sent a black member of his staff to Tiding's black constituents in Maryland. They wrote letters, sent telegrams, and generally protested against his disagreement with Hastie's appointment. William H. Hastie was confirmed on March 19, 1937.

Among those who supported Hastie during the hearings were Thurgood Marshall of the National Bar Association; William L. Houston, president of the Washington D.C. Bar Association; Victor H. Caniel, a native Virgin Islander; and Rufus G. Poole Hasties, a white colleague at the Department of the Interior. His mother and wife gave him moral support during this trying period. Hastie served as Federal District Judge in the Virgin Islands from 1937 to 1939.

Halfway through his term William Hastie resigned his federal position and became dean of the law school at Howard University. The following year, in 1940, Hastie moved to yet another post. He was appointed civilian aide to the secretary of war. Franklin D. Roosevelt, who was seeking an unheard–of third term, appointed him to the civilian aide post in the army. The jurist began his new position on November 1, 1940. He hesitated before he took the job because, in his own words, cited by Ware:

> I was reluctant not because of any lack of interest or because it was not an important area, but I was rather skeptical as to what [could be done by] a person with no authority of his own whom I was sure the military did not want serving in the Secretary's office.

Thurgood Marshall assisted Hastie in making the decision to take the job. Marshall reminded Hastie that there was no problem as long as the War Department understood that his purpose in becoming a magistrate was to fight against racial discrimination in the armed services. On December 18, 1940, an order went out to the chiefs of staffs and services and the general staff. According to *Ebony* for September of 1994, it said that "matters of policy which pertain to Negroes, or important questions arising thereunder, will be referred to Judge William H. Hastie, civilian aide to the Secretary of War, for comment or concurrence before final action." Hastie noted that the Secretary of War's letter of appointment omitted a commitment to integration within the armed forces. As a result, he immediately announced his intention to fight discrimination in the armed forces.

Judge Hastie resigned the civilian post in January of 1943 over the army's hostility and unwillingness to integrate its ranks. Correspondence from Colonel John R. Deane, secretary in the Office of the Chief of Staff, may have helped to spur his resignation. The colonel said in his letter, cited in the *New Yorker* for November 12, 1984:

> The intermingling of the races in messing and housing would not only be a variation from well established policies of the [War] department, but it does not accord with the existing customs of the country as a whole.

Hastie won some battles before he left the Armed Forces. He persuaded the Secretary of War to send the army's first black fighter squadron to Liberia, where they could play a larger role in the air war, and he convinced the American Red Cross to accept blood from blacks. The Red Cross, however, continued to label the blood black and white. When asked about his resignation, the jurist said he knew he had a job at Howard University waiting and that, as reported in *Ebony,* he did it "because I wasn't faced with hunger." Many viewed his act as courageous and believed he destroyed his career when he resigned. His letter of resignation, published in *Ebony,* included the following:

> Further retrogression is now so apparent [in the Air Forces] and recent occurrences are so objectionable and inexcusable that I have no alternative but to resign in protest and to give public expression to my views.

On January 31 when his resignation became effective, Hastie wrote several articles condemning the discriminatory policies of the military, especially the Air Force. The articles were published in a pamphlet in 1943 called *On Clipped Wings.* Upon his return to Howard University, Hastie assisted in preparing a successful legal campaign for the NAACP.

Joins Black Cabinet

Hastie received the Spingarn Medal from the NAACP in 1943 for his outstanding contribution "to the advancement of the Negro status." As a member of Franklin Roosevelt's "Black Cabinet," which included Robert C. Weaver, Robert Vann, Eugene Kinckle Jones, Mary McLeod Bethune, Lawrence Oxley, Edgar Browne, Frank Horne, and William Trent, he helped to form policies to help blacks progress in many areas, including housing and education. Unlike earlier black presidential cabinets, Hastie's group received paid appointments within the federal government.

In 1946 after a recommendation from an old friend, Harold Ickes, secretary of the interior, Hastie once again became a candidate for a government post. This time he was under consideration to succeed Charles Harwood as the first black governor of the Virgin Islands. At the time Hastie was the vice president of the Washington Committee for the Southern Conference on Human Welfare, the Washington Committee for the Community Planning, and the National Lawyers Guild. He had been chairman of the NAACP's legal committee and an editor of the *National Bar Journal* and the *Lawyers Guild Review.* He had been on the President's Caribbean Advisory Committee since 1942.

Hastie was questioned extensively by a subcommittee of the Senate Committee on Territorial and Insular Affairs, which opened hearings on his nomination. During the hearings, says Ware, he described himself as "a voteless resident of the District of Columbia, and I don't have any party affiliation." He also said, "I think that the American Constitution and laws are one of the great landmarks in world progress and in government, and I shall certainly hope and anticipate that we shall continue to be just that." After the "rather vigorous fight," as Hastie described the dispute over the nomination, the Senate confirmed him on May 1, 1946.

Hastie's tenure as governor extended for three years. During this period he helped to bring out the black vote for Harry S. Truman. After the election, President Truman asked Hastie what he wanted for his work in the presidential campaign. Hastie asked that Ralph J. Bunche be assistant secretary of state. However, Bunche declined the offer because he did not want to expose his family to Washington's racism and he thought he would be of greater service if he remained in the United Nations. Hastie did not ask a reward for himself. President Truman, nevertheless, nominated Hastie for a seat on the United States Court of Appeals. In October of 1949 he became the first black to sit on the bench of a U.S. Circuit Court of Appeals, which had jurisdiction for Pennsylvania, Delaware, New Jersey, and the Virgin Islands. Eventually, he became chief judge of the Circuit Court. He ended many years of public service on June 2, 1971, at the age of 66, when he retired from the bench in Philadelphia.

William H. Hastie died at Suburban General Hospital in East Norriton at the age of seventy–one. He served twenty–

one years on the appellate court, three of them as chief judge. He took the title of Senior Judge when he retired. He was awarded a number of honorary college and university degrees throughout his career, and he served as a trustee to Amherst College and Temple University.

Hastie was married to the former Beryl Lockhart. Their children, William H. Jr. and Karen Williams, are both lawyers. He had one granddaughter.

After he retired, Hastie, in a speech before the sixty–second annual convention of the NAACP, said the trend for blacks to "accept and encourage racial separatism as a desirable and potentially rewarding way of American life" must be halted. He believed this trend "can only lead to greater bitterness and frustration and to an even more inferior status than black Americans now experience." His speech also implied that young black and white Americans had become distrustful of the values of white society and emphasized that many in black society were absorbing and mimicking the destructive values of white society. He reminded the audience that it would not help black America to assume the worst traits of white America, suggesting that separatist goals would only keep the races further apart.

In essence, Hastie's speech remained consistent with his life's work: an attempt to bring integration, equality, and justice to all Americans.

REFERENCES

"Chronicles of Black Courage." *Ebony* 49 (September 1994): 72–78.

"He, Too, Spoke for Democracy." *Journal of Southern History* 55 (August 1989): 517–18.

"Judge. Exhibit at Harvard Law School Commemorating W. H. Hastie." *New Yorker* 60 (12 November 1984): 42–44.

"Judge William Hastie, 71, of Federal Court, Dies." *New York Times,* April 15, 1976.

McGuire, Philip. *He, Too, Spoke for Democracy.* New York: Greenwood Press, 1988.

"Public Interest Stirs Law Drive." *New York Times,* March 19, 1975.

"Rutgers Aide Traces 'Black Cabinet'." *New York Times,* October 28, 1973.

"Separatism Deplored by a Black Jurist." *New York Times,* July 8, 1971.

"Two Federal Judges Retire." *New York Times,* January 19, 1971.

[Untitled article.] *New York Times,* June 3, 1971.

Ware, Gilbert. *William Hastie: Grace Under Pressure.* New York: Oxford University Press, 1984.

COLLECTIONS

The William Hastie Papers are in the library of the Harvard Law School. Related collections are the Beck Cultural Exchange Center at the University of Tennessee, and at Howard University.

Mario A. Charles

Augustus F. Hawkins

(1907–)

Politician, Congressman

A soft spoken, articulate man whose service as a legislator in state and federal government spanned the years from 1935 to 1991, August F. Hawkins devoted his energy to issues of civil rights: employment, education, child care, housing, slum clearance, and age discrimination. In the California Assembly, and as the first black member of the House of Representatives from the Western part of the country, he was elected from districts populated by African Americans, Asian Americans, Mexican Americans, and white Americans, including Watts, the center of violent protests and rioting in 1965.

Augustus Hawkins, son of Nyanza Hawkins, a pharmacist, and Hattie Freemam Hawkins, was born in Shreveport, Louisiana, on August 31, 1907. Augustus, the youngest of five children, was ten when his father sold his business and moved the family to Los Angeles. The boy inherited the light complexion of his paternal grandfather, an Englishman, and grew into a handsome man, five feet, five inches tall, often mistaken for white. He worked in a drug store and in the post office during his high school years, and as a janitor in the girls' gymnasium when he studied at the University of California at Los Angeles (UCLA) for a B.A. degree in economics which he earned in 1931.

Hawkins's original intention was to enter graduate school at UCLA to prepare for a career in civil engineering, but the lack of sufficient financial support made it more attractive to take classes in the Institute of Government of the University of Southern California while he worked in the real estate business he set up with his brother, Edward. Before long, his increasing interest in the plight of minorities in his area led to political ventures in support of Upton Sinclair's unsuccessful campaign for governor of California and Franklin Delano Roosevelt's candidacy that ended with election to his first term as president of the United States in 1932.

First Political Office

In 1935 Hawkins won a seat in the California Assembly by defeating another African American, Frederick Roberts, longtime assemblyman. Contrary to his campaign rhetoric that Roberts's sixteen years in the assembly was too long, Hawkins's tenure stretched into more than a quarter of a century—from 1935 to 1962—and became the stepping stone to identical longevity in the United States Congress.

As an assemblyman, Hawkins was an influential figure in Sacramento, California's capital, sponsoring laws that reflected his concern about the status of the ethnic minorities in his district and working people in the state. Although he initiated or coauthored more than a hundred other laws, he is best remembered in the state for the five years of struggle leading to the passage of the Hawkins Fair Employment

Practices Act, signed in 1959. Hawkins used his willingness to work hard and his innate capabilities to chair powerful assembly committees that dealt with unemployment, labor and capital, rules, and public utilities.

When Hawkins went from the California Assembly to the U.S. House of Representatives in 1963, he was spokesman for the same constituency he had in the government of California, and brought to Washington his valuable legislative experience. Hawkins hoped that he could bring about more meaningful, more widespread changes at the federal level than in a state house. In April of 1970 Hawkins was cosponsor of the Elementary and Secondary Education Act, which improved the quality of education for children from lower income families and set guidelines for the antidiscrimination provisions of the 1964 Civil Rights Act. When Hawkins chaired the powerful House Education and Labor Committee, his charge was to monitor existing programs and provide legislation and funding for their operation at a time of severe budget cuts proposed by the Reagan administration. He opposed president Reagan's cuts in social programs, such as financial aid to students, grants to educational institutions, unemployment insurance, funds for school lunches, and job training. Hawkins's greatest success in the House was passage of the Humphrey–Hawkins Full Employment Bill in 1978.

Throughout his years in Congress, Hawkins pointed to failures in federal action. He emphasized that unemployment, lack of adequate education, and the sense of isolation among financially distressed people were the chief causes of disruptive behavior that effects the population as a whole. Over and over he pleaded for tax reform and encouraged citizens to be involved in the workings of their government at the grassroots level. He openly voiced dissatisfaction with military spending coupled with continued mistreatment of African American veterans returning from Vietman. A survey he requested confirmed that of five hundred and twenty–three higher–level positions in the Pentagon, only three were held by African Americans, and none were involved in decision making. During the war in Vietnam, Hawkins and William R. Anderson, Tennessee Representative, by their protest to President Richard M. Nixon, caused an immediate correction of the inhumane treatment of civilians in a prison in South Vietnam.

When Congressman Hawkins announced his plans to retire in January of 1991, he did so anticipating passage of the civil rights legislation that was ultimately signed on November 21 of that year. This was a fitting reward for a man whose sole purpose in public life was to better conditions for people without the means or the knowledge to take action for themselves. In retirement, he lives in Washington, D.C., engaged in tasks that mirror his tenure as an elected official. With characteristic energy, he now spends more time as director of the Hawkins Family Memorial Foundation for Educational Research and Development he founded in 1969. Supported by members of congress and educational institutions, the foundation formulates and implements policies aimed at more effective education of young people in preparation for employment. Such employment increases the chances for adult to be productive free from the problems that beset large numbers of minorities. No longer bound to the demanding and often unpredictable schedules in state and federal government, Hawkins maintains active membership in the NAACP and the Masonic Lodge. The widespread esteem felt for the Representative is shown by the honorary doctorates conferred upon him by twelve universities in states all over the country.

REFERENCES

Christopher, Maurine. *America's Black Congressmen.* New York: Thomas Y. Crowell Company, 1971.

Hawkins, Augustus F. Interview by Clyde Woods. "Black Leadership in Los Angeles" Oral History Project. University of California, Los Angeles, 1992, 1993.

"Hawkins Awaits Fate of Civil Rights Bill As His 28–Year Career Ends." *Jet* 78 (1 October 1990): 29.

"Hawkins Presents Papers." *Jet* 89 (29 April 1996): 22.

Pollock, Michael. "Social Spending: Gus Hawkins for the Defense." *Business Week* 2883 (March 4, 1985): 56.

COLLECTIONS

The Augustus Hawkins congressional papers are deposited in the UCLA Research Library's Department of Special Collections.

Dona L. Irvin

Robert E. Hayden
(1913–1980)
Poet, educator, editor

Through his meticulously crafted and highly thoughtful poetry, Robert Hayden explored human dilemmas, typically, but not always, in the context of race. He was a college professor throughout his career, doing most of his work at Fisk University in Nashville, Tennessee, and at the University of Michigan at Ann Arbor. In 1966 he won the Grand Prix de la Poésie at the First World Festival of Negro Arts in Dakar, Senegal. In 1976 he was appointed consultant to the Library of Congress of the United States, the first African American poet so honored.

Robert Earl Hayden was born August 4, 1913, in Detroit, Michigan. On June 10, 1940 he married Erma Inez Morris, a musician who had studied piano at Julliard. Their daughter, Maia, was born on October 5, 1942. He was raised by foster parents, William and Sue Hayden. His biological parents were Ruth Finn and Asa Sheffey. Asa Sheffey was a laborer. The Sheffeys had divorced by the time their son was born. Originally named Asa Bundy Sheffey, Robert occasionally visited each of the Sheffeys while he was growing up, especially his mother, who lived near and, at times, with the

Robert E. Hayden

Haydens. Although she was not educated herself, Ruth Sheffey supported her son's ambitions. She was a vivacious woman, a contrast to her son's foster family. William Hayden, a laborer, was a strict Baptist fundamentalist. Sue Hayden was less austere in manner and outlook than her husband. Although they were not highly educated, the Haydens did the best they could for young Robert. The family lived in an environment of poverty and danger in Paradise Valley, the ironic name for their Detroit inner–city community. Robert Hayden recalled in *Collected Prose* that in Paradise Valley, along with the "violence, ugliness, and cruelty,. . .there were people who retained. . .a sheltering spiritual beauty and dignity—my mother and my foster father among them—despite sordid and disheartening circumstances."

Very nearsighted even as a boy, Hayden was introverted, spending much of his time reading. He enjoyed playing the violin until he had to give it up because of his vision problems. Because of his weak eyesight, he transferred from the inner city's predominantly black Miller High School to predominantly white Northern High School where there were resources to assist students with visual problems.

Hayden's high school graduation from Northern in 1930 coincided with the beginning of the Great Depression, and the family had no money to send him to college. Unable to find work, he took some courses at Cass Technical High School, and in 1932, he entered Detroit City College (now Wayne State University) where he majored in Spanish. Although he left the college when he was just one semester hour short of graduation in 1936, he subsequently returned and received his B.A. in 1942.

From 1936 to 1938, Hayden worked as a researcher and writer with the Detroit unit of the Federal Writers' Project of the Works Progress Administration (WPA). Pontheolla Williams noted in *Robert Hayden: A Critical Analysis of His Poetry* that he "completed. . .[essays] on the anti–slavery activities in Detroit and. . .in Illinois" and that he "supervise[d] research into local history and folklore." In addition to providing him a livelihood during the Depression, the research proved relevant to Hayden's poetry, for he often meditated on the implications of historical figures and events. The experience also enabled him to learn more about other black writers affiliated with the WPA, notably Richard Wright, although unlike Wright, Hayden was not drawn to Marxist thought.

Hayden took some graduate courses at the University of Michigan in Ann Arbor during the summer of 1938. In 1942 he began full time graduate study there, and in 1944, he received his Master's degree. Hayden was a teaching assistant at the University of Michigan from 1944 to 1946, and from 1946 to 1969 he taught at Fisk University. After a brief period at the University of Louisville, he returned to the University of Michigan, his home base for the rest of his career. He held visiting appointments at the University of Washington, the University of Connecticut, Connecticut College, Indiana State University, and Denison University in Ohio.

In his youth, Hayden had joined his foster father's church, Second Baptist, but in 1943, he became a member of the Baha'i faith. In a 1977 interview in *Collected Prose,* Hayden explained the meshing of Baha'i tenets and his own beliefs. He wrote:

> I believe in the oneness of all people and I believe in the basic unity of all religions. I don't believe that races are important. I'm very suspicious of any form of ethnicity or nationalism; I think that these things are very crippling and are very divisive. These are all Baha'i points of view, and my work grows out of this vision.

Develops as a Writer

Hayden had become interested in writing while he was still in elementary school. Williams wrote that "he tried to rewrite the stories of plays and movies he had seen" and that while still in high school, he won an award for a short story entitled "Gold." He developed an interest in modern poetry as a teenager; he was especially drawn to Countee Cullen's work. Hayden's poem "Africa," published by *Abbott's Monthly* in 1931, is reminiscent of Cullen's "Heritage." According to *Collected Prose,* in 1941 Hayden met Cullen, who knew of his work and praised it during their conversation. Earlier, in the 1930s, Hayden had been thrilled to meet Langston Hughes, who read some of his poetry and encouraged him to find his own voice. Although the response dampened his spirits at the time, Hayden later recognized the accuracy and helpfulness of Hughes's critique.

As an apprentice volume, *Heart–Shape in the Dust* (1940) reflects Hughes's assessment. Even so, Hayden's merit as a poet was discernible, for the volume won the 1938 Jules and Avery Hopwood summer award at the University of Michigan. Hayden won another Hopwood award for ''The Black Spear,'' a poetry collection which to date has not been published. As a graduate student, Hayden was taught by W. H. Auden, who was a visiting professor at the University of Michigan. Hayden characterized the experience in *Collected Prose* as a marvelous one in that Auden's erudition and stimulation made him a memorable teacher. The two men subsequently maintained a warm, though not close, relationship.

Hayden received a Julius Rosenwald Fellowship in Creative Writing in 1947, during which time he worked on poems published in *The Lion and the Archer* (1948). The volume features six poems by Hayden and six by Myron O'Higgins. O'Higgins, a consultant and researcher at Fisk, had a Rosenwald Fellowship also. *The Lion* contains ''A Ballad of Remembrance,'' which became the title poem in a later volume. The cover art was provided by one of Hayden's students, William Demby, who was attending Fisk as a World War II veteran and who later became famous in his own right as a novelist. Hayden's next volume, *Figure of Time: Poems* (1955), consists of 14 poems: 11 new ones and three reprints. The work is illustrated by Aaron Douglas, who had come to prominence for his murals during the Harlem Renaissance and was on the faculty at Fisk.

Both *The Lion and the Archer* and *Figure of Time* were published by Hemphill Press, a small black press in Nashville. The volumes were part of the Counterpoise Series at Fisk, a project for which Hayden edited four books. The introductory leaflet to the series reflects Hayden's emphases in that it expresses opposition ''to the chauvinistic, the cultish, to special pleading, to all that seeks to limit and restrict creative expression.'' In phrasing consistent with Baha'i beliefs, the statement supports ''the oneness of mankind and the importance of the arts in the struggle for peace and unity,'' as noted in *Collected Prose.*

A Ballad of Remembrance (1962) contains some of Hayden's best known poems. ''Middle Passage,'' revised from earlier versions, is a key example. The poem focuses on the Amistad rebellion, in which Africans being brought to the Caribbean took over the ship meant to take them to slavery and eventually won their freedom in a United States court. The poem is a collage of types of materials, including journals, depositions, and hymns. A refrain characterizes the middle passage as a ''voyage through death/ to life upon these shores.'' Other often anthologized poems from the volume are ''O Daedalus Fly Away Home'' and ''Frederick Douglass,'' as well as ''Home to the Empress of the Blues,'' a tribute to Bessie Smith.

A section of *Ballad* draws on Hayden's time in Mexico, where he was based in 1954 and 1955, having received a Ford Foundation Fellowship. The sojourn enabled Hayden to draw on his earlier study of Spanish. Another section of the volume draws on childhood memories in poems such as ''The Whipping,'' ''Those Winter Sundays,'' and ''Summertime and the Living.'' *Ballad* was first published in London and then by the American firm October House as *Selected Poems* in 1966. ''Runagate Runagate,'' Hayden's stirring tribute to Harriet Tubman and the Underground Railroad, had been published earlier, but it was revised for *Selected Poems.*

Taken together, *A Ballad* and *Selected Poems* mark Hayden's maturity as a poet. The change in publishers and the international dimensions of publication also widened Hayden's audience. In 1966, *A Ballad of Remembrance* was awarded the Grand Prix de la Poésie at the First World Festival of Negro Arts in Dakar, Senegal. In the same year, Hayden was named poet laureate of Senegal.

Despite the accolades and greater fame in the sixties, Hayden was also subjected to negative criticism. At the Black Writer's Conference held at Fisk in 1966, Hayden was castigated by many of the conferees as the author of poems which were too erudite and too removed from political and social activism. The conference had been organized by John O. Killens, then writer–in–residence at Fisk. Hayden compared the experience at the Fisk conference to the criticism he received in college when he read his poems before the John Reed Club. There, according to *Collected Prose,* ''he was scathingly criticized for his lack of political awareness. And he was often accused of being too much the individualist and not willing to submit to ideology.'' In any case, the Fisk conference experience was painful. In 1969 Hayden resigned from the university.

Williams characterized Hayden's next volume *Words in the Mourning Time* (1970) as ''a cathartic work, his poetic response to the Fisk confrontation with the black militants, an affirmation of his humanism, and the rejection of what he sees as evil.'' The volume contains Hayden's tribute to Malcolm X, ''El–Hajj Malik El–Shabazz.'' The opening lines show Hayden's ''rejection of evil'' as well as his attention to central issues of the African American experience. In accessible, economical use of language, Hayden declares: ''The icy evil that struck his father down / and ravished his mother into madness / trapped him in violence of a punished self / Struggling to break free.'' The title poem in the volume ponders the meaning of the deaths of Martin Luther King and Robert Kennedy, and it mourns ''for America, self–destructive, self–betrayed.''

Hayden's other volumes are *The Night Blooming Cereus* (1972), *Angle of Ascent : New and Selected Poems* (1975), and *American Journal* (1978 and 1982). These works continue to demonstrate his maturity of thought and his concise crafting of language. The title, *American Journal,* for example, refers to the report of an extraterrestrial trying to discern American values. The alien observes that he will ''disguise myself in order to study them unobserved / adapting their varied pigmentations white black / red brown yellow the imprecise and strangering / distinctions by which they live by which they / justify their cruelties to one another.'' *American Journal* also includes ''The Snow Lamp,'' which focuses on Matthew Henson and his exploration of the North Pole, and ''Letter from Phillis Wheatley,'' which draws on Wheatley's letters to her black friend Obour.

Hayden was also a critic and editor. He wrote the preface to the reissue of Alain Locke's *The New Negro,* reissued by

Atheneum in 1968. He edited *Kaleidoscope: Poems by American Negro Poets* (1967), and for many years, he was the poetry editor for *World Order,* the Baha'i magazine. He collaborated with James E. Miller and Robert O'Neal in editing many Scott Foresman publications, including *American Models: A Collection of Modern Stories* (1973), *Person Place and Point of View: Factual Prose for Interpretation and Extension* (1974), *The Lyric Potential* (1974), and *The Human Condition: Literature Written in the English Language.* Another of Hayden's co–edited works, with David J. Burrows and Frederick Lapides, is *Afro–American Literature: An Introduction* (1971).

The city of Detroit recognized Hayden in 1969 for distinguished achievement by presenting him the Mayor's Bronze Medal. In 1970 he received an award from the National Institute of Letters for distinguished achievement in poetry. In 1975 he was elected a Fellow of the American Academy of Poets. This prestigious national honor was followed by another: his appointment as a consultant in poetry to the Library of Congress. He served two terms as consultant, 1976–77 and 1977–78. He was the first African American poet to hold the Library of Congress post.

Hayden held honorary degrees from Grand Valley State College in Allendale, Michigan, Brown University, Benedict College in Columbia, South Carolina, Wayne State University, and Fisk University. On January 4, 1980, he was among a group of American poets honored by President Jimmy Carter and Mrs. Carter at the White House. Hayden was too ill to attend a celebration held in his honor in Ann Arbor on February 24, 1980. He died the next day.

Although he saw the relevance of race to the human condition, Hayden refused to be limited in his subject matter. At the same time, he understood and demonstrated that poems on a racial theme inherently deal with the human condition. In an interview with John O'Brien for *Interviews With Black Writers,* Hayden summarized his philosophy. ''I am convinced,'' he said, ''that if poets have any calling. . .beyond the attempt to produce viable poems—and that in itself is more than enough—it is to affirm the humane, the universal, the potentially divine in the human creature.'' Hayden affirmed that calling unequivocally.

REFERENCES

Harris, Trudier, ed. *Afro–American Writers, 1940–1955.* Detroit: Gale Research, 1988.

Hatcher, John. *From the Auroral Darkness: The Life and Poetry of Robert Hayden.* Oxford, England: George Ronald, 1984.

Hayden, Robert. *American Journal.* New York: Liveright, 1982.

———. *Angle of Ascent: New and Selected Poems.* New York: Liveright, 1975.

———. *Collected Prose.* Edited by Frederick Glaysher. Ann Arbor: University of Michigan Press, 1984.

———. *Words in the Mourning Time.* New York: October House, 1970.

———, ed. *Kaleidoscope: Poems by American Negro Poets.* New York: Harcourt Brace Jovanovich, 1967.

Nicholas, Xavier, ed. ''Robert Hayden and Michael S. Harper: A Literary Friendship.'' *Callaloo* 17 (Fall 1994): 975–1016.

O'Brien, John, ed. *Interviews with Black Writers.* New York: Liveright, 1973.

Williams, Pontheolla T. *Robert Hayden: A Critical Analysis of His Poetry.* Urbana: University of Illinois Press, 1987.

COLLECTIONS

Robert Hayden's papers are at the National Baha'i Archives in Wilmette, Illinois.

Arlene Clift–Pellow

Roland Hayes

(1887–1977)

Concert tenor, arranger, voice instructor

Roland Hayes was a pioneer in removing racial barriers for ''singers of color'' throughout the world, encouraging and supporting younger artists such as Marian Anderson, Dorothy Maynor, and Paul Robeson. An outstanding vocal communicator, he was a recitalist and orchestral soloist of the highest order. F. W. Woolsey, in *The Black Perspective in Music,* wrote, ''Hayes was the only concert attraction [black or white] who could fill Carnegie Hall and Symphony Hall in Boston three times a season.'' His accomplishments and achievements were the result of hard work, perseverance, and faith in himself. Small in stature, Hayes was a giant in spirit. With his amazing vocal technique and spiritual singing quality, he would close his eyes, clasp his hands, and woo any audience.

Born in Curryville, Georgia, on June 3, 1887, in a cabin on the plantation where his mother had been a slave, Roland Wiltse Hayes was one of six sons and a daughter born to William and Fanny Hayes. His father, a sharecropper and a former slave as well, died when Hayes was 11 years old. Consequently, the boy spent most of his time working in the fields, only occasionally attending the poor country school for blacks.

After their father's death, Hayes and his brothers moved to Chattanooga, Tennessee, where he was a member of an African American youth quartet that sang for nickels and dimes at the train station. Factory work was his main source of income. At age 15, he met the African American pianist Arthur Calhoun, an Oberlin Conservatory student. Calhoun shared with Hayes his theoretical knowledge and introduced him to a white gentleman with a large collection of operatic recordings, including those of famed tenor Enrico Caruso. He

Roland Hayes

recognized Hayes's vocal abilities and encouraged him to pursue a career in music despite his mother's objections. Hayes set out for Oberlin but ran out of money in Nashville. He therefore enrolled at Fisk University, entering the preparatory department. Although he was 20, he was forced to enter the sixth grade.

Tuition, room, and board while at Fisk were earned by Hayes's work as a house boy and later as a butler. Through a misunderstanding, Hayes was dismissed from the school. Given no definite reason for such action, Hayes speculated that it was because he often sang for clubs and organizations, without requesting prior approval from the music department. Following the Fisk years, he lived and worked in Louisville, Kentucky, as a waiter at the exclusive Pendennis Club and sang arias at the Fourth Street movie theater. He also sang frequently at local black churches.

In 1911 Hayes was asked to join the Jubilee Singers—at that time a Fisk quartet—in Boston. (The Jubilee Singers and Fisk's music department were separate entities.) He remained in Boston after the other singers departed, studying with the noted basso Arthur J. Hubbard. While in the area, he studied academic subjects at Harvard University's extension school, supporting himself by working as a hotel bellboy and as a messenger for the Hancock Life Insurance Company.

Professional Career Launched

Hayes was ready for public appearances on a larger scale and in 1916 launched into four years of touring within the United States. According to Eileen Southern in *Biographical Dictionary of Afro–American and African Musicians,* Hayes appeared at concerts by black violinist Walter Craig in New York City, at Colored Musical Festival Concerts in Atlanta sponsored by black music patron Henry Hugh Proctor, and programs at black churches, colleges, and organizations throughout the south and east.

In 1917 Hayes dared to rent Boston's Symphony Hall for a recital, a first for an African American. He paid the $800 rental fee in advance, managing the concert himself. This was only the beginning of a stellar career—he enjoyed one success after another. But he could not secure a manager, most believing that the public would not support a black concert artist.

Hayes left for London in 1920, remaining there for five years. He studied German lieder (art songs) with composer, conductor, and song interpreter Sir George Henschel. One year following his arrival, he sang a command performance for King George V and Queen Mary at Buckingham Palace. This appearance resulted in a series of successes in Great Britain and throughout Europe. Of particular interest is the article "Roland Hayes in London, 1921" by Britisher Jeffrey P. Green that appeared in the Spring 1982 issue of *The Black Perspective in Music.*

A managerial contract was not difficult to secure upon his return from Europe. William Brennan, manager of the Boston Symphony, accepted the assignment. According to Warren Marr II, writing in *Crisis* 81:

> During the first year under that contract, Hayes sang thirty recitals. In his second year, he did 125, and southern managers had begun to complain that they had been left out. Soon he was singing in Birmingham, in Atlanta, and elsewhere across the South—always to unsegregated audiences.

Marr also noted that Hayes sang several concerts at Washington, D.C.'s Constitution Hall, to sold–out, non–segregated audiences several years prior to the incident involving Marian Anderson and the Daughters of the American Revolution (DAR). In 1939, the DAR denied Anderson permission to perform at the hall because of her race. A strong public outcry resulted in Anderson's appearance on the steps of the Lincoln Memorial in the nation's capital on Easter Sunday before an audience of 75,000.

Wins International Acclaim

Hayes was well–respected by the world's great performers—including the Spanish cellist Pablo Casals, English harpsichordist Myra Hess, and Fritz Kreisler, the Austrian violinist—all acquaintances established in Europe. It was Kreisler who urged Pierre Monteux, conductor of the Boston Symphony, to arrange an appearance of Hayes with the orchestra in 1923, another first for a person of African descent.

Hayes was the first of his race to receive international acclaim as a lieder singer, but he was also committed to the music of his people. *Current Biography* documented his feelings: "The Negro has his God–given music to bring to the sum total of good in the world. His future lies in the recognition of his heritage, the preservation of the songs of his fathers.''

Hayes married Helen Alzada Mann in 1932. They had one daughter, Afrika Fanzada. A dramatic soprano, she occasionally performed with her father and in the early 1960s was a member of the voice faculty of North Carolina Central College (now University).

Hayes's life was documented by Mackinley Helm in a biography entitled *Angel Mo' and Her Son,* published in 1942. The story is told in the first person, Roland Hayes speaking. His anthology of 30 African American spirituals was released in 1948, under the title *My Songs: Aframerican Religious Folk Songs Arranged and Interpreted by Roland Hayes.*

Throughout much of his professional life, the celebrated tenor continued to study: in London with Amanda Ira Aldridge (also known as Montague Ring and daughter of Shakespearean actor Ira Aldridge), with Theodore Lierhammer in Vienna, and with Gabriel Fauré, the famous French composer, in Paris. The consummate student became a university professor in 1950, when he joined the voice faculty of Boston University.

Hayes sang with leading orchestras in London, Paris, Amsterdam, Berlin, and Vienna, in addition to the principal orchestras in the USA. He was a leading tenor on two continents for more than half a century. His recital programs were ambitious, adventurous, and always accessible. A typical program would contain songs by Scarlatti, Monteverdi, Handel, Mozart, Beethoven, Schubert, Berlioz, Debussy, Saint–Saens, and a cycle of Negro work songs.

Two unfortunate incidents remained prominent in Hayes's memory. The first came when he faced a hostile audience in Germany at the end of World War I and was confronted by hissing upon the sight of an American black. Hayes patiently waited 20 minutes for silence, then sang Schubert's ''Du Bist Die Ruh.'' The result was overwhelming. The second came during the summer of 1942, when his wife was arrested in Rome, Georgia, near Hayes's birthplace. She and her daughter sat in an area reserved for whites. When her husband arrived to rectify the situation, he too was jailed and was beaten as well by the local police. According to *Current Biography,* upon his release he announced, ''I am not bitter toward anyone, and the humiliation is all on the other side. I am truly ashamed that this should happen in my native State. I love Georgia.''

On the occasion of his 50th anniversary on the concert stage, the world paid tribute. A recital was held at Carnegie Hall with Pablo Casals and choral director and university administrator Warner Lawson serving as cochairmen. Sponsor and financial beneficiary of the event was the American Missionary Association. Record numbers of blacks and many whites were in attendance. Dignitaries sent greetings, including the famed pianist Arthur Rubinstein and soprano Leontyne Price. Composer and music critic Virgil Thomson presented the American Missionary Association's first Amistad Award.

Many honors followed, including the Spingarn Medal of the NAACP in 1924, and the government of France's Purple Ribbon award ''for service to French music.'' In a ceremony at New York City's City Hall on the occasion of Hayes's 75th birthday, Mayor Robert F. Wagner presented Hayes with a scroll. Hayes died on January 1, 1977 at the age of 89.

A leading concert tenor during the 1920s, 1930s, and 1940s, Hayes excelled in the delivery of art songs, but also in the songs of his people. His life and career earned for him a firm place in history and a presence on the world stage.

REFERENCES

Carter, Marva Griffin. ''In Retrospect: Roland Hayes—Expressor of the Soul in Song (1887–1977).'' *The Black Perspective in Music* 5 (Fall 1977): 189.

Current Biography Yearbook. New York: H. W. Wilson, 1942.

Green, Jeffrey P. ''Roland Hayes in London, 1921.'' *The Black Perspective in Music* 10 (Spring 1982): 29–41.

Helm, Mackinley. *Angel Mo' and Her Son.* Boston: Little, Brown, 1942.

Hitchcock, H. Wiley, and Stanley Sadie, eds. *The New Grove Dictionary of American Music.* New York: Macmillan, 1986.

Hughes, Langston. *Famous Negro Music Makers.* New York: Dodd, Mead, 1955.

Marr, Warren II. ''Roland Hayes.'' *Crisis* 81 (June–July, 1974): 205–208.

Nichols, Charles H., ed. *Arna Bontemps–Langston Hughes Letters, 1925–1967.* New York: Dodd, Mead, 1980.

''Roland Hayes.'' Resume. 1966.

''Roland Hayes, 89, Concert Tenor, Son of a Former Slave, Is Dead.'' *New York Times,* January 2, 1977.

Southern, Eileen. *Biographical Dictionary of Afro–American and African Musicians.* Westport, CT: Greenwood Press, 1982.

———. *The Music of Black Americans: A History.* New York: Norton, 1971.

''Two Giants of Music World Dead.'' *The Richmond Afro–American,* January 4–8, 1977.

Woolsey, F. W. ''Conversation with Roland Hayes.'' *The Black Perspective in Music* 2 (Fall 1974): 179–85.

D. Antoinette Handy

George Edmund Haynes (1880–1960)

Social work educator, scholar, organization official

George Edmund Haynes, a social work pioneer, educator and administrator, civic leader, and advocate for urban black workers, is regrettably a neglected figure in African American history, specifically in the development of the social work profession. Though credited as a founder of the National Urban League and having established the first program in social work education at a predominately black institution of higher learning, his many accomplishments remain generally unknown beyond a small circle of social work educators.

Haynes was born during the brutal aftermath of the Reconstruction period in 1880 in Pine Bluff, Arkansas, to Louis and Mattie Haynes. His devoutly religious parents stressed education for their two children, George and Birdye, as a way to overcome the harsh conditions that most blacks of that era faced. After Louis Haynes died, Mattie Haynes moved the family to Hot Springs, Arkansas for the better educational prospects it offered her children. Shortly thereafter in 1893, young George was given the opportunity to visit Chicago to attend the World's Fair. This exposed him to the ideas of black intellectuals and activists, such as fiery orator Frederick Douglass, educator Anna Julia Cooper, and antilynching advocate Ida B. Wells, who spoke on various topics relating to racial progress and the future of the black race. This event affected Haynes's career aspirations. He returned to Arkansas determined to pursue an education and become instrumental in devising solutions to what was then called the "Negro Problem."

The absence of a high school for blacks in the state forced Haynes to leave the family to attend the Agricultural and Mechanical College in Normal, Alabama. After one year there he moved on to Fisk University Preparatory School in Nashville, Tennessee, in anticipation of enrolling in the college. Excelling in the rigorous classical curriculum that included Latin, geography, history, and mathematics, Haynes was accepted at Fisk in 1899. His high achievement earned him admission to Yale upon receiving his bachelor of arts degree from Fisk in 1903.

Although the Yale environment was not welcoming for the few blacks in attendance and was an unpleasant contrast to the supportive atmosphere of Fisk, Haynes found a brilliant mentor in sociologist William Graham Sumner, who guided his growing interest in the new field of sociology. Haynes rejected Sumner's Social Darwinist views, which attributed poverty to personal failure, and Sumner's bias against government help for the poor, but learned crucial methodology from his mentor and adapted many of Sumner's methods for his own use as a social scientist. Haynes graduated from Yale University in 1904 with a master's degree in sociology and then entered the Yale Divinity School. He continued his education by enrolling in summer courses at the University of Chicago in 1906 and 1907.

Haynes's first professional employment after graduation from college was with the Colored Department of the International Committee of the YMCA. This position allowed Haynes to merge his religious convictions with his social outlook by working to develop educational and leadership programs for young black men in urban areas. According to the social gospel to which Haynes subscribed, religion was best expressed through social action. He became an evangelist of sorts, taking that message to young men at black colleges throughout the South. He left the YMCA in 1908 to return to graduate school, with the intention of becoming more directly involved in studying the problems of the poor, especially those in urban areas. His interest in education led him to found the Association of Colleges and Secondary Schools in 1911. He also served as the association's first secretary.

George Edmund Haynes

Haynes enrolled at New York University's School of Philanthropy, which later became the Columbia School of Social Work. He received a doctorate in 1912, the first African American to earn that distinction at Columbia University. His dissertation study of the working life of blacks in New York City, "The Negro At Work in New York City" (1912), was an outgrowth of his work in organizations involved in easing the transition of black emigrants from the South.

Helps Establish National Urban League

Through his work Haynes became acutely aware of the many problems faced by the thousands of rural Southern blacks who streamed into the city in search of jobs and a new kind of social and economic freedom. Among his allies and coworkers in these organizations was an interracial group of black and white reformers and social service providers including the women and men who founded the National League for the Protection of Colored Women in 1906. This organization and others, such as the White Rose Mission founded by Victoria Earle Matthews in 1897, helped newly arriving black female workers who were often exploited by unscrupulous worker agents and employers. Haynes's network also included white social reformers Ruth Standish Baldwin and Frances Kellor, who encouraged his scholarly studies and proposals for social action to address the problems. Three of the organizations with which Haynes was involved—The National League for the Protection of Colored Women, the Committee on Urban Conditions among Negroes, and the Committee for Improving Industrial Conditions of Negroes—were the precursors of the National Urban League. which was founded in 1910 in New York under Haynes's leadership. He became the organization's first executive director and led the NUL into its prominent role as a policy–minded national advocate for the needs of the urban poor.

The philosophy that guided Haynes's social work agenda was found in his deep commitment to alleviating the burdens imposed on blacks by their history of servitude and victimization. He believed that poverty could be eradicated by attacking its root causes, rather than simply addressing the symptoms. Haynes viewed racism as a barrier to fighting poverty. For that reason he worked diligently to build networks of interracial alliance and cooperation. He was active in several interracial organizations, including the Association for the Study of Negro Life and History and the NAACP, of which he was a charter member.

As a scholar as well as a public policy advocate, Haynes foresaw the need for training a cadre of black social workers whose mission would be to serve these emerging urban clusters of mostly poor black workers. He also realized that most of the social work schools in the North did not readily admit black applicants. Therefore, in order to do effective social work among blacks, special skills and attitudes would need to be developed among social workers in these communities, whom he believed should live and work among the people they serve.

Develops Social Work Program at Fisk

Invited to join the faculty of Fisk University in 1910, Haynes accepted a professorship in social science and transferred his base of operation to Nashville, Tennessee. Haynes had decided to return to his alma mater because of its strategic location in the South and its superior academic standing. He believed that a Southern center was necessary in order to give credibility to the Northern–based work of the Urban League. During his years at Fisk, Haynes chaired the department of social science and developed a pioneering program in social work education. While at Fisk Haynes also introduced the first course ever taught at the collegiate level on the history of black Americans. He preferred to stress education over training because of his belief that thorough preparation rather than narrow specialization was the best approach in developing effective black social workers. His views on education resembled W. E. B. Du Bois's concept of the "talented tenth," a leadership class of educated blacks who would use their skills to uplift the race, although he also believed that vocational training would help elevate black workers. Under Haynes's direction Fisk became a preeminent institution for social work education. His program combined rigorous academic training with fieldwork that focused on the surrounding black community of Nashville. He cultivated working relationships with several local social service agencies while stressing his ideal of interracial cooperation. This helped him place his students to gain the necessary field experience.

Not content to have Fisk remain the only Southern black college offering a social work education, Haynes used the model he had developed for the National Urban League to design a program of affiliations with other black colleges that would bring them into the orbit of social work education. The NUL, in return, provided fellowships to promising students from these colleges to pursue advanced degrees in social work. Haynes was a frequent presenter at conferences and meetings dealing with the condition of black workers. He used these occasions to lecture on the importance of blacks and whites working together to ameliorate the injustices caused by white racism. His work at Fisk allowed Haynes to combine his advocacy role with his scholarly and administrative work, as well as to serve his profession and the NUL, where he remained national director until 1918.

Other Venues

While on leave from Fisk between 1918 to 1921, Haynes joined the United States Department of Labor as Director of Negro Economics. He hoped that his scholarly studies and copious data collection on the condition of the black labor force would influence government and social policy. The Wilson administration, however, was generally unsympathetic toward blacks. Haynes expanded his sphere of activity by working not only with leading figures in government, but also with charitable organizations such as the Federal Council of Churches. In 1921 he began a long tenure as executive secretary of the Department of Race Relations of the Federal Council of Churches. One of his initial acts was to direct a survey of religious life in black churches. He also promoted the concept of interracial clinics, which he touted as a way to diffuse racial tensions in the volatile postwar years. While with the council he established Race Relations Sunday—the second Sunday of each February—the forerunner of Brotherhood Week. Haynes held the position with the Council of Churches until 1947.

Meanwhile, Haynes continued to research the causes of urban ills and their solutions. Following the Chicago race riot of 1919, Haynes traveled to that city to study the riot's causes. The six–day riot allegedly started when a black man took a swim in an area of a public beach that was unofficially for whites only. Haynes concluded that the riot was simply the inevitable result of the long neglect of the worsening race relations caused by competition for jobs and deteriorating economic factors.

Leaving government in 1921, Haynes began gathering data on conditions in African countries. His interest in Africa resulted in his appointment with the YMCA as a regional consultant in South Africa from 1942 to 1955. He traveled to different African states collecting and disseminating data. This role catapulted him into the international spotlight. In 1950 Haynes published *Africa: Continent of the Future,* which presented his years of documented research on Africa. Haynes returned to academia as lecturer at the City College of New York from 1950 to 1959. He also taught the first course in black history at CCNY.

Haynes is generally accorded recognition by the profession of social work, especially for his development of the National Urban League's focus on social work at the local level. His initiatives in developing social work education at Fisk and his encouragement of programs at other predominately black colleges and universities warrant him a special place among pioneers in the profession. As an activist and administrator, Haynes absorbed the ideas of the Progressive Era and put them to work on behalf of disempowered urban blacks, who are today called the underclass. Haynes recognized that society's security is predicated upon how we treat those who are most vulnerable and most in need. His writings, teachings, and organizational activism all emphasize that the nation as a whole cannot truly advance until the standard of living is raised for all Americans. He also contended that people should be treated on the basis of worth and performance rather than on race.

Haynes was an important figure in the cultural aspects of black history from the mid–1920s through the early 1930s. By 1931 the influence of the Harmon Foundation on black culture rivalled that of the Julius Rosenwald Fund. Haynes and Alain Locke played major advisory roles with the Harmon Fund and its funding for African American artists, writers, and other professionals. In January of 1926, Harmon gave prizes to blacks for their work in literature, music, fine arts, industry, science, education, and race relations. Locke and Haynes are credited for the success of the first all–black art exhibition held on January 28, 1926, at New York's International House, sponsored by Harmon.

In addition to the titles earlier noted, Haynes's published works include *The Negro at Work during the World War* (1921) and *The Trend of the Races* (1929). Haynes also wrote entries on black Americans for the *Encyclopedia Britannica* in 1929 and 1941. He contributed articles to the *Social Work Yearbook* and to numerous professional journals.

Haynes's numerous affiliations included membership on the boards of trustees of Fisk University, Dillard University, and of the State University of New York—its first black member. He was a member of the American Association for the Advancement of Science, the American Association of Social Workers, and the National Conference of Social Welfare. He was also a member of Grace Congregational Church in New York City, served as vice–chairman of the Board of Home Missions, and as vice–moderator of the General Council of the Congregational Christian Churches.

In 1910 Haynes married fellow Fisk graduate Elizabeth Ross, who worked in a similar program for black college students and urban communities in her role as the first black national secretary of the YWCA. Elizabeth Ross Haynes shared her husband's passion for using social welfare programs in the service of black progress and worked with him until her death in 1953. The couple had one son, George Edmund, Jr.

In 1955, two years after the death of his first wife, Haynes married Olyve Love Jeter, who worked with him and was responsible for collecting and preserving his manuscripts and correspondence. After a short illness, Haynes died in Brooklyn's King County Hospital on January 8, 1960. He was 79–years old.

In 1975 his adopted home town of Mount Vernon, New York, where he lived the last five years of his life, commemorated the ninety–fifth anniversary of Haynes's birth. The Mount Vernon Public Library established the George Edmund Haynes Memorial Collection, which consisted of books by and about blacks. In further recognition of his birth and his work, the mayor of Mount Vernon proclaimed August 11, 1975, George Edmund Haynes Day. As part of the 1980 Fisk University Commencement, the university library commemorated the centennial of Haynes's birth.

The importance of Haynes's life and work is best expressed by his widow, Olyve Jeter Haynes, who summarized his legacy in the *Mt. Vernon Daily Argus.* She stated, ''He was not dramatic, not a rabble rouser, and did not lead marches. He felt that moral suasion and the conference table were the steps to democracy for Negroes in the United States.'' Through that process, many organizations and institutions were transformed by his presence and his multifaceted work.

REFERENCES

Carlton, Iris. ''A Pioneer Social Work Educator.'' Ph.D. dissertation, University of Maryland, 1982.

Haynes, George Edmund. ''The Birth and Childhood of the National Urban League.'' *National Urban League 50th Anniversary Yearbook,* 1950.

Lewis, David Levering. *When Harlem Was in Vogue.* New York: Knopf, 1981.

Logan, Rayford W. Logan, and Michael R. Winston, eds. *Dictionary of American Negro Biography.* New York: Norton, 1982.

Perlman, Daniel. ''Stirring the White Conscience: The Life of George Edmund Haynes.'' Ph.D. dissertation, New York University, 1972. Ann Arbor, MI: University Microfilms, 1972.

''A Pioneer in Race Relations.'' *Mount Vernon Daily Angus,* May 8, 1975.

Weiss, Nancy J. *The National Urban League, 1920–1940.* New York: Oxford University Press, 1940.

Who's Who in Colored America. 5th ed. Brooklyn, NY: Thomas Yenser, 1940.

COLLECTIONS

The George Edmund Haynes Papers are located in the Fisk University Library and in the Beinecke Library at Yale University. Proofs of his publications and manuscripts are in the Schomburg Center for Research on Black Culture, New York City. Materials on Haynes can also be found in the Joel E. Spingarn Papers in the Moorland–Spingarn Research Center, Howard University, and in the National Urban League

Archives (1910–1965) in the Manuscript Division of the Library of Congress.

Audrey Thomas McCluskey

Lemuel Haynes
(1753–1833)
Patriot, minister

Lemuel Haynes

In the chronicles of black life in America, Lemuel Haynes was a trailblazer in society, religion, education, and the military. Haynes was one of the first blacks to defend his country during wartime and to denounce slavery publicly. According to a number of historians, he was the first black to pastor a white congregation and to receive an honorary master of arts degree. Indeed, Lemuel Haynes's life was extraordinary.

Haynes was born on July 18, 1753, in West Hartford, Connecticut. His white mother, from a respectable New England family, and his African father abandoned him. He was not given a parental surname; instead he was given the name of the owner of the house where he was born.

When he was only five months old, Haynes was taken to Middle Granville, Massachusetts, where he was designated an indentured servant until he was 21. Deacon Dave Rose and his wife raised Haynes. Rose, one of Granville's first settlers, was a farmer. Haynes credited Rose with teaching him religious principles, and, according to Timothy Mather Cooley in *Sketches of the Life and Character of the Rev. Lemuel Haynes,* he recalled that Mrs. Rose "had peculiar attachment to me: she treated me as though I was her own child. I remember it was a saying among the neighbors, that she loved Lemuel more than her own children."

During the day, young Haynes worked on the Rose farm and attended the district–school (which was only in session a few months each year). At night, he studied by firelight in order to learn more than was offered in school. According to Cooley, Haynes once told a schoolmate, "I make it my rule to know something more every night than I knew in the morning." During Haynes's boyhood, he was nearly killed twice: he was rescued from drowning and from an ox that would have killed him. Haynes attributed his escaping death to Providence.

A Black Patriot Speaks Out

One of the controversies during the American Revolution was the issue of black (slave or free) participation. Although blacks fought against the British as early as the battles of Lexington and Concord in April 1775, orders were sent to recruiting offices not to enlist blacks as of July 1775. However, a British bid for black soldiers led to a reversal of the order, and, in January, 1776, Congress approved the enlisting of free blacks. Most states then began enlisting blacks, whether slave or free. Approximately 5,000 of the 300,000 soldiers who fought in the American Revolution were black. Lemuel Haynes was among them.

Haynes's indentureship ended in 1774, and the 21–year old enlisted as a Minute Man. Haynes fought in the Battle at Lexington in April, 1775. In 1776, he volunteered for an expedition where he served as one of Ethan Allen's Green Mountain Boys (and one of three blacks) who captured Fort Ticonderoga from the British.

During Haynes's time as a soldier, he advocated that the American Revolution free the enslaved. Haynes wrote an essay entitled, "Liberty Further Extended," published in Newman's *Black Preacher to White America.* He argued:

> That an African, or in other terms, that a Negro may Justly Chalenge, and has an undeniable right to his freed Liberty: Consequently, the practise of Slave–keeping, which so much abounds in this Land is illicit.
>
> There is Not the Least precept, or practise, in the Sacred Scriptures, that constitutes a Black man a Slave, any more than a white one.
>
> Shall a mans Couler Be the Decisive Criterion whereby to Judg of his natural right? or Becaus a man is not of the same couler with his Neighbour, shall he Be Deprived of those things that Distuingsheth him from the Beasts of the field?

> Men were made for more noble Ends than to be Drove to market, like Sheep and oxen. . . Because he is a human Being: and the immutable Laws of God, and indefeasible Laws of nature, pronounced him free.

Although the essay was unknown and unpublished until 1983, its creation, in approximately 1776, was some 53 years earlier than the publication of David Walker's *Appeal.* In 1801, 51 years ahead of Frederick Douglass' Fourth of July speech in Rochester, New York, Haynes addressed an Independence Day audience in Rutland, Vermont. In his speech, ''The Nature and Importance of True Republicanism,'' also published in *Black Preacher,* he cited slavery's effects: ''Nay–but being subjected to slavery, by the cruel hands of oppressors, they have been taught to view themselves as a rank of beings far below others, which has suppressed, in a degree, every principle of manhood.'' Haynes's speech was published that same year. Thus Lemuel Haynes dared to use pen and voice to condemn slavery a half–century earlier than the landmark antislavery protests by Walker and Douglass.

During his ministerial career, Haynes did not hesitate to express his views on other political issues including Federalism, the War of 1812, and New England secession.

Former Indentured Servant Becomes God's Servant

After serving in the Continental Army, Haynes returned to Granville and continued farming. He declined an offer to attend Dartmouth College. Instead, he studied Latin and Greek with several pastors and taught school.

On November 29, 1780, several ministers pronounced him qualified to preach. When Haynes accepted the pastorship of a new congregational church in Granville later that year, he began a distinguished 53–year ministerial career characterized by his serving as pastor of at least five white congregations: Granville, Massachusetts (1780–1785—Haynes was officially ordained November 9, 1785); Torrington, Connecticut (1786–1788); West Rutland, Vermont (1788–1818); Manchester, Vermont (approximately 1818–1821); and Granville, New York (1822–1833).

Haynes's endeavors as probably the first black American to pastor white congregations brought him national and international recognition. Some of his sermons and manuscripts were published in his lifetime. His most famous were ''Universal Salvation,'' an 1805 attack on Universalism that appeared in more than 70 editions, and ''Mystery Developed'' (1820), a narrative of a famous murder case, which is an early example of a short story by a black writer. During Haynes's 30–year tenure at the West Rutland Church, membership increased significantly. His advice on theological matters was sought by the presidents of Yale University and Amherst College. In 1804, Haynes became the first black American to receive an honorary master of arts degree, awarded by Middlebury College.

Haynes died on September 28, 1833. He was survived by his wife, the former Elizabeth Babbit, a white schoolteacher who was a parishioner at Haynes's first church in Granville, Massachusetts. Nine of Haynes's ten children survived him, including three sons: a farmer, a lawyer, and a doctor. His son Samuel was one of the doctors consulted during Haynes's final illness.

Centuries after his death, Lemuel Haynes is remembered as a man who accepted the challenges of his time. He sought America's independence, freedom for the enslaved, and greater spirituality for all.

REFERENCES

Barksdale, Richard, and Keneth Kinnamon, ed. *Black Writers of America: A Comprehensive Anthology.* New York: Macmillan, 1972.

Christian, Charles M. *Black Saga: The African American Experience.* Boston: Houghton Mifflin Co., 1995.

Cooley, Timothy Mather. *Sketches of the Life and Character of the Rev. Lemuel Haynes, A.M.* 1837. Reprint, New York: Negro Universities Press, 1969.

Logan, Rayford W., and Michael R. Winston, eds. *Dictionary of American Negro Biography.* New York: Norton, 1982.

Newman, Richard. *Lemuel Haynes: A Bio–Bibliography.* New York: Lambeth Press, 1984.

———, ed. *Black Preacher to White America: The Collected Writings of Lemuel Haynes, 1774–1883.* Brooklyn: Carlson Publishing, 1990.

Salzman, Jack, David Lionel Smith, and Cornel West, eds. *Encyclopedia of African–American Culture and History.* New York: Simon and Schuster/Macmillan, 1996.

Linda M. Carter

James Augustine Healy

(1830–1900)

Religious leader

The oldest of ten children born to a slave mother in Georgia, James Healy was a member of a remarkable family. James and two of his brothers became the first African American Catholic priests. James Healy himself became a bishop, and his brother Patrick Healy became a member of the Society of Jesus (Jesuits). Patrick Healy was the first African American to obtain a doctorate degree, and he served as president of Georgetown University. His sister, Eliza Healy, joined an order of nuns and became a mother superior, as well as a practical and successful school director. Another brother, Michael Healy, ran away to sea and had a very colorful career in Pacific waters, becoming a ship captain in the organization that later became known as the Coast Guard.

James Augustine Healy was born on April 6, 1830, to Michael Morris Healy and his light–skinned slave consort, Mary Eliza Smith, on a plantation seven miles north of Macon, Georgia. James Augustine, the first born, was followed by nine siblings: Hugh Clark in 1832, Patrick Francis in 1834, Alexander Sherwood in 1836, Martha Ann in 1838, Michael James in 1839, Eugene in 1842 (who died in infancy), Amanda Josephine in 1846, Eliza in 1846, and a second Eugene (1849?).

James Healy's father, Michael Morris Healy, was born in County Roscommon, Ireland. He deserted from the British army while serving on garrison duty in Nova Scotia around the end of the War of 1812. He made his way to Georgia and in 1828 was able to purchase land near Macon, which he built into a prosperous plantation. Not long after, he entered into a union with Mary Eliza Smith, even though interracial marriages were illegal in Georgia. That union was later accepted by the Catholic church as a valid marriage and posed no impediment to the religious vocations of any of his children. Under Georgia law at that time emancipation remained well nigh impossible, and since the children took on the slave status of their mother, Michael Healy took steps to ensure their future by sending them north to be educated.

James Healy was the first to go, in the fall of 1837, followed by Hugh and Patrick; they were educated in Quaker schools, first on Long Island and then in Burlington, New Jersey. Michael Healy drew up a will in 1845 whereby he arranged to have his property in Georgia disposed of and the proceeds invested for the benefit of his children. He left instructions that his wife should be sent to live in a free state and receive an annuity of $120 a year. By that time only Michael and Josephine were still in Georgia. An 1847 codicil made arrangements for two additional children born after the original will was drawn up.

James Healy did not find the years in the Quaker schools agreeable. He was sensitive to slurs about his African American ancestry as well as the prevailing strong prejudice against Roman Catholic Irish immigrants, even though the Healy children were not yet baptized themselves. (Similar racist remarks caused one of Healy's brothers to run away from school on more than one occasion.) In 1844 Healy along with three of his brothers entered the newly–founded, Jesuit–run College of the Holy Cross in Worcester, Massachusetts. Their father enrolled them on the advice of John Bernard Fitzpatrick, coadjutor bishop of Boston, who also arranged to have one of the Healy daughters boarded with his own sister. Up to this point Michael Healy's Catholicism seems not to have had much influence on his children.

A Catholic Education

Not long after joining the Catholic school, the Healy brothers were baptized. James Healy entered the school in the second year of a six–year secondary–and–college program. He distinguished himself academically, and within the first two years he decided on his religious vocation. He decided against becoming a Jesuit in the order of his mentors, and instead opted for seminary training because of the swarthiness of his skin which, according to his perception, posed difficulties for him in undertaking the novitiate at Frederick, Maryland. (One of Healey's lighter–skinned brothers did become a Jesuit.) In 1849 James Healy graduated from college, and he was ranked first in his class. (Healy's degree was officially from Georgetown University in Washington, D.C., since Massachusetts refused to charter Holy Cross until much later). In 1874 the school awarded Healy a doctor of divinity degree at its first commencement under a state charter.

That fall James Healy entered the Sulpician Seminary in Montreal, Canada. He was preparing to take minor orders of the Catholic priesthood in the spring of 1850 when he learned of his mother's sudden death on May 19. Michael Healy's death soon followed on August 29. The Healy will was probated without any problem, and Hugh Healy—who was working in New York City—made the trip to Georgia to bring the three remaining Healy siblings north. The timing of his parents' death caused great uncertainty for Healy, because he was required, in preparation for his minor orders, to submit certain documentation about himself, including the record of his baptism and the marriage license of his parents. James Healy's difficulty regarding the legitimacy of his parents' marriage was ultimately resolved, and he received minor orders in 1851. He then transferred in 1852 to the Sulpician Seminary in Paris, France, to continue his studies.

Healy at that point envisioned himself teaching theology as a career, but he never attained that goal. One of his younger brothers who was enrolled at a seminary in Montreal decided to quit that institution and join Healy in Paris in the fall of 1853. The younger Healy's departure for Paris led to a tragic accident that changed the elder brother's future. Hugh Healy, who was working in New York City and looking after the family concerns, saw his younger brother off to Paris from the pier on September 1, and then went on his customary rowing excursion, waving at the ship as it passed him by on its way out of the harbor. As Hugh Healy waved, a steamboat swamped and sunk his rowboat. He swallowed polluted water as he swam to the safety of shore, and died of typhoid 16 days later. The death of his brother caused James Healy to change his plans for further study. He completed his final year of study for the priesthood, was ordained on June 10, 1854, and returned to the United States.

A Boston Ministry

Healy's first assignment in Boston was as an assistant to a parish priest, although his friend and superior, Bishop John Bernard Fitzpatrick, would soon make use of the young priest's talents in other ways. Healy eventually served the bishop, first as secretary and then as chancellor for 11 years. In addition to the heavy clerical duties involved in his various appointments, Healy shouldered his family responsibilities by providing a home for the younger members, eventually on a farm at Newton, Massachusetts. He also took steps to settle the estate. Under Michael Healy's will, his slaves were to be leased out until the youngest child reached his majority (about 1870) and then were to be sold outright. With the consent of his co–heirs, James Healy arranged to have the sale immediately, and the estate was concluded in 1861 when final payments were transferred north.

By December of 1854 Healy became Fitzgerald's personal assistant with a charge to organize the chancery office. Additionally Healy served as pastor of Saint Vincent's. Part of his work for the bishop was to respond to especially virulent anti–Catholic sentiments in Massachusetts, where the Know–Nothing nativist party had secured an overwhelming victory in the 1854 state elections. This climate of animosity gave urgency to many of Healy's ongoing concerns including his strong support for an orphanage for Catholic children. At that time some Catholic orphans were placed far away with Protestant families in western states, and those who were placed in public institutions were cut off from their religion because of discriminatory legislation against Catholics. As late as 1874, in conjunction with his testimony against a proposition to tax churches, Healy lamented and politicized the fact that by law Catholics could not hold services in any public institution including the jails; the laws went so far as to forbid the administration of the last rites to persons who were dying in these establishments.

On June 24, 1855, Healy became chancellor of the diocese, and in 1857 he became vicar general. In his various roles he was both popular and effective. In late 1859 Fitzgerald undertook to build a new cathedral because shifting urban patterns made the original location increasingly less suitable. The original cathedral was sold, but with the outbreak of the Civil War the construction of a new facility became impractical. Fitzpatrick's health meanwhile was declining, and finally in 1862 his doctors ordered him to take a full year's rest. Healy in turn became rector of the new temporary cathedral and received full power of attorney to act for Fitzpatrick.

Healy himself was not in robust health, and he continued to overwork himself. In June of 1863 he left, on doctor's orders, on a tour of Europe and for six months of rest. He visited Rome, saw Fitzpatrick, and discussed the future of his younger brother who was then completing his studies in Europe. Fitzpatrick returned to Boston in the late summer of 1864; he died on February 13, 1865. When Fitzpatrick's successor, Joseph Williams, took office in March, Healy was assigned as pastor of St. James; he assumed his position on April 1. Sherwood Healy, who was also overworking himself and ruining both his eyesight and his health at a newly established seminary in Troy, New York, attracted the attention of the new bishop. After performing various services for Williams, including that of theologian at the First Vatican Council, Sherwood Healy assumed James Healy's former position as rector of the Boston cathedral in September of 1870.

Both James and Sherwood Healy were extremely popular, highly visible, and very effective priests in the diocese, although their racial background was bruited about; one rumor claimed that the African American cook at the rectory was in actuality the Healys' mother. The gossip had no significant impact on their being accepted by most Catholics. The Healy siblings did however experience prejudice within the church. For example, Josephine Healy ultimately joined an order of nuns in Montreal after she was denied admission (by a Southern–born mother superior) to the order of Good Shepherd nuns in 1874. Still the Healys enjoyed remarkable success in the church. Patrick Healy, the first African American Jesuit and the first to earn a doctoral degree taught at Georgetown University in Washington from 1866 on, was president of that university between 1874 and 1882, and was the first African American president of a Catholic institution of higher education. Eliza Healy had a notable career as an educational leader; she once saved a school on the verge of financial collapse. Sherwood Healy and a second Healy sister who also became a nun both died relatively young. In a completely different sphere, Michael Healy, who ran away to sea when he was 15, had an outstanding career on the Pacific and Alaska coast in the U.S. Revenue Cutter Service, forerunner of the Coast Guard. He was reputedly one of the models for the captain in Jack London's novel *The Sea Wolf.*

Even taking into account the historical period, some fault the Healys for their apparent rejection of their African American heritage. This caused some sharp reactions in retrospect during the 20th century. Cyprian Davis, a 20th–century black monk and historian, said in his book *The History of Black Catholics in the United States,* of the three Healys who were priests:

> [They] did not enter into solidarity with either the African American community as such or even the black Catholic community. . . . They never used their position to champion the cause of their fellow blacks. Nor did they ever give their fellow blacks the opportunity to bask in the reflected glory of their own noteworthy achievements.

The Healys' racial background was general public knowledge, but it was rarely discussed and remained at the level of gossip. In his book *Bishop Healey: Beloved Outcast,* Foley quoted a description of James Healy written by one of his parishioners at St. James:

> I remember Father Healy. He was a colored man, and I remember it was quite well known and talked about that he was one. But if he had any such thing as an inferiority complex concealed about his person, his Irish congregation never discovered it, for he ruled them—and they were not easy to rule. My recollection of him is of an undersized man, slight, good–looking, with a fringe of whiskers showing above his Roman collar, soft–spoken but decisive in both speech and manner, and a mighty good business man.

James Healy remained at St. James for nine years, during which time he undertook the building of a new church. It was just such parish duties as building a church, plus his intercessions for charities, and his political involvements which contributed to Healy's prominence in the church. It was believed that both James and Sherwood Healy's names were on the lists of candidates submitted to Rome to fill two vacant sees in Hartford, Connecticut, and Portland, Maine, in 1874. On February 12, 1875, James Healy was appointed second bishop of Portland at which time he resigned as the pastor of St. James. On April 5, Sherwood Healy took over the parish of St. James, along with the task of seeing to the completion of the new church. At age thirty–eight, Sherwood Healy had excellent prospects for future promotion, but death cut short his career. On August 23 he suffered two severe lung hemorrhages. He lingered but finally died on October 21.

Serves as Bishop of Portland

James Healy served as bishop of Portland for 25 years. After some initial difficulties with an order of teaching nuns, the Sisters of Mercy, he enjoyed good relations with his flock. (The sisters eventually became very devoted to their bishop.) The diverse diocese was spread across the states of Maine and New Hampshire. It included French–speaking members from Canada, Irish immigrants, and Native Americans.

One sharp tussle with a local priest caused Healy some problems at the outset. Healy sought to relieve the priest from his parish in large part because of the man's handling of a church building fund. The priest appealed to Rome, with a claim that Healy had violated canon law. Healy lost the case when his opponent employed an adept canon lawyer. The maligned priest even published in Europe an account of how Healy, a bishop, had mistreated him. Healy became so upset that he offered his resignation, once in the fall of 1878 and again when his appeal failed. Both times he was refused. Eventually a compromise was reached: in 1880 the priest was reinstated with the understanding that he would resign immediately, although the affair eventually dragged on much longer than was first envisioned. One result of this fracas was that Healy became meticulous in his attention to, and documentation of, diocesan affairs during the last 20 years of his tenure.

Even as bishop in Maine, Healy faced anti–Catholic sentiment once again—on his first round of visitation he found one of the churches destroyed by arson. Typical of the prolonged struggle between Protestants and Catholics was his effort to minister to Catholic youth imprisoned in the state reformatory. This matter was not resolved until 1898. Since much of the anti–Catholic agitation was supported by various secret societies, Healy adamantly opposed Catholic involvement in any such organizations, including initially the Knights of Labor, an early union organization.

Outside of his diocese Healy was fully accepted by his fellow bishops. At the Third Plenary Council of Baltimore in 1884, he was not a major figure, but he did propose some compromises on thorny issues, and in terms that were ultimately accepted by Rome. He was also chosen to be a member of the newly reshaped Commission for the Negro and Native American Missions. When New Hampshire was made into a separate diocese in 1884, Healy had the satisfaction of seeing his own nominee—Denis Bradley, Healy's former chancellor—become its bishop. His reputation as a speaker grew to a point that he was in great demand, even outside his own diocese.

Healy's heavy pastoral duties were interrupted from time to time by serious illness. In 1877 his doctors ordered him to rest in a milder climate and so avoid the rigors of a Maine winter. By the end of his life he regularly left Maine for the winter. In addition to the problems with his throat and his lungs, the condition of his heart also caused concern. He suffered a stroke that interfered with his ability to speak in June of 1893. Although he recovered completely, he spent the whole of the next year resting and traveling. He was then able to resume his episcopal duties with due attention to his health.

In June of 1900 James Healy celebrated his 25th anniversary as a bishop. Then on August 3 he had a mild heart attack which was initially misdiagnosed as indigestion. The following day he had a more massive heart attack. He died on August 5.

After a funeral service in the cathedral, he was interred in the Catholic cemetery just outside Portland. When Healy's will was probated, it was discovered that he was poorer than he had been when he first became a bishop.

James Healy achieved the almost impossible feat of largely evading the restrictions placed on African Americans during his time. In so doing he developed his potential and assumed a leadership role not only among the many siblings in his family, but also among his peers, in a society resolutely bent on denying opportunity to any person labelled black.

REFERENCES

Davis, Cyprian. *The History of Black Catholics in the United States.* New York: Crossroad, 1990.

Foley, Albert S. *Bishop Healy: Beloved Outcast.* New York: Farrar, Strauss, 1954. Reprint, New York: Arno Press and the *New York Times,* 1969.

———. *God's Men of Color.* New York: Farrar, Strauss, 1955.

Logan, Rayford W., and Michael R. Winston, eds. *Dictionary of American Negro Biography.* New York: Norton, 1982.

Smith, Jessie Carney, ed. *Notable Black American Women.* Detroit: Gale Research, 1992.

COLLECTIONS

Principal collections are in the Portland, Maine, diocesan archives and in the archives of Holy Cross College, Worcester, Massachusetts.

Robert L. Johns

Fletcher Henderson
(1898–1952)
Musician, bandleader

Fletcher Henderson was a major figure in the history and development of jazz. The big band era and the swing movement began with innovations in ensemble music pioneered by Henderson, his arrangers, and the musicians in his band. Their inspiration came from a historical legacy—the musical inventiveness of the small group jazz styles of New Orleans—the group cohesiveness, collective improvisation, and swinging solos of men like King Oliver and Louis Armstrong.

A formal ensemble style thus evolved in Henderson's band: arrangements featuring a blend of dance band styles common among touring club bands of the 1920s and 1930s meshed with popular song melodies and flavored with a taste of New Orleans gumbo in jazzy solos that showcased the artistry of the leading players.

Fletcher Hamilton Henderson Jr. was born in Cuthbert, Georgia, on December 18, 1898. His mother was a pianist and music teacher; his father, also a pianist, was principal of Randolph Training School, an industrial high school. Young Fletcher studied piano with his mother for seven years, with daily practice times firmly mandated by his father. He was well grounded in music theory and sightreading and developed an excellent sense of pitch, as did his younger brother, Horace, and sister, Irma. After his primary and secondary schooling, Fletcher graduated from Atlanta University in 1920 with a major in chemistry and mathematics. While in college, he participated in music and had a few band jobs.

Henderson moved to New York City after college, hoping to go on to graduate study and start a career in chemistry. Finding employment in this field was difficult, however, and soon he found his career taking a decided turn to music. He took a job as a song demonstrator with Handy and Pace Music Company–Publishers. The firm was founded by W. C. Handy, composer of the first published blues songs, and Harry Pace, a Memphis businessman. Pace soon established Black Swan, the first black–owned recording firm. As a skilled pianist with ample music talents, Henderson took on greater responsibilities, putting together ensembles, arranging, and scheduling recording sessions. Under his mother's tutelage, his training as a pianist focused on classical music. This served as a good foundation, enabling Henderson to adapt to necessary changes in repertoire and styles that this new occupation required.

In 1921, Henderson accompanied and promoted a tour for one of Black Swan's recording artists, blues singer Ethel Waters. She insisted on a firm, blues oriented accompaniment, similar to the driving style of James P. Johnson. She urged Henderson to study this style, and suggested that he listen to Johnson's piano rolls. Henderson obliged, and no doubt this opportunity broadened his grasp of an aspect of pianistic technique with which he was only noddingly familiar.

Fletcher Henderson

Recording engagements and band venues often called for enlarging the ensemble, which in turn led to additional jobs. One of these was an engagement at the prestigious New York dance hall, Club Alabam in 1923. Following a year at this location, Henderson moved the band in 1923 to the Roseland Ballroom lasting until about 1931. These were essentially dance band jobs, featuring the instrumentalists in Henderson's band plus an occasional lead singer.

Growth During the 1920s

Henderson was married in 1925 to Leora Meaux, a trumpeter and bandleader who sometimes sat in with the band. Engagements were plentiful during this period, and the band often spent weeks on the road. Despite personnel changes, Henderson was able to keep his group together. New music was needed and he and his principal arranger, Don Redman, were up to the task. Together they built a standard repertoire of excellent arrangements and developed the group cohesion and style for which the band became well known. In particular, the strong brass and reed sections and the band's outstanding arrangements became their calling cards and the envy of many musicians as well as other bandleaders.

The band was considerably strengthened by an astute personnel move by Henderson: famed trumpeter Louis Armstrong joined the group in 1924 and stayed for a year. Armstrong's addition was felt in several ways, first by the addition of a major entertainer, soloist, and vibrant personality, next by the New Orleans jazz flavor he brought to his solos and to the group, and finally by his contribution to the strength of the brass section. After Armstrong left in 1925, others within the section, notably Tommy Ladnier and Buster Bailey, continued his innovations. Another source of the band's strength was Coleman Hawkins who developed into an outstanding jazz stylist during his years with Henderson.

The music itself followed a standard format of dance tunes, popular songs, and novelty numbers. Within this context Redman introduced many innovations. He used melodic call–and–response interchanges between the brass and reed sections as well as plentiful injections of short riffs by sections and solo musicians. Next, he encouraged improvisation by leaving blank spaces to be filled with short, improvised solos. Another feature was his use of three clarinets together for a short section solo. Redman and Henderson also incorporated an improvised feeling into the orchestrated parts.

When Redman left in 1927, Henderson hired Benny Carter as arranger. He also used borrowed charts, exchanged music with other bands, altered ''stock'' published arrangements to suit the band, and eventually assumed the role of arranger himself. He matured greatly in this capacity, contributing many outstanding works to jazz history. Times were not good for the music business, however. There was much competition, and engagements were no longer so plentiful.

Going on the Record

Henderson's detractors often pointed to a lack of decisiveness at crucial times. The band regularly arrived late for engagements, particularly on the road. Discipline seemed to be a problem, as well as personnel changes. Sometimes a lack of precision was present, or musicians were not ready to begin a song. In 1928 a Philadelphia engagement featuring Vincent Youman's music was scheduled. Henderson had been injured prior to the engagement, but decided to continue. For the engagement, Henderson's band was augmented by a number of additional musicians. Henderson was asked to step down as conductor, and several of his musicians were peremptorily replaced. The musicians were angry on principle, some alleging racism, and several left the band. Despite these and similar problems, there can be no argument that the band continued to produce music with feeling and brought a fresh, new sound to jazz.

A milestone was reached in 1931 when John Hammond became interested in the group, and arranged for a recording session in 1932 for Columbia Records. This session called attention to the group's new songs, including ''Honeysuckle Rose,'' ''New King Porter Stomp,'' and ''Underneath the Harlem Moon.'' Their reputation spread abroad as the recordings were heard in England. Due to the enthusiastic reception of the band's music in England, Coleman Hawkins, Henderson's lead saxophone soloist, was offered regular employment and left the band. At about this time, however, Benny Goodman became aware of the group's new approaches to jazz, and purchased several of the band's arrangements.

Henderson began to struggle at this time, buoyed somewhat by the Goodman purchases. When Benny Goodman offered him the opportunity in 1939 to work with his band as arranger and occasional pianist, including work with the Goodman Sextet, he accepted. Henderson's personal career declined from this point. He occasionally returned to bandleading in the 1940s, and went on tour with Ethel Waters one final time in the late forties. He suffered a paralyzing stroke in 1950, and died on December 31, 1952.

Henderson's musical contribution can best be summarized within the context of the standard danceband repertoire of the day and the changes that followed on his efforts. He left a substantial legacy of more than 300 recordings to his credit dating back to his days with Black Swan. Many good selections are available on compact discs and longplaying records. Led by Henderson's band and others to follow, the dance band era and swing movement had a profound impact on popular music in general, an influence that lasts to this day.

REFERENCES

Alkyer, Frank, ed. *Down Beat; 60 Years of Jazz.* Milwaukee: Hal Leonard Corp., 1995. 26–27, 253.

Allen, Walter C. *Hendersonia; The Music of Fletcher Henderson and His Musicians.* Highland Park, NJ: Allen, 1973.

Berendt, Joachim E. *The Jazz Book.* Westport, CT: Lawrence Hill, 1975.

Bushell, Garvin. *Jazz from the Beginning.* Ann Arbor: University of Michigan Press, 1988.

Collier, James L. *The Making of Jazz.* Boston: Houghton Mifflin, 1978.

''Fletcher H. Henderson.'' Obituary. *New York Times,* December 31, 1952.

Fox, Charles, Peter Gammond, and Alun Morgan. *Jazz on Record.* Westport, CT: Greenwood Press, 1978.

Hadlock, Richard. *Jazz Masters of the 20's.* New York: Macmillan, 1965.

Hammond, John. ''Salute to Fletch.'' *Negro Digest* 9 (August 1951): 95–97.

Harrison, Max, Charles Fox, and Eric Thacker. *The Essential Jazz Records.* Vol. 1. Westport, CT: Greenwood Press, 1984.

Hodier, Andre. *Jazz: Its Evolution and Essence.* New York: Grove Press, 1956.

Jones, LeRoi. *Blues People.* New York: Norton, 1963.

Kernfeld, Barry, ed. *New Grove Dictionary of Jazz.* New York: Macmillan, 1988.

Magee, Jeffrey. ''Revisiting Fletcher Henderson's 'Copenhagen.''' *Journal of the American Musicological Society* 48 (Spring 1995): 42–66.

Peretti, Burton. *The Creation of Jazz.* Urbana: University of Illinois Press, 1992.

Ploski, Harry A. and James Williams. *Reference Library of Black America.* New York: Afro–American Press, 1990.

Southern, Eileen. *The Music of Black Americans.* 3rd ed. New York: Norton, 1997.

Swenson, John, ed. *The Rolling Stone Record Guide.* New York: Random House, 1979.

Tirro, Frank. *Jazz: A History*. New York: Norton, 1977.

Darius L. Thieme

Warren E. Henry
(1909–)
Scientist, inventor, educator

Warren Elliot Henry is recognized as a scientist of international eminence in the understanding of the basic properties of magnetic materials and superconductivity. His classic experiment, done at the Naval Research Laboratories, provided decisive evidence that allowed easy differentiation between two rival theories of low temperature magnetic phenomena. In particular, this experiment gave proof of space quantization. The resulting plots of "magnetic moments" versus magnetic field/temperature appear in elementary and advanced texts and reference books when the quantum nature of paramagnetic ions is discussed.

The Henry family had its roots in Alabama. Henry's father, Nelson Edward Henry, was born in Selma and his mother Mattie Viola McDaniel was born in Ramer. While both of his parents were teachers, Henry's father was also a farmer who organized his farm operations based on the scientific principles championed by George Washington Carver of the Tuskegee Institute. Warren Henry was born February 18, 1909, in Evergreen. He was followed by four brothers and two sisters. Four of his siblings became teachers, while two entered the ministry. Henry married Jeanne Sally Pearlson, of Cambridge, Massachusetts in New York in 1957. Their marriage produced one child, Eva Ruth, born in 1959.

From about 1912 to 1920, Henry attended the grammar school where his parents taught. He transferred in the seventh grade to a school run by a local black church in Greenville. To earn his high school diploma, he transferred again in his senior year to the Alabama State Normal School in Montgomery. It was here that Henry took his first formal courses in science. In 1927 he enrolled at Tuskegee Institute where he received a bachelor of science degree in 1931. For the next several years, he was a teacher and high school principal in Atmore, Alabama. From about 1934 to 1937, Henry was enrolled in the graduate chemistry program at Atlanta University, then accepted a part–time teaching position at Spelman College. He then returned to Tuskegee Institute as an instructor in the chemistry department. In 1937 Atlanta University conferred on him a master of science in organic chemistry. The following year, he entered the doctoral program at the University of Chicago and received a doctorate in physical chemistry in 1941.

Henry's academic performance and research studies at the University of Chicago were outstanding. His dissertation consisted of two parts. The first described the invention and construction of a device to measure extremely small changes in temperature that take place in an ongoing chemical reaction. The second part applied this device to an actual system and measured temperature changes as small as one ten–millionth of a degree.

Joins MIT's Radiation Laboratory

In 1941 Henry took a position at Tuskegee Institute as an assistant professor in the chemistry department. His excellent qualifications allowed him to also teach physics. In particular, he taught special physics courses to the young men training to be Army Air Corps officers. These men would form the 99th Pursuit Squadron and later become known as the Tuskegee Airmen of World War II.

Henry returned to Atlanta University and Spelman College in the summer of 1943 to teach courses in chemistry and physics. However, his stay was cut short by an invitation from the Massachusetts Institute of Technology to join the staff of its top secret facility: The Radiation Laboratory. There he did research on the electrical and magnetic properties of germanium, designed radar components such as video amplifiers and antijamming devices, and designed test equipment. The overall goal of the group in which he worked was to greatly improve the performance of the then current radar systems and create new systems for special purposes. During one emergency, Henry worked without stopping for 36 hours to complete the design of a special amplifier which was to be part of a new system for use on warships. His amplifier worked perfectly from the first day of its installation on ships. When the war ended, Henry participated in a massive writing project to document the work done at the Radiation Laboratory and continued in the basic research program of the new MIT Electronics Laboratory. This new assignment consisted of working out the heat dissipation tests for an advanced helium liquefier, and collaborating on experiments on the microwave skin effect in superconductors and the low–temperature electrical and mechanical properties of germanium.

In 1946 Henry returned to the University of Chicago as a research associate in physics at the Institute for the Study of Metals. In addition to teaching at the university, his research provided the answer to a challenging problem of critical importance to military aviation. The military's use of jet aircraft was then in its infancy. After a number of crashes it was determined that the major cause was "metal fatigue" of the main wing support. The metal fatigue was a consequence of the repeated flexing of the wings when the aircraft flew at high speed. If the failure time for the wing support could be predicted in advance, mechanics could replace it and thus prevent a crash. Henry's previous work, done for his doctoral research, provided him with the tool required to solve this problem. It was well known that repeated bending of a piece of metal causes its temperature to rise in the neighborhood of the area of greatest stress and, as a consequence, the metal weakens. In particular, the faster the temperature change, the faster the metal will fatigue and break. Henry used his doctoral research techniques to test various sample wing supports made from different metal alloys, and determined which alloy had the best mechanical properties. Further, he was able to make estimates of how long his wing support would last before replacement was required. The latter issue was very important since too early replacement would be expensive for the military.

In 1947 Henry acceptedthe position of professor and acting chair of the physics department at Morehouse College in Atlanta, Georgia. On an exchange basis, he taught a course in atomic structure at Atlanta University. During the 1947–48 academic year, he provided special personal tutoring for those students who were failing his physics classes and urged all his students to work hard, for this was the price of being a good scientist.

Joins Naval Research Lab

Morehouse College could not provide the equipment and related support for Henry's research, so in 1948 he accepted a position at the United States Naval Research Laboratory located in Washington, D.C. At the Naval Research Laboratory Henry began a strong research program in the study of magnetic structures of materials and their properties at low temperatures. Much of his efforts were directed toward development of the needed instrumentation required to conduct these studies, as Henry explained in articles in the *Review of Science Instruments* and the *Review of Modern Physics.* In *W. E. Henry Symposium Compendium,* Hattie Carwell described Henry's work:

> While at NRL he developed, and published, a mathematical expression for computing the dimensions of a liquid helium cryostat of specified performance characteristics. He used such cryostats of his improved design to make magnetic measurements on a wide range of materials in high magnetic fields produced by a strong–field magnet he helped to construct. This magnet was originally designed by Francis Bitter of MIT, but it was later improved on by Dr. Henry while at NRL.

Carwell noted further that Henry's measurements of the magnetization of paramagnetic salts earned him immediate international acclaim. She pointed out:

> Because of the accuracy, the number of data points, and the precision of fit to the Brillouin function, these results demonstrated beyond a shadow of doubt a positive proof of spatial quantization of the free paramagnetic ions. . . . Dr. Henry published many more papers on high field magnetization at low temperatures while at NRL, but the first papers are the classics and will be used by scientists and writers for many years to come as a demonstration of special quantization.

The secure establishment of his research career in physics at the NRL gave Henry time to engage in another of his cherished activities—teaching. His availability was brought to the attention of the physics department at Howard University. During 1954–58, he taught a number of courses in solid state physics there.

Accepts Position with Lockheed

In 1960 Henry accepted a position with the Lockheed Missile and Space Company in Palo Alto, California, as a senior staff scientist in the electronic sciences division. He used his expert knowledge in magnetics and cryogenics to solve various problems in aeronautical and spacecraft design. He also discovered several new superconductors, a new type of magnetic behavior, and initiated the theoretical study of the correlation of magnetic–electrical anomalies with the optical properties of special materials. His efforts led to useful applications in the detection of submarines, electronic guidance systems for missiles, and a significant breakthrough in a device to measure magnetic fields in outer space.

Henry moved to the Advanced Systems, Information Technology, Research and Development Division in 1963. He held the same responsibilities in this position as those in the previous division. In 1967 an additional title was added: senior staff scientist in the Advanced Concepts Division of Advanced Programs. This new position carried with it the responsibility of bringing into being new concepts and combinations of old concepts relating to space and related activities, and carrying out similar programs in the areas of aeromechanics, magnetics, cryogenics, electronics, and oceanographics.

In 1968 Lockheed granted Henry a one–year leave so he could teach as a visiting professor in the physics department at Howard University. During this time, Lockheed paid him half of his regular salary. At the end of the 1968–69 academic year, Henry accepted the position of tenured professor of physics at Howard.

The Howard University Years

Henry immediately began a research program to continue his previous work in magnetics and low temperature physics. From California, he brought equipment that was made specifically for him by Lockheed and the physics department at the University of California at Berkeley. Also, the Naval Research Laboratory had saved the equipment from his earlier work done there and he was allowed to borrow it for installment at Howard University.

For the 1971–72 academic year, Henry served as acting chair of the physics department. During this time many of his efforts were devoted to administering the department. However, he continued his research activities and produced two students who obtained a doctorate in physics. He resumed his academic and research duties full time in the fall of 1972, continued to teach courses in solid state physics, and provided mentoring to hundreds of undergraduate and graduate students. With his guidance, four students received a Ph.D. and ten earned M.S. degrees in physics during his tenure at Howard University.

Although Henry formally retired from Howard in 1977, he stayed on full time for an additional five years. During his tenure at Howard, Henry also headed a Task Force on Environmental Studies, chaired the Committee on Preservation and Protection of Creative Ideas and Work of Faculty, and served as coordinator of the affiliation between Howard University and the University of California at Berkeley.

Henry's concerns about the lack of African Americans seeking careers in scientific research led to his affiliation in 1974 with a program at Howard University called the Minorities Access to Research Careers funded by the National Institutes of Health. This program gives students in their junior and senior years of college the opportunity to conduct research under the direction of a faculty member. Students usually spend summers in the research laboratories of either the federal government or at other universities. Henry provided a leadership role in organizing a weekly seminar for these students where eminent persons in the natural sciences would present their latest research results and discuss other science and career–related issues such as which undergraduate courses should be taken, how to succeed in graduate school, and how to write a research paper.

In an earlier program, also funded by the National Institutes of Health, Henry mentored a number of students by allowing them to train in his research laboratory. This effort led to many oral and poster presentations at both local and national scientific meetings by Henry and the students.

Warren Henry is a renaissance man. He has over a half century of accomplishments in research, scholarship, teaching, service, and mentoring. While his major inventions were not patented, several of them, such as the metal Dewar for liquid helium and the magnetic–moment lift, allowed major advances to take place in the study of magnetic materials at low temperatures. His scientific work has received both national and international recognition. For example, he was both a participant and discussant at the 1976 International Conference on Magnetism held in Amsterdam, and he was invited to give a paper on magnetism at the December 1976 American Physical Society Meeting at Stanford University.

Henry has had an extraordinary amount of scientific and personal interaction with other world–class scientists. During his career, he has taken courses and seminars, held scientific discussions, and/or done experiments with more than 14 nobel laureates. Along with these associations, he has done distinguished scientific work at some of the most important research laboratories in the United States. In most of these laboratories, Henry was generally the sole African American employed at the level of true scientific involvement in the activities of these institutions. Often blatantly racist policies existed for all non–white workers. Respect from the scientific community and Henry's public no–nonsense stance against racist practices generally forced his employers to change their policies. This paved the way for other African American workers and scientists to follow.

Henry is a respected elder in the world scientific community, a master teacher and mentor, and a person who continues to light up the lives of others. He lives in Washington, D.C.

REFERENCES

''African–American Physicist Tells His Story.'' *Oakland Tribune,* October 20, 1997.

Carwell, Hattie, ed. *W. E. Henry Symposium Compendium.* Berkeley: Lawrence Berkeley National Laboratory, LBNL–41185, September 19, 1997.

Henry, Warren E. ''A Finite Difference Treatment of a Liquid Helium Cryostat Problem.'' *Journal of Applied Physics* 22 (1951): 1439–40.

———. ''Some Magnetization Studies at Liquid Helium Temperatures and Strong Magnetic Fields.'' *Review of Modern Physics* 25 (1953): 163–64.

———. ''Spin Paramagnetism of Cr+++, Fe+++, and Gd+++ at Liquid Helium Temperatures and in Strong Magnetic Fields.'' *Physical Review* 88 (1952): 559–62.

———, and Robert L. Dolecek. ''A Metal Dewar for Liquid Helium.'' *Review of Science Instruments* 21 (1950): 496–97.

Kessler, James H., J. S. Kidd, and others. *Distinguished African–American Scientists of the 20th Century.* Phoenix: Oryx Press, 1996.

Kittel, Charles. *Introduction to Solid State Physics.* 6th ed. New York: Wiley, 1986.

COLLECTIONS

The personal and professional papers of Warren E. Henry are in his possession. A number of his awards, associated letters, photographs, and other materials are on display at and/or held by the Moorland Spingarn Research Center of Howard University. An oral history interview conducted in the 1970s with Ronald E. Mickens is in the Special Collections of the Fisk University Library. CNN Cable News has a video tape of an interview with Henry, done in conjunction with the Warren E. Henry Symposium held at Lawrence Berkeley National Laboratory, Berkeley, California on September 20, 1997.

Ronald E. Mickens

Matthew A. Henson
(1866–1955)
Seaman, explorer, author

Matthew A. Henson is believed to be the first person to reach the North Pole. Although explorer Robert Peary's claims cast doubt on this first–time achievement by Henson, he was nonetheless an extraordinary explorer.

Matthew Alexander Henson was born on August 8, 1866, just a few months after the end of the American Civil War, in Charles County, Maryland. By the time he was 11, he had run away from home to find relief from a cruel stepmother and a strict household. Eventually he ended up in Washington, D.C., where he worked in a restaurant for his aunt, Janey Moore. While working in the restaurant, he sporadically attended the N Street Elementary School.

Excited by sea stories he had heard from a man called Baltimore Jack, Henson walked to Baltimore and positioned himself around the Baltimore waterfront. At age 12, he was hired as a cabin boy on the *Katie Hines,* a ship bound for China under the command of Captain Childs. The captain took an interest in Henson, and everyday, after Henson completed his assigned tasks, the captain declared school in session in his cabin. He taught Henson reading, writing, basic mathematics, and navigation. Outside the captain's cabin, Henson learned about prejudice and hatred from a drunken sailor who beat him up. This unprovoked attack was his first experience of racism. Childs reassured him that what happened to him was not his fault. As it turned out, this negative experience was turned into a positive one.

Henson developed a close relationship with the captain. Over the next six years Henson would travel around the world and visit China. On a return trip to Baltimore, the captain died of a fever and was buried at sea. Henson, aggrieved by the death of his friend, did not want to sail under another captain. When the ship reached Baltimore, he found a job but was unsatisfied. For four years he worked at odd jobs and eventually returned to Washington, D.C. He was working as a stock boy when he met Lieutenant Robert Peary.

Travels with Robert Peary

In 1887 Peary hired Henson to accompany him to Nicaragua to survey a canal route. It was on this trip that Peary discovered that Henson knew how to prepare a survey chart and had experience as a seaman. After completing this assignment, Peary renewed his interest in exploring the North Pole and formed an expedition. Henson was one of the first persons Peary invited on this expedition. Many people from different nations at this time were working toward reaching the North Pole as well.

Peary was able to convince the navy to allow him a one–year leave to head the expedition. Due to inadequate finances, he was forced to rely on volunteers. Frederick Cook of Brooklyn volunteered to become the expedition's surgeon. In 1891 Henson and Peary started on their trek for the North Pole. It was Henson's first attempt to reach the North Pole and Peary's second. Henson's skills as a carpenter were helpful in the construction of the base camp and sledges. Because of Henson's skin color the native Eskimos thought he may be from a neighboring tribe. Sensitive to their culture, he learned their language, which proved invaluable on their expedition. The native people also taught him how to load a sledge, kill a walrus, treat frost–bite, and manage a food supply. More

Matthew A. Henson

importantly, they taught him to drive a team of huskies. This first expedition with Peary, however, failed.

In August 1892 Peary and Henson went on a lecture tour to raise money for another attempt to reach the North Pole. In the spring of 1893, Peary and Henson were once again ready to begin another expedition. This attempt failed as well. Four more unsuccessful attempts were made. By now, Henson, age 40, had fallen in love with Lucy Ross. Before sailing again in July 1905 Henson promised to marry Ross when he returned. Upon returning from another unsuccessful attempt to reach the North Pole, Henson, as he had promised, married Ross. Not long after their marriage, Henson and Peary had geared up again for another North Pole expedition. Unlike the previous expeditions, this one was successful.

At the outset of the seventh expedition, there were six Americans and 19 Eskimos. However, the last 173 miles were covered by Henson, Peary, and four Eskimos. Peary chose Henson as his companion on the final phase of the expedition. According to the *Negro Digest,* Donald Macmillan, one of the Americans on the expedition, commented that Henson was chosen because "he was of more real value than all the rest of us put together." Peary also chose Henson undoubtedly due to their shared experiences on the six previous expeditions. On at least two occasions Henson had saved Peary's life: Henson rescued Peary when he was attacked by an enraged musk ox and on another occasion saved him from starvation. Peary paid Henson the highest compliment when he admitted, as quoted in the *Negro History Bulletin,* "He is my most valuable companion. I could not get along without him."

Henson and Peary Discover the North Pole

Now at age 53, Peary was unable to keep pace with the rugged demands of the last miles of the expedition. He was exhausted and disabled due to the loss of nine of his toes during previous expeditions. Therefore, he sent Henson. Peary and the four Eskimos trailed behind him. Forty–five minutes later Peary, driven on a sled by four Eskimos, arrived. Through careful observations and calculations, Peary claimed the discovery of the North Pole. On April 6, 1909, Henson and Peary planted the American flag.

The following day Peary was interviewed. He praised Henson for his courage, adaptability to the climate, loyalty, mastery of the Eskimo language, and skills in sled building, driving, and igloo construction. After the expedition, Peary received national and international fame, while Henson was unfortunately forgotten. Despite Henson's dedication, loyalty, sacrifice, and skills, he received no credit or fame. He lived his life in virtual obscurity. He was able to find work only as a parking attendant and later as a messenger boy in New York's Custom House. At age 70, Henson, having been appointed by President Howard Taft in 1913 as a clerk, retired on an annual income of $1,020. Quoted in *Ebony,* Henson once told a *Baltimore Sun* reporter,''I was fit as ever, and the retirement pay of $1,020 a year meant that Lucy could not retire with me. But we got along.'' Many bills were presented to Congress specifying that Henson, like Peary, should receive a medal and a pension, but all failed.

By 1912 Henson had written a book entitled *The Negro at the North Pole.* In it he discussed his experiences while trying to reach the North Pole. The *Pittsburgh Courier* quoted Henson who wrote of his experiences:

> As I stood there at the top of the world and thought of the hundreds of men who had lost their lives in the effort to reach it, I felt profoundly grateful that I, as the personal attendant of the commander, had the honor of representing my race in the historic achievement.

It was not until 1937 that Henson was finally recognized for his monumental accomplishment. In that year, he became the first African American member of the New York Explorers Club. On January 28, 1944, Henson received a belated medal in honor of the members of the expedition. The Chicago Geographical Society, in 1948, paid tribute to Henson, 81, by awarding him with a gold medal. President Harry S. Truman, in 1950, honored Henson in a ceremony at the Pentagon. The year before his death in 1954, he received a citation from President Dwight D. Eisenhower at the White House. Posthumously, the state of Maryland, in 1961, passed a bill providing for a permanent plaque honoring Henson to be placed in the State House at Annapolis, Maryland.

Henson died at age 88 of a cerebral hemorrhage. His surviving relatives were his wife, Lucy Henson, and a sister, Eliza Carter of Washington, D.C. The Hensons had no children. His funeral was held at the Abyssinian Baptist Church, and Adam Clayton Powell Jr. delivered the eulogy. Although Henson's last dying wish was to be buried next to Admiral Peary in Arlington National Cemetery, his body was buried in an unmarked grave in New York. Since Henson was not a veteran, it required an act of Congress to grant his wish. A number of Henson admirers had long sought to have him buried in Arlington. Notable among these was S. Allen Counter, who was notified in October of 1987 by the Department of the Army that Henson's remains would be moved to Arlington. Thirty–three years later, Henson, who died on March 9, 1955, was granted his wish. Following the work of Counter and the North Pole Family Reunion Committee, based at Harvard University, in 1986 efforts were underway to bring descendants of the Henson and Peary families together. On June 1, 1987, some 200 members of these families and guests assembled in Harvard's Memorial Hall for a family reunion banquet. On April 8, 1988, the family members and supporters were on hand for Henson's reburial.

Conflicting accounts concerning Peary's and Henson's discovery of the North Pole have been made public. Wally Herbert claimed in *The Noose of Laurels* that Peary's original diary—actually a log of his journey—and astronomical observations had been inaccessible until 1984, when the Peary family was persuaded to release these and other private materials for scholars to study. Herbert retraced the tracks of Peary's 1909 journey and concluded that some of Peary's diary entries conflicted with each other and that Peary's observations were faked. Herbert further assessed that Peary wanted fame and sought a promotion and retirement with the rank of rear admiral. In *North Pole Legacy,* Counter also discussed some of the controversy and noted that the new, ''damaging evidence'' troubles many African Americans. Counter confirmed that Peary and Henson did, in fact, record and confirm their navigational information in numerous sources.

Henson, a man described as the single most important member of Peary's team, gave unselfish devotion and dedication to a death–defying achievement. Although recognition was slow in coming, Henson never revealed any anger or regrets. He was proud to represent his race in this historic accomplishment.

REFERENCES

Counter, S. Allen. *North Pole Legacy: Black, White, and Eskimo.* Amherst: University of Massachusetts Press, 1991.

Forman, Harrison. ''Idol of the Arctic.'' *Negro Digest* 10 (June 1951): 32–42.

Frisby, Herbert M. ''Cover: Matthew Henson Memorial.'' *Negro History Bulletin* 25 (May 1962): 195–96.

Herbert, Wally. *The Noose of Laurels: Robert E. Peary and the Race to the North Pole.* New York: Atheneum, 1989.

''Matt Henson: Black Explorer is Part of Controversy in Film 'Race to the Pole.''' *Ebony* 39 (November 1983): 80–84.

''Matthew Henson Buried: Explorer First to See Pole.'' *Pittsburgh Courier,* March 19, 1955.

COLLECTIONS

The Peary Archives, including the famous Peary Diary that gives an account of the 1909 expedition are in the National Archives in Washington, D.C.

Patricia A. Pearson

Alonzo F. Herndon
(1858–1927)
Entrepreneur, philanthropist

Alonzo F. Herndon

Born a slave, Alonzo Franklin Herndon, founder and president of Atlanta Life Insurance Company, became one of the first prosperous black entrepreneurs in America in the years following Reconstruction. A man of great economic and social leadership, he made a fortune and also gave much back to Atlanta's black community.

Sophenie Herndon, an enslaved woman, gave birth to Alonzo Franklin Herndon on July 21, 1858, on a farm near Social Circle, Georgia. His only sibling Thomas was born two years later. His white father, whose name was listed as Abe on Alonzo Herndon's death certificate, owned the Herndon farm. Atlanta's richest black man by the turn of the century left no written record of his years of living in slavery. He does, however, in a brief autobiographical account stored in the Herndon Family Archives, "Alonzo Herndon Remembers," describe life for himself, his brother, and his mother immediately after the Emancipation:

> My mother was emancipated when I was seven years old and my brother Tom five years old. She was sent adrift in the world with her two children and a corded bed and [a] few quilts. She hired herself out by the day and as there was no money in the country, she received as pay potatoes, molasses, and peas enough to keep us from starving. Our former master finally allowed us to take shelter in a one room log cabin with four other families. My mother had only her bed space under which she stowed her daily earnings in potatoes or peas or molasses.

Along with his mother, the grandparents, Carter and Toma, helped to shape the mind of the young visionary as he worked on the former master's farm from the age of seven to 13. Between 13 and 16 years—now paid money for his labor—he continued working for his former master. His earnings of $25 for the first year, $30 for the second, and $40 for the third went to his mother. From his meager earnings, Herndon always managed to save a part because at an early age his vision projected him beyond the enslaved beginnings. He wrote in his autobiographical account, "I was some twenty years old and decided to seek my fortune in a broader field."

In spite of little formal education, vision and thrift inspired Herndon's life. Of his formal education Herndon says in his autobiographical account, "For my knowledge of books and the world was gleaned during these twenty years of life, in twelve months of schooling which constitutes all the schooling I ever had. I received this twelve months teaching in doses of five weeks a year." Herndon realized that farming would not propel him towards his dream, for his savings only amounted to $11 after years on the farm. When he was about 20, the future founder and president of Atlanta Life Insurance Company sneaked away from his mother, grandparents, and the farm. After working at odd jobs in small towns, he learned barbering, then one of the main professions of black men and sources of employment and business in the segregated South.

From Jonesboro to the Crystal Palace

Herndon glimpsed success with the opening of his first shop in Jonesboro, Georgia. But seeking expansion opportunities, he left Jonesboro and worked throughout the state as a barber from approximately 1878 to 1882, saving his money and earning the respect of the people in the various communities by being always "careful, conscientious, polite and tactful," as he wrote in his biographical note. His journeyman barbering ended in Atlanta after short stays in Rome, Georgia, and Chattanooga, Tennessee. In the city of Atlanta, he realized his dream of becoming a first–class barber and prominent businessman. "I came to Atlanta with the determination to succeed," he wrote.

With such determination and his experience, Herndon joined with the most prominent black barber in Atlanta, Dougherty Hutchins, a successful businessman before the Civil War. Within a few years, Herndon operated a five–chair shop under his own name. By the time his mother died at the age of 61 on June 3, 1892, Herndon had a budding reputation as a barber, businessman, and as a good human being, always thinking about the welfare of others. By 1893 Herndon owned three more barbershops. Although his first undertakings in barbering were to black customers, the barbershop for which he was known throughout the South was The Crystal Palace, located at 66 Peachtree Street. The elegant barbershop with its 25 chairs and 20 baths and showers opened to a non–black clientele in 1902. Herndon's wealth allowed him to travel to Europe to refine his barbering techniques in order to serve his clientele in the best way possible. The beveled plate glass that he saw in Paris on the Avenue de l'Opéra was copied and placed in his barbershop. European furnishings, including gold mirrors, bronze and crystal chandeliers bought during his trips, white marble walls and floors, and porcelain barber chairs underscored the uniqueness of the barbershop. The Crystal Palace simulated in a sense the black establishments like the Paschal's restaurant in Atlanta made famous by its clients.

In the barbershop, frequented by the judges, lawyers, doctors, and political figures, Herndon, a sagacious businessman, knew how to benefit from his access to many of the important men of the city and state. As his business grew, Herndon started to build a real estate empire which before his death included some 100 houses and a large block of commercial property in the black business district on Auburn Avenue.

As a sign of the times in which Herndon lived, black businesses, especially in the South, were vulnerable to racism. For example, in spite of his respect in both the white and black communities, Herndon's business was not spared the Atlanta race riot of 1906. The Crystal Palace was damaged, four of the barbers injured, and a bootblack kicked to death.

Becomes Insurance Magnate

Herndon's wealth and reputation as an ethical and honest businessman afforded him a privileged position in the business community. Two ministers, Peter James Bryant and James Arthur Hopkins, approached Herndon to purchase the Atlanta Benevolent and Protective Association, which according to Alexa Benson Henderson in *Atlanta Life Insurance Company* was "set up along the lines of an insurance society . . . essentially a burial association providing a death payment that ranged from ten to fifty dollars." Herndon agreed to purchase it for the price of $140. So, in 1905 Herndon entered into the insurance business as a neophyte but surrounded himself with a staff of some of the most capable people in the insurance business. With additional acquisitions, the Atlanta Benevolent and Protective Association became the Atlanta Mutual Insurance Association. As evidence of Herndon's business acumen, at the end of 1905 the company operated 23 offices in Georgia, offering insurance to blacks who could not find it at white companies. In 1915 his insurance business extended to Alabama with more than $1 million of insurance in force.

Herndon demonstrated a keen sense of the insurance environment and its potential pitfalls. This understanding pushed him to seek measures to protect the company and its policyholders. "Anxious to put the company in a position to achieve greater viability," wrote Henderson, "Herndon took steps in 1916 to increase the capital and improve its standing among individual companies." The control of the insurance company changed from policyholders to shareholders with Herndon owning most of the shares. In 1922 another reorganization resulted in a name change to the present Atlanta Life Insurance. The company's growth was characterized by its purchase of many small black insurance companies which kept ownership and control in the hands of blacks, an important element of Herndon's philosophy. In an advertisement in the *Southern News* for August of 1927, Atlanta Life noted its vital presence in the black community:

> It has over half a million dollars invested in school houses. Roads and institutions for public good. It has over $100,000 invested in the homes of our people. It gives employment to over 1,000 men of our race including Physicians, Lawyers, Printers, Accountants, Stenographers, Business Executives, Clerks and Agents.

Three years before his death, the company operated in Florida, Kentucky, Kansas, Missouri, Tennessee, and Texas.

Herndon possessed three qualities that marked him as an astute businessman: good judgment, thrift, and a concern and compassion for his community of employees, customers, and associates. A program brochure for Atlanta Life, located in the Herndon Room, noted: "Wherever or whenever we have something of which we are proud and joyful we always like to share that pride and joy with our people." He undoubtedly instilled this quality in his workers. An unpublished written tribute to Herndon on his 59th birthday, also in the archives, points out that "he always emphasized what he saved more than what he earned." In a publication in the archives entitled "A Personal Tribute to My Co–Workers," Herndon wrote, "They handle daily the hard–earned dollars of policy holders and always account for every penny."

Herndon never used his vast wealth to cushion himself from social, political, and philanthropic obligations in regards to the advancement of the black community. Herndon's notoriety in the business and black community invited many people to seek him out. The *Southern News* for August of 1927 reported that "No one can truthfully say that any deserving man ever came to Mr. Herndon for assistance that was refused. His sympathy extended to all who were in distress. Hundreds of people benefited by his wealth and generosity that the world will never know about." Specifically, many in the black community of Atlanta remember him for his generous donations in the service of children and working mothers. Herndon financed orphanages and nurseries, one of which bore his name.

Life Outside of Atlanta Mutual

Herndon was active in the Southview Cemetery Association, Atlanta Loan and Trust, and Atlanta State Savings Bank. A founder of Gate City Drug Company, Auburn Avenue's first black–owned drugstore, he provided a home for other black businesses and organizations, including one of the earliest black–owned hotels, in the Herndon Building located at 251 Auburn Avenue.

The prominent black business leader was sought out by both prominent leaders of the time, Booker T. Washington and W. E. B. Du Bois. At the first conference of the National Negro Business League, which Washington organized in 1890, Herndon was present as a delegate from Atlanta. Apparently he followed Washington's self–help philosophy, often lecturing on the topic. Although Herndon and Du Bois were among the 29 founders of the Niagara Movement in 1905 and attended the founding meeting that Du Bois called, he showed no continuing interest in the group, even as it grew into the NAACP.

In 1893 Herndon married Adrienne McNeil, a beautiful and talented woman born in Augusta, Georgia. At Atlanta University she was the only black woman faculty member; she and W. E. B. Du Bois were two of only three blacks on the faculty. The Herndons had one child, Norris Bumstead Herndon, who was born on July 15, 1897, and died in June of 1977. Adrienne Herndon died in 1910, months before the mansion that she had helped design was completed. After that, the stern Alonzo Herndon doted on his child and taught him the insurance business beginning from a very young age. Norris Herndon graduated from Atlanta University in 1919 and earned an M.B.A. from Harvard in 1921. Later, as vice–president, he aided his father in reorganizing the company.

After his first wife died, Herndon married Jessie Gillespie of Milwaukee, Wisconsin, in 1912. She also later served as vice–president of Atlanta Life. Alonzo Herndon, however, remained president of Atlanta Life until his death in 1927, at the age of 69. Jessie Herndon, together with her stepson, continued the philanthropic tradition of her late husband until her death in 1947. After his father died, Norris Herndon, who was nearly a recluse, succeeded him.

From October 23, 1993, to August 31, 1995, the Atlanta History Center celebrated his achievements in an exhibit entitled "The Herndons: Style and Substance of the Black Upper Class in Atlanta, 1880–1930." Above Auburn Avenue hangs a permanent banner of Alonzo Herndon, his wife, and only son Norris, adding to their permanent presence just a block away from Herndon Plaza. The walls of his Beaux Arts Classical mansion, completed in 1910 and now open to the public, chronicles his brilliant personal and professional life.

Norris Connally, a grand nephew of Herndon, now serves on the board of Atlanta Life. In an interview, he remembered visiting the Herndon home as a child, and playing with his cousin Norris, and the uncle's generous gifts of antiques to his mother.

The Atlanta Life Insurance Company, the second largest black insurance company in the United States, stands as a monument to the accomplishments in the business world of its founder and president until his death, Alonzo F. Herndon.

REFERENCES

"Alonzo Franklin Herndon." *Southern News* 4 (August 1927): 2.

Connally, Norris. Interview with Rosa Bobia, May 1997.

Henderson, Alexa Benson. *Atlanta Life Insurance Company: Guardian of Black Economic Dignity.* Tuscaloosa: University of Alabama Press, 1990.

Ingham, John N., and Lynne B. Feldman. *African–American Business Leaders.* Westport, CT: Greenwood Press, 1994.

"Thinking Men." *Southern News* 4 (August 1927): 7.

COLLECTIONS

The papers of Alonzo Herndon are in the Herndon Family Archives, Herndon House, 587 University Place, Atlanta, Georgia.

Rosa Bobia

James Hewlett

(fl. 1820s)

Actor, entertainer

Little is known of James Hewlett, who tried to make his way as an actor and musician between the 1820s and the mid–1840s. Surprisingly, one of the meager remnants of his existence is a portrait of him in the role of Richard III in 1821. Hewlett was the principal actor of the African Grove Theater, the first black theater in the United States, which led a precarious existence at the corner of Beeker Street and Mercer Street in New York City from the summer of 1821 to the summer of 1823.

Hewlett came from a New York family of mixed descent. His sister Elizabeth's mother was a white woman named King and her maternal grandmother was a white woman named Bartlett. The family may have originally come from the West Indies—James McCune Smith, the family physician, said Hewlett was born in the islands in an 1860 article quoted by Marshall and Stock—but Hewlett's two known sisters, Elizabeth and Mary, were apprenticed to the Quaker Mott family, apparently in New York City.

By 1816 James Hewlett was singing professionally. In that year, Henry Brown, former steward of a Liverpool liner, set up a tea–garden on Thames Street and Hewlett was one of his entertainers. Hewlett kept his day–time job; at one point he seems to have been a waiter at the City Hotel. James McCune Smith says he was "a very fine singer for the time" and "he added by degree dramatic exhibitions to the entertainments." In addition to singing, he gradually developed a reputation for a performance presenting imitations of several actors in very different dramatic roles. Smith describes the performer as "a mulatto of middle height, with sharp features, and a well–set coal–black eye." Hewlett followed the fashionable crowd to Saratoga in the summer and gave performances in a hotel there. According to Smith, his handbills described him as "Vocalist, and Shakespeare's proud Representative [who] Will Give an Entertainment in Singing and Acting." Hewlett, like his younger and more famous contemporary, Ira Aldridge, was an avid frequenter of the gallery of the Park Theater, New York's leading dramatic venue.

The success of Henry Brown's tea–garden or ice cream garden, which, despite the names, sold strong liquor–led him to set up a rough wood theater seating from 300 to 400 people on Mercer Street, charging a quarter for admission. As in all contemporary theaters, the evening's entertainment offered a mixture of music, dance, and plays. A handbill for a benefit performance for James Hewlett is reproduced in both the *Annals of the New York Stage* and *The Music of Black Americans.* The October 1, 1821 performance opened with ten songs, seven of which were sung by Hewlett himself. Then followed a performance of *Richard III,* starring Hewlett. Actors doubled roles, and the play was severely cut due to the limited number of performers available. Next came a two person pantomime, with Hewlett as one of the characters. Finally, there was a ballet devised by Hewlett, who was also one of the four dancers. The notices of Hewlett's performances, all by whites, are condescending, but he pleased his audience.

The performances at the African theater drew whites as well as blacks, and a portion of the auditorium was set aside for whites. The rowdiness and noisiness of the audiences led to complaints by neighbors and gave the police an excuse to close down the theater from time to time. Defiance of a police ban led to Hewlett and others being arrested after one of the performances of *Richard III.* They were released after promising not to continue but soon began giving performances again. Shortly before the African Grove closed for good, in June 1823, it produced for the first time in the United States a play written by a black author, *The Drama of King Shotaway,* written by the owner and manager Thomas Brown. Hewlett played the lead in the play which dramatized an insurrection on the West Indies island of St. Vincent.

Scattered traces of Hewlett appear after 1823. He tried his luck in England some time between 1823 and 1825, billing himself afterwards as "The New York and London Coloured Comedian." In 1826 he joined Frank Johnson, the Philadelphia band leader, in benefit concerts and appears to have gone to England for a second time after giving a performance at an improvised theater in Brooklyn on February 3. On September 28, 1826, Hewlett gave a performance at New York's Spruce Street Theater. In 1831 he gave a benefit performance on March 7 in New York City. There was another at Columbian Hall on September 22; Mrs. Hewlett, presumably his wife, played the piano.

The last definite trace of Hewlett is in Martin Delany's 1852 book *The Condition, Elevation, Emigration, and Destiny of the Colored People of the United States* under the name James Ulett. Delany says he performed several times at the Richmond Hill Theater in 1836. Delany writes, "Mr. Ulett was not well educated, and consequently, labored under considerable inconvenience in reading, frequently making grammatical blunders, as the writer noticed in a private rehearsal, in 1836, in the city of New York. He, however, possessed great intellectual powers, and his success depended more upon that, than his accuracy in reading. Of course, he was a great delineator of character, which being the principal feature in a comedian, his language was lost sight of in common conversation." Delany concludes with all we know about Hewlett's final years, "Mr. Ulett died in New York a few years ago."

James Hewlett deserves to be remembered for his attempt to build up a black theater in the United States. Possibly the first recorded slave song, "Opossum Up a Gum Tree," was sung at the African Grove Theater. The singer was young Ira Aldridge (1807?–1867), who was later to become a leading Shakespearean actor in Europe. Hewlett never achieved the fame of Aldridge, but that was not for want of trying.

REFERENCES

Delany, Martin Robison. *The Condition, Elevation, Emigration, and Destiny of the Colored People of the United States.* Philadelphia: The Author, 1852.

Lyons, Maritcha Rémond. *Memories of Yesterdays: All of Which I Saw and Part of Which I Was.* Unpublished autobiography. New York: Schomburg Center for Research in Black Culture.

Marshall, Herbert, and Mildred Stock. *Ira Aldridge.* New York: Macmillan, 1958.

Odell, George C. D. *Annals of the New York Stage.* Vol. 3. 1928. Reprint, New York: AMS Press, 1970.

Southern, Eileen. *Biographical Dictionary of Afro–American and African Musicians.* Westport, CT: Greenwood Press, 1982.

———. *The Music of Black Americans.* 2d ed. New York: Norton, 1983.

Robert L. Johns

A. Leon Higginbotham Jr.

(1928–)

Jurist, educator, author

A. Leon Higginbotham Jr. is one of six black jurists to be appointed to preside over a U.S. Court of Appeals. His commitment to the legacy of his mentor, Thurgood Marshall, in the struggle for equal justice for minorities, women, and the poor, has made him a leading civil rights advocate and scholar. In September 1995 President Bill Clinton presented Higginbotham with the Presidential Medal of Freedom, the nation's highest civilian honor. According to *Contemporary Black Biography,* the White House characterized Higginbotham as a "highly respected judge and academic" who has "worked tirelessly to advance the needs of those who have long been denied access to the American Dream." Quoted in *The Boulé Journal,* Thurgood Marshall commenting on Higginbotham's career said, "I think he is a great lawyer and a very great judge. Period."

Aloysius Leon Higginbotham Jr. was born on February 25, 1928, in Trenton, New Jersey, to Aloysius Higginbotham, a factory worker, and Emma Lee Douglass Higginbotham, a maid. The Higginbotham household possessed only two books: a Bible and a dictionary that someone had found in the trash. Young Higginbotham attended Ewing Park, a black segregated public elementary school, and integrated an all–white high school. As an adolescent, he worked as a hotel busboy, shoe store porter, and laborer. He excelled in school, demonstrating great skill in logic and language. A serious student, one summer he regularly rode his bicycle nearly 20 miles to be tutored.

At age 16 Higginbotham left home to begin his undergraduate studies at Purdue University. Initially, he showed interest in becoming an engineer, but an incident involving unfair housing for black students changed his mind and his life forever. Higginbotham requested heated accommodation in a campus dormitory for black students who were residing in the attic of an old house. Purdue's president, Edward Charles Elliot, replied as quoted in the *American Bar Association Journal* for September 1996, "Higginbotham, the law doesn't require us to let colored students in the dorm. We will never do it. And you either accept things as they are or leave the university immediately." Higginbotham said in the same source, "I am a lawyer today because of Dr. Elliott's negative motivation. I felt that I could not go into engineering, that I had to challenge the system."

Higginbotham transferred to Antioch College in Ohio where he met, and on August 21, 1948, married his first wife Jeanne L. Foster. Prior to receipt of his B.A. in sociology from Antioch College in 1949, Higginbotham successfully applied to Yale University School of Law. After graduating with an LL.B. in 1952, he served as a law clerk in the office of Justice William Curtis Bok in Philadelphia until 1953, when he was admitted to the Bar of the Commonwealth of Pennsylvania. During this time, Higginbotham's commitment to ending racism grew in response to witnessing Thurgood Marshall argue the *Sweatt v. Painter* case. This case contested the University of Texas School of Law's denial of admission to blacks.

Higginbotham served briefly as an assistant district attorney for Philadelphia County and in 1954 became a partner in the law firm Norris, Green, Harris, and (later) Higginbotham. He remained there until 1962 while simultaneously holding posts as a special hearing officer for the U.S. Department of Justice. In 1963, Higginbotham became the youngest commissioner on the Federal Trade Commission.

In 1964 President Lyndon Johnson appointed Higginbotham to serve as a U.S. District Court judge of the Eastern District of Pennsylvania at Philadelphia. Several of his law clerks later became influential figures in national politics. These clerks included Representative Eleanor Holmes Norton; Edward Dennis, head of the Criminal Division of the U. S. Department of Justice; Gilbert Casellas, chairman of the Equal Employment Opportunity Commission; and Kathleen Cleaver, former Black Panther who became an attorney and professor at Harvard University. For 13 years Higginbotham served as a jurist and lectured at university law schools nationwide. Serving as a visiting professor, he held posts at Wharton Graduate School at the University of Pennsylvania in 1970, the University of Hawaii in 1973 and 1974, and Yale University in 1975.

Named Federal Appeals Judge

In 1977 President Jimmy Carter appointed Higginbotham judge of the U. S. Court of Appeals for the Third Circuit (Philadelphia). He was the third person of African descent to become a federal appeals judge. During the time that he served in this position he continued lecturing, accepting a post at the University of Michigan in 1978. A few of his many administrative appointments included trustee of Thomas Jefferson University (1966–78) and Yale University (1970–76), the board of overseers of the University of Pennsylvania Law School (chairman, 1979), and citizen regent of the Smithsonian Institute. He is also a distinguished member and fellow of the American Bar Foundation and a member of the American Philosophical Society, the American Academy of Political and Social Science, and Christian Street Branch YMCA. The recipient of more than 80 honorary degrees and numerous honors and awards, Higginbotham has remained committed to public service.

As an academician, Higginbotham has written more than 100 published articles. In 1978 he received national acclaim for his book *In the Matter of Color: Race and the American Legal Process* (New York: Oxford University Press, 1978). In this book Higginbotham approached the sensitive issues of racism, its origins, and its influence on the American legal system from the perspective of an African American jurist. Citing numerous examples from the legal histories of Georgia, Massachusetts, New York, Pennsylvania, and Virginia, he argued that "The branding of any groups as inferior or less than human on the basis of color was not inevitable. There were sufficient legal, theological, and philosophical foundations upon which a more uniformly just and human social structure could have been built.''

In a review of this work Eugene D. Genovese, a renowned historian, wrote in the *New York Times Book Review,* ''Judge Higginbotham's main argument is that the law became an active agent, in not merely a passive reflection on the enslavement of most blacks, and the suppression of the rest; that it paved the way for new and greater atrocities within and without the law.'' The significance of Higginbotham's book can be measured through the author's awards from both literary and legal associations. The American Bar Association awarded him the Silver Gavel Award, and the National Bar Association bestowed him with a literary award. In addition, *In the Matter* earned Higginbotham the Frederick Douglass Award from the National Association of Black Journalists, an award from the National Conference of Black Lawyers, and a nomination for the American Book Award in 1981.

Since its publication in 1978, *In the Matter* continues to be used as a text at the undergraduate level in social science disciplines ranging from African American studies and American history to political science and philosophy. Additional works published by Higginbotham include an anthology entitled *Documents on Race and the American Legal Process.* His most recent work, *Shades of Freedom: Racial Political and Presumptions of the American Legal Process* (1996) again examined issues of race in relation to the American legal process. Next, he plans to write his autobiography.

Upon retiring from the bench in 1993, Higginbotham has focused his efforts on lecturing, counseling, and writing. His explanation to Lincoln Caplan in the *American Bar Association Journal* of his reason for leaving the bench was, ''I wanted to use my legal talent without the constraints necessarily imposed by the judiciary. I wanted to be able to focus on. . .what I thought were the significant issues confronting America.'' In 1994 Harvard University appointed Higginbotham as the first Public Service Professor of Jurisprudence at its Kennedy School of Government. He also joined Harvard's Afro–American Studies faculty, which included Henry Louis Gates Jr., Cornel West, and Evelyn Brooks–Higginbotham, the judge's second wife.

In 1994 top white executives at Texaco Incorporated were caught on tape making racist remarks about blacks and then plotted to destroy the tape. The company agreed to spend $176.1 million to settle a race discrimination lawsuit. Texaco hired Higginbotham in 1996 to advise the company on human resources and diversity. Higginbotham told *Jet* magazine that he looked forward to the assignment and was ''confident that Texaco wants to eradicate any of the inequitable vestiges of the past and make the company a model of equity and fairness.''

Higginbotham was awarded the Presidential Medal of Freedom in 1995, the nation's highest civilian honor. In July 1996 Higginbotham received the Spingarn Medal from the NAACP. Past recipients of this honor include Martin Luther King Jr., Colin Powell, Rosa Parks, and Langston Hughes. Higginbotham considers this award to be the most important of his life.

A tall, distinguished gentleman, Higginbotham is referred to in the *ABA Journal* as ''a lawyer's lawyer, versatile and measured—guiding institutional clients through legal mazes one day, filling the role of public advocate the next, cultivating the rising generation as a teacher, writer, and mentor.'' In the *ABA Journal,* he noted his hope that an emerging American leadership will mandate social justice by understanding that ''the law and its instruments are shapers; they can be used to eliminate injustice or to sustain it.''

Current address: Harvard University, Cambridge, MA 02138.

REFERENCES

Caplan, Lincoln. ''Judging Leon Higginbotham.'' *American Bar Association Journal* 82 (September 1996): 71.

Contemporary Authors. Vol. 110. Detroit: Gale Research, 1984.

Contemporary Black Biography. Vol. 13. Detroit: Gale Research, 1997.

Higginbotham, A. Leon Jr. *In the Matter of Color: Race and the American Legal Process.* New York, Oxford University Press, 1978.

———. *Shades of Freedom: Racial Politics and Presumptions of the American Legal Process.* New York: Oxford University Press, 1996.

''Judge A. Leon Higginbotham, Jr. to Advise Texaco on Diversity Matters.'' *Jet* 91 (16 December 1996): 6.

New York Times Book Review, June 18, 1978.

Who's Who among African Americans, 1996–97. 9th ed. Detroit: Gale Research, 1996.

Gregory Williams

Jesse Hill Jr.

(1926–)

Corporate executive, entrepreneur

Jesse Hill Jr. built a national career from monumental successes in the business, civic, and political arenas. He helped to shape modern–day Atlanta. Lured by the example of Alonzo Herndon, founder and president of Atlanta Life Insurance Company, as well as the reputation of the city of Atlanta as a progressive one for African Americans in 1949, Hill turned down other job offers in order to work at Atlanta Life. At the age of 22, Hill began a career with the insurance company that would span more than four decades.

Hill was born May 30, 1926, in St. Louis. His maternal family's southern roots can be traced to great–grandparents born in slavery near Mt. Bayou, Mississippi. Recently, Hill discovered that his great grandfather preached in a church in

Jesse Hill Jr.

the Mt. Bayou area bearing his last name, Dennis Chapel. The church may still exist. By the turn of the century, his grandparents had moved to St. Louis. Major Dennis and his wife, Mary Speaks Dennis, were the parents of 15 children. Hill's mother, Nancy Dennis Martin, was the oldest. Of his father, Hill would only say in a 1997 interview, ''I knew him.'' As the eldest, Hill's mother had to forego a high school education to earn money to help support her 14 siblings. Later, as a divorcee living with her parents, she worked as a laundress—a job she held for 30 years—to educate Hill and his sister, Mertice.

In St. Louis during the Great Depression, Hill's grandfather, described by business writer Ernest Dolsedolph in the *Atlanta Journal Constitution* as ''a veritable 1930's conglomerate,'' was a role model for Hill, who as a young man worked alongside him. Hill said in an interview, '' My grandfather, who always encouraged us to go into business, was a pioneer entrepreneur in south St. Louis where I grew up. He developed a business moving and hauling furniture called the Dennis Moving and Furniture Company. In addition to that, in the summer he sold ice and watermelons from a horse–drawn wagon and in the winter, he sold coal.'' After his grandfather's death, two of Hill's uncles continued the family business intermittently until the early 1990s.

Hill demonstrated his entrepreneurial aptitude early. He explained in an interview, ''Even before I finished elementary school, I had my own little business. In working with my grandfather, I acquired several wagons pulled by hand and I, as one of the first recyclers, would collect bottles, rags, newspaper, garments, copper, brass, and iron. An outlet company would purchase these things. I would have other boys who would use my wagons and work for me. So I got an early start in business.''

Hill also had a newspaper business. He said in an interview, ''I also sold all the black newspapers from around the country, the *Pittsburgh Courier,* the *Chicago Defender,* the *Michigan Chronicler.* The *Norfolk Journal and Guide* before we had an *Ebony* or *Jet.* I would receive them in the mail and sell them on the weekend.'' Growing up in the thirties in Missouri, Hill learned valuable lessons of sacrifice, thriftiness, and the great effort it took to eke out a living.

Hill obtained a bachelor's degree in mathematics and physics from Lincoln University in Missouri in 1947 and received a master's degree in business administration with an emphasis in actuarial science from the University of Michigan in 1949.

Business and Civic Involvement

In 1973 Norris B. Herndon, the son of the Atlanta Life founder Alonzo F. Herndon and owner of 80 percent of the company stock, stepped down as president. He promoted Hill, the vice president and chief actuary, to the position of president and chief executive officer. Hill led Atlanta Life to its highest level of growth in assets and shareholder value.

In addition to his responsibilities at Atlanta Life Insurance Company, Hill involved himself in the African American community. During his first three years in Atlanta, he became the superintendent of the Sunday school at Big Bethel African Methodist Episcopal Church, a position he held for over 25 years. He was secretary of the Atlanta Business League and a very active voter–registration worker for the Atlanta Negro Voters League, an important group for the expanding civil rights movement. In 1952 his distinguished service was recognized by the African American community. The Butler Street YMCA, Hill's first residence in Atlanta, was unused to honoring a person so young. ''My. . .grandparents and mother instilled in me that in service and giving you grow and receive,'' he said in a 1997 interview.

By Hill's own admission, the civil rights movement first propelled him to prominence in Atlanta. He told the *Atlanta Journal Constitution* in 1986, ''If I have stature, a lot of it had to have come from the civil rights movement.'' His work in voter registration increased when he accepted the chairmanship in the 1950s of the All–Citizens Registration Committee—a committee formed in 1946 to increase black voter registration. As chairman from the early fifties to the mid–sixties, Hill aided black Atlanta's quest for political power. He stated in a 1997 interview, ''[It] was a legendary committee which was the key to substantial increase in voter registration in Atlanta. Of my many civic experiences, that was the most vital and probably contributed more to the pursuit of dignity and empowerment for African Americans in Atlanta.'' The committee registered 50,000 African Americans.

In the late 1950s and early 1960s, the struggle to desegregate southern institutions intensified and Hill's association with the Atlanta Committee for Cooperative Action accelerated his participation in civic and community affairs. The ACCA was a group of like–minded businessmen and educators who came together informally to challenge Georgia's segregated colleges and universities. It published *A Second Look,* a study that proved that Atlanta was not as enlightened as it seemed since neither buses nor places like libraries were integrated in the city. He helped the cause of Charlayne Hunter–Gault and Hamilton Holmes by fighting for a year and a half to make them the first African Americans to desegregate the University of Georgia. According to Calvin Trillin in *An Education in Georgia,* "Hill called around the country to find the Turner High School principal, whose signature was required on the application form and who had left for the summer. Hill went to the Fulton County Courthouse with Charlayne and Hamilton towing their pastors along as references." Hill wrote hundreds of letters to the University of Georgia on the students' behalf. Trillin quoted Hill as saying, "They wouldn't tell you anything. . .. It was like pulling teeth."

Hill and the ACCA—despite the disapproval of the old leadership—supported the Atlanta University Center students in their 1960 attempt to desegregate lunch counters in public places and stores like Rich's, the largest department store in the city. He explained the nature of that support in 1997: "In Atlanta, I guess I'm thought of mostly for my coordinating and securing bail bonds for the release of students who were arrested during protests and demonstrations. We were able to provide the bond in such a manner that in many instances I could sign the bonds personally without putting up property or money." In *Atlanta Life Insurance: Guardian of Black Economic Dignity,* Alexa Henderson called Hill a high energy, "dynamic, articulate, skillful negotiator," who inaugurated a new era in race relations in Atlanta.

Hill went further in his leadership activities of the student movement, founding the *Atlanta Inquirer* in 1960. He pledged, along with other members of the ACCA, to fill the void that existed in the reporting of news in the African American community. The *Atlanta Inquirer*'s motto, "To seek out the truth and report impartially without fear or favor," was a forceful statement of its intent to give voice to the student protest movement. According to Hill, a big break came when an association of African American real estate agents pulled their advertisement out of the local African American newspaper and instead supported the *Atlanta Inquirer.* Although Hill is no longer associated with it, the newspaper is still published, 37 years after its first issue.

The vigorous activities in the civil rights movement and his corporate advancement during the sixties spotlighted Hill's leadership ability throughout the country. By the end of the sixties, Hill was chief actuary and vice president. The National Insurance Association elected him as their president in 1969.

Political Campaigner

The early 1970s were banner years for Hill. When Sam Massel won the Atlanta mayoral election in 1969, Hill was given credit for delivering the black vote. Hill was in the thick of several elections. He served as campaign chairman for Andrew Young, who in 1972 became the first African–American elected to Congress since Reconstruction. Gary M. Pomerantz wrote in *Where Peachtree Meets Sweet Auburn* that "Young's victory solidified Hill's political power in black Atlanta. Hill's name lent credibility, money and more than a few votes." Although he did not initially support him, Hill eventually became Maynard Jackson's campaign manager in Jackson's bid against Massell to become the first African American mayor of Atlanta in 1973.

Two other events in 1973 also contributed to Hill's ascendancy in Georgia and in the nation. At the age of 77, Norris Herndon, the son of founder Alonzo Herndon, tapped Hill as his successor. Hill considers the appointment the highlight of his business career because Herndon exhibited such confidence in him. As the third president of the company Hill became the CEO of the largest stockholder life insurance company or financial institution controlled or managed by African Americans. Then Hill began a series of firsts: Governor Jimmy Carter appointed him to the Georgia Board of Regents, the first African American regent in the Georgia State University system. Hill served two seven–year terms. A decade after the sit–in movement, Hill became the first African American elected to the board of directors for Rich's department store. In the early seventies, Hill was called upon by the president of the Federal Reserve Bank and the Georgia State Banking Commissioner to coordinate recapitalization of Citizens Trust. Hill succeeded in securing funds to keep the largest African American bank in Atlanta solvent. For 14 years, Hill served as chairman of the Board of Directors of the Martin Luther King Center for Non–Violent Social Change.

Enters National Politics

By the late 1970s, Hill's participation in politics had reached the national level. He was a premier fundraiser and campaigner for President Jimmy Carter, who became a close friend. Hill was appointed to the Presidential Georgia Campaign Steering Committee. President Carter offered him a cabinet post, which he declined. If Carter had won a second term, Hill would have considered the move to Washington. As a frequent visitor to the White House, Hill had the President's ear concerning the status of minority businesses in Georgia and around the nation. Hill served on the presidential advisory committee on wage guidelines and was chairman of the advisory board of the Minority Business Resources Center of the Department of Transportation. Hill and his wife have been White House dinner guests of six presidents.

"Atlanta Building New Bridges" is the theme Hill adopted in 1977 when at the age of 51 he became the first African American to head a major metropolitan Chamber of Commerce in the United States. The *Atlanta Journal Constitution* described his achievements in 1977: "He has been at the heart of much of Atlanta's progress in the past two decades. He also carries great political influence with close ties to Atlanta city government leaders, as well as the Georgian in the White House. . .President Jimmy Carter. He is known far and wide as a business and political mover and shaker.''

Hill and Atlanta Life Insurance stepped triumphantly into the decade of the eighties. Atlanta Life employed 1,500 people, had 60 offices in 12 states, had more than 800,000 policyholders, and the highest net earnings of any African American business in the nation. The celebration of the seventy–fifth anniversary of the company in September 1980 coincided with the opening of their six–story $10 million headquarters with President Jimmy Carter in attendance. Its location at the corner of Auburn and Courtland Streets stands as encouragement for the revitalization projects of the ''Sweet Auburn'' business district. Hill's leadership has pushed Atlanta Life into new areas. The decade was characterized by new acquisitions, aggressively pursued, such as that of the Mammoth Life and Accident Insurance Company. Other ventures not related to insurance represented new frontiers for the company.

Hill's leadership was informed by what the *Atlanta Journal Constitution* in 1977 called ''a well–groomed combination of economics and politics with subcategories of civic duty and church service.'' In recognition of that leadership Hill has received numerous awards. He received the Chief Executive of the Year Award from the Atlanta Business League in 1988 and in 1991 he was inducted into the Atlanta Business Hall of Fame. The University of Michigan awarded him its prestigious Business Leadership Award in 1987, and followed it with an honorary doctorate degree in the spring of 1996.

After 20 years of leadership, Hill retired as CEO of Atlanta Life in 1993 but stayed on as chairman of the board until 1995. He remains on the board of the Herndon Foundation, which owns more than 73 percent of Atlanta Life stock. He is the largest individual shareholder of the company. His retirement at Atlanta Life has given Hill more time to pursue other business and civic interests. He is joint owner of Concessions International, a food and beverage business which operates in 12 of the nation's airports. He sits on numerous boards including those of Delta Airlines and Knight–Ridder newspapers. Another of his projects is chair of the Blue Ribbon Committee for the NAACP 1998 National Convention, to be held in Atlanta.

''It is hard to imagine the absence of a personality like Hill,'' wrote Ernst Holsendolph in the *Atlanta Journal Constitution* in 1995. ''A consoling thought is that he will not disappear but merely retreat a bit.''

Retirement also gives Hill more time to be a grandfather to Jessica, Jonathan, Mark, John, Zachary, and Michelle. Following military service in South Korea, Hill flew to Holquin, Cuba, in 1955 to marry the woman whom he first met at Big Bethel AME church, Juana Azira Gonzales, a registered nurse. By 1959 the Hills were parents of two daughters, Nancy Mercedes and Azira Dominga. His two daughters are college graduates. Nancy received a B.A. in Journalism from her father's alma mater, Lincoln University in Missouri. Azira graduated from Harvard, the Yale School of Management, and the Emory Law School.

Jesse Hill came to Atlanta to associate himself with an historic company and to make a difference in the lives of others. He succeeded at both endeavors. ''There isn't anyone in town,'' stated Andrew Young in the *Atlanta Journal Constitution* in 1987, ''who helps more people in more ways and who has a deeper personal concern for people.'' In fact, one has to acknowledge his place in history as a man who worked to bring dignity and economic power especially to the African Americans and who ushered in a new business direction for his company. Known for decades as the most influential African American businessman and civic leader in Atlanta and the United States, Hill stated in 1997, ''my work with people in both the Black and white community and my position at Atlanta Life Insurance gave people confidence in me, and along with that respect.'' Hill is Atlanta's and America's success story.

Current address: 1325 Angel Fall Lane, SW., Atlanta, GA 30311–3666.

REFERENCES

'''Dynamo' At the Chamber.'' *Atlanta Journal Constitution,* December 16, 1977.

Henderson, Alexa. *Atlanta Life Insurance: Guardian of Black Economic Dignity.* Tuscaloosa: University of Alabama Press, 1990.

———. ''A Twentieth–Century Black Enterprise: The Atlanta Life Insurance Company, 1905–1975.'' Ph.D. dissertation, Georgia State University, 1975.

Hill, Jesse. Interview with Rosa Bobia, August 5, 1997.

''Hill Stresses Success of Public–Private Partnership to Aid Needy.'' *Atlanta Journal Constitution, October 24, 1987.*

''Jesse Hill: Leading by Example.'' *Atlanta Journal Constitution,* April 9, 1955.

''Jesse Hill Often 'First Black Who. . . .''' *Atlanta Journal Constitution,* April 8, 1977.

''The Long Road to Success.'' *Atlanta Journal Constitution,* January 26, 1986.

''A Newspaper is Born.'' *Atlanta Inquirer,* July 31, 1960.

Pomerantz, Gary M. *Where Peachtree Meets Sweet Auburn: The Saga of Two Families and the Making of Atlanta.* New York: Scribner, 1996.

''The Shaping of Atlanta.'' *Atlanta Journal Constitution,* August 14, 1987.

Trillin, Calvin. *An Education in Georgia.* Athens: University of Georgia Press, 1964.

COLLECTIONS

Jesse Hill's papers are located at the Atlanta Life Insurance Company office in Atlanta.

Rosa Bobia

Chester Himes
(1909–1984)
Writer

Chester Himes drew on a vast range of experiences during his prolific and often frustrating writing career. As a boy, he became familiar with life on college campuses. As a young man, he was convicted of armed robbery and served seven and a half years in the Ohio State Penitentiary. Although he began his writing career in prison, he often had to support himself after his parole through menial jobs. For the last 30 years of his life, he lived in Europe, spending most of his time in Spain. He pioneered the writing of detective novels featuring black policemen. He is the author 16 novels (not including translations, revised books, or his unfinished final work), approximately 70 short stories and sketches, two autobiographical volumes, and several essays. His works are typically pessimistic, reflecting Himes's own struggles.

Chester Bomar Himes was born July 29, 1909, in Jefferson City, Missouri, the youngest of the three sons of Joseph Sandy and Estelle Bomar Himes. Their other children were Edward and Joseph. Himes was married twice, first to Jean Johnson in 1937. They separated in 1951 and later divorced. In 1965 he married Lesley Packard.

At the time of his birth, Himes's father was head of the Mechanical Department and a teacher of blacksmithing and wheelwrighting at Lincoln Institute—later University—in Jefferson City, Missouri. When Chester was four years old, the family left Jefferson City for Cleveland, where they lived for about two years. Over the next seven years, they lived in several Southern locations. Joseph Himes was a teacher and administrator at Alcorn Agricultural and Mechanical College in Alcorn, Mississippi, and then at Pine Bluff Agricultural and Mechanical College in Pine Bluff, Arkansas. One year, while his father stayed at Alcorn, Himes's mother took the children to Augusta, Georgia. There, she taught at Haines Institute, where she had relatives on the faculty.

Although he was a professor, Joseph Himes's areas of specialty were a legacy of his descent from slaves who did manual labor. His dark skin contrasted with his wife's light complexion. Estelle Bomar Himes took pride in the fact that her ancestors, house servants, were related to the master's family by blood. Less tolerant of racial discrimination than her husband, she taught her children at home when they lived in Mississippi, rather than expose them to poorly funded and firmly segregated schools. Overall, Himes's parents had many conflicts based on different temperaments and color and class prejudices as they struggled to deal with economic hardships in a racist society. They separated in 1928 and eventually divorced.

When Himes was about 12 years old, his bother Joe was blinded in an accident for which he felt responsible. The chemistry experiment which led to the accident had been Chester's idea, but because of some misdeed on his part, his mother forbade him to assist. The family was turned away from the white hospital in Pine Bluff, and the black hospital lacked the expertise needed. To make certain that Joe received adequate care, his parents took him to Barnes Hospital in St. Louis. The family subsequently moved to St. Louis and lived there for almost two years to facilitate Joe's follow–up treatments. They moved back to Cleveland after nothing more could be done for Joe in St. Louis. In Cleveland, Joseph Sandy Himes could find work only as a janitor and handyman.

Chester Himes

Youthful Mistakes

Himes graduated from Glenville High School in 1926. Working in a hotel that summer to earn money for college, he fell down an elevator shaft. He was so severely injured that the doctors did not expect him to be able to walk again. He received compensation checks from the hotel for several years after the accident. He entered Ohio State University in Columbus in the fall of 1926, where he enjoyed playing the role of "big man on campus," especially to the relatively small number of black students enrolled. He neglected his studies, however, later recalling in *The Quality of Hurt* that he was "depressed by the white environment." He had expected to be dismissed by the end of the first quarter as a result of his poor grades. He certainly had the potential to achieve: he learned later that he earned the fourth highest score on the entrance examinations that year.

When Himes returned to Cleveland for the Christmas holidays, he became heavily involved with the night life, including gambling and selling whiskey, and he developed a reputation for violence. He returned to the university, but he was indeed dismissed in the spring of 1927.

Back in Cleveland, Himes continued his wild lifestyle, and the next September he returned to Columbus in a stolen car. He was arrested after he wrote bogus checks, using as identification a university student's identification card which he had found. He received a two–year suspended sentence, with the stipulation that if he committed any crime in Ohio in the next five years, he could be sentenced to serve the two years. Soon after leaving Columbus in early November 1928, Himes was arrested for an armed robbery he committed in Cleveland Heights. He had robbed an affluent white couple after learning of their jewels and other belongings from their talkative chauffeur. Himes's sentence was 20 to 25 years of hard labor in the Ohio State Penitentiary.

Himes wrote in *The Quality of Hurt* that he ''grew to manhood'' during his incarceration: ''I was nineteen years old when I went in and twenty–six years old when I came out. . . . I learned all the behavior patterns necessary for survival, or I wouldn't have survived, although at the time I did not realize I was learning them.'' He had been a gambling boss in prison, and he generally maintained a position of power as a result of his defiant attitude.

Struggling and Writing

Himes began to write while in prison. In *The Quality of Hurt,* he noted that his first publications were with black periodicals: ''the *Atlanta World,* the *Pittsburgh Courier,* the *Afro–American,* the *Bronzeman, Abbott's Monthly* and other similar publications.'' In 1934 *Esquire* magazine published his short story ''Crazy in the Stir'' as well as ''To What Red Hell,'' based on a deadly prison fire at the Ohio State Penitentiary in 1930.

By the time he was paroled in 1936, Himes knew he would make a career choice of writing. He wrote in *The Quality of Hurt*:

> No matter what I did, or where I was or how I lived, I had considered myself a writer ever since I'd published my first story in *Esquire*. . . . Foremost a writer. Above all else a writer. It was my salvation, and is. The world can deny me all other employment, and stone me as an ex–convict, as a nigger, as a disagreeable and unpleasant person. But as long as I write, whether it is published or not, I'm a writer, and no one can take that away. ''A fighter fights, a writer writes,'' so I must have done my writing.

In 1937 Himes married Jean Lucinda Johnson, whom he had known since the 1920s. He described her in *The Quality of Hurt* as ''the most beautiful brownskin girl'' he had ever seen. He was unable to find suitable work for a long time, a major disappointment since he wanted to support his wife well. The Great Depression was still having its effect, adding to the difficulty black men had in finding decent jobs at any time. Himes worked with the Works Progress Administration (WPA) as a laborer, research assistant in the Cleveland Public Library, and as a writer on the Ohio Writers' Project.'' One of his assignments was to write the history of Cleveland for the guide to the city.

With the termination of the WPA itself in 1941, Himes was again without work. He and his wife moved to Los Angeles, where he was able to find only low–level jobs, usually as a laborer in shipyards. In 1944 he received a Julius Rosenwald Fellowship, and they relocated to New York City. The fellowship enabled him to finish *If He Hollers, Let Him Go,* published in 1945. The novel draws heavily on Himes's experiences in Los Angeles. In *The Quality of Hurt* he termed *If He Hollers* a ''bitter novel of protest'' written ''from the accumulation of [his] racial hurts.'' The protagonist, Bob Jones, is a young black man who is unable to move ahead in a racist society. He courts a middle class light–skinned woman who does not understand his more bitter attitude. Jones advances somewhat in his dockyard job, but he is defeated when a white woman accuses him of rape though, in fact, he has spurned her advances. At the end of the novel, Jones is forced to join the army in the midst of World War II. The book was the most successful critically and commercially of Himes's novels published in the United States before he became an expatriate.

In 1945 Himes and his wife lived in northern California on a ranch owned by Jean's brother, Hugo. Himes worked on *The Lonely Crusade,* which was published in 1947. The novel's protagonist, Lee Gordon, is a black man of integrity who tries to carry out his union leadership activities fairly. The Communist Party tries to use him, as do the capitalist forces resisting union power. Gordon's marriage breaks apart in the face of interracial tension. Although Gordon never abandons his principles, the implication at the end of the novel is that he will be killed. Reviews of *Lonely Crusade* were overwhelmingly negative. Himes said in *The Quality of Hurt* that all groups—the Communists, the NAACP, and the unions among them—were equally hostile in their responses.

From 1946 to 1953, Himes's home base was New York, with some time in New England locales, often as the caretaker of estates. In 1948 he spent most of the summer in Saratoga Springs, New York at Yaddo, the writers' retreat. He was drinking heavily at the time, and overall, the Yaddo experience was not a happy one. It was during this time that he delivered a speech in Chicago on ''The Dilemma of the Negro Writer.'' The talk ''sought to tell the truth,'' Himes recalled in *The Quality of Hurt,* but his assessment met a cold reception from the white audience.

In the summer of 1950, Himes conducted a creative writing seminar at North Carolina College in Durham where his brother Joe was on the faculty. Despite his blindness, Joe Himes had graduated magna cum laude from Oberlin College and had gone on to receive a Ph.D. in sociology from Ohio State University. He had a distinguished career as a university professor. Himes's visit was a success, despite his initial hesitations about being in the South. In 1951 Chester and Jean Himes separated and they later divorced.

Cast the First Stone (1952) was Himes's third novel, but it existed in an earlier form in the 1940s. The original version, called *Black Sheep,* had a black protagonist. *Cast the First Stone*'s protagonist, Jim Monroe, is white, and the novel's plot focuses on attitudes toward homosexuality among prisoners. Himes himself avoided sexual abuse in prison because of his reputation to be very violent if necessary. James Lunquist noted in *Chester Himes* that the responses to the *Cast the First Stone* were mixed, some of them commending its "competence, its intensity, and its accuracy; but several reviewers were apparently greatly disturbed by the love scenes."

Expatriate Years

Himes had been growing increasingly frustrated with the critical reactions to his books and the lack of fair financial treatment by American publishers. He used the money he received from the publication of *Cast the First Stone* to leave the United States and in 1953 he sailed for France. Richard Wright, whom he had known in New York, assisted him in getting settled. Himes traveled to several locations, including London, before making Spain his home base in 1954. He often visited Paris and other European locations for short periods thereafter, however. He met his second wife, Lesley Packard, in Paris in the early 1960s. An Englishwoman, she was at that time working as a librarian and also writing a shopping column for the Paris edition of the *New York Herald Tribune.* Himes made a few business trips to the United States in connection with publishing and film matters, but he never made it his home after 1953.

As was the case for Richard Wright, Himes continued to draw on his experiences in America in works he wrote abroad. In *The Third Generation* (1954) Himes explored the conflicts of color and class which characterized his family. Lunquist noted that Himes began work on the novel in the 1950s after his visit to North Carolina. There, Himes reviewed notes his mother had made about tracing her family tree. Reception of *The Third Generation* by reviewers was for the most part positive, although some of them pointed out weaknesses in characterization and organization.

Himes's next novel, *The Primitive* (1955), is a story of lust and violence between a black man and a white woman. The nucleus for the book occurred in Himes's own life before he left New York, although, unlike the novel, the actual episode did not end in the death of the woman. Most reviewers were turned off by the thoroughgoing sordidness of the situation. On the other hand, in an interview with John A. Williams, Himes identified *The Primitive* as his favorite book. Himes noted that it was written in 1954 when he was in Mallorca, Spain, for the year and he had no distractions, adding, "I wrote [*The Primitive*] out of a completely free state of mind from beginning to end; where I saw the nuances of every word I put down." The subject matter of *The Primitive,* the potential for violence in the relationships between white women and black men, is also a central theme in much of Himes's other work. An early example is the tension between Bob Jones and Madge, the white woman, in *If He Hollers Let Him Go.* In *The Quality of Hurt,* Himes observed, "The final answer of any black man to a white woman with whom he lives in a white society is violence." Throughout his life, Himes continued to be aware of and affected by the negative reactions black men often faced if they were with white women. In his autobiographies, Himes wrote candidly of his own experiences in such situations.

Although Himes's detective novels grew out of financial need, the works—importantly—also gave him a chance to depict black men not as victims but as the dispensers of violence. Himes explained to Williams, "After all, Americans live by violence, and violence achieves—regardless of what anyone says—. . .its own ends." The novels' recurring main figures, New York police detectives Grave Digger Jones and Coffin Ed Johnson, do not suffer at the hands of others. As Mark Sanders observed in *The Oxford Companion to African American Literature,* "Himes adopts standard detective fiction formula, but uses it to posit black violence as a response to oppressive conditions. Jones and Johnson. . .[use] violence according to their own sense of propriety, and mete out justice in ways often independent of conventional, legal, or judicial practices."

For Love of Imabelle (1957) was the first of the detective novels. The French version, *La Reine des pommes,* won the Grand Prix du Roman Policier in 1957; a revised English version is titled *A Rage in Harlem.* Most of Himes's works in the genre were published first in French by the Paris firm Gallimard. Other books featuring the detectives are *Il pleut des coups durs* (1958) translated as *The Real Cool Killers* (1959, 1969), *Couche dans le pain* (1959) translated as *The Crazy Kill* (1959, 1968), *Tout pour plaire* (1959) translated as *The Big Gold Dream* (1960, 1968), *Imbroglio negro* (1960) translated as *All Shot Up* (1960, 1969), *Ne nous énervons pas!* (1961) translated as *The Heat's On* (1966) and republished as *Come Back Charleston Blue* (1974), *Retour en Afrique* (1964) translated as *Cotton Comes to Harlem* (1965, 1966).

Final Works

Two novels featuring Jones and Johnson, *Blind Man with a Pistol* (1969) and *Hot Day, Hot Night* (1970), were originally published in English. *Come Back Charleston Blue* and *Cotton Comes to Harlem* received even wider popularity when they were made into movies in the 1970s. Recognition of Himes's work in the genre is also indicated by the Chester Himes Black Mystery Writers Conference, which, according to an announcement in *The Black Scholar,* scheduled its second annual meeting for the spring of 1998.

Two other books by Himes which were first published in French are *Uneaffaire de viol* (1963) published in the United States as *A Case of Rape* (1984) and *Dare–dare* (*Run Man, Run*) (1966). *A Case of Rape* is an investigation of the events leading to the death of a white woman after a period of intense sexual activity; black men are her accused killers. The novel is atypical for Himes in that it is set in France, where Himes found racial tensions heightened during the Algerian war for independence. Himes explores once again his mingled themes of interracial sexual taboos and violence. *Run Man Run* shows the forces arrayed against a young black student who is hounded for a murder he did not commit. The policeman pursuing him has actually committed the murder, and the young man has no chance.

Himes turned to humor most fully in *Pinktoes* (1962), which satirized liberal and wealthy blacks and whites whose preoccupation with sex leads to hilarious consequences in supposedly elite society. The novel, which drew on Himes's experiences when he was a Rosenwald Fellow, was published in France in 1963 under the title *Mamie Mason.*

Over the course of his career, Himes wrote approximately 70 short stories, sketches, and dramatic pieces. These are usually relatively brief, straightforward vignettes which retain Himes's emphasis on reality with a tendency toward pessimism. In *Black on Black: Baby Sister and Selected Writings* (1973), "Baby Sister" is a key example of that pessimism. The story, written in dramatic form, focuses on incest as well as violence, with no positive solution to any of the problems.

The Collected Short Stories of Chester Himes (1990) provided greater access to Himes's short works than had been possible previously. In 1997 Gallimard published two volumes of his short stories translated into French by Lili Sztajn: *Une Messe en Prison* (*A Mass in Prison*) and *Le Paradis des Cotes de Porc* (Pork Chop Paradise). *Plan B,* which Himes was working on when he died, was published posthumously, originally in French and subsequently in English. In *My Life of Absurdity* Himes described it in its early stages as being "about a real black revolution in which my two black detectives split up and eventually Grave Digger kills Coffin Ed to save the cause."

Himes died on November 12, 1984, in Moraira, Spain. He is buried in nearby Benisa. Himes's two autobiographies, *The Quality of Hurt* (1973) and *My Life of Absurdity* (1976) are frank, informative works for understanding the rage that Himes felt and which is reflected in most of his protagonists. In all his work, Himes wrote with unstinting clarity. His style is deliberately blunt, and the extent of brutality and hopelessness, as in *The Primitive,* is often overwhelming. Although like most of his protagonists Himes may have found the odds against him overwhelming, he never surrendered.

REFERENCES

Andrews, William L., Frances Smith Foster, and Trudier Harris, gen. eds. *The Oxford Companion to African American Literature.* New York: Oxford University Press, 1997.

Bell, Bernard. *The Afro–American Novel and Its Tradition.* Amherst: University of Massachusetts Press, 1987.

The Black Scholar 27 (Spring 1997): 74.

Bloom, Harold, gen. ed. *Twentieth Century American Literature.* Vol. 4. New York: Chelsea House Publishers, 1986.

Blumenfeld, Samuel. "Chester Himes, noir sur blanc." *Le Monde,* December 26, 1997. Le Monde des livres/ La librairie électronique. World Wide Web. http:// www.lemonde.fr

Fabre, Michel. "*A Case of Rape.*" *Black World* 21 (March 1972): 39–48.

———. *From Harlem to Paris: Black American Writers in France, 1840–1980.* Urbana: University of Illinois Press, 1991.

———. "A Selected Bibliography of Chester Himes' Work." *Black World* 21 (March 1972): 76–78.

Fuller, Hoyt. "Traveller on the Long, Rough, Lonely Old Road: An Interview with Chester Himes." *Black World* 21 (March 1972): 4–22, 87–98.

Harris, Trudier, ed. *African American Writers, 1940–55.* Detroit: Gale Research, 1988.

Himes, Chester. *Black on Black: Baby Sister and Selected Writings*: New York: Doubleday, 1973.

———. *The Collected Short Stories of Chester Himes.* Foreword by Calvin Hernton. New York: Thunder's Mouth Press, 1990.

———. *My Life of Absurdity: The Autobiography of Chester Himes.* Vol. II. Garden City, NY: Doubleday, 1976.

———. *Plan B.* Jackson: University Of Mississippi Press, 1993.

———. *The Quality of Hurt: The Autobiography of Chester Himes.* Vol. I. Garden City, NY: Doubleday, 1971.

Lundquist, James. *Chester Himes.* New York: Frederick Ungar Publishing Co., 1976.

Milliken, Stephen F. *Chester Himes: A Critical Appraisal.* Columbia: University of Missouri Press, 1976.

Reed, Ishmael. "Chester Himes: Writer." *Black World* 21 (March 1972): 24–38, 83–86.

Williams, John A. "My Man Chester Himes: An Interview with Chester Himes." *Amistad I.* New York: Vintage Books, 1970.

Arlene Clift–Pellow

Eric H. Holder Jr.

(1951–)

Federal deputy attorney general, judge

Eric H. Holder became the highest–ranking black American law enforcement official in U.S. history in 1997 when he earned unanimous confirmation by the Senate as deputy attorney general. When President Clinton appointed him U.S. attorney for the District of Columbia in 1993, he was also the first black American to hold that post. In each of these positions Holder has demonstrated a desire to bridge the communication gap between racial communities while, at the same time, he proved his intolerance for violent crime by cracking down on criminal activity.

Born in Queens, New York, on January 21, 1951, Eric H. Holder Jr. is the son of Eric H. Holder Sr. and Miriam R. Yearwood Holder, emigrants from Barbados. Holder graduated from Manhattan's Stuyvesant High School and then entered Columbia University. While in college, he became involved with a needy community by spending Saturday mornings at the Harlem youth center and guiding youth on city tours. He also became affiliated with the national organization Concerned Black Men. Holder majored in American history and graduated from Columbia in 1973 with a bachelor's degree. He then studied law at Columbia and graduated in 1976, passing the New York Bar in 1977.

Immediately after receiving his law degree, Holder joined the Department of Justice's Public Integrity Section in Washington, D.C., as a trial lawyer. He helped prosecute high–level cases involving noted public figures who had been accused of corruption. During his tenure from 1977 to 1988, Holder prosecuted FBI agents, organized crime figures, politicians, and others. In 1988 President Ronald Reagan appointed Holder associate justice of the Superior Court of the District of Columbia, a position he held until 1993.

Holder's success and favored position among politicians led to his selection in late 1993 by President Bill Clinton as U.S. attorney for Washington, D.C., making him the first black to hold the position. He faced a major case involving Dan Rostenkowski, an influential Democratic congressman from Illinois and chair of the House's Ways and Means Committee, who was indicted on charges of misuse of official House accounts. Citing Holder's indictment of Rostenkowski, the *Philadelphia Tribune* reported that, in the matter of public policy, Rostenkowski had tremendous power over some major legislation. The *Tribune* also said that Rostenkowski was "very effective at making the intricate machinery of the White House work for him." Holder said in the *New York Voice* that the congressman had "about fourteen do–nothing employees on the House payroll . . . mainly handling such chores as mowing his lawn."

As U.S. attorney, Holder fought discrimination in lending in an area bank. In 1994 he was involved in the Clinton Administration's settlement of an unprecedented case against a bank in Chevy Chase, Maryland, that refused to market its services in minority neighborhoods, particularly by declaring black areas off–limits—a practice known as "redlining." Holder said in the *New York Voice* that the bank neglected "whole segments of a neighborhood" and that the practice devastated the lives of individual citizens as well as the entire community. The bank violated the federal Fair Housing Act, declared the Justice Department.

In 1996 Holder increased the pressure on violence in the District of Columbia, where biased–related crimes had become a serious problem. He told the *Washington Informer* that there is no place in society "for cowardly attacks on residents simply because they are Black, Latino, Jews or Asians." He declared that Asian business owners were targeted because of their nationalities, not simply because they were merchants.

Holder also worked to facilitate dialogue between Asian and African American communities. *Asian Week* quoted excerpts from his little–noticed speech given in 1995 when one of Holder's deputies was sworn in as president of the Asian American Bar Association. Holder said, "At a time when many other business owners ignobly fled from the city to the suburbs, Asian business owners stepped in and filled a void." He praised the owners for their goods and services and their pursuit of the "American dream." He then urged Asian Americans to extend their reach to the entire community to show that they have a full stake in the community.

Holder remained highly visible as U.S. attorney for the District of Columbia. He often spoke at local schools and organizations.

In April of 1997 President Clinton nominated Holder as deputy attorney general, the post immediately under Attorney General Janet Reno. At Senate hearings on June 13, Holder clearly stated his opposition to the death penalty. Quoted in the *New York Times* on June 14, 1997, he said, "I am not a proponent of the death penalty, but I will enforce the law as this Congress gives it to us." Of his impending confirmation which would make him the first black official in the second–highest post at the Justice Department, he said that the position would give him an opportunity "to help foster a dialogue between our diverse peoples about the issue of race in the hope that we can work to heal the racial divisions that have bedeviled this nation since its inception." After Holder was confirmed by the U.S. Senate, Reno, quoted in *Jet* on August 11, 1997, called him "one of the nation's most respected and qualified enforcement officials." She noted his wealth of experience and determination to safeguard streets and neighborhoods against violence. He was sworn in office in 1997 during a ceremony at the Justice Department, becoming the highest–ranking black law enforcement official in American history.

Holder is married to Sharon Malone, an obstetrician, and they have one daughter, Maya. Holder remains highly visible as an important law enforcement official and continues to speak out against issues of injustice and violence.

Current address: Deputy Attorney General, 950 Pennsylvania Ave. NW, Washington, DC 20530–0001.

REFERENCES

"Another Blow to the U.S. Congress: A Death." *Philadelphia Tribune,* August 2, 1994.

"City Officials Warn of Increase in Hate Crimes." *Washington Informer,* October 30, 1996.

"Clinton Administration Obtains Unprecedented Settlement in Lending Discrimination Case." *New York Voice Inc./ Harlem USA,* September 21, 1994.

Contemporary Black Biography. Vol. 9. Detroit: Gale Research, 1995.

"Holder's Swearing–In." *Jet* 92 (22 September 1997): 6.

"Justice Department Nominee Faces Little Opposition." *New York Times,* June 14, 1997.

"U.S. Senate Confirms Eric Holder Jr. as Deputy Attorney General; No. 2 Post At Justice Department." *Jet* 92 (11 August 1997): 32.

Who's Who in America. 50th ed. New Providence, NJ: Marquis Who's Who, 1996.

Wu, Frank H. "Letter from Washington: Getting Along." *Asian Week* 17 (6 October 1995): 9.

Jessie Carney Smith

Jerome "Brud" Holland
(1916–1985)
Educator, college president, diplomat, business executive

Brud Holland is perhaps known best as the president of two black colleges, an ambassador to Sweden, and a member of numerous corporate boards. He achieved several firsts as an African American. Holland was the first black member of the football team at Cornell University and later became the first black member of the university's Board of Trustees. When he was elected to the latter position, he also became the first black board member of an Ivy League school. In 1972 he became the first black member of the New York Stock Exchange's Board of Directors. He is notable for his ambition and determination, and for his success in varied fields.

Brud Holland was born Jerome Heartwell Holland on January 9, 1916, in Auburn, New York. He was one of thirteen children—ten girls and three boys—born to Robert H. and Viola Bagby Holland. Only five of these children survived to adulthood, and Jerome was the only one to attend college. The father, Robert Holland, was the son of an enlisted member of the Civil War Union Army's United States Colored Troops. Robert Holland had resided in Ithaca, New York, prior to moving to Auburn, where he struggled to support his large family by working as an itinerant repairman, handyman, yard worker, and gardener. Viola Holland supported his efforts to make ends meet by working in a local rope factory while also nurturing the family. Within the close–knit Holland family, young Jerome became known as "Brud"—a vernacular or idiomatic term for brother. This is the name by which he was generally recognized throughout his life.

Holland grew up in a town where blacks were a very small minority. First–generation Italians and Polish and second– and third–generation Irish lived there as well. They were generally poor but helped each other. "You weren't conscious of racial prejudice as such, but you were conscious of race," he recalled in the *Ebony Success Library.* "My parents were very religious people, strong in church memberships, and they belonged to many of the fraternal organizations, which in those days were extremely popular in the Negro community," he added.

Holland was ambitious from a young age and refused to be thwarted from his goals in the face of adversity and discrimination. His initial hopes of being admitted to Cornell University to receive a college education were dashed. Although he had acquitted himself well as a student and a football star during his years at Auburn High School, Cornell's admission's said that he lacked the necessary academic credentials. Determined to be admitted, Holland spent a year obtaining the credentials needed. He met this goal and enrolled at Cornell in 1935, only to meet racial discrimination when he arrived. Holland and other black students were not allowed to live in the campus dormitories. Instead, Holland found housing in the basement of a white fraternity house where he was employed as a maintenance man. Although he worked two additional jobs to pay his way through college, he excelled in academics and athletics. He earned recognition as a member of the Alpha Schmack Junior Honor Society and the Sphinx Head Senior Honorary Society.

Holland also won recognition for his athletic talent. He was the first African American in Cornell's history selected to be a member of its football team. His life as a varsity football player mirrored his other degrading campus experiences. Although his teammates included some of the white men from the fraternity house where he lived and worked, when off the football field they lived separate lives. When the team traveled he was unable to enter the segregated restaurants and hotels where his team members ate and lived. Eventually, Cornell's football team refused to play some games in areas where Jim Crow practices prevailed against Holland.

Holland reminisced in *Black Opportunity* about this period of his life:

> In the Spring of 1939 I was a member of the senior class of Cornell University. My grades were considered good, and I had been elected to the Junior and Senior Honorary societies. I was a member of the football team, and perhaps a rather prominent member as I was selected as left end on several All–American teams in 1937 and 1938. In all modesty, I was recognized as an outstanding campus citizen.

Holland was a superior blocker and defensive performer who dazzled crowds of spectators, many of whom lined up to shake his hand after the game. Edwin Bancroft Henderson wrote that Holland, who was six–feet one–inch tall and weighed 207 pounds, was "one of the greatest ends ever seen at the school and will long be remembered as the player who made the end–around play famous." Henderson noted that he was listed in a Cornell football manual as "a member of the University's all–time football team." His football legacy was secured when he was subsequently recognized and rewarded as an inductee of the National Football Foundation College Hall of Fame, and as a Charter Member of Cornell's Sports Hall of Fame in 1978.

In 1939 Holland graduated with honors from Cornell with a bachelor of science degree. He continued his studies at Cornell for two additional years, and earning a Master of Science degree in sociology in 1941. Meanwhile, he joined the faculty of Lincoln University in Pennsylvania as an instructor in sociology and physical education and assistant football coach, where he worked from 1939 to 1942.

From 1942 to 1946 Holland was director of personnel for the Sun Shipbuilding and Drydock Company of Chester, Pennsylvania. The next year he was personnel consultant for the eastern division of General Foods Corporation in Rochester, New York. He began to study toward a Ph.D. in sociology at the University of Pennsylvania while also working at Tennessee Agricultural and Industrial State University in Nashville. Between 1947 and 1951 he was director of the Division of Political and Social Sciences and end coach of the football team. He earned a doctoral degree in sociology from the University of Pennsylvania in 1950. His doctoral dissertation was on wartime integration of blacks into the shipbuilding industry and reflected insights that he gained while employed at Sun Shipbuilding. He moved again and took a job in Philadelphia as a Pete Memorial Foundation consultant, where he worked from 1951 to 1953. At that point he decided to try his hand at college administration at the top level.

Heads Two Black Colleges

Holland was appointed president of Delaware State College, Dover, in 1953. "No one else wanted it. The school was in a hopeless state and I was told by the governor to either build it up or close it," he told *Ebony Success Library*. At Delaware State Holland found time to conduct research and publish several studies, "A Study of the Employment Status of the Negro Population in the State of Delaware," "Patterns of Negro Residency in Delaware," "A Study of the Health Status of the Negro in Delaware," "A Sociological Analysis of the Situational Complex Confronting the State of Delaware Relative to Implementing the Desegregation of Public Schools," and "New Horizons in Guidance." Not only had Delaware State gained a fine president and scholar, Delaware had gained an educator who was interested in that state.

Holland left Delaware State College on an upward course with several new buildings and innovative educational programs to accept the position of the ninth president of Hampton Institute (now University). He and his family arrived in Hampton in the summer of 1960. During his inaugural address on April 29, 1961, Holland made clear the vision that he had for Hampton. Among his goals, Holland aimed to provide a first–class education in liberal arts, teacher education, business, applied science and technology; to aid foreign countries through economic and technical assistance projects and educational programs; and to experiment with new, innovative teaching techniques.

Holland, who had faced racial discrimination when he was entering the work force, intended to prepare Hampton graduates to so impress employers that they could not be denied opportunities because of their race. He recalled his treatment at Cornell in *Black Opportunity*:

> During the months before graduation scores of industrial recruiters visited the Cornell campus. With a single exception, every member of the senior class who had compiled a record similar to mine was interviewed and offered one or more jobs. I was that exception. Nobody interviewed me. Nobody offered me a job. I am a Negro.

Holland envisioned Hampton as a pace where recruiters and prospective employers would visit and offer students jobs, and where graduates would not face the humiliating experience he had known at Cornell.

Another one of Holland's objectives as president of Hampton was international aid. Holland's global perspective led him to travel to the Middle and Far East, Africa, the Caribbean and Europe. His involvement with the Council for African Training and the Agency for International Development (AID) led him to focus upon Sierra Leone, Africa, in the 1960s. In the fall of 1961 Holland—with AID funding and support from Sierra Leone's Prime Minister Margai—involved Hampton faculty, staff, and students in the Kenema/Batkanu project. The project aimed to assist Sierra Leone in raising the educational and socioeconomic level of its people through increased agricultural output, building construction, and educational programs in mathematics, education, mechanics, and other subjects. Holland also supported educational programs in Liberia, Africa, and the Virgin Islands.

During his tenure at Hampton, Holland added twelve new buildings to the campus and spurred alumni to increase their financial support of the school. He guided the college through a successful $18 million Centennial Campaign Drive, increased the institutional endowment to a new high of $40 million, established two endowed chairs, expanded the faculty, doubled faculty salaries, and boosted the enrollment to a new high.

Students benefited from a number of curricular changes and improvements under Holland's decade of leadership, including new programs in computer technology, mass media, cooperative education, and the Business Executive and Scientist in Residency program. In 1967 the undergraduate program in nursing won accreditation from the National League of Nursing.

Like students on many other college campuses, Hampton's students became active in the civil rights protests of the late 1960s. They raised issues and concerns about being oppressed and powerless in administratively controlled "bastions of high education." For four days in April of 1968 hundreds of Hampton students occupied the administration building, closing the school. Although they demanded Holland's resignation, he refused. Nevertheless, this experience led to a career reevaluation. He said in the *Afro–American Encyclopedia,* "In all candor the contemporary college scene encourages me to reconsider the moral and ethical reasons for continuing in an administrative capacity."

Becomes Ambassador to Sweden

Holland resigned as Hampton's president in January of 1970, following an announcement that President Richard M. Nixon had appointed him to be America's Ambassador to Sweden. He invited the Hampton Institute Choir to perform in Sweden during his tenure there and served as a model ambassador of goodwill. Unfortunately, on one occasion in April of

1970, he realized he was not as far away from home as he thought, when a group of anti–American protesters chanted ''Nigger go home,'' according to *Jet* magazine. Amid such racial insults as well as demonstrations and physical threats from those who opposed America's involvement in the Vietnam War, Holland remained ambassador to Sweden until the fall of 1972. He returned to the United States and maintained a highly visible public profile, establishing an office in New York City and devoting himself to the many major corporate boards to which he was elected. He also spent considerable time on the lecture circuit.

In 1972 Holland became the first African American member of the Board of Directors of the New York Stock Exchange, where he served until 1980. Soon afterward other major businesses and academic institutions that were criticized for not having black board members sought out his expertise. Holland joined numerous other boards, including that of Cornell University. He became the first black board member of Cornell and of any the Ivy League school. At one time his board memberships totaled twenty–three—an unprecedented number for a black at that time. These included the American Telephone and Telegraph, General Foods, Union Carbide, Federated Department Stores, Chrysler Corporation, Continental Insurance Company, Manufacturer Hanovers Trust Company, General Cigar Company, National Urban League, United Negro College Fund, American Arbitration Association, Pan American Bancshares, National Advisory Committee on Television, the Council on Foreign Relations, and the Johnson Foundation. He was a member of the Board of Corporators of Massachusetts Institute of Technology, a member of the President's Commission on All Volunteer Armed Forces, and on the Board of Governors of the American National Red Cross. In addition, he was a member or officer of numerous national, social, civic, fraternal, educational, and philanthropic organizations. Holland was a Carnegie Corporation grantee in 1964, a Danforth Foundation grantee in 1968, and a fellow of the American Academy of Arts and Sciences.

In recognition of his achievements, the high school stadium in his hometown of Auburn, New York, was named in his honor. Other honors included the Annual Salvation Army Award (1968), the NCAA Theodore Roosevelt Award, the Charles Evan Hughes Award from the National Conference of Christian and Jews (1972), and the Silver Anniversary All–American Award from *Sports Illustrated.* Among those institutions that awarded Holland an honorary degree were Northeastern University (1965), Hobart and William Smith Colleges (1965), Union College (1966), University of Cincinnati (1966), Colgate University (1969), Washington University in St. Louis (1970), Washington and Lee University (1971), Columbia University (1972), Adelphi University (1973), Tuskegee Institute (1977), and Morehouse College (1979). He also received an honorary degree from Hampton University and was awarded the United States Presidential Medal of Freedom, both of which were posthumously awarded in 1985.

Holland had married soon after he left Cornell and had two children, Jerome Jr. and Pamela. He was divorced about 1946. In 1949, while in Nashville, he married for a second time to Laura Mitchell, a Boston native and a psychology professor at Fisk University. They had two children, Lucy and Joseph. While at Hampton Laura Mitchell Holland taught psychology during one academic year and later served on the Virginia Governor's Commission on the Status of Women. She was an advocate of African American history and culture.

Holland died of cancer on January 6, 1985, and was survived by his wife Laura and four children. Holland left a legacy as a servant leader in higher education, in corporate America, and in his country. He had lived out the belief that he expressed in *Ebony Success Library*: ''Obstacles are no obstacles. There's always a way of getting something done.''

REFERENCES

Cooper, Jeanette. Telephone interview with W. Braxter Wiggins, February 17, 1998.

Ebony Success Library. Vol. II. Nashville: Southwestern Company, 1973.

Henderson, Edwin Bancroft. *The Negro in Sports.* Rev. ed. Washington, DC: Associated Publishers, 1939.

Holland, Jerome H. *Black Opportunity.* New York: Weybright and Talley, 1969.

Holland, Laura Mitchell. Telephone interview with W. Braxter Wiggins, February 27, 1998.

''Nigger Go Home.'' *Jet* 38 (30 April 1970): 4–5.

Pleasant, Mae Barbee. *Hampton University: Our Home by the Sea, An Illustrated History.* Virginia Beach: Donning Co., 1992.

Who's Who in America, 1982–83. 42nd ed. Chicago: Marquis, 1982.

Rywell, Martin, comp. and ed. *Afro–American Encyclopedia.* Vol. 4. North Miami, FL: Educational Book Publishers, 1974.

COLLECTIONS

The papers of Jerome Holland are in the Hampton University Archives.

W. Braxter Wiggins

James T. Holly
(1829–1911)
Religious leader, missionary, black separatist

James Theodore Holly had one simple main idea: the only way for blacks to flourish was to physically separate themselves from whites. Thus he was an ardent supporter of emigration, deciding on Haiti early on. During his brief career in the United States and Canada, he was an indefatigable laborer for his cause. Holly was also an ardent Christian, who gave just short of 50 years to building up an independent black Episcopal church in his adopted country.

Holly was born on October 3, 1829, in Washington, D.C., to Jane and James Overton Holly. He was the last of three sons and two daughters born to the couple, two of whom died very young. The Hollys had been free for several generations. The white father of James's great–grandfather, a Scotsman named James Theodore Holly, released from slavery his son, who bore the same name, in 1772. Holly and his brother Joseph followed their father's trade of shoemaking.

The Holly family was Roman Catholic, and Joseph and James may have received their initial instruction in a school for black children at their parish church, Holy Trinity. In 1837, they enrolled in the private school of John H. Fleet, a black physician. Then in 1844 the family—father, mother, and the three surviving children—moved to Brooklyn, New York. There Joseph established his own shop in 1845 and became involved in abolitionist circles. Between February and June of 1848 he published five articles on slavery in Frederick Douglass's *North Star.* Douglass was an escaped slave and leading black abolitionist.

Holly completed his apprenticeship as shoemaker in 1846. He also studied in the evenings and received instruction in mathematics and classical studies from a Spanish priest, Felix Varela of Transfiguration Church in New York City. Then in 1848 he found a job as clerk with the American Missionary Association through the good graces of white abolitionist Lewis Tappan. The job paid little money but provided valuable experience and contacts.

The elder Holly was dead, probably of the tuberculosis which afflicted other members of the family, by the time James, Joseph, their sister Cecilia, and their mother moved to Burlington, Vermont in 1850, the year a drastic new Fugitive Slave Act went into effect. The brothers set up as shoemakers. (James would also work at the trade later in life whenever finances became difficult; he even took it up again for a short while after he moved to Haiti.) The brothers clashed when they debated publicly before Burlington audiences about emigration and the efforts of the American Colonization Society to send freed blacks to Liberia: Joseph was opposed, but James approved.

Holly's first appearance in print was an article in Henry Bibb's *Voice of the Fugitive* on May 7, 1851, in support of emigration to Canada. A fugitive slave himself, Bibb was trying to persuade blacks to emigrate to Canada, and he called together a North American Convention of Negroes in Toronto in September of 1851. Holly could not attend, but on the final day the convention endorsed his plan for a league of blacks in North America and the Caribbean to defend their rights and lay the groundwork for emigration to Canada or the West Indies. Shortly thereafter, Holly became corresponding editor and traveling agent for Bibb's paper, a biweekly published in Windsor, Canada.

James T. Holly

Moves to Canada

Holly married Charlotte Ann Gordon of Burlington at an undetermined date. The couple undertook a six–week lecture tour in five eastern states in 1852 to build support for emigration to Canada. Bibb was not in Windsor when they arrived there. Holly immediately took on editorial responsibility for the paper. Bibb was now becoming very controversial as his support of the Refugee Home Society split the black community in Canada. The aim of the society was to buy a large block of land on which blacks could settle. Financial arrangements with those who bought land from the society, and the support of separatism came under fire. Mary Shadd, soon to become Mary Shadd Cary, and Samuel Ringgold Ward were adamantly opposed to it. They began to publish the *Provincial Freeman* to counter Bibb's paper. Frederick Douglass's *North Star,* published in Rochester, New York, was also in opposition. Joseph Holly was yet another opponent. In 1853 he moved to Rochester where he lent his support to Douglass, as well as publishing a book of poetry, *Freedom's Offerings.*

The Voice of the Fugitive ceased publication at the end of 1853, and Holly moved to Detroit with his wife and child. There he briefly taught school but received low marks for his many absences due to speaking engagements and for preaching the virtues of emigration to the children. Henry Bibb died in August of 1854, just before the National Emigration Convention in Cleveland. Holly was a delegate and very active in the convention. By now he had fixed on Haiti as a destination.

The year 1855 marked major changes in Holly's life. Joseph died of tuberculosis, and his mother joined his household. Holly had joined the Protestant Episcopal Church in 1852 at the urging of William C. Munroe, rector of a small black church in Detroit. A year later Holly was admitted as a candidate for holy orders and began private study with William Shelton of Detroit. On June 17, 1855, Holly became a deacon. His life goal was now set: he would lead a mass emigration of African Americans to Haiti, where he would work as a missionary to establish an independent and black Episcopal church.

Holly was able to find some private donations to finance a trip to Haiti, where he landed on August 3, arriving back in New York on September 8. Working occasionally as a laborer on the docks, he undertook a speaking campaign and collected money to support his family. He first delivered a lecture, "A Vindication of the Capacity of the Negro Race for Self–Government and Civilized Progress", in New Haven, Connecticut; this lecture was published in 1857.

Finding no encouragement for his missionary proposals, Holly accepted the rectorship of St. Luke's Episcopal Church in New Haven. He was ordained on January 2, 1855. The meager information on his family at this point in his life says only that two of his young children died shortly after the family's move to Connecticut. The following year, Holly succeeded Ebenezer Bassett, a future envoy to Haiti, as principal of the Whiting Street Public School, a position he held until the summer of 1859; he also opened a private school in the summer of 1858. When in 1859 he led a delegation to protest the second–rate conditions for blacks in the public schools, the school board's first step to improve the schools was to replace all black teachers with whites. That was not the only rebuff. An active Mason, Holly prepared a series of articles on Masonic ritual that attracted interest among white Masons until the racial identify of the author was discovered. By 1860, Holly was devoting almost all of his time to emigration.

Sets Course for Haiti

Holly never abandoned his plans for emigration, but began to seek new avenues of support when the second National Emigration Convention, meeting in Cleveland in August of 1856, would not single out Haiti as a favored destination without evidence of more solid support from the Haitian government than Holly could furnish, especially since Martin R. Delany was pursuing his scheme for African settlement. The church organization founded by Holly and William C. Munroe in July of 1856, the Convocation of the Protestant Episcopal Society for Promoting the Extension of the Church Among Colored People, did little to help blacks in the church or to forward emigration.

Holly began to seek help from whites. He approached Congressman Francis Preston Blair Jr. of Missouri, who proposed mass movement of blacks to the West Indies, but Blair's interest soon flagged. Then a new government in Haiti, that of President Fabre Geffrard, offered new inducements to immigration and appointed white abolitionist James Redpath to be the Haitian commissioner of emigration in the United States with a budget of $20,000, including his salary of $5,000. In 1860 Redpath hired Holly at a salary of $1,000 to recruit colonists among blacks; Henry Highland Garnet, a former slave, Presbyterian minister and black abolitionist, was also a recruitment agent. Redpath and Garnet worked together to gather emigrants in spite of Redpath's private disdain for Holly's supposed intellectual deficiencies, and the commissioner's tendency to shift the blame for any difficulties to his black employee.

Although opinion among black Americans was more favorable to emigration in 1860 than it had been previously, a battle broke out over the scheme. The most effective leader of the opposition, New York physician James McCune Smith, temporarily lost his newspaper outlet when Redpath bought the *Anglo–African.* On May 2, 1861, Holly and his company from New Haven, some 101 strong, set sail on a ship overcrowded by an additional company of 57 colonists. They arrived in Port–au–Prince on June 1. Tragedy soon followed. His mother and daughter died to be followed at Christmas by his wife and then an infant son who was the 43rd member of the party to die. While Holly held the group together, the fact that deserters were returning to the United States made Haiti an undesirable emigration destination for many.

Holly spent the next 50 years, lacking just a few months, in Haiti, with only a few short visits to the United States. In 1862 he married a New Haven woman, Sarah Henley, who had taken charge of the surviving children when he went to the United States to seek continued support. From his two marriages, Holly had a total of ten children who survived to adulthood; they achieved a remarkable record of education, producing several physicians. The only fervent church member to emerge was a daughter, and she had little scope for an active role in a male–dominated denomination.

In 1874 Holly became the first black bishop consecrated by the American Protestant Episcopal Church. He also became head of an independent church in Haiti. It was a difficult row to hoe. Converts were slow in coming, and he was dependent on the United States church for financial support, which was never generous. In addition, he was a "high church" man (stressing the liturgy and sacraments), and ran into difficulties with the "low church" men (evangelicals) who dominated the mission boards. Travel in Haiti was difficult, and Holly was a poor horseman. Periodic fires swept the capital and his church was burned several times. Dean, in *Defender of the Race,* summed up the state of his church at his death: " The total membership of the Orthodox Apostolic Church of Haiti in 1911 was barely 2,000 souls, ministered to by 12 priests and two deacons in 26 stations."

By the time his church burned in 1908, Holly was being forced to slow his pace by advancing age. In 1909, the President of Haiti and his entire cabinet attended the celebration of Holly's 35 years as a bishop, but later that year a commission which included three of his sons forced him to give up control of the church because of failing health and memory. Holly died in his sleep on March 13, 1911, and was buried in Haiti. His death was little noted in the United States.

Holly was consistent in his goal: the separation of blacks from whites. He was also constant in his attachment to a church whose American embodiment preferred to ignore blacks whenever possible. He did have the honor while attending the 1878 Lambeth Conference in England to be the first black to preach at Westminster Abbey, but recognition from white Episcopalians was usually begrudging at best. Of all the major African American leaders advocating emigration during the 1850s, he is the only one to remain permanently abroad.

REFERENCES

Bell, Howard H., ed. *Black Separatism and the Caribbean, 1860.* Ann Arbor: University of Michigan Press, 1970.

Burkett, Randall K., and Richard Newman. *Black Apostles.* Boston: G. K. Hall, 1978.

Dean, David M. Defender of the Race: *James Theodore Holly, Black Nationalist Bishop.* Boston: Lambeth Press, 1979.

Holly, Alonzo Potter Burgess. *God and the Negro.* Nashville: National Baptist Publishing Board, 1937.

COLLECTIONS

The major collection of materials on Holly is in the Archives and Historical Collections—Episcopal Church, Austin, Texas.

Robert L. Johns

Caspar A. Holstein
(1876–1944)
Entrepreneur, racketeer

Caspar Alexander Holstein, Harlem's "King of Policy" during the 1920's, supported education within the black community. He financed projects such as the Vincent Sanitarium to assist African American physicians in learning, paid the tuition of an African American student enrolled in Columbia University, and provided funding for the construction of the Caspar Holstein dormitory for girls in the Republic of Liberia. Holstein's generosity extended to support Marcus Garvey's black nationalist movement as well as Catholic and Jewish charities. As noted in *Opportunity* for October 1926, the magazine aimed "to stimulate and encourage interest in the serious development of a body of literature about Negro life," their scholarship became a yearly event because of Holstein's philanthropy. Its cash rewards, referred to as Holstein Prizes, were given to African Americans for short stories, plays, poetry, personal sketches, essays, and musical experience.

Caspar Holstein was born in Christiansted, the largest town on the island of St. Croix, on December 6, 1876. At the time of his birth St. Croix was under Danish rule; it is now one of the U.S. Virgin Islands. According to one report Holstein and his mother, Emily Holstein, moved to New York City in 1894. However, there is also evidence he traveled to New York without his mother. Emily Holstein may have died a few years earlier. After Holstein migrated, he may have lived in Brooklyn before he moved, making it home for the rest of his life. He attended school in Brooklyn and graduated from Boy's High School, completing the education he began in St. Croix.

One of Holstein's first employers in New York were the Christies, a prominent Brooklyn family for whom a street in New York City has been named. Holstein began work for the Southern aristocratic family after delivering a note to the right destination, although he was given an incorrect address by Mrs. Christie. Afterward, the family acknowledged Holstein's resourcefulness and hired him. Holstein's initial job in the household was to read to Mrs. Roe, the blind grandmother. This relationship blossomed into a lifetime friendship with the family. When Christie and his sister lost their fortune in the stock market crash of the 1920s, Holstein supported them. He paid for their apartment on West 93rd Street from 1921 to 1933 and maintained the quality of life they were familiar with. He buried them in Woodlawn Cemetery.

About that time Holstein also worked as a bellhop in a New York City hotel, where he placed bets for coworkers. Eventually, he enlisted in the United States Navy. Although the exact date of the enlistment is uncertain, writer Sadie Hall indicates that he served four years and eight months. Upon discharge he returned to his job as a bellhop, where it is believed he created a new betting method for policy numbers. He also studied embalming in Chicago.

Holstein believed blacks had the ability to progress through intellectual achievements that would result in social acceptance by white society. In 1926 he wrote in *Opportunity*:

> Having been all my life a firm and enthusiastic believer in the creative genius of the Negro race, to which I humbly belong, *Opportunity's* Contest to foster literary expression among Negroes has been a source of abiding interest to me. I honestly believe that it will go far towards consolidating the interests of and bridging the gap between the black and white races in the United States today. And particularly will it encourage among our gifted youth the ambition to scale empyrean heights of art and literature.

Holstein, however, was often at odds with the cerebral ideals he praised; he was at best a distant member of the scholarly circles. Although he contributed financially to *Opportunity* magazine's annual literary banquets where the Caspar Holstein Award was given in his honor, many leading figures of the Harlem Renaissance, such as Claude McKay and W. E. B. Du Bois, did not embrace his patronage.

Among Holstein's many and varied interests was the Turf Club at 111 West 136th Street where he sponsored prim

Caspar A. Holstein

affairs for people of diverse social, economic, and ethnic backgrounds. Holstein was also an Elk who gave generously to the Harlem community where he lived. His beneficiaries included numerous college and professional school students as well as Fisk and Howard universities. He never forgot the place of his birth, St. Croix, sending money to the island on numerous occasions and writing about repression in the Virgin Islands. Holstein was president of the Monarchs Lodge #45 a branch of the I.B.P.O.E. in Harlem and president of the New York Virgin Islands Association.

King of Policy Numbers

Schatzberg describes Caspar Holstein as a avid surveyor of the financial press, who one day sitting in his

> airless janitors closet, surrounded by brooms and mops . . . let out an uproarious laugh, and in general acted like a drunken man. That night when the pavement had been swept and the last clerk had gone he sat in the basement until dawn studying the clearing house totals in the papers he had saved religiously. He had them from a year back. The thought that the figures differed each day played in his mind like a wasp in an empty room . . . for six months he thought it over.

After analyzing the totals of the stock market reports of the clearing house for several months, Holstein devised a single scheme of selecting three digits, two from the first total and one from the second total, by an unvarying rule. Individuals then bet on the results of the clearing house at set odds. According to Sadie Hall's biographical sketch of Holstein, the play of the numbers which was loaded 999 to 1 (six dollars for a penny hit) attracted many Harlem blacks to Holstein's numbers racket. Harlemites also may have played the Italian Lottery which was centered on 115th street around First and Pleasant Avenues. There were no African American bankers or workers involved in the Italian operation.

Within a year after the system took off, Holstein owned three of the finest houses in Harlem, a fleet of expensive cars, a home on Long Island, and several thousand acres of land in Virginia. Holstein's new policy game appeared at a time when Jim Crow discrimination made it difficult for African Americans to earn a living, rents were doubled in black areas, and the overall economic circumstance of black Americans enticed many to bet and try to get rich. Holstein may have earned as much as $5,000 a day from the numbers played.

Holstein Kidnapped

As the policy game expanded, Caspar Holstein became a rich and well–known man. This notoriety led to his kidnapping on September 23, 1928, by white gangsters led by Vincent Cole. The gang demanded a ransom of $50,000 for Holstein's safe return, but people theorized there was a motive other than money for the kidnapping. They believed Holstein was told to get out of the policy business. Rumors circulated that implied Arthur Flengenheimer (Dutch) Schultz was moving in to Harlem to take over the numbers racket. Hearsay also implied that Max Romey, a part owner of the Sunset Beer Garden at 760 St. Nicholas Avenue, orchestrated the change.

The incident caused quite a stir. According to Allon Schoener in *Harlem on My Mind,* the *New York Times* of September 24, 1928 reported the case on its first page indicating that "Holstein, with an expert eye for a winning horse, amassed a fortune through spectacular plunges on the races." Rufus Schatzberg stated in *Black Organized Crime* that Holstein lost nearly $30,000 at Belmont Park racetrack during the week before his abduction. Newspaper coverage of the incident revealed an aspect of Harlem many whites were unaware of—that there were wealthy blacks who may have been involved with rackets.

Holstein's fortune diminished after he was kidnapped. Although Holstein was arrested on a complaint regarding policy numbers on December 23, 1935, the charge proved unfounded: he was out of the numbers racket. According to Sadie Hall in "Caspar Holstein," Holstein said, "[A]ll that stuff about me being a millionaire is posh, but the papers have reported it so often many people believe it." He also stated he was a real estate man living at 128 West 135th Street.

Some of the newspaper "dailies" of the period such as the *New York Times* supported his claim to be a businessman. They described him as a facile orator, a delver in politics who earned large sums of money in real estate, and as a successful handicapper. He was a loyal Democrat who contributed substantially to the party and wined and dined politicians and island leaders in his luxurious New York apartment. Holstein's real estate ventures included investments in mortgages through Louis Jacobson, 299 Broadway, which financed housing for blacks in Nepperham, New York, and give credence to his claim that he was indeed a real estate man. In 1938 when Fats Waller, the musician, was almost fatally shot, Holstein was called in for questioning about the incident since it occurred near his Turf Club. Police reports again suggested he was no longer a big player in the numbers game.

In addition to his business enterprise and his philanthropy, Holstein wrote several articles for *Opportunity* magazine, including "Congress and the Virgin Islands," "Senator Willis (Ohio) and the Virgin Islands," and "The Virgin Islands: Past and Present."

During his lifetime Holstein dressed fashionably in conservatively tailored suits, often of Irish linen. He often wore a fedora. He neither drank alcohol not smoked. He died almost penniless at the Harlem home of his life long friends, the Alverstone Smothergills, on April 5, 1944, after an illness of more than two years. His funeral was held on April 9 at Memorial Baptist Church in Harlem. He is buried in Woodlawn Cemetery in the Bronx. He had a number of prestigious friends who either attended his funeral or sent flowers. Among them were the U.S. District Attorney James Bough of the Virgin Islands, entertainer Bill Robinson Jr., and educator Moses Mims. His funeral drew some whites. Over two thousand people tried to view his body at the Memorial Baptist Church at 141 West 115th Street. Since his death a public housing project has been named for him in St. Croix, and the University of the Virgin Islands provides a scholarship in his name.

There are several versions of how the policy numbers racket began in Harlem. Most credit the Caspar Holstein with developing the scheme that continues to exist in some form today. Holstein used his wealth to assist the black community in numerous ways, including arranging summer trips on the Hudson for Harlem children. He is remembered as a sporting man of great generosity and ostensibly good intentions for black Harlem and the Virgin Islands.

REFERENCES

"Caspar Holstein Dies a Pauper." *New York Amsterdam News,* April 15, 1944.

"Caspar Holstein Dies At 67; Colorful Harlem Sportsman." *New York Amsterdam News,* April 15, 1944.

"Fails to Identify Kidnappers: Praises Their Kindness; Suspects Still held by Police." *New York Times,* September 25, 1928.

"Freed: M. Bernstein, P. Donohue, A. Dagustino, M. Schubert and R. Brown Held." *New York Times,* September 24, 1928.

Hall, Sadie. "Caspar Holstein." *Negroes of New York, 1939, New Biographical Sketches, A–Z.* Writers Program, New York City. Schomburg Center for Research in Black Culture, New York.

Hansen, Axel. *From These Shores.* Nashville: Privately Published, 1996.

Kellner, Bruce, ed. *The Harlem Renaissance: A Historical Dictionary of the Era.* Westport, CT: Greenwood Press, 1984.

"Negro, Believed Kidnapped in Harlem, by 4 White Men; Held for $50,000 Ransom." *New York Times,* September 23, 1928.

Schatzberg, Rufus. *Black Organized Crime in Harlem: 1920–1930.* New York, Garland Publishing, 1993.

Schoener, Allon. *Harlem On My Mind: Cultural Capital of Black America, 1900–1968.* New York, Random House, 1969.

COLLECTIONS

The Caspar Holstein collection of books by and about blacks is in the main library at St. Thomas, the Virgin Islands.

Mario A. Charles

Benjamin L. Hooks
(1925–)
Lawyer, organization leader, minister

Succeeding Roy Wilkins as the executive director of the NAACP, Benjamin Lawson Hooks served the association for more than 15 years. Among other issues, he stressed those pertaining to education and employment of blacks and other minorities in the United States. He is perhaps best known for his effective and persuasive oratorical skills; however, his diverse and successful career has included the fields of law, ministry, and public service.

Hooks was born on January 31, 1925, in Memphis, Tennessee. He was the fifth of seven children born to Robert Hooks Sr., co–owner, with his brother Henry, of a photographic business, and Bessie White Hooks. His paternal grandmother was Julia Hooks, who in 1917 had become one of the charter members of the NAACP branch in Memphis, Tennessee. Perhaps her involvement in the NAACP had a direct effect on her grandson's interest in the organization. His primary and secondary education were obtained at Porter Elementary School and Booker T. Washington High School in Memphis. After completing high school in 1941, he attended LeMoyne College (now LeMoyne–Owen College) in Memphis and Howard University in Washington, D.C. He received his J.D. degree in 1948 from DePaul University in Chicago. During World War II he served in the United States Army, where he was attached to the 92nd Infantry Division, an all–black combat unit.

Benjamin L. Hooks

Becomes First Black FCC Member

In 1949 Hooks began practicing law in Memphis and also became involved in community activities. One autumn day in September 1949 at the Negro County Fair in Memphis, Hooks's community activity led him to his future wife, Frances Dancy, a schoolteacher. Although their families had known each other for years, Hooks and Dancy had not seen each other since childhood. Hooks noticed her at the ice cream and sandwich booth where Dancy was helping her mother's friend, Mrs. Polk. According to Frances, Benjamin Hooks came to the booth and spoke to Polk but kept glancing in her direction. With the approval of her mother, the couple went on their first date to Tony's Inn, a popular restaurant on the south side of Memphis. After six months of dating, Hooks asked Frances Dancy to marry him. In the spring of 1951 they were married in an elaborate ceremony at Avery Chapel AME Church in Memphis, Tennessee.

Three years later, despite the fact that his father was unsympathetic to organized religion, Hooks became an ordained Baptist minister and pastor of the Middle Baptist Church in Memphis in 1956. He remained there until 1972. In 1964, however, he took on duties at the Greater New Mount Moriah Baptist Church in Detroit, where he also preached until 1972. Unable to preach at each church simultaneously, he alternated Sundays.

In 1961 Hooks became the assistant public defender for Shelby County, Tennessee. It was in this role as public defender that he came to understand fear. One day, while working on a civil rights case in Somerville, Tennessee, Hooks and several other lawyers were escorted out of town by sheriffs. Quoted in the *New York Times* for November 8, 1976, Hooks recalled, "I thought we were dead. . . . When I turned the curve I looked back and saw 75 or 80 cars behind us with shot guns hanging out the windows." Although a shot was fired, no one was injured.

In 1965 Tennessee Governor Frank G. Clement appointed Hooks to complete a judgeship in the Shelby County Criminal Court, thus making him the first black criminal court judge in Tennessee and the South since the Reconstruction period. The following year Hooks was elected to serve in this position for a full term. In December 1968 Hooks resigned the position to become president of the now defunct Mahalia Jackson Fried Chicken franchises. In *Jet* for December 1972, Hooks attributed the failure of these franchises to "long–haired brothers, with their hands up in a Black Power salute, shuffle right on by to Colonel Sanders Kentucky Fried Chicken."

In 1972 President Richard M. Nixon, fulfilling a campaign promise to select a black to serve as a member of the Federal Communications Commission (FCC), nominated Hooks to succeed Robert T. Barley, retiring after serving 20 years on the commission. Hooks, supported by Republican Tennessee Senator Howard Baker Jr., many civil rights leaders, and officials of numerous broadcasting organizations, was confirmed by the Senate. Hooks's first challenge occurred following his confirmation. He showed up an hour late for his first press conference. When asked about his tardiness, he explained in *Jet* for December 1972, "It has taken 38 years for us to get a Black commissioner, so I decided . . . to take all the time I wanted."

As the first black member of the seven–member FCC, an agency which grants and regulates radio and television licenses as well as telephone and telegraph services, Hooks complained that the black experience was portrayed inaccurately by the communication industry. Hooks noted in the same issue of *Jet* magazine that "unless we rob a bank or hold somebody up, we're not portrayed." He, therefore, favored preferential treatment for black ownership of radio and television stations. Robert A. DeLeon for *Jet* magazine quotes Hooks who said, "Black people in this country have a story to tell, and . . . if this story is told, this will be a better place to live."

Heads NAACP

After serving on the commission for four and a half years, Hooks decided there was nothing more he could do. On November 6, 1976, the board of directors of the NAACP unanimously elected Hooks as executive director, and he accepted. Hooks, a close colleague of Martin Luther King Jr., succeeded the retiring Roy Wilkins and took office on January 1, 1977. Hooks, according to the *New York Times,* was a "sophisticated charmer, a flamboyant preacher of the Southern Baptist school, and an intelligent man of many accomplishments." Hazel Dukes, president of the New York State

Conference of NAACP Branches and president of the National NAACP, described him in the April–May issue of *Crisis* as "a renaissance man, a man for all seasons. A man of deep spirituality . . . quiet dignity and boundless courage." Upon becoming the executive director of the NAACP, Hooks immediately focused on expanding and strengthening the organization's membership, programs, and funds. Hooks also indicated that under his leadership the NAACP would continue its focus on voting, unemployment, desegregation, education, and housing. Vowing that the NAACP would move in a new direction in pursuit of these same concerns,Hooks stated in *Ebony* (November 1978), "That the new direction has more to do with vitality [and]. . . style . . . but I am out to achieve the same things that . . . the NAACP has historically been after."

Hooks's three immediate goals were accomplished during his 15 1/2 years as executive director of the NAACP. One of his goals was to expand and strengthen the organization's membership. In accomplishing this goal, he focused on establishing more college chapters under his Youth and College divisions. He also focused on increasing the NAACP prison chapters and expanding on its Project Rebound program, which assisted parolees in readjusting to society in the areas of housing, employment, and providing other services. As a result, the organization was able to strengthen its membership from slightly less than 400,000 members to 500,000 members.

Hooks's second goal was to strengthen programs. Among the programs was Act–So (Afro–Academic Cultural Technological Scientific Olympics). The purpose of this program was to encourage black youths to strive for excellence and academic achievement through pride and competition. This program was recognized in over 500 cities for its creativity and viability. Also initiated were such programs as the Back–to–School/Stay–In–School Program, job readiness, SAT preparation, and the teacher competency test programs.

Strengthening the funding of the NAACP was the third goal. When Hooks succeeded Wilkins, the NAACP was $1 million in debt. By the end of 1978 the debt was reduced by half. By 1991 the NAACP had raised over $15.4 million, and when Hooks retired, the organization was debt free. Under Hooks's administration, the NAACP purchased the first home for the national headquarters in Baltimore, Maryland, a building owned by the organization.

There were also some legislative victories achieved during Hooks's administration. Among them were the Martin Luther King Holiday Bill; the Voting Rights Bill Extension; South African Sanctions Bill; and the 1991 Civil Rights Bill.

Retires and Receives Awards

For his diligent efforts, the NAACP presented Hooks at the 1986 National Convention the association's highest award, the Spingarn Medal. Six years later, Hooks informed the NAACP National Board of Directors that he would retire from the organization at the end of the contract year on April 1, 1993. In his statement to the board at the time of his announcement, Hooks, using the words of Roy Wilkins, indicated in *Crisis* for May 1992, "I intend to continue to fight for and with this organization as long as God gives health to this body."

Following his retirement he continued to provide service to the African American community by serving as senior vice–president of the Chapman Company, a minority controlled investment banking firm in Baltimore, Maryland; president of the National Civil Rights Museum at the site where Martin Luther King Jr. was assassinated in Memphis, Tennessee; and Distinguished Professor of the Benjamin L. Hooks Chair for Social Justice established in 1992 at Fisk University in Nashville, Tennessee. According to the *Memphis Tri–State Defender,* the chair was designed to "pass on the principles of leadership in public policy to future generations of civil rights leaders." Hooks, the chair's first occupant, served as a part–time lecturer at Fisk in the spring of 1995. His course focused on the social justice movements in the United States and was offered through both the Social Science Division and the W. E. B. Du Bois General University Honors Program.

Hooks's extensive work and long hours devoted to social and cultural projects were slowed down in 1994 when he had a massive heart attack. On September 10, 1994, he underwent a quadruple heart by–pass operation in a New Orleans hospital. He suffered the heart attack while attending the National Baptist Convention in Louisiana. Despite this setback and having to cut back his workload, in a short period of time he had returned to preaching in the pulpit.

On several occasions since retiring as executive director of the NAACP, Hooks has been asked if the civil rights movement and the NAACP are alive. He has responded by saying that the movement and the NAACP are very much alive. On August 22, 1996, the Progressive National Baptist Convention presented Hooks with the Martin Luther King Jr. Freedom Award for his years of service to the African American Community through the NAACP. In his acceptance speech he stated that prejudice lives. He noted in the *Washington Informer* for August 22, 1996, that "the country seems to be having a mental relapse. There are attacks on affirmative action due to the present conservative climate in this nation. This is just one of the major problems affecting African Americans."

Although Hooks has considerably reduced his workload, he is still active in the community and the church. He currently resides in Memphis with his wife, Frances. They have a daughter, Patricia Hooks Gray.

As executive director of the NAACP, Hooks was loyal to the basic purposes and principles of his predecessors, James Weldon Johnson, Walter White, and Roy Wilkins, in fighting against the entrenched Jim Crow policies during the heyday of the Civil Rights Movement. Like Wilkins, Hooks was concerned with eradicating bigotry and therefore became a strong and independent leader who championed civil and human rights.

Current address: Greater Middle Baptist Church, 4982 Knight Arnold Road, Memphis, TN 38118.

REFERENCES

African America: Portrait of a People. Detroit: Visible Ink Press, 1994.

"Ben Hooks Says Recovery Slowed by Reports of NAACP's Troubles." *Washington Afro–American,* December 10, 1994.

"Benjamin and Frances Hooks: How They Met and How He Proposed." *Ebony* 34 (February 1981): 92.

"Cabinet Secretary Says Many Key Civil Rights Groups Lead Changes." *Columbus (Georgia) Times,* April 12, 1994.

Delaney, Paul. "The Struggle to Rally Black America." *New York Times Magazine,* July 15, 1979.

DeLeon, Robert A. "Man Behind Changes to Make Radio, TV Relate to Blacks." *Jet* 43 (21 December 1972): 20–26.

"Dr. Hooks Lauded at Glittering Affair." *Crisis* 99 (January 1992): 23.

"1st Black FCC Member Gets Quick Senate OK." *Jet* 42 (15 June 1972): 8.

"Former Memphis Judge Named 1st Black on Federal Communications Post." *Jet* 42 (27 April 1972): 5.

Hawkins, Walter L. *African American Biographies.* Jefferson, NC: McFarland, 1992.

Hooks, Benjamin. "Publisher's Forward." *Crisis* 99 (April–May 1992): 4–5, 55.

Norment, Lynn. "New Life for an Old Fight." *Ebony* 34 (November 1978): 78–84.

"PNBC Denounces Clinton, Hear Jackson, and Honor Hooks." *Washington Informer,* August 22, 1996.

"Sophisticated Country Preacher: Benjamin Lawson Hooks." *New York Times,* November 8, 1976.

"TMC Donates $10,000." *Memphis Tri–State Defender,* February 22, 1995.

Who's Who among African Americans, 1996–97. 9th ed. Detroit: Gale Research, 1996.

Williams, James D. "Dr. Hooks to Retire after 15 Years as Executive Director." *Crisis* 99 (April–May 1992): 51–54.

Patricia A. Pearson

John Hope
(1868–1936)
College president, educator

John Hope was the first black president of Atlanta Baptist College, and the founding president of Atlanta University. He fostered improved race relations through service on numerous committees and was a staunch supporter of the YMCA and its work with black troops in France during World War I.

John Hope was born on June 2, 1868, in Augusta, Georgia. His grandmother, Alethea, was one of several slaves of Hugh Taylor, a prosperous plantation owner. Alethea, whose father was white, was the recognized mistress of a white man named Butt and was freed sometime before 1860. Of the seven children of Alethea, Mary Frances (Fanny) was the mother of John Hope; his father was James Hope. James Hope, a native of Scotland, was born in 1805 and accumulated sizable wealth as the proprietor of the Augusta Manufacturing Company, one of the South's few textile mills.

James Hope fell in love with the beautiful Fanny and lived openly with her. Their home was the center of socials attended by some of Augusta's white elite. With the Civil War imminent, James and his family left Augusta for New York City; they returned to Augusta and passed the war years. In 1867 James deeded the Augusta home to Fanny, and John Hope was born there a year later, in June. James Hope died in 1876; meanwhile, Fanny's family shared the benefits of white Augusta's aristocracy.

Fanny was nearly destitute after James's demise, as his white executors divested her of all except a small trust. John Hope became aware that he was "only another colored boy."

Young Hope was not resentful of white people though, despite the loss of his birthright. In 1881 he finished the eighth year in the Augusta public schools, where one of teachers was Lucy Craft Laney. Laney was a graduate of Atlanta University, and founder of the ground–breaking Haines Normal and Industrial Institute in Augusta for African American children. Hope worked as a clerk in a fashionable black–owned restaurant.

In 1886 Hope enrolled at Worcester Academy in Massachusetts. Hope insisted on being identified as black, although he could easily have passed for white. He joined in the school life of Worcester by serving on the debating team, being the editor–in–chief of the school's newspaper, and participating in sports. He graduated with honors and delivered one of the class orations in June of 1890. With the aid of a scholarship, Hope enrolled at Brown University in September. He continued his interest in journalism as a member of the editorial board of the *Brown Daily Herald* and founded an off—campus literary club, The Enquirers, which consisted of 15 young women. In 1894, at his commencement exercises, he was class orator and received the degree of bachelor of arts.

At Brown, Hope began to identify with the black people of Providence. His growing recognition of his blackness was aroused largely from the 1890 visit of John Mercer Langston to Providence. Langston was the first black American elected to public office, founder of the law school at Howard University, and a congressman from Virginia. Hope assisted in the organization of a public meeting and banquet as a member of the committee on arrangements. Hope faced the problem of being both a black man and an American citizen, and he decided that the time was at hand when gentility and ability should be acknowledged, regardless of color. Hope promoted this conviction for the rest of his life.

John Hope

Offered a post as a caucasian on the *Providence Journal,* for which he had done some reporting, Hope decided to shape his fortune with the black people of the South. He rejected an offer by Booker T. Washington to join the faculty at Tuskegee Institute in Alabama because he disagreed with some of Washington's ideas. Instead from 1894 to 1898 Hope chose to teach at Roger Williams University, a tiny black Baptist liberal arts college in Nashville, Tennessee. The faculty was mixed and the student body was coeducational; Hope taught natural sciences, Latin, and Greek.

Demands Social Equality

Hope visited Atlanta and heard Booker T. Washington's famous Atlanta Exposition Speech on September 18, 1895, and became more convinced than ever that he did not share Washington's opinions. On February 22, 1896, he revealed his convictions to a local debating team in Nashville. According to the *Dictionary of American Negro Biography,* he said, "If we are not striving for equality, in heaven's name for what are we living? . . . Now catch your breath for I am going to use an adjective: I am going to say we demand social equality." In the spring of 1896 in an address on "The Need of a Liberal Education for Us," cited in *The Story of John Hope,* Hope stated:

> The Negro must enter the higher fields. He must be prepared for advanced and original investigation. . . . Mere honesty, mere wealth, will not give us rank among the other peoples of the civilized world, and, what is more, we ourselves will never be possessed of conscious self–respect, until we can point to men in our own ranks who are easily the equal of any race.

Hope thus openly questioned the beliefs of Washington. Hope strove to combine diplomacy with conviction, however, when it came to the Washington phenomenon his diplomacy was taxed.

During his Christmas vacation in Chicago in 1897, Hope married Lugenia Burns on December 27, whom he had met while working there in 1893. Born in St. Louis, Burns had lived most of her life in Chicago and had done social work there. After their marriage she became friendly with the girls at Roger Williams University and started a class in physical education. The Hopes became the parents of two sons, Edward Swain, born in 1901, and John Jr., born in 1909.

Hope joined the faculty of Atlanta Baptist College in Georgia in 1898. In addition to teaching classics, he served as bookkeeper, introduced football in 1899, and coached for a few years.

W. E. B. Du Bois had joined the faculty of Atlanta University in 1897, the year before Hope assumed his duties at Atlanta Baptist College. Their friendship developed during the next 13 years, but Du Bois left in 1910 to join the NAACP. Their academic fervor brought them close together, and Hope was the only college president, black or white, to attend the 1906 Harpers Ferry meeting of the Niagara Movement. Hope was also the only college president to attend the protest meeting in May of 1909 in New York City which resulted in the founding of the NAACP.

Named College President

A month after his return from Harpers Ferry in 1906 Hope faced the savagery of the Atlanta race riot as he became the first black president of Atlanta Baptist College. He began actively to expand the enrollment and to seek financial support from northern philanthropic foundations. He demonstrated his ability to attract some of the leading black scholars to his faculty. For several years, when no other teacher was available, he continued to teach not only the classics but also logic, psychology, and ethics.

Atlanta Baptist was renamed Morehouse College in 1913 and Hope continued as president. He and Benjamin Brawley—a noted literary scholar whom Hope had lured as dean from Howard University and who had taught previously at Atlanta Baptist—organized the curriculum which laid the foundation for Morehouse's later reputation as the "College of Presidents" because of the number of graduates who became administrators of colleges.

Hope's activities continued to reach beyond the college campus boundaries. He was president of the National Association of Teachers of Colored Schools; a member of the advisory board of the NAACP; member of the executive committee of the National Urban League; honorary president of the Association for the Study of Negro Life and History; member of the board of managers of the Atlanta YMCA, and member of the city's Anti–tuberculosis Association. Hope inspected the treatment of black soldiers in France during the period from September of 1918 to July of 1919. Among his major recommendations was the replacement of white YMCA secretaries—who were generally disliked and distrusted by black soldiers and officers—with black secretaries. After a short return to Atlanta on Morehouse College business in May, Hope returned to France to oversee the work of black secretaries with the black soldiers. These secretaries were executives of the YMCA overseas installations. He accepted the establishment of separate rest areas as permissible because they were manned by black YMCA secretaries. Before he left France in July of 1919, Hope had been appointed a member of the field staff of the YMCA. Hope continued his interest in the Y until his death, giving support particularly to his friend Channing H. Tobias, a fellow YMCA leader.

World War I experiences left John Hope so disenchanted that he was hesitant to join the Commission on Inter–racial Cooperation then being organized by Will W. Alexander, a white southerner and former Methodist minister. After the commission elicited funds from a bond issue for the construction of a public high school for blacks, Hope accepted appointment on June 25, 1920. Lugenia Burns Hope became a member later and in 1932 Hope was elected president of the commission. The innumerable activities of the commission helped better race relations.

With the aid of considerable funds from the General Education Board and the American Baptist Home Mission Society, as well as black contributors, from 1920 to 1929 Hope built the "Greater Morehouse." He strengthened the administrative team at the college, and brought many stellar black scholars to the faculty. Among these notable additions was Benjamin Elijah Mays, who later became president of the college. The enrollment grew appreciably and new buildings were erected. Hope initiated cordial relations with Florence Matilda Read, the new white president of neighboring Spelman College and a pivotal person in the establishment of the new Atlanta University.

On April 1, 1929, the Board of Trustees of the new Atlanta University unanimously elected Hope president and on July 1, 1929, he became president of the first institution of higher education for African Americans offering only graduate work. He drafted a plan for the university, in cooperation with Spelman College and Morehouse College, to offer senior–graduate courses. On April 1, 1930, Hope submitted "The Six Year Plan," which proposed a graduate school, a school of business administration, a graduate school of liberal arts, a library school, a graduate school of social work through affiliation with the Atlanta School of Social Work, a department of music and fine arts, and more distant goals. The plan included recommendations regarding the architectural redesign of the three campuses, involving a new library, a president's house, a joint administrative building, and two graduate dormitories. The plan visualized the offering of masters degrees, and later the Ph.D. program. According to Clarence A. Bacote in *Atlanta University,* the school would "insist on the highest standards in the United States."

Hope in large measure realized these goals. He assembled the largest number of well–trained teachers in any predominantly black university except Howard. Among the most notable of these were historian Clarence A. Bacote; biologists Helene T. Albro of Spelman and Samuel M. Nabrit of Morehouse; English professors Nathaniel Tilman of Morehouse and William Stanley Braithwaite; Mercer Cook of Atlanta; Miss William Bryan Geter of Spelman; French professor Edward A. Jones of Morehouse; economist Brailsford R. Brazeal of Morehouse; Lorimer D. Milton, Jesse B. Blayton, and William H. Dean Jr., in the Department of Economics and Business Administration; and sociologist Ira de A. Reid.

The most notable appointment was that of W. E. B. Du Bois as guest professor in the Department of Economics and Sociology. In the fall of 1933 Du Bois began his second stint at Atlanta as professor of sociology. Hope was elated over Du Bois's decision to teach at the university. The two men had remained close friends over the years and also met in France in 1918 while Hope was a YMCA secretary and Du Bois was promoting his Pan–Africa concept.

These teachers and others less well–known but equally capable in many respects provided a high quality of work. Summer school (six weeks) was too short to enable students to complete requirements for the degree programs, but it permitted a sizable number of public school teachers to expand their knowledge and teaching skills.

In the summer of 1934 the Atlanta University Summer Theater surfaced under the guidance of Anne Cooke, the first theater in Atlanta to showcase African American plays. During a casual conversation with Cooke, a Spelman faculty member, Hope turned the talk to the restricted opportunity for blacks in the South to witness great plays with great artists because of segregation. The venture immediately succeeded and received a hearty response from the community and elsewhere.

When Hope accepted the presidency of Atlanta University it was with the understanding that he would remain president of Morehouse for two years after the affiliation. Close associates of Hope were deeply troubled about the strain under which he labored in his dual role and urged him to give up his position at Morehouse. Consequently, in the spring of 1931, Hope resigned his Morehouse responsibilities, after 25 distinguished years. In recognition of service, on June 1, 1931, 200 prominent African Americans assembled on the Spelman campus and toasted him "John Hope: Citizen of Atlanta."

The university's influence extended beyond the campus in outreach efforts. One of the most significant activities was directed by Lugenia Burns Hope and faculty members: a citizenship school sponsored by the NAACP to encourage blacks to register and vote. The project expanded throughout the South with the slogan "A Voteless People is a Hopeless

People.'' Hope supported his wife in this project and encouraged members of the faculty to serve on boards and commissions.

One of the most dramatic and significant events was the beginning of the first low–rent housing projects in the United States. As early as October of 1933 Hope urged the federal government to inaugurate a slum clearance project near the university. On September 29, 1934, Department of Interior Secretary Harold L. Ickes lit the fuse that dynamited the first house on the eighteen–acre site for the erection of the first government housing project for blacks in America.

Of the many honors conferred upon Hope, he probably most appreciated three: the 1929 Harmon Award for Distinguished Achievement in Education among Negroes, election as an Alumni member of Phi Beta Kappa (Brown University, 1919), and an LL.D. degree (Brown, 1935). He was also recognized with honorary degrees from Bates College, Bucknell University, Howard University, and McMasters University.

Following an attack of pneumonia, John Hope died in McVicar Hospital on the campus of Spelman College on February 20, 1936. Funeral services were held in the Morehouse Chapel, which was unable to accommodate the hundreds of people who had come to pay tribute to the celebrated educator. He was carried on the shoulders of students to a simple grave and buried beneath the window of his office on the Atlanta University campus. The NAACP recognized Hope's accomplishments with the posthumous award of the Spingarn Medal for 1935. In 1944, the Liberty Ship *John Hope* was launched from Richmond, California, as part of the World War II effort.

Hope was an extremely handsome, curly–haired, blue–eyed voluntary black, proud of his Scottish ancestry but dedicated to the pursuit of equality and justice for African Americans. He wore an easy confidence and rose to the top level of his aspirations. He laid secure foundations of an institution of learning in the South that offered blacks a higher education comparable to that obtainable in any other part of the country. His exploits entitle him to a foremost place among educational trailblazers.

REFERENCES

Bacote, Clarence A. *The Story of Atlanta University: A Century of Service 1865–1965.* Princeton, NJ: Princeton University Press, 1969.

Lewis, David Levering. *W. E. B. Du Bois: Biography of a Race, 1868–1919.* New York: Henry Holt, 1993.

Logan, Rayford, and Michael R. Winston, eds. *Dictionary of American Negro Biography.* New York: Norton, 1982.

Torrence, Ridgely. *The Story of John Hope.* New York: Macmillan, 1949.

COLLECTIONS

The John Hope Papers are located in the Atlanta University Center, Robert W. Woodruff Library, Atlanta.

Casper L. Jordan

George Moses Horton
(1797?–1883?)
Poet

The first American writer of syndicated features as well as the author of three collections of poetry, George Moses Horton became a man of letters while still a slave and thus helped establish the African American literary tradition. Hindered but not silenced by external circumstances, he became one of the first professional writers of any race in the South. In fact, Horton was often called a prodigy in Chapel Hill, North Carolina, where he sold his love poems to students and left a brief autobiography detailing his remarkable life that included friendships with students, university presidents, a governor, and army officers.

George Moses Horton was born in Northampton County, North Carolina, on the William Horton plantation, but since he was a slave the exact date of his birth was not recorded. According to his own account, he was the oldest child by his mother's second husband. He had five older half–sisters and eventually three younger sisters and one younger brother.

Sometime between 1800 and 1803 William Horton moved his family and slaves to Chatham County, North Carolina, where he purchased a farm. This move separated young George from his father but not from his mother and siblings. On the farm he was forced to tend cows. In his short autobiography, *The Black Poet,* he wrote:

> I here became a cow–boy, which I followed for perhaps ten years in succession or more. In the course of this disagreeable occupation, I became fond of hearing people read; but being nothing but a poor cow–boy, I had but little or no thought of ever being able to read or spell.

Teaches Himself to Read

Horton's ''little'' thoughts grew, however, and the solitude provided by tending cows enabled him to reflect, dream, and set goals more freely than if he had been a field hand. The first goal he set for himself was to learn the alphabet, which he did by hearing schoolchildren recite it and listening to people read. He also obtained an old speller and taught himself each letter by heart. Once he had learned to read the tattered spelling book, he moved up to the Wesley Hymnal that belonged to his mother. Because he already knew many of the songs from hearing them sung, he was able to match the words in the speller with the words in the songs. The poetry of these lyrics enchanted Horton, who noted in *The Black Poet:*

> At length, I began to wonder whether it was possible that I ever could be so fortunate as to compose in that manner. I fell to work in my head and composed several undigested pieces, which I retained in my mind, for I knew nothing about writing with a pen.

On Sundays, his only free day, Horton would review the old black speller and ponder the syllables; then he would read the Bible and the hymnal. The task he had set for himself, not just to read but to become a poet, was most ambitious for a slave. And yet, George Moses Horton did in fact fulfill his dream, carrying on the well–established oral tradition of his ancestors.

Horton's studies were soon interrupted when he was sent into the fields. But even there he did his work with his head in the clouds. Nights and Sundays were the only times he had for solitary reflection and poetic composition.

Journeys to Chapel Hill

Around 1815 George Moses was given to James Horton, the slave master's oldest son. He then made a request of his new master. He wanted permission to visit a university campus only four miles from the Horton plantation because he had heard that the students there loved poetry as much as he did, and he wanted to meet them. He did not tell his master that, however, so James Horton agreed that he could go as long as he did it on his free time and took along plantation products to sell.

Horton's first visit to the campus, which would have occurred before 1820, marked the beginning of his long association with the University of North Carolina at Chapel Hill. Legend has it that U.S. President James K. Polk, a member of the class of 1818, was one of the first students to encourage Horton. Soon he and others discovered that if given a subject Horton could create an extemporaneous oration.

Horton was determined to display his poetic talents and earn some money in the process. He was able to do so by composing acrostic love poems for the young men on campus. As he recalled in *The Black Poet:*

> Many of those acrostics I composed at the handle of the plough and retained them in my head (being unable to write) until an opportunity offered, when I dictated whilst one of the gentlemen would serve as my amanuensis. I have composed love pieces in verse for courtiers from all parts of the state, and acrostics on the names of many of the tip–top belles of Virginia, South Carolina, and Georgia.

Horton enjoyed a large and enthusiastic following that eagerly awaited his Sunday visits. As his popularity grew, so did his earning power. His compositions sold from 25 to 50 cents each. At one point he found it necessary to bargain with his slave master James and later with James's son Hall, paying them up to 50 cents a day for the freedom to continue visiting Chapel Hill. (When Horton became Hall's property, Hall demanded a dollar per day.) Thus he was able to keep producing lyrics such as these appearing in *The Black Poet:*

> Yon brook that babbles as it flows
>   Meandering through the lea,
> The charm of Nature richly shows,
>   But cannot charm like thee.

Publishes His Poetry

As might be expected, Horton benefited in other ways from his association with the university. In fact, it was at Chapel Hill in 1826 that he finally learned how to write down his own verses. His teacher was Caroline Hentz, an abolitionist from Massachusetts who was herself an author and the wife of a University of North Carolina professor, Nicholas Marcellus Hentz. She was so impressed by his poems that she submitted several of them to her hometown newspaper, the *Lancaster Gazette,* for publication. Horton's poems subsequently appeared in *Freedom's Journal* (the first black American newspaper) in 1828, the *Liberator* in 1834, and the *Southern Literary Messenger* in 1843.

In 1829, with the help of his friend Caroline Hentz, Horton published *The Hope of Liberty,* a collection of 21 poems that included his most famous work, "The Slave's Complaint." (The book was later retitled *Poems of a Slave* and bound with some of Phillis Wheatley's verses, then published in Philadelphia in 1837 and in Boston in 1838.) His hope was that it would earn enough money for him to purchase his freedom and move to Liberia, but the plan failed.

Producing a second volume of poetry also did not bring in much money toward the $250 Hall Horton had set as the purchase price for his slave. George Moses Horton then approached university president David Swain with two letters, one appealing to abolitionist William Lloyd Garrison for help in publishing a volume of poems and the other asking journalist Horace Greeley for money to buy his freedom. He asked Swain to forward both of the letters. Instead, Swain suppressed them.

In or around 1840, Horton married a slave woman owned by Franklin Snipes. She bore two children by Horton, a son named Free and a daughter named Rhody. Both took their mother's last name.

Achieves Freedom at Last

The outbreak of the Civil War in 1861 brought to a close Horton's occupation as campus bard. The young men marched off to fight, and Horton himself would soon attain the freedom that had eluded him for so long. During the war, however, he began reciting his poems to Union Army officers and their troops, finding a patron in Captain Will H.S. Banks of the 9th Michigan Cavalry Volunteers. When the unit was mustered out in Lexington, North Carolina, Banks went with Horton to Raleigh, where they published *The Naked Genius,* a third collection of poems containing 45 earlier works and some 89 new ones written with the federal troops. But Banks returned to Michigan in 1866 and soon lost touch with Horton.

Little more is known of Horton's life. In 1866, he turned up in Philadelphia, where according to one tradition, he held jobs with various members of the Cobb family and continued to write. Near the end of his life Horton was forced to turn to prose in order to support himself. He adapted Bible stories by giving the characters new names and changing the events to fit the times. He sold his pieces to several magazines, Sunday school publishers, and journals simultaneously, and as a result many of his works appeared in several different publications at once.

There is no record of Horton's death in Philadelphia. An article in the *Charlotte Observer* dated June 4, 1933, and cited in *The Black Poet* suggests that he may have returned to the South before he died, presumably in 1883.

While no one is sure exactly how or when Horton died, one thing is certain—he lived a remarkable life. He wrote numerous poems and published three collections: *The Hope of Liberty* (1829), *The Poetical Works of George M. Horton, the Colored Bard of North Carolina* (1845), and *The Naked Genius* (1865). Another volume, *The Museum,* was never published.

Horton's life is testimony to the ability of the human spirit to soar above oppressive conditions and reject what is and strive for what ought to be. His life also demonstrates the extent to which racism, bigotry, and ignorance prevent people from becoming all that they can be. Had it not been for slavery, who knows what George Moses Horton would have achieved?

REFERENCES

Jackson, Blyden. *A History of Afro–American Literature.* Vol. 1. Baton Rouge: Louisiana State University Press, 1989.

Logan, Rayford W., and Michael R. Winston, eds. *Dictionary of American Negro Biography.* New York: Norton, 1982.

Redding, J. Saunders. *To Make a Poet Black.* Ithaca, NY: Cornell University Press, 1988.

Sherman, Joan. *Invisible Poets: Afro–Americans of the Nineteenth Century.* Chicago: University of Chicago Press, 1989.

Walser, Richard, ed. *The Black Poet, Being the Remarkable Story (partly told my [sic] himself) of George Moses Horton a North Carolina Slave.* New York: Philosophical Library, 1966.

Nagueyalti Warren

"Black Harry" Hosier

(1750?–1806)

Preacher, slave, servant

A circuit–riding preacher during the Colonial and early National periods in America, Harry Hosier covered the Methodist itinerant circuits from the Carolinas to New England and brought the gospel to slaves, free blacks, and poor and affluent whites. He was the first black to preach before a white Methodist congregation. Though uneducated, he was remarkably talented and unusually intelligent, had great retention, and was highly creative in his preaching. He has been called the most eloquent preacher of his time.

Most sources report that Harry Hosier (also spelled Hoosier, Hoshur, Hossier), familiarly known as was born a slave near Fayetteville, North Carolina. There exist no reports about his parents, except that they came from Africa and were enslaved. Hosier may have been the slave of Henry (Harry) Dorset Gough (?–1808), who owned a large plantation, Perry Hall, located northeast of Baltimore. Francis Asbury (1745–1816), founder of American Methodism, preached in that area in 1775 and 1776, and it is possible that Hosier heard him preach and was converted around that time. It has been suggested also that Hosier encountered Harry Evans (c.1740–1810), a black preacher from Virginia, who founded a Methodist congregation in Fayetteville about 1780. Hosier may have been a member of his church and possibly was converted there.

Whatever his early religious background or the circumstances of his freedom, Hosier became a free man and was converted to Methodism either before or after his freedom. He and Francis Asbury met sometime before 1780. According to the *Encyclopedia of World Methodism,* Asbury noted in his journal entry on June 29, 1780, that their meeting was "providentially arranged." In connection with his evangelistic campaign to reach slaves, Asbury went to Todd, North Carolina, near the Virginia line, on the previous day and might have encountered Hosier there. His diary entry, quoted by Warren Thomas Smith in *Harry Hosier,* noted: "I have thought if I had two horses, and Harry (a coloured man) to go with, and drive one, and meet the black people, and to spend about six months in Virginia, and the Carolinas, it would be attended with a blessing."

Integrates the Methodist Pulpit

Hosier became Asbury's servant, guide, and a circuit–riding preacher. Asbury's interest in Hosier was due to Hosier's rare qualities which, no doubt, Asbury had observed. Hosier was an eloquent speaker who, though uneducated, was intellectually alert, creative, and possessed a remarkable memory. Those who heard him preach were instantly impressed with his work. He preached with Asbury at the Fairfax Chapel in Falls Church, Virginia, as early as May 13, 1781. This made him the first black preacher to deliver a sermon to white Methodist church in America. As was customary with circuit–riders, Hosier adopted a recurring theme for his sermons. Though untrained, he spoke of the "barren fig tree." Thus far records fail to document earlier accounts of Hosier's preaching or joint services with Asbury. On May 21, 1781, Hosier preached to a black congregation who came long distances to hear him at a place called P. Hites. By October 27 that year, Asbury and Hosier were in Delaware preparing to return to Virginia. Asbury feared that Hosier was now unwilling to go with him, having been influenced by the praises of whites who heard him preach. According to *Harry Hosier,* he said, "I fear his speaking so much to white people in the city has been, or will be, injurious; he has been flattered, and he may be ruined."

"Black Harry" Hosier

When Thomas Coke came to America as Methodism founder John Wesley's representative, Asbury planned a preaching trip for him through Delaware, Maryland, and Virginia and assigned Hosier to serve as his guide beginning November 1784 (and again in 1786). As well, the journey introduced Coke to the work of the Methodists and prepared him for the historical Christmas Conference that was to come that year. After hearing Hosier preach during the trip, according to *Harry Hosier,* Coke wrote in his journal, "I really believe he is one of the best Preachers in the world, there is such an amazing power attends his preaching, though he cannot read; and he is one of the humblest creatures I ever saw."

The tour ended in time for the Christmas Conference held in Lovely Lane Chapel in Baltimore from December 24, 1784, to January 2, 1785. It was at this conference that the Methodist Episcopal church was formally established in America and a permanent relationship was established between white and black Methodists. Hosier was present. Unverifiable claims are made that Richard Allen, later the founder of the African Methodist Episcopal Church, was also there.

Hosier and Asbury traveled together in early autumn 1786, when they went to New York. In September, after Hosier preached his first sermon in New York at the John Street Church, the local press noted the work of the unlettered black man and his success in the pulpit. As they traveled, Asbury knew that the best way to insure a large attendance was to announce that Hosier would preach. Hosier's travels continued; he served as circuit guide for other religious leaders and bishops and preached with them as well. These included Richard Whatcoat, from 1786 to 1788, and Freeborn Garrettson in 1789. When Hosier and Garrettson reached Boston in July, Hosier boarded with Prince Hall (1735–1807), founder of the Prince Hall Masonic Order, the first black masonic lodge. Hosier also traveled with Jesse Lee in the 1790s. Lee virtually founded Methodism in New England and in 1796, with Hosier's help, established the Zoar Methodist Church in Philadelphia, called the oldest black Methodist congregation. In 1803 Hosier traveled with John Walker on the Trenton Circuit and spent subsequent years in Maryland and Pennsylvania. Hosier remained popular wherever he preached: at camp meetings, quarterly meetings, and love feasts.

Hosier's life as a circuit preacher was not trouble–free. A woman named Sally Lyons brought charges of an undisclosed nature against him in 1791; after a full hearing in October, he was declared not guilty. Rumors also circulated that Hosier "fell from grace" and became an alcoholic addicted to wine; it appears that he recovered from his alcoholism. Some writers claimed that the charge of alcoholism kept him from being ordained. Although Richard Allen was ordained a deacon in 1799, becoming the first black ordained in the Methodist church, and other black preachers were ordained around that time as well, Hosier was excluded.

Throughout his preaching career Hosier resisted learning to read or write. Instead, he memorized Biblical passages and hymns that he heard and repeated them accurately to his audiences. According to G. A. Raybold, in *Reminiscences of Methodism in West Jersey,* cited in *Harry Hosier,* Hosier lost his gift of preaching when he did try to read. He responded to this rumor by admitting, "I sing by faith, pray by faith, preach by faith, and do everything by faith; without faith in the Lord Jesus I can do nothing."

The History of the Negro Race in America noted Hosier's nickname obviously came from the fact that he was "very black." He was described further as "small in stature with brilliant, keen eyes." Sometime in May 1806 Hosier died in Philadelphia and his funeral was held on May 18. Black and white mourners attended his burial at the cemetery attached to the Old Zoar Church. Despite his contribution to American life as a powerful evangelist, gifted speaker, and participant in historical events in the Methodist church, it was not until recent times that Hosier was again recognized in the church. According to Marilyn McGee, black United Methodists now celebrate his work and memory through the Harry Hosier Club, a benevolent group named in his honor.

REFERENCES

Harmon, Nolan B., Albea Godbold, and Louise L. Queen. *The Encyclopedia of World Methodism.* Vol. 1. Nashville: United Methodist Publishing House, 1994.

Melton, J. Gordon, ed. *The Encyclopedia of American Religions.* Tarrytown, NY: Triumph Books, 1991.

McGee, Marilyn. Interview with Jessie Carney Smith, June 1, 1996.

Murphy, Larry G., J. Gordon Melton, and Gary L. Ward, eds. *Encyclopedia of African American Religions.* New York: Garland Publishing, 1993.

Shockley, Grant S., ed. *Heritage and Hope: The African–American Presence in United Methodism.* Nashville: Abington Press, 1991.

Smith, Warren Thomas. *Harry Hosier, Circuit Rider.* Nashville: Abington Press, 1981.

Williams, George W. *History of the Negro Race in America.* 1882. Reprint, Salem, NH: Ayer Company Publishers, 1989.

Jessie Carney Smith

Charles Hamilton Houston

(1895–1950)

Lawyer, educator

Charles Hamilton Houston

Charles Hamilton Houston played a principal role in defining and pacing the legal phase of the African American struggle against racial oppression from the early 1930s until his death in 1950. When the unconstitutionality of racially segregated public schools was argued before the Supreme Court of the United States in 1954 in *Brown v. Board of Education of Topeka* and *Bolling v. Sharpe,* ''there were some two dozen lawyers on the side of Negroes fighting for their schools,'' recalled Justice Thurgood Marshall in *Amherst Magazine.* ''Only two . . . hadn't been touched by Charlie Houston.''

As a teacher, litigator, and mentor from 1924 to 1950, Charles Houston trained hundreds of African American students at Howard University's Law School and advised scores of African American lawyers affiliated with the NAACP and its Legal and Educational Defense Fund. Between 1934 and 1949 Houston played a central role as the NAACP's staff special counsel, National Legal Committee member, and senior legal advisor, particularly in the conceptualization and implementation of a long–range strategic plan of litigation that ultimately led to favorable rulings in Brown and Bolling.

Houston formulated a philosophy that scholars call ''Houstonian Jurisprudence,'' which J. Clay Smith Jr. described in the *Howard Law Journal.* Houstonian Jurisprudence consisted essentially of use of the law for social change, which he identified as ''social engineering,'' and his fundamental beliefs regarding equality, freedom, and justice as the *sine qua non* of an ideal society. Veteran civil rights lawyers agree that Charles Hamilton Houston was the first ''Mr. Civil Rights.''

Charles Hamilton Houston was born in the District of Columbia on September 3, 1895, to William LePre Houston (1870–1953), a lawyer, and Mary Ethel Hamilton Houston (1867–1947), a hairdresser and former teacher. As an adult, Charles Houston was a handsome man who stood a little more than six–feet tall. He married twice. His first union in 1924 with Margaret Gladys Moran ended in divorce; there were no children. Following his divorce of 1937, Houston married Henrietta Williams. Charles Hamilton Houston Jr., their only son, was born March 20, 1944.

The Formative Years

The Houston family, especially Charles's parents and Clotill Houston, an aunt who was a school teacher, placed great emphasis upon education and excellence. Houston attended the District of Columbia's segregated public schools and in 1911 completed his studies at the M Street college–preparatory high school. Enrolling at Amherst College in 1911, he studied hard, earned high grades, was inducted into Phi Beta Kappa and graduated magna cum laude in 1915. He taught English for two years at Howard University in Washington, D.C., but during World War I joined the army and served as an officer from 1917 to 1919. Following his discharge, he enrolled in Harvard Law School and, from 1919 to June of 1923, studied with such eminent professors as Roscoe Pound and future Supreme Court justice Felix Frankfurter. Houston became the first African American editor of the *Harvard Law Review* in 1921, received his LL.B. with honors in 1922, and earned his doctor of juridical science degree in 1923. After additional studies in civil law at the University of Madrid in Spain and travels to northern Africa, Houston returned to Washington, D.C., in the summer of 1924.

In 1924 Houston was admitted to the District of Columbia bar, entered law practice, established with his father the firm Houston and Houston, and accepted a teaching position at Howard University Law School. His practice of law at Houston and Houston on F Street Northwest, in the District, consisted mainly of civil law but included some criminal cases. Both Houstons handled matters of domestic relations, personal injury, negligence, wills, and estates. Within a few years, however, Charles Houston added to the practice civil rights claims. He remained with the firm until his death in 1950, taking one leave of absence to direct a phase of the NAACP's special litigation campaign in New York. Among other partners subsequently named were William Henry Hastie, Joseph Waddy, and William Bryant, each of whom became a distinguished jurist. Juanita Kidd Stout, a secretary at the firm, was encouraged by Houston to pursue her interest in law, and became the first African American woman appointed to the Supreme Court of Pennsylvania.

Houston was an enthusiastic participant in civic activities in Washington, D.C., and a law teacher at Howard University's law school. Houston, with other attorneys in the District including J. Franklin Wilson and Louis R. Mehlinger, founded the Washington Bar Association in 1925. Houston held membership in both the National Bar Association and the National Lawyers Guild; the American Bar Association was not open to African Americans. In addition to membership in the national and local NAACP, Houston participated in the American Council on Race Relations, served on the District of Columbia's Board of Education, and was an advisor as well as counsel to the Consolidated Parents Group of Washington, D.C. In the evenings, he taught law students at Howard a range of courses from administrative law to jurisprudence. His views regarding the potential of Howard's law school and the service he might render as an educator led Houston to accept a special responsibility after only three years of teaching and practicing law. During 1927 and 1928 Houston conducted a Rockefeller–funded national survey on the status and activities of African American lawyers. His findings revealed a striking shortage of African American attorneys: in particular, few with the formal training and experience in constitutional law to handle effectively civil rights cases in the federal courts. After recuperating from a bout with tuberculosis, Houston directed his attention to this problem.

In 1935 Houston published findings regarding African American attorneys, his views on duties, and a challenge to African American law students and attorneys in the *Journal of Negro Education.*

Howard Law School and "Social Engineering"

Becoming resident vice–dean and later vice–dean of Howard's law school in 1929, Houston, with the approval of Howard's president Mordecai Johnson, implemented a plan to transform the evening law school into a full–time, fully accredited day school. Under Houston's leadership as vice–dean and chief educational administrator, the law school's curriculum took on a new form and emphasis consistent with Houston's view given in his manuscript, "Personal Observations on the Summary of Studies in Legal Education as Applied to the Howard University School of Law," dated May 18, 1929. Houston believed it was the duty of Howard Law School to "equip its students with the direct professional skills most useful to them" and to train them to become "social engineers." By 1932, Howard University Law School was an American Bar Association–accredited institution and a member of the Association of American Law Schools. Under Houston and his immediate successors, a highly trained faculty was assembled, including William H. Hastie, Leon A. Ransom, George E. C. Hayes, James Nabrit, and George Marion Johnson. These law professors, many of whom became Houston's life–long friends and associates in NAACP cases, embraced the school's new mission. Howard University Law School became virtually a laboratory for civil rights, and many Howard graduates became distinguished advocates for African Americans.

During his years at Howard in the late 1920s and early 1930s, Houston developed and began to teach his "social engineering" to Howard law students, among them Thurgood Marshall, Oliver Hill, and William Bryant. An element of Houstonian Jurisprudence, social engineering was grounded in beliefs about law in this society: first, that law could be used to promote and secure fundamental social change for the improvement of society; and second, that law was an instrument available to minority groups unable to achieve citizenship with full rights, opportunities, and privileges.

NAACP Special Counsel

In 1934, when Houston was approached by the NAACP and the American Fund for Public Service about addressing the legal status of African Americans, Houston applied social engineering to the task. First, he carefully studied both data amassed and a proposal for litigation in a report prepared earlier by Nathan Margold, a white NAACP lawyer trying to reverse the separate–but–equal policy established by *Plessy v. Ferguson.* Houston then presented to the NAACP and representatives of the American Fund for Public Service a long–range plan of protracted struggle to establish gradually anti–Plessy precedents through litigation and community involvement. Houston's plan, with modifications, guided attorneys of the NAACP and its Legal Defense Fund through the early 1950s as they sought to invalidate Plessy and have racial segregation declared unconstitutional. In 1934, a joint committee of the NAACP and the American Fund for Public Service invited Houston to direct a campaign of litigation against racial discrimination in public education and transportation. He served as part–time NAACP special counsel from October of 1934 to June of 1935 and full–time special counsel from July of 1935 to 1940, working in Washington, D.C., and New York City.

The first African American selected by the NAACP to join its staff as a salaried attorney to direct its legal affairs nationally, Houston handled a variety of legal matters that individuals and branches brought to the national offices of the NAACP. Beyond education cases, the most notable were unconstitutional denials of due process and jury discrimination, such as *Hollins v. Oklahoma* (1935) and *Hale v. Kentucky* (1938). Primarily, however, Houston designed and led a strategically planned campaign of litigation, education, and community activism, the ultimate goal of which he described in his address before the National Bar Association in 1935 as ''complete elimination of segregation'' in public education. He explained his rationale:

> No segregation operates fairly on a minority group unless it is a dominant minority. . . . These apparent senseless discriminations in education against Negroes have a very definite objective on the part of the ruling whites to curb the young and prepare them to accept an inferior position in American life without protest or struggle.

Throughout the legal campaign, Houston sought to develop a sustaining community interest in the program of civil rights. Houston publicized the campaign against discrimination in education, touring the South to film the inequalities in black public schools compared to white public schools. He encouraged community involvement, developed model procedures, regularly provided advice or collaborated with other African American attorneys throughout the states, argued cases, and contributed to the preparation of many cases in the state and federal courts. In many of these tasks, he was aided by Thurgood Marshall, who began service as assistant special counsel in 1936. By late 1938 when Houston was working out of his Washington, D.C., office, Marshall assumed responsibility for operations in New York City. He succeeded Houston as special counsel upon Houston's resignation in September of 1940.

As special counsel, Houston argued several cases attacking discrimination in public education before state and federal courts. Cases in which African Americans sought admission to state–supported law schools in Maryland and Missouri were especially significant as first and second steps in the assault upon *Plessy v. Ferguson.* During 1935 and 1936, Thurgood Marshall, who had himself been denied admission to the University of Maryland's law school, and Houston shared in the preparation and argument of *Murray v. University of Maryland.* On appeal, Maryland's highest court affirmed the Baltimore City Court's ruling that Murray's equal protection rights had been violated and ordered Donald Gaines Murray's admission to the tax–supported law school.

In 1938, Houston and St. Louis attorney Sidney Redmond won the NAACP's first major U.S. Supreme Court victory in the legal campaign *Missouri ex rel Gaines v. Canada* (1938). In *Gaines,* the Supreme Court carefully scrutinized the state's equal protection obligation to applicant Lloyd Gaines in providing separate but equal public education. It held that Missouri neither could meet its Fourteenth Amendment obligation of equal protection through provision of out–of–state scholarships, nor could the state constitutionally exclude an African American from the white state university law school if an equivalent black university did not exist.

Concurrently, Houston and Thurgood Marshall provided legal expertise and assistance to local teachers in Maryland and other southern states as they challenged inequality in the salaries of African American and white teachers. With local and national support, such teachers as William Gibbs of Maryland, Modjeska Simkins of South Carolina, and Melvin Alston of Virginia litigated their claims. When in *Alston v. Board of Education* (1940) the U.S. Supreme Court refused to hear the appeal of the Board of Education, the case established the principle that a difference in teachers' salaries based solely on race constituted a denial of equal protection.

Assault on Racial Discrimination Through Private Practice

The conditions of employment for African Americans as well as their education had long been a concern of Charles Hamilton Houston. Retaining his affiliation with the NAACP through membership on the National Legal Committee, Houston addressed education through the NAACP and employment through his private practice during the 1940s. Racial discrimination against African American railroad workers occasioned two other successful oral arguments before the U.S. Supreme Court. As general counsel to the Association of Colored Railway Trainmen and to the International Association of Railway Employees, Houston pursued their claims of unfair labor practices in federal and state courts. On the same day, Houston argued before the U.S. Supreme Court *Steele v. Louisville and Nashville* and a companion case, *Tunstall v. Brotherhood of Locomotive Firemen and Enginemen.* In March of 1944, the court handed down its opinions in *Steele and* Turnstall, both of which involved issues related to racism and representation. In *Steele,* the justices ruled that a white labor union authorized under the federal Railway Labor Act to serve as the collective bargaining representative for railroad firemen must fairly represent all workers regardless of race, including those African American firemen excluded from the white union's membership. *Steele,* a landmark decision, established the duty of fair representation, and *Tunstall* was decided on the same basis.

Addressing the continuing concerns of African American railroad workers, Houston also served as an attorney for the President's Fair Employment Practice Committee (FEPC) as it planned hearings on racial discrimination in the railway industry. From 1944 to December of 1945 Houston served on the FEPC, then dramatically resigned in 1945 when President Harry S Truman refused to issue an order barring racial discrimination by the Capital Transit Company of Washington, D.C. In his letter to Truman dated December 3, 1945, located in the NAACP Records, Houston chastised Truman for his failure ''to enforce democratic practices and to protect minorities'' in the nation's capital and observed that such failure ''makes [the government's] expressed concern for national minorities abroad somewhat specious.''

In his private practice throughout the late 1940s, Houston focused his attention on several aspects of racial discrimination in the nation's capital. Working often into the early morning hours, he sought to balance his obligations in such a way as to give serious attention to both the issues of his own community and national matters related to the NAACP Legal Defense Fund's continuing campaign against racial discrimination in education. He provided, according to Thurgood Marshall, indispensable advice and counsel concerning such education cases as *Sipuel v. Oklahoma State Regents* (1948), *Sweatt v. Painter* (1950), and *McLaurin v. Oklahoma State Regents* (1950).

Houston, as well, advocated civil rights in his *Afro–American* newspaper column, his public addresses, his work as an officer of the National Lawyers Guild, and his activities with Mary Church Terrell and other citizens concerned about enforcement of anti–discrimination public accommodations statutes in Washington, D.C. Through the firm, Houston represented African American residents of the District with civil rights claims pertaining to discrimination in housing and education. Insisting that racism must go, Houston appeared in oral argument before the U.S. Supreme Court on the issue of the constitutionality of racially restrictive covenants on property in Washington, D.C., in *Hurd v. Hodge* (1948), the companion case to *Shelley v. Kraemer* (1948). Especially noteworthy was his preparation of a strong, comprehensive brief against restrictive covenants, which drew on law, policy, and social science. Counsel to the Consolidated Parents Group of the District, Houston filed litigation that laid the foundation for *Bolling v. Sharpe* (1950), the District of Columbia's companion case to *Brown v. Board of Education* (1954).

Charles Houston's involvements in the struggle against racial discrimination left him little time for relaxation with family or his friends, among whom he counted Thurgood Marshall, William Hastie, Spottswood Robinson, Raymond Pace and Sadie Alexander, Walter White, Roy Wilkins, Juanita Jackson Mitchell, Z. Alexander Looby, and Juanita Kidd Stout.

In 1949 a heart condition caused Houston to be hospitalized. On April 22, 1950, acute coronary thrombosis—a relapse from his earlier heart attack—ended Houston's life. Among his survivors were his wife, Henrietta Williams Houston; their son, Charles Jr.; his father, William LePre; and his aunt, Clotill Houston. For Houston's funeral, Howard University's Rankin Chapel was filled to capacity. U.S. Supreme Court Justices came to pay their last respects to the man, whom Justice William O. Douglas in later correspondence to J. Clay Smith called "one of the top ten advocates to appear before [the Supreme] court." Interment in Lincoln Memorial Cemetery of Suitland, Maryland, immediately followed funeral services on April 26, 1950. Houston's high competence and success as an educator, constitutional lawyer, legal strategist, and advisor had an immediate impact on interpretation of the law and opportunities for African Americans as well as far–reaching consequences for the ongoing struggle for freedom of African Americans.

In June of 1950, Charles Jr. accepted for his father the NAACP's Spingarn Medal. The Board of Trustees of Howard University voted to name their law school after Houston, and in 1981 Thurgood Marshall participated in a ceremony for the unveiling of a bust in Houston's honor. Numerous African American law students' and lawyers' organizations now bear his name, as do several public schools.

REFERENCES

Douglas, William O. Letter to J. Clay Smith, April 19, 1974. In possession of Smith.

Hastie, William H. "Charles Hamilton Houston." *Negro History Bulletin* 13 (June 1950): 207–8.

Houston, Charles H. "Foul Employment Practices on the Rails." *Crisis* 56 (October 1949): 269–71.

———. "The Need for Negro Lawyers." *Journal of Negro Education* 4 (January 1935): 49–52.

———. "Proposed Legal Attack on Educational Discrimination." Typescript summary of address delivered to the National Bar Association. August 1, 1935. In possession of author.

Kluger, Richard. *Simple Justice.* New York: Alfred Knopf, 1976.

Logan, Rayford, and Michael Winston, eds. *Dictionary of American Negro Biography.* New York: Norton, 1982.

McNeil, Genna Rae. *Groundwork: Charles Hamilton Houston and the Struggle for Civil Rights.* Philadelphia: University of Pennsylvania Press, 1983.

———. "'To Meet the Group Needs': The Transformation of Howard University School of Law." In *New Perspectives on Black Educational History.* Edited by James Anderson and V. P. Franklin. Boston: G. K. Hall, 1978.

Meier, August, and Elliott Rudwick. "Attorneys Black and White." *Journal of American History* 62 (March 1976): 913–46.

Robinson, Spottswood. "No Tea for the Feeble." *Howard Law Journal* 20 (1977): 1–9.

Segal, Geraldine. *In Any Fight Some Fall.* Rockville, MD: Mercury, 1975.

Smith, J. Clay Jr. *Emancipation.* Philadelphia: University of Pennsylvania Press, 1993.

———. "Principles Supplementing the Houstonian School of Jurisprudence." *Howard Law Journal* 32 (1989): 493–504.

COLLECTIONS

The papers of Charles Hamilton Houston are in the Moorland–Spingarn Research Center, Howard University, Washington, D.C. He is also represented in the NAACP records located in the Library of Congress.

Genna Rae McNeil

William DeHart Hubbard
(1903–1976)
Olympic track star, public housing official

William DeHart Hubbard was the first African American to win an Olympic gold medal. At the 1924 Paris Olympiad, he placed first in the long jump competition with a leap of 24 feet, 5 1/8 inches. A year later he set a world record in the same event of 25 feet, 10 7/8 inches. Hubbard was the equivalent of Carl Lewis during the early 1920s.

Hubbard was born on November 25, 1903, in Cincinnati, Ohio. He began his track career at a time when African Americans were barred from participating in athletics professionally, especially those who were unable to attend college. Many public recreation facilities were for whites only with no facilities available for African Americans. However, in the early 1900s, African American athletic clubs were developed to fill the gaps left by the limits of black colleges and the scarcity of black athletes at white schools. These clubs provided African Americans with access to quality competition. However, these clubs were not accredited by the Amateur Athletic Union (AAU), and were recognized only with the sanction of authorities. In 1926 Hubbard finally secured the first such sanction. Clubs could now enter teams in AAU meets and, when certain minimum standards were met, they could hold meets themselves. Their status enabled them to attract the best runners as members.

In 1921 Hubbard enrolled at the University of Michigan. During his college career Hubbard held the national and collegiate titles in the long jump and the hop, skip, and jump. He won the first of his six national championships in 1922. In 1924 he stepped into the annals of history when he became the first African American to win a gold medal, taking first place in the long jump at the Paris Olympics. At the 1925 Intercollegiate American Amateur Athletic Association Championships in Chicago, his final competition as a Michigan undergraduate, he won the 100–yard dash with a time of 9.8 seconds, and set a world record in the long jump. Hubbard had the best mark of his career in 1927 when he jumped 26 feet, 2 1/4 inches, but the mark was not recognized as a world record because the takeoff board was one inch higher than the surface of the landing pit. According to *Champions in the Makings*, "Hubbard was a premier short sprinter." When he raced in the 60–yard indoor sprint, his quick pickup made him practically unbeatable. His jumping technique gave him a comparatively short (100 feet) approach run and may have been the shortest run of all world record holders. "He followed a theory that the running distance be limited by a jumper's ability to generate top speed."

Injuries stopped Hubbard from competing after graduating from college, but he was able to defend his Olympic title at the 1928 games in Amsterdam. In 1957 Hubbard was inducted into the Drake Relays Hall of Fame and in 1959 the Helms Foundation Hall of Fame. He was also inducted into the Black Athletes Hall of Fame in New York City.

William DeHart Hubbard

From 1927 to 1941, Hubbard worked with the Cincinnati Public Recreation Commission, followed by an appointment to the Cincinnati Metropolitan Housing Authority. He and his family moved to Cleveland, Ohio, in 1942, where he became race relations advisor to the Federal Public Housing Authority. In this position he spearheaded a continuing fight for better minority group housing. He also served as an advisor to the Ohio Association of Real Estate Brokers and was an active member of the National Committee Against Discrimination. Still involved in athletics, Hubbard was successful professionally and prominent in Cleveland bowling circles. He retired from the Federal Housing Authority in 1969 and in that year the DeHart Hubbard Scholarship Fund for needy students was established at Central State University.

In the mid–1970s, Hubbard suffered a series of strokes and abandoned his community services because of ill health. He died June 23, 1976, in Cleveland, Ohio. He was survived by his wife Audrey; three children, Ezelle, Carolyn and Alton; and three grandchildren, Michael, Patricia and William. Hubbard was elected to the National Track and Field Hall of Fame in 1979.

REFERENCES

Ashe, Arthur R., Jr. *A Hard Road to Glory: A History of the African–American Athlete 1919–1945.* New York: Warner Books, 1988.

Clift, Virgil A., and W. Augustus Low. *Encyclopedia of Black America.* New York: McGraw–Hill, 1981.

Jordan, Payton, and Bud Spencer. *Champions in the Making: Quality Training for Track and Field.* Englewood Cliffs, NJ: Prentice–Hall, 1968.

Page, James A. *Black Olympian Medalists.* Englewood, CO: Libraries Unlimited, 1991.

Salzman, Jack, David Lionel Smith, and Cornel West, eds. *Encyclopedia of African–American Culture and History.* New York: Macmillan Reference Library USA/Simon and Schuster Macmillan, 1996.

"Whatever happened to . . . De Hart Hubbard?" *Ebony* 31 (March 1976): 140.

Young, A. S. "Doc." *Negro Firsts in Sports.* Chicago: Johnson Publishing Co., 1963.

Sheila A. Stuckey

Langston Hughes

(1902–1967)

Writer, editor, columnist, lecturer

Langston Hughes achieved fame as a poet during the burgeoning of the arts known as the Harlem Renaissance, but those who label him "a Harlem Renaissance poet" have restricted his fame to only one genre and decade. In addition to his work as a poet, Hughes was a novelist, columnist, playwright, and essayist, and though he is most closely associated with Harlem, his world travels influenced his writing in a profound way. Langston Hughes followed the example of Paul Laurence Dunbar, one of his early poetic influences, to become the second African American to earn a living as a writer. His long and distinguished career produced volumes of diverse genres and inspired the work of countless other African American writers.

Born James Langston Hughes on February 1, 1902, in Joplin, Missouri, a mining town, the young Hughes lived among well–educated African Americans. His parents, Carrie Mercer Langston Hughes and James Nathaniel Hughes, separated before Langston could know his father, but his extended family provided him with shelter and clothing plus education, heritage, and culture. Carrie Hughes, who enjoyed literature and theater, then moved with her baby into the home of her mother, Mary Sampson Patterson Leary Langston, who was born free in North Carolina and educated at Oberlin College in Ohio. From her side of the family came distinguished forebears whom Langston Hughes proudly acknowledged in his first autobiography, *The Big Sea.* Mary Patterson's first husband, Sheridan Leary, died with John Brown's raid at Harpers Ferry. Her second husband, Charles Langston, was an ardent abolitionist, and his brother, John Mercer Langston, earned three degrees from Oberlin College, passed the Ohio bar, and represented a Virginia district in the U.S. Congress.

Early Years

Although his youth was marked with transition, Hughes extracted meaning from the places and people whence he came. The search for employment led his mother and step–father, Homer Clark, to move several times. Hughes moved often between the households of his grandmother, his mother, and other surrogate parents. One of his essays claims that he has slept in "Ten Thousand Beds." Growing up in the Midwest (Lawrence, Kansas; Topeka, Kansas; Lincoln, Illinois; Cleveland, Ohio), young Hughes learned the blues and spirituals. He would subsequently weave these musical elements into his own poetry and fiction.

In a Cleveland, Ohio, high school, Hughes was designated "class poet" and there he published his first short stories. He became friends with some white classmates, yet he also suffered racial insult at the hands of other whites. He learned first–hand to distinguish "decent" from "reactionary" white folks, distinctions he would reiterate in his book *Not Without Laughter* and in his "Here to Yonder" columns in *The Chicago Defender.* Seeking some consolation and continuity in the midst of the myriad relocations of his youth, he grew to love books. His love of reading developed into a desire to write as he sought to replicate the powerful impact other writers from many cultures had made upon him. In his writing, Hughes accomplished an important feat. While others wallowed in self–revelation as a balm for their loneliness, Hughes often transformed his own agonies into the sufferings endured by the collective race and sometimes all of humankind.

After graduating from Central High School in Cleveland in 1920, he moved to Mexico City to live with his father for one year. His mother fumed about his departure, and his father offered him little warmth. Yet, with his unique gift for writing, Hughes turned the pain engendered by his parents' conflict into the noted poem, "The Negro Speaks of Rivers," published by *Crisis* in 1921.

Hughes gathered new impressions and new insights about race, class, and ethnicity in Mexico, where his ability to speak Spanish and his appearance often allowed him to blend in. Even Americans who would not have spoken to him in Cleveland or Kansas City would converse with him as a "Mexican" on the train. Although brown skin no longer remained an obstacle in Mexico, Hughes saw that poverty still reached many Mexicans. Numerous works, including a children's play, capture fragments of Hughes's days in Mexico.

When he left his ambitious father in Mexico, Hughes was expected to earn an engineering degree at Columbia University. Breaking abruptly with his insulted father, in the first of many brave and daring moves, Hughes withdrew from Columbia in 1922, and one year later he began his world travels. He visited several ports in Africa and he worked as a dishwasher in a Paris cabaret. Poems and short stories capture some of his impressions abroad. He sent a few of the pieces

Langston Hughes

back home, where they were published, enhancing his growing reputation as a writer.

When financial strain ended his travels, Hughes returned to the United States. He once again attempted various forms of work, this time in Washington, D.C., where his mother had moved. Besides blue–collar work, he also served briefly in the office of publisher and historian Carter G. Woodson. Although he respected Dr. Woodson's significance to the African American community, Hughes did not like the eye–strain or the detail of his assignments. Nevertheless, he continued to write. In 1925 he won first prize in poetry in *Opportunity* magazine. He also met writer Carl Van Vechten, who assisted Hughes in securing a book contract with publisher Alfred A. Knopf. Hughes also enjoyed his "discovery" by poet Vachel Lindsay as the "busboy poet."

Begins Publishing Books

Hughes's first volume of poetry, *The Weary Blues,* appeared in 1926. That same year, Hughes returned to college, this time as an older student and an acclaimed poet at the nation's first African American college, Lincoln University, in Pennsylvania. Spending any available weekend soaking up theater and music in nearby New York City, Hughes satisfied academic requirements during the week. A second volume of poetry, *Fine Clothes to the Jew,* was published in 1927. The Harlem Renaissance was in full bloom, and Hughes became one of the celebrated young talents who flourished during this era. Some controversy attended his celebrity, however. Not all blacks relished his use of dialect, his interpretation of blues and jazz, or his vivid and sensitive portrayals of workers. Hughes faced harsh criticism, including his designation not as poet laureate but as the "poet low–rate" of Harlem.

As Hughes completed his years at Lincoln University in 1929, he also completed his first novel, *Not Without Laughter,* published in 1930. Still receiving financial assistance from Charlotte Mason, the patron he shared with Zora Neale Hurston and Alain Locke, among others, Hughes also accepted her advice regarding the contents and tone of the novel. He expressed disappointment with the completed novel, but the text remains in print, retaining uplifting representations of the diverse populations within the black community.

In 1930, however, Hughes separated from the control and the financial support of Mason. His integrity meant more to him than any luxuries her wealth could provide, thus, as with the break from his father, Hughes abandoned financial security in search of his own goals. When Mason disapproved of him, Hurston and Locke, who remained loyal to her, dropped from Hughes's list of associates.

Following the advice of Mary McLeod Bethune and sponsored by an award from the Rosenwald Foundation, Hughes began to tour the South with his poetry. Highly regarded as a reader, handsome and warm in person, Hughes gained many readers and admirers during his tours. He also visited the Scottsboro Boys in Alabama, who were accused of raping a white woman. Hughes created poetic and dramatic responses to the men's plight and the mixed reactions of the American public.

In 1932, Hughes went to Russia with a group of African Americans to assist with a film project that never bore fruit. When the project dissolved, most of the participants returned to the United States, but Hughes set off to explore the Soviet Union. In his own observations of the Soviet Union, Hughes saw many reasons to appreciate communism. Thus, while many other American writers were attracted to socialistic perspectives during the depression years, Hughes openly praised practices he had observed in the Soviet Union: no "Jim Crow," no anti–semitism, and education and medical care for everyone. He wrote numerous poems to capture those travels, and later, in both his *Chicago Defender* column and in his second autobiography, *I Wonder As I Wander* (1956), he recorded impressions of his travels. Following the journey to the Soviet Union, Hughes completed work on his first volume of short stories, *The Ways of White Folks* (1934). In 1936 he received a Guggenheim Foundation fellowship and worked with the Karamu House in Cleveland, Ohio, on several plays. His interest in theater continued in New York, where he founded the Harlem Suitcase Theater in 1938. A 1941 Rosenwald Fund fellowship further supported his play writing. However, he also moved into another genre. His interesting family heritage, his remarkable travels, and his participation in African American culture led to his first autobiographical volume, *The Big Sea* (1940).

World War II Efforts

When the United States plunged into World War II, Hughes escaped military service, but he put his pen to work on behalf of political involvement and nationalism. Writing jingles to encourage the purchase of war bonds, and writing weekly columns in *The Chicago Defender,* Hughes encouraged readers to support the Allies. His appeals remained consistent with the "Double–V" campaign upheld by the black press: victory at home and victory abroad. Hughes encouraged black Americans to support the United States in its goals abroad, but he encouraged the government to provide for its own citizens at home the same freedoms being advocated abroad. A fictional voice emerged from these columns, that of Jesse B. Semple, better known as "Simple." While the character initially appeared as a Harlem everyman who needed encouragement to support the racially segregated U.S. armed forces, Simple evolved into a popular and enduring fictional character. The first volume of stories to develop from Simple's appearances in the *Chicago Defender* was published by Simon and Schuster in 1950, *Simple Speaks His Mind.*

Works in the Theater

Hughes retained his interest in theater, working with Kurt Weill and Elmer Rice to develop a musical adaptation of Rice's play *Street Scene.* The musical opened on Broadway in 1947, where it enjoyed a brief run that proved financially beneficial to Hughes.

Another significant theatrical collaboration involved William Grant Still, the first black composer in the United States to have a symphony performed by a major symphony orchestra, the first to have an opera produced by a major company in America, and the first to conduct a white major symphony orchestra in the Deep South. They collaborated on *Troubled Island,* based on the life of Jean Jacques Dessalines of Haiti, which Hughes had transformed from a play to a libretto. Hughes was in Spain reporting on the Spanish Civil War for the *Baltimore Afro–American* while Still adapted his libretto for an opera. Yet the project finally reached completion and opened in New York in 1949.

During the 1940s Hughes's poetry also continued to be published: *Shakespeare in Harlem* (1942), *Fields of Wonder* (1947), and *One–Way Ticket* (1949). He also engaged in some translation projects involving both French and Spanish texts. Hughes's success as a writer were acknowledged through the award of one thousand dollars from the American Academy of Arts and Letters in 1945. With his friend Arna Bontemps, he edited *The Poetry of the Negro* (1949).

The 1950s brought the Cold War and the horrors of Senator Joseph McCarthy's subcommittee on subversive activities. With his published record of socialistic sentiments and his public associations with known Communists, Hughes endured several years of attacks and boycotts. In 1953 he received a subpoena to testify about his interests in communism. Holding fast to his own dream of sustaining his career as a writer, Hughes salvaged his image as a loyal American citizen by insisting that the pro–Communist works he had published no longer represented his thinking. Although he bravely challenged authority figures earlier in his life, in this situation he acted to protect his chosen profession. He retained speaking engagements and his works continued to sell, but he lost the respect of some political activists. Communists bitterly resented the way he abandoned professed members of the party, including W. E. B. Du Bois and Paul Robeson, whom Hughes had lauded in earlier decades. Hughes chose self–preservation and sustained his career as a writer.

Frenzied Work Pace

A career as a writer often led Hughes to accept multiple book contracts simultaneously, thereby imposing upon himself an arduous schedule of production. Correspondence housed in the Beinecke collection at Yale University, in the Special Collections of Fisk University, in the Schomburg Center for Research in Black Culture, and collected in the

Charles Nichols edition of *Arna Bontemps–Langston Hughes Letters, 1925–1967* (1980) reveal Hughes's frantic pace of writing, editing, revising, and publishing from the 1950s to the end of his life. He began to offer juvenile histories, including *Famous American Negroes* and *The First Book of Rhythms* in 1954, and *The First Book of Jazz* and *Famous Negro Music Makers* in 1955. He collaborated with photographer Roy De Carava on *The Sweet Flypaper of Life* in 1956, and in the same year he wrote *Tambourines to Glory, The First Book of the West Indies,* and his second autobiography *I Wonder As I Wander.*

Hughes's character Jesse B. Semple continued to thrive, appearing frequently in his weekly column in the *Chicago Defender.* A second book, *Simple Takes a Wife* (1953) and a third, *Simple Stakes a Claim* (1957), led to a musical version, *Simply Heavenly,* which ran on Broadway in 1957.

The last ten years of Hughes's life were marked by an astonishing proliferation of books: juvenile histories, poetry volumes, single genres anthologies (*Laughing to Keep From Crying* [short stories], 1952; *Selected Poems,* 1957; *The Best of Simple,* 1961; and *Something in Common and Other Stories,* 1963); a collection of genres (*Langston Hughes Reader,* 1958); and an adult history of the NAACP (*Fight for Freedom,* 1962). Hughes edited *An African Treasury* (1960); *Poems from Black Africa, Ethiopia, and Other Countries* (1963); *New Negro Poets: U.S.A.* (1964); and *The Best Short Stories by Negro Writers* (1967), in which he became the first to publish a short story by Alice Walker. Some of his efforts in drama were collected by Webster Smalley: *Five Plays by Langston Hughes: Tambourines to Glory, Soul Gone Home, Little Ham, Mulatto, Simply Heavenly.*

Hughes was inducted into the National Institute of Arts and Letters in 1961, the year he published his innovative book of poems to be read with jazz accompaniment, *Ask Your Mama: 12 Moods for Jazz.* During the 1950s he also recorded an album of himself reading some of his earlier verse, accompanied by jazz great Charles Mingus.

Hughes shifted his weekly newspaper column from *The Chicago Defender* to *The New York Post.* While Hughes had never shunned aggressive politics, he was mistaken for a timid accomodationist. Readers' letters revealed ignorance about his consistently positive appreciation of black people and culture and his consistently fair treatment of people of all races and cultures. Resilient even to the end of his life, Hughes withstood accusations that he foolishly joked about racial turmoil. He endured the hostile criticism, but in 1965 he ended his 22–year tenure as a newspaper columnist.

Hughes's death on May 22, 1967, apparently resulted from infection following prostate surgery and two weeks of treatment at the New York Polyclinic Hospital. Memorial services followed many of his own wishes, including the playing of Duke Ellington's "Do Nothing Till You Hear from Me."

The works of Hughes continued to appear even after his death. He had prepared *The Panther and the Lash* (1967), a collection of poems, but it was not published until after his death. Collaborations such as *Black Magic* (with Milton Meltzer, 1967) and a revision of the 1949 anthology, *The Poetry of the Negro 1746–1970* (edited by Hughes and Arna Bontemps, 1970) were published, acknowledging his contributions and lamenting his death. Subsequent years have brought *Good Morning Revolution,* a collection of radical verse and essays (edited by Faith Berry, 1973); *Collected Poems,* a comprehensive and well–indexed chronological collection of his poetry (edited by Arnold Rampersad and David Roessel, 1994); *The Return of Simple,* a new collection of his Jesse B. Semple tales (edited by Akiba Sullivan Harper, 1994); *Langston Hughes and the Chicago Defender,* a collection of his non–Simple newspaper columns (edited by Christopher C. De Santis, 1995); and *Langston Hughes Short Stories,* retrieving previously unpublished short stories and collecting some now out of print (edited by Akiba Sullivan Harper, 1996).

Hughes never married and never had children. Yet, through his writing and through his generosity as a "dean" of literature, he nurtured scores of writers and left behind an enduring legacy of literature. Over twenty years after his death, on the eighty–ninth anniversary of Hughes's birth in 1991, amid great celebration by noted writers such as Maya Angelou and Amiri Baraka, his cremated remains were interred beneath the commemoratively designed "I've Known Rivers" tile floor in the Schomburg Center for Research in Black Culture in Harlem. Visitors to this noted research center may see this floor, pay respects to his remains, and remember the man.

REFERENCES

Barksdale, Richard K. "Langston Hughes: His Times and His Humanistic Techniques." In *Black American Literature and Humanism.* Edited by R. Baxter Miller, Lexington: University Press of Kentucky, 1981.

———. *Langston Hughes: The Poet and His Critics.* Chicago: American Library, 1977.

Bloom, Harold, ed. *Modern Critical Views: Langston Hughes.* New York: Chelsea House, 1989.

Clarke, John Henrik. "Langston Hughes and Jesse B. Semple." *Freedomways* 8 (Spring 1968): 167–69.

Davis, Arthur P. *From the Dark Tower: Afro–American Writers 1900 to 1960.* Washington, DC: Howard University Press, 1974.

———, and Saunders Redding, eds. *Cavalcade: Negro American Writing from 1760 to the Present.* Boston: Houghton Mifflin, 1971.

———, J. Saunders Redding, and Joyce Ann Joyce, eds. *The New Cavalcade: African American Writing from 1760 to the Present.* Vol. 1. Washington, DC: Howard University Press, 1991.

Dickinson, Donald C. *A Bio–bibliography of Langston Hughes: 1902–1967.* 2nd ed. Hamden, CT: Archon Books, 1972.

Drake, St. Clair, and Horace R. Cayton. *Black Metropolis.* Vol. 2. New York: Harbinger/Harcourt, Brace, and World, 1962.

Emanuel, James A., and Theodore L. Gross, eds. *Dark Symphony: Negro Literature in America.* New York: Free Press, Collier–Macmillan, 1968.

Gates, Henry Louis Jr., and K. A. Appiah, eds. *Langston Hughes: Critical Perspectives.* New York: Amistad, 1993.

Harper, Donna Akiba Sullivan. "Achieving Universality through Simple Truths." In *Langston Hughes: The Man, His Art, and His Continuing Influence.* Edited by James Trotman and Emery Wimbish Jr. New York: Garland Pub., 1995. 119–29.

———. "The Complex Process of Crafting Langston Hughes's Simple, 1942–1949." Ph.D. dissertation, Emory University, 1988.

Hughes, Langston. *The Big Sea.* Reprint, New York: Hill and Wang, American Century Series, 1963.

———. *I Wonder as I Wander: An Autobiographical Journey.* 1956. Reprint, New York: Hill and Wang, American Century Series, 1964.

———. *Not Without Laughter.* 1930. Reprint, New York: Knopf, 1971.

———. *The Return of Simple.* Edited by Akiba Sullivan Harper. New York: Hill and Wang, 1994.

Meltzer, Milton. *Langston Hughes: A Biography.* New York: Thomas Crowell, 1968.

Mikolyzk, Thomas A. *Langston Hughes: A Bio–Bibliography.* Westport, CT: Greenwood, 1990.

Miller, R. Baxter. *The Art and Imagination of Langston Hughes.* Lexington: University Press of Kentucky, 1989.

Mullen, Edward J., ed. *Critical Essays on Langston Hughes.* Boston: G. K. Hall, 1986.

Nichols, Charles H., ed. *Arna Bontemps–Langston Hughes Letters, 1925–1967.* New York: Dodd, Mead, 1980.

O'Daniel, Therman B., ed. *Langston Hughes: Black Genius.* New York: William Morrow, 1971.

Rampersad, Arnold. *The Life of Langston Hughes; Volume I: 1902–1941; I, Too, Sing America.* New York: Oxford University Press, 1986.

———. *The Life of Langston Hughes; Volume II: 1941–1967; I Dream a World.* New York: Oxford University Press, 1988.

Thompson, Anthony. Interview with Donna Akiba Sullivan Harper, Atlanta, GA, October 1985.

Trotman, C. James, and Emery Wimbish Jr., eds. *Langston Hughes: The Man, His Art, and His Continuing Influence.* New York: Garland, 1995.

COLLECTIONS

Langston Hughes's books are housed in a special collection in the Langston Hughes Memorial Library on the campus of Lincoln University in Pennsylvania. Hughes's correspondence and manuscripts are in the James Weldon Johnson Collection, Beinecke Rare Book and Manuscript Library, Yale University and in the Schomburg Center for Research in Black Culture, New York Public Library.

Donna Akiba Sullivan Harper

William Alphaeus Hunton (1863–1916)

Founder, organizer, administrator, orator, writer

The life work of William Alphaeus Hunton and the subsequent desegregation of the YMCA are inextricably linked. Hunton pioneered the organization, growth, and development of YMCAs, fostering the membership of young African American men and boys. His commitment and dedication provided opportunities for the development of leadership and organizational skills in the membership which led to a network of self–help and a sense of community for African American men, women, and children across the country.

William Alphaeus Hunton was born free on October 31, 1863, in Chatham, Canada, the sixth son of eight children born to Stanton and Mary Ann Conyers Hunton. Stanton Hunton had been a slave in Virginia, but the mistress of the plantation aided in his education. Stanton Hunton made three attempts to escape but was unsuccessful; around 1840 he purchased his freedom. He traveled north and by 1843 had settled in Chatham, Ontario. Stanton Hunton's older brother, Ben, was a slave in Natchez, Mississippi, until Stanton purchased his freedom and brought him to Chatham. Stanton Hunton was a stalwart support of abolitionist John Brown, and the Hunton home was a safe haven on the Underground Railroad. Little is known about William Hunton's mother except that she was a free black from Cincinnati. She died when William was only four years old.

William Hunton and his siblings were raised by their father and maternal grandmother, both of whom were very religious. They passed on their Christian beliefs and values to the children, also instilling in them a strong work ethic. These teachings would remain a guiding force in Hunton's life.

Hunton completed high school and graduated in 1884 from the Wilberforce Institute of Ontario. After graduation he worked as a public school teacher in Dresden, Ontario, until May of 1885, when he accepted an appointment as a probation clerk in the Department of Indian Affairs in Ottawa. It was there that Hunton joined the Ottawa YMCA, where he became the chairman of the Boy's Work Department.

In contrast to the YMCAs in the United States, those in Canada provided an almost fully interracial environment. It is possible that he was the only member of African descent in the Ottawa YMCA. This environment and the positive YMCA experiences in Canada reinforced Hunton's Christian belief in the brotherhood of man.

Hunton was very active in the Ottawa YMCA, attending meetings, lectures, and conferences. In 1886 he attended a conference in Hamilton, Ontario, where Edwin D. Ingersoll, a field secretary of the International Committee spoke of the association's need for young and better trained men for association work. After his speech he offered to talk with any young men who had an interest in this training. Hunton was among 22 who responded. Though somewhat shy, Hunton shared with Ingersoll some of his personal background and his interest in Christian fellowship as well as his feeling of being drawn to this work.

Ingersoll persuaded Richard C. Morse, executive secretary of the International Committee, to hire Hunton for the YMCA post in Norfolk, Virginia. Final negotiations included a salary settlement and accommodations for Hunton in Norfolk. Hunton accepted the position.

Building Bridges

In January of 1888, William A. Hunton began his work among ''colored men'' in Norfolk, Virginia, the first African American to be employed as a secretary for the YMCA. The YMCA's basic purpose was to develop the body, mind and spirit of young men and boys who were vulnerable to the pitfalls of newly found urban life. Bringing these concepts to this new field of work among black men who were considered even more innately susceptible to negative forces was seen as a challenge.

Addie Hunton described the setting in which William Hunton began his work in 1888. She wrote in *William Alphaeus Hunton*:

> the small city of Norfolk, Virginia, was chosen as the first laboratory, but its selection was neither by chance nor choice, except from God. A year before, a small band of young colored men had felt the need of spiritual comradeship and had united for prayer and meditation. . . .

Addie Hunton also pointed out that they formed the prayer group so that Hunton could ''conduct this first experiment.'' Because of it he became ''the first employed secretary of the Young Men's Christian Association for work among colored men.''

Hunton remained general secretary at the Norfolk YMCA for approximately three years. During that time, he achieved many goals: establishing literary and debating societies, a library, educational classes, a choral club, and a Bible study group. The latter was very important to him because of his strong belief in the importance of religion in a young man's life. The Bible study group also served to challenge the barriers between the various denominations among the membership.

In addition to his basic intelligence, Hunton brought many indispensable skills and abilities to his work. He was very analytical, evaluating situations and speculating upon consequences with a focus on improving services for the young men and boys in the association. He kept excellent records of the various activities and provided written reports to the association's board of directors and to the International Committee. Hunton's works also included the many daily tasks that kept the association operational. Hunton was most bothered by the inadequate facilities for the many activities. He was able to articulate these needs at the twenty–eighth convention in Philadelphia in May of 1889. As the first African American secretary to address an association's convention, he pointed to inadequate funding for the 41 ''colored'' associations and added, as quoted by Charles Wesley, in *A Historical Study of Y.M.C.A. Services to Colored Youth*, ''not one of our forty–one Associations has a building of its own, or a gymnasium, or baths, or a lecture hall capable of seating over 200 people. The average current expenses of those Associations last year was not quite one hundred dollars.''

Of the groups with whom Hunton worked, he found great satisfaction in his interactions with the student members from the Presbyterian Mission School. In fact he preferred work with the students as compared to the overall city work. Hunton always believed that African American college men would provide the best leadership for their own associations across the country.

In January of 1890, Hunton visited all of the ''colored'' associations across the country. It was the beginning of the period of Jim Crow, especially in the deep South. Hunton, who had not experienced racism in Canada, became more keenly aware of what African Americans were facing every day throughout the country. Even the association for which he held such hope had not changed its basic policy of segregation, nor did it financially assist the African American associations to any significant degree.

As Hunton continued his visits to the African American colleges and city associations around the country was well as his own work in Norfolk, the very taxing schedule and responsibilities made it obvious that more than a part–time effort was needed for the job. Then Hunton was named secretary on the staff of the International Committee and became its first African American secretary.

Working Alone

In 1891, Hunton officially assumed all the responsibilities for his new position. He would continue his work alone until 1898. During these years, Hunton's traveling schedule took him to several Southern states and to New York, New Jersey, Washington, D.C., Maryland, Massachusetts, and as far west as Kansas. His meetings involved strategy sessions for fund raising, membership drives, financial assessment, and Bible sessions, as well as student training and advising. It was his selflessness and the intensive hard work to which he devoted himself that made Hunton so greatly loved by the African American students and staff and respected by many of his white colleagues.

Hunton's observations and evaluations led to the publication of *First Steps*, a pamphlet written for the YMCA giving four basic suggestions to avoid the pitfalls of organizing and successfully sustaining the work of the ''colored'' association. His primary admonition was ''make haste slowly.'' Hunton was responsible for this and other kinds of intensive counseling and advisement at every association site he visited.

The work involving YMCA city associations was for African American men of the general community, most of whom were only 25 to 30 years away from emancipation. Many had no family in the cities, no skills, and many were illiterate. Nevertheless, they needed social support and the African American associations were places of social and spiritual refuge. Given the general low income, financial support from the community was minimal, and the policy of the YMCA national body restricted support of local associations.

Hunton realized, however, that his work would not succeed if there was no financial assistance from the National Board. Hunton wrote to the International Board on behalf of the African American associations that needed financial assistance. Hunton's schedule was exhausting and his responsibilities were so overwhelming that at times they even affected his health.

In 1890, while in Norfolk, Hunton met Addie Waites, the daughter of a YMCA supporter. She was 15 years old and he was 27. He began a correspondence with her as he travelled and continued his work. In 1893 they were married and subsequently had four children of which only the two younger children, William Jr. and Eunice, survived.

Addie was an intelligent young woman who had attended Boston Girls and Latin School and a Spencerian Business College in Philadelphia. She had taught at a vocational school in Normal, Alabama. She entered the marriage with an understanding of Hunton's commitment to his work. She made his life's work hers as well. She wrote in *Pioneer Prophet,* "I did most of Mr. Hunton's secretarial work and went with him to conferences when possible, looking after details and advising and inspiring him."

Although his wife's assistance was indispensable, Hunton needed someone who was active in YMCA work to assume secretarial responsibility for city associations. On April 20, 1892, Hunton met Jesse E. Moorland who was then the secretary for the association for African American men in Washington, D.C. Hunton was impressed with Moorland and the Washington program. He felt that Moorland should join him on the International staff, but it would be six more years before the International Committee hired Moorland as the second full time secretary. Moorland would assume the responsibilities for the city associations and Hunton would continue developing and strengthening the college associations.

The Spanish–American War in 1898 was also a very serious time for Hunton and the YMCA. The YMCA became involved nationally, setting up tents at each of the army and navy military camps. Regrettably, no provisions were made for the African American troops. Hunton, aware of this inequity, organized tent units in various states for them.

After the war, many of the men involved became permanent secretaries in the work of the association. This did not relieve the pressure of Hunton's responsibilities related to the YMCA's African American division. Finally, in October of 1898, the International Committee hired Jesse E. Moorland, who became the second African American international secretary. Moorland had graduated as valedictorian from Howard University's theological seminary and pastored churches in Nashville, Tennessee and Cleveland, Ohio. He had also been acquainted with YMCA work while at Northwestern Normal University and was appointed secretary of the African American association in Washington, D.C., while at Howard University, where he had previously met Hunton.

Working for the Future

In 1898 Moorland assumed responsibility for the operational side of the city work, and Hunton became fully involved with the college associations. Hunton realized the need for a third international secretary who would supervise the organizational phase of the work, specifically the new college groups. He also developed the philosophy of self–help for the African American YMCAs and laid the groundwork for their organization and development. He was deeply aware of the YMCA's commitment to segregation, north and south.

Despite these impediments, Hunton continued to travel to associations in cities and on campuses developing and strengthening the network among them. The growth in the number of associations brought requests for general secretaries to organize programs and membership. There was a tremendous need for qualified full time secretaries and it was Hunton's task to motivate and recruit the kind of men who would provide leadership in these positions. The work was demanding and the remuneration was low, requiring of these potential leaders an understanding of the associations' purpose and commitment. Although he was married, Hunton felt single men were more appropriate for the work because of the long hours and its itinerant nature. Above all, they needed the type of professional training available only at that time to white secretaries. As early as 1890, Hunton had espoused the need for professional training for the African American secretaries.

Unfortunately, at this point, Hunton did not have the funds nor the time to launch a separate training program. The YMCA had a few training schools which were open to African American secretaries, but did not encourage their application. The few who were admitted found that they could not afford to continue the program. Despite these problems, in 1905 Hunton was successful in bringing in George Edmund Haynes as the third African American international secretary. In 1907 Hunton, Haynes, Moorland, and several general secretaries formed the Summer Secretarial Institute. In his September 1908 report, Hunton enthusiastically commented on the meeting of the training session of secretaries held in Asheville, North Carolina. Subsequently, the institute was renamed the Chesapeake Summer School. Although open to all YMCA secretaries, the enrollment and faculty were predominantly African American.

Added to the small cadre of international secretaries was John B. Watson, whose youth and position as a college instructor was of particular importance to the program. Over a 15–year period, Hunton was responsible for selecting men to serve on the International Committee and to work with either the colleges or city associations.

Building for the Future

The turn of the century was the beginning of a period of intense activity revolving around the purchase of real estate in preparation for the construction of "colored" YMCA buildings. Hunton and Moorland were committed to the building program which would provide space for dormitories, swimming pools, libraries, study, and recreation rooms. Similar accommodations were already available to white members. At that time, of the 21 African American city associations, only five owned buildings: Baltimore, New Haven, Norfolk, Richmond, and Springfield, Ohio.

During the first decade of the twentieth century, Hunton and Moorland campaigned vigorously across the country to promote the building campaign. Their work was supported on a national level by the fund–raising impetus of philanthropists such as George Foster Peabody, Julius Rosenwald, and John D. Rockefeller Sr. The building campaigns would establish segregated YMCAs headed by white city boards but administered by black staff and committees. The continued increase in the number of student and city associations, however, spurred the growth in the number of YMCA buildings constructed for black members.

Hunton's responsibilities involved attendance at the many conferences and conventions on the local level. The International Conferences brought together YMCA administrators and supporters representing many nations to discuss the current status and future of the association and to honor those who had made a significant contribution in service to the association. In 1894 Hunton attended the Golden Jubilee of the World's Young Men's Christian Association, held in London, England. Of singular significance was his participation at the World's Student Christian Federation Conference in Tokyo, Japan, in 1907 where he presented a paper and also addressed public school officials. He had the opportunity to visit many provinces in Japan. Hunton also visited China and attended the China Centenary Missionary Conference in Shanghai. A visit to Korea completed his trip. In 1913, when he led a black delegation to the World's Student Christian Federation Conference at Lake Mohonk, New Jersey, many foreign delegates were people whom he had met in England and Japan.

Hunton was reportedly a fine orator. Of particular importance were the speeches he gave at the International Conventions of Young Men's Christian Associations. In 1893 he gave an address before the Thirtieth International Convention entitled, "The Growth and Prospects of Association Work Among Colored Young Men." In 1902 another speech entitled, "The Providential Preparation of the American Negro for Mission Work in Africa," was delivered before the World Wide Evangelization Convention, in Toronto, Canada. These speeches have been published. Other publications include *Association Work Among Colored Men, The Colored Men's Department of the Young Men's Christian Association,* and *First Steps.*

By 1905 both Hunton and Moorland began to show the strain of their tremendous work responsibilities. Both men became ill with malaria. Although they recovered, Hunton remained in a weakened condition. By 1914 he was diagnosed with tuberculosis. He attempted to continue with a modified schedule, but he was unsuccessful. He convalesced at Saranac Lake for a time but subsequently returned to his Brooklyn home where he died on November 26, 1916. He is buried in Cypress Hills Cemetery in Brooklyn.

During his stewardship, from 1888 to 1915, Hunton strengthened YWCA service to blacks by bringing other blacks into YMCA work as international secretaries, organized conventions, participated in the YMCA building program, saw the number of professional YMCA secretaries increase, and increased memberships in African American YMCAs nationwide. He was a highly influential figure in the YMCA movement and instrumental in its impact on the black community.

REFERENCES

Alexander, Jesse N, and Leo B. Marsh. *Selected Black Leaders of the YMCA.* Washington, DC: Association for the Study of Afro–American Life and History, 1978.

Arthur, George. *Life on the Negro Frontier.* New York: Association Press, 1934.

Bartlett, Lester W., Ralph M. Hogan, and Alden W. Boyd, eds. *The Y.M.C.A. Executive Secretary. An Analysis of the Activities of the Secretary Who is Responsible for the Administration of a Local Y.M.C.A.* Chicago: University of Chicago Press, 1929.

Franklin, John Hope. *From Slavery To Freedom. A History of Negro Americans.* 4th ed. New York: Alfred A. Knopf, 1974.

Hopkins, Howard C. *History of the Y.M.C.A. in North America.* New York: Association Press, 1951.

Hunton, Addie W. *William Alphaeus Hunton, A Pioneer Prophet of Young Men.* New York: Association Press, 1938.

Hunton, William Alphaeus. "Association Work Among Colored Men." *Intercollegian* 32 (November 1909): 34–36.

———. "The Colored Men's Department of the Young Men's Christian Association." *The Voice of the Negro* 2 (June 1905): 388–95.

———. *The Growth and Prospects of Association Work Among Colored Young Men.* An address by W. A. Hunton at the Thirtieth International Convention of Young Men's Christian Associations. Indianapolis, Indiana, May 10–19, 1893, 1–2. New York: International Committee of the YMCA, 1893.

———. *The Providential Preparation of the American Negro for Mission Work in Africa.* Proceedings of the World Wide Evangelization: The Urgent Business of the Church. New York: Student Volunteer Movement for Foreign Missions, 1902.

Logan, Rayford W., and Michael R. Winston, eds. *Dictionary of American Negro Biography.* New York: Norton, 1982.

Mjagkij, Nina. *Light in the Darkness: African Americans and the YMCA, 1852–1946.* Lexington: University Press of Kentucky, 1994.

Salzman, Jack, David Lionel Smith. and Cornel West, eds. *Encyclopedia of African–American Culture and History.* New York: Macmillan Library Reference USA/Simon and Schuster Macmillan, 1996.

Wesley, Charles H. *A Historical Study of Y.M.C.A Services to Colored Youth.* An Address delivered by Dr. Charles H. Wesley at the National Conference of Laymen and Secretaries, Bordentown, New Jersey, Sunday Morning, July 14, 1949, 6–11. Historical Library, Young Men's Association Christian Associations.

Williams, Bruce. Interview with Juanita R. Howard, June 20, 1996.

Y.M.C.A. Yearbook, 1888. New York: International Committee of the YMCA, 1888.

COLLECTIONS

William A. Hunton's personal papers and literary effects are housed in the YMCA Archives at the University of Minnesota, St. Paul, and in the Schomburg Center for Research in Black Culture in New York.

Juanita R. Howard

I

Elmer S. Imes
(1883–1941)
Scientist, inventor, teacher, scholar

Elmer Samuel Imes was the first black scientist to make a significant contribution to physics. His work had a major impact on the understanding and interpretation of quantum phenomena during the period from 1919 to 1925. He also made contributions to physics instrumentation through his construction and improvements to infrared spectrometers. During his lifetime, his research was extensively quoted and referenced in leading scientific journals in the United States and Europe by physicists and chemists studying the properties and molecular spectra of diatomic molecules.

The Imes family had its American roots in the southern central region of Pennsylvania. William L. Imes wrote in *The Black Pastures* that the family were ''rugged farming folk'' and had ''free black ancestry running back several generations,'' even in the latter part of the nineteenth century. Elmer Samuel Imes's parents, Benjamin Albert Imes and Elizabeth Wallace, met in Oberlin, Ohio, and were married there. Benjamin graduated from Oberlin College in 1877 and in 1880 obtained his divinity degree from Oberlin Seminary.

Elmer Samuel Imes was born October 12, 1883, in Memphis, Tennessee. Two other brothers, Albert Lovejoy and William Lloyd, soon followed. William Lloyd became a prominent theologian and had a distinguished career serving as pastor in northern churches as well as dean of the chapel at Fisk University.

Imes attended grammar school in Oberlin, Ohio, from about 1889 to 1895 and the Agricultural and Mechanical College High School in Normal, Alabama, from about 1895 to 1899. He then enrolled at Fisk University, where he received the B.A. degree in 1903. For the next several years he taught physics and mathematics at Albany Normal Institute in Albany, Georgia. He then returned to Fisk University around 1910, where he remained until 1915. During this time Imes completed academic work for the master of arts degree and also served as an instructor in science and mathematics.

With his M.A. degree, Imes reached the limits of what Fisk University could offer in terms of research. Since he was black, clearly any additional studies would have to be done at an institution outside the South. In 1915 he enrolled in the doctoral program in physics at the University of Michigan. Imes's academic work during his first year was of such high quality that he was offered a graduate fellowship for the remainder of his study there.

Elmer S. Imes

At the University of Michigan, Imes began his research under the guidance of Professor Harrison M. Randall. Just prior to Imes's arrival, Randall had gone to Germany to work in Professor Friedrich Paschen's spectroscopy laboratory. There he concentrated on the production, characterization, and measurement of the infrared region of the spectrum. Returning to Ann Arbor, Randall and his students began to design and build infrared spectrometers of higher resolving power and to build more sensitive detectors. The most notable of his students was Imes.

New Field of Scholarship Opened

Gary Krenz in *LSA Magazine* cited Randall and Imes for publishing in 1919 a single work that ushered in a new field of research, ''the study of molecular structure through the use of high–resolution infrared spectroscopy. Their work revealed for the first time the detailed spectra of simple–molecule gases, leading to important verification of the emerging quantum theory and providing, for the first time, an accurate measurement of the distances between atoms in a molecule.''

Imes received a doctorate degree in physics in 1918, and his dissertation was published in the *Astrophysical Journal* in

1919. Some extensions of this work appeared in a short joint paper that Imes published with Randall in 1920 in *Physical Review*. The fundamental significance of Imes's research was clearly stated by professor Earle Plyler in 1974:

> Up until the work of Imes, there was doubt about the universal applicability of the quantum theory to radiation in all parts of the electromagnetic spectrum. Some held that it was useful only for atomic spectra (electronic spectra); some held that it was applicable for all electromagnetic radiation. . . . Imes's high resolution work on HCl, HBr and HF was the first clear–cut experimental verification of the latter hypothesis, namely, that the rotational energy levels of molecules are quantized as well as the vibrational and electronic levels. . . . Thus, Imes's work formed a turning point in scientific thinking, making it clear that quantum theory was not just a novelty, useful in limited fields of physics, but of widespread and general application.

The significance of Imes's results was immediately recognized by major quantum scientists in both America and Europe. In the decade after 1919, his *Astrophysical Journal* paper would be extensively cited in research papers and reviews of the research literature on rotational–vibrational spectra of diatomic molecules. Within a very short time, discussions of Imes's work began to be incorporated into standard textbooks on modern physics. In each of these books, Imes's rotational–vibration spectrum of the fundamental absorption bands of HCl was prominently displayed. Imes's work also provided early evidence using molecular spectra for isotopes.

An interesting insight into how Imes was viewed by the scientific community can be obtained from a letter of professor Youra Qualls of Tuskegee Institute:

> I worked for Dr. Imes as secretary in either my junior or my senior year in college. At the time Dr. Imes was writing a history of physics. One of the delightful tasks I assumed was going through foreign science journals to note references to the work of "Imes of the U.S.A." My French and German were elementary by his standards, but I was able to keep up with this chore reasonably well. I mention it only to say that Dr. Imes was, I believe, far better known abroad than he was in his own country.
>
> To pursue the last sentence I will recall an incident occurring several years after my graduation. I was teaching at Langston University in the year that Dr. Charles S. Johnson became Fisk's president. On my way to Fisk for the inauguration, I met a Dr. Nielson, Dean of the Graduate School of Sciences at the University of Oklahoma. As Dr. Nielson and I talked, Dr. Imes's name came into the conversation. He told me that he had become familiar with the work of "Imes of the U.S.A." during his student days in Denmark but that he had never known that Imes was a Negro.

In further recognition of his outstanding research achievements, Imes was elected at the University of Michigan to membership in Sigma Xi, a national honor society for scientific research.

An Engineer and Intellect in New York

A year after receiving his doctorate, Imes married Nella Larsen on May 3, 1919, in New York. Their marriage produced no children, and they eventually divorced in Nashville, Tennessee, on August 30, 1933. Larsen was a gifted writer of the Harlem Renaissance. In 1930 she was the first African American female creative writer to win a Guggenheim Fellowship.

Imes spent the 1920s working in and around New York in several capacities as an engineer and applied physicist: as a consulting physicist(1918–22); a research physicist with the Federal Engineers Development Corporation (1922–24); with the Burrows Magnetic Equipment Corporation (1924–27); and as a research engineer at E. A. Everett Signal Supplies (1927–30). His applied research and engineering activities resulted in four patents concerned with determining the electrical and magnetic characteristics of certain materials and constructing instruments to measure these properties accurately.

During this New York period, Imes's own scholarly and literary interests, as well as his marriage to a well–known writer of the Harlem Renaissance, brought him in contact with many members of the African American intellectual and power elite throughout the 1920s. These figures included W. E. B. Du Bois, Charles S. Johnson, Arna Bontemps, Langston Hughes, Richard Nugent, Aaron Douglas, Walter White, and Harlem Renaissance benefactor Carl Van Vechten. Many of these same people would appear again in Imes's life during the 1930s through their connection to Fisk University.

The Return to Fisk University

The prevailing economic situation and possibly a conflict with his employer at the E. A. Everett Signal Supplies Company led Imes to consider returning to Fisk University at the close of the 1920s. After protracted negotiations with Thomas Elsa Jones, president of Fisk University, Imes returned to the university as professor and chair of the department of physics. He immediately began to reorganize the undergraduate physics curriculum and made preliminary studies for the initiation of a full–fledged graduate program.

During Imes's tenure at Fisk (1930–41), he and his students were involved in several research projects using X–rays and magnetic procedures to characterize the properties of various materials. Several students were sent to the University of Michigan during the summers to learn X–ray techniques, and Imes spent at least one summer at New York University carrying out experiments on magnetic materials. He also continued his research in infrared spectroscopy and returned to the University of Michigan for several summers to conduct experiments on the fine structure of the infrared rotational spectrum of acetylene.

Imes was active in several professional societies including the American Physical Society, American Society for Testing Materials, and the American Institute of Electrical Engineers. He would often attend national meetings of these organizations in the larger northern cities or in Canada. Another measure of his standing in the scientific community is indicated by his listing in the sixth and later editions of *American Men of Science.*

A major concern of Imes's was the training of students, and a number of his students enrolled at the University of Michigan. James R. Lawson earned a Ph.D. in 1939 for work focusing on infrared spectroscopy, and Lewis Clark graduated with an M.S. degree in physics.

As part of the Negro intellectual elite, Imes felt that the students at Fisk, as well as his friends and colleagues, should be exposed to the general outlines and themes of science. To this end, he developed a course called ''Cultural Physics'' and wrote a book–length manuscript to be used in it. The manuscript presents a general summary of the history of science, beginning with the Greeks and continuing up to the early part of the twentieth century.

In addition to his duties as chair of the department of physics, which included detailed work on the design of a new science building, Imes carried out an extensive correspondence with other researchers, equipment designers, and manufacturers. He was also heavily involved with both the academic and social affairs of Fisk University, including being in charge of and running various films for the university community, participating in the planning and execution of the Annual Spring Arts Festival, and serving on various scholarship and disciplinary committees.

Imes's tenure at Fisk was marked by a national scandal over his involvement with a white administrator at Fisk. This situation, as well as other complications, eventually led to his divorce from Nella Larsen on August 30, 1933.

Near the end of the 1930s, Imes's health deteriorated, and he returned to New York to be treated for cancer. He died on September 11, 1941. Imes's obituary in *Science* was written by his friend and scientific colleague W. F. G. Swann:

> In the death of . . . Imes science loses a valuable physicist, an inspiring personality and a man cultured in many fields. . . . His thesis . . . [dealt with] infra–red spectra, a subject on which he has acquired an international reputation. . . . It was the writer's privilege to become acquainted with Professor Imes in his graduate student days at the University of Michigan, where his research laboratory was a mecca for those who sought an atmosphere of calm and contentment. Imes could also be relied upon to bring to any discussion an atmosphere of philosophic soundness and level headed practicalness. . . . In his passing, his many friends mourn the loss of a distinguished scholar and a fine gentleman.

REFERENCES

Davis, Thadious M. *Nella Larsen: Novelist of the Harlem Renaissance.* Baton Rouge. Louisiana State University Press, 1994.

''Fisk Professor is Divorced by N.Y. Novelist.'' *Baltimore Afro–American,* October 7, 1933.

Fuson, Nelson. Notes taken of Dr. Earle Plyler's [Professor Emeritus of Physics, Florida State University] Symposium Talk at the Fisk Infrared Institute's 25th Anniversary Celebration, August 16, 1974.

Imes, Elmer S., ''Measurements of the Near Infra–Red Absorption of Some Diatomic Gases.'' *Astrophysical Journal* 50 (1919): 251–76.

Imes, William Lloyd. *The Black Pastures.* Nashville: Hemphill Press, 1957.

Krenz, Gary D. ''Physics at Michigan: From Classical Physics to Nuclear Research, 1888–1938.'' *LSA Magazine* 12 (Fall 1988): 10–16.

Qualls, Youra. Letter to Ronald E. Mickens, April 20, 1982.

Randall, Harrison McAllister, and Elmer S. Imes. ''The Fine–Structure of the Near Infra–Red Absorption Bands of the Gasses HCl, HBr, and H F.'' *Physical Review* 15 (1920): 152–55.

Swann, W. F. G. ''Elmer Samuel Imes.'' *Science* 94 (26 December 1941): 600–601.

COLLECTIONS

The papers of Elmer Imes are in the Carl Van Vechten Collection, Manuscript Division, New York Public Library; the Carl Van Vechten Collection, Beinecke Library, Yale University; and in the Special Collections Department, Fisk University Library. A manuscript copy of Imes's article ''Measurements of the Near Infra–Red Absorption of Some Diatomic Gases'' is also in the Fisk collection.

Ronald E. Mickens

Rex Ingram
(1895–1969)
Actor

Intelligent, talented, handsome, and debonair, Rex Ingram brought to the Broadway stage and Hollywood screen black masculine dignity that was rare in the age of servile, dense, and dim–witted black characters who shuffled along in self–demeaning roles. Ingram's role as De Lawd in *Green Pastures* made him immensely popular, and his career spanned 50 years. According to film historian Donald Bogle, ''Ingram was able to express a gentleness, an overriding interest and sympathy in all of mankind''—the one advantage he had over Paul Robeson, with whom he was often compared.

The son of a riverboat fireman, Rex Ingram was born on October 20, 1895, on a houseboat on the Mississippi River near Cairo, Illinois, when his mother, on her way home from a visit with relatives in Natchez, Mississippi, went into labor. At least this is the story that he told on many occasions. Ingram is said to have grown up working with his father on the steamer *Robert E. Lee,* and enrolled in Northwestern University in 1912; he was the first black man to earn a Phi Beta Kappa key at the school. In 1919 he reportedly graduated with a medical degree from Northwestern University Medical School. However, there is no record of his ever having attended Northwestern. Unless he attended under another name, one must assume this story was part of the thespian's facade. His family background and childhood remain a mystery.

Ingram claimed that he headed for California in 1919, where he sailed for 18 months as a crewman on a windjammer, returning in 1920. Ingram often told the story of his discovery by a talent scout. Quoted in the *New York Times,* he explained:

> My career as an actor was quite by chance. I was standing on a Hollywood corner waiting to cross the street, when I was discovered by a movie talent scout. I was persuaded that I was just what they needed to play a native of the jungles in the Tarzan pictures. What I thought would be a short diversion from my work as a physician became my career.

In his first film, *Tarzan of the Apes* (1918), Ingram was cast in a bit part. He appeared in many other Tarzan films and in the silent films *The Ten Commandments, The Big Parade, Salome,* and *King of Kings.* While he was in Hollywood, Ingram worked a number of jobs between films in order to support himself. According to *Ebony,* he claimed to have been called ''the greatest Negro heavyweight prospect since Jack Johnson'' when he fought professionally in California in 1921.

Ingram moved from California to New York City in 1928. In 1929 he made his stage debut on Broadway in David Belasco's *Lulu Belle,* and he played in *Porgy and Bess* on Broadway in 1933. *Goin' Home* (1932), *Stevedore* (1933), *Marching Song* (1934), and *Once in a Lifetime* (1935) were other off–Broadway shows in which he performed small parts.

In 1933 Ingram played a small part in the film *Emperor Jones.* More successful on screen than on stage, Ingram's first big break came in 1936 when he was cast as De Lawd in the film version of *The Green Pastures.* Richard B. Harrison played De Lawd in the stage play, and Ingram was in awe of his performance. Ingram recalled how he got the part in an article he wrote for *Ebony* magazine: ''Harrison's final collapse in 1935 in his dressing room at the 44th Street Theater in New York took place in my presence. I was there discussing the play with him and reading over lines from the part of Adam. . . . He was rushed to a hospital where he died.'' A national casting call was issued for the part left vacant by Harrison's death. As reported in *Ebony,* Ingram knew he had the part when the secretary at Warner Brothers called him and said ''Good morning, Lawd.'' He also played Adam and Hezdrel in the film.

Rex Ingram

Fame and Fortune Begin

Initially, Ingram was fearful of playing the part of God and doubted his own abilities to create a fictional portrayal of a spiritual ideal. But as he worked on the part his confidence increased. Ultimately the role produced what *Ebony* called a ''remarkable spiritual experience'' for the actor. *The Green Pastures* won more recognition for his performance than it did for that of any other actor. Bogle stated that in the film ''Ingram soared above all the sequences, all the characters, all the pageantry.''

Rex Ingram married Francine Everett in 1936. Also an actor, Francine was born in 1920, became a chorus girl at sixteen, married, and lost her husband when he was killed in an accident. The 17–year–old widow came to the Works Progress Administration Federal Theater Project looking for a job, where she met Ingram. The couple moved to Hollywood, but Ingram was forced to keep moving back and forth between Hollywood and New York to keep his commitments in plays and films. In the *Ebony* article he described it as ''great fun,'' but it must have played havoc with his marriage, which ultimately ended in divorce.

As Ingram's fame soared, he promised himself not to accept any more roles that were demeaning to blacks. He recognized the powerful influence of the entertainment media and wanted to help rather than retard the process of black freedom and acceptance in America. That he had no work for two years and was forced into bankruptcy speaks not only to the dearth of decent roles for black actors, but also to the difficulty they faced trying to maintain their artistic integrity.

A break came in 1938 when Ingram was cast by the Federal Theater Project as Christopher in the play *Haiti.* Brook Atkinson remarked on how infrequently Ingram was given an heroic part to play. He concluded in the *New York Times* that in *Haiti* ''Mr. Ingram gives a rattling good performance.'' The greatest moment in Ingram's life occurred when he sang the hit song, ''Franklin D. Roosevelt Jones,'' in the 1938 Music Box Production of *Sing out the News.* Mary McLeod Bethune, Eleanor Roosevelt, and President Roosevelt greeted him back stage and the president complemented him on his singing.

Ingram's fine performance in *The Green Pastures* led to his role as Jim in MGM's 1939 production of *Adventures of Huckleberry Finn.* With the character of Jim, Ingram wanted to promote the message of brotherhood. He played the part of Nigger Jim without becoming servile. Instead, he was powerful and heroic. Of his performance Bogle wrote: ''with his large chest and thick biceps Ingram seemed so powerful that audiences knew there were no chains strong enough to hold him down.''

Rex Ingram became an international star when in 1940 he was chosen to play the role of the Genie of the Lamp in the British film *The Thief of Baghdad.* For his efforts he earned $2,500 a week for 14 months. He returned to Hollywood in 1941, where he performed in *Talk of the Town* (1942); *Cabin in the Sky* (1943); *Sahara* (1943), in his opinion the most heroic role he was ever cast in; *Fired Wife* (1943); *A Thousand and One Nights* (1948); and *Moonrise* (1948).

The Fall and Return from Grace

In 1948 Ingram's bright career plunged into darkness when, as reported in the *New York Times,* he was arrested for transporting a minor, a 15–year old white girl from Salina, Kansas, across state lines for immoral purposes. He pled guilty to the charges and was sentenced to an 18–month jail term. He served ten months before being released on parole. As a result of the indictment Ingram lost his home in Warm Springs Canyon, California, and was forced to give up his role in the play *Set My People Free.* He suffered greatly from bouts of depression and self–doubt, but he refused to give up or go into seclusion.

In the article, ''I Came Back From the Dead,'' Ingram described for *Ebony* his return to the limelight after his troubles with the law. ''I stepped out on that stage with a cold sweat breaking out all over me. I will never forget the reception the audience gave me. It was deafening. They roared, clapped, cheered, and whistled for nearly two minutes, yelling 'come on, Rex.' I felt good.'' The audience he described was in the Las Palmas Theater in Los Angeles; the year was 1951, and Rex Ingram was making his first appearance since 1948 in Nick Stewart's *Christopher Columbus Brown.*

The way back was not easy, and Ingram never achieved again the stardom he lost resulting from the 1948 incident. However, he did manage find to work, playing an African chief in *Ramar of the Jungle* (1952) and appearing in *Anna Lucasta* (1958), *God's Little Acre* (1958), *Elmer Gantry* (1960), *Your Cheating Heart* (1964), and *Hurry Sundown* (1967). In 1957 he appeared on Broadway in the all–black production of *Waiting for Godot.* He appeared in the television shows *Daktari, I Spy, Gunsmoke,* and *Playhouse 90.* His last role was for *The Bill Cosby Show.*

Ingram smoked a pipe and made a hobby of collecting them; he owned about 500 pipes. He had a heart attack and died at his home in Hollywood on September 19, 1969, leaving behind his second wife, Dena, daughter Gloria Wagner, and two grandsons. He was 73 years old. He is remembered for his long career as an actor and for enhancing the black male image on stage and in film.

REFERENCES

Bogle, Donald. *Blacks in American Film and Television.* New York: Fireside, 1989.

———. *Toms, Coons, Mulattoes, Mammies, and Bucks.* 3rd ed. New York: Continuum, 1994.

Ingram, Rex. ''I Came Back From the Dead.'' *Ebony* 10 (March 1955): 48–58.

''Rex Ingram, the Actor, Dies in Hollywood at 73.'' *New York Times,* September 20, 1969.

Sampson, Henry T. *Blacks in Black and White.* 2nd ed. Metuchen, NJ: Scarecrow Press, 1995.

Nagueyalti Warren

J

Hulan Jack

(1905–1986)

Politician

When Hulan Jack was elected president of the Borough of Manhattan in 1953, he became the most powerful, highest paid, and highest ranking elected black official in the United States. His election signaled integration of the powerful New York Democratic political machinery known as Tammany Hall. An astute leader and skilled in all aspects of precinct politics, Jack's political finesse opened the door for other black politicians who succeeded him as borough president, including Dudley Edwards and Percy Sutton. Before he was elected president of Manhattan, Jack spent thirteen years in the New York State Assembly as a representative from Harlem. He soon became a power broker and a man of influence within the Democratic party, spending fifty years as a Democrat and thirty of those years leading the New York based New Deal Democratic party.

Born December 23, 1906, Hulan Edwin Jack Sr. was the son of Ratford Edwin and Emily George Jack. At birth, he was baptized in the Roman Catholic Church. His father, a teacher and minister, moved the family frequently to accept various ministerial posts. By the time Hulan Jack came to the United States at the age of seventeen, his family had lived in the Caribbean Islands of St. Lucia, where he was born, as well as St. Vincent, British Guiana, Chaparra, Cuba, and Bridgetown, Barbados. The Jack family included two other sons and two daughters. Of his developmental years, Jack later recalled in *Fifty Years A Democrat* that his "mother and father did everything in their power to give their children a good background in the traditions of the West Indies." Rigor, hard work, and discipline were the hallmarks of his parental training.

A supporter of the Marcus Garvey movement, Hulan Jack's father began making trips to the United States during the early 1900s to participate in Garvey–led, political activities. Garvey, himself a West Indian immigrant, was the guiding spirit of the Universal Negro Improvement Association. The association was based on equality and racial pride in the African heritage. In its early days, the Garvey movement embodied many elements of a radical working class ideology. Just how much of an impression Jack's father's political activities had on his son is hard to say, but Jack noted that his father always came back from the United States "inspired" after attending the Garvey meetings.

In 1923, at the age of 17, Hulan Jack accompanied his father to New York, the state that became his home for over sixty years. Once in New York, the young Jack began executing a three point plan he had set for himself upon learning he was coming to the United States: to acquire an American education, find work sufficient to sustain himself, and to participate in politics. He enrolled in night classes and earned a high school diploma in 1929. Subsequently, Jack completed three years of study towards a bachelor's degree in business administration in the New York University system.

After a relatively short period of time, Jack acquired work with the Samuel J. Redlech Paper Box Plant. While his hopes were to get a "good job," he soon found that his duties were confined to those of a janitor, box cutter, and factory porter. Determined to acquire more responsible duties, he became an astute observer of the workings of the machine end of productions, and within three months on the job, was moved into the machine–related area of the company. Later, he entered the sales end of the company and served as a vice–president for sales.

During his first year, the atmosphere at the plant was filled with speculation that union workers were planning to stage a strike, although a union strike did not occur for almost a year. As a nonunion employee, Jack continued going to work during the strike. An astute observer, he noted that despite the strike, the workers' salaries did not increase and their working conditions did not improve. A group of black workers, totally unfamiliar with the workings of the plant, was brought in to break the strike. These new workers were fired as soon as the strike ended. Watching these events, Jack learned much about black disenfranchisement in the American economic labor system.

Nearly ten years would pass before Jack was asked to join the union. Activities surroundings the strike, his most memorable experience with racism, doubtlessly heightened his consciousness about the importance of effective political representation. Despite the obvious failure of this strike, Jack was convinced that trade unions, under proper organization and leadership, could be effective mechanisms for improving the working conditions and quality of life for all Americans. Jack had quickly assessed life in America. As he wrote later in *Fifty Years a Democrat,* he had concluded that "in this country the Negro man or woman must resolve to use his or her capacities to the fullest, and to exercise patience, mutual respect, and unfettered good will toward all in the struggle for the progress of the American Negro Minority." He had resolved to fight racism and discrimination. This resolution led Jack into politics. Citizenship was a prerequisite for action. Thus, Jack began the application process and took the oath of citizenship in 1931.

By 1934 Jack had met the woman he intended to marry. Gertrude Hewitt, a native of Virginia, became his wife that same year. They had one son, Hulan Edwin Jack Jr. Following a brief illness in 1937, Gertrude Jack died and her body was returned to Virginia for burial in the Hewitt family cemetery. Four years later on March 27, 1941, Jack marred Almira Wilkinson, a resident of New Jersey, who became his life–long companion. They had one daughter, Julienne. Throughout his political career and beyond, the Jack family remained residents of Harlem.

Pivotal Roles as a Politician

The announcement of a black man's election to the Manhattan Borough presidency in 1953 focused international attention on Manhattan, for with Wall Street within the hub of its boundaries, the Borough was considered one of the world's strongest financial centers. The Manhattan's size, population density, municipal budget, and the range of authority and number of employees made it more important than other Boroughs comprising New York City.

A strong advocate for constituency–based representation at both the neighborhood and district levels, Jack began his political activity in the 1930s by attending neighborhood political meetings. It was during the 1930s that millions of black voters began leaving the Republican party to vote for the Democratic candidate for President, Franklin D. Roosevelt. As a consequence, there was a growing recognition within the Democratic party of the power potential of black voters. After carefully studying both the formal and informal sides of precinct politics, Jack stepped forward in 1940 when the Democratic machine decided to nominate a black candidate to match the bold move of the Republicans who had nominated a black candidate to represent Harlem in the New York State Assembly. Jack won and served as assemblyman from 1941 to 1953.

By the late 1940s a new era of political involvement for black people was at hand. The endless hours that Hulan Jack and other black leaders, such as Adam Clayton Powell Jr., had invested in training their constituencies in the workings of the two party political system were paying off. The net effect was a more involved, sophisticated, and supportive voter base. There were black representatives in New York at the local, state, and congressional levels. In the 1957 election, for example, the Manhattan Borough president's seat was sought by three other black candidates besides Hulan Jack, these being a Republican nominee, an Independent Democratic nominee, and a Liberal Democratic nominee. Jack was elected first Manhattan Borough president in 1953.

During his first term as borough president, Jack displayed skills of a visionary and long–range planner. During his tenure, major improvements to the borough's infrastructure took place. These included multimillion dollar investments in street repairs, transportation systems, sewers, and other public services. The availability of public housing was greatly increased as well. Jack proved to be politically savvy and for the most part was perceived as effective in his work. In 1957 he was elected to a second four–year term. It was during this second term that he ran into political problems. Convicted for accepting an illegal gift valued at $4,500, Jack resigned in disgrace in 1960. The charges against him were bitterly criticized by his constituency and thought to be the effect of radical discrimination. In *The Negro Politician — His Success and Failure,* Edward Clayton pointed out that "the struggle to stay atop the political pinnacle is a constant one in the lives of Negro politicians, beginning almost from the day they start working within the party as doorbell ringers and sometimes ending abruptly in complete political exile." He used Jack as an example, calling him a man "who invested twenty years of his lifetime in making a success of his career only to have it shattered because he unwillingly allowed a contractor to pay for the redecorating of the apartment in which he and his family lived."

After resigning reluctantly in 1960 as borough president, Jack remained an active worker and leader within the Democratic party, and he spent a lot of effort trying to clear his good name. His sentence was suspended. Ultimately, he cleared his name with constituents but was unable to have the conviction over turned.

Tammany Hall political machinery was under attack by a segment of the Democratic party known as "Reformers" during Jack's second term. Precinct politics had become as notorious for political corruption as for effectiveness in addressing the needs of its constituency. Winds of change were sweeping the country, and Tammany Hall was unable to insulate itself from that change. Precinct politics were radically altered and black public officials like Jack, formerly praised for learning how to work within the system, became ostracized and labeled Uncle Tom's. Eventually, the enormous power vested in individual borough presidents was combined and vested in the newly created Office of the New York City mayor.

Despite his conviction, Jack retained his Democratic party leadership role until 1972. In 1968 he reentered politics, winning an election to the New York State Assembly as the representative from Harlem. By 1970 he was again under political scrutiny, this time for conflict of interest charges related to a community service firm in which he was a partner. A grand jury was convened to hear the charges and weigh the evidence. Jack was convicted and sentenced to three months in a minimum security prison. Eventually he was publicly exonerated, but his political aspirations had come to an end with the conviction. After a lifetime of service to the Democratic party, Jack began working towards a restructuring of the Democratic party while in retirement.

In 1980 Hulan Jack became a political consultant to Lyndon LaRouche, an Independent candidate for the U.S. Presidency. In his last public political appearance, a nationally televised campaign address by Lyndon LaRouche, Jack endorsed LaRouche. LaRouche's main platform, restructuring of the American and, subsequently, the world economy, hit upon several areas that Jack had addressed in earlier years.

On December 19, 1986, Hulan Jack died quietly. He was eulogized by his only son, Hulan Jack Jr., a physicist and licensed engineer in New York City. His political success in

New York City paved the way for other black politicians who followed him and also brought him national attention as a ranking black official.

REFERENCES

Clayton, Edward T. *The Negro Politician—His Success and Failure.* Chicago: Johnson Publishing Company, 1964.

Encyclopedia of New York City. New Haven, CT: Yale University Press, 1995.

Jack, Hulan. *Fifty Years A Democrat: The Autobiography of Hulan E. Jack.* New York: New Benjamin Franklin House, 1982.

Smith, Jessie Carney. *Black Firsts.* Detroit: Gale Research, 1994.

Stone, Chuck. *Black Political Power in America.* New York: Dell Publishing, 1968.

Anne S. Butler

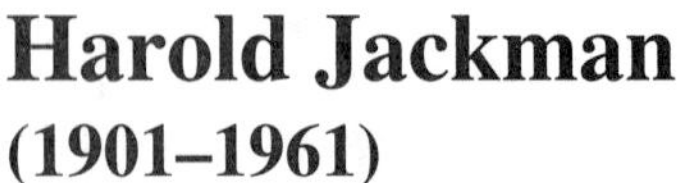

Harold Jackman

(1901–1961)

Educator, model, editor, bibliophile, theater cofounder, playwright, bibliophile

Harold Jackman

The Harlem Renaissance was an extraordinary flowering of African American arts and letters that took place in New York City's Harlem in the 1920s and 1930s. Harold Jackman helped to create the history and culture of the Renaissance through his association with the leading figures of the time and his involvement in the intellectual ferment of the era. A skillful journalist, he was associate, contributing, or advisory editor of two black literary magazines. He help promote black theater by becoming a founder of the Nego Experimental Theatre Company. preserved the culture of the period by recording detailed accounts of many of its significant events, by founding a literary and artistic collection at Atlanta University in Atlanta, and by contributing to African American collections elsewhere. Regina M. Andrews wrote in *Harold Jackman* that his interest in the creativity of his contemporaries ''surmounted racial lines, classic periods and lives of those who had a story to tell in verse, drama, on canvas, or clay.''

Jackman has been called a West Indian; in fact, he was born in London, England, in 1901. He grew up in Harlem and was educated in New York City's De Witt Clinton High School. He graduated from New York University, and received a master of arts degree from Columbia University. Jackman later became a junior high school history teacher in the local schools.

Considered handsome and distinguished looking both in his younger and later years, he worked part–time as a model while attending NYU and received fan mail from all over the world. He continued to model after college, and in his later years he depicted dentists, doctors, lawyers, and business executives. Painter Weinold Reiss published his portrait of Jackman in the March 1925 issue of *Survey Graphic* titled ''Harlem: Mecca of the New Negro.''

Jackman had a close relationship with poet Countee Cullen. In addition to being Cullen's very competent bridge partner, the literature of the Harlem Renaissance suggests that the two men loved each other. David Lewis wrote in *When Harlem Was in Vogue* that ''Cullen was uninterested in women and preferred the company of Harold Jackman'' and that Jackman adored his ''adoptive father,'' Frederick Cullen. After Frederick Cullen performed the wedding ceremony for his son and W. E. B. Du Bois's daughter, Yolande, on April 9, 1928, with Jackman as best man, the three men sailed for France on June 30, without the bride, leaving her to travel on her own.

Glittering Social Scene

Whatever the Jackman–Cullen relationship, it brought him into the company of the leading figures, both artists and patrons, of the era. In the late 1920s, for example, Jackman attended photographer and writer Carl Van Vechten's soirées, as well as parties that A'Lelia Walker held at her residence, the Dark Tower, and elsewhere. In fact, Bruce Kellner wrote in *Carl Van Vechten* that Jackman, Cullen, poet Langston Hughes, and the book's subject were among a regular group who had a standing invitation to attend Walker's parties.

Jackman, who often showed dignitaries around town, recalled in an interview with A. C. Sterling for "Those Were the Fabulous Days," published on October 11, 1952, *Pittsburgh Courier* and cited in Kellner's work previously noted:

> One couldn't help being impressed with the brilliance of the evenings. . . . Literature, politics, painting and music were always discussed. Something interesting was constantly happening. Madame Walker made certain that there was almost more than enough elegant dishes and drinks to go around.

Walter White, a black author and advocate, and his wife also held "formidable parties" where future Republican presidential candidate Wendell Wilkie, Van Vechten, noted attorney Clarence Darrow, writer Claude McKay, Langston Hughes, Cullen, and Jackman were among the honored guests. Jackman's apparent religious interests led him on visits to the little storefront churches in Harlem and to church services held in homes. There Jackman, along with Cullen, Hughes, Walker, and Arna Bontemps, poet and novelist, witnessed the swaying and hand clapping of the worshippers.

Jackman took the story of the Harlem Renaissance to London and Paris, where the recounting of the cultural arts of Harlem aroused great interest. Princess Violette Murat, a descendant of Napoleon, was so impressed with Jackman and the cultural movement that she and a contingent of friends visited Harlem to witness the cultural scene for themselves.

Jackman even appeared in literary works. For example, Cullen dedicated his poem "Heritage" to Jackman. In *The Harlem Renaissance Remembered,* Bontemps voiced the suspicion that other poems by Cullen might have been similarly dedicated. Byron Kasson, the hero and fictional black writer in Van Vechten's book, *Nigger Heaven,* fit Jackman's physical description. Jackman is also said to be present "thinly veiled" in Wallace Thurman's *Infants of the Spring.*

Jackman's journalistic talents were evidenced in his work as associate editor from 1935 to 1937 of the literary magazine *Challenge,* founded in 1934 by Dorothy West, the editor. He was also contributing editor, later an advisory editor, of *Phylon* from 1944 until his death.

Editor and Director

Jackman's flair for drama came to the fore in the Harlem Experimental Theatre Company which he helped to found in 1929 under the guidance of Dorothy R. Peterson. Regina Anderson (Andrews), Loften Mitchell and Dorothy Peterson were among the cofounders and directors; Andrews was also executive director. This forerunner of Harlem's little theater movement met in the 135th Street Library basement in Harlem, bringing together black actors, craftsmen, and playwrights. Among the actors were Clarence Streyhorne, Ira DeA. Reid, William Pickens, Alta Douglas, and Robert Dunmore. Jessie Fauset Harris was a leading spirit of the theatre, while Alain Locke, author and educator, and W. E. B. Du Bois were members of the board. Four months after the group was founded, Jackman directed the first performance, *Plumes,* by Georgia Douglas Johnson.

Many of the Harlem Renaissance figures established lasting friendships. The Jackman–Bontemps relationship was an example. After they met in 1924, the two corresponded after Bontemps left Harlem for Huntsville, Alabama, and elsewhere. From Alabama, he sent Jackman copies of his books, and they were still corresponding in 1943 when Bontemps moved to Fisk University in Nashville to become university librarian. In 1960, Bontemps sought out his friend's assistance for one of his research projects. Apparently the results were superior, Jackman producing detailed information with names, sidelights, and other useful information. Jackman considered opening a research service, but did not live to pursue it.

Establishes Cullen Memorial Collection

Jackman saw the need to collect and preserve materials by and about African Americans. Already an inveterate collector, by the late 1920s he began sending materials to Atlanta University. His relationship with Cullen endured until the latter's death in 1947. Jackman requested that Atlanta University name the collection as a memorial to Cullen, who had a great interest in the race as well as faith in its future. The collection emphasized contemporary life but included rare, older items as well. Jackman also solicited materials from his friends to be added to the collection. Among the largest contributors, in addition to Jackman, were Dorothy Peterson, Hughes, Van Vechten, and author Owen Dodson. After Jackman died, the collection was renamed the Countee Cullen–Harold Jackman Memorial Collection. Jackman's sister, Ivy Jackman, then deposited materials in the collection including over 300 titles from his estate.

Jackman assisted Van Vechten in gathering important black works, including manuscripts and books, for the James Weldon Johnson Memorial Collection at Yale. He also allowed him to unearth buried treasures in his own library for the Yale collection. Either through gifts from Jackman's library or through his efforts, he contributed to the development of collections at Fisk University Library and the Schomburg Collection of the New York Public Library.

Among Jackman's affiliations were life member and executive board member of the Negro Actors Guild. He was said to have been active in numerous artistic and literary movements begun in Harlem.

Jackman was considered handsome and distinguished looking both in his younger and later years. Weinold Reiss recognized Jackman's good looks when he painted the portrait published in the March 1925 issue of *Survey Graphic* titled, "Harlem: Mecca of the New Negro." Reiss labeled the painting, "A College Lad" (sometimes also called "A Young Student").

In a letter to Rosey Poole dated June 29, 1934, and quoted in *Harold Jackman,* Jackman described himself as "inclined to obesity, though not quite there, given to laughing at the wrong time, and so well looking that not even when I am sick do I excite the least bit of sympathy." He continued: "I always wished I were: tall, solemn and a bit tubercular.'' While vacationing in Maine, Jackman died on July 8, 1961.

Jackman's legacy was perpetuated in several ways. In January 1962, a three–day series of memorial lectures was held in Harlem. The John Hay Whitney Foundation and Harlem's Market Place Gallery were underwriters of the series. A Harold Jackman Memorial Committee was established to honor him and to carry on his work as collection–builder. His friends and supporters solicited letters for a published tribute to him. Nora D. Holt wrote that ''he wore the mantle of a princely gentleman with ease.'' Dorothy West wrote that ''his passionate interest in Negro art and letters, his unceasing participation in their promulgation were his life style.''

An authority on arts and letters, Jackman, who had great capacity for loyalty and deep friendship, is remembered for his association with the brilliance of the Harlem Renaissance era and his involvement in the major artistic movements in Harlem and greater New York. He moved in artistically creative circles in both America and Europe. Dodson wrote in *Harold Jackman* that Jackman ''brought to Harlem and to New York City especially, the cosmopolitan air of England and the Continent.'' He also loved what we later called ''Black Power in the arts,'' wrote Dodson, and helped to bring about ''freedom in the arts.'' Jackman's work helps to round out that of the artists, writers, dramatists, and other creative figures of that period. *Renaissance Man from Louisiana* describes his impact on the nation in commenting on his death: ''American letters had lost a giant'' and ''the already thinning ranks of the Harlem Renaissance writers had been invaded once more.''

REFERENCES

Anderson, Jervis. *This Was Harlem.* New York: Farrar Straus Giroux, 1981.

Bontemps, Arna. *The Harlem Renaissance Remembered.* New York: Dodd, Mead, 1972.

Ferguson, Blanche E. *Countee Cullen and the Negro Renaissance.* New York: Dodd, Mead, 1966.

''Harlem: Mecca of the New Negro.'' *Survey Graphic* 6 (March 1925).

Harold Jackman Memorial Committee, comps. *Harold Jackman.* Atlanta: Atlanta University, 1973.

Jones, Kirkland C. *Renaissance Man from Louisiana: A Biography of Arna Bontemps.* Westport, CT: Greenwood Press, 1992.

Kellner, Bruce, ed. *Carl Van Vechten at the Irreverent Decades.* Norman: University of Oklahoma Press, 1968.

———. *The Harlem Renaissance: A Historical Dictionary of the Era.* New York: Methuen, 1984.

———, ed. *Keep A–Inchin' Along.* Westport, CT: Greenwood Press, 1979.

Lewis, David Levering. *When Harlem Was In Vogue.* New York: Knopf, 1981.

Lowe, W. Augustus, and Virgil A. Clift, eds. *Encyclopedia of Black America.* New York: McGraw–Hill, 1981.

''Male Models.'' *Ebony* 14 (May 1959): 90–95.

Mitchell, Loften. *Voices of the Black Theatre.* Clifton, NJ: White, 1975.

Sinnette, Eleanor Des Verney, W. Paul Coates, and Thomas C. Battle, eds. *Black Bibliophiles and Collectors: Preservers of Black History.* Washington, DC: Howard University Press, 1990.

Smith, Jessie Carney, ed. *Notable Black American Women.* Detroit: Gale Research, 1992.

Van Jackson, Wallace. ''The Countee Cullen Memorial Collection at Atlanta University.'' *Crisis* 54 (May 1947): 140–42.

Van Vechten, Carl. *Nigger Heaven.* New York: Knopf, 1926.

COLLECTIONS

In Jackman's honor, the Countee Cullen–Harold Jackman Memorial Collection is available in the Woodruff Library, Clark Atlanta University. The collection includes Jackman's personal library. Of special importance is a series of day books dated back to 1926 that Jackman kept to document many significant events of the era.

Jessie Carney Smith

Jesse L. Jackson

(1941–)

Human rights activist, minister, political appointee, speaker, organization official

Jesse L. Jackson has been called one of the most eloquent speakers of our time. His speeches have galvanized people around the world into action; they have served as catalysts for boycotts, marches, voter registration drives, and social action organized to combat acts of injustice. His negotiations have brought home hostages from abroad and have forged new paths in employment. From humble beginnings, he has risen to greatness.

Jesse Louis Jackson was born to Helen Burns, then 16 years old, and Noah Robinson, on October 8, 1941. At the time, Burns lived with her mother Matilda, who at the age of 13 had given birth to Burns as the result of an interlude with a grocer's son from a nearby community. Burns, a gifted singer, had aspirations of attending college on one of the five music scholarships that had been offered to her. Instead, she made preparations for a career in cosmetology while raising her son. Living conditions in the Greenville, South Carolina, community were uncomfortable for the Burns family, as Robinson was Burn's married neighbor.

In Greenville, like many communities in the South, African Americans with financial stability lived in close proximity to those less well off. Noah Robinson, Jackson's

Jesse L. Jackson

father, lived a comfortable life as a cotton grader for John J. Ryan and Sons, a white–owned textiles firm, and a boxer. Robinson offered his wife and two sons, Noah Jr. and George, a comfortable existence, but finances were tight for the Burns family living directly next door. Matilda Burns, Jackson's grandmother, is said to have marched over to the Robinson household on numerous occasions demanding that Robinson purchase certain necessities for his child. She also insisted that her grandson have "legitimacy," so Robinson gave him the name of his own father, Jesse Robinson. Louis, Robinson's middle name, was passed on to his son as a further act of legitimization.

During Jackson's early childhood, Robinson and his family moved to another section of town. Before her son's third birthday, Helen Burns married Charles Jackson, a shoe shine attendant at a local barber shop. Young Jackson regarded him as his father, and later as a teenager, he was formally adopted by the World War II veteran. After serving in the U.S. Army in World War II, Charles Jackson worked as a janitor. A promotion and a transfer to the post office building in Greenville provided more money for the family enabling them to move to Fieldcrest Village, a nicer community than the residence of Jackson's youth.

Throughout Jackson's youth, the message of community responsibility was reinforced. He has referred to his community and extended family in Greenville as a "triangle of care." He learned the importance of community service from his mother as she voluntarily ordered groceries for an illiterate elderly neighbor. One year during the Christmas season when Helen Jackson was sick and Charles Jackson was unemployed, this same neighbor reciprocated by ordering six bags of groceries for the family so that they could have an ample holiday. By the age of nine, Jackson was tending to the needs of other less fortunate members of his community by volunteering to read the newspaper to illiterate adults. Jackson also knew the value of hard work. He delivered stove wood with a relative, caddied at Greenville's country club, and waited tables at an airport restaurant. He was so energetic that he earned the nickname "Bo Diddley" from his neighbors.

Greenville was home to Furman University and Jackson's mother did laundry for the college's fraternity members, washing and ironing for 20 cents per item. As a youngster, Jackson and his friends found a way to capitalize on college events by selling soda and peanuts to football spectators. They also offered to watch the cars of these spectators for a fee. After performing a hard day's work, Jackson and his contemporaries would sit on a grassy mound so that they, too, could watch the games. They did not know that the section where they sat was called "the Crow's Nest" by Furman's undergraduate students.

As a child, Jackson longed to attend Furman. Understanding the importance of education, he worked diligently as a student at Sterling High School. While there, he demonstrated extraordinary athletic prowess, playing football, baseball, and basketball. Upon graduating in 1959, he was offered a contract to play baseball with the Chicago White Sox. He declined the offer, but soon after, he received a football scholarship to attend the University of Illinois. Finding the racial climate smothering, he left, transferring to North Carolina Agricultural and Technical State University in Greensboro.

Assumes Leadership Role Early

Jackson assumed leadership positions early in life, becoming involved in numerous civil rights activities as an undergraduate. In 1963 he was responsible for leading a ten–month demonstration that included marches, sit–ins, and boycotts at area establishments where African American patrons were unwelcome. His inspiration to agitate came from myriad people, places, and situations, like Asa Philip Randolph who, just five months prior to Jackson's birth, threatened to march on Washington, D.C., with one thousand activists to protest discrimination against African Americans in the war industry. Jackson's fellow students recognized his persuasive abilities and elected him president of the North Carolina Intercollegiate Council on Human Rights. He was also elected student body president and joined the Omega Psi Phi Fraternity.

During his senior year of college, Jackson married the former Jacqueline Lavinia Brown; and upon completing a bachelor's degree in sociology in 1964, he was named field representative for the southeast region of the Congress on Racial Equality (CORE). He held this position for one year before leaving the South for Chicago. In 1965 Jackson studied theology on a Rockefeller grant at the Chicago Theological Seminary at the University of Chicago. There he participated in activities staged by Chicago's Coordinating Council of Community Organizations, an umbrella group for civic and civil rights organizations. He served as the director of field activities from 1965 to 1966. It is through this position that he became allied with a young minister from Georgia by the name of Martin Luther King Jr.

Jackson left the seminary to join King's Selma, Alabama, campaign against injustice. In 1966 he joined the Southern Christian Leadership Conference (SCLC). He assumed the position of Chicago coordinator for SCLC's Operation Breadbasket from 1966 to 1967 and became the director of special projects and economic development of SCLC. Receiving an appointment from King, he assumed the role of national director of Operation Breadbasket from 1967 to 1971. The organization, which was founded in 1957, helped African Americans gain thousands of jobs and business opportunities. Through SCLC, African American small business owners secured contracts with white and black suppliers, producers, and vendors. Recognizing the power of the African American dollar, Jackson, through the SCLC, threatened to boycott corporations with lax racial hiring practices.

In 1967 the Atlantic and Pacific (A & P) supermarket chain pledged to hire 770 African American Chicago residents. When the promise of following through on this pledge looked bleak, Jackson called a boycott of the chain. Two weeks later, 40 of the supermarkets situated in African American communities were the sites of boycotts and pickets. Fourteen weeks into the demonstrations, A & P signed a pact in which they promised to use African American extermination and janitorial services. A & P also vowed to invest funds in local African American banking institution.

Linked to Martin Luther King Jr.

Through agitation and SCLC's regular Saturday morning rallies, Americans became aware of the course of action to facilitate African American empowerment. Thousands attended these rallies where Jackson inspired the crowds. Jackson's name became linked with King's and the two became quite close. When trouble called, they responded, which led them to Memphis, Tennessee, in 1968.

African American sanitation workers were striking as a result of grievance they filed against the city of Memphis. They formed a union and lobbied for better working conditions, but Memphis mayor Harry Loebe refused to grant them an audience, threatening to fire them if they failed to return to work. Responding to the pleas by community activists, King, Jackson, and others went to lobby for equal rights for the workers. They went under the banner of peace, but violence met the organizers as they stood on the balcony of the Lorraine Motel. There, on April 4, 1968, King was assassinated, leaving 26–year–old Jackson, and the nation, stunned.

On April 5, 1968, an angry Jackson marched into a City Council meeting in Chicago wearing the blood–splattered sweater that he had worn at King's side the day before. He addressed the Council members and Mayor Richard Daley, who made a commitment to uphold the nonviolent goals and practices for which King stood.

During Jackson's crusades to right racial wrongs, his spirituality was heightened. Ordained a Baptist minister on June 30, 1968, he followed in the footsteps of twins Jesse and Jacob Robinson, his paternal grandfather and great–uncle. Jesse Robinson (1865–1923) preached joint sermons with his brother during which they referred to each other as "Blessed Buddy." As a guest of D. S. Sample, Jackson delivered his first sermon at Long Branch Baptist Church, his mother's church in Greenville. Present at this event were his mother, stepfather, and father, among others. After ordination, Jackson took the position of associate minister at Fellowship Baptist Church.

Jackson continued to work with Operation Breadbasket, the economic arm of the SCLC. Under his leadership, Operation Breadbasket sponsored the first Black Expo, a convention that featured speakers such as business owners who displayed their products, described their services, and detailed ways to start and maintain businesses.

Jackson was such a vocal activist that the entire nation began to focus attention on him and his projects. In 1969 he received honorary doctorates from Lincoln University in Pennsylvania and Chicago Theological Seminary. In 1970 he received honorary doctorates from Oberlin College, Howard University, and North Carolina A & T, his alma mater.

Founds Operation PUSH

When turmoil began to rock the foundation of SCLC, Jackson resigned in December 1971 after disputes with Reverend Ralph Abernathy, who had become president of SCLC in April after King's death. Despite differences of opinions with the SCLC leadership, Jackson remained optimistic. On December 25, 1971, Jackson founded Operation PUSH (People United to Save Humanity). He recognized that not only were African Americans living in blighted conditions, but people around the world suffered in poverty and oppression.

Jackson's willingness to embrace all people regardless of color, may stem from his own diverse ethnic background. While one of his great–grandmothers was a slave, she was also part Cherokee. One of his grandfathers was one–half Cherokee. One of Jackson's great–grandfathers, a sheriff of Greenville County, was an Irish plantation owner. The man who helped Helen Burns deliver Jackson on that October day was a white doctor for whom Matilda Burns worked. Jackson knew that to embrace and uplift African Americans, he had to simultaneously embrace other groups as well.

In the name of love for all people, Jackson continued to lobby for human rights through Operation PUSH. He gained such popularity that a poll conducted in the early 1970s indicated that he was one of the most recognizable figures in America. Forging new paths, he was able to produce national agreements with Burger King and Kentucky Fried Chicken, under which the corporations would provide more jobs for African Americans. He also called for the development and expansion of financial institutions that are owned and operated by African Americans.

In 1972 PUSH came to agreements with General Foods and Schlitz Breweries, which totaled over $150,000. The funds were to be channeled into employing African American labor, purchasing goods and services from African American–owned businesses, and investing in African American banking institutions. Other companies that agreed to build pacts with Jackson and Operation PUSH were Seven Up, Coca Cola, and Heublein. By 1986, under his aegis, Operation PUSH was expanded to 14 metropolitan areas including New York, Los Angeles, Memphis, and Columbus, Ohio.

Over time, Jackson's activism expanded more into the political realm. In 1972, unhappy with the slate of delegates elected to the Democratic National Convention, Jackson challenged Richard Daley on the grounds that the party reform rules had been violated. These charges were made because Jackson observed that young people, women, and African Americans were underrepresented. The outcome was that members of Jackson's group were granted delegate positions.

Jackson also dreamed of building a bridge between Africa and America. In the same year, Jackson visited Liberia, West Africa, to discuss the possibility of African American dual citizenship.

Education has been an important part of Jackson's scope. He developed a program under Operation PUSH called PUSH for Excellence, or PUSH EXCEL, which was designed in 1976 to aid in the motivation of African American students. Through PUSH EXCEL, he lobbied for the rights of each child to receive a free, quality education regardless of where the child lived.

Other organizations that were developed under the umbrella of Operation PUSH are the PUSH Commercial Division and the PUSH Minister's Division. The PUSH Commercial Division aids in developing African American businesses by making private and public sector funds available to entrepreneurs seeking domestic and foreign opportunities. The PUSH Minister's Division is an organization of ministers who understand the need for justice based on equity and righteousness.

During the 1980s the focus of Operation PUSH shifted to monitoring Affirmative Action programs in large corporations. This was an important move for the organization, as the decade of the 1980s was marred by attacks on the gains that African Americans had made. This demonstrated the flexibility of the organization and its ability to adapt to the times.

Seeks the U.S. Presidency

In 1984 Jackson did what few African Americans attempted before him. He sought the presidency of the United States of America, as did abolitionist and orator Frederick Douglass, who sought a place on the Republican ticket in 1888. In preparation for his campaign, Jackson launched voter registration drives in 1983, which took him through the southern region of the United States. He was called the first serious contender for the position, as he vied for the Democratic nomination. During his run, Jackson embodied the hopes of many African Americans, capturing 80 percent of the African American vote. In the primaries, as he ran against Walter Mondale and Geraldine Ferraro, Jackson garnered 21 percent of the total primary and caucus votes. Although he garnered 3.5 million votes, it was not enough to win the Democratic nomination.

In 1986 Jackson formed the National Rainbow Coalition to act as the political arm of Operation PUSH; it was devoted to social justice, education, mobilization, and empowerment. One way of seeking empowerment for African Americans was to support progressive politicians on the local level. Again, Jackson championed voter registration, this time registering two million new voters. In his speeches, he reminded them of their duty as Americans, but more specifically, he reminded them of their obligation as African Americans whose ancestors were brutally attacked and murdered as they sought suffrage.

During the 1980s Jackson's activism, moral strength, and eloquence aided him in gaining power. He was regarded as a highly spiritual man, who transcended denominational and religious differences, and in 1988, Jackson was again a presidential candidate. The outcome of this bid for the Democratic nomination against Massachusetts governor Michael Dukakis was more favorable for Jackson than 1984 had been. Advised by Ron Brown (who later chaired the Democratic National Committee and was appointed Secretary of Commerce), Jackson collected seven million votes—double the total of his 1984 campaign, while Dukakas collected ten million votes. Jackson's count included 12 percent of the white vote, which was three times the number of white supporters he had in 1984. In 14 primary elections, he placed first. He placed second in 36 others. That year, he served as one of the speakers at the Democratic National Convention in Atlanta. At his side were his wife Jacqueline, his daughters Jacqueline and Santita, and sons Jesse Jr., Yusef, and Jonathan.

Although many people have supported Jackson's outspokenness on issues he championed, some have not been so supportive. In 1988 a white Missouri couple was arrested while plotting to assassinate the civil rights leader.

The year 1990 ushered in wonderful successes for Jackson. He was elected to the position of shadow senator of the District of Columbia. Though some perceived this position to be largely ceremonial, holding no real power, Jackson has lobbied for statehood for the District of Columbia. Also in 1990, Jackson's persuasive abilities spurred the release of numerous hostages after the Iraqi invasion of Kuwait. The hostages held by Iraq's president, Saddam Hussein, were granted asylum after Jackson held negotiations with the leader.

In 1991 Jackson visited Hamlet, North Carolina, where 25 people had perished in a blaze at a chicken–processing plant. The plant, which was owned by Imperial Foods, was in violation of safety codes, thus causing the deaths and the 70 injuries that ensued. Addressing the Democratic National Committee in Los Angeles' Biltmore Hotel in 1991, Jackson told of the horrors he had witnessed at the facility. Jackson also spoke of the treatment of Gulf War veterans, encouraging those in attendance to rally for health care and home loans for the veterans, and education loans for veterans and their children. As usual, his speech met with resounding applause.

Jackson chose not to seek the presidency again in 1992. Instead, he directed his efforts toward voter registration. In March, with the sentiment that President George Bush had neglected urban America, Jackson challenged presidential hopefuls Bill Clinton, then governor of Arkansas, and Edmund G. Brown, former governor of California, to take a stand against the violence plaguing American cities. Together, in New Haven, Connecticut, the three men joined hands at Trinity Temple Church to begin a march in honor of the six young men murdered in New Haven during an 18–day period, paying tribute to all of the children in America slain by senseless acts of violence.

With transportation provided by the Democratic National Committee, Jackson maintained a frantic pace throughout the election year. By mid–October, Jackson had visited 27 states. To each state, Jackson brought a similar message—to take advantage of the constitutional right to vote. With stirring speeches on such topics as the North American Free Trade Agreement (NAFTA), Jackson captivated audiences in Western states. Jackson marched with supporters to voting booths set up in Colorado, one of the two states where the general election spans a period of a few weeks.

In 1996 PUSH celebrated its twenty–fifth year of service with a Sterling Anniversary Convention in Chicago. The theme, "Opening New Doors," was echoed throughout the three–day gathering. Present at the event, among others, were Roland Burris, former Illinois attorney general, Willie Barrow, minister and chairman of the board of Operation PUSH, publisher John H. Johnson, communications mogul Thomas Burrell, and Ingrid Saunders Jones, chair of the Coca–Cola Foundation and vice–president of corporate external affairs for the Coca–Cola Company. It was here that Jackson announced the merger of Operation PUSH and the National Rainbow Coalition to form the Rainbow PUSH Action Network.

Although Operation PUSH has maintained a focus on economic development, the National Rainbow Coalition has focused on political action and racial parity. Through the newly merged organizations, Jackson intends to take advantage of potential economic growth in the Pacific Rim. Recognizing a great imbalance in the number of African American–owned import businesses, Jackson is dedicated to expanding opportunities for advancement, especially by establishing chapters of the Rainbow PUSH Action Network abroad in countries like China, Indonesia, and Japan.

Jackson has maintained a hectic pace while writing a syndicated newspaper column, hosting a round table discussion group airing on cable television, publishing books, and negotiating with countries and corporations alike. President Bill Clinton recognized his importance in international affairs and in October 1997 appointed him as special envoy for the promotion of democracy in Africa.

Part of Jackson's ability to persuade the masses is rooted in his firsthand knowledge of problems that continue to plague a large portion of the underclass—discrimination, poverty, and single parenthood. Descended from an illiterate grandmother, he understands what it is like to become a first–generation success. Jackson compellingly arouses moral passion in both Americans and supporters abroad.

REFERENCES

"At Edge of Campaign, Jackson Labors on the Democratic Victory." *New York Times,* October 20, 1992.

The Ebony Success Library. 2 vols. Nashville: Southwestern Company, 1973.

Frady, Marshall. *Jesse: The Life and Pilgrimage of Jesse Jackson.* New York: Random House, 1996.

Hughes, Langston, Milton Meltzer, and C. Eric Lincoln. *A Pictorial History of Black Americans.* 5th rev. ed. New York: Crown Publishers, 1967.

"The 1992 Campaign; Jackson Leads Candidates in Protest Rally." *New York Times,* March 23, 1992.

"The 1992 Campaign: Jesse Jackson; on Sidelines of the Presidential Race, Jackson Turns to Local Campaigns." *New York Times,* July 26, 1992.

"PUSH Celebrates 25th Anniversary." *Ebony* 52 (December 1996): 46–50.

"Rev. Jesse Jackson is Sworn In As Clinton's Special Envoy to Africa." *Jet* 92 (27 October 1997): 4.

Salley, Columbus. *The Black 100: A Ranking of the Most Influential African–Americans, Past and Present.* New York: Citadel Press, 1993.

Wexler, Sanford. *An Eyewitness History: The Civil Rights Movement.* New York: Facts on File, 1993.

Nicole L. Bailey Williams

Maynard H. Jackson
(1938–)
Lawyer, mayor, entrepreneur

An historic first in southern politics took place on January 7, 1974, when a young black man became mayor of a city in the deep South. A top–notch attorney, Maynard Jackson turned Atlanta into a financial center and distribution hub by expanding international convention facilities, constructing the world's largest airport, and reducing crime. When he left office after his first two terms, Atlanta was listed in the *Places Rated Almanac 1981* as the best major city in which to live and work. While his insistence on Affirmative Action angered many whites, he sought to ease racial tensions by reminding people of the 1960s slogan that proclaimed Atlanta as a city too busy to hate.

Maynard Holbrook Jackson Jr. was born in Dallas, Texas, on March 23, 1938. He was the third of six children,

Maynard H. Jackson

two boys and four girls, born to Maynard Jackson Sr., a Baptist minister, and Irene Dobbs Jackson, a college professor. Jackson's paternal great–great grandfather, Andrew Jackson, was a slave who bought his own freedom and founded the Wheat Street Baptist Church in Atlanta, Georgia. His maternal grandfather was John Wesley Dobbs, a well–known Republican and Freemason who founded the Georgia Voters League. Jackson's maternal aunt is the noted soprano Mattiwilda Dobbs. Jackson's father was the first black candidate to run for the local board of education in Texas. His mother earned a doctorate in French from the University of Toulouse in France.

When Jackson was seven years old, his family moved to Georgia. His father became the minister of Friendship Baptist Church, and Jackson enrolled in Atlanta's segregated schools. At David T. Howard High School, Jackson was friends with Vernon Jordan, who would become director of the National Urban League. Jackson played football and ran track. He was an excellent student who at 14 completed the tenth grade and won a Ford Foundation Early Admissions Scholarship to Morehouse College. He also received the Glancy Fellowship which helped cover his fees.

At Morehouse Jackson majored in political science and history. He continued to play sports, and during the summers he worked at a variety of jobs including waiter, bartender, and one summer he went to Connecticut to pick tobacco. He graduated from Morehouse College in May 1956 with a bachelor of arts degree. At 18 Jackson did not know what to do with himself. His parents offered but two choices, either he would go to school or to work. Jackson chose the latter.

Jackson's first job was as a claims examiner for the Ohio State Bureau of Unemployment Compensation in Cleveland. He left this position in 1958 to work for the P. F. Collier Company selling encyclopedias. The job required frequent moves. In three years he lived in Boston, Cleveland, and Buffalo. According to *Current Biography,* Jackson was once described by a television news commentator as a man with a "toothpaste grin that can light up a room." Apparently his smile and good looks—Jackson is six feet three inches tall, light brown in complexion, with black hair and green eyes—helped him to work his way up to assistant district sales manager, earning $30,000 a year.

Working helped Jackson grow and clarify his goals. In 1961 he entered North Carolina Central University Law School. While Jackson was a student there the New York Bar Association named him one of the outstanding debaters in the United States. Jackson received his J.D. degree and graduated cum laude in June 1964. Moving back to Atlanta, he passed the Georgia bar in 1965. Jackson accepted a position as general attorney with the National Labor Relations Board. He also joined the Emory Community Legal Services Center in Atlanta, where he provided free legal assistance to needy clients.

A Summons to Action

While he was still in law school, Jackson married Burnella "Bunnie" Hayes Burke. The couple's first child, Brooke, was born April 8, 1968, the day of Martin Luther King Jr.'s funeral. It was a cathartic moment for Jackson. When he first learned of King's assassination, he was driving home from work. He arrived home to find his entire family in tears. Jackson recalled in the April 1988 *Ebony* that "there was a great shared fear, a gut–wrenching fear. It was not related to any fear for our own well–being, but just a fear for the future." Jackson felt that King's death was a summons to action. For three days he wrestled with his grief over King's death and with the issue of how best to act. He concluded in the same source "that politics, though imperfect, was the best available nonviolent means of changing how we live." Jackson believed that had King lived, he would have moved inevitably toward political involvement and economic development.

On the day of King's funeral and with the birth of his first child, Jackson made the decision to go into politics. Still he took no action. Then on June 5, 1968, Bobby Kennedy was shot; memories of King's death rushed back reminding him of his commitment. Jackson quit his job and borrowed $3,000 to run for the United Stated Senate against incumbent Herman Talmadge.

Although Jackson lost the race for senator, he made an impressive showing, proving to himself and others that Georgia was ready for a black politician. In his campaign for vice–mayor in 1969, Jackson made a concerted effort to win the black community. He visited three or four black churches every Sunday. On October 7, 1969, election day, Jackson busses took voters to the polls. His hard campaigning paid off when he won one third of the white vote and 99 percent of the black vote. Jackson unseated his opponent, Milton Farris, a white businessman who had served on the Board of Aldermen for 15 years.

Sworn in on January 5, 1970, as the first black vice–mayor of Atlanta, Jackson was also president of the Board of Aldermen. He and two of his colleagues formed Jackson, Patterson, and Parks, the city's first black law firm, of which Jackson was a senior partner.

Jackson began campaigning for mayor long before he announced his candidacy on March 28, 1973. Running against him were 11 other hopefuls, including Sam Massell, the incumbent and the city's first Jewish mayor. Jackson won 46.6 percent of the votes and Massell 19.8 percent.

In the runoff campaign, Jackson stressed that race was not an issue. He told the electorate that he intended to serve all of the people of the city of Atlanta. Massell, on the other hand, deliberately made race an issue. Quoted in the *New York Times,* he said, "I'm very definitely addressing myself to the fears of the white community. Maynard Jackson scares white people, not because he is a black man, but because he's the racist in this campaign."

Massell's two weeks of racially divisive campaigning backfired. He lost the election to Jackson who won 59.1 percent of the votes. Maynard Jackson was the youngest mayor in the history of the city and the first black mayor in a major Southern city as well as the first black mayor of a capital city. In his victory speech, Jackson was grandly eloquent, a style that was to become his trademark. Quoted in the *New York Times,* he told an enthusiastic crowd, "We have risen from the ashes of a bitter campaign to build a better life for all Atlantans."

In his first term as mayor, Jackson faced a formidable task. Shifting the balance of power from whites to a balance representing all of Atlanta's citizens was difficult. Jackson, however, was aggressive in his position as mayor. In May of 1974, when Jackson tried to fire Police Chief John Inman, Inman went to court challenging the mayor's authority. In the end Inman lost his job as chief. Still another problem arose when Jackson appointed A. Reginald Eaves to the office of Public Safety Commissioner. Eaves had been accused of using his political influence inappropriately. When he recruited blacks for the police department critics called it reverse racism. Jackson refused to fire Eaves. In 1976 statistics showed that crime was significantly decreasing, forcing some people to concede that Jackson had acted appropriately.

The threat of unsolved crimes, however, almost jeopardized Jackson's outstanding achievements as mayor. Near the end of his second term, Atlanta became the focus of nation–wide attention due to the serial murders of black children. The unsolved murders caused widespread alarm. The Federal Bureau of Investigation became involved, and Jackson imposed curfews and sponsored benefits to help the victims' families. In 1981 Wayne B. Williams was captured and convicted of the crimes, enabling Jackson's record in crime reduction to survive.

The Politics of Inclusion

Jackson's first two years in office can accurately be described as a period of inclusion for black people who had historically been excluded. He aggressively confronted the issue of racial inequality. The building of Hartsfield International Airport offers the best example of his "politics of inclusion," because he insisted that blacks get at least 25 percent of the action, or there would be no airport. He refused to back down. Jackson recalled in the December 1980 *Ebony* that he was subjected to "severe and continuous castigation, vilification and condemnation" for his stance. He insisted that minority participation was a criteria for going forward with the massive plan to construct the world's largest airport, and also said in the *Ebony* article, "the word minority should not mean women. Women are an oppressed group, but they are not a minority; they are over 51 percent of the population." Jackson stated explicitly that minority could not include white women, and he insisted that by minority he meant the inclusion of African Americans.

Jackson often was called a Don Quixote chasing the illusion of equality, justice, and fairness. In the name of all three, he ignored the charges that including blacks would cost more and slow down production. At the mayor's insistence 71 of the 200 firms hired to construct the facility were black. A workforce of 1800 consisted of at least 800 blacks. For the airport's $450,000 art collection, 50 percent were by black artists. Blacks own a number of concession stands and other airport businesses. The airport opened on time and within budget, giving the final shock to Jackson's critics.

Unable to seek a third consecutive term, Jackson returned to work as an attorney and was the Atlanta partner with Chapman and Cutler, a Chicago–based firm. He decided to run for office again in 1989. This was an all–black race, including Jackson, Michael Lomax, and Hosea Williams. Lomax dropped out early in the campaign, and Jackson won the election with a four–to–one majority over Williams.

The Second Time Around

Jackson found that the issues had grown to include ones he had not faced during his first two terms in office. The AIDS crisis, homelessness, rising crime, and lack of federal funds were among the many problems he faced as mayor. Aware of the many pressing social issues, Jackson focused his efforts on creating a healthy business climate to stimulate the economy and improve the conditions of the poor. In 1994 Atlanta hosted the football Super Bowl, and Jackson played a crucial role in helping to bring the 1996 Olympics to his city. For the first time in the history of the games, many jobs and profits went to black companies, black workers, and black institutions of higher education. More than 30 percent of all Olympic–related ventures were awarded to African Americans.

In 1994 Jackson's term ended, and he declined to run again. While it was rumored that Jackson would run for national office, it is unlikely. In 1992 Jackson was hospitalized to undergo multiple bypass heart surgery. He served as consultant for the Summer Olympics in 1996 and is now president and CEO at Jackson Securities.

Jackson was named by *Time* magazine as one of 200 Young American Leaders in 1975, and as one of 100 most successful blacks by *Ebony* in 1976. He is a member of the following organizations: the National Conference of Christians and Jews, National Organization of Women, National Welfare Rights Organization, NAACP, Urban League, National Gun Control Center, and a member of Alpha Phi Alpha Fraternity. He has received honorary degrees from Morehouse College, North Carolina Central University, and Delaware State College.

Having divorced "Bunnie" Burke in 1976, Jackson married Valerie Richardson on October 7, 1977. They have four children and live in the Cascade Heights area of southwest Atlanta. He has been a successful politician who set new heights both for the South and for blacks and a major force in the economic development of Atlanta.

Current address: Jackson Securities, Inc., 100 Peachtree Street NW, Suite 2250, Atlanta, GA 30303.

REFERENCES

Anderson, Kristine F. "Atlanta's Jackson Back In Familiar Mayor Role." *Christian Science Monitor,* September 12, 1991.

Berry, Bill. "The Airport that Maynard Built." *Ebony* 36 (December 1980): 52–58.

Boyer, Richard, and David Savageau. *Places Rated Almanac (1981): Your Guide to Finding the Best Places to Live in America.* Chicago: Rand McNally, 1981.

Chappell, Kevin. "The 3 Mayors Who Made it Happen." *Ebony* 51 (July 1996): 66–72.

Contemporary Black Biography. Vol. 2. Detroit: Gale Research, 1993.

Current Biography 1976. New York: H. W. Wilson Co., 1976.

"Maynard Jackson Wins in Atlanta." *New York Times,* October 5, 1989.

Turner, Renee D. "The Day King Died." *Ebony* 43 (April 1988): 133–138.

Nagueyalti Warren

Michael Jackson

(1958–)

Entertainer, humanitarian

Michael Jackson, often referred to as the most electrifying entertainer of the twentieth century, is a charismatic performer who composes many of his songs and choreographs most of his dances. His phenomenal album and video sales and personal appearance attendance figures have led to great wealth, and his humanistic interests have earned widespread admiration. Jackson's offstage life remains beset by eccentricities and personal insecurities that began at an early age, when his childhood was usurped almost completely by his astounding music career.

Michael Jackson was born on August 29, 1958, in Gary, Indiana, to Joseph and Katherine Jackson. Katherine Jackson, an adept musician who plays the clarinet and piano, was a wife and homemaker until she and Joe divorced in 1982. The children were Maureen, Sigmund "Jackie," Tariano "Tito," Jermaine, LaToya, twins Marlon and Brandon (Brandon lived less than twenty–four hours), Michael, Janet, and Stephen Randall "Randy."

Joe Jackson, former drummer and guitarist in a group that specialized in blues, guided the development of his children's talents through the early years and built the foundation for their future triumphs as musicians. Joe Jackson's vision of his sons' potential made him demand that they devote a large portion of their waking moments to music. He installed microphones in the home and held long hours of rehearsals, leaving no time for activities outside of class time and homework. Jackson's father often resorted to strict discipline and severe beatings, which eventually caused young Jackson to resist and later become withdrawn. Nevertheless, after three years of training, Joe Jackson allowed the brothers, Jackie, Tito, Jermaine, Marlon, and Michael, to appear in public as "The Jackson Five." Five–year–old Michael was the star soloist and dancer, executing routines patterned after James Brown and Sammy Davis Jr.

The Jackson Five won their first local talent show at Roosevelt High School in Gary and other competitions in rapid succession. Before long, Jackson developed a never–resolved conflict between a love for music, and the unrelenting pressure to strive towards perfection that would haunt him throughout adulthood.

Rise of the Jackson Five

The first big break for the Jackson Five came in 1968 when they appeared in an amateur night competition in Harlem's Apollo Theater, the coveted springboard for African American artists. Their highly successful concert caught the attention of Suzanne dePasse of Motown, the influential black–owned record company, and its president, Berry Gordy. Motown arranged to move Joe Jackson and his sons to Los Angeles in November of 1969, to establish residence in that entertainment center. When the boys joined Motown, they followed in the footsteps of Diana Ross and the Supremes, Stevie Wonder, Gladys Knight and the Pips, and other African American singing stars. Gordy took a personal interest in the young boys and hired a consultant to teach them the social graces of correct dress, proper speech, polite conversation, and gentlemanly table manners.

In 1969 the brothers made their debut Motown album, *Diana Ross Presents the Jackson Five,* which included the hit single, "I Want You Back." Before the end of 1971, they had

Michael Jackson

three more singles that sold over a million copies and were on the top of the pop charts: "ABC," "The Love You Save," and "I'll Be There." At age eleven, Michael Jackson's professional career and his public image were making strides, but he was still a lonely boy yearning for the companionship of his contemporaries.

The Jackson Five's national television debut in 1969 was in a Miss Black America beauty extravaganza, but their appearance on the highly rated *Ed Sullivan Show* shortly afterwards extended their audience to the entire country. Jackson and his brothers received invitations from other weekly programs whose fans were both young and old. Johnny Carson chatted with them on the *Tonight Show,* and so did Dick Clark on *American Bandstand.* They were welcomed on Don Cornelius's *Soul Train* and joined Diana Ross and the Supremes on *Hollywood Palace.*

Their rapidly growing popularity was reflected by the emerging interest of the media as their faces graced the covers of *Look, Life, Newsweek, Saturday Evening Post, New York Times Magazine,* and *Rolling Stone.* Motown protected their youthful clients from sensationalism and encouraged a portrayal of Michael Jackson as the lovable baby of the group with a charming personality, skill with the sketching pad, and a love of books. With an astounding rise in popularity, the Jackson Five concerts drew audiences of as many as 115,000 enthusiastic cheerers. They soon drew tons of fan mail, gifts to their door, and crowds wherever they went. Joe Jackson sought to safeguard his family from the public glare by purchasing a guarded estate in the San Fernando Valley, within reach of Los Angeles and Hollywood.

The brothers' first television special, *Goin' Back to Indiana,* was aired in 1971, with Bill Cosby, Diana Ross, Tommy Smothers, and Bobby Darin as supporting artists. An animated cartoon series with characters based on the Jackson brothers was released soon afterwards. In 1972, while still singing with the Jackson Five, Michael Jackson stepped out alone for the first time, with a solo album, *Got to Be There,* and a single record, "Ben." Three of the songs from *Got to Be There* were listed among the top–ten list of that year. Wanting more control over the direction of their careers and more artistic freedom, the Jackson Five severed ties with Motown and signed with Epic Records in 1974. With a new name, the Jacksons, they gave concerts, recorded together, and starred in a CBS television show during the summer of 1976. Eventually Michael Jackson would sever ties with his brothers and embark on a solo career.

Begins Career as Solo Entertainer

Michael Jackson began his solo career not by singing but by acting. He played the scarecrow in the 1977 movie *The Wiz.* The film was a critical and box office failure, but Jackson's performance did receive some praise. When he reached twenty–one, he cut all business connections with his father, and with a keen eye for business, assumed total responsibility for his career. His first major step was to join composer and producer Quincy Jones in a productive collaboration that pooled their expertise to create musical offerings of superior quality for years to come. Their first dual venture was the album *Off the Wall,* with sales topping the seven million mark at home and abroad.

In 1982, the Jones and Jackson collaboration produced a phenomenal second album, *Thriller,* that catapulted Jackson to superstar status. *Thriller* sold over 40 million copies and became the highest–selling album in history. *Thriller* presented Jackson as a coy sex symbol and demonstrated his talented dancing skills. He electrified the 50 million viewers of the 1983 *Motown 25* television special by singing and dancing to one of the album's songs, "Billie Jean," while wearing a black fedora, one white glove, and pants that ended above his ankles. The moonwalk was born and forever became his trademark, along with his one sequined glove. The distinctive attire was as much a topic of discussion as the melody, the lyrics, and the choreography.

Having established his reputation as an entertainer independent of his brothers, Jackson continued to compose, record, sell albums, and appear before live and television audiences of increasing sizes. However, as his success continued, so did his feelings of isolation. He rarely went out socially. His music and the microphone became his life. His immense wealth afforded him a fairy–tale sanctuary called Neverland, which is known for its child–like attractions that encourage Jackson to relive a childhood lost during his early rise to fame.

The first floor of Neverland reflects his love of art, literature, and music, with paintings, books, and a piano. The second and third floors are furnished for the pleasure of children, with toys, games, miniature trains, and room for slumber parties. Outside is an amusement park with rides, lakes, boats, and gardens to delight the terminally ill children who come to enjoy the beauty through the Make a Wish Foundation. The busy entertainer spends time whenever possible with each child, enjoying the pleasures of childhood he never experienced. Jackson's love of animals is apparent in the zoo that occupies a large portion of his 2,700–acre estate. His personal favorites are monkeys, chimpanzees, and snakes. Bubbles, his pet chimp, and Muscles, the boa constrictor, often travel with him.

Jackson has made numerous philanthropic gifts to educational and humanitarian organizations. Nearly 100 scholarships have been awarded through the fund, which was set up from his gifts to the United Negro College Fund. He used the $1,500,000 settlement from the Pepsi corporation for burns he suffered making an elaborate commercial for the company to establish the Michael Jackson Burn Center. He embarked upon a 15–country tour of Europe, Africa, Asia, and Australia, with proceeds designated for his Heal the World Foundation, a charity for children. Neverland hosted an art auction sponsored by the South African Council of Churches in its fight against apartheid. In 1985, at a time of widespread starvation in Ethiopia and the Sudan, Michael Jackson joined Lionel Ritchie to compose the heart–stirring song, "We Are the World." With the assistance of Quincy Jones, they arranged for famous pop artists to make a video that netted millions of dollars for relief in those African countries.

Fisk University presented an honorary doctorate of humane letters to Jackson, and he has been honored by Tuskegee University, the NAACP, and the Urban League. For his musical contributions, Jackson has earned numerous Grammy awards, with eight conferred in the 1984 ceremonies, including a special Award of Merit.

Aside from his musical ability, Jackson has shown his business acumen by purchasing the Sly Stone catalogue and securing, for the sum of $47.5 million, copyrights to the Beatles' songs. In return, he collects royalties each time a song composed by these artists is used for films, airplay, live performances, commercials, and stage productions.

Jackson and his brothers undertook a "Victory Tour," a symbolic final appearance together with fifty–five shows scattered over a broad section of the country, for five months from July to December of 1984. Discouraged by initial misgivings related to business and personal problems and staging difficulties, Jackson was not pleased with his personal performance but was greatly gratified by the audience response.

In answer to questions about the difference in his youthful facial features and his unique appearance, Jackson admitted to rhinoplasty and further cosmetic surgery to add a dimple to his chin. He explained the lightening of his complexion, however, to a skin pigmentation disorder called vitiligo, for which he has sought medical treatment.

There have been special points of happiness in Jackson's life as well as times that undermined his contentment. The high points offstage come from his assistance to children and institutions of higher education, and from the warm reception and honors he received throughout the African continent. A low point in family relations required all of his diplomatic abilities to steer clear of involvement in the suit filed in 1990 by his mother against sister LaToya, seeking to reclaim her 25 percent interest in the family's Encino mansion. The sharpest challenge to his serenity came in 1993 in the form of accusations of child molestation. In the face of unconvincing proof of guilt, he chose a financial settlement instead of a costly, time–consuming court battle.

A few months after the settlement, the media announced the secret marriage of Jackson and Lisa Marie Presley, daughter of singer Elvis Presley. The marriage, seen by much of the public as a possible distraction from the still–fresh court publicity, took place on May 26, 1994, in the Dominican Republic. Jackson's hopes that this would be the start of a life of tranquility were shattered when Lisa Marie filed for divorce in January of 1996. In November of the same year, Jackson married Debbie Rowe, his plastic surgeon's nurse, in Sydney, Australia. Debbie Jackson gave birth to their son, Prince Michael Jackson, in Cedars–Sinai Medical Center in Los Angeles on February 12, 1997.

Jackson's influence has been felt internationally because of his talent and ingenuity as an entertainer, and because his interests spread into subjects having to do with children, education, and peace and justice for all people. Rather than adhere to current trends, he creates his own physical presentations that fit his unique personality and the style of his music. He has been called "The King of Pop" because of his enormous record sales and concert sell–outs. He helped put music television (MTV) on the map with his heavily choreographed and elaborate videos. Many young stars in the music industry are indebted to Jackson, for he is a true fashion, music, and video pioneer.

Current address: c/o Sandy Gallin, Gallin–Morey–Addis, 8730 Sunset Blvd., Penthouse W, Los Angeles, CA 90069.

REFERENCES

"Citing Irreconcilable Differences, Lisa Marie Presley Files for Divorce from Michael Jackson." *Jet* 89 (February 5, 1996): 62.

Jackson, Michael. *Moonwalk.* New York: Doubleday, 1988.

Johnson, Robert E. "Eyewitness Report on Michael Jackson's Tour Inside Africa." *Jet* 81 (March 16, 1992): 10.

———. "A New and Revealing Look at Michael Jackson. *Ebony* 43 (June 1988): 176–82.

Nicholson, Lois P. *Michael Jackson.* New York: Chelsea House, 1994.

"Report: Baby Boy for Jackson." *Oakland Tribune,* February 13, 1997.

Taraborrelli, J. Randy. *Michael Jackson: The Magic and the Madness.* New York: Birch Lane Press, 1991.

Dona L. Irvin

John E. Jacob
(1934–)
Organization and corporate executive

For over 30 years John Jacob has been in high profile positions that gave him visibility, enabled him to direct activities that enhanced the black race, and made him a role model for young black men. As head of the National Urban League, his activities included negotiating agreements with corporate and foundation leaders that provided important benefits for blacks. Now as vice–president and chief communications officer of Anheuser–Busch Companies, he works with senior managers, the board of directors, and a 15–member policy committee, he promotes the company's products, primarily beer, in a manner that balances the health concerns and alcohol consumption risks of minority communities with the needs of Anheuser–Busch.

John Edward Jacob was born on December 16, 1934, in Trout, Louisiana, to Emory and Claudia Sadler Jacob and grew up in Houston, Texas. His father was a Baptist minister who supplemented his income as a carpenter and construction worker. The family, including Jacob's four brothers, was poor in material possessions but adhered to strict moral standards and codes of conduct. Jacob received an E. E. Worthing scholarship that enabled him to attend Howard University in Washington, D.C., and graduate in 1957 with a bachelor's degree in economics. After serving in the U.S. Army and rising to the rank of second lieutenant, Jacob returned to the nation's capitol to work as a postal service clerk and pursue graduate studies. Jacob was frustrated because his abilities to rise were thwarted by his race. In *Contemporary Black Biography* he is quoted as saying: "I hated the work, I went to work mad, I came home mad." He improved himself by continuing his education and in 1963 earned a master of social work degree from Howard. He was already working in the Baltimore Department of Public Welfare as a public assistance caseworker and was promoted to the position of child welfare supervisor.

In 1965 Jacob began what would be a 29–year career with the Urban League, one of America's premier civil rights organizations. Jacob's first position was with the Washington, D.C., Urban League as director of education and youth incentives. Within five years he had moved up the ranks as Northern Virginia branch office director, associate executive director, and director of the social work field work student unit. During the 1967 summer riots, Jacob's organizational skills came to the fore because of his management of the branch's Project Alert. This was a program that enabled inner city youth to assume leadership positions as contact people for neighborhood residents who needed assistance from the branch and social service agencies equipped to deal with tensions arising from the riots. The Washington branch served as a model by participating in development programs under Jacob's leadership. He gained recognition for his expertise in forging alliances with government and private agencies such

John E. Jacob

as the Ford Foundation. In 1970 Jacob relocated to San Diego to serve as executive director of that city's Urban League and in 1975 returned to Washington for a four–year stint as president of the local branch. In 1979 he was appointed executive vice–president of the National Urban League. In 1980 Vernon Jordan, the National Urban League's chief executive officer, was the victim of an assassination attempt, and Jacob served in his stead while Jordan recuperated. When Jordan retired and ended his ten–year tenure in 1982, Jacob succeeded him as national president.

Transfer of Leadership

Jacob's leadership style was markedly different from Jordan's for reasons other than just their personalities. Jordan was a lawyer who focused on negotiations with persons. While openly repudiating the Nixon administration's racial policies, Jordan still forged lasting personal and professional relationships in the White House that immediately benefited the league's programs and later benefited his own future goals.

Jacob faced the challenge of having to fill Jordan's shoes on January 1, 1982. His inaugural speech included his topmost goal, as quoted in the *Negro Almanac*: "This is my goal as I assume this important post: to make a difference." Early on, Jacob began to increase the league's visibility by criticizing the Reagan administration's budget cuts, holding a firm line against blacks willing to compromise in the battle for racial gains, and updating and upgrading league interests. One of the most pragmatic programs devised by Jacob was the

1985 Male Responsibility Campaign, one that stressed responsible sexual behavior by black teenage males. Another community involvement effort initiated to refocus on black survival values and create a black cultural and historical base was the Crime is Not a Part of Our Black Heritage program. In this same vein, the league also initiated a Stop the Violence campaign as a means of combating black–on–black crime. The funding for all such program effort was derived from a source that was distinctly a Jacob creation. He is credited with establishing the National Urban League's Permanent Development Fund that has been worth as much as $15 million and, at the time of his retirement, was worth at least $8 million. One education initiative that evolved from the fund was a partnership with Merrill–Lynch that deposits $2,000 annually for 12 years into individual bank accounts for 250 minority youth who will be graduates in the year 2000.

Jacob emphasized private sector funding for entry–level job training programs, federal government subsidized public works and job training programs, league–financed monetary support to the poor regardless of race, and support of economic boycotts. During the Bush Administration, Jacob proposed an urban Marshall Plan with the nation's military budget to be cut and $50 million transferred to fund minority training programs. After Bush vetoed the Civil Rights Act of 1990, Jacob's affirmative action efforts were thwarted by leaders who favored self–reliance efforts. Jacob, too, stressed self–reliance and self–help programs in neighborhood and community programs but he understood that federal assistance would always be needed to fund training programs for minorities and the poor of any race.

One of Jacob's greatest strengths has been his skill at networking and forging alliances. He regularly scheduled annual gatherings with corporate and foundation leaders whose advice and feedback enabled him to think more creatively in planning league programs and fund raising ventures. Earl Graves, *Black Enterprise* chief executive officer, and Virgis Colbert, senior vice–president of plant operations for Miller Brewing Company, have long been advisors whose input, along with that of other influential leaders, enabled Jacob to negotiate agreements beneficial to black communities. One such effort resulted in a $1.3 million donation to Los Angeles for job programs and other aid following the 1992 riots.

As with other organizational leaders, Jacob failed to realize all his goals. Matthew Scott quoted him in *Black Enterprise* as saying:

> As great as I think efforts in education have been, we simply have too many efforts going. . . . If we decide which one piece of this problem we want to take on, we could have a national impact far greater than the individual community impacts that we have had.

A New Challenge

As executive vice–president and chief communications officer of Anheuser–Busch Companies, since 1994, Jacob directs the company's communication activities with a decided focus on community, industry, and public concerns. As the author of a syndicated weekly newspaper column, "To Be Equal," he also enjoys exposure in over 600 newspapers.

Jacob's skills are tested by the seemingly dichotomous goal of the company's need to increase domestic beer sales to minority consumers while resisting aggressive advertising specifically targeted in low income and black and Hispanic communities, where alcohol consumption is known to contribute to disproportionately higher rates of alcohol–related health problems. On the one hand, Jacob fights against disclosure of alcohol content as one of the company's most potent malt liquor products accounts for nearly five percent of total sales. On the other, he stresses moderation in drinking. (Anheuser–Busch is also a leading maker of non–alcohol brews with a nearly 50 percent share of this market.) Jacob focuses too on publicizing the company's vast network of non–alcohol related subsidiaries, especially the family–oriented Busch Entertainment sector, which manages the Busch Gardens Sea World and Cypress Gardens theme parks.

A Life of Service

In 1986 Jacob was arrested for leading a demonstration of some 1,500 anti–apartheid supporters at the South African embassy. Less active and safer activities have been corporate board memberships with such groups as the Local Initiatives Support Corporation, A Better Chance, New York Hospital, National Advertising Review, D.C. Legal Aid Society, and Howard University, where he has served as chair of the board. Jacob has also served as a member of the D.C. Manpower Service's Planning Advisory Council and of the Judicial Nominating Commission for the U.S. District Court, and the U.S. Circuit Court of the District of Columbia. He is a life member of Kappa Alpha Psi Fraternity (1954). He has served as director of the National Conference of Christians and Jews (1983–88), member of the Rockefeller University Council (1983–88), corporate director of the New York Telephone Company (1983), the Continental Corporation (since 1985), and Coca–Cola Enterprises (since 1986).

Jacob has received numerous awards and honors, including the Whitney M. Young Award, Washington Urban League (1979); Attorney Hudson L. Lavell Social Action Award, Phi Beta Sigma Fraternity (1982); Achievement Award, Zeta Phi Beta Sorority (1984); National Kappaman Achievement, Durham Alumni Chapter of Kappa Alpha Psi (1984); Presidential Scroll, St. Augustine College (1987); and United Way of America's National Professional Leadership Award (1989). He has also received honorary degrees from Old Dominion University (1983), Fisk University (1984), Lafayette College (1985), and in 1986 from Tuskegee and Central State universities. In addition to his stint in the army, Jacob served in the U.S. Army Reserve with the rank of captain (1957–65). He was awarded the Airborne Parachutist Badge in 1958.

Jacob has been married to Barbara Singleton Jacob, an accountant, since 1959 and is the father of a daughter, Sheryl Renee. He is also a registered Democrat and an Episcopalian.

His view of America in the future was cited in *Contemporary Black Biography:*

> America has only one hope of entering the 21st century as a world power and a global economic force. That is its ability to achieve racial parity and to make full use of the African Americans and minorities it has so long rejected.

Jacob is a worthy role model for minorities as well as all Americans who strive to rise on their merits, not their race and color.

Current address: Executive Vice–President, Anheuser–Busch Companies, Inc., One Bush Place, St. Louis, MO 63118.

REFERENCES

''Anheuser–Busch Names New Executive Vice President.'' *New York Voice/Harlem USA,* June 22, 1994.

Contemporary Black Biography. Vol. 2. Detroit: Gale Research, 1992.

Devarics, Charles. ''Washington Update.'' *Black Issues in Higher Education* 10 (10 February 1994): 12.

Franklin, John Hope, and Alfred A. Moss Jr. *From Slavery to Freedom.* 7th ed. New York: McGraw–Hill, 1994.

Garth, William. ''Bill's Business.'' (John E. Jacob Named VP & COO at Anheuser–Busch Companies, Inc.) *Chicago Weekend* 37 (19 June 1994): 1.

Graves, Earl G. ''Where the Action Is.'' *Black Enterprise* 25 (30 September 1994): 9.

Negro Almanac. 5th ed. Detroit: Gale Research, 1989.

''New Urban League Leadership to Take the Helm.'' *Washington Informer,* May 25, 1994.

Scott, Matthew S. ''Climbing Jacob's New Ladder.'' *Black Enterprise* 25 (September 30, 1994): 128.

''Top Black Corporate Directors.'' *Ebony* 52 (January 1997): 38–48.

Who's Who among African Americans, 1996–97. 9th ed. Detroit: Gale Research, 1996.

Dolores Nicholson

Daniel ''Chappie'' James Jr.

(1920–1978)

Military officer

Daniel ''Chappie'' James Jr., also known as the ''Black Eagle,'' was one of the original Tuskegee Airmen. He later distinguished himself as an outstanding pilot and leader who became the first black in history to be promoted to the rank of four–star general. He was also commander–in–chief of the North American Air Defense Command (NORAD) and Aerospace Defense Command. In these positions James was responsible for safeguarding all of North America against enemy combat and missile attacks.

Daniel James Jr. was born on February 11, 1920, in Pensacola, Florida, to Daniel James Sr. and Lillie A. Brown James. He was the youngest of seventeen children. James's father was a lamplighter and later a gas plant worker. His mother, who placed a high value on education, started a school of her own to give her children and others a good start in life. From her James learned to strive for success and regard education as a means of getting ahead. After he left his mother's school he attended Washington High School, from which he graduated in 1937.

James then enrolled at Tuskegee Institute (now University), in Alabama. There he excelled as an athlete and a campus leader, picking up the nickname ''Little Chappie'' along the way. In 1942, during his senior year, he was expelled from Tuskegee for fighting. Twenty–seven years later, in 1969, he actually graduated from the school.

Completes Pilot Training at Tuskegee

With World War II raging in Europe and the Far East, James began training to become a pilot while he was still a student at Tuskegee under the auspices of the government–sponsored Civilian Pilot Training Program (CPTP). As a result of Public Law 18, which was passed in April 1939, the CPTP had been established in six black institutions of higher learning: Howard University, Hampton Institute, North Carolina Agricultural and Technical College, Delaware State College, West Virginia State College, and Tuskegee Institute. James, a commander pilot, thus began his career as one of the famed Tuskegee Airmen, as men in the black air force unit were called. He remained at Tuskegee from March 1942 until January 1943, graduating number one in his class.

Commissioned a second lieutenant in the Army Air Force, James was assigned to the 477th Bombardment Group, a newly created black unit stationed at Selfridge Field near Detroit, Michigan. Although he and his fellow black cadets had trained as combat pilots, they were not given an equal opportunity to fly on account of the racist attitudes that permeated society and the military during the 1940s. James and his unit never made it overseas despite the fact that some men had received extensive aerial instruction in Europe.

After World War II ended in 1945, James remained in the service, determined to fulfill his dream of becoming a general. In 1948 President Harry S. Truman ordered the end of segregation in the United States armed forces. The following year, James reported for duty with a fighter group stationed at Clark Air Force Base in the Philippines, where his arrival was met with much dismay and racism. James was determined not to allow people's attitudes to discourage him from pursuing his goals, however. As quoted by Neil Super in his biography

Daniel ''Chappie'' James Jr.

Daniel ''Chappie'' James, he said: ''I came to compete on an equal basis, and if they were going to try to hinder me with racism, I was going to overcome it through the power of excellence that my mother had taught me.''

In 1950 James was involved in a serious crash that occurred just after takeoff. Flying in a two–seater T–33, he and a fellow pilot experienced a flameout at an altitude of 50 feet, and the pilot was knocked unconscious. James was able to rescue himself and the other pilot before the plane was consumed by fire, but he received severe burns that kept him in the hospital for several weeks. He was subsequently awarded a Distinguished Service Medal for valor.

Heads Integrated Combat Unit

In 1951 James was sent to Korea, where he continued to display exceptional skill as an airman. After leading F–51 and F–80 fighter aircraft on a mission in support of the United Nations ground force near Nanchonjom, South Korea, he flew 101 additional combat missions during his six–month tour of duty in Korea and was promoted to captain. His proficiency earned him flight leader status and later the Distinguished Flying Cross.

James left the Far East in 1952 as a proven combat pilot. He was then assigned to Otis Air Force Base on Cape Cod, Massachusetts. James was promoted to major in 1952, and the next year he became a commander leader of his own black squadron. He was also the first African American to be given command of an integrated combat unit in the United States. A passionate orator who especially enjoyed working with and speaking to young people, James was named Young Man of the Year in 1954 by the Massachusetts Chamber of Commerce.

In 1956 James was promoted to lieutenant colonel before leaving for Air Command and Staff College (ACSC) at Maxwell Air Force Base in Alabama. After his graduation the following year, he was assigned to Air Force headquarters at the Pentagon as a staff officer.

Between 1960 and 1964, James was stationed at the Royal Air Force (RAF) base in Bentwaters, England, as director of operations and squadron commander in the 81st Fighter Wing. In 1962 he was assigned as squadron commander over a U.S. overseas air base that was also located in Bentwaters.

In 1964 James headed back to the United States for a two–year stint as director of operations for the 4453rd Combat Crew Training Wing at Davis–Monthan Air Force Base in Arizona. That same year, he was promoted to colonel.

In Vietnam between 1964 and 1967, James served as director of operations and vice commander of the 18th Fighter Tactical Wing in Ubon, Thailand. As a wing vice commander, he flew 78 combat missions over North Vietnam in 1967.

Speaks Openly Against Racial Discrimination

While James showed skill and diplomacy in handling racial stereotypes in his personal relationships, he was quite outspoken about eliminating discriminatory practices affecting blacks in the armed forces. Yet he rejected violence as a means of obtaining racial equality in the United States. To James, the fact that black had gained the right to fight in the Vietnam War was an important step toward securing their acceptance as Americans. According to James R. McGovern in *Black Eagle,* the intensely patriotic James once told a *New York Times* reporter that he was an American first and a black man second.

In 1967 James earned nationwide recognition for his essay ''Freedom—My Heritage, My Responsibility.'' Published in *Stars and Stripes* as part of a contest, it earned him the George Washington Freedom Foundation Honor Medal. An excerpt from his essay reflects his feelings about his country:

> This is my country, and I believe in her, and I believe in her flag, and I'll defend her, and serve her, if she has any ills, I'll stand by her and hold her hand, and through her wisdom and her consideration for the welfare of the entire nation, things are made right again.

After his tour of duty in Vietnam ended, James was reassigned as vice commander at Eglin Air Force Base in Florida. He was also in great demand as a speaker. In general, he focused his remarks on the American effort in Vietnam.

In August 1969 James was made commander of the 33rd Tactical Fighter Wing at Eglin Air Force Base in Libya, North

Africa, the largest American air base outside the United States. From 1969 to 1970 he was stationed in the Libyan Arab Republic as base commander of the 7272nd Flying Training Wing.

In March 1970, James was assigned to the Pentagon as Deputy Assistant Secretary of Defense for Public Affairs. He was then promoted to brigadier general in July 1970 and to major general in August 1972.

Promoted to Four–Star General

In 1973 James became vice commander of the Military Airlift Command with headquarters at Scott Air Force Base in Illinois. He was promoted to lieutenant general in 1974 and to full general on September 1, 1975, making him the first black to hold that rank in the history of the armed forces.

James's last assignment took him to the mountains of Wyoming, where he served as commander–in–chief of North American Air Defense Command (NORAD), the entity responsible for all U.S. and Canadian strategic aerospace defense forces. In this position James directed the surveillance and air defense of North American aerospace and provided warning and assessment of attacks on the continent by bombers and missiles.

In September 1977 James suffered a mild heart attack. He retired from the Air Force on January 26, 1978, after 35 years of service. Several weeks later, while fulfilling a speaking engagement in Colorado, he suffered a massive heart attack and died on February 25. He was buried in Arlington National Cemetery.

Among James's survivors were his wife, Dorothy, whom he had married on the Tuskegee campus on November 3, 1942, and three children—Danice, Claude, and Daniel III. In May of 1987, the Daniel ''Chappie'' James Center for Aerospace Science was dedicated in his honor at Tuskegee University.

James's legacy was one of perseverance in the face of racism, dedication to duty, and love of country. He refused to allow adversity or any other obstacle to stand in his way. Education, hard work, and belief in oneself, he maintained, made it possible for a person to achieve anything.

REFERENCES

''Blacks set Milestones in U.S. Military Service.'' *Jet* 71 (17 November 1986): 16.

''Chappie is a Four–Star Salute.'' *San Diego (California) Union,* February 17, 1991.

Craig, John. *Chappie and Me: An Autobiographical Novel.* New York: Dodd, Mead, 1979.

Francis, Charles E. *The Men Who Changed a Nation: The Tuskegee Airmen.* Boston: Branden Pub. Co., 1988.

General Daniel ''Chappie'' James, Jr. Learning Packet. Maxwell Air Force Base, AB: National Headquarters, Civil Air Patrol, 1988.

McGovern, James R. *Black Eagle: General Daniel ''Chappie'' James, Jr.* Tuscaloosa: University of Alabama Press, 1985.

Phelps, Alfred J. *Chappie: America's First Black Four–Star General: The Life and Times of Daniel James, Jr.* Novato, CA: Presido Press, 1991.

Rose, Robert A. *Lonely Eagles: The Story of America's Black Air Forces in World War II.* Los Angeles: Tuskegee Airmen, 1976.

Super, Neil. *Daniel ''Chappie'' James.* New York: 21st Century Books, 1992.

COLLECTIONS

Most of James's papers and literary effects are housed at Maxwell Air Force Base in Alabama. Some items, such as letters, tapes, interviews, speeches, and memorabilia, are in the Daniel ''Chappie'' James Center for Aerospace Science at Tuskegee University.

Alice M. Baker

Vernon D. Jarrett

(1921–)

Journalist, radio and television producer and moderator, lecturer, writer

An articulate, outspoken journalist, Vernon D. Jarrett is one of the nation's foremost newspaper, television, and radio commentators on issues of race, politics, urban affairs, and African American history. He has been a reporter and feature writer for the *Chicago Defender,* the *Pittsburgh Courier,* and other newspapers as well as a writer for the Associated Negro Press. He has written numerous radio shows delineating the black experience and describing the effect of worldwide events on black people.

Jarrett was born on June 19, 1921, to Annie Sybil Jarrett and William Robert Jarrett in Saulsbury, Tennessee, a place in Hardeman County not far from the Mississippi border. His parents were children of former slaves in Hardeman County; between them his parents spent a combined total of 104 years teaching in the public schools of West Tennessee. Jarrett's older brother—his only living sibling—at one time served as president of Atlanta University and as a visiting professor of literature at Oxford University in England.

In 1941 Jarrett graduated from Knoxville College, Knoxville, Tennessee, with a B.A. degree in history and sociology. He studied journalism at Northwestern University in 1946 and in 1956 continued his training at the University of Kansas City in Missouri, where he studied television writing and produc-

Vernon D. Jarrett

ing. Later, in 1959, he enrolled at the University of Chicago and studied urban sociology.

Jarrett's teaching experience includes being visiting associate professor of history at Northwestern University from 1968 to 1970. He also taught a television course in American history at City Colleges of Chicago from 1968 to 1971. He began his career in journalism in 1946 as general assignment reporter for the *Chicago Defender.* Jarrett became the first black syndicated columnist for the *Chicago Tribune* in 1970, writing three times weekly for the opinion and editorial page. From 1983 to 1996 he was columnist and a member of the editorial board of the *Chicago Sun–Times.*

Since 1968 Jarrett has been a talk–show host, producer, and commentator for WLS–TV, channel 7, an ABC–owned station in Chicago. He was first moderator for the show *Black on Black,* featuring interviews with outstanding black personalities. Later the show was renamed *For Blacks Only,* and still later the hour–long show became known as *Face to Face with Vernon Jarrett.* He began in 1996 *Jarrett's Journal,* aired on WVON–AM in Chicago, the city's only black–owned radio station, which he continues. Jarrett is one of the station's five owners.

Jarrett has participated in numerous national and international media productions. He was one of five journalists selected by the *MacNeil–Lehrer Report* to analyze the final 1992 presidential campaign debate involving President George Bush and presidential candidates Bill Clinton and Ross Perot. In 1996 when the British Broadcasting Corporation produced *The Promised Land,* a five–part television series on black migration to the North during and following World War II, Jarrett was a featured commentator for four of the shows. He has also narrated in a PBS series on *The Great Americans,* assigned to the episode on Harry S. Truman. In September of 1998 he is scheduled to appear in the PBS special *Soldiers without Swords,* the history of the black press in America.

The veteran newsman has appeared on ABC–TV's *Nightline* with Ted Koppel, the *NBC Evening News* with Dan Rather, NBC's *Meet the Press,* CBS's *60 Minutes,* the *MacNeil–Lehrer Report,* and CBS's *Night Watch.* He has also appeared on Canadian television's *Good Morning, Canada.*

For the 125th anniversary of the birth of W. E. B. Du Bois, on February 23, 1993, Jarrett convened at Fisk University in Nashville a group of black scholars and journalists to commemorate Du Bois's birth in a memorial seminar. He also moderated other seminars in honor of Du Bois held elsewhere. He served on the National Committee to Commemorate the centennial birth of Paul Robeson on April 8, 1998.

Jarrett's numerous memberships include the board of governors of the Chicago Chapter of the National Academy of Television Arts and Sciences. He was successful in establishing several professional organizations to promote the work of blacks and black journalists and organized other efforts to support black causes. For example, in 1976 he founded the Chicago Association of Black Journalists. He is a founder and member of the National Association of Black Journalists and served as its second president from 1977 to 1979. Jarrett, who admits that he is a radical and fiery journalist, was a founder in 1977 of the Monroe Trotter Group, an association comprising distinguished black journalists. Established at Harvard University, the organization is named for William Monroe Trotter (1872–1934), an elite militant integrationist, journalist, and important black spokesperson in the early twentieth century.

Jarrett is founder and chair of ACT–SO (Afro–Academic, Cultural, Technological and Scientific Olympics), which the NAACP's national office adopted in 1977 as one of its major programs. ACT–SO, now active in over 1,000 cities and towns, is designed to give young black academic achievers recognition similar to that given athletic stars. Jarrett is a member of Society of Professional Journalists, the YMCA, and the national advisory board of the Rosa Parks Institute in Detroit. He is also curator of the Oral History Department of the Rosa and Raymond Parks Pathways to Freedom Program for Youths. He is a member of the NAACP and serves on the editorial board for *Crisis* magazine, the organization's official journal. Since 1997 he has been a member of the Advisory Board for the Race Relations Institute at Fisk University.

Volunteer services occupy much of Jarrett's time. They include vice–president of the Chicago Citizens Schools Committee, devoted to improving public schools. He is writer–in–residence at Chicago's Jean Baptiste Point DuSable Museum of African American History.

Nominated for Pulitzer Prize

Since 1972, Jarrett has had the signal honor of being nominated seven times for the Pulitzer Prize in journalism for his work for the *Chicago Tribune* and the *Chicago Sun Times.* In 1976 and 1977 he was a juror to select the Pulitzer Prize winners. He has won numerous awards for his reporting. He was a professional scholar at the Freedom Forum's First Amendment Center at Vanderbilt University in Nashville, Tennessee, in 1995. He is conducting research on the philosophies of black crusaders at the turn of the century for *The Jericho Continuum,* a book of essays. His second book in progress, *But We Had Each Other,* describes his life growing up in Tennessee, "when all black children were the sons and daughters of all black parents," as he said in an interview. Spurred by a family who instilled in him a strong sense of racial pride, Jarrett felt superior to the white children in the private homes where he worked weekends as a houseboy and yard–keeper from the eighth grade until he went to college. Among the vignettes included in the book is the story of Harriet Combs, his maternal grandmother and a slave, who learned to read by eavesdropping when a tutor came to teach the mistress. Though the practice was forbidden and later discontinued, the mistress taught Combs to write as well.

Jarrett has received more than 100 awards and special recognitions from professional, civic, religious, business, and educational institutions and organizations. Among these, he was the first recipient of the NAACP's James Weldon Johnson Achievement Award in 1994. In 1979 he was named one of the nation's top five communicators in *Ebony* magazine's national poll of black leaders. He is the recipient of the American Civil Liberty Union's James P. McGuire Award (1988); the National Black Book Business and Professional Award (1990), presented annually by *Dollars and Sense* magazine; and the Lifetime Achievement Award from the National Association of Black Journalists (1991). He also received the NABJ's Award of Merit as founder and second president and in 1997 was honored with its President's Award. Jarrett received the National Association of Black School Educator's President's Award (1993). He holds honorary degrees from Lake Forest College of Illinois and Chicago State University.

Now senior fellow in the Great Cities Institute at the University of Illinois, Chicago, Jarrett also continues to lecture widely and gives keynote addresses for educational, civic, and other groups. He continues to write and to speak out forcefully on matters of race, saying that "racism is an invention." On this issue he said in an interview:

> Racism in America was manufactured, legalized, and glorified, and finally made acceptable by individuals who profited from it. It is not inborn and it required extraordinary effort [to survive], aided by the pulpit, academics, arts and letters, the media, the legitimate stage, the cinema, along with the enforcement powers of all levels of governments—backed by the violence of the mob.

Jarrett and his wife Fernetta H. Jarrett, a retired public school teacher, reared two sons—Thomas S. Jarrett, cameraman and sound engineer with WLS–TV in Chicago, and William R. Jarrett, a physician and surgeon, now deceased. Jarrett's career continues to be punctuated by numerous activities that help address issues of civil and human rights.

Current address: 6901 South Oglesby Avenue, Chicago, IL 60649.

REFERENCES

Ebony Success Library. Vol. 1. Nashville: Southwestern Company, by arrangement with Johnson Pub. Co., 1973.

Jarrett, Vernon. Interview with Jessie Carney Smith, February 12, 1998.

Stein, M. L. *Blacks in Communication.* New York: Julian Messner, 1972.

"Vernon Jarrett." Biographical sketch in files of the Race Relations Institute, Fisk University.

Who's Who among African Americans, 1998–99. 10th ed. Detroit: Gale Research, 1997.

Jessie Carney Smith

Blind Lemon Jefferson

(1897–1929)

Musician, composer, singer

Blind Lemon Jefferson was an early blues singer and composer, who wrote many of his own songs and played the the guitar. His recordings were popular all over the country and influenced many later blues singers. Blues musician and guitar stylist Aaron "T–Bone" Walker led Jefferson about the streets of Dallas as a youth and it is probable that Leadbelly (Huddie Ledbetter), another blues giant, also spent an appreciable amount of time with Jefferson. Many traditional blues musicians sang his songs or adaptations of them and show evidence of the influence of his guitar playing as well. Jefferson's songs and pieces of his songs have been found on down home blues recordings as late as the 1950s.

Lemon Jefferson was born on a farm near Couchman, in Freestone County, Texas, in July of 1897 to Alec and Classie Banks Jefferson. Classie Banks had two sons from a previous marriage: Clarence and Izakiah. She and Alec Jefferson had seven children: Francis, John (their first son), Martha, Mary, C. B., Gussie Mae, and Lemon (their second son). Lemon was born blind. In 1907 John was killed after he fell from a slow–moving train where he had been playing.

By the time Jefferson was 14–years old, he had already begun to develop his musical gift. Since playing on the street for money was one of the few options open to a blind, black

Blind Lemon Jefferson

young man in those days, he began to play his guitar and sing in Wortham. In time Jefferson became a popular local entertainer.

In 1917, when he was 20, Jefferson went to Dallas to try his luck. Since he could not immediately make enough money to support himself by singing and he weighed 250 pounds, Jefferson worked in Dallas theaters as a novelty wrestler. As soon as he could, he gave up this sideline to become a popular singer in Dallas and surrounding areas. While in Dallas, Jefferson spent many nights in brothels, playing and singing until he had collected enough money for liquor and a girl.

Jefferson frequently visited home in his car, for which he hired a driver. Around 1922 or 1923, he married a local girl named Roberta, who is remembered as a quiet, mousy woman who seldom knew the whereabouts of her husband. Their son Miles was born sometime between 1924 and 1926.

Jefferson was travelling extensively by the mid 1920s. He ventured as far east as Alabama and as far south as the coast of Texas. His musical abilities flourished, but his lifestyle was destructive. He would spend the money he earned in one night on liquor or a woman. The following day he would be recovering from a hangover and trying to earn enough money for his next meal.

Begins Recording Career

Sammy Price, a black pianist who had studied with Portia Washington (Booker T. Washington's daughter), was working in a Dallas music store during this period. He had heard Jefferson play as early as 1917 in Waco and knew him from the Dallas streets. Impressed with Jefferson's ability and aware of the success of other blues singers on record, Price recommended the singer to Paramount Records.

Jefferson went to Chicago in the spring of 1925 and cut two songs, but the record was not released until the summer of 1926 after his later records had become hits. In February 1926 Jefferson recorded again, and Paramount began advertising "Booster Blues" and "Dry Southern Blues" in April. This recording was a success, making Jefferson the first Southern self–accompanied blues singer to record hits. Despite all his success in selling records, Jefferson received very little in return. For example, his first and most successful producer, J. Mayo Williams, would have a little money, liquor, and a prostitute waiting for the musician at the end of each session.

In 1927 Jefferson recorded two songs for Okeh Records, but then returned to Paramount. By now he was running out of country material and began to record a more urban kind of blues, often with obvious double meanings in the lyrics. In an attempt to reach a larger audience, on three recordings in 1927 he even sang to the piano accompaniment of George Perkins. In four years of recording Jefferson completed 79 blues singles for Paramount and two for Okeh. In addition, he recorded some religious songs under the pseudonyms of Deacon L. J. Bates and Elder J. C. Brown.

In late 1929 Jefferson was playing at parties in Chicago and recording, albeit with diminishing success, nearly every month. In December 1929, he was found dead on a Chicago street. Jefferson recorded "Empty House Blues" for Paramount earlier that day. The session ended after dark and Jefferson left the studio saying that he was going to play for a house party. What happened then is unclear. One account said he suffered a heart attack on the way to the party and then froze to death; another that he was drunk when he left the house party, lost his way, and fell into a gutter where he froze to death.

Paramount arranged to have his body sent to Texas, and he was buried in the Wortham Negro Cemetery. His death did not go unnoted; Emmet Dickenson recorded a sermon, "Death of Blind Lemon," for Paramount. Heeding the plea of his song "See That My Grave Is Kept Clean," fans placed and dedicated a grave marker on October 15, 1967. Jefferson was inducted into the Blues Foundation's Hall of Fame in 1980.

Blind Lemon Jefferson left behind a legacy of recordings. While several later blues musicians have mimicked his vocal style, it is his guitar playing that was especially influential. According to *The Big Book of Blues:*

> Jefferson constructed intricate melodic structures punctuated with irregular phrasing that often expanded standard tempo patterns. He also used, to great effect, single–string arpeggios, repeating bass runs on the lower strings, and interesting jazzlike improvisation, which gave his style wonderful color and charisma.

REFERENCES

Charters, Samuel B. *The Country Blues.* New York: Rhinehart, 1959. Reprint with new introd. by the author, New York: Da Capo, 1979.

Cohn, Lawrence, and others. *Nothing But the Blues.* New York: Abbeville Press, 1993.

Encyclopedia of Southern Culture. Chapel Hill: University of North Carolina Press, 1989.

Harris, Shelton. *Blues Who's Who: A Biographical Dictionary of Blues Singers.* New Rochelle, NY: Arlington House, 1979. Reprint, New York: Da Capo, 1981.

The New Grove Dictionary of American Music. 4 vols. New York: Macmillan 1986.

Oliver, Paul. *The Story of the Blues.* Radnor, PA: 1969.

Palmer, Robert. *Deep Blues.* New York: Penguin, 1981.

Santelli, Robert. *The Big Book of Blues.* New York: Penguin, 1993.

Robert L. Johns

Charles S. Johnson

Charles S. Johnson
(1893–1956)
Sociologist, college president, civil rights leader

Charles S. Johnson conducted pathbreaking sociological research in the South for over three decades. Based at Fisk University in Nashville from the late 1920s to the mid–1950s, he wrote and supervised many studies with the same purpose: to show in depth how the pervasive system of racial discrimination and the socioeconomic structure in which it was embedded deprived black Americans of their fundamental rights to justice and equality of opportunity. There were many other facets to his distinguished career. In 1920 he wrote the greater part of the most comprehensive report of a race riot ever published to that date. Also at that time, as research director of the National Urban League and founding editor of its journal *Opportunity,* he was a pivotal figure in the support of young black writers and artists.

Charles Spurgeon Johnson was born on July 24, 1893, in Bristol, Virginia. His father, Charles H. Johnson, son of a slave, had been educated by his former master along with the master's own son and had then been sent to Richmond Institute (now Virginia Union University) for his divinity degree. He and his wife, Winifred Branch Johnson, arrived in Bristol in 1890; the Johnson pastorate there lasted for forty–two years, during which time the Reverend Johnson built a large, imposing church whose spire towered over the town. Bristol had very limited educational opportunities for blacks, so Charles Spurgeon, the oldest of five children, went to Wayland Baptist Academy, affiliated with Virginia Union University. He completed his degree at Virginia Union in three years, with distinction, in 1916. The widespread poverty and racial discrimination in the black community in Bristol and Richmond turned him in the direction of sociology and the University of Chicago.

Though he never completed a doctorate at Chicago, Johnson gained a wealth of research experience that served the rest of his career. His mentor and most important teacher was Robert E. Park, who was a leading member of the so–called Chicago school, with its emphasis on the integration of broad sociological theory and the actual social conditions in an urban–industrial setting.

Park, as president of the Chicago Urban League, arranged Johnson's appointment as research director of the league, but Johnson's studies of the Great Migration and the state of race relations in the industrial North were interrupted by war. Johnson enlisted in 1918 and served in battle in France as a regimental sergeant major. Returning to Chicago in 1919, he found himself in the midst of one of the worst race riots in our history. The commission formed in the wake of the riot chose him as associate executive director. Its report, *The Negro in Chicago* (1922), was largely Johnson's work, and established a benchmark for all subsequent studies in its realistic portrayal of the social infrastructure underlying the riot as well as the major problems blacks faced in employment, housing, education, and social services. The report reinforced Johnson's emerging credo: that systematic, disciplined research would arm the advocates for change—he among them—with the essential facts to undergird the combat against racism and the quest for justice. In 1921, the national office of the Urban League appointed him research director.

Serves Bridging Role in Harlem Renaissance

From 1921 until 1929 Johnson conducted many more community studies in the Chicago mode; they were largely factual but the facts themselves constituted an indictment of racial injustice. Moreover, in editing *Opportunity,* he brought to public attention the work of leading social scientists, black and white, who exposed the pseudo–science, misconceptions, and stereotypes that served as a rationale for racial prejudice and discrimination. Finally, in a broader cultural context, Johnson devoted himself to connecting the rising young black writers and artists in Harlem with publishers and sponsors downtown, a bridging role essential to the Harlem Renaissance and making him, as much as Alain Locke, "midwife" to the Renaissance. The bridging role would stand him in good stead for many years afterward in the South as he shuttled so often from Nashville to New York to Chicago in search of funding from a Rosenwald or Rockefeller foundation to further sociological research. Perhaps his attention to cultural matters stemmed from his growing awareness of how slowly progress for blacks was taking place in employment. As historian David Levering Lewis noted, "If the road to the ballot box and jobs was blocked, Johnson saw that the door to Carnegie Hall and the New York publishers was ajar." Langston Hughes, Zora Neale Hurston, Ethel Nance, Arna Bontemps, and many others in this movement have testified to Johnson's importance.

All the same, through the years in New York, Johnson remained attached to his primary goal: to return to the South and undertake the most comprehensive study possible of the racial system of the region as prelude to action against it. In 1929 he left the league to take a position directing social science studies and a department of race relations at Fisk University. He had a threefold purpose in mind: to create at Fisk a social science faculty and a center for research in race relations unique in the country; to construct through that research a full, historically–grounded portrayal of the institutional racism of the region; and to make effective use of these countless studies to help bring about social change in the racial system. In this last dimension, Johnson proposed to work with a coalition of white southern liberals and moderates at both the regional and national levels. For this program of collaboration with whites he has been strongly criticized, in particular by a number of black sociologists in the next generation who have found him too conservative, too autocratic in his control of funding and fellowships, and too deferential to the white liberals and the white establishment in advancing the program of the "Fisk Machine."

In Johnson's own time, W. E. B. Du Bois saw him as cautious and possibly reactionary, and E. Franklin Frazier was scornful of his dependence on the white philanthropic elite. (Ironically, the three black sociologist founding fathers are joined together in the American Sociological Association's Du Bois–Johnson–Frazier award for distinguished work in race relations.) Johnson, defined as a conciliatory realist, had little choice but to work with his white associates within the hard confines of segregation in the South. Only after *Brown v. Board of Education* in 1954, the Supreme Court decision striking down racial segregation in the public schools, was there sufficient leverage for the coalition to join with the younger black militant leaders in a full–scale direct strategy against the southern racial fortress. Johnson had no illusions about all of this. Years before *Brown,* he denounced segregation publicly, resisted it when it affected him personally, and continued to hope for integration—though without loss to the distinctive structure and culture of the black community. In 1942, in the celebrated Durham (North Carolina) Statement, of which he was one of the chief architects, he insisted on unequivocal wording on ending segregation.

For over nearly three decades, Johnson largely succeeded in carrying through what he intended to do on all three dimensions of his program. As a national center for social science research on race relations, Fisk came to rival the only other comparable institution, the University of North Carolina, which was equipped with far greater resources and financial support. A striking proportion of the next generation of black social scientists were trained by Johnson at Fisk. He brought in distinguished scholars from this country and abroad, including Park after his retirement from Chicago.

Establishes Race Relations Program

Johnson directed innumerable research studies of race relations in both southern and northern communities. His annual institutes of race relations were a dramatic innovation in the South of that era. National leaders and scholars and local and regional activists came together on an interracial basis on the Fisk campus to plan strategies for change. He forged an unprecedented relationship with other southern sociologists in the service of research; in 1946 his colleagues elected him president of the Southern Sociological Society.

In the outpouring of books, monographs, and articles produced from the Nashville base, three stand out and retain their value today. *Shadow of the Plantation* (1934), which Johnson himself called his favorite book, is a study of the nearly feudal tenant farm system in one Alabama cotton county, Macon, in the early 1930s. Some six hundred black families were held in such thrall that, as Johnson noted, "nothing remains but to succumb or to migrate." In the study of this ultimately doomed but still functioning system, Johnson called for decisive federal government intervention to curb the worst inequities. *Shadow* also endures (it was reprinted once again in 1996) because it weaves into the sociological data poignant, moving commentary by the tenants themselves. As one informant summarizes, "We jest can't make it cause they pay us nothing for what we give them and they charge us double price when they sell it back to us."

At the end of the decade Johnson published *Growing Up in the Black Belt* (1941), an analysis of black youth in six southern counties, including Macon, which showed that while a black boy or girl could grow up within a firmly structured community, he or she could not escape "the shadow of the white world." *Growing Up* has been notable for its rejection of the concept of caste governing Southern race relations. For Johnson, as for Oliver Cox and other sociologists, it was extremely important to show that change, however slow, not permanent subordination as in the presumed model from India, was the central issue. Racial segregation in all its forms would eventually crumble, not from a withering away of caste in the far future, but from active social protest from those subordinated and from vigorous governmental action. Pending such changes, it was equally important to show how deeply entrenched segregation in the South, the whole system of separate and unequal, made racial discrimination seem all–pervasive and intractable, indeed resembling something like a caste system. *Patterns of Negro Segregation* (1943), Johnson's comprehensive compendium of the endless ways in which this cruel system played out a half century ago, remains the standard reference volume.

Johnson's other books, unlike the three just described, were more general. They surveyed the state of race relations at various times and usually concluded with a plea for using democratic channels to press for further change. They rarely ventured into deeper theory as seen, for example, in some of the work of Du Bois and E. Franklin Frazier. That was in keeping with his basic ethos: systematic research to be then placed at the service of those leaders, black and white, who would advance the struggle to change public policy and achieve a greater degree of racial equality. One exception occurred, however, early on. In 1930, just as his large–scale study, *The Negro in American Civilization,* appeared, he was appointed to conduct an investigation into forced labor in Liberia for the League of Nations. Liberia, nominally independent but virtually economically dependent on the United States, was imposing a kind of slavery on its own people, an irony not lost on Johnson and others who thought about their African roots. His book, *Bitter Canaan,* published posthumously many years later (1987), revealed Johnson departing from his usual cool and detached sociological posture to give us at once a history of Liberia, a study forming the basis for reforming the forced labor system, and a moving personal memoir.

The building of the social sciences at Fisk, and the extensive research program in race relations in the South, formed the platform from which Johnson advanced the third goal of the Nashville years: the sidelines activism, or, as Lewis Jones, his outstanding student and later his close friend, described it, his "strategy of indirection" in the endless struggle for civil rights at both the regional and national levels. Regionally, Johnson worked to form organizations to combat racism in the South. Among them were the Southern Regional Council (SRC) and the Southern Conference for Human Welfare (SCHW). SRC sought to be as mainstream as an interracial organization could be in the era of segregation. Johnson was a prime mover in its formation and eventually helped persuade it to move against segregation, but by then it had been overtaken by events and by the nonviolent direct–action strategy of newer civil rights groups. SCHW, much more militant than SRC, helped to unite labor and civil rights groups in a common effort at economic and racial change, but Johnson's hopes for it eventually faded as it was constantly hounded by the southern establishment. At all events, these organizations, whether deemed radical or liberal, represented the only options in the South before the onset of the more dynamic civil rights coalition of the 1960s.

Nationally, Johnson served on a multitude of commissions and presidential initiatives—for example, that of Franklin D. Roosevelt on farm tenancy policy, Harry S. Truman's on organizing UNESCO, and on an educational program for postwar occupied Japan. Beyond such assignments, Johnson worked closely with allies in Washington, D.C., including both well–placed white New Dealers such as Will Alexander and Clark Foreman, and with an informal Black Cabinet made up of black leaders such as Mary McLeod Bethune and Walter White. The objective was to persuade the administration, generally uninterested in civil rights and wary in any case of crossing conservative southern Democrats, to move ahead on civil rights.

The Washington group had little access—they really had only two committed and influential allies at the highest level, Harold Ickes, Secretary of the Interior, and Eleanor Roosevelt—and they often failed in attempting to get an antilynching law or elimination of the poll tax. On occasion, however, the strategy worked. Johnson, Will Alexander, who was perhaps the most important southern white liberal and in the late 1930s and director of the Farm Security Administration (FSA), and Edwin R. Embree, director of the Julius Rosenwald Fund, wrote a landmark report, *The Collapse of Cotton Tenancy* (1935), on the plight of southern tenant farmers. Skirting the racial issue entirely, they proposed "rehomesteading" or settling tenants on their own property in "huge numbers." Eventually, their proposal became law, the Bankhead–Jones Farm Tenancy Act of 1937. Administered by the FSA, the program did not touch "huge numbers," but in this case, Alexander saw to it that, unlike many New Deal measures, at least there was mostly racial fairness and equity in the distribution of assistance.

In his last ten years, as Fisk's president (1946–56), Johnson devoted more time to the college and less to sociological research or activism. He strengthened the academic program, continued to receive substantial support for Fisk from the foundations, and helped to enhance the reputation of Fisk. Internally, the record was less impressive, due in part to his frequent absences and also to his rather reserved and stiff personality, which resulted in somewhat distant and formal relationships with faculty and staff. His reserve and occasional brusqueness with others had been a hallmark through the years in Nashville, though he could be warm and outgoing with close friends such as Langston Hughes and Aaron Douglas of Renaissance days.

Charles S. Johnson died October 27, 1956, as he was traveling to a meeting of the Fisk board of trustees in New

York. He is buried in Nashville's Greenwood Cemetery. Johnson was survived by Marie Antoinette Burgette Johnson, a teacher in music and theater, whom he married before leaving Chicago for New York thirty–five years earlier. He also left four children: Charles II, Robert, Patricia, and Jeh. His son Robert carried on his work in sociology.

As Fisk's first black president with most of his significant sociological work behind him, Johnson continued his lifelong advocacy for change in the racial system. In the role of research–advocacy, which he called his "sidelines activism," he collaborated closely with the small band of southern white liberals who were in a more open and strategic position than he was to press for change such as national legislation to end lynching or aid the embattled black and white farmers in the South. John Egerton rightly said of him, "Throughout the thirties and forties into the fifties, only a small number of black Southerners (and even fewer whites) were able to stay in the region and fight their way to national recognition in the long campaign for racial equality. Charles S. Johnson was one of them."

Johnson's critics have stated that as a national civil rights leader he had not matched the militancy of a Du Bois or a Frazier. It has been an unfair assessment. Given the far greater racial discrimination and constraints on black counter assertion in the South, he and the southern white liberals with whom he worked did what they could with what they had in resources and power. Lester Granger, then executive director of the Urban League and an old friend, rendered a more judicious verdict in the *New York Amsterdam News:* "He had all of the normal man's ambition, naturally, but the main purpose of his life's work was always clear; it was to dissipate the ghost of social superstition by letting the light of social facts stream in."

REFERENCES

Egerton, John. *Speak Now Against the Day: The Generation Before the Civil Rights Movement in the South.* New York: Knopf, 1994.

Johnson, Charles S. *Bitter Canaan: The Story of the Negro Republic.* New York: Transaction Books, 1987.

———. *Growing Up in the Black Belt.* Washington, DC: American Council on Education, 1941. Reprint, New York: Schocken Books, 1967.

———. *Patterns of Negro Segregation.* New York: Harper and Brothers, 1943.

———. *Shadow of the Plantation.* Chicago: University of Chicago Press, 1934.

Lewis, David Levering. *When Harlem Was in Vogue.* New York: Knopf, 1981.

New York Amsterdam News, November 9, 1956. Typescript of untitled article, Charles S. Johnson Papers, Fisk University.

Robbins, Richard. *Sidelines Activist: Charles S. Johnson and the Struggle for Civil Rights.* Jackson: University Press of Mississippi, 1996.

COLLECTIONS

Charles S. Johnson's personal papers, those of the Social Science Research Center, the Race Relations Institutes, and from his office as president of Fisk University are in Special Collections, Fisk University Library.

Richard Robbins

Frank Johnson

(1792–1844)

Composer, bandleader, orchestra leader, musician

Frank Johnson was a highly celebrated American composer and bandleader of the first half of the nineteenth century. Eileen Southern in her essay "The Philadelphia Afro–American School" summarized his importance as a composer and performer, saying that Johnson was a role model for both his white and black contemporaries. In addition to publishing music in 1818 when he was 26, he imported from Europe new music for his "'friends and patrons' to dance to." Johnson introduced new instruments to Philadelphia musical society, including the important Kent bugle; he trained his musicians to perform military dance and sacred concert music which they played locally and elsewhere; and he "lifted his dance music onto the concert stage with his promenade concerts." The first American to take a music group to Europe for a performance tour, he achieved numerous other professional firsts that made him a legendary figure in the field of music. Among these, he was the first to develop a "school" of black musicians; he also introduced the promenade concert to the United States. Johnson was the first African American to win wide acclaim as a musician in the United States as well as in England, the first to hold formal band concerts, and the first to produce racially integrated concerts in this country.

Little is known about Johnson's early life. He was born Francis Johnson in Martinique, the West Indies, in 1792. In 1809 he settled in Philadelphia, Pennsylvania, and first received public notice in 1818. At that time G. Willig published Johnson's *Six Sets of Cotillions.* The next year Johnson became the leader of a dance band that played at numerous public and private balls. According to Robert Waln's *The Hermit in America on a Visit to Philadelphia,* cited in Eileen Southern's *Biographical Dictionary,* he was listed as "sole director of all serenades" and "inventory–general of cotillions." He played for events for the elite and at leading schools of dance in Philadelphia. Although the details of his training are not given, it is said that he studied trumpet with black bandleader Mathew "Matt" Black and, after the War of

Frank Johnson

1812, may have had his start in Black's band. He also appears to have studied with Richard Willis, who directed West Point's military band for the U.S. Army.

Johnson became an accomplished keyed bugle–player and violinist. He led several military bands; one of these, the Third Company of Washington Guards, was organized following the War of 1812; other regiments hired the band after the company disbanded. In 1821 his small military band became associated with the Philadelphia State Fencibles regiment, an elite group. This association continued for many years. By the 1820s Johnson was a skilled musician and played the French horn exceptionally well; he played other instruments as well. However, when the band played for dances, string instruments replaced the winds that had been used. For special concerts, however, Johnson added such instruments as the bell harmonicon and harp. For these purposes the band was then called "Johnson's Celebrated Cotillion Band" or "Johnson's Fine Quadrille Band." After introducing keyed brass instruments to his musicians, Johnson led the group by the mid–1830s to become a brass band. He became an accomplished instructor and astute business manager, enabling him to identify good musical talent and to seek men of high artistic ability.

Beginning in 1824 Johnson's bands underwent several reorganizations and by 1832 reached the forefront as the leading military band in Philadelphia, playing at all famous military and other parades and fashionable functions in that city. In fact, when General Lafayette visited Philadelphia in 1824, Johnson's band was engaged to play at the Lafayette Ball. His band performed at black affairs as well and gave concerts at black churches in Philadelphia, New York, and Boston. The band also performed at black social functions, including balls and festivals, and at black funerals as well.

Eileen Southern wrote in "The Philadelphia Afro–American School" that Johnson "stood tall in the center of a Philadelphia School" that included William Appo, William Brady, Aaron J. Connor, and others. Those in his early band included Johnson's brothers–in–law William and Joseph Appo (William was a music teacher in New York), Edward D. Roland (successful violin teacher), Aaron J. R. Connor (composer of vocal and instrumental music) Francis V. Seymour, William Brady (skilled composer of sacred music), Joseph G. Anderson, and others of similar ability. Anderson, later Johnson's successor, was an all–around performer, director, instructor, composer, and band trainer for black regiments of the Union Army during the Civil War.

Plays for the Queen

Johnson and his band traveled to Europe in 1837 for six months, and his group gave its first concert in London that December. Thus, his was the first African American band to give concerts abroad. The group gave a command performance before Queen Victoria at Windsor, and he received from the queen as a token of her appreciation a silver bugle. Johnson learned the musical styles and forms used in Europe and became particularly fascinated with Johann Strauss's waltzes. He brought these styles home with him and during the Christmas season introduced the "Promenade concert" to Philadelphians in 1838, establishing a permanent tradition in the United States.

Like other musicians of that time, Johnson spent his winters in Philadelphia where his band performed during the fashionable activities of the season. He also operated a music studio. In summers, however, his band played at such stylish resorts as Saratoga Springs, New York; Cape May, New Jersey; and White Sulphur Springs, Virginia.

In 1838 Johnson embarked on a tour that included Toronto, Canada, and St. Louis, Missouri. However, conditions of slavery prevented him from touring or teaching in the deep South. While traveling elsewhere he gave instruction to a large number of black bandsmen as well as to white and black students of music. Although he left over 200 published pieces, many of the numerous manuscripts that he had written were lost. According to Southern's *Biographical Dictionary,* though none of his band pieces is extant, he did "cotillions, quadrilles, marches, and other dances, sentimental ballads, patriotic songs, operatic arrangements, and even minstrel songs." His music was popular for decades after his death and includes such well–known pieces as "Bird Waltz," "Philadelphia Grays' Quickstep," "Star–Spangled Banner Cotillions," and the "Voice Quadrilles."

In 1843 and 1844, when the minstrels were flourishing, Johnson became involved, however modestly, when he did an arrangement of "Jim Dandy." He may even have had a direct contact with the Virginia Minstrels.

In his short life, Johnson had surrounded himself with music, both with bands and fine players and in the music room he maintained in his home. *A Gentleman of Much Promise,* edited by Philip English Mackey and quoted by Southern in *The Music of Black Americans,* described what one wealthy white student saw in Johnson's house:

> The wall was covered with pictures and instruments of all kinds, and one side of the room was fixed with shelves whereon were thousands of musical compositions, constituting a valuable library. Bass drum, bass viols, bugles and trombones lay in admirable confusion on the floor; and in one corner was an armed composing chair, with pen and inkhorn ready, and some gallopades and waltzes half finished.

After Johnson held the first racially–integrated concert in the United States, in Philadelphia on December 29, 1843, and continued with a series of such concerts in early 1844, he became ill about March 1844. The kind and gentle man died two months later, on April 6, and was buried on April 9 in the cemetery of St. Thomas African Church at the corner of Fifth and Adelphia streets in Philadelphia. The silver cornet given to him by Queen Victoria lay on his casket during the procession. His famous brass band followed him in the procession and continued to play at his grave. As widely celebrated as he was, with one or two exceptions his mourners were black. His wife, Helen Johnson, survived him. In 1980 Johnson was elected posthumously an honorary member of the Artillery Corps Washington Grays at Philadelphia. He was a talented and versatile figure in music whose bands, compositions, and performances influenced the musically talented of those who followed him. While there were other black bandleaders during Johnson's time, he seemed "to dwarf other black bandmasters of the time," concluded Southern in *The Music of Black Americans.*

REFERENCES

Cromwell, John W. "Frank Johnson's Military Band." *Southern Workman* 29 (September 1900): 532–35.

"In Retrospect: Black Musicians and Early Ethiopian Minstrelsy." *The Black Perspective in Music* 3 (Spring 1975): 77–99.

Southern, Eileen. *Biographical Dictionary of Afro–American and African Musicians.* Westport, CT: Greenwood Press, 1982.

———. "Frank Johnson of Philadelphia and His Promenade Concerts." *The Black Perspective in Music* 5 (Spring 1977): 3–30.

———. *The Music of Black Americans.* 2nd ed. New York: Norton, 1983.

———. "The Philadelphia Afro–American School." *The Black Perspective in Music* 4 (Spring 1976): 238–49.

Trotter, James Monroe. *Music and Some Highly Musical People.* Boston: Lee and Shepard, 1878.

Yee, Shirley J. *Black Women Abolitionists.* Knoxville: University of Tennessee Press, 1992.

Jessie Carney Smith

J. Rosamond Johnson (1873–1954)

Composer, entertainer

J. Rosamond Johnson composed many widely popular songs, as well as some more ambitious works. With his vaudeville partner Bob Cole, he made an important contribution to the pre–World War I flowering of the black musical theater. A trained musician, he was an excellent pianist and singer and had a long and successful performing career on the stage. He made a significant contribution to the preservation of the black musical heritage by his work with spirituals, much of it done with his brother, James Weldon Johnson. The song–writing trio of Bob Cole and the Johnson brothers did much to do away with black stereotypes in the musical theater and to increase the opportunities for black musicians in the field of popular music.

Johnson was born on August 11, 1873, in Jacksonville, Florida, the third and last child of James Johnson and Helen Louise Dillet Johnson. The older children were Marie Louise born in 1868 and James William—later W. and in 1913 Weldon—born in 1871. Helen Johnson, hoping for a girl, had chosen the name Rosamond. When a son arrived, she added John to Rosamond, but her son was known as Rosamond to all his intimates. At the time of Rosamond's birth, James Johnson was a waiter in a resort hotel, and Helen Johnson was a schoolteacher. The family was loving and cultured.

Johnson grew up protected by his older brother whom he soon surpassed in music. Following in his brother's footsteps, he attended the local Staunton School, where his mother taught. When Johnson finished, he did not follow his brother to college. Instead he went Boston in 1890 to study music at the New England Conservatory; he planned to support himself by working at the trade he had learned, cigar making. He became a trained musician and a good singer and pianist. In 1896 he joined the company of *Oriental America* and toured for a year. He won plaudits for his fine baritone voice in the operatic portion of the show. Most observers said he was a baritone, but Maude Cuney–Hare, who heard him in later years, said he was a basso cantante—a bass with a light and high voice.

In the spring of 1897, Johnson returned to Jacksonville, where he set himself up as a music teacher on a level much above the previous itinerant music masters. Charging high fees, he quickly established himself and attracted many students. He also worked as organist and choirmaster of a large Baptist church and taught music once a week at the Baptist Academy. He had published two moderately successful pieces before his return home, and he began to set some of the poems of his brother, who was now principal of Staunton School, to music. The two brothers collaborated on a comic opera, and during the summer of 1899 went to New York. The work was not produced but the brothers attracted favorable attention from producers and music publishers. They also met Bob

Cole, already an established vaudeville star and the Johnsons and Cole wrote their first song together, "Louisiana Lize," and sold it to May Irwin, an established white performer, for $50.

The most famous song of the Johnson brothers had a casual beginning in Jacksonville. Unable to write a suitable poem on Lincoln for recitation at a Lincoln's Birthday program at the school, James Weldon Johnson decided to write a song to be sung by 500 school children. Rosamond set the song, it was presented, and the brothers forgot about it. The song went back with the students to their schools and churches and spread. Within twenty years it was sung in black schools throughout the South, largely passed on by typed or printed copies, which were often pasted in the backs of songbooks and hymnals. "Lift Every Voice and Sing," the Johnson brothers' song, became known as the Negro National Anthem.

The Johnson brothers visited New York again in the summer of 1900. They formed an informal songwriting partnership with Bob Cole which lasted for seven years—until James Weldon was named consul—and produced over 200 songs. The arrangement allowed for occasional work with other people. In May of 1901, there was a major fire in Jacksonville, which destroyed much of the city including Staunton School. Fortunately, the Johnson home was spared. Shortly after the fire, James Weldon Johnson was accused of dating a white woman who was actually a light–complexioned African American. After narrowly escaping being lynched, the two brothers soon left for New York, where they were in close contact with the major black musicians and entertainers in the city. Since the start of the new school year would be delayed because Staunton had to be rebuilt, the Johnsons were able to prolong their stay through the end of the year.

Collaborates on Hit Songs

Bob Cole and the Johnson brothers made substantial contributions to three white shows, *The Belle of Bridgeport, Champagne Charlie,* and *The Supper Club.* They also wrote the money–making hit "The Girl with the Dreamy Eyes" for Anna Held, music comedy star and wife of Florenz Ziegfeld. Eventually more than 30 Cole and Johnson songs appeared in white shows between 1900 and 1914. Cole and the Johnson Brothers were following in the footsteps of Gussie L. Davis, the first black musician to win success on Tin Pan Alley, and they signed a three year exclusive contract with music publishers Jos. W. Stern and Co. The newly rebuilt Staunton School was ready to open in February of 1902, and James Weldon Johnson returned south. Rosamond stayed in New York, and two months later was performing in vaudeville with Bob Cole, beginning with a salary of $300 a week.

Cole and Johnson came on stage in evening clothes and pretended to discuss a program for entertaining a party. Johnson played Paderewski's Minuet on the piano and then sang "Still wie die Nacht;" then they sang a program of original songs like "Mandy," "Tell Me, Dusky Maiden," and "Under the Bamboo Tree." This remained the basic format for the very successful Cole and Johnson act over the years. They were also successful abroad. For example, on their first European tour in 1905, Cole and Johnson played for eight weeks as headliners at London's Palace theatre.

Towards the end of the summer of 1902, after the end of the shortened school year at Staunton, James Weldon Johnson resigned his principalship and established himself in New York. Cole and the Johnson brothers were now at the height of their fame in the entertainment business. Their song, "Under the Bamboo Tree," based on the spiritual "Nobody Knows the Trouble I've Seen," sold 400,000 copies of sheet music in the first year of publication. Rosamond did the adaptation with some qualms about creating a pop music hit from a deeply meaningful spiritual. Bob Cole's name appeared alone on the music. After some discussion the songwriting team signed a three–year contract to work exclusively for Klaw and Erlanger, who were major producers of Broadway musicals. They wrote several shows for Klaw and Erlanger such as *Humpty Dumpty,* a success, and *In Newport,* which was their first flop. Singers vied for their songs. The white singer who refused songs from the group was very rare. At the height of their success, Cole and the Johnson brothers were each earning $25,000 a year in royalties for their songs. Rosamond Johnson's eminence was recognized when he joined Bob Cole, Bert Williams, George Walker, James Reese Europe, and six other prominent black performers as a founding member of "The Frogs," a benevolent and social organization in 1908.

In 1904 James Weldon Johnson got involved in political activities for the Republican party. Cole and the Johnson brothers wrote campaign songs for Theodore Roosevelt. In addition to "You're All Right, Teddy," they waved the Bloody Flag yet one more time with a song celebrating the Civil War heroism of William H. Carney, "The Old Flag Never Touched the Ground." Eventually in 1906, James Weldon Johnson was rewarded for his political involvement with an appointment as consul to Venezuela, which effectively removed him from active involvement in show business.

Cole and Johnson were featured in *The Shoo–Fly Regiment,* an all–black musical which appeared in 1907 and ran for two seasons. Among the stereotypes challenged in this show was the one which said blacks could appear only in comic love scenes. In 1909, Cole and Johnson presented *The Red Moon* which incorporated Native American elements along with black. Both shows, conducted by James Reese Europe, were well–received and drew appreciative audiences, but problems booking theaters minimized their financial success. Even at this early date, many second–string theaters—the only kind available to black shows—were converting to motion pictures, and the competition forced ticket prices lower so that even full houses did not always generate enough revenue to support a large theatrical company. Still *The Red Moon* toured for nearly a year.

At the end of the tour, Bob Cole's health was poor, but he recovered after a rest and returned to inaugurate a new vaudeville act. In 1910 Cole had a breakdown. He was found singing and dancing in the street and taken to Bellevue. The first diagnosis, general paresis caused by the late stages of syphilis, was changed by later examiners to a nervous breakdown. Regardless of the true diagnosis, Cole appeared to be on his way to recovery, when he drowned himself in the spring of 1911.

Continues Without Cole

Johnson seemed to have taken the death of Bob Cole very hard. It was early 1912 before he began performing in vaudeville again, this time with Charles Hart, a successful broad comic. The act was successful but did not last long. Before the act disbanded, it had a long engagement in a London revue, *Come Over Here,* at the Hammerstein Grand Opera House in London. Johnson married Nora Floyd, previously one of his piano students in Jacksonville, in London on July 13, 1913. Rosamond and Nora Floyd Johnson had two children, Donald and Mildred.

In 1914 Johnson returned to New York where he worked at the Music School Settlement for Colored Children; Johnson held a successful concert in Carnegie Hall on April 12, 1915, in support of the school, but the school closed six months later. Just before the concert, the black school board members kicked out the white members, effectively cutting off white philanthropy. It is not known whether Johnson led or merely acquiesced in this decision. At present, Johnson's career, for the rest of his long life, is only imperfectly known. It is certain that he continued his involvement in music. He worked on an edition of *Blackbirds* in England in 1936.

Johnson's documented shows in New York include *The Harlem Rounders* (1925), *Fast and Furious* (1931), *Porgy and Bess* (1935), and *Cabin in the Sky* (1941). He appeared in these shows and also is said to have worked on them in some musical capacity. He also appeared in the stage play *Mamba's Daughters* (1939). He continued to appear in acts like J. Rosamond Johnson's Quartet, active in 1930. There were songs by Johnson in revues like Bill Robinson's *Brown Buddies* (1930) and the short–lived *Fast and Furious* (1931), which featured a stage appearance by Zora Neale Hurston. Johnson did a choral version of Gershwin's *Rhapsody in Blue* for *Rhapsody in Black,* starring Ethel Waters (1931). Johnson also directed a 42 voice chorus for Bessie Smith's only film, the two–reel *St. Louis Blues* (1929). The evidence of Johnson's activity is at present hit or miss, but it is clear that he remained an active professional musician.

Johnson's skills as an arranger are evident in many printed collections of music. He arranged almost all of the songs in the collections he did with his brother, *Book of American Negro Spirituals* (1925) and *Second Book of American Negro Spirituals* (1926). Other collections of arrangements include *Rolling Along in Song* (1937), *Sixteen New Negro Spirituals* (1939), and *The Album of Negro Spirituals* (1940). He arranged upwards of 150 traditional songs. For two or three years after 1925, he toured in the United States and Europe with tenor Gordon Taylor, presenting programs of spirituals. Taylor had previously been a member of Johnson's act The Inimitable Five. There were also Johnson songs taken up by concert artists. Paul Robeson recorded Johnson's setting of Paul Laurence Dunbar's "Lil' Gal" as well as "Sence You Went Away" to a text by Johnson's brother. The latter song was also a part of the repertory of famed Irish tenor, John McCormack. "African Drum Dance," published in 1928, was performed in 1930 by the Omaha Symphony Orchestra.

J. Rosamond Johnson died in his sleep on November 11, 1954, at his home at 437 West 162nd Street, New York. Death was due to a heart condition. After the funeral at Saint Philip's Church, he was buried in Mt. Hope cemetery.

Johnson belongs to an important generation of African American musicians. His achievements merit fuller consideration. His contributions to the black musical stage have received considerable attention, but much of his life remains in obscurity. At least one of his works seems destined to survive for the foreseeable future. "Lift Every Voice and Sing" remains a very moving piece.

REFERENCES

Badger, Reid. *A Life in Ragtime.* New York: Oxford, 1995.

Gordon, Taylor. *Born to Be.* New York: Covici–Friede, 1929.

Hitchcock, H. Wiley, and Stanley Sadie, eds. *The New Grove Dictionary of American Music.* New York: Grove's Dictionaries of Music, 1986.

Johnson, J. Rosamond. "Why They Call American Music Ragtime." *Black Perspective in Music* 4 (July 1976): 260–64. Originally in *The Colored American Magazine* 15 (January 1909): 636–639.

Johnson, James Weldon. *Along This Way.* New York: Viking, 1933.

———. *Black Manhattan.* New York: Knopf, 1930.

Kellner, Bruce, ed. *The Harlem Renaissance.* New York: Methuen, 1984.

Logan, Rayford W., and Michael R. Winston, eds. *Dictionary of American Negro Biography.* New York: Norton, 1982.

Riis, Thomas L. *Just Before Jazz.* Washington, DC: Smithsonian Institute Press, 1989.

"Rosamond Johnson, 81, Buried at Mt. Hope Cemetery." *New York Age* (20 November 1954).

Sampson, Henry T. *The Ghost Walks.* Metuchen, NJ: Scarecrow Press, 1988.

Southern, Eileen. *Biographical Dictionary of Afro–American and African Musicians.* Westport, CT: Greenwood Press, 1982.

Woll, Allen. *Black Musical Theatre.* Baton Rouge: Louisiana State University Press, 1989.

Robert L. Johns

Jack Johnson
(1878–1946)
Boxing champion

Jack Johnson withstood the effects of racism and its limitations on boxing opportunities, to become the first African–American heavyweight boxing champion, in the world. In his career, he lost only five of ninety–seven bouts. A fearless man, his flamboyant and colorful lifestyle made him one of the most despised men, in America. He has been called by some experts the greatest boxer of his weight class.

Johnson was born John Arthur Johnson, in Galveston, Texas on March 31, 1878, the son of Henry and Tina Johnson. He was the third child in a family of six that included an older sister, Jennie, born in 1875, Henry, born in 1880, Fannie, born in 1885, and Charles, born in 1887. There were three other children who had died at birth. Johnson married his first wife, Mary Austin, in 1898. He then married Etta Terry Duryea, in 1909. His third wife, Lucille Cameron, and he were wed, in 1913. Johnson married his fourth wife, Irene Marie Pineau, in 1924.

Johnson's father was born into slavery. His mother was 19 years younger than her husband. Johnson's father worked at a variety of jobs including: woodcutter, saloon porter, and janitor for the East Side School district. He owned his house and provided for his family as well as he could.

Young Johnson attended public school, in Galveston. After being protected by his sister several times in school fights, his mother admonished him to not come home again without having defended himself and he followed her command. Johnson later participated in the Battle Royal, a sport for white spectators, where several young African American boys were blindfolded and placed in the ring to fight each other until only one remained. Johnson was often the winner, in this humiliating event. One young African American boy with one leg fought in the events and sometimes boys fought naked.

Several other experiences toughened Johnson's resolve. He was employed as a laborer and dock worker and often had fights with the men on the docks and back streets. When the circus was in town, he also fought the circus boxers. Although Johnson could not keep a steady job, he was attracted by boxing. Seeking better employment, he went to Dallas, in the early 1890s, where he worked in a carriage painting shop operated by Walter Lewis, a prominent local boxer who helped him strengthen his boxing skills. Johnson's performance encouraged him to consider boxing as a career. He continued to fight when he returned to Galveston and became known as a skillful fighter. When he was 15, he was victorious in his first regular ring battle, a sixteen–rounder, in a large, open field before a sizable crowd. His boxing prestige was enhanced when he beat a local and dangerous bully, Dave Pierson. Johnson was 16 and Pierson was a grown and toughened man. News spread, and people asked others if they heard what ''Lil Arthur'' had done. Later on, after he became prominent in the sports world, writers made him known the world over as ''Lil Arthur.''

Jack Johnson

Johnson's early boxing records in Galveston are sketchy, since he was not a top fighter. He won many local fights but needed recognition beyond that level. He went to Chicago to learn the tricks of the trade and, while he was there, he worked as a sparring partner. On March 7, 1899, Johnson was given a chance for a real fight against an African American boxer, Klondike Haynes. Suffering from malnutrition, Johnson quit the match in the fifth round and later returned to Galveston.

Joe Choynoski, a well–known fighter at that time, moved to Galveston and worked in the field of athletics. In his prime, Choynoski fought John L. Sullivan, Tom Sharkey, Jim Jeffries, and Joe Walcott. After defeats from Kid McCoy, Walcott, and Sharkey, Choynoski needed an incentive to compete again and rising boxers offered him that challenge. Johnson, an upward–moving boxer, would offer him a chance to return to glory. Since prize fighting was illegal in Texas, both men were jailed after their fight, in 1901. The jury wanted them freed while the judge wanted them in jail and a compromise was reached. The bond was reduced to one thousand dollars and twenty–four days in jail. Johnson left the city, in that year.

In the early 1900s, less than 50 years from the end of the American Civil War, African Americans were not considered equal to whites. Even though several African Americans, such as Jim Molineaux, had preceded Johnson in the ring, boxing still remained illegal, in many states. Also, many whites did not like the idea of African Americans physically beating white men. The financial rewards, however, were great for those willing to take the chance. Between 1902 and 1907, Johnson had 57 registered and successful fights in such cities as Boston, Philadelphia, Pittsburgh, Los Angeles, San Francisco, and Chicago. He fought in countless matches and exhibitions that were not officially recorded. He fought some of the leading African American heavyweights such as Joe Jeannette, in a six–round match, in Philadelphia, on May 9, 1905, where no decision was rendered and then Johnson lost to him, in the second round, on November 25. In 1906, Johnson defeated Sam Langford, the "Boston Tar Baby," in a fifteen–round match, in Chelsea, Massachusetts, on April 26, 1906. By then, Johnson looked confidently ahead to winning the world's heavyweight title. Although he demonstrated strength, speed. And skill, sports writers and boxing authorities questioned his claim to higher ring honors solely based on his race. On July 17, 1907, Johnson knocked out Bob Fitzsimmons, the 1897–1899 heavyweight champion. Racism was alive in the ring. Jeffries succeeded Fitzsimmons as the undefeated heavyweight champion, in 1905, but refused to fight Johnson because he was African American. After Tommy Burns beat Marvin Hart, Jeffries gave Burns the "title."

In 1908, amid many verbal exchanges in the ring, Johnson defeated Burns in the fourteenth round to win the heavyweight championship, in Sydney, Australia. Later, Johnson fought Tony Ross, Jack O'Brien, Al Kaufman, and middleweight champion Stanley Ketchell. Ketchell knocked Johnson down but Johnson rose up, gathered his faculties, and knocked out Ketchell.

While Johnson was liked in many white circles, his arrogance and ego had become a problem. He loved racing automobiles, but was not considered a racer. In the years to come, he faced reckless driving charges in many states. At one point, he was ordered to stay in jail, in San Francisco, for 25 days, for driving recklessly.

During this period, Johnson had fought all eligible fighters, but white boxing fans were not satisfied because the champion was black. The search was on for the "great white hope." In 1910, the Johnson–Jeffries fight was to be held in San Francisco, but due to a legality, the fight was moved to Reno, Nevada. On July 4, Johnson defeated Jeffries, the former champion who had been enticed to enter the ring again. Race riots occurred in cities around the country where African Americans were rejoicing and whites were angry. Songs were written about Johnson, in celebration of the win.

Johnson fought in many cities, toured with burlesque shows, and had an entourage of followers including white women. He had married, Mary, his childhood sweetheart, from Galveston, and his only African American wife, in 1898. She left him, in 1901, and he gained the reputation of womanizer. Johnson acknowledged, in his book, *Jack Johnson In the Ring and Out,* that there had been countless women in his life who had shared his triumphs and suffered with him during moments of disappointment. Later, he married, Etta, one of his main followers, in 1909. However, the pressure of his consorting with other white women, many of them prostitutes, became too much for her and, on September 11, 1912, she committed suicide at the Cafe de Champions. Crowds continued to follow him, including the prostitutes Belle Schreiber and Hattie Watson. Johnson bought a home on Wabash Avenue, in Chicago, and established a business, Cafe de Champions. On numerous occasions he entertained women, in his guest rooms, at the business.

Johnson grieved, but within a year's time, he again, married another white woman, Lucille, in 1913. Both were detained in jail prior to the marriage. Johnson was charged with abduction and she was held in an effort to prevent the marriage, but an African American minister married them anyway.

Government officials were enraged with Johnson because of his blatant arrogance and his flaunting of white women, who were prostitutes. A young woman named Harriett, a close white prostitute friend of Johnson's, was 18 when their affair began. The Mann Act was passed charging unlawful transportation of minors across state lines. A trial was held and white prostitutes, who knew him, testified on his behalf, but he was convicted. On June 4, 1913, Johnson was sentenced to a year and a day in jail and was fined one thousand dollars. He had been convicted under a law that was not even in effect at the time of his supposed violation.

Heads for Europe

Johnson left the United States for Paris and later England. However, after his credit ran out and fights could not be booked, he resorted to wrestling. In 1915, he fought Jess Willard, in Cuba. At the beginning of the fight, Johnson was in control, but as the rounds went on, Johnson began to tire and, in the twenty–sixth round, Willard knocked him out and he lost his crown. Johnson claimed later that he threw the fight but that story was not upheld. Johnson thought that, after the fight, he could return to America but his visa was denied and he had to return to Europe. He lived in Spain, where he established an advertising agency that eventually failed, and he returned to boxing.

In 1919, after World War I, Johnson left for Cuba and Mexico. While in Mexico, he had the support of General Venustiano Caranza, President of Mexico. When Caranza was killed, the new Mexican president did not favor Johnson. In 1920, Johnson was returned to America, and into the hands of law officials. He was imprisoned in Leavenworth for violating the Mann Act , before his 1913 escape to Europe. In 1924, he and his third wife divorced and he promptly married his fourth wife, Irene, who was also white. She remained with him, until he died.

Johnson wanted to return to boxing and fight Jack Dempsey, but Dempsey's stipulation did not meet his qualifications. He was allowed a bout in Mingo, West Virginia, but the Ku Klux Klan threatened to disrupt the fight and it was canceled. After several unsuccessful attempts to return to the ring, Johnson's career ended in Juarez, Mexico, where Bob Lawson, an African American boxer, knocked him out. Later, Johnson told stories about his life at Herbert's Museum in

New York, where there were other sideshow features such as a snake handler and a flea circus.

For one dollar a match, at the 1933 World's Trade Fair, in Chicago, he was used as a punching bag for young boys who wanted to box the former champion. Johnson became involved in political activities, by campaigning for Al Smith and Franklin Roosevelt. Later on, he served as a trainer.

Johnson did not like Joe Louis. He claimed that Louis held his left hand too low, was not balanced, and could not properly land his fists. Just as Johnson had forecasted, Louis' weaknesses caused Max Schmelling to knock him out, but Louis returned and defeated Schmelling, in 1938.

Tall in stature, Johnson had smooth, dark skin and a solid frame. He shaved his head which became a trademark. He was quick in the boxing ring and known for his style of defense. Even though he married three white women, in his early days he was friends with two African American women, his first wife and Clara Kerr. His free spirit and actions throughout life defied the prevailing racial attitude in America.

Johnson's joy for the sport of automobile racing led to his death. He lost control of the car he was driving fast near Franklington, North Carolina, on June 10, 1946. He died that same day, in St. Agnes Hospital, in Raleigh, from injuries sustained from the accident. He was buried in Graceland Cemetery, in Chicago. In 1954, Johnson was inducted into the Boxing Hall of Fame. In 1968, a Broadway show debuted about his life. It was entitled *The Great White Hope* and starred James Earl Jones. The show received rave reviews and several awards.

In a period of American history when racism was so strong and the hatred for African Americans was widely manifested, Johnson, the first African American heavy weight champion, fought his way to victory in over ninety wins and five losses. Johnson's fight extended beyond the ring. Through the years, Americans and Europeans denied him access to the ring or made such access a political issue. He would have surpassed his record, but the fighters could not agree on the conditions for the bout.

REFERENCES

Ashe, Arthur R., Jr. *A Hard Road to Glory: A History of the African–American Athlete 1919–1945.* New York: Warner Books, 1988.

Chalk, Ocania. *Pioneers of Black Sport.* New York: Dodd, Mead, 1975.

Henderson, Edwin Bancroft. *The Negro in Sports.* Washington, DC: Associated Publishers, 1939.

Johnson, Jack. *Jack Johnson: In the Ring and Out.* 1927. Reprint, Detroit: Gale Research, 1975.

Logan, Rayford W., and Michael R. Winston, eds. *Dictionary of American Negro Biography.* New York: Norton, 1982.

Mays, Benjamin E. *Born to Rebel.* Athens: University of Georgia Press, 1971.

Roberts, Randy. *Papa Jack: Jack Johnson and the Era of White Hopes.* New York: Free Press, 1983.

Young, A. S. ''Doc.'' *Negro Firsts in Sports.* Chicago: Johnson Publishing Company, 1963.

Barbara Williams Jenkins

James Weldon Johnson

(1871–1938)

Writer, activist, lyricist, diplomat, critic, educator, lawyer, editor

James Weldon Johnson achieved great success in a remarkably varied number of fields. Early in his career, he was a successful high school principal in Florida, a diplomat in Central and South America, and a lyricist on Broadway. He achieved pioneering breakthroughs in law and in publishing, even though he devoted a relatively brief amount of time to those fields. He wrote the words to ''Lift Every Voice and Sing,'' widely known as the Negro National Anthem. As an important civil rights activist, Johnson held major leadership positions in the NAACP from 1916 until 1931. From 1932 until 1938, he taught at Fisk University in Nashville, Tennessee. Within the period 1934–37, he also held a visiting faculty appointment at New York University. He received the Spingarn Medal in 1925 and a Julius Rosenwald Fellowship in 1929. He held honorary degrees from Atlanta University, Talladega College, and Howard University.

Johnson's achievements as an author have earned him a secure place in American literature. His major creative works include *The Autobiography of an Ex–Colored Man* (1912) and *God's Trombones* (1927). He was also an excellent anthologist and literary critic, as demonstrated in *The Book of American Negro Poetry* (1922; reissued 1931). His non–fiction works such as *Black Manhattan* (1930) and his autobiography *Along This Way* (1933) are valuable chronicles, for Johnson's talents, experiences, and temperament made him an excellent commentator on his times.

James Weldon Johnson was born on June 17, 1871, in Jacksonville, Florida. His original middle name was William, but he changed it to Weldon in 1913 on the grounds that William, in combination with the other two names, was too commonplace.

Johnson's parents were James and Helen Louise (Dillet) Johnson. James Johnson was born free in Richmond, Virginia, in 1830 and as a boy went to New York City to work. Largely self–taught, he worked as a headwaiter in major hotels during much of his adult life. Later, he became a minister. Helen Dillet Johnson was born in Nassau, Bahamas, in 1842 and came to New York City with her family when she was a girl. In addition to a Bahamian background, her family

James Weldon Johnson

also had roots in Haiti. A talented singer, she and James Johnson met in New York about 1860. He followed her to Nassau after she had returned there with her family during the American Civil War, and they were married in Nassau in 1864. They were still in Nassau in 1868 when their first child, Marie Louise, was born; she was to live less than two years. James Johnson had by then moved his family to Jacksonville, Florida, in search of better economic opportunity. James Weldon Johnson was their second child. The third child, John Rosamond, known as Rosamond, was born in 1873. Rosamond Johnson achieved significant fame in his own right as a musician, and he and James Weldon collaborated on many successful projects.

Johnson's mother, identified by Keneth Kinnamon in the *Black Writers of America: A Comprehensive Anthology* as "the first black woman public school teacher in Florida," was a major influence on his education. In addition to providing extensive guidance for her sons at home, she was also one of their teachers at the Stanton School, the public elementary school for colored children. Because there was no high school in Jacksonville that blacks could attend, Johnson attended Atlanta University's preparatory school starting in 1887.

In the summer of 1886, Johnson worked for Thomas Osmond Summers, a white physician. As a result, Johnson came into contact with a wide range of books and with the perspectives of a freethinking intellectual. The young Johnson also traveled with Summers to Washington, D.C., another broadening experience. In *Along This Way,* Johnson wrote that Summers provided his "first worthwhile literary criticism and encouragement."

By the time he received his baccalaureate degree from Atlanta University in 1894, Johnson had experienced a variety of other opportunities to expand his formal study. He attended the 1893 Chicago World's Fair, where he heard presentations by Frederick Douglass and by Paul Laurence Dunbar. Also in the summers prior to his graduation, Johnson was part of a male quartet that toured extensively in New England.

Perhaps his most deeply affecting experiences occurred in the summers of 1891 and 1892 when as a young teacher, he saw firsthand the living conditions for rural blacks near Hampton, Georgia. In *Along This Way,* he cited the experience as central to his understanding and lifelong commitment:

> I was anxious to learn to know the masses of my people, to know what they thought, what they felt, and the things of which they dreamed; and in trying to find out, I laid the first stones in the foundation of faith in them on which I have stood ever since.

Early Career Achievements

In the fall of 1894, Johnson accepted an offer to become principal of the Stanton School back in Jacksonville. After only one year, he was able to extend the curriculum to include the secondary school years. He did so without fanfare or fighting with bureaucracy. The consequences were nonetheless highly significant, for thereafter black students would not have to leave Jacksonville for a high school education.

Despite his busy schedule as an educator, Johnson founded a newspaper, the *Daily American,* in 1895. The paper allowed Johnson to share his insights on race–related issues in editorials. It folded after eight months.

Perhaps not surprisingly for a man who said in *Along This Way* that he found "spare time" contrary to success, Johnson's wide–ranging vision in the same period led him to another career entry point even as he continued as the Stanton principal. After studying law with attorney Thomas A. Ledwith, he passed the Florida bar examination in 1897. In *Along This Way,* Johnson notes, "This was the first time in Duval county, and, for all I could learn, in the state of Florida, that a Negro had sought admission to the bar through open examination in a state court." With a friend from childhood, Judson Douglass Wetmore, Johnson practiced law from 1898 to 1901, but never as his sole occupation.

Also at the turn of the century, Johnson was developing yet another area of work. His mother had seen to it that both of her sons developed their artistic—especially musical—talents and a special appreciation for African American culture. In 1900 the brothers collaborated in the writing of "Lift Every Voice and Sing," known widely as "the Negro National Anthem." They wrote the song—Rosamond the music and James Weldon the words—practically overnight for a school choir performance in honor of Lincoln's birthday. The song spread through those who learned it as school children and who in turn taught it to others after they became teachers. In *Along This Way,* Johnson wrote, "Nothing that I have done has paid me back so fully in satisfaction as being the part creator of this song."

Music was soon to play an even larger role in Johnson's life. He spent the summers of 1899 and 1900 in New York City becoming oriented to musical theater. He helped write song lyrics for his brother and Bob Cole, who was a performer, producer, and composer. Rosamond and Cole were already finding success as a team in the world of New York vaudeville and theatre.

Johnson resigned as the Stanton School principal in 1902 and moved to New York to devote himself full time to Broadway work. In *Along This Way,* he noted that the Johnsons and Cole "partnership lasted seven years, in which time we wrote some two hundred songs that were sung in various musical shows on Broadway and 'on the road.'" The Johnson brothers and Cole wrote such popular songs as "Under the Bamboo Tree," "The Maiden with the Dreamy Eyes," "Mandy," and "Oh, Didn't He Ramble." In *The Book of American Negro Poetry,* Johnson identified "Ramble" as a "jes' grew" song, the melody having been in the public domain; the trio's contribution was to add words to the verses. The team also wrote songs for full–length musicals including *Humpty Dumpty* and *The Sleeping Beauty and the Beast.*

In 1905 James Weldon accompanied his brother and Bob Cole on their performing tour. Despite their celebrity, the three were not able to find decent lodging in Salt Lake City, an incident that remained so indelibly with Johnson that 23 years later he refused to leave the train station in that city when he led an NAACP delegation to a California meeting; others in the group used the layover time to tour the city. Johnson had a more pleasant experience later in 1905 when he traveled to Europe with Johnson and Cole.

From 1903 to 1906, Johnson studied at Columbia University, where he worked with literary scholar Brander Matthews, who knew of Johnson's Broadway achievements, and Johnson described his relationship with Matthews in *Along This Way* as "warm and lasting." Before Johnson became more widely known as a writer, however, he moved into yet another field.

Enters Consular Service

Between 1904 and 1912, Johnson held two diplomatic posts. As treasurer of the Colored Republican Club in New York, a task pressed upon him by Charles W. Anderson, he became what he described in *Along This Way* as "the recognized colored Republican leader of New York." Anderson encouraged Johnson to apply for a post in the U.S. Consular Service. Johnson served as U.S. Consul in Puerto Cabello, Venezuela, from 1904 to 1909. His second post in Corinto, Nicaragua, meant an advancement in grade but carried more problems than the Venezuelan post. He found the duties more extensive, and he encountered several incidents of racial prejudice from white Americans visiting the country. He served during a time of revolution in Nicaragua, which concluded with U.S. Marines landing in the country.

From his consular posts, Johnson courted Grace Nail, who was in New York City. They were married there in 1910. She traveled back to Nicaragua with him, staying almost two years before returning to New York—Johnson's wish for her to safeguard her health. Johnson resigned his consular appointment in 1912, when it seemed clear that he would not be allowed to advance to an appointment in the Azores.

In 1914 Johnson returned briefly to journalistic writing when he became editor of established black newspaper, *The New York Age.* His work, primarily that of a contributing editor, was well–received by readers. Having taken on the post largely for financial reasons, he moved on once it was clear that the job could not provide full–time support.

Serves the NAACP

Johnson's next major career was as a civil rights activist at the NAACP, where he served in major leadership roles. Hired as the organization's first field secretary, he sought and received approval to organize branches in the South, by no means a routine endeavor at the time. His travels, starting in Richmond, Virginia, in 1917, laid the groundwork for increasing dramatically the number of southern chapters by 1919. The NAACP led many protest activities in the post–World War I period, which was marked by lynchings and riots. In 1919, for example, Johnson led a delegation to see President Woodrow Wilson in protest of the courtmartialing and death sentences meted out to black soldiers following a racially based conflict in Houston, Texas.

Johnson twice served as acting secretary of the NAACP before becoming its first non–white executive secretary in 1920. In his first year as executive secretary, Johnson visited Haiti to investigate reports of harsh treatment of that country's citizens following occupation by the U.S. Marines in 1915. Johnson deemed the imperialistic move by the U.S. government unjustified. He was nonetheless careful in his investigations not to compromise the safety of Haitians who felt they or their families would be in danger if they spoke freely. Warren G. Harding used Johnson's critical assessment of the U.S. presence in Haiti in his 1920 presidential campaign.

Johnson led the NAACP's efforts to have the Dyer Anti–Lynching Bill passed by Congress in 1922. The bill passed the House of Representatives, but stalling by Republicans, supposed allies, kept the Senate from voting on the bill. Nonetheless, Johnson felt the efforts of the NAACP had been successful in placing the issue in the forefront of Americans' thinking. In working relentlessly for voting rights and in investigating many other discriminatory actions, Johnson worked so vigorously that he was twice overcome with exhaustion, once in 1926 and again in 1929.

In 1927 Johnson was the lecturer in a week–long seminar at the University of North Carolina at Chapel Hill, an unusual opportunity for an African American at that time. In 1929–30, on leave from the NAACP, he was able to concentrate on traveling and writing as a result of receiving a Julius Rosenwald Fellowship. He attended a conference in Kyoto, Japan, sponsored by the American Council of the Institute of Pacific Relations. He spent time in Toyko as well, and on the return trip, he visited Hawaii.

The Writings

Even as he pursued his many other careers, Johnson was honing his skills as a writer. Cited in *Along This Way,* his first poem published in a major magazine (*Century* 1900) was in dialect: "Sence You Went Away." The poem was later set to music by Rosamond Johnson, and it was a concert favorite of many soloists, including Paul Robeson. In 1913 *The New York Times* published Johnson's poem "50 Years," which had been commissioned in honor of the fiftieth anniversary of Lincoln's signing of the Emancipation Proclamation.

Johnson began to write *The Autobiography of an Ex–Colored Man* (1912) at Columbia University and finished it in Venezuela. He chose to publish it anonymously so that it would be read as though it was indeed an autobiography of someone who was continuing to pass for white. However, the narrative is fictional. In *Black Writers,* Keneth Kinnamon pointed out that Johnson's friend Judson Douglass Wetmore was the prototype of "the ex–colored man." Johnson identified himself as the author when the book was reprinted in 1927. He wrote his own autobiography, *Along This Way,* to help distinguish his life from that of the narrator's in *The Autobiography.* In 1917 he published a collection, *Fifty Years and Other Poems,* which included some new but mostly previously published poems.

Johnson published many important works during the 1920s, the main decade of the Harlem Renaissance. Indeed, Johnson's preceding works embraced and illustrated themes and forms given prominence by many of the younger writers. *The Autobiography* incorporated the "tragic mulatto" theme, although Johnson's approach emphasized not so much a convincingly plotted novel as an opportunity for commentary on many phases of attitudes and situations related to race relations.

It was during the 1920s as well that the Johnson brothers compiled and arranged *The Book of Negro Spirituals* (1922) and *The Second Book of Negro Spirituals* (1925). In 1926 these works were published in one volume as *The Books of American Negro Spirituals.* In his prefaces to these volumes, James Weldon Johnson paid tribute to the beauty and power of the songs and to their anonymous creators. His poem "O Black and Unknown Bards" (1908) had expressed similar appreciation.

God's Trombones: Seven Negro Sermons in Verse (1927), perhaps Johnson's premier creative achievement, paid tribute to the "old–time Negro preacher." The work grew out of his visits to many churches as part of his NAACP speaking tours. "The Creation" (1920) was the first of the seven sermons Johnson wrote, after hearing an especially dynamic sermon by a minister in Kansas City, Missouri. Johnson completed the other *God's Trombones* selections in late 1926. He deliberately avoided the literary, plantation dialect which he felt had only two stops: pathos and humor. Johnson used colloquial language in an effort to convey the dignity and beauty of the sermons. He also conveyed the rhythm of the sermons without strict rhyme schemes. Aaron Douglas, the muralist whose work became prominent during the Harlem Renaissance, provided the illustrations for the original edition of *God's Trombones.*

Johnson's anthology, *The Book of American Negro Poetry* (1922; 1931), begins with a perceptive historical introduction. Johnson's brief headnotes to each poet provide informative critical assessments. The second edition includes writers who came to be known in the 1920s such as Langston Hughes, Countee Cullen, and Gwendolyn Bennett. Johnson noted that many of these younger writers, notably Hughes and Sterling Brown, were to some extent able to overcome the limitations traditionally part of dialect poetry.

During the 1930s, Johnson published several major works of nonfiction. His experiences on Broadway and his ongoing interest in a range of settings and people made *Black Manhattan* (1930) a very informative source for learning about the history of New York in the pre–Harlem Renaissance years. Like *Black Manhattan, Along This Way* provided a valuable historical record, for Johnson was directly involved in a wide range of significant events. Although Johnson included personal views and details, *Along This Way* is less an autobiography than a memoir. Reticence on the topic of his private life reflects his focus in his writing overall: a concern with issues. That concern is clear in *Negro Americans, What Now?* (1934), which addresses social and political topics with emphasis on various strategies for achieving racial integration. Johnson did not completely move away from poetry in the thirties. The title poem in *Saint Peter Relates an Incident of the Resurrection Day: Selected Poems* (1935) explored the absurdity of racial discrimination when the unknown soldier turns out to be "colored."

In 1932 Johnson began his appointment as the first Adam K. Spence Professor of Creative Writing at Fisk University. He held this post until his death. In *Along This Way,* Johnson wrote of enjoying the more contemplative life of the university setting as well as enjoying interaction with students.

Johnson married Grace Nail on February 10, 1910. They had no children. Grace Johnson was the daughter of successful Harlem real estate entrepreneur John B. Nail. James Weldon Johnson died in Wiscassett, Maine, on June 26, 1938, as a result of injuries received in a car–train accident. Although injured seriously, Grace Johnson survived the crash. Johnson's funeral was held at Salem Methodist Church in Harlem on June 30, 1938. The Reverend Frederick Cullen, Countee Cullen's father, officiated. He is buried in Greenwood Cemetery in Brooklyn, New York.

The term "Renaissance man" applies to James Weldon Johnson in its most comprehensive sense. Born less than ten years after the end of the Civil War, he mastered a remarkable number of professions. He was an agnostic who demonstrated in his creative efforts a profound respect for the Christian faith embraced by the majority of African Americans. Although he can be identified as a "race man," he was not limited in his outlook nor was he bitter, despite being a victim of both personal and institutional discrimination on many occasions. He had a well–justified sense of confidence as a talented, intelligent human being. His achievements are outstanding in both quality and in range.

REFERENCES

Barksdale, Richard, and Keneth Kinnamon, eds. *Black Writers of America: A Comprehensive Anthology.* New York: Macmillan, 1972.

Fleming, Robert E. *James Weldon Johnson.* Boston: G. K. Hall, 1987.

———. *James Weldon Johnson and Arna Bontemps: A Reference Guide.* Boston: G. K. Hall 1987.

Harris, Trudier, ed. *African American Writers, 1940–1955.* Detroit, Gale Research, 1988.

Jackson, Miles Jr. ''James Weldon Johnson.'' *Black World* 19 (June 1970): 32–34.

Johnson, James Weldon. *Along This Way: The Autobiography of James Weldon Johnson.* New York: Viking, 1933.

———. *The Book of American Negro Poetry.* New York: Harcourt Brace and World, 1922.

———. *God's Trombones: Seven Negro Sermons in Verse.* New York: Viking Press, 1927.

———. *St. Peter Relates an Incident of the Resurrection Day: Selected Poems.* New York: Viking, 1935.

———. *The Selected Writings of James Weldon Johnson.* 2 vols. Ed. Sondra K. Wilson New York: Oxford, 1995.

Levy, Eugene. *James Weldon Johnson: Black Leader, Black Voice.* Chicago: University of Chicago Press, 1973.

Logan, Rayford, and Michael R. Winston, eds. *Dictionary of American Negro Biography.* New York: W. W. Norton, 1982.

COLLECTIONS

The James Weldon Johnson Collection at the Beinecke Rare Book Collection at Yale University includes a major portion of the Johnson papers. Other materials are located in the Fisk University Library. The NAACP Papers, housed in the Library of Congress, are a further major resource.

Arlene Clift–Pellow

John H. Johnson

(1918–)

Entrepreneur, publisher, insurance company executive

John H. Johnson began life in poverty and worked his way up the economic ladder to become a wealthy businessman of international reputation. Founder of Johnson Publishing Company and such spinoffs as Ebony Fashion Fair and Ebony Cosmetics, he is the first successful black publisher to emerge after World War II. Among his publications is *Ebony* magazine, the most widely circulated and most popular black magazine, one that has continuously worked to eradicate negative stereotypes and replace them with positive black images. Through Johnson's leadership, Johnson Publishing Company consistently has been ranked among the nation's leading black businesses.

John Harold Johnson was born in a tin–roofed shotgun house in Arkansas City, a mill town in rural Arkansas, on January 19, 1918. His mother, Gertrude Johnson, was born to former slaves in Lake Village, Arkansas, and had a third–grade education. Raised in poverty, she worked in the fields and kitchens of the Mississippi Valley. After moving to Arkansas City, she worked as a domestic; she was married first to Richard Lewis and had a daughter, Beulah. After the marriage failed, ''Miss Gert'', as she was known, married Leroy Johnson, a laborer who worked in the local sawmill and on the levee. Gertrude Johnson promised her close friend, Johnnie Ford, that she would name her second child ''Johnnie,'' regardless of the child's gender; thus, John Johnson, born 14 years after his half–sister, was christened ''Johnnie.''

Johnson grew up in a two–parent home, where there was little money but great love. His mother, a short, forceful woman, dominated the household. Johnson's father, whom Johnson did not know well, traveled to levee camps up and down the Mississippi River and was killed in a sawmill accident when his son was eight. After that, Gertrude Johnson married James Williams, who delivered groceries for a bakery shop. The community of Johnson's youth was a strong one, where, as customary in may black areas of that era, the adults monitored and supervised the children of the community.

To help compensate for James Williams's small income, both Johnson and his mother worked; his mother operated field kitchens for a dredging company crew. She also served levee camps by doing laundry and cooking for the laborers. Young John Johnson, who accompanied his mother, learned the art of washing and ironing clothes early on.

Succeeds Against the Odds

Johnson was educated in Arkansas City Colored School, graduating in June of 1932. The city offered no public high school; since the family was poor, Johnson could not follow the traditional black option in Arkansas of attending boarding school in Pine Bluff or Little Rock. That summer both Gertrude and John Johnson continued to cook, wash, and iron for the levee camps, sometimes for as many as 50 men. Johnson wrote in his autobiography, *Succeeding Against the Odds,* that he became a master cook. When she was certain that the family was financially unable to move to Chicago, where Johnson could enter high school, Gertrude Johnson Williams made her son repeat the eighth grade rather than run wild on the streets or continue with menial work. He was advised that he would repeat that grade as many times as necessary until they had enough money for the move. Neighbors thought that arrangement was strange and that the mother was ''crazy for making sacrifices for a boy who would never amount to anything anyway,'' Johnson wrote.

Although the nation was in the middle of the Great Depression and unemployment in Chicago was high, in July of 1933, when he was 15, John Johnson moved to Chicago

John H. Johnson

with his mother; by agreement, his stepfather stayed in Arkansas. They roomed in a building at 5610 Calumet, on the South Side, where Gertrude Williams's daughter Beulah had also rented a room. Gertrude Johnson found a job as a domestic. By late 1933 Johnson, his mother, and his sister moved to an apartment at 5412 South Parkway. Soon afterward his stepfather joined them. His stepfather was unable to find a job, and his mother lost her job in the garment industry. Therefore, from 1934 to 1936 the family lived on public assistance, or relief, as it was known then.

In September of 1933 Johnson entered Wendell Phillips, a virtually all–black high school. By accident, he skipped the ninth grade and started school in the tenth grade with a view toward becoming a journalist. Later on he edited the school newspaper, the *Phillipsite,* and was sales manager of the yearbook, the *Red and Black,* presiding officer of the student council, leader of the student forum and the French Club, and junior and senior class president. Still poor, Johnson could not afford bus fare and walked to school in the bitter–cold months. His homemade suits and pants, his thick down–home country accent, and his bow legs made him the target of classmates' laughter. After running home crying to his mother, she solved at least a part of the problem. She persuaded a woman who was her employer and whose son was about Johnson's size to give her some of his old suits. Almost instantly, Johnson became one of the school's best dressed students. He resented the treatment he received and decided to retaliate by beating his classmates in the classroom and during extracurricular activities. He began to frequent the Fifty–eighth Street branch of the Chicago Public Library, where Vivian Harsh was in charge, and read widely in black history and literature, such as works by W. E. B. Du Bois and Booker T. Washington and the poetry of Langston Hughes. He also studied self–improvement books, such as those by Dale Carnegie. Johnson wrote in his autobiography, "Faith, self–confidence, and a positive mental attitude: These three were the basic messages of the self–help books that changed my life." He stood before his home mirror and practiced making speeches and approaching girls. When he began to speak out more in class, he amazed his classmates.

Students at Wendell Phillips High School transferred to a newly–constructed facility named Jean Baptiste Pointe DuSable after their school had burned down. Johnson's classmates at the two schools included several who became well known: singers Nat "King" Cole and Dorothy Donegan, comedian Redd Foxx, and entrepreneur Dempsey Travis. There was also Charles Murray Jr., son of Murray Hair Pomade founder, who rode to school in a chauffeur–driven limousine.

Near commencement time, with the persuasion of his white civics teacher Mary Herrick, Johnson changed his name from Johnnie to John, picked a middle name out of the air, and from then on was known as John Harold Johnson. He graduated from DuSable in 1936. At the school's commencement on June 11, Johnson was the only student chosen to speak and gave an impressive talk on "Builders of a New World." The *Chicago Defender* printed a notice of his impending speech, giving Johnson his first press coverage. Johnson graduated with "a fistful of honors" and a 200–dollar scholarship to the University of Chicago, he explained in his autobiography.

Johnson was asked to speak at a routine Urban League luncheon for outstanding high school students also held in 1936. One of Johnson's heroes, legendary business leader Harry H. Pace, who was president of Supreme Life Insurance Company and head of the New York–based Pace and Handy Music Company, was the main speaker. After Pace's speech, Johnson complimented him on his remarks and, in turn, Pace complimented Johnson on the good reports he had heard on his high school performance. When Pace learned that Johnson needed a part–time job to help finance his college education, he offered Johnson work in his company. Johnson wrote in his autobiography that the meeting with Pace changed and defined his life.

Eighteen–year–old Johnson reported to Pace's office on September 1, 1936, to begin a part–time job for $25 a month while he attended the University of Chicago part–time as well. He benefited from his experience with the company's executives, who included journalist and business manager Truman K. Gibson, attorney Earl B. Dickerson, and physician Midian O. Bousfield. When Johnson drove Pace to the bank each day, he used the time to question Pace about business and success. "Not a week goes by that I don't recall and use some lesson that I learned from him and other Supreme executives," Johnson pronounced in his autobiography. For a few months Johnson was assistant editor of *The Guardian,* the company's monthly newspaper. Pace was the paper's editor. In 1939 Johnson was promoted to editor, which placed the ambitious young man in a strategic position. Although Johnson intended to study for a law degree, he found Supreme Liberty Life so exciting that he dropped out of college and worked full–time.

In 1940 John Johnson met Eunice Walker, daughter of a prominent Selma, Alabama, physician and granddaughter of a founder of Selma University in Alabama. Walker was then a student at Talledega College in Alabama who was vacationing in Chicago. They married in Selma on June 21, 1941. Later they adopted two children, John Harold Jr., who died of sickle cell anemia when he was 25, and Linda (now Linda Johnson Rice).

Begins Publishing Venture

The world's events of that era set the stage for the beginning of Johnson's publishing venture. When World War II began, Johnson registered for the draft but was never called. During that period a new level of black consciousness arose. Pace gave him the task of reading magazines and newspapers and preparing a digest of events in the black world—an assignment that changed Johnson's life. Johnson became so knowledgeable about black achievement that he was often called on to give a digest of black news. He determined that he should begin a publication to pass on to the public the information he had garnered for Pace.

When Johnson considered publishing a magazine to summarize articles about black life, he sought the advice for Roy Wilkins, head of the NAACP, who tried to dissuade him. Writing about the experience in *Standing Fast,* Wilkins reported: "I knew the almost continuous financial difficulties *The Crisis* had had, and I told him that in my opinion, the time was not right to venture into the field. Fortunately, Johnson ignored me and began publishing *Negro Digest* in November 1942."

Johnson set up office in the corner of Earl Dickerson's law library in the Supreme Life Insurance Company's building, using 3507 South Parkway as his address for the Negro Digest Publishing Company. He wrote letters to policy holders of Supreme Life offering charter subscriptions at two dollars each. He needed 500 dollars for postage, and, with collateral, he could get it from Citizens Loan Corporation. With his mother's permission, he put up her new furniture as collateral for a $500 loan, then was able to mail his letters. On Sunday, November 1, 1942, his new publication, *Negro Digest,* was officially published. It was similar in name and format to *Reader's Digest,* but differed in that *Negro Digest* published complete reproductions of articles from the white and black press. Johnson described his reaction in his autobiography: "When I held the first copy of the magazine in my hand, I had a feeling of relief, exhilaration, and fear. I hadn't realized the true potential of the magazine until that moment, and I was overwhelmed by the idea that the life and death of this sixty–eight page baby was in my hands."

Johnson distributed 3,000 copies of the magazine to his prepaid subscribers but needed to sell the remaining 2,000 to pay his bills. He negotiated with Charles Levy Circulating Company, Chicago's biggest magazine distributor, and was finally able to obtain Levy's financial backing. He also broadened the journal's distribution by pushing it in places neglected by major distributors: mom–and–pop outlets, black–owned distributors, such as Chicago's National News Company. He made a profit on the first issue; otherwise, he admitted in his autobiography, there would have been no second issue.

Leaves Supreme

In 1943 Johnson was on leave from Supreme. Until 1944 he and his full–time secretary were *Negro Digest*'s only two employees; he disguised this fact and listed the names of relatives on the masthead. As the magazine grew in popularity, Johnson included a regular feature called "If I Were a Negro," and posed the question to major figures like Pearl Buck, Orson Welles, Edward G. Robinson, and Marshall Field. He also persuaded Eleanor Roosevelt to write the column for one issue, which was the cover story in October of 1943. After that, circulation jumped almost overnight, from 50,000 to 100,000. "We never looked back," wrote Johnson in his autobiography. "I was making so much money that I didn't know what to do with it," he continued.

In late 1943 Johnson bought his first building, located at 5629 South State Street. He made other longtime personal investments such as a three–story apartment home for himself and his wife, with space for his mother and stepfather. He bought cars for his mother, mother–in–law, and himself and his wife. He also expanded his staff and hired his mother, who remained on his staff from 1943 until she died in 1977.

Negro Digest grew, setting new records for a black magazine. Johnson said in his autobiography that he "didn't start a business to get rich—I started a business to provide a service and to improve myself economically." Now that the future of *Negro Digest* was assured, Johnson turned his attention to a new venture, the founding of *Ebony* on November 1, 1945, and to publishing its first book, *The Best of Negro Humor,* which Johnson edited. Johnson wrote in his autobiography that November became his signature month; *Negro Digest* was first issued in that month, were *Ebony* and other publications that followed.

Johnson knew that black people wanted to see themselves in pictures. *Life* magazine, then popular in the black community, was not geared to black people and black issues. He knew that blacks at that time in particular needed to see positive images of the race. According to the November 1995 issue of *Ebony,* published during its 50th–year celebration, "*Ebony* became the mirror of the struggle of rights activists. . .to desegregate rail and bus transportation, lunch counters, public schools. . .hotels and motels."

After considering several names for the new journal, Johnson's wife, Eunice Johnson, suggested "ebony" as the title. "It means fine black African wood," she explained in Johnson's autobiography. John Johnson added, "the name means. . .a tree, the hard, heavy, fine black wood that the tree yields, *and* the ambience and mystique surrounding the tree and the color."

The first run of *Ebony,* 25,000 copies, sold out in a few hours and Johnson immediately printed that number again. Immediately the journal moved ahead of *Negro Digest* and became the most widely circulated black journal in America, yet *Negro Digest* subsidized *Ebony.* No advertisements were used at first; to make a profit, however, he had to look for advertisers, and was able to secure contracts from major white companies, such as Zenith, Swift Packing Company, Armour Foods, Quaker Oats, Elgin Watch, and the makers of Chesterfield and Old Gold cigarettes. By then *Ebony* was in competition with another black magazine, *Our World.* When the latter magazine went into bankruptcy, Johnson bought it for 14,000 dollars. He hired one of *Our World*'s staff photographers, Moneta Sleet Jr., who later, still with *Ebony,* became the first black photographer to win a Pulitzer Prize (for the well–publicized, touching photograph of Coretta Scott King and children at Martin Luther King Jr.'s funeral). In retelling the 50–year history of *Ebony* in the November 1995 issue, Johnson was quoted as saying of its founding:

> We wanted to give Blacks a new sense of somebodiness, a new sense of self–respect. We wanted to tell them who they were and what they could do. We believed then—and we believe now—that Blacks needed positive images to fulfill their potentialities.

Johnson hired other black talent around 1948 and 1949 as writers, including Era Bell Thompson, Edward T. Clanton, Roi Ottley, and Doris Sanders. By then there were close to 100 full–time employees and over 4,000 independent distributors.

Forms Johnson Publishing Company

The firm's name, Negro Digest Publishing Company, was changed to Johnson Publishing Company in 1949 with corporate headquarters at 5125 Calumet. Book publishing had been suspended after its first book was published in 1945 until the Book Division was established in 1961 with book publishing resuming in 1962. The division first published such works as Paul Crump's *Burn Killer Burn,* Lerone Bennett's *Before the Mayflower,* Freda DeKnight's *The Ebony Cookbook,* and Doris Saunders's *The Ebony Handbook.* In time, the book division ventured into a variety of publications, including a number of children's books. Johnson raided black newspaper staffs and added to his staff photo editor Basil Phillips; writers Lerone Bennett Jr., Robert E. Johnson, and Simeon Booker; and society editor Geri Major.

Negro Digest was suspended in 1951 but revived in 1961 as a literary quarterly. In May of 1970, *Negro Digest* became *Black World,* which released its last issue in April of 1976. Spinoffs from Johnson's firm include the annual Ebony Fashion Fair, a traveling fashion extravaganza that home economist Freda DeKnight started in September of 1958 as the Ebony Fashion Show. Two thousand people attended the first show, and ten additional shows were held that year. The world–popular Ebony Fashion Fair showcases beautiful black women and men as models wearing exquisite, designer clothing. In succeeding years, other sponsors such as local Urban League chapters, sororities, and the NAACP were added. Eunice Walker Johnson became the director. The show annually produces thousands of subscribers for *Ebony* and *Jet* and raises millions of dollars for charity.

Between 1945 an 1972 Johnson produced other spinoffs: *Tan Confessions,* started in November of 1950 as a true–confessions magazine and later developed into a women's service magazine; *Proper Romance*; and *Jet,* a pocket–size weekly news magazine launched on November 1, 1951, that also contains special features. (The first issue of *Jet* sold out quickly and became a collector's item.) The firm also published *Hue,* a publication similar to *Jet* offering feature stories (which was abandoned in 1951); *Beauty Salon*; *Ebony Jr.,* designed for children between six and 12; *Ebony Man,* launched in 1985, and featuring grooming, appearance, and lifestyle issues for young black men; and *Ebony South Africa,* marking the company's expansion into the international publishing.

Diversifies

Fashion Fair Cosmetics, the world's largest black–owned cosmetics company, is a subsidiary of Johnson Publishing Company. Its forerunner was Johnson's mail–order company called Beauty Star, founded in about 1946, which sold wigs, vitamins, clothing and other products. Johnson advertises its products in *Ebony.* His company also owns Fashion Fair Cosmetics and Supreme Beauty Products.

In December of 1971 Johnson Publishing Company moved into its new eleven–story headquarters on Michigan Avenue, located ten blocks north of it old facility at 1820 South Michigan, which he bought and renovated in 1949. The new structure was the first black–owned building in Chicago's Loop.

Johnson had little contact with Supreme Life Insurance Company from 1943 to 1957. Later on he bought 1,000 shares of its stock and in 1974 was elected chairman and chief executive officer. He admitted in his autobiography that this gave him "a great sense of personal and corporate satisfaction," for he held the only two jobs he had in his life. He also serves as president of WLOU Radio Station and has bought and sold three other stations. When he purchased his first station in 1972, WGRT, he became the first black to own a radio station in Chicago.

Later, Johnson entered the television market and, with white sponsors, offered two major shows, Ebony Music Awards and the American Black Achievement Award. The white coproducers backed out, Johnson bought them out, broadened the format, and began sponsoring the annual ABAA show. His daughter Linda Johnson Rice runs the weekly variety show, the *Ebony/Jet Showcase* aired on a number of television stations.

During his legendary career, Johnson has served on a number of boards, including the Dial Corporation, Zenith Radio Corporation, and Chrysler Corporation. He is a trustee of the Art Institute of Chicago and a director of the Magazine

Publishers Association. He is recipient of the John Russwurm Award, National Newspaper Publishers Association, 1966; Spingarn Medal, NAACP, 1966; Communicator of the Year Award, University of Chicago Alumni Association, 1974; and Columbia Journalism Award, 1974. In 1975 he accompanied the U.S. Vice President Nelson Rockefeller on a goodwill tour to nine African countries. He received the National Press Foundation Award, 1986, and that same year *Black Enterprise* gave his firm the Number One Black Business Award. Johnson was inducted into the Black Press Hall of Fame in 1987. Other awards that followed were the Founders Award from the National Conference of Christians and Jews; the Mass Media Award; Distinguished Service Award, Harvard University Graduate School of Business Administration, 1991; and numerous others. He was inducted into the Chicago Journalism Hall of Fame in 1990. *Black Enterprise* for June of 1997 named Johnson one of its five marathon men, or "captains of the industry,"—those who have been on *BE*'s 100 list since the list was started 25 years ago; Johnson's company always finished near the top.

John H. Johnson never forgot his struggle from poverty to wealth; he demonstrated this when he hired Jesse Jackson. Although the date is not mentioned, in his autobiography Johnson remembered hiring Jackson "when he first came to Chicago, penniless, unemployed, and unknown." For this experience, Jackson refers to him affectionately as "Godfather." Johnson's mission now is to see Johnson Publishing Company grow. He told *Black Enterprise* for June of 1997 that he will seize all new opportunities and embrace technology to get were he needs to be. "Never say never about new things," he said. Although he has no plans to retire, his daughter, company president, Linda Johnson Rice, will play an increasing role in managing the company.

Current address: Publisher, Chairman, Chief Executive Officer, Johnson Publishing Company, Incorporated, 820 South Michigan Avenue, Chicago, IL 60605.

REFERENCES

Bennett, Lerone, Jr. *Before the Mayflower.* Chicago: Johnson Publishing Co., 1987.

Contemporary Black Biography. Vol. 3. Detroit: Gale Research, 1993.

"The *Ebony* Story." *Ebony* 51 (November 195): 80–86.

Ingham, John N., and Lynne B. Feldman. *African–American Business Leaders.* Westport, CT: Greenwood Press, 1994.

Johnson, John H., with Lerone Bennett Jr. *Succeeding Against the Odds.* New York: Warner Books, 1989.

Joyce, Donald Franklin. *Gatekeepers of Black Culture: Black–Owned Book Publishing in the United States, 1817–1981.* Westport, CT: Greenwood Press, 1983.

Whigham–Désir, Marjorie. "Marathon Men." *Black Enterprise* 27 (June 1997): 104–118.

Who's Who among African Americans, 1996–97. 9th ed. Detroit: Gale Research, 1996.

Wilkins, Roy, with Tom Mathews. *Standing Fast: The Autobiography of Roy Wilkins.* New York: Viking Press, 1982.

COLLECTIONS

The papers of John H. Johnson and those of Johnson Publishing Company are in the company's library but are not open to the public.

Jessie Carney Smith

Joshua Johnson
(1765?–1830?)
Painter

One of the most significant pioneering black American artists, Joshua Johnson—sometimes spelled "Johnston"—was a prolific portrait artist who produced more than 80 paintings in Baltimore at the turn of the nineteenth century. He became noted for his delightful, albeit stiff, depictions of wealthy Marylanders, replete with props and tack–studded Federal–style furniture.

Johnson's exact date and place of birth and death are unknown, as are his parents' and any siblings' identities. He may have been a Caribbean immigrant who settled in Baltimore (his name first appears in city records in the 1790s), or perhaps a freed slave once owned by the Peale family of painters; he was listed as a "Free Householder of Colour" in the city directory of 1817. There seems to be no death or burial records for him, but he probably died after 1824 since that is the last year he appeared in Baltimore municipal documents. Johnson's wives' surnames are unknown. He wed Sarah before 1798. They had two daughters who died in childhood, and three sons, who were baptized Catholic and grew up in Baltimore. Johnson married Clara (or Clarissa), who likely survived him, before 1803. Since Johnson appears in various directories as both black and white, he was apparently light–complexioned and of mixed heritage.

Virtually nothing is known of Johnson's early life. Given his stylistic affinity with Charles Willson Peale, Peale's son Rembrandt, and his adopted nephew Charles Peale Polk, however, he may well have studied with them or closely observed their work. Charles Peale Polk's father, as a privateer in coastal shipping, may have transported slaves in the South. He owned a French–speaking boy whom Peale wanted to buy; art historian Carolyn Weekley proposed the youth was Johnson. Peale already had two slaves, though he held abolitionist views and later freed Moses Williams, noted for his cut silhouettes. While the Peales had a more vibrant palette, similarities between the work of Johnson and the Peales include the stiff treatment of sitters' eyes, mouths, hands, and poses, and use of thin paint and props.

In 1798 Johnson advertised his work in the *Baltimore Intelligencer,* claiming that as a "self–taught genius" he had ''experienced many insuperable obstacles in the pursuit of his studies.'' He described himself as a limner, a nonacademic, portrait painter in a naive style.

Johnson depicted white working and middle classes, but his commissions largely came from prosperous, slave–holding families, often headed by merchants and seamen. Applying paint thinly in a restrained, yet silvery, palette, he excelled in rendering women wearing sheer bonnets, lace collars and cuffs, and white Empire–style dresses; men in suits and waistcoats amidst books and writing materials; and children with red shoes and coral jewelry holding cherries or strawberries, accompanied by pet dogs or butterflies. Sitters with candid gazes so frequently appeared elegantly posed on tack–studded furniture that scholars nicknamed him the ''brass tack artist.''

Johnson's best known family portraits are *Mr. and Mrs. James McCormick and Their Children* (1804–1805), *Mrs. Hugh McCurdy and Her Daughters* (1806–1807), and *Mrs. Thomas Everette and Her Children* (1818). His finest paintings of children (over half of his oeuvre) include *Letitia Grace McCurdy* (1900–1802) *Charles John Stricker Wilmans* (1803–1805), *Portrait of Edward Pennington Rutter and Sarah Ann Rutter* (1804), and *The Westwood Children* (1807). Johnson's later work demonstrates his skill in expressing familial relationships through gestures and poses such as an adult's arm about a child's shoulders or waist or a baby's hand upon a parent's chest. He may have derived attention to details of coiffures and clothing from a French Caribbean background. Three–quarters poses, theatrical drapery, and open windows are characteristics gleaned from conventional British portraiture.

Although Baltimore claimed many abolitionists and a large, free black community, it seems Johnson depicted few African Americans, who were less likely able to afford paintings. Yet Johnson's most important work is *Portrait of Daniel Coker* (1805–1810), a portrayal of the important Methodist, abolitionist founder of the African Bethel church, and advocate of African emigration. The artist painted a bust of the light–skinned, escaped slave with an aquiline nose and downward slanting eyebrows in a feigned oval. Johnson's only portrayal of a known white abolitionist is that of Dr. Andrew Aitkin (1804–1807).

While locally renowned during his lifetime, it was only in the 1940s that Johnson came to prominence when retired physician, genealogist, and historian Jacob Pleasants Halls identified 21 of his portraits. Since Johnson rarely autographed his works—his only signed piece is *Portrait of Sarah Ogden Gustin* (1798–1802)—Halls documented his works through stylistic analysis, oral histories, newspaper advertisements, and Baltimore housing, tax, professional, and church directories. Since then, Johnson's works have been featured in solo exhibitions at the Municipal Museum of the City of Baltimore (1948, curated by Pleasants) and the Abby Aldrich Rockefeller Center with the Maryland Historical Society (1987), and they have been avidly collected by major museums and private individuals.

Johnson's work is in the Abby Aldrich Rockefeller Folk Art Center, the National Gallery of Art, the Evans–Tibbs Collection, Hirschl and Adler Folk Art Museum, the National Museum of American Art, the Corcoran Gallery of Art, the Metropolitan Museum of Art, the Whitney Museum of American Art, the Municipal Museum of the City of Baltimore, the Maryland Historical Society, the Archdiocese of Baltimore, Queen Anne's County Historical Society, the Newark Museum, Bowdoin College Museum of Art, the Museum of Early Southern Decorative Arts, the Chrysler Museum, the American Museum in Britain, and in numerous private collections. While there is no repository of Johnson's papers, the visual legacy that this trailblazing artist created is significant, engaging, and substantial.

REFERENCES

Bearden, Romare, and Harry Henderson. *A History of African–American Artists from 1792 to the Present.* New York: Pantheon Books, 1993.

''Early Black Painter.'' *Colonial Homes* 8 (September–October 1982): 124–127, 164–165.

Hartigan, Lynda Roscoe. *Sharing Traditions: Five Black Artists in Nineteenth–Century America.* Washington, DC: Smithsonian Institution, 1985.

Hunter, Wilbur Harvey Jr. ''Joshua Johnston: 18th Century Negro Artist.'' *American Collector* 17 (February 1948): 6–8.

Pleasants, J. Hall. ''Joshua Johnston, the First American Negro Portrait Painter.'' *Maryland Historical Magazine* 37 (June 1942): 121–49.

Weekley, Carolyn J., Stiles Tuttle Colwill, and others. *Joshua Johnson: Freeman and Early American Portrait Painter.* Baltimore: Maryland Historical Society, 1987.

Theresa Leininger–Miller

Mordecai W. Johnson
(1890–1976)
College president, educator, minister

Mordecai Wyatt Johnson, born in humble circumstances in a small Southern town, rose to be one of the most highly respected clergymen, educators, and orators of his time. As a clergyman, he was like a prophet who boldly proclaims the word from on high. For 34 years (1926–1960) he was president of Howard University, Washington, D.C., where he made significant contributions not only to the university, but to the larger community as well. As an educator, he molded Howard University into the ''Capstone of Negro Education'' it had proclaimed itself to be. As an orator, he was one of the most effective platform presenters America has produced.

The son of former slaves, Mordecai Wyatt Johnson was born on December 12, 1890, in Paris, Tennessee. His father, Wyatt Johnson, was a preacher and mill worker. He was a strict disciplinarian who set rigorous standards for his son's chores and behavior. His mother was a domestic employed by one of the prominent families in town. She was kind and gentle, and demonstrated a keen interest in her son's education. Wyatt Johnson's first marriage to Nellie Biass produced three children: Jonas W., Dora, and Sallie. Three years after his first wife's death in 1885, Wyatt Johnson married Carolyn Freeman, a woman 30 years his junior. Mordecai was the only child of their union. His physical appearance made it possible for him to pass over into the white world. Nevertheless, he chose to remain in the societal status into which he was born.

Johnson's formal education began in a small elementary school in his native town. From there he went to Roger Williams University in Nashville, then to Howe Institute in Memphis and later transferred to the Atlanta Baptist College (now Morehouse College) where he completed his secondary and undergraduate education. During his college career, he was a member of the debating team and the Glee Club, a star athlete in three sports and quarterback of the football team. Offered a faculty position at the college upon graduation, he taught English and economics and served a year as acting dean. He maintained a profound interest in economics throughout his career—an interest that was apparent in some of his major addresses. After one year of teaching, he continued his education at the University of Chicago, where he received a second A.B. degree, and at the Rochester Theological Seminary in Rochester, New York, where he earned the B.D. degree. At Rochester he was profoundly influenced by the great "social gospel" advocate, Walter Rauchenbusch. His experiences there made an indelible impact upon his thinking and his entire career.

After a brief stint as secretary of the western region of the Student YMCA in 1917 he became pastor of the First Baptist Church in Charleston, West Virginia, where he served nine years. During that time, he founded a chapter of the NAACP and a Rochdale Cooperative, from which his parishioners and the community could purchase supplies at reduced prices. In 1921 he took a leave of absence from his church to study for a year at Harvard University Divinity School where he received the degree of master of sacred theology. At his graduation in June of 1922, he was chosen to represent the Graduate School at the university commencement. His speech on that occasion was entitled "The Faith of the American Negro." It resulted in his establishing a close relationship with Julius Rosenwald, the prominent philanthropist who was president of the Sears, Roebuck Corporation. Rosenwald was later to play a substantial role in helping Johnson realize some of his later administrative goals.

Becomes President of Howard University

At the age of 36, Johnson was elected the 11th, and the first African American, president of Howard University. He took the position in a crucial period in American history and especially in the history of African Americans. It was 1926 and the United States was enjoying the prosperity that had begun with the close of World War I in 1918. Business was booming and the economy was so strong that many thought progress inevitable. What was known as the Harlem Renaissance was in full swing, with the creative talents of African Americans expressed in literature, music, and art. The philosopher Alain Locke chronicled this era in his landmark book, *The New Negro.* It was a time of great expectations.

Mordecai W. Johnson

Ever since the establishment of schools for freedmen by white missionaries from the North following the Civil War, most of these institutions had been headed by Caucasians, as had Howard from its inception in 1867. Johnson's election to the presidency was hailed with pride by the black community at large. But he found an institution that, in many ways, did not measure up to the standards associated with a first–class university.

Financial Stability First

Johnson's first major responsibility was to assure the financial undergirding of the university. Since 1879 Congress had given some subsidies to the school, but the amounts were by no means adequate to the need nor were they assured each year. Encouraged by Johnson's leadership and his vision for the university, Louis C. Cramton, representative from Michigan, and other sympathetic lawmakers pushed through Congress a law providing annual support. This act in 1928 was of monumental significance for the future of the university. In recognition of this development, the NAACP awarded Johnson the Spingarn Medal, its highest honor.

Johnson set out to raise the quality of each of the schools in the university, starting with the medical school, one of only two in the nation to which African Americans were admitted without prejudice based on race. His first financial goal was to raise $250,000 to match a challenge grant by the General Education Board (GEB) toward a new building and endowment for the medical school, and an additional $180,000 for equipment. With help from Rosenwald, the arduous solicitations of alumni, medical faculty members, and an additional grant by the GEB, Johnson was able to announce at his first commencement as president that the campaign had been successful.

Johnson's primary concern, however, was raising the standards of the law school. When he assumed the presidency, it was a night school taught by men whose primary occupation was the practice of law during the day. With the advice of Associate Justice Louis D. Brandeis of the U.S. Supreme Court, Johnson made contact with top law schools for recommendations of their leading African American graduates to recruit for teaching at Howard. Brandeis pointed out that the bases for fighting racial discrimination were already embedded in the Constitution. What was needed, he said, was for lawyers to be prepared to base their arguments before the Court precisely upon the guarantees in the document. This proved to be significant advice not only for the development of the law school at Howard, but for affecting race relations throughout the country.

Johnson appointed Charles Hamilton Houston, a Phi Beta Kappa graduate of Williams College, with LL.B. and S.D.J. degrees from the Harvard Law School, as dean of the law school. Hamilton took the view that African American lawyers must see themselves as "social engineers." He and his colleagues developed high standards for students at the law school. Its most notable graduate was Thurgood Marshall, who became the first African American Associate Justice of the Supreme Court. At the law school, attention was given to research and intense analysis of litigation involving civil rights that had been or might be brought before the Court. It was no accident that Marshall, using the approach suggested by Brandeis, won 29 of the 32 of the civil rights cases he argued before the Court. These successes may be attributed in large measure to Mordecai Johnson's determination to make the Howard Law School the matrix out of which progress in the welfare of African Americans could be achieved. His role in its development was one of his major contributions to American life.

Controversy and Criticism

The first half of Johnson's tenure at Howard was marked by controversy. There were those who felt that it was unconscionable for the board of trustees to select a Baptist preacher who had no terminal academic degree and very little experience as a teacher and administrator in higher education. They maintained that he was not qualified to lead a great university. Johnson's administrative style was a source of animosity exhibited by some of the faculty and staff at Howard. Some accused him of being a dictator, of having a "messianic complex," and of being unyielding in the positions he took. Indeed, in one of his sermons he expressed the view that God had chosen individuals for certain purposes from the beginning of time. It would not be surprising if he believed that God had chosen him for a special mission. At this point in the development of some segments of higher education, it was not unusual for the charge of dictatorship to be made against college presidents.

Certain faculty and staff members maintained a continuous barrage of derogatory charges against Johnson during the first half of his administration. He persevered without responding. Through all the controversy he had the confidence and support of the trustees in constantly raising the level of support and the standards of the university. He made fruitful contacts with the major foundations, especially the Julius Rosenwald Fund, GEB, and the Federation of Jewish Charities. At the same time, he was able to attract top talent. During his administration, it was said that at Howard was the greatest collection of African American scholars to be found anywhere. Alain Locke, a philosopher and a Rhodes Scholar from Harvard, and Ernest E. Just, the internationally famous cell biologist, were already on the faculty when Johnson came. Added to them were, among others, Ralph Bunche, professor of political science and later a Nobel Laureate; Charles Drew, who perfected the use of blood plasma; Percy Julian, a noted chemist; Rayford Logan, a leading historian and an authority on the Caribbean; Abram Harris, an outstanding economist, and Sterling Brown, professor of English and a noted poet.

Johnson raised millions of dollars for new buildings and for upgrading all of the schools. Each segment boasted a strong curriculum. National honor societies, including Phi Beta Kappa, were established on campus. In addition, salaries were constantly increased and a favorable working environment was established. Johnson prided himself on upholding the standards and principles of academic freedom. During the era of the Communist scare, the House Un–American Activities Committee conducted investigations of certain faculty members and programs. Because Johnson spoke out favorably on certain aspects of the Russian government, there were those who accused him of being a Communist or a sympathizer—an accusation that he firmly denied.

Johnson was one of the university presidents who were possessed of strong leadership and personal magnetism. He ranked with William J. Hutchins, president of the University of Chicago; William H. P. Faunce, president of Brown University; and Abbot Lawrence Lowell, president of Harvard. Such men were not merely academic administrators, but national leaders, always in demand for counsel on issues of national interest.

As an Orator

One of the outstanding orators of his time, Johnson had a phenomenal memory and could speak without notes for as long as 45 minutes, yet was able to hold audiences spellbound because of his engaging speaking style and the content of his message. He traveled 25,000 miles a year speaking principally on racism, segregation, and discrimination. Early in his career, he was frequently in demand to lead religious–emphasis–weeks in colleges. He was the annual speaker on Education Night at the National Baptist Convention, USA, and a regular on the program at the Ford Hall Forum in Boston. In 1951 he was a member of the American delegation to the North Atlantic Treaty Organization (NATO) that met in London. On that occasion he was selected to speak on behalf of his sub–committee at the plenary session of the gathering. He pleaded for the favored nations to consider the plight of the underprivileged and dispossessed people of the world, and stressed the need for a sense of justice that the nations should display with those under their domination.

Always Johnson was prepared to tackle the difficult social issues, especially those to do with racial injustice. It was after hearing Johnson speak following his visit to India and an audience with the Mahatma Gandhi that Martin Luther King Jr. became convinced that nonviolent resistance was the best philosophy for African Americans to follow in their effort to end segregation and racial discrimination.

The Later Years

Johnson retired from the presidency of Howard University in 1960 after 34 years of service. He had brought the university a long way from where he found it in 1926. He had greatly expanded the campus, building a library and new structures for several schools within the university. Finances were sound. Enrollment increased from 2,000 in 1926 to more than 10,000 in 1960. In the larger world, some walls of segregation against which he had fought had begun to crumble.

Johnson married Anna Ethelyn Gardner of Augusta, Georgia, in 1916. To them were born five children: Carolyn, Mordecai Jr., Archer, William, and Faith. After her death in 1969, he married Alice Clinton Woodson, and settled in Washington, D.C. He died on September 10, 1976 at the age of 86.

As a clergyman, educator and orator, Mordecai Wyatt Johnson made a positive difference in the thousands whose lives he touched. Present generations are the heirs of his legacy.

REFERENCES

Boulware, Marcus H. *The Oratory of Negro Leaders: 1900–1968.* Westport, CT: Negro Universities Press, 1969.

Butler, Jenifier Bailey. ''An Analysis of the Oral Rhetoric of Mordecai W. Johnson; A Study of the Concept of Presence.'' Ph.D. dissertation, Ohio State University, 1977.

Hill, Richard H. *History of the First Baptist Church of Charleston, West Virginia.* Charleston: Privately printed, 1934.

Locke, Alain. *The New Negro: An Interpretation.* New York: A. and C. Boni, 1925.

Logan, Rayford. *Howard University: The First Hundred Years, 1867–1967.* New York: New York University Press, 1969.

McKinney, Richard I. *Mordecai, The Man and His Message: The Story of Mordecai Wyatt Johnson.* Washington, DC: Howard University Press, 1998.

Muse, Clarence L. ''An Educational Stepchild: Howard University and the New Deal.'' Ph.D. dissertation, Howard University, 1989.

Winston, Michael. *Education for Freedom. The Leadership of Mordecai Wyatt Johnson, Howard University, 1926–1960. A Documentary Tribute to Celebrate the Fiftieth Anniversary of the Election of Mordecai Wyatt Johnson as President of Howard University.* Washington: Howard University Archives, Moorland–Spingarn Research Center, May 5, 1976.

COLLECTIONS

Johnson's papers are on file at the Moorland–Spingarn Research Center at Howard University. Also on file there is a videotape of a ''Symposium Celebrating the Centennial Birthday of Mordecai W. Johnson, January 12, 1990,'' a record of ''Addresses by Former Professors at Howard University and Carolyn Johnson Graves, the daughter of Mordecai Wyatt Johnson,'' and a microfilm copy of ''Selected Items in the Julius Rosenwald Fund Archives in the Amistad Research Center'' from the originals in the Fisk University Library.

Richard I. McKinney

Rafer Johnson

(1935–)

Olympic medalist, public service worker

Rafer Johnson, the first African American to carry the American flag in the opening ceremonies of the Olympic games, holds a gold and a silver medal for his performances in decathlon events in 1956 and 1960. He is honored for his physical strength and stamina, academic success, and his dynamic contributions to the welfare of all people, especially African Americans. A hurdler, sprinter, and broad–jumper, he was called the nation's greatest all–round track and field athlete in the 1960s.

Rafer Lewis Johnson was born in Hillsboro, Texas, on August 18, 1935, the oldest of Lewis and Elma Johnson's six children. Lewis Johnson, a machinist, moved the family to Dallas when Rafer Johnson was two, then to Kingsburg, in the San Joaquin Valley of California, eight years later. They lived in a boxcar until Edward Fishel, a white man, offered a house and employment for the father as a machinist and the mother as a domestic worker. Backed by their benefactor's refusal to accede to demands that he remove the Johnsons from his property and his business, the family became accepted members of the community.

Johnson lettered in baseball, basketball, football, and track and field at Kingsburg High School. A well–trained, disciplined competitor, he amassed impressive records: .400 batting average in baseball, 17–point average in basketball games, and an average of nine yards each time he carried the football. In his senior year Johnson came in first in the 120–yard high hurdles, and second in the 220–yard low hurdles in the 1954 California State championship meet. He went on to take third place in the decathlon competition of the Amateur Athletic Union (AAU).

Inspired by that success and by the feats of Bob Mathias, gold medal winner in the 1948 and 1952 Olympics, Johnson began to concentrate on the most demanding contest of all—the grueling two–day competitions of the decathlon: javelin, shot put, discus, broad jump, high jump, pole vault, 110–meter hurdles, and races of 100 meters, 400 meters, and 1,500 meters. Scoring is tabulated in points based on the contestant's skills, track conditions, and previous records.

After high school in 1954, Johnson, an excellent student, chose an athletic scholarship at the University of California at Los Angeles (UCLA) from the many offered to him. His body had developed to six feet three inches, 200 pounds, with a 35–inch waist, the slender legs of a sprinter, and the torso muscles of a weight lifter. He was a quiet, modest man who never fell below a 3.0 grade point average while playing on the basketball and track and field teams, pledging a predominantly Jewish fraternity, heading three honorary societies, and acting as president of the student body.

During his college years, Johnson's reputation spread internationally. He became decathlon champion in March of 1955 at the Pan–American Games in Mexico; in a meet in Kingsburg he set a decathlon world record for most points amassed in a single competition in June of 1955, and he won both the National Collegiate Athletic Association (NCAA) and AAU decathlon titles. He progressed to the 1956 U.S. Olympic team in the decathlon and long jump events in Melbourne, Australia. Because of injuries he did not compete in the long jump, but won his first medal, the silver, by finishing second in the decathlon to Milton Campbell's Olympic record of 7,937 points. In May of 1958, in a USA–USSR meet, Johnson defeated Vasiliy Kuznetsov.

Johnson received a bachelor of arts degree in physical education from UCLA in 1959, and continued to train for the 1960 Summer Olympic Games in Rome, Italy. There his toughest challenger was Chuan–Kwang Yang, from Taiwan, a former teammate at UCLA. The two friends had competed in track meets before, always ending with similar win–lose statistics and point totals. In Rome, Johnson led Yang with a slight margin of 67 points just before the final event, the 1,500–meter run. Luckily for Johnson, when Yang won that race, his total was not sufficient to equal Johnson's figure of 8,392, a new world record that secured the Olympic gold medal for Johnson.

Rejecting an attractive offer from the Los Angeles Rams to play professional football, Johnson retired from athletic competition in 1960. His interests branched out into different areas, among them appearances in seven Hollywood movies. A staunch supporter of Senator Robert F. Kennedy's campaign for the presidency, Johnson was standing near the candidate when Kennedy was assassinated at the 1968 California Democratic primary. Johnson and Roosevelt Grier, another African American athlete, pinned down the attacker.

Aware of the symbolism of the exchange, Johnson accepted the torch from the next–to–last bearer, Gina Hemphill (granddaughter of Jesse Owens, who was a track star in the 1930s) and brought it into the Los Angeles Coliseum to signal the opening of the 1984 Summer Olympic Games. He ran the remaining distance to light the flame overcome by emotions that reflected the honor to himself and other African American athletes.

Tributes to Johnson include: Sportsman of the Year by Sports Illustrated Magazine in 1958; both the Sullivan Award for outstanding amateur athlete and Associated Press's Athlete of the Year nomination in 1960; national Track and Field Hall of Fame in 1974; and U.S. Olympic Hall of Fame in 1983.

Johnson has a history of public service with Special Olympics nationally and in California, the Amateur Athletics Foundation, the Hershey Youth Program for youth physical fitness, and the Kennedy Foundation. In business, he has been an executive with Continental Telephone in Bakersfield, California, and the organizer of Rafer Johnson Enterprises.

Johnson married Elizabeth Ann Thorsen, then a director of the Kennedy Foundation, in 1972. They have two children, Jenny and Josh.

Johnson holds a place of honor for his accomplishments as student leader, collegiate and Olympic athlete, and a man committed to the physical and mental health of people all over the country. Rafer Johnson has opened doors for people restricted by economic, physical, or cognitive limitations to participate in athletic activities.

In retirement, Johnson lives in Sherman Oaks, California.

Current address: c/o Special Olympics Southern California, 6071 Bristol Parkway, Unit 100, Culver City, CA 90230.

REFERENCES

"Big Man on Campus." *Ebony* 14 (May 1959): 53–58.

"Great Olympics Moments." *Ebony* 47 (March 1992): 52.

Henderson, Edwin B. and the Editors of *Sport* Magazine. *The Black Athlete, Emergence and Arrival.* New York: Publishers Company, 1976.

"One Man Track Team." *Ebony* 11 (July 1956): 46–49.

Porter, David L., ed. *African–American Sports Greats.* Westport, CT: Greenwood Press, 1995.

Rhoden, William C. "An Olympic Hero's Variation on Success." *Emerge* 6 (October 1994): 63.

Rust, Edna, and Art Rust Jr. *Art Rust's Illustrated History of the Black Athlete.* Garden City, NY: Doubleday, 1985.

Dona L. Irvin

Robert L. Johnson

(1946–)

Television executive, entrepreneur

Robert L. Johnson established the first and only firm that provides basic cable television programming by and about blacks. The founder, chairman, and chief executive officer of Black Entertainment Television, he took BET to the stock market in 1991, making it the first black–owned firm to join the New York Stock Exchange. He holds the controlling share of a major diversified media giant.

Robert Louis Johnson was born on April 8, 1946, in Hickory, Mississippi, a rural town 25 miles west of Meridian. The Johnson family moved to the industrial farming town of Freeport, Illinois, where both parents worked in local factories to provide for their large family. Johnson and his siblings were taught to be self–sufficient. As the ninth of ten children, Johnson told Beverly Smith in a 1992 interview on CNN's *Pinnacle* that he had "a lot of brothers and sisters that I could sort of pick on if I had to for whatever information."

Robert L. Johnson

Johnson hoped to become a fighter pilot in the U.S. Air Force but could not meet the physical requirements and concentrated instead on his studies and on college. A good student in high school, he graduated with honors in history and entered the University of Illinois on an academic scholarship, graduating in 1968 with a bachelor's degree in history. Although he lacked the usual qualifications, Johnson was considered a worthy enough risk to be admitted to Princeton University's Woodrow Wilson School of Public and International Affairs in 1969. He graduated sixth in his class in 1972 with a master's degree in public administration.

While at Princeton, Johnson established connections that led to a job as press secretary for the Corporation for Public Broadcasting. After joining the U.S. Army Reserve during the Vietnam War, he became public affairs officer at the Corporation for Public Broadcasting. Johnson then worked as director of communications for the Washington Urban League, press aide for the District of Columbia's city councilman Sterling Tucker, and press secretary for Walter Fauntroy, the District's nonvoting delegate to Congress. From 1976 to 1979 Johnson was vice–president of government relations for the National Cable and Television Association (NCTA).

Founds Black Entertainment Television

While at NCTA, Johnson developed the idea of starting a cable network company to promote black characters, thought, and philosophy primarily for African Americans. According to the A. C. Nielsen ratings, black viewers watched an average of 70 hours of television per week—compared to 48 hours for whites—but in the late 1970s no networks carried programming specifically for blacks, nor were blacks shown in powerful, dominant roles. He persuaded his NCTA supervisor to promise him a $15,000 consulting contract, which he used to secure a matching loan from the National Bank of Washington. He then borrowed $320,000 from John C. Malone, head of Denver–based Tele–Communications Inc. (TCI), one of the nation's largest builders of cable systems. Malone and TCI also paid him $180,000 for a 20 percent share in the new network.

On January 25, 1980, Black Entertainment Television, which Johnson created from the basement of his home, made its debut on cable with *A Visit to the Chief's Son,* a two–hour movie with an all–black cast that drew an audience of 3.8 million homes in 350 markets. At first, BET kept expenses low by showing low–cost programs that would appeal specifically to blacks, using such black film subjects as *Lady Sings the Blues.* Free music videos from record companies were aired by 1982, and BET soon added blacks stars, talk shows with black hosts and guests, and black college sports.

BET struggled with several consecutive years of losses. In 1982 Johnson took on a new partner, Taft Broadcasting Company. In 1984 Home Box Office, a cable subsidiary of Time Incorporated (now Time Warner), invested in BET because of its 24–hour telecasting and 7.6 million subscribers. In spite of phenomenal growth, by 1989 BET was still the smallest and least carried of all cable networks. The company also faced legal setbacks from competitors. Johnson began another cable venture in 1984, District Cablevision Incorporated, intended to wire homes and serve the District of Columbia. TCI owned 75 percent of the new company, however, and competitors filed suit to prevent a monopoly, causing more financial pressure. By 1986, the financial burden was eased, but BET did not pay back its investors until 1989.

Traded on New York Stock Exchange

Johnson then established BET Holdings Incorporated, the parent company of BET, and on October 30, 1991, BET became the first black–owned corporation listed on the New York Stock Exchange. Although by then three other black firms had gone public with their stock, none had remained on the public market or had been listed by the NYSE. According to *Current Biography,* the day BET was listed, investors "bid the price up to more than $23 a share, and BET (which reported $9 million in earnings in 1991) had acquired a market value of $475 million." Then Johnson sold 375,000 of his own shares and, in a single day, earned $6.4 million. His net worth after 11 years of work from the increased value of his controlling interest reached more than $104 million. Although the company lost some ground when investors questioned his subscriber count, BET sold some of its stock, clarified the number of subscribers, and later recovered some of its losses. Commenting on his financial progress, the *Network Journal* for June 30, 1995, quoted Johnson's statement to CNN: "Black people will become powerful in this country when they obtain power through control of economic wealth."

The company took a bold step in 1995 by moving its 350 employees to a new $15 million building in Washington's northern industrial corridor. In April of 1995, Johnson added a 50,000–square–foot film and video production facility, one of the largest of its kind on the east coast. In the *Network Journal* for June 30, 1985 Tony Chapelle cited Johnson's plans to become "the preëminent provider of information entertainment and direct marketing services to the Black community."

By 1995, BET reached 41.3 million households. By 1996 the cable network, still the core of the company's holdings, had a children's literature hour, public affairs show, weekly show for teenagers, town hall meetings, and music videos. BET also owned the Cable Jazz Channel and ventures in Africa and England.

In 1996, BET launched the nation's first black–controlled cable movie premium channel, BET Movies/STARZ!3, which offered a lineup of classics that included *To Sir with Love* as well as the newer *Pulp Fiction* and Spike Lee's *Clockers.* Johnson told the *Los Angeles Sentinel* for October 3, 1996, "What we're doing is something that's unique. We're branding movies that appeal to an audience that has demonstrated a tremendous amount of interest in viewing film entertainment." Encore Media Corporation, a cable and satellite movie provider, is another TCI–controlled company. That venture is intended to develop and exhibit black–oriented feature–length films and expand pay–TV households in urban markets.

In 1991 BET acquired controlling interest in *Emerge* magazine, which is aimed at young adults, and began publishing *YSB* (*Young Sisters and Brothers*), which appeals to adolescents. BET also established a radio network in 1994 which provides news and music to urban stations nationwide.

In addition to his business ventures, Johnson also founded the Metropolitan Cable Club in 1981, a forum for the exchange of information in the telecommunications industry, and served as its president and later a member of its board. He has also served as a board member of the Ad Council, the Cable TV Advertising Bureau, Minorities in Cable, the National Cable Television Association (NCTA), the Walter Kaitz Foundation, and the Board of Governors of the National Cable Academy. Among his awards are the Presidential Award, NCTA (1982); the NAACP's Image Award (1982); the Capitol Press Club's Pioneer Award (1984); the Business of the Year Award from the Washington, D.C., Chamber of Commerce (1985); the Executive Leadership Council Award (1992); and the Turner Broadcasting Trumpet Award (1993).

Described as intensely ambitious and foresighted, Johnson has also been characterized as gregarious, easygoing, graceful, personal, bright, and articulate. He wears a thick gold bracelet and custom shirts and usually works 15 hours a day during his six–day work week. On January 19, 1969, Johnson married Sheila Crump Johnson, now the BET's executive vice–president for corporate affairs, with whom he has a daughter, Paige, and a son, Brett.

In 1996, Johnson pledged $100,000 to Howard University to help support the School of Communication, and the school responded at its twenty–fifth anniversary gala by awarding Johnson the Messenger Award for Excellence in Communications. Jannette Dates, the school's interim dean, praised Johnson for his success and his support of the school. Quoted in the *Washington Informer* for November 6, 1996, Dates summed up Johnson's success:

> [H]e showed America that an African American from a not very privileged background can, with the strength of his intelligence and hard work, take a small beginning and become a tremendous success. He has also succeeded in communicating an array of new images of African Americans that are different from those that were portrayed over the years past.

Current address: Black Entertainment Television, 1232 31st Street NW, Washington, DC 20007.

REFERENCES

"BET Launching First Black Cable Channel." *Los Angeles Sentinel,* October 3, 1996.

"BET Links with Encore Media to Create First Black Movie Channel." *New York Amsterdam News,* October 5, 1996.

"BET's CEO Donates $100,000 to Howard." *Philadelphia Tribune,* October 29, 1996.

Brown, Janice Frink. "Black Entertainment Television Opens Plush Corporate Headquarters." *Washington Afro–American,* July 1, 1995.

"Businessman Honored for Success in D.C. Community." *Washington Informer,* November 6, 1996.

Chapelle, Tony. "Entrepreneur Makes BET and Wins." *The Network Journal* 4 (30 June 1995): 8–10.
Contemporary Black Biography. Vol. 3. Detroit: Gale Research, 1993.
Current Biography Yearbook. New York: H. W. Wilson, 1994.
Curry, George E. "A Birthday Celebration." *Emerge* 6 (31 October 1994): 1.
Edmond, Alfred, Jr. "Milestones in Black Business." *Black Enterprise* 25 (30 June 1995): 352.
Perl, Peter. "His Way." *Washington Post Magazine* (14 December 1997): 8–13, 23–27.
"Spike Lee Will Be BET Spokesperson: Filmmaker/Actor Hosts Premiere Week of Black Movie Channel." *Philadelphia Tribune,* January 3, 1997.
Trescott, Jacqueline. "Fifteen Years and Rising for BET's Star." *Emerge* 6 (30 September 1995): 66–67.

Jessie Carney Smith

Sargent Johnson
(1887–1967)
Sculptor, ceramist, printmaker

As one of the most prominent artists of the San Francisco Bay area, Sargent Johnson aimed to show the vast spectrum of African American beauty. In 1935 the *San Francisco Chronicle* quoted him as saying:

> It is the pure American Negro I am concerned with, aiming to show the natural beauty and dignity in that characteristic lip and that characteristic hair, bearing and manner; and I wish to show that beauty not so much to the white man as to the Negro himself. . . . The Negroes are a colorful race; they call for an art as colorful as they can be made.

Exhibits and commissions with the Harmon Foundation and the Federal Arts Project (FAP), respectively, provided him vehicles to promote his works. Consequently, he became one of the leading sculptors during the Harlem Renaissance era. Like Richmond Barthé, Augusta Savage, Elizabeth Prophet, Aaron Douglas, and others, Johnson's work projected African culture and racial pride during this period.

Sargent Claude Johnson was born on October 7, 1887, in Boston, Massachusetts, the third of six children of Anderson Johnson of Swedish ancestry and Lizzie Jackson Johnson of African American and Cherokee ancestry. Anderson Johnson died in 1897 and Lizzie Johnson in 1902. An uncle, Sherman William Jackson of Washington, D.C., took the children in when their father died. His wife, May Howard Jackson, a sculptor of repute, guided Johnson's first efforts in claymodeling, but the children were soon sent to live with their maternal grandparents in Alexandria, Virginia. There Sargent continued his modeling in clay by copying tombstones. When the grandparents could no longer care for the children, they were dispersed. Johnson spent the rest of his childhood at an orphanage run by the Sisters of Charity in Worcester, Massachusetts.

Johnson studied art at the Worcester Art School and went to the Bay area in 1915 with savings earned from work with the Sisters of Charity. He did further studies at the A. W. Best School of Art and the California School of Fine Arts. The sculptors Beniamino Bufano and Ralph Stackpole are often referred to as his major instructors.

Johnson's first exhibits were with the San Francisco Art Association in 1925. He won recognition in the city for his work. An undated San Francisco newspaper clipping in the Harmon files reports that no choice could be made between Johnson's *Forever Free,* a sculpture of mother and child, and his former art instructor Beniamino Bufano's *Torso.* From 1928 to 1935 he exhibited with the Harmon Foundation. In these exhibitions he won prizes for *Sammy,* a bust of a black boy, and other busts, such as *Chester.* Many of his early pieces were in glazed ceramic, and he also exhibited drawings.

From 1928 to 1933 the Harmon Foundation was a major force in the careers of black artists in general and presented five successful exhibitions that focused the public on the professional accomplishments and the needs of these artists. Correspondence in the Harmon Files shows that the foundation was very instrumental in promoting Johnson's career. The foundation not only exhibited his works but also provided him with materials on black culture and achievements, advised and recommended him for awards such as the Guggenheim Fellowship for further study, promoted articles on him in the *American Magazine of Art,* and sympathized with him during family problems.

Johnson and the Renaissance

During the 1920s, great changes in the entire structure of American society occurred. Many black writers and artists expressed racial and cultural themes in their works. This period became known as the Harlem Renaissance. Artists like Aaron Douglas used black themes in paintings and book illustrations, while Richmond Barthé and Johnson, the two most prominent sculptors of the late 1920s and 1930s, based most of their art in plaster, bronze, and ceramic on African masks and other cultural motifs. In 1936 Alain Locke, one of the most important intellectuals of the Renaissance, described Johnson's art: "For purely sculptural qualities Johnson's simplified surfaces are admirably adapted; and his African quality is very suited for racial characterization."

Johnson attempted to stylize black subjects as the ancients had stylized their art. As reported in the *Black Times* of Albany, California, Johnson said this about his art in the 1930s:

> I am producing strictly a Negro Art, studying not the culturally mixed Negro of the cities, but the more primitive slave type as existed in this country during the period of slave importation. Very few artists have gone into the history of the Negro in America, cutting back to the sources and origins of the life of the race in this country.

Johnson felt such work was of the utmost importance to black people and disliked the number of black artists who worked in the style of white Europeans. He explained:

> I am interested in applying color to sculpture as the Egyptian, Greek and other ancient people did. . . . I am concerned with color, not solely as a technical problem, but also as a means of heightening the racial character of my work.

Federal Arts Project and Collection

During the 1930s Johnson served as a supervisor on the Work Progress Administration's Federal Arts Project. The FAP gave black artists an opportunity to practice their craft and to be paid for doing so. Some of Johnson's most significant works commissioned by the FAP were the 1939 entrance reliefs and mosaic murals on a promenade deck for the Maritime Museum of Aquatic Park, the two eight–foot–high sculptures of Inca Indians seated on llamas for the 1939–40 Golden Gate International Exposition's Court of Pacifica, and a cast–stone frieze made for the George Washington High School Athletic Field in 1942. About this time Johnson began producing many well–received lithographs. During a visit to Mexico he became fascinated by black pottery made locally, and produced numerous small figures in the material. In 1947 he began to produce large panels from porcelain on steel. Over the next 20 years, he had many commissions for works in this medium. The largest, 78 by 39 feet, was commissioned by a Reno gambling casino. Constants in Johnson's work were his use of color for his sculpture and his readiness to experiment and adopt new techniques.

Johnson was able to sell his works to private collectors and museums as fast as he made them due to his experience working in an art gallery, where he learned the techniques of buying and selling, meeting buyers, and learning what they really wanted.

In 1915 Johnson married Pearl Lawson of Georgia whose father was a white Englishman and mother a French Creole. Their only child was Pearl Adele. Johnson died in Mt. Zion Hospital in San Francisco on October 10, 1967, when he was 80–years old. Funeral services were held on October 14 in Estrella Mortuary on 1115 Valencia Street in San Francisco.

A major sculptor in the San Francisco Bay area, Johnson contributed greatly to the field of art, particularly black art. As other artist during the Harlem Renaissance period, most of his works expressed racial themes. Its focus was to raise the consciousness of Americans about black culture beyond stereotypical views. Through his art he wanted to project a simplistic style appealing to the common man; his works touched broad spectrums of society both nationally and internationally.

REFERENCES

Anacostia Neighborhood Museum. *Barnett–Aden Collection.* Washington, DC: Smithsonian Institution Press, 1974.

Arvey, Verna. "Sargent Johnson." *Opportunity* 17 (July 1939): 213–14.

Bearden, Romare, and Harry Henderson. *A History of African–American Artists.* New York: Pantheon, 1993.

Butcher, Margaret J. *Negro in American Culture.* New York: Knopf, 1973.

Cederholm, Theresa D. *Afro–American Artists: Bio–bibliographical Directory.* Boston: Trustees of the Boston Public Library, 1973.

"Colorful Race Demands a Colorful Art." *Albany, California Black Times,* March 4–10, 1971.

Dallas Art Museum. *Black Art Ancestral Legacy: African Impulse in African–American Art.* New York: Harry N. Abrams, 1989.

Driskell, David C. *Two Centuries of Black American Art.* New York: Knopf, 1976.

"Fighting Cultural Segregation: Negro Artists Gain Recognition after Long Battle." *Pittsburgh Courier,* July 29, 1950.

Herring, James V. "Negro Sculptor." *Crisis* 49 (August 1942): 262.

Locke, Alain. *Negro Art Past and Present.* Washington, DC: Associates in Negro Folk Education, 1936.

Logan, Rayford W., and Michael R. Winston, eds. *Dictionary of American Negro Biography.* New York: Norton, 1982.

Negro Artists. New York: Harmon Foundation, 1935.

Salzman, Jack, David L. Smith, and Cornel West, eds. *Encyclopedia of African–American Culture and History.* New York: Macmillan Library Reference USA/Simon and Schuster Macmillan, 1996.

San Francisco Chronicle, October 6, 1935.

"Sargent Johnson." *Negro History Bulletin* 2 (March 1939): 50–52.

"Sargent Johnson Retrospective." *ABA: A Journal of Affairs of Black Artists* 1 (1972): 22.

Thiel, Yvonne G. *Artists and People.* New York: Philosophical Library, 1959.

COLLECTIONS

Correspondence and dated and undated newspaper clippings pertaining to Sargent Johnson from 1931 to 1952 are in the papers of the Harmon Foundation located at the Library of Congress, Washington, D.C. His art is located in the Aaron Douglas Collection, Amistad Research Center, Tulane University; Fine Arts Gallery, San Diego; the Oakland Museum; Van Vechten Gallery, Fisk University; Howard University; National Museum of American Art; Smithsonian Institution;

Schomburg Center for Research in Black Culture; and in other public as well as private collections.

Ruth A. Hodges

Absalom Jones
(1746–1818)
Religious leader

Absalom Jones rose from slavery to become the first black Episcopal priest and principal founder of St. Thomas, the first black Episcopal church. Through hard work he earned a place among the most affluent blacks in Philadelphia. His position as religious leader also propelled him into the spotlight as a community leader.

Jones was born a slave in Sussex, Delaware, on November 6, 1746. As a small child he was a house servant, earning tips which enabled him to buy a primer, a spelling book, and a New Testament. He learned to read by begging instruction from anyone who would help. In 1762 his mother, five brothers, and sister were sold, and Jones was taken to Philadelphia, where he worked in a store and learned to write. His spelling remained poor, however. In 1766 he was allowed to go to school at night for a brief period; there he learned the practical mathematical skills needed in trade. He grew into a stocky, dark–complexioned man of medium height and affable disposition.

Jones married a slave belonging to Sarah King in 1770. With donations and borrowed funds he raised 30 pounds to purchase her freedom, and Sarah King forgave the balance of ten pounds. Jones's duties were becoming increasingly onerous due to the growing family of his master, but he worked until midnight or later to aid his wife in her tasks and to earn money to repay the money borrowed to buy her freedom. In 1778 he began to ask to purchase his own freedom, but he was not manumitted until October 1, 1784. He remained with his former master as a wage worker.

Jones used the money he had saved to buy his freedom to buy a small house and lot in 1788, taking advantage of the Revolutionary War inflation to exchange his hard currency for the Continental money used to make the purchase. Fearing that his master could claim his property, Jones urgently pleaded to buy his freedom. After he was freed, he built two small rental houses on his lot.

Jones became a licensed Methodist lay preacher sometime around 1786, focusing on teaching and pastoral work. In May of 1787 Jones joined African American religious leader Richard Allen and others in forming the Free African Society. The society was set up to provide economic and medical aid to African Americans, advocate abolition, and maintain channels of communication with African Americans in the South.

Absalom Jones

The men soon discovered, however, that the racism they hoped to eradicate existed in the very religious body in which they operated. In November of 1787 Jones, Allen, and friends kneeled for prayer at what they thought were their new seats in the recently constructed gallery of St. George's Methodist Church only to have a sexton try to pull Jones to his feet and move him and the others to different seats despite pleas to wait until prayers were over. Prayers ended before the sextons resorted to force, and Jones and his friends rose and left the church for good.

Jones continued his association with the Free African Society while Allen became impatient, stopped attending meetings, and was dismissed on June 20, 1789; Jones, perhaps because of his friendship with Allen, did not sign the committee report recommending the action. In September of 1790 the society decided to hold religious services, which began in a rented room on January 1, 1791. Under Quaker influence the meetings began with 15 minutes of silence. Shortly thereafter the group decided to organize a church and to buy a lot to build on. Sometime during the year a special meeting of the group was held to discuss denominational affiliation; the leaders adopted the titles of elders and deacons of the African Church, choosing a regularly ordained white Episcopalian to officiate for them.

Jones and Allen cooperated in the task of collecting and burying the dead during the smallpox epidemic of 1793, which must have delayed the construction of the church building. The African Church of St. Thomas was dedicated on July 17, 1794. Negotiations with the white Episcopalians resulted in an agreement which stipulated that the church be received as an organized body, that the members retain control of their own affairs, and that a member be licensed as a lay reader and, if fit, become their minister. The public announcement of St. Thomas's reception into the Episcopal Church was made from the pulpit on October 12, 1794.

As the unofficial leader of the church, Jones seemed an obvious choice as a lay reader. After becoming lay reader in 1794, he was ordained deacon on August 6, 1795. While most Episcopalian deacons were required to possess a knowledge of Greek and Latin prior to ordination, this requirement was waived for Jones. The church, however, was not permitted to send a clergyman or delegates to church conventions. Jones became a the first black episcopal priest in 1804.

Jones was active in education and the community. He became head of the Masonic lodge founded in Philadelphia in 1798. In 1799 and 1800 he participated in petitions to the state legislature and Congress. Jones had conducted a school before the formation of St. Thomas, and in 1804 the vestry established a school that continued until 1816. In 1809 he joined Richard Allen and James Forten—a wealthy sail–maker, community leader, and member of St. Thomas's vestry—in forming the Society for the Suppression of Vice and Immorality. The society's hostility to liquor foreshadows that of later temperance organizations. The same three men also worked together to rally the African American community for the defense of Philadelphia during the War of 1812.

It is possible that Jones was one of the five local clergymen who ordained Richard Allen as the first bishop of the African Methodist Episcopal Church on April 11, 1816. In January of 1817, Jones was present at the first mass meeting of African Americans—a gathering that may have numbered as many as 3,000—at Allen's Bethel Church to denounce the plans of the American Colonization Society to transport free blacks to Africa.

Jones died on February 13, 1818, at the age of 71. He was buried in the churchyard of St. Thomas after his funeral on February 16. Absalom Jones had led his church for 22 years, with his vocation as a religious leader of African Americans stretching back even farther. Although Jones was also a community leader, the main thrust of his efforts was in the sphere of religion. The inscription on his tomb aptly sums up his life:

> To the memory of the Rev. Absalom Jones, who, born a slave, and becoming possessed of freedom by good conduct, and rendered respectable by a course of virtuous industry, was principally instrumental in founding the African Church of St. Thomas.

REFERENCES

Bragg, George Freeman Jr. *History of the Afro–American Group of the Episcopal Church.* Baltimore: Church Advocate Press, 1922.

George, Carol V. R. *Segregated Sabbaths.* New York: Oxford, 1973.

Logan, Rayford W., and Michael R. Winston, eds. *Dictionary of American Negro Biography.* New York: Norton, 1982.

Wesley, Charles H. *Richard Allen: Apostle of Freedom.* Washington, DC: Associated Publishers, 1935. Reissued, 1969.

Robert L. Johns

Eugene Kinckle Jones

(1885–1954)

Social welfare organizer

The fundamental need for economic enfranchisement and access to social welfare programs designed to meet the specialized needs of African Americans set the stage for the life of Eugene Kinckle Jones, cofounder and first field secretary of the National Urban League. A man of foresight and commitment, he dedicated 39 years of his life to improving race relations by bringing blacks and whites together to work towards common goals. His leadership on Roosevelt's ''Black Cabinet'' was instrumental in the creation of equal employment opportunities for the waves of migrating workers and essential social programs for black youth.

On July 30, 1885, Eugene Kinckle Jones was born in Richmond, Virginia, to parents who were both educators. His father, Joseph Endom Jones, was born to a slave, educated at Hamilton Academy, and received his bachelor's degree from Colgate in 1876. He was one of the first blacks in the state of Virginia to complete a college education. For 47 years, Joseph E. Jones taught at the Richmond Theological Seminary (now Virginia Union University). His mother, Rosa Daniel Kinckle Jones, was the daughter of free black parents. She was educated in private schools, Howard University, and the New England Conservatory of Music. Rosa Jones taught music for 40 years at Hartshorn Memorial College. This lineage placed Jones in the black bourgeoisie of Richmond.

While Jones grew up in times of segregation, racial antagonism and the Jim Crow era, he was also exposed to a black community that fostered racial pride, supported business ventures, and inspired political action. His early exposure to the ease with which his parents socialized with white members of their respective faculties was one of the influences that shaped his developing personal social philosophy.

Jones earned a bachelor's degree from Virginia Union University in 1906, where he was both a player and manager for the baseball and football teams. He began work on his master's degree at Cornell University in 1906. He had originally planned to major in civil engineering; however, realizing the limited employment opportunities for African Americans in the field of engineering, he chose sociology as his major. While at Cornell, he became the first initiate of the first black college fraternity, Alpha Phi Alpha. He went on to

Eugene Kinckle Jones

become the fraternity's first president and organized the first two chapters at other colleges, as well as the first graduate chapter. Jones earned his master's degree in 1908 at Cornell University. He wrote his graduate thesis on the progress of the American Negro since emancipation. Quoted in the definitive history of the National Urban League entitled *The National Urban League 1910–1940,* one of Jones's professors at Cornell, W. R. Willcox, described him as having "...an alert mind, a sober judgment, much diligence and ability as a student." Willcox continued, "He is thoroughly gentlemanly in bearing and conversation, has ability as well as training in research work and could meet people of both races tactfully and easily."

Jones married Blanche Ruby Watson in 1909 and was a family man. They had two children, Eugene Jr., who became a lawyer, and Adele, who became a social worker. Jones, a tall, light–skinned man with fine features and a well–trimmed mustache, lived with his family in Flushing, Long Island. While very little is known of his private life, it is said that he loved to play tennis and acquired an impressive collection of trophies. This son of a professor of music was himself a musician.

The life of Eugene Kinckle Jones is inextricably intertwined with the history of the National Urban League. In 1911, after teaching high school for two years in Louisville, Kentucky, Jones received an invitation from George E. Haynes, professor of social sciences at Fisk University, to work for the Committee on Urban Conditions among Negroes, one of the organizations that merged to form the National League on Urban Conditions among Negroes. Jones was named field secretary of the committee which, in 1920, became known officially as the National Urban League.

For the next 30 years Jones established the league's structure and programs. Under Jones's leadership the Urban League developed an interracial approach to the racial problem, including programs for social and economic development, opportunities for employment as civil servants, partnerships with management and labor, and use of black workers in support of national defense production needs. His advancement of the network of the organization was propelled by the migration of African Americans from the South to the North during World War I. It was at his urging that breakthroughs occurred in the abandonment of the policy of racial exclusion in the American Federation of Labor.

In addition to the social programs of the National Urban League, two literary accomplishments occurred during the Jones administration. In 1922 the league began publishing the magazine *Opportunity: Journal of Negro Life.* Many of the famous writers of the Harlem Renaissance were published in the magazine; winners of league–sponsored literary contests included Countee Cullen, Langston Hughes, and E. Franklin Frazier. In 1926, Jones was instrumental in the New York Public Library's acquisition of the Arthur Schomburg Collection of African American historical and cultural materials which is now one of the world's greatest repositories for such materials.

During the depression years of the 1930s, African American advisors were appointed to departments and agencies of the federal government to address the response of the Roosevelt Administration's New Deal to black concerns. Secretary Dan Roper of the Department of Commerce appointed Jones as the advisor on Negro affairs. He and a number of other black advisors became known, unofficially, as the Black Cabinet. During this time, from 1933 to 1937, Jones was on leave from the National Urban League. T. Arnold Hill, then director of industrial relations, was left in charge of the organization. Jones made frequent trips from Washington to New York to monitor the organization's programs. Gradually, he reduced his governmental activities, choosing instead to return to the helm of the league in 1937.

Jones was stricken with tuberculosis and worked intermittently from the spring of 1937 until 1941. He was then granted a one year leave of absence which was indefinitely extended. He assumed the title of general secretary until 1950 and relinquished the position of executive secretary to Lester B. Granger. In the *National Urban League 40th Anniversary Year Book,* Jones said of this unique organization:

> The League's importance is seen, first, in its contribution to Social Work; second, in its influence in raising the hopes and enlarging the opportunities for Negroes in America; and finally, in its patriotic service to the nation, recorded chiefly in its work of production during the two world wars, by helping to corral available Negro manpower and to bring to it a high point of efficiency.

On January 11, 1954, Eugene Kinckle Jones died in New York, leaving in his wake a legacy of service and an indelible inscription on the history of African Americans as evidenced by the strength of the organizations he helped to establish, the National Urban League and the Alpha Phi Alpha Fraternity.

REFERENCES

Jones, Eugene Kinckle. *The First Forty Years of Service to the American People.* National Urban League 40th Anniversary Year Book, 1950. New York: National Urban League, 1951.

"Kinckle Jones, 68, of Urban League." *New York Times,* January 12, 1954.

Lowery, Charles D., and John F. Marszalek, eds. *Encyclopedia of African–American Civil Rights: From Emancipation to the Present.* New York: Greenwood Press, 1992.

Ovington, Mary White. *Portraits in Color.* New York: Viking Press, 1927.

Parris, Guichard, and Lester Brooks. *Blacks in the City: A History of the National Urban League.* Boston: Little, Brown, 1971.

Weiss, Nancy J. *The National Urban League 1910–1940.* New York: Oxford University Press, 1974.

Ann C. Sullivan

Frederick McKinley Jones
(1893?–1961)
Inventor, refrigeration engineer

A mechanical genius whose inventions have improved the quality of life for humankind worldwide, Frederick McKinley Jones built radios, movie sound tracks, and gained a national reputation as inventor of refrigeration systems that revolutionized the food transportation industry.

Jones was born in Cincinnati, Ohio, around 1893. His mother died when he was an infant; his father died when he was nine–years old. Father Ryan, a Catholic priest in West Covington, Kentucky, took him in after his father's death. He encouraged Jones's early interest in machines. Jones was obsessed with cars, especially everything under the hood. By the time he was 20–years old, he could convert ordinary cars to racers and keep them in mint condition. His special gifts were an insatiable curiosity, an ability to decipher and decode the mechanical workings of virtually any machine, and the common sense to seek out expert advice when stumped by a problem.

Jones was first an automobile mechanic, then foreman at an autoshop. From 1912 to 1913, he was in hotel maintenance. His skills were soon noticed by Oscar Younggren, a hotel guest from Minnesota who offered him the position of master mechanic of his farm implement company. Jones accepted the position and moved to Hallock, Minnesota, where his duties were to repair and maintain farm equipment and cars. For the next 18 years, Jones left Hallock only to serve in World War II.

According to an article in the *Saturday Evening Post,* Jones returned to Hallock after the war because it was a place where "a man. . .[was] judged more on his character and ability than on the color of his skin." Not only could he earn a living there, but he could become involved in social and civic activities. Jones played in the village band, sang in a local quartet, fished and hunted, worked on his inventions, and became an amateur race car driver. He raced on the dirt track circuit until 1925, when his increasing nervousness convinced him that he was tempting fate too often. An accident while going into a turn at 100 miles per hour helped him make the final decision to end his fledgling racing career.

The "Talkies"

In addition to his many activities, Jones also served as Hallock's movie projectionist. By the late 1920s the death knell had sounded for silent movies, but equipment needed to convert to sound movies was prohibitively expensive for Hallock's lone theater owner. Using parts and equipment from Younggren's shop, Jones built a sound track unit that cost less than $100 and was superior in sound quality to more expensive, commercial versions. By the 1930s these machines had become obsolete with the advent of the film sound track, and again Jones invented a device for less money and better quality. News of these two inventions spread and in 1930 he was hired by Joseph Numero, owner of Cinema Supplies, a motion picture equipment manufacturer.

Numero's Minneapolis based company was experiencing difficulty keeping up with the rapid changes in motion picture equipment. Jones's sound track inventions propelled Numero's company to the forefront of the industry and in 1939 Numero successfully sold the business to Radio Corporation of America (RCA). While working at Cinema Supplies, Jones invented a movie ticket dispensing machine and achieved his first patent. This machine is still in use today.

The Pinnacle of Success

Jones's greatest achievement began with a rash promise Numero made to a friend in the trucking industry. Harry Werner, during a game of golf with Numero, challenged a third player, a man in the air conditioning business, to construct something that would prevent Werner from losing profits whenever his perishable products, such as poultry, spoiled during long distance transportation. When the man declined the challenge, Numero jokingly proposed building a refrigerator for Werner's trucks. Werner took Numero's proposal seriously, however, and when he bought a new aluminum truck, he sent it to Numero to have a refrigeration unit measure and fitted.

According to the *Saturday Evening Post,* Numero remembered "I expected to give it a quick once over and tell

Werner it couldn't be done. But Jones beat me to it. He climbed into the trailer, made some measurements and calculations, and popped his head out to announce he guessed he could fix up something. And we were stuck with it.''

After several experiments, Jones invented a shockproof refrigeration unit which mounted to the forehead of the truck. This unit became the cornerstone of the United States Thermo Control Company founded by Numero and Jones, now full partners, which grew into a $3 million business. Jones's refrigeration invention was patented in 1940 and the company manufactured air coolers for virtually every mode of transportation. Jones's invention revolutionized the transportation industry.

Despite having attained only a sixth–grade education, Jones proved capable of working with the staff of Thermo Control, many of whom were university trained engineers. His way of thinking and problem solving were unconventional, however. According to an article in the *Saturday Evening Post* describing Jones, ''Most engineers start at the bottom of a project and work up, but Fred takes a flying leap too [sic] the top of the mountain and then backs down, cutting steps for himself and the rest of us as he goes.'' Jones was well known for his impatience with incompetence, shoddiness, and over–reliance on the mechanics of an answer without looking at the real thing, but he was also compassionate and never fired an employee.

During World War II, Jones was classified as an electrician and earned the rank of sergeant. He designed portable cooling units that were used in military hospitals and at the front to keep blood serum, medicine, and food at appropriate temperatures. They were also used in airplane cockpits, B–29 engine nacelles, and ambulance planes. Jones designed the refrigeration systems for army and marine field kitchens. Nearly 70 percent of Jones's patents were awarded for refrigeration equipment.

After the war, in addition to running his business, Jones served as consultant to the Defense Department and the U.S. Bureau of Standards. He died in Minneapolis on February 21, 1961, of lung cancer and was buried at Fort Snelling National Cemetery. In 1974 Jones was posthumously inducted as a member of the American Society of Refrigeration Engineers, and in 1977 he was inducted into the Minnesota Inventors Hall of Fame.

REFERENCES

Burt, McKinley, Jr. *Black Inventors of America.* Portland, OR: National Book Co., 1989.

Hayden, Robert C. *Eight Black American Inventors.* Reading, MA: Addison–Wesley, 1972.

Logan, Rayford W., and Michael R. Winston, eds. *Dictionary of American Negro Biography.* New York: Norton, 1982.

Spencer, Steven M. ''Born Handy.'' *Saturday Evening Post* (May 7, 1949): 153–55.

Dolores Nicholson

James Earl Jones
(1931–)
Actor

''Papa used to tell me my child–voice was beautiful, like a bell. I grew up listening to the music of Southern voices, the rich oral testimonies guised in stories told on the porch of Papa's or at my great–grandfather's Home House. The storytellers in the family could mesmerize us with the high drama of our family tales or with vivid local gossip. . . . I grew up with the spoken word,'' wrote James Earl Jones in his autobiography. He became a multi–award winning actor known for his booming, legendary basso voice and as one of America's foremost classical actors. Jones exemplifies self–reliance and dignity in his choice of roles for the stage, screen and television. He lends nobility to his performances but considers acting as just a job. He works in every genre from classic to contemporary. In his more than 30–year career, Jones has appeared in some 64 films, 56 plays, dozens of television productions, and numerous audio recordings.

A midwife delivered Jones by oil lamp in Arkabutla, Mississippi, on January 17, 1931, to Ruth Williams Jones and Robert Earl Jones—their only child. Jones's maternal grandparents, John and Maggie Connolly, raised him in rural Mississippi, 30 miles south of Memphis, and provided the only stability he knew in his childhood. He saw his mother, an itinerant tailor, only occasionally. His father, Robert Earl Jones, left the family and farming before the son's birth. This was during the depression and both parents set off in search of work. His father went to work in Memphis as a prizefighter, earning a living as ''Battling Bill Stovall.'' Later he gave up his boxing career to try acting, after being a sparring partner of Joe Louis in USO (United Service Organizations) films during World War II. James moved with his grandparents to Dublin, Michigan, at around the age of five, when they sought better schools for their children and grandchildren. Eventually his grandparents formally adopted him and made a home in rural Michigan. In a 1981 *New York Times* article, James notes, ''My grandmother was a highly dramatic person. Her bedtime stories, when I was a child, were not about little lambs. Or carrying buckets uphill. Her stories were about hurricanes, lynchings and rapes. The dramatic things that had happened in her past.''

The move to Michigan was preceded by a visit to Memphis, where Jones's grandfather planned to return him to his mother to live but relented when Jones refused to let go of his safe haven in the family car. Jones never forgot the fury of that unexplained moment and it took its toll on the young child. ''A world ended for me, the safe world of childhood,'' he wrote in his autobiography. ''There was so much I could not ask or say. The move from Mississippi to Michigan was supposed to be a glorious event. For me it was a heartbreak, and not long after, I began to stutter.'' In Michigan, Jones

James Earl Jones

soon developed a stutter so serious that he could only communicate with his teacher and classmates with notes. On a CNN television program in October of 1993, Jones said, ''I spoke to the animals on the farm but language as social intercourse, I abandoned it because it was too painful and too embarrassing to try to talk as a stutterer. Its very difficult and as a young child I couldn't handle the embarrassment. I gave up speech.''

Jones was virtually mute for about eight years, from age six to 14. With the help and encouragement of his high school teacher, Donald Crouch, he joined the debating team. Crouch gave his star pupil a bound copy of Ralph Waldo Emerson's essay ''Self–Reliance.'' Crouch forced Jones, who was still mute, to recite in class a poem Jones had written and to defend himself against an erroneous charge of plagiarism. As Jones read the poem without difficulty, both knew that the written word had been a haven for Jones, the stutterer, and they began to work together to recapture Jones's ability to speak.

From then until he graduated, in his spare time alone, he would read Shakespeare aloud. He first heard Shakespearean verse when a visiting uncle raised his voice to the outdoors and recited Marc Antony's speech from Julius Caesar. His speech problems as a child have imbued him with a deep appreciation of the spoken language. Although Jones had the body of an athlete, ran some track, and for four years played basketball, he poured his energies into learning to speak again. ''I could not get enough of speaking, debating, orating—acting,'' he wrote in his autobiography. People were enchanted with his deep, strong voice. that he had. Jones had become popular as well; he was an officer on the student council, a class officer, and yearbook editor.

In 1949 Jones won the Regents Alumni Scholarship to the University of Michigan. He also received an award as public speaking champion. He had originally planned a medical career but failed his first anatomy course. He changed his focus to drama. His professional debut was in *A Sleep of Prisoners.* He also played the leading roles in Michigan productions of *Deep Are the Roots* (his campus debut in 1949) and *Othello.* He did part–time work as a brick mason to supplement his scholarship and was in the ROTC (Reserve Officer Training Corps). There were several productions at the Manistee Michigan Summer Theatre in which James was cast. He failed to take his final examinations at the end of his senior year at Michigan, and thus did not graduate with his 1953 class.

Jones entered the U.S. Army and was sent to Rangers training camp. During the two years of compulsory service, Jones saw active duty in Korea. In the army from 1953 to 1955, he became a first lieutenant and was on his way to a captaincy. While he was stationed at the Cold Weather Training Command, he almost decided to make the Army his career, but his regimental commander suggested that he explore options in civilian life. He was 21–years old before reuniting with his father, Robert Earl, a long–time actor. One summer he went to New York to see his father, who took him to see a Broadway play, his first. After the army, James went to New York City. Robert invited his son to move in with him, and they pursued their separate acting careers. They often worked together as janitors in several Broadway theaters. In 1955 Jones enrolled in an extension program and completed his B.A. degree at the University of Michigan. He also worked with a speech teacher and concentrated on articulation and voice control. Financed by the G.I. Bill, and with help from his part–time job, Jones also attended the American Theatre Wing and, after studying with Lee Strasberg and Tad Danielewsky, he received his diploma in 1957.

On Broadway

Jones's Broadway debut came in 1957 in *The Egghead.* His first big–time New York role was in *Wedding in Japan* that same year. In 1958 Jones played the butler in *Sunrise at Campobello.* His first leading role was in *The Pretender* (1959–60). He read a newspaper advertisement about a role in a play, off–Broadway, went in for an audition, joined the cast and eventually took over the lead from Ivan Dixon. In 1961 Jones acted with his father in *Moon on a Rainbow Shaw* for which he received a Theatre World Award in 1962. According to *Reader's Digest,* the best acting advice came from his father: ''Pay attention to the little things actors do.''

Jones believes that the turning point of his career was the role of Deodatus Village in the 1961 off–Broadway production of Jean Genet's drama of race relations, *The Blacks.* What was special about the play, Jones told the *Los Angeles Times,* ''was the heightened consciousness about racial politics, about liberty and freedom. There was a strong focus on the issues. I am of a generation that included Lou Gossett, Roscoe Lee Browne, Raymond St. Jacques, Cicely Tyson, Billy Dee

Williams . . . many of us ended up in *The Blacks,* and it put us all on the map.''

For seven years, beginning in 1960, Jones appeared with the New York Shakespeare Festival Theater in *Macbeth* (1962), *Othello* (1963), and *King Lear* (1963), among many others. He received the Drama Desk award for best performance for his 1964 *Othello,* and won the Vernon Rice Award for his 1965 version of Shakespeare's tale of the Moor. In 30 months, Jones had appeared in 18 plays, an unheard–of pace for a New York actor. In 1962 he won the Daniel Blum Theatre Award for Most Promising Personality in *Moon on A Rainbow Shawl.* Barbara Lewis's description of Jones in a 1977 *Encore American and Worldwide News* critique of *Oedipus Rex,* said:

> But towering over the merit of the play is James Earl Jones. Belonging to that long line of Black tragedians beginning with James Hewlett and including Ira Aldridge, Charles Gilpin, and Paul Robeson, Jones possessed a superb stentorian quality. His words eject piercingly into the air ahead of him, resounding with full echoes and surprising clarity. His energy and presence have a crackling wit and a volatile imagination.

Great White Hope

In 1967 Jones received his first widespread critical and public recognition when he was cast as the fictional boxer Jack Jefferson in a Washington, D.C., production of Howard Sackler's Pulitzer Prize–winning play *The Great White Hope.* He rose to stardom in the 1968 Broadway version of the play in the role of Jack Johnson, the first black heavyweight boxing champion. His searing portrayal earned Jones his first Tony Award and made him an overnight national celebrity. The role also brought him a Drama Desk award for outstanding performance. Jones's appearance in the film version of the play two years later brought him an Academy Award nomination. The Hollywood Foreign Press Association titled him ''Most Promising Actor'' and gave him a Golden Globe award for his performance. The wave of adulation and sycophancy was too much for Jones. After playing Jack Johnson for a year on Broadway, and after completing the role in the film of *The Great White Hope*—a box office disappointment—Jones suspended his career. He went to Los Angeles for a year's worth of concentrated therapy at the Primal Institute. There he was forced to consider his childhood and family relationships.

Jones won his first Drama Desk Award in 1970 for his part in Lorraine Hansberry's *Les Blancs.* In 1974 he got the Golden Globe Award and an NAACP Image Award for the play *Claudine.* On Broadway, he had a powerful presence in such works as *Emperor Jones* (1964), *The Blood Knot* (1964), an Obie Award–winning role in *Baal* (1965), *Happy Ending* (1966), *A Day of Absence* (1966), Athol Fugard's *Boesman and Lena* (1970), *The Iceman Cometh* (1973), *Of Mice and Men* (1974), *Paul Robeson* (1977), *Hedda Gabler* (1980), *A Lesson from Aloes* (1980), and *Master Harold and the Boys* (1982). He returned triumphantly to the stage in August Wilson's Pulitzer Prize–winning play *Fences* (1987). This role, which he starred in for three years, brought him another Drama Desk award, Antoinette Perry award, Outer Critics Circle award, Drama Critics award, and a Tony award for Best Actor.

Beginning with *Dr. Strangelove* (1964), Jones has performed in dozens of films. These include *The Comedians* (1967), *King: A Filmed Record, Montgomery to Memphis* (1970), *The Man* (1972), *Claudine* (1974, for which he was nominated for a Golden Globe Award), *The River Niger* (1975), *The Bingo Long Traveling All–Stars and Motor Kings* (1976), *A Piece of the Action* (1977), *Coming to America* (1988), *Field of Dreams* (1989), *Matewan* (1984), *Cry the Beloved Country* (1985), *Gardens of Stone* (1985), *Soul Man* (1986), *Hunt for Red October* (1990), *Sneakers* (1991), *Patriot Games* (1992), *Sommersby* (1993), *Meteor Man* (1993), *Clear and Present Danger* (1994), *Cry the Beloved Country* (1995), and *A Family Thing* (1996). Jones has never listened to conventional wisdom about what roles he should take. He told *Saturday Review,* ''Because I have a varied career, and I have not typecast myself, nobody knows what I'm going to do next. They don't know if I'm going to drop 20 pounds and play an athlete. They don't know whether I'm ready to be a good guy or a bad guy.''

Jones has a long television history. In 1965 he was the first African American actor with a continuing role on a daytime soap opera, *As the World Turns.* In the Ron Ely *Tarzan* series, Jones played an African chieftain. He appeared on the George C. Scott series *East Side, West Side* and also in *The Defenders* and *Lamp Unto My Feet.* In 1973 he hosted the variety series *Black Omnibus.* He portrayed Alex Haley in *Roots: The Next Generation* and had the lead role in the 13–week television series *Paris* (1979). Jones won two Emmy Awards in 1991 as Best Actor in a Drama Series for the television series, *Gabriel's Fire* (1990–92), and as Best Supporting Actor in a Mini Series or Special for the cable movie, *Heat Wave.* The BBC featured Jones in their mini–series *Jesus of Nazareth* and *Signs and Wonders.* The television dramas *Under One Roof* and *Harris and Company* showcased Jones as head of an extended family. Other television films include *The Cay* (1974), *The Atlanta Child Murders* (1984), and *The Vernon Johns Story* (1994).

The Voice, the Man, the Honors

We can now hear his powerful voice dramatically stating, ''This is CNN,'' before all the cable network's station breaks and in 1998 on *An American Moment* on CBS television. The voice is most memorable as that of the evil Darth Vader in the *Star Wars* film trilogy—*Star Wars* (1977), *The Empire Strikes Back* (1979), and *Return of the Jedi* (1983)—and as King Mufasa in the movie, *The Lion King* (1994). His voice is very much in demand for narrations and other recordings. He is often approached to record messages for fans' answering machine tapes. He has recorded the King James version of the New Testament, poetry by Langston Hughes and e.e. cummings, and American documents with Orson Welles, Henry Fonda, and Helen Hayes.

Jones was the recipient of *The Village Voice* Off–Broadway award in 1962. He received a Grammy Award in 1976 for best spoken word recording. He was inducted into the Black Film Makers Hall of Fame at the fourth annual Oscar Micheaux Awards ceremony in 1977. He received the Medal for Spoken Language from the American Academy and Institute of Arts and Letters in 1981. He received the 1990 Jean Renoir Award for his career. In 1992 Jones received the National Medal of Arts from President George Bush for outstanding contributions to the cultural life of the country. In that same year, Jones received the NAACP Best Actor Award and its Hall of Fame Image Award. He has also received two ACE Awards (cable television), Tony Awards and many nominations from the People's Choice Awards and Golden Globe Awards, and the Helen Hayes Award to mention a few. He was elected to the Theatre Hall of Fame in 1995. He is honored for his vigorous yet sensitive performances and for his ability to enrich the hearts and minds of his audiences. Jones told CNN's *Sonya Live* that:

> I did not set myself up to be any particular kind of actor. I wanted to be a character actor. I wanted to keep myself available for a variety of roles, both in type of character and in size of role. And I enjoy these days, doing cameo roles. I find it difficult to wait around for the one big juicy role. I would like to just keep working in roles that interest me and that are meaningful.

James Earl Jones's career has not been without controversy or free of politics. His critics have not always been happy with his choice of roles. Dozens of African American writers, artists, educators, religious and political leaders protested Jones's one man show, *Paul Robeson.* In a two–page advertisement in the January 11, 1978, issue of *Variety,* the play by Phillip Hayes Dean was labeled a ''pernicious perversion of the essence of Paul Robeson.'' Paul Robeson Jr. denounced the play as a distortion of his father's life. Celebrities, including Maya Angelou, Gwendolyn Brooks, and James Baldwin, formed the National Ad Hoc Committee to End the Crimes Against Paul Robeson. Jones countered that the committee was engaged in censorship.

Jones has actively participated in national politics and campaigns. In 1962 President John F. Kennedy appointed him to the Advisory Board of the National Council on the Arts. In 1979 Jones received the Mayor's Award of Honor for Arts and Culture from New York City. Jones testified before the House Appropriations Subcommittee on the Interior protesting proposed budget reduction of the National Endowment for the Arts in 1981.

Jones is divorced from the actress Julienne Marie Hendricks, whom he wed in January of 1967. He married Cecilia Hart on March 15, 1982; she had played his Desdemona. They have one son Flynn Earl, born in 1983. At nearly six feet, one inch tall, James Earl Jones is a large man with green eyes. He is a converted Catholic and an avid watcher of television. Interested in the arts, Jones has played the bugle, painted, and done a little sculpting. Much of the year, the Jones family lives on farms in upstate New York and north of Los Angeles. In his long and impressive career, James Earl Jones has played, among other things, a mentally handicapped disabled man (*Of Mice and Men*), a garbage man (*Claudine*), a famous boxer (*The Great White Hope*), a soldier (*Othello*), and a king (*King Lear*). He likes to play basic characters dealing with universal problems. He is a realist. His realistic approach to life and his craft translates well to the stage and screen. Jones, who tends to play heroic roles, has long been one of America's best role models and premier actors. Although he is often called to deliver speeches at functions and awards ceremonies, ''the stage is what I do best,'' he wrote in his autobiography. In addition to being exceptionally talented as an actor, much of his success has come because, as he wrote in his autobiography, he ''never traveled to anyone else's drumbeat.''

Current address: c/o Bauman and Hiller, 5750 Wilshire Boulevard, PH 5, Los Angeles, CA 90036.

REFERENCES

Black, Doris. ''James Earl Jones: Finest Serious Black Actor Confounded By His Success.'' *Sepia* 25 (August 1976): 24–32.

Burg, Robert. ''Young Actor on the Way Up.'' *Negro Digest* 15 (April 1966): 26–31.

Culhane, John. ''How James Earl Jones Found His Voice.'' *Reader's Digest* 145 (July 1994): 121–23.

Current Biography Yearbook. New York: H. W. Wilson, 1969.

Friedman, Sonya. ''James Earl Jones.'' *Sonya Live* (October 8, 1993): Transcript #398–2. Lexis–Nexis (online subscription service). 1998.

Green, Michelle. ''The Struggle to Be James Earl Jones.'' *Saturday Review* 9 (February 1982): 22–27.

''James Earl Jones: Actor Still Climbing.'' *Ebony* 20 (April 1965): 98–100, 104.

''James Earl Jones: How Does an Actor Make His Statement As An Artist?'' *New York Times,* December 10, 1980.

''James Earl Jones.'' [Interview.] *EM: Ebony Man* 6 (December 1990): 16–19.

''James Earl Jones Prepares to Map the Tormented Soul of Othello.'' *New York Times,* August 2, 1981.

Jones, James Earl. ''Jack Johnson is Alive and Well. . .On Broadway.'' *Ebony* 24 (June 1969): 54– 61.

———, and Penelope Niven. *Voices and Silences.* New York: Charles Scribner's Sons, 1993.

Lewis, Barbara. ''Oedipus Rex, King James Version.'' *Encore American and Worldwide News* 6 (4 April 1977): 39.

''The Un–retiring James Earl Jones; The Actor Isn't Leaving the Stage, Just Curtailing His Involvement in Serious Dramas in Favor of Less Taxing TV Roles.'' *Los Angeles Times,* September 2, 1990.

Kathleen E. Bethel

Jones, James Francis Marion.
See Jones, Prophet.

Laurence Clifton Jones
(1884–1975)
School founder, school administrator

Laurence Clifton Jones founded and was first principal of Piney Woods Country Life School in the Black Belt of rural Mississippi, once an area of ignorance, superstition and bare existence. He made it possible for thousands of black children to receive elementary and high school teaching, and helped the men and women of the area improve their lives without formal study. He founded the school on faith and left it with several buildings spread over thousands of acres of land. Jones became known affectionately as "The Little Professor of Piney Woods."

Laurence Clifton Jones

Laurence Clifton Jones was born November 21, 1884, in St. Joseph, Missouri. Although he was the only son of John Q. and Lydia Foster Jones, he had several sisters. Jones's life work was governed by his home training. His father, a tall, striking, part–Castilian man, was head porter at the Pacific Hotel in St. Joseph, where he also owned and operated a barbershop. John taught his son the dignity of labor and the wisdom of holding a practical outlook on life. His fragile, Wisconsin–born quadroon mother instilled in her son the idea that to do well according to one's strength was not ambition, but duty. Jones lived a life that was governed by his home training.

Early Education

Laurence Jones had his first job beyond the home when he was in elementary school. He worked at the largest barbershop in town assisting the porter as a shoe shine boy. The book Robinson Crusoe, the first book other than the Bible that impressed him deeply, also shaped his future. He was affected by the story of the resourceful hero who overcame physical obstacles by making things by hand to fit his needs.

Jones grew up knowing his family's expectations: that he would be a lawyer, doctor, editor, minister, professor, or congressman. He was expected to have all the traits of his ancestors. His maternal great–grandfather was born a slave in Virginia, purchased his freedom while still a young man, and moved to Pennsylvania. His maternal grandfather, Robert Foster, was born there. Since blacks were denied admission to public schools in Ohio at that time, Foster, who later moved to Michigan, established an interracial and interreligious school with some of his brothers and sisters for their children in 1848. In his autobiography, Jones wrote that the institution might have been the first school established in the country for industrial training of black youth.

Although racial segregation existed in Missouri, Jones read widely at the St. Joseph Public Library. He studied in the local schools and attended the white high school, but became dissatisfied with his training there and went to Marshalltown, Iowa, where he worked in restaurants and hotels to support himself. He received his diploma in 1903, the first black graduate of the school. Jones planned to work his way through Central Iowa Business College, but that summer he met a representative from the Iowa State University who persuaded him that he should study there instead. He entered the school that fall, worked his way through college, and graduated with honors in 1907 with a bachelor of philosophy degree.

In his junior year at Iowa State, Jones was assigned a theme on the work of educator and founder of Tuskegee Institute, Booker T. Washington. He read Washington's works and became fascinated with his philosophy and success. After graduation, Jones was offered a position at Tuskegee. However, he decided that he would cast his lot in the Piney Woods area and build a school for black youth. Although the salary was smaller than what Tuskegee offered, he thought the need for his service was greater in Hinds County.

The "Little Professor" Founds a School

Jones visited the plantation home of one of his students in the Piney Woods of Mississippi near Braxton, between Jackson and Gulfport. Although he made unsuccessful appeals to local church conventions to start a school in the area, he decided that he would cast his lot near Braxton and build a school for black youth. Moral conditions in the community were higher than he expected, yet the changes that a school could effect in the community were clear and demanding. When Hinds County closed its school in May 1909, Jones set out for Piney Woods. He had taught in the South for two years and invested $400 of the $490 he had earned into land for the new school. In preparing to open the school, he walked between 18 and 20 miles a day in Rankin and Simpson counties, visiting homes, churches, and neighborhood meetings, to talk with the rural people about rotating crops, sanitary cooking, and the importance of education. The residents of the area wanted their children to receive an education, but knew of no way to provide it. One local group had saved money for a school for 15 years, but they would not trust their savings to "Fesser" Jones, as they called him, because he was a "furriner."

By 1910, Jones had started his school. According to Jones's autobiography, his purpose was "to establish, maintain, and develop a country–life school." In accordance with this, his first students—three boys—received their education while seated on logs underneath a cedar tree. The number of students soon grew to 29. The school continued to grow as Jones recruited two of his former students from Hinds County as teaching assistants. The group built bonfires to keep themselves warm as the weather cooled, but the open–air school was less conducive to learning at these times. The construction of Taylor Hall, named after a local resident who donated $50 and 40 acres of land, marked the beginning of indoor classes. He also received local support and solicited funds from his friends in Iowa and elsewhere, enabling him to officially found the Piney Woods Industrial School on May 17, 1913.

Jones worked diligently and earned the trust of both whites and blacks in the community. At the beginning of each school year, parents, students, faculty, and the community at large came to the school's opening day to hear what "Fesser" had to say. According to Beth Day in *The Little Professor of Piney Woods,* Jones told the group at the beginning of the fifth year: "In the glow of a bonfire five years ago, before we had adequate shelter, I saw many of your faces light up with a new understanding of the meaning of education as we studied our books and practiced our manual training. . . . We need a sentiment to guide us over the rugged road we must travel if we are to reach success." Jones then scanned the crowd and asked them to describe what the school meant to them. One by one they rose to speak, as if they had been appointed, and told their stories of what education and the school meant to them and their families. One local resident remarked, "This school jus' beats everything."

Even though he had the moral support of the community, Jones continued to secure monies and equipment from outside sources to operate the school. He received little, if any, money from students' tuition. Many of the students were so poor that they came to class with all of their worldly possessions in a knapsack. Some students offered poultry, eggs, corn meal, butter, or small change in exchange for an education. In 1911, Jones received funds to purchase a press so that he could promote the school by publishing a monthly newsletter, *The Pine Torch.* The paper bore the slogan "Give the people light—they will find the way."

Personal Development

Jones's personal life underwent significant changes at this time. On June 29, 1912, he married Grace M. Allen, whom he met while a junior in college. They had two sons, Turner Harris, born May 6, 1914, and Laurence Clifton Jr., born December 10, 1917. Grace Allen Jones had graduated from Burlington High School and traveled in the interest of Eckstein–Norton School in Kentucky. She also taught in Missouri for a while, completed a course at Elliott's Business College in Burlington, and in 1902 founded the Grace M. Allen Industrial School. She studied public speaking and elocution at Ziegfield Musical College in Chicago. Needless to say, when she joined the Piney Woods faculty, she brought useful skills and valuable expertise. She taught English, formed mothers' clubs to work with women in the community, assisted her husband with farmers' conferences, and went on fund raising trips with him. In 1914 Laurence and Grace Jones signed on as lecturers on the Redpath Chautauqua Circuit. By the end of the decade, Jones had a Chautauqua contract to visit over 80 towns. At some point he was the first representative for rural schools in Mississippi. The State Department of Education appointed Jones and five others to work out a course of study for accrediting black schools in the segregated system.

Around 1918 Laurence Jones assisted with a revival. On the third night of his address he used phrases drawn from military life and operations, referring to life as a battle and stressing that black people must stay on the firing line and fight ignorance, poverty, and superstition. Several white men who heard this part of his speech spread the news that Jones was urging the group to "rise up and fight the white people." Around noon the next day an angry mob of about 500 men came to the church where Jones was speaking, threw a rope over his head, tightened the noose, and took him to a lynching sight. Eventually, an elderly man wearing a Confederate button persuaded the mob to release him.

That same year Piney Woods graduated its first class from the Normal Department. A review of the careers of the graduates of 1918 and 1919 indicated that some graduates had gone on to work as teachers and educational supervisors, while others studied in mainstream institutions. The farmers' conferences continued, and during the ten years of their existence the farmers purchased over 6,000 acres of land in the vicinity of the school. By 1921 the school had over 200 students in the boarding department, representing 38 counties in Mississippi. In addition to traditional book learning, industrial work, and religious instruction, the students participated in clubs and literary societies in order to give them an opportunity for self–expression and creativity.

Singing Groups Become Musical Messengers

To sustain the school, fund raising was essential, and Jones used a variety of means to obtain the monies needed. In 1921 Jones organized several small vocal groups of male and female students called the Cotton Blossom Singers, who became the best–known ambassadors or musical messengers for the institution. The singers traveled first in an open touring car donated for their use, but by 1927 they traveled in a larger and more functional "house car." The singers toured all parts of the United States, promoting the school while raising money for its survival.

Inspired by the success of the all–girl white orchestras of the time, such as the Ina Ray Hutton orchestra, in the late 1930s Jones organized a group he called the International Sweethearts of Rhythm. The young women members ranged in age from 14 to 19. He hired black women master teachers and conductors to lead the singers. By 1939 they appeared at dances, fund raising events, conventions, resorts, and at other gatherings and sites throughout Florida, Texas, California, New York, Virginia, and the Carolinas. In late summer of 1940 they signed a week's engagement at the famous Apollo Theater in New York City. In August 1940 they placed third in the large band division contest held at the New York City World's Fair. The Sweethearts severed their relationship with Piney Woods in early April 1941.

Takes on New Responsibilities

By 1929 Jones persuaded the state to relocate the school for blind black youth to Piney Woods. The department suffered from underfunding until 1945 when Helen Keller visited Piney Woods and appealed to the state legislature for adequate aid. At that time a new facility was set up in Jackson. Still, many of the students returned to Piney Woods to complete elementary, high school, and normal school programs. By the end of the 1930s Piney Woods still had a department for blind children as well as 500 other students.

The appeal for funds would not end. In December 1954 Jones's plight had been heard elsewhere. Ralph Edwards celebrated ''The Little Professor of Piney Woods'' and his story on the then–popular television program *This is Your Life.* Edwards asked one million people to send one dollar each to the school. Donations ranged from five cents from a young girl to $500,000 from the Brooklyn Dodgers baseball team. Within two months, $625,000 had been received. The show was aired again in July 1955, to widen the appeal. ''I did not expect the public to be so generous,'' Jones said in *Ebony* magazine.

During World War I Jones was in charge of the thrift stamp campaign among blacks in Mississippi. He worked in Rankin and Simpson counties for the American Red Cross. He was assistant director of the Armenian Relief campaign for Mississippi and was the secretary of the First United War Work Drive for blacks in the state. Among his various professional and service affiliations, Jones was a member of the State Executive Committee on Negro YMCA work, vice–president of the Mississippi Association of Teachers in Colored Schools, a member of the executive committee of the National Negro Press Association, and a member of the Kappa Alpha Psi Fraternity.

Jones retired from the presidency of the school following the 1974–75 school year, but came to his campus office daily and continued to travel on school business. He died of a massive stroke in St. Dominic Hospital in Jackson, Mississippi. His children and a sister, Nellie Boss, survived him.

From its crude and inconspicuous beginning as an open–air school within Mississippi's Black Belt, Jones built a school that earned international acclaim. Along the way, he transformed the lives of thousands of young people and their parents as he trained ''the head, the hand, and the heart.''

REFERENCES

Day, Beth. *The Little Professor of Piney Woods.* New York: Julian Messner, 1955.

Handy, D. Antoinette. *Black Women in American Bands & Orchestras.* Metuchen, NJ: Scarecrow Press, 1981.

Jenness, Mary. *Twelve Negro Americans.* New York: Friendship Press, 1936.

Jones, Laurence C. *Piney Woods and Its Story.* New York: Fleming H. Revell Company, 1922.

''Miracle of Piney Woods.'' *Ebony* 10 (October 1955): 36–41.

''Piney Woods School Founder Dr. Laurence C. Jones Dies.'' *Jet* 48 (31 July 1975): 8.

Rogers, Tommy. ''The Piney Woods Country Life School: A Successful Heritage of Education of Black Children in Mississippi.'' *Negro History Bulletin* 39 (September–October 1976): 611–14.

Jessie Carney Smith

Jones, LeRoi.
See Baraka, Amiri.

Prophet Jones
(1907–1971)
Religious leader

Prophet Jones was one of a swarm of cult leaders who built successful churches in the mid–twentieth century. Better than most others, he succeeded in attracting widespread attention from the media. His church was primarily based in urban areas of the North and attracted a disproportionate number of women. He struck a chord among many African Americans until morals charges resulted in a sharp decline in his influence.

James Francis Marion Jones was born in November 1907 in a Birmingham, Alabama, slum. His father was a railroad brakeman who abused his mother, Catherine L. Jones, a teacher and modiste. James Jones claimed that his first prophecy at age two was that his father would return home bloody from a slight accident. The son developed an intense relationship with his mother, and was rarely separated from her. She sewed most of Jones's elaborate costumes to his own designs. Her death in 1951 marked a major turning point in his life.

Jones grew up in a Holiness church, Triumph the Church and Kingdom of God in Christ, and began preaching regularly when he was 11. What schooling he obtained had little effect: he said that God forbade him to read any human book. Jones traveled about evangelizing for the church in the Midwest and the South with little success until he arrived in Detroit in 1938. There he built up a profitable church by 1944. When questions about control of the church and its assets arose, God told him on September 28, 1944, he claimed, while he was standing in his pajamas under a streetlight to found his own church, the Church of the Universal Triumph the Dominion of God.

This church centered on Jones and his ability to cure and prophesy. He was also a strong preacher capable of speaking for five hours at a stretch. According to his teachings death was not a necessary event, and he refused to hold funerals. In the year 2000 history would come to an end, and all persons then living would become immortal and live on a paradisiacal earth. A seven–day feast called Philamathyu celebrated his birthday, replacing Christmas for his followers. Jones published a handbook of strict rules for his followers. In addition to forbidding smoking, drinking, attending another church, or marrying without the Prophet's consent, these rules included according to *Ebony* in 1950:

> the proper way to bow and curtsy before the royal family [the Joneses], and how to wire the Prophet in case of tumor. Social clubs, coffee, tea and illegitimate children are forbidden. Women must wear girdles in public, and all must own swim suits. Steam baths should be taken often, a laxative once or twice a week.

A major drawing card of Jones's church was his ability to heal, and persons he helped gave him lavish gifts, like his famed $13,500 white mink coat, which came from two Chicago schoolteachers. According to Marguerite Cartwright, he told their supposedly dying mother to "make four trips to the Gary, Indiana, bus station and swallow water from the bathroom tap." Grateful followers even gave him three children. Freely offered donations were not always enough; *Ebony* said in 1956 that Jones was known to lock his followers in the church if the offering fell short of what he felt appropriate. In return for support Jones bestowed titles on all of his followers; his apparent favorite in 1956 was "Prince" Douglas Rogers, a very handsome young man according to *Newsweek.*

Jones's claim to prophecy was also very important to his followers and to the media, which spread his fame. Jones said that God spoke to him in his right ear in a breeze. He prophesied both for his own followers and issued annual predictions for print publications. As late as 1969, a considerable time after his heyday, *Ebony* included him among the astrologers giving predictions for the upcoming year.

The Prophet Makes a Splash

Jones was a charismatic cult leader. He supported his preaching, healing, and prophesying by a flamboyant worship and lifestyle. A six–foot tall, thin Jones dressed for his services in gaudy silk robes and feathers; one of his gowns was a replica of the wedding dress of England's Queen Elizabeth. He wore an earring in his left ear—the one not used by God. Even in a conventional suit he wore a ring on each finger of his left hand and several bracelets on his left wrist, including one with 812 diamonds. His home, Dominion Residence, was a 54–room mansion staffed with 12 servants aided by volunteers from his congregations. (Jones never married.) One bedroom of his mansion was dedicated as a shrine to his deceased great and good friend, James Walton, who was a member of Jones's "trinity," along with Jones himself and Jones's mother.

It is difficult to estimate the institutional base Jones built up. There were supposedly 362 of his Thankful Centers in 45 states and 16 countries. He claimed two or three million followers. These numbers are apparently wild exaggerations. It does appear that the great majority of his followers were women. Beginning in 1940 Jones reached followers through a radio broadcast on WKMH, which was aired at 1 a.m. in 1950. The radio program always began with a strong patriotic message, including the National Anthem and the Pledge of Allegiance. Television followed later; for a year he broadcast for an hour beginning at 12 a.m. Monday morning. His fame reached a wide audience when *Life* magazine published articles on him on two different occasions.

Jones began to run into trouble in the mid–1950s. Debts piled up; he faced an extortion attempt. A gunman attempted to force an interview, and there was a bombing threat against his home. The personal threats in early 1956 may have been connected with his announced plan to move his headquarters to exclusive Grosse Pointe, Michigan. Debtors began to seize his assets. The Internal Revenue Service filed liens against him, eventually collecting $12,000 on the mink coat and other personal property. What finally brought the edifice down were two morals charges in 1956, when he was first arrested for sexually molesting two boys. (Jones said they were in his bedroom to discuss music instruction.) Then he was accused of soliciting sex from a policeman. Jones collapsed and was found to be suffering from ulcers. Although he was not found guilty, his reputation and his church were in ruins.

A remnant of Jones's church nonetheless survived. *Jet* estimated at the time of his death that there were between 100 and 200 followers, mostly women, in 36 churches. In comparison with his heyday, Jones was poor in a relative sense. He still had considerable assets although it was difficult to separate church and personal property. Jones suffered a stroke in September of 1970 which left him paralyzed and almost bereft of speech. He died in Detroit on August 13, 1971. He was survived by two aunts, Ardella Simmons and Lubertha

Clay, and an uncle George Lynch. Since Jones feared burial, his body was placed in a crypt near that of his mother in Elmwood Cemetery.

Jones was one of the so–called ''big three'' among black cult leaders of his era. The other two were ''Sweet Daddy'' Grace of New York, who purchased Jones's Detroit mansion and died worth a claimed $26 million, and Father Divine of Philadelphia, whose assets were reputed to be on the order of $8 million. These three all had in common the ability to attract media attention through their flamboyant claims and behavior. Jones's life was colorful, but he tapped a genuine vein of religious feeling among blacks and a few whites.

REFERENCES

Cartwright, Marguerite. ''Observations on Community Life, III: I Visit Prophet Jones.'' *Negro History Bulletin* 18 (January 1955): 88–89.

DuPree, Sherry Sherrod. *Biographical Dictionary of African–American, Holiness–Pentecostals, 1880–1990.* Washington, DC: Middle Atlantic Regional Press, 1989.

''Mink–Minded Prophet Dies; Successor Sought.'' *Jet* 40 (2 September 1971): 20–23.

Murphy, Larry G., J. Gordon Melton, and Gary L. Ward, eds. *Encyclopedia of African American Religions.* New York: Garland, 1993.

Payne, Wardell J. *Directory of African American Religious Bodies.* Washington, DC: Howard University Press, 1991.

''Prophet Jones.'' *Ebony* 5 (April 1950):67–72.

''The Prophet Threatened?'' *Newsweek* 47 (13 February 1956): 90–91.

''The Rise and Fall of Prophet Jones.'' *Ebony* 11 (October 1956): 63–66.

Robert L. Johns

Quincy Jones

(1933–)

Composer, arranger, musician, producer entrepreneur, civil rights advocate, humanitarian

A multi–talented entertainer, Quincy Jones became one of the most acclaimed artists in the world of contemporary music. His 50–year career was described by *Billboard Magazine* for December of 1995 as a distinctly American odyssey, embracing music in all its dimensions—as an art, a business, and a catalyst for social change and spiritual renewal. Jones's extraordinarily diverse and successful career included his roles as a prolific composer, arranger, conductor, instrumentalist, record producer, major record label executive, magazine founder, television and movie producer, humanitarian, civil rights advocate, and entrepreneur. Always exploring and experimenting with new musical idioms, Jones masterfully blended swing, pop, soul, jazz, rhythm and blues, hip–hop, classical, African, Brazilian, and world music into award–winning compositions and arrangements.

Quincy Delight Jones Jr. was born March 14, 1933, in Chicago, the son of Quincy Delight Jones Sr. and Sarah Jones. A native of South Carolina, Quincy Jones Sr. moved to Chicago seeking a better life, free of the racial bigotry and segregation that were commonplace in the South. Unfortunately, Sarah Jones suffered chronic mental illness and spent most of her life in mental institutions or under a doctor's care. Life in Chicago was tough for the Jones family without the care and nurture of a wife and mother. Sarah and Quincy Jones Sr. were divorced after the birth of their younger son, Lloyd. The senior Jones remarried and moved to Bremerton, Washington, just outside Seattle, with his new wife Elvira and their blended family of her three children and his two sons. Jones's father and stepmother eventually had five children together. After several years in Bremerton, the family moved into Seattle in 1948.

In Bremerton, Jones was the only African American student in the class and had no problems. Unlike Chicago where there were black and white gangs that controlled certain areas and restricted access to them based on race, Jones's experience in Bremerton was extremely positive and completely integrated. Seattle was also a city where Jones and his brothers and sisters played, fought, and interacted with white children with no apparent difficulty because of their race. These early positive experiences contributed to Jones's belief in the dignity and worth of all humanity without regard to race, creed, or color.

Early Years

In Chicago, there was not much music in the Jones household, and Jones exhibited no real interest in music. Seattle was where Quincy Jones's love affair with music began to emerge and grow. Encouraged and inspired by his father, who was not a musician, Jones developed his musical interest primarily through the public schools and the local black churches. Initially, he helped to organize a choir at one of the local churches and began learning to sing spirituals. He started playing the piano, joined the high school band and became its student manager. As a band member, Jones experimented with a variety of instruments. He played percussion, French horn, baritone, alto saxophone, clarinet, trombone, tuba, and eventually the trumpet. With his musical talent awakened, Jones became an active member of every musical group at his high school. He played with the orchestra and dance band and sang with the chorus. During this time, he became increasingly interested in jazz. While still in high school and only 15 years old, Jones wrote his first suite, ''From the Four Winds.''

During the swing era, many big–name stars, including great African American musical talents, performed in Seattle. Jones attended these performances and was an apt pupil. He listened, observed, asked questions, and learned a lot from such musical giants as popular local bandleader Bumps

Quincy Jones

Blackwell, Cab Calloway, Billie Holiday, Count Basie and his septet, and the phenomenal trumpet player Clark Terry of the Duke Ellington orchestra. Other musical influences included Lester Young, Dizzy Gillespie, and Charlie Parker. However, it was another teenager, blind since the age of six, a transplant from Albany, Georgia, who arrived in Seattle in 1950, who had the biggest overall influence on Quincy Jones. Ray Charles played the piano, organ, alto–saxophone, and clarinet; he was a gifted composer and arranger, and he sang the blues in a unique soulful manner. Ray Charles taught Jones methods for arranging for big jazz bands, voicing horns, writing polytones, and even how to read and write in Braille. Their special relationship fostered almost half a century ago remained intact and Jones and Charles always were best friends.

In 1950, after graduating from high school, Jones won two scholarships to study music at the University of Seattle and Boston's renowned Schillinger's House of Music (which is now known as Berklee College of Music). He attended the University of Seattle for only a short period of time. He then went to Boston, partly because it was close to New York, where he studied at the Berklee School of Music for almost a year. He immersed himself in classes, sometimes taking as many as ten in one day, and worked in local clubs as a semi–professional musician. On weekends, Jones and other students made forays to New York to hear jazz greats such as Art Tatum, Thelonious Monk, Charlie Parker, Miles Davis, Charles Mingus, and others who embraced the bebop style. After Jones reached his eighteenth birthday, Lionel Hampton again invited him to join his big band. Jones left Berklee with the intention of returning to school after a short stint with the Hampton band, but he never did. Instead, Jones toured with the band as a trumpeter, arranger, and sometime–pianist off and on from 1951 to 1959.

Tours with the Lionel Hampton Big Band

From 1951 to 1953 the Hampton band toured major cities in every state in the United States. During his tour with the band, Jones realized that he was not likely to become one of the premiere trumpet soloists of jazz; rather, his talent would be directed toward the overall sound of music through composing and arranging. The first of Jones's compositions recorded by the band was "Kingfish," which included Jones playing a rare trumpet solo. During this same period two of Jones's compositions, "Waitbait" and "Brownie Eyes" were featured on a solo album by the fellow band member, Clifford Brown.

In September of 1953 the Hampton band began an extensive European tour, that included nightly concerts, frequent matinees, and considerable travel from one venue to the next. The tour included Oslo, Stockholm, Brussels, and Paris. Even with the band's demanding performance schedule, Jones wrote prodigiously and recorded in spite of Hampton's threat to fire summarily any band member who recorded independently. The recording sessions were held surreptitiously either very late at night or early in the morning when the musicians were tired, but Jones's scores were so good and player–friendly that they energized the musicians. The undercover recording sessions were important to the musicians because they gave them an opportunity to showcase their talent, to expose more Europeans to jazz, and to supplement their earnings from the tour. Among Jones's original compositions that have become classics recorded during this European tour were "Stockholm Sweetnin'," "'Scuse These Bloos," "Keeping Up with Jonesy," and "Evening in Paris."

The tour ended without incident over the undercover recordings, but all of the musicians knew that once the records were released they would be fired. Eleven of Hampton's band members resigned upon their return to New York, including Jones. By this time Jones had also become a father and he settled in New York.

Quincy Jones's devotion to music and commitment to his much heralded career success took a toll on his personal life. Each of his three marriages ended in divorce. The break–up of his third and longest marriage to actress Peggy Lipton was especially difficult. Jones's five children were: Jolie, the oldest daughter born during his first marriage to Jeri Caldwell; Martina–Lisa and Quincy III, offspring of his second marriage to Ulla, a Swedish woman; and Kidada and Rashida, his daughters of Peggy Lipton.

Jones and the Recording Studio

Jones's career shifted to the recording studio where he did a lot of jazz and commercial recordings as a freelance arranger. He wrote charts for James Cleveland, the king of gospel, Benny Carter, LaVern Baker, Chuck Willis, Dinah

Washington, Johnny Mathis, and even Lionel Hampton. He also arranged a series of albums for musicians whom he admired and respected including Clark Terry, Sonny Stitt, George Washington, and Cannonball Adderley. His work with Dinah Washington, arranging and doing some original songs, was fortunate because it provided a very important connection between Jones and Mercury Records.

In 1956 Jones received the New Star Arranger award in the *Encyclopedia of Jazz* poll. In that same year he organized and arranged tunes for big band leader Dizzy Gillespie for a State Department tour of the Middle East and South America. Jones left the tour in order to write and spend time with his family, but shortly after his return to the United States he was asked to make a big band album of his own jazz compositions by ABC–Paramount. This was something Jones had been wanting to do for a long time. The now classic *This is How I Feel about Jazz* contained three of Jones's songs from the European recording. Though he had more than enough work as an arranger and as an occasional composer, Jones was disappointed with the overall quality of music in the 1950s. He was also frustrated because he was still primarily relegated to supervising the rhythm and horn sections. Jones jumped at the opportunity to become its staff arranger and director of musical operations of Barclay Disques in Paris, Mercury's French distributor. At Barclay he tackled a variety of projects, had the necessary resources to complete them successfully, and finally got his chance to write strings. He learned all he could about the recording business at Barclay while continuing his own music studies with Nadia Boulanger, France's most revered music teacher.

Upon his return to New York, Jones had a dream offer to arrange the score for a new Broadway show, *Free and Easy,* to organize his own big band, and then go to Europe with the show. He was to break the show in, in Holland, Belgium and France and then meet Sammy Davis Jr. in London; work the show three weeks there; and then come back to Broadway and open for two years. This was a fantastic way to start a big band with outstanding well–paid musicians and to keep them together. Simultaneously, Jones took advantage of the opportunity to compose and arrange an LP for Count Basie, *One More Time,* that proved to be one of Basie's best–ever recordings. During the same period, Irving Green offered Jones and his new big band a recording contract and this resulted in *The Birth of a Band,* one of the most well–liked big band albums of all times. The European tour got off to a good start, and it closed. Jones now had responsibility for meeting a weekly payroll of $4,800 with no agent, no manager, and no work. In desperation and in order to get his band and their families back to the United States, Jones hocked the publishing interests on all his copyrights. The entire episode left Jones exhausted, burned out, and broke.

From Mercury to Hollywood

Irving Green, the president of Mercury Records, Inc., was familiar with Jones from his earlier sessions with Dinah Washington and his recent success with *The Birth of a Band* LP. Green offered Jones a position with Mercury as staff arranger and talent developer. Jones accepted the offer because he was able to keep his band together to play when concerts came along, pay off debts, and learn more about the commercial side of the industry. Prior to joining Mercury, Jones scored the major part of an album for ABA Paramount featuring his longtime friend Ray Charles.

During his tenure at Mercury, Jones acquired the nickname "Q" was promoted to vice–president, becoming the first African American executive in the recording industry at a major label, won his first Grammy in 1963 for his Count Basie arrangement of Ray Charles's *I Can't Stop Loving You* and scored the biggest successes in the company's history when he produced Lesley Gore, who became a winner of ten gold discs representing 10 million singles sales with LP follow–ups. Jones's successes at Mercury allowed him the flexibility to take other occasional prestige jobs such as conductor and arranger with Frank Sinatra and Count Basie for the classic, *Sinatra at the Sands.*

Jones was a pioneer in breaking down barriers in the music industry. As an avid movie buff, he had one more unrealized professional goal and that was to score soundtracks for movies. In 1965 Jones left Mercury and moved to Hollywood in order to increase his chances for work scoring movies. Jones succeeded in landing the job of writing the score for Sidney Lumet's independent film, *The Pawnbroker,* the first of his major motion picture scores. Though the movie was critically acclaimed and won an Academy Award for Best Actor, it was not a box office hit. It was nearly a year before Jones had another job scoring a feature film, *Mirage,* which was not a financial success. Jones finally got a break when he was asked to score *The Slender Thread* and *Walk Don't Run.* Both movies were financially successful, and Jones had made his mark by infusing movie music with jazz and soul. During this period, Jones had more work than he could handle writing music for films, such as *In Cold Blood, In the Heat of the Night,* and *For the Love of Ivy,* and themes for television productions like *Ironside* and *The Cosby Show.* His *Ironside* theme was the first synthesized–based pop theme song. Despite his accomplishments in scoring music for films and television and several Oscar nominations, the awards eluded him. Over time, writing the musical scores became less enjoyable and more of a grind. When A & M Records asked Jones to make an album, his first in four years, he readily agreed. The resulting album, *Walking in Space,* received a Grammy for the best performance by a large group, in 1969. His follow–up album in 1970 was *Gula Matari* which also won a Grammy for the best instrumental composition and best instrumental arrangement.

For Jones 1974 was a high point in his career but also a low point in his life. His new album release, *Body Heat,* caused a sensation in pop music circles; sales exceeded one million in the United States alone, and Jones received his first gold disc for the album. In the midst of such good fortune, disaster hit and Jones suffered a cerebral stroke caused by a ruptured aneurysm. Surgery was required and in preparing him for surgery a second aneurysm was discovered on the opposite side of the brain. Two surgeries were performed without complications within several weeks of each other.

After a convalescent period, which kept him out of the studio, doctors pronounced Jones fully recovered by February 1975, six months after his first aneurysm was discovered.

With his health restored and a new lease on life, Jones was extremely busy for the remainder of the 1970s. He produced several albums with the Brothers Johnson and received his first platinum record. He also wrote the musical score for the television miniseries *Roots,* which had the highest viewer ratings in history when it first aired in January 1977.

In 1977, while working on *The Wiz,* Michael Jackson and Jones joined forces to cut a state–of–the–art pop album, *Off the Wall,* which blended disco rhythms, pop tunes, and clever arrangements with Jackson's fantastic singing. The album sold more than seven million copies.

During the 1980s Jones continued to concentrate on recording and producing other artists. He formed Qwest Records, a fifty/fifty joint venture with Warner Bros. His records featuring an eclectic assortment of recording talents, including The Winans, a gospel duo; R&B vocalists Tevin Campbell, Tamia, Keith Washington, and Ernestine Anderson; spoken–word artist D–Knowledge; veteran jazzman Milt Jackson; and veteran entertainer Ray Charles.

Jones teamed with Michael Jackson again to produce another mega album, *Thriller,* which sold more than 40 million copies, making it the best selling album in recording history. Jones broke into film making as co–producer of the 1985 motion picture, *The Color Purple,* which was nominated for 11 Academy Awards. In that same year Jones brought together 40 of the world's biggest recording stars to record *We Are the World* for USA for Africa to raise money to feed the victims of Ethiopia's drought and resulting famine.

Listens Up

Jones started off the decade of the 1990s with a bang. His life and career were chronicled in the critically acclaimed Warner Bros. Film, *Listen Up: The Lives of Quincy Jones.* He continued to produce and win awards, but was more involved with expanding his business interests and developing a multimedia conglomerate. His landmark album, *Back on the Block,* was named Album of the Year at the 1990 Grammy Awards. The album was the first fusion of the be bop and hip hop musical styles and brought together legendary artists such as Miles Davis, Dizzy Gillespie, Ella Fitzgerald, and Sarah Vaughan with rap artists such as Ice T, Big Daddy Kane, and Melle Mel. Similarly, his 1993 recording *Miles and Quincy Live at Montreux,* won a Grammy for best large jazz ensemble performance.

On the business side, Quincy Jones and David Salzman, who had worked together to produce the incredibly successful *An American Reunion* concert at the Lincoln Memorial, the first official event of the 1992 presidential inauguration, merged their companies to form QDE (Quincy Jones–David Salzman Entertainment) in 1993. QDE was a co–venture with Time Warner in which Jones and Salzman equally share a 50 percent interest with Time Warner controlling the remaining 50 percent. Jones served as co–CEO and chairman of the new company which had a broad–ranging, multi–media focus including programming for network, cable, and syndicated television; motion pictures; magazine publishing; live entertainment; direct response marketing; and interactive projects for home entertainment and educational applications.

QDE launched *Vibe,* a magazine which was the brainchild of Jones. It was conceived as an entertaining chronicle of contemporary cool, targeted to young urban consumers. QDE and Time Life's Custom Publishing Division issued *African Americans Voices of Triumph,* a three–volume hard–back set highlighting the scientific, cultural, and social achievements of African Americans.

In the feature film area, QDE had a number of projects in active development and a "first look" agreement with Warner Bros. Pictures. Jones continued his work in television as the creator and executive producer of the popular sitcom, *Fresh Prince of Bel–Air* and as executive producer of another sitcom, *In the House,* starring rapper L.L. Cool J. The most recent addition to his television repertoire was Fox Television's *Mad TV.* QDE also had special commitments with NBC–TV and CBS–TV for pilot series and specials. QDE was also tapped to produce the sixty–eighth annual Academy Awards show, the world's most watched awards show on March 25, 1996.

The Quincy Jones and David Salzman collaboration continued in the interactive arena with the formation of QD7, a joint venture with multi–media publisher 7th Level to develop and publish interactive multi–media titles. The first release was *Q's Jook Joint,* a CD–ROM project chronicling the history of African American music through a retrospective of Jones's broad and diverse career.

Still in an expansion mode, Jones became involved with television broadcasting through a partnership with Tribune Broadcasting, Hall of Fame football player and radio station owner Willie Davis, television producer Don Cornelius, and television talk show host Geraldo Rivera to form Qwest Broadcasting, a minority–controlled broadcasting company. With Jones at the helm as the company's chairman and chief executive officer, the group purchased stations WATL–TV in Atlanta and WNOL–TV in New Orleans for a reported $167 million. These purchases made Qwest Broadcasting one of the largest minority–owned broadcasting companies in the country.

The combination of Jones's phenomenal creative talent, entrepreneurial instincts, practical business acumen, and his passionate love of music have positioned him as one of the most powerful people in the entertainment industry. The evidence of his unparalleled contributions to the music scene is apparent with the numerous awards and citations bestowed upon him for excellence in his field including 26 Grammy Awards, the most of any living honoree in the history of the award. He won an Emmy Award for his musical score of the *Roots* television miniseries and was a seven–time Oscar nominee. The Academy of Motion Picture Arts and Sciences honored Jones with their Jean Hersholt Humanitarian Award. Quincy Jones's talents were recognized around the world and he was the recipient of the Republic of France's renowned

Legion d'Honneur, the Republic of Italy's Rudolph Valentino Award, and the Royal Swedish Academy of Music's coveted Polar Music Prize.

A musical giant, Quincy Jones was a product of the swing era and a survivor of the bebop era who continued to have an impact on contemporary music. Jones was the consummate jazz musician, composer, arranger, conductor, record producer, and multi–media executive.

Current address: c/o William Morris Agency, 151 El Camino Drive, Beverly Hills, CA 90212.

REFERENCES

"The Dude as Artist: Discography." *Billboard* (50th Anniversary Issue, December 1995).

Horricks, Raymond. *Quincy Jones.* New York: Hippocrene Books, 1985.

Kallen, Stuart A. *Quincy Jones: I Have a Dream.* Edina, MN: Abdo and Daughter, 1996.

Newsmakers: The People Behind Today's Headlines. Detroit: Gale Research, 1990.

"Quincy Jones Biography: Multi–Media Entrepreneur." *Billboard* 107 (16 December 1995): 46.

"Quincy Jones Introduction." *Billboard.* Internet, December 26, 1996.

Reynolds J. R. "Currently Quincy." *Billboard* 107 (16 December 1995): 42.

Ross, Courtney Sale, ed. *Listen Up The Lives of Quincy Jones.* New York: Warner Books, 1990.

Rowland Mark. "The Billboard Interview." *Billboard* 107 (16 December 1995): 23–28. 40, 48, 50.

Paulette Coleman

Scipio Africanus Jones
(1863?–1943)
Lawyer, civil rights activist, politician

Scipio Africanus Jones

Scipio Africanus Jones was the first black lawyer entrusted with a major case by the NAACP. In a half–century of law practice in Arkansas, Jones was an effective advocate for black rights. He was also actively involved in politics and a noted community leader.

Jones was born about 1863, the son of a white man and a slave named Jemmima Jones. He grew up with his mother and her husband, Horace Jones, in Tulip, Arkansas. He went to local schools. He had moved to Little Rock by 1881 when he enrolled in the preparatory department of Bethel College (now Philander Smith College) and then attended Shorter College, from which he received a degree in 1885. He then taught school and sought legal training. Since the law school of the University of Arkansas was closed to blacks, he read law under white lawyers and was admitted to the bar in 1889. He opened practice and won a reputation as an able lawyer. Several fraternal organizations used his services, and he became national attorney general of the Mosaic Templars of America. He added business activities to his work as a lawyer, organizing, for example, the Arkansas Realty and Investment Company in 1908 and serving as chairman of the People's Ice and Fuel Company, the only black ice company in the United States. In April 1915 he was elected special judge to the Little Rock Municipal Court.

Jones was also active in Republican politics, resisting strenuously the efforts of the "Lily Whites" to exclude blacks from the party. In 1902 he helped put together a black slate of candidates in Little Rock, and in 1920 the "Black and Tans" even put up a black candidate for governor. He was a delegate to the Republican National Convention in 1908, 1912, 1928, and 1940. In addition to politics, he was active in community affairs, serving, for example, as head of the board of managers of the Aged and Orphan's Industrial Home in Dexter, Alabama.

Jones's wider reputation rested on his handling of civil rights cases. An early concern was the handling of county convict labor which was a system where prisoners worked out their fines at 50 cents a day by working for contractors. The system was rife with abuse; Jones sued a Mississippi–based contractor for false imprisonment. The contractor stopped business when he realized the costs of defending the suit. Jones also persuaded a progressive, though racist, governor, Jeff Davis, to remedy the situation by raising the rate and abolishing board charges for days not worked. He was a leader in the successful fight against the passage of a ''grandfather'' voting clause. Jones also attacked the exclusion of blacks from juries and helped obtain a state appropriation to support blacks seeking professional training who had to study out–of–state because of the segregation in Arkansas schools.

Defends in Elaine Riot Case

Jones's most famous case was the defense of the 12 blacks sentenced to death because of the Elaine race riots in October 1919. That summer had been marked by violence directed against blacks in major urban centers like Chicago, Omaha, and Indianapolis. The most plausible account is that blacks in Phillips County organized a labor union and hired a lawyer with the aim of obtaining an account of profits and debts—the plantation system in force claimed that black tenants always owed money when the cotton was sold. The blacks sought aid from a white Little Rock lawyer, U.S. Bratton. Whites attacked a meeting at a church, shooting out the lights; blacks returned fire, apparently killing a white man. Amid wild rumors of a planned black insurrection, local whites and the federal troops, called in to restore order, killed perhaps 250 blacks in the next week. In an atmosphere of hysteria, the trial on November 3 at the county seat of Helena condemned 12 men to death and 67 to prison terms of from one to 21 years. The court–appointed attorney for the blacks offered no defense, and the jury took five minutes to reach its verdict.

A former Confederate soldier who was now one of the state's most prominent lawyers, George W. Murphy, undertook to handle the appeals process on behalf of the NAACP. Jones joined Murphy as the representative of the local Citizens Defense Fund Commission, which eventually spent more money than the NAACP. Initially, the NAACP and its leading white lawyers were suspicious of Jones's abilities because of his race, but after receiving assurances of his competencies from persons like Monroe N. Work of Tuskegee, the NAACP and the CDFC began a cooperation which was not always easy.

The Arkansas Supreme Court granted a new trial to six of the men condemned to death and upheld the sentences of the other six. During the second trial in Helena, Murphy fell gravely ill, dying a short time later, and Jones had to handle the case alone in an atmosphere so hostile that Jones slept in a different house every night of the week the trial lasted. On the last night he drove his car into the country and walked three miles from where he parked before knocking on a door and asking for refuge. The six men were again condemned.

Jones then handled the appeals and subsequent trials of all 12 defendants until he successfully petitioned the U.S. Supreme Court to hear an appeal of the case of the six men who had not been granted a new trial. Moorfield Storey of the NAACP argued the case before the court. On February 19, 1923, the court issued a landmark decision, extending the Due Process Clause of the Fourteenth Amendment to cover the conduct of state criminal trials. The six men not involved in the appeal were released with no further trial, and the state governor granted the other six men a conditional pardon on January 14, 1924, the day before he left office. In four years of efforts, Jones had finally saved the lives of 12 men and had contributed to opening a major change in constitutional law. In so doing, he had materially contributed to the vitality and fund–raising ability of the NAACP.

Jones married twice. His marriage to Carrie Edwards in 1896 produced one child, Hazel. After his first wife's death, he married Lillie M. Jackson, of Pine Bluff, Arkansas. This union was childless. He died at home of arteriosclerosis on March 28, 1943. Funeral services were held at Bethel AME Church, and he was buried in Haven–of–Rest Cemetery. The white school board of North Little Rock named the black high school in his memory. Jones had done his best in a full life to change his society for the benefit of African Americans.

REFERENCES

Bush, A. E., and P. L. Dorman. *History of the Mosaic Templars of America—Its Founders and Officials.* Little Rock: Central Printing Co., 1927.

Cortner, Richard C. *A Mob Intent on Death.* Middletown, CT: Wesleyan University Press, 1988.

Logan, Rayford W., and Michael R. Winston, eds. *Dictionary of American Negro Biography.* New York: Norton, 1982.

National Association for the Advancement of Colored People. *The Arkansas Cases.* New York: NAACP, 1922.

Ovington, Mary White. *Portraits in Color.* New York: Viking, 1927.

Williams, C. Fred, and others, eds. *A Documentary History of Arkansas.* Fayetteville: University of Arkansas Press, 1984.

Robert L. Johns

Scott Joplin
(1868?–1917)
Composer

Scott Joplin was a talented musical composer who first made his mark as a writer of rags. His most famous work, ''Maple Leaf Rag,'' has remained a standard since its composition. Although Joplin faded from the public's memory for several decades after his death, the revival of interest in ragtime led to his rediscovery; and he is now recognized as an important influence on American music.

The 1994 biography of Scott Joplin by Edward A. Berlin revealed that much of what was previously believed about

Scott Joplin

Joplin's life is unreliable, beginning with his birth date. In 1942 his surviving heir (who might also have been his widow), Lottie Stokes Joplin, told the American Society of Composers, Authors, and Publishers (ASCAP) that Joplin was born November 24, 1868, in Texarkana, Texas. The place is almost certainly wrong since Texarkana did not yet exist, and the date is also suspect. Lottie Joplin did not give a birth date for the death certificate in 1917, and her memory was faulty by 1942 when she gave the death date as April 4, 1919, not the April 1, 1917, on the certificate itself.

Scott Joplin was born sometime before the middle of 1868 in northeastern Texas. His father Giles Joplin, a laborer, was born a slave in North Carolina about 1842; his mother Florence Givens Joplin, a laundress and domestic worker, was born free in Kentucky about 1841. In the 1880 census, when the family was living in Texarkana, the children were listed as Monroe (b. 1861?), Scott, Robert (b. 1869?), Jose (Osie, b. 1870?), William (1876?–1902), and Johnny (really Myrtle, a girl, b. 1880). Florence Joplin played the banjo and sang, and Giles Joplin played the violin; brothers Robert and William became professional musicians and performers like their older brother, Scott; all three played the violin.

The year 1875 is possibly the date the family established itself in Texarkana; a plausible tradition suggests that at the age of seven Scott was permitted to play the piano in a house where his mother worked as a domestic. Florence Scott not only appears to have been active in seeking out opportunities for her talented son's musical education, she became the principal support of the family when Giles Joplin left her for another woman in the early 1880s.

Scott Joplin studied music with several local teachers; the most important seems to have been a German immigrant, identified as Julius Weiss, who had a profound influence on Joplin by giving him free lessons of high calibre and by introducing him to European art music. Joplin was musically active in his mid–teens, teaching guitar and mandolin, playing for dances, and performing in a vocal quartet which performed at area venues.

Leaves Texarkana

Different sources place the date that Scott Joplin left Texarkana between 1885 and 1889. Evidence is lacking, however, to substantiate claims that he travelled extensively as a honky–tonk pianist before settling in St. Louis some time in the late 1880s. While extensive travels are probable, little is known of these years. One documented account places him in Texarkana in the summer of 1891. He was a member of the newly formed Texarkana Minstrels, who attracted unfavorable comments from the press when they performed on July 30 at a show advertised as a benefit to raise funds for a Jefferson Davis memorial. There is a tantalizing hint that Joplin may have first moved to Sedalia to attend high school. Some accounts suggest that he choose to settle in the town because his limited pianistic skills circumscribed his opportunities as a performer in larger centers.

Nevertheless, Joplin visited Chicago during the 1893 World's Columbian Exposition. There he met Otis Saunders, a mulatto who could pass for white. The two became friends, travelled to St. Louis, and then went to Sedalia late in 1893. In Sedalia Joplin became involved in the musical life of the community, playing for dances and in at least two brothels—the fame of Sedalia's red–light district endured until the outbreak of World War II.

In addition to being an active local musician, Joplin traveled extensively. He and two of his brothers were members of the Texas Medley Quartet, actually a double quartet, from 1894 to 1895. Some idea of the extent of Joplin's travels during these years is suggested by the place his music was first published. Two pieces appeared in Syracuse, New York, in 1895 and three in Temple, Texas, in 1896. Joplin also furthered his education by taking classes at Sedalia's George R. Smith College—unfortunately details are lacking since college records were destroyed in a fire. Joplin attracted a number of young, enthusiastic students, and he continued to teach throughout his life. In Sedalia there was Arthur Mitchell (1881?–1968), later a major ragtime composer; Scott Hayden, who collaborated with Joplin on several pieces; and a white 15–year runaway, S. Brunson Campbell (b. 1884?), another musician who later became a source of information and misinformation about Joplin.

The "Maple Leaf Rag"

Ragtime, which in its simplest form set a syncopated treble against a regular duple bass, was developing rapidly in the mid–1890s in both instrumental and vocal forms. (The vocal forms fell under the label of ''coon songs.'') Joplin was not the innovator of the genre but established himself as a refined composer of instrumental rags. His first major success was the ''Maple Leaf Rag,'' the only piece that did not drop out of sight during the long period of neglect that followed his death. (In 1936 Alain Locke, the leading black scholar and critic of his era, would identify Joplin as a white composer in *The Negro and his Music.*)

Berlin gave five different versions of how Joplin and his publisher, John Stark (b. 1841), came into contact. Although the ''Maple Leaf Rag'' bears the imprint of Sedalia, Stark had already moved to St. Louis, where he soon established a music publishing company, which later moved to New York. Joplin had learned caution in dealing with publishers and was represented by a lawyer when he signed a contract with Stark on August 10, 1899. His contract specified royalties of one cent on each copy of the sheet music. After a slow start the piece became and remained a steady best–seller, so Joplin was probably receiving some $600 a year from this one piece, more than the average yearly wage for a working man.

In addition to becoming famous as composer of the ''Maple Leaf Rag,'' Joplin married before he left Sedalia for St. Louis some time before the summer of 1891. Belle Jones Hayden (1875?–1930) was the widow of Joe Hayden, brother of Scott Hayden, Joplin's student. The 1900 Census lists Belle Jones and Scott Joplin as lodging at the same address—she had a child from the earlier marriage living elsewhere. (Two other children from this marriage had died by this date.) From the union between Belle Jones Hayden and Joplin, there was one child who died in infancy. This was Joplin's only known offspring. The marriage, legal or consensual, was over by 1903.

Little information exists about Joplin's other two marriages. In January 1904 Joplin went to visit relatives in Texas and Arkansas. In Little Rock, Arkansas, he met Freddie Alexander (b. circa 1875); Joplin and Alexander were married in her parents' Little Rock home on June 14. Joplin and his new wife moved to Sedalia where she died of pneumonia on September 10, 1904.

Joplin's last union was with Lottie Stokes (d. 1953). The date and even the existence of a valid marriage is in doubt. In April 1910 Joplin gave his marital status to the census–taker as widower, and no women lodgers lived at his address. Lottie Stokes Joplin gave the date of the wedding as June 18, 1910. However, no wife is listed among the 38 guests at a party honoring Joplin on the occasion of the publication of *Treemonisha* on June 14, 1911, and on October 13, 1913, she signed the document making her co–owner of the Scott Joplin Music Publishing Company as Lottie Stokes. Nonetheless, she was considered Joplin's widow and legal heir after his death. There is some further shadow on her reputation. She supported herself by renting apartments and then subletting the rooms and was partial to boarders in show business. However, some of the space in her apartments was used for short–time rentals for sexual purposes and one source even characterized her as a procuress.

Extends Musical Ambitions

From the publication of the ''Maple Leaf Rag'' on, Joplin continued to issue a steady stream of pieces, not all rags. Despite their individual excellence none of the following works achieved the continuing popularity of the work that first brought him fame. Despite John Stark's habit of paying royalties, Joplin turned increasingly to different publishers to seek better terms, and he finally decided to establish his own music publishing company in 1913. Until about 1907 he was based in the Midwest, principally in St. Louis, although his exact movements are difficult to trace.

Joplin was dissatisfied with his high reputation as a composer of rags: his ambitions ran to longer musical theater forms, ultimately to opera. His first effort at a longer piece was ''Ragtime Dance,'' a presentation of different dance steps for a vaudeville audience, performed in Sedalia in the fall of 1899. Stark did not publish this work, which had nine pages rather than the four pages normal for sheet music, until 1902. Joplin himself wrote the lyrics, which were probably perceived as offensive.

In 1903 Joplin produced a full–length ragtime opera, *A Guest of Honor,* again writing music and lyrics. He assembled a company of 32, which put on a try–out performance in East St. Louis before undertaking a Midwestern tour. At some point during the tour financial disaster struck, and the company was stranded. Not only did Joplin lose much money, it seems probable that the music was lost at this point. It is also possible that Joplin tried to forget the work entirely, since he never mentioned that *Treemonisha* was in fact his second opera.

Treemonisha

By the time of the production of *A Guest of Honor,* Joplin had almost entirely stopped appearing as a performer, living off his income as a composer and teacher. He established himself in New York City in July 1907. There he attracted occasional newspaper coverage. He was active over the years, for example, in the Colored Vaudeville Benevolent Association. Despite his musical ambitions, Joplin seems to have had little contact with James Reese Europe and other leading New York musicians like J. Rosamond Johnson and Will Marion Cook.

Joplin completed *Treemonisha* sometime in 1910. Again he wrote the libretto for this three–act opera. Finding no publisher willing to risk issuing the work, Joplin published the 230–page piano–vocal score himself on May 19, 1911. Despite an extraordinarily favorable article in the *American Musician and Art Journal,* Joplin struggled the next few years to get a production. It was first announced that there would be a staging in Atlantic City in November 1911. Joplin rushed to complete the orchestral score (now lost), assembled a cast, and began rehearsals; however, the production was canceled. To salvage something, Joplin rented a hall and put on an informal performance, accompanying the performance himself. There were about 17 persons in the audience, and no backer was impressed enough to furnish production funds. This is the only performance of *Treemonisha* in Joplin's lifetime. (This production is most plausibly placed in 1911 rather than in 1915.) There is evidence that Joplin revised the opera in 1912; the revisions did not survive.

Through the end of 1913 Joplin continued to have hopes for a production. An abbreviated performance set for New Jersey in the spring of 1913 fell through as did another scheduled in Harlem's Lafayette Theater in the fall. Joplin heard only one orchestrated number from the opera. On May 5, 1915, there was a rather unsatisfactory performance of the ballet from Act 2 by the students of the Martin–Smith Music School of Harlem.

Joplin published his last work *Magnetic Rag* in 1914. (Later publications are of earlier compositions.) By the most probable date of the meeting of Eubie Blake and Joplin in late 1915, Joplin was in an advanced stage of tertiary syphilis, barely able to pick out a tune on the piano. Joplin entered the hospital in mid–January 1917 and was transferred to a mental hospital at the beginning of February. He died in Manhattan State Hospital on April 1.

After his death, Joplin dropped out of public awareness, remembered only as the composer of ''Maple Leaf Rag.'' There are reports of extensive manuscripts, which have disappeared. He was not rediscovered until the 1960s, when a major revival of interest in ragtime took place. Under the stimulus of the score of the movie *The Sting,* which featured Joplin's music, his name appeared on the lists of best–sellers for both classic and popular recordings in the 1970s. *Treemonisha* premiered on January 28, 1972, in Atlanta and received much favorable notice. Several more productions followed, including one on Broadway in 1975. In 1976 Joplin received a special Bicentennial Pulitzer Prize for his contribution to American music. In 1983 his likeness appeared on a U.S. postage stamp. If Joplin's music is no longer on the music charts, he remains a major presence in American culture.

REFERENCES

Berlin, Edward A. *King of Ragtime.* New York: Oxford, 1994.

Blesh, Rudi, and Harriet Janis. *They All Played Ragtime.* New York: Knopf, 1950.

Curtis, Susan. *Dancing to a Black Men's Tune: A Life of Scott Joplin.* Columbia: University of Missouri Press, 1994.

Logan, Rayford W., and Michael R. Winston, eds. *Dictionary of American Negro Biography.* New York: Norton, 1982.

COLLECTIONS

There is a small collection of items relating to Scott Joplin in the Fisk University Library as well as the unpublished notes of Harriet Janis for *They All Played Ragtime.*

Robert L. Johns

Michael Jordan

(1963–)

Basketball player

Professional basketball hero and superstar Michael Jordan, sometimes called ''His Airness,'' is known worldwide as a phenomenal player who has brought success to the Chicago Bulls and the National Basketball Association (NBA). His versatility as an entertaining, skillful, and hard–driving athlete who appears to soar through the air as he winds his way through opponents and heads for the basket makes him an appealing player who draws crowds wherever he plays. He has focused tremendous attention to basketball as well as to the products he endorses.

Born in Brooklyn, New York, on February 17, 1963, Michael Jordan is the fourth child of James Raymond and Delores Peoples Jordan. He has two brothers, James Roland and Larry, and two sisters, Delois and Roslyn. The parents lived in Brooklyn for a short time, then returned home to Wilmington, North Carolina, where Michael Jordan was raised. James Jackson was an equipment supervisor for General Electric, then became owner of a retail business, while Delores Jordan was a customer–service supervisor at a bank. Lynn Norment wrote in *Ebony* that Delores and James Jordan ''wanted to rear children with strong moral character, confidence, high self–esteem, and who would feel that they would accomplish whatever goals they set.'' Love was predominant in the Jordan household. Michael Jordan and his siblings followed rules and attended to family chores. At times, however, young Michael was able to persuade his brother Larry to do his chores, sometimes paying for his service. At family dinners, the Jordan children were encouraged to discuss school and other activities. ''Church, like school, was not an option,'' wrote Norment.

Young Michael Jordan was always unselfish, happy–go–lucky, and competitive, and he preferred older playmates. He worked hard to achieve the goals that he set for himself in basketball. Using a backyard court that James Jordan built for sons Michael and Larry, the young men played one–on–one with each other and competed with friends as well. Since Larry was taller, Michael Jordan developed a fierce determination to win. The hustle that he developed earned him the nickname ''Rabbit.''

Michael Jordan played Little League baseball but at first was too small for the varsity basketball team at his school, Laney High. At the beginning of his sophomore year he made the basketball team but was soon cut. That same year he played on the football team for a brief period, played baseball, and ran track. He grew rapidly between his sophomore and junior year—from 5'11'' to 6'3''—and became a promising basketball player. He already had the ability to high–jump. At the end of his junior year, Jordan played with the summer Five Star Basketball Camp in Pittsburgh, where big–time college prospects trained. Before his senior year began, he had

Michael Jordan

accepted a scholarship offer from the University of North Carolina at Chapel Hill. By then Jordan had grown to 6'6''. Meanwhile, his high school coach, Clifton Herring, encouraged him further and drove him to the gymnasium for extra practice during his senior year. The more Jordan practiced, the more proficient he became.

In 1981 Jordan enrolled at UNC to pursue a major in geography. He roomed with Buzz Peterson, a white reserve player who later introduced Jordan to golf. In turn, Jordan taught Peterson to play pool. Jordan was a starter for UNC in his freshman season who scored low but was brilliant in clutch situations. He had the inspiration and support of his parents, who attended his games in Chapel Hill and on the road. He scored a jumper from the corner for coach Dean Smith's Tarheels, giving them a one–point victory over Georgetown and Smith his first title in his 24–year career at UNC. Jordan and Dean Smith had mutual respect and a special rapport that has lasted over the years.

Jordan was voted the Atlantic Coast Conference Rookie of the Year for 1981–82 and, due to his winning shot, was nicknamed ''Superman'' and ''Last Shot.'' In 1982–83 he was unanimously chosen All–American. Twice *The Sporting News* named him College Player of the Year, in 1982–83 and 1983–84. *Current Biography* quoted *The Sporting News* for 1983 in its description of Jordan, who developed a technique that still characterizes him: ''He soars through the air, he rebounds, he scores . . ., he blocks shots, he makes steals. Most important, he makes late plays that win games.''

Jordan toured with various All–Star teams in the summer of 1983, and he was a star in the Pan American Games held in Caracas, helping the U.S. basketball team win a gold medal. The next summer he was a member of the U.S. Olympic team under Bob Knight's leadership and won the gold medal at the Los Angeles games.

Becomes a Chicago Bull

The Chicago Bulls had made no National Basketball Association playoffs since the 1980–81 season. By 1984 they needed a star to pull themselves out of the doldrums and chose Jordan third in the pro draft of college players. He accepted their seven–figure five–year contract, dropped out of UNC after three years, and became an instant success as a professional player. Although his parents wanted him to get his college degree first, they continued to support him and attended his games. The Bulls saw an 87 percent increase in attendance, while attendance at their opponents' buildings soared also. In the 1984–85 season, Jordan led the NBA in points and was named Rookie of the Year and winner of the Seagram Award for NBA's best player. He was also a starter for the All–Star game that year.

A foot injury in 1985–86 caused Jordan to sit out all but 18 games. When he rejoined the team, the Bulls began to win again. Although Jordan scored 63 points in the game, the Bulls lost the playoffs to the Boston Celtics on April 20, 1986. *Current Biography* quoted Celtics superstar Larry Bird's comment about Jordan's high scoring that Jordan might really be ''God disguised as Michael Jordan.'' He won the All–Star vote for 1986–87 as well as the slam–dunk championship in the NBA All–Star weekend in Seattle in February 1987. Again in April 1987, Jordan scored 61 points at Chicago Stadium, but the Bulls lost to the Atlanta Hawks. He then became the second basketball player behind Wilt Chamberlain to pass the 3,000 points mark in a season. After he signed a lucrative contract with Nike to promote their sportswear, the ''Air Jordan'' athletic shoes became a hot item and led to endorsement contracts with McDonald's, Wilson sporting goods, Coca Cola, Chevrolet, Johnson Products, and Excelsior International, which made ''Time Jordan'' watches. He began to visit schools and hold basketball clinics.

With the added talent that Michael Jordan provided, the Bulls continued to develop and in 1991 won the NBA championship over the Los Angeles Lakers. The Bulls were the first team in 30 years to win three consecutive NBA championships, defeating the Portland Trail Blazers in 1992 and the Phoenix Suns in 1993. Jordan was named NBA Finals Most Valuable Player in each of the championships. He then led the first U.S. Olympic basketball team of professional players to the 1992 Olympics. The ''Dream Team,'' as they were called, won the gold medal in the Olympics in 1992 and again in 1996.

Although satisfied with his career performance and his position at the top, Jordan announced his retirement from professional basketball on October 6, 1993, and aimed to move on to something else. He emphasized, however, that he would not close the door to basketball permanently. Jordan's retirement came three years before he had planned, but it followed the untimely death of his father in the summer of 1993. During an apparent car theft, his father had been brutally murdered in North Carolina. In his struggle to deal with the tragedy, he tried his hand at professional baseball with the farm team for the Chicago White Sox. Even though he was unsuccessful as a player, he stimulated a new interest in baseball and drew crowds wherever he played.

Jordan returned to the Bulls in March of 1995. He won his fourth NBC Finals Most Valuable Player (MVP) Award in June of 1996 when he led the Bulls to victory over the Seattle SuperSonics for their fourth title in six years. Overcome with emotion after the win, he grabbed the ball, dropped to the floor, then staggered into the dressing room, where he dropped to the floor again and cried. The victory had taken place on Father's Day, and the memory of his deceased father was painful. Afterward Jordan left the gym to be alone. He won his fifth MVP award in May of 1998.

On March 12, 1997, Jordan moved past the record set by former Boston Celtic John Havlicek to become the NBA's sixth all–time leading scorer. In the Bulls' game with the Celtics that night, Jordan scored 32 points for a career total of 26,399. He continues to average 30 points per game and has scored at least 50 points in 37 games—the latest on April 27, 1997, in a postseason game with the Washington Bullets. Chicago's Ron Harper told the Associated Press in the *Nashville Tennessean* for April 28, 1997, "M. J. is M. J. We allow him to do his thing. If he wants to take over a game there is nothing Scottie [Pippen] can say or Phil [Jackson] can say to stop it." Jordan said in the same article: "That's my job. That's what I get paid the big bucks for. I want to win. I want to win another championship."

In June of 1997, when the Bulls defeated the Utah Jazz to win their fifth crown, Jordan received another NBA Finals MVP Award. Quoted in the Nashville Tennessean for June 14, 1997, he said of the Jazz: "They just keep getting bigger and bigger, and we keep winning and winning." The Bulls completed another championship season on June 14, 1998, when Jordan carried the team on his back by scoring 45 of their 87 points, including the game winning shot with five seconds left in game six against the Utah Jazz. Jordan again was the obvious choice for Most Valuable Player.

When the NBA held an All–Star Weekend in Cleveland, Ohio, in February of 1997, Jordan made All–Star history by recording the first triple double, with 14 points, 11 assists, and 11 rebounds. During halftime, the NBA's 50 greatest players in history were announced; 47 legendary players gathered at mid–court wearing their team jackets. Quoted in *Jet* for February 24, 1997, Jordan, who was one of the 50 honored, told the *Chicago Sun–Times,* "Those early stars are responsible for getting this league off the ground."

In 1991 and again in 1993, the NBA investigated allegations that Jordan had been involved in gambling activities at card games and on the golf course. The NBA, however, ended its probe without uncovering evidence of wrongdoing. Jordan continued to win games for the Bulls and to gain widespread respect. He is known for sticking out his tongue as he contemplates his free throw and for chewing gum rapidly as he plays.

During his career Jordan received numerous other awards and recognitions. He started for the NBA Eastern Conference All–Star Team 11 times; was NBA scoring leader ten times (1987–1993 and 1996–1998); and won NBA Defensive Player of the Year honors in 1988. In 1991 *Sports Illustrated* named Jordan "Sportsman of the Year." On February 8, 1998, Jordan played in what might have been his final All–Star game. Despite feeling ill, he led all scorers with 23 points to help the Eastern Conference team win. For his performance, he won his third career All–Star MVP award.

According to *Jet* magazine for May 19, 1997, Michael Jordan, Colin Powell, and Tiger Woods were named the most popular Americans in a *Wall Street Journal*/NBC Poll. Powell had the lead, followed by Woods and Jordan.

In 1996 Jordan starred in an animated children's film, *Space Jam,* his first movie. In addition to earning about $32 million from his 1996 contract with the Bulls, Jordan makes millions from endorsing such products as athletic wear, beverages, food, and underwear. He has been the subject of numerous books.

Jordan also gives back to the community. He established the Michael Jordan Foundation and for seven years has contributed to numerous charities through it. In fall 1996 Jordan and his mother opened the James Jordan Boys and Girls Club and Family Life Center in Chicago, endowed by $2 million from Jordan and $5 million from the Bulls. The club offers educational, cultural, medical, and child care opportunities and maintains a computer learning center, community health center, and youth and sports leagues.

The six–foot six–inch tall Jordan has a slim, athletic build and an effervescent smile. He shaves his head, sometimes wears an earring, and is well–dressed whenever he is out of uniform and before the public. He is also an avid golf player who demonstrates skill in that game as well. In 1989 he married Juanita Vanoy, whom he met in 1985. They live in Chicago with their three children, Jeffrey, Marcus, and Jasmine.

Jordan dazzles crowds wherever he plays. His artful method of handling a basketball and ability to defy gravity by appearing to float in the air have been said to transcend professional basketball. A versatile guard who slam–dunks, hits the long shot, and has a successful fade–away shot, Jordan is regarded by many as the best professional player in the history of his sport.

Current address: c/o The Chicago Bulls, One Magnificent Mile, 980 North Michigan Avenue, Suite 1600. Chicago, IL 60611.

REFERENCES

"By Jordan's Rules." *Nashville Tennessean,* April 28, 1997.

Contemporary Black Biography. Vol. 6. Detroit: Gale Research, 1994.

Current Biography Yearbook. New York: H. W. Wilson, 1987.

"High Five for Bulls." *Nashville Tennessean,* June 14, 1997.

Jordan, Michael. *Rare Air: Michael on Michael.* Ed. by Mark Vancil. San Francisco: Mark Vancil, 1993.

''Jordan Named MVP Again after Stellar Regular Season.'' *Nashville Tennessean,* May 19, 1998.

''Jordan Passes Havlicek as Bulls Beat Celtics.'' *Nashville Tennessean,* March 12, 1997.

''Jordan Rules.'' *Nashville Tennessean,* February 9, 1998.

''Mission Accomplished.'' *Nashville Tennessean,* June 17, 1996.

''NBA All–Star Weekend Celebrates 50 Greatest Players; East Tops West in All–Star Game.'' *Jet* 91 (24 February 1997): 52–54.

Norment, Lynn. ''We Didn't Set Out to Raise a Superstar.'' *Ebony* 52 (May 1997): 150–58.

''Powell, Woods, Jordan Most Popular Americans.'' *Jet* 91 (19 May 1997): 5.

Jessie Carney Smith

Vernon Jordan

(1935–)

Lawyer, civil rights leader, presidential adviser

Vernon Jordan

Since 1960, Vernon Jordan has been an influential figure in America. His accomplishments in the areas of civil rights, law, and politics characterize him as an agent of change. When he became head of President Bill Clinton's transition team, he was the first black placed in such a position. He has served as advisor to President Bill Clinton, becoming one of the most influential voices in Clinton's administration. The black community, corporations, politicians, and on a larger scale, America and the international community, have benefited from his talents.

Vernon Eulion Jordan Jr. was born on August 15, 1935, in Atlanta, Georgia. The elder Jordan was a postal clerk at Fort McPherson, Georgia, and his wife, Mary Belle Griggs Jordan, the daughter of a sharecropper, started a catering business during the depression years and transformed it into a successful endeavor that catered to Atlanta's elite. During his boyhood years, Vernon, along with his older brother, Warren, and his younger brother, Windsor, assisted with the catering business. The family lived in the University Homes Project, the nation's first federally–funded housing complex, until Vernon was 13. The Jordans then purchased a home.

Jordan attended segregated schools in Atlanta. At David T. Howard High School, he played basketball, was class orator, and performed in the school band along with Maynard Jackson, who, years later, became Atlanta's mayor. After graduating with honors in 1953, Jordan entered DePauw University in Greencastle, Indiana where he majored in political science and minored in history and speech. During his freshman year, Jordan won the Margaret Noble Lee Extemporaneous Speaking Contest and played on the freshman basketball squad; during his sophomore year, he won the Indiana Interstate Oratorial Contest, and he placed third nationally for his ''The Negro in America'' speech. Jordan, who served as a fraternity representative to the student senate and vice–president of the Jackson Club (its members were the six Democratic students at DePauw), was the sole black student in his class and one of five black students at DePauw. He also appeared in campus productions, including a play written about Southern racism. During his undergraduate years, Jordan worked as a waiter on campus (he once served then Vice–President Nixon who spoke at DePauw) and in Atlanta in the summers, where he also chauffeured a former mayor. After earning his B.A. degree in 1957, Jordan enrolled in Howard University's Law School where he was circuit vice–president of the American Law Student Association (ALSA) and a member of ALSA's board of directors. While at Howard, he met Shirley Yarbrough who became his wife on December 13, 1958. Jordan was awarded his J.D. degree in 1960.

Begins Law Career While Focusing on Civil Rights

Upon graduating from law school and returning to Atlanta, Jordan became a law clerk in the office of David Hollowell, a prominent civil rights attorney. Television correspondent Charlayne Hunter–Gault reminisced in *In My Place*:

> Not every Black lawyer at Howard wanted to practice civil–rights law, but those like Vernon prepared to, because, as he explained it, ''in those days, civil–rights law was at the cutting edge of change in

> the South. And the South was home, and I wanted to be home and be a part of that change." He then added, "And, of course, I wanted to join Hollowell. He was *the* civil–rights lawyer."

Hunter–Gault met Jordan during a 1960s landmark desegregation lawsuit; Hollowell and an Atlanta civil rights organization recruited two black students, Charlayne Hunter and Hamilton Holmes, to apply to the University of Georgia (UGA) in efforts to force the state of Georgia to comply with the Supreme Court ruling on desegregation. Jordan was a member of Hollowell's legal team that traveled 75 miles daily from Atlanta to Athens, Georgia, researching the school's records until Jordan found the crucial evidence indicating that the university had prevaricated concerning Hunter and Holmes's rejected admission applications. The Federal District Court ordered the University of Georgia to admit the two students. When Hunter arrived on the UGA campus for the first time, she was escorted by her mother and Jordan. *Current Biography* for 1972 described the occasion. "Using his body as a shield, Jordan personally forced a path through an angry white mob, so that Charlayne Hunter . . . could enter the university's grounds."

From 1961 to 1963, Jordan held his first leadership position with a civil rights organization as the field secretary for the Georgia Branch of the NAACP. His responsibilities included organizing and coordinating the activities of the local branches. In 1962, he led a successful boycott against stores in Augusta, Georgia, that refused to hire blacks. Julian Bond, another well–known civil rights leader who during the early 1960s, was a leader of the Student Non–Violent Coordinating Committee (SNCC), remembered Jordan's courage in *Vanity Fair*:

> Part of his job involved going into these little rural towns where there was some danger in being a black man in a suit, let alone a black man from the N.A.A.C.P. Being seen in a suit, driving a car, in some of these little counties where everyone knows each other, was a real act of courage.

In 1964, Jordan joined with Wiley A. Branton, a prominent civil rights lawyer, in the practice of law in Pine Bluff, Arkansas. Branton was counsel for the Little Rock Nine, who desegregated Central High School in Little Rock. Jordan then succeeded Branton as director of the Southern Regional Council's Voter Education Project (VEP). During his four–year tenure, the number of black voters increased tremendously. The number of black elected officials increased from 72 to 564. Jordan and the Voter Education Project played significant roles in implementing the Voting Rights Act of 1965. Jordan's activities on behalf of VEP catapulted him to the status of nationally known civil rights leader. Concurrently, other black leaders began to recognize his mediating skills. During this period, Jordan was a member of President Johnson's National Advisory Committee on Selective Service (1966–67), and he participated in the 1966 White House Conference, "To Fulfill These Rights."

In 1965, Jordan served as an attorney and consultant for the U.S. Office of Equal Opportunity in Atlanta. He was then appointed as a fellow at Harvard University's John F. Kennedy School of Government during the 1969–70 academic year. Although he considered running for the fifth congressional seat in Atlanta, Jordan instead accepted the executive directorship of the United Negro College Fund, a New York–based organization established in 1944. Although his tenure was brief—1970 to 1971—contributions increased by the unprecedented amount of ten million dollars, while Jordan was executive director.

Heads the National Urban League

On January 1, 1972, Jordan succeeded the late Whitney Young Jr. as executive director of the National Urban League. Under Jordan's guidance, the league expanded its mission as it sponsored, among other activities, voter registration drives in northern and western cities, employment training, housing, health, and educational programs, as well as efforts to resolve conflicts between black communities and police departments. The *Urban League Review,* a policy review journal, first appeared in 1975, and the following year marked the debut of *The State of Black America,* the Urban League's annual report.

Jordan was able to broaden the league's aims because he doubled its operating budget after successfully seeking increased funds from the federal government and corporate contributors. As a result of his work with corporations, Jordan joined the board of directors of numerous corporations and organizations, including American Express, American Museum of Natural History, Bankers Trust of New York, Celanese Corporation, Clark College, J. C. Penney, John Hay Whitney Foundation, National Multiple Sclerosis Society, National Urban Coalition, New World Foundation, Rockefeller Foundation, Twentieth Century Fund, and Xerox. He also continued to receive federal appointments, including the American Revolution Bi–Centennial Commission (1972), Presidential Clemency Board (1974), and Advisory Council on Social Security (1974).

While Jordan had forged extremely positive relationships with the corporate world and philanthropic organizations, he endured less than harmonious associations with several presidential administrations. Jordan audaciously criticized the Nixon and Carter administrations. He chided the Nixon Administration for its neglect of black America's concerns with employment, education, housing, and other areas. The Carter administration also came under attack when Jordan felt that President Carter failed to honor his campaign promises to blacks. Jordan became an early critic of the Carter Administration, and he warned the president not to take the black vote for granted.

Traveling to promote the Urban League was a frequent activity for Jordan. On May 29, 1980, he returned to a Fort Wayne, Indiana hotel after delivering a speech at the league's local chapter. Outside the hotel, a shot from a hunting rifle narrowly missed Jordan's spinal column as it seriously wounded him; he fell on the parking lot with a fist–sized hole in his back. As he waited to be rushed to the hospital, according to

African American Biographies, he thought of the advice his mother gave him while he was in college: "Son . . . if you trust Him, He will take care of you." Jordan spent nearly five hours in surgery and three months in Fort Wayne and New York hospitals. President Carter was one of Jordan's visitors during his hospitalization. On August 18, 1982, a white supremacist was acquitted by a federal grand jury after eight hours of deliberation; since then he admitted he shot Jordan. This same man killed two black joggers in Salt Lake City, Utah, three months after he shot Jordan, and in 1981, he was found guilty and received multiple life sentences for the joggers' murders.

After recovering completely from the attempted assassination, Jordan returned to his office in September, 1980. One year later, he announced his decision to resign from the Urban League effective December 31, 1981. While some people thought Jordan's decision had been influenced by his recent ordeal, he asserted that he had only intended to head the league for ten years. Some individuals assumed that Jordan was turning his back on civil rights; years later he countered, as reported in *Vanity Fair,* "I'm not a general, but I'm still in the army."

Becomes a Powerful Washington Insider

After resigning from the National Urban League, Jordan joined the prestigious law firm of Akin, Gump, Strauss, Hauer, and Feld, where he was a senior executive partner. Jordan worked at the Washington, D.C., office of the Dallas–based firm. Akin Gump employs approximately 250 lawyers in its Washington office and is one of the city's most powerful law and lobbying firms. Jordan advised corporate clients on Washington legislative and regulatory concerns and also supervised the firm's lobbyists.

Jordan's direct communication with U.S. presidents continued. In 1989 President Bush appointed him to his Advisory Committee for the Points of Light Foundation. Jordan unsuccessfully attempted to persuade Bush to sign the 1990 Civil Rights Bill. Two years later, he offered advice to Bush and presidential candidate Clinton on their responses to the Los Angeles riots.

Jordan, who had known Clinton since the 1970s and was one of his closest friends, encouraged Clinton's presidential bid since his days as Arkansas's governor. He was an important adviser to Clinton during the 1992 campaign; for example he helped select Al Gore as vice–president. After Clinton won the November election, he appointed Jordan—who chaired the 1990 transition team of Sharon Pratt Dixon when she won Washington, D.C.'s mayoral race—co–chairman of his transition team. This marked the first time in American history an African American headed a presidential transition team. He was instrumental in selecting cabinet officers and other key appointments. When Jordan was offered the position of attorney general, he declined. He emerged, however, as one of the most powerful figures in the Clinton Administration, as he continued to advise the president on domestic and foreign policies.

Numerous honors and recognition were bestowed upon Jordan. He received honorary degrees from 55 colleges and universities including his alma maters, DePauw University—he was previously awarded DePauw's Old Gold Goblet for outstanding achievement—and Howard University. Jordan acted as a trustee of various organizations including the Brookings Institute, DePauw University, Ford Foundation, Howard University, LBJ Foundation, and the NAACP Legal Defense and Educational Fund. Jordan was a major behind–the–scenes player in the corporate shakeup of 1993 when a new chairman was selected for IBM. He exerted influence in many corporate boardrooms as a director of at least nine national and three international boards. General Colin Powell, in the July 14, 1996, *New York Times,* commented on his friend's status, "He's in rarefied company, where his race is no longer a stereotype that has to be chopped down, and that says something about the America he works in and that he lives in."

Jordan is described as a charming, witty, sophisticated, tall, handsome man who was always impeccably dressed. According to *Current Biography* for 1972, his friend Andrew Young, the former Atlanta mayor, once identified Jordan as "a cross between Harry Belafonte and Sidney Poitier."

Jordan's first wife, Shirley, died in December 1985 after a 20–year battle with multiple sclerosis. Their daughter, Vickee, worked in public relations in New York. On November 22, 1986, he married Ann Dibble Cook, a former assistant professor at the University of Chicago School of Social Work, who sits on several corporate boards. Jordan had three stepchildren: Antoinette, Mercer, and Janice Cook. The Jordans divided their time between homes in Washington and Martha's Vineyard, Massachusetts.

In *Vanity Fair,* Jordan viewed his life as "a continuum. . . . If you have some notion that sitting on X, Y, or Z board makes me forget how I got there . . . or the people I met along the way, then you have totally miscalculated me." Vernon Jordan was a modern–day pioneer who advanced the civil rights of black Americans and expanded their presence in political and corporate circles.

Current address: Akin, Gump, Strauss, Hauer and Feld LLP, 1333 New Hampshire Avenue, NW, Suite 400, Washington, DC 20036–1564.

REFERENCES

"Being Intimate With Power, Vernon Jordan Can Wield It." *New York Times,* July 14, 1996.

Christian, Charles M. *Black Saga: The African American Experience.* Boston: Houghton Mifflin Co., 1995.

Contemporary Black Biography. Vol. 3. Detroit: Gale Research, 1993.

Current Biography Yearbook. New York: H. W. Wilson, 1972.

Current Biography Yearbook. New York: H. W. Wilson, 1993.

Hawkins, Walter L. *African American Biographies: Profiles of 558 Current Men and Women.* Jefferson, NC: McFarland, 1992.

Hunter–Gault, Charlayne. *In My Place.* New York: Farrar Straus Giroux, 1992.

Salzman, Jack, David Lionel Smith, and Cornel West, eds. *Encyclopedia of African–American Culture and History.* New York: Macmillan Library Reference USA/Simon Schuster Macmillan, 1996.

Who's Who among African Americans, 1996–97. 9th ed. Detroit: Gale Research, 1996.

Who's Who in America 1996. New Providence, NJ: Reid Reference Co., 1995.

Williams, Marjorie. "Clinton's Mr. Inside." *Vanity Fair* 56 (March 1993): 172–75, 207–13.

Linda M. Carter

E. J. Josey

(1924–)

Librarian, writer, activist

E. J. Josey was the first African American male to be elected president of the American Library Association (ALA). He was also cofounder of the Black Caucus of the American Library Association. Outspoken against racism in the library profession and in society, he is a highly regarded educator and library leader.

On January 20, 1924, Elonnie Junius Josey was born to Willie and Frances Josey in Norfolk, Virginia. Popularly known as E. J. to friends and colleagues around the world, he was the eldest of a five children. Although the family was poor, often without enough food to eat or enough fuel to heat their home, the Josey children were encouraged by their mother to develop their creative talents. Josey studied organ at what was then Hampton Institute and played for churches in the area on a part–time basis to earn extra money for himself and the family. A shy but bright child, he graduated at 16 from the segregated I. C. Norcom High School in Portsmouth, Virginia.

Josey was drafted after the start of the Second World War and served in the army from 1943 until his discharge on March 12, 1946. He decided to further his education and enrolled in the Howard University School of Music in Washington, D.C. There he came under the influence of such intellectual giants as Sterling Brown, John Hope Franklin, E. Franklin Frazier, William Hansberry, Alain Locke, and Rayford Logan. These men impressed him with the importance of studying and maintaining black history. Based on their influence, Josey made the decision to change his major to history.

After graduating from Howard, Josey enrolled in a master's degree program in history at Columbia University. Because his degree did not help him win a teaching job in the summer of 1950, to help finance his education, he worked part–time in the journalism library at Columbia for the next two years. While in this position, he became interested in library science as a profession.

The librarians under whom Josey worked at Columbia observed his aptitude and promise and recruited him to librarianship. He received his master's degree at the library school of the New York State University at Albany. While there his education was enriched by working in the New York State Library.

Nearly 45 years of Josey's life were devoted to active service to the library profession. Josey joined the staff of the Free Public Library of Philadelphia in 1953, his first job as a librarian. Because of the blatant racism he encountered on the job there, however, he remained for only one year, then accepted a position as history instructor at Savannah State College in Georgia. He did well as an instructor, but his real desire was to return to library work so he left Savannah after a year to accept a position as director of the library and professor at Delaware State College in Dover. In July 1959, after four productive years, Josey returned to Savannah State as director of the library.

Upon his return to Savannah, Josey established a Library Lecture Series, a Great Books Discussion Group, and the National Library Week convocations. These programs are credited with having brought large numbers of whites onto the Savannah State College campus for the first time. In keeping with his lifelong devotion to human rights, Josey also supported the Savannah State College students who initiated sit–in demonstrations at lunch counters following those by North Carolina Agricultural and Technical College students in Greensboro. This foray into the civil rights movement eventually led to his fights in 1964 and 1965 to make the American Library Association live up to its commitments to its black members and for the library associations in Alabama, Georgia, Louisiana, and Mississippi to admit African Americans.

In 1966 Josey accepted the position of Associate in the Academic and Research Libraries in the New York State Education Department. Later, he advanced through two promotions to chief of the Bureau of Specialist Library Services. During his first years in New York Josey focused on the development and upgrading of services provided by the 216 academic and research libraries in the state. He was instrumental in establishing the state's 3Rs program, a regional approach to cooperative library networking geared to the needs of research and university scholars, and oversaw the implementation of the New York State Interlibrary Loan Program. Another important achievement during this period was Josey's assumption of the editorship of *Bookmark.* His outstanding performance throughout his tenure in New York established him as a national leader in the field.

Josey's dedication to civil rights within librarianship was matched only by his dedication to the movement within the larger society. He was elected vice president of the Albany, New York, branch of the NAACP in 1980 and in 1981 he was elected president. He was instrumental in leading fights to put substance in the city's and county's affirmative action programs and helped organize the minority contractors in the area. His leadership in opposing South African apartheid by spearheading protests in the Albany area of entertainers who had performed in South African added greatly to the national boycott.

Josey retired from his New York State position in 1986 to embark on a new career as professor in the University of Pittsburgh School of Library and Information Science. He was well prepared to join the teaching ranks. As the library director at both Savannah and Delaware State colleges, he taught library–related courses to the general student body. He also was deeply involved in research and published several books and hundreds of articles throughout his career. Josey became a faculty member in North America's largest library school in the fall of 1986 and remained in that position until his retirement in 1995.

Heads American Library Association

When he joined the American Library Association (ALA) right out of library school in 1952, Josey began to familiarize himself with its history and operations. His study of issues confronting the association and his ability as a spokesperson resulted in his election to council in 1970, to the executive board in 1979, and to the presidency of the ALA in 1983. He was the third black and the first black male to head the association. After his year in that highest office, he returned to membership on council.

Josey attended his first Annual Conference of the American Library Association in Kansas City in 1957. He gained prominence in American librarianship during the stormy period of the 1960s and 1970s. He had become concerned that the ALA was unresponsive to black librarians, and he participated in the debates that resulted in updated and strengthened operations and goals for the association. The one exception to his criticism of ALA's responsiveness to black concerns was the association's adoption of a policy not to meet in cities where black librarians would be denied hotel accommodations. The policy had been adopted as a result of the treatment African American librarians received at the 1935 Richmond Annual Conference. Thus, in 1962, when he spoke before conference attendees to congratulate the association for adopting a resolution on individual membership and chapter status, an era of unprecedented activism was born that went far in preparing the profession to face the challenges of an emerging multiethnic, multilingual global society. However, it was at the 1964 Conference when Josey submitted and won approval for a motion that disallowed ALA staff members from attending, in their official capacity or at the expense of the ALA, the meetings of state associations unable to meet fully the requirements of chapter status in the ALA. The motion was the beginning of a revolution within the association to make it responsive to all its members. In the following year Josey became the first African American member of the Georgia Library Association.

The late 1960s and early 1970s found ALA rent by dissension from various groups whose purpose was to democratize the governance structure of the association and initiate policy change. Groups like the Congress for Change, Librarians for 321, and the Social Responsibilities Round Table began to resemble other critical groups which had influenced the association's development during its 100–year history and forced the group's council and executive board to deal with divisions threatening secession, mounting financial crisis, deteriorating relationships with publishers, and the loss of key staff at headquarters in Chicago.

In 1968 Josey met with Effie Lee Morris to discuss their mutual frustration with the slowness of the ALA in addressing black members' concerns. In 1969, after being appointed to the 1969–70 ALA Nominating Committee, Josey arranged to meet with black librarians at the 1970 midwinter meeting to discuss the need for identifying excellent black candidates and responsible white candidates to run for council in the 1971 elections. The librarians who met with Josey agreed to submit names for potential council candidates, and it was decided that a formal organization of black librarians was needed to represent the groups' concerns. Josey was elected their first chairman.

Founds Black Caucus

When the Annual Conference of the American Library Association was held in Detroit in 1970, the Black Caucus of the ALA was established. Josey was one of its founders. As noted in the *Handbook of Black Librarianship,* its purpose was to address the many issues facing the nation and the hesitancy of the library profession to respond to the problems of ''institutional racism, poverty, the lack of educational, employment and promotional opportunities for black and other minorities.'' A ''Plan of Action'' to move the association forward in dealing with the identified problems was called for, and, according to the handbook, the caucus succeeded in having the ALA Council pass a resolution ''that the libraries and/or librarians who do in fact, through either services or materials, support any such racist institutions be censured by the American Library Association.'' The action was taken to put ALA on record as deploring the new private schools throughout the South that were established to avoid racial integration, but relied on libraries and other schools to help meet their library and information service needs.

In June of 1983 Josey was rewarded for his many years of service to the ALA through active participation as chair of many committees and many years on the association's council and executive board. The membership of the oldest and largest library association in the world elected him president. The first African American male to serve at the helm of this prestigious organization, Josey was inaugurated as president of the ALA in Dallas, Texas, in June of 1984.

Under the theme ''Forging Coalitions for the Public Good,'' Josey moved to develop coalitions with other organizations to foster public sector support for libraries and their institutions. Highlights of his presidential year included the appointment of a Commission on Public Sector Support for Libraries to develop strategies designed to increase public support for libraries. This effort led to the eventual establishment of the ALA Development Office in 1991. Another highlight was the joint meeting of the Black Caucus of ALA and the Kenya Library Association in Nairobi, Kenya, one week prior to the conference of the International Federation of Library Associations. After completing his tenure as ALA president, Josey remained on the executive board as immediate past president.

Among the numerous honors that Josey has received are the ALA Black Caucus Award for Distinguished Service to Librarianship in 1979 and the Distinguished Alumni Award for Contributions to Librarianship from the School of Library and Information Science at the State University of New York in 1981. He received the President's Award from the NAACP in 1986 and the ALA Equality Award in 1991. He also holds four honorary doctorates.

In retirement Josey remains a key figure in American librarianship and an inspiration to hundreds whose lives he has influenced.

Current address: c/o School of Library and Information Science, University of Pittsburgh, Pittsburgh, PA 15260.

REFERENCES

Contemporary Black Biography. Vol. 10. Detroit: Gale Research, 1996.

Josey, E. J., ed. *The Black Librarian in America.* Metuchen, NJ: Scarecrow Press, 1970.

———, and Ann Allen Shockley, compilers and eds. *Handbook of Black Librarianship.* Littleton, CO: Libraries Unlimited, 1977.

Arthur C. Gunn

Percy L. Julian
(1899–1975)
Scientist, educator, entrepreneur, inventor

Percy L. Julian is recognized worldwide as a productive organic chemist, a trailblazer whose discoveries are important in medicine and industry. Julian began his brilliant career as a college chemistry teacher and progressed to research in an industrial laboratory, then to the establishment of his own business. His contributions include creating the synthesis of chemicals that made less expensive and readily available pharmaceutics for patients, in the form of physostigmine and cortisone.

Percy Lavon Julian, the oldest of six children by James Julian, a railway mail clerk, and Margaret Julian, a school teacher, was born on April 11, 1899, in Montgomery, Alabama. His father was a strict disciplinarian and a perfectionist, barely tolerant of less than top performance from his children. Young Percy, an excellent student, responded to the encouragement of his father to develop his early interest in science. Since there were no public high schools for black students in

Percy L. Julian

Montgomery in the early 1900s, he went from the small elementary school to a mission school that had been established for ex-slave children after the Civil War. When his parents saw the lack of motivation and challenge there, they sent him to the State Normal School for Negroes in his hometown.

After Julian graduated from normal school and was contemplating college, he read about the accomplishments of St. Elmo Brady, the first African American to earn a Ph.D. in chemistry. The young man took this news as inspiration to continue his study of science. Although he had not attended an accredited high school, he applied to colleges that seemed to offer the training he wanted. In 1916, when Julian was 17, he was admitted to DePauw University in Greencastle, Indiana, in the probationary status of ''sub–freshman.'' He took high school classes in the Ashbury Academy concurrently with freshman and sophomore courses at DePauw to achieve regular student classification. By the end of the second year, having fulfilled the secondary school admission requirements, Julian was a full–fledged college student. During this period, the Julian family moved to Greencastle, where each of the six children graduated from DePauw and began professional careers.

The reward of Julian's four years of long hours and hard work came in 1920 when he achieved a bachelor of science degree from DePauw. He ranked highest in grade point average of the class of 160 students, was named valedictorian, and was elected to Phi Beta Kappa. Entering graduate school was the next step in his ambition to emulate St. Elmo Brady's path to a doctorate in chemistry.

To Julian's disappointment, graduation proved to be the signal for racial restrictions that presented major challenges to his future plans. His record as a student was ample preparation to work as an assistant teacher or research assistant while he was a graduate student, but the racial climate of the 1920s prevented him from following his classmates with similar aspirations and qualifications. Instead of giving him employment at a university reflective of his academic studies, Julian's advisors suggested that he consider teaching at a "Negro" school in the South, where a doctorate was not a requirement. Still nursing a desire for further study and a research position, he accepted an appointment to teach chemistry at Fisk University in Nashville, Tennessee. His department head was Thomas W. Talley, the professor who had encouraged Brady to enter the University of Illinois to work for his doctorate.

Julian taught at Fisk for two years, leaving in 1922 with the Austin graduate fellowship in chemistry to study at Harvard University in Cambridge, Massachusetts. One year later, in 1923, he was awarded a master's degree in organic chemistry. Again he had graduated with the best grades of any other student, but was still unable to find an appropriate teaching or research appointment to subsidize uninterrupted graduate course work. Julian remained at Harvard for three years after the master's degree without adequate support and made small progress toward the doctorate.

With diminishing faith that reliable financial assistance would come to his rescue, in 1926 Julian postponed further study and went to another small school. He taught chemistry to African American students in West Virginia State College's one–person department with almost nonexistent equipment and no staff. With no support services, he taught classes, swept and mopped the floors, did research, and performed every other chore for the classroom and laboratory. He was unable to pursue his research goals with the limited facilities at West Virginia State College. Still seeking advancement, he spent the next two years, from 1927 to 1929, at Howard University in Washington, D.C., lecturing in chemistry and developing that department.

At Howard, Julian revived his intense interest in research that had reached its peak during the first year at Harvard. He had begun by investigating the properties of proteins and the linkage of carbon atoms in plants and animals that results in the production of materials that can cure sickness in human beings. Julian wanted to understand the phenomenon of living cells creating materials with healing qualities, and then duplicate them. His ultimate goal was to produce synthetic materials more easily obtainable at lower costs, which would ease the financial burden of patients.

While Julian was at Howard, he secured a grant from the General Education Board and additional financial assistance from supportive friends to leave for Vienna, Austria, in June of 1929, to study with Ernst Spath at the University of Vienna. He lived in Spath's home and developed the deep friendship and supportive relationship between professor and student. Julian increased his knowledge of organic chemistry by studying the natural substances in soybeans that produce physostigmine, useful in the treatment of glaucoma. He joined a number of scientists in many countries who wanted to replace soybeans, an extremely expensive source of physostigmine, with a synthetic material having the same properties. After much perseverance, he finally received his Ph.D. from the University of Vienna in 1931, 15 years after graduation from high school and his initial commitment to follow St. Elmo Brady.

Percy L. Julian in his laboratory.

With doctorate in hand, Julian returned to Howard University in 1931, this time as head of the chemistry department, with two German assistants from the University of Vienna. The following year, 1932, he returned to DePauw to teach and conduct research on physostigmine, assisted by Josef Pikl, one of his assistants from Germany, and two senior students. With his research going strong, Julian briefly paused to wed Anna Johnson, a sociology teacher from Howard University, on December 24, 1935. They had three children. He continued the study of physostigmine and published the first of his monographs in the *Journal of the American Chemical Society*, attracting nationwide attention. Aside from the scientific significance of Julian's research, the article was notable because he was the first African American senior author of an article in a major chemistry journal in the United States. At DePauw, Julian came to a major breakthrough by developing a synthetic chemical similar to natural physostigmine.

Develops Treatment for Glaucoma

In a dramatic moment in 1935, in the presence of W. M. Blanchard, the school's dean, Julian made the crucial confirmation that the synthetic chemical sample produced in his laboratory, and contained in the test tube he held in his hand, had the identical melting point as the natural physostigmine in Pikl's cylinder. Julian had reached a discovery that had evaded scientists for almost a century. When chemists all over the world read of his success in the *Journal of the American Chemical Society,* congratulations poured in to acknowledge the importance of the synthetic drug in the treatment of glaucoma and other muscle conditions.

Disappointed, but not surprised when DePauw's faculty did not approve Blanchard's proposal to appoint him head of the chemistry department, Julian knew that opportunities for African Americans were still defined by racial attitudes regardless of stature in their field of work. Hoping for better conditions, Julian did not hesitate to accept the position of director of research at Glidden Company in Chicago, starting in 1936. Glidden, makers of paints, varnishes, metals, and industrial chemicals, knew the value of soybeans—specifically for casein, a protein that can be extracted from the beans—to manufacture paints in its large industrial laboratory, but wanted a less expensive synthesis to create the same product.

Julian did not succeed in making synthetic casein, but using a new factory and new equipment he designed himself, he extracted a protein substance similar to casein to be used to coat paper so that it would not absorb ink. This discovery proved to be a financial bonus that made a profit for Glidden of more than $100,000 in its first year. In the absence of synthetic casein, he found other valuable uses for soybean proteins, including Aero–Foam. Many lives were saved in World War II by this fire–fighting foam, which was effective in oil or gasoline fires on ships and planes when water was ineffective.

Julian experimented with another component of soybean oils—sterols—a substance found in human sex hormones, testosterone and progesterone, which regulate male and female sexual development and other human characteristics, including immunity against disease. Despite the difficulty in penetrating the oil to reach the sterols, Julian was successful in producing the hormones chemically instead of by the costlier method of using organs and secretions of cattle. Testosterone and progesterone are used primarily to help women during pregnancy, increase the virility of young or older men, treat infertility, and in some cases, treat women with breast cancer.

A Treatment for Arthritis

Perhaps Julian's greatest achievement came in 1949 at Glidden when he created a synthesis of cortisone, a hormone produced in the adrenal gland and useful for the relief of arthritis pain. Because natural cortisone from animal bile is not practical for widespread use due to cost, Julian's synthesis, cortexolone or Compound S, was widely acclaimed by the medical profession. Use of the synthesis is not confined to arthritis, but extends to allergies, asthma, and patients whose immune system may be overactive. Cortisone has become an inexpensive ointment to relieve itching caused by insect bites, poison oak, or poison ivy.

After 17 years of making great strides in research, Julian left Glidden in 1953. The next step was to open his own businesses. Julian Laboratories in Franklin Park, Illinois, started in 1954, and Laboratorios Julian de Mexico in Mexico City was established in 1955. He and his partner, organic chemist Russell Marker, learned that they could use the wild yams in Mexico for sterols, and within a short time developed a profitable business. Julian sold the firm in 1961 to Smith, Kline, and French, an American pharmaceutical firm based in Philadelphia.

Education, career success, standing in the international community, or other aspects of good citizenry did not insulate Julian and his family from racist incidents. In 1950, after they bought a home in the all–white suburb of Oak Park, Illinois, and not long after he had been named Chicagoan of the Year, the Julians received threatening telephone calls before they moved in, and it took fear of court action to persuade the water commissioner to turn on the water for the property. Once they settled in the house, a bomb thrown from a speeding car landed inside, but fortunately, no one was injured. In 1951, the Union League Club in Chicago refused entry to Julian, research director for the Glidden Company, to a luncheon for distinguished industrialists and scientists because of its policy against the presence of black people.

In semi–retirement, Julian conducted research but also started two small companies in 1964: the Julian Research Institute and Julian Associates. Although suffering from the effects of cancer of the liver and confined to a wheelchair, he still controlled the businesses and worked as a consultant for Smith, Kline, and French until he no longer had the strength. Julian remained active in his research until his death on April 19, 1975.

Numerous well–deserved honors have been bestowed upon Percy Lavon Julian: the NAACP's 1947 Spingarn Medal; the City of Chicago's 1950 Chicagoan of the Year award; an honorary doctor of science degree from Northwestern University in 1951; and the American Institute of Chemists' 1964 Honor Scroll award and its 1968 Chemical Pioneer award. In 1985, the Illinois state senate passed a resolution in tribute to Julian, the governor issued a proclamation in his honor, and the Oak Park, Illinois Elementary School District No. 97 renamed a junior high school after him. In 1990, Percy Julian and George Washington Carver were elected posthumously to the National Inventors Hall of Fame, culminating a ten–year crusade by the National Patent Lawyers Association, a group of minority lawyers. In 1994, the U.S. Postal Service sold stamps with his picture, honoring Julian's many achievements.

Julian's research had humane as well as commercial value; industrial plants could increase their production output and physicians could hasten the healing process by use of the pharmaceuticals that resulted. Although gratified by each of his successes, his biggest reward was to see the effects of his discoveries in the healing of patients, and to know that he had a part in lessening someone's suffering.

One measure of Julian's success as a research chemist is that he applied for and was granted more than 100 patents in the span of his career. The patents gave him the exclusive right to manufacture, use, or sell the results of his mental powers—inventions and designs he conceived in his fruitful years as a scientific investigator.

Julian leaves a legacy of dedication and perseverance for African Americans inside the scientific fields. He identified his life's work before he left high school, and learned to cope with setbacks by restructuring his immediate plan of action without abandoning the ultimate end. It was not always easy for the gifted man to put aside his personal disappointments without losing hope for what was ahead, but his experiences paved the way for African American professionals who would come after him.

REFERENCES

''Carver, Julian Named to Inventors Hall of Fame.'' *Jet* 77 (29 January 1990): 9.

Hayden, Robert C. *Seven African American Scientists.* New York: Twenty–First Century Books, 1992.

Jenkins, Edward S., ed. *American Black Scientists and Inventors.* Washington, DC: National Science Teachers Association, 1975.

''Oak Park, Illinois, Names School for Percy Julian.'' *Jet* 68 (3 June 1985): 23.

''Percy L. Julian's Fight for His Life.'' Ebony 30 (March 1975): 96.

Williams, Michael W., ed. *The African American Encyclopedia.* New York: Marshall Cavendish, 1993.

Yount, Lisa. *Black Scientists.* New York: Facts On File, 1991.

Dona L. Irvin

Ernest Everett Just
(1883–1941)
Biologist, educator, author

Ernest Everett Just was described in *Science* as the ''best investigator in the field of biology that his people [had] produced.'' He made lasting contributions to the study of cellular physiology, experimental embryology, and fertilization. He earned international recognition for his research into the embryological resources of marine biology. Among the few scientifically–trained people of color of his era, he served as professor and head of the Howard University Department of Zoology from 1912 to 1941 and taught physiology in the Howard Medical School from 1912 to 1920.

Just pioneered medical school education methods by incorporating research into medical instruction, for which Howard and numerous other institutions had traditionally relied on part–time practitioners. He achieved success early in his career and in 1915 won the NACCP's first Spingarn Medal. According to Keith R. Manning in *Black Apollo of Science: The Life of Ernest Everett Just,* the medal was to be awarded to an individual of ''African descent'' who had performed ''the foremost service to his race.'' In his examination of marine life reproductive systems, Just went beyond the naturalistic focus of many of his contemporaries by taking into account external environmental factors and holistic perspectives. As his career progressed, Just attracted the attention of wealthy philanthropists interested in supporting his work, thereby stimulating him to concentrate most of his energies on laboratory research.

Ernest Everett Just was born in Charleston, South Carolina, on August 14, 1883. He was the third of five children born to Mary Matthews Cooper Just and Charles Fraser Just. An older brother and sister died before Just was a year old; he grew up with younger siblings, Hunter and Inez. He grew up in Charleston, South Carolina, where his father and paternal grandfather had served as construction workers in the Charleston Harbor, building some of the largest docks in the region. He was raised by his mother; his father died when Ernest was only four years old. A devout Christian, Mary Just supported her family by opening a school in Charleston. She also established a farming and industrial cooperative near the phosphate fields along the Ashley River, an area eventually designated in her honor as Marysville. Just received his earliest formal education at his mother's school and at the age of 13 he enrolled in the academy of South Carolina State College at Orangeburg, a public school for blacks, where he remained from 1896 to 1899. Ernest Just was regarded as quite handsome with a broad and prominent forehead and slender frame; he was deeply sensitive, gentle, quiet, scholarly, and dignified. On June 26, 1912, he married Ethel Highwarden, a native of Columbus, Ohio, whom he had met shortly after both became instructors at Howard University. The couple had three children, Margaret, Highwarden, and Maribel.

Early Years as Student and Instructor

With strong encouragement from his mother, Just became an excellent student. He left South Carolina in 1899, working his way to New York on the Clyde Shipping Line. Reading the *Christian Endeavor World,* he learned about the Kimball Union Academy in Meriden, New Hampshire. He enrolled there in the fall term of 1900. He completed the four–year classical program in three years, edited the student newspaper, presided over the debating society, and graduated as the top student in the class of 1903.

Upon graduation Just moved to Hanover, New Hampshire, to study at Dartmouth College where he had been awarded a scholarship. As an undergraduate he continued his outstanding academic career, excelling in Greek and majoring in history and biology. He earned honors in history, biology, and sociology, and ''special honors'' in zoology; he was awarded a Rufus Choate Scholarship, and graduated *magna cum laude* in 1907 with a B.A. and membership in Phi Beta Kappa.

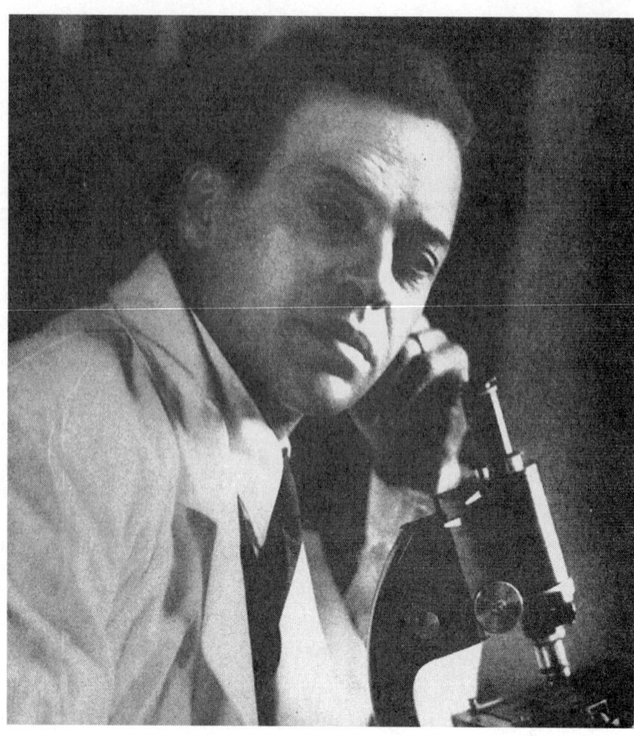

Ernest Everett Just

In the fall semester of 1907, Just was appointed instructor in English and rhetoric at Howard University; he taught first in the Teachers College and the Commercial College, then in the College of Arts and Sciences. He arrived during the rapidly expanding administration of Howard President Wilbur Patterson Thirkield (1906–1912). Thirkield strengthened professional education by organizing departments into schools as well as expanding instruction in music, theology, the natural sciences, and engineering. In this arena of reorganization and growth, Just applied his skills both in and out of the classroom. Well received as a teacher, he also founded the College Dramatic Club, the first such group at Howard, and collaborated with professors Benjamin G. Brawley and Marie Moore–Forrest on a number of dramatic productions that laid the foundation for later professional instruction in drama. Just was a founding member of Omega Psi Phi, a national fraternity of black students; he had succeeded in promoting the value of such organizations to Howard's white administrators.

In 1909 Just altered the course of his academic career, taking on graduate studies in biology at the Marine Biological Laboratory in Woods Hole, Massachusetts. President Thirkield had recognized in Just a keen intellect and induced him to abandon English, develop his scientific abilities, and plan to conduct research in the laboratories then under construction at Howard. Just continued his work during subsequent summers and earned a Ph.D. in zoology from the University of Chicago in 1916. He was influenced and supported greatly throughout his career by Chicago professor Frank R. Lillie, whom he assisted on an investigation of the breeding practices of sea urchins and marine worms.

Just published his first paper in the *Biological Bulletin* in 1912 and by the time he had completed doctoral studies he had published several more papers and was heavily engaged in teaching. While a professor in the medical school, he taught pharmacy, dental, and medical students in the mornings and zoology students in the College of Arts and Sciences in the afternoons.

Success and Recognition

Just's career took a new turn in 1920 when Frank Lillie introduced him to Julius Rosenwald, the famous philanthropist who supported Tuskegee Institute and built hundreds of YMCAs and school buildings for southern blacks. Rosenwald became concerned that a scientist of Just's stature was being denied access to the much better equipped research staff and facilities in the major public and private universities that were serving whites only. Thus began a series of grants, primarily in support of Just's research, by the Rosenwald Fund (1920–27, 1928–33), the Rockefeller Foundation (1925–30), the General Education Board (1928–33), the Carnegie Foundation (1934–35), and the Oberlaender Trust (1936), administered by the National Research Council. With such strong external support, Just was able to leave the Medical School faculty while retaining headship of the department of Zoology, and was allowed to spend six months—sometimes more—of each year at Woods Hole. This schedule testified to Just's stature as a scientist and scholarly production soon followed. While associated with Howard's medical school from 1912 to 1920, Just published nine papers but over the next ten years he wrote 38 papers and a book, *General Cytology,* with Frank Lillie, T. H. Morgan, and others.

Just focused on experimental embryology, investigating parthenogenesis, cell division and mutation, and fertilization. He experimented with the detection of electrochemical reactions in cells, reproducing the histological features of human cancer cells. His work on hydration and dehydration in cellular physiology influenced the treatment of nephritis and edema. According to the *Dictionary of American Negro Biography,* he claimed to be the first scientist to have "increased the number of chromosomes in a mammal." In *Science* magazine Lillie, his mentor, colleague, and friend, described Just's work as so complicated that it would become a "theme for study for many years to come." Manning wrote in *Black Apollo of Science* that Just had become "*the* current authority on fertilization," conducting research essential to an understanding of heredity and eugenics.

By the late 1920s Just had begun to synthesize his findings in an effort to define the physics and chemistry of protoplasm and to integrate his basic laboratory research into the study of general biology. He presented the conceptual components of these theories in 1930 as one of only 12 zoologists invited to Padua, Italy, to address the General Session of the Eleventh International Congress of Zoologists. He proposed that by analyzing the physiochemical processes of ectoplasm—studying the interactions between inner cellular substances and the external environment—one could begin to understand evolution and, indeed, life itself. His results subsequently appeared in German in *Naturwissenschaft* and in English in the *American Naturalist.*

According to Just, the direction of his research and the results he produced represented a revolution in thinking about biology. Not surprisingly, his reputation continued to accelerate. He was selected to be a member of the Washington Academy of Science and the New York Academy of Sciences (later in life), was named vice–president of the American Society of Zoologists, and was appointed to the editorial boards of *Biological Bulletin, Cytologia, Journal of Morphology, Physiological Zoology,* and *Protoplasma: Zeitschrift fuer Physikalische.*

Philanthropic support allowed Just to abandon the Marine Biological Laboratory at Woods Hole and to spend much of his leave time in European research laboratories. He was a guest researcher and the first American to work at the Kaiser Wilhelm Institut für Biologie, Berlin, regarded by many as the world's leading research laboratory, and the Stazione Zoologica in Naples. In Germany Just became associated with Harnack Haus and the great German theologian Adolph von Harnack. Von Harnack rekindled the zoologist's interest in theological issues that had lain dormant since his youth, thereby planting ideas later developed in Just's studies of biology and philosophy.

Local Discontent and International Achievement

As his scientific prowess and his reputation grew, his relationship with his home institution, Howard University, deteriorated. Despite the annual leave policy, generous by the standards of most university scientists, he began to view his teaching responsibilities as particularly burdensome. This point of view differed from that of the university, which maintained that Just's Rosenwald grants had been intended not merely for Just's laboratory work but also for strengthening the department of zoology and further developing a cadre of black scientists at the graduate level. These issues weakened Just's relationship with Mordecai W. Johnson, Howard president from 1926 to 1960, casting a pall over the zoologist's closing years at his home institution.

Graduate programs in zoology at Howard had begun in 1929 and during the next four years attracted 15 students. Eight of these graduated with an M.S. degree, yet from 1933 to 1935, only one student was enrolled. Contemporaries compared the enrollment decline in zoology with the gradual increases in other subjects offered in Howard's graduate degree programs during the same period. Just claimed that Howard had never met its own responsibilities incurred by the Rosenwald funds: to strengthen the infrastructure—space, staff, students, and equipment—for laboratory research. Just argued that Howard was too impoverished as a university to support the training of graduate biologists and zoologists. A solid undergraduate program, which Just had long supported, was more within the range of Howard's financial resources.

Meanwhile, Just was increasingly attracted to Europe and sought foundation support that would allow him to sever his ties with Howard University. He had been welcomed graciously by the European scientific community, and he was inexorably drawn to the social, artistic, and cultural life of Germany, Italy, and France. Although he did not succeed in attracting the necessary funds, he remained adamant in his desire for association with European research centers. During a leave of absence of more than two and a half years, he worked at the Laboratoire d'Anatomie et d'Histologie Comparées at the University of Paris and at the Sorbonne's Station Biologique de Roscoff. In 1939 he published *The Biology of the Cell Surface,* a book that synthesized much of his laboratory research with new theoretical perspectives, and *Basic Methods for Experiments in Eggs of Marine Animals,* a handbook for laboratory techniques that further solidified his international stature in marine fertilization.

Just set himself apart from most research scientists in his pursuit of interdisciplinary relationships. He described the proper approach to the study of life as neither vitalistic nor mechanistic but rather, interactive and holistic, and he sought to connect the biological sciences with social philosophy. He studied the writings of philosophers G. W. F. Hegel, Immanuel Kant, and Ernst Mach and also explored connections with physicists such as Arthur Stanley Eddington, James Hopwood Jeans, Werner Heisenberg, Max von Laue, Max Planck, and Frederich Schröder.

Just's discontent with Howard University symbolized, in a sense, his quarrel with American society as a whole. He felt rejected by the major white universities, which denied him access to the facilities commensurate with his interests and abilities. Additionally, the infrastructure for scientific research at Howard failed to meet his expanding demands as a research scientist. He decried a racial context that accommodated black scientists as medical practitioners but not as laboratory researchers. He felt that European society offered much richer opportunities to pursue his interests. He sought to create a role for himself not as a black scientist whose parameters of intellectual and social activity would be constricted but rather as a scientist for the entire human race who could pursue his interests without being restrained by the repressive features of American life. Yet, he made a vital contribution to black America's response to a hostile society by advocating objective, scientific methods over the more subjective humanities as a method for pursuing equality of opportunity.

Final Struggles

As the decade of the 1930s drew to a close, Europe became a less hospitable place to live. The entire continent was being swept into war. The Nazis overran France and in August of 1940 interned Just in a camp, probably at Chateaulin. In 1939 Just had divorced his wife and married Hedwig Schnetzler, a philosophy doctoral student he had met in Berlin. In 1940 they would have a daughter, Elisabeth. Fortunately, his wife's family was well–connected politically and succeeded—with the aid of officials from Brown–Boveri, an industrial giant with outlets in Germany and

Switzerland—in securing his release. Soon thereafter, Just and his wife sailed for America.

Just was also suffering financially, since he had chosen to remain in Europe without the benefit of consistent income. He never gave up seeking foundation support for his research overseas but the philanthropic interests had increasingly come to favor graduate education for black scientists and physicians over laboratory work in basic fields such as biology and zoology. The best hope for Just became the unattractive option of returning to Howard University.

In 1938 Just had appealed to the university for back pay since 1933, claiming that a 1920 agreement gave him a second semester leave each year without a salary reduction, and he also sought retirement income. He had contracted cancer and was able to secure sick leave at half–pay for the spring semester of 1938 out of ''consideration for his long services to the University,'' according to Rayford W. Logan in *Howard University: The First Hundred Years.* Yet in October of 1938, the Executive Committee at Howard agreed only to sick leave at one–third pay and the committee rejected his retirement claim, arguing that it would not be fair to Just to retire him on a small amount at age 55. Clearly, Howard had hoped to return him to full time service in order to strengthen the university's scientific programs. Just was given leave without pay for 1939–40 but was reinstated at full pay for 1940–41, the last academic year of his life. Just died of cancer on October 27, 1941, at the Washington, D.C. home of his sister Inez and was buried in Washington in the Lincoln Cemetery.

Financial concerns and a debilitating disease marred the closing years of a remarkable life. Possessed of a superior and disciplined intellect, Just was destined for success as a scientific researcher. As the years progressed, he continually pressed for opportunities to pursue his research and to live out his dreams unfettered by the racism of an oppressive American society. He faced the dilemma common to black intellectuals—whether to be known as a black scholar or simply as a scholar. The ambiguities of his final years indicate a less than satisfactory resolution to this dilemma, despite the national and international stature of his scientific achievements.

REFERENCES

Fontaine, W. T. ''Philosophical Implications of the Biology of Dr. Ernest E. Just.'' *Journal of Negro History* 24 (1939): 281–90.

Lillie, Frank R. ''Ernest Everett Just, August 14, 1883, to October 27, 1941.'' *Science* 95 (2 January 1942): 10–11.

Lips, Julius E. ''Ernest E. Just, An American Negro Scientist.'' *Opportunity* 20 (September 1942): 265–67.

Logan, Rayford W. *Howard University: The First Hundred Years, 1867–1967.* New York: New York University Press, 1969.

———, and Michael R. Winston, eds. *Dictionary of American Negro Biography.* New York: Norton, 1982.

Manning, Kenneth R. *Black Apollo of Science: The Life of Ernest Everett Just.* New York: Oxford University Press, 1983.

COLLECTIONS

The Ernest Everett Just Papers are housed in the Manuscript Division of the Moorland–Spingarn Research Center, Howard University.

John Mark Tucker

Ulysses S. Kay
(1917–1995)
Composer, educator

Ulysses S. Kay was one of the most outstanding composers of twentieth–century classical idioms. His works were conducted by leading conductors and played by leading orchestras. He studied composition with some of the major pedagogues in the twentieth century, including Howard Hanson, Paul Hindemith, Otto Luening, and Bernard Rogers. William Grant Still encouraged him early on to become a composer and remained a mentor. He received commissions for works from the Juilliard School of Music in New York, the National Symphony, and Opera/South, among many others. He composed over 135 pieces, including operas, piano music, orchestral and choral works, and chamber music. He wrote scores for television and for films. In his music, he used many styles ranging from spiritual–like melodies through neoclassicism to the atonal sounds of his contemporaries.

Kay's works were highly regarded. Nicolas Slonimsky wrote in *American Composers Alliance Bulletin* that, his ''musical language was that of enlightened modernism.'' As a consultant for Broadcast Music Incorporated (BMI), Kay influenced publishing decisions and other issues. His career began to accelerate after a performance of his orchestral overture, *Of New Horizons,* by the New York Philharmonic in Lewisohn Stadium in New York on July 9, 1944. Significant awards followed, giving him the recognition and exposure that his music needed to insure his future success. He received many honorary doctorates later in life for his contributions to American classical music, and in 1979, the American Institute of Arts voted him into membership.

Kay was born on January 7, 1917, in Tucson, Arizona. He died on May 20, 1995, at home in Teaneck, New Jersey. He was the son of Elizabeth Davis Kay and Ulysses S. Kay, and he had one sister. He was the nephew of the New Orleans jazz legend and cornet player, Joe ''King'' Oliver, who influenced him in his formative years.

Education and Influences

Kay's father was a barber who loved to sing. His mother, Elizabeth, played the piano. His father used to sing ballads, hymns, work songs, and songs he created to his son to keep him entertained. His sister played the music of the nineteenth–century Polish composer, Frederic Chopin, on the piano in their home. His uncle, Joe Oliver, determined that young Ulysses should study the piano before Oliver would teach him to play the trumpet, so he studied piano with William A. Ferguson. At school, he learned to play the violin. His sister helped him discover the saxophone while he was a student at Dunbar Junior High School. He loved jazz and the sounds of the saxophone, so he temporarily gave up the piano and the violin to study that instrument. At Tucson Senior High School, he played in the marching band, sang in the glee club, and played saxophone in jazz orchestras whenever he could. In 1934 he graduated from high school and enrolled at the University of Arizona in Tucson. He received his bachelor of music degree with training in public school music in 1938.

Kay encountered the music of Hungarian composer and pianist Béla Bartók as part of his piano study with Julia Rebeil, and he was schooled in music theory under John L. Lowell at the university. He later said that those experiences gave him a completely new perspective on the field of music composition. He received a scholarship to the Eastman School of Music in Rochester, New York, and he enrolled there as a graduate student in 1938. He earned a master's degree in 1940, studying composition with Bernard Rogers and then with Howard Hanson until 1941.

In Rochester, Kay first heard his works performed, including *Sinfonietta* in 1939, *Oboe Concerto* in 1940, and *Dance Calinda* in 1941. In the summer of 1941, Kay had the opportunity to study composition with Paul Hindemith at the Berkshire Music Center in Tanglewood, Massachusetts. He continued his studies with Hindemith at Yale University from 1941 to 1942.

The War and the Middle Years

In 1942 Kay enlisted in the U.S. Naval Reserves in World War II and served three and a half years as a musician second class in Quonset Point, Rhode Island. He played the flute, saxophone, and piccolo in the Navy band. He played the piano in dance orchestras. In addition, he was able to continue arranging and composing. A significant work of Kay's from this period was the orchestral overture, *Of New Horizons* in 1944, written in the neoclassical style, which brought him to the attention of the critics.

Kay's *Suite for Orchestra* in 1945 received a prize from BMI, the first of many to come. The following year, *A Short Overture,* also for orchestra, earned the George Gershwin Memorial Award. It was first performed in Brooklyn, New York, on March 31, 1947, conducted by Leonard Bernstein. Kay composed *Suite,* for strings, in 1947.

Kay received the first of many awards designed to give him more time to compose in 1946. The Alice M. Ditson Fellowship supported him during one year of creative work. BMI elected him to full membership in 1947. In 1947–48, he received the Julius Rosenwald Fellowship and a grant from the National Institute of Arts and Letters, and he traveled to Europe. One of his orchestral compositions from 1948, *Portrait Suite,* based on sculptures by Henry Moore, Jacob Lipschitz, and Wilhelm Lehmbruch, received the Phoenix Symphony Orchestra Award.

From 1946 through 1949, he attended Columbia University as a composition student of Otto Leuning. He completed a movie score for the motion picture, *The Quiet One,* in 1948, and subsequently arranged a concert suite from that score. The suite was premiered in New York in 1948.

On August 20, 1949, he married Barbara Harrison. Their three children are Melinda Lillian, Virginia, and Hillary. From 1949 until 1952, he lived in Italy with two Prix de Rome awards covering the years 1949–1952 and a Fulbright grant for 1950–51. His *Concerto for Orchestra* was completed in 1948. In 1950, while he was still in Italy, he wrote *Symphony in E,* his first major symphonic work.

A consulting position with BMI lasted from 1953 until 1968. The major completed composition of 1952 was *Three Pieces After Blake,* for soprano and orchestra. In 1953 the *Concerto for Orchestra* (1948), which was written in Italy, premiered in Venice by the Teatro La Fenice Orchestra conducted by Jonel Perlea. *Six Dances* for string orchestra and *Serenade* for full orchestra followed in 1954. The next year he composed his first one–act opera, *The Boor.* He wrote a second one–act opera, *Juggler of Our Lady,* in 1956.

In 1958 Kay went to the Soviet Union on a cultural exchange program with the first delegation of American composers. Included in this distinguished group were Roy Harris, Peter Mennin, and Roger Sessions. A concert of music by these composers was played by the Moscow State Radio Orchestra. He ended the decade of the 1950s with a large piece for soprano, baritone, chorus, and orchestra, called *Phoebus, Arise.*

Kay's first major work of the 1960s was *Choral Triptych,* for chorus and string orchestra in 1962. In 1963 he was commissioned to write "tranquil music" for a project Edward B. Benjamin sponsored, and the result was *Umbrian Scene. Umbrian Scene* was later recorded by the Louisville Orchestra. In the same year he wrote two more major works, *Fantasy Variations,* for orchestra, and *Inscriptions from Whitman,* for chorus and orchestra. Lincoln College in Lincoln, Illinois, presented him with the first of many honorary doctorates in music in 1963.

Kay received a Guggenheim Fellowship in 1964–65, and he composed *Emily Dickinson Set* for women's chorus and piano. In the same year, his original score was heard on the television special, *An Essay on Death,* a tribute to John F. Kennedy. It was telecast over WNET in New York on November 19. He wrote the film scores for two television documentaries for *The Twentieth Century* series on CBS, "F.D.R.: Third Term to Pearl Harbor," and "Submarine!," and another documentary called *New York: City of Magic.*

In 1965 Kay was a visiting professor at Boston University. Bucknell University in Lewisburg, Pennsylvania, awarded him his second honorary doctorate in music in 1966. In 1966–67 he was a visiting professor at the University of California at Los Angeles. He wrote *Markings* in 1966, an essay for orchestra that took its title from Dag Hammarskjöld's book, published posthumously. *Markings* was dedicated to the former United Nations Secretary General, who had been killed in a plane crash. It has been recorded by the London Symphony Orchestra.

The Golden Years of Commissions

Kay received a permanent appointment to the faculty of the Herbert H. Lehman College of the City University of New York in 1968. That year, the Atlanta Symphony under the direction of Robert Shaw commissioned him to write a piece for them. *Theater Set* premiered in Atlanta on September 26, 1968, on the opening night of the concert season. Kay said that the piece was a tribute to show music, without quoting any themes directly.

Kay's alma mater, the University of Arizona at Tucson, conferred on him an honorary doctorate in music in 1969. That year he received an honorary doctorate of humane letters from Illinois Wesleyan University in Bloomington, Illinois. In 1970 he composed a sextet for woodwinds and piano called *Facets,* which makes effective use of silence in the midst of sound. It was first performed at the Eastman School of Music on October 19, 1971. In 1972 he was named Distinguished Professor of Music at Lehman College, where he had been teaching since 1968.

Commissions for new works continued to pour in. The Juilliard School of Music commissioned a work in 1973 for five brass soloists and orchestra. The result was *Quintet Concerto.* For the American bicentennial, he wrote four major works, each on a different commission. The National Symphony received *Western Paradise,* for narrator and orchestra (1975). The Southern Regional Metropolitan Orchestra Managers Association, with a grant from the National Endowment for the Arts, got *Southern Harmony. Southern Harmony* was premiered by the North Carolina Orchestra on February 10, 1976. The music was inspired by American hymn tunes of the mid–nineteenth century.

The Princeton Theological Seminary and Presbyterian Church commissioned *Epigrams and Hymn,* also in 1976. Opera/South in Jackson, Mississippi, commissioned Kay's first full–length opera, *Jubilee,* based on Margaret Walker's book of the same title. The premiere of that work was on November 20, 1976, in Jackson. Dickinson College in Carlisle, Pennsylvania, gave him his fourth honorary doctorate in music in 1978. The Saratoga Performing Arts Center commissioned *Chariots* for orchestra in 1978, and that work received its premiere by the Philadelphia Orchestra with the composer conducting on August 8, 1979.

The University of Missouri at Kansas City awarded him an honorary doctorate in 1981. In August of 1982, he was a resident fellow at the Bellagio Study and Conference Center in Como, Italy. He retired from his position at Lehman College in 1988.

Kay's last major work was an opera titled *Frederick Douglass,* which he completed in 1991. The *Washington Post* cited his interview at the premiere of the work at Newark Symphony Hall with the New Jersey State Opera in April of 1991, when Kay said, "I wasn't composing operas to prove anything. I write out of interest, rather than trying to take on the cause of blackness or whatever."

Kay's numerous works can be divided into four broad categories by genre: dramatic works, orchestral works, vocal works, and chamber works. He withdrew some of his earlier pieces after he had achieved maturity. Most of his works are unpublished. Some of the published works are currently out–of–print.

Throughout his lifetime, Kay's musical styles defied categorization. They were not especially ethnic, nor did he strive to use folk music, jazz, or blues, as the basis for his work. In an interview in *The Black Composer Speaks,* he said in answer to a question about what features of his own music he saw as uniquely black, "I have nothing especially other than its expressive content." He often wrote in a neoclassical style with modern harmonies, like Prokofiev, Shostakovich, and Kabalevsky who worked in the Soviet Union, but he could just as easily write in an atonal idiom. He knew the system developed by Arnold Schoenberg for 12–tone music and could use those techniques if he felt they helped him accomplish his aesthetic goals.

Kay's mature style, according to Eileen Southern in the *New Grove Dictionary of American Music,* "is characterized by taut but warm melodies, complex polyphony, vibrant harmonic and orchestral coloring, and rhythmic diversity."

Photographs of Ulysses Kay show that he was a slight man, small in frame, and either bald or with short hair for most of his professional life. He wore glasses. He was often photographed with a conductor's baton in his hand. In the *Washington Post* scholar and musician Hildreth Roach described Kay as "a gentleman and a gentle man, highly intellectual, polite, and a bit shy. He was surprised and delighted that people would perform and listen to his music."

Kay benefited from the multitude of achievements in the field of classical music of William Grant Still. With more formal education and more earned degrees in music than his mentor and friend, Kay was able to open doors in the academic world that his predecessor could not. When Still died in 1978, the title of "Dean of Afro–American Composers" was passed to Kay. Kay became the bridge between the self–taught African American composer of European styles and an academic community in the United States trying desperately to create a style all its own. He was as much a part of the mainstream as any composer active in the middle decades of the twentieth century, and yet his music remained unique and not easily classified.

REFERENCES

Baker, David, Lida M. Belt, and Herman C. Hudson, eds. *The Black Composer Speaks.* Metuchen, NJ: Scarecrow Press, 1978.

Ewen, David. *American Composers: A Biographical Dictionary.* New York: G. P. Putnam's Sons, 1982.

Hitchcock, H. Wiley, and Stanley Sadie, eds. *The New Grove Dictionary of American Music.* London: Macmillan, 1986.

"Obituaries." *Who's Who Among African Americans, 1996/1997.* 9th ed. Detroit: Gale Research, 1996.

Slonimsky, Nicolas. *Baker's Biographical Dictionary of Musicians,* 7th ed., rev. New York: Schirmer Books, 1984.

———. "Ulysses Kay." *American Composers Alliance Bulletin* 7 (Fall 1957): 3.

Southern, Eileen. *The Music of Black Americans.* Rev. ed. New York: Norton, 1983.

"Ulysses Kay: A Musical Odyssey." *Washington Post,* May 28, 1995.

Wyatt, Lucius R. R. "Ulysses Kay's *Fantasy Variations*: An Analysis." *Black Perspectives in Music* 7 (Spring 1977): 75–89.

Carolyn L. Quin

William Melvin Kelley

(1937–)

Novelist, essayist, short story writer

William Melvin Kelley's writing career is rooted in the oppositions of race in American culture. Focusing on the ways in which both racial integration and the examination of racism have simultaneously and systematically shaped American culture, Kelley's fiction portrays black individuals who are unable to escape being defined by a society that imagines a singular black experience. In attempting to explore the effects of racism on both the society and the individual, Kelley creates fictional situations that bend space, time, and language to tell novel yet familiar tales that explore the relationships between race and African American identity. His career as a novelist, essayist, and short story writer spanned both the civil rights movement, with its emphasis on the place of blacks in America, and the Black Arts Movement, with its emphasis on nationalism and the links between African and African American culture.

William Melvin Kelley was born on November 1, 1937, in New York, to William Kelley, an editor, and Narcissa Agatha Garcia Kelley. Growing up in the Bronx, Kelley discovered the incongruities of race at an early age. Kelley's grandmother, a mulatto, was not identifiably black, and her father was the first Confederate officer to die in the Battle of Bull Run. Kelley's parents, believing that integration was the answer to racial problems in America, were the only black

William Melvin Kelley

family in a predominantly Italian neighborhood. He attended the Fieldston School, a private, predominantly white high school in New York. In 1957 Kelley entered Harvard, where he planned to prepare for a law career. By 1959, however, he had abandoned his plans to become a lawyer. After studying with novelist John Hawkes and poet Archibald MacLeish at Harvard, Kelley decided to write fiction for a black audience whom he described as being in, but not *of,* American society. Kelley married Karen Isabella Gibson, a painter and designer, in 1962. They have two daughters, Jessica and Cira Tikaiji.

Even before his first novel, *A Different Drummer,* was published in 1962, Kelley had established himself as a promising writer. He had been awarded the Dana Reed Prize for the best undergraduate piece published in a Harvard undergraduate journal in 1960. While working on his first novel, he received fellowships from the Breadloaf and New York writers conferences and support from the John Hay Whitney Foundation. With the appearance of *A Different Drummer,* Kelley, then 25, was awarded the Richard and Hilda Rosenthal Award of the National Institute of Arts and Letters. It was clear from *Drummer* that Kelley's fiction would be shaped by the contradiction between the American dream and the realities of the American experience for black people. Kelley clearly posits in *Drummer* that societal change can be effected by nonviolent protest.

Kelley's later works reflect his continued concern with the place of blacks in American culture, but they also illustrate Kelley's recognition that integration could never resolve America's racial problems, a position he clarifies in his collection of short stories, *Dancers of the Shore,* published in 1964. Like Kelley, the characters of that novel are empowered by explorations of African American history that they are able to reclaim and, thus, rewrite. After 1964, his focus on history enabled Kelley to explore ways in which black Americans examine the relationship between their self–concept and African culture and reject stereotypes that have historically defined them in American culture.

In the late 1960s, Kelley resolved to emphasize the relationship between African and African American culture. For him, individual African American experiences were related to the experiences of African Diaspora people all over the world. Like many African American writers before him, Kelley's experiences abroad, particularly those in Rome and in Paris, cemented his understanding of America's preoccupation with race.

Travels "Everywheres"

Kelley's third novel, *A Drop of Patience,* was written in Rome in 1965. Like the writers of the Harlem Renaissance and the Protest Period, Kelley noted that racial differences and social definitions were perceived differently in Europe. In keeping with Kelley's emphasis on the value of African American culture, the protagonist finds solace and psychological wholeness when he rejects the white world. *A Drop of Patience* rejects the cultural currency of whiteness and emphasizes the centrality of African American culture in the process of defining the black self.

After returning to the United States in 1965, Kelley was appointed author–in–residence at the State University of New York in Geneseo, where he again redefined his focus. The early 1960s were a particularly tense time in American race relations. Kelley became an increasingly outspoken critic of American life, speaking and writing about the ways in which racism permeated America's history. Later that year, Kelley returned to Europe to attend the Royaumont seminar on black literature. Paris offered Keeley an opportunity to obtain another perspective on American racism as well as to explore his African roots and the importance of Africa in the lives of African Americans.

In 1967 Kelley returned to France with his family. His exploration of African cultures led him to develop a language that could adequately represent African American culture and represent the distance between white and black in America. His subsequent writings use linguistic patterns derived from a number of African Diaspora sources. In , Kelley turned to the values of white America, emphasizing white immorality and African American empowerment. In the inability of the white and black characters to understand each other, Kelley emphasizes that language and history are central to understanding the racial situation in America.

Although Kelley never traveled to Africa, he studied numerous African cultures and continued to explore the possibilities of language. Following his sojourn in Paris, Kelley moved his family to the Caribbean. Each new view from abroad challenged him to create a means through which he could communicate with a black audience who could discern the unique language patterns he was formulating and understand his rejection of standard English. Galvanized by his exploration of language and culture, Kelley emulated James Joyce's *Finnegan's Wake* in *Dunfords Travels Everywheres.* Written partly in standard English and partly in a lexicon derived from Bantu, black English vernacular, and the slang associated with Harlem, *Dunfords* examines the lives of dual protagonists who, like Kelley, discover the extent to which American racism has misdefined them. Racial and sexual stereotypes define the protagonist's relationship with his "white" companions as he travels through fictional country in which the color of one's clothing defines social differences.

At the center of William Melvin Kelley's art is a powerful commitment to revise the history of America that seeks to misrepresent black identity. Kelley's work reveals a preoccupation with black subjectivity and a rejection of American culture's preoccupation with hierarchical racial categories.

After the publication of *Dunfords Travels Everywheres,* Kelley turned towards political rather than creative expression of his convictions.

Current address: The Wisdom Shop, PO Box 2658, New York, NY 10027.

REFERENCES

Abrahams, Willie E. "Introduction." *dem.* New York: Collier Books, 1969.

Black Writers: A Selection of Sketches from Contemporary Authors. Detroit: Gale Research, 1989.

Fabre, Michel. *From Harlem to Paris: Black American Writers in France, 1840–1980.* Urbana: University of Illinois Press, 1991.

Harris, Trudier. *From Mammies to Militants: Domestics in Black American Literature.* Philadelphia: Temple University Press, 1982.

Sheila Smith McKoy

B. B. King
(1925–)
Musician

B. B. King has been a major figure in the development of the blues tradition. A forerunner in the change from country to urban blues, his technique of playing the electric guitar as a solo instrument influenced a whole generation of young guitar players. Henry Pleasants in the *Grove Dictionary of American Music* characterizes King's high tenor voice as "the finest among blues singers." In addition to his musical talent, King is lauded for his ability to communicate with his audiences. Those who know him best admire him as a man as much as they admire his music.

Riley B. King was born on September 16, 1925, to Albert King and Nora Ella Pully King in a sharecropper's cabin between Itta Bena and Indianola, Mississippi. Albert King was an orphan who named his son after a brother who had disappeared. A second child died in infancy. Around 1930 Nora Ella King left her husband and moved back to the area her family had come from near Kilmichael, Mississippi. Although King lived from time to time with his mother and her two other husbands, he lived most of the time with his maternal grandmother, Elnora Farr, who sharecropped on a farm near Kilmichael. He was present when his mother died during the summer of 1935 at nearby French Camp. According to Charles Sawyer, she told her son: "If you are always kind to people, your kindness will be repaid, one way or another. And you will be happy in your life." Her admonition made a profound impression on him.

Nora Ella King and her mother were deeply religious Baptists who had a profound influence on King, as had Archie Fair, brother–in–law of Nora Ella King and pastor of a Holiness church near Kilmichael. By the time he was eight or nine, King was lead singer in the congregational worship at the Holiness church. His uncle also taught him the basics of playing the guitar. The moral precepts he learned in church remained a foundation of his character, although he privately became a skeptic about some church doctrine. Another major influence on King's moral development was the local schoolmaster, Luther Henson, who valued self–esteem and self–improvement.

Elnora Farr died on January 15, 1940, probably of tuberculosis. King stayed on in her cottage and took an acre of land to raise cotton and pay off his debts. That fall he moved to Lexington, Mississippi, to live with his father and his father's new family. Two years later King rode his bicycle back to Kilmichael, where a white cash tenant, Flake Cartledge, took him in. King was put up in a shed and ate with the family while he worked for his keep.

Begins Musical Career

Before his departure from Kilmichael in 1940, King had formed a gospel group with his cousin, Birkett Davis, and Walter Doris Jr. Davis had moved to Indianola, Mississippi, and in the spring of 1942 King joined him there with a guitar he purchased for $2.50. King went to work for Johnson Barrett, who farmed a thousand acres, as a sharecropper and tractor driver, for which he earned a dollar a day. With Birkett Davis and others, he joined a gospel singing group, The Famous St. John Gospel Singers. King soon discovered that he could earn more money by playing and singing the blues on the street in neighboring towns and cities on Saturday evenings than he could by singing gospel music on Sundays. On November 26, 1944, he married Matha Denton. The combination of agricultural work and marriage secured him an exemption from the World War II draft and allowed him to pursue a career in music.

B. B. King

Eager to leave the farm and try to make a living as a musician, King left for Memphis in May 1946 with $2.50 in his pocket and his guitar. His plan involved getting in touch with his cousin, Bukka (Booker T.) White, an established blues musician. King found that Memphis was full of young guitar players who were just as good or better than he was. Bukka White nevertheless took the young man in and found him a job. For ten months King devoted himself to improving his guitar playing under White's mentorship. Unable to adopt White's slide technique of playing the guitar because his hands were too large, King discovered a way of slurring pitch by stretching the strings. During his stay in Memphis, King participated in amateur night competitions at the Palace Theater.

Forced to return to Mississippi to fulfill his responsibilities to his wife and clear up a debt, King worked as a sharecropper in 1947 and 1948. King returned to Memphis where he became acquainted with Sonny Boy Williamson II (Rice Miller), who had a 15–minute radio program on radio station KWEM in West Memphis. Placing King in his program as a substitute for a conflicting gig, Williamson offered him an opportunity to play a song on the radio. The proprietress of the Sixteenth Street Grill then offered King a position as a regular performer. King then secured an opportunity to play for Nat D. Williams, the pioneering disc jockey at radio station WDIA, which had just gone to an all–black format. Finding King unpolished but talented, Williams allotted him a ten–minute unpaid spot advertising Pepticon, a tonic, and King became the Pepticon Boy. He was now in a position to send for his wife.

As his popularity grew, WDIA made King a disc jockey on his own show, *Sepia Swing Club.* Originally billed as the ''Beale Street Blues Boy,'' he soon became Blues Boy King, which was shortened to B. B. King. King became the first person at WDIA to be sponsored by a national advertiser, Lucky Strike cigarettes. King ended his association with WDIA in 1953, when the demands associated with touring became too great.

Early in his career, while King was performing a gig in Twist, Alabama, he named his most famous guitar Lucille. There was a fight over a woman named Lucille, and a tipped–over space heater caused a fire that claimed two lives. Once King was safely outside, he realized that he had left his guitar behind. He reentered the burning building and rescued the instrument. The Blues Foundation, based in Memphis, now offers the Lucille Award to an aspiring blues musician.

In 1949 King recorded four sides for Bullet Records. Although the records were only successful locally, they led to his contract with the RPM label. King remained with this label for ten years. Once again, King reaped only local fame from the six RPM records he recorded in 1949.

Wins Fame Among Black Audiences

The increasing pressures and demands of King's career led him to hire Robert Henry, a Memphis pool hall owner and entrepreneur, as a business manager. In the closing days of 1951, RPM's seventh record of King's music reached number one on Billboard's rhythm and blues charts and remained there for 15 weeks. Due to the success of this album, Universal Artists signed King and booked him at the Howard Theater in Washington, D.C., the Royal Theater in Baltimore, and the Apollo Theater in Harlem. King thus began a national tour that lasted six months. Three years earlier, he was earning $22.50 a week driving a tractor. Now, he earned $2,500 a week. King spent his new wealth extravagantly, a habit which has continued throughout his career. He is also considered generous with his friends and loves to gamble.

The strain of success became too much for the Kings' marriage to endure and they divorced in 1952. Over the years, King acknowledged fathering eight children with other women. His daughter Shirley grew up on the farm near Memphis that King had bought for his father. To the others, King gave his name and accepted financial responsibility for their welfare. He also has five ''informally adopted'' children.

Around 1953 King ended his business relations with Robert Henry, who was unversed in the music business beyond the Mississippi, Tennessee, and Arkansas area, and signed with Maurice Merrit, a Texan. With a steady string of records selling around 100,000 copies and dependable audiences, King found reliable back–up musicians and began touring again. The pace was demanding—in 1956 King played 342 one–night stands. This pace continued into the 1980s.

During King's early days of touring, he and his 15 to 20 person crew traveled in a bus that they dubbed ''Big Red.'' Touring was difficult for black musicians, who faced discrimination when traveling in the South. Touring also included the risk of injury due to accidents on the road. For example, King's bus was involved in a fiery crash in Texas in 1958. Although King was not on the bus and no passengers were killed, the insurance on the bus had lapsed that weekend and King had to pay a liability of $100,000. King has been involved in other automobile accidents. In 1961 he was thrown through a windshield and his right arm was cut to the bone. After treatment he managed to go on and fulfill his engagement, using his left hand to play his electric guitar. This incident illustrates King's determination to honor his engagements, which is a constant of his career. Only in recent years has King slackened the pace of his work. In 1990 he was hospitalized in Las Vegas because of diabetes. This forced him to miss dates at the New Orleans Jazz and Heritage Festival.

On June 4, 1958, King married for a second time. His wife, Sue Carol Hall, was just 18, 15 years younger than King. In 1966, the marriage ended primarily because of tensions brought about by King's constant touring.

Besides the dissolution of his marriage, King had other problems in 1966. The IRS put a $78,000 lien on his income, and his bus was stolen. More important still was King's suspicion that he was at an impasse in his music career. Although King was still touring, selling records in modest numbers, and appearing before black audiences, he had been unsuccessful as an opening act for the Rolling Stones, who had insisted on using him because of their veneration for his guitar playing. The audience booed his slow blues opening numbers and he had not been well received by white audiences during the prior two concerts.

At the same time other black performers were achieving the rewards of crossover stardom. Black rock and roll performers had won recognition since the 1950s on; Motown, with its black recording stars, was achieving major successes in popular music. Still, contemporary blues was almost completely confined to black audiences. Many young blacks were beginning to perceive King's music as old–fashioned. (Today his audiences are 90% white, a fact King deplores because he feels that black youth are neglecting their heritage.) Eventually, many white music enthusiasts, collectors, and folk singers began searching out old–time black blues performers after becoming dissatisfied with the contemporary urban blues musicians and their electronically amplified instruments.

Becomes a National Star

In 1965 white artist Bob Butterfield and his group (two of the five backup people were black) released the first amplified blues album to have mass distribution; it was a steady seller rather than a one–time hit and attracted attention to black Chicago blues players. Players, especially guitar players, began to attract attention, a trend furthered by Charles Keil's *Urban Blues* (1967), which included a chapter on B. B. King. Moreover, a small coffeehouse in Cambridge, Massachusetts, achieved renown by booking performers like Butterfield, Muddy Waters, and Howlin' Wolf. Word of this success opened other venues across the country.

For King the breakthrough came a little later in 1968. When he received a standing ovation from a largely white audience at San Francisco's Fillmore West even before he played a single note; this occasion marked his first successful appearance before a white audience. Soon thereafter, "The Thrill is Gone" became a hit, peaking at number 15 on the pop charts, King's highest rating ever. Subsequent records and albums would regularly make the charts, but never higher than number 28.

When King hired new manager Sidney A. Seidenberg, a New York accountant who had been keeping his books, Seidenberg immediately began to upgrade the performer's career by moving King to Associated Booking, renegotiating his contract with ABC records, and raising his minimum booking fee. (King changed labels in 1978 when MCA absorbed ABC.) Top jazz clubs and rock venues now featured King. Perhaps just as important in building a new long–term audience were his appearances on college and university campuses, where he became extremely popular. Guest host Flip Wilson invited him to the *Johnny Carson Show,* and other television talk shows soon followed. King's appearance on the *Ed Sullivan Show* on October 8, 1970, serves as a symbolic marker of his complete breakthrough to the mass audience.

King's music maintained a stable level of popularity from that point. He toured Australia and Europe in 1971, did a world tour in 1972, and was invited by the Soviet government to perform in the USSR in 1979. King, who has also performed in community theaters and in Las Vegas, primarily attracts middle–aged, middle–class Americans, although his music has touched a much broader audience. In 1973, Tougaloo awarded him an honorary doctorate, as did Yale University in 1977.

King is also active in philanthropy. In addition to his appearances at benefit concerts for such organizations as the NAACP and the National Coalition for the Homeless, he was one of the cofounders of the Foundation for the Advancement of Inmate Rehabilitation and Recreation in 1971. In 1982 he donated his collection of 20,000 records, which includes 7,000 rare blues 78s, to the Center for the Study of Southern Culture at the University of Mississippi.

In 1971 King received his first Grammy as Best Rhythm and Blues Performer for "The Thrill Is Gone." He later received Grammies for Best Ethnic or Traditional Recording in 1982, 1984, 1986, and 1991. In 1987 he was inducted into the Rock 'n' Roll Hall of Fame. The Grammies' sponsor, the National Academy of Recording Artists and Songwriters (NARAS), gave King a Lifetime Achievement Award in 1988. In 1990 he was awarded the Presidential Medal of Freedom and a star on Hollywood's Walk of Fame. In that same year he rode on the Mississippi float in the Rose Bowl Parade and in the following year led the Sula Social Aid and Pleasure Club float at the Mardi Gras parade in New Orleans. In 1991 King opened the 350 seat B. B. King's Memphis Blues Club in Memphis, Tennessee. When King visited Pope John Paul II during a special audience at the Vatican for artists in the Vatican's 1997 Christmas concert, he donated his famous guitar and 50–year companion, "Lucille," to the

Pope. The NARAS Lifetime Achievement Award has perhaps summed up his lifetime achievement by asserting that King is "one of the most original and soulful of all blues guitarists and singer, whose compelling style and devotion to musical truth have inspired so many budding performer, both here and abroad to celebrate the blues."

Current address: c/o Sidney A. Seidenberg, 1414 Avenue of the Americas, New York, NY 10019.

REFERENCES

Cantor, Louis. *Wheelin' On Beale.* New York: Pharos Books, 1992.

Cohn, Lawrence, and others. *Nothing But the Blues.* New York: Abbeville Press, 1993.

Harris, Sheldon. *Blues Who's Who.* New Rochelle, NY: Arlington House, 1979. Reprint, New York: Da Capo, 1981.

King, B.B., with David Ritz. *Blues All Around Me.* New York: Avon Books, 1996.

The New Grove Dictionary of American Music. New York: Macmillan, 1986.

"Newsmakers." *Jet* 93 (12 January 1998): 25.

Norment, Lynn. "B. B. King Talks About the Blues and History." *Ebony* 47 (February 1992): 44–50.

Oliver, Paul. *The Story of the Blues.* Radnor, PA: Chilton, 1969.

Rock Movers and Shakers. Santa Barbara, CA: ABC–Clio, 1991.

Sawyer, Charles. *The Arrival of B. B. King.* Garden City, NJ: Doubleday, 1980.

Who's Who among Black Americans. 8th ed. Detroit: Gale Research, 1994.

Robert L. Johns

Martin Luther King Jr.

(1929–1968)

Civil rights leader, minister

At the age of 26, Martin Luther King Jr. took up the leadership role that would fill the rest of his life. He furthered the stubborn determination of black Americans to break down the limits of a racist society. His strategy of nonviolent protest brought passage of far–reaching federal legislation that undermined southern efforts to enforce segregation through local laws. His vision of a just and equal society where race would be transcended fired the imagination of many Americans.

Michael King Jr. was born on January 15, 1929, in the Atlanta home of his maternal grandfather, Adam Daniel Williams (1863–1931). He was the second child and the first son of Michael King Sr. (1897–1984) and Alberta Christine Williams King (1903–1974). Michael Jr. had an older sister, Willie Christine (b. 1927), and a younger brother, Alfred Daniel Williams (b. 1930). The father and later the son adopted the name Martin Luther, after the religious figure who founded the Lutheran denomination.

The family background was rooted in rural Georgia. A.D. Williams was already a minister himself when he moved from the country to Atlanta in 1893. There he took over a small struggling church with some 13 members, Ebenezer Baptist. In 1899 Williams married Jennie Celeste Parks (1873–1941). The couple had one child that survived, Alberta Christine, M.L. King Jr.'s mother. A.D. Williams was a forceful preacher who built Ebenezer into a major church.

Michael King Sr. came to Atlanta in 1918. He had known the hard life of a sharecropper in a poor farming country. His father, James Albert King (1864–1933), was irreligious, became an alcoholic, and beat his wife, Delia Linsey King (1873–1924). In the fall of 1926, Michael Sr. married Alberta Williams after a courtship of some eight years. The newlyweds moved into A. D. Williams's home.

When Williams died in 1931, Michael King Sr. followed in his father–in–law's footsteps as pastor of Ebenezer Baptist Church. King, too, became a very successful minister. The King children grew up in a secure and loving environment. As King Jr. said in "An Autobiography of Religious Development," an essay written for a class at Crozer Seminary when he was 23: "It is quite easy for me to think of a God of love mainly because I grew up in a family where love was central and where lovely relationships were ever present."

King Sr. was inclined to be a severe disciplinarian, but his wife's firm gentleness—which was by no means permissive—generally carried the day. The parents could not, of course, shield the young boy from racism. King Sr. did not endure racism meekly; in showing open impatience with segregation and its effects and in discouraging the development of a sense of class superiority in his children, King Sr. influenced his son profoundly.

King Jr. entered public school when he was five. On May 1, 1936, King joined his father's church, being baptized two days later. His conversion was not dramatic—he simply followed his sister when she went forward. A period of questioning religion began with adolescence and lasted through his early college years. He felt uncomfortable with overly

Martin Luther King Jr.

emotional religion, and this discomfort initially led him to decide against entering the ministry.

Jennie Williams, King Jr.'s grandmother, died of a heart attack on May 18, 1941, during a Woman's Day program at Ebenezer. The death was traumatic for her grandson, especially since it happened while he was watching a parade despite his parents' prohibitions. Distraught, he seems to have attempted suicide by leaping from a second–story window of the family home. He wept on and off for days and had difficulty sleeping.

King studied in the public schools of Atlanta, spent time at the Atlanta Laboratory School until it closed in 1942, and then entered public high school in the tenth grade, skipping a grade. After completing his junior year at Booker T. Washington High School, he entered Morehouse College in the fall of 1944 at the age of 15. Since the war had taken away most young men, Morehouse, a men's college, turned to young entrants in desperation.

Attends Morehouse

The five–foot seven–inch tall King was a ladies' man and loved to dance. He was an indifferent student who completed Morehouse with a grade point average of 2.48 on a four–point scale. At first King was determined not to become a minister, and he majored in sociology. Under the influence of his junior–year Bible class, however, he renewed his faith. Although he did not return to a literal belief in scripture, King began to envision a career in the ministry. In the fall of his senior year he told his father of his decision. King Jr. preached his trial sermon at Ebenezer with great success. On February 25, 1948, he was ordained and became associate pastor at Ebenezer.

King decided to attend Crozer Theological Seminary in Chester, Pennsylvania, a very liberal school. King rose to the challenges of Crozer, earning the respect of both his professors and classmates. In addition to becoming the valedictorian of his class in 1951, he was also elected student body president, won a prize as outstanding student, and earned a fellowship for graduate study. During this time, King also rebelled against his father's conservatism and now made no secret about drinking beer, smoking, and playing pool. He became enamored of a white woman and went through a difficult time before he could bring himself to break off the affair.

During his last year at Crozer, King began to read the iconoclastic theologian Reinhold Niebuhr. Niebuhr and his challenge to liberal theology—and thus, to King's own ideas at the time—became the most important single influence on King's intellectual development, far surpassing his later interest in Mahatma Gandhi. After being accepted for doctoral study at Yale University, Boston University, and in Edinburgh, Scotland, he enrolled in graduate school at Boston University in the fall of 1951.

As King pursued his graduate studies, he also sought a wife. Early in 1952 he met Coretta Scott, an aspiring singer. She was the daughter of Obie and Bernice Scott, born in Heiberger, Alabama, on April 27, 1927. Growing up on her father's farm, she learned to work hard before attending Antioch College. King's parents opposed the marriage at first, but King prevailed and the marriage took place in June of 1953. King Jr. and Coretta had four children: Yolanda (b. November 17, 1955), Martin Luther III (b. October 23, 1957), Dexter (b. January 30, 1961), and Bernice Albertine (b. March 28, 1963).

In September of 1954 while still working on his dissertation, King became pastor of the Dexter Avenue Baptist Church in Montgomery, Alabama. King completed his Ph.D. dissertation comparing the religious views of Paul Tillich and Henry Nelson Wieman, and was awarded the degree in June of 1955. In November of 1990, scholars confirmed that significant parts of King's dissertation had been taken from the work of a fellow student, Jack Boozer, and one of the subjects of his dissertation, Paul Tillich.

The Montgomery Bus Boycott

On Thursday, December 1, 1955, Rosa Parks refused to give up her seat on a Birmingham bus, setting off a chain of events that catapulted King to world fame. Several groups within Montgomery's black community decided to take action against segregated seating on the city buses. The NAACP, the Women's Political Council, the Baptist Ministers Conference, and the city's African Methodist Episcopal (AME) Zionist ministers united with the community to organize a bus boycott. After a successful beginning of the boycott on Monday, the Montgomery Improvement Association (MIA) came into being that afternoon, and King accepted the presidency. His oratory at that evening's mass meeting roused the crowd's enthusiasm, and the boycott continued. It took 381 days of struggle to bring the boycott to a successful conclusion.

As MIA leader, King became the focus of white hatred. On the afternoon of January 26, King was arrested for the first time, spending some time in jail before being released. About midnight he was awakened by a hate phone call. As he sat thinking of the dangers to his family, he had his first profound religious experience. As he wrote in *Stride Toward Freedom:*

> At that moment I experienced the presence of the Divine as I had never experienced Him before. It seemed as though I could hear the quiet assurance of an inner voice saying: "Stand up for righteousness, stand up for truth; and God will be at your side forever."

On January 30, the King home was bombed. The bombing inspired the MIA to file a federal suit directly attacking the laws establishing bus segregation. In the second half of February the white establishment decided to arrest nearly 100 blacks for violating Alabama's anti–boycott law. These arrests focused national attention on Montgomery. King was arrested, tried, and convicted on March 22. The following weekend he gave his first speeches in the North.

In April, the U.S. Supreme Court struck down laws requiring bus segregation. Montgomery's mayor refused to yield. After long legal procedures, the Supreme Court's order to end bus segregation was served in Montgomery on Thursday, December 20, 1956. Despite jeopardized jobs, intimidation by the Ku Klux Klan, police harassment, and bombings, the success of the boycott became apparent when King and several allies boarded a public bus in front of King's home on December 21, 1956.

King was in Atlanta when five bombs went off at parsonages and churches in Montgomery in the early morning of January 10, 1957. On this date, a two–day meeting was scheduled to begin in Ebenezer Baptist Church to lay out plans to create an organization to maintain the momentum of the movement for change throughout the South. King returned to Montgomery to inspect the bomb damage, and was present for only the final hours of the meeting. In a follow–up meeting in New Orleans on February 14, the group adopted the name Southern Christian Leadership Conference (SCLC) and elected King president. King made his first trip abroad to attend the independence ceremonies in Ghana on March 5, 1958. In June, King received the NAACP's Spingarn Medal for his leadership.

King and his organization became increasingly estranged from the NAACP's Roy Wilkins, who feared the effect of another mass black organization on the NAACP's branches in the South and also disapproved of the SCLC's call for direct action. Nonetheless, King pressed forward and the SCLC's plans for a voter registration drive beginning in 1958 went forward. In need of a capable organizer at the Atlanta office, the SCLC's first choice was Bayard Rustin, who was a very effective worker but also vulnerable to smears because of his homosexuality. Rustin found a role at SCLC in a less visible position. Ella Baker came to Atlanta to take Rustin's place and shouldered much of the initial burden of organizational work for the SCLC. In spite of her efforts, the 1958 Lincoln Day launch of the voter registration drive failed to attract much attention, and the SCLC seemed on the point of disappearing.

As King was writing his book on the Montgomery boycott, *Stride Toward Freedom,* he benefited from the very frank criticism of white New York lawyer Stanley D. Levinson, who became one of King's most trusted advisors. Levinson was also a key factor in the FBI's later surveillance of King: there were allegations of a connection between Levinson and the Communist Party that formed one of the legal bases for wiretaps of King's telephone communications. FBI chief J. Edgar Hoover ordered those wiretaps as well as surveillance of King, of King's advisors outside the SCLC, and of their relationships to Communism and homosexuality. The FBI hoped to use the information to discredit King and his organization.

In June of 1958, King joined A. Philip Randolph, Roy Wilkins, and National Urban League leader Lester B. Granger in an unsatisfactory meeting with President Dwight D. Eisenhower. In September King was again arrested in Montgomery as he tried to enter a courtroom. King decided to serve his 14–day jail sentence for refusing to obey an officer rather than pay the $14 fine. He avoided jail time, however, as the police commissioner paid the fine to avoid the publicity King would have garnered. After this police incident, while at a book signing, King was critically stabbed by a deranged black woman.

King spent some time convalescing. In early February of 1959 he, his wife, and his biographer, Lawrence D. Reddick, embarked on a busy 30–day trip to India, sponsored by the Gandhi Memorial Trust. Through much of the year, SCLC floundered in the face of organizational and financial problems, aggravated by the lack of a clear goal beyond voter registration. On November 29, 1959, King announced his resignation from Dexter Avenue Baptist Church to move to Atlanta to take on full–time responsibilities at SCLC.

The Sit–ins Begin

Student activism provided the spark that gave new life to the Civil Rights Movement. On February 1, 1960, four students from North Carolina Agricultural and Technical College (now University) demanded service at a Woolworth lunch counter in Greensboro and continued to sit after their demands were refused. The sit–ins spread rapidly across the South. The first contact between the students and the SCLC occurred on February 16, 1960, as King delivered a well–received speech at a meeting held in Durham to coordinate more sit–ins. As soon as King returned to Atlanta, he discovered he was under indictment for perjury on his Alabama state tax forms. The ongoing legal procedures would be a matter of great concern to King until an all–white jury returned a verdict of not guilty on May 28, after a three–day trial.

Ella Baker, who realized she could not continue her active leadership role at SCLC much longer, arranged a meeting of student leaders at Shaw University beginning on April 15. King had the votes to establish the student movement as a branch of the SCLC but did not wish to alienate Baker, who aimed at an independent organization. Thus, the Student Nonviolent Coordinating Committee (SNCC) came into existence. Nonetheless, as the sit–ins continued, the adult leaders continued to quarrel; in particular, Roy Wilkins of the NAACP was still very unhappy. Rustin offered to resign from SCLC and King accepted. Ella Baker also left, with bitter feelings on both sides.

On October 2, 1960, King reluctantly joined a renewal of sit–ins at Rich's Department Store in Atlanta. King was arrested and spent his first night ever in jail. A compromise freed all participants except King, who was held as being in violation of the terms of probation for an earlier traffic ticket. Sentenced to a four–month term in prison, he was taken to the state prison at Reidsville, Georgia. Presidential candidate John F. Kennedy called Coretta Scott King to express sympathy, and continued legal efforts secured King's release after eight days in jail. On March 10, 1961, in spite of his private reservations, King spoke in favor of a compromise desegregation plan for Atlanta and won the support of the student organizers, who previously had vociferously labeled the plan a sell–out.

On May 4 the Congress on Racial Equality (CORE) launched the Freedom Rides, inaugurating a new phase in the struggle. On May 14 in Anniston, Alabama, the Freedom Riders encountered violent resistance. After further major trouble in Birmingham, they arrived in Montgomery on May 20 to be beaten by a white mob. At a Montgomery rally on May 21, King called for a large–scale nonviolent campaign against segregation in Alabama. A white mob surrounded the church where the rally took place, and the participants could not leave until about six the following morning.

King continued a heavy speaking program, bringing in sizable amounts of money to finance SCLC. In August SCLC joined SNCC, the NAACP, the National Urban League, and CORE in establishing the Voter Education Program (VEP). Over the next years considerable friction surfaced between VEP and SCLC over the SCLC's handling of money and its lackluster efforts in some areas. The leading organization of black Baptists also attacked King at this time. Under its leader, Joseph H. Jackson, the National Baptist Convention opposed the sit–ins. In August, Jackson held back an attempt by younger ministers to replace him and denounced King in very strong terms. This dispute eventually led King's supporters to form a rival organization, the Progressive Baptist Convention. At the same time King was involved in a dispute with SNCC over funding. The students felt SCLC owed SNCC part of the funds King's organization raised.

The Albany and Birmingham Challenges

In November of 1961 SNCC's attempt to establish a voter registration drive in Albany, Georgia, became a major learning experience. King made his first personal effort in December; in August of 1962, he gave up the attempt to break down segregation there. The police chief of Albany discerned that the real threat to segregation came from the use of violence, which would provoke federal intervention. He broke the momentum of the protest, and cooperation between SNCC, SCLC, the NAACP, and local blacks broke down in mutual recrimination.

In December the bombing of a Birmingham church drew King's attention to that city. Not only did Fred Shuttleworth's Alabama Christian Movement for Human Rights appear so well–established as to reduce the possibility of friction between various black factions, Birmingham's public safety commissioner, Eugene "Bull" Connor, was an ideal opponent. A staunch segregationist with a hot temper and little judgment, Connor was sure to make hasty mistakes and resort to violence.

The campaign got off to a shaky start, but Connor, now a lame–duck but clinging to office, helped immensely by unleashing police dogs to attack marchers. In a series of meetings King was able to bring local black leaders to his support—he had belatedly discovered that Shuttleworth was distrusted by many—but problems remained. An intense discussion of strategy with his coworkers ensued. If King did not get himself arrested, he would seem to be making the same kind of retreat that had happened in Albany; if he did, he risked being cut off from the movement at a crucial juncture. After 30 minutes of solitary prayer, King announced his decision to court arrest.

Having been arrested, King passed a difficult first night in solitary confinement, but over the next few days, events began to justify his decision. National support grew and money for bail flowed in—Harry Belafonte, for example, managed to raise $50,000. President Kennedy again made the gesture of telephoning his sympathy to Coretta Scott King.

Before he was released from jail nine days after his arrest, King read an open letter signed by eight white clergymen who denounced demonstrations. King set down a 20–page response called ''Letter from Birmingham Jail.'' This document became the most quoted and influential of King's writings. To keep the demonstrations going, James Bevel now recruited schoolchildren who began to march on May 2. Six hundred people went to jail that day. In a few days Connor turned fire hoses as well as dogs on the demonstrators. On May 10, under pressure from the White House, white businesses made some concessions to black demands. Since King found it increasingly difficult to restrain his followers from violence, he accepted the rather weak concessions and declared victory.

In the wake of Birmingham, King turned his attention to a march on Washington as a way of keeping up pressure for federal civil rights legislation. There were long and difficult negotiations between all parties concerned before the August event came into being.

On August 28, 1963, King won his gamble for a massive nonviolent protest in the nation's capital, even as events in the country seemed to be outpacing nonviolence. The peaceful demonstration drew some 200,000 blacks and whites to the steps of the Lincoln Memorial, and King delivered his most famous public address, the ''I Have a Dream'' speech.

As King kept up a hectic schedule of engagements and speeches, the FBI increased its surveillance. The strain on his family life was so great that he and Coretta King had a telephone quarrel, duly recorded by the FBI. The problems in SCLC continued: staff frictions made it difficult to settle on plans for future direct action. On July 2, 1964, the movement celebrated a victory as President Lyndon B. Johnson signed a new Civil Rights Act. Still, problems were mounting. A white backlash grew in the North and South, and the Ku Klux Klan indulged in increased violence in the South.

FBI director J. Edgar Hoover was determined to discredit King; in November of 1964 the FBI sent King a tape of one of his encounters with another woman, along with a note recommending suicide. Rumors of King's infidelities had circulated since the early 1950s but remained principally speculative until Ralph Abernathy's book, with its frank admission of adulteries, brought the matter into the open in 1989.

In October of 1964, as a result of extreme fatigue, King entered a hospital in Atlanta. It was at the hospital that King learned he had received the Nobel Peace Prize for 1964. He was 35–years old. Earlier that year, King became the first black American to be named *Time* magazine's ''Man of the Year.'' Journalists and politicians from around the world turned to King for his views on a wide range of issues. However, as King stated in his Nobel acceptance speech, he remained committed to the ''twenty–two million Negroes of the United States of America engaged in a creative battle to end the long night of racial injustice.''

In the wake of the Civil Rights Act of 1964, SCLC determined to target obstacles to voting, and Selma, Alabama seemed to be the right place to begin. SCLC dramatized its point on national television on May 7, 1965, when the attempt to march from Selma to Montgomery was brutally stopped by the police. President Johnson then asked Congress for a voting rights bill, which was passed in August. This was also the month that revealed the depth of black frustration outside the South. A civil disturbance in the Watts section of Los Angeles lasted six days and cost 34 lives, ushering in a period of several years of endemic urban unrest.

It was not clear how SCLC and King could move from their civil rights work in the South to addressing the economic problems of poverty in the North and elsewhere. In 1966, King undertook a Campaign to End Slums in Chicago. After nine months the campaign ended in failure. King discovered the liberal consensus on race relations stopped short of fundamental economic change. In addition, President Johnson's preoccupation with the war in Vietnam undermined government attention to internal reforms.

King took a stance against American involvement in Vietnam. His position in the Civil Rights Movement was under challenge, and the whole movement fell apart. SNCC began to repudiate him in June of 1966 as members adopted the slogan ''Black Power,'' while rejecting white allies and calling for the use of violence. In October King announced plans for a new initiative in 1968, the Poor People's Campaign. King wanted to recruit poor men and women from urban and rural areas—of all races and backgrounds—and lead them in a campaign for economic rights.

In an attempt to raise money for the campaign, King accepted an invitation to speak in support of Memphis sanitation workers on March 18, 1968. A mishandled demonstration on March 28 collapsed in disorder. King planned a new, better–organized demonstration and gave a very moving address to an audience of 500 at Memphis Temple on April 3. He spoke of and accepted the possibility of his own death, a recurring theme in his speeches. The following evening, shortly after 5:30 p.m., King was shot and killed on the balcony outside his motel room.

King's assassination led to disturbances in well over 100 cities and, before the violence subsided on April 11, the deaths of 46 people (mostly African Americans), 35,000 injuries, and 20,000 people jailed. On April 9 King's funeral was held in

Ebenezer; in addition to the 800 people crammed into the sanctuary, a crowd of 60,000 to 70,000 stood in the streets. He was buried in Southview Cemetery, near his grandmother. On his crypt were carved the words he often used:

Free At Last, Free At Last
Thank God Almighty
I'm Free At Last.

In 1986 Martin Luther King Jr.'s birthday became a national holiday. While alive, King became the symbol of hope for African Americans and for America as a whole that brotherhood and sisterhood could be obtained. The quintessential black leader, King's legacy reminds one of how far America has come, and how far it still has to go.

REFERENCES

Abernathy, Ralph. *And the Walls Came Tumbling Down.* New York: Harper and Row, 1989.

Baldwin, Lewis V. *There Is A Balm in Gilead.* Minneapolis: Fortress Press, 1991.

Branch, Taylor. *Parting the Waters.* New York: Simon and Schuster, 1988.

Carson, Clayborne, ed. *The Papers of Martin Luther King, Jr.* Berkeley: University of California Press, 1992.

Current Biography Yearbook. New York: H. W. Wilson, 1957.

Fairclough, Adam. *Martin Luther King, Jr.* Athens: University of Georgia Press, 1995.

Franklin, John Hope, and August Meier, eds. *Black Leaders of the Twentieth Century.* Chicago: University of Illinois Press, 1982.

Garrow, David J. *Bearing the Cross.* New York: William Morrow, 1986.

King, Coretta Scott. *My Life with Martin Luther King, Jr.* New York: Holt, Rinehart, and Winston, 1969.

King, Martin Luther Jr. *Stride Toward Freedom.* New York: Harper, 1958.

King, Martin Luther Sr., with Clayton Riley. *Daddy King: An Autobiography.* New York: William Morrow, 1980.

Lewis, David L. *King: A Critical Biography.* New York: Praeger, 1970.

Miller, Keith D. *Voice of Deliverance.* New York: Free Press, 1992.

Oates, Stephen B. *Let the Trumpet Sound.* New York: Harper and Row, 1982.

Reddick, Lawrence D. *Crusader Without Violence.* New York: Harper, 1959.

Smith, Jessie Carney, ed. *Notable Black American Women.* 2 vols. Detroit: Gale Research, 1992, 1996.

COLLECTIONS

The papers of Martin Luther King Jr. are in the Special Collections Department of Boston University and in Martin Luther King, Jr. Library, and Archives in Atlanta, Georgia.

Robert L. Johns and Leslie Norback

King, Riley.

See King, B. B.

Thomy Lafon

(1810–1893)

Entrepreneur, philanthropist

A philanthropist and entrepreneur who rose from poverty to wealth, Thomy Lafon was a successful broker and real estate investor in New Orleans whose efforts as community activist and philanthropist began before the Civil War. After accumulating wealth through his own frugality and wise business ventures, he donated his fortune to individuals and to religious, charitable, and educational institutions in the city.

Born in New Orleans on December 28, 1810, a free man of color, Thomy Lafon was the son of Pierre Laralde, who was probably French or of black and French extraction, and Modest Foucher, who may have been of Haitian descent. While little is known about Lafon's early life, Laralde probably deserted the family when Lafon was a young child. Thus far, records do not show how the name Lafon was obtained. Although the family was poor, Lafon managed to secure an education and became fluent in English and French, leading to the speculation that he was partially educated in Europe.

At some point Lafon became a school teacher. By some accounts he sold cakes to workmen along the wharves as well. His rise to wealth had its roots in his business activities before the Civil War began, while he was still in his thirties. According to *African–American Business Leaders,* the New Orleans city directory listed Lafon as a merchant in 1842, with a business located at 387 Rampart Street. By other accounts he had operated a small drygoods store on Orleans Street about 1850, and by 1861 he had moved his business to 97 Exchange Street. Although the exact location and dates of his business may be questioned, it is certain that he kept the same business location during the war, and by 1867 the city directory shows that he had a new business address, 16 Exchange Place, and lived at 242 Ursuline. The 1868 directory identified him as a "broker." Until 1870, he was considered the city's second leading black broker. At some point he also loaned money to others at "advantageous rates of interest." He was highly successful in real estate investments; by 1860 his property was worth $10,000.

Apparently Lafon was an astute businessman. In the decade of the 1860s he concentrated on real estate and land speculation, including swampland, buying $60,000 in property and selling $20,000. By 1870 he had increased his wealth to $55,000. He continued to buy and sell real estate, adding to his wealth. A community activist and social leader, Lafon and other free blacks banded together during the decade prior to the Civil War and were leaders of the Radical Club of New Orleans. They supported the Union troops but also demanded that blacks have voting rights and access to white schools. They helped to support and run *The Tribune,* the South's first black newspaper after the war. In time, however, their efforts failed as black rights in New Orleans and the South eroded.

As free blacks began to face the increasingly hostile whites in New Orleans, Lafon concentrated on his private life and philanthropy. After investigating requests for financial assistance, he was always known to give freely to those in need. He was a devout Roman Catholic who firmly believed in the church's mission and in religious and charitable donations. His charities included the American Anti–Slavery Society, the Underground Railroad, and the Catholic Indigent Orphans Institute. He also supported two institutions that he founded: the Lafon Orphan Boy's Asylum and the Home for Aged Colored Men and Women.

A tall, gaunt man of olive complexion, regular features, and steel–grey and straight hair, Lafon has been described as physically weak with an emaciated look. He carried himself with utmost dignity and was always courteous. Although he was exceptionally frugal and shunned extravagance—a fact that contributed to his ability to accumulate wealth—he was always impeccably dressed in expensive clothing that consisted of a frock coat, a top hat of beaver, and a cane. Although he acquired several fine houses, he chose to live in a shabby, humble cottage with his sister, his sole companion and adviser. At his death on December 22, 1893, his will provided for his sister, several relatives and friends, and religious and charitable institutions including the Catholic Institute for the Care of Orphans, the Louisiana Asylum, Charity Hospital, Straight University and New Orleans universities, and to the city of New Orleans. His worth was estimated at half a million dollars.

In honor of his benevolence, Lafon's name is connected to a number of institutions in New Orleans and several parishes in the state. In 1898 the Thomy Lafon Public School was dedicated, becoming the first school in New Orleans named for a black man and the second named for a black person. He was also listed on the Wall of Fame at the 1939–40 World's Fair in New York with other blacks, Native Americans, and foreign–born Americans who had made notable contributions to the nation's culture and progress. He is remembered in Louisiana as one of the most popular and charitable black people the state has known.

REFERENCES

Blassingame, John. *Black New Orleans, 1860–1880.* Chicago: University of Chicago Press, 1973.

Ingham, John N., and Lynne B. Feldman. *African–American Business Leaders: A Biographical Dictionary.* Westport, CT: Greenwood Press, 1994.

Logan, Rayford W., and Michael R. Winston, eds. *Dictionary of American Negro Biography.* New York: Norton, 1982.

Malone, Dumas, ed. *Dictionary of American Biography.* New York: Charles Scribner's Sons, 1943.

Murray, Florence, compiler and ed. *The Negro Handbook.* New York: Wendell Malliet and Co., 1942.

Murray, J. M. "Thomy Lafon." *Negro History Bulletin* 7 (October 1943): 6, 20.

Perkins, A. E., ed. *Who's Who in Colored Louisiana.* Baton Rouge: Douglas Loan Co., 1930.

COLLECTIONS

Rudimentary information on Thomy Lafon may be found in records at St. Louis Cathedral and at the City Hall in New Orleans. His will is in the office of the Clerk of the Civil District Court for the Parish of New Orleans.

Frederick Douglas Smith Jr.

John Mercer Langston

John Mercer Langston
(1829–1897)
Lawyer, congressman, diplomat, educator, orator

On April 22, 1855, when John Mercer Langston was elected clerk of Brownhelm township in his adopted state of Ohio, he became the first known African American elected to public office in the United States. In 1890, after an election marred by charges of fraud and intimidation, Langston took his place as a member of the Fifty–first Congress of the U.S. House of Representatives from the Fourth Congressional District of Virginia. Despite his prominence and achievements as an attorney, elected official, educator, author, orator, and diplomat, Langston was a man for whom race was often determinative.

Langston's autobiography, *From the Virginia Plantation to the National Capitol,* stated "John Mercer Langston was born upon a plantation located three miles from Louisa Court House, in Louisa County, Virginia, on the 14th day of December in 1829." Langston was the youngest of four children born to the wealthy white plantation owner and Revolutionary War captain, Ralph Quarles, who was in his sixties, and his beautiful former slave, Lucy Jane Langston, who was in her forties. In 1806 Quarles manumitted Lucy Langston and her daughter, Maria, whom he had fathered. According to the terms of the manumission reprinted in Langston's autobiography, the mother and daughter were "free persons at liberty to go where they please and to exercise and enjoy all the rights of free persons." Lucy Langston took the terms literally in the matter of her legal and sexual freedom; she had three children—William, Harriet, and Mary Langston—who were born after manumission, and whom Quarles did not father. After this hiatus Quarles and Lucy Langston resumed their relationship and together bore Gideon, Charles Henry, and John Mercer Langston.

Unlike many of the liaisons between slave owners and their female slaves, the relationship between Captain Quarles, a bachelor, and Lucy Langston was lasting and open. Such forbidden relationships often produced resentment and shame in the offspring. This was not so for John Mercer Langston, who reconciled his difficult racial legacy. Cheek and Cheek noted in *John Mercer Langston*:

> In casting his father as a lonely man of conscience, rather than as an immoral slaveholder taking lustful advantage of his human property; his mother as intelligent and loving, accepting her lot "with becoming resignation," (even as he omitted explicit reference to her outside sexual involvement), Langston cloaked his parents with respectability, aristocracy, and affection. Heaven approved their union, because church and state would not.

While Quarles lived, his position and wealth protected his family. Upon his death in April of 1834, Quarles bequeathed to each of his three sons a one–third share of his estate which included some 2,030 acres, his personal property, his cash, and his stocks, which they were to receive upon reaching the age of 21. Quarles named four influential and wealthy white men of Louisa County to serve as executors. A short time later, Langston's mother, Lucy Jane Langston, died. She was buried on the plantation beside her one–time master and longtime lover, Ralph Quarles, according to his directions.

The Formative Years in Ohio

The untimely death of his parents left Langston an orphan of means at age four. His older brothers took him to live with William Gooch, one of the executors of the estate, who had recently moved to Chillicothe, Ohio. His guardians, the Gooch family, lovingly embraced and protected Langston as a full family member. He was even called Johnnie Gooch and educated at the best schools Chillicothe had to offer.

In 1839 William Gooch, lured by the claims of opportunity in Missouri, was caught up in the westward expansion. He sold his Chillicothe properties, purchased land in Missouri, and made plans to relocate his entire family, including Langston, to Missouri. There was one problem: Missouri was still a slave state. William Langston, John's half–brother, took the extraordinary action of instigating *habeas corpus* against Gooch, seeking to have Gooch removed as guardian of John Mercer Langston and to prevent his brother's relocation to Missouri. Because Missouri was a slave state, John Langston's freedom and inheritance would have been in jeopardy. William Langston prevailed. The court prevented the Gooch family from taking John Mercer Langston out of its jurisdiction to Missouri and named Richard Long, a New England Puritan abolitionist who had purchased the Gooch's farm, as the young lad's new guardian.

As a light–skinned mulatto who had been raised in a white privileged environment, Langston did not fully understand all that had gone on about him. The only thing this child of nine years of age knew with certainty was his anger and heartbreak over the loss of his only true friends, the Gooch family. He mourned them and desperately hoped to be reunited with them.

Langston's life with the Long family was radically different—much more strict, severe, and labor–focused—from his life with the Gooch family. Richard Long was preparing Langston to be a hardworking black man, driving a horse and cart, and working in the fields. This experience was in sharp contrast to Langston's years with the Gooch family where he was being groomed to be a gentlemen, his life being filled with such pleasures as books, games, dogs, and a lot of love and affection. He had lived with the Longs for approximately a year and a half when his older brother Gideon sent for Langston to come live with him in Cincinnati, one of the most segregated and violently anti–abolitionist cities in Ohio. Cincinnati was home to a large, growing, youthful population of blacks who were often skilled artisans and craftsmen.

The Cincinnati Years

The Cincinnati years were important ones for Langston, for it was then that he was totally immersed in a black community for the first time in his life. His brother Gideon Langston was one of the leaders of black Cincinnati. As a bachelor who owned a barbershop and the city's only black–owned livery stable, Gideon was not the ideal person to care for a growing adolescent. He arranged for his younger brother to live with a fellow community leader, John Woodson, and his family. Woodson impressed upon those in his household and anyone else who would listen the importance of industry, morality, temperance, and virtue. Langston attended church and Sabbath school regularly at Bethel AME Church where Woodson was superintendent. He also attended the school, operated by two black ministers, where he was one of the star pupils.

Racial tensions mounted in Cincinnati during the spring and summer of 1841. On the night of September 3, 1841, a marauding white mob assaulted blacks on the streets of Cincinnati and unleashed a barbarous and deadly attack on the homes and businesses of black people in the section of town where Langston lived with the Woodsons. After razing a black confectioner's store and shouting down the mayor, who attempted to disperse the mob, the white rioters continued their advance into the black neighborhood. The well–armed blacks courageously defended their families, homes, and businesses. Their defense succeeded; the white mob retreated; and the struggle continued, but with different tactics. After the riot the whites used the enforcement of the infamous Black Laws as another way to control and weaken Cincinnati's black citizens. These laws required bonding, return of all fugitive slaves, repudiation of the doctrines and activities of abolitionists, and most immediately, the total disarmament and arrest of black lawbreakers. Raiding whites resorted to vigilantism, rounding up and arresting hundreds of black men, even though they had complied with the Black Laws.

After the riots, Langston moved from his former residence with the Woodsons to the home of William W. Watson and his family. With this move he was closer to school and to his older brother Gideon. William Watson was an industrious man of considerable means who owned a barbershop and bathhouse. Langston continued his formal studies, but worked in his landlord's businesses on the weekend.

The Cincinnati years were very important in Langston's growth and maturation. It was in Cincinnati that he experienced the power of black self–determination. In that city he was also exposed to some of the best oratory and antislavery rhetoric which, no doubt, helped him develop his own eloquence as a public speaker. Langston returned to Chillicothe in the spring of 1843, two years after he had arrived in Cincinnati, the city that indelibly shaped his philosophy about black freedom and empowerment.

The Oberlin Years

In Chillicothe Langston requested that the probate court name his half–brother, William, as his guardian. His request was granted, but because William was a bachelor, he boarded his youngest sibling with Harvey Hawes and his wife, a well–to–do black couple with substantial land holdings. In November of 1843, John Langston enrolled in the Chillicothe black school, where he was taught by two of Oberlin's early black students, George Vashon of Pittsburgh and William Cuthbert Whitehorne of Jamaica. (Vashon later became Oberlin College's first black graduate in 1844.) The two so favorably impressed Langston that he aspired to attend the preparatory department of Oberlin Collegiate Institute. William, Langston's older half–brother and guardian, was against the idea. Because of his success as a carpenter, William felt should learn a trade. With much prodding from William's younger half–brothers, Charles and Gideon, and Langston's teacher, George Vashon, William consented to a year of preparatory school at Oberlin.

Langston's admission to Oberlin continued a family tradition begun in 1835 when his older brothers, Gideon and Charles, had enrolled in the preparatory, thus becoming the first blacks to enroll at Oberlin. After a brief teaching stint in Chillicothe following the conclusion of his first year in the preparatory department, Langston returned to Oberlin and completed his preparatory course in time to be admitted to the college in the fall of 1845. He graduated with a B.A. in August of 1849.

After graduation from Oberlin, Langston pursued his ambition of becoming a lawyer, but the odds were against him. Up to that time, only three blacks had gained entry into the American legal profession, but Langston was determined nonetheless. By late December of 1849, Langston had begun studying law with abolitionist lawyer Sherlock J. Andrews of Cleveland. Andrews supplied Langston with the necessary legal textbooks and was to have provided occasional explication, but that arrangement was soon terminated. Next Langston sought admission to Ballston Spa, a law school in Saratoga County, New York, at the urging of a college friend who was a law student there. Langston was denied admission because of his race.

Langston indignantly rejected suggestions that he pass for a Spaniard, a Frenchman, or a Latin American or that he sit silently outside the regular classroom in the recitation area and slowly nudge his way closer into the classroom, if no one objected. He subsequently applied to Timothy Walker's noted Cincinnati Law School and was again rejected because it was believed that white students would not feel at home with a black classmate. He did not give up on his goal of becoming a lawyer, but rather he channeled his energies and idealism into black protest and reform through the Ohio black convention movement.

The Ohio black convention movement was said to be the most aggressive and sustained of the various black movements in the northern states. From 1837 until the outbreak of war, there were 21 conventions in Ohio. The agendas for the conventions ranged from organizing privately–funded black schools to acquiring common school privileges, and from repealing the Black Laws to full enfranchisement of blacks. Because the conventions often coincided with the opening of the state legislature, the conventions were often held in Columbus. The conventions were important training grounds in democracy, leadership, and political organizing; they were clearinghouses of vital information on land, markets, and employment, and on strategies for dealing with local or statewide issues; and they were confidence building and affirming to the dignity and worth of black people. The outstanding oratory of the Ohio state convention movement inspired listeners to recommit themselves to the struggle for freedom, justice, and equality for blacks.

In the fall of 1850, Langston enrolled in the Theology Department at Oberlin. While pursuing his theology degree and continuing his involvement with the Ohio black convention movement, Langston began to embrace and articulate a black nationalist consciousness. Langston and his allies vigorously condemned African colonization, but advocated emigration to form separate black communities in areas ranging from Canada to the West Indies. Emigration was to be the means by which blacks could achieve self–determination and nationalism based on self–respect, self–help, self–defense, solidarity, and insistence on the rights of all people. For his support of emigration, Langston incurred the wrath of Frederick Douglass and other abolitionists. He continued to wrestle with the pros and cons of emigration, black destiny, and black nationhood, privately, for the next several years.

Regardless of his interest in emigration, Langston felt compelled to work against slavery and injustice. Langston was gaining a considerable reputation as a political leader. In Oberlin he spoke out against the antiblack political planks of the Whigs and Democrats. In the summer of 1852 Langston became a supporter of the Free Democratic Party, primarily because of its seemingly fair treatment of blacks. The party recognized black convention delegates, elected Frederick Douglass as secretary, condemned the Fugitive Slave Law, and called for diplomatic relations with Haiti. Langston campaigned tirelessly throughout the state for the Free Democratic candidates. However, Langston's association with the Free Democrats was disappointing and grew strained when the party refused to endorse a resolution for black enfranchisement. Later, however, the Free Democratic state convention adopted a platform that endorsed black suffrage.

Langston's political activism on behalf of the Free Democratic Party put him in contact with Philemon Bliss, a leading attorney and newspaper publisher from Elyria, who agreed to allow Langston to study law in his office. The Free Democratic Party was antislavery and worked to suppress legislation or public sentiment which was oppressive as they vigorously denounced Ohio's political disenfranchisement of blacks. Langston's law studies began in the fall of 1853, shortly after he completed his degree in theology, at Oberlin. A committee of three from the five–member district court examined Langston thoroughly 12 months later on all aspects of the law. The examiners unanimously certified that Langston possessed the intellectual qualifications to discharge the duties of an attorney, and that he was of appropriate moral character and age. On the other hand, the examiners felt they could not qualify a black man to practice law because of existing laws which did not allow blacks to sue whites. However, they relied on an 1842 state supreme court decision, which said a ''nearer white than black'' mulatto was entitled to the rights of a white man. Deemed white enough, Langston was admitted to the Ohio state bar in September of 1854.

By 1854 Langston had become an opponent of emigration and a believer in a more humane, just, and integrated society in America. His participation as speaker and official in the State Convention of Colored Citizens of Ohio, the Colored National Convention at Rochester, New York, in July of 1853, the Ohio Anti–Slavery League, and the American Anti–Slavery Society which he addressed in May of 1854, helped to gain him wider recognition not only in the antislavery cause, but also as an advocate of colored schools with colored teachers in Ohio and for the importance of black commerce.

After some initial success as a lawyer, Langston began to contemplate marriage. He found his ideal mate in Caroline Wall of Rockingham, North Carolina. Like Langston, Caroline was the child of a white father—Colonel Stephen Wall, a planter and state senator—and a slave mother, Jane. Unlike Langston, Caroline bore her father's name. Caroline Wall combined the accepted feminine virtues with intelligence, education, a degree of independence, and racial commitment. In 1850 Caroline Wall and her sister Sara enrolled at Oberlin's preparatory department before matriculating at the women's collegiate level the next year. It was as Oberlin students that Caroline Wall and Langston met. After a measured courtship, they were married on October 5, 1854, at the home in Oberlin where Caroline boarded. After her marriage, Caroline Wall Langston completed her studies at Oberlin and graduated in 1856. Their first child, Arthur Dessalines Langston, was born on August 3, 1855, in Brownhelm, Ohio, only four months after Langston was elected clerk of Brownhelm township. In the spring of 1856 when his term as township clerk expired, Langston moved his young family to Oberlin where they lived until 1871.

In Oberlin, John and Caroline Langston expanded their family to include Ralph Eugene, born in 1857. Their first daughter, Chinque, was born in 1858, but died two and half year later. A second baby girl, Nettie De Ella, was born in 1861; and 1864 marked the arrival of the couple's third son and last child, Frank Mercer.

Becomes Lawyer and Elected Official

Upon reaching his majority in 1850, Langston purchased several parcels of land. Some of the land was intended to produce rental income for him, and a lush 50 acre farm near Lake Erie in Brownhelm township was to be his homestead. The newly–accredited lawyer became the first black inhabitant in the all–white abolitionist community of 1,200. The rigors of his theological studies; his total engrossment in the law; and the extensive lecturing, campaigning, and reform activities related to his ongoing commitment to racial advancement had taken a toll on his health. The cure for Langston's condition was two years of fresh air and physical exercise, to begin immediately after he completed his legal studies. The farm provided the necessary environment for his physical recovery, but it also established him as an independent, self–reliant yeoman farmer. The farm also served as an additional source of income should his law practice fail.

One week after he moved into his new home in Brownhelm, one of the town's leading attorneys, Hamilton Perry, asked Langston to assist in a very important case in which Perry's client was being sued for immediate possession of the house which he occupied. The plaintiff was represented by a far more experienced lawyer. Langston was ecstatic about the prospect of representing his first client, even as an assistant.

Langston conducted the cross–examination, presented the defense witnesses, and gave the summation, performing brilliantly. Spectators came from all of the surrounding areas to see and hear a black lawyer in court. The jury rendered a unanimous verdict for the defendant and Langston's future as a successful full–time lawyer with a lucrative practice was secure from that day forward.

Langston's status and stature in the Brownhelm community was evident when he was nominated for town clerk by the Independent Democrats. He handily won the election on April 2, 1855, more than 60 votes ahead of his ticket. With this victory, Langston became the first black elected to public office by popular vote in the United States. As a result of his triumph at the polls, Langston was invited to address the May meeting of the American Anti–Slavery Society, a very prestigious invitation and a speaking engagement he would long treasure. The speech was reported and published in the daily papers of New York and the leading journals and periodicals of the antislavery societies. In 1856, after the expiration of his term as clerk of Brownhelm, Langston moved his family to Oberlin where set up his law practice late in the fall of 1856. He continued his political activism, lectured widely on equal suffrage, and maintained an active relationship with his alma mater and its students. One year later on April 6, 1857, Langston was elected clerk of Russia township, his new home. It was the first time that abolitionist and fairly progressive Oberlin had ever elected a black to public office. The next year Langston was elected a member of the council of the incorporated village of Oberlin for two years, and in 1860, Langston was elected a member of Oberlin's first Board of Education, where he served successively for 11 years.

Langston handled many criminal cases; perhaps the most famous was his defense of Mary Edmonia Lewis, a black student at Oberlin, who was accused of poisoning her two white fellow boarders in 1862. The case aroused many passions on the campus and in the community. The accused girl was condemned by the majority of blacks in Oberlin; she was brutally beaten; and an attempt was made on the life of her lawyer, Langston. Subsequently, Mary Lewis was acquitted on the grounds of insufficient evidence. Later in life Edmonia Lewis, as she became known, was acknowledged as one of America's outstanding sculptors and the first African American sculptor of note.

In 1867, at the invitation of General Oliver O. Howard, Langston was asked to serve as inspector–general of the Freedmen's Bureau with responsibility for the schools of the freed people of the country. He traveled extensively in this position. Also in that year, he was admitted to practice before the U.S. Supreme Court. During the Civil War, Langston recruited black soldiers for the 54th and 55th Massachusetts and the 5th Ohio Regiments.

The Washington, D.C., Years

In 1869, because of his success as a lawyer and national statesman, Langston was offered a professorship in the Law Department of Howard University. Upon his arrival at Howard, he at once became dean of that department with responsibility for organizing it into a first rate law school. The school opened on January 6, 1869. Langston was dean of that law school for seven years. Because he served with such marked efficiency and success, Langston was asked to assume additional duties. He served as vice president and acting president of the university from 1873 to 1875, his last two years at Howard. While serving as vice president, Langston asked for clarification on his authority and responsibility, because of opposition he was receiving from white trustees. The board of trustees gave him the same authority as the school's president Oliver O. Howard. Howard resigned on Christmas Day 1874, and Langston was among five candidates nominated to succeed him. On that day also, Langston tendered his resignation as vice president, but informed the board on January 12, 1875 that he would serve as acting president for the remainder of the school year. On June 16, 1875, Langston renewed his resignation, but he also added his resignation as dean of the Law Department. The board tabled the resignations and proceeded to elect a new president. George Whipple, the white candidate, whom Langston had known at Oberlin College, had received ten votes and Langston four votes; the board was divided exactly along racial lines. At an Executive Committee meeting on July 2, 1875, with only three white members present, Langston's resignations were accepted. One of the Executive Committee members present that day, Edward P. Smith, was elected president on December 16, 1875, because of Whipple's resignation in July of that year.

Langston's enormous abilities, so ably demonstrated at Howard University, were recognized by President Ulysses S. Grant, who appointed Langston a member of the Board of Health of the District of Columbia, where he served for seven years. Later, in 1877, Langston was appointed by President Rutherford B. Hayes as United States Minister Resident and Consul–General to Haiti. He served in that post for eight years and all records indicate that he did so very conscientiously, having mastered the French language and the local customs. He also served as Charge d'Affaires to San Domingo during the same period.

Desiring to return to the United States, Langston resigned from his diplomatic position in January of 1885 to return to the practice of law. Despite his exemplary service, Langston had to petition the Court of Claims to recover $7,766 in salary withheld from him after diplomatic salaries were reduced by the House Appropriations Committee. In 1886 the U.S. Supreme Court ruled in his favor.

Upon his return to the United States in July, Langston did not return to the law. He had been unanimously selected by the Board of Education of Virginia to serve as president of the three–year–old Virginia Normal and Collegiate Institute in Petersburg, Virginia, now known as Virginia State University. He accepted the position and did much not only to place the institution on a solid foundation, but to make it one of the leading institutions in the country. He served until 1887, when control of the institute's board of visitors passed into Democratic hands.

In 1888 Langston ran for the U.S. House of Representatives from Virginia's Fourth Congressional District as an independent because he had been denied the Republican nomination. The initial results showed that Langston had lost by 641 votes to the Democratic candidate, Edward C. Venable, in an election fraught with irregularities. Langston challenged the election results and won after almost two years in litigation.

On September 23, 1890, the House, with almost all of the Democratic members absent, declared Langston the winner and seated him in Venable's place for the remainder of the Fifty–first Congress. Democrats boycotted Langston's swearing–in. Even so, he became the first black U.S. congressman elected from the Commonwealth of Virginia. Because the court challenge was so protracted, Langston had only a week to take up his duties before returning to his district to campaign for reelection. In that election he was defeated by the Democratic challenger James Epes by some 3,000 votes. On March 3, 1891, Langston's congressional career ended. In 1892 the Republicans asked Langston to run again for Congress, but he declined on the grounds that the Republicans were more likely to win in the Fourth District with a white candidate.

In his remaining years, Langston divided his time between Petersburg and Washington. He kept in touch with politics and worked on his autobiography which was published in 1894 under the title *From the Virginia Plantation to the National Capitol.* Other publications by Langston include *Freedom and Citizenship: Selected Lectures of Ho. John Mercer Langston* (1883) compiled by J. E. Rankin. Langston died of apoplexy at his home on Fourth and Bryant Streets in Washington, D.C. on November 15, 1897 and was buried in Woodlawn Cemetery in that city. His survivors included one daughter, Nettie (Mrs. James C. Napier); three sons—Arthur, Ralph E., and Frank Mercer; and several grandchildren.

After 108 years, the Commonwealth of Virginia recognized John Mercer Langston as one of its distinguished native sons with a historic marker in his birthplace of Virginia's Louisa County.

REFERENCES

Cheek, William, and Aimee Lee Cheek. *John Mercer Langston and the Fight for Black Freedom, 1829–65.* Urbana: University of Illinois Press, 1989.

Langston, John Mercer. *From the Virginia Plantation to the National Capitol.* 1894. Reprint, New York: Johnson Reprint, 1968.

Logan, Rayford, and Michael R. Winston, eds. *American Negro Biography.* New York: Norton, 1982.

Simmons, William J. *Men of Mark.* Cleveland: Geo. M. Rewell, 1887.

COLLECTIONS

The John Mercer Langston Papers are located in the Special Collections at Fisk University.

Paulette Coleman

Lewis Howard Latimer
(1848–1928)
Inventor, author

Lewis Howard Latimer

Lewis Howard Latimer devised an inexpensive method for manufacturing filaments for the electric incandescent lamp, thus, making the lamp affordable to the public and revolutionizing the electric light industry. A man of diversity, he not only patented a number of inventions; but he also was a writer, painter, and civil rights activist.

Latimer was born in Chelsea, Massachusetts, on September 4, 1848. He had two older brothers, George A. and William H., and one sister, Margaret. His parents, George W. and Rebecca Smith Latimer, were former slaves from Norfolk, Virginia. They were married around February of 1842 but, given their slave status, they could not live as a married couple. The couple escaped from Norfolk on October 4, 1842, aboard a ship bound for Boston. Latimer's mother, a dark 22 year old mulatto, posed as her husband's servant. Four days later, they arrived in Massachusetts, where they lived in fear of being discovered as runaway slaves. During the brief period of the recapture of Latimer's father, abolitionists kept his wife in hiding.

Latimer's father became famous for his efforts to be released from jail. He also worked with abolitionists to prevent other fugitive slaves from being recaptured. The abolitionists held protests, which Frederick Douglass and Charles Lenox Remond attended, which attacked Judge Lemuel Shaw's denial of a jury trial for Latimer's father, to determine whether or not he should be returned to his master. Later on, William Lloyd Garrison and Douglass raised funds to purchase Latimer's father's freedom. The abolitionists' protests led to a Massachusetts law which barred judges and other law enforcement officials from involvement in the return of fugitive slaves. The case even influenced the passage of the 1850 Fugitive Slave Act.

The Early Years

Since his family was very poor, young Latimer went to work at an early age to help earn money for the family's survival. He worked with his father as a paper hanger and also sold newspapers, including William Lloyd Garrison's *Liberator.* The fear of being kidnapped, or concern about the state of the family's finances, or perhaps for another reason, Latimer's father abandoned his family when his son was ten years old. Glennette T. Turner noted in *Lewis Howard Latimer* that, although they did not know of his whereabouts, Latimer's father remained close to his family and watched over them. In 1894, Douglass wrote to Latimer about having seen Latimer's father.

Whenever he could, young Latimer attended primary school, then Phillips Grammar School. He was a good student who enjoyed reading, creative writing, and art. He even skipped a grade due to his academic performances. However, after his father left, he quit school and worked full–time, to support his mother. His two brothers were sent to the Farm School, a state institution, where they worked for room and board. A family friend took care of his sister. For a while Latimer lived with his mother. He was sent to the Farm School when she decided to go to work as a ship's stewardess.

Latimer and one of his brothers ran away from the Farm School and returned home to find their mother and sister living together. Now 13–years old, Latimer worked as a waiter, held odd jobs in a private home, and served as office boy for a law firm. On September 13, 1864, Latimer, pretending to be older than he really was, joined the U.S. Navy. His brothers had already joined the Union forces. Latimer served as cabin boy on the *U.S.S. Massasoit* and saw action on Virginia's James River, near the area where his parents had been slaves. When the war ended, Latimer returned to Boston and was honorably discharged on July 3, 1865.

The Young Inventor

After a difficult search for employment, Latimer was hired, for three dollars a week, as office boy for Crosby and Gould, a firm of patent lawyers in Boston. He became fascinated with the draftsman's drawings and watched carefully to see what tools were being used in the process. He purchased a used book on drawing, and then saved enough money to buy used drawing tools as well. At night, he practiced the drawings until he felt he had mastered the art.

In time, Latimer was promoted to junior draftsman, then chief draftsman, often providing working models of inventions to accompany the drawings. At times he managed the business when his employer was away. He received $20 a week for his work, five dollars less than the other draftsman. By now, he knew how inventions were patented and wanted to become an inventor himself. He received his first patent in 1874, when he and W. C. Brown co–invented the water closet used on trains.

Works with Bell and Edison

Around this time, Latimer met Alexander Graham Bell, a teacher at a local school for the deaf located near Latimer's office. Bell asked Latimer to draw a schematic for the machine he wanted to use to transmit sounds through wires. On March 7, 1876, Bell was granted a patent for the world's first telephone.

In 1879, after unsuccessful employment with another patent lawyer, Joseph Adams, Latimer moved to Bridgeport, Connecticut, where he lived with his married sister. He met Hiram S. Maxim, who founded and was chief electrician and founder of the U.S. Electric Lighting Company. Maxim was also the inventor of the automatic machine gun which bore his name. Maxim hired Latimer as his assistant manager and draftsman. Latimer learned a lot about electric lights, and, after Thomas Alva Edison invented the electric light bulb in 1879, Latimer experimented on ways to improve it, by lengthening the life of the bulb, thus, making it affordable for homes and small industries.

Latimer moved, with Maxim, to New York City, in spring 1880, and continued to work as a draftsman. He also produced carbon filaments for electric lamps. After hundreds of attempts, he improved the filaments which made light bulbs less costly, thus revolutionizing the electric light industry. In September 1881, Latimer and Joseph V. Nichols received a patent for an incandescent electric lamp that became known as the Maxim electric lamp. According to Turner, Maxim used the invention without permission. On January 17, 1882, Latimer's process for manufacturing carbons was patented. The patent as well as those for other Latimer inventions were assigned to his employer, the U.S. Electric Lighting Company, which received all profits from sales.

Prolific Inventor

Between 1881 and 1882, Latimer was much in demand for his knowledge of electric lighting. He helped to install some of the first Maxim incandescent electric light plants in New York City, Philadelphia, and Canada, and supervised the production of the carbon filaments that were needed. After that, he was assigned to the task of installing incandescent and arc lighting in the railroad stations and yards in Montreal and New York City. From there, he went to London to build an incandescent lamp factory for Maxim, setting up Weston Electric Light Company and completing his work much sooner than expected.

Latimer left Maxim in 1883, shortly after returning to America. Although Maxim was a highly successful company, Latimer was forced to accept employment with smaller companies. He worked for several electric firms, including the Acme Electric Company of New York City, where he manufactured the Latimer Lamp. In 1884, he joined the Edison Electric Light Company, frequently traveling across America dealing with lawsuits that the Edison Company filed for illegal use of its patents, including suits against Maxim. He became the chief draftsman and patent expert for the company. In 1882, after several mergers, Edison became General Electric Company.

Latimer's creative curiosity continued. He devised a way to make elevators safe by preventing them from falling. On March 24, 1896, his patent for locking racks for hats, coats, and umbrellas was granted and his invention was used in public places such as restaurants and hotels. He patented a book support to keep books upright by supporting either the tops or bottoms of books, and devised an apparatus for cooling and disinfecting, which was used in apartments, hospitals, to keep conditions, of the buildings, cooler and more sanitary.

In 1896, the Edison and Westinghouse companies merged to establish the Board of Patent Control. Latimer, then, became chief draftsman and expert witness for the board, serving until it was dissolved in 1911. Although his eye sight had begun to fail when he was around 46, he remained productive. He joined the engineering firm of Hammer and Schwartz, in 1911, and retired from there, in 1924.

Civil Rights Activist

Between 1896 and 1906, Latimer was involved in civil rights activities. One of his friends was Richard Theodore Greener, the first African American to graduate from Harvard University. Greener encouraged Latimer to become involved in national civil rights issues, and in particular, to attend the 1895 meeting of the National Conference of Colored Men, in Detroit. Although unable to attend, Latimer wrote a spirited statement endorsing the convention and cited reasons why it should be held. According to Turner, Latimer wrote, "The community which permits a crime against its humblest member to go unpunished is nursing into life and strength a power which will ultimately threaten its own existence."

Latimer wrote to a number of well–established men of the time. Through correspondence, Greener introduced him to Booker T. Washington. Washington expressed his interest in having Latimer draft a "layout" for Tuskegee Institute's buildings and grounds. In 1902, Latimer wrote to the Brooklyn School Board in support of Samuel R. Scottron, whose re–appointment to the board was not confirmed.

In 1906, Latimer began to assist the Henry Street Settlement in New York City by teaching evening classes in English and mechanical drawing to newly–arrived Eastern European immigrants.

Latimer was a writer as well. In 1890, he published his first book on electric lighting, *Incandescent Electric Lighting: A Practical Description of the Edison System,* published by D. Van Nostrand & Company. The book was well received. Latimer also wrote music and poetry, including love poems to his wife. He was an artist as well. He made drawings of people he had observed and illustrated bookplates for his personal library. He corresponded with the National Association of Negro Authors and sent some of his poems to composer J. Rosamond Johnson, hoping they would be set to music.

In 1908, Latimer helped to found the Unitarian Church, in Flushing, New York. For many years, he was active in the George Huntsman Post of the Grand Army of the Republic (GAR), which was comprised Civil War veterans of the Union Army and Navy. He was honored as one of the 28 charter members of the Edison Pioneers, which was founded in 1918, to honor men who created the electrical industry.

Latimer married Mary Wilson of Fall River, Massachusetts, on November 10, 1873. She was an intelligent woman who encouraged her husband's efforts. They had two daughters, Louise Rebecca and Emma Jeanette. His wife died in 1924 and was buried, in her hometown. Latimer's eyesight, as well as his health, continued to fail. He was paralyzed on one side by a stroke on one side. In 1925, in honor of his 77th birthday, his daughters arranged to publish his poems in a book called *Poems of Life and Love,* printed in a limited edition. He recognized the beauty of the black woman in one of his love poems, "Ebony Venus," which was re–published in his biography:

Let others boast of maidens fair,
Of eyes of blue and golden hair;
* * * *
O'er marble Venus let them rage,
Who set the fashions of the age;
Each to his taste, but as for me,
My Venus shall be ebony.

Latimer died at home in Flushing, New York, on December 11, 1928, when he was 82. He was buried near his wife. At his death, Edison Pioneers historian William Miron Meadowcroft was among those who wrote tributes. Published in the biography *Lewis Howard Latimer,* Meadowcroft said: "We hardly mourn his inevitable going . . . so much as we rejoice in pleasant memory at having been associated with him in a great work for all peoples under a great man." He called Latimer broadminded, intellectually and culturally versatile, a linguist, and a devoted husband and father. Latimer's memory has been preserved in several exhibitions: the Henry Ford Museum in Dearborn, Michigan featured a Latimer lamp; the Museum of Science and Industry in Chicago prepared a traveling invention called "Black Scientists and Inventors;" and the Queens Historical Society has another. The General Electric Foundation provides an annual scholarship for minority students called the Latimer Achievement Award. A public school, in Brooklyn, was named after him, on May 10, 1968. It was to commemorate his success as inventor of economical carbon filaments which helped to facilitate the spread of electric lighting.

REFERENCES

Bowman, John S., ed. *The Cambridge Dictionary of American Biography.* New York: Cambridge University Press, 1995.

Haber, Louis. *Black Pioneers of Science and Invention.* New York: Harcourt and Brace, 1970.

Hayden, Robert C. *Eight Black American Inventors.* Reading, MA: Addison–Wesley, 1972.

Klein, Aaron E. *Black Scientists and Inventors in America.* Reading, MA: Addison–Wesley, 1971.

Mather, Frank Lincoln, ed. *Who's Who of the Colored Race: A General Biographical Dictionary of Men and Women of African Descent.* Chicago: Mather, 1915.

McFeely, William S. *Frederick Douglass.* New York: Norton, 1991.

Turner, Glennette Tilley. *Lewis Howard Latimer.* Englewood Cliffs, NJ: Silver Burdett Press, 1991.

COLLECTIONS

The papers of Lewis Latimer are in the Schomburg Center for Research in Black Culture, New York City.

Jessie Carney Smith

T. K. Lawless

(1892–1971)

Dermatologist, philanthropist

T. K. Lawless was a renowned dermatologist who made a lifetime commitment to provide medical and financial assistance to people throughout the world. Theodore Kenneth Lawless was born December 6, 1892, in Thibodeaux, Louisiana, to Alfred Lawless Jr. and Harriet Dunn Lawless. Shortly after his birth, his parents moved to New Orleans. Lawless's father, a prominent Congregational minister, and mother were well known for their generosity, and their willingness to give and share with others had a significant impact on their son. Known by his friends as "T. K.," he was often described as "versatile and unassuming."

Lawless attended Straight College, the only institution in New Orleans where blacks could acquire a secondary education at that time. In later years, Straight and New Orleans

T. K. Lawless

University merged to become Dillard University. He continued his undergraduate education at Talladega College in Alabama where he received an A.B. degree in 1914. Lawless attended the University of Kansas medical school and then entered Northwestern University in Chicago, Illinois, where he earned an M.D. in 1919 and an M.S. in 1920.

Contributes as Teacher and Doctor

After a one year fellowship of dermatology and syphilogy at Massachusetts General Hospital in Boston, Lawless completed his postgraduate training at the University of Paris, the most prestigious dermatology school in the early 1920s. While there, he ran out of money and asked his father for assistance. His father told him that he would send the money under the condition that he promised to be the best in his profession. Lawless agreed and worked diligently to make his father's request a reality.

In 1924, returning to the United States, he started his practice and maintained a dermatology clinic in a predominantly black neighborhood in Chicago. In the same year he began teaching dermatology at Northwestern University Medical School where he served as an instructor until 1941. While at Northwestern he established the first clinical laboratory for dermatology.

As an instructor and researcher, Lawless made significant contributions to the field of dermatology. His research was published in such scholarly publications as *American Journal of Dermatology, Journal of Laboratory and Clinical Medicine,* and the *Journal of the American Medical Association.* He worked diligently towards finding a cure for leprosy and made several advances in the treatment of both leprosy and syphilis. As a physician, Lawless's skills were sought by both blacks and whites and he was often consulted by other doctors for assistance with difficult cases. Lawless was noted for his equal treatment of patients regardless of class or race; according to an article in *Ebony,* he charged all his patients the same three dollar fee.

Works as Philanthropist

Evidence of Lawless's generosity and care for others can be traced to the beginning of his career. As a young doctor at Northwestern, he found the funds necessary to assist a black student who was to be denied graduation due to outstanding financial obligations. As Lawless's practice grew and his wealth increased, he donated funds for a research laboratory, equipped with the latest technology, at Provident Hospital in Chicago. In addition he supported several Jewish related causes in appreciation for the support he received from Jewish physicians when he sought letters of reference to study in Europe; of the 12 references he received, 11 were from Jewish physicians.

Other philanthropic acts included: the establishment of the Lawless Department of Dermatology in Beilison Hospital, Tel–Aviv, Israel; the T. K. Lawless Student Summer Program at the Weizmann Institute of Science, Rehovoth, Israel; the Lawless Clinical and Research Laboratory in Dermatology of the Hebrew Medical School, Jerusalem; Roosevelt University's Chemical Laboratory and Lecture Auditorium, Chicago; and Lawless Memorial Chapel, Dillard University, New Orleans. The chapel was built in honor of his father.

Lawless was an astute businessman and used his financial resources to make wise investments. He was a director of the Supreme Life Insurance Company and the Marina City Bank as well as a charter member, president, and associate founder of Service Federal Savings and Loan Association in Chicago.

Lawless was also affiliated with several professional organizations, including the American Medical Association, the National Medical Association, the American Association for the Advancement of Science, and various state and local medical societies. He was an associate examiner in dermatology for the National Board of Medical Examiners and served as consultant to the U.S. Chemical Warfare Board. He was also well respected for his service on the National Advisory Committee for the Selective Service, a committee formed to address the problems people in the medical profession.

For his professional and philanthropic contributions, Lawless was widely honored. He received honorary degrees from Talladega College, Howard University, Bethune–Cookman College, Virginia State University, and the University of Illinois. Among his prestigious honors were the Distinguished Service Award of Phi Beta Kappa, the Citation of the Weizmann Institute of Science (Rehovoth, Israel), the Greater Chicago Churchman Layman–of–the–Year Citation, the Citation of the United Church Board for Homeland Ministries, NAACP Spingarn Medal for 1954, and the Golden Torch Award of the City of Hope.

In 1970 at his seventy–eighth birthday celebration on Dillard University's campus, Lawless shared the philosophy that directed his life:

I sought my soul,
But my soul I could not see,
I sought my God, but my God eluded me,
I sought my neighbor, and I found all there.

Lawless died in Chicago on May 1, 1971, after a long illness. His funeral was held at the Lawless Memorial Chapel at Dillard University and he was buried in Mount Olive Cemetery in the Lawless family mausoleum. The renowned dermatologist devoted his entire life to others. He used his talents to heal the sick and his resources to enhance the lives of others.

REFERENCES

"Doctor With Big Heart." *Ebony* 13 (January 1958): 51–56.

Garrett, Romeo B. *Famous First Facts about Negroes.* New York: Arno Press, 1972.

Low, W. Augustus, and Virgil A. Clift, eds. *Encyclopedia of Black America.* New York: McGraw–Hill, 1981.

"Medical History: Theodore Kenneth Lawless, M.D., M.S., D.Sc., LL.D. 1892–." *Journal of the National Medical Association* 62 (July 1970): 310–12.

Robinson, Wilhelmena S. *Historical Afro–American Biographies.* New York: Publishers Company, 1976.

"Skin Wizard of the World." *Ebony* 1 (February 1946): 7–13.

Theodore Kenneth Lawless: Tributes and Response on the Occasion of his Seventy–Eighth Birthday, December 6, 1970. Dillard University, New Orleans, LA.

Theodosia T. Shields

Jacob Lawrence
(1917–)
Artist, educator

Jacob Lawrence has become one of the most acclaimed African American artists of the twentieth century. His work is characterized by small scale tempera and gouache paintings of genre scenes of African Americans and their sociopolitical struggles. His work is often organized through a series, typically accompanied with a simple text which serves as a narrative, based on the artist's careful research. Lawrence has been classified as a social realist and the style of his work is associated with Cubism.

Jacob A. Lawrence was the eldest of three children born to Jacob and Rosa Lee Lawrence on September 17, 1917, in

Jacob Lawrence

Atlantic City, New Jersey. Lawrence's father worked as a railroad cook and as a coal miner while his mother was employed as a domestic worker. The family moved to Easton, Pennsylvania, where Lawrence and his siblings were born. Jacob Lawrence's parents separated when he was seven years old. At that time, Rosa Lee Lawrence and her children moved to Philadelphia and the children were temporarily placed in a foster home. They reunited with their mother in Harlem in the early 1930s after she found employment.

At the age of 12, Lawrence was enrolled at Public School 89, and concurrently at the Utopia (Settlement) House which offered after–school classes in arts and crafts. The center was directed by Harlem artist Charles Alston, who immediately recognized Lawrence's artistic abilities. His first projects consisted of abstract drawings based on decorative patterns and designs observed in his home, and papier mache masks and cardboard dioramas using crayons and poster paints. Lawrence attended Frederick Douglass Junior High School and Commerce High School through the 11th grade.

During the Great Depression, Lawrence's mother lost employment and the family was forced to go on welfare. Lawrence dropped out of high school in order to take odd jobs to support his family. He was temporarily employed by the Civilian Conservation Corps to plant trees, build dams, and drain swamps in upstate New York.

Between 1932 and 1934, Lawrence studied again with Charles Alston at the Harlem Art Workshop, located at the 135th Street Library in Harlem. He continued to study under Alston and painter and sculptor Henry Bannarn at 306 West

141st Street, which became known as a central gathering place among Harlem artists. Those who frequented the site were commonly known as "the 306 Group," consisting of artists, musicians, poets and writers from Harlem, New York, and Europe. Lawrence also met Augusta Savage, a noteworthy sculptor and teacher who became instrumental in art education in Harlem as the director of community art programs for children and adults. Lawrence attributed his greatest formative influences to Alston, Bannarn, and Savage. During his early years in Harlem, Lawrence also came into contact with such noteworthy individuals as Romare Bearden, Gwendolyn Bennett, Bob Blackburn, Aaron Douglas, W. E. B. Du Bois, Ralph Ellison, Langston Hughes, Ronald Joseph, Gwendolyn Knight (who became the artist's wife), Norman Lewis, Alain Locke, Claude McKay, and Arthur Schomburg.

Lawrence was influenced by Asian wood block prints, and the work of Breughel, Daumier, William Edmonson, Giotto, Goya, William Gropper, George Grosz, Kathe Kollwitz, Jose Clemente Orozco, Diego Rivera, and David Siqueiros due to the importance these artists placed on documenting human emotion through historical, social, and cultural references. Lawrence was also keenly aware of the work of Arthur Dove, Georgio de Chirico, and Charles Sheeler who represented the growing American Modernist movement and its European counterpart.

Rise to Fame

In 1937 Lawrence was awarded a scholarship to the American Artists School in New York City, where he attended classes for two years. There he was instructed by Eugene Moreley, Anton Refregier, Philip Reisman, and Sol Wilson. During the evenings, Lawrence frequented Alston's studio as well the studios of other prominent Harlem artists. The artist made his public debut in April of 1937, at an group exhibition sponsored by the Harlem Artists Guild, at the 115th Street Public Library. Lawrence exhibited several paintings at the American Artists School the following month in conjunction with the Harlem Artists Guild. He was represented alongside his mentors Alston and Bannarn in both shows.

Savage managed to help Lawrence secure WPA (U.S. Works Progress Administration) Easel Project in 1938 lasting 18 months. Lawrence was contracted to complete two paintings every six weeks. It was during this time that he produced his first major works of art and established himself as a leading African American artist. In 1938 the artist initiated another series, *The Life of Frederick Douglass,* which was completed in 1939.

Lawrence was given his first one–man show in February of 1938, at the age of 20, at the YMCA in Harlem. The artist debuted his genre paintings of Harlem, depicting street and interior scenes done in 1936–37. The paintings were small, done with tempera and poster paint on brown wrapping paper. His early style was characterized by the use of flat shapes, frontal or profile views of people displaying overt gestures with mask–like faces, props that punctuate the organization of the figures, and an expressive portrayal of human emotion—attributes which would become his signature as an artist. Around 1937, upon the recommendation of Bearden, Lawrence became interested in using casein tempera (ground pigment, casein—milk protein, and ammonia) on gessoed hardboard panels. This change of medium allowed Lawrence to create a chalky, fresco–like appearance in his paintings.

At the YMCA, where Lawrence often played pool, he met "Professor" Charles Siefert, historian of African culture and art. Siefert introduced Lawrence to African and African American resources at the New York Public Library (currently known as the Schomburg Center for Research in Black Culture), which had an enormous influence on the artist. In 1935 Siefert took Lawrence to an important exhibition of African art at the Museum of Modern Art in New York City. Siefert possessed a vast library specializing in African and African American subjects which he made available to Lawrence. Due to the inspiration of Siefert, the artist developed a series of paintings in 1937 of the Haitian revolutionary Toussaint L'Overture, consisting of 41 panels.

Early in his career, Lawrence developed a very disciplined manner of working on his series projects. First, he conceives of a theme and begins to experiment with ideas that lead to sequentially structured compositions. The artist completes a final pencil drawing for each painting in the series. He then paints one color at a time, proceeding from dark to light in each of the individual paintings that constitute the series before continuing with the next color. Works contained within a series are normally accompanied by a text usually in the form of a narrative. Due to Lawrence's documentary use of images and captions combined, his work bears a similarity to photojournalism, which has been a popular form of media throughout the twentieth century.

In 1939 the artist had another exhibition at the American Artists School, which was reviewed favorably in *Art News.* That same year, Lawrence's *Toussaint L'Overture* series was shown for the first time at the De Porres Interracial Council headquarters, and again at an exhibition cosponsored by the Harmon Fund at the Baltimore Museum later that year. The series was reproduced, in part, in the March of 1939 issue of *Survey Graphic* and reviewed favorably by the *Baltimore Sun.* The same year, Lawrence's *Toussaint L'Overture* series was again shown at the American Negro Exhibition in Chicago, where Lawrence was honored with a second prize and medal.

In 1940 Lawrence's work was included in several exhibitions including group shows at the Harlem Community Art Center, Columbia University, and the Library of Congress. Beginning that year, Lawrence received a Rosenwald Grant for three consecutive years. This opportunity allowed the artist to move into a studio on 125th Street in New York City. There he began a series of images about black migration in the United States. He developed 60 panel paintings between 1940 and 1941, entitled *The Migration of the Negro.* In this series, the artist depicted the mass exodus of blacks from the rural South to the industrial North from the early 1900s until the 1940s.

The Middle Years

In 1941 Lawrence married Gwendolyn Knight, whom the artist met as a teenager in Harlem. Knight is originally from the West Indies and is also an artist. She has been a major force behind the artistic achievements of her husband throughout his career. They have no children. After their marriage, the couple lived in New Orleans for one year, during which time Lawrence began his *John Brown* series under the sponsorship of a Rosenwald Grant for a second consecutive year. Lawrence's *Migration* series was represented along with the work of Tanner, Alston, Johnson, Pippin, and Bearden in an exhibition at the Downtown Gallery entitled, ''American Negro Art: 19th and 20th Centuries'' in December of 1941. At the age of 24, Lawrence became the first black artist to be sponsored by a prominent New York City art gallery. Concurrent with the exhibition, *Fortune* magazine featured 26 color reproductions from the series. The entire series was purchased, half by the Museum of Modern Art and half by the Phillips Collection. The *Migration* series achieved popular success and is touted by scholars as the artist's greatest single artistic achievement.

Lawrence was introduced to many leading contemporary artists including Davis, Dove, Marin, O'Keeffe, Pippin, Scheeler, Shahn, Tobey, and Weber through his association with Edith Halpert, owner of the Downtown Gallery. The artist was featured in numerous exhibitions at the Downtown Gallery beginning in 1942 for a period of 20 years.

The artist began his *Harlem* series in 1942, again supported by a Rosenwald Fellowship. Lawrence joined the U.S. Coast Guard in 1943. Both of Lawrence's commanding officers, captain J. S. Rosenthal and lieutenant commander Carltin Skinner, encouraged the artist to continue his painting while fulfilling regular duties as a steward's mate. Rosenthal promoted Lawrence to the position of combat artist. Ultimately, Lawrence became the official Coast Guard painter. During his 26 months in the service, Lawrence produced approximately 48 paintings in a series entitled, *Coast Guard.*

After completing his obligations with the military, Lawrence resumed painting the history of African American people in 1945. He was saluted by *New Masses* magazine for his contribution to the arts in 1946. Funded by a Guggenheim Fellowship between 1946 and 1947, Lawrence completed a series that documented his memories of World War II. While working on the series the artist was featured in two shows—one at The Phillips Collection and the other at ACA Gallery in New York. The artist was invited by Joseph Albers to teach at Black Mountain College in North Carolina during the summer of 1947. Due to Albers's influence, Lawrence became absorbed in formal considerations based on Bauhaus principles of art and design. That same year, *Fortune* magazine commissioned the artist to do a series of ten paintings on postwar conditions in the South. In 1948 the artist exhibited the *Migration* series at the Eight Annual Exhibition of the Art Institute of Chicago and was awarded a silver medal.

Lawrence became psychologically depressed during the late 1940s due to his enormous success and the lack of recognition of his colleagues. Finally in July of 1949, Lawrence committed himself to Hillside Hospital in Queens, New York, to receive treatment for depression. During his stay from 1949 until 1950, the artist completed a series entitled *Hospital,* consisting of 11 panels. Lawrence actively resumed painting after his recovery. He began working on genre scenes of Harlem and a series entitled *Theater,* consisting of 12 panels. Soon thereafter, he began a series depicting the history of war and conflict in America entitled *Struggle—History of the American People* between 1955 and 1956. Thirty panels were completed of 60 originally projected.

The artist began teaching at Pratt Institute in 1955, where he stayed for 15 years, while also teaching concurrently at other institutions. He has also taught at the Art Students League, New York City; Brandeis University; The New School for Social Research; Skowhegan School of Painting and Sculpture; California State University at Hayward; and the University of Washington at Seattle. He retired from teaching.

The Mature Years

In 1960 Lawrence was given a retrospective by The American Federation of the Arts. He visited Nigeria at the invitation of the American Society of African Culture (AMSAC) and the Mbari Club of Artists and Writers of Ibadan once briefly in 1962 and again for eight months in 1964. He gained enormous insight about African aesthetics and design during his early years in Harlem and in Africa, which is evident in his work throughout his career. During his stay in Africa, Lawrence produced a series of paintings entitled *Nigeria.* He initiated a series of paintings based on the theme of civil rights in the South from 1961 to 1969.

In the late 1960s, Lawrence was commissioned by Windmill Books (Simon and Schuster) to direct a book project. He chose the life of Harriet Tubman. The book consisted of 17 of Lawrence's paintings accompanied with original verse. Some of the imagery in Harriet and the Promised Land (1968) was taken directly from Lawrence's *Harriet Tubman* series of 1939. Lawrence illustrated three other books: *Aesop's Fables* (1970), *Hiroshima* (1983), and *One Way Ticket* (1948). Lawrence completed a number of illustration projects including three covers for *Time* magazine, a poster for the 1972 Olympics in Munich, a silk screen poster in 1977 for a fund raising campaign to offset the expenses of President Jimmy Carter's inauguration, as well as several other poster projects.

In 1973 Lawrence was commissioned by the state of Washington to paint a mural about the life of George Washington Bush—the first black elected to the Washington legislature in 1889—at the State Capital Museum in Olympia. Lawrence was honored with a major retrospective at the Whitney Museum of American Art in 1974 and again at the Seattle Art Museum in 1986. In 1975 the Founders Society of the Detroit Institute of the Arts commissioned Lawrence to do an edition of silk screen prints of the *John Brown Series* from 1941.

Although Lawrence has painted throughout his career mostly with water–based materials, during the past several decades he has increased his use of media to include prints, drawings, and murals composed of enamel, as seen in the *Games* mural for the Kingdome Stadium in Seattle (1979), his *Exploration* mural at Howard University (1980), and a second mural for Hampton University, *Origins* (1984). During the 1970s Lawrence created several paintings based on the theme of libraries. In 1982 he was commissioned to produced a series of silkscreen prints for Limited Editions Club of New York City in collaboration with author, John Hersey.

In 1994 Lawrence completed a series of paintings based on the theme of the supermarket. The major theme of Lawrence's most recent works during the past two decades has been building, reflecting his love for manual craftsmanship, and tools. Lawrence collects antique tools and is an expert on their forms and functions. He uses his intimate knowledge about the subject of tools and hand labor throughout these thematically linked works.

Lawrence has received numerous awards during his career, including election in the Hall of Fame for Great Americans, 1976; nominated commissioner, National Council for the Arts, 1978–84; American Academy of Arts and Letters, 1983; NAACP (National Association for the Advancement of Colored People) 3rd Annual Great Black Artist's Award, 1988; College Art Association Distinguished Artist Award, 1988; National Medal of Arts, presented by President George Bush, 1990; National Art Club Medal of Honor, 1993; and the American Academy of Arts and Sciences, 1995.

In addition to the small gouache paintings based on themes organized as a series which characterize the artist's work, Lawrence has also produced a number of drawings, prints, murals, posters, and illustrations revealing his personal and cultural heritage. He prefers water-based paints and small brushes and usually paints small scale works on paper or gessoed panels. He has contributed a legacy of art revealing the expression, challenges, and rewards of black culture and society. He has immortalized his aesthetic philosophy and imagery through his involvement as a teacher. Lawrence was a child and adolescent during the prime of the Harlem Renaissance, survived the Depression, served in World War II, experienced post–war reconstruction and the Civil Rights Movement of the 1950s, 1960s, and 1970s, and his lifetime has nearly spanned the century. Jacob Lawrence has been proclaimed by critics as the divine translator of the history of the African American experience through art.

Lawrence and his wife have resided in the state of Washington since 1971.

Current address: c/o Francine Seders Gallery, Limited, 6701 Greenwood Avenue North, Seattle, WA 98103.

REFERENCES

King–Hammond, Leslie, and Joan Whitney Payson. *Jacob Lawrence, An Overview: Paintings from 1936–1994.* New York: Midtown Payson Galleries, n.d.

Perry, Regenia A., and Kinshasha Holman Conwill. *Free Within Ourselves: African–American Artists in the Collection of the National Museum of American Art.* Washington, DC: National Museum of American Art, Smithsonian Institution, 1992.

Stamey, Alison. Interview with Betty Lou Williams, June 13, 1997. Francine Seders Gallery, Limited.

Wheat, Ellen Wheat. *Jacob Lawrence: American Painter.* Seattle: University of Washington Press, 1986.

COLLECTIONS

Institutions that house historical information on Jacob Lawrence include the Archives of American Art, Smithsonian Institution, Washington, DC; Museum of Modern Art, New York City; Schomburg Center for Research in Black Culture, New York City; Syracuse University; New York Public Library; University of Washington; and the Whitney Museum of American Art.

Jacob Lawrence is represented in numerous museum collections including the Baltimore Museum of Art, Brooklyn Museum, Dallas Museum of Art, Detroit Institute of Arts, Hirshhorn Museum and Sculpture Garden, Metropolitan Museum of Art, Museum of Fine Arts in Boston, Museum of Modern Art (New York), National Gallery of Art, New Orleans Museum of Art, Philadelphia Museum of Art, The Phillips Collection, Portland Art Museum, St. Louis Art Museum, Seattle Art Museum, Toledo Museum of Art, Virginia Museum of Art, Whitney Museum of American Art, and a number of colleges and universities throughout the United States, particularly black institutions of higher learning.

Betty Lou Williams

Lee, Don L.
See Madhubuti, Haki.

Spike Lee

(1957–)

Filmmaker, screenwriter, actor

Spike Lee's recognition as a key black filmmaker in the American movie industry followed his first film in 1986. Since then he has become the nation's most successful and popular black director. His against–the–odds achievements opened doors for other black filmmakers. Winning acclaim for his accurate and unstereotyped depictions of black culture, Lee's goal has been to create films that capture the black experience. According to *Current Biography,* he stated his mission ''to put the vast richness of black culture on film.''

Shelton Jackson Lee was born March 20, 1957, in Atlanta, Georgia to William ''Bill'' Lee, a jazz composer and bassist, and Jacqueline Shelton Lee, an art teacher. His mother, who died in 1977 of cancer, nicknamed him ''Spike'' as toddler, evidently alluding to his toughness. Spike grew up the oldest three brothers, David, Cinque, and Chris, and one sister, Joie. The family moved from Atlanta shortly after Lee's birth and lived briefly in Chicago. In 1959 they moved to Brooklyn's predominantly black Fort Greene section. Jacqueline Lee provided a rich cultural upbringing that included plays, galleries, museums, movies. Bill Lee saw that the family experienced music, occasionally taking them to his performances at the Blue Note and to other Manhattan jazz clubs.

After graduating from John Dewey High School in Brooklyn, Lee majored in mass communications at his father's and grandfather's alma mater, Morehouse College in Atlanta. At Morehouse Lee took an interest in filmmaking, and upon graduation in 1979, was awarded a summer internship with Columbia Pictures in Burbank, California. In the fall, he returned to New York to attend New York University's Institute of Film and Television, Tisch School of the Arts. One of the few blacks in the school, Lee's first year at NYU was not without controversy. For his first year project he submitted a ten minute film, *The Answer,* that told of a young black screenwriter who remade D. W. Griffith's *The Birth of a Nation.* A pointed critique of the racism in Griffith's silent film, the faculty was displeased with his work, saying that he had not yet mastered ''film grammar.'' Lee suspected, however, that they took offence to his digs at the legendary director's stereotypical portrayals of black characters. An assistantship in his second year provided full tuition in exchange for working in the school's equipment room.

Lee earned his master's in filmmaking from NYU in 1982, and as his final film project, he wrote, produced, and directed *Joe's Bed–Stuy Barbershop: We Cut Heads.* His father composed the original jazz score, the first of several he created for his son's films. The film was set at a barbershop in Brooklyn's Bedford–Stuyvesant neighborhood that serves as a front for a numbers running operation. The Academy of Motion Picture Arts and Sciences awarded Lee the 1983 Student Academy Award for best director. The Lincoln Center's New Directors and New Films series selected the film as its first student production.

Upon graduation two major talent agencies signed Lee, but when nothing materialized, he was not surprised. In a *New York Times* interview, Lee said that it ''cemented in my mind what I always thought all along: that I would have to go out and do it alone, not rely on anyone else.'' Even though the honors enhanced his credibility, they did not pay the bills. In order to survive, Lee worked at a movie distribution house cleaning and shipping film.

At the same time, he tried to raise funds to finance a film entitled *Messenger,* a drama about a young New York City bicycle messenger. However, in the summer of 1984, a dispute between Lee and the Screen Actor's Guild forced a halt in the production of his first film. The Guild felt the film was too commercial to qualify for the waiver granted to low–budget independent films that permitted the use of nonunion actors. Lee felt that the refusal to grant him the waiver was a definite case of racism. Unable to recast the film with union actors, he terminated the project for lack of funds. Lee told *Vanity Fair* that he had learned his lesson: ''I saw I made the classic mistakes of a young filmmaker, to be overly ambitious, do something beyond my means and capabilities. Going through the fire just made me more hungry, more determined that I couldn't fail again.''

Spike Lee

Film Career Launched

With the disappointment of *Messenger* behind him, Lee needed a film with commercial appeal that could be filmed on a small budget. His script for *She's Gotta Have It* (1986) seemed to fill the bill. The $175,000 film was shot in 12 days at one location and edited in Lee's apartment. The plot follows an attractive black Brooklyn woman, Nola Darling, and her romantic encounters with three men. Lee played one of the three suitors, Mars Blackmon. In the comedy Lee poked fun at the double standard faced by a woman is who involved with several men. After the film's successful opening at the San Francisco Film Festival, Island Pictures agreed to distribute *She's Gotta Have It,* beating out several other film companies. At the Cannes Film Festival it won the Prix de Jeuness for the best new film by a newcomer. A success in the United States, it eventually grossed over $7 million.

Lee based next film, *School Daze* (1988), on his four years at Morehouse College. Set on a college campus during homecoming weekend, it explores the conflict between light–skinned and dark–skinned blacks. Those with light skin have money, expensive cars, and "good hair." The ones with darker skin are "less cool" and had "bad hair." Lee aimed to expose what he saw as a caste system existing within the black community. Lee began filming at Morehouse, but after three weeks the administration asked him to leave citing his negative portrayal of black colleges. Lee finished filming at Atlanta University. *School Daze* opened to mixed reviews but was a box office success, ultimately grossing $15 million. However, Lee's efforts to explore a complex social problem offended some, while others applauded.

Do the Right Thing (1989) opened with even more controversy. It portrays simmering racial tensions between Italians and African Americans in Brooklyn's Bedford–Stuyvesant section that erupt when a white police officer kills a black man. Some critics said Lee was endorsing violence and would hold him partly responsible if audiences rioted upon seeing the film. Lee stated that he did not advocate violence, but intended to provoke discussion. The Cannes International Film Festival included a screening of the film and the Los Angeles Film Critics gave it an award for best picture. *Do the Right Thing* received Golden Globe nominations for best picture, best director, best screenplay, and best supporting actor, but failed to win in any category. It was also nominated for an Academy Award for best original screenplay and for best supporting actor. It lacked a nomination for best picture despite its high acclaim. According to Lee, in *Jet* magazine, "the oversight reflects the discomfort of the motion picture industry with explosive think pieces." It cost $6.5 million to produce and grossed $28 million.

Lee's father inspired the main character and wrote the score for *Mo' Better Blues* (1990). A jazz trumpeter—who might be based on Lee's father, Bill Lee—tries to balance his love of music with his love of two women. However, Lee said the film was about relationships in general and not just the relationship between a man and a woman. He wanted to portray black musicians not dependent on drugs or alcohol.

Jungle Fever (1991) had another provocative theme, that of interracial sex. It also explores color, class, drugs, romance and family. A black married architect and an Italian American secretary are attracted to each other through the sexual mythology that surrounds interracial romance. At the end of their affair, they admit that they were just "curious," but not before both are at odds with their families. Color, class, drugs, romance, and family are all dealt with in this movie. Lee noted that whether the movie endorses or rejects interracial romance is not the point.

Next Lee directed a film on the life of Malcolm X. He knew from the start that it would be controversial. Warner Brothers originally chose Norman Jewison to direct the film. When Lee announced publicly that he had a problem with a white man directing the film, Jewison agreed to step down. Lee problems began early on with a group called the United Front to Preserve the Memory of Malcolm X and the Cultural Revolution. Their objections were based on their analysis of Lee's "exploitative" films. Others doubted that Lee would present a true picture of Malcolm X. After reworking the script, Lee battled with Warner Brothers over the budget. He requested $40 million to produce a film of epic proportions. Warner offered only $20 million. By selling the foreign rights for $8.5 million and kicking in part of his $3 million salary, Lee made up the difference by getting backing from black celebrities such as Bill Cosby, Oprah Winfrey, and Michael Jordan, much to Warner's embarrassment. Under Lee's direction, *Malcolm X* was released in 1992, grossing $48 million. It played a major role in elevating the black leader to mythic status, portraying him as a symbol for the extremes of black rage as well as for racial reconciliation.

Lee wrote *Crooklyn* (1994) with his sister, Joie, and brother, Cinque. Originally a short story by Joie, Cinque encouraged her to turn it into a screenplay. Joie and Cinque had planned for their own company to make the film, but after reading it, Spike was interested in producing it. The black family in Brooklyn during the 1970s sounds a lot like the Lees, but Joie Lee warned not to assume it is autobiographical. It is an unusual film, lacking a dysfunctional family, violence, gangs, and drugs. Instead, it follows the struggles and strengths of a family despite odds and obstacles.

In direct contrast to *Crooklyn* is *Clockers* (1995), Lee's intimate but violent look at the inner–city drug trade. Adapted from Richard Price's novel, initially the film was to be directed by Martin Scorcese and focus on the story's police murder investigation. However, Scorcese had other commitments, and Lee took over. He shifted the emphasis to the relationship between two brothers. One is on the "up and up" and the other is a clocker (a street level worker in the drug trade, always ready at any hour to provide crack.) Lee concentrated more on the bonds that connect black men rather than making another "gangsta" movie.

Lee released two films in 1996. The first, *Girl 6* (1996) had a cast and crew made up mostly of women. It follows a struggling actress who takes a job for a phone–sex line. Her sense of reality deteriorates when the calls begin to matter to her, and she eventually hits rock bottom. Reviews were not favorable, one critic wrote that this was the worst film Lee had made. Lee's tenth film in as many years was an investigation of the Million Man March of 1995. *Get on the Bus* (1996) details the voyage of 12 men from Los Angeles to Washington, D.C., to take part in the march. They represent the diversity of male African Americans, and Lee contrasted the men's speeches and debates so that the differences and tensions between them are intensified. Made in 18 days, *Get on the Bus* cost $2.4 million. Its entire budget came from black male investors who were inspired by the march's message.

Films Stir Controversy

Lee's earlier films courted controversy that helped maximize profits, but critics have said that since *Malcolm X* Lee has been less discerning, and his films have not done as well at the box office. However, his willingness to tackle sensitive issues of relevance to the black community has made his films profitable, awakening the industry to untapped market. Lee seems to be misquoted often, and finds it a nuisance to explain things he did not say. He would rather be out of the papers than see false claims. He told *American Film,* "All I want to do is tell a story. When writing a script I'm not saying, 'Uh–Oh,' I'd better leave that out because I might get into trouble. I don't operate like that." His goal is to prove that an all–black film directed by a black person can be of universal appeal.

In keeping with his interest in encouraging others who want to enter filmmaking, Lee established a minority scholarship at New York University's Tisch School of the Arts in 1989, and he also supports the College Fund/UNCF.

Lee is about five–feet six–inches tall and has a mustache and small beard. He wears glasses. Lee is a dedicated New York Knicks fan and has been known to plan film projects around the Knicks' basketball schedule. Associates describe him as possessing a fierce determination and unshakable self–confidence. Philip Dusenberry of New York advertising agency BBDO said of Lee in *Business Week,* "You get the impression that Spike is a devil–may–care kind of guy, but he's also a shrewd self–promoter." Other long–time associates told *Ebony* that Lee, "is an obsessive workaholic who seems intent on cramming a lifetime of work into a few short years." Lee is unusual in the filmmaking business in that he not only writes, directs, and produces, but also acts in all his films—although most of his roles are marginal. He does not consider himself an actor, but feels it creates box office appeal.

Lee makes no apology for his success and defends himself against charges of commercialism. His motivation for business investments comes from Malcolm X's philosophy that blacks need to build their own economic base. Lee was recognized as a marketing phenomenon and multimedia star only four years after his surprise hit, *She's Gotta Have It.* His first enterprise, Forty Acres and a Mule Filmworks, moved from his apartment to a remodeled Brooklyn firehouse in 1987. With tongue in cheek, Lee says the name reflects the arduous struggle he went through to make *She's Gotta Have It.*

In addition to his films, he has written several books that recount his experiences as a director. He has also produced music videos for Anita Baker, Miles Davis, Michael Jackson, and Branford Marsalis, among others. In 1988 he produced and directed a television commercial for Jesse Jackson's presidential campaign.

Lee also has his own collection of promotional movie merchandise, such as baseball caps, t–shirts, posters. Beginning with a rapidly expanding mail–order operation, Lee opened his retail store, Spike's Joint, in 1990.

Lee directed commercials for Levi's $20 million campaign for its 501 Jeans, as well as for Nike, The Gap, Barney's of New York, Philips Electronics, Quaker Oat's Snapple, and Ben & Jerry's ice cream. Appearing in Nike commercials with Michael Jordan, Lee was criticized for making Nike's expensive Air Jordans such a status symbol that many young people reportedly were stealing from each other. According to *Business Week,* Lee dismissed the charges as "thinly veiled racism." He also appeared in television commercials for Taco Bell and Apple Computer, and in print ads, "Milk. Where's your mustache?" for the National Fluid Milk Processors. He recorded the voiceover for a television ad for Topps Stadium Club basketball cards; a special set of "Spike Says" insert cards feature Lee's commentary on ten of the National Basketball Association's biggest stars.

Lee served as executive producer for several films, marketed his own comic book line, and directed short films for *Saturday Night Live* and MTV. His Forty Acres and a Mule Musicworks, which joined MCA Records in 1994, has been responsible for his movie soundtracks. In 1994, the TNT cable network signed Lee to be executive producer of the documentary *Hoop Dreams.* In 1995 Columbia Pictures TV signed him as one of several filmmakers in a series of one hour documentaries, "American Portraits" for the Disney Channel.

In late 1996, Lee joined DDB Needham Advertising to form a new ad agency, Spike/DDB. Their agreement called for Lee to direct urban–oriented commercials for a variety of clients. He previously worked with DDB on an educational spot for the College Fund/United Negro College Fund.

Lee married attorney Tonya Linnette Lewis, in October of 1993. They met in September of 1992 during the Congressional Black Caucus weekend in Washington D.C. Their daughter, Satchel Lewis Lee, was born in December of 1994. She was named after legendary black baseball star Satchel Paige. In May of 1997 their son, Jackson Lee, was born.

Known as one of the most original and innovative filmmakers in the world, Lee presents the different facets of black culture. He is quick to admit, however, that there are those in the black community among his detractors. Lee says that he is neither a spokesman for 35 million African Americans nor tries to present himself that way. He will probably continue to court controversy, but with his savvy and salesmanship skills, Spike Lee will remain a significant influence in the entertainment world.

Current address: Forty Acres and a Mule Filmworks, 124 DeKalb Avenue, Suite 2, Brooklyn, New York 11217

REFERENCES

Contemporary Black Biography. Vol. 5. Detroit: Gale Research, 1994.

Croal, N'Gai. "Bouncing Off the Rim." *Newsweek* 127 (22 April 1996): 75.

Current Biography Yearbook. New York: H. W. Wilson, 1989.

Darling, Lynn. "The Lees on Life." *Harper's Bazaar* 127 (May 1994):81–82.

"Doing the Job." *Sight and Sound* 3 (February 1991): 10–11.

Fitzgerald, Sharon. "Spike Lee: Fast Forward." *American Visions* 10 (October/November 1995): 20–26.

"Freeman, Washington Get Oscar Nods, Lee Snubbed." *Jet* 77 (5 March 1990): 54–55.

Hawkins, Walter L., ed. *African American Biographies.* Jefferson, NC: McFarland , 1992.

Hirshey, Gerri. ''Spike's Peak.'' *Vanity Fair* 54 (June 1991): 70, 80–92.

Kroll, Jack. ''Spiking a Fever.'' *Newsweek* 117 (10 June 1991): 44–47.

Newsmakers. Detroit: Gale Research, 1988.

''A Revealing Look at Spike Lee's Changing Life.'' *Ebony* 49 (May 1994): 28–32.

''Spike Lee Makes his Movie.'' *New York Times,* August 10, 1986.

Sharkey, Betsy. ''Knocking on Hollywood's Door.'' *American Film* 14 (July/August 1989): 22–27, 52–54.

''Spike Lee Does a Lot of Things Right.'' *Business Week* no. 3172, (6 August 1990).

Tate, Greg. ''Spike Lee.'' *American Film* 11 (September 1986): 48–49.

Flossie E. Wise

Carroll M. Leevy

(1920–)

Medical researcher, educator, administrator, humanitarian

Carroll M. Leevy

Carroll Moton Leevy, a physician, has been honored throughout the world as a pioneer in the research, diagnosis, and treatment of liver diseases and for his interest in the social as well as the physiological needs of patients. He is presently a distinguished professor at the University of Medicine and Dentistry, New Jersey Medical School (UMDNJ), and director of its Sammy Davis Jr. National Liver Institute, a center established in recognition of the value of Leevy's work in that field.

Leevy was born on October 13, 1920, in Columbia, South Carolina, to Isaac and Mary Leevy, then teachers in rural schools. His father graduated from Hampton University, his mother from South Carolina State College. In later years they first operated a department store in Columbia, then a funeral home and ambulance service. One of four children in the family, Leevy grew up with the example of his community–minded parents, knowing that in the family tradition, he would continue his education to prepare for a professional career. His sister Marion died while she was a student at South Carolina State College; his brother Isaac, a funeral director, died in 1979; sister Ruby Leevy Johnson is vice–president of Leevy's Funeral Home in Columbia, South Carolina.

Before he was school age, Leevy gave the first indication of his interest in medicine by voicing admiration of the efficiency of the pediatrician who cured his severe case of pneumonia. When he worked in his father's mortuary during adolescence, he observed the loss of life in the African American community due to inadequate facilities and medical personnel and vowed to become a doctor who considered the factors of racism contributing to the high death rate of black people. In high school he was part of humanitarian projects in school, the youth group of his church, and a Boy Scouts troop, and he took an early step toward his career by working with his chemistry teacher to complete a well–produced paper on isotopes. When he graduated with honors from Booker T. Washington High School in Columbia, he had been on the school's debating team and held the offices of president of his class, chair of the science club, and editor of the student newspaper.

Leevy enrolled as a premedical student in Fisk University in Nashville, Tennessee, and paid most of his expenses through a scholarship and a clerical job provided by the National Youth Administration (NYA). As president of the Student Christian Association, and vice–president of the Southeastern YMCA Field Council, Leevy did his part to eliminate racial discrimination and segregation in the campus neighborhood. These efforts—not always successful—and the 1940 experience of a totally integrated summer conference in Lisle, New York, inspired his life long intent to contribute to the solution of social and economic disadvantages in addition to conquering medical problems. He graduated from Fisk summa cum laude in 1941 and enrolled in the University of Michigan Medical School in the fall of that year. At Michigan he supplemented his finances with a fellowship from the Kellogg Foundation and from a job waiting tables.

While Leevy was in the first year of medical school, President Franklin D. Roosevelt nominated Leevy for membership on the National Advisory Committee of the NYA. His charge was to observe inadequacies in education and health care in segregated NYA units. He presented his findings in NYA conferences at Hyde Park and in meetings at the White House and received assurance from Eleanor Roosevelt and Mary McLeod Bethune that the discrepancies would be corrected. Unfortunately the recommendations fell victim to the pressing demands of World War II.

Commitment to Medical Education and Research

In 1942, his second year at Michigan, Leevy went into the Army Specialized Training Program. Its monthly stipend relieved the financial pressure and freed him for full–time clinical experience and strict attention to his studies. This rewarding exposure ended with his firm decision to specialize in medical education and research.

Following the award of the M.D. degree in 1944, Leevy completed the final four years of preparation for medical practice with a one–year medical internship and a three–year medical residency, each at the Jersey City Medical Center of UMDNJ, in Newark, New Jersey. The policy of segregated housing for African American staff at the center meant that Leevy and his fellow black trainees suffered the indignity of assignment to quarters in the basement of the Tuberculosis Hospital. Leevy also saw bigoted racial attitudes at the center reflected in the way some of the medical personnel reacted to their African American patients. In spite of these insults and his efforts to soften their effects, it was a successful period of professional growth for Leevy.

Leevy spent the first year at the center in a rotating internship in the Emergency Service, treating patients from the diverse citizenry of the state, in pediatrics, orthopedics, and internal medicine, and further sharpened his emerging skills as a diagnostician. During the next phase of training—resident physician—he first taught pharmacology to interns. He simultaneously conducted research in fluid metabolism in heart and liver failure and reported the findings in the *Journal of the American Medical Association.*

Publication of the work attracted broad attention to him as a developing medical researcher and led to his appointment as Chief Resident Physician. In this graduate level program, and with the advantage of continued study with excellent instructors, Leevy investigated the severity and the frequency of diabetes in patients with a history of liver trouble related to alcoholism. As a reward, he received the Modern Medicine Prize for introducing a new era in medicine by providing consistent follow up and other advancements in the treatment for that previously neglected group of patients.

At the end of the residencies in 1948, Leevy became director of Clinical Investigation and Outpatient Department at the center. His first actions were to diversify the staff by adding minority and female staff members and broaden the program by instituting postgraduate courses and setting up a research department. He established relations with the Medical Society of New Jersey, the National Medical Association (the organization of African American physicians), Tuskegee Institute (now University), Howard University, and Meharry Medical College. To stress the social implications of medical practice, he invited Charles Drew, Martin Luther King Jr., and other African American notables to address the staff.

Leevy's participation in UMDNJ was interrupted by a stint in the U.S. Navy at St. Albans Naval Hospital in Virginia. As a lieutenant commander, he developed a liver center at the hospital, and he discovered better ways to diagnose liver tumors. He then went to Harvard Medical School for a year of teaching and research but came back to UMDNJ for intensive work in hepatology that produced further significant understanding of the functions of the liver and liver diseases.

Leevy has taught thousands of premedical and post doctoral students from all over the world in his laboratories and classrooms. His teaching and administrative appointments at UMDNJ have been associate professor of medicine, professor of medicine, and chairman of the Department of Medicine. Since 1984 Leevy has been scientific director at the Sammy Davis Jr. National Liver Institute, and from 1989 to the present he has been a distinguished professor of medicine at UMDNJ. The UMDNJ–based institute is dedicated to research in prevention and treatment of liver disorders. His son, Carroll Barboza Leevy, a graduate of Johns Hopkins Medical School and associate director for clinical affairs is a valued part of the research team.

Leevy has lectured in medical schools in North America, Latin America, Europe, Africa, and Asia. From 1956 to 1992 he appeared in scientific television shows in the United States, Canada, and China. A prolific writer, Leevy is the author of six books on liver disease widely used for research and teaching, editor and contributor to numerous books, and author of more than 500 articles and papers. He sits on a large number of scientific boards, and is a much sought after reviewer for journals specializing in his field.

Leevy has a well established international reputation for his leadership in medical organizations, principally the American Association for Study of Liver Diseases (president, 1970), the International Association for Study of the Liver (president, 1986–88), the International Hepatology Informatics Group, and the Association for Academic Minority Physicians, a society he helped to establish.

Leevy holds honorary doctorates from Fisk University (1981), the New Jersey Institute of Technology, and the University of Nebraska (1989). His additional awards include: Robert H. Williams Distinguished Chairman of Medicine Award, Association of Professors of Medicine, 1991; and the Distinguished Service Award and the American Association for the Study of Liver Diseases, 1991. In 1991 he was named master in the American College of Physicians. Leevy also received the National Medical Association Centennial Award, 1995; and Distinguished Achievement Award, Association for Academic Minority Physicians, 1995.

Leevy's nonmedical service includes: University of Cape Town Fund, South Africa, since 1982; life membership, NAACP; National Urban League since 1960; and Congregational Church, Short Hills, New Jersey, from 1974 to the present. He is a member of Phi Beta Kappa and Alpha Omega Alpha. Leevy made a major contribution to the community as chairman of the Concerned Citizens of Newark. Working with citizens, city officials, and medical professionals, he was the main force in the development of the Newark Agreement. Under this agreement, the federal government allowed the location of the medical school in Newark. He was involved in the implementation of the agreement, seeing that the government's mandated improvements in health care for the community and ethnic and gender diversity in the medical staff were carried out.

On February 4, 1946, Leevy married Ruth Secora Barboza, a chemist who worked with him at St. Albans Naval Hospital and at Harvard Medical School. They have a son, Carroll Barboza Leevy, a physician, and a daughter, Maria Leevy, a creative writer living in New Jersey.

Carroll Moton Leevy is honored as a specialist in all matters having to do with the liver and as a man of integrity, whose interests extend into the social factors that determine the quality of life. In his laboratories, he has made discoveries that saved lives, and in his classrooms he passed his knowledge to new and continuing students for continuity into the future.

Current address: 35 Robert Dr., Short Hills, NJ 07078.

REFERENCES

American Men and Women of Science, 1995–96. 19th ed. New Providence, NJ: Bowker, 1994.

"Disciples of Hippocrates." *Black Enterprise* 5 (February 1975): 22.

Kessler, James H., J. S. Kidd, and others, eds. *Distinguished African American Scientists of the 20th Century.* Phoenix: Oryx Press, 1996.

Leevy, Maria. *Carroll M. Leevy M.D.* Unpublished manuscript in Carroll Leevy's possession.

Sammons, Vivian O. *Blacks in Science and Medicine.* New York: Hemisphere Pub. Corp., 1990.

Who's Who among African Americans, 1996–97. 9th ed. Detroit: Gale Research, 1996.

Who's Who in America, 1996. 50th ed. New Providence: Marquis Who's Who, 1996.

Dona L. Irvin

William A. Leidesdorff

(1810–1848)

Pioneer, entrepreneur, civic leader

William A. Leidesdorff made a major contribution to history. A most remarkable feature of Leidesdorff's short life is that in the period of only seven years, from 1841–1848, he was to be a major player in California's development. He was intimately involved in the movement for annexation and a civic leader in San Francisco who greatly developed commercial enterprise in the area. He served as American vice consul, served on the City Council, and helped establish the first public school. Leidesdorff's personal correspondence also reveals a deep personal involvement in the political, social, and military intrigue leading to the annexation by the United States of the erstwhile Mexican province that is now the state of California.

William Alexander Leidesdorff was born on St. Croix Island in 1810. His father, William Leidesdorff, was a Danish planter and his mother, Anna Maria Spark, was of African descent. Their five children, in birth order, were William A., Frederik Laurentius, Alisa, Adriane, and Anna Christiane. On November 18, 1810, Leidesdorff was baptized in the Lutheran Church in St. Croix. He was confirmed in the same church on April 2, 1826. His parents were not married, but his father accepted Leidesdorff as a son and took legal action in 1837 to acknowledge him and name him as an heir. In 1834 Leidesdorff went to New Orleans to work in his father's cotton business. Leidesdorff took out naturalization papers on February 25, 1834, and was soon active in social affairs.

John Ingham and Lynne Feldman report a story in *African-American Business Leaders* that Leidesdorff and a local socialite apparently developed an amorous relationship that led Leidesdorff to propose marriage. On hearing of Leidesdorff's avowal of his black parentage, the young lady's father refused permission for the union, leaving Leidesdorff desolate. Speculation ensued that this led to his taking to a seafaring career, which eventually led to his trip around South America and on to California. Axel Hansen in *From These Shores* wrote that the young lady died "from a broken heart" shortly after Leidesdorff's departure.

Leidesdorff inherited his father's property following the elder Leidesdorff's death sometime about 1840. Subsequent travels took Leidesdorff to New York. He settled there, working as a ship's master on several voyages and engaging in shipping and commercial trading, with New York as his base and homeport. He later sailed to California in 1841 as captain of the *Julia Ann.* Upon his arrival in California, he settled in Yorba Linda (now San Francisco) and bought a lot at the corner of Clay and Kearny streets. He took Mexican citizenship in 1844, and also acquired a large land grant on the American River from the Mexican government.

Seafarer Becomes Public Leader

After settling in California, Leidesdorff soon established a new business in Yorba Linda. He purchased a city lot in 1843 and built a general store there. He continued also as a seafarer on the *Julia Ann,* sailing to the West Indies and other ports until the sale of the boat by its owner, J. C. Jones, in 1845. Thomas Larkin, the American Consul stationed in Monterey, soon became a close friend of Leidesdorff and appointed him vice consul for the port of San Francisco; his Mexican citizenship apparently was not an issue at that time. Matters became somewhat more clouded politically, as Cali-

William A. Leidesdorff

fornia was in the throes of a public debate. This debate soon erupted into a three–sided conflict between those who wanted to remain allied to Mexico, those who wanted independence, including the so–called ''Bear Flag'' group, and those who wanted the United States to annex California.

The correspondence between Larkin and Leidesdorff makes it clear that they were in the center of this controversy, especially after receiving a visit by the explorer, Captain John C. Fremont, who may have been ''scouting'' to determine the extent of public support for annexation. At all events, the annexation proponents in California and Washington, D.C. won out; President John Tyler declared war on May 13, 1846, and ordered the occupation of California. Locally, Captain John Montgomery led the U.S. troops who captured the port of San Francisco, and Leidesdorff personally led a party that neutralized the local fort and the Presidio. Leidesdorff translated the text of the Montgomery occupation and annexation proclamation into Spanish for public delivery, while at the same time accepting the Mexican flag and important papers from the fort for safekeeping.

With the establishment of democratic institutions, a city council was elected, on which Leidesdorff served as treasurer. He also served on several major committees, including the school committee, which laid the groundwork for the establishment of the first public school in San Francisco in 1848.

At this time Leidesdorff lived in a one–story cottage on the corner of California and Montgomery streets, considered the finest house in the town. Soon thereafter, he built the City Hotel, the first hotel in Yerba Buena. It was located on the lot where his first store was erected in 1843. The hotel subsequently became the center of social life in the community.

Intrigue followed Leidesdorff to his grave. Following his death in 1848, his close friend Thomas Larkin applied to be declared executor of his estate. Leidesdorff had died intestate and with an indebtedness of over $60,000, but soon the value of his estate skyrocketed, making Leidesdorff a postmortem millionaire. Larkin's claim was disallowed due to Leidesdorff's Mexican citizenship. Captain Joseph Folsom, meanwhile having purchased the rights to the estate from the family, contested in court for the executorship with the State of California, which had also laid claim. Folsom was eventually granted full rights by the courts, and that brought a final resolution to the matter.

There were numerous changes of political leadership and responsibility in San Francisco during Leidesdorff's last few years, but he prospered nevertheless in business and retained an influential position in public society. He entertained prominent visitors to the city in his residence, and he took an active part in establishing the new city. One can certainly say that he was a precise and efficient public official, at least to judge from the *San Francisco Town Journal.* His handwritten ledgers as treasurer provide a thorough record of all purchases for the period of his tenure, from major transactions for building equipment down to supplies costing only a few dollars. His reputation for responsibility and honesty is thus confirmed. His accomplishments in public life established his position as a pioneer leader in early California history.

Leidesdorff's appearance has been described variously. He has been called ''very swarthy,'' ''a Dansk–Mulat,'' and one showing no signs of black blood. Hubert H. Bancroft characterizes Leidesdorff in *The History of California,* ''[A]n intelligent man of fair education, speaking several languages; active, enterprising and public spirited; honorable for the most part in his transactions; but jealous, quick tempered, often quarrelsome, and disagreeable.''

Leidesdorff died suddenly of typhus on May 18, 1848, when he was 38–years old. He was buried in Mission Dolores. A short street in San Francisco is named in his memory, as are a street and a plaza in Folsom, California. An aggressive entrepreneur, Leidesdorff is credited with sailing the first steamboat on the West Coast, the *Sitka,* purchased from a Russian company in Alaska. He introduced horse racing and built the first hotel in the new city as well as a warehouse and an expansive personal residence. At the same time he was very active in real estate and carried on a burgeoning and successful commercial career as a merchant, trader, and shipper. Initially valued at $60,000 in debt, his estate was subsequently valued at $1.5 million, based on the deed to his property, adjoining John Sutter's on the American River. The high value was primarily due to the presence of gold on the land. Leidesdorff was a courageous nineteenth–century black settler whose work led to the Territory of California becoming the 31st state of the Union.

REFERENCES

Bancroft, Hubert H. *The History of California.* 4 vols. San Francisco: The History Company, 1884–1890.

Byington, Lewis F., ed. *History of San Francisco.* Vol. 1. San Francisco: S. J. Clarke, 1931.

Cowan, Robert E. "The Leidesdorff–Folsom Estate: A Forgotten Chapter in the Romantic History of Early San Francisco." *Quarterly of the California Historical Society* 7 (June 1928): 106–11.

"The First Negro Millionaire." *Ebony* 14 (November 1958): 50–54.

Hansen, Axel. *From These Shores.* Nashville, TN: Privately printed, 1996.

Ingham, John N. and Lynne B. Feldman. *African–American Business Leaders: a Biographical Dictionary.* Westport, CT: Greenwood Press, 1994.

Lapp, Rudolph M. *Blacks in Gold Rush California.* New Haven: Yale University Press, 1977.

Logan, Rayford W., and Michael R. Winston, eds. *Dictionary of American Negro Biography.* New York: Norton, 1982.

San Francisco Town Journal, 1847–48. San Francisco: Printed by H. S. Crocker Co., 1926.

Savage, William S. *Blacks in the West.* Westport, CT: Greenwood Press, 1976.

———. "The Influence of William Alexander Leidesdorff on the History of California." *Journal of Negro History* 38 (July 1953): 322–32.

———. "Intrigue in California (1846)." *Midwest Journal* (Winter 1949): 63–68.

Young, John D. *San Francisco: A History of the Pacific Coast Metropolis.* San Francisco: S. J. Clarke, 1912.

COLLECTIONS

The William Leidesdorff Papers, 1838–1848 (50 folders, 3 microfilm reels) are in the Library of Congress. The California Historical Society Library in San Francisco has a collection of his correspondence, account books, and personal papers dating from 1834 to 1848. Two other Leidesdorff collections are in the Bancroft Library, University of California, Berkeley, and at the Huntington Library, San Marino, California.

Darius L. Thieme

Leile, George.
See Liele, George.

David Levering Lewis
(1936–)
Educator, writer, historian

The decade of the 1990s has produced a new generation of intellectual leadership for this nation. These intellectuals have sought to make their work meaningful to members of their own circle, yet accessible to a general educated audience. David Levering Lewis, biographer, historian, scholar, and educator, holds a prominent place within a burgeoning group of prolific African American authors who, particularly in the last two decades, have written extensively about race, about their lives, about the lives of others, and about America. Lewis's masterpiece, a Pulitzer–prize winning biography entitled *W. E. B. Du Bois: Biography of a Race,* chronicles both the life and the times of one of the most brilliant and fertile minds of the twentieth century. This work, which won eight book awards, ranks Lewis among the nation's most gifted contemporary writers and thinkers.

In 1948, when 12–year David Lewis met the 80–year–old Du Bois, neither imagined how significant each eventually would become in the other's life. Since that time, Lewis has blossomed from a precocious young boy standing in the shadow of an intellectual giant into a gifted and versatile scholar who has written deftly in the areas of African American history, European history, and African history.

Lewis was born May 25, 1936 in Little Rock, Arkansas to educated parents, John Henry Lewis and Alice Ernestine Bell Lewis. When Lewis was very young, his parents moved the family to Wilberforce, Ohio, home of Wilberforce University. Growing up in a comfortable middle–class home and college community provided Lewis with the opportunity and the stimulation to concentrate on his intellectual development. Lewis's father, who was a high school principal and later a college president, provided his family with a library filled with a variety of works by authors ranging from Frederick Douglass and W. E. B. Du Bois to Pushkin and Alexander Dumas. During Lewis's early life he had the opportunity to meet and dine with some of the most prominent members of the African–American community when they came to perform or to speak at the college. Lewis remembers being inspired by Marian Anderson, Thurgood Marshall, and Adam Clayton Powell.

Perhaps even more significant in the development of Lewis's sense of racial pride was the story he often was told about how his father sacrificed his job as principal of Little Rock's Colored High School because of his unyielding insistence that the salaries of African–American teachers equal those of white teachers. Coming of age in the mid–1950s, Lewis's concept of the responsibility of being a young black man in America was born out of the socially marginal existence of middle–class blacks, who believed that their individual actions directly reflected upon the entire race. He wrote in "From Eurocentrism to Polycentrism, "published in

Historians and Race, that many middle class African Americans believed that "exemplary feats of professional and intellectual" accomplishments would somehow assuage racist attitudes toward the black community. Even so, it was his family and the middle class, black college communities which primarily nurtured in Lewis the security and confidence to believe in the potential of his own success. When Lewis was an adolescent, his father assumed the position of president of Morris Brown College in Atlanta. He enrolled his son in Booker T. Washington High School, the same high school Martin Luther King Jr. attended just a few years earlier. Like King, Lewis did not actually complete the high school program; instead, he entered the Ford Foundation–funded Early Entrants Program at Fisk University in Nashville.

When David Lewis went off to Fisk University in the fall of 1952, he had turned down a generous offer from his uncle, a prominent physician in Atlanta, for a free college education if he would study medicine. Instead, he majored in history and philosophy at Fisk. In his sophomore year, Lewis was president of the Early Entrants and treasurer of the Student Council. During his college years Lewis also developed an interest in international issues and affairs. As a member of the International Student Center, Lewis had the opportunity to read foreign newspapers and journals, view foreign films, and participate in lectures, panel discussions, and debates. This experience would serve him well when he later found himself studying in London and Paris.

Lewis's years of study were vintage years in the history department at Fisk. The faculty included noted historian of Jacksonian America, Ed Pessen, prolific historian of African American history, August Meier, and, particularly influential in Lewis's intellectual life, Theodore Currier, whose "bachelor abode on the campus," wrote Lewis in "From Eurocentrism to Polycentrism," was an "after–hours' classroom and tavern enveloped in smoke and throbbing with sessions about every conceivable historical topic." Lewis's years at Fisk coincided with the college presidency of the indefatigable sociologist Charles S. Johnson, who, through his work both as a scholar and an administrator, took the university to new heights of integrity, accomplishment, and reputation. Lewis graduated Phi Beta Kappa with a bachelor of Arts in history and philosophy in 1956.

In the fall of 1956, Lewis contemplated a legal career and enrolled in the University of Michigan Law School, but decided after a semester that he was more interested in pursuing graduate study in history. Immediately, he entered the graduate history department at Columbia University in New York City, focusing on U.S. history almost by default because the European history course he was most interested in taking was full. He wrote a thesis entitled "John Fiske: A Traditional Figure in American Social Darwinism" and was subsequently awarded an M.A. in history in the spring of 1958. Still very interested in studying European history, however, Lewis enrolled in England's London School of Economics. Here he focused his studies on Modern European and French history. His dissertation, "Emmanuel Mournier and the Politics of 'Moral Revolution': French Liberal Catholicism in Crisis, 1926–1952," was completed in the spring of 1962, and he was awarded a Ph.D. These were formative years in Lewis's intellectual development. He would conclude his tenure in graduate school with a decidedly academic interest in biography and European history. All the while he continued to develop the intellectual breadth and skills that would serve him well when he subsequently began scholarly work in U.S. history. The fall of 1962 found Lewis reporting to Fort Benning, Georgia, for military service in the U.S. Army. He served as a psychiatric technician in Landstuhl, Germany for a year.

Writes King Biography

After completing his brief stint in the military, Lewis officially began his career as a university professor and scholar. He already had one publication to his credit. Shortly after completing his M.A. at Columbia, he coauthored the work with August Meier. Lewis and Meier spent the summer of 1958 interviewing numerous members of Atlanta's black middle class, from doctors and lawyers to bankers and club women. The fruit of their labor was an article, "History of the Negro Upper Class in Atlanta," published in the *Journal of Negro Education* in 1959.

From 1961 to 1965, Lewis held lectureships at the University of Maryland Overseas Education Program, the University of Ghana in Africa, Howard University in Washington, D.C., and at the University of Notre Dame in South Bend, Indiana. In all of these positions, Lewis taught various aspects of European history, from the Reformation to Modern Europe. At Morgan State University in Baltimore from 1966 to 1970, Lewis found his first tenured position, teaching courses on the French Third Republic.

In March of 1968, Lewis received a request from one of the editors of Penguin Publishers to write a biography of Martin Luther King Jr. For several reasons, Lewis approached the offer with some skepticism. First, although his master's program had trained him well in the methodology of historical biography, most of his professional training as a historian had been in European history. Also, he feared that perhaps the editor had selected him believing that he possessed some special insight into African American history because he was black. Lewis noted in "From Eurocentrism to Polycentrism," however, that King's assassination "turned what would have been a digression [from his then–current interest and training] into a unique opportunity to write about the promise and the mirage of America as the land of opportunity." Despite his initial misgivings, Lewis dedicated a year of his professional life to researching and writing a biography of the slain leader of the Civil Rights Movement. Lewis concluded in *King: A Biography*: "Martin Luther King was a rare personality, endowed with an ample intelligence, great courage and convictions, and an arresting presence. . .an unusual man—who lived in an extraordinary time." Lewis received sharp criticism for the book initially because its original title, *King: A Critical Biography,* was misinterpreted to suggest a criticism of King's life. In general, however, it was well received by the much of the academic community. Success with the King biography notwithstanding, Lewis's primary interest continued to be in the field of European history.

In 1970 Lewis accepted an associate professorship at the University of the District of Columbia. His experience researching and writing the King biography gave him scholarly breadth such that he now taught courses in Modern Europe as well as in U.S. civil rights history. Remaining in this position for ten years, Lewis then accepted an appointment at the University of California, San Diego in La Jolla where he remained for five years.

Rutgers—the State University of New Jersey—created an endowed chair to honor the life and service of Martin Luther King Jr. in 1968, and in 1985 Lewis became the second recipient of the chair. Along the way to earning this singular distinction, Lewis amassed an impressive list of contributions and activities as a scholar, historian, and valued community member. He has been the recipient of fellowships from the Woodrow Wilson International Center for Scholars and the John Simon Guggenheim Memorial Foundation. He has been a National Humanities Center Fellow, and received a Fulbright travel grant. He has worked on important national councils and committees such as the American Council of Learned Societies and the American Association for State and Local History, which commissioned him to write the Bicentennial History of the District of Columbia. Concurrently, Lewis has been involved in a number of service activities, including trustee for both the National Humanities Center and People for the American Way. He is a founding member of the Committee for Policy on Racial Justice and a member of the American Historical Association.

Du Bois Biography Wins Awards

As a scholar, Lewis has published several other books since the King biography and numerous journal articles in European, African, and African American history. His biography, *W. E. B. Du Bois: Biography of a Race, 1868–1919* (1993) has garnered the most critical acclaim and praise of his works to date. This work not only won the 1994 Pulitzer Prize in biography but also the National Conference of Black Political Scientists Outstanding Book Award, the Bancroft Prize in American History and Diplomacy, the Phi Beta Kappa Ralph Waldo Emerson Award, and several others. When asked by *Booknotes* interviewer Brian Lamb why he wrote the Du Bois biography, Lewis noted that Du Bois's was "a large life that impinges upon so many issues. . ." and further stated that he hoped to "use the life not simply to address and retrieve the multifaceted personality of Du Bois, but to use it as a window onto much of the 20th century." To label Lewis's biography a success is an understatement. This biography is a work that is intellectually sound and analytically challenging, yet readable. Lewis has written an accessible biography of a man who was so formal and erudite in his life as to be inaccessible to many. Writing scholarly sound but "user friendly" history is particularly important to Lewis's conception of his mission as a historian. In the *Booknotes* interview he explained, "There is an urgency for historians like never before, to speak to the large public. And if we don't we are going to leave the terrain to the Disney Corporation, and journalists, who when they are good, they are superb. But historians have a training that is of value, and we have got to practice accessibility in our language and presentation."

Lewis has lived a busy life of outstanding service and uncompromising intellectual and scholarly excellence. He has taken his responsibility as educator and mentor most seriously. At Rutgers, Lewis teaches undergraduate as well as graduate students. One of Lewis's interviewers, Herbert Boyd, noted that in the course of an interview held in Lewis's Rutgers office, Lewis was interrupted several times by students coming by with various requests and problems. Boyd was impressed with how attentively Lewis listened to students' problems and concerns and how patiently he offered suggestions. Among his graduate students, Lewis's reputation is that of an outstanding sage, highly demanding, and remarkably apt in teaching students to both analyze books as well as create their own compelling analyses and narratives. Kenneth Janken, assistant professor of African–American Studies at the University of North Carolina at Chapel Hill and a former student, described Lewis in an interview with Houston B. Roberson as "a real task master who cares deeply about his students' minds and his students as human beings."

Lewis defies the traditional practice of history by writing fluently in unrelated fields. Whether writing an historical monograph about an obscure community in Africa or on an infrequently visited topic in French history or even biographies of larger–than–life civil rights leaders, Lewis possesses abundant historical poise, intellectual skill, and insight to accomplish the task.

Married to Ruth Ann Stewart, Lewis is the father of four children: Eric, Allison, Jason, and Allegra. Currently, he holds the distinguished Martin Luther King, Jr. chair at Rutgers University.

Current address: Department of History, Rutgers, the State University of New Jersey, New Brunswick, NJ 08903.

REFERENCES

The Black History World Today Transcript. Herbert Boyd, "David Levering Lewis" [n.d.] http://www.tbwt.com/bht/lewis~1.htm

Booknotes Transcript. Brian Lamb interview with David L. Lewis, January 2, 1994. http://www.booknotes.org/transcripts/10059.htm (last updated June 20, 1997).

Boyd, Herbert. "David Levering Lewis." [n.d.] http://www.tbwt.com/bht/lewis~1.htm.

Cimbala, Paul A., and Robert F. Himmelberg, eds., *Historians and Race: Autobiography and the Writing of History.* Bloomington: Indiana University Press, 1996.

Curriculum Vitae of David Levering Lewis, 1997.

Gates, Henry Louis Jr. "Second Thoughts: Leaders of the Sixties Talk about the Nineties." *New Yorker* 72 (6 May 1996): 59–62.

Hertzberg, Hendrick, and Henry Louis Gates, Jr. "The African–American Century: The Cultural Centrality of Blacks and Other Paradoxes." *New Yorker* 72 (29 April 1996): 9–10.

Janken, Kenneth. Interview with Houston B. Roberson, March 11, 1998.

Lewis, David L. *District of Columbia: A Bicentennial History.* New York: Norton, 1976, 1978.

———. "From Eurocentrism to Polycentrism." In *Historians and Race: Autobiography and the Writing of History.* Edited by Paul A. Cimbala and Robert F. Himmelberg. Bloomington: Indiana University Press, 1996.

———. *King: A Biography.* Champagne: University of Illinois Press, 1978.

———. *The Portable Harlem Renaissance Reader.* New York: Viking, 1994.

———. *Prisoners of Honor: The Dreyfus Affair.* New York: William Morrow, 1974.

———. *The Race to Fashoda: European Colonialism and African Resistance in the Scramble for Africa.* New York: Henry Holt, 1994.

———. *W. E. B. Du Bois: A Reader.* New York: Henry Holt, 1995.

———. *W. E. B. Du Bois: Biography of a Race, 1868–1919.* New York: Henry Holt, 1993.

———. *When Harlem Was In Vogue.* New York: Knopf, 1981.

The Oval. Fisk University Yearbook, 1953, 1954, 1955, 1956.

Robbins, Richard. *Sidelines Activist: Charles S. Johnson and the Struggle for Civil Rights.* Jackson: University of Mississippi Press, 1996.

Who's Who In America. New Providence, NJ: Marquis Who's Who, 1997.

Houston B. Roberson

Henry Lewis

(1932–1996)

Symphony orchestra conductor, opera conductor

Henry Lewis garnered international recognition during his eight–year tenure as music director of the New Jersey Symphony Orchestra. The appointment of a 36–year–old black conductor to the job had been a landmark event, one of a number of important firsts in Lewis's life and career, including being the youngest person and first black to play with the Los Angeles Philharmonic as a double bassist. He was ultimately responsible, however, for developing the New Jersey group from a small community ensemble of part–time musicians into a highly respected professional orchestra.

Henry Jay Lewis was born in Los Angeles on October 16, 1932. He was the only child of Henry Lewis Sr., an automobile dealer and real estate salesman, and Josephine Lewis, a registered nurse at Queen of Angels Hospital. Educated in parochial and public schools, he began studying the piano at age five and soon thereafter took up the clarinet and several brass and string instruments. (He also studied vocal technique.) Lewis began giving solo double–bass recitals while still in high school and conducted his junior and senior high school orchestras at graduation ceremonies. With his love of classical music as well as his tremendous natural aptitude, he knew even then that he wanted to pursue a career in orchestral music.

Although he had his mother's support, Lewis received little encouragement from his father. Rather than become a musician, his father wanted him to choose what he considered a "respectable" profession. He saw no future in music for blacks. Lewis decided to tackle the bass in order to gain a seat in the school's orchestra. Soon he began studying with Herman Reinshagen, the former principal bass of the New York Philharmonic who was then a member of the Los Angeles Philharmonic. It was Reinshagen who guided Lewis's development as a virtuoso bass player and solo recitalist.

Invited to Join Los Angeles Philharmonic

When he was 16, Lewis rented the Wiltshire–Eben Theatre for a solo recital. The Los Angeles Philharmonic's music director Alfred Wallenstein was in the audience, and he was so impressed by what he heard that he invited the young man to audition for the orchestra. He was soon accepted as a full–fledged member and remained with the group until 1954. His success had two unexpected benefits: his father finally realized that there was a future for a black in a symphony orchestra, and he won a full scholarship to the University of Southern California.

Although he amassed more than enough credits to graduate, Lewis left the university without a degree. The only degree program in his field was in music education, and his interests went beyond methodology. While still enrolled at the university, however, he met his future wife, opera star Marilyn Horne, whom he married in 1960. They divorced in 1979.

Lewis was drafted into the military in 1954 and was assigned to the Seventh Army Symphony, first as a bass player and then as music director. Based in Stuttgart, Germany, the group received privileged treatment as a special services unit attached to the general. They rehearsed constantly and played three or four concerts a week, some of which were recorded for broadcast.

On one occasion, Lewis attracted the attention of Eduard van Beinum, music director of Amsterdam's Concertgebouw Orchestra. Van Beinum became his mentor, and when his military duties were completed in 1957, Lewis returned to the Los Angeles Philharmonic, where van Beinum was then serving as guest conductor.

In 1959 Lewis founded the String Society of Los Angeles, which later became the Los Angeles Chamber Orchestra. The group played throughout California and in 1963 set out on an extensive tour of Europe under the sponsorship of the U.S. Department of State.

Lewis made his subscription series debut with the Los Angeles Philharmonic in 1961 after guest conductor Igor Markevitch cancelled due to illness. Soon thereafter he was appointed associate conductor of the orchestra and resigned from his chair in the bass section. He remained with the Philharmonic until 1965.

Makes Operatic Conducting Debut

Lewis made his operatic conducting debut in the inaugural season of the San Francisco Spring Orchestra. He was invited to return for several additional productions, then conducted opera performances in Boston, Montreal, and Vancouver. He conducted at La Scala opera house in Milan, Italy, in 1965 and in 1972 became the first black to conduct New York's Metropolitan Opera on what turned out to be his fortieth birthday. There were many subsequent engagements, including the Metropolitan Opera's 1975 tour of Japan.

Prior to his selection as music director of the New Jersey Symphony Orchestra in 1968, Lewis conducted virtually every major American orchestra as well as a number of orchestras throughout Europe. The list included the New York Philharmonic; the symphonies of Boston and Chicago; the orchestras of Philadelphia, Cleveland, Pittsburgh, Detroit, San Francisco, Buffalo, and Baltimore; all of the major London orchestras; the RAI orchestras in Rome, Turin, and Milan; and France's Nouvel Orchestre Philharmonique.

Appointed to Direct New Jersey Symphony Orchestra

In February 1968, Lewis was appointed music director of the New Jersey Symphony Orchestra, the top choice out a field of 150 candidates for the job. Black journalist and music critic Raoul Abdul wrote of the event in *Blacks and Classical Music:*

> When the president of the orchestra's board was asked whether Lewis' race had any bearing on his appointment, he answered, ''Almost none until we came down to the final selection and realized that Mr. Lewis was the best qualified of all the candidates.''

A writer for *Time* magazine noted:

> The orchestra insisted that it chose Lewis only because he was talented, and not because he is Negro. Still, in a city [Newark] with an estimated 55% Negro population and a recent history of racial frustration, the appointment seems astute sociologically as well as musically.

A commentator for *Newsweek* also praised the musical skill Lewis brought to the role. ''The big winner in this new appointment is not Henry Lewis,'' declared the reporter, ''but the New Jersey Symphony Orchestra in securing for themselves a musician of real distinction.''

During Lewis's tenure, the orchestra grew from a part–time ensemble to a thoroughly professional contract orchestra. The number of concerts it performed increased from 22 per season to more than 125 and its budget grew from $75,000 to $1,500,000. Attendance went up and artistic standards were raised. His goal was to place good music in reach of ordinary people. To achieve this, the orchestra performed throughout the state at various outdoor concerts, in ghettos, and in working–class neighborhoods. It also made appearances at more traditional venues such as Carnegie Hall in New York City and the Kennedy Center in Washington, D.C. Wrote McFadden: ''During his colorful, often tumultuous tenure with the New Jersey Symphony, acclaim followed almost everywhere, and Mr. Lewis took on other high profile appearances as a guest conductor.'' But such opportunities diminished after 1976 because he was black.

Conducts Throughout Europe

As other black conductors before him had done, Lewis turned to Europe. When he returned to guest conduct with the New Jersey Symphony in 1985, he was presented with a key to the city of Newark, a tribute from Mayor Kenneth A. Gibson and the Newark City Council, and a proclamation designating March 29 as ''Henry Lewis Day'' in Newark. Critic Michael Redmond declared in the *Newark Star Ledger:*

> More than any other music director in the orchestra's 63–year history, Lewis made the New Jersey Symphony what it is today . . . a first–class professional orchestra of national reputation, and an artistic entity that has set the musical standard for the entire state. . . . He left a legacy that has continued to enrich this state, even in his absence. And that is something to applaud, commemorate, and celebrate.

In his later years, Lewis worked extensively with the Netherlands Radio Orchestra. He also appeared with the Hamburg Opera in Germany, the Royal Opera at Covent Garden in London, the English National Opera, and opera companies in the French cities of Marseilles and Avignon, Lausanne, Switzerland, Wales, and Venice, Italy. In addition, he worked regularly with orchestras in Germany, France, Italy, Denmark, Poland, and England. In the United States he led productions with the San Francisco Opera and the New York City Opera. He returned to Los Angeles in 1986 to conduct *Salome* for the Music Center Opera's inaugural season.

In 1990 Lewis collaborated with director Simon Callow in developing a London production of *Carmen Jones.* It opened at the Old Vic in April 1991, and in 1992 it captured the coveted Olivier Award for Best Musical.

Despite these many accomplishments, Lewis stated in a 1989 telephone interview with researcher and arts consultant William Terry:

> It is striking to me that an American conductor can be so successful in terms of both reviews and employment in Europe, and can be so completely ignored here. I work eight months of the year, but it's all in Europe. The only work I get here is guesting, or as a replacement for a sick conductor.

Although he had suffered from lung cancer, Lewis ended up dying of a heart attack in his Manhattan home on January 26, 1996, at the age of 63. The only child of his marriage to Marilyn Horne survived him, a daughter named Angela.

Henry Jay Lewis's place in history as one of the most remarkable conducting talents of all time is assured. Left to posterity are many albums and compact discs, including complete recordings of Meyerbeer's *Le Prophete,* Massenet's *La Navarraise,* numerous examples of arias and opera excerpts done in collaboration with Marilyn Horne, and a memorable RCA recording with the London Philharmonic Orchestra and Leontyne Price, which captured a Grammy Award.

REFERENCES

Abdul, Raoul. *Blacks in Classical Music.* New York: Dodd, Mead, 1977.

"Baton Breakthrough." *Newsweek* 71 (26 February 1968): 93.

Current Biography Yearbook. New York: H.W. Wilson, 1973.

"First Again." *Time* 91 (23 February 1968): 94.

Handy, D. Antoinette. *Black Conductors.* Metuchen, NJ: Scarecrow Press, 1995.

"Henry Lewis, Conductor Who Broke Racial Barriers of U.S. Orchestras, is Dead At 63." *New York Times,* January 19, 1996.

"Lewis, First Black on Met Podium, Leads 'Boheme.'" *New York Times,* October 18, 1972.

"Metropolitan Engages 1st Black Conductor." *New York Times,* April 25, 1972.

Redmond, Michael. "Maestro Lewis Still Has His Magic Touch." *Newark Star Ledger,* April 1, 1985.

Schumach, Murray. "Negro Conducts Coast Symphony." *New York Times,* February 10, 1961.

Terry, William E. Telephone Interview with Henry Lewis. Detroit, New York, August 1, 1989. Personal files of William Terry, Brooklyn, N.Y.

D. Antoinette Handy

John R. Lewis
(1940–)
Congressman, civil rights activist

John R. Lewis has been a front–line agitator in progressive social and human rights struggles in the United States for over 30 years. A cofounder of the Student Nonviolent Coordinating Committee (SNCC), he was an advocate of nonviolent protest to bring about social change for blacks in segregated America, using sit–ins and Freedom Rides as tools. He was also active in voter registration drives. Now a U.S. congressman and a political activist, he is recognized as one of the most influential blacks in national politics.

The third child of seven sons and three daughters, John Robert Lewis was born in Pike County near Troy, Alabama, on February 21, 1940. His parents were first sharecroppers on the farm of Lewis's birth and then bought a 110–acre farm nearby and established a modest cotton and peanut business.

John R. Lewis

To supplement their income, Lewis's father Eddie also drove a school bus while his mother, Willie Mae, was a laundress.

The Lewises were devoutly religious. By age eight, young John displayed his dislike for picking cotton and handling chores on his family's farm, preferring to dream of becoming a minister. He practiced preaching sermons by addressing the flock in his parent's chicken house, and by the time he was ten he had developed a full ministry. He baptized new chicks and held funerals for those that died. By his mid–teens he had listened to the sermons of Reverend Martin Luther King Jr. broadcast over local radio each Sunday morning. Despite his shyness and stammering speech, he modeled himself after King and preached regularly to Baptist churches in the area.

After graduating from high school in 1957—the first member of his family to do so—he entered the American Baptist Theological Seminary in Nashville, Tennessee. The 17–year–old worked as a part–time janitor to support himself. The next year he enrolled in Fisk University. Concurrently enrolled in the two institutions, in 1961 he received a B.A. from the Seminary and he graduated from Fisk with a B.A. degree in religion and philosophy in 1967.

The bus boycotts that developed in Montgomery, Alabama, by then aroused Lewis's interest in civil rights activism. When Lewis and several other students were restrained from establishing a chapter of the NAACP on the Fisk campus, he found another outlet for his newly–developed interests. Activist and clergyman James Lawson, a divinity student at nearby Vanderbilt University, held workshops on nonviolent techniques each week from September through November of 1959. These workshops were sponsored by the Nashville Christian Leadership Conference and Fellowship of Reconciliation. Lewis became a faithful student in the class. He had also come under the tutelage of Septima Clark at Highlander Folk School in Monteagle, Tennessee. Clark taught adults to read and to become teachers, and held an experimental week–long ''citizenship school'' to teach unschooled, potential black voters. Lewis was one of 16 students from Tennessee State University, the American Baptist Theological Seminary, Meharry Medical College, Vanderbilt, and Fisk who launched a test sit–in in Nashville on February 7, 1960—two months before the well–known sit–ins were launched in Greensboro, North Carolina. The students were arrested but continued their sit–ins over the next few weeks. Reflecting on this experience, Lewis said in an interview published in *Southern Exposure*:

> I just felt . . . that it was like being involved in a Holy Crusade. I really felt that what we were doing was so in keeping with the Christian faith. . . . We didn't welcome arrest. We didn't want to go to jail. But it became . . . a moving spirit. Something just sort of came over us and consumed us. And we started singing ''We Shall Overcome,'' and later we started singing ''Paul and Silas bound in jail, had no money for their bail. . . .'' It became a religious experience that took place in jail.

Lewis was arrested five more times. The student movement received wide media coverage and public support, and passive resistance became an effective weapon against racial segregation. The movement's efforts, coupled with an economic boycott of local businesses by black and whites as well, led to desegregated lunch counters by June of 1960 in seven Tennessee cities.

Cofounds Student Nonviolent Coordinating Committee

In April of 1960 Lewis and several other college students followed up their experiences at sit–in demonstrations by founding the Student Nonviolent Coordinating Committee (SNCC). Lewis volunteered to participate in the Freedom Rides organized by the Congress of Racial Equality (CORE) in 1961 to protest segregated interstate bus terminals. Headed to New Orleans from Washington, D.C., on May 4, he and 12 freedom riders met resistance as segregationists attacked the students and in one instance burned their bus. After a cooling–off period, the rides continued, and on May 21 the students were assaulted again, this time in Montgomery, Alabama. Lewis was knocked unconscious by a club–wielding bigot, but continued his rides that summer, risking his life while insisting that nonviolence was an appropriate protest technique. Again their protest was successful; in September that year the Interstate Commerce Commission outlawed racial segregation in bus depots.

Lewis dropped out of college in June of 1963, when his fellow protestors elected him chair of the SNCC. He was reelected in 1964 and again in 1965. Clearly he was a recognized leader in the Civil Rights Movement. Although Lewis appears to have become more militant in his views, some of SNCC's recent recruits were at odds with his ideas. Lewis concentrated on the March on Washington to be held on August 23, 1963. With Whitney Young, A. Philip Randolph, Martin Luther King Jr., James Farmer, and Roy Wilkins, Lewis had become one of the ''Big Six'' leaders. In addition to being one of the planners of the march, Lewis was also one of the keynote speakers. His radical speech, quoted in *Current Biography,* warned the audience that the protestors aimed for meaningful legislation from Congress or ''the time will come when we will not confine our march to Washington. We will march through the streets of Jackson. . .Danville. . .Cambridge. . . Birmingham. But we will march with the spirit of love and with the spirit of dignity that we have shown here today.'' He believed that President John F. Kennedy moved too slowly and ensured too little legislation to guarantee the civil rights of black citizens.

In 1964 Lewis's work with the SNCC concentrated on demonstrations in the South. He also coordinated SNCC's voter registration drives and community action programs through the Mississippi Freedom Summer. The next year Lewis rejected his fellow SNCC workers' advice and helped Martin Luther King Jr. organize the Montgomery to Selma march across the Edmund Pettus Bridge in Selma, Alabama. The march was held on Sunday, March 7, 1965, and was one of the most dramatic events of the nonviolent effort. In a confrontation with 200 Alabama state troopers and sheriff's deputies, the 25 marchers led by Lewis and activist Hosea Williams were attacked, marking the event as ''Bloody Sunday.'' Lewis was beaten into unconsciousness. A subsequent march across the bridge two weeks later involving 3,200 protestors—including King, Ralph Bunche, and white and black sympathizers—led to the passage of the Voting Rights Act of 1965 that President Lyndon B. Johnson signed into law in August.

During his work with SNCC, Lewis was arrested 40 times and endured numerous physical attacks and bodily injury; nevertheless, he retained his philosophy of nonviolence. He became disillusioned after the Selma/Montgomery experience and believed that blacks were beginning to tire of nonviolent approaches. By 1965 he was caught up in the national controversy over the Vietnam War, denounced the draft, became a conscientious objector, and in early 1966 cofounded the Southern Coordinating Committee to End the War in Vietnam. President Johnson appointed Lewis a member of his council for the White House Conference on Civil Rights. His fellow SNCC workers, however, had become disenchanted with his approach to civil rights and began to support the ''Black Power'' principles that militant Stokely Carmichael espoused. After Carmichael defeated him in 1966 in his bid to head SNCC for a fourth term, he soon resigned membership because he felt the organization had departed from its original nonviolent principles.

Lewis remained active in the Civil Rights Movement, serving with the Field Foundation in New York as director of civil rights and child welfare activities. He returned to the South in 1967 to complete his Fisk University degree and also to direct the Atlanta–based Southern Regional Council's community organization projects to help the rural poor in the Nashville area. From 1970 to 1977 he directed the Council's Voter Education Project, succeeding Vernon Jordan, and adding nearly four million minorities to the voter rolls, including his 51–year–old mother.

In 1977 President Jimmy Carter appointed Lewis to direct more than 250,000 volunteers in the ACTION program, a federal volunteer agency concerned with economic recovery programs in the community. ACTION also was overseer of the Peace Corps, Vista, and other antipoverty programs. He remained there until 1980 when he became community affairs director for the National Consumer Co–op Bank in Atlanta.

Enters Politics

Lewis became interested in politics as early as 1977 when he sought the Fifth Congressional District seat vacated by Andrew Young. President Carter had appointed Young ambassador to the United Nations. Lewis lost the race, then entered politics again in 1981, when he succeeded in his bid for a seat on the Atlanta City Council. While seated, he advocated ethics and neighborhood preservation. He resigned in 1986 to run for Congress and was elected in November that year as representative of the Fifth Congressional District, defeating black Georgia state senator Julian Bond. He was reelected to a fifth term in Congress in November of 1994 by an overwhelming majority.

In Congress Lewis has been chief deputy minority whip since 1991 and has sat on the influential Steering and Policy Committee in the 102nd and 103rd Congresses. In the 104th Congress he has been a member of the House Ways and Means Committee and co–chair of the Congressional Urban Caucus.

Political observers praise Lewis for his work in Congress and predict a bright future for him in national politics, and the *National Journal* named him one of 11 "rising stars in Congress" in 1990.

In addition to his work in civil rights and in Congress, Lewis has also served as trustee of the Robert F. Kennedy Memorial Foundation. He has been a member of the Atlanta Board of Education's advisory committee of the biracial commission, and a member of the advisory boards of *Black Enterprise* and the Martin Luther King, Jr., Center for Social Change. He is a member of the NAACP, the American Civil Liberties Union, the Afro–American Institute, and numerous civil rights organizations. In 1972 *Ebony* magazine named Lewis one of the most influential blacks in the United States, and in 1974 *Time* magazine called him one of the 200 rising leaders in the country. His alma mater, Fisk University, awarded him a doctor of laws degree in May of 1990.

On December 21, 1968, Lewis married the former Lillian Miles; they have an adopted son, John Miles. A Baptist and Democrat, the soft–spoken Lewis has spent most of life as a champion of civil rights activities, first through nonviolent protest and now in the national political arena.

Current address: 229 Cannon House Office Building, Washington, DC 20515.

REFERENCES

Branch, Taylor. *Parting the Waters: America in the King Years 1954–63.* New York: Simon and Schuster, 1988.

Contemporary Black Biography. Vol 2. Detroit: Gale Research, 1992.

Current Biography Yearbook. New York: H. W. Wilson, 1980.

"John Lewis Biography." Office of Congressman John Lewis, Washington, D.C., n.d.

Lyon, Danny. "The Nashville Sit–Ins: Nonviolence Emerges." *Southern Exposure* 9 (Spring 1981): 30–32.

Powledge, Fred. *Free At Last? The Civil Rights Movement and the People Who Made It.* Boston: Little, Brown, 1991.

Wexler, Sanford. *The Civil Rights Movement: An Eyewitness History.* New York: Facts on File, 1993.

Who's Who Among Black Americans, 1996–97. 9th ed. Detroit: Gale Research, 1996.

COLLECTIONS

Information on John Lewis and the sit–ins and civil rights movement can be found in the SNCC Freedom Center Collection at the University of Illinois, Chicago Circle, and in the Braden Papers, Civil Rights Collection, State Historical Society of Wisconsin in Madison. Information regarding Lewis's activities in the Nashville movement are in the Special Collections at Fisk University Library in Nashville, Tennessee.

Jessie Carney Smith

Reginald F. Lewis

(1942–1993)

Entrepreneur, philanthropist

Reginald F. Lewis was a highly successful businessman who had the skill and ability to negotiate some of the most spectacular business deals ever. His purchase in 1983 of McCall Pattern Company and in 1987 of the $1 billion food giant Beatrice International made him one of the 400 wealthiest business people in the United States, worth in excess of $400 million. According to his obituary in *Time* magazine, "he preferred being called a 'success story' rather than an 'African–American success story.'"

Lewis was born in Baltimore, Maryland, on December 7, 1942. His father, Clinton Lewis, was a civilian technician for the Army Signal Corps. Later he became the proprietor of several small businesses and then entered the U.S. Navy. When Lewis was five years old, his parents separated. His mother, Carolyn Cooper Lewis, worked both as a waitress and a night clerk at a local department store to support herself and her small son. Later, she became a postal worker. After the separation, mother and son lived on Dallas Street in what Lewis called, in his autobiography *"Why Should White Guys Have All the Fun?,"* a "semi–tough" neighborhood. They had moved in with his maternal grandparents, Sam and Sue Cooper, where he became a favorite with Sam Cooper. Although the Coopers had only an eighth–grade education, they had strong values and taught young Lewis how to deal with people of different backgrounds and races. Carolyn Lewis was a major influence throughout her son's life and, according to his book, Lewis "always exhibited a fierce protectiveness toward her."

When he was seven, Lewis was enrolled in St. Francis Xavier, a Catholic elementary school on Central Avenue, about five blocks from his home. The Oblate Sisters of Providence, an order that Elizabeth Lang founded in Baltimore in 1829, ran the school and served as teachers there. Lewis, who was already strong–willed, had several encounters with his teachers and recalled that one of the nuns told him that he would never be more than a carpenter.

When he was about nine years old, Lewis's parents divorced and in 1951 Carolyn Lewis married Jean S. "Butch" Fugett Sr., a young soldier from a nearby base. The new family moved to the West Side where they bought a row house at 2802 Mosher Street. His five half–brothers and sisters came rapidly.

At age ten Lewis had his first job, selling the *Baltimore Afro–American,* for which he earned $15 to $20 a week. He sold that route to his friend, Dan Henson, for $30. Then Lewis worked for the more profitable *Baltimore News American.*

Denied admission to continue his studies in a Catholic high school because of weak test scores, Lewis had to deal with his rejection. He also drifted away from the church where he had served as altar boy. He entered Dunbar High School, located in East Baltimore, an overcrowded school with an excellent academic reputation and an all–black faculty who were dedicated to their students. There he became a serious student and developed a strong determination to succeed. A talented athlete since his earlier years, Lewis became captain of the baseball, football, and basketball teams. By then he had the physique of an athlete: he was five–feet ten–inches tall and weighed about 170 pounds with a well–developed upper body and muscular legs. Until he was 15, Lewis had assumed that he would have a career in professional sports, retire early, and become a lawyer or businessman.

Lewis's entrepreneurial finesse was developing as well. He worked at night in a drugstore, and from age 16 to 18 he spent his summers in a full–time job at a country club. During this time he also learned to read the stock market. He became image–conscious and never lost that trait. In high school Lewis adopted the then–current "collegiate" style of dress, wearing tweed jackets, tapered pants, loafers, and thin, British neckties. However, Lewis's heavy work schedule took its toll on his grades. He completed high school with a rank of 118th out of 196 graduates, but though not a brilliant student, he was intelligent, well focused, and already successful in managing a variety of commitments.

Lewis entered Virginia State College, Petersburg, on a football scholarship. A third–string quarterback during his freshman year, as he nursed a shoulder injury, Lewis's performance fell far short of that demonstrated in high school. After his freshman year, Lewis quit football and devoted himself to his studies. He became an avid reader of the *New York Times* and the *Wall Street Journal.* In his studies, however, he had serious problems with mathematics, twice receiving a failing grade. He worked throughout college, earning $500 a week on commissions from the sale of photographic services to elementary and high schools in Virginia. He learned to master salesmanship and found the key to success was to make successive calls and build on each successful sale.

Lewis turned his thoughts to graduation, then graduate school or law school. Based on his perfect grades in economics and strong letters of support, he was selected for a summer program at Harvard Law School in 1965, which opened the door to a new world for him. Determined to do well in the program and to impress his instructors, Lewis read widely in the field of law. He was so impressive in the program that the school offered him admission that fall. He had never completed an application to Harvard and said in his autobiography, "I'm told that I am the only person in the 148–year–history of Harvard Law who was ever admitted before he applied."

To finance Lewis's studies, Harvard arranged an educational loan for Lewis and gave him a check for living expenses as soon as he arrived on campus. For the first time in his school career he could study without concentrating on work as well.

In the summer of 1966, he went to Europe for the first time. In Paris he befriended Helge Strufe, a young Scandinavian artist, and later arranged for some of Strufe's paintings to be sent on loan to Harvard. Lewis also bought some of Strufe's paintings, which later formed a part of his magnificent and valuable art collection.

Lewis graduated from law school in 1968; that summer he began work with one of New York City's blue–chip law firms—Paul, Weiss, Rifkind, Wharton, and Garrison. He was assigned to the corporate law department where Arthur Goldberg and Theodore Sorensen were among the luminaries already employed. Two years later Lewis made a bold move; he left the firm and became a partner with Murphy, Thorp and Lewis, one of the first African American law firms on Wall Street. In 1972 Lewis hired Charles Clarkson, a white attorney, and the next year hired Diana Lee. The two new staff concentrated on the legal work while Lewis continued to develop the business. Clarkson said in Lewis's autobiography that "Everybody was afraid of Reg over the years and it got worse." By then he was a tough taskmaster who required the best from his staff at all times. He also worked long hours and set the pace for his staff.

In time Lewis bought out two of his law partners and assumed the firm's liabilities. Within a few years the firm's major clients included General Foods, the Ford Foundation, Equitable Life, and Aetna Life. While sources differ on the dates of founding, according to Lewis's autobiography his firm was renamed Lewis and Clarkson in 1978 and in 1979 moved to 99 Wall Street.

Purchases McCall Pattern Company

In 1983, when huge corporations were being dismantled and sold to the highest bidder, Lewis read in *Fortune* magazine that the McCall Pattern Company was owned by a multibillion dollar conglomerate, Norton Simon Industries. Founded in 1870 and based in New York City, it was one of the nation's oldest home pattern companies and employed over 580 people in its production facilities in Manhattan Kansas. McCall's was also the second–largest home pattern company in business. Lewis had represented Norton Simon in 1973 when it sold *McCall's* magazine. Lewis created TLC Pattern (the Lewis Company) on July 29, 1983, for the purpose of taking over McCall, and created a holding company called TLC Group, Inc. In his view, McCall's was worth at least $18 million. Lewis also studied the economics of the sewing pattern business and knew how the industry operated. He aimed to buy the firm, reduce expenses, then sell it in a few years to make a sizeable profit. For him the takeover was an emotional as well as financial transaction and the first real test of his ability to bring about a deal of this magnitude. But he was confident that he could.

On January 29, 1984, Lewis closed the deal, acquiring McCall Pattern Company for $22.5 million in loans, without putting up any of his own money. Company revenues totaled $51.9 million. Lewis became even more intense and driven as a business–developer and owner; he also operated the firm with an innovative hand. The company doubled profits in 1985 and 1986, earning $12 million and $14 million respectively. On June 18, 1985, he sold the Manhattan, Kansas, operation to a third party, then leased it back, creating millions on McCall's balance sheet and eliminating significant capital gains tax. In the process, Lewis became a wealthy man and a member of the industrial elite. He spent little time in his law practice. He believed that the best way to gain a significant return on his investment would be to sell his company. In 1987, three years after he purchased McCall's, Lewis sold the company for a ninety–to–one gain.

Two weeks before the McCall sale closed, Lewis learned that Beatrice International was to be sold at auction; Lewis and the TLC Group decided to go for the company. At the age of 44 and anxious about the superdeal, he decided to seek advice from his mother, whom he respected highly. With her approval of the project that he refused to name, he had the added strength that he needed.

On August 6, 1987, Lewis signed an agreement to acquire Beatrice International for $985 million. Lewis now headed the largest African American owned enterprise in the country. According to Lewis's biography, John H. Johnson of Johnson Publishing Company was furious that he was no longer atop the list of major African American owned companies and never gave Lewis's achievement the recognition it deserved. As a media blitz developed over the acquisition, Lewis said in his autobiography: "This is a success story due to the transaction, not because of my race. . . . Iacocca is not cast as an Italian–American businessman and Icahn is not a Jewish–American. Why should I be an African–American?"

Comprised of 64 companies located in 31 countries, Beatrice was indeed a giant in world food production. Its parent company was Beatrice Foods, this country's 35th largest industrial corporation. According to *African–American Business Leaders,* Beatrice Foods manufactured "over 8,000 product lines under more than 200 different brand names." *Black Enterprise* reported that the acquisition made TLC Beatrice "the first and only black–owned company to break the $1 billion revenues barrier." *Black Enterprise* in 1988 named TLC Beatrice BE Company of the Year.

Diagnosed with incurable brain cancer in late 1992, Lewis began to arrange for the orderly transfer of power to his half–brother, Jean S. Fugett Jr, a lawyer. Fugett became vice chairman with responsibility for running the company, and Albert M. Fenster was named executive vice–president for operations.

Lewis was talented in areas beyond the business field and was recognized for his work. In 1979 Mayor Edward Koch of New York appointed him to the Off Track Betting Corporation, where he served for four years. Among Lewis's honors and citations was the Distinguished Service Award from the American Association of Minority Enterprise Small Business Investment Corporations.

Although he was not an activist, Lewis would not tolerate any form of racism and was also aware of the plight of African Americans. He contributed to the campaign expenses of several black politicians. He met Jesse Jackson in 1984 when Jackson first ran for U.S. president and held a fund raiser for him at Fraunces Tavern. In 1988, when Jackson ran for the presidency again, Lewis was his largest contributor. The two had become close friends. Lewis assisted other black politicians, including New York City mayor David N. Dinkins, Virginia governor L. Douglas Wilder, and Los Angeles mayor Tom Bradley. Lewis's philanthropy continued. In 1992 he made a $3 million gift to the Harvard University Law School, at that time the largest gift from a single individual in Harvard's history. Harvard responded and on April 23, 1993, named its first building in honor of an African American, The Reginald F. Lewis International Center. Lewis also gave $1 million to Howard University, $50,000 to Morgan State University to establish the Reginald F. Lewis Scholarship, and sizeable gifts to his undergraduate school, Virginia State University, and to the New York chapter of Kappa Alpha Psi Fraternity, to which he belonged.

Lewis had deep–set, piercing eyes and a bushy moustache. Charming and at the same time difficult to approach, he was intensely private, prone to mood swings, and was his own harshest critic. He spoke French fluently, was a serious tennis–player, and an art collector. Lewis died of a cerebral hemorrhage on January 19, 1993, after suffering also from brain cancer. His survivors included his wife Loida Nichols, of the Philippines, an attorney whom he married in a lavish ceremony in Manila's Paco Roman Catholic church on August 16, 1969, and children Leslie Nichols and Christina Nichols. His funeral was held in St. Edward's Roman Catholic Church in Baltimore, around the corner from his home, on January 23. Among those who sent condolences were President Bill Clinton and Hillary Rodham Clinton. He was buried in Baltimore's New Cathedral Cemetery. A memorial service was held at the Riverside Church in Manhattan on January 25. His longtime friend David N. Dinkins, then mayor of New York, was among the hundreds of people who attended the rites. Opera diva and friend Kathleen Battle sang ''Amazing Grace.'' The iron–willed negotiator, who remained a private person, masterminded several spectacular business, amassed a fortune, and became head of the nation's largest African American business, had touched the world with his vision and his business success.

REFERENCES

Contemporary Black Biography. Vol. 6. Detroit: Gale Research, 1994.

Ingham, John N., and Lynne B. Feldman. *African–American Business Leaders.* Westport, CT: Greenwood Press, 1994.

Lewis, Reginald F. (finished posthumously by Blair S. Walker). *Why Should White Guys Have All the Fun?* New York: Wiley, 1995.

Obituary. *Time* (1 February 1993).

Scott, Matthew S. ''Black Business Loses a Star: Lewis Dies of Cancer.'' *Black Enterprise* 23 (March 1993): 17.

Jessie Carney Smith

George Liele
(1750?–1820)
Religious worker

Although the exact year of his ordination remains uncertain, George Liele was the first black ordained Baptist minister in the United States. Born a slave, Liele's religious enthusiasm led him to actively seek converts to, and build churches for, the Baptist denomination he loved. He amply demonstrated that one of the best ways to bring Christianity to slaves was through the ordination of black ministers and allowing blacks to build up their own churches.

George Liele did not know the year of his birth, but it is assumed to be about 1750. He was born to slave parents named Liele and Nancy in Virginia. His owner, Henry Sharp, took him to Burke County, Georgia, shortly before the American Revolution. This is also the approximate time that he married since he estimated that he was 20 or 21 years older than the oldest of his four children.

George Liele

About three years after arriving in Burke County, Liele was converted and baptized by Matthew Moore, pastor of the Baptist church where Henry Sharp was a deacon. Around this time, Liele's owner gave him permission to move up and down the Savannah River as an exhorter, preaching to slaves. He developed a semi–regular circuit, traveling from Augusta to Savannah several times a year until the outbreak of the Revolutionary War. This mission made Liele the first known black Baptist missionary.

By 1775, Liele was preaching at Silver Bluff, near Beech Island, South Carolina, to a group of eight slaves, who formed the first black Baptist church in the United States. This small group furnished three men, in addition to Liele, who later became noted ministers elsewhere: David George, the first minister of the Silver Bluff Church, founder of the First Baptist Church in Shelburne, Canada, and missionary to Africa; Jesse Peter (sometimes known as Jesse Galpin), who became a missionary to South Carolina and Georgia slaves, helped found the first black Baptist Church in Savannah in 1788, and led the remnant of the Silver Bluff Church across the river to Augusta to establish a church there; and Henry Francis, missionary and first pastor of Ogeechee Baptist Church in 1803.

Liele was cut off from the Silver Bluff Church and other places up river from Savannah in November 1775 when the British promised emancipation to all slaves who supported Great Britain during the Revolutionary War. It is important to note that Liele's owner was himself a loyalist who fought with the British. During this time, Liele preached at Tybee Island, at the mouth of the Savannah River, where slaves were protected by the British army. At the beginning of 1779, when the British occupied Savannah, Liele moved there.

George Galpin, the loyalist owner of the plantation where Silver Bluff was located, fled to Savannah, and David George, pastor of the Silver Bluff church, led fifty slaves to Savannah in 1779 in response to the British promise of freedom to slaves who fought for the British. In Savannah, they formed a Baptist church. George Liele served as pastor of the church, probably because Liele's position as a servant to a British officer made it easier for him to watch over the interests of the flock. The church was dispersed in 1792 when the British evacuated Savannah.

Moves to Jamaica

Around the time of the Revolutionary War, Henry Sharp granted Liele his freedom from servitude. However, Sharp's heirs did not accept this decision and tried to reenslave him. Liele was temporarily placed in a British prison until the issue could be resolved. The British supported Liele's quest for freedom and released him from prison. Liele and other members of the church decided to leave Savannah with the British. David George left Savannah for Canada. Another member of the Savannah church, Brother Amos, left for the Bahamas where he established a flourishing church at New Providence. Liele immigrated to Jamaica. To pay for his passage, Liele indentured himself to Colonel Kirkland, the British officer who freed him from prison. The ship leaving Savannah was delayed, which enabled Liele to return to the city for a final visit during which he baptized four persons: Andrew Bryan and his wife Hannah Bryan, Kate Hogg, and Hagar Simpson.

In Jamaica, George Liele again founded a black Baptist church. His hard work and the influence of the English governor to whom he had been recommended by Kirkland enabled Liele to work out his indenture in two years, after which he began to preach. He founded his church with four other persons from America and began to work among the black slave population. Within a few years he bought three acres of land just outside Kingston where he built a church. Later, he built a second at Spanish Town.

Liele's work was never easy. He suffered from financial problems since he worked among a destitute slave population. Moreover, Liele was constantly suspected of preaching sedition. He incurred the disfavor of the legally established Anglican Church by building up a body of dissenting believers. Liele was jailed twice—once on a charge of sedition, and for debt incurred in building a chapel. He was freed of the first charge due to lack of evidence, but remained in jail for the second charge until the debt was paid.

To overcome his difficulties Liele attracted the support of men like Stephen A. Cook, a member of the Jamaica Assembly, who won permission from the assembly for the church to function and helped Liele solicit funds from English Baptists. Liele worked as a farmer and carried goods with a team of horses and wagons to support himself and his family.

George Liele was the first ordained African American Baptist minister and the first known black missionary. His perseverance, faith, and ability to work well with others enabled him to draw significant numbers of blacks to the Baptist Church in the United States and Jamaica, an achievement so great that its effects are still felt today.

REFERENCES

Brooks, Walter H. ''The Priority of the Silver Bluff Church and Its Promoters.'' *Journal of Negro History* 7 (April 1922): 172–196.

Freeman, Edward A. *The Epoch of Negro Baptists and the Foreign Mission Board National Baptist Convention, U.S.A., Inc.* Kansas City, KS: The Central Seminary Press, 1953.

Logan, Rayford W., and Michael R. Winston. *Dictionary of American Negro Biography.* New York: Norton, 1982.

Love, E. K. *History of the First African Baptist Church.* Savannah, GA: The Morning News Print, 1888.

Simms, James M. *The First Colored Baptist Church in North America.* Philadelphia: Lippincott, 1888.

Woodson, Carter G. *The History of the Negro Church.* 1921. 2nd ed. Washington, DC: The Associated Publishers, 1945.

Robert L. Johns

Little Richard

(1932–)

Singer, entertainer

Little Richard changed the direction of American popular music by pioneering rock music in America and, through his success, helping black artists break into mainstream popular music. While he did not do this single–handedly, the contrast between his flamboyant image and exuberant performance of ''Tutti Frutti'' and the staid version by a well–scrubbed Pat Boone in vee–neck sweater and saddle shoes is convenient shorthand for the shift.

Richard Wayne Penniman was born in Macon, Georgia, on December 5, 1932, the third child of Leva Mae and Charles ''Bud'' Penniman. There were 12 children in the family: Charles, Elnora (Peggie), Richard Wayne, Marquette de Lafayette, Walter Maurice, Horace Dearcy (Tony), Robert Realdo, Leva La Leda (Sylvia), Artis Elaine (Elaine), Gail June, Freka Diedra (Peaches), and Peyton Larry. Both parents came from large families. Charles Penniman's father, Walter Maurice, was a preacher; Charles became a brick mason and later a small–time bootlegger and nightclub owner. He was killed

Little Richard

outside his establishment while his wife was pregnant with her last child. Leva Mae Penniman married when she was 14 and had her first child just before she was 16.

Although the family was not affluent, Charles Penniman was a good provider. Little Richard was known as a mischievous boy. In a statement in the Sawyer biography, *The Life and Times of Little Richard,* Leva Mae Penniman characterized her third child as:

> the most trouble of any of 'em. He was very mischievous, always getting up to tricks. He got a lot of whippings. He didn't get whipped for everything he did, mind, or he wouldn't be here now, cos he did something nearly all the time!

He was also loud and boisterous. In high school Little Richard took up the saxophone. His mother said he could be heard three blocks away and added:

> He was real good. I was glad, because before that he used to beat on the steps of the house and on tin cans and pots and pans, or whatever, and sing. He could really sing. But, oh my, the noise.

Penniman received a religious upbringing. His immediate family attended the New Hope Baptist Church, but he also attended services in Pentecostal, AME, and Holiness churches with other family members. He especially liked the exuberant worship practices of the Pentecostal and Holiness congregations. Penniman first sang before audiences in local churches in a gospel group called the Tiny Tots. He later sang in a family group, the Penniman Singers. His singing was good enough to earn him an invitation from Rosetta Tharpe, a notable gospel singer, to sing on stage during one of her shows in Macon.

Little Richard's childhood was complicated by his developing sexual orientation, which angered his parents and attracted unfavorable attention from his male contemporaries. By his early teens he was hanging out with the gay community. According to Sawyer's biography, Penniman explained:

> Daddy was always criticizing me for the way I walked and talked and for the people I was running with. He would get real mad at me. He'd say, ''My father had seven sons and I wanted seven sons. You've spoiled it, you're only half a son.'' And then he'd hit me. But I couldn't help it. That was the way I was.

Begins Performing

Little Richard was 14 when he ran away from home to join Dr. Hudson's Medicine Show. He later became a vocalist with B. Brown and His Orchestra, which played mainly in Georgia. He was uncomfortable with the band, so he joined Sugarfoot Sam from Alabama, a traveling show in which he appeared for the first time in women's clothes. After a brief stint with the King Brothers Circus, Little Richard returned home. He then joined the Tidy Jolly Steppers, and then the L. J. Heath Show, and finally the Broadway Steppers, which played in Birmingham on Thursdays and in Atlanta on Fridays. In all of these shows he continued to appear in drag.

After leaving the Broadway Steppers, Little Richard received his first recording break. On October 16, 1951, he recorded ''Every Hour'' for RCA, which became a local hit. However, in a pattern that became depressingly familiar to the singer, Billy Wright's cover for Savoy Records outperformed Little Richard's original. Still, Little Richard's reputation was growing. He worked with Percy Welch and his Orchestra, which widened his audience to include Kentucky and Tennessee. During this period he also learned to play the piano. On January 12, 1953, Little Richard recorded four more songs, none of which were major hits.

Four weeks later, Charles Penniman was shot to death outside his club, the Tip Top Inn. Since his eldest son, Charles, was serving with the Marines in Korea, the duty of supporting the family fell principally on Little Richard, who then took a job washing dishes at the Greyhound bus station in Macon. A local promoter, Clint Bradley, found him work as a musician again with a group called Little Richard and the Tempo Toppers. This group played in black clubs throughout the Southeast, with a long stay in New Orleans. Early in 1953 the Tempo Toppers moved to Houston, Texas, where they recorded four sides for Peacock Records. The records did poorly, and Little Richard blamed their lack of success on Peacock's president, Don Robey. Since Little Richard was uninhibited and spoke his mind freely, Robey, who was known as a violent person, beat him severely. Four more recordings on October 5, 1953, unreleased at the time, marked the end of Little Richard's association with Peacock Records and the Tempo Toppers.

After some solo work, Little Richard established his own backup group, including Charles "Chuck" Conners, a drummer, and Wilbert "Lee Diamond" Smith, pianist and saxophone player. These musicians provided Little Richard with the hard rhythm and blues backing he needed. After adding two more saxophonists, the band was named the Upsetters. Little Richard and the band developed a tremendous reputation in southern clubs. On one occasion, while the group was in Macon between gigs, Little Richard was arrested on a morals charge and told by the police to stay away from the community. The band stayed on the road following that incident.

In late 1955 Specialty Records decided to record Little Richard. Black entrepreneur Arthur N. Rupe had founded the label initially to supply records for the "race" market in southern California in the 1940s. The label's first major popular hit was Lloyd Price's "Lawdy Miss Clawdy," which sold a million records in 1952. Rupe had made Robert "Bumps" Blackwell music director for the company and sent him to New Orleans to record Little Richard. The first part of the session was too tame for Blackwell. During the break, however, Blackwell was won over after he heard Little Richard perform "Tutti Frutti." According to the standards of the time, the lyrics of "Tutti Frutti" were considered too obscene to record, so Blackwell hired Dorothy La Bostrie, a local songwriter, to write new words. Fifteen minutes before the end of the session, she came in with her version. There was just enough time to record it with Little Richard accompanying himself on the piano. The record became a major hit.

Records Several Hits

Little Richard then traveled to Hollywood to make personal appearances, leaving the band behind. James Brown was hired to replace him in the remaining engagements of the Upsetters. The future superstar could sing like Little Richard and wore the tall pompadour; otherwise, there was no physical resemblance between the two singers. Pat Boone and Elvis Presley also recorded their own versions of "Tutti Frutti"; Boone's version sold a million copies since white radio stations would not play Little Richard's original. As is common among most beginning musicians, Little Richard's recording contract was biased in favor of the recording company. Thus, he earned very little money from "Tutti Frutti" or any of his early hits. His financial reward came from personal appearances. Nonetheless, performances of "Tutti Frutti" by white singers did lead white teenagers to seek out the original, which eventually sold a million copies also. "Tutti Frutti" was followed by a second major hit, "Long Tall Sally." His recording successes continued with "Rip it Up" and "Ready Teddy."

Little Richard was in great demand for personal appearances, even in the South. During such performances his flamboyant image was deliberately adopted so that he would appear less threatening as a black male. The attempt to defuse conservative reaction did not always work; he was arrested during a show in Houston because of his long hair. Still, Little Richard roused audiences to a fever pitch. In Baltimore, for the first time ever, young women took off their panties and threw them at the stage. Shortly thereafter, Little Richard bought a house in Los Angeles and moved his family there.

The year 1956 marked Little Richard's first film appearance as movie producers rushed to exploit the new teen–age passion for rock and roll music. His first film was *Don't Knock the Rock,* which opened in January 1957. By now, Little Richard was at the height of his career. Despite his promiscuous lifestyle, he remained a Bible reader and could not escape an uneasy conscience due to his religious upbringing. A missionary of the Church of the God of the Ten Commandments, Wilbur Galley, made a tremendous impression on him and put him in touch with another musician turned evangelist, the former King of Mambo, Joe Lutcher.

Tired of being exploited by his recording company and promoters, plagued by problems with the Internal Revenue Service, and exhausted from a heavy performing schedule, Little Richard left show business in 1957. He broke off in the middle of a tour of Australia and returned to the United States. He did perform a farewell concert at the Apollo Theater for Alan Freed, the disc jockey and rock promoter.

Little Richard formed a ministry with Joe Lutcher called the Little Richard Evangelistic Team. He contacted several Seventh Day Adventists and took a Voice of Prophecy course. Advised to start a family, he married Ernestine Campbell, a young woman with a sheltered upbringing, on July 11, 1959. Characteristically, he was six hours late for his own wedding. Little Richard then entered Oakwood College, an Adventist school in Alabama, to pursue a three–year course to become an elder in the church. The stay was ultimately satisfactory to neither Little Richard nor the school. He skipped lectures or showed up late. While he enjoyed his Bible course, Little Richard gave up on his English course. When school officials discovered his continuing homosexuality and confronted him, he left the church.

Little Richard remained popular as a recording artist because Specialty Records released his previously unissued material, which did quite well. In September 1959, Little Richard recorded 20 religious songs for George Goldner. He did return briefly to rock in 1960 when he participated in a secret recording session to help his old band the Upsetters. A few years later Bumps Blackwell, who had left Specialty for Mercury, persuaded Little Richard to record an album, *Little Richard, King of the Gospel Singers,* under the musical direction of Quincy Jones. This album was released in early 1962. Around this time, Little Richard's arrest for a homosexual encounter in a bus station restroom helped convince his wife to end their marriage after two–and–a–half years.

Following his divorce, Little Richard accepted an offer of an English tour from British promoter Don Arden. It is not clear whether the two agreed on the kind of music Little Richard was to perform. Little Richard thought he was going to sing gospel, but Arden advertised a rock tour. For the first show in England, on October 8, 1962, Little Richard sang gospel music. It was not well received by the audience. For the second show, Sam Cooke, the opening act, gave an enthusiastically received rock performance. Little Richard's strong competitive instincts were aroused. When he took the stage, Little Richard gave a rousing performance of rock hits, signaling his return to secular music.

Upon his return to the United States, Little Richard spent the next several months in a state of indecision about returning to show business before accepting an invitation to do a second tour of England. The Rolling Stones served as his opening act. The end of this very successful tour was marked by the filming of a television program entitled "The Little Richard Spectacular," which appeared on Granada Television in May 1964.

Little Richard cut a new record for Specialty in April 1964 and then embarked on a third tour of England. Upon his return, he learned that the record had flopped. He then took two steps to revive his career: he decided to change his image by becoming even more flamboyant; and he hired Bumps Blackwell as his manager. He raised enough money to get a show together and go on the road again. (One of his guitar players was a young man named Maurice James, later known as Jimmi Hendrix.) Of his religious beliefs at the time, Little Richard explained in the Sawyer biography, "I was not in harmony with the church at that time. I still believed in what they taught, but I wasn't doing that then."

Little Richard's recording career was on a plateau; most of his records sold moderately well, but hits became elusive. He recorded an album of rock standards for Vee Jay called, "Little Richard's Back and There's a Whole lot of Shakin' Goin' On." Unfortunately, Vee Jay went out of business just after a new record "I Don't Know What You Got" showed signs of becoming a hit. Little Richard then signed with Okeh, which produced no hits for him. Although his act was well received in clubs, his gay image resulted in few television appearances.

In 1968 the touring finally began to pay off when Little Richard was offered a two–week engagement at the Aladdin Hotel in Las Vegas. The act was a hit, and his two shows a night became three; the hotel held him over for two more weeks and then signed him for another two weeks later that year. He received television exposure on the Pat Boone and Joey Bishop shows and, in August of this year, appeared at Fillmore East, Madison Square Garden, and a three–day rock festival in Atlantic City, where he was the final act, appearing immediately after Janis Joplin. Appearances on the Johnny Carson show, the Della Reese show, and a special on ABC television marked the ascending arc of his career. A visual record of Little Richard at this time is presented in a film of a 1969 Canadian rock festival, *Sweet Toronto,* released in Canada in 1971.

On February 3, 1970, Little Richard appeared at the Coconut Grove. In swift succession he appeared on the Dick Cavett show, the David Frost show, and the Mike Douglas show. In addition, "Freedom Blues" became Little Richard's first hit in 13 years, leading to his appearance on the cover of *Rolling Stone.*

The April 1973 film *Let the Good Times Roll* further documents Little Richard's performing style. While he was still a star of major proportions during its filming, his music was regarded as old–fashioned in a world dominated by rhythm and blues. Success began taking a heavy toll. At one point Little Richard confirmed rumors that he had stomach cancer; his disavowal when later tests turned out negative was not widely disseminated. Still he had a major alcohol and cocaine habit. By 1975 Little Richard was increasingly strung out and difficult to handle. His use of cocaine turned into a thousand–dollar–a–day habit. Not only was his personality affected, his performances began to deteriorate, and he had not seen his family for a year.

Evangelizes Nationwide

Little Richard withdrew from show business for a second time, retreating to the family home in Riverside where he spent several weeks alone in his bedroom with his Bible. In time, he returned to evangelical activities as a member of the Universal Remnant Church of God. In 1977 Little Richard became a salesman for the *Black Heritage Bible.* In 1979 he began a nationwide campaign, giving his testimony wherever asked. His frank manner of speaking offended some people. He was forthright in admitting his own homosexuality and condemning it on biblical grounds. Commenting on his attitude, he said, "I have rejected homosexuality. I have rejected sex. Now I get my thrills from the ministry." He gives an account of his redemption on the gospel album *God's Beautiful City* (1979).

In 1985 Little Richard went to England to record an album, *Lifetime Friend,* which was released by Warner Brothers in late 1986. Upon his return to Los Angeles, he was severely injured in an automobile accident and spent a month in the hospital.

Beginning in 1986 Little Richard once again became visible in the field of popular music. Although his religious beliefs have remained intact and he is fond of passing out religious tracts, he seems to have found some resolution between his religion and the flamboyant image he continues to present to the public. To the inevitable question on homosexuality, he told Parke Puterbaugh in a 1990 interview for *Rolling Stone* "I'm not against it. . . . I'm not down on any lifestyle, any shape, form or fashion. Whether God has sanctioned our lifestyle or not, we still have a right to do what we want. So I'm not putting anything down. Neither am I picking anything up! [*Chuckles*] And I'll leave it right there."

On January 23, 1986, Little Richard was among the first persons inducted into the Rock'N'Roll Hall of Fame. In that same year he made a brief appearance in the movie *Down and Out in Beverly Hills,* and recorded "Great Gosh A'Mighty" for the soundtrack, which reached number 42 on the pop chart. Little Richard continued to enjoy sustained success as he contributed to other movie soundtracks and appeared as a guest on commercial albums. He also appeared on the album *For Our Children* (1991), a charity benefit for the Pediatric AIDS Foundation on which he sang "Itsy Bitsy Spider." In 1989 he played Old King Cole in Shelley Duvall's production of *Mother Goose Rock'N'Rhyme* for the Disney Channel, and in 1995 he had a cameo role on the television program *Bay Watch.*

Two events in 1990 may symbolize Little Richard's present status. On June 21 he received a star on Hollywood's Walk of Fame, and on September 23 he gave his first concert in his hometown of Macon in 35 years. Although most of Little Richard's music has been available on records for years, Specialty Records reissued many of his recordings on compact disc in 1994. In that same year he was the recipient of the Rhythm and Blues Foundation's Lifetime Achievement Award. Perhaps nothing underscores Little Richard's universal appeal more than the success of the children's album he recorded for Disney in 1992. *Shake It All About,* a collection of 12 songs, sold 250,000 copies.

Little Richard made an important contribution to American popular music in the 1950s. On the basis of this early achievement he built an enduring career in popular music despite his retreats from show business to evangelism.

Current address: c/o BMI, 8730 Sunset Boulevard, Third Floor, Suite 300, West Los Angeles, CA 90069–2211.

REFERENCES

Current Biography 1986. New York: H. W. Wilson, 1986.

Encyclopedia of Pop, Rock and Soul. New York: St. Martin's Press, 1989.

Encyclopedia of Rock. New York: Schirmer Books, 1987.

Guinness Encyclopedia of Popular Music. 4 vols. Chester, CT: New England Publishing Associates, 1992.

"Little Richard Leads R&B Honorees." *Billboard* 106 (29 January 1994): 10, 103.

Puterbaugh, Parke. "Little Richard." Interview. *Rolling Stone,* No. 641 (15 October 1992): 154–155. (Reprint of April 19, 1990, interview for *Rolling Stone.*)

Rock Movers and Shakers. Santa Barbara, CA: ABC–Clio, 1991.

"A Session with Little Richard." *Life* 15 (1 December 1992): 48–50.

Sherman, Tony. "Little Richard's Big Noise." *Legacy* (February/March 1995): 54–56. [Supplement to *American Heritage* 46 (February/March 1995).]

White, Charles. *The Life and Times of Little Richard, the Quasar of Rock.* New York: Harmony Books, 1984.

Robert L. Johns

Little, Malcolm.
See X, Malcolm.

Alain Leroy Locke
(1886–1954)
Philosopher, arts patron, educator, writer

Alain Locke was a major interpreter of black art and culture during the first half of the twentieth century. He was a brilliant scholar whose activities helped give depth and coherence to the study of black culture, especially during the period of the 1920s known as the Harlem Renaissance.

Alain Leroy Locke was born on September 13, 1886, in Philadelphia, Pennsylvania, to a distinguished family with a long history in education. His parents, Pliny (1850–1892) and Mary (Hawkins) Locke (1853–1922), were descendants of educated free blacks residing in the North.

Alain's grandfather, Ishmael Locke (1820–1852), who attended Cambridge University in Great Britain, worked as a teacher in New Jersey and Liberia. While in Africa, he married a similarly employed educator. When they returned to the United States, Ishmael found employment as an administrator of schools in Rhode Island. Later he was headmaster at the Institute for Colored Youth in Philadelphia.

Pliny Locke graduated from the Institute for Colored Youth in 1867. He taught mathematics at the school for a couple of years, then traveled to North Carolina after the Civil War to teach freedmen. In the early 1870s, he obtained accounting jobs with the Freedman's Bureau and the Freedman's Bank in Washington, D.C. While in the capital he enrolled at Howard College, earning a law degree in 1874. Afterwards, he returned to Philadelphia where he taught at the Philadelphia School of Pedagogy and worked as a clerk in the U.S. Post Office.

When Pliny Locke died in 1892, his family was among Philadelphia's black elite. His widow, Mary Locke, was determined to keep it that way by continuing the Victorian upbringing of Alain, her only child. A teacher herself, she enrolled Alain in one of the pioneer Ethical Culture schools and started preparing him for a career in medicine. That vocation had to be abandoned when rheumatic fever permanently damaged Alain's heart. Mary Locke responded, however, by encouraging her son in the study of piano, violin, and books.

In 1902, Alain Locke, a brown–complexioned and delicate young man, graduated second in his class from Philadelphia's Central High School. Two years later, he graduated first in his class from the School of Pedagogy. In 1904 he entered Harvard University. Locke was elected Phi Beta Kappa and graduated magna cum laude in 1907 with degrees in philosophy and English. From Harvard, he traveled to England as the first black American to be named a Rhodes Scholar. After being denied admission to several Oxford colleges because of his race, Locke was admitted at Hertford College, where he spent the next three years studying philosophy, Greek, Latin, and literature.

Alain Leroy Locke

Although faced with racial discrimination in England, Locke's warmth, ironic humor, and zest for philosophical debate were not dampened. He found consolation among a small group of Africans residing in London. After completing his studies in England, Locke traveled to Germany to study philosophy at the University of Berlin in 1910. He continued his studies the following year in Paris at the College de France.

Lacking the job opportunities of whites with a similar education, Locke, upon his return to the United States in 1912, spent six months traveling in the South exploring job leads at black colleges. The sojourn had a lasting effect on Locke, who had been sheltered most of his life from the black world. Not only did he gain a firsthand look at the race problem in America, according to Kunitz and Haycroft, he also acquired "an avocational interest in encouraging and interpreting the artistic and cultural expressions of Negro life."

In 1912 Locke obtained an appointment as assistant professor of English and instructor in philosophy and education at Howard University. There, sharing with W. E. B. Du Bois the belief that educated blacks were duty–bound to uplift their race, he became a vocal proponent of the "Talented Tenth." In 1915, responding to Carter G. Woodson's alarming assertion that the Negro was receiving a mis–education, he petitioned Howard's white trustees to establish a course on race relations. But the trustees rejected his proposal, claiming it was incompatible with the institution's "nonracial" mission. Finding the trustees' decision unacceptable, the Howard chapter of the NAACP and the Social Science Club responded by sponsoring a series of lectures by Locke. In the lecture series, entitled "Race Contacts and Inter–Racial Relationships," Locke debunked the premise of white supremacist thought prevalent during that time. The essential message of the lectures was that racial temperaments are not traceable to biological factors, but instead, to "historical and social causes."

Philosophic Thought Expressed

In 1916, Locke returned to Harvard. There he completed his doctoral dissertation, "The Problem of Classification in the Theory of Value." In this treatise, Locke wrote that values have their origin in specific, culturally determined feelings and attitudes. These feelings and attitudes, he argued, affect logical judgments and yield "facts" or "reality" that are no more than what people interpret them to be. Thus, Locke explained, values are neither objectively true nor false and therefore cannot be set forth as either absolute or universal. Locke reasoned that because of the range and variety of human values, their validity or the appropriateness of the way they are being employed can only be determined by studying them in their own historical, social, and cultural context.

Although Locke revised his philosophic thought as he matured, the main assertions of his dissertation remained unchanged over the span of his life. His views eventually attracted the attention of other philosophical thinkers including Sidney Hook, Horace M. Kallen, and John Dewey. These major philosophers and others quoted Locke or included his writings on value theory in their publications. Noteworthy is Locke's "Values and Imperatives" in *American Philosophy, Today and Tomorrow,* edited by Kallen and Hook (1935), and "Pluralism and Ideological Peace" in *Freedom and Experience,* edited by Sidney Hook and Milton Konvitz (1947).

Locke as Art Promoter

In 1918 Locke became the first black American to receive a doctorate in philosophy from Harvard University. After that, he returned to Howard to chair the philosophy department and teach.

From Howard's campus, Locke continued to pursue his favorite pastimes: reading literature, viewing art, and attending plays by blacks. In the process of immersing himself in black cultural expressions, he noticed increasing evidence that the older generation of black writers and artists were imitating and even submitting to Anglo–Saxon superiority values. Locke became alarmed because such works, instead of advancing the status of the black race, were helping to maintain its subordinate position.

Seeing that accommodation and protest strategies were also faltering, Locke began to blend his thoughts on value theory with his views on art and race relations. Eventually he decided the most effective way to raise the status of black Americans was through producing literature and art reflecting the true life of black people. In his fussy and often overbearing manner, Locke began to urge his Negro friends to abandon the racial assumptions and images perpetuated by white society. In their place, he encouraged them to use black folk experience as the source material for their creative works.

The depth and breadth of the Negro tradition to which Locke alluded could not be ignored as black migrants from the South and the Caribbean region poured into northern cities following World War I. They brought with them a variety of colorful accents, languages, music, poetry, art, folklore, dance, fiction, and ideologies. The convergence of these expressions fostered a cultural awakening in many cities, including Chicago, Philadelphia, Washington, D.C., and especially New York City's Harlem community. Locke relished these developments and began traveling to Harlem with greater frequency.

Locke was welcomed into the company of black artists and writers who met regularly in Harlem's cafes and nightclubs. Always elegant in attire, he mesmerized his acquaintances with an incomparable display of learning, urbanity, and empathy. At the same time, he began contributing reviews of their work to *Survey Graphic,* the NAACP's *Crisis,* and the Urban League's *Opportunity.* After a few years, he had established himself as the "philosophical midwife" of Harlem's black literary, musical, artistic, and theatrical talent.

Locke carried his enthusiasm for Harlem's cultural awakening back to Howard's campus, where in 1922 he proposed Howard as the center for a national Negro theater. Although his activist bent and caring *hauteur* made him increasingly popular among students, it did not do anything to win him the favor of Stanley Durkee, Howard's white president. Durkee rejected Locke's proposal for a national theater. In 1924 he gladly granted Locke sabbatical leave to do archeological work in the Sudan and Egypt.

With Locke away, the president remained under pressure from students and faculty. Their grievances, however, escalated when Locke returned from Africa. In an attempt to get control of the situation, Durkee fired several faculty members, including the most vocal of them, Alain Locke.

With the freedom afforded by his unexpected departure from academia, Locke became more actively involved with New York's young black artists, writers, and intellectuals, as well as the city's white editors, publishers, and philanthropists. According to David Levering Lewis, he was often seen "walking with his quick step and unfurled umbrella from Hotel Olga along Lenox and Seventh avenues, riding the subway to Downtown meetings and luncheons." In 1925, Locke helped edit a special issue of *Survey Graphic* entitled "Harlem: Mecca of the New Negro." The edition received highly favorable reviews. Later that year, he edited *The New Negro* (1925).

The New Negro was a collection of poems, stories, essays, and pictures of African and American Negro art. Contributors to the anthology included W. E. B. Du Bois, Jean Toomer, and many younger artists and writers such as Langston Hughes, Zora Neal Hurston, Claude McKay, Countee Cullen, and Richmond Barthé. In introducing the book, Locke boldly offered this talent as evidence that a "New Negro" had arrived with a "new psychology" and that the "spirit was awake in the masses."

The New Negro was an instant success and caused a vogue among whites for black art and literature. Locke zealously exploited this interest. As spokesperson for the New Negro Movement, he organized many exhibitions of black art, helped found the Harlem Museum of African Art, and, with the support of philanthropists like Mrs. R. Osgood Mason, who wanted to preserve the Negro tradition from the debilitating effects of Western civilization, he obtained the backing that many striving black artists and writers needed in order to produce, exhibit, and publish. Noteworthy among those helped was Locke's protégé, Langston Hughes. Conversant in French, Locke also took to Europe his campaign to inform whites about black art and literature.

In addition to these promotional activities, Locke continued to edit anthologies of black art and literature. Of note, he edited *Four Negro Poets* (1927) and, with help from T. Montgomery Gregory, the first collection of Negro drama, *Plays of Negro Life* (1927). Locke also wrote many articles about black art. In his writings, he disputed the notion that black art was childlike and without technique by documenting the "African influence" on Matisse, Picasso, and other European artists. Also, he explained that black art, in addition to being beautiful, is educationally valuable because it instills an admiration of the black face and form and offers insight into the genius of the black mind.

Although Locke promoted black art to inspire blacks and change white racial attitudes, he chastised black artists who resorted to sensationalism and exhibitionism to make their work marketable. Similarly, he had disdain for artists, writers, and intellectuals who used art as propaganda to protest the injustice of discrimination. On this subject, Locke, in "Art or Propaganda" (1928), as cited by George Hall, wrote that using art for propaganda only "perpetuates the position of group inferiority even in crying out against it." The function and object of art, Locke reminded, is not protest—it is beauty and truth. Thus, he challenged black artists and writers to produce great art and literature as the protest against the attitude that allows discrimination to exist.

Locke as Interpreter of Cultural Expressions

In 1928 Locke returned to the full–time teaching of philosophy at Howard University. From its campus, he continued to write critical essays and began to write a series of annual reviews of black literature in *Opportunity.* In his first annual review, "1928: A Retrospective Review" (1929), cited in Jeffrey Stewart's anthology of Locke's works, he wrote disparagingly of the New Negro's "inflated stock" and predicted the "Negro fad" would soon end. A few months later, October of 1929, the stock market crashed, leaving black artists without their wealthy sponsors and causing Harlem's literary and artistic output to decline. In "We Turn to Prose" (1932), cited in Stewart's anthology, Locke praised *The Black Worker* by Sterling Spero and Abram Harris for marking "the beginning of the end of that hitherto endless succession of studies on the Negro *in vacuo.*" And in "Black Truth and Black Beauty" (1933), also cited by Stewart, Locke discussed a "score of books that cannot by any stretch be listed as 'literature of the Negro.'"

Some black writers resented Locke's critical tone. According to Stewart, one, Jessie Fauset, responded that "your criticisms . . . point most effectively to the adage that a critic is a self–acknowledged failure as a writer." Indeed, Locke was not an artist or literary writer. Yet, he responded, that was no excuse for him to be an apologist for creative work that lacked excellence and social consciousness. Later, when he stated in "Toward a Critique of Negro Music" (1934), cited by Stewart, that the evolutionary process of development in American black music should eventually produce an American classical music, he was attacked again, this time for being "elitist" and attempting to "concertize" black folk music.

Indeed, Locke's suggestion that black folk music had to advance to something "higher" before it is "vindicated" was a contradiction that he never reconciled to his critics' satisfaction. Nevertheless, Locke attempted to do just that in his famous Bronze Booklet, *The Negro and His Music* (1936), cited by Paul Joseph Bugett. In speaking of formal classical music and Negro idioms, such as the spirituals and jazz, he wrote that eventually they must "be fused in a vital but superior product." What was the "superior" product? According to Locke it was "neither racial, nor national, but universal music."

When the editorship of *Opportunity* changed in 1942, Locke discontinued his retrospective views. He continued to edit and write, especially on race relations and culture. With Bernhard J. Stern, he edited *When Peoples Meet: A Study in Race and Culture Contacts* (1942). The publication included analyses by Ruth Benedict and Margaret Mead. In the same year he edited a special edition for *Survey Graphic* that emphasized the necessity of ending racial privilege in the United States, Africa, and Asia. One of his most noteworthy articles during this period was "The Negro in Three Americas" (1944), which helped focus attention on the diverse African presence in the Western Hemisphere.

In 1946, when Locke resumed his annual reviews in *Phylon,* he used his philosophical insight into underlying issues and trends in black life to plot the future course of the arts and the social sciences. Thus, in "A Critical Retrospect of the Literature of the Negro for 1947" (1948), cited by Stewart, he expressed the hope that the international struggle for the rights of minorities would become the stuff of great literature. In "Wisdom De Profundis" (1950), Locke praised sociologists such as E. Franklin Frazier and historians like John Franklin Hope for focusing attention on the black experience in their respective fields.

Promotes Black Education

Locke's praise for the sociological and historical work of progressive black social scientists was certainly understandable. After all, for decades he had argued that the black folk experience and African past should be studied and made the primary material from which all categories of art are fashioned. For him, however, the study of black life did more than offer material for art; it also yielded solutions to life's problems. Thus, he urged educational institutions to expose their black students to all aspects of their heritage.

Beginning in the 1930s, after Mordecai W. Johnson had become Howard's first black president, Locke organized a succession of conferences at Howard in an effort to make the university an intellectual clearinghouse on issues concerning race. Simultaneously, he revived Howard's literary magazine, *Stylus,* and expanded the university's library, art gallery, and theater company by supplying them with material that had African and black American folk content. Concurrently, he urged administrators at black colleges to eradicate apathy toward the study of African and black American life by designing curricula that reflect these experiences.

Locke's views on education caught the attention of the American Association of Adult Education (AAAE), a predominantly white national organization. In 1933 the AAAE commissioned him to evaluate adult education centers in Harlem and Atlanta. In 1935 responding in part to the lack of black cultural expressions in such programs, Locke founded the Association of Negro Folk Education (ANFE). Nine highly acclaimed Bronze Booklets were published by the ANFE between 1936 and 1942. According to Logan and Winston, Locke wrote that the booklets were published to bring "within reach of the average reader basic facts and progressive views about Negro life." Booklets written exclusively by Locke include *The Negro and His Music* (1936), *Negro Art: Past and Present* (1937), and *The Negro in Art: A Pictorial Record of the Negro Artist and the Negro Theme in Art* (1940).

It is important to note that Locke's attempts to make black cultural expressions an integral part of education were not made to reinforce racial distinctiveness and separation. Instead, his object was to place learning "upon a broader cultural basis." Such a base, Locke held, would help critical minds to solve racial problems. To that end, Locke led the overhaul of Howard University's liberal arts curriculum during the late 1930s, integrating the major disciplines into a general education program. His innovative leadership was recognized in 1945 when the AAAE elected him as its president.

By the time World War II ended, Locke was one of the best known black scholars in the United States. He continued to promote his ideas by accepting appointments at the University of Wisconsin (1945–1946), the New School for Social Research (1947), and the City College of New York (1948). He also continued to contribute articles on value theory, art, and race to various publications, including *Crisis, Nation,* and the *Journal for the Study of Negro Life.* In addition, Locke remained a persuasive member of many professional organizations, including the American Philosophical Association, the International Institute of African Languages and Culture, and the Association for the Study of Negro Life and History.

In 1951, Locke obtained a grant from the Rockefeller Foundation to write a synthesis of his studies of black culture in America. Hospitalized because of a heart ailment, Locke was not able to work on the manuscript until he recovered. In 1953, he retired from Howard University, receiving the university's honorary degree of doctor of humane letters.

Locke moved to New York City, but his health continued to deteriorate. Having never married, he turned to a colleague, Margaret Just Butcher, for help with the manuscript. The next year, however, sensing he would not live through the summer, he gave his materials and plan for the publication to Butcher, telling her simply that if anything should happen to him, she was to "do the book."

On June 9, 1954, Alain Leroy Locke died in Mount Sinai Hospital at age 67. His body was cremated at Fresh Pond Crematory, Little Village, Long Island. He bequeathed his extensive African art collection and papers to Howard University. Margaret Butcher carried out Locke's last wish, publishing *The Negro in American Culture* in 1956.

During the first half of the twentieth century, Alain Leroy Locke was a persistent apostle of beauty and truth. Through various fields of art he urged blacks to discover, reflect on, and redefine who they are. In addition, he helped whites to comprehend the unity and equivalence underlying Anglo–Saxon and black cultural expressions. In the process, Locke freed many blacks and whites from the effects of racism and, in so doing, helped raise the status of the black race.

REFERENCES

African–American Encyclopedia. Vol 5. Miami: Educational Black Publishers, 1974.

Baker, Houston A. *Modernism and the Harlem Renaissance.* Chicago: University of Chicago Press, 1987.

Barksdale, Richard, and Kenneth Kinnamon, eds. *Black Writers of America: A Comprehensive Anthology.* New York: Macmillan, 1972.

Bugett, Paul Joseph. "Vindication as a Thematic Principle in Alain Locke's Writings on the Music of Black Americans." In *The Harlem Renaissance: Reevaluation.* Ed. by Amritjit Singh, William S. Shirver, and Stanley Brodwin. New York: Garland Publishing, 1989.

Butcher, Margaret Just. *The Negro in American Culture.* 1956. Reprint, New York: New American Library, 1971.

Hall, George. "Alain Locke and the Honest Propaganda of Truth and Beauty." In *Alain Locke: Reflections on a Modern Renaissance Man.* Baton Rouge: Louisiana State University Press, 1982.

Hedgepeth, Chester M. Jr. *African–American Writers and Artists.* Chicago: American Library Association, 1991.

Huggins, Nathan Irvin. *The Harlem Renaissance.* New York: Oxford, 1971.

Hughes, Langston, Milton Meltzer, and C. Eric Lincoln, eds. *A Pictorial History of Black America.* 2nd ed. New York: Crown Publishers, 1968.

Kamp, Jim, ed. *Reference Guide to American Literature.* Detroit: St. James Press, 1994.

Kunitz, Stanley J., ed. *Twentieth Century Authors: A Biographical Dictionary of Modern Literature.* New York: H. W. Wilson Co., 1955.

———, and Howard Haycroft. *Twentieth Century Authors.* New York: H. W. Wilson Co, 1942.

Lewis, David Levering. *When Harlem Was in Vogue.* New York: Knopf, 1981.

Linnemann, Russell J., ed. *Alain Locke: Reflections on a Modern Renaissance Man.* Baton Rouge: Louisiana State University Press, 1982.

Locke, Alain L. *The New Negro.* 1925. Reprint, New York: Macmillan, 1992.

Logan, Rayford W., and Michael R. Winston, eds. *Dictionary of American Negro Biography.* New York: Norton, 1982.

Page, James A. *Selected Black American Authors.* Boston: G. K. Hall, 1977.

Stewart, Jeffrey C., ed. *The Critical Temper of Alain Locke: A Selection of His Essays on Art and Culture.* New York: Garland Publishing, 1983.

COLLECTIONS

The bulk of Alain Locke's papers are in the Moorland–Spingarn Research Center at Howard University; others are in the Schomburg Center for Research in Black Culture, and in scattered repositories.

Cortez Rainey

Rayford W. Logan

(1897–1982)

Historian, educator, writer, civil rights activist

Rayford Wittingham Logan, a historian who specialized in the study of Haiti, black America, and colonial Africa, was often near the hub of African American political and intellectual life. He taught at Howard University in Washington, D.C., from 1938 to 1973, where his colleagues included United Nations representative Ralph Bunche, sociologist E. Franklin Frazier, philosopher Alain L. Locke, poet and literary critic Sterling A. Brown, and historians Charles H. Wesley and John Hope Franklin.

Born in Washington, D.C., in 1897, Logan attended the M Street High School, where his teachers included Harvard–trained historian Carter G. Woodson and Harlem Renaissance writer Jessie R. Fauset. Bright but unsure of his future, Logan entered the University of Pittsburgh to study engineering. After a year, however, he transferred to Williams College in Massachusetts, where he was allowed to attend classes but could not live in the school's segregated dormitories nor eat in the dining halls. At Williams, where his diligence earned him a Phi Beta Kappa key, Logan was attracted to the study of history but did not pursue his interest for almost a decade. Immediately after his graduation in 1917, Logan enlisted in a segregated army unit, winning the rank of first lieutenant through a competitive examination. Stationed in France at the front, Logan was deeply troubled by the treatment of African American soldiers in general and intensely offended by the slights he received as an officer, especially from white enlisted men who refused to salute him, black soldiers who disobeyed him because he was a light mulatto, and other officers who discriminated against or otherwise mistreated him.

Outraged by the state of American race relations, Logan applied for and was granted a discharge in France in 1919. He remained an expatriate for five years, enjoying the far less racially polarized social scene in Europe. Supported by successful speculations in the European stock market, he cultivated friendships with a variety of people, including expatriate black Americans. In 1921, when African American political and cultural leader W. E. B. Du Bois was planning the Paris session of the second Pan African Congress and needed an interpreter, Logan was recommended for the position by his former French teacher, Jessie Fauset. He continued to work for Du Bois as a translator during the 1923 and 1927 Pan African congresses.

Returning to the United States in 1924 with a fluent knowledge of French and Spanish and familiarity with several other European languages, Logan held a succession of teaching positions at Virginia Union University in Richmond (1925–30), Atlanta University (1933–38), and Howard University beginning in 1938.

While at Virginia Union, Logan met Ruth Robinson, a Richmond native who had graduated from the Virginia Normal and Industrial Institute in Petersburg, earned a bachelor's degree from Virginia Union in 1929, and completed a bachelor's degree in music at Howard University in 1941. An accomplished soprano, Ruth was the choir director at Virginia Union when they met. After their marriage in August of 1927, she performed mostly in the Washington, D.C., area, and in the early 1950s she had an opportunity to study opera in Paris. Although Logan encouraged his wife to polish her singing skills and occasionally perform, he wrote in his diary that they would ''have a friendly separation'' if she sought a professional music career.

Between teaching posts in 1932–33, Rayford Logan served as assistant to Carter G. Woodson at the Association for the Study of Negro (later Afro–American) Life and History headquarters in Washington, D.C. and succeeded him as director in 1950–51 after Woodson's death.

While at Virginia Union and Atlanta, Logan spent his summers and leave time earning a master's degree from Williams College in 1929 and another from Harvard in 1932. His Harvard doctoral dissertation on United States–Haitian relations, completed in 1936, was published by the University of North Carolina Press in 1941 as *Diplomatic Relations of the United States with Haiti, 1776–1891.*

Writes on Black Themes

Logan's book on Haiti was the first work of a prolific writing career. Others are *The Negro and the Post–World War* (1945), *The African Mandates in World Politics* (1948), *The Negro in the United States: A Brief History* (1957), *Haiti and the Dominican Republic* (1968), and *Howard University: The First Hundred Years, 1867–1967* (1969). His most recognized work, *The Betrayal of the Negro: from Rutherford B. Hayes to Woodrow Wilson* (1965), was originally published in 1954 as *The Negro in American Life and Thought: The Nadir, 1877–1901.*

Logan edited books about the Southern white press, W. E. B. Du Bois, and Frederick Douglass. He also brought together a group of black leaders that included Mary McLeod Bethune, Charles S. Johnson, W. E. B. Du Bois, Sterling Brown, Langston Hughes, and others as contributors to *What the Negro Wants* (1944). His journal and newspaper articles cover a wide range of subjects including Haitian politics, blacks in Spanish America, the United Nations and human rights, French Africa, the Civil War, South Africa, Liberia, the Sudan, British racial prejudice, segregated schools, Carter G. Woodson, James Weldon Johnson, and Pan Africanism. The *Dictionary of American Negro Biography* (1982), which he edited with Michael R. Winston, was completed by Winston just before Logan's death in 1982. In his diaries and papers Logan discussed his research, interaction with publishers, royalties, and book reviews.

Stimulates Founding of the Tuskegee Airmen

Political and civic activities converged in Logan's career through his leadership of the black professional men's fraternity Alpha Phi Alpha. As president from 1940 to 1945, he was offered many opportunities to speak before diverse audiences. During the early 1940s, Logan chaired the Committee on Participation of Negroes in the National Defense Program, which was especially concerned that black aviators should be trained to serve in the Army Air Force. In this position, Logan testified before Congressional committees and met with President Franklin D. Roosevelt. The committee successfully pressured the Army to train African American pilots; but the trainees, the now–famous Tuskegee Airmen, were segregated at the Tuskegee Air Base in Alabama. Logan also collaborated with black labor leader A. Philip Randolph in his proposed 1941 march on Washington to campaign for equal employment opportunities in defense industries for people of all races.

Logan's papers indicate his avid interest in Haitian issues, African colonialism, the United Nations' treatment of oppressed peoples, and segregation in the United States in the late 1940s. He met periodically with Francis (Kwame) Nkrumah of Ghana and Nnamdi Azikiwe of Nigeria, who both later became leaders of their independent African nations, and traveled to San Francisco in 1945 to cover the United Nations organizational conference as a newspaper correspondent for the black–owned *Pittsburgh Courier.* He was included in many subsequent sessions on the responsibility of the United Nations towards colonized African nations. Logan also helped YMCA officials in their nascent desegregation efforts. As an expert on Haitian affairs, he was regularly invited to Haitian diplomatic functions and was occasionally solicited by the

U.S. Department of State to aid in the analysis of Caribbean affairs.

Logan's diaries provide detailed accounts of the challenges faced by a black scholar in the years before integration. They also chronicle several crucial decades in the American civil rights movement and provide insight into a number of African American organizations as well as the lifestyle of the black elite in Washington, D.C., and elsewhere. As a dean, department chairman, and history professor, Logan recorded various meetings in his diaries as well as his interactions with Mordecai W. Johnson, the first black president of Howard, who served from 1926 to 1960. He also documented his treatment by railroad workers and white fellow passengers on his speaking trips. Always extremely affronted by the indignities of segregation, Logan referred to the Jim Crow system as "humiliating, degrading, tomfoolery." Consciously writing for posterity, (addressing infrequent comments to "Dear Reader"), Logan in his diaries was sometimes candid, often newsy, regularly critical, and occasionally witty. Of Walter White, the executive director of the NAACP, he wrote, "It's a damned shame that the whole Negro race must revolve around Walter."

Logan retired in 1964 to devote his time to writing the centennial history of Howard University. Ruth Logan died of a stroke two years later. Returning to Howard from 1971 to 1974 as a distinguished professor, he was extremely affronted by the black nationalist movement on the campus and at other schools throughout the United States. Logan was an avid integrationist who refused to sanction the black power movement. Although he referred to African Americans in his early diaries as "black," in later life he refused to use the term and preferred "Negro."

The foundation for both the civil rights and the black nationalist movements had been laid by the scholarship of historians such as Robert Logan. In his eulogy to Logan, John Hope Franklin summarized his contribution: "If he was the scholar's scholar, which indeed he was, he was also the student's scholar, the very epitome of scholarship and teaching."

REFERENCES

Janken, Kenneth Robert. *Rayford W. Logan and the Dilemma of the African–American Intellectual.* Amherst: University of Massachusetts Press, 1993.

COLLECTIONS

Logan's diaries, which span four decades from 1940 to 1982, are now located in the Library of Congress Manuscript Division. His correspondence and papers, including a manuscript autobiography, are located at the Moorland–Spingarn Research Center at Howard University in Washington, D.C.

Debra Newman Ham

Richard A. Long

(1927–)

Educator, writer, patron of the arts

Richard Long's career as scholar, teacher, recorder and interpreter of culture, and arts connoisseur, spans four decades. He is noted for his contributions to black studies, literature, art, music and dance, and his interdisciplinary approach to the understanding of race and culture not just in the United States but globally.

Richard A. Long was born February 9, 1927, in Philadelphia to Thaddeus B. and Leila Washington. As a skilled blacksmith, Long's father was able even during the Great Depression to care for his family, consisting of five boys—Richard was number four—and one girl.

Long began his education at the Arnold School, a segregated public elementary school. His early life was marred by the death of his mother when he was six years old. As soon as he was old enough to travel around by himself, at the age of ten or 11, Long visited the city's museums, galleries, and other cultural offerings, and was also an avid reader of American literature and history. Long credits his early exposure to the arts for creating his deep and abiding appreciation for the humanities.

Long attended high school in Columbia, South Carolina, where he was sent to live with an aunt. He enrolled in the first high school for blacks in Columbia, Booker T. Washington. Following his graduation from high school, Long returned to Philadelphia to attend college, entering Temple University as a 16–year–old freshman. Long became interested in philology and excelled in the study of the history of the English language. In 1947 he graduated with a B.A. degree in English. Long continued to study English at Temple, focusing on old and middle English and earning the master of arts degree in 1948. The young scholar then entered the doctoral program in English at the University of Pennsylvania, focusing on renaissance and medieval literature. He completed all but his dissertation.

During the summer of 1950, Long traveled abroad, spending three weeks in London, three in Paris. In the fall he returned to the United States and began his first teaching job at West Virginia State College near Charleston. However, Long had a growing impulse to learn about the world. He left the school, took a job with the federal government and moved to Washington, D.C. He then became an instructor in English and speech at Morgan State University in Baltimore in 1951. Long was off to Paris again in the summer of 1954 to study and was awarded a Fulbright scholarship to study at the University of Paris in 1957 and 1958. In 1964, he began the pursuit of his doctorate in linguistics at the University of Poitiers. Taking a leave from Morgan State, Long moved to Paris where he spent the year as a lecturer in English at Poitiers and completed his dissertation. His degree was awarded

Richard A. Long

in 1965. Long returned to Morgan State and was promoted to associate professor of English and speech. Instead, he accepted a position of professor of English and French at Hampton Institute (now University) in Virginia, where he was also made director of the college museum.

Docent Extraordinaire

At Hampton, Long worked tirelessly to bring the museum recognition. In the fall of 1967, almost upon his arrival there, he organized an exhibit to mark the college's Centennial. The exhibit contained contemporary African paintings as well as the famous collection of *Hampton Album* photographs which were published by the Museum of Modern Art in 1966. In November, Long arranged an exhibition of the college's "Primitive Art of Africa, North America, and Oceanic" collection at the Union Carbide building in New York City. During Black History Month in 1968, Long showcased a select number of African American artists including Aaron Douglas, Ellis Wilson, Hale Woodruff, and Beauford Delaney.

Long moved with lightning speed through the academy. *Negritude: Essays and Studies,* written with Albert Berrien was published in 1967. Highly respected in both the academic and arts world, knowledgeable about the black experience, and known for his energy and ability to make things happen, Long was recruited away from Hampton in 1968. Atlanta University needed a director for its Afro-American Studies Program, and Richard Long was the perfect candidate. Harvard was also in pursuit of an expert in Afro-American Studies and tried to recruit Long. He chose Atlanta, not so much for its reputation as a black mecca as for its warmer climate. He did, however, agree to give lectures at Harvard as a visiting professor, and commuted to Cambridge from 1969 through 1971.

Directing Black Studies

In 1968, when Long assumed his new position as professor of English and Afro-American Studies, black students nationwide were intoxicated by the concept of Black Power but still reeling from the assassination of Martin Luther King Jr. that year. They were demanding and getting black studies departments at highly esteemed, predominately-white institutions. In 1967, a college student quoted by Nathan Hare in the *Negro Digest,* said: "The confrontation between the black bourgeoisie stance and the stark, ugly reality of black life in America has, at long last, and inevitably, begun at the bastion of the black bourgeoisie." He was referring to Howard University in Washington, D.C.; but the confrontation did not begin and end there. At Atlanta University in Atlanta the cry for black studies was loud and clear. Long's 1971 report entitled, "Black Studies Year One," in *Report, Atlanta University Center for African and African-American Studies,* describes his efforts to establish a first rate program at the center.

On April 23, 1971, he addressed the College Language Association's (CLA) 31st annual convention in Tallahassee, Florida. Giving the presidential address (he served as president 1970–1971) he spoke on "The Future of Black Studies." Asserting that black studies was at once the question and part of the answer to the current crisis in American education, Long challenged the organization, comprised mostly of black educators, to become "stewards" of the black people's interest in education. Long said that if black studies was to survive and thrive in American education, it could not become prey to pragmatic solutions resulting in departments, a smorgasbord listing of courses, or in autonomous institutes. Part of the answer was to be found in general education programs. Otherwise, he wrote in the *CLA Journal,* black studies would run the risk of becoming "devices of resegregation, and therefore once more a triumph of the system over legitimate revendications." Long concluded his address by stating what could be called his credo: "The future of black studies lies in its contribution to the wholeness and sanity of the new view. For outside of the central direction of American education, black studies will slowly assume the status of a digression and a backwater."

As director for the Center for Black Studies at Atlanta University, Long made every effort to live up to the challenge he had issued to his colleagues. He worked to bring the study of black experience and culture from margin to center, and to make it part and parcel of the American mainstream. In 1981, Long published a series of essays, setting forth and further refining his concept regarding black studies, entitled, *Africa and America: Essays in Afro-American Culture.* He wrote that too much of the Black Power movement was governed by posturing and gesturing, and too little attention was paid to the intellectual groundwork needed to make the symbols meaningful. He concluded: ''Symbols improperly conceived and improperly used may do irreparable damage to a cause. The cause of black consciousness has been in no way exempt from this truth.''

Showcasing Arts and Culture

The underlying philosophy that governs Long's outlook is that knowledge is the one universal means for accomplishing anything. In his role as director of the Center for African and African American Studies, Long used several methods for disseminating knowledge specific to the black experience. In 1968 he founded the Triennial Symposium of African Art. These symposia have been conducted at Harvard (1971), Columbia (1974), Museum of African Art (Chicago, 1977), High Museum and Atlanta University (1980), University of Oklahoma (1983), University of California–Los Angeles (1986), Smithsonian National Museum of African Art (1989), and the University of Iowa (1992). In 1996 the Art Symposium was held in conjunction with the Summer Olympic Games in Atlanta.

Long founded the annual Conference of African and African–American Studies (CAAS) at Atlanta University in 1968, bringing together scholars in the field. Between 1968 and 1978, he established the New World Festivals of the African Diaspora. The first festival took place in Brazil in 1978; other have included Haiti, Surinam, and Barbados. In 1970, a commemorative exhibition honoring author and educator Alain Locke was held at the United Negro College Fund Building in New York. Long was the mastermind for this exhibit as well as for the 1978 Beauford Delaney retrospective exhibit at the Studio Museum in Harlem.

While director of African and African–American Studies at Atlanta University, Long produced several works that contributed greatly to the field of black studies. These include *Afro–American Writing: Prose and Poetry* (with Eugenia Collier, 1972); a second edition was issued in 1985. This book, appearing at a time when black literature classes were proliferating and texts were scarce, was one of the first used for teaching Afro–American literature.

Long's text for the book *Beauford Delaney: A Retrospective* brought to light the work of a virtually unknown but talented black painter. *Black Americana,* his pictorial history of African Americans, was published in 1985, and reissued as *African Americans* in 1993. In *Black Writers and the American Civil War* (1988), Long chronicled the war experiences of eight black men and women.

Long's ground–breaking work, *The Black Tradition in American Dance,* appeared in 1989. This richly illustrated book depicts the history of black dance from early minstrels through today. Long is also the author of many articles, chapters in books, and encyclopedia entries including those in the *Harvard Encyclopedia of American Ethnic Groups, Encyclopedia of Poetry and Poetics, The Black American Reference Book,* and *World Encyclopedia of Black People.* He has also produced a slender volume of poetry titled *Ascending Poems* (1975), which revealed his warmth and humor, a side of him that many may not recognize. As expressed in ''Niggers is People,'' his poems display a surprising wit:

Not a word, not a sound
Else you gone be put down
Don't smack gum, don't break wind
And if you ain't yet been,
Go!
Niggers is people.

Joining the Institute of Liberal Arts

In 1988 when Atlanta University was considering a merger with another University Center school, Clark College, Long was considering a move. He had served as adjunct professor in the Graduate Institute of Liberal Arts (ILA) at Emory University in Atlanta since 1973. The ILA was a natural academic home for Long. Offered an endowed chair in 1988, he became the Atticus Haygood Professor of Interdisciplinary Studies in the ILA

Long's research interests include Ramayana dance–drama and the politics of culture in Thailand, Java, and Bali. He is also researching the representation of Asian dance on the American stage. His research has taken him to many countries around the world, including Thailand and Bali. In 1992, Long received the Living Legend Award from the National Black Arts Festival, and in 1995, the National Conference of Artists Award by the Middle Atlantic Writers Association. He is a life member of the Modern Language Association, Modern Humanities Research Association, College Language Association, and Association for the Study of Afro–American Life and History. Long continues to share his knowledge through teaching and writing.

Current address: Graduate Institute of Liberal Arts, Emory University, Atlanta, GA 30322.

REFERENCES

Hare, Nathan. ''Final Reflections on a 'Negro' College.'' *Negro Digest* 17 (March 1968): 40–46.

Logan, Richard A. *Africa and America: Essays in Afro–American Studies.* Atlanta: Atlanta University Center for African and African–American Studies, 1981.

———. *Ascending Poems.* Chicago: DuSable Museum, 1975.

———. (text for) *Beauford Delaney: A Retrospective.* New York: Studio Museum in Harlem, 1978.

———. ''The Future of Black Studies.'' *CLAJ* 25 (September 1971): 1–7.

———. Interview with Nagueyalti Warren, Emory University, Atlanta, Georgia, May 22, 1996.

Nagueyalti Warren

Z. Alexander Looby
(1899–1972)
Lawyer, civil rights activist, educator, politician

Known as the "dean" of African American attorneys in Nashville, and nationally for his work as a civil rights attorney for the NAACP, Z. Alexander Looby traversed the state of Tennessee in the company of other attorneys, arguing against racial discrimination. In 1951 he and fellow attorney Robert E. Lillard became the first African Americans elected to Nashville City Council in 40 years.

Zaphaniah Alexander Looby, the son of John Alexander and Grace Elizabeth Joseph, was born in Antigua, British West Indies, on April 8, 1899. His mother died when Looby was six or seven years old, and his father passed away when he was fifteen. As a child, Looby avidly read such English authors as Shakespeare, Milton, and Kipling. He stayed around the magistrate court and listened to white barristers argue their cases and dreamed of becoming an attorney. After the death of his father, Looby signed on as a cabin boy on a whaling ship headed for the United States. In 1914 he arrived in New Bedford, Massachusetts. Eight years after his arrival, Looby earned his bachelor's degree cum laude from Howard University in Washington, D. C., and in 1925 received the bachelor of laws degree from Columbia University. The following year he earned a J.D. degree from New York University.

In 1926, the same year that he received his doctorate, Looby went to Fisk University in Nashville as assistant professor of economic law, and remained there for two years. An early advocate of economic self–determination among African Americans, Looby encouraged members of his race to prepare themselves to enter the domain of commerce and finance.

Admitted to the Tennessee bar in 1929, Looby practiced law in Memphis, for a short period. There he met Grafta Mosby, a school teacher, whom he married in 1934. Unwilling to abide by the racial constraints imposed in Memphis by political boss Edward H. Crump, Looby returned to Nashville. In 1931, he was appointed lecturer in medical jurisprudence at Meharry Medical College. A year later, in 1932, he founded the Kent College of Law (no longer extant), Nashville's first law school for African Americans since the old Central Tennessee College's department of law (1877–1911). In 1936 Looby became a naturalized American citizen.

Attacks Segregation

One of the first attacks against segregation in Tennessee's higher educational system was filed by Looby in 1937, in association with Carl Cowan of Knoxville and Charles Hamilton Houston of the NAACP Legal Defense and Educational Fund. This suit sought to secure the admission of William B. Redmond of Franklin, Tennessee, to the University of Tennessee's School of Pharmacy in Memphis. Although

Z. Alexander Looby

Looby lost the case, it indicated the litigious direction that African Americans would take in their struggle for equal access to public education. In the 1938 case of *Gaines, ex rel Canada v. Missouri,* the U.S. Supreme Court invalidated racially exclusionary state laws. The following year, Looby, along with Cowan, Houston, Thurgood Marshall, and William H. Hastie, filed suit seeking the admission of Joseph M. Michael to the University of Tennessee School of Law. Despite the Supreme Court's ruling in the Gaines case, the Tennessee court steadfastly held to its earlier ruling.

In 1943 Looby entered the field of politics when he ran for a seat on the Nashville City Council representing the Fifth Ward. When the ballots were counted, Looby had over 3,100 votes, while the next closest opponent was Alex M. Hines, a white man, with almost 2,500 votes. Two weeks later, Looby and Hines faced each other in a run–off election; Hines defeated Looby by 3,800 votes. The same year that Looby ran for public office, he was elected president of the James C. Napier Bar Association, an organization for African American attorneys in Nashville, a position he held until 1945.

In February of 1946, a race riot broke out in Columbia, Tennessee, set off by a fight between William Fleming, a white repairman, and James Stephenson, an African American former military serviceman. The State Highway Patrol and National Guard terrorized the African American community, beating and shooting a number of citizens. Thirty–one African Americans were indicted on charges resulting from the melee. Twenty–five of those arrested were charged with attempted murder of four police officers. To represent the accused African Americans, the NAACP hired Maurice Weaver, a white attorney from Chattanooga, Tennessee, and Looby. On October 4, 1946, an all–white jury found 23 of the defendants not guilty.

Attorneys Looby, Weaver, and Thurgood Marshall returned to Columbia in mid–November to litigate the murder charge against the two remaining defendants. They won acquittal for one and a reduced sentence for the other. Their successful defense of the accused incensed white law officials. As Marshall and Looby drove out of Columbia on their way back to Nashville, they were followed and stopped by a group of law enforcement agents with a search warrant for their vehicle. The attorneys were momentarily allowed to continue their trip back to Nashville and Looby took over the driving. About a mile down the road, they were stopped again. Both refused to answer questions about who was previously driving. The group of eight law officials wanted Marshall. They detained him and ordered Looby and the others to go the other way. Looby refused to leave Marshall to the whims of the officers, thereby thwarting their clandestine plans to lynch Marshall. Subsequently, they took Marshall back to Columbia and charged him with drunken driving. The presiding judge freed him. In an attempt to protect themselves from further harassment, Looby and Marshall left for Nashville in another car and had a local man drive Looby's car. After his close encounter with Tennessee's officers of the law, Marshall said, quoted in Rowan's *Dream Makers,* ''Looby was one brave man.''

Victory in the Courts

In 1950, Looby and co–counselors Carl Cowan and Avon N. Williams Jr. of Knoxville filed the Anderson County School desegregation lawsuit. The attorneys successfully argued *McSwain v. Board of Anderson County, Tennessee* all the way to the U.S. Supreme Court and won the court–ordered desegregation of Tennessee's public schools.

Viewing politics as a way to change an oppressive system, the following year Looby ran again for a seat on the Nashville City Council. This time, with no white opponent, Looby was elected. Attorney Robert E. Lillard, another contender in the race, defeated his white opponent, Charles Castleman, in the run–off election on May 24, 1951.

As a city council member and as legal leader of the NAACP, Looby was in the vanguard of the civil rights movement among African Americans in Nashville. He helped to desegregate public education in the city and county, as well as the public golf courses and restaurants. Looby won equal pay for African American school teachers, brought action that ended segregation in the courts, and successfully compelled city leaders to dismantle racially segregated visiting hours at the Parthenon, a replica of the Greek temple.

In 1953, Looby was joined in his law practice by his former intern and co–counselor in *McSwain v. Board* , Avon N. Williams Jr. Their professional association lasted until 1969, when Williams went to the Tennessee General Assembly as a state senator.

Fight Leads to School Desegregation

In 1955, after the 1954 U.S. Supreme Court's decision in the case of *Brown v. Board of Education of Topeka, Kansas,* that the desegregation of public schools begin with ''all deliberate speed,'' Looby and his law partner, in consultation with the NAACP and Thurgood Marshall, filed a class action suit against the Nashville Board of Education. The board based its school desegregation plan on the adjective ''deliberate,'' as opposed to the noun ''speed.''

The case *Robert W. Kelley, et al. v. Board of Education* was not heard until 1956, when William E. Miller, a federal district judge, ordered Nashville's Board of Education to prepare a plan for desegregation by January of the following year. In 1958, the board of education proposed and Miller approved the ''grade–a year–plan.'' However, Looby and his law partner objected to the generous student transfer provisions of the plan and appealed the case. Losing in the Court of Appeals, Looby and Williams appealed the case to the U.S. Supreme Court in 1959 but failed to obtain the required number of votes for a hearing. Although momentarily defeated, Looby and Williams never wavered in their resolve. Their tenacity was rewarded in 1971 when U.S.District Judge L. Clure Morton ordered a massive cross–town busing plan to desegregate Nashville's public schools.

In 1955, the same year that Looby filed the Nashville school desegregation case, he ran for reelection and retained his seat in the council. The following year, Looby was one of 78 NAACP members investigated by the Un–American Activities Committee of the U.S. House of Representatives. In addition to investigating anyone with possible connections to the Communist Party, the committee also listed as subversive anyone who promoted racial equality.

The Tennessee General Assembly passed enabling legislation allowing the state's four major cities to form metropolitan governments in 1957. Nashville mayor Ben West appointed Looby (one of two African Americans; the other, George S. Meadows, a pharmacist and community leader, was appointed by county judge Beverly Briley) to the charter commission. Because of constitutional questions and political maneuvering in March of 1961 the state legislature passed an amendment to the 1957 enabling act. The amendment allowed for the creation of a metropolitan charter commission by referendum. On August 17, 1961, city and county voters overwhelmingly endorsed the private act creating the commission. Subsequently, Looby became a member of the second charter commission.

Sit–ins Force Change

Because Looby effectively lowered the racial bar in Nashville and across Tennessee, he became the target of many threatening telephone calls and letters. Nonetheless, he continued his crusade for African American equality and justice. In May of 1959, voters returned Looby to the Nashville City Council for a third term. Six months later, Nashville leaders and college students began the frontal attack on Jim Crow (segregated) dining facilities in the downtown business and shopping districts. They conducted "test sit–ins" to confirm the stores' exclusionary racial policies in public dining accommodations. On February 13, 1960, African American students from the city's predominately black colleges and universities conducted their first full–scale sit–in. Two weeks later, law enforcement officials arrested more than 75 students. As their cases reached the court dockets, Looby and 12 other African American attorneys defended the young demonstrators. While the sit–in demonstrations continued and the trials proceeded, Looby's name appeared almost every day in the headlines of the city's newspapers, as well as in the Southern Regional Council's *Southern School News.* In the pre–dawn hours of April 19, 1960, Looby's home was bombed. He and his wife miraculously escaped with minor injuries. By mid–day, an assemblage of at least 3,000 persons marched from Fisk University to the public square, protesting the malicious bombing attack. During a spirited debate on the courthouse steps, Mayor Ben West recommended that lunch counters be desegregated. As civil rights leader Martin Luther King Jr. addressed a crowd of 4,000 at Fisk University the following day, when Looby entered the hall to take his seat, the massive audience rose to its feet to honor him. On May 10, 1960, Nashville became the first major southern city to desegregate its lunch counters when six of the seven targeted stores agreed to accommodate African Americans in their dining facilities. However, sit–ins resumed in November, as racist practices were still the custom in most eating establishments.

In 1964, Looby lost his temper during a hearing for 30 civil rights demonstrators. He and his law partner were held in contempt of court and fined. Refusing to pay the fines, the 64–year old Looby and Williams were immediately sentenced, taken into custody, and incarcerated in the Metro jail. Mayor Beverly Briley, however, arranged to have the pair's fines paid, and they were released.

In 1961 Nashville council member Looby was only one of four African American public office holders in Tennessee. The following year, he ran as a candidate for justice of the Tennessee Supreme Court, but was defeated in the state Democratic primary.

Two months earlier, on June 28, the citizens of Nashville and Davidson County voted to consolidate the city and county governments into one single unit, the Metropolitan Government of Nashville and Davidson County. On November 6, 1962, voters elected Looby, the only member of the charter commission running for office, to the newly created 20th district council seat.

Like other African Americans in Tennessee who belonged to the Republican Party, including prominent Memphis barrister Benjamin Hooks (later executive secretary of the NAACP), Looby, a member of the party for more than 40 years, left the Republican camp in 1964 and declared himself an independent because he could not accept the Republican stance on civil rights, the Republican platform, and Republican presidential nominee Senator Barry Goldwater.

From 1940 to 1945, Looby served as national president of Omega Psi Phi Fraternity, and was also a 33rd–degree Mason. In 1946, the *Chicago Defender* placed Looby on its honor roll of outstanding contributors to harmonious race relations. The NAACP's 1947 *Crisis* magazine cited him as an effective leader. In 1950 Looby was listed among notable persons of color in *Who's Who in Colored America.* When the J. C. Napier Lawyers Association was reconstituted in 1978, members renamed it the Napier–Looby Bar Association to honor Looby, one of its celebrated founding members. In addition to teaching at Fisk and Meharry, he also taught at Tennessee Agricultural and Industrial State University (now Tennessee State University).

In 1971, Looby retired from the Nashville Metropolitan Council, after serving for more than two decades. Health problems and partial confinement to a wheelchair aided in his decision to leave government. Only semi–retired, however, he continued working as a practicing attorney.

Looby was hospitalized in Hubbard Hospital of Meharry Medical College on January 12. He died on March 24, 1972, and was survived by his spouse. Funeral services were held for him at Holy Trinity Episcopal Churce; his remains were interred in Nashville's Greenwood Cemetery.

Metropolitan Nashville recognized the contributions of Looby in August of 1976, naming a library and community center on Metro Center Boulevard in his honor. Six years later and ten years after his death, the Nashville Bar Association, whose white members denied Looby's membership application in the 1950s, posthumously awarded a certificate of membership in his name. In 1991, the Tennessee Historical Commission placed a historical marker commemorating his legal, political, and civil rights accomplishments in front of the Looby Library and Community Center.

REFERENCES

Baker, George. "Man Behind the Move." *Tennessean Magazine,* April 16, 1961.

———. "No Place to Hide." *Tennessean Magazine,* April 23, 1961.

Beeler, Dorothy. "Race Riot in Columbia, Tennessee: February 25–27, 1946." *Tennessee Historical Quarterly* 39 (Spring 1980): 49–61.

Doyle, Don H. *Nashville Since the 1920s.* Knoxville: University of Tennessee Press, 1985.

Fleming, James G., and Christian E. Burckel, eds. *Who's Who in Colored America.* New York: Christian E. Burckel, 1950.

Greenberg, Jack. *Crusaders in the Courts: How a Dedicated Band of Lawyers Fought for the Civil Rights Revolution.* New York: Basic Books, 1994.

Hawkins, Brett W. *Nashville Metro: The Politics of City–County Consolidation.* Nashville: Vanderbilt University Press, 1966.

Hine, Darlene Clark. "Black Lawyers and the Twentieth–Century Struggle for Constitutional Change." In *African Americans and the Living Constitution.* Edited by John Hope Franklin and Genna Rae McNeil. Washington, DC: Smithsonian Institutional Press, 1995.

Laska, Lewis L. ''History of African-American Lawyers in Tennessee, 1868–1968.'' Unpublished manuscript, n.d., from the files of Lewis Laska, Tennessee State University.

Lovett, Bobby L., and Linda T. Wynn, eds. *Profiles of African Americans in Tennessee.* Nashville: Local Conference on Afro-American Culture and History, 1996.

Nashville Banner, July 3, 1946; March 23, 1956; November 17, 1969.

Nashville Globe, December 20, 1946.

Nashville Tennessean, May 13, 1943; May 27, 1943; August 10, 1946; January 2, 1947; May 10, 1951; May 11, 1951; February 24, 1956; July 18, 1964; February 20, 1983; February 9, 1986.

Nashville World, September 16, 1932.

Rowan, Carl T. *Dream Makers, Dream Breakers: The World of Justice Thurgood Marshall.* New York: Little, Brown and Company, 1993.

Scott, Mingo. *The Negro in Tennessee Politics and Governmental Affairs, 1865–1965: The Hundred Years Story.* Nashville: Rich Printing Company, 1965.

Shane, Mary D. ''The Negro in Commerce and Finance.'' *The Greater Fisk Herald*: 9, 13.

Summerville, James. *Educating Black Doctors: A History of Meharry Medical College.* Tuscaloosa: University of Alabama Press, 1983.

Williams, Avon N., Jr. Untitled manuscript, n.d., in the author's possession.

Wynn, Linda T. ''The Dawning of a New Day: The Nashville Sit-Ins, February 13–May 11, 1960.'' *Tennessee Historical Quarterly* 50 (Spring 1991): 42–54.

COLLECTIONS

The papers of Z. Alexander Looby are in the Fisk University Library, Special Collections.

Linda T. Wynn

Joe Louis
(1914–1981)
Boxing champion

Heavyweight boxing champion of the world from 1937 to 1949, Joe Louis proved to the world that, regardless of negative popular media representation, black fighters were not innately inferior to their white opponents. Black Americans honored him for his physical stamina and his reputation as a man of personal integrity. His victory over Max Schmeling in 1938 assured all Americans of their mastery over the Nazis in Germany.

Joseph Louis Barrow, the seventh child of Monrow and Lily Reese, was born May 13, 1914, in Lafayette, Alabama.

Joe Louis

The Barrow children were Susie, Lonnie, Eulalia, Emmarell, DeLeon, Alvanius, Joseph Louis, and Vunice. Munrow Barrow, a farmer, was confined intermittently as an epileptic to the Searcy Hospital for the Negro Insane in Mt. Vernon, Alabama. Lily Barrow worked long hours in the fields along with her older children and gave her sons and daughters a wealth of love and care. She gleaned strength from the support of Mt. Sinai Baptist Church.

With assurance that her husband was no longer alive, Lily married Patrick Brooks, father of eight, when Louis was a young boy. The blended family of 16 boys and girls moved to a larger house and lived together in as much peace as possible for that number of individuals in one dwelling. When relatives migrated from the South to the North and relayed the news of abundant employment in Detroit, Louis's mother, older brothers, and stepfather made the move to that city, leaving the younger children in the care of Louis's uncle, Peter Reese. Not long afterward, when Louis was 12, he and the others made the trip by railroad to join the family in Detroit. They began a new life in a house on Madison Avenue and Mulick Street.

Louis married Marva Trotter, a secretary and photographer, in 1935. She sued for divorce on grounds of desertion in 1945, but they remarried in 1948 and divorced again the same year. Their daughter Jacqueline, was born in 1943, and son, Joseph Louis Barrow Jr., in 1947. Louis's marriage to Rose Morgan, a successful Harlem business woman, lasted from 1955 to 1957. His third wife was Martha Malone Jefferson, the second African American woman to pass the bar in California. Married in 1959, she and Louis had no children, but Martha adopted four children of a New York prostitute, one said to have been Louis's.

Develops Boxing Skills

Not having any more interest in Dufield Elementary School or Bronson Vocational School in Detroit than he had in the one–room school of Mt. Sinai Baptist Church in Alabama, Louis dropped out of formal study before he finished high school and went to work in an automobile plant. Meanwhile, he spent every free hour at the Brewster Recreation Center developing his newly discovered boxing skills. Before long he left the plant to train full–time as a boxer under the name of Joe Louis. After a swift rise to the national amateur light heavyweight championship, he fought as a professional. With Julian Black and John Roxborough as managers and Jack Blackburn as trainer, Louis continued a winning record. He earned the heavyweight championship by defeating James Braddock on June 22, 1937. Thirteen of his 15 victories from 1938 to 1941 were by knockouts.

Louis fought in Madison Square Garden, Yankee Stadium, Comiskey Park, and all over the country. Among his highly rated challengers were Primo Carnera, Max Baer, Buddy Baer, Jack Sharkey, Bob Pastor, John Henry Lewis, Tony Galento, Billy Conn, Lou Nova, Arturo Godoy, Ezzard Charles, Jersey Joe Walcott, and Rocky Marciano. African Americans looked on with mixed loyalties when Louis fought black opponents Jersey Joe Walcott in December of 1947 and Ezzard Charles in September of 1950.

The best remembered bouts of Louis's career are the two with Max Schmeling, a symbol of the idea of Aryan supremacy proclaimed by the Nazis. When they met on June 19, 1936, the German—the first to knock Louis to the floor—delivered a knockout blow in the twelfth round to gain the decision. African Americans waited two years for Louis to claim victory by knocking Schmeling out in the first round. Black and white Americans were jubilant. They were dancing in the streets in big cities and small towns. Radio commentators and newspaper reporters praised Louis for his patriotism.

Louis volunteered for the U.S. Army in January of 1942 and received an honorable discharge as a sergeant on October 1, 1945, with the Legion of Merit Medal. He had fought title matches to benefit the army and naval relief funds, and 96 exhibition bouts. With fellow servicemen Sugar Ray Robinson and Jackie Robinson, Louis resisted the army's policy of segregated facilities and helped remove barriers that kept African American soldiers out of officer training school.

Again a civilian, Louis returned to boxing, but gave up his title on March 1, 1949, having lost only seven of 129 amateur and professional fights and knocking out his opponent 85 times and receiving only two knockout blows.

Financial and Emotional Difficulties

Louis used the money he earned from boxing to support his mother and siblings, contribute to black causes, maintain an entourage of well wishers, underwrite the Brown Bomber Softball team, and pay for his affluent lifestyle. Starting in the 1950s, a progression of financial problems led to years of difficulty with the Internal Revenue Service. When the government requested a large sum of unpaid taxes, Louis returned to the boxing ring, then went into professional wrestling for a short period. From these earnings and the largess of friends, he survived financially and negotiated a manageable repayment schedule with the IRS.

In 1970, when his wife Martha realized that, despite her efforts and the treatment of his doctors, her husband could not recover from deep emotional stresses, she obtained a court order for him to undergo five months of treatment in a psychiatric hospital. After that he served as a celebrity greeter in Caesar's Palace in Las Vegas, basking in the adoration of a public that remembered his greatness as a prize fighter.

An aortic aneurism struck in 1977, leaving Louis paralyzed and dependent upon a wheel chair for mobility. On April 12, 1981, Joe Louis died. Three thousand mourners attended the funeral in Caesar's Palace Sports Pavilion in Las Vegas. Sammy Davis Jr. sang, and Secretary of Defense Caspar Weinberger read a message from President Ronald Reagan. Frank Sinatra spoke, and Jesse Jackson gave a eulogy that ended with a rousing cheer for the departed champion. Well wishers lined the streets of Harlem as the cortege made its way to Arlington Cemetery.

Louis's Memory Lives On

Champion Joe Louis's memory lives through numerous public tributes. The U.S. Postal Service issued a Joe Louis Commemorative Stamp in 1993 to honor his excellence in boxing and his victory over Max Schmeling. The portrayal of Louis on a stamp only 12 years after his death represented the overwhelming devotion and respect of the American people for him.

By an act of Congress in 1982, the U.S. Mint struck a gold national medal with Louis's picture on one side and the dates of his championship on the other. In a Joe Louis Barrow Day—1984 ceremony in the White House, President Reagan presented the trophy to Louis's widow, Martha, with a speech of commendation.

Joe Louis Barrow Jr. hit the first ball on opening day in 1989 for the redesigned and renamed Joe Louis–The Champ Golf Course in Riverdale, Illinois, near Chicago. In a broader tribute, each hole in the course was named for well known African Americans, such as golfer Calvin Peete and tennis star Althea Gibson. Dignitaries from the area were on hand for the celebration, and children from one of the public housing projects came to learn about Joe Louis, who once lived in Chicago.

Although he was born in Alabama, Louis spent his adolescent years in Detroit, a city that has kept his memory alive with three memorials. There is a striking ten–foot Joe Louis statue in Cobo Hall, a gigantic sculpture of Louis's fist near city hall, and the Joe Louis Arena—rated by many as the best facility for hockey in the country.

African Americans were proud of Louis's rise from humble beginnings during a time when the public relegated black athletes to substandard categories. Most African Americans were proud of Louis's love for his family and accepted him as a paragon of clean living. His less than honorable exploits were never widely reported, and he managed to maintain a reputation of a grateful son who gave full credit for his success to his mother. Black Americans interpreted his victories as triumphs, recognizing Louis's boxing strategy and talent and his willingness to sacrifice for a specific goal.

Many Americans, black and white, preferred the low key, home spun persona of Joe Louis to the flamboyant lifestyle of the former African American heavyweight champion Jack Johnson. The contrasts in their personalities and perceptions have been the subject of wide discussion.

REFERENCES

Barrow, Joe Louis Jr. *Joe Louis.* New York: McGraw–Hill Book Company, 1988.

''Cobb, Louis and Howe.'' *Sport* 80 (May 1989): 60–61.

''Illinois Golf Course to Bear Name of Joe Louis.'' *Jet* 6 (11 September 1989): 51.

''Joe Louis Becomes First Boxer Honored On U. S. Postage Stamp.'' *Jet* 84 (28 June 1993): 48–51.

Louis, Joe. *Joe Louis: My Life.* New York: Harcourt Brace Jovanovich, 1978.

Mead, Chris. ''Triumphs and Trials.'' *Sports Illustrated* 63 (23 September 1985): 74–89.

Rochette, Ed. ''National Medals Provide Inexpensive Pieces of the Past.'' *Antiques and Collecting* 92 (February 1988): 71–72.

Vitale, Rugio. *Joe Louis.* Los Angeles: Melrose Square Publishing Co., 1979.

Williams, Michael W., ed. *The African American Encyclopedia.* New York: Marshall Cavendish, 1993.

Dona L. Irvin

Joseph E. Lowery

(1922–)

Clergyman, civil rights activist, organization official

President of the Southern Christian Leadership Conference (SCLC) from 1977 to 1997, Joseph Echols Lowery is one of the founding members of this civil rights organization and a veteran of nonviolent activism and protest. He marched with Martin Luther King Jr. in Birmingham and Selma and was sued by Alabama state officials for his civil rights activities. For almost half a century Lowery has ministered to the spiritual needs of African Americans and fought without violence but with determination for the human rights of blacks and all oppressed peoples.

Joseph E. Lowery was born in Huntsville, Alabama, on October 6, 1922. His father, LeRoy Lowery owned a store in the black community of Huntsville. His mother, Dora Fackler, was a part–time teacher at the local primary school and a full–time homemaker for Lowery and his younger sister Doris. The Huntsville of Lowery's childhood was a small cotton–mill town, governed mainly by the textile mill and its owner. Situated in the northeastern part of the state between Decatur and Scottsboro, the town's black population was small. In an interview, Lowery recalled once being extremely frightened when his mother pulled the shades down before night and locked the windows and doors because the Ku Klux Klan was riding through the neighborhood. His childhood memories were catalyst for his developing awareness and commitment to struggle for civil rights.

While Lowery's father was a small businessman and wanted his son to become one too, Lowery's great grandfather, Echols Lowery, had been a minister and the first black pastor of a United Methodist church in Huntsville. On his mother's side were African Methodist Episcopal ministers. The family attended Lakeside United Methodist Church where Echols Lowery had been pastor.

In 1928 Lowery enrolled at the local primary school and his mother sometimes taught his class. He entered high school in 1936 at Alabama Agricultural and Mechanical College's laboratory school, beginning with the ninth grade. He remembers the great influence A. M. Stevens, his physics instructor, had on him, not so much with regard to the subject matter of physics but in terms of what it meant to be a man and maintain dignity in the South. Another important role model at this time in his life was Samuel William, a minister who also taught economics and civics. It was perhaps William's grasp of the spiritual, economic, and civic issues of the day that led in part to Lowery's own concept of economic justice.

Coming to Terms with Southern Racism

Growing up in the cotton belt and not having to pick cotton gave Lowery a sheltered status from some of the most blatant forms of racism. He remembers, however, that he had a growing awareness of the problems between blacks and whites because of the stories his father told. He realized later that those stories were a form of socialization black parents used to try to prepare their children for the Southern culture, in which blacks were expected to know their place in society. One story he remembers his father telling involved white reaction to his owning a nice car. Once on a trip in the country with his wife he had a flat tire. As he was changing the tire he was accosted by a white who cursed him, demanding to know what he was doing to the car. Quickly Lowery's father replied that ole Miss was in the car and would not tolerate profane language. Hearing this the man apologized and changed the tire for the white lady sitting in the car. When they drove off, LeRoy Lowery and his wife had a good laugh.

As a high school student, Lowery became more acutely aware of the restrictions imposed on black people. The summer that he was 14 he entered his father's store to get some candy. As he left the store a large white policeman

Joseph E. Lowery

punched him in the stomach with a nightstick. After clubbing him, the policeman said, "Get back boy, don't you see a white man coming in?" Angry and driven by the ego only a fourteen year old manchild possesses, Lowery rushed home and got his father's pearl handle pistol, planning to return and demand respect with the power of the gun. Suddenly his father appeared in the doorway. Lowery explained that his father never came home in the middle of the day. The only day that he could ever remember his father being at home was Sunday. His father had not witnessed the insult his son had suffered and apparently did not know himself why he had come home in the middle of the day. Lowery believes it was Providence. After listening to his son, LeRoy Lowery called the mayor of Huntsville and complained. Lowery remembers his father's look of anger and frustration when the mayor informed him that there wasn't anything he could do about the ignorance of the policeman. Lowery vowed then to do something to change things when he grew up.

Lowery graduated from high school in 1939 and entered Knoxville College in the fall. He majored in sociology, but after his first year at the college he returned home and enrolled at Alabama Agricultural and Mechanical College in Normal, Alabama. As a junior Lowery transferred to Paine College in Augusta, Georgia, where he pledged the Alpha Phi Alpha Fraternity. His best subjects were history and sociology, but he continued to take a number of business courses in order to prepare himself for the career his father assumed he would pursue, that of a businessman.

Lowery graduated from Paine College in 1943 with a B.A. degree in sociology. It was becoming clear to him that he did not want to go into business. A friend of his father's had a newspaper in Birmingham and needed someone with a college degree to edit the paper for him. Lowery's first job out of college was as an editor for the *Informer* (now the *Mirror*), a black newspaper in Birmingham.

Answering the Call

Birmingham, Alabama, in 1943, had a large black population. Jim Crow laws there forbade such things as blacks and whites playing checkers or dominoes together. In spite of these laws, one million black Americans were fighting in World War II to make the world safe for democracy. As Lowery edited the newspaper, recording acts of violence against his fellow blacks, he felt that he was called to preach.

Lowery enrolled in Paine Theological Seminary in 1944. Attending part–time, he continued to work for the newspaper. LeRoy Lowery had big plans for his son that did not include becoming a minister, moving frequently, and flirting with poverty. In this regard LeRoy Lowery was among a vast majority of middle class blacks of his generation who had struggled to take care of their families and educate their children during the Great Depression. Because he knew his father wanted him to go into either law or business, Lowery was reluctant to tell him he had decided on entering the ministry. Lowery recalled in the *Journal Constitution* for June 14, 1992:

> One of my greatest fears when I felt called to preach was telling my father . . . I wanted him to hear me preach first. After he heard me, we had our talk and he said, "I have no objection."

Lowery met Evelyn Gibson, daughter of Harris and Marva Gibson, in Birmingham while he edited the newspaper. They were married in 1947. He graduated from the seminary in 1950, with a bachelor of divinity degree and was ordained in the United Methodist Church. His first assignment took him to Mobile, Alabama, where he was pastor at the Warren Street United Methodist Church from 1951 to 1961.

Lowery preached his first sermon as an ordained Methodist minister in 1948, at a small church in Birmingham. At the conclusion of the service he recalled in the *Journal Constitution* for June 14, 1992, that an elderly woman approached him and said, "Keep on. One day you're gonna be a good preacher." Not only did he become a good preacher, he became a politically astute advocate for poor and oppressed people, a fiery preacher intent on bringing about a transformation in the land of his birth.

When the Montgomery Bus Boycott began in 1955, Lowery was well positioned to be instrumental in the movement for change. He first met Martin Luther King Jr. through his friend and colleague, the Reverend Fred Shuttlesworth. Rosa Parks's refusal to give up her seat on a bus to a white man set into motion a chain of events that had been waiting to happen. The Montgomery Improvement Association (MIA), led by King, directed the boycott that brought the Jim Crow bus system to its knees in Montgomery. Recognizing the power of the ministerial group to galvanize masses of people to work for political change, King decided to establish another group in 1957, when the boycott ended segregation on public busses.

The Beginning of the SCLC

In January of 1957 Lowery was one of the preachers from ten southern states to meet in Atlanta at Ebenezer Baptist Church with Martin Luther King Jr. to discuss the formation of a new organization called the Southern Negro Leaders Conference. King was elected president and Lowery vice president. The name of this organization of black southern clergy changed within a few months to Southern Christian Leadership Conference (SCLC).

The purpose of the SCLC was to continue the struggle for civil rights in a nonviolent, organized manner utilizing the tactics of passive resistance, civil disobedience, and public protests and marches. King selected Shuttlesworth and Lowery because of their knowledge and experience in the state of Alabama. Lowery made good on his boyhood promise to change the way the white police treated black people. Among his many contributions to the SCLC was his effort in exposing police brutality and implementing the hiring of black police officers in Birmingham.

In 1959 Lowery and three other staff members of the SCLC, Shuttlesworth, Ralph Abernathy, and Solomon S. Seay Sr., were sued for libel by police commissioner Sullivan of Montgomery, Alabama. The suit resulted from an advertisement that Bayard Rustin, an SCLC leader, placed in the *New York Times* to raise funds for the Martin Luther King legal defense fund. According to Branch, the full–page advertisement said: "In Montgomery, Alabama, after students sang 'My Country Tis of Thee' on the State Capitol steps, their leaders were expelled from school, and truckloads of police armed with shotguns and tear gas ringed the Alabama State College campus." Rustin had concluded the advertisement by using the names of the SCLC officials. The Alabama attorney general charged that the ad libeled the officials it implicated.

The lawsuit caught Lowery completely by surprise as he was unaware of the advertisement and had not been informed that his name was to be used. The other defendants were equally caught off guard. Lowery said he had to make a concerted effort to not question his concern for saving the soul of America. An all–white jury in Montgomery, in spite of all of the evidence presented showing their innocence, brought back a verdict of guilty in the *Sullivan v. New York Times* suit and ordered the four ministers to pay $3 million. Lowery's automobile was confiscated and sold at a state–ordered auction, and other property was seized. The law suit was appealed all the way to the U.S. Supreme Court and the *New York Times* and the SCLC ministers exonerated.

In 1961 the United Methodist Church transferred Lowery to Nashville, Tennessee, where he served as an administrative assistant to Bishop Michael Golden. In Nashville he led sit–ins at lunch counters and in restaurants and led marches against local hotels and hotel chains that discriminated against blacks. In his position as assistant to Golden, Lowery attended the World Council of United Methodist Churches in London.

From 1964 to 1968, Lowery pastored St. Paul United Methodist Church in Birmingham. His return to Alabama followed the church bombings that left three young black girls dead. Lowery's ministry and his politics were never at odds. On his arrival in Birmingham blacks were arming themselves in order to protect themselves and their property. Wealthy blacks guarded their neighborhood, which was known as Dynamite Hill because of the numerous bombings that took place there. To the blacks of Birmingham, many of whom were members of his congregation, Lowery preached nonviolent activism. He did not expect blacks to simply pray for a change but to actively work to bring it about. Because he did not advocate violence, he was viewed as a moderate by many of the blacks in Birmingham. The SCLC was seen as a proactive group closer to the common people and far less passive than the NAACP. The SCLC under King's leadership and the assistance of Lowery made significant gains in Alabama.

Violence, however, was to be confronted at every turn. By 1968 the war in Vietnam, violent student protests, and urban riots seemed to mark the end of nonviolent activism. The final blow occurred when King was shot and killed in Memphis, Tennessee, while organizing a march for striking garbage workers. With the death of their leader the SCLC floundered. Lowery told Ron Harris in *Ebony* for November of 1979, "When we lost Martin we lost our thrust." Lowery went on to explain that "another problem was that many people thought that because lunch counters and busses had been desegregated, we had won the war, when actually we had only won a few battles. Then black organizations, including SCLC made a strategic move away from direct action and towards the political arena because that was where we thought the thrust should be." Lowery also pointed out that the press lost interest, which is the kiss of death to any popular movement.

Keeping the Dream Alive

In the summer of 1968, Lowery was transferred from Birmingham to Atlanta, Georgia, where he was minister of Central United Methodist Church. Ralph Abernathy had succeeded King as president of the SCLC and together he and Lowery worked to increase voter participation. Lowery had been successful in helping to get the first black city councilman of Birmingham, Richard Arrington Jr., elected. He used this experience in Georgia to help get the Student Nonviolent Coordinating Committee (SNCC), the student arm of SCLC, member Julian Bond elected to the Georgia legislature.

As minister of Central United Methodist, Lowery's congregation grew to over 2,500 members. The church is the oldest and the largest historically black United Methodist Church in Atlanta. Under his leadership the church constructed Central Methodist Gardens, a low and moderate income housing complex of 240 units.

In February of 1977, Ralph Abernathy resigned as president of the SCLC. There was a power struggle within the ranks of the organization, and Abernathy was viewed by some militant members as too passive and lacking in leadership. This opinion was voiced by Hosea Williams, a minister, Georgia State Representative, and former SCLC field director under King. Williams was considered to be radical in his views by SCLC moderates. They nevertheless, recognized some truth in his charges. Lowery, a leading moderate, was made acting president. Then at the convention in August of 1977, he became president by a unanimous vote.

Lowery inherited a $10,000 SCLC debt. The once thriving organization had gone from 11,000 chapters and affiliates to only 400. His first order of business was to restore the organization to financial stability and build membership. He planned to accomplish this by redefining the organization's goal and mission. Williams, who had been appointed executive director, a move to placate the militants, objected to the new direction the organization was taking. He also resented the fact that he had no check writing privileges. Williams accused Lowery of making the organization into a bourgeois group.

Lowery wanted a peaceful organization unified by a common goal. On March 21, 1979, he fired Williams on the grounds that he had not resigned from his seat in the Georgia state legislature to accept his full–time $20,000–a–year position at the SCLC. Williams immediately began a campaign against Lowery, charging that he was destroying the SCLC and betraying King's legacy. Hoping to influence the SCLC Board of Directors meeting in Washington, D.C., on April 10, 1979, Williams organized a protest. About 40 of Williams's supporters picketed the meeting, but the board sustained Lowery's firing of Williams.

Continuing to March for Freedom

From the time he took over as president, Lowery was intent on actively addressing issues of civil and human rights. Describing his first few months he said in *Ebony,* "First we went to Mississippi and jumped on the Southern Company for buying coal from South Africa. Then we went to North Carolina and marched for Ben Chavis. Next we went to Decatur, Alabama for Tommie Lee Hines." Hines was a black mentally–challenged youth convicted of the rape of a white woman, and Chavis was part of the Wilmington Ten, who were arrested in 1972 and convicted on conspiracy to murder charges.

In 1979, on another march in support of Hines, Lowery and his wife were almost shot when the Ku Klux Klan fired into the group of marchers, injuring four. Unlike the 1960s when no police action would have been invoked, 4,000 state troopers were ordered to protect the demonstrators when they marched again for Hines. Later that same year Lowery led a march in Birmingham, Alabama, to protest a white policeman's shooting of a black woman. In August of 1979, when Andrew Young, United States Ambassador to the United Nations, was forced to resign because he had met with Zehdi Terzi, the Palestine Liberation Organization's member at the United Nations, Lowery led the SCLC more prominently into global issues. Already the SCLC was protesting issues of civil and human rights in South Africa. On August 20 Lowery led a group of 11 SCLC officials to the UN to meet with Terzi and discuss the Arab–Israeli conflict and Young's resignation. The next day Lowery and his associates met with the Israeli ambassador to the UN. In a press conference following this meeting Lowery, assuming a nonpartisan stance, told *New York Times* for August 22, 1979, that the SCLC wanted to see peace in the Middle East. Under Lowery's leadership the SCLC involved itself in every issue foreign or domestic that was likely to affect black Americans.

Lowery led a peace–seeking mission to Lebanon in the fall of 1979. A delegation of ten black American ministers met with PLO leader Yassir Arafat. They would have met with Menachem Begin, Israeli Prime Minister, except he refused to receive the self–appointed diplomats. Lowery and the SCLC were criticized for daring to venture beyond domestic issues of civil rights. The criticism was neither unexpected nor new. Lowery had heard it all before as he reminded readers in the *Washington Post* for September 24, 1979. Lowery recalled that when King and the SCLC had denounced the Vietnam war, "People said, 'stay in civil rights issues—blacks don't know anything about foreign policy.'" What critics forgot and Lowery pointed out was that blacks have died disproportionately in U.S. wars. To American Jews who objected to his conversation with the PLO Lowery said in the *New York Times* for August 22, 1979, "Don't worry about who I talk to; worry about what I say. Who are you to tell us who we can talk to? To heaven with you."

The Longest March

In February of 1982, Lowery organized the longest civil rights march in history. On February 5, 4,000 supporters and civil rights leaders marched from Carrollton, Georgia, to Montgomery, Alabama, arriving on February 18 to protest the conviction of two black women in Carrollton for voting fraud and also to demonstrate the need for an extension of the 1965 Voting Rights Act. Lowery told the marchers it was time to move to a new mountain top from race to economics.

The 1990s marked the beginning of that new mountain top. Lowery focused the SCLC on economic justice, maintaining that the elimination of poverty will solve problems such as drug use and crime. Toward this end, the SCLC has established several projects, among them are Operation Breadbasket, a $90 million agreement with Shoney's to sponsor joint venture projects with black businesses and colleges. The SCLC established the Liberation Lifestyles project, designed to teach people to place materialism in perspective and to value the spiritual things. Lowery's most recent brain–child was the Gun Buy Back Program which paid cash for guns that people turn in, which was part of a larger project called Stop the Killing.

Lowery is the recipient of honorary degrees from Clark College (Massachusetts 1975); Morehouse College (1978); Miles College (1977); and Dillard University (1980). In 1990 he was awarded the Martin Luther King Jr., Nonviolent Peace

Prize. In the same year he was presented the Medal for Outstanding Professional Service in the field of civil and human rights by George Washington University. He received the NAACP's Lifetime Achievement Award in July of 1997, in recognition of his dedicated and commited service to human rights.

In 1992 Lowery retired as pastor of Cascades United Methodist Church where he served since 1986. Until 1997 he worked full–time with the SCLC, when he stepped down and was succeded by Martin Luther King III, son of the celebrated civil rights leader. He also chairs the National Black Leadership Forum, and is chairman of the Board for the Metropolitan Atlanta Rapid Transit Authority. He and his wife have three adult children, Cheryl, Karen, and Yvonne. Lowery has two adult sons Joseph Jr. and LeRoy II from a former marriage.

Lowery's genius as a leader has taken him to national and international prominence. From the Civil Rights Movement to the fight for economic empowerment, Lowery has provided the paradigm for sustained political action.

Current address: Southern Christian Leadership Conference, 334 Auburn Avenue, N.E., Atlanta, GA 30303.

REFERENCES

''After 45 Years, Rev. Lowery Says Amen.'' *Atlanta Journal Constitution,* June 14, 1992.

''Bishops Honor Fellow Pastor, and Civil Rights Leader Lowery.'' *Amsterdam News,* November 20, 1993.

Branch, Taylor. *Parting the Waters: America in the King Years.* New York: Simon and Schuster, 1989.

Contemporary Black Biography, Vol. 8. Detroit: Gale Research, 1995.

Current Biography 1982. New York: H. W. Wilson, 1982.

''The Fervent Preacher and the Palestinians.'' *Washington Post,* September 24, 1979.

Garrow, David J. *Bearing the Cross: Martin Luther King, Jr., and the Southern Christian Leadership Conference, 1955–1968.* New York: Morrow, 1986.

Harris, Ron. ''Dr. Joseph Lowery: The Man Who's Reinventing SCLC.'' *Ebony* 35 (November 1979): 53–56.

''Israeli at U.N. Criticize Blacks for Supporting P.L.O.'' *New York Times,* August 22, 1979.

''Lowery Blasts FBI For Spying On SCLC, Others.'' *Jet* 73 (15 February 1988): 4.

''Lowery: 'Economic Violence' Must End.'' *Atlanta Journal Constitution,* August 10, 1992.

Lowery, Joseph. Interview with Nagueyalti Warren, July 16, 1996.

''Lowery, Napper Lash Out at '2–Strikes' Plan.'' *Atlanta Journal Constitution,* September 23, 1994.

''Lowery Says Integration Put Blacks in 'Polluted Stream.''' *Atlanta Journal Constitution,* August 7, 1990.

''Rights Group Acts to Heal Moderate–Militant Rift.'' *New York Times,* August 19, 1977.

''SCLC Election May Reveal A Split in the Ranks.'' *Atlanta Journal and Constitution,* August 14, 1977.

''SCLC Leaders Hope to Rejuvenate Group.'' *New York Times,* February 27, 1977.

''SCLC President Receives NAACP Lifetime Achievement Award.'' SCLC National Magazine 26 (July/August/September 1997): 17.

Nagueyalti Warren

Sam Lucas
(1840–1916)
Entertainer, actor

The career of Sam Lucas encapsulates the possibilities open to blacks in show business during his lifetime. Beginning in minstrel shows, Lucas became a very good all–round performer. He was allowed to try his hand at the stereotypical role of Uncle Tom on the stage and in film. Eventually he made his mark in vaudeville and was also closely involved in the birth of black musical comedy.

Lucas was born on August 7, 1840, in Washington, Ohio. Sources give Milady as his original name. We know of one brother, Tony, who survived him. The only other information about his family is that AME church leader Reverdy Ransom calls him an uncle—Ransom's stepfather and family were also residents of Washington. In Tom Fletcher's *100 Years of the Negro in Show Business,* Lucas characterized his education as ''fair.'' Singing and dancing came naturally to Lucas, and he learned to play the guitar. Before the Civil War, Lucas was a barber and developed his life–long habit of dressing well. He also acquired a diamond ring and an expensive gold watch—portable wealth which made more than one trip to the pawn shop during his career to bail out stranded companies.

Lucas said that he served in the army during the Civil War. After the war his entertainment skills became more than a sideline, and he pursued a professional career. Part of his activity was playing and singing for passengers on river boats. Blacks had begun to form minstrel companies to compete with white blackface–performers in the 1850s, and after the war black–managed and black–staffed companies became increasingly popular. Lucas began working with them.

Lucas worked with Callender's Georgia Minstrels; George Callender took over the troop from George Hicks in 1872. Lucas also seems to have been a member of the troupe under Hicks, since he was listed as a former member when he joined Lew Johnson's Plantation Minstrels in May 1871. In mid–1874 Lucas was with Henry Hart's Colored Minstrels; Lucas was presented with a gold medal after a performance of this troupe in St. Louis. In 1875 he was in a skit with Callender's Georgia Minstrels. He also sang ballads, and his status as a star was such that he published *Sam Lucas' Plantation Songster* in Boston, probably also in 1875. A second effort, *Sam Lucas' Careful Man Songster,* appeared in Chicago in 1881.

Stars With Hyers Sisters

In 1876 with the Hyers Sisters' company he premiered in Boston the long–time standard song, "Grandfather's Clock (Was Too Tall for the Shelf)." A major hit, the song was performed years later as mourners left his funeral. Lucas claimed that he wrote the song and sold it outright to the persons whose names appear on the sheet music, but some critics doubt that Lucas actually wrote any of the songs he sang including his other hits "Carve Dat Possum" and "Turnip Greens." Lucas worked with the Hyers Sisters in at least three of the productions in their repertory—*Out of Bondage, The Underground Railway,* and *Princess Orelia of Madagascar.* He told Fletcher that his billing in the last was "The Hyer Sisters, starring Sam Lucas."

In 1878 one of theatrical entrepreneur Charles Frohman's travelling *Uncle Tom's Cabin* companies was in difficulties. By this date blacks had appeared in secondary roles in the play, but there had never been a black in a principal role. In an attempt to keep the company afloat. Frohman decided to try a novelty appeal, and Lucas became the first black to play the role of Uncle Tom. The show still did not make money, and Lucas's watch and diamond ring came to the aid of the stranded company in Cincinnati. Lucas continued to work in minstrel shows; in the 1879 season, for example, he was on tour in the South with Haverly's Genuine Colored Minstrels.

At some time in the 1870s Lucas married Carrie Melvin, a fellow performer, whose specialties were the violin and the cornet. Their only known child, Marie (d. 1947?), was old enough to sing on stage in Boston in 1883. Marie Lucas received an excellent musical education and became a notable band leader in the early twentieth century. The Lucases seem to have settled in Boston where Lucas organized the Hub Concert Company which was quite successful. Lucas and his wife also appeared together in vaudeville; they continued the act into the 1890s. Lucas also took other jobs as the occasion offered.

In 1890 Lucas began his association with a series of shows which would bring black musicals into existence. Lucas suggested the formation of a black burlesque company to white producer Sam T. Jack. The company's performances centered around a combination of variety turns, comedy, and elaborately costumed women. Lucas was in large measure responsible for hiring the talent, securing the material, and generally managing the company while Jack concentrated on the financial end. *The Creole Show* opened in the fall of 1890 and became a major attraction. Lucas and his wife remained with the company until the end of 1891.

In 1892 the Lucases appeared again in vaudeville, and in the summer of 1896 they returned to the United States from working abroad. That fall they appeared in A. G. Field's *Darkest America* company to great applause. Lucas also appeared in one or more versions of John Isham's *Octoroons* during the last half of the decade. From 1897 through early 1899 Lucas and his wife played vaudeville together and in early 1899 they also appeared with the Genuine Southern Specialty Company. In April of 1899 Lucas appeared in vaudeville with a different woman partner and at the end of September opened in Robert Cole and Billy Johnson's show, *A Trip to Coontown.*

This show was a landmark. It was the first full–length black musical comedy and the first black show to be a major draw for white New Yorkers. Lucas worked with the show through early 1901 when he joined the Alabama Troubadours Company, a large summer park–show. In late 1903 he was stage manager for P. G. Lowery's Nashville Students. Lucas may also have tried his hand at the restaurant business since he is named as a proprietor of the Smart Set Buffet and Palm Gardens in St. Louis in 1904. That year he also appeared with the white *Moonshiner's Daughter* company.

In 1905–06 Lucas appeared in the Ernest Hogan show *Rufus Rastus.* He next had a hit in "The Bode of Education" skit in Cole and Johnson's *Shoo Fly Regiment* from 1906 to 1908 and worked in their *Red Moon* (1909–1910). He then worked as a single in vaudeville until he retired from the stage in 1912. In 1914 Lucas became the first black to play the title character on film in a full–length film version of *Uncle Tom's Cabin.* According to Tom Fletcher, he caught a chill from which he never fully recovered by plunging into the river to rescue Little Eva.

Lucas died at his daughter's home on January 10, 1916, of an undiagnosed cirrhosis of the liver. He had suffered intermittent ill–health for the preceding five years. Lucas's only survivors were his brother Tony and his daughter Marie Lucas. His funeral was held at Mother Zion Church in Harlem. Called the "dean" of black performers and affectionately known as "Dad" to his fellow performers long before his death, Lucas had maintained a theatrical career remarkable for its longevity.

REFERENCES

Cuney–Hare, Maud. *Negro Musicians and their Music.* 1936. Reprint, New York: Da Capo, 1974.

Fletcher, Tom. *100 Years of the Negro in Show Business.* 1954. Reprint, New York: Da Capo, 1984.

Handy, D. Antoinette. *Black Women in American Bands and Orchestras.* Metuchen, NJ: Scarecrow Press, 1981.

Johnson, James Weldon. *Black Manhattan.* New York: Knopf, 1930.

Klotman, Phyllis Rauch. *Frame by Frame.* Bloomington: Indiana University Press, 1979.

"Sam Lucas, Veteran Performer, Is Dead." *New York Age,* January 13, 1916.

Sampson, Henry T. *The Ghost Walks.* Metuchen, NJ: Scarecrow Press, 1988.

Simond, Ike. *Old Slack's Pocket Reminiscence and Pocket History of the Colored Profession from 1865–1891.* 1891. Reprint, Bowling Green, Ohio: Popular Press, 1974.

Southern, Eileen. *Biographical Dictionary of Afro–American and African Musicians.* Westport, CT: Greenwood Press, 1982.

Toll, Robert C. *Blacking Up.* New York: Oxford, 1974.

Trotter, James M. *Music and Some Highly Musical People.* Boston: Lee and Shepard, 1878.

Robert L. Johns

John Roy Lynch

(1847–1939)

Congressman, lawyer, realtor

John R. Lynch was one of the most noteworthy blacks to hold political office in the South during the Reconstruction Era (1865–1877). Born of a slave mother and a white planter father on September 10, 1847, near Vidalia in Louisiana, John Roy Lynch overcame his humble beginnings to become a trailblazer for blacks seeking to enter the political arena. The young man who was born a slave in Concordia Parish became a magistrate at the age of 20, a legislator at 22, a member of the U.S. Congress at 24, a confidante of President Ulysses S. Grant at 26, and temporary presider at the 1884 Republican National Convention at the age of 36.

Lynch's early years are somewhat obscure, but some facts are known about this period in his life. His mother was a slave owned by the white plantation owner who was Lynch's father. Little is known about her, but she is depicted as a woman of high moral character in John Hope Franklin's *The Autobiography of John R. Lynch.* This union produced at least two other siblings—a brother named William and a sister whose name is unknown. Lynch's white father was apparently very concerned about the welfare of the family, as he made arrangements with a friend to free John Roy's mother and the children upon his death. But this friend proved to be false; when the father died suddenly, the mother and the children were sold to another plantation owner, Alfred V. Davis of Natchez, Mississippi. John Roy accustomed himself to the life of a slave, and got along well with his new master, who made him a favored body servant.

Lynch obtained his freedom in 1863 when Union forces occupied Natchez. The slaves knew that reaching the Union forces meant freedom. Lynch and other slaves on the Tacony Plantation decided to leave in search of the Union lines. It was perhaps this early contact with the Union soldiers as a camp employee and later as a cook on a naval vessel that caused Lynch to join the United States Army some 35 years later. He was 17–years old when he became free.

The job market during this era was extremely constrained, and, like many freed slaves, Lynch had to find a way to make a living away from the plantation. In 1866 he became an assistant at a photographic studio in Natchez, Mississippi. The proprietor of the studio was so impressed with John Lynch's abilities that, within one year of employing the former slave as a photographer and businessman, he turned the entire management of the studio over to Lynch.

John Roy Lynch

Having established himself economically, Lynch began working hard to make up for his lack of formal education. Although he attended night school for only four months while in the Union Army camp in 1863—which was as long as the night school for blacks in Natchez was open—Lynch, like most slaves, had limited or no access to education before emancipation. He worked hard to improve himself and obtain enough education to become a competitive player in the highly contentious society of the deep South during Reconstruction. Within a few years that perseverance paid off, and his newly–acquired skills propelled him into politics, public service, law practice, real estate, and the pursuit of historical studies

About this time, John Lynch began to dabble in politics, the arena where he was to make his greatest contribution. He became a magistrate at the age of 20. The Republican military governor Adelbert Ames appointed Lynch justice of the peace in Natchez from April to December 31, 1867. He served as a representative to the state Republican Convention held in Jackson, Mississippi, on July 1, 1869, and was also an assistant secretary to that Convention. He won his first elective office as a member of the Mississippi State House of Representatives in 1869, at age 22. He served on the National Emigration Aid Society Executive Committee, the Committee on Resolutions, the Committee on Public Education, the Committee on Elections, and the Elections and Military Affairs Committees of the State Legislature. In 1871 he was elected the Speaker of the House of Representatives. Lynch moved on to the national political scene in 1872 when he was a delegate to the Republican National Convention. He was elected later that year to the United States Congress, one of 22 African Americans to serve between 1870 and 1901. He served for two full terms and had more influence at the White House than any other black man until modern times. Within a year of leaving Congress, he was nominated and elected chairman of the 1884 Republican National Convention, the first African American to be elected to such a position, and the first to deliver the keynote address to the convention.

While in Washington, Lynch served on several congressional committees, and was renowned for his support of the 1875 Civil Rights Act which banned discrimination in public accommodations; it was declared unconstitutional in 1883. The violent overthrow of the Republican government in Mississippi in 1875 ended his congressional career, except for one additional year in 1882–83, the result of his victory in a disputed election. In *John R. Lynch,* James H. McLaughlin observed that "John R. Lynch began to use his writing and oratorical skills to convince the newly freedmen (ex–slaves) of their political rights, convincing them that they should exercise these rights."

Lynch held appointive offices in the federal government and the army under Presidents Benjamin Harrison, William McKinley, Theodore Roosevelt, and Howard Taft. President McKinley appointed him paymaster of volunteers in the Spanish–American War, with the rank of major in the U.S. Army. In 1901 he took this post in the regular army.

Lynch was married twice, first to Ella Somerville and later in 1911, having moved to Chicago after divorcing Ella, he married Cora Williams. No mention is made concerning any children from either marriage. He worked for 25 years as a lawyer and realtor in Chicago. He was the author of *The Facts of Reconstruction* (New York: Neale Publishing Company, 1913), a well–reasoned and informed defense of Reconstruction against a rising tide of historical criticism. John Roy Lynch died in 1939 of natural causes.

Lynch was the first black congressman from Mississippi and in 1884 he was the first black to preside over the Republican National Convention. His life exemplifies the courage, determination, and character necessary to strive against great odds.

REFERENCES

Appleton's Cyclopedia of American Biography. New York: D. Appleton and Co., 1888.

Barnes, William H. *Biographies of Members of the Forty–Third Congress.* Washington, DC: W. H. Barnes, 1875.

Christopher, Maurine. *America's Black Congressmen.* New York: Thomas Y. Crowell, 1971.

Franklin, John H., ed. *The Autobiography of John R. Lynch.* Chicago: University of Chicago Press, 1970.

Logan, Rayford W., and Michael R. Winston, eds. *Dictionary of American Negro Biography.* New York: Norton, 1982.

McLaughlin, James H. *John R. Lynch, The Reconstruction Politician.* Ball State University Press, 1981.

Miscellaneous Document No. 12, 47th Congress, 1st Session.

Sewell, George A. *Mississippi Black History Makers.* Jackson: University of Mississippi Press, 1977.

Simmons, William J. *Men of Mark.* 1887. Reprint, New York: Arno Press and the *New York Times,* 1968.

Wharton, Vernon L. *The Negro in Mississippi, 1865–1890.* Chapel Hill: University of North Carolina Press, 1947.

Thura Mack

M

Haki Madhubuti

(1942–)

Poet, essayist, educator, publisher

In his various roles as poet, essayist, teacher, businessman, Haki Madhubuti has consistently struggled to concretize his definition of black life, black survival, and commitment to the values that lead to cultural wholeness of the individual and the group. His works can be satirical, celebratory, and politically incisive. In a poem entitled "Gwendolyn Brooks," published in *Every Shut Eye Ain't Sleep,* dedicated to one of his mentors, Haki Madhubuti wrote:

> into the sixties
> a word was born. . . . Black
> & with black came poets
> & from the poet's ball points came:
> black doubleblack purpleblack.

Although these lines and others that ring numerous changes on the word "black" pay homage to Brooks, they also provide a context for the lifelong work of Haki Madhubuti. In the tradition of the poets of the Black Arts movement, Madhubuti has conveyed the essence of blackness; the promulgation of cultural values in the black community; and the expression of those spiritual, political, and physical values that lead to the health and survival of the community. The poem also reflects his inventive use of language, the rapid fire changes and riffs on the word that marks the style of a poet whose works are often meant to be performed. As revealed in his book *Killing Memory,* he has been guided by an attitude toward literature, in particular poetry, that says that

> the face of poetry must be fire erupting volcanoes,
> hot silk forging new histories,
> poetry delivering light greater than barricades of
> silence,
> poetry . . . preparing seers, warriors.

Haki Madhubuti, born Don L. Lee on February 23, 1942, spent his first year of life in Little Rock, Arkansas, his birthplace. His parents, Jimmy and Maxine Lee, left Arkansas, however, in 1943 and moved to Detroit. The move did not improve the lot of the family, for his father deserted them soon after the birth of Lee's sister, leaving his mother to rear the two children through a series of jobs that included domestic work and jobs as a bar maid. Madhubuti's mother died when he was 16, and her death resulted in another move for him when he went to live with his aunt in Chicago. His own family has had more stability; he has been married since 1974 to Safisha, a professor at Northwestern University. Together

Haki Madhubuti

they have three children: Lani, Bomani, and Akili. He is also the father of two children, Don and Mari, from two previous unions.

Madhubuti's formal education includes a high school diploma received in 1960 from Dunbar Vocational High School in Chicago. He earned his A.A. degree from Chicago City College and later an M.F.A. from the University of Iowa. During his lifetime, he has received various awards, including the National Endowment Grant for Poetry (1983), Distinguished Writers Award from Middle Atlantic Writers Association (1984), and the American Book Award (1991). He was named author of the year by the Illinois Association of Teachers of English, and he was the only poet chosen to represent the United States at the International Valmiki World Poetry Festival in New Delhi, India, in 1985.

Early Influences

Madhubuti's development as a man of letters can be traced back to the influence of his mother who, despite the precariousness of their existence, exposed him early to the wonders of the library in which he found works by black authors. He notes in *Black Men: Obsolete, Single, and Dan-*

gerous? that once his mother introduced him to the marvels of the Detroit Public Library, he was seldom without a book. From this introductory period, made particularly significant by his reading of Richard Wright's *Black Boy,* until his graduation from high school, he read other black writers including Chester Himes, Frederick Douglass, and Booker T. Washington. Although his initiation into the armed services was marred by a vicious reaction by his commanding officer to Madhubuti's reading of Paul Robeson's *Here I Stand,* his stint in the army also became a period of intense self–education in African American literature. He left the army in 1963, acquainted with the work of Gwendolyn Brooks, Claude McKay, and W. E. B. Du Bois. According to Madhubuti in "A Personal Journey," the library became a place where he found "new friends, uncritical friends. . . . Reading became as important as water and food."

Following his discharge from the army, he became an apprentice and curator at DuSable Museum of African History (1963–67), another significant step in his development; there he was under apprenticeship to Margaret Burroughs, an authority on black history and culture. During this period, he also enrolled in Wilson Junior College (now Kennedy–King College). Meanwhile, he was preparing himself for the disciplined life of the writer; from 1961 to 1966, he followed a strict regimen of reading a book a day and writing a book review of approximately 200 words. These activities were conducted while he held various jobs to sustain himself, including a few for the retail giants of Chicago—Speigel and Montgomery Wards, as well as a job in the post office.

First Poetical Expressions

Madhubuti's first volume of poetry appeared in 1966 with the publication of *Think Black.* Although he had not yet changed his name from Don L. Lee, the poems in this slim volume signaled the direction that this future prolific poet and essayist would take. Announcing himself to the world, the speaker of this volume reveals to the reader the year in which he was "born into slavery," thus indicating the political turn that much of the poetry would take. In this volume, which was originally self–published and self distributed, he defines himself unquestioningly as a black poet. He castigates America not only for its enslavement of black people, but also for its forced internment of the Japanese during World War II. One of the most frequently anthologized pieces from the book, "Back Again, Home" speaks to a sense of awareness and rebirth, a call to revolutionize one's thinking as Lee's persona realizes the fallacy of his own enslavement to the materialistic dream of upward mobility, an enslavement that resulted in his loss of self. This message remains a constant in Madhubuti's work. From the beginning, he has challenged values that are destructive of the individual and the culture and has called for the rejection of those values. The volume also reveals another dimension to Madhubuti's voice that expresses itself in a softer and more intimate poem such as "A Poem for Black Hearts."

In 1967, along with Johari Amini (Jewel Latimore), and Carolyn Rodgers, Madhubuti launched the Third World Press in the basement of his South Ada Street apartment in Chicago with seed money of $400. The Third World Press has the distinction of being the longest continuously operating African American press in America. Its inauguration signalled what is a distinctive element in Madhubuti's life as a man of letters—his role as an institution builder, particularly institutions which perpetuate the word and the world of ideas. This institution and others that were to follow became concrete representations of his political and philosophical positions, which stress self–reliance individually and culturally; e.g., building institutions within the community that supports the values of that community. He has noted the hypocrisy of criticizing the institutions of America while remaining dependent upon some of those institutions to convey his beliefs to the public.

As the 1960s ended, Madhubuti published two additional volumes of poetry: *Black Pride* (1968) and *Don't Cry, Scream* (1969). In addition, he started the Institute of Positive Education, a school offering two– to– eight–year–olds an Afrocentric education (1969). He also participated in the first Pan–African Festival in Algiers and became writer–in–residence at Cornell University.

The 1970s and Beyond: Expanding the Vision

The beginning of the 1970s saw the publication of *We Walk the Way of the New World* (1970), a collection of poems that continues and expands the themes from his earlier works. While a poem like, "Back Again, Home" speaks directly to rebirth on an individual level primarily, the title poem from this new volume speaks to a rebirth on the collective level. Referring to the black man's sojourn in America as the "dangercourse," the speaker notes the transformations that have occurred as the community marches toward nationhood. According to this poem, it has been a journey marked by elements of self–hatred, and enslavement to empty capitalistic values. As the layers are stripped away, the speaker's vision is one of black people having run the "dangercourse" emerging as "owners of the New World / the New World" (a world cleansed/transformed by a new people who no longer are corrupted by or corrupt the land/world). The vision articulated in this poem indicates the driving force behind Madhubuti's roles as poet, essayist, and institution builder—to keep before his audience those values that lead to renewal and survival. Continuing the trend in his previous volumes, *We Walk the Way of the New World* also contains poems that reveal a more intimate side. Such poems are included in the section entitled "Blackwoman Poems."

The decade of the 1970s also saw the publication in 1971 of *Directionscore: Selected and New Poems* as well as *To Gwen with Love,* a book he edited with Frances Ward and Patricia Brown. Of major importance was the publication of *Dynamite Voices: Black Poets of the 1960s,* also in 1971. It was a volume that provided a critical context for the writers of the Black Arts movement by one of the participants of the movement. Published by Broadside Press, the work allowed Madhubuti to articulate his definition of the black literary critic's role. While maintaining that the black critic must not be narrow in focus, Madhubuti clearly indicates that it is the black critic's role to reflect his or her grounding in the black experience that will enable the critic to develop standards of evaluation related to that experience. It was in 1972 that Madhubuti also started the *Black Books Bulletin.*

In 1973 Madhubuti decided to change his name from Don L. Lee to Haki Madhubuti, a name that means "justice," "awakening," and "strong" in Swahili. It was the year in which he became poet–in–residence at Howard University and during which *Book of Life* was published by Broadside Press. The introduction of *Book of Life* reveals a certain disillusionment on the part of the poet. He also uses the opportunity in this volume to admonish his audience to become independent and to understand the connection between the development of the black woman to her full potential and the development of the black nation to its full potential. In 1973 *From Plan to Planet* also appeared. Published jointly by Broadside Press and the Institute of Positive Education, the book had as its motivation the spiritual building of African minds. Therefore, seeking to transform and enhance the spiritual state of his audience, Madhubuti includes ruminations on such topics as self–hatred, money, power, sex, and drug addiction. The decade ended with the publication of *Enemies: The Clash of Races* (1978) and the launching of the African American Book Center.

The decade of the 1980s saw a continuation of Madhubuti's role as poet and the expansion of his role as critic. He wrote *Say That the River Turns: The Impact of Gwendolyn Brooks* (1984) and *Killing Memory, Seeking Ancestors* (1987). Third World Press spearheaded the African American Publishers Booksellers and Writers Association in 1989. In speaking of Africa, Madhubuti noted in the prologue to *Killing Memory* that the "land of sun has a special meaning" for him, although he was "not prepared for the land that gave birth to civilization." The prologue further indicates that Madhubuti's goal has been to move culturally from "negro to Black to African," a trip on which he as poet–seer–teacher seeks to guide others. Hence, the poem reflecting the second half of the title becomes another expression of the poet's role. "Seeking Ancestors," a poem written for the First Annual Egyptian Studies Conference in Los Angeles in February 1984, is divided into five parts focusing first on the "death traps" in American culture, juxtaposed with a rumination on the first people to use the triangle and cultivate the earth. There is a call for the storytellers to recall the memory of those people in order to call us to our better selves. Throughout Madhubuti's poetical career, he has sought to recall genius to the community, for there are poems devoted not only to Gwendolyn Brooks, but also to Hoyt Fuller, Malcolm X, and the nameless others in the community whose lives exemplify survival under difficult circumstances. His role as the "renamer," the "recaller of tradition," can also be seen in the style of much of his poetry which captures the rhythms of talk, accompanied by performance. Expanding his role as educator, Madhubuti began teaching at Chicago State during this decade (1984). He is currently professor of English there. That same year, he, an environmental engineer, and a lawyer founded the National Black Holistic Retreat of which he is director.

While Madhubuti has continued to write poetry in the 1990s, he has also enhanced his role as essayist. In 1990 he published *Black Men: Obsolete, Single, Dangerous?, African American Families in Transition: Essays in Discovery, Solution and Hope,* a book that addresses the issues that continue to threaten the survival of black men in America, along with advice on the solution to these issues. In 1991 Madhubuti's Third World Press was successful in adding Gwendolyn Brooks to its list of major authors. Responding to the upheaval caused by the Rodney King case in Los Angeles and to the ensuing unrest, Madhubuti edited *Why L.A. Happened: Implications of the '92 Los Angeles Rebellion* in 1993. This was followed by *Claiming Earth: Race, Rage, Rape, Redemption: Blacks Seeking a Culture of Enlightened Empowerment* (1994), a book that the author has described as a work about the development of one's own resources. Madhubuti's significance can be shown by a statement from this volume in which he declares that there is no separation between "my cultural self and my political, professional, business, familial, and writer selves." In his life and career, he has exemplified the individual's attempt to create a unified self and to live a holistic life, one not broken down into segments or fragments of person, poet, teacher, and entrepreneur, a life in which the self is imbued with the cultural values informed by the black experience.

Current address: Third World Press, 7822 South Dobson, P.O. Box 730, Chicago, IL 60619.

REFERENCES

Andrews, William, Frances Smith Foster, and Trudier Harris, eds. *The Oxford Companion to African American Literature.* New York: Oxford University Press, 1997.

Contemporary Authors. Vol. 73–76. Detroit: Gale Research, 1978.

Contemporary Literary Criticism. Vol. 73. Detroit: Gale Research, 1993.

Madhubuti, Haki. *Black Men: Obsolete, Single, Dangerous?* Chicago: Third World Press, 1990.

———. "Gwendolyn Brooks." In *Every Shut Eye Ain't Sleep: An Anthology of Poetry by African Americans Since 1945.* Edited by Michael S. Harper and Anthony Walton. Boston: Little, Brown, 1995.

———. *Killing Memory, Seeking Ancestors.* Detroit: Lotus Press, 1987.

———. "A Personal Journey: Race, Rage, and Intellectual Development." In *Praise of Our Fathers and Our Mothers: A Black Family Treasury by Outstanding Authors and Artists.* Edited by Wade Hudson and Cheryl Willis Hudson. East Orange, NJ: Just Us Books, 1997.

——— (Don L. Lee). *Think Black.* Detroit: Broadside Press, 1969.

——— (Don L. Lee). *We Walk the Way of the New World.* Detroit: Broadside Press, 1970.

Oliver, Stephanie Stokes. "Liberated Love." *Essence* 22 (July 1991): 93–107.

"Preaching the Power of the Printing Press." *Chicago Tribune,* January 31, 1992.

Johnanna L. Grimes–Williams

Monroe A. Majors

(1864–1960)

Physician, civil rights and political activist, editor, journalist, writer

A pioneer in the medical profession, Monroe A. Majors was credited with founding a drugstore and a hospital in Texas and with joining in the founding of pioneer medical societies for blacks in Texas and Chicago. He was the first black to pass the examination set by the California Board of Examiners, becoming certified to practice medicine in the state. He was as devoted to journalism, race relations, and political activism as he was to attending to the health care needs of his patients in such cities as Waco, Chicago, Decatur, Illinois, and Monrovia, California. He was known also for compiling the first comprehensive biographical work on black women, *Notable Negro Women,* that stood alone in the field for 100 years.

Monroe Alpheus Majors was born in Waco, Texas, October 12, 1864, the son of Andrew Jackson Majors and Jane Barringer Majors and the youngest of three children. The family moved to Austin in 1869 to provide better educational advantages for their children. He grew up in a strict tradition with parents who were firm about their children's attendance at Sunday school, church, and grammar school. Majors attended public schools first, then enrolled in West Texas College—a school managed by the Freedmen's Aid Society.

Apparently the Majors family exposed their children to a variety of cultural experiences. This was a time when minstrel shows flourished. Majors was impressed by the Georgia Callender Minstrels, hearing the singing of Billy Kersands, and the brass bands and minstrel parades. He observed his father's power in the community and ability to influence blacks to vote regularly, including his two sons when they were old enough to do so.

In 1874, when he was ten years old, Majors was appointed a page to the Texas State Legislature in Austin. There he developed a fascination for politics and a keen interest in the progress of black people that influenced him throughout life. He was impressed by the presence of 47 black members of the Texas House of Representatives and four in the Senate. He honed his reading skills and became an avid reader of newspapers and books. Particularly impressed by T. Thomas Fortune, who edited the *New York Age,* he may have been influenced by Fortune's journalistic skills when he later became a journalist himself.

Monroe A. Majors

Majors spent three years as a page, and, when his term expired, he worked in the Raymond House, Austin's best hotel. He met many of the well–known figures of the day, including abolitionist Henry Ward Beecher, Buffalo Bill, and Otis Skinner. He continued his work at the hotel while he attended college. From 1881 to 1883 Majors attended Tillotson College and Normal School in Austin, founded by the American Missionary Association. The school's president, Reverend W. Brooks, recognized Majors's talent, took a keen interest in him, and encouraged him to prepare for a profession. About 1882, when he was 18 years old, he was appointed assistant mailing clerk in the local post office.

As he prepared for a medical career, Majors moved to Nashville, Tennessee, and enrolled in a literary course at Central Tennessee College in 1883. Meharry Medical College had grown out of the school in 1876. He also entered Meharry in 1883 and graduated in 1886, when he was 21 years old, with an M.D. degree. He was salutatorian in a class of ten students. While in medical school, he helped support himself by working as postmaster and news reporter for the school. He also headed a department of penmanship at Meharry.

Black Medical Society Organized

Majors returned to Texas in 1886 and practiced medicine in Brenham, a small town located between Houston and Austin. He later became the first black to practice medicine in Calvert. He saw a need to unite the black physicians in the state and, in 1886, called a meeting in Galveston. Majors and 13 other physicians organized the state's first black medical society and the second black medical association in the country—the Lone Star Medical Association, later known as the Lone Star State Medical, Dental, and Pharmaceutical Association. (The Medico–Chirugical Society of the District of Columbia, organized in 1884, was the nation's oldest medical society for blacks.) He developed a keen interest in politics, but negative white reaction to black political power was growing. After whites in the area of Brenham drew up a list of all blacks who were to be killed, a member of the local Grand Army warned Majors that he was on the list and advised him to leave town immediately.

Majors moved first to Calvert and shortly afterward to Dallas. His departure had been timely; soon after he moved from Brenham, Majors learned that three blacks, including one of his friends, had been hanged. He taught school at an unnamed location in Texas for one year.

Relocating again in 1888, Majors set up practice in Los Angeles, where he was the first black to pass the examination of the California Board of Examiners; and, on January 26, 1889, he became certified in the state. He also became the first black to practice medicine on the Pacific Coast and west of the Rocky Mountains. In addition to his practice, he lectured at meetings of medical societies and at the Los Angeles Medical College. A talented man with skills in journalism, Majors became editor of the *Los Angeles Western News.* Still politically active, he used the newspaper to help blacks in Los Angeles secure appointments in areas where they had not been previously employed—the police force, city public works, and in the office of assessor and collector.

Majors returned to Waco in 1890, where he bought a house and used it for his medical practice, remaining there until 1895. Meanwhile, Robert Charles O'Hara Benjamin, the first black editor of the *Los Angeles Daily Sun,* encouraged Majors to compile a major work on black women. By the time he moved to Waco, he began the compilation that resulted in *Noted Negro Women: Their Triumphs and Activities,* published in Chicago in 1893. A work of such scope required the assistance of others who knew black women and their contributions. Majors wrote to Frederick Douglass, soliciting his help in extending the list. Douglass responded on August 26, 1892, saying that:

> We have many estimable women of our variety, but not many famous ones. . . . It is not well to claim too much for ourselves. Such extravagance invites contempt rather than approval. I have thus far seen no book of importance written by a Negro woman and I know of no one among us who can appreciably be called famous. This is in no way a disparagement of the women of our race. We stand too near a former condition to have any famous work in science, art, or literature, expected of us. It is not well to ship the paddle wheels before we have steam to move them.

Although Douglass did not "find it consistent" to expand the list, he agreed that many of the women on Majors's list were admirable, "cultured, refined, and ladylike," but would not consent that they were famous. His letter did not dissuade Majors from continuing the work. *Noted Negro Women* was published as a comprehensive work containing signed entries and listings of numerous black women who had gone unnoticed; until the 1990s it remained the most thorough account on the work of black women.

On April 23, 1893, Majors went to Chicago. While the reason for his temporary stay there is unclear, he remained for five months, returning to Waco in September. In Chicago he met Daniel Hale Williams, who founded Provident Hospital in 1891. He came in contact with great black leaders and intellectuals who had assembled in Chicago for an exposition, including Frederick Douglass. Majors, Charles S. Morris, and Paul Laurence Dunbar worked together to arrange forums to highlight the achievement of blacks. As U.S. Minister to Haiti, Douglass presided over the Haitian building and addressed over 8,000 people in Festival Hall. After Majors, Morris, and Dunbar helped Douglass organize his address, he began to call them his "three musketeers."

Founds Drugstore for Blacks

Majors continued his medical practice in Waco and from 1891 to 1894 lectured at Paul Quinn College, a black institution in Waco founded by the African Methodist Episcopal church. He also established a drugstore in Waco, becoming the first black to found a drugstore in the Southwest. Majors either founded or was instrumental in establishing Waco's Colored City Hospital as well. His political activities continued, as did his work in journalism. From 1893 to 1894, he edited the *Texas Searchlight.* Through this journal, he responded to W. Calvin Brann, who published a periodical called *The Iconoclast.* Brann used his publication to denounce black people, and his printing of one piece in particular, "The Mulatto Bastard," so incensed Majors that he took action immediately to stop its distribution. Majors and Norris Wright Cuney, Republication National Committeeman from Texas and Collector of Internal Revenue for the federal government, persuaded the Waco postmaster to stop distribution through mail.

In 1894, Majors was elected president of the organization he had helped to found earlier, the Lone Star State Medical, Dental and Pharmaceutical Society. He was elected chairman of the Board of Directors of the Texas Cotton Palace Exposition held in Waco in 1894. The exposition also held a special "Colored People's Day," which was well attended and a financial success. Quoted by W. Montague Cobb in the *Journal of the National Medical Association,* Majors commented on the affair:

> We were given full authority to deny to white folk the right to trespass on Negro rights. They wanted to dine at all of the restaurants and confectioneries on the Fair grounds and a hundred or more citizens came to me for charity. We let them see how it feels to be denied human rights.

So successful was his work as head of the organization that some local white citizens wanted him to become mayor of Waco.

Although the reason for his next move is unclear, in 1898 Majors relocated to Decatur, Illinois, and established a practice. Although the town already had a number of wealthy physicians, residents still welcomed Majors. About a month after his arrival his office was constantly crowded with patients. Race relations in Decatur were no better than they were in the Texas. Although Majors enjoyed prestige, popularity, and success, some residents began to resent him. The lynching of a black in Decatur three months prior to his arrival was fresh on the minds of many, particularly those who campaigned against the state's attorney who refused to stop the act. When the attorney became a candidate for Congress, the Democratic press talked with local residents about the matter; Majors, one of the influential residents, was among those interviewed. Accused of endorsing the Democrats, Majors began to receive threats and left Decatur.

Writings Are Published Widely

Majors remained in the Midwest, this time relocating to Indianapolis. His political activism continued. He worked with Republican George L. Knox who campaigned in a local race against Tom Taggart, a Democrat. When the Republicans won, Majors was named associate editor of the *Indianapolis Freeman,* a position he held from 1898 to 1899. He had already written articles for the paper beginning in 1896, and from that year until 1899, he continued to publish his works in the *Freeman.* He wrote poetry, a weekly advice column called "Majors Melange," and articles on a variety of topics, such as white terrorism, the advancement of blacks, the power of the press, crime, black physicians, and reminiscences of slavery.

Continuing his peripatetic tendencies, Majors returned to Waco in 1899 and resumed his practice. In 1899 and 1900, he was also superintendent of the hospital he had built—the Colored City Hospital, now officially run by the city. Majors would neither remain in Waco long nor curb his militancy toward racial oppression. He knew that he had to leave Waco, and he reasoned that the only place he could be fairly safe was Chicago.

Majors left the South permanently in 1901 and settled in Chicago, where he would maintain his medical practice until 1921. The relationship he had earlier with poet Paul Laurence Dunbar continued, and for 11 years the two remained close friends. Although the early location of his medical practice is unclear, in time he moved to the Loop district, becoming the first physician to maintain an office in that area. In Chicago he demonstrated the same zeal for medicine, writing, and political and civic involvements that he had shown elsewhere. In 1903, he bought a residence at St. Lawrence and 45th Street. Although the dates for many of his involvements are unknown, for two years he served on the city's board of health, having been appointed by two of Chicago's mayors. He promoted the organization of Chicago's black doctors into their own medical society, presumably resulting in the formation of the Cook County Physicians Association. He was a charter member of the organization.

In 1908, Majors served as commissioner of the Lincoln Day Centennial, which brought the well–known minister and orator J. W. E. Bowen to speak on the occasion. Later he chaired a grievance committee of Provident Hospital. In 1915, the governor of Illinois appointed him to the board of the Negro Half Century of Freedom and Progress exposition. He was national president of the National Negro Authors Association at Lincoln Center, an adjunct to the program of the Half Century Exposition. His organizational memberships throughout his lifetime included the Odd Fellows, Knights of Pythias, NAACP, United Brothers of Friendship, the National Business League, and the Texas Club. He was also a Thirty–second Degree Mason.

Majors continued to use his skill as a journalist as well. At the request of Booker T. Washington, from 1908 to 1911 Majors edited the *Chicago Conservator.* His editorials were also published in the *Chicago Broad Ax* and the *Chicago Defender,* and his poems appeared in such newspapers as the *Washington Bee,* the *Peoples Advocate,* and the *Colored American.* He also published "Ode to Frederick Douglass" (1917) and *First Steps to Nursery Rhymes* (1921), a book for black children. In addition to his contributions to journalism, poetry, and other disciplines, Majors was said to have originated the term "paralysis diabetes," known in medical literature.

In 1925, Majors awoke one morning to blindness. Due to racial prejudice, Northwestern University denied him admission. Although he paid the deposit of 1800 dollars and later, as required, obtained an endorsement from Daniel Hale Williams, who spoke to hospital officials of Major's importance to the black race, the denial stood. Majors was then readily treated at Presbyterian Hospital and received all courtesies normally given to a physician. He was charged only for board. Majors received one ophthalmic operation in 1926 and another in 1933. He was fitted for glasses, but in time his vision deteriorated again. He moved back to Los Angeles on March 4, 1933, and lived with relatives while he practiced medicine for two years. According to Logan and Winston in the *Dictionary of American Negro Biography,* he may have practiced also in Monrovia, California, until 1955. His health failing by then, he moved back to Los Angeles in 1956, where he died on December 10, 1960, of natural causes.

A staunch Republican, Majors was also a member of the Methodist Episcopal Church. While in California in 1889, Majors married Georgia A. Green of Oberlin, and had one daughter, Grace (Boswell), born March 29, 1890. His marriage in 1909 to Estelle C. Bonds resulted in the birth of a daughter, Margaret Jeanette, 1913–1972, who was to become a well–known composer, musician, and educator. Altogether, Majors had four wives. Quoted in the *Dictionary of American Negro Biography,* Majors's survivors recalled that he had "a rather disagreeable personality." Often called "big daddy," he was a known "ladies' man."

Monroe Majors, licensed in three states, practiced medicine in the late 1900s and well into the first half of the twentieth century. His legacy is in his pioneering medical practice, organization of two medical societies for black physicians, in journalism, and in the publication of the seminal work *Noted Negro Women.*

REFERENCES

Cobb, W. Montague. "Monroe Alpheus Majors, 1864– ." *Journal of the National Medical Association* 47 (March 1955): 139–41.

Douglass, Frederick. Letter to Monroe Majors, August 26, 1892.

Logan, Rayford W., and Michael R. Winston, eds. *Dictionary of American Negro Biography.* New York: Norton, 1982.

Majors, Monroe. *Noted Negro Women.* Chicago: Donohue and Henneberry, 1893.

Who's Who in Colored America. New York: Who's Who in Colored America Corp., 1927.

COLLECTIONS

The papers of Monroe A. Majors are in the possession of his granddaughter, Eleanor Boswell–Raine, in El Sobrante, California.

Jessie Carney Smith

Malcolm X.
See X, Malcolm.

Eugene Antonio Marino

Eugene Antonio Marino
(1934–)
Religious leader

Eugene Marino was the first African American Catholic Archbishop in the United States. He had an important symbolic and practical influence on black Catholics, who had long pressed both for an increased black leadership in the Church and for recognition of their special concerns. He proved to be an effective leader in the church. Unfortunately Marino's involvement in a sex scandal forced him to resign his office before the impact of his leadership could be fully felt.

Eugene Antonio Marino was born in Biloxi, Mississippi, on March 25, 1934, to Jesus Maria Marino and Irene Bradford Marino. He was the sixth of eight children. Jesus Marino was a baker, and Irene Marino worked part–time as a maid and cleaning woman. In spite of his father's Puerto Rican name and heritage, Eugene Marino grew up entirely in the African American community and spoke no Spanish. Early on, while he attended parochial school, he decided on his religious vocation.

After graduating from high school in 1952, he attended Epiphany Episcopal College in Newburgh, New York, the minor Josephite seminary. (The Society of St. Joseph of the Sacred Heart has ministered to blacks in the United States since 1871, striving, among other aims, to train black priests.) He entered the novitiate in 1955 and made his first profession in 1956. Marino attended St. Joseph's Major Seminary in Washington, D.C., in 1956, and earned his bachelor's degree in 1960. The following year he made his final profession to the Josephites, and he was ordained a priest on June 9, 1962. Along with his course of study, he also took summer school classes. After earning his degree he studied at Loyola University in New Orleans and took a master's degree at Fordham University in 1967.

Marino's first assignment as a priest was to teach at Epiphany Apostolic College. In 1968 he became spiritual director of St. Joseph's Major Seminary and in 1971 was elected the first African American vicar general or second–in–command of the Josephites. On September 12, 1974, he was consecrated auxiliary bishop of Washington, the fourth African American to become a bishop. As bishop, Marino did much to address the concerns of black Catholics. He was theologically conservative to moderate but was a strong advocate of programs to help the poor. In November of 1985 Marino became secretary of the National Conference of Catholic Bishops, another first for an African American and a distinct mark of recognition. He was instrumental in arranging a large meeting of black Catholics and Pope John Paul in the New Orleans Superdome during the pope's 1987 visit to the United States. It has been suggested that this success was a factor in Marino's appointment as the first African American archbishop in the United States on March 15, 1988. He said of himself as quoted in the *National Catholic Reporter* of November 10, 1989:

> Whether I like it or not, I happen to be . . . the highest–ranking spokesperson in the African–American Catholic church. And whether I attach a great deal of significance to that or none at all, it remains a fact. People will see me as someone who would have a special insight into concerns, challenges or problems of a black Catholic nature.

Marino quickly established himself as an effective and popular archbishop of the Atlanta archdiocese. One of the issues he addressed concerned the sexual misconduct of priests after a grand jury indictment of one priest on charges of child molestation. Marino issued strict new guidelines in response to the controversy. Ironically, his own conduct soon brought the issue of clerical celibacy to the forefront.

Marino was forced to resign his post in June of 1990 after evidence surfaced of an affair between Marino and a woman named Vicki Long. He began the relationship soon after he moved to Atlanta. Long had been involved with other priests and had filed a paternity suit against one in Columbus, Georgia, in 1987. (Blood tests showed the priest was not the child's father.) Marino went into counseling and dropped all contact with his former colleagues. Long claimed that she and Marino were secretly married in December of 1988; she filed for divorce and also attempted suicide. In April of 1993 Long claimed that she and Marino were reconciling.

Marino's fall was an occasion for sadness especially in view of his demonstrated abilities and his potential as a leader. Another African American, James P. Lyke, replaced Marino as archbishop in Atlanta.

REFERENCES

''Archbishop Eugene Marino Resigns after Relationship with Young Georgia Woman.'' *Jet* 78 (20 August 1990): 4–6.

Cheers, D. Michael. ''A Long–Awaited First.'' *Ebony* 43 (October 1988): 92–96.

Edwards, Robin T. ''Sanchez Not First U.S. Prelate Whose Reported Liaison Became Public.'' *National Catholic Reporter* 29 (19 March 1993): 7.

Golphin, Vincent F. A. ''Marino, Only U.S. Black Archbishop Resigns.'' *National Catholic Reporter* 26 (27 July 1990): 24.

Hansen, Susan. ''New Archbishop Marino's Goal: Gospel Standard.'' *National Catholic Reporter* 24 (25 March 1988): 1, 5–6.

''Marino Goes into Hospital Psychiatric Unit.'' *National Catholic Reporter* 26 (24 August 1990): 7.

''Marino Two–Year Affair Linked to Resignation.'' *National Catholic Reporter* 26 (10 August 1990): 4.

Moore, Trudy S. ''Ex–Bishop Marino and Vicki Long Reunite after Sex Scandal and Plan New Life Together.'' *Jet* 83 (5 April 1993): 32–37.

Murphy, Larry G., J. Gordon Melton, and Gary L. Ward, eds. *Encyclopedia of African American Religions.* New York: Garland, 1993.

Windsor, Pat. ''Atlanta's Marino Cuts the Mustard.'' *National Catholic Reporter* 26 (10 November 1989): 3–4.

''Woman, 27, Charges She Married Ex–Archbishop Marino Two Years Ago.'' *Jet* 78 (27 August, 1990): 14–15.

''Woman Says She Is Wed to Archbishop and She Will 'Stand By' Him.'' *Jet* 78 (3 September 1990): 12–13.

Robert L. Johns

Elijah P. Marrs
(1840–1910)
Minister, educator, political activist

Elijah P. Marrs was a man of the cloth, a leader of men, an advocate for the education of blacks, and a prominent participant in state politics. His early religious calling and an innate sense of the importance of education set his life on a path that led to great achievements and had a strong impact on the course of history of African Americans in Kentucky. His involvement in fighting railroad car segregation as a leader of the Anti–Separate Coach Movement of Kentucky, as well as his role in the founding of several churches and of what later became Simmons University, is a testament to his efforts on behalf of the African American community.

In his autobiography *Life and History of the Rev. Elijah P. Marrs, First Pastor of Beargrass Baptist Church, and Author,* Marrs, born in January of 1840 in Virginia, describes himself as the son of a free man, Andrew, and a slave mother, Frances, meaning he was born a slave. His first job in his master's house was as a dining room boy, followed by six years of working with his mother attending the cows. A turning point in the life of young Marrs occurred the day Marrs saw his father telling his minister that he had ''found religion.'' The observance of his father's conversion experience was the catalyst that led Marrs to profess his faith in Christianity at the young age of 11. Marrs also became convinced at this time that he was to prepare for his future by learning to read and write: ''Very early in life I took up the idea that I wanted to learn to read and write. I was convinced that there would be something for me to do in the future that I could not accomplish by remaining in ignorance.''

Marrs's Christian faith and his baptism were major factors in the removal of traditional barriers that prevented slaves from learning to read. He wrote in his autobiography:

> After my conversion and baptism I was permitted to attend Sunday–school and study the Word of God for myself. My master then removed all objections to my learning how to read, and said he wanted all the boys to learn how to read the Bible, it being against the laws of the State to write. We had to steal that portion of our education, and I did my share of it I suppose.

Marrs's ability to read benefitted the black community around him; when he picked up newspapers from the post office, he would read the articles and share the news regarding the war between the North and South with other slaves. Black soldiers who had enlisted in the Union Army entrusted Marrs to pick up the letters they sent home to their families, though this was a dangerous task in Confederate country.

Marrs decided to enlist in the U.S. Army, and, as he walked to Simpsonville, South Carolina, he convinced 27 men to join him. He joined the Army on September 28, 1864, and was assigned to Company L, Twelfth U.S. Colored Artillery. When his ability to read and write was brought to the attention of some of the officers, he was reassigned as the Third Duty Sergeant, Company L, 12th U.S. Heavy Artillery. His army career lasted until April 20, 1866. During the war he kept slaves informed of events by reading newspapers to them for long periods of time.

After the Civil War ended, Marrs and his brother Henry worked together raising crops and, as noted in his autobiography, doing "as much hauling as he could do at eight dollars per day." Eventually, friends convinced Marrs to go to Simpsonville to teach their children. He opened his first school on September 1, 1866, and taught in Lagrange and New Castle County until 1873. On August 3, 1871, Elijah P. Marrs married Julia Gray.

Marrs began his Christian ministry at this time and was granted a license to preach in 1873. With the support of his wife, Marrs entered Roger Williams University, a Baptist college in Nashville, Tennessee, in 1874, and became an ordained minister on August 22, 1875. Later that year, Julia Marrs fell sick and remained bedridden for five months. She died on April 9, 1876.

After the death of his wife, Marrs traveled to Cincinnati, where he attended the Republican National Convention of 1876. The convention nominated Rutherford B. Hayes, who was elected the nineteenth President of the United States. Frederick Douglass was also present at the convention. Marrs's travels were cut short when he received word from his brother Henry of plans to open a school. The brothers opened the Kentucky Normal and Theological Institute at Crescent Hill in Louisville in 1880, which later became Simmons University. Elijah Marrs became the school's first president.

Marrs was involved in state politics, the education and civil rights of blacks, and the ministry of the black Baptist church. He served as a delegate to every political convention held by African Americans in the state of Kentucky in the postwar era and was a prominent figure in the first election in which African Americans voted, held in 1870. He also sat on the state central committee of the Anti–Separate Coach Movement. He was a delegate to the first educational convention in Kentucky in 1868 and the first Convention of Colored Men in 1882 as well as the National Convention of Colored Men in 1883.

Marrs founded and served as pastor of the Beargrass Colored Baptist Church in Crescent Hills, Kentucky, from 1880 until his death in 1910. His life is weaved through the political, social, and theological history of blacks in the state of Kentucky.

REFERENCES

Howard, Victor. *Black Liberation in Kentucky: Emancipation and Freedom, 1862–1884.* Lexington: University Press of Kentucky, 1983.

Kentucky Encyclopedia. Lexington: University of Kentucky, 1992.

Lucas, Marion B. *A History of Blacks in Kentucky.* Vol. 1: *From Slavery to Segregation, 1760–1891.* Frankfort: Kentucky Historical Society, 1992.

Marrs, Elijah P. *Life and History of the Rev. Elijah P. Marrs.* 1885. Reprint, Miami: Mnemosyne, 1969.

Simmons, William J. *Men of Mark.* Cleveland: Geo. M. Rewell, 1887.

Smith, S. E., ed. *History of the Anti–Separate Coach Movement of Kentucky.* Evansville, IN: National Afro–American Journal and Directory Publishing Co., 1895.

Ann C. Sullivan

Wynton Marsalis

(1961–)

Jazz and classical trumpeter, composer, lecturer, promoter, educator

The rebirth of traditional jazz in the United States and throughout the world is unquestionably due to the efforts of one man more than any other, Wynton Marsalis. A master of both jazz and classical trumpet by his early twenties, Marsalis was, by his mid–thirties, the greatest active composer of music in the traditional, or pure, jazz style. Incredibly, he proved himself equally adept at developing his non–music skills—promoter, lecturer, educator—all of which he used effectively to crusade for his first love, jazz.

Wynton Marsalis was born on October 18, 1961, in New Orleans, Louisiana, and raised in the nearby town of Kenner. He was the second of six children born to Ellis and Dolores Marsalis. A renowned jazz pianist, Ellis Marsalis was the founder of, and an instructor in, the jazz program at the New Orleans Center for the Creative Arts. Dolores Marsalis was a one–time jazz singer and substitute teacher who gave up her career interests to devote her energies to raising her musically–talented children. Several of Wynton Marsalis's brothers were also successful professional musicians. Wynton Marsalis, a never–married bachelor, fathered three young sons.

Marsalis's introduction to music came early. Ellis Marsalis was so impressed with the musical development of eldest child Branford, who was exhibiting great skill on clarinet and

Wynton Marsalis

piano while only in the second grade, that he induced six–year–old Wynton to begin music lessons early as well. Ellis Marsalis, then playing for famed trumpeter Al Hirt, asked his boss for an advance to buy Wynton a trumpet. The Dixieland icon did not loan Ellis Marsalis the money; instead, he gave him one of his old trumpets to give to the boy. Wynton Marsalis made his debut the following year, playing ''The Marine Hymn'' at the Xavier Junior School of Music. Trumpet playing, however, interested Wynton less than did basketball and Boy Scouts, and he practiced irregularly.

Becoming Devoted to Music

At age 12, Wynton Marsalis's musical desire surged when he heard a recording by jazz trumpet great Clifford Brown. He dedicated himself to the mastery of the instrument and to the jazz idiom. An important step in that climb was becoming a student of John Longo at the New Orleans School for the Creative Arts. Longo, a trumpet player trained in classical music as well as jazz, encouraged his pupil to absorb the best from all musical styles. When not practicing, Marsalis began spending increasing amounts of time listening to recordings featuring the trumpet. Among these was a classical album by Maurice Andre, which proved an important incident in the young musician's life.

No longer content to focus solely on jazz, Marsalis began splitting his time between jazz and classical music. At fourteen, Marsalis won a statewide youth competition that resulted in his being a featured soloist with the New Orleans Philharmonic Orchestra, for which he played Franz Joseph Haydn's *Trumpet Concerto.* He made a second appearance with the orchestra at sixteen, playing Johann Sebastian Bach's *Brandenburg Concerto No. 2 in F Major.*

While in high school, Marsalis played first trumpet with the New Orleans Civic Orchestra. He also found time to play in a number of other bands, including the New Orleans Brass Quintet and the Creators. The latter was an eight–member funk rock group in which Branford Marsalis played the saxophone (his signature instrument). At seventeen, Wynton Marsalis went to Tanglewood, Massachusetts, to attend the Berkshire Music Center's summer school, which waived its usual eighteen–year–old age requirement. The result: he walked off with the Harvey Shapiro Award for Outstanding Brass Player.

Marsalis's devotion to music did not prevent him from being a stellar scholar as well. At Benjamin Franklin High School, Marsalis compiled a 3.98 (4.0 scale) grade point average on his way to becoming a National Merit Scholarship finalist. Offered scholarships to Yale University and other Ivy League institutions, he turned them down. Marsalis later said that he was tired of going to white schools and dealing with the ''racial vibe'' at them. He chose instead to accept a full scholarship from New York City's prestigious Juilliard School of Music.

Initially, while at Juilliard, Marsalis supported himself by playing with the Brooklyn Philharmonia and in the pit band for the Broadway hit *Sweeney Todd.* However, his experience as a jazz student at Juilliard was not what he had envisioned. He discerned at the school a bias against jazz, which increasingly bothered him. His disillusionment with Juilliard, however, did not prevent him from making outside contacts that would help establish him in the jazz world.

Renowned drummer Art Blakely was so impressed with Marsalis at a Manhattan club date that he asked the young trumpeter to spend his 1980 summer vacation as a member of the percussionist's own Jazz Messengers. Marsalis eagerly accepted. At only nineteen years old, he also became the band's musical director. It was during that tour that Marsalis began to attract national attention that resulted in his being dubbed a prodigy by the jazz press.

In 1981 Marsalis left Juilliard before earning a degree. By then, he did not have to look hard for work. He played off and on with Blakely, but perhaps more importantly, he caught on with jazz giant Herbie Hancock's V.S.O.P. quartet. (V.S.O.P., or Very Special Old Pale, occurred as initials on labels of some of Handy's works.) A pianist, Hancock and two members of his quartet had made up the rhythm section for Miles Davis's quintet in the 1960s, when Davis was changing the face of jazz. Marsalis spent the summer of 1981 touring Japan and the United States with V.S.O.P. and appeared on their album, *Quartet,* later that same year.

Marsalis's burgeoning talent not only caught the ears of established performers but those of jazz critics, as well. Marsalis was voted ''the talent most deserving of wider recognition'' in a 1981 *Down Beat* poll. His busy schedule of working for other, more noted performers paid off when

Columbia Records offered him a contract that year. The contract, however, contained an unusual clause that required him to record both jazz and classical music for the label.

Marsalis's first album came later that year. The recording eponymously titled *Marsalis* was produced by Hancock at Marsalis's request. It featured Hancock and the other V.S.O.P. members on several cuts, while Marsalis's brother Branford appeared on cuts throughout the album. Columbia pushed the disc aggressively and it sold over 125,000 copies, a huge hit by jazz standards. Wynton Marsalis then formed his own band, which included Branford in its early incarnation.

In addition to his new band's activities, Marsalis also appeared on several other albums that were released over the following year: the Jazz Messengers' *A La Mode;* Wayne Shorter's live double–album *Jazz at the Opera House*; *The Young Lions,* a recording of the 1982 Kool Jazz Festival; and Chico Freeman's *Destiny's Dance.* In addition, Wynton Marsalis was joined by his father and older brother for one side of the 1982 album *Fathers and Sons,* a tribute to traditional jazz, that featured father and son saxophonists Von and Chico Freeman on the album's other side.

Throughout 1982, Marsalis kept on the move. He brought traditional jazz back into vogue with tours of the United States, Europe, and Japan. During December, after an extended tour of the United Kingdom, Marsalis recorded his classical debut in London. He performed several concertos with Raymond Leppard and the National Philharmonic Orchestra. While there, Marsalis met one of his idols, classical trumpeter Maurice André, who said that the young musician was potentially the greatest classical trumpeter of all time.

While Marsalis's fame grew, there were also snipers who took aim at the successful young musician. Several critics claimed that Marsalis played with neither a depth of emotion nor a distinctive style. In a *New York Times Magazine* article on the rise of traditional jazz, Jon Pareles remarked that some critics took Marsalis to task "for sounding like an encyclopedia of jazz trumpet styles." In the same source, Marsalis countered by saying, "If you play trumpet and you don't sound like Miles (Davis) or Dizzy (Gillespie) or Clifford (Brown) or Fats (Navarro), you're probably not playing jazz. If you don't sound like somebody else, you sound like nothing." Most of all, critics seemed to draw comparisons between Marsalis and Miles Davis's mid–1960s sound while Davis was on the Blue Note label. This was not surprising considering that Marsalis had worked closely with Hancock, as well as with saxophonist Wayne Shorter, who played with Davis in the sixties.

Marsalis was becoming the premier spokesman for the then out–of–favor traditional jazz style, or what he often called "true jazz." In a pair of *Downbeat* interviews from 1982 and 1984, he was outspoken about fellow artists who had "defected" from true jazz. He dismissed anybody who attempted to blend jazz with rock or R&B, or who experimented with free–form or avant–garde approaches. His comments were sensational in the laid–back world of jazz, especially because they applied to just about every major artist in jazz at the time, including Davis and Hancock. They appeared all the worse for coming from an upstart twenty–one–year–old.

Coming into His Own

1983 proved a watershed year for Marsalis, for two reasons. One was that his quintet released its first album, *Think of One,* to rave reviews. The disc marked Marsalis's debut as a producer and included three self–composed tracks. In his *New York Times* review, Jon Pareles noted that while some cuts were still indebted to the sound developed at Blue Note in the 1960s, Marsalis was developing his own musical personality, especially in terms of tempo changes.

The other major event in 1983 was the simultaneous release of his classical album debut, the *Haydn/Hummel/ Mozart Trumpet Concertos.* The CBS Masterworks album included standard concertos by Franz Joseph Haydn, Johann Hummel, and Leopold Mozart. Marsalis believed that it was important for him to show that he could play music from the established repertoire in order to be taken seriously. The reviews for *Trumpet Concertos* may have been even more exuberant than they had been for *Think of One.*

Both albums were well–received by the public, each racking up sales of over 100,000 copies. The response to each one, by Marsalis's peers, proved to be an even bigger story in February 1984. Marsalis grabbed Grammy awards for best solo jazz instrumental performance and for best classical instrumental performance with orchestra. In the process, he became not only the first musician ever to win both awards in the same year, but the first to be nominated in both of those categories in a single year. The double win made him an instant celebrity, something that would never have happened had he won in only one category.

In 1984 Marsalis continued his hectic pace. In between his quintet's tours of the United States, Europe, and the Far East were jammed recording sessions, seminars, and festivals. During the summer, he played twenty–four concert dates with symphony orchestras in the United States, Canada, and England, working with the top conductors in each country. Despite the warm critical and fan reaction to his classical forays, Marsalis was quoted in interviews as wanting to give up classical music to focus his time and energies on jazz.

Marsalis also took time from his busy schedule to visit schools for the purpose of enlightening students on the merits of jazz, which he claims is the only thoroughly American high art form. He became known for giving lessons to any child that approached him carrying a horn. Many of those young players found that he was available to them long after their initial encounters. Marsalis stayed in touch, offering them playing tips over the phone, inviting them to gigs, or even giving them instruments. In 1987 he helped start a three–year jazz education program in the Chicago schools.

Also in 1987, Marsalis was a key figure in launching the annual Classical Jazz Festival at New York's Lincoln Center. His association with the summer jazz series later grew into other programs at the Lincoln Center, including a series of youth concerts.

Meanwhile, the recordings kept flowing out and awards kept flowing in. Despite his stated desire to leave classical music behind, he continued to release classical recordings. Two of those reflected his keen interest in the Baroque style: 1984's *Wynton Marsalis/Edita Gruberova: Baroque Trumpet Music* and 1988's *Wynton Marsalis: Baroque Music for Trumpets.* Among his many jazz recordings during the period were 1984's *Hot House Flowers,* 1985's *Black Codes (From the Underground),* 1986's *J Mood* and 1987's *Marsalis Standard Time, Vol. 1.* He was voted Jazz Musician of the Year in *Downbeat*'s reader's poll in 1982, 1984–86, and 1989, and received several other honors from fans and critics in related categories of the magazine's annual polls. He amassed a considerable Grammy collection, winning a total of eight trophies in the jazz and classical categories by the end of the decade.

Marsalis continued his almost non–stop touring. His band's lineup was amorphous, and evolved from a quintet to a septet during the period. He consistently spent around 300 days on the road annually, with play dates accounting for about 150 days a year and the rest filled with seminars, charity events or composing time. All the hard work paid off, however, as traditional jazz, spearheaded by the Marsalis thrust, underwent a rebirth of popularity.

In 1991 Marsalis became artistic director of Jazz at Lincoln Center, a year–round program he also founded, though the program proved a lightening rod for controversy. Critics railed over several points. They charged Marsalis with cronyism for hiring a staff that is majority black, and for providing his band with regular work there. He was labeled arrogant for presenting his own compositions there, and was regarded as elitist for programming only traditional jazz, while excluding experimental styles.

Marsalis contended those criticisms came predominantly from white critics. He fired back at his detractors by claiming that after decades of jazz programs being organized by whites, some of the white audience was not comfortable with seeing a black man with the power to exercise such decisions. He defended the use of his own band by stating that it was only fair, as his group contained some of the finest musicians in the world. As for performing his own compositions, Marsalis pointed out that his contract as artistic director required him to compose a new work each year. Finally, he was unwilling to budge on his musical tastes, as he contended that it was for his vision that he was hired.

Marsalis argued that most of the criticisms were the paternalistic notions of well–meaning, but unenlightened white writers who could not know what it is like to be black in America, nor to be able to understand the connection blacks have to a chiefly black artistic medium. "I'm not going to allow some reporter, who should be coming to our classes to learn what this music is, tell me what we should be doing," he said in a July 1994 *Ebony* article. "That's not going to happen. So they can carp, they can moan, they can all get together and write the same article. But I will never step up in public and act lower than what I was raised to act. And I won't be bowing to them and begging. I'm not going to do that."

Maturity and New Growth

By the early 1990s, Marsalis began realizing a new maturity, both in his performing talent and in his compositional skills. In fact, feeling that he had not given the Haydn, Hummel, and Mozart concertos the interpretive depth they deserved when he recorded them a decade earlier, he re–recorded them in 1994. This time he was happier with the results.

Marsalis's compositions got longer, as he was no longer satisfied to stay within a five– or six–minute format. That became evident in such early–nineties works as *Citi Movement* (a dance commission) and *In This House, On This Morning* (a Lincoln Center commission), pieces for his septet that included movements lasting over half–an–hour in length. He also began composing for groups other than jazz combos. *Six Syncopated Movements,* another dance commission, was a collaboration with New York City Ballet Director Peter Martins for pit orchestra. Tours and recorded versions of these works followed.

In early 1994, Marsalis tackled the biggest challenge of his composing career. In addition to writing the music, he served as his own librettist for the slavery epic *Blood on the Fields.* Commissioned by Lincoln Center, the complex twenty–two–section oratorio was written for jazz orchestra, ensemble and three vocal soloists. The three–and–a–half–hour work made its debut at Lincoln Center's Avery Fischer Hall on April 1, 1994, to a warm reception.

Marsalis became an author that same year with the publication of *Sweet Swing Blues on the Road,* a joint project with photographer Frank Stewart. In the book, Marsalis flavors his impressions of life on the road with tributes to legendary jazzmen and meditations on the nature of jazz. The following year he penned *Marsalis on Music,* a book on music fundamentals that accompanied a four–part PBS series of the same name. The book and series explain how basic elements of music are shared by different musical styles. Also included with the book was an audio CD that provided musical examples to clarify abstract concepts.

Marsalis disbanded his septet in early 1995 to devote more time to composing, to concentrate on the recording of *Blood on the Fields,* to develop the National Public Radio show *Making the Music* and to work on other projects. A few months later, Marsalis was ready to hit the road again and regrouped with a new quartet.

In 1996 Marsalis was among those profiled in *Time* magazine's "The Time 25: Time's Most Influential Americans." Also that year, the *Blood on the Fields* recording was released to great acclaim. The extent of that acclaim became clear the following April when Marsalis received the Pulitzer Prize for Music. It marked the first time a jazz composer had ever been so recognized since music was added as a category in 1943. In 1997, Marsalis was tapped for a five–year term on the 20–member New York State Council on the Arts, which promotes artistic endeavors statewide.

Marsalis continued to receive many awards, but in 1997 he was honored in a more unusual way. An $80,000 life–size bronze statue of the musician was erected in Marciac, France, a town of 1,200 residents that draws 125,000 fans each August to its jazz festival, to recognize his accomplishments. Marsalis showed his gratitude by composing the ninety–minute "Marciac Suite."

Slim, but with a round face, Marsalis sported a brush mustache and wire–rimmed glasses. Though approaching his late–thirties, he remained boyish looking. When appearing at public functions he preferred expertly tailored dark suits and standard neckties, especially for performances. At home, in his New York City, Upper West Side apartment, he was comfortable in sweats, or plaid flannel shirts. Neither a smoker nor a drinker, he tried to keep himself in shape for the long, road tours that were part of a successful musician's life. When life afforded the luxury, he grabbed his basketball, found a court and shot hoops for exercise and enjoyment.

In addition to spending his free time listening to recordings of other musicians–his apartment was lined with shelves of CDs—Marsalis spent hours reading. "Reading opens you up to worlds you have never known. It expands your conception of what's possible. It gives you a route of escape or a way to deal with a more intense reality," he said in an *American Visions*' interview that appeared in the June–July 1997 issue. Not surprisingly, he read countless books on music, including the densest theoretical works. However, his interests varied, ranging from poetry to essays to histories to novels. Marsalis counted Walt Whitman, Pablo Neruda, and Ralph Ellison among his favorite writers. He credited the book *The Fatal Shore: The Epic of Australia's Founding,* by Robert Hughes, for inspiring *Blood on the Fields.* He told *American Visions* "the book I still dig the most, in terms of high literature, is the Bible."

Marsalis's many non–music skills—lecturer, promoter, educator—brought with them numerous responsibilities that infringed on his time as a musician. Nevertheless, he was unwavering in his top priority. "My first responsibility is to develop musically," he said in a July 1996 *Stereo Review* interview. "I want to keep playing my horn, playing classical music on a higher level, to become a better jazz musician, to write better music. I like doing all these extra things, but I'm a musician, and it's important that that's where I spend most of my time."

Current address: c/o Agency for the Performing Arts, 9000 West Sunset Boulevard, Suite 1200, West Hollywood, CA 90069–5801.

REFERENCES

Alterman, Eric. "Jazz at the Center." *The Nation* 264 (12 May 1997): 8.

Carr, Ian, and Digby Fairweather, eds. *Jazz: The Essential Companion.* New York: Prentice Hall, 1987.

Current Biography Yearbook. New York: H. W. Wilson, 1985.

Jackson, Norlishia, and T. Brooks Shepard. "Summer Reading." *American Visions* 12:3 (June–July 1997): 28–35.

Labi, Nadya. "Blow Like Me." *Time* 150 (25 August 1997): 80.

LaBlanc, Michael L., ed. *Contemporary Musicians: Profiles of the People in Music.* Detroit: Gale Research, 1992.

Lacayo, Richard. "What Ever Happened to the Class of 1996?" *Time* 149: (21 April 1997): 70–71.

"Marsalis Tapped for Arts Council Seat." *Nashville Tennessean,* August 4, 1997.

Norment, Lynn. "Wynton Marsalis." *Ebony* 49 (July 1994): 44–50.

Pareles, Jon. "Jazz Swings Back to Tradition." *New York Times Magazine* (17 June 1984): 22–23, 54–55, 61–63, 66–68.

Russ, Ronald S. "Marsalis on Music." *Library Journal* 120 (December 1995): 111.

Smith, Ken. "Center Stage: Wynton Marsalis." *Stereo Review* 61 (July 1996): 104.

Stewart, Zan. "Blood Brothers." *Down Beat* 64 (May 1997): 26–28.

"Sweet Swing Blues on the Road." *The Economist* 334 (11 March 1995): 86.

"Time 25: Time's 25 Most Influential Americans." *Time* 147 (17 June 1996): 52–79.

Vigeland, Carl. "My Home Is the Road." *Down Beat* 62 (May 1995): 16–18, 20.

Who's Who in America, 1998. New Providence, NJ: Marquis Who's Who, 1997.

Kevin C. Kretschmer

Thurgood Marshall
(1908–1993)
U.S. Supreme Court judge, U.S. solicitor general, civil rights attorney, organization official

As chief attorney for the NAACP for 23 years, Thurgood Marshall used the courts to strike down racially discriminatory practices in voting, housing, transportation, teachers' salaries, graduate and professional education, public schools, and the administration of justice. Marshall's leadership enabled the NAACP to win 27 of 32 cases argued before the U.S. Supreme Court, an outstanding record of success. After four years as a judge on the U.S. Court of Appeals, Third Circuit, and two years' work as solicitor general, the chief trial attorney for the United States, Marshall served with distinction as an associate justice of the U.S. Supreme Court for 24 years. He was the first African American to serve on those two courts.

Thurgood Marshall was born July 2, 1908, in Baltimore, Maryland, the youngest of two sons of William Canfield

Thurgood Marshall

Marshall and Norma Arica Williams. William Marshall was a railroad dining car waiter, butler, then later chief steward in a private club located on Chesapeake Bay. Norma Williams was a school teacher as well as an accomplished musician who sang in opera and theater performances in Baltimore.

According to Marshall himself, in speeches and in interviews, his maternal great grandfather, whose name is unknown, was a slave captured in the Congo in the 1840s who was so rebellious and uncooperative that his master chose to free him rather than sell him to another slave owner. Marshall was named for his paternal grandfather who was told he needed two names to join the Union Army in the Civil War and chose "Thoroughgood" as his first name. By the second or third grade, Marshall disliked having to spell such a long name and convinced his mother to change it to Thurgood.

A strong sense of independence and a willingness to protest were a part of family tradition on both sides of Marshall's family. As he grew, his awareness of racial discrimination developed along with a determination to fight it. His father, explaining the meaning of the term, "nigger," ordered Marshall to fight anyone who called him that name.

Marshall attended the public schools of Baltimore. He frequently disobeyed authority and engaged in mischievous behavior. One grammar school principal had a unique way of punishing misbehaving students: he sent them to the basement with a copy of the U.S. Constitution with orders to memorize a particular section before returning to their classes. Marshall memorized the entire constitution by the time he left that school. He graduated from Douglas High School in 1925.

At the age of 17, Marshall entered Lincoln University in Pennsylvania in September of 1925. Several students from African and Asian nations were also enrolled, including the future president of Ghana, Kwame Nkrumah. Future band leader Cab Calloway and writer Langston Hughes were also classmates.

His mother wanted Thurgood Marshall to become a dentist; however, Marshall antagonized his biology teacher who eventually flunked him in the course, effectively ending his pre–dentistry studies. Marshall, at this time, was still a mischievous "cut–up" who liked practical jokes. He was part of the Weekend Club, a group of students who spent enormous amounts of time partying, drinking, and playing cards. In spite of his raucous behavior, Marshall read widely and maintained a B average. Marshall entered debates as a sophomore, led the debating team to an unbeaten record, and began to concentrate on studies in the humanities. He graduated cum laude in June of 1930, majoring in American literature and philosophy.

On a visit to a Philadelphia church, Marshall met Vivian "Buster" Burey, an undergraduate at the University of Pennsylvania. She captivated Marshall and they married when they were both age 21 on September 4, 1929, before Marshall's last semester at Lincoln. Vivian Marshall had a calming and steadying effect upon Thurgood Marshall. Their desire to have children was thwarted as Vivian Marshall had three or four miscarriages, never carrying a child to term. She died of lung cancer in February of 1955, after almost 26 years of marriage.

Marshall married Cecilia A. Suyat on December 17, 1955, a Hawaiian–born woman of Filipino ancestry. She worked as a secretary with the national office of NAACP. She became the mother of two children: Thurgood Jr. and John William.

Attends Law School

Marshall's parents were fully supportive of their son's efforts to get an education. They generously shared their home with Thurgood and Vivian Marshall while he attended law school. Marshall applied to the University of Maryland Law School but was denied admission because no blacks were eligible under the state's segregation laws. He decided to attend Howard University Law School in Washington, D.C.

At Howard, Marshall benefited from a sustained relationship with Charles Hamilton Houston, a remarkable individual who was the vice–dean of the law school. In 1927 Houston was the first black lawyer to win a case before the U.S. Supreme Court. Houston enlisted Howard law students to combat racial discrimination and injustices against blacks, and to change the image of black lawyers by endowing them with a social mission in addition to their commercial function. Marshall realized the importance of a legal education, studied with unusual dedication, and graduated first in his class in 1933. He received an LL.B. degree, magna cum laude, and was admitted to the Maryland bar in 1933.

From 1933 to 1936, Marshall was in private practice in Baltimore, handling some standard legal work, but he was especially attracted to cases involving discrimination or injustice, even when clients could not pay. He barely collected enough money to survive and incurred a debt of as much as $3,000 to $4,000. In 1934, he was appointed counsel for the Baltimore chapter of the NAACP.

Marshall, still incensed that he was denied the opportunity to study at the University of Maryland Law School, decided to help another black gain admittance. In 1935, with the help of Charles Hamilton Houston, he sued the University of Maryland to admit Donald Murray. Marshall proved that Maryland offered whites a legal education at a tax–supported university but provided no legal education to blacks. The court in Baltimore ordered Murray's admission to the University of Maryland Law School, and the Maryland Court of Appeals upheld the decision. Marshall's anger was long–lasting. While a member of the Supreme Court in 1980, Marshall declined to attend a ceremony in which the University of Maryland dedicated its new law library in his honor.

Fights Racial Discrimination

Houston and Marshall became instrumental in an NAACP campaign to end legal segregation in the South. In 1930 the NAACP was awarded a grant from the American Fund for Public Service, also known as the Garland Fund. Houston was hired in 1935 as special counsel, becoming, in 1936, a full–time NAACP attorney in charge of the campaign to end jury exclusion, unequal school funding, disfranchisement, residential segregation, and segregated transportation.

Desiring to use the law to advance the civil rights of blacks and needing a steady source of income, Marshall, in late 1936, accepted a position as assistant special counsel for the NAACP, or deputy to Houston. Marshall began work in the NAACP's national office in Harlem. In 1938, when Houston resigned for health reasons, Marshall, at age 30, took complete charge of the work, though his title was not changed to special counsel until May of 1939. In October of 1939 the NAACP created a new and independent organization to pursue its legal work—the NAACP Legal Defense and Educational Fund—to take advantage of new federal laws regarding tax–exempt status. Marshall was appointed director and, later, director–counsel of the Legal Defense Fund (LDF). He remained director–counsel of LDF until his appointment to the U.S. Court of Appeals in 1961.

Marshall followed the basic strategy established by Houston. Marshall was a great legal tactician and legal strategist who saw a current case as a stepping stone to a broader objective. He would not use a tactic merely to win a present case if the tactic might limit or conflict with the attempt to end all racial discrimination. Marshall traveled an average of 50,000 miles a year, speaking at NAACP meetings throughout the country, investigating lynching and racial discrimination cases, conferring with potential plaintiffs in lawsuits, preparing for court cases, and raising money to support the cases being pursued. Marshall decided which cases to pursue, supervised the preparation of cases, and coordinated appeals to higher courts. He personally argued many cases before the U.S. Supreme Court. Of 32 cases the NAACP argued before the U.S. Supreme Court, Marshall and the NAACP legal staff won 29.

Marshall's work in breaking down segregation and racial discrimination drew considerable opposition from white southerners, many of whom were accustomed to lynching or beating blacks who did not accept racial discrimination. Frequently the subject of verbal threats, Marshall was occasionally in actual physical danger. In some towns Marshall slept in a different house each night to avoid letting violence–prone whites know precisely where he was.

Wins for the LDF

Marshall and the LDF staff believed that an end to racial segregation in publicly–funded education would have the greatest overall, long–range impact for African Americans. Since the 1896 *Plessy v. Ferguson* Supreme Court decision, courts had employed the ''separate but equal'' theory to judge racial segregation as legal as long as the facilities were equal. Since no southern state provided a law school education or extensive graduate school education for black Americans, Marshall and the LDF concentrated on proving inequality in those areas as a prelude to attacking the legality of racial segregation itself. Still, some attention was given to overturning other forms of discrimination, using lawsuits in local, state, and federal courts.

In a series of cases undertaken from the 1930s through the 1960s, the NAACP lawyers tried to establish a record that would contribute to the overthrow of the racial segregation system. In 1938 the U.S. Supreme Court ordered the University of Missouri Law School to admit Lloyd Gaines. Federal court decisions set a broader precedent than did state, but Marshall successfully undertook actions in state courts to equalize the salaries of black and white teachers.

Other NAACP cases brought additional small steps and decisions which chipped away at the foundations of the racial segregation system. In *Smith v. Allwright,* 1944, the Supreme Court ordered that blacks be allowed to vote in primary elections in Texas. In *Morgan v. Virgini*a, 1946, the Supreme Court declared that interstate passengers entering the South could not be forced into segregated seating on public transportation, though it did not rule on state–required segregation for passengers traveling only within the state. In *Sipes v. McGee* and *Shelley v. Kraemer,* decided in 1948 by the Supreme Court, restrictive covenants keeping blacks and other minorities out of white protestant neighborhoods, were declared unenforceable by any court or government.

Two cases in 1950 provided a stronger legal basis to challenge the whole system of racial segregation in the South. In both cases, *Sweat v. Painter* and *McLaurin v. Oklahoma,* the Supreme Court's decision emphasized the importance of intangible qualities of education. Heman Sweat was ordered admitted to the University of Texas Law School by virtue of the fact that a newly established law school for blacks at Texas Southern University was not equal to the University of Texas because intangible qualities like reputation, professors, library, and student body made the University of Texas a better school. In the case of George W. McLaurin, who had been admitted to the University of Oklahoma doctoral program in education, the court ruled that efforts to segregate him in classes and elsewhere were also illegal.

In the *Brown v. Board of Education* case, 1954, the Supreme Court ruled that segregation itself was unconstitutional. NAACP lawyers employed sociological and psychological data to show the harm segregated school systems did to the personality development of black children in addition to the other inequalities in the dual system. Thus Marshall and the NAACP were able to show substantial inequality in both tangible and intangible aspects of the education offered to blacks. The Supreme Court not only declared that segregated schools were inherently unequal but also specifically overruled the ''separate but equal'' principle of the 1896 *Plessy v. Ferguson* decision, ordering that federal courts no longer use it. Marshall realized that if the Supreme Court declared ''separate but equal'' invalid for schools, it was only a matter of time until all forms of racial segregation by law were overturned.

In the following years, Marshall and the NAACP legal staff vigorously pursued lawsuits to implement school desegregation throughout the country. Marshall himself served as counsel for the Little Rock, Arkansas, school integration case in 1957. He also served as counsel for Autherine Lucy's successful court case ordering her admission to the University of Alabama in 1956. Though Marshall preferred carefully planned and logically chosen court cases to advance the cause of racial equality, he did begin to give legal assistance and support to the newly developing tactics of bus boycotts and sit–in demonstrations. Thus, when Martin Luther King Jr. and the Montgomery Improvement Association switched from merely demanding courtesy and better seating on buses to challenging bus segregation itself, Marshall wrote the legal brief to appeal the decision of a lower federal court to the Supreme Court and had NAACP counsel Robert L. Carter present the argument in court. Also, when college students were being arrested for trying to integrate lunch counters and other public facilities in the South, Marshall and NAACP lawyers represented over 1,200 demonstrators, eventually securing a valuable decision from the Supreme Court in *Garner v. Louisiana,* 1961, that peaceful sit–ins and protest demonstrations were a form of free speech and could not legally be stopped by arresting them for disturbing the peace.

Gains Appointment to U.S. Courts

On September 23, 1961, President John F. Kennedy nominated Marshall to be a judge on the U.S. Court of Appeals, Second Judicial Circuit, headquartered in New York City. Since Congress recessed four days later without acting on the nomination, Kennedy gave Marshall a recess appointment in October which allowed him to begin work with confirmation by the U.S. Senate to come later. Strong opposition from Southern senators surfaced and he was not confirmed until September 11, 1962, almost a year later. Mark Tushnet in *Making Constitutional Law* says that in almost four years on the Court of Appeals, Marshall wrote over ''130 opinions, in cases ranging from worker's compensation problems to complex tax deals to important constitutional issues.'' Because the court's caseload involved many ''relatively routine cases,'' Marshall had very little opportunity ''to develop a distinctive jurisprudence.'' None of Marshall's opinions were reversed by the Supreme Court and some of his dissenting opinions later became the basis of majority opinions of the Supreme Court. Tushnet concludes that ''Marshall had a reputation as a solid though unspectacular appellate judge'' on the Second Circuit.

The journey to the Supreme Court began shortly after Lyndon Johnson was elected President in 1964. Johnson was committed to civil rights for African Americans and wanted to be the first president to name a black to the Supreme Court. Johnson asked Thurgood Marshall to resign his lifetime appointment on the court of appeals, take a pay cut, and become solicitor general of the United States in preparation for the appointment to the Supreme Court. Marshall was confirmed by the U.S. Senate on August 11, 1965. The third highest position in the department of justice, the solicitor general serves as the government's chief attorney in cases before the Supreme Court. Marshall's job included deciding which cases the government should take to the Supreme Court and who should argue them. As solicitor general, he argued 19 cases before the Supreme Court and won 15 of them, including a challenge to the Voting Rights Act of 1965. His performance as solicitor general was considered good but not outstanding by most court observers.

Becomes First Black U.S. Supreme Court Justice

When Tom C. Clark resigned from the Supreme Court to avoid conflicts of interest when President Lyndon Johnson named Clark's son, Ramsey Clark, acting attorney general, Johnson nominated Marshall as associate justice of the U.S. Supreme Court in June of 1967; he was confirmed by the Senate in August of 1967 and was seated, at age 59, on October 2, 1967. Marshall became the first African American justice on the Supreme Court, serving from 1967 to 1991. Marshall, the grandson of a union soldier and the great grandson of a slave, became the successor of Tom Clark, the grandson of a Confederate soldier.

Evaluations of Marshall as a Supreme Court justice vary according to the expectations of the evaluator. Mark Tushnet in *Making Constitutional Law* offers considerable insight. He believes that Marshall made important contributions to constitutional law based upon ''the substantive vision of justice his work embodied.'' Marshall's whole career ''embodied the tradition of the lawyer–statesman,'' a term Tushnet explains as, "[a person] of practical wisdom" who is "devoted to the public good but keenly aware of the limitations of human beings and their political arrangements." Marshall, both as lawyer and as judge, used the law in a practical way "to shape a working solution to the pressing problems of social life." He also believed strongly that lawyers and courts should follow established procedures. Both in discussions preliminary to deciding cases and in questions from the bench during oral arguments, Marshall stressed to all that the contemporary context of issues and the background of the litigants must be factored into court decisions. His numerous dissents stressed these issues also.

Those who criticize Marshall's work as a Supreme Court justice fault him for not having written articles for law review journals or for not being interested in technical matters, such as taxes. Thus, according to the *Detroit Free Press* for June 28, 1991, "Law professors have rated Marshall 'average,' partly because he took little interest in difficult issues other than civil rights and individual liberties."

Marshall was an Episcopalian vestryman, a thirty–third degree Prince Hall mason, and a member of the Alpha Phi Alpha fraternity. On the personal side, *Time* magazine for June 23, 1967, said that Marshall was "a gregarious storyteller with a dry wit and a healthy thirst for bourbon and water" and one who was "equally comfortable drawling earthy tales in a self–mocking, chitlins–and–cornpone Negro dialect or arguing law in meticulously scholarly tones." He was a great storyteller or raconteur throughout his life. He used stories to make a point to colleagues or to illuminate a legal principle. Marshall developed cooking as a lifelong avocation after his maternal grandmother, Mary Eliza Williams, taught him to cook so that he would have a practical skill to help him earn a living, if necessary.

Marshall was awarded the NAACP's Spingarn Medal in 1946. He held honorary degrees from over 20 universities around the world. In 1992 Marshall was the first recipient of the American Bar Association's Thurgood Marshall Award, given to pioneers in law who have fought for personal liberty and civil rights. In his honor, the Thurgood Marshall Federal Judiciary Building was erected on Columbus Circle in Washington, D.C. The Thurgood Marshall School of Law and Law Library at Texas Southern University in Houston, Texas, was named to honor him.

Problems of declining health: glaucoma, hearing loss, and difficulty walking led to Marshall's decision to resign from court in June of 1991. He died on January 24, 1993.

In a career that spanned 58 years, Marshall achieved an enormous amount. His legal work in the civil rights movement demolished the intellectual and legal basis for the system of racial segregation. His work helped to establish a new standard of racial equality and equal opportunity. In his long career, Marshall evolved from civil rights lawyer to civil rights leader to national figure as a U.S. Supreme Court justice. Harvard University law professor Randall Kennedy, as quoted in the February 4, 1993, *Detroit News,* believes that "some of Justice Marshall's opinions . . . are far reaching and prophetic utterances and will be validated by historians looking back a century hence."

REFERENCES

Bigel, Alan I. *Justices William J. Brennan, Jr. and Thurgood Marshall on Capital Punishment: Its Constitutionality, Morality, Deterrent Effect, and Interpretation by the Court.* Lanham, MD: University Press of America, 1997.

Bland, Randall W. *Private Pressure on Public Law: The Legal Career of Justice Thurgood Marshall.* Port Washington, NY: Kennikat Press, 1973; 2nd ed. Lanham, MD: University Press of America, 1993.

"Civil Rights Champion Retires." *Detroit Free Press,* June 28, 1991.

Contemporary Black Biography. Vol 1. Detroit: Gale Research, 1992.

Davis, Michael R., and Hunter S. Clark. *Thurgood Marshall: Warrior At the Bar, Rebel on the Bench.* New York: Birch Lane Press, Carol Publishing Group, 1992.

Friedman, Leon, and Fred L. Israel, eds. *The Justices of the United States Supreme Court: Their Lives and Major Opinions.* New York: Chelsea House, Vol. 4, 1969; Vol. 5, 1978.

Goldman, Roger L. *Thurgood Marshall: Justice for All.* New York: Carroll & Graf, 1992.

Greenberg, Jack. *Crusaders in the Courts: How A Dedicated Band of Lawyers Fought for the Civil Rights Revolution.* New York: Basic Books, 1994.

Kluger, Richard. *Simple Justice: The History of Brown v. Board of Education and Black America's Struggle for Equality.* 2 vols. New York: Alfred A. Knopf, 1975.

McNeil, Genna Rae. *Groundwork: Charles Hamilton Houston and the Struggle for Civil Rights.* Philadelphia: University of Pennsylvania Press, 1983.

Mello, Michael. *Against the Death Penalty: The Relentless Dissents of Justices Brennan and Marshall.* Boston: Northeastern University Press, 1996.

"Opinions Reflected a Strong Belief in Tolerance, Equality." *Detroit News,* February 4, 1993.

Rowan, Carl T. *Dream Makers, Dream Breakers: The World of Justice Thurgood Marshall.* New York: Little, Brown, 1993.

"The Supreme Court: Negro Justice." *Time* 89 (23 June 1967): 18.

"Talking With Carl T. Rowan: The Kick in Marshall's Beef Stew." *People* 39 (22 February 1993): 79.

Tushnet, Mark V. *Making Civil Rights Law: Thurgood Marshall and the Supreme Court, 1936–1961.* New York: Oxford University Press, 1994.

———. *Making Constitutional Law: Thurgood Marshall and the Supreme Court, 1961–1991.* New York: Oxford University Press, 1997.

———. *The NAACP's Legal Strategy Against Segregated Education, 1925–1950.* Chapel Hill: University of North Carolina Press, 1987.

"Voice of the N.A.A.C.P.: Thurgood Marshall." *New York Times,* August 28, 1958.

De Witt S. Dykes Jr.

John Sella Martin (1832–1876)

Minister, abolitionist, organizational worker, journalist, politician

John Sella Martin was an important figure who was overlooked until the 1980s. As a prewar abolitionist leader, he was a relative latecomer to the movement since he escaped from slavery only in January 1856. He was an effective spokesman in Great Britain during the war, working hard and effectively to counter Confederate efforts to sway public opinion. His postwar work for the Colored National Labor Union and his editorship of *New Era* did not prove long–lasting, and his involvement in Louisiana politics was largely disastrous. Impatience, ill–health, and drug addiction were largely responsible for the dispersal of his efforts after the Civil War. For three years after the war Martin served as agent of the American Missionary Association in Great Britain and carried out his duties under quite difficult circumstances.

John Sella Martin was born in Charlotte, North Carolina, in September 1832. His mother, Wini–fred, was a mulatto slave owned by a Mrs. Henderson. Mrs. Henderson arranged a liaison between Winifred and her nephew, a Mr. Martin. This liaison produced a second child, Caroline, before Mr. Martin showed that he had no intention of marrying as his aunt wished. In her anger she sent him off to manage one of her properties in Virginia and sold Winifred and her two children to a slave dealer who took them to Georgia.

Dr. Chipley of Columbus, Georgia, bought the family, but it was broken up when Martin was about nine. He became the property of Edward Powers, a Northern money–lender, living in Columbus. Powers lived in a hotel, where Martin learned of free black patrons. Martin learned to read clandestinely from white playmates, bribing them with marbles. Powers discovered this and forbade him to continue to read for other members of the black community.

Martin wrote himself a pass and ran away to Troop County, Alabama, to visit his mother. Fearing her owner's brutality, she refused to escape with him. He was eventually discovered in her cabin and sent back to Columbus in irons. There he spent seven months in jail. A fellow inmate, a Mr. Green from Boston, taught him grammar, history, and arithmetic. Martin was freed from jail when his owner developed eye problems and needed someone to read for him. His services as reader and attendant resulted in a grant of freedom in his owner's will. Powers died in 1850, but his relatives were able to overturn the will.

In the next few years, Martin had a succession of owners, both black and white. For seven months he was owned by a slave trader. With a new owner he became a hairdresser on an Alabama riverboat. Both his manner and his learning made him restless to be free. In 1855 Martin began to plan his escape, following a quarrel with white employees jealous of his position as a steward on a Lake Ponchatrain boat. He had already acquired a set of free papers from an older black and, after some difficulty, eventually secured a job on a boat going from New Orleans to Saint Louis. He was refused a train ticket (in Cairo, Illinois), but a white man bought him one after a casual inspection of his papers. Martin arrived in Chicago on January 6, 1856.

Becomes Free

In Chicago Martin came into contact with Mary Ann Shadd and H. Ford Douglas, black abolitionists and supporters of black emigration to Canada, who were on a lecture tour. Under the aegis of Shadd and Douglas, Martin soon became known in abolitionist circles and delivered his first speeches in Illinois. Then he moved to Detroit, where he studied for the ministry under a local Baptist minister. He was ordained after a successful speaking tour in Michigan in the spring of 1857.

Martin's first ministerial position was at the Michigan Street Baptist Church in Buffalo, New York. He was actively involved in the community and in politics, working for the Liberty Party's candidate Gerrit Smith. Martin also married Sarah Martin, the daughter of a prosperous local farmer. In November 1859 Martin was called to the Joy Street Baptist Church in Boston.

During the three years Martin was at Joy Street Baptist, the congregation grew from 151 to 205 communicants. The position also helped him achieve national prominence. In August 1859, a New England black convention launched an attack on Henry Highland Garnet's African Civilization Society. Martin rose to defend the emigrationist organization. He then arranged a meeting in Boston at which Garnet had a chance to defend his position. Martin also experienced in April 1860 the full bitterness of the debate when he attended alongside Garnet a stormy New York meeting called expressly to condemn the African Civilization Society. Although Martin did not change his beliefs about emigration, he did not attend the subsequent New York meeting organized by Garnet, and he disassociated himself from the society in a letter of April 17 to the *Weekly Anglo–African.*

As prewar tensions rose, Martin became a leader in the Boston efforts to counter an increasingly vocal desire of many white merchants to reach an accommodation with the South. Massachusetts governor Nathaniel P. Banks vetoed an 1859 bill allowing blacks to serve in the militia. Martin and other blacks pressed for a reversal but without success. When pro–Southern whites broke up a meeting of support for John Brown at Tremont Temple in December 1860, Martin held a meeting at Joy Street Church the same evening. The militia prevented direct attack on the church, but could not provide protection for those leaving the meeting. Some blacks were assaulted, and some property was damaged. Not only did Martin support the abolitionists by opening his church to meetings during a period when mob violence was a real threat, he and other black leaders petitioned the state legislature to reject any compromise with the South. For a second time they tried to form a black militia company, only to be turned down.

Martin was downcast by the futility of his political efforts and the refusal of the North to admit that slavery was the cause of the war. In addition, his first child died in the early summer of 1861, and he suffered from a painful recurrent urinary tract infection. He decided to visit France in search of medical attention, but also took up the suggestion that the trip include an anti–slavery lecture tour of Great Britain to counter Southern propaganda efforts. In the end, he never went to France due to several painful flare–ups of his disease.

Martin left for London in early August of 1861. Since there was still little evidence that the abolition of slavery would result from the war, Martin had difficulty drumming up support for the Northern war effort. In November he concentrated on the evils of slavery. He also raised money to secure the freedom of his sister and her two children. He returned to the United States in February 1862 and after long negotiations purchased them, seeing his sister for the first time in 20 years. The three newly freed slaves settled first in Michigan and then moved permanently to Jamaica.

In the meantime, Martin was buoyed by developments on the national scene, in particular Lincoln's Emancipation Proclamation in September. His health was still a matter of great concern—his recurrent illnesses now included pleurisy. London would not seem to be a healthier city than Boston for him, yet Martin left his Joy Street church in January 1863 to return there to head a newly formed congregational church in a working class area of London's East End. He met with a cordial reception from his prospective communicants and built up a congregation. In addition he worked hard to counter continuing Southern propaganda through lectures and letters to newspapers. After a successful stay in Great Britain, Martin return to America in early 1864. This decision was reinforced by doctor's advice on the management of his continuing ill health.

Becomes Agent for the American Missionary Association

Upon Martin's return to the United States, he accepted the call to become minister of Shiloh Presbyterian Church in New York. There was some delay in taking up the post, however, and he was not inaugurated until February 1865. In April of that year the American Missionary Association (AMA) announced his appointment as its agent in Great Britain. The AMA's work had expanded immensely among the new freedmen as the war ended, and British contributions were urgently needed. As competing anti–slavery organizations gave way to competing freedmen's aid groups, rivalry among Evangelical denominations complicated matters in Great Britain. In addition, the reaction to the Morant Bay Rebellion in Jamaica of late 1865 unmasked wide anti–black sentiments in Great Britain. Martin had the knowledge and the prestige to steer the best possible course in this situation.

With some difficulty, Martin worked out an arrangement between the British Freed–Man's Aid Society and the AMA, opening the way to effective fund–raising for the latter. Still jealousy and backbiting among various agents and groups continued to be a major problem, as did the rising tide of racism. His efforts were beginning to pay off when Shiloh Church forced him to return to his pastoral duties in November of 1865, leaving a situation in Great Britain that took a turn for the worse.

Martin and the AMA had a falling out. The association had a debt of more than $30,000 in May and needed Martin's fund–raising abilities, so a compromise was reached. Martin resigned from Shiloh in April of 1866 and soon sailed for Great Britain as a special secretary for the duration of his 18–month mission. The difficulties of relations between the various organizations in both countries continued, and Martin's health worsened. Overall contributions from this second trip did not reach the level of those from the first in spite of all Martin's efforts. His greatest success was in Scotland.

By late 1867 Martin had apparently become addicted to the opium he was taking for relief of his pain. The addiction also seemed to contribute to wide swings in mood, and Martin's relations with the AMA became even more strained, although the association did recognize that he was the best man to be its agent. In early August 1868 Martin sailed for America.

Martin spent time at Saratoga, New York, caring for his health and negotiating with the Fifteenth Street Presbyterian Church in Washington, D.C., where he took up the pastorship toward the end of the year. He intended to influence political events in Washington. For example, he lobbied hard (and unsuccessfully) to have Frederick Douglass named minister to Haiti. Illness often undermined his efforts. For example, he could not take an active role in the National Colored Convention in January 1869, although he was elected to the executive board.

By the end of 1869 Martin was able to take part in the activities of the Colored National Labor Union, formed in response to the exclusion of blacks from the National Labor Union. The black organization held its first national convention in Washington, D.C., in December. As a member of the national board Martin argued for the full participation of women. Early hopes soon turned to disappointment as local organizations failed to take hold, and the movement was dead by 1872.

At the same time Martin was involved with the issue of schooling for blacks in Washington. In late November 1869 Martin enrolled his daughter in an all–white school; when the principal discovered she was black, she was sent home. This storm broke out in the midst of negotiations about schooling for blacks in the district. Martin's daughter was in fact legally enrolled. She was allowed to attend as a visitor for a while, and then the trustees suggested that she be classified as white and so continue. The final resolution of the case is not known, but the furor undermined any attempts to form mixed schools in the district and so postponed integration for many years.

In the meantime Martin and a group of black Washingtonians were trying to establish a national newspaper, the *New Era.* Martin became editor when Frederick Douglass turned down the position—Douglass was not yet ready to move to Washington and had doubts about the soundness of the paper's financial basis. (Douglass's son Lewis became chief compositor and head of the printing office.) By the time the first issue of the paper appeared in January 1870, Douglass had agreed to become corresponding editor. Soon after, Martin left Fifteenth Street Presbyterian Church, which was his last ministerial position. The *New Era* never quite met its operating expenses.

Returns to the South

When Sarah Martin became seriously ill, Martin solicited and won a position as a missionary for the AMA in Mobile so that his wife could live in a climate more suitable for her health. Sarah remained in Washington, however, when her husband went south in July. His plans to continue to edit the *New Era* from a distance proved impractical. Frederick Douglass was contracted to take over the paper at a considerable cost.

Martin henceforth turned to many expedients in order to support himself and make his mark, but his desire to live again in the South was a constant. He called on his connections for a federal patronage job. Rejected as a special agent of the Treasury Department, Martin became a Post Office Department special agent in Mobile. The appointment ended by late 1870 when Martin moved with his family to New Orleans.

Lectures at Straight University (now Dillard) won him fame, but little money. Martin found that Louisiana politics was dominated by a major quarrel between two factions of the Republican Party, complicated by a bitter dispute between black factions. Nonetheless Martin entered local politics in August 1871, supporting Governor Henry Clay Warmoth. Martin was rewarded with a nomination as a district school superintendent. Although Martin worked as superintendent for a while, the nomination was rejected by the legislature in February 1872.

Martin was a delegate to the National Convention of Black Republicans held in New Orleans in early 1872, but he was near to breaking away from the party. He moved to Shreveport. Finally in June he threw his support to liberal Republicans who had nominated Horace Greeley to run against Grant. The election in Louisiana resulted in the formation of two separate state governments, both claiming legitimacy. Martin did not claim his seat in one faction's legislature and remained in Washington, where he was soon accepted by his former political allies. He became editor of the *New National Era* in early February 1873, but the attempted reorganization of the paper failed, and Martin resigned when the rival *New Citizen* took over in October.

Martin remained involved in the fringes of Washington politics. He joined a lecture circuit in late 1873. Martin and George Downing, a caterer for Congressional events, became rivals for leadership in the National Council, a black organization lobbying for a civil rights bill. After bitter infighting that lasted a few months, Martin found a job in the middle of 1874 as a special agent for the Treasury Department in Shieldsboro, Louisiana, a small port near New Orleans. By the end of the year Martin was again living in New Orleans.

Martin was still associated with leading black circles in the city. He was a founder of the New Orleans Atheneum Club in early 1875 and served as president until a June reorganization. He was also a member of the Louisiana Progressive Club, which included important black politicians—and a few white ones—among its 36 members. In August he was a member of the Louisiana delegation to the Convention of Colored Newspaper Men held in Cincinnati. Martin was active in the convention, but unfortunately he gave a public speech praising former Louisiana Governor William Kellogg, head of one faction of Louisiana Republicans, which offended many Louisiana blacks.

Martin's movements after the convention are unknown. He may have spent some time in Massachusetts, since his wife and daughter were living there. It is known that he lost his treasury job. On August 11, 1876, he died from an apparent suicide in New Orleans.

John Sella Martin died at an early age, dissipating his talents towards the end of his life under the double influence of his illnesses and the opiates he was taking to control pain. His contemporaries recognized his abilities as a speaker, writer, and organizer—his constant advocating for the freedom and rights of African Americans was his greatest contribution.

REFERENCES

Blackett, R. J. M. *Beating Against the Barriers.* Ithaca, NY: Cornell University Press, 1989.

Logan, Rayford W., and Michael R. Winston, eds. *Dictionary of American Negro Biography.* New York: Norton, 1982.

Noel, Baptist Wriothesley. *Freedom and Slavery in the United States of America.* London: James Nisbet and Co., 1863.

Ripley, C. Peter, ed. *The Black Abolitionist Papers.* Vol. 1. Chapel Hill: University of North Carolina Press, 1985.

COLLECTIONS

The correspondence between Martin and the American Missionary Society is in the American Missionary Association Papers at the Amistad Research Center, New Orleans.

Robert L. Johns

Marycoo, Occramer.
See Gardner, Newport.

Charles Harrison Mason
(1866–1961)
Religious leader, church founder

By any standard Charles Harrison Mason was a remarkable person. The church that he founded, the Church of God in Christ, had a million members when he died and then grew to the fifth largest denomination in the United States with some seven million members in 600 congregations. Between 1982 and 1991 it grew by over 48 percent and brought Pentecostalism into the mainstream of American religion. A slim, articulate man, sporting a bow tie and a pencil–thin moustache, Mason had a profound knowledge of the Bible despite little formal education. He was also a spiritual leader who inspired others to share his vision. His church grew initially as he developed a doctrine and forms of worship with strong appeal to newly urbanized blacks.

Charles Harrison Mason was born on September 8, 1866, on the Price farm just north of Memphis in what is now the town of Bartlett, Tennessee, to Jerry (d. 1879) and Eliza Mason, former slaves of Prior Lee, a wealthy Baptist who had strong connections to Jackson, Mississippi. Mason's parents were tenant farmers and devout members of Missionary Baptist Church. From childhood until his baptism in the Holy Ghost at the age of 40, Charles Mason had frequent spiritual visions and dreams, such as vivid visual impressions of heaven and hell. In 1878 the Masons moved to Plumerville, Arkansas, where they worked on John Watson's plantation. Jerry Mason died of yellow fever the following year.

In late summer of 1880, C. H. Mason was very ill and nearly died. During this crisis, on Sunday, September 5, he felt the presence of God. His wife's biography explained he "got out of bed and walked outside all by himself. There, under the morning skies, he prayed and praised God for his healing. During these moments Charles renewed his commitment to God." Mason's baptism by his half–brother I. S. Nelson at Mt. Olive Baptist Church near Plumerville soon followed.

Mason subsequently traveled about in southern Arkansas as a lay preacher, especially to summer camp meetings. Mason was ordained and licensed to preach at Preston, Arkansas, in 1891. He did not immediately become a full–time minister. He married about this time, and his wife, Alice Saxton, daughter of the best friend of his mother, was strongly opposed to the idea. She divorced him after two years of marriage; Mason did not remarry as long as she lived. In 1903 Mason married Lelia Washington (d. 1936). They had eight children: Alice, Marie (who predeceased her father), Lelia, Charles H. Jr., Deborah Indiana, Julia, Ruth, and Arthur F. In 1943 Mason married Elsie Washington (b. c.1920), who survived him.

The failure of Mason's first marriage sent him into a depression so deep that he contemplated suicide at times. His

Charles Harrison Mason

mental state improved when in 1893 he read a newly published autobiography subtitled *The Story of the Lord's Dealings with Amanda Smith, Colored Evangelist.* Amanda Berry Smith (1839–1915) had had remarkable success in the United States and abroad, and her book was very popular, especially among blacks. Smith preached the doctrine of sanctification, which was soon to be institutionalized in holiness churches. Sanctification had many sources in nineteenth–century Protestantism but is ultimately traced back to John Wesley (1703–91), the founder of Methodism, who taught that believers could be freed from outward sin and perfected in love in this life. Many who take this position see the change as a process of growing in God's grace after conversion. According to holiness believers the normative expectation was an immediate change through a baptism of the Holy Spirit following the initial conversion experience when a believer first accepts Christ—in other words, immediate sanctification after justification. Mason preached his first sermon on sanctification at Preston in 1893, a sermon he often quoted from later.

Founds a Church

Mason entered Arkansas Baptist Institute on November 1, 1893, but withdrew the following January. Mason's belief in the literal truth of the Bible conflicted with the higher criticism of the Bible taught by Charles Lewis Fisher, a top graduate of Morgan Park Seminary (now the University of Chicago Divinity School). Mason's suspicions about the worldliness of African Americans who aspired to a middle class lifestyle contributed to his departure as well.

In 1895 Mason met Charles Price Jones (1865–1947). Jones came from an impoverished background much like Mason's, and his prospects in the church were bright. He entered Arkansas Baptist College in January 1888 to graduate in 1891. A powerful preacher, he was identified early on as a rising star in the denomination. Jones was a powerful preacher and hymn writer. He began preaching on holiness doctrine in 1895, holding a revival with Mason in that year at Mt. Helms Baptist Church and publishing a booklet on the subject in 1896. At this time the forced separation of the holiness movement from the parent Baptist church was nearly complete. Jones and Mason were in agreement on doctrine, and they worked together from 1895 to 1907. Between 1897 and 1899 the conflict with the Baptists became increasingly bitter. At a holiness convention held at Mt. Helms Baptist Church in 1898, Jones moved to change that church's name to Church of Christ Holiness, marking a complete break with his Baptist background and initiating a year–long legal struggle over control of the church property. The Jones faction lost the suit in January 1899 and was read out of the National Baptist Convention USA that fall. During this period Jones and Mason had been working in Holmes County around Lexington, Mississippi, making many converts and building a strong base there for a congregation.

Jones and Mason conducted a successful revival meeting in Lexington, Mississippi, in 1896. After meeting in a private house, the congregation found its first home in an abandoned cotton gin building. This was the first separate meeting place of the Church of God in Christ, a name Mason said was revealed to him as he was walking the streets of Little Rock in March 1897. That same year Jones and Mason moved their headquarters to Memphis, Tennessee, where the church was incorporated and chartered. Jones was general overseer and presiding elder, and Mason was co–leader and overseer of Tennessee.

Azusa Street and Beyond

Despite the success of the church, Mason still harbored doubts about the completeness of his own sanctification. News of the Azusa Street Revival in Los Angeles under William Joseph Seymour reached Memphis in 1906. In April 1907 Mason, along with church leaders D. J. Young and J. A. Jeter, joined many others traveling to Los Angeles to experience the revival. Seymour asserted that speaking in tongues, as the Apostles did at the first Pentecost, was the true sign of sanctification. This became a central doctrine for all of the modern Pentecostal movements, which received their initial impetus from this revival.

Mason spent five weeks at Azusa Street. Later he and Seymour would collaborate in spreading the word, together holding a revival in 1916 in Washington, D.C. At the Azusa Street Mission Mason had a vivid experience of God's Spirit, quoted by Clemmons thus:

> Some said, ''Let us sing.'' I arose and the first song that came to me was ''He Brought me out of the Miry Clay.'' The Spirit came upon me and the saints. . . . Then I gave up for the Lord to have His way with me. So there came a wave of Glory into me, and all of my being was filled with the Glory of the Lord. So when He had gotten me straight on my feet there came a light which enveloped my entire being above the brightness of the sun. When I opened my mouth to say ''Glory,'' a flame touched my tongue which ran down to me. My language changed and no word could I speak in my own tongue. Oh! I was filled with the Glory of the Lord. My soul was then satisfied.

In addition, he found new powers within himself, including the power to heal. E. W. Mason reported that on his return, Mason also had received the power ''to speak in tongues and interpret the same. [God] soon gave me the gift of interpretation—that is, He would interpret sounds, groans and any kind of spiritual utterance.''

Inspired by his new insight, Mason preached at a successful revival at Portsmouth, Virginia, before his return to Memphis in July of 1907. A white preacher, Glenn Cook, who was Seymour's business manager, had already brought tidings of the Azusa Street Revival to Mason's Memphis congregation. Inevitably, in August, the Church of God in Christ split. Jones, who was a very strong–willed man, refused to modify his holiness position and accept speaking in tongues. In 1909 Mason won the legal struggle for control of the charter and the name of the church. Jones and his supporters became the Church of Christ (Holiness) U.S.A.

The Pentecostal Assembly of the Church of God in Christ met in Memphis in November 1907. Membership was still mostly rural. There were three congregations from Tennessee, three from Arkansas, two from Mississippi, and two from Oklahoma. There were also about 12 other leaders from around the country, including some whites. Mason was elected General Overseer and Chief Apostle of the church that he would head for more than a half century. Mason had complete control but used his power with wisdom and discretion. The delegates agreed to hold a holy convocation every year from November 24 to December 14.

The Church Grows

Part of the church's appeal to working–class blacks was its adoption of practices ultimately deriving from Africa. These included active participation by the congregation in call and response preaching, testimony, spontaneous song, and dance. Instruments allowed in the church included drums and guitars. The church has been hospitable to the development of gospel music. Members of the church include Victor Records' most popular preacher and singer of sermons between 1926 and 1931, F. E. McGhee (d. 1972), and later gospel singers like Horace and James Boyer, the Winans, and Andrae Crouch.

The church did not systematically exclude whites. In what may have been a matter of convenience on their part, some 300 white preachers sought ordination from Mason before 1914; most led all–white congregations. (Ordination in a legally established church entitled ministers to half–price railroad tickets.) When in 1914 the white congregations broke away to form the Assemblies of God, Mason accepted an invitation to address the meeting. In the spring of 1916 Mason went to Nashville to conduct a camp meeting for whites. Southern mores soon put an end to black and white cooperation in evangelism, although a few whites did remain with the church. Maxwell quoted a Church of God in Christ leader: "A favorite saying of Mason's was that the church is like the eye: it has a little black in it and a little white in it, and without both it can't see." Mason did not abandon contact with whites, and in 1952 he was honored for his achievements at the Pentecostal World Conference in London, England.

During World War I, the U.S. government became suspicious of any group that failed to mimic its anti–German policies. Mason's insistence on pacifism in his church alarmed the authorities and led to his arrest on several occasions. The government's suspicions were not eased by William B. Holt, a blonde–haired man of German descent who was also Mason's aide and a fellow Church of God in Christ pastor. Holt was reported as being abusive toward authorities on one occasion when he arrived in Jackson, Mississippi, with $2,000 to bail Mason out of jail.

During the latter part of Mason's life, he bent his energies to the day–to–day life of the church. He sent out strong missionaries, male and female, to build churches. Undoubtedly there was criticism and friction, but Mason was an astute and charismatic leader, and his denomination maintained its cohesiveness with unparalleled growth.

Youth work began with the foundation of the Young People's Willing Workers in 1914, and foreign mission work began in 1922. In 1939 a bishop for foreign fields was appointed. Although ultimate control continued with Mason, the growth of the church and his own aging led to changes in the management of the church. Five overseers (the title was changed to bishop in 1957) were appointed in 1933, and in 1951 Mason set up a special commission to help him supervise the church.

While women were not allowed to be pastors and gave lectures from a subordinate rostrum rather than sermons from the pulpit, Mason used strong women like Lizzie Woods Roberson—Mother Roberson—who served as head of the women's division from 1911 to her death as an octogenarian in 1945. Her successor, Lillian B. Coffey (1896–1964) was also a heroine to the church, along with many other women. In the field of education, Arenia Conelia Mallory (1905–1977) served as second head of the Saints Industrial School and Academy, founded in 1918, until her retirement in 1976 and had a significant impact on education for blacks in her section of Mississippi, including the establishment of a junior college for blacks in Holmes County.

A monument to C. H. Mason is the 3,000–seat Mason Temple standing on a street named after him in Memphis, Tennessee. At the time it was built in 1946, it was the largest black–built religious structure in this country. (Martin Luther King Jr. delivered his last speech before the assassination in this building on April 3, 1968.) Mason died in Detroit on November 17, 1961. After lying in state and an elaborate funeral, he was buried in a marble vault in the foyer of the church.

For the members of his church, the real memorial of this remarkable church founder and leader is not found in his material achievements but in the spiritual gifts he brought to the world. In 1994 the all–white Pentecostal Fellowship of North America decided to disband. Leaders went to Memphis to repent for their exclusion of Church of God in Christ and other black Pentecostals. After the formal dissolution of the old organization, the new interracial Pentecostal Fellowship of North America selected Church of God in Christ bishop Ithiel Clemmons as its head. This selection demonstrated the importance of Charles Harrison Mason's leadership of the Church of God in Christ not only for black Americans but for Christians worldwide.

REFERENCES

Clemmons, Ithiel C. *Bishop C. H. Mason and the Roots of the Church of God in Christ.* Bakersfield, CA: Pneuma Life, 1996.

DuPree, Sherry Sherrod, ed. *The African–American Holiness Pentecostal Movement: An Annotated Bibliography.* New York: Garland, 1996.

———. *Biographical Dictionary of African–American, Holiness–Pentecostals,* 1880–1990. Washington, DC: Middle Atlantic Regional Press, 1989.

Mason, E[lsie] W[ashington]. *The Man, Charles Harrison Mason.* Memphis: [Church of God in Christ], 1979.

Maxwell, Joe. "Building the Church (of God in Christ)." *Christianity Today* 40 (8 April 1996): 22–28.

Murphy, Larry G., J. Gordon Melton, and Gary L. Ward. *Encyclopedia of African American Religions.* New York: Garland, 1993.

"One Million Followers Mourn Bishop C. H. Mason's Death." *Jet* 21 (14 December 1961): 18–21.

Payne, Wardell J., ed. *Directory of African American Religious Bodies.* Washington, DC: Howard University Press, 1991.

The Story of Bishop Charles Harrison Mason and the Development of the Church of God in Christ. Videotape. COGIC Publishing Board, 1993.

Who Was Who in America. Vol. 4. Chicago: Marquis Who's Who, 1969.

Robert L. Johns

Walter E. Massey
(1938–)
Physicist, college president, educator

The ninth president of Morehouse College, the nation's only historically black, all–male, four–year, liberal arts institution, Walter Eugene Massey is positioned to lead the school into the 21st century. A Morehouse alumnus, he is a nationally recognized scientist and educator, experienced administrator, scholar, and scientist who became known also for his work as director of the Argonne National Laboratory, a well–known scientific organization. As a black American his firsts include heading the American Association for the Advancement of Science and the National Science Foundation.

On April 5, 1938, in Hattisburg, Mississippi, Walter Eugene Massey was born the second son of Almar and Essie Nelson Massey. He has one brother, Almar Jr. Massey's father was a steel worker in the mills of Hattisburg. His mother taught elementary school. By the time Massey entered school he could already read. He attended Eureka primary school and during these years recalled in an interview with the author that it was his mother, not a school teacher, who influenced him. At Boykin Middle School, Massey first became interested in science. He studied at Royal Street High School, where he was part of the high school band.

Massey's high school mathematics teacher, Jimmy James, impressed by his student's unusual aptitude in mathematics, urged him to test for the early entry program at Morehouse College in Atlanta, Georgia. Massey recalled enjoying mathematics and manipulating numbers, but was most interested in excelling and using the power of his mind to escape from Mississippi. In an interview with the author he recalled, "Hattisburg was a small southern town where blacks could be, and often were, in real physical danger. Living that way can destroy one's self confidence and pride. You had to be so careful. I knew I was smart. It was my ticket out."

Massey passed the examination with high marks, received a Ford Foundation scholarship, and was on his way to college at the age of 16. He recalled that at Morehouse students from other parts of the South, Atlanta in particular, made fun of blacks from Mississippi. They called them backward, and said they came from "the sticks." He felt that he had a lot to prove. In fact, he remembered taking his first physics class because the Morehouse students said it was extremely difficult. "I'd never even heard of physics," he told an interviewer. The same was true of calculus. Thus, by taking the hardest courses the college had to offer, he hoped to erase the stigma of ignorance attached to Mississippians. While his determination insured his success, Massey credited Morehouse for its "ability to recognize a young man's potential rather than classify him by his background."

Massey graduated from Morehouse College with a bachelor of science degree in mathematics and physics in 1958. He spent the summer in New York studying at Columbia University and returned to Morehouse as instructor of physics in the fall of 1958. The 20–year–old instructor was younger than some of his students. Perhaps had it not been for the support and encouragement of his mentor, physics professor Sabinus H. Christensen, Massey would have left the academy. Because he had been taught well, however, he enjoyed teaching. During the summer of 1959, Massey taught physics at Atlanta University and made plans to attend graduate school.

In 1959 Massey won a National Defense Act Fellowship, which enabled him to attend Howard University for one year beginning in the summer of 1959. He also taught a course in physics there. In 1960 he was accepted to graduate school at Washington University in St. Louis, Missouri, and was awarded a National Science Foundation Fellowship.

Massey benefitted from the healthy influences of a number of mentors as he made his way through school. One such mentor was Eugene Feenberg, his dissertation advisor at Washington University. Massey chose to study theoretical physics. Again his choice was driven in part by how people would judge him. Recalling why he chose this field, Massey said in *Physics Today,* "So much depends on what people think of you. In theoretical physics, no one reading your papers would know if you were black or white. There's no such thing as black physics."

While conducting research for his thesis, Massey joined the research staff at Argonne National Laboratory in Argonne, Illinois. The laboratory is operated by the U.S. Department of Energy and is part of the university consortium including Washington University and the University of Chicago.

In 1966 Massey earned both his master of science degree and doctor of philosophy degree in physics. The title of his dissertation was "Ground State of Liquid Helium: Boson Solutions for Mass 3 and 4." After completing his research, Massey was retained by Argonne as staff physicist. He remained in this position from June of 1966 until September of 1968. Massey was offered a position as assistant professor of physics at the University of Illinois at Urbana in the fall of 1968. He accepted the position, moved, and reentered the world of academe.

The Physics of Life

Because of his academic discipline and the time it required to become competent in his subject, Massey missed the civil rights and black power revolutions taking place in the streets of America. He was either in the library or the laboratory. Yet Massey's commitment to intellect did not preclude his awareness of social issues. His desire to go to the University of Illinois campus stemmed from a need to reconnect with students and issues in ways he had not been able to as a student.

Massey's first night on the Illinois campus provided the opportunity. Two hundred and sixty–four black students had been jailed for protesting racism at the university. Massey was instrumental in acquiring their release. He said in interview that his philosophy regarding social commitment is "maximize your benefits to others. Positively affect others in whatever you do." Since his strengths are in the areas of mathematics and science, he seeks to help in that way. He is especially concerned about the numbers of black students who lack skills in these areas.

Remembering his own weak academic preparation in both subjects and knowing that without the guidance of caring mentors and the skills of good teachers he never would have majored in mathematics and physics, Massey helped to organize the Illinois Science and Mathematics Academy, a high school developed for gifted students. He also served as a trustee for the Academy for Mathematics and Science Teachers, a laboratory that has trained approximately 17,000 Chicago public school teachers. While at Illinois, Massey tutored and counselled many black students.

In Chicago Massey met a fashion model for print advertisements and local fashion shows and a Trans–World Airlines reservation clerk, Shirley Anne Streeter. Massey and Streeter were married on October 29, 1969. In January of 1970, the couple moved to Providence, Rhode Island, where Massey became associate professor of physics at Brown University.

At Brown Massey faced the same problem he had encountered in Illinois, black students with weak preparation in mathematics and science. He started the Inner City Teachers of Science Program (ICTOS), a program for undergraduates studying to become science teachers; then they would mentor and tutor urban students in their high school science classes. In 1975 Massey earned promotion to the rank of full professor of physics. His research on superfluid helium established his reputation as an outstanding scientist.

First Black Dean

In 1975 Massey became an American Council on Education (ACE) Fellow. The ACE fellowship provided for the training of administrators, usually for positions as college president. When Massey returned to Brown he was appointed dean of the undergraduate college. Argonne National Laboratory and the University of Chicago enticed Massey to leave Brown in 1979 with an offer to direct Argonne, with its $250 million annual budget and staff of 4,000 people. The offer also included a professorship at the University of Chicago.

At Argonne and the University of Chicago, Massey created the Argonne National Laboratory–University of Chicago Development Corporation. This organization acted as catalyst for transferring the technologies created at Argonne to industry and into the marketplace. He also worked to improve scientific education and headed the Chicago Mayoral Task Force on High–Technology Development.

In 1989 Massey became the president of American Association for the Advancement of Science, a 140,000–member organization that included 285 scientific societies. From his position as president, Massey was able to focus national attention on American science education. "If we look at the comparative performance of American students in science relative to that of their peers in other countries, we see that a great deal needs to be done," Massey said in *Contemporary Black Biography.*

Although he is a Democrat, Walter Massey was chosen by President George Bush in 1991 to head the National Science Foundation (NSF). Massey assumed the new position in March. The scientific community praised Bush's selection. In his role as director, Massey sought to continue to improve science education and increase the number of minorities and women in the field.

In April of 1993 Massey left the NSF to become provost and senior vice–president for academic affairs at the University of California System in Oakland, California. He remained in California until August of 1995, when he was appointed president of Morehouse College. He was inaugurated February 16, 1996. A southern Baptist, Massey described himself in an interview as "easy–going." He likes to dance and he loves jazz. He and his wife have two grown sons, Keith and Eric.

Recognized Scholar and Scientist

Walter E. Massey is the recipient of numerous honors and awards. The one he holds most dear is the award presented in 1992 by his undergraduate alma mater, the Bennie Trailblazer Award. In 1974 Massey was named Outstanding Educator of America and the following year he received the Distinguished Service Citation of the American Association of Physics Teachers for exceptional contributions to the teaching of physics. In 1988 he was awarded the Distinguished Service in Engineering from the University of Illinois College of Engineering. The Honorary Fellow Award, from the Society for Technical Communication was presented to Massey in 1989. In 1992 he received the Archie Lacey Memorial Award by the New York Academy of Sciences, the Distinguished Achievement Award from Morgan State University, as well as the Golden Plate Award from the American Academy of Achievement.

Massey has been awarded honorary Doctor of Science degrees from numerous institutions, and a Doctor of Humanities Honorary Degree from Mt. Sinai Medical School in New York, 1994.

Massey holds membership in the following professional organizations: American Academy of Arts and Sciences, American Association for the Advancement of Science, American Association of Physics Teachers, American Nuclear Society, American Philosophical Society, American Physical Society, New York Academy of Sciences, and Sigma Xi.

Massey is a man with a vision who overcame academic weaknesses to become a scholar and leader in the field of physics. Once in a leadership position, he turned his energies toward helping minority students overcome deficiencies in science. As a black college president, he is both a leader and role model for young African American men.

Current address: Morehouse College, 830 Westview Drive, S.W., Atlanta, GA 30314.

REFERENCES

Contemporary Black Biography. Vol. 5. Detroit: Gale Research, 1994.

Goodwin, Irwin. "Conversation with NSF's Walter Massey: Leaner Times, Meaner Times for Science." *Physics Today* 45 (August 1992): 51–58.

Lyons, Douglas C. "Pathfinders of the '80s." *Ebony* 44 (August 1989): 60–66.

Massey, Walter E. Interview with Nagueyalti Warren, June 17, 1996.

"U. of California says NSF Chief Will Become Provost in April." *Chronicle of Higher Education* 39 (3 February 1993), A–29.

Who's Who among African Americans, 1996–1997. 9th ed. Detroit: Gale Research, 1996.

Nagueyalti Warren

Samuel Proctor Massie Jr.

Samuel Proctor Massie Jr.

(1919–)

Chemist, educator, writer, college president, entrepreneur

Samuel P. Massie was the first African American professor at the U.S. Naval Academy in Annapolis, Maryland. He set such a high standard of excellence in teaching that 30 years later the U.S. Department of Energy sponsored a program to establish Chairs of Excellence in his name. The chairs provide $14.7 million to establish environmental engineering professorships at nine historically black colleges and universities, assisting these schools in producing cutting–edge minority engineers in the areas of environment and waste management.

Born in North Little Rock, Arkansas, on July 3, 1919, to Samuel and Earlee Massie, he has one brother, a physician. His parents taught in the segregated Arkansas school system. Massie married Gloria Thompkins of Philadelphia, whom he met at Fisk University. They have three sons, Herbert, James, and Samuel III.

Massie—nicknamed "Proc" to avoid confusion with his father—graduated from high school at the age of 13. Because of his youth and the family's limited finances, his parents delayed his entering college for a year. After that year, young Samuel earned his first degree, an A.A., at Dunbar Junior College in Little Rock. He received a B.S. in chemistry from the Arkansas Agricultural, Mechanical, and Normal College (now known as the University of Arkansas at Pine Bluff) in 1938, an M.S. in chemistry from Fisk University in 1940, and a Ph.D. in organic chemistry from Iowa State University in 1946.

After serving in World War II, Massie helped conduct research projects as a doctoral student on chemical warfare agents, the atomic bomb, and antimalarial drugs. Ironically, a job as a chemist, which he greatly desired, was unavailable to him. He returned to teach at Fisk. After two years, Langston University in Oklahoma offered him a full professorship, which he accepted. He later became head of the department.

Returning to Fisk several years later, he worked to strengthen the master's degree program, helping graduates to succeed in doctoral programs. In 1960 Massie moved to the National Science Foundation in Washington, D.C., and served part time as chairman of the department of pharmaceutical chemistry at Howard University. He left that position to assume the presidency of North Carolina College (now North Carolina Central University) in Durham in 1963, where he stayed for three years.

A pioneering career move came in 1966 when, at age 49, Massie was hired as the first African American faculty member at the U.S. Naval Academy in Annapolis, Maryland. There he spent most of his career inspiring students with his keen mind and sense of humor, challenging them to follow his lead. He chaired the academy's chemistry department from 1977 to 1981, and retired in 1993.

When Massie arrived at the Naval Academy, his race prevented him from buying a home nearby. In an interview, he said, "Bitterness closes doors." He bought a home several miles away and proceeded to change things. He co–founded the academy's black studies program and helped change a policy that denied journeyman positions to African American workers. He was appointed by five Maryland governors to serve as chairperson of the Maryland State Board of Community Colleges for 21 consecutive years, and worked as chairman of the Governor's Science Advisory Council for ten years. He also served for nearly ten years as a member of the Board of Visitors at Towson State University in Maryland and as a member of the Board of Trustees of the College of Wooster in Ohio for 21 years.

In addition to teaching, Massie has published widely in scientific journals. His 1954 article in *Chemical Reviews,* "The Chemistry of Phenothiazine" is considered a classic in the field. As a result of his research on phenothiazine, Massie was asked to speak at the American Chemical Society's International Conference in Zurich, Switzerland in 1955, and in 1960 was elected as national chairman of visiting scientists for the 90,000–member organization.

The following year the Manufacturing Chemists Association recognized him as one of the top six college chemistry teachers in the United States, and a 1975 Freedom Fund award from the NAACP local chapter went to him. At a White House Ceremony in 1988 he received a National Lifetime Achievement Award for his contributions to science, technology, and community service.

Massie felt particularly proud when recognized by two of the schools he attended because of the manner in which he was treated at the time.'separate but equal,'' he called it in an interview. One was the award of an honorary doctorate by the University of Arkansas in 1970, and in 1981 the Distinguished Achievement Citation by Iowa State.

Massie also has received honorary degrees from Lehigh University, Bowie State University, the University of Maryland Eastern Shore, the College of Wooster, and Fisk University, as well as the Henry A. Hill Award of the National Organization of Black Professional Chemists and Chemical Engineers. His fraternity, Kappa Alpha Psi, presented him its highest award—the Laurel Wreath—and in 1989 he was inducted into the National Black College Alumni Hall of Fame in the area of science.

In 1992 the Annapolis Chapter of the National Naval Officers Association established an endowment in his name to provide incentive scholarships to individuals from disadvantaged socioeconomic backgrounds in Anne Arundel County who would not otherwise have the opportunity to complete professional studies. At the Smithsonian Institution, a permanent, hands–on interactive video exhibit features Massie, helping to make his accomplishments known to future generations.

Massie was recognized by the American Chemical Society in 1996 as the person who had done the most to promote careers in chemistry among minority students. In presenting him their Dreyfus Award, the society gave $10,000 to Fisk University for their role in producing this inspiring educator. The Department of Energy named its chair of excellence in honor of Massie in 1997. He was honored again that year when the National Academy of Science hung his picture in its gallery. In 1997, Massie became vice–president for education of Bingwa Multicultural Software, a company that develops products to teach mathematics in the context of ethnic backgrounds.

Current address: 12203 Brittany Place, Laurel, MD 20708.

REFERENCES

Kessler, James H., et al. *Distinguished African American Scientists of the 20th Century.* Phoenix: Oryx Press, 1996.

Massie, Samuel P., Jr. Interview with Margaret D. Pagan, June 28, 1996.

McMurray, Emily J., ed. *Notable Twentieth–Century Scientists.* New York: Gale Research, 1995.

"National Headliners." *Jet* 93 (1 December 1997): 10.

Salzman, Jack, David L. Smith, and Cornel West, eds. *Encyclopedia of African–American Culture and History.* New York: Macmillan Library Reference USA/Simon and Schuster Macmillan, 1996.

Sammons, Vivian Ovelton. *Blacks in Science and Medicine.* New York: Hemisphere Publishing Corporation, 1990.

Who's Who among African Americans, 1996–97. 9th ed. Detroit: Gale Research, 1996.

Margaret D. Pagan

Jan E. Matzeliger
(1852–1889)
Inventor

Jan Matzeliger revolutionized the shoe manufacturing industry with his lasting machine patented in 1883. Although Matzeliger had little formal education and was a self–taught inventor, he made it possible to manufacture shoes rapidly with as much precision as the hand–laster.

Born in Paramaribo, Suriname, South America, on September 15, 1852, Jan Earnst Matzeliger was the son of a Netherlands–born engineer and a black Surinamese woman who probably came from West Africa. When he was three years old, Matzeliger began living with a paternal aunt. Later he became an apprentice in a government machine shop

Jan E. Matzeliger

where his father was superintendent and where he demonstrated a talent for mechanics and machine work.

In 1871, when he was 19 years old, Matzeliger left Suriname and became a sailor on an East Indian ship. After cruising for two years he disembarked permanently when the ship visited Philadelphia. He held a variety of odd jobs there before moving to Boston in 1876. In the winter of 1877 Matzeliger settled in nearby Lynn, Massachusetts, then the shoe manufacturing center of the country. Alone, poor, and barely able to speak English, he eventually found a job with Harney Brother's shoe factory, where he operated a McKay sole–sewing machine, then followed with other jobs such as work on a heel burnisher, on a buttonhole machine, and as a maintenance man. In odd hours he was a coachman in a West Lynn park.

Determined to communicate better, he enrolled in evening school and soon learned to speak English with barely an accent. At some point he developed a personal library, acquiring books on physics and other practical subjects, several Bibles, and other works. He also acquired a barometer, a set of drawing instruments, and other tools.

Matzeliger rented a room over the old West Lynn Mission where he had space to explore the possibility of improving the machinery he used at work. After observing hand–lasters, he began a ten–year project of designing and building a series of machines to revolutionize shoe manufacturing. For his first machine, which he built in 1880, he used pieces of wood, old cigar boxes, short pieces of wire, and other odds and ends, and six months later he had completed a crude model of a mechanical laster for shoes. (In shoe manufacturing, a ''last'' is a foot–shaped model that provides the form of the shoe.)

Invents Shoe Lasting Machine

Now assured that he was moving in the right direction, Matzeliger collected discarded parts, inoperable machines, and old castings and built a larger, simplified, and improved iron model. As he worked also as a maintenance machinist for a shoe manufacturer named Beal, he used a small space in the plant to work on his model. Extremely poor and living on a few cents a day, Matzeliger needed financial support for this work. He rejected financial offers that would result in giving up rights to his toe–folding device, then received support from two wealthy investors from Lynn who would own two–thirds of the invention. He was granted a patent on March 20, 1883, for his lasting machine. He continued work on the model, and by the spring of 1885 the prototype was ready to test. On May 29 the laster made a record run, lasting seventy–five pairs of women's shoes. He had revolutionized the shoe industry and lightened the load of the human laborer. His machine came to be known as the ''Niggerhead Laster.''

Still dissatisfied with the quality of his machine, Matzeliger used the money from his invention to begin a third and improved model, patented on September 22, 1891, for an application filed after the May 29 factory test. Since his local backers, C. H. Delnow and M. S. Nichols, were unable to raise enough money for large–scale production of the invention of 1885, they solicited the support of George W. Brown, agent for the Wheeler and Wilson Sewing Machine Company, and Sidney W. Winslow, who formed the Consolidated Lasting Machine Company. The company took over the inventor's patents and gave Matzeliger a large block of company stock. While the handlaster of the 1880s barely made fifty pairs of shoes in ten hours, Matzeliger's machine produced from 150 to 700 pairs in the same period. The demand for the new laster was so great that, by 1889, the company set up a school to train operators to use the device. It also led to a major concentration in the industry.

In his lifetime Matzeliger had begun a number of inventions, some patented after his death. These included a mechanism for distributing tacks and nails, October 12, 1883; nailing machine (improvements in tack and nail distribution and driving mechanism), February 25, 1879; and tack separating and distributing mechanism, March 25, 1890.

Matzeliger was also a religious man. After attempts to join a white church were unsuccessful because of his complexion, in 1884 he joined the Christian Endeavor Society, the North Congregational Church's youth group. Though not a member of the church at the time, he attended services, taught Sunday School, served on committees, and participated in fund raising activities. A multitalented man, he was a painter as well; in his spare time Matzeliger gave lessons in oil painting to one of his friends from his church organization.

Matzeliger has been described as a slender, handsome man with dark, slightly pock–marked skin. He always stood erect and was clean and neat. He was always polite, cheerful, and made friends easily. He customarily wore a rectangular lapel pin inscribed "Safe with Jesus."

In the summer of 1886 Matzeliger attended a rainy church picnic and contracted a nagging cold. He grew tired, weak, and became a semi–invalid; eventually the illness was diagnosed as tuberculosis. He continued to work, however, experimenting on a fourth model of his lasting machine. He and several of his friends moved into a house Matzeliger had purchased on Albany Street, where they nursed and cared for him. Nevertheless, he succumbed to his lingering illness, and on August 24, 1889, at age 37, he died in the Lynn Hospital. He was buried in the Pine Grove Cemetery in Lynn. His headstone is inscribed, "In Fond Remembrance," by his friends in North Church.

Matzeliger willed all of his holdings in the Union Lasting Machine Company and one–third of his interest in the Consolidated Lasting Machine Company to North Congregational Church, which early on accepted him as a member. He gave small blocks of Consolidated stock to the attending physician at Lynn Hospital and two–thirds of his holdings in Consolidated to 15 or more of his closest friends. He left his gold watch and chain, two of his paintings, his barometer, Bibles, and the rights to his "Safe Motor" (an invention in progress when he died) to a number of men and women who had loved him. He provided for an education at Amherst College and support to enter the ministry for his young art student of the Christian Endeavor group, and he left books, sketches, and drawing instruments to other young people.

While Matzeliger received praise for his work while he was alive, he may have received greater recognition after his death. In 1901 the Pan–American Exposition awarded him the Gold Medal and Diploma posthumously. The city of Lynn designated May 16, 1967, Jan E. Matzeliger Day, an activity sponsored by the local NAACP. On September 15, 1991, the U.S. Postal Service recognized Matzeliger's work, making him the first black inventor commemorated on a postage stamp. His name is permanently linked with the shoe manufacturing industry.

REFERENCES

Baker, Henry E. *The Colored Inventor, A Record of Fifty Years.* 1913. Reprint, New York: Arno Press and the *New York Times,* 1969.

Culp, D. W., ed. *Twentieth Century Negro Literature.* Naperville, IL: J. L. Nichols, 1902.

Hayden, Robert C. *Eight Black American Inventors.* Reading, MA: Addison–Wesley, 1972.

Kaplan, Sidney. "Jan Earnst Matzeliger and the Making of the Shoe." *Journal of Negro History* 40 (January 1955): 8–33.

Logan, Rayford W., and Michael R. Winston, eds. *Dictionary of American Negro Biography.* New York: Norton, 1982.

Malone, Dumas, ed. *Dictionary of American Biography.* New York: Charles Scribner's Sons, 1963.

Smith, Jessie Carney, ed. *Black Firsts.* Detroit: Gale Research, 1994.

Frederick Douglas Smith Jr.

Robert C. Maynard

(1937–1993)

Newspaper editor and publisher, journalist, reporter, social critic

As a high school dropout and newspaper reporter by age 16 and a freelance writer by age 19, Robert Maynard was the first black national correspondent for the *Washington Post* and later the first black editor–in–chief of a major American daily newspaper, the *Oakland Tribune.* He also helped train many minority journalists through an institute that he cofounded.

Born June 17, 1937, in Brooklyn, New York, Robert Clyve Maynard was the youngest of six children. Both his father, Samuel C. Maynard, a part–time lay preacher who also owned a small farm, and his mother, Robertine Isola Greaves Maynard, had emigrated from Barbados to the United States in 1919. Maynard grew up in the tough, predominantly black Bedford–Stuyvesant section of Brooklyn. Samuel Maynard instilled sound study habits in his children, taught them to strive for excellence, and encouraged a strong work ethic. Maynard had fond childhood memories of his family's dining room table, where he and his siblings exchanged ideas and reported what they had learned each day. As the youngest and last child to speak, Maynard began writing down what he wanted to say. Under their parents' tutelage, the children developed a lifelong love of knowledge, and Maynard developed a lifelong love for writing.

Discussing his father's influence on his life, Maynard told Pamela Noel in the June 1985 *Ebony*: "From him I learned that every task has to be approached in a certain way. You've got to determine the tools that are going to be required to do it and make sure you have those tools before you start." Maynard was also influenced by his father's wise real estate investments that led to the family's financial security and developed a keen business acumen of his own.

Maynard began writing when he was eight years old. After preparing an essay about a new wave of immigrants in his neighborhood, he brought home an old typewriter to facilitate his writing. Although the Maynard children knew the value their parents placed on education, only Robert Maynard chose not to pursue a college career. Instead, he cut classes at Brooklyn's Boys High School to spend his time at the editorial offices of the *New York Age,* a now–defunct black weekly paper, which published his first articles. The

Robert C. Maynard

newspaper so fully consumed Maynard's interest that by age 16 he had dropped out of school.

From a base in Greenwich Village, where he moved in 1956, Maynard continued to work for the *Age,* wrote freelance articles for local black weeklies, and mixed with well–known writers such as James Baldwin and Langston Hughes, who encouraged him to write. He also worked as a reporter for the *Baltimore Afro–American.* During this period he searched unsuccessfully for other employment, mailing out more than 300 resumes to white dailies and working at odd jobs to support himself. In 1961 Jim Hicks, editor of the *York (Pennsylvania) Gazette and Daily,* hired him as a police and urban affairs reporter, giving Maynard his first big opportunity. He covered a variety of stories, worked hard, and eventually was assigned to cover the civil rights movement in the South. Hicks also persuaded Maynard to apply for a one–year Nieman Fellowship for journalists at Harvard University. Maynard was selected for the prestigious award and spent 1966 taking courses in art, economics, music, and history. He returned to the *Gazette* in 1967 as night editor but soon left.

Joins the *Washington Post*

Ben Bradlee, a former editor of the *Washington Post,* spotted Maynard at Harvard in a seminar for Neiman fellows and recalled in the *Atlanta Journal Constitution* that he was ''confrontational, argumentative, mean, and skeptical, verging on the obnoxious.'' Bradlee no doubt recognized that Maynard was also a self–assured, outspoken, and talented reporter and writer. After Maynard's fellowship ended, Bradlee hired him, making him the *Post*'s first black national correspondent. He developed a high profile around Washington and was noted for his brash manner and stylish dress. Some found him arrogant, while others saw him as talented and charming. Maynard was an immediate success, had a wide range of contacts, and had free rein to report local and national news. He originated and wrote an eloquent five–part series on the growing black militancy, which was published in September of 1967. In 1972 he helped to cover the Watergate scandal—the illegal break–in of Democratic party offices by the Republican campaign committee during Richard M. Nixon's presidency—as well as its consequences.

Continuing at the *Post,* Maynard also worked part–time in 1972 for *Encore,* a new black monthly that reported news from a black perspective. In that year Bradlee appointed Maynard to an 18–month stint as ombudsman to monitor and report the Post's performance, fairness, accuracy, and clarity both internally and in editorials. He was also made an associate editor. In 1976 he was one of three questioners at the final presidential debate between President Gerald Ford and Jimmy Carter, the Democratic contender.

Maynard developed a strong interest in developing training opportunities for minority journalists. In 1972 he and Earl Caldwell, a black reporter for the *New York Times,* codirected a new summer training program in journalism at Columbia University, funded by the Ford Foundation. The program was discontinued two years later when the foundation withdrew its support. Dismayed, Maynard took a leave of absence from the *Post* in 1977 to found a similar program known as the Institute for Journalism Education at the University of California, Berkeley. He also established Jobnet, a liaison between potential employers and nonwhite journalists which by 1982 provided about one–fourth of all new minority journalists and by 1983 was the largest single source of minority journalists. Maynard chaired the program until 1979.

Shortly after he founded the institute, the Gannett newspaper chain hired Maynard as affirmative action consultant. In 1979 Gannett also appointed Maynard editor of its newly acquired *Oakland Tribune,* making him the nation's first black director of editorial operations for a major daily newspaper. At the *Oakland Tribune* Maynard hired minority journalists, including the first openly gay columnist, and brought new life into the paper. He increased the amount of local news, instituted community advisory boards, and focused on issues directly affecting the Oakland community. He offered a morning and afternoon edition and tried to appeal to everyone—from the upper middle–class in Walnut Creek to the blue–collar in Oakland.

First Black Owner of a Major Daily

In spite of his ambitious efforts, however, the paper struggled financially. Maynard cut the afternoon edition and managed to retain his staff. When Gannett decided to acquire a local television station in 1982, the Oakland Federal Communications Commission ruled that the newspaper had to be sold first. Using the newspaper company's real estate holdings as collateral, Maynard arranged two bank loans for a down payment of $5 million, gave Gannett a long–term promissory note for the $17 million balance, and bought the *Oakland Tribune* himself in April of 1983. As president of the board and owner of 79 percent of the paper's stock, he became the first black in the United States to have a controlling interest in a major, general–circulation city daily.

Although Maynard failed to make *The Tribune* a financial success—primarily because of Oakland's lagging economy and because the town was squeezed by prosperous San Francisco and the booming South Bay—his style permeated the newspaper, and the *Tribune* became a symbol of racial pride. It won numerous major awards, including a Pulitzer Prize in 1990 for its photographic coverage of the 1989 Bay Area earthquake. He and his wife sustained the paper with the help of $5 million in cash from the Freedom Forum, $4 million in guaranteed loans, and assistance in erasing the original debt to Gannett, now worth $31.5 million. But as matters worsened and Maynard became terminally ill, he sold the paper in 1992 to William Dean Singleton, owner of several newspapers in the Bay Area.

Maynard was active in many civic organizations. He served on the board of trustees of the Rockefeller Foundation, the Pacific School of Religion, the Bay Area Council, the Associated Press, and the Pulitzer Prize Committee. He was a member of the Oakland Chamber of Commerce, the Council on Foreign Relations, and the Sigma Delta Chi Society of Professional Journalists. He held honorary doctorate degrees from York College in Pennsylvania and the California College of Arts and Crafts. Maynard was a Democrat and a member of the Lutheran Church.

Maynard was also a family man. He had one daughter, Dori J., from his early first marriage and two children, David H. and Alex Caldwell, from his second marriage on January 1, 1975, to Nancy Hall Hicks, a well–known journalist for the *New York Times* who later became a lawyer.

In 1992 Maynard suffered a recurrence of the cancer first diagnosed and treated in the late 1980s. After selling his paper, he kept a full schedule as faculty member at the Institute for Journalism Education, writer of a syndicated column, and commentator on television news shows. After his death at home in Oakland on August 17, 1993, at the age of 56, his life was celebrated in the area and in Washington, D.C.

Ernst Holsendolph summarized his work in the *Atlanta Journal and Constitution*: "Maynard's values and point of view were embodied in his style of reporting. It was the shoe–leather kind, where reporters brush past the official spokesman and talk to the real people—the poor, the alienated and the lonely people, for whom there are few true representatives." In *Current Biography* for 1986, Holly I. West of the *Washington Post* commented that his "hunched shoulder swagger, a hip, big city strut from his youthful days in Brooklyn, telegraphs his brimming confidence." She observed that he lifted the spirit of friends and immobilized enemies with "his smoky voice and eloquence." Although fully committed to journalism, Maynard had other interests. Journalist Earl Caldwell, a longtime friend, called him a Renaissance man and noted his love of books, cooking for dinner parties, classic cars, photography, languages, and collecting fountain pens.

Maynard is remembered for blazing his way to eminence as a journalist and publisher and for opening up opportunities for minority journalists in newsrooms across the nation.

REFERENCES

Contemporary Authors. Vol. 110. Detroit: Gale Research, 1984.

Contemporary Black Biography. Vol. 7. Detroit: Gale Research, 1994.

Current Biography 54 (October 1993): 59.

Current Biography Yearbook. New York: H. W. Wilson Co., 1986.

"Give Me a Chance to Try." *Newsweek* 122 (August 30, 1993): 60.

"A Man Whose Life Made a Difference." *Atlanta Journal and Constitution,* August 22, 1993.

Maynard, Robert C., with Dori J. Maynard. *Letters to My Children.* Kansas City: Andrews and McMeel, 1995.

Noel, Pamela. "Robert Maynard: Oakland's Top Newsman." *Ebony* 40 (June 1985): 105–10.

Obituary. *New York Times,* August 19, 1993.

Schardt, Arlie, and Michael Reese. "Oakland's New Look." *Newsweek* 94 (24 September 1979): 89.

Who's Who among African Americans, 1992–93. 7th ed. Detroit: Gale Research, 1992.

Jessie Carney Smith

Benjamin E. Mays

(1894–1984)

Educator, scholar, clergyman, civic leader, public speaker

Benjamin Elijah Mays, the son of South Carolina slaves, overcame the obstacles of early twentieth century racial oppression and emerged as one of the leading African American educators in the United States. Receiving his doctorate from the University of Chicago in 1935, Benjamin Mays served as president of Morehouse College from 1940 to 1967, bringing it into the spotlight as one of the nation's most prestigious institutions of higher learning for African American men. Perhaps the most notable president of the college, he was known for his outstanding leadership and personableness with students and staff. As president, Mays had a great impact on shaping black higher education as well as some of the greatest African American leaders of this century, including civil rights leader Martin Luther King Jr. and the first African American mayor of Atlanta, Maynard Jackson. He was known as well as a great public speaker who was in constant demand.

Benjamin Mays, known also as "Bennie," was born to Hezekiah Mays and Louvenia Carter on August 1, 1894, near Ninety–Six, a small town in Greenwood County, South Carolina. Mays grew up the youngest of three sisters and four brothers. Hezikiah Mays, a proud man who resisted submissiveness to whites, earned a living as a renter, an occupation one step above a sharecropper, a prevalent occupation among southern rural blacks at the turn of the twentieth century. He owned his mules but rented his farm land by supplying bales of cotton to the white landowner. It was nonetheless difficult for the family to survive. The reality of being poor and black in a racist town may have contributed to the drinking binges of Hezekiah Mays. The binges often led him into violent outbursts and even physical attacks on Mays's mother. Louvenia Carter Mays, a deeply religious and outspoken woman, refused to acquiesce under the ranting and raving of Hezekiah Mays and exercised a strong determination to keep the family together. In many ways, she stabilized the family by leading them in prayer at the end of the day. Her strong Christian faith influenced Mays and served as hope for him and his siblings.

Benjamin E. Mays

In addition to family problems, racial turmoil and terrorism marred Mays's early years. At age five, he understood the danger that blacks constantly faced. When a group of armed white men cursed his father and made him salute them it went unchallenged. Such a confrontation most often resulted in a beating or loss of life. The previous year, this mob participated in the Phoenix Riot that started in Greenwood County and lasted for days, ending with the lynching of several blacks. Events of this nature led Mays to think about ways of overcoming a life of torture.

Learns Value of Church and Education

Although his mother was illiterate, she valued education and prayed that young Mays's desire to receive an education would be granted. At age six, he began attending the Brickhouse School, named for the nearby large brick house owned by a white man. Other family members and Mays's first teacher recognized a brightness in him that showed promise. He immediately became the star pupil and excelled from the praise and encouragement that he received from his teacher.

Despite Mays's intelligence and eagerness to learn, blacks in rural South Carolina had limited opportunities for eduction. He desired more school than the four months a year allowed to blacks by the Greenwood County school system. Black children learned of pain and fear early in life due to skin color. Mays realized that education was the only hope in changing his plight. Through his church, Mt. Zion Baptist, he learned about schools that would provide more education.

Mt. Zion Church played an important role in young Mays's life. In addition to praising his gifts and talents, the Mt. Zion community provided him with his first public speaking experience as an eight–year–old Children's Day speaker. He revered his pastor, James Marshall, and perceived him as a role model. Marshall and the congregation encouraged Mays to pursue his education outside of Greenwood County. Throughout the state and southern region, church–supported schools compensated for the education restrictions placed on black youth in Greenwood County. In 1909, after he convinced his father of the need to further his education, Mays, at the age of 15, traveled to McCormick, South Carolina, to attend The McCormick School, a Baptist association school strongly supported by his pastor and church.

Mays's brief stay at The McCormick School offered little more than the Brickhouse School. A minister and his wife taught and ran the school. Mays soon decided to enroll in a better school, South Carolina State College, in Orangeburg, South Carolina. With the blessings of his mother and ministers, Mays left for State College in the fall of 1911.

South Carolina State College proved to be a valuable institution with qualified teachers to assist Mays in his studies. His father, however, continued to call him home to help on the family farm. Mays viewed this as a hindrance from his goals and asked one of the professors to explain to his father the importance of completing the school year. His refusal to go home during the school year resulted in his father's withdrawal of financial support. Mays financed the rest of his high school education by working as a Pullman porter. The Pullman Railroad Company recruited students to work on the rail line during the summer months. In 1916, Mays graduated as valedictorian from the High School Department at South Carolina State College. Unfortunately, the time spent away from school on the farm caused him to graduate as an older student at the age of 21.

Embittered by personal encounters with South Carolina's racist whites and a system that denied opportunities for African Americans, Mays decided against attending college in the South. Moreover, Mays wanted to study at a white college in order to compete with whites, to prove the worth of a black person, and show that they could achieve great things. For Mays, a southern white school was not an option; southern white colleges and universities were not open to blacks in the early 1900s. Although not all northern schools were open to blacks, some had nondiscrimination policies regarding race. Bates College in Lewiston, Maine had such a policy. After attending Virginia Union for one year, Mays entered Bates College in the fall of 1917.

Bates College turned out to be wonderful experience for Mays, changing his views of white people. Mays observed that not all whites held negative views of black people or refused to have them as friends. Bates did not change his financial status, however. Having adequate funds to live in Lewiston continued to challenge him. In later years, Mays stated in *Born to Rebel* that "without Bates' concern for me, I would have never been able to meet my financial obligations for my three years there." The college assisted him with loans and work to pay his tuition and living expenses. The last two years Mays received academic scholarships for his expenses. In the spring of 1920, he graduated with honors from Bates College.

The following August in Newport News, Virginia, Mays married a high school friend, Ellen Harvin, who taught school in Clarendon County, South Carolina. Shortly after their wedding, Ellen Harvin Mays returned to South Carolina to resume her teaching and Benjamin Mays returned North to continue his work as a Pullman porter. Their marriage only lasted for two–and–a–half years, because Ellen Harvin Mays died in Atlanta in 1923 following an operation.

Teaching, Tampa, and Training

When Ellen Mays died, Benjamin Mays was teaching at Morehouse College in Atlanta. While doing graduate work in 1921 at the University of Chicago, John Hope, president of Morehouse, recruited him to teach mathematics. Mays taught in the department from 1921 to 1924. During these years, he also pastored a small Baptist church, Shiloh, located in the vicinity of Morehouse and Spelman colleges. After teaching and pastoring for three years, he decided to pursue his academic goals. His desire to finish graduate studies compelled him to return to the University of Chicago School of Religion in September of 1924. In the spring of the following year, he received the M.A. degree in New Testament studies. The lack of equality for African Americans and the problem of segregation continued to disturb him. The problems were particularly visible upon his return to South Carolina State College to teach the year following graduation.

The fall of 1925 provided a new job for Mays and a new friend, Sadie Gray. While working on his Ph.D. the following summer, Benjamin Mays married Gray. The marriage lasted for 42 years, until the death of Sadie Gray Mays in 1969.

Following the wedding, Mays decided to delay his studies one more time and pursue work with Sadie Gray Mays in Tampa at Florida's National Urban League. He assumed the position of executive secretary with the Family Service Association, where Sadie Mays was a case worker. Mays's direct contact with Tampa's white and black leaders, brought him prestige. However, the job proved to be extremely difficult. Given the many needs of African Americans in the 1920s and the high level of racial discrimination, the job's demands overwhelmed Mays. He also found himself frustrated and emotionally drained by daily encounters with racism and segregation. For example, southern whites refused to address blacks with the proper titles of "Mrs.," "Mr.," or "Miss." Mays insisted that he and others in his office address each other with these titles when receiving calls from whites.

Mays stayed with Tampa's National Urban League for two years and then decided to work with the national YMCA. For the next two years, Mays served in Atlanta as National Student Secretary of the YMCA. This position entailed working with students at black colleges in five southern states. He continued to protest racial segregation. The mid to late 1920s afforded him professional positions from which to whittle away at racial injustice.

In the late 1920s and early 1930s, Mays stood out as an African American leader, educator, and scholar. His academic expertise and leadership abilities, along with his training as a minister, allowed him to address the social and religious issues facing African Americans. Members of the Institute of Social and Religious Research, an agency funded by the Rockefeller family, recognized the exceptional qualities in Mays and asked him to direct a study of African American churches. Mays, along with Joseph Nicholson, a minister in the Colored Methodist Episcopal church, spent more than a year researching on 691 black churches in 12 large cities. The findings showed how the black church functioned to provide hope, pride and status to millions of black people faced with racism. In 1933, their findings were published in *The Negro's Church.*

In 1932 Mays returned to the University of Chicago to complete his graduate studies and earned his Ph.D. degree in 1935. It was indeed a major accomplishment for a black man to receive a Ph.D. in the 1930s, especially from one of the most reputable schools in the country. Before graduation, Mordecai Johnson, a graduate of Morehouse College and president of Howard University in Washington, D.C., offered Mays the deanship of the School of Religion. Mays accepted the position and worked to make Howard an outstanding institution among divinity schools.

From 1934 to 1940, Mays served as dean of Howard University's School of Religion. While serving as dean, Mays achieved a higher graduate enrollment, an adequate library, accreditation by the American Association of Theological Schools, and an improvement of the school's plant. Mays continued to show an interest in racism and race relations. In 1939, while leading a conference on Christian Youth and Race, he realized that the racism was not limited to the United States. He was disturbed to hear Christian delegates from South Africa boldly defend segregation as the will of God. His observance of such intolerance further challenged him to work against racism.

The Morehouse Years

With administrative experience and an international perspective, Mays ended his tenure at Howard University in 1940. He became the sixth president of the school that gave him his first teaching post, Morehouse College. He offered a bright vision to the school during a time of low morale.

Mays's administration did not follow business as usual. He understood the need for a larger endowment and higher salaries professors. Despite the fact that some of the students struggled to meet tuition costs, Mays initiated a strict policy where students paid their tuition and other school costs prior to attending classes. No student was allowed to graduate with outstanding debt. Mays's strict business mind and financial emphasis earned him the nickname, "Buck Bennie." Although Morehouse attracted good students, Mays worked to enroll even better students. He also realized a need for scholars on the faculty in order to prepare Morehouse students for competitive graduate schools. Several graduates of Morehouse returned to teach after earning doctoral degrees from prestigious graduate schools. They brought the kind of scholarship that Mays had outlined for the college. In the early 1940s, two Morehouse sons returned to teach, including Hugh M. Gloster, who succeeded Mays as president in 1967.

Mays recognized that the greatness of a college resides in its financial strength and community. He used his striking good looks and winning smile to encourage Morehouse alumni to increase their donations. He enjoyed an enormous amount of popularity as the college's president. Faculty and students alike saw Mays as personable and committed to the welfare and growth of the college. He emphasized that students possess strong values in his 1957 Ninetieth Anniversary of the College statement, quoted by Edward A. Jones in *A Candle in the Dark.* Mays said, "Morehouse has always encouraged the student to make maximum use of his mind . . . to [develop] integrity and sound character."

Mays inspired Martin Luther King Jr., who graduated from Morehouse in 1948. As a mentor, he advised King during seminary school and the early days of his civil rights leadership. Mays felt that the chapel gatherings at Morehouse brought them together. In *Born to Rebel,* Mays stated that he "was not aware how deeply he was impressed by what I said and did until he wrote *Stride Toward Freedom.* . . . In public addresses he often referred to me as his 'spiritual mentor.'" On April 9, 1968, Mays delivered the eulogy of Martin Luther King at the service on the campus of Morehouse.

King's great oratory skills were inspired by Mays's sermons, addresses, and lectures. An eloquent speaker, Mays captivated audiences with his engaging style and resonant voice. Throughout his career, countless people found inspiration in his speeches and words of wisdom. *Remembering Bennie Mays* stated that he may be remembered best for these words: "It is not a disgrace not to reach the stars, but it is a disgrace to have no stars to reach for. Not failure, but low aim is sin."

Mays greatly contributed to Morehouse's national reputation. As dean of Howard University's School of Religion, he strove to place historically black colleges and universities on the same plane as white institutions. In 1957 the Committee on Accreditation of the Southern Association of Colleges and Secondary Schools granted Morehouse College full membership. Mays achieved one of his major goals, which was, according to *A Candle in the Dark,* to place Morehouse "on equal footing with the best institutions serving white students." The second victory of this nature came in 1967 when Phi Beta Kappa gave a chapter to Morehouse. Mays was instrumental in providing Morehouse not only with a strong national reputation, but with international recognition as well. His contact with outside lending sources and philanthropists allowed the faculty to receive travel grants and scholarships. In the late 1950s, European Summer Travel Grants were awarded to many faculty families.

During his 27 years as president, Mays continually wrote and published. His first book, *The Negro's God,* was published two years before he assumed the presidency at Morehouse. In his book, *Seeking to Be a Christian in Race Relations,* Mays opposed the argument that segregation was a Christian institution by stating that "from its inception the Christian church had in its membership people of different nations, races and colors." The book also applauded the nonviolent civil rights demonstrations of the 1950s and 1960s. In 1960, Mays, along with the other Atlanta University presidents, supported the student activists and their statement on human equality by paying for their manifesto to appear in three Atlanta newspapers. After retiring from Morehouse, Mays wrote his autobiography, *Born to Rebel,* and a companion work, *The People Have Driven Me On.* He also wrote chapters in 15 other books, more than 70 magazine articles, and more than 1,000 articles for the *Pittsburgh Courier.*

In 1965 Morehouse's alumni magazine, *The Alumnus,* recognized Mays as the most effective president in Morehouse history. This issue outlined his accomplishments in expanding the institution and raising its standards. He increased the number of faculty members holding doctorates from 1.3 to over 54 percent. Forty percent of Morehouse graduates who earned doctorates were students under his presidency. He also expanded the campus to include 18 additional buildings. In 1967, after serving for more than a quarter of a century, Mays retired as Morehouse College's sixth president. The following year he served as a visiting professor at Michigan State University.

Mays served as president on Atlanta Board of Education and served from 1969 until his retirement in 1981. The same year Atlanta's city council named a high school and a street in his honor. The city council of Greenwood County, South Carolina, followed by naming Mays Crossroad after him. Mays also received 28 honorary degrees, including doctorates from Harvard, Boston, and Brandeis universities and from the school that he led for 27 years, Morehouse College. In 1984 Benjamin Mays died at his home at the age of 90.

On the 100–year anniversary of his birth in 1994, Morehouse College honored its revered president by dedicating the Benjamin Elijah Mays National Memorial. The memorial, completed in 1995, is located on the campus in front of the oldest dormitory, Graves Hall. It has a larger–than–life bronze statue of Mays, a plaza and a half–moon wall made of Georgia marble. The wall is engraved with selected quotations from his works. His remains, along with those of Sadie Gray Mays, are interred at this memorial. Also at this site are historical items, photographs, and letters held in a time capsule, which will be opened in the year 2095.

REFERENCES

Jones, Edward A. *A Candle in the Dark.* Valley Forge, PA: Judson Press, 1967.

Mays, Benjamin. *Born to Rebel: An Autobiography.* New York: Charles Scribner's Sons, 1971.

———. *Seeking to Be a Christian in Race Relations.* New York: Friendship Press, 1957.

''Remembering Bennie Mays.'' *The Alumnus: Morehouse College Alumni Magazine* 56 (Summer 1995): 18–21.

COLLECTIONS

The papers of Benjamin E. Mays are in the Moorland–Spingarn Research Center, Howard University, Washington, D.C.

Horace L. Griffin

Willie Mays

Willie Mays

(1931–)

Baseball player

For 22 years American baseball was graced with the presence of Willie Mays. He is known as the finest all–around player to pick up a bat. Because Mays could hit, throw, and run as well as—or better than—anyone, he became the prototype of the complete player and set a new standard for professional baseball.

William Howard Mays Jr. was born on May 6, 1931, in Fairfield, Alabama. He was the only child of William Howard and Anna Sattlewhite Mays. Both parents were only 16 years old at the time of Mays's birth. His father worked in the steel mill of the all–black town situated just 13 miles from Birmingham. Although the town was all black, all of the social services except the schools were white. The doctor who delivered Willie Mays charged the young parents a fee of $11 for his trouble. It is said that the doctor noticed the infant's exceptionally large hands which seemed to connect directly to his wrist without the customary tapering. Who would have suspected that those were the hands of a major league baseball hall–of–famer.

William Howard Mays Sr., himself a baseball player, was a pitcher for the Negro amateur leagues. Mays Sr. played catch with his son by the time the young boy was able to walk. The elder Mays inherited the name ''Cat'' from his own father, Walter Mays, known as ''Kitty Cat'' for his lithe style when playing the outfield with the Birmingham Black Barons of the Negro League. Willie Mays's mother was a former high school track star, making the future New York and San Francisco Giant heir to the athletic abilities of both parents.

When Willie Mays was three years old his parents divorced. He continued to live with his father who brought in a homeless woman to care for the three–year–old. Her name was Sarah, and Willie Mays called her Aunt. He also continued in close contact with his mother who remarried. She and her second husband, Frank McMorris, produced ten children. Willie Mays has two half brothers and eight half sisters.

In 1937 Willie Mays began his education in a segregated school in Alabama. His father coached Willie in the rudiments of baseball, and Mays's fondest memories were the weekends and vacations that allowed him the freedom to play ball, sit in the dugout when ''Cat'' played with the Industrial League, and listen to the older men talk about perfect strategy and winning techniques. In the fall of 1946, Mays entered Fairfield Industrial High School where his mother had been a track star. He took courses in the dry cleaning trade. Mays was a top athlete in high school. He played football and basketball, and ran track; the school had no baseball team. Had there been a baseball team it probably would not have challenged Mays who at 13 was already playing semiprofessional ball with the Gray Sox. At age 14 he played with his father as an outfielder on the Birmingham Industrial League—Willie played center field while his father played left field.

When Willie Mays was 16, his father called a friend, Lorenzo (Piper) Davis, the manager of the Black Barons. Davis arranged for Mays to try out for the team. Piper Davis, who became both mentor and coach to the baseball prodigy, signed Mays as a utility outfielder.

When school was in session, Willie Mays was allowed only to play on Sundays when the team was in the Birmingham area. During the summer, however, he joined the Black Barons on the road. Mays was on a team with men who were ten years his senior. He made his professional debut on July 4, 1948, in a doubleheader. The older men grumbled when Piper Davis put Mays into the starting lineup in the second game. Mays played center field and left field; he hit "one for three" balls on the average. He was good. Even those men who were determined to complain about any young rookie on the team were soon silenced by Mays's indisputable talent. Following his debut, Mays became the regular center fielder for the team. He spent the next two years with the Black Barons. During this time he sharpened his skills as a player.

Moves into Major Leagues

When Mays graduated from Fairfield High School on June 20, 1950, the New York Giants paid the Black Barons $10,000 for Willie Mays and paid Mays a personal bonus of $5,000.

Racial integration permeated the political agenda of the 1950s, as was characterized in a statement by Chief Justice Earl Warren of the U.S. Supreme Court—that separate but equal had no place in America. When Jackie Robinson "broke the color line" and joined major league baseball in 1945, black Americans applauded. Then Satchel Paige signed with a major league in 1948. When the Giants signed a teenager like Mays, the youngest black man ever signed by the "big leagues" (as the majors were called) some but not all saw it as a welcome opportunity. Others realized the potential jeopardy to the Negro leagues. Charles Einstein points out in *Willie's Time* that within two years of Mays's joining the Giants, two of the better Negro baseball leagues collapsed.

For Willie Mays baseball was a path of escape, out of the steel mills of a blatantly racist and segregated South, but soon after a Civil Rights Movement emerged with enough force to change the South and to call into question his own commitment to the cause. As Mays played his way up from poverty, he remained silent about racism and other injustice done to him and to other blacks. Twenty years after he graduated from Fairfield Industrial High School, a staunch segregationist sent the building up in flames; it was completely destroyed by a fire bomb to avert the impending integration of the school. In the course of the next decade and a half, the town of Fairfield would effectively disappear, and the city of Birmingham, Alabama would come to symbolize for the world the violent hatred of white racism unleashed on unarmed men, women, and children. For black athletes such as Mays who had attained success in the white society, the times were bittersweet.

Mays's first assignment with the Giants was with the Class B Inter–State League in Trenton, New Jersey. During the 1950 season he played 81 games with a .353 batting average. This earned him a promotion to the Minneapolis Millers, a Triple A American Association team also owned by the Giants. Mays's favorite baseball player was Joe DiMaggio. Mays studied DiMaggio and copied and practiced his swing, perfecting it with personal fineness. In 1951 Mays played 35 games; his batting average was .477; he hit eight home runs. His performance opened the door for his major league debut.

On May 25, 1951, Willie Mays became the number three hitter in the New York Giants' starting lineup; his position was center field. The game at Shibe Park in Philadelphia was disappointing for Mays who failed to hit the ball in the five times he was at bat, but manager Leo Durocher never doubted Mays's ability. Despite the batting slump, Mays's fielding remained phenomenal.

Willie Mays had escaped the grueling work of the Birmingham steel mills, but he had yet to escape the prejudice that caused Martin Luther King Jr. to dub Birmingham the most racist city in America. In the 1951 World Series, the presence of three black players in the outfield provoked an anonymous and racially charged note to the stadium press box. According to Einstein, the note read:

> Willie Mays is in a daze
> And Thompson's lost his vigor
> But Irvin whacks for all the blacks—
> It's great to be a nigger.

One year earlier, in 1950, racial bias in Sioux City had prevented Mays from joining the team there. In fact, had it not been for the lackluster performance of the New York Giants in 1951, Durocher might not have elevated Mays to the majors quite so quickly. Mays hit only .182 in the World Series that year but hit 20 home runs and achieved a .274 batting average for the season. He was named the National League Rookie of the Year for 1951. He was only 20 years old.

The Korean conflict of 1950–53 interrupted Mays's career. He was drafted by the U.S. Army in May of 1952. At the time when Mays entered the service, black people were not even allowed to drink from the same water fountain as whites in the South. Despite his success Mays was still one of only a few blacks in major league baseball. Mays went to help his country safeguard democracy abroad, while the failures and restraints on his own freedom prevailed in America. Mays's military career was without incident. He was stationed at Fort Eustis, Virginia and assigned to the physical training department. He continued to play baseball with the army team and was never stationed overseas.

Mays received an honorable discharge in March of 1954. The Giants were in Phoenix for spring training and when Mays rejoined them a reporter for *Newsweek* wrote, "A front–office official gloated: 'There's the pennant.'" Mays was back doing what he loved best, and the Giants captured the National League Pennant. They also won World Series against the Cleveland Indians in four straight games. It was during this series that Mays made the most talked about fielding play in World Series history. In the eighth inning of the first game, with the score tied at three, Vic Wertz of the Indians hit what should have been an extra–base hit that would have driven in more than one run; however, Mays caught the ball on the fly over his shoulder and, immediately wheeling around, threw back to the infield. This quick–thinking play allowed only one runner to reach home plate. The Giants promptly re–tied the game and then won it in the tenth inning.

In October of 1954, Mays was named Player of the Year by *Sporting News,* and in December the Associated Press poll of sportswriters and sportscasters voted him Male Athlete of the Year. He also received the 1954 B'nai B'rith Sports Award—a diamond–studded belt valued at $10,000, and he made appearances on the *Ed Sullivan Show* and the *Colgate Comedy Hour.* Although Mays achieved high visibility, he never developed airs. Whenever the Giants played in New York, Mays boarded at Mrs. Anne Goosby's rooming house in Harlem and he played street ball with the neighborhood youth.

In February of 1955, Mays moved to Englewood, New Jersey. In his home state of Alabama, the bus boycott started by Rosa Parks had gained world attention. That was the same year Emmitt Till, a 14–year–old, was lynched in Money, Mississippi. Mays never spoke out publicly about the racial events taking place in his home state and throughout the South. He adopted an apolitical stance and he focused his anger instead on the little ''white'' ball. He slugged at every pitch with all the power and fury he might have directed toward the enemies of black liberation, and he racked up 51 home runs in the 1955 season. Mays is one of only seven players in the history of baseball to hit more than 50 home runs in a single season. He is not a large man physically standing only 5 feet 11 inches tall; he always kept his weight around 175 pounds. For his size he was a surprisingly powerful hitter. He was also quick and able to run and steal bases, perhaps because of a healthy appetite. (Mays has also been described as a hardy eater.)

The end of 1955 brought to a close Mays's bachelor days as well as his relationship with Leo Durocher. Durocher, who was replaced by Bill Rigney as manager, had shown an exceptional interest in the young Mays, and treated him with fatherly kindness and respect.

In May of 1956 Mays married Marguerite Wendell. They adopted an infant son named Michael in 1958. That marriage ended in divorce in 1963. In November 1971, Mays married Mae Louise Allen.

New York fans loved Willie Mays, so when at the end of 1957 season the Giants moved to San Francisco, it was not an easy transition for Mays nor his fans. Californians were cool towards Mays. They already had a hero, a native son in the person of Mays's hero, the great Joe DiMaggio; they did not intend for anyone to upstage their hometown idol. Although they booed Willie Mays they could not ignore his skill and talent. He played every game as though it were the World Series. His brilliant performances, ready smile, and ''say hey!'' greeting, for which he was dubbed the ''Say Hey Kid,'' eventually won the hearts and admiration of San Franciscans.

Willie Mays catching a fly ball in the 1954 World Series.

In 1961 Mays turned 30. He had mastered the shifting winds at Candlestick Park, and hit four home runs in a single game, becoming only the fifth player to ever do so. In 1962 he took the Giants to another World Series, with 141 runs batted in. But 1963, framed in violence and tumultuous change, began with the June assassination of NAACP field secretary, Medgar Evers; a legendary civil rights March on Washington; and a September bombing that killed four young black girls at a Baptist church in Birmingham. The turbulent year finally ended with the murder of President John Kennedy and was for Willie Mays a year of personal upheaval as well. His first marriage had ended in 1961, but the court proceedings took place in 1963. In his autobiography, *Say Hey,* Mays wrote: ''Going through a divorce put an awful strain on me. The court hearings were going on during the '63 season . . . my financial state was a mess at the time of my divorce.''

In 1964 manager Alvin Dark appointed Mays captain of the Giants. The action by Dark was suspect because of the timing. Dark was embroiled in a controversy over racist comments he had made. As Jackie Robinson relates in his book, Dark, it seemed, was trying to repair his image. In essence he had said that blacks were moving too fast in the South and should slow their strides toward freedom. Mays, in his own autobiography, rallied to Dark's defense saying, ''I knew what Dark was saying. I was from the South, and so was he. I understood what he was talking about.''

Mays commented further that several months later Dark was quoted as saying, ''We have trouble because we have so many Spanish–speaking and Negro players on the team. They are just not able to perform up to the white ball player when it comes to mental alertness.'' Mays relates that he told the angry black and Hispanic players, ''We had a pennant to win. Forget what he said in the story. What was he like when it mattered?'' He succeeded in getting the men to play, but the Giants lost the pennant anyway.

Legend in Residence

Willie Mays hit 52 home runs in 1965. Herman Franks took over as manager of the Giants and Mays assumed the role as assistant, though without the official title. He also became the national spokesperson for the Job Corps. As usual Mays remained politically neutral and seemingly oblivious to the socio–economic and political world in which he played ball. In his book he observed, ''I seemed to have entered a new phase: legend in residence. With that hallowed status goes an insistence by some people that I also be able to solve the world's problems, or at least those troubling America. This, I refused to do. I had a narrow framework of operations I was comfortable with and that I enjoyed doing.'' When asked why he did not publicly support the Civil Rights Movement, according to the *Encyclopedia of African–American Culture and History,* he said: ''I don't picket in the streets of Birmingham. I'm not mad at the people who do. Maybe they shouldn't be mad at the people who don't.''

In 1965 it was black power not civil rights that disrupted the nation. The assassination of the Nation of Islam's Malcolm X in February, and the summertime riots in Watts in California, evoked no comment from Mays. When the violence hit home—that is when the situation affected baseball—and a curfew in San Francisco caused the closure of Candlestick Park, according to Mays he recorded the following:

> San Francisco was hit by some bad racial riots. Mayor Shelley asked the Giants to telecast their game with the Braves. A special feature of the broadcast was a tape–recorded message I read for the fans in which I didn't mention a problem. I didn't tell the youngsters to stay home. But I was credited with helping to calm the volatile situation. I simply said, ''Root for your home team. I know I'll be out there in centerfield trying my best.''

The Giants traded Mays to the New York Mets in 1972; they never indicated that a trade was being discussed. Instead, Mays found out from Red Foley, a New York reporter. Mays retired in 1973.

Mays was inducted into the Black Hall of Fame 1974, and in 1979 he was the sole player inducted into the Baseball Hall of Fame and only the ninth to succeed on the first nomination. In 1980 he was inducted into the San Francisco Hall of Fame. That same year he received the A. Philip Randolph Award.

Mays is an avid golfer with a nine handicap, and a neat dresser. He presides over Say Hey, Inc., a foundation for disadvantaged youth, and he enjoys talking to young people about the most important part of his life—baseball.

Current address: Say Hey Inc., 51 Mount Vernon Lane, Atherton, CA 94026.

REFERENCES

Contemporary Black Biography. Vol. 3. Detroit: Gale Research, 1993.

Current Biography Yearbook. New York: H. W. Wilson, 1955.

Einstein, Charles. *Willie's Time.* New York: Lippincott, 1973.

''He Came to Win.'' *Time* 64 (26 July 1954): 46–51.

''May Days.'' *Newsweek* 63 (4 May 1964): 86.

Mays, Willie, with Lou Sahadi. *Say Hey: The Autobiography of Willie Mays.* New York: Simon and Schuster, 1988.

Salzman, Jack, ed. *Encyclopedia of African–American Culture and History.* New York: Macmillan, 1996,

Sullivan, George. *Willie Mays.* New York: Putnams, 1973.

Nagueyalti Warren

Elijah McCoy
(1843–1929)
Inventor

One of the most noted black inventors in the United States, Elijah McCoy revolutionized the maintenance of locomotive and stationary engines by inventing a self–lubricating device—a small cup that supplied drops of oil to moving parts while they operated, thus increasing productivity. Although he received approximately 45 patents, most of them were for various lubricating devices, each representing an improvement over its predecessor. He became internationally known for his inventions. Born on March 27, 1843, in Colchester, Ontario, Canada, Elijah McCoy was the son of George and Mildred Goins McCoy, both former slaves in Kentucky who escaped to Canada in 1837. George McCoy joined the Canadian Army and, after his honorable discharge, received 160 acres of farmland in Colchester. Elijah McCoy completed grammar school and mechanical school while working on his father's farm. When Elijah McCoy turned 15, his father sent him to Edinburgh, Scotland, to study mechanical engineering. McCoy spent five years in Scotland, returning to Canada as a master mechanic and engineer. A year later he moved to the United States in search of work in his field.

McCoy accepted the best offer available, that of railroad fireman on the Michigan Central Railroad. Since wood was used in the engines, oil had to be applied to its steam chest to lubricate the machines; the workers stood on the running board and poured in the oil. Convinced that there was a better way to add lubrication, McCoy believed that he could provide the way.

McCoy began to experiment with automatic lubricators for steam engines. On June 23, 1972, he received patent No. 129,843 for his lubricator. He assigned his first patent to William and S. C. Hamlin of Ypsilanti, but retained the second for himself. Never satisfied with his work, McCoy

Elijah McCoy

continued to work toward a perfect invention. He granted his third patent, assigned on May 27, 1873, and his fourth, granted on January 20, 1874, to S. M. McCutchen and E. P. Allen of Ypsilanti.

According to the *Ypsilanti Commercial* of July 21, 1872, cited in *The "Real McCoy" of Ypsilanti,* local reaction to McCoy's inventions was mixed. One local engineer praised the device as "the very best lubricating cup I have ever used" while others objected to the invention, calling it "a nigger oilcup" invented by a "coon." Notwithstanding these objections, railroad officials accepted the device, and many came to Ypsilanti to talk with McCoy. The officials hired McCoy to supervise the installation of oilcups on locomotives and to instruct engineers and technicians on their use. Most of the railroad locomotives in operation in the United States between 1872 and 1915 were fitted with McCoy's lubricators. Steamships and factories also adopted his oil device. No piece of heavy equipment was considered complete unless the McCoy system was in place.

Folk etymology claims those who sought out his devices insisted that they wanted "the real McCoy," and nothing else. The evidence that the phrase "the real McCoy" originated in reference to Elijah McCoy's lubricating devices is inconclusive. A. P. Marshall emphasized in the introduction to *The "Real McCoy" of Ypsilanti,* "there have been several 'Real McCoys' in America's past. . . . We can be fairly certain that the term now means 'the real and authentic' thing."

McCoy continued to evolve his invention: between 1872 and 1876 he obtained six patents for lubricators and one for an ironing table. Apparently he interrupted his work for six years. By 1882 he had moved to Detroit and lived at 5730 Lincoln, later residing at 180 Rowens Street. Between 1886 and 1926 he was very productive; some sources claim that he received about 45 patents while others report that he received more than 50. All except eight of these were for lubricating devices.

In April of 1915 McCoy patented an invention that he called his best: the graphite lubricator. It reflected his continuous efforts to improve his lubricators and was designed to eliminate difficulties in oiling the superheater engine. To manufacture and market his lubricator, he organized the Elijah McCoy Manufacturing Company in 1920. Other patents granted McCoy included the steam dome for locomotives (June 16, 1885); scaffold support (June 4, 1907); valve and plug–cock (June 30, 1914); vehicle wheel tire (October 2, 1923); and a rubber heel (November 10, 1925). By 1923 he had become well–known throughout the manufacturing industry. His inventions also were patented in such foreign countries as Great Britain, France, Germany, Austria, and Russia.

Aside from his inventions, McCoy spent his time counseling Detroit's youth and encouraging them to apply themselves to hard work so that they, too, might become productive.

McCoy married Ann Elizabeth Stewart (1847–1872) on February 7, 1868. Nothing more is known about her life. On February 25, 1873, he married Mary Eleanora Delaney Brownlow, who was born in Lawrenceburg, Indiana, in 1846 and died in 1923. They had one child. A philanthropist and clubwoman, Mary McCoy had a profound influence on her husband's life and work. When he was 80–years old, McCoy was still active in the community. After 1926, however, his health began to fail. He was admitted to Eloise Infirmary, Eloise, Michigan, in 1928 and died on October 10, 1929. He was buried in Detroit.

According to A. P. Marshall, McCoy is among those important African Americans who died without due recognition in his era. It was only as a result of a resurgence of public interest in historical African American figures during the latter 1960s that his reputation achieved the prominence it merited. He is remembered as a pioneer inventor who helped increase the productivity of America's industrial machines.

REFERENCES

"Elijah McCoy (1843–1929)." *Ebony* 22 (December 1966): 157.

Hayden, Robert C. *Eight Black American Inventors.* Reading, MA: Addison–Wesley, 1972.

Malone, Dumas, ed. *Dictionary of American Biography.* New York: Charles Scribner's Sons, 1943.

Marshall, Albert P. *The "Real McCoy" of Ypsilanti.* Ypsilanti, MI: Marlan Publishers, 1989.

Michigan Freedmen's Progress Commission. *Michigan Manual of Freedmen's Progress.* Compiled by Francis H. Warren. 1915. Reprint, Detroit: John M. Green, 1985.

Smith, Jessie Carney, ed. *Notable Black American Women.* Detroit: Gale Research, 1992.

Who Was Who in America. Chicago: Marquis, 1968.
Who Was Who in America. Historical Volume 1607–1896. Rev. Ed. Chicago: Marquis, 1967.

COLLECTIONS

Biographical information, pictures, and models of Elijah McCoy's oil cup are in the files of the Ypsilanti Historical Museum and the Burton Historical Collection of the Detroit Public Library.

Frederick Douglas Smith Jr.

Wade H. McCree Jr.

(1920–1987)

U.S. Solicitor–General, judge, lawyer, educator

Wade H. McCree Jr.

Wade H. McCree Jr. devoted his career to the legal profession as the second black U.S. solicitor–general, and also as a judge in three different courts in the state of Michigan. He served first on the Wayne State Circuit Court, then in the U.S. District Court for the Eastern Division of Michigan and the U.S. Court of Appeals for the Sixth Circuit Court. He had a lasting concern for civil and human rights.

Born on July 3, 1920, in Des Moines, Iowa, Wade Hampton McCree Jr. was the son of Wade Hampton McCree Sr., a pharmacist and federal narcotics inspector, and Lula Hannah Harper McCree, a teacher and librarian who had worked with pioneer black educator Mary McLeod Bethune. The McCrees had another son and two daughters. The family lived in Des Moines until McCree Sr. became an inspector for the U.S. Food and Drug Administration and moved his family first to Hilo, Hawaii, then to Chicago and on to Boston. McCree Jr. graduated from Boston Latin School and planned to enter the University of Iowa until he learned that black students were denied space in the residence halls. He enrolled in Fisk University in Nashville, Tennessee, and graduated in 1941 summa cum laude with an A.B. degree. In 1942 he entered Harvard Law School on a scholarship, but his studies were soon interrupted when he was called to active duty as an enlisted man in the U.S. Army during World War II. He won the Combat Infantry Badge and the Bronze Star for combat in Italy. After four years of service during which time he won promotion to captain, McCree continued at Harvard Law School in 1946 and received an LL.B. degree in 1948, ranked twelfth in his class.

McCree practiced law in Detroit with Harold G. Bledsoe's firm. He and Bledsoe campaigned for G. Mennen Williams, who was elected governor of Michigan in 1948. Williams then appointed McCree to the State Workmen's Compensation Board as a Workmen's Compensation commissioner. In 1954 he appointed McCree a judge of the Wayne County Circuit Court, making him the second black to sit as a judge on a court of record in Michigan. He won reelection the year after his appointment and served in the position altogether for seven years, although naysayers predicted that a black judge would not win a county–wide election. While on that bench McCree encouraged able black lawyers to seek judgeships. He also was an adjunct faculty member of law schools at Wayne State University and the University of Detroit. President John F. Kennedy in 1961 appointed McCree to the U.S. District Court for the Eastern District of Michigan, where he served until 1966 when President Lyndon B. Johnson named him to the U.S. Court of Appeals for the Sixth Circuit in Cincinnati. He remained in that post until 1977, the first black to hold the position. While on that bench he was involved in several civil rights appeals that included school desegregation cases in Michigan, Ohio, and Tennessee and earned a reputation for being highly prepared.

Named U.S. Solicitor–General

McCree resigned from the appeals court to become solicitor–general under President Jimmy Carter, a position he held until 1981. He was the second of three blacks—the others were Thurgood Marshall, who was appointed in 1965, and Drew S. Days III, who was appointed in 1994. In the *Detroit Sunday News Magazine,* McCree defined the solicitor–general as "the architect of the federal government's appeal policy." Since the U.S. Supreme Court "makes law" for this country, the solicitor–general can affect law himself through the cases that he chooses to take to the high court. He argued a controversial case related to the Hyde amendment, the legal basis that Congress used to cut off federal support for Medicaid abortions. He argued the affirmative action case *Bakke v. the University of California at Davis,* the first major reverse discrimination case heard in the U.S. Supreme Court. In the case, Alan Bakke, a white applicant, challenged the university for refusing his application and accepting minority applicants who he contended were less qualified. In the final ruling, the Supreme Court, influenced by McCree's argument, ordered the school to admit Bakke but upheld affirmative action under certain guidelines. Quoted in the *Detroit News* for August 31, 1987, former attorney general Griffin Bell said that the case was "the most significant civil rights controversy to come before them (the judges) since the school desegregation cases of 1954."

When he left office as solicitor–general, in 1981 McCree was appointed Lewis Simes Professor of Law and the University of Michigan and brought with him a reputation as a distinguished jurist and public official. He taught courses on constitutional litigation, the legal profession, and constitutional law.

Beyond the classroom and courtroom, he served on numerous boards. He served the legal profession as member of more than 50 committees, councils, and boards. He was a fellow of the American Bar Association, a member of the Council of the American Law Institute, the Institute of Judicial Administration, the Executive Committee of the Association of American Law Schools, and the U.S. Judicial Conference Standing Committee on Rules of Practice and Procedures. He was a founding trustee of Friends School in Detroit; a trustee of Fisk University; a member of the visiting committees of Harvard Law School and Mercer University Law School; an overseer of Harvard College and the University of Pennsylvania Law School; and a member of the visiting committees of law schools at Wayne State University, the University of Chicago, Case Western Reserve, and the University of Miami. McCree was a member of the American, Michigan, Detroit, Wolverine and other bar associations; the NAACP, the Kappa Alpha Psi Fraternity, and numerous other religious, fraternal, civic, and social organizations. He held honorary degrees from more than 30 colleges and universities, including an LL.D. from Harvard in 1969.

As successful as he was, it is said that the primary disappointment that McCree experienced in his career was that he never served on the U.S. Supreme Court, where he thought he deserved a place. While on Michigan's law faculty, however, the U.S. Supreme Court did appoint him as a special master, which enabled him to hear three cases.

McCree had a broad range of interests: poetry, music, literature, and law. He had a love for education and the humanities as well as the law, and found a way to integrate these disciplines. In a commencement address in May of 1987 at the University of Colorado, quoted in the *Michigan Law Review,* he said:

> I prefer to think of the law as one of the liberal arts: liberal because it must be informed by the humanities and the social sciences, and art, because the principal task of a lawyer is dealing with uncertainties. Identifying them and crafting a response based upon his knowledge of structure even if he is ignorant of content.

The soft–spoken McCree has been described as consistently a man of integrity. He was a man of wisdom, intellect, and remarkable kindness; he had instant wit and charm. In the article "'Judge's Judge,'" his friends and associates said that humor was his hallmark. "He was able to use humor, such as his mastery of limericks, to diffuse tension" and was known to insert humor in the middle of a graceful argument.

After a brief illness, McCree died of cancer on Sunday, August 30, 1987, at Henry Ford Hospital in Detroit. He was survived by his wife, Dores B. McCrary McCree; daughter, Kathleen; twins Karen and Wade; one sister and one brother; and two grandchildren. The University of Michigan Law School honored him by devoting the *Michigan Law Review* for November of 1987 to his memory. Highly acclaimed by his faculty colleagues and students, McCree was fondly remembered by former governor G. Mennen Williams, who wrote that "few in our time have contributed as much to the human condition" as McCree. Lee C. Bollinger remembered, among other qualities, his striking gift of storytelling: he "entertained, amused, and bedazzled" his colleagues and students with a "bottomless cask of vintage stories." Judge Horace W. Gilmore wrote that he was "a fine lawyer and a fine judge" who was "always concerned with protecting the constitutional rights of all. . . . He was born to be a judge."

REFERENCES

Biography File, Michigan Biography Collection, Michigan State Library.

Clanton, Earl S., III. "Judge Wade Hampton McCree, Jr., 36th Solicitor General of the United States." *Kappa Alpha Psi Journal* 62 (April 1977): 60–63.

Funeral Program, First Unitarian Universalist Church, Detroit, Michigan, Thursday, September 3, 1987, in the author's files.

"'Judge's Judge' Wade McCree Helped Mold Law, History." *Detroit News,* September 1, 1987.

"Man of Law, Civil Rights, Wade McCree Dies at Age 67." *Detroit News,* August 31, 1987.

"McCree's Devotion, Intellect Praised." *Detroit News,* September 1, 1987.

Michigan Law Review 86 (November 1987): 217–65.

Stark, Al. "Mr. Wade McCree . . . For the Government." *Detroit Sunday News Magazine,* March 20, 1977.

De Witt S. Dykes Jr.

Claude McKay
(1890?–1948)
Writer, poet, editor

Claude McKay, Jamaican–born poet, novelist, essayist, and editor, is acknowledged by literary critics as a leading spokesman of the Harlem Renaissance or "New Negro" movement of the 1920s. Although McKay lived abroad during 12 years of this flowering of a new black aesthetic, his poems and novels reflect many social concerns voiced by other black intellectuals during a period of racial unrest and sense of alienation prevalent in a changing America following World War I. Because of his Jamaican background, however, McKay is also frequently viewed as an outsider to the main milieu of the Harlem Renaissance—a paradoxical artist whose clear sense of a West–Indian cultural heritage differed from the black American's search for a distinct identity within the U.S. mainstream. Immigrating to the United States in 1912 and joining the American expatriates in Europe just ten years later, McKay remained forever ambivalent about his adopted country. He did not become a U.S. citizen until April 13, 1940. In *Black Writers of America,* Richard Barksdale and Keneth Kinnamon quoted this fiery poet who lamented towards the end of his life that he was "a man who was bitter because he loved, who was both right and wrong because he hated the things that destroyed love, who tried to give back to others a little of what he had got from them and the continuous adventure of being a black man in a white society."

Claude McKay was born Festus Claudius McKay on September 15 in Sunny Ville, Jamaica. The exact year of McKay's birth is uncertain. For example, Harold Cruse, author of *The Crisis of the Negro Intellectual,* preferred 1890 but in a footnote suggested that 1889 or 1891 were also possible birth years. Barksdale provided the year 1889, while Tyrone Tillary in a 1992 "psychological" biography of McKay, *Claude McKay: A Black Poet's Struggle for Identity,* cited 1890. All three sources, however, agreed on September 15. McKay was the eighth and youngest surviving child of Thomas Francis and Hannah Ann Elizabeth Edwards McKay, who, although of the peasant class, lived comfortably. Wayne Cooper, author of *Claude McKay: Rebel Sojourner,* stated that the serious–minded Thomas Francis had married the gentle, teen–age Hannah Ann in 1870 following a brief courtship. After two years of marriage, the couple began their family. Of the eleven children born, only eight survived. From oldest to youngest, they were: Uriah, Mathew, Rachel, Thomas Edison, Nathaniel, Reginald, and Hubert. According to Cooper, Claude McKay "was named Festus Claudius, after a Roman governor and an emperor mentioned in the New Testament Book of Acts."

Tillary attempted to trace McKay's ambivalent or paradoxical personality back to McKay's childhood. He described the parents as having distinctly contrasting personalities. According to the biographer, Thomas Francis was a stern

Claude McKay

"fundamentalist" Baptist whose aloofness distanced him from his sensitive, youngest child. On the other hand, Hannah lavished warmth and affection on young Claude. Later in the poet's career, maintained Tillary, "McKay's love of his mother and of the natural habitat of Jamaica constituted his strongest and fondest memories of his boyhood." McKay's mother died in 1909, leaving him grief–stricken.

Influences on Intellectual Growth

From 1898 until 1901, Claude McKay lived with his oldest brother Uriah, an agnostic schoolteacher. In certain respects, this living arrangement was preferable to Claude McKay's austere home environment. McKay's brother, although strict, introduced Claude to the beauty of the printed word. Uriah enjoyed reading English classics and passed on this passion to his young charge. However, Claude McKay was also attempting to express in his own words his love for Jamaica, his homeland. Tillary stated that spiritually Claude McKay was nourished by the Jamaican folklife of Sunny Ville; McKay's homeland "remained a symbol of desired innocence to the poet." Providing a different perspective, Cooper attributed the social status and values of the family in a rural community to Claude McKay's artistic formation:

> By virtue of their superior economic position and Christian education, the dark–skinned McKays could claim a social position in Jamaican society akin to that of the traditional mulatto elite. They certainly distinguished themselves from their poorer neighbors and felt equal in every way to the

> colored elite, whose pretensions of superiority they scorned. As aspiring members of the middle class, the McKays were sensitive to any class discriminations based on skin color. . . . Claude would grow up suspicious and resentful of light mulattoes.

After returning to Clarendon Parish in 1901, McKay found several new role models who served as mentors or as father figures, as his brother Uriah had been. From 1901 until 1909, McKay also vacillated about a career. For example, from 1906 to 1909 he attended a trade school in Kingston with little or no enthusiasm. He returned home briefly, but after his mother died in 1909, McKay joined the police force in Kingston. While serving in the constabulary, McKay formed close relationships with someone known in McKay's writings only as ''Bennie'' and with an inspector on the force. Two separate poems,''To Inspector W. E. Clark'' and ''Bennie's Departure,'' recorded McKay's sorrow when each of these friends left. McKay's first volume of poetry *Constab Ballads* included the latter poem, quoted in part below and cited in Tillary's *Claude McKay*:

> De fateful day I member still
> De final breakin' o' my will,
> Again de sayin' o' good–bye,
> My poor heart's silent wilin' cry;
> My life, my soul my all
> be'n gone,
> And ever since I am alone.

While still serving on the police force, McKay met Walter Jekyll, an English aristocrat who was researching Jamaican stories. Jekyll was so impressed with McKay's poetry that he found a way to have a few printed in the *Daily Gleaner,* a local newspaper. Readers liked the poems, most of which were written in Jamaican dialect. Encouraged by Jekyll, McKay continued writing poems about Jamaica. By 1912 McKay had written two volumes of poetry—*Songs of Jamaica* and *Constab Ballads.* The poems earned the young Jamaican poet the Jamaican Medal of the Institute of Arts and Sciences. This award enabled McKay to seek his fortunes in the United States.

Immigration to America

In 1912, after a brief return to Sunny Ville in 1911, McKay immigrated to America, intending to earn a degree in agriculture at Tuskegee Institute in Alabama. According to David Levering Lewis in *When Harlem Was in Vogue,* however,:

> Rural Alabama turned out not to be the place for a fiery, black islander whose soft, lyrical voice was easily provoked into shrill profanity. He moved on to Kansas State College, almost immediately, more suitable for agriculture but not ideal for poetry, which by 1914, McKay had discovered he wanted to make his career after all. New York beckoned and money for the trip arrived from a white Jamaican patron.

Harlem in 1914 provided the intellectual and imaginative ferment for the aspiring poet. During the previous two decades and until 1920, Harlem had been a refuge for black Southerners seeking employment opportunities. The Great Migration began in 1915 as nearly two million black Americans fled the impoverished South and flocked to the urban North. This sudden influx of new workers brought attendant racial conflicts. Thus, the black American contended against the growing force of the Ku Klux Klan and other forms of racial hostility and violence.

According to Roger M. Valade III, author of *Essential Black Literature Guide,* ''This period of social upheaval and conflict inspired black intellectuals to reexamine their role in American society and their unique cultural heritage.'' McKay accepted the challenge, even though he was a young poet. The literary impetus was directed towards correcting many stereotypes of black people that had been promoted in earlier decades in art, literature, and the theater. Instead, the New Negro artists celebrated the black working class, a romantic return to the ''primitive'' past, protest against racism, and the black American's relationship with Africa.

In *The Life of Langston Hughes,* Arnold Rampersad provided information on the genesis of McKay's famous sonnet ''If We Must Die'':

> While he [Langston Hughes] had been in Mexico, black America had suffered a summer of bloodshed, notably in Chicago, that stirred Claude McKay in *The Liberator* to write his most memorable poem . . . exhorting blacks to go down fighting. . . . Between June and the end of the year [1919], Whites lynched seventy–six blacks; riots erupted in some two dozen cities.

From 1914 until characteristic wanderlust propelled him to Europe in 1919 and again in 1922, McKay was an angry, black literary voice in America. According to Tillary, once McKay moved to New York in 1914, his search for a literary publication amenable to his views led him in two directions. Initially, he was attracted to the radical publication *Masses,* which, however, rejected the young Jamaican poet's works. When this controversial voice ceased operating because of U.S. government scrutiny, it reappeared in 1918 as *The Liberator,* edited by Max Eastman. McKay's opportunities increased when Eastman, through Eastman's sister Crystal, became interested in McKay's poetry. Two of McKay's sonnets had already appeared in 1917 in *The Seven Arts,* edited by James Oppenheim, Waldo Frank, and Van Wyck Brooks. McKay used the pseudonym Eli Edwards. In 1919, with Eastman's reliable friendship to endorse him, McKay was able to have ''The Dominant White'' published in April and nine additional poems published in July—all in *The Liberator.*

By June of 1922, according to Barksdale, ''McKay was a key member of the editorial staff of *The Liberator,* and his name continued on the masthead through the final issue of October 1924. In addition to poems, he contributed essays and reviews to this important, radical journal.'' Although McKay had married Eulalie Imelda Edwards on July 30, 1914, and had one daughter from this union, the marriage had ended soon in divorce. The former wife and daughter, Rhue Hope McKay, returned to Jamaica after the marriage dissolved. Perhaps an underlying cause of the divorce was the financial hardship that McKay had endured after arriving in New York in 1914. According to Barksdale, at various times early in his career, the struggling writer worked menial kitchen jobs in hotels or held Pullman–waiter jobs.

In 1919 McKay, with the support of a patron, sailed to England, joining other American literary expatriates disillusioned with the American post–World–War I social unrest. Having been reared in Jamaica under British rule, McKay, according to Tillary, expressed for a long time a romantic notion of what this rule had been: positive and encouraging. For example, Claude McKay usually attributed the poverty and struggle of Jamaican peasants to economics, not to British oppression. Tillary quoted from a letter that McKay wrote to James Weldon Johnson in the late 1920s: "In my village, I grew up on equal terms with white, mulatto, and black children of every race because my father was a big peasant and belonged. The difference on the island is economic, not social." However, Tillary contended that an early unpublished autobiography *My Green Hills of Jamaica* fails to reveal facts to support McKay's professed idealism regarding his homeland. On the contrary, stated Tillary, "The Jamaica described in his *Green Hills* manuscript was never so idyllic, either during his childhood or at the time of the writing of the manuscript."

Only later in life did McKay express hostility towards the British when he visited England from 1919 until the spring of 1920. David Levering Lewis described the awakening:

> He discovered quickly that the average Briton had not the remotest idea that he and they shared at least a common culture of school and court, let alone any notion of equality between them. There was no more talk [i.e., by McKay] of Homeland England. England annealed the hatred within McKay, sending him back to America to become "among all black poets, . . . par excellence the poet of hate."

Lewis credited this bitter experience with racism as the cause of McKay's subsequent attraction to the social ideas of Marx, Lenin, and the Communist party even though McKay never joined the Communist party. Nevertheless, while in England, McKay was able to publish *Spring in New Hampshire,* a book of poetry. In 1922 this volume was reissued in an enlarged American edition retitled *Harlem Shadows.* The poems established McKay as a major writer of the Harlem Renaissance. Barksdale quoted I. A. Richards, a contemporary of McKay and a distinguished literary critic who wrote the preface to *Harlem Shadows,* who praised the book as "the best work that the present generation is producing in this country." The volume, which includes "If We Must Die," treats two of McKay's primary concerns: racism and violence towards black people in America and abroad.

In 1920 when McKay returned to America, he attempted to align himself with militant black intellectuals. David Levering Lewis described the difficulty in achieving this goal, given McKay's Jamaican background and, most importantly, given McKay's fierce determination to follow his own path. According to Lewis:

> The racial burden afflicting McKay was of the cruelest duality—of being *in* but not *of* two cultures. To most whites outside Greenwich Village, he was just another black man. But McKay also found himself estranged from Afro–Americans. W. E. B. Du Bois' *Souls of Black Folk* had shaken him "like an earthquake" when he read it as an agricultural student at Kansas State College. But meeting the flesh–and–blood Du Bois was "something of a personal disappointment. He seemed possessed of a cold, acid hauteur of spirit." Protesting that he "never had the slightest desire to insult Harlem society or Negro society anywhere," McKay succeeded without really trying.

In 1922 McKay again left America. Like so many writers of the Lost Generation, McKay looked towards France as the place to become most productive and most accepted as a writer. Staying in Paris, Toulon, Marseilles, or other French havens, McKay wrote copiously. For a while he lived in the former Soviet Union and in Africa as well. During these years, McKay wrote the following works: *Home to Harlem,* a novel (1928); *A Long Way from Home,* an autobiography (1927); and the novels *Banjo* (1929), *Gingertown* (1932), and *Banana Bottom* (1933). McKay's last nonfiction work was *Harlem: Negro Metropolis,* published in 1940.

Typical of McKay's writings, *Home to Harlem* celebrated the unencumbered rhythm of life of the black man's spiritual heritage. The novel, about Ray, an educated black man, trying to understand another black man, carefree Jake, a wartime deserter who returns to Harlem, elicited a range of reactions from black intellectuals. Frequently compared to Carl Van Vechten's *Nigger Heaven,* McKay's picaresque novel differed significantly from the former, according to Wayne Cooper: "It was the Harlem of the picaresque black wanderer, who found there 'down home folks' like himself trying as best they could to fashion their lives anew in an alien environment." The purpose of the Harlem Renaissance was to lift the black American's image from the shameful legacy of slavery. To the extent that his colleagues thought McKay had failed or succeeded, McKay's novel was denounced or praised. Tillary quoted from a March 1928 letter the enthusiastic response of Langston Hughes, McKay's junior, who wrote to Locke that the novel "must be the flower of the Negro Renaissance even if it is no lovely lily." McKay himself offered no apology for his graphic portrayal of the less favorable side of Harlem. David Levering Lewis quoted McKay's rebuttal to negative criticism, "I consider this book a real proletarian novel . . . but I don't expect the nice radicals to see that it is." McKay also denied any attempts to mimic *Nigger Heaven.*

In the September 29, 1928, issue of *Negro World,* Marcus Garvey condemned *Home to Harlem.* Garvey's searing, one–page article implied that McKay is like other black writers influenced by white publishers "to portray to the world the looseness, laxity, and immorality that are peculiar to our group; for the purpose of those publishers circulating the libel against us among the white peoples of the world, is to hold us up to ridicule and contempt and universal prejudice.'' Despite the range of critical responses, *Home to Harlem,* won the Harmon Gold Award for literature in 1929 and soared to the best–seller list after only 14 days. This inclusion marked the first time a novel by a black person had achieved such distinction.

McKay's final novel *Banana Bottom* was, according to Tillary, the Jamaican author's attempt to show that ''he was an artist of many moods and not simply of the primitive–exotic–picturesque.'' His theme, as in *Home to Harlem* and *Banjo,* was the prominence of folk over Western civilization. In addition, he uncharacteristically focused on a female main character.

Final Years and Return to America

In 1934 McKay returned to the United States, publishing few new works until his death in 1948. While still in Europe, stated Tillary, McKay had become solitary and had distanced himself from the Harlem–Renaissance circle. Except for Max Eastman and his patrons—the latter with whom he only grudgingly corresponded—McKay remained aloof. Tillary explained this change as due to McKay's increasing depression and bouts of dizzy spells and headaches. However, when McKay resettled in the United States, he established a friendship with the author Ellen Tarry, who led him to convert to Roman Catholicism in October of 1944.

Assessment of a Writer

Claude McKay's involvement in the rebirth of black literature during this period was itself paradoxical. For example, he fit easily into the white, avant–garde circles in New York, thus antagonizing many African American intellectuals. In addition, because McKay was Jamaican as well as much older than many African American intellectuals, his lack of exclusive political commitment to the Harlem Renaissance rendered him suspect. Harold Cruse cited Alain Locke's assessment of McKay:

> In 1937, his autobiography was reviewed by Alain Locke under the title ''Spiritual Truancy.'' There, Locke called McKay the ''playboy of the Negro Renaissance'' and accused him of ''chronic and perverse truancy'' and a ''lack of common loyalty'' for his stand–offish attitude towards the American Negro situation.

Nevertheless, sonnets such as ''Outcast,'' ''If We Must Die,'' and ''America'' evoke vividly the struggles, doubts, and aspirations of black people generally during this time period.

As a Harlem Renaissance poet of paradox, Claude McKay wrote sensitively and nostalgically about his homeland and, at the same time, bitterly about racism elsewhere. He seemed to develop love/hate relationships towards these environments that promised much but on experience and reflection denied dignity to black residents. Radical as well as romantic, McKay's poetry expressed this ambivalence—often ironically. For example, his poem ''The Harlem Dancer'' celebrates the exotic, calm grace of the ''half–clothed'' dancer: ''To me she seemed a proudly swaying palm.'' The lascivious eyes of the youth ''devour'' this graceful creature who sings hauntingly of far–away, tropical places. She herself reflects a calm beauty and serenity following a psychological storm. However, the sonnet ends with the abrupt, realistic lines:

> But looking at her falsely–smiling face,
> I knew her self was not in that strange place.

While in Chicago, McKay died on May 22, 1948, of a heart attack. His grave is located in Woodside, New York. As the quotations from ''The Harlem Dancer'' illustrate, McKay saw the good and evil influencing black society's experiences. Not all poems express such contradictions, of course. When writing poetry about Jamaica or novels of ''low–life,'' McKay captured the essence of the free but often socially maligned natural spirit. Furthermore, McKay's usual poetic structure is the sonnet but within that 14–line restriction, McKay's emotions range widely. Never acknowledging any indebtedness to prior authors' influence or even to any traditional sonneteer, McKay transformed the European sonnet structure into a vehicle to express the passionate yet paradoxical voice of the Harlem Renaissance.

REFERENCES

Barksdale, Richard, and Keneth Kinnamon. *Black Writers of America.* New York: McMillan, 1972.

Cooper, Wayne F. *Claude McKay: Rebel Sojourner in the Harlem Renaissance; A Biography.* Baton Rouge: Louisiana State University Press, 1987.

Cruse, Harold. *The Crisis of the Negro Intellectual.* New York: William Morrow, 1967.

Garvey, Marcus. ''*Home to Harlem,* Claude McKay's Damaging Book Should Earn Wholesale Condemnation of Negroes.'' *Negro World* (September 29, 1928): 11.

Lewis, David Levering. *When Harlem Was in Vogue.* New York: Oxford, 1981.

Locke, Alain. ''Spiritual Truancy.'' *New Challenge* 2 (Fall 1937) 81–85.

McKay, Claude. ''Why I Became a Catholic,'' *Ebony* 1 (March 1946): 32.

Rampersad, Arnold. *The Life of Langston Hughes.* Vol. I, 1902–1941. New York: Oxford, 1986.

Tillary, Tyrone. *Claude McKay: A Black Poet's Struggle for Identity.* Amherst: University of Massachusetts Press, 1992.

Valade, Roger M. III. *The Essential Black Literature Guide.* New York: Visible Ink Press, in association with the Schomburg Center for Research in Black Culture, 1996.

COLLECTIONS

The papers of Claude McKay are in the Beinecke Library at Yale University and in the Schomburg Center for Research in Black Culture in New York City.

Grace E. Collins

Floyd McKissick
(1922–1991)
Civil rights activist, lawyer, entrepreneur, city developer

A modern civil rights leader, Floyd McKissick believed that African Americans could never achieve equality unless they had political and economic power. A skillful and powerful leader for the Congress of Racial Equality (CORE), he assisted in the change of the organization's philosophy from nonviolence to advocation of the building of an African American base of power. His development of Soul City in Warren County, North Carolina, was to have been an experiment where all people could participate in the development of a new, harmonious city.

Floyd Boyce McKissick was born March 9, 1922, in Asheville, North Carolina to Ernest Boyce McKissick and Magnolia Ester Thompson McKissick. The McKissicks also had three daughters Geraldine, Frances, and Jean. Both parents were graduates of Livingston College in Salisbury, North Carolina, with the normal degree, a popular education degree at one time. To earn a living, Ernest McKissick became a bellman at the Vanderbilt Hotel in Asheville and Magnolia McKissick became a seamstress. Asheville, located in the western part of the state, was attractive vacation spot for the rich, especially the famous Vanderbilt family who developed the Biltmore Estate on the outskirts of the city. McKissick's maternal grandfather was a Methodist minister and his paternal grandfather was a Baptist minister.

Growing up in Asheville, Floyd McKissick had a normal childhood, playing baseball, going to church, joining the boy scouts, ice skating, attending school and, working at odd jobs. He built a wagon and created small jobs, such as delivering ice to the housewives. He also built wagons for other boys. Two childhood incidents etched a permanent picture of racism in his memory. While traveling with his aunt on the trolley car, he became inquisitive about the duties of the motorman, and when he and several white youngsters approached the motorman, the man told him he must learn to stay in his place. Another racial incident occurred when he was a boy scout. As he and other African American children were ice skating in a public arena, he moved too close to the rope that served as boundary between the white skaters and them. He was admonished, attacked by a white policemen, and taken to jail, although he was neither formally arrested nor held in custody. The memory of African American families who reacted as if he had done something wrong lingered after the experience with the policeman.

McKissick finished high school in Asheville and wanted to attend Morehouse College in Atlanta, Georgia, because the college offered pre–law courses. McKissick's interest in becoming a lawyer was sparked as a child by his maternal grandfather would have him practice as a minister and also act as a lawyer in mock trials.

Floyd McKissick

Struggle for Quality Education

McKissick worked a summer job and saved $40 for his tuition at Morehouse. Although he lacked $75 of the full amount, Morehouse admitted him. To help pay his college expenses, he was given a campus job as a waiter in the dining hall and became the personal waiter to W. E. B. Du Bois. Tobacco farms in the area provided jobs and helped many Morehouse students defray their expenses. McKissick joined the tobacco crews to earn money. Obtaining a college education was uppermost in McKissick's mind. Although he passed his subjects, the times were troublesome for all young men. World War II began in 1941; McKissick left school and enlisted in the army, serving as a sergeant in the European Theater; he also received a Purple Heart and five battle stars.

After the war, McKissick returned to his native state of North Carolina and served as youth chairman for the NAACP and worked for the Congress of Racial Equality (CORE). At that time CORE was pacifist group seeking racial equality. McKissick again faced the harsh reality of segregation when he joined CORE's Journey for Reconciliation Ride to test bus segregation in the upper regions of the South in 1947.

McKissick's application to the University of North Carolina's (UNC) law school was ignored. He worked for a year as a waiter and with the added support of the GI bill for education, McKissick returned to Morehouse for a year and achieved honor roll status. With two years of college behind him, he was eligible to enter law school. With the backing of Thurgood Marshall and the NAACP Legal Defense Fund, he filed a suit for admittance to the UNC's law school.

During the waiting period he enrolled in law school at North Carolina College (now North Carolina Central University) in Durham. At that time, graduate and professional schools were established in many parts of the South to train African Americans and keep them from attending the historically white institutions. The law school at NCC was one of these. While in law school, he joined others in pressuring the North Carolina legislature to appropriate more funds for the law school to meet accreditation requirements. Although they succeeded in obtaining money for the school to upgrade its facilities, the facilities were unequal to those of the white UNC at Chapel Hill. During McKissick's senior year in law school, UNC's law school admitted him, even though all of his credits were done at NCC. Quoted in *Contemporary Black Leaders,* he said: "Technically I finished North Carolina College because I had all my credits and honors *before* I got into the University of North Carolina." He was awarded a degree from UNC School of Law in 1951 and was the first black to receive a Doctor of Laws (LL.D.) degree from the school.

McKissick passed the state bar in 1952 and joined the law firm of Birt and Berry in Durham. After three years of general law practice, McKissick started his own firm; civil rights cases became one his specialties. He represented a wide variety of clients, including labor unions, and churches.

Leads CORE

McKissick served CORE as director of the Durham, North Carolina chapter. CORE had been founded in 1942 and McKissick began his stint with the organization in 1947. Called a maverick lawyer, he worked with the student activists in Greensboro who, in 1960, planned and initiated sit–in movements in Greensboro and other North Carolina cities.

McKissick held other important positions in CORE. He served as national chairman from 1963 to 1966 and represented the organization in the 1963 March on Washington. In 1966, when James Farmer left office, McKissick was unanimously elected national director of the organization at the CORE convention.

Under McKissick's leadership CORE, at first $4 million in debt, raised $1 million and was well on the way to financial solvency. McKissick's legal training was a positive factor in this financial gain. While at CORE, McKissick guided the organization through the alteration of its mission to emphasize African American empowerment.

With the passing of the Voting Rights Act and the imminent political shift of power in certain communities, African Americans had to be qualified to participate in the new process. After serving CORE for 18 months, McKissick was granted leave to begin a training program to help African Americans acquire responsible leadership skills to make political, economic, and social decisions. The program was financed by the Ford Foundation.

While living in New York, he formed the Floyd McKissick Enterprises and from this sprung assistance to other organizations to develop programs of empowerment. A march was organized from Memphis, Tennessee to Jackson, Mississippi to encourage blacks to vote. During the march, James Meredith was shot. McKissick, upon hearing the sad news, flew to Memphis and joined the march with other civil rights leaders in support of Meredith. Prominent in the march was Stokely Carmichael; it was at this time that Carmichael coined the phrase "Black Power" as the group walked along, and subsequently changed the negative connotation of the word "black" to positive.

Develops Soul City

During the early 1970s McKissick shifted his political orientation from Democratic to the Republican party. In 1972 he supported Richard M. Nixon for reelection as president, with the philosophy that African Americans should not depend on one party. Because of this political shift, many African Americans became disenchanted with McKissick.

Politically, McKissick had been a Democrat who tried to work within the system to bring about civil rights for African Americans. He became disenchanted when called to the White House for the signing of the Civil Rights Bill when nothing else was promised to his people. He may have felt that having the freedom to vote and partake of the public accommodations laws was enough for African Americans, believing that America is capitalistic and economic power is what runs the country.

McKissick secured more than $19 million federal funds and $8 million in state grants to form Soul City in Warren County, North Carolina, near the Virginia line. It was McKissick's dream that an integrated society could exist with self governance and healthy living, and the quality of life for society would be enhanced. Soul City was never completed.

Through his various positions as he moved ahead in the fight for equality, McKissick, maintained his association with the law. In 1990 Governor Jim Hunt of North Carolina appointed McKissick judge to the Ninth Judicial District of North Carolina. He was also a partner with his son in the firm, McKissick and McKissick and concentrated on civil rights litigation and personal injury.

McKissick was member of the District of Columbia Bar, the U.S. Supreme Court Bar, and the National and Southeastern Bar Association. Other memberships included the U.S. Advisory Committee, Association of Trial Lawyers, and the NAACP. He cofounded the North Carolina Center for the Study of Black History. Socially, he was a member of the Alpha Phi Alpha Fraternity.

In 1942 McKissick married Evelyn Williams; they had one son, Floyd Jr., and three daughters, Joycelyn, Andree and Stephine Charmaine. McKissick died April 21, 1991, after a bout with lung cancer. His funeral was held at Union Baptist Church in Durham and he was buried in Soul City. His widow continued to live in Soul City.

The legacy of Floyd B. McKissick is his work as champion of civil rights and economic power for African Americans. He confronted tough barriers in the struggle for equality, But he remained constant in his uphill climb for the civil rights of his people.

REFERENCES

Branch, Taylor. *Parting the Waters.* New York: Simon and Schuster, 1988.

Contemporary Black Biography. Vol. 3. Detroit: Gale Research, 1993.

Farmer, James. *Lay Bare the Heart.* New York: Arbor House, 1985.

Fax, Elton C. *Contemporary Black Leaders.* New York: Dodd, Mead, 1970.

Who's Who among Black Americans. 6th ed. Detroit: Gale Research, 1990.

Barbara Williams Jenkins

Elridge W. McMillan

(1934–)

Foundation executive, government official, educator

Elridge W. McMillan's early ambition to help his race led him to exceptional service and to recognition as a spokesperson in education, civil rights, and philanthropy. President of the Southern Education Foundation, he has concentrated his efforts towards improving the education of minorities and the disadvantaged, particularly in the South.

Born August 11, 1934, in Barnesville, Georgia, just south of Atlanta, McMillan is the youngest of three sons born to Agnes Boatwright McMillan, a former school teacher, and Marion Reynolds McMillan, Sr., a Methodist minister. As was customary of Methodist ministers, McMillan's family moved every three to five years. McMillan was an infant when his family left Barnesville, and he spent his early years in St. Marys, Sylvania, and Dublin, Georgia, where he graduated from high school. At 15, the family moved to Atlanta and McMillan entered Clark College there in the following year.

McMillan graduated with an A.B. degree in English in 1954. While pursuing his graduate degree at Teachers College, Columbia University, New York, during summer vacations, he taught seventh grade in the Atlanta public schools. In 1959 he received an M.A. degree in guidance and student personnel administration and was promoted to resource counselor for a division of the Atlanta public schools.

McMillan left the school system in 1965 to become the first African American hired by the newly created federal office, the Office of Economic Opportunity (OEO) where he remained for three years achieving a number of promotions.

Elridge W. McMillan

In 1968 McMillan joined the Southern Education Foundation (SEF) in Atlanta. The SEF was formed to promote equal and quality education primarily for blacks in the South. SEF is a merger of the John F. Slater Fund, the Virginia Randolph Fund, the Peabody Education Fund, and the Negro Rural School Fund. The Negro Rural School Fund, also known as the Jeanes Fund was established in 1907 by Anna T. Jeanes, a Philadelphia Quaker, in order to bring black master teachers to work in school systems in the rural South. Known as "Jeanes Teachers," they regularly visited the one–room schools in their districts to ensure the use of proper teaching methods and to evaluate the needs of the teachers and pupils. The *SEF News* for Spring 1994 reported that McMillan had early memories of Annie Daniels, a Jeanes supervisor, who along with McMillan's father, organized a small group of local black residents to register to vote in the early 1940s.

McMillan's career with the SEF began as a program associate. He was promoted to associate director in 1969, then to executive director in 1978. In 1983 when the foundation's organizational structure was revised, his title was changed to president.

McMillan recognized the need for various agencies concerned with equity to collaborate. Under his leadership, SEF was reorganized from a private foundation to a public charity allowing it to more effectively convene and facilitate collaborations and consortia to improve education for blacks in the South. For example, from late 1993 to 1995, SEF directed an initiative called Panel on Educational Opportunity and Post–Secondary Desegregation. Funds were obtained from the Ford Foundation to support the program. SEF later issued a report from the panel called *Redeeming the American Promise,* which was an in–depth study of the status of higher education for minorities in the South. From the 1980s and into the 1990s, SEF directed a Consortium on Teacher Supply and Quality involving six historically black colleges and universities and three graduate institutions. During this same period SEF directed the Black College Library Improvement Project, funded by the Andrew W. Mellon Foundation, to strengthen libraries in twenty black colleges and universities. Since 1994 SEF has also administered the Black Colleges Program, a national initiative of PEW Charitable Trusts designed to increase retention rates of students at ten black colleges and universities.

First Black to Chair Georgia Regents

In 1975 McMillan became a member of the Board of Regents of the University System of Georgia, a 16–member board that governs Georgia's 34 public colleges and universities. In 1986 he became the first black chair of the regents. In addition, McMillan is a trustee of Clark Atlanta University and executive secretary and trustee of The Herndon Foundation in Atlanta. He serves as director of the Atlanta Committee for Public Education. He is a member of several professional and service organizations including the President's Council of Tulane University, the Atlanta Action Forum, Association of Black Foundation Executives, Omega Psi Phi Fraternity, and 100 Black Men of Atlanta.

McMillan received honorary doctorates from Clark College in 1980 and Tuskegee University in 1994. When he received an honorary doctor of humanities degree from Claflin College in 1992, the school's president, quoted in the *SEF News* for February 1993, cited his ''sterling achievement in higher education and his continuing commitment to the service of the people of the region.'' McMillan has received numerous other awards. Among them, he won the State Committee on the Life and History of Black Georgians' Black Georgia of the Year Award in 1978 and the NAACP's W. E. B. DuBois Award in Education in 1979 and 1982. The Georgia Association of Black State Colleges honored him in 1995 with the Distinguished Service in Education Award and in 1997 with an award recognizing his support to the association and to black higher education in Georgia.

In 1968 McMillan married Marlania Kiner of Cincinnati; later they divorced. In an interview, McMillan called himself arrogant, but Grace Aarons, McMillan's executive assistant, sees him differently. She described him in ''Black History Month—History on the Making'' as ''an humble man, but one with stark determination to bring to fruition difficult but worthy causes which challenge him.'' In addition to his contributions in education in the South, which have also had a national impact, McMillan has been selfless in his service to people and to communities in Georgia, including the Warren Memorial United Methodist Church in Atlanta, where he sings in the sanctuary choir.

Current address: President, Southern Education Foundation, Inc., 135 Auburn Ave. NE, 2nd Floor, Atlanta, GA 30303.

REFERENCES

Aarons, Grace. ''Black History Month—History in the Making. Elridge W. McMillan—Humanitarian; Outstanding Educator.'' Office of Elridge W. McMillan, 1997.

———. Memorandum to Jessie Carney Smith, May 14, 1997.

''Biography. Elridge W. McMillan.'' April 1996. From the files of Elridge W. McMillan. n.d.

''Elridge W. McMillan.'' Biography notes. From the files of Elridge W. McMillan. n.d.

McMillan, Elridge W. Interview with Jessie Carney Smith, August 16, 1997.

''McMillan Receives Honorary Degree.'' *SEF News* 7 (February 1993): 2.

''Recalling the History of Black Education.'' *SEF News* 8 (Spring 1994): 3.

Who's Who among African Americans, 1998–99. 10th ed. Detroit: Gale Research, 1997.

Words in Action. Southern Education Foundation. Annual Report. Atlanta: 1996.

Jessie Carney Smith

Ronald E. McNair

(1950–1986)

Astronaut, physicist

In his brief career in the U.S. Space Program, Ronald McNair became the second black astronaut in space and the first black to lose his life while in flight. His outstanding academic achievements and expertise in physics and the specialized fields of chemical and high–pressure lasers led him to be selected in 1979 as a shuttle mission specialist for the National Aeronautics and Space Administration (NASA). He became known as a member of the crew for the ill–fated manned spacecraft *Challenger* launched in 1986.

Ronald Ervin McNair was born to Carl and Pearl McNair on October 21, 1950, in Lake City, South Carolina, a quaint little town that was typical of most pre–Civil Rights–era rural towns. He had two brothers Eric and Carl Jr. The McNairs were a highly industrious couple who taught their sons by words, examples, and deeds. The three boys were never asked or expected to do more than they witnessed their parents doing to provide for the family. Carl McNair Sr. was an automobile body repairman. He taught his sons this trade despite never making as much as $100 a week during their childhood. Pearl McNair was a high school teacher. In order to earn a master's degree in education from South Carolina State College, she made the 600–mile round trip to Orangeburg, South Carolina, during the years that her sons attended grade school. The McNair boys did farm work during summer months to supplement the family income.

Ronald E. McNair

Ronald McNair exhibited early promise of being a scholar. He could read and write before entering school and was considered a mechanical genius, which earned him the nickname of "Gizmo." The impetus for his early love of science was the Soviet launch of Sputnik, the first space satellite. In the first grade he was obsessed with Sputnik to the extent that he was observed looking skyward on a regular basis. At Carver High School McNair was a well–rounded student who excelled in athletics as well as in academics. When his peers carried Afro combs as expressions of their heritage, he carried a slide rule. In a posthumous tribute to him in *Ebony* magazine for August 1986, a former classmate said, "We all knew that Ron was smarter than the rest of us. We all knew that he was going to get that 100 on a test. However, his determination made the rest of us eager to study hard to at least get a 99."

Due to his intelligence, insatiable curiosity, and parent–instilled work ethic, McNair graduated as class valedictorian and was awarded a state scholarship to North Carolina Agricultural and Technical State University (NC A&T) in Greensboro. He was a discouraged freshman until a counselor urged him to seek a major in physics. Quoted in *Time* magazine, the counselor said, "I think you're good enough." In 1971 McNair graduated from NC A&T magna cum laude and was named a Ford Foundation Fellow and Presidential Scholar. He received a scholarship to continue his studies at the Massachusetts Institute of Technology (MIT).

Despite his outstanding achievements, McNair reluctantly accepted the MIT scholarship for graduate study. He overcame his initial hesitancy and excelled academically just as he had done in high school and in undergraduate college. In later years, as an experienced astronaut, McNair would counsel young people to persevere, to be prepared, and to believe in themselves. At MIT he had to heed that advice to overcome an obstacle that might well have devastated a less confident student. Near the end of his doctoral program, McNair lost all the data for his doctoral thesis, an accumulation of two years specialized laser physics research findings. This material was the result of collaborations with top–flight laser physicists from MIT and the École d'été Théorique de Physique at Les Houches, France. Despite this setback, he started again and produced a second set of data in less than a year. In an *Ebony* article for May 1986, his doctoral thesis adviser, Michael Feld, said McNair never complained about the misfortune and that "the second set turned out better than the first set of data. This was typical of the way he worked to accomplish goals."

In 1976 McNair completed all requirements for the Ph.D. degree in physics and joined the Hughes Research Laboratories in Malibu, California as a scientist. He was an acknowledged expert in the specialized fields of chemical and high–pressure lasers. His doctoral thesis was published in reputable technical journals and he wrote articles that were also accepted for publication. At the only professional job he would ever have outside of space science, McNair came across an application from the National Aeronautics and Space Administration (NASA) for shuttle personnel and decided to submit it. Although previous candidates traditionally had been test pilots, NASA had begun to consider scientists and McNair was confident that he was qualified. Once accepted, however, disaster struck when he was seriously injured in a car accident and warned that his recovery might interfere with the NASA start–up schedule. Following his own creed of perseverance, preparation, endurance, and self–belief, he was able to enter the program on time.

From Scientist to Astronaut

In August of 1979 McNair completed the training and evaluation course for shuttle mission specialists and began working at the Shuttle Avionics Integration Laboratory. Four years later, according to *African–American Biographies,* he was transferred to STS–11 and also served as a capcom for flights 41–G and 51–A in 1984. That same year his first space flight on *Challenger* orbited the earth 122 times and launched a $75 million communications satellite, an operation that required him to operate *Challenger*'s remote manipulator arms. Displaying the humor for which he was well known, McNair joked about trying to locate his tiny home town, while dressed in a beret, sunshades, and carrying a movie clapboard name tag inscribed "Cecil B. McNair." He had a total of three flights in 1984, including his service as a mission specialist aboard Mission 41–B, an eight–day flight that required deploying two communications satellites. In an *Essence* article, McNair described an incident he experienced during a flight in February of 1984:

> I was awakened by music being piped up from the Mission Control Center . . . [and] immediately recognized . . . my college alma mater . . . [and] glanced

at the N.C. A&T banner proudly affixed to the wall and 400 years of history quickly raced through my mind.

After the 1984 space shuttle flights, Lake City, South Carolina, honored its most famous son by renaming Main Street after him and embedding the imprint of his boots in a cement block that was placed in the city park he could not enter during his childhood due to racial restrictions.

The *Challenger* Tragedy

Although shuttle launches had become regular events, NASA and President Ronald Reagan envisioned a trip in space that would recapture the excitement and pride of the first space efforts and reestablish the United States as the premier world power in outer space. Not only would the 1986 *Challenger* carry the first private citizen into space, but that person would be a school teacher. Christa McAuliffe, a Concord, New Hampshire, high school teacher and mother of two, was selected from a pool of 11,000 applicants as the first educator to travel in space. This space flight was also notable due to the racial, ethnic, and gender diversity of the seven crew members.

On January 28, 1986, television sets the world over tuned to major network coverage of the Cape Canaveral, Florida, flight that began its climb into space at 11:38 a.m. A little over a minute later, millions of viewers, in addition to the site witnesses comprised of crew members' families, friends, and coworkers, watched in horror as *Challenger* exploded. As they watched, mesmerized by the awful beauty of the spectacle, white plumes of smoke slowly spiraled earthward and the finality of the doomed flight became apparent. All seven members of the crew died.

It has been said that political pressure was the impetus in deciding to grant clearance to launch the flight in questionable weather. NASA and the manufacturer of the O–rings knew that exposure to cold temperatures could cause fuel leakage, yet NASA was influenced by the publicity over the McAuliffe selection as a civilian crew member. Fourteen years prior to this fatal flight, the U.S. Space Program first allowed a manned spacecraft to be used without a launch escape system. These two factors were both preventable, yet it is claimed that both contributed to the deaths of the *Challenger* crew.

The Aftermath

Cheryl Moore McNair, Ronald's widow, was the first survivor to file a lawsuit against Morton Thiokol, manufacturer of the defective O–rings. She accused the company of deliberately failing to warn the astronauts about the defects. She reportedly received a settlement in excess of $1 million.

Ronald McNair and Cheryl Moore, a New York city native, had married in 1976. Their youngest child Joy Cheray was only 18–months old when her father died; her brother, Reginald, was just three–years old. After her husband's death, Cheryl McNair, and other surviving family members of Challenger victims, founded the Challenger Center for Space Science Education in memory of the entire mission crew. As the founding director, she continues to oversee programs designed to inspire and educate students and teachers in science and mathematics through space education. North Carolina A&T also named a science research center in McNair's honor.

As an academician and laser physicist, McNair was awarded three honorary doctorates and numerous commendations. He was a multitalented individual, who held a sixth–degree black belt in Karate and was an excellent saxophonist. He was dedicated to young people, his church, family, and community. When signing autographs, McNair always appended the message: ''Be your best.'' He had planned to begin a teaching career after his last space mission as a way to have greater impact on young people. In a personal mission to reach America's youth, McNair frequently spoke to school children and strove to help them understand the real meaning of courage. He de–emphasized the glamour and grandeur of such high profile positions as his own. He defined true courage, as quoted in *Contemporary Black Biography,* as ''enduring . . . persevering, the preparation and believing in one's self.''

McNair was eulogized by the President of the United States, the governor of South Carolina, his minister, and NASA officials at memorial services at NASA headquarters and at the Wesley United Methodist Church in Lake City. The last memorial service was held at McNair's home church, Antioch Missionary Baptist Church in Houston. Jesse Jackson, fellow North Carolina A&T alumnus and McNair's personal friend, provided the most meaningful eulogy, as reported in the May 1986 *Ebony*:

> To appreciate Ronald McNair, one needs to understand Lake City, S.C., a town several miles deeper than the country. Ron and his two brothers picked cotton, cucumbers, and chopped tobacco to help their family. But from that place, God chose a laser physicist to defy the odds of oppression.

REFERENCES

Cheers, D. Michael. ''Requiem for a Hero 'Touching the Face of God.''' *Ebony* 41 (May 1986): 82–94.

Contemporary Black Biography. Vol. 3. Detroit: Gale Research. 1993

''The Essence Guide to College Survival.'' *Essence* 17 (August 1986): 74.

Gray, Paul. ''Seven Who Flew for All of Us. *Time* 127 (10 February 1986): 33–34.

Hawkins, Walter L. *African–American Biographies: Profiles of 558 Current Men and Women.* Jefferson, NC: McFarland, 1992.

Haywood, Richette. ''Ebony Update.'' *Ebony* 51 (May 1996): 94.

Dolores Nicholson

James H. Meredith
(1933–)
Civil rights pioneer, writer, entrepreneur

James H. Meredith was a pioneer in the desegregation of higher education in the South. He became known during the civil rights era of the 1960s when he withstood bitter opposition and integrated the University of Mississippi. The involvement of the John F. Kennedy administration and the use of the military to effect Meredith's admittance and stay at the school brought international attention to the case.

Moses ''Cap'' Meredith named his son J. H. Meredith to prevent whites from calling him simply by his first name. It was not until 1950 when he enlisted in the Air Force that Meredith had to bow to regulations and give himself a full name; only then did he become James Howard Meredith. Meredith was born on June 25, 1933, in Kosciusko, Mississippi. He was the seventh of 13 children born to Cap Meredith. The elder Meredith had six children by his first wife. After she died, he married Roxie Smith, who later gave birth to J. H. Cap Meredith was a farm owner who grew cotton, corn, and other crops. When he was 12, young J.H. was baptized in Wesley Memorial Chapel, a Methodist church.

For 11 years Meredith walked more than four miles a day each way to Attala County Training School, the elementary and high school for blacks in the area. While white students were bussed to school, there was no school bus to transport the black students. None of his teachers held a college degree. In 1950, Meredith's junior year in high school, the Merediths sent their son away from the inferior, segregated schools in Kosciusko to St. Petersburg, Florida, where he lived with an aunt and uncle and attended Gibbs High School. He graduated in 1951, joined the U.S. Air Force, and spent the next nine years in the service as a clerk–typist. Stationed first in Kansas, he took extension courses at the University of Kansas around 1963, and in 1954 he enrolled at Washburn University in Topeka. He also studied at the U.S. Armed Forces Institute from 1954 to 1960 and while stationed in Japan from 1958 to 1960, he enrolled in the University of Maryland's Far Eastern Division.

Before leaving for Japan Meredith and his wife, Mary June Wiggins Meredith—whom he married in 1956—made arrangements to enter Mississippi's all–black Jackson State College (now University) as full–time students in September of 1960. James Meredith entered as an advanced junior in history and political science. By December of 1961, he had completed all requirements for his degree at Jackson State. He wrote in *Three Years in Mississippi* that the Legal Defense Fund, the Justice Department, the Federal Court of Appeals, and other groups advised him to not to graduate from Jackson State in order not to be declared ineligible for admission later to the University of Mississippi, also known as Ole Miss. Jackson State had ordered his diploma and a yellow tassel to

James H. Meredith

indicate that he was graduating with honors; his name was on the list of graduates. The only way to delay graduation was to refuse to pay a required fee of four dollars and 50 cents, which Meredith did. He continued to enroll in classes well after his class graduated in May of 1962.

Integrates Ole Miss

Inspired by the broadcast of President John F. Kennedy's January 20, 1961 inaugural address, Meredith decided the next day that he wanted to exercise his democratic rights and apply for admission to the University of Mississippi. He was now in his second quarter at Jackson State. He wrote to the registrar of the University of Mississippi and received application forms. On January 29 he went to see Medgar Evers, Mississippi's NAACP field secretary, who advised him to write to Thurgood Marshall of the Legal Defense and Educational Fund. In his letter to Marshall, reprinted in *Three Years in Mississippi,* Meredith said he wanted to make this move in the interest of his country, race, family, and himself. ''I am familiar with the probable difficulties involved in such a move as I am undertaking and I am fully prepared to pursue it all the way to a degree from the University of Mississippi,'' he wrote.

Meredith's application was filed on January 31, 1961; he also sent Thurgood Marshall his school records and a catalog of the University of Mississippi. Marshall turned the matter over to Constance Baker Motley of the Legal Defense Fund. Since he had missed the application deadline for entering in the second semester of 1960–61, Motley encouraged Meredith to look toward enrolling in September for the 1961–62 school year.

The prevailing racial attitude in Mississippi of that period led to numerous intimidations of blacks and some deaths. The student sit–in movement was in full swing and on March 27 students from nearby Tougaloo College were arrested for demonstrating at the Jackson Public Library. Other demonstrations followed, and the secret Mississippi Improvement Association for Students was organized. The MIAS also led the Jackson State College demonstrations. Meredith appears to have been involved in writing some of the organization's pamphlets, but said in his autobiography that he was not a member. The NAACP, of course, was involved in some of the protests. On June 12, 1961, Medgar Evers was assassinated outside his home in Jackson, which added fuel to the racial fire. The NAACP reacted to the continuous racial unrest and the denial of rights to blacks by proposing a march on Washington. When the NAACP's fifty–fourth annual convention was held in Chicago in that summer, two highly visible blacks denounced the march: J. H. Jackson of the National Baptist Convention, and James Meredith. Meredith called the march an example of lay intrusion in matters that should be handled by the five blacks then in Congress. According to Taylor Branch in *Parting the Waters,* the "already frosty audience booed Meredith for this iconoclastic suggestion." Meredith "lost his temper and scolded them as immature 'burrheads.'"

Meredith applied for admission to Ole Miss's summer term. On May 25, 1961, the school denied his application. After that, Motley filed a class–action suit in district court to allow Meredith to enroll in the university's summer term; the petition said he had been denied admission solely because of race. While the court ruled in favor of Ole Miss, the U.S. Fifth Circuit Court of Appeals in New Orleans overturned that decision and on June 25, 1962, Meredith's twenty–ninth birthday, the court ruled that Meredith be admitted to Ole Miss. After the state's several appeals—and summer school was over—the court issued a stay on September 10. On September 13, Justice Hugo Black issued an injunction against the university officials, ordering them to admit Meredith according to his application on file and enjoining them from excluding his admission and class attendance, and from any forms of racial discrimination.

Angered by the decision, Mississippi governor Ross R. Barnett defied the federal government on statewide radio and television with the promise that he would interpose the state's authority between the university and the federal judges. Quoted in *Before the Mayflower,* Barnett said, "There is no case in history where the Caucasian race has survived social integration." He said he would go to jail, if necessary, to prevent integration at the school. On September 20 and 25 the governor personally denied Meredith admission. On September 26, Mississippi's lieutenant governor Paul Johnson turned back Meredith and the federal marshals who escorted him. Barnett was found guilty of contempt of federal court on September 28, and the next day Johnson was found guilty of civil contempt. President John F. Kennedy responded with an executive order providing assistance in removing this unlawful obstruction of justice. Federal marshals escorted Meredith to his dormitory room on September 30. The National Guard and Army troops were ordered in to quell the violence that erupted on campus and to protect Meredith. Two men died, scores were injured, and over 200 protestors were arrested. Federal marshals ended their stay on campus, in August of 1963, when Meredith graduated and left the state, ending a period of his life that would be reflected in the title of his autobiography: *Three Years in Mississippi.* Meredith went on to receive a certificate of study from Ibadan University in Nigeria in 1965.

Marches Against Fear

On June 6, 1966, Meredith organized what he called a March Against Fear. This was an attempt to draw attention to black voting rights in the South and to help blacks overcome the fear of violence if they attempted to vote. The 220–mile march was along Route 51 from Memphis to Jackson. The second day of the march, near Hernando, Mississippi, white activist James Aubrey Norvell attempted to assassinate Meredith, filling his body with shotgun pellets. This triggered a march on the Mississippi capitol. Martin Luther King Jr., Floyd McKissick, Stokely Carmichael, and other civil rights demonstrators continued the march on June 7, ending it with a 30,000 person rally at the state capitol. It was during that week that Carmichael launched the Black Power movement.

Meredith was often in opposition to civil rights leaders. By the end of the 1960s he was in New York studying for his law degree at Columbia University and found time to become involved in politics. In addition to his earlier clash with the NAACP, he found resistance when he challenged Adam Clayton Powell, Jr. for his seat in Congress. Although the House of Representatives had censured Powell for his political and ethical behavior, he was still popular and widely accepted among his Harlem constituents. In 1966 Meredith's autobiography, *Three Years in Mississippi,* was published by Indiana University Press. In 1968, Meredith graduated from Columbia University's law school.

Returning to Mississippi in 1971, Meredith again felt the wrath of many blacks for failing to endorse popular Charles Evers, the black mayor of Fayette and the first black candidate for governor of that state. He was unsuccessful in his bid for public office five additional times during the 1970s. During this period he made a fairly good living from income earned from speaking engagements. He also formed the Reunification Under God Church and became involved in investment banking, sales, farming, and other activities that were not especially lucrative.

Meredith took an interest in college teaching and was unsuccessful in his attempt to land full–time jobs in that field in the state of Mississippi, including the much–preferred Ole Miss; however, he taught a course on blacks and the law at Ole Miss in 1984 and 1985. Later, he accepted a position as visiting professor in Afro–American Studies at the University of Cincinnati in Ohio. There he is said to have made undocumented charges of racial discrimination against college and city officials. When his contract was not renewed the next year, Meredith moved to San Diego in search of a high position with the Republican Party.

In 1989 North Carolina's conservative Republican senator Jesse Helms offered Meredith a $30,000–a–year position as domestic policy advisor, researcher, and writer. They dissolved the relationship later and by 1991 Meredith was in the news again, this time as endorser of former Ku Klux Klan leader David Duke, gubernatorial candidate in Louisiana.

Meredith began to devote more time to writing and research. In 1991 he established Meredith Publishing, located in Jackson, Mississippi, the outlet for his multivolume set, *Mississippi: A Volume of Eleven Books,* and other works. In 1996 Meredith launched another march. This time he called for a Black Man's March to the Library, which aimed to promote reading and the writing of standard English. Quoted in the *Los Angeles Sentinel,* he said, "The language spoken in the black community is not the language used in our education system. . . . Anyone not learning standard English will not excel in our education system." He set out from a Memphis library on June 1 for a repeat walk along U.S. 51 to reach Jackson on June 25, his sixty–third birthday. Slowed by prostate cancer surgery in April, he had to be driven the last 50 miles.

Attention was called to Meredith's historic work at Ole Miss when the film *Ghosts of Mississippi* was released in 1977. The film was an reenactment of the life of Medgar Evers, Meredith's close advisor in the integration of Ole Miss. In the fall of 1997 he created the Meredith Institute at Ole Miss, offering weekend classes to teach black American English. The program is closed to girls and women. The Institute is scheduled to open its Library School for Black Boys and Men in Jackson in January and another in February in San Diego.

Meredith had three children by his first wife: John Howard, Joseph Howard, and James Henry. Two years after the death of his first wife in 1989, he married Judy Alsobrooks, a television reporter in Cincinnati; their children are Kip and Jessica Howard. Although Meredith has demonstrated an interest in politics and writing, he is known primarily as the first black to graduate from the University of Mississippi.

Current address: Meredith Publishing Company, P.O. Box 10951, Jackson, MS 39289.

REFERENCES

Bennett, Lerone Jr. *Before the Mayflower.* 6th ed. Chicago: Johnson Publishing Co., 1987.

Branch, Taylor. *Parting the Waters.* New York: Simon and Schuster, 1988.

Contemporary Black Biography. Vol. 11. Detroit: Gale Research, 1996.

"'Ghosts of Mississippi': Poignant Re–enactment of Medgar Evers Case." *Sun Reporter,* January 9, 1997.

"Meredith Finishes March. . .Finally." *Los Angeles Sentinel,* July 4, 1996

Meredith, James. *Three Years in Mississippi.* Bloomington: Indiana University Press, 1966.

Salzman, Jack, David Lionel Smith, and Cornel West, eds. *Encyclopedia of African–American Culture and History.* New York: Macmillan Library Reference USA/Simon and Schuster Macmillan, 1996.

"U. Of Miss. Opens School for Blacks." *New York Times,* November 23, 1997.

Jessie Carney Smith

Ralph H. Metcalfe

(1910–1978)

Congressman, Olympic track star, coach, educator

Ralph H. Metcalfe's lifetime included the accomplishments of a major sports hero followed by the vicissitudes of a political career representing an inner city African American constituency. A high school and collegiate champion who went on to become an Olympic medalist, Metcalfe's guiding ethic embodied many of the values of good sportsmanship. Once referred to as "the world's fastest human," his career in politics followed broadly the model set up in sports competition. For Metcalfe, athletic competition featured teamwork, aggressive striving towards a clear goal, responding to challenges, a crusading spirit, and a willingness to share one's talents for a common purpose. Later in life, he projected these character traits on to his career as a politician and public servant.

As a Chicago councilman and a U.S. Congressman, Metcalfe was responsive to the needs of his constituents, including the underprivileged, who sought equal employment and a better quality of life. As a Congressman, he led numerous investigations into governmental activities and areas of social concern, health, and public safety. In these efforts, he earned the gratitude and continuing electoral support of his constituents.

Metcalfe was born in Atlanta, Georgia, on May 30, 1910, the son of Clarence and Mamie Holmes Metcalfe. He was their third child. The Metcalfes subsequently moved to Chicago, where young Metcalfe attended Doolittle Elementary School, Phillips Junior High, and Tilden Technical High School. His father worked in the stockyards and his mother was a dressmaker. Metcalfe held several part–time jobs to earn money and help family finances. Showing an early interest in sports, he joined the track team at 15, and four years later, in 1929, became a national interscholastic sprint champion. Upon entering Marquette University, he continued to enhance his athletic skills. He rose to the level of one of the world's fastest sprinters, and captained the track team by winning numerous competitions and equaling or setting the

Ralph Metcalfe (right) with Jesse Owens, 1936.

National Collegiate Athletic Association (NCAA) and world records in virtually every sprint category. Metcalfe was named the 1929 National Interscholastic Sprint Champion and National Collegiate Champion in 1932, 1933, and 1934. He was referred to as ''the world's fastest human.'' At Marquette, he was president of his graduating class, earning his bachelor of philosophy degree, in 1936.

While at Marquette, he was selected for the U.S. Olympic team, and competed in both the 1932 and 1936 Olympics. In 1933 and 1934, Metcalfe was a member of an invitational U.S. track and field team assembled to compete in international track meets in Europe and the Far East. In the 1932 Olympics, held in Los Angeles, Metcalfe competed in the 100 and 200 meter springs. In the 100 meters, decided by a legendary photo–finish, Metcalfe and Eddie Tolan finished in a virtual tie, with Tolan being declared the winner; both runners were credited with the Olympic record time, of 10.3 seconds. Thus, Metcalfe earned a silver medal in this race, and finished third in the 200 meters, earning a bronze medal. At the 1936 Olympics, in Berlin, he earned a silver and gold medal. Metcalfe barely lost the 100–meter sprint, finishing a close second, to Jesse Owens, in the Olympic record–tying time, of 10.3 seconds. Metcalfe then joined Owens on the 400–meter relay team, which won its race, in the world–setting time of 39.8 seconds. The German Chancellor, Adolf Hitler, was visibly chagrined when members of his ''master race'' were unable to defeat the ''upstart'' Americans, including Metcalfe and Owens, in several head–to–head competitions. Owens insisted that Metcalfe take the higher position in the medal photo for the 400–meter relay team (the position of honor), showing his esteem for Metcalfe's sportsmanship and team spirit. Metcalfe and Owens became lifelong friends.

Following the 1936 Olympics, he was appointed track coach and political science instructor at Xavier University in New Orleans, serving from 1936–42. On a leave of absence, Metcalfe completed his graduate studies in physical education at the University of Southern California, and received his master of arts degree in 1939. During 1942–43, he worked as an African American field consultant to the National Catholic Community Services and as the United Service Organization's (USO) mobile director. His responsibilities included planning and directing recreational and athletic programs in Anniston, Alabama, the communities of the Louisiana Maneuvers area, and in California, for men of the armed services on active duty or in training. For his achievements in these demanding tasks, in the field of recreation and morale for African American troops, he received the James J. Hoey Award for Interracial Justice in October of 1943. He received this jointly with Philip A. Murray, president of the Congress of Industrial Organizations (CIO).

Drafted into the U.S. Army, in 1943, Metcalfe served as a first lieutenant and physical training officer in the Transportation Corps in Louisiana. Well suited for his work, he was commended by his unit, and received the Legion of Merit award for program planning. He was discharged from service at Camp Grant, Illinois, in March of 1946. Returning to Chicago following military service, he was named director of the Department of Civil Rights, which was part of the Commission on Human Relations. He served there until 1949. Other public activities associated with athletics that he was involved with included: his service on the Illinois State Athletic Commission from 1949–52, and his service as co–chairman of the Third Pan–American Games Organizing Committee in 1959. He was later appointed by Vice–President Hubert H. Humphrey to the National AAU and NCAA Sports Arbitration Board. He was also appointed to serve on the President's Committee on Olympic Sports from 1975 to 1977.

On July 20, 1947, he married Madalynne Fay Young. They had one son, Ralph H. Metcalfe Jr., who was active in Chicago politics and in the Ralph H. Metcalfe Youth Foundation.

Enters Politics

Metcalfe's illustrious athletic career helped prepare him for the challenges he would later face in the public arena. In 1949, Metcalfe was named to the Illinois State Athletic Commission. His political career began in earnest with his position as Democratic Committee member for the Third Ward of Chicago from 1952–71. This was followed by his election as alderman and service on the Chicago City Council from 1955 to 1971, where he was elected president pro–tem in 1969. From 1952 to 1972, he served as delegate to the Democratic National Convention, and to the Illinois State Democratic Convention from 1953–72. He also served on the Chicago Planning Commission. In 1970, he was elected to the

U.S. Congress from the first district in Chicago. Metcalfe succeeded Congressman William L. Dawson. Metcalfe served there until his death in 1978. Congressman Metcalfe was widely known for his advocacy of citizens' rights, consumer protection, health care, job access, fair housing, and equal access to federal services. He earned the gratitude and support of his constituents, as was graphically illustrated by the electoral margin of his 1974 reelection. His winning majority set a record for the highest plurality achieved by a U.S. Congressman. An interesting and dramatic turn of events in Metcalfe's political life occurred in 1972, when he announced at a People United to Save Humanity (Operation PUSH) meeting that he had "turned black." The precipitating events were summarized in *Encore* magazine, Metcalfe was long thought of as a party regular, coming up through the ranks, earning support in his political ascendancy through his loyalty to Democratic party causes. He was upset by the criticism that he had become too cozy with Mayor William Daley's political machine. Initially profiting from Daley's strong support, he was sensitized by criticism that Daley had quickly forgotten pre–election promises to Metcalfe's district, which had contributed a strong voter turnout on Daley's behalf in the crucial close elections of 1960 and 1963. Then, when Martin Luther King Jr. did not win support for a rally and march in Chicago in 1966 Metcalfe was said to have used his influence, on Daley's behalf. Metcalfe was also alleged to have participated, at Daley's behest, in the opposition at the Democratic National Convention to the seating of the rival integrated Georgia state delegation led by Julian Bond.

In Metcalfe's defense, it was said that he was a regular Democratic party member following the leadership as a team player, in the tradition of his sports background. In this instance, he was working on behalf of his constituents. However, allegations of police brutality came forward, and Metcalfe heard of shootings and beatings occurring on his very doorstep that he, a Congressman, could do nothing to stop. He felt a deep sense of responsibility to his son and to his constituents to redress these wrongs. At the 1972 PUSH meeting, he declared his open support for African American causes, saying that, although he was tardy, it was "never too late to be black." Open warfare ensued on both sides. Metcalfe participated in the formation of the Concerned Citizens for Police Reform. Negotiations were held and promises elicited from Mayor Daley, but there were few practical results. Metcalfe then held Congressional committee hearings on the police brutality issue and turned up evidence of misuse of appropriated funds. As a result of this pressure, the Chicago Civil Service Commission instituted psychological testing for police officers; the police Special Operations Group was instructed not to disregard civil rights in their discharge of duties; and the minimum height for police recruits was reduced (thereby opening the ranks to more applications by women and minorities). Further, following newspaper allegations of police spying on community leaders, hearings and a Government Accounting Office study revealed that ten million dollars, partly derived from federally–appropriated funds, had been spent on undercover activities. Metcalfe promptly called for an end to such diversion of funds.

Stung by these actions, Daley fought back by trying to strip him of patronage, supporting an opposing candidate in the congressional election; and urging that Metcalfe be stripped of his committee seat. Metcalfe returned fire by handily winning the primary and the following election by a plurality of 91 percent (followed by 95 percent in 1974). These numbers were the highest in the Congress, and he returned to his committee seat. Metcalfe refused to support Daley's candidate in the 1972 race for Illinois Attorney General, Edward Hanrahan. Hanrahan had ordered the infamous police raid on the Black Panther Party headquarters in 1969, resulting in the death of party leader Fred Hampton.

Challenges Regulations Affecting African Americans

Following these encounters, Metcalfe turned to national as well as local issues of federal abuses affecting the underprivileged. His committee hearings on Alabama public health clinics revealed some 400 untreated syphilis patients who were African American, and the committee cited the Department of Health, Education and Welfare for failing to enforce guidelines requiring preventive health treatment for indigents. The Federal Aviation Agency (FAA) was studied next, and subsequently cited for not enforcing safety standards. The Federal Bureau of Prisons was cited for isolating inmates for up to three years and using mind control techniques to control prisoners. Ever vigilant, Metcalfe built an enviable record in Congress as a champion of public causes and was a person who was not afraid to take on political bosses, lobbyists, and federal agencies. Metcalfe was a member of the Congressional Black Caucus. He was Chairman of the House Panama Canal Subcommittee which set the groundwork for the negotiation of a new Panama Canal Treaty. With this record, he earned the support and affection of his constituents.

As a permanent contribution to society, he founded the Ralph H. Metcalfe Youth Foundation to support athletic, educational, and cultural programs. He was a member of the Black Athlete's Hall of Fame, the Helms Athletic Foundation, the Wisconsin Hall of Fame, the National Track and Field Hall of Fame, and the U.S. Track and Field Hall of Fame. He was a member of Amvets, the American Legion, the Chicago Urban League, the NAACP, the Cosmopolitan Chamber of Commerce, Alpha Sigma Nu, Alpha Phi Alpha Fraternity, the Masons, Elks, and the Varsity (Chicago; president, 1962), and served in 1963 as president of the Joint Negro Appeal.

Metcalfe's political career ended with the his sudden death of an apparent heart attack at home in Chicago on October 10, 1978. Burial was in Holy Sepulchre Cemetery in Worth, Illinois. His contribution was best summed up by the words of his friend and colleague, Congressman John Conyers of Michigan, who alluded to the parallels between his achievements in athletic competition and the challenges he met in the political arena. Conyers stated in *Freedomways* that Metcalfe, in his life's work, "summoned up the same courage that earlier had won him the admiration of the world for his athletic achievements. In the end, Ralph stood his ground, a moderate and reasonable man up against an immoderate and unreasonable political system."

REFERENCES

Chalk, Ocania. *Black College Sport.* New York: Dodd, Mead, 1976.

"Chicago South Side Boss Stepping Down." *The Milwaukee (Wisconsin) Journal,* September 11, 1969.

Christopher, Maurine. *Black Americans in Congress.* New York: Thomas Y. Crowell, 1976.

"C.I.O. Head, Famed Athlete Receive 1943 Hoey Awards." *The Catholic News,* October 30, 1943.

Conyers, John, Jr. "The Metcalfe Legacy A Personal Remembrance." *Freedomways* 18 (November 1978): 208–09.

———. "Remembrance of Things Past The Man Who Outran the Daley Machine." *Encore* 7 (20 November 1978): 38–40.

Henderson, Edwin B. *The Black Athlete.* New York: Publishers Company, 1969.

Memorial Tribute to Ralph H. Metcalfe. Washington, DC: Government Printing Office, 1978.

"Metcalfe Dies Alone in Chicago Amid his Struggle For Blacks." *Jet* 55 (26 October 1978): 6–9.

Scally, Sister Mary Anthony. *Negro Catholic Writers, 1900–1943.* Grosse Point, MI: W. Romig, 1945.

Smythe, Mabel M. *The Black American Reference Book.* Englewood Cliffs, NJ: Prentice–Hall, 1976.

Who's Who in America, 1978–79. 40th ed. Chicago: Marquis Who's Who, 1978.

COLLECTIONS

Personal documents of Ralph Metcalfe, including birth certificate, U.S. Army enlistment and service forms, recommendations and personal letters are in the Vivian G. Harsh Research Collection of Afro-American History and Literature, Chicago Public Library.

Darius L. Thieme

Albert E. Meyzeek

(1862–1963)

Educator, civil rights activist

Albert E. Meyzeek

Educator Albert E. Meyzeek was an outspoken activist in the integration movement in Kentucky early in the twentieth century. A champion of civil rights causes, Meyzeek helped to establish a colored branch of the YMCA, opened libraries to blacks, and fought to end segregation in education and in public facilities in Louisville.

Albert Ernest Meyzeek was born on November 5, 1862, during his mother's visit to relatives in Toledo, Ohio. His parents, John E. and Mary Lott Meyzeek, were residents of Toronto, Canada. Albert E. Meyzeek was of mixed parentage—his father was a white Canadian and his mother, a black American. Meyzeek's father was a champion of blacks and successfully won two law suits against the Indiana School Board forcing the abolishment of unhealthy and inadequate segregated schools. Meyzeek's maternal grandfather, John Lott, was one of the organizers of the Ohio River Underground Railroad. Lott filled his grandson's head with many tales of runaway slaves in their quest for freedom.

Shortly after his birth, Albert Meyzeek and his mother returned home to Toronto. He received his early years of schooling in Canada. Spending his formative years in Toronto, he acquired a strong British accent which he retained his entire life. In 1875 the family moved to Terre Haute, Indiana, and Meyzeek enrolled in Terre Haute Classical High School where he was the only black student in his class. He graduated as valedictorian of his class.

Meyzeek initially planned to become an attorney and began working in the law offices of Superior Court Judge Mack and United States Senator Daniel W. Voorhees. While studying school law, he learned that the Terre Haute School Board was in violation for not providing adequate schools for primary children. He sought a writ against the school board, and the case was quickly concluded with the district receiving an additional school facility. Deciding that law might not be too lucrative, he decided to enroll at the Indiana State Normal School. Meyzeek continued his studies and later received a bachelor's and a master's degree from Indiana University in Bloomington. In 1896 Meyzeek married Pearl E. Hill, who had been an elementary teacher in the public school system.

She was a very devoted Christian and faithful wife for Meyzeek.

50 Years as Educator

Beginning in 1884, Meyzeek taught school in Terre Haute, Indiana. He moved to Louisville in 1890 where he began an extraordinary tenure of more than 50 years of service in public education in Kentucky. He passed the state's comprehensive school principal examination and began his first principalship in Kentucky. This first appointment in Louisville was with the Maiden Lane School, which later became Benjamin Banneker School. He was soon transferred to Western Colored School and then to the Eastern Colored School, where he served as principal from 1891 through 1893. For the next three years he was the principal at Central High School where he expanded the curriculum from three to four years and established a reference library in the school.

In 1896 he was given two appointments, principal of the Eastern School District which included the Jackson Junior High School and principal of the Colored Normal School. While serving as principal of the Normal School over a 14 year period he trained three–fourths of Louisville's black teaching staff. As a school principal, he reorganized the internal structure, offered new courses, sought college educated teachers, established a school library, organized clubs for parents, and implemented discipline in his schools. When the enrollment in Jackson Junior High increased, Meyzeek decided to concentrate his energies at that institution. He remained principal of Jackson Junior High School until he retired in 1943, at which time he was presented with a gold watch and flowers at a testimonial banquet. Throughout his teaching career he sought opportunities to improve the schools in which he served. One of his accomplishments was having black schools named for notable persons of African descent.

Meyzeek was among the black educators who continuously sought to upgrade the quality of education for black children through the Kentucky Negro Education Association. He also served as president of the association in 1927. He was a member of Kentucky's State Board of Education from 1948 to 1956. While serving in this capacity, he advised the desegregation of the public school system. He was staunchly opposed to Kentucky's "Day Law," which prohibited black and white students from attending school together.

Leads Civil Rights Struggles

As an educator Meyzeek sought to provide educational opportunities for his students. On one occasion, he took his students to the Louisville Public Library; they were refused admittance. This incident resulted in Meyzeek's campaign to raise money for a branch Carnegie Library for blacks in Louisville. In 1907 the Western Colored Branch Library opened in a temporary location on Chestnut Street until the permanent facility was opened on October 29, 1908. The Western Colored Branch Library, located at Tenth and West Chestnut, is believed to be the first public library opened for blacks in the United States. This library was so successful that Meyzeek was able to convince white library officials to establish an additional branch library for blacks, the Eastern Colored Branch, which opened January 28, 1914. Although all the libraries in Louisville were integrated in 1952, the Western Branch Library still serves the needs of the people in that section of the city.

His library initiative was but one of Meyzeek's efforts to secure human rights for Louisville blacks. Meyzeek spearheaded drives to desegregate the General Hospital, protested against ordinances for segregation on public conveyances, worked to open the University of Louisville to blacks, and helped open a "colored" branch of the YMCA as early as 1892. He was also one of the founders of the Louisville Urban League, which he chaired for 29 years. Among his many other accomplishments, Meyzeek had the distinction of being one of the founders of a national black fraternity, Kappa Alpha Psi. He was the first man initiated into this Greek letter organization.

Meyzeek was also a successful businessman, serving as one of the founders of the Domestic Life and Accident Insurance Company in Louisville. The black–owned insurance company was to become one of the leading black businesses in Kentucky. Because of the Jim Crow laws, blacks in the city of Louisville were denied access to amusement opportunities until Meyzeek and others helped establish the Citizens Amusement Company and the Palace Theater Company of Louisville to remedy this situation. After Meyzeek retired from teaching he also worked as an assistant in the office of the Price Administration in Kentucky during World War II.

Meyzeek was a devout Episcopalian and a member of the Episcopal Church of Our Merciful Savior. At the time of his death on December 19, 1963, at the age of 101, he was the Senior Warden Emeritus of this church. Meyzeek was described by minister E. G. Harris in *Old War Horse of Kentucky* in the following manner: "Meyzeek's citizenship has been a blessing to our people. He is the last of the old fighting guard, often called 'Old War Horse of Kentucky.'" Meyzeek is buried in the Eastern Cemetery in Louisville.

On April 3, 1967, the Louisville Board of Education ordered that the Jackson Junior High School's name be changed to Albert E. Meyzeek Junior High School as a tribute to his numerous civic and educational accomplishments. It is now the Albert E. Meyzeek Middle School.

During his lifetime, Meyzeek proudly led the black people of Louisville in their struggle against social injustice and in their quest for civic improvements.

REFERENCES

Dunnigan, Alice A. *Fascinating Story of Black Kentuckians: Their Heritage and Tradition.* Washington, DC: Associated Publishers, 1982.

Horton, John Benjamin. *Old War Horse of Kentucky.* Louisville: J. Benjamin Horton and Associates, 1986.

Kentucky's Black Heritage. Frankfort: Kentucky Commission on Human Rights, 1971.

Kleber, John E., ed. *The Kentucky Encyclopedia.* Lexington: University Press of Kentucky, 1992.

Who's Who in Colored America. 5th ed. Yonkers, NY: Christian E. Burckel, 1938–40.

COLLECTIONS

An Albert E. Meyzeek clipping file is available at the Western Branch Library, and administrative records of his tenure in the Jefferson County School system are housed at the Educational Media Center for Louisville Public Schools.

Karen Cotton McDaniel

Kweisi Mfume

Kweisi Mfume

(1948–)

Congressman, civil rights leader, organization executive

As a teenager Kweisi Mfume was captivated by the fast–paced street life in West Baltimore. However, refusing to allow the negative forces of the inner city to suppress him, he became a leader in the black community, and served in the U.S. House of Representatives before becoming head of the NAACP.

Kweisi Mfume was born Frizzell Gray on October 24, 1948, in Turners Station, Maryland, a small town ten miles south of Baltimore city. He lived in a two–parent household headed by his mother, Mary Elizabeth Willis Gray, and Clifton Gray, who Mfume would later find out was his stepfather. The oldest of four children, he and his three sisters, Darlene, LaWana, and Michele, lived with their parents not far from the steel mills and shipyards on the Chesapeake Bay. Mary Gray worked on an assembly line for an airplane parts manufacturing company, as a maid, and at odd jobs to help support the family. Clifton Gray worked as a truck driver and, consequently, he was seldom home. The family was usually financially pressed.

Mfume spent the first 11 years of his life in the county atmosphere of Turners Station. Mary Gray was undoubtedly the greatest influence in her son's life. Because his stepfather spent most of his time on the road, his mother raised the children on her own. The family was grounded in the church and the children were expected to live their lives accordingly. Mfume's mother placed responsibilities on her son, particularly watching his younger siblings while she was at work. She knew he could handle the job, but she also knew that raising a boy to be a man was a hard task for a couple, and an even harder task for a mother whose husband was rarely home. The presence of a male role model was almost nonexistent. To provide good male role models, Mary Gray ensured that Mfume participated in Little League baseball and in a marching band. The instructors of these organizations were men who instilled in their charges discipline and a strong work ethic. They provided Mfume with a positive male presence in his life, which was important, because the father–son relationship did not develop between Gray and Mfume. When the two did have a chance to interact, Gray was often abusive; the friction may have stemmed from the fact that Kweisi was not his biological son. Gray's abusive nature was also displayed toward Mfume's mother, which fueled Mfume's anger toward his stepfather. One day in November 1959 Gray went to work and never returned.

Trying to raise four children and pay the mortgage became too much for the mother and in the spring of 1960 the family moved to West Baltimore. If Turners Station was a quiet sanctuary, Baltimore was its opposite. Mfume quickly adapted to his new surroundings. He sold newspapers to supplement the family's income and made new friends. It was during this period of that Mfume met Rufus Tate, a longtime friend of the family. The two made an instant connection and Tate also gave the family money when they were in a financial bind. The Grays always seemed to be struggling to keep things together and they moved frequently because they were unable to pay rent regularly.

Mfume's interest in politics was initiated in Baltimore. One evening in the fall of 1962 Mfume slipped out of the house and went down to the Fifth Regiment Armory to see President John F. Kennedy speak to the people of Baltimore. In his autobiography *No Free Ride: From the Mean Streets to the Mainstream,* Mfume wrote, "[I doubt if] there was a soul in the rally who wanted to be there more than [I], or who was as giddy and excited over Kennedy's vision of hope and progress as [I] was."

In 1964 Mary Gray learned that she had cancer and had little time to live. Her primary concern was the care of her children after she was gone. She and the rest of the family decided that the girls would live with their grandmother, and that Mfume would move in with his two uncles. During her illness she attempted to prepare her son for life after she was gone. She told the young Mfume that he was special and made him promise that he would never give up and that he would make something of himself. When she died in her son's arms one April evening, his life was changed forever. That night Rufus Tate came over to the house to offer his condolences to the family but also to reveal that he was his biological father.

At the age of 16 Mfume was cast into the world of adults. He had to support himself and he also felt obligated to provide for his sisters as well. He tried to work at two jobs and go to school, but the task was overwhelming. Without his mother's guidance, Mfume dropped out of school, had one unsuccessful marriage and several relationships with women, resulting in five children, all boys. Now, with children to feed, the little bit of money that he earned was insufficient to support his children and himself. Mfume began to hang out on street corners and running numbers. He began to associate with known hustlers, and his reputation as a hoodlum grew; he was picked up by the police several times. Mfume was engulfed by the street life, making fast money, drinking, gambling, and even carrying a gun.

Mfume's life was rapidly plummeting in the wrong direction. However, two major events occurred that Mfume believes turned his life around—both on the same street corner. The first was a chance encounter with Parren J. Mitchell, a Maryland congressman. The exchange between the two revolved around what Mfume was doing to help his people; Mitchell challenged Mfume to stop being part of the problem and to start becoming part of the solution. Although Mfume began to think about the encounter; it was not until the second event that Mfume began to change his life.

One night, as he was standing on the corner shooting dice with his friends, he saw a vision of his mother's face before him. Mfume believed that this represented a revelation from God that he should change his life; when the vision ended, he turned and left that corner and the street life for good.

Life Turns Around

After earning his Graduate Equivalence Diploma (GED) Mfume enrolled in the Community College of Baltimore. He also worked as a disc jockey at a local radio station owned by James Brown, and he volunteered to work on some local political campaigns. As a DJ, Mfume created a show called *Ebony Reflections,* which proved to be vastly different from other radio shows. He discussed issues that were of concern to the black community. Mfume played speeches of Malcolm X and Martin Luther King Jr. and poetry by Nikki Giovanni over jazz tunes.

Ebony Reflections provided Mfume with a forum for his political views. It was during this period that Mfume changed his name from Frizzell Gray to his present African name to reflect his cultural heritage. Kweisi Mfume means "conquering son of kings." Mfume graduated from the Community College of Baltimore in 1974 then entered Morgan State University, where he helped the Student Government Association to lobby for a university radio station—WEAA–FM.

In 1976 Mfume graduated magna cum laude from Morgan State and accepted a position there as a faculty member. He also served as program director of WEAA while he taught political science and communication courses. As station director and talk show host of WEAA, Mfume continued to voice his displeasure with Baltimore's local government. One caller suggested that he run for the Baltimore city council, and Mfume did.

In 1978 Mfume launched his campaign for the fourth district city council seat. It was a difficult campaign, seemingly headed nowhere due to lack of funds. Still Mfume's dedication to making a change captured the voters' interest, and his door–to–door campaigning showed people that he was willing to fight for his beliefs. Although the election was close, he won and represented the fourth district of Baltimore for seven years.

Mfume continued his education during his tenure on the city council, attending Johns Hopkins University where he earned a master's degree in the liberal arts in 1989. During his years of service on the city council, he gained the reputation for being an honest politician who would fight diligently for his constituents. Most importantly, he learned how to gain support for his ideas and how to select his battles.

The departure of Parren Mitchell from the Seventh Congressional District seat opened the door for Mfume to take his ideas to the federal level and to help more people. He won the congressional seat after a tough and slanderous campaign marred by attacks against his morality—a tactic that did not work. In 1987 Mfume went to Washington, D.C., where he was an active member of the House of Representatives for five terms. He served on three committees: Banking, Finance and Urban Affairs, Small Business, and the Select Committee on Hunger.

In Mfume's first term on Capitol Hill, he served as treasurer for the Congressional Black Caucus (CBC). Mfume steadily progressed up the leadership ladder in the CBC, gaining a higher position with each term; in 1993 he became the chairman. At the helm, Mfume changed the direction of the CBC, choosing to focus on economic empowerment and political networking. The caucus, which now had the power of an increased membership, was able to influence legislation in the House, such as tax breaks for the working poor. They also pressured President Bill Clinton to send U.S. troops to Haiti.

Heads NAACP

Mfume, however, believed that his accomplishments as a congressman were few and stated in a 1996 *U.S News and World Report* article, ''It's difficult to bring about the kind of change I want as an individual member of Congress. I could stay and do little or leave and do a lot.'' On February 20, 1996, Mfume resigned from Congress to become president and chief executive officer for NAACP. Mfume's first priority was to get the organization out of its seven–figure debt. In Mfume's first year as the president of the NAACP, he retired its debt and increased its membership. The organization was able to raise money from a variety of sources: members, foundations, and corporations. Mfume also expanded the scope of the organization to encompass problems facing those on the street corner as well as the legal battle against social, political, and economic injustice. He believes that the problems facing the black community are multidimensional and therefore require more than one perspective. This belief has resulted in Mfume asking other organizations to work with the NAACP to find solutions to these problems.

In his autobiography, *No Free Ride: From the Mean Streets to the Mainstream,* Mfume recalled his journey from the streets of Baltimore, his election to Congress, to his position as NAACP president. He has been at both the bottom and the top of the social order. He has endured suffering in his life with courage and a determination to succeed and correct the problems that were obstacles in his youth. Mfume's years of public service to the people of American reflect his commitment, especially to teenagers, providing hope as they learn to control their own destiny.

Current address: NAACP, 4805 Mt. Hope Dr., Baltimore, MD, 21215.

REFERENCES

Borger, Gloria. ''Up from the Street Corner.'' *U.S. News and World Report* 115 (9 August 1993): 33–35.

Bositis, David A. *The Congressional Black Caucus in the 103rd Congress.* Washington, DC: Joint Center for Political and Economic Studies, 1994.

''A Child of the Movement.'' *U.S. News and World Report* 119 (25 December 1996): 62.

Clay, William L. *Just Permanent Interests: Black Americans in Congress, 1870–1991.* New York: Amistad, 1992.

Howe, Rob, Sarah Skonik, and Don Hamilton, ''The Bootstrap Method.'' *Business Week* 45 (26 February 1996): 55–58.

Mfume, Kweisi, and Ron Stodghill II. *No Free Ride: From the Mean Streets to the Mainstream.* New York: Ballantine, 1996.

Stodghill, Ron II, ''From Table–Pounder to Inside Player.'' *Business Week* 307 (1 March 1993): 72–75.

Swain, Carl M. *Black Faces, Black Interests: The Representation of African Americans in Congress.* Cambridge: Harvard University Press, 1995.

Damien Bayard Ingram

Oscar Micheaux
(1884?–1951)
Filmmaker, novelist, farmer

A trailblazer for today's independent black filmmakers and a key figure in movie history, Oscar Micheaux was a pioneering filmmaker whose efforts produced 40 melodramas, social dramas, gangster movies, and musicals between 1918 and 1948. He was a novelist, publisher, producer, and distributor of his own books and films. He rejected the stereotypical roles for blacks and worked assiduously to create on–screen images that would counter the racist representations of black Americans. Micheaux was the one black filmmaker who survived the competition from Hollywood and even the Great Depression, making the successful transition from silent to talking motion pictures.

Oscar Micheaux was born in January of 1883 or 1884 in Metropolis, Illinois, a small town in Masac County near the Ohio River. He was one of 11 children born to Swan and Belle Micheaux. His parents were former slaves who had moved to Illinois from Kentucky when the Civil War ended. His father owned a small farm and his mother, having taught herself to read and write, taught school. An older brother, Lawrence, fought in the Spanish–American War under Teddy Roosevelt in 1898. He later contracted a disease and died in the service.

As a young man Micheaux was curious about the world around him and observed much. He spent a lot of time talking and listening to the black Pullman porters who worked on the Illinois Central railroad that came through his town. He heard stories about Chicago, New Orleans, and Harlem that fired his imagination. He was also told that in big cities he could make more money than he could ever hope to make in Metropolis.

In 1900, Micheaux decided to try his luck in Chicago. He worked in an automobile plant and in a coal mine for $1.25 a day before he arrived. Micheaux's older brother, William, was in Chicago and provided him a place to stay while he looked for work. Micheaux finally got a job pitching hay and moved to Wheaton, Illinois. Here he earned enough money to open his first bank account. In 1902, Micheaux obtained a job as Pullman porter, earning $40 a month. He increased his bank account to over $2,000. His travels from coast to coast gave him experience he would later draw upon to create his novels and movies.

Black Homesteader in South Dakota

With big dreams, Micheaux left the Pullman Company in 1906. He heard about government land being auctioned off in South Dakota, and decided to try his luck. Near the town of Gregory, South Dakota, he purchased a quarter section of land for $3,000 from Olivet Swanton. In 1909 he purchased another quarter section for $640. He now owned 320 acres of

South Dakota farmland. He was the only black homesteader in this section of South Dakota.

Farming proved successful for Micheaux. It seems he planted and harvested simultaneously by rotating the crops so one was ready for harvest at the time he was planting a different crop. Despite his unorthodox methods of farming, Micheaux had cultivated 120 acres of his land by the end of his first year, significantly more than any of his neighbors.

Micheaux's fame as a farmer spread as far east as Chicago, where he often visited. But life on the prairie was lonesome. He urged his friends to homestead in South Dakota but was unable to persuade them to leave the city. On March 19, 1910, Micheaux wrote in the *Chicago Defender*:

> The Negro leads in the consumption of produce, and especially meat, and then his fine clothes—he hasn't the least thought of where the wool grew that he wears and describes himself as being "classy." He can give you a large theory on how the Negro problem should be solved, but it always ends that (in his mind) there is no opportunity for the Negro. . . . I am not trying to offer a solution of the Negro problem, for I don't feel there is any problem further than the future of anything, whether it be a town, a state or race. It depends first on individual achievement, and I am at a loss to see a brilliant future for the young colored man unless he first does something for himself.

In 1909 Micheaux became enamored with a young school teacher from southern Illinois named Orlean McCracken. She was the youngest of two daughters of N. J. McCracken, presiding elder of the African Methodist Episcopal (AME) Church's southern Illinois district. When Micheaux was a young boy, the minister had been pastor of the AME church in Metropolis. After a long–distance courtship, Micheaux proposed marriage to Orlean. They were married in a small church in Chicago by the Reverend W. D. Cook on Thursday, April 20, 1910. Micheaux and his new wife left the same day for their home in Gregory, South Dakota.

From the beginning, the marriage was doomed. His city wife was unhappy in the isolated sod house without family or friends nearby. Farm work was hard and she was accustomed to teaching school; furthermore, his in–laws suspected Micheaux of marrying their daughter as a means of acquiring more land. To make matters worse, in March of 1911 their first child was stillborn. Micheaux's in–laws blamed him for not being with his wife when the child was born. Micheaux's absence was due to a farming accident. Several weeks later his wife left him, going back to Chicago with her father and sister. Micheaux went to Chicago several times to try to win her back but was unsuccessful.

The Birth of a Writer

Micheaux's days as a homesteader were drawing to a close. The droughts during the summer of 1911 severely damaged his crops, and he was unable to meet his mortgage payments. The *Gregory Times Advocate,* March 20, 1913, included the sale of one of Micheaux's quarter sections for the sum of $1888.27 by the Farmers and Traders Bank. The previous year, in June, the Royal Union Mutual Insurance Company had foreclosed on another section.

Despondent over his failed marriage and disappointed over the loss of his land, Micheaux was prompted to write a book describing his experiences. His book was titled *The Conquest* and was published in 1913 by the Woodruff Press in Lincoln, Nebraska. While the book was marketed as a novel, it actually was the autobiography of Micheaux with fictitious names and places. It details his early life in Metropolis, his job as a Pullman porter, and his experience in homesteading in the Rosebud section of South Dakota. The book presents an accurate account of how life was in this section of the United States from 1904 to 1913.

Months before the book was published, Micheaux was busy marketing it by himself. On April 3, 1913, the *Gregory Times Advocate* contained the following notice: "Oscar Micheaux was in the city Saturday taking orders for his book, *The Conquest*. . . . The editor had the opportunity to read the first chapter of the book, and can heartily recommend it as an interesting story if the first chapter is any criterion."

The book was so successful that Micheaux believed he could earn a living as a writer. By 1915 he had written another book, *The Forged Note,* published by Woodruff Press. To promote his second book, Micheaux went on an extensive tour, traveling to large cities including those in the South such as Atlanta, Memphis, and Birmingham. This novel was promoted as the literary sensation of the decade. In 1916 Micheaux moved to Sioux City, Iowa, and founded his own publishing company, Western Book Supply Company.

Micheaux's third book, *The Homesteader,* was published by his own company in 1917. This novel came to the attention of George P. Johnson, the booking manager of the Lincoln Motion Picture Company in Los Angeles, California. Johnson wanted to purchase the film rights to *The Homesteader.* Micheaux agreed to sell but insisted on two conditions that caused the deal to fall through. First, he wanted to go to Los Angeles and supervise the filming of the story. The second condition was set forth in a letter to George Johnson, written May 13, 1918, and quoted by Sampson: "By your circulars I note that your pictures appear to be limited to 3 reels, whereas I am sure this voluminous work could not be possibly portrayed short of eight reels, for it is a big plot and long story."

The closing of one door meant the opening of another for Micheaux. When the deal fell through with the Lincoln Motion Picture Company, Micheaux established the Micheaux Film and Book Company in Sioux City, Iowa, with a second office in Chicago. He sold stock in his company to the white farmers and businessmen he had known in South Dakota. The shares ranged in price from $75 to $100.

The Homesteader was produced as an eight–reel film with an all–black cast starring Charles Lucas in the leading role and Evelyn Preer as leading lady. All of the actors were members of the prestigious Lafayette Players of New York City. Many of the scenes were shot on location in Sioux City. According to the *Chicago Defender,* of the opening night in February of 1919:

> *The Homesteader,* the greatest of all Race productions . . . is a remarkable picture both as a story and photography; it tells of the troubles of a young man upon the sea of matrimony beginning where he gives up his real sweetheart as a matter of principle, marries another as a matter of accommodation and carries on through the details of a wedded life, made miserable for both parties by the hypocritical father of the girl—a preacher—who takes them both over the jumps, to the end that he is himself bumped off by the girl, who at the same time frees the young man from wedlock.

In 1921 Micheaux established another Chicago office at 119 West 132nd Street. He hired Joseph Lamy, a white man, for foreign distribution. The U.S. distribution office was in Chicago and supervised by his younger brother Swan Micheaux Jr. Micheaux's second film, *Within Our Gates* (1920), was controversial, containing a scene where a black man is lynched by a white mob in the South.

In 1920 there were no ratings for films; however, there was an Illinois State Board of Movie Censors. *Within Our Gates* was first rejected by this board because they feared it would incite a race riot. At a second showing, a number of prominent blacks were invited to the viewing, including representatives from the Associated Negro Press. While opinion was divided, the film was allowed to be shown for the first time in Chicago at the Hammon's Vendome Theater.

The controversy surrounding *Within Our Gates* did not prevent Micheaux from including lynching scenes in other movies. The 1921 release of *The Gunsaulus Mystery* was based on the actual case of Leo Frank, a young Jewish man convicted of killing a young white girl and lynched near Marietta, Georgia, in 1915. Controversy erupted when the film, patterned after the newsreel, showed Frank's body. The Jewish community found it objectionable. The black press responded to their outcry by pointing out that black people found W. D. Griffith's *Birth of a Nation* objectionable, yet it continued to be shown.

In 1924 Micheaux was again censored, this time by the Motion Picture Board of Censors in Virginia. *The Son of Satan* was banned in Virginia because of explicit language, even though it received rave reviews elsewhere. In the same year, Micheaux released *The Dungeon* and was criticized for his use of fair-skinned characters, although the use of such characters was a rather common practice at the time. D. Ireland Thomas, writing in the *Chicago Defender* for July 8, 1922, suggested that perhaps Micheaux was trying to book his film into white theaters. This was the case, as the black market was limited. Even though he had been able to sell his novels to whites, Micheaux never was able to penetrate the white theater market.

Discovers Paul Robeson

Micheaux had an unorthodox if not altogether bizarre way of identifying talented actors. Sometimes he would be struck by the person's gesture or some other intangible quality. Basically he trusted his intuition. Not only did he discover Lorenzo Turner, who starred in 14 Micheaux productions, he also cast Paul Robeson in his feature film debut. Robeson made his debut in *Body and Soul* (1925) at the New Douglas and Roosevelt Theaters on November 15, 1925. Robeson went on to become an actor and concert singer of international reputation.

Body and Soul suffered from a confusing plot but still received good reviews. The film dealt with a corrupt preacher who extorts money from gamblers and forces a young member of his church to steal money from her mother, and even includes a suggestion of rape. The subject matter caused the film to be censored in New York for its portrayal of the clergy. This forced Micheaux to edit the film, which, according to Bogle, made the plot all the more confusing. Outsiders suggest that Micheaux's personal experience with his former father–in–law may account for his virulent portrayal of ministers.

In 1926, Micheaux and Alice B. Russell, a stage and screen actor, married and made their home in Montclair, New Jersey. On March 1, 1927, Micheaux's brother, Swan, resigned from the Chicago office and took a job with the Agfa Raiv Corporation in Berlin, Germany. One biographer speculates that Micheaux forced his brother to resign because Swan had mismanaged the company and almost brought it to bankruptcy. The plot of Micheaux's film *The Wages of Sin* seems to support this theory. The 1927 film portrays a brother who owns a film company and gives his younger brother a position in the company, only to have the younger brother squander the company's money on women and entertainment.

As one might imagine, there were many problems to be faced by independent black filmmakers. Difficulty came when Swan left, forcing Micheaux to close the Chicago office. To save the company, Micheaux and his wife ran the New York office themselves. His wife kept the books, and he did all the film production: scriptwriting, directing, editing, and casting actors. Although he could not pay his actors large salaries, he was still able to get some of the top names of the day. Frequently he drew from his own family members and friends. His wife and her talented sister, actor Julia Theresa Russell, were often cast in lead roles.

Attempting to cut corners in every way he knew, Micheaux cut rehearsal time, used no retakes, and used local citizens as much as possible for extras. But on February 28, 1928, Micheaux was forced to file for bankruptcy in New York U.S. District Court. His assets were listed as $1,400 and his liabilities as $7,827. Financially, Micheaux was down but by no means out.

On the day that the court papers were filed, Micheaux was on the road promoting his two most recent films, *Thirty Years Later* and *The Millionaire.* As a result of his tenacity, in

1929 he reorganized his company, naming it the Micheaux Film Corporation. The officers were Oscar Micheaux, president; Frank Schiffman (white), vice president; and Leo Bracher (white), treasurer. Schiffman, the owner of several theaters in New York that catered to blacks, left after accusing Micheaux of misappropriating funds. It was not long before Micheaux was again running the company practically by himself.

Produces First Talking Feature Film

The first two films released by the newly reorganized company were *The Daughter of the Congo* (1930) and *The Exile* (1931). The former was a silent film with a musical soundtrack; the latter was the first all–talking feature film by a black independent filmmaker. For the two films Micheaux had an all–star cast. They were box office successes, but he was harshly criticized in the black press. Criticizing *The Daughter of the Congo,* Theophilus Lewis wrote:

> The first offense of the new film is its persistent vaunting of intraracial color fetishism. The scene is laid in a not so mythical republic in Africa. Half of the characters wear European clothes and are supposed to be civilized, while the other half are wearing their birthday suits and some feathers and are supposed to be savages. All the ignoble ones are black. Only one of the yellow characters is vicious, while only one of the black characters, the debauched president of the republic, is a person of dignity. . . . Even if the picture possessed no other defects, this artificial association of nobility with lightness and villainy with blackness would be enough to ruin it.

While some of Micheaux's themes were indicative of a lack of black pride, particularly regarding the affirmation of skin color, others appear out of synchronization with the conservative times in which they appeared. These usually were censored by the white establishment. *The Exile* is a case in point. In Pittsburgh, two members of the Censor Board objected to a scene that showed a white man trying to take advantage of a woman and then being thrashed by the black man who comes to her rescue. A later scene in the same movie showed a black man making love to what appeared to be a white woman.

The 1938 release of *God's Stepchildren* premiered at the RKO Regent Theater at 116th Street in New York, but after only a two–day run it was stopped. Again the issue was race. This time the Communist League and the National Negro League objected to the portrayal of color snobbery among blacks. Micheaux cut a scene that generated the most protest. As a result of the publicity generated by the controversy, the film did better than expected. Technically *God's Stepchildren* was one of Micheaux's best efforts. It was shot in the home of a friend, which meant the budget was substantially lowered.

The Notorious Eleanor Lee, released in 1940, was the last film to appear under the Micheaux Film Corporation label. Premiering in Harlem, the film opened to floodlights and a carpeted sidewalk. Colonel Hubert Julian, the well–known black aviator, was master of ceremonies and he was in formal dress, including top hat, white silk gloves, and a flowing cape. The movie, an exciting gangster story about a prize fighter, became a moderate success at the box office.

World War II forced Micheaux to cease productions because of the scarcity of talented actors and rising costs. During the war, Micheaux returned to his career as a novelist. Again he formed his own publishing company, the Book Supply Company, located in his home at 10 Morningside Avenue, New York City. Over a three–year period he wrote and published *The Wind from Nowhere* (1944); *Case of Mrs. Windgate* (1945); *Story of Dorothy Stanfield* (1946); and *Masquerade* (1947). All were successful, and many were sold by the author on the campuses of historically black colleges and universities.

In 1948 Micheaux unwisely invested a large sum of money to help finance *The Betrayal,* a movie adaptation of his book *The Wind from Nowhere.* Micheaux lost a fortune, which forced him back on the road to sell his books. At 67, he had crippling arthritis and depended on a wheelchair for mobility. While on a trip in Charlotte, North Carolina, Micheaux suddenly became ill and died in a local hospital a few days later, on Easter Monday, 1951. He was survived by his wife. The couple had no children.

On May 18, 1986, the Directors Guild of America posthumously presented Micheaux with the Golden Jubilee Special Directorial Award for his cinematic achievements. The following year, Micheaux was finally awarded a star on the Hollywood Walk of Fame. Of Micheaux's efforts, author and social commentator bell hooks has correctly written that Oscar Micheaux's work was a counter–hegemonic cultural production consciously created to disrupt and challenge stereotypical and racist representations of blacks. Despite criticism from both blacks and whites, Micheaux's films still remain an artistic view of black life in the past.

REFERENCES

Bogle, Donald. *Blacks in American Films and Television.* New York: Fireside, 1989.

———. *Toms, Coons, Mulattoes, Mammies, and Bucks.* New York: Continuum, 1994.

hooks, bell. ''Micheaux: Celebrating Blackness.'' *Black American Literature Forum* 25 (Summer 1991): 351–60.

Klotman, Phyllis R. ''Annual Film Quarterly Book Roundup: Black Cinema Treasures: Lost and Found by G. William Jones.'' *Film Quarterly* 46 (Summer 1993): 30–31.

Leab, Daniel. ''A Pale Black Imitation: All Colored Films.'' *Journal of Popular Film and Television* 4 (1975): 56–76.

Narine, Dalton. ''Black America's Rich Film History.'' *Ebony* 43 (February 1988): 132–138.

Sampson, Henry T. *Blacks in Black and White: A Source Book on Black Films.* Metuchen, NJ: Scarecrow Press, 1995.

Young, Joseph A. *Black Novelist as White Racist: The Myth of Black Inferiority in the Novels of Oscar Micheaux.* New York: Greenwood Press, 1989.

Nagueyalti Warren

Milady, Samuel.
See Lucas, Sam.

Dorie Miller

(1919–1943)

Serviceman, hero

Dorie Miller

An African American seaman became one of the earliest heroes of World War II in the Pacific arena. Dorie Miller was a messman in the disastrous first days of World War II in the segregated U.S. Navy. His courage and initiative during the attack on Pearl Harbor won him the Navy Cross and respect from the country he served honorably.

The son of Connery and Henrietta Miller, Dorie (or Doris) Miller was born on October 12, 1919, on a modest farm near Waco, Texas. As sharecroppers on a 28–acre cotton farm, his parents eked out a skimpy living. In his teen years, Dorie Miller had become a brawny young man who stood five–feet ten–inches tall and weighed over 200 pounds. He wanted to leave the farm, and when he was 19 he yielded to the call of a Navy recruiter in Waco who persuaded him to join the service.

Miller had little motivation to love the U.S. Navy. He had enlisted in a fighting service, and it had attached him—as it did all black sailors—to the most servile of jobs. His enlistment meant hard work at menial labor, since, until June 1, 1942, the messman branch was the only one officially open to African Americans. He was a mess attendant waiting tables aboard an all–powerful battleship and for some time thereafter had no chance to rise.

Brief training ashore, Miller was assigned to the *U.S.S. Arizona,* which, on December 7, 1941, was anchored in Pearl Harbor on the island of Oahu. It was a calm Sunday morning, and Miller was occupied with laundry on deck, when at 7:55 a.m. a formation of 353 Japanese dive bombers, level bombers, torpedo planes, and fighters, launched from six aircraft carriers, approached, to bring off the greatest surprise offensive in naval history. One–by–one the planes peeled off and plunged toward the *Arizona* and as the planes passed over the battleship, they released a devastating bomb.

After being knocked down, Miller managed to scramble to his feet; the reverberations of other blasts and the babble of machine guns broke the tranquility of the otherwise sluggish day. Although smoke and flames engulfed the harbor, Miller spotted someone lying on the captain's bridge. He ran to the spot; the wounded man was his commander, Captain Mervyn Bennion. There was blood on the deck from chest and stomach injuries as Bennion lay sprawled there. Although Miller could not stop the steady bleeding, he moved the captain to a safer place and sought medical assistance. As he moved the body toward a companionway, heedless of his own safety, bullets from an enemy plane continued their fire on deck.

Miller placed the officer near the deck's steel bulkhead as sailors and a medical corpsman treated the moribund captain. Although as a messman he was unauthorized to fire a gun, Miller crossed the bridge to a machine gun. He had been a crack shot with a squirrel gun back home in Texas, but had never been schooled in the use of a machine gun and had never fired one. Meanwhile, the enemy fire continued. The *Arizona* was the battleship most badly bombed and set afire. Bodies were scattered around the deck and some men jumped overboard as enemy planes flew low over the ship, firing upon the fleeing seamen.

Miller was knocked down by the exploding Japanese bombs. He might have leaped overboard as did many other members of the crew; instead, Miller rotated the machine gun on its base, fiddled with the gun, and squeezed the trigger as another plane flew over. When nothing happened, he released the jam, then fired successive bursts at an attacking aircraft. The Japanese plane that was his target erupted in flames and plunged into the sea. Miller was credited with dropping three more planes before his ammunition was spent. By now the *Arizona* was foundering and the gallant son of a Texas sharecropper was ordered to abandon ship.

Among the fearless and heroic stories that originated at Pearl Harbor that desperate day, Dorie Miller's was one least pleasing to a rancorous Navy command structure. Not that anyone could challenge the courage he demonstrated, or disavow his success, but such actions by a mess attendant and a black man were inconceivable. The U.S. Navy, saturated with the racist presumptions that blacks were inferior and of little account, was unhappy at having to recognize that a "Negro" could act heroically and fight effectively, especially of his own initiative. The Navy was even more hesitant to honor him publicly. Twelve weeks after Pearl Harbor, and in response to relentless pressure by newspapers and civil rights groups that stretched all the way to the White House, Dorie Miller was accorded the Navy Cross, "For his distinguished devotion to duty, extraordinary courage and disregard of his own personal safety." On June 10, 1942, when Miller was 22 years old, Admiral Chester W. Nimitz pinned the Navy's highest award for valor on his chest and advanced him to mess attendant first class. This was done on direct orders from President Franklin D. Roosevelt.

Miller received a hero's welcome ceremony in Waco and Dallas. He was greeted with deep satisfaction in New York's Harlem and in black communities elsewhere. He addressed a graduating class of noncommissioned officers at the Navy's Great Lakes Training School even though Miller and other African Americans were not deemed suitable for such training.

Mess attendant Miller was sent to Bremerton, Washington, to prepare as a cook. He resumed his old duty of waiting tables. On November 24, 1943, a Japanese submarine torpedoed the *U.S.S. Liscome Bay,* which sank at sea with most of her 712–man crew. Among them was Dorie Miller.

Segregation remained; not until June 1949 did the Naval Academy graduate its first black man. The ordeal of Miller in many ways mirrored more than three centuries of black struggle in the service of America. Nevertheless, Miller remains a celebrated figure for his gallantry during the bombing of Pearl Harbor.

REFERENCES

Hughes, Langston. *Famous Negro Heroes of America.* New York: Dodd, Mead, 1958.

Lee, Irvin H. *Negro Medal of Honor Men.* New York: Dodd, Mead, 1967.

Logan, Rayford W., and Michael R. Winston, eds. *Dictionary of American Negro Biography.* New York: Norton, 1982.

Richardson, Ben. *Great American Negroes.* Rev. ed., New York: Crowell, 1956.

Robinson, Wilhelmina S. *Historical Negro Biographies.* New York: Publishers Co., 1968.

Casper L. Jordan

Kelly Miller
(1863–1939)
Mathematician, sociologist, writer, journalist

Kelly Miller was a brilliant scholar and prolific polemicist on matters of race, education, and other public issues affecting the general welfare of African Americans from the late 1890s to the 1920s. He was a major force in the intellectual life of black America for nearly half a century. During his 44–year career (1890–1934) at Howard University, he was first a professor of mathematics, later a professor of sociology, and eventually dean of the College of Arts and Sciences. His role and influence at Howard were unparalleled, and Howard was sometimes referred to as "Kelly Miller's University."

Miller developed a national reputation as a lecturer, essayist, and newspaper columnist. He was probably the first African American scholar to become a syndicated columnist, primarily for the black press. Miller's column appeared weekly for nearly twenty years in the more than one hundred newspapers such as the *Pittsburgh Courier, Journal and Guide, Boston Chronicle, Afro–American,* and the *Washington Tribune.* It was estimated that he had access to more than half a million readers through these columns during the 1930s. Eisenberg wrote in the *Journal of Negro History* that Miller was not an "armchair observer," and that he traveled extensively at his own expense "speaking before teachers or Sunday church groups." Miller's discussions were "well attended, some by several thousands, and even white gatherings, unwilling to admit him as a member, heard him as a speaker."

Formally trained as a mathematician, Miller made the transition to sociologist with little difficulty in 1918. He embraced the new field of sociology because its discipline and rigor provided the possibility for an objective understanding of the race issue in America. As a sociologist, he wrote many scholarly articles for mainstream academic publications such as *Scientific Monthly, Atlantic Monthly, Educational Review* and *Journal of Social Sciences.* His earliest well–known scholarly work was a critical analysis, *Race Traits and Tendencies of the American Negro,* an 1896 work published under the auspices of the American Economic Association. This article argued that the alleged inferiority of blacks was genetically determined and was the cause of their social disorganization. Miller's career was devoted to matters of race because of its pervasive and determinative nature in American society.

Miller did not shy away from controversy, and some of his most notable essays, those contained in *Race Adjustment,* refuted racist theories about the innate inferiority of blacks. Miller believed, like many of his well–educated contemporaries, that blacks were an underdeveloped people but not an inferior people. He also believed that black underdevelopment would be overcome with education, self–reliance, good character, industry, and thrift. Miller emphasized this by pointing out the enormous progress blacks had made in spheres of endeavor in the 50 years after emancipation. He wrote in *The Primary Needs of the Race,* cited in W.D. Wright's article, "The Thought and Leadership of Kelly Miller," that "The world has now come to recognize that the Negro possesses the same faculties, powers and susceptibilities as the rest of mankind, albeit they have been stunted and dwarfed by centuries of suppression and ill usage."

Miller was born July 18 or 23, 1863 in Winnsboro, South Carolina, to Kelly Miller, a free black tenant farmer and veteran of the Confederate Army, and Elizabeth Roberts Miller. He was the sixth of ten children born to the couple. An uncle later became a member of the South Carolina legislature. Miller's early education was at a local school started during Reconstruction. There he attracted the attention of Willard Richardson—a minister, missionary, and teacher—because of his unusual abilities in mathematics. With the assistance of Richardson, in 1878 Miller was admitted to a much better and more established school, the Fairfield Institute, located in Winnsboro. In 1880 Miller was awarded a scholarship to Howard University's Preparatory Department. He completed the curriculum which emphasized Latin, Greek, and mathematics in record time.

Student Days at Howard and Johns Hopkins

While an undergraduate student at Howard, Miller passed the civil service examination and was appointed to a position as clerk with the U.S. Pensions Office. Miller was a good student and a diligent federal employee. In an unusual expression of love and gratitude, Miller used his earnings to purchase a farm for his parents which he gave them upon his graduation. After his graduation from Howard in 1886, Miller continued working for the Pensions Office to support himself and began studying physics, astronomy, and advanced mathematics with Captain Edgar Frisby, an English mathematician at the U.S. Naval Observatory. At the conclusion of that year of study, Miller asked Simon Newcomb, Frisby's boss at the National Observatory and a professor of mathematics at Johns Hopkins University, to sponsor his application for admission to that school. Newcomb recommended Miller's admission to the president of Johns Hopkins University, Daniel Coit Gilman. The request was significant because no black person had ever been admitted to the university. His application was presented to the board of trustees for action, and they agreed to admit Miller, consistent with the Quaker principles upon which the university was founded.

Miller was personally received by Gilman who assured him that he would be accorded the same rights, privileges, and access to facilities and programs as any other student at Johns Hopkins University. During his two years of study at Hopkins, Miller recounted, he experienced no overt hostilities nor classroom embarrassments. He described his treatment as "cool, calculated civility." Though Miller attended Hopkins from 1887 to 1889 as a graduate student, he did not complete his graduate degree because he was unable to meet the increase in tuition in 1889.

Miller returned to Washington, D.C., where he taught at the renowned M Street High School during the 1889–90 academic year. In 1890 Miller was appointed professor of mathematics at Howard University. This appointment launched an academic career that spanned more than four decades at that one institution of higher education. During those years, Miller subsequently received his A.M. (1901) and LL.D. (1903) degrees from Howard.

On July 17, 1894, Miller married Annie May Butler, a teacher at the Baltimore Normal School whom he had met while a graduate student at Johns Hopkins. They were the parents of five children—Isaac Newton, Paul Butler, Irene, May, and Kelly Jr.

From his position as a mathematics professor, Miller was successful in incorporating sociology into the college curriculum at Howard in 1895. From 1895 to 1907, Miller was professor of mathematics and sociology. Eventually, Miller taught sociology exclusively. Later, Miller played a pivotal role in building the department of sociology through his teaching and his leadership as the department head from 1915 to 1925. Miller was acting dean of the College of Arts and Sciences of Howard for one year, prior to his formal selection as dean. According to the *Dictionary of American Negro Biography,* Miller's appointment as acting dean in October of 1907, shortly after Booker T. Washington was elected a member of the university's board of trustees on May 28, 1907, was viewed by many as proof positive that the president had made a deal with Washington and his cohorts. There is no conclusive evidence to support or reject this proposition. What is known is that Miller was the most prolific and respected member of the undergraduate faculty. He agreed with the president's plans for Howard's future expansion, support from private philanthropic sources, and some accommodation with the trend toward applied sciences. Because of his status in the campus community and his support of the president's vision and philosophical position on Howard's future, Miller was the logical choice for dean. On January 21, 1908, Miller was appointed dean of the College of Arts and Sciences at Howard University.

Miller's impact at Howard was tremendous during the eleven years he served as dean. The old classical curriculum was modernized and redesigned to address the problems faced by blacks and to expand offerings in the natural and social sciences. Student enrollment increased, primarily through the efforts of Miller who traveled extensively lecturing at churches and high schools and promoting the educational opportunities available at Howard University. The enrollment at Howard increased at an annual rate of forty percent during Miller's tenure.

Miller believed in the systematic study of blacks and considered Howard the natural place for this kind of scholarly pursuit. Michael Winston wrote in *Dictionary of American Negro Biography:*

> Miller believed that Howard should become a center for studies of the American Negro and Africa, and continued to urge the inclusion of such courses in the curriculum. He envisioned the establishment of a "Negro–Americana Museum and Library." In 1914 he persuaded Jesse E. Moorland, a Howard trustee and alumnus, to donate to Howard his large private library on the Negro in Africa and the United States as a first step in the development of the proposed museum and research library.

The Moorland Foundation eventually became an important resource for scholarly studies on the Negro in the decades following the First World War.

In spite of the enormous contributions of Miller and other black academics at Howard, the presidency of that institution remained the exclusive domain of white men during Miller's time. Nonetheless, Miller was a strong advocate for the principle of black leadership at black universities given the exclusion of black professors from leadership roles in white universities. He was instrumental in uncovering the racist views of Howard's last white president, who had demoted Miller to dean of the Junior College (1919–1925) just before abolishing that college in 1925.

Miller became embroiled in a controversy with the first black president of Howard, Mordecai Johnson, who served from 1926 to 1960. The controversy was triggered by Howard University's Social Science Division's sponsorship of a conference with the Joint Committee on National Recovery that included Socialists and Communists on the program, and Miller's alarm at the growing number of communists and socialists who were joining the social sciences faculty at Howard. To Johnson, the issue was quite simply the university's right of academic freedom which encourages it to engage in discourse and inquiry which might involve individuals with views that are unpopular or outside the mainstream. Despite calls for a congressional investigation into "communistic teaching at Howard," the president vigorously defended the university's right to sponsor the conference and the sanctity of the academy as a forum for the free exchange and investigation of all ideas. Though his involvement in this controversy and his growing disillusionment with race relations of the era caused him some problems, Miller was still revered and respected, though he did not regain his earlier prominence on campus. His national reputation and stature were not severely affected by his battles with administrators at Howard.

When he retired in 1934, Miller held the post of Dean Emeritus. At the time of his retirement, sociology was undergoing a number of changes. Garraty and Sternstein wrote in the *Encyclopedia of American Biography* of a new sociology that was emerging on black college campuses, calling it "A myth–blasting social science that rejected the idea of a black cultural tradition in America; a sociology that permitted scientific detachment from the kind of dilemmas Miller tried to face."

Even after retirement, Miller continued to bring analytical rigor and discipline to his projects. Two of them were the revival of his plan to develop at Howard a research center and museum devoted to the documentation and preservation of black history and culture, and writing of his autobiography.

Philosophy and Activism Outside the Academy

Miller believed in racial self–reliance, self–help, pride, and unity. He encouraged professional and technical development, and the instillation of a strong sense of racial responsibility in young people. He also championed a prominent leadership role for the church. On this subject, W. D. Wright wrote in *Phylon,* "Miller wanted the Church to spread the ideas of thrift, economy, and industriousness to help inculcate the habits of self–sacrifice and saving, and to help mobilize blacks for economic and socio–cultural development." He also noted that in Miller's view "Religion furnishes the only sanction that can enable backward races to contemplate the trend of modern movements."

The Miller philosophy also held an important role for agriculture in the march to advance the race. He felt that agriculture was the basis for advancement of any underdeveloped group, with manufacturing coming later. Miller promoted the importance of blacks acquiring land, developing a strong separate rural economy, and developing their own enterprises and patronizing them. He decried northern migration and urban life as having a deleterious effect on the morals and values of black people.

Miller was often characterized as a reconciler, a harmonizer, and a straddler. His moderate leadership brought criticisms from all sectors, but according to Wright, "he was convinced that only a rational, moderate approach could help blacks make sustained and sure progress." Miller played an active role in the ideological debate between Booker T. Washington and W. E. B. Du Bois, believing that both industrial and higher education were necessary for the development of any race. Miller had worked with Washington while he served on the Howard University Board of Trustees and he had assisted Du Bois in editing *Crisis.* Miller had praise and criticism for the leaders and adherents of both camps, though he defended the more conservative position in one of his most celebrated essays, *Washington's Policy.* He saw himself as a mediator in the debate and sought to bring together both sides on common ground. Such a posture is often necessary but rarely appreciated, and Miller was criticized as indecisive and non–committal on this matter.

Like many intellectuals of his time, Miller believed that blacks had a right to education and he fought vigorously for that right. He was much less concerned with achieving a fully integrated educational system, because he felt integration would derail blacks from realizing their destiny. According to Wright in *Phylon,* Miller said that ''Integrated schools might make blacks spectators to the process of black development, rather than helpers.'' Miller was a strong crusader for the equality of blacks in all spheres of American life, including the equal right of blacks to vote. The ascendancy of Woodrow Wilson to the presidency, the perpetration of outrageous acts of violence against blacks, the challenge to traditional black middle class leadership posed by Marcus Garvey, and the post–World War I antiblack sentiment all converged to make for confusing and desperate times. Eisenberg wrote, ''No longer was the Washingtonian philosophy of industrial education and non–resistance widely accepted. . . . No one organization was sufficiently concerned with the general welfare of the race. Eisenberg also contended that ''the N.A.A.C.P. concentrated on legal matters and the National Urban League on city adjustment for rural families.''

In an attempt to develop a common approach to the persistent and perplexing problems facing blacks, in 1923 Miller called for a national ''Sanhedrin.'' The purpose of the proposed Sanhedrin, patterned after the highest ruling body and court of justice among the Jewish people in the time of Jesus, was to forge a sense of racial unity, pride, and consciousness among blacks, and to formulate a program to address the problems facing members of the race. The Sanhedrin was convened in February 1924 in Chicago. There were more than 500 delegates representing fifty organizations in attendance. The agenda was full, and proposals and resolutions were put forward on issues such as health care, aid to farmers and students, participation of women in civic affairs, conditions of urban life and many other pressing, though not politically charged issues. Initial reaction to the meeting was favorable. Critics, however, were vociferous in faulting the Sanhedrin for its silence on such vital issues as the Ku Klux Klan, labor unions, housing, and intermarriage, and its weak position on lynching, segregation, and industrial discrimination. Follow–up activities did not proceed well because of old schisms among the leaders, jealousies, inadequate planning, and Miller's inability to assume the duties of president on a full–time basis. These problems thwarted the development of a permanent organization.

Miller's Publications

Miller's most widely read essays and pamphlets were later compiled and published as books. Many of them were in the form of open letters or responses to hate–filled diatribes of prominent public figures. One of Miller's earliest successful pamphlets, published in 1905, was *As to the Leopard's Spots: An Open Letter to Thomas Dixon.* That pamphlet was followed a year later by Miller's response to the Atlanta race riot in 1906, *An Appeal to Reason on the Race Problem: An Open Letter to John Temple Graves.* In 1911, Miller wrote a very popular essay, entitled ''The Political Plight of the Negro,'' which appeared in *The Nineteenth Century.* He followed that with the publication of his Race Statesmanship Series which included his most widely distributed pamphlet, *The Disgrace of Democracy: An Open Letter to President Woodrow Wilson.* More than 250,000 copies of this 1917 work were sold. The government tried to limit distribution of the pamphlet, and it was prohibited from army posts.

In 1913 Miller began publishing *Kelly Miller's Monographic Magazine,* a compilation of essays on race and national affairs. This enterprise led to the publication of some of Miller's books though his most significant book, *Race Adjustment,* was published in 1908 before he began the magazine. His other significant books, *Out of the House of Bondage* published in 1914 and *The Everlasting Stain* published in 1924, were considered an outgrowth of Miller's monographic magazine. *Race Adjustment,* out of print for more than a generation, was reissued in 1968 as part of a series by Schocken Books on Negro History.

Miller died on December 29, 1939, at his home in Washington, D.C., after a heart attack. His funeral was held at the Andrew Rankin Memorial Chapel on the Howard University campus and he was buried at Lincoln Memorial Cemetery in Washington, D.C. His survivors included his wife and four of his children.

Miller was a dominant intellectual figure from the latter part of the nineteenth century to the early twentieth century. He understood racism and the need to protest. Miller believed in lawful protest, but refused to take a dogmatic position of either militancy or moderation. His numerous publications leave an indisputable legacy of Miller's commitment to the advancement of the race.

REFERENCES

Eisenberg, Bernard. ''Kelly Miller: The Negro Leader as a Marginal Man.'' *Journal of Negro History* 45 (July 1960): 182–97.

Garraty, John A., and Jerome L. Sternstein, eds. *Encyclopedia of American Biography.* 2nd ed. New York: HarperCollins, 1995.

Logan, Rayford W., and Michael R. Winston, eds. *Dictionary of America Negro Biography.* New York: Norton, 1982.

Lowery, Charles D., and John F. Marszalek, eds. *Encyclopedia of African American Civil rights: From Emancipation to the Present.* New York: Greenwood Press, 1992.

Meier, August. ''The Racial and Educational Philosophy of Kelly Miller, 1895–1915.'' *Journal of Negro Education* 29 (Spring 1960): 121–27.

Miller, Kelly. *Race Adjustment [and] The Everlasting Stain.* New York: Arno Press and the *New York Times,* 1968.

———. *Out of the House of Bondage.* 1914. Reprint, New York: Arno Press and the *New York Times,* 1969.

Ploski, Harry A., and James Williams, eds. *The Negro Almanac.* 5th ed. Detroit: Gale Research, 1989.

Schuyler, Robert Livingston, and Edward T. James, eds. *Dictionary of American Biography.* New York: Charles Scribner's Sons, 1958.

Wright, W. D. "The Thought and Leadership of Kelly Miller." *Phylon* 39 (June 1978): 180–92.

Paulette Coleman

Arthur Mitchell

(1934–)

Dancer, choreographer, educator, dance company founder

Arthur Mitchell

Arthur Mitchell was one of the first black Americans to become successful and internationally known as a classical ballet dancer. He was the first black principal dancer in one of the world's great dance companies, the New York City Ballet (NYCB), which he joined as soloist in 1955. To give minority students an opportunity to learn classical ballet, he founded and served as director of the Dance Theater of Harlem, demonstrating that blacks could succeed in the art and bringing international recognition to blacks as classical dancers.

Born in the Harlem section of New York City on March 27, 1934, Arthur Adam Mitchell was the son of Arthur Mitchell, a contract engineer, and Willie Mae Mitchell. He was the oldest of five children – two brothers, Herbert and Charles, and two sisters, Laura and Shirley. When he was ten, Mitchell joined a Police Athletic League glee club, where his training in the arts began. He attended the public elementary and junior high schools in his neighborhood. During his teenage years, Mitchell came under the influence of a street gang known as the Hilltop Lovers but was able to free himself from the gang's hold. "Education saved me," he told Robert Fleming for *American Visions.* A junior high school counselor saw him tap dancing at a social function and recognized that he had talent as a dancer. The counselor encouraged him to take dance lessons as well as audition to gain admission to New York's High School of Performing Arts. After studying tap dance for two years, he entered the school and majored in dance. At some point he also studied modern dance and ballet.

Mitchell performed jazz and modern dance in school concerts as well as with outside groups. Some of his teachers nudged him toward modern dance. He appeared in modern dance recitals with Nantanya Neumann and Shirley Broughton and with the Choreographer's Workshop. It was about this time that Mitchell crystallized his thoughts about a career in dance. "When I realized this, it gave me tremendous strength, energy, oneness, pride and sense of direction," he said in *American Visions.* On leave from school in 1952, his senior year, he went to Paris and appeared in a revival of *Four Saints in Three Acts,* a revival of the opera by Gertrude Stein and Virgil Thomson. He returned to New York and won the High School of Performing Arts's annual dance award, becoming the first male so honored. By now he had become interested in ballet and found it his greatest challenge. Mary Hinkson, one of his teachers and a black who had danced as soloist with the Martha Graham company, encouraged him to develop this interest in ballet. Hinkson encouraged Karel Shook, a teacher at Katherine Dunham's School of Dance, to teach Mitchell the techniques of ballet. According to Alvin Ailey in *Revelations,* at one time Mitchell lived with Shook on Thirty–Fourth Street and First Avenue. Since Mitchell's ankles were not yet strong and flexible enough, "he did a thousand *battements tendus* every night to stretch his feet and make his ankles more supple." Ailey visited Shook's place and spent considerable time with Mitchell and Shook. Upon graduation in 1952 Mitchell, who had received a scholarship to Bennington College, which offered a fine modern dance training program, chose instead to accept another scholarship and study at the School of American Ballet. He knew that the school, directed by renowned choreographer George Balanchine, was the main training ground for members of the New York City Ballet. Mitchell became Balanchine's student.

Racism found a place in the field of dance and for a while kept other black male dancers out of the field. For Mitchell, it meant that white parents objected to having him attend classes with their daughters and to performing duets with them in recitals. The school, however, held steadfast to its commitment to Mitchell and his rights as a student.

Mitchell continued to perform as a modern dancer while he studied. He danced with the Donald McKayle Company, the New Dance Group, and with Sophie Maslow's and Anna Sokolow's companies. He first appeared on Broadway in the musical *House of Flowers,* by Harold Arlen and Truman Capote, which opened on December 30, 1954, and which ran for 165 performances. Geoffrey Holder, Carmen De Lavallade, Pearl Bailey, Juanita Hall, Diahann Carroll, and Alvin Ailey appeared in the same production. It was the first Broadway appearance for Mitchell and Carroll. Mitchell left his role as understudy to become lead dancer four weeks later. He joined the John Butler Company in 1955, appearing on American television and in the European tour until he accepted the New York City Ballet's invitation to join the company.

Joins New York City Ballet

The principal dancer for the New York City Ballet from 1955 to 1969, Mitchell made his debut with the company in November of 1955 in *Western Symphony.* He became the first black dancer in a major ballet company. His career continued amid racial stirs: letters to the company protested its allowing a black man to dance with a white woman. When the company arrived to do television shows, producers tried to keep Mitchell from dancing. An interview in 1973, cited in *American Visions,* quotes Mitchell as recalling an insult he heard at a performance: "My God, they've got a nigger in the company, but you know, he's not bad." Balanchine remained firm in his statement that there would be no performance if Mitchell did not dance.

Balanchine, who admired Mitchell's talents, helped ensure Mitchell's early success with the company by choreographing a number of dances especially for him. Mitchell scored an early success in a *pas de deux, Agon,* which Balanchine created. According to *Current Biography,* this was "a ballet in which Stravinsky's highly complex score . . . matched by Balanchine's equally complex choreography." The ballet premiered on December 1, 1957, with Mitchell dancing with Diana Adams Mitchell. Mitchell continued to be cast in roles without regard to his color; he had white partners and at times he was cast as a black, for example, in *The Nutcracker* and *The Figure in the Carpet.*

Mitchell had another early success. His modern dance background, which had become highly expressive, led him to play the role of Puck in Shakespeare's *A Midsummer Night's Dream,* which Balanchine developed into the first full–length ballet created in the United States. Reviewing his performance in the *New York Herald Tribune* for January 28, 1962, cited in *Current Biography,* Walter Terry said of Mitchell: "As he trots about with his magical flower . . . Mr. Mitchell leads us into a world of delightful fantasy."

Mitchell's performances in jazz ballets for the New York City Ballet included Balanchine's *Clarainade* and *Ivesiana*; Jerome Robins's *Interplay,* and John Taras's *Ebony Concerto.* He appeared in several other ballets by Balanchine, including *Four Temperaments, Episodes,* and with Suzanne Farrell in the Balanchine–Stravinsky ballet *Orpheus.* He danced with Maria Tallchief in John Taras's *Piège de Lumière.*

When the NYCB was between seasons, Mitchell was engaged in other activities, such as William Dollar's Ballet Theatre Workshop and the Guy Lombardo production of *Arabian Nights* performed at the Jones Beach Marine Theatre. When the musicals *Carmen Jones* and *Kiss Me, Kate* were revived at New York's City Center, Mitchell appeared in them. He appeared on television, performing in such programs as the *Jackie Gleason Show, Look Up and Live, Camera Three,* and *Omnibus,* and for a long time appeared on nearly every major television variety show in the United States.

During this period as well, Mitchell began work as a choreographer, assisting Rod Alexander in arranging the dances for the Broadway musical *Shinbone Alley,* which opened on April 13, 1957, and lasted through 49 performances. That summer he was choreographer and a dancer at the Newport (Rhode Island) Jazz Festival. He was a member of the interracial dance group that was created for the Festival of Two Worlds held in Spoleto, Italy, in 1960. The next year he served at the festival as dancer, choreographer, and actor. He toured Europe and the Middle East, dancing at Convent Garden in London, La Scala in Milan, the Paris Opéra, and in such major cities as Tel Aviv, Athens, and Moscow.

Mitchell danced in the Metropolitan Opera production of *Orfeo* in March of 1962, and later that year went on the NYCB's tour of the Soviet Union. Again his performance in the *pas de deux* from *Agon,* this time with Allegra Kent, warmed up the cold audience in Moscow who had a special interest in the company's lone black dancer. Following that, when John F. Kennedy was inaugurated as President of the United States in 1961, Mitchell and Kent did a duet from Balanchine's *Stars and Stripes,* and in May of 1964 he danced the lead role in *Western Symphony* before President and Mrs. Lyndon B. Johnson at the Presidential Salutes in New York City and in Washington, D.C.

In 1965 Mitchell helped to organize and became artistic director of the American Negro Dance Company, which was scheduled to perform in the first World Festival of Negro Arts in Dakar, Senegal. Unable to raise the $130,000 needed for the tour, the plans were canceled.

Founds Dance Theater of Harlem

In the late 1960s Mitchell set up ballet companies in Italy, Senegal, Brazil, and elsewhere. He left the NYCB in 1972 to devote his energies to the black ballet company he had founded in 1969—the Dance Theater of Harlem.

By 1968 Mitchell had been commuting to Brazil for two years as he organized the Brazilian Ballet Company. On April 4, 1968, the day that Martin Luther King Jr. was assassinated, Mitchell was on his way to the airport for another flight to Brazil when he learned the shocking news. He told *Ebony* magazine for June of 1974: "By the time I got to the airport I was saying to myself 'Arthur, why are you going to Brazil when you should be doing something at home. . . .' I turned around, went back home, and started contacting folks about starting a school." Karel Shook, then master ballet and choreographer of the Netherlands National Ballet, his friend and former teacher, was among the first to be called.

Mitchell worked to establish the Dance Theater of Harlem, which was started in a loft in Greenwich Village in February of 1969. According to the 1974 *Ebony* article, the three–fold purpose of the school was "to train those desiring a career in dance and/or dance teaching; to provide professional dancers for a resident company for companies elsewhere; and to train young people as lighting experts, set and costume designers, choreographers, etc." There were only two professional dancers for the thirty students enrolled. The school moved to larger quarters, to the basement in Central Harlem's Church of the Master–space renovated with a $325,000 grant from the Ford Foundation. To match the grant, the troupe, founded about the same time the school was established, raised money by giving performances, their first on January 8, 1971, at the Guggenheim Museum. To attract students and stimulate an interest in the school, Mitchell said in the same article, "We would play the music real loud so that anyone passing by could hear it. Kids would come in and just sit on the floor and watch what we were doing. That's how we recruited, and it wasn't long before we had more than 400 students." The company made its first European tour that summer, appearing initially in the Festival of Two Worlds in Spoleto, Italy, then toured Italy, Belgium, and Holland.

Still the school needed money and space. Mitchell promoted the school throughout New York's cultural community and received positive response. The company received $109,000 from the Alva and Bernard F. Gimbel Foundation to purchase a spacious garage located on West 152nd Street, which was renovated and became their permanent home. The theater attracted students from as far away as Chicago and cities in the South; it also attracted students from low income families, many of whom had full stipends while others had very low fees. By 1976 1,300 students were enrolled while the company was comprised of 27 dancers. The school graduated a number of highly disciplined dancers, including Ben Vereen and Hinton Battle. Some of the principal dancers in the company were Lydia Abarca, Virginia Johnson, Lowell Smith, and Paul Russell.

The company also presented works by Mitchell, George Balanchine, Geoffrey Holders, and others. At first the company gained its greatest recognition in European capitals, where, according to Mitchell in James Haskins's *Black Dance,* the name "Harlem is an attraction. Harlem is a magic word. When you say *Harlem,* it fascinates everyone all over the world. Many times they'll say, 'Oh, are you the Globetrotters?' Or, 'Are you a basketball team?' But a lot of people come and say, 'Ah, it's ballet, but you know they're wonderful.'" The company has now gained greater recognition in the United States.

In the early 1990s the Dance Theater of Harlem met financial difficulties and lost the support of several of its major sponsors. To trim operations, Mitchell canceled some of the company's performances and furloughed fifty dancers and staff for six months. The company's financial health was restored when Mitchell persuaded some of the nation's largest firms, such as American Express and the Lila Wallace–Reader's Digest Foundation, to invest in the company. The theater finished the year in the black. It was now supported by the income it received from touring as well as from foundations. Quoted in *American Visions,* Richard Philip of *Dance Magazine* called Mitchell a pioneer and "a tremendous role model and teacher." The company's survival "is a miracle, largely due to Arthur Mitchell's determination and its wonderful performers," he said.

In addition to his dancing career, Mitchell was a dance educator. He taught dance at the Katherine Dunham School, the Karel Shook Studio, and the Melissa Hayden School, Cedarhurt, Long Island. He also taught at the Jones–Haywood School of Ballet in Washington, D.C. The predominantly black school was subsidized by the School of American Ballet and the Ford Foundation.

Highly recognized for his worth, Mitchell received a Certificate of Recognition from the Harold Jackman Memorial Committee in 1969. That same year Arthur Mitchell and the Dance Theater of Harlem received a special tribute from the Northside Center for Child Development. He received the Changers Award from *Mademoiselle* magazine, 1970; the twentieth annual Capezio Dance Award, 1971; and the National Medal of Arts in 1993. In 1994 he was named ambassador–at–large by the National Endowment for the Arts, and in 1994 he received a MacArthur Fellowship. Mitchell received the School of Ballet Lifetime Achievement Award in 1995.

Mitchell remained executive director and choreographer of Dance Theatre of Harlem, Everett Center for the Performing Arts, and continued the tradition that helped make him famous by the training of young blacks to become classical ballet dancers.

Current address: Dance Theatre of Harlem, Everett Center for the Performing Arts, 466 West 152nd Street, New York, NY 10031.

REFERENCES

Ailey, Alvin, with A. Peter Bailey. *Revelations: The Autobiography of Alvin Ailey.* New York: Carol Publishing Group, 1995.

"Ballet Star." *Ebony* 15 (November 1959): 122–26.

Contemporary Black Biography. Vol. 2. Detroit: Gale Research, 1992.

Current Biography. New York: H. W. Wilson, 1966.

"Dance Theatre of Harlem: Where Talent Abounds." *Ebony* 29 (June 1974): 106–113.

Fleming, Robert. "Arthur Mitchell and His Harlem Crusade." *American Visions* 7 (April/May, 1992): 48–50.

Haskins, James. *Black Dance in America.* New York: Crowell, 1990.

Hughes, Catharine. "Poet in Motion." *Ebony* 23 (October 1968): 210–17.

Morton, Carol A. "The Dance Theatre of Harlem: An Experience in Blackness." *Essence* 3 (May 1972): 58–59.

Who's Who Among Black Americans, 1996–97. 9th ed. Detroit: Gale Research, 1996.

Jessie Carney Smith

Clarence M. Mitchell Jr.
(1911–1984)
Administrator, civil rights activist, lawyer

Clarence M. Mitchell Jr. was a key participant in the movement to enact legislation ensuring the civil rights of African Americans. He worked quietly behind the scenes on Capitol Hill to win passage of major civil rights legislation between 1957 and 1968, including the Civil Rights Act of 1964, the Voting Rights Act of 1965, and the Fair Housing Act of 1968. As a lobbyist for the NAACP, Mitchell worked tirelessly to secure laws that would fight workplace and housing discrimination—laws which now stand as a legacy to his efforts.

Born March 8, 1911, in Baltimore, Maryland, Clarence Maurice Mitchell Jr. was the son of Clarence Maurice Mitchell Sr., a chef, and Elsie Davis Mitchell. As the eldest of six children, Mitchell, like his brothers and sisters, was taught the value of family, church, and respect for self and others.

Mitchell attended the Baltimore public schools and worked at night at a hotel to assist his family financially. Although there was very little time to play, he managed, under the sponsorship of the Young Men's Christian Association, to engage in amateur boxing under the name of "Shamrock Kid." In the spring of 1928, he graduated from Douglass High School and in the fall entered Lincoln University in Pennsylvania. While attending Lincoln University, Mitchell joined a debating team and eventually became its captain. By 1932, he completed his B.A. degree and began contemplating a career in medicine.

Mitchell returned to Baltimore, however, and accepted a job as a reporter at the *Baltimore Afro–American.* As a young journalist for the newspaper, Mitchell witnessed and reported on two lynchings on the eastern shore of Maryland in 1933. His vivid memory of these lynchings allowed him to testify before Congress.

Mitchell received his law degree from the University of Maryland Law School and later took graduate courses in social work at Atlanta University and the University of Minnesota. In 1937 he became executive secretary of the Urban League in St. Paul, Minnesota. On September 7, 1938, he married Juanita Elizabeth Jackson, the daughter of Lillie Mae Jackson, a well–known civil rights activist in Maryland. Juanita Jackson, like her husband, became a lawyer and a widely–known civil rights activist. The couple had four sons who carried on the Mitchell tradition of public service: Clarence Mitchell III, who became a Maryland state senator; Keiffer Jackson Mitchell, a physician; Michael Mitchell, who served as a Baltimore city councilman; and George Davis Mitchell, who was a law clerk in the family firm and a real estate executive.

While Mitchell worked at the St. Paul Urban League, many supporters recognized his potential as a leader. Among them was Robert Weaver, later the first Secretary of Housing and Development during Lyndon B. Johnson's administration. In 1941 Weaver recommended Mitchell to become the assistant director of Negro Manpower Service at the War Manpower Commission in the Department of Labor. In 1942, Mitchell became a member of the Fair Employment Practices Committee. This commission was formed as a result of action by A. Philip Randolph, president of the Brotherhood of Sleeping Car Porters, and Walter White of the NAACP. Together these two powerful men threatened a protest march on Washington, D.C., if action was not taken to further the hiring of African Americans in defense industries. President Roosevelt feared the possible violence and political embarrassment, so he issued Executive Order 8802, which set up a Fair Employment Practices Committee to receive and investigate any complaints of discrimination against African Americans in war industries. In 1945, the NAACP appointed Mitchell as its labor secretary in the Washington office to assist the executive secretary, Walter White. In 1950, Mitchell became the director of the Washington Bureau of the NAACP. As director of the bureau, he developed an effective working relationship with Democratic and Republican leaders. Due to his political astuteness and involvement in successful legislative matters, he was dubbed "the 101st Senator of the United States."

In addition to serving as the chief lobbyist for the NAACP, Mitchell also accepted the job of legislative chairman of the Leadership Conference on Civil Rights. Mitchell's first successful achievement as the director of the bureau occurred in 1957. Congress passed the Civil Rights Act of 1957, the first piece of civil rights legislation since Reconstruction. This act, among other things, created the U.S. Commission on Civil Rights and the Office of Assistant Attorney General for Civil Rights within the U.S. Department of Justice. Mitchell's advocacy of equal opportunity was not limited to civil rights legislation. His personal fight for equal opportunity propelled him to national prominence in 1956 when he was arrested for attempting to use a whites–only railroad terminal waiting room in Florence, South Carolina.

Seven years later the bureau achieved another milestone. Mitchell stood by as a witness when President Lyndon Johnson signed into law the Civil Rights Act of 1964, and the following year the Voting Rights Act of 1965. In 1968, Mitchell played a key role in lobbying for the passage of the 1968 Fair Housing Act, the final landmark civil rights legislation of the decade. After the passage of the 1968 civil rights bill, the Congressional Quarterly Service, cited in *Negro Heritage,* reported that Mitchell "was the catalyst who organized and kept together the forces that passed the bill." During his 28 years as civil rights lobbyist, he firmly believed that operating within the framework of existing legislation would bring about success. According to the *New York Times* on March 20, 1984, Mitchell once stated that "success usually comes from action based on facts rather than on vain hopes or groundless fears."

Mitchell's expertise on civil rights issues encouraged presidents from Harry Truman to Jimmy Carter to consult him. He also received many awards, including the NAACP's Spingarn Medal in 1969 for his achievements as a civil rights lobbyist, and the Medal of Freedom, the nation's highest civilian honor, presented to him by President Jimmy Carter in 1980.

In 1978, Mitchell's grueling schedule of 12–hour days came to an end with retirement. He decided to return to Baltimore to practice law. He carried on his commitment to public service in retirement by serving on the University of Maryland board of regents and as an advisor to the mayor of Baltimore. Almost five years after his retirement, the man who played a pivotal role in the passage of civil rights legislation of the 1950s and 1960s and the oldest brother of Parren J. Mitchell, then a U.S. Representative, died of a heart attack at the Maryland General Hospital on March 18, 1984. Although Mitchell died at the age of 73, the landmark legislation he helped to shape stands as his legacy.

REFERENCES

"Clarence M. Mitchell: Civil Rights Lobbyist, New Spingarn Medalist." *Negro Heritage* 8 (1969): 126–127.

"Clarence M. Mitchell Is Dead; N.A.A.C.P. Lobbyist Till '78." *New York Times,* March 20, 1984.

"Clarence Mitchell: The Man on the Hill." *Crisis* 87 (December 1980): 562.

"14 Win Medal of Freedom." *New York Times,* April 22, 1980.

"The Impact of Pure Brass: Clarence Mitchell, Jr." *Crisis* 83 (April 1976): 122–126.

"Rights Movement Leaders Gather in Memory of One of Their Own." *New York Times,* March 24, 1984.

Veteran Civil Rights Leader Clarence Mitchell Jr. Dies." *Jet* 75 (2 April 1984): 15.

Who's Who in America, 1980–81. 41st ed. Chicago: Marquis Who's Who, 1980.

Williams, Michael W., ed. *The African American Encyclopedia.* North Bellmore, NY: Marshall Cavendish, 1993.

Patricia A. Pearson

Loften Mitchell

(1919–)

Playwright, theater historian, writer

Loften Mitchell's first stage productions were the shows which he and brothers Louis, Melvin, and Clayton performed in the backyard of their home in Harlem. From these humble beginnings, Mitchell's talent for writing plays, screenplays, and novels commanded popular attention, and his works were widely performed. In addition to his writing, Mitchell's work as a theater historian earned him recognition as one of the chief custodians of the history of African Americans in the theater.

Mitchell was born April 15, 1919, in Columbus, North Carolina, to Ulysses Sanford Mitchell and Willia Spaulding Mitchell. In addition to his three brothers, he had one sister, Gladys. The family moved to Harlem before Loften Mitchell was a month old.

Mitchell married Helen Marsh in 1943, and they had two sons, Thomas and Melvin. They were divorced in 1956. He married Gloria Anderson in 1991.

Young Loften Mitchell's interest in the theater began at the vaudeville theaters of Harlem. He learned first–hand the promise of black theater as he observed at work such pioneering black artists as Dick Campbell, Ralph Cooper, Ethel Waters, Fredi Washington, and Canada Lee. Quoted by J. A. Jahnnes in *Afro–American Writers after 1955,* he said: "I dared to dream the long dream and others dared to encourage me . . . I saw in the theatre the elevation of human life." He also witnessed the negative stereotypes of African Americans in the American theater and later worked to remove such images in order to project real–life, positive images.

After finishing junior high, Mitchell enrolled in New York Textile High because he had been promised a job on the school newspaper. Realizing his need for training at an academic high school, he transferred to DeWitt Clinton High in the Bronx, where he graduated with honors in 1937. He found work as an elevator operator and delivery boy to support himself while he studied playwriting during the evening at City College of New York. Meanwhile he performed with the Rose McClendon Players in Harlem. A professor from Talladega College in Alabama helped him win a scholarship to study there, and Mitchell received his B.A. degree with honors in 1943. While at Talladega, he won an award for the best play written by a student. The play included the stories he had heard at the vaudeville houses while he was growing up in Harlem. It also became the basis for his critical work later published in 1967, *Black Drama: The Story of the American Negro in the Theater.*

After two years in the U.S. Navy as a seaman second–class during World War II, Mitchell enrolled as a graduate student at Columbia University in New York. There he studied playwriting with John Gassner from 1947 to 1951. In 1948 he accepted a job with the Department of Welfare as a social investigator, but continued to study during evenings. At this time he wrote one of his first commercially successful plays, *Blood in the Night* (1946), which was followed by *The Bancroft Dynasty* in 1948, and *The Cellar* in 1952. In 1957 he wrote *A Land Beyond the River,* a drama based on South Carolina pastor and schoolteacher Joseph DeLaine's historic court case, which ended segregation in public schools. The play enjoyed a long Off–Broadway run, and was published as a book. The following year Mitchell won a Guggenheim award, which enabled him to return to Columbia and write for a year.

Mitchell worked as a writer and actor for New York radio station WNYC's weekly program "The Later Years," (1950–1962). He also wrote a daily program titled "Friendly Advisor" for radio station WWRL in New York (1954).

A series of plays followed: *The Photographer* (1962), *Ballad of Bimshire* (1963), *Ballad for the Winter Soldiers* (1964), and *Tell Pharaoh,* which was televised in 1963 and produced on–stage in 1967. *Star of the Morning* (1965) dramatized the life of black comedian Bert Williams. Mitchell's most successful musical, a tribute to Harlem's entertainers written with Rosetta LeNoire and entitled *Bubbling Brown Sugar* (1975), opened on Broadway, traveled to the London stage, was nominated for a Tony Award for best musical, and was awarded the Best Musical Award in 1977. He also wrote *Cartoons for a Lunch Hour* (1978), *A Gypsy Girl* (1982), and *Miss Ethel Waters* (1983).

In addition to his plays, Mitchell never lost sight of the need for a written history of blacks in the theater. He wrote his most widely–read work, a study of African American theater entitled *Black Drama,* in 1967. In this collection of 12 essays, Mitchell discussed Charles Gilpin's work in Eugene O'Neill's *Emperor Jones* at the Provincetown Theatre in 1920. Mitchell stated that "This play, while offering one of the most magnificent roles for a Negro in the American theatre, is the first in a long line to deal with the Negro on this level. O'Neill obviously saw in the Negro rich subject matter, but he was either incapable or unwilling to deal directly with the matter." The work also examined the African Grove Theater of 1820, the Rose McClendon Players of 1939, and such outstanding artists as Ira Aldridge, Bert Williams, Paul Robeson, Sidney Poitier, and Ruby Dee.

Mitchell was a professor at State University of New York at Binghamton's theater department and the Department of African American Studies (1971–85), and professor emeritus from 1985 to the present. In addition, he wrote a novel, *The Stubborn Old Lady Who Resisted Change* (1973), and edited *Voices of the Black Theater* (1976). In *Voices,* Mitchell credited actor and writer Dick Campbell with shaping his career in the theater and introducing him to Ossie Davis, Frederick O'Neal, Alain Locke, W. C. Handy, and others who also promoted Mitchell's work or produced his plays. Regina M. Andrews, whose reminiscences are also recorded in *Voices,* gave Mitchell and other Pioneer Drama Group members access to the theater in Harlem's 115th Street Library where they performed two of his plays, *Cocktails* and *Cross Roads.* The group performed there again in 1946 to produce two more of Mitchell's plays, *The Cellar* and *The Bancroft Dynasty.*

In addition to being widely performed, Mitchell's plays earned him honors and awards. He won a playwriting award from the Research Foundation, State University of New York (1974), and the Outstanding Theatrical Pioneer Award from the Audience Development Committee in 1979.

An important figure who has made important contributions to the African American theater, Loften Mitchell's work as playwright and essayist preserves the work of black artists who preceded him as well as those whose genius, talents, and pioneering efforts were realized during his lifetime. He has documented an important part of black America's cultural development, in addition to contributing to that development through the body of his own written work.

Current address: 88–45 163rd St., Jamaica, NY 11432.

REFERENCES

Abramson, Doris E. *Negro Playwrights in the American Theater, 1925–1959.* New York: Columbia University Press, 1969.

Black Writers. Detroit: Gale Research, 1989.

Davis, Thadious M., and Trudier Harris, eds. *Afro–American Writers after 1955: Dramatists and Prose Writers.* Detroit: Gale Research, 1985.

Peterson, Bernard L. *Contemporary Black American Playwrights and Their Plays.* Westport, CT: Greenwood Press, 1988.

Ploski, Harry A., and Roscoe C. Brown Jr., eds. and compilers. *Negro Almanac.* New York: Bellwether Publishing Co., 1976.

Rush, Theressa G. *Black American Writers Past and Present.* Metuchen, NJ: Scarecrow Press, 1975.

Shockley, Ann A., and Sue P. Chandler. *Living Black American Authors.* New York: Bowker, 1973.

COLLECTIONS

The papers of Loften Mitchell are located at the State University of New York at Binghamton, the Schomburg Center for Research in Black Culture in New York, Talladega College, and Boston University.

Jacqueline Jones–Ford

Parren J. Mitchell

(1922–)

Congressman, civil rights activist, educator

Parren J. Mitchell, the first African American from Maryland elected to Congress, served as a member of the U.S. House of Representatives from 1971 to 1986. In Congress he was known as "Mr. Minority Enterprise" because of his efforts to promote economic empowerment in the black community and his support of legislation benefiting minority businesses. An influential and effective leader in the House of

Representatives, he helped organize the Congressional Black Caucus and served as its chairman in the late 1970s.

Mitchell was born on April 29, 1922, in Baltimore, Maryland, to Elsie and Clarence Mitchell. His father supported the family by working as a hotel waiter. Parren Mitchell was the ninth of ten children, three of whom died in childhood. The surviving children were Evelyn Mary, Clarence Jr., George Albert, Lorenzo William, Anna Mae, Parren James, and Elsie Julia.

Although the Mitchell parents were not community activists, they grounded their children in religion. They also taught them to respect education and to be driven by a sharp sense of self–pride. The Mitchells of Maryland became one of the country's most exceptional political families since the 1930s. Some family members entered politics while others made their impact felt in the civil rights arena. Parren Mitchell's older brother, Clarence M. Mitchell Jr., for example, was the Washington lobbyist for the NAACP for nearly two decades. In that capacity he helped push many civil rights bills through Congress during the 1960s.

After attending Baltimore public schools, Parren Mitchell entered the U.S. Army in 1942 and served as an infantry officer in the 92nd Infantry Division during World War II. He received a Purple Heart before he was discharged in 1946. Upon leaving the Army, he enrolled at Morgan State College as it was known then in Baltimore and, in 1950, he earned his bachelor's degree. In the same year, he successfully sued the University of Maryland to compel the university to accept him as its first African American graduate student. He completed his master's degree in sociology in 1952.

After graduation, Mitchell taught sociology at his alma mater, Morgan State College, during 1953 and 1954. From 1954 to 1957, Mitchell was supervisor of probation work for the Supreme Bench of Baltimore City. In 1963 he began his service as the executive secretary of the Maryland Commission on Interracial Problems and Relations, a commission formed to oversee the implementation of the state's new public accommodation law. Two years later, he became executive director of the Baltimore Community Action Agency, an anti–poverty program. In 1968 Mitchell returned to Morgan State College as a professor of sociology and assistant director of its Urban Affairs Institute.

Mitchell soon decided to throw his hat in the political ring. He ran unsuccessfully in the Democratic primary for Maryland's Seventh Congressional District seat in 1968. Two years later, however, he won the general election. This victory made him the first African American since 1898 elected to Congress from a state below the Mason–Dixon line.

Mitchell's career in Congress focused primarily on the economic empowerment of minorities. He urged African Americans to recognize the essential link between political power and economic power and worked to increase economic opportunities for minorities through strengthening and increasing minority economic institutions. Mitchell wrote major legislation that provided economic opportunities for minorities. In 1976 he attached an amendment to a Public Works Bill that compelled state, county, and municipal governments seeking federal grants to set aside ten percent of their funds to retain minority firms as contractors and subcontractors. He also introduced legislation in 1976 that required proposals from contractors to spell out their goals for awarding contracts to minority subcontractors. The law potentially provided access to billions of dollars for minority businesses. His amendment to the multi–billion dollar Surface Transportation Assistance Act of 1980 required that ten percent be set aside for minority businesses. It was primarily through Mitchell's efforts that minority businesses enjoyed tremendous increases in the procurement of government contracts.

During Mitchell's eight terms in Congress he served as whip–at–large; senior member of the House Banking, Finance and Urban Affairs Committee; chairman of its Subcommittee on Domestic Monetary Policy; chairman of the House Small Business Committee; chairman of the Task Force on Minority Enterprise; chairman of the Subcommittee on Housing, Minority Enterprise and Economic Development of the Congressional Black Caucus; and member of the Joint Economic Committee.

Mitchell left Congress in 1986 after serving 16 years. In 1998, he still served as chairman of the Minority Business Enterprise Legal Defense and Education Fund (MBELDEF), a nonprofit group he founded in 1980. The MBELDEF's mission is to counteract setbacks to minority business and provide a focus for minority economic development through the promotion of positive public and private policies, practices and innovations, and in particular, to aid the interests of minority businesses, in seeking full enforcement of present laws and defending against efforts to erode their effectiveness. The organization also seeks to promote minority business development through public education.

Mitchell's efforts have been widely honored. He accepted 14 honorary degrees, mostly doctorates. He has also received awards from more than 3,000 national and local consumer, civil rights, business, economic, and religious groups. Some of these diverse groups include the National Alliance of Black Educators, the Southern Christian Leadership Conference, the Morehouse College Alumni, the Joint Center for Political Studies, the Minority Contractors of Dayton, the Alaska Black Caucus, the Consumer Federation of America, the National Bankers Association, the National Association of Black Manufacturers, and the Martin Luther King Jr. Center.

A civil rights activist since his youth, Parren J. Mitchell has continued to be an advocate for civil rights. During his years as a member of the U.S. House of Representatives, he proved to be a gifted politician as well as an effective and influential legislator. Since leaving Congress, Mitchell has continued to promote and defend legislation beneficial to minority business.

Current address: Minority Business Enterprise Legal Defense and Education Fund, 220 I St. NE, #280, Washington, DC 20001.

REFERENCES

''Biographical Sketch of Parren J. Mitchell.'' Washington, DC: Minority Business Enterprise Legal Defense and Education Fund, n.d.

Clay, William L. *Just Permanent Interests: Black Americans in Congress, 1870–1991.* New York: Amistad Press, 1992.

McNeil, Thomas J. ''Parren J. Mitchell: Trailblazer from Black Baltimore.'' Master's thesis, Morgan State University, 1994.

Minority Business Enterprise Legal Defense and Education Fund. Washington, DC: MBELDEF, n.d.

Mitchell, Grayson. ''Maryland's Most Maverick Mitchell.'' *Black Enterprise* 7 (July 1977): 27–33, 54.

''Mitchell of Maryland: Standing Up, Speaking Out.'' *Washington Post,* February 1, 1976.

Ragsdale, Bruce A., and Joel D. Treese. *Black Americans in Congress, 1870–1989.* Washington, DC: U.S. Government Printing Office, 1990.

Salser, Mark R., ed. *Black Americans in Congress.* Portland, OR: National Book Company, 1991.

COLLECTIONS

The Soper Library at Morgan State University holds approximately 120 items in its Parren J. Mitchell Collection located in the Parren J. Mitchell Seminar Room.

Delphine Ava Gross

Tom Molineaux
(1784–1818)
Boxer

Tom Molineaux was a boxer whose prowess in the ring secured his freedom from slavery and culminated in a professional career in England. Although unsuccessful, Molineaux's attempts to win the British heavyweight championship contributed to his enduring reputation and led to his induction into the Boxing Hall of Fame.

Molineaux was born on March 23, 1784, in Georgetown, then an incorporated town in Maryland and now a prestigious residential area in the District of Columbia. As was the case with most slaves, the family name was derived from that of the plantation master, Algernon Molineaux, who soon moved to Richmond, Virginia. Tom Molineaux's father, Zachary, was so outstanding a boxer that he is credited as being the founder of boxing in America; Zachary's father was also a renowned boxer. When Zachary Molineaux died, the teenager assumed his father's position as chief handyman on the plantation as well as continuing to train as a boxer.

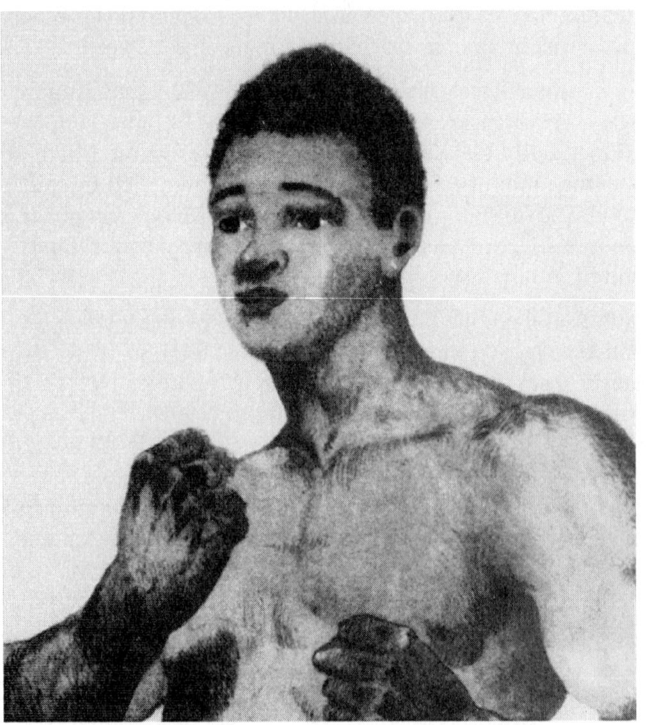

Tom Molineaux

In the years around the beginning of the nineteenth century, prowess as a boxer or jockey was a road to favorable treatment of a slave by a master with a love of sport and gambling. In *Pioneers of Black Sport,* Ocania Chalk wrote that, ''As a young man, [Molineaux] won his freedom and $100 dollars for his master when, on an adjoining plantation, he whipped a slave named 'Black Abe' who had been acknowledged as the toughest fighter around.'' In addition to his freedom, Molineaux received the then princely sum of $100.

When Molineaux defeated ''Black Abe,'' owned by Randolph Peyton, a neighboring plantation owner, he left the South forever with $500 in one pocket and his manumission papers in the other. He went to New York City and headed for the docks where he was hired first as a porter and then as a stevedore. His reputation was enhanced as he became known as ''master of the city's waterfront brawlers,'' according to Roi Ottley. He lived and worked near the old Catherine Markets which gave him proximity to merchant ship crews who were boxing aficionados. He soon learned from a sea captain that he could earn a good living as a boxer in England. In 1809, Molineaux left America and earned his passage working as a sailor on the *H.M.S. Bristol,* a merchant ship.

A New Life and Career

Soon after landing, Molineaux embarked on a professional career under the guidance of Bill Richmond. His new sponsor was a native Staten Islander born a free black and brought to England in 1777. Richmond's patron was General Percy, the future Duke of Northumberland, who had served as a commander during the British occupation of New York. By 1800 he had become a semi–professional boxer with fifteen recorded bouts of which two were losses. Richmond was extremely popular and enjoyed the patronage of the English nobility. Lord Camelford, an avid sports fan and fight–backer, hired him as his valet and helped establish him in the tavern business. When Richmond moved to London, he opened the Horse and Dolphin Tavern in St. Martin's Lane in Leicester Square and established a hotel on Whitcomb Street, Haymarket. Lord Byron was one of his admirers.

When Molineaux arrived in London, Richmond was in a position to be of service in furthering the novice boxer's career since he also conducted a boxing academy. Under Richmond's training regimen, Molineaux demolished his first opponents in eight consecutive bouts. They are often identified as "Unknown" or by false names because they feared being identified as losers to a black boxer. By then, Richmond felt that Molineaux was ready for a championship bout and openly challenged Tom Cribb, a recently retired champion, to return to the ring to fight his protégé. Cribb was the British bare–knuckle champion which was analogous to being world champion. The challenge was widely publicized since it was printed in the *London Times* and set for December 10, 1810, at Copthall Common near East Grinstead, Sussex. Molineaux was the loser by outright trickery but the accounts vary. According to Chalk:

> Tom Molineaux was bilked out of his rightful victory. Molineaux knocked Cribb down–and–out in the twenty–eighth round. Cribb's second, Joe Ward, leaped into the ring and accused Molineaux of having lead weights concealed in his hands. Meanwhile, the referee, Ap Rhys Price, exhorted the slowly reviving Cribb, "Now, Tom, now! For God's sake, don't let the nigger win. Remember the honour of old England."

Meanwhile, the timekeeper ignored the mandatory 30–second count, and Cribb lay senseless for two full minutes. After being revived, he recovered enough to beat Molineaux in the 40th round. Other accounts have the fight ending in the 33rd round; one has Molineaux hitting the ring post and fracturing his skull; another has Cribb's second biting Molineaux's thumb and arguing with Molineaux's second about rules. The most bizarre account is given by Budd Schulberg:

> As bloody black Molineaux waited to be proclaimed the first American and the first of his race to be champion of England, the toughs slashed through the ropes . . . the thugs saw to it that British honor was avenged. They broke Molineaux's fingers and tightened their own around his bull–like neck. . . . When order was restored, Cribb was refreshed, Molineaux was done in, and the Union Jack was ever so precariously at the top of the flagpole again.

Cribb retired again amid constant mutterings about the blatant and grave injustice done to Molineaux, the winner in the hearts of fair–minded Englishmen who cared about pugilistic skills, not skin color. Richmond demanded a rematch, the notice being printed in the Christmas Day 1810 issue of the *London Times.* Although it expressed Molineaux's sentiments about racial discrimination, a factor in his debatable loss, he did not write it since he was illiterate. Meanwhile, awaiting an answer, he did exhibition boxing with anybody willing to enter the ring. Unfortunately, he neglected to train properly and began enjoying the good life to the extent that he and Richmond parted company. On September 28, 1811, the rematch was held at Thistleton Gap, Wymondham. Molineaux's lack of commitment was described by Arthur Ashe: "When the day of the bout arrived . . . [he] reportedly consumed a whole chicken and a quart of ale just before going into the ring."

Cribb won by a knockout in an 11–round fight that lasted only nineteen minutes and ten seconds. He had earned $1,000 for the first bout and received $4,000 for the rematch under the winner–take–all Articles of Agreement. Molineaux left with a broken jaw and a subscription of $125 collected by ringside sympathizers. His loss, according to Schulberg, was "an allegory played again, this time before 25,000 mad–dog Englishmen."

Molineaux was defeated in both spirit and body and swiftly descended into a downward spiral that proved irreversible. He became an alcoholic and street brawler. He traveled throughout Scotland and Ireland as a boxing instructor and performed with a troupe of boxers and a circus. His last fight against a credible opponent was with George Cooper in 1815; it was over in less than twenty minutes, another blot on Molineaux's record. During the last year of his life, Molineaux was supported by black friends who were members of the 77th Regiment Band in Galway, Ireland. On August 8, 1818, he died in the regimental barracks, his body wasted from the ravages of tuberculosis and excessive drinking and malnutrition. Molineaux ended up penniless due to his own gullibility, lack of a formal education, and dependence on dishonest managers, trainers, and promoters. His worst mistake was becoming estranged from Bill Richmond who was greatly respected in life and greatly mourned at his death; unlike his protege, he did not die penniless or alone.

In 1958 Molineaux was inducted into *The Ring*'s Boxing Hall of Fame. According to Chalk, "Molineaux's career was a prototype of the lot of the black prizefighter in years to come, a legacy that he could no more control than he could change his slave heritage." On July 5, 1939, Molineaux's great–great nephew, John Henry Lewis, was knocked out by Joe Louis in the first heavyweight championship bout between two black fighters in America.

REFERENCES

Ashe, Arthur R. Jr. *A Hard Road to Glory.* 3 vols. New York: Warner Books, 1988.

Chalk, Ocania. *Pioneers of Black Sport.* New York: Dodd, Mead, 1975.
Henderson, Edwin Bancroft. *The Negro in Sports.* Rev. ed. Washington, DC: Associated Publishers, 1939.
Isenberg, Michael T. *John L. Sullivan and His America.* Urbana: University of Illinois Press, 1988.
Logan, Rayford W., and Michael R. Winston, eds. *Dictionary of American Negro Biography.* New York: Norton, 1982.
Oates, Joyce Carol. *On Boxing,* Garden City, NY: Dolphin/ Doubleday, 1987.
Odd, Gilbert E., ed. *Encyclopedia of Boxing.* New York: Crescent Books, 1983.
Orr, Jack. *The Black Athlete: His Story in America.* New York: Lion Books, 1969.
Ottley, Roi. *Black Odyssey: The Story of the Negro in America.* New York: Charles Scribner's Sons, 1948.
Schulberg, David. *Sparring with Hemingway and Other Legends of the Fight Game.* Chicago: Ivan R. Dee, 1995.

Dolores Nicholson

Irvin C. Mollison

Irvin C. Mollison
(1898–1962)
Attorney, scholar, judge

President Harry S Truman's appointment of Irvin C. Mollison to the post of associate judge of the U.S. Customs Court in 1945 was a history–making event. Mollison, however, had been making history since he left his native Mississippi to enter the best educational institutions outside the South and make his mark as a scholar. He went on to set legal precedents by convincingly arguing before the U.S. Supreme Court the unconstitutionality of racially restrictive covenants. His well–argued case marked the beginning of fair housing litigation that would challenge defacto segregation in the North.

Irvin Charles Mollison was born in Vicksburg, Mississippi, on December 24, 1898. His mother, Ida Welbourne Mollison, was a school teacher. His father, Willis Elbert Mollison, was one of the last black persons in Issaquena County, Mississippi, to hold a major public office after Reconstruction. He was elected circuit and chancery clerk in 1883. Mollison had two brothers, Walter A. and Welbourne A., and two sisters, Lydia and Ann. The family belonged to the Episcopal Church in Vicksburg.

Mollison attended Tougaloo Academy right outside the capital of Jackson, Mississippi. From Tougaloo he entered Oberlin College in Ohio in 1916, where he spent one year before gaining acceptance to the University of Chicago as a sophomore. At the university Mollison was inducted into Phi Beta Kappa honor society and graduated with honors in 1920. He was admitted to the University of Chicago Law School in the fall of 1920. Mollison graduated in 1923 and sat for the bar examination during the summer. He passed and was admitted to the Illinois Bar.

Mollison and several friends began a private law practice in Chicago. William L. Dawson and Herman Moore shared the law offices of Mollison, Moore and Dawson with him. Moore was later appointed a judge and assigned to the Virgin Islands; Dawson became a congressman. Both were instrumental in getting Mollison appointed to a federal judgeship.

Through a mutual friend, Mollison met socialite Alice Rucker, the daughter of Henry A. Rucker of Macon, Georgia. Rucker was a prominent politician. On August 26, 1930, Mollison and Alice were married in Chicago. The wedding was the social event of the year. In spite of the Great Depression, Mollison earned a good salary and the couple resided at 417 East 60th Street in Chicago. The Mollisons were model citizens. Alice Mollison devoted her time to volunteer work at Provident Hospital, where Mollison became secretary of the Board of Directors. In 1938 Mollison was appointed a member of the Board of Directors of the Chicago Public Library, and from January 1944 to October 1945 he served as a member of the Board of Education for the city of Chicago.

Mollison practiced law in Chicago for 20 years and was the lead attorney on the famous 1940 Hansberry Case, which he argued before the Supreme Court. In *Hansberry v. Lee,*

Lorraine Hansberry's father challenged the restrictive covenants in the city of Chicago that prevented black people from receiving fair housing opportunities. In the end Hansberry won his case, but the stress and strain of the long fight took its toll on him and he died of a heart attack.

In October of 1945 President Truman nominated Mollison for the position of associate justice of the U.S. Customs Court in New York. This federal judgeship carried with it a lifetime appointment. He was the first black person to be nominated for such a position within the continental United States. On Friday, November 10, 1945, Mollison's nomination passed the Senate without any dissenting votes. When asked on November 10, 1945, by *New Amsterdam* news reporter, Julius J. Adams, how he felt about his appointment, Mollison replied, "I deeply appreciate the honor. I do not regard this appointment as any particular personal recognition, but as a recognition of the race to which I belong."

In 1946 the Schomburg Center of the New York Public Library recognized Mollison for his contribution to better race relations for his participation in such groups as the Cook County Bar Association and the National Lawyers Guild. Mollison was also a lifetime member of the NAACP and a member of the National Urban League. In 1954, he and other African American leaders, resigned from the Urban League—charging that it had lost contact with the needs and wants of the people—in hopes of forcing the organization to take a more proactive stance with the political movements of the time.

After his appointment to the U.S. Customs Court, Mollison and his wife moved from Chicago to 670 Riverside Drive in New York City, but they continued to think of Chicago as home. Mollison commuted between the two cities and often held court in both. Returning from court in Chicago on May 5, 1962, Mollison suffered a massive heart attack and was found dead in his compartment on the Twentieth Century Limited train when it arrived at Grand Central Station. He was 63–years old.

Mollison was buried at St. Edmunds Episcopal Church in Chicago on Saturday, May 12, 1962. He was survived by his wife of 32 years, two brothers and two sisters. He had served the nation well by helping to eliminate racial restrictive covenants in housing. In honor of his achievements, a Chicago school was named the Irvin C. Mollison School in 1955. It is located at 4415 South King Drive.

REFERENCES

"Death Takes Judge Mollison and Louis Lantier." *Amsterdam News,* May 12, 1962.

"First Black Federal Judge in U.S. Takes Office." *Amsterdam News,* November 10, 1945.

"Irvin C. Mollison, U.S. Judge, 63, Dies." *New York Times,* May 6, 1962.

"Senate Gets Nomination of Mollison." *Amsterdam News,* October 13, 1945.

COLLECTIONS

Mollison's papers are housed in the Library of Congress and at the University of Chicago.

Nagueyalti Warren

Garrett A. Morgan
(1875–1963)
Inventor, businessman

An inventor and businessman who was active in the affairs of Cleveland, Ohio's black community, Garrett A. Morgan is widely known as the inventor of the gas mask. Although racism made it difficult for him to get the mask accepted, his invention saved countless lives during World War I.

Born on March 4, 1879, Garrett Augustus Morgan was the seventh of eleven children of Sidney and Elizabeth (Eliza) Reed Morgan. He grew up on a farm in Paris, Kentucky. His slave mother was part Indian and had been freed in 1863 by the Emancipation Proclamation. His father was the son of a Confederate colonel. With six years of education, when he was 14–years old, Garrett Morgan moved to Cincinnati, Ohio, where he was employed as a handyman for a prosperous landowner. Because he possessed little formal education, Morgan hired a tutor to assist him with his grammar skills.

In June of 1895 Morgan relocated to Cleveland, Ohio, destitute and friendless, where he remained for the rest of his life. He learned three trades and patented his many inventions. He would consequently possess a factory, a business earning a sizable annual profit, and a home.

Morgan began his work in Cleveland as a sewing machine adjuster for a clothing manufacturer. This position stimulated his lifelong preoccupation and skill with mechanical things. In 1907 he began to repair and sell sewing machines, the first of his several business enterprises. His business was so successful that, in 1909, he established a tailoring plant, the Morgan Skirt Factory, and hired 32 employees to produce coats, suits, and dresses.

Morgan's adaptability and ingenuity was further displayed when he discovered and perfected a human hair–straightening procedure. He had discovered the procedure by accident in 1905. To market the product, in 1913 he founded the G. A. Morgan Hair Refining Company. This company soon offered a complete line of hair–care products all bearing Morgan's label.

Morgan's National Safety Hood was his most notable invention, however. Morgan had played with the idea as early as 1912 and improved his original mask in the ensuing years. His patent application identified his safety helmet as a]"Breathing–Device." In 1914 he was awarded U.S. Patent No.

Garrett A. Morgan

1,113,675. On July 25, 1916, 250 feet below Lake Erie's surface, a discharge erupted in the Cleveland Waterworks tunnel. Workmen were trapped. Morgan and other emergency personnel wore early versions of Morgan's safety hood invention—later known as gas masks—and were able to rescue the endangered workers.

Manufacturers produced, and fire departments used, Morgan's invention, but he could not persuade black Clevelanders to invest in a company to help produce his safety hoods. He had to turn to the white community to help establish a manufacturing concern. He became the general manager of the National Safety Device Company. All other officers were white.

Morgan marketed his invention from state to state, frequently hiring white men to display his apparatus when visiting certain southern states. To hide his identity further, he "passed" as an Indian. He remained unsuccessful in his attempts to persuade blacks to invest in the stock of the company. The stock soared in price until it became widely known that Morgan was a black man, and then the mask was no longer produced or generally used. During World War I, however, the mask preserved American soldiers from lethal chlorine gas fumes on the battlefields.

Morgan's other major invention, a three–way automatic traffic signal, received a patent in 1923. The G. A. Morgan Safety System publicized the traffic control mechanism as "A better protection for the pedestrian, school children, and R. R. crossing." Morgan was granted patents for the traffic mechanism in Canada and England. In 1923 the General Electric Company bought the patents for his traffic signal for $40,000. With this money, Morgan bought a 121–acre farm near Wakeman, Ohio. There he established the exclusively black Wakeman Country Club and attempted to sell lots to develop Wakeman Heights, "a village of our own," according to his promotional cards.

In 1931 Morgan was an unsuccessful independent candidate for the City Council in Cleveland—his first and only try for public office.

After Morgan developed glaucoma in 1943, he made annual visits to the Mayo Clinic in Rochester, Minnesota, but they were of little use. He was left almost blind for the rest of his life. This disability notwithstanding, he designed new products. In 1961 he proposed a pellet to be placed in cigarettes to prevent a fire if the smoker fell asleep with the cigarette still burning. His other inventions included a woman's hat fastener, a round belt fastener for sewing machines, and a friction drive clutch.

Morgan was a shrewd entrepreneur and a concerned Cleveland citizen. He established in 1920, and published until 1923, a weekly newspaper, the *Cleveland Call,* to fill a vacuum of news coverage pertaining to black achievements in the white newspapers. He served as treasurer of the Cleveland Association of Colored Men until it merged with the NAACP. Morgan became a lifelong member of the NAACP. He sat on the committee for the Home for Aged Colored People and was a member of the governing board of the Phillis Wheatley Association, a social service organization for women.

Throughout his lifetime, Morgan received awards and citations for his inventions. In 1914 he won the First Grand Prize Golden Medal of the National Safety Device Company at the Second International Exposition of Safety and Sanitation. He held honorary membership in the International Association of Fire Engineers and also was cited by the U.S. government for his traffic signal. In September of 1963, a month after his death, Morgan received national acknowledgment at the Emancipation Centennial Celebration in Chicago. A public school in the Harlem section of New York City was named for him in 1976.

Morgan was married twice. His first marriage in 1896 to Madge Nelson, ended in divorce after two years. On September 22, 1908, he married fellow Clevelander Mary Anne Hassek, a Bohemian seamstress. Garrett Morgan died in Cleveland in August of 1963. After funeral services at the Antioch Baptist Church, he was buried in Lake View Cemetery, Cleveland. He was survived by his three sons, John P., Garrett A. Jr., and Cosmo H. and seven grandchildren. He had made a major contribution to the world with his chief inventions, the gas mask and the traffic light signal.

REFERENCES

Hayden, Robert C. *Eight Black American Inventors.* Reading, MA: Addison–Wesley, 1972.

Logan, Rayford W., and Michael R. Winston, eds. *Dictionary of American Negro Biography.* New York: Norton, 1982.

Mather, Frank Lincoln. *Who's Who of the Colored Race: A General Biographical Dictionary of Men and Women of African Descent.* Chicago: Mather, 1915.
Van Tassel, Donald D., and John J. Grabowski, eds. *The Encyclopedia of Cleveland History.* Bloomington: Indiana University Press, 1987.

COLLECTIONS

The Garrett Augustus Morgan Papers are deposited at the Western Reserve Historical Society, Cleveland, Ohio.

Casper L. Jordan

Morganfield, McKinley.
See Muddy Waters.

Ernest Morial

Ernest Morial
(1929–1989)
Mayor, politician, lawyer, judge

Ernest Morial, active both in law and in civil rights, was the first black assistant U.S. attorney and the first elected to the Louisiana legislature since the time of Reconstruction. His sound leadership eventually led to his election as the first black mayor of New Orleans. He proved highly effective in that position, fighting for the rights of minority business owners and helping to revitalize the city.

Ernest Nathan ''Dutch'' Morial was born October 9, 1929, in New Orleans, the youngest of six children born to Walter and Leonie Morial. His family considered him to be a beautiful baby, and when his father saw similarities between the baby on the Dutch–brand paint can and his son, he nicknamed Morial ''Dutch''. The nickname remained with Morial throughout his life.

Morial and his family were part of a light–skinned ethnic group commonly known as ''Creoles'' in Louisiana. Because of Morial's light complexion and straight black hair, blacks, whites, and Creoles often questioned his race. Morial, however, always thought of himself as black.

As a child, Morial was small, but very strong–willed. Since winning was very important, he accepted every challenge. His peers and teachers believed that he was destined for great things; his playmates called him ''The Great Morial.'' Quoted in the newspaper *Dixie,* one of his teachers once commented: ''I don't know what this little fellow is going to be but he's going to be something great.''

Because Morial's family was devoutly Catholic, his early education began at St. Louis Catholic school. He later attended Xavier Prep, a high school known as the most prestigious black Catholic school in New Orleans. When he was in the tenth grade, his parents transferred him to McDonogh 35, which had the reputation for being the best public school in the city for blacks.

At the end of his first year at McDonogh 35, Morial, thinking life at sea would be more exciting, decided to leave school to become a merchant marine, following in the footsteps of his older brother Walter. His brother Walter, however, convinced him to return to school and may have been responsible for turning his life around. Morial graduated from McDonogh in 1948. From there he entered Xavier University in New Orleans, the only historically black Catholic college in the country, and graduated in 1951 with a bachelor of science degree in business administration. With the support of his family, peers, and teachers, he entered the all–white Louisiana State University Law School in 1951. Although he was not the first black man to attend the school, in 1954 he became the first to graduate.

Morial began law practice in 1954 with his mentor and friend, A. P. Turead, a prominent civil rights lawyer and ''dean'' of Louisiana's black lawyers. The two were instrumental in bringing many desegregation suits to court and thereby dismantling many segregation practices and policies. At the same time Morial became involved with the New Orleans chapter of the NAACP and served as chapter president from 1962 to 1965. Under his administration the membership tripled from 2,000 to 6,000. He also held a position on the association's national relations committee.

From his involvement with the NAACP and civil rights issues, Morial developed an interest in entering the political arena in Louisiana. His first attempt to win a seat on the Louisiana Democratic State Central Committee in 1959 was unsuccessful. From 1965 to 1967 he was an assistant U.S. attorney, a first for a black man from Louisiana. In 1967 he was elected to the Louisiana legislature, the first black to hold such a position since Reconstruction. During his race for the legislature, he received the endorsement of the local papers of New Orleans, the *New Orleans State–Item* and the *Times Picayune*—again the first black given such recognition.

Morial was a highly successful legislator. He often engaged in behind–the–scenes politics in a quiet manner. Quoted by James Rosemary in "Personality: Dutch Morial," he once said of himself:

> It was just good common sense for me to resist the urge to jump–up and grab the microphone constantly. Many times, just the fact of my being for something . . . vocally would have caused others to be against it.

While in the legislature he served on the legislative committee and encouraged the governor to appoint a black to a seat on the criminal courts bench.

Morial was first appointed, then elected, as juvenile court judge for the Orleans Parish from 1970 to 1972. He was also judge of the Louisiana Court of Appeal, fourth circuit, second district, from 1972 to 1978.

On November 13, 1977, Morial was elected mayor of New Orleans. His election made news throughout the nation, and was important for several reasons. New Orleans was ranked fourth among cities containing the largest number of African Americans. New Orleans was the second largest port city in the country. Morial was the first black elected mayor of the city.

From the beginning of his administration, Morial accomplished great things for New Orleans and Louisiana. Serving two terms, from 1978 to 1986, he created the first Office of Economic Development to coordinate the city's efforts to retain and attract business and industry. He created the city's first office of Minority Business Development and appointed the first minority business enterprise counselor to assist small and minority–owned businesses in bidding for contracts with government agencies and to move minorities into the economic mainstream. He was responsible for the development of a new $60 million redevelopment of the riverfront area for retail use.

Morial was affiliated with many organizations and boards on the local, state, and national levels. He was a founding member of the Lawyer's Committee for Civil Rights in 1963. He served on the board of directors of the National League of Cities and the Tulane University board of governors. From 1968 to 1972 he was general president of the Alpha Phi Alpha Fraternity. He received Xavier University's Alumnus of the Year Award in 1977 and an honorary doctorate from the institution in 1978. From 1971 to 1980 *Ebony* magazine continuously named him one of the 100 Most Influential Blacks.

Morial died on December 24, 1989, of cardiac arrest due to a severe asthma attack and was buried in the St. Louis Cemetery #1 in New Orleans. He was survived by his wife, Sybil Haydel, daughter of a prominent physician in New Orleans, whom he married in June of 1955. His survivors also include the Morials' five children: Julie, Marc, Jacques, Cheri, and Monique. He is remembered as an influential leader in Louisiana who was instrumental in supporting the economic and political rights of African Americans and minorities.

REFERENCES

"Ecumenical Service for Ernest N. Morial." December 27, 1989.

James, Rosemary. "Personality: Dutch Morial." *New Orleans* 5 (April 1971): 52–56.

"The Kid Who Would Be Mayor." *New Orleans Times–Picayune–Dixie,* Part I, August 16, 1981; Part II, August 21, 1981.

Morial, Ernest N. *A View of the City: New Orleans, 1978–1984.* New Orleans, 1984. New Orleans Public Library, Louisiana Collection.

Rushton, Bill. *State Report: Louisiana, New Orleans Elects Black Mayor.* Chapel Hill, NC: Institute for Southern Studies, 1978.

Who's Who in America, 1980–81. 41st ed. Chicago: Marquis, 1981.

COLLECTIONS

The papers of Ernest N. Morial are in the Amistad Research Center, Tulane University, New Orleans. Additional information is in the Louisiana Collection of the New Orleans Public Library.

Theodosia T. Shields

E. Frederic Morrow
(1909–1994)
Lawyer, television executive, White House aide

First black to serve on the White House staff, E. Frederic Morrow was the grandson of an ex–slave. He fought for justice and racial equality for African Americans at a time when segregation and discrimination were accepted by many Americans as normal. Morrow's presence in the Commerce Department in 1953 paved the way for Ronald Brown who followed forty years later to become Secretary of Commerce.

Born in Hackensack, New Jersey, on April 20, 1909, Everett Frederic Morrow was the oldest son of John Eugene Morrow, a Baptist minister, and Mary Hayes Morrow. The family consisted of one daughter, Nellie Katherine and four sons, John H., William H., A. Eugene, and Frederic. Hackensack was a small town marked by racism. Describing his hometown, Morrow wrote in *Forty Years a Guinea Pig*:

> It does not take a high I.Q. to imagine what it meant to grow up Black in New Jersey in the Twenties and Thirties. With every recreational, social and economic Avenue closed to Black kids and the conspiracy in the school system to give them inferior education by relegating them to special classes a Black child's horizon was in the dust of the street.

Completing the public schools in New Jersey, Morrow entered Bowdoin College in Brunswick, Maine, in 1926. He claims his admission was based on an error. Bowdoin had already accepted its token black, Bill Dean, who would become Morrow's roommate. Morrow was mistaken for the scion of Dwight Morrow, also from New Jersey and senior partner of the Wall Street banking firm of J. P. Morgan. Morrow graduated in 1930 and began his career as a bank messenger, delivering stocks and bonds to banks and financial houses. Often he carried millions of dollars in negotiable bonds and stocks strapped to his arms. The messengers, with the exception of Morrow, were young, white men on their way to becoming bank presidents.

Morrow remained on the job six months before taking a position with the National Urban League to work with Lester B. Grange, executive secretary and editor of *Opportunity* magazine. He worked for the Urban League for two years, then moved to the NAACP. Morrow became a spokesperson and national field secretary for the NAACP and traveled throughout the South encouraging branches to organize and speaking to youth organizations.

In 1941 when the country entered World War II, Morrow, rather than waiting to be drafted into the segregated army, volunteered in order to take the 13 weeks of basic training and then enter Officer's Candidate School. He was sent to Fort Dix, New Jersey, the only black among the other 31 men who volunteered and the only one with a college degree. In 1941 Morrow was 31 years old, six feet one inch tall, and weighed 135 pounds. He passed the physical but was

E. Frederic Morrow

told he had failed the examination for Officer's training although he had scored a more than acceptable 155 on the I.Q. test. After 30 days in the army, Morrow was promoted to sergeant. He challenged the reported test results and demanded to retake the examination; he entered Officer's Candidate School at Fort Lee, Virginia. Morrow served in the 477th Composite Group with Colonel Benjamin O. Davis, Jr. as an information and education officer. He left the Army at the rank of major.

In October of 1945, using the GI Bill, Morrow entered law school at Rutgers University in New Jersey and graduated in September 1948, at which time there were fewer than 12 black attorneys in the state of New Jersey. After failing to pass the New Jersey Bar, he switched careers and became a writer for CBS television in New York. Morrow found working in television exciting and a good outlet for his creative talents.

Becomes Presidential Aide

At the end of summer 1952, Morrow was approached by Val Washington, a black Republican, to help improve the Republican image in the black community. Since the Roosevelt years, African Americans had overwhelmingly voted Democratic. Morrow, hoping to use the opportunity to make advancements for civil rights, requested a leave of absence from CBS, and went on the campaign trail with General Dwight D. Eisenhower as the only black in the Eisenhower's entourage. After winning the election, Eisenhower asked Morrow to be his aide. Morrow faced a dilemma. In *Forty Years* he wrote:

I was not a politician—merely a citizen vitally concerned about good government and the character and ability of those elected to administer it. I had hoped some day to run for Congress—but serving as a Black functionary in some administration did not cause the adrenaline to flow with vigor. On the other hand, what a fantastic offer and chance this was. I'd be the first Black in history to be an Aide to the President of the United States.

After much reflection, Morrow accepted the President's offer but racism prevented his appointment for two years. Morrow had already resigned from CBS and, according to *Forty Years,* felt himself to be "beached like a whale—high and dry on the sands of unemployment and with a loss of face." After threatening to embarrass the administration, Morrow was finally made advisor on business affairs in the Department of Commerce, a new position with policy making authority and prestige. Morrow was not appointed to the White House Staff until July 9, 1955, when he was made administrative officer for the Special Projects Group in the Executive Office of the President. A private swearing–in ceremony was held so as not to upset the many Americans opposed to his appointment.

Faces Sharp Criticism

The Emmett Till murder in Mississippi in 1955 led angry blacks to accuse Morrow of placating whites for his personal gain and forsaking the collective needs of African Americans. Morrow, indeed, felt like an apologist for the administration he was reluctant to support. In *Forty Years* he recalls, "I was an appointee who had sworn to serve the President and my country honesty[sic]. . . . I was also a Black keenly feeling the ills afflicting my race, many of which I had suffered from." As he had done while in the military, Morrow continued to push for the morally correct and democratic treatment of African Americans. As a result, he caught the raging anger from both whites, who resented his aggressiveness, and blacks, who charged he wasn't doing enough. Morrow was forced to realize his mistake in working for the Republicans after his tenure ended. When he attempted to sell his first book to publishers, he found that powerful party members had blacklisted him with all major American publishers. Finally he secured a publisher in 1963.

In 1960 when Morrow left the White House, he had trouble finding a job. He and his wife were social outcasts in the black community. His nephew, John H. Morrow, Jr., recalled in an interview that Morrow's often repeated motto, "keep on keeping on," got him through the rough times. He became vice–president of the African American Institute in New York, and went on to become the first African American vice–president of Bank of America, the largest privately owned bank in the world. Morrow was in charge of the international division monitoring foreign loans and business development.

On July 19, 1994, Morrow died at Mount Sinai Hospital in New York of complications resulting from a stroke. He was 88 years old. Morrow was survived by his wife of 37 years, Catherine Gordon Boswell Morrow; his sister, Nellie Parker, a retired teacher in Baltimore; and a brother, Dr. John H. Morrow, of Huntington Beach, California.

Morrow was a member of Alpha Phi Alpha Fraternity and the recipient of an honorary doctor of laws degree from Bowdoin College in 1970. He had devoted his life to breaking down racial barriers as White House Aide and in the banking industry.

REFERENCES

Branch, Taylor. *Parting the Waters.* New York: Simon and Schuster, 1988.

"E. Frederic Morrow, First Black Aide at White House, Dies." *Jet* 86 (8 August 1994): 16–17.

Morrow, E. Frederic. *Black Man in the White House: A Diary of the Eisenhower Years.* New York: Coward–McCann, 1963.

———. *Forty Years a Guinea Pig.* New York: Pilgrim Press, 1980.

———. *Way Down South Up North.* Philadelphia: United Church Press, 1975.

Morrow, John H., Jr. Interview with author, June 18, 1996.

COLLECTIONS

Morrow's papers from the White House period are in the E. Frederic Morrow Collection at the Eisenhower Library in Abilene, Kansas. Other papers are housed at Boston University.

Nagueyalti Warren

"Jelly Roll" Morton
(1885?–1941)
Composer, musician

"Jelly Roll" Morton was America's first great jazz composer and one of the foremost contributors to American music. A pioneering jazz musician and leader as well, Morton claimed to have invented the term jazz and the musical style itself at the height of the Swing Era in 1902 while he performed in New Orleans; there he began playing four beats to the bar instead of the two beats normally associated with ragtime. Morton incorporated a variety of melodic styles in his work. He was also an influential composer; his works were widely recorded, reaching a vast audience. Morton was the first jazz artist to write down his arrangements and, according to many scholars, the first to publish a jazz arrangement, "Jelly Roll Blues." His legacy was preserved in 1938 at the Library of Congress when Alan Lomax recorded eight hours of Morton's music and personal anecdotes. Eileen Southern's 1982 *Biographical Dictionary of Afro–American and African Musicians* calls this recording "perhaps the most important oral history of jazz ever issued."

The facts concerning Morton's early life remain in dispute, as he often embellished the truth about his life. He was born Ferdinand Joseph LaMothe (or Lamothe) either on September 20, 1885, sometime in 1886, or on October 20, 1890. His birthplace was in Gulfport, Louisiana, or Gulfport, Mississippi, or New Orleans. His light–skinned Creole father E. P. "Ed" LaMothe, whose last name has also been given as "LeMenthe" and "Lemott," was a carpenter and trombonist schooled in classical music who abandoned the family when Morton was a child. Morton's early childhood was spent in Biloxi and Meridian, Mississippi, but was raised in New Orleans by his godmother Eulalie Echo, and took the last name of his stepfather Willie Morton, who was a porter and trombonist. When Morton was three, his mother, Louise Monette, married William Mouton, later known as Morton. Morton's mother died when he was 15. His Aunt Lallie had the most (but not necessarily the best) influence on him, proudly taking him to saloons when she was at liberty and to jail when she was confined. It was there that he heard the inmates singing, which he considered his first musical inspiration. Another influence on Morton, which became a theme through his life, was voodoo, as practiced by his Aunt Lallie. She kept glasses of water around the house and Morton claimed that he heard voices coming out of them. At night chains rattled and sewing machines ran by themselves; Morton never lost his fear of voodoo and always kept holy water near his bed.

Morton's family respected opera musicians, but any other musician was considered a tramp. Morton was both a respected musician and a tramp, but he never played at the opera. His first instrument was made of two chair legs and a tin pan, but, to him its music sounded like a symphony. He played the harmonica at age five. He also played guitar, which he studied with a Spaniard, and trombone in the sporting houses of the New Orleans red–light district known as Storyville. He took up the piano as a teenager and studied under a black professor of music named Nickerson from St. Joseph's Seminary College in Saint Benedict, Louisiana. A chance meeting in 1902 with the famous New Orleans ragtime pianist Tony Jackson, who composed "Pretty Baby" and "The Naked Dance," determined the direction of his musical career. Morton began composing, and wandered to Tulsa, Chicago, and Mobile during the years of 1904 and 1905.

After leaving New Orleans permanently around 1906, Morton worked in Louisiana and Mississippi as a pianist, small–time pool hustler, card shark, and gambler. He made the incredibly vast sum of twenty dollars in tips on his first night. His aunt soon recognized the source of his new clothes, and kicked him out of her house so that he would not corrupt his younger sisters. James Dapogny wrote that it was his grandmother who, after learning about his work as a sporting–house pianist in New Orleans when he was about seventeen, drove him from the house; after then, Dapogny said he began to travel. He never returned to New Orleans after 1907.

"Jelly Roll" Morton

Composes the Blues

Morton moved around for a number of years, living in St. Louis, Mobile, Chicago, and elsewhere, and he earned a livelihood in a variety of ways. In 1908, for example, he moved to Memphis to work in a vaudeville show. In 1911 he was pianist for McCabe's Minstrel Troubadours in St. Louis and Kansas City. While in New York in 1911, he was said to have sported a diamond in his front tooth. He settled in Chicago for three years, managing a cabaret. He published his first composition, "Jelly Roll Blues," in 1915; the title is a reference to Morton's self–bestowed nickname, a slang term for female genitalia and sexual intercourse in general. This tune is one of the first jazz orchestrations ever published. It was soon followed up by Morton's "King Porter Stomp" in 1916.

Morton traveled to San Francisco, Chicago and Detroit in 1915, and for the next year he managed and performed in a hotel and night club in Los Angeles. Between 1917 and 1923 he traveled and performed from Tijuana, Mexico to Vancouver and Alaska. From there he returned to Los Angeles, where he worked as a boxing promoter, as a bandleader, and in other areas of entertainment. He prospered during this period, and was in partnership with Anita Johnson, whom he sometimes called his wife; there is no evidence that they were married. Johnson is said to have had some influence on two of his compositions; she also wrote the lyrics for "Dead Man Blues."

In 1923 Morton returned to Chicago where he spent five years as staff arranger for the Melrose Publishing House. He recorded as a solo pianist in Richmond, Indiana, in 1923 and 1924 (''London Blues,'' ''Grandpa's Spell,'' ''Milenburg Joys,'' ''Wolverine Blues,'' ''The Pearls'') and with a white group called the New Orleans Rhythm Kings. Sterling A. Brown wrote in *Black World* that Morton, a first-rate pianist, was one of the first blacks to play with a mixed band. During this period he recorded on the Victor label and his works sold well. Between 1926 and 1930, he recorded in Chicago and New York (''Kansas City Stomp,'' ''Sidewalk Blues,'' ''Smokehouse Blues,'' ''The Chant Mournful Serenade,'' ''Shreveport Stomp,'' ''Ponchatrain Blues'') with his band, The Red Hot Peppers (Kid Ory, trombonist; Johnny Dodds and Omer Simeon, clarinetists; Baby Dodds, drummer). Around this time he toured with W. C. Handy, playing second piano in Fate Marbele's band and fronting pianist Henry Crowder's band.

In 1927 he met Mabel Bertrand, a Creole from New Orleans, who worked as a showgirl in Chicago; they married the next year. She exerted some influence on his rather colorful life and career, and remained his wife, living in Harlem until his death in Los Angeles.

Morton moved to New York in 1928, at the peak of his success. He recorded with the Red Hot Peppers, and played for two months at Harlem's Rose Danceland. In 1929 he led an all-girl revue in Chicago. 1931 found him leading his own ensemble in Harlem, and in 1932 he was piano accompanist for several Harlem music shows. In 1934 he became the house pianist at the Red Apple Club in Harlem, and recorded with white trumpeter Wingy Manone.

Morton's recordings in New York never reached the commercial or artistic success of those recorded in Chicago. Popular interest in New Orleans jazz was at a low during the 1930s, and the Great Depression caused the collapse of the record industry. Also, Morton did not adopt the big-band style of New York musicians that was popular by then. Morton was virtually ruined financially by this collapse in his popularity and by his investment in a failed cosmetics company. During the period of 1930–35 Morton's dwindling success and prestige may have led to the abrasive personality and monumental self-esteem that he exhibited then. As a bandleader, his life was temporarily over. While a few of his earlier published compositions were played and sometimes recorded by other bands, Morton had no new music published until 1938.

Morton moved to Washington, D.C. in 1935 and played a two-year engagement at the Jungle Club. He managed a nightclub during 1937. Sometime in 1938 Morton moved back to New York, organized a music publishing company, and began performing and recording just in time to take advantage of a revival of interest in New Orleans style jazz.

According to Dapogny, in 1938 Morton was attacked in a night club in Washington, D.C. and wounded in his head and chest. This aggravated existing health problems, and the injuries affected him the rest of his life. During his days in Washington he had a five-week recording session with Alan Lomax, who recorded Morton's music and his commentary in the Library of Congress and helped to preserve his legacy. Also about this time, Roy Carew published some of Morton's music as a means of providing him some help. Morton began another solo career in 1939, but a heart attack forced him into the hospital. He also suffered from asthma. He had only modest financial success and was forced to accept a small check each week from Catholic Charities.

The following year he went to Los Angeles, hoping to claim an inheritance from his godmother as well as live in a climate that might benefit his health. He renewed his association with Anita Johnson, but also kept in touch with his wife, Mabel. In California he formed a new group, but was too sick to work. He entered Los Angeles County General Hospital in May and died eleven days later in Anita's arms, on June 10, 1941, of heart disease resulting from chronic high blood pressure. He was 50. Since he had remained a Catholic, a requiem High Mass was sung in his honor at St. Patrick's Church; his pallbearers were Kid Ory and his bandsmen. He was survived by his widow and two sisters. Morton's will, apparently prepared by another party for his signature, was probated on June 28, 1941; no mention was made of his wife, Mabel. His interest in Roy Carew's publications went to his sister, Améde Colas. He left whatever else he had of value, including royalties from Melrose, Southern Music Company, and the American Society of Composers, Authors, and Publishers, to Anita Johnson.

Morton was the subject of a loosely biographical Broadway musical by George C. Wolfe in 1992 entitled *Jelly's Last Jam.* In addition to his work as composer and bandleader, he was an excellent pianist who altered the early ragtime style, added other styles to ragtime, and demonstrated strength and grace that was uncommon. Dapogny said of Morton: ''During his lifetime, the intrinsic merit of Morton's work was not recognized. Among some, he may still be unappreciated; however, now at last his true value as a remarkable, unique composer and pianist, a musician who ranks among the very finest jazz has produced and who made important contributions to that genre, is becoming known.''

REFERENCES

Brown, Sterling A. '''Jelly Roll' Morton.'' *Black World* 23 (February 1974): 28–48.

Chilton, John. *Who's Who in Jazz.* Philadelphia: Chilton Book Co., 1972.

Cook, Bruce. *Listen to the Blues.* New York: C. Scribner's Sons, 1973.

Dapogny, James. *Ferdinand ''Jelly Roll'' Morton.* Washington, DC: Smithsonian Institution Press, 1982.

Feather, Leonard. *Encyclopedia of Jazz.* New York: Horizon Press, 1965.

Hughes, Langston. *Black Magic.* Englewood Cliffs, NJ: Prentice–Hall, 1967.

———. *Famous Negro Music Makers.* New York: Dodd, Mead, 1955.

Roach, Hildred. *Black American Music: Past and Present.* Boston: Crescendo Pub. Co., 1973.

Southern, Eileen. *Biographical Dictionary of Afro–American and African Musicians.* Westport, CT: Greenwood Press, 1982.

———. *Music of Black Americans.* New York: Norton, 1983.

Jacqueline Jones–Ford

Bob Moses

(1935–)

Civil rights activist, educator

Bob Moses was the right man for the time. Not everyone had the unwavering courage and indomitable commitment to take on the racist state of Mississippi in a fight to gain civil rights for black residents. Through the Student Nonviolent Coordinating Committee (SNCC), he organized and trained students for Freedom Summer in 1961, and, perhaps most important, he elevated the struggle from lunch–counter sit–ins to aggressive campaigns to educate and register black voters. As he combated the rabid hatred ingrained in the heart of Mississippi, he never gave up on his hope for improved conditions. His legacy extends beyond Mississippi, as he has become a role model to all who seek to challenge wrong without regard to the price.

Robert Parris Moses was born January 23, 1935, in New York's Harlem to Gregory and Louise Parris Moses. The couple had two other sons. Gregory Moses worked as a janitor at the 369th Armory in Harlem but greatly resented his job and station in life. His father, William Henry Moses, a well–educated and prosperous Baptist preacher, became seriously ill during the Great Depression and was unable to educate his younger children. Gregory Moses, angry that his older brother received an education and later became a college professor, stressed the value of learning to his sons.

Moses responded with enthusiasm. Before entering high school, he was given a city–wide examination. His score was so high that he was admitted to Stuyvesant High School for gifted students. He thrived in the seemingly race–free, liberal environment, becoming captain of the baseball team and senior class president before graduating in 1952. Moses then accepted a scholarship to attend Hamilton College, an exclusive liberal arts school in upstate New York. Moses was one of three black students at the college, and, in an environment where he was truly the minority, he was excluded from many of the social activities. Subsequently, Moses grew introspective and self–contained.

Nonetheless, Moses did not let this obstacle prevent him from learning all he could. He majored in philosophy and read Albert Camus in the original French version. He was attracted to Eastern philosophers and intrigued by pacifist thinking. The summer of his junior year he studied abroad, attending a Quaker workshop and living in France with pacifists who had survived World War II. Moses also studied with a Zen Buddhist monk in Japan before returning to school and graduating in 1956. That fall, Moses enrolled in a Ph.D. program in philosophy at Harvard University. Concentrating on analytic philosophy, Moses focused on mathematical precision instead of the more traditional philosophical questions regarding the nature of reality. He received the master of arts degree in 1957, and was due to continue in the program for the Ph.D. when his mother died suddenly and his father suffered a mental breakdown.

Bob Moses

Moses left school to work in order to pay for his father's care. He was hired as a mathematics teacher at Horace Mann High School, a private institution in New York. He was there when the sit–in movement started. A native New Yorker, Moses personally had escaped the horrendous but legal mistreatment of blacks by whites. What he knew of the South he had only heard second–hand or had seen in the media. What struck him as he watched the black students demonstrate was that the mood had changed; they were no longer fearful. Instantly, Moses made a connection. As he related in *The Promised Land*: "It made me realize that for a long time I had been troubled by the problem of being a Negro and at the same time being an American."

The Journey From Bondage

Moses was 25–years old in June of 1960 when he decided to go South and work with the Martin Luther King Jr. and the Southern Christian Leadership Conference (SCLC).

Arriving in Atlanta, he was asked to participate in a recruiting trip as a field representative for the newly formed SNCC. Although nothing in his background and training had prepared him for what he would encounter in the deep South, he volunteered.

Moses went to Cleveland, Mississippi, where he met the head of the local chapter of the NAACP, Amzie Moore. Moore convinced Moses that the best route to freedom for black people in Mississippi was through education and voter registration. The two men jointly developed a plan for registering voters.

Moses returned to New York later that year, and taught at Horace Mann High School. When school was out, he returned to Mississippi and was appointed SNCC field secretary for the state of Mississippi. Moses began to organize his voter registration campaign in McComb, the southwestern part of the state. From 1961 until the spring of 1963, Moses worked with a determination and commitment unrivaled by many other workers. Only 6,700 of 60,000 blacks in Mississippi were registered to vote, even though all of the black citizens there had attempted to register. That 60,000 had even attempted in a state where Medgar Evers, Emmett Till, and others had been murdered and lynched for less, was a testimony to Moses's influencing presence. Frightened black people followed his lead because they loved, trusted, and respected him.

Part of the reason for this high regard black Mississippians accorded Moses for his ability to control his emotions and remain focused, calm, and confident in the throes of danger. His legendary bravery is described by a SNCC worker in *Parting the Waters,* "I just didn't understand what kind of guy this Bob Moses is, that could walk into a place where a lynch mob had just left and make up a bed and prepare to go to sleep, as if the situation were normal."

By the summer of 1964, Moses was weary, battle–scarred, and disappointed with the civil rights movement, the way black and white workers were relating to each other, and the way his relationship with his wife, SNCC volunteer Dona Richards, was turning out. His last effort during "Freedom Summer" was to have the Mississippi Freedom Democratic Party (MFDP) delegates seated at the Democratic National Convention instead of the all–white state delegation. His effort was lost when the northern white liberals voted with their southern white counterparts to defeat MFDP's request.

Following the Democratic National Convention, Moses left SNCC. In 1966, he and Dona Richards divorced, and when Moses was drafted in July of 1966, he fled to Canada. He spent the next two years working various jobs and remarried. In 1968, Janet Jemmott, also a former SNCC field secretary, became his second wife. The couple moved to Tanzania where they remained until 1976.

Solving for *X*

Returning to the United States, Moses returned to Harvard to complete the program he had abandoned years ago. But his growing concern for black children with poor mathematics skills prompted him to once again abandon his degree program. He became a volunteer tutor in the school system, beginning with his own daughter's eighth grade class.

In 1982, Moses received a coveted McArthur Foundation Award, known as the "Genius" grant, that enabled him to establish the Algebra Project, a math–science program for inner–city and minority children. Centered in Cambridge, MA, the program now reaches 45,000 sixth through eighth grade students in 105 schools in the inner cities and rural South.

Three decades after Moses was beaten in Liberty, Mississippi, for trying to register voters, he returned to that state, this time to teach algebra. He does so with the same fearless determination that made him a hero of the Civil Rights Movement. Moses demonstrates the project in Jackson at Brinkley Junior High School, then drives north to the Delta Algebra Project in Indianola where he was arrested years before for taking sharecroppers to register to vote.

Algebra is important in a high–tech society for obvious reasons. For Moses, though, algebra is a philosophy, a way of looking at the world. It probably accounted for his calm in times of crisis. According to Bruce Watson in the *Smithsonian* magazine, Algebra means "the uniting of broken parts to restore a whole." It provides a way of coming to terms with the unknown. As such, it can account for Moses's philosophical approach to life. The murder of three civil rights workers in Mississippi in the summer of 1963 prompted Moses to reveal his philosophy to a group of upset volunteers. He said in the *Smithsonian* magazine: "You have to break off a little chunk of a problem and work on it, and try to see where it leads, and concentrate on it." In other words solve for *X*. That fundamental math principal, he argued, applied to life's problems as well.

The Algebra Project works because it enables students to attack problems in their daily lives. Moses calls the project a new version of civil rights, insisting that math literacy holds the key to full citizenship in the coming century. When he is not on the road demonstrating the Algebra Project, Moses resides in Massachusetts with his wife. They have three adult children. Moses has been a symbol of courage for those who fought for the freedom of black people through the various aspects of the Civil Rights Movement. He continues to work for the freedom of black people, this time black children whom he is helping to become literate through the Algebra Project.

Current address: 99 Bishop Richard Allen Drive, Cambridge, MA 02139.

REFERENCES

Branch, Taylor. *Parting the Waters: America in the King Years 1954–63.* New York: Simon and Schuster, 1988.

Chevigny, Bell Gale. "Mississippi Learning: Algebra as Political Curriculum." *Nation* 262 (4 March 1996): 16–21.

Michelmore, Peter. "Bob Moses's Crusade," *Reader's Digest* 146 (March 1995): 107–111.

Walter, Mildred Pitts. *Mississippi Challenge.* New York: Aladdin, 1992.

Watson, Bruce. ''A Freedom Summer Activist Becomes a Math Revolutionary.'' *Smithsonian* 26 (February 1996): 114–25.

Nagueyalti Warren

Walter Mosley

(1952–)

Writer

Walter Mosley has given mystery novel fans their first black hero with Ezekiel ''Easy'' Rawlins, private eye. Although Mosley had already earned his place on best–seller lists, presidential candidate Bill Clinton's 1992 endorsement of him as his favorite mystery writer certainly gave an additional boost to the writer's visibility. Considering that he had not published a word until 1990, Mosley's books have drawn both critical and popular acclaim for his depiction of black life as well as for the language he uses.

Walter Mosley

Born January 12, 1952, Mosley grew up in the Watts section of Los Angeles, the son of Leroy and Ella Mosley. His father, an African American from Louisiana, was a school custodian. His mother, whose white Jewish family had emigrated from Eastern Europe to New York, was a personnel clerk for the Los Angeles Board of Education. An only child, Mosley has said that his parents gave him a lot of security and that he has inherited qualities from both. In particular, he feels connected to his gregarious father, who died in 1993 of cancer, and says he would be willing to trade his fame to have his father back. His mother continues to be supportive, attending his book signings and readings when she can; and Mosley says that it is nice to have her there. In a 1992 interview in *People Weekly,* Mosley said that he absorbed storytelling skills from both sides of the family—Ella's, with their ''old Jewish stories about the czars and living in Russia, and Leroy's, with their Texas tales of violence and partying and eating and drinking.'' The family's rich oral history and great stories have provided a sound base for Mosley's writing.

Mosley graduated from high school in 1970. Anxious to leave Los Angeles, he attended Goddard College in Plainfield, Vermont. However, he was a lackadaisical student, spending more time hitchhiking around the country rather than attending classes. He soon was advised to leave. Eventually entering Johnson State College in Johnson, Vermont, he graduated in 1977 with a bachelor's degree in political science. For a short time Mosley continued graduate studies in political science at the University of Massachusetts but moved to Boston to be with dancer Joy Kellman, whom he married in 1987 (they were estranged as of 1998). Drifting from one job to another in the late 1970s and early 1980s, at various times he made and sold pottery, tried the catering business, and in 1982, began work as a computer programmer for Mobil Oil in New York.

Writing Career Begins

Mosley had been interested in writing since he was young, but had given up the idea. Strongly influenced by Alice Walker's *The Color Purple* and by French writers such as Camus, he began writing at night and on weekends. In an 1995 *Ebony* interview, Mosley said his growth as a writer began with a single sentence: ''On hot sticky days in southern Louisiana the fire ants swarmed.'' He remembers thinking, ''My gosh, That's a very good sentence.'' Signing up for night classes in the graduate writing program at the City College of New York in 1985, he studied with program head and novelist, Frederic Tuten. His first ''Easy Rawlins'' story, *Gone Fishin',* was rejected by 15 agents, but this did not dissuade him. By 1989 Mosley had completed *Devil in a Blue Dress.* He showed it to Tuten who passed it on to his agent, Gloria Loomis. Six weeks later Loomis had sold it to W. W. Norton. Published in 1990, it was made into a movie by the same title, which was released in 1995 and starred Denzel Washington and Jennifer Beals. Other ''Easy Rawlins'' novels quickly followed: *A Red Death* (1991), *White Butterfly* (1992), *Black Betty* (1994), and *A Little Yellow Dog* (1996) were all published by Norton.

Experienced writers usually advise novices to write about what they know best, so it is not surprising that Mosley has placed his character, ''Easy Rawlins,'' in the Watts community of his childhood. So far, six of Mosley's novels feature the ''reluctant'' detective, and there will probably be more to come. In the mystery genre, Mosley is unusual in that he has taken his character, Easy, from the late 1940s and with each novel moves him through various stages of his life. Each new book takes place about five years after the previous one. Mosley told *Publishers Weekly* in 1994, ''I love writing about Easy. He's always changing—his life, his children, his friends—and I learn more about writing with each book.'' Easy Rawlins, a down–on–his–luck World War II veteran, stumbles reluctantly into his sleuthing career in order to pay his mounting debts. Mosley sees his characters as composites. For example, he sees Easy as the endearing black everyman, a moral detective seeking the truth, who is used to expose the thin line between crime and business as usual. Mosley says he particularly loves his black men characters and he sees them as heroes.

In an 1992 article in *People Weekly* Mosley said, ''If I do it right, they tell a story which has all the political and social fabric entwined around them.'' He wants to write about black people as black people, not in relation to whites nor as victims, but as living their own lives. For Mosley, the story is the thing and messages about racism are secondary. His writing has been called multilayered with a depth not usually found in this genre.

In a departure from the ''Easy'' novels, Mosley's *RL's Dream* (1995) is a non–mystery about an elderly blues guitarist who is dying of cancer, and *Always Outnumbered; Always Outgunned: The Socrates Fortlow Stories* (1997) is a collection of short stories that address racial problems that the community faces. Both of these were also published by Norton. Several of Mosley's short stories have been published in magazines. ''The Thief'' appeared in *Esquire,* July 1995; ''Equal Opportunity'' in *Critical Quarterly,* Winter 1995: and ''Double Standard'' in the August 1995 issue of *Gentlemen's Quarterly.*

Even though *Gone Fishin',* Mosley's first novel, had initially been rejected by 15 agents in the mid–1980s, it became a hot property. Any number of publishers in the 1990s were willing to pay handsomely to have the manuscript. Mosley, however, chose Black Classics Press of Baltimore, a small independent African American publisher, hoping that other successful black writers will also consider black publishers. Waiving his advance, Mosley said, ''I'm not rich, but I realize this was like giving a black publisher a million dollars. And let me tell you, it feels good to give someone a million dollars.'' *Gone Fishin'* came out in January of 1997 and is dedicated to his father.

For outstanding mystery writing, Mosley received the John Creasey Memorial Award and the Private Eye Writers of America Shamus Award for *Devil in a Blue Dress.* It was also nominated by the Mystery Writers of America for the 1990 Edgar for best first novel. *White Butterfly* was also nominated for an Edgar and for Britain's Crime Writers' Association Gold Dagger Award.

Mosley has served on the board of directors of the National Book Awards and is a member of the executive board of the PEN American Center. He founded PEN's Open Book Committee whose purpose is to encourage mainstream publishers to hire more minorities. Mosley is troubled by what he calls passive racism in publishing. ''A lot of black people read, more than anybody thinks,'' he says in a *New Yorker* article.

Mosley has said he is humbly amazed at the ''hoopla'' generated by his work. When asked to tell about his life, he says that it is not very interesting in any kind of major way, and he thinks no one else would be interested. Lanky, pale–tan, and with an open face, he was described in a June 1994 *Esquire* article as ''a warm bearish fellow, almost naive in his sense of wonder about life.'' As a pastime, he collects comic books, which numbers about 6,000.

Walter Mosley is a writer with a unique voice and perspective, who, according to the *Baltimore Sun,* does what his father told him every man must do. ''Pay the rent and, if possible, love what you do to pay the rent.'' Mosley most definitely appears to be doing what he loves.

Current address: Publicity Department, W. W. Norton & Company, Incorporated, 500 Fifth Avenue, New York, NY 10110.

REFERENCES

''At Dinner with Walter Mosley; Heroes in Black, Not White.'' *New York Times,* June 15, 1994.

''Catching up with Walter Mosley.'' *Baltimore Sun,* July 12, 1996.

Contemporary Black Biography. Vol. 5. Detroit: Gale Research, 1994.

Current Biography Yearbook. New York: H. W. Wilson Co., 1994.

Gleick, Elizabeth. ''Easy Does It.'' *People Weekly* 38 (7 September 1992): 105–106.

Hogness, Peter. ''The Writing Life: How Walter Mosley Discovered His Audience—and the Voice of his Fiction.'' *Writer's Digest* 76 (March 1996): 8–9.

McCullough, Bob. ''Walter Mosley.'' *Publishers Weekly* 241 (23 May 1994): 67–68.

''Mosley's Moves.'' *New Yorker* 71 (7 August 1995): 27.

Muller, Gilbert H. ''Double Agent: The Los Angeles Crime Cycle of Walter Mosley.'' In *Los Angeles in Fiction: A Collection of Essays.* Edited by David Fine. Albuquerque: University of New Mexico Press, 1995.

Nathan, Jean. ''Easy Writer.'' *Esquire 121* (June 1994): 42.

Peterson, V. R. ''Living Easy.'' *People Weekly* 44 (30 October 1995): 42.

Reid, Calvin. ''Mosley to Do Early Mystery with Black Press.'' *Publishers Weekly* 243 (3 June 1996): 30.

Sherman, Charlotte Watson. ''Walter Mosley on the Black Male Hero.'' *American Visions* 10 (August–September 1995): 34–37.

Whetstone, Muriel L. ''Walter Mosley: Hollywood Discovers Best–selling Author.'' *Ebony* 51 (December 1995): 106–12.

Flossie E. Wise

Carlton Moss
(1910–1997)
Filmmaker, actor, writer, social critic, educator

Carlton Moss's pioneering efforts in the film industry spanned several decades. He protested first the absence, and later, poor treatment of blacks in films and the film industry. In 1944 he wrote *The Negro Soldier,* the first U.S. Army training film that favorably depicted blacks; it was used to introduce black and white soldiers to the importance of blacks in military history and to boost the morale of black troops. The film, along with Moss's wartime releases, *Team Work, Don't Be a Sucker,* and other works, also helped pave the way for blacks in the motion picture industry.

Born in Newark, New Jersey, in 1910, Carlton Moss grew up in Newark and in North Carolina as well, where he received his early education. Moss graduated from Morgan State College—now University—in Baltimore.

Soon after graduation, Moss began his career as an actor and writer. He formed "Toward a Black Theater," a troupe composed of actors from black colleges, which toured black campuses as well as New York City. While living in New York in 1932–33 he wrote a black drama for an NBC radio series called "The Negro Hour." Frederick W. Bond wrote in *The Negro and the Drama* that Moss "enhanced his prestige by presenting his dramalogues 'Careless Love,' 'Folks from Dixie,' and 'Noah'" over the NBC airwaves. Although the drama series was short–lived, those who acted on it became known as the Lafayette Players. Bond also noted his conversation with stage and screen actor Leigh Whipper in November 1937, who said "Moss is the best and most prolific writer in New York." A talented writer, actor, and teacher, Moss was selected from a large pool of candidates to teach drama in the early years of Roosevelt's New Deal Administration's work in Harlem. For seven years he was writer and actor for Community Forum, a radio talk show broadcast over radio station WEVD.

Moss became a fixture in the Federal Theater of the Work Projects Administration primarily because of his work as director of the Harlem Federal Theatre. The Negro Theater of this period came under the auspices of the Federal Theatre Project and had units in major cities such as New York, Boston, Chicago, Seattle, Philadelphia, San Francisco, and Los Angeles. The theater flowered under the guidance of a committee of black theatre workers: Edna Thomas, Harry Edwards, Gus Smith, Rose McClendon, and Carlton Moss. The committee members sought and helped to develop black actors and playwrights. Productions were directed by blacks such as Frank Wilson and Rose McClendon, by whites who included John Houseman, Elmer Rice, and Orson Welles, and by leaders in the theater elsewhere. The theater produced Moss's play, *Prelude to Swing*. Moss was also chief assistant to John Houseman at the Lafayette Theater in Harlem when Houseman and Orson Welles produced a Haiti–based adaptation of *Macbeth* in 1935, the Negro Theatre's first production. An instant success, *Macbeth* played for a long time in Harlem and then went on a lengthy tour.

In early 1942 Moss wrote *Salute to Negro Troops* which was first presented at Harlem's Apollo Theatre. According to *Split Image,* Moss formulated discrete subjects such as the social goals of black Americans, black workers in the war industry, and similar themes into this propaganda primer.

The Negro Soldier

Moss had important contacts. During World War II he was consultant to Secretary of War Harold Stimson and also served the War Department as information specialist for the Information and Education Division. His work with the War Department resulted in his writing and acting in several films. In *Slow Fade to Black,* Thomas Cripps wrote that "the single most significant marriage of art and politics was Moss's *The Negro Soldier.*" He called the work "a product of political pressure put upon the Army by John Houseman. . .; William Hastie of [Franklin D. Roosevelt's] 'black cabinet;' and Carlton Moss." Hastie's successor, Truman K. Gibson, advisor to the War Department on race matters, had compiled a list of what noted Hollywood film director Frank Capra, in *The Name Above the Title,* called "a thick dossier of sickening acts of discrimination against Negro troops in the South." The department had hired Gibson to investigate the work of the 92nd Division comprised of black troops who served in Italy, and who had received unfavorable press. Gibson gave his list to Frank Capra, executive producer of a series of training films for the army called *Why We Fight.* Capra, under pressure from officials in Washington, gave Moss the job of chronicling in film the work of blacks in the military in an effort to boost the morale of black soldiers. Capra wrote in *The Name Above the Title* that "Moss wore his blackness as conspicuously as a bandaged head." Over Moss's objections, Capra edited Moss's work over and over to eliminate "the angry fervor." Moss wrote the script for *The Negro Soldier,* was technical advisor, and appeared in the film as a preacher. The film traces the black soldier's participation in past wars, including Minutemen at Lexington and Concord, Prince Whipple and his service with George Washington, the Massachusetts 54th Regiment of volunteers in the Civil War, and black troops in World War I. The film also highlighted the work of such notable blacks as scientist George Washington Carver and track star Jesse Owens.

The Name Above the Title cited praise by the black press for the film. The *Pittsburgh Courier's* Herman Hill wrote: "An ultra favorable–opinion reaction by members of the fourth estate, indicated that the 45–minute picture might easily prove to be one of the most outstanding and factual characterizations of the Negro ever made." Abe Hill wrote in the *Amsterdam News,* "The movie succeeds in proving that this is the Negro's war. . . . If any child, white, black, or blue ever wants to know what in the world the Negro has been doing in this country for the past 300 years, let him spend 40 minutes seeing this picture and he will have learned a life's lesson." And Langston Hughes, then a columnist for the

Chicago Defender, wrote, "The War Department has just shown to the press the most remarkable Negro film ever flashed on the American screen. . . . It is distinctly and thrillingly worthwhile."

Its merits notwithstanding, both Peter Noble in *The Negro in Films* and Daniel J. Leab in *From Sambo to Superspade* have reported that the film was severely criticized. Noble found that the film minimized the role played by "a quarter of a million coloured soldiers who fought on the side of the Union During the Civil War." Leab wrote that the movie's coverage of blacks was "superficial." He quoted one critic who said the film was "pitifully, painfully mild." Leab continued, saying that "none of the real problems faced by blacks in the military were touched on. Relations between the races, whether in the armed forces or in civilian life, received no real examination." The War Department allowed the film to be distributed "in the most gingerly way possible," parceled out to regional distributions and then to exhibitors on request.

Moss went to Europe in 1944 and supervised the production of the documentary *Team Work,* a sequel to *The Negro Soldier.* Also released in 1944, the film highlighted the service of black soldiers in the ground, air, and sea forces of the army's battles in Europe, showed action shots from the beaches of Normandy, and stressed the important role of black troops in the Allied services. According to the *New York Times,* some film historians concluded that Moss's army documentaries had a powerful influence on black films generally, and that "no single film since D. W. Griffith's 1915 epic *Birth of a Nation* has had a more powerful influence on black movies, black movie roles and society than . . . Moss's . . . Army documentary, 'The Negro Soldier.'"

Moss's documentaries on the army were released to civilians after the war was over. The films showed the heroism of black soldiers and were seen as "a harbinger of racial progress," according to the *New York Times.* In fact, these documentaries were used to accelerate the push for racial desegregation. The United Auto Workers used *The Negro Soldier* to educate its members about an integrated work force that would follow. Moss's documentaries also inspired Hollywood to release films with black themes.

In 1949 Moss's friend, Stanley Kramer, hired him to help write Elia Kazan's movie *Pinky,* which portrayed a black girl who passed for white. Moss quit the project early because he felt the film was demeaning to blacks. Kramer also paid tribute to Moss in his 1949 film *Home of the Brave* by naming the black soldier who was the victim of racial discrimination "Moss."

After the war, Moss settled in West Hollywood where he monitored the work of the Hollywood scene. A strong–willed person who perhaps worked better as an independent filmmaker than as a collaborator, Moss almost always worked on his own terms. The *New York Times* wrote that he spent most of his career "turning out obscure industrial movies, training films and schoolroom documentaries with names like 'Happy Teeth, Healthy Smile.'"

Moss spent a year at Fisk University in Nashville, Tennessee, where he initiated a film program under the administration of David Driskell, head of the Art Department. With Moss on the faculty, Fisk became the first black college in the country to teach the art of film production. While at Fisk, Moss produced *Paul Laurence Dunbar* and *Missing Pages* and taught cinema courses as well. Later he taught similar courses at the University of California at Irvine.

Produces Award–Winning Films

As head of Artesian Productions in 1976, Moss produced and directed a film about Frederick Douglass called *The House on Cedar Hill,* referring to where Douglass lived in the Anacostia section of Washington, D.C. Moss was also a writer and the producer for Hollywood's Wexler Film Productions. In that position he produced *What About Tomorrow,* which earned him two awards: the Golden Eagle Award at the Cine Festival, and first prize at the U.S. Industrial Film Festival. Two other award–winning films that he produced while with Wexler were *Teeth Are for Life,* which earned him first prize at the Chicago Film Festival, and *Healthy Teeth, Happy Smile,* for which he won the Cris Award at the Columbus Film Festival, the Golden Eagle Award at the Cine Festival, and first place at the Edinburg Film Festival. Among Moss's other films were *All the World's a Stage, Gift of the Black Folk,* and *The Afro–American Artist.*

Moss was a versatile writer. Among his works were a monograph, *Negro Music Past and Present* and "The Negro in American Films," an article published in *Freedomways* in 1963. The latter work helps define further his commitment to blacks in the film industry. He wrote that while blacks "appeared in the first creative films ever made," for example, the slapstick comedy *Off to Bloomingdale Asylum* produced in France in 1902 and probably with black characters portrayed by whites, he found that the American motion picture industry "set the pattern for the handling of Negroes on the scene. The presence of colored people in American life, their second class status, often defined by local law, national customs and community mores, was a source of comedy for the early American motion picture producers." Rather than actually have blacks on the screen, the American motion picture used white actors in black grease paint to portray blacks as whites supposedly saw them: stupid, immoral, in roles that made blacks the target of cruel and insulting jokes, as slaves, and in other demeaning roles. He condemned D. W. Griffith's *The Birth of a Nation* (1915), which called for separation of the black and white races in America with whites as the rulers. The film, he said, "proved the power of the screen to mold and shape opinion." Still, Moss saw a new day coming for the blacks in American film.

On August 9, 1997 Moss died at a hospital near his home in Los Angeles. He was 88 years old. His wife had died several years earlier; his only survivors were his two sisters, Mary Moss and Phyllis Henderson. Moss remained a critic of black exploitation films and set an uncompromising course of making films to portray the black experience favorably. He was an inspiration to countless blacks in the film industry, from directors to stagehands.

REFERENCES

Bond, Frederick W. *The Negro and the Drama.* College Park, MD: McGrath Publishing Co., 1940.

Capra, Frank. *The Name Above the Title.* New York: Macmillan, 1971.

"Carlton Moss, 88, Who Filmed the Black Experience, Dies." *New York Times,* August 15, 1997.

Dates, Jannette L., and William Barlow, eds. *Split Image.* Washington, D.C.: Howard University Press, 1990.

Leab, Daniel J. *From Sambo to Superspade: The Black Experience in Motion Pictures.* Boston: Houghton Mifflin, 1975.

Moss, Carlton. "The Negro in American Films." *Freedomways* 3 (Spring 1963): 134–42.

Noble, Peter. *The Negro in Films.* Port Washington, NY: Kennikat Press, 1948.

Sampson, Henry T. *Blacks in Black and White.* Metuchen, NJ: Scarecrow Press, 1977.

Smith, Jessie Carney, ed. *Black Firsts.* Detroit: Gale Research, 1994.

COLLECTIONS

The Oral History Program of the Margaret Herrick Library Center for Motion Picture Study, located in Beverly Hills, California, contains an interview with Carlton Moss and other writers and directors.

Jessie Carney Smith

Archibald J. Motley Jr.

(1891–1981)

Painter

Archibald J. Motley Jr. was the first African American artist to depict urban social life of African Americans in art. Motley's painting celebrates the vitality of African American neighborhoods and lifestyles in the 1920s and 1930s. In *Chicago History,* Elaine Woodall wrote that Motley "did more to advance and shape the course of black art than any other painter of his day. . . . Motley provoked criticism both from blacks and whites "because he refused to depict the traditional black stereotypes and would not use painting as a vehicle for propaganda." Unlike his contemporaries, Cedric Dover wrote in *American Negro Art* that Motley "painted a period," or created paintings that evoked the history of an age.

Though associated with the period of the Harlem Renaissance, Motley spent most of his life in Chicago, and the majority of his work presented the urban lifestyle of Chicago's South Side. Motley's portraits demonstrate that he was a master of realistic painting, but, for the most part, Motley abandons the academic style to create evocative scenes of the joys of life in the city. Motley painted "people as scenes," explained Samella Lewis in *African American Art and Artists,* concentrating on actions rather than individuals. In painting against the stereotype of the subservient Negro, Motley found his style by incorporating some elements of a primitive, naive style. Throughout his career, Motley showed interest in capturing natural light and producing artificial light, especially in night scenes. Motley was also distinguished from many of his contemporaries and successors, including Jacob Lawrence, by his rendering of his fascination with shades of skin color. Even in the very populated street scenes, Motley presented a variety of skin tones rather than limiting his palette to a single color for African Americans.

Motley was born in New Orleans, Louisiana, on October 7, 1891. Before he was two–years old, his family, as a part of the northern migration of that era, moved to Chicago. In New Orleans, threats from white competitors forced Motley's father to abandon his general merchandise store and home. Motley spent most of the rest of his life in Chicago. His father, Archibald Motley Sr., was a porter and an early supporter and member of the Brotherhood of Sleeping Car Porters. Motley's mother, Mary Huff Motley, was a schoolteacher in Louisiana before she married. In Chicago, the Motleys lived in the Englewood neighborhood on Chicago's South Side. Englewood was a neighborhood comprised primarily of European immigrants, and the Motleys were one of the few black families in the neighborhood. In 1924, Motley married his high school sweetheart, Edith Granzo, the daughter of German immigrants who disowned her when she married Motley. He and Edith had one child, Archibald "Archie" J. Motley III. Motley's only sister, Flossie, had a son, Willard, who became a writer of naturalistic novels during the 1940s and 1950s. Willard spent a lot of time with Motley's family and wrote at least parts of his novels at the Motley kitchen table. Motley died January 16, 1981, in Chicago.

Training and Apprenticeship

In the Englewood elementary schools, many of Motley's teachers encouraged him in his drawing. After elementary school, Motley worked at a number of odd jobs, and, at 18, he entered Englewood High School, where he was an outstanding athlete in football and baseball. He played semiprofessional baseball on weekends. High school afforded Motley the opportunity for training in various kinds of drawing and sketching. After graduating from high school in 1914, Motley

Archibald J. Motley Jr.

was offered a full scholarship to study architecture at the Armour Institute by its president Frank Gunsaulas, an acquaintance of Motley's father. Motley turned down the scholarship to study at the Art Institute of Chicago. Gunsaulas, however, was impressed enough with Motley's talent that he paid his first year's tuition at the art institute. Motley excelled and earned a scholarship job to complete his formal training. In 1919, he returned to the institute a year after he had graduated to sit in on a class offered by George Bellows, one of his favorite artists.

After graduation from the art institute, Motley was unable to find work as an artist, partly because of racism. During this period, Motley made a conscious decision to paint only black subject matter. He wanted to help break down the traditional stereotypes of African Americans and depict his race undertaking a wide range of activities. As a student, Motley had suggested that the art institute use black models in class. A number of portraits, many of the them of family members, characterize this period of his career, revealing Motley's interest in imaging women of mixed racial ancestry. His skill in rendering features, including his subjects' hands, was exceptional. One of the most moving of his portraits is of his paternal grandmother, Emily Motley, when she was 82–years old, called *Mending Socks* (1924). This painting has been one of the most widely exhibited of the Motley's work and is probably his most popular. Motley himself considered it his finest portrait. His exhibited paintings earned him some local and national recognition, and he began offering private art lessons in 1926 to fellow African Americans, including the sculptor Richmond Barthé. Motley was named director of the Chicago No–Jury Society of Artists for the 1926–27 term, "quietly making history as the first ever black to hold this post," wrote Elaine Woodall.

Gains Wide Recognition

Motley showed some paintings in several of the art institute's exhibits and won the Frank G. Logan medal and prize for *A Mulatress* and the Joseph Eisendrath Award for *Syncopation* at an Art Institute exhibit in 1925. He was included in the prestigious "Paintings and Water Colors by Living American Artists" in the Newark Museum, as well as other exhibits in Illinois and New York. *Mending Socks* won the popular prize at the Newark Museum exhibit. Motley's biggest breakthrough occurred in 1928, when the New Gallery of New York City organized a one–person show of his work, the first one–person show of an African American artist since the 1908 exhibition of Henry O. Tanner's work. This show was created purely on the basis of Motley's distinction as an artist, since the organizers knew nothing about his race or his person until after the show had been arranged.

Motley was the first artist to appear on the first page of the *New York Times.* Upon the advice of George Hellman, director of the New Gallery, Motley had begun to create paintings with an African setting for his one–man show in 1928. Paintings like *Waganda Charm–Makers* and *Kikuyu God of Fire* incorporated the spirit of African myth. They have an eerily mystical quality, but they remain essentially realistic in style, if not in content. The direction which Motley takes with his art, however, is more clearly anticipated by paintings like *Black and Tan Cabaret* and *Syncopation,* two paintings that were part of the 1928 exhibit.

The Guggenheim Fellowship, which Motley received in 1929, afforded him the opportunity to go to Paris to study and work. Some of Motley's paintings of the Paris period, such as *Blues* and *The Jockey Club,* showed the characteristic style for which Motley became well known. These paintings exemplified the highly stylized characteristics of Motley's more famous genre scenes. His paintings in Paris and upon his return home captured black urban social life with characters involved in diverse situations. His characters were represented as strong and dignified. Many of his paintings teemed with life, as they were crowded with figures. As Motley exaggerated some of the physical features of his subjects, particularly the lips in paintings like *Lawd, Mah Man's Leavin'* (1940) or *Gettin' Religion* (1948), his types border on caricature. However, what was technically most significant in these paintings was Motley's lifelong interest in the depiction of light, both in its source and its quality.

Many of his paintings were evening or night scenes. Motley combined the natural light of the moon with artificial sources of light. Many of these cityscapes were dominated by a single color, usually a cobalt blue. In his depiction of city night life, Jontyle T. Robinson observed in *The Art of Archibald I. Motley, Jr.,* Motley demonstrated a particular interest in the role of music in black life and showed that black cultural innovations bridge "cultural boundaries that united people of different nationalities and races.'' Unlike Tanner, Motley was more interested in secular music than in spiritual.

When Motley returned to Chicago from Paris in 1930, the Great Depression was underway. Like many other artists of the period, he went to work for the Works Progress Administration (WPA). Motley planned a series of murals and paintings on ''The Evolution of the Negro'' and produced about 15 of these paintings dedicated to the history of African Americans. Throughout the 1930s and 1940s, Motley continued to produce the genre of paintings that became his trademark. When his wife Edith died on December 17, 1948, Motley had to go to work to support his mother and 14–year old son. He was employed at Styletone to created designs for hand–painted shower curtains. During the 1950s, he made several visits to Mexico to see his nephew Willard in Mexico, by this time a celebrity as a novelist. Most of the paintings produced during this period were of Mexican life and were dominated by yellows and aquas rather than the night–time blue of his Chicago scenes.

The First One Hundred Years: He Amongst You Who is Without Sin Shall Cast the First Stone: Forgive Them Father For They Know Not What They Do (1963–72), possibly Motley's last painting, was perhaps the only overtly political painting Motley created. It is a montage of many symbols covering the 100 years since the signing of the Emancipation Proclamation. Motley's earlier paintings captured the objective view of an observer of African Americans enjoying life, offering little information on the oppression they faced. This painting served as a powerful closing statement to his career. Motley was not unaware of oppression, but chose to paint the positive social elements that ought to be central to a community. Rather than focusing on the sources of restriction, his paintings become a joyous celebration of life of African Americans and their contributions to American society.

REFERENCES

Bearden, Romare, and Harry Henderson. *A History of African–American Artists from 1792 to the Present.* New York: Pantheon, 1993.

Donaldson, Jeff Richardson. ''Generation '306'—Harlem, New York.'' Ph.D. dissertation. Northwestern University, 1974.

Dover, Cedric. *American Negro Art.* New York: New York Graphic Society, 1960.

Driskell, David C. *Two Centuries of Black American Art.* New York: Los Angeles County Museum of Art/Alfred A. Knopf, 1976.

Estell, Kenneth. *African America: Portrait of a People.* Detroit: Visible Ink Press, 1994.

Hess, Elizabeth. ''The 'Other' Masters.'' *Village Voice* 33 (21 June 1988): 95, 111.

James, Curtia. ''Archibald J. Motley, Jr., at the High Museum at Georgia Pacific Center.'' *Art in America* 81 (March 1993): 116–17.

Jewell, Edward Alden. ''A Negro Artist Plumbs the Negro Soul.'' *New York Times Magazine* (25 March 1928): 8, 22.

Lewis, Samella. *African American Art and Artists.* Berkeley: University of California Press, 1990.

Porter, James A. *Modern Negro Art.* Washington, DC: Howard University Press, 1943. Reprint, 1992.

Robinson, Jontyle Theresa, and Wendy Greenhouse. *The Art of Archibald J. Motley, Jr.* Chicago: Chicago Historical Society, 1991.

Woodall, Elaine D. ''Looking Backward: Archibald J. Motley and the Art Institute of Chicago: 1914–1930.'' *Chicago History* 8 (Spring 1979): 53–57.

COLLECTIONS

Some of Motley's work is collected at the Chicago Historical Society; the most substantial collection is that of Archie Motley and Valerie Gerrard Brown; otherwise, the works are widely dispersed; many have been lost. Robinson and Greenhouse's book noted above is the most thorough source on the location of material.

Gordon K. Lee

Willard Motley
(1909–1965)
Writer

The 1947 publication of *Knock on Any Door* claimed for Willard Motley a lasting place in American literature. Motley's novel inspired a King Features comic strip, a movie starring Humphry Bogart, and rave reviews comparing Motley to the best writers of the naturalistic school. Though Motley wrote arresting prose detailing the slums and the problems of the urban poor, he did not include African Americans as central characters. Thus, while he may hold a place in the annals of American literature, his name often is excluded from the chronicles of African American writers.

Willard Francis Motley was born July 14, 1909, in Chicago, Illinois. Some sources list his date of birth as 1912. His father, Archibald Motley Sr., worked as a pullman porter on the Wolverine, a special train that ran between Chicago and New York City, and his mother Mary, called Mae by her family, was a housewife. The family lived on the South Side of Chicago at 350 West 60th Street. They were the only black family in the neighborhood. According to Motley's biographer Robert E. Fleming, Willard was born ''in a private white hospital and two weeks later baptized in the [Roman Catholic] cathedral.'' Motley had one older brother Archibald J. Motley Jr., the famous painter, and an older sister Florence, or Flossie as the family called her. As the only African American family in the all–white neighborhood, the Motleys were not perceived to be a threat. However, all was not perfect between the races and Motley related several events where his father was

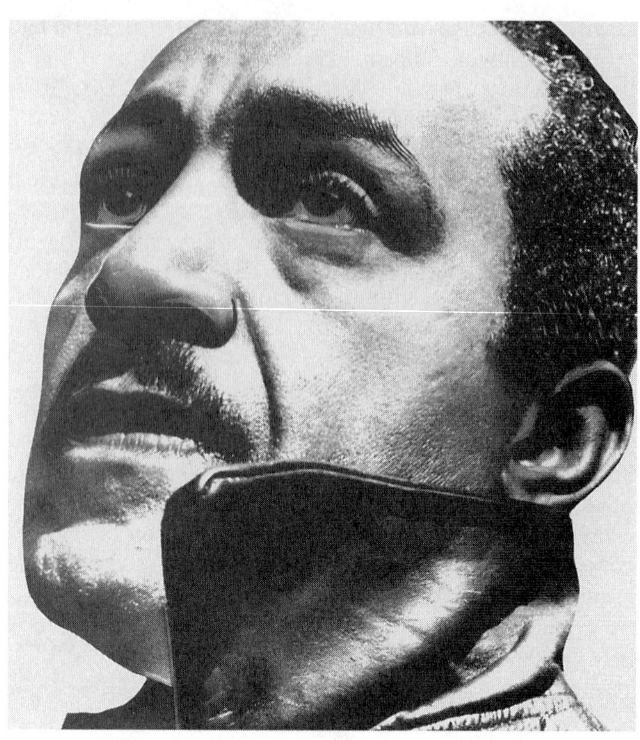

Willard Motley

angered by racists. But his distinctly middle–class background afforded Willard Motley a choice to accept the positive whites and to ignore the hostile ones, something his fellow black creative writers refused to do and for which Motley criticized them, accusing them of returning hate for hate.

Becomes Professional Writer

At 13 Motley began to write articles for the *Evening Post* and the *Chicago Defender.* He contributed to the children's pages, "Boys and Girls Post," and to *Dollar Ideas,* a first–person–account of how young people could earn money. Motley's first published short story appeared in the *Defender.* Titled "Sister and Brother," the story appeared in three parts on September 23, 30, and October 7, 1922. Motley became editor of a weekly column on the children's page, the *Defender Junior.* He had his own byline and photograph, complete with a pen name, Bud Billiken. His column was called "Bud Says." Motley established Billiken Club chapters throughout the city and called for submissions of poems, drawings, and letters. He wrote the column, answered letters, and sent birthday cards to members of the club, for which he earned three dollars a week. He continued to work as editor until July 5, 1924.

In 1924, Motley entered Englewood High where for the first time he was in a racially mixed environment. Grammar school, where he had been the only African American in his class, had not prepared him for the diverse culture of Englewood, which included young African American students who carried knives. However, he appears to have adjusted. He was highly active as a high school student, participating in football, intramural basketball and baseball, track, and boosters' club. He also wrote for the school newspaper and the yearbook. He graduated in January 1929. Following his graduation he continued to live with his parents and volunteered as assistant coach for the high school football team. He was unable to find a job due to the Great Depression, and he began to feel that his writing was suffering from the lack of material generated by his middle–class existence.

Hobo Trips and the Long Road to Success

To gather material for his writing, Motley decided he needed to travel. On July 3, 1930, he traveled to New York City on his bicycle. He owned a total of 51 cents, and the trip took 13 days. This was the first of many adventures he would embark on with little or no funds, content to travel as a hobo. While he was in New York, he submitted stories to *Colliers, Liberty,* and the *Chicago Times.* They were all rejected. His early success as a child had not prepared him for the difficulties of the publishing world. However, despite his disappointment, Motley continued to write and to travel.

In 1936 Motley made two trips out West, visiting Colorado, Idaho, and Wyoming, where he ended up in jail for trying to steal gasoline. He was able to produce publishable articles from these travels; but by 1936, his family with the exception of his mother, Mae, were still unsupportive of his artistic efforts. They thought he was a dreamer and a loafer, unwilling to accept the kind of jobs African American men were expected to take. Feeling stifled and frustrated at his lack of success in his chosen career, Motley moved away from his parent's home in 1939. He could afford only a slum apartment on Fourteenth and Union Street in Chicago. His rent was 12 dollars a month.

Shortly after Motley moved, he began visiting Hull House, an intellectual center for young artists, where he met William P. Schenk and Alexander Saxton. These men were important influences on his life and work. Saxton became his lifelong friend. By the fall of 1939, the three men had established *Hull–House Magazine.* At this point Motley's fictional style began to take shape. His creative writing centered on slum life and was realistic. In a 1941 entry in *The Diaries,* Motley writes, "The past year has brought so many new influences, ideas, perspectives into my life that I have, in the full sense, grown up." That year he was to complete three chapters of his novel, *Leave Without Illusions,* which became *Knock on Any Door.*

Knock on Any Door was first submitted to Harper's in 1943. It was rejected. But in April 1944 Macmillan gave Motley a contract and a small advance for his novel, which needed extensive revisions, and in 1946 Motley won both a

Newberry Library and a Rosenwald Foundation grant in order to complete it. Rewritten and published in 1947, the novel won immediate critical acclaim. However, none of Motley's later novels could compare with the standard set by his first. Part of the reason for his work's decline was that times were changing. Naturalism was giving way to modernism, and Motley's style failed to change.

Motley was not the only nor the first African American writer to focus on white characters. Both Frank Yerby and Alexander Dumas also contributed to this old but unpopular African American literary tradition. Nonetheless, African Americans were proud of Motley's success. They claimed him as a successful writer who was black if not a successful black writer. Motley's novels are *Knock on Any Door* (1947); *We Fished All Night* (1951); *Let No Man Write My Epitaph* (1958); and *Let Noon Be Fair* (1966). His other published works include ''The Education of a Writer'' (*New Idea,* Winter 1961); ''The Almost White Boy'' (*Soon One Morning,* ed. Herbert Hill, 1963); ''A Kilo of Tortillas, A Guaje of Pulque'' (*Rogue,* August 1964); and ''Give the Gentleman What He Wants'' (*Rogue,* October 1964).

Motley moved to Mexico in 1951 where he bought a house twelve miles from Mexico City. There he would remain until his untimely death on March 4, 1965, from intestinal gangrene. Though he never married, in Mexico Motley adopted two sons, Sergio and Raul. He is buried in Cuernavaca, Mexico.

REFERENCES

Fleming, Robert E. *Willard Motley.* Boston: G. K. Hall, 1974.

Giles, James R. ''The Emergence of Willard Motley in Black American Literature.'' *Negro American Literature Forum.* Vol. 4. (1970): 31–34.

Klinkowitz, Jerome, ed. *The Diaries of Willard Motley.* Ames: University of Iowa Press, 1979.

Major, Clarence. *The Dark and Feeling.* New York: The Third Press, 1974.

COLLECTIONS

Motley's papers (1957–1963) are housed in The Willard Motley Collection at the University of Wisconsin. Seventy–five cubic feet of uncatalogued material is on loan to Northern Illinois University. Photographs are available from the Motley estate. Contact Attorney Walter Roth (D'Ancona, Pflaum, Wyatt, and Riskind) at 30 North LaSalle Street, Chicago, Illinois 60602; (312) 580–2020.

Nagueyalti Warren

Robert Russa Moton

(1867–1940)

Educator, writer

Recognized as one of the most famous African American educators in America and a tireless promoter of racial progress, Robert Russa Moton was the second president of Tuskegee Institute. A protégé of Booker T. Washington, he was involved in many activities associated with racial advancement. During the early 1900s, Washington and Moton toured the southern states to fund–raise and promote industrial and vocational education. He was a political advisor on federal appointments to Presidents Wilson, Harding, Coolidge, Hoover, and Franklin D. Roosevelt.

Robert Russa Moton was born in Amelia County, Virginia, August 26, 1867, on a plantation, the son of Booker Moton and Emily Brown. Moton spent most of his early years on the Vaughan plantation in Prince Edward County. His mother was the cook in the ''big house'' and his father was in charge of the field hands. Moton was introduced to education at an early age. Emily Moton secretly devoted one hour each night to teaching her son how to read. She was one of the very few black women in the neighborhood who could read at all. For several years the secret that Emily Moton could read was kept, until Mrs. Vaughan, wife of the plantation owner, walked in one night during one of the learning sessions. Much to Emily Moton's surprise, Mrs. Vaughan was pleased at her discovery and said that she was very wise to teach her son to read. Mrs. Vaughan's youngest daughter Mollie soon took over and taught Emily Moton and young Robert for one hour every afternoon.

In 1880 Robert Moton moved to Surry County and secured work in a lumber camp to save money for school. He worked at the lumber yard for two years and became involved in politics. Moton enrolled in Hampton Institute in 1885. He failed the entrance examinations, but was offered a job in the saw mill. He worked there while attending night school, and was soon admitted to day school. After his junior year, he began teaching in Cottontown, Cumberland County, Virginia. During his time in Cottontown, Moton worked in the Prince Edward County superintendent's office in Farmville where he copied deeds and worked with legal contracts. After Moton expressed an interest in law, the superintendent gave him books to read and lessons in law. Moton soon gathered enough knowledge to pass the Virginia bar and received a license to practice law. He taught for one year before returning to Hampton and graduating in 1890.

After graduation, Moton was offered the position of commandant of the male student cadet corps at Hampton. He held the rank of major, a title he retained the rest of his life. Although he had intended to stay only two years in this position, he remained at his post for 25 years. It was during his years at Hampton that Moton began his association with racial progress.

Robert Russa Moton

In 1905 Moton married Elizabeth Hunt Harris of Williamsburg, Virginia. She died childless the following year. A few years later, Moton met Jennie Dee Booth, a graduate of Hampton and a teacher in the Whittier Training Institute at Hampton. The two were married on July 1, 1908, in a simple ceremony in Memorial Chapel on the campus of Hampton Institute. The Motons had five children: Catherine, Charlotte, Jennie, Robert, and Allen.

Heads Tuskegee Institute

After the death of Booker T. Washington on November 14, 1915, Moton succeeded him as principal of Tuskegee Normal and Industrial Institute. Moton said in his 1916 inaugural address, published in *Finding a Way Out*:

> In order that this institution shall continue to carry forward the ideas and ideals of its great Founder; in order that it shall keep the respect and confidence of the people of this land, we must first, everyone of us, principal, officers, teachers, graduates, and students use every opportunity and strive in every reasonable way to develop and strengthen between white and black people, North and South, that unselfish cooperation which has characterized Tuskegee from its very beginning.

Like Washington, Moton was also an adviser to the federal government on racial policies and the appointment of blacks to federal positions. Moton established close ties with Presidents Wilson, Harding, Coolidge, Hoover, and Roosevelt.

In 1908 Moton was elected president of the National Negro Business League, and continued to be re–elected for more than twenty years. During the period of World War I, Moton was instrumental in negotiating a loan of five million dollars from the United States government for use in Liberia. He was also very active in speaking on the subjects of war savings stamps, liberty loan drives, and the conservation of food.

After World War I, racial tensions escalated across the nation. Blacks who had gone to Europe to fight for democracy came home to race riots and lynchings. During the lynchings and riots in 1918, Moton helped form the Commission on Interracial Cooperation, which published annual lynching statistics. One of the many factors behind the increased violence concerned rumors that black soldiers had been cowards in the war, and had raped French women. Moton was sent to France to investigate the treatment of black troops and to publicize his findings to the United States. According to *Born to Rebel,* on April 19, 1919, the *Birmingham Pipe* carried the headline: ''Negro Soldiers Win Lasting Fame Despite the Whispering Gallery Shouts R. R. Moton of The Tuskegee Institute.''

The truth was, the number of Frenchwomen raped by black soldiers was highly exaggerated. There were seven men charged with rape and only two were found guilty and convicted. The percentage of rape among black soldiers was equal to that of all other soldiers. According to *Born to Rebel,* the *Birmingham Pipe* in its April 19, 1919, issue quoted Moton as saying:

> Your record has sent a thrill of joy and satisfaction to the hearts of millions of black and white Americans, rich and poor, high and low. Black mothers and wives, sweethearts, fathers, and friends have rejoiced with you and with our country in your record. You will go back to America as heroes as you really are. You will go back as you have carried yourselves over here in a straightforward, mannerly and modest way.

Moton's document did not stop the riots, but it did set the record straight. In 1920 he wrote about his findings in his autobiography, *Finding A Way Out.* Moton promoted the establishment of a hospital for black veterans. Following the war, black veterans returned home to the South with no health care facilities available for them. Officials at the Veterans Bureau began looking for a site to build a segregated hospital to serve the more than 300,000 southern black veterans. Perry states in *Health Quest* that ''this was the 1920's and the initial response from both black and whites throughout the South was lukewarm.'' Whites were determined that no black hospital would be established ''within spitting distance'' and blacks questioned whether ''the harsh social and political climate of the South was the best place to nurture a healthcare haven for black soldiers.''

In 1923 Moton's leadership resulted in the building of a veterans hospital for black soldiers. Tuskegee Institute donated 300 acres of land for the facility. The hospital was to be staffed entirely by African Americans and was to be a training ground for young black doctors, a plan that infuriated local whites who thought that it should be run by whites. The Veterans Bureau officials were convinced that there were not enough qualified black doctors or nurses to staff the hospital, and decided to hire a white staff. They also decided to hire "black nursemaids" so that white female nurses would not have to touch black men which was forbidden by Alabama laws at the time.

On February 12, 1923, the hospital was dedicated. The Veterans Bureau made Colonel Robert H. Stanley, a Southern white man believed to be a member of the Ku Klux Klan, the hospital's first chief administrator. The Klan created trouble for the hospital during its first year of operation. Many people involved with the facility received death threats, including Moton.

Blacks from the community, churches, and organizations such as the NAACP, convinced bureau officials and President Calvin Coolidge that the plan to hire an all–white staff was a bad one. In the summer of 1923, Coolidge ordered that the hospital staff only African Americans. The hospital got its first black administrator, Dr. Joseph H. Ward, in 1924. Until the hospital closed in recent years, it continued to serve a varied, though still predominantly black, veteran population. The 45–building complex became the third largest hospital in the state of Alabama.

In 1929 Moton wrote his most important book, *What the Negro Thinks,* a restatement of the Tuskegee formula to meet the demands of a better educated and race–conscious black middle class. In that work Moton decried racial discrimination in law and legislation, transportation, education, and housing, and advocated a civil equality of races who in social life should remain "ethnologically distinct." "As for amalgamation," Moton said, "very few expect it; still fewer want it; no one advocates it; and only a constantly diminishing minority practice it, and that surreptitiously."

In 1934 Moton retired from Tuskegee Institute. Published in *The Tuskegee Student,* his resignation letter to the board of trustees, written October 25, 1934, comments on the deliberation he gave to his decision to retire at the end of the academic year. By retirement he had completed 45 years in academia, of which 25 were at Hampton and 19 at Tuskegee. Already beyond the retirement age, he would not entirely divorce himself from the school, but believed that he could "better serve Tuskegee and the cause for which it stands, by spending my remaining years in an atmosphere removed from the pressure of official responsibility, and giving myself to the accomplishment of a few cherished objectives which I hope to make my final contribution to the cause which is dear to us all."

During Moton's presidency at Tuskegee, many changes occurred. Admission standards were raised and policies changed. An accredited junior college program was added and a four–year curriculum was in the planning stages. He established an ROTC program to train students for military careers. The method of financial support of the institution was changed from philanthropy to support by an endowment fund. Hampton and Tuskegee launched a joint campaign and were able to increase Tuskegee's endowment under Moton's administration from $1,945,000 to $7,704,000 at his death.

Throughout his life, Moton was a member of numerous organizations and societies. In 1908 he was elected trustee of the Jeanes Fund, an education trust, and secretary of the board. He was on the board of trustees of a number of black educational institutions including the People's Village School in Mt. Meigs, Alabama; the Industrial Home School for Colored Girls in Peak, Virginia; the Negro School for Boys in Hanover, Virginia; and Fisk University in Nashville, Tennessee. He was vice–chairman of the National League on Urban Conditions among Negroes, a forerunner of the National Urban League. He was a member of the executive committee of the Permanent Roosevelt Memorial movement and of the National Child Welfare Association; and he was made a member of the International Committee of the YMCA in 1919. In 1927 Moton was appointed to serve as a member of the Hoover Commission on the Mississippi Valley Flood Disaster, and founded the National Negro Finance Corporation in Durham, North Carolina. He was selected chair of the United States Commission on Education in Haiti by President Hoover.

Moton received honorary degrees from Oberlin College, Williams College, Harvard University, Virginia Union University, Wilberforce University, and Howard University. In 1930 he received the Harmon Award in Race Relations, and the NAACP Spingarn Medal in 1932 for distinguished service.

After retiring from Tuskegee Institute in 1932, he and his family returned to the Moton family estate at Holly Knoll, Capahosic, Virginia, where he died on May 31, 1940. He was buried at Hampton Institute.

Moton's family estate, Holly Knoll, was always a meeting place where black educators, politicians, and business people came to solve problems plaguing the black community. In later years, the site became the Moton Conference Center, home of the United Negro College Fund. The two–story Georgian–style mansion is listed in the National Register of Historic Places and is the only site owned by African Americans to be in the Virginia Historic Register. In 1993 the decision was made to close the center, after the facility became too expensive to manage.

Robert Russa Moton kept at the forefront of the advancement of the black race. Through his work as educational leader, he promoted the education of the race.

REFERENCES

Bell, Sallie M. Brown. "A Study of the Development of Tuskegee Institute under the Administration of Washington, Moton and Patterson." Master's thesis, Atlanta University, 1950.

Bullock, Ralph W. *In Spite of Handicaps.* 1927. Reprint, New York: Books for Libraries Press, 1968.

Harlan, Louis R., ed. *The Booker T. Washington Papers, 1889–95.* Vol. 3. Chicago: University of Illinois Press, 1974.

Marable, Manning. "Tuskegee Institute In The 1920's." *Negro History Bulletin.* 40 (November/December, 1977): 764–768.

Matthews, Basil. *Booker T. Washington.* Cambridge, MA: Harvard University Press, 1948.

Mays, Benjamin E. *Born To Rebel.* New York: Scribner's, 1971.

"Minutes from the Board of Trustee Meeting, October 26, 1934." *Tuskegee Student* (October 1934): 30.

Moton, Robert Russa. *Finding a Way Out.* New York: Doubleday, 1920.

———. *What The Negro Thinks.* New York: Doubleday, 1929.

Perry, Phyllis. "Tuskegee VA Center: Giving Black Veterans a Fighting Chance." *Health Quest: The Publication of Black Wellness* 4 (31 March 1994): 60.

Phillip, Mary–Christine. "UNCF Closes Moton Center." *Black Issues In Higher Education* 10 (18 November 1993): 32–3.

Salzman, Jack, David Lionel Smith, and Cornel West, eds. *Encyclopedia of African–American Culture and History.* New York: Macmillan Library Reference USA/Simon and Schuster Macmillan, 1996.

Smith, Jessie Carney, ed. *Notable Black American Women, Book II.* Detroit: Gale Research, 1996.

COLLECTIONS

Records of Moton's tenure at Hampton University can be found at Hampton University Archives, Collis P. Huntington Memorial Library, Hampton University. Records of his Tuskegee tenure, can be found in the Robert Russa Moton Papers, Hollis Burke Frissell Library, Tuskegee University, Tuskegee, Alabama. More information can be found in the following collections: The Moton Family Papers, Library of Congress, Washington D.C.; Records of the Agricultural Stabilization and Conservation Service (Record Group 145), the National Archives, Washington, D.C.; Robert Russa Moton Portrait Collection, Schomburg Center for Research in Black Culture, New York Public Library; National Negro Business League materials in the Albon L. Holsey Correspondence, Hollis Burke Frissell Library, Tuskegee University; Booker T. Washington Papers, Library of Congress; Records Collection, Southern Regional Office, National Urban League, Library of Congress.

Sheila A. Stuckey

Muddy Waters
(1915–1983)
Musician

Muddy Waters was a blues musician whose career stretched over forty years. As a child he learned the folk traditions of the down home blues, a development in black music that occurred roughly in the area of Mississippi called the Delta, which stretches south from Memphis, Tennessee, to Vicksburg, Mississippi, and from the Mississippi River to the hill country. In Chicago Waters built on the Delta tradition in a creative way by exploiting the use of electrically amplified instruments. This music developed into the Chicago blues. While Waters never became a major pop star, musicians in many different fields of contemporary music see in him a revered ancestor.

Muddy Waters was born McKinley Morganfield in Rolling Fork, Mississippi, on April 14, 1915, one of ten children. His father was sharecropper Ollie Morganfield, and his mother Bertha Jones. Waters's mother disappeared from his life when he was six months old; according to differing accounts, she either died or separated from Ollie Morganfield. Waters was then entrusted to his grandmother who lived nearby. Three years later she and her grandson moved north to the Stovall plantation in Coahoma County near Clarksdale. Even before the move, Waters had been nicknamed Muddy because of his fondness for playing in the mud. Because his family called him Muddy, the other children on the Stovall Plantation added "Waters" to his nickname. Although Waters did not particularly like the name, it stuck.

Waters had little formal schooling, having left school after the second or third grade. Some critics have attributed his mastery of the subtleties of blues playing to his dependence on learning through his ears. He was a master of slight variations in time and pitch that few musicians, even many who played in his bands, have been able to match. Waters told James Rooney:

> "But looks like my blues is so simple to play and then again it's hard. There's a lot of people say, 'Man, anybody can play that.' Then they get up to play and can't play. . . . Maybe I do it the wrong way, 'cause I'm kind of a delay singer, maybe. There's a lot of guys, if he ain't on the beat, he can't play it. But you've got to learn to play behind the beat a little. . . . A lot of people can't hear. They got a bad ear. . . . I'm lucky. I got a good ear. 'Cause that's what I works by—my ear."

Waters's first serious instrument was the harmonica, which he took up when he was 7. By the time he was 13, his playing was in demand at local social occasions like fish fries. When Waters was 17, he took up the guitar, and for $2.50 purchased the first of the three Sears Roebuck instruments he used before moving to Chicago. With his friend Scott Bohannon

Muddy Waters

(the spelling of the last name varies, even appearing as Brown), he formed a successful two–guitar team.

While influenced locally by older local blues artists like Charlie Patton (1891–1934) and Son (Eddie) House (1902–1988), broader influences reached Waters through records. He first had access to the phonograph through a neighboring woman, and later his grandmother bought one herself. Waters listened to popular recorded blues artists like Blind Lemon Jefferson (1897–1929), Memphis Minnie, Leroy Carr, Lonnie Johnson, and Tampa Red, as well as legendary local bluesman Robert Johnson (c. 1912–1938), whom he never met.

When he was 18, Muddy Waters married and moved out of his grandmother's house. Little is known of Waters's private life; during interviews, he spoke primarily of his music. According to *Blues Who's Who* there may have been a second marriage to a woman named Geneva in 1940. She died in 1973. A 1972 article in *Ebony* features a picture of Muddy Waters, Geneva, a son, and a great–granddaughter, Chandra. According to *Deep Blues,* in 1979 Muddy Waters married a third time to 25–year–old Marva Jean Brooks.

During the early 1940s, Waters's home became a juke house. People gathered there on Saturday nights to dance, gamble, and drink bootleg whiskey. Thus, music became a profitable sideline to his work on the plantation where he was earning 22 1/2 cents an hour as a tractor driver. In 1941 and 1942, he recorded for the folk music collector Alan Lomax; two of his songs from the 1941 session were issued on record by the Library of Congress.

Moves to Chicago

Increasingly dissatisfied with life on the plantation, Waters toured with the Silas Green tent show for a few weeks. He then lived for a brief period in Saint Louis with a woman other than his wife but returned because his grandmother needed his help. Having been cursed by the overseer when he asked for a raise to the 27 cents an hour earned by the top tractor drivers, Waters left Mississippi for Chicago in May 1943 with his grandmother's blessing.

In Chicago, Waters found a support network of family and friends. He lived with his sister and her husband, Dan Jones, for a week, then found a room on a lower floor of the same building. Two or three weeks later he moved in with cousins on the west side. It was during World War II so jobs were plentiful. In spite of the housing shortage, Waters found a four room apartment within the next two or three months. He escaped being drafted because of his illiteracy and poor eyesight. (He later improved his reading skills.) Waters found work playing the blues, first at house parties in his sister's flat and then at neighborhood bars for five dollars a night.

Waters acquired his first electric guitar in 1944 as a practical necessity to meet the need for loudness in noisy venues. Although he did not like it as well as the acoustic guitar at first, Waters was pleased by the fact that the bands he was associated with were the first to popularize the amplified Mississippi Delta blues sound. Previous bands used amplification simply for the guitar solos and turned the volume down for singing. Waters kept the guitar loud and amplified his voice over it. For balance the other instruments were likewise amplified. By the early 1950s, the resulting Chicago blues had become the most popular form of the blues and won wide audiences among blacks in the South and among recent transplants immigrants from that region in northern cities.

Waters's first apartment at 1851 West Thirteenth Street was near Maxwell Street, the center of blues in Chicago. Many guitarists played for tips on this street, relying on extension cords to power their instruments. Waters's first substantial gig was as a guitar accompanist to Eddie Boyd at the Flame Club in the mid–1940s. He met Sunnyland Slim (Albert Luandrew, 1907–) at the Flame Club. Waters and Slim soon began working together. By this time, Waters was earning 52 dollars a week from his music in addition to the money he earned from his day job as a truck driver.

In September 1946 Slim, who was the more established musician at the time, arranged for Waters to sing in a recording session for Columbia records, one of the two major companies doing blues recording for the black market. Nothing came of this session. Waters's big break did not occur until the following year when Slim, who had a recording session with Aristocrat records (Aristocrat later became Chess records when the Chess brothers bought out their partner in 1950), needed a guitarist. A friend tracked down Waters on his delivery route and, at the end of the session, Waters had recorded two songs in the modern blues style. Again these songs were not issued, although Waters did attract some interest within the music industry. In a later session, Waters abandoned the modern urban blues style, replacing it with more traditional songs from Mississippi. This record first went into outlets on Chicago's South Side and sold out within twelve hours. The record was selling so well that the record outlets charged $1.10 for a 79 cent record and limited sales to one per customer. More discs were pressed and these also sold well in Chicago and in the South. Waters ended his relationship with Chess in 1973 and sued for back royalties. He then switched to the CBS/Blue Sky label.

Forms a Band

By the end of 1948 Waters had his own band, which performed steadily in and around Chicago. He also began touring in the South. Waters attracted several talented musicians to his band and, while none of these musicians ever achieved stardom, many had distinguished careers. One of his colleagues, harmonica player Little Walter (Marion Jacobs), even outsold Waters during the 1950s. Despite the success of Waters's band, Chess refused to record the group until the middle of 1950. When the band finally did record, Waters's popularity increased dramatically.

From 1951 to 1958 Waters placed 12 records on the rhythm and blues charts. ''I'm Your Hoochie Coochie Man'' and ''Just Make Love To Me,'' both written by bass player Willie Dixon, were the only two to place among the top five on the chart. By the mid–1950s, however, audience tastes began to change as rock and roll captured young black and white listeners. Consequently, slow blues numbers went out of favor. Waters put down his guitar for a year or two beginning in 1955 to concentrate on singing, but his band continued to work five or six nights a week in and around Chicago and tour from time to time, most often to the deep South.

In 1958 Waters began his first tour of England. After the first concert, he had to turn down the volume of his music to better suit his audience. This tour and a second in 1962, during which he used an acoustic guitar when English audiences were better prepared for the electric instrument, were important in positioning Waters as a folk artist. On July 4, 1960, he appeared at the Newport Jazz Festival despite the fact that rioting had occurred the previous day. His reception was enthusiastic, and Chess issued an album of the performance.

Despite the efforts of his new manager, Bob Messinger, Waters did not enjoy wide popularity with white audiences until 1964. In that year, English groups like the Rolling Stones, who took their name from one of his songs, began recording covers of his songs. To benefit from his new popularity, Waters issued the solo acoustic album *Muddy Waters Folk Singer* in 1964.

Now reaching a plateau in his career, Waters was performing and recording for a largely white audience. Like many jazz and blues musicians, he was concerned with the lack of interest in blues music by young blacks. He told James Rooney:

> If I hadn't come to Chicago, I don't know who would have kept [the blues] alive. And we'll see who'll keep it alive after I've done made it through the scene. Most of them are into another scene now. We can't live always. Who's gonna take it? It's gotta come from the black people. They're ducking. They're running from it.

After 1968, Waters continued to be a steady seller on records as well as a respected live performer. Life on the road had its hazards, however. On October 11, 1973, Waters was severely injured in an automobile accident that killed three persons, including the driver beside whom he was sitting. Waters suffered a broken leg, fractured ribs, a sprained back, and a paralyzed right hand. He stayed in the hospital for three months and was forced into semi–retirement for two years. His first major live appearance after the accident was on November 25, 1976. Despite this accident, Waters was highly prolific, appearing five times on pop charts, with the albums *Electric Mud* (1968), *Fathers and Sons* (1969), with white bluesmen Paul Butterfield and Mike Bloomfield; *Hard Again* (1977), with producer Johnny Winter, on the new label Blue Sky; *I'm Ready*; and *King Bee* (1981). He won Grammy awards for Best Ethnic or Traditional Recording in 1972, 1973, 1976, 1978, 1979, and 1980. In August 1978 he played at the White House staff picnic during Jimmy Carter's administration. In 1980 he was inducted into the Blues Foundation's Hall of Fame, and in January of 1987 he was posthumously inducted into the Rock 'n' Roll Hall of Fame at the second annual induction dinner.

Waters died of a heart attack at his home in Chicago on April 30, 1983. As a songwriter and performer he left behind an impressive body of work. His recorded work is readily available from MCA, which purchased the Chess catalog and has issued a boxed set of all his recordings for Chess on compact discs, as well as his individual albums. Musically, Waters will be remembered for forging the link between deep Mississippi Delta blues and hard–edged, electric Chicago blues.

REFERENCES

The Big Book of the Blues. New York: Penguin, 1993.

Bims, Hamilton. ''Blues City.'' *Ebony* 27 (March 1972): 76–86.

Charters, Samuel B. *The Country Blues.* 1959. Reprint, New York: Da Capo, 1975.

Cohn, Lawrence, and others. *Nothing But the Blues.* New York: Abbeville Press, 1993.

Encyclopedia of Rock. New York: Schirmer Books, 1988.

Harris, Shelton. *Blues Who's Who.* New Rochelle, NY: Arlington House, 1979. Reprint, New York: Da Capo, 1981.

Obrecht, Jas. ''Muddy Waters: The Life and Times of the Hoochie Coochie Man.'' *Guitar Player* 28 (March 1994): 30–48, 72.

Oliver, Paul. *The Story of the Blues.* Radnor, PA: 1969.

Palmer, Robert. *Deep Blues.* New York: Penguin, 1981.

Rock Movers and Shakers. Santa Barbara, CA: ABC–Clio, 1991.

Rooney, James. *Bossmen: Bill Monroe and Muddy Waters.* New York: Da Capo, 1971.

Welding, Pete. "Muddy Waters: Last King of the South Side?" *Downbeat* 61 (February 1994): 32–36. Reprint of interview in October 8, 1964, issue.

Robert L. Johns

Elijah Muhammad
(1897–1975)
Religious leader, black nationalist

Elijah Muhammad achieved national prominence in the 1940s as the leader and self-proclaimed prophet of the Nation of Islam. The black militant group stood in sharp contrast to other civil rights groups of the era by advocating separation of the black and white races, while professing strong beliefs in the doctrine of self-sufficiency and certain laws of the traditional Islamic faith. As Muhammad promoted his religious beliefs, he also rearticulated the themes of black pride and black nationalism. He became an inspiration to many blacks disillusioned with the Civil Rights Movement as efforts to win legal equality did little to erase economic and social inequalities. As a vocal critic of white America, Muhammad drew sharp reactions to his radical position on race relations, which included a belief that whites were a race of devils bent on the destruction of the black race. But in spite of harassment from the government and infighting within the group, Muhammad nurtured the fractured Nation of Islam into an influential organization of considerable financial holdings that stood as a model of black entrepreneurship and self-reliance.

Elijah Muhammad was born Elijah Poole in Sandersville, Georgia, to William and Mariah Hall Poole on October 7, 1897. He was the sixth of thirteen children. William Poole was a sharecropper and second-generation Baptist minister with a local church. Mariah Poole worked as a domestic.

The family moved to Cordele, Georgia, in 1900. Elijah Poole received a meager formal education in the public school for blacks in Cordele. He may have left school as early as the fourth grade. At the age of ten he began chopping firewood and selling it in town to help support the family. Almost as soon as he began work, he had a traumatic formative experience. While carrying firewood to Cordele, he came upon the aftermath of a lynching. The lynching was a harsh lesson about the underlying violence which supported race relations.

At the age of 16 Elijah Poole left home and moved to Macon, Georgia. Over the next few years, he worked at whatever jobs were available. He was working for the Southern Railroad Company at the time he married Clara Evans (1898–1972) on March 17, 1919. Between 1921 and 1939, the marriage produced eight children. Two of the children had been born by the time the family moved to Detroit in April of

Elijah Muhammad

1924, joining the mass migration of blacks fleeing the oppressive economic and social conditions in the South.

Like many blacks, the Pooles did not find conditions in Detroit to be much better than in Georgia. They were forced to live in segregated housing and faced job and wage discrimination. Elijah Poole lacked the skills and connections to find steady work—his longest stint at one job was two years at the American Wire and Brass Company between 1923 and 1925. The Great Depression began early for African Americans. As the decade of the 1920s drew towards its close, Poole faced long bouts of unemployment. Eventually the family became recipients of public assistance. Poole became increasingly upset by his inability to support his family and sought relief in alcohol to the point that he would routinely pass out in gutters and alleys.

Meets W. D. Fard

Poole's life took a radical turn after he met the founder of the Nation of Islam, W. D. Fard. Accounts of W. D. Fard's background and life are widely at variance. According to police and FBI records he was born either in New Zealand or Portland, Oregon, on February 21, 1891. He used the names of Fred Dodd or Wallace Ford before becoming W. D. Fard upon his arrival in Detroit. His ethnic heritage may have included Polynesian ancestry, but in jail he always passed for white. He operated a cafe in Los Angeles in the 1920s. There were various contretemps with the law, and he ended up by spending three years in San Quentin prison for selling narcotics. Released from prison on May 27, 1929, he left for the East and ended up in Detroit. He worked at first as a retail salesman in the black community, and began organizing the Nation of Islam in 1930.

According to the Nation of Islam, Fard, known as Fard Muhammad to his followers, was born to a black father and a white mother in Mecca and charged with revealing the truth to the ''American So–Called Negroes.'' According to Andrew Claude Clegg in his book *An Original Man: The Life and Times of Elijah Muhammad,* shortly after meeting Fard, Poole asked, ''Who are you, and what is your real name?'' To which Fard replied, ''My name is Mahdi; I am God, I came to guide you into the right path that you may be successful and see the hereafter.''

Poole began learning the lessons, a series of questions and answers that the prospective member of the organization had to memorize, and was called to be a minister, receiving a new surname, Karriem, as a mark of his new status. His subsequent elevation to Supreme Minister, and, thus, Fard's second–in–command, was not long in coming.

Although the Nation of Islam followed the dietary and prayer laws of traditional Islam, the group diverged radically from that faith in ways which attracted the attention of the U.S. government and law enforcement agencies. According to the Nation of Islam doctrine, blacks were the original, superior race of humans on earth, and whites were the result of a biological experiment performed by an evil magician. As a result of their unnatural creation, whites were considered to be evil and destined for destruction at the hands of Allah. Until the time when blacks would be liberated from the oppression of the ''white devils,'' they were to remain separate from them. The Nation of Islam advocated a disciplined lifestyle, self–sufficiency, and an entrepreneurial spirit as a way to foster a strong sense of black pride.

The radical nature of the Nation of Islam's beliefs made the organization a target for police harassment. In November of 1932, police began to investigate a bizarre murder committed by a man with vague ties to the Nation of Islam, and used the opportunity to arrest Fard. When it became apparent that the persecution was only serving to make a martyr of Fard, the police ordered him to leave the city. Fard ignored the order and went into hiding, using the time to prepare Elijah Karriem to take over the organization. Fard bestowed on him the surname of Muhammad and appointed him as chief minister of Islam.

Fard's departure shattered the fragile unity of the Nation of Islam, and fierce factional fighting was acerbated by continuing police harassment. Elijah Muhammad took refuge from the struggles from time to time at Temple No. 2 in Chicago. Finally in April of 1934 he relocated the headquarters of the movement in that city. It was there that Muhammad had his last meeting with his leader in June of 1934 before Fard disappeared.

The Wilderness Years

In late 1935 another dissident movement, led this time by a younger brother of Elijah Muhammad and another assistant minister, Augustus Muhammad, attracted over three quarters of the members of the Chicago temple. By September Elijah Muhammad's faithful following had shrunk from 400 to 13, and he had to flee the city for fear of being murdered by the rival faction. Elijah Muhammad went first to Temple No. 3 in Milwaukee. What he may have at first envisioned as a short absence from Chicago stretched into seven years. During these years he made only infrequent and brief visits to Chicago to see his wife and children. He left Milwaukee after a few weeks and made Washington, D.C., his headquarters. There he applied himself to studying the 104 books on a list which Fard Muhammad had given him and began to proselytize discreetly. In 1939 he organized Temple No. 4 in Washington.

The activity in Washington attracted the attention of law enforcement agencies who infiltrated the group. The United States was preparing to take part in World War II, and the FBI was much concerned by the Muslim refusal to participate in war efforts, including a refusal to serve in the Armed Forces. The FBI arrested Elijah Muhammad on charges of failing to comply with the draft law on May 8, 1942, but their investigation seemed more concerned with finding evidence to support charges of subversion. Clara Muhammad and the Chicago Muslims scraped up enough money for bail, and Elijah Muhammad returned to Chicago as soon as he was freed on July 23 to avoid being arrested again.

The FBI took the offensive against the Muslims and also at least two other black groups it labeled subversive in September of 1942. They closed Temple No. 2 indefinitely and arrested thirty–eight male members, including Elijah Muhammad, for draft evasion. Muhammad and four others were also charged with sedition on extremely flimsy evidence. The charge was eventually dropped, but Muhammad entered the Federal Correctional Unit in Milan, Michigan, on July 23, 1943, to serve his sentence for draft evasion. The imprisonment lasted until August 24, 1946.

The Nation of Islam Grows

The FBI's attempts to disrupt the organization only served to strengthen the Nation of Islam. The remnant was very loyal and strongly committed. In addition, Elijah Muhammad gained great prestige and emerged from prison as the unchallenged leader of the movement.

It was at this period that the Nation of Islam took its first steps into the business world. The efforts began modestly in 1947 with a restaurant and a bakery in Chicago. Gradually, the organization became more affluent and more bureaucratic, even though growth was slow at first. In 1950 there were only about 286 members of the Nation of Islam Temple No. 2 in Chicago, but growth began to quicken. One of the most effective leaders to emerge from the rapid expansion was Malcolm X, who became minister of the New York temple in 1954.

Malcolm X was far more charismatic than Elijah Muhammad and a much better speaker. Along with a comparative lack of oratorical presence, Elijah Muhammad was physically unimpressive. He was delicately built, five–feet six–inches tall, and weighed less than 150 pounds; he also suffered from bronchial asthma, which sometimes interfered with his delivery of speeches. It even forced him to spend his winters in Phoenix, Arizona, for a number of years beginning in 1961. The celebrity of Malcolm X eventually came to surpass that of Elijah Muhammad, but the younger man remained steadfastly loyal for many years.

The seeds of two later problems can be traced to the mid–1950s. As the financial success of the Nation of Islam increased, seemingly well–founded rumors of the misuse of funds by insiders, especially family members of Elijah Muhammad, grew. At about the same time Elijah Muhammad began a series of liaisons with young women, fathering thirteen known children by eight different women. This dalliance seems to have slowed or stopped by 1962, but the knowledge of the extramarital affairs was widespread in the inner circles by then and contributed to the break between Elijah Muhammad and Malcolm X.

Black Power and Black Nationalism

In July of 1959 Elijah Muhammad began a trip to Africa, the Middle East, and Pakistan. Part of his aim was to gain recognition as an authentic Muslim leader and mute criticism of the Nation of Islam by orthodox Muslims in the United States. His fulfillment of the obligation to make a pilgrimage to Mecca during this trip meant that he was accepted as an authentic, albeit heterodox, Muslim.

WNTA–TV of New York showed a five–part documentary on the Nation of Islam on July 13–17, 1959. Produced by Mike Wallace and Louis Lomax and called *The Hate That Hate Produced,* the series presented a sensational and highly negative image of the group. According to Clegg, in an interview Elijah Muhammad ''confirmed for the record that he believed that the white man was the devil, that the so–called Negro would be resurrected by 1970, and that there would be some blood shed when the white world was destroyed.'' As a portent of the future, Malcolm X received more air time than Muhammad.

The program raised white alarm, led to condemnation of the Nation of Islam by civil rights organizations like the NAACP and the Southern Christian Leadership Conference (SCLC), helped recruit a substantial number of new black Muslims, and made Malcolm X a celebrity routinely sought out by the media for his comments on developments in the ongoing civil rights struggle. With its heightened visibility, the Nation of Islam became an inspiration for young blacks who felt that legislation like the Civil Rights Act did little to change racist attitudes and improve the economic conditions of blacks. The Nation of Islam had adopted a program of black pride, black separatism, and black economic development long before the slogan ''Black Power'' became a powerful rallying point for militants in the mid–1960s.

Nonetheless, the Nation of Islam remained politically conservative in spite of its rhetoric. It rejected political action; the overthrow of whites would come about through divine, not human, action. Survival was more important than armed self–defense. For example, with the blessing of Elijah Muhammad, Malcolm X and Jeremiah X, the Muslim minister in Atlanta, met with Ku Klux Klan leaders on January 28, 1961, to deflect Klan violence away from Muslims in the South on the basis of their shared hostility to integration.

When President John F. Kennedy was assassinated on November 22, 1962, Elijah Muhammad ordered his ministers to make no comment on the event to avoid a backlash against the Nation of Islam. Pressed by a reporter, Malcolm X could not refrain from saying, as Clegg and other sources report, ''being an old farm boy myself, chickens coming home to roost never did make me sad; they've always made me glad.'' Because of these remarks, Elijah Muhammad suspended Malcolm X from his ministry for 90 days, setting off a chain of events which would lead to a irrevocable break between the two leaders on March 8, 1963. On February 21, 1965, after a long war of words, Malcolm X was assassinated by members of the Nation of Islam. There is no proof that Elijah Muhammad directly ordered the assassination, but at the very least his anger and bitterness towards his protégé created a climate of opinion in the Nation of Islam that made the deed seem meritorious to members.

The Final Years

By 1965 Elijah Muhammad's health was becoming precarious. In addition to asthma, he now suffered from diabetes and high blood pressure. Nonetheless, he maintained a firm grip on the leadership of the Nation of Islam in spite of violent infighting in several mosques between 1971 and 1973, and some brutal murders of critics of the Nation of Islam. Suspicions regarding his role in the assassination of Malcolm X did not affect Elijah Muhammad's growing reputation. He was a role model to young black militants, even though his conservative family values and disapproval of such things as Afros, dashikis, and the use of drugs were very much out of tune with many in the rising generation. Not only was he seen as a champion of black nationalism, he offered an example of successful business operations as the Nation of Islam's financial empire grew. In addition, the Nation of Islam's success in rehabilitating young black prisoners won praise.

Clara Muhammad died in August of 1972. Elijah Muhammad was frail but still active until his health gave way suddenly in January of 1975. Entering Mercy Hospital in Chicago on January 29, he died on February 25. After the funeral at Mosque No. 2, the remains were interred in Glenwood Cemetery.

The Nation of Islam gave birth to two successors after Elijah Muhammad's death. Wallace (now Warith) D. Muhammad, Elijah's seventh child, took over the reins of the Nation of Islam. He quickly set about dismantling the rules and belief system and on October 18, 1976, changed its name to the World Community of Islam in the West. This national organization in turn was dissolved in 1985; each mosque became fully independent. Louis Farrakhan, the minister of the New York mosque who had by no means given up his fervent belief in Fard Muhammad's teachings, broke with

Wallace Muhammad in late 1977 and started his own organization under the old name, the Nation of Islam.

The religious heritage of Elijah Muhammad lives on directly in Louis Farrakhan's Nation of Islam. Indirectly, Elijah Muhammad did much to make profession of Islam acceptable to black Americans and led numbers to become orthodox Sunni Muslims. In many ways, his black nationalism revived the responses of nineteenth–century black nationalists and separatists in the context of the twentieth century. With his emphasis on black pride and black separatism, he played a major role in articulating racial concerns that still resonate in today's society.

REFERENCES

Clegg, Claude Andrew III. *An Original Man: The Life and Times of Elijah Muhammad.* New York: St. Martin's Press, 1997.

Lincoln, C. Eric. *The Black Muslims in America.* Boston: Beacon Press, 1961.

Magida, Arthur J. *Prophet of Rage: A Life of Louis Farrakhan and his Nation.* New York: Basic Books, 1996.

Muhammad, Elijah. *The Fall of America.* Chicago: Muhammad's Temple of Islam No. 2, 1973.

———. *Message to the Blackman in America.* Chicago: Muhammad Mosque of Islam No. 2, 1965.

Murphy, Larry G., J. Gordon Melton, and Gary L. Ward. *Encyclopedia of African American Religions.* New York: Garland Publishing, 1993.

X, Malcolm, with Alex Haley. *The Autobiography of Malcolm X.* New York: Grove Press, 1965.

Robert L. Johns

Eddie Murphy

(1961–)

Actor, comedian

Eddie Murphy, actor and comedian, exploded on the entertainment scene at the age of 19 as an extra for the comedy television show, *Saturday Night Live.* Taking full advantage of his brief solo opportunities in front of the camera, Eddie Murphy was clearly destined to be a star. "I try to be honest with my comedy and try to do things that I think are genuinely funny," he pointed out in *Jet* magazine for June 1994. "I try to be true to who I am. I don't think I've ever compromised who I am and I think I'm a funny guy." His innovative style has made him one of the most important comedic stars of his generation.

Edward Regan Murphy was born on April 3, 1961, in the Bushwick section of Brooklyn, New York. His mother Lillian Murphy was a telephone operator, and his father Charles Murphy was a New York City transit police officer, amateur comedian, and emcee. Eddie Murphy is a year younger than his brother Charles Jr. Murphy married Nicole Mitchell, a model, on March 18, 1993. They have three children, daughters Bria Liana and Shayne and son Myles Mitchell.

Murphy's parents separated when he was three years old. Soon after that, his mother became ill and was hospitalized. Young Eddie and his brother were sent to a foster home, a painful experience for him. Murphy has said that staying with a harsh woman was probably the reason he became a comedian. He refined his comic gifts by watching cartoons for hours and absorbing the mannerisms of the animated characters. He learned to do perfect imitations of their voices.

Murphy's father died when Eddie was eight years old, stabbed to death by his girlfriend. His mother married Vernon Lynch, a foreman at Breyer's Ice Cream factory and a boxing coach. The family moved to Roosevelt, a largely black middle–class suburb on Long Island, in 1970. Half brother Vernon Jr. later joined the family. Eddie Murphy was an early class cut up, using humor to be accepted. He fondly remembers in his biography *Murphy* his first comedy performance. "It was in the first grade. Our teacher said that whoever made up the best story would win an Eskimo Pie. I cracked the kids up with a story and won!" His childhood interests included hours of television, ventriloquism, art and music, karate, baseball, and astronomy. His comedic idol has always been Richard Pryor.

Murphy has performed in front of live audiences since he was 15. His first stage performance was on July 9, 1976 as host of a talent show at the Roosevelt Youth Center. He did a 15–minute impersonation of singer Al Green. Eddie Murphy frequently performed at school assemblies and, unknown to his parents, at after hours clubs. He worked harder on his jokes than his school work. A perennial summer school attendant, Murphy was forced to repeat the tenth grade; he went to night school and doubled up on classes. Voted the most popular boy in his class, he graduated from Roosevelt High School, New York City, in the summer of 1979.

For a short time Murphy teamed with a couple of white comedians in a novelty group called the Identical Triplets. He began performing regularly at important comedy clubs in New York, such as the East Side Comedy Club, the Improvisation, the Comic Strip, and Catch a Rising Star. The owners of the Comic Strip became his managers and helped him improve his timing, delivery, and material. He was performing at the Comic Strip in Fort Lauderdale, Florida, when he got word that the television show *Saturday Night Live* (SNL) was going to hire a black comedian.

Saturday Night Live

Murphy, at his mother's insistence, had already enrolled at Nassau Community College to study theater, but put school

Eddie Murphy

aside to audition for SNL. He waged a campaign to be seen by SNL's talent coordinator, sometimes calling three times a day pleading for a chance. After six auditions, he was hired as a feature player, earning $750 per show. The producer claimed that Murphy was too inexperienced to have a regular spot, and he received little air time during his first season. Murphy expressed his belief that he was the show's token black.

In 1980, when Murphy first auditioned for SNL, the show was entering is sixth season with new cast members and a new producer. An October 26, 1981, *New York Times* article proclaimed , "It has been less than a month since the debut of NBC's new and improved 'Saturday Night Live,' and Mr. Murphy has already revived a tradition . . . Eddie Murphy has stolen the show." His first character for SNL was the very militant critic Raheem Abdul Muhammed and his appearance was a big success. He soon became a regular cast member. For the 1983–84 season Murphy earned $30,000 for ten shows.

Murphy's trademark laugh is infectious and cannot be described or replicated easily. His impersonations of boxer Muhammad Ali, comedians Bill Cosby and Jerry Lewis, civil rights leader Jesse Jackson, entertainer Mr. T, and music stars James Brown and Stevie Wonder for SNL were hilarious. His characterizations included a grumpy Gumby, based on the animated television program; Mr. Robinson, an urban version of children's show host Mr. Rogers; Little Richard Simmons, a blend of the exercise guru and the legendary rock and roller; television huckster Velvet Jones; and, a grown up version of the "Little Rascals" character, Buckwheat. While these portrayals left audiences in spasms of laughter, Murphy says that he gave his characters serious thought. Sensitive to the power of racial stereotypes, Murphy has held fast to a commitment not to do anything that would be degrading to himself or to his people.

Major Motion Picture Star

Paramount Pictures signed Murphy for $200,000 to co–star as Reggie Hammond in Walter Hill's *48 Hrs* (1982) with Nick Nolte during the SNL's hiatus. The film was a big hit, making $80 million. The studio quickly signed him to a mutually–profitable, multipicture contract for $15 million. He formed Eddie Murphy Productions in 1983. Murphy delivered a series of films, consistently generating money at the box office: *Trading Places* (1983), *Best Defense* (1984), *Beverly Hills Cop* (1984), *Golden Child* (1986), *Beverly Hills Cop II* (1987), *Eddie Murphy Raw* (1987), *Hollywood Shuffle* (1987), *Coming to America* (1988), *Harlem Nights* (also director, producer, and screenwriter, 1989), *Another 48 Hours* (1990), *Boomerang* (1992), *The Distinguished Gentleman* (1992), *Beverly Hills Cop III* (1994), *Vampire of Brooklyn* (also coproducer, 1995), *Nutty Professor* (1996), *Metro* (also co–executive producer, 1997), *Doctor Dolittle* (1998), and *Mulan* (1998).

Murphy's HBO Special *Eddie Murphy Delirious* and other recordings of his comedy routines are big sellers on the home video cassette market. His albums include: *Eddie Murphy* (1982), *Eddie Murphy Comedian* (1983), *How Could It Be* (1984, the single "Party All the Time" was recorded with Rick James), *So Happy* (1989), *Distinguished Gentleman* (1992), *Love's Alright* (Motown, 1993), and *Metro* (1997).

Murphy's awards include the Image Award, entertainer of the year, NAACP, 1983; Grammy Award, best comedy album, 1984, for *Eddie Murphy: Comedian*; the People's Choice Award, favorite all–around male entertainer, 1985; People's Choice Award, best motion picture actor, 1989; NAACP Lifetime Achievement Award, 1991. He was honored with a commemorative stamp issued by the African nation Lesotho; he received the Heritage Award for career achievement, Soul Train Music Awards, 1993; the 2,067th star on the Hollywood Walk of Fame, 1996; and best actor award, National Society of Film Critics, for *The Nutty Professor,* in 1997.

Eddie Murphy has had his share of criticism over the years. His comedy routines have been labeled profane and controversial. He has been accused of women bashing, of being conceited, offensive, apolitical, and lacking singing talent. "I'm a cocky guy," says Eddie Murphy in his biography. "But there's no such thing as a humble entertainer. To tell you the truth, I don't know what makes me tick. I don't know what makes me happy or sad, what goes on in my mind. The only thing I'm secure about is that I'm funny."

Robin Carter described Murphy in *Sepia* as having "an appealing sort of innocence, despite his "street smarts and business acumen." He makes no attempt to "veil his real identity, he is straight forward and in the raw." He has "unassuming modesty." One notices the "grace of his confident stride, the manliness of his slender form, and the softness of his alert, brown eyes, and it is especially refreshing to see all of this splendor subdued behind an easy mannered charm . . . and a friendly smile."

Eddie Murphy's talent and charisma have fueled his career. He lives comfortably with his family at his New Jersey estate named Bubble Hill. His success came so quickly that it is often difficult to remember that he is still a young man with years of work on stage, screen, and television ahead for his legion of admirers.

Current address: Eddie Murphy Productions, 5555 Melrose Avenue, Los Angeles, CA 90038–3197.

REFERENCES

Carter, Robin. "Live: Eddie Murphy." *Sepia* 21 (May 1982): 21–23, 28–30.

Collier, Aldore D. "Eddie Murphy Returns as Axel Foley in *Beverly Hills Cop III.*" *Jet* 86 (13 June 1994): 56–59.

Davis, Judith. *The Unofficial Eddie Murphy Scrapbook.* New York: New American Library, 1984.

Eichhorn, Dennis P. *Murphy.* Seattle: Truman Publishers, 1987.

Gross, Edward. *The Films of Eddie Murphy.* Las Vegas: Pioneer Books, 1990.

"How an Amiable Youth Became a Star At 20." *New York Times,* October 26, 1981.

Leavy, Walter. "Eddie Murphy: Hollywood's $2 Billion Man Talks About His Marriage, *Beverly Hills Cop III* and the Joys of Fatherhood." *Ebony* 49 (June 1994): 100–102.

Lyons, Gene. "Laughing With Eddie." *Newsweek* 101 (3 January 1983): 46–48.

Ruuth, Marianne. *Eddie: Eddie Murphy From A to Z.* Los Angeles: Holloway House Publishing Co., 1985.

Wilburn, Deborah A. *Eddie Murphy.* New York: Chelsea House, 1993.

Kathleen E. Bethel

Isaac Murphy
(1861?–1896)
Jockey

African American jockeys played conspicuous roles in the horse racing circles of the nineteenth and early twentieth centuries, dominating thoroughbred racing from the Civil War until 1911. Isaac Murphy was the first jockey of any race to win back–to–back Kentucky Derbies and the first to win the Derby three times. He was one of the stellar jockeys of the era and one of the greatest riders in history, winning 44 percent of all races he rode.

Isaac Burns Murphy was born on the David Tanner farm in Fayette County, Kentucky. The date of his birth is uncertain; however, some sources use January 1, 1861 since all thoroughbred horses are assigned New Year's Day as their birthday. James Burns, Murphy's father, was a free black and a bricklayer. After a stint in the Union Army, Burns died in a Confederate prison camp. Murphy's mother, whose first name we do not know, moved her family to Lexington, where they lived with her father, Green Murphy. By Fall 1876 his mother had persuaded Isaac to assume the surname Murphy, in honor of his grandfather, a well–known auctioneer in Lexington.

Mrs. Burns worked in Lexington as a laundress for Richard Owings at the Owings and Williams Racing Stable, where in 1874 young Murphy, weighing a wiry 70–pounds, began to gallop the horses. In 1876 he received formal training in horsemanship from "Uncle" Eli Jordan, the black trainer at the stable. Murphy learned to be a hand rider rather than a whip rider and kept this riding style throughout his career. As a hand–rider, he sat low and forward, and as the horse moved its head the rider's hands moved forward and down in unison, the reins never drawing on the horse's mouth.

Wins the Derby

Murphy was one of a number of black jockeys who dominated horse racing during the nineteenth century. In the inaugural derby on May 17, 1875, which black jockey Oliver Lewis won, 14 of the 15 jockeys were black. Between 1875 and 1902, 14 black jockeys won the derby. Murphy rode his first race in Louisville on May 22, 1875. His first winning mount was Glentina, at the Crab Orchard Park in Lexington on September 15, 1876. His records were in most respects not excelled. He won 44 percent of all the races in which he rode: 1412 mounts, 628 winners. He is the only jockey to have won the Kentucky Derby, the Kentucky Oaks, and the Clark Stakes at one meet (1884), and the first rider to have won back–to–back Derbies (1890 and 1891). Jimmy Winkfield, another black jockey, tied Murphy's back–to–back Derby wins in 1902. Murphy's record of three Derby wins was not matched for 39 years, when Earl Sante tied it in 1930 and not surpassed for 57 years, when Eddie Arcaro, riding atop Citation, broke it in 1948.

At Saratoga, New York, in 1882 Murphy won an awesome 49 victories in 51 starts. He won three runnings of the Hindoo Stakes: 1883, 1885, and 1886 and on May 23, 1887, the Latonia Derby in Kentucky. He also won four of the first five runnings of the American Derby at Washington Park, Chicago: 1884, 1885, 1886, and 1888.

A few weeks before Murphy's 1884 Kentucky Derby victory on Buchanan, the feisty horse had nearly unseated him at the post in Nashville and then fled over the track. Only the

Isaac Murphy

owner's threat of suspension persuaded Murphy to ride Buchanan at the Derby. His agreement to ride caused Derby betting to rise as well and advanced the horse to the third favorite. While Buchanan threw Murphy again at the starting line before the race started, Murphy's skill prevailed and he won by two lengths. He won his second Derby in 1890 on Riley and his third on Kingman in 1891. Meanwhile, at the Coney Island Jockey Club, Sheepshead Bay, New York City, on June 25, 1890, Murphy had won by a head one of his most unforgettable races: a match with Snapper Garrison, whose final surges came to be known as a ''Garrison finish'' in horse racing.

Murphy was the undisputed king of jockeys and rode consistently for the top stables of the day. By 1883, he was earning $10,000 a year, commanding $25 for every winning ride, and getting $15 for every loss. Later his annual earnings increased to $15,000. His yearly earnings totaled nearly $25,000 by the time his career closed.

Murphy's career in horse racing had practically ended by 1891. He had a weight problem and during the off–season winter months his weight would reach 140 pounds. Murphy dieted arduously prior to the spring race meetings, and his body was vulnerable and subject to disease. When he raced at the Monmouth Handicap at Monmouth Park, New Jersey, on August 26, 1890, Murphy, dizzy and weakened from dieting, fell off his mount, Firenze, finishing last. Judges suspended him for being drunk, ignoring Murphy's weakened condition and claim that he had been drugged, and the clerk of sales's statement that Murphy was sober before the race. As Murphy rode in fewer and fewer races because of his weight problem, he began to purchase and train horses at the Lexington Association Track in a futile attempt to switch from jockey to trainer.

Murphy passed away on February 12, 1896, in Lexington. Most sources claim that he died of pneumonia while others say the cause remains a mystery. In ''Day of the Black Jockey,'' Jo Cavallo quotes Lynn Renau's assertion in her book, *Racing Around Kentucky,* that Murphy suffered from bulimia and that he had a lung infection ''caused by vomit he inhaled during the desperate routine jockeys call flipping.'' At his death, Murphy bequeathed a legacy of $30,000 to his only heir, his wife Lucy Osborn Murphy, whom he married in 1882. Murphy was the first jockey to be inducted into the Jockey Hall of Fame (1955) at the National Museum of Racing, Saratoga Springs, New York.

In 1967 Murphy's remains were removed from a neglected grave in Lexington and reburied with a marker at a gravesite in Man o' War Memorial Park, Fayette County, Kentucky, near the thoroughbred horse Man o' War. His marker, inscribed Isaac Burns Murphy, gives 1860 as his year of birth.

Logan and Winston quote a researcher who says that Murphy ''was considered the greatest judge of pace the country had ever seen, the near–perfect jockey who rode with his hands and heels and only drew his whip to satisfy the crowd. His integrity and honor were the pride of the turf.'' Jo Cavallo that the soft–spoken, gentle Murphy had long arms, a short waist, and strong legs. He was intelligent and had an uncanny sense of pace, and was a ''natural horseman.''

The segregation of blacks and whites outside the sphere of sports also invaded horse racing. In 1894, the Jockey Club was formed to regulate the profession, and blacks were systematically denied licenses. By 1910, only a few black jockeys were left. None made much money and few found much work. The last African American to ride in a Kentucky Derby was Jess Conley in 1911. Jo Cavallo observed, ''Horse racing is the only American sport in which the visible involvement of African–Americans has virtually come to an end.'' Murphy's stellar racing career, however, remains unmatched.

REFERENCES

Ashe, Arthur R. Jr. *A Hard Road to Glory.* Vol. 1. Washington, DC: Amistad Press, 1993.

Cavallo, Jo. ''Day of the Black Jockey.'' *American Legacy* 2 (Spring 1996): 22–32.

Churchill Downs News. Black Expo Edition. 1980.

Logan, Rayford W., and Michael R. Winston, eds. *Dictionary of American Negro Biography.* New York: Norton, 1982.

Rhoden, William C. ''Modern Lessons from the Old Black Jockeys.'' *Emerge* 6 (September 1995): 70.

Smith, Jessie Carney, ed. *Black Firsts.* Detroit: Gale Research, 1994.

Young, Andrew Sturgeon Nash. *Negro Firsts in Sports.* Chicago: Johnson Publishing Co., 1963.

Casper L. Jordan and Jessie Carney Smith

Daniel Murray
(1852–1925)
Librarian, bibliophile

Daniel Murray is an excellent example of a librarian of great position who, though not formally educated in his profession, made a singular imprint for himself at the Library of Congress during his lengthy tenure. In the 1923 *Report of the Librarian of Congress,* the then librarian, Herbert Putnam, deemed that Murray's "extraordinary record exceeded in the Library of Congress probably in but one single instance, was remarkable in the almost unbroken continuity and regularity of his attendance." However, regularity of attendance at the library was certainly not Murray's main claim to fame.

Daniel Murray

Daniel Alexander Payne Murray, librarian, bibliographer, and biographical researcher, was born on McElldery Street, near Asquith, in Baltimore, Maryland, March 3, 1852 (some sources say 1851), the youngest son of George, a free black, and Eliza Wilson Murray. His father was of Scotch–Irish stock and a descendant of the Earl of Murray, the half–brother of Mary Queen of Scots. Eliza Murray was unmistakably of Indian mixture. The baby Daniel was christened after Daniel Alexander Payne, his father's friend and the influential African Methodist Episcopal Church bishop who had pastored Baltimore's Bethel A.M.E. Church from 1845 to 1850. When Murray was about five years old, he entered a small primary school in the neighborhood; he later studied at other public schools in Baltimore and then entered the Unitarian Seminary in his hometown.

On April 19, 1861, Murray witnessed the Confederate attack on the Sixth Massachusetts Regiment in Baltimore during the Civil War. Murray spent his summers in Washington, D.C., with his half–brother, Samuel Proctor, a well–known caterer and keeper of the Senate Restaurant, then called the "Hole in the Wall." Around 1863 he also met President and Mrs. Abraham Lincoln. In 1879, Murray married Anna Evans of Oberlin, Ohio, an alumna of Oberlin College whose uncle and cousin had participated in John Brown's raid on Harper's Ferry. Seven children were the products of this union.

Joins Library of Congress

In 1871, when Murray was nineteen years old, Ainsworth R. Spofford, the Librarian of Congress, who knew of his relationship to Samuel Proctor, asked him to join the staff of the Library of Congress. From 1874 to 1897, he was personal assistant to Spofford. Under Spofford's guidance Murray augmented his knowledge, became skillful in several foreign languages, and acquired indispensable research proficiencies. For a short time Murray was appointed chief of the Periodical Division; his reason for leaving the position is unclear. He had a remarkable memory and knew the library's collection well. He was also an assistant librarian beginning in 1881, holding this post until his retirement from the Library of Congress in 1923.

During the 1890s Murray, Murray demonstrated his skill as a builder. He was involved in building a number of fine residences in Washington and in the Anacostia section of the District of Columbia. In 1894 he guided the remodeling of St. Luke's Church in the district. He also had a deep interest in industrial education and began to agitate for the introduction of industrial training in the black public schools. The *Colored American Magazine* called the Armstrong Manual Training Building on P Street "a monument to the energy of . . . Murray on behalf of industrial education in the District of Columbia."

In 1899, as the nation prepared for the American Exposition to be displayed at the 1900 Paris Exhibition, Murray was asked to provide a special demonstration on "Negro Literature." He startled the literary world by compiling a bibliography of over 2,000 books and pamphlets written and published by blacks. For his work Murray was heralded worldwide, since, until then, no one knew the breadth of black works. For this accomplishment he received honorable mention at the exposition. He was curator of a collection of Negro books and pamphlets that was the by–product of the exhibit; it later was called the Murray Collection. Murray edited his *Preliminary List of Books and Pamphlets of Negro Authors for the Exhibition*—an outstanding landmark of the African American experience. In his position at the Library of Congress, Murray's probe for materials by black authors and the drive to document their lives promoted an everlasting interest in black literature.

Authority on Black Bibliography

The Paris Exposition presentation on "Negro Literature" validated Murray's work as a specialist in black bibliography. Murray contemplated securing as many titles as possible for prospective preservation in the Library of Congress. As a result of his search, in January 1900 he produced a preliminary list. Seven years later he produced a similar bibliography of titles for the Jamestown, Virginia, Tercentenary. Murray also collected a personal library that he willed to the Library of Congress. This collection for some time served as the Library of Congress's "Colored Author Collection"—which became the basis for a black collection at the library.

As Murray amassed more titles, he felt constrained to write his *Bibliographia–Africana* that would include all known literature by black writers and give their biographies as well. Like other early black bibliophiles, through his work he aimed to eliminate concepts of racial inferiority and to demonstrate that blacks were intellectually accomplished.

Murray wrote an article for *Voice of the Negro,* publishing some of his work there. Known for his scholarship, expertise in serving library patrons, and his incredible memory, he was often sought out for information on black history and literature, to lecture before historical and literary societies, and to give evidence before the U.S. Congress.

The fertile lode of material that Murray located—a first among blacks searching for their pasts—motivated him to propose his *Historical and Bibliographical Encyclopedia of the Colored Race Throughout the World.* According to the prospectus for the encyclopedia, this work was conceived to chronicle in six volumes the race's "progress and achievements from the earliest period down to the present time." It promised "25,000 biographical sketches . . . a bibliography of over 6000 titles of books and pamphlets . . . a synoptical list of all books of fiction by Caucasian authors that deal with the race question and a list of nearly 5000 musical compositions by colored composers in every part of the world."

For this impressive task Murray requested some of the most celebrated and educated blacks to collaborate as assistant editors. Among those who agreed to aid Murray were John E. Bruce, Arthur A. Schomburg, John W. Cromwell, L. M. Hershaw, Bishop J. Albert Johnson, William S. Scarborough, and Richard Robert Wright Jr., and intellectuals from Africa and the Caribbean area. Twenty years of research was put into the undertaking, but it was never completed and published. The bulk of this material was bequeathed to the State Historical Society, Madison, Wisconsin.

Murray was renowned in Washington's social and civic affairs. For President William McKinley's second inauguration on March 4, 1901, Murray chaired the special activity customarily held for black people; he was also made president of the "Ball." He was a member of the National Commission to escort Admiral George Dewey to Washington to receive the accolades of Congress and a silver ceremonial sword after his Far Eastern victories. He wrote a new plan for assessing and collecting taxes, which was later enacted into law in the District of Columbia. Murray was a member of Philadelphia's American Negro Historical Society and of the Bethel Literary and Historical Society. He was the first black member of the Washington Board of Trade and was either a member or officer of the Washington Civic Center and the Oldest Inhabitants Association. He was also corresponding member of the Negro Library Association of New York City, of which Arthur A. Schomburg, John E. Bruce, and James Weldon Johnson were also members. He contributed articles to the *Voice of the Negro* and collaborated in writing *Banneker, the Afro–American Astronomer* (1921).

On December 31, 1922, Murray retired from the Library of Congress after fifty–two years. A man of medium build who stood about five feet eight–inches tall, he died of natural causes at his residence in Washington three years later, in 1925. His burial place is in Woodland Cemetery, and his widow Anna and seven children survived him.

Daniel A. P. Murray's dream of a Negro encyclopedia was parallel to that of W. E. B. Du Bois and Carter G. Woodson, who also made unsuccessful attempts to accomplish a multivolume reference work on the legacy of black people. Although his impressive research was never published, his position as a bibliographer of black literature makes him a pioneer in the black history movement.

REFERENCES

Jackson, Wallace Van. "Some Pioneer Negro Library Workers." *Library Journal* 64 (15 March 1939): 215–217.

Josey, E. J., and Ann Allen Shockley, eds. *Handbook of Black Librarianship.* Littleton, CO: Libraries Unlimited, 1977.

Leer, Daniel. Daniel Murray." *Colored American Magazine* 5 (October 1902): 432–40.

Logan, Rayford W., and Michael R. Winston, eds. *Dictionary of American Negro Biography.* New York: Norton, 1982.

Murray's Historical and Biographical Encyclopedia. Prospectus. Washington, DC: World's Cyclopedia Company, 1912.

Sinnette, Elinor Des Verney, W. Paul Coates, and Thomas C. Battle, eds. *Black Bibliophiles and Collectors.* Washington, DC: Howard University Press, 1990.

U.S. Library of Congress. *Report of the Librarian of Congress, 1923.* Washington, DC: Government Printing Office, 1923.

Who's Who of the Colored Race: A General Biographical Dictionary of Men and Women of African Descent. Chicago: Mather, 1915.

COLLECTIONS

The papers of Daniel A. Murray are at the Library of Congress, Washington, D.C.

Casper L. Jordan

Peter Marshall Murray
(1888–1969)
Physician

Peter Marshall Murray was a leading African American physician who worked to advance the status of black doctors throughout the United States. He was an early black member of the staff of Harlem Hospital. In addition to showing the professional skill that enabled him to rise to head the gynecological department of that hospital, he demonstrated leadership in the National Medical Association and in the local and national branches of the American Medical Association (AMA). As the first black doctor elected to the house of delegates of the AMA, Murray worked diligently and effectively to break down segregation in the local branches.

Murray was born on June 9, 1888, in Houma, Louisiana, to John L. and Louvinia Smith Murray; he was one of four children. John and Louvinia Murray early on moved to New Orleans, where John Murray worked as a stevedore and Louvinia Murray, as a laundress. Peter Murray stayed behind on his grandparents' farm until 1900. He then followed his parents to New Orleans, where he subsequently enrolled in the elementary department of New Orleans University, a Methodist Episcopal school that later merged with Straight University to become Dillard University. The young Murray graduated from the college department with a B.A. degree in 1910. (In 1955 he donated the carillon and clock for Dillard's new chapel as a memorial to his mother.)

Murray did not decide on a career until his senior year. His mother had found work at the New Orleans Women's Hospital and Infirmary. Impressed by the medical profession, she urged her son to become a doctor. Murray was initially rejected by Howard Medical School because he lacked a foreign language, but a summer's tutoring in German allowed him to enter the school in the fall of 1910.

Murray had to work to support himself and to send money home to his family. He worked as a night watchman and was able to do some studying on his job with the connivance of a helpful supervisor. Even so he had to rely on another student's notes for a course in anatomy taught when he had to be at work. He was able to pass the examination and receive credit for the course without attending classes. Murray graduated from Howard Medical School in 1914 with honors in surgery and obstetrics.

Murray became an assistant instructor in surgery upon graduation and in 1915 established a private practice in Washington, D.C. In 1917 and 1918 he served as medical inspector for the District of Columbia public schools, and in 1918 he became assistant surgeon–in–chief at Freedman's Hospital.

Besides establishing a professional career, Murray also established a family. In 1917 he married Charlotte Wallace (d. 1982), daughter of a medical graduate who had chosen the ministry instead of practicing medicine. A woman of beauty and charm, his wife possessed a very good contralto voice; she taught music in the public schools and was a soloist at leading black churches. There was one son, John Walker, who survived his father.

Peter Marshall Murray

With the friendship and support of leading members of the local medical establishment, Murray was favorably situated in Washington. Still, however flourishing and vibrant the local African American community, Washington was a southern city, characterized by rigid segregation. In 1920 the Murrays moved to Harlem in search of greater opportunities. Among the motives for the move was Charlotte Wallace Murray's desire for a more active music career; her aim seems to have been at least partially met since she did not stop singing in public until 1953.

In New York, Murray initially set up practice with Dr. Wiley Merlio Wilson, a slightly older friend. The Wiley Wilson Sanitarium opened at 135th Street and Seventh Avenue soon after Murray's arrival. This sanitarium came into existence because of the ever–present difficulty of black doctors in obtaining staff appointments in majority run hospitals. Murray maintained his connection with the clinic for 15 years and became very successful, attracting about 75 percent of referrals among black physicians.

Joins Staff of Harlem Hospital

Louis Tompkins Wright (1891–1952), a 1915 graduate of Harvard Medical School, was in 1919 the first of a small group of black doctors admitted to Harlem Hospital as adjunct visiting surgeons and physicians. Black presence at Harlem

Hospital did not grow rapidly although the public institution was in an area of the city that was rapidly gaining in black population. In July 1925 five black physicians were finally appointed to the staff, with the first black interns following in 1926. In 1928 Murray became a member of the staff at the rank of provisional assistant adjunct visiting member in gynecology. Murray rose to become director of gynecological service, from which he retired in 1953 after 25 years of service.

It is said that the problems of addressing black staffing at Harlem Hospital were acerbated by factional struggles between the graduates of white medical schools, led by Wright, and those of black medical schools, led by Murray. A 1930 reorganization of the hospital led to dismissal of many white staff physicians and the appointment of black doctors, but the problems were by no means resolved. Adam Clayton Powell Jr. made his first mark in politics in April of 1933 when he organized a public demonstration that upstaged an NAACP investigation of charges of racial discrimination at the hospital. Nonetheless Murray managed to make his way undeterred by the struggles.

After his retirement from Harlem Hospital in 1953, Murray served as director of obstetrics and gynecology at Sydenham Hospital. In 1954 Murray was named to the board of trustees of the State University of New York, and in 1958 he was appointed to the New York City Board of Hospitals, the oversight body for the city's 29 public hospitals. Murray was also a leader among Howard University alumni and served on the university's board of trustees from 1926 to 1962, serving in 1952 as chair of a committee that initiated far–reaching changes in the medical school. President John F. Kennedy appointed him to a newly formed Health Resources Advisory Committee in 1962.

Murray's public roles were supported by professional achievements. He was certified by the American Board of Obstetrics and Gynecology in 1931, a first for an African American. Over the years he published many articles in medical journals. He became a fellow of the American College of Surgeons and of the International College of Surgeons.

It was Murray's activities in professional organizations that attracted the most attention. In 1932 he was president of the segregated National Medical Association and served as chair of its publication committee from 1943 to 1957. Murray tried unsuccessfully to move the NMA to line up behind the American Medical Association's opposition to a national health insurance plan in 1949; in 1961 he was successful in persuading the organization not to support the King–Anderson bill, which aimed at providing medical care for the elderly. He had earlier joined the Medical Society of the County of New York, the largest component of the American Medical Association. He began serving on various committees as early as 1936. Twelve years of service in the local organization's governing body led to his 1950 election as the first black member of the national organization's house of delegates. During his 12 years' service there he pushed vigorously for the end of segregation in all AMA local branches. From 1954 to 1955 he served as president of the New York County organization.

Murray's activities brought him much recognition. The National Medical Association gave him its Distinguished Service Award for 1954. The New York Academy of Medicine presented him a plaque for distinguished service in 1969. He also received honorary degrees from New Orleans University (1935) and Lincoln University (1944).

Murray died on December 19, 1969, in New York City. His funeral was held at Saint Mark's Methodist Church, of which he had been a member. His wife, his son, and a grandson survived him. At his death he was revered as an elder statesman in medicine for his many varied contributions to the profession. In particular, he was remembered for his part in breaking down segregation in the American Medical Association.

REFERENCES

Bailey, A. Peter. *The Harlem Hospital Story.* Richmond, VA: Native Son Publishers, 1991.

Cobb, W. Montague. ''Peter Marshall Murray, M.D., 1888–1969.'' *Journal of the National Medical Association* 59 (January 1967): 71–74, 80.

''Dr. Peter Marshall Murray Receives Distinguished Service Award for 1954.'' *Journal of the National Medical Association* 46 (November 1954): 420–21.

Hamilton, Charles V. *Adam Clayton Powell, Jr.* New York: Atheneum, 1991.

The Kaiser Index to Black Resources, 1948–1986. Brooklyn, NY: Carlson, 1992.

Logan, Rayford W. *Howard University: The First Hundred Years.* New York: New York University Press, 1969.

———, and Michael R. Winston, eds. *Dictionary of American Negro Biography.* New York: Norton, 1982.

Morais, Herbert M. *The History of the Negro in Medicine.* New York: New York Publishers Company, 1968.

''Murray on Health Resources Advisory Committee.'' *Journal of the National Medical Association* 55 (January 1963): 72–73.

''Murray on New York Board of Hospitals.'' *Journal of the National Medical Association* 50 (May 1958): 213.

''Murray President of Medical Society of the County of New York.'' *Journal of the National Medical Association* 46 (July 1954): 274–75.

Who's Who in America. 31st ed. Chicago: Marquis Who's Who, 1960.

Who's Who in Colored America. 5th ed. Brooklyn, NY: Who's Who in Colored America, 1940.

COLLECTIONS

The Peter Marshall Murray papers are in the Moorland–Spingarn Research Center, Howard University.

Robert L. Johns

Clarence Muse

(1889–1979)

Actor, entertainer, composer, writer, director

Clarence Muse was an able actor, who worked in an era that did not favor opportunities for blacks in serious drama. He worked to establish legitimate theater for blacks from the early years of the twentieth century on. He acted in more than 200 Hollywood motion pictures, often playing stereotypical characters. He possessed an innate dignity that mitigated his portrayals, and he had occasion to demonstrate his versatility even within the confines of the studio system of his era. He also was a composer and writer. It is perhaps the diversity of his talents that is responsible for his being less famous than he deserves.

Clarence Edouard Muse was born in Baltimore on October 7, 1889, to Alexander and Mary Kellems Muse. Little is known about his early life before he graduated in 1911 from Dickinson University in Carlisle, Pennsylvania, with a bachelor of laws (LL.B.) degree. When he evaluated the opportunities open to black lawyers at the time he opted for an only slightly less difficult career in show business. He had a fine bass voice and found work in minstrel shows, tab shows—live entertainment offered between movies—and vaudeville. He started as a singing entertainer in New York on Hudson River boats and then in cafes in Palm Beach, Fla. Using money he won in a card game, he bought into a debt–ridden touring company with which he spent several years traveling the South. Muse was married and had a son by the time he moved to New York.

With a burning desire to become a serious actor, Muse seized the chance to replace Charles Gilpin in the Lafayette Players in early 1916 for a salary of $90 a week. As reported in her article in *The Theater of Black Americans,* Muse told M. Francesca Thompson that "he felt out of place as an 'Ethiopian' among all of the other 'high–yellow Negroes' in the company." The company also used older plays from the Broadway repertory since no stock of black plays existed at the time. Muse recalled an attempt to change his appearance with a blonde wig and white make–up. He had off–stage lines to say before his first entrance. The audience knew his voice and normal appearance and erupted when he stepped on stage. It took several minutes before the clapping and foot stomping died down.

Muse worked for several years with the Lafayette Players. One of his most celebrated roles was Dr. Jekyll and Mr. Hyde. He also had parts in the plays *Thais* and *The Master Mind,* to cite only two. In the 1920s he was often on the road with a touring company. He could have been working with one of the two touring companies established by the Lafayette Players before the end of 1917 or leading his own company. In 1922 he produced a nonmusical play by Flournoy Miller and Aubrey Lyles, *The Flat Below.* Tom Fletcher reported some movie making which seems to date from this period. Fletcher also claimed that Muse was an assistant director of a "colored" movie company The Harrison Dixon Film Company, designed to film stories written for the *Saturday Evening Post* by Harrison Dixon, a white man. Fletcher made a film with Muse and others in Vicksburg, Mississippi, where the white production crew got into trouble for addressing the black cast using the taboo word "mister." Muse also lived in Chicago, where he produced shows for the Royal Gardens. In 1927 Muse produced *Miss Bandanna,* which gave Moms Mabley her first starring role.

Goes to Hollywood

Muse was still trying to make his career in the live theater when he received a lucrative 12–week contract at $1,250 a week to appear in the first all–black talking film, *Hearts in Dixie* (1929)—it was also the film industry's second all–talking film. He played the role of Stepin Fetchit's father–in–law, Uncle Nappus. Now in his late forties, Muse decided to settle in Los Angeles, where he had a long career playing bit and featured roles in motion pictures. He also continued his activities in other areas, including the theater.

The Lafayette Players moved to Los Angeles in 1928 and survived there until 1932. Muse again worked with them, playing Dr. Jekyll and Mr. Hyde again and producing—along with Evelyn Preer—Dubose Heywood's *Porgy.* Muse also played the title role in the play. He produced in 1934 a memorial radio program for Preer on KRKD in Los Angeles. Later in the 1930s he worked with the Negro unit of the Federal Theater Project and directed one of its most successful productions in the west, Hal Johnson's folk opera *Run, Little Chillun,* which ran for two years. Muse continued to put together musical shows for clubs and theaters through the years.

Muse was a composer and lyricist himself and a member of the American Society of Composers, Authors and Publishers. His most famous song was "When It's Sleepy Time Down South." In 1932 Muse published *Way Down South,* an account of the life of entertainers in the south, written with David Arlen. About this time, he also wrote the pamphlet "The Dilemma of the Negro Actor," describing a perennial problem for the black actor. He could choose to be responsible to black audiences or to enjoy success in stereotypical roles. Under prevailing conditions, the former course meant that he or she ran the risk of not working at all.

In the more than 200 movies he made for the Hollywood studios, Muse played many different kinds of parts, from the rebellious slave in *So Red the Rose* (1935) to the more stereotypical domestic roles, some even as small as one or two lines. According to film historian Peter Noble there was a type called "a Clarence Muse part" in Hollywood. This was "a sort of uncle to the hero of the film, a kindly benevolent and altogether friendly person who helps to make the course run smooth." Donald Bogle wrote, "The fact that [Muse] played tom characters cannot be denied. The fact that he played them with great intelligence and thoughtfulness has often been overlooked."

Muse had a prominent role in the production of *Way Down South* (1939). He collaborated on the script with Langston Hughes, who found the discrimination in Hollywood particularly trying. Muse not only acted in a leading role, he co–directed the film with the official director, Bernard Vorhaus, and also contributed to the music. For many this film only continues the black stereotypes purveyed by Hollywood during this era. Muse wrote a more dignified role for himself in *Broken Strings* (1940), produced outside the Hollywood system. In it he played a concert violinist in conflict with himself and his son. This is probably his best role on film. Another independent film with which Muse was associated was *The Spirit of Youth,* starring Joe Lewis (1938), for which Muse wrote the song lyrics. In 1947 Muse worked on and in *The Peanut Man* in which he played George Washington Carver. This was a 45–minute film made for $50,000.

In the 1955–56 television season, Muse played Sam on "Casablanca," one of the three segments of *Warner Bros. Presents.* Although Muse slowed down in the mid 1950s, he was 83 when he appeared in *The World's Greatest Athlete* (1973) and 86, in *Car Wash* (1976). His very last appearance was in *The Black Stallion* (1979) the year of his death.

Muse lived long enough to see himself inducted into the Black Filmmakers Hall of Fame in Oakland, California, in 1973. In 1972 he received an honorary doctorate from Bishop College; his alma mater Dickinson College gave him an honorary doctorate of laws in 1978. He spent much of his later life on a ranch four miles from Perris, California, with his Jamaican–born wife Ena. Muse suffered a stroke and died a month later on October 13, 1979, in a hospital in Perris. He would have been 90 the following day.

Muse led a long life during which he sustained a career as an entertainer. He made a mark in the theater and in films and appeared on television in a series and on specials. A man of many talents, he also sang, wrote music, produced shows, and wrote in various forms. Physically a small man, his voice and presence allowed him to make an impression both on stage and in the mostly small roles to which he was confined by his times.

REFERENCES

"Birth of a Musical." *Ebony* 1 (April 1946): 47–50.

Bogle, Donald. *Blacks in American Films and Television.* New York: Garland, 1988.

———. *Toms, Coons, Mulattos, Mammies, and Bucks.* New York: Viking, 1973.

Fletcher, Tom. *100 Years of the Negro in Show Business.* 1954. Reprint, New York: Da Capo, 1984.

Hill, Errol, ed. *The Theater of Black Americans.* Englewood Cliffs, NJ: Prentice–Hall, 1980.

Kellner, Bruce. *The Harlem Renaissance.* New York: Methuen, 1984.

Klotman, Phyllis Rauch. *Frame by Frame.* Bloomington: Indiana University Press, 1979.

Mapp, Edward. *Directory of Blacks in the Performing Arts.* 2nd ed. Metuchen, NJ: Scarecrow Press, 1990.

Mason, B. J. "The Grand Old Man of Good Hope Valley." *Ebony* 27 (September 1972): 50–57.

Noble, Peter. *The Negro in Films.* 1948. Reprint, Port Washington, NY: Kennikat Press, 1969.

Null, Peter. *Black Hollywood.* New York: Carol Publishing Group, 1975.

"The Peanut Man." *Ebony* 2 (July 1947): 48–50.

Rampersand, Arnold. *The Life of Langston Hughes.* Vol. 1. New York: Oxford, 1986.

Sampson, Henry T. *Blacks in Black and White.* Metuchen, NJ: Scarecrow Press, 1977.

Southern, Eileen. *Biographical Dictionary of Afro–American and African Musicians.* Westport, CT: Greenwood Press, 1982.

Who's Who in America. 39th ed. Chicago: Marquis Who's Who, 1977–79.

Robert L. Johns

Isaac Myers
(1835–1891)
Labor leader, businessman

Isaac Myers was involved in the first attempts to organize unions among African Americans. He achieved a measure of success in Baltimore but was defeated in his endeavor to build a national organization. Nonetheless, he remained a political leader in Baltimore, a role which led to his employment with the federal government. He was also very active in civic affairs and in his church.

Myers was born free in Baltimore on January 13, 1835. He received an education in a private school run by John Fortie (1783–1859), a black Methodist Episcopal minister. In 1851 at the age of 16 he was apprenticed to James Jackson, a black caulker. Myers became a skilled workman before he began to work in 1860 for Woods, Bridges, and Company, which became the largest grocery company below the Mason–Dixon line during the Civil war. Myers set himself up as an independent grocer in 1864 but resigned the following year after a dispute with his business associates and returned to the shipyards.

Black caulkers in Baltimore had been organized since at least 1838 and they had successfully bargained with shipyard owners on wages and working conditions. The increase in immigration from Europe, however, brought an influx of white workers, who competed with African Americans for the jobs. The resulting tension between the two groups led to a series of riots directed against African Americans in 1858. Black caulkers continued to find work until October of 1865, when white shipyard workers went on strike to protest the presence of black workers. As a result, many black longshoremen and caulkers lost their jobs.

Traditional accounts say that Myers then conceived the idea of organizing an association to buy a shipyard. Myers was indeed one of the 15 founders of the company, but the prime mover seems to be black businessman John Henry Smith, who also served as cashier to the business. The company was capitalized for $40,000, with 8,000 shares at five dollars. Since most shipyard owners would have refused to sell to blacks, Smith approached white businessman William Applegarth, who leased property and then, on February 7, 1866, subleased it to the John H. Smith Company, which became the Chesapeake Marine Railway and Dry Dock Company, legally incorporated in 1868.

Some of the original stockholders seemed to have believed that the property had been purchased rather than leased for 18 years. The Chesapeake Marine Railway and Dry Dock Company soon employed 300 black caulkers and carpenters. It survived, due in part to government contracts, and the six–year mortgage was paid off on–schedule. In 1884, with the loss of its lease, the company went out of business. The success of the dry dock led to the collapse of the ban against black longshoremen, but owners tried to cut wages. Myers supported a strike and protest which restored the former rate of $2.50 a day.

Myers, who seems to have been an associate of Smith over the years and who was a fluent orator, thus appears to have been a vigorous proponent rather than the sole originator of the idea of operating a dry dock. It is perhaps due to Myers's visibility in the community and his later prominence in politics that his name was singled out for remembrance. Despite his shared role in the creation of one of the largest black–operated businesses of the era, the importance of his role in later union activities is undeniable.

After the shipyard was in operation, Myers became involved in a nationwide attempt to organize workers. He was one of nine African American delegates to attend the National Labor Union convention in 1869. There Myers called for unity between black and white workers. In December a Washington convention organized the Colored National Labor Union, a parallel organization, and Myers became its head. He made an organizing tour early in 1870. Black–white unity broke down at the August convention of the white organization when Myers refused to leave the Republican Party to form a new party or to join the Democrats. His speech defending continued black support of the Republican Party caused a sensation among the delegates. In the meantime, the national black organization had not been successful at the local level. At its second convention on January 8, 1871, Myers's term as president ended. The third convention in the fall of 1871 marked the end of this attempt to organize black workers.

Myers left the shipyard for government service as a messenger in the Customs Service in Baltimore. On March 7, 1870, he was named supervisor of mail service for the Southern states with his headquarters in Washington, D.C. His job also included laboring for the Republican Party, and in 1872 he campaigned vigorously in North Carolina, a state ravaged by violence directed against black political power. Even his job in the postal service had its dangers since it involved the detection of crime; he solved several notorious cases. In July of 1878, during an escape attempt by a prisoner he was escorting, Myers sustained a wound to the leg.

Myers left government service in 1879 to open a coal yard in Baltimore. In 1882 he was editor of the *Colored Citizen,* a weekly paper. This seems to have been a short–lived effort since he also went back to work for the government in that year, serving as a gauger until early 1887.

In 1888 Myers was secretary for the Republican campaign in Maryland. The same year he organized the first Maryland Colored State Industrial Fair; later he was supervisor of black exhibits for the State Agricultural and Mechanical Exhibition. He was also active in many other organizations. He was founder and president of the Colored Business Men's Association of Baltimore and organized the first building and loan association of the city. A past Grand Master of the Masons by 1889, he was also active in the Oddfellows and Good Samaritans. He wrote a three–act play *The Missionary.*

Myers was also a very active leader in his African Episcopal Methodist church, holding several positions at Bethel Church in Baltimore. For 15 years he was superintendent of Bethel's Sunday School. One of his last projects was an Aged Ministers Home. In 1889 he was elected president of an association which pledged to raise $50,000 to build the facility.

Isaac Myers married twice, first to Emma V. Myers (d. 1868). The oldest of their three children, George A., was born on March 5, 1859. Isaac Myers then married Sarah E. Deaver, daughter of a Baltimore butcher, possibly around 1875 since George was then a student in the preparatory department of Lincoln University in Pennsylvania. George Myers became a very influential black politician from his barbershop in the leading hotel in Cleveland, Ohio. Isaac Myers died at his home at 1218 Jefferson Street in Baltimore on January 26, 1891, from paralysis. He was buried on January 29 in a very well–attended funeral, said to be the largest for an African American in Baltimore.

Myers's attempts to organize unions for blacks collapsed because the racism of white workers made cooperation between blacks and whites impossible. Both sides lost, and blacks would long distrust organized labor. Beyond his efforts with unions, Myers was an important leader in his community.

REFERENCES

Bragg, George F., Jr. *Men of Maryland.* Baltimore: Church Advocate Press, 1925.

''A Colored Byrnes.'' *Indianapolis Freeman,* October, 12, 1889.

Graham, Leroy. *Baltimore: The Nineteenth Century Black Capital.* Lanham, MD: University Press of America, 1982.

James, Felix. ''The Civic and Political Activities of George A. Myers.'' *Journal of Negro History* 58 (April 1973): 166–78.

Logan, Rayford W., and Michael R. Winston. *Dictionary of American Negro Biography.* New York: Norton, 1982.

Matison, Sumner Eliot. ''The Labor Movement and the Negro during Reconstruction.'' *Journal of Negro History* 33 (October 1948): 426–68.

Thomas, Bettye C. ''A Nineteenth Century Black Operated Shipyard, 1866–1884: Reflections Upon Its Inception and Ownership.'' *Journal of Negro History* 59 (January 1974): 1–12.

Robert L. Johns

N

James C. Napier
(1845–1940)
Attorney, entrepreneur, politician, register of the U.S. Treasurer

James C. Napier

James C. Napier of Tennessee rose to national prominence as a political activist, an attorney, and an entrepreneur. A leader in the African American community, Napier was elected three times to the Nashville City Council. He served on the state executive committee of the Republican party and as a delegate to Republican national conventions. In 1911 he was appointed register of the U.S. Treasury by President William Howard Taft.

James Carroll Napier was born to William Carroll and Jane Elizabeth Watkins Napier near Nashville, Tennessee on June 9, 1845, one day after the death of former President Andrew Jackson. The Napiers had two other sons, Elias W. Napier and Henry Alonzo Napier, and one daughter, Ida M. Napier. William and Jane Napier's children were the grandchildren of Elias Napier, a wealthy white physician and iron producer from Dickson County, Tennessee.

The Napier family moved the family to the free state of Ohio when James Napier was approximately three years old. They remained in Ohio until 1855, when Napier's father brought his family back to Nashville where he established a commercial livery stable. Four years later because of William and Jane Napier's urgent desire for their children to have access to an education, William Napier, in partnership with other free persons of color, organized a school to educate the community's children. When white vigilantes forced the school to close, Napier sent his spouse and children back to Ohio where James C. Napier completed his basic education, and went on to Wilberforce University and Oberlin College.

Two years after the Civil War ended, Napier returned to Nashville where he served as a page in the upper chamber of the Tennessee General Assembly. From 1868 until 1870 he was one of three Davidson County claims commissioners appointed by Governor William G. Brownlow. As claims commissioner, Napier audited the petitions of those who lost their property through military intervention of the Confederate and Union armies.

On May 27, 1865, African Americans established the State Colored Men's Convention and upon his return to Nashville, Napier became an active member of the organization. In 1870 Democrats and white conservatives won control of the Tennessee General Assembly. The conservatives employed tactics of intimidation and violence against the newly emancipated black populace. In an attempt to combat the lawlessness, the convention sent a delegation to Washington, headed by Napier, to implore the Congress and President Ulysses S. Grant to abolish the conservative government and annul the 1870 state constitution. Napier appeared before the Reconstruction Committee of the Congress and gave testimony about the atrocious deeds of the Ku Klux Klan. Failing in the quest, the following year the group asked Congress to establish a national school system and to pass legislation to enforce the South's compliance with the Fifteenth Amendment.

Acting upon the advice of a family friend, John Mercer Langston—who in 1855 became the first African American to hold elective office, and who was dean of the Law School at Howard University—the Napier's emboldened their son to attend law school in the nation's capitol. In 1870 Napier entered Howard University's Law School. While at Howard, Napier supported himself working as a government clerk. In 1872 Napier received his degree with the nation's first class of African American law graduates. After being admitted to the bar of the Supreme Court of the District of Columbia, in the same year Napier returned to Nashville and was admitted to the Tennessee bar.

Joins Internal Revenue Service

In May of 1875 James Carroll Napier embarked upon a ten–year career with the Internal Revenue Service. He also successfully ran for a seat on the Nashville City Council in 1878, the same year that he married Nettie Langston, the daughter of John Mercer and Caroline M. Wall Langston, in Washington, D.C. According to some, the nuptial ceremony of James and Nettie Napier was one of the largest social affairs in 19th–century black Washington. Because of his marriage, Napier had close connections to the upper echelons of the nation's African American community. Later, James and Nettie Napier adopted an infant daughter and named her Carrie Langston Napier.

The Napiers returned to Nashville, and James C. Napier became one of the more powerful African American politicians and the most influential African American citizen in the community. During his tenure on the Nashville City Council from 1878 to 1889, over which he was the first African American to preside, Napier was instrumental in the hiring of the first black teachers for the public schools, the construction of the first modern black school buildings (Meigs and Pearl in 1883), and the implementation of public high school training for Nashville's black citizens. Napier used racial segregation to his advantage by insisting that black teachers and administrators be employed to staff the black schools. Also, he was instrumental in the appointment of the first black firefighters to the city's fire department.

Napier also attended to his law practice and real estate business. Napier's properties increased over a 20–year period to 17 holdings including Napier Court, an office building that was rented to black professionals.

Napier was very active in the political arena; he became one of the most devoted members of Tennessee's Republican Party. In 1882 he was elected to serve on the executive committee of the state Republican Party. He served as secretary of the committee for six years. The same year that he was elected to the executive committee of the state Republican Party, Napier unsuccessfully ran for a seat in the state legislature and for circuit court clerk of Davidson County.

Champion of African American Conciliation

In 1891 Napier met Booker T. Washington and they became close friends and associates. Proponents of the accommodationist point of view, the two believed racial progress could be accomplished through enterprise, moral virtues, and property acquisition. While Napier and Washington agreed on most issues confronting African Americans, their views differed on the issues of African American political activity and educational needs. Booker T. Washington seldom made public statements in support of African American political rights. In contrast to Washington, Napier fervently endorsed the rights of African Americans to retain the political power that they had attained. While Washington saw the value of higher education, he had no doubt that economic progress among African Americans could best be accomplished through education in the industrial arts. Napier, however, contended that both forms of education were necessary.

Margaret Murray Washington and Nettie Langston Napier were also close friends. Margaret Washington often spent two or more weeks each summer at *Ogedankee,* the Napiers' summer home on Nolensville Road outside Nashville.

In 1896, the same year that the Supreme Court legalized the "separate but equal" doctrine in its decision of *Plessy v. Ferguson,* Tennessee began preparations to celebrate its centenary. The all–white executive committee of the Tennessee Centennial Exposition formed a Negro department, and Napier was selected to chair the executive committee. On August 31, 1896, however, he resigned his position in a protest over the Negro building and the exhibits.

Two years after he resigned from the Tennessee Centennial Exposition, Napier ran for congress but lost his bid to represent the people of his district in the U.S. Congress. Napier organized in 1902 the first Tennessee branch of the National Negro Business League. The following year the league held its annual meeting in Nashville.

In that year the Tennessee State Railroad Commission extended the 1881 Jim Crow transportation statute to cover all forms of railroad travel. Napier protested to no avail. In 1905 Tennessee enacted a segregated streetcar law, and Napier and other business, political, and religious leaders founded the Union Transportation Company in an unavailing attempt to provide alternative transportation.

On November 5, 1903, J. C. Napier along with ministers Robert H. Boyd, Preston Taylor and William Haynes, J. B. Bosley, E. B. Jefferson, J. S. Ewing, J. W. Grant, and J. A. Cullom met to organize a bank. Each of the men in attendance pledged $100, and Napier further expressed his willingness to raise his pledge to $1,000 if the occasion should present itself to capitalize the banking venture. Two months later, on January 14, 1904, the One–Cent Savings Bank and Trust Company opened on 411 Cherry (now Fourth Avenue, North), in space provided by Napier. Napier served without compensation as cashier of the One–Cent Savings Bank's—now known as Citizens Savings Bank and Trust Company and now the nation's oldest continually operating African American bank.

While Napier was involved in business and political affairs, his wife Nettie Langston Napier concerned herself with issues facing women and children of the African American community. In 1907, she formed and became president of the Porter Homestead Day Home Club, an organization directed toward meeting the needs of Nashville's working poor. An active member of the National Association of Colored Women (NACW), she held various positions in the national organization, including president of the Douglass Memorial Fund. As director of the Committee of Colored Women, Nettie Napier worked for the Red Cross during World War I.

In 1908 James Napier began lecturing at Nashville's Meharry Medical College in medical jurisprudence. He continued until 1939 when he was appointed to the board of trustees of the philanthropic Anna T. Jeanes Foundation. Established in 1907, the fund sought the appointment of African American teachers to do industrial work in rural schools and to do extension work.

Named Register of the Treasurer

As a consequence of public patronage and his prominence in national Republican politics, Napier was offered a consulship to Bahia, Brazil, in 1908, and the position as minister to Liberia in 1910 by President William Howard Taft. Napier declined both positions. The following year, Napier accepted the position of register of the treasury of the United States.

While register of the treasury, Napier continued his campaign to procure federal funds due African Americans under the Morrill Acts of 1862 and 1890. In February of 1908, he and James Hardy Dillard of the Jeanes Funds met with president Brown Ayres of the University of Tennessee, Knoxville, to ascertain how the institution used its Morrill funds. Later, before a Washington, D.C. meeting of state superintendents, he underscored the lack of funding for black schools under the Morrill Acts and petitioned the group for its support in the equal dispensation of financial resources between black and white schools.

In 1909, the State of Tennessee announced plans to implement a system of state normal colleges. For many years, Napier and other leaders of the African American community had sought funding from the Tennessee General Assembly for public higher education for the state's citizens of African descent. When it was announced that plans were in the making to establish three white institutions of higher learning, Napier and others began lobbying and mobilized support from the African American community. The state legislature established three white normal schools and an Agriculture and Industrial State Normal School for African Americans.

The initial appropriations bill stipulated that $16,700 be given for the African American school and $33,430 be given for each white school. This disproportion in funding lasted for a number of decades. The act did not provide money to purchase land or build new schools. Napier, R. H. Boyd, Henry A. Boyd, Dock Hart, and Preston Taylor mobilized support to have the school located in Nashville. They launched a drive to raise funds for the purchase of a site and buildings. In 1910 a county bond referendum was defeated. Nonetheless, their efforts yielded results in 1911, when the State Board of Education selected Nashville as the site for Tennessee Agricultural and Industrial State Normal School (now Tennessee State University). Two years later, the state legislature passed a bill that granted to the newly established public school a share of federal funds, as set forth in the Morrill Act of 1890.

During the presidential election of 1912, Napier supported the incumbent, President William Howard Taft. Democrat Woodrow Wilson, a native Southerner, won the election. The first Congress of Wilson's presidential administration entertained the greatest deluge of proposed discriminatory laws against African Americans ever initiated by the legislature. While most of the proposed statutes failed to win passage, by the end of the year Wilson segregated African American federal employees by executive order and phased most of them out of the civil service. Under the order, blacks and whites were prohibited from using the same restroom facilities in the Treasury Department. Napier protested in vain, and after working under the new administration for almost seven months, in July of 1913 he resigned his position as register of the treasury in protest.

Napier returned to Nashville and continued his business, civic, political, and professional affairs. In 1914 he became president of the Nashville Negro Board of Trade (NNBT). Two years later, he was elected president of that group. Napier's presidency came at a time when African Americans were leaving the South because of legally sanctioned racial segregation, disenfranchisement, and a dearth of educational and employment opportunities. Believing that the mass exodus of African Americans from the South was deleterious to commerce, he appealed to league members and southern whites to work in concert to avert black migration.

Between 1918 and 1940, Napier remained active in many endeavors. He continued to practice law, lecture at Meharry, and perform his duties at Citizens Savings Bank and Trust Company.

In addition to serving on the Anna T. Jeanes Foundation, Napier also was a member of the board of trust at Fisk and Howard universities and Meharry Medical College. He helped to raise funds for the Colored Young Men's Christian Association and Fisk University. A member of Howard Congregational Church, Napier also served on its official board.

On June 9, 1932, the African American community paid homage to its prominent citizen when it celebrated Napier's 87th birthday at the African Methodist Episcopal (AME) Sunday School Union. Over 200 people came to celebrate the occasion and pay tribute to the venerable leader. Mary McLeod Bethune was numbered among the guests. In 1934, in honor of the Napiers' 56th wedding anniversary, students at Tennessee A and I State College produced and publicly presented for the couple a pageant entitled, "From African to America." The following year, Fisk University awarded James Carroll Napier an honorary Doctor of Laws degree—the second honorary degree awarded by the university.

Two years before his death, Napier was appointed to the Nashville Housing Authority by Mayor Thomas L. Cummings. In 1940 the Nashville Housing Authority suspended its rule not to name a public housing unit for a living person. The first public housing units completed for African Americans in the city were named in Napier's honor.

Nettie Napier died in 1939. One year and seven months later Napier himself died at his home on Sunday, April 21, 1940, at age 94. Funeral services were held three days later in the Fisk Memorial Chapel. On that day Fisk University, Tennessee Agricultural and Industrial State College (later University), the National Baptist Publishing Board, Citizens Savings Bank and Trust Company, and the Negro city schools suspended activities in remembrance of Napier. Napier was interred in Greenwood Cemetery between his wife, Nettie Langston Napier, and his daughter, Carrie Langston Napier. Other members of the Napier and Langston families are buried nearby.

Born during the era of slavery and an active participant during the Reconstruction period, James C. Napier spent his lifetime challenging the inequities imposed upon African Americans during the epoch of racial segregation. Napier, an early proponent of self–determination for members of his race, sought to maximize economic, educational, political, and social opportunities within the restrictive racial *modus operandi.* In 1970 the Metropolitan Historical Commission of Nashville and Davidson County paid tribute to its nationally renowned citizen of both the nineteenth and twentieth centuries when it placed a historical marker at the J. C. Napier Homes, 648 Claiborne Street, to commemorate his contributions to the city, state, and nation.

REFERENCES

Clark, Herbert. "James Carroll Napier: National Negro Leader." *Tennessee Historical Quarterly* 60 (Winter 1990): 243–252.

Doyle, Don H. *Nashville in the New South, 1880–1930.* Knoxville: University of Tennessee Press, 1985.

Foner, Eric. *Freedom Lawmakers: A Dictionary of Black Officeholders During Reconstruction.* New York: Oxford University Press, 1993.

Haley, James T., comp. *Afro–American Encyclopedia or The Thoughts, Doings, and Sayings of the Race.* Nashville: Haley and Florida, 1896.

Johnson, Terri, and Ophelia Paine, eds. *Andrew Jackson Slept Here: A Guide to Historical Markers in Nashville and Davidson County.* Nashville: Metropolitan Historical Commission of Nashville and Davidson County, 1993.

Lamon, Lester C. *Black Tennesseans, 1900–1930.* Knoxville: University of Tennessee Press, 1977.

———. *Black Tennesseans, 1791–1970.* Knoxville: University of Tennessee Press, 1981.

Logan, Rayford W. *The Negro in American Life and Thought: The Nadir, 1877–1901.* New York: Collier Books, 1954.

Lovett, Bobby L., and Linda T. Wynn, eds. *Profiles of African Americans in Tennessee.* Nashville: Local Conference on Afro–American Culture and History, 1996.

Mitchell, Reavis L. Jr. "Tennessee Centennial: The African American Community." *Leaders of Afro–American Nashville Series.* Nashville: Local Conference on Afro–American Culture and History, 1997.

Morton, Cynthia Neverdon. *Afro–American Women of the South and the Advancement of the Race, 1895–1925.* Knoxville: University of Tennessee Press, 1989.

Napier, James Carroll. Biography File, Special Collections, Fisk University Library.

Nashville Daily American May 26, 1890.

Nashville Tennessean April 21, 1940; March 2, 1988; December 2, 1992.

Obituary. *Journal of Negro History* 25 (1940): 400–401.

Scott, Mingo Jr. *The Negro in Tennessee Politics and Governmental Affairs: 1865–1965, The Hundred Years Story.* Nashville: Rich Printing Company, 1965.

Smith, Jessie Carney, ed. *Notable Black American Women.* Detroit: Gale Publishing, 1992.

———. *Black Firsts.* Detroit: Visible Ink Press, 1994.

Wynn, Linda T. "Building Confidence: The Survival of a Financial Institution." *The Courier* (Tennessee Historical Commission) 19 (February 1981): 4–5.

COLLECTIONS

The papers of James Carroll Napier are in the Fisk University Library, Special Collections.

Linda T. Wynn

William C. Nell (1816–1874)

Abolitionist, civil servant, community activist, historian, writer

William C. Nell was a major figure in Boston from about 1840 through the Civil War. On the national scene, he tended to be eclipsed by figures like Frederick Douglass and Henry Highland Garnet, but his role was hardly negligible. Among the many campaigns he led in Boston was one that resulted in the abolition of that city's segregated schools in 1854. As a journalist and letter writer he was an effective publicist for black causes. He was also an ardent supporter of integrated organizations and an active abolitionist. When the Anti–slavery Movement split in 1840, Nell remained loyal to the branch led by his fellow Bostonian, William Lloyd Garrison. He also contributed to black history by championing the memory of Crispus Attucks and writing the first extensive documented treatment of the history of African Americans in the United States.

Nell was born in Boston on December 20, 1816, to William Guion Nell and Louisa Nell. William G. Nell had recently established himself in Boston. He was a steward on the *General Gasden,* based in Charleston, South Carolina. A recent account reported that the ship was taken by British forces, and he spent time as a prisoner of war. His son claimed that the ship escaped capture and arrived in Boston on July 28, 1812. William G. Nell took up residence and became a tailor. A member of the First African Baptist Church (changed to First Independent Baptist Church in 1838), founded by Thomas Paul, he became a prominent black leader and, in 1826, was a founding member of the Massachusetts General Colored Association. He was an associate of David Walker, author of *Walker's Appeal.* Louisa Nell was a native of Brookline, Massachusetts.

William C. Nell grew up in a relatively privileged black family. He attended the segregated public school for blacks held in the basement of the African Baptist Church. There, in 1829, at the age of 13, he had one of the formative experiences of his life. The mayor of Boston, Harrison Gray Otis, and the chair of the School Committee, Samuel T. Armstrong, visited the school. They told Nell, Nancy Woodson, and Charles A. Battiste that they would receive prizes for excellence. White students so honored received silver Benjamin Franklin medals and attended a dinner held at Faneuil Hall. The three black students received autobiographies of Franklin in a small format but were not invited to the dinner. However, Nell attended as a waiter's helper. These events fixed in Nell's mind a determination to work against prejudice in the school system and segregation everywhere.

Even with his family background, Nell had to first overcome his low self–esteem. In an unpublished and undated typescript of the life of Nell by George W. Forbes (offered by James Oliver Horton), Nell responded to a question about his plans for his future: "What is the use of my trying to be somebody? I can never be anything but a nigger anyway."

Begins His Career

In spite of his cynicism, Nell showed promise for special achievement. In 1832, he was secretary of the Juvenile Garrison Independent Society, a self–help organization of black youth. He also demonstrated an ability to write and speak well and delivered a speech for the organization's second anniversary in October 1833. It appeared in the *New England Telegraph.* A year later he spoke at an anti–slavery oratorical exhibition. Nell worked as an errand boy for William Lloyd Garrison's *Liberator,* and, over considerable opposition, Garrison arranged to have him learn printing in the paper's shop.

While considerable evidence of his activities remain, it is not clear exactly how Nell supported himself as an adult before he became a postal employee in 1861. He clerked and read law for a period in the office of William L. Bowditch. Nell finally stopped law study because he would have to swear allegiance to the Constitution of the United States to become a lawyer, and he felt that it was immoral to support a government which condoned slavery.

There were intermittent, low–paying positions in later years. Between 1840 and 1843, Nell was office manager of the American Anti–Slavery Society, then headquartered in Boston. His position was terminated when funds became scarce. In 1847, Nell moved to Rochester, New York, where he became a printer for the *North Star.* His name was added to the paper's masthead, joining the names of Frederick Douglass and Martin R. Delany. The income of the paper barely met expenses. Nell's name was removed from the masthead on June 23, 1848. He ended his relationship with Douglass and severed his connection with the paper in 1851, when Douglass broke with Garrison.

Nell was a tireless journalist and wrote *The Colored Patriots of the American Revolution* in 1855. The book is the first history written by a black and founded on written documentation, which made it a groundbreaking effort. In spite of the importance of his work, his writing brought little income. Thus, it would seem that Nell relied for most of his life on work he advertised for in the December 11, 1848, *Liberator,* as reprinted by Robert P. Smith:

> William C. Nell offers his services as copyist, accountant, and collector. Particular attention given to preparing forms of agreement, deed, mortgages, etc., conducting correspondence, and any other department of writing. He will procure help for families, stores, etc., in which capacity his effort have generally proved satisfactory. He will attend to the delivery of parcels, circulars, etc., and any similar employment. . . . Terms moderate.

Nell finally found work with a steady income in 1861, when he became the first black to hold a position in the federal government. Boston postmaster John Gorham Palfrey defied the law forbidding the employment of blacks in the postal service to appoint him clerk, a position Nell held until his death.

In the decade after his graduation from school, Nell was active in many integrated organizations promoting racial equality. He was a member of the Boston Minor's Exhibition Society, the Young Men's Literary Society, the Boston Mutual Lyceum, the Histrionic Club, and the Adelphic Union Library Association. A gregarious and playful man, his company was welcomed by both adults and children regardless of race. His attractive personality and participation in organizations combined with his writing and oratorical skills made him a natural community leader. Through his contacts with the press, especially the *Liberator,* he was an effective publicist for the organizations and causes he supported.

Leads Push for School Integration

In 1840, Nell began the campaign that would make him famous. Boston blacks had long been dissatisfied by the quality of the education in the one segregated public school of the city open to them. Nell spearheaded a series of petitions to the school board. Since the petitions failed to produce the desired outcome, the next step was to file suit. Initiated in 1849 by future senator Charles Sumner and assisted by Robert Morris, the first black admitted to the Massachusetts bar, the suit failed in the Massachusetts Supreme Court. Nell then began to organize petitions at a state level rather than a city and continued to hold protest meetings. Finally, in the spring of 1855, the state legislature put an end to segregation in education, making Massachusetts the only state to do so before the Civil War.

In December of 1855, Nell was honored for his role in dismantling the segregated school system at a dinner organized by the black community and was awarded with a gold watch. Donald M. Jacobs offered in *Courage and Conscience* the words of escaped slave and abolitionist William Wells Brown regarding this occasion: "No man in New England has performed more uncompensated labor for humanity, and especially for his own race than William C. Nell.'' Many prominent white abolitionists were present. Harriet Beecher Stowe could not attend because she had suffered an accident, but she sent an autographed copy of *Uncle Tom's Cabin.*

School segregation was not the only issue Nell involved himself in. He worked for equal treatment among races in transportation, theaters, and other public venues. He managed to succeed in convincing some established to discontinue racist policies. Nell also was a founding member of the Freedom Association in 1842, a black group organized to help fugitive slaves. Nell and Robert Morris supported the merger of this group with the integrated Boston Vigilance Committee, founded in 1846. While Nell was generally a conservative Garrisonian, he reacted a bit more radically to racism as the nation moved toward the Civil War.

The passage of the Fugitive Slave Act of 1850 inspired Nell's campaign to recognize the heroism of Crispus Attucks, the black man killed in the Boston Massacre. In 1851, he led a petition to the legislature for a monument to Attucks. (A monument was erected 37 years later in 1888.) Soon afterwards, a serious illness during the winter of 1851–1852 caused a lengthy interruption in Nell's activities. Nell's campaign became more urgent for him after the Dred Scott decision of 1857, in which the U.S. Supreme Court declared that blacks were not citizens of the United States. He was able to persuade the city of Boston to proclaim the first Crispus Attucks Day on March 5, 1858, and he saw that the celebrations continued for several years.

In connection with the campaign to recognize Attucks, Nell produced, in 1851, a 23–page pamphlet entitled *The Services of Colored Americans in the Wars of 1776 and 1812.* After publishing an augmented second edition of the pamphlet in 1852, Nell expanded this work into a nearly 400–page book, *The Colored Patriots of the American Revolution,* published in 1855. This was the first work of black history based on written documentation, and it included material about many of Nell's contemporaries.

Nell was also active on the national level, but his commitment to integrated organizations and the Anti–Slavery Society, led by Garrison, alienated him from radical leaders. A reluctant participant in the Black Convention Movement because of its segregated nature, he signed the call for the national convention held in Henry Highland Garnet's church in Troy, New York, in October of 1847. Nell and the New England Garrisonians joined the New York City delegation led by James McCune Smith in an alliance forged by Frederick Douglass. This group formed a moderate block which outvoted Garnet on crucial issues.

Quarrels with Douglass

When Douglass broke with Garrison in 1853, Douglass and Nell came into direct conflict. They exchanged sharp words at the Rochester National Black Convention in July. John W. Blassingame reported that Douglass called him '''a hanger on' and a 'contemptible tool' of Garrison.'' This conflict spilled over into the first meeting of the newly created Black National Council. Nell supported Ohio activist William Howard Day in the factional infighting at this meeting and also at the July 1854 meeting that marked the of the effort to build this national organization.

Although Nell changed some of his views as the Civil War neared, he did not follow radical leaders like Garnet. Nell was among the blacks firmly opposed to Garnet's African Civilization Society in the late 1850s. In 1850 Nell rejected the anti–political stance of Garrison and ran as an unsuccessful Free Soil Party candidate for the Massachusetts legislature. In the late 1850s, Nell was active in the efforts, which came to nothing, to establish a black militia company, and during the war he was active in recruiting blacks for the army.

Garrison himself was moving in the same direction, and Nell displayed his loyalty in the last issue of the *Liberator* on December 29, 1865, through a two–page tribute to Garrison. The loss of this outlet for his journalism resulted in Nell's becoming less visible in his final years.

Little is known of the years before Nell's death. He continued to work at the post office, apparently without any advancement. In April of 1869, he married. He left a widow and two children when he died in 1874 of a cause noted as paralysis of the brain. Garrison delivered the eulogy at his funeral. Nell was buried in Forest Hills Cemetery. On September 18, 1989, a monument was placed at his grave.

According to William Wells Brown, Nell was ''of medium height, slim, genteel figure, quick step, elastic movement, a thoughtful yet pleasant brow, thin face, and chaste in his conversation.'' He was a well–known figure among the black elite of the first part of the nineteenth century and played an important role as a black abolitionist, especially in his native state.

REFERENCES

Blackett, R. J. M. *Beating Against the Barriers.* Ithaca, NY: Cornell University Press, 1989.

Blassingame, John W., ed. *The Frederick Douglass Papers.* Series 1, vol. 1. New Haven, CT: Yale University Press, 1982.

Brown, W[illia]m Wells. *The Rising Son.* 1874. Reprint, Miami, FL: Mnemosyne Publishing, 1969.

Daniels, John. *In Freedom's Birthplace.* Boston: Houghton Mifflin, 1914.

Horton, James Oliver. *Free People of Color.* Washington, DC: Smithsonian Institution Press, 1993.

Jacobs, Donald M., ed. *Courage and Conscience: Black and White Abolitionists in Boston.* Bloomington: Indiana University Press for the Boston Athenaeum, 1993.

Logan, Rayford W., and Michael R. Winston, eds. *Dictionary of American Negro Biography.* New York: Norton, 1982.

Nell, W[illia]m C[ooper]. *The Colored Patriots of the American Revolution.* 1855. Reprint, New York: Arno Press and the *New York Times,* 1968.

Pease, Jane H. and William H. *They Who Would Be Free.* New York: Atheneum, 1974.

Quarles, Benjamin. *Black Abolitionists.* New York: Oxford University Press, 1969.

Smith, Robert P. "William Cooper Nell: Crusading Black Abolitionist." *Journal of Negro History* 55 (April 1970): 182–99.

Schor, Joel. *Henry Highland Garnet.* Westport, CT: Greenwood, 1977.

Robert L. Johns

Huey P. Newton
(1942–1989)
Political activist, organization cofounder

Founder of the Black Panther Party, Huey P. Newton was a complex man determined to help African Americans gain their rightful place in the social structure of the United States. He was convinced that the best chances for success in the struggle for equal rights for black Americans depended upon a militaristic, nationalistic approach; this conviction was motivation for his part in bringing about the Black Panther Party for Self–Defense in 1966. The Panthers brought about a decrease in the brutality against African Americans in the Bay Area of California and gave young people a sense of identification with an organization that cared about them and other black citizens.

Huey P. Newton was born in New Orleans, Louisiana, on February 17, 1942. His father, Walton, came to Oakland in 1944 with the mass migration of blacks from the South to the West Coast to work in the defense plants of World War II. A year later, his mother, Amelia, followed with their children. Huey, then three, was the youngest of seven children. In his childhood, he was a junior deacon in Bethel Baptist Church, where his father was the minister. Newton graduated from Oakland Technical High School in 1959 with the reading skills of a primary student. Before graduation, Newton had already served a month in juvenile hall for gun possession and was well on his way to a life of dissipation and petty crime that led to alienation from his parents.

Newton knew that he must expand on his education before he could satisfy his growing desire to make a difference in his community. He began to tap his latent mental abilities by reading Plato's *Republic,* and with the help of his brother Melvin, the scholar of the family, Newton read the opus over and over until he could comprehend the meaning of each word. He enrolled in Merritt Community College in Oakland, earned an associate of arts degree, and then spent a semester at San Francisco Law School, not for a law degree, but to learn the intricacies of coping with law enforcement agencies. In his free time he attended meetings of the fledgling Afro–American Association, organized by the young attorney Donald Warden (now Khalid Al–Mansour).

Huey P. Newton

Although he was becoming better prepared academically and more sophisticated politically, Newton continued to run afoul of the law, sometimes using his own legal knowledge in court to avoid prosecution. He could not, however, escape the 1964 penalty of a month in solitary confinement with restricted nourishment in the Alameda County Jail for assault with a deadly weapon. Newton credited this experience in quietness with helping him learn to control his mind for clearer thinking.

Conception and Birth of the Black Panther Party

In 1965 Newton and fellow student Bobby Seale joined the Soul Students Advisory Council and the Revolutionary Action Movement at Merritt College in their efforts to bring classes in African American history to the college. They were soon disillusioned when those organizations rejected their proposed demonstration on campus with an open display of firearms. Unshaken from their belief in the power of guns, Newton and Seale set about formulating their vision of a well–armed self–defense group.

Newton and Seale began intense, systematic readings and discussions, concentrating on the examples of the Black Muslim movement and Robert Williams in the United States, Mao Tse–Tung in China, Frantz Fanon in the Caribbean and Africa, and Fidel Castro and Che Guevara in Cuba. On October 15, 1966, Newton and Seale opened an office on Fifty–eighth Street in North Oakland, and unveiled a ten–point platform that called for total redressing of the inequities in all areas of African American life in the United States. This was the official birth of the Black Panther Party for Self–

Defense. The well–conceived, all–encompassing doctrines of the organization covered employment, economic security, housing, education, dependable police protection without brutality, fair court hearings and release of all African American prisoners, exemption from military service, and a United Nations supervised vote to determine the destiny of black Americans.

Bobby Seale was the first chairman of the new group; Newton, the defense minister; and Eldridge Cleaver, minister of information. The Panthers, in black berets and black leather jackets, soon became a recognizable force and attracted young men seeking their own selfhood and ways to contribute to African American life. Driving cars equipped with cameras and tape recorders, they came to the aid of any African American they saw being interrogated by the police on the streets of Richmond, San Francisco, Berkeley, or Oakland. They were visible advocates for black citizens in need. The Panthers served breakfast to children, provided free medical clinics, escorted seniors to and from their homes, and operated a fully accredited elementary school in a predominantly African American part of Oakland.

The party attracted far–reaching attention from a case that involved a member, Denzil Dowell. Dowell had been fatally shot on April 1, 1967, by Contra Costa County Sheriff Department officers as he supposedly resisted arrest for automobile theft. Unable to accept the verdict of justifiable homicide, party members mounted protests that culminated with the appearance of 30 gun–bearing Panthers, clad in the usual black attire, on the steps of the state capitol in Sacramento on May 2, 1967. Law makers were inside debating passage of legislation to restrict use and ownership of firearms.

The twenty–four men and six women in the Panther group stood silently while Seale read, in Newton's absence, the leader's statement of resistance to the proposed law introduced by Representative Donald Mulford, a conservative Republican. That night, pictures of armed African Americans with bandoliers appeared on news broadcasts all over the country. The Mulford Law, known as the anti–Panther bill, was passed in July of that same year without delay and with few dissenting votes.

Three months later, on October 27, 1967, Newton was the central figure in a case where he was shot in the stomach, and an Oakland police officer, John Frey, was shot to death. Newton pleaded not guilty, but he was convicted of voluntary manslaughter with a sentence of two to fifteen years in prison. Nationwide cries of ''Free Huey'' led to two retrials on the grounds that the judge did not give proper instructions to the jury. Both trials ended with hung juries and case dismissal.

By the 1970s the Black Panthers were suffering from internal and external pressures. Cleaver, minister of information, and many of his supporters broke with the party. Major damage came from the FBI and CIA's spies within the inner circle and overt outside surveillance. It was suspected that informants from the drug world and from the Communist party were listening in as well. Gun battles with police took a toll on the lives of the membership. Such powerful opposition hastened the end of their effectiveness.

Newton's personal life continued to be a mass of problems stemming from court charges and prison sentences, compounded by drug and alcohol use. He was arrested on a variety of infractions—burglary, illegal possession of firearms, murder, manslaughter, and violation of probation. He fled to Cuba in 1974 to avoid prosecution but returned in 1977.

Newton completed study for a bachelor's degree and a Ph.D. in social philosophy from the Santa Cruz campus of the University of California in 1980. For his dissertation, ''War Against the Panthers: A Study of Repression in America,'' he drew upon his intimate knowledge of the ideals, challenges, frustrations, and successes of the organization he helped conceive.

The end of Huey Newton's life came in the early morning hours on August 22, 1989, after he had been found on a sidewalk in West Oakland, seriously wounded by gunshots to the abdomen and head. He was 47-years old. The fatal attack had come not near his home, but in the area where the Black Panthers had concentrated their efforts to improve the lives of its residents. Newton's assailant, Tyrone Robinson, an African American and alleged drug dealer, was reported to have told police that his motive was self–defense and an effort to elevate his status in the Black Guerrilla Family, an organization of black prison inmates. Convicted of first–degree murder, Robinson was sentenced to 32 years in prison.

On the day of the funeral, well–wishers and admirers packed the large sanctuary of the church Newton had joined in 1985, Allen Temple Baptist Church in Oakland. In the midst of her grief, Newton's widow Fredrika was aware that Newton had known he might die by violent action, but she took comfort in the value of his work for the people underrepresented in their society. The Reverends J. Alfred Smith Sr. and Jr., the Reverend Cecil Williams, the Reverend Frank Pinkard, Congressman Ronald Dellums, Bobby Seale, David Hilliard, attorney Charles Garry, who pleaded cases for Newton and the Panthers in scores of court appearances, H. Rap Brown, Erika Huggins, Elaine Brown, and Johnny Span paid public tribute to Newton and to the accomplishments of the political party he created.

Initially, the Panthers' support came from disillusioned veterans of the Vietnam war and younger people seeking means to uplift the race. Soon African Americans of all ages welcomed its success in decreasing the widespread police brutality in the Bay Area. While many people distrusted the party's methods, they saw the Panthers' constructive activities, such as its breakfast programs and independent schools, as contributing to racial progress. When Newton died in 1989, thousands expressed sadness over his ignominious end. His death symbolized the persistent social problems that plagued the very area that this man—known as politically shrewd and capable of motivating large numbers of Americans—tried to help.

Fredrika Newton established the Dr. Huey P. Newton Foundation in 1993 to keep the philosophy and contributions of Newton and the history and activities of the Black Panther Party alive.

REFERENCES

"Comrades in 'The Movement' Remember the Life of Huey Newton Killed In Oakland." *Jet* 76 (11 September 1989): 55.

Moore, Gilbert. *Rage.* New York: Carroll and Graf Publishers, 1993.

Newton, Huey P. *To Die For The People.* New York: Writers and Readers Publishing, 1973.

Newton, Michael. *Bitter Grain: Huey Newton and the Black Panther Party.* Los Angeles: Holloway House, 1991.

Williams, Michael W., ed. *An African American Encyclopedia.* New York: Marshall Cavendish, 1993.

COLLECTIONS

Information on Huey P. Newton is in the papers of the Black Panther Party at Stanford University in Stanford, California.

Dona L. Irvin

Robert N. C. Nix Sr.

Robert N. C. Nix Sr.

(1898?–1987)

Congressman, lawyer, politician

Robert N. C. Nix Sr. was the first African American elected to the U.S. House of Representatives from Pennsylvania. Though he is characterized by his opponents as lacking leadership, Nix worked quietly to achieve the goals of his constituency. His voting record supported those policies which were particularly favorable to African Americans and other poorly represented groups. A member of the Black Congressional Caucus from the time of its formation, Nix was not radical or especially outspoken. His moderate, quiet demeanor made him a target for those who felt he was not aggressive enough in promoting a national black agenda. His long political apprenticeship, made him aware of the way political machinery operated, and he believed he could accomplish more within the system than he could as an outsider.

Robert Nelson Cornelius Nix Sr. was born in Orangeburg, South Carolina, a middle child in a large family. His estimated date of birth is August 9, 1898. His parents were Sylvia and Nelson Nix. Nelson Nix was a former slave who earned a doctorate in mathematics and became the dean of faculty at State Agricultural and Mechanical College in Orangeburg, now South Carolina State College.

Nix moved and lived with relatives in New York City and attended a private elementary school in Harlem. He graduated from Townsend Harris Hall High School in New York City. He then attended Lincoln University in Chester County, Pennsylvania, where he received a bachelor's degree in 1921. While at Lincoln University, he was a member of the debating team, played football and baseball, and was an A student. One of the few African Americans admitted to the University of Pennsylvania Law School at that time, Nix received his law degree in 1924. After passing the bar exam, Nix began practicing law in 1925 and opened one of only two or three black law offices in Philadelphia at that time.

Nix married Ethel Lanier of Washington, D.C. They had one child, Robert N. C. Nix Jr., who became the first African American to head any state court when he became Chief Justice of the Pennsylvania Supreme Court. Nix and his son owned the law firm Nix and Nix until the younger Nix resigned in 1968 to become a Philadelphia judge.

Launches a Career in Politics

Nix became involved in the Democratic Party shortly after opening his practice. He was elected executive committee member of the Democratic Party for the Forty–fourth Ward in Philadelphia in 1932 and continued to serve in that capacity for many years. He served as chair from 1950–1958. One of his most important accomplishments during this period was working to get African Americans registered to vote. Nix's work led to Philadelphia gaining the highest percentage of voter registration among African Americans in the country. He persistently continued to work towards refining the registration laws and voting patterns of states where African Americans did not or could not vote.

Nix's involvement in the community was also demonstrated by his work as a special deputy attorney general for Pennsylvania's revenue department and as a special assistant deputy attorney general from 1934 to 1938. He continued to serve as a special assistant deputy attorney general for many years. Nix was later unanimously chosen leader of the Thirty–second Ward. He became a member of the Policy Committee and the Philadelphia Democratic Campaign Committee and cochair of the Inter–Relations Committee of the Democratic Campaign Committee in 1953. Nix was active in the NAACP and the Philadelphia Citizens Committee Against Juvenile Delinquency and Its Causes. In addition, he was a member of White Rock Baptist Church in Philadelphia and a member of the deacon board.

Pennsylvania's First Black Congressman

Nix's hard work in the community paid off when he was selected as a delegate to the Democratic National Convention in 1956 (and again in 1960 and 1964). Nix had run unsuccessfully for various offices before 1958. In *Black Man's America,* Simeon Booker equated Negro politics in Philadelphia with a plantation system: white overlords dominated the vote, and "no independent Negro [was] in politics in the city."

Nix ran for Congress in a special election in 1958, giving his birthdate as 1905, because he believed his true age could work against him. He won a seat in the House of Representatives and became the first black to represent a constituency in Pennsylvania. Nix's tenure in the U.S. House of Representatives was not without controversy, nor was it without accomplishment. Nix did not seek to bring attention to himself and was accused by his opponents as being too closely affiliated with the regular Democratic Party, as well as criticized for absenteeism and being out of touch with his constituency. However, he was known to spend his Saturdays in Philadelphia listening attentively to the requests of his constituents. Booker characterized him as "a painstaking lawyer but a lackluster lawmaker" who did little to lead any civil rights move. His first term in Congress was typical of a freshman representative. His proposed legislation dealing with issues, such as discrimination in the armed forces, hunger in underdeveloped countries, and unemployment, died in committee and never reached the floor. Nevertheless, Nix continued to address these issues. During his first term, he supported a congressional resolution to urge France to cease its conflict with Algeria. In *America's Black Congressmen,* Maurine Christopher noted his concern with unemployment as shown in his campaign in 1962, when Nix commented, "This is the richest and most technically advanced country in the world. . . . Every citizen should enjoy the opportunity to make a living consistent with his abilities and skills." According to Ragsdale and Treese in *Black Americans in Congress,* Nix sponsored bills to preserve the Philadelphia navy yard and to establish a "senior service corps" to employ people over age 60. Consistent with Nix's view of himself as a representative, he sponsored and supported legislation which helped his city and constituency that included many elderly and African Americans.

Continuing his interest in protecting voting rights, Nix proposed a bill that would reduce a state's representation in proportion to the qualified adults it denied voting rights to. The bill was blocked by the Judiciary Committee, but Nix continued to show his support of civil rights in other ways. Nix joined 16 other Democrats in attempting to bar the seating of the Mississippi delegation in January 1965 on the grounds that the elections were illegal, since many blacks were not permitted to register to vote in its district. In the succeeding session, Nix challenged the South Carolina delegation when it insisted South Carolina's voting registration was free and open. Nix argued that the state's requirement of literacy testing was not legal; 61 percent of blacks over 25 were school dropouts, so the literacy requirement was an obvious maneuver to disenfranchise blacks. Those blacks who attempted to register were intimidated.

Nix worked for the Voting Rights Act of 1965. Maurine Christopher described in *America's Black Congressmen* the effect of the act, "[it] suspended literacy tests and other restrictive devices and provided federal examiners to supervise registrations and elections in states with a history of disenfranchising minority–group citizens." Other areas Nix worked in were legislation regarding urban renewal and mass transportation and the fight to keep Congress from denying Adam Clayton Powell his seat in the Ninetieth Congress.

Though Nix could often be found standing at the back of the House observing the proceedings or conferring with his colleagues rather than taking a highly visible position, he developed the reputation of being an effective and powerful speaker. With tension growing in Washington as the date of Martin Luther King's 1963 March on Washington approached, Nix gave one of his most memorable speeches on the floor of the House. He urged:

> Ladies and gentlemen of the House of Representatives, I appeal to you to examine your attitudes toward the August 28 march in terms of the total cause of which that event is only a symbol. I urge you to take into consideration the fact that all men's civil and personal rights are of paramount importance at present; that they are not. . .subject to being rationed at the will of some so–called master group. I ask you to accept the inevitable; not because it is inevitable. . .but because it is right and no other course will protect the Negro or the Nation's future.

Nix also delivered the eulogy in the House for President John F. Kennedy.

As a freshman Representative, Nix was appointed to the Merchant Marine and Fisheries Committee and the Veterans' Affairs Committee, serving on both for two sessions. He was appointed to the Foreign Affairs Committee in 1961 and to the Post Office and Civil Service Committee in 1963, serving on these committees until he left Congress. In 1977, as ranking member of the Post Office and Civil Service Committee, Nix was expected to become the chair. His selection was contested by some of the younger members of the committee as well as some staffers, but was confirmed.

During the 1960s, the number of black representatives in Congress increased as a result of the Civil Rights Movement and redistricting legislation. Black members of Congress found it was difficult to reach their legislative goals as individuals and consequently formed the Congressional Black Caucus. The caucus grew and began to organize itself more strongly through fund–raising and keeping a professional staff. Nix was characterized and criticized as a moderate in the organization, which sought immediate results. According to Clay, Nix was a "congressman first, a Democrat second, and a black third." Quoted by Barker and McCorry in *Black Americans and the Political System,* Nix answered his critics,

> I've seen people come into this Congress feeling it was incumbent upon them to give everybody hell, talking about the wrongs and fancied wrongs that happen everyday. . . . They didn't correct a damn thing. . . . The legislation they sought to present to the House later on received little interest from any source. . . . In voicing your disapproval, you don't make your fellow member of Congress responsible for what you're condemning unless he is responsible. Nor do you condemn the whole white race.

Nix was sensitive to the charges made against him, and his voting record clearly demonstrated that he was dedicated "to ending the oppression of black people."

After Nix left Congress at age 80, he continued to be active in local ward politics until his death in 1987. Of his congressional career, according to his grandson, Nix was probably most proud of being the ranking member of the delegation which went to Mexico when he was chair of the Mexico–United States Interparliamentary Conference and of his long involvement with the Post Office and Civil Service Committee. More important to him than any of these accomplishments, though, was the success of his son, who was elected to serve as an associate justice on the Pennsylvania Supreme Court in 1972 and became Chief Justice 12 years later. The federal building named for Nix in Philadelphia serves as a monument to Nix's political accomplishments, both for his city and for his race.

REFERENCES

Afro–American Encyclopedia. Vol. 7. North Miami: Educational Book Publishers, 1974.

Barker, Lucius J., and Jesse J. McCorry, Jr. *Black Americans and the Political System.* Cambridge, MA: Winthrop, 1976.

Biographical Directory of the United States Congress 1774–1989. Bicentennial Ed. Washington, DC: Government Printing Office, 1989.

Booker, Simeon. *Black Man's America.* Englewood Cliffs: Prentice–Hall, 1964.

Christopher, Maurine. *America's Black Congressmen.* New York: Crowell, 1971.

Clay, William L. *Just Permanent Interests: Black Americans in Congress, 1870–1991.* New York: Amistad, 1992.

Congressional Directory. Eighty–sixth Congress, First Session. 1959. Washington, DC: Government Printing Office, 1959.

Nix, Robert N. C. III. Telephone interview with Gordon K. Lee, August 28, 1996.

Ragsdale, Bruce A., and Joel D. Treese. *Black Americans in Congress.* Washington, DC: Government Printing Office, 1990.

Salzman, Jack, David Lionel Smith, and Cornel West, eds. *Encyclopedia of African–American Culture and History.* New York: Macmillan Library Reference USA/Simon and Schuster, 1996.

"17 House Democrats Back Plan to Bar Mississippi Delegation." *New York Times,* December 24, 1964.

"16 Democrats Bid U.S. Act to Halt Algeria Conflict." *New York Times,* August 9, 1959.

Williams, Michael W., ed. *African American Encyclopedia.* New York: Marshall Cavendish, 1993.

COLLECTIONS

Nix's papers are housed at the Afro–American Historical and Cultural Museum in Philadelphia.

Gordon K. Lee

E. D. Nixon Sr.
(1899–1987)
Union leader, civil rights activist, railroad porter

On February 25, 1987, the city of Montgomery, Alabama, mourned the death of its leading black citizen and native son, E. D. Nixon Sr. Nixon's political and civic activities have been chronicled but the general public still knows little of his accomplishments. Nixon never sought fame and glory, only the opportunity to make his hometown a better place for its citizens to live lives free from the deleterious effects of segregation and second–class citizenship.

Edgar Daniel Nixon Sr., known simply as E. D., was born on July 12, 1899, in the shadow of Alabama's state capitol in Montgomery as the fifth of eight children of Sue Ann Chappell Nixon and Wesley Nixon. Until her death, when Nixon was eight years old, Sue Nixon worked as a maid and cook. Wesley Nixon, a Baptist minister, remarried and fathered nine other children. Nixon was sent to Autauga, Alabama, to live with his paternal Aunt Pinky, who was a staunch and devout Seventh Day Adventist and strict disciplinarian. Nixon's schooling was sporadic, because the one–room segregated school that went only to the eighth grade was ten miles from his aunt's house. When he was 14 years old, he became self–supporting and lived in Selma and Mobile where he worked on a street car line and in a grocery store. At other times, he did carpentry work, loaded boxes, and cleaned yards. Back in Montgomery, he worked in a local grocery store for a dollar a day and often had to sleep in kitchens when he was unable to afford a rented room.

E. D. Nixon Sr.

After working in the Union Station baggage room for some time, Nixon was hired as a sleeping–car porter. Realizing that his severely limited education would limit his advancement in employment, Nixon spent his spare time learning to read and write. Whenever he saw an unfamiliar word, he would write it down and look it up in a used dictionary he kept in his room. The young man also realized that job advancement would depend on his ability to get along with people and to conduct himself in a manner that would elicit respect from others. His physical presence was another incentive that caused others to be respectful, as he was a tall, dark–skinned man with big shoulders, big frame, and craggy face. In *Parting the Waters,* Branch described Nixon as having ''fists as big as eggplants and a coal–black face. [He was] not an educated or cultivated man.''

Nixon was a family man devoted to his wife, Arlet, his son, E. D. Jr., by his deceased first wife, Alease Curry Nixon. Arlet was from a well–do–do family from Pensacola, Florida, and Nixon met her on a train run. He always bragged that his wife had never worked and would never have to work, even after his death. His son, a folksinger known as Nick LaTour, lives in California and works in the theatrical field. Nixon owned his own home, a car, and property and never failed to point out that he enjoyed more material success and less debt than most of Montgomery's better educated blacks.

Influenced by A. Philip Randolph

Nixon was an ideal sleeping–car porter because he was accustomed to hard work and service to the public. He also had an insatiable curiosity about the world outside the South. Railroad travel provided an opportunity for him to see a world where black people were leaders. Nixon soon met the man who would exert the most influence on his life and future endeavors. In the late 1920s he was in St. Louis and heard A. Philip Randolph speak at the local YWCA, where Nixon stayed on overnight railroad runs. Randolph accused the Pullman Company of treating black employees as if they were chattel. An impressive speaker with an Oxford–tinged accent, Randolph fought the company for 12 years to gain recognition for a union called the Brotherhood of Sleeping Car Porters. When Nixon heard him, Randolph was urging the porters to form an alliance with him to fight for a guaranteed salary raise to $150 a month. Nixon was stunned because his monthly salary was only $72.50, and he supported the charismatic speaker by putting a dollar in the collection place. When he returned home, he was summoned to the manager's office and threatened for having attended the St. Louis meeting. Nixon informed the company manager that he had not only attended the meeting but, had, as well, joined the brotherhood and would sue the company if the threats continued.

When Nixon began as a sleeping–car porter, the job required working 11,000 miles a month or having one's salary prorated. Because of the varying times of departure on train runs, a porter might miss breakfast, lunch, or dinner on the train. In 1937 Randolph's brilliant and relentless tactics prevailed, and the Brotherhood of Sleeping Car Porters signed a contract with the Pullman Company. Nixon's branch, founded in the 1920s, became one of the first black locals in the nation.

Commitment to Montgomery

Randolph would be the key figure in honing Nixon's organizational skills, but he was not the catalyst for Nixon's burning desire to effect community action. When Nixon first met Randolph, he was already involved in local efforts to improve the quality of life for Montgomery's black citizens. He had made an unsuccessful attempt to get a swimming pool for blacks after two black children drowned while swimming in a drainage ditch. But it was his untiring contributions toward unionization that was the crucible in which Nixon was forged.

In 1928 Nixon helped organize state and local NAACP chapters in Alabama with Walter White and Roy Wilkins as constant mentors. During his tenures as state and local president, 21 branches were added to the state NAACP, and the local membership increased from less than 500 to nearly 3,000. In the 1930s he organized the Montgomery Welfare League to assist poor blacks in getting on welfare rolls. In 1941 he participated in planning the threatened National March on Washington, an effort that forced President Franklin D. Roosevelt to issue Executive Order 8802 that established the Fair Employment Practices Commission.

In 1944 Nixon organized the Montgomery Voter's League in his home. He was also president of the Progressive Democratic Association, an old–line black organization that was successful in getting blacks on the police force for the first time since Reconstruction. In that same decade, Nixon counseled the residents of Oak Park who were suffering from insect infestation due to the city's use of the park area as a dumping ground and storage area for manure. When the city refused to halt the practice, Nixon got two white lawyers to prepare a suit against the city, a tactic that worked. As NAACP president, Nixon had tried, in the 1940s, to challenge the legality of the city bus codes. Unfortunately, the woman chosen to be the plaintiff in the test case, Viola White, died while appeals dragged on for ten years after the 1944 filing.

Voter registration was always a local NAACP project. Rosa Parks wrote in her autobiography that she first met Nixon in 1943 when he persuaded an Alabama–born black lawyer in New York to come to Montgomery to teach blacks how to deal with state requirements for getting voter certificates. The legal and illegal tactics used by white registrars prevented Parks from receiving her certificate for two years. She had planned to file a suit. However, when Nixon and Arthur Madison, the New York lawyer, went with her, in 1945, she was finally successful. However, she still was forced to pay the one–and–a–half dollar poll tax that was retroactive for the 11 years between the legal voting age and her age.

In 1944 Nixon persuaded 750 blacks to march to the courthouse and demand their right to vote. The following year, he ran for a county seat on the Montgomery Democratic Executive Committee, an election he lost by only 200 votes. This was a historic milestone in that he was the first black to seek political office since Reconstruction. During World War II, Nixon used his influence and reputation as a leading black union leader to get Eleanor Roosevelt's assistance in getting a local USO club for black soldiers. When the club was established near the railroad station, someone else was hired to oversee USO activities and Nixon's efforts were largely ignored.

Despite the highly visible strides made to improve the quality of life for the black populace of Montgomery, Nixon felt snubbed by his own people, especially highly educated Alabama State College faculty, ministers, and those in the upper echelon of society. Nixon was a self–made man who lacked a college education. He was always one of the more outspoken blacks, and the black elite seemed annoyed by his neglect to use standard English and his frankness.

Nixon's main competitor and chief rival as a community activist was Rufus Lewis. Lewis represented the educated, Alabama State College, black power structure. He was a well–educated businessmand, a polished public speaker, and reputedly wealthy. Those who favored Lewis, considered Nixon to be uneducated, self–serving, and embarrassing as a public speaker. Nixon had more national alliances, however, including Eleanor Roosevelt, A. Philip Randolph, and the unions. Blacks, whether rich or poor, turned to him to post bonds when they got in trouble with police. For this reason, Bertha Butler, a friend and neighbor of Rosa Parks, called the Nixon home when she saw Parks being removed from the City Lines bus by a policeman and taken to the police station on the evening of Thursday, December 1, 1955. Parks called her husband to come for her, but Nixon had already called Clifford Durr, a local white attorney, who found out the charges and amount of bail. By the time Raymond Parks arrived, Nixon had paid the $100 bail bond and had Parks's trial date set for Monday, December 5, 1955.

There is controversy about the timetable of events and the roles of the principal players in the Montgomery Bus Boycott from the arrest until the day of the final court decision. Nixon knew that the time was right to test segregation laws. Rosa Parks's case was not the first Nixon had considered in using. Earlier Nixon had rejected the case of Claudette Colvin, a 15–year old black youngster who had been arrested on March 2, 1955. Nixon was convinced that Colvin was too unstable to withstand litigation procedures and could not elicit community support. No one could have doubts about Parks. She was neither too upper or lower class, and she was respected as an ardent church worker, wife and daughter, NAACP worker and employee, and loyal civic worker.

Boycott and the MIA

After Parks agreed to become the center of a test case, Nixon, according to Cox's biographical account, had a late night conversation with his wife. He said, ''You know, I think every Negro in town should stay off the buses for one day in protest for Mrs. Parks arrest.''

At 5:00 on Friday morning, December 2, 1955, Nixon called Ralph Abernathy and then his own pastor, H. H. Hubbard, both officials of the black Baptist Minister's Union. They agreed to the test case and proposed boycott. A third call was made to Martin Luther King Jr., new minister and new father. After making 18 additional calls, Nixon finalized plans for a meeting and prepared for his weekend train run to Chicago. He was quite secure in his belief that the idea for the proposed Monday, December 5, bus boycott was solely his and that he had set a solid foundation for it.

Nixon was unaware that an old adversary was implementing boycott plans. Jo Ann Robinson, Alabama State College English professor and Women's Political Council (WPC) president, secured access to the college mimeograph machine, an illegal move in the state of Alabama, and she and two students created fliers calling for a boycott on Monday. That Friday afternoon she and WPC members carried them all over the city.

The one–day boycott was more successful than anyone imagined. Nixon, Abernathy, and Edgar N. French, pastor of Hilliard Chapel AMEZ Church, met and laid the groundwork for a long–term boycott and a new, permanent organization that Abernathy named the Montgomery Improvement Association (MIA). In *The Walls Came Tumbling Down,* Abernathy discussed his initial preference for Nixon as leader, because of his authoritative and militant stance against injustice. This small group accepted Nixon's agenda, but Nixon declined to become leader and suggested King.

At the organizational meeting that afternoon, the proposed organizational name was accepted and Nixon's resolutions were adopted. Lewis distributed them without attaching the names of their proposers. Nixon was incensed and accused the men of being cowards. As he continued to attack their manhood, King entered. At that moment, Lewis nominated him for the presidency of MIA, a move that caused Nixon to wonder whether Abernathy and King had made an arrangement with Lewis.

381 Days of Struggle

The MIA elected Nixon treasurer. As a leading and widely known labor leader, he had the support of A. Philip Randolph and the major unions. The United Auto Workers' Union (UAW) contributed $35,000, and a labor union rally in New York's Madison Square Garden raised $18,000, in one night. During the two years of his tenure, Nixon cut checks totaling close to $500,000 for the MIA and the boycott. He also served as an unofficial legal advisor. Nixon also depended on Randolph to secure labor money and to recommend and send organizational experts down to assist the government. Bayard Rustin was one such person who came to Montgomery, but many MIA leaders were leery of associating with him because some ministers could not accept Rustin's homosexuality. Nixon was the exception. When MIA members were indicted for boycott activities, Rustin explained the finer points on how to be arrested and throw the police off guard. Nixon was the first to be indicted and, following Rustin's instructions, walked to the courthouse rather than waiting for the deputies to come to his home and arrest him. After his release on bond, the other indictees followed his example and the process became a big social affair that infuriated the sheriff.

Nixon deposited MIA contributions in banks over a wide geographic area so that the local banks and federal authorities could neither locate nor freeze the accounts. Nixon personally raised almost $100,000 during the boycott and always credited local white supporters who were sympathetic. One white man handed him $500 to secure a cash bond, and a group of white neighborhood businessmen each gave $1,000 to make bonds for those in need.

As the boycott movement progressed, Nixon began to feel that he was being pushed out. He continued to work hard and even had to defuse a potentially damaging financial scandal in the MIA. King and Abernathy were in California at an NAACP convention and unable to refute the charges of corruption. Nixon dealt with the matter while knowing full well that funds had been misappropriated because car–pool drivers and disreputable fuel dealers were cheating the MIA on gasoline charges.

A major breach in relations with King occurred when Nixon persuaded Randolph to invite King to testify before the platform committee at the Chicago Democratic National Convention. Nixon always felt that King never appreciated his efforts, especially his considerable success in getting UAW money to pay bills. In his autobiography, King claimed that Nixon had always overestimated his role in creating and developing the MIA and in initiating the boycott. In spite of friction between leaders, the crisis was over on Friday, December 21, 1956, when Nixon, King, Abernathy, and Glen Smiley, Rustin's successor, boarded the first desegregated bus in Montgomery at 6:00 a.m.

After the Boycott

The post–boycott MIA could never sustain the momentum created during the boycott. Once the buses were desegregated, King returned in 1960 to Atlanta to lead the Southern Christian Leadership Conference (SCLC) and the media followed him. Abernathy, who succeeded King as MIA leader, joined him in Atlanta, and Jo Ann Robinson, WPC president, left Alabama State College along with other prominent faculty who were also heavily involved in the boycott. Due to severe economic reprisals, Parks and her family were forced to leave Montgomery and move to Detroit. Nixon was hurt and upset at what he considered to be betrayal and desertion by the MIA big names; only Parks had a valid reason for leaving, in his estimation. Nixon continued to feel slighted and, in 1975, declined an invitation to the twentieth anniversary celebration.

In 1964 when he retired from the railroad union position, Nixon became director of community services for the Young Forte Village housing project, the number one crime area in the city. He supervised the installation of playgrounds and new street lights, secured city bus service and a branch post office, and planted trees. Gene Harvey conceived the idea of the E. D. Nixon Summer Olympics and Nixon made it a viable program for young people aged nine to 16. He also set up scout troops and acquired uniforms for all youth groups. This directorship was closely allied to his work with the United Parcel Service's national personnel manager, Walter Hooke. In 1968, as vice–president of the local Opportunities Industrial Center (OIC) center, Nixon assisted the new director in starting up a new program to serve black and white unemployed people.

One cause dear to Nixon's heart was the support of Natasha Hayes, a three–year–old cancer victim. In 1974 he set up the Natasha Hayes Fund to raise money for other sick children and personally raised nearly $7,000. Nixon also worked with the Alabama Coalition Against Hunger in the 1970s and assisted with senior citizen's programs. He served on the board of the Alabama State Red Cross and with the South Central Alabama Development Commission, the Central Alabama OIC, and on the Montgomery County Board of Pensions and Security. In 1975 he was appointed to the U.S. Commission on Civil Rights for the state of Alabama and served as its vice–president.

Later in life Nixon was a staunch supporter of governor George Wallace; he also made public attacks on the emerging black causes and movements. He criticized the SCLC for stealing the glory from local grassroots groups that had laid the foundation to deal with problems and issues before calling SCLC for assistance. His most vocal opposition was turned on the Black Power movement and its hypnotic slogans that, to Nixon, strongly favored racial separatism, the antithesis of all his life's work. His support of Wallace, for whom he cast ballots in 1958 and 1962, was the real issue that alienated Nixon from other civil rights leaders.

In 1965 the Militant Labor Forum sponsored a dinner to mark the tenth anniversary of the Montgomery Bus Boycott. By 1979 Nixon had received nearly 400 citations from state and local governments and national organizations. In December 1971 the Alabama House of Representatives adopted Resolution HR57 as commendation of Nixon's service to the state of Alabama. In August 1974 governor Wallace issued a proclamation commending Nixon's support of Alabama's youth. This was followed by a Montgomery mayoral proclamation, in 1977, honoring Nixon's community service. The Alabama State Historical Commission placed Nixon's Clinton Street home on the Alabama Register of Landmarks and Heritage in 1981. A self–educated man, Nixon was awarded four honorary doctorates, including one from Alabama State University in 1981. He began referring to himself, in writing, as "Dr. E. D."

Nixon was most gratified when he was recognized for 50 years of service at the local Holt Street Baptist Church in 1982. In 1983 his son celebrated Nixon's 84th birthday with a spectacular party that was a reunion of relatives and important people in Nixon's life. He also received the NAACP's Walter White Award in recognition of over 50 years of service to that organization. One of the greatest honors came when Nixon, although failing in health, attended the groundbreaking ceremony for the one–million–dollar E. D. Nixon complex for the elderly and handicapped in Tuskegee, Alabama, in January 1987. The complex was named for him at the special request of mayor Johnny Ford and dedicated in October 1987. In 1989 the Office of Minority Affairs in the Tennessee General Assembly started the E. D. Nixon Research Project which involved securing print materials that chronicled his life.

Nixon died on Wednesday, February 25, 1987, at Baptist Medical Center in Montgomery, from respiratory ailments and cancer. His funeral was held at Bethel Missionary Baptist Church and he was buried in Montgomery's Eastwood Cemetery on March 3.

In *The Origins of the Civil Rights Movement,* the roots of the Montgomery Movement are examined; the conclusion is that the movement was the collective vision of an uncharismatic, largely uneducated Pullman porter, the WPC membership of well–educated black women, and community organizations who turned to a charismatic leader after the movement had snowballed. Baldwin and Woodson quote Nixon's life–long defender, Joe Azbell, who said of him:

> Nixon's whole life was built around the impossible dream. Who would have believed a Pullman Car porter, born in poverty, would have such an important role in changing America and the world for black people.

REFERENCES

Abernathy, Ralph David. *And the Walls Came Tumbling Down.* New York: Harper and Row, 1989.

Anderson, Jervis. *A Philip Randolph: A Biographical Portrait.* New York: Farrar Strauss Giroux, 1973.

Baldwin, Lewis V., and Aprille V. Woodson. *Freedom is Never Free: A Biographical Portrait of E. D. Nixon, Sr.* Atlanta: United Parcel Service, 1992.

Bennett, Lerone, Jr. "The Day the Black Revolution Began." *Ebony* 32 (September 1977): 54–64.

Branch, Taylor. *Parting the Waters.* New York: Simon and Schuster, 1988.

Cox, Donald. "Edgar Daniel Nixon: Kingmaker." *Black World* 20 (February 1971): 87–98.

"E. D. Nixon, Leader in Civil Rights, Dies." *New York Times,* February 27, 1987.

"Freedoms, Great and Small." *New York Times,* March 1, 1987.

King, Mary. *Freedom Song.* New York: William Morrow, 1987.

Morris, Aldon. *The Origins of the Civil Rights Movement.* New York: Free Press, 1984.

Nixon, E. D. Sr. Letter to Mrs. J. R. Carr, October 9 1975. Copy in Special Collections, Tennessee State University.

———. Interview by Frank Adams, February 25, 1981. Transcript of Tape Recording. Copy in Special Collections, Tennessee State University.

Parks, Rosa, with James Haskins. *Rosa Parks: My Story.* New York: Dial, 1992.

Robinson, Jo Ann Gibson. *The Montgomery Buy Boycott and the Women Who Started It.* Knoxville: University of Tennessee Press, 1987.

"Voices of the Civil Rights Movement—Ethics and Morality." Transcript of E. D. Nixon, February 1, 1980 Cassette no. 21. Howard University, Washington, DC.

Wright, Roberta Hughes. *The Birth of the Montgomery Bus Boycott.* Southfield, MI: Charro Press, 1991.

COLLECTIONS

The E. D. Nixon Collection is located at Alabama State University in Montgomery. A reprint copy of the collection is in the Special Collections at Tennessee State University, Nashville.

Dolores Nicholson

Joseph "King" Oliver
(1895–1938)
Bandleader, musician

Joseph "King" Oliver was at the center of the new musical movement of the 1900s labeled "jazz." Raised in New Orleans, he absorbed an atmosphere strongly flavored with the sounds of Buddy Bolden, Bill Bailey, and the brass bands of New Orleans. He passed this heritage on to Louis Armstrong. Dizzy Gillespie, Bubber Miley, Cootie Williams, and Wynton Marsalis, among many others, owe much to his seminal innovations as a leader, soloist, and musician.

As a soloist, Oliver featured clipped phrases and technical showmanship with a hint of vaudeville theatricality. He also introduced new concepts of timbre as well as new mutes and lip techniques, including uncanny imitations of human and animal sounds. Oliver's groups helped crystallize the standard idiomatic structure of jazz. His bands were highly disciplined and noted for their close—often improvised—harmony, tight ensembles highlighting instrumental solos, and rhythmic "straight four" beat regularity contrasted with imaginative syncopation. Improvisation was uppermost in everything they did and stressed their underlying African folk heritage. Critical listeners also referred to their raw and vital sound, their joy, and their direct emotional appeal. Oliver's mentoring of Louis Armstrong gave the jazz world another legendary figure for many decades to come after Oliver's death in 1938.

The New Orleans Dixieland revival was in part initiated by the "rediscovery" in the 1940s of Oliver's first jazz recordings. These recordings in many ways served as definers of form, orchestration, and content for the various revival bands that followed in the 1940s, '50s and later, led by such musicians as Bunk Johnson, Wilbur De Paris, and, later, Al Hirt.

Joseph "King" Oliver was born near Abend, Louisiana, on May 11, 1885 (some sources give his birthplace as on or near Dryades Street, in New Orleans). When he was young, the family moved several times, to Dryades Street and other locations. His mother died in 1900, and he was raised by his older half–sister, Victoria Davis. He spent his formative years as a musician in New Orleans, and one of his early music teachers was bandleader Walter Kenchen. As a youth, he played in various local groups, first as a trombonist and later switching to cornet. Oliver lived in the same neighborhood as Kid Ory, the Dutreys, and other musical families; he and his friends all played music together virtually from childhood. Reports have Oliver playing professionally in various well–known New Orleans bands, beginning in about 1904 when he was nine. These included the Onward Brass Band, the Allen, Olympia, Melrose, Eagle band, and the Original Superior Orchestra. He took an early interest in young Louis Armstrong, giving him lessons and an instrument, helping him with jobs, and later recommending Armstrong as his replacement when he left Kid Ory's band to go to Chicago in 1918.

Well–known as a good ensemble musician, Oliver's first extended engagements were with the Four Hot Hands, from about 1912 to 1918. The band was led by early jazz pioneer Richard M. Jones. Next, he played with Kid Ory's Band in 1918. It was Kid Ory who first headlined him as "King" Oliver, and the nickname stuck. In 1918, former New Orleans bandleader and bassist Bill Johnson, who had moved to Chicago, called for Oliver to come north to join his band as lead cornetist. Many point to his union with the Johnson band and its subsequent developments as initiating the first full flowering of the Chicago jazz movement.

Playing at the Royal Gardens Cafe, this band and others to follow established a reputation for the transplanted New Orleans style, featuring a tight, highly syncopated ensemble sound and a blend of the raw folk blues sound of the South with the professional musicianship of the Northern big city environment. The blues, "stomp" song, ensemble brass band sounds, the instrumental solo, and the vibrant, lively New Orleans beans–and–rice flavor gave us a new music, called "jazz" which, in reality. had several points of origin.

Forms Creole Jazz Band

Leading his own band in 1920, King Oliver took the group on a west coast tour to San Francisco, Oakland, and Los Angeles in 1921, returning to Chicago in 1922. He then sought to add to his group's strength. He summoned Louis Armstrong from New Orleans to join his band in Chicago in 1922. He named the group King Oliver's Creole Jazz Band, and they went on to record the first seminal series of jazz recordings by an all–black band in 1923–24. In addition to Louis Armstrong, Oliver's band included several famous early jazz pioneers: Johnny Dodds, "Baby" Dodds, Lil Hardin Armstrong, Buster Bailey, Honore Dutrey, Bill Johnson, and Johnny St. Cyr.

Extremely popular in Chicago, the group attracted many area and visiting musicians to their sessions at Lincoln Gardens (the Royal Gardens, renamed) and the Plantation Lounge. Musicians listened attentively and often sat in. Some prominent musicians of the day commented admiringly about the band's "pure" New Orleans sound, high quality, technical command, raw emotion, and rhythmic drive. Their influence was felt by bandleaders and musicians alike, including Paul

Whiteman, Bennie Goodman, Bud Freeman, Fletcher Henderson, and Bix Beiderbecke.

By all accounts, a stern, sometimes gruff disciplinarian, Oliver was often affable and jovial otherwise. A good correspondent, his letters to friends and family show him to be of a positive nature, sensitive and caring, and not complaining about his ill fortune, even later in life.

Anecdotes abound concerning Oliver. He was a prodigious eater. His favorite lunch reportedly was half a dozen hamburgers and a quart of milk. He was also reported to have eaten twelve whole pies at one sitting on a bet. A man of powerful lungs and good embouchure (lip technique), he repeatedly engaged in ''cutting sessions'' with others; he and Armstrong were reported to have once engaged in a duel where together they played 125 consecutive choruses of ''Tiger Rag.'' He loved sugar, and reportedly ate sugar ''sandwiches,'' which inspired Clarence Williams to write ''Sugar Blues'' for him. As a soloist, he sometimes disguised his fingerings with a handkerchief and waited to the last minute to tell his partners some details about his coming solos or breaks.

Influenced Trumpeters

Oliver invented the first jazz plunger mute by combining a soda bottle with a bathroom plunger. He exploited the ''wah–wah'' technique using his hand in the bell of the instrument as well as by playing into a cocked (tilted) silver or tin–cup mute. In one caper based on this technique, he and his bass player Bill Johnson were said to have done a few choruses where they imitated a baby (Oliver, on cornet) crying and a nurse comforting the baby (Johnson on bass). His innovative use of the ''wah–wah'' effect, particularly on his trademarked solos in ''Dipper Mouth Blues,'' has influenced trumpeters, from Armstrong to Miley on down to the present day, and has found its way into classical music as well.

It is by his original group's recordings, that jazz lovers have come to respect its contribution to jazz history, and that of its leader. He first recorded in 1923 and produced some 36 sides that are historically significant to this day. King Oliver continued to record until 1930 for Gennett, Okeh, Paramount, Columbia, Vocalion, and Victor Records. These records marked the first regular series of jazz recordings by an all–black band. The 1923 sessions featured the band under its original title, King Oliver's Creole Jazz Band. Changes of musicians ensued, and later recordings were done by Oliver under the band title, Dixie Syncopators, or Savannah Syncopators, and other titles such as King Oliver and his Orchestra.

The first sessions, as described by Lil Hardin in Martin Williams' *King Oliver,* involved the use of techniques new to their day, but very primitive–sounding to current observers. The musicians clustered around, playing into a large horn, and the recording implement cut directly onto the revolving wax surface. Test pressings were done at that time to check for balance and placement, and then the master was cut. On reflection it seems almost amazing that a viable musical replica of the session emerged.

At all events, the engineers arranged the placement of the musicians in such a way that the two cornets (Oliver and Armstrong) were some distance away from the recording horn, with Armstrong the farthest away. The result was an acceptable balance, and the band's first recordings were cut. At one of these first sessions, the band cut ''Dipper Mouth Blues,'' which featured a three–chorus solo with use of the ''wah–wah'' effect by Oliver that soon became a standard for practice and even memorization by upcoming trumpeters. They also cut ''Chimes Blues,'' Louis Armstrong's first recorded solo, which also became a model, along with his later solos and those made after he left King Oliver.

An excellent analysis of these first recordings and their contribution to the development of jazz is given by Martin Williams in *King Oliver.* Fortunately, all of Oliver's recording have since been reissued. Composition by composition, Williams points to the polyphonic integration, sturdy tempos, strong leadership, and cohesion shown in their recordings, as well as the abundance of good solos and breaks, especially by Oliver and Armstrong. Williams praises their appeal to the ear through integration of the ensembles, and to the soul by way of their emotional content. In the latter respect, for example, he credits Oliver's ability to transform the emotional tone of a blues with his clever use of mutes. He characterizes the group's ''swing'' as consistent, positive and predictable, and credits the strength of sidemen Jonny Dodds and Honore Dutrey in their riffs and breaks, particularly on ''Froggie Moore,'' ''Dipper Mouth Blues,'' and ''Snake Rag.''

Critics contrast the first recordings by Oliver's original group as featuring the deep–rooted cohesive New Orleans flavor, and the next group of recordings (by the Dixie Syncopators) with more of an orchestral sound, with the role of the leader being more significant in terms of shaping overall balance. Williams contrasts Oliver's approach as a bandleader with that of Jelly Roll Morton, citing similarities and differences. One sees an attempt by Oliver, in adding reeds, to achieve homogeneity with a different blend of sound. In a way his approach also compares with that of Fletcher Henderson, while retaining the popularity of the New Orleans jazz flavor. In his recordings, one can also see his creative mind at work on the occasions where he accompanies another solo musician. A prominent example is his sympathetic call–and–response work with singer Sippie Wallace on ''Mourning Dove Blues.''

Although some reports aver that his best years as a musician were those spent in New Orleans prior to 1918, he had certainly reached a peak about 1925 in terms of his leadership strengths and personal popularity and that of his group. At this point, Armstrong soon left to begin his own career and began to surpass Oliver in public prestige. Jazz prominence diffused to a number of players, including Bix Beiderbecke, Dizzy Gillespie and Miles Davis.

Hitting the Road

After 1927 the original band had largely dispersed, although Oliver continued to record and lead ensembles. That was the year that Oliver shifted his focus to New York. Following some successful engagements, he was offered the job of providing the house band for a new night club, to be called The Cotton Club. Making a fateful choice, he declined the offer, and the engagement went to Duke Ellington. Oliver, however, played engagements in the region, and received a good recording contract with Victor, which was to extend to 1930. Next, he booked a tour of the Midwest, ending in Kansas City.

The years following 1930 brought a decline to Oliver's career, partly due to poor health, inadequate bookings, and unfortunate travel circumstances. He suffered from heart trouble and serious gum disease, and by 1935 he could not play his instrument, continuing, however, as leader. Particularly valuable to jazz history is the coverage of Oliver's last years as a bandleader, as reported in Allen and Rust's biography, *King Oliver.* The authors present a detailed coverage of Oliver's decline, including journals of about two years of road engagements with the wages paid, job sites, and accounts of accidents, cancellations, illness, but yet the constant hope of success. These can serve as an objective reportage of a typical musician's sometimes hard and sometimes gratifying life on the road during this period.

A tour of the South and Southwest was largely unsuccessful, with cancelled bookings, bus breakdowns, and salary cuts. Short engagements were scheduled, but illness and other circumstances brought an end to his active career. Finally, by 1936 Oliver had settled in Savannah, inactive in music, running a fruit stand and working as a janitor. His ill health soon closed in on him and he died of a cerebral hemorrhage at age 42 on April 8, 1938. His sister, Victoria Davis, assisted with funeral arrangements, and burial was arranged in Woodlawn Cemetery in New York, with Louis Armstrong, Clarence Williams, and a few other musician friends attending.

Perhaps his contribution is best summarized in his work as leader, soloist, and sensitive musician, as revealed in his recordings and the accounts of his performances. He gave his audiences joy, and his musicians hope, dignity and pride. Quoting Williams in *King Oliver,* "without Joseph Oliver, the feeling and form of his music and the techniques he found to express them, jazz would not have happened as we know it."

REFERENCES

Allen, Walter C., and Brian Rust. *King Joe Oliver.* London: Sidgwick and Jackson, 1958.

Anderson, Gene. "The Genesis of King Oliver's Creole Jazz Band." *American Music* 12 (Fall 1994): 283–303.

Berendt, Joachim. *The Jazz Book.* Westport, CT: Lawrence Hill, 1975.

Bushell, Garvin. *Jazz from the Beginning.* Ann Arbor: University of Michigan Press, 1988.

Harrison, Max, Charles Fox, and Eric Thacker. *The Essential Jazz Records.* Westport, CT: Greenwood Press, 1984.

Hitchcock, H. Wiley, ed. *New Grove Dictionary of American Music.* London: Macmillan, 1986.

Hodier, Andre. *Jazz; Its Evolution and Essence.* New York: Grove Press, 1961.

Jones, LeRoi. *Blues People.* New York: William Morrow, 1963.

Kernfeld, Barry, ed. *NewGrove Dictionary of Jazz.* London: Macmillan, 1988.

Larkin, Colin, ed. *The Guinness Encyclopedia of Popular Music.* London: Guinness Publishing, 1992.

Peretti, Burton. *The Creation of Jazz.* Urbana: University of Illinois Press, 1992.

Ramsey, Frederick Jr., "King Oliver and his Creole Jazz Band." In *Jazzmen.* Edited by F. Ramsey Jr. and Charles Edward Smith. New York: Harcourt, Brace, 1939.

Rose, Al. *I Remember Jazz.* Baton Rouge: Louisiana State University Press, 1967.

Souchon, Edmond, "King Oliver: A Very Personal Memoir." In *Jazz Panorama.* Edited by Martin T. Williams. New York: Crowell–Collier 1962. Reprint, New York: Da Capo Press, 1979.

Southern, Eileen. *Biographical Dictionary of Afro–American and African Musicians.* Westport, CT: Greenwood Press, 1982.

Williams, Martin T. *The Jazz Tradition.* New York: Oxford, 1970.

———. *King Oliver.* New York: Barnes, 1960.

Darius L. Thieme

Frederick D. O'Neal

(1905–1992)

Actor, theater organizer, playwright

Like the celebrated nineteenth–century abolitionist, writer, and statesman for whom he was named, Frederick Douglass O'Neal had a long and multifaceted public life. In a career in the entertainment industry that spanned more than 60 years O'Neal earned critical acclaim for his performance on stage, in films, and on television as well as numerous prestigious awards for acting and for service to his profession. In addition to acting, O'Neal was also praised for his work as a labor leader and as a theater organizer.

Born on August 27, 1905, in Brooksville, Mississippi, O'Neal was the sixth of eight children born to Ransome James and Minnie Bell Thompson O'Neal. O'Neal and his siblings enjoyed a middle class upbringing. Ransome O'Neal ran a general store called R. J. O'Neal and Son, a business begun by his father, Ransome O'Neal, Sr. Both Ransome and Minnie O'Neal had successful careers as well–respected teachers in the black community of Brooksville. They left their positions, however, in order to devote more time to raising a family and to running the family's general store. Renee Simmons noted in *Frederick Douglass O'Neal* that the two former teachers

Frederick D. O'Neal

stressed the value of a good education, an idea that Frederick O'Neal emphasized throughout his long career in the dramatic arts. He believed that "a good actor never stops learning."

Despite the racial tensions and discrimination that plagued Mississippi in the early part of the twentieth century, O'Neal described the 14 years he spent growing up there as happy ones. Simmons credits the future actor's positive attitude and "strong family structure" with enabling him to combat the racist attitudes of the Deep South. O'Neal, who felt called to the stage at the age of eight when he gave a recitation at the Brooksville School during one of the school's monthly performances for teachers and parents, received invaluable encouragement and advice from his father about pursuing his dreams and coping with racism. According to Simmons, Ransome O'Neal offered to help his son but cautioned:

> The only thing I ask of you is that you be the best in your particular field. . . . And if you are not successful, just remember it's not because you are a Negro, it's because you didn't take advantage of every opportunity. All of us have some kind of problem to overcome.

Perhaps this advice helped the 14–year–old O'Neal cope with his father's unexpected death on February 4, 1919, and his mother's subsequent decision to move the family to St. Louis, Missouri, in 1920. There they joined two of Frederick's older brothers, John and Harvey. O'Neal recalled in Simmon's work that his family had owned a great deal of property in Brooksville which they sold prior to the move to St. Louis. This change in his family's financial circumstances and location did not prevent him from pursuing his dream of becoming an actor nor from getting an education. His new job as a file clerk for Meyer Brothers Drug Company required him to switch from day to night school in order to earn his high school diploma in 1922.

Throughout the 1920s O'Neal continued to hold a variety of jobs and pursued his dream. During these years he worked as a clerk, farmer, bellhop, houseman, blacksmith, cowpuncher, and automobile salesman. He also became something of an entrepreneur. In 1926 he a man named Roy Glover started an advertising company. Three years later O'Neal struck out on his own to create the Arrow Parcel Delivery Service, whose slogan was "Service to the Point." In 1935 he teamed up with Louis White and established the short–lived Bootcraft Valet Service. From 1936 to 1937 he held the position of executive secretary for the St. Louis Negro Businessman's League. Acting remained his true interest, though the experience he gained from his various enterprises no doubt proved useful to him when be became a founding member of two significant African American theater groups, St. Louis's Aldridge Players and the American Negro Theatre.

Founds the Aldridge Players

In St. Louis O'Neal pursued his interest in theater and discovered his gift for managing and organizing theater groups. In 1920 he joined the St. Louis branch of the National Urban League because this group put on a play each year at the Old Odeon Theatre. Simmons wrote that the league's goals included "[sponsoring] the works of local Negro artists and other cultural affairs," improving race relations, and encouraging black theater artists. Among the plays O'Neal performed in as a member of the league were Shakespeare's *As You Like It* and *Black Majesty,* playwright John Vandercooks's version of the life of Henri Christophe, who rose from slavery to become the emperor of Haiti from 1811 to 1820. These often well–received productions inspired O'Neal to found the Aldridge Players in 1927 so the Urban League group could perform more frequently. The head of the league, John Clark, and Annie Turnbo Malone, the black hair care magnate, assisted him in this endeavor; O'Neal served as the group's executive director. He chose its name to honor the nineteenth–century African American Shakespearean actor Ira Aldridge; it later became known as the Negro Little Theatre of St. Louis. The group disbanded in 1940.

Like the Urban League, the Aldridge Players believed in the value of community service. In addition to staging about three plays a year, the group performed at the St. Louis YMCA as well as on college campuses, in high schools, in a Missouri prison, and for other community organizations in the St. Louis area. They also raised money for children's homes, college scholarships, and depression relief funds by holding an annual banquet and sponsored, along with other organizations, high school drama festivals and tournaments. O'Neal's energy, enthusiasm, and devotion to his profession and community accounts for much of the Aldridge Players' success. In an interview with Renee Simmons, Mercedes Spiller, a former member of the Aldridge Players, praised O'Neal's efforts to serve the African American people: "He has always been the person he is now. . .never waivered from his goals. . .determined to succeed and take others with him." The Aldridge Players were committed to supporting playwrights who wrote about African Americans and often performed plays written by members of its writers' group. Among the works the group presented were Georgia Douglas Johnson's *Plumes* and Paul Green's *Your Fiery Furnace* and *No'Count Boy.*

Cofounds the American Negro Theatre

In 1936 O'Neal met Harlem Renaissance writer Zora Neale Hurston who had stopped in St. Louis while on a cross–country lecture tour. Hurston advised him that if he wanted to become accomplished in the theater he needed to go to New York. O'Neal accepted her advice and reluctantly left his family, friends, and the Aldridge Players and moved to New York. He worked as a laboratory assistant during the day and took acting classes at night at the New Theatre School, from 1936 to 1940. He also received instruction at the American Theatre Wing and took private classes with Theodore Komissarzhevsky, Lem Ward, John Bond, Doris Sorrel, and Benjamin Zemach.

Although Hurston's advice proved sound, opportunities for aspiring African American actors were not as plentiful as O'Neal might have hoped. For example, political issues led to the end of the Negro Unit of the Federal Theatre Project because some politicians perceived the organization as a Communist–affiliated, leftist group. He joined the Rose McClendon Players, which, like the Federal Theatre Project, folded in 1939. In 1940 he and playwright Abram Hill founded the American Negro Theatre, whose acronym, "ANT" underscored the members' industriousness. O'Neal and Hill envisioned ANT as a collaborative theater group that would serve its artists and the Harlem community. Membership in ANT was open to people of all races, creeds, colors, and nationalities who passed an audition. Simmons wrote that O'Neal described ANT as "a theatre with a Black point of view. . .to involve the Harlem community as patrons, not necessarily as participants. Although the theatre intended initially to reflect the Harlem community, ANT never intended to be a segregated theatre." Throughout his career O'Neal continued to protest all forms of discrimination and segregation. During his years with ANT, O'Neal appeared in several of its productions, including *Three's a Family, Anna Lucasta, Henri Christophe, On Striver's Row,* and *Natural Man.* When *Anna Lucasta* moved to Broadway, O'Neal recreated his role as Frank and received rave reviews as well as the New York Critics Circle Award and the first Clarence Derwent Award for the best supporting male performance of the 1944 season. *Anna Lucasta,* with O'Neal in the role of Frank, was also performed in London and at the Civic Theatre in Chicago. Simmons observed that "O'Neal never forgot his obligation to the American Negro Theatre." ANT, which fostered the careers of Ruby Dee, Sidney Poitier, Harry Belafonte, Earle Hyman, Alvin Childress, Isabel Sanford, and Ossie Davis, among others, closed in 1951.

In addition to creating a successful theater company during his early years in New York, O'Neal married Charlotte Talbot Hainey, whom he met in 1941. The couple wed in 1942, and celebrated their fiftieth wedding anniversary a few months before the actor's death. They had no children. Shortly after his marriage, O'Neal was drafted into the U.S. Army. He was stationed at Fort Dix, New Jersey, and later at Fort Huachuca in Arizona. At the end of this service Private O'Neal received an honorable discharge, returned to New York, and continued his association with ANT.

Moves to Film and Television

In 1949 O'Neal moved from stage to screen, appearing in the Twentieth Century Fox film *Pinky,* directed by Eliza Kazan and produced by Darryl Zanuck. The movie also featured actresses Jeanne Crain and Ethel Waters. His success in *Pinky* led to roles in nine other movies, including a film adaptation of *Anna Lucasta* in 1959 with O'Neal once again playing the role of Frank. He also had a starring role in *Take a Giant Step* (1959). His co–stars in the film included Ruby Dee, Johnny Nash, and Beah Richards. He also appeared in *No Way Out; Tarzan's Peril; Something of Value; The Sins of Rachel Cade;* and *Free, White and 21. Strategy of Terror,* his last movie, was produced in 1969. His list of television credits include a CBS production of James Weldon Johnson's *God's Trombones,* a 1957 episode of *The Phil Silvers Show,* a 1957 Hallmark Hall of Fame version of *The Green Pastures,* and a 1959 production of the Langston Hughes play *Simply Heavenly.* From 1961 to 1962 he played a policeman on the NBC sitcom *Car 54, Where Are You?* His character was teamed with African American comedian Nipsey Russell. He made his last television appearance in a 1967 episode of *Tarzan* but continued to work on stage until the mid–1970s. O'Neal might have done even more work as an actor, particularly during the 1950s when his career had begun to take off, but he, like so many other American artists, was blacklisted during the anticommunist witch hunt led by Eugene McCarthy and the House Un–American Activities Committee.

Becomes President of Actor's Equity Association

Despite McCarthyism, O'Neal enjoyed a productive career as an actor, as his long list of stage, film, and television credits demonstrates. He also had a profound impact on the entertainment world through his efforts as a union activist and leader. O'Neal joined the Actor's Equity Association (AEA) in 1944. Prior to becoming its first—and to this date, only—African American president, a position he held from 1964 to 1973, he held several offices within the organization and served on numerous committees. Many of these committees addressed the concerns of African Americans, including the Hotel Accommodations Committee and Equity League Committee on Negro Employment. The 1964 Nominating Committee initially overlooked O'Neal, who was then the organization's first vice–president, for the office of president. Ordinarily the AEA's first vice–president's nomination for president had been automatic. This oversight prompted several members of the committee to file a minority report in protest of the committee's decision. As a result of their efforts, O'Neal's name was placed on the ballot. He received 1,872 votes, 282 more than were cast for his opponent, Eddie Weston. Before winning this election, O'Neal had also been serving for three years as the president of the Negro Actor's Guild, a position he resigned when he became the president of AEA.

A black man becoming president of an organization that was 96 percent white was no small feat. In a 1964 interview with *Ebony* magazine shortly after his election, O'Neal insisted that he won because of his experience, ability, and knowledge of the organization and not because of race: "The fact that I'm a Negro didn't play a decisive part in my election." Beginning with his early days with ANT, O'Neal had earned a reputation for being a even–tempered mediator, a skill he continued to put to good use before and after assuming the presidency of AEA. His patience sometimes frustrated his younger African American colleagues. Quoted by Simmons, one young, unnamed black actor told the *New York Times*:

> Sometimes I get mad at him. He's usually a mediator when the Negroes want a champion. We, the younger firebrands, feel we don't want to hear the other side when we're being burned. I didn't vote for him, but he's very qualified in general. It's a great thing for the union as such and he'll straighten out a lot of things and maybe help strengthen the union on the civil rights issue as well.

O'Neal did strive to end discrimination and segregation in the entertainment industry. In 1944, as chair of the AEA's Hotel Accommodations Committee, O'Neal worked to improve the housing situation for black actors performing with traveling groups. He also protested the existence of segregated theaters such as Washington's National Theatre, which permitted black actors to perform but refused to allow blacks to sit in the audience. By 1949 O'Neal's efforts had begun to pay off when some theaters in New York and Washington changed their policies. During the 1950s he wrote several articles for *Equity* magazine that addressed the issue of casting African Americans in roles that accurately represented their participation in American life and did not rely on stereotypes and caricatures. Realizing that African Americans were often overlooked for parts other than those that specifically called for a black actor, he also encouraged the entertainment industry to base their casting decisions on actors' abilities rather than on their race. He also became AEA's black theater historian and wrote articles for *Equity* that chronicled the contributions blacks had made to the dramatic arts.

This energetic, talented, and altruistic actor received many awards during his lifetime, among them the Motion Picture Critics' Award for *Anna Lucasta* in 1959, the Ira Aldridge Award, presented to him by the Association for the Study of Negro Life and History in 1963, the Negro Trade Union Leadership Council Humanitarian Award in 1974, and the Frederick Douglass Award in 1975. He was named NAACP Man of the Year in 1979, and received a special Paul Robeson Citation Award in 1985, and the Black Filmmakers Hall of Fame Award and Tribute in 1990. Also in 1990 the John F. Kennedy Center made O'Neal an American Theatre Fellow. He has also received several honorary doctorates.

On August 25, 1992, Frederick Douglass O'Neal died at his Manhattan home after a long bout with cancer. On September 15, 1992, many of his friends and colleagues gathered at New York's Shubert Theatre to celebrate the 86–year life of the man many called the "gentle giant" because of his physical stature and calm disposition. During this service, actor Ossie Davis, a former member of ANT, offered a tribute to O'Neal. Simmons quoted him in 1996. He said:

> The theatre into which I came had very specific qualities which, fortunately, it no longer has. America had fought a brutal, vicious war on the subject of racism. And there were a lot of people at that time who wanted to do something about it. . . . The thrust was led by people like Abe Hill and Fred O'Neal. . . . Fred O'Neal was always in the forefront of the struggle.

O'Neal's courage, determination, and vision of a world free from discrimination make him a giant not only in the entertainment industry, but also in the battle for justice and equality for all people.

REFERENCES

"Actors' New Boss: Frederick O'Neal Heads Actors' Equity Assn." *Ebony* 19 (June 1964): 58–63.

Current Biography Yearbook. New York: H. W. Wilson, 1946.

"Frederick O'Neal." http://www.bobwest.com/ncaat/oneal.html (last updated May 16, 1996).

Low, W. Augustus, and Virgil A. Clift, eds. *Encyclopedia of Black America.* New York: McGraw Hill Book Co., 1981.

Obituary. *Jet* 82 (14 September 1992): 60.

Simmons, Renee A. *Frederick Douglass O'Neal: Pioneer of the Actor's Equity Association.* New York: Garland Publishing, 1996.

Williams, Michael W., ed. *African American Encyclopedia.* Vol. 4. North Bellmore, NY: Marshall Cavendish Corp., 1993.

Candis LaPrade

Roi Ottley

(1906–1960)

Journalist, writer

Roi Ottley was objective in his writing, optimistic about race relations, and a champion of black people. In addition to his work as a writer of fiction and nonfiction, he was a foreign correspondent and journalist for the black and white press in America. He was the first African American journalist to receive a Rosenwald Fellowship, and was renowned for his contribution to interracial understanding.

Roy Vincent Ottley was born August 2, 1908 in New York City to Beatrice Brisbane and Jerome P. Ottley Sr. and educated at St. Bonaventure College (1926–27), the University of Michigan, and St. John's School of Law. In addition, he studied play writing at Columbia University (1934–35), article writing at the City College of New York, and black folk literature under James Weldon Johnson at New York University (1935–36).

While studying, Ottley decided writing would be his life's work. Following this decision, he worked for seven successive years for the *Amsterdam Star–News* as a reporter (1930), columnist (1932–37), and by 1935 editor, a position he held for two years. He was editor of the New York City Writers Project in 1937, and from 1937 to 1941 he was a freelance writer for such magazines as the *New York Times, Liberty, Mercury, Ebony, Common Ground, Travel, Collier, The Nation,* and *New Republic.* He was reporter for both the Columbia Broadcasting System and the British Broadcasting System in 1943. As his career expanded, in 1944 he became a foreign correspondent for *Liberty* magazine and the *New York PM* and in 1945 for the *Pittsburgh Courier* and the Overseas News Agency. With the *Liberty* assignment, he became the first African American war correspondent with a roving assignment and no deadline for a major white daily paper and a nationally known magazine. His career experiences grew to include that of columnist for the *Chicago Tribune* from 1945 to 1960 and publicity director for the National CIO War Relief Committee in 1943. He was also a social worker from 1932 to 1937.

Roi Ottley

Experiences of a Journalist

Ottley's overseas reporting included the Normandy invasion, the death of Mussolini, and the Arab French conflict in Syria. During his tenure abroad, there were interviews with prominent political leaders, such as Colonial Secretary Amery Count Carlo Sforza (a prominent Italian antifascist), Charles de Gaulle, and Sir Stafford Cripps and with religious leaders such as Pius XI. In the United States, his interviews included Gov. Herman Talmadge and Samuel Green, the Grand Dragon of the Ku Klux Klan (1949). As a writer for the *Tribune,* he wrote an analytical series addressing black issues in the 1950s.

As a war correspondent, Ottley traveled over 30,000 miles through Europe and Africa, visiting such destinations as Wales, Brittany, Normandy, France, Scotland, Belgium, Casablanca, Algiers, and Oran. In his travels he interviewed the leaders, but also met and lived with the common people to ascertain conditions, attitudes, hopes, and aspirations. His assessment of the war situation was evident in a 1944 interview with Llewellyn Ransom of the *People's Voice* following a six–month tour of the European war front. He said, "Imperialism has been shaken to its very roots because the world convulsion has dislocated society and changed human values, the darker races of the colonial world are making broad demands and getting them." In the same interview, he discussed race relations on the front and the vital role of blacks.

Later, Ottley's articles summed up his trip and the lessons it had taught him; article subjects and titles are indicative of some of the issues, such as the undervaluation of blacks, the universal oppression of people of color, and the desire of blacks to fight on the front line—for full participation in the war. These titles included "There's No Race Problem in the Foxholes" (January 1, 1945), "No Self–Rule in Sight for World's Colonial Peoples" (January 2, 1945), and "Negro GI Doesn't Want to Sit This One Out: An Open Letter to the War Department" (January 7, 1945). His reporting from the front includes an article in the December 1946 *Pittsburgh Courier,* "Tan GI's Attacked Unfairly" (December 28, 1946), in which he talks of a German scheme to remove all African Americans from Germany.

In 1956, as a writer for the *Chicago Tribune* after the war, Ottley wrote a series of articles on migration and one on voting. He won journalistic praise for his series on the migration of African Americans to northern cities in the 1950s. He asserted that they fled because of the racism and, even though prejudice existed in the North, there were more opportunities to overcome these acts and prosper. Discussed also in the April 29, 1956 Sunday *Tribune* are the problems and solutions which result from this flight from a "feudal to a modern way of life." He underscored the patriotism of the African American by citing that this mass movement was almost totally within, not outside the United States. Another of his series of articles addressed the political— the African American voter, the influences, the trends, the potential, the issues, and the changes in the new African American voter. The series was based on a political sampling of all strata of Chicago's African American community.

In addition, Ottley wrote human interest articles in which he presented African American achievers in Chicago. Among these were Leonard J. Livingston, president of the Jackson Mutual Life Insurance Company, which grew out of a burial society he and others began; Ottaway Owens Morris, the assistant general secretary of the metropolitan YMCA and the first black to be in a policy–making position in the Y's nearly 120 years in Chicago; J. Wesley Jones, one of the organizers of the National Association of Negro Musicians; and Philip C. Williams, obstetrician and gynecologist and the first African American admitted to membership in the Chicago Gynecological Society. Additionally, he wrote articles, some satirical, for the *Negro Digest* in the 1950s. Some of these were "Great Negro Lovers," published in the February 1951 issue, in which he said, "some of the greatest lovers of history have been darker than the much–ballyhooed Hollywood concept and their amours have been legion." Other examples of his satirical writing are, "What's Wrong with Negro Women," "Understanding White Folks," and "Behold the Innkeeper."

Writes of a New World

Ottley's travels, interviews, and articles addressing social subjects led him to write four nonfiction books. At the time of his death, he was nearing the completion of his first novel, *White Marble Lady,* which was published in 1965. His first book, *New World A–Coming: Inside Black America* (1944) earned him the distinction of being the first African American journalist to receive a Rosenwald Fellowship and made him the first African American to have a book published in the Houghton Mifflin Life–in–America series. The book also brought him recognition for his contribution to interracial understanding by both the *Chicago Defender* and the Schomburg Collection in New York City, and a radio program *New World A–Coming,* designed to promote racial harmony for which he won the Peabody Award. The book, published before a wave of race riots swept through American cities, presented African American history, problems, and hopes. Ottley believed that solving the problems of African Americans would solve the problems of all minority groups in the United States. He also felt that whites were not apathetic regarding the plight of minorities, but ignorant of the facts. He pointed out that the African Americans' desire to participate fully in American life and that their battle for equality was one shared and faced by races around the world. *New World A–Coming* was also published in Brazil and in England under the title *Inside Black America.*

In his second book, *Black Odyssey: The Story of the Negro in America* (1948), Ottley suggested the way in which African Americans respond to society directly impacted how the world reacted to them. Through records and interviews from both America and Europe, he chronicled the origin of African American slavery and other historical occurrences by fusing the involved individuals and events.

Ottley's *No Green Pasture* (1951), published in England in 1952, detailed his journeys abroad and cautioned people not to believe that Europe lacks racism. His last nonfiction book was *Lonely Warrior: The Life and Times of Robert S. Abbott* (1955), a biography of the founder and editor of the *Chicago Defender.* Robert Sengstacke Abbott is viewed by many as having initiated the existence of the modern African American press. Ottley showed him to be multifaceted: one who loved his race, provided a forum for young people, loved and wrote history, and called for the destruction of American race prejudice.

Ottley died in October of 1960, leaving behind his wife Alice L. Dungey Ottley, a native of New Orleans whom he married in 1951, and daughter, Lynne. The excerpt from a review written by John Chamberlain of *New World A–Coming,* which appeared in his obituary in the *New York Times,* is true of all of his writing. "He writes a vigorous prose, mingling history, humor, irony, drama and sober reflection . . . that explains the status and the wholly reasonable demands of the Negroes."

REFERENCES

Black Writers. 2nd ed. Detroit: Gale Research, 1994.
Current Biography Yearbook. New York: H. W. Wilson, 1943.
"*New World A–Comin*' Author Home from Wars." *People's Voice,* 1944, in the Moorland–Spingarn Research Center, Howard University, Washington, DC.
Obituary. *New York Times,* October 1, 1960.
Ottley, Roi. "Great Negro Lovers." *Negro Digest* 9 (February 1951): 37–43.

COLLECTIONS

Biographical information on Roi Ottley is in the vertical files in the Special Collections Department, Fisk University, and in the Moorland–Spingarn Research Center, Howard University.

Helen R. Houston

Anthony Overton
(1865–1946)
Entrepreneur, banker

In 1927 the *Chicago Bee* reported that Overton Hygienic Products Company employed over 150 African American people in its home and branch offices and manufactured 250 products—some for other countries including Egypt, Liberia, and Japan. Several years after its founding in 1922, the Douglass National Bank enjoyed deposits of $1,507,336. Victory Life Insurance Company, founded in 1923, enjoyed assets of $167,000 with a surplus of $157,000 and an income of $14,719 by the end of 1924. Within the first three years of operation, the insurance company opened branches in eight states and Washington, D.C. The man behind these companies was Anthony Overton.

Anthony Overton was born to Anthony and Martha DeBerry Overton on March 21, 1865, in Monroe, Louisiana. He attended public schools in Louisiana until leaving for Kansas, where he entered Washburn College in Topeka. In 1888 Overton received his bachelor of law degree from the University of Kansas Law School. On June 14 of the same year he married Clara M. Gregg, a resident of Lawrence, Kansas, in her hometown. The couple had four children, Everett Van, Mabel Helena (Fowler), Eva (Lewis), and Frances Madison (Hill).

Upon being admitted to the Kansas state bar in 1889, Overton began practicing law in November. Shortly thereafter, he received an appointment to preside on the bench of the Municipal Court of Shawnee County, Kansas. He retained this position for one year before moving to Oklahoma City in 1892, where he purchased a general store. While working as a merchant, Overton successfully ran for political office in 1892. He secured the position of treasurer of Kingfisher County, Oklahoma.

In 1898 the Overtons relocated to Kansas City, Missouri, where Overton founded Overton Hygienic Products Company with an initial investment capital of $1,960. The first product manufactured by the company was Hygienic Baking Powder. During the first nine months of business the company lost an average of $40 a month. Overton worked as a traveling salesman through this period, and his interpersonal skills and business savvy proved valuable, when the loss was soon recovered. In 1903 disaster struck as floods destroyed the business district of Kansas City. Overton Hygienic Products Company was not spared, and although its financial crisis was not known outside the firm, the company went bankrupt. After rebuilding, Overton decided to move his company to Chicago, which he did in 1911.

Chicago proved to be the right city for Overton Hygienic Products Company, as consumers seemed receptive to the new products that the company manufactured. The success was in part because of the racial segregation which existed and which forced African Americans to patronize primarily African American businesses. Nonetheless, consumers enjoyed the high quality of Overton's products such as flavor extracts, shoe polish, and toiletries that the company began producing. Under the name High–Brown Products, Overton Hygienic Products Company began manufacturing a full line of perfumes and cosmetics. Overton's integrity and racial pride compelled him to decline from manufacturing some popular items of the day including skin bleach and other such toiletries.

By mid–1912, Overton Hygienic Products Company had made $117,000 and had a product line that produced 52 items. The company's success enabled Overton to employ five salaried African Americans to market the products. Three years later the company was reported to employ 32 people full–time and to produce 62 products while holding capital of $268,000. Overton detailed the path to entrepreneurship in his 1915 book, *Successful Salesmanship.*

Anthony Overton

In 1916 Overton founded the *Half–Century,* a monthly variety magazine targeting primarily educated, conservative black women readers who enjoyed middle class status. The magazine contained general information, news reports, and items of cultural interest. Some sources suggest that the magazine was the precursor to *Ebony.* In *Half–Century* Overton reflected the concerns of Chicago's older black residents and questioned the wisdom of northern migration by massive numbers of blacks. Overton encouraged racial independence, race pride, and self–help for blacks. During the ''Red Summer'' of 1919, Overton was greatly distressed by the vicious racial violence directed against African Americans, especially since Chicago saw the most violent race riot. In his publication, he protested the violent episodes, and urged African Americans to join the NAACP as a vehicle of change.

By 1920 Overton Hygienic Products company grossed $1 million annually. The success of his cosmetics line put Overton in direct competition with other beauty supply greats of the day, including Madame C. J. Walker, whose business was based in Indianapolis, and Annie Turnbo–Malone, whose companies were based in St. Louis and Chicago.

With the success of his company well underway, Overton decided to diversify his business holdings by entering another field. After the completion in 1922–23 of the $250,000 Overton Building at 36th and State Streets, Overton began renting office space to professional African Americans. Among his clients were Walter T. Bailey, Chicago's first African

American architect, and the Theater Owners Booking Association, which represented and obtained performance engagements for African American talent. While these clients were important, the one client with which Overton had the most contact was the Douglass National Bank, which was probably situated on the first floor.

Helps Found Bank

Assisting Pearl Chavers, Overton helped to found Douglass National Bank in 1922. Douglass National Bank was one of the first African American–owned banks in Illinois. Another African American businessman named Jesse Binga opened Chicago's first African American–owned bank in 1921, but Binga's bank operated under a state charter while Overton's operated under a national charter. Douglass National Bank and other African American–owned banks filled a void in the banking industry. With Overton as the bank's president, business burgeoned. In its first year of business, receipts for deposits at the bank totaled $56,030. Never content with the extent of his endeavors, Overton decided to invade another field of business.

Overton founded Victory Life Insurance Company in 1923 with the goal of providing profitable employment opportunities for African Americans, creating estates, and providing money for widows and orphans. A staunch believer in dividend reinvesting, he invested his dividends in real estate through mortgages on the homes of Chicago's African Americans. This business move was probably carried out in cooperation with Overton's Great Northern Realty Company—which he had established sometime earlier—as the real estate industry in Chicago boomed between 1919 and 1929. By April of 1924, the company enjoyed a capital of $100,000 with a surplus of $50,000. Seven months later, assets at Victory Life Insurance Company totaled $167,000 and the company enjoyed a surplus of $157,000. During the same year, Dr. P. M. H. Savory and Dr. C. B. Powell, two members of New York's affluent African American society, visited two of Overton's businesses, Victory Life Insurance Company and Douglass National Bank. Impressed with what he saw, Savory invested $3,750 for 50 shares in Victory Life.

Overton's companies changed dramatically in 1925. With Overton as president, Victory Life opened offices in Kentucky, Maryland, Missouri, New Jersey, Ohio, Texas, Washington, D.C., and West Virginia. In April of the same year the *Half–Century* was discontinued and replaced by the *Chicago Bee.* Readership of the *Chicago Bee* was concentrated primarily on Chicago's South Side. The newspaper was in competition with the *Chicago Defender,* a publication that appealed to the masses. The *Chicago Bee,* which criticized the practices of the underclass, captured the attention to his involvement with the *Chicago Bee,* Overton financed two other publications, the *Chicago Whip* newspaper and *Champion* magazine.

Overton received good news in 1927. Bradstreet, an independent credit rating service, assessed the worth of Overton Hygienic Products Company at upwards of $1 million. Victory Life Insurance Company had also gained permission to practice business in the state of New York. It was the first Illinois company to gain admittance in over 20 years. This move may have been engineered by the influential doctors Savory and Powell. Between 1927 and February of 1932, the insurance company conducted $7 million of business transactions in New York alone.

By the end of the decade, America began to recognize the achievements of Anthony Overton. In 1927 Overton became the first businessman to be awarded the Spingarn Medal by the NAACP for helping to improve the lives of African Americans. He also won the Harmon Business Award given by New York's Harmon Foundation in 1928.

Business continued to flourish for Overton. Nineteen twenty–nine saw deposits at Douglass National Bank total $1,507,336. In the same year Overton erected the *Chicago Bee* Building as a newspaper office and an apartment building. This happy time would not last long. As a result of the stock market crash, Americans became fearful for their financial institutions. African Americans were no different. Douglass National Bank survived three frantic bouts with the bank's depositors and investors, but in 1931, a year prior to the bank's closing, deposits plummeted to $542,455. When it closed involuntarily in 1932, depositors received 38 percent of their holdings. This was the highest amount paid by any bank in the nation.

Control of Victory Life Insurance Company changed hands. In April 1933 Powell and Savory seized the reins of the company and changed the name to Victory Mutual Life Insurance Company. Overton conducted the operations of Overton Hygienic Products Company and the *Chicago Bee* newspaper from the *Chicago Bee* Building after abandoning the Overton Building. He continued to produce the newspaper into the 1940s.

Despite the turmoil that destroyed his companies, Overton's prudent financial decisions enabled him to spend his remaining days in considerable comfort. During his lifetime Overton had pursued a variety of interests, including politics but he excelled in the business world, building a business empire called the Overton Great Bee Victory Douglass Syndicate, or OGBVD. Aside from being active in business pursuits, Overton was a board member of the Chicago Urban League and the Young Men's Christian Association (YMCA). He was a 33rd degree Mason and held memberships in Knights of Pythias, Appomattox Club of Chicago, Sigma Pi Phi (the Boulé), and Alpha Phi Alpha Fraternity. He was an unpretentious man whose personal lifestyle reflected his modesty. He used practically all of his wealth to develop his enterprises. Overton died in Chicago on July 3, 1946.

REFERENCES

Adams, Russell. *Great Negroes Past and Present.* 3rd ed. Chicago: Afro–Am Pub. Co., 1969.

Bontemps, Arna. *100 Years of Negro Freedom.* New York: Dodd Mead, 1961.

Ingham, John N., and Lynne B. Feldman. *African–American Business Leaders: A Biographical Dictionary.* Westport, CT: Greenwood Press, 1994.
"Personal." *Journal of Negro History* 32 (July 1947): 394–96.
Poinsett, Alex. "Unsung Black Business Giants." *Ebony* 45 (March 1990): 96–100.
National Cyclopedia of American Biography. New York: James T. White, 1965.
Who's Who in Colored America. 5th ed. Brooklyn: Thomas Yenser, 1940.

Nicole L. Bailey Williams

Jesse Owens
(1913–1980)
Olympic track star, entrepreneur

Called the "world's fastest human," Olympic athlete and winner of four gold medals in 1936, Jesse Owens became a legend in his own time. He overcame crippling poverty, segregation, and racial discrimination to soar to the heights of his Olympic aspirations. Americans cheered, but when the games were over, Owens was forced to struggle in order to live the American dream.

James Cleveland Owens was born September 12, 1913, in Oakville, Alabama. His father, Henry Owens, was a sharecropper, and Emma Fitzgerald Owens, his mother, took in washing and ironed clothes in order to earn extra money. But the family lived in extreme poverty. Owens was the tenth of eleven children consisting of four sisters and six brothers.

As a child, J. C., as he was then called, was chronically ill. Inadequate housing, food, and clothing were injurious to Owens's health. Every winter he suffered from pneumonia and was never treated by a physician as there was no money for medical care. In the segregated town of Oakville, school for black children was a pastime. "We could only go to school when there wasn't anything [else] going on," Owens recalled in William Baker's *Jesse Owens.* Not surprisingly, he faced an academically troubled future. Owens's mother, naturally optimistic and enthusiastic in her outlook, encouraged Owens to dream. She also prompted her husband to move the family up North in order to provide a safer environment for her children.

From J.C. to Jesse

The move to Cleveland, Ohio, changed Owens's life. His father found work in the steel mills, as did his three brothers. Owens worked in a shoe repair shop after school and on weekends. For the first time in his life, he attended school regularly. He enrolled at Bolton Elementary School just three blocks from his house. As the now famous story goes, when the teacher asked Owens's name, he replied "J. C.," but she misunderstood his southern accent and thought he said Jesse. He did not possess the courage to correct her.

Jesse Owens

Owens later attended Fairmount Junior High School. Fairmount was integrated, mostly by immigrants and southern migrants like Owens. Emphasis was not on academics but rather on citizenship, manners, and behavior. This type of education—Americanization, as it were—would have a lasting effect on Owens, although it would not see him through the rigors of college.

Fairmount affected his life in other ways as well, for here he met two important people whose friendship lasted a lifetime. One was a pretty young girl named Minnie Ruth Solomon, whom he later married. The other was a white physical education teacher named Charles Riley. This teacher–turned–coach saw in the young student the talent Owens had once observed in his father. While Owens appreciated the things Coach Riley taught him, he recalled in *The Jesse Owens Story,* "The true beginning of my running really lay with my father. He was an expert on leg exercises because he was the champion runner in our county. . . . I used to watch him . . . for he had legs like no human being I'd ever seen and a way of running that resembled a cat." Owens would also learn to run like a cat, and Riley's training helped perfect the technique. Quoted by William Baker, Riley told Owens to run "like the ground was burning fire."

When Owens entered East Technical High School, Riley continued coaching him. The education that should have taken place at the high school did not. Instead, Owens received vocational training. Owens's homeroom teacher, Ivan Green, took an interest in him as a track and field star, but not as a pupil. Still, Owens was the only child from his large family to graduate from high school.

In 1929, Henry Owens was hit by a car. While he only sustained a broken leg from the accident, he was off work for three months and was required to take a physical examination before returning. The examination revealed that he was blind in one eye. This diagnosis forced him into chronic unemployment at the beginning of the Great Depression. His children dropped out of school in order to work. All hopes were pinned on Jesse Owens.

On August 8, 1932, Owens's first daughter, Gloria Shirley, was born to 16–year–old Ruth Solomon, who dropped out of school and found a job working in Wagner's Beauty Shop. According to Owens, he and Ruth secretly married in Erie, Pennsylvania, in the spring of 1935.

On May 20, 1933, Owens took the Interscholastic finals with a long jump measuring 24 feet, 3 and 3/4 inches, breaking the world record by more than 3 inches. In June of 1933, at the National Interscholastic Championship Track Meet at Stagg Field in Chicago, Owens jumped 24 feet, 5/8 inches in the long jump, ran the 220 race in 20.7 seconds, and ran the 100–yard dash in 9.4 seconds, which tied the world record. East Technical High School won the meet with 54 points, of which Owens contributed 30. Owens came home to a hero's welcome. The city of Cleveland greeted him with a victory parade. Because of his stellar athletic record, colleges from across the country tried to recruit Owens. Although his academic record was deficient, no one seemed to care as long as he kept running hard and fast.

The Buckeye Bullet

Despite all his offers from various colleges, Owens felt the need to be close to home. Charles Riley wanted Owens to attend the University of Michigan, and the black press informed Owens that Ohio State University was blatantly racist and being sued by the NAACP on behalf of two black students it refused to house. In the end the arrangement for him to work three jobs to pay his tuition and support his family led him to enroll in his state university.

Owens entered Ohio State University in October. Owens was barred from living on campus because of his race, but lived in a boarding house with other black students on East 11th Avenue, about a quarter–mile from the campus. High Street restaurants refused to serve blacks, and they were only admitted to one movie theater in the slum section of the town, where they were restricted to the back section of the balcony.

Owens rarely discussed the treatment he experienced in Columbus, but his classmates remembered. Charles Beetham, Mel Walker, and William Heintz recalled in Baker's *Jesse Owens* that Columbus was "a cracker town, just like Jackson, Mississippi." One event, however, stuck in Owens's memory. In *Blackthink* he recalled:

> I do remember riding in the Ford that day and not being able to keep down the bitterness that all the Negroes had to be in one car. Not that it wasn't natural in a way. . . . We'd won a lot of races for our team. I myself had set four world's records. . . . We were good enough to compete alongside the white athletes, but often not good enough to take showers with them afterwards or to ride with them on the way to the meets.

The *Chicago Defender* had warned Owens about Ohio and its university. But what made Jesse Owens a hero was not just his athletic ability but his unique way of looking at the world. Baker said that he was always able to see "a flower on the dung heap and cultivate it to his advantage." Owens turned discrimination into an opportunity to study almost without interruption. But in spite of his efforts, by the end of March of 1934, he was on academic probation.

Instead of securing the personal attention Owens needed to succeed academically, his coach arranged for him to address local school and service organizations every Wednesday at noon. The pattern of behavior Owens developed in order to make these public addresses would characterize his entire life. He learned to correct his bad grammar and to cover his limited experience with personal anecdotes, charm, and wit.

In addition to public speaking skills, Owens began to develop a personal magnetism, a charismatic personality. Under Coach Snyder's directions, he altered his running style. The Owens trademark was perfected. It was serious and quiet, without any hint of demonstrative gesturing; it was smooth and graceful, with Owens appearing to glide to victory. Owens's speed earned him the nickname "the Buckeye Bullet."

The Road to Gold

On May 5, 1935, Owens broke five world records at a meet held at the University of Michigan at Ann Arbor. Many track and field enthusiasts think of May 5, 1935, as the greatest day in track and field history. According to Baker, because of his achievements that day, Owens earned the title "the world's fastest human."

Owens returned to campus in the fall as elected captain of the Ohio State University Track Squad. He was the first black ever to captain a Big Ten team. There was only one problem facing Owens: his grades had not improved. Working toward a degree in physical education, he had managed to avoid rigorous mathematics and science courses for which he had no preparation; still, he was making little progress toward the degree. Owens, now with his name in record books, had to live up to his reputation.

The 1936 Olympics in Berlin was plagued by a boycott movement dating back to 1933. The Amateur Athletic Union (AAU) delegates voted to withhold American athletes from the Games unless the Nazis altered their treatment of German Jews. The American Olympic Committee disagreed with the conclusion of the AAU, insisting that it was wrong to mix politics and sports. The 1936 Games caused anger and protest not only from American Jews but from others as well. The black press pointed out that Nazi racism affected more than just the Jews. Blacks in Germany married to German women lived under legal and social discrimination. All the rhetoric surrounding the boycott revealed one irony: racist attitudes and practices in the United States were little different from the fascism of Nazi Germany. On December 8, 1935, the AAU reversed its earlier decision and voted for the American athletes to participate.

Owens had other problems to deal with. In December the AAU informed him that his name had been removed from the list of ten finalists for the Sullivan Award, a trophy presented annually to the top amateur athletes in the United States. The summer before, Owens had a problem with employment that rendered him ineligible for the award. The case was later dismissed, but not in time for Owens to be considered for the award, one of the most prestigious awards honoring the year's best amateur athletes. Following this disappointment was another. In the fall quarter, Owens had failed a psychology course. He was now academically ineligible to participate in the winter indoor track season.

On January 21, 1936, Ripley's *Believe It or Not* featured Owens's record–breaking performances of the previous spring. His performance during the spring of 1936 made him a favorite for the Olympics. In the final trials for the Olympic team, Owens finished first in the 100–meter and 200–meter sprints, and in the long jump. There were 66 Americans on the 1936 Summer Olympic track and field team. Ten were African American men and two were African American women: hurdler Tidye Pickett and sprinter Louise Stokes. The *Amsterdam News* for July 18, 1936, printed the following comment: ''Those who mourn the defeat of Joe Louis at the hands of the determined German, Max Schmeling, can find not only solace, but also genuine pride and appreciation in the results of the Olympic selections.''

Olympic Glory

The black community, stunned by Louis's defeat, pinned all of its hopes on Jesse Owens as he set sail the morning of July 15, 1936, on the *S.S. Manhattan* bound for Germany. When the games opened August 1, Owens fought to control his anger. Owens recalled in *The Jesse Owens Story,* ''I'd never had time to be a crusader. But when the hour came for me to compete, I was mad. I was angry because of the insults that Hitler and the other German leaders had hurled at me and my Negro teammates on the Olympic squad. I was angry for all the colored people back home.'' Owens knew he had to control the negative emotions or they would destroy his chance of winning.

Owens won in the 100–meter sprint, the 200–meter sprint, the long jump, and the 400–meter relay, collecting a total of four gold medals. In the long jump Owens broke his own record, clearing twenty–six feet, five and three–quarter inches. It would be twenty–five years before anyone would break his record. Although the German spectators gave Owens a standing ovation, controversy surrounded Adolph Hitler's reaction to his win. Hitler's legendary snub of Owens by refusing to shake his hand never actually occurred. It is true that on the first day when two Germans won they were summoned to Hitler's box where he shook their hands. As the day grew long and rain began to come, the black high jumper Cornelius Johnson won the gold. Just before the playing of the American national anthem, Hitler and his group of men walked out of the stadium. If anyone was snubbed, it was Johnson and not Owens. Owens did not win his gold medal until the next day, and by then Hitler had been told by the president of the International Olympic Committee that he would have to be impartial in his accolades. The American press, however, exaggerated the story. The *New York Times* headlines read, ''Hitler Snubs Jesse.'' Even though Owens initially denied it, apparently he tired of the constant denial and gave in, so the story continued to circulate. Baker reported in *Jesse Owens* that ''the American press shifted the focus of the snub yarn away from Cornelius Johnson onto Jesse Owens . . . [because] every new medal won by Owens enhanced his appeal as the target of Hitler's supposed insult.''

Ticker tape parades, autograph seekers, photographers, and reporters welcomed home the Olympic hero. Then suddenly the band stopped playing, and Owens faced American reality. He told *Ebony* in 1988: ''I came back to my native country and couldn't ride in the front of the bus. I had to go to the back door. . . . I wasn't invited up to shake hands with Hitler, but I wasn't invited to the White House to shake hands with the President, either.''

Worse, perhaps, than the discrimination Owens faced, were the misleading offers Owens received to pay him fantastic salaries for personal appearances. On the basis of these offers, Owens refused to tour Europe for post–Olympic Games as the AAU insisted that he must. He felt that he was being exploited, receiving no money, yet making money for the AAU. Coach Snyder supported Owens and advised him to return to the United States and cash in on the once–in–a–lifetime offers. The AAU suspended Owens. The best offer he received came from Ohio's premier black college, Wilberforce. They would pay him $2,800 a year to coach the track team. There was one obstacle. Owens would need his college degree.

Owens earned money the best way that he could, hustling his Olympic fame and turning professional. He campaigned for the Republican Party in the presidential election of 1936, and exhibited his speed by running at baseball games, county fairs, and carnivals. In 1937, his second daughter, Marlene, was born. With a growing family and aging parents, Owens felt pressured to earn money and security. He opened a dry cleaning business but went bankrupt. Finally, in 1940, with the birth of his youngest daughter, Beverly, Owens decided to return to Columbus to complete his degree. He enrolled at Ohio State, and paid his tuition by coaching track. The only degree Owens would obtain from Ohio State University was an honorary degree awarded in 1972. After four terms, he gave up. His cumulative grade point average was 1.07.

Owens decided to do what he did best besides running and jumping. He loved to talk, and he had a gift for oratory. He capitalized on this strength and went on the lecture circuit talking to young people about sports. He organized the Junior Olympic Games for youths in Chicago in 1956. Eventually he was able to open his own public relations firm and was said to have earned around $100,000 in 1970.

The Ire of Militant Blacks

The militancy characterizing the 1960s caught Owens by surprise. The son of an Alabama sharecropper, he was taught to grin and bear insults. His political stance had worked for him. A celebrated speaker, businessman, and Republican, Owens caught the fire of militant blacks for his opposition to the black American Olympic boycott and protest. Burned by charges that he was an ''Uncle Tom,'' Owens fought back, stating his case in a personal memoir, *Blackthink* (1970). In the book Owens assessed black militants and made the mistake of presuming that the reaction by Tommy Smith and John Carlos, who raised their fists in a Black Power salute at Mexico City's 1968 Olympics, did not strike a responsive chord with the majority of black people. In *Jesse Owens,* Baker summarized Owens's position: ''It was a view of the world, of success by means of the work ethic, and of the failure that reflects a flawed character.'' For blacks who had not made it in America, Owens said in *Blackthink* that they needed to ''fight harder to make equality work.''

While whites lauded the publication of Owens's book, blacks denounced him as insensitive to racism and the deplorable social conditions of most blacks. Owens received the praise of Republicans, and President Richard M. Nixon made him goodwill ambassador to West Africa. The letters of protest and outrage from angry blacks, however, weighed heavily on Owens's mind.

Owens's reflections led him to write another book, *I Have Changed* (1972), in which he retracted much of what he stated in *Blackthink.* In this book he defended the rights of blacks to protest racism and injustice and admitted that equality had not dawned for most black people who suffered from limited job opportunities, unfair housing, inferior education, poverty, and ill health. With this book, Owens made his peace with the black community, and with himself. He recognized he had much to learn from his daughters' and grandchildren's generations, when he wrote in this book, ''I'm still changing.''

The Last Mile

In December of 1979 Owens, who smoked a pack of cigarettes a day, entered the hospital complaining of fatigue. On December 12 he was diagnosed with lung cancer. On March 21, 1980, he was airlifted to the university hospital in Tucson, Arizona, where he and Ruth had lived since 1971. Owens died on March 31, 1980.

Flags flew at half–mast all over the state of Arizona, and Owens's body lay in the state capitol rotunda in Phoenix. Later his body was flown to Chicago for the funeral held in the Rockefeller Chapel of the University of Chicago. A steel gray casket draped with a white silk flag bearing five Olympic rings held the world's fastest human of 1936. Before he died, Owens, responding to reporters' questions regarding the upcoming Olympics, made a statement characteristic of his life and philosophy. Quoted by Baker, he said: ''The road to the Olympics doesn't lead to Moscow. . . . It leads to no city, no country. It goes far beyond Lake Placid or Moscow, ancient Greece or Nazi Germany. The road to the Olympics leads, in the end, to the best within us.''

In 1976, 40 years after his Olympic feat, Owens was invited to the White House to receive the Presidential Medal of Freedom from Gerald Ford. In 1979 he received the Living Legend Award from Jimmy Carter. In 1990, Owens's widow received a Congressional Gold Medal in his honor. Three campus buildings at Ohio State carry Owens's name, as does the athletic track. In 1982 the Jesse Owens International Indoor Track and Field Meet began in New York. Owens is an appealing hero for all Americans regardless of race or political persuasion because his is the perfect rags to riches story. He had moved from the cotton fields of Alabama to the well–paid, highly visible world of a businessman and international traveler and was a lovable hero on and off the track.

REFERENCES

Baker, William J. *Jesse Owens: An American Life.* New York: Free Press, 1986.

Bennett, Lerone. ''Jesse Owens' Olympic Triumph Over Time and Hitlerism.'' *Ebony* 43 (September 1988) 144–46.

''Bound for Berlin.'' *Amsterdam News,* July 18, 1936.

Contemporary Black Biography. Vol. 2. Detroit Gale Research, 1992.

Owens, Jesse, with Paul G. Neimark. *Blackthink.* New York: Morrow, 1970.

———. *I Have Changed.* New York: Morrow, 1972.

Sabin, Francene. *Jesse Owens: Olympic Hero.* New Jersey: Troll, 1986.

Nagueyalti Warren

Harry H. Pace

(1884–1943)

Entrepreneur, insurance executive, music publisher, record producer, educator, lawyer

Harry H. Pace has been described as "a man of many parts and a multitude of interests," a visionary, and a risk–taker. John Ingham and Lynne Feldman continued their description of Pace in *African–American Business Leaders,* calling him "bigger than life: the sort of individual who, if presented in fiction, would never be believed." All through his professional life, he had the knack of making good connections. He is known for his business ventures in black music publishing and for establishing the first major black–owned and –operated recording company, Black Swan. He was also a successful insurance company executive and cofounder, through the merger of three companies, of Supreme Life Insurance Company.

Harry H. Pace

Born in Covington, Georgia, on January 6, 1884, Harry Herbert Pace was the son of Charles Pace, a blacksmith, and Nancy Francis. Although his father died when Pace was an infant, Pace, a precocious child, was fortunate in his exposure to a good education. He worked his way through Atlanta University, receiving the A.B. in 1903.

In 1905, W. E. B. Du Bois founded the *Moon Illustrated Weekly,* a small magazine that became the precursor of the *Crisis,* the official organ of the NAACP. Du Bois, an influential black leader and intellectual, called Pace to Memphis to serve as business manager of the *Moon.* Pace put aside his dream of going to law school in order to join Du Bois, whom he had known in Atlanta, in the publishing venture.

Financial Genius

The *Moon* failed. In November of 1906, at age 22 and destitute, Pace was offered the position of professor of Latin and Greek at Lincoln University in Jefferson City, Missouri. He accepted, remaining there for a year. In 1907 he was urged to return to Memphis and join the staff of Solvent Savings Bank, at a reduction of salary from $100 a month to $83. When he assumed his duties as cashier, the bank's assets were around $50,000, with a deficit of $7,000. Within four years, the bank's assets had increased to $600,000 and his salary more than doubled to $200 a month.

In 1912, Du Bois attempted to persuade Pace to join him on the staff of *Crisis.* Pace, fearing a repeat of the earlier failure, instead accepted the position of secretary of Standard Life Insurance Company in Atlanta.

Under Pace's skillful leadership, Standard Life became the first black insurance company to sell ordinary life insurance, and the third to achieve legal reserve status. On its board were such persons as Emmett J. Scott, secretary to Booker T. Washington; Henry A. Boyd, of the National Baptist Publishing House in Nashville; Col C. Johnson, publisher of the *Savannah Tribune*; and John Hope, president of Morehouse College. Growth of the company was rapid.

In the fall of 1916, William F. Penn headed a group of petitioners, including Pace, John Hope, and Benjamin J. Davis Sr., who persuaded the board to abandon the plan to decrease the amount of education for black students. Anticipating further struggles to strengthen black education, the Atlanta branch of the NAACP was established with Pace as president, writer, and educator.

In June of 1917 Pace married Ethlynde Bibb. They had two children. While on his honeymoon in Jacksonville, Florida, he learned of a plot to oust him from his job. He remained with Standard for three years, then resigned. Then he headed to New York City for another exciting adventure.

Music Company Founder

The Pace–W. C. Handy relationship began while both were in Memphis. Handy wrote of the meeting in his autobiography:

> In 1907 I first became a tenant of the Solvent Savings Bank. The cashier of the bank was Harry A. Pace, a handsome man of striking personality and definite musical leanings. Pace had written some first rate song lyrics and was in demand as a vocal soloist at church programs and Sunday night concerts.

According to Handy, ''it was natural, if not inevitable,'' that the two men would partner to publish music because of their similar interests and social background.

In 1913 the two published ''Jogo Blues'' and ''The Girl You Have Never Met'' under the name of Pace and Handy Music Publishers. Pace then left for Atlanta to work for Standard Life. However, the two kept in touch and it was Pace who advised Handy to move the company to New York City. This was accomplished in 1918, and offices were opened on Broadway where only a few black publishing houses were located. Pace became president; Charles Handy, brother of W. C., vice–president; and W. C. Handy, secretary–treasurer. The distinguished band leader Fletcher Henderson was song–plugger and pianist, while the talented composer William Grant Still was chief arranger. The firm's first publication, ''A Good Man is Hard to Find,'' was a success.

Pace and Handy dissolved their partnership in January of 1921. The successor to the Pace and Handy Music Publishers, also known as the ''House of the Blues,'' was The Handy Brothers Music Company. Charles Handy became president and W. C. Handy secretary–treasurer.

Black Swan Records

Seeing opportunity in the recording industry, Pace formed the Pace Phonograph Corporation, the first black–owned and –operated recording company. In the same year, Black Swan records was created, a label featuring only ''coloured'' artists and named in honor of Mississippi–born, Afro–American singer Elizabeth Taylor Greenfield (d.1876), who was known as ''The Black Swan.''

Both Henderson and Still left Handy Brothers and joined Pace Phonograph. Within a short period of time, the staff had increased to 15 clerks, seven district managers, one thousand dealers and agents all over the country, and an eight–man orchestra. Shipping reached 2,500 records per day. However, getting the firm established was not easy; white record companies presented formidable competition. Following the somewhat successful release of several records, Pace's real breakthrough was in locating the young singer Ethel Waters. Her first two records were ''Down Home Blues'' and ''Oh Daddy.'' Within six months, half a million records had been sold, helping to bring the company out of the red. With the technical and artistic talents of Still, now musical director, and Henderson as recording manager, success appeared inevitable. During this period, wrote John H. Johnson in *Succeeding Against the Odds*, ''Pace discovered and gave the first crucial helping hand to more Black artists and leaders than any other American.'' He was the first to hire Henderson, Isabelle Washington, and Freddie Washington—both actresses—in addition to discovering singers Waters and Trixie Smith.

Pace decided to send Waters out on tour with Henderson's band, the Black Swan Jazz Masters. The success of this endeavor allowed Pace to buy a plant in Long Island City for use as a recording and pressing laboratory. According to Pace, Black Swan was selling 7,000 records a day, but could press only 6,000. Consequently, three more presses were ordered in 1923.

The advent of radio as a means of transmitting music at a much cheaper cost, however, meant problems for Black Swan as well as several white record companies. Fearing bankruptcy, Pace sold the company to Paramount Records. Eileen Southern wrote in the *Biographical Dictionary of Afro–American and African Musicians* that the Black Swan label ''forced white recording companies to do three things: to recognize the vast Negro market for recordings, to release 'race catalogues,' and to advertise in black newspapers.''

Prior to terminating his involvement in the recording industry, Pace found time to become active in African American politics. The early 1920s was the era of Marcus Garvey, a black nationalist who urged creation of an independent black nation in Africa. Pace was in the forefront of the anti–Garvey movement. He joined with other black leaders in condemning Garveyism as a philosophy not worthy of aiding the race.

Major Insurance Merger

In 1925 Pace, along with several other wealthy blacks, organized the Northeastern Life Insurance Company in Newark, New Jersey. He began to see benefits in uniting several major African American insurance companies, the weakness of one company being the strength of another. He believed in the black economic power that insurance companies could generate, both by providing job opportunities for blacks, and by developing a financial reservoir. In 1929, Northeastern Life Insurance Company of Newark, Supreme Life and Casualty of Columbus, Ohio, and Liberty Life Insurance Company of Chicago were merged. The new firm was called Supreme Life Insurance Company, with Pace as president and chief executive officer. Supreme Life was the largest black business in Chicago and the North.

Outside his insurance and music ventures, Pace was involved in many other activities. In 1930 he began studying for a law degree, an idea forfeited many years before when he joined Du Bois in their failed publishing venture. Upon graduation, he became a member of the law firm of Bibb, Tyree, and Pace, remaining with the firm until he died. Along the way, he was a prominent member of the National Negro Insurance Association, serving as president for one year, statistician for one year, and general counsel for four years. He wrote extensively on insurance issues, contributing articles to such publications as the *Crisis, The Messenger,* and *The Southern Workman.* He was a dedicated member of the Elks, having organized the first lodge in Memphis.

In 1933, U.S. Secretary of Commerce Roper appointed Pace to an advisory committee on black activities. He was assistant counsel to the Illinois Commerce Commission, served on the board of directors of the NAACP, and was a member of the local board of the Urban League. At one time he was secretary of the Georgia State Republican Committee.

Pace died in Chicago on July 26, 1943. He was involved with most of the prominent black Americans of his time, and was one of the most important figures in black social and economic history during the first part of this century. In the assessment of Ingham and Feldman, Pace was ''a giant of a man who slipped through the cracks of historical memory.''

REFERENCES

Dixon, Robert, and John Godrich. *Recording the Blues.* New York: Stein and Day, 1970.

Handy, W. C. *Father of the Blues: An Autobiography.* New York: Macmillan, 1941.

Ingham, John N., and Lynne B. Feldman. *African–American Business Leaders: A Biographical Dictionary.* Westport, CT: Greenwood Press, 1994.

Lewis, David Levering. *W. E. B. Du Bois: Biography of a Race.* New York: Holt, 1993.

Johnson, John H, with Lerone Bennett Jr. *Succeeding Against the Odds.* New York: Warner Books, 1989.

Partington, Paul G. ''The Moon Illustrated Weekly—The Precursor of the Crisis.'' *Journal of Negro History* 48 (July 1963): 206–216.

Sampson, Henry T. *Blacks in Blackface: A Sourcebook on Early Black Musical Shows.* Metuchen, NJ: Scarecrow Press, 1980.

Southern, Eileen. *Biographical Dictionary of Afro–American and African Musicians.* Westport, CT: Greenwood Press, 1982.

———. *The Music of Black Americans: A History.* 2nd ed. New York: Norton, 1983.

White, Walter. *A Man Called White: The Autobiography of Walter White.* New York: Viking, 1948.

D. Antoinette Handy

Alan Cedric Page

(1945–)

Football player, lawyer, state Supreme Court justice, humanitarian

Chosen in 1967 by the Minnesota Vikings as their first–round draft pick, Notre Dame's Alan Cedric Page went on to earn the Most Valuable Player award in the National Football League in 1971. Page gained athletic fame as one of four ''Purple People Eaters'' of the Viking's defense, assisting the team in winning 10 division titles and four Super Bowls from 1968 to 1978. Interestingly, Page viewed sports not as a goal, but as a job, a means to achieve an education. He told *Parade Magazine* in 1990, ''Even when I was playing professionally, I never viewed myself as a football player. There's far more to life than being an athlete.'' Page wanted to transfer his football stardom into a force that could effect positive change for children in education. For that reason, he established the Page Education Foundation (1988) to support education for children of color at risk of not continuing their education. With his athletic career behind him, Page entered the field of law, serving as assistant attorney general of Minnesota from 1987 through 1993, when he became an associate justice of the Minnesota Supreme Court.

One of four children of Georgianna Umbles and Howard Felix Page, Page was born on August 7, 1945, in Canton, OH. He has two sisters, Marvel and Twila, and a brother, Howard. His friends, neighbors, and family worked in a steel mill. His mother, a country club attendant, and his father, a bar manager, emphasized the importance of learning. They instilled strong values in him, and Page looked up to his parents as role models.

Page told *Parade Magazine* in 1994, ''I grew up in a family where education was valued. It was made clear to me by my parents that if I was going to be successful, if I was going to have a better life than they had, then I was going to have to perform in the classroom.'' And Page did perform academically, graduating from Central Catholic High School in Canton and then from the University of Notre Dame in 1967 with a B.A. in political science. At Notre Dame, Page was All–America defensive end, winning three letters, and in his final year at Notre Dame, Page was the first–round drive pick for the Minnesota Vikings. In the NFL, he played the position of a defensive tackle. He logged 15 NFL seasons with the Vikings and the Chicago Bears without missing a game, reflecting the strong work ethic instilled by his parents and good fortune to avoid serious injury.

While playing for the NFL, Page met and married Diane Sims. They have four children, Nina, Georgianna, Justin, and Khamsin, who have all shared their father's interest in continuing their education beyond high school, but not his passion for sports.

Page played professionally for the Vikings from 1967 to 1978, achieving recognition as the first defensive player in the

Alan Cedric Page

history of the NFL to receive the Most Valuable Player award in 1971. He received numerous awards and honors for his performance in the NFL. He became interested in running, so he dropped a few pounds, opting to use speed instead of muscle as a defensive player; however, the running triggered his move from the Vikings to the Chicago Bears, where he continued as a star performer until he retired at the end of the 1981–82 football season.

In 1979, he was the first active NFL player to complete a marathon. For several years, Page and his wife competed quite successfully in various races. Page told *Runner's World* that running "was really fun. And running became our social life, became our way of escaping, our way of relaxing." In 1987, Page completed the Edmund Fitzgerald Ultra–Marathon (62 miles). He continues to run about six miles daily, keeping his weight a trim 220 pounds for his six–foot four–inch frame.

Law Profession Appeals to Page

The fantasies of young Page went beyond the gridiron and into the courtroom. Page admired former Supreme Court Justice Thurgood Marshall and was a fan of the Perry Mason television show. He told Teresa Scalzo for *Minnesota:*

> I had dreams of being a lawyer. I didn't really understand what lawyers did, [but] the few lawyers I saw had big homes and drove fancy cars and didn't seem to work all that hard. Those are the kinds of things that appeal to a child growing up in an environment where friends and neighbors and family work in a steel mill every day. It seemed to me there had to be some alternative. That, coupled with the belief that there is some value in being able to solve problems.

While still employed full–time as a professional football player, Page attended the University of Minnesota full time, graduating in 1978. He joined the firm of Lindquist and Vennum and specialized in employment and labor litigation (1979–84). Page was Assistant Attorney General in Minnesota (1987–93) when elected to the National Football Hall of Fame in 1988.

Page's personal crusade reaches beyond the courtroom and into the classroom through the Page Education Foundation. Scholarship recipients complete a community service project related to education by tutoring K–8th grade children for eight to 10 hours each month of the school year while attending post–secondary school, thus creating a pyramid influencing younger students of color as mentors and role models. Page established the foundation in 1988 with a goal to increase the participation of minority youth in postsecondary education and work–readiness activities. The financial aid combined with community service stimulate hope and self–motivation. Jill Westberry told the *St. Paul Pioneer Press* about her tutoring, saying "The girl's father told me, 'I don't know what you're doing, but she's different person.'" After handing certificates to scholarship winners in 1992, Page said, "It's vital, if we're going to solve the problems of the community, for young people to be involved." The National Education Association (NEA) awarded the 1991 Friend of Education Award to Page for his work in encouraging minority students to stick with their education. Aetna also recognized Page's work by awarding him the Arthur Ashe Voice of Conscience Award. Arne H. Carlson, Governor of Minnesota, gave a Certificate of Commendation to the Page Education Foundation on April 25, 1995. Page further enhanced the Foundation by helping establish the Page/Kodak Challenge, a nationwide essay contest encouraging urban youth to recognize the importance of an education (1989–92).

The U.S. Jaycees selected him as one of America's Ten Outstanding Young Men in 1981. In 1990, Page was inducted into the Nike Walk of Fame. He was also inducted into Chicago's Inner City Sports Hall of Fame in 1991. The Notre Dame Alumni Association presented their 1992 Rev. Frederick Sorin Award to Page, commending him "for his vision and commitment to education . . . as a true son of Notre Dame." That same year, he received the NCAA Silver Anniversary Award and the East–West Game Babe Hollingsberry Award. In 1993, Page received the U.S. Sports Academy Theodore Roosevelt Meritorious Service Award and the WCCO Radio Distinguished Good Neighbor Award; he was also inducted into the College Football Hall of Fame.

Page is also very active professionally and in the community. In 1972, he was chairman of the Minnesota Council on Physical Fitness; state chairman of the United Negro College Fund in 1972, on the Advisory Board in 1984, and Telethon Co–host in 1984; state chairman of the American Cancer Society in 1978; board of directors, Chicago Association for Retarded Citizens, 1979–81; honorary co–chair, Child Care Works, 1984; and task force chair, Minnesota State Games, 1984. Page is a member of the American Bar Association, 1979–present; National Bar Association, 1979–present; Minnesota Minority Lawyers' Association, 1980–present; Advisory Board, League of Women Voters, 1984–91; Advisory Board, Mixed Blood Theater, 1984–present; Institute of Bill of Rights Law Task Force on Drug Testing in the Workplace, 1990–91; Board of Directors, Minneapolis Urban League, 1987–90; Minnesota State Bar Association, 1979–85, 1990–present; Board of Regents, University of Minnesota, 1989–92; and American Law Institute, 1993–present.

Page regularly speaks to minority students about the importance of education and, as he told the *Los Angeles Times,* he believes "being gifted with athletic ability makes one worthy of recognition; it does not make one a role model." He encourages adults to influence children to look at the values and good examples of hard work that decent Americans provide every day for "creating and sustaining hope for the future. These are not the heroes who offer hope with promises of winning the lottery, becoming a rap star or pulling down backboards and endorsement contracts in the NBA. These are simply men and women who get up every morning and do the things that citizens do," he said in the interview. About his own work ethic, Page told *The Sporting News* for December 7, 1992, "I've always had high expectations for myself."

Current address: Minnesota Judicial Center, 25 Constitution Avenue, St. Paul, MN 55155.

REFERENCES

Balzer, Howard. "Foursome Stakes Claim to Fame." *The Sporting News* 206 (8 August 1988): 36–37.

Fedo, Michael. "Close–Up: Alan Page the Defense (Doesn't) Rest." *Runner's World* 25 (February 1990): 30–32.

Page, Alan C. "We Become Whom We Emulate." *Los Angeles Times,* February 23, 1996.

"Page Scholarship Recipients Are Required to Give, Too." *St. Paul Pioneer Press,* June 24, 1992.

Pate, Eric T. "The View from the Bench." *The Sporting News* 214 (7 December 1992): 7.

Ryan, Michael. "He Gives Kids a Chance to Win." *Parade Magazine* (9 September 1990): 24.

Scalzo, Teresa. "Benched." *Minnesota* (November–December 1993): 36–39.

Schaap, Jeremy. "Now He Tackles Injustice." *Parade Magazine* (15 May 1994): 12.

Younger, Joseph D. "'The Future Is Yours.'" *Amtrak Express* (January/February 1992): 36–40.

Claire A. Taft

"Satchel" Paige
(1906–1982)
Baseball player, coach

"Satchel" Paige was a baseball pitcher who towered over the world of Negro League baseball from 1926 until 1947. During his most productive playing days, however, black players were forbidden entry into the major baseball leagues. On July 7, 1958, he became the first black to serve as relief pitcher in a major league game and the next year became the first black to pitch in the World Series.

Leroy Robert Paige was born July 7, 1906, in Mobile, Alabama. He was the seventh child of John Page, a gardener, and Lula Page, a washerwoman. (The family later added an "i" to its surname.) Paige's brothers and sisters included John Jr., Wilson, Julia, Ellen, Ruth, Emma Lee, Clarence, Inez, Palestine, and Lula. All 13 family members lived in a four–room house near the bay on South Franklin Street.

A formal education was not as highly regarded as bringing home money for food. Even though Paige was enrolled in W. H. Council School, from age seven he worked at the Mobile train depot. He took a pole and rope and carried satchels and bags for small change and earned his lifelong nickname "Satchel." As a child, Paige often skipped school and seldom studied. Wilbur Hines, the baseball coach of W. H. Council School, allowed Paige to play as an outfielder and first baseman. At age ten, during midseason, he pitched for the team after the starting pitcher became injured. Between work and baseball, he developed few close friendships and got into many childhood fights.

At age 12, while walking home from a ballgame, Paige was dazzled by a toy store display and pocketed a few toy rings and colored stones. On July 24, 1918, he was sentenced to five and one–half years at the Industrial School for Negro Children at Mount Meigs, Alabama. Ironically, the experience helped to develop his baseball skills; it also gave him the opportunity to receive the only formal, uninterrupted education of his life. He no longer had to work for food, help support his family, or worry about clothes or shelter. Before leaving the reform school, the coach of the baseball team saw his potential and encouraged him to take care of his arm and concentrate on baseball.

As a young man, Paige was tall and thin and appeared to be all arms and legs. He had already reached his adult height of six feet three and one–half inches and weighed 180 pounds. (He briefly picked up the nickname "The Crane" while at Mount Meigs.) When he was 17, he returned to Mobile to live with his mother; his father had died a year before his release. A month after returning home, Paige got a job picking up bottles and sweeping near Eureka Gardens. This was the semiprofessional ballpark of the all–black Mobile Tigers. His brother Wilson played as catcher or pitcher for the team. After watching a game, Paige introduced himself to the team manager as Wilson's brother and tried out for the team as a

''Satchel'' Paige

pitcher. He threw fast, controlled pitches that amazed the manager. He was given a dollar and told to return with his brother for the next game. He would earn a dollar for games he won and receive a keg of lemonade for games he lost. To earn additional income he started pitching for other teams. For a regular job, Paige started working at the ballpark of the white minor league team, the Mobile Bears. His reputation grew as a player and from 1924 until 1926 he won 30 games and lost only one.

Professional Baseball and the Negro League Years

After several semipro victories in 1926, Alex Herman, owner of the Chattanooga Black Lookouts (1926–27), asked him to pitch for the Negro Southern League team. On May 1, 1926, Paige made his professional pitching debut. His mother objected to his move to professional baseball. She was devoutly religious and viewed playing professional baseball, especially on Sundays, as a sin. Paige's old friend Alex Herman assured Paige's mother that part of his salary would be sent back home.

No regular statistics were kept in the Negro Leagues. In 1927, the manager of the best Negro Southern League team, the Birmingham Black Barons (1927–29) asked him to pitch. In 1929 Paige played winter baseball in the West Indies and Latin America. This continued throughout his career with the Negro leagues. In the spring of 1930, he played for the Elite Giants in Nashville and later in Cleveland. In the off–season Paige joined a barnstorming team called the Black Sox. Barnstorming referred to the practice of playing exhibition games around the country, especially in small towns and rural areas. The Black Sox team played some exhibition games against the Babe Ruth All–Stars, and Paige struck out superstars such as Babe Ruth and Hack Wilson.

In 1931 the Elite Giants disbanded during the Great Depression. However, Gus Greenlee, the owner of the Pittsburgh Crawfords (1931–34; 1936), hired him to pitch. In his first game he pitched a victory over the top Negro League team, the Homestead Grays. The Crawfords became a highly regarded team in the newly organized Negro National League. With the Crawfords, he won 21 straight games and pitched 64 scoreless innings. He also led the Crawfords to Negro National League championships. His teammates included five future Baseball Hall of Fame stars, James ''Cool Papa'' Bell, Oscar Charleston, Josh Gibson, and Judy Johnson. Large crowds came to see him pitch and both black and white fans compared his skills to those of Babe Ruth.

While playing for the Pittsburgh Crawfords, Paige's fame and spending habits grew. During this time he met a waitress at the Crawford Grill, Janet Howard, and married her on October 26, 1934. Denied many things as a poor child, Satchel developed a passion for spending money on his wife, clothes, cars, shotguns and fishing; he often had financial problems. Paige left the Crawfords after disagreeing with the owner, Gus Greenlee, over financial terms and began playing semipro baseball.

In 1934 Paige joined the Bismarck team in North Dakota, owned by Neil Churchill. This was the first time he had played baseball with white teammates. Due to racism, Paige and his wife could not find housing and lived in an old railroad freight car. Paige endured the hardships and pitched a winning game against the Bismarck's archrivals from Jamestown. During the off–season, he learned that he had been banned from the Negro Leagues for breaking his contract with the Pittsburgh Crawfords. He moved to the Southwest and formed his own barnstorming team, the Satchel Paige All–Stars. The team played in the California league against Dizzy Dean's major league exhibition team. At the time, Dizzy Dean was a fastball pitcher who dominated the major leagues. That season, Paige's All–Stars won four of the six exhibition games played against Dizzy Dean's All–Stars team. In one game he struck out one of the best major league hitters, Pepper Martin.

Returning to play for the Bismarck, he led the team to their first national semipro championship and was named most valuable player. While in North Dakota, he met some Sioux Indians who gave him a snakebite oil, which developed the sensation of heat; it became a favorite salve for his pitching arm.

In 1936 Paige returned to play for the Pittsburgh Crawfords, and his ban from the Negro Leagues was lifted. However, in the spring of 1937 Paige received an offer from the Dominican Republic to play for the Trujillo Stars. He and other teammates of the Crawfords found themselves playing in the middle of an intense political feud. The team of President Rafael Trujillo eventually won the national baseball tournament and was escorted by the army off the field. He hoped to return to play for the Crawfords, but a salary agreement could not be reached. The owner, Gus Greenlee, sold his contract to a team in Newark for which Paige never played.

Late in the summer of 1938 Paige pitched in the Mexican League. While playing in a game in Mexico City his shoulder snapped and the injury threatened his career. Unable to pitch, he called managers and owners for possible coaching positions. His reputation for jumping clubs, tardiness, and not showing for games made it difficult for him to find a job. Halfway through the season, Ralph Wilkinson, owner of the Kansas City Monarchs (1939–48), bought his contract from Newark, and Paige traveled with the Monarch's B team throughout the Northwest and Canada. In the summer of 1939 his pitching arm improved and he joined the Monarch's A team as the ace pitcher. The Monarchs went on to win the Negro American League title in 1939, 1940, and 1941.

In the 1940s the Kansas City Monarchs became the best team of the Negro Leagues; and Paige was the main attraction. In July 1942 he struck out his old teammate Josh Gibson in a game between the Monarchs and the Homestead Grays and won the Negro League World Series. Paige's teammates included Hilton Smith, "Lefty" LaMarque, Connie Johnson, Ted Strong, Newt Allen, and future Chicago Cubs coach John "Buck" O'Neil. In 1945, Jackie Robinson played with Paige as a rookie. In 1942 Paige became the highest– paid player in all of baseball after Hank Greenberg was drafted into military service. Whether in or out of the regular season, Paige used every opportunity to play baseball. His pitches were known by the names of jump ball, wobbly ball, blooper, drooper, and his famed hesitation pitch. He would stretch, plant his left foot forward, and hesitate to bring his arm forward right away. Batters would swing before he released the ball. Paige was a powerhouse talent who pleased fans with his trademark long, slow walk to the mound and an unusual windmill windup. After the United States entered World War II, Paige tried to enlist but was rejected because of his age. In order to contribute to the war effort, he visited military hospitals and camps.

The Major League Years

By 1943, it was obvious to the sports world that black players represented a reservoir of untapped talent for the major leagues. Entrepreneur Bill Veeck arranged to buy the Philadelphia Phillies. Veeck intended to hire black players including Paige. He informed his partner, Rudy Schaeffer, the editor of the *Pittsburgh Courier,* Wendell Smith, and promoter Abe Saperstein of his plan. A meeting in Chicago with baseball commissioner Kennesaw Mountain Landis sabotaged his plans. The commissioner ordered Phillies owner, Jerry Nugent, not to sell the team to Veeck. That same year Branch Rickey, the new manager of the Brooklyn Dodgers, asked his scout to look for good black players. Paige hoped to have an opportunity to play in the major leagues before his pitching arm and baseball skills diminished.

In July of 1943, Paige was honored at Wrigley Field while pitching for the Memphis Red Sox against the New York Cubans. The game was widely advertised and roughly 25,000 fans came to Wrigley Field to honor him. That same year, Paige and his wife Janet Howard divorced.

In 1945 while Paige was playing for the Kansas City Monarchs, rumors circulated that blacks were going to be allowed to play in the major leagues. One of the team's best rookies was Jackie Robinson. Branch Rickey of the Brooklyn Dodgers announced the signing of Robinson to play for the Montreal Royals of the International League. In 1947, Robinson started playing for the Brooklyn Dodgers and became the first African American to play in major league baseball.

On July 7, 1948, as president of the Cleveland Indians, Bill Veeck signed Paige to a contract. Two days later, Paige became the first African American to pitch in the American League as a relief pitcher against the St. Louis Browns. The Cleveland Indians went on to win the American League pennant. In his first three starts in the major leagues, Paige drew 201,829 fans and set nighttime attendance records in Chicago and Cleveland.

Paige became the first African American to pitch in a World Series in 1948 and was named Rookie of the Year and Most Valuable Player. On October 24, 1948, he was honored with a Satchel Paige Day in Los Angeles. Paige received a special Helms Award for pitching excellence. He was appointed to the 1952 and 1953 American League All–Star teams.

The Hall of Fame and His Road to Glory

After 22 years, Paige overcame the segregation and racism of American baseball and reached his dream of playing in the major leagues. At the age of 42, he became the oldest rookie in the history of major leagues by joining the Cleveland Indians (1948–1949). His baseball career and personal life were fulfilling. A year earlier, he married his second wife, Lahoma Brown, on October 12, 1947, in Hayes, Kansas. She had a daughter by a previous marriage, Shirley Long, but produced six other children with Satchel, Pamela, Carolyn, Linda, Robert, Lula, and Rita.

In 1951 Bill Veeck sold the Cleveland Indians and bought the St. Louis Browns. Paige joined the Browns on July 17, 1951, and stayed through the 1953 season. From 1954 until three days before his death, Paige participated in baseball through pitching, coaching, barnstorming, and personal appearances.

In August of 1971, Paige was inducted into the National Baseball Hall of Fame as a Negro League star. A protest over separate housing of the plaques caused commissioner Bowie Kuhn and Paul Kerr, the president of the National Baseball Hall of Fame, to give full membership to Paige. His plaque is now housed with those of other great baseball stars.

By the 1980s, Paige had developed emphysema and heart problems. On June 5, 1982, he was honored by the Kansas City Royals and threw out the first pitch of the game. Three days later, Paige died of a heart attack and was buried in Kansas City, Missouri.

Satchel Paige is remembered as one of baseball's most exciting pitchers in the old Negro leagues. As his plaque in the National Baseball Hall of Fame reads, he proved to be a "legend among major league hitters."

REFERENCES

Ashe, Arthur R., Jr. *A Hard Road to Glory.* New York: Amistad Press, 1988.

Humphrey, Kathryn Long. *Satchel Paige.* New York: Franklin Watts, 1988.

Paige, LeRoy (Satchel). *Maybe I'll Pitch Forever: A Great Baseball Player Tells the Hilarious Story Behind the Legend.* Garden City, NY: Doubleday, 1962.

Riley, James A. *Biographical Encyclopedia of the Negro Baseball Leagues.* New York: Carroll and Graf Publishers, 1994.

Rubin, Robert. *Satchel Paige: All–Time Baseball Great.* New York: G. P. Putnam's Sons, 1974.

"Satchel." *New York Times,* June 10, 1982.

"Satchel Paige, Black Pitching Star, is Dead at 75." *New York Times,* June 9, 1982.

Thorn, John, and Pete Palmer, eds. *Total Baseball: The Ultimate Encyclopedia of Baseball.* 3rd ed. New York: HarperPerennial, 1993.

Saundra P. Peterson

Charlie "Yardbird" Parker
(1920–1955)
Musician

Charlie "Yardbird" Parker was one of the greatest jazz figures to appear on the American jazz scene. Raised and nurtured as a musician in the vibrant musical climate of Kansas City, he soon migrated to New York City where he earned the respect of jazz fans and critics alike. Folklore, tales, suppositions, and questions abound concerning many aspects of his life and career.

One can paint a picture of stark contrasts in telling Parker's story. In some ways, he led a life of majesty, playing gigs in some of the top jazz venues, including Birdland, named after Parker. In his day, that was only club named for a contemporary jazz artist. He was virtually worshipped by musicians and jazz fans alike for his talent, his improvisatory genius, and his innovative contributions to music. He preached the gospel of a new music with his horn and inspired numerous young musicians to follow in his tracks. Saxophone students to this day memorize his solos and improvisations. In other ways, Charlie Parker lived a life shared with the

Charlie "Yardbird" Parker

homeless by sleeping on the street, riding subways to the end of the line and back, pawning valuables, and borrowing money, clothes, and even musical instruments.

One can best describe Parker's musical force as a tree, deeply rooted in Kansas City soil. Improvised solos were a feature of Kansas City Jazz in the 1920s and 1930s. The solos fit snugly into the standard three–part song form, where the soloists took middle choruses between ensemble renditions of the song. The solos emphasized embellishments and variations over the fixed harmonic changes of the song. Improvisation, running the chord changes, arpeggios, and virtuoso displays were also featured, and these root elements highlighted the jam sessions that young Parker watched, studied, and eventually led. Parker's particular model was saxophonist Lester "Prez" Young. He learned quickly, studying all of Young's available records and noting his approach to technique: breathing, embouchure, support, reeds, fingering, intonation, everything. Riffs—short, repeated ensemble solos—were a Kansas City band trademark, and these were incorporated into Parker's solos as well.

Parker was tutored in scales and harmony by his musical colleagues, including Tommy Douglas, Buster "Prof" Smith, and others. When he moved to New York, he heard Art Tatum's piano renditions at the Chicken Shack, a local bar. These inspired Parker, and during practice sessions with guitarist Biddy Fleet, he experimented with rhythm and wove the upper intervals of chords into a new melodic countermelody above the chord changes. By long and arduous practice, he built a strong technical foundation to the point where, at his height, he had no peer as a master of his instrument.

Disparity was common in Parker's lifestyle. He loved food—particularly chicken, hence his nickname, "Yardbird," a country name for chicken. He also suffered from serious ulcers, in all probability one of the causes of his death. He had a consuming lust for female companionship, and tales of his sexual prowess are legendary. As a heroin addict and an alcoholic, he often seemed to his friends to be on a quest to live life to the extremes. He seemed to believe only in the "now." It is surely a testament to his strong constitution that he was able to accomplish so much in his music, while taxing his body so severely.

Charles Christopher Parker Jr. was born in Kansas City, Kansas, on August 29, 1920, the son of Addie and Charles Parker. The family moved to Kansas City, Missouri, when he was eight or nine, and he entered Crispus Attucks Grammar School. He went to Lincoln High School in 1933, and came under the tutelage of Alonzo Lewis, the band director. Parker's father was a vaudeville entertainer and often played piano at home, but found it difficult to get good performing jobs. He eventually drifted away from the home in about 1931 and found employment as a railroad chef. His mother worked various jobs as a charwoman to keep the family together.

Begins Jazz Career Early

In the early 1930s, Kansas City was a thriving metropolis under the dominance of the Pendergast political machine. As a rail hub, cattle and wheat market, and entertainment center, Kansas City had a vibrant night life in its many clubs. It was the home base for many jazz orchestras that toured throughout the center of the country, including the Bennie Moten Count Basie Orchestra, Andy Kirk's Clouds of Joy, and Jay McShann's Orchestra. Leading musicians who hailed from Kansas City included Lester Young, Herschel Evans, Ben Webster, and Jo Jones. Many writers have claimed it as the home of the after–hours jam session. It was within this lively musical milieu that young Parker began to develop as a musician.

After Alonzo Lewis, Parker's band director, introduced him to the baritone horn, alto horn, and, briefly, the tuba, his mother bought him his first instrument, an alto saxophone. This brought about a profound change, not only in Parker's life, but in the course of black music history. His family lived in a neighborhood near the city's entertainment center and its many jazz venues, and his high school friends were mostly young aspiring musicians. In his sophomore year, his mother got another job working the night shift at the Western Union Company's downtown office. This left young Charlie Parker relatively free of supervision in the evenings, and he began spending most of his time listening to jazz in the clubs, well into the early morning hours. Musically, he developed quickly; he began playing professionally and joined the musician's union in 1934, when he was about 14. His schooling suffered, however, as he devoted most of his attention to the saxophone and to learning jazz.

Parker's most influential friends included pianist Lawrence "88" Keyes; bassist Gene Ramey from Lincoln High; local professional drummer Jesse Price; and local junk merchant "Old Man" Virgil. Virgil often provided Parker with a dose of worldly wisdom and served as an alter–ego, conscience, and partial father figure, as well as the butt of Parker's frequent practical jokes. Parker's sweetheart, Rebecca Ruffing, soon graduated from Lincoln High, and they decided to get married. The Ruffing family moved in with the Parkers, and Charles Parker's son, Leon was born in 1936.

Fate soon provided an ironic turn to Parker's fortunes. In a road accident after an out–of–town gig in Eldon, Missouri, over the Thanksgiving holiday, the car in which Charles was riding overturned in a ditch coming out of a curve on an icy road. One of Parker' friends was killed in the accident. Parker suffered injuries but chose to be treated at home. A favorable insurance settlement followed, and Parker was able to buy a new Selmer saxophone; a substantial boost to his musical development. At a later time, he was treated for pain from the accident and drugs were prescribed; perhaps contributing to his ensuing addiction.

Parker's marriage began to sour, and he left for Chicago in 1938. Seeking to improve his career opportunities, he pawned his saxophone for travel funds. He met saxophonist Goon Gardner, who took him in and helped him with odd jobs. He was also in touch with Buster "Prof" Smith, the Kansas City bandleader who had since moved to New York. Parker decided to follow Smith, and so he hitched a ride on a band bus bound for New York. Arriving there, he stayed with Smith for a time. Gigs were not easy to obtain, and he took a job dishwashing at the Chicken Shack where pianist Art Tatum provided entertainment. It was here that he heard Tatum's advanced musical ideas, and these were to prove pivotal for Parker. Also at this time, one of his out of town gigs took him to Annapolis, Maryland, where his mother sent word of his father's death. Parker rushed home to Kansas City for the funeral.

New Jazz Created

Parker stayed in Kansas City for a time, he and Rebecca Parker divorced, and in 1939 he was hired to work with the newly formed Jay McShann Orchestra. The band toured the region and then headed for a southern tour, finally ending up in New York in 1942. When McShann took the group back to Kansas City, Parker elected to stay in New York. At this point, the new musical style called "bop" evolved in a series of after–hours jam sessions, and Parker was at the center of the new movement. The movement evolved around a nucleus of like–minded musicians seeking new modes of expression: Parker, trumpeter Dizzy Gillespie, pianist Thelonius Monk, drummer Kenny Clarke, drummer Max Roach, trumpeter Miles Davis, and saxophonist John Coltrane.

The first formative sessions took place at two "after–hours" clubs, Minton's and Monroe's. After a period of experimentation, clashing, and blending of personnel and personalities in free–wheeling "cutting" session challenges, Parker and Gillespie soon solidified their dominance of the field. Their blend of talent and technique gave the new music its trademark "hot" flavor of high–power, high–speed technical display laced with clipped phrases, unexpected turns of melody, rhapsodic improvisatory twists, and humorous scat singing. In short, jazz gave birth to a new child, thanks, in part, to Parker.

Jazz musicians at that time earned their principal livelihood as members of organized bands and in recording sessions. For Parker, these included engagements with Earl Hines's orchestra in 1943, and Billy Eckstine's orchestra in 1944–45, with frequent out–of–town gigs, recording dates, and tours in the South and Midwest. In 1943, he married Geraldine Scott of Washington, D.C. After returning to New York for an engagement with Gillespie at The Three Deuces, a tour was arranged by promoter Billy Shaw that took Parker to California in December of 1945.

Several important recording sessions were held in California, as well as engagements at Billy Berg's jazz club and a major concert organized by Norman Granz at Philharmonic Hall in Los Angeles—dubbed "Jazz at the Philharmonic." A major mishap occurred at this point in Parker's career. After a strenuous Dial recording session in July of 1946, he had a physical and mental breakdown at his hotel, and was committed to the Camarillo State Hospital. Very likely, drug abuse, his physical condition, fatigue, and stress contributed to his collapse. His friends rallied to his side. Doris Sydnor, a friend from New York, and Ross Russell of Dial Records were instrumental in gaining his release into Russell's custody. Parker subsequently moved to New York with Sydnor in 1947, and they moved in together near the entertainment district. Although Parker and Geraldine Scott never divorced, in 1948 he married Sydnor in Tijuana.

Showing resilience, Parker recovered his strength and also enjoyed his new marriage. Parker had become somewhat of a legend in his own time at this point. Billy Shaw presented him with an invitation and engagement at the International Jazz Festival in Paris in 1949, together with a number of the most respected jazz figures of the day: Flip Phillips, Tad Dameron, "Hot Lips" Page, and Sidney Bechet, among others. Later that year Shaw designed and built a new jazz club, and named it "Birdland," in honor of Charlie Parker. Parker, of course, played at the opening on December 15, 1949, and many times in subsequent years.

Parker's travels next took him on tour in the South, and then to Sweden in late 1950, where he was a great success. He stopped in Paris on the way home, and was urged by jazz writer Charles Delauney to schedule a major concert appearance there. He suffered a physical collapse, however, attributed to severe ulcers and left Paris quickly without cancelling the engagement. He apologized graciously to the Paris concert audience by a radio hookup from New York, where he was interviewed on Leonard Feather's jazz show. He was hospitalized in New York and diagnosed as suffering from peptic ulcers.

Parker and his wife, Sydnor, had since drifted apart, and he and Chan Richardson began living together in 1950. They had dated previously, and she had visited him in California earlier. They lived as common–law man and wife, and this relationship lasted until shortly before his death. Richardson had a daughter, Kim, from another relationship, and she and Parker had two children: a daughter, Pree, in 1952, and a son, Baird, in 1953.

Parker next traveled on a Jazz at the Philharmonic tour to Europe in 1951–1952. Following recording sessions and short tours, another tour in California was organized in 1954 with the Stan Kenton Orchestra. Although the tour was successful, a personal tragedy occurred. While visiting with sculptor Julie MacDonald in Hollywood and sitting for a head sculpture, he heard of the death of his daughter, Pree. Losing his two–year–old daughter to pneumonia deeply affected Parker. He blamed himself for being an inattentive parent. He rushed home for the funeral, and took his family to Cape Cod for some quiet time alone.

Several engagements ensued in 1954, including an unfortunate one at Birdland. Parker was featured with an ensemble including string orchestra, and was displeased with the arrangements and the performance. He abruptly dismissed the musicians and cancelled the performance. This, of course, did not sit well with the musicians or the management. Following the occasion, he became very upset, had a serious argument with Richardson, and attempted suicide. He was admitted and treated at Bellevue Hospital. Following his release, he was engaged for a Jazz at the Philharmonic Concert on September 25. The concert went well, but he felt stress once again and had himself readmitted to Bellevue.

Following his release, Parker tried to regain physical and spiritual control, but became openly despondent, speaking to friends of suicide, and at times living as a street person. He was able to play at the "Open Door" Jam session early in 1955, hosted by writer Bob Reisner, and Parker persuaded a prominent artist agency to get him a few bookings. They arranged for a Birdland gig in March, followed by a Boston engagement on March 9. The group opened well enough, but at the concluding Saturday performance, on March 5, his pianist, Bud Powell, was drunk and unable to perform. This caused a disastrous scene, with Parker cancelling the performance.

Parker retreated from the immediate scene, seeking to gather his energies. On March 9, he headed toward Boston, but only got as far as the apartment of a close friend, the well–known socialite and supporter of the arts, Baroness Pannonica de Koenigswarter. Charles "Yardbird" Parker died late on Saturday night, March 12, 1955, in the Baroness's New York apartment. It was several days before the news reached "the streets" of New York City. When it did, rumor accompanied fragmentary truth, and graffiti began appearing in Harlem and Greenwich Village, saying "Bird Lives," emphasizing the aura of mystery surrounding Parker's death. He left, however, an impressive legacy of recordings and inspiration for musicians and music lovers to contemplate.

Doris Parker, presumed to be legally married to Charlie Parker, was named administrator of his estate. Matters did not rest, however, as protracted law suits followed over the rights to his compositions, recordings, and royalties. Geraldine Scott, then living in Anderson, West Virginia, successfully petitioned to become administrator. In 1962, Parker's estate was divided among Geraldine Parker, the Parker children, Addie Parker (his mother), and Doris Parker.

Excellent lists of Parker's recordings may be found in the Woideck and Russell biographies. Virtually all of his recorded works are available on cassettes and CDs, and transcriptions of his solos are available from a number of sources, published and archival. Some of his most memorable compositions include "Cherokee," a Kansas City favorite; "Embraceable You" "I Got Rhythm" (particularly the version with the incredible duet solo with Dizzy Gillespie); "Parker's Mood"; and "Koko."

REFERENCES

Alkyer, Frank. *Down Beat: 60 Years of Jazz.* Milwaukee: Hal Leonard, 1995.

Berendt, Joachim. *The Jazz Book.* Westport, CT: Lawrence Hill, 1982.

Bregman, Robert, Leonard Bukowski, and Norman Saks. *The Charlie Parker Discography.* Redwood, NY: Cadence Jazz Books, 1993.

Cerulli, Dom, Burt Korall, and Mort L. Nasatin, eds. *The Jazz Word.* New York: Ballantine Books, 1967.

Feather, Leonard. *The New Edition of the Encyclopedia of Jazz.* New York: Bonanza Books, 1960.

Frankl, Ron. *Charlie Parker.* New York: Chelsea House, 1993.

Garland, Phyl. *The Sound of Soul.* Chicago: Henry Regnery, 1969.

Gillenson, Lewis W., ed. *Esquire's World of Jazz.* New York: Thomas Y. Crowell, 1974.

Gray, Martin. *Blues for Bird.* Victoria, BC: Ekstasis Editions, 1993.

Hirschmann, Thomas. *Charlie Parker: kritische Beitrage zur Bibliographie sowie zu Leben und Werk.* Tutzing, Germany: H. Schneider, 1994.

Hitchcock, H. Wiley, ed. *The New Grove Dictionary of American Music.* New York: Macmillan, 1986.

Hodier, Andre. *Jazz: Its Evolution and Essence.* New York: Grove Press, 1956.

Jones, LeRoi (Amiri Baraka). *Blues People.* New York: William Morrow, 1963.

Kernfeld, Barry, ed. *The New Grove Dictionary of Jazz.* New York: Macmillan, 1988.

Koch, Lawrence. *Yardbird Suite: A Compendium of the Music and Life of Charlie Parker.* Bowling Green, OH: Bowling Green State University, 1988.

Koster, Piet, and Dick M. Bakker. *Charlie Parker.* Alphen aan den Rign, Netherlands: Micrography (Golden Age Records), 1976.

Miller, Mark. *Cool Blues: Charlie Parker in Canada, 1953.* London, ON: Nightwood Editions, 1989.

Owens, Thomas. *Charlie Parker: Techniques of Improvisation.* Master's thesis, University of California, Los Angeles, 1974; Ann Arbor, University Microfilms, 1975.

Reisner, Robert Grove. *Bird: The Legend of Charlie Parker.* New York: Da Capo Press, 1975.

Roach, Hildred. *Black American Music: Past and Present.* Malabar, FL: Kreiger Publishing Co., 1992.

Russell, Ross. *Bird Lives; The High Life and Hard Times of Charlie (Yardbird) Parker.* New York: Charterhouse, 1973.

Southern, Eileen. *Biographical Dictionary of Afro-American and African Musicians.* Westport, CT: Greenwood Press, 1982.

———. *The Music of Black Americans.* 2nd ed. New York: Norton, 1971.

Williams, Martin. *The Jazz Tradition.* New York: Oxford University Press, 1970.

Woideck, Carl. *Charlie Parker: His Music and Life.* Ann Arbor: University of Michigan Press, 1996.

Darius L. Thieme

Gordon Parks

(1912–)

Photographer, writer, filmmaker, composer, musician

Gordon Parks is a creative genius, an award–winning photographer, writer, and film maker. All told, Parks published 12 books, including three autobiographies. He is a composer of orchestral music and film scores, plus he wrote a ballet, *Martin,* about Dr. Martin Luther King Jr. In his many endeavors Parks further earned a reputation as a renaissance man. He was the first African American photographer to work at *Life* and *Vogue* magazines, and the first African American to work for the Office of War Information and the Farm Security Administration. Additionally, Parks was the first African American to write, direct, and produce a film for a major motion picture company. His film, *The Learning Tree,* was among the 25 films placed on the National Film Registry of the Library of Congress in 1989. Parks in his 1990 memoir, *Voices in the Mirror,* admitted that, "I've liked being a stranger to failure, since I was a young man and I still feel that way. I'm still occupied with survival; still very single–minded about keeping my life moving—but not for fame or fortune."

Gordon Parks rose from a childhood of poverty in a segregated society, yet he never exploited his background as vindication for poor performance. Likewise he refused to bow to convention. He excelled in multiple artistic fields, and he used his creative talents to better the world around him. He was born Gordon Roger Alexander Buchanan Parks on November 30, 1912, in Fort Scott, Kansas, to Andrew Jackson and Sarah Ross Parks. Parks, the youngest of 15 children, described his parents as hard working, always providing, and God fearing people who were forgiving, compassionate, and active models of love.

Parks attended a segregated elementary school, and in high school the school he attended was integrated, although it

Gordon Parks

maintained exclusive and discriminatory policies toward black students. African American students were barred from attendance at social functions and from participation in sports. The school further dismissed any aspirations beyond the menial for its children of color. Yet Parks maintained in *Voices in the Mirror* that he was "taught how to live honorably and how to die honorably."

Parks's mother died when he was 16, an event that changed his life and catapulted him into the world unexpectedly. He moved to St. Paul, Minnesota, to live with his sister and her family, but he had altercations with her husband. After a brief period, Parks was evicted by his brother-in-law and found himself thrust upon his own resources, homeless in a cold Minnesota winter, with very little money. For nearly a week he spent his nights riding the trolley line from St. Paul to Minneapolis and back again. Parks, who demonstrated some musical talent even as a youngster, eventually acquired a job playing the piano nightly in a brothel for tips. He held the job for two years. Then, in 1929, he got a job as a busboy. Parks wrote of those times in his memoir; he said that he worked in a "Minnesota club as a busboy in the day, and [as] a general lackey at night." He nurtured a desire to succeed, and he became an avid reader at the club's library. However, he was forced to seek employment again and to quit high school when the "panic and depression [the Great Depression]" set in. Parks resumed his employment as a bordello pianist. There, he once said of himself, "[T]he music I fed them was filled with my mood, and it seemed to soothe their souls. Friends began calling me 'Blue,' because of the blues I played." One of the numbers frequently requested of Parks was "No Love," a song that he composed after an argument with his future wife.

Parks moved to Chicago for a brief while, but he returned to St. Paul where a white band leader, Larry Funk, heard Parks play his composition "No Love." Funk was taken by the music. He not only played the song on national radio, but he also invited Parks to join and travel with the band. Parks accepted the offer, and he stayed with the group until 1933 when the band dissolved in New York. Parks once again was jobless and broke. He soon joined the Civilian Conservation Corps, but he left that employment in 1934 and returned to Minneapolis. Upon his arrival he worked as a waiter, but he wished to promote his song writing. The following year, he took a job once again as a pianist and he used the opportunity to showcase his own tunes. In time he became a waiter on the North Coast Limited, a transcontinental train, which to him represented the "Minnesota Club on Wheels." It was on this job, while riding the train, that he was inspired to become a photographer.

Develops Talent for Photography

Parks's interest in photography was triggered while leafing through magazines one day, on a run on the North Coast Limited. He related his experience in *Voices in the Mirror* wherein he explained that he found one article in particular with photographs of migrant farm workers. The pictures, taken by photographers of the Farm Security Administration, depicted "stark, tragic images of human beings caught up in the confusion of poverty. . . ." The images, he went on to write, "saddened me." He began to read more about photography and to visit art museums, to study the works of others. Ultimately it was a newsreel of the Japanese bombing of the U.S. gunboat *Panay,* by photographer Norman Alley, that affected Parks the most. After viewing the film he was "determined to become a photographer." Three days later, he bought his first camera: a $7.50 Voightlender Brilliant. Parks said, "[The camera] was to become my weapon against poverty and racism." Parks's first photographs immediately attracted the attention of the Eastman Kodak Company, which sponsored a showing of Parks's pictures in the company show windows.

Parks studied art and learned to capture and to convey powerful images with his camera. Because of his work on the North Coast Limited, he frequently found himself in Chicago during layovers on train runs between Minneapolis and Chicago. Whenever he was in Chicago he occupied himself by taking photographs of the people and the tenements of the city's south side. The pictures were reminiscent of the ones of migrant workers that had inspired him earlier, and the subject of the Chicago tenements developed into a particular favorite of Parks. Those early pictures foreshadowed what was to become his documentary style, a style that would mature remarkably soon after, when Parks relocated from St. Paul to become a full-time resident of Chicago.

While still in Minnesota Parks approached Frank Murphy, the owner of a women's store in St. Paul, about displaying some photographs in Murphy's store windows. Parks had seen some pictures in *Vogue,* and he wanted to try his hand at fashion photography. Murphy agreed to display Parks's pictures which were eventually seen by Marva Louis, wife of Joe Louis—heavyweight boxing champion of the world. She urged Parks to move to Chicago where he could profit not only from her encouragement but also from her well-connected lifestyle and her involvement with the South Side Community Art Center. Parks's itinerary in Chicago included "photo shoots" of Chicago's wealthy society matrons, as well as visits to the south side slums, where he captured many poignant moments with his camera.

In 1941 Parks's eloquent depictions of Chicago's poor earned him a Julius Rosenwald Fellowship. He was the first photographer to be so honored. For his fellowship Parks was apprenticed for one year to Roy Emerson Stryker at the Farm Security Administration in Washington, D.C. Parks was appalled at the bigotry and racism that permeated the bureau, and he set about to document the conditions with his camera. He took one particularly memorable photograph of Ella Watson, a poor, black, government charwoman, posed against the U.S. flag with broom and mop in hand. The Farm Security Administration was later absorbed by the Office of War Information, and Parks was assigned to Selfridge Field in Michigan to cover the newly formed 332nd Fighter Group—a squadron of black pilots.

Parks resigned from federal employment in 1944 and moved to New York City. In New York he applied for work with *Harper's Bazaar* and was rejected because of racial prejudice. With the intervention of a fellow photographer, Edward Steichen, however Parks secured casual-ware assignments for *Glamour* magazine. Six months later he received an assignment with *Vogue.*

While freelancing at *Vogue,* Parks joined Roy Stryker's photography team at Standard Oil Company in New Jersey. Parks's work with Standard Oil involved photographing corporate officials, and he was also assigned to develop a documentary series on rural America. Privately, Parks created a photographic essay on gang life in Harlem, and he used this piece, which focused on a young gang leader named Red Jackson, to secure a position on the staff of *Life* in 1948. Parks remained with *Life* until 1972. During that time he completed over 300 assignments. He used his art to document poverty in Harlem and Latin America, as well as the 1960s black civil rights movement in the United States. He did articles concerning the Black Panthers (a militant civil rights organization), the Ingrid Bergman-Roberto Rosellini love affair, Broadway shows, personalities, fashion, and politics. Some of Parks's works from those years include "Crime Across America", and the "Death of Malcolm X". Phil Kunhardt Jr., then an assistant managing editor at *Life,* told *Smithsonian* magazine of Parks at that time: "[A]t first he made his name with fashion, but when he covered the racial strife for us, there was no question that he was a black photographer with enormous connections and access to the black community and its leaders. He tried to show what was really going on there for a big, popular, fundamentally conservative white magazine." Kunhardt further concurred with Malcolm X's autobiography: "Success among whites never made Parks lose touch with black reality."

Book Publishing Emerges

In addition to his photography, Parks began to draw word pictures and thus embarked on a second career as a writer. In his earlier works he incorporated his knowledge of photography. He published his first book in 1947—an instructional manual entitled *Flash Photography.* That book was followed by a second manual in 1948, *Camera Portraits: Techniques and Principles of Documentary Portraiture.* In time, while he continued to work at *Life* he was encouraged to write about his early life in Kansas, and out of that beginning he developed his best-selling novel, *The Learning Tree,* which was published in 1963. *The Learning Tree* is a fictionalized account of his own childhood in Kansas. The book ends with the death of his mother. As fiction, the book tells the story of a black family in a small Kansas town during the 1920s. The story focuses on a young boy named Newt Winger. Parks related in his third autobiography *(Voices in the Mirror)* that the title and the inspiration for the novel grew out of his recollection of a conversation he had with his mother when he was young. He asked her whether the family had to stay in Fort Scott forever, to which his mother replied, "I don't know, son, . . . but you're to let this place be your learning tree. Trees bear good fruit and bad fruit, and that's the way it is here. Remember that."

In 1966, Parks published the first of three autobiographies, *A Choice of Weapons.* It tells of his struggle to survive whole after his mother's death. The title "came to him after President John F. Kennedy's assassination," according to Parks. Quoted in *Afro-American Writers after 1955,* Saunders Redding said that, "It is [a] perceptive narrative of one man's struggle to realize the values (defined democratic and especially American) he has been taught to respect." The theme of the book is evident in an article in the *Detroit News* in which Parks said, "I have a right to be bitter, but I would not let bitterness destroy me. As I tell young black people, you can fight back, but do it in a way to help yourself and not destroy yourself." Following this first autobiography he combined the imagery of two art forms, poetry and photography, for a subsequent book entitled *Gordon Parks: A Poet and His Camera* which appeared in 1968.

During the 1970s Parks published three more books combining photographs and poems: *Gordon Parks: Whispers of Intimate Things* and *In Love,* in 1971, and *Moments Without Proper Names* in 1975. The latter book portrays the unique suffering of African Americans and offers a response to the pain. In *Afro-American Writers after 1955,* Parks said of the book, "[T]he first part . . . says more of what I want[ed] to say, what I felt was necessary to say. The back part . . . is the beauty part. It is simply what it is—the beautiful moments." In 1971, he also published *Born Black,* a collection of essays on personalities of the black struggle for civil rights including Malcolm X, Martin Luther King Jr., Huey Newton, and Stokeley Carmichael. In the various essays Parks included a discussion of the black Nation of Islam, as well as the situation of a family in Harlem. From 1970 to 1973 Parks was also involved in the founding of *Essence* magazine for black women.

Parks is particularly skillful at interweaving his various interests and endeavors, as is illustrated by his book *Flavio* which was published in 1978. The book evolved from a photo essay that Parks developed in 1961 while on assignment from *Life* to document the poverty in Rio de Janeiro. This he did by scrutinizing an impoverished family, the Da Silvas. The Da Silvas had a 12–year–old son, Flavio, who was dying of bronchial asthma and malnutrition. The original photo essay, ''Freedom's Fearful Foe: Poverty,'' appeared in the June 16, 1961 issue of *Life*. Public response to the article was overwhelming; people sent money and offers of adoption. Most significant, as Parks related in *Voices in the Mirror,* was an offer from ''the Children's Asthma Research Institute [in Denver]: without charge we will definitely save him. All you have to do is deliver him to our door.'' As a result of the publicity Flavio was brought to Denver for treatment and eventually returned home in good health. Parks remained in contact with Flavio, and out of the experience came the award–winning biography of Flavio.

In 1979 Parks produced a second installment of his own life story, *To Smile in Autumn, A Memoir,* which spans the years from 1944 to 1978. *Afro–American Writers* said of the book, ''[I]t combines passages from his poems, journals, and letters with recollections of wives, children, lovers, and career assignments.''

In 1981 he published a second novel, *Shannon.* Unlike *The Learning Tree,* the novel *Shannon* was targeted at adults. It is an historical novel, set in New York. The book chronicles the O'Farrell family's rise to prominence; it broached a variety of social issues: the labor problems of World War I, the powerful influence of the Catholic Church in the Irish community, and the conflict between the rich and the poor.

Parks's third memoir, *Voices in the Mirror,* was published in 1990. In it he offered a retrospective overview of his life, from his poor beginnings in Kansas to his many triumphs both in America and abroad. In 1996 in *Glimpses Toward Infinity,* Parks's twelfth book, this talented and artistic author incorporated poetry, photography, and something new—samples of his own paintings.

Film and Music Careers Develop

During the years when Parks worked at *Life,* he discovered yet another creative outlet—a film career. Initially he served as a consultant on several Hollywood films. Eventually he produced his first film, a documentary on Flavio, after which he made three other documentaries, including *Diary of a Harlem Family* and *Mean Streets.* He was the first African American to produce, direct, and score a film for a major Hollywood studio: Warner Brothers. The film, released in 1960, was *The Learning Tree* based on Parks's original novel of the same title. Donald Bogle in *Blacks in American Films and Television* divides Parks's films into two general categories: commercial dramas, and personal ''romances.'' In the first category, *Shaft* and *Shaft's Big Score,* were released in 1971 and 1972 respectively. Also among Parks's commercial dramas was *The Super Cops* released in 1974 in which he focused on contemporary men of action caught up in urban life. Parks's first film, *The Learning Tree* was also the first of his personal romance films, followed by *Leadbelly* in 1976 and, to some degree, *Solomon Northrup's Odyssey* in 1984. Most of Parks's films, excluding *The Super Cops,* present assertive black males facing those social and political elements that rob them of their manhood. In *Voices in the Mirror,* Parks recounted his disappointment with Hollywood as he struggled to get Paramount to distribute and promote *Leadbelly,* the story of the folk and blues singer Huddie Ledbetter. Parks also produced an autobiographical film, *Gordon Parks: Moments Without Proper Names,* which was televised on PBS in 1988.

Parks wrote many musical compositions including blues tunes and popular songs in his early career and frequently incorporated his music into his films. Conversely, he wrote several film scores and then adapted the music afterward for their separate release. Among these were *Tree Symphony* from *The Learning Tree,* and ''Don't Misunderstand'' from *Shaft's Big Score.* He composed *Concerto for Piano and Orchestra, Piece for Cello and Orchestra, Five Piano Sonatas* and *Celebrations for Sarah Ross and Andrew Jackson Parks.* He created the music and libretto for a five–act ballet entitled *Martin* in 1989. The ballet, which was a tribute to Martin Luther King Jr., premiered in Washington, D.C. *Martin* later aired on national television on King's birthday in 1990. Parks was the executive producer of the television presentation. He also directed and photographed a documentary that preceded the ballet. He blended his multiple interests in photography and music yet again when he produced a portrait of jazz musicians for a 1996 issue of *Life.*

Wins Awards and Honors

Parks was honored many times for his bold and creative visions. He was named Photographer of the Year by the American Society of Magazine Photographers in 1960, and in 1964 he received the Philadelphia Museum of Art Award and the Art Directors Club Award. That same year he won the Mass Media Award and an award for outstanding contributions to better human relations; both awards were bestowed by the National Conference of Christians and Jews Brotherhood in 1964. Two years later, in 1966, he received a Notable Book Award from the American Library Association for *A Choice of Weapons.* The following year, in 1967, he received the Nikon Photographic Award for promotion of understanding among nations of the world. Parks received an Emmy Award for best television documentary for his *Diary of a Harlem Family* in 1968, and in 1970 he was honored with the Carr Van Anda Award from Ohio University School of Journalism. He was inducted into the Black Film Makers Hall of Fame in 1973. The list goes on: Spingarn Medal from the NAACP in 1972; first place at the Dallas Film Festival in 1976 for *Leadbelly*; Christopher Award for best biography in 1978, for *Flavio*; and Guild for High Achievement from the National

Urban League in 1980. The NAACP Hall of Fame Award and the Frederick Douglass Gold Medal went to Parks in 1984, and he received the American Society of Magazine Photographers Award in 1985. Parks was the Kansan of the Year in 1985, and for that distinction he received the Governor's Medal of Honor from the State of Kansas. In 1988 he received both a Commonwealth Mass Communications Award and a National Medal of Arts.

Between 1968 and 1996 Gordon Parks received honorary degrees from 13 separate institutions: Maryland Institute of Fine Arts in 1968; Pratt Institute in 1981; Syracuse University School of Journalism in 1963; Boston University School of Public Communication in 1969; Colby College in 1974; Lincoln University in 1975; Rutgers University in 1980; Kansas City Art Institute in 1984; Art Center College of Design in 1987; Hamline University in 1987; American International College in 1988; Savannah College of Art and Design in 1988; and the University of the District of Columbia in 1996.

John F. Kennedy High School in New York City honored Parks with a media center in his name, and The Learning Tree Schools were established in his honor. In January of 1998 *Jet* announced that the Stockton School in East Orange, New Jersey was renamed to become the Gordon Parks Academy—a magnet school of radio, animation, film, and television.

Personal Notes

Parks married Sally Alvis in 1933. The couple, who divorced in 1961, had three children: Gordon Parks Jr.; Toni Parks Parson; and David Parks. Parks Jr. the first born, was a film director like his father. He died tragically in an airplane crash in 1979 while filming on location in Africa. In 1962 Parks married Elizabeth Campbell—They have one daughter, Leslie, and they were divorced in 1973. Parks's third marriage, in August of 1973 to Genevieve Young, also ended in divorce, in 1979. Parks has three grandchildren (Alan, Gordon Parks III, and Sara) and one great granddaughter, Dannah.

Parks, who resides in New York City, is still trying to find the meaning of life. He is still in love with life, because ''nothing is more noble than a good try,'' according to Parks in the ''Epilogue'' to *Voices in the Mirror.* He revealed further that he has ''been given several names—Mr. Dreamer, Mr. Striver, and . . . Mr. Success . . . the first two fit rather well; the third has a slight feel of discomfort.'' He summed up his life in *Visions* as follows:

> I've known both misery and happiness, lived in so many different skins it is impossible for one skin to claim me. And I have felt like a wayfarer on an alien planet at times—walking, running, wondering about what brought me to this particular place, and why. But once I was here the dreams started moving in, and I went about devouring them as they devoured me.

Current address: c/o Ben Benjamin, Creative Management Associates, 9255 Sunset Boulevard, Los Angeles, CA 90069.

REFERENCES

Bogle, Donald. *Blacks in American Films and Television: An Encyclopedia.* New York: Simon and Schuster, 1988.

Contemporary Authors. New Revision Series, Vol. 26. Detroit: Gale Research, 1989.

Contemporary Black Biography. Vol. 1. Detroit: Gale Research, 1992.

Harris, Trudier, and Thadious M. Davis, eds. *Afro-American Writers after 1955.* Detroit: Gale Research, 1984.

Moore, Deedee. ''Shooting Straight: The Many Worlds of Gordon Parks.'' *Smithsonian* 20 (April 1989): 66–77.

''New Jersey School Named for Gordon Parks.'' *Jet* 93 (19 January 1998): 23.

Parks, Gordon. *Voices in the Mirror: An Autobiography.* New York: Doubleday, 1990.

''Seeing through Eyes Born Poor and Black.'' *New York Times,* September 21, 1997.

COLLECTIONS

The Gordon Parks collection was donated to the Library of Congress.

Helen R. Houston

Charles H. Parrish Sr.

(1859–1931)

Educator, minister, school founder, college president, activist

Charles H. Parrish Sr. proved that the American dream for success can become a reality through his persistence and ambition. Born a slave, he advanced from an errand boy to become a university president. He was notable for his achievements in education, religion, and social activism—separate arenas that overlapped in Parrish's personal philosophy. Parrish headed the Eckstein Norton Institute, a center for the industrial education of blacks, and two black colleges, Lynchburg Baptist University and Simmons University. He was a pastor for 45 years and was active in turn-of-the-century civil rights politics. He founded and served as president to the Louisville, Kentucky, NAACP.

On April 18, 1859, in Lexington, Kentucky, Charles Henry Parrish Sr. was born to Hiram and Harriet Hall Parrish, the slaves of Jeff Barr and Beverly Hicks. Hiram Parrish, a deacon of the First Baptist Church, was a teamster. His wife Harriet was an accomplished seamstress and, according to her son, a woman of strong character to whom he attributed his success. Charles, the oldest of the Parrish children, had one brother and one sister.

Charles H. Parrish Sr.

As a child, Parrish and his siblings regularly attended Sunday school at the First Baptist Church. Parrish learned to spell and read through the church literacy programs. When he was six, his family received their freedom and he began public school at the freedmen's school in Lexington. Parrish spent his early years in training in the Baptist church, which he had joined at the age of twelve. In 1872 the church made him church secretary, a position he held for eight years in addition to a position as teacher in the Sunday school. He was also elected as clerk of the deacon board and church clerk.

Parrish's experiences teaching Sunday school made him aware of his own limited learning, so he became committed to getting a liberal education. Because of his family's impoverished state, he was forced to quit school to work as a porter in a general store from 1874 to 1880. Ambitious and determined, every free moment of his time was spent studying.

Parrish's desire for an education also became a subject of his prayers. Finally, his father agreed that he could quit work to attend the Nashville Institute for the fall term of 1878. However, his father died March 11, 1877, which left young Parrish responsible for his mother and two siblings. Reluctantly, Parrish decided to postpone his educational plans and to devote his energies to providing for his family. On July 22, 1879, Parrish again suffered a tragic loss with the death of his mother. Overwhelmed with family responsibilities and stricken with grief, his schooling was no longer a priority. He decided to focus his attention and affection on his little thirteen–year–old sister, whose education and future became his greatest desire. Unfortunately, tragedy struck for the third time, and she too died in June of 1880. With his life savings depleted and his time consumed with work, Parrish saw no way to complete his personal educational goals.

William J. Simmons, who was then pastor of the First Baptist Church in Lexington, had witnessed the hardships that Parrish had suffered. When Simmons was called to Louisville to the Kentucky Normal and Theological Institute (later known as State University and finally as Simmons University), he took Parrish with him. Finally, on September 13, 1880, Parrish began his education.

Both Parrish and the institute, which the General Association of Negro Baptists had created in Kentucky, were struggling financially, and Parrish worked diligently to improve the status of both. He completed the Normal School course of studies in 1882, receiving the highest honor—a gold medal. Then he began the college program, which he completed in 1886 with an A.B. degree in theology. Parrish worked his way through college by holding many jobs, including student teacher, bookkeeper, and tutor, and still managed to become the first valedictorian of the college. While in college, he was elected delegate to the National Convention of Colored Men in 1883 and to both the Republican State Convention and the Colored Educational Convention in 1884. Because of his dedication and his exemplary personal character, the university professors and trustees appointed him secretary and treasurer of the university as well as guardian of the students. He subsequently became professor of Greek. In 1889 he completed a master's degree at State University and in 1898 received an honorary doctorate of divinity. In 1915 he received his LL.B. from Central Law School in Louisville and in 1923 the LL.D. degree.

While Parrish was pursuing this educational path, he also pursued a spiritual one. On January 2, 1886 Parrish was ordained. In September of that year he became the pastor of the Calvary Baptist Church in Louisville, a role he served for 45 years until his death.

Heads Three Schools

Throughout his life, Parrish was involved in the leadership of a number of educational institutions. In 1890 William J. Simmons and Parrish founded the Eckstein Norton Institute in Cane Spring, Kentucky, 29 miles from Louisville. In the fall of 1890, following Simmons's sudden death, Parrish became the second president of Eckstein Norton, which stressed industrial education. For the April 1893 issue of the *AME Zion Church Quarterly,* Parrish wrote, "Industrial education reduces the abstract theories of the school room to practical realities, and shows the actual and intimate relationship existing between book lore and the actualities of real life." The funding for the Eckstein Norton Institute came from the support of white businessmen who promoted industrial training for blacks. The school closed in 1912.

In 1907 Parrish became president of Lynchburg Baptist University in Virginia. One year later he founded the Kentucky Home Society for Colored Children, also serving as its president. Parrish became president of State University in 1918 and served in this capacity until his own death in 1931.

As president, he made many improvements in the school, including changing the name to Simmons University in honor of its founder. He also provided a valuable contribution to education as the vice president of the Central Law School. He served as president of the Kentucky State Teachers' Association from 1895 to 1897 and was the secretary of the board of trustees for the Lincoln Institute in Lincoln Ridge, Kentucky.

Represents Louisville Blacks and American Baptists

Parrish was in the forefront of Louisville's black civil rights leadership, and when Kentucky African Americans met in Frankfort to form the Anti–Separate Coach Movement, he was selected as the chairperson of the resolutions committee in 1893. Parrish was also selected to serve as the spokesperson to meet with the governor.

Not only did Parrish serve as a spokesperson for Kentucky blacks, but he also served as a voice for American blacks in 1904 when the National Baptist Convention sent him as a delegate to the World's Sunday School Convention in Jerusalem. The following year he attended the World's Baptist Congress in London and later visited Germany, preaching in seventeen German towns. He was elected to the World's Missionary Convention in Edinburgh, Scotland, in 1910. Beginning in 1914, Parrish served as the president of the Joint Commission of American Baptist Theological Seminary in Nashville for ten years. In 1915 the National Baptist Convention sent him as a messenger to Baptists in Jamaica, and he was baptized in the Caribbean Sea while there.

In 1923 Parrish was an American delegate to the Baptist World Alliance Meeting in Sweden. He was named to the executive committee at the Stockholm meeting, being one of two blacks on the eight–member committee. Also he contributed to the Baptist Church as president of the Executive Board of the General Association of Negro Baptists of Kentucky and as recording secretary of the Foreign Mission Board of the National Baptist Convention.

Parrish's community involvement included active membership in several social and fraternal organizations, including the Masons, Knights of Pythias, Mosaic Templars, Foresters, Odd Fellows, Royal Neighbors, Good Samaritans, and the United Brothers of Friendship.

In December of 1913, Parrish called together a group of black leaders and formed the Louisville NAACP, which was officially recognized in 1914. He was elected as president of the organization. Later, in his capacity as a member of both the NAACP and the Commission on Interracial Cooperation, Parrish became involved in protests against residential segregation and city park segregation practices. At Parrish's request, NAACP national speakers Chapin Brinsmade and Joel Spingarn spoke at a rally in protest of the Louisville city ordinances. Parrish served on the NAACP's executive board until 1920, when he resigned because the chapter rejected his moderate stance on segregation.

Parrish demonstrated his business acumen in Louisville in the positions of vice–president of the Mammoth Life and Accident Insurance Company for thirteen years, director of American Mutual Savings Bank for two years, and director of First Standard Bank for five years. Other business involvement in the community included his work with the Louisville Negro Business League, of which he served as president.

Parrish's professional affiliations included membership in the American Geographical Society, the American Sociological Society, and the Southern Sociological Congress. In 1912 Parrish was elected Fellow of the Royal Geographical Society in London, England.

Parrish wrote the handbook for Baptist Churches, *What We Believe,* in 1886. Other pamphlets Parrish published include: *God and His People, The Gospel in the Adjustment of Race Differences, Oriental Lights for the Teacher, Travels in the Holy Land,* and *Aspirations of Christian Africa.*

On January 26, 1898, Parrish married Mary Virginia Cook, a native of Bowling Green, Kentucky. Mary Parrish, a devout Christian, became a well–known speaker, journalist, and teacher at the Eckstein Norton Institute in Cane Spring, Kentucky. The marriage produced one child, Charles Henry, Jr., on January 12, 1899. Parrish, his wife, and their son resided on Sixth Street in Louisville, in the heart of the black community. Following his parents' legacy, in 1950 Charles Jr. became the first black hired to the faculty by a southern white institution, the University of Louisville. Charles Parrish, Sr.'s contribution to both the educational and Baptist Church communities is unsurpassed. During his lifetime, Parrish's prominence as a church leader became worldwide. In Kentucky Parrish played a pivotal role in advancing educational opportunities and civil rights for African Americans. The people of Louisville respected him as educator, activist, businessman, and minister. He died on April 8, 1931, and was buried in the Louisville Cemetery.

REFERENCES

Dunnigan, Alice A. *Fascinating Story of Black Kentuckians: Their Heritage and Tradition.* Washington, DC: Associated Publishers, 1982.

Johnson, W. D. *Biographical Sketches of Prominent Negro Men and Women of Kentucky.* Lexington: Standard Print, 1897.

Kleber, John E., ed. *The Kentucky Encyclopedia.* Lexington: University Press of Kentucky, 1992.

Richings, G. F. *Evidences of Progress among Colored People.* 4th ed. Philadelphia: George S. Ferguson Co., 1897.

Simmons, William J. *Men of Mark: Eminent, Progressive, and Rising.* Cleveland: Geo. M. Rewell, 1887.

Wright, George. *Life behind a Veil: Blacks in Louisville, Kentucky, 1865–1930.* Baton Rouge: Louisiana State University, 1985.

COLLECTIONS

The papers of Charles H. Parrish are housed in the Ekstrom Library, Archives and Records Center, the University of Louisville, Louisville, Kentucky.

Karen Cotton McDaniel

Frederick D. Patterson

(1901–1988)

Veterinarian, educator, college president, fund raiser, organization founder

Frederick D. Patterson was a major influence on the development of higher education for African Americans through his presidency of Tuskegee Institute, his creation of the United Negro College Fund, and his leadership of the Phelps Stokes Fund. As third president of Tuskegee Institute, he built upon the models established by his predecessors, Booker T. Washington and Robert Russa Moton. He expanded on their ideas, creating unique solutions to financial problems that plagued black private colleges from the Great Depression through most of the civil rights era. Private black colleges were struggling to provide education for the youth of the African diaspora in America during a time of segregation. Through the United Negro College Fund (UNCF), the nation's first collective fund–raising organization in higher education, Patterson inspired them to struggle together.

Frederick D. Patterson

Frederick Douglass Patterson was named after the black hero in whose Anacostia neighborhood he was born in Washington, D.C., on October 10, 1901. He was the youngest of six children of Mamie Brooks Patterson and William Patterson. His remains were cremated following his death at home in New Rochelle, New York, on April 26, 1988. He was survived by his wife, Catherine and son, Frederick II.

Within 11 months of his birth, Patterson's mother died of tuberculosis, and one year later, his father succumbed to the same disease. William Patterson's will contained the stipulation that his children be cared for and educated by designated families of Washington D.C.'s black community. In return for their care, he offered his family's household furniture, library, and china. Julia Dorsey, an elderly ex–slave who had moved with the family from Texas, cared for the youngest child, Frederick. She raise him in her home until the eldest child, Wilhelmina, known as Bessie, took sole responsibility for him.

Despite their recent move, the father's wishes were fulfilled. Both Mamie and William Patterson originally came from Texas and both studied at Prairie View State Normal and Industrial Institute, a state school in Prairie View, Texas. William Patterson's Texas career included time as a high school principal, a teacher trainer and a publisher of the *Calvert Texas Republican.* While in Texas, he passed the U.S. government clerk examination; he, his wife, their five children, and some of their relatives and friends, including Julia Dorsey, moved as a group to the nation's capitol. Once in Washington D.C., William discovered that, due to his race, his clerical appointment paid at a lower rate, a messenger's salary. Unwilling to accept this discrimination, he enrolled in Howard University Law School and graduated just as his wife gave birth to Frederick. Before William Patterson could practice, he died, leaving six children.

Bessie Patterson, then a student pianist, raised Frederick in Anacostia in a loving, secure environment. The second oldest child, Lucille, married and the older boys, John, James, and Lorenzo attended St. Paul's, a vocational school in Lawrenceville, Virginia. When Bessie completed her studies, she took Frederick back to Texas, where she felt they might fare better than in the East. She taught music at several schools and, when it was possible, kept her brother with her. With the help of various friends and family, she managed his care. Later she kept her 12 year old brother with her full–time when she obtained a position teaching music at Prairie View, her parents' alma mater. Frederick Patterson enrolled in Prairie View after spending a few terms in the elementary school at Sam Houston College.

Becomes a Veterinarian

Voted the "Least Likely to Succeed" by his eighth grade classmates, Patterson remained an unresponsive student at Prairie View Agricultural and Mechanical College until he came in contact with Edward B. Evans, veterinarian to whom Patterson was assigned as a student worker. Evans had a degree in veterinary medicine from Iowa State University. When it was time for Patterson to go to college, he wanted to follow the route of his idol, and become an Iowa State University–trained veterinarian. With Bessie's blessing, but lacking the fees for even the first term's study, Patterson left for Ames, Iowa, and enrolled in Iowa State in the fall of 1919. Racial discrimination prevented him from living in the college dormitories; he could not eat on campus either. Instead, he lived in an apartment with several other black students, most of whom were World War I veterans. The veterinary medicine course was rigorous and Patterson struggled initially. Meanwhile, he supported himself by working at various jobs—rug cleaner, delivery truck driver, waiter, elevator operator, and porter. He served in the U.S. Army Reserve Officers' Training Corps (ROTC), which helped pay his college tuition.

One summer, Patterson's ROTC obligation took him to an army installation in Carlisle, Pennsylvania, where he found himself one of two black reservists among the thousands of ROTC students. Although all these student soldiers trained and bunked together, the dining hall was segregated. Many whites wanted to sit near the blacks, so that they could get their leftover food.

Following graduation with a degree in veterinary medicine from Iowa State University in 1923, Virginia State College in Petersburg offered Patterson a job teaching veterinary students. During the next few years, he returned to Iowa State to obtain his master's degree in veterinary medicine—an undertaking paid for by the General Education Board.

In 1932 Patterson was appointed to the faculty at Tuskegee Normal and Industrial Institute (later Tuskegee Institute and now Tuskegee University) in Tuskegee, Alabama, to practice and teach in its agriculture division, where the famous George Washington Carver, was conducting his research. The two men began a friendship that lasted until Carver's death in 1943.

Always looking to advance his skills and his career options, Patterson taught only a few terms at Tuskegee before he enrolled in a doctoral program in bacteriology at Cornell University in Ithaca, New York. When he returned to Tuskegee with a doctorate, he was the their first faculty member to earn this advanced degree. Soon, the deanship of the Agriculture School was his, along with a sizeable veterinary practice and increasing prominence in the Tuskegee Institute community.

As a scientifically–trained teacher of veterinary subjects to students studying nursing, home economics, and agriculture, Patterson offered more advanced subjects. He instituted new practices in the care and treatment of the animals in Tuskegee Institute's farms and programs. Patterson also worked with the Moveable School's staff of experts. The U.S. Department of Agriculture created the program, consisting of a specially constructed truck to display agriculture, home economics, child care, and nutrition information. Patterson sometimes accompanied the Moveable School as it traveled around to the communities of black agricultural workers in Macon County, near Tuskegee Institute.

Becomes Tuskegee's Third President

Tuskegee's president, Robert Russa Moton, respected Patterson's abilities and work. When Moton retired in 1935, Patterson was favored as successor. The Board of Trustees sustained Moton's endorsement, and Patterson became president–elect at 34 years old. Even before his formal installation, Patterson was already an important part of the Tuskegee scene. He married Catherine Elizabeth Moton, one of Robert Moton and Jennie Dee Moton's daughters, in June of 1935, a few months prior to his inauguration as Tuskegee's third president.

As president, Patterson struggled to find the programs and practices that would upgrade Tuskegee as a school and provide Tuskegee students the occupational skills that ensured them jobs. Earlier, Tuskegee students had studied agriculture and home economics. They had opportunities to study plumbing, shoemaking, and nursing as well as English, history and biology. Approaching the second half of the twentieth century, however, Patterson wanted students at Tuskegee to have the technical skills necessary to compete in the job market, even a usually segregated one. The new Patterson administration created the Commercial Dietetics program to train students for readily–available jobs as chefs in hotels, restaurants, and at resorts across the United States. It also provided internships around the country for students apprenticing in the food preparation field. Program graduates found work that paid salaries equal to those of Tuskegee graduates who became teachers. *Service,* a magazine for the men and women of the various service occupations allied with the dietetics program, was published in cooperation with the program and circulated around the United States during the 1930s and 1940s.

Even more acute than the need to supply cooks for the nation was the need to make veterinary education available to black students of the segregated South. For the most part, the field of veterinary medicine excluded blacks. The black agricultural population of the United States was concentrated in the South, where the schools of veterinary medicine—and the universities in which they were located—denied them admission. Patterson used these exclusionary practices as a basis for creating the Southern Regional Education Board (SREB), his answer to educational discrimination. Some Southern states funded public schools that excluded blacks from training in particular fields. With the SREB those states were required to pay school fees for the out–of–state education of blacks who studied in those fields. Since veterinary medicine was available for whites but not blacks in the South, Patterson worked to establish an accredited school of veterinary medicine at Tuskegee, one that black students around the nation could attend. It continues as the only veterinary school ever founded at black college.

Consistent with the Tuskegee tradition of seeking black faculty to demonstrate black excellence and diversity, Patterson recruited an all–black veterinary medicine education faculty. The recruiting of students and building the physical plant were directed by Patterson with the assistance of Edward B. Evans, who served briefly as dean of Tuskegee's new School of Veterinary Medicine. The new school achieved accreditation and, within a few years, graduated more black veterinarians—both male and female—than all other veterinary medicine schools in the country combined. These veterinarians, too, worked in a segregated society, but whites did not object to paying blacks for veterinary services.

Tuskegee's program in Commercial Aviation and its School of Engineering were also created during Patterson's

Tuskegee tenure, in 1939 and 1948 respectively. Unlike some, Patterson never doubted that black people could fly planes and be engineers if opportunities for training existed. The Tuskegee aviation program remained the most famous of the opportunities that Tuskegee produced during the Patterson years. Patterson's efforts made the famed Tuskegee Airmen possible. He established the Commercial Aviation program to train Tuskegee students as pilots, and learned to fly himself. After determining that the new U.S. Army Air Corps—the predecessor of today's Air Force—would not be racially integrated, Patterson lobbied to have a training program for military pilots established at Tuskegee. The resulting federal airfield and training program created a supply of black men, including commercial aviators, who became the celebrated black fighter pilots of World War II, the Tuskegee Airmen.

Creates and Develops the United Negro College Fund

Patterson battled with the serious budgetary problems that stood in the way of the institutional growth that he sought for Tuskegee Institute. He studied the conditions of other schools as well. Patterson conducted an informal survey of black college presidents in the early 1940s that yielded some interesting results. According to these educators, their institutions' financial condition was as bad as or worse than Tuskegee's. Based on that information, Patterson developed a speech on the subject for presentation to a local social organization; later, he crystallized his thinking about the financial state of black private colleges into a proposal for colleges to do fund raising together. Thus, the idea for the United Negro College Fund was born.

Patterson wrote a column in the *Pittsburgh Courier* and he used that space to present his idea to black America. He received encouragement in conversations and through the mail, and soon he called a meeting in 1943 of more than a dozen presidents of private black colleges, including Benjamin E. Mays of Morehouse College, Albert Dent of Dillard, David Jones of Bennett, Florence Read of Spelman, Thomas Elsa Jones of Fisk, Mordecai Johnson of Howard, and Rufus Clement of Atlanta University.

The black colleges lacked the endowments that provided some of the operating funds that wealthier white colleges used to maintain and develop their institutions. In the past, many black colleges relied on substantial contributions from white philanthropists to supplement modest student fees to constitute their operating budget. With a newly–instituted federal income tax and a change in philanthropists' attitudes, contributions for black colleges were not coming from the usual contributors in the expected amounts. Patterson proposed to raise money from the broader base of Americans who were concerned with the plight of these students. He focused on the nation as a whole, not just to a few rich individuals, to meet the challenge to educate all youth—regardless of color—by supporting their educational institutions and thereby increasing the national strength.

The idea that the group of black private college presidents agreed to was a one–time joint effort to raise operating funds for their colleges by waging a national campaign. The group agreed to work together using the name the United Negro College Fund, obtained an office and staff in New York City, and began an institutional effort that is now over 50 years old.

Enlisting the endorsement of John D. Rockefeller Jr., the colleges launched that first campaign in 1944 and raised more than they hoped, nearly $800,000. The number of the fund's member colleges increased and by the time Patterson ended his active involvement with the fund more than a dozen years later, there were 41 private black colleges who identified with the slogan "A mind is a terrible thing to waste." In addition to the annual campaign for operating funds, the College Fund successfully raised capital funds.

At Tuskegee, Patterson continued to practice educational innovation while studying educational administration at Stanford University. When he left Tuskegee Institute in 1953, he had raised its status from an advanced high school to that of an accredited college with graduate programs and divisions.

Patterson left the presidency of Tuskegee to take on the presidency of the Phelps Stokes Fund in New York City. The Phelps Stokes Fund worked primarily in the fields of education and housing, and when Patterson began in 1953, he concentrated on issues of African education. In the same way that he brought his knowledge of science to the presidency of Tuskegee, Patterson brought his knowledge of vocational and technical education to the challenge of planning education for Africans of soon–to–be independent nations.

Troubleshooting African Education and Civil Rights

For 17 years Patterson traveled three or four times a year to East and West Africa, conferring with heads of state of Nigeria, Sierra Leone, and Ghana, and meeting with educators at the University of Liberia, the University of Ibadan in Nigeria, and at Makerere College in Kampala, Uganda. Patterson's expertise lay in his years of experience planning technical education at Tuskegee and in observing educational planning and development at the UNCF–member colleges. Africans needed Patterson's expertise in developing the training programs for technical jobs traditionally held by European colonials. Patterson helped a government decide, for example, how many nursing and medical schools it needed to build. Plumbers, agronomists or soil scientists, veterinarians, and nurses were all needed in a continent that lacked educational institutions to train Africans for these jobs. The nation reexamined the long colonial tradition of sending Africans abroad to be educated. Everyone could not be sent to England or America to be educated. Africa had to educate its own. Patterson helped governments decide when, where, and how educational infrastructure should be developed to make African–trained professionals reality.

Africans sometimes found it difficult to obtain graduate education in the United States was sometimes difficult for Africans. Patterson involved Phelps Stokes in helping make more graduate education possible for Africans. The fund developed programs to assist those Africans attending graduate schools in specific technical fields with spending money, transportation expenses, and support for their families in the United States.

As head of the Phelps Stokes Fund, Patterson also served a unique role in the civil rights struggle of the 1950s and 1960s. Patterson hosted meetings at Robert Russa Moton's mansion in Capahosic, Virginia, so that student civil rights leaders could meet with corporate executives who continued to discriminate against African Americans in their businesses. Capahosic was one of the few sites where integrated meetings could be held in the South. UNCF–member schools also held their meetings there. With its picturesque holly trees, view of the Capahosic River, and Patterson's leadership, the conference center provided a forum for discussing the pressing race issues of the day. These meetings produced concessions on the part of the corporate representatives and further elevated the importance of black college students in negotiating the removal of barriers of segregation.

When Patterson retired from the presidency of Phelps Stokes in 1970, he decided to attack a problem that disturbed him for over 30 years—that of building the endowment of black colleges. He formulated an idea, the College Endowment Funding Plan (CEFP), by which black colleges like the 41 UNCF members as well as public colleges, with significant support from the insurance industry, can solicit and build endowment. This increased endowment provides increased interest, which gives colleges more money with which to operate programs, pay faculty and staff, and provide assistance for students.

On June 23, 1987, President Ronald Reagan awarded the Presidential Medal of Freedom, the highest civilian honor the United States bestows on its citizens, to Frederick Patterson. Ten months later, as Patterson worked to refine aspects of the College Endowment Funding Plan and finish his autobiography, *Chronicles of Faith,* he died. Patterson was awarded the Spingarn Medal of the NAACP posthumously in 1988.

Frederick Douglass Patterson was a giant on the landscape of higher education in twentieth century America. He worked tirelessly to increase both funds and curriculum for black colleges. His contributions to Tuskegee Institute, to black technical education and to educational opportunity in general, his gift of the UNCF, and the global focus of his work at the Phelps Stokes Fund all merit recognition for a creative and pioneering legacy.

REFERENCES

College Endowment Funding Plan. Washington, DC: American Council on Education, 1976.

F. D. Patterson. Obituary. *New York Times,* April 17, 1988.

Goodson, Martia Graham, ed. *Chronicles of Faith: The Autobiography of Frederick D. Patterson.* Tuscaloosa: University of Alabama Press, 1991.

Patterson, F. D. Interview. United Negro College Fund Oral History Project, Oral History Research Office, Columbia University, 1980.

Phelps Stokes Fund and Its Work, July 1, 1963–June 30, 1965. New York: Phelps Stokes Fund Report, n.d.

Williams, T. S.. *Development of a Black Professional School: The School of Veterinary Medicine as an Educational Institution and as a Sociocultural System: An Historical Study, 1940–1970.* Tuskegee, AB: Carver Research Institute, 1977.

COLLECTIONS

Patterson's papers are housed at the Smithsonian Institution. The papers of the Phelps Stokes Fund during Patterson's administration are at the Schomburg Center for Research in Black Culture.

Martia Graham Goodson

Daniel A. Payne
(1811–1893)
Religious leader, educator, historian, college president

Daniel A. Payne is a key figure in 19th–century black history. For him religion, morality, education, and racial progress went hand in hand. As a religious leader, he was involved in the rapid expansion of the African Methodist Episcopal (AME) Church throughout the nation. He influenced the denomination to adopt the goal of educating its clergy. He fostered the education of African Americans by acquiring and rebuilding Wilberforce University as the first black–owned and controlled institution of higher learning. His ideal of uplifting humanity through morality and education reinforced the belief system of the emerging black middle class.

Daniel Alexander Payne was born in Swinton Lane (later Princess Street), Charleston, South Carolina, on February 24, 1811, to London and Martha Payne. London Payne's father was white and of English heritage. London Payne was a slender brown man, five feet eight inches tall. He was reportedly born free in Virginia but later was kidnapped and sold as a slave in South Carolina. London Payne died in 1815, when Daniel was about four and a half years old. Martha Payne was a slim, light–brown skinned woman of medium height and mixed heritage: her grandparents were Native American and black. She, like her husband, was a devout Christian, and she took Daniel Payne to class meetings after the death of his father. She died when her son was nine and a half. Payne was then raised by his great–aunt, Sarah Bordeaux.

At the age of eight, Payne entered the Minors' Moralist Society's school where he stayed for two years. (The society was an organization of free blacks devoted to helping poor black children.) He studied for three years under Thomas S. Bonneau, the most popular black teacher in Charleston at the

Daniel A. Payne

time. At age 12, Payne was apprenticed as a carpenter; five and a half years later he spent nine months working for a tailor.

Payne's thirst for knowledge was stimulated by the *Self–Interpreting Bible* of John Brown. Brown, of Haddinton, Scotland, had taught himself Latin and Greek as a poor youth. Payne was inspired by Brown's example and was determined to continue his own education by reading every book he could get his hands on.

At the same time his religious development was unfolding. He joined a Methodist class at the age of 15 and underwent a conversion experience when he was 18. Shortly after his conversion he had a vision that determined the shape of the rest of his life. In his autobiography, *Recollections of Seventy Years,* he tells of a feeling of hands pressed against his shoulders; he heard an inner voice. The voice said, ''I have set thee apart to educate thyself in order that thou mayest be an educator to thy people.''

Opens First School

Payne opened his first school in 1829. He taught three free children by day and three slaves by night for a total income of $1 a month, not enough to support himself. Through the charity of a slave woman, Mrs. Eleanor Parker, he was able to survive the year. He nearly stopped teaching after the first year but persevered with greater success in the years to come. By 1834 his school, with 65 students, was the most popular of the five schools for blacks in existence at the time in Charleston.

Payne also continued his own education, studying geography, English grammar, astronomy, mathematics, and botany through the standard textbooks of the time. He further incorporated into his studies Greek, Latin, French, and drawing. It was during those years, in 1832, that Payne permanently injured his eyesight by observing a total eclipse of the sun with his naked eye.

In the summer of 1834, Payne's educational endeavors came to the attention of the white community when a group of whites discovered some of his students on a plantation collecting zoological specimens. They gave the boys an ''impromptu examination'' and were greatly impressed with how well the students performed. In his autobiography Payne quotes a young doctor in the group of whites as saying, ''Why, pa, Payne is playing hell in Charleston.''

The South Carolina legislature launched an assault against the education of all black people, free or slave, in late 1834 by setting penalties for any black who taught other blacks to read or write. A penalty was set, up to $50 dollars in fines and a whipping of up to 50 lashes. For whites caught teaching blacks, the penalties were doubled. Although other black schools continued to operate quietly in Charleston, Payne left the city on May 9, 1835 and traveled north.

Payne arrived in New York with several letters of introduction in hand. He met most of the leading blacks in the city, and he also sought interviews with white clergymen, most of whom advised him to prepare as a missionary to Africa. One exception was Lutheran minister Daniel Strobel, who was looking for a young black man to train at a seminary in Gettysburg. Strobel assured Payne that he would not have to accept Lutheran doctrines or to go to Africa to be admitted.

Payne spent two successful years at Gettysburg, but a recurrence of his eye problems made it impossible for him to continue his studies and graduate. The president of the seminary, S. S. Schmucker, suggested that while the Lutherans would willingly accept Payne as a minister, he would be more useful to the AME Church. Payne left the seminary and traveled to Philadelphia with the intention of joining the AME Church, but was dissuaded by a friend. The friend warned Payne of opposition within the AME Church to an educated clergy. As Payne recounted in his memoirs:

> it was a common thing for the preachers of that Church to introduce their sermons by declaring that they had ''not rubbed their heads against college–walls,'' at which the people would cry, ''Amen!'' They had ''never studied Latin or Greek,'' at which the people would exclaim ''Glory to God!'' They had ''never studied Hebrew,'' at which all would ''shout.''

Payne heeded his friend's warning. He was licensed by the Franklin Synod of the Lutheran Church in June 1837 and was ordained two years later.

Since there were no vacancies for a Lutheran minister at the time of his ordination, Payne accepted an offer from a Presbyterian church in East Troy, New York, with the permission of the Lutheran synod. The small black church had 40 to

50 members. Soon after his arrival, Payne became a delegate to the convention of the National Moral Reform Society, a black organization in Philadelphia. Contact with white abolitionists Theodore Weld and Lewis Tappan, along with other members of the American Anti–Slavery Society, led to an offer for Payne to become one of the society's public lecturers. After spending time in prayer, Payne decided to decline the offer because it conflicted with his ministry.

Payne's ministerial career was soon interrupted nonetheless. On December 31, 1837, he injured his throat while preaching and lost his voice for nearly a year. In addition, a serious illness kept Payne confined to his bed from January to April of 1838. He resigned his pastorate and spent some time in Carlisle, Pennsylvania, where he had previously taught Sunday school while in the seminary. He began teaching again and, by early 1840, his teaching endeavors had met with great success. By 1843, he had acquired 60 students. It was also during those years in Philadelpha that his contact with leading members of the AME Church successfully dissolved Payne's prejudices against the denomination. He joined the AME Church in the winter of 1841 and became a local preacher in the spring of 1842. By May of 1843, he was fully accepted as a minister.

Begins Ministerial Career

Payne accepted the pastorship of Israel AME Church in Washington, D.C., in June of 1843. He intended to return to his school in Philadelphia after one year. After posting the bond of $1,000 required for black ministers in the District of Columbia, however, he threw himself into the work at hand with great energy. He also published a series of essays, "Epistles on the Education of the Ministry," in the *African Methodist Episcopal Church Magazine* from April 1843 to March 1884. In the articles, he pressed for the education of the clergy, thus continuing an effort which he had begun in 1842, when his resolution in favor of the education of the ministry was passed at an annual AME conference. The storm of criticism raised by his proposal for a course of studies for prospective ministers was such that he was reluctant to attend the General Conference of 1844 until he was urged by Senior Bishop Morris Brown.

Upon initial consideration by the conference, Payne's resolution to draw up a course of study for the ministry was overwhelmingly rejected. However, it passed the next day with the staunch support of Bishop Brown. Payne was named to chair the Committee of Education, which was charged with the task of creating a reading program.

In 1845 Payne was transferred to Baltimore, where he remained until 1850. Shortly after his arrival, he added the responsibilities of a school to his extensive pastoral duties. The church grew steadily and a new building was erected. Payne also worked to reduce the role of uninhibited singing and praying groups at Sunday worship services so that the congregation's behavior would more closely resemble white middle class norms. He steadfastly opposed what he considered the extravagant and inappropriate behavior of praying bands with their bush meetings, ring dancing with clapping hands and stomping feet, and what he calls in his autobiography "cornfield ditties." Education and uplift, as he saw it, would remain constants in his work.

In 1847 Payne married Julia A. Ferris. She died within the year, shortly after giving birth to a daughter who lived only nine months. There were also problems in the church arising from the transfer of property to a newly independent local church, as well as from Payne's continuing efforts to change AME worship practices. Payne prevailed in his pursuits, but not quickly enough to prevent physical violence. Payne was himself attacked during the controversy by a club–wielding woman—he suffered no injury.

As a result of these problems, Payne wished to escape pastoral duties for a while and devote his energies to historical research. The request was refused, but Bishop William Paul Quinn reduced Payne's pastoral responsibilities and appointed him to a smaller congregation; the Ebenezer Station church near Baltimore, which Payne had helped to become independent. However, the membership of Ebenezer refused to accept him. Payne used this rejection as justification to devote his time to collecting historical materials. After preaching at a funeral service for his colleague Bishop Morris Brown in 1849, Payne spent the next two years visiting every church in the denomination to gather historical documents. He supported himself, in part, by giving lectures.

As a result of his activities, Payne was tapped as a candidate for bishop. He had previously refused to allow himself to be considered but it was obvious that, with the death of Morris Brown, the AME church needed more than one active bishop besides William Paul Quinn. On May 7, 1852, Payne and Willis Nazery joined Quinn as bishops. The three men divided the church into three jurisdictions and agreed to rotate among themselves every two years. Payne took charge of the Philadelphia Conference and the newly formed New England Conference as he began the very active life of a bishop.

In 1854, Payne married for a second time. His new wife, Eliza J. Clark, had three children from a previous marriage. They lived in Cincinnati for one year, but Payne wanted to move his family to a place that had better schools and higher moral standards. Payne and his family ultimately settled in Tawawa Springs, three and a half miles from Xenia, Ohio. This was the site chosen by the white Methodist Episcopal church for their school for blacks. On July 3, 1856, Payne moved to what was to be his permanent home. The Methodist Episcopal School, named Wilberforce University, opened that October. (Payne pointed out in his autobiography that it was the white Methodists who chose the name "university" for what began as an elementary school.) Payne served as one of the institution's 24 trustees and as a member of its executive committee.

Buys Wilberforce University

Wilberforce University closed in June of 1862, its finances strained due to the outbreak of the Civil War. On March 10, 1863, the Methodist Episcopal Church offered to sell the school to the AME Church for $10,000. When pressed by leaders of the Methodist Episcopal Church for an immediate answer, Payne agreed to buy the school. By the following June, the first payment of $2,500 was made, and Wilberforce reopened in July under AME auspices with Payne as president. Payne would continue in the combined role of bishop and Wilberforce University president until 1876.

The first three installments of the loan had been paid when Wilberforce's central building was burned down by an arsonist on April 14, 1865, the same day that President Abraham Lincoln was assassinated. The school overcame this setback largely through the continued fundraising efforts of Payne, who raised $96,000 for the school during his presidency. Payne was a vigorous president who built Wilberforce into a college–level institution. The school awarded its first bachelor degrees to students from the theological department in 1870.

During the time he was involved with Wilberforce, Payne's duties as a bishop also required great dedication. In the midst of the Civil War, he gained an audience with Abraham Lincoln on April 14, 1862, at which time he urged the President to sign the emancipation bill for the District of Columbia. Lincoln signed the bill two days later. The following year, Payne visited the American Missionary Association schools in Virginia and organized AME churches in that state and in Tennessee. The final defeat of the Confederacy opened the entire South to missionary work, and the AME church expanded rapidly.

Travels and Later Years

In 1867 Payne made his first trip to Great Britain in search of funding for Wilberforce University. While he received a cordial reception, he found it very difficult to secure promises of funding. As a result, the trip was a disappointment. While in Europe, Payne attended a meeting of the Evangelical Alliance in the Netherlands, and he spent several months in Paris. He returned just in time to attend the AME General Conference in 1868. Payne traveled to Europe a second time in 1881 as a delegate to the Ecumenical Conference in London. He was a very active participant at the conference—he delivered documents and presided over one of the sessions.

Although Payne always worked tirelessly, he was never a robust man. Over the years, he suffered several bouts of prostration brought on by overwork. In 1873, he contracted cholera. In 1883, he took a fall in his home, and malaria attacked his body for several months in 1886. In time, he decided that he could no longer endure the harsh Ohio winters and he established a winter home in Jacksonville, Florida, in 1883. People who met him during those years remember Payne as a slight man, weighing no more than 100 pounds, with a shrill voice.

As he grew older, Payne had other concerns in addition to his health. For example, he found many young men in the AME Church, especially those from the South, to be impatient and disrespectful. He was disgusted by what he perceived as politicking in elections for bishops at the General Conventions—he seems to have half–believed the rumors of "vote buying." He also feared the church was overextending its commitment to education, that it created too many new colleges without sufficient assurance of financial backing.

At the same time, Payne found reasons to look back on his own career with pride. In 1881, he was denied first–class accommodations and put off a train from Jacksonville. At the time, Payne was a highly respected leader in the AME Church, and the incident inspired protest meetings as far away as Baltimore. His efforts to improve education were instrumental in building up a cadre of learned blacks. His church expanded enormously, and he saw an increase in members who were writers as evidence of the rise in literacy.

Payne's crowning accomplishments were his two major literary endeavors—a history of the AME Church and an autobiography. Although *Recollections of Seventy Years* (1888) was assembled and edited from his materials by others, it remains a valuable account of the man and his era. His *History of the African Methodist Episcopal Church,* published in 1891, remains a valuable resource over 100 years later.

Payne died in Wilberforce, Ohio, on November 29, 1893. Alexander Wayman, senior bishop of the AME Church, presided at Payne's funeral in Baltimore. Fannie Jackson Coppin, head of Philadelphia's Institute for Colored Youth, was among the speakers. In May of 1894 Henry M. Turner unveiled a monument over Payne's grave in Laurel Cemetery. One of the speakers at the occasion was Frederick Douglass.

Daniel Alexander Payne devoted his life to his church and to the education of blacks. He set his goals to evangelize, educate, and uplift, and he saw that his dream was shared by many before his death. His literary works remain essential documents for understanding the black history of his times.

REFERENCES

Graham, Leroy. *Baltimore: The Nineteenth Century Black Capital.* Lanham, MD: University Press of America. 1982.

Handy, James A. *Scraps of African Methodist Episcopal History.* Philadelphia, PA: AME Book Concern, n.d.

Logan, Rayford W., and Michael R. Winston, eds. *Dictionary of American Negro Biography.* New York: Norton 1982.

Malone, Dumas. *Dictionary of American Biography.* New York: Charles Scribner's Sons, 1943.

Payne, Daniel Alexander. *History of the African Methodist Episcopal Church.* Nashville: AME Sunday–School Union, 1891.

———. *Recollections of Seventy Years.* Nashville, TN: AME Sunday School Union, 1888.

Robert L. Johns

Pembroke, Jim.
See Pennington, James W. C.

I. Garland Penn
(1867–1930)
Educator, journalist, religious worker

I. Garland Penn was a unique man of the church. He was not an ordained minister, or had even received formal training, yet he worked fervently and faithfully for the advancement of the church. His work extends beyond local boundaries, as he participated on a national level for the Methodist Episcopal Church. Penn, like most of his generation, believed that education was one of the principal means for improving the lot of African Americans. He actively and passionately pursued that goal by working in the Sunday school and effecting change on the national level. His name lives on as the writer of a book on the African American press which has served as a standard reference text on the subject for more than a century.

Irvin Garland Penn, who seldom spelled out his first name, was born to Isham and Maria Irvine Penn in New Glasgow in Amherst County, Virginia, on October 7, 1867. He was the oldest of five children, one of whom, William Fletcher Penn, also achieved eminence when he graduating from Yale University Medical School in 1897. William Fletcher (b. 1870) established practice in Atlanta, Georgia, where his brother was living at the time. There the physician became the step–father of Louis Tompkins Wright (1891–1952), who in turn became a very prominent physician in New York City and chairman of the board of trustees of the NAACP from 1935 until his death.

Isham and Maria Penn moved to Lynchburg about 1872 in order to give their children a good education. Penn went to school in Lynchburg until the fall of 1883 when financial difficulties kept him out a year. He landed a job as a teacher in Bedford County , but was able to return to the Lynchburg Colored High School the following year. In 1886, he was one of five members of the first graduating class of the school.

After graduation, Penn taught school in Amherst County and continued to work as a newspaperman. He had written for the weekly paper, the *Lynchburg Laborer,* since 1885 and in 1886 became editor and part–owner. The following year, he became a teacher at Payne School in Lynchburg and his partner, P. H. Johnson, took over management of the paper and renamed it *Laboring Man.* Unfortunately, the paper did not survive. Penn soon became principal of the school, a position he held until 1895. In 1890, he received a degree from Rust College in Holly Springs, Mississippi, a Methodist Episcopal–sponsored school. *Who's Who in Colored America* says the degree was an M.A. , which might well be an honorary degree. Wiley College in Marshall, Texas, awarded Penn an honorary degree in 1908.

On December 26, 1889, Penn married a fellow faculty member at Payne School, Anna Belle Rhodes (1865–1930), a graduate of Shaw University. Only two poems by Anna Belle Rhodes are extant and they were published in M. A. Majors's

I. Garland Penn

Noted Negro Women: Their Triumphs and Activities. Majors credited her with valuable—and previously unacknowledged—work on her husband's first book. The marriage produced seven children: Wilhelmina (Mrs. Franklin, b. 1890), I. Garland Jr. (b. 1892), Georgia S. (Mrs. Williams, 1894–1924), Elizabeth H. (b. 1896), Louise (Mrs. Sandipher, b. 1898), Marie (Mrs. Miller, b. 1900), and Anna Belle (Mrs. Maxwell, b. 1903).

Penn's journalism experience motivated him to compile and publish a sweeping history of the black press, a very ambitious project for a man only 24–years old. *The Afro–American Press and Its Editors* appeared in 1891. The first part describes more than 170 African American periodicals, beginning with the first, *Freedom's Journal,* which started in 1827. The second part includes biographical sketches of many journalists and newspaper contributors. For more than a century, the work has been must–reading for those seeking information about the black press.

Religious Leader

Originally, the Penn family was connected with the Colored Methodist Episcopal Church, a group that emerged from the Methodist Episcopal Church South in 1870. As adults, Penn and his brother, Fletcher, were members of the Methodist Episcopal Church, a largely white denomination. The change in denomination may have been due to more appealing activities at the Jackson Street Methodist Episcopal Church. Penn said in *Seven Graded Sunday Schools,* that he entered that church's Sunday school at the age of five. By the age of 15, Penn was its secretary and soon became a teacher and then superintendent.

Penn's identification with the Jackson Street Church was probably strengthened by the fact that during the week the building housed the public school of which he was principal. In 1888, he delivered a stirring talk at the Washington Conference meeting in Baltimore. The Washington Conference was the separate administrative body for blacks in the Methodist Episcopal Church. The following year, he spoke at the Annual Conference of the Colored Methodist Episcopal Church, urging the establishment of a normal and theological school in Virginia.

The Jackson Street Congregation was a strong church with 800 in the congregation and 600 in the Sunday school. Penn was the recording secretary when the church vigorously supported the creation of the Virginia Collegiate and Industrial Institute, which began operation near Lynchburg in 1893. When the Washington Conference met in Lynchburg in 1892, Penn was selected as a lay delegate to the quadrennial General Conference of the Methodist Episcopal Church. Before his death, Penn would be elected lay delegate ten consecutive times in a span of 40 years, a unique distinction.

At this first convention, Penn supported the election of a black bishop. It was not until 1920 that the church selected its first two black bishops for service in the United States, Robert E. Jones (1871–1960) and Matthew W. Clair Sr. (1865–1943).

Educational Work for the Church

By 1895, the Methodist Episcopal Church offered full-time employment to Penn, but he first accepted the position of national commissioner of Negro exhibits at the Cotton States and International Exposition held in Atlanta. Penn issued the invitation to speak to Booker T. Washington, who gave his famous "Atlanta Compromise" speech. This is the most remembered event of the exposition, but Penn also presided over the founding meeting at the First Congregational Church of the National Medical Association, the leading professional organization for black physicians.

In 1897, Penn became assistant general secretary of the Epworth League, a national effort of the Methodist Episcopal Church to further the education of blacks. He held this position until 1912. He lived in Atlanta but traveled nationwide. In 1912 Penn became one of the two corresponding secretaries of the Methodist Episcopal Freedmen's Aid and Southern Education Society and relocated to Cincinnati, Ohio, following in the footsteps of M. C. B. Mason, the first black to hold that position. In 1924, when the board was restructured, he became secretary of endowment and promotion for the Negro Schools.

In his work for the church he performed such outstanding services as helping Wiley College recover from a disastrous 1918 fire and negotiating in 1923 the merger of Cookman Institute and Daytona Normal and Industrial Institute with Mary McLeod Bethune as president of the new institution. It later became Bethune–Cookman College. Penn also served as a trustee of many educational institutions, such as Wiley College, Clark University, and Gammon Theological School of Atlanta, and Walden College of Nashville, and as a member of the Joint Commission on Unification of the Methodist Episcopal Church from 1892 to 1928.

Penn died on July 22, 1930 at the age of 63; the cause of death is unknown. His wife preceded him in death a month earlier. There were 12 speakers at his funeral at Calvary Methodist Episcopal Church in Cincinnati, including the two black bishops and one white one. Penn was buried next to his wife in the Colored American Cemetery.

Nothing Penn produced after the *Afro–American Press and Its Editors* matched the importance of that work. There was a brochure of 81 pages, *The Reasons Why the Colored Man Is Not in the World's Columbian Exposition* (1893). In addition, he was coeditor of an informational work of some 700 pages, *The College Life* (1895), and of the proceedings of a youth religious and educational congress, *The United Negro* (1902). Most of his later writing was for correspondence, reports, and speeches he was required to prepare. Still he was tireless in the pursuit of educational opportunities for African Americans. For more than 30 years he occupied a key position in the Methodist Episcopal Church and did much to shape the church's efforts in the education of blacks.

REFERENCES

Bearr, David W. C. "I. Garland Penn: Truth–Hunter and Pathfinder." *Virginia United Methodist Heritage* 22 (Spring 1996): 23–35.

Brawley, James P. *Two Centuries of Methodist Concern: Bondage, Freedom and Educations of Black People.* New York: Vantage Press, 1974.

Culp, D. W., ed. *Twentieth Century Negro Literature.* Napierville, IL: J. L. Nichols, 1902.

Hartshorn, W. N., ed. *An Era of Progress and Promise.* Boston: Pricilla Publishing, 1910.

Hurlbut, Jesse Lyman, ed. *Seven Graded Sunday Schools.* New York: Eaton and Mains, c.1893.

Logan, Rayford W., and Michael R. Winston, eds. *Dictionary of American Negro Biography.* New York: Norton, 1982.

Murphy, Larry G., J. Gordon Melton, and Gary L. Ward, eds. *Encyclopedia of African American Religions.* New York: Garland, 1993.

Smith, Jessie Carney, ed. *Notable Black American Women.* Detroit: Gale Research, 1992.

Stowell, Jay S. *Methodist Adventures in Negro Education.* New York: The Methodist Book Concern, 1922.

Who's Who in Colored America. New York: Who's Who in Colored America, 1927.

"A Worthy Representative of His Race." Obituary. *The Christian Advocate,* July 31, 1930.

Robert L. Johns

Penniman, Richard Wayne.
See Little Richard.

James W. C. Pennington
(1807–1870)
Minister, abolitionist

James W. C. Pennington was a leading abolitionist. Unlike most escaped slaves, he managed to secure an education that he valued highly. This led him to become a very effective speaker, writer, and fundraiser for the cause, both in America and abroad. He spoke widely, wrote two short books, saw several of his sermons and addresses printed, and contributed to newspapers. Unfortunately, his career ran into problems when he was only 47, and he died in poverty and neglect.

James William Charles Pennington was born Jim Pembroke on a farm on Maryland's Eastern Shore to slave parents named Brazil and Nelly, in January of 1807. It was said that his grandfather was a Mandingo prince bought by slavers, around 1746. At the death of their first owner, James Tilghman, in 1807, their new owner, Frisby, Tilghman's son took Pennington, his mother, and his older brother, to a farm in Washington County, near Hagerstown. This move broke up the family unit until Tilghman consented to buy Pennington's father. By the time of Pennington's flight, in 1828, he had 11 brothers and sisters, all owned by Tilghman except for his older brother, Robert, who had been sold and lived six miles away.

In 1816, Pennington was hired out to a Hagerstown stone mason with whom he remained for about two years. Back at the farm Pennington became an assistant to the blacksmith and, in a few years, became a capable blacksmith himself. Pennington worked on the farm as a blacksmith until the spring of 1828, when he was sold. Shortly afterwards, Tilghman repurchased him and set him to work as a carpenter. The relations between master and slaves were deteriorating. Tilghman beat Pennington's father with little provocation, and, shortly thereafter, Pennington, himself, was beaten. The whole family, 13 of the 33 slaves on the farm, became suspect. Telling no one, Pennington decided to escape. Blackett quoted from Tilghman's description of the fugitive: Pennington was 5'5'' high very black, square and clumsily made'' with a down look, prominent reddish eyes, and mumbles or talks with his teeth closed.''

Pennington set out on Sunday, October 28, 1828. The escape itself was arduous, and Pennington had to escape from custody when he was taken near Reistertown, Maryland. When he finally arrived in Adams County, Pennsylvania, he was directed to the home of a Quaker farmer, William Wright, who gave him work on his farm and began his education. Just

James W. C. Pennington

in time to evade the attention of slave catchers, Pennington was sent on to Chester County, Pennsylvania, where he spent seven months before moving to Brooklyn, New York. There he worked as a coachman and pursued his education, in evening schools and private tuition.

In 1829 Pennington was converted, becoming a Presbyterian. He achieved his first public notice when he addressed a meeting of Brooklyn African Americans called to protest a formation of a Brooklyn chapter of the American Colonization Society, in the summer of 1831. The persons, at the meeting, immediately selected Pennington as their delegate to the first annual Negro Convention, held in Philadelphia a week later. Pennington continued to be active in the following three conventions.

Turning his mind to what he could do to help the slaves, Pennington decided on the ministry. While he was making remarkable progress studying on his own, he had a chance to become a schoolteacher near Brooklyn in late February or March of 1834. He was appointed at a salary of $200 a year. In his narrative, Pennington underlined the value of education to him:

> There is one sin that slavery committed against me, which I can never forgive. It robbed me of my education; the injury is irreparable. . . . It cost me two years' hard labour, after I fled, to unshackle my mind; it was three years before I had purged my mind of slavery's idioms; it was four years before I had thrown off the crouching aspect of slavery; and now the evil that besets me is a great lack of that

general information, the foundation of which is most effectually laid in that part of life which I served as a slave.

Enters the Ministry

Pennington taught in Newtown for two years and then in Hartford, Connecticut, for three. In Hartford, he studied for the ministry under great difficulties. In 1837, he was ordained and returned to Newton as an assistant minister in a Presbyterian Church. He then took charge of a newly founded Congregational church. In July of 1840, Pennington moved to head the Talcott Street Colored Congregational Church, in New Haven, where he remained, until 1847.

In 1840, Pennington tried to revive the convention movement, in abeyance since 1835, with no success. From the time of his arrival in Hartford and continuing for the next four years, Pennington and his wife Harriett worked to keep afloat the North African School, one of the two local schools open to African Americans. The promotion of education was a constant in his life. In the early 1850s, he was an active member of the New York Society for the Promotion of Education among Colored Children. In conjunction with his teaching, Pennington published one of the earliest histories of blacks, a hundred page booklet called *A Text Book of the Origin and History. . .of the Colored People,* in 1841. Despite its name, the book is too advanced to serve as an elementary school text.

Pennington worked to advance the cause of African Americans, and his fellow ministers, who twice chose him to head the Hartford Central Association of Congregational Ministers, eventually recognized his efforts. He was one of the few African Americans prominent in the leadership of the American and Foreign Anti–Slavery Society, which was founded in 1840, in opposition to the policy of moral suasion. The faction of abolitionists headed by William Lloyd Garrison maintained it. In 1841, he became first president of the African American–organized Union Missionary Society, one of the organizations that united to form the American Missionary Association, in 1846.

In 1843, the Connecticut State Anti–Slavery Society named him as a delegate to the World's Anti–Slavery Convention; and the American Peace Society appointed him delegate to the World's Peace Convention, both of which were held in London that year. Pennington gave a long address to the antislavery convention that attracted much attention in antislavery circles, and spoke extensively throughout Great Britain.

As Pennington's celebrity grew, his status as a fugitive slave became more critical; a letter published in an antislavery newspaper in November of 1844 inadvertently disclosed his secret. Pennington began negotiations to purchase himself and his parents. The negotiations came to nothing, and it seemed that Tilghman no longer owned Pennington's parents. In August of 1845, Pennington was granted a two–year leave of absence by his church to pursue a classical education. By the end of that year, he went to Jamaica for a short visit. Pennington later used his position, as the chair of the Commerce Committee at the Negro National Convention of 1847, to press for closer commercial ties between people of African decent in Jamaica and African Americans in the United States.

Pennington's first wife, Harriet, died at the age of 36 in June of 1846. Pennington continued his studies and pressed for the revocation of the white–only voting clause in the Connecticut State constitution. Voters rejected the change overwhelmingly, in 1847.

Dejected by the rebuff of African American manhood in Connecticut, Pennington focused on new opportunities. In 1847, he accepted the pulpit of Shiloh Presbyterian Church in New York City left vacant by the death of Theodore S. Wright. On May 17, 1848, Pennington married Elmira Way in Hartford.

Publishes Slave Narrative

Shortly before the Fugitive Slave Act of 1850 became law, Pennington—increasingly fearful for his safety—appealed to John Hooker of Hartford to negotiate for his freedom. After some delay, Pennington went abroad, in the summer of 1849, to counter the activity of the American Colonization Society, which was pointing to the recent independence of Liberia as proof of the success of its goals. On May 27, 1851, Pennington's freedom was won for $150, which was paid in Maryland to the estate of his owner. In England, Pennington published an account of his early life and his escape from slavery. It was entitled, *The Fugitive Blacksmith.* The book was a great success that reached a third edition, in 1850, soon after its publication. He also gave many well–received anti–slavery lectures and attended the second World Peace Conference held in Frankfort. His efforts were recognized when he became the first African American to receive an honorary doctorate of divinity, which was awarded by the University of Heidelberg in December of 1849.

Pennington also fell under suspicion of collecting money under false pretenses. He alleged to have continued to collect money to buy his freedom when he had already raised the necessary funds. The charges of mishandling funds were never substantiated although Pennington's own account, in *The Fugitive Blacksmith,* was not quite straightforward. He did seem to have used money collected on his behalf to aid the flight of his father and two brothers to Canada.

Returning to New York, Pennington continued his anti–slavery and civil rights work, as well as accumulating property. He became a landlord. Throughout 1852, he continued his assault on the American Colonization Society, both as a member of New York City's Committee of Thirteen and in his presidential address to the state's African American convention. Pennington had long been an active member of the Underground Railroad as an agent in Hartford, fund–raiser in Great Britain, and member of the New York Committee of Vigilance. Surprisingly enough, he seemed to have been responsible for the first major failure of the railroad, when he allowed his brother and two nephews to be retaken, in the summer of 1854. (Pennington later arranged for their purchase). As a result, the Philadelphia committee of the railroad refused to trust its New York counterpart for some time following this incident

Forced to Resign from Shiloh Church

In early 1855, Pennington formed the New York Legal Rights Association to de–segregate public transportation. He brought suit after being forcibly removed from a streetcar on May 24. He lost the suit, in December of 1856. Around this time, he was also running into difficulties that undermined his leadership position. The un–verified charges about mishandling money were bothersome, but not a major source of concern to fellow African Americans. His acceptance of the position of moderator, of the Third Presbytery, of New York, in 1853, was a major blow. It was one thing to be a member of a church which accepted segregation; it was quite another to join a governing body of such a church. Pennington might have survived the storm of criticism if his alcoholism had not become public knowledge in 1854. After a long struggle, Pennington was forced to resign from Shiloh Church in December of 1855.

Pennington then returned to Talcott Street Church in Hartford for two years, and in mid–1858 he officiated again at the Newton Presbyterian Church and taught school in the village, positions he had held more than 20 years earlier. Pennington was still contributing to the press in November of 1859, when he printed an editorial defending John Brown in the *Anglo–African Magazine,* but his influence was in sharp decline. After flirting briefly with Henry Highland Garnet's African Civilization Society at the end of the decade, he became a firm opponent. In October of 1861 Pennington left for Britain where he met with little success. In June of 1862 he was sentenced to a month of hard labor, by a Liverpool court, for shoplifting a book.

In November of 1864 he joined the African Methodist Episcopal (AME) Church. In October of 1865 he went to Natchez, Mississippi, where he spent about a year doing missionary work for the church. By the beginning of 1867, he was minister of the Newbury Congregational Church in Portland, Maine. In 1869 the Presbyterian Committee of Missions for Freedmen gave him an appointment in Jacksonville, Florida. There he had a salary of $200 a year, the same amount he was paid for his first teaching position in Newton. At his death, on October 22, 1870, the church he founded had 36 members. No family member was present when he died, and none of the major African American papers noted his death.

As with many early African Americans, the details of Pennington's private life are imperfectly known. His public life revealed him to be one of the leading abolitionists of the first half of the nineteenth century, a role to which his slave experience gave weight. He also insisted on education and evangelism as key elements in the efforts to raise up African Americans. His gifts as orator and teacher were undermined by alcoholism, and he was almost forgotten when he died.

REFERENCES

Armistead, Wilson. *A Tribute for the Negro.* Manchester, England: William Irwin, 1848.

Blackett, R. J. M. *Beating Against the Barriers.* Ithaca, NY: Cornell University Press, 1989.

Logan, Rayford W., and Michael R. Winston, eds. *Dictionary of American Negro Biography.* New York: Norton, 1982.

Malone, Dumas, ed. *Dictionary of American Biography.* New York: Scribner's, 1943.

Pennington, James W. C. *The Fugitive Blacksmith.* 3rd ed. London: Charles Gilpin, 1850.

Ripley, C. Peter, ed. *The Black Abolitionist Papers.* Vol. 1. Chapel Hill: University of North Carolina Press, 1985.

Simmons, William J. *Men of Mark.* Cleveland: Geo. M. Rewell, 1887.

Sterling, Dorothy, ed. *Speak Out in Thunder Tones.* Garden City, NY: Doubleday, 1973.

Still, William. *The Underground Rail Road.* Revised Edition. Philadelphia: Wm. Still, 1883.

Robert L. Johns

Edward J. Perkins

(1928–)

Diplomat, ambassador

As the first African American ambassador to South Africa, Edward J. Perkins is widely respected for his skills as a leader, negotiator, and communicator. His perseverance and determination have helped to promote positive change in South Africa and destroy the apartheid system. Working his way up the government hierarchy, Perkins spent his entire career in the federal government. His emphasis on professionalism has enabled Perkins to withstand the roller coaster ride that often distinguishes leaders working in the foreign service.

Edward Joseph Perkins was born on June 8, 1928, in Sterlington, Louisiana, as the son of Edward Joseph Perkins Sr. and Tiny Estella Noble Holmes and raised in rural Louisiana. After attending a black–only two–room school in the south, Perkins waited almost 40 years before continuing his education, choosing to enlist in the U.S. Army. From 1958 to 1966, Perkins served with the Army and Air Force Exchange Service in Japan and Taiwan. While there, he met and married Chinese born Lucy Chen–mei Liu on September 9, 1962. They have two daughters, Katherine Karla Shih–Tsu and Sarah Elizabeth Shih–Yin.

Perkins first attended Lewis and Clark College, but transferred to the University of Maryland and graduated in 1968 with a bachelor's degree in political science. While in school, he took a job in the U.S. Foreign Service's Agency for

International Development, where he remained until 1970, when he became assistant director for management on the U.S. Mission to Thailand. After two years, he served as staff assistant in the Office of the Director General of the Foreign Service. He quickly rose to become a personnel officer and served as such from 1972 to 1974.

As he continued to climb through the ranks, Perkins furthered his education. He attended the University of Southern California (USC), where he earned a masters degree in Public Administration in 1972. In 1978, still at USC, Perkins completed his doctorate degree.

Perkins advanced in his career by working for the Bureau of Near Eastern and South Asian affairs as an administrative officer for a year. From 1975 to 1978, he was a management analysis officer for the U.S. Department of State. From there, Perkins became counselor for political affairs for Accra, Ghana, in 1978–1981; deputy chief of mission in Monrovia, Liberia, from 1981 to 1983; and then director of the Office of West African Affairs for the U.S. Department of State from 1983 to 1985. Through all of this, he found time to study French at the Foreign Service Institute in 1983.

Becomes Ambassador

In 1985, Perkins achieved his diplomatic goal when President Ronald Reagan appointed him ambassador of Liberia. He entered the West African country in an era when Liberians were growing increasingly frustrated with their government. Samuel K. Doe, Liberia's dictator at the time, threatened anyone that sought to change the political conditions in his country. Perkins's job was to foster economic reform and democratization there while preserving America's strategic and technical assets. Ultimately, the United States withdrew assistance while Perkins was ambassador, and Liberia entered into one of its bleakest periods in history.

One year later, Perkins was appointed ambassador to South Africa. He faced a different challenge. In Liberia, Perkins dealt with the evils of one man; in South Africa the problems were imbedded in the entire political system. America, particularly the Reagan administration, was criticized for its inattention to the situation. For this reason, Perkins was sent to South Africa to confront the issue. South Africa, however, did not welcome Perkins, and he was greeted with a deal of resentment upon his arrival in South Africa. As noted in *Contemporary Black Biography,* many newspapers in South Africa labeled Perkins's newest position as nothing more than a "transparently racist appointment." Government opponents there believed that this was a job Perkins should have turned down. However, Perkins, avoiding publicity, slowly changed the public attitude that he was a powerless black appointee by meeting with black opposition groups and traveling to black villages. He encouraged his staff to visit these villages as well, hoping they could better comprehend the distressing differences and ravaging effects on South Africa's blacks.

Perkins even went beyond that. He mandated that all embassy functions include representatives from all races. He placed high priority on establishing relations with a broad base of people. His efforts were rewarded. By the time he left the post in 1989, he had become an active participant in efforts to improve conditions in South Africa, bringing a sense of pride to the Reagan Administration while helping to reduce the many racist policies rampant in that country.

After completing his time in South Africa, he was sworn in as director general of the Foreign Service and director of personnel. During the ceremony, Perkins emphasized his commitment to open communications. In 1992, President George Bush appointed Perkins as the U.S. ambassador to the United Nations. His time at the U.N. was brief. In 1993, President Bill Clinton replaced him with Madeleine Albright. He was given a new appointment, ambassador to Australia. Perkins remained in that position until he retired in August of 1996.

In addition to numerous honorary degrees, Perkins has received many awards during his career. In 1967, the Agency for International Development honored him with its Meritorious Honor Award. He received the Department of State's Superior Honor Award in 1983. In 1985, he received the Eastern Region Award from the Kappa Alpha Psi Fraternity for his achievement in foreign affairs. He received the Presidential Meritorious Service Award in 1987 and the Presidential Distinguished Service Award from Bush was bestowed upon Perkins in 1989. Retired Superior Court Judge William S. Thompson presented to Perkins a plaque from the Judicial Council of the National Bar Association "for integrity and courage" during his diplomatic service in South Africa. Perkins also received a number of honorary degrees: University of Maryland, 1990; St. John's University, 1990; Beloit College, 1990; and University of Southern California, 1995. Perkins has served on the board of visitors for the National Defense University and the board of directors of Lewis and Clark College. He is a member of the Navy League, the American Society for Public Administration, Veterans of Foreign Wars, Kappa Alpha Psi Fraternity, and Sigma Pi Phi Fraternity (the Boulé).

Big in size and distinguished in demeanor, Perkins can best be described as charismatic, self–disciplined, and poised. Perkins, who is honest and demonstrates solid political skills, maintained a good working relationship with President Reagan and his political appointees. His strategy as ambassador included listening to all sides and keeping Americans informed of the political situations in South Africa. Perkins has been criticized, however, as being too soft–spoken and too anxious to follow the policies of the U.S. administration. In spite of it all, Perkins rose to meet the challenge. No other U.S. ambassador before him had worked as closely with the black community. Because of this, along with his participation in various protests and demonstrations, the first African American ambassador to South Africa established his credibility. Known by many as a first–class professional, Perkins is a leader who truly made a difference.

Current address: U.S. Department of State, Washington, DC 20520.

REFERENCES

Ambassador Edward J. Perkins Sworn in as Director General of Foreign Service and Director of Personnel. Washington, DC: U.S. Department of State Bureau of Public Affairs, October 5, 1989.

Booker, Simeon. ''Edward Perkins, U.S. Envoy to S. Africa, Reveals His Cold War Against Apartheid.'' *Jet* 5 (18 April 1988): 32–33.

Contemporary Black Biography. Vol. 5. Detroit: Gale Research, 1994.

''Inside the U.N. Security Council.'' *San Francisco Chronicle,* November 7, 1993.

''Lawyers' Award Finally Reaches UN Ambassador.'' *Jet* 82 (12 October 1992): 11.

Nelan, Bruce W. ''New Man in the Townships.'' *Time* 128 (23 February 1987): 58.

Riccucci, Norma M. '''Execucrats,' Politics, and Public Policy: What Are the Ingredients for Successful Performance in the Federal Government?'' *Public Administration Review* 55 (May 1995): 219–30.

Who's Who among African Americans, 1996–97. 9th ed. Detroit: Gale Research, 1996.

Who's Who in America, 1996. 50th ed. New Providence, NJ: Marquis Who's Who, 1995.

Williams, Michael W., ed. *The African American Encyclopedia.* New York: Marshall Cavendish, 1993.

Lori Michelle Muha

Harold R. Perry

(1916–1991)

Priest, bishop

Harold R. Perry, a Divine Word priest of the Roman Catholic Church, has been called a man of many firsts. The most important of these history–making distinctions came when he was the first black American Catholic in the twentieth century to be appointed a bishop in the United States. He was named auxiliary bishop of the Archdiocese of New Orleans in the fall of 1965 by Pope Paul VI and consecrated January 6, 1966. Symbolizing the church's demonstrated witness of brotherhood, this appointment foretold the great changes in the role black Catholics would play in both the church and the country. He also was the first black clergyman to deliver the invocation at an opening session of the U.S. Congress. This was on July 8, 1963, and appropriately was for the 88th Congress that passed the civil rights bill. In 1964 he became the first black Superior of the Society of the Divine Word's southern province, which was a first of its kind for any major religious order.

Devout Catholic Upbringing

Harold Robert Perry was born in Lake Charles, Louisiana, October 9, 1916, the oldest of six children in a family of devout Catholics. His parents were of French–Creole ancestry and were third generation Catholics. His father, Frank J. Perry, was a rice mill worker and his mother, Josephine Petrie Perry, was a domestic cook who at one time had worked in the rectory of Sacred Heart Church. Even though Frank and Josephine Perry did not complete high school, they encouraged all of their children to succeed. Harold's brother Frank A. Perry became a surgeon and was a professor at Meharry Medical College in Nashville, Tennessee. His other brothers, James and Fred Perry, became dentists; and his sisters Thelma Perry White and Verlie Perry Kennedy, teachers. The family's home was surrounded by Catholic institutions which played an important role in their lives. Sacred Heart Church was just across the street, and the parish schools were less than a block away. Their neighbors were Italian, Irish, black, and white, and even though the children played together they did not attend church or school together. The racial attitudes of Harold Perry's parents were broad, and in an interview in *Ebony* in 1966, he recalled that ''they taught us not to resent white people. 'Be sure,' they would caution, 'that there is no prejudice on your part.''' This advice was to follow him throughout his life.

Perry completed his elementary education in 1930 at Sacred Heart School in Lake Charles. He had decided at age 12 that he wanted to be a priest. He later said that he was lucky and had never had a doubt that the priesthood was the right thing for him. Supported and encouraged by his family as well as by the zealous pastor of Sacred Heart Church where young Perry was an altar boy, he applied for entrance into several seminaries. Many of the Catholic orders did not accept blacks, but this early experience of racial discrimination and rejection failed to embitter him or dissuade him from the pursuit of his goal. Quoted in the *Washington Post* for January 30, 1966, he said, ''Until then, it had not occurred to me that my race would be a handicap in anything I wanted to do.'' He was finally accepted by the Society of the Divine Word, a missionary order that actively recruited blacks and was the first to train black priests in the United States. Because of the Depression, the Perry family could not finance their son's seminary years, but one of the priests came to his rescue and paid his tuition for the first four years. The Blessed Sacrament Sisters, who considered Perry a prize pupil, also helped by buying the clothes he would need.

Perry entered St. Augustine Seminary in Bay St. Louis, Mississippi, in the fall of 1930. Completing high school in 1934 and staying in the college department until 1937, Perry was the only one of his original class of 26 to finish. Upon his graduation, he was sent to the Holy Ghost Mission House in East Troy, Wisconsin, to make his novitiate for the Society of the Divine Word. In 1938 Perry began his major theological studies at St. Mary's Seminary in Techny, Illinois, and in 1939 returned to St. Augustine's to complete his studies. On June 21, 1943, he made his final profession and was ordained into the priesthood on January 6, 1944, in Bay St. Louis. After

Harold R. Perry

14 years of study Perry became the 26th black to be received into the ministry of the Catholic Church in America.

Father Perry served eight years as an assistant pastor in a number of churches. His first assignment, lasting from 1944 until 1948, was at Immaculate Heart of Mary in Lafayette, Louisiana. He then moved to Our Lady of Perpetual Help in St. Martinsville, Louisiana, and then to St. Peter's in Pine Bluff, Arkansas where he stayed until 1951. His next post was St. Gabriel's in the all–black town of Mound Bayou, Mississippi. In 1952, Perry was appointed to his first pastorate. As founding pastor of St. Joseph's, he was responsible for developing the independent and newly established parish for the 1,000 black Catholics in Broussard, Louisiana, a town that had a total Catholic population of 3,000. He not only served as pastor but supervised, over a period of two years, the building of a church, a rectory, and a parochial school. Perry returned to St. Augustine Seminary in 1958 and served as its rector until 1963. By that time there were 130 faculty members and students at the integrated seminary. He later told the *Washington Post* for January 30, 1966, "I felt that I ran a relaxed community where anyone felt free to speak his mind. I was surprised to learn, after leaving, that some considered me a bit strict. I like to see a man give an honest day's work." To his credit Perry was recognized as being a leader in a quiet, dignified way, with an unswerving loyalty to the church and compassion for all members.

In 1964 Perry's faith and attitude, plus a willingness to work, led to his being named Superior of the Society of the Divine Word's southern province, thus becoming the first black man to hold such a position for a major religious order. Included in his jurisdiction were schools in Texas, Louisiana, Mississippi, and Arkansas. In addition, he was responsible for Divine Word missions and missionaries, 37 parishes, a coeducational high school in Lafayette, Louisiana, and the St. Augustine Seminary at Bay St. Louis.

Becomes Bishop

In the fall of 1965, Father Perry was in Rome to attend the consecration of his good friend Bishop Carlos Lewis of Panama. Upon his arrival at the Rome airport, he was immediately escorted to the Vatican where he was told that the Holy Father wished to make him the first black bishop in the United States and that he would be auxiliary to Archbishop Philip M. Hannan in the New Orleans diocese. The newly appointed bishop was quite excited and called it the great surprise of his life. He said in the *New York Times* for January 7, 1966, "When the Holy See appointed a Negro bishop, I had two surprises—one that I had received the appointment and two, that New Orleans was the place I was to serve." Introducing his new assistant at a Rome press conference, Hannan said in the *New York Times* for October 4, 1965, "He is singularly qualified by his learning, diverse pastoral experience and solid piety to assume the duties of his office." When asked if a black prelate could succeed in Louisiana, according to the *New Orleans Times Picayune* for July 18, 1991, the confident Perry replied, "I was effective as a priest. I expect to be effective as a bishop." He down–played his appointment as a symbol with racial overtones, preferring to think of it as being chosen because of his qualifications. He said that his work would be to meet and serve the needs of everyone in the archdiocese. Perry was consecrated in New Orleans' St. Louis Basilica, January 6, 1966, by Archbishop Egidio Vagnozzi, apostolic delegate to the United States. After his consecration as bishop, Father Perry also served as pastor of St. Theresa of the Child Jesus, rector of the National Shrine of Our Lady of Prompt Succor, and pastor of Our Lady of Lourdes until he retired in 1985 due to failing health.

The impact of Father Perry's elevation to bishop raised fears that his installation would create bitter racial dissention in the Louisiana Catholic community because many remembered the stiff resistance and sometimes violent response to the 1961 desegregation of parochial schools in the New Orleans archdiocese. Reactions this time were more favorable with only a few exceptions. Local, state and national leaders welcomed and congratulated Perry and he received positive messages from north and south, from both black and white, and from Catholics, Protestants and Jews. His appointment did bring out a few dissidents. At the procession preceding Perry's installation as bishop, there were those who picketed, in particular, a woman who had been excommunicated in 1962 for her rebellious stand against integration in the Catholic Church. Perry said he knew she would be there and said in *Current Biography,* "There are some who feel as she does and they certainly have a right to their opinion." He also told the *New York Times* for January 7, 1966, that the segregationist pickets "were not representative of the people of New Orleans and cause them great embarrassment."

Even though his appointment came during the civil rights struggle, Perry noted that his duties were never defined by his race but that he felt he had a special obligation to black people. Quoted in the *New Orleans Times Picayune* for July 18, 1991, he said, ''I thought it was, in a sense, a burden, but at the same time it was an opportunity to do something very good for the church and for my people.'' He emphasized that he would be no civil rights crusader nor would he participate in demonstrations but reserved the right to speak against injustice. He told the *Washington Post* for January 30, 1966, ''There were some who thought that since the Protestants have an outspoken leader for civil rights, I would perform the same function for the Catholic Church,'' he said, ''But I am not the Catholic answer to Dr. Martin Luther King.'' Not wanting to be a crusader did not mean Bishop Perry did not understand black identity and black pride. Ultimately, both King and Perry passionately believed in the same things—justice and peace—and would spare no effort to combat racism and to tear down segregation.

Bishop Perry felt that the greatest need of the black community was a program of social justice that would overcome the deficit in education and skills that would be necessary to gain back the confidence that had been destroyed by discrimination. After his consecration, Perry told the *Washington Post* for January 30, 1966, ''The great problem is to enable Negroes to qualify for the opportunities open to them. Education is the key. This is a very long haul. This is where the real work comes in. There will be those who want everything now, whether they are qualified or not but that is unreasonable.''

Active in Many Organizations

Throughout his priesthood Perry was active in both secular and religious organizations. He also wrote several articles on early African saints for the St. Augustine Messenger and contributed to the Catholic publications Shield and the Claverite. For 40 years he was a member of the Knights and Ladies of St. Peter Claver, a predominantly black Catholic service organization and had served as its national chaplain. He was a technical adviser to the Air Force's chief of chaplains, a member of Loyola University's Board of Regents and Xavier University's Board of Trustees, a member of the episcopal committee of the Society for the Propagation of the Faith, and was on the boards of the National Urban League, the National Catholic Conference for Interracial Justice, the Catholic Interracial Council, and the National Catholic Conference of Bishops. In 1963 he was among a group of 250 religious leaders of all faiths invited to the White House by President John F. Kennedy to discuss peaceful desegregation of public accommodations. Perry received honorary degrees from 13 colleges and universities including Loyola University and Notre Dame Seminary in New Orleans and Xavier in Cincinnati. At a 1967 dedication ceremony conducted by Cardinal Francis Spellman, a new community center and auditorium for the St. Mark the Evangelist church and school of Harlem was named Bishop Perry Hall in his honor. In 1970 he received a citation for outstanding work on the Governor's Commission on Law Enforcement and Administration of Criminal Justice for Louisiana, and in 1971 was co–recipient of the Hoey Award for Interracial Justice. In January of 1991, just months before his death, Perry was honored with a special Mass to celebrate the silver jubilee of his ordination as bishop.

Perry was five feet eight inches tall and tended to be stocky. He was described as a scholarly man, but one with a quick wit, ready laughter, and an endearing personality. He was humble and many were impressed by his quiet self–assurance and sincerity. His interests included photography, golf, swimming and tennis, and he was a fan of the Chicago Bears football team. He also is said to have enjoyed a good meal.

Perry died Wednesday, July 17, 1991, at a health care center in Marrero, Louisiana. He was 74. He had been on extended sick leave since 1985 suffering from complications due to Alzheimer's disease. A funeral Mass was held July 22, 1991, at St. Louis Cathedral in New Orleans, and burial was in St. Louis Cemetery. Speaking at Perry's funeral, his good friend Bishop Joseph Francis, called him a ''reconciler.'' Quoted in the *New Orleans Clarion Herald* for August 1, 1991, he said that Perry 'spent a lifetime trying to reconcile people with God and with one another. This role is the most difficult of all to play because it is fraught with risks. It takes a lot of courage to stand up and insist that judgments on persons and events must often be deferred and mercy and an openness to truth be given a chance to surface.'' ''No one will ever know what he had to endure as the first black bishop,'' Archbishop James P. Lyke of Atlanta said in the same source, and Auxiliary Bishop John H. Ricard of Baltimore pointed out that ''Bishop Perry was the personification of the changes that were taking place in the church and society. Bishop Perry took the brunt of the resistance.''

Harold Perry was a great inspiration for black Catholics and was admired by most for his mild, non–militant manner. His humble but dignified acceptance and love, regardless of color or ethnic origin, can only serve as a model of persevering efforts to turn away from racism in the mind and heart. He was said to be the right kind of person to be a pioneer. A woman recruited by Perry as an organist, perhaps characterized him best when she said in the *New Orleans Times Picayune* for July 23, 1991, ''I loved him. He was the kind of person, if you didn't know he was a bishop, you wouldn't know.'' His quiet courage and unfailing dignity served him well during his 47 years in the priesthood.

REFERENCES

''Bishop Harold R. Perry, 74, Dies; First Black Prelate in the Century.'' *New York Times,* July 19, 1991.

''Bishop Perry Eulogized as Priest, Prophet.'' *New Orleans Clarion Herald,* (1 August 1991): 6–8.

''Cardinal Spellman Dedicates New Center in Harlem.'' *New York Times,* February 21, 1967.

Current Biography Yearbook. New York: H. W. Wilson, 1966.

Foley, Albert S. ''Father Harold R. Perry, S.V.D.'' In *God's Men of Color.* New York: Arno Press and the *New York Times,* 1969.

"Historic Actions in the Church: LA. Negro Priest Appointed Bishop." *Negro History Bulletin* 29 (December 1965): 65–66.
"Mass to Honor Pioneer Black Bishop." *New Orleans Times Picayune,* January 12, 1991.
"Negro is Installed as a Bishop in New Orleans." *New York Times,* January 7, 1966.
"Negro Named a Bishop; Gets New Orleans Post." *New York Times,* October 4, 1965.
"Perry's Humility Remembered." *New Orleans Times Picayune,* July 23, 1991.
"Perry's No Catholic Dr. King." *Washington Post,* January 30, 1966.
"Pioneering Bishop Harold Perry dies at 74." *New Orleans Times Picayune,* July 18, 1991.
"Roman Catholics: Historic Bishop." *Time* 86 (8 October 1965): 70.
Scally, Sister Mary. *Negro Catholic Writers: 1900–1943.* Detroit: Walter Romig, 1945.
Thompson, Era Bell. "Bishop Harold Perry: Man of Many Firsts." *Ebony* 21 (21 February 1966): 62–70.

Flossie E. Wise

Frank Petersen Jr.

Frank Petersen Jr.
(1932–)
Military officer

Frank Petersen Jr. was the first African American marine pilot and the first African American marine to attain the rank of brigadier general. As an accomplished fighter pilot and dedicated leader, he served his country in both the Korean and Vietnam wars, earning numerous medals and decorations for his bravery. In addition to his impressive fighting record, Petersen became known for his ability to inspire the men who served under him, nurturing many military careers.

Frank Emmanuel Petersen Jr. was born March 2, 1932, in Topeka, Kansas, to Frank Emmanuel Petersen Sr. and Edith Sutthard Petersen. He was educated in the Topeka public schools and attended Washburn University for one year before joining the U.S. Navy in 1950 as a seaman apprentice. He entered the Naval Aviation Cadet Program in 1951 and began flight training school. Upon completion of training there in 1952, he accepted a commission as a second lieutenant in the U.S. Marine Corps.

Petersen continued his education much later, receiving his bachelor of science degree in 1967, and his master's degree in international affairs in 1973, both from George Washington University. He also attended the Amphibious Warfare School in Quantico, Virginia; the Aviation Safety Officers Course at the University of Southern California; and the National War College in Washington, D.C.

As Petersen began his military career, he had a two–fold purpose in mind: first, he thought that the Navy would afford him the opportunity to do extensive traveling; and second, he wanted to earn money to pay for his college education. Early in his navy career as a seaman apprentice, Petersen was inspired by the first black navy aviator, Jesse Brown, who lost his life on assignment in North Korea. Petersen saw Brown as a hero who endured rigorous training in flight school. Petersen felt that he, too, could accomplish such a task.

In 1952, Petersen became a second lieutenant in the United States Marine Corps at the age of 20, becoming the Marine's first African American pilot. He was also designated a navy aviator. He received flight training at the U.S. Naval Air Station in Pensacola, Florida, at another base in Corpus Christi, Texas, and at the Marine Corps Air Station in Santa Ana, California.

During this period Petersen met another great military figure, air force captain Daniel "Chappie" James, who later became the first African American four–star general. At a time when Petersen needed encouragement to continue his career goals, James made himself available and provided the inspiration that Petersen needed.

On active duty during the Korean War, Petersen was a fighter attack pilot and flew 64 combat missions in 1953. For his outstanding performance, he received six air medals and the Distinguished Flying Cross, the most prestigious aviation medal. In addition to his impressive flight performance, Petersen earned the admiration and respect of the men he led and always made time to provide counseling to African

American men. His dedication to those under him inspired some to call him "godfather."

Petersen began another tour of duty in 1968 when he proudly served in Vietnam. He led marine Fighter Attack Squadron 314, a tactical air squadron, becoming the first African American to lead a tactical air squadron in the Navy or Marine Corps. As commander, he demonstrated great leadership in battle by flying 290 missions against enemy positions.

While serving as commanding officer, Petersen was injured during an attack in North Vietnam in August of 1968. With one engine on fire and only partial control of his crippled fighter, he flew his plane to friendly territory before fire engulfed the aircraft. Due to the fire burning throughout the control systems, Petersen was forced to eject from the aircraft, suffered a wound, and received a Purple Heart for this action.

Even after the Vietnam experience, Petersen continued to serve his country with distinction. In 1979 he was selected for promotion to brigadier general and later advanced to the rank of major. He was promoted to lieutenant general in 1986.

After 38 years in the Marines, including over 300 combat missions and more than 4,000 hours in fighter attack aircraft, he retired in 1988 with many decorations and commendations including 20 individual medals for combat valor. He had the distinct honor of holding the senior ranking aviator's designations of the Marines, the Silver Hawk, and the Navy's Gray Eagle. He was also designated a navy aviator and was the senior ranking pilot in both branches of services from 1985 to 1988, and was senior pilot in the U.S. Armed Services from 1986 to 1988.

After many years of active military duty, Petersen continued his association with the military in retirement. In 1988 he became commanding general of the Marine Corps Development and Education Command, a training center in Quantico, Virginia, where he was responsible for the Marine's Principal Advanced Education and Training command. The center base houses 5,000 marines and provides training for security personnel affiliated with the Marines, the Federal Bureau of Investigation, and drug enforcement agents.

Petersen's affiliations with boards and organizations are numerous. Since 1960 he has been affiliated with the Tuskegee Airmen; from 1990 to 1992 he was a member of the board of directors for the National Aviation Research and Education Foundation, and currently serves as the vice–president of DuPont Aviation. Other affiliations include National Bone Marrow Foundation; Higher Education Assistance Foundation; Opportunity Skyway; Institute for the Study of American Wars; Montford Point Marines; and the Business Executive for National Security.

Petersen exemplifies the qualities of a marine as well as one who has enjoyed life's experiences. Asked about his career in an interview for *Ebony* magazine in 1986, he responded: "In summarizing my career, I would have to say I've had a hell of a lot of luck in the sense of being in the right places at the right times, and receiving those assignments that made me competitive." Notwithstanding his luck, Petersen also brought to his military assignments courage, dedication, and a sense of duty that led him to excel. Divorced from Eleanor Peterson, he lives in Stevenville, Maryland, and has five children: Gayle, Dana, Frank III, Lindey, and Monique.

Current address: DuPont Aviation, New Castle County Airport, 199 North DuPont Highway, New Castle, DE 19720.

REFERENCES

Estell, Kenneth, ed. *Reference Library of Black America.* Vol. 2. Detroit: Afro–American Press, 1975.

Fleming, Robert. "Col. Frank Petersen 'The Godfather' in Line for Star Rank." *Encore* 8 (2 April 1979): 22.

Greene, Robert Ewell. *Black Defenders of America, 1775–1973.* Chicago: Johnson Pub. Co., 1974.

"Lt. General Frank E. Petersen. Top Man at Quantico." *Ebony* 42 (December 1986): 140–46.

Who's Who among African Americans, 1996–97. 9th ed. Detroit: Gale Research, 1996.

COLLECTIONS

Petersen's official biographical records and other data are in the Division of Public Affairs, Headquarters, Marine Corps, Washington, D.C.

Theodosia T. Shields

William Pickens
(1881–1954)
College administrator, orator, activist, government official

William Pickens was one of the most popular black Americans of his time and one of America's most important civil rights leaders from 1915 to 1945. Pickens, the second black to receive a Phi Beta Kappa key from Yale University, returned to his native South and began a career in college teaching and administration before devoting his efforts full–time to the civil rights movement. He used his oratory and writing talents in his efforts to promote the NAACP and the culture of black America. At age 60 he accepted a governmental position where he encouraged African Americans to buy savings bonds.

William Pickens was born on January 15, 1881, in Anderson County, South Carolina. He was the sixth of ten children and the first son born to Jacob and Fannie Pickens, two former slaves who gained their freedom in the 1860s. The Pickenses worked primarily as tenant farmers, and the family moved more than 20 times before William's 18th birthday. At various times, Jacob Pickens also worked as a hotel employee,

William Pickens

bartender, henchman for a white politician, section hand, brakeman, and fireman, while Fannie Pickens was employed as a cook and washerwoman. Jacob also served as superintendent of his Baptist church's Sunday School.

Jacob and Fannie Pickens worked hard to provide better living conditions and educational opportunities for their offspring. During that time, black children attended segregated schools, and children of tenant farmers frequently experienced interruptions in their formal schooling when it became necessary for them to work in the fields alongside their parents. Thus, William did not have the opportunity to attend a school that offered nine months of instruction until September of 1891, and his attendance prior to the Christmas recess that year was sporadic because he had to miss school in order to pick cotton. Once the new year began, however, 11–year–old William zealously attended school. In his first autobiographical effort, *The Heir of Slaves,* Pickens remembered the day when his mother planned to keep him home from grammar school in order for him to help her. Pickens wrote:

> I was deeply in love with school and study. . . . She never tried it again—I cried and pleaded as if my heart would burst. The prospect of missing my classes for a day seemed to me absolutely unbearable. It seemed that it would tear down all that I had builded.

His mother grabbed a switch, but even the threat of physical pain could not prevent Pickens from protesting until she relented. He commented further, "I can see now that she was rather proud of the event, for never again did she make any arrangement that would keep me out of school for a day." After that incident, Pickens never missed another day from school for the next seven years.

Fannie Pickens and her eldest son recognized the importance of education and so did her husband, but she died in 1894. Jacob Pickens struggled to keep his family together. His friends criticized him for allowing his oldest son to remain in school. Nonetheless Jacob Pickens worked overtime to support his family. He did not order his son to quit school.

During his last year of grammar school, William Pickens was hired as a ferryman on the Arkansas River. That following summer he saved $40, almost his total wages, hoping to finance his high school education although there was no public high school in his district. He applied to a Little Rock high school, passed each entrance examination with a perfect score, and was admitted. He used his summer savings to pay the $2.50 fee charged to students who did not live in that school district. During Pickens's first year, he continued to work on the ferry, but during his second year in high school, he was employed at a barrel and keg factory where another employee constantly tried to hit Pickens in the head with barrel pieces. Pickens was forced to remain alert hour after hour, yet he wrote in *The Heir of the Slaves* that he regarded his tormentor:

> [A]s one of my appointed teachers who, whether he willed it or not, gave me (somewhat against my will, too) a most valuable mental and moral discipline. . . . All summer he kept up his attack; all summer I kept up my defense. If I experienced any feeling like hatred in the beginning, it was very soon all lost, and I came to look upon the daily action as a *contest* in which it was 'up to me' to win.

Pickens's excellent aptitude for his studies was frequently a source of amazement to nonblacks. The summer prior to his senior year in high school, he worked as a janitor at a business college for white males. The students were surprised when they discovered that Pickens could easily comprehend their schoolwork. Pickens recalled in *The Heir of Slaves* that, during his senior year, a local newspaper reported that he was "a Negro boy that possessed the language of the Romans although he had the color of Erebus." In a separate incident, during that same year, when an attorney visited Pickens's school, he invited Pickens to meet his (the attorney's) partner in order to prove to the partner that a black person could be fluent in Latin. When all was said and done, Pickens was the valedictorian of his high school at the commencement exercises in June of 1899. He delivered a 40–minute speech.

Begins Association with Academia

After high school graduation, Pickens passed the state teachers' examination and obtained a license to teach first grade, a position that many of his peers would have accepted because it paid $40 to $50 a month. However with his father's approval, Pickens rejected the position—Father and son were in agreement on the importance of completing college.

Pickens wrote to G. W. Andrews, the president of Talladega College in Alabama, seeking admission. Talladega was a college for white males. It was built by slaves in 1852. In 1867 the school became a black college with white administrators and faculty. Andrews did not send Pickens a letter of admission; instead the white man suggested that Pickens could have "hope." Thus Pickens spent the summer, along with his father, working on the new railroad under construction in Arkansas.

At the start of the fall semester, Pickens arrived at Andrews's doorstep with nothing more than $50 and hope. The greatly astonished Andrews, who had forgotten about Pickens, was so impressed with the young man's determination that he granted him admission and mentioned Pickens's struggle over adversity in a "chapel talk" that same morning. Talladega's dean examined Pickens in classical literature and enrolled him in the sophomore class.

Pickens majored in foreign languages and worked in the college library to pay his way through school. He won several literary prizes and an oratorical contest during his very first year at Talladega. Due to his oratorical talents, 19–year–old Pickens spent the summer of 1900 with four other Talladega students on a fund raising tour for the Christian missionary college. The other students sang, and Pickens delivered his award winning speech, "Negro Evolution," which soon appeared in print due to public demand.

During one of his trips, he met Booker T. Washington on a train. The two were traveling to a meeting of the American Missionary Association where they were both scheduled to speak. Washington shared his Pullman with Pickens, and some passengers thought he was Washington's son.

On another journey, Pickens had the opportunity to travel to Yale University. He was so impressed with the institution that his next educational objective was to attend Yale. In 1902 Pickens graduated from Talladega but declined an offer to teach Latin at a high school. Again he wanted more education, and his goal remained Yale University. Pickens had relatives in Chicago, so he traveled there, found employment at Gates Ironworks, and saved money to travel to Yale and support himself for several weeks in the hope that he would find a job at Yale to help finance his education. While in Chicago, he met the eminent poet Paul Laurence Dunbar who maintained a correspondence with Pickens throughout his student career at Yale.

That fall Pickens entered Yale where he was one of a very small group of black students. His first semester found him working part–time in a kitchen at the Young Men's Christian Association (YMCA) to pay his tuition. By the end of the semester, he had distinguished himself as an "A" student and was exempted from tuition expenses for the remainder of his studies at Yale.

Pickens again majored in foreign languages. After winning the Ten Eyck Prize in oratory, he managed to quit his job at the YMCA. He also received a congratulatory letter from former President Grover Cleveland. Pickens graduated from Yale in 1904 and was only the second black to receive a Phi Beta Kappa key from Yale.

Pickens was offered a lucrative contract by a New York lecture bureau to tour America and Europe for three years, but after obtaining advice from several individuals including Dunbar, who had toured as a lecturer, Pickens declined the offer. He believed that as an African American, he could be more useful as an educator. Although Pickens continued to accept speaking engagements, he spent the next 16 years on the faculties of various black colleges.

Pickens was offered a teaching position at Tuskegee Institute (now Tuskegee University), but he declined. He chose Talladega instead and taught classics and sociology at his alma mater from 1904 to 1914. Pickens was one of a very few black teachers there.

In 1905 Pickens married the former Minnie Cooper McAlpine, a graduate of Tougaloo College in Mississippi. Prior to her wedding she taught at the American Missionary Association school in Meridian. The couple's three children were born in Talladega. During Pickens's last two years at his alma mater he served as the president of Alabama's State Teachers' Association. Pickens also traveled to Europe with his wife, and he frequently socialized with Booker T. Washington. Time and again the two men were featured speakers together at the same events.

Pickens then spent one academic year (1914–15) as head of the department of Greek and sociology at Wiley University in Marshall, Texas. While there he experienced two racial confrontations that might easily have ended in bloodshed or death. The first incident occurred when a white man challenged Pickens over a six dollar debt owed to Pickens; although the man had a gun, Pickens did not back down and the harasser drove away. The second incident took place when Pickens was returning from an NAACP speaking engagement in New York. Instead of riding in the train's Jim Crow section, Pickens demanded that his Pullman ticket be honored despite the conductor's warning that he would be killed if he insisted on staying on the train. Before retiring for the night, he asked the black porter to warn him if anyone approached his berth. According to Pickens's own recount of the incident in *Bursting Bonds,* he harbored little hope of surviving the night:

> I had no expectation of seeing the light of day again. . . . Worry would be useless, so I slept, with the finger of my right hand coiled over the trigger of a deadly weapon. . . . I think I would not have gone into this car if I had *known* that it would cost me my life and destroy the life of others. But being in was another thing, and being bullied out was impossible. I remembered my boyhood in Arkansas: that just twenty years before I had defied death there, when an officer had drawn a Colt's pistol to shoot me because I was fighting for respect to my sister—and I had kept right on fighting.

Needless to say, Pickens survived the night. In 1915 he left Wiley University to accept an offer to become the first black dean at Morgan College (now Morgan University) in Baltimore. Zora Neale Hurston, the well–known author, met Pickens when she attended Morgan's high school division and remembered him fondly in her autobiography, *Dust Tracks on a Road,* where she described him as understanding: "I was prepared to be all scared of him and his kind. I had no money and no family to refer to. I just went and he talked to me. He gave me a brief examination and gave me credit for two years' work in high school and assigned me to class." Little did Hurston realize how closely Pickens's educational experiences mirrored her own in determination. Hurston mentioned in her autobiography that Pickens served as her oratorical coach, and she placed second in a speech contest. She also provided readers with a glimpse into Pickens's harmonious family life.

In 1918 Pickens was promoted to vice–president at Morgan. That same year Wiley College awarded him with an LL.D. degree. Pickens remained at Morgan until 1920.

Becomes Key Figure in the NAACP

Pickens resigned from academia in order to become more active in the civil rights movement. Years earlier in July of 1905 he met with 28 other black intellectuals and leaders in Fort Erie, Ontario. The group, headed by the dynamic W. E. B. Du Bois, called for an end to all forms of racial discrimination and demanded full rights for blacks. The organization, viewed as the forerunner to the NAACP, was known as the Niagara Movement and remained operational for five years.

In 1910 the NAACP was established. Pickens was one of the association's founding members, one of its most successful recruiters during his tenure with the organization. He was also one of the NAACP's most influential forces who, along with Du Bois, James Weldon Johnson, and Walter White, molded the NAACP into America's most potent civil rights organization. While still working at Morgan in 1914, Pickens along with NAACP chairman Joel E. Spingarn established a Louisville, Kentucky branch of the association and challenged Jim Crow conditions in Memphis in 1915.

In 1920 the NAACP appointed Pickens as assistant field secretary. Thus, when the academic year ended at Morgan, Pickens and his family moved to New York. It was the era of the Harlem Renaissance. The Pickenses were extremely active in their community's social and cultural affairs.

In his capacity as field director and later as director of NAACP branches, Pickens continued to recruit new members and to assist in establishing new branches. He served as a liaison between the national headquarters and its several branches, solicited funds, and completed special projects. Among his varied activities he investigated lynchings, gathered firsthand evidence of racial discrimination, and successfully lobbied to the U.S. Congress. His lobby effort, at the onset of the First World War, won the support of more than 300 congressmen and resulted in the establishment of a black officers' training facility at Fort Des Moines, Iowa.

Pickens had become one of America's most important black leaders whom William Andrews called in the introduction to *Bursting Bonds* "one of the half–dozen best–known black men of his time." Pickens was a featured speaker at many NAACP sponsored events such as the 1915 Convention and the 1919 National Conference in Lynchburg, Virginia. Pickens also spoke on behalf of the NAACP and/or about race relations at numerous events held by other organizations. In *Fight for Freedom,* Langston Hughes discussed Pickens and praised his oratorical talents, calling him:

> ". . . [A] man of the people" with a powerful voice, a jolly face, and a smile "like a lighthouse in the sea," Pickens became one of the most popular platform orators in America. Although he had received his Phi Beta Kappa key at Yale, Pickens never lost the common touch and was not adverse to using colloquial English in his talks. He had at his command a vast number of humorous stories to send his audiences into gales of laughter.

In addition to his talent for oratory, Pickens publicized his thoughts via the printed page. His memoirs, *The Heir of Slaves* and *Bursting Bonds,* published in 1911 and 1923 respectively, are important contributions to the genre of black autobiography. These writings document the experiences of one of the great pioneers of the 20th century civil rights movement. Pickens published *The New Negro* in 1916, a collection of his essays centered around the theme of black Americans' right to full citizenship. From 1919 to 1940, Pickens reached his largest audience as a contributing editor and syndicated columnist of the Associated Negro Press, the largest black news syndicate in the United States. Pickens's weekly articles were published in more than 100 black newspapers.

In 1937 Pickens took a one–year leave of absence from the NAACP in order to lecture at adult education centers for the Federal Forum Project. In 1941, on leave again from the NAACP, he was appointed director of the International Section of Treasury Department Savings Bonds (War Bonds). Four years later, blacks had purchased approximately $1 billion worth of bonds. Pickens retired from the Treasury Department in 1950.

Pickens continued as a consultant to the Treasury Department on a part–time basis. All the while he wrote, lectured, and traveled. On April 6, 1954, while Pickens and his wife were traveling home from South America and the Caribbean, Pickens died after suffering a heart attack on board the *S. S. Mauretania.* He was buried at sea.

Pickens was survived by his wife of 49 years and their three children: William Jr., Harriet, and Ruby. All three had graduated from college, and Harriet achieved distinction in her own right as the first black woman to receive an officer's commission in the Navy Women's Auxiliary (WAVES).

William Pickens's legacy to his children and to all black Americans included a passion for learning and a fervent desire to advance his race.

REFERENCES

Avery, Sheldon. *Up from Washington: William Pickens and the Negro Struggle for Equality, 1900–1954.* Newark: University of Delaware Press, 1989.

Hughes, Langston. *Fight for Freedom: The Story of the NAACP.* New York: Norton, 1962.

Hurston, Zora Neale. *Dust Tracks on a Road.* 1942. Reprint, New York: Harper Perennial, 1991.

Logan, Rayford W., and Michael R. Winston, eds. *Dictionary of American Negro Biography.* New York: Norton, 1982.

Pickens, William. *Bursting Bonds.* 1923. Reprint, *Bursting Bonds; the Heir of Slaves.* Bloomington: Indiana University Press, 1991.

———. *The Heir of Slaves.* 1911. Reprint, *Bursting Bonds; the Heir of Slaves.* Bloomington: Indiana University Press, 1991.

———. *The New Negro: His Political, Civil and Mental Status and Related Essays.* 1916. Reprint. New York: Negro Universities Press, 1969.

COLLECTIONS

The Pickens Papers are located at the Schomburg Center for Research in Black Culture, New York Public Library.

Linda M. Carter

Bill Pickett

(1870–1932)

Wild West show performer, cowboy

Bill Pickett was a major star of rodeos and Wild West shows and the inventor of a unique style of bulldogging in the first years of the twentieth century. He was the first black working cowboy, and spent his life in that career.

Willie M. Pickett was born to Thomas Jefferson Pickett and Mary Virginia Elizabeth Gilbert Pickett on December 5, 1870, in the Jenks–Branch community about 30 miles northwest of Austin, Texas, in Travis County. He was the oldest of 13 children born to the couple between 1870 and 1890. Thomas Pickett was born a slave in 1854 in Louisiana, as his owners moved from South Carolina to Texas. The racial heritage of both parents was mixed and included Native American ancestry. After the Civil War ended slavery, Thomas Pickett moved his family to a small holding near Austin sometime in the early 1870s and began to raise vegetables for market. His oldest son, Bill, went to a rural school through the fifth grade.

About the time Bill Pickett finished his schooling in 1881 at the age of 11, he learned from observing cattle dogs a method of controlling cattle. Bulldogs had originally been bred to control bulls by biting their sensitive muzzles and holding on. Pickett discovered that he too could subdue cattle by biting; as an adult he leaped from his horse, seized the steer by the horns, and pulled the head back to the point where he could bite the upper lip. The animal would be immobilized and follow as he dropped to the ground, with the animal often landing on top. This technique is forbidden in modern bulldogging—now officially called steer wrestling—which involves much lighter animals weighing between 400 and 750 pounds. Pickett faced steers between 800 to 1,100 pounds. Naturally, he lost teeth and was frequently injured; although he tried to work in spite of damage to his body, he was sidelined on one occasion for nine months. Over the years he estimated that he bulldogged some 5,000 head.

Pickett and several of his brothers worked on ranches around Austin and became skillful cowboys. The Picketts moved to Tyler, Texas, around 1888. There, between 1888 and 1890, five Pickett brothers offered their skills at breaking horses. Pay for cowhands was low—about five dollars a week with board. Thus, in Austin around 1886, Bill Pickett rode bucking horses on Sunday afternoons to amuse bystanders and picked up some extra cash by passing the hat. He also gave occasional demonstrations of his method of bulldogging, which amazed spectators to whom it was completely new, especially since Pickett was not a large man. At five feet, seven inches, he weighed 145 pounds.

For some years Pickett worked on various ranches around Tyler. On December 2, 1890, he married Maggie Williams. The Picketts had nine children, Sherman, Nannie, Bessie, Leona, Boss, Willie, Kleora Virginia, Almarie, and Alberdia. The two sons, Sherman and Boss, died in infancy, but all the girls reached adulthood. The family lived in Tyler, where Pickett was a deacon of the Tyler Baptist Church. Pickett took any farm and ranch work available, including cotton picking, and supplemented the family diet by hunting. Sometime in the late 1890s he became blind for eleven months; when the condition cleared up, his eyesight never troubled him again.

Bill and Tom Pickett gave exhibitions of bulldogging at the first Tyler county fair in 1888. It is not clear when Bill Pickett began to tour extensively. Lee Moore, a local rancher, managed his touring, and Pickett made appearances in many Texas towns before making extensive out–of–state engagements beginning in 1900. After the 1902 season, Pickett had a new manager, Dave McClure, who took Pickett to major events like the 1904 Cheyenne Frontier Days celebration. Coverage by a national magazine pushed Pickett and his bulldogging technique into the spotlight.

Joins 101 Shows

Ex–Confederate soldier George W. Miller and his three sons had built a very large and profitable ranch near Ponca City, Oklahoma, called the 101. To entertain a convention of editors, the Miller brothers staged a wild–west show on their ranch on June 11, 1905. The show attracted some 65,000 persons to the specially built facilities. Pickett's current manager, Guy ''Cheyenne Bill'' Weadick, a major influence in the development of the modern rodeo, brought to the event his star bulldogger, now billed as ''The Dusky Demon.''

The 101 Ranch staged another show in 1906. By now the Millers liked the money the shows brought in and were ready to develop a traveling show. In 1907 they signed a contract with Pickett, who maintained his relationship with the 101 for the rest of his life.

The Picketts moved to accommodations on the ranch, but the family later settled in Ponca City. Pickett lived on the ranch and visited his family when he could. For a traveling cowboy, family life became secondary. From 1907 through 1913 Pickett toured with the 101 show in the United States, with an occasional foray into Mexico. He appears to have been earning about six dollars a week plus board for his efforts in the shows, and during the winters he did regular ranch work. In the winter of 1913 the show went to South America and then to England. All the horses were seized by the British government at the outbreak of World War I, and the troupe had difficulty in booking passage home. At the close of the 1916 season, the Millers ended their shows, which had contributed to the $800,000 profits of the 101 Ranch between 1908 and 1916.

Pickett now did ranch work at the 101 Ranch, with occasional rodeo appearances. In 1920 he moved with his family to Oklahoma City. While his family was happy there, he was not. In 1924 he moved back to the 101. The ranch was now experiencing hard times, so he had no regular salary but asked for money as he needed it. A new 101 show went on the road in 1925 but with little financial success; the shows limped along to an end in 1931.

After a brief illness, Maggie Pickett died in a hospital on March 14, 1929, and was buried near Norman, Oklahoma. Bill Pickett was now left alone since all of his daughters had married and left home. In 1931, the 101 Ranch went into receivership. In March of 1932 a horse kicked Pickett in the head. After a fourteen–day coma, he died on April 2, 1932. After a funeral held on the porch of the main residence of the 101 on April 5, he was buried about three miles away on the ranch.

Bill Pickett's skill as a bulldogger can be seen in a film short, *The Bulldogger,* preserved in the Library of Congress. Pickett received posthumous recognition. On December 9, 1971, he was the twentieth person and the first black inducted into the National Rodeo Cowboy Hall of Fame in Oklahoma City. The North Fort Worth Historical Society unveiled a bronze statue of him in 1987. Millions more people became aware of him when the Postal Service issued a commemorative stamp in March of 1994. Bill Pickett was a living legend. He was a brave and innovative man who revolutionized the rodeo. A living legacy is his family, Pickett had 215 living direct descendants in 1994.

REFERENCES

Hanes, Bailey C. *Bill Pickett.* Norman: University of Oklahoma Press, 1977.

Johnson, Cecil. *Guts: Legendary Black Rodeo Cowboy, Bill Pickett.* Fort Worth: The Summit Group, 1994.

Robert L. Johns

Samuel R. Pierce Jr.

(1922–)

Lawyer, government official

Samuel R. Pierce Jr.'s talents and intellect have been his vehicles to a life of distinction. In high school and college, he was recognized for his impressive athletic ability as well as his keen intellect. Many of his accomplishments carved new roles for those of his race. Pierce was one of the first black Americans to argue a case before the U.S. Supreme Court, to become a partner of a major New York City law firm, and to serve as a director of a Fortune 500 company. Pierce gained national attention in the 1980s when he became the Secretary of Housing and Urban Development (HUD) and consequently, the Reagan administration's highest–ranking black American appointee.

Samuel Riley Pierce Jr., the oldest of Samuel and Hettie Elenor Armstrong Pierce's three sons, was born on September 8, 1922, in Glen Cove, Long Island, a New York City suburb. His father parlayed his job at Nassau Country Club into a valet service for its members prior to becoming the owner of a dry–cleaning business and real estate investor. According to *Current Biography,* ''To his son Samuel, he passed on a belief in self–sufficiency, a drive to excel, and a partiality for the Republican Party.''

Pierce's desire to excel was evident early on. As a high school student in Glen Cove, he was a sports editor of his school's newspaper, football player, captain of the basketball team, Long Island 100–yard–dash champion, and senior class salutatorian. Pierce was awarded a scholarship to Cornell University where he was a member of the football team and was elected to Phi Beta Kappa during his junior year. Pierce also was the first black athlete to play football against the U.S. Naval Academy. Subsequently, he was named to the Long Island Athletic Hall of Fame.

World War II interrupted Pierce's career as a scholar athlete. He served in North Africa and Italy and was the only black American agent in the U.S. Army's Criminal Investigation Division in the Mediterranean Theater of Operations. In 1946, Pierce was discharged from military duty.

Pierce resumed his studies at Cornell and received his B.A. degree with honors in 1947. Two years later, Pierce, who was president of Cornell's Law School Association, received a J.D. degree from Cornell followed by an LL.M. degree in

Samuel R. Pierce Jr.

taxation from New York University's School of Law in 1952. Years later he was awarded a number of honorary degrees, including a LL.D. from New York University's School of Law.

Begins Law Career

Pierce's law career began in 1949 as an assistant in the office of Frank Hogan, a Manhattan district attorney, until 1953. For the next two years, Pierce was an assistant U.S. attorney for the Southern District of New York. In 1955 he became the first African American to serve as assistant to the Under Secretary of Labor. In 1956–57 Pierce was associate counsel and later counsel to the House Judiciary antitrust subcommittee. Then he returned to the world of academia. In 1957–58 he was a Ford Foundation fellow at Yale University's Law School, and from 1957 to 1970 adjunct professor at New York University's School of Law.

During the 1950s, Pierce became increasingly involved in the Republican Party. He was New York Representative Kenneth Keating's campaign treasurer for his 1958 U.S. Senate race. In 1959 and 1960 Governor Nelson A. Rockefeller appointed Pierce to vacancies on New York County's Court of General Sessions, and each time, Pierce unsuccessfully sought election to full 14–year terms.

Pierce then joined Battle, Fowler, Stokes and Kheel where from 1961 to 1970 and 1973 to 1981, he was an associate and later partner. Pierce was the first black American partner of a major New York City law firm. Litigation, labor, tax, and antitrust law were his specialties.

Pierce continued to advance in the legal world, yet he found time to participate in legal, employment, economic, and administrative endeavors on behalf of black Americans. In 1961 he joined the legal team that defended civil rights leaders, including Martin Luther King Jr., and the *New York Times* in a libel suit filed by Alabama officials over an advertisement. Pierce argued the case before the Supreme Court, and the result was the 1964 ruling in their favor. During 1963–64, he was a member of a New York City panel, appointed by the mayor, that sought increased construction industry jobs for blacks. He was a founder of the Freedom National Bank in 1964, the first commercial bank in the state of New York with a majority of black officers. During the next two years, Pierce chaired a committee that attempted to improve operations of a Harlem antipoverty agency, Haryou Act. Also in 1966, Mayor John Lindsay appointed him to a panel that recommended judicial appointments.

Mayor Robert Wagner and Governor Rockefeller appointed Pierce beginning in the 1960s, to various boards, respectively. In 1964 he became a board member of U.S. Industries, the first black American to serve as a director of a major national and international company in the United States.

Advances Politically

In the mid–1960s, according to the *Encyclopedia of African American Culture and History,* J. Edgar Hoover, the director of the Federal Bureau of Investigation, identified Pierce "as a preferable 'moderate' alternative to more 'radical' black leaders such as Roy Wilkins and the Rev. Dr. Martin Luther King, Jr." Thus a number of influential individuals saw Pierce as an asset. He joined the Committee of Black Americans for Nixon and Agnew, and after the election, he rejected an offer to become chairman of the Civil Service Commission in the Nixon Administration; however, from 1970 to 1973, he served as general counsel to the Treasury Department. Pierce was the first black American to hold a subcabinet post in the Treasury Department where he supervised 900 lawyers, negotiated the legal terms of a $250,000 federal loan guarantee for the Lockheed Aircraft Corporation, and helped develop the Administration's 1971 wage–price freeze. In 1973 he received the Treasury Department's Alexander Hamilton award, the department's highest honor.

Upon Pierce's return to his New York City law firm in 1973, he was named to a panel charged with investigating the causes of the city's July 1977 blackout, and a mediation panel that negotiated a contract for city transit workers in 1978. Serving on the American Stock Exchanges's board of governors in 1977 and 1979, Pierce also sat on the boards of General Electric, International Paper, and Prudential Insurance. He also served as a trustee of Cornell, Hampton and Howard universities, and Mt. Holyoke College.

In 1980 Pierce was selected by President–elect Ronald Reagan as Secretary of Housing and Urban Development (HUD). Pierce initially declined; self–evaluation led him to consider his talents and background more compatible with the office of Attorney General or Secretary of Labor. He later acquiesced, however, and was sworn in on January 23, 1981.

Takes the Helm at HUD

Upon assuming leadership of HUD, Pierce attempted to improve the department's management and efficiency. He reduced staff by 21 percent for a savings of $129 million annually, improved financial forecasting and investing of Federal Housing Administration insurance funds resulting in $2.8 billion investment income between fiscal years 1981–88. Pierce initiated the administration's first debt collection program in order to reduce the $1.6 billion to HUD.

At the first meeting of the Organization for Economic Cooperation and Development in Paris in 1983, Pierce was elected chairman of OECD's Urban Affairs Ministers Conference. He was the first American to serve as UAM's chairman, and in 1986 became the first person ever to be re–elected.

Pierce has been described as Reagan's most effective cabinet member. Indeed Pierce appeared to support the majority of the budget cuts and asserted that the administration's efforts would improve the slumping housing industry as well as the economy. As a result, he argued, the poor would benefit more from an improved economy than from HUD programs.

Yet Pierce did not automatically rubber–stamp every Reagan item. He persuaded the president to reverse his decision to eliminate the Urban Development Action Grants program in fiscal 1982; this program used governmental funds to generate private investment in cities. In addition, he blocked a plan that attempted to limit FHA home mortgage loans.

Initiates New Policies

During Pierce's tenure, he replaced costly Section 8 New Construction with a voucher system that enabled poor people to afford existing housing, upgraded housing for low–income families, increased housing for the poor by facilitating new construction for which HUD funds had been committed, and continued new housing construction for the elderly and handicapped while implementing cost containment measures. In addition, he took steps to increase the number of FHA and Government National Mortgage Association mortgages, curbed the escalating cost of new homes for middle–income families through HUD's Joint Venture for Affordable Housing with communities, increased the number of public housing units, and established five programs to aid the homeless.

HUD's *New Directions in Housing and Urban Policy* concluded that under his leadership, "The Department continued and reinforced its support of equal housing opportunity and aggressively pursued strengthened enforcement of the nation's fair housing law." By the time the administration left office in 1989, "the assisted housing debt had been reduced to less than $200 billion; at the same time, the number of assisted families had increased from 3.2 million in 1981 to 4.3 million by the end of 1988." In the late 1980s, HUD became the object of increased scrutiny. Pierce was forced to resign in 1989 and was investigated, but never charged, for wrongdoing as HUD's secretary. Later, a number of his close associates were indicted for fraud, bribery, and lying to Congress. In 1993 and 1994, two of Pierce's chief assistants, Lance Wilson and Deborah Gore Dean, were sentenced to six months and twenty–one months in prison respectively.

In 1989 Samuel Pierce received the Martin Luther King Jr. Salute to Greatness award, the Reagan Revolution Medal of Honor, and the Presidential Citizens Medal. In addition, Pierce began an association with the Turner Corporation as a consultant.

Since 1948 Pierce has been married to Barbara Penn Wright who through the years has maintained her career as a physician in New York City. The Pierces have one daughter, Victoria.

Current address: 16 West 77th Street, New York, NY 10024.

REFERENCES

Current Biography Yearbook. New York: H. W. Wilson, 1982.

Pierce, Samuel R. Interview with Linda M. Carter, March 6, 1997.

Salzman, Jack, David Lionel Smith, and Cornel West, eds. *Encyclopedia of African–American Culture and History.* New York: Macmillan Library Reference USA/Simon Schuster Macmillan, 1996.

U.S. Department of Housing and Urban Development. *New Directions in Housing and Urban Policy: 1981–1989; A Review of the Activities and Programs of the U.S. Department of Housing and Urban Development.* Washington, DC: HUD, 1989.

Uzell, Lawrence A. "The Unsung Hero of the Reagan Revolution." *National Review* (9 December 1988): 29–31.

Who's Who among African Americans, 1998–99. 10th ed. Detroit: Gale Research, 1998.

Linda M. Carter

P. B. S. Pinchback

(1837–1921)

Politician, businessman, newspaper editor

P. B. S. Pinchback is principally remembered as the first black governor of a state. Others know him best as an impressive grandfather who had an overwhelming effect on his grandson, Jean Toomer, the Harlem Renaissance writer.

His life and career illuminate many aspects of the nineteenth–century South, and he was a major figure in Reconstruction politics.

Pinckney Benton Stewart Pinchback was born in Macon, Georgia, on May 14, 1837, to William Pinchback (d. 1848), a white planter, and Eliza Stewart (1814–1884), his very fair–skinned mulatto slave. P. B. S. Pinchback could have passed for white, and one of his sisters in fact did. Although William Pinchback appears to have been already married, his relation with Stewart was a long–term, stable one and produced ten children, most of whom died young. She gave birth to their first child in 1829, and six more preceded P. B. S. Pinchback, although only two lived. By 1887 only P. B. S. was still living. In 1835 or 1836 William Pinchback took Stewart to Philadelphia and freed her and her children.

William Pinchback established himself on a new plantation in Holmes County, Mississippi. In 1846 the nine–year–old P. B. S. and his older brother Napoleon (b. 1830) were sent to a school in Cincinnati for children of mixed racial heritage. When William Pinchback died in 1848, his provisions for Stewart and his children were ignored. To escape reenslavement, Stewart and her five living children went to Cincinnati. About a year later, Napoleon became mentally ill and was confined to an asylum. At age twelve, P. B. S. found work on canal boats traveling between Cincinnati and Toledo. He eventually worked on boats on the Mississippi and Missouri Rivers from 1854 on.

Pinchback rose to become a steward on steamboats but combined his work with gambling. He was the protégé of George H. Devol, who wrote, "He was my boy. I raised him and trained him. I took him out of a steamboat barbershop. I instructed him in the mysteries of card–playing, and he was an apt pupil." The propensity to gamble never left Pinchback. In spite of the limitations imposed by racial status, he developed an assertive personality and was prepared to resort to force to defend his rights. Kerman and Eldridge quote from Jean Toomer, who observed that his grandfather did things with dash and flair. "[He was] masculine, active, daring, full of energy, vital, never ill, hearty eating, hearty laughing, drink enjoying, able to command, clean, upstanding, forceful, intelligent, well–dressed, well–kept, well–off, noble in bearing, serious, fun–loving, stormy if need be, full of feeling, a grand speaker, a center of influence and attraction, having many friends, much exciting business, and an air of adventure.

Pinchback established himself in New Orleans, where he married Nina Hethorn (c. 1854–1928), who was also nearly white. Two of their six children died young; the survivors were Pinckney (b. 1862), Bismark (c. 1864–1924), Nina (1866–1909), and Walter, (b. circa 1868).

The Civil War interrupted river traffic on the Mississippi. Pinchback's boat was at Yazoo City when he left it and made his way through the blockade to New Orleans. On May 16, 1862, he got into a fight with his brother–in–law, who was wounded. Pinchback made bail in the civil court but was arrested again and tried by the occupying Union military authorities. On May 25 he began serving a two–year sentence

P. B. S. Pinchback

for assault with attempt to murder. In August he was released to enlist in the First Louisiana Volunteers, and he was soon engaged in recruiting for other formations. On October 12, the Second Regiment of Louisiana Native Guards entered the army with Pinchback as its captain. He insisted on his rights as an officer and refused to ride on segregated streetcars. On September 3, 1863, he resigned in frustration at the army's reluctance to accept black officers. A few weeks later he tried again for a military position, raising a company of cavalry, but again was denied a commission. A final attempt to secure a commission in 1865 fell through because the war ended; Pinchback was in Washington, D.C., on this quest when Lincoln was assassinated.

Enters Politics

In 1865 as he was returning home, Pinchback spoke out in Alabama about the postwar treatment of blacks. Congressional Reconstruction now gave him the opportunity to enter politics. He turned down an appointment as Inspector of Customs at New Orleans, but in April 1867 he organized the Fourth Ward Republican Club3 and subsequently become a member of the Republican state committee. He was elected to the state constitutional convention in the fall of 1867 and became a prominent leader. He worked to establish full civil rights for blacks in the new constitution. The following April he was elected to the state senate under the new constitution. He at first lost the election 899 to 819 but won in a re–count, a pattern he would repeat in many of his subsequent elections. In May he served as a delegate–at–large to the Republican National Convention in Chicago, and he would be a delegate to many more over the years. He turned down another federal appointment in 1869 to remain in the state senate.

Pinchback actively pursued wealth in these years. One avenue was to use inside information about the actions of the legislature, which violated no current norms of political behavior. He also made an inflated profit from dubious projects such as the state–incorporated Mississippi Packet Company, an undertaking that did not survive long. He also engaged in business enterprises, notably commission and cotton factorage activity, as part of the firm Pinchback and Antoine. That enterprise was a success until 1873, when he and C. C. Antoine, a Senate colleague, quarreled about profits arising from the sale of land for a park to the city of New Orleans. Antoine felt he had been cheated out of $40,000 of the profit from the transaction. In December 1870, Pinchback and Antoine began to publish the *New Orleans Louisianian.* Pinchback soon became sole owner of the paper, which continued until 1881. Another source of Pinchback's wealth was his ownership of shares in the extremely corrupt Louisiana Lottery, which was finally abolished in 1892.

In March of 1871, Pinchback became director of schools for New Orleans, a post he held until 1877. Involvement in city politics was another avenue for both public service and profit. Pinchback maintained a lavish lifestyle, and the wealth he accumulated during this period supported his family in great style until late in his life, when his continued gambling depleted his resources. His family spent their summers in the North, most often at Saratoga, New York, because of the excellent horse racing venues. When unequal treatment of blacks became a problem on railroads, he made strong protests and on at least one occasion simply hired a private car.

Becomes Governor of Louisiana

Politics in Louisiana became very complicated as the Republicans split into factions and unreconstructed whites threatened Republican rule. The sudden death of the black lieutenant governor, Oscar P. Dunn, led to Pinchback's election on December 6, 1871, to the positions of president pro tem of the state senate and lieutenant governor. This choice also made him head of the New Orleans police. In August 1872 Pinchback received the Republican nomination for governor, but he withdrew from the race in a compromise with another Republican faction, receiving instead the nomination for congressman–at–large. The Republicans won the election in November, and Pinchback won his House seat. Events before the election involved Pinchback in a losing railroad race with Governor Henry Clay Warmoth. Both he and the governor were out of the state at the same time. The legislature passed legislation favored by Pinchback and his faction of the Republican Party but initially opposed by Warmoth, who did sign it later on although too late to mend his political fences. If Pinchback reached the state capital first, he would have had the power to sign it into law as acting governor. It seems to have been fortunate that Pinchback met the governor along the way and turned back since it is claimed that men were posed along the railroads to see that he did not reach Louisiana alive.

On December 6, 1872, just over a month before Warmoth's term as governor ended, the newly elected legislature met. There were many contested elections, but Pinchback swore in all senators whose elections were certified by the Republican–controlled returning board. He maintained that his action allowed the Republicans to retain control of the senate for four more years.

On December 9, Governor Warmoth was impeached. As president of the senate, Pinchback thus became governor—a first for an African American. He held the office until January 13, 1873, when the next elected governor took office.

On January 15, 1873, Pinchback was elected to a full six–year term as senator by the state senate, thus becoming a member–elect of both houses of Congress, but the effort to claim his congressional seats was prolonged and ultimately unsuccessful. The Senate denied him the seat on March 8, 1876, although in July it allowed him the pay and mileage due a senator for the time before his refusal, a sum of $16,666. The House gave the seat to his opponent in the final days of the session.

Career Declines

An appointment as Louisiana Commissioner to the Vienna Exposition allowed him to spend three months touring Europe beginning in May 1873. On January 13, 1875, the Louisiana senate elected him senator again in case of a vacancy in an effort to strengthen his still–pending claim on the seat. He had the political support to be elected a delegate to the 1876 Republican National Convention and also to become president of the state party convention. In 1877 Pinchback supported Democratic governor F. T. Nicholls, one of two people who claimed to have won the election. Both Republican and Democrat candidates were sworn in under near civil war conditions. In return, Pinchback was appointed to the State Board of Education. In 1879 he was appointed to the Internal Revenue Service but soon resigned to serve in the new state constitutional convention. In that body his support of the creation of a segregated school, Southern University, resulted in a major break between Pinchback and the Creole community, which was not willing to accept any form of segregation. From 1883 to 1885 he served on the board of trustees of the school. Pinchback's final federal appointment in Louisiana was as surveyor of customs for New Orleans on February 24, 1882, a position he held until July 2, 1885. There is also evidence that he later worked in a civil service position for the Internal Revenue Service in Boston in 1910–11, when he was trying to recoup his fortune. In the fall of 1885 he entered law school. He was admitted to the Louisiana Bar on April 10, 1886, but there is no record that he ever practiced.

Around this time Pinchback's income from investments was about $10,000 a year. About 1892 he moved from Louisiana to Washington, D.C., where he built an imposing house. Pinchback was a domineering patriarch and in spite of his attention to their education his sons achieved no great distinction. Pinchback's daughter Nina defied him to marry Nathan Toomer on March 29, 1894, but Toomer deserted his wife even before the birth of their son, Eugene, on December 26. Pinchback's grandson, best known as Jean Toomer, author of *Cane,* grew up in his grandfather's house, which was sold in 1906. After spending time in Brooklyn and elsewhere, the Pinchbacks and Jean Toomer returned to a Washington apartment in 1909, when Toomer's mother died.

By 1912 the Pinchbacks were living in an apartment on U Street. In 1920 Jean Toomer persuaded his grandfather to give him an allowance of five dollars a week and let him live in the apartment while Toomer wrote. The grandparents were very frail by this time, and Toomer had to run the household. In 1921 Pinchback entered a nursing home. He died on December 21, 1921, and was buried in Metairie Ridge Cemetery, New Orleans, but by that time he was almost forgotten in New Orleans. His son Walter and grandson Jean were the only family members present at the sparsely attended New Orleans funeral.

P. B. S. Pinchback was a man who loved to gamble and who easily attracted attention, both favorable and unfavorable. Although he was not averse to using his political activities to enrich himself, he steadfastly defended the rights of other African Americans. Although his courage is beyond question, he could not prevail in the increasingly unfavorable political and social climate of the end of Reconstruction. In many ways he personified the ideals of Southern manhood, insisting on his right, for example, to ride streetcars assigned to whites. New Orleans streetcar employees would remove white patrons from the cars, leaving him to ride in isolation, completely unperturbed. In his pride and assertiveness Pinchback yielded to few.

REFERENCES

Bontemps, Arna. *One Hundred Years of Negro Freedom.* New York: Dodd, Mead, 1961.

Devol, George H. *Forty Years A Gambler on the Mississippi.* Cincinnati: Devol and Haines, 1887.

Haskins, James. *Pinckney Benton Stewart Pinchback.* New York: Macmillan, 1973.

Ingham, John N., and Lynne B. Feldman. *African–American Business Leaders.* Westport, CT: Greenwood Press, 1994.

Kerman, Cynthia Earl, and Richard Eldridge. *The Lives of Jean Toomer.* Baton Rouge: University of Louisiana Press, 1987.

Logan, Rayford W., and Michael R. Winston, eds. *Dictionary of American Negro Biography.* New York: Norton, 1982.

Malone, Dumas, ed. *Dictionary of American Biography.* New York: Charles Scribner's Sons, 1943.

Simmons, William J. *Men of Mark.* Cleveland: Geo. M. Rewell, 1887.

COLLECTIONS

The major collection of Pinchback papers is in the Moorland–Spingarn Research Center, Howard University, Washington, D.C.

Robert L. Johns

Horace Pippin
(1888–1946)
Painter

Horace Pippin is considered the most important African American painter of the first half of the twentieth century. He was a self–taught artist who reached a height of artistic achievement, fame, and recognition that few artists, regardless of race, attain. His contribution to art history and American painting is significant. Pippin's rural upbringing helped to shape his unique way of seeing the world as he recorded what he observed on paper, canvas, and board. He reinvented and interpreted without sentimentality and with a level of reality that made his work modern in concept. Although modernism in art may not have been a conscious concern of Pippin, his approach to painting assesses the internal and external factors of the modernistic thought. His sensitive and insightful portrayals of African Americans have helped to document aspects of daily life in the African American community that had previously been unrecorded in the art world.

Pippin, one of three children, was born in West Chester, Pennsylvania, on February 22, 1888. His mother, Harriet Johnson Pippin, was a domestic worker. Little is known about his father, Horace Pippin, Sr. We do know that he did not play a vital role in the family's life to the extent that later in life Pippin would say that he did not know his father at all. When Pippin was still very young, his mother moved the family to Goshen, New York, where she had relatives and knew that she would be able to support herself and her family.

As he grew up in Goshen, a relatively small, supportive community, Pippin was surrounded by relatives and friends. In this pleasant rural setting, Pippin's keen sense of observation and his way of seeing the world, people, and their interaction with each other, took shape. Undoubtedly, this environment strongly influenced his painting style. Pippin attended a one–room, segregated school where he constantly drew illustrations. Frequently his handiwork appeared on his homework or on in–class assignments. Although his teachers were not always pleased with this practice, they, along with others in the community, recognized his abilities and encouraged him to develop his talent.

With this support, Pippin learned that his work was liked and appreciated. This encouraged him to hone his artistic skills. In 1902 Pippin's formal education ended when his mother became ill. He quit school to work odd jobs to help support the family; he remained the breadwinner until his mother died in 1908. By 1912 Pippin had left Goshen and relocated to Patterson, New Jersey, where he continued to work an assortment of jobs. One job, a mover of oil paintings, gave Pippin the opportunity to examine up close numerous oil paintings and provided him firsthand knowledge of fine art.

The tall, dark–brown complected Pippin was a man of strong build. He was deeply religious, thoughtful, quiet at

Horace Pippin

times, and had a wonderful sense of humor. His personality and demeanor made him generally well liked by all who knew him. Though a fine human being, this minimally educated, poor black man was, by most standards, just ordinary. Like other ordinary people, he probably would have passed through life with little notice. However, his talent as an artist always set him apart and has given him a place in art history.

Pippin was patriotic and willing to fight for his country. This being the case, immediately after the United States entered World War I, Pippin enlisted. He was assigned to the Fifteenth Infantry. A dedicated and conscientious soldier, before setting off for Europe he was given the rank of corporal. The 15th Infantry Regiment, an all–black volunteer regiment, became the 369th Colored Infantry Regiment of the 93rd Division of the United States and was under French command. In 1918, while on active duty, Pippin was wounded in his right shoulder which left him unable to raise his right arm above his shoulder. As a result, Pippin spent several months in the hospital and then was honorably discharged in 1919. Because of the 15th Infantry's outstanding service, France awarded him the Croix de Guerre.

During his 14 months in the army, Pippin was very prolific, producing numerous sketches of the French landscape, soldiers, and the war environment. Unfortunately, few of these drawings are extant because Pippin destroyed them as the U.S. security regulations demanded. He returned to the United States disabled, with only a small war pension and very disillusioned with life in general. Not only was he unable to work to support himself, but he could not engage in his most prized pastime—arts and crafts projects. Unsure about his future, with little or no prospects for his life, in 1919 Pippin returned to the familiar environment of West Chester, Pennsylvania, the place of his birth.

On November 21, 1920, not long after his return to West Chester, Pippin married Jennie Ora Featherstone, twice widowed with a six–year–old son. Pippin and Jennie had no children together. Jennie Pippin owned a house and took in washing to supplement Pippin's pension. The marriage spurred Pippin to move forward and find a way to reconcile his war experiences. At this point, he began to paint war scenes from memory. This artistic activity, though difficult for Pippin because of his handicap, became a form of therapy. He devised a method of holding materials, which enabled him to strengthen his arm. In about a year, Pippin was able to regain a level of control and could hold a paint brush again.

Artistic Works Noticed

Pippin's artistic pursuits and development were being supported by family, friends, and associates. In 1937 he started to display his work in local shops in his area. It was at one such display that art critic and historian Christon Brinton viewed one of the "Cabin in the Cotton" series of paintings (1935–1944). Brinton was moved by the work and decided it should reach a larger audience. As a result of Brinton's backing, Pippin was included in an exhibition of self–taught artists curated by Holger Cabill, head of the WPA art projects at the Museum of Modern Art in New York. Also included in the exhibit were works by French artists Henri Rousseau, and Camille Bombois and by American artists Edward Hicks, John Kane, and Joseph Pickett. Between 1937 and 1946, Pippin's work received praise in the press from art critics and collectors.

Unlike many self–trained artists, Pippin was very versatile in his subject matter. He painted portraits from his imagination and memory, religious themes, still lifes, war scenes, rural scenes, street scenes, interiors, and flowers. His interests and focus were unlimited. What touched him as an individual made its way into his paintings. Organization of the composition and balance in color were vital aspects in Pippin's work. For example, Pippin's "Cabin in the Cotton" series went through many different metamorphoses. At times the picture area would be organized so that the viewer only saw the cabin from the vantage point of an outsider—not invited and unnoticed—or in another of the cabin paintings, the composition allows the viewer to enter into the cabin and become a participant in the life of the subject. There is always a focus on detail in Pippin's work. It is as if at times every blade of grass, every brick and tree, had to be just so, Pippin was so interested in assisting viewers to experience the work. In the painting *West Chester Court House* the foreground, middleground, and most of the background are active with an array of squares, rectangles, shapes, textures, and sizes structuring the work into an ordered scene. The viewer understands the significance of this building and really the smallness of the only figure, a small African American paperboy. In such works Pippin's observations become social commentary.

Pippin died of a stroke on July 6, 1946, and his wife, who had been committed to a mental institution in 1944, died ten days later.

Horace Pippin is considered an important figure in African American art history. His works are in the permanent collections of the Metropolitan Museum of Art, Whitney Museum of American Art, Hirshorn Museum, Phillips Collection, Philadelphia Museum of Art, Pennsylvania Academy of Fine Arts, San Francisco Museum of Art, and numerous private collections and galleries.

REFERENCES

Bearden, Romare, and Harry Henderson. *A History of African–American Artists: From 1792 to the Present.* New York: Pantheon, 1993.

Bogle, Donald, ed. *Black Arts Annual, 1987–1988.* New York: Garland Publishing, 1989.

Crane, Aimee, ed. *Portrait of America.* New York: Heparin Press, 1947.

hooks, bell. *Art on My Mind: Visual Politics.* New York: New Press, 1995.

Powell, Richard. *Black Art and Culture in the 20th Century.* London, England: Thames and Hudson, 1997.

Stein, Judith. *I Tell My Heart: The Art of Horace Pippin.* New York: Universe Publishing, 1993.

Alicia M. Henry

James O. Plinton Jr.

(1914–1996)

Business executive, pilot, instructor

James O. Plinton Jr. is known for achieving a number of firsts in flight: he was one of the first blacks to complete the U.S. Army Air Corps's Central Instruction School, the first black top executive for a major airline, and the first black to co–organize and operate a passenger and cargo airline outside the United States. In 1957 Trans World Airlines (TWA) hired him as executive assistant to the director of personnel and industrial relations. In this position, he hired the airline industry's first black flight attendant and the first black airline pilot.

Plinton was born on July 22, 1914, in Westfield, New Jersey, to Mary Williams Plinton and James O. Plinton Sr. Plinton's parents instilled in him the importance of working hard at a young age. He and his brother were required to help their father in his dental laboratory. Plinton said in *Black Enterprise,* "The ability to work hard is a gift from God."

Although Plinton's father wanted him to pursue a medical career, he attended Lincoln University in Lincoln, Pennsylvania, and graduated in 1935 with a bachelor's degree in biology. After service in the Merchant Marines and at the U.S. Post Office, Plinton went on to the University of Newark's Civil Pilot Training Program where he received a commercial pilot's license and a flight instructor's rating.

Aviation Career Takes Flight

The only black in a class of 35 trainees, no one but Plinton believed he would complete the training. In fact, the head of the school's Aeronautic Division spent a half hour telling him about the obstacles he would face trying to get through the program. Plinton persevered and successfully completed the primary course with honors. He was also selected with the top one fourth of his class to receive secondary training. Upon completion of the course, he was one of the six men selected from over two hundred qualified applicants to receive the cross–country and instructor training courses. In February 1941 he was sent to Tuskegee Institute (now University) as one of the first black flight instructors for the first black fighter squadron, the 99th Pursuit Squadron. There he trained about 150 pilots, many of whom fought in World War II and became known as the Tuskegee Airmen. Plinton loved aviation, and with a lot of hard work he moved up quickly. By the end of 1943, he had become assistant director of the Division of Aeronautics at Tuskegee under G. L. Washington, and was placed in charge of the War Training Service Program. He was also in charge of Airport No. 1 at Tuskegee and served as assistant chief pilot.

Plinton was then selected by the U.S. Army Air Forces Training Command to be one of the four black pilots sent to Central Instructors School to be trained and commissioned as advanced army flight instructors and service pilots. Plinton took first place when the selections were made, and after graduation three months later, he was assigned with three colleagues as the first black Army flight instructors at Tuskegee Advanced Army Air Base. His most famous student was Daniel "Chappie" James Jr. of the black 99th Pursuit Squadron and the armed forces's first black four–star general.

After training and piloting during World War II, Plinton lived and worked extensively in the Caribbean. In 1944 he helped organize Andesa, the national airline service in the Republic of Ecuador. He was invited in 1948 to the Republic of Haiti where he established and operated Quisqueya Ltd., an inter–island commercial flight service based in Kingston, Jamaica. While there as a guest of the government, he also built and operated the Haitian American Dry Cleaners and Laundry, the first modern dry cleaning and laundry chain in Haiti, with just $5,000. His business grossed $250,000 annually. After 11 years in Haiti, Plinton returned to the states.

First Black Executive of a Major Airline

In 1957 Plinton was hired at Trans World Airlines (TWA) as a top executive in personnel and industrial relations, becoming the first black executive of a major U.S. airline. In this position, he was able to hire the first black flight attendant and the first black pilot for a major airline.

In 1964 Plinton negotiated landing rights for TWA in the African nations of Kenya, Tanzania, and Uganda. While working in East Africa, he became interested in wild game hunting, and in 1968 he organized an all–black, 21 day safari in East Africa, which included fishing, sightseeing and hunting.

Plinton's most creative accomplishment while at TWA was his development of a marketing plan targeting specific groups according to economic levels, social interests, age, professional status, and ethnicity. TWA did not buy the plan. In 1971, when Plinton was unreasonably passed over for a promotion to a vice–presidential position that he thought he deserved, he decided to leave TWA. He then joined Eastern Airlines as vice–president for special marketing affairs. In 1975 Plinton assumed the dual position of vice–president for urban and international affairs. The next year he became vice–president for marketing development. In this position, Plinton was responsible for reorganizing Eastern's international division. He retired from Eastern Airlines in 1979.

Plinton's successful career won him numerous awards and recognition over the years. Fisk University honored him with a doctorate of laws degree in 1978 and Embry–Riddle Aeronautical University honored him with a doctorate in aeronautical science. He received the National Order of Honour, and also National Order of Labor from three different Haitian presidents. Other awards include: Distinguished Service Award, Lincoln University in Pennsylvania; Outstanding Man of the Year Award in Marketing, Long Island University; Outstanding Achievement in Aviation, Negro Airmen International; President Kenneth David Kaunda Award for Humanism; and the CHIEF Award, Association of Independent Colleges and Universities of Florida.

Plinton's other affiliations were numerous, and he was a member or officer of many organizations and boards. Plinton was a charter member of the Negro Airmen International (1958–96) and director of the Caribbean Tourism Association (1972–79). He was president, vice–chairman, and community chairman of the board for the YMCA of the United States (1973–81). He was on the board of various other organizations including the Embry–Riddle Aeronautical University (1976–96) and the Miami Museum of Science and Space Transit (1988–96) to name a few.

Plinton's most recent position was chair of the board at Tacolcy Economic Development Corporation in Miami, Florida. He died of cancer on July 4, 1996, at Lake Wales Medical Center Extended Care Facility in Lake Wales, Florida, at age eighty–one. He was survived by his wife Kathryn, whom he married in 1952 while she was secretary to the General Consulate to the Netherlands. The Plintons had two children: James Norman and Kathryn Ann Breen. Plinton was a pioneer in the airline industry, having served for 40 years either as pilot, flight instructor, or executive.

REFERENCES

''Career Guide: Opportunities and Resources For You.'' *Ebony Success Library,* vol. 3. Chicago: Johnson Publishing Co., 1973.

Clift, Virgil A., and Augustus W. Low. *Encyclopedia of Black America.* New York: McGraw–Hill, 1981.

James, Dalton. ''James O. Plinton, Jr., Eastern Airlines.'' *Black Collegian* 8 (March/April 1978): 47.

''James Plinton Jr., 81, Broke Color Barriers at U.S. Airlines.'' *New York Times,* July 14, 1996.

''James Plinton Jr., Pioneer Airline Exec, Dies At 81.'' *Jet* 90 (29 July 1996): 57.

Thompson, Era Bell. ''African Safari.'' *Ebony* 24 (February 1969): 114–22.

Ward, Francis. ''Jim Plinton's Flight to Corporate Success.'' *Black Enterprise* 10 (September 1979): 59–60.

Who's Who among African Americans, 1996–97. 9th ed. Detroit: Gale Research, 1996.

COLLECTIONS

Information on James O. Plinton is located in the Alumni files at the Langston Hughes Memorial Library at Lincoln University, Lincoln, Pennsylvania.

Sheila A. Stuckey

Sidney Poitier

(1927–)

Actor, director, producer

Sidney Poitier has served as a model and door–opener for African American actors such as Denzel Washington, Yaphet Kotto, Morgan Freeman, Laurence Fishburne, and Samuel L. Jackson, to follow. *Contemporary Biography* called him ''the first black man to be given a succession of serious, dignified roles in Hollywood films.'' According to the *African American Encyclopedia,* he created dignified, educated African American characters and stimulated audiences to question the stereotypical portraits of blacks. He was also ''praised and ridiculed for portraying the well–spoken and noble but nonthreatening African American during a period when African American frustration at racism was a major news.'' As a result of his performance in *Lilies of the Field* (1963), he became the first African American in U.S. film history to win an Oscar for best actor. In 1995 he was awarded the Kennedy Center Honor for lifetime achievement in the performing arts and, according to *Jet* magazine, he was ''praised by fellow actor Paul Newman for his pilgrimage of startling grace. . . . 'He has changed the face of film itself.'''

Sidney Poitier, the youngest of seven children, was born prematurely in Miami, Florida, on February 20, 1927, to Reginald James and Evelyn Outten Poitier. His parents were

Sidney Poitier

uneducated tomato farmers who had come to Miami from Cat Island in the Bahamas to sell their tomatoes. They returned to the Bahamas when Poitier was three months old. Growing up he was poor and received a limited education.

In an attempt to insure a better life for his son, Poitier's father sent him to Miami in 1943 to live with his brother Cyril. Because of his defiance in the face of racism, he soon had to leave Miami to insure the safety of his brother's family for the Ku Klux Klan was looking for him. Under the cover of night, he left Miami for New York with summer clothes and three dollars. Once in New York, he secured a job as a dishwasher. However, the cold weather was too much for his summer wardrobe; he enlisted in the army saying he was 18, not 17. He returned to civilian life after one year and 11 days of service.

Poitier married Juanita Marie Hardy, a dancer, on April 29, 1950, and they were divorced in 1965. On January 23, 1976, he married Joanna Shimkus, an actress. Poitier had six children: Beverly Poitier Henderson, Pamela, Sherri, and Gina from the first marriage; Anika and Sydney from the second marriage.

Stage Performance

Upon his discharge from service, Poitier returned to New York and secured another dishwashing job. His interest in acting, which began as a youngster viewing such stars in films as Tom Mix, Gene Autrey, Wild Bill Elliott, and Roy Rogers, was again aroused. He saw an advertisement for the American Negro Theatre in Harlem's *Amsterdam News* calling for actors to audition and answered the ad. Due to his poor reading ability, accent, and lack of training, he was turned down by the director and cofounder of the American Negro Theatre, Frederick O'Neal. This rejection served as an impetus for Poitier's development; he was determined to prove himself. Thus, he learned to speak properly, to rid himself of his accent, and to read. Six months later, following these efforts, he reauditioned and became a student of acting at the American Negro Theatre. In *Blacks in American Films and Television* Bogle said that he ''became part of a group of post–World War II new–style black actors that included Harry Belafonte, Ossie Davis, Ruby Dee, Earle Hyman, and Lloyd Richards.''

The theater presented one or two productions a year designed to promote the work of new students and the work in 1945 was *Days of Our Youth.* Poitier wanted the part of Liebman, but Harry Belafonte was brought in even though he was not a student at the theater. This led to a clash between two men, who would later become friends. Due to the petition of his classmates, however, he was cast as Belafonte's understudy. The Broadway director James Light was invited to critique an evening's rehearsal; Belafonte was unable to appear and Poitier had to step in. Following the evening's rehearsal, Light presented his plan for the play *Lysistrata* with an all–black cast and offered Poitier the part of Polydorus. He accepted and made his first Broadway appearance in 1946 in *Lysistrata.*

In the first performance of the play, Poitier was petrified; instead of saying his lines in the correct order, he began with line three, went to line seven, and was never able to recoup. Even though he was devastated, the audience found the performance hilarious and, according to Poitier in *This Life,* some reviewers saw him as ''the only saving grace of the evening'' and praised his ''acute comedic approach to the part of Polydorus.'' As a result of this performance, he garnered the role of Lester in *Anna Lucasta* (1947) and toured with the play in 1948. In 1959 he appeared as Walter Lee Younger in *A Raisin in the Sun* directed by Lloyd Richards, a portrayal which has been praised for the emotional power of the performance. Other stage performances include *On Striver's Row, You Can't Take It With You, Rain, Freight, The Fisherman, Hidden Horizon,* and *Riders to the Sea.*

Film Performance

Poitier made his greatest impact in motion pictures during the 1950s and 1960s. His first film appearances were training films for the army; one of them was *From Whom Cometh My Help* (1949), an Army Signal Corps documentary. He made his first Hollywood appearance in 1950 in *No Way Out*; his character was a noble, educated, dedicated young doctor. Bogle said in *Blacks in American Films and Television,* ''By his very presence, by his basic sense of self, he was flipping movie history upside down.'' In spite of the fact that there had been other black actors demonstrating both action and intelligence and performing serious roles prior to Poitier, they did not become ''leading dramatic actor[s] working *consistently* in American films.'' In 1955 he appeared in *Cry, the Beloved Country,* an adaptation of the novel of the same name by Alan Paton, as the Reverend Msimangu. Part of the film was set in South Africa; Poitier traveled to Africa were he was an indentured laborer and learned about South African society and black people.

In the 1950s as well, Poitier appeared in *Red Ball Express* (1952), *Go, Man, Go* (1954), and *Blackboard Jungle* (1955). The latter film, according to Bogle in *Blacks in American Films and Television* represents ''one of his most exciting roles as a rebellious high school student.'' He also appeared in *Goodbye, My Lady* (1956), *Band of Angels* (1957), and *Something of Value* (1957). *Edge of the City* (1957) and *The Defiant Ones* (1958) changed his career and established him as a star. In *Blacks in American Films and Television,* Bogle said that, in the latter film, he was ''sometimes angry, sometimes explosive and almost always likable . . . [and] proved himself one of the screen's most talented dramatic actors.''

Bogle suggested in *Toms, Coons* that there were three reasons for Poitier's rise in the 1950s while other actors failed. First, ''for the mass white audience, Sidney Poitier was a black man who had met their standards . . . For black audiences he was the paragon of black middle–class values and virtues.'' Second, ''in many respects his characters were still the old type that America had always cherished.'' Third, ''Poitier became a star because of his talent. He may have played the old tom dressed up with modern intelligence and reason, but he dignified the figure.'' He appeared in three other movies during the 1950s: *Mark of the Hawk* (1958), *Virgin Island* (1958), and *Porgy and Bess* (1959).

The 1960s found Poitier the subject of controversy. Militants in the African American community did not approve of his roles, which were often seen as white creations and denied him realistic romantic relationships. His performance as Walter Lee Younger in *A Raisin in the Sun* (1961) earned him an Antoinette Perry Award nomination for best actor in a drama. His other movies of the 1960s included *All the Young Men* (1960), *Paris Blues* (1961), and *Pressure Point* (1962). For low budget picture *Lilies of the Field* (1963) he received ten percent of the profits, an Oscar for best actor in a drama, and a Golden Globe nomination for best actor. *The Long Ships* (1964), *The Greatest Story Ever Told* (1965), *A Patch of Blue* (1965), and *To Sir, With Love* (1967). The last two received some negative black audience response, for following the Oscar, Bogle wrote in *Blacks in American Films and Television* that there was a shift in his audiences ''from a social philosophy of cultural integration and assimilation to one of cultural naturalism and separatism.'' However, his most controversial picture of the period was *Guess Who's Coming to Dinner* (1967); other pictures of the period included *In the Heat of the Night* (1967), *For Love of Ivy* (which was the result of his original idea, 1968), and *The Lost Man* (1969).

In the 1970s Poitier's career seemed to begin to wane. However, he appeared in movies such as *They Call Me Mister Tibbs* (1970), *The Organization* (1971), *Buck and the Preacher* (1972), *A Warm December* (1973), *Uptown Saturday Night* (1974), *Let's Do It Again* (1975), and *A Piece of the Action* (1977). His movie credits in the 1980s included *Shoot to Kill* (1988) and *Little Nikita* (1988). In the 1990s he appeared in *One Man, One Vote* in the role of the South African President Nelson Mandella. The film tells the story of the negotiations that led to South Africa's first all–race election in 1994.

Becomes Producer and Director

In *This Life,* Poitier pointed out his powerlessness. ''I was not in control of the film business. I was not even in control of my career in the film business beyond making a decision to play or not to play in a given piece of material. Furthermore, nothing in the material from which I had to choose had anything to do with the kind of family life thousands of . . . guys lived.'' This realization and a deluge of negative criticism following *To Sir With Love, In the Heat of the Night,* and *Guess Who's Coming to Dinner,* led him to the crossroad of his career. Poitier needed to work behind the camera in order to serve the African American community and provide more positive images. It is behind the camera that images can be altered, decisions made, and audiences impacted. Thus, in *This Life* Poitier reported on his move toward involvement when he, along with Barbara Streisand, Steve McQueen, and Paul Newman—all members of the Creative Management Associates—formed the First Artists Corporation. Each artist agreed to make at least three films in a six–year period. Each artist retained artistic control. At the same time, Poitier entered into an agreement with Columbia Pictures to produce and star in two films that they would distribute.

Poitier's first major directing effort resulted in *Buck and the Preacher* (1972), which he and Harry Belafonte coproduced and costarred. In 1973 he directed a romance entitled *A Warm December.* His most successful directing and acting effort in the 1970s was with Bill Cosby in a series of comedies. These included *Uptown Saturday Night* (1974), *Let's Do It Again,* and *A Piece of the Action* (1977). The success of these films encouraged Poitier's confidence in his ability to anticipate what audiences wanted to see. Thus, the 1980s found him engaged solely in directing such films as *Stir Crazy* (1980), *Hanky Panky* (1982), and *Fast Forward* (1985).

Television Appearances and Writing

Poitier appeared in features such as *Separate but Unequal* (1991) receiving an Emmy and Golden Globe nomination, *Sneakers* (1992), and *Children of the Dust* (1995). He appeared on numerous television episodes, including *The New Bill Cosby Show* (1972). Additionally, he participated in numerous television specials: *The Night of 100 Stars II* (1985), *The Spencer Tracy Legacy: A Tribute to Katherine Hepburn* (1986), *Bopha!* (Narrator, 1987), *The Kennedy Center Honors: A Celebration of the Performing Arts* (1989), *Celebrate the Soul of American Music* (syndicated, 1991), *AFI Salute to Sidney Poitier* (also known as *The 20th Annual American Film Institute Life Achievement Award,* (1992), *The*

19th Annual Black Filmmakers Hall of Fame (syndicated, 1992), and *An American Reunion: New Beginnings, Renewed Hope* (also known as *An American Reunion: The People's Inaugural Celebration,* (1993).

In 1986 he wrote the original story *For Love of Ivy.* In 1980 he published his autobiography, *This Life.* He told his life story with humor, courage, candor, and honesty. He detailed his life from the time of his birth to his work as producer and director, offered advice to actors, discussed Hollywood and the filmmaking business, and made observations about child rearing and the conditions of the young. He collaborated with Carol Berman in 1988 to write *The Films of Sidney Poitier.*

Poitier's honors and awards are numerous. Among them are the Georgia Cini Awards from the Venice Film Festival For *Something of Value* (1958); in that same year he received an Academy Award nomination for best actor, Silver Bear Award, Berlin Film Festival, New York Film Critics Award, best actor, and British Academy Award, best foreign actor, all for *The Defiant Ones*; William J. German Human Relations Award, American Jewish Congress (1966); Golden Apple Star of the Year Award, Hollywood Women's Star Press Club (1967). In 1968 He was knighted by Queen Elizabeth II. Other honors and awards include the Male World Film Favorite, Knight Commander of the British Empire (1974); Coretta Scott King Book Award, American Library Association Social Responsibilities Round Table For *This Life* (1981); Cecil B. De Mille Award, Hollywood Foreign Press Association (1982); Pioneer Award at the Black Oscar Nominees Dinner (1989); the American Film Institute's Lifetime Achievement Award (1992); the Kennedy Center Award for lifetime achievement (1995); and the Black History Maker Award by New York's Associated Black Charities (1997).

While Poitier was appointed as the Caribbean Islands' Japanese ambassador in November of 1995, it was not until 1997 that a ceremony was held at the Imperial Palace in Tokyo where he presented his credential to Emperor Akihito. He will work out of an office in the Foreign Ministry in Nassau, the Bahamas.

Poitier has greatly impacted Hollywood both on and off screen. He began working when African American actors, directors, and producers were few and little recognized. He moved to the point that Bogle says in *Blacks in American Films and Television* happened in the 1980s: "he remained the most important black actor ever to have appeared in American motion pictures . . . and almost singlehandedly changed Hollywood's image of black America." Because of his contributions to the film industry, African Americans are seen on both sides of the camera in roles which are often very different from those earlier stereotypical, nonthreatening, paragons of virtue, emotionless, and or lifeless African American characters presented by Hollywood.

Current address: Verdon Productions, Ltd., 9350 Wilshire Boulevard, Suite 310, Beverly Hills, CA 90212. Agent: Martin Baum, Creative Artists Agency, 9830 Wilshire Boulevard, Beverly Hills, CA 90212–1825.

REFERENCES

"Actor Sidney Poitier and Bluesman B. B. King among Kennedy Center Honorees in D.C." *Jet* 89 (18 December 1995): 61.

Bogle, Donald. *Blacks in American Films and Television: An Illustrated Encyclopedia.* New York: Simon and Schuster, 1989.

———. *Toms, Coons, Mulattoes, Mammies, and Bucks: An Interpretive History of Blacks in American Films.* New Expanded Ed. New York: Continuum, 1989.

Contemporary Theatre, Film, and Television. Vol 7. Detroit: Gale Research, 1989. Vol. 14, 1996.

Poitier, Sidney. *This Life.* New York: Knopf, 1980.

"Sidney Poitier Becomes Bahamas' Ambassador to Japan." *Jet* 91 (5 May 1997): 6–7.

"Sidney Poitier, Jessye Norman, and Ed Bradley Honored at New York's Associated Black Charities Black History Makers Award Dinner." *Jet* 91 (3 March 1997): 52–53.

Williams, Michael W., ed. *The African American Encyclopedia.* Vol. 5. New York: Marshall Cavendish, 1993.

Helen R. Houston

Poole, Elijah.
See Muhammad, Elijah.

Salem Poor
(b. 1747)
Revolutionary War patriot

A "Negro Man Called Salem Poor . . . in the late Battle at Charlestown, behaved like an Experienced officer, as Well as an Excellent Soldier. . . . In the Person of this *sd* [said] Negro Centers a Brave & gallant Soldier" reads a portion of the December 5, 1775, "Recommendation of Salem Poor" to members of the General Court of the Massachusetts Bay, assembled at Cambridge. This recommendation of recognition, signed by 14 colonial army officers, was entered into the court record on December 21, 1775, and January 2, 1776, thus assuring 28–year–old freedman Poor's place in the military annals of the American Revolution. Details of this patriot's personal life, however, are scant.

The first record of "Salem Boy, servent [*sic*] to John and Rebecca Poor" is found in the year 1747, when he was baptized in the North Parish Congregational Church in Andover (now North Andover), Massachusetts. His youth and early manhood were spent in servitude on the Andover farm of John Poor and his son, John Poor, Jr. Salem obviously was industrious and on July 10, 1769, in his twenty–second year, had accumulated 27 pounds "lawful money" to purchase his freedom from John Poor Jr. The Instrument of Manumission, however, was not entered into Andover court records until February of 1772.

In August of 1771, Poor married a woman named Nancy Parker, "a half breed Indian servant in the family of Capt. James Parker," according to papers in the Charlotte Helen Abbot Collection of the Andover Historical Society. Another mention of Salem and Nancy is found in the North Parish Congregational Church records: a son, Jonas, was born to Salem and Nancy Poor, and he was baptized on September 29, 1776, in the church. No record of other children has yet been located. Nor has a record been found of Salem Poor's occupation, if he returned to Andover after he concluded his service with the Continental Army on March 20, 1780, or the place and year of his death and burial site. Most information on Salem's life concerns his service in the Andover Militia and the Continental Army.

In March of 1774, after the Continental Congress designated certain units of the Massachusetts militia to serve as "Minutemen," the Massachusetts Committee of Safety permitted black volunteers to join town and village companies. A number of free black men promptly enlisted, and one was Salem Poor. Poor enlisted in the First Andover Company as a private and, like other militia minutemen, was trained to respond at a minute's notice to British aggression.

As rebellion continued to foment within the Massachusetts Bay Colony, British Military Governor Thomas Gage was ordered to destroy the rebels' military stores at Concord. At midnight on April 19, 1775, as British troops marched from Boston toward nearby Concord, the alarm was spread. After a confrontation at Lexington in which the British troops killed eight minutemen and wounded ten others, the British soldiers then moved to Concord, where they encountered another group of minutemen at Concord North Bridge. The Americans fired what became known in history as 'The Shot Heard Round the World.' The short battle saw the rout of the British, who retreated.

Shortly after the British retreat from Lexington, minuteman Salem Poor enlisted under Captain Samuel Johnson in the Fifth Massachusetts Regiment on April 24, 1775. To strengthen their hold on Boston, which they controlled, the British planned to seize and fortify nearby Dorchester Heights and Charlestown peninsulas. Americans heard of the British plans and decided to forestall the British troops. On June 16, 1775, Colonels Israel Putnam and William Prescott led patriot militia to construct a redoubt on Breed's Hill; the British were amazed to see the fortifications the following morning and set out to reclaim the peninsula. British Major General William Howe commanded 2,400 soldiers. Not until the third assault were they able to overwhelm the fortifications, taking very substantial casualties.

During the retreat, Salem Poor saw British Lieutenant Colonel James Abercrombie, who had led the elite grenadiers at Breed's Hill (later known as the Battle of Bunker Hill), "mount a redoubt and wave his arms in triumph; the colored lad aimed and fired, and then watched the British officer topple over," wrote Andover historian Sarah L. Bailey in *Historical Sketches of Andover.* The death of Abercrombie, like that of British Major John Pitcairn, reputedly killed by another black patriot, Peter Salem, further undermined the morale of British soldiers and strengthened the resolve of the patriots.

Attitudes about the use of black soldiers varied in the course of the struggle. General George Washington, commander of the Continental Army, ordered on July 10 that no additional black men were to be recruited into the army. On December 30, 1775, he revoked that order in response to British offers of freedom to slaves willing to serve under the British flag. The latter directive was approved by the Continental Congress on January 16, 1776. Salem Poor, however, was never away from active duty more than a few months at a time, as shown by his extensive military record from 1775 to March 20, 1780, listed in the official Revolutionary War Militia Rolls in Volume XII of *Massachusetts Soldiers and Sailors of the Revolutionary War:*

> POOR, SALEM, Andover. Private, Capt. Benjamin Ames's co., Col. James Fry's regt.; company return dated Oct. 6, 1775; *also,* order for bounty coat or its equivalent in money, dated Boston, Dec. 13, 1775; *also,* Private, Capt. Abram Tyler's co., Col. Edmund Phinney's regt.; muster roll dated Garrison at Fort George, Dec. 8, 1776; enlisted May 14, 1776; *also,* list of men raised to serve in the Continental Army from 1st Andover co., as returned by Capt. Samuel Johnson; residence, Andover; engaged for town of Andover; term, 3 years, to expire Jan. 1, 1780; *also,* list of men mustered by Nathaniel Barber, Muster Master for Suffolk Co., dated Boston, May 11, 1777; Capt. Alexander's co., Col. Wigglesworth's regt.; *also,* Private, Major's co., Col. Calvin Smith's regt.; Continental Army pay accounts for service from May 20, 1777, to March 20, 1780; *also,* Capt. Nathaniel Alexander's co., Col. Edward Wigglesworth's regt.; return [year not given] mustered by Maj. Barber; *also,* same co. and regt.; muster roll for May, 1778, dated Camp Valley Forge; *also,* same co. and regt.; muster roll for June, 1778, dated Camp near White Plains; *also,* same co. and regt.; pay roll for Oct., 1778; *also,* Maj. John Porter's co., (late) Col. Wigglesworth's regt. Commanded by Maj. Porter; muster roll for March and April, 1779, dated Providence; enlisted April 20, 1777; enlistment, 3 years.

Salem Poor's military service attests to the fact that he was not among the 5,000 African Americans who lost their lives in the eight–year War for American Independence—and who are memorialized by a bronze sculpture in Pennsylvania's Valley Forge National Historical Park—but he was among the 500 black sharpshooters in the Continental Army who spent the legendary frozen winter of 1777–78 with

General George Washington in his Valley Forge encampment. He also served in the crucial battles of White Plains, New York, and Providence, Rhode Island. Only one instance is recorded of Salem Poor having been commended for his bravery, the submission of the petition of recommendation in December 1775. Two hundred years later Poor's valor was publicly recognized. On March 25, 1975, as part of the United States Postal Service's Revolutionary War Bicentennial series of stamps entitled "Contributors to the Cause," a commemorative ten–cent stamp was issued in recognition of "Salem Poor—Gallant Soldier."

REFERENCES

Bailey, Sarah Loring. *Historical Sketches of Andover.* 1880. Reprint, Andover, MA: Andover Historical Society, 1990.

Boatner, Mark M., III. *Encyclopedia of the American Revolution.* New York: McKay, 1959.

"Contributors to the Cause." Washington, DC: U.S. Postal Service, March 25, 1975.

Foner, Jack D. *Blacks and the Military in American History.* New York: Praeger, 1974.

Kaplan, Sidney, and Emma N. Kaplan. *The Black Presence in the Era of the American Revolution, 1770–1800.* Greenwich, CT: New York Graphic Society, 1973. Rev. ed. Amherst: University of Massachusetts Press, 1989.

"Lexington Concord Staff Ride Field Study" for Military Science Department of Worcester Polytechnic Institute, Worcester, MA. http://www.wpi.edu/Academics/Depts/MilSci/BTSI/lexcon/lexcon_fld.html (last modified October 1, 1997).

"Manumission Paper of Salem Poor, July 10, 1769." Phillips Library of Peabody Essex Museum, Salem, MA.

Maslowski, Pete. "National Policy toward the Use of Black Troops in the Revolution." *South Carolina Historical Magazine* 73 (January 1972). From the author's files.

"Monument to Patriots of African Descent." *Valley Forge National Historical Park.* Plymouth Meeting, PA: Valley Forge Convention and Visitors Bureau, 1996, http://www.valleyforge.org.

Nell, William Cooper. *The Colored Patriots of the American Revolution.* 1855. Reprint, New York: Arno Press, 1968.

"Poor Family Records" and "Vital Records of Andover to 1850," Charlotte Helen Abbot Collection of Andover Historical Society Museum and Research Center, Andover, MA, http://www.town.andover.ma.us/commun/research.htm#historical.

"Poor, Salem, Andover." In *Massachusetts Soldiers and Sailors of the Revolutionary War.* Vol. 12. Boston, MA: Secretary of the Commonwealth and Massachusetts Archives, 1904.

Quarles, Benjamin. *The Negro in the American Revolution.* Chapel Hill: University of North Carolina Press for the Institute of Early American History and Culture, Williamsburg, VA, 1940. Second edition, 1961.

"Recommendation of Salem Poor." *Journal of the House of Representatives of Massachusetts* 51, Part II, 1775–1776. Commonwealth of Massachusetts State Library, Boston.

"Staff Ride Glossary" for Military Science Department of Worcester Polytechnic Institute, Worcester, MA. http://www.wpi.edu/Academics/Depts/MilSci/BTSI/glossary.html (last modified June 11, 1997).

"Worcester Polytechnic Institute Breed's Hill/Bunker Hill Staff Ride," for Military Science Department of Worcester Polytechnic Institute, Worcester, MA. http://www.wpi.edu/Academics/Depts/MilSci/BTSI/hill/hill.html (last modified June 11, 1997).

Ilene Jones–Cornwell

Ted Poston
(1906–1974)
Journalist, civil rights activist, writer

One of the first African Americans to work full time at a big–town white daily, Ted Poston encouraged the development of black journalists both by stimulating talented young blacks to enter the profession and by persuading newspaper publishers to hire them. He protested segregationists' activities through the press and used the press to promote civil rights. Poston was described in *Crisis* as a great reporter as well as "a matchless raconteur." To his friends, Poston was a master of oral. Through his published short stories, he gained importance as a writer.

Theodore Roosevelt Augustus Major Poston, known as Ted, was born in Hopkinsville, Kentucky, on July 4, 1906, to Ephriam Poston, a newspaper publisher, and Mollie Cox Poston. He was the younger brother of Ulysses and Robert Lincoln Poston, who also became writers. Ted Poston's career started early. In 1922 he began working as a copy clerk for his father's newspaper, the *Contender,* in Hopkinsville, continuing there until the paper was forced to move out of town because it was considered too controversial. Poston was educated in the segregated schools of Hopkinsville. He received his bachelor's degree in 1928 from Tennessee Agricultural and Industrial State College, later known as Tennessee State University, in Nashville. He did further study in writing at New York University.

Breaks Barriers in Journalism

After college, Poston apparently spent some time in Savannah, Georgia. Then he rode a cattle boat to New York, where his brother Ulysses had joined Alfred E. Smith's campaign as Democratic candidate for president. Through

Ulysses's influence, Poston was hired for a $150–a–week job as a writer for Smith's campaign in New York City. After the Democrats lost, Poston went to work as a dining car waiter for the Pennsylvania Railroad as well as a columnist for the *Pittsburgh Courier.* When the stock marked crashed in 1929, he moved to the *New York Amsterdam News,* his first full–time job.

Although Poston was bitterly anti–Communist, in 1932 he and several other young black artists and writers traveled to Moscow for work on an ill–fated film project, *Black and White,* that Russia's Meschrabpom Film Corporation was to develop. He returned to the United States still bitter toward Communism. Poston advanced to city editor of the *Amsterdam News* around 1934. In the mid–1930s, Poston covered Thomas E. Dewey's raids on numbers rackets in Harlem. His part in leading a strike to unionize the *Amsterdam News* led the owners to fire him in 1936. It was amidst the Great Depression, and, like many writers, Poston took a job with the Works Progress Administration.

In the late 1930s he signed on as a space writer (30 cents an inch) for the *New York Post,* becoming the first African American to write full time for a New York daily and one of the first to work full time with a big–town, white–owned daily. His hiring was contingent upon his success in finding a first–page story for the next issue of the paper. In his search, Poston headed to his home in Harlem. As he left the subway he saw a group of blacks chasing a white man. The chasers turned out to be the protectors or "angels" of M. J. "Father" Divine—a charismatic and sensational black preacher and healer—who were driving out the white man as he tried to serve notice of an impending lawsuit. The *Post* ran the story and hired Poston, who remained with the newspaper until his retirement in 1972.

Poston was assigned to cover New York City Hall. White journalists there shunned him and compared notes without asking him to join them. After he learned to scoop them on stories, they accepted Poston and his talent. His assignment at city hall led Poston to cover racial issues as well as some of the most noted political personalities of the time, such as political boss Huey Long of Louisiana and 1940 Republican nominee for president Wendell Wilkie. *Newsweek* noted that, as Wilkie shaved in a hotel bathroom, Poston "took the only available seat."

On leave from the *New York Post* from 1940 to 1945, Poston worked as a New Deal publicist in Washington, D.C., and developed a close relationship with Harry S Truman, who offered him a job as special assistant to the president. During his Washington years Poston was a public relations consultant for the National Advisory Defense Commission, Office of Production Management, War Production Board, and the War Manpower Commission. He also headed the Negro News Desk in the Office of War Information's news bureau in Washington.

Assignments in the South for various periods during his career placed Poston in dangerous, sometimes life–threatening situations. He was required to report to the *New York Post* every night so that his office would know that he was still alive. In order to cover the Scottsboro trial in Alabama, involving a white woman's false charge of rape by a group of young black men, Poston dressed shabbily and obtained phony identification as an itinerant preacher. When angry whites caught him mailing a package to New York City and questioned his actions, he produced his preacher's identification and was left unharmed. He wrote about the experience in April 1944's *Negro Digest* under the title "My Most Humiliating Jim Crow Experience." He also covered the Montgomery Bus Boycott in 1955, when racial tensions were still high. A close encounter with death was reported in *Jet,* September 3, 1959. While visiting in Daisy Bates's home in Little Rock, hoodlums fired at the home and narrowly missed Poston. His newspaper, the *Post,* took a $50,000 insurance policy on him before he left Arkansas.

Writes Short Stories

In addition to his newspaper work, Poston wrote a number of short stories, many of them autobiographical or about the plight of black Americans. He wrote articles and reviews for a number of periodicals, including *Ebony,Nation,New Republic,Saturday Review,* and *Survey.* His work is represented in a number of anthologies, including *The Negro Caravan* (1970), *Black Joy* (1971), and *The Best Short Stories by Negro Writers: An Anthology from 1899 to the Present* (1967). He was also a contributor to *Race and Media* (1967). In 1991 Kathleen A. Hauke compiled his stories under the title *The Dark Side of Hopkinsville: Stories by Ted Poston.* Earlier Poston had written the stories, humorous accounts of his childhood, under the same title.

Poston was honored for his work as journalist and writer, and for the risks he took to cover accounts of racial problems in the South. In 1950, after covering a racial discrimination trial in Tavares, Florida, he received the Heywood Broun Memorial Award—a $500 cash price and a citation—from the American Newspaper Guild. He had been responsible for uncovering a missing witness whose important testimony led to freedom for a black laborer accused of murder. He was one of the first black reporters to win the award. Poston's success and national recognition as a journalist sparked activity among a group of liberal white publishers who launched a national talent hunt for talented black journalists. They contacted Poston for leads, and the search led to a job offer for journalist Carl Rowan, a promising find. Poston commented in the November 1955 issue of *Ebony*: "First they're shocked, then they think that a Negro who is working for a white newspaper must be a helluva guy."

In 1950 Poston received Long Island University's George Polk Award, again for covering racial discrimination in Florida. Poston's handling of news of the anti–black rioting in Groveland, Florida, in 1950 earned him an award from the Irving Geist Foundation. For promoting interracial tolerance, the Newspaper Guild of New York honored Poston in 1950, and Beta Delta Mu gave him the Unity Award in 1951.

Around this time Long Island University in New York awarded him the George Polk Memorial plaque for best national reporting. In 1972 the City of New York awarded Poston its distinguished service medal. He also received distinguished service plaques from the boroughs of Brooklyn, Bronx, and Queens. He belonged to the NAACP, Stuyvestant Community Center, Grand Street Boys, the Newspaper Guild (Washington, D.C., chapter), and the Omega Psi Phi Fraternity. Poston was a Baptist and an independent Democrat.

After Poston retired in 1972, Black Perspective, his professional organization, honored him for professional excellence and the work that he did for other black journalists. He had enjoyed writing autobiographical accounts of his youth and his early life in Hopkinsville and planned to return there to continue his work, but failing health prevented him from doing so. In the winter of 1973 traveled to St. Thomas, Virgin Islands, in order to work on his autobiography. While there he suffered a mild case of amnesia and wandered the streets for three days. He returned to Brooklyn and seemed to be recovering satisfactorily when he died suddenly on January 11, 1974, while chatting with friends in his Brooklyn home. He was buried in Kentucky. In 1935 Poston married Miriam Rivers and in 1941 he married Marie Byrd Jackson; both marriages ended in divorce. In 1957 he married Ersa Hines Poston, a career public servant in New York, who survived him.

Poston, spindly, mustached, and tall, is remembered as a pioneer journalist who protested racial discrimination through his writing and who helped other black journalists advance in their profession. Poston was noted for outstanding coverage of many of the NAACP's crucial civil rights battles. In March of 1974, *Crisis* quoted the *New York Post's* obituary of Poston, calling him a "legendary reporter." The same article quoted Roy Wilkins, who hailed Poston as a "highly skilled reporter with the determination and courage to follow his story into the eye of the storm."

REFERENCES

Black Writers. 2nd ed. Detroit: Gale Research, 1994.

Crisis Editorials. *Crisis* 81 (March 1974): 77–78.

David, Jay. *Black Defiance.* New York: William Morrow, 1972.

"Good News." *Crisis* 57 (April 1950): 235.

Kellner, Bruce, ed. *The Harlem Renaissance.* New York: Methuen, 1984.

"Milestones." *Time* 103 (21 January 1974): 43.

"New York Beat." *Jet* 16 (3 September 1959): 63.

Obituary. *New York Times,* January 12, 1974.

"Poston's Success Sparked Search for Negro Newsmen." *Ebony* 11 (November 1955): 79.

"The Press." *Newsweek* 33 (11 April 1949): 61–62.

Stein, M. L. *Blacks in Communications.* New York: Julian Messner, 1972.

"Ted Poston Gets Journalism Citation." *Jet* 3 (2 April 1953): 48.

"Ted Poston Succumbs at His Brooklyn Home." *Jet* 45 (31 January 1974): 5.

Who's Who in Colored America. 7th ed. Yonkers–on–Hudson, NY: Christian E. Burckel, 1950.

Jessie Carney Smith

Alvin F. Poussaint
(1934–)
Psychiatrist, educator, author

It is unusual in America for a physician to have national name recognition. It is even more unusual for a black psychiatrist to have both a name and a face that are recognized by the general public. Alvin F. Poussaint is a well–known public figure associated with family and children's issues, and an expert on the impact of racism and those whom it affects. Poussaint has spent much of his life at an educational institution where he has consistently kept African Americans, and particularly African American children, at the center of his concerns.

Alvin Francis Poussaint was born in East Harlem in New York City on May 15, 1934, the seventh of eight children of Harriet Johnston Poussaint, a homemaker, and Christopher Poussaint, a printer and typographer. From the time he began school until he finished medical school, Alvin Poussaint was educated at schools in Manhattan. He was raised as a Roman Catholic. Poussaint contracted rheumatic fever at the age of nine, an event that he credits with having changed his life. It gave him months of exposure—three months in a hospital and two months in a convalescent home—to doctors and nurses, influencing him to consider becoming a physician. Physically restricted, Poussaint got lost in the world of books, and when he returned to school he was an avid student. Later, while many of his friends—including a brother with whom he shared a bedroom—became drug addicts, Poussaint aimed himself toward achievement.

While in junior high school, a teacher suggested that Poussaint take a competitive test for admission to one of New York's special public high schools. Poussaint was accepted at the prestigious Stuyvesant High School, a predominantly white public school for gifted students with high academic potential. There he was very active in student life, doing creative writing and editing a literary magazine. He taught himself to play the clarinet, saxophone, and flute. While he was in high school, his mother died of cancer. After Poussaint graduated from Stuyvesant, his father wanted him to go to college locally. Poussaint attended Columbia University, with a four–year New York Regents Scholarship paying his tuition. At Columbia, he continued to excel academically.

At home, however, things were stressful. Poussaint told *Child* magazine, "I didn't come home until the [Columbia]

Alvin F. Poussaint

libraries closed. That way I had minimal dealings with my [heroin–addicted] brother. But he stayed up late, and it was at night that he did his shooting up. So I was constantly picking him up off the floor, taking the needle out of his arm, dealing with a lot of his craziness, and, on the other hand, trying to help him if I could.'' Nor was the social scene at Columbia appealing. According to Poussaint in *Contemporary Black Biography,* while in college ''social situations were awkward, there being a prevalent feeling among [white students] that blacks shouldn't come to social events. . . . They didn't expect you to show up at the dance.''

Poussaint graduated from Columbia in 1956 and won a full scholarship to medical school, the only black person in the entering class of 86 students. Because his room and board were paid, he was able to move away from home. But then, Poussaint told *Child* magazine, he had to face the ''isolation and indignities of being the only black student at the Cornell University Medical College, where [his] mother had given birth to him as a charity patient.'' Observations about racism and its impact on blacks and whites, which began in high school and continued throughout Poussaint's college and medical school career, eventually fueled his professional interests.

In 1960 Poussaint received his M.D. from Cornell and then trained at the University of California in Los Angeles (UCLA) from 1960 to 1964, first as an intern at the Center for the Health Sciences, and later as a resident and chief resident at the Neuropsychiatric Institute. After UCLA, where he earned an M.S. in 1964, Poussaint turned his attention to the South and the Civil Rights Movement.

As southern field director of the Medical Committee for Human Rights (1964–65) based in Jackson, Mississippi, Poussaint headed a staff of volunteer medical workers and private citizens. They provided medical care to civil rights workers in the South and worked to desegregate health facilities there. Poussaint left Mississippi in 1966 and joined Boston's Tufts University Medical School faculty as director of a psychiatry program in a low–income housing project in Boston, Massachusetts. Since that time, most of Poussaint's career has been centered in the Boston area.

Poussaint was first appointed to the faculty of Harvard Medical School in 1969. He has remained there and, since 1993, has been clinical professor of psychiatry. In addition, he served as the director of student affairs at the school. He has been affiliated with the Massachusetts Mental Health Center in Boston and has been senior associate in psychiatry at the Judge Baker Children's Center in Boston, where he is director of the Media Center.

Writes on Black Issues in Psychiatry and Society

Poussaint's professional writings have ranged from clinical studies of bed wetting, low back pain, and epilepsy, to studies of motivation, behavioral science teaching, black suicide, and grief response. In particular, Poussaint has been a pioneer contributor to the discussion of issues surrounding the nurturing of black children. His articles have appeared in publications such as the *Journal of Negro Education, University of Chicago School Review, Psychiatric Opinion, Rehabilitation Record, Journal of Medical Education,* and *American Journal of Psychiatry.* He has written and served as co–author of chapters in books on minority group psychology, the black child's self–image, interracial relations, and black–on–black homicide. He has also contributed to several psychiatry textbooks, professional journals, and other publications.

In an attempt to bridge the gap between professional psychiatry and lay people in the African American community, Poussaint offers a psychiatrist's perspective of how early education can be used to fight racism in an article published in *Ebony* magazine in October of 1970, entitled ''Why Blacks Kill Blacks,'' which was the basis for a book of the same title, published in 1972. Since then he has been a regular contributor to the popular magazine.

Two *Redbook* articles in 1971 and 1972, both written with James P. Comer, marked the starting point for much of Poussaint's most important and popular writing. The first article answered questions that black parents most frequently ask about rearing a black child in a predominantly white society. The second discussed what parents must do to rear their children free from prejudice. Response to the two articles eventually led to the publication of the book *Black Child Care,* written by both Poussaint and Comer. In 1992 Poussaint and Comer revised their book, retitled *Raising Black Children,* maintaining its question–and–answer format and focusing on nurturing black children at various developmental stages. They also collaborated in writing a weekly newspaper column, *Getting Along,* from 1970 to 1985, with United Features Syndicate.

Poussaint's writings center on creating, nurturing, and combating attacks on healthy black self–image. Whether addressing individuals, families, or the black community as a whole, Poussaint focuses on being proactive rather than reactive in the face of racism and stereotypical assumptions that impact the lives of blacks.

Receives Wide Professional Acclaim

Poussaint is a fellow of the American Psychiatric Association, a fellow of the American Association for the Advancement of Science, a member of the American Academy of Child and Adolescent Psychiatry, and a fellow of the American Orthopsychiatric Association. In 1971 he was a founding member of Operation PUSH (People United to Service Humanity) and served on the boards of trustees for more than a dozen years.

Various government agencies have used Poussaint's services as a consultant. These include the Department of Health, Education, and Welfare; the FBI; the State Department; the White House; and several conferences on civil rights and on families and children.

Poussaint has also been an active consultant to media. He was script consultant on the pioneering *Cosby Show,* which made Poussaint's name known in households worldwide. He was also NBC's production consultant to the spin–off television show, *A Different World.* He has been a consultant to the Congressional Black Caucus and a member of congressional and medical delegations to the People's Republic of China and to Cuba. He was a member of Action for Children's Television, the Boston University School of Social Work, and a Project Interchange seminar for American leaders in public policy held in Israel.

Poussaint has continuously served on the editorial board of publications such as *Black Scholar, Victimology: An International Journal, Journal of African American Male Studies, Young Sisters and Brothers Magazine, HealthQuest: The Publication of Black Wellness,* and *Nurture: The Magazine for Raising Positive Children of Color.* He has been a member of the editorial board of the Council on Interracial Books for Children, *Education Today,* the Urban Family Institute, Memorial for Our Lost Children, Facing History and Ourselves, and *Get Real: Televised Rap Music Forum and Youth Anti–Violence Campaign,* among others.

Poussaint belongs to the boards of the National Association of African American Artists and the 21st Century Commission on African American Males; he formerly served on the board of Wesleyan College. Poussaint co–chaired the Jesse Jackson presidential campaign in Massachusetts in 1983–84. Since 1993, he has been national co–director of the Lee Salk Center at KidsPeace.

Poussaint has received numerous awards and honors, including recognition from the Southern Christian Leadership Conference, Cornell University Medical College, Medical Committee for Human Rights, and Northeastern University's Center for the Study of Sports in Society. He has also been recognized with an American Black Achievement Award from Johnson Publishing Company; a Medal of Honor and an Award for Outstanding Service from NAACP chapters, and a media award from the Gay and Lesbian Alliance Against Defamation. He has been recognized by the Jewish Family and Children Services of Kansas City, the Baltimore Health Department, and Morgan State University.

Poussaint has been director for the Media Center at the Judge Baker Children's Center in Boston. Founded in 1994 by Poussaint, the Center produces children's programming and advises the communications industry through message research and advocacy for responsible media. Through the work of the Media Center, the Judge Baker Children's Center has become the first mental health center in the United States to produce a national television pilot, *Willoughby's Wonders,* a program based on contemporary knowledge of psychosocial development in children. This educational show for six– to eight–year–olds features an urban soccer team that explores themes of teamwork, inclusion, and individuality, as well as teaching the social skills of cooperation, empathy, and persistence.

Poussaint is now married to Tina Young. His career as a physician, a psychiatrist, an educator, a writer, and an agent of social change has been a successful one. He has increased public awareness of today's mental health challenges. Through his work in and on the media, Poussaint has raised the public's consciousness of the child, particularly the black child, as a television viewer who sees on the screen a representation of life that profoundly affects his or her psychological and social development. Because Poussaint believes that raising a child is everybody's business, his work implores adults to be responsible with children, families, and the media.

Current address: Judge Baker Children's Center, 3 Blackfan Circle, Boston MA 02115.

REFERENCES

Annual Report. Judge Baker Children's Center, 1995.

Comer, James P., and Alvin F. Poussaint. *Black Child Care.* New York: Simon and Schuster, 1975.

Contemporary Black Biography. Vol. 5. Detroit: Gale Research, 1994.

"Cosby Show's Advisor Brings Parenting Tips to Workshops." *Detroit Free Press,* March 18, 1994.

Lamb, Yanick, "Lessons from Life: Two Leading Child Psychiatrists Discuss How They Beat the Odds—and How Your Child Can, Too." *Child* 8 (June/July 1993): 100–102, 126–29.

Poussaint, Alvin F. *Why Blacks Kill Blacks.* New York: Emerson Hall, 1972.

"What's the Biggest Problem Facing Families Today?" *USA Today,* July 8, 1992.

Martia Graham Goodson

Adam Clayton Powell Jr.
(1908–1972)
Minister, councilman, congressman, civil rights activist

For his front–line civil rights activity that spanned more than three decades, Adam Clayton Powell Jr. was respectfully called "Mr. Civil Rights." Yet *The New York Times* editorialized when Powell died in 1972 that the former New York councilman, congressman, and minister "took as the measuring rod for application of his talents the grossest of white standards for personal and political success" and had become "lost in a sea of cynicism and self indulgence, leaves no lasting heritage." Notwithstanding the mixed reaction to his activities, Powell was a powerful, colorful, and effective religious, political, and civil rights leader.

Adam Clayton Powell Jr.'s entire life was an enigmatic paradox, rooted in his tri–racial heritage of African American, Caucasian, and Native American ancestors. According to Powell's 1971 autobiography, *Adam by Adam,* his paternal grandmother, Sally, was a Negro–Indian woman whose first child, born on May 4, 1865, "had been sired by a white slaveowner named Powell" in Franklin County, Virginia, just above the northern border of North Carolina. Shortly before the birth of her baby, Sally was given shelter by a former slave named Dunn (first name unknown), who rented a one–room log cabin and was a share–cropper farmer. Sally and her child lived in Dunn's cabin until November of 1867, when she married mulatto farmer Anthony Bush. In 1875 they moved their family—which included Sally's firstborn son, Adam Clayton—to Fayette County, West Virginia. During the time they share–cropped on the banks of the Knawha River in Fayette County, Anthony Bush adopted the surname Powell, possibly taking the name of the small village of Powellton at the western edge of the county.

At the age of 13, young Adam Clayton Powell Sr. met his future wife, Mattie Fletcher Shaffer, who had been born in 1872 in Fayette County to Samuel and Eliza Wilson Buster. Adam Clayton Powell Sr. finally married Mattie in 1889, when she was 18 and he was 25.

By the time Powell Sr. married Mattie, he had totally reformed his life. After eight years in West Virginia leading a dead–end existence as a bum, a drunkard, and a gambler, he finally had to leave the state in August of 1884 to avoid being murdered. In March of 1885 he was converted in a Baptist church in an Ohio mining town. An avid scholar of the Bible, he became secretary of the church's Sunday school. In 1888 he was given a full scholarship to attend Wayland Seminary and College in Washington, D.C., from which he graduated four years later. After a year as an itinerant minister, Powell Sr. became permanent pastor of Immanuel Baptist Church in New Haven, Connecticut, in the fall of 1893. Here the first Powell child, a daughter Blanche, was born in 1898, and, ten years later, Adam Clayton Powell Jr., was born on November 29, 1908.

Adam Clayton Powell Jr.

Father Heads Church

Just before Powell's birth, his father accepted the call to become the seventeenth minister of the Abyssinian Baptist Church. Founded in 1808 in New York City, the church was considered "the mother church of the Baptists of the North." The Powell family relocated to West 40th Street near the church in midtown New York when Powell Jr. was just six months old in May, 1909.

After settling his family in a temporary home, and later in a brownstone house on 134th Street, the minister firmly established himself as the church's spiritual leader and made his presence felt in the surrounding urban community. After the dedication of the new Abyssinian Baptist Church in Harlem on May 20, 1923, an impressive cathedral–type church, the Powells moved into a ten–room penthouse atop the new church buildings. Later they resided in a three–story brownstone house on 136th Street. In this insulated cocoon of upper–middle–class affluence, young Adam Powell—fair of skin with blond hair and hazel eyes, like his sister Blanche—was the focal point of the household.

"I was spoiled, utterly and completely," Powell wrote in his autobiography, as he recalled the nurturing of his youth. "But let me blame it on the women . . . because women have always spoiled me." This preferential treatment was extended with his becoming "sickly"—symptoms indicated tuberculosis—just before his sixth birthday, which necessitated constant care over the following six years. "I was enfolded in the attentions of the three women [mother Mattie, sister Blanche, and housekeeper/cook Josephine] who figured so importantly in my childhood. What a wonderful womb to live in."

For young Adam Powell, his "being so light–skinned that he could 'pass' for white" resulted in an extremely active and diverse social life during his basketball–oriented years at Townsend Harris High School, from which he graduated at age 16, and as he entered City College of New York (CCNY) in 1925. He continued to devote his energy to basketball and extracurricular activities, ignoring his studies and focusing on "having a good time, going to parties, drinking, smoking, [and] being spoiled by women in new ways." Although he failed three subjects, his father's friendship with the college president resulted in a waiving of the suspension rules; Adam Powell was allowed to return for a second semester at CCNY in 1926. "My father, who worshipped scholarship . . . could not understand the transition I was going through," recalled Powell. "He did not remember his teen–age experiences as a bum, a gambler, and a drunkard back in Rendville, Ohio. And I, not knowing at that time he had gone through a similar period in his own life, rebelled against his 'holier–than–thou' attitude and his Calvinism."

Adam Powell's continued enjoyment of a "playboy's social life" and the colorful night life of the arts renaissance in Harlem kept him on a collision course with disaster. He reached that goal in 1926 when he again failed at CCNY during the second semester. That winter his sister Blanche—"my real love . . . my Princess"—died of a ruptured appendix. Powell was devastated by the loss, and his world crashed around him. Depressed and mourning, he returned home.

Finds Religion

In what Powell described as a "tremendous vacuum" and an "aching void," he moved through several temporary jobs that summer—drifting, gambling, partying, and womanizing—until he reached a pivotal turning point in his life. One of his father's friends convinced him to enter Colgate University in upstate New York, far from the "madding crowd" of Harlem. At Colgate, he entered "passing" for white and was paired with a white roommate. Then as his racial mixture was discovered, he was abruptly rejected by the white students. "This was the first time in my life that deep discrimination had touched me directly," he wrote in his autobiography. "It came as a tremendous shock to me." But it also awakened his "race consciousness" and aroused his sensitivity to racial inequities, previously unseen or blindly ignored.

As he applied himself to his studies and his grades consistently improved, Powell began to lean toward attending medical school—until the last half of his senior year. In February of 1930, during a late–night study session, he had a religious experience, and he decided to enter the ministry. He preached "a trial sermon" on the night of Good Friday, 1930, at Abyssinian Baptist Church in Harlem. The following week, the church's board of deacons granted him a license to preach. Adam Powell Jr., following his graduation from Colgate and acceptance to Union Theological Seminary, became the church's assistant pastor, business manager, and heir apparent to the leadership of Abyssinian when his father retired.

At the time of Powell's spiritual awakening, he was dating Isabel Washington, a Cotton Club performer who had arrived on Broadway to become a shining star in the drama, *Harlem.* She was separated from her husband and had a son, so her involvement in Powell's life was disapproved by his family and the hierarchy of Union Seminary. Powell refused their demands that he eliminate Washington from his life. He left the seminary and enrolled in Columbia University, where he received a Master of Arts degree in religious education in 1932. In March of 1933 he married Isabel Washington and adopted her son, Preston, as his own. The young couple devoted their dual energies to the church's busy life as Powell administered Abyssinian's adjacent four–story community center, which operated a full–time morning–to–night program seven days a week. Powell's growing awareness of social and economic discrimination and the need to eliminate discriminatory employment practices led to his seeking and securing governmental assistance for an Unemployed Section and Adult Education (USAE) program in the center.

Powell's fight to secure jobs for his congregation expanded to the pages of Harlem's *Amsterdam News,* where he began contributing a regular column, "Soap Box," in 1935. Powell inherited the mantle of leadership as the eighteenth minister of the church when his father retired in 1937 after 29 years as pastor of Abyssinnian. Powell brought his campaign for black employment and economic justice to the pulpit. Assuming an increasingly active role as a political catalyst, he helped establish the Greater New York Coordinating Committee for Employment (GNYCCE), that brought together several coalitions pursuing the same goal of eradicating economic and social discrimination. In 1939 the GNYCCE organized a picket line protesting discriminatory hiring practices at the New York World's Fair resulting in the establishment of a quota system, which guaranteed 50 jobs for blacks during the fair—and the GNYCCE later participated with the United Negro Bus Strike Committee to picket for a quota system to facilitate the hiring of black bus drivers, an effort which achieved success in 1942, when blacks were finally hired as New York City bus drivers.

Becomes a Politician

Riding the crest of his popularity in Harlem, Powell declared his candidacy for the New York City Council in late 1941. He reorganized the GNYCCE as the People's Committee for political equality to handle his campaign. The election results placed him third in a field of 99 candidates, and at the age of 33 he was seated on the city council. The following year he was co–founder and editor–in–chief of a Harlem newspaper, *People's Voice,* to which he transferred his column, "Soap Box," from the *Amsterdam News.* When a Twenty–second Congressional District was reapportioned for Harlem the next year, Powell used his newspaper to announce his candidacy for Congress, stressing his platform of fair employment, the elimination of poll taxes, and declaring lynching a federal crime. The 1944 primary election handed the Democratic nomination to Powell and he was elected, unopposed, in the general election. He took his seat in Congress the following January and began a long, albeit controversial, career of 23 years (1945–67, 1969–70) in the U.S. House of Representatives.

As this new chapter opened in Powell's life, an old chapter ended. His wife Isabel, who probably was aware of her husband's involvement with jazz pianist Hazel Scott, separated from Powell in 1944. The couple divorced in 1945 and that August Powell married Hazel Scott, with whom he would have a son, Adam Clayton "Skipper" Powell III, in 1946.

From 1945 to 1955, Powell and Chicago's William L. Dawson were the only African Americans in the Congress. As black veterans of World War II returned to U.S. society, strengthened by military combat and imbued with a new sense of dignity and pride, they found segregated conditions unchanged in America. Powell immediately championed the veterans' and fellow blacks' demands for equal access to education, housing, and transportation, publicly condemning all forms of segregation and discrimination. Although he felt his congressional role was primarily symbolic at first, his uncompromising stand against racism garnered increasing media attention. He became one of the most vocal and effective leaders in the accelerating civil rights movement from the post–war era through the 1950s and early 1960s, earning the appellation of "Mr. Civil Rights."

In 1949 Powell chaired the subcommittee of the House Committee on Education and Labor and presided over hearings during May 10–26 to investigate discrimination in employment due to race, color, religion, or national origin. Findings supported the provisions stipulated in House Resolution 4453, the Federal Fair Employment Practice Act, and companion bills to prohibit discrimination in employment were enacted.

Encounters Political Stumbling Blocks

Powell developed into an astute politician during the 1950s anti–Communist McCarthy era, but he mistakenly switched political horses in mid–stream. Although an elected Democrat, he supported Republican Dwight D. Eisenhower after his 1952 election as President, hoping to advance legislation for civil rights within the administration. His actions incurred behind–the–scenes wrath of a number of Democrats. Coincidentally, in 1953 Powell became the subject of a tax–fraud investigation. In 1956 he campaigned for Eisenhower's re–election, which may have had a significant impact on the administration's support of the Civil Rights Act of 1957, the first federal civil rights law since Reconstruction. The act set up the Commission on Civil Rights to investigate charges of civil rights violations, and created the Civil Rights Division in the Department of Justice to enforce federal civil rights laws and regulations. This sweeping legislation apparently added fuel to the flame under the boiling cauldron of conservatives, both Northern and Southern, who awaited their opportunity to discredit Powell. This opportunity arrived in 1958 when Powell, impatient with the administration's failure to take further action on civil rights initiatives, lambasted the Eisenhower administration. This imprudent move, according to historian Charles Hamilton, "broke the carefully constructed bridge" between Powell and Eisenhower's staff and supporters, leaving him ostracized by angry Republicans and a vulnerable target for disgruntled Democrats.

A grand jury indicted Powell for tax evasion and fraud in the spring of 1958—charges that he denied—and powerful New York Democrats began a movement to "purge" Powell from the Democratic Party. After expending considerable effort, Powell managed to defeat the movement to expel him from the Democratic Party. He was re–elected to the Congress as a Democrat. His mounting troubles, however, did not wane.

In 1960, as public attention was focused on the Presidential race of Democrat John F. Kennedy and Republican Richard Nixon, Powell's trial on tax–evasion charges unfolded. Two charges were found ungrounded and the verdict on a third charge was hopelessly deadlocked in jury deliberations, so the case was dismissed. Whatever satisfaction Powell must have felt upon being absolved of tax fraud was small compared to the upheaval he faced later in the year. After 15 years of stormy marriage, Hazel Scott Powell divorced her husband. Powell found consolation in his staff secretary, Yvette Diago. She had come to Washington to work on Powell's staff "at the lowest point in my life," wrote Powell, "when friends turned their backs on me, when politicians were out to purge me, when enemies in high places were out to get me." They married late in 1960. They would remain married for five years and have a son, Adam Diago Powell.

In the eventful year of 1960, Powell became chairman of the powerful House Committee on Education and Labor, serving in that position for seven years. Under his direction, the committee helped pass 48 pieces of social legislation involving a monetary outlay of more than $14 billion. Among this legislation were the 1960 Civil Rights Act, the 1961 Minimum Wage Bill, the Manpower Development and Training Act of 1962, and five bills in 1964: the Anti–Poverty Bill, the Juvenile Delinquency Act, the Vocational Education Act, the National Defense Act, and the Civil Rights Act.

Even as many of Powell's long–championed civil rights bills came to fruition and passed into law, Powell's conduct became more and more erratic. "Powell, especially after he became chairperson of a major congressional committee in 1961, flaunted his power. He boasted of his influence and taunted his detractors," wrote his biographer, Charles Hamilton. "He used the weapons of ridicule to put down the segregationists, and this made him that much more objectionable to friend and foe alike. His friends wished he would be less of a show–off, less openly arrogant, and less obviously opportunistic.'' Historian Richard Bardolph observed in 1974, ''His absenteeism, his boastful attitude, and his colorful private life disappointed many reformers and offended many congressmen.''

Although Powell was first regarded as ''a symbol of Negro success,'' according to Bardolph, ''his downfall began in 1960, when he refused to pay a slander judgment rendered against him for defamation of a Harlem woman's character by his remarks on a television show.'' Powell, who did not appear in court while the jury deliberated over the libel suit filed by ''alleged bag woman Esther James,'' was found guilty of slandering the woman and ordered to pay damages in the amount of $46,500. Incensed by what he considered a grave injustice, the congressman set into motion a long series of appeals, and the case stretched on until December of 1968. Powell refused to pay the damages judgment. He was later ''found guilty of criminal contempt of court and fled to the Bahamian island of Bimini to avoid arrest,'' wrote Bardolph.

During the protracted legal maneuvering to reverse the Esther James's judgment, Powell became the target of multiple attacks from other fronts. Senator John Williams of Delaware castigated him on the floor of the Congress in 1963 for personal misconduct and misuse of government funds. In 1967 the House subcommittee that was investigating Powell's handling of funds of the powerful Committee on Education and Labor made several serious charges against the congressman and revoked his chairmanship of the committee. The House then voted (307–116) to deny him his congressional seat. As Powell filed suit to challenge the legality of the action, a special election was held in Harlem to fill the ''vacant'' seat. Powell was re–elected *in absentia* by a huge majority. The following year, as Powell devoted his energy to ministerial duties at Abyssinian Church and gave frequent lectures on college campuses, the United States Supreme Court agreed to accept his case. The eventual ruling two years later found that Powell's exclusion from the Congress was unconstitutional. Not waiting for an official judicial pronouncement, Powell announced his candidacy for re–election. A resounding show of support came from ''indignant Harlemites who were not going to be told by [white majority] Congress who they should select,'' wrote Hamilton, and Powell won his seat in the House in 1968. In early 1969, after friends helped Powell pay the remainder of the slander judgment to Esther James, he was again seated in the Congress. ''They [members of the Congress] intended to let me back in, but there had to be one last punishment to show the world they were vigilant,'' wrote Powell. ''The final agreement was to permit me to be admitted if I would accept a $25,000 fine and the loss of my 22 years of seniority. I could not refuse the terms.''

Powell's return to the political arena was bittersweet. He was diagnosed as having prostate cancer in 1969. Although he announced his retirement from politics, by 1970 he had changed his mind and decided to seek re–election to the House. By then, he was considered an ineffective legislator and his record of frequent absences from the Congress had earned censure from his own constituents. As a result, he had four challengers for the Eighteenth Congressional District seat and he lost the Democratic nomination to Harlemite Charles B. Rangel, who then was elected the new congressman in November.

Stunned by his defeat after 23 years as Harlem's congressman, Powell returned to Bimini in the Bahamas, where his live–in companion, Darlene Expose Hine, resumed taking care of the debilitated crusader. Cancer took a heavy toll, and his health declined rapidly. In April of 1971, Powell announced to his Abyssinian congregation that he was stepping down as minister and would spend his coming days writing another book about his life. A year later, he suffered complications from prostate surgery and was immediately transported by air to Jackson Memorial Hospital in Miami, Florida. There he died that night, on April 4, 1972.

Powell's funeral was held several days later at the Abyssinian Baptist Church in Harlem. Then Darlene Expose Hine, in keeping with Powell's wishes, had his body cremated and scattered his ashes over the waters off South Bimini. Adam Clayton Powell Jr. then passed from life into legend.

Although the flamboyant minister, congressman, and civil rights activist won numerous awards and honors for his achievements—including the renaming of Harlem's Seventh Avenue to Adam Clayton Powell Jr. Boulevard and the addition of his name on the towering Adam Clayton Powell Jr. State Office Building—and his controversial life was recorded on reams upon reams of newsprint, the man himself still remains an enigma, an inexplicable paradox. The *New York Times* rushed to judgment when Powell died and pronounced that his life on earth left ''no lasting heritage,'' but Powell's role as one of the earliest, most tenacious crusaders for minority civil rights speaks to the fallacy of the *Times*'s statement.

REFERENCES

Bardolph, Richard. ''Powell, Adam Clayton, Jr. (1908–1972).'' *The World Book.* Vol. 15. Chicago: Field Enterprises Educational Corp., 1974.

Berry, Mary Frances. *Black Resistance/White Law.* New York: Appleton Publishers, 1971.

Contemporary Black Biography. Vol. 3. Detroit: Gale Research, 1993.

Ebony Pictorial History of Black America; Volume II: Reconstruction to Supreme Court Decision, 1954. Nashville: Southwestern Company (by arrangement with Johnson Publishing Company) 1971.

Hamilton, Charles. *Adam Clayton Powell, Jr., The Political Biography of an American Dilemma.* New York: Macmillan, 1991.

Hampton, Henry, Steve Fayer, and Sarah Flynn, eds. *Voices of Freedom.* New York: Bantam Books and Blackside, 1990.

Hickey, Neil, and Ed Edwin. *Adam Clayton Powell and the Politics of Race.* New York: Fleet Publishing Company, 1965.
Jacobs, Andy. *The Powell Affair: Freedom Minus One.* New York: Bobbs–Merrill, 1973.
''King vs. Powell.'' Editorial. *New York Times,* April 6, 1972.
Powell, Adam Clayton, Jr. *Adam by Adam.* New York: Dial Press, 1971.
Powell, Adam Clayton, Sr. *Against the Tide.* New York: Richard R. Smith, 1938.
''Rebuke for Powell.'' *New York Times,* January 10, 1967.
Whalen, Charles and Barbara Whalen. *The Longest Debate, A Legislative History of the 1964 Civil Rights Act.* New York: New American Library, 1985.
Wright, J. Leitch, Jr. *The Only Land They Knew.* New York: Free Press, 1981.

Ilene Jones–Cornwell

Colin Powell

Colin Powell

(1937–)

Military leader

A four–star general in the U.S. Army, Colin Powell has been appointed to high positions in both Republican and Democratic administrations. He was the first black national security advisor and the first chair of the Joint Chiefs of Staff. The mastermind behind the United States's involvement in the Persian Gulf War, he was involved in Operations Desert Shield and Desert Storm. Later he was pursued vigorously by the Republican Party as a vice–presidential candidate in the 1996 presidential elections. He continued to enjoy high visibility, as attested to in the *Wall Street Journal*/NBC news poll for 1997 which identified him as the most popular American.

Born on April 5, 1937, in Harlem, Colin Luther Powell is the son of Jamaican immigrants Luther Powell and Maud Ariel McKoy Powell. After immigrating to the area when he was in his early twenties, Luther Powell was a gardener on estates in Connecticut and a building superintendent in Manhattan who worked to become foreman of the shipping department of a garment manufacturer. Maud Powell, a seamstress in the garment district, was a staunch supporter of the International Garment Workers Union. At the time of Colin Powell's birth, his parents lived on Morningside Avenue, then moved to other locations before settling at 952 Kelly Street in the Hunts Point section of the South Bronx when Colin Powell was six. While his parents worked, his maternal grandmother, Alice McKoy, took care of Powell and his only sibling, Marilyn, who was five and a half years older. When he was in college, his family left their decaying neighborhood and moved to their own house on Elmira Avenue in Queens.

Even though Powell came from a close–knit family and had a secure childhood, he was surrounded by and couldn't help but observe the rough life of the streets and the struggles others suffered because of the Great Depression. His neighborhood was racially–mixed, consisting of Jewish, Irish, Polish, Italian, black, and Hispanic families. Most of the black families there had roots in Jamaica, Trinidad, Barbados, or other West Indian islands.

When Powell was promoted from the third to the fourth grade in Public School 39, he was placed in the bottom form, known as ''Fore Up,'' meaning that he was *considered* a slow learner as were many black students. He was not an athlete but enjoyed street games and kite fighting. He studied piano briefly, then flute, but gave up both. When he was 14–years old, Powell had his first job at Sickser's, a baby furnishings and toy store.

In high school, Powell played on the basketball team, ran track, and for a short time was involved in the Boy Scouts. He had no special interest in either. In February 1954, two months before he was 17, Powell graduated from an accelerated program at Morris High School. He was accepted at both New York University, a private school, and City College of New York (CCNY), a public college. He chose the latter because of lower costs. To help support himself, he continued to work at various jobs on weekends and vacations, including work with the International Brotherhood of Teamsters, Local 812, and a bottling company.

At CCNY, he joined the Reserve Officer's Training Corps (ROTC) and after being courted for membership by three military societies, joined the Pershing Rifles, the precision drill team. He found the ROTC appealing and considered the Pershing Rifles an elite group. He also enjoyed the discipline, structure, camaraderie, and sense of belonging that the Pershing Rifles provided. During his last three years of college, the drill hall became his universe and on weekends he spent up to seven hours there in practice. He remained a mediocre student through college but pulled up his grades with straight A's in ROTC. Upon graduation from CCNY, in 1958, with a B.S. in geology and the honor of Distinguished Military Graduate, he was commissioned a second lieutenant in the army.

In his autobiography, *My American Journey,* Powell acknowledged an "unpayable debt" to the New York City public system of education. He said, "I typify the students that CCNY was created to serve, the sons and daughters of the innercity, the poor, the immigrant." Although he had a C– average, Powell added that he:

> emerged from CCNY prepared to write, think, and communicate effectively and equipped to compete against students from colleges that I could never have dreamed of attending. If the Statue of Liberty opened the gateway to this country, public education opened the door to attainment here. . . . I am, consequently, a champion of public secondary and higher education.

Army Career Begins

Powell's career in the U.S. Army began in 1958, with basic training in Fort Benning, Georgia, followed by his first assignment overseas, to the Third Armored Division in West Germany, for a tour of Gelnhausen, located near Frankfort. He was indoctrinated into army life and learned that in the 48th Infantry, the care of the men was the main concern. By the end of the year, he was promoted to first lieutenant. After completing a two–year tour ending in late 1960, he was sent to Fort Devens, about 30 miles west of Boston and was assigned to the First Battle Group, Fourth Infantry, Second Infantry Brigade.

By 1961 Powell had completed the required three years of service for his ROTC experience. He knew that he was well–suited to the military and never considered leaving it. While stationed in Fort Devens, he went on a blind date with Alma Vivian Johnson, a Birmingham native, and they developed a lasting friendship that led to marriage on August 25, 1962. In the summer of 1962 Powell, was sent to Fort Bragg, North Carolina, for training as a military advisor, then to war in South Vietnam for his first tour of duty. While patrolling the Laos border with an infantry battalion, he stepped into a trap and injured his foot, for which he was awarded a Purple Heart. Later that year he was awarded the Bronze Star.

Returning to the United States early in 1963, Powell had difficulty locating housing for his family in the Columbus, Georgia, area near Fort Benning, where he had been assigned. They lived in nearby Phoenix City, Alabama, instead. He had a similar experience earlier at Fort Bragg. He was also denied service at a drive–in hamburger joint unless he went to the back window. He refused to succumb to such racial discrimination. At Fort Benning, Powell completed a month–long Pathfinder course for paratroopers. Pathfinders were an elite within an elite group. He graduated number one in the class and added the Pathfinder insignia to his Combat Infantryman's badge, airborne wings, and other decorations. After this stint, Powell was assigned to the Infantry Board at Fort Benning, where he tested new weapons and designed RAM (Reliability, Availability, and Maintainability) standards for the test. He completed the Infantry Officers Advanced Course in May of 1965, ranking first among his class of 200. He returned to the Infantry Board after completing a course for instructors and receiving an oak leaf and a promotion to major.

Powell remained at Fort Benning almost three years, then moved to Fort Leavenworth, Kansas, in the spring of 1967. He entered the Army's Graduate Civil Schooling Program and was ranked among the top infantrymen in his class. From July of 1968 to July of 1969 Powell was reassigned to Vietnam, to the resurrected World War II Twenty–third Infantry Division known as Americal. He was executive officer of the Third Battalion, First Infantry, Eleventh Infantry Brigade. He was injured during a helicopter crash landing and received a Soldiers Medal for bravery in helping rescue injured men from the burning wreckage.

Powell entered graduate school at George Washington University in Washington, D.C., and graduated with a master's degree in business administration in 1971. He had earned all A's and one B, in computer logic. After receiving his degree, Powell was urged to study for a Ph.D., but he was eager to return to the army. In July of 1971, he was assigned to the Pentagon where he reported to lieutenant general William E. DePuy, who headed the office of the assistant vice chief of staff of the army. Powell became a White House Fellow for 1972–73, assigned to the Office of Management and Budget (OMB), then headed by Caspar Weinberger. He served briefly under Frank C. Carlucci, then under Fred Malek. He refused an opportunity to remain at OMB another year, returning to the army after he had completed his assignment.

In 1973 Powell was assigned to Camp Casey in South Korea to help obstruct a possible attack by North Korea. When he returned to the United States in September of 1974, Powell was temporarily assigned to the Pentagon until his National War College (NWC) classes, for which he had been selected, began in August of 1975. In an accelerated program, he was promoted to full colonel in February of 1976, midway through the NWC. He missed the last two months of training because of a new assignment, but graduated with distinction. Powell took command of the Second Brigade of the 101st Airborne Division at Fort Campbell, Kentucky, remaining there until 1977. He said in his autobiography that he wanted to remain at Fort Campbell to become chief of staff of the

101st Airborne. Instead, he was called back to Washington where he was assigned to the Office of the Secretary of Defense during President Jimmy Carter's administration.

Becomes a High–Ranking General

On June 1, 1979, Powell's formal promotion ceremony to brigadier general was held. President Carter made major shakeups in his cabinet, removing Joseph Califano as Secretary of Health, Education, and Welfare, and James Schlesinger as Secretary of Energy. He assigned Charles Duncan to take over the Department of Energy. Duncan asked Powell to join his transition team, and for a brief period in 1979 Powell became Duncan's executive assistant.

When the 1980 elections were held, Powell chose to vote for Ronald Reagan instead of supporting Carter as he had done in 1976. In April of 1980 Iranian students had seized 53 Americans as hostage in the American embassy in Tehran and held them captive for five months. This incident highly influenced Powell's decision to advocate Reagan instead of Carter. Powell wrote in his autobiography that "the Carter Administration had been mauled by double–digit inflation and the humiliating spectacle of the Americans held hostage in Iran." When Reagan took office, Powell had an opportunity to become undersecretary of the army, but chose to "go back to doing what brigadier generals are supposed to do," as he wrote in his autobiography.

Powell was assigned as assistant division commander for operations and training for the Fourth Infantry Division (Mechanized), Fort Carson, Colorado, remaining there from 1981 to 1983. In August of 1983, Powell became deputy commander of Fort Leavenworth, Kansas, and headed an operation called CACDA, or Combined Arms Combat Development Activity. Those who held the position previously, found that it served as a launchpad to higher ranks. On June 19, 1983, the last days of his CACDA tour, Powell was promoted to major general. He spent only 11 months in Fort Leavenworth, then returned to Washington as military assistant to Secretary of Defense Caspar Weinberger from 1983 to 1986. In 1986, when U.S. Congress declared that the covert sale of arms to Iran was in this country's interest, Powell wrote to National Security Council head, Admiral John Poindexter, that Congress had to be notified about the sale. Poindexter ignored the memorandum. When a scandal arose about the covert sale; however, Powell was found to have acted within the law and kept his credibility.

On March 26, 1986, Powell received a third star that went with his new job as commander of the Fifth Corps in Frankfort, West Germany, where he had been assigned in 1986 to command 75,000 troops. On December 31, 1986, he formally gave up command and on January 2, 1987, was back in Washington as deputy assistant to President George Bush for national security affairs. Powell reorganized the National Security Council (NSC) staff and also chaired its policy review group. Powell was promoted to national security advisor on November 5, 1987. On September 20, 1988, Powell was the first national security adviser to receive the Secretary's Award, given for "distinguished contributions to the development, management, or implementation" of American foreign policy. He remained in the position until 1989.

Powell was promoted to chairman of the Joint Chiefs of Staff in 1989, the top position in the military and became a four–star general. While Powell was at Fort Leavenworth, the U.S.–based forces had been organized into two commands: FORSCOM, or U.S. Forces Command, and TRADOC, or Training and Doctrine Command. Now as chair of the Joint Chiefs of Staff, Powell directed what he called in his autobiography "one last command," or command of FORSCOM. Through his command, Powell successfully oversaw Operation Desert Shield in 1990, where massive numbers of troops and supplies were moved to Saudi Arabia. He also directed the successful Operation Desert Storm, the offensive option developed alongside the defensive stance. Six weeks later, President Bush announced from the Oval Office that Kuwait had been liberated, Iraq's army had been defeated, and U.S. military objectives had been realized.

Powell's position also involved him in such activities as the Haitian refugee problem, or Operation Safe Harbor; the establishment of camps for Haitian refugees, a plan which Powell rejected; and by early 1992 the reduction of the armed forces by 25 percent. He also had a number of speaking engagements, including the 1992 commencement address at Fisk University in Nashville, Tennessee, which was Alma Powell's alma mater 35 years earlier. Quoted in his autobiography, Powell talked to those gathered about family and diversity: "We must remember that America is a family. There may be differences and disputes in our family. But we must not allow the family to be broken into warring factions. . . . I want you to find strength in your diversity."

Powell retired from the military in September of 1993. Powell's retirement was a colorful affair broadcast nationally from the parade ground at Fort Meyer, Virginia. President Bill Clinton presented him the Presidential Medal of Freedom with Distinction, the nation's highest civilian award.

After his retirement, Powell rejected George Bush's appeal to serve as his running mate in the 1996 presidential elections. Instead he devoted himself to writing his autobiography (published in 1995), traveling the lecture circuit, and serving on business, corporate, and academic boards. Powell was generally regarded as a mobilizer, racial healer, and great leader. In accordance with such goals, he chaired President Clinton's volunteer program for improving children's lives, called the President's Summit for America's Future. In the April 21, 1997, issue of *Time,* Powell said "I have arrived at the point in my life where I am trying to use what I have been given by my nation to help the nation." The President's summit kicked off the program on April 27, 1997, in Philadelphia, where Powell, Clinton, and former presidents George Bush and Jimmy Carter stood together on the steps of Independence Hall. They called for America to unite through volunteer service in what the *Nashville Tennessean* for April 27, 1997, identified as "an effort organizers hope will improve by the end of 2000 the lives of at least 2 million of America's 15 million poor children.''

In an interview for *Meet the Press* held during the President's Summit for America's Future initiated on April 26, 1997, Powell said that he was comfortable and satisfied in private life; he is convinced that he made significant contributions while involved in politics and is now making important contributions as a private citizen. *Time* magazine named him one of the most influential people in America for 1997. When asked, ''Is it fair to say that you will not be a candidate for president in the year 2000?'' he responded, ''The assumption is fair.''

In private life, the Powells are regular worshipers at St. John's Episcopal Church in McLean, Virginia. Although Alma Powell was baptized a Congregationalist, she became an Episcopalian while she and her husband were at Ft. Leavenworth. The Powells have three children—Michael Kevin (b. March 23 1963), Linda (b. April 16, 1965), and Annemarie (b. May 20, 1969).

Powell stands six–feet one–inch tall and weighs around 200 pounds. He is calm, mild–mannered, skilled in dealings with civilians and military personnel, and carries himself in a military manner. He gives careful attention to detail. He is neither humble nor a bragger; he is a confident man. Throughout his life he has maintained a special fondness for automobiles and mentioned them frequently in his autobiography.

Colin Powell is a significant figure in military history. Although he is not regarded as a race man, he is an important role model for blacks in mainland America, including the West Indian immigrant. He achieved greatness because he prepared himself well for the work that he liked best, the military, and executed his assignments with dignity and exactness.

Current address: 909 N. Washington St., Suite 767, Alexandria, VA 22314.

REFERENCES

Contemporary Black Biography. Vol. 1. Detroit: Gale Research, 1992.

Current Biography Yearbook. New York: H. W. Wilson, 1988.

Klein, Joe. ''Heartbreaker.'' *Newsweek* 126 (20 November 1995): 36–41.

Powell, Colin. Interview, *Meet the Press,* NBC Television, April 26, 1997.

———, with Joseph E. Persico. *My American Journey.* New York: Random House, 1995.

''Time's 25 Most Influential Americans.'' *Time* 149 (21 April 1997): 40–66.

''Powell, Woods, Jordan Most Popular Americans.'' *Jet* 91 (19 May 1997): 5.

''Summit Turns Volunteer Dream into Reality.'' *Nashville Tennessean,* April 27, 1997.

Thomas, Evan. ''The General's Lady.'' *Newsweek* 126 (20 November 1997): 37–40.

''Why He Got Out.'' *Newsweek* 126 (20 November 1997): 42–45.

Jessie Carney Smith

Awadagin Pratt

(1966–)

Concert pianist

In 1992 a new star burst onto the American concert scene. Awadagin Pratt, the first black performer to win the coveted Naumburg International piano competition, began a professional career that was to become both wide–ranging and very demanding. He has joined a company of established black artists, including Jessye Norman, Kathleen Battle, Andre Watts, and Paul Freeman, who have garnered prominent places before the concert–going public both here and abroad.

Awadagin Pratt was born in Pittsburgh, Pennsylvania, on March 6, 1966, and began studying piano when he was six years old. In 1975 his family moved to Normal, Illinois, where his parents, Mildred and Theodore Pratt, were professors of social work and nuclear physics, respectively. For Awadagin and his younger sister, Menah, the home environment included a strict regimen of piano and violin lessons, tennis lessons, and regular practice sessions. Attending public schools in Normal, he was active in athletics, and was on the tennis team at Normal Community High School, played doubles tennis with his sister, played on basketball teams, and competed in local sports tournaments.

Pratt's interest in music soon deepened, and upon graduation from high school, he enrolled at the age of 16 at the University of Illinois, majoring in music and studying piano, violin, and conducting. In 1986 he enrolled on scholarship at the Peabody Conservatory of Music in Baltimore. He continued in their study program, earning performance diplomas in piano and violin in 1989 and a graduate performing diploma in conducting in 1992. He thus became Peabody's first student to earn three performance diplomas.

Continuing in private study, Pratt began preparing for a concert career. He entered the 1992 Naumburg International piano composition and won first prize, the first black American to win this prestigious award. After several major concert successes, he was awarded the Avery Fisher Career Grant in 1994, and his full–time concert career continued at a rapid pace.

Initially featured in recitals and concerto performances as a Beethoven interpreter, his concert career took him to New York, Washington, D.C., Chicago, and Los Angeles. He appeared on the September of 1994 PBS television concert honoring Mystislav Rostropovitch, broadcast live from the Kennedy Center in Washington, D.C. A concert appearance at

Awadagin Pratt

the White House, at the invitation of President and Mrs. Bill Clinton, followed. Concert appearances with major symphony orchestras during the 1994–95 season included performances with the New York and Los Angeles Philharmonic orchestras, the National Symphony Orchestra in Washington D.C., and the Minnesota Orchestra. He also performed with the Atlanta, St. Louis, and Cincinnati Symphony orchestras. Pratt made his debuts at Chicago's Ravinia Festival, Cleveland's Blossom Music Festival, and the Caramoor Music Festival in the summer of 1995.

Pratt had a full and demanding schedule as well during the 1995–96 concert season, including debut appearances as soloist with the Pittsburgh, Detroit, and New Jersey Symphony orchestras and the Buffalo Philharmonic, and return engagements with the Atlanta, St. Louis, and Seattle symphony orchestras. In addition to recital appearances at New York's Lincoln Center and the Kennedy Center, he also made his recital debut in Capetown, South Africa, in December of 1995. On February 23–24, 1996, his tour schedule brought him to Nashville, Tennessee, where he performed the Saint-Saens 4th Piano Concerto with the Nashville Symphony Orchestra.

Following a debut appearance at the Aspen Festival in the summer of 1996, he traveled to Japan for recital and concert appearances in Osaka and Tokyo in September of 1996. His demanding schedule resumed during the 1996–97 season, with engagements with the New York Philharmonic and National Symphony Orchestras and recitals at Orchestra Hall in Chicago, the Dorothy Chandler Pavilion in Los Angeles, and the Tonhalle in Zurich.

Pratt signed a recording contract with Angel/EMI in 1993 and has since released three CD–recordings. The first two are recital albums, with the initial album, *A Long Way from Normal,* released in 1994, featuring works by Brahms, Bach, Franck, and Liszt. The next album, released in 1996 was an all–Beethoven album of sonatas. His third album, *Live from South Africa,* featuring works for piano, was released in January of 1997.

Pratt has presented a challenging persona in his visage, his appearance on stage, his manner of addressing his instrument, and in the general aura he projects. He makes full use of the tonal nuances and sound spectrum available from his instrument to interpret his varied repertoire. His is a forceful presence; in dreadlocks, he evokes something of the free spirit of one of his favorite composers, Ludwig van Beethoven. He evinces controlled energy, dressing comfortably, often in turtle–neck and slacks and seldom in tuxedo, leaving himself free to marshal and direct his considerable technical abilities for interpreting the music. He sits low, on a specially designed bench, for greater control, directing his energies forward towards his instrument. He offers his audiences fresh approaches and is often rewarded with their enthusiastic praise. As for the music critics, for the most part he has had excellent reviews, with many writers commenting on his stage presence, command of pianistic technique, and his ability to convey both breadth and depth in his interpretations.

Pratt's repertoire has been wide. Centered initially in the German classicists—Beethoven, Mozart, and Bach—he also features the Romantics and French nineteenth century composers. Principally presented in concert and on records as a piano soloist with orchestra as well as in solo recitals, he has occasionally appeared as a conductor, both from the piano and before the orchestra in symphonic works. He has also performed in chamber music programs. His concerts over a span of less than five years (1992–97) have taken him to four continents to audiences in the major cities of the United States, Europe, South Africa, and Asia, with three major CD albums to his credit. Pratt shows great promise of standing in the forefront of our interpreters of the classical repertoire for the piano. In addition, he will make a mark as a symphonic conductor. Awadagin Pratt currently resides in Albuquerque, New Mexico.

Current address: IMG Artists, 420 West 45th St., New York, NY 10036.

REFERENCES

"Artful Awadagin; Pratt Strikes an Original Chord in the Precise World of Classical Piano." *Charlotte Observer,* October 1, 1995.

"Awadagin Pratt, as Conductor and Soloist, Personalizes Rubati." *Amsterdam News,* September 21, 1996.

Chang, Yahlin. "The Piano Man's Not with a Band; in Every Way, Awadagin Pratt Defies Stereotype." *Newsweek* 128 (25 November 1996).

Hasson, Bill. "A Long Way from Normal." Record review. *American Visions* 9 (October–November 1994): 48.

IMG Artists Presskit, and 1997 update.
McCardell, Charles. "A Salute to Slava." Concert review. *American Record Guide* 57 (September–October 1994): 58.
"A Mother Enjoys Life's Sweet Song." *Nashville Tennessean*, May 28, 1997.
"Now He's a Player." *People* 38 (17 August 1992): 71.
"Piano Sontas Nos. 9, 7, 30 and 31, Ludwig van Beethoven; Awadagin Pratt, Piano." Record review. *Chicago Sun Times*, March 31, 1996.
"Piano Virtuoso Pratt's a Classical Beauty." *Bermuda Royal Gazette*, January 24, 1997.
Pratt, Menah. Interview with Darius Thieme. May 23, 1997.
"Pratt Recital is Rich Prelude to a Brilliant Future." *Detroit Journal*. December 12, 1966.
"Pratt Secures Critics' Interest." *Nashville Tennessean*. February 23, 1996.
"Symphony Stages Franch Works with Finesse." *Nashville Banner*. February 26, 1996.
Stearns, David Patrick. "Classical Music." Record review. *Stereo Review* 59 (September 1994): 109.
Woolford, Pamela. "A Glimpse At a Unique Classical Musician." *Crisis* 101 (July 1994): 49–51.

Darius L. Thieme

J. C. Price

J. C. Price
(1854–1893)
Minister, college president, educator, orator

J. C. Price, college president, orator, temperance advocate, and minister, was an internationally famed leader who was largely forgotten by the twentieth century. Price, through hard work and devotion, was highly instrumental in establishing Livingstone College, a school for ministers in North Carolina. He dedicated his short life to the service of God and the uplift of the black race.

Joseph Charles Price was born February 10, 1854 in Elizabeth City, North Carolina. His mother was Emily Pailin Dozier, a freeborn black woman who exerted great influence on her son. He inherited her looks, temperament, patience, and unwavering Christian faith. Price's father was a shipbuilder's slave named Charles Dozier. Unfortunately, his master sold Price's father; Price saw him in Baltimore, Maryland, years later. Emily Dozier later married David Price, the man whose name the young boy used. Her new husband treated her son as his own.

Price was legally free since his mother was born free, but the status of poor free blacks was little better than that of slaves in the state of North Carolina. The mother and her son moved in 1863 to New Bern, North Carolina. There they were in an area governed by federal troops and Price could seek an education with less opposition from the racially prejudiced Southern society of the time. His first venture into the federally–occupied city of New Bern led him to St. Peter's African Methodist Episcopal Zion (AMEZ) Church Sunday School where he was warmly welcomed by the school administration despite his shabby appearance. When the children laughed at his ragged clothes, bare feet, and awkward outbursts of curiosity, Thomas C. Battle, the superintendent reprimanded them with a prophetic warning that they would be willing and happy to shine his shoes one day.

The St. Peter's AMEZ Sunday School was the first training ground for Price who soon excelled in basic oratorical skills, singing, and public demeanor. Walls cites Battle as saying of him, "he became at once the example for the whole school." Price's first educational experience was at the parochial school that met in old St. Andrew's Chapel, the predecessor to St. Peter's AMEZ church, and then at St. Cyprian Episcopal School which was governed by the Boston Society. According to Walls, his most notable characteristic was love as observed by John C. Dancy, one who knew Price best: "He loved and he was loved . . . it was with him a religion . . . it [was] Godlike." Price began to receive praise and school honors, but his pride was always tempered by an exceptional sense of maturity.

At the age of 17, Price assumed his first educational position. While still teaching, he entered Shaw University in nearby Raleigh. Although he did not graduate, two events occurred there that had tremendous impact on Price's life. He was called on to debate James H. Harris, a leading state political orator who had criticized young men. Price so successfully refuted the claim that his oratorical skills attracted great attention in the state's capitol. The second event was Price's conversion and acceptance of God's call to the ministry. Price was received at the same church where he had been a faithful and outstanding Sunday School student, the church of his mother—St. Peter's AMEZ Church. Price was licensed in 1875 in the North Carolina Conference.

Price realized that he yet needed more than Shaw University could offer if he were to fulfill his destiny, to uplift, educate, and lead his people to Christ. He eventually left Shaw, and entered Lincoln University in Pennsylvania, spurning a $1,200 salaried position offered him by a congressman.

Price's four years at Lincoln were highlighted by his ranking of "first" each year and being named valedictorian at graduation. As a senior, Price began junior year theological studies at Lincoln University School of Theology and completed the three–year program in two years. During his seminary years he was also ordained an elder and elected delegate to the AMEZ General Conference.

One person whose role was crucial in backing Price's education and the future development and growth of Livingstone College was William E. Dodge, a Christian philanthropist, New York merchant, prominent Republican and Lincoln University trustee. Price became Dodge's protégé and expressed his gratitude privately and publicly. Dodge provided Price with a scholarship to finance his education at Lincoln. Dodge also introduced Price to wealthy English friends who financially assisted Price's efforts in establishing and maintaining Livingstone College. In later years Dodge gave the men's dormitory at Livingstone College, Dodge Hall, which is still in use.

Leadership Role Begins

After Price's graduation from the Lincoln University School of Theology, he returned to his home state as a temperance lecturer under the financial aegis of William E. Dodge. The official campaign had begun in Raleigh and Price's reputation had already been established while he was a student at Shaw. Price increased his visibility by becoming a delegate to the 1881 Ecumenical Conference in London, England. At the Ecumenical Conference, Price spoke on the subjects of Methodism, the temperance movement, and race issues of the times. He toured the country for the purpose of securing funding for Zion Wesley Institute, a new school in Concord, North Carolina to train black ministers, of which he had become an honorary board member. Zion Wesley Institute would eventually move to Salisbury and become Livingstone College.

Price took the fund raising task under the aegis of Bishop James Walker Hood, the founding father of the AMEZ Church in North Carolina and a civil rights leader during the Reconstruction era. Hood had known Price from the time Price's mother moved the small family to New Bern. Hood's request that Price devote an entire year to fund raising activities changed the course of the new Lincoln graduate's life. As a fund raiser, Price was highly successful with the venture, netting $10,000 for the fledgling college.

While Price was overseas in England his mother died back in the United States. This tragic event was somewhat offset by his courtship of and subsequent marriage to Jennie S. Smallwood of Beauford, North Carolina. They had met years before in New Bern. After her parents died, she became the ward of a New York abolitionist family who enrolled her at Scotia Seminary in Concord, North Carolina. Shortly after Price's return from England, the couple married and became parents of five children: William and Louise, who died as young adults; Josephine, who later married Richard W. Sherrill, long–time general manager of the AMEZ Publishing House in Charlotte; Joseph Crummell Price, named in honor of Alexander Crummell, the most famous Episcopal priest during his father's lifetime; and Alma.

From Zion Wesley to Livingstone

Price returned from England with the funds needed to support Zion Wesley Institute, which had originally opened in December 1879. The principal, Cicero R. Harris, supervised four teachers and three students. By the time of Price's return in 1881, and despite an enrollment of 24 students, the school had already suspended operations due to lack of operating funds. Zion Wesley was now apparently one of a number of failed AME Zion schools like Rush University in Fayetteville, North Carolina, and others in Birmingham, Alabama, Middleton, Pennsylvania, New York State, and Ohio.

Hood averted another failure by relocating Zion Wesley from Concord to Salisbury when the citizenry there made an offer of $1,000 to purchase 40 acres of land and an existing two–story building located on the property. In September 1882 the school reopened with five students. Price took charge. He was able to influence a number of his professional colleagues to make sacrifices and join him at Zion. Edward Moore, the Lincoln salutatorian of 1899, gave up a principalship with a promised salary increase. William Harvey Goler received no salary for the first year. A native of Halifax, Nova Scotia, Goler had been a classmate and confidant of both Price and Moore at Lincoln University. It would be Goler's sad duty to deliver Price's eulogy some ten years later.

In *Joseph Charles Price,* Walls characterized Price as a Christian realist who emphasized conscience, intellect, skill, and industry with the educational slogan of "heart, head, and hand." Walls credits Price with founding "the first purely Negro institution in the South and in the country."

In 1877 the name of Zion Wesley Institute was changed to Livingstone College. Like several other black schools, however, Livingstone was always open to all people of widely varying levels of education. Because illiterate and semi–literate students were being admitted with qualified applicants, grammar and high school classes were offered alongside the advanced classical curriculum. In 1884 the curriculum comprised four courses of study: the Grammar School and Normal, Theological, and Classical Studies. There was also an Industrial Department that offered carpentry, brick laying, and other trades for young men, and cooking, needlework, dressmaking, and other trades for young women.

Price had a goal that was reasonable and politically correct for the time. As stated by Walls, "Livingstone . . . [would be] a bridge between the two extreme ideas, teaching the industries with classical and professional branches, while teaching religious subjects to serve the needs of the church that was sponsoring it." Price had to travel widely and utilize his powers of oratory to raise funds to supplement AMEZ General Conference appropriations. In 1888 the conference promised $6,000 to Livingstone College. In an annual report in the year before his death, Price praised Livingstone as being the only Southern institution of color that truly represented "Negro Self Help." There was no state aid for the school, and the college paid a higher percentage towards its own support than any of its sister institutions. Although Price was a commanding presence on campus as teacher, administrator, and mentor to faculty, students, and staff, fund raising was his primary function. Among his greatest philanthropic successes were contributions collected from Collis P. Huntington, the railroad magnate, and Leland Stanford, a builder and philanthropist who had high regard for Price.

Price had a phenomenal gift of oratory. Josephus Daniels of Raleigh and a U.S. Ambassador to Mexico and Secretary of the Navy in the Wilson Cabinet regarded Price and Booker T. Washington as the most remarkable blacks of their day. He wrote in the Introduction to Walls's biography, "The Negro, Price, the child of slavery, as black as any black man in Africa, made as great strides in his short life with his race in the school and in the pulpit as Lincoln made in his notable career."

Price refused career advancement offers that could have made him a wealthy man and left his family comfortable. He was offered the AMEZ bishopric in 1884 and 1888 but declined to run in spite of a groundswell of support. It was declared that he was the only minister who did not want to be a bishop. In 1888 President Grover Cleveland offered Price the post of Minister Plenipotentiary to Liberia. Price declined the offer stating he believed he could do more good for his people in Salisbury.

The Final Years

Price's life may have been shortened by the enormous pressures he faced to keep Livingstone afloat. Clearly, an annual appropriation of $6,000 from the AMEZ General Conference, forthcoming or not, was insufficient to maintain a college. Price also remained active in the temperance movement. Letters to his wife describe fund–raising trips far from the small town of Salisbury during the harshest months of the year. Despite the many philanthropic gifts given to Livingstone because of Price, detractors openly and covertly opposed him. He had made enemies as early as 1884 by opposing Hood while winning the battle to broaden the educational programs. From then on he had to literally fight to gain church and internal support and to rebuff repeated attempts at subverting his position of leadership.

Booker T. Washington reaped the benefits of many of Price's ideas on education. David Levering Lewis said that W. E. B. Du Bois believed that Washington's ascendancy was due first to acclamations of the white race, and secondly to his adeptness at synthesizing Price's advocacy of vocational education and racial conciliation. Lewis characterized Price as, "[A] spellbinding orator . . . perhaps the only serious rival of Booker T. Washington for the mantle of paramount race spokesperson." Two years after Price's death, Washington's star ascended with his appearance at the Cotton States and International Exposition in Atlanta; what Price started, Washington finished. In *Along This Way,* James Weldon Johnson also compared Price with Washington. Johnson invoked race exemplars and described Price as, "broad shouldered, vigorous, radiating vitality, jet–black and handsome, renowned as an orator and educator and who, had he not died young, might have rivaled Booker T. Washington for the leadership of the Negro race."

When the World's Congress of Races at the Columbian Exposition convened in Chicago in 1893 three weeks before his death, Price had been invited as the "race" speaker, but he was dying by that time, having been diagnosed with Bright's Disease some six months prior to his death, although he was still traveling as late as two weeks before his final confinement. When school opened in early October, Price rallied to attend Sunday School and participate as superintendent and then, on Monday, to attend Devotional Services. In an unbelievable show of strength and courage, he attended Tuesday and Wednesday meetings to be with his students. Then his doctor insisted that he remain at home. On October 21, 1893, he called for his family while still lucid, but shortly thereafter the effects of the disease caused his rapid decline and death.

On the campus of Livingstone College are the Price Mausoleum, a favorite hide–and–go–seek spot for countless numbers of neighborhood children, and the Price Memorial building. Joseph Charles Price High School, opened in the 1920s for Salisbury's black youth, was a casualty of integration in the city, but the building still stands. Across the nation are many AMEZ churches bearing the name of Price. But the greatest legacy is the thousands of Livingstone College graduates from both the college and seminary who lived exemplary lives of service modeled after that of their founder.

REFERENCES

Franklin, John Hope. *George Washington Williams: A Biography.* Chicago: University of Chicago Press, 1987.

Howe, Minnie. Unpublished Journal. Salisbury, NC, February 14, 1923.

"In Honor of the Oldest Living College Graduates and the Founder's Family." Centennial Issue. July–September 1980.

Johnson, James Weldon. *Along This Way: The Autobiography of James Weldon Johnson.* 1933. Reprint, New York: Penguin Books, 1990.

Lewis, David Levering. *W. E. B. Du Bois: Biography of a Race (1868–1919).* New York: Henry Holt, 1993.

Pritchard, Myron T., and Mary White Ovington. *The Upward Path: A Reader for Colored Youth.* New York: Harcourt, Brace and Howe, 1920.

Roundtree, Louise M. *An Annotated Bibliography on Joseph Charles Price (1882–1893): Founder of Livingstone College.* Salisbury, NC 1960. Revised 1963.

———, ed. "The American Negro and African Studies." A Bibliography on the Special Collections in Carnegie Library, Livingstone College, Salisbury, NC, 1968.

———, ed. *The Brief International Story of Livingstone College.* Prepared in the Centennial Year. Salisbury, NC, 1980.

Trent, W. J., Jr., ed. *The 1930 BLUE BEAR.* Salisbury, NC: Livingstone College, 1930.

Walls, William Jacob. *Joseph Charles Price: Educator and Race Leader.* Boston: Christopher Publishing House, 1943.

Yandle, Paul. "Joseph Charles Price and His 'Peculiar Work.'" Part I. *North Carolina Historical Review* 70 (January 1993): 40–56.

COLLECTIONS

According to Yandle, Price's papers are on loan from his family to Wake Forest University Library Rare Book Room, Winston–Salem, North Carolina.

Dolores Nicholson

Charley Pride

Charley Pride

(1938?–)

Singer, baseball player

The first black star at the Grand Ole Opry and a country music superstar, baritone Charley Pride began his career in the black baseball leagues but later became a singer when he was denied a position in professional baseball. He overcame problems of race caused both by blacks and whites to become a leading country music artist.

Although there are discrepancies in his birth year, most sources indicate that Charley Frank Pride was born on March 18, 1938, in Sledge, Mississippi, a small town about 60 miles south of Memphis, Tennessee. He came from a family of 11 children–eight boys and three girls. The oldest were from the first marriage of his mother, Tessie B. Stewart Pride. Charley was the second child born to his mother and Mack Pride. While his father named him Charl Frank, his birth certificate gives his name as Charley.

The Prides lived in a three–room house where the children slept three and four to a bed, alternately with head to foot. "Many a time, I was awakened in the night by toes jabbing me in the face," Charley wrote in his autobiography, *Pride.* Charley and his siblings worked in the cotton fields on the farm where Mack Pride was a sharecropper. He continued: "I always had the feeling that there was something else I was supposed to do, something besides following in my father's footsteps and being another sharecropper working another man's land and growing old with a cotton sack around my neck."

Pride grew up in a dysfunctional family. His father's parents had abused their eight children and Mack beat his children with a strap. Although Pride's mother tried to protect her children, his father was unrelenting. Pride later acknowledged that his father was "not unfeeling," but unable to express himself in a normal way. In *Pride,* the singer tells of the ambivalent feelings he had toward his father: he did not like him, but he loved him and Pride regrets that their relationship lacked warmth and tenderness.

Pride became fascinated with radio at an early age. He especially liked the *Grand Ole Opry* program that was broadcast live from Nashville on Saturday nights. Pride learned to sing the country and western songs just like his favorite stars, mimicking the sounds and dialects of Roy Acuff, Eddie Arnold, Ernest Tubb, and Hank Williams. When he sang country music at home, his family thought he was extending his ability to imitate sounds, as he had done with animals and the British, Irish, and other accents he heard on the radio.

The first country music Pride heard live was on the streets of Sledge, when he was about five years old. A local merchant, Sander's Grocery Store, used the music on Saturday afternoons to attract customers. Pride later became interested in playing the guitar, saved most of his earnings, and—when he was 14 years old—bought his first guitar, an inexpensive Silvertone. When he inadvertently left his guitar outside one night and rain, heat, and humidity destroyed it, Pride was without an instrument for a while.

Pride continued to tinker with musical instruments. He folded paper around a comb and hummed against it to make musical sounds. He also rigged a crude one–string steel guitar as he tacked nails into the wall, strung bailing wire between them, tightened the wire, and plucked the strings either by finger, metal, or a glass jar or bottle.

Early Career in Professional Baseball

Pride was quickly becoming restless. Jackie Robinson had become a baseball star with the Brooklyn Dodgers in 1947 and Pride thought that, he too, could have a future in baseball–not with the Negro leagues, as they were called, but with the major leagues.

Pride graduated from Sledge Junior High School in 1954 and headed for Memphis to play baseball the following spring. While some sources claim that Pride played for Detroit, according to his autobiography he became a pitcher for the Memphis Red Sox of the Negro American League, had a one–year stint with the Birmingham Black Barons, then returned to the Red Sox. During his baseball career, Pride's team played postseason games against such stars as Elston Howard, Monte Irvin, Willie Mays, Hank Aaron, and Warren Spahn. In off–seasons he returned to Sledge to complete his high school education.

In November 1956 Pride was drafted into the U.S. Army. After basic training, he was sent to quartermaster school at Fort Carson, Colorado, and remained there, assigned to Special Services. In December 1956, he married Rozene Cohran of Oxford, Mississippi. They eventually had three children: Craig, Dion, and Angela. He spent 14 months in the military, was discharged, and returned to the Memphis Red Sox. Pride was hopeful that a major league baseball team would offer him a contract, but none was offered. In the spring of 1960, Pride moved his family to Missoula, Montana, where he signed with the Missoula Timberjacks of the Pioneer League. Pride also worked with the American Smelting & Refining Company beginning in 1960 and played on its baseball team, the East Helena Smelterites.

For a brief time, Pride played with the semipro Amvets in Montana and sang the national anthem over the public address system before ballgames, and if time permitted he tacked on one or two country tunes. He also sang at local bars. Baseball, however, remained his passion. He tried out the New York Mets and the Los Angeles (now Anaheim) Angels, but was unsuccessful. Pride wrote in his autobiography, ''Since leaving home, baseball had been my obsession. I had pursued it with a single–mindedness that left me with little capacity for anything else–except family, and at times I'm sure even that part of my life suffered from my infatuation with the diamond.''

Begins Career as a Country Singer

After failing to win a spot on the New York Mets roster in 1963, manager Casey Stengel offered Pride a bus ticket to Montana. Pride accepted the offer, but routed himself through Nashville. While there, he arrived at Cedarwood Publishing Company–the firm Woodrow ''Red'' Sovine, who had heard him sing in Missoula, advised him to contact. While at Cedarwood he met Jack Johnson, who had been looking for a black country singer and encountered Pride by accident. After listening to Pride sing a few songs, Johnson was impressed and, according to Pride's autobiography, commented ''I can do something for you.'' He wanted to change Pride's name to George Washington W. Jones III, a name Johnson considered appropriate for a black singer. ''There ain't gonna be no name changing. My name is Charley Frank Pride,'' the singer replied adamantly.

Pride hired Johnson as his manager and returned to Missoula. In late 1965, he signed a recording contract with RCA records. Jack Clement, Pride's producer, decided that Pride's first released single would be ''Snakes Crawl at Night.'' However, Pride wanted the song ''Just Between You and Me'' to be his first release. Pride eventually concluded that neither RCA nor Clement wanted a black country and western singer to sing love songs. He was also prevented from recording one of his favorite songs, ''Green Green Grass of Home,'' because one line included the words ''there runs Mary/hair of gold and lips like cherries.'' The prevailing attitudes of the time held that a black man could not sing about a blond girlfriend, or trouble would follow. When ''Just Between You and Me'' was released in 1966 and began climbing the charts, Pride knew that he was headed for success. A few months after the release of ''Just Between You and Me,'' Pride traveled to Detroit and appeared on stage with country stars Merle Haggard, Buck Owens, and Red Foley.

The Detroit concert did not assure Pride a place in country music. In fact, he still faced an uphill struggle. The Civil Rights Movement had made some people edgy about protests and sit–ins. Many nightclub managers feared that violence might erupt if they booked Pride. Those who heard Pride perform, however, loved him. Around this time he appeared at Chicago's prestigious Club Rivoli, singing the first night to a crowd of 80 and the next night to a capacity of 800. Pride's early music career continued to be difficult and he felt anxious about being accepted in the various cities where he performed. Race was often an issue. In his autobiography Pride revealed an incident that occurred at the end of show in Texarkana—a town that straddles the Arkansas and Texas border. A man approached him and said, ''I'm the Grand Wizard of the Ku Klux Klan here.'' Before Pride could gain his composure the man added, ''I just want to shake hands with a man.'' Pride had yet another experience when he made his first USO tour in Germany, where, by choice, black and white soldiers sat on separate sides of the room. Black soldiers heckled him mildly because he sang country music. ''When you gonna do one for us brothers?'' he was asked. He replied: ''I'm singing for my brothers on this side of the room and for my brothers on this side. I told you in the beginning. I'm not James Brown. I'm not Sam Cooke. I'm Charley Pride, country singer. I'm just me and that's what you get.''

By 1966, Pride's career was on the upswing. He attracted large crowds and several country music publications named him the Most Promising Male Artist. He sang before the Country Music Convention in Nashville in October that year and received a standing ovation. Pride joined the Willie Nelson tour, which he believed "opened some doors, partly because it dispelled a lot of anxieties about the race factor" as they performed in areas known for being segregationist strongholds. His continued popularity allowed him to tour with Faron Young, Ernest Tubb, and Buck Owens.

Pride's touring was interrupted briefly in 1968 when he suffered from manic depression resulting from a brain chemical imbalance. Pride refused to take medication for this condition and by 1982, the depression had recurred. After he was hospitalized for depression in 1989, Pride finally came to terms with his illness and began taking the prescribed medication.

Appears on Grand Ole Opry

Charley Pride became the first black singer to perform at the Grand Ole Opry in Nashville in January 1967. That evening, he sang "Snakes Crawl at Night" and a Hank Williams number, "I Can't Help It If I'm Still in Love with You." By this time Pride's first recorded album, *Country Charley Pride,* was a best seller. His first gold album was *The Best of Charley Pride,* released in 1969; it moved to number one on country charts in 1970. Pride continued to release albums and nearly all nine of those released between 1970 and 1972 appeared on country and pop charts; six of the albums won gold record awards. Since then, 12 of Pride's 40 LPs have gone gold in the United States.

Pride's popularity soared from the 1960s onward as his singles (numbering over five million) topped the record charts and became the most frequently played songs on country and western stations. As a result, Pride toured widely and appeared on a number of television programs, including *The Lawrence Welk Show, Hee Haw, The Tom Jones Show,* and *The Johnny Cash Show.* In 1970 he won his first Gold Single Award for "Kiss an Angel Good Morning," which was his first crossover song and his biggest country hit, reaching the Top 20 on the pop charts. On October 10, 1971, he was the only double winner at the Country Music Association's presentation at the Grand Ole Opry, when he was named Entertainer of the Year and Male Vocalist of the Year. The Music Operations of America presented him with the Entertainer of the Year award a short time later. Pride won two Grammy Awards in 1971 when his album *Did You Think to Pray* was named Best Sacred Performance and his single "Let Me Live" was named Best Gospel Performance. He won a Grammy again in 1972 for *Charley Pride Sings Heart Songs.* In 1976 Pride received the American Music Award's Favorite Male Vocalist in Country Music. In 1980 *Cash Box* magazine named him the Top Male Country Artist of the Decade (for the 1970s) and Top Male Vocalist on the country list in 1985.

Pride dissolved his contract with RCA records in 1985 and joined a new label, 16th Avenue Records. The first record he cut on the new label, "Have I Got Some Blues for You" moved into the Top 10 on the *Billboard* charts. Pride also began playing in Branson, Missouri—now one of the major entertainment centers in America—in 1992 and has since opened his own theater there. He returns to Nashville for the annual celebration, Fanfare, which enables fans to meet country stars in person.

Charley Pride has earned the love and respect of country music fans as well as music lovers generally. He has a special concern for young singers who are entering the country music field.

Current address: Charley Pride International Fan Club, PO Box 670507, Dallas, TX 75367–0507.

REFERENCES

The African American Almanac. 6th ed. Detroit: Gale Research, 1994.

The Comprehensive Country Music Encyclopedia. New York: Random House, 1994.

Current Biography Yearbook. New York: H. W. Wilson Co., 1975.

Ebony, March 1967.

Ebony Success Library. Vols. 1–2. Nashville: Southwestern Publishing Co.

Pride, Charley, and Jim Henderson. *Pride: The Charley Pride Story.* New York: William Morrow, 1994.

Southern, Eileen. *Biographical Dictionary of Afro–American and African Musicians.* Westport, CT: Greenwood Press, 1982.

Stambler, Irwin, and Grelun Landon. *The Encyclopedia of Folk, Country & Western Music.* 2nd ed. New York: St. Martin's Press, 1983.

Who's Who among Black Americans, 1994–95. 8th ed. Detroit: Gale Research, 1994.

Jessie Carney Smith

Henry Hugh Proctor

(1868–1933)

Minister, writer, lecturer

Henry Hugh Proctor, a promotor of racial pride among blacks, spent a lifetime working to strengthen the spiritual, social, and cultural life of black people. He called the African American spiritual black people's great gift to the world. He promoted black Congregationalism, fought disenfranchisement, and worked to improve race relations. Although he embraced the concept of self–help—but not in the same vein as Booker T. Washington—he also successfully raised funds in the white community, securing funds from wherever he could to support the community outreach activities of his church.

The youngest of two brothers and two sisters, Henry Hugh Proctor was born on December 8, 1868, in a farm cabin near Fayetteville, Tennessee. His father, Richard Proctor, was born a slave in South Carolina, and his mother, Hannah Murray Proctor, was born a slave in Mississippi. They met in Alabama before the Civil War, moving to Tennessee and working as sharecroppers after they were freed in the 1860s. The Proctor family moved some miles away to another farm cabin in Clifton before young Henry started school. Proctor began his education in a rural school five miles from their Clifton home, which was open for only three months a year and between crops. It was here that he gave his first speech, at a closing exhibition, and that he heard his first sermon–the building served as a church as well as a school.

Proctor was 12–years old before he saw a town, Fayetteville, some 12 miles away with a population of 2,000. The family later moved there, where schools were better and the term ran for nine months. Young Proctor completed the school course and was an apprentice in the county district schools, first as an assistant then as teacher at a little school on Pea Ridge, where he earned $25 a month. Later he became principal of his school in Fayetteville.

The experiences of seeing the city lights of Fayetteville earlier and his conversion to Christianity later own made a mark on Proctor. After the conversion, he became anxious to increase his education. In 1884 he entered Central Tennessee College in Nashville for one term and in the same year transferred to nearby Fisk University. Having lost his savings when the banks failed, Proctor worked his way through school by digging ditches, setting type, teaching, preaching, and contributions from friends in the North.

Among Proctor's schoolmates were scholar and activist W. E. B. Du Bois and Margaret Murray—later the wife of the influential black leader Booker T. Washington—whom Proctor introduced to the county where he lived and where she taught school. Among the faculty and administrators who shaped his life were Henry S. Bennett, who organized the Congregational Church at Fisk, and the school's president Erastus Milo Cravath, a Christian statesman. It was at Fisk that Proctor was called to the Christian ministry. After graduating from Fisk seven years later in 1891 with a B.A. degree, Proctor entered Yale University Divinity School. During his three years at Yale, Proctor and the three other black divinity school students who were there each year formed a quartet and sang "Negro melodies" in churches throughout New England. Proctor wrote in his autobiographical sketches, *Between Black and White,* "I sometimes say I dug my way through Fisk and sang it through Yale." His graduating thesis at Yale was on the theology of slave songs of the South, subsequently published in Hampton Institute's *Southern Workman.* He was graduated from Yale in 1894, and was one of eight students the faculty chose to speak on graduation day. His address on "A New Ethnic Contribution to Christianity" was later published in *The Congregationalist.*

Henry Hugh Proctor

Proctor married Adeline Davis, a fellow student at Fisk and also a faculty member there earlier, in 1893. They had five children: Henry Hugh, Muriel, Lillian, Roy Cravath, and Vashti Adeline.

Ordained into the Congregational ministry, Proctor was appointed pastor of the First Congregational Church on Houston Street in Atlanta, where he served until 1920. The church was one of the largest and best–known black churches in America. He reached Atlanta on Memorial Day to serve a church founded one year before he was born. Its ministers were from New England, graduates of Yale who organized Storrs School—the first school for blacks in Georgia. The American Missionary Association (AMA) founded the church in 1867 in the Storrs School facility, following its practice of building a church beside each of its schools.

Helps Organize NCCWACP

In 1903 Proctor and George W. Henderson, a professor at Straight University in New Orleans (which later became Dillard University), organized the National Convention of Congregational Workers among the Colored People (NCCWACP). The convention brought together young blacks from all over the country who were church and school workers in Congregational churches. The convention worked to help black Congregational churches support themselves and to improve the theological education programs in those schools founded by the AMA. The AMA, founded by the Congregational church, established six black colleges in the South, including Dillard and Atlanta University, and a number of elementary and high schools for blacks. Proctor was president of the convention from 1906 to 1908 and corresponding secretary from 1908 until his death in 1933.

While attending a NCCWACP convention in Memphis in 1906, Proctor learned of the Atlanta Riot which broke out on Saturday, September 22, and lasted for one week. He returned home to the find that many Atlantans had been killed or wounded. Meanwhile, Proctor and white attorney Charles T. Hopkins, a native–born Southerner, met to plan strategies for easing the racial tension. They called in 20 whites and 20 blacks who formed the Interracial Committee of Atlanta and worked together until peace was restored. This marked the beginning of a movement for interracial cooperation in the South, as other cities adopted their plan. Some blacks misinterpreted Proctor's actions, accusing him of producing the riots because a week earlier he had warned the city council that "city blood would run in the streets" if the local dives (disreputable entertainment establishments) were not closed. The local press also printed false information. All the time Proctor's aim had been for peace.

In his struggle for racial harmony and uplift of the black race, Proctor began to confer with Booker T. Washington, having met him when he came to Atlanta to deliver the Cotton States and International Exposition Speech in 1895. Washington regularly spoke at Proctor's church and was a guest in his home, helped raise money for the church, and was one of his correspondents. It was Proctor who promoted Washington's speaking engagements in Georgia. The connection also led Proctor to leading people in the North, who helped him secure funds for his new church. Proctor witnessed harmonious work between Washington and W. E. B. Du Bois, although the two had opposing views on race matters. Sometimes the two men went to Proctor's house at night where they conferred on plans that were afterward put into practice. Proctor wrote in his autobiographical sketches, "They are the right and left wings of a great movement. Just as a bird must have both wings for successful flight, so must any movement have the radical and conservative wings." Proctor believed that people needed a broadness of spirit to work together for racial unity. "This spirit of cooperation, not only between the various wings of the race but also between white and black, was perhaps the chief contribution the First Congregational Church of Atlanta made to social betterment during the quarter of a century of my pastorate," he continued.

Proctor built in Atlanta a new church facility that he called an "industrial temple" that aimed to address the spiritual, physical, and social needs of the community. Washington spoke at the groundbreaking in 1908. The new building offered an employment bureau, Sunday school, and such facilities as a kindergarten, library, a ladies' parlor, reading room, model kitchen, sewing room, gymnasium, and gallery. The auditorium had a seating capacity of 1,000. In the absence of local YMCA and YWCA (Young Men's and Young Women's Christian Associations) facilities for blacks in Atlanta, the church filled an important gap in social services as well. It also maintained the Avery Home for Working Girls—the first such home in the world opened by any church for young black girls—and carried on mission work in the slums. The church also supported the Carrie Steele Orphanage in Atlanta, and Proctor served on its board of directors. Presidents Theodore Roosevelt and William Howard Taft were among the notable personalities who visited the church services.

It was at Proctor's church that the first temperance society in Georgia was established. For admission applicants were required to sign a pledge of total abstinence from alcohol as were all members of the church. Proctor was an advocate of cultural activities as well and considered music a vital part of church and everyday life. Since black residents were denied admission to Atlanta's operas that had attracted the great stars of the Metropolitan Opera, in 1910 Proctor organized the Atlanta Music Festival Association to bring the best black musical talent to the city, to instill racial pride, and to promote the black musical heritage. Among the performers appearing first at the Municipal Auditorium–Armory and later in the auditorium at First Congregational Church were Harry T. Burleigh, Anita Patti Brown, Lulu Vere Childers, Samuel Coleridge–Taylor, Will Marion Cook, Roland Hayes, Clarence Cameron White, and Carl Diton. On programs as well were choirs and choruses from black colleges, including those from Morehouse College, Tuskegee Institute, Howard University, and the Fisk Jubilee Singers.

The Church and Black Aristocracy

First Congregational Church was not without critics, nor was Proctor. John Dittmer in *Black Georgia in the Progressive Era* charged that Atlanta's black aristocracy was attracted to the church and that Proctor and other light–skinned persons had "exclusive mulattoes in their society and for their associates." The chief contemporary "mulatto–baiter" was journalist Benjamin Jefferson Davis Sr., who wrote editorials for his *Atlanta Independent,* quoted in Dittmer. In *Aristocrats of Color,* Willard B. Gatewood quoted Davis who said that the black upper class of Atlanta, most of whom were members of Proctor's church, was comprised of "the artificials, the superficials, the seemers, would–bes, race leaders, posers, wish–I–was white social sets, [and] educated idlers." Further, Gatewood claimed that elitism "was perhaps inherent in Congregationalisn" at that time.

According to Du Bois in *Social and Physical Conditions of Negroes in Cities,* quoted by Gatewood, Proctor proclaimed in 1897 that "We must come into close personal touch with the masses." To those who object, presuming that the common people will "presume upon our social reserve," he added that "there is not the least danger in the plainest people mistaking our kindly interest as an invitation to our private social functions. . . The immaculate swan comes in spotted from the vilest sewer." He continued by saying "you can not elevate society by lifting from the top; you must put the jackscrews under the mudsills of society. Put the unfailing dynamics of friendly visitation under the homes of the poor and the whole people will rise." By the time Proctor left the Atlanta assignment, he had built the congregation from 100, when he arrived, to 1,000 members.

In the 1890s Proctor, a Republican, worked with Du Bois, Washington, and other black leaders to protest the illegal segregation of blacks on Pullman cars. They were unsuccessful in their attempts to persuade the Georgia legislature to overturn the segregation law enacted in 1899 that extended the Jim Crow practice, which continued until after World War II. Proctor, along with other black leaders such as businessman Alonzo F. Herndon, politician Henry L. Rucker, and educator George A. Townsend, was involved in political agitation in 1907, petitioning legislators to defeat an amendment requiring registrants to meet one of five specific qualifications to be able to vote.

A number of successful black leaders, including Proctor, Du Bois, and John Hope of Morehouse College, were men of great racial pride. They knew of all–black towns, such as Mound Bayou in Mississippi, and discussed the possibility of establishing a black colony on the Georgia coast, near Brunswick.

In 1919 in the aftermath of World War I, the War Department asked Proctor to go to Europe as a chaplain to boost the morale of black troops there. He visited France and spoke to more than 275,000 black soldiers during his 4,000–mile trip. Returning home in 1920, he was called to the Nazarene Congregational Church located at Lefferts Place and Grand Avenue in Brooklyn. Under his leadership membership grew from 160 to more than 1,000.

Proctor was assistant moderator of the National Council of the Congregational Churches of the United States in 1904–06. During this same period he was vice–president of the Urban League of Brooklyn and of the Brooklyn Lincoln Settlement. He was vice–president of the AMA from 1906 to 1909 and a member of the American Board of Commissioners for Foreign Missions from 1923 to 1930. From 1926 until his death, he was moderator of the New York City Congregational Church Association, the first black to hold this distinction. Proctor was also highly active in the alumni program of his alma mater, Fisk University, particularly in the 1920s and early 1930s. He set up and directed the first concerted efforts at organized fund raising that, once launched in the early 1920s, brought in enough nickels, dimes, and pennies from the national black community to reach $100,000 and save Fisk from financial disaster. In 1926 Proctor became one the first three alumni elected to the board of trustees.

Proctor lectured widely and became known for his address on ''The Burden of the Negro.'' He contributed frequently to the *American Missionary* and the *Congregationalist.* In 1931 his series on ''Negro Migration from the South'' was published in the *New York Herald Tribune,* which had requested the articles. In addition to *Between Black and White,* he wrote *Sermons in Negro Melody,* published in 1916. He was founder of the *Georgia Congregationalist,* later called *The Congregational Worker*—the official organ of black Congregationalists. In recognition of his early achievements, in 1904 Clark University in Atlanta awarded Proctor an honorary Doctor of Divinity degree. He died on May 12, 1933, in Brooklyn.

Proctor was an influential leader who rose to prominence after Atlanta's race riots as a peacemaker, and led his church to become a viable social force in the black community.

REFERENCES

Biography File, Special Collections, Fisk University Library.

Dittmer, John. *Black Georgia in the Progressive Era, 1900–1920.* Urbana: University of Illinois Press, 1977.

Foster, Lemuel L. ''Statement Read by Andrew J. Allison At Dr. Proctor's Funeral.'' *Fisk News* 6 (April 1933): 4–7.

Gatewood, Willard B. *Aristocrats of Color.* Bloomington: Indiana University Press, 1990.

Grant, Donald L. *The Way It Was in the South: The Black Experience in Georgia.* New York: Carol Publishing Group, 1993.

Harland, Louis R., and Ramond W. Smock, eds. *The Booker T. Washington Papers.* Vol. 5, 1899–1900. Urbana: University of Illinois Press, 1976.

Johns, Altona Trent. ''Henry Hugh Proctor.'' *Black Perspective in Music* 3 (Spring 1975): 25–32.

Logan, Rayford W., and Michael R. Winston, eds. *Dictionary of American Negro Biography.* New York: Norton, 1985.

Malone, Dumas, ed. *Dictionary of American Biography.* New York: Charles Scribner's Sons, 1943.

Murphy, Larry G., J. Gordon Melton, and Gary L. Ward, eds. *Encyclopedia of African American Religions.* New York: Garland Publishing, 1993.

Proctor, Henry Hugh. *Between Black and White.* 1925. Reprint, Freeport, NY: Books for Libraries, 1971.

Richardson, Joe M. *A History of Fisk University, 1865–1946.* University: University of Alabama Press, 1980.

Who's Who in Colored America. 1927. Vol. 1. New York: Who's Who in Colored America Corp.

COLLECTIONS

The papers of Henry Hugh Proctor are in the Amistad Research Center, Tulane University, New Orleans.

Jessie Carney Smith

Samuel D. Proctor

(1914–1997)

Minister, educator, public servant, orator

Educator, theologian, social activist, and Christian icon Samuel D. Proctor was a powerful public speaker who quickly won over an audience by making difficult concepts understandable. When he delivered a message he spoke to all age groups and genders because he was able to weave contemporary thought with the abiding faith that he lived by and believed. Proctor believed in the inherent good of humanity and rejected the negative image that appeared in the media as accurate descriptions of the African American community. He chided us to recall success mechanisms that have worked for us in the past and to renew the most powerful of them all, faith. He spoke of hope.

Samuel Dewitt Proctor was born on July 13, 1914, to Velma Gladys Hughes Proctor and Herbert Proctor. His parents were students together at Norfolk Mission College just as his maternal grandparents had been when they met and married. Proctor and his five siblings grew up in a loving home that had a strong spiritual foundation. His family was active in church life. Aunts and uncles sang in the choirs and played the organ in several churches. Four of his uncles were pastors and two of the largest churches in Norfolk were founded by his great–grandfather Zechariah Hughes. Proctor recalled in *The Substance of Things Hoped For* that "Church and family were like a seamless garment." For the Proctors, all facets of their religion were "as close as breathing and nearer than hands and feet." Proctor recalled that, "We never sat down to eat anything—a bowl of oatmeal, a piece of buttered spoon bread, a chicken leg—without bowing our heads and mumbling a fast prayer."

Proctor attended Virginia State College on a music scholarship and graduated in 1942 with the A.B. degree. He had been an outstanding student and skipped three grades, putting him in college at the same time as his older sister and brother. Although money was a problem, Proctor's faith and hard work helped him to succeed.

Samuel D. Proctor

Preacher and Professor

Proctor's career was threefold; heading a church, teaching theology, and serving the public. In 1943 he was ordained to the ministry. He was a graduate student at the University of Pennsylvania in 1944–45 and also received a B.D. degree from Crozer Theological Seminary in 1945. During his year at Crozer he was the only black student. Proctor was the pastor of the Pond Street Church in Providence, Rhode Island, from 1945 to 1959. In 1945–46 he spent four days of each week attending to his duties at Pond Church and the other three studying for a doctorate at Yale University in New Haven. He ultimately transferred from Yale to Boston University to be closer to his family and graduated in 1950 with the Th.D. degree. Proctor soon found that as a minister with a formal education he would be responsible for nurturing his congregation's spiritual growth and also would be involved in social activism. Soon after he was called to the Pond Street Church he became a leader in the efforts to pass a Fair Employment Practices Act in the Rhode Island legislature. During a return visit to Crozer in 1950, he met Martin Luther King Jr., a student there at the time, and established a relationship with him that remained intact over the years.

From 1949 to 1950 Proctor was dean of the School of Religion and professor of religion and ethics at Virginia Union University, which was founded less than a mile from the plantation his grandmother grew up on as a slave. He continued to teach at the school and lectured widely and by 1953 he was vice–president of Virginia Union University. While he was vice president he was invited by the American Baptist Foreign Mission to join a team of clergy which was to implement the transfer of institutions under American control to the control of indigenous people. Their job was, in consultation with the Burmese and Indian missions, to put in place the procedures for transition.

Proctor was president of Virginia Union from 1955 to 1960. In 1960 he moved to North Carolina to become president of the Agricultural and Technical College of North Carolina, as it was known then. He was president of the college until 1964, but was on leave from 1963 to 1964 while he served as the associate director of the Peace Corps in Nigeria and Washington, D.C. From 1964 until 1965 he was the associate general secretary for the National Council of Churches. From 1965 through 1966 he worked in the Office of Economic Opportunity as special assistant to the director and director of the North East Region. For the following two years, 1966–68, Proctor was president of the Institute for Service to Education. He came back to academe at the University of Wisconsin as dean of special projects for a year, 1968–69. He then moved on to Rutgers University in 1969 and was professor of education in the graduate school until 1984, when he became professor emeritus. While at Rutgers, he also held the position of senior minister of the Abyssinian Baptist Church from 1972 until 1989. He succeeded Adam Clayton Powell Jr., who kept the Abyssinian Baptist Church in the forefront of the civil rights struggle. Proctor continued the tradition. Under his leadership the church created the

Abyssinian Housing Development Program which provides over 50 housing units to needy families in Harlem. Proctor also invited the New York Philharmonic to give annual concerts at the church.

Proctor's Philosophy

In 1966 the National Board of the Young Men's Christian Association published Samuel Proctor's *The Young Negro in America: 1960–1980,* in which Proctor acknowledged African Americans' need for literacy and skill development and showed a keen understanding of the young African Americans of that period. Proctor did not excuse violent behavior but understood the genesis of the frustration that black youth were experiencing at that time. He saw blacks as human, and with all of the strengths and frailties that come with being mere mortals. In a chapter from *The Young Negro In America: 1960–1980* entitled ''Outliving the Stereotype'' he noted that in spite of their reputed docility blacks were not more naturally non–violent that any other group. ''A sophisticated theory of non–violence,'' he wrote, ''is the result of tireless spiritual discipline such as Gandhi's, and what makes us think that the Negro is more capable of such discipline than the Klansman?''

Proctor believed that there is enough room in American society for diversity. In the *Young Negro in America* he insisted that people not be given immutable labels based upon race. He told all Americans that outliving the stereotypes does not mean the diminishing of their heritages. It means ''stepping out of the mire of bad statistics in those matters that affect any and all Americans, mortality rates, crime rates, financial competence, educational attainment, and political participation.'' The title of Proctor's most recent book, *Substance of Things Hoped For: A Memoir of African–American Faith* came from Paul's letter to the Hebrews (''Now faith is the substance of things hoped for, the evidence of things not seen''), and encapsulated his belief that religious faith has sustained African Americans and remains the key to survival and improvement.

Proctor was recognized widely for his work. His awards include: the Distinguished Service Award, State University of New York at Plattsburgh (1966); the Outstanding Alumnus Award, Boston University; the Rutgers Medal for Distinguished Service; and 45 honorary degrees from colleges and universities. In addition to the books mentioned above, he wrote *Sermons from the Black Pulpit* (1984), *The Epistle to the Abyssinians and Other Sermons of Inspiration* (1977), and *Preaching about Crisis in the Community* (1988).

While speaking to students at Cornell College in Mount Vernon, Iowa, on Wednesday, May 25, 1997, Proctor suffered a heart attack. He died the next day in Mercy Medical Center, Cedar Rapids, Iowa. He also had suffered an attack earlier, in 1979, and had been hospitalized then. He was 75 years old when he died. Proctor and his wife, Bessie Louise Tate Proctor, had been married for 52 years and lived in Somerset, New Jersey. His funeral was held a week after his death, at the church he had pastored, Abyssinian Baptist Church in Harlem. He was survived by his wife and by four sons—Herbert, of Roselle, New Jersey; Timothy D., of Durham, North Carolina; Samuel T., of Detroit, Michigan; and Steven, of Brunswick, New Jersey. His survivors also included five grandchildren; a great–grandson; one sister, Harriet Tyler of Philadelphia; and one brother, Oliver W. Proctor. Samuel D. Proctor was well known as a quiet activist and a charismatic orator who even in his retirement years was one of the most sought after speakers in America. Comments made at Proctor's funeral, quoted in the *New York Times* for May 31, 1997, characterized his work: Lawrence Carter, dean of the chapel at Morehouse College, said that ''He never wasted a sentence,'' and Jesse Jackson said, ''He came preaching and teaching, and he left preaching and teaching.''

REFERENCES

''Johnson Adds Four Poverty Aides; Proctor Will Head Office Here.'' *New York Times,* September 13, 1964.

''Preachers Turn Out to Honor Samuel Proctor.'' *New York Times,* May 31, 1997.

Proctor, Samuel D. *My Moral Odyssey.* Valley Forge, PA: Judson Press, 1989.

———. *The Substance of Things Hoped For: A Memoir of African–American Faith.* New York: G. P. Putnam's Sons, 1996.

———. *The Young Negro in America.* New York: National Board of the Young Men's Christian Association, 1966.

———, and William Watley. *Sermons from the Black Pulpit.* Valley Forge, PA: Judson Press, 1984.

Salzman, Jack, David Lionel Smith, and Cornell West, eds. *Encyclopedia of African–American Culture and History.* New York: Macmillan Library Reference USA/Simon and Schuster Macmillan, 1996.

''Samuel Proctor, 75, Ex–Pastor of Abyssinian Baptist Church.'' *New York Times,* May 26, 1997.

''Teachers Taught About the Negro.'' *New York Times,* December 5, 1965.

Who's Who among African Americans, 1996–97. 9th ed. Detroit: Gale Research, 1996.

Audrey Williams

Gabriel Prosser

(1775?–1800)

Slave, insurrectionist

Virginia slave Gabriel, popularly known as Gabriel Prosser, was the primary leader of what is considered to be earliest attempt at a large–scale slave revolt on U.S. soil. Despite months of careful planning, the attack on Richmond failed disastrously. Prosser and a number of his co–conspirators were captured, tried and hanged.

Gabriel Prosser was born to an African–born mother about 1775 in Henrico County, Virginia. He grew up a slave of Thomas H. Prosser, a tavern keeper and landowner who had a reputation for being a brutal master. Gabriel Prosser had at least two brothers, Martin and Solomon, who also lived on the Prosser estate. A blacksmith by trade, he was regularly lent out to persons in nearby Richmond and the surrounding area. He was married to a woman named Nanny.

A large man, Prosser stood about six–feet two–inches tall. He was missing two front teeth, and had several scars on his head. His mistress is credited with teaching him reading and writing (the education of slaves was not tightly restricted at the time). What he lacked in education, Prosser was said to make up for in common sense. A deeply religious man, he was strongly influenced by the Bible, especially Old Testament stories of liberation and vengeance. Emulating Samson, the hero of the Book of Judges whose superhuman strength was due to his flowing hair, Prosser wore his hair long.

Planning a Revolt

Rumors of insurrections were not uncommon in Virginia, both before and after the American Revolution. Buoyed by knowledge of the new country's documents of liberty, black slaves were inspired to win freedom for themselves, as well. By 1800, several slaves were independently recruiting others to join their ranks for a massive slave rebellion in central Virginia. The leader of these loosely affiliated groups was a slave named Jack Bowler, also known as Jack Ditcher. How long this unfocused plan was active is uncertain. By the spring of 1800, Prosser had certainly become involved in it.

As Prosser's involvement increased, his leadership abilities emerged. Before long, the 25–year–old was regarded by many as the movement's leader. Eventually, a vote was taken to determine who should be in charge, Prosser or Bowler. Prosser easily won the majority of votes cast; Bowler was made the second in command.

Prosser spent months planning the attack, which focused on capturing Richmond, the state's new capital. Often he would spend Sunday, his day off, in Richmond to become familiar with its layout and size up its defenses. (Before this and other early–nineteenth–century revolts, slaves had much more freedom of movement than they did subsequently.)

Slaves often gathered in the vicinity of the brook bridge on the Prosser property for religious occasions, fish fries and barbecues. These events proved excellent opportunities, or covers, for recruiting conspirators and passing information. On Sunday, August 10, there was much discussion among the plotters concerning the date for their rebellion. Some wanted to delay it indefinitely, while others, including Prosser, were ready to take action. Prosser drafted his brother Martin, a preacher, to persuade the conspirators to act quickly. Martin quoted Bible passages and cited pragmatic reasons such as available food from the impending harvest, the last weeks of warm weather, and inactive slave patrols to convince the crowd to accept late August as the target date for the assault. The slave army assented and agreed to meet the following Sunday to firm up details.

Prosser's plan called for a three–pronged attack on Richmond, a city of about 8,000 white residents. An army of more than 1,000 slaves would gather on the night of August 30, a Saturday, at the Brook Swamp on the Prosser estate, about six miles northwest of Richmond. They would march behind a banner invoking the American, French, and Haitian Revolutions, emblazoned with the words ''Death or Liberty.''

The first group would set fire to the dockside warehouse district on the southern end of the city. That would force residents to leave their homes to fight the blaze, while diverting their attention from the heart of the city. Meanwhile, the other two columns would attack from the north with the intention of capturing the capitol building, seizing the contents of the arms depositories and kidnaping the governor, future–president James Monroe. The bridges leading into Richmond would be secured in order to allow other slaves safe passage into the city to join their numbers, while keeping whites from surrounding areas from sending a counter force into the city. Prosser's plan also included killing all the whites in Richmond, save Frenchmen, Methodists, Quakers, and poor women without slaves, groups deemed sympathetic to their cause.

The conspirators had a small amount of ammunition ready for the assault. Ten pounds of gun powder had been purchased, and Prosser and Martin had made nearly a peck of bullets. In the meantime, their brother Solomon, a blacksmith on the estate, had turned six scythes into 12 crude but effective swords. Many of the force were to carry crossbows, spears, or heavy clubs until they managed to acquire firearms during their pillaging.

Prosser was effective in organizing the necessary forces, once estimating that he would be able to amass a force of 10,000 slaves in the course of the attack (the area around Richmond was believed to be home to 32,000 slaves). He also made plans to contact the Catawba Indians to invite them to join his ranks once the attack got underway.

If all went as planned, Prosser expected a spontaneous revolt to erupt in all parts of the state. Prosser advocated the initial slaughter of whites in the hope that a campaign of terror would demoralize whites and paralyze their will to resist. Later, after accomplishing his initial objectives, he planned to show mercy on nonbelligerent whites. In fact, he thought that poor whites might be persuaded to join in the fight against the rich, who kept them down as well.

Many historians believe that Prosser thought that a general revolt would force Monroe to concede to his terms. He wanted either a new country for freed blacks within the state's boundaries, or, at the very least, the liberation of the state's slaves along with a guarantee of clearly defined political rights. Some historians maintain that Prosser had much larger goals in mind. They believe that he was prepared to go county by county to free all the slaves within the state's borders and then, after stabilizing his gains, aid similar revolts in neighboring states.

The Revolt Betrayed

On the day of the proposed attack, two slaves of the Chopart family, Tom and Pharaoh, went to Mosby Chopart and informed him of the impending events. Chopart then contacted Governor James Monroe. Despite having to overstep his authority to muster the militia, Monroe quickly took action. A 30–man guard was sent to the penitentiary where the public arms were held, a 20–man guard was placed at the magazine, and a 15–man guard stood watch at the Capitol. Patrols were sent to reconnoiter key routes to the city.

At noon it had begun to rain. By evening, the main road leading to the city from the Prosser property was flooded. Torrential rains, possibly the result of an off–coast hurricane, were filling low areas to the point of virtually isolating the Prosser estate. Making their way to the city was now all but impossible for the attack force. Prosser and his lieutenants postponed the assault to the next night and disbanded the group.

The next morning, another slave informed his master, William Mosby, of the plot. Mosby also went to Monroe with the information. Before the insurgents could be reassembled, more militiamen were summoned and set loose on the countryside around the Brook Swamp.

Dozens of slaves were rounded up. The authorities were amazed at the apparent size of the conspiracy, as each newly questioned slave implicated ever more of their number. It soon became clear to the whites that they could not hang all the insurrectionists; doing so would decimate the slave population, causing a labor shortage.

Monroe made Richmond an armed camp in the hope of discouraging any further slave uprisings. He also offered $300 rewards for the capture of Prosser and Jack Bowler. After hiding out for several days, Bowler was talked into surrendering by a black man named Peter White. White was shocked when he received only $50 in reward money; the $300 had been meant for whites only.

Prosser managed to elude his pursuers for two weeks before boarding the schooner, Mary, on September 21. The three–masted ship had run aground about four miles below Richmond. The captain of the ship, Richardson Taylor, was a Methodist antislavery advocate with a largely black crew. Although informed of Prosser's identity and the $300 reward, Taylor did nothing to collect. Instead, he headed downriver to Norfolk. Once there, two of the slave crewmen, Billy and Isham, notified authorities of Prosser's whereabouts in order to collect the reward money. The ship was boarded and Prosser was placed in chains.

Prosser put up no resistance, but told his captors that he would confess only to Monroe. He was taken back to Richmond and on September 27 was brought before Monroe at the governor's mansion, where a crowd had gathered outside. Monroe was disappointed, however, when Prosser stoically kept silent, being unwilling to give up the names of his co–conspirators in order to protect them. He was then taken to the penitentiary, a building he had hoped to capture nearly a month before. He maintained his silence during visits from a committee of council members and from Monroe himself.

On October 3, Prosser was tried, convicted, and sentenced. He was given a brief stay of execution in the hope that he would divulge details of the plot. He remained silent. Four days later, on October 7, Prosser and Bowler were hanged. In all, 35 slaves were hanged for their part in the attempted uprising.

What has become known as the Gabriel Insurrection had serious ramifications. Whites in the antebellum (pre–Civil War) South, slave holders or not, were never at ease again. Their fears resulted in legislation to outlaw the education of slaves and to restrict the movements of blacks, both slave and free. Overseers began treating slaves ever more brutally and with even less concern for their general welfare. Conversely, the Virginia legislature passed a resolution in late 1800 in an attempt to persuade the national government to purchase lands to the west that would be set aside for free blacks and dangerous slaves to colonize. The resolution was revived in 1801, 1802, 1804, and 1816. That sentiment eventually prompted the creation of the American Colonization Society. Led by Henry Clay, the society was an influential organization up to the start of the Civil War.

Many modern historians believe that Prosser's plan would have worked had it not been for the catastrophic weather. Even with Monroe's prior knowledge of the revolt, the size of Prosser's force should have been enough to overwhelm the several dozen men who guarded a few key points in the city. Despite the magnitude of his actions, the name Prosser was all but forgotten in the nineteenth century. Whites, fearing that other blacks would emulate him, kept his name out of the public record. Nevertheless, folk stories kept his name alive among blacks. Through exhaustive research, twentieth–century historians have been able to uncover the role Prosser actually played in an important episode in American history. In so doing, Prosser has gained the fame he deserves.

REFERENCES

Kimball, William J. "The Gabriel Insurrection of 1800." *Negro History Bulletin* 34 (November 1971): 153–56.

Marszalek, John F. "Battle for Freedom—Gabriel's Insurrection." *Negro History Bulletin* 39 (March 1976): 540–43.

Salzman, Jack, David Lionel Smith, and Cornel West, eds. *Encyclopedia of African–American Culture and History.* New York: Macmillan Library Reference USA/Simon and Schuster Macmillan, 1996.

Williams, Michael W., ed. *The African American Encyclopedia.* New York: Marshall Cavendish, 1993.

Kevin C. Kretschmer

Robert Purvis
(1810–1898)
Abolitionist

A member of the tiny Northern pre–Civil War black elite, light–skinned enough to pass for white, and further set apart by substantial wealth, Robert Purvis was nevertheless an ardent and tireless advocate for the abolition of slavery and full rights for African Americans. His home outside Philadelphia was a stop on the Underground Railroad, the network which helped runaway slaves escape to free States and Canada. After the Civil War, he continued to speak out even as social and political changes dimmed the high hopes raised by Emancipation.

Robert Purvis was born on August 4, 1810, to William Purvis and Harriet Judah. His mother was a free woman of color and 22–years his father's junior. Although the two were not legally married, Purvis acknowledged the three children of the union, William Jr., Robert, and Joseph. According to the traditional account, Harriet was the daughter of a German, Baron Judah, and a freed slave, Dido Badaraka, who had been kidnapped from Morocco. A recent account traced her ancestry more prosaically to the ''Turks,'' a community of very mixed descent established near Stateburg, South Carolina. This group of light–skinned people shunned the label of ''black'' even though they were legally counted as free persons of color.

William Purvis (1762–1826) was an Englishman who emigrated to the United States about 1790 and became very wealthy as a cotton broker. The elder Purvis sent Robert and his brothers to Philadelphia to attend a private school in 1819 and moved there himself shortly after. He died of typhus seven years later, leaving Robert some $70,000. To all of his children he left a heritage of antislavery sentiment. When William Jr. died of tuberculosis in 1828, his share of the estate was divided between the two surviving brothers. Further property would came to Robert in 1869 on the death of his mother.

Settling Down

Purvis completed his formal education by spending a brief period at the recently founded Amherst College in Amherst, Massachusetts, and another brief period at a Pittsburgh academy. In Philadelphia, the Purvis brothers found a warm welcome in the home of James Forten Sr., who became like a father to them. Forten, a very wealthy businessman, and

Robert Purvis

his family were vitally interested in the struggle for the rights of African Americans. He eventually became father–in–law to Robert, who married Harriet Forten in 1831, and to Joseph, who became the husband of Sarah Forten in 1838.

Robert and Harriet probably lived with the Fortens until Purvis bought a house on Lombard Street in 1832. Their first child, William, was born in 1832. He would die in 1857, of tuberculosis like his brothers Joseph and Robert Jr. Between 1837 and 1848, seven more children were born to the couple: Joseph Parrish, Harriet, Charles Burleigh, Henry W., Robert, Granville Sharp, and Georgianna. Their mother herself died of tuberculosis in 1875. Purvis later married Tacy Townsend, a white Quaker from Byberry, a community near Philadelphia.

Purvis's growing family was matched by his growing wealth. He was a shrewd investor, especially in real estate in and near Philadelphia. In 1843 the Purvises purchased a farm in Byberry, where he set himself up as a gentleman farmer engaged in raising fancy poultry and fine horses–the bulk of his wealth was invested elsewhere. The Byberry farm became the family home, and Purvis spent most of his time there after the Civil War. Two of the portraits displayed in the Byberry house reflected Purvis's dedication to the abolitionist cause. One was a portrait he commissioned of Joseph Cinque, leader of the slave rebellion aboard the slave ship *Amistad* in 1839. The other was that of John Brown, the antislavery activist who led an abortive raid on Harper's Ferry, Virginia.

Securing an adequate education for their children was a matter of great difficulty for African Americans of the era. Even with their wealth, the Purvises found the problem hard to solve. In one instance, Purvis took a stand and won a victory. This was in 1853 when the Byberry school board decided to exclude blacks. Purvis went on a tax strike, which proved to be very effective, given the amount of taxes he paid. The board decided to reverse its decision. The Purvises, however, did not send their children to the local school; even after blacks were readmitted, segregated seating and other forms of discrimination continued.

In both the home on Lombard Street and at Byberry, the Purvises were noted for their hospitality. They entertained many guests over the years, including clandestine visitors to a carefully hidden secret room in the Byberry home, which was a stop on the Underground Railroad.

Works for Abolition

The Purvises and the Fortens were all ardent abolitionists. Robert Purvis made his first antislavery speech in 1827 at the age of 17; by 1832 he had become a seasoned lecturer. In that same year, he formed a lasting friendship with William Lloyd Garrison, an editor, lecturer and abolitionist leader. Along with Garrison and others, Purvis was a founding member of the American Anti–Slavery Society in Philadelphia in December 1833, and one of only three black delegates among a total of 63 drawn from 11 states. The summer after the founding of the antislavery society, Purvis left his wife and newborn son at home while he traveled to Great Britain to further the cause of abolition, his only trip abroad before the Civil War. Purvis had the usual difficulty faced by blacks in obtaining a passport, a document which said the bearer was a citizen of the United States. (He may have been the first black to obtain a passport, a document that blacks did not routinely receive until the administration of Abraham Lincoln.) Purvis was also the only black member of the older Pennsylvania Society for Promoting the Abolition of Slavery from its founding in 1775 until 1859.

The Cause Is Set Back

Between 1839 and 1844, the span of its existence, Purvis was president of the Vigilance Committee of Philadelphia, an organization to help fleeing slaves. From shortly after its founding, it was a de facto all–black organization. When the committee ceased its work, individual members continued their efforts to help refugee blacks. Purvis was later the only chair of the interracial successor organization, the General Vigilance Committee, active between 1852 and 1857. Purvis served as president of the Pennsylvania Anti–Slavery Society from 1845 to 1850, stepping down after four terms.

Helping fugitive slaves was not the only matter of concern to northern blacks. Purvis led efforts to oppose the undermining of the status of blacks in Pennsylvania. While the effort in 1833 to defeat legislation severely limiting the settlement in Pennsyania of free blacks from other states was successful, the cause suffered a setback when the new state constitution of 1838 disenfranchised blacks. Purvis was also active in the Colored Convention movement, which held annual conventions from 1830 until 1835, then continued sporadically thereafter.

Purvis was active in many different areas of reform. Some involved efforts on the behalf of blacks, such as creating better educational opportunity. But he also worked on behalf of temperance in the fight against the consumption of alcohol, women's rights, and prison improvement. His wife ardently supported his efforts. Along with school teacher Sarah Mapps Douglass and two of her sisters, Sarah and Margaretta Forten, Harriet Forten Purvis was one of the four black founding members of the Female Anti–Slavery Society of Philadelphia in 1833.

Purvis participated in the Philadelphia Library Company of Colored Persons, founded in 1833, and the Gilbert Lyceum, of which he and his wife were founding members in 1841. This literary society was almost unique in its day for being open to both men and women.

As the country drifted towards civil war, Purvis, like most of his black contemporaries, became increasingly bitter and less committed to the pacifism urged by Garrison. He gave vigorous vent to his disillusionment with American government at the protest meeting in response to the U.S. Supreme Court's controversial *Scott v. Sanford* decision in 1857 that had the effect of making slavery legal in all the territories. He was co–chair of the mass meeting held in Philadelphia two years later on Martyr Day, December 2, 1859, the day John Brown was hanged for his leadership of the Harper's Ferry raid. Purvis did not come around to full support of the Union war effort until the Emancipation Proclamation was issued in 1863.

In spite of his disenchantment, Purvis was vigorously opposed to the attempts of Henry Highland Garnet to further the movement in the mid–1850s to resettle blacks in a location outside the United States. This position was constant throughout his life and led him to oppose Henry McNeal Turner's post–Civil War colonization plans. Another constant was Purvis's opposition to voluntary segregation in the form of all–black organizations.

Continues to Speak Out After Civil War

Purvis continued to be a respected leader after the Civil War although less active. In spite of the fact that he did not participate in social life—he disapproved of both drinking and dancing, as well as other frivolous diversions—his name is the fourth most often mentioned in the William Dorsey collection of newspaper clippings covering the latter part of the nineteenth century in Philadelphia. Purvis was further isolated by his economic position as a wealthy black. Furthermore, by temperament and breeding, he was out of sympathy with the corruption that often characterized politics at both the national and local level. Since he had no stake in patronage, he found it easy to break with the Republican Party as early as 1874 and become an independent in politics. In 1884 he supported Benjamin Butler's Greenback–Labor Party.

Purvis continued to be a vigorous spokesman for protest. For example, at a meeting called by the Afro–American League to protest the massacre of 20 blacks in Carrolton, Mississippi, on March 17, 1888, Roger Lane, author of the book, *William Dorsey's Philadelphia and Ours,* quoted Purvis as saying: ''My blood boils when I see the gingerly, mealy–mouthed way in which the press of my country has treated the subject.'' Purvis also tried to improve on the mostly ineffectual efforts to increase local job opportunities for African Americans.

Purvis died of a stroke on April 15, 1898. He was the last surviving founder of the American Anti–Slavery Society. Poet and Abolitionist John Greenleaf Whittier much later remembered his first impression of Purvis in 1833. Quarles, in *Black Abolitionists,* quoted Whittier as saying, ''I think I have never seen a finer face and figure, and his manner, words, and bearing were in keeping. Who is he, I asked.'' Although Purvis's situation in life was much different than that of most blacks, he used his wealth and abilities to further the cause of abolition and uplift. He could well have withdrawn to a life buffered by his wealth, perhaps even concealing the racial identity assigned him by society. But he chose not to shirk what he saw as his duty and fought vigorously for the dignity of African Americans, a label he would have rejected for himself, preferring simply American.

REFERENCES

Barksdale, Richard, and Keneth Kinnamon. *Black Writers of America.* New York: Macmillan, 1972.

Borome, Joseph A. ''Robert Purvis and His Early Challenge to American Racism.'' *Negro History Bulletin* 30 (May 1967): 8–10.

Brown, William Wells. *The Black Man.* 1865. Reprint, Miami: Mnemosyne, 1969.

Johnson, Pauline C. ''Robert Purvis.'' *Negro History Bulletin* 5 (December 1941): 65–66.

Lane, Roger. *William Dorsey's Philadelphia and Ours.* New York: Oxford, 1991.

Logan, Rayford W., and Michael R. Winston, eds. *Dictionary of American Negro Biography.* New York: Norton, 1982.

Quarles, Benjamin. *Black Abolitionists.* New York: Oxford, 1969.

Smith, Jessie Carney, ed. *Notable Black American Women.* Detroit: Gale Research, 1992.

Still, William. *The Underground Rail Road.* Rev. ed. Philadelphia, Wm. Still, 1883.

Robert L. Johns

Benjamin A. Quarles
(1904–1996)
Historian, scholar, educator, administrator, writer

In his classic volume, *The Negro in the Making of America,* Benjamin A. Quarles wrote, ''If, strictly speaking, there is no such thing as Afro–American history, it is because this past has become so interwoven in the whole fabric of our culture.'' Quarles was one of the most important historians of the twentieth century. He is credited with revising historians' understanding of the involvement of blacks in U.S. history. As an educator for more than 45 years, Quarles was celebrated nationally for his academic achievements.

Benjamin Arthur Quarles was born on January 23, 1904, in Boston, Massachusetts. His parents were Arthur Quarles, a Boston subway porter and Margaret O'Brien Quarles. He was older than his four siblings—Ruth, Henry, Lorenzo, and Ann. As the first born in the family, he was given certain responsibilities even as a youth, such as bringing books from the library for his mother. This introduced him to the institution which would serve as a catalyst for his pioneering research in African American history. Libraries played a central role throughout his lifetime.

While growing up in Boston, Quarles worked at menial jobs but took advantage of the cultural and historical opportunities that the city offered him. He graduated from English High, the oldest public high school in the United States. After high school he worked as a porter during the summer on steam boats that traveled between Boston and Bar Harbor, Maine. In the winter months he worked as a bellhop in Florida.

The 1920s marked the height of the Jazz Era and the beginning of the Harlem Renaissance which brought about a new black pride and awareness that permeated the nation's cities. It was during this period that Quarles decided to change the direction of his life. During one of his summer trips down the eastern seaboard, he visited a friend at Shaw University, a small black school in Raleigh, North Carolina. Impressed with the atmosphere at Shaw, he took his savings and enrolled in that institution in 1927, at the age of 23. Later, Quarles decided during a Christmas recess that he would pack up his belongings and leave school for good. After a few weeks at home in Boston, however, he changed his mind. At Shaw, he became a student leader and debater. It was during his sophomore year that he was introduced to black history by an inspiring white female teacher, Florence Walter. In an interview with the *Baltimore Afro–American* on February 19, 1977, Quarles noted that, ''I had heard the name Crispus Attucks killed in the Boston Massacre and spoken of as the first American to die in the Revolution, but I never knew that there was such a thing as black history.'' He noted the absence of black history classes in the Boston schools, and observed that blacks ''were systematically taught, consciously and unconsciously, that there was nothing that you needed know other than that there were slaves and they were freed and they had created something of a problem and we were still adjusting to the problem.'' Quarles's interest in the subject of African American history would become a lifelong passion.

Quarles continued his study of history, and he was graduated as class valedictorian in 1931. With the aid of a Social Science Research Council Fellowship financed by the Rosenwald Fund, he continued his education, pursuing graduate studies at the University of Wisconsin–Madison. While at the University, Quarles wanted to delve deeper into the relatively untouched territory of black history. His first graduate professor informed him that black people should not study their own history because they would be too biased, turning it into propaganda. Quarles challenged his professors who gave him the opportunity to study his own history. He proved to them that black historians could write their own history objectively.

In 1933 Quarles graduated with a master's degree and returned to Shaw University as instructor of history. He taught at Shaw from 1935 to 1939. During his tenure there, Quarles met his future wife, Vera Bullock, of Greensboro, North Carolina. In 1937 they were married and the following year their daughter Roberta was born. Quarles continued his doctoral studies at the University of Wisconsin. He was awarded the prestigious Rosenwald Fellowship in 1937 and another Rosenwald Fellowship in 1938. This was a significant academic honor for Quarles because, as noted by historians August Meier and Elliott Rudwick in *Black History and the Historical Profession,* ''the Rosenwald Fund awarded few fellowships to historians, and a considerable portion of this assistance went to postdoctoral research rather than to facilitating the earning of advanced degrees.'' He would receive another Rosenwald Fellowship in 1945 to continue postdoctoral work.

Quarles published two scholarly articles, ''The Breach Between Douglass and Garrison,'' *Journal of Negro History* (April 1938) and ''Frederick Douglass and John Brown,'' *The Rochester Historical Society Publication* (1939) while he was working on his dissertation.

By 1939 Quarles and his family had left North Carolina and moved to New Orleans. After securing a teaching position at Dillard University, he rose through the ranks from professor (1939–46) to dean of instruction (1946–53). In 1940 he earned his Ph.D. degree in history. He wrote his doctoral dissertation on the life and career of Frederick Douglass. He published a major biography of Frederick Douglass in 1948.

Quarles's first wife died suddenly in 1951. He married Ruth Brett of Murfreesboro, North Carolina, a year later. He met her while she was the dean of students at Fisk University. In 1953 Quarles moved his family to Baltimore, Maryland, to assume a position as chairman of the department of history and political science at Morgan State College. In 1954 his second daughter, Pamela was born.

Quarles spent most of his career teaching, writing, and researching. At Morgan State, Quarles's administrative duties did not curtail his passion for scholarship. His administrative skills assisted him in developing the department of history into one of the most noted departments on campus. He remained chairman of the department until 1968. Quarles was slender and tall, a gentle giant. Shy and quiet, he was a modest man, and always polite. He wore spectacles and a fedora, and he was always the gentlemen who tipped his hat when approached by students and adults. History was his passion and students would engage him for hours on this subject. He always had time to talk with them.

During his tenure at Morgan, in addition to his teaching responsibilities, he increased the faculty and expanded the curriculum. His innovative approach to teaching and writing history allowed him to keep abreast of new trends in the field. His discipline and skill at budgeting his time showed in the numerous publications that he produced. He published seven of his major works during his appointment at Morgan.

Influences Attitudes Toward Black Achievements

Quarles's success as a teacher and scholar spread beyond the walls of historically black institutions. His teaching and research ultimately changed the way the nation viewed the achievements of African Americans in U.S. history. Quarles was a pioneer in the field of African American historical scholarship and he consistently stressed throughout his works the achievements of African Americans in America.

Quarles's lifelong mission was to analyze and correct the historical record which excluded African Americans from the historical equation. Quarles also was one of the first historians to consider the historical role of women in his works, including his discussion of their accomplishments in *The Negro in the Making of America* (1964) and *Black Abolitionists* (1969). His pioneering research validated the need to write and study African American history, and as a visionary, Quarles knew the importance of women's history. He stated in a June 1976 *Washington Post* article that women's history is "an attempt to place in proper perspective and proper importance an element that has not found its proper niche. And it will become more popular as an academic discipline."

A prolific writer, Quarles wrote ten books and many journal articles. His books include: *Frederick Douglass* (1948), *The Negro in the Civil War* (1953), *The Negro in the American Revolution* (1961), *Lincoln and the Negro* (1962), *The Negro in the Making of America* (1964), *The Black Abolitionist* (1969), *Black History's Diversified Clientele* (1971), *Allies for Freedom: Blacks and John Brown* (1974), *Black History's Antebellum Origins* (1979), and *Black Mosaic* (1988). He was coauthor of a number of other works.

Quarles may be best known for his biography and for his many articles about the life and times of Frederick Douglass, but historian Rosalyn Terborg–Penn, who worked with Quarles at Morgan, stated in a tribute to him at the Smithsonian in 1996 that many of his colleagues and students believed that his most seminal work was the book *Black Abolitionists.* "In this revisionist study published in 1969, he challenged the traditional interpretation that abolitionists were primarily white reformers."

Quarles also published 70 shorter pieces, 11 chapters in books, 26 encyclopedia entries, five documentary sources, 12 introductions to reprints, and 107 book reviews. In all his important studies, Quarles placed blacks at the center rather than on the periphery of major events and movements in American history. In recognition of his scholarship and scholarly works, Quarles received numerous honorary degrees from more than a dozen colleges and universities.

Quarles belonged to many professional and civic organizations. From 1947 until 1951 he was secretary of the New Orleans Urban League. He served as a member of the New Orleans Council of Social Agencies (1949–51), and vice–president of the Urban League (1949–51).

Among the many recognitions of Quarles's scholarship are the American Historical Society's Senior Historian Scholarly Distinction Award (1988) and the Smithsonian Institution's National Museum of American History Lifetime Achievement Award (1996). Quarles was the first professor at Morgan State College to receive the distinction of being named Teacher of the Year (1964), and he was awarded the honor of Distinguished Professor by the State of Maryland that same year. On February 26, 1989, Morgan State University dedicated the Benjamin A. Quarles Afro–American Studies Room in Soper Library in his honor.

Other awards and honors received by Quarles were: President Adams and Rosenwald Fellowships (1937); Rosenwald Fellowships (1938, 1945); Social Science Research Council Fellowships (1942, 1957); the Organization of American Historians' Huggins Carlist Award; and the Carnegie Corporation Advancement Teaching Fellowship (1944; 1947). He was named Honorary Consultant, American History, Library of Congress (1949–51) and Guggenheim Fellow (1959). He was honored by Phi Alpha Theta (1967); and named Vice President Emeritus, Association for the Study of Afro–American Life and History (1971); and to the American Council of Learned Societies (1976–78). He was an honorary fellow of the Mark Twain Society, and a member of Phi Alpha Theta history honor society.

Quarles also served on numerous boards and advisory committees, including the U.S. Office of Education, Library Services (1964–66); the State of Maryland Commission on

Negro History and Culture (1969); and the *Journal of Negro History* editorial board (1971). Quarles was on the editorial advisory boards for the Booker T. Washington, Frederick Douglass, and Lydia Maria Child papers projects. He was also a member of the Association for the Study of Afro–American Life and History, the American Antiquarian Society, and the Maryland Historical Society.

Throughout his academic and professional career, Quarles became a mentor to future historians and scholars. His friends and colleagues were numerous, including scholars from all over the country such as Carter G. Woodson, Charles Wesley, John Hope Franklin, Dorothy Porter Wesley, August Meier, Lorenzo Greene, Louis Harlan, Roland McConnell, Rosalyn Terborg–Penn, John Blassingame, James McPherson, Leslie Fishel Jr., and Dorothy Sterling.

In 1974 he retired as a distinguished professor of history from Morgan State University although he continued to research and publish scholarly works well into his eighties. Quarles's academic career was based on pursuing truth. It was his love of this liberating pursuit that he passed on to his students and his colleagues. Fellow historians Meier and Rudwick assessed Quarles's achievements when they wrote that:

> Quarles revised black history by correcting the omissions and distortions in American history textbooks. He chronicled the advanced nature of African cultures, discussed slave revolts and the constructive side of Reconstruction, and presented the achievements and contributions of blacks as early American explorers, as highly skilled craftsmen in the antebellum period, and as citizens and soldiers from Crispus Attucks to World War II.

On November 16, 1996, at the age of 92, Quarles died of a heart attack at Prince George's Hospital Center in Maryland. A memorial service was held at the Episcopal Life Care Community in Mitchellville, Maryland, where he had lived with his wife, Ruth Brett, for eight years. In lieu of a traditional funeral, his body was donated to the State Anatomy Board located in Baltimore, Maryland.

''His consistent theme that blacks, rather than being passive objects of white actions, were themselves major actors in the struggle for their own freedom and influential shapers of American history'' as noted by Meier in his introduction to *Black Mosaic,* was an important truth for Quarles, a truth he researched meticulously. His longtime friend and colleague, historian John Hope Franklin, quoted in the *Baltimore Sun* for November 19, 1996, said of Quarles, ''I can say categorically and without fear of contradiction that Benjamin Quarles was one of the finest, most original historians of his generation.'' His pioneering research validated the need to write and study African American history. The *Baltimore Sun* for November 24, 1996, summarized his importance by observing that ''Quarles' legacy will be remembered as one of the first historians to fairly and objectively portray the contributions and struggles of blacks and whites in colonial America as inextricably intertwined.'' The *Sun* went on to confirm that his work had ''helped to legitimatize and recognized the field of black history in the academy.''

Quarles was a pioneer who helped to revise the history of African Americans in the nation and their role in world civilization. His commitment to scholarship in African American history can be summarized by his own words in the program of the dedication of the Quarles room at Morgan State University, ''I sensed that this was a field in which one might find information that was new and fresh. I was not disappointed.''

REFERENCES

Baltimore Evening Sun, February 19, 1983; July 20, 1985.

''Benjamin A. Quarles Dies; Authority on Black History.'' *Washington Post,* November 18, 1996.

''Benjamin Arthur Quarles, 92, Scholar of Early Black–American History.'' *New York Times,* November 20, 1972.

''Black Focus Today.'' *Baltimore News American,* November 23, 1996.

''Black Historian Finds Field Healthy.'' *Baltimore Sun,* February 13, 1978.

Black Writers: A Selection of Sketches from Contemporary Authors. Detroit: Gale Research Inc., 1987.

''Books and Authors.'' *Baltimore Sun,* May 25, 1952.

Cattell, Jacques, ed. *Directory of American Scholars.* 3rd ed. New York: Bowker, 1957.

''Dedication of Quarles Room.'' Program. Morgan State University, February 26, 1989.

''Dr. Benjamin Quarles, Scholar, Author and Historian Dies.'' *Baltimore Afro–American,* November 23, 1996.

''Dr. Quarles Guest Lecturer at Naval Academy.'' *Baltimore Afro–American,* February 19, 1977.

Fisher, Vivian. *Register of the Benjamin A. Quarles Papers.* Beulah Davis Special Collections Department, Morgan State University, 1995.

Meier, August. ''Introduction: Benjamin Quarles and the Historiography of Black America.'' *Black Mosaic: Essays on Afro–American History and Historiography,* by Benjamin Quarles. Amherst: University of Massachusetts Press, 1988.

Meier, August, and Elliot Rudwick. *Black History and the Historical Profession, 1915–1980.* Urbana: University of Illinois Press, 1986.

''Metro.'' *Baltimore News American,* February 6, 1972.

Morgan State College. *Bulletin,* 1953–1974.

''Name Dropping.'' *Baltimore News American,* September 3, 1972.

Quarles, Benjamin. *The Negro in the Making of America.* 2nd rev. ed. New York: Collier Books, 1987.

''Quarles: From Black's Roots Comes Self–Esteem.'' *Baltimore Sunday Sun,* February 13, 1977.

Salzman, Jack, David Lionel Smith, and Cornel West, eds. *Encyclopedia of African–American Culture and History.* New York: Macmillan Library Reference USA/Simon and Schuster Macmillan, 1996.

''A Scholar, a Writer, a Gentleman.'' *Baltimore Sun,* November 24, 1996.

''A Sense of Self Out of the Past.'' *Washington Post,* June 18, 1976.

Terborg–Penn, Rosalyn. ''Benjamin Quarles'' *Mind On Freedom.* Smithsonian Institution, February 1996: 12–13. Special Collections, Morgan State University.

Thorpe, Earl E. *Black Historians: A Critique.* New York: William Morrow, 1971.

Who's Who among Black Americans. 5th ed. Lake Forest, IL: Educational Communications, Inc., 1988.

COLLECTIONS

The papers of Benjamin Quarles are located in the Beulah M. Davis Special Collections Department, Soper Library at Morgan State University. Vertical file materials of newspaper clippings and the ''Quarles Memorial Convocation Program, Celebrating The Life and Legacy of Dr. Benjamin A. Quarles,'' February 6, 1997, are also located in the Special Collections Department.

Vivian Njeri Fisher

A. Philip Randolph
(1889–1979)
Union organizer, labor leader

A. Philip Randolph is one of the most important black labor leaders of his era. Early in life he became a socialist, and as part of his efforts to further the cause, he edited the *Messenger* from 1918 to 1927. Randolph then turned his efforts to leading the Brotherhood of Sleeping Car Porters to recognition as a bargaining agent, in a 12–year struggle. Using the power and reputation he had acquired in the struggle, Randolph called for a March on Washington in the summer of 1942 to protest government indifference to black rights in the war effort. The prospect of this protest resulted in a major advancement for the civil and economic rights for blacks.

Asa Philip Randolph was born on April 15, 1889, two years before his brother James Jr., in Crescent City, Florida, to James William Randolph (1864–1924) and Elizabeth Robinson Randolph (c. 1872–1926). James William Randolph, originally of Montecello, Florida, received some education in a school set up by white Northern Methodist missionaries. He became a tailor and then an AME minister. The elder Randolph served only small and poor churches and always had to work at other jobs in the effort to make ends meet. In 1884 he was appointed to the church in Baldwin, Florida. The following year he married the youngest Robinson daughter, who was one of the best students in his Sunday school class. She was only 13–years old and two years later gave birth to their first son James William Jr., who died in 1928.

The Randolph family was desperately poor, and there were few books in the house. Randolph Sr. insisted that his sons spend part of every afternoon reading. By example, he instilled pride in their black heritage. Later, as the position of blacks in Jacksonville worsened, he would not let his sons read in the segregated facilities of the public library or use the segregated streetcars.

When Asa Randolph entered Cookman Institute, a Methodist school, in 1903, he blossomed intellectually, displaying great ability in literature, public speaking, and drama. In addition, he became a star baseball player and a fine singer. At his graduation in 1907, Asa was chosen class valedictorian.

Since the family lacked money to send their sons on to any university, their prospects for jobs were limited. Even though they were not good prospects for the ministry, they pretended to undergo the conversion experience and joined the church. For four years Randolph held a series of menial jobs in Jacksonville. He maintained his intellectual interests and gave public readings, sang, and acted in an amateur dramatic group. He also continued to read. Although Randolph did not continue to follow Du Bois's lead in later years, he told Jervis Anderson that the *Souls of Black Folk* was "the most influential book he ever read." In early 1911 Randolph told his parents that he was going to New York for a few months; he did not confide in them that his goal was to become an actor nor that the move was likely to be permanent.

A. Philip Randolph

Arrives in Harlem

Randolph and a Jacksonville friend, who returned to Jacksonville some eight months later, arrived in Harlem in April, 1911. When their money ran out, they sought out the menial jobs available. Randolph's pattern of work in these early years is exemplified by a 1914 stint as a waiter on a boat traveling between New York and Boston. Randolph first used his verbal skills to talk himself into a waiter's job but was nearly fired the first day when it became clear that he did not have the experience he claimed. Placed on probation for the rest of the trip, he was proud to be fired for trying to organize the waiters and kitchen help on the return trip. In these years

Randolph worked just long enough to scrape together some money, and he tried, usually with little success, to raise his fellow workers' consciousness of their exploitation.

Toward the end of 1911, Randolph sought contact with educated blacks by frequenting the Epworth League, a young persons' organization at Salem Methodist Church, pastored by Frederick Cullen, foster father of poet Countee Cullen. Randolph had absolutely no interest in religion. He also participated in the theater club, memorizing much Shakespeare and presumably acquiring the "Harvard" or "Oxford" accent characteristic of him in later life. He also maintained his lifelong habit of dressing impeccably. Randolph abandoned his plans to become an actor in the face of his parents' horrified reaction when he finally broached the subject to them.

Randolph had discovered that City College offered bright young New Yorkers a free education. His enrollment in February 1912 marked a turning point in his life. In addition to the courses he began taking, he now came in contact with the thriving student radicalism of the campus and adopted the belief in socialism that would be a major influence in his life. In addition to his usually short–lived jobs, the longest being a stint of several months as a porter for the Consolidated Gas Company, Randolph organized his own discussion and political action group, the Independent Political Council.

In 1914 Randolph met Lucille Campbell Green (1883–1963); they married in November. Green was one of the first beauty salon operators trained by Madame C. J. Walker when Walker came to New York in 1913. In addition to becoming very successful in her profession, Green became a close friend of Walker and her daughter. Superficially Lucille and Asa Randolph were very different; she was as gregarious as he was reserved and formal. Nonetheless, the marriage was a great success, and Asa Randolph had a reputation of undeviating fidelity. During the last ten years of her life, when Lucille Randolph was confined to a wheelchair, her husband read to her every evening when he was home and sat by her bed at night holding her hand when she was in pain. They had no children.

Becomes an Agitator

Toward the end of 1916 Randolph and his close friend, Chandler Owen, joined the Socialist Party. Emulating Hubert H. Harrison (1883–1926), the St. Croix native who had the reputation of being the father of radicalism in Harlem, they became soap–box orators at the corner of Lenox Avenue and 135th street. Randolph became an accomplished orator, holding listeners' attention with his fine baritone voice. In January 1917, Randolph and Owen were invited to edit a monthly magazine for the Headwaiters and Sidewaiters Society of Greater New York. Randolph now adopted as his byline the form of his name under which he became famous, A. Philip Randolph. Randolph and Owen published the *Hotel Messenger* for eight months before being fired.

Randolph and Owen began a new magazine, now simply called the *Messenger,* which appeared in November 1917. It managed to survive until 1928 although it never made money and did miss a few issues. From a high circulation of 26,000 in 1919, it struggled to reach 5,000 in the 1920s. After Owen lost interest in socialism and left for Chicago toward the end of 1923, the overall quality of the magazine declined. Under George Schuyler, who joined Randolph as second member of the staff in 1924 and soon became de facto managing editor, the magazine focused more on black culture than on politics by publishing the early short stories of Langston Hughes and many poems of Georgia Douglass Johnson.

The *Messenger* was at the center of a shifting group of radicals, including W. A. Domingo; Lovett Fort–Whitman; Abram L. Harris, later a Howard University economist; Robert Bagnall, the NAACP's director of branches; William Pickens, NAACP field organizer; Wallace Thurman, fiction writer; and Theophilus Lewis, drama reviewer. During World War I, the magazine took an uncompromising antiwar stance. In August 1918 Randolph and Owen were arrested in Cleveland during an antiwar speaking tour. The judge felt that the youthful–looking "boys" were both too young and, as blacks, not smart enough to have written the incriminating articles in the *Messenger,* so he released them. In late 1919 during the postwar Communist scare, a report of the Justice Department, as cited by Anderson, characterized the *Messenger* as "by long odds the most able and the most dangerous of all Negro publications."

In addition to their involvement with the *Messenger,* Randolph and Owen were busy in politics. They organized the first socialist club in Harlem in support of socialist Morris Hillquit's campaign for mayor of New York. In losing the election, Hillquit appeared to have drawn 25 percent of the vote in Harlem. In 1920, Randolph ran for state comptroller and won 202,361 votes, only a thousand less than socialist presidential candidate Eugene V. Debs. After another losing campaign for secretary of state in the next election, Randolph never ran for office again.

The war years marked the peak of socialist influence in the black community. The educated "Talented Tenth" tended to be socially conservative and seek their advantage through white patronage and the Republican Party. The black masses were not attracted by the idea of joint class–based activities with white labor because of the long history of anti–black discrimination in the union movement. While blacks did discover that Randolph and the Socialists were correct in asserting that participation in the war effort would lead to no gains, the widespread postwar disillusionment furthered recruitment by the more spectacular black nationalism of the Marcus Garvey movement.

Randolph and Marcus Garvey began their relationship with cautious cooperation, but Randolph later joined other black leaders in opposing Garvey in 1920, especially as rumors of financial irregularity in the finances of Garvey's Black Star Line began to circulate by the end of the year. On September 5, 1922, after Garvey had been indicted for mail fraud, Randolph received the left hand of a white man in a package with a cover letter ostensibly written by a member of the Ku Klux Klan threatening dire consequences to Randolph if he did not come to terms with Garvey's Universal Negro Improvement Association (UNIA). (The circumstances were never elucidated.) In response, the *Messenger* stepped up its attacks on Garvey, although Randolph was not one of the eight prominent blacks who signed a letter of January 25, 1923, to the Attorney General urging the government to act against Garvey and UNIA with vigor. Randolph's associate, Chandler Owen, however, was one of the signers and the probable instigator of the letter since the return address on the letter was that of the *Messenger.*

Randolph and the Sleeping Car Porters

By 1925 Randolph had achieved no success in any of the political or trade unions he had founded over the years; all were defunct. Except for the continued publication of the struggling *Messenger,* at the age of 36 Randolph seemed at a dead end in his career. Then Ashley L. Totten, a Pullman porter, asked Randolph to speak to a group of porters about trade unions and collective bargaining. Some time after Randolph delivered a successful talk, he was asked by Totten and other dissatisfied porters to help them form a union. Randolph published articles on Pullman porter grievances in the July and August issues of the *Messenger* and then took on the role as their leader. The Brotherhood of Sleeping Car Porters was unveiled at a mass meeting on August 25, 1925.

Porters in New York were initially enthusiastic. In Chicago, headquarters of the Pullman Company and base for the largest number of porters, reaction was more hesitant. Randolph, however, was able to recruit the support of Milton Price Webster. Randolph and Webster differed in most things except for their devotion to building up a union. Randolph had the ability to work with people of differing temperament and opinions. Over the years the two men developed a close working relationship characterized by mutual trust.

In its opposition to the union, the Pullman Company could rely on a network of informants and the support of most of the leaders of the black community. Union activity eventually led to firings. The passage of the Railway Labor Act on May 20, 1926, gave railroad workers the right to organize and slowed the erosion of membership. The struggle between union and company now went to a Board of Mediation. A complete impasse resulted in the mediation board's calling for arbitration in the summer of 1927, but arbitration was not required by the law and the Pullman Company refused to budge. The Brotherhood was not strong enough to support a strike, so a 1928 strike vote was only a tactical weapon in a struggle that the union again lost. The nearly 7,000 members in 1928 declined to strike in 1932. Randolph worked hard to sustain the organization, even leading the Brotherhood into the American Federation of Labor (AFL) in 1928.

The chance to revitalize the Brotherhood came in the wake of the election of Franklin D. Roosevelt when new legislation gave increased power to railroad unions, but unfortunately not to the porters' organization. As a common carrier, the Pullman Company was not covered by the new legislation, which was amended in 1934. After a new wave of firings by the Pullman Company and another attempt to set up a company union, the Brotherhood of Sleeping Car Porters was finally recognized in the summer of 1935 as the legal bargaining agent for porters, the first black union to achieve this status. Two years of effort followed before the company began bargaining in good faith and finally came to terms on August 25, 1937, the twelfth anniversary of the establishment of the Brotherhood.

From Union Organization to Civil Rights

Randolph always connected his union activities to a broader vision of economic and social progress for blacks. In 1935, Howard University sponsored a conference on economic conditions for black Americans. From this meeting grew a new organization, the National Negro Congress, to further "progressive" programs affecting blacks. Randolph became the first president of the organization, whose first meeting was in February 1936. He warned implicitly against dependency on Communists in the presidential address he wrote but did not deliver in person. By the third convention of the congress in 1940, Communists had indeed come to dominate, and Randolph publicly resigned.

In 1940 the issue centered on the war against Hitler and Fascism. Randolph supported the struggle against Nazism, while the Communists, in the wake of the pact between Stalin and Hitler, were against war preparations. As the United States built up its ability to carry on a war, blacks continued to suffer discrimination in employment and housing, as well as segregation in the armed forces. Randolph was not happy with the modes of protest used so far, such as public statements and conferences with officials including the president. In December 1940, he decided on more direct action in the form of a march on Washington. As leader of the coalition formed to further the march, Randolph issued a public call in March 1941 for a demonstration on July 1. Alarmed by the prospect of 100,000 blacks converging on Washington, the administration sought to dissuade Randolph. In a meeting with the president on June 18, Randolph maintained his refusal to call the march off. Executive Order 8802 was hammered out and issued on June 25. A Fair Employment Practices Committee was set up to oversee the workings of the order, which forbade discrimination in employment in defense industries and government. To the dissatisfaction of younger and more militant persons who were pushing also for desegregation in the armed forces, Randolph stood by his pledge to the president and called off the march. The March on Washington organization held together long enough to hold a series of mass rallies in different cities during the summer of 1942 before it began to disintegrate in the face of bitter criticisms by some blacks.

A new chance for Randolph to lead the effort to effect significant changes for African Americans occurred with the passage of the 1947 Draft Act. Since segregation continued to be the rule in the armed forces, Randolph formed an organization that became known as the League for Nonviolent Civil Disobedience Against Military Segregation; Bayard Rustin, who became one of Randolph's closest collaborators, served as its executive secretary. With Hubert Humphrey leading a floor fight for a strong civil rights plank at the Democratic

National Convention, which was also being picketed by blacks led by Randolph, President Harry S Truman measured his need for black votes in the upcoming election and issued Executive Order 9981 on July 26, 1948. While the language of the order was ambiguous, Truman issued a clarification saying that it did indeed abolish segregation in the armed forces.

In spite of all his efforts in the AFL, Randolph made only slow progress in combating racial prejudice in the labor movement. He did not follow John L. Lewis of the United Mine Workers into the CIO. It was the 1950s before some laggard AFL unions began to allow blacks to join. When the AFL and CIO united in 1955, the new organization adopted a more progressive stance on blacks in unions. Randolph joined Willard Townsend of the CIO as one of the two blacks on the Executive Committee. Although Randolph and George Meany—who became president of the AFL in 1952—would develop deep admiration for each other from the beginning, the relation was forged in bitter confrontation. After a clash with Meany at the AFL convention, Randolph formed the Negro American Labor Council in 1959. The council could not claim great success as militant blacks pushed for an independent black labor organization on one side while on the other, white racism remained well–entrenched in some unions and locals. Randolph resigned from the council in 1964. Still, on the national level, the AFL–CIO became a strong lobbyist for civil rights legislation in the mid–1960s, and it now continues to sponsor the A. Philip Randolph Institute to monitor black affairs in labor.

Decline in railroad passenger service had made the Brotherhood of Sleeping Car Porters a moribund union, so Randolph's influence depended more and more on his personal prestige. Beginning in the 1950s, Randolph became a respected elder statesman rather than the most visible black figure in the political world of the United States.

Randolph performed one last major service to the Civil Rights Movement. Early in the 1950s, Randolph had worked with Martin Luther King Jr. to support mass demonstrations in Washington, such as the Prayer Pilgrimage, although these demonstrations attracted little attention. In 1962 he consulted with King and then told Bayard Rustin to organize a 100,000–person demonstration on August 23, 1963. At the insistence of Roy Wilkins of the NAACP, Randolph took on the job of national director for the march but also insisted on retaining Rustin as organizer. Again it was Randolph who said no to President John F. Kennedy, who held a meeting to try to get the march cancelled.

As the years passed, Randolph became increasingly frail. After he was mugged in his Harlem apartment building in the summer of 1968, he was moved to a safer apartment. He became weaker and had a heart condition that caused him to faint. Randolph died in New York on May 16, 1979, at the age of 90.

Since Randolph's achievements are written large in history, two honors will stand for many. In 1971, Harvard University conferred an honorary degree on this socialist and activist, and in 1989 his likeness appeared on a postage stamp issued for Black Heritage Month.

In the last major speech of his career, Randolph was the first person to address the 200,000 people assembled by the March on Washington at the Lincoln Memorial on August 28, 1963. Anderson cites this speech, in which Randolph summarized the goals he pursued throughout his life, civil rights and economic justice:

> But this civil rights revolution is not confined to the Negro, nor is it confined to civil rights, for our white allies know that they cannot be free while we are not, and we know that we have no future in a society in which six million white and black people are unemployed and millions live in poverty.

REFERENCES

Anderson, Jervis. *A. Philip Randolph.* New York: Harcourt Brace Jovanovich, 1973.

Brazeal, Brailsford R. *The Brotherhood of Sleeping Car Porters.* New York: Harper, 1946.

Contemporary Black Biography. Vol. 3. Detroit: Gale Research, 1993.

Current Biography Yearbook. New York: H. W. Wilson, 1951.

Dalfiume, Richard M. *Desegregation of the U.S. Armed Forces.* Columbia: University of Missouri Press, 1969.

Franklin, John Hope, and August Meier, eds. *Black Leaders of the Twentieth Century.* Urbana: University of Illinois Press, 1982.

Garfinkel, Herbert. *When Negroes March: The March on Washington Movement in the Organization Politics for FEPC.* Glencoe, IL: Free Press, 1959. Reprint with a new preface by Lewis M. Killian, New York: Atheneum, 1969.

Harris, William H. *Keeping the Faith.* Urbana: University of Illinois Press, 1977.

Kellner, Bruce, ed. *The Harlem Renaissance.* New York: Methuen, 1984.

Kornweibel, Theodore. *No Crystal Stair.* Westport, CT: Greenwood Press, 1975.

Pfeffer, Paula F. *A. Philip Randolph, Pioneer of the Civil Rights Movement.* Baton Rouge: Louisiana State University Press, 1990.

COLLECTIONS

Much early material was destroyed in a fire during the 1930s. Major collections are the Chicago Division of the Brotherhood of Sleeping Car Porters Papers at the Chicago Historical Society and those from the New York headquarters in the Library of Congress, Washington, D.C. Many of the personal files once at the A. Philip Randolph Institute, formerly of New York City and now of Washington, D.C., are now in the Library of Congress.

Robert L. Johns

Charles B. Rangel
(1930–)
Congressman, lawyer

Charles B. Rangel is one of the most influential members of the U.S. House of Representatives. For more than three decades, he has represented the 15th Congressional District in the New York City neighborhood of his birth. A liberal Democrat, Rangel emerged in the 1970s as one of the most powerful African American politicians in the United States. A Korean War hero, a defender of the poor and disadvantaged, and an antidrug crusader, Rangel is a dedicated politician. His negotiation skills, his coalition building, and his overall mastery of the art of politics have made Charles Rangel one of the most charismatic and politically adroit African American leaders of the twentieth century.

The son of Ralph and Blanche Mary Wharton Rangel, Charles Bernard Rangel was born June 11, 1930, in the Harlem community of New York City. He was the second of three children, the others Ralph Jr. and sister Frances. ''Mrs. Blanche'' was a well–known civic worker and ''Mom'' to many young people growing up in Harlem. Blanche Rangel worked in the city's garment center and was active in the affairs of the International Ladies Garment Workers Union until her retirement in 1965. Rangel barely knew the father who he says physically abused his mother, never held a job, and left the family when Charles was six. His mother cleaned house, worked as a home attendant, and cut threads off shoulder pads coming off a factory assembly line. When he was eight, he too went to work, in a neighborhood drug store, delivering prescriptions and pouring castor oil into small bottles from five–gallon cans. Rangel attended the public schools in Harlem, P.S. 89 (now P.S. 175), Junior High School 139, and DeWitt Clinton High School. He always worked, but by the time he was in high school he was often truant and occasionally driven home by the police. At 16 he quit school to sell shoes, and drifted until he went into the U.S. Army.

Rangel served in the U.S. Army's Second Infantry Division (503rd Artillery) in Korea from 1948 to 1952. He was awarded the Purple Heart and Bronze Star for Valor after being wounded while bringing some 40 men out from behind Chinese lines. Rangel received U.S. and Korean Presidential Citations and four Battle Stars while serving in combat. He was honorably discharged with the rank of staff sergeant. After his military duty, he returned to New York but found he could get little more than a menial job. One day, as he lugged boxes in the garment district, it began to rain, and he spilled his cargo. ''I looked at those boxes all over the street and thought, 'There's got to be something better than this,''' he recalled in a speech before the National Urban League many years later. Rangel completed high school in 1953.

Rangel had difficulty persuading the Veterans Administration to underwrite his higher education. On the strength of an aptitude test, officials insisted that he apprentice to become either an undertaker or an electrician. Instead, Rangel became an honor student, using the G.I. Bill to receive his B.S. in business administration from the New York University School of Commerce in 1957, the first in his family to graduate from college. He completed his LL.B. from St. John's University School of Law in 1960 as a dean's list student under a full three–year scholarship. Rangel continues to be committed to the G.I. Bill, which supports education and job training, noting the difference it made in his life.

Charles B. Rangel

Before earning his law degree, Rangel served as a legal assistant in the New York County district attorney's office from 1953 to 1959. For the last two years of that period, he was a special investigator for the Local Elections' Fraud Bureau. Rangel then joined the law firm of Weaver, Evans, Wingate, and Wright. He was admitted to practice in the courts of the state of New York in 1960. He earned a key appointment when Attorney General Robert F. Kennedy named him assistant U.S. attorney in the U.S. Federal Court, Southern District of New York in 1961. In the next five years, he served as legal counsel to the New York City Housing and Redevelopment Board, with the Neighborhood Conservation Bureau, legal assistant to Judge James L. Watson, associate counsel to the Speaker of the New York State Assembly, general counsel to the National Advisory Commission on Selective Service, and counsel to the President's Commission to Revise the Draft Laws.

As a child, Rangel's role model was his maternal grandfather, a courthouse elevator operator who always wore his uniform and badge home and knew all the judges and promi-

Charles B. Rangel (at microphone) with members of Black Caucus, 1980.

nent lawyers. When his grandfather wanted to continue working at his Civil Service job past the mandatory retirement age of 70, the young Rangel stopped by the local political club to ask for help in the matter. They told him that if he wanted to change policies he had to go into politics. Soon after that he got involved in politics himself, mostly, he said, because he had seen how puny the competition was. In an address to the annual convention of the National Urban League, Rangel spoke of his sense of history and unity, remembering that blacks have worked together from cotton fields to the battlefields in Europe and Asia, giving their blood while keeping faith that full equality will come.

Begins Political Involvement

In 1966 Rangel, a legal advisor to many figures in the Civil Rights Movement, was elected to represent the 72nd District, Central Harlem, in the State Assembly. Rangel served as a New York State Assembly member from 1967 to 1971. His voting record reflected his liberal views. He supported the liberalization of abortion laws and legalization of the lottery. During this time, he became friendly with former Manhattan Borough president Percy Sutton and governor Nelson Rockefeller, both of whom helped his career. In 1964 Rangel and Sutton founded the John F. Kennedy Democratic Club on West 130th Street in Harlem. In 1969 Rangel sought the Democratic nomination for New York City Council president. As the only citywide African American candidate, Rangel ran last in a six–man field.

Former New York City mayor David Dinkins and secretary of commerce Ronald Brown also shared his friendship and confidence. Rangel once worked as a clerk in Harlem's famed Hotel Theresa, which Brown's father then managed.

In 1969 Rangel turned his attention to national issues in his endorsement of the first nationwide protest day against the Vietnam War. His growing interest in national affairs led him to run for a seat in the U.S. House of Representatives. He headed a four–way congressional primary field and ousted Harlem's flamboyant and once–powerful Congressman Adam Clayton Powell Jr., whose career in Congress was then in eclipse on charges of misusing public funds. Rangel sensed that Harlem would want to replace Powell with someone who could produce more for the district. Rangel defeated him by a slim margin (150 votes) in the Democratic primary. He unseated Powell gently, avoiding harsh frontal attacks, building productive political alliances and working extremely hard.

Handily elected to the 92nd Congress on November 3, 1970, Rangel was sworn in on January 3, 1971, representing the 19th (now 15th) Congressional District of New York. He has been reelected to each succeeding Congress. His district covers the neighborhoods of East and Central Harlem, Central Park West, the Upper West Side, Roosevelt Island, and Washington Heights–Inwood. One of the original seats of African American political power, Upper Manhattan has seen demographic changes. Non–Hispanic blacks continue control, partly because of low Hispanic (mainly from Puerto Rico and the Dominican Republic) voter participation rates. In the 1990 census, African Americans comprised some 47 percent of the district's population, whites 28 percent, and others 26 percent.

As a first–year member of the House, Rangel was appointed to the Select Committee on Crime. Just out of the U.S. attorney's office in New York where he had tackled the famed French Connection heroin case, Rangel had long labored on the drug–fighting front. Because of the large number of heroin addicts in Harlem (an estimated 30,000 in 1970), Rangel made elimination of the heroin trade his top priority in his first term in office. He was influential in passing the 1971 amendment to the drug laws that authorized the president to cut off all military and economic aid to any country that refused to cooperate with the United States in stopping the international traffic in drugs. He was a member of the House Select Committee on Narcotics Abuse and Control from 1976 to 1982 and was a natural choice as chairman from 1983 to 1993. He is a leading American strategist in the international war against drugs, traveling hundreds of thousands of miles to inspect possible drug sources and check on enforcement of agreements to ban crop growth. Rangel continues tackling the drug problem with legislation, congressional hearings, speeches, and discussions with anyone who will listen. His criticism of the government has at times distanced him from the executive branch, and he was banned from a 1986 White House drug conference. At the start of the 103rd Congress in 1993, the House voted against reauthorizing the committee on narcotics.

Legislative Leader

Rangel served as chair of the Congressional Black Caucus 1974–75. He was a member of the House Judiciary Committee in 1973–74 when it voted to impeach President Nixon. In 1975 Rangel became the first African American to serve as a member of the House Ways and Means Committee, chairing the Select Revenue Measures Subcommittee. Ways and Means is responsible for overseeing the apportioning of government revenues with jurisdiction over the Social Security and Medicare systems, welfare, taxes, trade, and tariffs. Two years later, his colleagues in the New York Congressional delegation voted him the majority whip for New York State.

In the 1970s Rangel voted along liberal lines on House legislation. He voted to end the U.S. bombing of Cambodia, against funding the B–1 bomber and nuclear carriers, and against the deregulation of natural gas. He voted for busing for school integration, federal assistance for abortions, for auto pollution controls, and the creation of a consumer protection agency. At the end of the decade, Rangel was a member of the Democratic Steering and Policy Committee, which nominates committee chairs and proposes the party's legislative priorities. In 1983 Rangel was appointed a deputy whip for the House Democratic leadership.

Rangel is regarded as the most pragmatic of the senior African American members of Congress. He is the one most likely to choose modest but tangible help for his constituents over an opportunity to express outrage. He has lived some problems of his district and that makes him an effective spokesperson for distressed areas. Having grown up poor, the memories of standing in line for surplus food are still fresh in his mind. During his seventh term, Rangel played a key role in getting Congress to approve: a $4.6 billion emergency jobs and recession–relief bill, the $165 billion Social Security bailout bill, a $54 billion Housing and Urban Development appropriation, money for the Caribbean Basin Initiative, a national holiday for Martin Luther King Jr., legislation extending the free surplus food program ($50 million) and jobless benefits ($56 million), and an extension of the Civil Rights Commission.

As a senior member of the Congressional Black Caucus, Rangel may be its most effective lobbyist. He has acquired clout, the kind he said African American leaders demand. He told the *Afro–American,* "Black leaders are putting both major parties on notice that they no longer will be satisfied with promises of more social programs and appointments to secondary posts. We want to sit at the seat of power and we expect full participation."

In 1984 Rangel was one of the few nationally prominent African American Democrats to bring muscle behind the Rainbow Coalition presidential campaign of Jesse Jackson. He considered running for mayor of New York City in 1985. Nearly 25 years after his election to Congress, Rangel faced a challenge from Adam Clayton Powell IV, the son of the man he once defeated. For 13 of 14 House elections, Rangel has won with better than 95 percent of ballots cast; in his first election in 1970, he won with 87 percent of the vote.

In 1987 Rangel introduced measures in Congress to have the black nationalist leader Marcus Garvey exonerated of mail fraud charges on which he was convicted in 1924. That same year, Rangel was defeated in his bid for the majority whip's job in the House of Representatives. In 1997 Rangel cosponsored the African Growth and Opportunities Act, which establishes an economic forum and creates Overseas Private Investment Corporation Funds, a $150 million equity fund, and a $500 million infrastructure fund.

Rangel survived a 1993 House banking scandal to win reelection to a 12th term in Congress. The Justice Department cleared him of any criminal wrongdoing for 64 overdrafts at the closed bank. He has been the top Democrat on the Joint Committee on Taxation since 1995, and in 1996 became the ranking member of the House Ways and Means Committee, but lost his bid to become committee chairman. He is the senior Democrat on the Trade Subcommittee on Ways and Means, and a member of its Human Resources Subcommittee. He pays particular attention to trade with the Caribbean and Africa, and the development of the Harlem International Trade Center. Since 1995 Rangel has been a member of the Congressional Advisory to the U.S. Trade Representative and the President's Export Council.

Rangel is a favorite speaker much in demand, a frequent commentator on political talk shows, and has written a weekly column in the *New York Courier.* While he fights for traditional Democratic constituencies, such as the poor, cities, and organized labor, Rangel is also sensitive to the needs of business, especially New York City's financial community. He has created programs that benefit low income and minority constituents by offering incentives to businesses that invest in urban communities. In promoting trade and commerce, Rangel wants corporations to back job training and educational programs for the disadvantaged. He is the principal author of the $5 billion Federal Empowerment Zone demonstration project to revitalize urban neighborhoods. He is also the author of the Low Income Housing Tax Credit and has championed the Targeted Jobs Tax Credit. Education, jobs, and training continue to be his mantra.

Almost six–feet tall, portly, and gravel–voiced, Rangel is very much the Old World–style gentleman yet one who sprinkles his sentences with mild profanity. He is known as a fair and strong negotiator and mediator, with an extraordinary sense of good humor. He is acutely embarrassed, he said, to see the New Deal falling apart while he is on the job. Rangel spends most of his time in Washington. He returns on weekends to New York City, where he lives in a Harlem brownstone with his wife, Alma Carter, a former social worker, whom he married on July 26, 1964. He has said that he loved her at first sight on the dance floor of Harlem's Savoy Ballroom. They have two children, Steven and Alicia. Alma Rangel is the co–chair of the Congressional Black Caucus Spouses and participates in many civic and community organizations. Rangel does not look forward to retirement. He has no hobbies and is unable to relax after the third day of a vacation.

Current address: 2330 Rayburn House Office Building, Washington, DC 20515.

REFERENCES

''Congressman Charles Rangel May Run for New York Mayor.'' *Afro–American,* November 26, 1983.

Contemporary Black Biography. Vol. 3. Detroit: Gale Research, 1993.

Current Biography Yearbook. New York: H. W. Wilson, 1984.

''New Man From Harlem.'' *Time* 95 (6 July 1970): 19.

Norment, Lynn. ''Charles Rangel: the Front–line General in the War on Drugs.'' *Ebony* 44 (March 1989): 128–31.

''Nothing from Nothing: The Meaning of the Powell–Rangel Race.'' *The Village Voice,* September 13, 1994.

Rangel, Charles. ''Remarks of Rep. Charles Rangel, (D–NY), National Urban League Conference, Washington, DC.'' Transcript of speech, August 8, 1989. *Federal News Service.* Lexis–Nexis (online subscription service). November 23, 1997.

''Rangel's Voice: Stronger Than Ever; Dean of Delegation Furious Over Cuts.'' *New York Times,* May 16, 1995.

Rubin, Alissa J. ''Many–faceted Rangel Positioned to Become House Deal Maker.'' *Congressional Quarterly* 54 (7 December 1996): 3335–3340.

Who's Who in America. 52nd edition. New Providence, RI: Marquis Who's Who, 1998.

Kathleen E. Bethel

Reverdy C. Ransom
(1861–1959)
Religious leader, civil rights activist

Reverdy C. Ransom was a major force in the history of the African Methodist Episcopal (AME) Church. One researcher ranks him alongside such church leaders as Richard Allen, Daniel Alexander Payne, and Henry McNeal Turner. Ransom worked hard to shape his church to meet the challenge of the mass migration and urbanization of blacks. At the same time he strove to maintain the intellectual vitality of the church and worked against tendencies which could well have ended by fragmenting it. He was also a vigorous leader in the search for civil rights and promoted his goals by a great mass of writing.

Reverdy Cassius Ransom was the son of Harriet (Hattie) Johnson and an unknown father, who was probably white. This inference is based on Ransom's red hair and statements he made in his significantly titled autobiography, *The Pilgrimage of Harriet Ransom's Son.* In it he flatly stated that he knows nothing of his paternal lineage. Of George Warner Ransom, he said in carefully chosen words: ''[He] gave me a sur–name for which I have always given him grateful thanks. This rather silent, taciturn man was a father to me for more than fifty years.'' Reverdy Ransom was born on January 4, 1861, in the two–room log cabin of his maternal grandmother, Lucinda in Flushing, Ohio. Lucinda was brown skinned and a very intelligent woman who had learned to read in her native Virginia, where she had been held in semi–slavery although legally free. After she came to Ohio she bought a house and large plot of ground in Flushing, a largely Quaker settlement. Harriet Ransom, a woman Reverdy Ransom described as having ''a light bronze complexion, with clearly cut features,'' was Lucinda's only daughter by a Native American—Lucinda's other children had a different father.

Reverdy C. Ransom

Ransom lived at his grandmother's place until he was four. Then, presumably after his mother's marriage to Ransom, she took him to board with his paternal grandparents, Louis and Betsy Ransom on a small farm near Old Washington, Ohio. Reverdy Ransom retained vivid memories of the farm although he felt unwelcome among the numerous Ransom children and was always hungry. The arrangement seems to have been a form of day care since he speaks of sharing his mother's room at night. The family attended the local African Methodist Episcopal Church. Despite their attachment to the church, the temperance movement had not touched them, and they gave watered whiskey even to the young toddlers. Ransom himself continued to drink as an adult, much to the scandal of more conservative church members. He learned to read during his time in Old Washington in a segregated local school held in the AME church building.

About 1869 Ransom and his mother made a final move together to Cambridge, Ohio, an important rail junction, where both George and Harriet Ransom lived for a long time, died, and were buried. Ransom early imbibed his mother's aspirations for him. He attended the inadequate local school for blacks; at 13 he tried to get into the white public school but was refused. He wrote: "Sometimes when I would voice the ideals and aspirations my mother had inspired, my companion would point to me in derision as a 'white folks nigger.'"

Attends Wilberforce

Ransom sought learning wherever he could, sometimes working in exchange for lessons. He became a teacher when he was the only black to take advantage of a local summer normal school. He taught two years in country schools, saving his money from these and other jobs to put aside enough to attend Wilberforce. His mother mortgaged the house to supply the rest. The plans almost fell through because of his early marriage. Ransom married Leanna Watkins, a domestic, on February 17, 1881; they had a son, Harold George Ransom, born November 4, 1881. The couple drifted apart after Ransom left Cambridge for Wilberforce, divorcing on February 1, 1886, and the son spent the first eight years of his life with Ransom's mother.

Wilberforce students tended to be older then than now and very serious about their studies and their religion. Ransom not only made good the deficits in his education, he also came into contact with a galaxy of black intellectuals. In particular he came to the attention of influential men like Bishop Daniel A. Payne and future bishop Benjamin W. Arnett, his early patrons. These men were leaders in a church in which a formerly dominant northern branch was losing influence to a rising southern branch—a very approximate summary of a much more involved situation.

During his first year Ransom had his conversion experience in the privacy of his room. This is an example of how he faced two ways in his religious life; caught between old ways and new, he felt the need to be converted, but he had resisted going to the mourner's bench in his own church to publicly receive the faith. He later felt the worship of the silent congregation in his New Bedford church was cold, but after he tried to emulate the emotional appeal of a folk preacher from Kentucky who nearly sang his sermon to the great enthusiasm of the congregation at North Street Church in Springfield, Ohio, he meekly accepted the rebuke of a woman parishioner. As he wrote in his autobiography, she said, "That is all right for him, but we don't want our minister to make himself ridiculous by any such performance."

The following year Ransom attended Oberlin College on a tuition scholarship, working at odd jobs to support himself. Ransom found that black students were barred from many aspects of campus life. When he helped organize a protest against the plan to impose segregation of black women in the women's dining hall, he lost his scholarship even though the requirement for seating at a separate table was abandoned. Poverty and the necessity to work prevented much association with fellow black students like Ida Gibbs and Mary Church except for John Alexander, a future West Point appointee, who was also poor.

Ransom felt the call to preach—his stepfather, who had not yet become a Christian, told him he was a fool who would lead a life of poverty. Harriet Ransom sold her cow to give her son the money to begin at Wilberforce again, and after four years of struggle and deprivation, he managed to earn his B.D. degree in June of 1886. His progressive and heretical views on the Trinity and other doctrines, which he took care to conceal, could have landed him in serious trouble with his dogmatic elders. When he delivered his commencement speech on "Divine and Civil Law" to great applause, his mother forced her way onto the platform to embrace him.

Ransom had spent the year before his graduation as preacher at a church at Selma, Ohio, for a salary of $109, making the 12– mile trip on Saturdays and Mondays. There he met Emma S. Comer, whom he married in 1886. She was an ideal minister's wife and a woman of no mean achievement who died in 1941. They had one son, Reverdy Cassius Jr. In 1943 Reverdy married a third time to Georgia Myrtle Teal, who was dean of women at Wilberforce before the marriage.

Begins Life Work

In his first assignment after graduation, Ransom was transferred to the Pittsburgh Conference and assigned to a church in Altoona, Pennsylvania. It had 13 members, most of them old, and his compensation averaged five dollars a week. His new wife joined him at the beginning of his second year. Ransom was ordained on October 14, 1888, by Bishop Daniel A. Payne, who assigned him to Allegheny Mission in what is now North Pittsburgh. When Ransom asked Payne for a different assignment after discovering the mission had only five in its congregation: he wrote that the bishop "stamped his foot and shaking his trembling fingers at me said, 'Begone! Leave my presence! There are people there.'"

Ransom soon built up a congregation, discovering in the process the need for social services among the slum dwellers he was ministering to. He also broke with tradition when he refused to expel the organist, who had become pregnant; he supported her and married her to the child's father some months later. Ransom bought a house in a desirable neighborhood on Chartiers Street and after moving the house back, built a small church on the lot. Indignant white neighbors stoned the house, nearly killing his infant son.

Assigning new ministers to difficult and poor churches was a tradition of the denomination. In September of 1890 Payne transferred Ransom without notice to the Ohio Conference and gave him the affluent North Street Church in Springfield, Ohio. Buggies lined the street for two blocks on both sides of the church on Sundays. In Springfield Ransom was able to assist poet Paul Laurence Dunbar in launching his career by selling 100 copies of Dunbar's first book after church services, helping him pay the printer's bill.

In spite of his prosperity, Ransom looked frail. He was six–feet, two–inches tall weighing between 170 and 180 pounds; in his book on AME bishops Wright says he was "of light brown complexion with a few freckles, reddish hair and mustache." Singleton described him in 1936 as "very tall . . . stringy, gaunt, and lean" with a "shrill, musical voice." Daniel Payne anxiously questioned Ransom about his parents' and his own health and constitution before sending him to St. John's in Cleveland, Ohio, in 1893. Payne died shortly afterwards, and Arnett became Ransom's most powerful patron.

Ransom conducted a revival at St. John's in the spring of 1894, baptizing nearly 300 persons. In that year he also initiated a practice which spread widely by organizing the first Board of Deaconesses in the AME, probably a first in any black denomination. He was also becoming noted as a powerful orator and preacher and making useful contacts with white politicians and philanthropists. In 1896 Ransom attended his first General Convocation, where he was disgusted by the electoral corruption and the general disorder, rising at times to physical violence, which had come to characterize the meetings.

In that year Arnett offered either of the two principal churches in Chicago to Ransom, who chose Bethel. There Ransom built a local and national reputation as he did his best to adapt the AME to changing urban conditions, especially the mass migrations which were undercutting the influence of all old–line Protestant denominations, both black and white. Ransom formed, for example, the Men's Sunday Club which met in the afternoon to spread culture, a similar organization for women, some of whom also worked as voluntary social workers, and outreach programs for children, including a kindergarten.

Arnett found the money to enable Ransom to launch the Institutional Church and Settlement House in 1900. This Chicago center offered a wide range of services to the community. It generated great excitement in 1903 when a bomb exploded near Ransom's office after he had launched an attack on the numbers racket. The nature of the opposition to Ransom's experiment excited in the church is caught by a remark of his successor at Institutional Church, J. W. Townsend. In *87 Years Behind the Black Curtain,* R. R. Wright quoted Townsend as saying that he aimed to, "make it a regular A.M.E. Church, to cut out the social foolishness, and bring religion back."

Attacks Booker T. Washington

On the national scene Ransom joined the revived Afro–American Council in 1898, becoming the secretary. The second meeting was held in his Chicago Church. There he rose to publicly rebuke Booker T. Washington, but his motion to remove Washington's name from membership went down to defeat amid great tumult. Even W. E. B. Du Bois, scholar, activist and later Washington's great opponent, felt the attack was untimely, and Ransom had to retreat and make his peace temporarily. Ransom did not even bother to attend the 1900 session when Washington's supporters took over the organization completely.

Unfortunately Arnett was transferred to another district in 1900, and Ransom came under increasing attack inside the church. His new bishop, Abram Grant, an ardent Booker T. Washington supporter, forbade him to preach on Sunday mornings at the Institutional Church on the grounds that he was undermining attendance at regular AME churches such as Bethel—headed by Archibald J. Carey, a very ambitious rival. Senior Bishop Henry McNeal Turner rather highhandedly revoked the ban. When Ransom could not come to a satisfactory agreement about his assignment with the next bishop, C. T. Shaffer, he simply walked out of the conference. Arnett, bishop in New England, appointed him first to New Bedford and then in 1905 to Charles Street AME Church in Boston.

In Boston Ransom allied himself closely with William Monroe Trotter, who was vehemently opposed to Booker T. Washington. Ransom joined the Niagara Movement, organized in 1905 by Du Bois and others. The following year Ransom was the center of sensational stories in the press. He was traveling by train to Huntsville, Alabama, to give the commencement address at Agricultural and Mechanical College on May 28, 1906, when a white woman asked him a question in French to which he gave a brief reply. Two rabid white men then forced him from the first–class car into the segregated car, claiming that Ransom had been passing himself off as a foreigner and flirting with a white woman. William H. Councill, the college president who had the reputation of being so conciliatory towards whites that he made Booker T. Washington sound like a militant, saw that Ransom was sent packing as soon as possible and subsequently denied that the school had ever invited Ransom to speak, falsely claiming that it was the fault of the alumni council.

Arnett died in 1907, and Henry McNeil Turner, who took over some of Arnett's responsibilities, rather gingerly arranged to transfer Ransom to New York City. Ransom did not abandon his militancy about civil rights nor his willingness to try new directions in his new assignment. At Bethel AME Church he showed liberality by encouraging black entertainers to come to the church—show business was in his family since famed entertainer Sam Lucas, a member of the original Georgia Minstrels, was his uncle.

While Ransom had many enemies in the church, he had also allies and supporters. In the 1912 General Convention he was elected editor of the *AME Church Review,* a position he held until 1924. He tried to maintain the magazine as a significant intellectual periodical. Since he did not find the job a full–time one, he also established a mission, the Church of Simon of Cyrene, in the worst black slum in the city—the Tenderloin—where he ministered to prostitutes, petty criminals, and derelicts. In 1918 he ran for a seat in Congress, defying the local Republican party leaders. They managed to have his election petition thrown out on the grounds that it lacked a sufficient number of valid signatures so that he had to run as a write–in candidate.

In the 1920 General Convocation Ransom made a good showing in the elections for bishops and in 1924 at the age of 63 he was finally elected bishop. He moved back to Wilberforce, where he lived in the house, Tawana Chimney Corner, rebuilt by Arnett after an 1895 fire. He still had many battles to fight in the church in addition to administering his assigned districts. In 1928 he led the battle to move bishops who had managed to build up fiefdoms in districts that some had controlled for 16 years. That battle was not resolved until 1936. Not all of Ransom's energies were concentrated on his own church. In 1934 he founded the Fraternal Council of Negro Churches, which became a vigorous and successful lobbying organization in the 1940s and early 1950s under the leadership of Baptist William H. Jernigan.

From 1932 to 1948 Ransom served as chairman of the board of trustees of Wilberforce University, another bone of contention between Northerners who saw Wilberforce as the denomination's flagship educational institution and Southerners who were trying to build up their own colleges. A complicating factor in the case of Wilberforce was the role of the state of Ohio, which supplied funds for some programs. Although Ransom saw financial stability return to school during the depression, the ultimate outcome left him angry and bitter. In 1948 after an acrimonious quarrel AME's Wilberforce and Ohio's Central State University existed side by side.

A final, bitter struggle in the church involved Bishop David Henry Sims. Beginning in 1940 he was charged with defrauding his followers and oppressing church members. It was not until 1946 after several court battles as well as extensive church discussion and action that the issue was resolved by Sims's removal. Even that decision had to be upheld by a court decision the following year.

One side effect of Ransom's move back to Ohio was his involvement in state Democratic politics which led to his appointment as the first black commissioner on the Ohio Board of Pardon and Parole; he held the position from 1936 to 1940. In that year he opened the Democratic National Convention with a prayer, and the next year Roosevelt appointed him a member of the Volunteer Participation Committee in the Office of Civil Defense. In 1948 Ransom stopped supervising districts; at his request he remained an active bishop as director of the Bureau of Research and History. He retired as an active bishop in 1952 and died at his home in Wilberforce in 1959 at age 98. He is buried in Wilberforce.

Born just before the Civil War broke out, Revery Ransom lived long enough to see the beginnings of the Civil Rights Movement he had done so much to prepare. In between these eras he led a full life devoted to his religion and to the improvement of conditions for African Americans. He ended the introduction to his autobiography by saying: ''We ask not that others bear our burden, but do not obstruct our pathway, and we will throw off our burdens as we run.''

REFERENCES

Burkett, Randall K., and Richard Newman. *Black Apostles.* Boston: G. K. Hall, 1978.

Encyclopaedia of the African Methodist Episcopal Church. 2nd. ed. Philadelphia: Book Concern of the A.M.E. Church, 1947.

Lincoln, C. Eric, and Lawrence H. Mamiya. *The Black Church in the African American Experience.* Durham: Duke University Press, 1990.

Logan, Rayford W., and Michael R. Winston, eds. *Dictionary of American Negro Biography.* New York: Norton, 1982.

Ransom, Reverdy C. *The Pilgrimage of Harriet Ransom's Son.* Nashville: Sunday School Union, [1949?].

Singleton. George A. *The Romance of African Methodism.* New York: Exposition Press, 1952.

Wright, R. R. *The Bishops of the A.M.E. Church.* Nashville: The A.M.E. Sunday School Union, 1963.

———. *87 Years Behind the Black Curtain.* Philadelphia: Rare Book Company, 1965.

Robert L. Johns

James T. Rapier
(1837–1883)
Congressman, farmer, government official

James T. Rapier was a congressman from Alabama during Reconstruction. Coming from a unique family background, he was well–prepared for his political career, which also led to federal appointments that he fulfilled with integrity and efficiency. In his personal affairs, especially cotton planting, he displayed the business acumen which characterized his family.

James Thomas Rapier was born free in Florence, Alabama, on November 13, 1837, the fourth and last child of John H. Rapier Sr. (1808–1869) and Susan Rapier (1811–1841). His older brothers were Richard G. (1831–1895?), John H. Jr. (1835–1865?), and Henry (1836–1859?). Little is known of Susan Rapier except that she was from Baltimore and born free, which also made her children free. She may also have been partly white, since a son later labelled himself a quadroon. After her 1841 death in childbirth, John H. Rapier Sr. began a relationship with a slave named Lucretia (1826–1864?)—whom he could not marry because marriage between free and slave blacks was forbidden by state law—and had five more children who became free only at the end of the Civil War.

John H. Rapier Sr. was the oldest son of a remarkable slave woman known as Sally (1790–1849). In Virginia she had two sons, John and Henry (1817–1888?), by John Thomas (1788–1834?), the son of her white owner. She was brought to Nashville with her two sons by an heir who was probably the children's father. There she was able to hire out her time, first as a cleaning woman and then as a very successful laundress. She also had a third son, James P. Thomas, by John Catron (1786–1865), a future justice of the U. S. Supreme Court. In spite of her legal status, Sally lived as though she were free and worked for her children's freedom. She saw that they were all trained initially as barbers.

John H. Rapier Sr. was hired out in 1818 to a barge man and entrepreneur, Richard Rapier, who founded Florence, Alabama, in the following year. Richard Rapier provided for John H. Rapier's freedom, and the young man became free by legislative act in 1819. He settled in Florence as a barber, and by 1860 was considered the tenth wealthiest free black in the state. Sally advised her second son, Henry, to escape to the North. Henry Thomas became a barber in Buffalo, New York,

James T. Rapier

but he eventually moved to Canada, where he took up farming. Sally then arranged to purchase her youngest son's freedom. After completing his apprenticeship in 1846, James P. Thomas became a very successful Nashville barber, and mother and son operated their businesses out of the same house. In 1851, after his mother's death in a cholera epidemic, he won recognition for his freedom and exemption from the state law which required freed blacks to leave the state.

James T. Rapier had ample opportunity to know his grandmother and youngest uncle when he and his brother John lived with them in Nashville while attending a clandestine school for blacks. John H. Rapier Sr. encouraged his sons to leave the South. After going to school in Canada, Richard and Henry went to California to seek gold in 1855. After quarrelling with his brother, Henry dropped permanently out of sight, but Richard farmed in California for 25 years afterward. John Rapier Jr. led an adventurous life. After engaging in private military action with William Walker in Central America, he ended up in Minnesota, where he became a journalist and occasional poet before exploring the possibilities of Haiti and Jamaica in the early 1860s. After receiving securing medical training, he became an assistant surgeon at Freedmen's Contraband Hospital in Washington, D.C.

James T. Rapier worked on river boats from 1854 to 1856, enjoying a life of hard work, drinking, fighting, and women—much to his father's disgust. The son agreed to attend school in Buxton, Canada, which had begun as a utopian black community and grown into a prosperous town of more than 2,000 inhabitants by the early 1860s. His uncle Henry farmed there, and his father had bought land there.

James Rapier began school in the fall of 1856 but did not change his lifestyle until April of 1857, when he became a convert to Methodism. Schweninger cited John Rapier Jr.'s comment on the conversion: "Letter from James. Buxton, Professed Religion. Damned Fool." James Rapier spent another year at Buxton, and then in 1860 he attended a normal school in Toronto, receiving a teaching diploma in early 1863. He returned to Buxton to teach, and in late 1864 he returned to Nashville.

Returns to the South

Rapier found he could do little to help the blacks who had crowded into the city because of the war. He did some reporting for a Northern newspaper, and in 1865 he rented land in Maury County and raised a cotton crop. At a convention calling for black suffrage in Nashville on August 7–8, 1865, he emerged as a leader. This call for suffrage attracted little support in the North, and throughout the South state legislatures were passing laws aimed at maintaining white control over former slaves. In 1866 Rapier rented several hundred acres of prime land near Florence and became a major cotton planter.

In March of 1867 laws passed by the U.S. Congress began a new era in Reconstruction. To begin the process of reordering the South under these laws, Rapier called a meeting of Lauderdale County freedmen on April 24 to select a black voter registrar. The assembly chose John H. Rapier Sr. A month later James Rapier called a meeting to select a black nominee to the state's first Republican convention, and again he was the spontaneous and unanimous choice.

Rapier was named a vice–chairman of the convention, which met in Montgomery on June 4, 1867, and he helped draw up the party platform. Because of his attendance there, he was absent during a bitter dispute about the seating of an antiblack white federal judge as a delegate, a foretaste of the factional divisions that would characterize the party during Reconstruction. Rapier was nominated for the state constitutional convention and during the election on October 1–3 was the only black elected in his district, coming in near the top of the polls. The convention met on November 5, but Rapier did not achieve his goals of a relatively lenient disfranchisement clause for former rebels and specific guarantees of black rights, especially rights to equal access in public accommodations. Alabama reentered the union under its new constitution on June 25, 1868.

Rapier campaigned actively for Ulyssses Grant in the fall. This activity was not without danger—at one point a meeting was broken up by horsemen wearing white hoods. Soon afterward he faced even more serious danger. A freedman, the father of Illinois congressman Oscar DePriest, warned him that he had been accused of burning down the Tuscumbia Female Academy near Florence. Rapier escaped with only the loss of his crop and his steamboat woodyard, but the three other accused blacks, all active in politics, were arrested and lynched the following day. Rapier spent the next year as inconspicuously as possible in a Montgomery boarding house. In August 1869 he returned to Florence to be with his ailing father, who died of stomach cancer on September 18. James Rapier served as executor of his father's will and assumed responsibility for his younger half–brothers and half–sisters, who except for one were all still minors.

Rapier made the decision to stay in the South and continue his efforts in politics. In late 1869 he went to Washington as a delegate to the first National Negro Labor Union Convention. In the spring of 1870, he undertook a speaking tour to celebrate the adoption of the Fifteenth Amendment, and he won the Republican nomination for secretary of state. A director of the Alabama and Chattanooga Railroad System immediately offered him $10,000 to withdraw. Rapier persisted but lost by 5,000 votes due to the hostility of many white Republicans and a campaign of violence directed against black voting.

Rapier worked hard to try to build a labor union to improve conditions for blacks; he was especially concerned by the poor schooling available to blacks as well as the prevalence of debt peonage, a system under which tenants perpetually borrowed money from the landlord in order to plant their crops and live until harvest time. He had been elected a vice–president of the national organization in 1869, and he organized a state convention which met on January 2, 1871. In the same month he led a delegation to the second national convention. By the time the Alabama organization met again in January 1872, it had become clear that the local organization, like the national one, was doomed by the lack of effective political support.

President Grant appointed Rapier Assessor for the Second Revenue District in April of 1871, the highest patronage position yet given to a black in Alabama. The appointment aroused much hostility, and Rapier had to fight off charges of misconduct within his office later in the year. In October he attended the Southern States Negro Convention in Columbia, South Carolina, a meeting which attracted many prominent black Southern politicians. Rapier was unable to persuade the convention to endorse the reelection of Grant. In spite of continued white violence, Rapier felt confident that the Republicans would carry Alabama in the 1872 elections.

Becomes Congressman

Rapier launched a campaign for the congressional nomination from the Second District, which included Montgomery. To support his quest, he launched the first black–owned and black–operated newspaper in the state, the *Republican Sentinel,* on April 1, 1872. He was influential in rallying the state Republican party behind Grant. Winning the nomination in August, he won the November election with the support of nearly all 18,000 eligible black voters and of 1,500 white voters.

The new Congress would not convene until December 1873. In early 1873 Rapier was appointed commissioner to the Fifth International Exposition in Vienna, Austria. He fell ill shortly before his scheduled departure, but after several weeks in bed, he undertook the trip to Europe, where he spent five months. On December 1 he took his seat in Congress.

Although Rapier was a conscientious congressman, an increasingly conservative tide was sweeping the Congress and the country, and the session's major civil rights legislation failed.

In July of 1874 Rapier launched his campaign for renomination. Despite boisterous factional fighting at the convention, he was again nominated. Because of white violence, bribery, and other voting irregularities, however, Rapier lost the election. He returned to Washington for the lame duck session of Congress which produced a much–weakened civil rights act. In Alabama, conservative whites had consolidated their control of the state by the middle of 1875 through rearranging congressional districts and passing legislation that made it easier for white plantation owners to supervise voting by their tenants.

By this time, the Republican party had effectively split into two factions. Rapier rented land in Lowndes County and sought the nomination for the new Fourth District in opposition to the black incumbent Jarral Haralson. After Rapier received the Republican nomination, Haralson ran as an independent but withdrew from the campaign after Charles Shelley, sheriff of Selma and the Democratic nominee, arrested him on a charge of vagrancy, waved a derringer in his face, and verbally abused him for two hours. In the heavily black district, the final count was Shelley, 9,624 votes; Haralson, 8,675; and Rapier, 7,236.

Rapier turned to cotton growing, but he did not lose his interest in politics. In 1878 he again backed a newspaper, the *Republican Sentinel and Hayneville Times.* He was also nominated collector of internal revenue of the Second District, a prime political prize, and in July 1878 was confirmed despite vigorous opposition.

In early 1879, in response to oppressive economic and social conditions in the South, a large mass emigration of 50,000 blacks from the South was underway, headed in the direction of Kansas. Rapier attended the Southern States Emigration Convention at Nashville. On May 6, Rapier was the first speaker and supported the emigration. On May 9, he brought in a drafted statement of support for the emigration for consideration by the convention. He consistently supported emigration until the end of his life, even visiting Kansas to explore conditions for emigrants there, and did not back down in two days of testimony before the Senate Committee on Emigration in 1880, during which he denounced Alabama laws oppressing black tenant farmers.

In the deadlocked Republican convention of 1880, which eventually turned to dark horse James A. Garfield, Rapier was a stalwart supporter of John Sherman. He also visited Kansas again and purchased land there. He continued his interest in cotton planting and in 1882 earned a net profit of $5,000. Although he won praise for his work for the Treasury Department, he was suspended from his duties in September 1882. His health was by now visibly deteriorating, and he finally submitted his resignation just after he had been told he would be retained in office. Rapier died of pulmonary tuberculosis on May 31, 1883. He had never married, and his uncle John P. Thomas, an affluent real–estate owner in St. Louis, had his remains transferred there, where he was buried in Cavalry Cemetery in an unmarked grave.

In his short life of 45 years, Rapier had the good fortune to have a loving and close family who helped him secure a good education. Like other members of his family, he developed considerable entrepreneurial skills. He tried his best to secure black rights through his political activities in his native state; but in spite of his own financial success, he ended his life by urging his fellow black Alabamians to seek opportunity elsewhere.

REFERENCES

Christopher, Maurine. *America's Black Congressmen.* New York: Thomas Y. Crowell, 1971.

Logan, Rayford W., and Michael R. Winston, eds. *Dictionary of American Negro Biography.* New York: Norton, 1982.

Rabinowitz, Howard N., ed. *Southern Black Leaders of the Reconstruction Era.* Urbana: University of Illinois Press, 1982.

Schweninger, Loren. *James T. Rapier and Reconstruction.* Chicago: University of Chicago Press, 1978.

———. "A Slave Family in the Ante Bellum South." *Journal of Negro History* 50 (January 1975): 29–44.

COLLECTIONS

Rapier family papers are in the Moorland–Spingarn Research Center at Howard University, Washington, D.C.

Robert L. Johns

William J. Raspberry

(1935–)

Newspaper columnist, television commentator, teacher, speaker

William J. Raspberry is a Pulitzer Prize–winning journalist who writes a syndicated column for the *Washington Post.* Discussing his professional philosophy in the *American Journalism Review,* Raspberry wrote, "I believe journalism can change the world and can save the world. I think any particular journalist is very unlikely to do much of either. And yet we ought to . . . as a matter of routine, behave as though we have the power to nudge the world in one direction or the other."

William James Raspberry was born in Okolona, Mississippi, on October 12, 1935. He has one brother and three sisters. Both of his parents were educators: his father, James Lee Raspberry, taught shop, and his mother, Willie Mae Tucker Raspberry, taught English. On November 12, 1966,

William J. Raspberry

Raspberry married Sondra Patricia Dodson, and they have three children: Patricia D., Angela D., and Mark J. When away from his job, William Raspberry enjoys reading murder mysteries, attending plays and movies, and spending time with his family.

The Making of a Journalist

Raspberry credits his accomplishments as a journalist to the training he received early in life. His parents instilled in him a love for reading, helped him to develop a positive approach to life, and taught him to think logically. In *Looking Backward at Us* he described reading as the "passport to a world that was otherwise beyond my reach" and as a foundation for his ability to write. "It was my unquestioned belief that books were full of information and excitement and pleasure that kept me reading, that expanded my curiosity and (though I didn't know it at the time) got me ready for writing."

Raspberry's education helped prepare him for a career in journalism. The elementary and secondary experiences provided the fundamentals of grammar, but he truly learned to write on the job. At Indiana Central College, now the University of Indianapolis, Raspberry changed his major several times, from mathematics to history, then English. For a time he was a pre–seminary student. During the summer before his senior year, he worked for the *Indianapolis Recorder.* Here he dealt with information that he considered important and had an audience that he thought needed the information. He worked at capturing and maintaining the interest of his audience. Here he learned to give human form to statistics. He had to explain why matters were important, to consider all sides of a controversy, and to understand that one may embrace a point of view that differs from one's own.

Raspberry worked four years at the *Recorder* as reporter, proofreader, and then managing editor. "It constituted my journalism school," he has said in *Contemporary Authors.* In 1960, he was drafted into the army. Stationed in Virginia, he served as a public information officer in Washington, D.C. When he completed his service, he took a job as a teletypist for the *Washington Post.*

Raspberry realized that his writing skill needed to be honed and actively sought opportunities to strengthen his craft. After a year at the *Post,* he asked for a job as copy editor and then spent his time analyzing other people's writing in order to improve his own. His talent and hard work were recognized by Joe Paull, one of the *Post*'s assistant managing editors. The young reporter recalled in the *American Journalism Review,* "The big announcement came when he told me, 'Starting Monday, you're doing obits.'"

Successful Career Emerges

In 1966 Raspberry began writing a column for the *Post,* after initially declining the assignment in fear that he would run out of ideas. More than 30 years later, he is still writing and still credits his parents with influencing the content of his articles. He wrote in *Looking Backward at Us,* "It was from my mother, the English teacher and amateur poet, that I learned to care about the rhythm and grace of words; it was from my father, the shop teacher, that I learned neither end tables nor arguments are worthwhile unless they stand solidly on all four legs." In 1971, the editors promoted the column, originally titled "Potomac Watch," to the editorial page, and it became syndicated in 1977.

As early as 1974, Raspberry had gained a reputation as the most respected black journalist on any white newspaper in the country. His colleagues speak well of his work. He has been considered thoughtful, mannerly, and well–meaning with a calming tone. In the *American Journalism Review* he was called "a wise and careful person," while Raspberry has described himself as a "solutionist." He said in *Editor and Publisher* for February 2, 1991, "I try to talk . . . from the point of view of sharing the problems—not coming down from the mountain to bestow wisdom." That attitude is recognized by his readers. One writer stated in *Christian Science Monitor,* "Raspberry's signature writing style—is to wrestle with himself on paper, exposing his own struggle to resolve tough issues." His writing style has been described as incisive, probing, and lucid.

Raspberry has also engaged in other aspects of his journalism profession. From 1973 to 1975 he served as a television commentator for station WTTG in Washington, and as a discussion panelist for WRC–TV from 1974 to 1975. He also has taught journalism classes at Howard University and has lectured on race relations and public education. He has written articles for popular magazines, but he is most at ease with his chosen work, writing newspaper columns. He likes being able to write about issues while they are ''hot'' and in the public's mind. He added in *Contemporary Authors* that

> the advantage of writing a column is that it's a living organism. It grows and you can bend it and shape it from one day to the next. I haven't reached hard conclusions about a lot of things that interest me. But each column can take it one developmental step further.

That process of bending and shaping has brought many awards to Raspberry. The Capital Press Club granted him its Journalist of the Year award in 1965 for his coverage of the Los Angeles Watts riot. The Federal Bar Association gave him its Liberty Bell Award for his ''outstanding community service in promoting responsible citizenship.'' In 1994 he received the Pulitzer Prize for commentary. Then in 1995, the National Society of Newspaper Columnists presented Raspberry its Lifetime Achievement Award.

Raspberry has served on a variety of professional committees and groups. Since 1984 he has held membership on the board of advisors for the Poynter Institute for Media Studies. In 1985 he became a member of the board of visitors for the University of Maryland School of Journalism. He has been a juror for the Robert F. Kennedy Award, and from 1979 to 1986 he served as a member of the Pulitzer Prize Board. He belongs to the Capital Press Club, the National Association of Black Journalists, the Gridiron Club, and Kappa Alpha Psi Fraternity. At least four universities have awarded him honorary degrees: Georgetown University, the University of Maryland, the University of Indianapolis, and Virginia State University.

In speeches to journalists, Raspberry urges educators to teach students good citizenship, and he encourages reporters to be sensitive to the people they write about and to tell the story straight. He exercises his own concern for individuals not only in the words he writes but also by being receptive to readers' ideas and by frequently assisting people with their problems outside the confines of his column. He has a particular concern for the black youth of the nation. According to the *American Journalism Review,* he believes that racial strife ''helped to produce a generation of children who saw themselves not as bright, capable youngsters with the ability to take control of their own destinies but as essentially helpless victims of a racism they could do nothing about.''

In a lecture at Kansas State University, published in *Vital Speeches of the Day,* Raspberry espoused ''mutual fairness'' and stressed that one should focus on problems rather than on enemies. He described seeking out enemies as a game for pessimists and noted that ''identifying problems is both optimistic and healing. The whole point of delineating problems is to fashion solutions.''

Raspberry is a well-respected, fair, insightful, and competent journalist who helps to shape the opinions of his readers primarily through his articles in one of the nation's leading newspapers, the *Washington Post.*

Current address: Washington Post Co., 1150 15th St., NW, Washington, D.C. 20071–0002.

REFERENCES

Astor, David. ''William Raspberry Talks about His Work.'' *Editor and Publisher* 124 (2 February 1991): 36–38.

———. ''Writer Wants to See What Is Going Right.'' *Editor and Publisher* 128 (24 June 1995): 118–19.

Contemporary Authors, Vol. 122. Detroit: Gale Research, 1988.

Contemporary Black Biography. Vol. 2. Detroit: Gale Research, 1992.

Fibich, Linda. ''The Solutionist.'' *American Journalism Review* 16 (May 1994): 28–33.

Germani, Clara. ''A Black Journalist Looks at Civil Rights Today.'' *Christian Science Monitor* 85 (15 January 1993): 10.

''The *Post*'s Lone Ranger.'' *Time* 104 (16 September 1974): 48.

Raspberry, William. ''Crisis of Community: Make America Work for Americans.'' *Vital Speeches of the Day* 61 (1 June 1995): 493–96.

———. *Looking Backward at Us.* Jackson: University Press of Mississippi, 1991.

Stein, M. L. *Blacks in Communications: Journalism, Public Relations and Advertising.* New York: Messner, 1972.

———. ''Good Citizens Make Good Reporters.'' *Editor and Publisher* 127 (3 September 1994): 28–29.

Marie Garrett

Charles Lewis Reason

(1818–1893)

Educator, abolitionist

For more than half a century, Charles Lewis Reason was a community leader in New York. As teacher and principal, he touched the lives of generations of black youth. He also was a prominent leader in the abolitionist movement and was the first black American to hold a college professorship. He helped build Philadelphia's Institute for Colored Youth into a premier school.

Charles Lewis Reason was born on July 21, 1818. His parents came from the West Indies in 1793—Michiel, from Martinique and Elizabeth from Haiti. Charles Reason had at least two brothers, Elwer and Patrick. Patrick (1816–1898) became a noted engraver and lithographer who was active in the New York African American community until he moved to Cleveland in 1869. All three brothers received an education at the African Free School where their classmates included

Charles Lewis Reason

such figures as Henry Highland Garnet, James McCune Smith, Ira Aldridge, and Alexander Crummell.

At the age of 14, Charles Reason began his teaching career as a monitor under the supervision of another long–time and influential New York teacher, John Peterson. Saint Philip's Episcopal Church chose Reason for seminary training, but his fate was the same as that of Isaiah de Grasse and Alexander Crummell: the New York bishop barred him from the theological seminary because he was black. As a result of this injustice, Reason resigned from St. Philip's.

Reason earned a college degree at Central College in McGrawville (now McGraw), New York, a school officially opened on September 4, 1849, by the American Baptist Free Mission Society. The school was quick to recognize his learning and teaching ability. In October of that year, he became professor of belles lettres, Greek, Latin, and French, as well as adjunct professor of mathematics. (Two other blacks became professors at the school before it went bankrupt in 1859 and closed in 1861: William G. Allen and George Boyer Vashon.) In 1852 Reason became head of the Institute for Colored Youth in Philadelphia. He took with him Grace A. Mapp, an 1852 graduate of Central and the first black woman to complete a degree in a four–year college course.

Reason was instrumental in building a struggling manual training school into perhaps the best academic school for African Americans during the first half of the nineteenth century. When he left to return to New York in 1855, the number of students had increased from six to 118. This change of residence seems to coincide with his third marriage, to Clorice Esteve Reason, who maintained a pre–Civil War salon frequented by the serious and high–minded, and also ran an extensive business making ice cream. She died before her husband. (Nothing is known of his previous marriages.)

Reason was passionate about equal rights for African Americans throughout his life. While still in his teens, he joined with other youth of his age like Henry Highland Garnet and George Downing to form the Young Men's Convention in 1837. The goal of the Convention was to challenge the restrictive suffrage provision of the New York State constitution, which set a $250 property requirement for voting by blacks and none for whites. Older black leaders like Samuel Cornish, Philip Bell, and Charles Ray joined in the protest, and the foundation for civil rights agitation in the state grew from this effort. Together with Henry Highland Garnet, Reason served as secretary of the 1840 state convention of blacks which pressed for suffrage. He was an organizer of the New York Society for the Promotion of Education Among Colored Children, which gained control of black schools in 1847. In spite of their early partnership, Reason and Garnet divided on the issue of the colonization of Africa. While Garnet favored an emigration of African Americans to Africa, Reason spoke out against colonization, and on April of 1849 he was a speaker at a two–day meeting called to denounce the American Colonization Society.

Reason continued his abolitionist work while he was in Philadelphia during the early 1850s. He was a member of the General Vigilance Committee, which aided the work of the Underground Railroad. Reason also condemned white abolitionist Lucy Stone for addressing a segregated audience in 1854.

When the idea of black emigration came to the fore again in the 1850s, Reason was constant in his opposition. In New York on April 12, 1860, Reason and George Downing held their own in a debate with John Sella Martin and Henry Highland Garnet who were advocating the emigration program of Garnet's African Civilization Society.

Reason was also a contributor to newspapers and an occasional poet of some competence as evinced by his four surviving poems. Reason's life is even less fully documented after the Civil War than before it. He retired from teaching in 1890 when he was 72–years old and died at his residence, 242 East 53rd Street, New York, on August 16, 1893, from nephritis and heart disease. He is buried in Greenwood Cemetery.

A light–colored and very handsome man, Reason won high praise from those who knew him, from Daniel A. Payne, who first met him when Reason was 20, to Maritcha R. Lyons, a former student and herself a master teacher. Payne says that Reason also contributed more than words to black causes. When Payne approached well–off New York African Americans for funds to build a museum at Wilberforce, Reason and his wife were the only ones to make contributions—both gave $25.

Reason made his most lasting contribution as a teacher. Payne stated that he watched many teachers here and abroad, "but I have seldom met his equal, never his superior." In addition, Reason was a constant supporter of black causes and a worker for abolition who won the respect of his black contemporaries for his efforts over the years.

REFERENCES

Blassingame, John W., ed. *The Frederick Douglass Papers.* Vol. 2. New Haven: Yale University Press, 1982.

Logan, Rayford W., and Michael R. Winston. *Dictionary of American Negro Biography.* New York: Norton, 1982.

Lyons, Maritcha Remond. *Memories of Yesterday.* Unpublished autobiography. Harry H. Williamson Papers. Schomburg Center for Research in Black Culture.

Payne, Daniel Alexander. *Recollections of Seventy Years.* Nashville: AME Sunday School Union, 1888.

Pease, Jane H., and William H. *Those Who Would Be Free.* New York: Atheneum, 1974.

Quarles, Benjamin. *Black Abolitionists.* New York: Oxford, 1969.

Sherman, Joan R. *Invisible Poets.* Urbana: University of Illinois Press, 1974.

Simmons, William J. *Men of Mark.* Cleveland: George M. Rewell, 1887.

Robert L. Johns

J. Saunders Redding
(1906–1988)
Writer, critic, educator, scholar

J. Saunders Redding

J. Saunders Redding, often called the "dean of Afro American scholars," was constrained like other African American artists of his day. He was unable to devote all of his time to his craft and his work options were few. However, he transcended the limitations. Redding's writing reveal that he was an integrationist. He believed African American culture and the American experience were so interdependent, one could not be studied without the other. His study then was across racial and national boundaries. *A Scholar's Conscience* called his egalitarian attitude an outgrowth of his upbringing: hearing his father read from the Bible and *The Crisis,* his grandmother recite from *The Book of Common Prayer,* his mother quote the poetry of Whittier and Whitman, and his college teachers demonstrate Hugh Blair's Lectures on Rhetoric and Belles Lettres. Because of his independent thinking, he was not swayed by fashionable literary movements and was often at odds with other critics.

James Thomas Saunders Redding was born October 3, 1906, in Wilmington, Delaware. He was the third of seven children born to Lewis Alfred, a postal service worker, and Mary Ann Holmes Redding, a school teacher turned housewife; both were graduates of Howard University, who impressed upon their children the value of education. Redding spent one year at Lincoln University in Pennsylvania and then transferred to Brown University where he earned both a bachelor of philosophy (Ph.B.) in 1928 and a master of arts (M.A.) in 1932. His performance was so outstanding at Brown that he met the requirements for Phi Beta Kappa. Due to the racism of the 1920s, however, it was not until 1943, after he had made a name for himself, that he was awarded the honor. He pursued further graduate study Columbia University in 1933–1934. In 1929 he married Esther Elizabeth James; to this union was born Conway Holmes and Lewis Alfred II.

Begins Teaching Career

In spite of Redding's negative feelings about African American colleges, he taught at a number; however, he was dismissed from his first teaching job because of his attitude. *A Scholar's Conscience* noted that "during his early career he found black college administrators a bulwark against positive action, liberal or even independent thought, and spiritual and economic freedom." He was an instructor at Morehouse College (1928–1931) and Louisville Municipal College (1934–1936). From 1936 to 1938, he served as head of the English department at Southern University and from 1938 to 1943, he was chairman of Elizabeth City State College's English department. In 1943, he became professor of English and American literature at Hampton Institute. He served in this capacity until 1955, when he was named the James Weldon Johnson Professor of Literature and Creative Writing.

In 1966, he became the director of the Division of Research and Publication for the National Endowment for the Humanities and from 1970–1988 served as its curator. Redding, like so many Americans, benefited from the 1968 unrest and thrust to have African American inclusion on white college campuses. From 1968 to 1969, he was a member of the faculty at George Washington University; he lectured widely, and in 1970, he became a member of the English department at Cornell University, the first Afro–American to be appointed the rank of professor in the College of Arts and Sciences and the first to hold an endowed Chair. He became the Ernest I. White Professor of American Studies and Humane Letters Emeritus in 1975.

From 1944 to 1950, he was visiting professor at Brown University. In 1952 Redding had a three–month lecture assignment in India for the Department of State. Then in 1962 he spent several months on a lecture tour to African universities under the auspices of the American Society of African Cultures. The Africa tour caused him to recognize the misconceptions about the continent and their source and, according to *A Scholar's Conscience,* to say, ''I no longer believe in the Africa I was taught to believe in'' and ''whatever political sophistication I have is not enough to cope with the sophisticated politics of Africa.'' From these experiences he found material that he used in his writing.

Writes Nonfiction Works

Redding's experience as writer and critic included both nonfiction and fiction, books, essays, and short pieces and shared editorship. His first book, *To Make a Poet Black* (1939), was an attempt to provide a critical and historical overview of African American literature and to place the authors and works in what *A Scholar's Conscience* called ''a compendium of Afro–American literary history.'' He spoke of this work as, ''written with a mind for the problems of students, . . . [and he] hoped that the odor of scholarship attaches to it so slightly as to give the book some appeal to popular taste; for ultimately literature, if it is to live at all, must be in the strictest sense popular.''

For nearly three decades, his work, with the exception of his first short story, ''Delaware Coon'' and his novel *Stranger and Alone,* was written under the name Saunders Redding. However, yielding to the urgings of family, ''he restored the 'J' to his by–line.'' For his second book, *No Day of Triumph* (1942), he was commissioned by the University of North Carolina and financed by the Rockefeller Foundation to chronicle black life in the South. The book provides autobiographical information as well as a picture of pre–World War II southern blacks. *No Day of Triumph* earned him commendation from Richard Wright for moving away from the concept of the Talented Tenth—W. E. B. Du Bois's term for the black American intelligentsia—and also the North Carolina Historical Society's 1944 Mayflower Award for Distinguished Writing by a resident of the state.

In 1950 he wrote *They Came in Chains: Americans from Africa,* a history beginning in 1619. His 1951 publication *On Being a Negro in America* was an attempt to purge that which was unhealthy in him and America. He wanted to end the necessity to always address the race issue, for ''the human spirit is bigger than that'' and he was ''tired of giving up . . . [his] creative initiative to these demands.'' Further ''this piece [was to] stand as the epilogue to whatever contribution . . . [he had] made to the literature of race.''

As a result of his exchange lectureships in India in 1952, Redding published several pieces. One of these was *An American in India: A Personal Report on the Indian Dilemma and the Nature of Her Conflicts* (1954) in which he reported some of his discoveries; racialism, colonialism, what *A Scholar's Conscience* called ''an urge to defend America,'' and ''the color of [his] skin . . . was . . . [a] touchstone'' in his journey. *The Lonesome Road: The Story of the Negro's Part in America* (1958, reprinted in 1973) was commissioned for the Doubleday Mainstream of American Series. He again presents the history of African Americans, this time by way of biographies of 12 achievers, known and little known. His 1967 work, *Negro,* explored historical events up to the civil rights unrest and legislation of the 1960s. Potomac Book commissioned the work for its U.S.A. Survey Series.

Other nonfiction works include *Men and the Writing of Blacks* (1969) and *Negro Writing and the Political Climate* (1970). Redding was a contributor to many publications, the author of the introduction to a book of essays and sketches on W. E. B. Du Bois (1963) and on the social protest writing of Langston Hughes (1973). He coedited *Reading for Writing* (1942) and *Cavalcade: Negro American Writing from 1960 to the Present* (1971). The latter, a seminal work, was in response to the need for a text for African American studies.

Becomes Fiction Writer

Redding's fiction includes short stories in the *Brown University Quarterly.* One of which was the ''Delaware Coon'' (December 17, 1928); it was reprinted in the June 1930 issue of *Transition: An International Quarterly for Creative Experiment.* ''A Battle Behind the Lines'' was published in the January 9, 1958, issue of the *Reporter.* His third published book was a novel, *Stranger and Alone* (1950). Initially, it was to be part of a trilogy. The main character, Shelton Howden, is the product of miscegenation, confused about his identity and ultimately the betrayer of his race. Critics were said to be more receptive to the book than the reading public; according to *A Scholar's Conscience,* even his friend Arthur P. Davis called this novel, ''perhaps his most glaring mistake in judgment.''

Redding wrote a weekly book review column for the *Afro–American* from 1946 to 1966. His book reviews critiqued works by both black and white writers like James Baldwin, Ernest Gaines, Paula Marshall, Gwendolyn Brooks, John Hope Franklin, William Faulkner, John Dos Passos, Ernest Hemingway, and Herbert Aptheker. His book reviews were on arts, humanities, and the social sciences. His work as literary critic also appeared in the *American Scholar, Phylon, Atlantic Monthly, New York Herald,* and *Saturday Review of Literature.*

The high quality of Redding's work led to many accolades. He was a Guggenheim fellow twice (1944–1945, 1959–1960), received the New York Public Library citation for outstanding contribution to interracial understanding (1945, 1946), National Urban League citation for outstanding achievement (1950) and a Ford Foundation fellowship at Duke University (1964–1965) and at the University of North Carolina. He received honorary degrees from Virginia State College (1963), Hobart College (1964), University of Portland (1970), and Wittenberg University (1977). Others have been granted by Dickinson College, Brown University, and the University of Delaware. From 1973 to 1977 he was honorary conservator of American culture, Library of Congress.

Faith Berry's evaluation of his work in *A Scholar's Conscience* is a fitting tribute to his memory: "He is perhaps the writer of his generation who best represents and comes closest to explaining, the hopes and conflicts of American democracy in a multiracial society."

REFERENCES

Berry, Faith, ed. *A Scholar's Conscience: Selected Writings of J. Saunders Redding, 1942–1977.* Lexington: University Press of Kentucky, 1992.

Contemporary Authors. New Revision Series. Detroit: Gale Research, 1988.

Redding, J. Saunders. *On Being Negro in America.* New York: Charter Books, 1962.

———. *To Make a Poet Black.* Ithaca, NY: Cornell University Press, 1988.

COLLECTIONS

Redding's papers are located at Brown University in Providence, Rhode Island.

Helen R. Houston

Ira De A. Reid
(1901–1968)
Sociologist, scholar, educator

A researcher and educator of first rank, Ira De A. Reid studied the black experience in the United States and abroad, recording facts and figures and using his scholarship to help remedy the conditions of poverty, ignorance, and oppression.

Born on July 2, 1901, in Clifton Forge, Virginia, Reid was the son of the Daniel Augustine, a Baptist minister, and Willie Roberta James Reid. Reid spent his early childhood in Harrisburg and Philadelphia, Pennsylvania. He attended the public schools in Germantown, outside of Philadelphia. Before Reid could complete high school, his father was transferred to a church in Savannah, Georgia. Unable to attend the public schools of Georgia because there were no high schools for blacks, Reid enrolled at Morehouse Academy. However, in 1917, after Reid had entered Morehouse College, his father died. His mother, who was from West Virginia, moved the family back there.

Reid joined the military in 1917 during World War I. He attempted to enter the Colored Officers Training Camp at Fort Des Moines, Iowa, but was rejected. After the war ended, Reid returned to Morehouse College and received his bachelor of arts degree in 1922. He had become interested in the study of sociology as an undergraduate. As a discipline, sociology was new, yet it seemed to offer what no other field of study had attempted—a means by which one could study and perhaps understand the causes and results of a racist society.

Reid wanted to advance his education, but needed to earn money. His first job following graduation was as director of Texas College's high school in Tyler, Texas, a position he held for one year. In the summer of 1923 he enrolled in classes at the University of Chicago, but by the fall he had returned to his mother's home where he taught at Douglass High School in Huntington, West Virginia. In 1924 Reid won a fellowship from the Pittsburgh Urban League and began working as industrial secretary of the New York Urban League. At the same time he studied for a master's degree at the University of Pittsburgh. The energy with which he pursued several tasks simultaneously was to characterize his entire life and career.

Reid earned the master of arts degree in sociology in 1925. That same year on October 15 he married Gladys Russell Scott. They had one child, Enid Harriet, born August 15, 1928. While working with the Urban League in New York, Reid conducted research on Harlem churches. The result of his research was "Let Us Pray," an article published in *Opportunity* in September 1926. Charles S. Johnson, director of research for the National Urban League and editor of *Opportunity,* resigned in 1928. Reid succeeded him and remained director and editor until 1934. He resigned to accept a teaching position at Atlanta University where he worked with W. E. B. Du Bois.

Reid studied and surveyed racial problems in Troy and Albany, New York, in 1928 during his tenure with the National Urban League. In 1929 he surveyed Denver; he spent 1930 and 1931 compiling data on blacks in New Jersey; and he surveyed Baltimore in 1934. The National Commission on Law Observance and Enforcement commissioned Reid to study criminal behavior in 1934. The results of this study were published as *A Study of 200 Negro Prisoners in Western Penitentiary, Pennsylvania.* Reid directed a federal survey of white–collar and skilled workers in 1937, and from 1937 to 1941, he was consulting social scientist on minorities for the Social Security Board. Between 1940 and 1942, Reid was consultant on minorities for the War Manpower Commission.

In 1939, Reid received the Ph.D. degree in sociology from Columbia University. In the same year he published his dissertation entitled *The Negro Immigrant, His Background, Characteristics, and Social Adjustments 1899–1937.* Reid studied at the London School of Economics in 1939 on a Julius Rosenwald grant.

Many of the problems Reid uncovered through his research he believed could be rectified through education. His idea for an adult education program at Atlanta University was a step in this direction. In 1942 Reid became director of the People's College, and when Du Bois retired in 1943, he became department chair and editor of *Phylon.*

Teacher by Popular Demand

In 1946 Reid was invited to lecture at Haverford College in Pennsylvania. He went there as visiting professor of sociology, teaching three days a week. He also was visiting professor of educational sociology in the School of Education at New York University. What had started out as a one year stint at Haverford College became, at the insistence of the students, a permanent appointment as professor and chair of the department of sociology and anthropology in 1947. Not only was Reid an outstanding and energetic researcher, he incorporated his enthusiasm for research with his love for students and teaching creating a winning combination.

Reid was the first black assistant editor of the *American Sociological Review* from 1947 to 1949. He served on the Advisory Commission to the U.S. Department of Labor between 1946 and 1948, and was asked to serve as consultant on higher education for the Trusteeship Division in the United Nations in 1949. From 1951 to 1954, Reid commuted from Pennsylvania to New York where he was visiting professor at the New York School of Social Work, Columbia University. In 1956 he edited *Racial Desegregation and Integration.* In June 1956, Gladys, his wife of 30 years, died. Reid married Anne M. Cooke on August 12, 1958.

Reid spent a good part of his later years abroad. In 1962 he traveled to Nigeria where he served as visiting director of the department of extra–mural studies at the University College of Ibadan. The following year he became Danforth Distinguished Visiting Professor of Sociology at the International Christian University in Tokyo, Japan. He returned the summer of 1963 as visiting professor at Harvard University. In 1965 Reid was consultant for the American Council on Education.

In 1966 Reid became professor emeritus at Haverford College and was inducted as an honorary member into Phi Beta Kappa. He was a fellow in the American Association for the Advancement of Science; a fellow and member of the executive committee of the American Sociological Association and served as vice president of ASA. He had been president of the Eastern Sociological Society in 1955. Reid was also associate director of the Division of Race Relations for the American Missionary Association in 1943. He was a member of the Board of Directors of the American Cancer Society and a trustee of the National Urban League. He received honorary degrees from Morehouse College in 1953 and from Haverford in 1967.

Reid's publications include: *Negro Membership in American Labor Unions* (1930); *The Negro's Relation to Work and Law Observance* (1931); *The Negro in New Jersey* (5 vols. 1932); *The Problem of Child Dependency Among Negroes* (1936); *The Negro Community of Baltimore* (1935); *Adult Education Among Negroes* (1936); *The Urban Negro Worker in the United States: 1925–1936* (1938); and "The Church and Education for Negroes," in *Divine White Right,* edited by Trevor Bowen, 1934.

Suffering from emphysema, Reid died at Bryn Mawr Hospital in October of 1968. He had made a difference in education, sociology, and research, particularly for the black American community. A researcher in the tradition of W. E. B. Du Bois, Reid looked for facts to argue and explain human society and its behavior. He was able to take the facts and figures of his intense research and translate them into information useful to students and to policy makers.

REFERENCES

Bacote, Clarence A. *The Story of Atlanta University.* Atlanta: Atlanta University, 1969.

Current Biography 1946. New York: H. W. Wilson, 1947: 503–505.

Logan, Rayford W., and Michael R. Winston, eds. *Dictionary of American Negro Biography.* New York: Norton, 1982. 519–520.

Reid, Ira De Augustine. *In a Minor Key: Negro Youth in Story and Fact.* New York and Washington, DC: American Council on Education, 1940.

Obituary. *Negro History Bulletin* 31–32 (November 1968): 8.

Nagueyalti Warren

Charles Lenox Remond
(1810–1873)
Abolitionist

Charles Lenox Remond was the first black hired to lecture by the American Anti–Slavery Society. A member of a notable family of entrepreneurs and abolitionists, he was unwavering in his support of abolition. His role was somewhat overshadowed by Frederick Douglass, who surpassed him in popularity on the lecture circuit, and by his steadfast adherence to William Lloyd Garrison's American Anti–Slavery Society. Nonetheless, he became increasingly outspoken as the Civil War approached. He was always firm in his rejection of separatist black organizations, even as a temporary expedient.

Remond was born in Salem, Massachusetts, on February 1, 1810. He was the oldest son of the eight children, two boys and six girls, of John and Nancy Lenox Remond (1788–1867). John Remond emigrated from Curaçao in 1798 and became a hairdresser, merchant, and caterer. He became a U.S. citizen on May 2, 1811. Nancy Lenox Remond was a cakemaker.

Remond was educated in the public schools of Salem and apparently trained as a barber. Around 1853 Remond married his first wife, Amy Matilda Williams Cassey, who was the daughter of Peter Williams Jr., the first black Episcopal priest in the city of New York. Remond married Elizabeth Thayer Magee after the death of Amy in 1856. They had four children: a daughter and three sons. Remond's small and irregular income placed the family in poverty. Elizabeth worked as a seamstress and also solicited loans from white abolitionist Wendell Phillips to keep the family afloat.

Charles Lenox Remond

Becomes an Abolitionist

Remond's activities in the abolitionist and reform movements began early. It is probable that he was involved in the black Massachusetts Anti–Slavery Society, the first state antislavery organization, from the time it was founded in 1832. This was also the year black women of Salem, including his mother and several sisters, founded the Female Anti–Slavery Society of Salem, the first women's antislavery organization. Both organizations later merged.

In 1834 he was a delegate from Massachusetts to a national black convention in New York. He also attended a meeting of the Rhode Island Anti–Slavery Society in 1837. Remond appears to have moved to Newport, Rhode Island, along with his parents, who went there in 1835 to seek an education for their youngest daughter, Sarah, in a private black school. The older Remonds moved back to Salem in 1841.

In 1838 Remond's oratorical skills won him a position as the first African American lecturer for the American Anti–Slavery Society. He undertook a tour of Maine, Massachusetts, and Rhode Island for the society with Ichabod Codding, a clergyman. Remond spoke in most states in the North, but the major part of his activities centered in New England.

In 1840 Remond joined white abolitionists William Lloyd Garrison, Nathaniel Peabody Rogers, and Lucretia Mott as a delegate from the American Anti–Slavery Society to the World Anti–Slavery Convention in London. During an eventful sea voyage, Remond was forced to sleep in the steerage. When the delegates arrived, they discovered that the convention refused to seat women. As a result they protested by sitting in the gallery as observers.

Remond lectured in Great Britain for 19 months with great success. On his return to the United States, he found that Garrison had hired Frederick Douglass to speak for the cause. Douglass undertook his first speaking tour for the Massachusetts Anti–Slavery Society in the company of Remond. The powerful oratorical skills of Douglass upstaged Remond's speaking, and the two men eventually quarrelled.

In February of 1842 Remond successfully addressed the Legislative Committee of the Massachusetts House of Representatives and helped secure legislation favorable to blacks. On October 30 of that year, Remond had his first major experience of audience hostility as a proslavery crowd howled at him and Frederick Douglass as they tried to address a meeting in Faneuil Hall called to protest the arrest of fugitive slave George Latimer, the father of the noted inventor. As tensions on the issue of slavery rose in the nation, Remond found hostile audiences common.

At the National Convention of Colored Citizens in Buffalo, New York, in April 1843, Remond was part of the forces which combined to reject Henry Highland Garnet's resolution in support of slave revolts. This position reflected his adherence to William Lloyd Garrison's principle of moral suasion. Remond occupied several positions in Garrisonian organizations. From 1843 to 1849 he was on the board of managers of the American Anti–Slavery Society. From 1845 to 1850 he was president of the Essex County Anti–Slavery Society and vice–president of the New England Anti–Slavery Society.

Sarah Remond began to speak on abolition as early as 1842. She joined her brother as a paid lecturer on the antislavery circuit in 1856. In June 1856 he opened a temperance dining room to supplement his income, but he did not give the venture much personal attention since he was still traveling extensively. When his wife Amy died on August 15, 1856, his moroseness and ill–temper became a trial to those around him.

Advocates Insurrection

With Garrison's tacit blessing, Remond began to change his position, becoming more militant. In 1848 he helped organize the Free Soil Party. The passage of the Fugitive Slave Act of 1850 dashed his hopes for a peaceful abolition of slavery. In 1854 he called for the dissolution of the Union and shortly thereafter called for slave insurrection. Still, in speeches of this period, he opposed separatist organizations. In 1863 he accepted a paid job as recruiter for the black 54th Massachusetts Regiment, and in 1865 he spoke against the dissolution of the American Anti–Slavery Society.

In 1866 Remond moved to South Reading (now Wakefield), Massachusetts. The previous year he had been employed as a streetlight inspector in Boston and in 1871 he became a clerk in the Boston Custom House, a position he held until the time of his death from tuberculosis on December 22, 1873. His health had been noticeably deteriorating for the previous 18 months. His second wife and at least two of his children, a daughter and a son, had died previously. Another son died in 1881 at the age of 20. William Lloyd Garrison joined fellow abolitionists John T. Sargent and Wendell Phillips to conduct the funeral service.

Remond was a significant leader in the abolition movement. Some of his contemporaries found him temperamental and oversensitive. Still, his steadfastness, single mindedness, and hard work led to important contributions to the antislavery cause.

REFERENCES

Billington, Ray Allen, ed. *The Journal of Charlotte L. Forten.* New York: The Dryden Press, 1953.

[Garrison, Wendell Phillips, and Francis Jackson Garrison.] *William Lloyd Garrison.* 4 vols. Boston: Houghton, Mifflin, 1894.

Logan, Rayford W., and Michael R. Winston, eds. *Dictionary of American Negro Biography.* New York: Norton, 1982.

Malone, Dumas, ed. *Dictionary of American Biography.* New York: Scribner's, 1943.

Pease, Jane H., and William H. Pease. *They Who Would Be Free: Blacks' Search for Freedom, 1830–1861.* New York: Atheneum, 1974.

Quarles, Benjamin. *Black Abolitionists.* New York: Oxford, 1969.

Ripley, C. Peter, ed. *The Black Abolitionist Papers.* Vol 1. Chapel Hill: University of North Carolina Press, 1985.

Smith, Jessie Carney, ed. *Notable Black American Women.* Detroit: Gale Research, 1991.

Stevenson, Brenda, ed. *The Journals of Charlotte Forten Grimké.* New York: Oxford, 1988.

Wallace, Les. "Charles Lenox Remond: The Lost Prince of Abolitionism." *Negro History Bulletin* 40 (May–June 1977): 696–701.

Yee, Shirley J. *Black Women Abolitionists.* Knoxville: University of Tennessee Press, 1992.

Robert L. Johns

Hiram Rhoades Revels
(1827–1901)
Minister, educator, U.S. senator

Hiram Rhoades Revels is renowned for being the first U.S. Senator of African American descent. Coming out of the turbulent times of the Civil War and Reconstruction years, Revels distinguished himself as a religious leader and educator among black Methodists. Associated with the African Methodist Episcopal (AME) Church and the Methodist Episcopal (ME) Church, North, Revels labored as an itinerant preacher and missionary, traveling widely through the Midwest, the border states, and the South, eventually settling in Mississippi. Revels was one of only a few college–educated black men in America before 1860 and proved himself a leader of his people through a long and varied career. Even though his temper and bearing could be characterized as cautious and conciliatory, Revels steered a remarkable path from grass–roots Methodist preacher to national political leader, celebrated as a symbol of the new black political power that flowered in the South after the Civil War. Elected to the U.S. Senate as a Republican from Mississippi in 1870, Revels served during the years 1870–71, completing the unexpired term of Jefferson Davis.

Revels was born in Fayetteville, North Carolina, on September 27, 1827. Due to the vagaries of record keeping in those years, little is known about Revels's parentage or family, other than the fact that he was born of free parents in a slave state. Even the year and date of his birth have been disputed. By being born a free black, Revels escaped the hardships and deprivations of slavery, though he was well aware of its effects from having lived in association with enslaved people for many years. In the early 1850s, Revels married Phoeba A. Bass of Zanesville, Ohio, and the couple raised six daughters.

Revels had an early love of learning and knowledge, and he pursued his education in a determined fashion. Beginning at the age of eight or nine, Revels attended a private elementary school in Fayetteville conducted by an intelligent free black woman. At the age of 15, Revels and his family moved to Lincolnton, North Carolina, where for a time he practiced the trade of a barber. Within two years Revels decided to move to

Hiram Rhoades Revels

Indiana, a free state, where he could continue his education and escape the restrictive laws placed upon education for blacks in the South. Revels arrived in Indiana about 1844, and he enrolled at Beech Grove Seminary, a Quaker school located near Liberty in Union County. Revels soon became deeply involved with the teachings of the African Methodist Episcopal (AME) Church. Among black Methodists, the AME Church was the most populous and dynamic group; during the nineteenth century it grew and extended its reach as a potent religious and educational force in free black communities.

Becomes Methodist Minister

Now aiming toward a career in the ministry, Revels moved to Drake County, Ohio in 1845 and spent a year studying theology in a black seminary. In his autobiography in the *Midwest Journal,* Revels explained, ''Here I studied more earnestly than I had done before in order to keep pace with the more advanced students, and I was successful in the undertaking, and greatly benefited by attending that school.'' At about the age of 18, Revels decided to commit his life to religious and educational work. Soon after, he began to preach. At the conclusion of this period of his training, probably in 1845, Revels received ordination as a minister in the AME church. Revels's first pastorate was probably a position at the AME church in Richmond, Indiana. In August 1849, the AME church ordained Revels as an elder in the Indiana Conference. By this time, Revels had become well known as a teacher, lecturer, and preacher throughout the states of Indiana, Illinois, and Ohio.

Like most Methodist ministers, Revels was an itinerant lecturer and preacher. He traveled extensively and preached in both slave and free states. He most often preached to free black congregations, but he also ventured further afield and preached and taught among the slave populations. He stated in his autobiography, ''I labored as a religious teacher and educator in Indiana, Illinois, Kansas, and to some extent in Kentucky, Tennessee, and Missouri, during which, at times, I met with a great deal of opposition. I was imprisoned in Missouri in 1854, for preaching the gospel to Negroes, though I was never subjected to violence.''

In 1853 Revels accepted a pastorate in an AME church in St. Louis, Missouri. During his first year there, however, Revels fell into a heated dispute with Bishop Daniel A. Payne and some members of his congregation. As a result of the rift, Revels withdrew entirely from the AME church and for a time became a Presbyterian, accepting a pastorate at the Madison Street Presbyterian Church in Baltimore, Maryland. But he did not remain so for long. By 1855 Revels returned to the AME church and determined as well to continue his education by enrolling in theology courses at Knox College in Galesburg, Illinois. Revels remained at Knox College for two years before he returned to Baltimore and accepted a pastorate at an AME church in 1857. Revels may have been drawn to Baltimore because his brother, Willis Revels, also an AME minister, served as the pastor of AME Bethel Church in Baltimore at the time. Soon after his arrival, Revels became the principal of a high school for black students in Baltimore.

Upon the outbreak of the Civil War in 1861, many in the free black communities in the northern states rallied to the Union war effort. This was also true in Baltimore, where Revels assisted in the organization of black volunteers. Since black men were not allowed to enlist as soldiers until late 1862, it is probable that Revels assisted in organizing black work battalions that supported Union armies in the early years of the War. Revels returned to St. Louis in 1863, where he established a school for freedmen. He also helped to recruit and organize the first black regiment of soldiers from Missouri. During the following year, Revels accompanied the Missouri regiment to Vicksburg, Mississippi, where 70,000 to 80,000 soldiers were encamped at the time. While there, Revels assisted the provost–marshall in caring for the black populations distressed by the dislocations of war.

With the end of the Civil War in April 1865, enslaved blacks had at last won their freedom, but with freedom came a host of problems. Foremost among them were public health, poverty, and illiteracy. Working with the Freedmen's Bureau and other charitable organizations in Mississippi, Revels lent his hand to aid the freedmen. Revels did extensive pastoral work among the freedmen in the Vicksburg and Jackson areas. He preached and taught, helping to establish several churches and schools in the region, especially in Jackson.

During the winter of 1865, Revels left the AME church and joined the Methodist Episcopal (ME) Church, North. Probably Revels wished to continue his work in the emancipated South, and this Methodist denomination possessed considerably more influence and offered more resources for work in the southern states. Revels's first assignment with the ME church, North, came with a call to Leavenworth, Kansas. In late 1866, Revels transferred to another ME church in Louisville, Kentucky, where he stayed for about a year, then accepted a brief assignment in New Orleans. Finally he took a position in Natchez, Mississippi in 1868, where he led a growing ME church. The following year, Revels assumed the position of presiding elder of the ME church, North, serving the Mississippi Conference.

Enters Politics

Implementation of the Reconstruction Act of 1867 as well as the passage of the Fourteenth and Fifteenth Amendments to the Constitution opened the way for extensive black participation in local and national politics. Revels's life and fortunes took a dramatic turn as he reluctantly entered the arena of Mississippi politics. In late 1868, provisional military governor Adelbert Ames appointed Revels for a term on the Natchez city Board of Aldermen. The following year, his friend, John R. Lynch, another well–known black Mississippi political figure from Natchez, persuaded him to enter his name as a candidate for state senator, representing Adams County. When the county Republican caucus convened in December 1869, Revels hesitantly accepted the nomination as a compromise candidate in a deadlocked election. The following month the newly–elected Mississippi legislature gathered at Jackson for its first session. Blacks in the Legislature comprised a conspicuous minority of 34 members of a total of 140. The presiding officer invited Revels to open the session with a prayer. ''That prayer,'' remarked John R. Lynch in *The Facts of Reconstruction,* ''—one of the most impressive and eloquent prayers that had ever been delivered in the Senate chamber,—made Revels a United States Senator. He made a profound impression upon all who heard him.''

A primary task before the Legislature was to fill three vacancies in the U.S. Senate. Two slots would complete unexpired terms, and the third would shortly follow with a full six–year term. The black minority caucus pressured the body to choose a black man to fill at least one seat. Revels was untried and mostly unknown in politics, but he impressed all his peers with his intelligence, dignified bearing, and articulate expression. Thus it was that Revels, without pursuing or expecting high political office, captured the nomination to fill the short, unexpired term. At the time, the Republican nomination was the equivalent to being elected, and Revels prevailed with a large majority vote. Like a rising star, Revels, at the age of 44, ascended in an extraordinary fashion to one of the highest political offices in the nation.

Upon his arrival in Washington in February 1870, Revels naturally attracted a great deal of attention. Several newspaper accounts offered descriptions of his appearance and personal qualities. They noted a tall, dignified, and portly man, of benevolent expression and pleasant, impressive voice. He was distinct and convincing in his speech. On the Senate floor, however, Revels received a mixed reception. A protracted debate ensued over Revels's credentials and eligibility to serve. After three days of discussion and argument, Revels at last received acceptance with a 48–8 final vote. In a dramatic moment, with the Senate galleries packed with onlookers waiting in anticipation, Revels came forward to deliver a short, dignified, and self–assured acceptance speech. It was a symbolic gesture signifying a new political era for America's Congress.

Given that Revels served as a new man in a brief term that lasted a little over a year, his accomplishments in the Senate were few. He introduced several minor bills, presented a number of petitions, and served on the Committee on Education and Labor and the Committee on the District of Columbia. None of the bills he sponsored gained passage into law. He did address the Senate effectively on several occasions, on such topics as the readmission of Georgia (March 16, 1870) and the construction of levees in Mississippi (January 11, 1871). Revels also spoke out, however unsuccessfully, for the integration of public schools in the District of Columbia. Coinciding with his Senate term, Revels conducted an extensive lecture tour, traveling throughout New England, New York, and the Midwest, often speaking to large and appreciative audiences.

Revels's political philosophy could be characterized as accomodationist. His political actions bespoke his conservative and conciliatory nature. In his second address to the Senate on May 17, 1870, Revels advocated amnesty for the former Confederates, provided they pledged loyalty to the government of the United States. Though a Republican, he was not a ''radical.'' Rather, he professed a reform–minded outlook toward racial advancement, one that advocated self–improvement through religious education, temperance, and high moral character. Revels did not agitate for the civil and political rights of blacks. In one incident, however, Revels did use his Senate office to successfully aid black mechanics who were barred employment at the U.S. Navy Yard. Through his intercession, black tradesmen gained jobs and equal treatment.

At the conclusion of his Senate term in March of 1871, Revels returned to Mississippi, where he accepted an appointment as president of the newly–established Alcorn University (now Alcorn State University), the first land grant college for black students, located near Rodney, Mississippi. Revels left Alcorn briefly in 1873 to serve as interim Secretary of State for Mississippi. The following year Revels resigned from the Alcorn presidency to avoid dismissal by Governor Adelbert Ames, a political enemy. He then moved with his family to Holly Springs, Mississippi, where he reentered the ministry, serving as pastor to the local ME church.

Revels's accomodationist views, his anger with Ames, as well as his alienation from the Republicans due to what he perceived as widespread corruption in Mississippi government, all led him to openly campaign for several Democrats during the elections of 1875. That benchmark year in Mississippi politics, the Democrats, through systematic intimidation and violence against the majority black population and white Republicans, swept the Republicans from office. When the U.S. Senate's Select Committee interviewed him in 1876 during its investigation into fraudulent practices in Mississippi during the elections of 1875, Revels testified falsely on behalf of the Mississippi Democrats. This political turnaround cost Revels his Holly Springs pastorate as well as the backing of many of his previous black supporters. Mississippi's new Democratic governor, John M. Stone, reappointed Revels to the presidency of Alcorn University in July 1876. In sum, Revels served as president of Alcorn for nine years. In declining health, he retired from his position in 1882. Revels and his family once again returned to Holly Springs. There, in semi–retirement, he taught theology courses at Shaw, later Rust University, in Holly Springs, and resumed his religious work as a presiding elder in the ME church, North, Upper Mississippi District. Revels died of a stroke while attending a conference of the Methodist Episcopal Church, North, in Aberdeen, Mississippi, on January 16, 1901. He was buried near his home in Holly Springs, Mississippi.

Revels was one of a significant group of Southern black ministers who entered politics in the Reconstruction era. His reluctant entry into politics proved most remarkable in that he succeeded so quickly, rose to such high office, and earned the respect and admiration of his colleagues, black and white. Although his accomplishments as a black political leader were limited, Revels ably blazed a trail others might follow.

REFERENCES

Borome, Joseph H., ed. ''The Autobiography of Hiram Rhoades Revels Together with some Letters by and about Him.'' *The Midwest Journal* 5 (1953): 79–92.

Graham, John H. *Mississippi Circuit Riders, 1865–1965.* Nashville: Parthenon Press, 1967.

Gravely, William B. ''Hiram Revels Protests Racial Separation in the Methodist Episcopal Church (1876).'' *Methodist History* 8 (1970): 13–20.

Lynch, John R. *The Facts of Reconstruction.* New York: Neale Publishing Co., 1913.

McFarlin, Annjennette Sophie, ed. *Black Congressional Reconstruction Orators and their Orations, 1869–1879.* Metuchen, NJ: Scarecrow Press, 1976.

Singer, Donald L. ''For Whites Only: the Seating of Hiram Revels in the United States Senate.'' *Negro History Bulletin* 35 (March 1972): 60–63.

Smith, Samuel Denny. *The Negro in Congress, 1870–1901.* Chapel Hill: University of North Carolina Press, 1940.

Thompson, Julius Eric. ''Hiram R. Revels, 1827–1901: A Biography.'' Ph.D. dissertation, Princeton University, 1973. Reprint, New York: Arno Press, 1982.

Walker, Clarence E. *A Rock in a Weary Land: The African Methodist Episcopal Church During the Civil War and Reconstruction.* Baton Rouge: Louisiana State University Press, 1982.

Wharton, Vernon Lane. *The Negro in Mississippi, 1865–1890.* Chapel Hill: University of North Carolina Press, 1947.

COLLECTIONS

The papers of Hiram Revels are distributed in three archival collections. His handwritten 14–page autobiography is in the Carter G. Woodson Collection at the Library of Congress. A group of Revels's letters are included in the Charles Sumner Papers at the Houghton Library, Harvard University. His personal scrapbook comprising newspaper clippings and personal memorabilia, as well as a selection of his letters, are in the Revels Papers at the Schomburg Center for Research in Black Culture of the New York Public Library.

Kenneth Potts

Willy T. Ribbs

(1956–)

Race car driver

In 1991 Willy T. (William Theodore) Ribbs Jr. made history as the first African American driver to compete in the famed Indianapolis 500. He was born in San Jose, California, the son of William Theodore ''Bunny'' Ribbs Sr., an amateur road–racer in the late 1950s and early 1960s, and Geraldine Henderson Ribbs. From 1973 to 1975 Ribbs attended San Jose City College in California. He began his racing career in 1977 at the age of 21. Ribbs attended driving school in England and was determined to make a name for himself. When asked by an interviewer for *Road and Track* why he chose to start his career in England, Ribbs replied, ''Because it's the University of Motor Racing. I want to be the best, so I race with the best.'' He joined a team called Scorpion Racing and was an immediate success, placing first in six of 11 races, which earned him the title ''Star of Tomorrow'' by corporate sponsor Dunlop. He was also named International Driver of the Year and won the British Sports Writers Award.

Because of a lack of funds for racing, Ribbs utilized his boxing abilities by entering boxing matches at prizefighting clubs in the East End of London. He always emerged the winner, with enough money to pay for his next race. He even became acquainted with Muhammad Ali during one of the great heavyweight champion's frequent trips to London and later trained with Ali's former aide, Drew ''Bundini'' Brown.

Although Ribbs has enjoyed success in his racing career, the road to success has not been an easy one. In 1978 he returned to the United States and made his debut at the Long Beach Grand Prix, where he drove in a warmup race for young drivers and finished in tenth place. At this time in his career, Ribbs had earned a reputation for being outspoken and boastful. He was quoted in *Contemporary Black Biography* as saying, ''The way I drive cars is so smooth it puts chills on the arms of any person watching. I'm ultra–fast, aggressive and smooth.'' His attitude and a traffic ticket for driving down a one–way street offended officials at a NASCAR race in Charlotte, North Carolina, and Ribbs's entry was withdrawn. He was ineligible to compete for the next three years.

In 1981 Ribbs met Jim Trueman, owner of Truesports at Laguna Seca in Monterey, California. Trueman was the former owner and president of Red Roof Inns. For the next three years, Ribbs drove for Red Roof Inns in a semi–pro series. Ribbs has credited Trueman as the "man who saved his career." Two years later, Ribbs met Neil DeAtley, a wealthy contractor who assembled a two–car team of racing Trans–Am Camaros. The International Motorsports Association's series was sponsored by Budweiser, so financing was not a problem. Ribbs was signed as the number two driver and was teamed with the road racing veteran David Hobbs driving the number one car. The team was a successful combination with Ribbs winning five races and Hobbs winning four. Ribbs was named Trans–Am Rookie of the Year.

In 1984 Ribbs ran into trouble again when he was suspended from the team and fined $1,000 for fighting with competitor Bob Lobenberg, whom he claimed had tried to push him off the track during warmups in Atlanta. Discussing the altercation and ensuing penalty, Ribbs commented in *A Hard Road to Glory,* "[I]f you let somebody get away with it once, it could go again and the next time it could be your life. I don't take any nonsense, I don't care if it's Lobenberg or Mario Andretti." He switched to the Roush Racing team and drove Ford Capris for the remainder of the 1984 Trans–Am season. With more wins (17) than any other Trans–Am driver during 1984 to 1986, Ribbs became the leading money winner in Trans–Am history.

Cancellation of Plans to Qualify

With all of these victories, Ribbs announced that he would become the first black driver at the Indianapolis 500. He went to Indianapolis and constructed a deal with boxing promoter Don King as his manager. King was able to obtain Miller Brewing Company as sponsor, but the last minute preparation and lack of speed forced Ribbs to withdraw from the race.

In 1987 he was afforded the opportunity to compete in the International Motorsports Association (IMSA) GTO sedan racing series and won the manufacturing championship for Toyota. He was named IMSA Driver of the Year for 1987 and 1988. Yet once again, he was suspended by the IMSA for hitting another driver. It seems that Ribbs's controversial career may have contributed to his inability to attract major corporate sponsors over the years.

A Second Chance

Still unable to attract a corporate sponsor, in 1989 Ribbs drove a developmental IMSA GTP Eagle HF Prototype. He was offered the chance to drive in several PPG Cup races in Ray Neisewander's Raynor team. In 1991 Ribbs improved his PPG Cup season, finishing seventeenth in points in nine starts with Walker Motorsports team. The Walker team was backed financially by Derrick Walker and entertainer Bill Cosby. In his second try, Ribbs qualified for the team with only 45 minutes left in the final six–hour qualifying session. He still lacked corporate sponsorship—until the Friday before the race, when McDonald's announced that it would provide sponsorship for Walker Motorsports. This historic race made Ribbs the first African American driver to race at the Speedway. After the 1991 Indianapolis 500, Walker managed to enter the Detroit Grand Prix, but again there was no corporate sponsorship. At this junction, Ribbs had become discouraged and did not know if he wanted to continue his racing career. Nevertheless, he finished eleventh in the 1991 Detroit Grand Prix driving a Cosworth–powered Lola and earned $47,280.

In recent years, Ribbs has continued to drive for Walker Racing (the name changed from Walker Motorsports in 1993). In 1993, with the help of Cosby and a $7 million sponsorship from Service Merchandise Company, Ribbs raced a second time in the Indianapolis 500. Bill Cosby told *Jet* magazine, "A man who has worked so hard for this opportunity will now be on an equal playing field, he will no longer be a first–class racer driving a third–class car with a third–class engine." He finished twenty–first in the race. That year he started in 13 races with Walker Racing in a competitive season with full–time sponsorship from Service Merchandise and Pepsi. In 1994 he started 15 races with Walker Racing and scored a season–best finish of seventh at Michigan. Since 1994, Ribbs has been racing on the Championship Auto Racing Teams circuit and according to a 1997 article in the *Rocky Mountain News,* Ribbs planned to form an Indy Racing League team, with sponsorship from singer Pat Boone. In 1997 as well, Ribbs knew that NASCAR was reportedly anxious to bring more minorities into the sport, but he had not been called to race as he had hoped.

Through the years, Ribbs has won numerous awards and honors: Dunlop Star of Tomorrow Champion Europe, 1977; International Driver of the Year Europe, 1977; British Sports Writer Award Europe, 1977; Trans–Am Rookie of the Year, 1983; winner of 45 percent of races entered since 1983; winner of the 1985 Trans–Am series opener in Phoenix (10 victories in 25 Trans–Am starts); 17 victories in 39 Trans–Am starts; five International Motorsports Association victories; three–time 1986 Norelco Driver Cup Award winner; Proclamation of Willy T. Ribbs Day, City of Miami, 1984, City of Atlanta, 1984, and City of St. Petersburg, 1987; Interamerican Western Hemisphere Driving Champion, 1984; Motorsports Press Association All–American Drivers Award, 1984–85; Phillips Business Systems GTO Driver of the Year, 1987 and 1988; SCCA Trans–Am All–Time Money Earner, 1988; and first African American driver to compete in Indianapolis 500, 1991.

Ribbs married Suzanne Hamilton in 1979. He has two children, Sasha and William Theodore Ribbs III. He still enjoys boxing with such heavyweights as Ray Mercer to keep in shape. Columbia Pictures and actor Michael Douglas purchased the rights to Ribbs's life story for a future movie. He occasionally appeared as an extra on the set of the television series *The Cosby Mysteries.*

Current address: 2343 Ribbs Lane, San Jose, CA 95116.

REFERENCES

Ashe, Arthur R., Jr. *A Hard Road to Glory: A History of the African–American Athlete since 1946.* New York: Warner Books, 1988.

"Bill Cosby Inks $7 Million Racing Pact to Help First Black to Drive in Indy 500." *Jet* 84 (24 May 1993): 50–52.

"Black Driver Ribbs Waits for a Call." *Nashville Tennessean,* June 3, 1997.

Contemporary Black Biography. Vol. 2. Detroit: Gale Research, 1992.

Salzman, Jack, David Lionel Smith, and Cornel West, eds. *Encyclopedia of African–American Culture and History.* New York: Macmillan Reference Library USA/Simon and Schuster Macmillan, 1996.

Shaw, Jeremy. "Willy T. Is Back." *Road and Track* 44 (August 1993): 130–31.

Stocker, Scott. "Crash Not Enough to Keep Luyendyk out of Race." *Rocky Mountain News Online,* http://www.denver–rmn.com/sports/other/0629irlnt.htm (29 June 1997).

Who's Who among African Americans, 1996–97. 9th ed. Detroit: Gale Research, 1996.

"Willy T. Ribbs." *1995 Indy Carnival Home Page,* http://www.gwb.com.au/gwb/indy.html (20 March 1995).

Sheila A. Stuckey

Richard, Little.
See Little Richard.

Willis Richardson
(1889?–1977)
Playwright, writer, director, drama historian, educator

Pioneer black dramatist Willis Richardson was the first black to have a play produced on Broadway and possibly the first black to edit collections of plays for children. The height of his success came early in his career. The characters in his works represented a range of black types, from the cultured to the uncultured, and from the financially successful to the tenement dweller, all geared to show the struggles, shortcomings, visions, and hopes of black people.

Born on November 5, 1899, in Wilmington, North Carolina, Willis Richardson was the son of Willis Wilder and Agnes Ann Harper Richardson (sources differ on his date of birth). He attended public elementary school in Washington, D.C., from 1899 to 1906, then entered M Street High School, where he studied from 1906 to 1910. He accepted a position as clerk and mechanic with the U.S. government in 1911.

While in high school, Mary Burrill, one of his teachers who was also an aspiring playwright, encouraged Richardson to write plays. He was encouraged further in 1916 when he saw Angelina Grimké's play *Rachel,* presented under the auspices of the NAACP. From 1916 to 1918 Richardson studied poetry and drama through a correspondence course. In his article "The Hope for Negro Drama," published in the *Crisis* in 1919, Richardson saw black drama emerging. Although some plays written by then included black characters, he hoped for plays to show "the soul of a people," adding that "the soul of this [black] people is truly worth showing." Richardson acknowledged his interest in playwriting and cited black plays for their educational value. It was during the Harlem Renaissance that he emerged as a dramatist.

In 1920 Richardson contributed dramatic sketches for children to the *Brownie's Book,* edited by W. E. B. Du Bois. His first play to be staged was *The Deacon's Awakening,* in 1921 at St. Paul, Minnesota. Richardson showed his work to Alain Locke and Montgomery Gregory, both in charge of the Howard University Players. Although the Howard players wanted to present some of Richardson's one–act plays, the school's white president denied them permission for fear that the propaganda in the work might damage the university's reputation. Locke and Gregory referred Richardson to Du Bois, then editor of the *Crisis,* a magazine that was then sponsoring plays and productions.

First Broadway Play by Black Playwright

Black Theatre USA discussed the problem that the Howard Players encountered. Du Bois advised Richardson to contact Raymond O'Neil's Ethiopian Art Players in Chicago. O'Neil already had begun searching for an African American folk play to produce along with Oscar Wilde's *Salome.* In 1923 the Ethiopian Art Players staged a triple offering that included Richardson's *Chip Woman's Fortune,* in Chicago, Harlem, and at the Frazee Theater on Broadway. This was the first time the work of a black dramatist was produced on Broadway.

Richardson's success continued. In 1924 the Howard Players presented his *Mortgaged* (the first play they staged by a black playwright). In 1925 the Karamu House staged his *Compromise,* and in 1926 the Krigwa Players produced his *Broken Banjo.*

Among other plays written by Richardson are *Bold Lover, The Curse of the Shell Road Witch, The Dark Haven,* and *The Rider of the Dream. Crisis* published a number of Richardson's plays. In 1930 Richardson's first anthology appeared, *Plays and Pageants from the Life of the Negro,* published by Associated Publishers. In 1935, his and Mae Miller's *Negro History in Thirteen Plays* was published by

Associated Publishers. Richardson's collection of plays for children was published 20 years later, in 1955, under the title *The King's Dilemma.*

During his lifetime, Richardson wrote nearly 30 one–act plays and almost a dozen three–act plays, most of which black schools and colleges produced. His most famous work was *Chip Woman's Fortune.* His criticism, poetry, and one short story were also published. Richardson joined the ranks of such writers and directors who helped build black drama as Owen Dodson, Melvin Tolson, and Thomas Pawley. He taught black drama at several black colleges in the South and was an instructor in drama at Morgan State College (now Morgan State University).

Richardson received the Amy Spingarn Prize for drama in 1925 for his play *The Broken Banjo* and in 1926 for his three–act drama *Bootblack Lover,* both staged under the auspices of the *Crisis.* In 1928 he received the Edith Schwarb Cup from the Yale University Theater. His memberships included the Authors League of America, Dramatists Guild, Harlem Cultural Council, and the NAACP.

Writing about black plays in *Black American Writers Past and Present,* Richardson expressed disappointment that black groups continued to stage plays that depict blacks as pimps, prostitutes, dope pushers, street walkers, and "the corner dudes." He noted: "Before my first play, *The Chip Woman's Fortune,* was staged on Broadway in 1923, Black actors were put upon the stage to be laughed at. Now, they are put upon the stage to be pitied or scorned." He was disheartened that black professional actors ignored the plays he wrote about the "better class, respectable, Afro–American families."

After 43 years in government service, with the U.S. Bureau of Engraving, Richardson retired in 1954 and continued to live in Washington, D.C. He married Mary Ellen Jones on September 1, 1914, and they had three daughters: Jean Paula, Shirley Antonella, and Noel Justine. He died in 1977, ending a colorful career as participant in the black theater movement and promoter of black lives and black American history through plays.

REFERENCES

Barksdale, Richard. *Black Writers of America.* New York: Macmillan, 1972.

Brawley, Benjamin. *Negro Genius.* New York: Dodd, Mead, 1937.

Hatch, James V., and Ted Shine, eds. *Black Theatre USA.* Revised and expanded ed. New York: Free Press, 1974.

Kellner, Bruce, ed. *The Harlem Renaissance: A Historical Dictionary for the Era.* New York: Methuen, 1984.

Rush, Theresa G. *Black American Writers Past and Present.* Vol. 2. Metuchen, NJ: Scarecrow Press, 1975.

Richardson, Willis. "The Hope for Negro Drama." *Crisis* 19 (November 1919): 338–39.

Scally, Mary Anthony. *Negro Catholic Writers, 1900–1943; A Bio–Bibliography.* Detroit: Walter Romig, 1945.

Jessie Carney Smith

Wilson C. Riles
(1917–)
Educational administrator

Wilson C. Riles is a dedicated and sensitive educator, whose integrity as an independent thinker catapulted him to the top of his field. In 1970, he was the first African American elected to a statewide office in California when he was elected state superintendent of public instruction and director of state education. His ideas and beliefs changed the face of education in California. Riles helped direct nationwide attention to the many facets of early childhood education.

Wilson Camanza Riles was born June 27, 1917, near Alexandria, Louisiana, a backwoods sawmill town where turpentine was distilled from resin. He was the only child of Wilson Roy Riles and Susie Anna Jefferson Riles. Wilson Riles married Mary Louis Phillips, a school teacher, on November 13, 1941. They had three sons, Michael Leigh, Wilson C. Jr., Phillip Gregory, and a daughter Narvia (Mrs. Ronald Bostick).

Riles's father worked as a crew chief in a turpentine camp; his family was poor. Quoted in *Essence,* he said, "My parents had me rather late in life. They loved me so, I had a secure, early childhood. Being poor, I was spoiled in a nonmaterial way." His mother died when he was nine and his father passed away two years later. He was taken in by the Bryants, a childless couple who had been friends of his parents.

Riles was determined to better himself. There were only four accredited black high schools in Louisiana, and he planned to attend one in New Orleans. With the support of the congregation in his African Methodist Episcopal Church, he was able to attend the high school of his choice. He said in *Who's Who in America*:

> Is growing up in rural Louisiana during the depression as an orphan, poor and black, attending a segregated school, a handicap? I have never thought so. Maybe it's because of the superb teachers who never let me feel sorry for myself. As I recall, some did not even have college degrees, but they believed I could learn. Because they did, it never occurred to me that I couldn't. Forrest Paul Augustine, the principal, admonished us to get as much education as we could because, "that is one thing no one can ever take away from you." I chose education as a career because those humble public schools gave me a chance. I want all boys and girls to have a chance, too.

After graduation, the Bryants moved to Flagstaff, and he went with them. He worked his way through Arizona State College with a job under the National Youth Administration program for $100 a month. With a full class load, he also earned an additional $15 a month working in the cafeteria. As the only black student at the school, he would arrive at each

Wilson C. Riles

class early so other students could make their seat selections around him. Wilson graduated with a major in education and minors in business education and history.

Riles's first teaching job was on an Arizona Apache Indian Reservation at Pistol Creek; it paid $100 a month, as much as his old college job. Wilson taught 12 children, whose parents were black laborers leasing land in the area and working for a lumber company. White, African American, and American Indian children were each taught in separate facilities. It was at a Flagstaff church that he met Mary Louise Phillips. She was on spring break visiting an aunt. Phillips was teaching in Phoenix, a place where married women could not teach. Riles commuted weekends for seven months until they secretly wed in November of 1941. He spent three years at Tuskegee during World War II in the Army Air Corps before returning to school at Northern Arizona University to earn an M.A. in school administration in 1947.

After 14 years as a teacher and administrator in the Arizona public schools, the Rileses moved to Los Angeles in 1954, where Riles became executive secretary of the Pacific Coast region of the Fellowship of Reconciliation, a pacifist organization. Through his work with the California Department of Education on equal opportunity for school personnel, he became head of the department's Bureau of Intergroup Relations in 1958. In 1965, he was named associate superintendent of the California State Department of Education to head a $100 million a year Federal Compensatory Education Program aimed at improving the education of children from low income families. He did so well that he was asked to serve on Urban Education Task Forces for Presidents Johnson and Nixon. In 1969, he was promoted to the position of deputy superintendent of public instruction for programs and legislation.

Unhappy with the incumbent superintendent, an ultra conservative who had tried to drastically slash state support of public education, Riles decided to seek the top position. Few thought he had a chance to win. The job was controversial, and the two–term incumbent was politically connected. Riles waged a strong campaign, though, traveling throughout the state and winning support of the major newspapers and the major education organizations. In the 1970 statewide election he polled 3.25 million votes—more than any black man ever received in a single election in the United States. Riles ran without organizational ties, without advance financial backing, and without a political base. Surprisingly, he won with a half million plurality over his well–identified white opponent. In 1971, Riles became the superintendent of public instruction for the State of California. Riles stated his educational belief for a 1972 in *Essence* article:

> To carve education down to its barest dimensions, it is the process of seeking after the truth. Its purpose is to teach one to think rationally. The end product should provide one with some options and enable one to have some choice about what he wishes to do with life. Education and freedom must go hand in hand—they are inseparable.

Riles directed the country's largest education system from his office in the state capital. The job only paid $35,000 a year, but was the overseer of 4.5 million school children in more than 1,100 school districts. He was responsible for an annual budget of $2.5 billion and his administrative staff numbered more than 2,300. During his first term, Riles so impressed the voters of California that in 1974 they reelected him with an unprecedented 70 percent of the vote in a field of seven candidates. He served as state superintendent for 12 years. In that capacity, he also served as an ex–officio regent of the University of California and as a trustee of the California State University and Colleges.

Receives Spingarn Medal

In 1973, Riles received the Spingarn Medal, the highest award from the NAACP. Its publication, *Crisis* stated that:

> As superintendent of public instruction, he restored the nonpartisan nature of his office and pulled together the diverse factions within the educational field with exceptional administrative skill.

A major priority of Riles has always been early childhood education. He was able to restore the confidence of the state legislature in his department, he unified the education profession into a single lobby, and he pushed through the largest school aid measure in the state's history. During his tenure, Riles designed an early childhood education program, expanded federal programs to help disadvantaged children, developed a master plan for special education for disabled children in California, and started a school improvement program, which set up parent and teacher councils in many schools trying to open up the system and give parents a voice in their children's education.

In 1983, Riles established Wilson Riles and Associates, an educational consulting firm providing expertise in executive searches, intercultural relations, school improvement strategies, public speaking, management reviews, and corporate services. He is director emeritus of Wells Fargo Bank and has served on numerous councils, commissions and committees. He is a member of Phi Delta Kappa, the education honor society. Riles has received nine honorary doctorates and many awards for public service and leadership. At six–feet four–inches tall, with deep brown skin, gray hair and mustache, Riles is an imposing figure with a warm smile and confident manner. His efforts as an educational administrator have made a difference in California and beyond. Now, as an educational consultant, he shares his expertise with other groups ranging from schools to corporate America.

Current address: Wilson Riles and Associates, 400 Capitol Mall, Suite 1540, Sacramento, CA 95814–4407.

REFERENCES

Assagai, Mel. "Wilson Riles—a 'Black Anglo–Saxon?'" *Encore American & Worldwide News,* February 21, 1978.

"California's New Education Boss." *Ebony* 26 (May 1971): 54–62.

Davis, Bruce C. "Dr. Wilson Riles." *Essence* 3 (August 1972): 62–63, 77.

"Educator Named Spingarn Medalist." *Crisis* 80 (June–July 1973): 211.

"Elects First Black to Head California's Education Post." *Jet* 39 (19 November 1970): 13.

Warner, Mary. "Wilson Riles Educates the California Child." *Sepia* 29 (February 1980): 24–30.

Who's Who among African Americans, 1998–99. 10th edition. Detroit: Gale Research, 1997.

Who's Who in America. 50th ed. Wilmette, IL: Marquis, 1996.

"Wilson Riles Speaks Out." *Black Enterprise* 8 (July 1978): 35–38.

Kathleen E. Bethel

Paul Robeson
(1898–1976)
Singer, actor, activist, lawyer

Paul Robeson, a great American singer and actor, spent much of his life actively agitating for equality and fair treatment for all of America's citizens as well as citizens of the world. Robeson brought to his audiences not only a melodious baritone voice and a grand presence, but magnificent performances on stage and screen. Although his outspokenness often caused him difficulties in his career and personal life, he unswervingly pursued and supported issues that only someone in his position could effect on a grand scale. His career flourished in the 1940s as he performed in America and numerous countries around the world. He was one of the most celebrated persons of his time.

Paul Leroy Robeson was born in Princeton, New Jersey, on April 9, 1898, the fifth and last child of Maria Louisa Bustill and William Drew Robeson. During these early years the Robesons experienced both family and financial losses. At the age of six Paul and his siblings, William, Reeve, Ben and Marian suffered the death of their mother in a household fire. This was followed a few years later with their father's loss of his Princeton pastorate. After moving first to Westfield, the family finally settled in Somerville, New Jersey, in 1909, where William Robeson was appointed pastor of St. Thomas AME Zion Church.

Enrolling in Somerville High School, one of only two blacks, Paul Robeson excelled academically while successfully competing in debate, oratorical contests, and showing great promise as a football player. He also got his first taste of acting in the title role of Shakespeare's *Othello.* In his senior year he not only graduated with honors, but placed first in a competitive examination for scholarships to enter Rutgers University. Although his other male siblings chose all–black colleges, Robeson took the challenge of attending Rutgers, a majority white institution in 1915.

In college between 1915 to 1919, Robeson experienced both fame and racism. In trying out for the varsity football team, where blacks were not wanted, he encountered physical brutality. In spite of this resistance, Robeson not only earned a place on the team but was named first on the roster for the All–American college team. He graduated with 15 letters in sports. Academically he was equally successful, elected a member of the prestigious Phi Beta Kappa Society and the Cap and Skull Honor Society of Rutgers. Graduating in 1919 with the highest grade point average in his class, Robeson gave the class oration at the 153d Rutgers Commencement.

With college life behind him, Robeson moved to the Harlem section of New York City to attend law school, first at New York University, later transferring to Columbia University. He sang in the chorus of the musical *Shuffle Along* (1921) by Eubie Blake and Noble Sissle, and made his acting debut in 1920 playing the lead role in *Simon the Cyrenian* by poet Ridgely Torrence. Robeson's performance was so well received that he was congratulated not only by the Harlem YMCA (Young Men's Christian Association) audience but also by members of the Provincetown Players who were in the audience. While working odd jobs and taking part in professional football to earn his college fees, Robeson met Eslanda "Essie" Cardozo Goode. The granddaughter of Francis L. Cardozo, the secretary of state of South Carolina during Reconstruction, she was a graduate of Columbia University and employed as a histological chemist. She was the first black staff person at Presbyterian Hospital in New York City.

Paul Robeson

The couple married on August 17, 1921, and their son Paul Jr. was born on November 2, 1927.

To support his family while studying at Columbia Law School, Robeson played professional football for the Akron Pros (1920–1921) and the Milwaukee Badgers (1921–1922), and during the summer of 1922 he went to England to appear in a production of *Taboo,* which was renamed *Voodoo.* Once graduating from Columbia in 1923, Robeson sought work in his new profession, all the while singing at the famed Cotton Club in Harlem. Offered an acting role in 1923 in Eugene O'Neill's *All God's Chillun Got Wings,* Robeson quickly took this opportunity; he had recently quit a law firm because the secretary refused to take dictation from a black person.

Although *All God's Chillun* brought threats by the Ku Klux Klan because of the play's interracial subject matter and the fact that a white woman was to kiss Robeson's hand, it was an immediate success. It was followed in 1924 by his performances in a revival of *The Emperor Jones,* the play *Rosanne,* and the silent movie *Body and Soul* for Oscar Micheaux, an independent black film maker. In 1925 Robeson debuted in a formal concert at the Provincetown Playhouse. His performance which consisted of Negro spirituals and folk songs was so brilliant that he and his accompanist, Lawrence Brown, were offered a contract with the Victor Talking Machine Company. Encouraged by this success, Robeson and Brown embarked on a tour of their own, but were sorely disappointed. Even though they received good reviews, the crowds were small and they made very little money. What Robeson came to know was that his talents in acting and singing would serve as the combined focus of his career.

Acting and Singing Career

Robeson's acting career started to take off in 1928 when he accepted the role of Joe in a London production of *Show Boat* by Jerome Kern and Oscar Hammerstein. It was his singing of "Ol' Man River" that received the most acclaim regarding the show and earned him a great degree of attention from British socialites. Robeson gave concerts in London at Albert Hall and Sunday afternoon concerts at Drury Lane. In spite of all this attention, Robeson still had to deal with racism. In 1929 he was refused admission to a London hotel. Because of the protest raised by Robeson, major hotels in London said they would no longer refuse service to blacks.

Much attention was given to Robeson's acting and singing and he was embraced by the media. The *New Yorker* magazine in an article by Mildred Gilman referred to Robeson as "the promise of his race," "King of Harlem," and "Idol of his people." Robeson returned briefly to America in 1929 to perform at a packed Carnegie Hall. In May of 1930, after establishing a permanent residence in England, Robeson accepted the lead role in Shakespeare's *Othello.* This London production at the Savoy Theatre was the first time since the performance of the great black actor Ira Aldridge in 1860 that a major production company cast a black man in the part of the Moor. Robeson was a tall, strikingly handsome man with a deep, rich, baritone voice and a shy, almost boyish manner. The audience was so mesmerized by his performance in *Othello* that the production had 20 curtain calls.

Accolades for outstanding acting and singing performances were prevalent during the 1930s in Robeson's career, but his personal and home life were surrounded by difficulties. His wife Eslanda "Essie," who had published a book on Robeson, *Paul Robeson, Negro* (1930), sued for divorce in 1932. Her actions were encouraged by the fact that Robeson had fallen in love and planned to marry Yolande Jackson, a white Englishwoman. Jackson, whom Robeson called the love of his life, had originally accepted his proposal but later called the marriage off. It was thought by some who knew the Jackson family well that she was strongly influenced by her father, Tiger Jackson, who was less than tolerant of Robeson and people of color in general. With his marriage plans cancelled, Robeson and his wife came to an understanding regarding their relationship, and the divorce proceedings were cancelled.

Activism

Robeson returned to New York briefly in 1933 to star in the film version of *Emperor Jones* before turning his attention to the study of singing and languages. His stay in the United States was a short one due to his treatment by the racist American film industries and because of criticism by blacks regarding his role as a corrupt emperor. Upon returning to England, Robeson eagerly immersed himself in his studies and mastered several languages. Robeson along with Essie became an honorary members of the West African Students' Union, becoming acquainted with African students Kwame Nkrumah and Jomo Kenyatta, future presidents of Ghana and Kenya, respectively. It is also during this time that Robeson played at a benefit for Jewish refugees which marked the beginning of his political awareness and activism.

Robeson's inclination to aid the less fortunate and the oppressed in their fight for freedom and equality was firmly rooted in his own family history. His father William Drew Robeson was an escaped slave who eventually graduated from Lincoln College in 1878, and his maternal grandfather, Cyrus Bustill, was a slave who was freed by his second owner in 1769 and went on to become an active member of the African Free Society. Recognizing the heritage that brought him so many opportunities, Robeson, between 1934 and 1937 performed in several films that presented blacks in other than stereotypical ways. He acted in such films as *Sanders of the River* (1935), *King Solomon's Mines* (1937) and *Song of Freedom* (1937).

On a trip to the Soviet Union in 1934 to discuss the making of the film *Black Majesty,* Robeson not only had discussions with the Soviet film director Sergei Eisenstein during his trip but was so impressed regarding the education against racism for schoolchildren that he began to study Marxism and Socialist systems in the Soviet Union. He also decided to send his son, nine–year–old Paul Jr., to school in the Soviet Union so that he would not have to contend with the racism and discrimination Robeson confronted in both Europe and America.

Robeson continued acting in films confronting stereotypes of blacks while receiving rave reviews for his success in singing ''Ol' Man River'' in the 1936 film production of *Show Boat.* He also embarked on a more active role in fighting the injustices he found throughout the world. Robeson cofounded the Council on African Affairs to aid in African liberation, sang and spoke at benefit concerts for Basque refugees, supported the Spanish Republican cause, and sang at rallies to support a democratic Spain along with numerous other causes. At a benefit in Albert Hall in London, Robeson is quoted in Philip Foner's *Paul Robeson Speaks* as saying ''The artist must elect to fight for freedom or slavery. I have made my choice. I had no alternative.'' This statement echoed a clear and focused direction of Robeson's personal and professional life.

In 1939 Robeson stated his intentions to retire from commercial entertainment and returned to America. He gave his first recital in the United States at Mother AME Zion Church Harlem where his brother Benjamin was pastor. Later on in the same year Robeson premiered the patriotic song ''Ballad for Americans'' on CBS radio as a preview of a play by the same name. The song was so well received that studio audiences cheered for 20 minutes after the performance while the listening audience exceeded the response even for Orson Welles's famous Martian scare program. Robeson's popularity in the United states soared and he remained the most celebrated person in the country well into the 1940s. He was awarded the esteemed NAACP Spingarn Medal (1945) as well as numerous other awards and recognitions from civic and professional groups. In the American production of *Othello* (1943), Robeson's performance placed him among the ranks of great Shakespearean actors. The production ran for 296 performances—over ten months—and toured both the United States and Canada.

Robeson's political commitments became foremost in his life as he championed causes from South African famine relief to support of an antilynching law; in September 1946 he was among the delegation that spoke with President Harry S Truman about antilynching legislation. The meeting was a stormy one as Robeson adamantly urged Truman to act, all the while defending the Soviet Union and denouncing United States' allies. In October of the same year when called before the California Legislative Committee on Un–American activities, Robeson declared himself not a member of the Communist Party but praised their fight for equality and democracy. This attempt at branding him as un–American was successful in causing many to distrust his political commitments. Regardless of these events, Robeson decided to retire from concert work and devote himself to gatherings that promoted the causes to which he had dedicated himself.

In 1949 Robeson embarked on a European tour and in doing so spoke out against the discrimination and injustices that blacks in American had to confront. His statements were distorted as they were dispatched back to the United States. Although Robeson got mixed responses from the black community, the backlash from whites culminated in riot before a scheduled concert in Peekskill, New York, on August 27, 1949; a demonstration by veteran organizations turned into a full–blown riot. Robeson was advised of this and returned to New York. He did agree to do a second concert on September 4 in Peekskill for the people who truly wanted to hear him. The concert did take place but afterwards a riot broke out which lasted into the night leaving over 140 persons seriously injured. With such violence surrounding Robeson's concerts, many groups and sponsors no longer supported him.

By 1950 Robeson had received by so much negative press that he made plans for a European tour. His plans were abruptly halted because the United States government refused to allow him to travel unless he agreed not to make any speeches. With no passport and denied his freedom of speech abroad, Robeson continued to speak out in public forums and through his own monthly newspaper, *Freedom.* Barred from all other forms of media, his own newspaper became his primary platform from 1950 to 1955. His remaining supporters encompassed the National Negro Labor Council, Council on African Affairs, and the Civil Rights Congress. The NAACP openly attacked Robeson while other black organization shunned him in fear of reprisals. Undaunted by these negative responses, Robeson traveled the United States encouraging groups to fight for their rights and for equal treatment. Even though he suffered from health as well as financial difficulties, Robeson held firm to his convictions and published in 1958 his autobiography *Here I Stand* through a London publishing house.

On May 10, 1958, Robeson gave his first New York concert in ten years to a packed Carnegie Hall. When the concert was over, he informed the audience that the passport battle had been won. From 1958 to 1963 Robeson traveled to England, the Soviet Union, Austria, and New Zealand. He was showered with awards and played to packed houses throughout his travels. After being hospitalized several times throughout his trip due to a disease of the circulatory system, Robeson returned to the United States. Much had changed since the Civil Rights Act of 1957 and school integration were in full enactment. Robeson was welcomed on his return by *Freedomways,* a quarterly review which saw him as a powerful fighter for freedom. A salute to Robeson was given in 1965 which was chaired by actors Ossie Davis and Ruby Dee along with writer James Baldwin and many other admirers.

Eslanda ''Essie'' Robeson died of cancer in 1965 at the age of 68 and Robeson went to live with his sister Marian in Philadelphia. He remained in seclusion until he died there on January 23, 1976; on his 75th birthday four days later a ''Salute to Paul Robeson'' was held in Carnegie Hall. Paul Leroy Robeson's funeral was held at Mother AME Zion Church in Harlem before a crowd of 5,000.

On February 24, 1998, Robeson received a posthumous Grammy lifetime achievement award. His honors are numerous, as Robeson's life is being depicted through exhibits, film festivals, and lectures. Upon the centennial of his birth on April 9, 1998, at least 25 U.S. states and several countries worldwide hosted celebrations of his life and work in every conceivable manner.

Paul Robeson was truly a man who saw a commitment to the oppressed, and particularly black people, as a much more profound calling than the accolades he received for his astonishing talents. His extraordinary voice and engaging acting abilities would have undoubtedly brought him more fame, fortune, and approval than the activist role he pursed instead. It is because of this clear vision of justice that he is remembered as a great American and a great citizen of the world.

REFERENCES

Duberman, Martin B. *Paul Robeson.* New York: Alfred A. Knopf, 1988.

Foner, Philip S. *Paul Robeson Speaks: Writings, Speeches, Interviews 1918–1974.* New York: Brunner/Mazel Publishers, 1978.

Jackson, Kenneth T., and others, eds. *Dictionary of American Biography.* Supplement Ten, 1976–1980. New York: Charles Scribner's Sons, 1995.

''Robeson Receives Posthumous Grammy.'' *New York Times,* February 25, 1998.

Southern, Eileen. *Biographical Dictionary of Afro-American and African Musicians.* Westport, CT: Greenwood Press, 1982.

Williams, Michael W., ed. *The African American Encyclopedia.* New York: Marshall Cavendish, 1993.

COLLECTIONS

Paul Robeson's papers are in the Robeson Family Archives, Moorland Spingarn Research Center, Howard University, Washington D.C.

Leańtin LaVerne Bracks

Bill ''Bojangles'' Robinson
(1878?–1949)
Dancer

Bill ''Bojangles'' Robinson became one of the most popular and beloved performers of his day. His combination of tap dancing, songs, telling jokes, and imitating natural sounds proved a popular one for audiences for many years. It is claimed that some of his contemporaries were superior in dancing ability and had a wider range of steps, but he was the acknowledged master in appealing to the public. Despite the bright smile he featured in his act and his public benefactions, Robinson had a darker side. He was often difficult to work with and was also a compulsive gambler prone to violence. He resented the racism he faced, but his reputation has suffered from charges he was an Uncle Tom, especially because of the stereotypical roles he played in motion pictures which still appear on television with some regularity.

Robinson was born Luther Robinson in Virginia, possibly in 1878—all Richmond city government records were destroyed in 1885. State records offer two Luther Robinsons, born 1877 and 1876, neither of whose parents have the names attributed to Robinson's parents. Their names are given as Maxwell and Maria Robinson; both died before 1885. There may have been an older sister. There certainly was a younger brother, named William. As a child Luther Robinson beat his brother up and appropriated his name and then called the younger sibling Percy, a name that stuck. Percy Robinson was blind and living in Fayetteville, North Carolina, when his brother died.

The children's grandmother, Bedilia Robinson, did not want to accept responsibility for them; apparently some sort of joint custody was arranged because the boys seem to have lived with her and another relative for awhile. Robinson's grandmother was a strict Baptist who sternly disapproved of dancing. All Robinson retained from her religious convictions was a distaste for all religion. He found a younger sidekick named Lemmeul V. ''Eggie'' Eggleston and spent much of his time on the streets. The two picked up odd jobs, shined shoes, and danced in the streets for pennies. If there was any formal schooling for Robinson, it had little effect. He was illiterate. His second wife is reputed to have taught him to read and write his name.

Bill "Bojangles" Robinson

Robinson had a quick temper and often got into fights. He also engaged in petty crime. He is supposed to have earned his nickname from a local hatter, Lion J. Boujasson—whose name came out Bojangles in local speech. Robinson allegedly stole a beaver hat from the man. This account, derived from a childhood friend, is not universally accepted.

Robinson ran away to Washington, D.C., about 1890 with a older local white youth, Lemuel Gordon Toney, who was later known by the stage name Eddie Leonard. Toney had show business ambitions and planned to use Robinson as a "pick" in his act. "Picks"—short for pickaninnies—were cute and talented black youngsters used as support for the star of the act. Around 1892 Robinson got a job as a pick in the show *The South Before the War.* After a year he outgrew the job and had to continue to scramble to survive. He acquired his first knife and razor scars. Often wounded in fights because of his quick temper, he never missed a performance because of an injury. For example, he opened *Brown Buddies* in 1930 with his arm in a sling—he had been shot accidentally by the police as he chased a purse snatcher. Tom Fletcher stated in *100 Years of the Negro in Show Business* that his fights were never vicious, but for others, Robinson had a reputation for having a nasty disposition. Marshall and Jean Stearns wrote in *Jazz Dance,* "Youngsters did not say hello to Robinson unless they knew him pretty well, and he clearly enjoyed his reputation of being a tough guy." He is not known to have ever caused a death with the revolver he carried, although it figures prominently in several stories about him. Given the potential for difficulties with the law, Robinson later devoted time and effort to ingratiating himself with police departments in the cities where he played and to maintaining good relations with them.

Establishes Himself in Show Business

In 1900 Robinson was appearing with another young dancer, Theodore Miller; the pair was making more of an impression at the time with their singing than with their dancing. Robinson began to build a reputation as a dancer by winning a buck and wing contest against formidable competition in a contest held every Friday evening by the *In Old Kentucky* troupe, which was playing in Brooklyn. He continued to seek work with a variety of partners when Miller stopped performing in 1901. Robinson probably first worked with his most famous partner, George C. Cooper, in the summer of 1900.

The arrangement between Cooper and Robinson became lasting in 1902 when Cooper, an established vaudeville star, decided to permanently replace his former partner, who had taken to drink. At first Robinson did not dance and played the ragged fool to Cooper's natty straight man. Still the two men were appearing on the Keith circuit, one of the best in vaudeville. It was six months before Robinson was billed under his own name; the two finally became Cooper and Robinson on January 10, 1903. Robinson continued as a clown and expanded his role over the years. Cooper and Robinson remained together as a successful and well–paid team until 1914, introducing a new act every year and achieving success abroad. The relationship was not always easy because of Robinson's off–stage behavior. Cooper often had to stand bail for Robinson, who was constantly getting into trouble, usually because of his gambling.

On November 14, 1907, Robinson married Lena Chase, who was 22–years old and wanted to become a schoolteacher. The marriage got off to a rocky start and eventually broke down. On March 21, 1908, Robinson was arrested for armed robbery. On September 30 he was sentenced to 11 to 15 years in prison. As a result of a retrial with new evidence, a jury took 15 seconds to acquit Robinson early the next year, but he had spent time in jail. In the first part of January of 1909 Cooper and Robinson were back on the road.

For the next six years the act played the Keith and the Orpheum circuits with sustained success. Robinson attained equal status with Cooper and took off the clown outfit. Robinson was famed for his professionalism on the stage, but offstage his life continued to be unstable. Gambling, drinking, and absence all took a toll on his marriage. By 1916 Robinson and his wife had separated, but they did not divorce until 1922, just days before Robinson's second marriage.

In Des Moines in 1914 Robinson hit a policeman over the head with a cue stick in a poolroom brawl, and Cooper used this latest escapade as a reason to break up the act. The decision may really have come about because of money problems—Robinson would gamble the act's earnings away—or because of tensions over Cooper's decision to marry a white woman. Robinson may well have foreseen the consequences imposed by the era's racism. After the marriage

Cooper was able to work only in black theaters for many years.

Robinson now had the good fortune to become a client of agent Marty Forkins. It was only Robinson's death that ended the association with this top–flight agent. With an eye for publicity, Forkins invented a completely bogus story of how the two met and set about building Robinson up as a solo vaudeville act. The rule had been that blacks were acceptable on the white circuits only as a pair. There could also never be more than one black act on a bill. Forkins found Robinson a job as dance instructor for the white chorus girls at the Marigold Gardens Theater in Chicago with the understanding that Robinson would also be allowed to perform a solo act. After about a year, he began to work small–time houses in the midwest. A growing reputation made him a major attraction on the Keith circuit within about three years.

Robinson performed at training camps during World War I, increasing his audience exposure. In 1918 he introduced his staircase dance, which he did not invent, but the routine did not become an invariable feature of his act until about 1924, when he had a portable staircase made.

Marries Second Wife

It was about 1920 or 1921 that Robinson met Fannie Clay, who became his second wife. Clay, who was some 20 years younger than Robinson, had come to Chicago from Tennessee to study pharmacy. She was working in a Walgreen's drug store. The store's manager was one of Robinson's loan sources. The manager was not there one day, and Robinson persuaded Clay to lend him money. He repaid the loan within a month and began to flirt. Chronically short of funds due to his gambling, he stole her favorite jeweled pin. When he returned the pin and admitted his guilt, she berated him. However, instead of ending the relationship—they were not yet dating—she helped him out. Eventually Robinson began to send her money while he was on tour. She opened a bank account in his name. After several months of long distance courting, Robinson complained of the high cost of the follow–up phone calls he made to make sure she received his telegrams and asked her to join him in Minneapolis. She did. They married as soon as it was legally possible, and she took on the job of trying to bring some order into his life. As a result of her efforts, from 1921 on his career is easily followed in his scrapbooks. The couple had no children, so she could travel with him and serve as his personal manager.

Gambling was always a major problem. Robinson did not smoke or drink, but he ate four to eight quarts of vanilla ice cream a day. He was meticulous about his wardrobe yet tended to leave his expensive sheet music lying about the theater. Five–feet seven–inches tall, he was a perfect size 38 and bought his suits off the rack. He ran through 20 to 30 pairs of dancing shoes a year.

Billed as "The Dark Cloud of Joy," Robinson worked steadily in vaudeville with increasing success between 1914 and 1927. In the summer of 1926 he toured Europe. Most years until 1925 he worked 52 weeks a year. In that year he began the practice of not working during World Series week. Robinson was an avid Yankee fan and a very good ball player himself. He also used his athletic abilities for publicity purposes by winning races in which he ran backward. He would run 75 yards backward against persons running 100 yards forward and usually win. Robinson held the unofficial world record for running backward until 1977.

Marty Forkins foresaw the demise of vaudeville as talking motion pictures appeared, beginning with *The Jazz Singer* in 1927. Thus he encouraged Robinson's appearance in *Blackbirds of 1928.* Robinson won wild acclaim from theatrical critics and found a new, upscale audience. The play ran for 518 performances, and he took up residence in Harlem's Dunbar Apartments. Robinson did not go on tour with the show but returned to vaudeville. As a gesture toward settling down in one place, he now performed mostly in New York and up and down the East Coast. In 1930 he appeared in the musical *Brown Buddies.* Robinson received very good reviews although the show was weak and closed after only 113 performances.

In a search for new outlets for performing Robinson began to explore film. He did a dance number in *Dixiana* (1930) for RKO. The all–black film *Harlem is Heaven* (Herald Pictures, 1933) played to black audiences. Robinson then appeared in a vaudeville music revue, *Hot From Harlem,* which opened at New York's Palace Theater on February 13, 1932. The following year the revue's name became *Goin' to Town.* A new version of *Blackbirds* in 1933 was not saved by Robinson's dancing. In 1934 he appeared in a Vitaphone short, *Black Orchids.*

Robinson was, in the meantime, building his reputation as a public benefactor. He was generous to people down on their luck. He played an estimated 3,000 benefits during his lifetime, and made gestures like giving Richmond, Virginia, $1,200 to put up traffic lights at a busy intersection in a black neighborhood. In 1933 he was given the honorary title "Mayor of Harlem."

None of Robinson's success protected him from racial slights, however. He did not always endure them patiently but fought back on occasion, sometimes even pulling out his gun. Robinson actively helped young men like Roy Wright, one of the Scottsboro boys accused of rape in 1931, paying for a vocational course after Wright won release in 1937. Toward the end of his life he regularly attended the Monday morning lineup at a local police station and tried to help young men he felt should not be there.

On occasion Robinson affected public policy. A member of the Elks, he used his influence with New York mayor James J. Walker to win permission for the organization to hold a convention in the city in 1926 despite opposition from the white Elks. Around 1946 or 1947 he managed to have blacks and whites play in a Miami benefit before a black and white—albeit segregated—audience. This was a step toward the relatively early desegregation of performances in that city.

Stars In Major Motion Pictures

Robinson had his first major breakthrough in film in 1935 when he appeared in *The Little Colonel* with Shirley Temple. For this performance he taught the child star a version of the step dance. He did dance numbers in *Hooray for Love* (RKO, 1935) and *The Big Broadcast of 1937* (Paramount, 1935) and played Will Roger's servant in *In Old Kentucky* (Fox 1935). There were roles in more Shirley Temple films for Twentieth Century Fox: *The Littlest Rebel* (1936) and *Rebecca of Sunnybrook Farm* (1938). He also choreographed her film *Dimples* (1936) and performed a number in her film, *Just Around the Corner* (1938).

In January of 1936 Robinson's appendix was removed in a Los Angeles hospital. By this time the Robinsons were spending several months of every year on the west coast, and soon a house designed by Paul Williams was being built for them. That fall he opened the new downtown Cotton Club in New York in September and remained there through late January. During that period a gala celebrated Robinson's 50 years in show business. His next film, *One Mile From Heaven,* co–starring Freddi Washington, was a flop.

Robinson was awarded the *Mirror*–Ted Friend Gold Medal in 1937 for his ability, personality, and public appeal. He was also named honorary president of the Negro Actors Guild when it was formed that year. In June the city of Richmond, Virginia, held Bill Robinson Day. Tributes and awards came in increasing numbers in the following years.

In September of 1938 Twentieth Century Fox dropped Robinson and nine other actors. Robinson returned to the Broadway stage in early 1939 in Mike Todd's *Hot Mikado,* which was a big hit but had a short run on Broadway. Robinson did two shows at the Cotton Club in addition to his stage performance. When a shorter version of the show played first two and then three shows a day in Flushing Meadow Park in connection with the World's Fair, Robinson still did two shows at the Cotton Club. Included in the cast of the musical was Elaine Plaines, a young dancer from Brooklyn. Plaines was shy and 40 years younger than Robinson. Robinson was not a womanizer but he had fallen in love with her. He was not quite openly courting her, and she stayed behind when *The Hot Mikado* went on tour.

Over the years Robinson was a guest on many radio programs and later wouldf be seen on television; he was a great favorite of Ed Sullivan. He was still finding steady work as the forties began but smash hits proved more elusive. In late 1940 he joined the otherwise all white revue *All in Fun,* which closed after three performances. In early 1941 Robinson tried to revive Harlem night life by opening the Mimo Professional Club on 132nd Street. It did not flourish long under his management. He also threw himself into the war effort, performing for war bond rallies and at military camps. For some months he worked in a revival of *The Hot Mikado.*

Robinson returned to the west coast to star in *Stormy Weather,* which opened in 1943 to bad reviews but had good box–office receipts. His co–star, Lena Horne, had some very harsh words for him. In his book, *On the Real Side,* Mel

Bill "Bojangles" Robinson with Shirley Temple.

Watkins quoted Lena Horne's daughter, Gail Lumet Buckley. Buckley stated that her mother felt he was "one of the biggest Uncle Toms in show business." Buckley went on to say, "As far as Lena was concerned, nothing. . .could make up for Bill Robinson. He carried a revolver, was poisonous to other blacks, and truly believed in the wit and wisdom of little Shirley Temple."

After filming *Stormy Weather,* Robinson began to work on the revue *Born Happy* in Los Angeles and summoned Elaine Plaines to appear in it. Fannie Robinson demanded a divorce, which was granted on June 19, 1943, in Nevada. The divorce was friendly, and many who knew about the situation felt that if Fannie had not forced the issue, the marriage would not have ended. Robinson married Plaines on January 27, 1944, in Columbus, Ohio. He soon became very attached to Elaine's mother, addressing her as Mother, and spent as much or more time at his in–laws' home in Brooklyn than he did in his own Harlem apartment.

Robinson continued to work in spite of his failing health although his new wife and mother–in–law did manage to persuade him to work less and take vacations. He needed the money: he had very little to show of the immense sums he earned during his lifetime. At his death his entire estate was probated at $24,000 in life insurance. There were signs of a developing heart problem, and he suffered a series of unacknowledged, slight heart attacks. He developed cataracts and took care never to wear in public the heavy glasses he needed after the operation. On April 24, 1948, Robinson suffered his first major heart attack at a benefit for the American Heart Association. He quickly resumed activities, but in March of

1949 he had a second heart attack and was essentially confined to his mother-in-law's Brooklyn home until he entered Columbia Presbyterian Medical Center on November 14. There he died on November 25.

Friends arranged and paid for his funeral, which was said to be the largest the city had ever had with some 100,000 attendees in the church and the streets around it. Sixty thousand people viewed the body as it lay in state at the 369th Regiment Armory. Harlem schools were dismissed for a half day, and it is claimed that a million people lined the streets of Manhattan to see the procession which took his body from the Abyssinian Baptist Church, where the funeral was held, to Evergreen Cemetery in Brooklyn, where he was buried.

Robinson became one of the major stars of his age. His career lasted long enough to be documented on film and on recordings of radio broadcasts. Early on Robinson coined a phrase to describe a felicitous state of affairs, and it sums up the happy emotion he wished to inspire in his audiences through his energetic and attractive stage personality: ''Everything is copacetic.''

REFERENCES

Fletcher, Tom. *100 Years of the Negro in Show Business.* New York: Burdge, 1954. Reprint, New York: Da Capo, 1984.

Haskins, Jim, and N. R. Mitgang. *Mr. Bojangles.* New York: William Morrow, 1988.

Johnson, James Weldon. *Black Manhattan.* New York: Knopf, 1930.

Klotman, Phyllis Rauch. *Frame by Frame.* Bloomington: Indiana University Press, 1979.

Logan, Rayford W., and Michael R. Winston, eds. *Dictionary of American Negro Biography.* New York: Norton, 1982.

Sampson, Henry T. *The Ghost Walks.* Metuchen, NJ: Scarecrow, 1988.

Stearns, Marshall, and Jean Stearns. *Jazz Dance.* New York: Macmillan, 1968.

Watkins, Mel. *On the Real Side.* New York: Simon and Schuster, 1994.

Woll, Allen. *Black Musical Theatre.* Baton Rouge: Louisiana State University Press, 1989.

Robert L. Johns

Frank Robinson

(1935–)

Baseball player and manager

Named general manager of the Cleveland Indians in 1975, Frank Robinson was the first African American to serve as the general manager of a major league baseball team. In his career as an athlete he played for a number of other teams, including the National League Cincinnati Reds and the American League Baltimore Orioles, and was the first black named the Most Valuable Player in both leagues. He won the triple crown in 1966—the most home runs, most runs batted in, and the highest batting average—the first black player to hold the honor.

Robinson was born August 31, 1935, in Beaumont, Texas, the only child of Frank and Ruth Robinson. The Robinsons lived in Sisdale, Texas, 20 miles from Beaumont. Ruth Robinson had three previous marriages and nine children from those unions. Other children who can be identified are Johnny, Silvester, Robertha, Ellyson, and Raymond. The Robinsons divorced when Frank was an infant, and Ruth Robinson later moved to Almeda, then to Oakland, California. She and young Robinson lived in the homes of her other children until she saved enough money to get an apartment, and then a house. Robinson grew up in a neighborhood in West Oakland where black, Hispanic, and Asian residents apparently mixed well.

Robinson's long interest in baseball perhaps stemmed from the bat and mitt he received when he was one year old. He continued to play as a youngster and fondly remembered a Mrs. Rosso, who supervised the playground where he played ball. On other occasions he went to her home so he could go along with her when the playground opened. He especially enjoyed summer months for the experience he gained in recreational baseball games.

Robinson grew to become a tall, gangling, and skinny loner. When not playing ball, and as funds permitted, he devoted his leisure time to attending movies. He attended McClymonds High School where his schoolmates were Kurt Russell, Vada Pinson, and Bill Russell, all well-known athletes later on. Robinson starred on the basketball team and for a while was a defensive back in football, but he considered these sports simply something to do while he waited for baseball season to open. He was cautious when playing sports outside his main interest because he did not want to chance the injuries. He played third base and tried his hand at pitching but became an outfielder; he made the All-City Baseball Team for three years. Bobby Mattick, a baseball scout, recognized his baseball talent early on.

While in high school, Robinson and his classmates learned the meaning of respect and honesty. Robinson disliked school work and considered it unimportant; he graduated from McClymonds High School in 1953 with less than a brilliant record. He signed with the Cincinnati Reds, and for the 1953 season was assigned to their Class C team in Ogden, Utah.

Robinson went through a series of training camps, played in various cities in that state, then went to the South and eventually ended up in Columbia, South Carolina, with the Sally League. From this league he went to the major league and completed all of its training programs. All along the way he played various positions and hit different kinds of balls. Each venture was a learning experience as was the racism that he now faced.

Frank Robinson

In the early 1950s segregation was the rule; therefore, as an African American baseball player, Robinson had to find accommodations in black neighborhoods, staying in boarding houses, private homes, and the YMCA. He ate at black restaurants, and when the team traveled, the white baseball players had to bring sandwiches to the black players because they could not leave the bus. Although conditions improved when he moved to the major leagues, racism still prevailed.

First Black Manager in Major League Baseball

Robinson's break into the major leagues was a long–awaited dream, but the climb was tough. He continued to hit well despite receiving numerous injuries. Sometimes he fell into a slump, but managed to come out of it. His relationships with the baseball managers were rocky, even after a very good season. The Cincinnati Reds called him in 1956, at a time when he had a dazzling record on the field. He batted .290 and knocked in 83 runs. As a rookie he had a record–tying 26 home runs. From 1956 to 1965 Robinson played with the National League's Cincinnati Reds. *Current Biography* called him a ''problem player'' who had ''inscrutable moods'' but was a ''perennial All–Star.'' Still, in 1961 he helped the Reds win their first pennant in two decades. Although Robinson and the Reds' general manager, Bill DeWitt, were at great odds, Robinson compiled an impressive record with the team and received a salary of $60,000. He has been a successful player and manager with other teams as well.

Traded to the American League's Baltimore Orioles in 1965, the right fielder remained there as player until 1971. He led the team to victory in the 1966 World Series—their first ever—in a four–game sweep by scoring two home runs. He received a salary of $100,000. In 1966 as well, Robinson became the first black baseball player to win the triple crown—the most home runs, most runs batted in, and the highest batting average. During the winter months between 1968 and 1971, he managed the Santurce Cangrejeros, a high–calibre team of the Puerto Rican League. In spring 1971 he managed a major–league all–star team that defeated the New York Yankees in an exhibition game.

Robinson was traded to the Los Angeles Dodgers in 1971. Already with a career home run record of 586, while with the Dodgers he was ranked fourth on the list of home–run hitters. He played with the California Angels from 1973 to 1974. He was a player with the Cleveland Indians in 1974 and was named manager of the Indians in 1975, becoming the first black manager of a major league baseball team. He was named manager of the Rochester Red Wings in 1978. He coached the Baltimore Orioles from 1978 to 1980 and then left to serve as manager of the San Francisco Giants in 1981. He left the team in 1984. He returned to the Orioles as coach from 1985 to 1987. Robinson was named Orioles' manager from 1988 to 1991, then assistant to the general manager from 1991 to 1997.

In 1997 Robinson was appointed director of baseball operations for the six–team Arizona Fall League. He is also special projects consultant to the baseball commissioner, making him the ninth black executive in the central office of major league baseball.

Highly honored in the field of baseball, Robinson was named National League Rookie of the Year, 1956; and member of the All–Star Team, 1957, 1959, 1961–62, 1965–71, and 1974. In 1982 while he was with the San Francisco Giants, and again in 1988 after returning to the Orioles, Robinson was named American League Manager of the Year. He was named the Most Valuable Player of two leagues: the National League in 1961 and in the American League in 1974. In 1982 he was inducted into the Baseball Hall of Fame.

Robinson had grown up in baseball with no commitments outside the sport. Beside assisting his mother financially, he bought cars and lived freely. Marriage in October 1961 to Barbara Ann Cole brought stability into his life; he had to learn how to compromise and to budget. When his children Kevin and Nichelle were born, and when they adopted son Frank Kevin, he knew he had come full circle. Robinson is six–feet one–inch tall, muscular, and has been described in *Current Biography* as ''confident, in a relaxed way'' with a ''wry sense of humor.'' Although it is said that he is ''not outgoing,'' he provided moral support and encouragement to young players.

Especially in his early career he posed threats at bat and in the field, then endured racial retaliation in the form of injuries from infielders. Nevertheless, baseball legend Frank Robinson broke racial barriers in American baseball and set records both as a manager and as a powerful player.

Current address: Assistant General Manager, Baltimore Orioles, Oriole Park at Camden Yards, 333 W. Camden Street, Baltimore, MD 21201.

REFERENCES

Anderson, Dave, and Frank Robinson. *Frank.* New York: Holt, Rinehart, Winston, 1976.

Contemporary Black Biography. Vol. 9. Detroit: Gale Research, 1995.

Current Biography Yearbook. New York: H. W. Wilson, 1971.

''People.'' *Jet* 92 (2 June 1997): 20.

Robinson, Frank, with Al Silverman. *My Life Is Baseball.* New York: Doubleday, 1968.

Smith, Jessie Carney, ed. *Black Firsts.* Detroit: Gale Research, 1994.

Who's Who among African Americans, 1998–99. 10th ed. Detroit: Gale Research, 1996.

Barbara Williams Jenkins

Jackie Robinson

Jackie Robinson
(1919–1972)
Baseball player, activist

Honored internationally as the central figure in baseball's ''Noble Experiment,'' Jack Roosevelt Robinson, known in the world of baseball as Jackie Robinson, took the first steps toward integrating the sport's major league teams when he signed a contract to play with the Brooklyn Dodgers in 1947. This gigantic stride, which prepared the way for the legendary feats of Willie Mays and Henry Aaron, was an early harbinger of the significant changes in contract negotiations, compensation, and general status of professional athletes addressed half a century later in the 1994–95 baseball strike. His individual challenge to the accepted policies of organized sports demonstrated that change was possible through the concentrated effort of a player's union.

Jackie Robinson was born in Cairo, Georgia, on January 31, 1919. His parents were Jerry Robinson, a plantation farm worker, and Mallie, a domestic worker. There were five children in the Robinson family: Edgar, Frank, Mack, Willa Mae, and Jackie. Frank—his youngest brother's greatest fan—and Edgar are no longer alive, but Mack and Willa Mae still live in Pasadena, California. Mack, Robinson's early role model, a world–class sprinter, came in second to Jesse Owens in the 200–yard dash in the 1936 Olympics. Jerry Robinson left his wife and children, never to return, when Jackie was six months old. When she was 30 and Jackie 13 months old, Mallie, a deeply religious woman who believed in the possibility of advancement for herself and her children, set out by railroad to start a new life in Pasadena. Mallie Robinson washed and ironed clothes for well–to–do people and had to augment her meager earnings with welfare relief. Money was limited, but Jackie never felt deprived of her love and attention.

Despite the absence of some of the more arduous racial conditions of Georgia, Pasadena had similar restrictions—the movies were segregated, African Americans could swim in the municipal pool and attend the YMCA only on designated days, and some eating places were closed to black people. From the teachings of his mother, however, Robinson learned important lessons of self–respect and self–confidence.

Carl Anderson, a neighborhood automobile mechanic, pointed Robinson in the right direction when the young boy engaged in petty misbehavior with his friends. Karl Downs, youthful minister of Robinson's Methodist church, paced the sidelines whenever his protégé was on the playing field and counseled him when his athletic, social, or academic life became burdensome. Encouraged by his mother and his mentors and by the exhilaration of successes in sports, Robinson turned more and more of his energies to the playing fields.

Introduction to Sports

Robinson's first competitive game took place when his fourth–grade soccer team played the sixth graders. Then came football, tennis, basketball, the track team, and table tennis. In athletics he had more freedom to relate to people on equal terms, with less emphasis on race and more on body development, coordination, and performance level. Because of his skill as a football quarterback, .400 baseball player, and exceptional broad–jumper, Robinson was accepted as a friend by white team mates, attended the same schools, and visited back and forth in each other's homes. Still, with added age and broadened experience, Robinson saw that athletic success did not guarantee full freedom in the racially and economically unequal American society. Opposing players often reminded him of his race by rougher–than–necessary hits, arguments, and racial slurs.

Robinson won letters in football, baseball, basketball and track at Muir Technical High School and Pasadena Junior College. When he left the latter in 1939, he declined attractive offers from universities nationwide and chose the University of California at Los Angeles (UCLA), just an hour's drive from his mother's home in Pasadena. Robinson's honors at UCLA were impressive: for two years highest scorer in basketball competition in the Pacific Coast Conference, national champion long jumper, the school's first athlete to letter in four sports, All–American football halfback, and varsity baseball shortstop. He left college in 1941 because of financial pressures, not many units from a bachelor's degree.

Directly after UCLA, Robinson worked for a few months as an athletic director in the National Youth Administration, in Atascadero, California. Driven by a growing, overwhelming desire to play professional sports, Robinson went to Hawaii in the fall of 1941 to join a semiprofessional, racially integrated football team, the Honolulu Bears. On weekends he was a member of the team, and during the week a construction worker. At the end of the short season, he returned to the United States in December 1941, right after the Japanese attack on Pearl Harbor that took the nation into war.

In 1942, Robinson was drafted into the U.S. Army and sent to a segregated unit in Fort Riley, Kansas, where under existing policy he could not enter Officer's Candidate School. After protests by heavyweight boxing champion Joe Louis, then stationed at Fort Riley, and other influential persons—including Truman Gibson, an African–American advisor to the secretary of war—black men were accepted for officer training. Upon completion of the course of study, Robinson was commissioned as a lieutenant in 1943.

A racially charged incident at Fort Hood, Texas, threatened to discredit Robinson's service record, when in defiance of a bus driver's command to go to the rear of the bus, he refused to leave his seat. Robinson, a lifelong teetotaler and non–smoker, was charged, originally, with public drunkenness, conduct unbecoming an officer, and willful disobedience. With a public outcry by fellow service men, the NAACP, and the black press, led by the *Pittsburgh Courier* and the *Chicago Defender,* the court martial ended in exoneration. However, instead of going to meet with black soldiers in the European Theater of Operations as he desired, Robinson's next assignment was athletic director to new recruits at various camps in this country. He left the service in November 1944 with an honorable discharge.

For a while Robinson coached a basketball team at what is now Houston–Tillotson College, in Austin, Texas, but the genesis of his professional baseball career came in 1945, when he signed with the Kansas City Monarchs of the Negro American League for $400 a month. In this league, which included such luminaries as Satchel Paige, Josh Gibson, and ''Piper'' Davis, Robinson was treated with reverence because of his overall playing skills, speed, and batting average that approached .400.

Major League Contract

Even though playing with the Monarchs had the hardships of long, uncomfortable bus rides from town to town, uncertain away–from–home accommodations, low pay, poor playing fields, and the humiliation of the prevailing discrimination and segregation, this was the perfect springboard for Robinson's debut into the major leagues of baseball. It was the arena where he attracted the attention of Branch Rickey, who opened the door for him.

Before he decided on Robinson, Rickey, a devout Christian, and president of the Brooklyn Dodgers, had searched nationwide for the ideal African American man, one talented enough to play on major league teams and well–enough adjusted within himself to withstand the attacks sure to come in the racially prejudiced setting. Rickey had scouted Robinson with the Monarchs and was impressed enough to meet with him for a personal assessment.

Rickey interrogated Robinson extensively for three hours on August 28, 1945. In a dramatization of hotel, restaurant, and game situations, he glared at Robinson, shouting demeaning words and phrases while observing his reactions. At the end he quoted the Biblical passage that advises turning the other cheek. Satisfied that Robinson met the tests of ability, stamina, and tolerance, Rickey exacted a promise of extreme patience and forbearance for three years, then offered him a contract. On October 23, 1945, Rickey made the historic announcement that Jackie Robinson, a black man, would play for the Montreal Royals, the minor league affiliate of the Brooklyn Dodgers. Satchel Paige gave a ringing endorsement of Robinson as the best possible selection for ''The Noble Experiment.''

In the midst of the 50th celebration of Robinson's debut as a Dodger, former players spoke publicly of votes by most National League teams whether to go on strike when the black man took the field. Had it not been for the leadership of Rickey, National League President Ford Frick, Baseball Commissioner Albert B. ''Happy'' Chandler, and players like Stan Musial, the course of professional baseball might have taken a different turn.

In the winter of 1946, while Robinson was playing with Montreal, he married Rachel Isum. They met as students at UCLA. Her greatest interest was her future as a registered nurse, his a career in professional sports. Because Rachel was not an avid sports fan, nor initially overwhelmed by the attention of a college super star, it took some time for the relationship to develop. They were married six years after the initial introduction. A year after his death, Rachel Robinson founded the Jackie Robinson Foundation to provide motivational and financial support to minority students and maintain an archive of material relating to his career. She lives in Connecticut, still a major force in the foundation's success.

Robinson Jr., the oldest of their children, born in 1946, was killed in an automobile accident in 1971. Sharon, born in 1950, is a midwife, living in Stamford. Her brother, David, two years younger, operates a coffee farm in Tanzania, East Africa.

At the end of one year with the Montreal Royals, the Brooklyn Dodgers brought Robinson up from the minors to open the 1947 season. The team won the league title and Robinson finished with a .297 batting average, a league–leading 29 stolen bases, and the title of Major League Rookie of the Year.

After Robinson had kept silent for the agreed time, he began to speak up when pitchers narrowly missed his head, fans shouted epitaphs, or obscene mail came to his home. He fought the denial of equal service in eating and sleeping quarters, or wherever he faced discrimination. Finally, the curative effects of time and recognition of Robinson's value to the team caused the majority of players to settle into the spirit of cooperation. With Robinson on the roster, the Dodgers won National League pennants in 1947, 1949, 1952, 1953, 1955, and 1956. In 1955 they defeated the New York Yankees in the World Series.

When the Dodgers decided to trade Robinson to the Brooklyn Giants after the 1956 World Series, he retired from the game, declining to join his team's archrivals from the same city. It was a fitting time for the star to leave—with a .311 lifetime batting average, and 197 stolen bases over his career.

Robinson's induction into baseball's Hall of Fame in 1962 was a cause of celebration for black people around the world. He chose his wife, Rachel, his mother, Mallie, and his friend, Branch Rickey, to flank him in the Cooperstown award ceremony. This highest possible recognition of Robinson's skill and service was a symbol of victory to African Americans in the continuing struggle against injustice, proof that black Americans are as capable as any others.

Robinson's Hall of Fame plaque records the highlights of his brilliant career. With the Brooklyn National League 1947 to 1956, he was the leading National League batter in 1949 and holds the fielding mark for second baseman, playing 150 or more games with .992. He led the National League in stolen bases in 1947 and 1949 and was named Most Valuable Player in 1949. He is joint record holder for most double plays by second basemen, 137 in 1951. He led second basemen in double plays from 1949 through 1952.

After Professional Baseball

After baseball, Robinson headed the personnel office of the New York–based restaurant chain, Chock Full O'Nuts. He took an active role in the Harlem YMCA and other social and community organizations, and was a key figure in establishing and nurturing Harlem's African American–owned and –controlled Freedom Bank—now defunct—through its initial period in the mid 1960s. Despite black America's pride in Jackie Robinson's strength as a trail blazer, his exceptional performance on the baseball diamond, and his high visibility in community efforts, he was not free from controversy or from disagreement with other popular African American figures. While Robinson had deep affection for rights leader Martin Luther King Jr. and felt the pain of his suffering, he knew that his own temperament was not suited for King's nonviolent demonstrations. He preferred to volunteer time as head of fund raising drives for churches in Georgia destroyed by arsonists.

Robinson embraced King's dream of equality but used an issue of his syndicated newspaper column that appeared in the 1950s and 1960s, mostly in the *New York Post* and the *New York Amsterdam News,* to air his disagreement with his stand against the war in Vietnam. King telephoned Robinson and explained his motivation for the opposition. After their long talk, Robinson had not been persuaded to accept King's stance but understood why King, a champion of nonviolence in our South, could not condone armed conflict in Asia.

To Robinson, civil rights advocate Malcolm X was a talented man with a message of promise for African American youth but hampered by a philosophy based on hatred. In a much publicized war of words the two men feuded over Malcolm's characterization of Ralph Bunche, former undersecretary to the United Nations, as a man muzzled by white people who had put him in that position. Robinson defended Bunche's integrity, and Malcolm X criticized successful African Americans who distanced themselves from the struggle for equal rights. Malcolm X's and Robinson's goals were identical, but their approaches took divergent routes.

At one time Robinson resigned from the NAACP, citing its failure to listen to younger, more progressive black people. Nevertheless, he was labelled an "Uncle Tom" by black militants who resented what they interpreted as Robinson's identification with a conservative, affluent white society.

In 1949 the House Un–American Activities Committee subpoenaed Robinson to rebut singer, actor, and political activist Paul Robeson's declaration that African Americans would not support this country in a war with the Soviet Union. In his autobiography, *I Never Had It Made,* published shortly before he died, Robinson defended his 1949 testimony that he would not desert his country based on "a siren song sung in bass." He disavowed the phrasing, which he then saw as an insult to the older, wiser Robeson, a hero to the people for whose causes he had made meaningful sacrifices.

Robinson's political alliances were unlike those of most African Americans who shied away from the Republican Party. He campaigned for Democrat Hubert Humphrey in the presidential primary, yet he chose Republican Richard M. Nixon over John F. Kennedy in the 1960 general election. When Robinson compared his observations of the two candidates for president long after the election, he regretted he had not chosen Kennedy. During the campaign, Nixon was friendly and charming in private meetings, and seemed interested in the civil rights of African Americans. Robinson saw no tangible evidence of Nixon's sympathy for the struggle in the South. On the other hand, when Robinson met Kennedy, he wondered whether the Democrat's failure to make eye contact as they talked was due to an unspoken prejudice. Robinson's fears disappeared with the news of Kennedy's public objections to the persecution of Martin Luther King. Robinson came to the belated conclusion that Kennedy was the better man.

New York Governor Nelson Rockefeller, a Republican, named Robinson Special Assistant for Community Affairs in 1966, with the responsibility of improving the governor's popularity among residents of Harlem. In response to criticism, Robinson defended his membership in the Republican Party as a way to make heard the otherwise ignored voice of black opinion.

In protest against baseball's failure to add African American managers and front office personnel, Robinson declined to participate in the 1969 old timers game. Three years later, he came to Dodger Stadium in Los Angeles for ceremonies to mark the 25th anniversary of his first major league contract. By that time the effects of heart disease, diabetes, and failing eyesight were apparent. Still a handsome, proud man, nattily dressed in a business suit, his hair was totally white, and his gait was noticeably slower.

Jackie Robinson's last public appearance was on October 15, 1972, at Riverfront Stadium in Cincinnati, when he threw out the first ball in the 1972 World Series. Nine days later, rescuers were unable to revive him from what would be the fatal heart attack that struck when he was 53–years old in his Stamford home on October 24, 1972. His funeral was held on October 27, 1972, at Riverside Church in New York. The pallbearers were all sports figures: Ralph Branca, Larry Doby, Junior Gilliam, Don Newcombe, Pee Wee Reese, and Bill Russell. On its way to Cypress Hills Cemetery, the procession passed through Harlem and Bedford Stuyvesant where thousands lined the route. They were paying tribute not only to Robinson's athletic abilities, but to him as the symbol of opportunities for African Americans in professional sports without limitations of race. He had withstood the pains and frustrations of the trailblazer while giving record–breaking performances on the field of play, leaving lasting encouragement to players who followed long after he retired.

REFERENCES

Frommer, Harvey. *Jackie Robinson.* New York: Franklin Watts, 1984.

Harris, Mark. "Where've You Gone, Jackie Robinson?" *Nation* 260 (15 May 1995): 674.

Rampersad, Arnold. *Jackie Robinson: A Biography.* New York: Knopf, 1997.

Robinson, Jackie. *Baseball Has Done It.* Philadelphia: Lippincott, 1964.

———. *I Never Had it Made.* New York: G. P. Putnam's Sons, 1972.

Tygiel, Jules. *Baseball's Great Experiment.* New York: Vintage Books, 1983.

Williams, Michael W., ed. *An African American Encyclopedia.* New York: Marshall Cavendish, 1993.

Dona L. Irvin

Robinson, Luther.
See Robinson, Bill "Bojangles."

Randall Robinson
(1941–)
Civil rights activist, lawyer

Randall Robinson is an activist who believes that peoples of color around the world need support and representation. Additionally, he believes that one person can make a difference. The validity of his beliefs can be seen in the significant roles played by African Americans in foreign policy decisions to peoples of color spearheaded and guided by Randall Robinson.

Randall Robinson was born in Richmond, Virginia, on July 6, 1941, to educators Maxie Cleveland, a high school history teacher, and Doris Robinson Griffin, a teacher and housewife. In the *Black Collegian,* Robinson has credited his father with being "a real pillar" for him. He was educated in the public schools of Richmond, where he and his brother Max—the first African American network television news anchor—were coached as players on the Armstrong High School basketball team. As a result of his athletic skills, in 1959 he won a basketball scholarship to Norfolk State College (later University) where he was politically active and dropped out of college in his junior year. Following this, he was drafted into the army and spent his tour of duty in Georgia. When he returned, he attended Virginia Union University in Richmond from which he graduated in 1967 with a B.A. in sociology. Upon graduation, he entered Harvard University Law School. He also joined a campus protest against apartheid in South Africa. In 1970 he was awarded a law degree and won a Ford Foundation fellowship that allowed him to work in Tanzania.

From 1972 to 1975 Robinson was community development division director of the Roxbury Multi–Service Center in Roxbury, Massachusetts. In 1975 he moved to Washington, D.C., to become staff assistant to William L. Clay, U.S. representative from Missouri, and was responsible for writing

Randall Robinson

policy pronouncements. From 1976 to 1977 he served as staff attorney for the Lawyer's Committee for Civil Rights under Law Compensatory Project in Washington, D.C. His responsibility was to examine the legal requirements for compensatory education as given in Title 1 of the Elementary and Secondary School Act. During this period he was administrative assistant to Michigan representative Charles Diggs; as a staff member for Diggs, he joined a congressional team on its visit to South Africa and witnessed the dehumanizing effects of apartheid.

TransAfrica and TransAfrica Forum

Following his visit to South Africa, he and the Congressional Black Caucus at a Black Leadership Conference, recognizing the absence of African voices in international policy making and the general neglect of black countries, established an advocacy group. Thus, in 1977 TransAfrica came into existence with Randall Robinson as its executive director and founder, a position he still holds. Robinson admits that the times have been lean but at no time has he entertained the idea of leaving the organization. The success of the group is reflected in its achievement. As he works for contemporary issues, he also recognizes the need for establishing what he called in the June 7, 1993, issue of *Jet* "an institution to hand on to the next generation." He saw this as "the *only* way you can address serious problems in our time." To this end, in 1993 the TransAfrica headquarters, which is African America's only foreign policy home in the world, was dedicated. The foreign policy library and resource center is named in honor of tennis legend Arthur Ashe, who had worked for black liberation. With its concern for both the present and the future, it is a lobbying agency as well as a center for research and education. TransAfrica holds annual conferences and a series of seminars on foreign policy. The organization also publishes two quarterlies, *TransAfrica Forum* and *Issue Brief.*

In addition, TransAfrica maintains an educational affiliate known as TransAfrica Forum, which was established in 1981 and collects and disseminates information and helps plan U.S. foreign policy affecting black areas throughout the world. Ed Lewis, publisher of *Essence,* serves as its president. Through conferences, publications, and educational programs, it examines political injustices that television news coverage has ignored.

TransAfrica has often used tactics which were used by civil rights activists of the 1960s, including hunger strikes and sit–ins. Utilizing these strategies, Robinson was instrumental in bringing the plight of South Africa and Haiti to the attention of the world. This is in keeping with the focus of the organization, which is concerned with both Africa and the Caribbean. It has lobbied, testified, and asked for more overall aid to Africa and to those countries which are working toward democracy; at the same time, TransAfrica asks for a decrease in aid for those countries which evidence a disregard for, or problems with, human rights.

Robinson's commitment to the work and guiding principles of TransAfrica is evidenced in his actions and successes. In the mid–1980s, he helped establish and coordinate the Free South Africa Movement, which had as one tactic protesting in front of the South African embassy for over a year. Among the protestors were such famous people as Mary Frances Berry, Walter Fauntroy, Arthur Ashe, Harry Belafonte, the daughter of President Jimmy Carter, and two of the children of Senator Robert Kennedy. More than 5,000 were arrested. The protestors demanded the release of Nelson Mandela and other political prisoners and a repeal of South Africa's Apartheid rule and laws. Robinson's fight led to the Comprehensive Anti–Apartheid Act of 1986 which was passed in spite of President Reagan's veto.

In the 1990s Robinson entered into a 27–day hunger strike to protest the U.S. policy toward Haiti, the return of Haitian refugees, and the admission of Cubans to this country. This action led to the deposing of military leaders in Haiti and the reinstatement of exiled President Jean–Bertrand Aristide. Robinson and other prominent African Americans protested for democracy in Nigeria outside the Nigerian embassy and protested against unfair American policies in the Caribbean at the office of the U.S. trade representative in Washington, D.C., by dumping 2,000 pounds of bananas on the doorstep.

According to the TransAfrica report for February 29, 1996, in addition to the above, in the last 17 years the organization has spoken out against human rights violations in Liberia, Zaire, Kenya, Malawi, and Ethiopia; spearheaded the struggle to maintain economic sanctions against Zimbabwe;

facilitated meetings between American policymakers and foreign leaders; and organized meetings between African American leaders and Secretary of State James Baker on apartheid, famine relief, and human rights. According to the TransAfrica report, the goal for the organization under Robinson and deputy director Maryse Mills, is to "pursue all opportunities to create an understanding among policymakers and assist in the formulation of constructive U.S. foreign policy as it affects Africa and the Caribbean."

Robinson's awards of recognition and appreciation include the National Association of Black Journalists' Community Services Award; Africa Future Award presented by the U.S. Committee for UNICEF; the Humanitarian Award from the Congressional Black Caucus and another from the Martin Luther King Jr. Center for Non–Violent Social Change; the Hope Award from the National Rainbow Coalition; the Drum Major for Justice Award from the Southern Christian Leadership Conference; and the Trumpet Award for International Service by the Turner Broadcasting System. He has also been recognized by the Johnson Publishing Company, Omega Psi Phi Fraternity, WJLA Channel 7, Alpha Kappa Alpha Sorority, Jackie Joyner–Kersee Community Foundation, and the Howard University Hospital. Honorary degrees have been awarded by such institutions as Columbia College, Delaware State College, Morehouse College, North Carolina Agricultural and Technical State University, Ohio Wesleyan University, the University of the District of Columbia, and the University of Massachusetts, Amherst.

In 1987 Randall Robinson married Hazel Ross Robinson, a foreign policy adviser. From his first marriage, to librarian Brenda Randolph, he has two children, Anikie and Jabari.

Robinson has not hesitated to put his life and well–being on the line in his effort to involve African Americans in international affairs and to keep before the public the plight of Africa and the Caribbean.

Current address: TransAfrica, 1744 R Street NW, Washington, DC 20009.

REFERENCES

Chapelle, Tony. "Randall Robinson and TransAfrica: Standing on the Frontline." *Black Collegian* 21 (September–October 1990): 96, 168–69.

Contemporary Black Biography. Vol. 3. Detroit: Gale Research, 1993.

"Randall Robinson." Biographical Statement, *TransAfrica/TransAfrica Forum.* Fax to Helen R. Houston, June 26, 1996.

"Randall Robinson's TransAfrica Dedicates New Building." *Jet* 84 (7 June 1992): 33–34, 38.

"TransAfrica/TransAfrica Forum." Black Information Network World Wide Web. (http://bin.org/assocorg/transafr/transafr.htm) Accessed February 26, 1996.

"Transafrica Forum Home Page." (http://www.igc.apc.org/transafrica/) Accessed June 2, 1997.

Helen R. Houston

Sugar Ray Robinson

(1921–1989)

Boxer, entrepreneur, philanthropist

Sugar Ray Robinson was considered by many boxing experts the best prizefighter in history. He was known for his boxing artistry and knockout power with either fist. Ranked number one in *The 100 Greatest Boxers of All Time,* Bert Randolph Sugar noted, "Robinson could deliver a knockout blow going backward. His footwork was superior to any that had been in boxing up to that time. His hand speed and leverage were unmatchable." Robinson recorded 175 victories and 110 knockouts with only 19 losses, and he held titles in the welterweight and middleweight divisions of boxing. Robinson believed that boxing was the art of self–defense, and he patterned his style of fight against the opponent's style. An observer of his fighting described him as "the sweetest fighter . . . sweet as sugar." He was the five–time middleweight champion of the world.

Walter Smith Jr., later known as Sugar Ray Robinson, had no middle name and was just called "Junior" by his family. He was born May 3, 1921, on McComb Street in Detroit, Michigan, in a rented wooden frame house. His father, Walker Smith, and his mother, Leila Marie Hurst Smith, migrated to Detroit from Dublin, Georgia, with two daughters, Marie (b. 1917) and Evelyn (b. 1919). The couple were seeking relief from poverty as small farmers growing mostly cotton, corn, and peanuts. In Detroit, his father found work in construction during the day and sewer projects at night. He worked six days a week from early morning until midnight. His mother worked as a chambermaid at the Statler Hotel.

In Detroit at age ten, Robinson often visited Brewster Center Gymnasium to see a neighbor, an aspiring young amateur fighter named Joe Louis. After the separation of his parents two years later, Robinson moved with his mother to Harlem in New York City. His mother worked as a laundress and young Robinson ran errands for a grocery store, sold driftwood, shined shoes, and danced for pennies on the sidewalks. At 14 he met George Gainford at the Salem Crescent gym and began boxing. Since Robinson was underage for his first fight, Gainford gave him the American Athletics Union card of another amateur fighter, Ray Robinson. From that point, Walter Smith used the name Sugar Ray

Sugar Ray Robinson

Robinson. Gainford would remain his trainer and manager throughout his boxing career. Under Gainford, Sugar Ray won 85 consecutive fights with 69 victories by knockouts. This included a win over the undefeated future Featherweight Champion Willie Pep. Curt Horrman supplied Robinson's financial backing.

Robinson's boxing career growing, he attended DeWitt Clinton High School for three years but did not graduate. He ended his amateur career by winning Golden Gloves tournaments in 1939 and 1940 in featherweight and lightweight divisions.

The Professional Boxing Years

In October of 1940 Robinson had his first professional fight with Joe Echevarria at Madison Square Garden. Robinson won the match with a left hook in the second round. The headline fight was Fritzie Zivic versus Henry Armstrong. At the time, Armstrong was the reigning welterweight champion and a black star. Armstrong, Joe Louis, and Robinson represented a trio of the first great black boxers.

By 1942 Robinson had matches with Marty Servo, the lightweight champion, Sammy Angott and Izzy Jannazzo, both leading lightweight contenders, and knocked out Fritzie Zivic. He also fought Jake La Motta for the first time. He earned ''Fighter of the Year'' honors. Robinson was 5–feet, 11–inches tall and weighed in between 144 to 160 pounds.

In March of 1943 Robinson was inducted into the army as a sergeant in Joe Louis's boxing troop. The troop gave exhibition fights for army camps and hospitals. Shortly before a European tour of duty, he woke up in Halloran Army Hospital on Staten Island with amnesia from a fall. Two months later he received an honorable discharge from the army. During this time he met and married Edna Mae Holly of Miami, Florida, on May 29, 1943. The couple had a son, Ray Jr.

During the following years, Robinson was often called the fastest fighter pound–for–pound. Jack Dempsey and others regarded him as the leader in the welterweight class. He wanted a shot at the championship after Marty Servo retired shortly after a non–title loss to Rocky Graziano. Robinson beat Jake La Motta, Vic Dellicurti, Izzy Jannazzo, and Sammy Angott. Robinson was then matched against Tommy Bell for the vacant welterweight championship. In Madison Square Garden in December of 1946, he won the welterweight title in a 15–round bout against Bell. In a series of matches to defend his title, he fought Jimmy Doyle in Cleveland on June of 1947. A year earlier, Doyle had a rough fight with Art Levine and suffered cerebral damage. His health condition was unknown when the fight between Doyle and Robinson took place. In the eighth round, Jimmy Doyle received fatal injuries. Robinson contemplated quitting boxing but returned to the ring after turning over 80 percent of the purse to Doyle's family. He continued to defend his title and fought Kid Gavilan at Yankee Stadium in September of 1948 and Bernard Docusen in Chicago in June of 1949. In the fifth successful defense of his title, he fought Charlie Fusari in Jersey City in August of 1950. Robinson donated his purse to the Damon Runyon Cancer Fund.

Robinson toured Europe and defeated the former European middleweight champion, Jean Stock, and the middleweight champions of the Netherlands (Luc Van Dam), France (Jean Walzack and Robert Villemain), and Germany (Hans Stretz). He was known as the ''boxing idol of Europe.'' In 1950 the New York Boxing Writers Association voted Robinson the outstanding boxer of year. He won the J. Neil Memorial Plaque.

Soon after this honor, Robinson won the world middleweight championship from Jake La Motta in Chicago on February 14, 1951. The estimated stadium and television audience for this fight was 30 million people. On February 5, 1943, La Motta handed Robinson his first loss in 123 professional fights. This would be Robinson's only loss from the late 1930s to the early 1950s. On July 10, 1951, Robinson lost the middleweight championship to Randy Turpin, a black British fighter. Two months later Robinson regained the title on September 12 in New York by a knockout in the tenth round. Robinson successfully defended his title against Carl ''Bobo'' Olson and Rocky Graziana. In 1951 he won the world middleweight championship by defeating Kid Marcel in France.

On June 25, 1952, Robinson lost a fight to Joe Maxim for the Light Heavyweight crown. After this fight he retired from the ring for 22 months and went into show business as a tap dancer before regaining the middleweight title from Carl ''Bobo'' Olson. By 1957 Robinson had fought Gene Fullmer twice, losing the first bout and winning the second. That year he lost a fight with Carmen Basilio, but in 1958 regained the middleweight title from Basilio. At age 44, Robinson announced his retirement on December 10, 1965.

The Golden Years

After retirement, Robinson moved with his second wife, Millie, to Los Angeles, California. He enjoyed golfing, dancing, and playing the drums. He was inducted into the Boxing Hall of Fame in 1967 and two years later, in 1969, he founded the Sugar Ray Robinson Youth Foundation for inner city children of Los Angeles. He held extensive real estate and business holdings in New York, Cleveland, Detroit, and Chicago. Well known for his philanthropy, Robinson estimated that he gave $4 million to family, friends, and charities. He donated his purse to the Damon Runyon Cancer Fund, the Hearst Veterans Fund, the National Foundation for Infantile Paralysis, the B'nai B'rith, and the Cancer Society of France.

Robinson died from Alzheimer's disease and diabetes on April 12, 1989, at Brotman Medical Center in Culver City, California. Five–time middleweight champion of the world, Robinson was a boxing artist with knockout power in both fists. One of the greatest prizefighters of all times, he had quick, powerful hand speed and an unmatchable self–defense.

REFERENCES

Current Biography. New York: H. W. Wilson Company, 1951.

Current Biography CD–ROM. New York: H. W. Wilson Company, 1996.

Fleming, G. James, and Christian E. Burckel, eds. *Who's Who in Colored America.* 7th ed. New York: Yonkers–on–Hudson, 1950.

Reference Library of Black America. Detroit: Gale Research, 1997.

Robinson, Sugar Ray, with Dave Anderson. *Sugar Ray.* New York: Viking Press, 1971.

"Sugar Ray Robinson, Boxing's 'Best,' Is Dead At 67." *New York Times,* April 13, 1989.

Saundra P. Peterson

J. A. Rogers

(1883?–1965)

Historian, writer, journalist

In a pioneering attempt to recover the Black African historical presence which had been excluded, ignored or misrepresented by mainly white historians, Joel Augustus Rogers, known simply as J. A. Rogers, devoted more than 50 years of his life to corrective research and revisionary scholarship. Almost entirely self–educated, he mastered several foreign languages–among them French, German, Portuguese and Spanish—tirelessly traveled and extensively researched library and museum archives in Europe and Africa, and became one of the most prolific writers of his time. His works reached a broad audience in the African American community, even though they were widely ignored by the white academic world.

The exact date of J. A. Rogers's birth is not known, but he is thought to have been born December 6, 1883, in Negril, Jamaica. Some sources claim that he was born in September of 1880. He was the only child of Samuel and Emily Johnstone Rogers. Other facts concerning his early life are scarce and the information is often unreliable.

After childhood, Rogers's life is better documented. After serving four years in the British army, Rogers immigrated to the United States in 1906, although he did not become a citizen until 1917. He lived for many years in the heart of Harlem at 37 Morningside Avenue, where he accumulated a magnificent library and entertained a wide group of interesting guests.

In 1917 the mainstream publishing house of M. A. Donohue & Company, Chicago, eventually going through four editions, released Rogers's first book, *From Superman to Man.* Rogers published a fifth edition himself in 1941. The book reveals how white historians have rewritten history to exclude, ignore, or recast black achievements by ascribing the achievements to Europeans. Rogers's lack of proper scholastic credentials added to the difficulties of getting his work published that he already faced as an African American writer, forcing him to publish much of it himself. His research led him to radical conclusions, which challenged the generally accepted views concerning race and the identity of African Americans. Few of his scholarly contemporaries granted him any recognition, except to challenge the accuracy of his work. Although some historians later confirmed his claims, they still left Rogers largely unacknowledged.

It is not surprising that no institution of higher learning in the United States conferred an honorary degree upon Rogers; however, he was elected to membership in the Paris Society of Anthropology in 1930, and in the same year he was one of the speakers at the International Congress of Anthropology which was opened by Paul Doumer, then president of France. He was also a member of the American Geographical Society, and the Academy of Political Science.

In 1930 Rogers attended the coronation of Emperor Haile Selassie I of Abyssinia, and during the Italian invasion of Ethiopia (1935–36) he covered the conflict for the *Pittsburgh Courier* as a war correspondent. Although several sources claim that he was the first African American war correspondent, two others preceded him: Thomas Morris Chester, who was correspondent for the *Pittsburgh Press* during the Civil War; and Ralph Waldo Tyler, who was the first and only African American war correspondent during World War I.

J. A. Rogers

A partial listing of Rogers's literary credits includes: *As Nature Leads: An Informal Discussion of the Reason Why Negro and Caucasian Are Mixing in Spite of Opposition* (1919); *The Ku Klux Spirit* (1923); *One Hundred Amazing Facts About the Negro, With Complete Proof* (1934), which ran to 24 editions; *World's Greatest Men and Women of African Descent* (1936); *The Real Facts About Ethiopia* (1936), which grew out of his firsthand experiences as foreign correspondent for the *Pittsburgh Courier* during the Italian invasion; *Your History From the Beginning of Time to the Present* (1940); the monumental *Sex and Race* (three volumes, 1941–44), which documents miscegenation throughout world history and which ran to nine editions; *World's Great Men of Color* (two volumes, 1946), which gives 200 biographies dating from 3000 B.C. to 1946 A.D. and was republished in 1972; *Nature Knows No Color Line* (1952); and *Africa's Gift to America* (1959), which discusses the role of African Americans in the development of the United States. He also contributed articles to *The Journal of Negro History, Crisis, Survey Graphic, American Mercury,* and *Messenger* magazine. At one time he was contributing editor of the latter publication. For many years Rogers was the writer of an illustrated feature for the *Pittsburgh Courier* entitled ''Your History.''

Perhaps W. E. B. Du Bois in the preface to *The World and Africa* (1974) gave the most accurate evaluation of the work of Rogers:

> I have learned much from James [sic] A. Rogers. Rogers is an untrained American Negro writer who has done his work under great difficulty without funds and at much personal sacrifice. But no man living has revealed as many important facts about the Negro race as has Rogers. His mistakes are many and his background narrow but he is a true historical student.

In fact, Rogers's works were more widely read than those of Du Bois and historian Carter G. Woodson because many black barbershops and other popular gathering places provided his books for their customers. Du Bois also wrote the following for the dust jacket of *Sex and Race*: ''The person who wants in small compass in good English and in an attractive form the arguments for the present Negro position should buy and read and recommend to his friends *From Superman to Man.*'' Another illustrative comment by the Catholic Board for Mission Work Among the Colored People is to be found on the inside jacket of *Sex and Race*: ''There are more objections against the colored race answered in this book more satisfactorily and convincingly than in any book we have read upon the question.''

Rogers continued to work on a number of manuscripts until his death at St. Clare's Hospital in New York City on March 26, 1965, after a very brief illness following a stroke; his funeral was kept secret at his request. His widow, Helga Bresenthal Rogers; a half–brother, Jan H. Rogers; and a half–sister, Constance Hall, survived him. Although he was a journalist and novelist, J. A. Rogers is remembered most as an historian and for his numerous writings that aimed to bring to the forefront the contributions of blacks in the United States and abroad. His books and personal library are at Fisk University.

REFERENCES

Davis, Arthur P., and Michael W. Peplow, eds. *New Negro Renaissance.* New York: Holt, Rinehart and Winston, 1975.

''Negro Genius Throughout the Ages in the Old and New World.'' Flier, Special Collections, Fisk University Library, n.d.

Ottley, Roi. *New World A–Coming.* Boston: Houghton Mifflin, 1943.

Ploski, Harry A., and Roscoe C. Brown Jr. *Negro Almanac.* New York: Bellwether, 1967.

Rush, Theressa G. *Black American Writers: Past and Present.* Metuchen, NJ: Scarecrow Press, 1975.

Sandoval, Valerie. ''The Bran of History: A Historiographic Account of the Work of J. A. Rogers.'' *Schomburg Center for Research in Black Culture Journal* I (Spring 1978): 5–7, 16–19.

Smith, Jessie Carney. *Black Firsts.* Detroit: Gale Research, 1994.

Thorpe, Earle E. *Black Historian.* New York: Morrow, 1971.

Turner, W. B. ''J. A. Rogers: Portrait of an Afro–American Historian.'' *Black Scholar* 6 (January–February 1975): 32–39.

Who's Who in Colored America. 7th ed. Yonkers–on–Hudson, NY: Christian E. Burckel, 1950.

Jacqueline Jones–Ford

Carl Rowan

(1925–)

Journalist, government official, author, scholar

Carl Thomas Rowan, syndicated columnist, overcame poverty to transcend the limitations of racism imposed on people of color. He excelled as a journalist for major newspapers, as a ground–breaking official in government, and in various strata in society. He was the first black or one of the first in many occupational positions. In the "Foreword" to his memoir, *Breaking Barriers,* he described his life experiences as opportunities in a "blessed lifetime of being thrust onto the ramparts where freedom was challenged by tyranny."

Carl Rowan was born in Ravenscroft, Tennessee, a dying coal mining town, on August 11, 1925, to Thomas David and Johnnie Bradford Rowan. Soon after his birth the family moved to McMinnville, Tennessee, to improve their economic condition. The move failed due to the Great Depression, and the family suffered great economic hardship. Young Rowan often had to augment the family income through various menial jobs. In his autobiography he described this time as one of living in a home where there were no clocks or watches, "no electricity, no running water, no toothbrushes, . . . no telephone, no radio and no regular inflow of money." In spite of the crushing poverty, he excelled in school. From 1938 to 1942, Rowan attended Bernard High School, a tiny and ill–equipped school built by the Julius Rosenwald Fund, where his teacher, Bessie Taylor Gwynn, forced and encouraged him to pursue excellence, to maintain his own standards, and not to be swayed by others. He wrote in his autobiography that she told him, "Never waste time fretting about what you *don't* have. Just make the most of what you *do* have—a brain." As a result of this encouragement, he graduated as both valedictorian and class president and moved to Nashville, Tennessee, to work and attend college. Originally he intended to attend Fisk University, but his limited finances prohibited this.

In 1942, aided by an anonymous doctor, Rowan enrolled in Tennessee State University where he was again influenced and encouraged by teachers. Frances Thompson, an art instructor, encouraged Rowan to think big. At the first class meeting, she asked the students to predict what grade they would earn in the class; Rowan predicted a "C." After she lectured him, he changed his prediction to an "A." This gave him a "new measure of self–esteem," he wrote in his autobiography. Other professors were equally important in his development. Merle Eppse and George W. Gore encouraged him to take the national examination for admission to the Navy's V–12 program in preparation to become an officer candidate at midshipman school. He passed the examination and after a long wait received orders to report to Washburn Municipal University in Topeka, Kansas.

Carl Rowan

In the Military

According to Rowan's autobiography, he officially reported on November 1, 1943, to Washburn Municipal University where he was assigned as the sole black in a unit of 335 sailors. This began Rowan's self–liberation by presenting him with "new horizons of opportunity and potential achievement." While at Washburn, he encountered much racism but said, "I felt sorry for the decent young white men who were straining not to commit any racial faux pas that might get them in trouble." During this time at Washburn, he encountered whites using terms which in many instances seemed pejorative but which he understood to be "meaningless clichés" and to which he did not take offense. Even when there was an obvious act of bigotry, he diffused tension without any show of rage. According to the *Nashville Tennessean* for January 16, 1991, this began his philosophy throughout his career, "You don't break any barriers by being strident. . . . The key is to be insistent and to use language that any reasonable person can understand." Ultimately, he was commended for his handling of himself and a possibly volatile situation.

After a period, the navy transferred him to Northwestern University in Evanston, Illinois. Since blacks were not permitted to live on campus, however, he was retransferred to Oberlin College in Ohio. From Oberlin he was sent to the Naval Reserve Midshipman School at Fort Schuyler in the Bronx. At age 19, he was commissioned an officer, one of the first 15 blacks to earn a commission in the navy. Rowan was assigned to sea duty on the *U.S.S. Mattole.* Two months later he was transferred to the *U.S.S. Chemung* and given deputy command of the communication division. He ended his naval career in 1946.

Journalism Calls

Following the navy, Rowan returned to Oberlin College because of the credits he had earned there while in the navy and because the college allowed him to study in a ''safe'' environment. He earned an A.B. degree in mathematics in 1947 with a desire to earn an advanced degree in journalism. His desire to become a journalist was solidified by the way in which that racial incidents were reported. One of the events that shaped his decision took place in South Carolina where in 1946, Isaac Woodard, a black U.S. Army sergeant who had served in the South Pacific, was beaten by lawmen, denied medical treatment, and blinded, while the perpetrators of the crime were acquitted. The failure of the press to tell the truth of the white brutality, to condemn the injustice of both the treatment and the courtroom proceedings, and to provide news for the black community led Rowan to say in his autobiography, this ''as much as any event, stilled my resolve to be a writer to bust open the lily–white journalistic establishment in America.''

Rowan became a freelance writer for the *Baltimore Afro–American* while at Oberlin. He continued to write for the *Baltimore Afro–American* and took on additional assignments for the *Minneapolis Spokesman* and the *St. Paul Recorder* while a graduate student at the University of Minnesota.

After graduating with an M.A. in journalism in 1948, Rowan became a copyeditor for the *Minneapolis Tribune.* In addition to his thriving career, Rowan married Vivian Louise Murphey, a public health nurse, on August 2, 1950. The Rowans had three children together: Barbera, Carl Thomas Jr., and Geoffrey. In 1950 he also became the first general assignment black reporter for the paper and one of only five black journalists in the United States. His resolve as a journalist was not to limit himself to being a black reporter giving news only on black issues and events but to be a reporter to present ''truths that only . . . [he could] tell,'' he wrote in his autobiography.

To this end, Rowan proposed to this editor that he be sent to the South to report on ''what it means to be a Negro in the Postwar [World War II] South.'' This series comprised 18 articles, the result of a 6,000–mile trek through 13 states and was entitled ''How Far from Slavery?'' The series which details the racism Rowan encountered in his travels, won the Sidney Hillman Award for the best newspaper reporting in 1951; the Minneapolis Junior Chamber of Commerce cited him for service to humanity; the curators of Lincoln University in Jefferson City, Missouri, cited him for high purpose, high achievement, and exemplary practice in the field of journalism; and the Minneapolis Jaycees named him the Minneapolis Outstanding Young Man of 1951. His first book, *South of Freedom,* grew out of these articles and later, a follow–up visit to the South led to another book, *Go South to Sorrow* (1957). He also wrote a series of articles entitled ''Jim Crow's Last Stand,'' that was carried in many papers and designed to inform people about the issues involved in the *Brown v. Board of Education* case. This led to the Sigma Delta Chi Award for the best general reporting in the nation in 1953.

In 1954 Rowan was invited by the United States Department of State to travel to India and lecture on the role of a free press in a free society. His stellar performance caused Secretary of State John Foster Dulles to ask him to extend his visit and present his speech in Southeast Asia. Upon his return, he wrote a series of articles about India and Pakistan for the *Minneapolis Tribune.* He returned to Asia to cover the Bandung Conference. His second book, *The Pitiful and the Proud* (1956), grew out of these Asian travels. Again he was chosen to receive the Sigma Delta Chi Journalism Award, this time for his India series, ''This is India.'' In 1956 he was again awarded the Sigma Delta Chi medallion, this time, according to his autobiography, for ''the best foreign correspondence of 1955 for . . . [his] articles on Southeast Asia and . . . coverage of the Bandung Conference.'' With this award he became the first journalist to receive the Sigma Delta Chi Award in three consecutive years.

By 1957 his byline was published regularly in the *Saturday Evening Post, Redbook, Look, Reader's Digest,* and *Ebony* ''on subjects as diverse as how Viv and I taught our children about race to what Negroes really wanted and whether they were ready for equality,'' he reported in his autobiography. Other assignments included United Nations correspondent for the *Minneapolis Tribune,* a series on the American Indian (''Our Unknown Neighbors''), and articles in *Ebony* on Paul Robeson, ''Has Paul Robeson Betrayed the Negro,'' in which he attempted to counteract the biased treatment of Robeson in the press. He wrote about John F. Kennedy and Richard Nixon, and on the Civil Rights Movement in the South. In 1961 he resigned from the *Tribune.*

Receives Federal Assignment

President John F. Kennedy asked Rowan to become the Deputy Assistant Secretary of State for Public Affairs (1961–63). With this appointment, Rowan became the first black to hold such a high position in government. From 1963 to 1964 he served as U.S. Ambassador to Finland, based in Helsinki. In 1964 following the assassination of John F. Kennedy, he returned to Washington, D.C., and was appointed director of the U.S. Information Agency. He was charged with ''telling America's story,'' as he wrote in his autobiography. With this appointment, *Contemporary Biography* said that he became ''the highest ranking black in the federal government and the first to ever attend National Security Council meetings.'' In 1965, due to disillusionment, efforts to compromise him and his principles, and an inability to work with President Lyndon Johnson any longer, Rowan resigned his USIA position and returned to his career in journalism.

Following Rowan's resignation from government, he agreed to write three columns each week on a subject of his choice for the *Chicago Daily News* and Publishers Newspapers Syndicate and to do three three–minute television commentaries each week for Westinghouse Broadcasting. He was also under exclusive contract to *Reader's Digest.* As a syndicated columnist Rowan broke yet another barrier; he had his own daily radio program, *The Rowan Report,* and made regular appearances on the television program *Agronsky and Company* (1976–1988). He was a regular panelist on *Meet the Press* and *Inside Washington.*

In 1986 Rowan wrote and produced a documentary program *Justice Thurgood Marshall: The Man,* which looked at the ways in which Marshall changed the racial climate in this country. Rowan hosted and helped produce, with Jeanne Bowers, a program entitled "Searching for Justice: Three American Stories" for the Gannett Corporation at WUSA–TV in celebration of the anniversary of the U.S. Constitution in 1987.

In addition to his other activities, Carl Rowan has written seven books. These include *Wait Till Next Year: The Life Story of Jackie Robinson* (1960), *No Need for Hunger* (1962), *Just Between Us Blacks* (1974), *Race War in Rhodesia* (1978), *Breaking Barriers: A Memoir* (1991), *Dream Makers, Dream Breakers: The World of Thurgood Marshall* (1993), and *The Coming Race War in America: A Wake Up Call* (1996).

Prolific and insightful, Rowan's works have generated him many awards in addition to those mentioned. Rowan has won the American Teamwork Award, the National Urban League (1955); Distinguished Achievement Award, Regents of University of Minnesota (1961); Communications Award in Human Relations, Anti–Defamation League B'Nai B'Rith (1964); and the "Best Book" citation from the American Library Association in 1953 for *South of Freedom* and in 1956 for *The Pitiful and the Proud.* In 1954 he received the Distinguished Service Award from the Capital Press Club and the National Brotherhood Award from the National Conference of Christians and Jews and in 1968 he was given the Elijah P. Lovejoy Award. The Capital Press Club named him Washington Journalist of the Year (1978). In the same year, *Ebony* presented him with the American Black Achievement Award and he received the George Foster Peabody Award for *Race War in Rhodesia.* In 1987 he received the Alfred I. DuPont Columbia University Silver Baton Award for his television documentary *Thurgood Marshall: The Man* and was named annual president of the prestigious journalist's group, the Gridiron Club. He has been inducted into both the Sigma Delta Chi Hall of Fame and the Black Journalists Hall of Fame. In addition to being awarded an honorary Doctor of Letters degree from Oberlin College in 1962, he has received numerous other honorary degrees. In 1993 the Lynch Annex Elementary School in Detroit was renamed in his honor to become the Carl T. Rowan Community School.

The Controversy of Carl Rowan

During his career, Rowan achieved many awards and recognition but his career was not without controversy. In a time when fear emanated from the FBI, Rowan not only spoke out against J. Edgar Hoover but also called for his firing. "The kind of abuse and contempt for the law in the [Martin Luther] King [Jr.] and Muhammad Ali eavesdroppings becomes almost inevitable when a man is left in a key job as long as Hoover has been. Hoover ought to be replaced–immediately," he wrote later in his autobiography. Another source of controversy is that in both his articles and his memoir, he spoke out against Ronald Reagan. He said in his autobiography that he wrote "at least a hundred columns excoriating Ronald Reagan" and he was one of the few journalists in the land to write bluntly that Reagan's agenda "is neither fair nor humane, but cruelty covered up by glib clichés." His independence and adherence to what he believed to be right led to his reporting of truths regardless of the consequences. As a result of this stance, he has been both praised and criticized, earning both respect and disdain. In 1988, there was a robbery attempt at his home in Washington, D.C., and Rowan, a frequent advocate of gun control, shot and wounded the intruder. For this, he was charged with possessing an unregistered firearm, charges which were later dropped. Rowan accused Mayor Marion Barry of retaliation because of Rowan's criticism of Barry's administration as corrupt.

The *Washington Post,* cited in *Contemporary Black Biography,* called Rowan "the most visible black journalist in the country." As cited on the jacket of his memoir, the *New York Times Book Review* called him "a prophet with honor on both sides of a biracial society divided against itself." Rowan continued his fight against racism. He said, as cited in the *Nashville Tennessean* for March 19, 1997, that "until we can either educate or somehow force people to face the truth, there isn't going to be any tranquillity in this society." In a 1992 commencement address he said, according to the *Nashville Tennessean* for April 19, 1992, that "learning has liberated more people than all of the armies ever put together by man" but also asserted "while a lot of change has taken place and barriers broken . . . [in American society], bigotry is on the upsurge again, aided and abetted by politicians from the White House down."

Current address: 1101 7th Street, NW, Washington, DC 20036.

REFERENCES

Contemporary Black Biography. Vol. 1. Detroit: Gale Research, 1992.

Current Biography Yearbook. New York: H. W. Wilson, 1958.

"For Rowan, Victory Overcomes Bitterness." *Nashville Tennessean,* January 16, 1991.

"Racism Won't Be Erased Soon, Author Asserts." *Nashville Tennessean,* March 19, 1997.

Rowan, Carl T. *Breaking Barriers: A Memoir.* New York: HarperCollins, 1991.

"Rowan Recalls Marshall as Lawyer, Friend, Storyteller." *Nashville Tennessean,* February 12, 1993.

"Rowan to Warn TSU Grads to Close Doors." *Nashville Tennessean,* April 19, 1992.

Salzman, Jack, David Lionel Smith, and Cornel West, eds. *Encyclopedia of African–American Culture and History.* New York: Macmillan Reference Library USA/Simon and Schuster Macmillan, 1996.

Tennessee Biographical Dictionary: People of All Times and Places Who Have Been Important to the History and Life of the State. New York: Somerset Publishers, 1994.

Helen R. Houston

David Ruggles

(1810–1849)

Abolitionist, hydrotherapist, editor, entrepreneur

David Ruggles was active in many areas. He was a grocer, bookseller, editor, and, most importantly, a daring secretary of the New York Vigilance Committee, helping fugitive slaves and defending the rights of those wrongly held as slaves. When his health failed, he spent the end of his short life as an important hydrotherapist, espousing a novel medical treatment involving the use of water.

Ruggles was born on March 15, 1810, in Norwich, Connecticut, to David and Nancy Ruggles, who were both free. He was the eldest of five children: four boys and a girl. Ruggles received a good elementary education in Norwich, and, in 1827, at the age of 17, he moved to New York City.

In New York Ruggles lived first at 15 Chapel Street. By 1829 he was a butter merchant and grocer and continued in that trade until 1833. He then became a traveling agent for the abolitionist paper the *Emancipator.* He demonstrated a talent for public speaking and writing. He addressed audiences in support of the paper and published six articles in it. Since he still needed to earn a living, he opened a bookstore in 1834, where he sold antislavery works and stationary and engaged in activities like printing, book–binding, and composing letters for persons unable to write. He was the first African American bookseller, and, in 1834, he was the first black to appear in the imprint of a book when he published *The "Extinguisher" Extinguished.* His second published work, the following year, was *The Abrogation of the Seventh Commandment by the American Churches,* with the same imprint. *An Antidote for a Poisonous Combination,* two pamphlets published together, appeared in 1838, with a different publisher.

Ruggles's bookstore at 67 Lispenard Street was burned in September 1835, but he continued to live at the same address and act as an agent for abolitionist papers. He also espoused other causes. Although he had sold spirits in his grocery store, in 1835, Ruggles was an officer of the New York City Temperance Society, founded in 1829 by Samuel Cornish. The following year he was appointed as a fund–raiser for the newly founded Phoenix High School, an institution to provide better educational opportunities for blacks.

At a large meeting of "Friends of Human Rights," on November 20, 1835, Ruggles was chosen as secretary. He became a member, along with William Johnson, Robert Brown, George Barker, and J. W. Higgins, of the New York Committee of Vigilance, which was formed as a result of the meeting. Other prominent blacks soon joined. Ruggles's most important occupation was as secretary and leading spirit of the New York Committee of Vigilance.

Ruggles was one of the most aggressive and daring defenders of both escaped and former slaves. He boldly entered houses to question the status of persons held as slaves and appeared at hearings before magistrates, who in general were favorable to slave–holders. Ruggles also took fugitive slaves under his own roof and assisted them to safety. Perhaps the most famous fugitive he aided was Frederick Douglass (still using the name Bailey), whom he sheltered for several days in September 1838, and who was married to Anna Murray Douglass in his residence by James W. C. Pennington, himself a fugitive slave.

When Ruggles was arrested for the first time on December 28, 1835, on the charge of assault, he suspected that this was an attempt to send him into slavery in the South. In another case involving a fugitive slave, Thomas Hughes, who allegedly stole $9,000, Ruggles was thrown in prison in April 1838 and held overnight because a friend, possibly Samuel Cornish, refused to stand bail. For 17 months he stood accused of a major crime until he was discharged without a trial in November 1839. The hardships of this period probably contributed greatly to undermine his health.

Breaks with the Committee of Vigilance

Before his imprisonment, Ruggles was already undergoing strained relationships with members of the Committee of Vigilance. The financial affairs of the committee were difficult, and expenses chronically outran funds. Ruggles did not keep adequate records, and he fell under suspicion of misappropriating funds. His tactics did not always win approbation from his more conservative colleagues. In particular, Samuel Cornish, a fellow member of the executive committee and editor of the *Colored American,* did not approve of Ruggles's attempt to rescue a fugitive slave by force in 1836. Relations between the two men reached the breaking point the following year when Cornish published, on October 17, 1837, a letter by Ruggles claiming that John Russell, a black lodging–house operator, had forced three Africans to go on board a ship bound for New Orleans after an attempt to sell them in New York was unsuccessful. Russell sued the paper for libel and won. Since Cornish had accepted Ruggles's account as true without verification, he blamed Ruggles for the paper's ensuing difficulties. Members of the Committee of Vigilance lined up in support of Cornish.

In January of 1839, Ruggles was forced to resign as secretary of the organization. His health was broken, and he was losing his eyesight. His career as an antislavery activist was also essentially over, and he was near destitution. He tried his hand at publishing a quarterly newspaper, *The Mirror of Liberty,* which managed only four issues before its end in 1840. In that year, Ruggles tried to revive the National Black Convention Movement, in abeyance since 1835. He called for a meeting to be held in New Haven, Connecticut, in August

1840, to start an organization called the National Reform Convention of the Colored Inhabitants of the United States. This meeting drew disapproval from black leaders, and only five delegates and 20 observers attended.

In 1841 Ruggles was involved in two cases involving discrimination in transportation. A mass meeting of blacks in New Hartford protested Ruggles's beating by a steamer captain from whom he had tried to buy a first class ticket. He then sued the New Bedford and Tauton Railroad when he was forcibly removed from the all–white first class car. He lost the case.

Remaining in New York until 1842, Ruggles lived at 62 Leonard Street. By that time his health was deteriorating; and doctors predicted his death within six weeks. In the fall of that year, Lydia Maria Child, a celebrated white abolitionist, gave him lodging in Northampton, Massachusetts. This town was a center for abolitionists who had formed a commune called the Northampton Association of Education and Industry. Ruggles was accepted as a member of the commune and gradually regained his health by following a self–administered course of hydropathy, a regimen that had been recently devised in Germany involving rest, diet, and the application of water in various forms. He received written instructions from Dr. Robert Wesselhoeft, a German emigre physician practicing in Cambridge, Massachusetts.

After some 18 months, Ruggles regained much of his health. His eyesight remained poor but adequate enough to allow him to move around without assistance. He claimed to have developed an acute sense of touch which he featured as a diagnostic tool in his later practice. Since Ruggles had the equipment devised for his own treatment, he now treated other patients. He was called ''doctor'' by his patients, including white abolitionist William Lloyd Garrison, who underwent a course of treatment at his hands in 1848. Another famous patient was Sojourner Truth in 1845.

Ruggles became a successful hydrotherapist. By March 1849, he had acquired 112 acres of land by purchase and lease and erected a number of buildings. The principal building had 20 rooms with separate treatment facilities for men and women. There were no vacancies in his establishment when he died in the presence of his mother and sister on December 26, 1849, of an acute inflammation of the intestines. He was buried in Norwich, his birthplace.

Ruggles deserves notice as a vigorous polemicist and antislavery worker, as well as a pioneer hydrotherapist. In both roles he left a decided mark on his era.

REFERENCES

Blackett, R. J. M. *Beating Against the Barriers.* Ithaca, NY: Cornell University Press, 1986.

Logan, Rayford W., and Michael R. Winston, eds. *Dictionary of American Negro Biography.* New York: Norton, 1982.

Pease, Jane H., and William H. Pease. *They Who Would Be Free.* New York: Atheneum, 1974.

Porter, Dorothy B. ''David Ruggles, An Apostle of Human Rights.'' *Journal of Negro History* 27 (January 1943): 23–50.

Quarles, Benjamin. *Black Abolitionists.* New York: Oxford, 1969.

Sterling, Dorothy, ed. *Speak Out in Thunder Tones.* Garden City, NY: Doubleday, 1973.

Robert L. Johns

Bill Russell

(1934–)

Basketball player, coach

In 1980 the Professional Basketball Writers Association named Bill Russell the greatest player in the history of the National Basketball Association (NBA). Known as a defensive center, Russell changed forever the way basketball is played by creating defensive strategies that have become standard. Playing for the University of San Francisco, Russell was part of a team that won two National Collegiate Athletic Association championships and 55 straight games. After college he helped the United States win a gold medal in the 1956 Olympics in Melbourne. As player and coach for the Boston Celtics (1956–1969), Bill Russell won 11 championships including an unprecedented and unequaled eight in a row. In addition to leading the league in rebounding for four seasons, he was awarded the NBA's Most Valuable Player trophy five times: 1958, 1961, 1962, 1963, and 1965. He was the first African American to coach in the NBA. Russell's competitive spirit has also engaged civil rights issues. As a player, he angered many people when he spoke out about a quota system in the NBA, but his remarks, it has been argued, brought an end to the NBA's unacknowledged quota system.

William Felton ''Bill'' Russell was born in Monroe, Louisiana, on February 12, 1934, to Charles and Katie Russell. He has one brother, Charlie, who is two years older. In 1956 Russell married his college sweetheart, Rose Swisher. Russell and Rose have three children: William ''Buddha'' Felton Jr., Jacob, and Karen Kenyatta. In 1969 Russell left the marriage, and in 1977 he married Didi Anstett.

When Russell was nine, his family moved to Oakland, California, to escape the overt racism of the deep South. Russell recounted that Oakland was like heaven compared to Louisiana, but poor living conditions and racial prejudice were still a part of life. Three years after the move to Oakland, Russell's mother died. Mr. Charlie, as Bill refers to his father, gave up the small trucking business that he had built up with farmers in the San Joaquin Valley and took a job in a foundry so that he would be closer to home to raise his two sons.

Bill Russell

Russell suffered a deep depression following the death of his mother. He eventually started reading and learned about Henri Christophe, the slave who led a successful revolt against the French and became emperor of Haiti. This made an indelible impression on the young Russell, and Christophe became one of Russell's lasting heroes.

Preparation for Greatness

In the eighth grade, Russell could not make the home room basketball team, was cut from the football team, and failed in an attempt to become a school cheerleader. At predominantly black McClymonds High School, the junior varsity coach George Powles convinced Russell, gangly and uncoordinated, to try out for the team, then carried him as the sixteenth member of a 15–member junior varsity team, so Bill had to share a jersey with another player. Working at his game on the playground and at the boys' club, by his senior year Russell developed some of those skills for which he has become well–known. A scout for the University of San Francisco saw him play and offered a scholarship to Russell, who apparently played the game of his life. USF was the only school to offer Russell a scholarship.

Because Russell graduated from high school in January, he had the opportunity to join a traveling squad, the California High School All–Stars, which toured the Pacific Northwest and British Columbia playing exhibition games. While a member of this team, Russell worked on some of the techniques which later made him the master of defense. Riding the bus and the bench, Russell began to imagine himself performing particular actions that he saw others performing on the court. This technique enabled him to develop his rebounding and shot–blocking. By the time he enrolled in USF in the fall, he was on his way to becoming a dominant player. At USF he was a roommate with K. C. Jones. Both Russell and Jones went on to play and coach in the NBA.

During Russell's sophomore year, the team did not have a spectacular year (14–7 was their record). During the junior season would be different; the team lost early on to UCLA, 47–40, but then started to win, including a win over UCLA the week following the loss. USF won 55 straight games during Russell's junior and senior years and two NCAA championships.

Russell's potential to dominate defensively under the basket led to two rule changes in NCAA basketball: the free–throw lane was widened from six to 12 feet, and shots could no longer be blocked after they had started downward toward the basket. Because his USF teammates were deliberately firing flat shots so that Russell could stuff the ball in the basket, the new rule designed to move centers a little further from the basket was called the Russell rule. Though Russell did not have the statistics that many professional teams were looking for in a big man, a number of teams were interested in him. Red Auerbach and the Boston Celtics performed some pre–draft finagling to put themselves in a position to draft the six–foot ten–inch Russell, a choice Auerbach was criticized for. Russell chose not to sign with Boston right away because he wanted to play for the U.S. Olympic team in December 1956, which won the gold medal. When Russell returned to the United States, he married Rose Swisher, then moved to Boston. Auerbach signed Russell to a contract for $19,500, making him the highest paid rookie in the NBA.

The Bill Russell Era

Bill Russell was crucial to the Celtics' success. Before his arrival, Boston had never won a championship. With Auerbach's coaching (beginning in 1950), the Celtics made the playoffs, but were unable to crack the top. The first year that Russell was with the team, however, the Celtics won their first championship. They went on to win 11 championships over the next 13 years. Russell was honored with five Most Valuable Player trophies.

What Russell brought to the Celtics was a new, winning style of defense. He also brought an emphasis on team play rather than individual success. Though Russell's statistics were not as impressive as those of his primary rival, Wilt Chamberlain, he garnered win after win for his team. So impressive was Russell's presence that the 13 years he played for Boston became known as the ''Bill Russell Era'' of basketball.

In Russell's second year with the Celtics, they lost the championship to St. Louis after Russell injured his ankle in the third game and was lost for the rest of the series. However, the Celtics reeled off eight successive championships, perhaps the most impressive dominance by a single team of any sport at any time. Red Auerbach's confidence in Russell paid off for the team.

When Auerbach decided to retire in 1966, he chose Russell as his successor. At the time of the announcement, the Celtics had lost the opening game of the championship series with the Los Angeles Lakers. Boston came back to win yet another championship and sent Auerbach out as a winner. Russell's first year as coach was a difficult one, and the Celtics finished second to Philadelphia in the regular season and lost to Philadelphia again in the semifinals of the playoffs. The string of championships had come to an end at eight. In the next two seasons, though, the Celtics came back to reclaim their title.

In 1969 Russell announced his impending retirement, and the Celtics won a thrilling series against the Lakers. Russell retired the same way he came in, a champion, with 11 NBA titles in all, a feat unprecedented and unequaled in any professional sport.

More than a Basketball Player

During his years in Boston, Russell was more than a great basketball player. Lessons he learned from his father were to be a man and to be proud of his heritage. These are lessons he never forgot when he became a celebrity. In *Go Up for Glory,* Russell revealed that when he dies, he would like the following inscription: "Bill Russell. / He was a man." In Boston Russell was active with the NAACP and the Boston public schools to try to improve the lives of children in underprivileged neighborhoods. In 1959, as a liaison of the U.S. Department of State, Russell went to Africa as ambassador of basketball and good will. He invested in the economy of Liberia by buying a rubber plantation and providing jobs for Liberians.

As early as 1958, Russell was outspoken in accusing the NBA of having an unwritten quota system, explaining that no team had more than three African Americans. Russell is credited with paving the way for more African Americans to join the NBA. In 1964 Russell expounded further on racism within professional basketball and around the country. He suggested that the media were complicit in this quota system by the way they treated the athletes based on race. A black, Russell said in the January 18, 1964, *Saturday Evening Post,* is fooling only himself if he thinks that his own life, regardless of fame or wealth, is separate from "the total condition of the Negro." The racial situation in the United States at that time required solidarity among black people. According to Russell, a black person's only weapon is to keep pushing, to keep rocking the boat: "We have got to make the white population uncomfortable and keep it uncomfortable, because that is the only way to get their attention."

Not all sports fans were enamored with Russell's forthrightness. When he referred to basketball as a child's game played by men, Russell was identifying life outside of the basketball court as most important. He conducted integrated basketball clinics in Jackson, Mississippi, following the death of Medgar Evers. Russell commented in *Go Up for Glory,* "I believe that I can contribute something far more important than mere basketball." William Kunstler, who was representing some jailed Freedom Riders at the time Russell went to Mississippi, recounted in *Sports Magazine,* "As I recall, Russell was the only professional athlete who demonstrated enough interest in the deep South civil rights struggles of the early Sixties to come take a look at what was happening in the arena." Russell's family became a target of racial violence in their nearly all–white neighborhood in Reading, Massachusetts.

With other black athletes in 1967, Russell met with Muhammad Ali about his decision not to serve in the U.S. military. Coming out of that meeting, Russell was convinced of Ali's sincere faith and the belief that Ali would be all right. He told *Sports Illustrated* for June 19, 1967, "I'm not worried about Muhammed Ali. He is better equipped than anyone I know to withstand the trials in store for him. What I'm worried about is the rest of us."

A sore point with many for Russell's fans has been his refusal to sign autographs. For him, they represent a meaningless piece of paper that suggests an artificial closeness between the player and the fan. He would prefer to shake a person's hand because it is more personal. Russell disdains how autograph–signing seems to elevate one person above another.

When Russell left the Celtics, he took up, among other activities, acting, golfing, being a color–commentator for televised NBA games, filling in as a talk–show host, and lecturing on college campuses. As a color–commentator, Russell's style, according to *Life* for February 25, 1972, was pure Russell: "loose, confident, skillful and precise. . . . You know exactly when he's disgusted, exactly when he's bemused, exactly when he's bored."

In 1974 Russell was the first black player to be elected to the Basketball Hall of Fame. Russell protested his enshrinement partly on the basis of the hall's history of racism, partly on the basis that it is a form of self–aggrandizement which is not good for one, and partly because it is primarily a political and self–serving organization whose standards are too low. He was inducted despite these objections.

Russell has held two additional coaching positions in the NBA. He became coach and general manager for the Seattle Supersonics in the summer of 1973. In his second year the Supersonics made the playoffs for the first time in the franchise's history. In the four years that he was with this team, he increased the level of play, but not enough to satisfy either himself or the owner of the Supersonics. There was a lot of contention among the players, a far cry from the unselfish play of Russell's years with the Celtics. In 1987 Russell came out of retirement again to coach the Sacramento Kings, but this relationship was even more short–lived. After a disappointing partial season, Russell stepped down. Losing hurt too much, he said. Russell continued as the vice–president of operations with the Kings to help build the foundation for the franchise.

Bill Russell will be remembered primarily for his contributions to basketball, particularly for his shot–blocking and rebounding skills. He also opened doors for others in basketball by openly criticizing the league's unacknowledged quota system so that today over 60 percent of NBA players are African American. Russell, tremendous competitor that he is, recognized that basketball is not an arena of absolute importance. His actions in the community and the nation established a precedent for social responsibility among those in a position to effect change. Following the examples of his heroes like his father and Henri Christophe, Russell knows what it means to be a man and shows others the way.

Current address: Sacramento Kings, 1 Sports Parkway, Sacramento, CA 95834–2301.

REFERENCES

Afro–American Encyclopedia. Vol. 8. North Miami: Educational Book Publishers, 1974.

Brown, Roy B., ed. "Bill Russell." In *Contemporary Heroes and Heroines.* Detroit: Gale Research, 1990.

"Coach Russell." *Newsweek* 67 (2 May 1966): 72–73.

Current Biography. New York: H. W. Wilson, 1975.

Cyclops. "Eagle and Stork and Real Prince." *Life* 72 (25 February 1972): 8.

Devaney, John. *The Story of Basketball.* New York: Random House, 1976.

Grimsley, Will, and The Associated Press Sports Staff. *101 Greatest Athletes of the Century.* N.P.: Associated Press, 1987.

Henderson, Edwin B., and the editors of *Sport. The Black Athlete: Emergence and Arrival.* Cornwell Heights, PA: Publishers Agency, 1978.

Klein, Dave. *Pro Basketball's Big Men.* New York: Random House, 1973.

Kunstler, William M. "Bill Russell." *Sport Magazine* 77 (December 1986): 39.

Linn, Edward. "I Owe the Public Nothing." *Saturday Evening Post* 237 (18 January 1964): 60–63.

Lupica, Mike. "The Dipper's Lament." *Esquire* 109 (May 1988): 53–58.

McCallum, Jack. "The King at His New Court." *Sports Illustrated* 67 (16 November 1987): 36–39.

Rein, Richard K. "Catching His Second Wind, Ex–Celtic Legend Bill Russell Scores Now as a Social Critic." *Sequel* 13 (14 January 1980): 78.

Rogin, Gilbert. "We Are Grown Men Playing a Child's Game." *Sports Illustrated* 19 (18 November 1963): 74–78.

Russell, Bill, with Taylor Branch. *Second Wind: The Memoirs of an Opinionated Man.* New York: Ballantine Books, 1979.

Russell, Bill, with Tex Maule. "I Am Not Worried about Ali." *Sports Illustrated* 26 (19 June 1967): 18–21.

Russell, Bill, as told to William McSweeny. *Go Up for Glory.* New York: Berkely, 1966.

Russell, Bill, with Bob Ottum. "The Psych . . . and My Other Tricks." *Sports Illustrated* 23 (25 October 1965): 32–34.

Shapiro, Miles. *Bill Russell.* New York: Chelsea House, 1991.

Gordon K. Lee

John Brown Russworm (1799–1851)

Journalist, abolitionist, colonizer, editor

John Russworm is noted as one of the first African American college graduates and an editor of the first African American newspaper, *Freedom's Journal.* When he announced his support of African colonization in 1829, his American career ended in a storm of controversy. In Africa he enjoyed a solid career, establishing the first newspaper in Liberia and becoming governor of Maryland Colony, later part of Liberia.

John Brown Russworm was born on October 1, 1799, in Port Antonio, Jamaica, to an unidentified slave mother. His father was a white American merchant, John Russworm, who raised him as free. In 1807 the younger John Russworm, then called John Brown, went to Quebec for schooling. Russworm Sr. settled in Portland, Maine, in 1812, and in 1813 married Susan Blanchard who demanded that the boy be given the family name and treated as a family member. She maintained her position after her husband's death in 1815 and her remarriage.

John Brown Russworm entered Hebron Academy in Hebron, Maine, in 1819, and then in September of 1824 went to Bowdoin College from which he graduated on September 6, 1826. He was the third African American to graduate from an American college. (The first was Alexander L. Twilight, Middlebury College, 1823. The second, Edward Jones, graduated from Amherst two weeks before Russworm.) The noted author Nathaniel Hawthorne was among his classmates at Bowdoin where Russworm was considered an industrious rather than a brilliant student.

Russworm taught at Primus Hall's school in Boston, probably before his graduation, after which he went to New York City where he became involved with the planning of a black newspaper designed to answer the scurrilous attacks on African Americans in white papers. With Samuel Cornish as senior editor, Russworm became an editor of *Freedom's Journal,* the first edition of which appeared on March 16, 1827. From its inception the paper supported abolition and opposed the colonization of Africa, a controversial belief that free African Americans should return to Africa and start colonies there. Cornish resigned as editor to become an agent of the New York African Free Schools, and Russworm became sole editor on September 14, 1827. Some critics point to the decline in the quality of the paper after Cornish's departure as a major factor in its eventual failure. In addition, like most pre–Civil War black newspapers, *Freedom's Journal* faced continuous financial problems.

Before accepting the position on *Freedom's Journal,* Russworm had turned down an attractive offer from the American Colonization Society, although he had leaned towards emigration to Haiti in his Bowdoin commencement address. During the course of his editorship, his equivocation

John Brown Russworm

about emigration was evident only in the lack of anticolonization material until he made an open but qualified declaration of his favorable opinion on February 14, 1829, and then declared unequivocally on March 7 "our rightful place is in Africa."

The resulting uproar forced Russworm to resign. His farewell editorial appeared on March 21. He accepted the position of superintendent of schools in Liberia offered by the American Colonization Society. Russworm arrived in Monrovia in November of 1829. In addition to establishing a school, he also edited a paper, the *Liberia Herald,* the first issue of which appeared on March 6, 1830. This was the first newspaper in Liberia and the third in West Africa.

In addition to his work as an editor, Russworm accepted political appointments. From 1830 to 1834 he served as colonial secretary of Liberia. In 1834 he moved to Cape Palmas in Maryland Colony. He became governor of Maryland Colony in 1836 and held that position until his death on June 17, 1851. According to Huberich, he was an outstanding success as an administrator, and he received a warm welcome from the Colonization Society when he visited the United States in 1848. Nonetheless, he faced continuing vilification by the abolitionist press throughout his life. At his death his wife Sarah McGill Russworm and four of his five children survived Russworm. A monument to him was erected at Cape Palmas and a nearby island bears his name.

Russworm's importance in African American history rests on the relatively brief period he was editor of *Freedom's Journal.* He is a more substantial figure in the history of Liberia where he was a pioneering black official who laid the foundation for the eventual incorporation of the Maryland Colony into Liberia.

REFERENCES

Brewer, William M. "John B. Russworm." *Journal of Negro History* 13 (October 1928): 413–422.

Foner, Philip, ed. "John Brown Russworm, A Document." *Journal of Negro History* 54 (October 1969): 393–397. Russworm's 1826 commencement address, "The Condition and Prospects of Hayti."

Gross, Bella. "Freedom's Journal and The Rights of All." *Journal of Negro History* 17 (July 1932): 241–286.

Huberich, Charles Henry. *The Political and Legislative History of Liberia.* 2 vol. New York: Central Book Company, 1947.

Logan, Rayford W., and Michael R. Winston, eds. *Dictionary of American Negro Biography.* New York: Norton, 1982.

Malone, Dumas, ed. *Dictionary of American Biography.* New York: Scribner's, 1943.

Robert L. Johns

Bayard Rustin

(1910–1987)

Pacifist, civil and human rights activist

For more than a half century, Bayard Rustin masterminded and implemented national and international activism on behalf of humanity. Active in the American Pacifist Movement and an advocate of nonviolence, Rustin once spent 28 months in a federal prison and was jailed periodically as he consistently campaigned for world peace and brotherhood. Rustin supported India's quest for independence from Britain and freedom movements in various African countries, but his universally acknowledged organizational and tactical skills were best utilized in various civil rights movements. Hailed by Columbus Salley in *The Black 100* as the "resident theoretician and practitioner of the modern civil rights movement," Rustin was intimately involved in the creation of two organizations: the Congress of Racial Equality (CORE) and the Southern Christian Leadership Conference (SCLC) He was also involved in the implementation of milestone events including the Freedom Rides through the South, the Montgomery Bus Boycott, and the 1963 March on Washington where Martin Luther King Jr. delivered his "I Have a Dream" speech. As an adviser to King, *Contemporary Black Biography* said that Rustin "provided much of the organizational know–how, political savvy, and theoretical underpinning for King's civil rights victories." In addition, Rustin was the first black American leader to urge that black priorities shift from protest to politics.

Bayard Taylor Rustin was born March 17, 1910, in West Chester, Pennsylvania. At age 11, Bayard discovered he was not the youngest of Janifer and Julia Davis Rustin's eight children; he was their grandson, whom the Rustins adopted soon after his birth. Julia Davis felt that his teenage mother, Florence, was ill–prepared for maternal responsibilities. Davis was a rarity; she was an African American Quaker, and she instilled her religious values along with a sense of social commitment in young Bayard.

Rustin attended the all–black Gay Street Elementary School and West Chester Junior High School. When he entered West Chester Senior High, enrollment was approximately 600; only a few students were black. Rustin excelled in academics and athletics—basketball, track, tennis, and football—and participated in many extracurricular club activities including the history, French, science, drama, and glee clubs as well as the chorus. Few of his black peers remained at West Chester long enough to graduate.

Although in *Strategies for Freedom* Rustin described West Chester as a town "rich in the history and culture of Negro Americans. . . [and] an important stop on the Underground Railroad," it was an enclave of segregation and the birthplace of Rustin's social activism. Rustin's civil rights campaign, which spanned more than five decades, began as early as his high school years. Blacks were barred from department stores, restaurants and the local YMCA, and they were required to sit in movie theater balconies. Rustin, however, sat in the white section of the Warner Theater and was promptly arrested. In *Bayard Rustin,* Jervis Anderson called the experience "the first of more than twenty–five arrests he was to log in a near lifetime of social protest." Rustin led a number of his black classmates into West Chester's segregated facilities, where they were usually thrown out. On one occasion, his high school football team traveled to its competitor's home town, and on the eve of the game, Rustin presented his coach with an ultimatum: he threatened that the black players would not participate in the game unless they were moved from their segregated accommodations. The coach acquiesced, and the black team members were moved to the same location that housed their white teammates.

As a tenor soloist in his high school's chorus, Rustin participated in a competition held at Temple University where West Chester High's chorus won all–state honors. The presentation of the award, however, was delayed until Rustin's age was verified. The judges were so impressed with his voice, they assumed he was older. When Rustin graduated from West Chester High, he ranked nineteenth in a class of 100 and was the first black recipient of the D. Webster Meredith Prize for excellence in public speaking.

Although Rustin attended several colleges, he never received a degree. He was enrolled as a music major at Wilberforce University where he was the first tenor and principal soloist of the Wilberforce Quartet. The group traveled extensively as ambassadors and fund raisers for the university. He then transferred to Cheyney State Teachers College—now Cheyney University—where he was an excellent debater, the chorus's chief soloist, and the featured vocalist of the Cheyney State Quartet. However, lack of funds to continue his undergraduate education and the onset of the Great Depression sent Rustin to New York where he enrolled in free evening classes at the City College of New York.

Bayard Rustin

Rustin held various jobs during his earliest days in New York, including part–time usher at a movie theater, substitute teacher at Benjamin Franklin High School, part–time director of a Harlem Youth Center, and waiter. His considerable vocal talents led to his occasional hiring as a last minute replacement for vocalists at the Apollo Theater. He also sang backup for Leadbelly in cafes. He appeared in the chorus of *John Henry,* the all–black musical that starred Paul Robeson and served a stint in Josh White's vocal quintet after *John Henry* closed. White's group recorded *Chain Gang,* an album of blues and work songs.

Rustin traveled as a member of White's quintet for approximately two years. During his trips, he recruited for the Young Communist League (YCL), which he had joined because of its commitment to Southern racial struggles. According to Taylor Branch in *Parting the Waters,* "His qualities made him an ideal organizer. He could entertain crowds with speeches or songs, write pamphlets skillfully, and run a meeting. Fearless, unattached, able to get along with whites and Negroes alike, Rustin rose quickly as a youth recruiter for the Communist Party." In 1941 he was designated the leader of a campaign against segregation in the military, but in June of that year, orders came from Moscow for the American Communist Party to focus on World War II and to abandon its civil rights commitments. A disenchanted Rustin resigned from the Communist Party.

Also in 1941, Rustin helped A. Philip Randolph, head of the Brotherhood of Sleeping Car Porters and one of the most influential black American leaders of his era, plan a march on Washington movement in an effort to gain equal access to defense jobs; Rustin served as a youth organizer. Randolph cancelled the march, however, after President Roosevelt signed an order eliminating racial discrimination in defense jobs.

Becomes Pacifist and Civil Rights Activist

Randolph was instrumental in Rustin's introduction to A. J. Muste, a leading pacifist and head of an international pacifist organization, Fellowship of Reconciliation (FOR). In 1941 Muste appointed Rustin FOR's field secretary for youth and general affairs, a position that required Rustin to travel throughout the United States to promote the Gandhian principles of nonviolent struggle for social change. College students were among Rustin's most receptive audiences.

In 1942 Rustin's FOR colleague, James Farmer, founded the Congress of Racial Equality (CORE); CORE was sponsored by FOR. According to *Contemporary Black Biography,* ''At the heart of CORE's philosophy was the idea of 'nonviolent direct action'. . . . Interracial in its membership, CORE's activities focused on challenging racial discrimination in public accommodations and transportation.'' Rustin, a charter member of CORE, served as its first field secretary. Until 1955, Rustin was an influential member of FOR and CORE: he held various offices in both organizations, conducted weekend and summer seminars on nonviolence and race relations, and undertook national speaking tours on behalf of FOR and CORE.

During his travels, Rustin frequently encountered racial discrimination. Each time his reaction was the same as it was when he was in high school: he campaigned for civil rights. When an Indianapolis restaurateur refused to allow him to eat in her establishment, Rustin persuaded her to participate in his experiment. The owner agreed to serve Rustin a hamburger once he stipulated he would leave if any white patron protested. No one objected to Rustin's presence, and consequently the owner treated him like any other restaurant customer. In another 1940s incident, Rustin was invited to speak at a church in Ohio. The event's organizers, assuming that their guest speaker was white, saw Rustin sitting in the auditorium, mistook him for a janitor, and asked him if he had seen Rustin in the building. They were shocked when they realized their mistake. Thus, these encounters became opportunities for Rustin to encourage whites not to make assumptions about blacks.

On another occasion in the late 1940s, Rustin traveled to St. Paul, Minnesota. Although a reservation had been made for him, the hotel's desk clerk would not honor it. Rustin announced he would spend the night in the hotel's lobby, and others joined him in his impromptu sit–in. Early the next morning, the hotel's management offered him one of the best rooms. Rustin refused and stayed with a white family instead. Also during the 1940s, Rustin organized a sit–in at a YMCA cafeteria in Washington, D.C., which only allowed blacks to eat in the kitchen. Attempting to drive Rustin and his fellow protestors away, the cafeteria's management poured ammonia in the air–conditioner. Rustin phoned the fire department, telling them the kitchen was on fire. The fireman arrived and reprimanded the management; the sit–in continued and eventually the cafeteria was desegregated. Regardless of the incident, Rustin used his keen intellect, organizational talents, and tactical skills as he continued his campaign for civil rights.

Although Rustin advocated and practiced nonviolence, he was not always its recipient. For example, during the summer of 1942, he boarded a bus in Louisville, Kentucky, bound for Nashville, Tennessee. When Rustin was ordered to move to the back of the bus, he refused and was beaten and arrested, enduring physical pain to promote the causes of nonviolence and racial equality. During World War II, Rustin applied for and was granted classification as a conscientious objector because he was a Quaker. Three years later, when the draft board ordered him to take a physical examination, as required, he refused. According to Jervis Anderson, Rustin felt that the draft board was inconsistent in its treatment of religious and nonreligious conscientious objectors, and he chose to risk the penalty of federal imprisonment rather than work at a hospital as a known objector. He spent 28 months in an Ashland, Kentucky, penitentiary. While imprisoned, he taught English and music to his fellow white and black inmates and sought to end segregation among the inmates. Rustin continued as an activist for CORE and FOR after his release from prison. In April 1947 Rustin and George Houser led the first Freedom Rides in the South in an effort to test the 1946 Supreme Court ruling that banned segregated interstate travel. Rustin and Houser described their trip as a Journey of Reconciliation (JOR), and they were part of an interracial team of eight blacks and eight whites. When they boarded buses in the Southern states, the black activists sat in front seats while their white colleagues occupied rear seats. When bus drivers told them to move, they refused by asserting their right to sit anywhere as interstate bus passengers. When they were arrested, they phoned the local NAACP and lawyers, were assisted, and continued on the JOR. There were fewer arrests than expected, and the JOR was relatively peaceful until the activists traveled to Chapel Hill, North Carolina, where they encountered what Jervis Anderson called ''the most frightening threat of violence'' and were charged with violating segregation laws. Rustin was sentenced to 30 days on a chain gang. Rustin and Houser viewed the JOR as a success because it set a precedent for future nonviolent Southern protest. There was an unanticipated outcome as well. Rustin wrote an article entitled ''Twenty–Two Days on a Chain Gang,'' which was published in the *New York Post.* His detailed, firsthand account of the horrors of the chain gang sparked interest in prison reform in North Carolina.

Rustin's involvement in India's quest for independence won him recognition as an international activist. According to *Contemporary Black Biography,* ''Rustin participated in India's movement for independence from Britain, gaining an international reputation as a political strategist that took him to India to work for Gandhi's Congress party and to Africa to assist Kwame Nkrumah, an activist for African self–rule who became the first prime minister of the Gold Coast.'' Rustin did more than support Indian and African causes while abroad. As head of the Free India Committee, he was frequently arrested for picketing outside the British Embassy in Washington, and he cofounded the American Committee on Africa in the 1950s to fight colonialism and apartheid.

In addition to his reputation as an activist, by now his social life was coming under scrutiny in some circles. While Rustin accepted the fact that he was a homosexual and in 1953 served a jail term on a morals charge in Pasadena California, political organizations and other groups did not accept his orientation.

Meets Martin Luther King Jr.

Although Rustin campaigned for worldwide human rights, he made his greatest contributions in the civil rights arena. On December 1, 1955, Rosa Parks refused to move to the back of a bus in Montgomery, Alabama. She was arrested, and four days later, the Montgomery Improvement Association (MIA) began a boycott of all Montgomery buses. Rustin offered Martin Luther King Jr. his services.

Rustin worked diligently, generating publicity material, composing songs for mass meetings, organizing car pools, soliciting funds from northern supporters, and handling other activities. When he returned to New York, he formed an In Friendship organization there which continued his fund raising endeavors. Through In Friendship, Rustin staged a rally at Madison Square Garden that raised $20,000 for MIA, and on the first anniversary of the boycott, held a concert featuring Tallulah Bankhead, Harry Belafonte, Duke Ellington, and Coretta Scott King at the Manhattan Center. Rustin's greatest contribution to the boycott was his practical experience in nonviolent protests; he advised Martin Luther King Jr., who until then had only studied Gandhian philosophy. Now King was able to convert theory into practice. The Montgomery Bus Boycott ended in the same month of its one–year anniversary with the Supreme Court desegregation decision. According to Jervis Anderson, Rustin viewed the boycott as ''a post–Gandhian contribution'' to the theory and practice of nonviolence since the black leaders had not yet become pacifists.

In 1957 Rustin, along with Ella Baker and Stanley Levison, founded the Student Christian Leadership Conference (SCLC). Anderson wrote that Rustin, envisioned SCLC as a vehicle ''that could translate what we had learned during the bus boycott into a broad strategy for protest in the South,'' advocate direct nonviolent action, and be led by Southern blacks. King was elected SCLC's leader and, according to *Contemporary Black Biography,* Rustin continued to advise him: ''Rustin. . . helped the emerging leader by briefing him for meetings, drafting speeches and press releases—in short, by giving the younger man the benefit of his experience as a political tactician and of his connections with wealthy civil rights supporters.'' King emerged as the eminent civil rights leader while Rustin was the tactical genius of the movement from the mid–1950s to the mid–1960s.

Rustin's relationship with King was beset with problems. From the beginning, a number of members of the Montgomery Improvement Association objected to Rustin's involvement in the bus boycott and his association with King because of his former affiliation with the Communist Party and his personal life. These objections were later shared by various SCLC members. However, it was not until 1960 that Rustin was forced to disassociate with SCLC and King because of the politically motivated demands of Adam Clayton Powell Jr., the New York Congressman. In 1964, one year after his successful organization of the March on Washington, Rustin was reinstated as a key advisor to King although they disagreed on such issues as the Vietnam War, King's attempt to restore peace in the Watts section of Los Angeles after the 1965 riots, and King's plan to take the civil rights movement north to Chicago. Still, King respected Rustin's political judgment.

In 1964, when King was awarded the Nobel Peace Prize, Rustin was part of the delegation that traveled to Norway for the awards ceremony. Rustin was asked to plan the group's itinerary.

Organizes March on Washington

A. Philip Randolph revived his idea of a massive march on the nation's capital and asked Rustin, who had successfully organized the SCLC's Prayer Pilgrimage to Washington in 1957 and the Youth Marches for Integrated Schools in 1958 and 1959, to plan the event. As the national coordinator of the march and with a mandate to motivate at least 100,000 individuals to participate, Rustin adroitly brought together for the first time all the prominent civil rights leaders and groups in one of the largest protest events in the history of the United States. After the 1963 March on Washington, Rustin continued to serve as a strategist and tactician to black American leaders. However, his emphasis shifted from street protests and mass demonstrations to political intervention.

In 1965 the A. Philip Randolph Institute (APRI) was founded and Rustin was appointed the institute's executive director. Continuing to travel and lecture across the country, he guided the APRI's operations including sponsoring voter registration drives as well as conferences, supporting political candidates, and advising civil rights leaders. In the early 1970s, Rustin stepped down from his position as APRI's executive director and became its honorary president although he remained involved in policy making and other activities. Rustin was an elder statesman with an active schedule of lecturing and advising in the 1970s and 1980s as he continued to crusade for civil rights in the United States and human rights abroad. In 1975 Rustin founded the Black Americans to Support Israel Committee. In 1986, one year before his death, he created Project South Africa in an effort to provide financial support to promote democracy. One month before his death, Rustin traveled to Haiti to determine the potential for democratic elections in that country.

When Rustin returned to New York after his week–long mission to Haiti in late July, he became ill. Over the next several weeks, he was misdiagnosed several times before exploratory surgery revealed he had a perforated appendix. Two days later, on August 24, 1987, Bayard Rustin died. More than 1,000 people attended his memorial service on October 1, 1987, at the Community Church in Manhattan. Over the Memorial Day weekend in 1988, Rustin's ashes were interred at a private residence in upstate New York.

Among Rustin's many awards were the Council Against Intolerance in America's Thomas Jefferson Award for the Advancement of Democracy in 1948, the Pittsburgh Branch of the NAACP's Man of the Year Award in 1965, the Trade Union Leadership Council's Eleanor Roosevelt Award in 1966, and the Howard University Law School's Liberty Bell Award in 1967. He received the National Council of Churches' Family of Man Award in 1969, the National Council of Jewish Women's John F. Kennedy Award in 1971, and the Urban League's Lyndon Johnson Award in 1974. The Catholic Interracial Council of New York presented him with the John LaFarge Memorial Award in 1981 and he received the Defender of Jerusalem Award in 1987. Rustin received honorary degrees from Brown University, Clark College, Columbia University, New York University, and Yale University.

Bayard Rustin deserved each accolade he received. While many of his contemporaries were frequently in the media spotlight, Rustin consistently labored in the background. Armed with his intellect, eloquence, dignity, and organizational and tactical skills, Rustin influenced and inspired individuals, nations, and generations in his quest for peace and social justice.

REFERENCES

Anderson, Jervis. *Bayard Rustin: Troubles I've Seen.* New York: Harper Collins, 1997.

Branch, Taylor. *Parting the Waters: America in the King Years 1954–63.* New York: Simon and Schuster, 1988.

Contemporary Black Biography. Vol. 4. Detroit: Gale Research, 1993.

King, Coretta Scott. *My Life with Martin Luther King, Jr.* New York: Holt, Rinehart and Winston, 1969.

Rustin, Bayard. *Down the Line: The Collected Writings of Bayard Rustin.* Chicago: Quadrangle Books, 1971.

———. *Strategies for Freedom: The Changing Patterns of Black Protest.* New York: Columbia University Press, 1976.

Salzman, Jack, David Lionel Smith, and Cornel West, eds. *Encyclopedia of African-American Culture and History.* New York: Macmillan Library Reference USA/Simon Schuster Macmillan, 1996.

Salley, Columbus. *The Black 100: A Ranking of the Most Influential African-Americans Past and Present.* New York: Citadel Press, 1993.

Shaw, Thomas M. *Bayard Rustin As Art Collector.* Catalog. Union: Kean College of New Jersey, n.d.

Young, Andrew. *An Easy Burden: The Civil Rights Movement and the Transformation of America.* New York: Harper Collins, 1996.

Linda M. Carter

S

David Satcher

(1941–)

Physician, U.S. Surgeon General, medical school president, educator, research center administrator

David Satcher, an expert in sickle cell disease as well as an advocate for a wide range of health concerns from teen–age smoking to childhood immunization to AIDS, became the first African American head of the Centers for Disease Control in 1993. In 1998 he was the second of his race to become Surgeon General of the United States. The U.S. Senate confirmed Satcher's position as ''America's top doctor'' on February 11, 1998, after a five–month political stall following his nomination. He was the first person in over three years to fill the post, one that has fueled national controversy over abortion and family values.

Satcher was born on March 2, 1941, and grew up on a farm west of Anniston, Alabama. His father, Wilmer Satcher, was a foundry worker and his mother, Anna Satcher, a homemaker; neither attended school beyond the elementary level. Of their ten children, including one adopted daughter and one set of twins, eight survived childhood. David was the third youngest of the surviving children. Wilmer and Anna Satcher were strong believers in education and, unlike many other farm families of that period, never kept their children out of school to work the farm. All eight went to college or trade school. The Satcher parents were deeply religious as well. Wilmer Satcher studied the Bible, which helped him to perfect his reading. Each Sunday the family worshiped at Mt. Liberty Baptist Church, where David Satcher taught a Sunday school class. His religious training and upbringing continued to guide him through life.

When he was two years old, Satcher had his first brush with disease, nearly dying of whooping cough. This may have been a defining moment for him, as it gave him his first encounter with lessons of race and disease prevention that ultimately would shape his medical career. He was attended by a black doctor on house call to the ramshackle four–room wooden farm house in rural, segregated Alabama where the Satchers lived. His eldest sister, Lottie Washington, told the *New York Times* for September 13, 1997, ''I remember the doctor telling my mother that he wouldn't live until the next day.'' Hearing through family lore the story of his survival, Satcher determined early on that he wanted to be a doctor.

As a child, Satcher was a serious student who enjoyed reading. Lottie Washington, who still lives in Anniston, told the *New York Times* for September 11, 1997: ''Even when he rode the bus to school, he would read the whole time while the other kids played and talked.'' He demonstrated an early interest in medicine and a ''desire to see things get well'' as a student at the all–black Thankful Junior High School. Robert Satcher told the *Nashville Banner* that, during this period his brother David attended to a disabled chicken. ''He got the chicken and put this splint on it and put tape around it, and the chicken got well.'' As the Satcher children worked the fields on the forty–acre farm, the brothers took *Reader's Digest* with them and read and quizzed each other during their rest periods. Their interest in reading had been stimulated by their school principal, who encouraged the parents to provide reading materials for them at home over the summer months.

David Satcher

Satcher continued his education at the segregated Calhoun County Training School in Hobson City, where chemistry and science teacher James A. Dunn encouraged him to consider a career in science. Satcher joined the track team and sang in the school choir. He spent his weekends at work at the foundry where his father was employed, but he put academics first and graduated at the top of his class. He entered Morehouse College in Atlanta on a full scholarship and worked odd jobs to help support himself. Still he had time to serve as president of the student government association his first year. The college president, Benjamin E. Mays, had a strong influence on Satcher as well as many other students there. According to brother Robert, as reported in the *Nashville Banner,* Mays told Satcher, ''With your potential, the sky's the limit.'' In 1963 Satcher graduated Phi Beta Kappa with a B.S. degree. He entered Case Western Reserve University in Cleveland, Ohio, and in 1970 was the first black there to earn both an M.D. and a Ph.D. simultaneously in cytogenetics—the study of chromosomes. He was also elected to membership in Alpha Omega Alpha, the prestigious national honor society in medicine. After completing a residence at Strong Memorial Hospital at the University of Rochester, Satcher began his medical career at the King–Drew Sickle Cell Center, a research center in Los Angeles, where he remained from 1971 to 1979. He was associate director of the center from 1973 to 1975, and assistant professor and interim chairman from 1974 to 1975. He was also professor and chairman of the department of family medicine at the King–Drew Medical Center during the 1970s. During his stay in Los Angeles he was assistant professor at the University of California, Los Angeles and interim dean at the Charles R. Drew Postgraduate Medical School. He operated a free clinic at the Second Baptist Church in the Watts section of the city from 1974 to 1979. In 1979 he returned to Atlanta to chair the community medicine department at the Morehouse School of Medicine. He taught his students to practice medicine among the urban poor, where few physicians were to be found.

Becomes Medical School President

Satcher's outstanding career did not go unnoticed, nor did his belief in bringing health care to those who needed it most. He left Morehouse in 1982 to become president of Meharry Medical College and executive officer of its Hubbard Hospital. Meharry was historically significant; it had trained about 40 percent of the nation's black physicians and dentists. Now the medical school and hospital were financially strapped and the hospital, which had too few patients to train its residents, ran the risk of losing its accreditation. Satcher moved swiftly to turn things around. Extensive help came from the federal government when President Ronald Reagan approved $55.6 million in aid for the school. The hospital also expanded its affiliations with area hospitals. Hubbard Hospital, the school's teaching facility, provided extensive treatment to Nashville's indigent—the poor of all races—without adequate compensation from the city. To ease the burden, Satcher developed a plan to merge the hospital with the city–owned Nashville General Hospital. Although the move touched strong racial cords, the merger was approved and, according to many, led to the survival of the historically black medical school. Its success was a monument to Satcher's vision. While at Meharry, Satcher also founded the *Journal on Health Care for the Poor and Underserved,* the only publication of its kind in the nation.

Heads Centers for Disease Control

Health and Human Services Secretary Donna Shalala appointed Satcher to head the Centers for Disease Control in 1993, making him CDC's first black director. She told the *Atlanta Journal and Constitution* that he would bring to his new role ''world–class professional stature, management skills, integrity, and preventive health care experience.'' Satcher took over the CDC on January 1, 1994, amidst troubled times. Hundreds of jobs had to be cut to reduce the budget, and the agency was under fire for alleged job discrimination. By his various actions, Satcher kept the CDC in the national spotlight. He forced some veteran employees to retire and hired women and minorities to replace them. He was the driving force behind President Bill Clinton's apology to survivors of the Tuskegee experiment of 1932–72, in which many black men with syphilis were left untreated. Perhaps his greatest mark at CDC was the center's shift in emphasis from infectious diseases to the leading health issues of today, such as cancer, heart disease, and prevention of injury.

On Friday, September 12, 1997, President Clinton nominated Satcher to become the nation's top doctor—the U.S. Surgeon General—as well as assistant secretary of health and human services, in charge of health policy. He handily met the test of his confirmation hearings before the Senate Committee on Labor and Human Resources. Quoted in the *New York Times* for September 13, 1997, Satcher said, ''I want to be the Surgeon General who reaches our citizens with cutting–edge technology and plain, old–fashioned straight talk.'' He continued, ''Whether talking about smoking or poor diets, I want to send messages of good health to our cities and suburbs, our barrios and reservations, and even our prisons.'' His nomination was well received on Capitol Hill; he had the endorsement of the American Medical Association as well. Some supporters even called him ''squeaky clean,'' with an unblemished record.

Among those groups objecting to his nomination was the National Rifle Association; it took issue with the CDC's research on guns and violence and opposed the center's use of tax dollars for research the NRA called ''political advocacy.'' There were expected rumblings over the joint CDC and National Institutes of Health studies of AZT and pregnant women in Africa and Asia. When Satcher supported President Clinton's position on all issues related to health care and social issues, including Clinton's views on partial birth abortions, this threw up a red flag for some politicians. On Sunday, November 9, 1997, Senate Majority Leader Trent Lott announced plans to hold up Satcher's nomination until 1998 because he failed ''the Republican litmus test on partial birth abortions.'' The *Nashville Tennessean* for November 12, 1997, criticized the move, saying that Lott was ''playing politics at the expense of a decent, reputable physician and a respected public servant who shouldn't have to be treated with such disregard.'' According to *Jet* for December 1, 1997, Senator Ted Kennedy confirmed that ''some senators had put holds'' on Satcher's nomination until 1998.

Satcher withstood the fracas and five months after his nomination was confirmed as Surgeon General by a 63–35 vote in the Senate. He was sworn in to office on February 13 as U.S. Surgeon General as well as assistant secretary for health at the Department of Health and Human Services. While he had realized his dream, he acknowledged in the *Nashville*

Tennessean for February 14, 1998, that the American dream did not end there. Satcher thanked the Senate "for conducting such a lively and healthy debate." He added, "when it comes to public health, what unites us is greater than what divides us."

Satcher has been involved with a number of professional organizations. Among his numerous memberships are the Institute of Medicine, National Academic of Sciences, and Alpha Omega Alpha. During President Clinton's first term, Satcher was advisor to Hillary Rodham Clinton's health–care task force. His awards have been numerous as well. While in Los Angeles, Satcher received the Watts Grassroots Award for community leadership in 1978. In 1986 he was elected to the Institute of Medicine and the National Academy of Sciences. He was named Nashvillian of the Year in 1992, and in 1994 *Ebony* magazine awarded him the black achievement award. The next year Satcher received the Breslow Award in Public Health. In 1996 the American Medical Association honored Satcher with the Nathan Davis Award. Satcher, along with nine federal, state, and local government officials, received the honor for promoting the art and science of medicine and improving public health. The December 1996 issue of *Jet* recognized Satcher for his "efforts in a 1996 report which states that physical activity reduces the risk of dying prematurely from heart disease and reduces the risk of developing high blood pressure, diabetes, colon cancer, and alleviates feelings of anxiety and depression." He practices proper diet and exercise in his life.

Satcher's first wife, Anniston native Calli Herndon, died of breast cancer in 1976. They had four children, Gretchen, David, Daraka, and Daryl. In 1978 he married poet Nola Richardson of Los Angeles. They now live in a home reserved for the surgeon general on the grounds of the National Institutes of Health in Bethesda, Maryland. In addition to his administrative duties, Satcher spends his time sifting through a flood of speaking requests from domestic and foreign sources and filling as many as he can. He especially enjoys taking photographs with young children while he is dressed in his double–breasted navy blue uniform with gold epaulets and brass buttons. He told the *New York Times* for April 21, 1998, that the uniform as well as his position excites children and that "young children want to take a picture with the Surgeon General." Satcher, who spent much of his career making quiet progress in community medicine, preventive care, and public health particularly for African Americans, is now also an advocate for the health of all Americans. Toward this end he encourages citizens to bear responsibility for improving their own health.

Current address: U.S. Surgeon General's Office, 5600 Fishers Lane, Rockville, MD 20857.

REFERENCES

"Bio of Dr. David Satcher." *New York Times,* September 11, 1997.

Booker, Simeon. "Ticker Tape." *Jet* 93 (1 December 1997): 10.

"CDC Chief Chosen as Surgeon General." *New York Times,* September 13, 1997.

"CDC Chief: Prevention Will Be Key." *Atlanta Journal and Constitution,* August 21, 1993.

"Challenges Face New CDC Chief." *Atlanta Journal and Constitution,* August 21, 1993.

Contemporary Black Biography. Vol. 7. Detroit: Gale Research, 1994.

"David Satcher Proud to Be Nominated as 'America's Doctor.'" *New York Times,* September 13, 1997.

"Determined Family Pushed Satcher to Strive for Goals." *Nashville Banner,* February 11, 1998.

"Don't Make Satcher a Political Pawn." Editorial. *Nashville Tennessean,* November 12, 1997.

"Dr. David Satcher, CDC Director, Honored by American Medical Association." *Jet* 91 (23 December 1996): 14.

Foster, Henry W., with Alice Greenwood. *Make a Difference.* New York: Scribner, 1997.

"Profile of Dr. David Satcher." *New York Times,* September 11, 1997.

"Satcher Is Looking like a Shoo–in." *Nashville Tennessean,* October 5, 1997.

Satcher, Robert. Telephone interview with Jessie Carney Smith, February 26, 1998.

"Satcher Takes Office, Notes Tough Fight on Nomination." *Nashville Tennessean,* February 14, 1998.

"Surgeon General Nominee Confirmed, Filling a 3–Year Void." *New York Times,* February 11, 1998.

"Tiptoeing Through the Mine Fields of Health Policy." *New York Times,* April 21, 1998.

Who's Who among African Americans, 1998–99. 10th ed. Detroit: Gale Research, 1997.

Jessie Carney Smith

Arthur Alfonso Schomburg

(1874–1938)

Bibliophile, library curator, writer

The work of Arthur Alfonso Schomburg, a distinguished black bibliophile, is a tribute to the world of scholarship and is preserved in one of the world's largest repositories of materials for the study of peoples of African descent—the Schomburg Center for Research in Black Culture in Harlem. A self–taught historian with a remarkable memory, he worked to inspire racial pride both through his organizations and through the encouragement of study and research on black themes.

Schomburg was born on January 24, 1874, to Carlos Féderico Schomburg, a German–born merchant, and Mary Joseph, a black midwife and washer woman. On January 28 of

Arthur Alfonso Schomburg

that year, young Schomburg was baptized Arturo Alfonso. Although the story of his birth and early childhood is often conflicting and mysterious, Schomburg chose not to clear up many of the mysteries. According to his biographer, Eleanor Des Verney Sinnette, he knew little about his father. He identified his mother as born free in St. Croix, Virgin Islands, in 1837; she was educated at the elementary level and later became a midwife. He had one sister, Dolores María, known as ''Lola,'' who was born in San Juan and was 14 years older than he. Both maternal grandparents were born free in St. Croix.

Although the only primary schools available to him in San Juan charged tuition, Schomburg may have attended, but did not complete his work at the Instituto de Párvulos, a Jesuit school. Schomburg also claimed to have attended the Institute of Popular Teaching, or Institute of Instruction in San Juan. There are also statements that he was completely self–educated.

During his childhood, Mary Joseph either remained in San Juan and sent Arturo to the Virgin Islands to live with her parents to attend school, or she moved to the Virgin Islands with him. In either case, he had friends in St. Croix and St. Thomas, joined a debating team there, and according to his biographer, Schomburg claims, without documentation, that he attended St. Thomas College.

Schomburg was preoccupied with his own heritage and is said to have become curious about his past through a literary club in Puerto Rico, where history was a favorite topic of discussion. When whites spoke of the accomplishments of their Spanish ancestors, he became curious about his own ancestors and about people of color in Puerto Rico and the Caribbean. Haitian revolutionary Toussaint L'Ouverture was one of his early heroes. He began to read widely in areas of his interest, both in Spanish and English, and developed a lifelong interest in Caribbean and Latin American history.

By adolescence, Schomburg was described in his biography as ''somewhat self–effacing, soft–spoken . . . of medium height with a café au lait complexion, soft curly brown hair, and rather large, limpid, warm brown eyes.'' While Schomburg was in the Virgin Islands, he became more curious about Puerto Rico's and Cuba's struggle for independence than his own heritage. He knew that he needed to leave the islands to become educated, and he had considered either a career in medicine or a place in the revolution. He may have returned to San Juan to work as a printer to earn money to travel north. Aged 17, Schomburg left the Caribbean for New York City, arriving on Friday, April 17, 1891, with letters of introduction to cigarmakers in Manhattan verifying his experience as a typographer. He settled on the lower east side of Manhattan.

To sustain himself while attending night school at Manhattan Central High School, Schomburg held various jobs—elevator operator, bellhop, printer, and porter. He sustained his interest in the Puerto Rican struggle for independence and on April 3, 1892, when he was 18–years old, he became a founding member and secretary of a political club, Las Dos Antillas (The Two Islands), that assisted in Cuba's and Puerto Rico's independence. His last major involvement in the movement came on August 2, 1898, when a meeting was held in which the revolutionary support groups disbanded. His interest later shifted from the Cuban and Puerto Rican movement to the freedom of people of color everywhere. Later, however, he severed his ties with the Puerto Rican community and from then on lived as a black man, or ''a Puerto Rican of African descent,'' as he became known.

Schomburg became active in fraternal organizations, first in freemasonry through El Sol de Cuba Lodge, No. 38, founded by Cuban and Puerto Rican exiles. By 1911 he was elected master; later the organization was renamed the Prince Hall Lodge to honor Prince Hall of Cambridge, Massachusetts, the first black accredited Mason. While serving as master, Schomburg gathered and organized the Masons' documents, papers, books, pamphlets, correspondence, photographs, and other items, and was largely responsible for preserving the black lodge's early history. From 1918 to 1926 he was grand secretary of the Grand Lodge of New York and in 1925 became a Thirty–third Degree Mason.

For a while Schomburg may have considered becoming a lawyer. From 1901 to 1906 he worked with the New York law firm Pryor, Mellis & Harris and, according to his biographer, led others to believe that he was studying toward a degree from the firm by ''reading law.'' After he was denied permission to take the New York State Regents examination to qualify for a ''law certificate,'' he left the clerk–messenger position and became messenger for the Latin American department of Bankers Trust Company in lower Manhattan. He rose in rank to become supervisor of the mailing department before retiring in 1929 on a medical disability.

Collects Black Materials

Schomburg's interest in collecting evidences of black history became apparent in 1911, when he began to collect rigorously and systematically. He had met John Edward Bruce (Bruce Grit), journalist, lay historian, and bibliophile, and joined the Men's Sunday Club that Bruce founded. The club meetings usually included some discussion of racial issues as well as books, and the members raised funds to purchase items on black history for the club's library. In April of that year, Schomburg and Bruce co–founded the Negro Society for Historical Research, which would greatly influence black book collecting and preservation as well as the study of African American themes. In 1914 Schomburg became a member of the American Negro Academy (ANA), founded in 1897 by Alexander Crummell, where he met such black scholars as W. E. B. Du Bois, Alain Locke, Kelly Miller, and Carter G. Woodson. This affiliation furthered Schomburg's interest in collecting black materials. In 1922 he was elected fifth president of the ANA. Since the ANA was based in Washington, D.C., Schomburg was primarily an absentee president; his friend John W. Cromwell attended the executive committee meetings and provided direct supervision of the organization until he died in 1927. In time, Schomburg became unhappy with the ANA, lost his enthusiasm for the weakening organization, and received little comfort for his efforts. He held the office until the ANA dissolved in 1929.

Schomburg was in New York when the Harlem Renaissance was at its peak. If he had not known them already, he came in contact with such luminaries as Claude McKay (who became his closest friend), Walter White, and James Weldon Johnson. He had great respect for Marcus Garvey and supported many of Garvey's principles of black development. The Harlem Renaissance period provided fertile ground for Schomburg to promote his interest in black themes and stimulated further his interest in collecting black books. The rigor with which Schomburg collected was manifest in the sizeable collection that he gathered. He sought out materials from booksellers throughout the United States as well as in Europe and Latin America. By 1925 he had acquired 5,000 books, pamphlets, manuscripts, prints, etchings, and other items. When the New York Public Library opened the Division of Negro Literature, History, and Prints at the 135th Street Branch in May that year, he sold his collection for $10,000 to the Carnegie Corporation to be placed in the new library. His collecting practices continued. He sailed for Europe on June 25, 1925, in search of missing pieces of black history to strengthen his collection now at the library.

Schomburg's close relationship with Charles Spurgeon Johnson, who had headed the Department of Research and Investigations for the National Urban League and edited the league's official journal, *Opportunity,* and by 1928 chaired the Social Science Department at Fisk University, led to Schomburg's position in 1929 as curator of the Negro Collection in the university library. During his brief tenure at Fisk, Schomburg established a distinguished collection similar to his own, then left in 1932 to become curator of the Division of Negro Literature, History, and Prints at the New York Public Library (renamed in 1973 the Schomburg Center for Research in Black Culture). Continuing to travel extensively, he spoke at conferences and before other groups to solicit materials for the collection. The same meticulous care was used in developing the collection that he used in building his private library, and was instrumental in building an impressive collection of rare and current books and materials for the library that he now served. Schomburg sought support for the collection wherever he could, using friends such as Langston Hughes to locate materials during Hughes's travels, and persuading black writers, composers, artists, and others to contribute works. He also built a network of people who led him to materials in this country or abroad, or purchased them in his stead. Schomburg did what he could to persuade the library system to purchase items for the collection, and when the library refused to pay for materials he had ordered improperly, he often paid for the works himself. He also organized two notable exhibitions—one on the achievements of blacks, and a traveling exhibition of African art and handicrafts.

Writes on Black Themes

Schomburg's interest in the black experience was expressed also in his writings. Although he had little formal training and clearly was not a good writer, influential black intelligentsia respected his potential for enhancing scholarship. Such scholars as W. E. B. Du Bois, Charles Spurgeon Johnson, and Alain Locke edited his works carefully to make them more readable. Schomburg also promoted the study and research on black themes in the nation's black colleges, as seen in his essay ''Racial Integrity: A Plea for the Establishment of a Chair of Negro History in Our Schools, Colleges, etc.,'' published in 1913 in Nancy Cunard's work, *Negro.* His publications also included such works as ''A Bibliographical Checklist of American Negro Poetry'' (1916) and ''Economic Contribution by the Negro to America,'' published in 1916 as an occasional paper of the American Negro Academy. He also published articles in *Crisis, Opportunity, the Messenger, Negro World, Negro Digest, the A.M.E. Review, New Century,* and *Survey Graphic.*

Once highly visible through 30 organizations to which he belonged, his memberships included the Urban League, the NAACP, and the Negro Writers' Guild. In time Schomburg became disenchanted with black organizations—often because of a dispute—and resigned. He became annoyed with the black intelligentsia as well, sometimes because of trivial matters, sometimes because he felt overlooked, or merely due to dissatisfaction with another person's point of view. In time he removed himself from the limelight.

On June 30, 1895, Schomburg married Elizabeth ''Bessie'' Hatcher, a fair–skinned beauty from Staunton, Virginia, and they lived in the San Juan Hill section of New York. They had three sons, Maximo Gomez, Arthur Alfonso Jr., and Kingsley Guarionex. After Bessie Schomburg died in 1900, he married Elizabeth Morrow Taylor on March 17, 1902, a native of Williamsburg, North Carolina. She died early, leaving two young sons, Reginald Stanfield and Nathaniel

José. All of his children lived with their respective maternal relatives—Bessie's in Virginia and Tennessee, and Elizabeth's in Virginia and New Jersey. About 1914 Schomburg took a third wife, Elizabeth Green, a nurse and friend of Bessie Schomburg's sister, and they had three children—Fernando, his only daughter, Dolores Marie, and Plácido Carlos.

Schomburg, who was of medium build, had remarkable energy and determination. His health began to fail in late 1936, and his pace was slowed. As late as 1938, Schomburg expected to continue his speaking engagements and attend meetings. He developed a dental infection, however, that required extraction. After that he became ill, failed to respond to treatment, and on June 10, 1938, died at Brooklyn's Madison Park Hospital. After a private funeral held on June 12 at Brooklyn's Siloam Presbyterian Church, Schomburg was buried in Cypress Hills Cemetery in Brooklyn.

Charles Spurgeon Johnson's tribute to Schomburg at a memorial service held on June 8, 1939, serves as a summary of his work. He called the Schomburg Collection a "visible monument to the life's work of Arthur Schomburg. It stands for itself, quietly and solidly for all time, a rich and inexhaustible treasure store for scholars and laymen alike, the materialization of the foresight, industry and scholarship" of Schomburg.

REFERENCES

Contemporary Black Biography. Vol. 9. Detroit: Gale Research, 1995.

Johnson, Charles Spurgeon. "Arthur A. Schomburg." *The Speeches of Charles Spurgeon Johnson.* Vol. 6. Unpublished. Nashville, Fisk University Library, February 1959.

Logan, Raymond W., and Michael R. Winston, eds. *Dictionary of American Negro Biography.* New York: Norton, 1982.

Moss, Alfred A., Jr. *The American Negro Academy.* Baton Rouge: Louisiana State University Press, 1981.

"Notes." *Journal of Negro History* 23 (July 1938): 392–408.

Sinnette, Eleanor Des Verney. *Arthur Alfonso Schomburg: Black Bibliophile and Collector.* Detroit: The New York Public Library and Wayne State University Press, 1989.

———, W. Paul Coates, and Thomas C. Battle, eds. *Black Bibliophiles and Collectors.* Washington, DC: Howard University Press, 1990.

COLLECTIONS

Schomburg's personal papers and private library are in the Schomburg Center for Research in Black Culture, New York City. Additional materials are scattered and are in the possession of the Schomburg family; others are included in the Thomas Elsa Jones Papers and the Charles S. Johnson Collection, Fisk University Library; the Arthur Schomburg Papers, the John Edward Bruce Collection, and the John Wesley Cromwell Collection in the Moorland–Spingarn Research Center at Howard University; the James Weldon Johnson Collection and the Claude McKay Papers at Yale University; the Henry P. Slaughter Collection, the Robert W. Woodruff Library, Atlanta University Center, and elsewhere.

Jessie Carney Smith

Dred Scott

(1795–1858)

Slave, litigator

In 1857, Dred Scott, plaintiff in the momentous court case *Scott v. Sanford,* became the most famous slave of his time. The chief issue in the case was whether Scott, in fact, was a slave. The outcome of the case, decided by the United States Supreme Court, not only determined Scott's legal status, but also the prior and then current legal status of all African Americans in the United States.

Dred Scott was born to slave parents in Southampton County, Virginia, in 1795. According to the *Dictionary of American Negro Biography,* Scott was listed as Sam on the Virginia Tax Lists of 1818 and was the property of Captain Peter Blow and, following Blow's death, John Moore. Sometime between 1834 and 1848 he changed his name to Dred Scott.

Between 1827 and 1830, Blow moved his family and slaves to St. Louis, Missouri. Following the death of Peter Blow in 1831, his son Charles sold Sam for $500 to John Emerson in 1833. Emerson was then a surgeon in the U.S. Army stationed at Jefferson Barracks, Missouri. While the servant of Emerson, Sam was taken to Illinois for three years–a free state established under the Northwest Ordinance of 1787–and Wisconsin for two years–a territory in which slavery was prohibited by the Missouri Compromise. Emerson, like other military personnel, disregarded the law and brought along slaves.

In 1836, with Emerson's consent, Scott married Harriet Robinson, a slave girl recently purchased by his owner. Harriet was Scott's second wife; his first wife had been sold. The following year Emerson was stationed at Fort Gibson and the Scotts became hired servants until they returned to Jefferson Barracks in 1838. At this time, Scott became the body servant of Colonel Henry Bainbridge.

The following year Scott's first daughter, Eliza, was born during a journey to St. Louis, and their second daughter, Lizzie, was born at Jefferson Barracks in Missouri. Meanwhile, in 1843, Emerson died and left all of his property to his widow, Irene Sanford Emerson. Irene Emerson never contemplated emancipating Scott. Upon moving to Massachusetts in the mid–1840s, she left Scott in St. Louis. It has been speculated that Irene Emerson did not free Scott because her father, who was appointed executor of her inheritance, sup-

Dred Scott

ported slavery. Scott, with the help of Taylor and H. T. Blow–the wealthy sons of his initial owner–attempted at various times to purchase freedom for himself and his family, but to no avail.

With the financial assistance of H. T. Blow, Scott approached two attorneys, Burd and Risk, who helped the Scotts sue for their freedom in county court. They sued for their freedom on the grounds of assault and false imprisonment. They asked for damages of $10,000. The Scotts lost this case, but a new trial was set for December 2, 1847. In 1847 Scott filed suit in the state circuit court of St. Louis, Missouri, and won on the grounds that he had been carried into the free state of Illinois and the free territory of Wisconsin. However, in 1852, the state supreme court reversed the decision.

While the case was pending, Irene Emerson married Dr. Calvin Clifford Chaffee, a strong anti–slavery supporter. Calvin Chaffee, the sons of Peter Blow, and Irene Emerson's brother, John A. Sanford, who had moved to Missouri, provided financial assistance to the Scotts in their quest for freedom. In 1853 Scott filed a new suit, this time against Sanford. To assure a favorable outcome for Scott in the new court case, the plaintiff and the defendant agreed to say that Scott's ownership had been transferred to Sanford. It could be said that the matter was between two citizens, *Scott v. Emerson* (which was later named *Dred Scott v. Sanford*) and therefore was a case for the federal district court. Once the suit was filed the clerk inadvertently misspelled Sanford's name, thus changing it to Sandford. After Scott lost this case, his attorneys, based on a writ of error, appealed to the United States Supreme Court.

On March 6, 1857, the United States Supreme Court ruled against Scott. Chief Justice Roger B. Taney, writing the decision of the court, ruled that Scott was not legally a citizen and therefore could not bring suit in the courts, and that since the Missouri Compromise was unconstitutional, slave owners could take their slaves to the territories and retain ownership of them. The outcome of the case was twofold: it determined the legal status of all African Americans as not being citizens of the United States; and it held that the Missouri Compromise of 1820 was unconstitutional.

Immediately following the 1857 decision, Irene Chaffee gave title of the Scotts to Taylor Blow, who freed them. Afterwards Scott worked for Theron Barnum and his wife, owners of the famous Barnum Hotel in St. Louis, as a porter. He died of tuberculosis in St. Louis on September 17, 1858, and was buried in Wesleyan Cemetery. Until 1957, his grave remained unmarked. In recognition of the importance of the Dred Scott case, the courthouse where Scott's trial was held, located at Broadway and Market in St. Louis, is now a museum.

REFERENCES

Davis, John P., ed. *The American Negro Reference Book.* Englewood Cliffs, NJ: Prentice Hall, 1966.

"Dred Scott's Children." *Ebony* 9 (April 1954): 83–86.

Drotning, Phillip T. *A Guide to Negro History in America.* Garden City, NY: Doubleday, 1968.

Estell, Kenneth. *African America: Portrait of a People.* Detroit: Visible Ink Press, 1994.

Franklin, John Hope, and Alfred A. Moss. *From Slavery to Freedom.* New York: McGraw–Hill, 1994.

Logan, Rayford, and Michael R. Winston, eds. *Dictionary of American Negro Biography.* New York: Norton, 1982.

Malone, Dumas, ed. *Dictionary of American Biography.* New York: Charles Scribner's Sons, 1935.

Ploski, Harry, Otto J. Lindenmeyer, and Ernest Kaiser. *Reference Library of Black America.* New York: Bellwether Publishing, 1971.

Romero, Patricia W. *I Too Am America: Documents from 1619 to the Present.* Cornwells Heights, PA: The Publishers Agency, 1976.

Sanders, Doris E., ed. *The Ebony Handbook.* Chicago: Johnson Publishing Co., 1974.

"St. Louis to Build Memorial to Dred Scott." *Jet* (October 1, 1953): 7.

COLLECTIONS

The Dred Scott Collection is located in the Missouri Historical Society at the Jefferson Memorial in St. Louis. It includes the Blow Manuscripts, legal reports of the county, state and federal governments, and various newspaper articles pertaining to Dred Scott in 1857 and 1858.

Patricia A. Pearson

Emmett Jay Scott
(1873–1957)
Editor, college administrator, political activist

Emmett Jay Scott has been hailed as a statesman and a diplomat. Although he had a wide and varied career, he was probably best known for his close association as confidante and advisor to Booker T. Washington at Tuskegee Institute in Alabama. There he devoted himself to furthering Washington's goals and played a major role in the intrigues by which Washington dominated black organizations and media in the early 1900s. He has been called the chief architect of what came to be known as the "Tuskegee Machine." He was an active political operator, both locally and nationally for many years.

Emmett Jay Scott was born February 13, 1873, in Houston, Texas, to Horace Lacy Scott, a blacksmith and civil service employee, and Emma Kyle Scott. He graduated from Colored High School in Houston at age 14, and from 1887 to 1890 attended Wiley College, a small Methodist school in Marshall, Texas. Holding a variety of jobs to help pay his way, Scott carried mail from the Marshall post office to the Wiley campus, chopped wood, fed the school hogs, and was a bookkeeper in the president's office. Most sources say that he did not graduate although he received an honorary M.A. from Wiley in 1901. In 1918 he also received honorary LL.D degrees from both Wiley and Wilberforce University in Ohio for his achievements.

After spending three years at Wiley, Scott worked as a janitor in a Houston office building but dreamed of becoming a journalist. He became an assistant janitor and messenger for the white daily newspaper, the *Houston Post.* His talents were recognized at the *Post,* and he was given increasing responsibilities as a copy writer and classified columnist and eventually had his chance as reporter. He stayed with the *Post* for three years. When the paper changed hands in 1894, the new owner objected to a black's employment above the janitor level. Even though Scott retained his position, this experience led him to help found and edit a black weekly newspaper, the *Texas Freeman.* Leaving the *Freeman* in 1897, Scott served as special assistant to Booker T. Washington, founder and president of Tuskegee Institute, until Washington's death in 1915. He stayed on as the institute's secretary until 1919. In April of 1897 Scott married Eleanora J. Baker, the daughter of newspaperman Henry Baker of Galveston, Texas. They would have five children: Emmett Jay, Jr., Evelyn Bernice Payne, Clarissa May Delaney, and twins, Horace and Leonora Kyle Garland.

Scott was by nature a worshiper of heroes. In the 1890s he was greatly influenced by Norris Wright Cuney, the leading black politician in Texas. Through Cuney he became involved in Republican politics and established an affiliation that lasted the rest of his life. He took advantage of this opportunity to become schooled in diplomacy as well as

Emmett Jay Scott

political intrigue and to prepare for sensitive work. When Cuney retired, Scott looked for another hero and found him in Booker T. Washington. In his 1895 Atlanta Exposition speech (also known as the Atlanta Compromise speech), Washington counseled that blacks should stop agitating for rights in return for job opportunities. Scott was in full agreement and not only wrote glowing editorials to that effect, but also began a column in the *Texas Freeman* on Tuskegee news. This caught Washington's attention, and through Scott's influence and persuasion, he accepted an invitation to speak to a citywide audience in Houston. A large crowd of both blacks and whites attended, impressing Washington with Scott's ability to organize. Washington had been looking for an assistant who would be capable of assuming great responsibilities and upon meeting Scott, was impressed with his talent and dependability. Eleven days after the Houston speech, Scott received a letter from Washington offering him a position as his personal secretary. After some initial indecision, Scott accepted and moved to Tuskegee in September of 1897.

The Tuskegee Years

Scott's employment marked the beginning of Booker T. Washington's national power as the African American political and educational leader, which W. E. B. Du Bois later called the "Tuskegee Machine." Scott became the closest private adviser to "the Wizard" as he called Washington, and became so submerged in Washington's personality that it was often difficult to determine which one had written certain correspondence. He seemed to instinctively understand Washington's thinking. Some people thought Scott overstepped his bounds when he attacked those who disagreed with Washington's ideas. Many felt also that Scott unduly interfered in the affairs of the black press and black rights organizations. Evidence suggests, however, that the two men were in full agreement about the way these matters were handled. In "The Story of My Life and Work," published in the *Booker T. Washington Papers* Washington wrote, "Mr. Scott understands so thoroughly my motives, plans and ambitions that he puts himself into my own position as nearly as it is possible for one individual to put himself into the place of another, and in this way makes himself invaluable not only to me personally but to the institution."

As Washington's secretary, Scott greatly influenced and dominated the Tuskegee Machine, an intricate, nationwide web of institutions in the black community. In Louis R. Harlan's book, *Booker T. Washington: The Making of a Black Leader 1856–1901,* he discusses the machine's control of the black press through subsidy and purchase. Espionage was practiced on a broad scale, as was involvement in secret activities. It also tightly controlled black political patronage. Much of its power came from influence over white philanthropists and federal patronage appointments. Scott's status brought him into contact with many of the nation's leaders, enabling him to further Washington's philosophy of accommodation. Seen as a rather limited program that accepted segregation and opposed black militancy, it proved unacceptable to Du Bois and other militant blacks. The Tuskegee faithful, including Scott, considered accommodation both moral and necessary. They believed that commitment to Washington's accommodation philosophies was essential to prevent whites from attacking blacks, especially in the South. It was also felt that having a single leader—Washington—was necessary so the race's already meager influence would not be weakened further.

The Tuskegee Machine continued to function after Washington's death in 1915. Emmett Scott was the obvious successor to head Tuskegee Institute, but he was passed over in favor of Robert R. Moton, who was chosen by the largely white board of trustees. The ambitious Scott was probably bitterly disappointed. Many wrote him expressing their dismay, but Scott professed his satisfaction with the situation. Scott stayed on at Tuskegee as secretary, but his loyalty to Moton was in question. The suspicion that he was interested only in his own advancement was hard to overcome.

In 1917, after the United States had entered World War I, any rivalry between Scott and Moton was temporarily suspended when Scott was appointed special assistant to the Secretary of War by President Woodrow Wilson at Moton's suggestion. Scott advised the secretary on matters affecting black soldiers, holding this responsibility from 1917 through 1919. According to his own book, *Scott's Official History of the American Negro in the World War,* his appointment was called by Kelly Miller of Howard University "the most significant appointment that has yet come to the colored race." Some hoped that this would be an immediate cure for all racial ills in America, but Scott was quick to emphasize that his job was to advise in matters primarily affecting the interests of black draftees and soldiers. He also was to counsel and assist in looking out for their families and dependents. In fact, he later said that this work—looking after allotments, allowances, compensation, and war risk insurance for black soldiers and their families—was the most satisfying aspect of the job for him. Even his detractors admitted that he was an effective go–between and that he was able to raise the morale of the black soldiers.

Scott's first assignment proved successful when he was able to ensure that equal and impartial application of Selective Service Regulations was available for blacks and whites alike. Through Scott, training in military science and tactics was provided for blacks, and he was also instrumental in the formation of the Reserve Officers Training Corps (ROTC) in a number of black educational institutions. Because of Scott's perseverance, the racial tension caused by the pressure of greater numbers of black troops in the military was lessened. This was especially true for those encamped near large cities. Scott's experience led to the 1919 publication of his book, *Scott's Official History of the American Negro in the World War.*

Leaves Tuskegee

After the war, many blacks believed that their loyal service would help bring democracy to the South, but they knew they needed a leader. Scott's ambition was to be that leader. There were those who admired the way he promoted Washington, but they doubted his ability to promote himself. He ingratiated himself with northern blacks, only to alienate his southern associates. Carl S. Matthews, in the *South Atlantic Quarterly* noted Scott's complaint when he returned to Tuskegee: "every time I turn around there seems to be the thought on somebody's part that—in one way or another—I ought to be 'supplanted or eliminated.'"

Scott made the break with Tuskegee in June of 1919, when he became secretary–treasurer and business manager of Howard University in Washington, D.C., until 1934. Scott was Howard's most important black administrator until 1926, when Mordecai Johnson was selected as the university's first black president. Scott and Johnson did not have a peaceful association. Scott was said to be dissatisfied with Johnson's dictatorial policies and procedures, and Johnson thought Scott's work was highly incompetent. Although Johnson's criticism of Scott did not reflect the views of the majority of the trustees, the animosity continued for years. In 1932 because of the growth of the university, the Board of Trustees voted for reorganization of the by–laws. As a result, Scott became the secretary of the board and of the university, and the duties of treasurer went to someone else. Even though Scott had been able to withstand Johnson's attacks, Johnson finally succeeded in his determination to be rid of him. At its April 1938 meeting, the board did not reelect Scott as secretary but suggested that since he had just passed his sixty–fifth birthday, he be retired effective June 30, 1938. Scott, in a prepared statement, was not able to convince the board to let him stay on. He regarded his dismissal as improper and illegal, and he filed suit against the university in June of 1938.

During his tenure at Howard, Scott was a member of a committee that developed a retirement system which became effective during Johnson's administration. He also served on a committee whose recommendations resulted in salary increases for faculty and administrators and another that provided a procedure for electing the first alumni trustee. After leaving Howard, Scott worked as a public relations consultant in Washington, D.C. During World War II, aided by influential Republican contacts, Scott became director of employment and personnel relations for shipyard Number Four of Sun Shipbuilding and Dry Dock of Chester, Pennsylvania. The all–black yard was famous for building navy hospital ships and barges under government contract. He also organized blacks in the yard and in the area for the Republican party.

Scott served in many organizations over the years. He was secretary for the National Negro Business League from 1900 to 1922, secretary of the International Conference on the Negro in 1912, and for almost 30 years was a member and secretary of the Southern Education Foundation. He was a member of the first District of Columbia parole board. Active in the YMCA, Scott was a member of the Interstate Committee of Maryland, Delaware, and the District of Columbia, and of the National Conference on Colored YMCA Work. He also was the first black elected vice–president of the National Council of the YMCA.

Political Life

A staunch Republican since the 1890s, Scott actively entered politics in 1924, serving on an advisory committee for the Republican convention. He was a member of the Republican State Committee for the District of Columbia, assistant publicity director for the Republican National Committee from 1939 to 1942, and was a member of the public relations staff for every national convention from 1928 through 1948. He served as a specialist on blacks and as an advisor on racial matters to the Republican national chairman. His association with the Republican Party lasted until his death.

In 1909 Scott was one of three U.S. commissioners appointed to go to Liberia. Their mission was to analyze the country's diplomatic and economic difficulties. The report that Scott wrote, *Is Liberia Worth Saving?,* strongly influenced the United States's decision to establish a protectorate over Liberia. Scott's other acknowledged early publications included *Tuskegee and Its People* (1910), written with Booker T. Washington, and *Booker T. Washington, Builder of a Civilization* (1916), written with Lyman Beecher Stowe. The latter was a laudatory biography that personified Washington's beliefs and goals. His 1920 monograph for the Carnegie Endowment for International Peace, *Negro Migration during the War,* was a study of the migration of more than 400,000 blacks from the South to the North in the three years following the war's outbreak.

Emmett Scott was involved in a variety of business activities over the years. In 1915 he pushed for the production of a feature film that would challenge the image of blacks as presented in D. W. Griffith's, *The Birth of a Nation.* It was to be called *The Birth of a Race* and was to be based on Booker T. Washington's *Up from Slavery.* This venture, however, was ill–fated from the start. Scott's attention was drawn elsewhere when he was appointed special advisor to the Secretary of War. Financed by the sale of stock, the production suffered from many delays and in the end was an entirely different picture than Scott had envisioned. *The Birth of a Race* opened in December of 1918 to unfavorable reviews.

Scott shared Washington's views that blacks who achieved success in business would be respected by whites and would be given political and civil rights. He came to know the business community well through his years as organizer and secretary of the National Negro Business League. Most of his ventures in the 1920s and later years included real estate, insurance and banking. All were under black management and primarily served black customers and clients.

Scott has been described as being small with delicate features, light skinned, and impeccably attired. He wore pince–nez glasses, and his colleagues characterized him as "suave." He was both feared and admired by his associates over the years. Scott died December 12, 1957, in Washington, D.C., ending a public career that spanned more than half a century. He was 84 years old and had been a patient at Freedmen's Hospital for more than a year.

Although many people thought Emmett Scott might assume national leadership among blacks after Washington's death, he was unable to do so. In fact, by the 1920s, he had little voice except in education circles. Eventually he may have become somewhat pessimistic, doubting whether black men could expect equality. Scott played a significant role in the civil rights struggle of the early 1900s. The role he had hoped for later in his career diminished as the NAACP came to the fore. Still, he was a major figure alongside Booker T. Washington and continued to have an important voice in the channeling of white philanthropy to black education.

REFERENCES

"Do You Remember Emmett J. Scott?" *Negro Digest* 8 (May 1950): 91.

"Dr. Scott Dies at 84." *Washington Afro–American,* December 14, 1957.

"Emmett J. Scott, Educator, Was 84." *New York Times,* December 14, 1957.

Garraty, John A., ed. *Dictionary of American Biography.* Supplement 6. New York: Charles Scribner's Sons, 1980.

———. *Encyclopedia of American Biography.* New York: Harper, 1974.

Harlan, Louis R. *Booker T. Washington: The Making of a Black Leader.* New York: Oxford University Press, 1972.

Leab, Daniel J. "All–Colored—But Not Much Difference: Films Made for Negro Ghetto Audiences, 1913–1928." *Phylon* 36 (September 1975): 321–339.

Logan, Rayford W. *Howard University: The First Hundred Years 1867–1967.* New York: New York University Press, 1969.

Logan, Rayford W., and Michael R. Winston, eds. *Dictionary of American Negro Biography.* New York: Norton, 1982.

Lowery, Charles D., and John F. Marszalek, eds. *Encyclopedia of African-American Civil Rights, from Emancipation to the Present.* New York: Greenwood Press, 1992.

Matthews, Carl S. "The Decline of the Tuskegee Machine, 1915–1925: The Abdication of Political Power." *South Atlantic Quarterly* 75 (Autumn 1976): 460–469.

The National Cyclopaedia of American Biography. Vol. 43. New York: James T. White, 1961.

Scott, Emmett Jay. *Scott's Official History of the American Negro in the World War.* Chicago: Homewood Press, 1919.

———. "Twenty Years After: An Appraisal of Booker T. Washington." *Journal of Negro Education* 5 (October 1936): 543–54.

Washington, Booker T. "The Story of My Life and Work." In *The Booker T. Washington Papers.* Ed. Louis R. Harlan and John W. Blassingame. Vol. 1. Urbana: University of Illinois Press, 1972.

COLLECTIONS

The Emmett Jay Scott papers are held in the Morris A. Soper Library of Morgan State University in Baltimore. Much material is also included in the Booker T. Washington Papers at the Library of Congress.

Flossie E. Wise

Wendell Scott
(1921–1990)
Automobile racer

The first and only black driver to win a National Association for Stock Car Aauto Racing (NASCAR) Winston Cup race (then called the Grand National), Wendell Scott gained fame first in the segregated South, then throughout the nation, as an important contender in the predominantly white sport of stock car racing. Although inferior equipment as well as racial prejudice marred his racing career, in his lifetime Scott had over 500 racing starts.

Born in Danville, Virginia, on August 21, 1921, Wendell Scott grew up in that city's "Crooktown" section and later worked as a driver for a local taxicab company (he may have owned the company). He served for a while in the U.S. Army's 101st Airborne unit as a paratrooper. After his discharge, Scott returned to Danville and hauled moonshine from illegal stills to the fairgrounds. He told Sylvia Wilkinson in *Dirt Tracks to Glory,* "My liquor car would do 95 in second gear, and 118 in high. Back then there wasn't a police car in Danville that could go over 95." Scott's interest in racing

Wendell Scott

began in 1949 as he regularly watched races at the Danville Fairgrounds Speedway. His entry into racing came in 1950 when the operator of the fairground racetrack wanted to attract more people the races. Scott said in *Dirt Tracks,* "He went down to the police department to find out which black boys had speeding records. He walked in, and they told him if you're looking for a black boy to drive a car, then you're looking for Wendell Scott." The police knew Scott's racing ability well, having chased him often throughout southern Virginia as he hauled moonshine. For his equipment, Scott borrowed the "liquor car" that he had sold his brother-in-law when the car "got too hot" for him to use.

That same year Scott bought a used racecar and tried to enter it in the amateur NASCAR event at Bowman-Gray Stadium in Winston-Salem, North Carolina. Racing officials, who did not recognize his race because of his light skin and steely eyes, required him to add a safety belt before he could enter. As he attempted to purchase a belt, he was told that he could not race. Scott knew why.

Scott returned to Danville and was approached by a promoter in the old Dixie Circuit, not recognized by NASCAR, who asked if he wanted to drive. Scott accepted and during the next four years won 128 entries in the amateur and modified races. His racing career began at the Danville Fairgrounds Speedway, where he was track's the first black racer.

Races in NASCAR

In 1954 Scott was accepted in NASCAR's Modified Division and added more victories to his record. In this division drivers were allowed certain major changes in their cars that were not allowed in the Grand National. Strengthening his racing career to become one of the South's most popular stock car race drivers, he set a neck–breaking pace at major speedways in Virginia and North Carolina. By 1958 he was one of the leading contenders at the weekly races in Norfolk. He won the 1959 NASCAR Sportsman championship at the Richmond Southside Speedway and State of Virginia.

In 1961 Scott reached the big time: he entered NASCAR's premier division, the Grand National Circuit, and made his GN debut at the Spartanburg, South Carolina, Fairgrounds. In five of his GN races he finished in the top ten and in 1962 had 11 top finishes. By 1964 he was known throughout the country and, in 30 races, had finished in the top ten a total of 19 times. He raced in the World 600 in Charlotte in 1964, starting in fortieth place and finishing in ninth place to set a Grand National record for a fortieth–place starter. His win in the GN 100–mile race at Jacksonville, Florida, on December 1, 1963, in which he drove a 1962 Chevrolet, was his biggest win and his first and only GN victory. Richard Petty came in second. Scott was the first and only black to win the GN trophy, now called the NASCAR Winston Cup. Promoters and NASCAR officials denied him public glory at the race, refused him the NASCAR trophy in public view, and eventually awarded him a makeshift trophy—an inexpensive block of wood.

Racial incidents of this kind marred Scott's early career. Until 1961 racial prejudice kept him from qualifying for the GN circuit tour. Racing inspectors required more of Scott than of the white drivers, such as repairing chips in his car's paint. During his first five years of driving, fellow competitors maneuvered to run his car off the track while crowds jeered him. During the racial unrest in Birmingham, Alabama, in the 1960s, Scott hurried from a race after threats were made to turn his car over and burn it. In 1971, a white promoter of the Charlotte Motor Speedway reneged on his promise to provide Scott a "first class car" to use at the CMS, no doubt bowing to pressure from white drivers. In time, however, Scott received enthusiastic cheers for his crowd–pleasing style of driving. He also constantly turned to help fellow drivers in distress.

Perhaps the greatest threat to Scott's success was his inability to afford adequate equipment, forcing him to drive used cars and leaving him victim of constant car troubles. He never had a new racer. Apparently a superior mechanic, he repaired his inferior equipment and kept his cars in as good condition as he could. Nearly all of his earnings went to repair his cars. He always felt that with new equipment he would always come out on top. But racing was central to him. He told *Sepia* magazine: "Racing is in my blood. It takes a light head and a heavy foot to be a racer. I guess I have both."

Looking back on the difficulties he had in his racing career, Scott said in *Dirt Tracks to Glory,* "I really never could say racing was good to me, because I never made enough money where I could go and buy anything I needed. . . . The most I ever got . . . was around $7,000. One year I did get $13,000 from the Firestone Tire and Rubber Company for running Firestone tires. . . . I never started racing because I thought it would be easy."

"A stock car racer has to have skill, common sense, a knowledge of his car, luck, and a whole lot of guts," Scott told *Ebony* in 1966. "There is always the chance of a pileup, and that can cause not only injury but death." Although Scott had a close call in a 37–car pileup at the Daytona speedway in 1960, his injury in an 18–car pileup at the Talladega races in 1973 ended his career. After retiring from full–time racing, he continued to drive. In his lifetime he made over 500 racing starts and had 128 career wins in sportsman and modified races. He had 506 GN starts and was in the top ten NASCAR starts 147 times. In point championship standings, he was sixth and tenth both in 1966, ninth in 1968, and ninth in 1969. Some sources ranked Scott alongside such racing greats as A. J. Foyt and Mario Andretti, who competed at the most notable of all racing events, the Indianapolis 500. While earlier in his career Scott had considered that race too, he never attempted it.

In addition to a racing career, Scott owned an automobile repair shop, which he ran when he was not on the racetrack. A religious man, Scott often worried that his racing interfered with his obligations at North New Hope Baptist Church, where he was a member. Although he had hauled moonshine earlier, Scott repoirted in *Dirt Tracks to Glory,* "I never drank a drop of liquor in my life. I just hauled it." He was also a nonsmoker and was bitterly opposed to drugs. Scott's driving career was showcased in 1977, when the film *Greased Lightning,* starring Richard Pryor and featuring Pam Grier, was released. Scott served as technical consultant to Third World Cinema, the production company for the film.

For his pioneering work, Scott received a number of honors, including the State of Florida Citation for Outstanding Achievements (1965); honorary Lieutenant–Colonel–Aide–de–Camp Honor via the Governor of Alabama State Militia (1970); the first Curtis Turner Memorial Achievement Award (1971); Schafer Brewing Company Achievement Award (1975); Muscular Dystrophy Association Award for Achievements, Roanoke, Virginia (1981); Virginia Skyline Girl Scout Council Award for outstanding contributions (1985); Danville, Virginia, Citizenship Award (1985); and Early Dirt Racers Driver of the Year Award (1990). In 1977 Scott was inducted into the Black Athletes Hall of Fame. He also became president of the Black American Racing Association and was an honorary lifetime member. He also received proclamations from Atlanta, Georgia, and Danville, Virginia. In 1986 and Mayor Seward Anderson of Danville declared August 8, 1990, Wendell Scott Day. According to *Jet* for January 23, 1998, he was honored again in Danville, when the street where he had lived was renamed Wendell Scott Drive.

After being hospitalized several times in 1990 for high blood pressure, kidney problems, and later a six–month–bout with spinal cancer, Scott died in Danville's Memorial Hospital on Sunday, December 23, 1990, at age 69. He was survived by his wife, Mary, whom he married about 1944, three sons, four daughters, and 15 grandchildren. The General Assembly of Virginia passed a resolution officially mourning Scott's death and recognizing him as a trailblazing sportsman and a man of skill, dedication, and perseverance. He had broken the racial barrier in stock car racing with a NASCAR win.

REFERENCES

Ashe, Arthur R., Jr. *A Hard Road to Glory: A History of the African-American Athlete Since 1946.* New York: Warner Books, 1988.

Claes, Cynthia. "NASCAR's Wendell Scott Dies of Cancer at Age 69." *Autoweek* 41 (7 January 1991): 55.

"Dixie's Daredevil on Wheels." *Ebony* 15 (May 1960): 61–64.

"Johnson, Fox Got to Dodge; Wendell Gets First Victory." *Southern Motor Sports Journal* 2 (5 December 1963): 1–3.

"Racer Wendell Scott in Hospital." *Danville Register and Bee,* August 3, 1990.

"Stock Car Racer Reaches Bigtime." *Ebony* 21 (May 1966): 61–66.

"A Street for Scott." *Jet* 93 (26 January 1998): 54.

Wendell Scott Fact Sheet, n.d. Files of the Virginia–North Carolina Piedmont Genealogical Society, Danville, VA.

"Wendell Scott Rides with Death and Glory." *Sepia* 12 (16 May 1963): 68–71.

Wilkinson, Sylvia. *Dirt Tracks to Glory: The Early Days of Stock Car Racing as Told by the Participants.* Chapel Hill, NC: Algonquin Books, 1983.

Wright, Buddy. "Local Driving Legend Scott Dead at 60." *Danville Register and Bee,* December 24, 1990.

COLLECTIONS

Biographical material on Wendell Scott, including articles, tributes, articles, death notices, and other items, may be found in the Virginia–North Carolina Piedmont Genealogical Society, Danville, Virginia.

Frederick Douglas Smith Jr.

William Joseph Seymour (1870–1922)

Religious leader

A May 27, 1997, article in the *New York Times* described a revival begun Father's Day 1995 at the Brownsville Assembly of God in Pensacola, Florida as probably the longest running since:

> a one–eyed preacher in Los Angeles named William Seymour called on God to sweep clean the souls of Azusa Street. The famous Azusa Street Revival began in 1906 and ran for three years, and is largely responsible for the growth of the Pentecostal movement which now has some 20 million members in the United States and more than 200 million around the world.

The article did not state, and it is possible that many do not know, that Seymour—the catalyst for the establishment of the modern Pentecostal movement, including the predominantly black Church of God in Christ and the predominantly white Assemblies of God denominations—was an African American.

William Joseph Seymour was born on May 2, 1870, in Centerville, Louisiana, to Simon and Phyllis Salabarr Seymour. Not much is known of his early life except that he had little education but several visions of God. While the outline of events in his early manhood is clear, sources differ on exact details and dates. About 1890 he moved to Indianapolis, where he was a waiter in a hotel. He attended a black congregation in the predominantly white Methodist Episcopal Church. In 1900 Seymour moved to Cincinnati. There Martin Wells Knapp, a former Methodist minister, induced him to join the Evening Lights Saints, a revivalist Holiness group which focused on Christ's return to set up his kingdom on earth, an event they believed imminent.

This church, a mainly black offshoot of the Church of God of Anderson, Indiana, was one of the many Holiness churches that came into being during the middle of the last decade of the 19th century. Their common theme was the proclamation of the doctrine of sanctification. Sanctification had many sources in 19th–century Protestantism but is ultimately traced back to John Wesley, the founder of Methodism, who taught that believers could be freed from outward sin and perfected in love in this life. Many who take this position see the change as a process of growing in God's grace after conversion, but for Holiness believers the normative expectation was an immediate change through a baptism of the Holy Spirit following the initial conversion experience when a believer first accepts Christ, in other words, immediate sanctification through a fire baptism from the Holy Spirit after justification through repentance and Christ's water baptism.

Ordained as a Minister

In Cincinnati an attack of smallpox left Seymour blind in one eye. He seems to have used a glass eye in later life. His recovery from the disease led to his decision to become an itinerant preacher, and in 1902 he was ordained by the Church of God. From 1903 on his wanderings as an evangelist took him to Chicago, Georgia, Mississippi, Louisiana, and then to Texas. His family had moved to Houston, and Seymour settled there. In the summer of 1905 Seymour was replacement pastor for Lucy Farrow, a female Holiness minister and niece of black abolitionist Frederick Douglass, during her absence. Farrow spoke in tongues, a new experience for him. (Some sources use the spelling Farrar.) Farrow's gift was all the more exciting since like many Holiness adherents he believed that glossolalia, or speaking in unknown tongues, was a sign of the imminent coming of the Last Days.

Farrow had worked in Topeka, Kansas, as a servant for Charles Fox Parham, a white evangelist who was now running a Bible school in Houston and who taught that speaking in tongues was indeed a central sign of the working of the Holy Spirit. She urged Seymour to contact Parham to learn more. Parham was a racist who allowed Seymour to listen to classes through the window of the classroom or, in case of rain, through the open door. There is considerable controversy about the extent of the influence of Parham on Seymour, whose attendance at the school may have been very short; estimates range from a few weeks to a few days. What is sure is that Parham's racism deeply offended him; Seymour believed that the coming together of blacks and whites in worship was another sign of the arrival of the Last Days.

It seems probable that Parham's teaching merely confirmed Seymour in a belief about the centrality of speaking in tongues as sign of the working of the Holy Spirit. Otherwise, there were sharp divergences between the two. Parham had very liberal ideas on marriage and divorce and is even seen by some as the source of a free love movement in the early 1900s in midwest Pentecostalism; Seymour did not approve of divorce or sexual license. Parham did not believe in overly emotional worship; Seymour adhered to African American traditions of highly demonstrative worship. Most importantly, Parham did not believe in complete sanctification as a second work of grace.

The differences were sharply underlined in October of 1906 when Parham seized upon an invitation from Seymour to address the congregation at the Azusa Street Mission in Los Angeles to deliver an attack on Seymour's doctrine and worship practices. Clemmons wrote in *Bishop C. H. Mason,* citing Parham's words, "'God is sick at His stomach' due to the 'animism' [Parham] perceived in the enthusiastic worship. . . . [He] openly expressed his disgust at the mix of whites with blacks, and the failure of blacks to recognize their 'place.'"

Leader of the Azusa Street Revival

In Houston, Seymour met Neely Terry, a woman from Los Angeles, who thought he sounded like Julia M. Hutchins, formerly of the Second Baptist Church in that city. In the spring of 1905 the authorities of the Baptist Church invited Hutchins and eight other families to stop attending services because of their strong Holiness views. Since the church Hutchins established after her expulsion by the Baptists needed a pastor, she may have accepted a recommendation to invite Seymour made by Terry on her return to Los Angeles.

Other accounts imply that he traveled to Los Angeles on his own, attracted by Terry's description of what was happening there. There is also a claim that he received some financial help from Parham. In any case, he passed through Denver on his way there, and made a very bad impression on white evangelist Alma White and the students of her Bible school. White utterly rejected the doctrine of sanctification and was dismayed by his praying. As cited by Cox in *Fire From Heaven,* she wrote: "I felt that serpents and other slimy creatures were creeping around me. After he had left the room, a number of the students said they felt he was devil possessed. . . . In my evangelistic and missionary tours I had met all kinds of religious fakirs and tramps, but I felt he excelled them all."

In Los Angeles on February 22, 1906, Seymour preached in Hutchins's church both the necessity of establishing a multiracial community and displaying glossolalia as signs of the work of the Holy Spirit. Shocked by the addition of speaking in tongues to Holiness doctrine, Hutchins locked him out of the church, perhaps for the afternoon service after his first sermon and certainly within a week. (Seymour eventually came to modify his insistence on the importance speaking in tongues and accepted Hutchins's position that glossolalia was a gift but not necessarily the central and most important.)

Seymour began to hold services in the home of Mr. and Mrs. Richard Asberry, at 214 North Bonnie Brae Avenue. (The name is also given as Asbery and Asbury.) Neither he nor his followers had yet experienced speaking in tongues. In early April the experience came. One account says the first to speak in other tongues under his guidance was Jennie Evans Moore, his future wife, on April 6. She may have simply been the first woman on April 9, since another report says that the first person was Ed Lee at that date. According to this version, Seymour had summoned Lucy Farrow from Texas to work with the women. According to the eyewitness testimony reprinted by Tinney in his article on Seymour in *Black Apostles,* Farrow rose from the dinner table at Lee's house, saying, "'The Lord tells me to lay hand on you for the Holy Ghost.' And when she laid her hands on him, he fell out of his chair as though dead, and began to speak in other tongues." When they entered the evening prayer meeting a little later, the six persons already there also began to speak in tongues. The excitement continued to mount for three days straight, and finally Seymour spoke in tongues himself on April 12.

As news of these events spread, numbers attending the meetings quickly outgrew the premises. The noise and crowds attracted police attention. Nearby at 312 Azusa Street there was a very run–down building, originally constructed as the first African Methodist Episcopal church in Los Angeles and now in very poor condition after serving as a warehouse and then a livery stable. The area was now mostly given over to business so there were few persons living nearby to complain of the noise generated by the meetings.

The building was hastily cleaned out. The pulpit was on the level of the congregation and made of two boxes nailed together—on occasion Seymour would put his head into the top compartment of the boxes as he prayed privately. Seating was benches made of planks nailed on barrels. Seymour lived on the second floor of the building, which also had a room where prayer was held 24 hours a day. Services began at this site on April 14.

Earthquake Hits During Revival

Excitement mounted to the point that the *Los Angeles Times* gave coverage to the revival on April 18, the day of the great San Francisco earthquake. The belief that the earthquake had been predicted at the mission only increased crowds.

Some came from curiosity, but many came in search of salvation and healing, both physical and spiritual. By the beginning of May more than a thousand persons a day sought out the revival. Through 1909 the Azusa Street Mission held three services a day with prayer meetings 24 hours a day.

Seymour's vision of a racially unified community seemed to be fulfilled as blacks, whites, and Hispanics came together to pray and worship. As word of what was happening spread, people from all over the United States and from abroad came. Many pastors and spiritual leaders, especially from black and white Holiness churches, came to investigate, found the Spirit, and took Pentecostal teachings back to their own churches, where they found enthusiastic supporters and launched Pentecostal churches. As quoted by Clemmons, Charles H. Mason, leader of the Church of God in Christ, tells what they found:

> Then I gave up for the Lord to have His way with me. So there came a wave of Glory into me, and all of my being was filled with the Glory of the Lord. So when He had gotten me straight on my feet there came a light which enveloped my entire being above the brightness of the sun. When I opened my mouth to say 'Glory,' a flame touched my tongue which ran down to me. My language changed and no word could I speak in my own tongue. Oh! I was filled with the Glory of the Lord. My soul was then satisfied.
>
> Much of the revival at Azusa Street involved familiar elements in Holiness teachings except for the stress on speaking in tongues. A major novelty was the size and interracial character of the crowds, although blacks remained the most numerous. The mission staff was mixed.

Seymour took steps to institutionalize the mission by incorporating it at the beginning of 1907 as the Pacific Apostolic Faith Mission, Los Angeles. (At this date, the word 'apostolic' in a church name did not imply a rejection of belief in the Trinity as it often did a few years later.) In September of 1906 he began to publish a newspaper whose national and international circulation shortly reached 20,000.

The Fire Dies Down

In about three years the crowds diminished. Hopes for the immediate arrival of the Last Days died down, and it is also possible that Seymour's own energy was flagging. By 1908 white Pentecostals began to separate from black. Few congregations had ever been genuinely integrated, and in face of prejudice from nonmembers, especially in the South, some white groups like the Pentecostal Fire Baptized Holiness Church encouraged black groups to form a separate denomination. Many of the some 300 whites ordained by the predominantly black Church of God in Christ split off to go into the Assemblies of God and elsewhere.

In Los Angeles, too, whites were moving into all–white Pentecostal churches, and attendance at the Azusa Street Mission fell off. A sharp blow came when Seymour quietly married Jennie Evans Moore on May 13, 1908; the marriage had immediate repercussions for the church publication. At its peak in March of 1907 *The Apostolic Faith* newspaper had 50,000 subscribers all over the world. In the wake of the marriage, white Clara Lum, administrative assistant for the newspaper, left for Portland, Oregon, with the mailing list of the paper. Although the paper soon died under her editorship, Seymour could never recover the list.

Although jealousy is commonly given as the reason for Lum's departure, she said she rejected the idea of any marriages when the Last Days were so near. The church she founded with Florence Crawford in Portland is still flourishing.

Other tussles put a strain on the church. In 1911 William H. Durham, a white preacher, tried to take over the mission. He had been left to occupy the pulpit while Seymour was traveling. Not only did Durham vie with Seymour for control of the congregation, he proclaimed theological positions in contradiction to those of Seymour. When he was finally forced out of the building, he took some 600 members with him.

Then in 1913 a Trinitarian controversy erupted in Los Angeles and cut sharply into Seymour's remaining congregation. A Pentecostal camp meeting introduced the new oneness doctrine. Traditional Christian teaching maintains the Trinity as three distinct persons in one God; oneness or Jesus only maintains there are just three names for one single person in God. This position attracted 300 of those attending the meeting, including all of the blacks. Since many of the those African Americans attended Azusa Street, Seymour's congregation fell off to about 20.

In 1915 Seymour published a book of discipline for his church, *The Doctrines and Discipline of the Azusa Street Apostolic Faith Mission of Los Angeles,* and he took the title of bishop. He still called for an interracial church but now stipulated that the leadership must be black. Although Seymour continued to travel and evangelize for the rest of his life, speaking principally to black audiences, he was gradually fading out of sight. Around 1916 he evangelized from New York to Virginia in the company of Church of God in Christ leader Charles Harrison Mason. Here and there, there are still churches, both Church of God in Christ and others, which trace their founding to direct impetus from Seymour, including a cluster in Virginia.

Seymour died of a heart attack on September 18, 1922. Jennie M. Seymour became pastor of the church. In 1930 she had to fend off another attempt by an outsider to take it over. The struggle grew so intense that on January of 1931 the police padlocked the building. The dispute was finally settled in the courts. She died in 1936. No trace of the original building exists; the site was a shopping plaza a few years back. A few offshoot churches survive on the West Coast. Some of the churches Seymour founded in the East have now formed an ecumenical association, United Fellowship of the Original Azusa Street Mission, with headquarters in Jefferson, Ohio.

William Seymour's life appeared to end in a minor key, marked by near failure. Except for the three years from 1906 to 1909 there is little to make him stand out from many other earnest pastors and evangelists. During those three years, however, he played a vital role. All over the country people were engaged on spiritual quests leading towards Pentecostalism. Seymour provided the spark which led to the explosive growth of the Pentecostal movement and in so doing changed Christianity over the face of the entire planet.

REFERENCES

Burkett, Randall K., and Richard Newman, eds. *Black Apostles.* Boston: G. K. Hall, 1978.

Clemmons, Ithiel C. *Bishop C. H. Mason and the Roots of the Church of God in Christ.* Bakersfield, CA: Pneuma Life, 1996.

Cox, Harvey. *Fire From Heaven.* Reading, MA: Addison–Wesley, 1995.

DuPree, Sherry Sherrod, ed. *African–American Holiness Pentecostal Movement: An Annotated Bibliography.* New York: Garland, 1996.

———. *Biographical Dictionary of African–American, Holiness–Pentecostals, 1880–1990.* Washington, DC: Middle Atlantic Regional Press, 1989.

Murphy, Larry G., J. Gordon Melton, and Gary L. Ward, eds. *Encyclopedia of African American Religions.* New York: Garland, 1993.

Payne, Wardell J., ed. *Directory of African American Religious Bodies.* Washington, DC: Howard University Press, 1991.

"Revivalism Finds a Capital in a Florida Church." *New York Times,* May 27, 1997.

Sanders, Cheryl J. *Saints in Exile: The Holiness–Pentecostal Experience in African American Religion and Culture.* New York: Oxford, 1996.

Robert L. Johns

Bernard Shaw

(1940–)

Television journalist, reporter

A pioneer black news anchor in cable television, Bernard Shaw is a highly visible black television journalist. While he is known for the delivery of news on other networks, he has distinguished himself more recently on prime–time reports for CNN. He is noted for his persistence, dedication, penetrating questions, and for incisive reporting on breaking news.

Bernard Shaw was born May 22, 1940, in Chicago, to Edgar Shaw, a housepainter and railroad employee, and

Bernard Shaw

Camille Murphy Shaw, a housekeeper. To nourish his keen interest in current affairs, Edgar Shaw brought home Chicago's four daily newspapers, weekly news magazines, and books, which Bernard Shaw read regularly. He developed high regard for journalists and newsmakers with a particular interest in Edward R. Murrow on CBS. By the time he was 13, Murrow had become Shaw's role model.

Journalistic Aspirations

Determined, dedicated and ambitious, Shaw, decided that he wanted to be a broadcaster. On Sundays, at the bookstore buying the *New York Times,* he would converse with Clifton Utley, a Chicago commentator and father of television journalist Garrick Utley. Later he visited newsrooms to talk to writers to learn about the profession. Shaw's involvement in various school activities at Dunbar High School helped prepare him for the world of broadcasting. He produced and announced the daily high school radio program and served on the debating team.

Since his parents could not afford to send him to college, he joined the Marine Corps in 1959 after high school graduation and served until 1963. Marines learn discipline, and Shaw knew that their regimentation would help him succeed in pursuing his interests.

While stationed in Hawaii in 1961, he was persistent in trying to talk to Walter Cronkite who was in Hawaii to filming *The Twentieth Century.* After he made more than 30 phone calls to Cronkite's room, Cronkite grudgingly agreed to give him a few minutes to talk about a news career. They talked for a half hour. They have remained friends since that time.

After his discharge from the Marine Corps, Shaw enrolled at the University of Illinois, Chicago Campus, and majored in history. Maintaining his interest in broadcasting, he worked without pay in the wire room at WYNR–radio in Chicago while continuing to carry a full schedule of classes. When the station changed its name from WYNR to WNUS and its format from rhythm and blues to all news, he later received $50 a day as a reporter.

Becomes a Television Journalist

Shaw began his career as a reporter with WYNR/WNUS radio in Chicago, where he worked from 1964 to 1966. In 1965 he was a news writer for WFLD Television in Chicago. He returned to radio from 1966 to 1968 as a reporter for WIND, owned by Westinghouse Broadcasting Company. After the assassination of Martin Luther King Jr. in 1968, Shaw was chosen by the King family to accompany King's body from Memphis to Atlanta, but he had to decline the offer because WIND wanted him back in Chicago. With a year left in college, he made a difficult choice between completing his degree and accepting a promotion with the station and a transfer to Washington, D.C. He accepted and was WIND's White House correspondent from 1968 to 1971.

Shaw moved to the Columbia Broadcasting System (CBS) as a news reporter in Washington, D.C., from 1971 until 1974, then as a correspondent from 1974 to 1977. By 1977 he hoped to expand his experience and utilize his knowledge of Spanish. After CBS rejected his offer to become a Latin American correspondent, Shaw moved to American Broadcasting Company (ABC) in Miami as chief of the Latin American Bureau until 1979. In 1980 Shaw was appointed chief Washington correspondent at Cable News Network (CNN), making him the first black anchor there.

Breaking news stories have been important for Shaw through the years. He was assigned to report on the Chicago riots of 1968. He was one of few journalists to report on the Jonestown mass suicide in Guyana of Jim Jones and his followers in 1978. He covered the Nicaguaran Revolution in 1979. He joined the major television networks in 1987 in a nationally televised interview with President Ronald Reagan. In 1988 he moderated the second presidential debate in Los Angeles. The Tiananmen Square uprising by Chinese students and other protestors in May 1989 was captured by Shaw and Dan Rather. In Baghdad in 1991, Shaw provided 16 and a half hours of continuous coverage on the Persian Gulf War from the Al–Rashid Hotel. Shaw, Peter Arnett, and John Holliman were the only newsmen reporting because communications channels from the other major networks had been halted. Other breaking coverage by Shaw was of the Tokyo Economic Summit of President Bill Clinton in July 1993 and the Los Angeles Earthquake of January 1994.

Shaw is thorough in his inquiring. During several political campaigns he asked tough questions of the candidates, such as Michael Dukakis, George Bush, and Dan Quayle. Through the years his excellent performance has paid off: CNN, which he was hesitant about joining in 1980, became a top television news show. Shaw is rated as a top news anchor with Tom Brokaw of NBC, Peter Jennings of ABC, and Dan Rather of CBS.

Shaw has been honored with prestigious awards over the years for his news reporting. He received the 1989 Emmy Award for News and Documentaries, for outstanding coverage of a single breaking news story of the National Association of Television Arts and Sciences, and the 1990 Award for Cable Excellence for best news anchor. For his work in Baghdad in 1991, he was bestowed with the George Foster Peabody Broadcasting Award and the Cable ACE Award from the National Academy of Cable Programming for best newscaster of the year. He also received the 1991 Lowell Thomas Electronic Journalistic Award, the 1991 David Brinkley Excellence Communication Award from Barry University, the 1994 Walter Cronkite Award for Excellence in Journalism and Telecommunication, and the William Allen White Medallion for Distinguished Service from the University of Kansas in 1994.

Shaw married Linda Allston on March 30, 1974, and they have two children—Amar Edgar, and Anil Louise. Shaw, tall, slim–framed, with graying hair and a deep resonant voice, is an avid reader. He tends his rose garden in his spare time. He also believes in philanthropy and has given over 130,000 dollars to the Bernard Shaw Endowment Fund, under the aegis of the University of Illinois Foundation. In order to be prepared for covering the news, he believes that reading widely is essential. According to *Current Biography,* in 1961 Walter Cronkite advised him "to read omnivorously and to remain open and curious about all facets of human existence." Shaw has followed that advice and continues to make reading a priority.

Persistence, dedication, and hard work pay off for Bernard Shaw. Although television does not have an abundance of African American journalists, Shaw's tenacity, determination, and credentials opened doors for him and led him to a highly visible position with CNN television.

Current address: Principal Washington Anchor, CNN America, Inc., CNN Building, 820 First St. NE, 11th Floor, Washington, DC 20002.

REFERENCES

Black Writers. Detroit: Gale Research, 1989.

Contemporary Authors. Vol. 119. Detroit: Gale Research, 1987.

Contemporary Black Biography. Vol. 2. Detroit: Gale Research, 1992.

Current Biography. New York: H. W. Wilson, 1995.

Dates, Jannette L., and William Barlow, eds. *Split Image: African Americans in the Mass Media.* 2nd ed. Washington, D.C.: Howard University Press, 1993.

Barbara Williams Jenkins

George I. Shirley
(1934–)
Opera singer, educator

George Shirley began his singing career as the first black member of the U.S. Army Chorus and went on to become the first African American tenor to sing under contract with the prestigious Metropolitan Opera. He has performed grand opera roles in the world's most distinguished opera houses and has sung with the world's great orchestras in a long career which combines recording, performing, and teaching.

George Irving Shirley was born in Indianapolis, Indiana, on April 18, 1934, to Irving Ewing and Daisy Shirley. His was a musical family; his father played guitar, piano, and violin, and his mother sang. Shirley showed early promise as a singer and entered a radio contest at the age of five, singing a popular Bing Crosby song. His prize was his first recording of himself. When his parents moved to Detroit the following year, young George continued to sing in church and school and also played baritone horn in a community band. Although his talent was recognized, Shirley never sought an operatic career during his youth. He seemed destined instead for music education and was urged to become Detroit's first black public school music teacher.

Shirley completed his early schooling in Detroit's schools and did well at Northern High School, earning excellent grades in music and other subjects. To supplement his musical training, his parents sent him to the Ebersol School of Music for six years. Following high school graduation, he attended Wayne State University and earned his B.S. degree in music education in 1955. He stayed at Wayne State for a year of graduate studies and taught school before his induction into the army in 1956. Shirley married his high school sweetheart, Gladys Lee Ishop, on June 24, 1956.

Following basic training at Ft. Leonard Wood, Missouri, Shirley thought of serving in the army band program until he and a few army buddies decided to audition for the U.S. Army Chorus. Captain Loboda, director of the chorus, accepted him as the first black member of the famed touring and performing ensemble. Urged by army buddies, he began private study with Themy Gerogi, who recognized his talent, and extended his army service in order to continue his studies.

In his three years with the Army Chorus, Shirley also sang regularly with the choir at Vermont Avenue Baptist Church in Washington, D.C., and elsewhere. In 1959 an Army Chorus friend, Ara Berberian, who also later developed an operatic career, told him that a tenor was needed for the Turnau Opera Company at a summer resort in New York's Catskill mountains. Shirley was hired and made his operatic debut in the role of Eisenstein in Johann Strauss's *Die Fledermaus.*

Shirley next came to the attention of Boris Goldovsky, a renowned opera conductor and teacher, who urged him to attend the Tanglewood Music Center and participate in Goldovsky's summer opera school. This experience, too, proved valuable and was influential in advancing Shirley's career. Encouraged by Goldovsky, Shirley entered and won the American Opera Auditions in Cincinnati. Opportunities followed to sing in Milan and Florence, where he made his European debut in the role of Rodolpho in Puccini's *La Bohème.*

George I. Shirley

Returning to America Shirley won first prize in the Metropolitan Opera Auditions in New York in 1961, the first black tenor to win this national competition. He also earned the praise of the *New York Time*'s music critic who attended the auditions. The prize was a $2,000 scholarship plus performances. A feature television performance on *The Bell Telephone Hour* followed, and then he debuted with the Metropolitan Opera in October of 1961 in the role of Ferrando in Mozart's *Così Fan Tutte.*

Joins the Met

With his professional operatic career under way, Shirley began studying with Cornelius Reid in New York. He became the first black singer to perform under contract with the Metropolitan Opera, where he performed regularly for 11 years. Among his accomplishments during his first decade with the Metropolitan Opera were major roles in more than 20 operas, including Adorno in *Simon Boccanegra;* a costarring role with Renata Tebaldi; Fenton in *Falstaff,* with Franco Guarrera in the title role; Rodolpho in *La Bohème;* and Don Jose in *Carmen.* He also sang regularly with the New York

City Opera, Opera Society of Washington, D.C., Santa Fe Opera, and the Spring Opera of San Francisco. Performances in other countries included *Don Giovanni* at London's Covent Garden, *The Magic Flute* at the Glyndebourne Festival, and solo performances with the New York Philharmonic, the Philadelphia Orchestra, and the Boston Symphony.

In 1972 Shirley suffered a professional setback when he was called on to substitute at the Metropolitan Opera for the Italian tenor Franco Corelli, who was not available to sing the title role in Gounod's *Roméo et Juliette* for the opening of the fall season. As reported in the *Washington Post* on July 29, 1979, Shirley felt prepared vocally but not mentally for the role. The *New York Times* music critic panned his performance, severely shaking his confidence.

A period of profound self–examination followed from which Shirley emerged to resume his career. Successful performances were recorded at major halls, and he was soon in demand again. He sang in the American premiere of Cavalli's *L'Egisto* in 1975, the role of Loge in *Das Rheingold* at London's Royal Opera under the direction of Colin Davis in 1976, and the role of Romilayu in the New York City Opera's world premiere in April 1977 of Kirchner's *Lily.* He also sang in Stravinsky's *Oedipus Rex* with the Houston Symphony in 1977, which had been his first operatic performance twenty years earlier as a student at Wayne State University.

In May 1977 his made his debut at the esteemed La Scala, Milan, as Pelléas in Debussy's *Pelléas et Melisande.* In recent years he has been featured regularly in major roles with the Deutsche Oper of Berlin, appearing with them on their 1988 tour of Japan and singing the role of Pluto in Offenbach's *Orpheus in the Underworld* in 1990. In 1990 he also sang in the premiere of Richard Strauss's *Friedenstag* in New York's Carnegie Hall with the Collegiate Chorale and performed as soloist with the Mormon Tabernacle Choir on CBS radio.

Shirley has recorded frequently for RCA, Columbia, Decca, Angel, Vanguard, and Phillips Records. In addition, he has recorded tenor arias for the Laureate Series of Music Minus One records. In 1968 he received a Grammy Award for his performance in the prize–winning recording of Mozart's *Così Fan Tutte.* He has performed as a soloist with the London Symphony under Lorin Maazel, the Chicago Symphony under Sir Georg Solti, and the Boston Symphony under Seiji Ozawa. His awards include an honorary doctorate from Wilberforce University (1967), the National Arts Club Award (1960), Il Concorso di Musica e Danza, Vervelli, Italy (1960), the Concert Artist's Guild Competition, the Symphony Saintpaulia's Lifetime Achievement Award (1995), and many others.

George Shirley has been a professor of voice and a member of the artist faculty of the University of Michigan, Ann Arbor, since 1987. He has also served as adjunct professor of voice at Long Island Community College, artist–in–residence at Morgan State College, humanist–in–residence at Howard University, and professor of voice at the University of Maryland from 1980 to 1987.

In a difficult career, George Shirley's achievements have been remarkable. He was the first black high school music teacher in Detroit, the first African American member of the U.S. Army Chorus, the first black tenor to win the Metropolitan Opera Auditions, the first African American tenor to sing under contract at the Metropolitan Opera, and the first black to sing major operatic roles at many of the theaters where he has performed. Early in his career, he was compared to black tenor Roland Hayes, who did not have the repertoire or the opportunity to sing grand opera. His favorite roles from his extensive repertoire are Pelléas, Rodolpho, Don Jose, Ottavio in *Don Giovanni,* Tamino in *The Magic Flute,* and Herod in *Salomé.*

Shirley has long been concerned with the difficult problems faced by young black singers— racism as well as troubling arguments concerning dramatic realism, culture, and character. In an *Opera News* article, "The Black Performer," he speaks frankly of the obstacles he encountered and offers advice to young performers. He and Therman Bailey, a New York singer and voice teacher, have formed an organization, Independent Black Singers, to assist young aspiring singers. George Shirley takes seriously his role as advisor, believes it to be God's design, and feels blessed to be chosen.

Current address: School of Music, University of Michigan, Ann Arbor MI 48109.

REFERENCES

Abdul, Raoul. *Blacks in Classical Music.* New York: Dodd, Mead, 1977.

Amsterdam News, November 4, 1995.

Baker's Biographical Dictionary of Musicians. 8th ed. Revised by Nicholas Slonimsky. New York: G. Schirmer, 1992.

Hitchcock, H. Wiley, ed. *New Grove Dictionary of American Music.* New York: Macmillan, 1986.

"Leading Man at the Met." *Ebony* 21 (January, 1966): 84–91.

"Names, Dates and Places." *Opera News* 41 (December 18, 1976): 7.

Ploski, Harry A., and Williams, James. *The Negro Almanac.* 5th ed. Detroit: Gale Research, 1989.

Roach, Hildred. *Black American Music.* 2nd ed. Malabar, FL: Krieger Publishing Co., 1992.

Secrist, Merle. "Starring George Shirley—Again." *The Washington Post Magazine* (29 July 1979): 10–13.

Shirley, George. "The Black Performer." *Opera News* 35 (January 1971): 6–13.

———. Interview with Darius L. Thieme, February 16, 1998.

———. Letter to Darius L. Thieme, February 16, 1998.

Southern, Eileen. *Biographical Dictionary of Afro–American and African Musicians.* Westport, CT: Greenwood Press, 1982.

———. *The Music of Black Americans.* 3rd ed. New York: Norton, 1997.

Turner, Patricia. "Afro–American Singers." *Black Perspective in Music* 9 (Spring 1981): 73–90.

"Welcome to Tenorland—George Shirley." E–mail from George Shirley to Darius Thieme, February 1998.

Who's Who in America, 1986–87. 44th ed. Chicago: Marquis, 1986.

Darius L. Thieme

Charlie Sifford

(1922–)

Professional Golfer

Although he is a golf champion, it is not his golf game that makes Charlie Sifford notable. It is his 50–year insistence on being a professional golfer that makes him stand out. He refused to accept the segregation of the golf courses, golf associations, and golf tournaments that kept the elitist professional sport all white. As a result of his resistance, Sifford eventually became the first full–fledged black member of the Professional Golf Association and winner of golf tournaments on the PGA Tour across the country. Nonetheless, Sifford was still excluded from some southern PGA tournaments and once had to sue in order to collect a first prize of $100,000 and a new car when he shot a hole–in–one at a match in Los Angeles, California.

Charles Luther Sifford was one of six children of Eliza and Roscoe Sifford of Charlotte, North Carolina. He was born June 2, 1922, and has been married to the former Rose Crumbley since 1947. They are the parents of two sons, Charles Jr. and Craig.

By the time his father insisted that young Charlie Sifford join him working at a Charlotte fertilizer plant, Charlie had already learned that by caddying after school he could earn almost as much in tips on the golf course as his father was bringing home from his full time job at the plant. He and other young black men carried the golf bags of white golfers around the links of the nearby Carolina Country Club in the days before golf carts had wheels or were mechanized. After beginning work at age ten, Sifford quickly earned a reputation as an outstanding caddy who not only carried bags but who also could assist golfers in improving their game. At 13, he was earning $1.50 a day after school caddying two rounds for golfers who would especially seek Sifford out to carry their heavy bags of clubs and balls. He eventually worked at the fertilizer plant with his father for one day, lifting 110–pound bags of manure. He never returned. He went back to the sport of golf.

A Good Caddy

Sifford described his life as a caddy in his autobiography, *Just Let me Play:*

> I was a good caddy because the game was so important to me. I knew everything about the golf course, like where the trouble was, where the bad lies were, which direction to best approach each green, and how each putt would break. I made it a point to know the strengths and weaknesses of the player I was caddying for and to suggest ways that would keep him out of trouble that he couldn't handle.

Golf has been Sifford's passion since he began playing at the Carolina Club on Mondays when the course was closed to members and caddies were allowed to play. When he was 14 he was good enough to shoot a two–under–par 70, winning a caddies' tournament in 1936.

Sifford continued to improve his game, not only by playing against caddies and the golfers for whom he caddied; he also felt that he challenged his game by betting on his matches. He usually won. By age 17, he was better than most of the golfers at the country club.

Eventually Sifford's skills forced him to leave both his job and Charlotte. As an eleventh–grade student, Sifford's golf game was generating complaints among the members of the country club who felt that he was too good a player. The club's management suggested to Sifford that he might be in physical danger on the golf course if he continued to play. He wrote in *Just Let Me Play,* ''For the first time in my life, the white people rose up to try to stop me from playing. It was a situation that I would face my entire career in golf.''

After a racial incident in which Sifford was called a ''nigger'' and responded, he left Charlotte on a bus to live with family in Philadelphia. When his uncle looked at him like he was crazy and, according to his book, asked him who he thought was ''gonna be playin' golf out here in 30–degree weather?'' that Sifford realized that golf and caddying were not the year–round activities in Pennsylvania that they were in North Carolina. In Philadelphia, Sifford eventually played golf on his first public golf course, Cobbs Creek, and worked at a nine–to–five job at the National Biscuit Company. He was drafted into the U.S. Army in 1943 and served in Okinawa, playing on an Army golf team. When he returned to the United States, Sifford married and made up his mind to become a professional golfer. He said in his book, ''I had no teacher, no mentor, and no sponsor, but I had a challenge before me. I knew that it wouldn't be easy, but that was okay. It was the challenge of making it that drove me on.''

Very few black people were able to make a living playing professional golf. Golf courses, country clubs and tournaments were segregated and so was the Professional Golfers Association (PGA). This organization of white men who played golf professionally—for money from sponsors of golf tournaments—had a Caucasians–only rule in its by–laws, a provision which excluded Sifford from membership. In addition, certain matches, Opens and Invitationals were not usually ''open'' to blacks and did not often invite them. Many white golfers had sponsors who would support them financially before they played well enough to win money at tournaments. Sifford never had a sponsor.

These same restrictions had prevented other black professional golfers—Ted Rhodes, Bill Spiller, Zeke Hartsfield,

Howard Wheeler and others—from competing for prize money. For Sifford, golf was possible because his wife was employed, and she and their son lived with her mother in Philadelphia.

At this time, in the early 1950s, there were only three white tournaments that black golfers were allowed to enter: the Los Angeles Open, the Tam O'Shanter in Chicago, and the Canadian Open in Toronto. Thus excluded, black players competed instead in the National Negro Open, a mini–tour for blacks sponsored by the United Golf Association. This competition had limited prize money and was played on inferior municipal courses on weekends, yet it was popular with both men and women golfers including sports and entertainment figures who were attracted to the contests. The National Negro Open was the first time Sifford was surrounded with black people who loved the game as much as he did.

Six–Time Negro Open Winner

Sifford was a six–time winner of the UGA National Professional title, including a streak of five tournament victories in a row between 1952 and 1956. These wins were not, however, enough to provide a living.

Unlike other professional sports, Sifford's paycheck depended on his personal performance on a particular day or series of days. Sifford couldn't win money unless he could play; and he couldn't play unless racial barriers and attitudes were crushed. He needed time to continue to improve his game and the opportunities to play as often as his white competitors, who were admitted to tournaments based on membership in the all–white PGA, on invitations from corporate or club sponsors, or because they had been top money winners in previous contests.

Golf is a solitary game. Golfers are not surrounded by friends to cheer them on during tournaments. When Sifford was allowed to play, the racially tense environments—which included hostile officials and sponsors—threatened to break the intense concentration Sifford needed to play well: to read the ball's position on the golf course, to select the right club, and to execute the necessary stroke.

A great opportunity to improve his game came when Sifford got a job that required him to play golf. Popular singer Billy Eckstine hired Sifford as valet, golf teacher, and golf partner. From the mid–1940s to the mid–1950s, when Eckstine was at the height of his popularity, Sifford toured with the singer in the winter and played golf on the UGA Tour in the summer. Often riding all night to their next engagement, Eckstine's entourage would arrive in a city in the morning. After a few hours sleep, Eckstine and Sifford would play golf early in the day, then prepare for Eckstine's evening performance in the afternoon. This routine allowed Sifford to play golf regularly, and to play at courses made available to Eckstine by local people who wanted to befriend the entertainer. Sifford was able to improve his game, with Eckstine helping Sifford's career by giving him time off, and sometimes entrance fees, to enter tournaments.

Sifford's first professional win was in July of 1951 at the all–black Southern Open, a tournament played at Atlanta's Lincoln Country Club, a nine–hole municipal course that allowed blacks to play. The first prize was $500.

Much of the progress made in integrating professional golf was initiated by well–known black figures in other sports, including Joe Louis, whose prestige helped his voice be heard where others' might not. Louis—even before Eckstine hired Sifford—traveled with his own golf pro, Ted Rhodes. In January of 1952, Joe Louis tested the racial restrictions of the PGA by declaring his intention to play in the San Diego Open, a tournament on the PGA Tour which had never been open to blacks. To make good his threat to play in the San Diego Open, however, it was necessary for Louis to play a qualifying round in Phoenix, Arizona. Louis and three other amateurs joined black pros Sifford, Bill Spiller, and Ted Rhodes. These men were unable to stay in hotels, eat in restaurants in Phoenix, or use the locker room, showers, or snack bar of the Phoenix Country Club, where the tournament was played. "We vowed that if we had to compete to qualify," Sifford wrote in his book, "we'd play our hearts out and force them to enter us in the tournament. They couldn't deny us if we played well on their course."

Split into two groups, they were sent out as the first group to tee off in the morning, only to find the cup at the first hole filled with human feces. This outrage affected Sifford's game to the point that he failed to qualify, as did most of the other blacks. However, it further heightened his determination to confront the Caucasian–only PGA policy that prevented him from playing in the tournaments that could let him demonstrate his golf skills and earn a living as a golfer. In 1955, he earned about $1,500 from the limited tournaments in which he was able to play.

Being able to compete in only a fraction of the important tournaments continued to hamper Sifford's development as a player. He was nearly 40 years old and was still barred from the lucrative and intense golf competition for which, except for race, he was otherwise qualified.

In 1957, after seasons of struggling to keep his head above water, Sifford became the first black man to win a tournament on the PGA Tour when he won $2,000 for his play at the Long Beach Open at the Lakewood Golf Course in California. Sifford called the win "the one that won the home"—the first house he and his wife bought, in Los Angeles. Rose Sifford and Charles Jr. moved to California, allowing the family to be together. Rose got an office job. The rules of segregated golf were so capricious that, in the week following his victory at the Long Beach Open, Sifford was not allowed to enter another PGA tournament. This pattern of playing in some tournaments and being barred from others continued until the early 1960s.

Fights Caucasian–Only PGA Rule

Another athlete, Jackie Robinson, used a 1959 newspaper column to bring Sifford's exclusion from professional golf to even more public attention. Robinson reminded readers that the President of the United States, Dwight D. Eisenhower, well known for his love of golf, was a member of the all–white Augusta National Golf Club. He observed that although Sifford was able to play in many other tournaments in California, he was not invited to play in either the Bing Crosby tournament at Pebble Beach or the Palm Springs Desert Golf Classic. As quoted in Sifford's book, Robinson concluded that golf, known as the sport of gentlemen, ''is the one major sport in America today in which rank and open racial prejudice is allowed to reign supreme . . . [applying] the ungentlemanly and un–American yardstick of race and color in determining who may and may not compete.'' According to Robinson, ''Not only should court action be considered, but I feel the issue is one for a thorough investigation by the Civil Rights Commission.'' Joe Louis's continuing concern for Sifford's exclusion from professional golf was demonstrated when, as Jackie Robinson reported, Louis sent a telegram to Vice President Richard Nixon stating that, with regard to world–wide concern about ''swastikas painted on churches and synagogues . . . similar swastikas are being painted on every green at the Palm Springs course'' in Nixon's home state of California when golfers like Sifford were excluded from that tournament.

The PGA remained unresponsive. Finally, when threatened with action by the California Attorney General, who personally supported Sifford's desire to play professional golf freely in the state of California, the PGA offered Sifford tentative status as an approved player in 1961. He would have to play in 25 tournaments a year for the next five years to become a full–fledged member of the PGA. Even with this concession from the PGA, Sifford was still barred from playing the southern and southwestern PGA–approved tournaments. ''I had paid my $65 dues to the PGA, but that didn't mean I was automatically entered into every tournament,'' he wrote in his book. For example, Sifford's applications to play in New Orleans, Puerto Rico, Pensacola, St. Petersburg, Palm Beach and Wilmington, North Carolina, were turned down.

Sifford's first PGA tournament in the South was in North Carolina in 1961 at the Greensboro Open, played at the Sedgefield Country Club, where he finished a impressive fourth and won $1,300, despite anonymous late night phone threats daring him to play, and despite being followed around the course on the first round of play by drunken whites who taunted Sifford with profanity and racial insults. Following the Greensboro tournament, Sifford was again denied entry into several PGA events. Nonetheless, by playing well when he was allowed to compete, Sifford finished in the top 20 in nearly every tournament and managed to stay in the top 60 money winners for the year. This record permitted his temporary PGA card to be renewed for a year.

Sifford remained approved—by being among the top 60 money winners on the PGA Tour for the five years the PGA required before granting him a Class A PGA membership in 1964. In fact, Sifford was in the top 60 from 1960 to 1974. Though some events in the South were still closed to him, Sifford did well, winning the Puerto Rican Open in 1964 and the Hartford Open in 1967. However, it was his 1969 first place finish in the famed Los Angeles Open that marked the first major victory by a black golfer in a PGA event.

By the late 1960s and early 1970s, the age of entering golfers was dropping and their backgrounds had changed significantly. They were now coming to the professional ranks after playing in college, already groomed for a professional career. In contrast, blacks seldom had those opportunities and Sifford, for example, who got his start as a black caddy, was nearly 50 years old when PGA tournaments opened up for him. Even these good times were, according to Sifford, short–lived. In his autobiography, Sifford observed, ''A scant six years after I had been on top of the golf world by winning the L.A. Open, I was out of the game. My total tour earnings were $341,345 for a lifetime of work.''

When the PGA Seniors competition for older golfers began, Sifford actively competed, winning the PGA Seniors Championship in 1975 and the Suntree Classic in 1980. His career earnings on the PGA Senior Tour totaled $800,000.

Golf continued to find ways to treat Sifford and the few other black PGA golfers—Lee Elder and Calvin Peete—differently from white golfers. The most prestigious tournaments—the Masters, the Ryder Cup, and the Legends of Golf—continued to be all–white. Also, unlike white players whose records were not as good, Sifford was unable to make money from endorsements. For example, Sifford began smoking a cigar when he was 12 years old, and always played golf with a cigar stuffed in the corner of his mouth. He was known for the cigar, but no cigar manufacturer ever offered him an opportunity to do an endorsement. Nor did he get offers to do advertisements or to do commentary on golf broadcasts. He was not offered the chance to get paid to appear at corporate annual golf outings. In fact, at a tournament in Los Angeles in 1986, after shooting a hole–in–one, Sifford had to sue and win a jury verdict in order to collect the hastily–withdrawn prizes—a new Buick Riviera and $100,000. It was Sifford's largest single paycheck.

Reaching the end of his active golfing career, and after considerable searching for work, the Siffords moved to Cleveland, Ohio, where both Charlie and Rose worked at the Sleepy Hollow Country Club. ''Up to then, no blacks had ever been allowed near the place,'' he wrote in his book. They worked without salary; instead, they made money by running the golf shop that sold golf paraphernalia and lessons, and rented golf carts. With his wife's help, Sifford was able to keep the long hours required of the job as well as play a few tournaments.

Although he was the first black person to win membership in the PGA, Sifford rejected the label, ''The Jackie Robinson of Golf.'' He wrote in his autobiography, ''If I was the Jackie Robinson of Golf, I sure didn't do a very good job of it. . . . Jackie was followed by hundreds of great, black ballplayers who have transformed their sport. . . . But there are hardly any black kids coming up through the ranks of golf today.'' Despite Sifford's pessimism about the future for blacks in golf, it is clear that his example forced American attention to be focused on the bastion of segregation that golf has been. His victories over discrimination in golf and his ''just let us play'' attitude inspired thousands of black golfers who loved the game and who had been excluded from full participation.

In 1988, the Siffords left Ohio for a suburb of Houston, Texas, where Charlie is a member of the Deerwood Country Club. He continues to play golf.

Current address: Charlie Sifford, c/o Professional Golf Association, Box 109601, 100 Avenue of Champions, Palm Beach Gardens, Florida 33418.

REFERENCES

Ashe, Arthur R. Jr. *A Hard Road to Glory, A History of the African–American Athlete Since 1946,* New York: Warner Books, 1988.

''Charlie Sifford Breaks PGA Race Barrier, Professional Golf Association.'' *Pittsburgh Courier,* April 19, 1960.

Contemporary Black Biography. Vol. 4. Detroit: Gale Research, 1992.

''Negro, Charlie Sifford Wins Long Beach Open.'' *Norfolk Journal and Guide,* November 16, 1957.

Sifford, Charlie, with James Gallo, *Just Let Me Play, The Story of Charlie Sifford, the First Black PGA Golfer.* Latham, NY: British American Publishing, 1992.

Martia Graham Goodson

William J. Simmons
(1849–1890)
Religious worker, educator, journalist, college president, writer

William J. Simmons

William J. Simmons accomplished much in his brief life. He spent most of his childhood in dire poverty as a fugitive slave. Through great efforts he achieved a college education and became an educator and a Baptist minister. As an educator he had great impact on black education in Kentucky. As a minister he created a large national organization of black Baptists. A noted writer and newspaper and magazine editor, Simmons's greatest editorial achievement was as editor and author of a valuable collection of biographies.

William J. Simmons was born to slave parents Edward and Esther Simmons on June 29, 1849, in Charleston, South Carolina. While he was young, his mother escaped to Philadelphia with three small children: William, Emeline, and Anna. Although an uncle, Alexander Tardiff, a shoemaker, cared for the fugitives as best he could, the family suffered from poverty and constant threats to their newfound freedom. At one time, Esther and her children were sick with smallpox in the back room of a garret while Tardiff faced questioning by slavehunters in his workshop's front room.

Tardiff went to sea for two years, while Esther Simmons worked as a washerwoman in Roxbury, Pennsylvania. Upon Tardiff's return, they moved to Chester where slave catchers soon appeared, and mother and children had to hide in Philadelphia again. Tardiff then found a job as a shoemaker in Bordertown, New Jersey. The family continued to live in dire poverty. The children did not go out to work, nor did they attend public school. Tardiff, who had been educated in Charleston under Daniel A. Payne, provided Simmons with instruction.

In 1862 Simmons was apprenticed to a Bordertown dentist, Leo H. DeLange. Soon Simmons could handle much of the routine work himself. He tried to enter a dental school in Philadelphia but was rejected because of his race. On September 16, 1864, Simmons ran away and joined the army. He witnessed the final stages of the Civil War in Virginia and was discharged on September 13, 1865. For the next two years he worked as an assistant to an African American dentist in Philadelphia and then went back to Bordertown.

In Bordertown in 1867 Simmons became a Christian and joined the white Baptist church there, becoming the only black member. When he felt called to the ministry, the church paid his expenses for three years of education. In September 1868 he entered the northern university of Madison (now Colgate) and then transferred to Rochester. Eyestrain, brought on by studying Greek, caused him to stay out of school for two years. In 1871 Simmons entered Howard University, graduating with an A.B. degree in 1873. During his senior year, he walked seven miles a day to teach school, drilled the Cadet Company for an hour in the late afternoon, and attended classes at night. Simmons graduated as salutatorian of his class, and managed to save $300. His abilities as a teacher had led to his appointment as principal of one of the schools where he taught, Hillsdale Public in Washington, D.C., before his graduation.

After his graduation in 1873, Simmons went to Arkansas and secured a teaching certificate but returned to teach at Hillsdale for the school year. On August 25, 1874, Simmons married Josephine A. Silence of Washington. This marriage produced seven children: Josephine Lavinia, William Johnson, Maud Marie, Amanda Moss, Mary Beatrice, John Thomas, and Gussie Lewis.

Simmons then moved to Florida in September. There he invested in land and oranges. These efforts were not rewarding, so Simmons became principal of Howard Academy, a county official, and chairman of the Republican county campaign commission. He was ordained a deacon and licensed to preach in 1879. He pastored a small church and was ordained the night before he left Florida.

Heads Louisville School

Simmons returned to Washington in 1879 to teach but left later that year to become pastor of First Baptist Church of Lexington, Kentucky. Then in September 1880, he became president of the Normal and Theological School in Louisville, an institution sponsored by the General Association of Colored Baptists in Kentucky. The school was in dire condition: it had two teachers, thirteen students, and no money. He built up the institution, which was renamed State University in 1883 and, after Simmons's death, Simmons University. By 1891 the school had 250 students and half of the faculty had college degrees. The college department remained small, around 20, graduating two or three students a year.

The school did not absorb all of his energy, however. On September 29, 1882, Simmons became editor of the *American Baptist,* a Louisville–based newspaper. His efforts for this paper were recognized in 1886 when Simmons was elected president of the Colored Press Association. He widened his editorial efforts in 1888 by founding a magazine, *Our Women and Children,* which used the talents of many able women as subeditors and authors. Simmons's most enduring effort as an editor and writer came in 1887 with *Men of Mark,* a volume of biographical sketches.

Simmons was also involved in many organizations, secular and religious. In 1883 Simmons convened and organized the Baptist Women's Educational Convention of Kentucky, which did much to support State University. In 1886 Simmons summoned the meeting in Saint Louis, which organized the American National Baptist Convention, of which he became the first president, serving until 1890. Besides organizational skills, Simmons had great abilities as a speaker and was often asked to address conventions and schools, appearing before both black and white audiences.

In 1885 a meeting of the black teachers of Kentucky drew up a list of various grievances. Simmons was made chairman of a committee of 20 to present the petition to the state legislature. He made a strong presentation to the legislature's Joint Committee on Grievances and Propositions. One result of this protest was the state's foundation of a state normal school for blacks.

In 1890 Simmons suddenly resigned from State University to found Eckstein Norton Institute, an industrial training school, at Cane Springs in Bullit County, Kentucky. He took with him some of the top teachers from State, including Charles H. Parrish, Mary V. Cook (later to marry Parrish), and Ione E. Woods. Simmons fell ill in May 1890 and died at Cane Springs on October 30 of complications related to heart disease. His funeral was held in Louisville on November 3 with interment at Cane Springs the following day.

Simmons's untimely death marked the end of an active and productive life. In a short time, Simmons had made his mark as a religious leader, an educator, editor, and writer.

REFERENCES

Hartshorn, William Newton, ed. *An Era of Progress and Promise, 1863–1910.* Boston: Priscilla Publishing Co., 1910.

Logan, Rayford W., and Michael R. Winston. *Dictionary of American Negro Biography.* New York: Norton, 1982.

Lucas, Marion B. *A History of Blacks in Kentucky.* 2 vols. n.p.: Kentucky Historical Society, 1992.

Parrish, Charles. *Golden Jubilee of the General Association of Colored Baptists in Kentucky.* Louisville: Mayes Printing Co., 1915.

Simmons, William J. *Men of Mark.* Cleveland: Geo. M. Rewell, 1887.

Robert L. Johns

Henry Proctor Slaughter (1871–1958)

Publisher, organization official

Henry Proctor Slaughter, a career employee of the Government Printing Office, is noted for developing one of the best and largest collections of materials by and about African Americans. Slaughter was born to Sarah Jane Smith and Charles Henry Slaughter in Louisville, Kentucky, on September 17, 1871. After his father's death when Slaughter was six–years old, he hawked newspapers to help provide for his widowed mother and his brother and sister. This was the beginning of Slaughter's lifelong interest with the written word.

Slaughter graduated salutatorian of his class at Central High School in Louisville. After graduation, he became an apprentice printer for the Champion Publishing Company which put out the *Louisville Champion* newspaper. He was promoted several times and by 1894 he was foreman of Champion Publishing and manager of the *Lexington Kentucky Standard.* According to an article in the *Colored American,* Slaughter was characterized as making ''logical speeches, having a trenchant pen and strong hand at the helm of the Standard.'' While at Champion, he worked with Horace Morris, the grandmaster of the Kentucky chapter of the Prince Hall Masons, a black fraternal organization. His association with Morris probably influenced his later involvement with fraternal organizations.

Slaughter attended Livingstone College in Salisbury, North Carolina, founded in 1879 by the African Methodist Episcopal Zion (AMEZ) church. To help support himself, he taught a class in printing at the college and worked as manager and foreman of the AMEZ Publishing House. George W. Clinton, editor of the *Star of Zion,* the official organ of the AMEZ church, recognized Slaughter's excellent editorial and managerial skills.

In 1896 Slaughter moved to Washington, D.C., where he was the first African American to take the examination for the position of compositor at the Government Printing Office (GPO). He was initially appointed to the Agricultural Division and remained with the GPO in various capacities until his retirement in 1937. Some of the positions he held included proofreader, monotypist, linotypist, compositor, and machinist.

Throughout his career, Slaughter was actively involved in fraternal, professional, and political organizations. He was very active in the Odd Fellows and was continuously elected to serve on the board of directors of the Odd Fellows Hall Association in Washington, D.C. He also edited the *Odd Fellows Journal* from 1910 until it ceased publication in 1937. He achieved thirty–third–degree status in the Prince Hall Masons. He was a member of the GPO Typographical Union, whose membership included only 20 African Americans out of about 1,600 total members. Well respected by both blacks and whites, Slaughter was the only black elected to chair the ''Chapel,'' a section of the union. A longtime Republican, Slaughter served on inaugural committees for presidents William McKinley, Theodore Roosevelt, William Howard Taft, and Woodrow Wilson. In addition, he was secretary of the Kentucky Republican Club in Washington.

Slaughter was also committed to the idea of lifelong learning. Although he never practiced, he earned both a bachelor's and master's degree from Howard University's School of Law while working at the GPO. He was a member of the American Negro Academy which was founded by Alexander Crummell in 1897 to promote literature, science, and art and to foster higher education. He was also a member of the Mu–So–Lit Club, the Labor Day Bunch, and the Pen and Pencil Club. Slaughter greatly enjoyed his participation in these various organizations and was known as a liberal host, often preparing elaborate meals for his organizations' meetings.

Slaughter also remained an active journalist throughout his career. He was staff correspondent for the *Lexington Kentucky Standard* in Louisville, and contributed articles to the *Philadelphia Tribune,* the *American Baptist,* and the *A.M.E. Church Review.*

Slaughter, above all else, was a collector. He concentrated on collecting books, pamphlets, music, photographs, prints, and manuscripts relating to the history of black life and culture and spent a small fortune in his forty years of collecting. He was known for his success as a black bibliophile and for his expertise on black subjects. At one time his library numbered more than 10,000 volumes. In addition to books, Slaughter maintained a file of 100,000 newspaper clippings and 3,000 pamphlets on the history of race relations and slavery. According to Clarence A. Bacote, Slaughter owned by 1945 one of the best and largest libraries of materials by and about blacks.

Slaughter, who lived at 1264 Columbia Road in Washington, D.C., filled three floors and a basement of his Washington, D.C., townhouse with books, many of which he acquired from a friend. He also purchased many volumes from English booksellers, retaining the sales slips to document their cost. He filled the tops of dressers and small bookcases in all his bedrooms with rare books, then built bookstacks on the top floor to house his books on slavery and the Civil War, which he had cataloged. Some of his books had fine bindings, among them an early edition of the poet Phillis Wheatley.

Through his membership in the American Negro Academy, Slaughter associated with other collectors of black works and in 1915 helped to organize the Negro Book Collectors Exchange for the purpose of centralizing all literature written by people of color.

In 1946 Slaughter made the decision to sell his collection because of the safety hazards imposed by its physical size. Two universities attempted to purchase it but Slaughter, who was perhaps influenced by his friendship with Rufus E. Clement, then president of Atlanta University, sold it to the university for $25,000. Slaughter knew the school would provide the proper care for the collection and would be accessible to scholars as well.

Slaughter had married twice. On April 27, 1904, he married Ella M. Russell of Jonesboro, Tennessee. After she died on November 2, 1914, he married Alma R. Level of Chicago on November 24, 1925. The marriage ended in divorce.

Slaughter died in Washington, D.C., on February 14, 1958, after a brief illness. His body was cremated on February 18. He was survived by a sister, Ida S. Gray of Louisville, and three nephews.

During his lifetime Slaughter associated with people of all races. Trustworthy, diplomatic, and friendly, his friends included bishops, ministers, political figures, scholars, and bibliophiles. His love for books and the written word was manifest in all his work, but most importantly in his building of the nation's finest private collections of books on Negroana.

REFERENCES

Bacote, Clarence A. *The Story of Atlanta University: A Century of Service.* Princeton, NJ: Princeton University Press, 1969.

Josey, E. J., and Ann Allen Shockley, eds. *Handbook of Black Librarianship.* Littleton, CO: Libraries Unlimited, 1977.

"Kentucky Leader." *Colored American* 10 (May 10, 1902): 1, 4.

Logan, Rayford W., and Michael R. Winston, eds. *Dictionary of American Negro Biography.* New York: Norton, 1982.

Mather, Frank Lincoln, ed. *Who's Who of the Colored Race.* Chicago: Mather, 1915.

Sinnette, Elinor Des Verney, W. Paul Coates, and Thomas C. Battle, eds. *Black Bibliophiles and Collectors.* Washington, DC: Howard University Press, 1990.

COLLECTIONS

The Slaughter collection is housed at the Atlanta University Center, Robert W. Woodruff Library.

Casper L. Jordan

Moneta J. Sleet Jr.

(1926–1996)

Photojournalist

In 1969 Moneta J. Sleet Jr. became the first African American male and the first African American photographer to win a Pulitzer Prize. He served as staff photographer for the Johnson Publishing Company for over four decades, covering some of the most important events of twentieth-century history. Sleet's Pulitzer Prize–winning photographic portrait of Coretta Scott King and her youngest child, Bernice, was taken during Martin Luther King Jr.'s funeral. In one split second Sleet captured what words could never adequately express. Whether he was creating images of celebrities or the largely anonymous, all were "photographed with the care and sensitivity that are Moneta Sleet trademarks," in the words of an *Ebony* article of January 1987.

Sleet was born in Owensboro, Kentucky, to Moneta J. and Ozetta L. Sleet on Valentine's Day in 1926. When he was quite young his parents gave him a box camera, and his love for photography began at that moment. He was the official photographer in high school and at Kentucky State College (now University) where he received a B.A. degree in business administration in 1947. Before graduating, he served in the U.S. Army during World War II and earned the rank of staff sergeant.

In 1948 Sleet was hired to teach and set up a photography department at Maryland State College (now the University of Maryland, Eastern Shore). In 1949 he moved to New York City to pursue graduate studies in photography and journalism. He supported himself as a sportswriter for the *Amsterdam News* and as a photographer for *Our World* while attending the School of Modern Photography and Columbia University. He earned a master's degree in journalism from New York University in 1950. In 1955 *Our World* ceased publication, and Sleet was hired as staff photographer for the Johnson Publishing Company. For more than 40 years, readers of *Jet* and *Ebony* magazines had access to a privileged view of the black experience because of the photojournalistic efforts of Sleet and his cohorts.

Sleet extended his visual insight beyond the United States. His assignments took him to Africa, Europe, and South America. He captured the moment in history when several African nations gained their independence and was always in the forefront of the Civil Rights Movement in America's Deep South. Some of his most memorable works were taken at the 1963 March on Washington, the 1965 Selma to Montgomery March, and the 1963 Independence Day celebrations in Nairobi, Kenya. Sleet also accompanied Martin Luther King Jr. to Norway for his acceptance of the Nobel Peace Prize. Former heads of state photographed by Sleet include Emperor Haile Selassie of Ethiopia, Prime Minister Kwame Nkrumah of Ghana, President William Tubman of Liberia, and Prime Minister Jomo Kenyatta of Kenya. His signature moment came at King's funeral in Atlanta in 1968, when he photographed Coretta Scott King and daughter Bernice grieving. The work brought him worldwide recognition. In addition to photographs of the powerful and famous, Sleet also captured the likenesses of countless unnamed citizens all across America.

In 1971 Sleet and Gwendolyn Brooks, a poet and fellow Pulitzer Prize winner, returned to Montgomery, Alabama, where Rosa Parks's refusal to move to the back of the segregated bus had sparked the Civil Rights Movement of the 1950s and 1960s. Sleet's photographs complemented Brooks's original text, "In Montgomery." In addition to taking photographs of Alabama flags and civil rights sites, Sleet also included everyday scenes depicting ordinary citizens living ordinary lives at Dexter Avenue Baptist Church; the Midtown Holiday Inn, where blacks and whites swam together; the State Senate Chambers, where the first black page proudly stood at attention; and in the office of E. D. Nixon, the unsung hero of the Montgomery Bus Strike.

Paying the Price

Forty years of experience as a professional photographer exacted a heavy price for Sleet. In an *Ebony* interview in January 1987, Sleet said, "It's not an easy life, so it's important to have a family who understands. I have been very fortunate." His family consists of his wife of nearly 50 years, Juanita Harris Sleet, and his two sons and a daughter, Gregory, Michael, and Lisa.

Sleet paid a price for working solely for black publications. The white media has always overshadowed or ignored the efforts of black journalists and photographers. The great majority of Sleet's photographs could never have been eligible for a Pulitzer since magazines cannot submit entries for the prize. His famous King funeral photograph happened to be shot for the funeral press pool and reproduced by wire services for use in papers all over the world, making his nomination possible.

In his career Sleet faced another dilemma. As a black man, his travels with Martin Luther King Jr. and to civil rights events caused him to be less than totally objective in his pursuit of photojournalistic truth. According to *Contemporary Black Biography,* when questioned about the compassion and sensitivity readily evident in the King funeral photograph, he responded:

> I must say that I wasn't there [at the major civil rights demonstrations] as an objective reporter. To be perfectly honest I had something to say or at least hoped that I did, and was trying to show one side of it—because we didn't have any problem finding the other side. So I was emotionally involved. That may not be a good school of journalism, but that's the way I felt.

There was certainly no question of total objectivity whenever Sleet photographed King and his family. In 1956 he took one of the earliest family photographs when Yolanda King, the oldest child, was a baby held in her mother's arms as the family posed on the steps of Dexter Avenue Baptist Church in Montgomery. His close association with King resulted in one of the largest collections of King's photographs ever made. This is in addition to coverage of the Civil Rights Movement where he photographed King in more professional settings. In all of his work, Sleet aimed to be sensitive to the reality of the moment.

The first exhibition of his work was a 1970 one–man show sponsored by the Alpha Kappa Alpha Sorority in the City Art Museum of St. Louis, Missouri, and in the Detroit Public Library. Sleet's second exhibition took place 16 years later and was cosponsored by the Johnson Publication and the Phillip Morris Companies. It opened at the New York Public Library. The initial two–year run in four cities was expanded due to requests for bookings in additional cities. The 125–photograph retrospective included the best of the King family photographs as well as those of world–renowned figures in politics, world affairs, and show business. Other exhibitions have been held in the Black History Museum in Hempstead, New York, the Studio Museum in Harlem, and the Metropolitan Museum of Art. In 1983 an exhibition of his work was mounted at major museums and included photographs of such greats as Muhammed Ali, Haile Selasie, Stevie Wonder, Jomo Kenyatta, and Billie Holiday.

Besides the 1969 Pulitzer Prize, Sleet received the following awards and honors: Citation for Excellence, Overseas Press Club of America, 1957; photojournalism awards, National Association of Black Journalists, and commendation from the National Urban League, both in 1978; and induction into the Kentucky Journalism Hall of Fame at the University of Kentucky, in 1989. Sleet was a member of the NAACP and the Black Academy of Arts and Letters.

After working on assignment for *Ebony* magazine at the 1996 Olympics in Atlanta, he returned to his home in Baldwin, N.Y. and was diagnosed with cancer. He died on Monday, August 31, at Columbia–Presbyterian Medical Center when he was 70–years old. In addition to his wife and children, he is survived by three grandchildren and one sister, Emmy Lou Wilson of Detroit. His funeral was held at the Unity Church of Christianity in Long Island, New York's Valley Stream community. He was buried at Calverton National Cemetery, Calverton, Long Island. Lerone Bennett, who had worked with Sleet for 41 years, told *Jet* that Sleet was "a major witness, perhaps the greatness witness of our greatest 50 years. . . . He was there, he had a camera and an eye, and he saw it all. . . . And in the end, the witness became the subject, and the picture–taker became a picture and a promise and a truth."

Sleet was a perpetual optimist known for his gentle nature and engaging personality. He was able to make others smile when they preferred otherwise. Until his death, he continued to photograph for the Johnson Publication Company, reflecting the sensitivity and care for which his work has become known. In 1996 the *New York Times* capsuled his career by saying that he "brought his camera to a revolution and ended up capturing many of the images that defined the struggle for racial equality in the United States and Africa."

REFERENCES

"Backstage." *Ebony* 51 (January 1996): 21.

Brooks, Gwendolyn, and Moneta Sleet. "In Montgomery: Pulitzer Prize–Winning Poet, Photographer View City Famed in Civil Rights Flight." *Ebony* 26 (August 1971): 42–48.

"Communications." *Jet* 89 (29 April 1996): 24.

Contemporary Black Biography. Vol. 5. Detroit: Gale Research, 1994.

Ebony Pictorial History of Black America. Vol. 3. *The Civil Rights Movement to Black Revolution.* Nashville: The Southwestern Company, 1971.

Ebony Success Library. Vol. 1. *1,000 Successful Blacks.* Nashville: The Southwestern Company, 1973.

"Image Maker: The Artistry of Moneta Sleet, Jr." *Ebony* 62 (January 1987): 66–68.

"Moneta J. Sleet, Jr., Pulitzer Prize–Winning Photographer, Eulogized in New York." *Jet* 90 (21 October 1996): 12–18.

"Moneta Sleet, Jr., 70, First Black to Receive Pulitzer." *New York Times,* October 2, 1996.

Tweedle, John. *A Lasting Impression: A Collection of Photographs of Martin Luther King, Jr.* Columbia: University of South Carolina Press, 1983.

Who's Who among African Americans, 1996–97. 9th ed. Detroit: Gale Research, 1996.

Dolores Nicholson

Robert Smalls
(1839–1916)
Naval hero, congressman

"Oh Lord, we entrust ourselves into thy hands. Like thou didst for the Israelites in Egypt, Please stand over us to our promised land of freedom.'' Quoted in *Crisis* magazine, this was the prayer uttered by Robert Smalls as he made a bold and heroic escape to freedom during the Civil War. Smalls was an enslaved man who took his dream of freedom and turned it into reality by commandeering the Confederate steamer, *The Planter,* and sailing the vessel to Union forces and freedom. He would go from slave to naval captain, state legislator, and U.S. Congressman.

Robert Smalls was born on April 5, 1839, in the McKee family slave quarters in Beaufort, South Carolina. His mother, Lydia Smalls, was born a slave on the Ashdale Plantation and was brought to John McKee's home as a house servant to take care of his five children. Here Lydia Smalls was given adequate food and clothing. She was treated well, but she never mistook kindness for freedom.

Robert Smalls's father is unknown. It is said that his father could be one of two men, either Moses Goldsmith, a merchant in Charleston, or most probably, according to the Smalls family, John McKee, her master. It is clear that Robert Smalls's father was a man of European descent.

Smalls was raised in the McKee house on Prince Street and was well liked by John McKee and his family. Henry McKee, John's son, inherited Robert and Lydia Smalls upon John McKee's death in 1848, and Robert was Henry's favorite servant. Some of Robert Smalls's duties were tending McKee's horses, rowing his boat on outings, and carrying his bow on archery expeditions.

Although mother and son were treated kindly, Lydia Smalls did not want him to forget that a slave was still a slave. Historians believe that Lydia Smalls forced young Robert to watch slaves being beaten in the front yard of Beaufort jail. She made him watch slave auctions as well. She wanted her son to understand the fate of African Americans within the system of slavery.

In 1851 Henry McKee bought CobCall Plantation near Charleston and took Robert Smalls to live there. Smalls made an arrangement to hire himself out, agreeing to pay McKee a set price of $15 a month. On December 24, 1858, Smalls, at only 17, married his first wife, Hannah Jones, a slave of Samuel Kingman. Jones was 14 years older and worked as a hotel maid. Smalls made an arrangement with his wife's master to purchase her time for seven dollars a month and also to purchase freedom for his wife and child at a price of $800 for both. Their first child, Elizabeth Lydia Smalls, was born on February 12, 1858.

In Charleston Smalls did everything from working at the Planter's Hotel to working as a lamplighter for the city of Charleston. He also worked for a Charleston rigger, John Simmons, for one year. Smalls gained invaluable knowledge about sailing and sailmaking and during that year became a superior sailor.

Robert Smalls

Smalls already knew the harbors and waterways of South Carolina and Georgia seacoasts better than most seamen. By the time the Civil War came, he had pored over many maps and charts of the waterways, mastering them in order to maneuver after the onset of the war. He made extra money transporting goods by boat, but it was his expert sailing skills and knowledge of the waterways that would aid him in his journey for freedom.

In 1861 John Ferguson employed Smalls on the cotton steamer, *The Planter.* He made $16 a month, $15 of which would go to Henry McKee. Smalls supplemented his income by engaging in trade on the side. *The Planter* was approximately 150 feet long and could hold up to 1400 bales of cotton. During the war the ship was under the command of Brigadier General Roswell S. Ripley commanding second military district of South Carolina. The Confederate government chartered the steamer, and it was converted into a special dispatch boat for Ripley.

Seeks Freedom

Smalls and his black crewmen met late at night at Robert Smalls's house to talk about how to hijack *The Planter* and sail their way to freedom. They discussed different options, but it was ultimately decided that Smalls would plan the escape because he had the best knowledge of the waterways.

The crew promised to obey him and be ready at a moment's notice.

That day came on May 12, 1862. The white crew of *The Planter* entrusted the steamer to their black slaves, while they went into town on an unauthorized leave. Among the white crew members who left were: the captain, C. J. Relyea; the chief engineer Zerich Pitcher; and mate Samuel Smith. Once the white crew members went on shore, Smalls jumped into action. Smalls alerted his black crew: two engineers, John Smalls (no relation) and Alfred Gradine, as well as Abraham Jackson, Gabriel Turno, William Morrison, Samuel Chisolm, Abraham Allston, and David Jones. The crew then collected Robert Smalls's wife and child, along with four other women and two other children. At approximately 3:00 a.m. Smalls and his crew stole *The Planter* from the dock in front of the home and office of Brigadier General Ripley. Robert Smalls knew all the signals necessary to fool the Confederates. His biggest obstacle was passing Fort Sumter.

Smalls uttered a prayer as they were approaching Fort Sumter; otherwise there was complete silence. Smalls and his crew were afraid a Confederate Army officer at the fort would question the early departure of *The Planter,* but no one did. *The Planter* continued on until it was out of firing range of the harbor forts. As they moved upstream, they ran up the white surrender flag and sailed toward the United States Navy fleet.

Smalls sailed toward the closest ship, the *U.S.S. Onward.* Captain Nicholas of the *Onward* sent his crew to *The Planter* and ordered them to bring the officers of the vessel to him. Robert Smalls told Captain Nicholas of his ordeal with slavery, his willingness to serve for the Union Navy, and his desire to be free. In order to check out his story, and to verify this was not a Confederate trick of some kind, Nicholas ordered his men to search *The Planter.* All the captain's crew found were the five women and three children aboard the vessel.

Although the story seemed incredible to Captain Nicholas, he referred Smalls to Admiral Du Pont. On May 13, 1862, Robert Smalls told his story and delivered his cargo of Confederate artillery to Admiral Du Pont and the federal authorities. Du Pont thought very highly of Smalls and his act of heroism.

Smalls, once an obscure slave, was now attracting national attention. His story was a blow to the Confederacy's morale and an encouragement for the Union. Smalls was appointed a pilot in the United States Navy and assigned to *The Planter.* He was invaluable to the navy because he was familiar with the channels and bays of South Carolina, Georgia, and Florida.

Smalls could not be enlisted directly into the Federal Navy because, according to some sources, enlisted men had to be graduates of naval school. He was commissioned as a second lieutenant, Company B, 33rd Regiment, U.S. Colored Troops. He engaged in 17 battles during the Civil War; one of the most famous was in December of 1863. *The Planter* sailed through the Stono River, near Folly Creek in South Carolina and was fired upon by the Confederates. The white commanding officer, Captain Nickerson, panicked and hid in the coal bunker of the ship. Smalls took control of the ship and brought the vessel out of firing range and back to port.

Smalls received a promotion due to his heroism at Folly Creek. He was the first and only African American during the Civil War to hold the title of captain in the U.S. Navy. Smalls's second daughter, Sarah Voorhees, was born on December 1, 1863, about the time Smalls received his promotion. Smalls was also named the commanding officer of *The Planter* until he was discharged from service on June 11, 1865. The demobilization of *The Planter* and the end of the Civil War ended Smalls's service to the United States Navy.

In 1866 Robert Smalls and his crew finally received their prize money. Smalls received an award of $1500 and the rest of the crew received $500 each. Normal awards during war were half of the appraised value of the ship which the Navy set at $15,000. In actuality the value of the ship was nearer $75,000.

Smalls would give an additional 25 years of service to his state and his country, this time in the political arena. His political career started prior to his leaving the U.S. Navy. In 1864 Smalls, who had become one of the most prominent men in South Carolina, moved back to Beaufort and was sent as a delegate to the Republican National Convention. He was also committed to aiding African American advancement during the Reconstruction Era. In 1867 he purchased a two–story building in Beaufort to serve as a school for African American children. Since he felt education was the key to his race's advancement, it became one of Smalls's greatest crusades.

Smalls himself had a limited education. What reading and writing skills he had, he acquired after the Civil War with the help of a schoolteacher named Miss Cooley. He spent nine months studying many hours a day to learn basic skills.

Becomes U.S. Congressman

During the Reconstruction Era, Smalls continued to be one of the most celebrated African Americans in South Carolina. In 1866 he became a delegate to the South Carolina state Constitutional Convention. He was instrumental in pushing a section of the state constitution that would include mandatory education for all of South Carolina's children.

Smalls was elected a Republican member of the state house of representatives in 1868 and served until 1870. He was then elected to the state senate for an additional four years. In addition to his service to the state government, he kept up with his military interests. Smalls held the commands of lieutenant colonel, brigadier general, and major general in the South Carolina State Militia. His service to the militia ended in 1877, when the Democrats took power in the state government.

In 1875 Smalls left the state senate to accept a seat in the U.S. House of Representatives. During his time in office, Smalls continued to represent his constituency to the best of his ability. Some of his biggest concerns were securing funds for the restoration of the Beaufort library, the redistribution of confiscated lands held by the government to South Carolina constituents, and the promotion of measures to construct telegraph lines in South Carolina. The time that Smalls and his African American contemporaries spent trying to secure basic human rights for African American people left them little opportunity to initiate innovative legislation.

North Carolina Congressman James E. O'Hara sought to push through a measure in Congress that would adequately compensate Smalls and his crew for capturing *The Planter.* He also made a motion to finally have Smalls's name placed on the retired navy list with the rank of captain. Both measures were blocked.

Smalls lost his congressional seat from 1880 to 1881. After his defeat in 1880, he contested the results, and won back his seat in 1881. He was in the House of Representatives until 1887, serving during the 44th, 45th, 47th, 48th, and 49th Congresses. Smalls lost his wife Hannah in 1883, after the close of the 47th session of Congress. The cause of death was unrecorded. In 1890 Smalls married Annie Elizabeth Wiggs, a 34–year–old schoolteacher. She died only five years later in 1895. They had one son, William Robert, born in 1892. Smalls ended his career by becoming a customs collector, but he also worked actively with the Republican Party in South Carolina. His last public service occupation was collector of Beaufort, an appointment he received from President William McKinley. He held that post until Smalls died at 1:30 a.m. on February 23, 1915, in his Prince Street home, formerly belonging to Henry McKee, which he purchased during the Reconstruction Era. He had suffered from failing health for over two years, with malaria, rheumatism, and diabetes. Smalls was survived by his three children, Elizabeth Lydia, Sarah Voorhees, and William Robert.

Although Smalls has never received the acclaim that his contemporaries Booker T. Washington and Frederick Douglass achieved, his accomplishments are still worthy of recognition and celebration. He was indeed small in stature but great in terms of his contributions to South Carolina and American history.

REFERENCES

Miller, Edward A. *Gullah Statesman: Robert Smalls from Slavery to Congress, 1839–1915.* Columbia: University of South Carolina Press, 1995.

Rosbrow, James M. ''The Abduction of the Planter.'' *Crisis* 56 (April 1949): 106–107.

Taylor, Alrutheus A. ''Negro Congressman a Generation After.'' *Journal of Negro History* 7 (April 1922): 127–77.

Uya, Okon Edet. *From Slavery to Public Service: Robert Smalls, 1839–1915.* New York: Oxford University Press, 1971.

Ingrid Irene Sabio

James McCune Smith (1813–1865)

Physician, abolitionist, journalist

James McCune Smith was the first African American to earn a medical degree. He established his practice in New York City, where he was a prominent civic leader and abolitionist. In conjunction with his medical practice, he established what may be the first pharmacy run by a black American. He was also a noted speaker and writer. As a journalist, he briefly edited the *Colored American,* wrote a column for Frederick Douglass's paper, and edited the *Weekly Anglo–African.*

Smith was born on April 18, 1813, in New York City. One account asserted that both his parents were fugitive slaves from Charleston, South Carolina. Another claimed that his mother was freed so that she could testify in a trial. They were of mixed descent, and their son was light complexioned. The father, Samuel, was a merchant in New York. Smith was educated at the African Free School, where at the age of 11 he was selected to deliver an address on the occasion of a visit to the school by Lafayette, the French hero of the American Civil War, on September 10, 1824. Two more of his school exercises, a journal for the navigation class and a drawing of Benjamin Franklin, were exhibited along with the address to Lafayette at the American Convention for Promoting the Abolition of Slavery in Baltimore in November of 1828. (Other school work exhibited today includes a short poem and a ''Dialogue with W. H.'' on the importance of attending school.)

Since no college in the United States was open to Smith, Peter Williams, the black rector of Saint Philip's Episcopal Church, helped him attend Glasgow University, Scotland, in 1832. Smith earned a bachelor's degree there in 1835, a master's in 1836, and a doctorate of medicine in 1837. He was an active member of the Scottish anti–slavery movement, serving as an officer of the Glasgow Emancipation Society. Smith interned briefly in Paris, in 1837, before returning to the United States.

Smith established a successful medical practice, treating not only blacks in New York. His wealth led to a mansion on Sixth Avenue, as well as charges of elitism and snobbery. For some 20 years he served on the staff of the Free Negro Orphan Asylum. He also established, in 1837, a drugstore at 93 West Broadway and eventually opened another at 65 West Broadway. These pharmacies also served as training grounds for several black pharmacists. The back room of the second store contained a library and served as a meeting place and club for prominent black men.

Little information was documented on his private life. A marriage to a woman named Malvina produced four children, three of whom died of illness within a six–week period during the summer of 1854. At his death, Smith was survived by a widow and five children.

James McCune Smith

Supports Black Manhood Suffrage

Although Smith was prominent in local affairs and was a vigorous supporter of the Underground Railroad, his reputation developed out of his involvement in the movement for black manhood suffrage in New York state. Blacks were prevented from voting by a property–ownership qualification. Smith worried that efforts by blacks without white assistance might prove counterproductive. Therefore, he attended the 1840 State Convention of Blacks, at which he raised the issue with reservations about the wisdom of holding the convention in the first place. In February of 1841, Smith appeared before the state legislature alongside Henry Highland Garnet to argue for removal of any restrictions to black manhood suffrage. (Smith also favored women's suffrage, and, in 1853, he called for a state women's rights convention to be held in Rochester.) Chances for black manhood suffrage seemed more favorable in 1846, after a convention to revise the state constitution put the issue to a vote. Smith campaigned vigorously, but a 224,000 to 85,000 vote defeated the proposal. He also worked hard in 1860 to eradicate the abolition of the property requirement, but was again defeated by voters.

Smith's work for suffrage brought him into contact with the wealthy white abolitionist Gerrit Smith. In 1846, Gerrit Smith contributed 120,000 acres of land to distribute among black heads of families, and Smith was one of three blacks chosen to select the recipients.

Smith recognized early on that the aims of white and black abolitionists were not always the same. Even before his return to the United States, Smith pointed out in the *Liberator* in the summer of 1838 that white abolitionists pressed for freedom from slavery for Southern slaves but accepted segregation and non–voting status for Northern blacks. Even though Smith was prominent in the deliberations of the American and Foreign Anti–Slavery Society, founded in 1840, he noted that it was dominated by whites.

As time went on Smith became more convinced that the struggle to achieve emancipation and civil rights for blacks was primarily the responsibility of blacks. In the 1852 meeting of the American and Foreign Anti–Slavery Society, Smith attacked prominent abolitionists like Lewis Tappan for refusing to hire a black sea captain and John Rankin for refusing to give a $500 loan to a black who wanted to open a drugstore. Beginning in 1854, Smith continued for nearly a year accusing white abolitionists of insincerity in the column he wrote for Frederick Douglass's paper. At the same time Smith became aware of a gap between black leaders and the people and, in 1855, lamented the apparent futility of his and his colleagues' efforts to effect real change and represent black people.

Smith initially opposed the efforts of leaders like Henry Highland Garnet to align black voters behind the single issue of abolition in his Liberty Party. In the 1844 state black convention, Smith was one of the leaders of the opposition to Henry Highland Garnet's efforts to commit delegates to the support of his party. However, in 1848 Smith became a supporter of Garnet's party and widened his political efforts, organizing blacks on a national level. In 1853 his call for a national federation was adopted by the National Black Convention, but the plan soon miscarried due to factionalism.

In the mid–1850s, Smith, Frederick Douglass, Henry Highland Garnet, and Jarmain Loguen organized the remnants of the Liberty Party into the Radical Political Abolitionists, a group that would soon disappear. One cause of the party's failure was the split over the colonization of American blacks outside of the United States. Smith continued his stand against colonization throughout his lifetime. Smith's radicalism grew. In 1859 he abandoned his calls for political action and predicted the immanence of a slave insurrection. As late as August 22, 1861, when the Civil War was getting underway, Smith was unwilling to follow the lead of other abolitionist leaders and rally to the support of Lincoln.

Smith was also prominent in the fields of education and journalism. In the 1847 National Negro Convention, Smith and Alexander Crummell led the New York City delegation that pressed for the creation of an academically oriented black college. Although the resolution passed by a vote of 26–17, the project never got beyond the planning stage.

Smith began his work in journalism in late 1838, when he took over most editorial responsibility for the *Colored*

American. He resigned in June of 1839. Beginning in 1848 he supported Frederick Douglass's efforts in journalism both as a distribution agent and as an unpaid columnist for Douglass's paper. In 1859, he launched the *Weekly Anglo–African,* an offshoot of an existing monthly publication. Drawing upon the contributions of many prominent blacks, the paper was national in scope. Unfortunately, it did not survive long.

Smith wrote several works. These include a pamphlet, *A Lecture on the Haytien Revolution* (1841); ''Life and Labors of Rev. Henry Highland Garnet,'' a long introduction to Garnet's *A Memorial Discourse* (1865); and several lengthy periodical articles including ''The Influence of Climate Upon Longevity'' (1846), a defense against an attack written by John C. Calhoun.

In 1863, Smith was appointed professor of anthropology at Wilberforce University. He could not take up the position, however, because of his failing health. He died in his Williamsburg home on November 17, 1865.

Smith was distinct as the first black to earn a medical degree and probably the first to open a pharmacy with a career of service in the efforts for black advancement. His work as abolitionist, political leader, and journalist were important in the struggle for black empowerment in the United States.

REFERENCES

Andrews, Charles C. *The History of the New York African Free–Schools.* 1830. Reprint, New York: Negro Universities Press, 1969.

Lyons, Maritcha Rémond. *Memories of Yesterday.* Unpublished autobiography. Henry H. Williamson Collection. Schomburg Center for Research in Black Culture.

Malone, Dumas, ed. *Dictionary of American Biography.* New York: Scribner's, 1943.

Morais, Herbert M. *The History of the Negro in Medicine.* New York: Publishers Company, 1970.

Nell, William C. *The Colored Patriots of the American Revolution.* 1855. Reprint, New York: Arno Press and the *New York Times,* 1968.

Pease, Jane H., and William H. Pease. *Those Who Would Be Free.* New York: Atheneum, 1974.

Quarles, Benjamin. *Black Abolitionists.* New York: Oxford, 1969.

Sterling, Dorothy, ed. *Speak Out in Thunder Tones.* Garden City, NY: Doubleday, 1973.

Robert L. Johns

Smith, Walter Jr.

See Robinson, Sugar Ray.

Charles C. Spaulding (1874–1952)

Insurance executive, entrepreneur, civic leader

From the time Charles Clinton Spaulding was recruited by the fledgling North Carolina Mutual Life Insurance Company as company manager until his death in 1952, he was the dominant force who ruled supreme over the largest black business in America at that time. It had assets then of nearly $38 million and insurance in force of over $179 million. Spaulding was always a salaried employee of the company who never owned company stock and whose final estate was worth some $200,000. He was a man who believed in both self–help and racial solidarity.

Charles Clinton Spaulding was born on August 1, 1874, in Columbus County, a rural area west of Wilmington and near Whiteville and Clarktown, North Carolina. It was populated by freeborn blacks who first settled there in the early nineteenth century. They were descendants of Wilmington–based plantation slaves. Spaulding's father, Benjamin McIver Spaulding, was an extraordinary man who was a farmer, blacksmith, cabinetmaker, artisan, Reconstruction–era county sheriff, and community leader. He did not place a high priority on education for his ten children, who all worked on the family farm and helped their mother with household chores. Spaulding's mother, Margaret Moore Spaulding, was the sister of Aaron McDuffie Moore, the man who would shape his nephew's young adulthood. Although Spaulding credited his father as being his role model because of the post–Emancipation life he created for himself and the lessons he imparted to his son on the farm, it was his uncle who gave him a home in Durham, North Carolina, in 1894, and urged him to get an education. Moore was a physician who founded a hospital and commanded respect from white civic and business leaders because of his philanthropical and religious activities, and his sterling character. He was also very fair–skinned so he could pass for white.

In Durham, at the age of twenty, Spaulding went to Whitted Grade School for two years and earned the equivalent of a high school diploma. He worked as a dishwasher, bellhop, waiter, and cook in the home of a rich white family to support himself while attending school. After graduation, in 1898 he secured a job as manager of a cooperative grocery store, a venture started by twenty-five black Durhamites, all of whom withdrew their initial investments at the first sign of financial problems. Although Spaulding was left with no stock on the shelves and three hundred dollars worth of bills, the failure was not attributed to his management.

During this time, Aaron Moore and a group of six other investors had organized an insurance company, North Carolina Mutual and Provident Association, that was chartered in 1898. This prominent group included John Merrick, a former slave and a barber, real estate speculator, and extension worker for the Grand Order of True Reformers, a leading

Charles C. Spaulding

secret fraternal order and benefit association founded in 1897; and James Shepard, founder of the National Religious Training School of Durham, now North Carolina Central University. The True Reformers, according to Frazier, was the most notable organization set up to create business undertakings and serve as a role model for fledgling black businesses. By 1900 the insurance company was in deep trouble and neither Merrick nor Moore, who had bought out the other original investors, could manage the business due to their professional pursuits. They knew of Spaulding's entrepreneurial talent and offered the position of general manager to Spaulding, who needed a job and so accepted. In 1900 he also married Fannie Jones, a home office clerk who would become the mother of their four children before her death in 1919.

In a two–dollar–a–month rented desk space in the corner of a doctor's office, Spaulding worked as janitor, agent, and general manager. The company was in dire straits because the first policyholder died shortly after being insured for $40 on a 65–cent premium. The company also faced the problem of not being able to bond workers because of racial discrimination. Since this was a state charter requirement, the owners were forced to establish their own firm, the Southern Fidelity Trust. Ingham and Feldman quoted others' descriptions of Spaulding as a ''go–getter [and] natural born salesman.'' In Black Leaders, Weare also described him as an irrepressible optimist with a ''quick mind'' and ''boundless energy.'' He represented the ''New Negro'' of that era. He was the complete antithesis of Merrick, who often displayed the requisite behaviors of one whose livelihood depended on the goodwill and largesse of white clients:

> John Merrick would say ''Thank you, sir'' for every fifty–cents tip that came his way. . . . But not Spaulding. Lean, Cassius–like, he seldom smiled. He sought no tips. All he asked of life was an open field and a fair change. He was strictly business.

Spaulding was a door–to–door salesman who would stand on street corners to sell policies, and more policies needed to be sold because Merrick and Moore had to pay the dead policyholder's beneficiaries $40. Spaulding always displayed the claim receipt to prove that the company had a history of financial stability. As a recruiter, he was successful in amassing a large sales force of teachers and ministers, who always needed to supplement their meager incomes. While this expansion increased premium income, it also increased expenses, so Spaulding was by no means becoming wealthy. The next three years were indeed precarious ones due to sickness and death claims in addition to higher office and travel expenses. Because Merrick and Moore earned independent incomes, they were able to pay claims and expenses out of their pockets. Finally, in 1903, premiums began to exceed claims, and two decisions heralded their growing prosperity. First, Spaulding was put on salary at $15 a week, and next, the triumvirate decided to expand by aggressively advertising their product.

The Rise of North Carolina Mutual

In 1903 Moore and Merrick's decision to hire Spaulding was justified because of his move to publish a company newspaper that would serve the dual purpose of benefitting the black community and advertising their business. The Duke family donated a printing press, and a newspaper called the *North Carolina Mutual* became a reality. Another highly successful venture was the distribution of advertising novelties such as black art calendars. By 1904, Spaulding had significantly upgraded the company by expanding into other states and expanding the range of offerings. Because industrial insurance was more expensive for policyholders and more costly to administer, Spaulding began offering industrial straight life policies.

The company showed its viability as a new office building was constructed on a street separating black and white Durham. By 1906, additional property had been purchased and the building enlarged to house the insurance offices, Moore's medical offices, fraternal order offices, a drugstore, a barbershop, lawyers' offices, the newspaper offices, clothing stores, a tailor shop, and a black bank—the Farmer's and Mechanics Bank founded in 1908.

By 1913, Spaulding's leadership had resulted in the bank's reaching the level of ''old line legal reserve'' status, a definite indication of company stability and respectability. By 1916 the company territory had extended northward to Virginia, Maryland, and the District of Columbia. By 1924 the parent company's umbrella covered a fire insurance company, a savings and loan association, a Raleigh branch bank, a mortgage company, and a finance corporation.

Spaulding's first wife died in 1919 and the following year he married Charlotte Garner of Newark, New Jersey, reportedly the only person able to influence him in any way. Merrick also died in 1920, but the company was both stable and expanding its services and offerings to the black community. Spaulding was elevated to secretary–treasurer of the firm, now named the North Carolina Mutual Life Insurance Company. In 1923 Moore died and Spaulding became president, an office he held until his death 29 years later.

Becomes Civic Leader

In 1920 Spaulding was the overseer for the construction of North Carolina Mutual's marble–trimmed, six–story home office building. Its impact on Durham was described by Weare in Black Leaders:

> By the end of the 1930s the Mutual had taken on a cultural legitimacy that transcended Negro business. . . . The company served as a landmark in the minds of visitors and townspeople, blacks and whites, and in the collective psyche of the community. . . . As long as it stood six stories tall as a black institution in a southern town of squat warehouses and dimestores, and in the white rather than in the black business district, it commanded attention. . . . It came to represent in the white mind a self–delusory promise of what the black community might be. The black success was made over into a white success, even a sectional success. Durham offered three glittering examples of Southern achievement: Duke University, American Tobacco, and the North Carolina Mutual—three satisfying symbols of the New South.

Spaulding was the living black symbol of the New South largely because his power in the black community was firmly lodged in his ability to get from powerful whites what black Durham needed and to secure patronage from white powerbrokers. He became the determinant of who got what in nearly every arena of black life in Durham. Spaulding's power base was North Carolina Mutual, a black company that white economic sanctions could not affect.

Spaulding utilized his church, the White Rock Baptist Church, as a contact base for insurance agents and, in turn, North Carolina Mutual financed the church and thus had a major say in the hiring and firing of ministers. He controlled Lincoln Hospital, built by Moore, Merrick, and the Duke family, as chairman of the board of trustees. One collaborative relationship was between Spaulding and James E. Shepard, former original partner in the insurance company and founder–president of the predecessor of North Carolina Central University. In 1944 Shepard made overtures to the white state legislature to make his school the first publicly–supported black liberal arts college in the South, and was supported by Spaulding at legislative hearings.

With Louis Austin, editor of the Durham–based Carolina Times, Spaulding averted what could easily have been an adversarial relationship because Austin, like Spaulding, could not be controlled by blacks or whites. A self–avowed town radical, according to Weare in *Black Leaders*, in the community Austin was regarded as "that nigger communist from Massachusetts."

Although they were polar opposites in terms of personality and politics, Spaulding and Austin respected one another and so created a complementary relationship that allowed the two to come together as a solid front to gain benefits for Durham's black citizenry. Each man benefitted from this reciprocity. Spaulding could help Austin in securing loans by letting bank officials think he controlled the paper by controlling Austin. The alliance, in turn, made Spaulding more acceptable to Durham's black working class.

Spaulding was on the board of trustees of Howard and Shaw universities in Washington, D.C., and Raleigh, N.C., respectively, and the Oxford, North Carolina, Colored Orphanage, and worked tirelessly to save other black institutions from extinction. On a political level, he was appointed to the State Council of Unemployment and Relief at the onset of the Great Depression and had access to Franklin D. Roosevelt's "Black Cabinet," and also served on Herbert Hoover's Federal Relief Committee. In *Black Leaders*, Weare said that, in the 1930s, Spaulding "emerged as a racial statesman." In 1931 Spaulding became the first black elected to the board of the Slater Fund and also functioned as a regional broker for the Rosenwald Fund. His influence was so widespread that he successfully spearheaded a fund–raiser in black Durham to build Duke University's Gothic Chapel. The fact that Duke was totally segregated was not an issue since even the few blacks who donated money, as well as those who abstained, knew that Spaulding's gesture could later be used as a bargaining chip to benefit black Durham. Another power base was his appointment as national chairman of the Urban League's Emergency Advisory Council. This was coordinated by the league and the federal government with a goal of drumming up black support for the National Recovery Administration and other New Deal agencies during Franklin D. Roosevelt's Administration.

Despite his seemingly magic touch, not even Spaulding could work miracles and his notable failures were in the realm of discrimination in many federal programs because of the multi–tiered layers of racist bureaucracy that were totally immune to his charm, reputation, or political connections. After a series of local and national events that were personally painful and humiliating, Spaulding began to realize the need for a local black political base. On one occasion in the early 1930s, he was assaulted by a white drugstore clerk who was not arrested by the Raleigh police despite Spaulding's stellar reputation in the white community. He became the head of the Durham Committee on Negro Affairs (DCNA), an organization that was still, in the 1980s, a viable political factor in the local black community at large. The foci of the DCNA were economic welfare, civic rights, and electoral politics. Major successes were mostly political. The DCNA, in tandem with Austin's *Carolina Times*, endorsed candidates and voter registration, community education, and political independence. Spaulding's membership on the executive committee of the Atlanta–based Commission on Interracial Cooperation afforded him the opportunity to work and converse with southern white liberals in the first half of the twentieth century.

Spaulding's community affiliations were numerous. He was president of the Farmers and Mechanics Bank, a trustee of the Morrison Training School for Boys of North Carolina, a deacon and trustee of White Rock Baptist Church, a member of the Knights of Pythias and the Masons, treasurer of the National Negro Bankers Association, a founding member and first president of the National Insurance Association in 1921, and vice–president of the United Negro College Fund; he was a member of the National Committee of the Urban League, the Southern Education Foundation, the Chambers of Commerce of New York City and Durham, and the Kappa Alpha Psi Fraternity. In 1926 he received the Harmon Award for creativity in business and industry. He held honorary degrees from Atlanta University, Shaw University, and Tuskegee Institute (now University).

Spaulding died in Durham of heart failure on his seventy–eighth birthday, on August 1, 1952, before the full flowering of the civil rights era. Upon his death, Durham's mayor declared the day of the funeral to be one of respect for his memory and deeds. Over three thousand crowded into the White Rock Baptist Church auditorium and the overflow spilled out on the lawn and sidewalks. The memorial address was given by Mordecai Johnson, then president of Howard University, and Spaulding was buried afterward in Beechwood Cemetery.

In 1980 Spaulding was posthumously inducted into the National Business Hall of Fame by *Fortune* magazine and Junior Achievement. Spaulding's overwhelming presence was attested by a prominent executive as quoted by Ingham and Feldman in African–American Business Leaders:

> There was never nobody behind C. C. Spaulding. [He] was his own man in every way. The only somebody that governed him just a teensey weensey little bit was his wife . . . and when I say teensey weensey, I mean teensey weensey.''

Spaulding was a role model for black racial and economic progress nationwide. The great measure of Spaulding's leadership was that his death, like those of Moore and Merrick, only occasioned sadness and a sense of loss, but not an upheaval in the company's ongoing success. His son, Asa, the Kennedys, and Clements created a successful transition, and North Carolina Mutual Life Insurance Company still stands as tribute to a 20–year–old general manager who made good the beneficiaries' claim at the death of the first policyholder.

REFERENCES

Franklin, John Hope, and August Meier, eds. *Black Leaders of the Twentieth Century.* Urbana: University of Illinois Press, 1982.

Frazier, E. Franklin. *Black Bourgeoise: The Rise of a New Middle Class in the United States.* New York: Macmillan, 1962.

Haynes, George E. *The Trend of the Races.* New York: Council of Women for Home Missions and Missionary Education Movement of the United States and Canada, 1922.

Ingham, John N., and Lynne B. Feldman. *African–American Business Leaders: A Biographical Dictionary.* Westport, CT: Greenwood Press, 1994.

Kranz, Rachel C. *The Biographical Dictionary of Black Americans.* New York: Facts on File, 1992.

Logan, Rayford W., and Michael R. Winston, eds. *Dictionary of American Negro Biography.* New York: Norton, 1982.

Weare, Walter. *Black Business in the New South: A Social History of the North Carolina Mutual Life Insurance Company.* Durham, NC: Duke University Press, 1993.

Who's Who in Colored America. Vol. 1. New York: Who's Who in Colored America Corp., 1927.

———. 7th ed. Yonkers–on–Hudson, NY: Christian E. Burckel, 1950.

COLLECTIONS

The C. C. Spaulding Collection is at the North Carolina Mutual Life Insurance Company's office building in Durham.

Dolores Nicholson

William Henry Steward

(1847–1935)

Editor, publisher, church leader, activist

William H. Steward was a nationally known Baptist layman who distinguished himself as the publisher and editor of the *American Baptist* for 56 years. He was not, however, only a religious leader, as his work with civil rights activities in Louisville made him one of the most recognized persons in that city for half a century.

Born July 26, 1847, in Brandenburg, Kentucky, of slave parents, Steward and his family moved to Louisville when he was a youngster of ten. Although it was legally against the law to teach blacks to read and write, Steward attended a private church school at the First African Baptist Church under the leadership of Henry Adams and William H. Gibson, both ministers, and R. T. W. James. Steward became a teacher in the public ''colored'' school in Frankfort in 1867; he also taught in Louisville's public and private schools, beginning in

William Henry Steward

1872 at the Eastern Colored School. Steward began his employment as a messenger and then as a purchasing agent with the Louisville and Nashville Railroad in 1875. Appointed as Louisville's first black postman in 1876, Steward's route was in an affluent white neighborhood. This route provided Steward the opportunity to establish alliances with influential whites, which he maintained throughout his life.

In 1875 Steward was elected chairman of the Board of Trustees of State University, the Kentucky black Baptist college. He held the board position at State University (later known as Simmons University) until his death. Steward was called the pioneer of the black Baptists in Kentucky because of his commitment to the denomination. At a time when the university was in financial need, he donated hundreds of dollars to them to insure the school's success. In *Evidence of Progress Among Colored People,* Richings describes him as follows: "William Steward is one of those clear–headed and bright–minded men peculiar to Kentucky. His work as a journalist is most creditable. He is the editor and publisher of the *American Baptist,* published at Louisville, Ky."

On April 23, 1878, Steward married Lexington native Mamie F. Lee, who was a music teacher at State University. Mamie Steward was also an excellent organist and pianist and devoted to the Baptist church. She was elected president of the Baptist Women's Educational Convention, which served to recruit youths to State University, secure funds to pay for the university's property, build a dormitory for girls, and develop a greater missionary spirit among members. The Stewards had four children: Lucy B., Jeannette L., William H. Jr., and Caroline A. Steward was a highly devoted family man and the *American Baptist*'s office was always within a few blocks of the family home. Although he had a housekeeper, Steward walked to his home each day for lunch at 1:00 p.m. to be there when his children arrived home from school at 1:30 p.m. He loved celebrating anniversaries and was especially proud of his 50th anniversary in 1928. At the time of his death Steward also had three grandchildren: Steward Picket, and Elizabeth and Myrtle Black.

Becomes Editor and Publisher

A devout Baptist since his baptism in 1867 in the Kentucky River, Steward was involved in all aspects of his denomination's activities on local, state, and national levels. In Louisville's Fifth Street Baptist Church, he served as the superintendent of the Sunday School, a member of the board of deacons, leader of the church choir, and as a trustee. In 1879 Steward purchased the *Baptist Herald* and began publishing the *American Baptist,* the official organ of the American National Baptist Convention, which he continued for 56 years. He served as secretary of the General Association of Colored Baptists in for years beginning in 1877. He also served as secretary of the National Baptist Convention for 14 years.

Steward was active in many educational and racial uplift movements in Louisville and the state of Kentucky. He was vice president of the National Afro–American Council and president of the National Afro–American Press Association in the 1890s. Steward vigorously participated in the Unity Lodge No. 12 Masonic Fraternity where he served as its Master Eminent Commander of Cyrene Commandary and as the Worshipful Grand Master of the Jurisdiction of Kentucky.

Steward worked with such Kentucky contemporaries as Albert E. Meyzeek, physician Ellsworth E. Underwood, and minister and college president Charles H. Parrish on local civil rights issues. Steward was also a friend and follower of Booker T. Washington with whom he frequently corresponded seeking advice on the Kentucky situation. Like Parrish, Steward was very moderate in his views and believed that blacks could accomplish their goals by working with influential whites in Louisville. Through his connections with Louisville's prominent whites, Steward received several important positions. As a member of the Colored School Board of Visitors, he controlled the employment of black school employees from the mid–1890s to 1910. Through his influence and position in the Republican Party, Steward helped blacks secure high–level patronage jobs when Republicans were elected to various offices. In 1897 Steward was appointed as a judge of registration and election for the Fifteenth Precinct of the Ninth Ward in Louisville. He was the first person of color to hold this position in Kentucky. When Louisville officials finally agreed to hire black firemen and policemen in the 1920s, all blacks had to receive Steward's approval to be hired.

Steward worked with many black lawyers, doctors, ministers, and business professionals to fight inequities in

Louisville. As professionals, their hours were more flexible and, therefore, provided them the opportunity to pursue race issues. Steward and Ellsworth E. Underwood were among the leaders of the Anti–Separate Coach Movement, which fought Jim Crow laws in Kentucky in the 1890s.

In December of 1913, Steward and Parrish called together a group of black leaders and formed the Louisville NAACP, which was officially recognized in 1914. Later Steward, as a member of both the NAACP and the Commission on Interracial Cooperation, whose purpose was to improve race relations and elevate the status blacks, became involved in protests against residential segregation and city park segregation practices. Steward remained involved as a member of the NAACP's executive board until he resigned in 1920 because the chapter had rejected his moderate stance on segregation.

In 1930, two years prior to his retirement, Steward began preparing his successor William Howard Ballew, a minister, and to make arrangements for the transfer of the *American Baptist* to the General Association of Baptists. In 1933, some 18 months prior to his death, with written permission from family members and a payment of one dollar, Steward transferred the paper's ownership to the General Association. Steward personally remained responsible for all previously incurred indebtedness of the paper. Steward died on January 3, 1935, and was interred in the Louisville Cemetery.

During his lifetime, Steward played a pivotal role in the advancement of racial equality in the city of Louisville and the state of Kentucky.

REFERENCES

Dunnigan, Alice A. *Fascinating Story of Black Kentuckians: Their Heritage and Tradition.* Washington, DC: Associated Publishers, 1982.

Kleber, John E., ed. *The Kentucky Encyclopedia.* Lexington: University Press of Kentucky, 1992.

McKinney, Victor Jr., ed. *The American Baptist Centennial Volume: The History of a Kentucky Institution, 1878–1978.* Louisville: American Baptist, 1978.

Parrish, Charles H., ed. *Golden Jubilee of the General Association of Colored Baptists in Kentucky: The Story of 50 Years' Work from 1865–1915.* Louisville: Mayers Printing Co., 1915.

Richings, G. F. *Evidences of Progress among Colored People.* 4th ed. Philadelphia: George S. Ferguson Co., 1897.

Simmons, William J. *Men of Mark.* Cleveland: Geo. M. Rewell, 1887.

Smith, S. E., ed. *History of the Anti–Separate Coach Movement of Kentucky.* Evansville: National Afro–American Journal and Directory Publishing Co., c.1895.

Wright, George C. *A History of Blacks in Kentucky.* Vol. 2. *In Pursuit of Equality, 1890–1980.* Frankfort: Kentucky Historical Society, 1992.

———. *Life Behind a Veil: Blacks in Louisville, Kentucky, 1865–1930.* Baton Rouge: Louisiana State University Press, 1985.

COLLECTIONS

The personal papers of William Steward remain with family members, and the records of activities of the *American Baptist* remain with the paper in the office in Louisville. Other records of his association with Simmons University are housed in the archives of the University of Louisville.

Karen Cotton McDaniel

William Still
(1821–1902)
Abolitionist, reformer, writer, businessman

Although William Still is best known as the primary documenter of the Underground Railroad, it should be remembered that he also participated with courage and intelligence in the momentous events that led up to emancipation. Following the Civil War, Still channeled his reform efforts into civic and charitable activities with Philadelphia's black community. Through these achievements Still has left his mark as an important black leader and reformer of nineteenth century America.

''Like millions of my race, my mother and father were born slaves, but were not contented to live and die so,'' William Still wrote in the *Underground Railroad.* He continued, ''My father purchased himself in early manhood by hard toil. Mother saw no way for herself and children to escape the horrors of bondage but by flight. Bravely, with her four little ones, with firm faith in God and an ardent desire to be free, she forsook the prison–house, and succeeded, through the aid of my father, to reach a free state. Here life had to begin anew.''

William Still was born on October 7, 1821, the eighteenth child of Levin and Sidney Steel, both former slaves. Still's father was a Maryland slave who went north after purchasing his own freedom. Still's mother escaped bondage with her four children in order to rejoin her husband. Slave hunters soon recaptured her, but she escaped a second time in 1807. The couple relocated to the remote pine barrens of Shamong in southern Jersey. It was here, near Medford, in Burlington County, New Jersey that William was born. To prevent recapture, they changed their surname to Still, and Sidney took the name Charity as a new given name.

As a boy, Still assisted his father with the work of the family farm. He had little formal education, with the equivalent of one to two years of public schooling. Still left home at the age of 20, and, in 1844, ventured to Philadelphia, home to one of the largest free black population in the northern states. Upright, ambitious, and largely self–taught, Still at first

William Still

drifted from job to job until friends recommended him for the position of clerk at the office of the Pennsylvania Society for the Abolition of Slavery in 1847. That same year, Still married Letitia George. The couple raised four children: Caroline, Ella, William W., and Robert.

Works in the Underground Railroad

From his lowly post at the Anti–Slavery Society office, Still rose to become one of the preeminent black proponents and participants of the secretive but highly significant operations of the Underground Railroad. The designation "Underground Railroad" became the accepted metaphor for the widespread effort to assist runaway slaves with their escape through the northern states en route to safe havens in Canada and elsewhere. Workers of the Underground Railroad actively hid the fugitives, providing them with shelter, food, supplies, and occasionally, legal aid and transportation to the next station.

In December of 1852 a group of Philadelphia abolitionists, most members of the Pennsylvania Anti–Slavery Society, formed a local General Vigilance Committee. The name "vigilance" connoted the action arm in Underground Railroad work. They appointed Still secretary and chairman of this four–man committee, and charged the group with the task of raising funds and "attending to every case that might require their aid . . . and keeping a record of all their doings." The Fugitive Slave Law enacted in 1850, made the act of assisting a runaway slave a federal offense. The law compelled citizens, under punishment of fine and imprisonment, to aid in the recapture and return of escaped slaves. It brought the horrors of slavery home to both blacks and whites of the free states. Thus Still and his co–workers took organized actions that not only endangered themselves but also defied and thwarted the law.

The Philadelphia station was a key link in the eastern seaboard route of the Underground Railroad, and under Still's direction the Vigilance Committee aided nearly 500 fugitive slaves between the years 1852 and 1857. Still's capability for quick and creative actions, his leadership and communication skills, as well as his close attention to detail, contributed to this achievement. As secretary of the Philadelphia General Vigilance Committee, Still interviewed and recorded the personal histories of each fugitive slave, especially those with remarkable adventures en route to the North. He later used these narratives to compile a book documenting the history of the Underground Railroad which was published in 1872. Still gave the book a lengthy title, *The Underground Railroad; a Record of Facts, Authentic Narratives, Letters, etc., Narrating the Hardships, Hairbreadth Escapes, and Death Struggles of the Slaves in their efforts for Freedom, as Related by Themselves and Others, or Witnessed by the Author.* The work, nearly 800 pages in length, was a sprawling compendium of facts, stories, letters, news articles, and various data on the characters and events of the Underground Railroad, all based on Still's records, memory, and experience. It reflected Still's ardent desire to record accurately for history the often heart–rending and moving accounts of slaves striving for freedom. It also confirms and documents the active commitment given the antislavery cause by the free blacks in northern cities, as exemplified by the antislavery workers in Philadelphia. Still's book is unusual and remarkable in the fact that its author was a primary black participant in many of the events recounted therein. It also deserves praise in that Still allowed the fugitives to speak in their own words and describe their own motives and actions. Thus, it has the feel of truth and authenticity.

Still maintained close contact with former slaves who had settled in Canada. During the 1850s he acted as an agent for, and contributed articles to, two black Canadian abolitionist newspapers: Henry Bibb's *Voice of the Fugitive,* and Mary Ann Shadd Cary's *Provincial Freeman.* Still toured western Canada in 1855 to examine the condition of black communities and wrote a report refuting the charge that fugitives were unable to cope with freedom.

In 1859 Still wrote a persuasive letter to the newspaper, *North American and United States Gazette,* that initiated a campaign to integrate Philadelphia's street car lines. Rules of access required black citizens to ride only on the front platform of the street car. The campaign came to an eventually successful conclusion in 1867, when the Pennsylvania legislature passed an act ending the discrimination. However, Still's conduct in advocating change gave rise to harsh criticism from some members of the black community. Still defended his actions in an address, later printed in pamphlet form, titled *A Brief Narrative of the Struggle for the Rights of the Colored People of Philadelphia in the City Railroad Cars.*

With the outbreak of the Civil War in 1861 Vigilance Committee work ceased. Even though Still resigned from his position in the Anti–Slavery office, he continued to be active in the effort to aid the newly freed slaves, including a large influx of ''contrabands,'' slaves freed as a result of the invading northern armies. With the sponsorship of the Pennsylvania Anti–Slavery Society, abolitionist leaders organized an employment office for freedmen in 1862. Still agreed to head the agency, and under his guidance the office helped hundreds of former slaves find jobs and housing, and to locate lost relatives. However, the onslaught of requests for aid overwhelmed the agency, forcing Still to resign his position after six months. The office eventually merged with three other similar organizations to become the Freemen's Employment Agency.

Business and Civic Pursuits

From the beginning, Still was an entrepreneur, living out his own self–help philosophy. He augmented his wages with a series of business ventures, most notably as a dealer in coal, ice, and stoves to the local community. His house served as a boarding–house when needed. During the war years he won a profitable government contract as a sutler, or supplier, to Camp William Penn just outside Philadelphia where black soldiers were stationed and trained. Drawing on his business acumen, Still sold and distributed copies of *The Underground Railroad* on a subscription basis, using an elaborate system of agents. Thus, the book found wide distribution, and through three editions and multiple printings, sold thousands of copies.

In much of his later life, Still dedicated himself to improving the health and welfare of Philadelphia's black community. He kept his ties with the former Pennsylvania Anti–Slavery Society, which later continued its work as a philanthropic association. He served as a member of the Freedmen's Aid Commission, remained active in community affairs, and served on the boards of a number of black charitable and welfare institutions. During the 1870s and 1880s, Still devoted his energies to guiding and directing the Home for the Aged and Infirm Colored Persons in Philadelphia. A devout member of the Berean Presbyterian Church, Still helped found a Mission Sabbath School in North Philadelphia, and in 1880, he worked to establish an early branch of the Young Men's Christian Association (YMCA) for Philadelphia's black youth. Still died in Philadelphia on July 14, 1902, at the age of 81.

REFERENCES

Gara, Larry. *The Liberty Line: the Legend of the Underground Railroad.* 1961. Reprint, Lexington: University of Kentucky Press, 1996.

Lane, Roger. *William Dorsey's Philadelphia and Ours.* New York: Oxford, 1991.

Pease, Jane H. and William H. *They Who Would be Free: Blacks' Search for Freedom, 1830–1861.* New York: Athenaeum, 1974.

Quarles, Benjamin. *Black Abolitionists.* New York: Oxford, 1969.

Ripley, C. Peter, ed. *The Black Abolitionist Papers.* 5 vols. Chapel Hill: University of North Carolina Press, 1985–92.

Siebert, Wilbur H. *The Underground Railroad from Slavery to Freedom.* New York: Macmillan, 1899.

Simmons, William J. *Men of Mark: Eminent, Progressive, and Rising.* Cleveland: Geo. M. Rewell, 1887.

Still, William. *An Address on Voting and Laboring, delivered at Concert Hall, Tuesday evening, March 10th, 1874.* Philadelphia: Jas. B. Rogers Company, Printers, 1874.

———. *A Brief Narrative of the Struggle for the Rights of the Colored People of Philadelphia in the City Railway Cars. . . Read before a large public meeting held in Liberty Hall, Lombard St. below Eighth, April 8th, 1867.* Philadelphia: Merrihew and Son, Printers, 1867.

———. *Still's Underground Rail Road Records, With a Life of the Author.* Rev. ed., containing a short biography of Still written by James P. Boyd. Philadelphia: Betts and Company, 1883.

COLLECTIONS

The bulk of Still's personal papers, including his vigilance committee journals and personal letters, are housed in the William Still Papers at the Historical Society of Pennsylvania.

Kenneth Potts

William Grant Still
(1895–1978)
Composer, arranger, conductor

Hailed as the ''Dean of African American Composers,'' William Grant Still had a long and distinguished career as a composer, arranger, and conductor. As a composer of classical music, he was considered the leader of the first generation of African American composers in the twentieth century. He believed that folk music was the richest source for the sounds needed to make American music stand apart from the European models that had dominated composed music. In his attempt to be instrumental in defining an ''American sound,'' Still spent his life collecting, studying, and analyzing the many melodies and rhythms of the ethnic groups that make up the Western hemisphere. Although he arranged folk songs, especially African American spirituals, for various instrumental and choral combinations, he used the scales and rhythms derived from them as his primary source of inspiration in his larger forms. Unlike other American composers who based entire symphonic works on quotations of folk themes, Still chose to compose his own melodies and to harmonize them using the richly stacked chords of jazz and blues. He wanted to elevate the blues by using its characteristic structures in symphonies, ballets, and operas, and, at the same time, express the unique qualities of the music of his people.

Only a fledgling composer and arranger during the artistically active period known as the Harlem Renaissance, Still nevertheless absorbed the philosophies of the group of intellectuals who made up that circle. Well–read, he often chose literary sources for his inspirations. The writings of Alain Locke, Paul Laurence Dunbar, and W. E. B. Du Bois had a profound effect on Still's musical compositions and his personal aesthetic choices. Langston Hughes was a personal friend and collaborator, whose poetry and prose Still set to music. Always searching for authentic sources for the music of Africa and African cultural holdovers in the New World, Still worked with Zora Neale Hurston for a time after her folklore–collecting expeditions to the Caribbean in the 1930s. He subscribed to the notion set forth by the Czechoslovakian composer Antonin Dvořák in the late nineteenth century that the source for an original American sound in symphonic music could be found in the music of African Americans.

Born in Woodville, Mississippi, on May 11, 1895, William Grant Still Jr. was the only child of Carrie Lena Fambro Still (1872–1927) and William Grant Still Sr. (1871–1895). His father, a native of Woodville and a graduate of Alcorn Agricultural and Mechanical College in Lorman, Mississippi, taught mathematics, played the cornet, and was the leader of a popular brass band. His mother, who was from Atlanta, Georgia, taught English, played the piano, and later established a Shakespearean circle where she produced the English writer's plays. William Grant Still Sr., died when his son was an infant, and Carrie Still remarried in 1904. William Grant Still Jr. married Grace Dorothy Bundy on October 4, 1915. They had four children, William Bundy, Gail Lynton, June Allen, and Caroline Elaine. The couple separated in 1931 and divorced in 1939. Later that year Still married Verna Arvey, a Jewish woman who was a native of Los Angeles. They had two children, Duncan Allan and Judith Anne.

William Grant Still

Formative and Explorative Years

Following the untimely death of his father, Still and his mother moved to Little Rock, Arkansas, where his grandmother and aunt lived. He was raised by his mother, his grandmother, Anne Fambro—who had been a slave—and his stepfather, Charles Benjamin Shepperson, who joined the household when William was about nine years old. Shepperson introduced him to opera on Red Seal records and took him to recitals. Still studied the violin arduously while he was in high school, and he was valedictorian of his class in 1911 at M. W. Gibbs High School, where his mother taught English.

When Still entered Wilberforce University in Ohio at the age of 16, he realized that music would be his vocation. He taught himself to play all the instruments of the band and orchestra. He also led the band program while he was a student, composed music, had a recital of his own works, and formed a string quartet in which he played the cello. He was greatly inspired by a concert tour by Samuel Coleridge–Taylor, the African British composer who had been educated at the Royal Academy of Music in London. Still obtained an oboe from a mail–order house and taught himself to play it. Eventually he began to get jobs playing oboe, violin, and cello in dance orchestras in Columbus, Cleveland, and Dayton, Ohio. In the summer of 1916, he worked for W. C. Handy, the "Father of the Blues," at his Memphis publishing firm and performed in the South on tour with Handy's band. Still made the first arrangement of Handy's *St. Louis Blues* for the band.

When his inheritance from his father came to him on his twenty–second birthday, Still used the money to attend Oberlin Conservatory of Music to study theory and composition. He studied with Friedrich Lehmann and George Whitfield Andrews. In 1918, he enlisted in the U.S. Navy as a mess attendant. When naval personnel discovered that he could play the violin, he entertained in the Officers' Mess, playing the popular tunes of the day. After his discharge, he went to Port Newark, New Jersey, to work in a shipyard. He and his wife had two children by then, so he returned to Columbus, where he knew he could find work as a musician. He briefly attended Oberlin again until 1919, when W. C. Handy asked him to come to New York to work as an arranger in the Pace and Handy Music Publishing Company.

The New York Years

In New York, Still wrote stock arrangements for dance bands and jazz groups and arranged spirituals for chorus and piano. He also performed on oboe, violin, and cello, usually on the road with Handy's touring bands. In May of 1921, he earned a spot playing oboe in the orchestra of Noble Sissle and Eubie Blake's show, *Shuffle Along,* the first highly successful all–black musical theatre production in New York. The cast included Paul Robeson, Caterina Jarboro, Florence Mills, and Josephine Baker. When *Shuffle Along* went on the road to Boston in July of 1922, Still took advantage of the opportunity to study composition privately with the American composer, George Chadwick, who was the director of the New England Conservatory of Music. When the show moved on to Chicago in October, Still and his wife returned to New York, where Still took a position with Harry Pace's Pace Phonograph Company which issued recordings on the Black Swan label. Still did arrangements for artists who recorded on the label. He also conducted the orchestra and produced recordings for others.

Still was promoted to musical director when Fletcher Henderson took another position. Still's first recorded original compositions were made on the Black Swan label. Under the pseudonym Willie M. Grant, he wrote the songs "I Want To," "How I Got Dem Twilight Blues," "Love Me in Your Own Time," and "Go Get It." His earliest recorded spiritual arrangements date from this period. In March of 1924, Pace sold the Black Swan label to Paramount and Still's job ended.

In 1923, when the avant–garde French composer Edgard Varèse offered a scholarship in composition to an aspiring African American composer, Still had responded. His study with Varèse lasted from 1923 until 1925 and led to the premieres of his first works in the International Composers' Guild Concerts. The connections he made through Varèse and his circle of contemporary composers launched his career as a classical composer. The earliest works from this period included "Death Song," (1921) based on a poem by Paul Laurence Dunbar, "From the Journal of a Wanderer" (1924), "From the Black Belt" (1924), "From the Land of Dreams" (1925), "Levee Land" (1925), written especially for Florence Mills, and sketches for the suite, "Africa" (completed in 1930).

Still's reputation as an orchestrator and arranger grew to such an extent that he eventually worked for Don Voorhees, Clarence Williams, Lucketh Roberts, and Paul Whiteman in addition to Handy. In the 1920s, his orchestrating credits included the musical productions *Runnin' Wild* (1923), *Dixie to Broadway* (1924), *Creole Follies, Struttin' Time, Earl Carroll's Vanities, Americana,* and *Rain or Shine* (1928).

Even while he was actively arranging for others, Still continued serious composition, and he completed his first ballet, *La Guiablesse,* commissioned by Ruth Page and the Chicago Allied Arts in 1926. *Darker America* (1926) premiered in 1926 with Eugene Goossens conducting on an International Composers' Guild concert. In 1927 Jessie Zachary performed three of Still's songs, "Winter's Approach" (1926), "The Breath of a Rose" (1927), and "Mandy Lou" (1927), in a concert at the New School for Social Research in New York. Still and his wife, Grace Bundy, collaborated on a popular song, "No Matter What You Do," which was published.

In 1928 Still was notified of his selection to receive the second of the William E. Harmon Awards for Distinguished Achievement among Negroes in Music. He became a charter member of the Pan American Association of Composers founded by Edgard Varèse, Henry Cowell, and Carlos Chavez. Other members included Ruth Crawford, Howard Hanson, Roy Harris, Charles Ives, and Heitor Villa–Lobos.

From 1929 to 1930, Still completed about 118 arrangements for the Paul Whiteman Orchestra and spent about a year in Hollywood, California with that group as their arranger for the *Old Gold Hour,* a radio program. He composed original works for Whiteman's band as well. He completed several classical works during that time, including a ballet, *Sahdji,* based a the story by Bruce Nugent—also known as Richard Bruce—which had been published in Alain Locke's *The New Negro* (1925). *Sahdji* had its premiere performance by the Rochester Philharmonic Orchestra under Howard Hanson in 1931.

Back in New York and temporarily out of work, Still brought together his sketches for his *Afro–American Symphony,* which he finished in 1930. It premiered in Rochester, New York, at the Eastman School of Music on October 28, 1931. Based on the melodies and harmonies of jazz and blues, and the first symphony ever to use a banjo, it became his most famous composition and his most enduring.

In 1931 Still signed a contract with Willard Robison to work in radio as an arranger and conductor. He wrote arrangements for *Willard Robison's Deep River Hour* on WOR radio in New York. In addition, his arrangements were played over WNAC and WEEI in Boston. Eventually, he became the conductor of the orchestra for that program.

Still's professional life began to accelerate in 1933. His works were being played in Europe and his composition, *The Deserted Plantation,* was performed at The Metropolitan Opera House by The Paul Whiteman Orchestra. His ballet, *La Guiablesse,* was produced in Rochester with an all–white cast and in Chicago with an all–black corps de ballet and white principal dancer, Ruth Page, who had originally commissioned the work. In 1934 the African American dancer Katherine Dunham performed the ballet in Chicago. Still also did an arrangement for a recording of the young singer and member of "The Rhythm Boys," Bing Crosby.

Active Years in California

Still's life as a composer changed dramatically when he received a Guggenheim Fellowship for composition in 1934, which was renewed in 1935 and 1938. He received permission to move to California—instead of going to Europe as most fellows did—to compose an opera. Completed in 1935, *Blue Steel* was based on a story by Carlton Moss with a libretto by Harold Bruce Forsythe. Still completed several other pieces including *Quit Dat Fool'nish* for solo piano, *Dismal Swamp, The Black Man Dances,* and *Lenox Avenue.* In 1936, he joined the American Society of Composers, Authors, and Publishers (ASCAP) and also wrote the score for the movie, *Pennies from Heaven,* starring Bing Crosby. He worked as a composer, arranger, and orchestrator in film for the major studios off and on from 1936 to 1943.

In 1937 Still completed *Symphony in G Minor,* subtitled "Song of New Race." He also finished the first of two volumes of spiritual arrangements for Handy Brothers Music. He began to work on his opera, *Troubled Island,* based on a story by Langston Hughes, in 1937. He would not completely finish the opera until about 1942.

Still received a commission in 1938 to write the theme music for the 1939 New York World's Fair. The result was a piece that has been published under three titles: *Rising Tide, Victory Tide,* and *Song of a City.* The next year, with the encouragement of his second wife, Verna Arvey, who was a concert pianist, he wrote his first significant solo piano collection, *Seven Traceries.* In 1939 Still received a Julius Rosenwald Foundation Fellowship, which allowed him to compose for another year without seeking other employment.

In 1940 Still collaborated with Katherine Garrison Chapin on a cantata, *And They Lynched Him on a Tree,* and with Zora Neale Hurston in a collection of folk song settings, called *Caribbean Melodies.* The next year, he wrote *Plain–Chant for America,* also with Chapin, and another opera, *A Bayou Legend.* Howard University awarded him an honorary doctorate, the first of eight he would eventually receive.

Still was associated with the film, *Stormy Weather,* for a while in 1943, when he resigned because the producers changed the point of view for the film. When he was hired he understood that the film would be about the achievements of blacks in music. When it turned out to be all popular music, Still quit the movie. After that he did some freelance orchestrating for Dmitri Tiompkin, until he began to have trouble with his eyes.

Still wrote some of his most ambitious works in 1943 and 1944, including "Bells" for solo piano, *In Memoriam: The Colored Soldiers Who Died for Democracy, Suite for Violin and Piano, The Festive Overture of 1944,* and *Poem for Orchestra. Songs of Separation,* his only song cycle, was written in 1945. The following years brought *From the Delta* for band (1945), *Pastorela* (1946), Symphony No. 4, *Autochthonous* (1947), *Danzas de Panama* (1948), *From a Lost Continent* (1948), and *Miniatures for Flute, Oboe, and Piano* (before 1948).

Discouragement and Final Success

By late 1948 preparations had begun for the premiere of the Hughes and Still collaboration, *Troubled Island,* by the New York City Opera. Still was so busy with preparations and excited about seeing his lifelong dream fulfilled that he did not write any new music. The first of three performances was on March 31, 1949 and was recorded for broadcast in Europe through the Voice of America. Still's work was the first opera composed by an African American to be performed by a major New York opera company. Before that performance, the Metropolitan Opera and the New York City Opera had only selected works by European composers.

After the production of *Troubled Island,* Still wrote two more operas, *Costaso* (1949–50) and *Mota* (1951). Opera was Still's first genre of choice, but staging them was so enormously expensive that he did not see another of his operas produced until 1974, four years before his death. In the years that followed, Still's works other than his operas were performed widely and broadcast on radio in the United States and Europe. He spent his days arranging some of his older works for different combinations of instruments, especially if someone had expressed an interest in performing a piece. "Summerland from Three Visions," one of his most popular short pieces, exists in at least 12 arrangements done by the composer as demand dictated. Still also wrote arrangements, songs, and piano pieces for music education textbooks and piano instruction methods.

In 1953 Still received the Freedoms Foundation Award for his work, *To You, America!* In 1954 he received an honorary doctorate from Bates College. That year he wrote a work for children that defines the focus of his later years, *The Little Song that Wanted to be a Symphony,* for narrator, voices, and orchestra. Ruth Watanabe noted in "Program Notes," *Thirty–Eighth Annual Festival of American Music* that Still said the melody "would bring friendship to American children of many different racial groups. . .[the theme] gives up its idea of becoming a symphony in order to make the children of America happy and to bring them together in harmony and brotherhood." Still spent many days in schools in his later years lecturing about his works, about American music and its debt to African origins, and about brotherhood and bringing the races together.

In 1958 Still wrote an original work for solo harp and orchestra, *Ennanga,* with themes based on African folk music. In 1959, he "officially" retired by ending the diary entries that he had made since about 1938. Despite that decision, he fulfilled two commissions from the American Accordionists Association in 1960, resulting in "Aria" and "Lilt". In 1961 the American Guild of Organists commissioned a piece for organ, *Reverie.* During the sixties, Still arranged folk songs into the groups known as *Folk Suites Nos. 1–4* and *Folk Suite for Band.* He won a prize from the National Federation of Music Clubs for *Peaceful Land.* His last opera, *Highway 1, U.S.A.,* which was a reworking of an earlier work called *A Southern Interlude* (1942), was performed by the University of Miami Opera in 1962. Recognition in his later years came in the form of honorary doctorates from the University of Arkansas, Pepperdine University, the New England Conservatory of Music, the Peabody Conservatory of Music, and the University of Southern California at Los Angeles.

Still died in Los Angeles on December 3, 1978. His deep sense of the importance of a spiritual life can be summed up by noting the inscription he added to the manuscripts of so many of his compositions: "With humble thanks to God, the Source of Inspiration." Still was a pioneer in the early years of twentieth–century American classical music, not only for African Americans, but for all Americans. His incorporation of jazz and blues elements into his compositions, his use of folk music, and his willingness to be the first, make him the greatest of his generation and a model for generations to come.

REFERENCES

Arvey, Verna. *In One Lifetime.* Fayetteville: University of Arkansas Press, 1984.

Southern, Eileen. ''Conversation: With William Grant Still.'' *The Black Perspective in Music* 3 (Special Issue No. 2, May 1975): 165–75.

———. *The Music of Black Americans: A History.* Rev. ed. New York: Norton, 1983.

———, comp. ''William Grant Still: List of Major Works.'' *The Black Perspective in Music* 3 (May 1975): 235–38.

Still, Judith Anne, Celeste Anne Headlee, and Lisa M. Headlee–Huffman, eds. *William Grant Still and the Fusion of Cultures in American Music: Centennial Edition.* 2nd ed. rev. Flagstaff, AZ: Master–Player Library, 1995.

Still, Judith Anne, Michael Dabrishus, and Carolyn L. Quin. *William Grant Still: A Bio–Bibliography.* Westport, CT: Greenwood Press, 1996.

Still, William Grant, interviews by R. Donald Brown, November 13, 1967, and December 4, 1967.

———. Unpublished Typescript, ''Negro Serious Music.'' Edited by Judith Anne Still.California Black Oral History Project. Fullerton: California State University.

Watanabe, Ruth. ''Program Notes,'' *Thirty–Eighth Annual Festival of American Music,* Rochester, NY, May 2, 1968.

COLLECTIONS

The largest collection of manuscripts and papers relating to William Grant Still can be found in the William Grant Still and Verna Arvey Papers at the University of Arkansas Libraries, Fayetteville, Arkansas. The collection also contains audio tapes and memorabilia. Photocopies of all of the scores available through William Grant Still Music will be placed with the University of Northern Arizona by June of 1998. The Fisk University Library contains an audio tape of an interview with Still as part of the oral history collection.

Carolyn L. Quin

Carl B. Stokes
(1927–1996)
Mayor

''For a brief time in Cleveland, I was the man of power. I had what no black man in this country has had before: direct control of the government of predominantly white population,'' said Carl Stokes in his autobiography *Promises of Power.* This self–assessment captures the uniqueness of the election of Carl Burton Stokes to the office of mayor of America's eighth largest city in 1967. He served two two–year terms from 1967 to 1971 before deciding that the city's deteriorating racial and political climate mitigated against a third try for that office.

The great–grandson of a slave, Carl Stokes was born in a poor black neighborhood in Cleveland, Ohio, on June 21, 1927. He and his older brother, Louis Stokes, were raised by their widowed mother, Louise Stokes, a domestic worker. Their father, Charles Stokes, was a laundry worker who died at the age of 39, when Carl was two years old. The family of three lived in a dilapidated two–family house, sharing one bed. When Cleveland became the first city in America to build public housing, the Stokes family were among the first to move into the new housing units. Their new apartment provided amenities such as hot water, a washing machine, and a separate bed for their mother. The brothers carried newspapers and worked in neighborhood stores to earn money to help support the family. Especially important to young Carl was the housing project's recreation center which introduced him to art classes, organized sports, the opportunity to play on the championship ping–pong team, and access to a world beyond his confined neighborhood.

Although he was a capable student, at age 17 Stokes dropped out of East Technical High School. (East Technical High School is known for graduating Olympic track athletes Jesse Owens and Harrison Dillard.) Lured by the diversions of street life, Stokes mastered the rules of survival and became a pool hustler and gambler. He also worked in a foundry. At 18 he joined the U.S. Army and served in Europe near the end of World War II. Stokes returned home in 1946 with a changed attitude, determined to finish school and raise his standard of living. According to the *Washington Times,* Stokes heeded his mother's advice to, ''[G]et something in your head so you won't have to work with your hands like I worked with my hands.'' Stokes used the G.I. Bill to return to East Tech, complete high school, and to finance his enrollment at West Virginia State College.

Stokes studied at West Virginia State from 1947 to 1948. He returned to Cleveland to enroll at Western Reserve University in 1948, where he stayed until 1950. He did not complete his bachelor's degree. He landed his first professional job, as a liquor enforcement agent, in 1950. Stokes credited this job with opening his eyes to the politics of race in the North. The job required him to close down illegal liquor operations in the black community but prohibited him from enforcing the same law against white establishments. Stokes held this job for three years before leaving Cleveland to attend the University of Minnesota Law School, where he earned a bachelor of science degree in law. Stokes completed his LL.B. degree at the Cleveland Marshall School of Law, working as a probation officer during the day and attending classes as night.

After graduating with a bachelor of science in law and passing the bar examination, Stokes opened a joint law practice in Cleveland in 1957 with $120 and his brother as a partner. The brothers primarily represented black defendants

Carl B. Stokes

in automobile accidents, criminal proceedings, and police misconduct cases. During this same period Carl Stokes began his political career and charted a methodical path to elective office. He managed the successful campaign of a local black man, Lowell Henry, for a seat on the city council and cultivated relationships with black politicians and businessmen. These men, who became his mentors and advisors, included William O. Walker, the influential publisher of the city's weekly black newspaper, the *Cleveland Call and Post.*

In 1958 Stokes's political connections led to his appointment as assistant city prosecutor by Cleveland mayor Anthony Celebreeze. He also became active in the early days of the Civil Rights Movement in Cleveland, serving on the executive board of the local chapter of the NAACP and joining the Urban League and other black civic organizations. Stokes widened his base and expanded his contacts by joining the mostly white Young Democrats Club. This organization attracted young men under 35 who were interested in becoming active in party politics. The base of Stokes's political support, however, was cultivated and sustained within the black community. In 1962 his charisma, political skills, and ability to cross racial lines helped him to win a seat in the Ohio General Assembly, becoming the first black Democrat to hold that office. He twice won reelection and served until he was elected mayor of Cleveland in 1967.

While in the Ohio General Assembly Stokes worked with NAACP lawyers in filing the law suit that reached the U.S. Supreme Court and resulted in the redistricting plan that created the Twenty–first Congressional District. His brother Louis Stokes, one of the attorneys who argued the case, ran for election in the new district and won. He has represented the district since 1968. The Twenty–first Congressional District Caucus, named for the new district, was organized in 1970 to maximize black political clout in local and national elections.

First Black Mayor of a Major City

Stokes's first campaign for mayor of Cleveland ended in a narrow defeat. He ran as an independent and lost to Democrat Ralph S. Locher by only one percentage point, less than 3,000 votes. Stokes viewed this losing campaign for mayor in 1965 as the height of his political career because of the pure energy levels and dedication of his supporters, although the lessons learned were not fully reaped until two years later. He ran again in 1967 as a Democrat, defeating Locher in the party primary. Stokes went on to defeat Republican Seth Taft, grandson of the former U.S. President William Howard Taft, in the general election. In the two–year interim, Stokes had firmed up his base of black support and gained a foothold among white liberals and the Cleveland business establishment. In the 1967 election Stokes won 50 percent of the vote in a city with a 37 percent black population. He won 15 percent of the white vote and over 90 percent of the energized black vote. ''My task,'' stated Stokes in *Vital Speeches,* ''was to maximize my black vote, get as many white votes as I could, and to minimize white–fear reactions that would cause a majority voter turn–out for my white opponent.''

Stokes's victory made him the first black mayor of a major city in America. His victory also served as an endorsement of coalition building across racial and class lines. He became an instant national celebrity and the prototype of an emerging generation of urban black politicians who solidified their base of support among blacks while reaching out for the support of white liberals and the business community. Stokes became a spokesperson for revitalizing America's inner cities. He warned the nation about the impending urban crisis caused by the loss of jobs, housing, and hope. His national stature was confirmed by his election in 1970 to the presidency of the National League of Cities, an organization composed of mayors and city and county officials.

The Stokes administration was defined by an attempt to increase city services in underserved communities. His goal, Stokes said, was not to deny services to any neighborhood, but to equalize services to all neighborhoods. Among his initiatives were the building and revitalizing of public housing, expansion of recreational programs, an increase in city income tax to finance social programs such as school funding and water purification, and making the city service work force more reflective of the racial diversity of Cleveland. He also opened city hall jobs to blacks.

Many of Stokes's long range goals were stymied by the eruption of an urban rebellion in July 1968, only months after he took office. Glenville, the northeast neighborhood where the Stokes brothers launched their law practice, was the scene of a shootout between the city police and a black nationalist group headed by Fred Ahmed Evans. The night–long confrontation between police and the black nationalists resulted in the death of six black civilians and three white police officers. To quell the accompanying riot, Mayor Stokes ordered all white police officers removed from the area and replaced them with black officers, who at that time comprised only seven percent of the police force. Although the riot abated after several days, an outcome favored by the added presence of the National Guard, the political fallout lingered and clouded the rest of Stokes's tenure as mayor.

Further damage was done when it was later revealed that $6,000 dollars from the mayor's innovative program, Cleveland Now!, organized to build housing, promote jobs creation, and provide recreation and summer jobs for youth, was paid to the black nationalist group implicated in the Glenville shootout. Although Stokes won reelection in 1969, the Glenville shootout weakened the good will toward his administration and created distrust of the city government among some white allies, and a lasting friction among the Stokes administration, the police department, and a recalcitrant city council. In a desperate last attempt to ease the antagonism and assert authority over the police department, Stokes hired retired black general Benjamin O. Davis Jr. as safety director. General Davis's crisp military style and inability to relate to the diverse population of Cleveland quickly alienated him from the mayor and important segments of the city's population. Davis resigned from the top law enforcement job after less than a year. Stokes soon announced that he would not seek a third term in 1971.

In assessing his political fortunes following the Glenville uprising, Stokes later made the following observation in *Vital Speeches*:

> ''The political damage was deep and proved to not be reversible. A major, innovative public–private sector program that depended upon and had been receiving funding from the business community, dried up. The racial lines in the city council hardened and the passage of any legislation of significance became the occasion for confrontation and obstruction that had no relation to the subject of the bill. Any hope of softening the long–established racial divisions in the city was over. The bright promise of the partnership of a young, black mayor and a majority white city population being able to fashion new ways of racial cooperation was not to be.

Stokes left Cleveland in 1972 to become the first black news anchor in the New York City area. He worked for WNBC television for eight years and served as urban affairs editor and foreign correspondent in Africa. He returned to Cleveland in 1981 and joined a prestigious law firm, serving as general counsel for the United Auto Workers. Stokes reentered the political arena in 1983 and was elected judge of the municipal court. His attempt to become housing court judge in 1989 was rebuffed by voters, although he retained his seat on the municipal court until 1994, when President Bill Clinton appointed him ambassador to the Seychelles, a cluster of islands in the Indian Ocean off the cost of Africa. Stokes left the Seychelles on a medical leave–of–absence after he was diagnosed with cancer of the esophagus in 1995.

In 1973 Simon and Schuster published Stokes's political biography, *Promises of Power.* Stokes contributed articles to *Tuesday Magazine,* the *Cleveland Press and Plain Dealer, Playboy, Social Science Quarterly, Vital Speeches,* and other publications. Among the honors and awards Stokes received for his work as politician and journalist were an Emmy for outstanding individual craft in feature reporting. Among the academic institutions awarding Stokes an honorary degree were Boston University, Tufts University, Oberlin College, Wilberforce University, and North Carolina Agricultural and Technical State University.

Stokes was married four times. His first marriage to Dayton, Ohio native Edith Shirley Smith ended in 1953. Stokes's marriage to Fisk University graduate Shirley Edwards in 1958 produced three children—Carl Jr., Cordi, and Cordell. The couple divorced in 1973. He married Raija Kostadinova of Finland in 1981. They also divorced but then remarried in 1993. Stokes had an adopted daughter, Cynthia, and a stepson, Sasha Kostadinova from that marriage.

Stokes succumbed to cancer of the esophagus on April 3, 1996, at the Cleveland Clinic in his hometown. The handsome, charismatic Stokes became a symbol of a changing America in the late 1960s as he overcame racial barriers in politics and in television. Following Carl Stokes's death, Louis Stokes summed up his brother's importance in the April 3, 1996, issue of the *New York Times,* saying that Carl Stokes ''inspired black Americans to aspire to higher political office all over the country.''

REFERENCES

''Carl Stokes, Public Official Who Broke Racial Barriers, 68.'' *New York Times,* April 3, 1996.

''Living Legacy Award Dinner.'' *Washington Times,* December 11, 1995.

''Past Glory Has Faded for Stokes.'' *New York Times,* December 3, 1989.

Stokes, Carl B. *Promises of Power: A Political Autobiography.* New York: Simon and Schuster, 1973.

———. ''Racial Equality and Appreciation of Diversity in Our Urban Communities: How Far Have We Come?'' *Vital Speeches* 59 (1 April 1993).

Weinberg, Kenneth G. *Black Victory: Carl Stokes and the Winning of Cleveland.* Chicago: Quadrangle Books, 1968.

Who's Who among African Americans, 1996–97. 9th ed. Detroit: Gale Research, 1996.

Audrey Thomas McCluskey

Leon H. Sullivan

(1922–)

Minister, civil rights leader, entrepreneur

In his 38 years as pastor of Zion Baptist Church in Philadelphia, Leon H. Sullivan has accomplished much in his quest for civil rights and his battle against urban decay. He has not only pastored an urban congregation that grew from 500 to 6,000 members, he established an anticrime group that numbered 20,000 volunteers, created a youth employment program that yearly placed 1,000 teenagers in jobs, and organized 400 ministers to encourage their congregations to boycott companies that practiced discrimination in hiring. Sullivan founded a major job training program that mushroomed into a national and international operation. He founded an investment group which not only built inner city housing and shopping centers but formed a major aerospace supply agency as well. Sullivan is also responsible for generating a set of guidelines for American corporations doing business in South Africa. Since his retirement in 1988, this influential national and international figure has focused on battling African hunger, unemployment, and illiteracy.

Leon H. Sullivan

Leon H. Sullivan was born October 16, 1922, in Charleston, West Virginia. His young parents separated and later divorced. As a result, Sullivan was raised by his grandmother, who introduced him to Christianity during his childhood. Sullivan attended segregated elementary and secondary schools in Charleston, and his family moved 11 times before he became an adult.

When Sullivan was only ten years old an incident occurred that affected him profoundly. He sat down at a drugstore counter and was about to order a soft drink when he was told to stand; he could not sit there. Sullivan described the impact of this incident in his 1969 book, *Build Brother Build.* He wrote, ''That was my first real confrontation with bigotry, prejudice and discrimination. I stood on my feet; and at that moment as I stood there, glaring back at the big man's burning eyes, I decided that I would stand on my feet against this kind of thing as long as I lived. I have kept my word. I am still standing on my feet. And I will stand on my feet until I die.'' Sullivan entered many such establishments on his personal quest for justice, only to be refused service. One of his desegregation efforts had a different outcome. He entered a restaurant he described as a ''greasy spoon'' where a section was reserved for blacks who could order food but could not eat there. Sullivan, who was now in the tenth grade, recited the Constitution's Preamble, to the astonishment of the restaurant's patrons and owner. The owner rewarded him with a free meal and announced he was welcome to eat there whenever he wanted; Sullivan became a regular customer.

By the time Sullivan was 13, he was six feet tall. He initially viewed his height as a handicap, until his status as a star high school basketball and football player won him an athletic scholarship to West Virginia State College. At West Virginia State, he played basketball and football and was involved in numerous activities including the student council, the literary society, the John Dewey Society, black history groups, and the newspaper guild.

Chooses Dual Mission

During Sullivan's sophomore year in college, his grandmother's health deteriorated and death was soon imminent. He described the experience and his reaction in *Build Brother Build.* As Sullivan looked around his grandmother's room and noticed poverty's effects, she instructed: ''Leonie, help your people. And don't let this kind of thing happen to anybody else.'' The following Sunday, Sullivan, speaking to a youth group in Huntington, West Virginia, realized that his life's work would be as a minister.

Two men served as Sullivan's mentors in his quest to become a minister: Moses Newsome and Adam Clayton Powell, Jr. Sullivan met Newsome, a young minister, soon after his grandmother's death. Newsome taught Sullivan theology, arranged for his ordination, and helped him obtain appointments at two churches where he pastored on alternate Sundays. During this period, Sullivan continued his college studies as well as sports activities. He volunteered to be an army chaplin during World War II but was rejected because of his youth. Instead, he obtained a job in an ordinance plant in order to help the war effort.

During the spring of 1943, the same year Sullivan graduated from college, he met Powell, pastor of Abyssinian Baptist Church in New York City and future congressman.

Powell, who had accepted an offer to preach at one of Sullivan's churches on his way to a NAACP meeting, was impressed with Sullivan, and persuaded him to move to New York after graduation.

Sullivan's two years in Harlem were productive. On Powell's recommendation, Sullivan became the first black American coinbox operator for Bell Telephone Company. He met A. Philip Randolph, president of the Brotherhood of Sleeping Car Porters, which is recognized as the first black American union. Randolph was the originator of the March on Washington Movement, and the 21–year–old Sullivan was elected president of the National March on Washington Movement. According to Sullivan, Randolph was his third mentor. He wrote in *Build Brother Build,* "Mr. Randolph tutored me as a father would, in movement tactics and philosophy. It was from him that I learned much of the art of massive community organization, and he taught me the meaning of nonviolent direct action. I have used that method since then in all of my protest programs. Mr. Randolph was preaching the doctrine long before it became popular across America."

In his capacity as march president, Sullivan also worked with noted civil rights activist Bayard Rustin. Regardless of other demands on his schedule, Sullivan, along with his dentist friend Lawrence Ervin, spent Friday and Saturday evenings delivering street corner civil rights orations; their only props were a ladder and an American flag.

Sullivan then became a supply minister at the Rendall Presbyterian Church. In the mid–1940s, he developed a rapport with neighborhood gang members and was instrumental in organizing a June 1944 meeting at the church where 400 gang members negotiated peace terms for themselves and the community. Mayor Fiorello LaGuardia soon became familiar with Sullivan's accomplishments and frequently consulted him on Harlem matters. Sullivan, after persuading LaGuardia that more black Americans should be added to the police force, recruited 100 black men who became police officers within one month. These new officers and Sullivan, along with support from prizefighters Sugar Ray Robinson and Joe Louis, created a youth recreational center.

Sullivan resigned from Rendall Presbyterian in order to accept Powell's offer to become assistant minister at Abyssinian Baptist. He also worked on Powell's successful campaign to gain a New York Congressional seat. Sullivan credits Powell with instructing him in church matters and politics.

In 1945 Sullivan received a degree from Union Theological Seminary. He also married Grace Banks and they moved to New Jersey, where Sullivan assumed the pastorate of First Baptist Church in South Orange. Under his leadership, membership increased. Sullivan was elected president of the South Orange Council of Churches and continued to work in the community, especially with young people. During this period, Sullivan continued his educational pursuits: he received a master's degree in religion from Columbia University in 1947 and did postgraduate work in educational and social psychology, community organization, religious philosophy, and religious education. Years later, Sullivan earned a doctor of divinity degree from Virginia Union University.

In 1950 Sullivan resigned from First Baptist and moved to Philadelphia where he assumed the pastorship of Zion Baptist Church. Sullivan's goal of building an effective community ministry was compatible with Zion Baptist's history of community involvement, dating from its founding in 1882. As in South Orange and Harlem, the young minister continued to make the community's youth a priority. For example, when Sullivan encountered five boys loitering on a street corner, he invited them to play basketball with him at a nearby gym. After playing basketball, Sullivan invited them to visit Zion Baptist. The boys attended church the following Sunday and were eventually baptized by Sullivan. Due to the influence of Sullivan and Zion Baptist, the members of this group, which included dropouts and juvenile delinquents, all later became men of distinction in the areas of education, employment, government, or professional sports.

In 1953, three other boys met a different fate; they were murdered on the steps of a YMCA building. Motivated by this urban tragedy, Sullivan established the Philadelphia Citizens Committee Against Juvenile Delinquency and Its Causes. Only one year later, 20,000 volunteers were involved in crime–fighting efforts. In recognition of Sullivan's founding of the Philadelphia Citizens Committee, the National Junior Chamber of Commerce designated him one of America's ten outstanding young men; Sullivan received his award from Vice–President Richard Nixon.

Citing employment opportunities as an antidote to juvenile delinquency and frustration, Sullivan established a youth employment office at Zion Baptist that placed 1,000 young people yearly in jobs. In 1957 the Freedom Foundation hailed Sullivan's program as the United States' most effective privately developed youth program. Sullivan did not become complacent, however; his program could not find jobs for thousands of youth due to discriminatory hiring practices. Sullivan wrote public officials including the mayor of Philadelphia and the President of the United States and asked for their help in ameliorating black unemployment, but their responses were insignificant.

Once again, community adversity led to the creation of a new Sullivan project, the Selective Patronage Program (SPP). Four hundred black ministers in Philadelphia sought improved black employment opportunities at various companies. When their requests were denied, they urged their congregations to boycott the offending establishments until their minimum requests were granted. Between 1959 and 1963, as a result of SPP, black Philadelphians gained more than 2,000 jobs. Successful SPPs were also conducted in Boston, Detroit, New York, and elsewhere, and corporations boycotted included Coca–Cola, Esso, Gulf Oil, and Sun Oil. In 1962 Sullivan traveled to Atlanta, at Martin Luther King's request, to familiarize the city's ministers with the SPP strategy. Consequently SPP was the inspiration for King and Ralph Abernathy's Operation Breadbasket, a program that was later headed by Jesse Jackson. As a result of the success of SPP and Sullivan's earlier endeavors, *Life* magazine proclaimed him one of 100 outstanding young adults in America.

Founds Opportunities Industrialization Center

Although proud of SPP's phenomenal employment accomplishments, Sullivan realized that while it had opened employment doors for blacks at previously segregated companies, another problem existed. There were numerous positions for secretaries, machinists, computer workers, and others, yet many blacks lacked the skills needed for these jobs. Thus, Sullivan founded the non–profit Opportunities Industrialization Center (OIC) in 1964. He persuaded city officials to allow him to convert a vacant jail in North Philadelphia into OIC's training center; five additional training centers were later established in other sections of the city. Initially there was no governmental funding for the program, so financial contributions and equipment were solicited from the community, congregations, and private sector businesses.

OIC students' learning did not begin at the training center. First they were enrolled in OIC's prevocational effort, the Feeder Program (FP), located in an old synagogue near the training center. Since many OIC students had dropped out of school and/or had low levels of self–worth, the FP was designed to increase their self–esteem and ambition through instruction that included minority history, literacy, English as a second language (for foreign–born Americans), and consumer awareness as well as personal grooming and deportment. After completing the FP, students attended an OIC training center where they gained skills in such areas as drafting, power machine operating, electronics, sheet metal work, machine shop, chemical laboratory technician training, teletype operating, and restaurant practices. OIC found employment for students upon completion of training and provided further training to those who requested it.

OIC became the fastest growing manpower program in the United States. In 1967 there were 70 OICs in the United States, and centers were being established in Africa. That same year, President Lyndon Johnson visited an OIC training center in Philadelphia. In the late 1960s, an American president traveling to another city to visit a program generated by black Americans was a rare occurrence. By 1969, 1,500 trainees were enrolled in Philadelphia while national OIC attendance was 20,000. Columbus Salley cited additional statistics in support of OIC's success in *The Black 100.* He wrote, "OIC has grown. . .to over one hundred training centers throughout the United States; OIC International. . . has established training centers in twelve African countries, and several centers in the Philippines and Eastern Europe; OIC has trained more than one million American men and women, with over 800,000 finding employment, and generated about $15 billion in annual income in the United States. . ..

Although federal funding for OIC greatly diminished during the Reagan Administration, leading to program and budget reductions, OIC training programs still exist in 80 cities in the 1990s.

Establishes Zion Investment Associates

In 1962 Sullivan sought 50 volunteers from his congregation who would contribute ten dollars monthly for 36 months in an investment cooperative program he called the 10–36–50 Plan. Two hundred church members initially responded, and thus Zion Investment Associates (ZIA) was formed. For the first 16 months, the ten–dollar contributions from the 200 investors were placed in a non–profit trust for scholarships and charitable donations for the community and anyone in need, regardless of race. The contributions of the final 20 months were channeled into a profit–making investment corporation that purchased various properties in Philadelphia. In 1964 ZIA bought a $75,000 apartment building. One year later ZIA broke ground on Zion Gardens, a million dollar garden apartment complex. In 1967 ZIA broke ground on a four–acre site named Progress Plaza, a $1.7 million shopping center which became the largest black American–built, –owned, and –managed shopping center. ZIA later built Progress Haddington Shopping Plaza, another urban shopping center. A multimillion–dollar facility known as the Progress Human Service Center was also built and managed by ZIA. In addition the group built Opportunities Tower I and Opportunities Tower II, $8 million dollar senior housing complexes.

ZIA ventured into other areas. With a $400,000 grant from the Ford Foundation, it built an entrepreneurial training center at Progress Plaza. In 1968, with financial support from the General Electric Corporation, Progress Aerospace Enterprises, the first black–owned aerospace company was formed; it became a major aerospace supply agency. Also in 1968, ZIA opened Progress Garment Manufacturing Enterprises.

ZIA experienced remarkable growth. Four hundred new members joined in 1965, and in 1968 3,000 more investors were added. That same year, there were 10,000 names on ZIA's membership waiting list. Over the years as membership increased, ZIA was transformed from a church–based group into a community–based organization and ultimately into a national association.

Creates Sullivan Principles

In 1971 Sullivan joined General Motors' Board of Directors. As the corporation's first black director he was instrumental in expanding GM's black American employment and dealerships. His concern for improving economic and social conditions extended beyond American shores. In 1977 he created the Sullivan Principles, a code of conduct for American corporations operating in South Africa designed to guarantee fair treatment for black South African employees.

The original six guidelines were: nonsegregation of work, comfort, and eating facilities, fair employment practices for all; equal pay for equal work, supervisory, administrative, clerical, and technical job training for blacks and other nonwhites, an increased number of supervisory positions for blacks and other nonwhites, and an improved quality of life for employees outside of the workplace. In 1984 Sullivan added that American corporations in South Africa were required to attempt to overturn apartheid, to allow black workers employment mobility, and to provide adequate employment housing near the workplace. Also by 1984, Sullivan had successfully used his position as a GM board member to ensure that GM as well as 149 of the 150 American corporations investing in South Africa were observing the guidelines.

In 1988 the Sullivans, parents of Howard, Julie, and Hope, moved to Phoenix, Arizona after Sullivan assumed the position of Zion Baptist's pastor emeritus. Sullivan's retirement from Zion Baptist allowed him to spend more time focusing on African concerns. In the late 1980s, he urged American corporations to sell their South African investments, and he called on the United States government to impose sanctions against South Africa. Eventually the Sullivan Principles, along with the withdrawal of international businesses from South Africa and international sanctions, proved to be key elements leading to apartheid's end.

Sullivan strove for African improvement in other ways as well. During the 1980s, he founded the International Foundation for Education and Self–Help (IFESH)to fight illiteracy, hunger, and unemployment in Africa and to promote African self–reliance. Sullivan organized and cochaired the first African and African American Summit, held at Abidjan, Ivory Coast, in April, 1991; the conference's findings were the subject of a United States Senate Subcommittee on Africa hearing. In October 1991 Sullivan presided at the United Nations Day for Africa, an event he initiated in order to focus on debt relief for Sub–Saharan African countries.

Many honors and awards have been bestowed upon Sullivan. He holds honorary doctorates from more than 30 institutions including Dartmouth College, Princeton University, Temple University, Yale University, and the University of Pennsylvania. Other educational honors include the Leon Howard Sullivan Chair at the University of Wisconsin, established in 1976, and the Leon Howard Sullivan Scholarship Fund at Bentley College in Massachusetts, established in 1988. Among his many awards are the American Exemplar Medal (1969), the NAACP's Spingarn Medal (1971), and the Franklin D. Roosevelt Four Freedom Medal Award (1987). In 1991 Sullivan received the Presidential Medal of Freedom, America's highest civilian award, and the Distinguished Service Award, the Ivory Coast's highest honor. GM is not Sullivan's only board membership; he is also a member of the Mellon Bank Corporation Board of Directors.

Leon Sullivan is a worthy recipient of these numerous awards and tributes. He has pioneered and preached self–help strategies to the world. His prolific accomplishments have made lasting national and international contributions to the improvement of the human race.

Current address: Progress Plaza Shopping Center, 1501 North Broad Street, Philadelphia, PA 19122.

REFERENCES

Contemporary Black Biography. Vol. 3. Detroit: Gale Research, 1993.

Hawkins, Walter L. *African American Biographies.* Vol. 2. Jefferson, NC: McFarland, 1994.

Salley, Columbus. *The Black 100: A Ranking of the Most Influential African Americans, Past and Present.* New York: Citadel Press, 1993.

Salzman, Jack, David Lionel Smith, and Cornel West, eds. *Encyclopedia of African–American Culture and History.* New York: Macmillan Library Reference USA/Simon and Schuster Macmillan, 1996.

Sullivan, Leon H. *Build Brother Build.* Philadelphia: Macrae Smith, 1969.

Linda M. Carter

Louis Sullivan
(1933–)
Medical school president, physician, government official

As the highest–ranking African American in the Bush Administration, Louis Wade Sullivan presided over the largest federal agency, the Department of Health and Human Services, and administered its $500 billion annual budget. His position on preventive medicine, campaign against smoking, and manipulation of budget cuts to preserve health care programs for the poor and minorities demonstrate his unwavering commitment to the poor and underserved. He also played a major role in establishing the Morehouse School of Medicine, the third medical school at a historically black institution in the United States.

Lou Sullivan, as he is called by family and friends, was born in Atlanta on November 3, 1933. He was the youngest of two sons born to Walter Wade, a mortician, and Lubirda Elizabeth Priester Sullivan, an elementary school teacher. While their children were still young, the family moved to the small town of Blakely, Georgia, where whites of the small town south of Macon did not welcome the middle–class Sullivans. Walter Sullivan and his wife fought the bigotry and racism they encountered by establishing the Blakely chapter of the NAACP.

Sullivan and his older brother Walter Jr. were sent back to Atlanta to attend school and lived with family friends during the school year. Their father once was shot and wounded for his active resistance to white domination in Blakely. As Walter Sullivan Jr. told the *New York Times,* "They stayed in that little town for twenty more years to prove a point: that whites couldn't run them out."

In 1950 Sullivan entered the freshman class at Morehouse College, where he undertook the premedical curriculum and graduated magna cum laude in 1954. He received a scholarship to Boston University Medical School and entered in the fall of 1954. Sullivan worked his way through medical school

Louis Sullivan

by waiting tables to earn extra money for expenses not covered by his scholarship.

During the fall semester of his second year, Sullivan married Eve Williamson, an attorney, on September 30, 1955. He was also elected class president twice. The only black person in his graduating class, Sullivan ranked third and graduated cum laude, earning his medical degree in 1958. He was accepted into the internship and residency program at New York Hospital–Cornell Medical Center in New York City.

In 1960 Sullivan received a fellowship in pathology at Massachusetts General Hospital in Boston. The following year he earned a postgraduate research fellowship at Thorndike Memorial Laboratory at Harvard University Medical School. He became instructor of medicine at the Harvard Medical School in 1963 and in 1964 was appointed assistant professor of medicine at the New Jersey College of Medicine, where he remained until 1966.

Sullivan returned to Boston in 1966 to become codirector of hematology and assistant professor of medicine at the Boston University Medical Center. He was promoted to associate professor of medicine in 1968 and became a full professor in 1974. At Boston University, Sullivan became a renowned hematologist specializing in blood disorders linked to vitamin deficiencies.

The Morehouse Project

A planner and goal–setter, Sullivan intended to become chair of a department in a prominent medical school by the age of forty–five. Instead, at forty–two, he found himself involved with a group of his Morehouse friends and alumni who wanted to expand opportunities for African Americans to attend medical school. Only two historically black medical schools still existed in the United States—Howard University in Washington, D.C., and Meharry Medical College in Nashville, Tennessee. The 1978 case of *Bakke v. University of California* challenged affirmative action regarding medical school admissions, and doors that had swung open in the wake of civil rights and affirmative action were swinging closed.

The Morehouse doctors recruited Sullivan to address this growing problem. Resigning from his tenured position as professor of medicine and physiology in 1975, Sullivan left Boston to return to his native state. At Morehouse in 1978, he created a two–year medical program at the historically black Atlanta University Center College which prepared students to attend accredited medical schools wherever they could gain admission. He was appointed dean of the school when it was still a two–year program connected to Morehouse College.

Sullivan's dream, however, was to build a full–fledged medical college. Soliciting help from the U.S. Congress, Fulton County Commission, Atlanta City Council, and local business and civic leaders, he proved so persuasive and successful in his quest for funding that he even won the support of conservative white state legislators. In spite of his criticism of the Ronald Reagan Administration's cutbacks in federal aid to education, he secured large federal grants for the school.

Former provost of Atlanta University Prince Rivers underscored Sullivan's crucial role in the establishment of Morehouse School of Medicine when he told *New York Times* reporter Ronald Smothers, "When government agencies deal with black institutions, they have to have confidence in the individuals, because they don't have confidence in the institutions. Lou Sullivan, as a researcher and scholar, is in a class by himself, and he was able to build that confidence."

By 1981 Sullivan's work paid off with the creation of the Morehouse School of Medicine, the third predominantly black medical school in the United States. Under Sullivan's leadership, the school, which is independent of Morehouse College, began active research programs on a wide range of health problems affecting the black community, such as sickle–cell anemia, hypertension, certain forms of cancer, low birth weight, and high infant mortality rates. Since its inception, 89 percent of the school's students have passed second–year national examinations, and 99 percent have passed fourth–year exams.

Pro–Life or Pro–Choice

When George Bush was elected, he considered appointing Sullivan Secretary of Health and Human Services, the largest of the federal agencies. When Bush's intentions became public, however, controversy followed almost immediately.

Sullivan's credentials as a hematologist, researcher, and physician, and his leadership at Morehouse School of Medicine made him eminently qualified, but opposition to his nomination arose over his stand on abortion. As soon as news leaked of Bush's intended nomination of Sullivan, the National Right to Life Committee—the largest anti–abortion group in the country—expressed strenuous opposition.

In a December 18, 1988, interview in the *Atlanta Journal and Constitution,* Sullivan was depicted as supporting a woman's right to chose abortion as an option. In the same newspaper on the following day, however, Sullivan contradicted his statement and said that he was opposed to the use of federal funds for abortions. Because Bush had campaigned on an anti–abortion platform and had been elected with the support of anti–abortion groups, rumors arose that Bush might withdraw Sullivan's nomination.

In a move that angered and disappointed many pro–choice groups, Sullivan released a statement to the press on December 18, 1988, reversing his position: "I wish to emphasize that in the area of abortion, my personal position is that I am opposed to abortion except in the case of rape, incest or threat to the life of the mother." Still, the NRLC remained opposed to Sullivan's nomination.

In spite of the abortion battle, Sullivan was confirmed as the new Secretary of Health and Human Services on March 1, 1989. His abrupt reversal on the abortion issue did not mean that he had abandoned his personal convictions, as some Georgians suspected when conservative Republican Newt Gingrich enthusiastically supported Sullivan for the job. As Sullivan's friend and colleague, Marian Wright Edelman, executive director of the Children's Defense Fund, asserted in the *Congressional Quarterly,* "He will be one who is very sensitive to the medically underserved."

One week after his confirmation, Sullivan again alienated conservative Republicans by endorsing community programs that distributed free hypodermic needles to drug users in exchange for ones that might be contaminated with the AIDS virus. In the *New York Times* for March 9, 1989, Sullivan elaborated: "I don't subscribe to the view that [distributing free needles] condones drug abuse. If this is a strategy that shows promise of helping to arrest the spread of AIDS, I think this is something that does deserve a chance for an appropriate trial." Both President Bush and anti–drug czar William J. Bennett had publicly stated their opposition to needle–exchange programs. Again Sullivan changed his public position in order to act on his private beliefs.

Working for Minority Health Care and Disease Prevention

Sullivan told *New York Times* reporter Julie Johnson that minority health care and preventive medicine were his top priorities. He requested and received $42.9 million for the 1990 fiscal year from Richard G. Darman, director of the Office of Management and Budget, for scholarships and research aid to selected medical schools whose funding had been cut by the Reagan Administration. Sullivan also asked for and received $25 million more for occupational health programs that mainly benefit minorities and had been cut 37 percent by Reagan's budget.

Sullivan altered his noncommittal reputation when he fought to prevent budget–cutting that would eliminate health care programs for minorities and the needy. The issue for which he will be remembered, however, is his stance on cigarette smoking. Sullivan attacked smoking and the advertising tactics used by the tobacco industry. In an angry speech directed at the R. J. Reynolds Tobacco Company, Sullivan revealed that the company's new brand of cigarettes specifically targeted black teenagers and caused the company to cancel the product. When the Republicans failed to win reelection to the White House, Sullivan returned to his position as president of Morehouse School of Medicine in 1993.

Sullivan is a member of the National Academy of Sciences, American Society of Hematology, American Society for Clinical Investigation, Phi Beta Kappa, and Alpha Omega Alpha honor societies. Sullivan and his wife have three grown children—Paul, a physician; Shanta; and Halsted. In his role as president of Morehouse School of Medicine, Sullivan's mission has not changed from his original intent—to train health care providers for service in poor and underserved communities.

Current address: Morehouse School of Medicine, 720 Westview Dr. SW, Atlanta, Georgia 30310.

REFERENCES

Congressional Quarterly 46 (24 December 1988): 3578.

Contemporary Black Biography. Vol. 8. Detroit: Gale Research, 1995.

Current Biography Yearbook. New York: H. W. Wilson, 1988.

"Health Chief Seeks to Aid Minorities." *New York Times,* April 25, 1989.

"The Importance of Dr. Sullivan." *New York Times,* December 23, 1988.

Wheeler, David L. "Sullivan, Nominee for Health and Human Services Post, Seen Likely to Follow Bush's Lead on Major Issues." *Chronicle of Higher Education* 35 (4 January 1989): A17, A–22.

Nagueyalti Warren

Percy E. Sutton

(1920–)

Lawyer, civil rights activist, lecturer, public official, television executive

Evidence that Percy Sutton is an effective and popular community leader is not difficult to find. Eighty percent of New York City's voters elected him Manhattan Borough president in 1966. Although officially retired, he still delivers nearly one lecture or speech every week to college students, business leaders, government officials, and international groups. He serves on the boards or executive committees of several nonprofit organizations and businesses. The founder of a company that owns and operates radio stations and cable TV systems, he has said that African Americans must influence or control elements of the broadcast and news media in order to liberate themselves, and to have a significant impact on the political processes of this nation.

Percy Ellis Sutton was born on November 24, 1920, in San Antonio, the youngest of 15 children of Samuel J. and Lillian Smith. His father, who was born in slavery, initially became a farmer and later advanced himself to principal of Phyllis Wheatley High School in the then–segregated San Antonio school system. His mother was also an educator. Both parents were determined that their children would be provided the best opportunities possible. Each of their 12 surviving children went to college, and the children themselves helped each other to complete their educations, with the older ones giving financial support to the younger ones. Sutton married the former Leatrice O'Farrel in 1943. His children, Pierre and Cheryl Lynn, work in his radio and television business.

Percy E. Sutton

Distinguished Family

All of Sutton's siblings became distinguished citizens in their respective professions and communities. An older brother, Alexander Carver, a minister, taught him to be concerned about other people. His deceased brother Oliver, his former law partner, became a judge on the New York State Supreme Court. Another brother, G. J., was the first black man from San Antonio to sit in the Texas House of Representatives. The Institute of Texas Cultures of the University of Texas at San Antonio honored the Sutton family in its permanent exhibit depicting African Americans who have made significant contributions to the state's development.

The *New York Post* for September 17, 1966 reported that a traumatic experience at age 13 contributed to Sutton's firm commitment to the civil rights struggle. "I was passing out some NAACP (National Association for the Advancement of Colored People) pamphlets and this big cop comes up and says 'Nigger what are you doing out of your neighborhood?' and then he proceeded to beat the hell out of me." He remembered his father's admonition and was guided by it then and throughout his life: "Suffer the hurts, but don't show the anger, because, if you do, it will block you from being able to do anything effectively to remove the hurts."

Supporting himself by doing odd jobs, Percy Sutton attended three historically black universities without earning a degree: Prairie View Agricultural and Mechanical College in Texas, Tuskegee Institute in Alabama, and Hampton Institute in Virginia. He also learned to fly, and earned money as a stunt pilot at county fairs. Since he was already a flyer, when World War II (1939–45) came along, he attempted to enlist in the Army Air Corps. Rejected by southern white recruiting officers, he quickly moved to New York City where his enlistment was accepted. Serving with the famous Tuskegee Airmen, Sutton won combat stars as an intelligence officer with the 332nd Fighter Group's black 99th Pursuit Squadron in the Italian and Mediterranean theaters of operation.

Honorably discharged from the Air Corps as a captain, Sutton entered Columbia University School of Law on his GI Bill benefits. While at Columbia, he earned his living as a part–time dishwasher, bellhop, and waiter. He subsequently switched to Brooklyn College School of Law so that he could study and hold down a full–time job at the same time. He served first as a clerk in the general post office and then as a subway conductor. He received his law degree in 1950 and passed the New York bar the next year.

Sutton served again in the military during the Korean War as an Air Force intelligence officer in Washington, D.C. Later, he became the air force's first black trial judge advocate. He left the service for the second time in 1953 and returned to New York City to begin his legal and political career.

Later that same year, Sutton, with his brother Oliver and George Covington, set up a law partnership on 125th Street, the hub and heart of Harlem, and began his practice of law in the continental U.S. and the Virgin Islands that spanned over 40 years. He served for many years as attorney to civil rights activists Malcolm X, and after Malcolm's death he continued to represent Malcolm's widow, Betty Shabazz, and the Shabazz family. He and former New York City mayor David Dinkins also defended Malcolm Shabazz, the 12–year–old grandson of Betty, who set a fire in 1997 that caused his grandmother's death. The Sutton and Covington law firm, always socially conscious, handled many cases free of charge. In the South in

1963 and 1964, when there were massive arrests of civil rights workers, the firm represented more than 200 defendants. Sutton himself served as a consultant to the Student Nonviolent Coordinating Committee.

Political Arena

After a succession of positions in the New York branch of the NAACP, Sutton was elected its president in 1961 and again in 1962. He took part in many civil rights sit–ins and demonstrations during his NAACP leadership days, and about the same time, began to develop an interest in politics. Unfortunately, his early political efforts were not too successful. After 11 years (1953–1964) of losing elections for Democratic party district leader, assemblyman, and New York City councilman, he finally began to develop a solid political base. In 1963, along with future–U.S. Congressman Charles Rangel, he helped form an insurgent Harlem Democratic political club with nearly a thousand volunteer workers. Initially called the John F. Kennedy Club, this organization later became the Martin Luther King Jr. Club. The new club helped propel Sutton into the New York State Assembly in the November 1964 election; he took his seat in the lower house of the New York legislature on January 1, 1965.

Sutton's charismatic personality and eloquence as a speaker were recognized when he was selected spokesman for the 13 black assemblymen in the 165–member assembly. Under his leadership, black assemblymen, who had formerly been discriminated against in legislative assignments, became members of every major committee. One was even made majority whip.

As an assemblyman, Sutton was a major supporter of state funding to build the New York Public Library's Schomburg Center for Research in Black Culture, located at 135th Street and Malcolm X Boulevard (Lenox Avenue). Another legislative initiative was the Search for Education, Elevation, and Knowledge (S.E.E.K.) program, which enabled promising students from disadvantaged backgrounds to enter college. In 1966, he was voted Assemblyman of the Year by the Intercollegiate Legislative Assembly.

In 1966, after Constance Baker Motley stepped down from her job as Manhattan Borough president to accept a federal judgeship, the New York City Council chose Sutton to fill her unexpired term. Elected and re–elected borough president in his own right by the overwhelming majority of New York voters, he was for 11 years (1966–77) the highest elected African–American official in the state. By law at that time, he had two votes on New York's Board of Estimate, the executive body responsible for allocating money to run all of the city's public service departments. The borough presidency was what its occupant made of it, and Sutton, a sophisticated tactician, knew how to exert political clout.

Because Sutton had to deal with a largely white constituency, he took time to visit parts of Manhattan where few blacks, even politicians and appointed city officials, ever appeared. He would often take walks at dawn through the neighborhoods, dresssed casually and accompanied by his personal assistant, talking with residents and seeking advice on how to represent all the people in his district more effectively.

Owner of Cable, Radio, Newspaper

In addition to a variety of business activities, Sutton is chairman of Queens Inner Unity Cable System (QUICS), a cable television system in New York City. He is the major founder of the Street Literacy Clinic and the Magic of Learning, a computer–based, interactive, multimedia learning system that teachers use to help young people improve basic skills in reading, writing and functioning in the language of their environment.

In 1968, Percy Sutton withdrew from the U.S. Senate race to support former New York City councilman Paul O'Dwyer in his effort to take away the Senate seat of Jacob K. Javits. In 1972, long before most politicians considered it politically wise to do so, he openly opposed the American military build–up in the Vietnam War. He supported U.S. Senator George McGovern, the "peace" candidate for president of the United States.

As Manhattan Borough president, Sutton gained a national reputation as an expert on urban problems, among them crime in the inner cities. On December 10, 1972, he chaired a public hearing on crime in Harlem, sponsored by the Haryou Act Community Corporation. He expressed the view that effective police and judicial work, together with cooperative effort by the city government to eliminate problems of housing, unemployment and drug traffic, were needed to solve the problem of urban crime.

In 1971, with his brother Oliver and Clarence B. Jones, he was co–founder of the Inner City Broadcasting Corporation which purchased radio station WLIB–AM, making it the first black–owned station in New York City. The company also produces videos for entertainment companies around the country. In the same year he formed a black group called AMNEWS which purchased the *New York Amsterdam News*, the second largest black weekly in the United States. The *Amsterdam News* is currently owned by publisher and editor Wilbert A. Tatum.

Advisor and Counselor

Sutton is an advisor or counselor to many African American institutions, including Harlem Hospital and the United Black Association. In the 1984 and 1988 presidential campaigns of civil rights advocate Jesse Jackson, he was legal advisor, fund raiser and confidant to the candidate. He serves as guest lecturer or "politician in residence" on college campuses, treating the subjects of communications and high technology, finance, business law, and politics at City College of New York, Princeton University, and elsewhere.

Sutton left public office in December 1977, after losing a Democratic primary bid to become mayor of the city of New York. Upon his retirement in 1991, he became chairman emeritus of City Broadcasting. Since then, the corporation has been run by the Sutton children and other family members. No longer active in the political arena except for financial support of candidates and causes, he supports many legal, business, human rights, civil rights, and trade and service organizations and efforts, including the New York Council of the National Boy Scouts of America. Sutton is also vice chairman and board member of the Greater Harlem Chamber of Commerce and is also affiliated with the Harlem Business Alliance.

In January of 1995, Sutton became a member of a delegation of leading American business people selected by U.S. Secretary of Commerce Ron Brown to represent the United States at the Group of Seven (G–7) Nations roundtable meeting on Telecommunications and High Technology in Brussels. The G–7, comprising the United States, Japan, Germany, Great Britain, France, Italy, and Canada, are the world's major industrial democracies. Sutton was selected by his European colleagues to attend follow–up discussions in Brussels and Washington, D. C. In May 1996, he served as a U.S. delegate to the G–7 and developing nations Intelligence Technology Conference in Midrand, South Africa.

Sutton has received hundreds of national, international and local awards honoring his contributions in the fields of communications and high technology, human rights, civil rights, business and philanthropy, among them the NAACP's Spingarn Medal.

Sutton, the consummate politician, knew how to exert political clout. Knowing the meaning of power, he passed on this knowledge to those he mentored, among them former mayor David N. Dinkins. Though retired, Sutton continues to give the community the benefit of his talents and expertise in politics, business, and communication.

Current address: Inner City Theatre Group, 361 West 125th Street, Suite 213, New York, NY 10027.

REFERENCES

Inner City Theatre Group. ''Biographical Sketch of Percy E. Sutton.'' July, 1996.

''Percy Sutton's Secret—'I like people.''' *New York Post,* September 17, 1966.

Riley, Clayton. ''Percy Sutton: Power Politics—New York Style.'' *Ebony* 28 (November 1972): 165–75.

Who's Who among African–Americans, 1996–97. 9th ed. Detroit: Gale Research, 1996.

Vivian D. Hewitt

Benjamin Tucker Tanner

(1835–1923)

Church leader, editor, journalist

Benjamin Tucker Tanner was a leading intellectual in the African Methodist Episcopal (AME) Church at the end of the nineteenth century. As a bishop of the church, Tanner committed himself to the moral uplifting of the many congregations he served; as the editor of the oldest continuously published black newspaper, he sought to build up the intellectual capacities of his readers. Tanner used his leadership skills to benefit the African American community, and to dispel the stereotype that African Americans were incapable of higher thinking.

Tanner was born in Pittsburgh, Pennsylvania, on December 25, 1835, to Hugh S. and Isabel Tanner. The Tanner children—which included Benjamin and his three sisters, Arena, Nancy, and Mary—took advantage of the schooling available to them. Benjamin Tanner trained as a barber and used his skills in that profession to support his mother after the death of his father.

Tanner continued his schooling at Avery College—a school for blacks in Allegheny (now North Pittsburgh)—and studied there between 1852 and 1857, apparently first in the preparatory department followed by one year of the college course. He converted to Christianity in 1856 and spent three years at Western Theological Seminary beginning in 1857. He received an honorary M.A. degree from Avery in 1870 while Henry Highland Garnet headed the school. In the later 1870s Wilberforce University gave him an honorary doctorate of divinity.

On August 14, 1858, Tanner married Sara (Sadie) Miller (1840–1914). She was the daughter of Charles Jefferson Miller, the mixed heritage son of a white planter in Winchester, Virginia. Benjamin and Sarah Tanner had seven children who lived to become adults; two others died as infants. The adult children were Henry Ossawa (1859–1937), Hallie (1863–1901), Mary Louise (1865–1935), Isabella (Belle) (b. 1867), Carlton (1870–1930), Sara (Sadie) Elizabeth (1873–1900), and Bertha (b. 1878). The children were a remarkable group. Henry Ossawa became an important painter; Hallie Tanner Johnson became the first woman with a medical degree licensed to practice in Alabama; and Carlton became a minister and missionary in South Africa. Mary Louise married Aaron Mossell, the first African American graduate of the University of Pennsylvania School of Law, and was the mother of Sadie Tanner Mossell Alexander, a noted lawyer

Benjamin Tucker Tanner

who was one of the first three black women to earn a doctorate. Sara married one of the first African American doctoral graduates from the University of Pennsylvania, and Belle was an AME minister.

Tanner became a deacon and elder of the AME church in May of 1860. His first assignment was in Sacramento, California, but efforts to raise money for passage fell through. His bishop, Daniel A. Payne, then placed him with the Fifteenth Street Presbyterian Church in Washington, D.C., where he stayed for 18 months. He worked regularly at least six hours in his study at the church but still found time to babysit his son.

In 1861 Tanner founded a Sunday school for freedmen in the naval yard in Washington. In April of the following year he moved to the Alexander Mission on E Street for the AME, an assignment which roused local opposition to such an extent that the building had to be guarded by soldiers, and in 1863 he moved to the Georgetown church where he successfully retired the $300 debt. A brief stint at Bethel Church in Baltimore followed in 1866. He soon resigned to head a proposed AME school in Fredericktown, Maryland. It is not clear that plans for the school were realized, but Tanner did organize a school for the Freedmen's Society in Frederickstown.

In 1867 he published a very substantial work of more than 450 pages, *An Apology for African Methodism,* which contained history and a description of the current state of the church. Throughout his life he continued to be a productive writer on church and African American subjects. In 1868 the church found the right position for this man who seemed as interested in teaching as in preaching: editor of the church's weekly newspaper, the *Christian Recorder,* then, as it is now, the oldest continuously published black paper. Tanner held this position for 16 years until 1884.

As editor of the *Christian Recorder,* Tanner was based in Philadelphia. In 1872 he purchased his permanent home, an eight–room house at 2708 Diamond Street in North Philadelphia, near the Morris Brown Mission, where the family worshiped. While the newspaper was principally devoted to church affairs, it did contain material of interest to African Americans in general. Tanner made his first trip abroad when he traveled to the Methodist Ecumenical Conference of 1881 in England.

The newspaper did not completely fulfill Tanner's ambitions. He aimed at developing a quarterly periodical of substantial content. In 1888 the General Conference allowed him to establish the *AME Church Review.* In the following four years he built the publication into the leading black intellectual publication. Tanner felt obliged, however, to sever his connection with the periodical in 1892, when he was elected bishop.

Tanner undertook the arduous duties of administering church districts, shifting to a new one every four years. His responsibilities as bishop ran from Canada to Florida and from New England to Colorado. He organized annual conferences in East Tennessee (1901) and West Florida (1906); in 1901 he briefly served as dean of Payne Theological Seminary in Wilberforce, Ohio. In 1901 Tanner was again delegate to a Methodist Ecumenical Conference in England. In 1908 he was a delegate to the Tri–Council of Colored Methodists, meeting counterparts from the AME Zion church and the Colored (now Christian) Methodist church. Tanner retired as active bishop in 1908. He requested and received half–salary for his retirement, the first bishop to do so.

Tanner was still a vigorous man and he maintained his active interest in church affairs in his retirement. Sara Tanner died in 1914. Benjamin Tanner died at his home of natural causes at midnight, January 15, 1923. His elaborate funeral was held at Union AME Church on January 20.

At the time of his death Tanner could take pride both in his own achievements and those of his children. In the AME Church he stood firmly for education and the uplifting of the African American community. He is a prime example of an intellectual who vigorously carried out Daniel A. Payne's program of intellectual development within the church.

REFERENCES

Arnett, B[enjamin] W., ed. *The Budget for 1884.* Dayton, OH: Christian Publishing House, 1884.

"Bishop Tanner Dead in Philadelphia." *New York Age,* January 20, 1923.

Logan, Rayford W., and Michael R. Winston, eds. *Dictionary of American Negro Biography.* New York: Norton, 1982.

Mathews, Marcia M. *Henry Ossawa Tanner.* Chicago: University of Chicago Press, 1969.

Simmons, William J. *Men of Mark.* Cleveland: Geo. M. Rewell, 1887.

Smith, Charles Spencer. *A History of the African Methodist Episcopal Church.* Supplemental Volume. Philadelphia: Book Concern of the AME, 1922.

"The Tanner Family." *Negro History Bulletin* 10 (April 1947): 147–52, 167.

Wright, R. R. *The Bishops of the African Methodist Episcopal Church.* Nashville: The AME Sunday School Union, 1963.

Robert L. Johns

Henry Ossawa Tanner (1859–1937)

Painter

Henry Ossawa Tanner is remembered as the first African American artist to receive national and international recognition for his work. His life, actually, is dotted with many firsts. He was one of the first African American artists to attend the Philadelphia Academy of the Fine Arts, the first African American artist to exhibit in the Parisian Salon, and the first African American artist and among only a handful of American artists named chevalier of the Legion of Honor from the French government. Tanner's excellent draftsmanship, superb coloring, subtle lighting technique, and painstaking glazes in a variety of works have amazed art critics for more than a century. His accomplishments during the late nineteenth and early twentieth centuries created a sense of pride within the African American art community and fostered new hope for the acceptance of African American art in the United States.

Born on June 12, 1859, in Pittsburgh, Pennsylvania, Tanner was the first child of Philadelphia native and African Methodist Episcopal Bishop Benjamin Tucker Tanner (1835–1923) and Sarah Elizabeth Miller (1840–1914), the granddaughter of a plantation owner. Tanner's mother was one of eleven children born to a slave named Elizabeth and freeman named Charles Jefferson Miller, in Winchester, Virginia. After Henry, his parents had six additional children: Halle (1864–1901); Mary Louise (1865–1935); Isabella (b.1867); Carlton M. (1870–1933); Sarah Elizabeth (1873–1900); and Bertha (1878–1962). Tanner's parents instilled the value of religion, education, and a solid work ethic in their children. These values had a lasting impact on Tanner as well as his younger siblings. All of the Tanner children were well educat-

Henry Ossawa Tanner

ed, intimately involved in the church, and pursued professional careers. For example, Halle Tanner became the first woman allowed to practice medicine in Alabama. Tanner married Jessie Macauley Olssen (d. 1925) on December 14, 1899, a white woman of Swedish–Scottish ancestry from San Francisco who was widely admired for her beauty and musical talents. The couple had one son, Jesse Ossawa, born September 25, 1903, in New York City.

Tanner's Early Years

It was during the period when the Tanners were living at 2708 Diamond Street in North Philadelphia that Henry Tanner discovered his love of painting. The year was 1872 and Tanner, at age thirteen, was a young student in the Roberts Vaux Consolidated School for Colored Students. According to Tanner, he and his father were taking a leisurely stroll in the park near their home when he observed, for the first time, an artist painting a landscape. Later in 1909, Tanner described what he considered a crucial turning point in his life. Quoted in *The Art of Henry O. Tanner,* he said:

> The subject the artist had chosen was a middle distance hillside with a magnificent elm in bold relief. Showing my lack of comprehension of what the artist was trying to do, I asked my father: ''Why does he not have a spy–glass that he can see that big tree more distinctly? Why does he get so far away?'' It was this simple event that, as it were, set me on fire. Like many children, I had drawn upon my slate to the loss of my lessons, or all over the fences to the detriment of the landscape, but never had it crossed my mind that I should be an artist, nor had I ever wished to be. But, after seeing this artist at work for an hour, it was decided on the spot, by me at least, that I would be one, and I assure you it was no ordinary one I had in mind.

That night, Tanner pleaded with his parents for 15 cents to purchase a set of dry colors and a few paint brushes. The next day, tools in tow, he set off to the exact spot that he had seen the artist working the day before. He began sketching and never stopped. Unfortunately, Tanner lived in an era offering few options for an aspiring artist to receive formal training in the United States. There were even fewer artists of American African descent, such as Robert Duncanson (1821–1871), Edward Mitchell Bannister (1826–1901), and Edmonia Lewis (c.1845–c.1912), who were actively pursing this profession.

Initially, Tanner's father discouraged Tanner from becoming a professional artist, instead encouraging him to work in a family–owned flour business as an apprentice. At first, Tanner agreed and took an apprenticeship in 1878. Within a year, though, Tanner fell seriously ill and was forced to resign. After convalescing at Rainbow Lake in New York, his parents acquiesced and supported his dream of becoming a painter.

Tanner wasted no time. In 1879, at the age of 21, he enrolled at the oldest and most respected art school in the country, the Pennsylvania Academy of the Fine Arts. Although the Academy had no racial restrictions, Tanner was the only African American student attending. While there, he studied under the Philadelphia realist painter Thomas Eakins (1844–1916), a professor of drawing and painting. Eakins's interest in exploring the depths of the human soul in introspection influenced Tanner's artistic style.

In 1885, Tanner left the academy but remained in Philadelphia to establish himself as a professional artist. In addition, he wanted to earn enough money to travel to Europe to further his artistic training. Sadly, Tanner was unable to raise the needed funds to make the trip. So, in 1889, he relocated to Atlanta, Georgia, and opened a photography gallery and ''art room'' but that venture flopped.

During the period when Tanner was operating what he once referred to as ''that miserable gallery,'' his work caught the attention of Mrs. Hartzell, wife of Bishop Joseph Crane Hartzell, a trustee of Atlanta's Clark University, a Methodist school. Mrs. Hartzell so admired Tanner's work that she introduced him to her husband who in turn offered him a position as art teacher. Tanner accepted, and sold his gallery. Before starting the new position, he made a brief trip to North Carolina's Blue Ridge Mountains.

Tanner took his camera, hoping to pay for his small rented cabin and other expenses with the photos he shot. Tanner recalled in the Mathews biography *Henry Ossawa Tanner,* ''I made photos of the whole immediate region—a most lovely country and as no photographer had ever visited it before, they were a success, and my hard times—very hard times—vanished as the mountain mists do before the sun.''

The Paris Years

Although Tanner had enjoyed a few small successes in America—exhibiting at both the Pennsylvania Academy of the Fine Arts (April 1881) and the National Academy of Design, New York, (April 1885)—he still longed to travel abroad and study art in Europe. He also knew that Europeans were much more tolerant of racial differences than Americans. The Bishop and his wife were empathetic to his plight and, in 1891, purchased all of Tanner's paintings for $300, enough for him to make the journey to Europe.

Tanner fell in love with Paris, an artist's paradise, instantly. He enrolled in the Académie Julien, a popular private art school, studied under French artists Jean–Joseph Benjamin–Constant and Jean–Paul Laurens, and joined the American Art Students' Club. Tanner's stay in Paris, however, was short–lived. During the summer of 1893, he contracted typhoid fever and was forced to return to the United States to recuperate.

Back in America and fully recovered, Tanner attended the World's Columbian Exposition in Chicago where he presented the paper "The American Negro in Art" at the Exposition's auxiliary Congress on Africa. He also participated in the exposition's special show of 100 American art students for which he submitted the serene genre painting of an elderly man instructing a young boy on the art of banjo playing, entitled, *The Banjo Lesson,* 1893. *The Banjo Lesson* was one of 40 works illustrated in the show. In 1894, Tanner continued to paint using the themes of deep contemplation and transference of knowledge from the old to the young, exemplified in his painting of an elderly man and a boy blessing their meal, entitled *The Thankful Poor.*

In a statement made in Philadelphia after his return to the United States, Tanner addressed his newfound interest in the depiction of African Americans. Writing in the third person, Tanner explains in *The Art of Henry O. Tanner:*

> Since his return from Europe he has painted mostly Negro subjects, he feels drawn to such subjects on account of the newness of the field and because of a desire to represent the serious, and pathetic side of life among them, and it is his through that other things being equal, he who has most sympathy with his subject will obtain the best results. To his mind many of the artists who have represented Negro life have only seen the comic, the ludicrous side of it, and have lacked sympathy with and appreciation for the warm big heart that dwells within such a rough exterior.

After selling *The Thankful Poor* to Philadelphia patron John T. Morris in 1894, Tanner used the money to return to Paris. That same year, Tanner achieved another first: he painting, *The Music Lesson,* earned him acceptance to exhibit in the Parisian Salon. Between 1895 and 1904, Tanner remained in Paris at a rented studio–apartment and became a member of the American Art Association of Paris. During that period, Tanner entered his first large scale religious painting, *Daniel in the Lion's Den,* to the salon. The painting was awarded an honorable mention.

The success of *Daniel in the Lion's Den* diverted Tanner's attention from portraying African American genre scenes. Pleased with *Daniel in the Lion's Den*'s success, Tanner immediately began another biblical painting, *The Resurrection of Lazarus.* News of his latest project caught the attention of Rodman Wannamaker, a fellow member of the American Art Club and a representative of his family's business in Paris. Wannamaker was so impressed with its religious feeling that he offered to pay Tanner's expenses to the Holy Land to expose him to the locations Tanner was painting. In April of 1897, Tanner submitted *The Resurrection of Lazarus* to the salon and then embarked upon his journey. Tanner traveled to Palestine, Egypt, and made stops in Europe on his return. After a brief summer visit with his parents in America, he returned to Paris where he discovered that out of the 3,263 works submitted to the salon, *The Resurrection of Lazarus* was awarded a medal. More important, the French government purchased the painting for the Musée de Luxembourg, and that action launched Tanner as an internationally acclaimed artist.

The years following were particularly fruitful. In 1900, Tanner received widespread recognition and praise for a painting, *Nicodemus Visiting Jesus.* It was exhibited at the Pennsylvania Academy of the Fine Arts, awarded the Lippincott Prize, and purchased for the Temple Collection. He also was awarded the silver medal for *Daniel in the Lion's Den* at the Exposition Universelle, Paris. In 1903, Tanner began the first of a series of paintings entitled "Mothers of the Bible," for reproduction in *Ladies Home Journal.* Four paintings, *Sarah, Hagar, Rachel,* and *Mary,* were successively illustrated in the monthly journal from September through December of 1903.

In the spring of 1904, Tanner helped found the Société Artistique de Picardie in the artist colony at Le Touquet–Paris–Plage, Pas–de–Calais. In April, he was awarded the silver medal for *Daniel in the Lion's Den* at the Louisiana Purchase Exposition, and in 1906 he received the second–class medal for his work, *The Disciples at Emmaus*—which was later purchased by the French government. That same year, his painting, *Two Disciples at the Tomb,* was awarded the Harris Prize for "the most impressive and distinguished work of art of the season," and was purchased for the permanent collection of the Art Institute of Chicago.

Between 1908 and the onset of the first World War in 1914, Tanner's Parisian reputation reached the United States. In 1908, Tanner joined the Paris Society of American Painters, and visited Algiers and Tangiers. That October he visited the United States for his first solo exhibition at America Art Galleries in New York. In April of 1909, he was elected, along with artist Mary Cassatt and George Bellows, to the National Academy of Design, and in 1911 attended a solo exhibition at Thurber Art Galleries, Chicago. In 1913 Tanner was elected president of the Société Artistique de Picardie. Between January and March of 1913, Tanner returned to America to attend both a solo exhibition at Thurber Galleries and a conference of the NAACP in Philadelphia.

At the onset of the first World War, Tanner and his family were residing in the small town of Trépied, located near Etaples, Pas–de–Calais (Artois). The war soon shattered their tranquil life. Added to the turmoil was the death of his mother in August of 1914. In the midst of these events, Tanner found it increasingly difficult to paint. To relieve his feelings of helplessness and despair, he became heavily involved in relief work. In the fall of 1917, Tanner submitted a proposal to the embassy of the United States of America that called for the utilization of vacant land around hospitals and base depots for raising potatoes and other garden vegetables by convalescent patients. The American ambassador in Paris, William G. Sharp, presented the proposal to the American Red Cross and Tanner was granted the position of lieutenant in the Department of Public Information. He was later granted the title of assistant director of Farm and Garden Services. Tanner served in the American Red Cross from December of 1917 until June of 1919, during which time he received permission to sketch activities in the war zone.

Reputation Soars

After leaving the service of the American Red Cross, Tanner did not immediately resume his painting. Instead he concentrated on resting from the pressures from his war work, repairing his house in Trépied, and attending to legal and financial affairs.

Still, Tanner was gaining admiration and respect as an artist among African Americans. Overall, a majority of African Americans viewed Tanner as a role model event though there were those who were critical of his lack of interest in painting black subjects. In fact, in 1922 a group of African American artists and teachers in Washington, D.C., honored Tanner, according to art historian Marcia Mathews, by sponsoring and ''extensive Negro art exhibition, including paintings by Tanner himself, in the studios of Dunbar High School.''

Interestingly, Tanner did not perceive himself to be a ''Negro'' painter but, throughout his life, maintained an interest in Americans of African descent. And Tanner often met with African artists such as William Edouard Scott, Hale Woodruff, Palmer Hayden, Laura Wheeler Waring, William H. Johnson, James A. Porter, Elizabeth Prophet, and Aaron Douglas, giving them advice on their art and careers. He also participated in exhibitions featuring African American art, such as the New York Public Library's 135th Street branch exhibition in August of 1921—the first major exhibition of African American artists in the United States—which contained two works by Tanner: *Christ Washing the Feet of the Disciples* and *The Good Shepherd.*

In 1923, Tanner's life was altered by two major events: the death of his father, Benjamin Tucker Tanner on January 15; and the French government naming him chevalier of the Legion of Honor. After his father's death in December, Tanner visited the United States for the last time, remaining in America until March 22, 1924. During that period, he accepted a commission from Cheyney Training School for Teachers, Cheyney, Pennsylvania, and painted *Nicodemus Coming to Christ.* On September 8, 1925, his wife died at Etaples and was buried at Sceaux near Paris. The following year, Tanner's son Jesse accepted a position with the geophysical department of the Anglo–Persian Oil Company and by October was diagnosed with ''nervous exhaustion.'' He was forced to leave his position; Tanner cared for his son, nursing him back to health.

In October of 1927, Tanner was elected full academician of the National Academy of Design. Three years later he joined the European chapter of American Artists Professional League and received the Walter L. Clard prize for his painting *Etaples Fisher Folk* and exhibited in the Members Prize Exhibition at the Grand Central Art Galleries, New York City. In 1932, he joined the Allied Artists of America, New York. In June of 1934, he moved to his last studio–apartment on 43 rue de Fleurus. On May 25, 1937, Henry Tanner died in Paris and was buried in the same cemetery in France as his wife.

Tanner's legacy as an artist who overcame the barriers of racism to pursue his goals of artistic excellence is alive in the hearts and minds of scholars, artists, and art aficionados around the world. Even in death, Tanner's work continues to break new ground. As recently as October of 1996, Tanner's achievements as an artist were honored by the White House when, at the request of President Bill Clinton and Hilary Rodham Clinton, the White House acquired *Sand Dunes at Sunset, Atlantic City.* This was the first painting by an African American artist to be a part of the White House permanent collection.

REFERENCES

The Art of Henry O. Tanner (1859–1937). Organized by the Frederick Douglass Institute, in collaboration with the National Collection of Fine Arts, Smithsonian Institution.Washington, DC: The Institute, 1969.

Bearden, Romare, and Harry Henderson. *A History of African–American Artists: From 1792 to the Present.* New York: Pantheon Books, 1993.

Boime, Albert. ''Henry Ossawa Tanner's Subversion of Genre.'' *The Art Bulletin* 75 (September 1993): 415–41.

Mathews, Marcia M. *Henry Ossawa Tanner: American Artist.* Chicago: University of Chicago Press, 1969.

Philadelphia Museum of Art. *Henry Ossawa Tanner.* New York: Rizzoli, 1991.

Riggs, Thomas, ed. *St. James Guide to Black Artists.* Detroit: St. James Press, 1997.

Skeel, Sharon Kay. ''A Black American in the Paris Salon.'' *American Heritage* 42 (February/March 1991): 76–83.

White House Press Release. ''White House Announces Acquisition of Henry Ossawa Tanner Painting for Permanent White House Collection.'' October 22, 1996.

Tuliza Fleming

Marshall W. "Major" Taylor
(1878–1932)
Athlete

"Major" Taylor became the world champion bicycle rider and the first American–born black champion in any sport. Popularly known as the "fastest bicycle rider in the world" until he retired in 1910, Taylor overcame racism in cycling to become the first black member of an integrated professional athletic team, the first black to have a commercial sponsor, the first black to establish world records, and the first black to compete regularly in an open, integrated annual athletic championship.

Born in Indianapolis on November 8, 1878, Marshall Walter Taylor was one of eight children: five girls and three boys. His father, Gilbert Taylor, married his mother, Saphronia Kelter, when they lived in Kentucky, and several of their children were born there. Both parents were freeborn, although their parents had been slaves who moved into the free state of Indiana near the time of the Civil War.

Around 1887 Gilbert Taylor, an experienced horseman, became coachman for the Southard family, wealthy white residents of Indianapolis. Gilbert Taylor took his son Major to work with him on occasions, mostly when the horses needed exercising. Major and the Southard's young son Daniel, who were about the same age, became best friends, playmates, and companions. The Southards furnished young Taylor's clothing, and he and Daniel began to dress alike. Taylor mixed with Daniel's friends, also from wealthy families, and learned to ride bicycles along with them, using the bicycle the Southards had bought him.

The Southards provided Taylor with a private tutor who taught him to read and write. Gradually he set aside the values he learned on his family's farm, alienated himself from his family, and became accustomed to the customs and comfort that go along with wealth. Apparently he lived with the Southards and visited his family occasionally on weekends. His siblings resented his fine clothes, different speech, and cultured ways. When the Southards moved to Chicago, however, and the Taylors refused to let their son go along, Taylor's life was shattered. He wrote in his autobiography, *The Fastest Bicycle Rider in the World,* "I dropped from the happy life of a 'millionaire kid' to that of a common errand boy, all within a few weeks."

Taylor amused himself and the city residents by becoming a trick bicycle rider. He showed off his tricks outside a bicycle store in town and drew such a crowd that the police were called to break up the congestion. Soon he left his five–dollars–a–week newspaper route and began work for the store, Hay and Willis, receiving a $35 bicycle and six dollars a week. In addition to his custodial duties, Taylor dressed in uniform and was booked to give an exhibition of trick and fancy riding.

Marshall W. "Major" Taylor

Taylor's employers sponsored a ten–mile race each year and awarded a gold medal to the winner. Taylor went to witness the event, and Hay asked him to ride with the group, thinking that he would inject a bit of humor for the thousands of observers. According to *The Fastest Bicycle Rider,* he said "I know you can't go the full distance, but just ride up the road a little way, it will please the crowd, and you can come back as soon as you get tired." Hay's words had made Taylor determined to go the distance; he won the first prize, the gold medal that he had seen and admired earlier in the Hay and Willis store. He finished the race about six seconds ahead of the scratch man and collapsed on the roadway. When the 13–year–old Taylor was revived, the gold medal was pinned on his chest.

Taylor's next race was in an event for boys under 16, held in Peoria, Illinois, in the summer of 1892. At that time the city was the hotspot for bicycle racing. Then 14, he came in third but was encouraged by the crowd's reaction. Taylor wrote in his autobiography, "Little did I imagine then that the next time I appeared on this track that I would be greeted as the Champion of America and it is a safe bet that nobody else imagined so."

In the spring of 1893 Taylor left Hay and Willis and went to work for H. T. Hearsey, whose bicycle store on North Pennsylvania Street was much more established. Although he did general work in the store, his principal occupation was as teacher of bicycle riding. While in Hearsey's employ, Taylor regularly won races, including a 75–mile road race from Indianapolis to Matthews, Indiana. The first prize was a house lot located in the center of Matthews. Taylor gave the deed to his mother. Unfortunately prevailing racial prejudice of the time made its mark: crack riders of the day resented the presence of a black rider. He was barred from competing on any track in Indianapolis after he broke Walter Sanger's one–mile record on the Capital City track a few months before the 75–mile race. He won races in Lexington, Kentucky, sponsored by black residents and drawing the fastest riders from Louisville, St. Louis, Chicago, and Cincinnati.

Shortly after the 75–mile race Taylor began to work for Louis D. "Birdie" Munger, a great retired cyclist and was employed in practically every department in his firm, the Munger Cycle Manufacturing Company. Munger was aware of Taylor's success as a rider and teacher. The two grew close. According to Taylor's autobiography, when a member of the firm asked why Munger "bothered with that little darkey," Munger said that Taylor was unusual and had the makings of a champion. "I am going to make him the fastest bicycle rider in the world," Munger promised. To give Taylor greater speed as a racer, Munger built him a 14–pound bicycle, the lightest and best that he could produce. Taylor also was inspired to greater performance by meeting with racing legend Arthur August Zimmerman.

Because of racial prejudice, members of Munger's firm objected strenuously to the attention he gave Taylor. Munger left the firm and established a bicycle factory in Worcester, Massachusetts. Taylor joined him and soon began to impress local residents with his riding tricks, including climbing steep inclines. In the fall of 1895 he raced in Worcester, Massachusetts, having joined the Albion Cycle Club of black riders. After the factory moved to Middletown, Connecticut, in 1896, he soon raced against top amateur cyclists, making his debut at a state heat sponsored by the League of American Wheelmen in New Haven. His professional debut came in the winter of 1896 when he raced the half–mile open handicap at Madison Square Garden, easily becoming the winner.

Becomes First Black World Champion Bicycle Rider

In 1898, backed by the Sager Gear Company, Taylor rode the Sager chainless bicycle for the fastest mile in the history of cycling at that time. On Thursday, August 10, 1899, at Montreal's Queen's Park track, Taylor, who was just over five feet tall, became the world champion bicycle racer, the first black American champion in any sport, and the second black world champion in any sport. (In 1890, Canadian–born George Dixon became world champion bantam–weight boxer.) In 1900 Taylor won heats at Terre Haute, Indiana; Erie, Pennsylvania; and elsewhere. Quoted in his autobiography, the *Erie Dispatch* for September 17, 1900, wrote: "Major Taylor is not as light in complexion as [black boxer] George Dixon, but he is a dandy in dress and he has a muscular development that is the envy of every slim–jim that sees him."

During his racing career in the United States, Taylor often faced overt racial prejudice. He was often refused permission to enter a race, and according to an unidentified newsclipping in his scrapbook, cited in *Major Taylor,* in 1898 his life was threatened in Savannah, Georgia. The threatening letter read "Mister Taylor, if you don't leave here before 48 hours, you will be sorry. We mean business. Clear out if you value your life." The letter was signed "White Riders."

Around 1899 Taylor found himself caught in a political war between racing associations seeking control of professional racing: the League of American Wheelmen (LAW) and the rival National Cycling Association (NCA). Taylor also announced earlier that he would not race on Sundays for religious reasons. He was lost in the shuffle for power as the LAW relinquished its power to the NCA. Taylor had been suspended earlier, both by the NCA and the American Racing Cyclists Union (ARCU) for breaking a contract and for deserting the ARCU for the LAW. In 1900 he was reinstated into both organizations.

Taylor visited Europe from March through June of 1901 and entered 25 races, winning 21 firsts. This was the apex of his racing career. His victories in Europe caused his popularity to soar, and the daily press gave him wide coverage. He raced against the best sprinters in Berlin, Copenhagen, Geneva, Toulouse, Bordeaux, and elsewhere, including nearly every European capital. Finally he rose above the shadow of racial prejudice.

Although he returned to the United States in 1901, through the spring of 1904, Taylor raced almost continuously in Europe and the United States. Wherever he traveled he enjoyed celebrity status. He was not unbeatable, however, and lost races to some of his outstanding contemporaries. Since he chose not to ride on Sundays, he was unable to compete for the world championship in 1902 and 1903.

On March 21, 1902, he married Daisy Victoria Morris, a tall, slim, striking woman who was the daughter of a black mother and a white father. She was older than Taylor, having been born in Hudson, New York in January 28, 1876; she was raised by her mother and educated at the private Hudson Academy. Her place in the cultured and educated world and in prominent social circles contrasted from Taylor's farm background, yet his reputation in Worcester and his wealth made him a suitable pick. Their only child, Rita Sydney, known as Sydney, was born in Sydney, Australia, on May 11, 1904. Taylor became deeply committed to John Street Baptist Church in Worcester. He also kept a neat workshop at home and whenever seen beyond the home he was impeccably dressed, wore a hard straw hat, and carried a cane.

Taylor had raced almost continuously since he was 15, except in 1905 and 1906 when he retired briefly. The worst accident in his career, a crash in Bordeaux in 1907, gouged and burned the full left side of his body, but he recovered. His last season in Europe was in 1909. As his career began to fail, Taylor grew despondent. At the end of his European tour, he beat the reigning champion of France, Victor Dupré, which gave him some consolation. He had competed throughout the United States, Europe, and Australia. He raced in Salt Lake City in the summer of 1910. Quoted in *Major Taylor,* the *Salt Lake Tribune* called him "the highest priced bicycle rider in the world." The spark had left his performance however, and Taylor retired from racing in 1910, when he was 32 years old.

Criticized for retiring so early, Taylor wrote in his autobiography:

> Little did they realize the great physical strain I labored under while I was competing in these sixteen years of trying campaigns. Nor did they seem to realize the great mental strain that beset me in those races, and the utter exhaustion which I felt on the many occasions after I had battled under bitter odds against the monster prejudice, both on and off the track. In most of my races I not only struggled for victory, but also for my very life and limb.

After retiring he engaged in a series of ventures to earn a living. He invented a wheel divided into independently sprung sections to provide efficient cushioning and by 1912 tried to put the wheel into production. By 1914 the Major Taylor Manufacturing Company was formed, with Taylor and his old friend Fred Johnson of Iver Johnson Company as co–owners. The company was unsuccessful. Taylor undertook five or six more business enterprises, all related to the automobile industry or metal manufacturing. He built the Excello Manufacturing Company to make automobile oils with operated in Worcester between 1913 and 1915 and then closed. After that, Taylor had financial difficulty, working as salesperson, machinist, and in other odd jobs. He formed other business partnerships that also failed. Taylor gradually left public life and became withdrawn and uncommunicative.

The amount of Taylor's savings from racing is unclear. One source claimed he saved about $35,000 while another concluded he had about $75,000. There appears to be no doubt that he was comfortable financially. In addition to cash, he had assets of a fine house and other property in Worcester, an automobile, numerous possessions from travels abroad, and other investments.

In September of 1917 Taylor reentered public life for one last race an old–timers heat at the Newark velodrome called the ''Rheumatic Stages for Aged Bikers.'' He won the race.

By 1923 Taylor began to write his autobiography *The Fastest Bicycle Rider in the World.* The book was not published until 1929 (although the date printed in the book is 1928). It was self–published under the imprint of Wormley Publishing Company. His health as well as his marriage deteriorated, and he was unable to earn enough money to support his family. His savings were depleted, and he liquidated his assets to pay his living expenses. He began to peddle his book in 1929 but earned little money from sales. The Taylors broke up sometime in 1930. His final years were spent in Chicago, the last stop on his book–selling tour. Impoverished, he roomed at the YMCA and was out of touch with his wife and daughter.

In the mid–1920s Taylor had suffered from shingles, which damaged his heart and kidneys and led to coronary and renal complications. He died on June 21, 1932, at age 53, in the charity ward of Chicago's Cook County Hospital, of nephrosclerosis and hypertension, with chronic myocarditis as a contributory cause. His body was unclaimed for a week, then buried at public expense in a pauper's grave in Mount Glenwood Cemetery. In 1948, 16 years after his death, several former bicycle racing greats formed the Bicycle Racing Stars of the 19th Century, based in Chicago, and on learning about the circumstances of Taylor's burial, moved to bring him the proper final recognition. Frank Schwinn, owner of the Schwinn Bicycle Company, financed Taylor's reburial in a more desirable part of the cemetery, the Memorial Garden of the Good Shepherd. A bronze plaque was installed at the dedication service. On Sunday, May 23, 1948, when the service was held, 100 people gathered at the new site and lay flowers and an American flag on his grave. Ralph Metcalfe, 1932 Olympic winner, gave the keynote address, and 1936 Olympic winner Jesse Owens was among those in attendance. The plaque summed up his importance:

> World's champion bicycle racer who came up the hard way without hatred in his heart, an honest, courageous, and god–fearing, clean–living, gentlemanly athlete. A credit to his race who always gave out his best.

REFERENCES

Ashe, Arthur. *A Hard Road to Glory.* Vol 1. New York: Warner Books, 1980.

Menker, Frank G. *The Encyclopedia of Sports.* South Brunswick, NJ: A. S. Barnes, 1975.

Ritchie, Andres. *Major Taylor.* San Francisco: Bicycle Books, 1988.

Taylor, Marshall W. ''Major''. *The Fastest Bicycle Rider in the World.* 1928. Reprint, Freeport, NY: Books for Libraries Press, 1971.

Williams, G. Grant. ''Marshall Walter Taylor (Major Taylor), the World–Famous Bicycle Rider.'' *Colored American Magazine* 5 (September 1906): 336–45.

Jessie Carney Smith

Edward S. Temple

(1927–)

Track coach, educator

Edward S. Temple, head Tigerbelles track and field coach at Tennessee State University for 44 years, is known for his accomplishments. During his tenure as coach, 40 members of his team won 23 Olympic medals—13 gold, six silver, four bronze—for the United States, won 34 National Team titles, 30 Pan–American medals, and 39 of the 40 women received undergraduate degrees. Additionally, he was head coach for two Olympics and was inducted into numerous halls of fame.

Edward Stanley Temple was born September 20, 1927, in Harrisburg, Pennsylvania, the son and only child of Christopher Richard, a federal government worker, and Ruth Naomi Temple, a local government worker. His grandparents had a major role in his rearing and saw that he went to the Baptist church every Sunday. In his early years, he was interested in music and even played the trumpet in the junior high school band. Music took a back seat to athletics, however, when he entered John Harris High School, where he was all–state halfback in football and the first African American captain of the track and basketball teams. Upon graduation, he had many opportunities for higher education and had made a decision to attend Pennsylvania State University.

Tom Harris, a neighbor, encouraged Temple to attend Tennessee State Agricultural and Industrial College (now Tennessee State University) in Nashville, Tennessee. When he heard that Leroy Craid, Temple's arch rival from William Penn High School, was planning to attend, Temple knew that he did not want to miss what was happening at this unknown institution. When the young men arrived, they found no track program and had to compete against each other. In spite of the lack of track, Temple chose to remain, major in physical education, and minor in sociology. In his junior year, he met Charlie B. Law of Hartsville, Tennessee, who became his wife in 1950 (they have one child Edwina) and later in his career provided a home away from home for the Tigerbelles; she was mother, advisor, and confidante.

Edward S. Temple

That same year he graduated and began applying for coaching positions. At almost the same time, the Tennessee State University coach accepted another position and recommended Temple to Walter S. Davis, the college president, as track coach. Davis suggested to him that he pursue the master's degree and work in the campus post office in addition to coaching. In his autobiography, *Only the Pure in Heart Survive,* Temple said he began coaching both the men's and women's track team, on half a track, a budget of $64 for "equipment, track shoes, uniforms, travel, everything," three or four men, and two women: Jean Patton and Frances Newburn. This was also the first year the United States had a women's team for the Pan–American Games; Patton was one of the members. Not only were facilities and monies almost nonexistent, but this was also the time of segregation in the South. Temple remarked in his autobiography: "We didn't go anywhere for meets except Tuskegee and Alabama State. That's as far as we could go. Then, with segregated restaurants and restrooms, we'd have to pack lunches and head for the fields when we traveled. We'd all squeeze into my car and take turns driving. I had to be the chauffeur, coach, trainer, and manager until Earl Clanton came along and helped me out." The team received its first scholarship in 1967 and in 1978 "a decent track facility."

Coaches the Tigerbelles

As the coach, Temple began recruiting runners. His first recruit was Mae Faggs, who in 1948 had been a member of the Olympic team and held the national indoor 200–meter title. In spite of a number of problems, she remained under his leadership and soon became, according to Temple, the catalyst for the Tigerbelle program and the one who taught him more than anyone else about coaching women. In 1955 he coached the Tigerbelles to their first national and integrated championship.

To supplement his income while coaching, Temple refereed sports events; it was at a basketball game at Burt High School in Clarksville, Tennessee, that he saw Wilma Rudolph who was to gain Olympic fame and glory. He recruited her to become a part of the summer training program he instituted to strengthen the Tennessee State University program and to develop young talent. Two others who participated in the program were Wyomia Tyus and Edith McGuire. Temple wrote in his autobiography, "Many [of the] girls . . . excelled in several sports. Most of them played high school basketball. Rudolph, Tyus, McGuire, and Chandra Cheeseborough were all as good in basketball as they were in track."

Temple claims he had no Olympic aspirations when he became the coach. Yet, there was at least one Tigerbelle on every U.S. Olympic 4 x 100–meter relay team from 1952 through 1984. The 1956 and 1960 foursomes were made up of Tennessee State University runners. Temple wrote that "they have the distinction of being the first American team to have all its members make up a USA Olympic 400–meter relay team twice [1956 and 1960]." The Tigerbelles have included such outstanding performers as Mae Faggs, Wilma Rudolph, Wyomia Tyus, Madeline Manning, Lucinda Williams, Martha Hudson, Barbara Jones, Rathy McMillan, Isabelle

Daniels, Edith McGuire, Willye B. White, and Chandra Cheeseborough. Temple believes Tyus has not received the recognition she deserves for winning back–to–back gold medals in the 100–meter dash in the Olympics and setting new world and Olympic records. The Tigerbelles under the leadership of Coach Temple won 23 Olympic medals: 13 gold, six silver, and four bronze. Additionally, his Tigerbelles won 34 National Team titles, 30 Pan–American Games medals, and eight became National Track and Field Hall of Fame inductees. These stellar performances from his 40 women Olympians were the result not only of his teaching, but also his discipline, and his model.

Young women were always to conduct themselves as ladies in both carriage and appearance, and they were to treat practice as a serious business—no chatter and frivolity. In describing his philosophy, Temple said in his autobiography, "I never run around hugging any of my girls. We maintain a coach–athlete relationship and it stays that way. Track is a business and I try to handle it as a business in all situations. For instance, I show no emotions if they win." For his part, he was objective, a fanatic about time, a strong disciplinarian, and he never missed a practice when he was in town. The emotional congratulations and hugs were left to his wife, Charlie B. He is even reported to have left more than one of his runners stranded who arrived two minutes late when the team was scheduled to leave at a designated time.

Above all, Temple constantly reminded the women they were ladies first, students second, and athletes third. At the sports banquets as much emphasis was placed on scholastic achievement as on trophies. Girls were to maintain at least a C+ average and not one ever flunked out. This discipline and philosophy resulted in 39 out of the 40 women who went to the Olympics achieving one or more degrees and serving as teachers, doctors, coaches, public speakers, ministers, entertainers, and community leaders.

Temple's athletes remember his teaching, his discipline, his concern, and his sayings posted on his walls and emphasized in their years with him. Three of these were: "If you are not part of the solution, you are part of the problem"; "There's a lot we could learn if we weren't already convinced we knew it all"; and "What the fool does in the end, the wise man does in the beginning." In his autobiography, he notes that there were certain characteristics he observed in most of his superstars: they were the quiet type, nonchalant, junk food eaters, had common sense, adjusted to adversities, liked to sleep a lot, and the mother was the dominant figure in their lives.

Coaches Olympic Teams

As a result of his outstanding record as head coach of Women's Track and Field at Tennessee State University from 1951 to 1994, Temple garnered international exposure and acclaim. He was head coach for the U.S. women's Olympic track and field team two consecutive times—1960 in Rome, Italy, and 1964 in Tokyo, Japan; he was an assistant coach in the 1980 games in Moscow (which the United States boycotted). This made him the first coach in history to coach three U.S. Olympic women's track and field teams. He was also a member of the United States Olympic Committee between 1960 and 1984.

Temple was the head coach of the National Junior Women's Track Team at the dual meet with Romania in Bucharest and the first ever Junior Championships held in Athens, Greece, in 1986. In 1982 and 1986, he was the head coach for USA Junior Women's Team, the Pan–American Games; the coach for the Amateur Athletic Union Women's Team on its European Tours in 1978 and the 1970 tour of Germany, USSR, and Romania; coach for the Pan–American Games in 1959 and 1975; the U.S. Track and Field Team's European Tours, 1958, 1960, and 1970. He was the coach for the first meeting of the USA and USSR (1958) in Moscow, and of the USA vs The People's Republic of China (1975).

In 1995, Temple received the Tennessee Sports Hall of Fame's Board of Directors Award and the Nashville Women's Political Caucus's Good Guy Award in recognition of men who have supported the progress of women in all different walks of life. He was honored by the USA Olympic Committee for his many contributions to the Olympic Movement in 1994; in the same year, he received the Track and Field Master Coach Award for contributions to the sport of track and field, as a coach and educator of coaches. Other honors and awards include the state of Tennessee's Sportsfest Award for outstanding achievement in track and a commitment to excellence (1993); the first Joseph Robichaux Memorial Award for outstanding contributions to the advancement of women's track and field (1992); induction into the National Track and Field Hall of Fame (1989); the *American Visions* magazine's Salute to the Black Olympic Coach 1988); the Athletic's Congress/USA President's Award (1986); induction in the Harrisburg Central Area Chapter of the Pennsylvania Sports Hall of Fame (1985); the Black Athletes Hall of Fame (1977); and the Tennessee Sports Hall of Fame (1972). Additionally, he has life membership in the Amateur Athletic Union (awarded by the Southeastern AAU Association) and is a member of the Helma Hall of Fame.

In 1998 the Edward S. Temple Track was dedicated at Tennessee State University and in 1989, the Ed Temple Boulevard in Nashville was dedicated. The NCAA Track and Field Coaches Association established in 1993 the Edward Temple Award to be given annually to the Female Track and Field Athlete. On February 16, 1996, a plaque citing Temple's accomplishment was unveiled at his alma mater: John Harris High School in Harrisburg, Pennsylvania. The awards and recognition amassed by Temple have in no way changed the man and his humility. He constantly gives credit and praise to others. Walter S. Davis, the women, other coaches, and especially Charlie B. Temple—his wife and "assistant coach" and support throughout his coaching and teaching career.

Two descriptions of Edward S. Temple which appear in the early part of his autobiography are indicative of the man and how others view him. The first is by B'Lou Carter, who said: ''He is a strict disciplinarian, yet a gentle person; he is humorous, yet all business. Temple is unashamedly patriotic and has been an excellent goodwill ambassador all around the world. He is a man of quiet determination and integrity. He can be very formal, yet he is at his best with his own comfortable colloquial way of talking.'' The second and one of the strongest testimonials in the book and is made by Wilma Rudolph, who says that Temple's life has been filled with his family and the Tigerbelles at Tennessee State University and that she sees him as the foundation on which women's track and field has been built. She also attributes to his work the significance of being the ''cornerstone for the likes of Title IX,'' which guarantees gender equity in educational sports programs. Truly, Coach Temple's women athletes are a reflection of the man.

Current address: 2628 Delk Avenue, Nashville, TN 37208.

REFERENCES

Temple, Charlie B. Interviews with Helen R. Houston, June 20, July 12, September 8, 1995.

Temple, Ed. *Only the Pure in Heart Survive.* Nashville: Broadman Press, 1980.

COLLECTIONS

The Edward S. Temple Papers and memorabilia are located in the Special Collections Department, Brown–Daniel Library, Tennessee State University, Nashville, Tennessee.

Helen R. Houston

Clarence Thomas

(1948–)

U.S. Supreme Court judge, lawyer, administrator, jurist

Clarence Thomas challenged the traditional black agenda of strong governmental support for civil rights and social and economic justice to become the second African American to sit on the U.S. Supreme Court.

Thomas was born on June 23, 1948, in Pin Point, Georgia, an impoverished settlement of a few dozen black families. When he was two years old just before his brother was born his father, M. C. Thomas, deserted the family, leaving Leola Anderson Thomas (1931–) to raise the boys and their older sister Emma.

Clarence Thomas

Leola Thomas naturally struggled to feed and clothe her children. Her trials continued when the shack in which they lived without electricity or plumbing went up in flames. She moved with the children to a dingy one–room apartment in a Savannah slum, but finding the squalid neighborhood intolerable, she sent the children to live with relatives. Clarence Thomas was sent across town to live with her father.

Roots of Conservative Thought

Seven–year–old Clarence Thomas arrived at the East 32nd Street home of Myers Anderson (1907–1983) toting a grocery bag containing his hand–me–down clothes. At Myers's home he found a safe neighborhood, the comfort and luxury of a clean home, three good meals a day, and his own bedroom. Most importantly, he found a grandfather who had already decided that he was going to instill in the boy an ethic of individual effort and achievement. According to Macht, Anderson told him, ''You're going to get up every morning and work hard all day. If you're not going to do that, then you're going to leave.''

Myers was a good example of a 'self–made' man. In Savannah he built a pushcart and started hauling firewood, kerosene, and coal across the city's cobblestone streets. Later he bought a truck and expanded his delivery business.

Myers had a work ethic that made him rigid and demanding. He required that Thomas be seated for breakfast by seven o'clock every morning. He made him do house chores, help with deliveries and work on his family's farm. In addition, he constantly told Thomas that crime, welfare, alcohol, and laziness were his enemies, and that hard work, discipline, education, and moral conduct were his priorities.

Shortly after Thomas arrived, Myers enrolled him in Saint Benedict's Elementary School, a school for black boys run by white Franciscan nuns. According to Macht, Myers let Thomas know right from the beginning that he would accept no excuses for failure: "These are the rules: Your teachers are always right. . . . If they [the nuns] beat you in school and you come home and complain about it, you'll get another one."

Thomas excelled at St. Benedict's. The school's white nuns drilled him in the traditional subjects and bolstered his self–esteem. At predominantly black St. Pius X High School, where students constantly teased him about his dark skin, the learning experience was the same. These Catholic schools made such an impression on Thomas that he became an altar boy at St. Benedict's Catholic Church. Eventually he decided to enter the priesthood.

For a short time Thomas attended St. John Vianney Minor Seminary, distinguishing himself academically and in sports, before entering Immaculate Conception Seminary in Missouri in 1967. As one of only a handful of blacks, he tried to ignore the white seminarians' racial slurs. According to Macht, Thomas would later recall, "I was determined not to see every slight or criticism as discrimination or bigotry. Once you get in the habit of doing that, you disempower yourself; your attitude becomes: No matter what I do, discrimination will prevent me from doing well." But in 1968, when he overheard a student saying, "That's good, I hope the SOB dies," in response to the news that Martin Luther King Jr. had been shot, Thomas packed his bags and left the seminary.

A nun persuaded him to enroll at the College of Holy Cross, a Jesuit school in Worcester, Massachusetts. As one of only six blacks in his freshman class, Thomas resented the perception on campus that he and his black classmates had been admitted because of their race rather than their abilities. He found that perception difficult to overcome. Some black students showed an aversion to studying; others allowed self–doubt to defeat them and dropped out. Thomas agonized over these developments because he felt they were helping to confirm the black students' uncertainties and the widely held belief of their inferiority.

Although usually withdrawn, Thomas participated in protests against the Vietnam War, served as treasurer of the school's Black Student Union, and studied the philosophies of Booker T. Washington, Malcolm X, and the Black Panthers. In 1971 he graduated from Holy Cross with honors and a degree in English. The day after graduating, he married Kathy Ambush, a shy black student attending a local college.

Although Thomas was invited to attend several law schools after graduating, he applied to Yale University. Instead of allowing him to compete openly with whites for admission, Yale used an affirmative action program to admit him and 11 other black students. Thomas, resented the admission procedure and told classmates that he was not at the school because of its benevolence; he was there because he was qualified, like the white students.

Yale's admissions policy indelibly affected Thomas's outlook. More influential though were the ideas of Thomas Sowell, a conservative black economist. After reading Sowell's, *The Economics and Politics of Race,* which discussed the unintended effects of affirmative action programs, Thomas began remarking to friends that such programs were racist because they help to perpetuate the notion that without preferential treatment blacks cannot compete and attain the same level of excellence and achievement as whites. Blacks, he asserted, could accomplish those virtuous ends by themselves, through their own efforts.

Emboldened by a spirit of self–reliance after graduating with a law degree from Yale in 1974, Thomas joined fellow black graduates in looking for work. Macht quoted Thomas's recollection of this experience: "The perception was that you were never qualified, even if you were in fact overqualified. Prospective employers dismissed our grades and diplomas, assuming we got both primarily because of preferential treatment." John C. Danforth, however, the Republican attorney general for Missouri, was impressed with his credentials and appointed Thomas as an assistant attorney general.

Thomas moved to Missouri with his wife and son, Jamal. Two years later, after Danforth was elected to the U.S. Senate, Thomas went to work as an attorney in the law department of the Monsanto Corporation. By 1979 he was back with Danforth, who had asked him to come to Washington, D.C., as his legislative assistant.

Promotes Conservative Ideas

When Thomas arrived in Washington, the country was reeling from a downturn in the economy. Amid rising rates of inflation, unemployment, and crime, a debate ensued about whether the liberals' economic and social policies were at fault. Thomas joined the discussion.

Thomas unabashedly remarked to associates that he thought government measures that treat blacks as a "disadvantaged" people were harmful. He noted that measures such as affirmative action, welfare, and busing, instead of improving conditions in the black community, actually promote black unemployment, the breakup of black families, low performance by black students, and a sense of inferiority among blacks in general. Fusing his own experiences with the ideas of Booker T. Washington, Malcolm X, and Thomas Sowell, he suggested that the best remedies for the problems of the black community were hard work, self–reliance and self–sufficiency.

Liberal blacks and whites with whom Thomas conversed thought Thomas's views were appalling. To them, his opinions showed that he was not committed to the black community, and they reacted by ridiculing and shunning him. Thomas, however, accustomed to being excluded at white schools, sought solace through association with the Lincoln Institute and other conservative policy groups that shared his views.

In 1980 Thomas flew to San Francisco to attend a meeting of black conservatives. There he ended up giving an interview to a *Washington Post* reporter in which he urged blacks to leave the ideological plantation of liberalism. Thomas's comments caught the attention of Ronald Reagan, the Republican presidential nominee.

After entering the White House, President Reagan nominated Thomas to be assistant secretary for civil rights in the Education Department. While at the agency, Thomas and his wife Kathy divorced, leaving him with custody of their son. Less than a year later, in 1982, the president nominated Thomas to be chairperson of the Equal Employment Opportunity Commission.

The EEOC had been one of the major accomplishments of the Civil Rights Movement. The EEOC which the Reagan Administration saw as a classic example of excessive government gave blacks and women greater access to employment.

In his first case as EEOC chairperson, Thomas sued General Motors for discrimination in the workplace and in 1983 forced the automaker to agree to a $42.5 million settlement, the largest settlement in EEOC history. But as the EEOC began to handle other cases, he signaled his intention to change the agency's approach. According to Macht, Thomas announced, "I do believe in compensation for actual victims, [but] not for people whose only claim is that they are members of a historically oppressed group."

Civil rights, women's, and labor group leaders correctly took these comments to mean that the EEOC would no longer use class action suits and affirmative action methods like quotas, hiring goals, and timetables to force companies to promote and hire more minorities. The new policy angered them. Members of the Congressional Black Caucus refused to meet with Thomas to discuss EEOC matters. Other black leaders criticized him, saying that he did not "think black." White liberals called him a traitor to his race, women, and the working class.

Unfazed, Thomas, in addressing the graduates at Savannah State College in 1985, spoke admiringly of the black tradition of individual effort and disparagingly of affirmative action. As quoted by Crovitz in his introduction to *Clarence Thomas: Confronting the Future,* Thomas said:

> I had the benefit of people who knew they had to walk a straighter line, climb a taller mountain and carry a heavier load. They took all that segregation and prejudice would allow them and at the same time fought to remove those awful barriers. . . . You all have a much tougher road to travel. Not only do you have to contend with the ever–present bigotry, you must do so with a recent tradition that almost requires you to wallow in excuses. You now have a popular national rhetoric which says that you can't learn because of racism, you can't raise babies you make because of racism, you can't get up in the morning because of racism. Unlike me, you must not only overcome the repressiveness of racism, you must also overcome the lure of excuses. You have twice the job I had.

Despite ongoing criticism, in 1986 Thomas was confirmed for another term as EEOC chair. Afterwards, he married Virginia Lamp, a white labor relations attorney from Nebraska. Over the next three years, he continued to retool the EEOC to match the conservative philosophy of the Reagan Administration.

During this period Thomas became more conservative in his views. As quoted by the Congressional Black Caucus Foundation in *Court of Appeal,* Thomas accused civil rights leaders and their liberal Democratic allies of "generating self–perpetuating social ills." Democrats in Congress, however, responded to his polices and rhetorical assaults by disapproving his budget requests for EEOC.

Eventually criticism of Thomas shifted from his policies and rhetoric to his management of the EEOC. According to Phelps and Winternitz, a Senate investigation of the EEOC found that the agency's enforcement of antidiscrimination laws "had seriously deteriorated over the last five years." and that Thomas had allowed over 13,000 cases of discrimination to lapse.

Despite such criticism, Thomas steadily gained favor within the Republican Party. In 1989, near the end of his term, the newly elected Republican president, George Bush, started looking for someone to fill a seat on the U.S. Court of Appeals for the District of Columbia. President Bush wanted a nominee who would help carry out the Republican agenda from the court. That agenda called for dismantling affirmative action programs, outlawing abortions, and reviving the death penalty.

Thomas had long sought a federal judgeship as a way to get out of the politics surrounding the EEOC. So when Bush offered him a seat on the bench, he quickly accepted. During his Senate confirmation hearing, Thomas adeptly portrayed himself as a supporter of judicial restraint rather than an apostle of conservative ideology. His testimony achieved its intended result. The U.S. Senate confirmed him to be a judge on the appeals court.

Appointed to Supreme Court

Thomas had been on the bench for only 15 months when Justice Thurgood Marshall announced his retirement. Four days later, July 1, 1991, President Bush presented Thomas to the nation as his nominee to replace Marshall on the Supreme Court.

Members of the Alliance for Justice a powerful coalition of liberal civil rights, women's, labor, and civil liberties groups, including the NAACP were stunned by Bush's selection. They feared that Thomas, if confirmed, would join other conservative justices in overturning landmark civil and abortion rights decisions. The alliance launched a vigorous campaign to block his confirmation. In spite of its efforts to prove that Thomas's character and philosophy made him unsuitable for the court, his prospects for confirmation remained favorable.

Seated in the ornate Senate Caucus Room at the witness table, in front of the Senate Judiciary Committee's dias on September 10, Thomas began giving testimony that allayed concerns about his views on civil rights, privacy rights, and civil liberties. As the hearing neared an end, the majority of the all–white, male committee was prepared to recommend him to the full Senate. Then the committee chairperson, Democratic Senator Joseph Biden, received confidential documents concerning sexual misconduct that Thomas had allegedly engaged in while serving at the Education Department and EEOC. Democratic members of the panel considered using these allegations put forth by Anita Faye Hill to sink his confirmation. The senators, fearing that public disclosure of the allegations by them would backfire, decided not to mention them in further questioning.

The allegations did, however, erode support for his confirmation. Split seven to seven on whether to confirm him, the committee sent his nomination to the floor without a recommendation and without informing other senators of Hill's allegations. As the Senate was concluding debate and preparing to vote, someone on the Judiciary Committee leaked details from the documents to the press. Hill's sexual harassment charges were immediately swept up by the news media and carried across the country, causing a public uproar and dooming Thomas's chances for confirmation. Inundated with calls from women critical of its handling of the charges, the Senate decided to postpone its vote on Thomas so that the Judiciary Committee could hold hearings on Hill's allegations.

When the hearings reopened in the Senate Caucus Room, October 11, they were carried live by ABC, CBS, NBC, and C–span to a record television audience. In his opening statement to the committee, Thomas said emphatically, "I have not said or done anything that Anita Hill has alleged." He complained that his reputation had been ruined and told the panel that he had come before it to clear his name. Hill, also a Yale law school graduate who since leaving EEOC had become a tenured law professor, addressed the committee next. An attractive black woman, she stunned television viewers by giving graphic testimony about sexual comments that she claimed Thomas made to her about pornographic films and his sexual prowess.

When Thomas returned to the hearing room, he angrily denied "each and every single allegation." Moreover, barely concealing his contempt for Democratic senators, he called the proceedings "a high–tech–lynching for uppity blacks who in any way deign to think for themselves, to do for themselves, to have different ideas, and it is a message that unless you kowtow to an old order, this is what will happen to you. You will be lynched, destroyed, caricatured, by a committee of the U.S. Senate rather than hung from a tree."

The committee completed its hearing three days later, but without reaching a conclusion about whether Hill's charges were true. When the full Senate convened, it voted 52–46 to confirm Thomas. On October 18, Thomas, at age 43, was sworn in as Associate Justice of the U.S. Supreme Court.

Justice Thomas lives on a five–acre estate in Virginia with his wife. Each day, he drives to the U.S. Supreme Court building in Washington, D.C. There, he works long hours reviewing cases, writing opinions, and voting on the constitutionality of state and federal laws. In his free time, he speaks to black students, encouraging them to work hard, make the most of opportunities open to them, and to persevere when faced with difficulty. And he shares with them the wisdom of his grandfather: "Old man *can't* is dead. I helped bury him."

Clarence Thomas urges blacks to overcome bigotry in the United States by embracing the principle of "self–sufficiency" rather than "victimization." In the process, he stirred debate within the black community over the usefulness of liberal traditions and the effectiveness of the established civil rights agenda. Of particular note, he did what he said self–reliant black people could do attain a high level of achievement in America.

Current address: Supreme Court Justice, Clarence Thomas, Supreme Court of the United States, 1 First St. NE, Washington, DC 20543–0001.

REFERENCES

Chrisman, Robert, and Robert L. Allen, eds. *Court of Appeal: The Black Community Speaks Out on the Racial and Sexual Politics of Clarence Thomas vs. Anita Hill.* New York: Ballantine Books, 1992.

Danforth, John C. *Resurrection: The Confirmation of Clarence Thomas.* New York: Viking, 1994.

Macht, Norman L. *Clarence Thomas.* New York: Chelsea House Publishers, 1995.

Mayer, Jane, and Jill Abramson. *Strange Justice: The Selling of Clarence Thomas.* Boston: Houghton Mifflin, 1994.

Phelps, Timothy M., and Helen Winternitz. *Capital Games: Clarence Thomas, Anita Hill, and the Story of a Supreme Court Nomination.* New York: Hyperion, 1992.

Thomas, Clarence. *Articles and Speeches by Clarence Thomas.* Washington, DC: Lincoln Institute for Research and Education, 1991.

———. *Clarence Thomas: Confronting the Future: Selections from the Senate Confirmation Hearings and Prior Speeches.* Introduction by Gordon Crovitz. Washington, DC: Regnery Gateway, 1992.

United States. Congress. Senate. Committee on the Judiciary. *Nomination of Judge Clarence Thomas to be Associate Justice of the Supreme Court of the United States: Hearings before the Committee of the Judiciary, First Session.* Washington, DC: U.S. Government Printing Office, 1993.

———. Committee on Labor and Human Resources. *Nomination: Hearing Before the Committee on Labor and Human Resources, United States Senate, Ninety–Ninth Congress, Second Session on Clarence Thomas of Missouri, to be Chairman of the Equal Employment Opportunity Commission, July 23, 1986.* Washington, DC: U.S. Government Printing Office, 1986.

Cortez Rainey

Franklin A. Thomas

(1934–)

Lawyer, foundation executive, humanitarian

Franklin A. Thomas, a successful leader in urban renewal, was named president of the Ford Foundation, making him the first African America to head a major philanthropic foundation. Through his work with the foundation, he helped needy communities, supported cultural and educational institutions, and aided in civil rights activities in the United States and abroad.

Born in Brooklyn on May 27, 1934, to West Indian parents James and Viola Atherley Thomas, Franklin Augustine Thomas was the youngest of six children; he grew up in the Bedford Stuyvesant neighborhood. His father, a laborer, died when Franklin Thomas was 11. To support the family, his mother worked as a housekeeper and during World War II as a machinist. Franklin Thomas and his wife, Dawn Conrada, divorced in 1972. Franklin is the father of four children—Keith, Hillary, Kerrie and Kyle.

Thomas came from a family that fostered racial pride. He also developed close ties in his West Indian community. He was a good student and a Boy Scout leader at Concord Baptist Church. He played basketball on the local courts and later was an outstanding basketball player at Franklin J. Lane High School in Brooklyn, where he was a star center. He turned down sports scholarships to several institutions and accepted an academic scholarship at Columbia University. While there, he won a basketball scholarship. He became captain of the basketball team, a first for an African American in the Ivy League. He was voted the league's most valuable player in 1955 and 1956. He also completed Reserve Officers' Training Corps (ROTC) training at Columbia.

In 1956 Thomas earned his bachelor's degree from Columbia. His ROTC training earned him a commission in the U.S. Air Force, where he served as a navigator with the Strategic Air Command. He left the military with a rank of captain, joined the air force reserve, and in 1960 enrolled in the Columbia Law School, receiving the LL.B. degree with moot court honors in 1963. In 1963 and 1964 Thomas was an advisor with the Federal Housing and Home Finance Agency in New York's regional office and was admitted to the state bar the following year. From 1964 to 1965 he was assistant U.S. attorney for the Southern District of New York.

After serving as deputy police commissioner for legal matters of the New York City Police Department from 1965 to 1967, Thomas was named president and chief executive officer of the Bedford Stuyvesant Restoration in 1967. He was in private practice in New York from 1977 to 1979.

Franklin Thomas's experiences in working with groups making a difference prepared him for the challenge at Ford Foundation. At the helm of the Bedford Stuyvesant Restoration Project, he pulled together community groups to work toward the same goals in improving the inner city community. Having grown up in Bedford Stuyvesant, Thomas was familiar with the community and its constituents therefore assisted him in providing direction for its restoration. During Thomas's tenure of ten years with the project, job training, jobs, mortgages, housing, businesses, cultural/community facilities were provided to the community. It was a success for urban renewal in a nation that reaped rewards for its citizens. Thomas directed a budget of $63 million implementing the restoration project. Franklin Thomas became nationally known and was widely sought after his successful venture. This included a cabinet offer from President–elect Jimmy Carter as Secretary of Housing and Urban Development, which he declined. After leaving the Bedford Stuyvesant Restoration project in 1977, he returned to the practice of law. Then for a nine–month period he filled in as president of the John Hay Whitney Foundation. He also chaired the Study Commission on United States Policy Toward Southern Africa and wrote the foreword to its report *Time Running Out* (1981).

Thomas served on the Board of the Ford Foundation two years, from 1978 to 1980, prior to becoming chief officer in 1980. A nationwide search was undertaken involving many major pools of talent, but Thomas was offered the position and he considered it a challenge.

The Ford Foundation, one of the country's largest philanthropic organizations, was in financial trouble at the time. Its assets dropped significantly from $4 billion to $2.8 billion due to the decline in the stock market. Thomas directed a study of the foundation's programs and services over an 18 month period and found ways to reduce expenditures. As result of his findings, the foundation eliminated some staff positions, closed programs in selected overseas offices, and redirected program goals.

Under his 20 year leadership at the foundation, he directed the reorganization of the foundation and helped it focus on action–oriented studies. He sought partnerships with corporations in providing financial resources. Areas funded were Third World rural poverty, urban renewal, and human rights activities. There was a deemphasis on education, foreign policy, and immigration studies.

Thomas left the foundation in 1995; the next year he became head of the TFF Study Group, a non–profit organization formed to assist in the development of South Africa. His report, *Time Running Out,* for which Thomas received widespread attention, served as the impetus to the formation of the TFF Study Group. In addition to Thomas, Mildred Fierce and Wayne Fredericks were members. The report was first published in 1983, updated in 1991–92, and was the result of the Study Commission on U.S. Policy Toward South Africa which Thomas co–chaired.

The six–foot tall, brown–skinned Thomas has received numerous awards, including the Lyndon Baines Johnson Award, 1974; the John Jay and Alexander Hamilton Awards from Columbia College, 1983; the James Kent Medal from Columbia University Law School; the Columbia University Medal of Excellence in 1976, and Council on Foundation's 1995 Distinguished Grantmaker Award.

Franklin Thomas's interest in improving humanity and making a difference continues through participation on major boards. In 1969 he became one of the first two black members of Columbia University's Board of Trustees. Other board memberships included Columbia Broadcasting Corporation, Cummins Engine Company, Citicorp, Allied Stores, and New York Life Insurance Company.

In recognition of his work, Thomas received honorary degrees from Yale University (1970), Fordham University (1972), Pratt Institute (1974), Pace University (1977), and Columbia University (1979).

Thomas's success in guiding projects has made a difference and helped to improve the quality of life for many people. Humanitarian projects guided by Thomas are results–oriented, highly visible, and qualitative. He has made a positive impact on the lives around him.

Current address: TFF Study Group, 595 Madison Ave., New York, NY 10022.

REFERENCES

Contemporary Black Biography. Vol. 5. Detroit: Gale Research, 1994.

Current Biography. New York: H. W. Wilson, 1981.

Who's Who among African Americans, 1996–97. 9th ed. Detroit: Gale Research, 1996.

Barbara Williams Jenkins

Jesse O. Thomas

(1883–1972)

Educator, government official, civic worker

Known for his widespread contributions as a civil rights leader, Jesse O. Thomas was a social worker and an educator whose influence was felt in metropolitan centers of the country and from state to federal governments. One of his major positions was as field secretary of the National Urban League, concentrating in states in the South.

Born in McComb, Mississippi, on December 21, 1883, Thomas was the son of Jefferson Thomas and Amanda Johnson Thomas. From the public schools of McComb, he entered Tuskegee Institute, founded in an old church in Tuskegee, Alabama, in 1881 by its first teacher and principal, Booker T. Washington.

Impressed by his brilliance, self–confidence, and speaking ability Washington invited Thomas to give an address at the 1910 dedicatory celebration of Thompkins Hall, named after a generous benefactor, Charles E. Thompkins, of Connecticut. The just completed, well–designed dining hall, the largest structure on campus, had a seating capacity of 2,300. Appearing on that occasion in his senior year was a distinct honor for Thomas. Not long afterward, in 1911, he received a bachelor's degree. Subsequently, when his impact upon the welfare of African Americans had become apparent, a financial award was given annually in the name of Jesse O. Thomas to a student of Tuskegee who exhibited exceptional academic achievement.

After graduation, Washington asked Thomas to use his talents as field secretary for his alma mater with headquarters in Rochester, New York. From 1912 to 1916 he was a nationwide representative of Tuskegee and president of the national alumni association and was closely involved with the institute, which later became Tuskegee University.

Thomas ended his ties with Tuskegee in 1916 and took the job of principal of Voorhees Normal and Industrial Institute in Denmark, South Carolina. Under his leadership Voorhees developed a new curriculum with courses of study that qualified its graduates for certification to teach in that state without the formality of state administered examinations. After two years at Voorhees, Thomas went to his first government assignment, supervisor of Negro economics of New York in 1918, working in the office of the New York State Department of Labor. At the same time, he was an examiner in the United States Employment Service in New York City.

In 1919 Thomas went to the National Urban League, where he spent most of his career. The Urban League, whose mission is to study and make advancements primarily in the economic status of African Americans, is a companion organization to the NAACP whose scope envelopes all aspects of black life in the United States. Thomas's training, interest, and experience was excellent preparation for the post of field secretary for the league's southern division. He traveled by rail to cities mostly in the South, meeting with local African American leaders, spreading the philosophy of the Urban League, and setting up branches in the larger cities in places such as Los Angeles, Miami, Little Rock, Richmond, and New Orleans. One of the largest and best supported chapters was in Atlanta—in Thomas's thinking, a model for other branches.

Aside from the time consuming duties of organizing and supporting local chapters, Thomas was successful in encouraging the African American middle class—teachers, businessmen and other professionals—to subscribe to *Opportunity,* the League's magazine, a counterpart to the NAACP's *Crisis.*

While employed by the Urban League, Thomas continued his own education by studying as a graduate student at the New York School for Social Work intermittently from 1919 to 1923. During this period he was the primary organizer of Atlanta University's School of Social Work, the first institution established to teach the skills of social work to African Americans. The idea of the school and the impetus for its creation came to life in the 1919 conference of social workers in New Orleans, when Thomas initiated discussion about the dearth of qualified black workers in every state of the union.

Once in operation, he occupied a seat on the school's board of directors to guide its progress and insure its success.

Thomas resigned from the Urban League in 1940 after serving a year as acting executive secretary, having replaced the incumbent, Eugene Kinckle Jones, who was disabled by illness. Thomas then became the National Red Cross's first African American employed in policy–making status, classified as special assistant director of domestic relations.

Thomas's community involvement depicted the breath of his interests and the extent of his commitment to improvement in the quality of life for black Americans. The proof was in his association with organizations that represented business, social work, education, and economic development. He was a delegate to the First Session of the International Conference of Social Work, in Paris, France, in 1928. In the same year, he served on the Mississippi Flood Relief Committee. Thomas was a member of the Committee on Economics and Industry of the National Conference on Social Work. When he was in college he pledged to Omega Psi Phi Fraternity.

Jesse O. Thomas died in 1972 in Sacramento, California, at age 86, survived by his wife, Nellie, and one daughter, Anne Thomas Braxton. Starting in a small town in Mississippi, then progressing to cities all over the United States, and overseas to France, Thomas earned a reputation as a man whose accomplishments in the advancement of civil rights are widely respected. His motivation was rooted in concern about the plight of underprivileged and underrepresented African Americans who did not have the advantage of education, work skills, health care, or knowledge about how to make the most of life in the face of difficult circumstances.

REFERENCES

''Founder of Atlanta League, School of Social Work Dies.'' *Jet* 25 (16 March 1972): 18.

Weiss, Nancy J. *The National Urban League 1910–1940.* New York: Oxford University Press, 1974.

Who's Who in Colored America. New York: Who's Who in Colored America Corporation, 1929.

Dona L. Irvin

Howard Thurman

(1900–1981)

Theologian, clergyman, mystic, civil rights advisor

Known as one of the great mystics and theologians of the twentieth century, Howard Thurman gained prominence both as an influential African American pastor and as a religious leader of faith and nonviolence throughout the world. After serving as pastor of the Church for the Fellowship of All Peoples, Thurman became Dean of Marsh Chapel and Professor of Spiritual Resources and Disciplines at Boston University, becoming the first African American to hold such a leadership position in ministry at a major white university. His early achievements as a spiritual leader and writer enabled him to be one of the most compelling religious figures in America. Moreover, it was Thurman's application of Mahatma Gandhi's philosophy of peace and nonviolence in his ministry that proved to be a valuable resource for Martin Luther King Jr. and other ministers involved in the Civil Rights Movement of the 1950s and 1960s.

Howard Washington Thurman was born at the turn of the twentieth century on November 18, 1900, in Daytona Beach, Florida, to Saul Solomon Thurman, a railroad worker, and Alice Ambrose, a domestic for the wealthy white families of Daytona Beach. He was their second child and only son. Perhaps no family member had a stronger impact on Thurman's life than his maternal grandmother, Nancy Ambrose. He developed a special bond with this grandmother and often reflected upon her religious devotion and inner strength. Her strong constitution became a major source of support for the family following the deaths of his father and stepfather while he was still a child.

By all accounts, Thurman's mother was a devout Christian who, along with her mother, taught Thurman the importance of spiritual values and compassion for others. According to Luther Smith in *Howard Thurman: The Mystic as Prophet,* Thurman's revered grandmother ''was the first to teach Thurman that spirituality sustains one in the midst of life's many predicaments.'' His grandmother's teachings about spirituality found support in the faith community of the Mount Bethel Baptist Church, where his mother and grandmother were members. In addition, ''Grandma Nancy'' instilled in young Thurman a sense of self–worth that enabled him to deal with the bitter experiences of racial segregation and discrimination in the south. Thurman's thirst for knowledge can also be attributed to his grandmother's nurture. Although illiterate, she appreciated the importance and value of education and understood it to be a means of liberation.

Works for His Education

Thurman and the black community of Daytona were also influenced by another strong advocate of education during the early 1900s, Mary McLeod Bethune. She had founded Bethune College in Daytona for young African American women, with meager funds from the sale of sweet potato pies. The school later merged with the Cookman Institute, an all male school, and changed its name to Bethune–Cookman College. In *With Head and Heart,* Thurman stated that ''the very presence of the school, and the inner strength and authority of Mrs. Bethune, gave boys like me a view of the possibilities to be realized in some distant future.'' As a result of this influence, he desired more education than the seventh–grade limit reserved for blacks in Daytona. Thurman's grandmother appealed to Daytona's school authorities that he be allowed to complete the eighth grade. The authorities complied and

Howard Thurman (left) with O. D. Foster and T. K. Zoo, 1952.

extended the eighth grade to Daytona's blacks based on Thurman's fine performance.

Despite Thurman's acumen, public high school was not an option for him or any black child in Daytona. There were only three high schools for blacks in the state of Florida. Several private church–supported schools also provided high school education for blacks. From among these Thurman chose Florida Baptist Academy in nearby Jacksonville. He would live with relatives and work to pay for his school and living expenses. Although his mother and grandmother both supported his pursuit of education, they could not provide much more. The death of his father and stepfather left the family with very little money.

Black and poor, Thurman encountered another obstacle to his attempt at getting a high school education when he arrived at Daytona's train station on the day he was to leave for Florida Baptist Academy. After purchasing his ticket, he had no money to pay for the shipping of the trunk containing his clothes and other belongings. Thurman, upset by the apparent end of his high school dream, began to cry at the railway station. It was at this moment that Thurman's hope came from an unknown black man. After inquiring about Thurman's dilemma, as noted in Thurman's book *With Head and Heart,* the man responded by saying, "If you are trying to get out of this damn town to get an education, the least I can do is to help you. Come with me." He took Thurman to the ticket agent and paid for the trunk. This generous man did not say another word to Thurman, but simply turned and disappeared down the railroad track. Thurman never saw him again.

After finishing his studies at Florida Baptist Academy, Thurman enrolled at Morehouse College in Atlanta, Georgia, in the fall of 1919. Morehouse, an institution founded by the American Baptist Missionary Society for the education and training of African American men planning careers in education and ministry, had begun to earn a reputation as the preeminent institution for refining the mind and character of the nation's brightest young black men. Instrumental in that effort was the school's first African American president, John Hope. He, along with Samuel Archer, who was dean, and distinguished faculty members such as Benjamin Mays and sociologist E. Franklin Frazier (who served as Thurman's professors) contributed to Thurman's intellectual development. In 1923 Thurman graduated from Morehouse with a B.A. degree. His love for religion and philosophy had been significantly enhanced at Morehouse. After much thought about his future professional career, Thurman decided to enter Rochester Theological Seminary in the fall of the year.

Rochester Theological Seminary proved to be a challenging experience. Rochester was one of few schools that would admit blacks during the 1920s. Thurman was one of two blacks in the 1926 entering class. Thurman faced many challenges at Rochester. The climate of Rochester became the first for this Florida native. Although Thurman had spent a summer in New York while attending Morehouse, he had not lived in the North during the fall and winter months. The overall environment seemed quite foreign to him. The faculty members and student body were quite different from the intimate family circle that existed at Morehouse. George Cross, however, perceived special abilities in Thurman and encouraged him to work to his fullest potential. While a seminary student, Thurman began to work as a minister at the First Baptist Church in Roanoke, Virginia, during the summer months.

In the spring of 1926 Thurman graduated from Rochester Theological Seminary. The following week, on June 11, 1926, he married Kate Kelley, a graduate of Spelman College, the women's counterpart to Morehouse College in Atlanta. Hours after the wedding, the new couple left in order for Thurman to assume his first church appointment, Mt. Zion Baptist Church in Oberlin, Ohio, a community centered around the progressive Oberlin University. During what would become a brief pastorate, Howard and Kate had their first child, Olive Katherine, in 1927. They did not experience the role as parents together for very long, however. Kate soon developed an illness that claimed her life in December of 1930. The extended illness and death of Kate left Thurman severely depressed. With an infant and no wife, family members assisted Thurman in his daughter's care. Thurman turned to travel as a way to rid himself of his loneliness.

Two years later on June 12, 1932, Thurman married Sue Bailey, a collegiate secretary for the national board of the YWCA, at Kings Mountain, North Carolina. She shared similar experiences with Thurman. Bailey was a graduate of Spelman College, where she had known mutual friends of Thurman while he attended Morehouse. She had also received her master's degree from Oberlin University in the town of Thurman's first church. They had one daughter, Anne, who was born in 1933.

After post–professional study at Oberlin and Haverford, Thurman joined the faculty of his alma mater, Morehouse College. In addition to his teaching responsibilities, Thurman took over duties as chaplain of Morehouse's daily chapel services. This experience enabled him to further his professional career.

In 1931 Thurman joined the faculty at Howard University's School of Religion in Washington, D.C. It was not long before Thurman was appointed dean of Howard's Rankin Chapel. He would serve as professor of theology and dean of Rankin Chapel from 1932 to 1944. The dean of the School of Religion was Benjamin E. Mays. A graduate of the University of Chicago, Mays worked diligently to place Howard's School of Religion as a reputable divinity school in the country. Thurman's ministry as dean of chapel would contribute toward that end. The chapel program was of strong quality with a recognition for other religious traditions. Mays and Thurman became life–long friends and held great respect for each other. According to Cason Hill in *The Alumnus,* Mays referred to Thurman as one who "generated in the minds of young negroes the idea of freedom. . . . When they heard or read [him], for the first time they experienced a free man and his freedom was contagious."

Develops Christian Ministry of Nonviolence

Thurman's tenure as dean of Rankin Chapel introduced an ecumenical religious experience to the university community. Having studied under the mystic scholar, Rufus Jones, Thurman had developed an inclusive understanding of religion. Thurman's worship experience took on various innovative and creative styles. For example, meditation would often become the centerpiece of the worship. According to *The Alumnus,* Thurman provided "stretches of time for meditation, a quiet time for prayers . . . a service that would permit greater freedom for the play of creative imagination." Thurman had begun to appreciate the varieties of religions and religious experiences and had a strong desire to provide a religious ritual which reflected the diversity of worshippers. He began evening chapel or vesper services called the Twilight Hours. These services introduced various elements of worship, including liturgical dance.

Much of this wider vision of religion and worship resulted from Thurman's experience of serving, in 1935, as chair of a delegation of African Americans who went on a "pilgrimage of friendship" to India, Burma and Ceylon as guests of the Student Christian Movement. This trip was sponsored by the YMCA and YWCA International Committee which acted on behalf of the World Christian Student Federation. Sue Bailey Thurman, who had served as collegiate secretary for the YWCA, accompanied him, along with another couple. The trip allowed Thurman to address some crucial issues around Christianity and racial oppression as well as to deepen his commitment to pacifism, a philosophy that opposes war and violence as a means to settling disputes. He began to hone his belief that religion could be a tool for bringing the human family together. Just as he understood how religion had been used to institute slavery and racial segregation and discrimination, he believed that religion could function as an oasis to foster love and a community of equality through nonviolence.

Thurman recognized the importance of nonviolence and adopted this philosophy as central to Christian ethics. The trip to India and a 1936 meeting with Mahatma Gandhi further shaped his philosophy on nonviolence, which had taken root while he was a college student and a member of the Fellowship of Reconciliation, an organization designed to end war, international and social conflict through the practice of non–violence. In October of 1943, Thurman received a letter from Alfred Fisk, a Presbyterian minister and philosophy professor at San Francisco State College, requesting that he provide him with a seminary student to assist him in organizing an interracial congregation. The student who Thurman recommended declined the offer and Thurman decided to take on this project to begin an interracial church. Thurman's request was accepted and he left with his wife to assist in the founding of the church.

Founds Church for All Peoples

The Church for the Fellowship of All Peoples went much farther than a church of white and black Christians. It served as a place of worship for individuals from various backgrounds, including a significant number of Japanese Americans, individuals from a diversity of religious backgrounds, humanists and a wide range of other people whose only common denominator was their belief in God. This church allowed Thurman to experiment with his belief that religion could bring people together in the work for peace on earth. As cofounder and pastor, Thurman gave to the congregants some of the same unique spiritual experiences that he had shared with the parishioners at Rankin Chapel. As he wrote in *With Head and Heart,* he offered "liturgical dance; a dance choir; English Handbell Choir and art exhibits." For Thurman, the primary goal of this church and the Christian church in general was to create a climate of unity and wholeness, countering the divisions and separation that destroy community.

In the midst of the beauty surrounding San Francisco, racial bigotry, segregation and discrimination existed as they did elsewhere in the United States. The Fellowship Church served as a challenge to these racist practices. Several members encountered opposition to the ideals and practices that they created within their religious community. One church member was warned by the management at her apartment complex that it would not be possible for her to have "minority" members at her home. A crisis resulted when she ignored the prohibition and invited them. Thurman witnessed the deep–seated racism of the society as well. He found that he was in a closed world, very different from the world that he experienced at the Fellowship Church.

In his pastoral ministry to the ill and dying, Thurman noticed the absence of African American physicians. He encountered hospital staff members who did not know how to respond to an African American clergyman in a position of authority visiting white patients. He found the same attitude when he officiated at funerals of deceased white members. These experiences provided insight into the need for the Fellowship Church to continue the work of transforming a society of intolerance and exclusion.

Thurman's ministry received recognition outside of the San Francisco community and made an impact on Harold Case, president of Boston University. He was interested in Thurman implementing a similar ministry at Boston University's Marsh Chapel. Thurman would have a joint appointment with the School of Theology and Marsh Chapel, similar to the position he had held at Howard University. In 1953 Case offered the position to Thurman and he accepted. He resigned from the full–time pastorate at the Church for the Fellowship of All Peoples and prepared to move to Boston. In 1953 Thurman became the first African American to be dean of chapel at a major white institution of higher learning.

Thurman would not only be the first African American dean of chapel but the first to conduct chapel services in a nontraditional way. His eastern meditations would set a precedent for chapel services at the university. His past experiences as pastor of an integrated church and dean of a university chapel prepared him for this new setting.

Thurman later discovered there was opposition to his coming, both on racial and theological grounds. Harold Case, however, was committed to Thurman's appointment. As dean of the chapel, Thurman enjoyed a position that allowed him to use his nontraditional approaches to ministry and worship and to preach sermons to a diversity of populations, including students from neighboring campuses. Some students found Thurman's dark imposing presence and pensive looks awe inspiring while others observed this appearance as intimidating. Thurman responded to these reactions with a determination to help worshippers transform into more peaceful and loving individuals.

Thurman maintained an openness to a variety of approaches. He knew that Case's attraction to his becoming dean of the chapel had to do with his creativity. Thurman took advantage of the new media in society. There were radio broadcasts of the services and a television program titled *We Believe,* a daily series of religious talks shared by religious leaders in the Boston area. These television talks received a positive response and enhanced the ministry that Thurman had begun at the chapel.

In addition, Thurman provided the chapel with liturgical dance and artistic liturgies and his mystic trademark of long meditations and silence. Thurman's deanship at the Marsh Chapel of Boston University flourished. In *With Head and Heart* he described the ministry at Marsh Chapel as having "opportunities for the communal celebration of life and death and for the widest range of the human experience." Thurman viewed his ministry as enhanced by his wife, Sue Bailey Thurman. She insisted that once each month the 65–member choir join her and her husband for dinner. The chapel provided a home for the many international students on campus. Thurman's religious worship of silence and meditation paralleled practices in such eastern religious faiths as Buddhism and Hinduism, which were the religious traditions of many of the students. In an effort to allow Thurman time to travel and respond to other needs of the university, two anonymous San Francisco friends gave a substantial contribution to Boston University to underwrite Thurman's salary for three years and to provide him with a new office and a secretary. Thurman's last years at Marsh Chapel ended a productive ministry. In 1993 Life magazine named him one of the country's 12 greatest preachers. The Thurmans spent their last years at Boston traveling. Thurman had a leave–of–absence from the university while Boston searched for his replacement as dean. Their years at Boston ended with two trips around the world, spending time in both Nigeria and Israel. In addition, they went to Japan, the Philippines, Egypt, Hong Kong, and

Hawaii. The third year Thurman was minister–at–large, which involved some work with Marsh Chapel.

After officially retiring from Boston University in the summer of 1965, Howard and Sue Thurman returned to San Francisco for him to chair the Howard Thurman Educational Trust Fund. In *They Looked for a City,* Walter Fluker defined the trust as ''a charitable and eleemosynary foundation that provides a channel for the enlistment of funds for those who share the dream of community.'' Throughout the latter part of his life, Thurman devoted his efforts to the trust and to teaching the principles that he had lived and taught throughout his career.

Thurman wrote more than 20 books on spirituality and social consciousness. Some of the more popular works are *Jesus and the Disinherited, The Creative Encounter: An Interpretation of Religion and Social Witness*, and *The Luminous Darkness: A Personal Integration of the Anatomy of Segregation and the Ground of Hope.* The church for which he had become famous was highlighted in his book, *Footprints of a Dream: The Story of the Church for the Fellowship of All People.* In 1979 Thurman wrote his life story, *With Head and Heart: The Autobiography of Howard Thurman.* His belief in nonviolence as a tool for peace and community can be found throughout his works.

In 1981 Thurman died in his San Francisco home. The Howard Thurman Trust is now being run by Sue Bailey Thurman. She solicits funds from those individuals who have the same vision as her husband. In Thurman's hometown, Daytona Beach, Florida, there is the Howard Thurman home. This home has become a symbol of hope for youth and reminds those who visit of the need for community service.

Several memorials are dedicated to Thurman's life and thought. Boston University has established the Howard Thurman Center as a part of the Martin Luther King Jr. Center. As well, there is a Howard Thurman Listening Room located in the basement of Marsh Chapel at the university. This room holds a glass encasing of Howard Thurman's possessions while he was dean of Marsh Chapel. Visitors may listen to the sermons given by Thurman while he was dean. Mozella Mitchell, in *The Human Search,* located more than 100 Howard Thurman Listening Rooms in the United States and abroad. They have been established in churches, college chapels, prisons, and other institutions.

Morehouse College has erected a monument in his honor, located to the right front of the Martin Luther King Jr. Memorial International Chapel. It is a 73–foot bell tower surrounded by a reflecting pool and eight flags. Each of the flags has a golden eagle symbolizing the presence of God. On the outside of the obelisk is a bronze plaque of Thurman and excerpts of his writings. His ashes are interred in the tower.

Inside the chapel at Morehouse College is the Howard Thurman Listening Room. There is also at Morehouse a Howard Thurman Chapel of the Inward Journey. Thurman is remembered for his religious leadership and for his nonviolent approach to civil disobedience.

REFERENCES

Fluker, Walter. *They Looked for a City: A Comparative Analysis of the Ideal of Community in the Thought of Howard Thurman and Martin Luther King Jr.* Lanham, MD: University Press of America, 1989.

''The Many Unforgettable Faces and Facets of Howard Thurman '23.'' In *The Alumnus: Morehouse College Alumni Magazine* 56 (Spring 1995): 16–19.

Mitchell, Mozella, ed. *The Human Search: Howard Thurman and the Quest for Freedom.* New York: Peter Lang Publishers, 1992.

Smith, Luther E. *Howard Thurman: The Mystic as Prophet.* Washington, DC: University Press of America, 1981.

Thurman, Howard W. *With Head and Heart: The Autobiography of Howard Thurman.* New York: Harcourt Brace Jovanovich, 1979.

COLLECTIONS

The papers of Howard Thurman are at Boston University and in the Colgate Rochester Divinity School at Colgate University. There is also at Colgate the Howard Thurman Papers Project.

Horace L. Griffin

Wallace Thurman

(1902–1934)

Novelist, playwright, ghostwriter, journalist

As the *enfant terrible* of the New Negro Movement in Harlem, Wallace Thurman's criticism stung the old guard by challenging their standards of aesthetics and pointing out their biases, but his *Fire!*—a literary journal—burned ever so briefly. Yet his life and works remain a symbol and legacy of that period of artistic genius known as the Harlem Renaissance.

Wallace Henry Thurman was born in Salt Lake City, Utah, on August 16, 1902, the son of Oscar and Beulah Thurman. Little is known about his childhood. It is rumored that he had an American Indian grandmother who married a Jewish peddler. Whether this is true or not, Thurman's African ancestry was quite evident. He was often described as very dark skinned. Thurman attended the public schools in Salt Lake City, graduating from high school in 1919. He graduated from the University of Utah in 1922, completing early the premedical curriculum and scoring high in chemistry and pharmacy. In 1923 he enrolled for post–graduate work at the University of Southern California in Los Angeles, where he spent a year studying and perhaps trying to gain acceptance within the elite society of African Americans at the predominantly white university. Dorothy West recalled in ''Elephant's Dance: A Memoir of Wallace Thurman'' that Thurman ''hated Negro society, and since dark skins were never the fashion among Negro upper classes, the feeling was occasionally mutual.'' Ostracized by whites and lighter skinned blacks, Thurman, like the heroine of his first novel, did not return to USC but remained in Los Angeles where he sought to establish himself as a journalist. He was a reporter for the *Los Angeles Sentinel,* a local African American newspaper, and had his own column entitled *Inklings.*

Thurman read about the widely heralded New Negro Movement, or the Harlem Renaissance, taking place in New York. He also met and was influenced by Arna Bontemps, who would later become a major figure in Harlem. In 1924 in an effort to promote a similar movement on the West Coast, Thurman established his own literary magazine, *The Outlet.* The journal lasted only six months but marked the first of his many efforts to be a successful publisher. Thurman left Los Angeles in 1925 and moved to New York City.

In New York Theophilus Lewis, a good friend and mentor, helped Thurman obtain work as a reporter for the *Looking Glass,* another short–lived publication. But his experience as a reporter and editor enabled him to become managing editor of the *Messenger* in the spring of 1926. In 1917, A. Philip Randolph and Chandler Owen founded the *Messenger* for the purpose of addressing economic and political issues related to the African American community. Sometimes, however, they published short stories and poetry by new African American writers. When Thurman became its managing editor, he accepted the first short stories of Langston Hughes and other people that Thurman in ''Negro Artists and the New Negro'' claimed ''still retained some individual race qualities and who were not totally white American in every respect save the color of skin.'' Thurman left the *Messenger* in the fall of 1926 to accept a position as the circulation manager for a white–owned monthly, *The World Tomorrow.*

Thurman and Langston Hughes became close friends and expressed the ideas of a new school of young writers that came to be known as the Harlem Renaissance. In *The New Negro: Thirty Years Afterward,* Charles S. Johnson called Locke ''dean of this group of fledgling writers of the new and lively generation of the 1920's.'' The group included Zora Neale Hurston, Aaron Douglas, Gwendolyn Bennett, John Davis, Bruce Nugent, Arna Bontemps, Nella Larsen, Dorothy West, Countee Cullen, Claude McKay, Jessie Fauset, Rudolph Fisher, and Jean Toomer.

Artistic *Fire* Takes Hold

In the summer of 1926 the New Negro group of young writers and artists decided to establish their own journal. Thurman was chosen as editor for several reasons, not the least of which being that he had a full–time job and could put up the funds and also obtain credit. The name for the journal, Hughes revealed in *The Big Sea,* was to suggest ''that it would burn up a lot of old, dead conventional Negro–white ideas of the past, *épater lebourgeois* into a realization of the existence of the younger Negro writers and artists, and provide us with an outlet for publication not available.''

Fire! cost $1,000 to produce, and Thurman provided most of the funds. Today the journal is recognized as being the first really influential African American little magazine of the twentieth century. Both obscene and revolutionary, *Fire!* made Thurman one of the most daring small journal editors. But despite being hot—''melting steel and iron bars, poking livid tongues between stone apertures and burning wooden opposition with a cackling chuckle of contempt,'' as Thurman wrote in the foreword in November 1926—*Fire!* survived only one issue. Only a few bookstores in Greenwich Village stocked the journal. African American critics of the old guard hated it, attacking the editor and all of the contributors; and *Fire!* seems to have escaped the notice of white critics entirely.

Thurman, who had already angered many readers with his 1925 criticism of the New Negro in *The Looking Glass,* was again upbraided for his editorial about Carl Van Vechten's *Nigger Heaven.* He wrote in *Fire!,* ''Some time ago, while reviewing Carl Van Vechten's lava–laden *Nigger Heaven,* I made the prophecy that Harlem Negroes, once their aversion to the 'nigger' in the title was forgotten, would erect a statue on the corner of 135th Street and Seventh Avenue, and dedicate it to this ultra–sophisticated Iowa New Yorker.'' He concluded with the prediction that ''Mr. Van Vechten will be spoken of as a kindly gent rather than as a moral leper exploiting people who had believed him to be a sincere friend.''

Thurman spent the next four years paying the printer for *Fire!* His health was failing, but his desire to establish a publication that would afford a wider outlet for young African American writers than did *The Crisis, Opportunity,* and the *Messenger* would not let him quit trying. He tried again in 1928 with *Harlem, A Forum of Negro Life.* This publication folded after only two issues. In 1927, however, many of his articles appeared in prestigious publications, including the *New Republic, Independent, The World Tomorrow, The Bookman,* and *Dance Magazine,* which helped establish Thurman as a critic, albeit a caustic one.

Thurman, always in debt and often unemployed, began to suffer the physical effects of his bohemian lifestyle. He had a swollen thyroid and other infected glands that required surgery. Yet he lived and drank gin like water. One of the best descriptions of Thurman's lifestyle came from Arthur P. Davis of Howard University, who was a college student in New York during the Harlem Renaissance. Davis recalled in ''Growing Up in the New Negro Renaissance'' that

> The Campus boys ... found parties at Wallace Thurman's house in 139th Street ... far more exciting than those at the Dark Tower [home of A'Lelia Walker, heiress of the Madam C. J. Walker empire]. Thurman was a charming host with a hearty laugh and a keen sense of the phony. His parties tended to have a broader social mixture than those at the tower. There one found in addition to writers and artists, truck drivers and other workers,

theatrical people from downtown, and always, it seems, a disproportionate number of white girls. The sky was the limit at Thurman's parties.

In 1928, Thurman found employment with McFadden Publications on its editorial staff, probably the first African American to hold such a position with a large New York publishing firm. Langston Hughes's description of his friend in *The Big Sea* makes it clear why Thurman was chosen for the job: "He was a strangely brilliant black boy who read everything, and whose critical mind could find something wrong with everything he read. Thurman had read so many books because he could read 11 lines at a time."

The Blacker the Berry the Sweeter the Juice

Thurman's first novel was published by Macaulay Company in 1929. *The Blacker the Berry the Sweeter the Juice,* a title taken from African American folklore, blew the lid off intra–race color prejudice and self–hatred. Largely autobiographical, the novel with its ironic dedication "To Bulah [Thurman's mother], the goose who laid the not so golden egg," focused on the life of Emma Lou, an intelligent, middle class young woman with very dark skin. Like Thurman, Emma is from the West, goes to Los Angeles and then to New York. Constantly scorned because of her color, she resorts to using bleach creams and hair straighteners. Reviewed in both the *New York Times Book Review* (as a novel about a "coal black nigger") and the *New York Herald Tribune Books,* the novel failed to win critical acclaim. V. F. Calverton, *Tribune* critic, wrote in "The Negro Writer," "As a literary effort it is without distinction." What distinguished the novel, however, was its subject matter—a theme that would remain with the black experience and come under harsh examination during the black aesthetic movement of the 1960s.

In addition to editing, Thurman became a ghostwriter for *True Story* and other magazines and books and a reader for Macaulay Publishing Company. He also worked as a playwright. *Harlem: A Melodrama of Negro Life in Harlem,* Thurman's first play written in collaboration with William Jourdan Rapp, premiered on Broadway on February 20, 1929. The play received mixed reviews and complaints from old guard African Americans that it focused too much on the low–life in Harlem. The play enjoyed over 90 performances in New York, however, and went on to play in Chicago and in Los Angeles. Based on a short story Thurman had written and published in *Fire!* entitled "Cordelia the Crude," the melodrama centered on a southern family's move north into urban crime and poverty. The play also examined prejudice against West Indians by American blacks. The following year Thurman collaborated with Rapp on *Jeremiah, the Magnificent,* a three–act play that was performed only once after Thurman's death. Neither play was published.

In 1932 Thurman's second novel was published. *Infants of the Spring,* with a title from a line in Shakespeare's *Hamlet,* was a sardonic debunking of the New Negro Movement. Often credited with coining the word *Niggerati* to describe the African American *literati,* Thurman exposed the bohemianism plaguing creative artist—infants in a well–spring of opportunity. It seems Thurman's bitterness was uncontrolled in this novel, for he, like Raymond in his novel, is consumed by self–hatred. Hughes's insight into the psyche of his friend was most revealing because he understood that Thurman liked being black but hated the scorn it brought him; he was attracted to bohemianism, but thought it wrong to be a bohemian. "He liked to waste time," Hughes wrote in *The Big Sea,* "but he always felt guilty wasting time. He loathed crowds, but he hated to be alone."

The Interne, Thurman's third and final novel, was written in collaboration with Abraham L. Furman. It treated the problems found in an urban hospital and has more than an African American focus. This last novel was published in 1932.

In 1934, Thurman signed a contract with Bryan–Foy Productions to write a scenario for *Tomorrow's Children,* a picture on sterilization, and another screenplay, *High School Girl* (1935). The first screenplay was banned in New York because of its sexually explicit content.

Wally, as he was called by his friends, became ill in California and returned to New York in May 1934. He was diagnosed with tuberculosis, but he continued his destructive life style and collapsed at his own reunion party in July of 1934. He was taken to City Hospital on Welfare Island, the very hospital he had written about in *The Intern.* Six months later he died, on December 22, 1934. On Christmas eve, Louise Thompson, Thurman's ex–wife, along with a host of Harlemites including Countee Cullen, Dorothy West, Aaron Douglas, and Walter White, attended his funeral at the Levy and Delany funeral parlor at 211 West 134th Street. Thurman was buried in Silver Mount Cemetery on Staten Island. An obituary, "Death Claims Noted Writer," published in the *New Amsterdam* newspaper, listed Mrs. A. L. Jackson, grandmother; Mrs. Bulah Dorsey, mother; and Arthur Jackson, uncle, all residents of Salt Lake City, Utah, as survivors.

Thurman did not win acclaim for the technical brilliance of his literary works; however, because of his sincere, veracious, and poignant themes and a lifestyle that epitomized the bohemian era, he will never be forgotten. Only rarely is a book written about this famed era without the mention of Thurman, for in remembering him, the creative and rebellious spirit of artistic fire is celebrated.

REFERENCES

Bloom, Harold, ed. *Black American Prose Writers of the Harlem Renaissance.* New York: Chelsea House, 1994.

Calverton, V. F. "The Negro Writer," in *Black American Prose Writers of the Harlem Renaissance.* New York: Chelsea House, 1994.

Chidi, Ikonne. *From DuBois to Van Vechten.* London: Greenwood, 1981.

Davis, Arthur P. "Growing up in the New Negro Renaissance," *Negro American Literature Forum 2* (Fall 1968): 53–55.

"Death Claims Noted Writer." *Amsterdam News,* December 29, 1934.

'''Dynasty' and Some Other Recent Works of Fiction.'' *New York Times Book Review* 17 (March 1929): 6.

Hughes, Langston. *The Big Sea: An Autobiography.* New York: Knopf, 1940.

Johnson, Charles S. *The New Negro: Thirty Years Afterward.* Washington, DC: Howard University Press, 1955.

Logan, Rayford W., and Michael R. Winston, eds. *Dictionary of American Negro Biography.* New York: Norton, 1982.

Singh, Amritjit, William S. Shiver, and Stanley Brodwin, eds. *The Harlem Renaissance: Revaluations.* New York: Garland, 1989.

Thurman, Wallace. *The Blacker the Berry.* New York: Macaulay, 1929.

———. ''Cordelia the Crude.'' *Fire!* 1 (November 1926): 17.

———. ''Harlem Facets.'' *The World Tomorrow* 10 (November 1927): 465–67.

———. *Infants of Spring.* New York: Macaulay, 1932.

———. *Jeremiah the Magnificant.* Unpublished. New York.

———. ''Negro Artists and the Negro.'' *New Republic* 52 (31 August 1927): 37–39.

———. ''Negro Poets and Their Poetry.'' *Bookman* 67 (July 1928): 55–61.

———. ''Nephews of Uncle Remus.'' *Independent* 119 (24 September 1927): 296–98.

———, and Abraham Furman. *The Interne.* New York: Macaulay, 1932.

———, and William Jourdan Rapp. *Harlem.* Unpublished. 1929.

West, Dorothy. ''Elephant's Dance: A Memoir of Wallace Thurman.'' *Black World* 20 (November 1970): 79–80.

COLLECTIONS

Wallace Thurman's papers, unpublished plays, and letters are housed in the James Weldon Johnson Collection at Yale University. The play, *Jeremiah the Magnificant,* and photographs of Thurman are available in the Schomburg Center for Research in Black Culture, New York City.

Nagueyalti Warren

Charles Albert Tindley

(1851–1933)

Minister, composer

Charles Albert Tindley was famed in his lifetime for being one of the most powerful preachers in Philadelphia. He is known as a hymn writer with a powerful influence on the performers and composers who created gospel music, from Lucie Campbell to Thomas Dorsey. His hymns are found in many hymnals, and some have even entered the folk tradition in both black and white churches.

Charles Albert Tindley was born on July 7, 1851, to Charles Tindley, a slave, and (H)ester Miller Tindley, who was free, in or near Berlin, Maryland. The elder Charles Tindley was the slave of Joseph Brindell, whose farm was near Berlin. Charles Albert Tindley's mother died while he was young. His mother's sister, Caroline Miller Robbins, raised him until he was old enough to be hired out. Although he was set to work alongside slaves, his free status was recognized.

Tindley did not go to school but taught himself to read. He wrote in his 1932 *Book of Sermons* quoted by Bernice Reagon, ''I could read the Bible almost without stopping to spell out the words.'' About 1868 when he was 17, he married Daisy Henry (d. 1924). They had eight children, several of whom displayed decided musical talent. In 1927 he married Jenny Cotton, who survived him.

Tindley moved to Philadelphia in 1875, staying first with his aunt, Julia Miller. Her father Arnold Miller had purchased his own freedom and then that of his family, including Charles Albert Tindley's mother. Julia Miller contributed to that effort after she gained her freedom and moved to Philadelphia.

Tindley worked first as a hodcarrier, carrying mortar to bricklayers, and also as sexton at the John Wesley Methodist Episcopal Church. Tindley became pastor of this church some 25 years later, when it was called the Bainbridge Street Church. He worked at improving his education and, in 1885, asked to join the Methodist Episcopal church's segregated Delaware Conference, which included Delaware, Maryland, New Jersey, and Pennsylvania. After a probationary appointment in Cape May, New Jersey, Tindley was ordained deacon in 1887 and elder in 1889. He had a variety of assignments in the conference and became presiding elder of the Wilmington District in 1900. He was a delegate to the denomination's general convocation every four years from 1908 until his death and was nominated for bishop in 1916 and 1920.

In 1902 Tindley was appointed to the Bainbridge Street Church, which then had a congregation of 130; he remained with the congregation for the rest of his life. The church moved to East Calvary Church on Broad Street in 1906. Tindley's prowess as a preacher strained the capacity of the building—his congregation now numbered some 5,000, and he attracted a large number of whites on Sunday evenings. Late–comers to any service had to stand. In the early 1920s Tindley undertook to build a new 3,200–seat church, later named Tindley Temple, which opened in 1925 shortly after the death of his first wife.

The new building was still crowded with a membership of close to ten thousand with 5,000 active, but the congregation was poor. Finances remained a major problem, and the bank threatened foreclosure in 1930. The church called in a popular revival minister, G. Wilson Becton, to conduct a crusade. Becton did help the finances but when he was forced out for being too flamboyant, he took some 3,000 of the congregation with him. Tindley was by this time in poor health. Gangrene set in after an injury to a foot in early 1933. After two weeks in the Frederick Douglass Hospital, he died on July 26, 1933.

The worship style of Tindley Temple had deep roots in the black religious tradition. The congregation behaved like that of a Baptist or Pentecostal church, giving loud vocal and physical responses in worship—Tindley Temple had a second rail on the balcony to prevent worshippers feeling the spirit from falling over.

Tindley came from one of the earliest areas evangelized by Methodists and one of the most persistent in retaining African elements in worship. African Methodist Episcopal bishops Daniel Payne and Levi Coffin had great difficulty there in suppressing ring dances and praying bands in the churches of their denomination. The praying band tradition continued in Tindley's church as worshippers gathered in the church basement on weeknights to sit in a circle and pass the night in singing and praying. Tindley's background gave him his power as a preacher. He knew what poor black emigrants from the country sought in their worship, and he had the gift of reaching his audience. He also had an impressive physical presence, being six–feet two–inches tall and weighing 230 pounds.

During his preaching, Tindley would break into song, with the congregation joining him in singing the chorus. He continued the message of his preaching in his hymn texts and had the gift of finding simple yet impressive music to set them. Tindley was a musical illiterate and appears to have held text and music for several hymns in his head, dictating them to the transcriber as a group. He published eight pieces in C. Austin Miles's *New Songs of the Gospel* in 1901; they had considerable success. By 1926 he published 34 more with an additional few appearing after his death. In 1905 he joined three Methodist bishops to form the Soul Echoes Publishing Company, which published *Soul Echoes: A Collection of Songs for Religious Meetings,* consisting mostly of his pieces, and in 1916 he joined his sons and others in forming the Paradise Publishing Company to publish *New Songs of Paradise! No. 1.* The sixth in the series includes all of his work as well as a few doubtful items.

Among the hymns, some, such as ''Stand By Me'' and ''We'll Understand It Better By and By,'' became popular among white congregations as well. In Reagon's collection of articles, Horace C. Boyer identifies nine songs, including these two, as standards of the gospel repertory. Inasmuch as gospel music is mostly characterized by performance practice, it is not clear how far Tindley and his church choir had moved in that direction. Still his music lends itself to the gospel performing style, and Thomas A. Dorsey, the ''father of gospel music,'' is explicit in acknowledging a debt to Tindley. A contemporary might well have considered Charles Albert Tindley only as a powerful preacher and minister. He drew large numbers of poor urban blacks, and also some whites, to hear his message. His heritage today, however, is to be found in church hymnals and gospel performances.

REFERENCES

Murphy, Larry G., and others, eds. *Encyclopedia of African American Religions.* New York: Garland, 1993.

Reagon, Bernice Johnson, ed. *We'll Understand It Better By and By.* Washington, DC: Smithsonian Institution, 1992.

Spencer, Jon Michael. *Black Hymnody.* Knoxville: University of Tennessee Press, 1992.

Robert L. Johns

Channing H. Tobias
(1882–1961)
Organization official, minister, social worker, civic leader

A vocal champion for the rights of African Americans, Channing H. Tobias became a distinguished social worker, Young Men's Christian Association (YMCA) leader, and organization official. In 1946 he became the first black director of the Phelps Stokes Fund. The ''mystery man of race relations,'' as he was referred to in *Ebony,* was a crusader for racial understanding and cooperation worldwide and worked through his various organizations to bring about the realization of equality for humankind.

Born on February 1, 1882, in Augusta, Georgia, Channing Heggie Tobias was the son of Fair J. Tobias, a coachman who had studied at Atlanta University, and Belle Robinson Tobias, a domestic servant. The father was of black and French extraction while the mother was of black and Native American ancestry and passed along to her son some of the facial features of her ancestral strain. Tobias and his only sibling, an older sister, were raised by relatives or friends while their parents worked his sister with their paternal grandmother and Tobias with a widowed illiterate friend of his mother, who saw to it that he regularly attended Sunday school and church service. His mother died when Tobias was 12–years old.

Channing Tobias received his early education at Haines Institute in Augusta, Georgia, then for three years studied at Paine Institute (now Paine College), also in Augusta, and received a B.A. degree in 1902. Tobias became interested in the ministry, and in 1900 he was ordained a minister in the Colored Methodist Episcopal Church (now the Christian Methodist Episcopal Church). Continuing religious studies, he received his bachelor of divinity degree from Drew Theological Seminary, Madison, New Jersey, in 1905. He spent the first six years of his working career at Paine as professor of biblical literature, but interrupted his work there in 1908 for study at the University of Pennsylvania. In 1910 Tobias married Mary Pritchard whom he met while both were students at Paine. They had two daughters, Belle and Mary.

In his autobiography published in *Thirteen Americans,* Tobias acknowledged the influence of spiritual advisors on

Channing H. Tobias

his development, including George Williams Walker, president of Paine Institute when Tobias attended it; Lucius H. Holsey, a bishop who advised him at the time he decided to study theology; Henry Anson Buttz, a Greek scholar and president of Drew University when Tobias was a student; and Alfred Faulkner, a church historian. Tobias called Julius Rosenwald and Mahatma Gandhi two people of great character who were outside his church but influenced significantly his religious beliefs. He was impressed by Rosenwald's contribution to the education of black children in the South by eventually building 5,000 modern schools. He knew Gandhi from their first meeting in Renigunta, India, when, in 1936 to 1937, Tobias was on his way to the World Conference of YMCAs in Mysore as chair of the Committee on Race Relationships and one of a 12–member delegation from the United States. He also traveled to the Near and Far East. Gandhi and Tobias discussed the race problems in America. Tobias noted their conversation in *Thirteen Americans.* When asked for his advice or encouragement for American blacks who were struggling for freedom, Gandhi told him of his struggle in South Africa and said, "All I can say is that there is no other way than the way of nonviolence not of the weak and the ignorant but of the strong and the wise." Tobias concluded that no teacher of his Christian faith had impressed him as Gandhi had, "because he was the living embodiment of what he taught," and that people of different faiths had to "find common ground on which to stand as they seek the realization of truth." While at the conference in Mysore, Tobias attacked both the YMCA and the world conference, saying that the United States and South Africa were practically the only countries in the world that allowed racial exclusion in their YMCAs. He brought before the conference a resolution from the Committee on Race Relationships to end segregation.

Becomes YMCA Leader

Tobias had become interested in the work of the YMCA and in 1911 left teaching after William Alphaeus Hunton recruited him as student secretary of the International Committee of the YMCAs. He held the position until 1923. He attended the Paris section of the Second Pan–African Congress in September 1921. He was a delegate and speaker at the World Conference of YMCAs held at Helsingfors, Finland, and from there traveled to other YMCA centers in Europe. In 1923 he was elected senior secretary of the Colored Men's Department of the National Council, which Hunton had founded, and held the position until 1946. While on an assignment for the YMCA, he was almost lynched near Metter, Georgia, by a mob of inflamed whites who carried him off the train he was riding, convinced that he had shot a white man; the conductor persuaded the mob that they had the wrong man. He was not embittered by the experience but kept race relations at the forefront of his work efforts. He was delegate and chairman of the Committee on Race Relations, World Conference of YMCA centers in Egypt, Palestine, Ceylon, China, Japan, and Hawaii in 1937. By the time he was 63 years old, he had to retire from the YMCA, according to its policy, but continued his membership on the International Committee.

Tobias moved to the Phelps Stokes Fund and from 1946 to 1953 served as its first black director. He worked to support the fund's mission—the improvement of educational opportunities for blacks. He turned down dozens of offers for political and other appointments. In 1946, for example, he rejected President Harry Truman's offer to become Minister to Liberia, saying that he had committed himself to the Phelps Stokes Fund. He remained with the fund for ten years, then left to become chairman of the NAACP's board of directors. He increased membership in the association to a new high and saw many of its anti–discrimination goals reached. When he retired from that position in 1959, he was named chairman emeritus.

Although he was widely recognized as a liberal, Tobias acknowledged in *Ebony* that he was a "liberal without qualifications." Throughout his life he had been a member of the Republican Party. In 1941, however, he had become more active in politics and was the Fusion Party's candidate for the New York City Council. Tobias withdrew and threw his support to Adam Clayton Powell Jr. He declined nomination for the same office again in 1943, after the Executive Committee of the Republican Party designated him as their candidate. He campaigned for Roosevelt in the 1944 race and spoke at several rallies for the president, including the Liberal Party rally. He declined to support the Eisenhower–for–President campaign in 1948 and threw his support to Henry A. Wallace.

A popular speaker, Tobias lectured often on race relations and spoke before many YMCAs, other organizations, and academic institutions throughout the United States. In 1951 he spoke before the Sixth General Assembly of the

United Nations. Later President Harry S Truman nominated him as an alternate delegate to the Sixth General Assembly, which stirred some controversy because he was black. He praised President Truman for his civil rights fight and for appointing a President's Committee on Civil Rights. Tobias became so vocal that, according to the *Dictionary of American Negro Biography,* "like other outspoken leaders, he was accused of being a Communist" merely because he spoke out. He was said to have "a record of connections with flagrant Communist fronts exceeded by few other individuals in the files of the House Committee on un–American activities." The charges were groundless, and he served as alternate delegate from 1951 to 1952.

In addition to his talent as a speaker, Tobias wrote widely. His autobiography was published in 1953 in *Thirteen Americans,* where, prompted by the impending destruction of humankind in the atomic era, he stressed the importance of the interfaith religious approach to resolving problems of human relationships at home and abroad. He believed that no one religion or denomination is adequate to express the desires of all nations, races, and peoples of different cultural backgrounds. He wrote:

> Men always have and doubtless will approach truth from different angles. Therefore, Lutherans will continue to be Lutherans; Baptists will continue to be Baptists; Catholics will continue to be Catholic; Jews will continue to be loyal to the Jewish faith; but at the same time it is possible for all to be striving to discover some means by which they may speak with one voice and more with united action for satisfying those deep yearnings of the human heart that are common to all nations, races, and tongues.

His views were also given in his speeches published in journals or separately reprinted.

Condemns Segregation in the Armed Forces

In his lifetime, Tobias was clear in his views toward World War II, conditions for blacks during and after the war, and race relations in general. He kept in touch with war issues through his membership in the National Advisory Committee on Selective Service, the Joint Army and Navy Committee on Welfare and Recreation, and the National War Fund's board of directors. Tobias also worked through the Committee on Overseas Relief and Reconstruction and the Commission on a Just and Durable Peace. He called for an end to segregation in the armed forces, discrimination against black nurses in the war, compliance with Government Order 8092 of the Federal Employment Practices Commission that barred discrimination in industries holding war contracts, and the end of segregated blood plasma in the army and navy as practiced by the Red Cross.

In time, Tobias became widely accepted as an elder statesman, a recognition that led to close contact with the White House and other areas of government. For example, he, Walter White, and A. Philip Randolph met with President Franklin D. Roosevelt to discuss the status of blacks in the armed forces and in war industries. Again in 1944 he was spokesperson for a committee that conferred with Roosevelt on the maintenance of an interracial policy in the provisions for black servicemen in rest centers to be established by the U.S. Army.

Tobias opposed segregation in schools and in public transportation. After the war, when problems of reconversion and unemployment emerged, he lashed out again on behalf of blacks. He was asked to help draft New York State's fair employment act later known as the Ives–Quinn bill that was designed to bring about fairness in employment practices. The first law of its kind passed by any state, the bill became effective in July 1945. Tobias worked through numerous organizations to address the concerns of African Americans, including the NAACP (as vice–president and board member), the Council on African Affairs, New York City's Mayor's Committee on Race Relations, the American Council on Race Relations, the New York Chapter of the Southern Conference on Human Welfare, and the Federal Council of Churches. He worked extensively in community organizations to improve race relations; for example, he was associate director of the Commission on Interracial Cooperation from 1935 to 1942 and chaired the National Freedom Rally held in Madison Square Garden in 1943 and 1944. He was a successful and independent man whose interests lay outside public office. Quoted in *Ebony,* he said, "The secret of any success I might have had is independence. By this I mean independence in approaching public issues. I have deliberately and repeatedly turned down offers to accept public office."

In 1942 Tobias was administrator of the New York State War Finance Committee. Henry Morgenthau Jr., former Secretary of the Treasury, nominated him to the board of directors of the Modern Industrial Bank in New York City. He was elected to membership and at some point became the first black elected to the board of a major bank. He held many other appointments, including member of the Board of Trustees and later chair of the board, Hampton Institute (now University), and Howard University, where he served from 1931 until his death in 1961. Howard recognized him as one who could "calm ruffled waters." Other board memberships were at Paine College and the Phelps Stokes Fund, Palmer Memorial Institute, Wiltwyck School for Boys, the Marshall Field Foundation, Jessie Smith Noyes Fund, and the American Bible Society. He was an editorial advisor of the *Protestant Digest* and a member of the editorial board of the *Protestant Voice.*

Honored widely for his work, his honors date back to 1928 when he received the Harmon Award for Religious Service. He was named to the Honor Roll of Race Relations the Schomburg Collection, New York Public Library in 1943; to the Chicago Defender Honor Roll in 1944; and received the Spingarn Medal in 1948 for his vitality, courage, and long and rich experiences in race relations. Tobias received many honorary degrees from such institutions as: Gammon Theological Seminary, Morehouse College, Jewish Institute of Religion, New School for Social Research, and New York

University. At the latter he was the first black to received an honorary degree from that institution.

Tobias was called an impressive man with an imposing stature; he was light in complexion. After a lengthy illness, he died on November 5, 1961, in New York City Hospital. His funeral was held at Riverside Church on November 8, where Morehouse College President Benjamin E. Mays delivered the eulogy and, according to *Crisis,* called him "a man of integrity, conviction, sincerity, character and courage . . . [who also] walked in the tradition of the Hebrew prophets." He was buried in Woodlawn cemetery in the Bronx. Tobias's first wife had died in 1949, and on March 31, 1951 he married Eva Gassett Arnold, who survived him. He also left his two daughters from his first marriage.

In his career Tobias influenced thousands of young people throughout the United States and abroad. An educator as well as a Christian and social justice statesman, Tobias worked to bring about equal rights for all people.

REFERENCES

Current Biography. New York: H. W. Wilson, 1945.

Finkelstein, Louis, ed. *Thirteen Americans: Their Spiritual Autobiographies.* New York: Institute for Religious and Social Studies, Jewish Theological Seminary of America, 1953.

"Last Rites Held for Channing H. Tobias." *Crisis* 68 (December 1961): 636–37.

Logan, Rayford W. *Howard University: The First Hundred Years.* New York: New York University Press; Issued Under the Auspices of Howard University, 1969.

———, and Michael R. Winston, eds. *Dictionary of American Negro Biography.* New York: Norton, 1982.

Mjagkij, Nina. *Light in the Darkness: African Americans and the YMCA, 1852–1946.* Lexington: University of Kentucky Press, 1994.

Murphy, Larry G., J. Gordon Melton, and Gary L. Ward, eds. *Encyclopedia of African American Religions.* New York: Garland Publishing, 1993.

"Mystery Man of Race Relations." *Ebony* 6 (February 1951): 15–21.

Who's Who in Colored America. 7th ed. Yonkers–on–Hudson, NY: Christian E. Burckel, 1950.

COLLECTIONS

The papers of Channing H. Tobias are in the YMCA of the USA Archives, the University of Minnesota, St. Paul.

Jessie Carney Smith

Jean Toomer
(1892–1967)
Writer, philosopher

Writer and philosopher Jean Toomer—whose closest associates in the early 1920s included fellow American writers Sherwood Anderson, Waldo Frank, and Hart Crane—is one of the most intriguing figures in U.S. and African American literary history. For decades following the success of his single full–length book, *Cane* (1923), he disappeared from the view of those who expected him, in subsequent works, to become a formidable figure in American letters. That promise was never fulfilled and from the late 1920s through the early 1960s even his whereabouts were unknown among his best friends prior to the publication of *Cane.* Although contemporary critics, most of whom also consider *Cane* a spectacular achievement, have meticulously searched his writings between the late 1920s and the early 1950s, no one has discovered anything to suggest that after 1923 Toomer had any desire or attempted to build a name for himself among the literati of his generation. To the contrary, while he continued to write for a long time, he deliberately severed himself from their world, rejecting the voice of the poet for that of the philosopher and prophet. In spite of that, today, the wide recognition of his early work links him inextricably to the writers of the Harlem Renaissance. *Cane* is an extraordinary text, the story of its author's deflection from literary art, and contemporary scholarly interest in his subsequent writings have generated hundreds of essays and close to a dozen books by new critics seeking to resolve the riddle of Toomer's genius and the roots of his disillusionment with the literary enterprise he knew.

Nathan Eugene Toomer, the son of Nina Pinchback Toomer and Nathan Toomer, was born in Washington, D.C., on December 26, 1894, in Pennsylvania. His maternal grandfather, P. B. S. Pinchback, was a controversial figure in Reconstruction–era politics. A Southerner by birth and upbringing, son of a mulatto slave and her master who manumitted the second family he kept in addition to his legal wife and children, Pinchback was a fiery figure who served as a commissioned officer in the Corps d'Afrique, a black regiment in the Civil War, then as local and state senator, and later as lieutenant governor of Louisiana for a short period. In the early 1890s, he moved with his wife, the former Nina Hethorn, sons Bismarck and Walter, and daughter Nina from their New Orleans mansion to Washington, D.C. His eldest child, Pinckney, a graduate of the University of Pennsylvania and already a pharmacist, was by then well established in Philadelphia. In Washington, Pinchback built a house in a new development in an almost all–white area of the city. As in New Orleans, the Pinchbacks lived elegantly under a patriarch who held close control over his family and conducted his political and social lives with great flair.

Less is known about Toomer's paternal ancestry. His father, Nathan, was born in North Carolina in 1841, but spent

Jean Toomer

much of his life in Georgia. The son of a mixed–blood woman and a successful planter, it is not clear whether he was free–born or a slave. Like Pinchback, he loved the display of luxury. Toomer's mother, Nina, attended finishing school in Massachusetts and, in her early adult years, engaged in writing poetry, playing the piano, and other ''womanly arts,'' in preparation for a brilliant marriage. When she fell in love with Nathan Toomer, her father's disappointment was great. Toomer was 27–years older than his bride–to–be and only four years younger than Pinchback, he had been married previously, and the father believed that the suitor was fiscally unreliable and an unscrupulous businessman. Specifically, he believed Toomer was a gambler. Pinchback did not prevent the marriage, however, which took place on March 29, 1894, but his fears later proved well founded. Three months after the wedding, without making explicit explanations, Nathan Toomer left his pregnant new bride and did not return until three days before the birth of their son, Nathan Pinchback Toomer, on December 26 of that year. Six weeks later he left again, and although he returned after several months, in October 1895 he disappeared altogether. His desertion of Nina and her son left the young woman no recourse but to return to her father's house where she and the young boy were financially dependent on him. Among other things, they were forced to endure his edict that Nathan Toomer's name never be mentioned under his roof. In addition, although Nina rejected her father's wish to take legal steps to change her son's name, informally, he became Eugene Pinchback. In school and college he called himself Eugene Pinchback Toomer. At age 25, when he began to write, he renamed himself Jean Toomer. Many years later he reverted to Nathan Jean Toomer (to clarify his gender) and sometimes used N. Jean Toomer as his official signature.

During his early years in his grandfather's house, Jean Toomer lived in an extended family. The group included his mother, grandparents and his uncle Bismarck, who remained at the family home until he married in 1905. He described Bismarck as a gentle intellectual, who was a disappointment to his father because he did not have a successful public career but instead engaged in mundane clerical jobs by day while he read, wrote stories, or drew at night in his room. Toomer loved his uncle's books much more than his school books, and as he got older, he found in this quiet man a great source of knowledge and information. He was also aware that his mother loved him and they occasionally went on special outings. However, probably emotionally and financially overwhelmed by the changes in her life, she gave him less time than he wanted from her. With his grandmother, the relationship was constant, warm, and sympathetic until her death in 1928, and later he paid special tribute to her quiet strength. What impressed him most about her was that in spite of his shortcomings, he knew she never lost faith in him. As for his grandfather, he fully enjoyed the time he spent with the older man especially after he was old enough to sit at the table when his grandfather was at supper in the evenings. Toomer loved to listen to the stories that Pinchback told of himself and was thrilled when Pinchback occasionally took the child downtown to have lunch with his political associates who ''made much over me,'' Toomer wrote. When, as sometimes happened, in the evenings, he was allowed into his grandfather's bed he always found a very sympathetic ear to tell about school and his friends. Later in ''Earth Being,'' one of his many autobiographical essays, his memories of the old man as he was growing up were of an affectionate but loving tyrant with his family who was ''indomitable'' in the world of business. In speaking of his own search for independence in those early years, he characterized his relationship to the adults in his world as one in which he was in a struggle to gain conquest over them: he conquered his nurse at age three, his mother and grandmother at seven, but he did not conquer his grandfather until Pinchback died.

In 1906, Nina Pinchback Toomer remarried and she and her son moved to New Rochelle, New York. In Washington he was accustomed to having many friends, but in New York he found it difficult to form new relationships. Nor did he respond positively to the overtures his stepfather made to him. Instead of displaying his usual gregariousness, he was withdrawn and introspective, spending most of his time with books and in other solitary activities. He read novels and works of ancient chivalry about Sir Galahad and Sir Lancelot, he bicycled, swam, fished, and sailed alone. He also did very well in school. Then his life changed again when in 1909 his mother died of complications following minor surgery. The following year, at age 15, he returned to the Washington home of his grandparents to discover that reverses in their financial situation had led to a reduction in their style of living and to become aware of the physical deterioration of the ageing couple. Now, instead of an almost all white community, Toomer lived in a racially mixed neighborhood where interestingly, he was pleased with the increase in emotion, rhythm, color, and gaiety that characterized the lives of the black residents of the area. Nevertheless, in spite of the changes and although he was full of adolescent anxieties, during his first year back his performance in school signaled a successful transition from New York to Washington.

Unfortunately, the ease of that return did not last long for Jean Toomer. During his high school years problems of teen sexual anxieties and racial identity assailed him. Having no one in whom he could confide his feelings, he was guilt–ridden over the first and searched for a rationale to resolve the second. Although in physical appearance Jean Toomer's racial heritage was unclear, he perceived the small portion of African heritage on both sides of his family as a social disadvantage. By the time he was ready for college in 1914 he decided to disavow claims to either white or black blood, and to find a place for himself as an individual in the world with no racial designation. He would be only an American. So strong was this desire in him, that for college he chose to separate himself from everyone he knew, and he entered the University of Wisconsin–Madison the summer of 1914, with plans to study scientific agriculture.

During his first year at Wisconsin, he discovered that he had no intentions to study agriculture, and at the same time he had a sense of failure in his social life. He left soon after the beginning of the spring term. Toomer repeated that pattern many times in the following four years, attending six separate educational institutions between 1914 and 1918, and never remaining sufficiently long at any of them to complete a degree, not even the two–year program at the College of Physical Training in Chicago that he commenced in 1916. Always he began enthusiastically, but after a short time he became disillusioned. Most unfortunately, this period in his life coincided with the steady slide of the Pinchbacks into failing health and economic poverty while Toomer, unreasonably, continued to depend on them for financial support. Bitter arguments over money between himself and his grandfather lasted until Pinchback's death in December of 1921. During these years, Toomer's academic interests ranged from medicine to literature. Like many of the writers of the Lost Generation, he saw the world falling into chaos as a result of many new technological advancements, and he was searching for a way to halt the disintegration. At different times he embraced science, philosophy, history, or literature, and with each embrace he convinced himself that he had discovered the philosophical system capable of responding to the breakdown of the collective human experience that was reflected in his own. Each such discovery stimulated a period of intense study on his part followed by one of abject disillusionment and a painful readjustment to await the exhilaration of the next new discovery.

The *Cane* Years

The first breakthrough out of that quagmire occurred for Toomer in 1919. In the spring of that year he lived in New York, where he met and became friends with radical and literary personalities. Residing in Greenwich Village in close contact with writers like Waldo Frank and editor Lola Ridge, and following an intensive regimen of wide reading in American and European contemporary and canonical literature, he decided on a literary path. Not surprisingly, although he managed to complete a poem, "The First American," during the winter of 1920–1921, his failure in his earliest attempts to find a literary voice of his own left him frustrated. Then, in the fall of 1921, not having been in the South before, Toomer agreed to go to Sparta, Georgia, for a short time, as a substitute head teacher in a small rural school. There, for the first time in his life he met poor rural black people and experienced what he later called the "root life" of those people. Listening to the spirituals and folksongs, he believed he was in contact with the swiftly disappearing pristine spirit life of black people, a life that was being lost to technology and urbanization. Here, for him, was the true art of living. Toomer was so moved by the experience that two months later, on the train returning to Washington, he began to compose *Cane.* Remaining in close contact with Waldo Frank, who read and critiqued his writing, his enthusiasm for the project lasted from the fall of 1921 through December of 1922, when the first draft of the book was complete. In addition to his relationship with Frank, by then he had contact with a wider literary circle, including black writers like Claude McKay and James Weldon Johnson, and his name was appearing in print.

The first major journal to carry Toomer's work was the *Crisis,* where "Song of the Son" (also in *Cane*) his most anthologized piece, appeared in April of 1922. Claude McKay's interest in his work led to the appearances of three others in the fall of the same year in the *Liberator.* Jessie Fauset, Sherwood Anderson, Georgia Douglas Johnson and John McClure, editor of *Double Dealer,* were among those who took a keen interest in Toomer's budding career in 1922. Along with the poetry and short stories that he wrote in that time, as a result of his trip to Georgia, Jean Toomer recognized possibilities for drama in black folk and urban life. Working in two different styles, in the early 1920s he wrote two plays, *Balo* a one–act folk drama, and *Natalie Mann,* a full–length expressionist play about black middle class life in Washington. The first named, which had a brief stage life at the famous Howard Theatre during its 1923–24 season, gave a positive although far from romantic view of black folk life, while the second examined the negative aspects of urbanization on the lives of those blacks who fall victim to its destructive aspects. Interestingly, a major theme in this play was black male domination of black women, and Toomer positions himself not only as the champion of women, but also as their liberator. While *Natalie Mann* had too many flaws to make it worthy as living life theater, as Toomer's experimentation with expressionism, it placed him in the forefront of American drama in the 1920s, and linked his name with such formidable figures of the time as Eugene O'Neil and Pulitzer Prize–winner Paul Green, a North Carolina white who wrote plays about blacks.

Cane, a slim volume of prose narratives, poetry, and one dramatic piece, was published in September of 1923, and Jean Toomer became one of a group of avant garde writers anxious to change the contemporary American literary status quo. In

New York, in addition to Waldo Frank, the group included Hart Crane and Van Wyck Brooks. Toomer's achievement received high praise from this coterie of his peers. *Cane* was his effort to express the feelings he experienced during his first confrontation with the black folk culture. Critics are still drawn to it for the depth of that expression and for the author's magnificent use of language. Vivid, sometimes mystical, sometimes sensuous, and sometimes spiritual, its lyrical qualities encompass the contradictions of violence, beauty, joy, and the pain of what it meant to be poor and black in the American South or middle class and black in the segregated American North in the early part of this century.

The book has three parts. In the first, Toomer faces the black and white South where, in spite of the victimization of blacks by whites which creates a world in complete imbalance, black people struggle to retain their humanity. For example, Toomer's lush nature imagery continually reminds readers of the possibilities of a universe that transcends the forces of human injustices. In this section, the lyricism in the work is most pronounced. In the second section, the writer looks to the urban experience in Washington, D.C., and Chicago. As we might expect of Toomer, the dominant feature of this part of the book is the harshness of both the setting and the lives of those who reside in the cities. Although not relentlessly negative, the section foregrounds a people who, unlike those in Section I, have lost touch with the spirit of their ancestral heritage as much as they have with the natural landscape. Section III of *Cane* embodies the search for a return to black roots with full knowledge of what has already been irretrievably lost. The best hope for a positive future for the collective black self, Toomer suggests, rests with the poet who will be the source of reconciling the past with the present. The book concludes on this note, as the rise of the morning sun announces a new day. Taken as a whole, the book makes a very strong statement in favor of literary art as a curative to the chaos of the modern era.

Cane was favorably reviewed in such journals as the *New Republic,* the *Crisis,* and *Opportunity,* and by Allen Tate in the *Nashville Tennessean.* Besides the reviews, ''Blood Burning Moon,'' the story of a lynching that concludes the first part of the book, appeared in the prestigious *The Best Short Stories of 1923.* Toomer's admirers, white and black, including W. E. B. Du Bois, hailed it as the promise of a new day for black literature in America. Although sales of the book were small, the door to a career as a literary artist stood open to Jean Toomer, but he turned his back on it. By the beginning of 1924 Jean Toomer had once again decided that the road he had taken was not the one to the ends he sought.

After all the disruptions in his life and his failures to find his way in the world, the success of *Cane* was most gratifying to Jean Toomer's family, especially to his grandmother and his Uncle Bismarck. Indeed, Toomer's correspondence of the period, with Waldo Frank in particular, indicate that as he wrote his book he felt his many ''scattered'' parts coming together as a result of his Georgia experiences. He often wrote of the black experience as part of his own. He also spoke enthusiastically of plans for future writing projects, ostensibly continued outgrowths of the first Southern experiences. Unfortunately for him, his sense of ''wholeness'' through the evocation of blackness in the literary process was only temporary, and extremely short–lived. Even more conclusively, he never returned to explore personal or social concerns through literary art. Prominent among his complaints against his friends in the literary world at that time was his continuing ambivalence toward his racial identity, an issue that eventually caused an irreparable rift between him and Frank who, in writing the introduction to *Cane,* extolled the ''new Negro Writer.'' Toomer's unhappiness over the inability of others to see him as a multiracial being without special allegiances to any of his bloodlines, also affected his feelings toward his publisher Horace Liveright who advertised *Cane* as the work of a ''colored genius.'' In the end, Toomer turned away from the world he had worked hard to win, and this time he looked toward the thoughts of George Gurdjieff, the Eastern mystic, who promised what Toomer longed to achieve: harmony with self and the universe.

The Gurdjieff Years

George Gurdjieff appeared in the western world in the early 1920s, during the psychologically–confused, post–World War I era, and attracted the attention of prominent intellectuals such as poet T. S. Eliot and architect Frank Lloyd Wright. Gurdjieff's philosophy embodied a system for human development that promised his followers they would find meaning to living (internal harmony) through the attainment of higher consciousness. His ideas constituted a union of selective tenets of Eastern philosophy and Western theory into a system best described as a ''work'' with philosophical and psychological bases that engage the physical, mental, and emotional centers of human activity. Hard physical work, music, dancing, and gymnastics are also integral to the system. After some time in Moscow and St. Petersburg, he set up an institute outside of Paris, near Fontainbleau, where Europeans and Americans flocked to him. At best, Gurdjieff's reputation remains controversial. His followers praised him; others who knew him called him a charlatan and a demonic character.

Soon after learning of Gurdjieff, Toomer plunged headlong into that ''work'' and remained intensely committed to it for a decade. Although that intensity lessened in subsequent years, he never completely relinquished its hold on him. In the summer of 1924, as he would do for several successive summers, he went to the institute where he participated in the physical restoration of buildings that were in great disrepair and learned as much as he could about the system. Back in the United States that fall, he visited Harlem hoping to establish his own Gurdjieff group. While the Harlem writers still held him in respect because of *Cane,* even those who were interested in the new teachings could not afford the investment of time and money that the system required. Consequently, Toomer left New York in 1925 for Chicago's Gold Coast district, where for several years he successfully led Gurdjieff groups. At the end of the summer of 1931, during which Toomer conducted a Gurdjieff experiment in cooperative living in Portage, Wisconsin, he married Margery Latimer, a novelist from the area who had been a member of the group.

Sadly, ten months later, following the birth of their daughter who was given her mother's name, Margery Latimer was dead.

In 1934 two significant events occurred in Jean Toomer's life. First, he officially broke with Gurdjieff and then he remarried. In his letter to the man he had avidly followed and whose work he promoted for a decade, he explained that the changes he anticipated in taking on the roles of husband and father made it impossible for him to continue to give the time that was needed to be a teacher of Gurdjieff's system. He married Marjorie Content and the couple, with his daughter, settled in Pennsylvania Dutch Country. That marriage lasted until Toomer's death in 1967.

Although Jean Toomer rejected the pursuit of a literary career in 1923, he did not give up writing. As proof, the Beinecke Collection of his papers at Yale University contains more than 30,000 individual items. While his post–1923 efforts earned him little in publications, between that year through the mid–1940s, he wrote energetically and attached traditional generic names to his productions. Thus, his extensive corpus includes items he called poetry, short stories, novels, plays, partial autobiographies, as well as essays, pamphlets, correspondences, and other miscellany. Stories of the rejections he received from editors and his frantic appeals to be heard during those years of his life are well known to critics. Only once more did he experience qualified success, when, in 1936, his long poem ''The Blue Meridian,'' appeared in the last of *The New Caravan* anthologies. Unlike *Cane,* which emerged from his spontaneous response to a momentous event in his life and took less than two years between its conception and publication, this poem, first conceived in 1914, was 22 years in the making. An earlier version, ''The First American,'' finished in the winter of 1921–22, was never published. The later version is a carefully considered and reasoned idealistic statement regarding racial homogeneity in America, but unlike most of the writings of this period of his life, this one combines literary merit with social concerns. The influences of Walt Whitman, Hart Crane, and Gurdjieff on Toomer are all visible in ''Blue Meridian'' which sings all Americans of all races and groups coming together in a cultural/aesthetic melting pot:

It is a new America
To be spiritualized by each new American.

Unfortunately for Toomer, the poem received no critical attention. The ideas in ''Blue Meridian'' encompass Toomer's comprehension of what it would feel like to be wholly integrated into the membership of the human race, unhindered by labels that inevitably create simplistic and prejudicial categories that separate groups of people from each other.

By the mid–1930s, unable to make the progress he wished toward inner harmony through higher consciousness, Jean Toomer began to experience new self–doubts. Although his marriage to Marjorie Content was good, giving him love, the stable family he lost after his mother's death, and the resources that freed him from life–long financial difficulties, his search for wholeness remained unfulfilled. In 1936 the family had moved from Marjorie's New York home to a farm outside of Doylestown, Pennsylvania, where with time, space, and the opportunity to think, write, and explore the possibilities for the life he wanted, he expected fulfillment. His deep desire then was that with the financial help of his father–in–law, he would establish a Gurdjieff–like ''institute for the development man [sic]'' on the farm. In a preliminary step to that goal, Toomer read, wrote copiously, and often gathered his friends to the farm where he held sessions on greater self–understanding and character development. He had rejected Gurdjieff the man but continued to cling to Gurdjieff's philosophies and principles, which permeated his spiritual, psychological, and social writings. He endured great disappointments over the constant flow of rejections these brought from publishers.

Without giving up Gurdjieff's lessons, by the late 1930s Toomer was again exploring other systems of thought. By then he was associated with the Quakers and for much of the rest of his life he lectured and wrote extensively for them. He had also read and given thought to the works of Aldous Huxley and Irish mystic and poet A. E. (George William Russel). In 1939, he became convinced that he needed to travel to India, where he believed there were teachers who held the secret of how to tap into large quantities of universal energy to achieve higher consciousness. Taking his family with him on a physically arduous trip financed by his wife's father, a trip made more difficult with the onset of World War II while they were there, Toomer spent nine months traveling in India in another unsuccessful bid to discover the secrets of nature that eluded him. Through the 1940s, although his health began to deteriorate, he continued to write—novels, short fiction, drama, autobiographies, poetry and non–fiction prose—as he explored other writings that promised internal harmony. Among other things, he read the literature of Scientology and went into Jungian psychoanalysis. His search was long and thorough, but yielded no rewards. Increasing ill health—painful arthritis, eye troubles, and alcohol–related problems—along with his great disappointment in not being able to make his voice heard in writing fueled his unhappiness. He believed, with some justification, that his physical symptoms reflected his internal tensions but was incapable of changing the situation. On March 10, 1967, he died. The cause was listed as arteriosclerosis. Coincidently, his old friend, Waldo Frank, died in New York only three months before he did.

The Legacy

Toomer's reputation rests solidly on *Cane,* the book he tried to put behind him. The most widely known of the writers in the African American tradition, like Charles Chesnutt, Paul Laurence Dunbar, James Weldon Johnson, Zora Neale Hurston, and W. E. B. Du Bois, at best made limited impression on American literature in their time. *Cane* was different. It resounded across racial lines in 1923, bringing African American literature to a new frontier. Unfortunately, with Toomer's disappearance from the literary world in the late 1920s, the book also disappeared for more than three decades. The interest it sparked following its rebirth in the mid–1960s fully assures it a permanent place in the American literary tradition.

Much of the credit for the successful literary recovery of Toomer and *Cane* goes to Harlem Renaissance writer Arna Bontemps, library director at Fisk University during the 1960s, whose efforts were most responsible for the removal of the vast collection of Toomer's unpublished works from his home to Fisk University's archives during that decade. Since then, a number of late twentieth century scholars have looked to and beyond *Cane* to locate Toomer inside of the literary tradition and to make his writings available to others. Among these, the late Darwin T. Turner did the earliest contemporary scholarship on the elusive Toomer and piqued the interest of dozens of others who continued his work. While none of the later writings, of which a large number are now in print, have yet captured as wide an interest as the book, they are subjects of scholarship. *The Collected Poems of Jean Toomer* (1988), edited by Robert B. Jones and Margery Toomer Latimer, offers the student "a study in the phenomena of the spirit." Written over a period of more than three decades, from 1919–1955, these poems dramatize, as only poetry can do, the writer's consciousness. Jones's philosophical study, *Jean Toomer and the Prison–House of Thought, A Phenomenology of the Spirit* (1993) and Rudolph Byrd's *Jean Toomer's Years with Gurdjieff* (1990) provide useful insights into Toomer's mind. Nellie Y. McKay's *Jean Toomer, Artist: A Study of His Literary Life and Work* (1984) examines *Cane* against the background of Toomer's life through the publication of the book and his subsequent struggles to achieve internal harmony. There is no question that Jean Toomer's work has gained the respect of a large number of late twentieth–century scholars and readers. As a writer and philosopher, his place in the canon is now secure.

REFERENCES

Byrd, Rudolph P. *Jean Toomer's Years with Gurdjieff.* Athens: University of Georgia Press, 1990.

Jones, Robert B., and Margery Toomer Latimer, eds. *The Collected Poems of Jean Toomer.* Chapel Hill: University of North Carolina Press, 1988.

———. *Jean Toomer and the Prison–House of Thought: A Phenomenology of the Spirit.* Amherst: University of Massachusetts Press, 1993.

Kernan, Cynthia Earl, and Richard Eldridge. *The Lives of Jean Toomer, A Hunger for Wholeness.* Baton Rouge: University of Louisiana Press, 1987.

McKay, Nellie Y. *Jean Toomer, Artist: A Study of His Literary Life and Work.* Chapel Hill: University of North Carolina Press, 1984.

Toomer, Jean. *Cane.* Edited by Darwin T. Turner. New York: Norton, 1988.

COLLECTIONS

The manuscript collection of Jean Toomer's papers, originally placed at Fisk University, are now located at the Beinecke Library at Yale University.

Nellie Y. McKay

Monroe Trotter
(1872–1934)
Publisher, editor, civil rights activist

An elite militant integrationist and one of America's most important black spokesmen of the early twentieth century, Monroe Trotter was a diligent man whose work has been called the precursor of the Civil Rights Movement of the 1960s. Most of his significant work was done before he was 40–years old. He was active in a number of local groups, most of which were forums for militant race activities. A journalist as well, Trotter was a founder of *The Guardian,* an organ dedicated to equal rights of black Americans.

The first two children of James Monroe Trotter and Virginia Isaacs Trotter died in infancy. Virginia Trotter left Boston for her parent's home on a farm near Chillicothe, Ohio, to give birth to her third child, William Monroe Trotter. He was born April 7, 1872. She returned to Boston when he was seven months old. Of the Trotter's three children who survived—the other two were Maude and Bessie—Monroe was the only son and the favored child. He grew up in suburban Hyde Park, which until the 1890s was predominantly white.

James Monroe Trotter, a demanding patriarch, may have steered his son to become a career protest leader. By age five, Monroe Trotter, as he was known throughout life, knew that race work would be an important part of his future. Although surrounded by whites in the community and at work, James Trotter was highly race–conscious. He had been a lieutenant in the Civil War and recorder of deeds (1897–98) for the federal government. In Boston he worked in musical promotions, as an agent for the local telephone company, and had a real estate business. He had an interest in politics as well. In 1878 his noted work *Music and Some Highly Musical People* was published; it was a tribute to black musicians and became a classic. Monroe Trotter was a good student and led his class academically both at Hyde Park Grammar School and Hyde Park High School. He was the only black in his high school class and was elected president of his senior class. Influenced by his mother, he had considered becoming a minister, received some training by the pastor of the white First Baptist Church of Hyde Park, but he also respected his father's strong dislike for his religious leaning and gave up the idea. In James Trotter's view, as a black minister his son might not fight the world's race problems but would serve a segregated congregation instead.

Trotter worked as a shipping clerk in Boston after graduating from high school. He entered Harvard University in 1891. His father's death the next year thrust him into a new role, as head of the household. At Harvard, however, he won scholarships for the next three years and worked during summer months to supplement his income. He was active in the church, played tennis, and rode his bicycle around Cam-

Monroe Trotter

bridge and Boston. Although he steered clear of frivolous college activities, he did belong to the Wendell Phillips Club, the YMCA, and the Prohibition Club. He was an organizer and president of the Total Abstinence League for undergraduates. He was a serious student who studied hard and took extra courses as well. He ranked third in his freshman class and never lower than eighth in his college career. During his junior year Trotter became the first black in the university's history elected to Phi Beta Kappa. He graduated in June of 1894 with an A.B. degree, magna cum laude.

Already one of Boston's young luminaries in black society—now more so with his Harvard degree—Trotter was a member of the Boston Bachelors as well as the Omar Khayyam Circle. The latter was an exclusive literary group for blacks that met at the home of Maria Baldwin, a school teacher in Cambridge.

Neither his Harvard degree, his academic record, nor his exclusive background could combat the racial discrimination that he soon encountered. Trotter wanted a business career in real estate but in the meantime he worked as a clerk for an industrial fair. Until he opened his own business in 1899 as insurance agent and mortgage negotiator for mostly white clients, he worked variously as a shipping clerk for a Boston bookseller, an indexing clerk for the Boston Book Company, a statistical clerk for a genealogist, and as an employee of Holbrook and Company, a Boston real estate firm.

On June 27, 1899, Trotter married petite, vivacious, Geraldine Louise Pindell—known as ''Deenie''—of Boston, who had a family background of racial militancy. They had known each other since childhood and dated while Trotter was at Harvard. They had no children and never wanted any.

Trotter began to dabble in politics. He worked for Republican municipal candidates and was alternate delegate from his ward at several political conventions. He volunteered as assistant registrar of voters in Boston. Conditions for blacks in the South had worsened and the attitude of Southern whites toward race was spreading north. Although race leader and educator Booker T. Washington rose to prominence, his policies and public statements were too moderate and conciliatory for some blacks. By the turn of the century, Trotter decided it was time for him to address matters of race in another style.

Feuds with Booker T. Washington

Trotter and other black elites organized the Boston Literary and Historical Society in March of 1901. The Society provided a forum for them to discuss race matters. Trotter was also one of three blacks who founded a weekly newspaper in Boston, *The Guardian.* The others were William H. Scott, a minister and leader of the Massachusetts Radical Protective Association of which Trotter was a member, and George W. Forbes, an outspoken man who in the 1890s worked on another Boston newspaper. *The Guardian,* which Trotter financed, was first published on November 9, 1901, and appeared every Saturday. It was not designed to turn a profit but to address the needs and aspirations of black America and was the mouthpiece through which the anti–Bookerites spoke. At the time it was the only channel for publicizing national black agitation.

Trotter and Washington were from vastly different backgrounds: Trotter was born free while Washington was born a slave. While they disagreed on racial policy—Trotter was a militant while Washington was an accommodationist—they agreed that education for blacks was essential. Trotter argued for the long–range implications of education, that education was needed to prove the intellectual ability of the race, and that blacks should have access to the highest form of education. Washington, however, stressed the immediate advantages of education and believed in industrial training as a route to a good job. Washington saw Trotter as corrupt. Trotter saw Washington as one who sought power, wanted to be a political leader, and could not tolerate criticism of his approach to black progress.

Trotter's camp, who called themselves ''radicals,'' were talented, elitist, and generally better educated than Washington's followers, who were called ''Bookerites.'' There were prominent blacks on both sides. At that time, however, race men W. E. B. Du Bois and Kelly Miller had not chosen between the two groups. Agitation between the camps continued and came to a head on July 30, 1903. Washington spoke to a crowd at Columbus Avenue African Methodist Episcopal Church, sponsored by the local branch of the National Negro Business League. As Trotter stood on a chair and presented a list of race questions to Washington, the police escorted him and his sister, Maude Trotter, from the church and arrested them; their mother bailed them out. Charges against his sister were later dropped, but Trotter was tried, convicted, and fined 25 dollars; he also served a 30–day jail sentence. While he was imprisoned, Trotter's friends and his wife continued to publish *The Guardian.* The church incident came to be known as "The Boston Riot." The Trotter and Washington camps became even more hostile. Forbes left the paper to be replaced by Du Bois.

Trotter continued to affiliate himself with change groups. After the riot he founded the Boston Suffrage League in 1903. In April of 1904 the league sponsored a protest meeting at Faneuil Hall and planned a convention in New England that fall. In Providence that October, blacks from Massachusetts, Connecticut, and Rhode Island formed the New England Suffrage League and elected Trotter president. In addition to suffrage activities, the group endorsed anti–lynching legislation, federal aid to southern schools, integrated seating on interstate carriers, among other issues.

Niagara Movement and the NAACP

The Washington camp enjoyed the success of the Afro–American Council and the National Negro Business League; both organizations contributed to Washington's power. Trotter knew there was a need for radical mobilization among his own camp. He and his followers then organized the National Negro Suffrage League and elected a Richmond lawyer, James H. Hayes, president. Meanwhile, in 1905 Du Bois invited 29 blacks from all over the country—all anti–Bookerites—to a small hotel in Fort Erie, on the Canadian side of Niagara Falls, for a conference in support of freedom and growth of the black race. They formed the Niagara Movement with Du Bois serving as general secretary and Trotter as head of the Press and Public Opinion Committee. Du Bois and Trotter drafted a "Declaration of Principles," a radical document that the members endorsed. Although he had supported women's suffrage, when Du Bois organized a woman's auxiliary to the movement early in 1906, Trotter initially opposed the group, but later relented. Deenie Trotter then joined, but the Trotters' affiliation lasted only until 1907 when they both resigned. The movement faced other problems, however, and in 1909 it merged with the NAACP. Trotter attended the founding conference in New York, and had limited contact with the organization for a few years. He then severed his relationship, having become estranged from the local leadership and at odds with the two early NAACP leaders, Oswald Garrison Villard and Du Bois. He was also unable to accept the fact that whites provided both leadership and financial support to the organization.

In the meantime, Trotter was a founder of the National Equal Rights League (NERL) in 1908 and worked through the organization for a number of years to agitate for black rights. Those who could not accept the NAACP had the NERL as an alternative.

Trotter and Du Bois supported Woodrow Wilson for president but found him less supportive of blacks than they had envisioned. Among other actions, Wilson rejected black advisors, supported segregationist policies in federal office buildings, and kept blacks out of key civil service positions. In protest, Trotter led a delegation to the White House to meet with Wilson and he and the President engaged in a heated argument for 45 minutes, until Wilson ordered the group to leave. The incident was publicized in newspapers such as the *New York Times,* the *Boston Evening Transcript,* and the black *New York Age.* In the *Age,* James Weldon Johnson praised Trotter for taking a stance but condemned the way he did it.

Protests Racial Film

D. W. Griffith's viciously racist film *The Birth of a Nation* was shown at the White House in February of 1915 by arrangement of Thomas Dixon, who wrote the book on which the film was based. Although President Wilson praised the film, Trotter vehemently protested it, especially when it was to be shown at Boston's Tremont Theatre. Trotter and ten others were arrested for attempting to ban the Boston showing, which Trotter called a rebel play. Though banned in Chicago, St. Louis, all of Ohio, and areas in Massachusetts, the film still ran in various theaters in Boston for over six months. When attempts were made to return the film to Boston in the spring of 1921, Trotter again gathered his forces, including the Knights of Columbus and the NAACP, and was instrumental in having the censorship law affecting moving pictures passed in Massachusetts. This time he was successful in banning the film.

While in 1901 Trotter owned, through inheritance, property all over Boston, by 1908 he had run into financial difficulty. Advertisers in his paper owed him money which he was unable to collect. He obtained a second mortgage on his Dorchester home where he and his wife had lived, and the next year sold his last two houses. He worked long hours and took no vacation. His wife did all she could to handle the bookkeeping, subscriptions, and other newspaper matters. When the influenza epidemic ravaged the nation in the fall of 1918, she succumbed to it on October 8; she was barely 46. Trotter concentrated on *The Guardian* after that and for several years continued to publish her photograph in the paper. Still, he could not make a go of the paper without her and it lost its former intellectual caliber and literary touch.

Trotter turned back to the Republicans and supported their presidential candidate, Warren G. Harding. On race matters, Trotter clung to his old ideas, concentrated his efforts in the Boston area, and in time was left in the dust of the new black leaders and their activities. He continued to work with the NERL but apparently did not fully embrace the increasingly powerful NAACP. He and the NERL rejected Marcus Garvey and his work. He deplored Garvey's references to African heritage and use of the word "Negro." Instead, Trotter always used the terms "Colored American," "Colored people," or "Afro–American." After 1919 he refused to use "Negro" in *The Guardian*'s editorials. Trotter also remained outside the cultural activities that occurred as the Harlem Renaissance.

In his last years Trotter continued his attempt to collect from his advertisers. He even resorted to dances, picnics, and other benefits to raise money for *The Guardian.* A few of his friends did contribute to the paper. By 1934 he shared an apartment at 41 Cunard Street with benefactor Mary Gibson and her son. In the early morning of his sixty–second birthday, unable to sleep, he went to the roof of the building where his family believed he lost his balance and fell to his death; some sources claim his death was an apparent suicide.

Although at times Trotter's historical significance has been obscured, he was an important figure in the first third of this century, consistently using protest to remove barriers to racial integration.

REFERENCES

Fox, Stephen R. *The Guardian of Boston.* New York: Atheneum, 1971.

Puttkammer, Charles W., and William Worthy. ''William Monroe Trotter.'' *Journal of Negro History* 43 (October 1958): 298–316.

Who's Who in Colored America. Vol. 1. New York: Who's Who in Colored America Corporation, 1927.

COLLECTIONS

The papers of William Monroe Trotter are in the Mugar Library at Boston University. Trotter materials can also be found in the papers of Woodrow Wilson and William McAdoo at the Library of Congress.

Jessie Carney Smith

Ture, Kwame.
See Carmichael, Stokely.

Henry McNeal Turner
(1834–1915)
Religious worker, emigrationist, educator

A leading member of the African Episcopal Church, Henry McNeal Turner was important in establishing the denomination in Georgia and Africa. He was also a leading advocate of his era for the emigration of African Americans to Africa. Often viewed simply as a precursor to later exponents of black nationalism, like Marcus Garvey, he was actually an important figure in African American history.

Turner was born free in Newberry Court House, South Carolina, on February 1, 1834, to Hardy and Sarah Turner (d. 1888). His father was the son of Julia Turner, a white plantation owner, and her black superintendent. His maternal grandmother, Hannah Greer, told her grandson that her husband, David Greer (d. 1819), was the son of an African king, enslaved but then set free because of his royal birth. Hardy Turner died while his son was a child. Henry McNeal had a sister who died young and two more half–siblings from his mother's marriage to Jabez Story.

Henry McNeal Turner

Under state law Turner was apprenticed out several times as a boy. He worked in the cotton fields alongside slaves but vigorously resisted whippings, a punishment to which free blacks were not legally subject. He disliked his apprenticeships to a blacksmith and a carriage maker and ran away at least once. When Sarah Turner married Jabez Story around 1848, she and her son moved to join him in Abbeville. Turner was hired to do janitorial work in a lawyers' office when he was 15 and by his 20s was a beginning carpenter.

Although Turner's mother made efforts for him to be taught to read earlier, his education dates from his job at the law office in Abbeville about 1819. In direct violation of state law, they instructed him in elementary subjects except for English grammar. Converted to Christianity on June 12, 1844, and joining the Baptist church, Turner's mother influenced him spiritually. He was also stirred by Methodist preachers at summer camp meetings near Abbeville between 1848 and 1851 and admitted to the Methodist Church in 1848. As documented by Angell, Turner described his conversion experience, ''I fell upon the ground, rolled in the dirt, foamed at the mouth and agonized under conviction until Christ relieved me by his atoning blood.''

In 1851 Turner was licensed as an exhorter and in 1853 as a preacher. In December of 1854 he acquired a guardianship certificate after naming a white man to vouch for his good behavior and he could travel as an evangelist. The splits between Northern and Southern Baptists and Methodists had the effect of easing Southern fears of separate black churches after the 1840s, and supervision of the religious activities of blacks became more relaxed, except in South Carolina due to the experience of the Denmark Vesey conspiracy of 1822. Turner thus found semi–independent black urban churches in the South, especially in Georgia, which he soon came to prefer. From 1853 to 1858 Turner preached throughout the South, visiting South Carolina, Georgia, Alabama, Louisiana, and Mississippi. A spell–binding speaker, he attracted both blacks and whites to his sermons.

On August 31, 1856, he married Eliza Ann Peacher, aged 19 and the daughter of a leading house builder in Columbia, South Carolina. The marriage between Turner and his first wife produced 14 children before her death in 1889. Only four lived to adulthood, and only two survived their father: John Payne (b. March 1, 1859) and David Milchon, sometimes called McNeal by his father (b. October 31, 1860). His daughter Victoria died in childbirth in 1892, and daughter Josephine died after an operation for an internal tumor in 1897.

In 1893 Turner married Martha DeWitt of Bristol, Pennsylvania. She died in early 1897. In 1900 he married Harriet Wayman, the widow of a fellow AME bishop. She died by 1907. On December 3, 1907, Turner married Laura Pearl Lemon, a divorced woman, in the face of considerable opposition from the Council of Bishops and his own grand–daughter Charlotte Lankford. Born about 1880 Laura Pearl Lemon had been hired as Turner's assistant secretary in June of 1897 and became chief secretary in 1900. She also became an assistant editor of *The Voice of the People,* Turner's newspaper, head of the missionary department of Morris Brown College, and president of the Women's Home and Foreign Missionary Society of Northern Georgia. Turner's fourth wife died at the age of 35, about five months after his death in 1915. He had no children from his final three marriages.

Turner had an extremely patriarchal view of marriage. Ponton explained, "as a husband he made provision for every enjoyment and comfort for the woman he selected as the partner in life, so that no complaint could come to him from her to retard him in his God–given work. . . . His will was the supreme law and the controlling influence of his home."

Joins AME

In New Orleans in 1857 Turner met Willis H. Revels, pastor of St. James Church, who told him of Richard Allen and the African Methodist Episcopal Church. Turner made no immediate attempt to join, and it has been suggested that during this time he was still working out the freedom of his wife, who was probably a slave. He spent the next year continuing to work for the Southern Methodists. In particular he did outstanding work alongside three white Methodist ministers in a revival in Athens, Georgia, in April and May of 1858, where Turner claimed 100 converts. At the revival, marked by a quiet intensity of prayer unlike the emotionalism of Turner's own conversion, he preached by invitation to the white students and professors of the University of Georgia.

Around summer's end Turner traveled with his wife to St. Louis to join the AME church at its annual conference in August of 1858. Although his desire to join an all–black church was genuine, it may not have been the only motive for the move. The Turners were part of a wider emigration of free blacks from the South just before the Civil War.

Turner's rise within the denomination was rapid. From 1858 to 1860, he pastored two small churches in the Baltimore conference and endeavored to supplement his education. Then he led Union Bethel in Baltimore from 1860 to 1862 and Israel Church in Washington, D.C., from 1862 to 1863. He was ordained deacon in April of 1860 and elder in 1862. He continued to build an outstanding reputation in the church through his work in the AME Book Concern, his selling and writing for the *Christian Recorder,* and his participation on the conference's Committee of Missions. In Washington he joined the Prince Hall masons and cultivated white politicians like Charles Sumner as he carried out extensive renovations on the church building. He displayed a rigidity and refusal to back down even in the face of majority opposition in his conduct of quarterly meetings of local AME ministers. His diaries show that a real anxiety about the possibility of damnation underlay his outer show of confidence, and he retained his belief in the literal existence of Hell until the end of his life.

Turner came to the conclusion that black troops should fight for the Union by the end of 1862. When the Emancipation Proclamation was issued on January 1, 1863, Turner joined other blacks to recruit soldiers. The First Regiment of the United States Colored Troops came into being by summer, and Turner applied to become its chaplain. William Hunter, an AME minister from Baltimore, also had turned in an application for a position as chaplain. Hunter entered the army on October 10, 1863, and Turner received his commission on November 6.

Turner suffered a series of illnesses during the first few months he was in the army, culminating in a severe attack of smallpox in February of 1864. After fighting in Virginia, his regiment was part of the forces which captured Fort Fisher, North Carolina, in January of 1865.

Turner was thus positioned to join in the competition between the AME and the AME Zion churches for the allegiance of blacks in North Carolina. (AME Zion mostly prevailed in North Carolina.) In Georgia in December of 1865 Turner took on organizing his church, continuing efforts which had begun a year earlier but which were faltering because of the death of one prominent missionary and the departure of the other. Turner decided to resign his commission and soon afterwards left the Freedmen's Bureau. Until 1871 Turner devoted tremendous energy to the organization and development of the AME Church in Georgia. He became church superintendent of the state from 1866 to 1871. Akin to the position of bishop, his job involved almost constant travel and preaching. For a while, there was limited cooperation with the ME Church South: both denominations were eager to forestall the activities of the ME Church North in the state. The ME Church South agreed that its black congregations could leave to join the AME Church but retained control of church properties. The adherence of established congregations to the AME and a vigorous revival movement among all denominations black and white in 1866 brought in many new members. Soon this growth revealed the problem of the low supply of experienced and literate black ministers. Turner met this need by waiving the requirements for literacy and even for a thorough knowledge of the Bible. He appointed many temporary preachers, presenting the successful among them to the Annual Conference for Ordination.

Enters Politics

In addition to carrying out his heavy work load as a minister, Turner became heavily involved in Reconstruction politics from 1867 to 1871. His disappointments in the political sphere intensified his distrust of whites and convinced him later that separation of the races and black emigration could be the only hope for black empowerment. He threw the resources of his church into organizing the Republican Party in Georgia. Thirty–six blacks, including six AME ministers, were elected to the state constitutional convention, which met from December of 1867 to March of 1868.

Striving to improve relations with whites, Turner pursued a conciliatory conservative policy during the convention. He even favored a full pardon for Jefferson Davis and voted against inserting in the constitution a provision that blacks could hold office. However, his politics did little to attract white allies and stimulated hostility from all sides. Nevertheless, Turner won election to the subsequent legislature, and the failure of conciliation became increasingly evident. The legislature voted to expel black members by an 83 to 23 vote with black members forbidden to vote on the issue. Turner rose to denounce the decision in a three–hour speech on September 3, 1868.

It was now clear that any political power for blacks in Georgia rested on support at the national level, and that state support disappeared with the end of Reconstruction in Georgia in 1871. Klu Klux Klan terror tactics and Democratic Party efforts to deny the ballot to blacks combined with the factional infighting in the Republican Party contributed to the demise of political power for blacks.

In the legislative elections of 1870, Turner appeared to have won election to the legislature by 17 votes, but his margin of victory disappeared in a fraudulent recount. He would subsequently serve a while longer in a legislative session held under military guard to ratify the Fifteenth Amendment.

In Macon, Georgia, his position was undermined by a virulent quarrel with Republican J. C. Swayze, editor of the *Macon American Union.* Swayze and Turner had been reluctant allies, but they eventually broke when Turner was appointed postmaster in Macon in May of 1869, and the entire staff of the post office walked off the job. As the controversy swirled, Turner was seen in Macon in July, in the company of Marian Harris, a prostitute whom he had known since 1867 and with whom he had been seen in Atlanta, Philadelphia, and Washington. She was carrying $1,800 in phoney Bank of New Jersey notes and was arrested. Turner was then accused of conspiring with her to pass counterfeit money. After a three–day hearing the charges against him were dismissed. Swayze published more allegations about financial improbity of Turner and privately circulated some of Turner's correspondence containing obscenities. Turner was forced to resign from his government position. The white community soon forgot about him and the scandal, but the allegations of infidelities with Harris and other women undermined his position among some blacks.

Turner's political involvement brought trouble to the church. The ME Church South—predominantly white–controlled—no longer cooperated with the AME and supported the formation of the Colored [now Christian] Methodist Episcopal Church in January of 1869. The ME Church South used its control of titles to church property as a lever. The rate of growth in the AME Church dropped from 5,000 to 500 new members a year. On the positive side the AME Church became completely independent and viewed much more favorably by black Baptists.

In 1872 Turner became pastor of St. Philip's in Savannah, a post he held for the four years. He was responsible for the completion of a new church building. He was also involved in local life, delivering and publishing several lectures, and active as a Mason. He completed a new hymnal, published in 1876, and a church standard through the 1890s. He continued to be active in the conference without completely abandoning politics. While his position of inspector in the U.S. Custom House excited little animosity, he was unsuccessful in an attempt to be elected coroner.

Becomes an Emigrationist

As conditions for blacks in the South worsened, Turner was also beginning to take a pro–emigration position. At first he did not focus exclusively on Africa, but the desire to Christianize the continent finally led him to select it as a destination for American blacks. By 1873 his pronouncements in favor of emigration were emphatic enough to be challenged by Northern blacks like Frederick Douglass, and Turner began to move closer to the American Colonization Society. In 1876 he became a lifetime honorary vice–president of that organization, whose formation in 1816 had sparked the first national black protest movement.

In that year, too, Turner won election to head the AME publishing concern, based in Philadelphia, which was in difficult financial straits. Turner gave the concern high visibility, but his hectoring of ministers who did not subscribe to the *Christian Recorder* and his extensive absences traveling did not relieve the financial pressures. After a sheriff's seizure of the concern's property in February of 1878, Theodore Gould was brought in as deputy, and together he and Turner did much to stabilize the operation. In his travels Turner became increasingly attuned to the problems of black farmers, especially the practice of debt peonage. He supported emigration to Liberia on the ship *Azor* in 1878. The efforts of mass black migration to Kansas, culminating in the spring of 1878, also received Turner's blessing.

Turner was one of the candidates of Southern members of the AME for election as bishop in the General Conference of 1880. Since Daniel A. Payne, the best known and most respected bishop, believed the allegations about Turner's sexual and financial irregularities, he was firmly against Turner's election. AME Southerners prevented the charges against Turner from being heard on the convention floor and elected their candidates. Having carried the election of their candidates and securing regional representation in the national leadership, the Southern blacks could now split among contending factions. In order to avoid an open quarrel that might have damaged the church, Payne consecrated Turner bishop, and the two buried their public differences. Turner was the proposer of the celebration of Payne's thirtieth anniversary as a bishop in August of 1882. Although there would be disagreements among the men over the following years, Payne presided at Turner's 1893 marriage to Martha DeWitt just a few months before his death in November.

As a bishop Turner presided over various districts for terms of four years. He established his home in Atlanta. While his rough comments on ideological opponents might suggest that he would run into difficulties, Turner was a successful bishop, skilled at managing his ministers and even called in to resolve disputes in other episcopal districts. To offer guidance in ecclesiastical disciplinary matters, he published *The Genius and Theory of Methodist Polity* in 1885.

Concerned with what he perceived as a decline of piety, Turner favored the return of revival meetings. While he did not approve of shouting in regular church services, he did wish to continue the emotionalism of the camp meetings of his youth. In 1895 he became senior bishop of the denomination as a result of the death of older bishops and, in 1896, returned as bishop of Georgia. Turner became chair of the Morris Brown Board of Trustees from 1896 to 1908, but his efforts for industrial education were unsuccessful. As a respected, but controversial elder, he was perceived as conservative by the rising generation of ministers. One of Turner's forward–looking initiatives, however, was overturned by the church in 1887: his 1885 ordination of a woman, Sarah Ann Hughes of North Carolina.

Turner maintained that doctrinal differences strengthened a church and he gradually came to a liberal position on the Bible, holding that not all parts are equally inspired. In 1895 he stated that a new translation of the Bible by and for blacks was needed. Thus he initiated some of the themes of black theology. Aroused by the implicit racism in the religious language of whites, Turner declared, as cited by Angell, "The devil is white and never was black." In 1895 he told a black Baptist convention in Atlanta, "God is a Negro." Angell quoted his defense of this statement in the *Voice of Missions*:

> *We have as much right* biblically and otherwise to believe that God is a negro, as you buckra or white people have to believe that God is a fine looking, symmetrical, and ornamented white man. . . . Yet we are not stickler as to God's color, any way, but if He has any we would prefer to believe that it is nearer symbolized in the blue sky above us and the blue water of the seas. . .but we certainly protest against God being a white man or against God being white *at all*.

Turner's attempts to build racial pride rested on his conviction that the first humans were black. An unfortunate counterpart of his high estimation of blacks was the fierceness of his denunciations of those who did not live up to his ideals. This intransigence made him many enemies.

Fosters African Missions

Turner also pushed for increased missionary activity in Africa as opportunities opened up there. Turner gave concrete expression to his evangelization hopes when he made his first trip to Liberia, where he received an enthusiastic reception, in late 1891. To support the mission work, he organized a new women's auxiliary, the Woman's Home and Foreign Missionary Society, to abet the efforts of an older, mostly Northern Women's Parent Mite Missionary Society. Between 1892 and 1900 Turner organized missionary societies in 11 annual conferences. Two of his wives, Martha DeWitt Turner and Laura Lemmon Turner, were very active in the organizations. He continued to speak in favor of emigration to Africa at a convention he organized in Indianapolis in 1893. However, he faced opposition from the majority of those in attendance.

In Liberia Turner's missionary efforts were weakened by the personality defects of Alfred L. Ridgel in Liberia (Ridgel probably committed suicide in September of 1896 by leaping off a river boat). Turner also quarreled with the Sierra Leone missionary John R. Frederick, who in 1897 left the AME church in disgust, taking his congregation with him. Although the AME church survived in these countries, Turner personally became very unpopular.

New possibilities opened in South Africa, where the independent Ethiopian Church, founded by Africans, sought to unite with the AME in 1896. By the time Turner visited Africa in 1898, many Africans were almost ready to consider him a Messiah. He took vigorous steps to organize the AME Church there. As he had earlier in Georgia, he ordained ministers with little regard to their education. He also took the controversial step of naming African James D. Dwane as vicar bishop, a sort of missionary bishop, subject to later approval by the church. The action and Dwane's character were attacked although Turner's action was sustained. However, Dwane broke with the AME and sought admission to the Anglican Church taking along several ministers just as the Boer War broke out in late 1899. The AME finally agreed to appoint missionary bishops to work in South Africa in 1900, naming Levi Jenkins Coppin and Marcellus Moore.

Turner's position on emigration was becoming increasingly unpopular, especially when the white–owned International Migration Society took two shiploads totaling more than 500 blacks to Liberia in 1895 and 1896. The airing of the complaints of emigrants and returnees contributed to the unfavorableness of emigration. Turner ceased coupling emigration and missionary work in the later part of the decade.

Other events further injured Turner's career. In 1900 Robert Charles of New Orleans, who was an agent for the paper Turner edited for the AME, the *Voice of Missions,* killed several policemen before being captured and lynched. Turner was forced to give up the paper as a result, but promptly launched his *Voice of the People* as a replacement. When he tried to raise money to buy ships to carry emigrants to Africa in 1903, the attempt was a dismal failure with no more than $1,000 raised.

As the tide of antiblack violence and lynching rose, in 1897 Turner caused a stir when he advocated that every black man in the United States keep several guns in the house. In 1906 his disgust with America led to his famous statement about the flag, which was reprinted by Angell, "to the Negro in the country, the American flag is a dirty and contemptible rag. Not a star in it can the colored man claim, for it is no longer the symbol of our manhood rights and liberty."

In 1899 Turner suffered a mild stroke from which he seemed to have completely recovered. Still he became increasingly fragile after the turn of the century although he continued to work diligently. Despite the controversy caused by his fourth marriage in 1907, his new wife's care and protection aided in prolonging his life. He was not given a district to supervise in 1908, but was appointed church historiographer. However, he did little in this position. In 1912 he was named to supervise Michigan and Canada. On his way to a church conference in Ontario, he collapsed from a massive stroke on the ferry to Windsor, Ontario, on the early morning of May 8, 1915, and died a few hours later. It is estimated that 25,000 persons viewed his remains in Atlanta before the funeral ceremony on May 19. He was buried in South View Cemetery.

Turner inspired controversy for his support of emigration to Africa but also gained much respect for his vigorous and effective leadership in his church. He focused on the problems of poor Southern blacks in a way than many of his contemporaries did not, and themes that he first articulated have present–day relevance in black theology.

REFERENCES

Angell, Stephen Ward. *Bishop Henry McNeal Turner and African–American Religion in the South.* Knoxville: University of Tennessee Press, 1992.

Chirenje, J. Mutero. *Ethiopianism and Afro–Americans in Southern Africa, 1883–1916.* Baton Rouge: Louisiana State University Press, 1987.

Litwack, Leon, and August Meier, eds. *Black Leaders of the Nineteenth Century.* Urbana: University of Illinois Press, 1988.

Ponton, M. M. *Life and Times of Henry M. Turner.* Atlanta: A. B. Caldwell, 1917.

Redkey, Edwin S. *Black Exodus.* New Haven, CT: Yale University Press, 1969.

———. "'Rocked in the Cradle of Consternation.' A Black Chaplain in the Union Army Reports on the Struggle to Take Fort Fisher, North Carolina." *American Heritage* 31 (October/November 1980): 70–79.

Turner, H. M. *Speech on the Eligibility of Colored Members to Seats in the Georgia Legislature.* Augusta, GA: E. H. Pughe, [1868].

COLLECTIONS

Surviving papers and memorabilia are in the Moorland–Spingarn Research Center, Howard University.

Robert L. Johns

Nat Turner
(1800–1831)
Slave, liberation theologian, insurrectionist

In mid–afternoon on Monday, August 22, 1831, in the fields outside Jerusalem—the country seat of Southampton, Virginia—armed black men led by Nat Turner were in hot pursuit of white southerners under the command of Captain Alexander P. Peete. At the last minute, Peete's men were rescued by reinforcements dispatched from Jerusalem. Turner's forces fell back to Major Thomas Ridley's plantation where he assembled 40 men for the assault on Jerusalem. Before he settled down to sleep for the night, he was attacked, losing half his forces. Thus ended the Nat Turner insurrection, the most famous slave revolt in American history.

Nathaniel Turner was born October 2, 1800, to African–born slaves of Benjamin Turner, a wealthy plantation owner in the Tidewater region of southeast Virginia bordering North Carolina. Whether or not his mother, Nancy, had tried to kill him at birth rather than raise him in slavery, as writers of the Work Projects Administration study, *The Negro in Virginia,* contend, Nat Turner's birth was a troubled one which left its imprint.

By his own account, recorded in his famous *Confessions* to his counsel Thomas Gray, Turner's childhood contained prophetic circumstances that he, his family, and the slave community, believed marked him for the "great work" he was to perform. "Being at play with other children, when three or four years old," he recollected to Gray:

> I was telling them something, which my mother overhearing, said it had happened before I was born—I stuck to my story, however, and related something which went, in her opinion, to confirm it—others being called on were greatly astonished, knowing that these things had happened, and caused them to say in my hearing, I surely would be a

> prophet, as the Lord had shewn me things that had happened before my birth. And my father and mother strengthened me in this my first impression, saying in my presence, I was intended for some great purpose, which they had always thought from certain marks on my head and breast.

Turner was close to his grandmother, "who was very religious." By his example, Turner's father, an African who had on many occasions tried to escape from slavery, gave him the example of a black man who refused to be enslaved. Finally succeeding in his endeavor to run away, he emigrated to Liberia, where, according to John Cromwell, "it is said his grave is quite as well known as that of Franklin, Jefferson or Adams is to the patriots of America."

Although Thomas Gray maintained that Turner's mother taught him to read, it is not likely that this African–born woman was literate. Turner confessed that "the manner in which I learned to read and write, not only had great influence on my own mind, as I acquired it with the most perfect ease, so much so, that I have no recollection whatever of learning the alphabet—but to the astonishment of the family, one day, when a book was shewn to me to keep me from crying, I began spelling the names of different objects." Turner's precociousness became a source of wonder to the slave community.

Growing from a precocious youth into adulthood, Turner's physical appearance and demeanor were powerfully marked by the daily brutalities of plantation slave labor and the spiritual vocation of his prophetic calling. Small in stature with "distinct Africa features," Nat Turner was roughly five feet six to eight inches tall, weighing approximately 160 pounds, bright complexioned, but not a mulatto. He was broad in the shoulders from working in the fields, with broad feet and a knock–kneed, brisk, energetic step. He had a moustache and goatee. The strongest contrast of physical features that one would encounter upon meeting Nat Turner would be between his deep–set eyes that sparkled from his constant fasting and meditation, and the two deep scars that stretched across his temple and the back of his neck, punctuated by a large knot on his right arm.

Unrest and Revelations

Systematic or isolated, slave unrest was pervasive in Southampton County over the period from Nat Turner's birth to his revolt. No matter how widespread slave unrest had become, however, Nat Turner's insurrection broke on an unsuspecting white populace precisely because white authorities treated the pattern of slave violence against masters as isolated, criminal activity, instead of as antislavery acts of resistance.

The 1820s were a stormy period of transition in the United States, particularly for the plantation economy of the South. Stephen Oates notes that a severe depression in 1819 and a downward spiraling of agricultural prices lasted four years. Farmers and planters in Virginia, which was especially hard hit, sold their excess off to the Deep South. "The Panic hurt Samuel Turner [the son of Benjamin Turner and Nat's owner at the time], too, but he balked at selling his Negroes. Instead he hired an overseer to get more work out them and to manage the estate more efficiently."

The flogging that Nat Turner received at the hands of Samuel Turner's overseer impelled him to run away to the Flat Swamps. He avoided slave patrollers for 30 days and nights, then returned of his own free will to Samuel Turner's house because of the prophetic revelations he experienced while suffering the exposure, fasting, and deprivations of the wilderness.

After experiencing the conflict between the voices of heaven that bid him to return to his master and the voice of his earthly community that chastised him for returning, Turner then prophesied the battle on Jerusalem's fields: "I had a vision—and I saw white spirits and Black spirits engaged in battle, and the sun was darkened—and I heard a voice saying, 'Such is your luck, such you are called to see, and let it come rough or smooth, you must surely bare it.'" The toil of laboring in the fields played a crucial part in the unfolding drama of Turner's revelations, inasmuch as it was while laboring that his spiritual visitations took place. The very process of toiling in the fields provided the terms of reference for Turner's prophetic rhetoric. He says that it was while working at the plow that the spirit came to him; that blood appeared on the leaves of the corn stalks; that he experienced his prophetic sense of the "great work" he was to perform; and finally, that he struck a new covenant.

In the midst of the 1821–23 depression, Samuel Turner died, once again raising the anxiety of his slaves that they would be sold into the dreaded plantation despotism of Georgia. Nat, valued at $400 as a prime field hand, was sold to Thomas Moore. Though little is known of Turner's young wife, Cherry, it is at this point that we come across her name for the first time. We do know that sometime after his return from the Flat Swamp, he and Cherry married. On Samuel Turner's death, Cherry was sold to Giles Reese.

Nat and Cherry Turner had three children, a daughter and two sons, though slavery prevented them from living together as husband and wife.

Having married into the wealthy Francis family, Thomas Moore was an ambitious young plantation farmer on the rise. With 720 acres of his wife's family's land to work, Moore worked his field hands hard to raise productivity and efficiency in an effort to overcome depressed cotton prices.

Around this time, Turner began to style himself a Baptist preacher and started conducting his own "praise meetings" in 1825. He continued to fast, meditate, and sequester himself from others, while continuing the relentless toil and intense work pace under Thomas Moore. The physiological impact of this grueling regimen and self–deprivation had its hallucinatory effects. The wretched conditions of slavery led Turner to read the Christian story of Jesus back into the violent stories of Old Testament retribution and redemption. The blood of atonement to be spilled for the sins of slavery would be that of

Nat Turner, captured in the forest [engraving].

the white slavemasters and their families on behalf of black slaves.

Unorthodox Ministry

Droughts, crop destruction, and forest fires marked the year 1826, phenomena of which Turner claimed foreknowledge. He would preach to slaves in Jerusalem one Sunday, go down to Cross Keys to preach the following Sunday, while on other Sabbaths he preached at Bethlehem Crossroads. His labors for Thomas Moore and his itinerant travels as a preacher gave him a knowledge of Southampton's terrain that few men had. By 1827, Turner had identified some 20 or so men, slave and free, whom he could trust with the meaning of his revelations. They met together after praise meetings, and prepared for the great "mission" that Turner told them God had in store for them.

One other episode in the young preacher's ministry intensified the contradictions and freedom in which his mind moved and released itself from his earthly conditions of toil and suffering. A white overseer from a nearby plantation, Etheldred Brantley, sought the salvation of the young prophet for some unspecified, yet unpardonable, sin for which whites refused to forgive him. Brantley accepted Nat's forgiveness, ceased his forbidden behavior, then strangely came down with a case of bleeding boils. Nat convinced him to fast and pray with him for nine days, after which Brantley was healed. The young preacher then announced that he would baptize Brantley and himself at Pearson's Mill Pond before a large assembly of black and white onlookers. While the white dove Turner prophesied would descend from heaven and land on his head never materialized, the greater social miracle in the minds of his black followers was that a white man would be baptized by a black man.

Despite all the rejoicing at this miracle and the unprecedented esteem it brought the young prophet, Nat Turner was still the chattel of Thomas Moore.

From this violent contradiction between free black mind and social enslavement came, on May 12, 1828, the most definitive revelation of Turner's fast–induced visions:

> I heard a loud noise in the heavens, and the Spirit instantly appeared to me and said the Serpent was loosened, and Christ had laid down the yoke he had

> borne for the sins of men, and that I should take it on and fight against the Serpent, for the time was fast approaching when the first should be last and the last should be first.

In other words, Turner was told to cut down his enemies with their own weapons.

Because Turner kept his own counsel, divulging the details of the mission neither to his wife nor his followers, he escaped the fate of betrayal that had bedeviled so many other slave insurrections. The actual plans of his mission were not shared with anyone until the eve of the uprising.

In 1828, Thomas Moore unexpectedly died. His widow married a local wheelwright named Joseph Travis the following year. With the slaves Travis brought with him when he moved his carriage business to the Moore plantation, the slave population increased to 17. By all accounts, including Turner's, Joseph Travis was a "good master."

The conditions of unrelenting toil and suffering were the ground from which rebellion grew. However, as necessary as the material crisis was in bringing slave ferment to the point of insurrection, the revolt still relied on the contingency of a "sign" to signal Nat that his work was to commence. This sign came in February of 1831 when an eclipse of the sun occurred, causing a great stir among blacks and whites alike in Southampton, indeed, up and down the eastern seaboard. Taking the eclipse to be his long awaited sign and "immediately conceiving the seal to be removed from his lips," observed William Drewry, "he communicated the work to be done to his four confidants—Henry Porter, Hark Travis, Nelson Williams, and Sam Francis."

All of these men were intensely disaffected with their circumstances, all belonged to the slave church underground, and all four were field hands like Nat. Hark Travis was chief among Nat's lieutenants. He belonged to Joseph Travis, and before that to Thomas Moore, and so was a good friend of Turner's. Hark was a physically powerful and handsome man whom whites considered a "black Apollo." Nelson Williams was the property of a small farmer, Jacob Williams, against whom, along with his white overseer, Nelson bore an intense grudge. Nelson was also a powerful conjurer, eschewing traditional Christianity. Henry Porter and Sam Francis were chosen by Nat for their dogged loyalty to him.

Nelson and Hark were given the rank of general, and the responsibility of plotting the logistics of the insurrection using a crude map of Southampton County drawn by Turner with berry juice. They compiled a list of 18 trusted slaves who could be relied upon when the rebellion began. Turner and his four lieutenants settled on July 4 as their day of judgment.

Turner fell sick as the Fourth of July approached, and the insurrection was postponed. Dreadful doubts about his bloody mission shook his resolve. As he told Gray in the *Confessions*:

> Many were the plans formed and rejected by us, and it affected my mind to such a degree, that I fell sick, and the time passed without our coming to any determination how to commence—Still forming new schemes and rejecting them, when the sign appeared again, which determined me not to wait longer.

On Saturday, August 13, the morning sun grew strangely dim as atmospheric changes caused it to change colors—green, blue, and then white. Stranger yet, later that afternoon a black spot seemed to appear on the face of the sun. To Turner it looked as though a black hand was stretched across the surface of the sun. Interpreting these natural phenomena as his final sign, Turner and his comrades chose the night of August 21 as the moment to commence their "work of death." Sunday, the day after the black spot appeared on the sun, Turner convinced some slaves at a church meeting to participate in his plot, telling them "that as the black spot had passed over the sun, so would the Blacks pass over the earth." Despite his guarded secrecy—even his four closest comrades did not know the specifics of his plan—the word was out in the slave quarters that something large was about to happen.

General Nat Turner's Fray

On the afternoon of Sunday, August 21, Turner's four lieutenants—Hark, Nelson, Henry, and Sam—met together at Cabin Pond on Giles Reese's land for a final feast of roast pig and apple brandy. They were accompanied by two recruits, Jack Reese and Will Francis. While the men ate and drank they made their final plans for the insurrection. Turner not present for most of the barbecue arrived later with an air of mystery about him. He appeared before his men wearing his old hat and with his deep-set eyes shining from having fasted and meditated in preparation for the task they were to commence. Seeing Will Francis among his cadre for the first time, Turner asked him why he had come to this place. Will answered that his life is worth no more than the others and that his liberty was just as dear, adding that he too intended to get his freedom or die trying.

After a day of church, eating and drinking, the whites were settled in for the night. Turner depended on the swiftness of his forces and the element of surprise in unleashing the forces of Jubilee. "Sometime in the previous week," Stephen Oates gathered, "Nat had seen his wife and had given her his sacred papers—the list of followers, the drawings of the crucifix and the sun."

The first blow was struck at the plantation of Joseph Travis, Turner's own master. Turner and his men hit the Travis farm around 2 a.m. Monday morning, August 22. The whole household of five whites was dispatched by the insurrectionists. Turner struck the first blow, his hatchet, however, glanced off Joseph Travis' head before, as Nat Turner confessed, "Will [Francis] laid him dead, with a blow of his axe, and Mrs. Travis shared the same fate, as she lay in bed."

Procuring several guns and rounds of ammunition, Turner proceeded to drill the insurgents in military formation in the barnyard of the Travis plantation. They also assigned themselves military commissions, with Turner made general.

From Sunday night through Monday morning, the insurgents, their numbers grown to 15 with seven on horseback, swept through the Southampton countryside from plantation to plantation carrying out their bloody work. Turner's plan was to instigate a general insurrection. Marching on the Francis plantation, the insurgents were joined by nearly all of the family slaves. Five slaves from the Edwards plantation joined as well. The rebels spared the lives of Mrs. Harris, a widow, her children and grandchildren on the appeals of one of the insurrectionists, Joe Harris. At the Wiley farm, the white women were hidden in the woods protected by their slaves.

By nine o'clock the force had grown to 40 and they had covered a three mile radius, from the point of origin of the insurrection at the Travis farm. General Nat Turner rode in the rear of an armed cavalry of 20 mounted men who swept down on plantation and farm house with a swiftness that surprised and terrorized the residents. In the end 63 whites were killed by Turner's forces. At its height, the force increased to more than 60 men armed with guns, axes, swords, clubs and pikes. Turner's swift strikes brought him within three miles of the county seat of Southampton, at Jerusalem. However, having come so near to Jerusalem, Turner reluctantly conceded to the wishes of his lieutenants, who wanted to go in search of fresh recruits for the assault on the county seat.

The Monday night attack upon his forces at the Ridley plantation following his retreat from Jerusalem fields, signaled the final unraveling of Turner's fortunes. Realizing that his tactical advantage had been spent, Turner retreated into hiding, after directing his forces to rendezvous back at the Travis plantation. Upon returning there, he ran into white patrollers. Believing that he had been betrayed, at this point Turner gave up all hope of renewing his campaign, and turned attention to his personal survival. Constructing a hideout beneath a pile of fence rails on the Travis plantation and provisioning himself from the old plantation, Turner remained underground for six weeks.

White Terror, White Panic

In that time, a reign of white terror engulfed the Virginia Tidewater, and extended throughout the South. Whites retaliated indiscriminately and brutally against the black population, slave and free. In all, over 200 black men, women, and children were killed in the white backlash. The panic of 1831 extended into 1832 as false reports and rumors spread of blacks on the move. So frenzied were southern white anxieties over the events in Southampton that there were Nat Turner sightings everywhere, often simultaneous ones at some distance from each other.

Ten weeks after his August insurrection, Nat Turner was captured by Benjamin Phipps, who didn't even recognize Turner. Phipps happened upon Turner near the dug–out den to which Turner had moved after his hideout at the Travis plantation had been discovered by a hunting dog.

After his capture on October 30, Turner was taken the next day to Jerusalem where he was tried on November 5, before a board of magistrates. In the interim between his arrival at Jerusalem and his trial, Turner gave his famous deposition, published as the *Confessions of Nat Turner,* to his attorney Thomas Gray. The *Confessions* were published by Gray and carried a lithograph sketch of Nat Turner by a former Norfolk artist, John Crawley. Over 50,000 copies of the *Confessions* were sold only a few weeks after coming off the press.

Turner gave his confessions November 1–3 in the county jail at Jerusalem. All those convicted in connection with the insurrection had been executed or deported from the state of Virginia before October 1 (four of them boys), except Turner, who was still at large. Two slave women, Charlotte and Lucy, were identified as participants in the rebellion. Lucy was executed on September 26, the only woman hanged among those executed. In all, 53 of the 70 or so slaves connected with the insurrection were tried before the county court, beginning September 8.

Turner offered no testimony, nor did he instruct his attorney to present any argument on his behalf. The court found him guilty and sentenced him to hang on Friday, November 11, 1831. A little more than a month after his thirty–first birthday, Turner was hanged from a tree in Jerusalem. At his execution, he exhibited calm composure, and declined an offer to address the immense crowd that had assembled for the event. His firmness of resolve extended to the hanging itself: not a limb or muscle was observed to have moved in his body.

White depravity also extended beyond Turner's death. Without betraying the least bit of outrage, William Drewry reported that "the bodies of those executed, with one exception, were buried in a decent and becoming manner. That of Nat Turner was delivered to the doctors, who skinned it and made grease of the flesh. His skeleton was for many years in the possession of Dr. Massenberg but has since been misplaced."

It was the idea of freedom itself that was the animating force in the Nat Turner insurrection. Nat Turner and his four comrades proved that the idea of freedom transcends the limitations of the given circumstances and laws. In answer to Thomas Gray's questions regarding his knowledge of plans for other insurrections or knowledge of a reported insurrection in North Carolina, Gray recorded in the *Confessions* that Nat "denied any knowledge of it." Instead, when Gray "looked him in the face as though [to] search his inmost thoughts, he replied, 'I see sir, you doubt my word; but can you not think the same idea [freedom]. . .might prompt others, as well as myself, to this undertaking.'"

REFERENCES

Brawley, Benjamin. *A Social History of the America Negro.* New York: Macmillan, 1921.

Cromwell, John W. "The Aftermath of Nat Turner's Insurrection." *Journal of Negro History* 5 (April 1920): pp. 208–234.

Drewry, William S. *Slave Insurrections in Virginia (1830–1865).* Ph.D. dissertation. Johns Hopkins University. Washington, DC: Neale Company, 1900.

Duff, John B., and Peter M. Mitchell, eds. *The Nat Turner Rebellion: The Historical Event and the Modern Controversy.* New York: Harper and Row, 1971.
Foner, Eric, ed. *Nat Turner.* Englewood Cliffs, NJ: Prentiss–Hall, 1971.
Higginson, Thomas Wentworth. *Black Rebellion.* New York: Arno Press, 1969. Originally published as *Travellers and Outlaws.* New York: C. T. Dillingham, 1888.
Oates, Stephen B. *The Fires of Jubilee: Nat Turner's Fierce Rebellion.* New York: Harper and Row, 1975.
Pease, Jane H., and William H. Pease. *They Who Would Be Free: Blacks' Search for Freedom, 1830–1861.* New York: Atheneum, 1974.
Raboteau, Albert. *Slave Religion: The ''Invisible Institution'' in the Antebellum South.* New York: Oxford University Press, 1978.
Schwarz, Philip J. *Twice Condemned: Slaves and the Criminal Law of Virginia, 1705–1865.* Baton Rouge: Louisiana State University Press, 1988.
Turner, Lucy Mae. ''The Family of Nat Turner, 1831 to 1954.'' *Negro History Bulletin* 18 (March 1955): 127, 146; (April 1955): 155–58.
Turner, Nat. *The Confessions of Nat Turner. . . As made to Thomas R. Gray.* Baltimore: Thomas R. Gray, 1831. Appendix to Henry I. Tragle, ed. *The Southampton Slave Revolt of 1831.* Amherst: University of Massachusetts Press, 1971.
Wish, Harvey. ''American Slave Insurrections before 1861.'' *Journal of Negro History* 22 (July 1937): 299–320.
Work Projects Administration (WPA). *The Negro in Virginia.* 1940. Reprint, New York: Arno Press, 1969.

Lou Turner

Ralph Tyler
(1859–1921)
Editor, journalist, government official

Ralph Tyler was a noted journalist of the late nineteenth and early twentieth centuries whose work became widely known when he reported on race relations and migration in the South, and later, in 1919, when he became the first and only black correspondent covering World War I. Although the war ended three months after his assignment, he was largely responsible for the news accounts of black soldiers in France during the final months of the war, particularly on the final day before the armistice was signed.

Born in Columbus, Ohio, in 1859, Ralph Waldo Tyler was the son of James S. and Maria McAfee Tyler and the oldest of eight children. He worked as teacher, clerk, postal carrier, clerk, and stenographer. To prepare himself as a stenographer, Tyler spent long hours studying shorthand and

Ralph Tyler

apparently became proficient. His training would serve as his passage into journalism. While pushing a mop as a janitor in the newsroom of the *Columbus Dispatch,* a white newspaper, at a time when all editorial offices had closed, he encountered William D. Brickell, the owner, who sought a staff member to take a letter. After Tyler offered his assistance, took a letter in shorthand, and then typed it, Brickell was so impressed that he told him to ''put down that mop . . . for good.'' This was the beginning of Tyler's career as a journalist.

In 1888 Tyler was appointed stenographer of the *Dispatch.* Since he worked closely with the editor, he learned the many details of newspaper work. He supplemented his meager income with funds earned in the barbershop that he operated and by waiting tables in the diner car of the Columbus–Cleveland train. He developed an interest in politics, particularly legislation that affected blacks and the appointment of blacks to office. In 1893 Tyler, a member of the Republican Party, and George A. Myers, a black leader in Republican politics in Ohio, began correspondence that would continue for three decades or more. Myers became Tyler's confidant, advisor, and backer. By 1896 Tyler's interest in politics had deepened while his interest in journalism continued. When he attended the Republican National Convention in St. Louis that year, he seized an opportunity to report the proceedings when the *Dispatch*'s reporter became too intoxicated to do his work. The press carried his articles under the byline of the regular reporter. Nevertheless, his work became widely known.

After that, Tyler's journalism career blossomed, and black newspapers sought his work. At some point he became society editor for the *Dispatch* and continued to work as secretary to William D. Brickell and confidential secretary to Robert F. Wolfe, who published both the *Dispatch* and the *Ohio State Journal.* According to the *Negro Digest,* Tyler had a clever and readable style that made him invaluable to the owners. Good journalism at that time frowned on court notoriety in the press. Tyler drew on his friendships with local servants who had pipelines to the most distinguished families through which the news would flow. He wrote dignified and glowing accounts of parties and other social affairs describing in detail the dresses the women wore. He earned the admiration and respect of this readers, as well as his fellow workers and his employer.

After 17 years, Tyler left the *Dispatch* because the paper changed ownership. From 1901 to 1904 he was a reporter for the *Ohio State Journal* in Columbus. He continued his extracurricular writings. His affiliation the newspapers brought him in contact with many influential journalists. In December 1905, using the pseudonym Olga Louise Cadijah, he wrote a pamphlet on race relations. His writings also included an Arabian romance, "The Love that Could Not Sin," published in 1908 in *The Colored American Magazine.*

By now Tyler's interest in political office had come to full blossom. He campaigned for a position as consul in a South American country, but was unsuccessful. While working as stenographer for Robert F. Wolfe, he became friendly with educator and school founder Booker T. Washington, of the Tuskegee Institute. When President Theodore Roosevelt asked Washington to find a black to fill the $5,000–a–year post as auditor in the Navy Department, Washington recommended his friend in Columbus. Tyler had already been Roosevelt's active supporter. His responsibilities for the Navy included settling all of the department's accounts, including those of the secretary of the navy. Tyler served for nine years, first under Roosevelt, then under President Howard Taft, and briefly under President Woodrow Wilson. In order to win editorial support for Taft during the 1908 Republican presidential campaign, he carried Republican funds to black newspapers in the Midwest, and was rewarded with the ability to influence black appointments that rivaled Washington's power.

A surge of racial discrimination that came with the Wilson Administration prompted Tyler to write a story for the *Washington Evening Star.* Tyler ignored the warnings of his friends that an article on racial discrimination under the Wilson Administration was foolish, insisting that he had a story to tell. According to the *Negro Digest,* when he left Washington, he had a letter from Franklin MacVeagh, Secretary of the Treasurer, dated March 1, 1913, that read: "I have learned in years of official and personal relations to entertain a high respect for your public service and your personal character. You have been throughout, an official who has had my confidence and esteem."

After leaving Washington in 1913, when black officeholders were purged from their positions, Tyler became national organizer for the National Negro Business League set up in 1900 under the direction of Booker T. Washington. In this capacity he traveled throughout the country for the league and black businessmen. He wrote accounts of his travels and conditions for blacks, particularly in the South, for the American Press Association, which in 1914 began to syndicate his columns. He also worked closely with Washington's personal secretary, Emmett J. Scott. Tyler's work in the South stimulated him to study black migration to the North and to write and publish his findings in journals and newspapers. Tyler's interest in politics continued, and some sources called him a shrewd politician. In February 1916 he petitioned to run as delegate–at–large to the Republican National Convention in Ohio. He garnered good support, with more than 30,000 votes, but was unsuccessful in his bid.

Named War Correspondent

Tyler returned to Washington, D.C., as secretary of the National Colored Soldiers Comfort Committee near the time the United States declared war on Germany in April 1917. He was present when Emmett J. Scott, special assistant to the secretary of war, called together black newspaper editors in June 1918 to discuss the role of black journalists in the war. They agreed that an experienced black journalist should be sent to France to report on activities and conditions of black soldiers then serving in World War I. Moreover, they agreed that the black press of America needed first–hand and accurate information on the precise conditions under which blacks worked and fought in France during wartime.

The Committee on Public Information announced on September 16, 1918, the appointment of Tyler as a regularly commissioned war correspondent, making him the first and only black official war correspondent. He was to serve under General John J. Pershing, commander–in–chief of the American Expeditionary Forces overseas. Tyler brought with him a wealth of experience and wide contacts with white correspondents already serving at the front. As well, his three sons were serving at the front in France. The Committee on Public Information was to receive Tyler's reports, then forward them to Scott for editing and distribution to the national black press. The war ended less than three months after Tyler's appointment.

During the last months of the war and for a period after the armistice was signed, Tyler wrote valuable and interesting first–hand accounts of black soldiers in France. According to *Scott'sOfficial History of the American Negro in the World War,* Tyler reported on the final fighting, written one day before the armistice took effect:

> The colored troops who took part in the last battle of this war acquitted themselves splendidly, fought valiantly, and with such precision and order as to earn for them high praise. . . . The "Buffaloes" suffered not a single casualty—not one wounded or killed. . . . The 366th, 265th, 351st Machine Gun, and 167th Field Artillery, all colored, engaged in this final battle of the war.
>
> After the signing, the black soldiers, just out of the trenches, began cheering and singing songs and

hymns such as ''Swing Low, Sweet Chariot'' and ''Hail, Hail, the Gang's All Here.''

After the war, Tyler returned to Ohio and for the remainder of 1919 lectured widely on the work of black soldiers in the war. He became editor of the *Cleveland Advocate* in April 1919, associate editor of the *Columbus Ohio State Monitor,* and wrote for newspapers in Chicago and New York as well. Around the same time he sued a restaurant in Springfield, Ohio, that denied him service because of his race, and won $100 in damages.

Tyler died of apoplexy at his home in Columbus, Ohio, on June 2, 1921, at the age of 62. His funeral was held at his home on June 4, followed by burial at Greenlawn Cemetery. His widow, three sons, two brothers, and two sisters survived him. Tyler's death attracted national attention and tributes from many who knew his work and recognized his talent. According to the *Negro Digest,* James Faulkner wrote in the *Cincinnati Enquirer* that Tyler was a remarkable man with unusual talents, and that men of all races were affected by his loss. Faulker said, ''always he preferred reasonableness to force and in the end he accomplished more by his quiet persistency than . . . with noise and threats.'' The *San Antonio Sentinel,* also quoted in the *Negro Digest,* recognized Tyler as ''a real man of letters and cultured gentleman'' who ''wielded a trenchant pen.''

Tyler successfully climbed the ranks in journalism, from janitor in a newspaper office to society writer, war correspondent, and editor. He is best known for his assignment as journalist during World War I, when he reported on the activities of black soldiers in France.

REFERENCES

Harlan, Louis R., and Raymond W. Smock, eds. *The Booker T. Washington Papers.* Vol. 6, 1901–02. Urbana: University of Illinois Press, 1977.

Logan, Rayford W., and Michael R. Winston, eds. *Dictionary of American Negro Biography.* New York: Norton, 1982.

Scott, Emmett J. *Scott's Official History of the American Negro in the World War.* Chicago: Homewood Press, 1919.

Wilson, Brad. ''The Mop Boy Who Became Society Editor.'' *Negro Digest* 7 (June 1949): 3–6.

COLLECTIONS

The George A. Myers Papers at the Ohio Historical Society, Columbus, contains correspondence between Ralph Tyler and Myers. Letters, reports, and statements from Tyler relating to the U.S. Auditor's Office are in the General Records of the Department of the Treasurer, Record Group 56, National Archives, Washington, D.C.

Jessie Carney Smith

Edward Ellsworth Underwood
(1864–1942)
Physician, minister, editor, civil rights leader, politician

Edward Ellsworth Underwood

Edward Ellsworth Underwood, a Frankfort, Kentucky, physician, was highly respected throughout the state because of his zealous involvement with the NAACP and the Anti–Separate Coach Movement, which worked to abolish Kentucky's segregated railroad policy. Underwood was born June 7, 1864, in Mt. Pleasant, Ohio, to Johnson P. Underwood, a well known and distinguished minister in the African Methodist Episcopal (AME) Church in Ohio, and Harriet Clanton Underwood. Edward Underwood was educated by a highly regarded professor, J. L. Champ, in the segregated elementary public schools in Mt. Pleasant, Ohio. After completing this program of study, Underwood's family was able to enroll him in the white high school, from which he graduated in three years finishing third in his class, in 1881.

Underwood taught in the Emerson Colored School, in Ohio, from 1881 to 1888. While teaching, Underwood became licensed to preach in the African Methodist Episcopal church at the young age of 19. Because of his eloquent delivery, the "boy preacher" acquired a reputation as an orator and became highly desired by churches. Underwood had always been devoted to his faith and worked endless hours in the church. He served as the superintendent of the St. John's Sunday School in Cleveland for three years and served as secretary of the Ohio Sunday School Institute.

In 1891 Underwood completed his medical degree at Western Reserve University in Cleveland, Ohio. He moved to Frankfort, Kentucky, where he began practicing medicine on March 4, 1891. He sustained a lucrative medical practice in Frankfort from 1891 until his death in 1942. For four years, 1897–1900, Underwood served as Frankfort's assistant city physician, the only black appointed to the position. Other professional involvements included his position as the president of the State Medical Society of Kentucky and his memberships in the National Medical Association and the Kentucky Medical Association. Underwood was also secretary of the U.S. Board of Pension Examining Surgeons. In 1911 he established the People's Pharmacy and was selected as the school physician for the students at Kentucky State College.

Underwood was active in many community organizations and worked to improve conditions for people of his race. He was one of the leaders of the Anti–Separate Coach Movement, which fought Jim Crow laws in Kentucky in the 1890s. He also served as the executive secretary of the State Executive Committee for this movement. In 1898 Governor William Bradley appointed Underwood to the Board of Trustees of Kentucky State Normal School, now Kentucky State University. In April of 1919, Underwood was one of the founders of the Frankfort NAACP branch and was elected as its first president. He was chairman of the Frankfort Inter–Racial Commission and the State Committee of the Inter–Racial Commission, and an active member of the Frankfort Negro Business League. He also served as the president of the Franklin County (Frankfort, Kentucky) Colored School of Agriculture and Industrial Association. Within the church, Underwood served on the Board of Stewards of the St. John AME Church. He was a lay member of the Annual Conference and a lay delegate to the General Conference of the AME Church in 1920 and 1924 in Kentucky.

Throughout his life Underwood worked on the editorial staff of various newspapers. Beginning in Cleveland, Underwood was employed with the *Cleveland Gazette* for several years. He also wrote editorials for the *Pioneer Press,* and *The Old Fellows Signal* in West Virginia. In 1891, in Frankfort, while practicing medicine, he began editing another black newspaper, the *Blue Grass Bugle,* which he served for ten years. Additionally, he worked as educational editor of the *Lexington News.* In 1906 he wrote the *History of the Colored Churches of Frankfort,* which contained photos and descriptions of church programs, building histories, and lists of members of the four black churches.

Like many prominent blacks of his period, Underwood belonged to various fraternal organizations and secret societies including the Knights of Pythias, the Free Masons, the Grand United Order of Odd Fellows, and the United Brothers of Friendship. Underwood's association with the Knights of Pythias began in 1913. Within the Pythian organization, he was president of the board of directors of the Pythian Mutual Independent Association of Kentucky, was a member of the W.B.F. National Pythian Temple and Sanitarium Committee and was the Supreme Keeper of Records and Seal.

Politically active in the Republican Party, while in Mt. Pleasant, Ohio, Underwood was elected without opposition to the Jefferson County Republican Central Committee in 1887. In 1888 Underwood defeated four white opponents to be elected to the Mt. Pleasant City Council. In Kentucky, Underwood was organizer and president of the State League of Colored Republican clubs and a member of both the Republican City and County Committees of Frankfort and Franklin County. Kentucky Governor Bradley appointed Underwood in 1895 as a member of the Kentucky Commissioners of the Cotton States and International Exposition in Atlanta and to represent the state at the Tennessee Centennial in Nashville in 1897.

On July 3, 1895, Edward E. Underwood married Sara J. Walker, who was a teacher in the Frankfort public school system at the time of their marriage. They had two children, Ellsworth Walker and Robert McPherson. Edward Ellsworth Underwood was a leader for the African American people of Kentucky. He rose to the challenges of a segregated society and helped to improve conditions and provide new opportunities for his people.

REFERENCES

Dunnigan, Alice A. *The Fascinating Story of Black Kentuckians: Their Heritage and Tradition.* Washington, DC: Associated Publishers, 1982.

Johnson, W. D. *Biographical Sketches of Prominent Negro Men and Women of Kentucky.* Lexington: Standard Print, 1897.

Mather, Frank Lincoln, ed. *Who's Who of the Colored Race.* Chicago: Mather, 1915.

Smith, S. E., ed. *History of the Anti–Separate Coach Movement of Kentucky.* Evansville, IN: National Afro–American Journal and Directory Publishing Co., c.1895.

Who's Who in Colored America. 4th ed. Brooklyn, NY: Thomas Yenser, 1937.

Wright, George C. *A History of Blacks in Kentucky.* Vol. 2. Frankfort, KY: Kentucky Historical Society, 1992.

Karen Cotton McDaniel

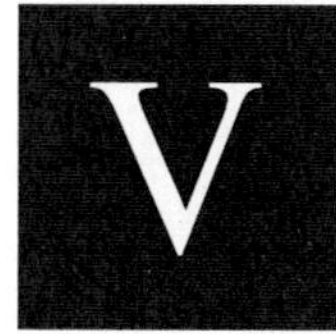

James Van DerZee

(1886–1983)

Photographer

James Van DerZee did not start out to become a well–known ''picture–takin' man.'' Although trained initially on the piano and the violin, photography came to fascinate him, from the time he won an unsophisticated camera in a selling contest until he grew to become an important chronicler of contemporary African American life and culture. While he did not receive public acclaim until he was 82 years old, his legacy includes some 125,000 pictures, negatives, and glass plates that document how a sizeable number of urban black people—men, women and children—lived in America's twentieth century.

Born in Lenox, Massachusetts, on June 29, 1886, James Augustus Joseph Van DerZee was the second of six children of John and Elizabeth Van DerZee, who had formerly been butler and maid for General Ulysses S. Grant. He was raised in a comfortable, close–knit family where art and music were considered as important as the ''three R's.'' Van DerZee wed three times. His first marriage, to Kate Brown in 1907, ended in divorce. He fathered two children by her—a son, Emil, who died at age one, and a daughter, Gladys, who died at age 15. His second wife, Gaynella Greenlee, whom he married in 1920, died in 1976. Shortly after her death, he met Donna Mussenden, whom he married on June 15, 1978. Van DerZee died May 15, 1983, at age 97, in Howard University Hospital, Washington, D.C. The university had awarded him an honorary doctoral degree the day before.

Mainly a self–taught photographer, Van DerZee as a young teenager began taking pictures with the simple camera he had won in 1900. Later, after buying a better camera, he took many photographs of his family and friends, experimenting with lighting, composition, and background. These, together with pictures of his high school friends, form a large part of his earliest work.

In 1906 Van DerZee moved to New York City, intending to become a musician. Reared as an Episcopalian, he joined St. Mark's Methodist church because he knew some of the members there. In 1915 he converted to Catholicism. Shortly after his 1907 marriage to Kate Brown, the couple moved to Phoebus, Virginia, to be near her relatives. Working at the nearby Chamberlain Hotel, he took pictures on the side for the Whittier School, a prep school for Hampton Institute, Hampton, Virginia. Whittier students and teachers greatly appreciated his photographs and music, but after less than a year in Phoebus, the Van DerZees returned to New York. In New York, Van DerZee gave private lessons in violin and piano. First violinist in the John Wanamaker Orchestra, he formed the Harlem Orchestra and played in various musical groups, including Fletcher Henderson's band.

James Van DerZee

Van DerZee's first full–time job in photography came in 1915 as a darkroom assistant earning five dollars a week at the Gertz Department Store in Newark, New Jersey. When his boss was away on holiday, he became the photographer. Popular with the customers because he took time to pose them, the job gave him technical experience which he put to good use when he opened his first studio, Guarantee Photos, at 109 West 135th Street, the hub of the growing Harlem community at the time. Later, he opened other studios at 2065 and 2077 Seventh Avenue and finally settled at his GGG Studio, 272 Lenox Avenue, named for his second wife. In these studios, he took thousands of photographs of everyday life in Harlem, the cultural capital of African Americans in the 1920s and 1930s.

Equal Attention to All

Van DerZee photographed entertainment celebrities, including Bill ''Bojangles'' Robinson, Mamie Smith, Florence Mills, Countee Cullen, the Mills Brothers, and Hazel Scott. Athlete subjects were Jack Johnson, Harry Wills, ''Kid'' Chocolate, Sam Langford, and Joe Louis. Ministers included Adam Clayton Powell Sr., Adam Clayton Powell Jr., Father Divine, and Daddy Grace. Business leaders such as Madam C. J. Walker and Madam Sarah (Sara) Spencer Washington of the Apex School of Beauty Culture also had their portraits taken by him. He became the official photographer for Marcus Garvey's Back–to–Africa movement, the United Negro Improvement Association. Whether the subjects were famous or just average people, Van DerZee gave each the same careful attention. With business flourishing, he photographed soldiers, family gatherings, weddings, communions, graduations, holidays, children, parades, conventions, and rallies.

In the 1930s, calendar companies needing pictures of African American subjects turned to him. Through calendars of his own, he also promoted his business. Some of his funeral pictures, a genre prominent in Harlem in the 1920s and 30s, were published in 1978 in *The Harlem Book of the Dead.*

A considerable drop–off in business, due primarily to the popularity of inexpensive cameras and the opening of competing studios, caused him to stop taking pictures professionally in the 1960s. While walking in Harlem, Reginald McGhee, director of photographic research for the 1968 ''Harlem On My Mind'' exhibition at the Metropolitan Museum of Art, happened upon the GGG Studio. There he discovered Van DerZee and his treasure trove of photographs. Van DerZee contributed more photographs to the Metropolitan Museum of Art's ''Harlem On My Mind'' exhibit than anyone else.

Though Van DerZee gained celebrity status from the Met's exhibit, his economic downward turn in the 1970s caused him to lose his home and the GGG Studio. He and his wife Gaynella moved to a small apartment on West 94th Street. Meanwhile, McGhee convinced Van DerZee to turn over his thousands of negatives, prints and glass plates to the James Van DerZee Institute established in 1970 at 103 East 125th Street. In 1976, the Institute moved to the Metropolitan Museum of Art, with McGhee as its director.

Resumes Photography

With the help of his third wife, Donna Mussenden, Van DerZee reopened his studio in 1980 and resumed taking photographs after a lapse of 25 years. His major subjects at the time—Bill Cosby, Muhammad Ali, Miles Davis, Eubie Blake, Lou Rawls, and Romare Bearden—considered it an honor to sit for a Van DerZee portrait. By 1981 the James Van DerZee Institute and the bulk of the photographer's collection were housed at The Studio Museum in Harlem. Currently, The Studio Museum at 144 West 125th Street houses the largest public holding of Van DerZee's work, while his widow, Donna, maintains the largest privately held collection.

Van DerZee's photographs have been exhibited in many galleries and museums throughout the nation, including the Studio Museum in Harlem and the National Portrait Gallery in Washington, D.C. In 1978 President Carter gave him a Living Legacy Award in recognition of his contribution to the documentation of African American life. That same year, he received the Pierre Toussaint Award from Cardinal Cook at St. Patrick's Cathedral, New York. Besides the honorary degree awarded him by Howard University, he received the same honors from Seton Hall University in 1976 and Haverford College in 1980. He received honors from the American Society of Magazine Photographers and the International Black Photographers. The Metropolitan Museum of Art made him a Fellow for Life.

Reginald McGhee wrote in the introduction of his book *The World of James Van DerZee* that he ''was a photojournalist long before the word came into existence.'' Said McGhee, ''I have studied the works of photographers whom I consider to be masters . . . and in my opinion the name of James Van DerZee should be added to [that] distinguished list.''

REFERENCES

Contemporary Black Biography. Vol. 6. Detroit: Gale Research, 1994.

Haskins, Jim. *James Van DerZee: The Picture–Takin' Man.* New York: Dodd, Mead, 1979.

McGhee, Reginald. *The World of James Van DerZee: A Visual Record of Black Americans.* New York: Grove, 1969.

''Noted Harlem Photographer Is Dead.'' *New York Times,* May 16, 1983.

Van DerZee, James, Owen Dodson, and others. *The Harlem Book of the Dead.* Dobbs Ferry, NY: Morgan and Morgan, 1978.

Who's Who among Black Americans, 1980–81. 3rd ed. Northbrook, IL: Who's Who Among Black Americans, 1981.

Who's Who in America, 1980–81. 41st ed. Chicago: Marquis, 1980.

Willis–Thomas, Deborah, ed. *Black Photographers, 1840–1940: An Illustrated Bio–Bibliography.* New York: Garland, 1985.

COLLECTIONS

Van DerZee's works are located at the Luna Gallery, Washington, D.C.; Metropolitan Museum of Modern Art, New York; Schomburg Center for Research in Black Culture, New York, New York; and Studio Museum in Harlem, New York. Van DerZee's wife also has a personal collection.

Vivian D. Hewitt

Robert L. Vann
(1887–1940)
Journalist, lawyer, politician, civil rights activist, editor

A leader in twentieth–century black journalism and editor of the *Pittsburgh Courier,* Robert Vann made that newspaper an advocate of social change for blacks and built it into the nation's leading weekly black newspaper at the time. Although he was active in the legal and political life of Pittsburgh, it was through journalism that he made his most significant contribution.

The story of Robert Lee Vann is recounted in detail by his biographer, Andrew Buni, in *Robert L. Vann of the Pittsburgh Courier.* While Vann's papers and those of his wife who succeeded him in the newspaper business might facilitate other interpretations of his life, the papers were destroyed after her death on June 9, 1967. Vann was a man of sleek black hair, light, coppery skin, and a strong straight nose, who stood five–feet eight–inches tall. He was born on August 27, 1879, in the small, rural town of Ahoskie, North Carolina, in the predominantly–black community of Hertford County. Vann's mother, Lucy Peoples, was the daughter of Fletcher Peoples and Martilla Holloman, former slaves who remained in the area after the Civil War and ran a general store in Ahoskie. As a teenager, Lucy Peoples was a local domestic. She named her son "Robert Lee" in honor of his great–grandfather and gave him the surname of the Albert Vann family, her first employer. She retained her maiden name.

Robert Vann may have been born out of wedlock. His father may have been Joseph Hall, a local black field hand who lived with Lucy Peoples on "Old Dr. Mitchell's Farm" when Vann was a young child. It is possible also that Vann's father was white. After Hall deserted the family, Lucy Peoples and her young son, then six years old, relocated to the John O. Askew farm in nearly Harrellsville. There they lived in a kitchen cabin separated from the main house and slept on beds near the stove.

Vann found life on the Askew farm comfortable and pleasant, due to John Askew's acceptance of him and Vann's freedom to share toys and horses with the Askew children. As well, life among whites in the area provided an atmosphere of relaxed race relations. Vann's mother provided him discipline and religion, and when he was 13–years old saw that he was baptized in the Wiccacon River, the place of baptism for the New Ahoskie Baptist Church. Mary Askew, her employer's wife, helped mold Vann's character and shaped his early education.

Vann enrolled in the Springfield Colored School, a crowded, one–room building, where the sessions ran from December to March, perhaps to allow time for the black children to work in the farm fields. By age 12, he graduated from the school and at the 1892 commencement exercises recited the first of many poems he would write in his lifetime.

Robert L. Vann

When his mother married John Simon, a local dirt farmer, and moved to Simon's shack in the Red Hill area, Vann's world was shattered as this new life offered little in comparison to the tranquility he had known with the Askews. His plans to move on to secondary school that fall were given way that year to work at the Red Hill farm, or to work as a hired hand on nearby farms. In the fall Vann entered Waters Training School in Winton, a private, Baptist–run institution, where he studied intermittently due to lack of money. He moved to the campus where he remained until graduation in 1901 as class valedictorian. To strengthen his academic preparation, in fall 1901 he entered Wayland Academy in Richmond, the preparatory school for Virginia Union University, receiving his diploma sometime in 1902.

Vann enrolled in the college program at Virginia Union but was more a practical joker and frivolous student than a serious one. He continued to write poetry, however, and published it in the *University Journal.* At Union Vann developed friendships with two students who, like himself, became prominent later in life: J. Max Barber, later editor of *The Voice of the Negro* and opponent of Booker T. Washington, and Eugene Kinckle Jones, a radical and executive secretary of the National Urban League. On the ideological spectrum, Vann was in tune with Jones, not Barber. While in Richmond Vann mingled with the city's black elite and learned the social graces.

Vann left Virginia Union at the end of the term in 1903. His reasons for leaving are uncertain; however, he may have been disturbed over the deteriorating racial conditions in the South. Certainly he was influenced by Booker T. Washington's autobiography, *Up From Slavery,* which helped strengthen his ideas on racial pride and economic self–help. He moved to Pittsburgh and enrolled in Western University of Pennsylvania, entering as a sophomore on an Avery Scholarship. Aware of the difficulties Vann might face as a black, the school's registrar tried to persuade him to register as an Indian student, but he refused. He also was introduced to the black genteel and was quickly accepted.

For two years Vann contributed regularly to *The Courant, A Journal of the Student Body of Western University of Pennsylvania,* and in his senior year was elected editor–in–chief—the first black to hold the position. While he registered to vote when he arrived in Pittsburgh three years earlier and voted regularly, in 1906 Vann became active in Republican politics, attended party meetings and rallies, and worked hard for the party's unsuccessful mayoral candidate, William Magee. Some years passed before Vann considered a place for himself on the Republican machine. Since Vann had continued to write poetry, he was asked to write the class poem that he recited at his 1906 graduation.

Vann's interest in journalism had been spurred earlier by experiences at the *Richmond Planet,* strengthened by his work with *The Courant,* and stimulated by his Virginia Union friend Max Barber. Without financial support, however, he was unable to attend the Pulitzer School of Journalism in New York as he wanted. Instead, Vann entered Western's School of Law, financing his studies by working as a dining car porter. He completed his law degree in June of 1909, and on December 18 of that year, passed the bar. He opened a small office at 433 Fifth Avenue in a predominantly white business neighborhood. On February 17, 1910, he married Jesse Ellen Matthews, whom he met on Pittsburgh's South Side while in his senior year of law school. She was the daughter of Civil War veteran William H. Matthews and Mary Jane Matthews.

Vann became one of Pittsburgh's five black attorneys. Although he chose to specialize in criminal law on the belief that the black community needed such expertise, his practice was unrewarding. Instead, he worked on legal problems such as property claims, wills, and cases that paid small fees. To supplement his income, he turned to the newspaper business and politics.

Birth of the *Pittsburgh Courier*

In March of 1910 Robert Vann was asked to provide legal advice for the *Pittsburgh Courier,* which Edwin Nathaniel Harleston had founded and first published on January 10 that year. As well, Vann contributed articles and poems to the weekly issues that were published. The paper was incorporated on May 10, 1910, when Vann officially became legal counsel and received ten shares of stock in lieu of a fee. Although the black community needed a newspaper of its own, the *Courier* struggled to stay alive. After Harleston resigned in the fall of 1910 because he had no equity in the paper, Vann accepted editorship. He had already edited his school's newspaper while a student at Western University of Pennsylvania and contributed regularly to the *Courier* since it was first published. Although the pay was low, the position enhanced his law practice by making his name widely known in the community.

The newspaper continued to struggle until 1914, when the staff moved to larger quarters and hired Ira F. Lewis, a North Carolina native whom Vann met two years earlier. He was to write sports news, but became successful immediately selling advertisements. The circulation nearly doubled within a year. Later Lewis became business manger, a position he held until Vann died.

Vann used the *Courier* to crusade for improvement in all facets of black life—housing, health, education, employment crime, politics, and other areas. He called for blacks to form their own financial institutions; he called for more black physicians; he pleaded for the establishment of a black hospital to serve the community. As well, Vann used the paper to combat distortions of blacks in the white press and, in general, to provide to the black community local news on blacks that the mainstream press ignored. The paper also published news from their home states to the new black immigrants from the South.

Enters Politics

By 1917 Vann and other blacks had gained some political strength and candidates for public office could not ignore them. Vann defected from the political machine in favor of E. V. Babcock and was responsible for persuading large numbers of voters to elect him mayor. His reward was his appointment as assistant city solicitor on March 1918.

Both the *Courier* and Vann backed the country's entry into World War I and hoped that one result of the war would be improvements in life for the nation's blacks. Since he was too old for the war, Vann did what he could on the home front by working in Liberty Loan drives, YMCA rallies, and Red Cross campaigns. Emmett J. Scott, special assistant to the Secretary of War, Newton Baker, appointed him to the "Committee of One Hundred." The committee of black spokesmen reported on conditions blacks faced in the armed services and in the nation. Vann worked with the committee to formed a black National Publicity Bureau that publicized wartime achievements of blacks. Vann also was successful in the appointment of Ralph Tyler as the first black war correspondent on the front line to report on the deeds of blacks.

Vann had a temperate attitude toward the Houston riot of August 23, 1917, involving soldiers of the Twenty–fourth Infantry and the white police. He wrote in defense of the hanging of the alleged black perpetrators yet condemned the mistreatment of black soldiers who were abused in southern towns. He reacted moderately to the Chicago race riot of July 17, 1919, set off when a black youth was stoned on Lake Michigan, saying that riots cause economic loss and that race riots were futile and damaged the whole society.

In January of 1920 Vann began an adventurous journalistic project when he published *The Competitor: The National Magazine.* With Vann as editor, Ira F. Lewis as secretary, and Elliot C. Alexander as president, the journal sought nationwide readership. Authors represented in the work were James Weldon Johnson of the NAACP; R. R. Moton, president of Tuskegee Institute; Emmett J. Scott, secretary–treasurer of Howard University; Archibald Grimké, former minister to Santo Domingo; and Eugene Kinckle Jones, Vann's schoolmate from Virginia Union. Although Vann worked desperately to save the journal, it ceased publication after 18 months of debt. The *Courier* joined the Associated Negro Press in November 1925 and used the services of Washington–based Louis Lautier, who also supplied coverage to the *Baltimore Afro–American* and the *Chicago Defender.*

After two unsuccessful attempts to be elected judge of the Court of Common Pleas of Allegheny County, Vann turned more attention to the *Courier,* improving it tremendously by hiring capable news staff and strengthening its appeal. In 1925 he hired George Schuyler to write "Views and Reviews" for the editorial page. In 1925 Vann sent him to tour the South for nine months and write a series of on–the–road observations. When the tour ended in 1926, Schuyler's articles and his circulation drives resulted in an increase in readership of at least 10,000. In 1927 historian and writer Joel A. Rogers began to write special feature articles based on his observations; Walter White wrote "The Spotlight," or weekly book reviews, news articles, and theatricals; and W. Rollo Wilson, formerly with the *Pittsburgh American,* began a popular feature sports section called "Sports Shots."

Vann hurled editorial daggers toward James Weldon Johnson and W. E. B. Du Bois for reasons that are unclear, perhaps using the attack to enhance the circulation of his paper. He made a number of charges against Johnson and the NAACP; for example, he claimed that Johnson used monies from the Garland Fund to support his pet projects rather than those that would benefit the entire race and accused Johnson of literary insensibilities. He also claimed that Du Bois, an NAACP officer, used $5,000 to fund a questionable study of education in South Carolina. The Johnson–Vann feud ended only after Johnson's death in 1938; even then, Vann refused to attend his funeral. Vann and Du Bois apparently settled their dispute, and by the mid 1930s Du Bois was a regular contributor to the *Courier.*

After A. Philip Randolph organized the Brotherhood of Sleeping Car Porters to force the Pullman Company to treat black porters fairly, the *Courier* became the union's strongest supporter. By 1928, however, Vann and Randolph were at great odds. On April 14 Vann called for Randolph's resignation. Randolph refused, and the *Courier* became a critic of the Brotherhood rather than a supporter. According to Andrew Buni, Vann's biographer, the real cause of the dispute was that Vann wanted control of the Brotherhood for himself.

Vann continued his political activities, but he became disenchanted with the Republican Party and by 1932 he had become a Democrat. His support of Franklin D. Roosevelt in the 1932 elections led to his appointment to the U.S. Department of Justice as special assistant to the Attorney General. He held the position from 1933 to January of 1936, when his resignation became effective. Though Vann remained Roosevelt's supporter, he had become frustrated and disappointed with his assignment and felt that the appointment was made to silence him.

Following his stint in Washington, the *Courier* enjoyed unprecedented circulation. Vann built a momentum for the paper that continued after his death. From the new, modern printing plant that he built in 1929, the paper was in position to grow. Its size increased from 16 to 20 pages and by 1930 the paper was published in four editions—local, northern, eastern, and southern. Between 1930 and 1935 Vann found new topics of great interest to spark circulation. Since his paper fought to build self–respect and racial pride, it attacked the popular "Amos and Andy" radio show that started in 1929. Beginning February 15, 1930, Marcus Garvey wrote short–lived weekly articles on the Universal Negro Improvement Association but used the article mainly to defend his own actions. The paper also publicized the famous Scottsboro case of the early 1930s, which involved several black youth in Alabama who were accused of raping a white woman. Vann supported the NAACP in its efforts to defend the youth. The paper's feature stories also included those from W. E. B. Du Bois, who had left the NAACP's *Crisis* magazine.

Vann covered the 1936 Olympics in Berlin and reported on the great black athletes Ralph Metcalfe, Cornelius Johnson, and Jesse Owens, who won a total of eight medals. Owens won four to become the outstanding Olympic performer. By the next year Vann was enjoying a good life and a good income from his law practice as well. The *Courier* continued to flourish. He became vice–president of the all–white Associated Weekly Publishers of Allegheny County and was named its general counsel.

In February of 1938 Vann and the *Courier* launched an intense campaign for better treatment of blacks in the armed services and published an open letter to President Roosevelt about the crusade. Believing that total integration of the services would not occur, Vann called for an all–black army division. He asked Percival Prattis, the *Courier*'s city editor, to survey congressmen, newspaper editors, and educational and religious leaders to obtain their opinions and published their responses in his paper. The NAACP joined the fight against racial inequality in the armed services, but called for total and immediate integration; however, Charles Hamilton Houston, the NAACP's special counsel, sided with Vann. The National Bar Association worked to end exclusion of blacks in the National Guard. Other groups launched similar fights.

On May 6, 1939, Vann founded his own company, the Interstate United Newspaper Company, which aimed to help black newspapers obtain national advertising. His goal was to take business from similar firms run by whites and to start a self–help economic enterprise for blacks.

Although Vann had wanted to join the Pittsburgh Chamber of Commerce for some time, it was not until 1939 that he was invited to membership. The Pittsburgh organization had been regarded as a the most powerful and influential of all chambers. While Vann had become its first black member, his failing health prevented him from active work in the organization.

Vann became seriously ill with abdominal cancer in early 1940. Surgery arrested his condition, yet Vann was not optimistic about his future and gave some consideration to writing his memoirs. He used the little energy he had left to support Wendell Willkie's bid for the presidency of the United States. He did not live to see the election results. He entered Pittsburgh's Shadyside Hospital on October 14, 1940, where he died on October 24. That same day Roosevelt announced the nomination of Colonel Benjamin O. Davis for promotion to brigadier general, the first black so honored.

The press eulogized Vann as one who rose from obscurity, conferred with presidents, and became an internationally–known publisher and editor. The *Courier* carried a ''Memorial Supplement'' for a full week, publishing letters and condolences that were received. Vann was buried at the end of October in a mausoleum that he had designed in Homewood Cemetery. He was surrounded by stained glass windows depicting three phases of his life: The Book of Knowledge, representing education; the Scales of Justice, representing his legal career; and the Gutenberg press, for his newspaper career. A bronze plaque in his honor was placed at the entrance of the Pittsburgh Courier Publishing Company.

To honor Vann and his contributions, a school in Ahoskie, North Carolina, and one in the Hill District of Pittsburgh were named for him. Vann left funds to establish scholarships at Virginia Union University and the University of Pittsburgh. As well, Virginia Union erected the Robert L. Vann Memorial Tower to honor the fallen giant. In recognition of his fight to integrate the armed services, on October 10, 1943, the Liberty Ship *Robert L. Vann* was launched.

The life of Robert L. Vann was rich and rewarding, not only for himself but for the thousands of readers of the *Pittsburgh Courier.* Through his leadership, the paper reached wide acclaim and brought news to the black community where it had been lacking. He was as much a crusader for racial justice as he was an advocate for enlightening the entire community through the press.

REFERENCES

Buni, Andrew. *Robert L. Vann of the Pittsburgh Courier.* Pittsburgh: University of Pittsburgh Press, 1974.

Jessie Carney Smith

Melvin Van Peebles
(1932–)
Novelist, playwright, screenwriter, director, actor, composer, stock market trader

Melvin Van Peebles breaks barriers and stereotypes with his books, films, and music, creating works with a radical, political, or, as he was quoted in *Variety,* ''sociological edge,'' raising awareness of racial prejudice and societal problems among all groups. He began his first career in the U.S. Air Force as a navigator–bombardier, continued in civilian life as a portrait painter, a cable car driver in San Francisco who made three films and a pictorial book, a journalist in Paris who wrote books and screenplays in self–taught French, an author of novels and screenplays, a producer and director of film and stage plays, and an actor. Above all, he may be looked at as a renaissance man and contemporary jack–of–all–trades who is never at a loss when faced with the need to take another direction. His film *Sweetback* earned him recognition as the ''godfather of independent black film.'' He was also called ''the grandfather of rap,'' for his musical compositions with talk–singing.

Edwin Griffin and Marion Van Peebles were married in Longview, Texas. Their son Melvin Van Peebles was born on August 21, 1932, in Chicago. Marion Van Peebles was a hard worker from Georgia who taught himself to read. Becoming a small businessman in Chicago, he was able to send son Melvin away to college after he graduated from Thornton Township High School in 1949. Van Peebles graduated with a degree in literature from Ohio Wesleyan University in Delaware, Ohio. A partial scholarship with ROTC led, 13 days after graduation, to three and a half years as an officer in the Air Force. The young lieutenant returned to civilian life, discovering his expertise as radar operator, bombardier, and navigator on a jet bomber useless in gaining work with civilian airlines who still refused to hire minorities.

Van Peebles met his wife Maria Marx in California. They moved to Mexico where their first son, Mario, was born. The family grew to include a daughter, Megan, before the Van Peebles moved to Amsterdam. Later, Van Peebles moved to Paris to work on films. His second son, Melvin, was born there.

Growing tired after a few months of the confinement of painting portraits for a living, the family returned from Mexico to settle in San Francisco where Van Peebles found a new challenge while driving cable cars. Heeding the inquiries of patrons eager to learn more about the cable cars he wrote *The Big Heart,* a sentimental pictorial book on cable cars, in 1957. Ruth Bernard took the photos. In 1957 Van Peebles also decided to expand in another direction, films. His first feature movie turned into three 11–minute shorts, a borrow–the–camera, listen–to–the–friend, learn–on–the–way project. Hollywood rejected the films, while Van Peebles rejected its offer of an elevator operator or dancing job.

Melvin Van Peebles

Having been a celestial navigator and having studied radar, physics, and astronomy in the service, Van Peebles decided to expand those interests by working toward a Ph.D. in astronomy in Amsterdam. There, he studied with the Dutch National Theatre and toured as an actor in Brendan Behan's play *The Hostage.* A letter from Henri Langlois, an associate of Cinémathèque, telling him he should be making films and inviting him to Paris, interrupted his new life. He accepted the invitation and the red carpet treatment but was not offered a job, so once again he taught himself a new language to continue his writing in French as well as English.

Making a Living in France

Not knowing French nor having friends in Paris, Van Peebles initially did whatever he could to earn a living. His inquisitiveness gained him work as a crime reporter, and finally he became editor of *Fara Kiri,* France's version of *Mad* magazine. Having learned that a French writer could have a film director's card, he wrote five novels in French. His first book, *Un Ours pour le F.B.I.* (1964), *A Bear for the F.B.I.* (translated in 1968), tells of racial problems in the life of a middle–class American black. Seeking American writers, an American literary agent found Van Peebles and asked him to write a black book with rage. In response, he wrote *Un Américan en Enfer* (1965), about George Abraham Carver, a black prisoner accidentally killed by falling rocks. In hell, Carver and other blacks are treated well, causing greater hell to the white residents there. The agent wouldn't publish it; however, the book was finally published in the United States in 1976 as *The True American.* He wrote a collection of short stories, *Le Chinois du XIV* (1966) and two short novels, *La Fête à Harlem* (1967) and *La Permission* (1967). Qualified for a French director's card, Van Peebles received financial assistance from the French Ministry and a private citizen, allowing him to make his first feature film, *La Permission* (*The Story of a Three–Day Pass*), a bittersweet story of a black soldier's harassment from his army buddies for his affair with a French woman. This film eventually took him back to the United States.

Van Peebles brought *The Story of a Three–Day Pass* to the 1967 San Francisco Film Festival as the delegate of France. The film won Critic's Choice award for best film, finally opening the door in the United States for a black film director. Columbia hired Van Peebles to direct and write the score for *Watermelon Man* (1970), a humorous tale that laughs with, not at, people. The watermelon man, a bigoted white insurance agent used to racing a commuter bus each morning, wakes up black one day.

Creative Beyond Film

Brer Soul, Van Peebles's first album, uses minimalist music and monotone talk–singing to tell stories of black street life. On September 26, 1968, A&M released the album featuring metered musical monologues before DJ King Stitt, U Roy, the Last Poets, and Gil Scott–Heron came along to further develop what is referred to as rap. Timothy White quoted Van Peebles in *Billboard:*

> When I was growing up in the streets of Chicago, a brer was a bro, a homeboy. . . . The idea of doing a record employing the Brer Soul character arose back in 1967, when I returned to this country after living for several years in Holland and France. From abroad I knew the ferment of the civil rights movement, but I was struck when I got back here that almost none of the black popular or protest music mirrored the black experience *per se.*

The words are accompanied by funky jazz music. Again quoted in *Billboard,* Van Peebles said, "In each song, I wanted to describe a part of life rarely seen." This desire to reproduce less visible parts of life, ghetto or street life, characterizes Van Peebles focus in his creative efforts. He later directed and supervised the editing of *Funky Beat* (Arista Records), a music video by rap group Whodini, and composed the music and lyrics for *The Apple Stretching. Ghetto Gothic* (1995), his ninth album, portrays the mellowed Van Peebles.

Three Broadway plays show Van Peebles's creativity, ingenuity, and expertise. He wrote the books, music, and lyrics as well as produced and directed *Ain't Supposed to Die a Natural Death* (1971), which portrays street life including frank and controversial discussions of lesbians and prostitution and adapts the recordings from *Brer Soul.* The attendance of black celebrities increased attendance and the life of the play, performed 325 times. *Don't Play Us Cheap* (1972) is a comedy about Harlem life, which he adapted for film in 1973, using his own company, Yeah, Inc. Between them the plays gained 11 Tony nominations and a featured cover story in the

New York Times Magazine Section. In 1973 Van Peebles toured the United States with his one–man show *Out There by Your Lonesome.* Van Peebles third Broadway play, *Waltz of the Stork,* came out in 1982. He and son Mario both acted in the play. He also did off–Broadway plays *Champeen* (1979) and *Kickin' the Science* (1992).

Turning to television, Van Peebles wrote two scripts produced as television films for NBC. *Just an Old Sweet Song* came out in 1976. Van Peebles's teleplay *Sophisticated Gents,* filmed in 1979, came out in 1981. Nine boyhood friends, members of a black athletic team, reunite after 25 years to honor their old coach and discuss how their lives have been affected by their color. Another teleplay by Van Peebles, *The Day they Came to Arrest the Book,* is a 1987 Emmy award winner. Van Peebles has also written other teleplays for adult audiences.

Preferring the freedom from studio control and making his own choices of material and messages, Van Peebles found his own financing for his next film, *Sweet Sweetback's Baadasssss Song* (1971, Yeah, Inc.), which made Variety's list of all–time moneymakers. *Sweetback* paved the way for blaxploitation films with super stud–type heroes portraying action and violence against the establishment, allowing black urban audiences to fantasize about power and retribution. Van Peebles wrote the script and music, produced, directed, and starred in *Sweet Sweetback's Baadasssss Song,* which he made in three weeks with nonunion help. He passed out leaflets on street corners, promoting the film as "Rated X by an All–White Jury," and he dedicated it to "All the Brothers and Sisters who have had enough of The Man." Audiences advertised it by word of mouth, and their attendance placed the film on *Variety*'s list of moneymakers. Sweetback, a pimp in a brothel, chooses to avenge the beating of a youth by two white policemen. He turns revolutionary, stomps the policemen unconscious, and runs, eventually, to his freedom in Mexico, showing the audience a black who fought The Man and won. Eventually *Sweetback* took in $10 million, becoming one of the highest–grossing independent films of its day. Van Peebles recalled in *Jet,* "My film, *Sweet Sweetback,* was made mandatory viewing for the Panthers by Huey." He recalled Newton saying, "*Sweet Sweetback* blows my mind every time I talk about it because it's so simple and yet so profound."

Van Peebles worked on the American Stock Exchange for three years, learning enough in that time to pass the exam to become a stock trader. He was its only black trader. His experiences in option trading led to a series of weekly television commentaries in New York and to the writing of *Bold Money: A New Way to Play the Options Market* (1986), which explained trading in easy–to–understand language. *Bold Money: How to Get Rich in the Options Market* (1987) followed.

Father and Son Work Together

Mario Van Peebles made his screen debut in *Sweet Sweetback's Baadasssss Song.* Years later, he asked Van Peebles if they could make another film together, which Mario wrote. They worked together on *Identity Crisis.* The comedy film stars Mario and features a gay French couturier popping in and out of a black rapper's body. Van Peebles produced and directed the film in 1989. Then father and son are coauthors of the book *No Identity Crisis.* These "Block and Chip" productions offered the elder Van Peebles the opportunity to share his expertise with son Mario. Later they collaborated on *Panther,* portraying the earlier rage of *Sweetback* as they retell the political activities of the 1960s and early 1970s. In 1993 Van Peebles acted in the film *Posse,* an all–black Western written by Mario Van Peebles.

Van Peebles wrote, produced, acted in, and coedited *Panther* (1995), directed by son Mario. Like *Sweetback,* this film empowers the black community just as the community empowers its artists by going to performances. The film reviews the history of the Black Panther Party for Self–Defense, founded in 1966. Van Peebles has held benefit concerts on behalf of the party. Quoted by Karen G. Bates in *Essence,* Van Peebles pointed out that "Nothing has changed! The gravity then is parallel with the gravity of our situation now." Mario Van Peebles added:

> One of the biggest things Dad brought to this film was the whole parallel between the then and now of drugs and alcohol being brought into the Black community. These same communities that were insisting on power to the people have been flooded with alcohol and drugs; they've been medicated. And the gangs have inherited the bravado of what might have been Panther life—but without the ideology to understand what their actions are.

The time line of the movie ends around 1969 to 1970, allowing, according to Michael Robinson in *American Visions,* "a stirring affirmation of black masculinity, an image of what the Panthers could have, and maybe should have, been."

In 1986 Van Peebles acted in the television series *L.A. Law.* In 1987 he acted in *Jaws: The Revenge. In Calm at Sunset* (1997), a Hallmark television presentation, Van Peebles portrayed the character of the mature sage rather like he did in an earlier film, *Taking Care of Terrific* (1988). In the television miniseries remake of Stephen King's *The Shining* (1997), Van Peebles's strong supporting role is also one of a mature sage. In real life he continues as the mature sage in his relationships with his children and colleagues. Van Peebles is known for being outspoken, full of ideas, and playfully deceptive. He is usually pictured with a giant cigar, reflecting the appetite metaphor he often uses in his writing. Mario and Megan Van Peebles work in the entertainment world; Melvin Van Peebles works in the business world in New York City.

Van Peebles is a member of the Directors Guild of America and the French Directors Guild. He was awarded first prize from the Belgium Festival for *Don't Play Us Cheap.* Hofstra University awarded him an honorary doctorate in humane letters in December of 1994.

In a telephone interview with Claire Taft he told of his oft repeated saying, "The golden rule is that he who has the gold makes the rules.'' This has dictated Van Peebles's preference for financing his own work, allowing him to produce that which is most important, right, and necessary to him. He led the way for independent African American cinema. His attitude is reflected in his article on the Margaret Mead Film and Video Festival. He wrote:

> Our species is still alive and kicking. We are still the same ol' ragtag band of rascals and dreamers, still tussling with the environment to survive, searching for equilibrium, for place (whatever that means), and when our bellies are full enough, moving on to the next priority, still trying to make sense of life, trying to transform that survival into meaningful existence.

''Grandfather of rap'' and ''godfather of modern Black Cinema,'' Van Peebles continues to write, publish, direct, act, and do the unexpected, but people always find him open and accessible.

Current address: c/o Simon and Schuster, 1230 Avenue of the Americas, New York, NY 10020–1586.

REFERENCES

Bates, Karen Grigsby. ''Power to the Peebles.'' *Essence* 26 (June 1995): 58–59, 112–14.

Cohn, Lawrence. ''Van Peebles Returns to Filmmaking after Decade–Long Sabbatical.'' *Variety* 334 (8–14 February 1989): 11.

Cripps, Thomas. ''Sweet Sweetback's Baadasssss Song and the Changing Politics of Genre Film.'' In *Close Viewings: An Anthology of New Film Criticism.* Edited by Peter Lehman. Gainesville: University Press of Florida, 1990.

''Father–Son Duo Team Up to Make New Movie Panther.'' *Jet* 88 (22 May 1995): 32–35.

James, Darius. ''Black Pop's O.G.'' *Grand Street* 13 (Summer 1994): 150–60.

Newton, Edmund. ''Sweet Stock Picker.'' *Black Enterprise* 17 (October 1986): 84–88.

Robinson, Michael. ''The Van Peebleses Prowl Through the Panthers' History.'' *American Visions* 10 (April 1995): 16–18.

Salzman, Jack, David Lionel Smith, and Cornel West, eds. *Encyclopedia of African–American Culture and History.* New York: Macmillan Library Reference USA/Simon and Schuster Macmillan, 1996.

Van Peebles, Melvin. *Identity Crisis: A Father and Son's Own Story of Working Together/Melvin and Mario Van Peebles.* New York: Simon and Schuster, 1990.

———. ''Margaret Mead Film and Video Festival: Rascals, Survivors, Dreamers.'' *Natural History* 104 (October 1995): 56–57.

———. *Panther.* New York: Thunder's Mouth Press, 1995.

———. *Sweet Sweetback's Baadasssss Song.* New York: Lancer, 1971.

———. Telephone interview with Claire A. Taft, December 1996.

White, Timothy. ''Rap Roots: The Story of Brer Soul.'' *Billboard* 104 (11 July 1992): 3.

Zimmerman, Paul D. ''Stud on the Run.'' *Newsweek* 72 (10 May 1971): 116, 118.

Claire A. Taft

James Varick
(1750?–1827)
Religious leader

James Varick was one of the leaders in the creation of separate black churches. He played an important role in the formation of the African Methodist Episcopal (AME) Zion Church, a major black denomination. He also served as its first supervisor.

James Varick was born about 1750 near Newburgh in Orange County, New York. His mother was a slave of the Varicks or Van Varcks. She was later freed. His father, Richard, was born in Hackensack, New Jersey, where he was baptized in the Dutch Church. The family lived in New York City while James Varick was young. He acquired an elementary education in New York schools.

By trade Varick was a shoemaker. Later he also worked as a tobacco cutter. Since the church with which he was associated did not pay its preachers for many years, he worked at his trades to support himself and his family. About 1790 he married Aurelia Jones. The couple had four sons and three daughters.

The important events in Varick's life were associated with his religious avocation. Varick joined the John Street Methodist Church in New York City at an early date, possibly in 1766 the year after the church held its first meeting. Varick seems to have been licensed to preach by this group although he does not appear among the licensed preachers of the early Zion church as given by Christopher Rush, the second supervisor or bishop, in his 1844 history of the denomination.

As early as 1780 black members of the John Street Church were holding separate class and prayer meetings. In 1796 Varick was among those black leaders who established separate meetings on a firmer footing. The group met for prayer on Sunday afternoons and heard preachers and exhorters on Wednesday evenings in a house in Cross Street, which they remodeled to hold these meetings. Then in 1799 the group decided to erect a building and form a separate church.

In October of 1800 the African Methodist Episcopal Zion Church, a wooden building at the corner of Church and Leonard Streets, was dedicated. (The name of the mother church, Zion, was officially added to the denomination's name in 1848.) In March of 1801 the church was formally incorporated under New York law. This incorporation placed

James Varick

the church and its property firmly under the control of the trustees, who were required to be of African descent.

Since the church had preachers but no ordained minister, white ministers preached on Sunday afternoons and Wednesday evenings and supplied a morning communion service on the second Sunday of every month. The church thrived. It acquired a burying ground in 1807 and laid plans to buy the lots it had leased along with another adjacent one and to erect a new brick church to replace the original building.

In 1820 as Zion was engaged in erecting its new church, which had the effect of scattering the congregation among a number of temporary meeting places, a competing black denomination appeared in the form of Richard Allen's African Methodist Episcopal Church, which was trying to build up a national organization from its Philadelphia base. After the Allenites were rebuffed by Zion, they organized their own New York church in Mott Street. Yet not all members of Zion were completely estranged from the Allenites, and Varick himself opened a meeting for Allen during the dedication ceremonies. Further negotiations between the two denominations failed, however, leaving a considerable amount of bitterness on both sides.

It was after this that Varick reappeared in a leadership role in the Zion church. In Rush's account, the trustees met at Varick's house in July of 1820 and decided to pursue the ordination of black ministers, allowing Zion to dispense with white ministers. Varick must have been coming to the fore in church affairs earlier than this, but his name does not appear on early documents.

A general meeting of the church on August 11, 1820 resulted in two decisions: a refusal to join Allen and a refusal to return to white control. The problem of elders for the separate church now became crucial. On September 13, 1820, Abraham Thompson and James Varick were selected by the congregation to become elders and they began to act immediately, holding communion services. A book of discipline for the new church was ready for printing by November 1. The denomination acquired churches outside of New York City, but its growth did not match that of Richard Allen's group.

At the first convention of the new denomination in June of 1821, Varick was appointed district chairman, an interim supervisory position for the whole denomination. Finally, on June 17, 1822, white Methodist elders ordained Abraham Thompson, James Varick, and Leven Smith. James Varick then officially became supervisor of the church on July 30, 1822, and was reelected again in 1824. (The title bishop was not adopted until later).

In addition to his purely ministerial duties, Varick ran a school first in his home and then in the church building. He was the first chaplain of the New York African Society for Mutual Relief (1810) and a vice–president of the African Bible Society (1817). In 1821 he was a member of the group of blacks who petitioned the state constitutional convention for the right to vote. He supported the establishment of *Freedom's Journal,* the first black newspaper, in 1827.

On July 4, 1827, the thanksgiving service for the final abolition of slavery in New York was held in Zion church. On July 22 Varick died at his home. Originally he was buried in the Colored Union Cemetery (now Woodlawn). His remains now repose in the crypt of the African Methodist Episcopal Zion Church in Harlem.

As is the case with many early figures, it is difficult to clearly discern all the elements of Varick's career. Although his name appears only sporadically in early records, his leadership role in the creation of the African Methodist Episcopal Zion denomination is attested to by his selection as its first supervisor. His influence continues to the present day. His church is now the second largest black Methodist group.

REFERENCES

Hood, J. W. *One Hundred Years of the African Methodist Episcopal Zion Church.* New York: AME Zion Book Concern, 1895.

Logan, Rayford W., and Michael R. Winston, eds. *Dictionary of American Negro Biography.* New York: Norton, 1982.

Malone, Dumas, ed. *Dictionary of American Biography.* New York: Scribner's, 1943.

Moore, John Jamison. *History of the A. M. E. Zion Church in America.* York, PA: Teachers' Journal Office, 1884.

Rush, Christopher. *A Short Account of the Rise and Progress of the African M. E. Church in America.* Reprint, New York: Christopher Rush et al., 1866.

Wheeler, B[enjamin] F[ranklin]. *The Varick Family.* Mobile, AB: The Author, 1906.

Robert L. Johns

George Boyer Vashon
(1824–1878?)
Teacher, lawyer, writer

George Boyer Vashon is among the small number of well-educated blacks who faced the difficult task of trying to make a career in a society mostly determined to keep blacks in inferior positions. He tried first for the law, which ultimately proved frustrating. He then turned to teaching. Vashon left behind a small body of poetry, accomplished enough to give rise to regrets that he did not write more.

George Boyer Vashon was born on July 25, 1824, in Carlisle, Pennsylvania. He was the only son of John B. Vashon (c.1792–1854) and his amiable but anonymous wife. There were two older daughters. John Vashon was born in Norfolk, Virginia, to a white father and a mulatto mother. He was a sailor in the War of 1812. In 1822 he moved from Virginia to Carlisle, Pennsylvania, and in 1829 to Pittsburgh, where he prospered as a barber and eventually became proprietor of the City Baths. An ardent abolitionist, he was a friend and financial supporter of abolitionist William Lloyd Garrison.

John Vashon was active in providing for the education of blacks in Pittsburgh. In addition to founding the first Anti-Slavery Society in Pittsburgh in 1833, he helped set up the African Education Society in 1832. George Vashon first appeared in a public role in 1838, when the 14-year-old was secretary of the newly-founded Juvenile Anti-Slavery Society, the first in the United States.

In 1840 George Vashon entered Oberlin College, becoming the first black graduate of the school in 1844. While he was pursuing his degree, he taught in Chillicothe, Ohio. There he taught and became a role model for John Mercer Langston, later a congressman from Virginia. Vashon also helped Langston to settle in Oberlin when the younger man continued his education there.

After his graduation from Oberlin, Vashon read law in Pittsburgh with Walter Forward (1786–1852), a lawyer, a former congressman, and an important politician. In late 1847 Vashon tried in vain for admittance to the bar in Pennsylvania. Disgusted, he decided to go to Haiti. On his way there, he stopped in New York where he took the bar examination and was admitted to that state's bar on January 11, 1848. Vashon

George Boyer Vashon

taught at College Faustin in Port-au-Prince until he returned to settle in Syracuse, New York, in the late summer of 1850. There he practiced law for four years.

Vashon drew upon his Haitian experiences when writing the line poem "Vincent Ogé," which deals with the unsuccessful revolt of free persons of color in 1790–91. It appeared in *Autographs for Freedom* in August 31, 1853. "Vincent Ogé" was followed in 1864 by a second poem, "A Life-Day," which in its 126 lines does not rise to the level of the first. The 108 lines of "Ode on the Proclamation of the Fifteenth Amendment," read by Vashon at Israel Church, Washington, D.C., on April 13, 1870, completes his known poetic work.

In the fall of 1854 Vashon took up the position of professor of belles lettres and mathematics at Central College, an integrated abolitionist school in McGrawville, New York. (He was the third African American to serve on the faculty.) After spending three years there, Vashon returned to Pittsburgh and there married Susan Paul Smith (1838–1912), the granddaughter of Thomas Paul, the celebrated Boston Baptist minister. The marriage produced seven children.

George Vashon became principal and teacher in Pittsburgh's segregated schools for blacks. He held these positions until 1864 when he became principal of Avery College, a school for blacks, just outside Pittsburgh. Then in the fall of 1867 he moved to Washington, D.C., to take up a position as solicitor for the Freedman's Bureau. On October 8, 1867, he was appointed as a teacher in the Evening School of Howard University's Normal Department. He thus became the first black appointed to the faculty of the university, although not in a regular department. The salary was to come from tuition, but the nine students known to have attended provided an income of less than $25 a month. Vashon's connection with Howard ended in September of 1868 when the school seems to have been shut down.

In 1869 Vashon took a prominent role in the National Convention of the Colored Men of America, held in Washington, D.C. on January 13–16, 1869, and worked with the following organization through the next year. In 1870 he was a frequent contributor to the *New Era,* an ultimately unsuccessful attempt to establish a black newspaper of national scope in Washington. Unfortunately, after this flurry of activity there is a dearth of information for the last years of Vashon's life.

Vashon then taught at Alcorn Agricultural and Mechanical College (now University) in Mississippi. In the *Dictionary of American Negro Biography,* Joan R. Sherman gave the dates as 1874 to 1878. No records of Vashon's affiliation with the school survived, and this last period in his life remains obscure. There is also no record of Vashon's death in the state archives, but he seems to have died in Mississippi in October of 1878.

In *The Rising Son,* William Wells Brown described him as "of mixed blood; in stature, of medium size, rather round face, with a somewhat solemn countenance, a man of few words—needs to be drawn out to be appreciated." George Boyer Vashon belongs to the small group of pre–Civil War educated blacks. While much of his life was spent as a teacher, he was also an activist from the early days of the Abolition Movement. Although his life was closely circumscribed by prejudice, by example and personal effort he tried to advance the cause of all blacks.

REFERENCES

Brown, William Wells. *The Black Man.* 4th ed. Boston: Robert F. Wallcutt, 1865.

———. *The Rising Son.* Boston: A. G. Brown and Co., 1876.

Cheek, William, and Aimee Lee Cheek. *John Mercer Langston and the Fight for Black Freedom, 1829–65.* Urbana: University of Illinois Press, 1989.

Delany, Martin Robison. *The Condition, Elevation, Emigration, and Destiny of the Colored People of the United State.* 1852. Reprint, New York: Arno Press and the New York Times, 1968.

Griffiths, Julia, ed. *Autographs for Freedom.* New York: J.C. Derby, 1854.

Langston, John Mercer. *From the Virginia Plantation to the National Capitol.* Hartford, CT: American Publishing Company, 1894.

Logan, Rayford W. *Howard University: The First Hundred Years.* New York: New York University Press, 1969.

Logan, Rayford W., and Michael R. Winston, eds. *Dictionary of American Negro Biography.* New York: Norton, 1982.

Merrill, Walter M., ed. *The Letters of William Lloyd Garrison.* Cambridge, MA: Harvard University Press, 1971–.

Nell, Wm. C. *The Colored Patriots of the American Revolution.* 1855. Reprint, New York: Arno Press and the New York Times, 1968.

Quarles, Benjamin. *Black Abolitionists.* New York: Oxford, 1969.

Sherman, Joan R. *Invisible Poets.* Urbana: University of Illinois Press, 1974.

Smith, Jessie Carney, ed. *Notable Black American Women.* Detroit: Gale Publishing, 1992.

Robert L. Johns

Denmark Vesey
(1767–1822)
Carpenter, liberation theologian, slave insurrectionist

Denmark (Telemaque) Vesey bought his freedom for $600 from Captain Joseph Vesey, a retired Bermuda slave trader, in 1800 after winning $1,500 in Charleston's East–Bay Lottery. Vesey achieved fame as the revolutionary organizer of what John Killens in the introduction to *The Trial Record of Denmark Vesey* called, "the most elaborate insurrectionary project ever formed by American slaves." Vesey's life and thought was a product of the ideas and forces of freedom in an age of revolution that stirred the souls of the enslaved and the free alike.

Among the cargo of 390 slaves that Captain Joseph Vesey took on board his schooner *Rebecca* during one of his slave trading voyages between Charleston, South Carolina, and Cap Francais, Santo Domingo (Haiti), in 1781, was a handsome 14–year old boy. The officers on Vesey's ship were impressed with the boy's intelligence and alertness. Giving him the name of the Greek mythological hero Telemaque (Telemachus), the son of Odysseus who traveled the world over in search of his father, Captain Vesey's crew adopted the boy as the ship's mascot until their arrival in Santo Domingo. Upon weighing anchor at Cap Francais, the commercial trading in slaves for rum and other goods took precedence over any attachment to the bright young man. He was sold, as was the rest of Captain Vesey's human cargo, to one of the island's planters.

Although it is not known whether Vesey was born on St. Thomas or in Africa, the corruption of the name Telemaque into Denmark may not have been as a result of black pronunciation—as most accounts contend—but derived from the fact that St. Thomas was, with the rest of the Virgin Islands, a possession of Denmark. Since the Danes were trafficking Africans taken captive in Guinea, Telemaque's roots may be found in that West African area. Regardless of the reason, Telemaque came to be pronounced and spelled "Denmark."

After the passage of three months to a year, Captain Vesey's commercial slave trading brought him again to Haiti, where he was made to repossess Vesey from his irate owner who had it certified by the island's medical officer that he was unfit due to unexplained seizures. Black abolitionist and essayist Archibald Grimké speculated in his 1899 paper for the American Negro Academy, *Right on the Scaffold,* that Telemaque's epileptic fits "were in truth feigned, and therefore the initial *ruse de guerre* of that bright young intelligence in its long battle with slavery." Three years later, Captain Vesey settled in Charleston, South Carolina, to become a slave broker and ship merchandiser.

In all, Telemaque remained with Captain Vesey for 20 years, until the old slave trader's retirement. By the time he had come of age, Vesey had opened his own shop as a master carpenter and had come to be known by Charlestonians as Denmark Vesey.

White Masters, Black Masters

Despite his own personal success as a tradesman and the respect that brought him from white and black Charlestonians alike, it was the irreconcilable contradiction of being a "free" black man in a slave society and the amoral status of Charleston's free black slaveowning community which impelled him toward his rendezvous with history. When white and mulatto slaveowning refugees fled from the Haitian Revolution for American Southern cities like Charleston in the 1790s, Captain Joseph Vesey was instrumental in aiding them. This represented his young bondsman's second brush with the Haitian Revolution (the first brush being the year Vesey participated in pre–Revolutionary Haiti in 1781). Haitian mulatto slaveowners were joining a free black society in which, according to the 1820 census, 72 percent of free black households owned slaves. Although some had bought relatives and were unable to emancipate them legally under South Carolina law, many Charleston area blacks were engaged in the commercial slave trading of their own people for labor and profit.

Such a moral corruption of Charleston's free black community, in which Vesey was a prominent member, strengthened his resolve to uproot slavery. For no matter where he moved in Charleston's free black community, he was confronted with black slaveowners. The African Methodist Church he attended on Anson Street was located in a neighborhood of black masters, and black slaveowners lived next to his residence at 56 Bull Street. Charleston was known for its black slaveowning elite. Because dark skin was associated with slave status, a premium was placed on light–skin among the city's African American slaveholding elite. The most "color struck" organization among Charleston's mulatto elite was the Brown Fellowship Society, formed in 1790. Several members of the Brown Society would play the most treacherous role in the defeat of the Vesey insurrection.

Around 1818 Vesey set out in earnest to organize a massive slave insurrection along the lines of the Haitian Revolution. Along with Vesey's revulsion at rubbing elbows with Charleston's black slaveowning elite, there were two other circumstances much closer to home that set his foot firmly on the path of revolution.

At the time of his planned insurrection, Vesey had been a resident of Charleston for 40 years and had amassed wealth estimated at $8,000. Grimké reported that he married seven times to slave women and had a "plurality of children," many of them step–children. None of his children, however, were born free by the laws that governed slavery in the state of South Carolina. Children born of a slave mother and a free father were still the property of the slave owner, and the master of a slave woman married to a free man set the period of visitation between husband and wife. That he quite possibly had no knowledge of his own forebears, and that his own fathering of children only added to the wealth of slave masters and to the destruction of the black family "ate deep into Vesey's mind," Grimké noted.

One other accumulation of racist indignities left Denmark Vesey "ravished of manhood," according to Grimké, and drove him toward his plunge to freedom. In 1815, 5,000 black parishioners resigned enmasse from Charleston's white–dominated Methodist Church and transferred their membership to the newly formed African Methodist Church. The white Methodist backlash in 1817 led to the indiscriminate arrest of 469 black Methodists on false charges of disorderly conduct. Again, in 1818, 140 black Methodists were charged with violating laws prohibiting the education of slaves without the supervision of whites. In 1820, petitions by black freedmen to conduct religious services without the presence of whites was rejected, and, in 1821, white authorities again warned black clergy and laity not to educate slaves.

In addition, a set of government restrictions, fines and taxes designed to severely limit the mobility of Charleston's free black population, were imposed. The enactment of a set of anti–black laws in 1820 prohibited the entrance of free blacks into the state of South Carolina and placed restrictions on South Carolina free blacks reentering the state; a $50 tax was levied on free blacks; and heavy licensing fees were imposed on black artisans to curtail their competing with white artisans and workers.

Organization, Pan–Africanism, African–Americanization

As a free, self–employed carpenter, Vesey came under the weight of all of these restrictions. As a deacon in the African Church, he felt the repressive whip of the white Methodist backlash. The intersection of all of these developments in the life and thought of Denmark Vesey shaped his revolutionary perspective.

At the same time, according to Grimké, "the sundry religious classes or congregations with Negro leaders or local preachers, into which were formed the Negro members of the various churches of Charleston, furnished Vesey with the first rudiments of an organization.'' Vesey took advantage of the organizational space that the banned African Church afforded slaves and freed blacks to meet. Along with churches, religious and ethnic organizations like the Gullah Society and the African Association, as well as artisans' shops where Africans worked, organized venues for the discussion of ideas and strategies for liberation.

The most important aspect of Vesey's method of enlisting recruits to his bold plans for liberation, however, was his ability to look past the seemingly docile exterior of Charleston's ''contented slaves'' and recognize the force and reason of revolution in the enslaved African. That was particularly evident in the case of two of his chief lieutenants, Ned and Rolla Bennett, who were the trusted bondsmen of South Carolina's governor Thomas Bennett.

Vesey, who spoke several languages, including African languages, achieved an historic first in the organization of a liberation movement, in that he made it a principle to organize along pan–African lines. His pan–Africanism reflected another feature of his organizational strategy—namely, bringing together forces from the city and the countryside. In that way he sought also to combine a tightly–knit, disciplined cadre with the elements of spontaneous revolt that he expected to provoke in the larger slave population. Vesey traveled as far as 100 miles from Charleston to recruit slaves to his undertaking and engaged the help of other agitators to aid him in organizing forces on the sea islands of St. James' and St. John's. While much of the leadership of the insurrection came from the class of slave artisans in the city, Vesey knew that its success depended on the blacks in the countryside. Isolated rural blacks were distinct culturally from whites.

Vesey, however, had to contend with the problems arising from African American diversity from the vantage point of organizing an extensive insurrection involving the city and the countryside. He therefore drew his underground cadre of organizers from the artisans and mechanics of Charleston's slave community. Most were literate, well versed in the political debates of the day, and often communicated through written correspondence. Some, like Monday Gell, ''could read and write with facility, and thus attained an extraordinary and dangerous influence over his fellows,'' according to Peter Wood in *Black Majority.*

Following two years of relentless agitation in Charleston's slave community, Vesey began the practical planning of the insurrection in 1821 from his home at 56 Bull Street. The extent and depth of the underground organization of the Vesey insurrection is a credit to the five lieutenants that made up his inner circle: Peter Poyas, Ned and Rolla Bennett, Monday Gell, and Gullah Jack. Like Vesey, these men were extraordinary products of the monumental social forces and contradictions in the South that were inexorably driving American society towards civil war. Peter Poyas was a ''first–rate ship carpenter''; Monday Gell hired himself out and kept a shop where he made harnesses; Ned and Rolla Bennett handled Governor Bennett's state house and family estate; and Gullah Jack was an African conjuror and medicine man.

The Principles and the Plan

From Poyas's lips came the dire principle for organizing among Charleston's slave community: ''Take care and don't mention it (the plot) to those waiting men who receive presents of old coats from their masters or they'll betray us,'' Grimké wrote. Recruitment proceeded apace as money was collected in the city for raising forces in the countryside. Weapons were bought as well as manufactured in large quantities by smiths. Vesey neglected his carpentry business as he made more recruiting trips into the countryside to enlist foot soldiers for his war of liberation. By some estimates, Vesey's organized forces grew to the impressive number of 9,000 blacks; the plan was that tens of thousands of more slaves would rise up spontaneously to join the general insurrection. (Because Vesey and his comrades immediately burned all the documents pertaining to the insurrection once they got word that the plot had been discovered—especially the meticulous lists that he and each of his lieutenants kept of men they had enlisted—we shall never know for certain the full extent of the conspiracy.)

Ned Bennett organized blacks drawn from the ranks of Charleston's apprenticed slave butchers, in part because of their access to their master's horses. Mingo Harth, another lieutenant, organized another contingent of 4,000 blacks from the countryside to be deployed along Charleston's South Bay. Since the Atlantic slave trade continued to illegally bring Africans into South Carolina's Low Country, the Angolan root doctor Gullah Jack was made responsible for organizing a revolutionary force from this community. Slave barbers in Charleston were enlisted to create wigs and false whiskers to disguise the insurrectionists as they moved on the whites guarding the Charleston arsenal on the moonless night that Vesey had chosen for the assault.

A key organizational principle of the insurrection was its pan–African cooperation. According to Stuckey, the Vesey conspiracy was a unique demonstration of ''the very process by which Africans were being transformed into a single people.'' Monday Gell, an Ibo; Mingo Harth, a Mandingo; Gullah Jack, an Angolan who organized ''Gullah Company;'' Tom Russell, a smith and a conjuror's apprentice to Gullah Jack; and Vesey, all claimed membership in Charleston's various African ethnic associations and religious societies. Stuckey contended that these provided the organizational basis for the ''ethnic companies'' that Gell, Harth, and Gullah Jack led. There was, besides these bands, a French language company.

On the ground, Vesey's plan for realizing this goal called for an attack on the city of Charleston coming from six different quarters. The plan was dependent on the element of surprise and the rapid seizure of strategic buildings and positions around the city, such as the U.S. arsenal, the governor's mansion, and the city's main guardhouse. The timing of the insurrection was also critical. Vesey timed the attack for midnight, Sunday, July 14, 1822.

Vesey had observed that whites seasonally abandoned the city during the summer for vacations and resorts, and July 14 would also be a moonless night. The crucial factor in Vesey's plan was that the Sunday date meant "that large bodies of slaves from adjacent plantations and islands went to visit the town without molestation, whereas on no other day could this have been done. Thus, without exciting alarm, did Vesey plan to introduce his Trojan horse or country bands into the city," Grimké explained.

On the evening of May 25, on Fitzsimmons Wharf, young William Paul recklessly presumed much too much about the racial solidarity that he faithfully believed bound him to Colonel Prioleau's mulatto bondsman, Peter. Colonel Prioleau's man was surely one of "those waiting men. . .who received presents of old coats from their masters." It was to this "waiting man" whom William Paul confided that Charleston stood on the threshold of the largest slave rebellion in American history.

Fearful and beside himself with the enormity of the information given him, Peter Prioleau Desverney sought the council of the free mulatto tin plater, slaveowner, and Brown Society member William Pencil, who urged him to tell his secret to his master. On Pencil's advice, Colonel Prioleau's man committed the first of several acts of betrayal that would be the undoing of Vesey's elaborate plan of insurrection. For his act Desverney was manumitted and granted a lifelong annuity of $50 by the state of South Carolina and exemption from taxation.

The first arrest, interrogation, and confession of a conspirator, William Paul, took place on May 30, leading to the arrest of Mingo Harth and Peter Poyas on May 31. So limited was the knowledge that any conspirator had about others involved or about any other aspect of the plan, that there was very little to which William Paul could actually confess. When brought before the authorities, Mingo Harth and Peter Poyas exhibited such composure that their captors were disarmed and compelled to release them, although they were kept under surveillance until more evidence could be gathered. The authorities were once again thrown off guard by the steeled composure of Ned Bennett, who shrewdly used his status as the personal slave of the governor and volunteered to be interrogated. According to Killens, "Blacks handled themselves with such composure when arrested and questioned that some of the authorities were inclined to believe that the entire plot was the figment of an overactive imagination."

Vesey and his comrades were not dissuaded or disoriented by the breach of secrecy. Instead, Vesey moved the date of the insurrection up one month to June 16. In the meantime, white Charlestonians were in a heightened state of anxiety for another five or six days, when the second and most decisive act of betrayal was committed by what Grimké called that "distrusted class of 'waiting men,' whose highest aspirations did not seem to reach above their masters' cast off garments."

Still not convinced that there was no threat, the white authorities enlisted a spy to infiltrate the slave underground of night meetings and church discussions. For this they promised a 45–year old smith and African Church deacon, George Wilson, his freedom and the false promise of his wife and son's emancipation if he brought them hard evidence of a conspiracy. On June 14 Wilson provided the most damning proof of the planned insurrection, complete with the date, time, logistics, and principal leaders.

Upon receiving word of this most serious breach of their plans, Vesey and the other leaders hastily met on the night of June 15, decided to postpone the uprising, and immediately sent word to the countryside to call off the march on the city. As it happened, this last directive came too late. When one of the armed contingents managed to arrive in Charleston by canoe on the appointed day, Vesey got word to the rebels to disperse and wait for further orders. On Sunday, June 16, when masses of blacks from the countryside entered Charleston, they found that the city was occupied by five companies of federal troops and an assortment of local militias.

From June 14 to their arrests, Vesey and his lieutenants were under surveillance. The arrest of ten slaves, including Poyas and Rolla, Ned, and Batteau Bennett, June 17–18, instantly sent Vesey into hiding. On June 19, a secret court of two magistrates and five freeholders began hearings that lasted until July 26. Vesey was arrested on June 20 at the home of his wife Beck. Gell was arrested on June 27 and Jack on July 5.

"Die Silent": The Aftermath

Arrested and held in the Charleston Work House, Vesey and Peter Poyas concerned themselves with the protection of the revolution and with minimizing any risk to the lives of their recruits. The stoic steadfastness of the leadership of the insurrection before the white authorities, and the fact that they disclosed none of the names of the thousands they had enlisted, with the exception of Monday Gell, signified that these revolutionaries saw it as their fundamental duty to protect their followers. This heroic sense of responsibility for the lives of people is what made Vesey and his co–leaders the martyrs of 1822. Because they were willing to risk their lives to free people, they saw it as their obligation to "die in silence" to protect the lives of people.

Vesey came before the Court of Lionel H. Kennedy and Thomas Parker, the two sitting magistrates in the case, on June 23, the day after his arrest. Found guilty, after a week of secret and often coerced testimony against them, Vesey, Poyas, Rolla, Ned, and Batteau Bennett, and Jesse Wood, one of Vesey's aides, met their death on the gallows early in the morning of July 2 between the hours of six and eight a.m., on a place called Blake's lands, near Charleston. The most fitting epitaph to Vesey and his comrades was that even after their execution, Jack, who was still at large, was in the midst of carrying out the planned insurrection when he was arrested on July 5. He was tried, and executed on July 12.

Only Gell, one of Vesey's chief lieutenants, betrayed and turned state's evidence to save himself from hanging. The confessions of Gell, Charles Drayton, and Harry Haig led to the most extensive arrests of alleged insurrectionists (upwards to 60 slaves were arrested on the basis of the testimony of these three men). As a consequence of the disclosures by these three men, Charleston's white rulers were provided with the means to send their most chilling "terror of example" to the black community, when, on Friday morning, July 26, the state of South Carolina executed 22 men on the gallows. This gruesome spectacle was carried out in the most public space in Charleston at the intersection of King and Calhoun streets, also known as the Lines. The corpses of the men were left hanging in public display "on the Lines," for three days. The families of the executed men were not allowed to claim their bodies, instead, the authorities handed them over to surgeons for dissection.

By the end of the Vesey affair, 131 men had been charged; 35 men had been executed; and 32 were deported (some, like Prince Graham, demanded to be repatriated back to Africa); the rest were imprisoned, or had the charges against them dropped. Gell and his two co–informants had their death sentence commuted and were deported. Desverney, upon being manumitted by the state of South Carolina for his act of treachery, became an upstanding member of Charleston's free black community by marrying into the Brown Society's elite of mulatto slaveowners.

Despite the identification of segments of Charleston's free elite with the white slaveholding aristocracy, it was not sufficient to head off the backlash of white repression which came down like a razor–strap on free black Charlestonians. A law, directed at what whites perceived as the communications network of slave rebellions, restricted free blacks, especially free seamen, coming into Charleston. It was the successful legal defense against the federal attempt to strike down this state restriction on black mobility, which became the earliest articulation of the Southern states' rights argument which would lead to the Civil War.

By 1832, the South Carolina legislature voted for the Ordinance of Nullification, in which the state of South Carolina recognized "No tribunal upon earth above her authority." The nullification ordinance was the culmination of a series of constitutional confrontations between South Carolina and Washington that commenced with the Negro Seaman's Act of 1823 in response to the Vesey affair. Thus had Vesey set in motion the chain of events that would lead to the American Civil War and the realization of his revolutionary aim—the abolition of slavery?

The slaves who bore witness to those days of heroism, treachery, and terror, June and July of 1822, kept alive the memory of Vesey's daring act of liberation. According to Dickson Bruce and Israel Nesbitt, "As narratives collected from former slaves by the Federal Writers's Project in the 1930s show, some slaves in South Carolina had kept the Vesey story alive throughout the antebellum period and drawn inspiration from it." The Vesey House, at 56 Bull Street, was declared a National Historic Landmark, on May 11, 1976, but is not open to the public. Martin Luther King often recited the immortal lines that James Russell Lowell wrote at the time of the hanging of John Brown for leading a raid, inspired by Vesey, on the arsenal at Harper's Ferry:

> Right forever on the scaffold,
> Wrong forever on the Throne,
> Yet that scaffold sways the future.

REFERENCES

Freehling, William W. "Denmark Vesey's Antipaternalistic Reality." In *The Reintegration of American History: Slavery and the Civil War.* New York: Oxford University Press, 1994.

Grimké, Archibald H. *Right on the Scaffold, or the Martyrs of 1822.* Occasional Papers No. 7. 1901. Reprint, New York: Arno Press, 1969.

Higginson, Thomas Wentworth. *Black Rebellion.* New York: Arno Press, 1969.

Johnson, Michael P., and James L. Roark. *Black Masters: A Free Family of Color in the Old South.* New York: Norton, 1984.

Killens, John Oliver. Introduction to *The Trial Record of Denmark Vesey.* Boston: Beacon Press, 1970.

Koger, Larry. *Black Slaveowners: Free Black Slave Masters in South Carolina, 1790–1860.* Jefferson, NC: McFarland, 1985.

Lofton, John M. "Denmark Vesey's Call to Arms." *Journal of Negro History* 33 (October 1948): 395–417.

———. *Denmark Vesey's Revolt: The Slave Plot That Lit a Fuse to Fort Sumter.* Kent, OH: Kent State University Press, 1983.

Nesbitt, Israel. "Looking Back To Vesey's Insurrection." In *The American Slave: A Composite Autobiography XI.* Supplement 1, series 1. 12 vols. Westport, CT: Greenwood Press, 1977.

Savage, Beth L., ed. *African American Historic Places.* National Register of Historic Places. National Park Service, U.S. Department of the Interior. Washington, DC: The Preservation Press, 1994.

Starobin, Robert S., ed. *Denmark Vesey: The Slave Conspiracy of 1822.* Englewood Cliffs, NJ: Prentice–Hall, 1970.

Stuckey, Sterling. "Agitator or Insurrectionist?: Remembering Denmark Vesey." *Negro Digest* 15 (February 1966): 28–41.

———. *Slave Culture: Nationalist Theory and the Foundations of America.* New York: Oxford University Press, 1987.

Wade, Richard C. *Slavery in the Cities: The South, 1820–1860.* London: Oxford University Press, 1964.

Wish, Harvey. "American Slave Insurrections Before 1861." *Journal of Negro History* 22 (July 1937): 229–320.

Wood, Peter. *Black Majority: Negroes in Colonial South Carolina from 1670 through the Stono Rebellion.* New York: Knopf, 1974.

Woodson, Carter G. *Free Negro Owners of Slaves in the United States in 1830, Together with Absentee Owner-*

ship of Slaves in the United States in 1830. Washington, DC: Association for the Study of Negro Life and History, 1924.

Lou Turner

U. Conrad Vincent

(1892–1938)

Physician, hospital founder, reformer

U. Conrad Vincent made medical history by developing the varicocele operation for surgery of varicose veins connected to the testicle and ovary. He was the first African American to serve an internship and residency at Harlem's Bellevue Hospital and later opened a proprietary hospital in Harlem to provide health services for African Americans.

Born on January 5, 1892, in Raleigh, North Carolina, Ubert Conrad Vincent was the son of Andrew and Cora F. Vincent. His father was a minister, educator, and later dean of the School of Theology at Shaw University in Raleigh. His mother was born in Wilson, North Carolina, and taught domestic science at Shaw. Of the Vincent's 14 children, U. Conrad was the second of the eight children who survived.

After attending Chavis High School in Raleigh, Vincent entered Shaw University where he remained an honor student until he graduated in 1914. Then of slight build, the left–handed Vincent exercised his athletic talent and became a second baseman in college. He became friends with Max Yeargan, who was known later for his work with the YMCA. In 1914 Vincent entered Leonard Medical School at Shaw and remained until the medical unit closed in 1915 due to the impending loss of accreditation. He was then admitted to the University of Pennsylvania Medical School. He worked each summer as a Pullman porter to support himself. His work also took him to Saratoga Springs in upper New York State, a resort for the wealthy. A number of Howard University's medical graduates also worked there each summer. He received an M.D. degree from the University of Pennsylvania Medical School in 1918.

Since Philadelphia's hospitals were closed to blacks for postgraduate training, Vincent was matched with Bellevue Hospital in New York City for his internship. Once his photograph arrived and hospital officials saw that he was black, his application was rejected. Pressure from a New York State assemblyman and intervention by a professor at the University of Pennsylvania led to Bellevue's acceptance of Vincent, but not until October of 1918. He then became the first African American intern at Bellevue Hospital. After he completed his internship, he served a residency at the hospital from 1919 to 1920 under Edward L. Keyes, a leader in the field of urology.

While resident surgeon at Bellevue, Vincent developed a procedure known as the varicocele operation to correct a varicose condition of the veins of the spermatic cord or ovaries. His method was published in textbooks, including Keyes's standard text on urology. Many who used the texts or knew about the procedure were unaware of Vincent's race. Keyes also wrote to Vincent on February 18, 1920—his letter was published in Montague Cobb's article in the *Journal of the National Medical Association*—commenting on the efficacy of Vincent's method. Cobb noted that:

> it is a tribute to the anatomists under whom [Vincent] studied that in the first year after he graduated . . . [he] was sufficiently anatomically oriented to develop a surgical technique soundly based on anatomy, which became a permanent contribution.

On February 11, 1919, Vincent was licensed to practice in New York state.

On April 23, 1920, Vincent married Naomi Tulane of Montgomery, Alabama. The Vincents had four children: Ubert Conrad Jr., Silvia Naomi, Jacqueline Tulane, and Barbara Patricia, who were between the ages of four and 15 when their father died. A sociable man, Vincent enjoyed the theater, particularly musical comedy. Using his tenor voice, he often sang in parlor circles. Still a sports enthusiast, he also returned to Philadelphia annually for the Penn Relays. Though a modest man, he bought a flashy Stutz Bearcat automobile and a summer cottage at Oak Bluffs on Martha's Vineyard.

From 1929 to 1930, Vincent did a rotating internship at Freedmen's Hospital in Washington, D.C., after which he moved to Harlem where he spent the rest of his life. He opened a practice in rented rooms at 209 West 135th Street, prospered, and with funds from his father, purchased the building. In 1923 he moved to 251 West 138th Street, on what was known as "Strivers' Row" and became one of the first blacks to live there. Although Harlem Hospital was city–owned, its staff was white until 1920, when Louis T. Wright became the first African American appointee. In 1925, Vincent was appointed to the staff as an attending surgeon in the Division of Urology. Five years later, in March of 1930, he was dropped from the staff due to reorganization. After vigorous protest, in 1933 he was appointed head of the urological service. Claims that he "resigned" a short time later came under scrutiny by the NAACP, especially since the hospital had been the center of agitation and recrimination for some time.

Citing an article in the *New York Times,* Cobb wrote that by age 35, Vincent had the largest practice of black physicians in New York. Among his patients were the dancers the Nicholas Brothers and musicians Eubie Blake, Noble Sissle, and Lottie Gee. He still faced the racism against black physicians in New York City and across the country and that barrier forced many of them to open proprietary hospitals. On March 17, 1929, the beginning of the Great Depression, he opened Vincent's Sanatorium located in a five–story building he bought at 2438 Seventh Avenue between 137th and 138th streets. His Bellevue supervisor, Edward L. Keyes, was a member of the new hospital's advisory board. Vincent determined that the hospital would be a community facility. The press gave wide coverage to the two–day opening activities and tours of the 50–bed facility. Vincent H. Tulane, his father–in–law and owner of a drug store and grocery in Montgomery, Alabama, was superintendent. A series of circumstances beyond his control, including his own illness and the effects of the Stock Market crash of 1929, caused the hospital to fail; it closed on September 30, 1930. He moved his practice to his home, prospered again, then became ill again in August of 1938 with a kidney infection. He died on December 18, 1938, when he was nearly 47–years old.

Vincent's busy life left little time for much else, however, he was a member of the Harlem Surgical Society and the Medical Society of the County of New York. He was highly respected by the medical profession, particularly blacks; he was keenly interested in the welfare of the community residents and through his work on the staff of Harlem Hospital he gave great service to Harlem's poor. Vincent was a gifted man who contributed to the health of countless of patients, including the poor as well as affluent blacks in Harlem and New York.

REFERENCES

Cobb, W. Montague. ''Ubert Conrad Vincent, B.S., M.D., 1892–1938.'' *Journal of the National Medical Association* 67 (January 1975): 73–80.

Vincent, Jacqueline Tulane. Telephone interview with Jessie Carney Smith, July 1997.

Jessie Carney Smith

Walcott, Louis Eugene.
See Farrakhan, Louis.

David Walker
(1796?–1830)
Abolitionist, protest writer

The life of David Walker was very short and imperfectly recorded. Little suggests that he was destined for widespread fame until he published and distributed a protest work in 1829. This act made him famous in his time, and his small book has resonance down to the present day.

Walker was born on September 28, probably in 1796 or 1797. The brief history of his life in Henry Highland Garnet's 1848 edition of Walker's *Appeal to the Colored Citizens of the World* gives 1785 as the year of Walker's birth, but also states that he died at the age of 34. Recent researchers are inclined to believe that the given age at death is correct. Walker was born in Wilmington, North Carolina, the son of a slave father and a free mother. His mother's status meant that he was also free. His father died before he was born.

Nothing is known of his early life except that Walker developed a hatred of slavery and decided to leave the South. According to his own statements, he then traveled over much of the South and the West, which in his days meant as far as Tennessee. He mentioned two events from that period in the *Appeal*—reading two articles in a Southern newspaper and visiting a Methodist camp meeting near Charleston—that seem to place him in Charleston in 1821. This opens the possibility that he was in contact with Denmark Vesey, a fellow free black, a fellow Methodist, and chief planner of a slave insurrection discovered just before it was to begin the following summer. This contact must remain unproven, however, since Walker's name occurs nowhere in the documents about the revolt. It is also possible that he spent some time in Philadelphia before settling in Boston.

In 1825 Walker established himself in Boston; his appeared in the city directory, where he was listed as a clothes dealer at the City Market. In 1828 his place of business was at 20 Brattle Street, and he moved the following year to number 40 in the same street. He operated a new and used clothing store. In 1828 he and two other used–clothes dealers were charged with receiving stolen goods and tried. However, all three kept good records and were acquitted because they could show that they had accepted the items in good faith.

Beginning in 1827 Walker resided on Belknap Street (now Joy Street). He was a faithful member of the May Street Methodist Church, which was organized under black exhorter Samuel Snowden in 1818 and acquired its first permanent building on May Street in 1823. Snowden and the Baptist minister, Thomas Paul, were the only two black ministers in Boston. (Although Walker expressed great admiration of Richard Allen, the African Methodists did not have a church in Boston until 1833.)

Walker quickly began to make his mark in the Boston African American community. He was active in the Massachusetts General Colored Association, a early black organization devoted to abolition of slavery and to full equality. In his mind this association was a nucleus for a national mass organization of all blacks. Along with Thomas Paul, Walker was one of the two agents in Boston of *Freedom's Journal,* the first black newspaper, which began publication at the end of March 1827. One of Walker's speeches before the General Colored Association appeared in the paper on December 19, 1828. As reprinted by Wilentz in *Davis Walker's Appeal,* Walker was already sounding the theme of the *Appeal*:

> Shall we keep slumbering on, with our arms completely folded up, exclaiming every now and then, against our miseries, yet never do the least thing to ameliorate our condition, or that of posterity? . . . Ought we not to form ourselves into a general body, to protect, aid, and assist each other to the utmost of our power . . .?

In 1828 Walker married Eliza. It has been suggested that Garnet's omission of her maiden name in his account of Walker's life may indicate that she was a fugitive slave. A daughter was born to the couple, but she died of lung fever just a few days before her father. Walker's only surviving child, Edwin (1831?–1910), later one of the first two blacks elected to the Massachusetts legislature in 1866, was born posthumously.

According to Garnet, Walker was "prepossessing, being six feet in height, slender and well proportioned. His hair was loose, and his complexion dark." He was militant and courageous. When friends urged him to flee to Canada after the storm raised by his tract, he replied, according to Garnet, "I will stand my ground. *Somebody must die in this cause.* I may be doomed to the stake and to the fire, or to the scaffold tree, but it is not in me to falter if I can promote the work of emancipation."

Walker assured his fame by publishing *Appeal, in Four Articles, Together with a Preamble, to the Colored Citizens of the World, But in Particular, and Very Expressly to Those of the United States of America.* The title page carried the date of September 28, 1829. Although this was the third protest published by an African American in 1829—George Moses Horton, a North Carolina slave poet had published some stanzas on freedom and Robert Alexander Young's *Ethiopian Manifesto* had appeared a short time earlier—it caused consternation in the South, where the first copies arrived before the end of the year. The third edition of the *Appeal* with more revisions and additions appeared in June 1830.

One of the reasons for the resonance of the *Appeal* was its effective distribution. Walker took steps to see that it reached the South. Tantalizing hints, again falling short of proof, imply that the distribution may have been more systematically organized than we can now know. Of the copies distributed by individuals and not mailed, many appear to have gone by ship. Copies have been discovered in Savannah, Georgia; Charleston, South Carolina; Richmond, Virginia; New Orleans, Louisiana; and several cities in North Carolina. Some white men living in the region were involved. Elijah H. Burritt, a white printer in Milledgeville, Georgia, was forced to flee because he had obtained copies of the work for distribution. The alarm was general in the South, and state legislatures passed laws against seditious publications. In the North, rumors claimed that Southerners were offering $3,000 for Walker dead and $10,000 for him alive in the South.

Walker died suddenly on August 3, 1830, at his home. On January 22, 1831, the *Liberator,* a militant anti–slavery weekly newspaper edited by William Lloyd Garrison, published a letter from "A Colored Bostonian," alleging that Walker had perished at the hands of slaveholders. Apparently many blacks in Boston believed this to be true, but there is no convincing evidence that the death was not natural. There probably now exists no evidence to prove decisively either conclusion.

Walker's *Appeal* offers a convenient date for the beginning of the sectional hostility that culminated in the Civil War. The South began to move toward white solidarity on the issue of slavery; the North saw the beginnings of the abolitionist movement, which would slowly overcome that region's indifference to the issue. William Lloyd Garrison, who began publishing the *Liberator* in 1830, was influenced by Walker although he could not agree with him on all points. In turn, Walker's son bore Garrison as a middle name. Generations of black militants beginning with Henry Highland Garnet, who republished the *Appeal* in 1848, have found inspiration in Walker's work.

REFERENCES

Aptheker, Herbert. *"One Continual Cry."* New York: Humanities Press, 1965.

Garnet, Henry Highland. *Walker's Appeal, with a Brief Sketch of His Life.* 1848. Reprint, Nashville: James C. Winston, 1994.

Jacobs, Donald M. *Courage and Conscience: Black and White Abolitionists in Boston.* Bloomington: University of Indiana Press for the Boston Athenaeum, 1993.

Logan, Rayford W., and Michael R. Winston, eds. *Dictionary of American Negro Biography.* New York: Norton, 1982.

Malone, Dumas, ed. *Dictionary of American Biography.* New York: Scribner's, 1943.

Nell, William C. *The Colored Patriots of the American Revolution.* 1855. Reprint, New York: Arno Press and the New York Times, 1968.

Wilentz, Sean, ed. *Davis Walker's Appeal.* Rev. ed. New York: Hill and Wang, 1995.

Robert L. Johns

Leroy T. Walker

(1918–)

Educator, Olympic coach, Olympic administrator

A pioneer Olympic coach, Leroy T. Walker was the first African American to become president of the U.S. Olympic Committee (USOC). He was the Olympic head track coach for teams from Ethiopia, Israel, Trinidad–Tobago, Jamaica, and Kenya and served as chairman of key Olympic committees. Walker served as vice–president and director for the Atlanta Committee for the Olympic Games. He was first a successful college administrator, having served as track and field coach, department head, chancellor for university relations, and university chancellor.

Leroy Tashreau Walker, the youngest of 13 children, was born June 14, 1918, in Atlanta, Georgia, to Mary and Willie Walker. His father worked on the railroad and died when Walker was a youngster; then the older children assisted the family as caretakers. Walker moved to New York City while he was a young boy and lived with an older brother in Harlem. He grew up in the city doing odd jobs and going to school. In 1936, determined to receive a college education, Walker enrolled at Benedict College in Columbia, South Carolina, on an athletic scholarship. He was considered a top athlete and a good student. After graduation in 1940, he enrolled in the graduate program at Columbia University and received a master's degree in physical education in 1941. His dream was medical school, but the only two African American medical schools, Howard University and Meharry Medical College, had long waiting lists. Apparently he gave no consideration to other medical schools. In 1957 Walker earned a Ph.D. degree in biomechanics from New York University.

Walker began his professional career in 1941 at his alma mater, Benedict College, as chairman of the physical education department and coach for basketball, football, and track and field. In 1942 Walker moved to Bishop College in Marshall, Texas, assuming a similar position. For two years, 1943 to 1945, Walker served in the same positions at Prairie View Agricultural and Mechanical College.

Walker accepted a challenging position at North Carolina College in Durham, North Carolina, (now North Carolina Central University) and while there in his early years he coached basketball, football, and track and field teams and served as chairman of the physical education department. Later his successful coaching techniques brought considerable publicity to the track and field teams. Many of his athletes performed in each Olympics between 1956 and 1980. From 1974 to 1983 Walker served as vice chancellor for university relations and from 1983 to 1986 as chancellor of North Carolina Central University. He retired as chancellor and was named chancellor emeritus in 1986, after serving the institution for 40 years.

Olympic and Other International Involvements

During his North Carolina Central years, Walker served in various capacities beyond the institution. He was program specialist with the Cultural and Exchange Program of the Department of State in 1959, 1960, and 1962. Other international experiences included director of program planning for the Peace Corps in Africa, 1966–68. He was cofounder of the annual Pan African–USA track meet. This event is a bridge between African American and African track athletes. Having ceased in 1982 due to the political uprisings in South Africa, the meet was reestablished in 1994. Walker's involvement with the Olympics also earned him a variety of responsibilities, such as coach for the Ethiopian, Israeli, Trinidad–Tobago, Jamaican, and Kenyan teams for the Olympic games and later as head coach of U.S. Track and Field teams for the Montreal Olympic Games in 1976.

With the Olympics organization, he served the U.S. Olympic Committee as chair of committees, a member of the board of directors, and treasurer, from 1988 to 1992 and president in 1992. While serving as treasurer, the contingency fund increased by $43 million. While serving as president, several controversies arose: his support for the 2000 Beijing Olympic games, the Tonya Harding attack on skater Nancy Kerrigan, and the charge against the U.S. Olympic Committee for its lack of appropriate minority hiring.

In 1992 Walker was vice president and director of sports for the Atlanta Committee for the Olympic Games (ACOG) with a handsome six figure salary. When the presidency of the U.S. Olympic Committee became vacant, he was top choice for the position and gave up his salaried position with ACOG to assume the nonsalaried, but prestigious post.

Walker was active in other organizations and served in leadership positions, including U.S. Track Association, American Association for Health, Physical Education and Recreation Department, and the International Association of Athletic Federations. He is a member of the National Association of Intercollegiate Athletics, the Central Collegiate Athletic Association, Sigma Delta Psi, Alpha Phi Omega, and the Omega Psi Phi Fraternity. Walker is a writer as well. His three books are *Manual of Adapted Physical Education,* 1960; *Physical Education for the Exceptional Student,* 1964; and *Championship Techniques in Track and Field,* 1969.

Walker received numerous awards in recognition of his leadership qualities. These include the James E. Shepard Outstanding Teacher Award, 1964; Achievement Award, Central Intercollegiate Athletic Association, 1967; Distinguished Alumnus Award, Benedict College, 1968; Distinguished Service Award, Kiwanis International, 1971; recognition from the City of Durham, 1971, and from the Durham Chamber of Commerce, 1973; the Governor's Ambassador of Goodwill Award, 1974; and the Max Gardner Award, 1976. He was elected to the HC Hall of Fame, 1975; South Carolina Hall of Fame, 1977; and the National Association Sport and Physical Education Hall of Fame, 1977. Walker received the Robert Giegengack Award, the Athletic Congress's highest award. He was named Role Model Leader at North Carolina State University, 1990. He received the Achievement in Life Award, Encyclopedia Britannica. He was elected to the Athletic Congress Hall of Fame; Helms National Hall of Fame; U.S. Olympics Hall of Fame; and the Mid–Eastern Athletic Conference Hall of Fame.

Walker, a widower, was married to Katherine Walker who died in 1978. They had two children, Leroy Jr. and Carolyn. Walker's contributions to education and sports have spanned more than 40 years. He earned a reputation as a coach, administrator, scholar, consultant, and leader. Through his busy schedule as collegiate coach and administrator, he enhanced the participation of people of color in the Olympics. For international competition, he performed as coach, consultant, and administrator, having become the first African American to serve as president of the U.S. Olympic Committee. Respected among his peers at North Carolina Central University, he achieved the highest position there as chancellor at the university.

Current address: 2525 Meridan Parkway, Suite 230, Durham, NC 27713.

REFERENCES

''Introducing Dr. LeRoy T. Walker USOC President.'' *Ebony* 49 (June 1994): 38–42.

Salzman, Jack, David Lionel Smith, and Cornel West, eds. *Encyclopedia of African–American Culture and History.* New York: Macmillan Library Reference USA/Simon and Schuster Macmillan, 1996.

Who's Who among African Americans, 1996–97. 9th ed. Detroit: Gale Research, 1996.

Barbara Williams Jenkins

Moses Fleetwood Walker
(1857–1924)
Baseball player, activist, inventor, entrepreneur

Moses Fleetwood Walker was the first black to play major league baseball. Unfortunately, he played at a time when blacks were being driven into segregated teams and leagues. It would be more than a half–century before another black—Jackie Robinson—donned a major league uniform.

Walker was born on October 7, 1857, in Mount Pleasant, Ohio, to Moses W. Walker (1820–1891) and Caroline O'Harra Walker (1822–1893). The family background is somewhat confusing. Weldy W. Walkers' death certificate lists his mother's name as Maria Simpson. This name was supplied by Moses Fleetwood's son Thomas, who 15 years earlier had told a coroner that he did not know the name of his grandmother. These circumstances lead to speculation that the last three children may have had a different mother. Alternatively, although all records say that Caroline O'Harra was born in Ohio, Maria Simpson may have been a slave name she concealed. Of course, Thomas Walker may have simply been mistaken.

Moses Fleetwood (known as Fleet to the family) was the fifth or sixth of seven children: Cadwallader (b. 1844), William O. (1846–1918), Mary B. (b. 1849), Sarah M. (1851–1916), Lizzie (b. 1857), Moses Fleetwood, and Weldy Wilberforce (1860–1937). It is possible that Lizzie, who shares the 1857 birth date and who is absent in the 1870 census, was a twin sister. Both parents were of mixed racial heritage. His father was a cooper (barrel–maker) when Moses Fleetwood was born.

By 1860 Moses W. Walker moved to Steubenville, Ohio, where he became the first black physician in that city. Almost certainly, whatever medical training he had was through the apprentice system. His two youngest sons were educated in Steubenville. The city had a segregated school for blacks until at least 1872 but the schools seem to have been integrated shortly afterwards because Moses Fleetwood and his brother Weldy are listed as graduates of Steubenville High School.

Although his medical practice brought relative affluence to his family, by 1870 Moses W. had become a Methodist Episcopal minister. In 1877–78 he served the Second Methodist Episcopal Church in Oberlin, Ohio, leaving there for a post in Jeffersonville, Indiana, before returning to Steubenville by 1880.

In 1877 Moses Fleetwood enrolled in Oberlin's preparatory program, entering Oberlin in the fall of 1878. Moses Fleetwood began his college career with excellent grades which declined during the three years he spent at Oberlin as he turned his attention to girls and more especially to baseball. While he was not the first black baseball player at Oberlin—that honor goes to an unidentified player in 1865—he and his brother were members of the first varsity baseball team in 1881. The team played only five games, but Moses Fleetwood's skills in a 9–2 victory over the University of Michigan were so impressive that he was invited to move to that school to play ball.

During the summer of 1881 Walker had his first recorded racial incident in baseball. He had been hired to catch for the White Sewing Machine Company of Cleveland. In July at Louisville, Kentucky, he was refused breakfast at a local hotel. Then the Louisville Eclipse team refused to take the field if he played.

Walker entered Michigan in the spring of 1882 to play baseball and study law. By this time one of his sweethearts, Arabella Taylor (1863–1895) of Xenia, Ohio, was pregnant. Walker and Taylor were married in Hudson, Michigan, in July 1882. Their first child, Cleodolinda Dewers, was born in December. Two more children completed the family: Thomas Fleetwood (1884–1939) and George Wise (b. 1886). Arabella Taylor Walker died in Steubenville, Ohio, on June 12, 1895.

In the spring of 1898, Moses Fleetwood Walker married again. His bride, Ednah Jane Mason, was born in Albany, Ohio, in 1861. She graduated from Oberlin in 1884. After teaching school for a while, she moved to Chicago where she ran a grocery store and meat market. Her 1888 marriage to William George Price ended either by death or divorce and she returned to live with her parents in their Oberlin home in 1897. There were no children from the Walker–Mason marriage.

Becomes Professional Ball Player

In the spring of 1882 Walker played for a University of Michigan team much strengthened by his presence and which won 10 of its 13 games. That summer he played professional ball for the New Castle, Pennsylvania, Neshannocks, sustaining his reputation as a catcher. When he returned to the university, Weldy joined him. Both brothers pursued their studies for a while longer, but the lure of professional baseball ultimately proved too great for them to finish their degrees.

Moses Fleetwood Walker played his first full season of professional ball in 1883 for the Toledo club in the Northwestern League. There he demonstrated his durability as a barehanded catcher, only occasionally using slightly padded lambskin gloves. The fact that players were paid only when they played encouraged him to continue playing even with split and bleeding fingers. It is not known how much he was paid, but one estimate put his earning power at $2,000 a year, a large income by contemporary standards. During the season there occurred the first of a series of incidents between Adrian "Cap" Anson and Walker. Anson managed the Chicago White Stockings of the National League and was a virulent racist. He refused to play an exhibition game in Toledo if Walker played. Anson backed down this time when it came to a question of forfeiting his team's share of the gate receipts, but he would carry his point in later years.

The success of the Toledo team's season was such that they moved to the American Association the following year,

Moses Fleetwood Walker (middle row, far left), with Oberlin College's varsity baseball team.

retaining Walker's services. Thus in 1884 Walker became the first black to play on a major league team. (The American Association had won this status in an 1882 agreement with the National League to refrain from raiding.) The season promised difficulties for Walker. Not only was there another exhibition game scheduled with Cap Anson's team, but the schedule took the team to Louisville and other Southern cities. Walker faced the full array of the problems confronting black players at the time.

Walker apparently began by accepting the problems caused by his race, but towards the end of his career he met refusal of service and accommodation by suing. Since most of the suits were in local courts, the record here is far from complete. Not only did Walker have to face hostility off the field from people in the stands, he had problems with some of his teammates. For example, in this 1884 season star pitcher Tony Mullane refused to take signals from his catcher so Walker stopped giving them and never knew what kind of pitch to expect. Mullane pitched to Walker 42 times that season and despite the situation the two were fairly successful working together. Mullane was not alone in his prejudice over the course of Walker's career.

The exhibition game with Anson's club fell through, so another confrontation was put off until another year. Walker's season was marked by injuries, including a broken rib. In addition, the Toledo team ran into financial difficulties and had to cut expenses, so Walker was released at the end of the season. It would be 63 years before there was another black major league player. In December 1884 Walker took a position as a postal clerk in Toledo.

Nonetheless, Walker was able to spend five more seasons in baseball. It is impossible to pinpoint when his problems with alcohol began but by the end of his career, he was drinking hard. In 1885 he was first with the Cleveland team in the Western League. In April he was the person selected to be charged in a test of Cleveland's ordinance against Sunday baseball. His case was won, but another case later that season resulted in affirming the ban. Cleveland would not have Sunday games until 1910. When the Cleveland team went broke in June, Walker went to a team in Waterbury, Connecticut, where he also spent the following year.

In 1887 Walker went to Newark of the International League to catch for black pitcher George Washington Stavey. The pair had great success. Walker was probably earning

$200 a month. This was more than the $12 to $18 a week of players on the all–black professional teams that were coming into existence as black players were squeezed out of formerly integrated teams. Cap Anson again forced Walker out of an exhibition game and was vociferous in his opposition to a possible offer to the black catcher–pitcher pair by a major league team. (Anson is also supposed to have blocked another offer to Walker on a different occasion.) The International League took note of rising anti–black sentiment and voted to bar all black players in July but rescinded the decision when it became public. During the off–season the league settled on an informal quota of one black per team.

Syracuse won an exception to the league rule when Walker jumped to that team for the 1888 season. The second black player, Robert Higgins, left before the end of the season. During this time Walker was arrested for possessing a loaded gun behind the stands when he was thrown out of a game in Toronto—he was on the bench but not suited up—along with a number of Toronto fans. He was again at Syracuse in 1889 to become the last black in the league until Jackie Robinson. Syracuse released him on August 23, leaving only three blacks whose careers on white baseball teams continued for a while longer.

In evaluating Walker's ability as a player, his biographer David W. Zang feels that changes in the game make use of Walker's statistics meaningless as a basis for comparison. Instead he points to the fact that Walker played professional baseball for seven years in the face of a rising tide of prejudice that included fellow players refusing to cooperate with any black teammate and umpires who admitted to making close calls regularly go against black players.

Faces Murder Trial

After leaving baseball, Walker continued to live in Syracuse, one of less than 900 blacks in a population of 88,000. He found work as a postal clerk. Inspired by the failed attempts of a former Syracuse University professor to make an explosive artillery shell, Walker believed he had solved the problem and won a patent for his idea on August 18, 1891. Before the patent was issued he was on trial for murder. On Thursday, April 9, 1891, shortly after four in the afternoon he killed Irish bricklayer Patrick ''Curly'' Murray with a knife during a street brawl. Walker himself was injured on the back of his head, according to his account, by a thrown stone. All parties were drinking, and testimony by witnesses varied dramatically. By the time Walker came to trial on June 1, the charge was reduced from first to second degree murder. On June 3 he was acquitted. He then returned to Steubenville, where he worked again as a postal clerk, now handling registered mail on a railroad run.

Between 1891 and 1895 he suffered many personal losses. His father, who had separated from Caroline Walker and lived in Detroit, died in May 1891. Caroline Walker died of a throat disease in December 1893, and his wife died of cancer on June 12, 1895. On September 19, 1898, just four months after his marriage to his second wife, Ednah Jane Mason Price, Walker was arrested on charges of stealing from the mails. Over three years he established a pattern as the only railroad employee in eastern Ohio to lose regularly letters he had directly received but did not claim to have dispatched. Although he made good the monies lost, investigators suspected him of borrowing from the mail to meet personal needs. The postal inspectors' trap did not run as smoothly as planned, but Walker was convicted and sentenced to a year in prison. His appeal for a presidential pardon was rejected.

On his release Walker returned to Steubenville where he took up residence at the Union Hotel at 105–7 Market Street. He or some family member ran the hotel and its billiard parlor until the death of his son, Thomas Walker, in 1939. In 1902 he and his brother Weldy briefly published a newspaper, *The Equator,* however no issues survive. There are also records of Walker traveling with his wife, singing and showing slides of the Spanish–American War in March 1902 and then traveling for some months later that year to give kinescope exhibitions. In 1904 he acquired the Cadiz Opera House, which he operated until he retired in 1922. This theater, opposite the court house, offered live entertainment and movies.

Walker entertained a mostly white clientele. Blacks were segregated in a balcony. Whatever he privately thought of the racist content of the shows he presented, he booked live minstrel shows and appears to have exhibited *Birth of a Nation.* He again demonstrated his mechanical ability by inventing devices to make the change from reel to reel smoother. Although Cadiz was dry, he continued to drink privately. He and his wife continued the lodge activities they had begun in Steubenville.

In 1908 Walker revealed another side of himself when he published a 48–page booklet, *Our Home Colony: The Past, Present, and Future of the Negro Race.* In this work he called for forced return of all blacks to Africa. He denounced racial mixing and blamed black women with their alleged low morals more than their white partners for miscegenation. This man who had married two women who appeared nearly white also denounced the fixation of black women on white standards of beauty. Of all groups he rated lowest, however, it was mulattos like himself.

Walker was living in Gallipolis, Ohio, during the ten months during which this work appeared. It is possible that Walker and his brother Weldy were planning on organizing emigration themselves. Zang quoted Weldy Walker as stating his occupation on a 1908 questionnaire from Oberlin as ''General Agent for 'Our Home Colony' and Liberian emigration.'' If so the brothers' plans left no further trace.

Ednah Jane Walker died in Cadiz of chronic nephritis on May 26, 1920. Walker sold the Opera House on March 1, 1922, but his retirement was short–lived. Within a month he tried running a theater in Cleveland, but that enterprise failed after three months. At the time of his death from lobar pneumonia on May 11, 1924, he was working as a clerk in a billiards parlor. His body was brought back to Steubenville, where he was buried beside his first wife.

Moses Fleetwood Walker had to be excluded from competing with whites in baseball since the prevailing racist ideology said blacks were always inferior and any evidence to the contrary had to be suppressed. On an ideological level he turned to black nationalism. But his voice was muted and seems to have had little impact. Ironically, his career ended as it began—entertaining largely white audiences, first by his baseball skills and then as theater operator.

REFERENCES

Peterson, Robert. *Only the Ball Was White.* Englewood Cliffs, NJ: Prentice Hall, 1970.

Walker, M. F. *Our Home Colony: The Past, Present, and Future of the Negro Race in America.* Steubenville, OH: Herald, 1908.

Zang, David W. *Fleet Walker's Divided Heart.* Lincoln, NE: University of Nebraska Press, 1995.

COLLECTIONS

The Oberlin College Library has an extensive collection of primary and secondary materials about Walker.

Robert L. Johns

Fats Waller

(1904–1943)

Pianist, composer, band leader

A major figure in American music, Fats Waller was one of those special talents that burn brightly and then were extinguished all too soon. In just 39 years, he created a musical legacy that still lives on today. His talent seemed to know no bounds. As a jazz pianist he was considered one of the best, if not the best, of the famous New York stride pianists of the 1920s, a group that included such luminaries as James P. Johnson, Eubie Blake, and Willie ''The Lion'' Smith. As a composer he penned such notable hits as ''Ain't Misbehavin','' ''Honeysuckle Rose,'' ''Squeeze Me,'' and ''Black and Blue,'' songs that remain a standard part of the jazz repertoire. As a singer and band leader, he became one of the first African American artists whose popularity transcended racial boundaries.

Waller was born Thomas Wright Waller on May 21, 1904, in New York City. His parents, Edward Martin and Adeline Lockett Waller, had 11 children, only five of whom survived childhood. Waller was the fourth–born of these five.

Fats Waller

Waller married Edith Hatchett in 1920, and, in 1921 they had a son, Thomas Waller Jr. The couple divorced in 1923, and, in 1926 Waller married Anita Ruthford, who bore him two sons, Maurice and Roland Waller.

Waller's parents grew up in Virginia, but after their marriage in 1888, they moved to New York City in hopes of finding greater opportunity and freedom. Waller's parents were devout Baptists, and, upon arriving in New York, they settled in Greenwich Village to be near the Abyssinian Baptist Church which was located there. Waller's began work as a stable hand, but he eventually saved up enough money to buy a wagon and team of horses and start his own cartage business. A hard–working man, he soon made the business successful enough to enable him to support his family comfortably. The Wallers were a close family, and religion played a large role in their daily life. Waller's father became a deacon and then chairman of the Board of Deacons and superintendent of the Sunday School at the Abyssinian Baptist Church. His wife sang in the choir and accompanied the singers on the organ and piano. When the church moved to Harlem in the early 1900s, the Wallers followed, moving to 134th Street where young Waller was born.

Waller's musical talents emerged at a young age. His first exposure to music came through the church as he listened to his mother accompany the choir. He began piano lessons at the age of six, and, though he showed little interest in learning scales and music theory, his remarkable ear allowed him to reproduce popular songs perfectly after hearing his teacher play them only a few times. As his musical proficiency grew, he was asked to play the piano for his classmates as they marched into assembly and then was chosen as the pianist for the school orchestra. Waller was growing physically during this time as well. Though he had not yet attained his eventual height of six feet, and weight of over 280 pounds, he was already big enough that his classmates affectionately dubbed him "Fats," the nickname by which he was known to everyone but his parents, for the rest of his life.

Harlem was alive with music during this period, and Waller became fascinated by the jazz he heard all around him at the local clubs and cabarets. This disappointed his father, who thought of jazz as "devil's music" and had hoped his son would become a classical pianist. By 1918 Waller realized that his real musical education had to come from outside of school, so he convinced his father to let him drop out of high school to pursue his musical career. He discovered the Lincoln Theater in Harlem, a movie and vaudeville theater with a pianist who accompanied the silent films and an organist who accompanied the acts. Enthralled by the music he heard there, Waller quickly became a regular. The pianist at the Lincoln, Mazie Mullins, noticed his interest and befriended him, and before long Waller was sitting beside her as she played and filling in for her on her breaks. In 1919 when the Lincoln's regular organist suddenly became ill, Waller was hired to replace him for ten days. He was a hit in his first music job, and he later quipped in Maurice Waller and Anthony Calabrese's book *Fats Waller,* "At the end of those ten days, I had learned more music than in all the time before I started." When the regular organist left the Lincoln later that year for a better–paying job, Waller was hired as the permanent replacement for the then impressive salary of $23 a week.

Studies with James P. Johnson

The following year proved to be a pivotal one for Waller. First came tragedy in the family. His mother had been suffering from diabetes for years, and, in 1920, finally succumbed to the disease. Waller and his mother had always been close, and her death left him disconsolate. Feeling unable to remain living in the family household after her death, he moved in with a friend, Russell Brooks. The loss of one close relationship led to the beginning of another. The Brooks had a player piano and an ample supply of piano rolls by James P. Johnson. In his grief, Waller threw himself into Johnson's music, listening to the piano rolls daily and slowing them down so he could mimic the movement of the keys with his fingers. Seeing Waller's dedication, Brooks arranged a meeting between Waller and Johnson. This meeting began an association that was to change Waller's life forever.

Waller could not have chosen a better mentor. James P. Johnson was the acknowledged king of the stride piano, a style of jazz that grew out of ragtime and demanded great technique and creativity. Though Waller was not yet fully–formed musically at the time of their first meeting, Johnson recognized his young pupil's talent. As Waller later described in Waller and Calabrese's *Fats Waller:*

> At first James P. didn't say much. He just let me play. Then he'd tell me to do this, or try that, and I did. Before I knew it, he was sitting on the stool next to me, making that piano rock. He'd play trills and strong bass figurations. He taught me more in an afternoon than I had learned in ten years.

Waller continued to study with Johnson for the next two years, and, as his piano–playing blossomed under Johnson's tutelage, his career began to follow suit. Their teacher–student relationship gradually developed into one of equals, and Johnson introduced Waller to Willie "The Lion" Smith, Eubie Blake, and the other great New York stride pianists of that era. With Johnson's backing, Waller began making his own piano rolls and working regularly at cabarets and rent parties, functions where tenants in Harlem would raise money for their rent by providing food, liquor, and music in their apartment for a modest admission fee. Between playing cabarets and rent parties at night and the Lincoln Theater during the day, Waller soon established himself as one of the top pianists, in New York.

While Waller's career was a success in the early 1920s, his marriage to Hatchett was not. The couple married soon after the death of Waller's mother. But, as time went on, their differences made the marriage unworkable. Waller was an ebullient man with a large appetite for fun, food, and liquor while his wife was a quiet woman and a devout Baptist. As Waller's musical career developed, she became increasingly frustrated with her husband's late hours and carefree lifestyle, and, by 1922, they separated and were later divorced. Their parting was not an amicable one, and, for the rest of his life, Waller found himself in legal trouble for refusing to make his alimony payments regularly. Waller married Ruthford in 1926, and the couple remained happily together for the rest of Waller's life.

Gains National and International Acclaim

For the rest of the 1920s, Waller continued his artistic growth and success. He began writing songs in 1924, and immediately displayed a remarkable gift for composition. "Squeeze Me," the second song he wrote, became a big hit in 1924, and he went on to write over 400 songs by the end of the decade. Many of them were co–written with his long–time lyricist, Andy Razaf, including such classics as "Ain't Misbehavin'" and "Honeysuckle Rose." In the latter part of the 1920s, Waller composed for the musical theater, writing the scores for such hit shows as *Keep Shufflin'*, in 1928, and *Hot Chocolates*, in 1929. His recording career also flourished during this period, both as a pianist and an organist. By the end of the 1920s, Waller was one of the most popular performers in New York.

The triumphs continued for Waller in the 1930s. As the new medium of radio became popular, he used it as a springboard to national fame, appearing on the shows "Paramount on Parade" and "Radio Roundup" from 1930 to 1931 and then starred for two years on WLW in Cincinnati. It was also in 1930, that Waller began singing in performances and on recordings at the urging of Joe Davis, his music publisher. His distinctive phrasing and infectious personality proved irresistible to audiences. With his boundless musical talent and quick wit he was a natural for radio, and his appearances won him countless new fans, both African American and white.

By the mid–1930s, Waller was an international star, and he remained so until his death in 1943. He toured Europe twice with resounding success in the late 1930s, and besides making several short movies with his band, Fats Waller's Rhythm, he appeared in three feature–length films, *Hooray for Love* and *The King of Burlesque*, both of which were released in 1935, and 1943's *Stormy Weather*. With his natural showmanship and charisma he handled himself well in all of them, and, in *The King of Burlesque,* he managed to strike a blow against the prevailing racism of that time. As his son, Maurice Waller, remembered in his book *Fats Waller*:

> The original script of *The King of Burlesque* called for Dad to play a Stepen Fetchit part. He objected vehemently to his part and the way blacks in general were treated by the film. After long and vehement arguments, the producer gave in.

By 1943 Waller was at the height of his fame and success, but finally his huge appetite for food and liquor caught up with him. While returning by train from Hollywood after a West Coast tour, he contracted bronchial pneumonia, and, when the train reached Kansas City on the morning of December 15, his manager discovered him dead in his sleeping compartment. He was 39.

Condolences and testimonials to Waller the musician and Waller the man flooded in from around America and the world. Louis Armstrong reportedly cried all night long upon learning of the death of his friend and colleague. Waller's funeral in Harlem was one of the largest ever held there. Thousands of people attended the funeral, filling the church and lining the streets outside. Adam Clayton Powell Jr. gave the final eulogy. Quoted in *Fats Waller,* he said, "Because God gave him genius and skill, he in turn gave the world laughter and joy for its difficult and lonely hours. Thomas Waller and his songs shall live again."

Powell's words were prophetic. Waller's music did indeed live on. Songs like "Ain't Misbehavin'," "Honeysuckle Rose," and "Jitterbug Waltz" remain standards. A new generation came to appreciate the full breadth of Waller's talents when *Ain't Misbehavin',* a Broadway musical based on his compositions, opened in 1978. The show was yet another triumph for Waller and his music. It won the New York Drama Critics Circle Award for best musical and three Tony Awards, including best musical. It ran for 1,604 performances. Contemporary audiences had the opportunity to experience Waller's genius again in 1996 when the Pointer Sisters organized a successful revival of *Ain't Misbehavin'*.

Waller's place in America's musical history was secure. A large man with an even larger talent, he left his indelible mark on American music as a composer, keyboardist, singer, and band leader. In 1981 the City of New York placed a commemorative plaque in memory of him at the site of the Harlem apartment house where he spent his childhood. This memorial was well–deserved, but Waller's most enduring legacy was his music, which will live on for as long as jazz and popular music were played.

REFERENCES

Contemporary Musicians: Profiles of the People in Music. Vol. 7. Detroit: Gale Research, 1992.

James, Edward T., ed. *Dictionary of American Biography.* Supplement Three. New York: Charles Scribener's Sons, 1973.

Kernfield, Barry, ed. *The New Grove Dictionary of Jazz.* London: Macmillan, 1988.

Kirkeby, Ed, Duncan P. Schiedt, and Sinclair Traill. *Ain't Misbehavin': The Story of Fats Waller.* New York: Dodd, Mead, 1966.

"Plaque in Harlem a Memorial to Fats Waller." *New York Times,* August 19, 1981.

"Pointers Get Joint Jumpin' for *Ain't Misbehavin'.*" *Columbus (Ohio) Dispatch,* March 6, 1996.

Salzman, Jack, David Lionel Smith, and Cornel West, eds. *Encyclopedia of African–American Culture and History.* New York: Macmillan Reference Library USA/Simon and Schuster Macmillan, 1996.

Shipton, Alyn. *Fats Waller: His Life and Times.* New York: Universe Books, 1988.

Thompson, David. *Fats Waller.* Alexandria, VA: Time–Life Books, 1980.

Vance, Joel. *Fats Waller: His Life and Times.* Chicago: Contemporary Books, 1977.

Waller, Maurice, and Anthony Calabrese. *Fats Waller.* New York: Schirmer Books, 1977.

Arthur W. Buell

Eric Walrond

(1898–1966)

Writer, journalist

Eric Derwent Walrond was a key participant in the Harlem Renaissance, one of the twentieth century's most important cultural eras. Walrond wrote a number of essays, reviews, and short stories that appeared in many well–known periodicals during the early and mid–1920s. His collection of ten short stories of West Indian life, *Tropic Death* (1926), heralded his ascension as a notable Harlem Renaissance writer.

Walrond was born in Georgetown, British Guiana (now known as Guyana), in 1898; his father was Guyanese and his mother was Barbadian. In 1906, eight–year–old Eric and his mother moved to a small, rural settlement near the town of Black Rock in Barbados after the elder Walrond abandoned them. The settlement was owned by Mrs. Walrond's father.

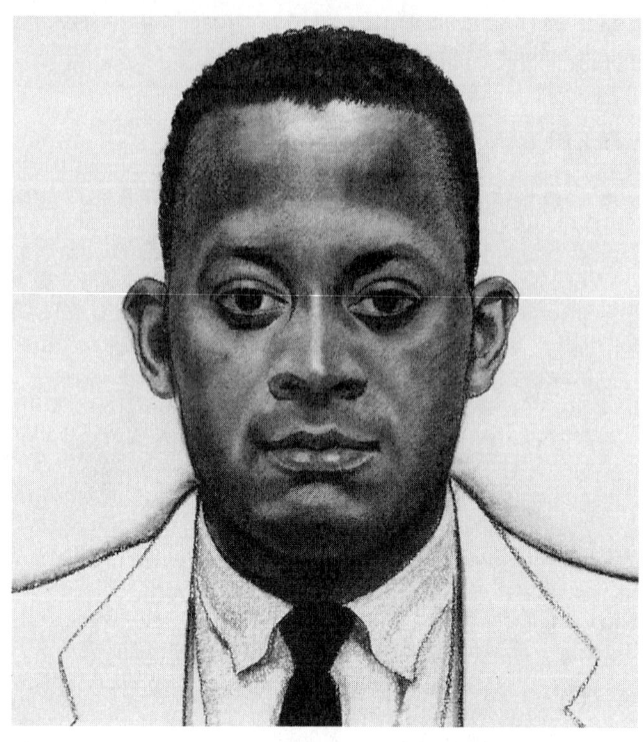

Eric Walrond

She had previously endured the stigma of marrying outside of her class; then she had to cope with the myriad problems of being deserted by her husband and raising her son without the support of his father.

Young Eric's formal education began at St. Stephan's Boys' School in Black Rock. In 1910 his educational environment changed. Thousands of West Indian and Guyanese men were hired to dig the Panama Canal and it is assumed that the senior Walrond was one of them. Eric and his mother moved to the Canal Zone where a reconciliation was sought. Although her marital efforts were futile, mother and son settled in Colon. Eric attended the public schools there, and as a result, the boy who had been reared under British tradition was now immersed in Spanish culture and became bilingual. He completed his secondary education with private tutors from 1913 to 1916.

Walrond's schooling prepared him for employment as a secretary or stenographer, and his first job was as a clerk in the Health Department of the Canal Commission at Cristobal. In his second job, Walrond made use of his strong interest in journalism; he was hired by the *Panama Star and Herald,* an important newspaper in the tropics. He was employed as a news, court, and sports reporter from 1916 to 1918.

Later in 1918, the 21–year–old Walrond moved to New York. His initial efforts to continue his journalistic career by working at a Harlem newspaper were unsuccessful. From 1922 to 1924, Walrond attended City College of New York (now known as City University of New York), and from 1924 to 1926, he took creative writing courses at Columbia University. During those years, Walrond wanted to support himself by working as a secretary. During his formative years in Barbados and Colon, Walrond experienced little, if any, racial discrimination. Thus he was appalled by the numerous New York employment rejections that were race–motivated. He eventually secured secretarial and stenographer positions with the British Recruiting Museum, an architect, and the superintendent of the Broad Street Hospital.

The Harlem Renaissance

Walrond relinquished the hospital job in order to resume his career in journalism during the earliest days of the Harlem Renaissance. This was the era during the 1920s and early 1930s that marked the prolific production of black American literary, artistic, and musical works. Most of the era's writers, including Walrond, were born elsewhere, and their creations did not always center on Harlem, yet Harlem was the acknowledged focal point of the movement symbolizing an attitudinal awakening of black Americans. Redefining black American identity was a major concern of Harlem Renaissance authors. They blended literary talent with awareness of their racial heritage and progress in their effort to present realistic images of black life.

Walrond's most productive years as a writer coincided with the Harlem Renaissance. He was a co–owner, editor, and reporter of the *Brooklyn and Long Island Informer,* a black American weekly publication from 1921 to 1923. He concurrently served as an associate editor of *Weekly Review.* In 1923, Walrond became an associate editor of *Negro World,* the weekly newspaper of Marcus Garvey's Universal Negro Improvement Association. His tenure with *Negro World* ended two years later when Walrond became disenchanted with Garvey's leadership abilities. His next position was at *Opportunity,* a publication of the National Urban League. Walrond was *Opportunity*'s business manager from 1925 to 1927. *Opportunity* and *Crisis,* published by the NAACP, were the two major periodicals of the 1920s that consistently included the work of Harlem Renaissance writers. During the early and mid–1920s, Walrond's articles, reviews, and short stories appeared in both magazines as well as other well–known periodicals including *Argosy, All–Story Magazine, Current History,* the *Independent,* the *Messenger, New Age, New Republic, Saturday Review of Literature, Smart Set, Success Magazine,* and *Vanity Fair.* One of Walrond's most memorable essays is "The New Negro Faces America," (*Current History,* 1923) in which he criticizes the philosophies of W. E. B. Du Bois, Marcus Garvey, and Booker T. Washington, asserts that each leader lacks what the black race needs, and offers characteristics of a new black identity.

As a key participant in the Harlem Renaissance, Walrond encountered some of the twentieth century's most prominent black Americans. W. E. B. Du Bois, editor of *Crisis*; editor Charles S. Johnson of *Opportunity;* novelist Jessie Redmon Fauset, literary editor of *Crisis;* and literary critic Alain Locke are generally recognized as the mentors of the Harlem Renaissance. They eloquently voiced the need for a black American attitudinal awakening, created works that set the era's tenor, and promoted the works of new and/or younger authors. Since Walrond's works appeared in *Crisis* and *Opportunity,* Du Bois, Johnson, and Fauset sanctioned his writing ability. Additional approval of Walrond's talent came in 1925 with the landmark publication of *The New Negro,* an anthology of Harlem Renaissance writing edited by Locke; Walrond's short story, "The Palm Porch," is included.

Opportunity provided a publishing outlet for young writers. Further, editor Charles Johnson promoted their talents by awarding *Opportunity*'s prizes for creative achievement in May 1925 at a banquet in New York attended by more than 300 people. Prizes were awarded according to genre. In the category of short story writing, Walrond won third prize for "Voodoo's Revenge." Langston Hughes, arguably the most famous Harlem Renaissance figure, met Walrond at the banquet.

Walrond's talent facilitated his entry into Harlem social life. In a Fisk University oral history transcript cited in *When Harlem Was in Vogue,* Ethel Nance, Charles Johnson's secretary, offered glimpses into Walrond's personality and physical appearance:

> He was always bringing someone to Harlem. . .or if people wanted to come they would say, "Get in touch with Walrond and he'll see that you meet interesting people." You would think of him as being tall; he may not have been six feet. He had flashing eyes; his face was very alert and very alive.

Another Harlem Renaissance figure, Dorothy West, wrote in *The Richer, the Poorer,* "Countee Cullen, Langston Hughes, Zora Neale Hurston, Bruce Nugent, Rudolph Fisher, Jean Toomer, Eric Walrond were the new names."

Wallace Thurman, another young member of the Harlem Renaissance, wrote a satirical novel about the activities of his contemporaries. In his *Infants of the Spring* (1932), Walrond was portrayed as a character named Cedric Williams. Thurman had high praise for Walrond. He wrote, "Next to arrive was Cedric Williams, a West Indian, whose first book, a collection of short stories with a Caribbean background, . . . marked him as one of the three Negroes writing who actually had something to say, and also some concrete idea of style."

Tropic Death was Walrond's most critically acclaimed work. In this collection of ten stories with Caribbean settings, Walrond takes his readers on journeys of humanity where poverty, famine, racism, and relationships are exposed, and sudden death is prevalent. There are no happy endings in *Tropic Death,* as children, women, and men are victims of the environment. Walrond's writing style has been described by various literary critics as avant–garde, realistic, naturalistic, impressionistic, gothic, and autobiographical. *Tropic Death* won praise from Du Bois, Hughes, and Walrond's other Harlem Renaissance contemporaries, including poet, professor, and literary critic Sterling Brown. In *The Negro in American Fiction,* Brown cited *Tropic Death* as a "brilliant first book. . . . Gifted with a power of description, Walrond gives us, for the first time, a vivid sense of Negro life in the tropics below the Gulf stream." Walrond was 28 when *Tropic Death* was published in 1926 and was considered one of the most promising younger talents to emerge from the Harlem Renaissance.

Life After *Tropic Death*

Walrond left his position at *Opportunity* in 1927, and the next year he was awarded a John Simon Guggenheim Memorial Foundation Award and a Zona Gale scholarship at the University of Wisconsin in order to complete a book about the Panama Canal and French involvement with the project. Boni and Liveright, publisher of *Tropic Death,* announced its intent to publish this manuscript, tentatively titled *The Big Ditch.* Although rumors circulated, according to *When Harlem Was in Vogue,* that Walrond "had squandered the stipends and written nothing," he in fact conducted extensive research for the book in the Caribbean in 1928 prior to traveling to London and Paris on an extension of the grant.

Walrond came in contact with other Harlem Renaissance figures while abroad. Artist and writer Richard Bruce Nugent saw Walrond at a London railway station in 1929 and after arriving in Paris that same year, Walrond became a member of the African–American enclave there, shared a studio with Countee Cullen, and attended numerous parties. He returned to the United States in 1931 to visit his parents in Brooklyn. Upon his return to France, Walrond resided in a small village near Avignon. He spent the rest of his life in France and England.

Walrond's publications during his European years included an article about a Panama financial scandal which appeared in a Madrid magazine, short stories and an interview in French magazines, short stories and one article in the *Black Man,* a Garveyite magazine. Fewer details are known about Walrond's personal life. He was married twice, and he had three daughters: Jean, Dorothy, and Lucille. Walrond died in 1966 in London, where he was working on a book about the Panama Canal.

Eric Walrond remains one of the Harlem Renaissance's most enigmatic figures. Regardless of the many unanswered questions concerning Walrond's professional and personal affairs, such as why he stopped publishing in America and whether or not any unpublished manuscripts are extant, Eric Walrond's journalistic and literary works are enduring testimonies to his talent.

REFERENCES

Bone, Robert. *Down Home: A History of Afro–American Short Fiction from the Beginning to the End of the Harlem Renaissance.* New York: Putnam's, 1975.

Brown, Sterling. *The Negro in American Fiction.* 1937. Reprint, New York: Atheneum, 1969.

Contemporary Authors. Vol. 125. Detroit: Gale Research, 1989.

Fabre, Michel. *From Harlem to Paris: Black American Writers in France 1840–1980.* Urbana: University of Illinois Press, 1991.

Lewis, David Levering. *When Harlem Was in Vogue.* New York: Oxford University Press, 1989.

Locke, Alain, ed. *The New Negro.* 1925. Reprint, New York: Atheneum, 1968.

Sinnette, Elinor Des Verney. *Arthur Alfonso Schomburg: Black Bibliophile and Collector.* Detroit: New York Public Library and Wayne State University Press, 1989.

Thurman, Wallace. *Infants of the Spring.* 1932. Reprint, Boston: Northeastern University Press, 1992.

Walrond, Eric. ''The New Negro Faces America.'' *Current History* 17 (February 1923): 786–788.

———. *Tropic Death.* New York: Boni and Liveright, 1926.

West, Dorothy. *The Richer, the Poorer: Stories, Sketches, and Reminiscences.* New York: Doubleday, 1995.

Linda M. Carter

Douglas Turner Ward

(1930–)

Playwright, director, producer, critic, theatrical company cofounder

Douglas Turner Ward is sometimes called the ''father of the modern black theater.'' His career has been tied closely to the Negro Ensemble Company (NEC), which he cofounded in 1967. His work has promoted the careers of a number of black actors and black playwrights and has led to significant new directions in the black theater.

Ward was born on a sugar cane and rice plantation near Burnside, Louisiana, on May 5, 1930, the only child of Roosevelt and Dorothy Short Ward, who worked as field hands on the plantation. When he was ready for school, young Ward was sent to nearby New Orleans to live with a relative and attend a two–room, one–teacher school. Already a gifted reader, Ward advanced in grades rapidly. When Ward was eight the family relocated to New Orleans, where Roosevelt Ward worked first as a fork lift operator and later as foreman on the docks. After World War II white laborers returned to man the docks, and Roosevelt Ward lost his job. He afterward joined his wife, who worked as a seamstress, in establishing a tailoring business in their home.

Ward read widely and accelerated his education. By the time he was 12 he had entered high school—the all–black New Orleans Catholic high school, or Xavier University Prep—where he participated in track and played football. After graduation, he spent the year 1946–47 at Wilberforce University in Xenia, Ohio, and continued to play football. He had set his sights on a football scholarship and transferred to the University of Michigan for the 1947–48 year. He had studied journalism, but after a knee injury disrupted his athletic career he began to skip formal classes and to spend his time in the college library where he became an avid reader. He admitted in *Essence* that he had also become involved in ''radical political movements.'' In 1948, when he was 18, Ward left college and set out for New York City, where he lived with an aunt. He continued his involvement with a left–wing political activist group by distributing leaflets on street corners and writing for the *Daily Worker.* Inadvertently, his involvement launched his career in the theater.

Soon Ward found his niche. After he wrote satirical sketches to provide some relief during heated political meetings and then a cantata based on slave rebel Nat Turner's life, and received overwhelming positive responses, he knew that he wanted to work in the theater. He was now only 19–years old. Ward worked as a journalist from 1948 to 1951. In 1951 he was arrested for draft evasion and jailed in Louisiana for three months. He was required to remain in Louisiana for two years; later the Supreme Court overturned the conviction. During the wait he spent his time around working–class blacks—in pool halls and backrooms—where he learned their dialogue.

Ward returned to New York but left political activism behind. Now he wanted to know acting from the actor's perspective, so he studied at Paul Mann's Actors' Workshop from 1955 to 1958. He was first understudy and then replacement for Robert Earl Jones—father of actor James Earl Jones—as Joe Mott in a 1956 revival of Eugene O'Neill's *The Iceman Cometh,* and then in a revival of *Lost in the Stars.* He first appeared on Broadway in 1959, where as understudy to Sidney Poitier, he had a bit part in Lorraine Hansberry's *A Raisin in the Sun.* Then he played the major role of Walter Younger and toured with the play in 1960 and 1961. Other plays in which he appeared during this period were *The Blacks* (1961–62) and *Pullman Car Hiawatha* (1962). He was an understudy for a role in *One Flew over the Cuckoo's Nest* (1963) and appeared in *Rich Little Rich Girl* (1964), *The Blood Knot* (1964), and *Coriolanus* (1965). During the 1960s he also appeared in a number of television shows, including *Dupont Show of the Month, East Side/West Side,* and *Studio One.*

Ward had begun to write plays early on. He showed one of them to his friend, actor Robert Hooks, and beginning November 15, 1965, Hooks produced two one–act comedies, *Day of Absence* and *Happy Ending* at St. Marks Place Theatre. The two plays ran for 500 performances and won a Vernon Rice–Drama Desk Award and an Obie Award (Off–Broadway's most prestigious prize). Public Broadcasting Laboratory later produced *Day of Absence* on educational stations.

Cofounds Negro Ensemble Company

Black theater as well as Ward's career was affected significantly by Ward's article, ''American Theater: For Whites Only?,'' published in the *New York Times* for August 14, 1966. The article came at a time when black talent in the theater was low. In the article he stressed the need for a permanent black theater in America that would not be a segregated or separatist theater but a home–base for black artists. The theater, he added, would concentrate on black themes but would include and interpret good drama wherever it originated. Whites could participate in the theater as well, but in Ward's view, blacks were responsible for providing an outlet for exploring their own experience. George McBundy of the Ford Foundation was impressed by the article, resulting in a three–year grant of $1,200,000 from the foundation to Ward, Hooks, and producer Gerald Krone to found and support the Negro Ensemble Company. Hooks, who stayed with the company until 1970, was managing director; Krone was administrative director; and Ward was artistic director. NEC became a vehicle for the production of works by many black playwrights as well as for Ward's own writing and acting. With the exception of the first productions which were by white writers—Peter Weiss's *Song of Lusitanian Bogey* and Richard Lawler's *Summer of the Seventeenth Doll,* which opened in 1968—the next 20 years would be devoted to producing plays written by black Americans as well as by Caribbean and African playwrights.

Controversy surrounded the theatre's beginning: black leaders protested because the theater was located at St. Marks Playhouse and not in Harlem. They also opposed the presentation of plays by white writers to open NEC's productions.

Ending the 1968 season, however, were Nigerian playwright Wole Soyinka's play *Kongi's Harvest,* about an imaginary African state, and *Daddy Goodness,* a humorous fable by Richard Wright and Louis Sapin. Ward directed the latter play. NEC gained wide acclaim for its production in 1969 of Lonnie Elder's tragicomedy *Ceremonies in Dark Old Men.* Ward received the Vernon Rice Drama Desk Award for his role in the play as a Harlem widower who engaged in such rituals as checker games and bootlegging. In April of that year, NEC made its London debut at the Aldwych Theatre.

Ward wrote and acted in the play *The Reckoning,* which Hooks Productions staged on September 4, 1969, in cooperation with NEC; it ran for 94 performances. NEC presented Ward's one–act play *Brotherhood* on a double bill with *Day of Absence* on March 17, 1970. Throughout the 1970s, Ward devoted most of his time to administrative and production work of NEC. Still, he produced a short piece, *The Redeemer,* presented at Actors Theatre of Louisville. In the mid–1970s, NEC produced for ABC–TV and the Public Broadcasting System two of its most celebrated plays, *Ceremonies in Dark Old Men* and *The First Breeze of Summer.*

Other plays presented by NEC include Joseph Walker's *The River Niger,* one of NEC's biggest successes. Ward directed the play and appeared in it as well; the production won a special Tony Award for achievement in 1968–69 and an Obie Award in 1973. The play ran on Broadway and set attendance records on tour in Philadelphia, Washington, D.C., Chicago, and Detroit. NEC also presented Lesli Lee's *The First Breeze of Summer* (1975); Charles Fuller's *The Brownsville Road* (1976); Steve Carter's *Nevis Mountain Dew* (1978); Samm–Art Williams's *Home* (1979 and moved to Broadway in 1980); and Charles Fuller's *A Soldier's Play* (a Pulitzer Prize–winner in 1982).

In 1980 NEC moved to larger quarters on West 55th Street. Two years later, under Ward's leadership, NEC and the Hartford Stage Company developed a working relationship to expand NEC's reach.

According to *Black Theatre USA,* through the years, NEC trained and provided work for numerous black actors of note, including Frances Foster, Roscoe Lee Brown, Rosalind Cash, Cleavon Little, Denise Nichols, Richard Roundtree, Roxie Roker, and Esther Rolle. NEC began to struggle when federal and private funding decreased. The company was homeless by 1992 and ceased production but not before it had introduced to the world a variety of high quality black writing, acting, and producing. It had also spawned many black theater groups nationwide, including the D.C. Black Repertory Company, the Urban Arts Corps of New York, the Kuumba Workshop of Chicago, and the Paul Robeson Players of Los Angeles.

Now divorced, in 1966 Ward married Diana Hoyt Powell, who later became an editor, and they had two children. Ward has been called a versatile playwright and actor whose work embraces a wide range of black experiences. He has made an immense contribution to the black theatre.

Current address: Agent: William Morris Agency, 1325 Avenue of the Americas, New York, NY 10019.

REFERENCES

''American Theatre: For Whites Only?'' *New York Times,* August 14, 1966.

Current Biography Yearbook. New York: H. W. Wilson, 1976.

Davis, Thadious M., and Trudier Harris, eds. *Afro–American Writers after 1955.* Detroit: Gale Research, 1984.

Hatch, James V., and Ted Shine, eds. *Black Theatre USA.* Rev. and expanded ed. New York: Free Press, 1996.

Mitchell, Loften. *Black Drama: The Story of the American Negro Theatre.* New York: Hawthorne, 1967.

Peterson, Maurice. ''Douglas Turner Ward.'' *Essence* 4 (June 1973): 44–45, 75.

Ribowsky, Mark. '''Father' of the Black Theater Boom.'' *Sepia* 25 (November 1976): 67–78.

Who's Who among African Americans, 1998–99. 10th ed. Detroit: Gale Research, 1997.

Jessie Carney Smith

Samuel Ringgold Ward

(1817–1866?)

Abolitionist, religious worker, journalist

A tall, very dark man with an imposing physical presence, Samuel Ringgold Ward was one of the leading black orators in the abolition movement. He was uncompromising in his demand for the immediate end of slavery and did not hesitate to point out the racism he encountered among some white abolitionists and churches. A Congregational minister, he added journalism to his activities in support of antislavery.

Ward was born in the Eastern Shore section of Maryland on October 17, 1817, to slaves, Ann and William Ward. His father was of pure African descent. A fugitive slave, William ward lived in Cumberland County, New Jersey, from 1820 to 1826, in New York City from 1826 to 1938, and in Newark from 1838 until his death at the age of 68 in May 1851. Although he undertook any available work, he was primarily a house painter. Ann Ward, born about 1786, was a widow about ten years older than her husband with a dark complexion and straight hair. She was a formidable woman, weighing 184 pounds and stronger than most men. She was also an excellent money manager who was allowed to hire her time out. Ward was the second of three sons; the oldest died before his birth. His younger brother, Isaiah Harper Ward, was born in New Jersey on April 5, 1822, and died on April 16, 1832. His mother died on September 1, 1853, and his father died in May 1851.

Ward was a sickly child. When he was about two his father was wounded and beaten, and Ann Ward expressed her displeasure to her owner in no uncertain terms. Her owner did not dare attempt to whip her, but she felt that she would be sold as soon as her son became healthy. In 1820 she decided to escape. Her husband first hesitated, then followed her lead.

Ward's parents settled at Waldron's Landing near Greenwich, New Jersey, in 1820. As part of their efforts to protect their precarious freedom, they were silent about their origin and Ward's birthplace although they were open about his brother's birth in a free state. Although Ward guessed at their status, his parents never told him directly that he had been born a slave. (His mother told Ward's wife in 1841 or 1842.) As a child, he witnessed the fugitive slave problem in his own family: in 1826 a cousin was re–enslaved but later made a successful escape; in 1828 two of his cousins were taken back to the South and never heard from again.

The Wards stayed in Waldron's Landing until the area experienced a rash of slave–catching. Moving to New York City, they spent their first night, on August 3, 1826, with the parents of future black abolitionist Henry Highland Garnet, who were relatives. Ward attended the Free African School on Mulberry Street along with schoolmates who were later leaders in the Anti–slavery Movement: Garnet, Alexander Crummell, and Charles Lewis Reason.

Ward's work in the Anti–slavery Movement began in 1833 when he found a job as a clerk for inventor Thomas L. Jennings and later for abolitionist David Ruggles. On July 7, 1834, his attachment to the antislavery cause was strengthened when he was beaten by members of a mob after attending an antislavery meeting and arrested while those who beat him went free. At the same time, Ward underwent a religious conversion and for the next few years he taught school and set his sights on the ministry. In 1836, Ward taught school in Newton, New York where he followed the work of abolitionist James W. C. Pennington. He then moved to Newark, New Jersey to teach. It was there where he met and married Emily E. Reynolds of New York in January 1838 and saw the birth of his first child, Samuel Jr., in October 1838. Although little is known of his family life, by 1855 there seems to have been three more children: William Reynolds, Emily, and Alice.

Samuel Ringgold Ward

Becomes Antislavery Activist

The New York Congregational Association licensed Ward to preach in May of 1839. In November of that year he became a traveling agent of the American Anti–Slavery Society and later the New York Anti–Slavery Society. Ward delivered his first public speech in 1837 and soon became as respected an orator as Frederick Douglass, James Pennington, Henry Highland Garnet, and Alexander Crummell.

In April of 1841 Ward became minister of a white Congregational church in South Butler, Wayne County, New York, and was formally ordained and installed in September. He withdrew from this pastorate in 1843 because of a throat disease, and in December went to Geneva, New York, where he was treated, began to study medicine with two local doctors, and spoke occasionally in a local church.

By 1844 Ward recovered fully. He was able to campaign vigorously in 1844 for the antislavery Liberty Party, and in 1846 he became pastor in Cortland Village, New York. Beginning February 14, 1849, he edited a newspaper, *The Impartial Citizen,* published in Syracuse, New York. After suspending publication briefly in June 1850, the paper moved to Boston and struggled until finally folding in 1851. In that year Ward moved to Syracuse, where he became involved in the "Jerry rescue."

Jerry McHenry, a fugitive who had lived in Syracuse for some time, was seized in broad daylight on October 1, 1851. After a group of blacks stormed the combination jail and courthouse and rescued him he was rearrested in the late afternoon. Ward visited the fugitive and gave a speech to the crowd assembled outside. Later that evening the crowd reassembled and effected a rescue. In the aftermath, 12 blacks and 14 whites were indicted. Nine of the 12 blacks escaped to Canada, including Ward and prominent black abolitionist Jermain W. Loguen.

By December of 1851, Ward had been hired by the Anti-Slavery Society of Canada and undertook a strenuous program of speaking and writing on its behalf. He had just published the introductory issues of another newspaper, *The Provincial Freeman,* when he was asked to go to England to raise funds for the society. Appearing in that country the year after the publication of *Uncle Tom's Cabin,* Ward attracted much attention and received patronage from some members of the nobility as well as from British abolitionists. Throughout 1853 and 1854 Ward continued to work in England. While there, a Quaker, John Candler, gave him 50 acres of land in Saint George Parish, Jamaica and in 1855, after publishing *Autobiography of a Fugitive Slave,* he moved there. Perhaps because of Ward's outspoken nature, the white leaders of the Canadian Anti-Slavery Society did not treat him with the respect he desired. The end of his stay in England was marred by charges that he defrauded a tradesman.

Unfortunately the records of Ward's presence on the island of Jamaica are meager. In Kingston, Ward pastored a small congregation of Baptists until early 1860, when he moved to Saint George Parish. He is said to have had considerable political power in Kingston, but he did not thrive in his new venture outside the city. He appears to have died in great poverty in 1866 or soon thereafter. No copy of his final work, *Reflections Upon the Gordon Rebellion,* published in 1866, is known to exist.

Ward was one of the most vigorous and outspoken leaders of his era. He moved people with his powerful oratory and writing. His struggle was compounded by the unrelenting racism surrounding him. Although he headed two predominantly white churches, he faced discrimination as a black even within the abolition movement. He was not, however, a person willing to hold his tongue or compromise his determination.

REFERENCES

Logan, Rayford W., and Michael R. Winston, eds. *Dictionary of American Negro Biography.* New York: Norton, 1982.

Malone, Dumas, ed. *Dictionary of American Biography.* New York: Scribner's, 1943.

Pease, Jane H., and William B. Pease. *Those Who Would Be Free.* New York: Atheneum, 1974.

Ripley, C. Peter. *The Black Abolitionist Papers.* Vol. 1. Chapel Hill: University of North Carolina, 1985.

Ward, Samuel Ringgold. *Autobiography of a Fugitive Negro.* 1855. Reprint, Chicago: Johnson Publishing House, 1970.

Winks, Robin W. *The Blacks in Canada.* New Haven: Yale University Press, 1971.

Robert L. Johns

William Warfield

(1920–)

Vocalist, actor, music educator

Perhaps no other male vocalist is associated more closely with the roles he has portrayed than the renowned concert artist William Warfield. Warfield's repertoire includes arias and songs from stage works, opera, oratorios, classical songs, spirituals, folksongs, and narrations. He has performed concert engagements in numerous countries on three continents, and toured for the U.S. State Department on several occasions. In 50 years of recording and performing, he has become best known as the successor to Todd Duncan in the title role of Gershwin's *Porgy and Bess,* and for singing "Joe" in *Showboat.*

William Caesar Warfield was born in West Helena, Arkansas, on January 22, 1920, the eldest of five sons of Bertha McCamey and Robert Warfield. His father was a Baptist minister, and some of his earliest musical experiences were of singing in his father's church choir. When William was young, his father moved the family to Rochester, New York, where William attended primary and secondary school. A good student, William studied the piano from an early age, and began voice lessons during high school. In his senior year won the District Award in 1938 for the National Music Educators League vocal competition. In the finals of this competition in St. Louis, he won the first place award—a scholarship to the music school of his choice. He chose the Eastman School of Music, where he majored in voice and received a bachelor of music degree in 1942.

After service in the U.S. Army during World War II, Warfield returned to Eastman, intending to earn a master's degree and become a teacher, but his plans were interrupted when auditions for Harold Rome's upcoming Broadway show, *Call Me Mister* came to his attention. He auditioned and was accepted for the national touring company of the show. Two other musical engagements followed—Heywood's *Set My People Free* in 1948, and Blitzstein's *Regina* in 1950.

During this time he also began studying voice privately with Yves Tinayre and Otto Herz, under the auspices of the American Theatre Wing's Professional Training Program. Otto Herz, an accomplished teacher–coach and pianist who accompanied Warfield on many subsequent concerts, and Tinayre, a specialist in song literature and early church music,

William Warfield

helped him prepare repertoire for his forthcoming debut recital. The recital, at New York's Town Hall on March 19, 1950, was well received by critics.

Invitations quickly followed for appearances at home and abroad, and the 1950s brought for Warfield several rewarding experiences as well as points of transition in his growing career. The Australian Broadcasting Company invited him to tour the continent in a series of 35 concerts and recitals from June through September of 1950, including performing with the five principal symphony orchestras in Australia's major cities. While in Australia on tour, he agreed to a contract with MGM studios for the starring role in the movie version of Jerome Kern's *Showboat.* Warfield and soprano Leontyne Price then agreed to sing what would become signature roles: the title roles in Gershwin's *Porgy and Bess.* The show was scheduled to rehearse for its opening in 1952 in the United States, tour in Europe, and return for a final Broadway production.

After returning to the United States, he and Leontyne Price married. They began their new life together in 1952, as performers with joint leads in a work they both came to love, *Porgy and Bess.* Next came a serious decision for Warfield, concerning his continuance under contract with Columbia Artists management. A series of pivotal meetings took place. The producers of *Porgy and Bess* asked Warfield to sever his Columbia Artists contract and agree to an exclusive contract with *Porgy and Bess,* but Warfield declined. Warfield resumed his concert schedule and left the cast before their return for their New York City opening, at the Winter Garden on March 9, 1953.

Next came serious discussions for both Warfield and his wife regarding their career directions. Leontyne Price had been offered a Metropolitan Opera debut as "Aida." Peter Herman Adler, director of the NBC Opera Theatre, urged strongly against accepting "The Met's" offer. He predicted for her an important career as one of opera's alltime great divas. He advised Price to sidestep this offer and pursue a more conservative course, developing her repertoire more fully in Europe and then coming back to "The Met" fully prepared and able to "call her own shots."

For Warfield, professional advice went the other way. There was a sentiment leaning towards opera, but the feeling was that he already had a sterling reputation in the musical theater, founded on dramatic strengths as well as his vocal security. The argument was that forsaking his already proven successes in this respect to embark on untried territory in another and very demanding performing area was not wise and perhaps perilous, and he was advised to remain in musical theater. Both parties heeded the proffered advice, and prospered on their separate tracks.

Their marriage eventually suffered under the strain of two diverging and highly demanding careers. Warfield and Price separated in 1958 and divorced in 1972, but remained close friends and confidants. Memorable joint performances for Price and Warfield included a Philadelphia joint recital in 1954 with Otto Herz at the piano, flavored with selections from *Porgy and Bess* as well as operatic and song literature. The famous "lost Messiah" followed a 1956 performance of Handel's *Messiah,* featuring both artists, with the Philadelphia Orchestra under Eugene Ormandy, in which Eileen Farrell's voice was later substituted for Price's in the published recorded version, due to contractual obligations of both Leontyne Price and the orchestra.

Career Soars

Warfield's career expanded rapidly in the 1950s. He toured as soloist with the Philadelphia Orchestra in 1955 and continued on tours sponsored by the U.S. State Department in 1956, 1958, and 1959 to West Africa, the Near East, Europe, Asia, Australia, and Cuba. He frequently recorded and appeared on television, and starred as "De Lawd" in Marc Connely's *Green Pastures* in 1957 and 1959 on NBC Television. He also began to study technique with Metropolitan Opera performer Rosa Ponselle and he sang at her funeral in 1971.

In 1961 a revival of *Porgy and Bess* starring Warfield was staged by the New York City Opera Company. The work was repeated in 1964, and Warfield led the cast in a Vienna Volksoper production during the years from 1965 to 1972. *Showboat* was staged in New York City's Lincoln Center in 1966, and performances also followed at the Volksoper in Vienna during 1971–72. He performed at the Casals Festival in Puerto Rico in 1962 and 1963. He appeared at the Athens Festival in 1966, and at the Pacem in Terra II Convocation in Geneva in 1967. In 1972 he sang in a production of Puccini's *Gianni Schicchi* in Central City, Colorado. A recital for the

Duke Ellington Center on March 24, 1975, in New York's Carnegie Hall, commemorated the 25th anniversary of his debut recital in Town Hall in 1950. The full house included Marian Anderson, Roland Hayes, and Hall Johnson, who each played an influential role in his career and artistic development.

Warfield's talent as an actor is brought forward in many ways during his career in his characterization of various dramatic roles. These skills are also emphasized in works where he takes a speaking part—for example in his interpretation of Aaron Copland's *A Lincoln Portrait,* which uses excerpts of Abraham Lincoln's speeches. He has narrated in performances of this composition several times over the years with various orchestras, and his recording of the work with the Eastman Philharmonia Orchestra earned him a Grammy Award in the ''Spoken Word'' category in 1984. Other recordings of the work were made, including one with the New York Philharmonic Orchestra under conductor Leonard Bernstein, in 1986. He also narrated it at the Copland memorial concert in April of 1991 at Lincoln Center. Warfield also narrated the premiere performance of Jonathan Brace Brown's *Legacy of Vision,* with text selected from Martin Luther King Jr.'s ''I Have A Dream'' speech. It was first performed by the Nashville Symphony, conducted by Karen Lynn Deal with Warfield as narrator, at the symphony's annual Martin Luther King Jr. tribute concert on January 19, 1997.

In 1991 Warfield gave a joint recital with Robert McFerrin in St. Louis. Both artists included favorite works from opera, musical comedy, and classical songs. Warfield has also performed and narrated as a soloist with the Jim Cullum Jazz Band and on the PBS ''Riverwalk'' series from 1989 to 1998, which included performances of the band's jazz version of *Porgy and Bess,* selections from *Showboat,* and the *Harlem Rhapsody.*

In 1974 Warfield accepted a position as professor of music at the University of Illinois, School of Music in Urbana. He retired in 1990 as chairman of the voice faculty and has since been a visiting professor at Eastern Illinois University and an adjunct professor of music at Northwestern University. His academic honors include the Alumni Citation from the Eastman School of Music (1954), New York City's Handel Medallion (1974), and honorary doctor's degrees from the University of Arkansas (1972), Lafayette University (1977), Boston University (1982), Augustana College (1983), and James Milliken University (1984).

Warfield has been active in the National Association of Negro Musicians, serving as its president in 1984. He has served also as a board member of the Lyric Opera of Chicago and the New York College of Music; a trustee of the Berkshire Boys Choir; a member of the music panel of the National Association for the Arts, and a judge for the Whittaker Vocal Competition of the Music Educator's National Conference. His awards, dedicated service to education, and long performing career are a testimony to his contribution to the arts in America.

Current address: 247 East Chestnut Street, Apartment 701, Chicago, IL 60611–2405.

REFERENCES

Abdul, Raoul. *Blacks in Classical Music.* New York: Dodd, Mead, 1977.

Fellowes, Myles. ''Building Programs and Program Building.'' Interview with William Warfield. *Etude* 73 (February 1955): 13, 51, 55.

Hitchcock, H. Wiley, ed. *New Grove Dictionary of American Music.* New York: Macmillan, 1986.

Southern, Eileen. *Biographical Dictionary of Afro–American and African Musicians.* Westport, CT: Greenwood Press, 1982.

Thompson, Oscar, editor–in chief. *The International Cyclopedia of Music and Musicians.* 10th ed. Edited by Bruce Bohle. New York: Dodd, Mead, 1975.

Turner, Patricia. ''Afro–American Singers.'' *Black Perspective in Music* 9 (Spring 1981): 73–90.

———. *Afro American Singers.* Minneapolis: Challenge Productions, 1977.

Warfield, William. *William Warfield: My Music and My Life.* Champaign, IL: Sagamore, 1991.

Who's Who among African Americans, 1998–99. 10th ed. Detroit: Gale Research, 1997.

Who's Who in America. 52nd ed. New Providence, NJ: Marquis Who's Who, 1997.

''William Warfield.'' In *Riverwalk* internet site. http://www.riverwalk.org/warfield.htm (last updated April 14, 1998).

Wibkin, Angela. ''Success Story; Warfield Joins Symphony for MLK Tribute.'' *Nashville Business Journal* 13 (January 13, 1997): 15.

Darius L. Thieme

Booker T. Washington

(1856–1915)

School founder, college president, educator, community leader, organization founder, writer

As the first national black leader after the end of slavery, Booker T. Washington articulated the conservative values such as self–help and hard work, while eschewing public political participation and agitation for equality of the New South and the nation. In so doing, he created a space for the education of blacks. He reminded the South and the nation that an educated black citizenry would benefit the entire nation. Thus, he called for an education that would teach the dignity of labor, for Washington believed that the mass of black people would earn their living working with their hands. His emphasis on industrial education took hold for both blacks and whites. Washington also worked, albeit behind the scenes, to make sure that blacks maintained their share of the political patronage from the Republican party. He also insisted that blacks take advantage of every economic opportunity possible. In addition, he constantly reminded the South that the region could not progress and leave eight million blacks behind, for, regardless of how much progress the South made, without corresponding black advancement, it would remain behind the other sections of the nation.

Booker Taliaferro Washington, who saw himself as the successor to Frederick Douglass in the black community and on the national level, especially in the Republican party, was born into slavery on April 5, 1856, on James Burroughs's farm near Hale's Ford, Virginia, to Jane Ferguson, a slave for Burroughs. Ferguson had an older son, John. Later she would marry a black man, Washington Ferguson, also a slave, by whom she had one daughter, Amanda. Washington spent the first nine years of his life in slavery on the Burroughs's farm. His life was not easy because Burroughs was not a wealthy planter.

Because his mother spent so much time cooking for the Burroughs family, she had little time for her own children. Yet in both of his autobiographies, *The Story of My Life and Work* published in 1900, and *Up from Slavery,* published in 1901, Washington remembered his mother fondly. In such an environment, food was at best skimpy. Thus, when his mother would cook the occasional chicken for her children, Washington would later write that even though the chicken may have been taken from Burroughs's yard, it was not stealing, for his mother had no other choice. Rather, she was doing the best that she could under the circumstances to take care of her children.

As Louis Harlan observed in *Booker T. Washington: The Making of a Black Leader,* the end of slavery was one of the defining moments in Washington's life. The end of the Civil War brought freedom without any resources. Former slaves were left to fend for themselves. Since there was no land settlement, former slaves had to return, in many instances, to their former masters.

At the end of the Civil War the family consisted of Booker, John, Amanda, their mother, and stepfather. Washington's stepfather, Washington Ferguson, had left the plantation in order to find work in the salt mines, and the family soon joined him in Malden, West Virginia. Soon after the family moved to West Virginia, Washington's mother adopted an orphan boy who became James B. Washington.

The trip to West Virginia was a memorable one for the young Washington, even though a great deal of hardship was connected with it. As Washington remembered it years later, the trip was made in a wagon and took about ten days. He and his siblings had to walk a great deal of the way; the whole family slept out in the open. Washington's stepfather had secured employment in the salt and coal mines in Malden, a place that was not conducive to nurturing the aspirations of a child who wanted an education. In fact, the area was very primitive and, instead of attending school, Washington and his brother John were forced to work in the coal and salt mines

Booker T. Washington

alongside their stepfather. Thus, for a while at least, attending school was out of the question.

In spite of the drudgery of working in the salt and coal mines and the primitive nature of his surroundings, it was in Malden that Washington would have his first chance to attend school, even if it would be sporadic. Washington's stepfather allowed him to attend school for a half day. On his first day in school, according to his later recollections in *The Story of My Life and Work,* Booker added the surname that he would make famous:

> The first day I entered school, it seems to me, was the happiest day that I had ever known. The first embarrassment I experienced at school was in the matter of finding a name for myself. I had always been called ''Booker,'' and I had not known that one had use for more than one name . . . . When he [the teacher] came to me he asked for my full name, and I told him to put me down as ''Booker Washington,'' and that name I have borne ever since.

Because Washington was unable to attend school long, even for a half day, because his stepfather needed his labor, his mother helped him to secure employment as the houseboy for General Lewis Ruffner's family. Both Ruffner and his wife Viola made a profound impression on the young Washington. Viola Ruffner taught him the importance of cleanliness and order. Washington was an apt and eager pupil. Years later he would write in *The Story of My Life and Work* that ''Mrs. Ruffner gave me the most valuable part of my education. Her habit of requiring everything about her to be clean, neat and orderly, gave me an education in these respects that has been most valuable to me in the work that I have since tried to accomplish.'' Washington worked for the Ruffners four years, that is, until he went to Hampton Institute.

Former Slave Enters Hampton

It was in the coal and salt mines that Washington first heard about Hampton Institute. He learned that a poor student could pay his or her way by working at this new school. Washington was determined to reach Hampton and the education that he so strongly desired. Thus, in early October of 1872, with the blessing of his mother and brother John, Washington left for Hampton, Virginia. He was 16–years old with only a few years of sporadic schooling. He had, however, a strong desire to learn and to please those who could help him to accomplish his goal. What is clear from his stay with the Ruffners was Washington's desire to please those who had placed their trust in him, especially if they were white. Consequently, in going to Hampton Institute, a school founded in 1868 by the American Missionary Association to educate newly freed blacks, Washington was going to a school that would build on what Viola Ruffner had taught him. The journey to Hampton was not easy. He rode when he had money and walked when he did not. By the time he arrived in Richmond en route to Hampton, he was penniless.

Hampton was a good place for the young Washington to develop. The school taught both normal school classes for teachers and trades as well. The school's founder and first principal, Samuel Chapman Armstrong, believed that African Americans were a backward race who had to be taught skills that would make them useful citizens. In a word, Armstrong did not believe in social equality. Because of Armstrong's beliefs about black people, every aspect of the students' lives was closely regimented. And yet, Washington thrived in this environment, and Armstrong, in a real sense, became Washington's father figure.

Washington spent three years as a student at Hampton under Armstrong's influence. According to Louis Harlan in *Booker T. Washington: The Making of a Black Leader,* Armstrong and Hampton transformed Washington. Armstrong became for Washington the ideal of father and leader. Washington later wrote in *The Story of My Life and Work*:

> After I had been at Hampton Institute a day or two I saw General Armstrong, the Principal, and he made an impression upon me of being the most perfect specimen of man, physically, mentally, and spiritually, that I had ever seen, and I have never had occasion to change my first impression. In fact as the years went by and I came to know him better, the feeling grew.

Along with admiration for Armstrong, Washington absorbed much of his philosophy, including its racist aspects.

While at Hampton, Washington worked and studied hard. The teachers were dedicated and Washington responded to their teaching in a very positive way. He absorbed not only the subjects that he was taught; he also absorbed the strict New England way of life that was an integral part of the atmosphere of the school. He got his first chance at public speaking at Hampton, too. He says that it was at Hampton that he was also introduced to the use of two sheets on the bed and to the toothbrush. As principal of Tuskegee he would insist on the toothbrush along with the use of two sheets as a mark of transformation. Later, he would spend 1878–79 at Wayland Seminary in Washington, D.C., a liberal arts institution, but it was at Hampton that Washington was shaped into the man that would create Tuskegee Institute and become the first national black spokesperson for the New South.

After graduating from Hampton, Washington taught in Malden from 1875 to 1877. During his short stint as a public school teacher, Washington prepared several of his students for Hampton Institute, including his brother John. Probably in the fall of 1878, Washington entered Wayland Seminary where he studied for an academic year. His autobiographies do not say why he studied there. Washington, D.C., was the first large city Washington would live in, and, at the age of 22, this young man found the city wanting. For one who had been trained at Hampton, the city was downright sinful. In addition to the sinful nature of city life, Washington would later write in *Up from Slavery* that he saw young black men who had very little, trying to make an impression that they were men of worth. Washington, for the remainder of his life, would remain hostile to cities. He believed that people should be near the soil, where they earned their living by the sweat of their brow.

After his year's stay at Wayland, Washington returned to West Virginia in the spring of 1879. During the interval, before he took a job at Hampton on January 10, 1879, it is not clear what he was doing. Louis Harlan has suggested in *Booker T. Washington: The Making of a Black Leader* that Washington may have been studying law. At any rate, Washington must have been pleased to receive a call from his alma mater and his beloved mentor, Samuel C. Armstrong. He taught at Hampton from 1879 to 1881.

In 1881 he received a call to open a school in Alabama, and Washington accepted the call to become principal of this new school. After he had been recommended by Armstrong to Alabama school officials, Washington made his way into the Deep South for the first time. This was for the young 25–year old Washington a leap into the unknown. He already had a blueprint for his school in mind; he would build a second Hampton in the heart of the Black Belt, a section of the South that had been profoundly shaped by slavery and where the shadow of the plantation was still present.

Establishes Tuskegee Institute

On July 4, 1881, Washington opened the doors of Tuskegee Normal and Industrial Institute to black students. He was the only teacher, and he taught under very harsh conditions. He may have been making a statement by opening the new institution on the nation's birthday. Even before the school opened, Washington set about to establish cordial relations with local whites. In fact, the school had been the product of cooperation between blacks and whites, a result of a political compromise of sorts between black voters and white Democrats. To win seats in the Alabama legislature, Colonel Wilber F. Foster, a Democrat seeking a Senate seat, and Arthur L. Brooks approached Lewis Adams, an African American businessman, requesting his aid in getting black voters to support them. In order to get blacks to cast their votes for the two Democrats, Lewis requested a normal school for blacks to be built in Tuskegee. Once the men were in office, they delivered on the promise, and on February 10, 1880, Governor Rufus W. Cobb signed the bill establishing the school at Tuskegee. When Washington arrived on the scene in 1881, there were no school buildings. He had only the $2,000 from the state of Alabama promised for salaries.

Washington was aware of those in the white community who were opposed to any type of school for blacks; therefore, he sought to win the friendships of both white and black, for he knew if the school were to succeed it had to be accepted by the entire community. It is to Washington's credit that the school did thrive in such an unlikely place. From the start, Washington sought to allay fears of the whites that his school would make blacks unfit for useful work.

Washington's success in making Tuskegee an important institution in Alabama and in the nation can be attributed to his skill in negotiating the racial divide. The educational program that Washington espoused also contributed to the school's survival. The school would be both normal and industrial. Students would learn how to work with their hands as well as learn how to teach. Like Hampton, Tuskegee had to take students, some who had been slaves, and make them self–reliant individuals.

By all accounts, the first years of the school were extremely difficult. Because most of the students were poor, the school could only charge minimal fees. In addition, Washington made it clear that all students would work to help pay their way, thereby cutting down on the cost of operating the school. Coupled with the poverty of the students was the school's lack of funding to construct the buildings needed to accommodate the students. Here Washington turned to Armstrong and Hampton for assistance. Additionally, Olivia Davidson joined him as a teacher and principal of girls. Along with Washington, she worked to make Tuskegee Institute a success. She would also become Washington's second wife in 1885 and the mother of his two sons, Booker Taliaferro Jr. and Ernest Davidson. Olivia Davidson Washington died in 1889.

Washington married his first wife, Fanny Norton Smith, on August 2, 1882. They had one child, Portia Marshall Washington, born in 1883. Fanny Washington died in 1884. Washington's third wife was Margaret James Murray, a graduate of Fisk University in Nashville, Tennessee, whom he married in 1892. No children were born to this union, but Margaret became a mother to Washington's two sons. Like his second wife, Margaret James Murray devoted herself to working with Washington at the school. She also worked to improve the lives of poor black women in Tuskegee and in Macon County by teaching them how to prepare wholesome meals, to care for their homes and children, and themselves.

While Washington himself was a devoted family man, he did not have the time that he desired to spend with his children, for he was always busy raising money for the school. He never received enough money from the state of Alabama to pay salaries; therefore, he was always on the lookout for wealthy friends who could assist Tuskegee. One such friend of the school and one of Washington's closest advisors was William H. Baldwin Jr., vice–president of the Southern Railroad. He not only served the school as a trustee, but he worked with Washington to put the school on a sound business basis.

Washington built Tuskegee Institute into a normal and industrial school. As noted, the school was very much like Hampton but with a difference. Hampton had mostly white administrators and faculty, Tuskegee had an all black staff, from administrators down to the faculty to the workers who maintained the grounds. Washington took note of everything on the campus; how the teachers taught, how the students were fed, how the grounds were maintained and, how many industries on the campus were running properly. Nothing was too small for him to notice. He believed that the students and faculty should produce what was needed, and only purchased what they could not produce themselves.

Tuskegee Institute prepared its students to be teachers in the public schools as well as to be skilled craftsmen and women. Washington also wanted the students who attended and graduated from the school to make a difference in the communities where they worked. Thus, beginning in the 1890s some of Tuskegee's students established small schools patterned after Tuskegee.

As Tuskegee grew and became more secure, Washington's reputation as a wise leader also grew. Whites in both sections of the country felt that he was leading back people in a safe and productive path. In his addresses and published essays, Washington told black people to grasp the opportunities that they had rather than constantly complain about what they did not have. He encouraged blacks to start businesses and buy homes and farms and become useful and productive citizens. He also encouraged black people to make friends with sympathetic whites in their communities. He said very little about black participation in the political process, because he felt political rights would come in due time as blacks acquired education, character, and property. Washington felt that blacks should accommodate themselves to the prevailing conditions, that the time for agitation and protest was over, and black people had to take advantage of the opportunities that were possible.

Takes a Compromise Position

As Washington became more popular in the larger society, he became more conservative in his utterances. He seldom criticized whites in public, yet he was always ready to blame black people for what he felt were their shortcomings. On September 18, 1895, Washington, who had been chosen to speak at the Cotton States and International Exposition in Atlanta, reiterated much of his New South philosophy in an address that has been dubbed the "Atlanta Compromise" speech by many of his critics. While telling his white audience what it wanted to hear, he said that black people had started at the wrong place in their quest to take advantage of freedom. They had started with politics rather than with learning how to till the soil to the best advantage, starting businesses, and buying homes. Moreover, he said that African Americans were not too concerned about social equality; instead, the ability to earn a living was far more important. Thus, in terms of social interaction whites and blacks could be as separate as the fingers of the hand, but in terms of economic development and mutual progress for both races, they could become one. If both races heeded his vision for the New South, of casting down their buckets where they were, the South would indeed become the new garden of Eden. The address was well–received by whites and blacks, and Washington became the national black leader. He was consulted by those in power on what was best for black people.

Less than two years after he became the chosen black leader, Washington hired Emmett Jay Scott, a graduate of Wiley College, and journalist from Texas to be his personal secretary. Scott was an excellent choice; he was intelligent, hard–working, and completely loyal to Washington. It was Scott who made it possible for Washington to create the Tuskegee Machine, an organization with political clout given by control over philanthropy that went to black institutions and by the few political appointments that went to blacks. Washington used the power that he amassed between 1895 and 1910 to reward his friends and punish those he perceived to be his enemies. He did not allow for debate among those blacks who rejected his program. He made every effort to destroy those individuals that he saw as his enemies.

Even as he counseled the masses of black people to forego politics, Washington was very political. He had even consulted with President Grover Cleveland, but his greatest influence as an advisor came during the Theodore Roosevelt Administration (1901–1908). It is safe to say that no black person received any political appointment without Washington's approval. And yet, Washington, as much as possible, insisted on working behind the scenes. He did not want white southerners to know the extent of his influence, especially those who never quite trusted him for building the most popular institution in Macon County, Alabama. In spite of Washington's public stance of a lowly educator trying to find a niche that would make his race indispensable in the New South, during the period between 1877 and 1913 Washington enjoyed his role as the "Wizard," as Scott and other loyal black men called him. He firmly believed that black people could accomplish more by working behind scenes with whites of good will than they could accomplish by protesting. In the face of rising violence against blacks, Washington asked them to be patient and work harder to improve their economic lot.

Washington did work to help other black schools receive some of the funds that were given by northern philanthropists. In addition, Washington served on the board of trustees of Fisk and Howard. He also pushed, in his way, for increased funding for black public education, yet he wanted and received the lion's share of the funds for Tuskegee and the schools that followed his philosophy of emphasizing industrial education instead of stressing their liberal arts programs. For example, John Hope, the president of Morehouse College, never received large sums of money from Northern philanthropists and, when he tried to raise money to build Sales Hall in 1910, Washington used his influence to help Hope receive the money only after Robert R. Moton encouraged him to do so. Of course, Hope had been active in the founding of the Niagara Movement and the NAACP; Washington opposed both organizations.

As Washington became a national figure, he not only received important requests for speaking engagements, but magazines and journals also requested articles from him on a variety of topics, especially on the state of race relations. Because Washington was a busy man and did not have the time to write, he employed a host of ghost writers to churn out article after article. One such writer was Robert E. Park, who later became a professor of sociology at the University of Chicago. Emmett J. Scott also wrote newspaper articles for Washington.

Much of the writing was done for the moment and reflected no profound thought on any of the problems of the day. Nevertheless, Washington's autobiographies are worth reading even today. *The Story of My Life and Work* was published in 1900 for a subscription book audience, and the bulk of the writing was done by Edgar Webber, a young black journalist. He did not, however, serve Washington well. There were many errors in *My Life and Work,* which famed newspaper editor T. Thomas Fortune made an effort to correct. Despite the errors and poor qualities of the printing and the writing, the book sold well. In it Washington gave details about his life that would not be found in the more popular *Up from Slavery.* Washington was dissatisfied with the book because he did not have the time to give it the close supervision that he would give *Up from Slavery.*

Even as *The Story of My Life and Work* was being peddled by subscription agents, Washington was negotiating with Lymann Abbott, editor of the *Outlook,* to publish a series of autobiographical articles in that journal. While Louis Harlan and John Blassingame suggested in their introduction to volume one of *The Booker T. Washington Papers* that *Up from Slavery* was also ghost written, it may be that Washington supervised the project so closely that Max Thrasher, who worked with Washington on the book, can not in the strict sense be called a ghost writer.

At every turn of writing *Up from Slavery* Washington was there. He even wrote drafts of the book based on the dictations that he had given Thrasher. As the book appeared in the *Outlook,* it was well received by the reading public, for it was one of the outstanding success stories of the times. Washington made it clear that with hard work and the help of sympathetic whites, along the way, he had become a useful citizen. Washington's story of an almost self–made man resonated with a reading public.

Near the end of his life, Washington did speak out against the difficulty that black people in the South were having in affirming their basic rights as citizens. He noted that blacks in the North could vote, while, for the most part, blacks in the South could not. He also felt that blacks were not being given a fair chance.

As a leader and educator between 1881 and 1915, Washington should be viewed in the context of his times but with a difference. Born during the era of slavery and coming of age during Reconstruction, Washington was very much aware of the violence against black people, especially during and after Reconstruction. From his own experiences, he believed that black people needed white friends to protect them against the lawlessness of the mob. In fact, from Washington's point of view, blacks could not survive without the help of whites of good will.

As Louis Harlan noted in *Booker T. Washington: The Wizard of Tuskegee,* all of Washington's role models were conservative white men who believed that black people had to be led in the proper paths. Black people had to make themselves useful in the New South by focusing on their obligations rather than on their rights. The South needed workers, and blacks were excellent workers. Thus, in those areas such as owning land, saving money, buying homes, and establishing businesses, black people had to take advantage of what the South offered. To be sure, Washington did not create the racial problems of his time. He merely sought to ease them. He believed that black people would ultimately be an integral part of the American body politic, but until that time arrived, they had to develop themselves in every area possible.

Feeling that agitating for rights would be counterproductive, he counseled blacks to make the best of the situation in which they found themselves, for, if they worked hard, things would get better.

One of Washington's chief shortcomings, however, was his inability to share or divide leadership. He had to be in control at all times. In this context, Oliver C. Cox, who taught at Tuskegee, may be on target in suggesting that Washington functioned as the favorite slave, standing between the black community and the whites in power. "The favorite slave," according to Cox, "was frequently very firm in dealing with the rank–and–file of his class for being remiss in their duties. Indeed, one feels constantly that Washington never fully lost the attitude of a favorite slave." And yet, Washington did build an institution, something that most of his detractors did not do, that stands like his autobiographies as a sign for the absent leader, still in our midst chiding and provoking controversy.

From the time he left Malden, West Virginia, for Hampton Institute in 1872 until the day of his death at his home on the campus of his beloved Tuskegee Institute, Washington was always working, always on the move. He took few vacations, for he had to keep an eye on what was taking place on campus and in black America. He seemed to have been afraid that something would go awry if he were not on hand. Thus, when he collapsed in New Haven on October 25, 1915, of overwork, nervous exhaustion, and arteriosclerosis, Washington knew his time was near, and it is very understandable that he wanted to die at home, a place that was the length of his shadow. When he died on the morning of November 14, 1915, one of the most important men in the South had left the scene. He had been the most important black leader since Frederick Douglass.

REFERENCES

Andrews, William. Preface to *Up from Slavery,* by Booker T. Washington. New York: Norton, 1996.

Baker, Houston A., Jr. *Modernism and the Harlem Renaissance.* Chicago: University of Chicago Press, 1987.

Bond, Horace Mann. *Negro Education in Alabama: A Study in Cotton and Steel.* 1939. Reprint, New York: Octagon Books, 1969.

Cox, James M. *Recovering Literature's Lost Ground: Essays in American Autobiography.* Baton Rouge: Louisiana State University Press, 1989.

Cox, Oliver C. "The Leadership of Booker T. Washington." In *Great Lives Observed: Booker T. Washington,* edited by Emma Lou Thornbrough. Englewood Cliffs, NJ: Prentice–Hall, 1969.

Harlan, Louis R. *Booker T. Washington: The Making of a Black Leader, 1856–1901.* New York: Oxford University Press, 1972.

———. *Booker T. Washington: The Wizard of Tuskegee, 1901–1915.* New York: Oxford University Press, 1983.

———, and others, eds. *The Booker T. Washington Papers.* 14 vols. Urbana: University of Illinois Press, 1972–89.

Spencer, Samuel R. *Booker T. Washington and the Negro's Place in America.* Boston: Little, Brown, 1955.

Washington, Booker T. *Up from Slavery: Autobiographical Writings.* In *The Booker T. Washington Papers,* edited by Louis R. Harlan and John Blassingame. Vol 1. Urbana: University of Illinois Press, 1972.

COLLECTIONS

The majority of Booker T. Washington's papers are in the Library of Congress; however, some are still in the Tuskegee University library.

Frank T. Moorer

Denzel Washington

(1954–)

Actor, humanitarian

Denzel Washington is a leading actor with a reputation for selecting quality roles. He earned his place in Hollywood through superb performances, and when he won an Academy Award for Best Supporting Actor in the film *Glory,* he became the fifth African American to win an Academy Award. He has been named one of American's ten favorite actors.

Denzel Washington was born on December 28, 1954, in Mount Vernon, New York, to Denzel Washington, a Pentecostal minister, and Lennis Washington, a beautician and a former gospel singer. He grew up in an integrated neighborhood that bordered the Bronx where he associated with West Indians, Italians, as well as blacks, and learned much from the different cultures. He, his older sister Lorice, and younger brother David were brought up in a disciplined home. Washington's mother influenced and grounded her children through solid values and activities with groups such as the Boys Club and the Young Men's Christian Association (YMCA). When he was 12, Denzel Washington worked part–time delivering clothes to the cleaners and brushing the clothes of clients in the barbershop his mother co–owned.

Washington's parents divorced when he was 14–years old, an event that devastated the young man and led to behavioral problems. He rejected religion and became unruly, just the opposite of what he had been. To help curb his behavior, his mother sent him to Oakland Academy, a private preparatory school primarily attended by wealthy white children in upstate New York. He achieved excellence in baseball, track, football, and basketball. He also played piano in a local black band called the Last Express.

Washington entered Fordham University in 1972 to begin work on a college degree in pre–medicine. To pay his expenses, he acquired several loans and ran an after–school baby–sitting service at a Greek Orthodox Church in Upper Manhattan. He dropped out of school one semester due to poor grades and worked at the post office and then as a trash collector, but soon returned to Fordham. During a summer job at a camp, he made a recitation on stage that set the direction of his career. He was lauded for his natural acting ability and enrolled in a theater workshop. Changing his career plans, he dropped pre–medicine as a major and embraced journalism. While at Fordham he starred in two student drama productions, *The Emperor Jones* and *Othello.* In 1977 he had a professional offer to act in *Wilma,* the story of track star Wilma Rudolph, a movie made for television. Meanwhile, Washington completed his college degree with a double major in drama and journalism.

Becomes Professional Actor

With his goal now set in a new direction, acting became a focus for Washington. He began his study of professional acting at the American Conservatory Theater in San Francisco. He won key roles in *Man and Superman* and *Moonchildren.* The class size was reduced after a tough competition, but Washington retained a place in the program. He was a quick learner and as school progressed Washington, who then believed he had learned the techniques necessary for good acting, missed class often. He left the conservatory at the end of his first year, with two remaining, and moved to Los Angeles to try professional acting.

Unsuccessful in Los Angeles, Washington moved back to his mother's house in Mount Vernon. While attending an off–Broadway play, he ran into Pauletta Pearson, whom he met briefly when the two played in *Wilma.* Their relationship grew; Pearson moved into the Washington home and later they married. His wife gave him the encouragement that he needed during his frustrations in the 1970s.

Denzel Washington

Washington landed a role in the social comedy *Carbon Copy* (1981), which flopped at the box office. Believing that he would not fulfill his dream of becoming an actor, he accepted a job at an urban recreation center teaching sports and acting to children. One week before he was to report to work, he auditioned for and landed the role of Malcolm X in *When the Chickens Come Home to Roost,* which played at the Henry Street Settlement Arts for Living Center. Washington studied hard for the role, learned to imitate Malcolm X, and even dyed his hair red. He appeared in the Negro Theatre Ensemble's production of *A Soldier's Play,* which offered Washington the chance to play another major role. For his performance with the Negro Ensemble Theater, critics acclaimed his acting and honored him in 1982 with the Obie Award and the Outer Circle's Critic Award. These two performances led his career in an upward turn in the 1980s.

Washington appeared with several African American productions, including *The Might Gents* and *Ceremonies in Dark Old Men.* Returning to Shakespeare, he acted in *Coriolanus* as Aedilus, through the Black and Red Ensemble production for the Shakespeare–in–the–Park program.

Washington did other work for television, appearing in *License to Kill* and *Flesh & Blood.* He declined a number of movie offers that would have required him to play negative roles such as a pimp or druggie. He accepted an offer to play a doctor in the television program *St. Elsewhere* and believed that the part would cast him as a positive role model for young blacks. During the series' full run, from 1982 to 1986, he played the Yale–educated Phillip Chandler.

Washington took breaks from *St. Elsewhere* to appear in movies. In 1984 he starred in *A Soldier's Story,* based on a play of the same title. Most of the original cast of the play were in the movie. He appeared in *Power* (1986), which set out to expose the problems of the media. In 1987 he acted in a powerful and moving story portraying the martyred Steve Biko, a South African activist, in *Cry Freedom.* This film received mixed criticism; some critics felt that too little emphasis was on Biko and too much focus was on the white newspaper editor Donald Woods. Washington's excellent performance in *Cry Freedom* earned him the nomination in 1987 for an Academy Award as Best Supporting Actor and the NAACP's Image Award for best supporting actor.

Using the same preparation techniques as for *When Chickens Come Home to Roost,* he immersed himself in tapes and speeches about Steve Biko. Physically, he changed his appearance to somewhat resemble Biko, removing caps from his teeth and adding several pounds to increase his weight.

Washington appeared in two other movies, *For Queen and Country* (1988) and *The Might Quinn* (1989), before landing a role in *Glory* (1989). The film details the story of African American soldiers trained to fight in the Civil War, the Fifty–fourth Massachusetts Volunteer Infantry unit formed in 1863 by white colonel Robert Gould Shaw of Boston. Many Americans felt that African Americans could not fight in the Civil War. However, the courage and strength of these men under Shaw's supervision enabled them to fight an heroic battle ending in the July 18, 1863, attack on Battery Wagner, a key fortification of Charleston, South Carolina. Denzel Washington played the part of Trip, a former slave, who had become angry, tough, and bitter from his slave experiences. As in previous movies Washington prepared by reading first–hand accounts of even he was to portray. Quoted in his biography, *Denzel Washington,* he said, "It was difficult to break myself down and become a primitive man; that was the challenge of this part." This role brought his second Academy Award nomination for Best Supporting Actor, and his first Oscar.

Although Washington consistently received moving and stirring roles to play, he rejected a part the 1980s film *Platoon,* because he wanted to play a Native American rather than a black. Washington claims both ethnic groups in his background.

Director Spike Lee tailored the role of jazz musician Bleek Gilliam for Denzel Washington in *Mo Better Blues* (1990). The story depicted an African American jazz trumpeter—who might be based on Lee's father, Bill Lee—who tries to balance his love of music with his love of two women. The critics were mixed in their reviews, but Washington's performance was outstanding. Utilizing his familiar training techniques for the role, Washington, engaged himself in the character of Miles Davis by learning to play a trumpet and staying in the company of this legendary musician.

Washington next appeared in the 1990 comedy–drama, *Heart Condition.* It is the story of a white detective who receives the heart of black lawyer Washington, who acted as the ghost. Washington moved on to *Ricochet* (1991), then to *Mississippi Marsala* in 1992. For the latter film he won the NAACP's Best Actor Award.

In 1992, Washington and Lee collaborated as actor and director for the powerful movie *Malcolm X.* His extraordinary performance in this stirring movie earned him the Academy Award's nomination for Best Actor, the NAACP Image Award for Best Actor, and the Berlin Film Festival's Award. The film was named the best picture for 1992, a plus for Spike Lee and Denzel Washington. In addition, Washington won the New York Film Critic's Circle Award, Best Actor; the Boston Society of Film Critic's Award, Best Actor; and Chicago Film Critic's Award, Best Actor.

Washington continued to receive offers for movie roles. He appeared in three films during 1993; *Much Ado About Nothing,* a film version of Shakespeare's comedy; *The Pelican Brief,* the story of a newspaper reporter's investigation of the assassinations of two Supreme Court justices; and *Philadelphia,* the story of a homophobic lawyer who learns about life and love from his AIDS–stricken client. In 1995 he acted in *Crimson Tide,* an action film in which he was a young, Harvard and U.S. Naval Academy–trained executive officer aboard a beleaguered nuclear submarine further beset by mutiny, and *Devil in a Blue Dress,* in which he played a private detective who, after wrestling with racism, reconfirms his American dream. His next venture was the military drama *Courage Under Fire,* a story of a lieutenant colonel, played by Washington, and his command in the Persian Gulf. The officer gave an order to fire during the night on what he thought was the enemy; later the officer found out that the unit fired on was one of his own.

In 1996 Washington starred in *The Preacher's Wife,* with singer Whitney Houston. It was an adaption of the old movie classic, *The Bishop's Wife,* about a church couple. More recently, he turned down a role in *Amistad,* telling USA Weekend, "I ain't putting no chains around my neck. I'm not in the mood." He did accept a role in both Gregory Hoblit's *Fallen* and Spike Lee's *He Got Game.* He is booked for roles through the year 2000. A Harris Poll, cited in *USA Weekend* in January of 1998, listed him the tenth most popular movie star.

Handsome, suave, tall, and brown skinned, Denzel Washington is considered the next Sidney Poitier. He works with the Boys and Girls Club and does commercials for the national organization. He has given generously—$1 million—to the Children's Fund of South Africa and $2.5 million to his church, the Church of God, in Los Angeles. In 1997 he won the Whitney M. Young Award from the Los Angeles Urban League for outstanding community activities, especially with youngsters.

Denzel and Pauletta Pearson Washington are the parents of four children: John David, Katta, Malcolm, and Olivia. A family man, he finds time to coach the football team of John David, Katta's basketball team, and to enjoy his wife's gourmet meals and holiday traditions. They live in a Beverly

Hills home built by black architect Paul Williams. Washington believes in religion and family. Quoted in his biography, he said: "I always try to have my family with me when I am out in public." He wants to show that "black people can have families," thus helping to remove negative stereotypes of the one–parent black family. During a family visit to Africa in summer of 1995, the Washingtons renewed their marriage vows, in a ceremony performed by archbishop Desmond Tutu. Although Washington receives many accolades, he strives to remain unaffected by them.

Washington's trademark for success in portraying a character has been to learn as much about the individual as possible, including his social, historical, and political environments and displaying physical traits. With this kind of dedication and zeal to be true to the character, Washington has established himself as a leading actor in the movie industry.

Current address: Attention Sandy Rice, Publicist, PMK Public Relations Inc., 955 South Carrillo Drive, No. 200, Los Angeles, CA 90048.

REFERENCES

Brode, Douglas. *Denzel Washington: His Films and Career.* Secaucus, NJ: Carol Publishing Group, 1997.

Current Biography Yearbook. New York: H. W. Wilson, 1992.

"Denzel Washington, Black Matinee Idol." *Washington, D.C., Times,* February 2, 1990.

Nelson, Jill. "No More Mr. Nice Guy?" *USA Weekend* (9–11 January 1996): 4–5.

Salzman, Jack, David Lionel Smith, and Cornel West, eds. *Encyclopedia of African–American Culture and History.* New York: Macmillan Library Reference USA/Simon and Schuster Macmillan, 1996.

Who's Who among African Americans, 1996–97. 9th ed. Detroit: Gale Research, 1996.

Barbara Williams Jenkins and Jessie Carney Smith

Harold Washington
(1922–1987)
Lawyer, politician

The first black mayor of Chicago, Harold Washington was an astute politician who also served as a state representative and state senator. He changed the city by reducing its budget deficit and hiring more minorities in visible positions, including the first black police chief.

Harold Washington was born to Roy Lee and Bertha Washington on April 15, 1922, in Chicago, Illinois. His birth

Harold Washington

at Cook County Hospital was a graduation present for Roy Lee Washington Sr., who earned his law degree from the then Chicago Kent College of Law in June of 1922. Later in the year, Roy Washington passed the Illinois bar examination and subsequently opened a law office in the city to begin serving Chicago's public. He would also work as a clergyman.

Harold Washington attended Felsenthal Elementary School on South Calumet Avenue. Harold's brother Edward made sure that his younger brother was not intimidated often by the school's bullies. In 1932, at the age of ten, young Harold began to work as a window cleaner, often earning a nickel for two windows washed. His parents allowed him to save his money and, in the end, he had enough to order Charles Atlas's muscle–building kit through which he built his muscles and was able to defend himself against all bullies.

By 1933 Harold's father, now divorced, had been ordained an African Methodist Episcopal minister. Bertha Price Washington left Roy after the birth of their fourth child. The Washington family moved from their South Parkway address to South Vincennes, where Mahalia Jackson and other well–known black gospel singers also lived; the Washington home was also next to the famous Ebenezer Baptist Church. In 1935 Roy Washington was remarried, to Arlene Jackson, a school teacher and a music instructor, and the Washingtons moved to South Indiana Avenue.

When the Washingtons moved to a larger home on East 44th Street in Chicago, young Harold met and fell in love with Nancy Dorothy Finch, who lived on the third floor of their apartment building. They would eventually marry. Nancy and

Harold attended both Forrestville Elementary and DuSable High School together. At Forrestville, Harold idolized Charlotte Roland, a teacher who made a great impression on the future mayor of Chicago. He was also influenced by his DuSable High School English teacher, Jeannette Triplett, who, according to Florence H. Levinshon in *Harold Washington: A Political Biography,* "didn't take any stuff, and students had to produce in her class." DuSable harmony and voice teacher Mildred Bryant Jones, a good friend of W. E. B. Du Bois, made sure that Washington enrolled in the school's Glee Club. At the library, head librarian Vivian Harsh had an effect on Washington. Her collection of books brought him in contact with the works of Du Bois and Carter G. Woodson, the founder of America's Black History Month celebration. Washington was an avid reader. In high school, Washington was a good at sports, participating in Chicago's 1939 sports championship. He also played on his neighborhood baseball team, the Falcons.

In 1934, Washington, at age 12, learned a lot about Chicago's electoral politics. Black Republican Congressman Oscar DePriest lost his reelection bid to Arthur W. Mitchell, who became the first black Democrat to serve in Congress. Washington's father, an associate minister of Chicago's Bethel African Methodist Episcopal Church, openly supported Mitchell's electoral campaign. The senior Washington gave political speeches on Mitchell's behalf at AME churches on both the south and the west sides of Chicago.

Washington joined the Civilian Conservation Corps in 1939. His first paid employment took him to Michigan to plant evergreen trees and to do limestone quarrying. He later served over three years in the army. When he was 18, Washington and his high school sweetheart, Nancy—only 17—obtained parental approval to get married; the wedding was performed by Washington's father in May of 1941 in his living room.

After the army, when Washington entered Roosevelt University and later Northwestern University Law School, he used his G.I. Bill benefits to pay for his education. As an undergraduate he majored in political science and economics. In the fall of 1949, he was the only black admitted of the 185 freshman to the Northwestern law school class. As an undergraduate and later in law school, Washington was an excellent student. It was, therefore, not very surprising that in his junior year at Roosevelt he was appointed a part–time class lecturer in political science. In his senior year, Washington was a full–time teaching assistant in the department, working directly under political science professor Dale Pontius.

His paycheck from teaching was not enough to make ends meet, so Washington and his brother, Roy Lee Jr., established a decorating and maintenance service. They drummed up business from fellow students and professors by advertising on the Roosevelt University bulletin boards. Both brothers also did decorating, plumbing, carpentry, and plastering jobs at the apartment building owned by their father in Chicago's South Side. Washington studied hard in law school and graduated in 1952. Two years earlier, Washington divorced his wife. Upon graduation from Northwestern University School of Law, Washington first served as an assistant city prosecutor in Chicago from 1954 to 1958. As the only black arbitrator for the Illinois Industrial Commission for six years between 1958 and 1964, he made plans to open a private law practice. This he did, and the practice flourished until he plunged himself full time into Illinois politics. He ran as a Democrat for the Illinois State House of Representatives and, on January 6, 1965, he was sworn in at Springfield, Illinois, as a freshman in the House.

Chicago's First Black Mayor

Washington served in the Illinois House from 1965 to 1976. In 1977 he was elected to the state Senate, where he served until 1980. He worked hard with fellow state representatives to leave his mark on Illinois politics. His major accomplishments included helping to establish the Illinois Fair Employment Practices Commission and helping win recognition of Martin Luther King Jr.'s birthday as a state–wide holiday. From 1980 to 1983, he served in the U.S. House of Representatives. Washington won a very tight mayoral race in 1983 to become the first black person to occupy that position in Chicago history.

Washington's election was not an easy one. His Republican opponent was a Chicago insurance millionaire and former state legislator, Bernard Epton. Before facing Epton, Washington first had to overcome other hurdles in his own Democratic primary by beating both incumbent mayor Jane Byrne and candidate Richard M. Daley, a Cook County state attorney and the son of former mayor Richard J. Daley. Washington was 61 at the time of his victory and in top form. Melvin G. Holli and Paul M. Green explained Washington's win in *Bashing Chicago Traditions: Harold Washington's Last Campaign*: "Harold Washington beat Bernard Epton in 1983 because he carried all of the black vote and some of the white vote; Bernard Epton lost because he carried almost all of the white vote and none of the black vote."

As the mayor of Chicago, several of Washington's achievements stand out. He brought about deficit reduction in city budgeting, increased hiring of minorities and, for the first time, the appointment of a black police chief. Unfortunately, his administration was rife with political in–fighting. Before he could complete his first term as mayor, Washington died of a massive heart attack on November 25, 1987.

Many observers and commentators have assessed Washington's political fortunes favorably. Holli and Green described Washington's impact on Chicago as a political maverick. They wrote, "Harold Washington rushed upon the Chicago political scene like an angry burning ember on tinder–dry prairie grass, and he ignited a political prairie fire that burned fiercely in 1983, profoundly altering the 'natural order' of things and changing the political ecology of power." Washington was a major figure in Illinois politics, particularly in Chicago, but died before he could achieve greater successes. The main public library building in Chicago is named in his honor.

REFERENCES

Holli, Melvin G., and Paul M. Green. *Bashing Chicago Traditions: Harold Washington's Last Campaign.* Grand Rapids, MI: W. B. Eerdmans, 1989.

———, eds. *The Mayors: The Chicago Political Tradition.* Carbondale, IL: Southern Illinois University Press, 1995.

Kleppner, Paul. *Chicago Divided: The Making of a Black Mayor.* DeKalb: Northern Illinois University Press, 1985.

Levinshon, Florence H. *Harold Washington: A Political Biography.* Chicago: Chicago Review Press, 1983.

Travis, Dempsey. *"Harold": The People's Mayor: An Authorized Biography of Mayor Harold Washington.* Chicago: Urban Research Press, 1989.

Yvette Alex–Assensoh

Walter E. Washington
(1915–)
Mayor, lawyer, housing administrator

Walter E. Washington

After serving as housing administrator in Washington, D.C., and in New York City, Walter Washington was appointed mayor of Washington, making him the first African American mayor of a major U.S. city. President Lyndon B. Johnson appointed him to the position when the three man commission heading city government became a one man position. He was reappointed by President Richard Nixon and then was elected to the office of mayor. Chief Judge H. Carl Moultrie, of Washington D.C.'s Superior Court, paid high tribute to him in the *Washington Post* for May 10, 1979, saying that "few men have accomplished in a lifetime what Walter Washington accomplished in ten years. Few men walked with kings and associated with royalty yet kept common touch. . . . Few men can boast that they received a burning city and left it on its way to recovery."

The great–grandson of a slave, Walter Edward Washington was born April 15, 1915, in Dawson, Georgia, his mother's hometown. The only child of William L. Washington and Willie Mae Thornton Washington, he grew up in Jamestown, New York. His father worked in factories and ran a hotel valet shop. His mother taught school.

After completing his public school education in Jamestown, Washington enrolled at Washington, D.C.'s Howard University. He studied public administration and sociology, receiving his B.A. in 1938. Then he engaged in graduate study at American University. Early in his career, he attended evening school at Howard University's law school and earned his L.L.B. in 1948.

25 Years with the Housing Authority

Washington began work in 1941 with the capital city's Alley Dwelling Authority, which became known a couple of years later, as the National Capital Housing Authority (NCHA). He served first as a junior housing assistant and from 1945 to 1950 as housing manager. His tasks included arranging housing for the military in the District of Columbia area during World War II. From 1951 to 1961, he filled various executive roles within the organization. In 1961, President John F. Kennedy named Washington executive director of the agency. He was the first African American to hold the position.

For five years Washington led the NCHA. He worked to provide housing for the city's poor and, according to the *Washington Post* for November 27, 1966, he also sought to help the people of Washington "become good neighbors." Whether in the slums or among administrators and politicians, Washington worked "by creating confidence and goodwill." He enlisted the expertise of the city's best architects to design public housing. Described as "forever inventive," he built a program to encourage private builders to renovate old homes and sell them to the housing authority. A *Washington Post* article for September 7, 1967, credited Washington with "new ideas that are now accepted practice in public housing: day–care centers, job counseling and financial advice, credit unions and tenant councils."

New York's Mayor John V. Lindsay recognized the administrator's accomplishments and invited Washington to join his cabinet. On November 22, 1966, he assumed chairmanship of the New York Housing Authority. The *New York*

Times described Washington's accomplishments during his tenure there in an August 25, 1967, article. "Washington settled a major strike of public housing employees, introduced 'scattered–site' housing, leasing and renting of units, modern design and his 'turnkey' concept of private construction for later public use." These were concepts that he had developed during 25 years of service in the nation's capital. His colleagues found him "uniformly charming, easy to work with, and determined to make his point."

Jason Nathan, New York's housing and development administrator, spoke of Washington's commitment to low–income families. In the *Washington Post* for September 7, 1967, Nathan said, "His real impact has been in the area of innovation, involvement of the people in low–rent projects and in summer programs." Over 400,000 people took part in recreation programs he established. He made a personal commitment to responding to citizen concerns, taking time to meet with over 60 tenant groups, and scheduling the meetings so that participants would not have to miss work.

Elected Mayor of Washington, D.C.

Washington's residence in New York was brief. He left the NYHA when President Lyndon B. Johnson appointed him sole commissioner of Washington D.C., a city formerly headed by a three–man commission. When Washington assumed office on September 28, 1967, he became the first African American head of a major American city. Richard M. Nixon re–appointed Washington to the position twice, in 1969 and in 1973, and the city elected him to office for a four–year term in 1975. In the *Washington Post* for September 7, 1967, President Johnson stated, "We have found a man who can provide the leadership, the vision, the understanding and the talent to move the Capital City forward, steadily and surely . . . a strong and authentic voice for the people of the district." When he assumed the role of mayor, Washington accepted a decrease in salary, from $35,000 to $28,500. He named crime, employment, and welfare as his priorities.

Early in his tenure as mayor, Washington appointed task forces to study the city's problems and advise him. In his first few hours in office, he met with 300 marchers protesting the cut of anti–poverty funds. According to the *Washington Post* of November 8, 1967, five groups, a total of 21 people, focused on the issues of "housing and community development, transportation, human resources, economic development and 'environmental protection.'" Washington remained actively involved with the people whose welfare was entrusted to him. Throughout his term in office, he gathered information by employing John Lindsay's style of walking the streets of the city, talking with people. When conflicts arose, he worked with all parties involved to reach solutions. The *Washington New Observer* for February 27, 1993, said that he "set a tone for the city that calmed the fears of business people, reassured a doubting Congress and convinced citizens that the city could manage itself. . . . His regard and respect for each and every individual, his calm demeanor, kept the city cool."

Probably his most challenging responsibility was to restore peace during the rioting that followed the assassination of Martin Luther King Jr. in 1968. He applied this similar calm and considerate approach in dealing with many other difficult situations.

Washington was unable to solve all of the city's problems, of course, but at the end of 11 years in office, he elevated the city from the rubbles of the 1968 riots to a place where people were proud to live. He had also built a $40 million surplus in the treasury. In the *Washington Post* for December 31, 1978, one of Washington's advisers observed, "In his own style, he created a feeling that Washington is not a dead city, that it's going to overcome its problems and rebound."

Leads Distinguished Private Life

After completing his service as mayor, Washington entered private life as a Washington partner for a New York City law firm, Burns, Jackson, Miller, and Summit. He had acquired a number of honors along the way. At least 16 universities and colleges granted him honorary degrees. Among his more distinctive awards are the following: The National Civil Service League named him recipient of its Career Service Award in 1973; Howard University Law School's Alumni Association granted him its Distinguished Service Award in 1974; and the Greater Washington Board of Trade bestowed its Man of the Year Award to him in 1983. The American Civil Liberties Union added its Judge Egarton Award in 1984.

Washington's record of service in various organizations is equally impressive. He served on the advisory board of the U.S. Conference of Mayors and as vice chairman of the National League of Cities' Human Resources Committee. He acted as vice president of the United Community Funds and Councils of America. He was a trustee of the John F. Kennedy Center for Performing Arts. He served on the board of directors of the Washington area Boy Scouts of America, the United Planning Organization, and the Big Brothers of America.

On December 26, 1941, Washington married Bennetta Bullock, daughter of the minister of Washington D.C.'s Third Baptist Church. Bennetta Washington holds a doctorate in guidance and counseling from Catholic University. An educator and social worker, she served as principal of the capital city's Cardoza High School and then as director of the National Women's Job Corp. The Washingtons have one daughter, Bennetta Jules–Rosette. Bennetta Washington died in 1991, and Walter Washington is now married to Mary Burke, a former regional economist under Robert C. Weaver, Secretary of the Department of Housing and Urban Development. She was a member of the cabinet of Hugh Carey, governor of the State of New York, serving as director of the Women's Division.

The *Washington Post* for November 27, 1966, described Washington as "a bit reserved at first but easily relaxed when he senses that you sincerely share his concerns and enthusiasms, always meticulously dressed and always impeccably polite, cuts a fine figure of a man.'' His career has proven him to be not only polite, but a man with an active concern for the welfare of others.

Washington told the *Washington Post* for September 24, 1993 about his career. ''Of my 50 years of service to the city, nothing's been more rewarding than my work in the neighborhood. . . . If you can strengthen your block, you can build a neighborhood, and if you fix the neighborhoods, then you have a city.'' His commitment at both the neighborhood and city levels is representative of this philosophy.

When he retired from his office as mayor, Washington told the *Washington Post* for December 31, 1978:

> What I would like to be remembered for is that Walter Washington changed the spirit of the people of this city, that he came in as mayor when there was hate and greed and misunderstanding among our people and the races were polarized . . . and in the span of just a little over a decade he had brought people together through love and compassion, had helped bring about home rule . . . and had helped people have more meaningful, satisfying and enjoyable lives.

A city and its people felt the impact of such leadership and concern.

Current address: 1025 15th Street NW, Washington, DC 20005.

REFERENCES

Bair, Frank, ed. *Biography News.* Detroit: Gale Research, 1972.

Current Biography Yearbook. New York: H. W. Wilson, 1969.

''Due for Post in Capital.'' *New York Times,* August 25, 1967.

''Enjoying Life without City Hall.'' *Washington Post,* May 10, 1979.

George, Emmett. ''Big Upset in Washington Politics.'' *Sepia* 27 (November 1978): 17–23.

Lantz, Ragni. ''D.C. 'Mayor' Walter Washington: LBJ's Prescription for Our Ailing Capital.'' *Ebony* 5 (March 1968): 72–77.

''Mayor Recalls Era of Tumult.'' *Washington Post,* December 31, 1978.

''The Mayor Who Isn't.'' *Newsweek* 76 (31 August 1970): 78–79.

''The Pride of the Neighborhood.'' *Washington Post,* September 24, 1993.

''2 Experts Will Study Problems of District.'' *Washington Post,* November 8, 1967.

''Walter E. Washington.'' *Washington New Observer,* February 27, 1993.

''Walter Washington: Back Home.'' *Washington Post,* September 7, 1967.

''Well, At Least New York Needs Him Even More.'' *Washington Post,* November 27, 1966.

Marie Garrett

Waters, Muddy.
See Muddy Waters.

André Watts

(1946–)

Concert pianist

André Watts is the first African–American concert pianist to achieve international superstardom. Critics have called Watts electrifying, sensational, daring, colorful, imaginative, powerful, and a supervirtuoso. One of today's celebrated superstars, Watts burst on the Philadelphia music scene at age nine and the world music scene at age 16. He has subsequently performed all over the globe, always receiving rave reviews. Born June 20, 1946, in Nuremburg, Germany, the son of an African American career soldier, sergeant Herman Watts, and a Hungarian mother, Maria Alexandra Gusmits, Watts lived in Europe, mostly near army posts, until the age of eight. A change in his father's military assignment caused the family to move to the United States and settle in Philadelphia.

The family unit remained intact until 1962, when Herman and Maria were divorced. Maria Watts insists that it was not a question of the husband deserting the family. André remained with his mother, whom he credits with considerable influence in his development. In an interview for the *New York Times Magazine,* Watts described his mother as '' a very sharp woman. She never tells me that my performances are unqualified successes, always picks out some obscure passage that needs polishing.'' Maria Watts worked to support herself and young André, first as a secretary and later as a receptionist in an art gallery.

Watts began studying the violin at age four. By the time he was six he made it known that his preference was for the piano, so his mother, a pianist herself, gave him his first lessons. As is frequently the case, he loved to play but hated to practice. When his habit persisted, his mother began relaying stories of her countryman, pianist and composer Franz Liszt, emphasizing the fact that he practiced faithfully. Liszt soon became Watts's hero, and he even adopted Liszt's bravura playing style.

In Philadelphia, Watts went first to a Quaker school, then to a parochial one, then to Lincoln Preparatory School. He was also enrolled at the Philadelphia Academy of Music, where he studied with Genia Robinor, Doris Bawden, and Clement Petrillo, graduating in June 1963. It is said that with his huge hands, he always painted in full colors.

Watts entered his first competition at age nine, competing with 40 other gifted youngsters for an opportunity to appear in one of the Philadelphia Orchestra's Children's

André Watts

Concerts. Watts won the competition and with this accomplishment successfully launched his career. He performed a Franz Joseph Haydn piano concerto. At age ten, he performed the Felix Mendelssohn G minor concerto with the Robin Hood Dell Orchestra and at 14, Cesar Franck's *Symphonic Variations,* again with the Philadelphia Orchestra.

When Watts was 16, he auditioned at Carnegie Recital Hall before three New York Philharmonic assistant conductors and Leonard Bernstein's secretary. The group applauded his audition performance, moving him on to the maestro himself—Bernstein—and the finals, where things went equally well. Watts had little awareness of what this event could make possible. Watts recalled the experience several years later for journalist Norman Schreiber, Watts said:

> Hey my teacher was there; my mother was there; they were going to be really bummed out if I played like a pig. I would feel miserable. I also realized it would be good for you if other people like your playing.

Watts played Liszt's E–flat Concerto at Lincoln Center with the New York Philharmonic, conducted by Leonard Bernstein. A *Young People's Concert,* the program was taped three days earlier than it was shown on CBS television on January 15, 1963. Bernstein introduced the young pianist to the national audience. Less than three weeks after he was soloist for the *Young People's Concert,* Bernstein asked Watts to substitute for an ailing Glenn Gould, who was the scheduled soloist for the New York Philharmonic's regular subscription concert on January 1, 1963. Again Watts performed the Liszt E flat Concerto. So spectacular was this performance that he made international headlines and Columbia recorded an LP entitled, *The Exciting Debut of André Watts. Time* magazine quoted the liner notes:

> . . . Andre approached the piece as a tone poem. In scherzo passages, he had the speed and power necessary to dignify his delicately poetic ideas of the slow pianissimos. His singing tone stayed with him in every mood of his varied approach, and when he had sounded his final cadenza, the whole orchestra stood with the audience to applaud him. Even the Philharmonic fiddlers put down their bows and gustily clapped hands.

Enters Concert Life

Following his debut, Watts's manager restricted him to a limited number of engagements: the first year, six concerts; the next, 12 concerts; the next 15 concerts, and so on. His mother and manager, decided that his entry into concert life would be gradual. In addition, success would not isolate him from his classmates. His English and American history instructor, Roy Cusumano wrote in *International Musician,* ''he became friendlier and more responsive.'' Gradually the number of concerts increased, reaching 150 by the mid–1970s. By then Watts was performing about eight months out of the year. In the late 1990s, he fulfilled roughly 100 engagements per year, divided between concert appearances and solo recitals.

Though he attained celebrity status at an early age, Watts continued to study with the noted pianist and teacher Leon Fleisher. Following high school graduation, Watts began to study part–time for a bachelor of music degree at Peabody Institute in Baltimore, where Fleisher was a member of the faculty. He graduated in 1972.

In July 1963, Watts appeared at New York City's Lewisohn Stadium with Seiji Ozawa and the New York Philharmonic, performing Camille Saint–Saen's Concert No. 2 in G minor. In September 1963, he again performed the Liszt concerto at the Hollywood Bowl. He opened the 1964–65 National Symphony Orchestra's season in Washington, D.C., performing the Saint–Saens concerto. He returned to New York in January 1965 to perform Chopin's Concerto No. 2 in F minor with the Philharmonic.

Watts made his European debut in a London performance with the London Symphony Orchestra in June 1966. Shortly thereafter he appeared with the Concertgebouw Orchestra in Amsterdam, Holland. In October of the same year, he made his New York recital debut, opening the Great Performers Series at Philharmonic Hall. He made his debut in Berlin, Germany, also in 1966, when he performed with the Berlin Philharmonic under the leadership of Zubin Mehta.

Watts embarked on a three–month world concert tour beginning in September of 1967, under the auspices of the U.S. Department of State. He celebrated his twenty–first birthday by signing a long–term exclusive contract with CBS

Records. By 1969 he was on a full–scale concert schedule, booked three seasons in advance.

Makes Public Impact on Television

Anniversaries were becoming more and more frequent. Though only 30 at the time, he celebrated his tenth consecutive appearance in Lincoln Center's Great Performance Series at Avery Fischer Hall in 1976. Since he was the first classical artist to make his initial public impact through television, the producers believed that his should be the first solo recital televised live in its entirety from Lincoln Center. Watts's relationship with television in the field of classical music is unique. His PBS Sunday afternoon telecast in 1976 was the first solo recital presented on *Live from Lincoln Center* and the first full–length recital to be aired nationally in prime time. The 1988–89 season offered a televised concert featuring the Shostakovich First Piano Concerto, performed with the Philadelphia Orchestra, with Watts doubling as piano soloist and program host.

In June and July 1974 he made a five–week tour of Japan and made summer appearances at the Hollywood Bowl, Ambler, Ravinia, and Concord festivals. Between recitals and orchestral appearances throughout the United States, there were two European tours during the 1975–76 season. Unlike many other protégés, Watts lived up to his early promise and was a greater sensation as time moved on. A 1975 press release from the Judd Concert Bureau described Watts as:

> Serious–minded and worldwise. . .Watts dresses conservatively and comes on rather like a mature college professor as he talks soberly of the artist's responsibilities to society. He is not for the gimmick of any kind, plays his programs straight and shies away from publicity not specifically related to his metier. . . .

Watts decribed the playing experience to James Conaway of the *New York Times*:

> My greatest satisfaction is performing. The ego is a big part of it, but far from all. Performing is my way of being part of humanity—of sharing. I don't want to play for a few people, I want to play for thousands. . . . There's something beautiful about having an entire audience hanging on a single note. I'd rather have a standing ovation than have some chick come backstage and tell me how great I was.

In 1964 the National Academy of Recording Artists and Sciences presented Watts with a Grammy Award and in February 1973 he was selected as *Musical America's* Musician of the Month. Other honors and awards include honorary doctorates from Albright College and Yale University, the Order of the Zaire from that African country, and a University of the Arts Medal from the University of the Arts in Philadelphia.

Still in great demand after performing more than 30 years, Watts was asked by Mark Adams for the *Washington Post* about the 1991 winner of the Naumberg Piano Competition, "a black whiz kid with dreadlocks named Awadagin Pratt." Watts's response was, "This is not an unfillable position." Thirty–three years after his first recording, 1995 and 1996 reviewers still raved over Watts's performances of Tchiakovsky's Piano Concert No. 1, Saint–Saens's Piano Concerto No. 2 with the Atlanta Symphony, MacDowell's Piano Concerto No. 2, and Liszt's Piano Concertos Nos. 1 & 2 with the Dallas Symphony.

At age 50, Watts remains one of the world's "greatest in demand" pianists, both as recitalist and concert soloist. He continues to perform on the world's most important concert stages and with the world's most celebrated orchestras and conductors.

Current address: c/o IMB Artists, 22 East 71st Street, New York, NY 10021.

REFERENCES

Conaway, James. "Andre Watts on Andre Watts." *New York Times Magazine* (19 September 1971): 14–26.

"Concert: Andre Watts Plays Mozart." *New York Times,* August 13, 1987.

Current Biography Yearbook. New York: H. W. Wilson, 1968.

Cusumano, Roy. "The Prep School Days of Andre Watts." *International Musician* (April 1969): 5, 21.

The Exciting Debut of Andre Watts. Liner Notes, Columbia Records 1963, MSS 64458.

Hiemenz, Jack. "Musician of the Month, Andre Watts." *Musical America* 23 (February 1973): 4–5.

Press Material, Judd Concert Bureau, 1975.

Schreiber, Norman. "My Lunch with Andre." *Amtrak Express* (April/May 1989): 20–24.

Southern, Eileen. *Biographical Dictionary of Afro–American and African Musicians.* Westport, CT: Greenwood Press, 1982.

"Watts Plays for the Millions." *New York Times,* November 26, 1976.

"Watts's Incidental Achievement." *Washington Post,* April 16, 1993.

D. Antoinette Handy

Robert C. Weaver
(1907–1997)
Government official, scholar, labor and housing specialist

Robert Weaver spent a lifetime dedicated to public service and in 1966 became the first African American in history to serve as a Cabinet officer with his appointment as Secretary of Housing and Urban Development under President Lyndon B. Johnson. After beginning his federal service in 1933 at the Interior Department, he soon earned respect as one of the country's foremost experts on labor, housing, and race relations, becoming an influential advisor to President Franklin D. Roosevelt. Later he moved into academia, making important contributions as a scholar, lecturer, college president, and board member of public and private organizations. In his public career, he served as an official in government at the federal, state, and city levels for more than 50 years.

Robert Clifton Weaver was born in Washington, D.C., on December 29, 1907, the son of Mortimer Grover, a postal clerk, and Florence Freeman Weaver. His grandfather, Robert Mortimer Freeman, was a member of the first graduating class of Harvard's dental school and the first African American to earn a degree in dentistry. Weaver was also a nephew of the black composer and musician Harry Burleigh. Robert Weaver had a brother, Mortimer, who became an assistant professor at Howard University and died suddenly at the age of 23. Robert Weaver credits his mother with inspiring the children to intellectual achievement. Weaver married Ella V. Haith on July 18, 1935, and they had one adopted son, Robert C. Weaver Jr., now deceased.

Robert Weaver grew up as one of seven African American families in a Washington suburb, and he and his brother had to travel an hour and a half every day to attend school. Even before he graduated in 1925 from Dunbar High School in Washington, D.C., he demonstrated his skill and capacity for hard work. By his junior year he was a paid electrician, and he operated his own electrical business in his senior year. Weaver attended Harvard University, where he majored in economics and received a B.S. (cum laude) in 1929, an M.S. in 1931, and a Ph. D. in 1934.

Robert Weaver made a major contribution to this country in Franklin D. Roosevelt's administration, when he was one of the academics brought to Washington by the New Deal. He served in the Department of the Interior in several official capacities from 1934 to 1938, first as an aide to Secretary Harold Ickes—one of many positions he filled as advisor on black affairs to an agency head. He was an influential member of Roosevelt's ''Black Cabinet,'' a group of blacks working in the Roosevelt administration that had been called together in August 1936 by Mary McLeod Bethune, who enjoyed a friendship with Eleanor Roosevelt and was one of the few blacks who had access to the President. The group organized two national conferences on black problems. The first, held in January 1937, produced a report that had very little influence on administration policy, but the group's pressure secured important advancements for blacks in housing and employment.

The most dramatic effect of Weaver's influence in the Roosevelt Administration is said to have occurred days before the 1940 presidential election. Roosevelt's press secretary had an altercation with a black policeman after a major campaign speech by Roosevelt in New York's Madison Square Garden. White House aides contacted Weaver at midnight about how to repair the damage this incident might cause among black voters. Weaver suggested that more than a speech was necessary and transmitted some recommendations. Within 48 hours the nation had its first black general, Benjamin O. Davis Sr., a

Robert C. Weaver

black assistant to the Selective Service director, Campbell Johnson, and a black civilian aide to the Secretary of War, William Hastie.

Weaver continued to hold government positions after leaving his initial post in the Interior Department. From 1938 to 1940 he served as special assistant to the head of the National Housing Authority, Nathan Strauss. In 1940 he was assistant to Sidney Hillman at the National Defense Advisory Commission. During World War II, he served on the War Production Board and the Negro Manpower Commission, promoting the cause of integration in industry and greater participation by black workers in the war effort.

Turns Service at State and Local Level

In 1944, feeling that the implementation of antidiscrimination measures was proceeding too slowly, he left national government to serve the city of Chicago as executive director of the Mayor's Committee on Race Relations. When he left Chicago, he plunged into a variety of sometimes overlapping positions in teaching and service as a government and organization official. From 1945 to 1948 he was director of community services for the American Council on Race Relations.

In 1946 he was called to serve in the United Nations Relief and Rehabilitation Administration and worked in several official capacities in the Ukraine, U.S.S.R., including as deputy chief of mission. Returning to Chicago, he entered academic life as a visiting lecturer at Northwestern University in Evanston, Illinois, in 1947–48 while also serving on the board of the Metropolitan Housing Council and as an officer of the American Council on Race Relations. From 1949 to 1955 Weaver was director of the Opportunity Fellowships program of the John Hay Whitney Foundation. He also served on the national selection committee of the Fulbright Fellowship program, the fellowship selection committee of the Julius Rosenwald Fund, consultant to the Ford Foundation, and as chair of the faculty selection committee of the United Negro College Fund.

Further involvements in academia continued. Weaver taught summer school at Columbia University Teachers College (1947 and 1949) and the New School for Social Research (1949) and also served as visiting professor at New York University School of Education from 1948 to 1951. After leaving his cabinet post, he was president of Bernard M. Baruch College in 1969–70, a branch of New York University. From 1971 until he retired in 1978, he was Distinguished Professor of Urban Affairs at Hunter College. He has also been an invited lecturer at many other schools.

Weaver continued his active involvement in politics when the Democrats returned to power in New York in 1955. He initially went to Albany as Deputy State Rent Commissioner and later became the first black in the state cabinet when he became Commissioner, a position he held until January of 1959. From June to December in the following year he was vice–chair of the New York City Housing and Development Board. New mayor Robert F. Wagner wanted Weaver to follow Hulan Jack as Manhattan Borough President after Jack's conviction on charges of conflict of interest, but President–elect John F. Kennedy intervened to name him director of the Federal Housing and Home Finance Agency. Weaver achieved great success in coordinating the activities of five subordinate agencies. Kennedy tried to make the agency a cabinet department in 1961, but his attempt was blocked by Congress because of his obvious plan to name Weaver to head the new department. President Lyndon B. Johnson succeeded in creating the Department of Housing and Urban Development four years later.

Becomes Housing Secretary

On January 13, 1966, President Lyndon B. Johnson appointed him Secretary of the newly created U.S. Department of Housing and Urban Development (HUD), and he was sworn in five days later. A strong believer in the positive social values of urban development, he set an example by living in an apartment development in Capital Park, an urban redevelopment area in Washington, D.C., during his tenure as Secretary of HUD. Among his major responsibilities was the coordination of activities and functions among the Federal Housing Authority, Small Business Administration, Government National Mortgage Administration, and the Model Cities Program, with policy direction by the Department of Housing and Urban Development. In addition, he advocated a greatly expanded role for the federal government in all areas affecting urban development, towards the goal of finding long–range solutions to the nation's urban problems. Weaver left government service when Richard Nixon became president in 1968. He then served in academic positions until his formal retirement from Hunter College in 1978.

After leaving government service, he continued to serve on the boards of businesses such as the Metropolitan Life Insurance Company (1969–80) and the Bowery Savings Bank (1969–80) as well as those of educational and public institutions such as the visiting commission of the Harvard University School of Design (1978–83), the New York City Conciliation and Appeals Board (for rent control) (1973–84), the board of Mount Sinai Hospital and Medical School (1970–97), and the executive committee of the board of the NAACP Legal Defense Fund (1978–97). In addition, he was chairman of the board of the NAACP in 1960–1961. Civic concerns led him to serve as president of the National Committee Against Discrimination in Housing (1973–87). His distinguished position in American life was recognized by his election to the American Academy of Arts and Sciences in 1985.

Weaver was also a productive scholar who wrote four books and 185 articles. *Contemporary Biography* quoted him as saying, "When I can't relax . . . then I feel real frustrated and start writing." In his scholarship, as in public service, he focused on the role and function of government at several levels and the interrelationships among these levels. His views were wide–ranging and unabashedly liberal, calling for an expanded role for the federal government in urban development, integration of the federal service at all levels, and the expansion of opportunity in housing and employment for the urban poor of all races. He singled out segregation in housing as the root cause of segregation and consequent discrimination in many other areas.

Among his innovative ideas for urban renewal and housing was the concepts of government intervention through financial offsets, easing of loan requirements, government loan guarantees, and tax incentives to broaden the base of home ownership through direct federal participation while encouraging private investment and development. Always a forward–thinking problem solver, he called for planners to anticipate future needs. His critiques frequently postulated solutions for problems he projected would need solutions five or ten years in the future. For example, he suggested that city planners note the current lack of land for public use in the nation's major cities and seek to acquire marginal lands for public use many years beyond the horizon of current city planning. Another innovative concept called for balanced urban planning, which allows functions and inputs to be shared between government, industry, and private and public organizations. He also pointed to the need for balance in sharing expertise, funds, and responsibilities between federal, state, and city institutions. He acknowledged, too, the divided loyalties, trusts, and suspicions that frequently cause difficulties in such partnership attempts.

Weaver's research was often informed by his extensive background in Franklin D. Roosevelt's administration working for greater participation by African Americans in the nation's work force—particularly during World War II—in wartime industry, in the military, and in the federal service itself. His practical experience resulted in many published studies of this very broad topic, including *Negro Labor* (1946).

Weaver was a member of Omega Psi Phi Fraternity and received more than thirty honorary doctorates. Among his numerous other recognitions and awards were the Spingarn Medal of the NAACP, 1962; Russwurm Award, 1963; Albert Einstein Commemorative Award, 1968; Merrick Moore Spaulding Achievement Award, 1968; Award for Public Service, U.S. General Accounting Office, 1975; New York City Urban League's Frederick Douglass Award, 1977; election to the Hall of Fame of the National Association of Home Builders, 1982; the M. Justin Herman Award, National Association of Housing and Redevelopment Officials, 1986; and the Equal Opportunity Day Award, National Urban League, 1987.

Weaver died at his New York City home on July 17, 1997. His wife died in 1991, and their son Robert Jr. died in 1962. Robert C. Weaver's life reflected a deep personal commitment to serve the public. Active over a period of many years in governmental, academic and civic pursuits, he advocated respect for differences and the sharing of responsibilities for improving the quality of life for all Americans.

REFERENCES

Adams, A. John, and Joan Martin Burke. *Civil Rights.* New York: Bowker, 1970.

Bardolph, Richard. *The Negro Vanguard.* 1959. Reprint, Westport, CT: Negro Universities Press, 1971.

Contemporary Black Biography. Vol. 9. Detroit: Gale Research, 1995.

Current Biography Yearbook. New York: H. W. Wilson, 1961.

Ploski, Harry A., ed. *Reference Library of Black America.* Vol. 1. New York: Afro–American Press, 1990.

"Robert C. Weaver, 89, First Black Cabinet Member, Dies." *New York Times,* July 19, 1997.

Weaver, Robert C. *Negro Labor: A National Problem*: New York, Harcourt, Brace, 1946.

———. "Negro Labor Since 1929." *Journal of Negro History* 35 (January 1950): 20–38.

———. "The Role of Government in Improving the Urban Environment." In William Zisch, Paul O. Douglas and Robert C. Weaver. *The Urban Environment: How It Can Be Improved.* New York, New York University Press, 1969.

———. *The Urban Complex: Human Values in Urban Life.* Garden City: Doubleday, 1964.

Who's Who among Black Americans, 1996–97. 9th ed. Detroit, Gale Research, 1996.

Who's Who in America, 1994. 48th ed. New Providence: Marquis Who's Who, 1993.

Who's Who in American Politics, 1995–96. 15th ed. New Providence: Bowker, 1995.

Darius L. Thieme

Robert Wedgeworth Jr.

(1937–)

Library administrator, educator, organization executive

The first black to become executive director of the American Library Association (ALA), Robert W. Wedgeworth Jr. has spent his career as a librarian, library administrator, and library education and organization leader. He was the first black dean of the library school at Columbia University. Later he became the first black library director at the University of Illinois, Urbana, the largest public university research library in the United States and the third largest of all American university research libraries after Harvard and Yale. He was the first non–European to head the International Federation of Library Associations and Institutions in more than 60 years.

Wedgeworth was born July 31, 1937, in Ennix, Texas, the son of Robert Sr. and Jimmie Johnson Wedgeworth. He completed an A.B. degree at Wabash College, Crawfordsville, Indiana, in 1959 and an M.S. in library and information science at the University of Illinois in 1961. He began his library career at the Kansas City Public Library in Missouri as a cataloger from 1961 to 1962. In 1962 he moved to Park College, Parksville, Missouri, as an assistant librarian. Following a year as acting head librarian at Park College, he accepted a position as head librarian at Meranac Community College in Kirkwood, Missouri, a suburb of St. Louis, in 1964 and remained until 1966.

In 1962 the ALA selected Wedgeworth as one of about 75 librarians to serve as staff for "Library 21," a library–of–the–future exhibit at the Seattle World's Fair. The group was given special training in automated data processing techniques. The experience was a major factor in his appointment as assistant chief acquisitions librarian at Brown University library in July of 1966, with a special assignment to introduce library automation to the Brown libraries. From 1966 to 1969 Wedgeworth managed the domestic and foreign acquisitions activities at Brown while developing an automated acquisitions and fund accounting system. As a Council on Library Resources fellow, he studied the Western European book trade in the summer of 1963.

Wedgeworth moved to Rutgers University, New Jersey, in the fall of 1969 to do advanced studies in librarianship and teach in the Graduate School of Library Service. In 1971 he became an assistant professor at Rutgers. He left library education to become executive director of the ALA in August of 1972, becoming the first African American to be appointed to a high–level position in the association. He would later note that well into the 1970s, few African American librarians had been appointed to ALA committees and few elected to council.

Wedgeworth assumed the leadership role at ALA at a time of internal strife. The association was rent with dissension from groups such as the Congress for Change, Librarians for 321.8, and the Social Responsibilities Round Table, all of which had the democratization of ALA as their objective. During this time the association's council and executive board dealt with threats of secession from various divisions, a mounting financial crisis, deteriorating relationships with publishers, and the lack of key personnel at ALA headquarters.

The situation demanded a leader who was both competent and patient, receptive and cautious, and youthful and strong. By 1974 it was clear that Wedgeworth was the right person to lead the ALA, and the strength of his leadership was evident by increased memberships. Conference attendance reached a new high: 14,382 persons registered for the 1974 conference in New York City. In San Francisco in 1975, attendance was the second highest in ALA history with 11,606 persons registered.

Following his appointment as executive director, Wedgeworth began working towards democratizing the ALA and making it more visible and credible nationally and internationally. Under his leadership the association grew from 28,000 members to over 40,000. He was able to rebuild the headquarters staff, bring the deficit under control, and secure a new headquarters building with 50,000 square feet of space. During his 13–year tenure he also supervised directly the accreditation process for graduate programs in library and information science in the United States and Canada and launched several initiatives aimed at strengthening the association.

Wedgeworth studied the ALA prior to his appointment as executive director to show the extent to which African American librarians had been excluded from the group's higher levels. He concluded that black members lacked authority and organization within the association. He suggested that black librarians join forces with the Social Responsibilities Round Table to create a separate power base that could be combined with an important decision–making unit within ALA. Such an association would call attention to the lack of an effective African American voice within ALA and professional opportunities for African American librarians. The result of Wedgeworth's study was the establishment of the ALA Black Caucus.

In 1982, while in his ALA position, Wedgeworth was also a visiting professor at the School of Library Science, University of North Carolina at Chapel Hill. He left the ALA in 1985 to become dean of the School of Library Service, Columbia University, until 1992, when the university announced that the school would close. In 1992 Wedgeworth moved to Urbana, Illinois, where he became interim librarian at the University of Illinois. He was appointed university librarian and professor of library administration in November of 1993.

In his more than 30 years as a librarian, library educator, and association executive, Wedgeworth created and edited two major reference works: *ALA Yearbook,* published from 1976 to 1985; and the *ALA World Encyclopedia of Library and Information Services,* third edition, 1985. In addition, he wrote numerous articles on international librarianship, international book trade, copyright, management, information policy, and information technology. He conducted studies of the book trade in Western Europe, Latin America, and South Africa, and in 1989 produced *The Starvation of Young Black Minds: The Effects of the Book Boycotts in South Africa.*

Wedgeworth served as a member of the board of trustees of the Newberry Library, Chicago, and, beginning in 1987, he was the public member of the Accrediting Council of Journalism and Mass Communication. He also chaired the Advisory Committee of the Office of Information Technology of ALA. Other advisory council memberships included the Center for the Book, Library of Congress; Princeton University Libraries; Stanford University Libraries; and Gannett Center for Media Services. He was a trustee of the American Library in Paris from 1986 to 1992, and since 1988 has been a trustee of Wabash College, Indiana.

Wedgeworth was elected to the executive board of the International Federation of Library Associations and Institutions (IFLA) in 1985. He was elected president of the federation in 1991 and reelected in 1995. With headquarters in the Netherlands, IFLA represents over 1,400 library associations and institutions in over 140 countries. He has been Honorary President of the IFLA since 1997.

Wedgeworth received many honors and awards, including honorary doctorates from Mary Park College in 1973, Atlanta University in 1982, Western Illinois University in 1983, and College of William and Mary in 1988. He was named the Most Distinguished Alumnus of the University of Illinois, Graduate School of Library and Information Science, for 1991, and in 1989 he received the prestigious Joseph Lippincott Award from the ALA. Wedgeworth received the Medal of Honor from the International Council of Archives for work in fostering cooperation between libraries and archives. When he was named recipient of the Melvil Dewey Award from the ALA in 1997, Janet Swann Hill, award jury chair, commented in *American Libraries* that Wedgeworth ''seemed a natural choice. . .because of the parallels in his career [with] that of Melvil Dewey.''

Reflecting on his career, Wedgeworth told *American Libraries,* ''I've been extremely fortunate in my choice of career at a time that was critical in the life of several major institutions.'' Looking back with pride on his work with the ALA, Columbia University, and IFLA, he called experiences ''highlights in terms of opportunities.'' He also revealed that he was looking forward to the second half of his career, to becoming more involved in academic librarianship and returning to editing the *World Encyclopedia of Library and Information Services.* He told *American Libraries* that he would like to be remembered for ''changing people's lives by creating more opportunities for them to participate and to develop.''

Wedgeworth is married to Chung–Kyun, a systems librarian, and has one daughter, Cicely Veronica.

Current address: University of Illinois at Urbana–Champaign, 230 Library, 1408 West Gregory Drive, MC–522, Urbana, IL 61801.

REFERENCES

ALA Yearbook. Chicago: American Library Association, 1976.
"They Won! And Did It ALA's Way." *American Libraries* 28 (September 1997): 70–74.
"Voice of 30,000 Librarians: Robert Wedgeworth, Executive Director of American Library Association, Seeks to Make Librarians Visible." Ebony 28 (June 1973): 107–12.
Who's Who among African Americans, 1998–99. 10th ed. Detroit: Gale Research, 1997.
Who's Who in America, 1996. 50th ed. New Providence, NJ: Marquis Who's Who, 1996.

Arthur C. Gunn

Charles H. Wesley
(1891–1987)
Historian, minister, educator

Charles H. Wesley

Charles H. Wesley, a Harvard–trained historian, was a multi–talented individual who wrote books and articles relating to the history of African Americans in the United States, including pioneering studies on labor history and biographies of historic black leaders such as Richard Allen and Prince Hall. He worked as an educator and dean at Howard University, as the president of Wilberforce and Central State universities in Ohio, and as president and executive director of the Association for the Study of Afro–American Life and History. He was also a leading churchman, serving as the pastor of Ebenezer and Campbell African Methodist Episcopal (AME) Churches in Washington, D.C., and ministering as presiding elder for all of the American Methodist Episcopal churches in the Potomac District.

Born in Louisville, Kentucky, on December 2, 1891, to Charles Snowden and Matilda Harris Wesley, young Charles Harris Wesley received solid religious and academic training. His grandfather was a sexton in Quinn Chapel African Methodist Episcopal Church, where Wesley was baptized. He attended Louisville public schools. After attending Central High School from 1904 to 1906, he transferred to the academy of Fisk University where he studied from 1906 until 1907, when he was admitted to college. At Fisk Wesley excelled academically as well as in music, drama, and sports. He even performed with the Fisk Jubilee Singers for a brief period in 1909. Deeply drawn to the study of black history by George Edmund Haynes, a black professor at Fisk who was a pioneer social worker, Wesley decided to make black history his life's work.

Graduating from Fisk in 1911 at 19 years of age with a major in classics, Wesley received a university fellowship from Yale University in New Haven, Connecticut, where he studied history and economics for two years. He graduated with a master of arts degree in 1913 and was recruited to teach at Howard University in Washington, D.C. In addition to his academic accomplishments, in 1913 Wesley also joined the Zeta Chapter of Alpha Phi Alpha Fraternity in New Haven.

Wesley's first job at Howard was as instructor of history and modern languages with a salary of $700. From the beginning of his 30–year stint at Howard, Wesley remained active in many other endeavors at the same time. At Howard he introduced fascinating and popular lectures on the role of African Americans in United States history. His first few years as an instructor were filled with a variety of activities. In the summer of 1914 Wesley traveled to France to study French and music at the Guilde Internationale in Paris but his trip was cut short by the outbreak of World War I. From 1914 to 1915 he studied at Howard's law school. On November 25, 1915, Wesley married Louise Johnson of Baltimore, Maryland. The couple remained together for almost 50 years until Louise Wesley's death in 1973. The union produced two girls, Louise and Charlotte.

The year after his marriage, Wesley joined a fledgling scholarly group called the Association for the Study of Negro Life and History (ASNLH). Founded by Carter G. Woodson, who had received a doctorate from Harvard in 1912, the association was dedicated to the scholarly pursuit of black history and culture. Woodson encouraged Wesley in his research by publishing some of his articles in early issues of the association's organ, the *Journal of Negro History.* These include "The Struggle of Haiti and Liberia for Recognition" (October 1917), "Lincoln's Plan for Colonizing the Emancipated Negroes" (January 1919), and "The Employment of

Negroes as Soldiers in the Confederate Army'' (July 1919). In subsequent years Wesley wrote many more articles for the journal.

Historian Becomes Minister

The year 1918 brought several changes in Wesley's life. He was promoted to assistant professor of history at Howard, became engaged in war relief work with the YMCA, and accepted the directorship of the choir at the Metropolitan AME Church in Washington, D.C. Wesley was also the director of the Men's Glee Club at Howard. A church leader who observed Wesley's musical leadership at Metropolitan urged him to enter the ministry. He complied. In 1918 he was assigned to Ebenezer AME Church in Georgetown where he served until 1923.

Wesley was officially ordained and admitted as a minister in 1921. He served in the District of Columbia as the pastor of Campbell AME Church from 1923 to 1927 while also serving as the chief secretary of the Baltimore Annual Conference of the AME Church from 1922 to 1929. These and other church duties led to his appointment as presiding elder of the Potomac District in 1928. In this position he oversaw the work of the pastors and officers in 20 to 25 churches until 1938 when he resigned. While working with the AME church, he published a biography of the denomination's founder entitled *Richard Allen: Apostle of Freedom* (1935).

In addition to his success with writing and in the church, at Howard University Wesley was a rising star. He became an associate professor in 1919. As a recipient of the Austin's Teacher's Scholarship from Harvard University in 1920, Wesley spent the 1920 to 1921 school year in Cambridge, Massachusetts, while commuting biweekly to his church. He completed his doctorate in history at Harvard in 1921. Vanguard Press in New York published Wesley's dissertation in 1927. Entitled *Negro Labor in the United States, 1850 to 1925,* this work became a classic in the emerging field of black history. Wesley was the third black man to receive a doctor of philosophy degree from Harvard. The first two were W. E. B. DuBois and Carter G. Woodson, both in history.

Wesley returned to Howard to serve as professor of history and chair of the history department from 1921 to 1942. The first black historian to be a recipient of a John Simon Guggenheim Fellowship, Wesley spent 1930 and 1931 in England researching the role of blacks in the abolition movement and the history of emancipation in the British empire. During the next few years, Wesley wrote *The Collapse of the Confederacy* (1935). He also served as the director of the summer school program at Howard in 1937, as acting dean of the College of Liberal Arts from 1937 to 1938, and as dean of the graduate school from 1938 to 1942.

Wesley worked diligently with his fraternity in many capacities and between 1931 and 1964 was elected president of Alpha Phi Alpha ten times. In 1929 Howard University Press published Wesley's *History of Alpha Phi Alpha: A Development in Negro College Life.* This work enjoyed a long life with many editions. Because of his history of Alpha Phi Alpha, Wesley was later sought out to prepare histories of other organizations. A few of these titles include *A History of the I. B. P. O. E.* (1956), *History of Sigma Pi Phi: First of the Negro–American Greek–Letter Fraternities* (1969), *The History of the Prince Hall Grand Lodge of Free and Accepted Masons of the State of Ohio, 1849–1971* (1972), and *The History of the National Association of Colored Women's Clubs: A Legacy of Service,* (1984).

Heads Black Colleges

As a result of his prolific scholarship and excellent administrative abilities, Wesley was named president of Wilberforce University in Wilberforce, Ohio, where he served from 1942 to 1947, and then of Central State University in the same city from 1947 to 1965. William Peters Robinson, Sr., a member of the ASNLH executive council, wrote the introduction for a series of essays by Wesley published by ASNLH in 1969 entitled *Neglected History: Essays in Negro History by A College President.* In it Robinson stated that the essays represented Wesley's ''ceaseless search for the truth and for setting the record straight against . . . falsifications'' which represented the African American as a ''pariah.'' Wesley himself wrote that he and the association would ''continue to make contributions to historical truth until recognition has been given to the unrecognized.''

Wesley remained active with the historical community by serving as the president of ASNLH from 1950 to 1965 and as executive director of the association from 1969 to 1972. Writing of the accomplishments during the years that Wesley was executive director in a 1983 issue of the *Negro History Bulletin,* J. Rupert Picott stated that in 1969 the ASNLH hosted over 4,000 delegates and visitors ''from across America'' at its annual convention. In 1970 the association purchased new quarters in Washington, D.C., at 1401 14th Street, Northwest. ASNLH officially changed its name to the Association for the Study of Afro–American Life and History (ASALH) and received a Ford Foundation Grant for program expansion in 1972.

Three years after his first wife's death, on November 30, 1978, Wesley married Dorothy B. Porter, the renowned bibliographer of African Americana, whose resourcefulness and foresight caused the Moorland–Spingarn Collection at Howard University to become one of the most celebrated repositories for black history in the world. Together, the Wesleys continued to do research. In his retirement years Wesley published *Prince Hall: Life and Legacy* (1977) and *Henry Arthur Callis: Life and Legacy* (1977), in addition to the institutional histories mentioned earlier.

During his lifetime Wesley received many honorary degrees and was a member of numerous organizations including Phi Beta Kappa, American Association of University Professors, the Masons, American Historical Association, Southern Historical Association, and American Antiquarian Society.

After a short illness, Wesley died August 16, 1987, just a few months before his ninety–sixth birthday. Although

Wesley's works have received mixed reception from reviewers, none has doubted his productivity and pioneering spirit as a historical scholar. In addition to his numerous books, he regularly published articles, spoke before audiences, and remained active in a wide variety of scholarly and secular organizations. His versatility in areas such as music and linguistics served him well as he dedicated his life to recognition for the unrecognized.

REFERENCES

Contemporary Authors. Vols. 101, 123. Detroit: Gale Research, 1981, 1988.

Conyers, James L., Jr. *Charles H. Wesley: the Intellectual Tradition of a Black Historian.* New York: Garland, 1997.

Harris, Janette Hoston. "Charles Harris Wesley, Educator and Historian, 1891 to 1947." Ph.D. dissertation, Howard University, April 1975.

Meier, August, and Elliot Rudwick. *Black Historians and the Historical Profession.* Urbana: University of Illinois Press, 1986.

Obituary. *New York Times,* September 2, 1987.

Obituary. *Washington Post,* August 22, 1987.

Thorpe, Earl E. *Black Historians: A Critique.* New York: William Morrow, 1971.

Wesley, Charles H. *Neglected History.* Wilberforce, OH: Central State College Press, 1965.

Winston, Michael R. *The Howard University Department of History.* Washington, DC: Howard University Department of History, 1973.

COLLECTIONS

Information on Charles H. Wesley is in the Vertical File, Moorland–Spingarn Research Center, Howard University, Washington, D.C.

Debra Newman Ham

Cornel West

(1953–)

Philosopher, scholar, educator, writer

Henry Louis Gates, in *Emerge* magazine, has called Cornel West "our black Jeremiah." West is a new breed of black scholar, erudite but also accessible, an intellectual but equally an activist who seeks to define black intellectual responsibility. In *The Ethical Dimensions of Marxist Thought,* West challenges black scholars with questions regarding political action and commitment. He asked:

> How do we put the fundamental issues of employment, health and child care, housing, ecology, and education on the agenda of the powers that be in a world disproportionately shaped by transnational corporations and nation–state elites in a global multipolar capitalist order? How do we keep a focus on these issues while we fight racism, patriarchy, homophobia, and ecological abuse? What effective forms of progressive politics can emerge in this new moment of history?

Such challenging questions mark West as a philosopher and prophet grounded in present–day realities; structured by the black experience, his vision of what ought to be is fueled by, in his own words in the reference above, "the Christian ethic of love–informed service to others."

Cornel West was born in Tulsa, Oklahoma, on June 2, 1953. He was the youngest son in a family that included his two sisters, Cynthia and Cheryl, and an older brother, Clifton III. His father, Clifton L. West Jr., was a civilian Air Force administrator. His mother, Irene Bias West, taught elementary school and later became a school principal. West's grandfather, Clifton L. West Sr., was pastor of Tulsa Metropolitan Baptist Church.

West grounds his childhood experience in the social and political milieu of post–World War II America. No one, West insists, has escaped the effects of European modernity, for at one point Europe dominated and controlled more than two–thirds of the world's people. He calls the world he grew up in the "American century," a term borrowed from Henry Luce. In *The Ethical Dimensions of Marxist Thought,* West defined it as "a period of unprecedented economic boom in the United States, the creation of a large middle class . . . and a mass culture primarily based on African American cultural products."

Born into this world, West saw his father and mother earn a living while demonstrating to him the ideals of dignity, integrity, and humility. During the late 1950s, the family moved to Sacramento, California. West's grounding in Christian theology took place during this period of his life. According to *The Ethical Dimensions of Marxist Thought,* the Christian narratives, symbols, rituals, and concrete moral examples provided him with "existential and ethical equipment to confront the crises, terrors, and horrors of life." West came to understand an aspect of Christianity that moved him from passivity to activism.

Political Action

West's first important political action took place when he marched with his family in a civil rights demonstration in Sacramento in 1963. He was ten years old. This would later influence him when, as a high school student and class president, he and his best friend, Glenn Jordan, organized a strike of students demanding courses in black studies. The strike was city–wide and brought positive results.

Cornel West

In 1970, West entered Harvard University in Cambridge, Massachusetts. He understood clearly who he was and why he was there. Of his college experience, he recalled in his book:

> I became part of the first generation of young black people to attend prestigious lily–white institutions of higher learning in significant numbers. . . . Owing to my family, church, and the black social movements of the 1960s, I arrived at Harvard unashamed of my African, Christian, and militant decolonized outlooks.

At Harvard, West became involved in social activities which actually were social actions. He participated in a breakfast program for low–income children in the Jamaica Plains area of Boston and made weekly visits to the Norfolk State Prison. As a member of the Black Student Organization in 1972, he participated in the protest against Harvard's interest in the Gulf Oil Corporation. The demonstration resulted in the takeover of Massachusetts Hall, including president Derek Bok's office.

West studied government under Martin Kilson, one of the few black professors at Harvard during the early 1970s. According to Kilson, in the New York Times Magazine, West was "the most intellectually aggressive and highly cerebral student [he had] taught in . . . 30 years at Harvard." Kilson arrived at Harvard in 1959. West credits Harvard for broadening his world view.

West majored in philosophy and then changed to the Near Eastern languages and literature department, where he studied the Hebrew and Aramaic languages. Focusing on history and social thought, West doubled up on his courses in order to graduate a year early. He received his bachelor of arts degree magna cum laude in 1973.

Wanting to further his studies in philosophy, West applied to and was accepted by the philosophy department at Princeton University. In 1975, West earned a master of arts degree from Princeton and continued to study for his Ph.D., which he earned in 1980. After completing his course work for his doctorate, West became an assistant professor of philosophy and religion in 1977 at Union Theological Seminary in New York, where he remained until 1984, when he accepted a position at Yale University.

West believed that his move to Yale Divinity School gave him the opportunity to reflect on the crisis in American philosophy and social thought. While West valued and cultivated the life of the mind, he by no means became disconnected from the world of active demonstration and protest. In fact, when he arrived at Yale, the campus was embroiled in two issues: one, the movement for a union of clerical employees, and the other, objection to Yale's investments in South African companies.

Critical Thought and Focused Action

West was no arm–chair revolutionary (1960s term for intellectuals). He took to the streets with the mass of protesters, and when he was arrested and jailed, he said, as noted in his book, "My arrest and jail . . . served as a fine example for my wonderful son, Clifton, quickly approaching adolescence"—an example his son followed as a progressive student body president of his predominately black middle school in Atlanta. West was married twice, with each ending in divorce. Clifton is the son of his first marriage and lives in Atlanta.

In the spring of 1987, West was angered by the Yale administration which denied his request for a leave–of–absence and insisted that he teach a full load, two courses at Yale. West had made prior arrangements to teach three courses at the University of Paris in the spring of 1987, anticipating his leave from Yale. When his leave was denied, West commuted every five to seven days between New Haven and Paris from February to April. While teaching abroad, he was amazed at the lack of knowledge regarding American philosophy and African American intellectual thought in particular.

West returned to the United States with a fiancee, Elleni Gebre Amlak, an Ethiopian, and a new job. He left Yale and returned to Union. After only a year at Union, he again went to Princeton where he was professor of religion and director of the Afro–American Studies Program.

The Crisis of Leadership

In returning to Princeton West wanted to form a critical mass of black scholars, with Toni Morrison at the center, in order to address the problems plaguing Americans approaching the century's end. West's vision of the coming millennium is one of social chaos and self–destruction unless Americans seize the moment, and, as noted in his book, galvanize "demoralized progressives and liberals across racial, class, regional, age, and gender lines."

Writing and publishing since the 1970s, West had many important books in print when in 1993 Beacon Press published his first best seller, *Race Matters.* In this book, perhaps more accessible to the general reading public than his more philosophical works, West scrutinizes race and cultural diversity and pronounces the political body terminally ill. Healing, however, is within our capabilities. West's prescription for society's ills is love.

In 1994 Henry Louis Gates, the W. E. B. Du Bois Professor and director of Afro–American Studies at Harvard, recruited West to come to Harvard. West and his wife now reside in Massachusetts.

West is a member of the editorial collective for Boundary 2: An International Journal of Literature and Culture. He also writes a column for *Tikkun,* a Jewish journal.

West has written the following books: *Black Theology and Marxist Thought* (1979); *Prophesy Deliverance! An Afro–American Revolutionary Christianity* (1982); *Prophetic Fragments* (1988); *The American Evasion of Philosophy: A Genealogy of Pragmatism* (1989); *The Ethical Dimensions of Marxist Thought* (1991); *Beyond Eurocentrism and Multiculturalism* (1993); and *Race Matters* (1993). He is coeditor of *Theology in the Americas* (1982); *Post–Analytic Philosophy* (1985); and *Out There: Marginalization of Contemporary Cultures* (1990). West and bell hooks together have written *Breaking Bread: Insurgent Black Intellectual Life* (1991), and he and Henry Louis Gates have edited *The Future of the Race* (1996).

In 1982, West joined the Democratic Socialists of America. He has served on the national political committee for seven years and became its honorary chairperson. A popular scholar in great demand as a speaker, Cornel West is an important black intellectual known for his challenging and provocative views on social and political issues.

Current address: Department of Afro–American Studies, Harvard University, Cambridge, MA 02108.

REFERENCES

Boynton, Robert S. "Princeton's Public Intellectual. *New York Times Magazine* (15 September 1991): 6, 39.

Contemporary Black Biography. Vol. 5. Detroit: Gale Research, 1993.

Gates, Henry Louis. "Affirmative Action." *Emerge* 7 (March 1996): 24–29.

West, Cornel. *The Ethical Dimensions of Marxist Thought.* New York: Monthly Review Press, 1991.

Who's Who Among Black Americans, 1996–97. 9th ed. Detroit: Gale, 1996.

Nagueyalti Warren

Charles White
(1918–1979)
Painter

Artist Charles White was a painter and printmaker whose works reveal his concern with such issues as racism, social injustice, poverty, and the lives of ordinary black men and women. At a time in art history when the art world's focus was on the Abstract Expressionist movement, White remained true to his own artistic vision and continually challenged his own artistic development in order to express his message clearly.

Charles White Jr. was born on April 2, 1918, in Chicago. His parents, who never married, were Ethel Gray and Charles White Sr. Gray, a domestic worker from Mississippi, had moved North and met White's father in Chicago. White Sr., a Creek Indian, worked in construction. White's parents' union lasted only a few years after his birth; then they separated. Gray later married Clifton Marsh, a postal worker. Marsh was an excessive drinker, and ultimately Gray became the sole financial support of their household. For White, his stepfather was a disruptive presence. The marriage ended in divorce during White's early teens.

White has said in *17 Black Artists,* "From the time I was seven I never wanted to do anything but paint." This focus and determination early on served him well. Even though they were poor, Gray was determined that her son would have a better life than hers had been. She enrolled White in music and art classes and tried to expose him to different experiences. White excelled in art and received numerous awards.

High school was generally a frustrating period for White. During his high school years, while reading for pleasure, he read Alain Locke's *The New Negro* and was greatly influenced by the work. From Locke's book White learned of the many contributions black Americans have made to the development of American culture. He had learned none of this in the public school system and resented what he considered blatant omissions in his education. He began to speak out in classes questioning why teachers taught so little about black history. This reportedly annoyed his teachers, who knew nothing about the contributions of blacks to American history and culture. White soon found himself at odds with most of his teachers and began skipping most of his classes with the exception of art. The art instructors liked and encouraged him. They also recognized his artistic talent and continually entered his works in different competitions, many of which he won. He was offered scholarships at two schools, Chicago Academy of Fine Arts and Frederick Mizer Academy of Art. However, upon discovering that he was black, both institutions denied him admission.

White, however, was not deterred by this racism and continued to work. During this time he was greatly influenced by Mitchell Siporin and Edward Millman, who were socially active artists in Chicago. Their interest was in social realism, the focus of their work being on people in urban environments. They introduced him to the works of Mexican mural painters, allowed him to visit their studios, and would often critique his work. Such encouragement and mentoring continued and paid off when White won first prize in an art competition. White would have graduated from high school in 1936 but because of his truancy remained an extra year and graduated in 1937. For White, 1937 was a good year. In May he was accepted into the Art Institute of Chicago. White had to overcome serious financial obstacles while studying at the Art Institute and still completed his training a year ahead of schedule.

Paints Murals

After finishing his course of study at the Art Institute, White qualified for the Works Progress Administration as an artist. This period was very rewarding for him. During his WPA days he completed many murals with figures of such historical black Americans as Sojourner Truth, Frederick Douglass, George Washington Carver, and Booker T. Washington. The work was very stylized with strong geometric shapes. These murals provided powerful visual communication about historic African Americans who had been involved in leading their people and shaping the history of this country. Unfortunately, many of the WPA murals have been printed over or covered over. Even though most have been destroyed, fortunately a mural titled *Contribution of the Negro to American Democracy* is at Hampton University. White exchanged ideas with other gifted black artists: Eldzier Cortor, Archibald Motley, Charles David, Bernard and Margaret Goss, Gwendolyn Books, Elizabeth Catlett, Richard Wright, Willard Motley, Gordon Parks, and Katherine Dunham.

Marries Elizabeth Catlett

In 1941 White married Elizabeth Catlett, relocated to the South where Catlett was head of Dillard University's art department, and won a Rosenwald Foundation Fellowship. Life in the South was a new experience for White. Here he noticed that people, the pace of life, sounds, and smells were all different from those he had experienced in the North. He began to appreciate the uniqueness of Southern living, however, and as result of the new experiences later changed the way he portrayed black Americans.

By 1942 White and Catlett had moved to New York City and immersed themselves in the art scene. White studied at the Art Student League. His studies there, coupled with his experiences in the South, were the catalysts that initiated a change in the style of his work. During this period he exhibited extensively, moved freely in the close–knit black art scene, and became increasingly well known.

Life for White changed in 1943 when he was drafted into military service and assigned to an engineer regiment where he painted camouflage. A year later White became ill and was diagnosed with tuberculosis; he spent the next three years recuperating in Beacon, New York, at the Veterans Administration Hospital. His time there was unproductive as far as his painting was concerned, but he did spend many hours reading and rereading the classics as well as modern literature. By 1947 White was well and once again painting. He had a solo exhibition which was reviewed in the *World Telegram,* where he was referred to as:

> a mature, powerful, articulate talent. He paints Negroes, modeling their figure in blocky masses that might have been cut from granite. He works with tremendous intensity. His subjects are militant, fiery, strong, they are symbols rather than people—symbols of his race's unending battle for equality.

In the fall of 1947 White and Catlett moved to Mexico. There they studied at Esmeralda School of Painting and Taller de Grafica Popular Workshop. Of this experience White said in *A History of African American Artists*: "I saw artists working to create an art about and for the people. This has been the strongest influence in my whole approach. It clarified the direction in which I wanted to move."

White and Catlett divorced; soon afterward, White's recurring respiratory problems returned, and he had lung surgery in New York. He remained hospitalized for one year and after his release from the hospital was active again, showing at galleries and interacting with other artists in and around New York City.

In 1950 White married Frances Barrett, a social worker. They adopted two children, Jessica and Ian, in 1963 and 1965. The Whites traveled in Europe, where White's work had already a considerable following. In the countries they visited, White was received as a distinguished artist and invited to lecture and jury shows. The attention in Europe opened more doors for White back home in the United States. Still seeking some respite from White's health problems, the Whites moved to Altadena, California, in the mid–1950s. He died on October 3, 1979.

Today Charles White is recognized among artists as a master draftsman and skilled artist. His mature style mainly depicts a composition with one or several figures. His ability to communicate the complexities of the black persona through his compositions tends to challenge the viewer to interact with the images and inevitably evokes strong emotional responses.

REFERENCES

Bearden, Romare, and Harry Henderson. *A History of African–American Artists from 1792 to the Present.* New York: Pantheon, 1993.

Fax, Elton C. *17 Black Artists.* New York: Dodd, Mead, 1971.

McElroy, Guy C., Sharon F. Palton, and Richard J. Powell. *African–American Artists 1880–1987.* Washington, DC: Smithsonian Institution, 1989.

Powell, Richard. *Black Art and Culture in the 20th Century.* London: Thames and Hudson, 1997.

White, Frances Barrett, with Anne Slott. *Riches of the Heart.* New York: Barricade Books, 1994.

COLLECTIONS

Charles White's work is collected in a number of museums and galleries, including the Metropolitan Museum of Art, Whitney Museum, the Art Institute of Chicago, Howard University Gallery of Art, Atlanta University, Hampton University, and in private galleries and collections.

Alicia M. Henry

Clarence Cameron White
(1880–1960)
Composer, violinist

Clarence Cameron White

Clarence Cameron White was one of the country's outstanding composers and violinists of the first half of the twentieth century, with performances to his credit at the principal concert halls in the United States and Europe. His concert tours as a violinist received critical acclaim, and he was rated highly among concertizing artists of his period. As his musical career developed, a series of fortunate meetings with several of the most outstanding persons of African descent in the arts—Will Marion Cook, Harry T. Burleigh, Paul Laurence Dunbar, and the Afro–British composer Samuel Coleridge–Taylor among them—brought impetus and inspiration to his progress. As a composer, his works emphasized African American themes, flavored by the spiritual and folk heritage. An interest in Haitian history and folklore also was a source of inspiration, providing the basic material for the plot of his opera, *Ouanga.* As an educator, he exerted a positive influence, chairing several music departments and enjoying a fruitful career as a teacher.

White was born August 10, 1880, in Clarksville, Tennessee, the son of James W. and Jennie Scott White (Edwards and Mark give the date as August 10, 1879). His father was a doctor and the principal of Clarksville High School. White's father died when he was two, and he and his mother went to live with her parents in Oberlin, Ohio. During her youth, his mother had studied violin, and was an 1867 graduate of Oberlin Conservatory of Music. Therefore Oberlin was a congenial place for her. One White's most memorable early musical experiences was being taken by his mother to a performance of the *Messiah* at the Oberlin Conservatory.

White began his early education in Oberlin. Showing musical aptitude, he took violin lessons beginning when he was eight and was a boy soprano soloist in the church choir. Then his mother decided to resume her teaching vocation and obtained a job as a teacher in Chattanooga, Tennessee. She subsequently remarried, and White happily accepted her husband, William H. Conner, as a ''second father.'' In 1890 White's stepfather accepted a new position as a medical examiner in the Government Pension Office in Washington, D.C., and this became his family's new home.

Completing his primary and secondary school education in the Washington, D.C. schools, White continued his musical studies as well. He began to study violin at age 12 with Will Marion Cook, noted black composer and violinist, a pupil of the legendary German violin virtuoso, Joseph Joachim. White's first encounter with Cook must have been somewhat traumatic for White. Accompanying his mother to a concert in Washington, he was very interested in the fact that Cook was scheduled to perform. To White's chagrin, however, he slept, missed Cook's performance, and created a minor disturbance at the event. Cook took an interest in the youth, however, asked to meet him, and offered violin lessons. White profited greatly from his tutelage.

Trains with Luminaries

White's first performances as a violinist began at this time in area churches. He also began the study of music theory and completed his first composition, a piece for violin and piano. His accompanist was a talented young pianist, Beatrice Warrick. They were later to marry, in 1905. White also studied violin during this period with the accomplished teacher, Joseph Douglass (the son of Frederick Douglass), and played in his orchestra. His studies in 1894–95 included classes at Howard University.

White enrolled at Oberlin Conservatory of Music in 1896 and studied there until 1901. He participated in a full and rigorous program, including playing in the student orchestra as a first violinist. At the time, he was the only black student in the orchestra. He received a boost in his musical career when a family friend obtained an invitation for him to play for President William McKinley at the White House.

After leaving Oberlin to pursue his career, he studied and played for two years in Boston, New Haven, and New York, and met and received the warm support of Paul Laurence Dunbar and Harry T. Burleigh. At a 1902 concert in New York City he was fortunate to meet Booker T. Washington, who invited him to perform at Tuskegee Institute in Alabama. The support and encouragement of these exemplary individuals was very meaningful to White at this juncture in his life. He also heard about a scholarship award available at the Hartford School of Music, competed in 1902, won the award, and studied violin at the school for a year.

In 1903 White took a position as violin teacher, registrar, and vice president of the Washington Conservatory of Music, directed by his fellow Oberlin graduate, Harriet Gibbs. He remained there until 1907. In 1905 he and Beatrice Warrick were married. White also taught in the Washington, D.C., public schools and continued to concertize regularly. During 1904 White had a memorable meeting with the noted Afro–English composer Samuel Coleridge–Taylor. He had corresponded with the composer and received some of his compositions while a student at Oberlin. During Coleridge–Taylor's visit to the United States in 1904, White was able to accompany the composer on tour, and played Coleridge–Taylor's "African Dances" for violin and piano.

White's experiences during Coleridge–Taylor's tour led White to visit London and study composition with him in the summer of 1906. A return to London from 1908 to 1910 was made possible by an E. Azalia Hackley scholarship. During this period he continued his study of composition with Coleridge–Taylor, studied violin with Michael Zacharewitsch, participated in concerts as a violinist in the renowned Croydon String Players Club, and concertized often with Coleridge–Taylor.

White returned to the United States for a concert tour during 1910–11, including a visit to Chicago and to the Washington Conservatory for its June commencements in both 1910 and 1911. Upon Coleridge–Taylor's death on September 2, 1912, White published a eulogy in the *New York Age* for September 26, 1912, in which he gave a warm tribute to the composer's outgoing personality, generosity, personal inspiration, and kindness towards youth.

The White family moved to Boston in 1912. White was active in the Boston public schools from 1912 to 1923, and conducted the Boston Victoria Concert Orchestra from 1914 to 1924. He also concertized frequently during this period, returning to Oberlin in 1911 and in following summers to prepare for his concert tours. He also was active as a composer; his *Bandana Sketches* for violin and piano were published by Carl Fischer in 1918, followed by *Cabin Memories,* and *From the Cotton Fields,* 1920–21.

Organizes Black Music Association

White was one of the original organizers of the National Association of Negro Musicians, together with R. Nathaniel Dett and Nora Holt. He circulated letters proposing the organization in 1916, and joined in preparing for the organization's first national convention in 1919. He later served as the association's president (1922–24) and a member of the board of directors. He also joined the American Society of Composers, Authors and Publishers (ASCAP) in 1924.

White next served as director of the Music Department at West Virginia State College from 1924 to 1930. His concert activities continued, including directing and recording with the Men's Glee Club. At West Virginia State he met John Matheus, professor of Romance languages, and they developed a joint interest in Haitian folklore and history. Supported by the Harmon Foundation, they traveled to Haiti during the summer of 1928 to gather material. Their collaborative efforts resulted in a two–act play, *Tambour* (written by Matheus with incidental music, including a ballet number, "Meringue," by White) and the opera, *Ouanga* (libretto by Matheus and music by White). The plot of the opera is based historical events in the life of the Haitian emperor Dessalines, a Christian, and his struggles against voodoo religious practices then prevalent in Haiti, the capture of his beloved, Defilee, and his assassination.

A Rosenwald Fellowship in 1930 for study abroad enabled completion of the opera in Paris, where White studied composition and orchestration during 1931 and 1932 with Raoul LaParra. During White's stay in Paris, a string quartet composed by him—based on Negro themes, with the movements entitled "Prelude," "Dawn," "Jubilee," and "Hallelujah"—was played by faculty members at the Ecole Normale de Paris. The performance likely marked the first public performance in Paris of a classical work by a black composer since the days of the Chevalier de Saint–Georges in the eighteenth century.

Heads Hampton Institute

In June of 1932, while still in Paris, White was announced as the new director of music and conductor of the Hampton Singers at Hampton Institute in Virginia, succeeding R. Nathaniel Dett. When White returned to the United States in November of 1932, a concert performance of excerpts from his just–completed opera *Ouanga* was given under the auspices of the American Opera Society of Chicago. White received the David Bispham Medal for music immediately following the performance, becoming the thirty–fifth recipient and first black American awardee.

Performances of *Ouanga* began to take place following its initial reading in Chicago. In 1938 the Illinois Symphony performed the overture of the opera. The first staged production of *Ouanga* was sponsored by the Burleigh Musical Association in South Bend, Indiana, and held on June 10–11, 1949. It was warmly received. Next, the Dra–Mu Negro Opera Company of Philadelphia performed the work fully staged with costumes and ballet on October 27, 1950. Two New York concert performances of the opera, with ballet, followed in 1956. The performances were given by the National Negro Opera Company on May 27, 1956, at the Metropolitan Opera House, and at Carnegie Hall on September 29, 1956. The cast included McHenry Boatright, Juanita King, and Carol Brice, with a young Judith Jamison in the ballet corps. The conductor was Henri Elkan. Reviews, particularly of the Philadelphia performance, were uniformly good, with praise of the staging, singing, and music.

White's work at Hampton continued during 1932–35. His frequent concerts with the Hampton Singers were well received, and featured radio broadcasts, including a series of four broadcasts in 1935 on the NBC Red Network and a performance at the White House for President Franklin D. Roosevelt. White resigned as director of music at Hampton Institute following a board–of–trustees mandated reorganization of the music program, and the family moved to Elizabeth, New Jersey.

In 1937 White was named a music specialist for the National Recreation Association, established by President Roosevelt under the aegis of the Works Progress Administration. The association's responsibility was to offer aid in organizing community arts programs. An important accomplishment for White was holding a regional conference in West Chester, Pennsylvania, for local organizers seeking to establish music programs in their communities. A culminating event of the 1937 conference was the founding of a community chorus to sing a series of public concerts. Later, in 1946, White was invited to conduct a chorus at the June Music Festival in Cincinnati. Members included those who had participated in the chorus organized by White in 1937. White's work with the National Recreation Association involved frequent travel during the period of 1937–41, visiting and working with community groups.

White's life's work in music continued during his later years. His wife and close companion of 36 years died at their home in Elizabeth, New Jersey, in October of 1942. Beatrice had accompanied him on many of his travels, and they appeared frequently over the years as piano and violin recitalists. They had two sons who predeceased their mother. White soon moved to New York and in 1943 remarried to Pura Belpre, a writer and librarian in the New York Public Library. White remained active in concerts, composing and arranging music from his home and studio in New York until his death of cancer on June 30, 1960, at Sydenham Hospital.

During his lifetime, White received several prestigious awards. He was presented an honorary Master of Arts degree from Atlanta University in 1928 and an honorary doctorate of music from Wilberforce University in 1933. In addition to the Rosenwald Foundation and David Bispham awards previously mentioned, he received the Harmon Foundation prize for music in 1927. His *Elegy* for orchestra received the Benjamin Award for tranquil music in 1954, garnering a $1,000 prize and a premiere performance by the New Orleans Philharmonic Symphony Orchestra, conducted by Alexander Hilsberg. With more than 100 compositions to his credit, his works have been played by renowned violinists Jascha Heifetz, Albert Spaulding, and Fritz Kreisler, by symphony orchestras in Boston, Washington, D.C., and New Haven, and by the Goldman Band and U.S. Marine Corps Band. His compositions and arrangements include *Forty Spirituals,* many of which remain in the concert repertoire, as well as *Bandana Sketches* and *Cabin Memories* for violin, *Legende d'Afrique* for violoncello, and a *Concerto* in G minor for violin.

White will long be remembered for a career in which he greatly enhanced the role of the African American musician and composer. Reaching forward from an interest in themes expressive of his heritage, he contributed a broad variety of music to his audiences. He was also a role model for continuing to expand the possibilities for the African American on the concert stage, particularly through the scope of the music presented—from solo songs to instrumental performance to grand opera.

REFERENCES

Abdul, Raoul. *Blacks in Classical Music.* New York: Dodd, Mead, 1977.

"Clarence Cameron White." Obituary. *New York Times,* July 2, 1960.

Cuney–Hare, Maud. *Negro Musicians and Their Music.* New York: DaCapo Press, 1974.

Edwards, Vernon, and Michael Mark. "In Retrospect: Clarence Cameron White." *Black Perspective in Music* 9 (Spring 1981): 51–72.

Hitchcock, H. Wiley, ed. *New Grove Dictionary of American Music.* New York: Macmillan, 1986.

Logan, Rayford W., and Winston, Michael R., eds. *Dictionary of American Negro Biography.* New York: Norton, 1982.

"Opera: Ouanga, Voodoo in Haiti." Review. *New York Times,* May 28, 1956.

Robinson, Wilhelmena. *Historical Negro Biographies.* New York: Publishers Co., 1968.

Shirley, Wayne D. "In Retrospect: Letters of Clarence Cameron White." *Black Perspective in Music* 10 (Fall 1982): 189–212.

Southern, Eileen. *Biographical Dictionary of Afro–American and African Musicians.* Westport, CT: Greenwood Press, 1982.

———. *The Music of Black Americans.* 3rd ed. New York: Norton, 1997.

Who's Who in America, 1952–1953. Chicago: Marquis, 1952.

Who's Who in Colored America. Vol. 1. New York: Who's Who in Colored America Corp., 1927

Who's Who in Colored America. 7th ed. Yonkers, NY: Christian E. Burckel, 1950.

COLLECTIONS

An extensive collection of White's letters, papers, and music manuscripts is housed at the Schomburg Center for Research in Black Culture, New York Public Library. A collection of the composer's letters is at the Library of Congress, Music Division, Washington, D.C., as are copies of most of the composer's published compositions. An additional repository the composer's materials is the Moorland–Spingarn Research Center at Howard University, Washington, D.C.

Darius L. Thieme

Walter White

(1893–1955)

Civil rights worker, organization executive, writer

When Walter White became leader of the National Association for the Advancement of Colored People (NAACP), the organization's priorities had been set. His contribution was to move those priorities forward. During his lifetime and in large part due to his efforts, lynching ceased to be a common event. His courage, energy, and hard work did much to bring the problem of race relations in the United States to the center of the political stage. It was at White's urging that President Harry Truman set up a Civil Rights Committee whose report, "To Secure These Rights," was reflected in civil rights planks in the 1948 platform of the Democratic National Convention and set a political agenda for liberals. When the Supreme Court dismantled school segregation in *Brown v. Board of Education* shortly before White's death, he could look with pride at a long legal campaign led by the NAACP.

Walter Francis White was born on July 1, 1893, in Atlanta, Georgia, to George White and Madeline Harrison White. Walter White, the fourth child, had an older brother, George Jr., the oldest child, and five sisters, Alice (Glenn), Olive (Westmoreland), Ruby, Helen, and Madeline, the youngest child. George White Sr. came from Augusta, Georgia, and attended Atlanta University's high school.

Walter White began his autobiography, *A Man Called White,* with the statement: "I am a Negro. My skin is white, my eyes are blue, my hair is blond. The traits of my race are nowhere visible upon me." All members of the White family were light–skinned. Walter White's maternal grandfather was a Dr. E. Harrison, white. Caroline Bond Day gives White's mother's heritage as one–sixteenth black, one–sixteenth Indian, and seven–eighths white, and Day estimates that his father was one–fourth black and three–quarters white. When George White Sr. was struck down by an automobile in 1931, he was taken unconscious to the white side of the hospital—only when a brown–skinned son–in–law made inquiries about him was George White taken to the much inferior black side, where he died 17 days later.

In addition to skin color, the family's education, home ownership, and aspirations set it apart from the black masses.

Walter White

Its religious affiliation was also not widely shared—they were members of the First Congregational Church, which was just a half block away from the family home. The pastor of the church during White's youth and young manhood was famed black minister Henry Hugh Proctor (1868–1933), a Fisk classmate of W. E. B. Du Bois and holder of a B.D. degree from Yale University. After the Atlanta riots, Proctor led his church into extensive social work, constructing the first gymnasium open to the community as well as the first church–sponsored home for black girls, the Avery Home for Working Girls.

George White Sr. saw to the family's religious training in a nearly Puritan tradition, with long family prayer sessions on Sunday. White's childhood was generally happy. As he grew older, he sought a job as a bell–hop in a leading downtown hotel. In his first hotel job he inadvertently passed as white.

In his autobiography Walter White ascribed his firm identification as an African American to his experiences in the September 1906 Atlanta race riot. White and his father witnessed episodes of violence on Saturday, September 7, the first day of the riots, as they made his father's rounds to collect the mail. The following evening, the neighborhood prepared for the visitation of the mob. Walter White heard the son of their grocer yell, "That's where that nigger mail carrier lives! Let's burn it down! It's too nice for a nigger to live in!" Very quietly, George White said then, "Son, don't shoot until the first man puts his foot on the lawn and then—don't you miss." Fortunately, shots rang out from a house further down the street and the mob turned aside.

White attended high school at Atlanta University—there were no public high schools for blacks. He then attended the college, receiving his degree in 1916. We know little of his experiences at university other than that he was a member of the debating society, played football—"not too good football," he says in his autobiography, possibly since he was only five–feet seven–inches tall—and was president of his graduating class. In the summer of 1915, he gave up hotel work to sell insurance for the Standard Life Insurance Company, headed by Harry Pace, who later set up a music publishing company and then founded Black Swan records. Since Atlanta had been pretty thoroughly canvassed by this time, White devoted much of his effort to selling in rural areas. This gave him valuable first–hand experience of the conditions of rural blacks. During the following school year, White worked part–time for the insurance company and then accepted a job as a clerk upon graduation.

In 1916, the Atlanta school board decided to cut out the seventh grade in black schools to save money to be used for white schools just as it had previously cut out the eighth in 1914. White grasped eagerly at the suggestion that blacks form a local branch of the NAACP to spearhead a protest; when the branch was formed, Pace was president and White, secretary. Their protests to the school board set in motion a series of actions that eventually led to the establishment of Atlanta's first high school for blacks in 1920.

James Weldon Johnson was invited to address the first public mass meeting of the NAACP. White was called upon to deliver an unplanned speech and gave a fiery address. A friend said much later, as reported by Kahn, "When human rights are involved . . . Walter is never at a loss for a word. Or even several paragraphs." Johnson had dinner with the Whites before he left Atlanta and closely questioned Walter. Johnson later wrote Walter White to offer him a job as assistant secretary in the NAACP's New York office. White hesitated. The organization was in a shaky condition, and he would take a reduction in income. Physician Louis T. Wright (a future chair of the NAACP board and White's personal physician in New York in later years) and White's father urged him to accept the offer. In his autobiography, White quoted his father as saying:

> Your mother and I have given you . . . the best education we could afford, and a good Christian home training. . . . Now it is your duty to pass on what you have been given by helping others less fortunate to get a chance in life. I don't want to see you go away. I'll miss you. But remember always, God will be using your heart and brains to do His will.

Joins National NAACP Office Staff

White took up his duties in New York on January 31, 1918. Originally, he was to perform clerical and office duties, but on February 12, he and James Weldon Johnson read of a terrible lynching in Estill Springs, Tennessee. White volunteered to go to the scene and, passing as white, make an investigation. This investigation in Tennessee was the first of many occasions that he risked his life. In the summer of 1919, as White investigated a disturbance in which as many as 200 blacks may have been killed, he was identified and barely escaped lynching in Phillips County, Alabama. After some years, White's fame became too great for him to continue his undercover investigations. The dangers he ran as a result of his efforts to combat racism were principally but not solely from whites. White had some close calls also when blacks identified him as white in tense racial situations. He narrowly escaped a bullet in the aftermath of the 1919 Chicago riots.

White undertook a very active pattern of work for the NAACP. In the ten years following 1918, he made personal inquiries into 41 lynchings and eight race riots. In Tulsa he was even drafted as a temporary deputy sheriff on the basis of his appearance. White worked assiduously in publicizing his findings. Under the tutelage of James Weldon Johnson, he developed great skills as a lobbyist. There was always much travel and many speaking engagements. For example, in 1919 Waldron says White covered 26,000 miles and spoke 86 times; Waldron added that this pace picked up in subsequent years: in February of 1927, White spoke 17 times and had several conferences in a 12–day span.

In addition to his work for the NAACP, White's horizons also expanded as he developed wider intellectual interests. Here again his mentor was James Weldon Johnson, who became a close friend. On February 15, 1922, White married Leah Gladys Powell, a fellow member of the NAACP staff; the marriage produced two children, Jane (b. 1923) and Walter Carl Darrow (b. 1927).

In 1922, White made negative comments about a novel on blacks by a white author in a review for *Smart Set.* The magazine's editor, H. L. Mencken, challenged him to do better. Mary White Ovington lent her Massachusetts cottage to the Whites during the summer of 1922, and during 12 days of intense work, White produced the draft of *The Fire in the Flint.* The novel was about the return of a Southern–born doctor to his hometown where he is eventually forced to confront racism head on. Within the novel, the doctor is burned at the stake because of a false claim that he had raped a white woman, his sister is raped, and his brother murdered by whites. The sensational nature of the material led to the novel's garnering extensive reviews and good sales for a first novel when it was published in 1924 by Knopf. White's second novel, *Flight,* published in 1927, attracted less attention. This novel ended with the heroine's decision to rejoin the black community after passing as white. White thought his third novel would be a three–generation work based on his own family. In June 1927, using the money from a Guggenheim Fellowship Grant, White took his family to France for a year to work on the book. Away from the United States, White's attention was drawn to the racial situation in his native country and he devoted much of his time to an analysis of the causes of lynching. The book which resulted, *Rope and Faggot,* was published in 1929. White eventually wrote about 45,000 words of the family novel, some two–thirds of the whole.

Becomes "New Negro"

Alain Locke chose White as one of the contributors to *The New Negro* (1925), one of the Harlem Renaissance's defining works. White's role in the Renaissance went far beyond writing. In his prominent position he was active as a link between people and as a promoter of works. Black writers and white sympathizers met at parties. Carl Van Vechten contacted White after reading *The Fire in the Flint.* He and White became friends, and White introduced him to other Harlem writers and artists. Other aspects of White's efforts on the behalf of artists and writers are amply represented in the NAACP files. For example, the poet Claude McKay used White as one of his main contacts in Harlem over the years, and White assiduously promoted his favorite black poet, Countee Cullen. In music, White's activities succeeded in attracting a larger audience to one of Paul Robeson's early recitals, helping to launch his career.

White's absence in 1927–28 during the time he held the Guggenheim indirectly led to his advancement at the NAACP. James Weldon Johnson began to overwork himself. In the spring of 1929, Johnson took a leave of absence from the NAACP. During Johnson's absence, White was very effective as one of the three acting secretaries. White helped the NAACP to win an important victory in 1930—the defeat of Herbert Hoover's nomination of John J. Parker of North Carolina to a seat on the U.S. Supreme Court. As White explained in his autobiography, Parker had declared in 1920, "The participation of the Negro in politics is a source of evil and danger to both races and is not desired by the wise men in either race or by the Republican Party of North Carolina."

Parker's nomination was defeated by one vote in the Senate. The unprecedented protest campaign organized by the NAACP, especially by black voters in Northern and border states, was credited for the defeat. The political power of the NAACP was enhanced by the role of blacks in the defeat of several Parker supporters in subsequent elections.

A frail Johnson resigned on December 17, 1930, and White became executive secretary in his place, a position he held until his death. By now the NAACP had institutionalized the goals which were central to White's activities for the rest of his life. It investigated and publicized lynchings, it attacked racial injustice in the courts, and it lobbied against segregation in the legislatures.

The NAACP was now faced with the problems of severely declining revenues. It was heavily dependent on memberships for funding, and the Depression following the stock market crash of October 1929 cut sharply black earning power and also philanthropic contributions. By 1934 the organization was on the verge of financial collapse.

Becomes Executive Secretary of the NAACP

White was named executive secretary of the NAACP at the same board meeting that made Joel E. Spingarn president. The relation between the two men shaped the administrative history of the organization between 1930 and 1935. White had consulted Spingarn, who was then an editor at Harcourt and Brace, about his first novel in 1922. Spingarn continued to offer advice and encouragement to White over the years, but they did not address each other on a first name basis until 1932. Spingarn took the lead in formulating the NAACP's financial policies, especially from 1930 to 1933. Although White appears to have been a meticulous record keeper, Spingarn took up a large role in financial affairs and retrenchment. The financial measures brought about a rift between White and the other salaried executives; all attacked White in a signed memorandum presented to the board in December 1931, charging him with presenting false information to the board. The financial crisis had reached such a point in mid–1933 that Roy Wilkins, then assistant secretary, was placed on half salary and Robert W. Bagnall, director of branches since 1919, was fired and his position abolished.

The financial crisis had a major effect on the relations between White and W. E. B. Du Bois, the editor of *Crisis,* which were not good to begin with. In 1929, the magazine began to lose money. Du Bois struggled to retain his editorial autonomy as the board formed a committee to supervise the magazine. Significantly, all signers of the December 1931 memorandum to the board attacking White withdrew their signatures except Du Bois. It is not clear what the reasons were for the intense dislike the two men took to each other beginning sometime in the 1920s. Du Bois and White, however, were both proud men with a considerable measure of vanity. Since Spingarn wished to retain Du Bois as editor of the *Crisis,* these struggles were patched up in 1933.

Du Bois then stepped up his ultimately futile efforts to change the goals of the NAACP. In January 1934 he endorsed voluntary self–segregation in an editorial in *Crisis.* In February, Du Bois refused to publish White's heated reply affirming absolute opposition to segregation in any form, even though White had incorporated some softening changes suggested by Spingarn. On April 9 the board rejected separate statements on segregation proposed by Du Bois (two members supported him) and by Spingarn. The board then adopted a position condemning segregation without resolving the question of whether black churches and schools were to be considered forms of forced segregation. For this and other reasons, Du Bois severed all connection with the NAACP by July and White took over management of *Crisis,* appointing Roy Wilkins, now assistant secretary, editor.

Another attempt to change the goals of the NAACP by a group of young intellectuals also came to nought. One of the leaders, Abram Harris of Howard University, was elected to the board in 1934. Harris led a board committee to draft a plan for a reorganization intended, among other things, to change the way the board operated and to address the economic problems of working–class blacks. Harris and his supporters won only a partial victory on board changes, and the economic plan entailed costs the organization could not support. Harris was chagrined to learn that the proposed economic plan was almost the same as the program of the Urban League.

One result of the internal struggles was the resignation of Joel E. Spingarn as chairman of the board in 1935—he remained president of the association until his death in 1939, when his brother followed him in the now largely ceremonial position. His replacement was Louis T. Wright, a distinguished black surgeon and White's personal physician. (Wright once saved White's life by carrying him seven blocks to the hospital and operating on him for appendicitis.) This change shifted power into White's hand; for approximately the next 15 years, he was essentially in sole control of the NAACP. In 1937 he received the organization's Spingarn Medal.

Continues the Battle

One of White's major achievements dates from 1935. He was instrumental in securing a foundation grant which enabled the NAACP to hire Charles Hamilton Houston, a noted black lawyer. Although the legal department retained a degree of independence from White's control, Houston led a brilliant team, including such persons as William H. Hastie and Thurgood Marshall, which undertook a legal campaign to dismantle legal segregation culminating in *Brown v. Board of Education* in 1954, shortly before White's death.

White's life involved much hard work, with great attention to detail, travel, and writing. In later years he seems to have been the almost indispensable black representative on advisory committees, being involved in such matters as the formation of the United Nations in 1945 and serving as a delegate to the General Assembly of the United Nations in Paris in 1948. He wrote articles for major magazines like *Saturday Evening Post* and *Reader's Digest.* He wrote a regular column for the *Chicago Defender* and a syndicated column for the *New York Herald–Tribune.* When he was called on to investigate the condition of black troops during World War II in 1943 to 1945, he became a war correspondent for the *New York Post* and produced another book, *A Rising Wind.* His final book, *How Far the Promised Land,* was published in 1955 after his death.

In the late 1940s about five percent of blacks 18 or older were members of the NAACP, a formidable pressure group. This gave White considerable leverage as a lobbyist; all politicians may not have loved him but he was feared where he was not liked. A gregarious man, he was on a first name basis with many members of Congress and with at least five of the nine Supreme Court justices. As a lobbyist he was forthright in expressing his opinion and notorious for his refusal to compromise his principles. This is proven by his refusal to accept a compromise offered by President Roosevelt on an anti–lynching bill, as well as by his vigorous opposition to the establishment of a segregated flight training program at Tuskegee during World War II, just as he had opposed segregated training camps for black officers in World War I. Roy Wilkins sums up his impression of White's temperament by saying, "he was brash, outgoing, effusive, a great salesman, propagandist, and maker of friends."

White published his autobiography, *A Man Called White,* in 1948. A very interesting and well–written work, it reflects the institutional and representational side of Walter White and concentrates on race relations in the first half of the twentieth century.

In an acrimonious meeting on his return to the NAACP in 1950, the board retained White as executive secretary but gave Roy Wilkins the responsibility for day–to–day operations and made Wilkins report directly to the board. With lessened power, White continued to formulate broad policy and serve as spokesperson for the NAACP.

White died of a heart attack on March 21, 1955. After a large funeral at St. Martin's Episcopal Church in Harlem, his remains were cremated at Ferncliff Cemetery, Hartsdale, New York. He was survived by his widow and two children.

For at least a quarter of a century, Walter White and the NAACP claimed the attention of white Americans as the voice of black Americans. White must receive great credit for making black concerns visible to the majority community and helping to build a liberal consensus on race relations. In addition to leading the NAACP to important legal victories, White initiated great changes in public attitudes, opening the way to the further gains of the civil rights era.

REFERENCES

Black Writers. Detroit: Gale Research, 1989.

Cannon, Poppy. *A Gentle Knight.* New York: Rinehart, 1956.

Day, Caroline Bond. *Negro–White Families in the United States.* Cambridge, MA: Peabody Museum of Harvard University, 1932.

Kahn, E. J., Jr. "The Frontal Attack." *New Yorker* 24 (September 4, 1948): 28–38; (September 11, 1948): 38–54.

Kellner, Bruce, ed. *The Harlem Renaissance.* New York: Methuen, 1984.

Lewis, David Levering. *When Harlem Was in Vogue.* New York: Knopf, 1981.

Logan, Rayford W., and Michael R. Winston, eds. *Dictionary of American Negro Biography.* New York: Norton, 1982.

Ovington, Mary White. *The Walls Came Tumbling Down.* New York: Harcourt, Brace and World, 1947.

"Poppy Cannon White, 69, Dead." *New York Times,* April 2, 1975.

Ross, B. Joyce. *J. E. Spingarn and the Rise of the NAACP, 1911–1939.* New York: Atheneum, 1972.

Waldron, Edward. *Walter White and the Harlem Renaissance.* Port Washington, NY: Kennikat Press, 1978.

White, Walter. *A Man Called White.* New York: Viking, 1948.

Wilkins, Roy, with Tom Mathews. *Standing Fast.* New York: Viking, 1982.

COLLECTIONS

Walter White's papers are in Sterling Memorial Library of Yale University. Much material is also in the NAACP papers in the Library of Congress, including copies of much of the correspondence.

Robert L. Johns

Albery Whitman
(1851–1901)
Poet, minister

Albery Whitman is regarded by many as the most talented black poet of the nineteenth century. While much of his verse shows the influence of other poets, he was technically skilled and rose to passages of great power in spite of his tendency to diffuseness. He also attempted long narrative poems, which are more characteristic of his work than short lyrics. Despite the assiduous labors of his grandniece Ernestine G. Lucas in her family history *Wider Windows to the Past,* much of Whitman's life remains in the shadow. Fire destroyed the courthouse in the county of his birth and also his home in Atlanta, making it difficult to trace the life in detail.

Albery Alson Whitman was born on May 30, 1851, in Hart County, Kentucky, the second child of Caswell and Caroline Bronner (sometimes Brawner) Whitman. Family historian Lucas prefers the spelling Alberry, but when the first name appears in full in the signature under the frontispiece and on the title page of his books, it is written Albery. There were four other children: Richard Gillem (1848–92); David Whitfield (c. 1855–c. 1890); Julia Catherine (1858–1952); and Robert Taylor (1862–1945). Caswell Whitman was a slave born in Missouri, but the status of Caroline Bronner is in doubt. Lucas believes that she was a slave but writes that Caroline was raised in Lexington, Kentucky, by a free family to whom she had been entrusted by her mother. The mother is said to have feared the loss of her free papers. If Caroline's mother was indeed free, Caroline and her children were not slaves. Of course if Caroline could not prove free birth, she may well have been a *de facto* slave. Albery Whitman himself stated that he was born a slave.

Caswell and Caroline Whitman were both very light complexioned. Lucas reported a contemporary description of their second son by James Corrothers in *In Spite of the Handicap,* which said, "Whitman was a tall, fine–looking man, and could easily have passed for white." The older Whitmans were dead by the mid–1860s, but they left a heritage of religion and striving to their children. Three Whitman brothers became African Methodist Episcopal ministers—Richard, Albery, and Robert, although Robert never became the pastor or a congregation. Richard Whitman attended Wilberforce as did Albery, who only managed to spend about six months there. This was long enough for Albery to become thoroughly impressed with Daniel Alexander Payne, the AME bishop and president of the school, who became a role model. The only other notice of schooling for Albery Whitman is some seven months in a school in Troy, Ohio, while he was working on the railroad there. His educational attainments were greater than the actual 18 months we know that he attended school would suggest at first glance. Family tradition claims that he could read when he was three, and his first publication of poetry was about 1871 (the publication is no longer extant).

Albery Whitman

Whitman married Kate "Caddie" White (1861–1908). She was a very light–skinned woman, who was probably the daughter of an AME minister and born in Bowling Green, Kentucky. They had four children: Caswell (1876–1936), Mabel (1879–1942), Essie Barbara (1882–1963), and Alberta (1887–1964). The daughters were famous entertainers as the Whitman Sisters. In *Wider Windows to the Past* Lucas clears up one area of confusion: Alice Hart Whitman, who also starred as a Whitman sister, was adopted. Alice died in 1969 but was some years older than the age of 61 given in the death notices.

The census of 1870 places Whitman in Troy. He worked on the railroad while attending school. The time in Troy was followed by a year of teaching in Carysville, Ohio, and then another year of teaching in Hart County, Kentucky. He spent six months teaching at Wilberforce in the early 1870s. At some point he became an AME minister; his first assignment seems to be the South Street AME Church in Zanesville, Ohio, where he successfully oversaw the completion of a new brick church in 1876. The following year he went to Springfield, Ohio, where he spent some 18 months and was again active in building a new church.

While he was in Springfield, Whitman published his third volume, *Not A Man and Yet a Man* (1877). In the preface to the work Whitman identified himself as the general financial agent of Wilberforce University and stated that he published the work in furtherance of the aim of the school "to inspire and increase in the pupil self–respect, self–control and self–development." In addition he indicated that a portion of the sales proceeds from the book would go to the school. There was some talk of sponsorship of a trip abroad by a wealthy Springfield resident, John H. Hinton. Whitman may have still been an Ohio resident in 1879, when he delivered a lecture on ''Men of Our Times'' in Bellefontaine. An admission charge of 35 cents suggests his drawing power as a speaker.

The 1880 census lists Whitman as living in Danville, Kentucky, with his wife, two children, and his sister Julia. He was identified as a minister and his wife as a seamstress. Whitman was active in the 1880 AME conference in Richmond, Kentucky, where he preached the missionary sermon.

Moves West

In the early 1880s Whitman apparently moved to Osceola, Arkansas, where one of his daughters was born; a little later he and his siblings are found in Kansas. William J. Simmons, in *Men of Mark* reports that in 1887 Whitman was living in Kansas and was in poor health. Whitman later pastored churches in Wichita and North Lawrence; The Lawrence, Kansas, *City Directory* of 1890–91 lists Whitman as minister of Saint James Church; he owned a home there that was in possession of his widow until 1906. Some time later he was in Grayson, Texas, when he supplied an affidavit concerning property in Kansas. Traces of his movements disappear for the next few years, but during his final years he was in Georgia. Whitman was in Savannah, where he led St. Phillips, before moving to Atlanta, where he pastored Allen Temple. Whitman was on a speaking engagement in Anniston, Alabama, when he contracted pneumonia, dying within the week, on June 29, 1901. He was buried in Southview Cemetery, Atlanta.

Whitman the poet published extensively. No copies of *Essay on the Ten Plagues and Miscellaneous Poems* (c. 1871) survive. The following volumes were: *Not a Man and Yet a Man, with Miscellaneous Poems* (1877), *The Rape of Florida* (1884), which was revised as *Twasinta's Seminoles* (1885); a republication of *Twasinta's Seminoles* in 1890 with *Not a Man and Yet a Man* and a collection of shorter poems; *The World's Fair Poem* (1893); and *An Idyl of the South* (1901). Many critics rate him as the most important black poet between Phillis Wheatley and Paul Laurence Dunbar, although that assessment could be challenged by supporters of Frances Ellen Watkins, whose contemporary fame was certainly greater.

Technically proficient, Whitman typically wrote long narrative poems. *Not a Man and Yet a Man* has about 5,000 lines. *The Rape of Florida* is in Spenserian stanzas, which Whitman was the first black poet to use. Blyden Jackson summarized his estimation of the poet in *Afro–American Writers before the Harlem Renaissance* by saying, ''His verse was often too long, too digressive, and shallowly facile. Yet his poetry should be read for the many lines that display his original genius.''

Whitman was a notable public speaker, famed for his sermons and lectures. Sources say that his career in the church was hindered by alcoholism. Lucas, his grandniece, denies that he was an alcoholic, and it is possible that he may have simply been stigmatized as a result of a refusal to endorse total abstinence. Still his temperament and situation as described by Reverdy C. Ransom, who knew him, are compatible with a seeking for solace in alcohol:

> Whitman had a lively imagination and emotional temperament; and a musical voice. He knew how to draw upon his endowment as occasion required. When he brought this to bear upon the audience of our people, a bedlam of emotional enthusiasm always ensued. The man, I think, was lonely. There were few among us with whom he could have communion of mind and spirit. His work in the ministry was largely concerned with drudging tasks for which he had little interest, and no enthusiasm. . . . One of our greatest American tragedies is the fact that the buried talents of black men and women are not permitted to emerge because of race and color prejudice.

REFERENCES

Harris, Trudier, ed. *Afro–American Writers before the Harlem Renaissance.* Detroit: Gale Research, 1986.

Lucas, Ernestine G. *Wider Windows to the Past.* Decorah, IA: Anundsen Publishing, 1995.

Ransom, Reverdy C. *The Pilgrimage of Harriet Ransom's Son.* Nashville: Sunday School Union, n.d.

Simmons, William J. *Men of Mark.* Cleveland: Geo. M. Rewell, 1887.

Whitman, A[lbery] A. *Not a Man and Yet a Man.* Springfield, OH: Republic Printing, 1877.

Robert L. Johns

John Edgar Wideman
(1941–)
Novelist, short fiction writer, essayist, critic, teacher

When John Edgar Wideman appeared on the literary scene, many critics hailed him for his craftsmanship–his experimentation with the novelistic form and the allusive quality of his writing aligned him with so–called mainstream writers past and present. Coming at a time when much attention was paid to writers of the Black Arts Movement writers who eschewed art for art's sake, who espoused the political purpose of art in which the message was of primary importance and therefore, forceful and direct, this writer seemed out of step with his contemporaries too allusive, too convoluted in style. In fact Wideman's early works, while introducing some of his recurring themes, show his indebtedness to writers such as T. S. Eliot and James Joyce, a reflection of his academic training perhaps. In an interview for *Swing Low: Black Men Writing,* he said that he ''once thought he would like to write books that both his family in Pittsburgh and literary scholars could read and enjoy,'' hence the complexity of his style. However, as a writer who is still evolving, his aspirations have shifted somewhat. In the same source, he claimed, ''I'd settle for writing books that just my family [can] read and enjoy. . . . Any literary scholar who has good sense will enjoy them (i.e., his works) too.'' This shift reflects the twofold nature of Wideman's significance within the African American literary tradition. His attention to craft and his experimentation with the form of the novel put him within the tradition of Jean Toomer, Ralph Ellison, and other twentieth–century writers who have contributed to the dynamism of this genre.

But just as importantly, increasingly through his fiction, Wideman has captured the voices and experiences of the past–African American and African–bringing them into the present and preserving them in the face of devastation. In serving as a chronicler of events and as a preserver and conservator of family history and African American culture, Wideman has learned that he does not have to give up his artistic goals in turning to African American culture as the source of language and technique. In fact, according to *Blackness & Modernism,* he could ''talk about the most complicated, sophisticated and intense moments and understandings and characters in the Afro–American idiom.''

John Edgar Wideman was born June 14, 1941, to Edgar and Bettye French Wideman in Washington, D.C. He spent his early years in Homewood, a section of Pittsburgh, where his family moved soon after his birth. When Wideman was in high school, the family moved again, this time to Shadyside, a predominantly white neighborhood unlike Homewood. As revealed in his memoir *Fatheralong,* Wideman's father, a native of South Carolina, served in World War II. The father also attended the University of Pittsburgh for a brief time on GI benefits and worked at various jobs, including those of waiter and welder. While the memoir paints a picture of a father–son relationship that was quite distant, his father's influence can be seen in certain tendencies in the writer's life, for Edgar Wideman was quite good at sports, an ability which John Wideman showed during his high school years. The father was also a voracious reader, especially of pulp westerns. The athlete/intellectual–writer are components of John Wideman's evolution as well. In fact, he had aspirations toward a basketball career early in his life.

His mother was raised in Homewood, which Wideman described in *Brothers and Keepers* as a ''close–knit, homogeneous community where relationships were based on trust, mutual respect, common spiritual and material concerns.'' It is Homewood, in particular the spiritual geography of this community, which has become significant in the development of the writer's vision. In addition to John, the Wideman siblings include Gene, Robby, Letitia, and David. As for his own family, John Wideman married Judith Ann Goldman in 1965, and they have three adult children: Daniel Jerome, Jacob Edgar, and Jamila Ann.

John Edgar Wideman

Wideman's early education was in the public schools of Pittsburgh. He attended Peabody High School, graduating as valedictorian of his class. He has noted that during his early years the Pittsburgh Public Library was significant to his development, for it gave him entry into a world beyond Homewood. In the Carroll interview, he referred to the library as his ''tourist office'' so that when he began to think about writing ''what I had learned from reading fertilized and organized the beginning of that process.''

Following his graduation from high school, Wideman entered the University of Pennsylvania, graduating with a bachelor's degree in 1963. Although from his high school days Wideman had evidenced a certain athletic talent, his academic abilities were just as apparent, for following his graduation from college, he attended Oxford University as a Rhodes scholar. In 1966 he graduated from Oxford with a bachelor of philosophy degree in eighteenth–century literature.

Wideman's career as a university instructor began in 1966 at his alma mater, the University of Pennsylvania, where he remained until 1974. During this period he served in other capacities, including assistant basketball coach (1968–72) and notably as director of the Afro–American Studies Program, which he initiated. In 1975 he assumed a post at the University of Wyoming at Laramie where he was professor of English until 1986. Currently he is professor of creative writing and American studies at the University of Massachusetts at Amherst.

Since the beginning of his tenure as a university instructor, Wideman has served the arts community. In 1968 he became a National Humanities Faculty consultant in numerous states as well as a consultant to secondary schools across the country. In 1976 he made a lecture tour of Europe and the Near East under the auspices of the U.S. Department of State. In addition, during that same year, he was a Phi Beta Kappa lecturer.

Wideman has received many accolades in recognition of his literary and academic achievements. In addition to the Rhodes Scholarship, he was the 1963–66 Thouron Fellow at Oxford University and from 1966 to 1967 he was a Kent Fellow at the University of Iowa, where he attended the creative writing workshop. In the seventies, he received awards for his athleticism and his literary talent. In 1974 he was named to the Philadelphia Big Five Basketball Hall of Fame; he received the young Humanist Fellow Award in 1975. In the eighties, Wideman received the Pen/Faulkner Award for fiction for *Sent for You Yesterday* (1984); a National Book Critics Circle Award nomination for *Brothers and Keepers* (1984); and the John Dos Passos Prize for Literature from Longwood College (1986). In this decade, the awards have continued with another PEN/Faulkner Award for *Philadelphia Fire* (1990) and a MacArthur Prize Fellowship (1994). He was also a National Book Award finalist for *Fatheralong; A Meditation on Fathers and Sons* in 1995.

A Man of Letters

At age 26 in 1967, Wideman published his first novel. The book *A Glance Away,* published while he was a young instructor at the University of Pennsylvania, showed his modernistic bent but also focused on one of his recurring figures. James Coleman referred to this book as evidence of Wideman's "mainstream modernism as it focuses on a Caucasian intellectual who is alienated from both the black and white communities." *Hurry Home,* published in 1970, is still considered modernistic in its style; however, the focus here shifts to the black intellectual.

The Lynchers, published in 1973, deals ostensibly with the aborted attempt by young black males to lynch a policeman in the South. For Wideman, however, the real subject of the book is the imagination. He noted in *Interviews with Black Writers* that this element of humanity is a "natural preoccupation because the imagination plays such a powerful role in the relationship between blacks and whites in America, which is also a predominant theme in my work." What matters in *The Lynchers,* he continued in *Interviews,* is the act that "certain social realities have pushed their characters to, [and the] attitudes [that] are taken by both blacks and whites."

As Wideman was finding his fictional voice, he was also defining that voice in critical articles published in such scholarly magazines as *Black Literature Forum, Callaloo,* and *American Poetry Review.* Here and in this third book Wideman reflects an expanded focus in his evolution as a writer. Whereas he acknowledges the echo of T. S. Eliot in *A Glance Away,* the first novel, he had begun at this point to immerse himself in the work of black writers and had started teaching a course in black literature. As he noted in *Interviews with Black Writers,* such exposure became crucial to his development, for it "awakened a different . . . self image and the whole notion of a third world. The slave narratives, folklore, and the novels of Richard Wright and Ralph Ellison have been most important to me. . . . Toomer's *Cane* as an individual work was very important . . . because of its experimentation and open form."

The Homewood Trilogy and Beyond

Anyone familiar with the work of Wideman is aware that the Homewood community, the land of his mother's family and his orientation to the world, figures prominently. Beginning with *Hiding Place* (1981) and continuing with *Damballah* (1981) and *Sent for You Yesterday* (1983), Wideman expands his vision of that community and its traditions. While the author cautions against an overzealous search for parallels with the actual place, it is clear that the community has come to stand for sustaining values in a world fraught with evidence of change and collapse. Wideman has noted that in spite of what appeared to be the Eurocentric influences in his early work, he had never really left the world of his family, for, he noted in *Swing Low,* that it gave him "a very powerful sense of identity and support," which he took to Oxford and beyond. He continued, saying that the community provided a strong preparation for life because it was a "very wise and historically grounded community."

It is significant that in *Damballah* (a collection of short stories), that sense of community extends back to Africa, thus establishing and reestablishing the link that was broken with the advent of slavery, a break that was physical, but not necessarily spiritual, as symbolized by the figure of Orion. The collection ends with "The Beginnings of Homewood," which further underscores the link that has been reestablished through the powers of the writer's imagination. The interplay of the real world and the fictive world becomes evident as these stories of freedom, perseverance, and strength of family and community become an occasion for the author's rumination on the fate of his brother who is now serving time in prison. The book opens with an address "To Robby" in which the author said, "These stories are letters. Long overdue letters from me to you. I wish they would tear down walls." The story of Sybella Owens, the African–the great–great–great grandmother whose escape from slavery, whose push for freedom is a "struggle that doesn't end"–is a tale that connects not only with Robby's story but also with the readers' stories.

In discussing the significance of the intellectual–writer as character in his work, Wideman noted that the novelist or writer is "a storyteller, and it is the process [of storytelling] that is going to knit up the culture . . . the storytelling tradition/activity is crucial to survival, individual survival, community survival." This indicates further Wideman's significance, for he places the writer/storyteller at the center of culture as preserver, as healer.

The 1980s also marked the appearance of *Brothers and Keepers* (1984) which, although not a novel, has certain novelistic features. Technically, it is a biography of his brother's life, but becomes a story of Wideman's life and a rumination on the relationship between these siblings whose lives have taken two distinct directions. Wideman said in *Blackness and Modernism* that the book was intended to help his brother ''legally [and], spiritually but at the same time to help myself. . . . I had separated myself from the larger Black community [although] I was still in contact in important, sustaining, natural ways.'' The decade would close with the publication of *Reuben* (1987), a work that draws on African cosmology, traditions, and myth, and *Fever* (1989), a collection of short stories.

Writing into the 1990s

Continuing to focus on the devastation in the urban landscape and the people, Wideman published *Philadelphia Fire* in 1990. The book deals with the city's bombing of the MOVE headquarters which had been ordered by Wilson Goode, the black mayor. This work was followed by *The Stories of John Edgar Wideman* in 1992 and *Fatheralong* in 1995. The latter book is the second technically nonfictional work (although fiction and nonfiction tends to blend and merge in his books), and it continues themes noted earlier; that is, family relationships, connections, identity/definitions. The work describes a trip back in time and space taken with his father to his father's ancestral land Promised Land, a small black community outside of Greenwood, South Carolina. It becomes an occasion to ponder questions of identity and definitions of father and son/self. Meditating on the significance of the journey, the author stated, ''I know my father's name, Edgar and some of his fathers' names, Hannibal . . . Jordan. . . . I know the name of a place, Greenwood, South Carolina.'' *Fatheralong* then becomes a metaphorical/spiritual sojourn of the author/the father/African Americans through suffering, resignation with the hope of finally seeing/knowing the father, that is, learning the f(F)ather's name.

The Cattle Killing, published in 1996, shows that Wideman is continuing to develop and expand themes from his past works. It returns to the violence of the urban environment and the destruction of black youth/black people. It picks up the disintegrated family as the main character thinks about the city landscape that he must traverse in order to visit his father who lives alone, in an area known as the Hill, an area which his mother fears because of the dangers lurking there. The connection is made between the fate of black youth/black people who shoot each other and the killing of the Xosha cattle that are ''slaughtered by a starving people, dreamless and broken, dying as their cattle had died, exiled from the ark of safety that had been home and culture and heritage.'' Again, it is the writer–intellectual who performs the act of healing through his imagination/vision, who through his art joins the past and present, linking the stories of struggle/freedom wherever black people inhabit. Near the close of the book, the author averred that in ''Pittsburgh, Chicago, Los Angeles . . . up and down the land in the cities, there are funerals and rallies and each is a story, a celebration and mourning . . . different stories . . . that are one story . . . Romona [Africa] lights her candle passes it to Mandela . . . [who] passes it to the ghost of a woman finding herself.''

John Edgar Wideman's significance to African American literature and culture is evidenced in his continuing evolution as a writer. As he evolves, he not only records the sources of devastation to the individual, family, community within the urban landscape, but he also finds within that community those sources of sustaining values both past and present. In refining his own voice and vision he creates and re–creates stories that are crucial to the healing of the self and the community.

Current address: Department of English, University of Massachusetts Amherst, Amherst, MA 01002.

REFERENCES

Andrews, William, Frances Smith Foster, and Trudier Harris, eds. *The Oxford Companion to African American Literature.* New York: Oxford, 1997.

Carroll, Rebecca. *Swing Low: Black Men Writing.* New York: Crown Trade Paperbacks, 1995.

Coleman, James W. *Blackness & Modernism: The Literary Career of John Edgar Wideman.* Jackson, MS: University Press of Mississippi, 1989.

Contemporary Authors. Vol. 42. Revised series. Detroit: Gale Research, 1992.

Lustig, Jessica. ''Home: An Interview with John Edgar Wideman.'' *African American Review* 26 (Fall 1992): 453–57.

Mbalia, Doneatha Drummond. *John Edgar Wideman: Reclaiming the African Personality.* Toronto: Associated University Presses, 1995.

O'Brien, John, ed. *Interviews with Black Writers.* New York: Liveright, 1973.

Wideman, John. *Brothers and Keepers.* New York: Henry Holt, 1984.

———. *The Cattle Killing.* New York: Houghton Mifflin, 1996.

———. *Damballah.* New York: Avon Books, 1981.

———. *Fatheralong: A Meditation on Fathers and Sons, Race and Society.* New York: Vintage Books, 1995.

———. *Philadelphia Fire.* New York: Henry Holt, 1990.

———. *The Stories of John Edgar Wideman.* New York: Pantheon Books, 1992.

Johnanna L. Grimes–Williams

L. Douglas Wilder
(1931–)
Lawyer, governor, politician, radio talk show host

When Beulah and Robert Wilder named the ninth of their ten children after the poet Paul Laurence Dunbar and the abolitionist, author, and statesman Frederick Douglass, they could not have known that one day he would join his famous namesakes on the roll of pioneering African American leaders. Born January 17, 1931, in Richmond, Virginia, Lawrence Douglas Wilder became the nation's first elected African American governor when he defeated his white Republican opponent J. Marshall Coleman in a hard–fought race.

Wilder grew up in Church Hill—a segregated Richmond neighborhood—in a house his parents built in 1923 for $2,875. Years later, during his 1989 gubernatorial campaign, Wilder often commented on the two miles that separated his family's home on 28 and P streets and Richmond's Capitol Hill, where both the Governor's Mansion and the Jefferson–designed statehouse are located. Quoted by Margaret Edds in *Claiming the Dream,* he said: "It's a short distance to walk, but it's a mighty, mighty mountain to climb." Nevertheless, Wilder's biographer Edds described the years he spent living in the two–story frame house with his parents and his seven surviving siblings six sisters and one brother as poor but happy.

Robert Judson Wilder Sr., born 21 years after the Civil War's end to James W. and Agnes Johnson Wilder, a couple once forced by slavery to live on separate plantations. Robert Wilder Sr. supported his wife and children by working as a salesman for Southern Aid Insurance, the nation's oldest black–owned insurance company although he had planned to become a lawyer. He and his brother Charles, who wanted to be a physician, agreed that Beulah and Robert Wilder would mortgage their home to pay for Charles's medical school. Charles, in turn, would use his medical practice to support his brother's preparations for a legal career. Charles's unexpected death at age 32 prevented Robert Sr. from realizing his dream. From Robert Wilder, Douglas—as his mother insisted he be called—learned industry, discipline, and frugality, the last in particular being a trait he has used to his advantage when campaigning for political office.

Although Wilder's strict but loving father provided him with guidance and a positive role model, his mother, Beulah Olive Richards Wilder, whom Donald Baker characterized in *Wilder: Hold Fast to Dreams* as a "tee–totaling Christian woman," played the most significant role in shaping the character and self–confidence of her son. According to Edds, Beulah Wilder often told Douglas Wilder he was "a special little boy." In the same source, Wilder's sister, Agnes Nicholson, described her mother and brother as "the best of friends" who enjoyed spending time together working crossword puzzles, reading, and talking.

Some of the credit for Wilder's successful career as a lawyer, state senator, lieutenant governor, and governor must also be given to his hard–working Church Hill neighbors and to the unique experiences this poor but tight–knit African American community offered the bright, ambitious young boy. In addition to performing numerous chores around the family home, Wilder shined shoes, shot pool, sang in the choir of Richmond's First African Baptist Church, attended George Mason Elementary School, and worked as a newspaper salesman for the *Richmond Planet,* a weekly black newspaper later called the *Richmond Afro–American.* At Billy's Barber Shop, a place Wilder would later call "my stadium," Wilder began to hone his oratorical skills. Edds told of one of the barbershop's regular customers, Arthur Burke, who remembered another patron telling young Douglas Wilder: "You should be a lawyer. You argue too much and you tell the biggest lies in the world."

L. Douglas Wilder

At the age of 12, Wilder skipped the eighth grade and entered Richmond's segregated Armstrong High School. In addition to working in a downtown office building running an elevator, Wilder maintained a lively social life and participated in many of Armstrong's extracurricular activities, including the Cadet Corps, the cheering squad, and the senior play. He also served as artist and cartoonist for the school's newspaper and yearbook. Wilder graduated from Armstrong High School in 1947.

Although Wilder was a good enough student to be elected to the National Honor Society, he had not distinguished himself sufficiently to earn a college scholarship. For financial reasons and because his parents would not grant permission for their 17 year old son to enter the U.S. Navy, Wilder enrolled at Virginia Union University, a black liberal arts college founded soon after the Civil War and located in Richmond, as a chemistry major with the intention of becoming a dental surgeon. His mother gave him $25 of the $100 he needed for a semester's tuition. He earned the rest as a waiter at Richmond hotels and country clubs, jobs he continued to hold in order to pay his way through college.

An indifferent student who perhaps devoted too much time to his social life, Wilder graduated with a bachelor's degree in chemistry in August of 1951 after repeating a calculus course in order to raise his grade–point average to meet the graduation requirements. In spite of his lack of direction as a college student, Wilder considered his years at Virginia Union to have been instrumental to his political success. At the dedication of Virginia Union University's $7.5 million L. Douglas Wilder Library and Learning Resource Center on February 14, 1997, he was quoted in the *Richmond Times Dispatch* as saying that ''But for Virginia Union, I could never have been governor of any place or anything. . . . I could never have really believed in myself.''

Though Wilder had yet to settle on a profession, in August of 1952, a year after receiving his college diploma, he embarked on a new phase of life. He was drafted into the army and sent to Korea as a member of A Company, First Battalion, 17th Infantry Regiment, 7th Division. While stationed in Korea, Wilder began to display leadership qualities and to speak out openly against racism. Private Wilder, appalled that his fellow African American soldiers' seemed to be passed over for deserved promotions, arranged for them to meet with the battalion commander, Major Earl C. Acuff. His political skills were evident at this meeting and African American soldiers began receiving promotions; Wilder himself became a corporal.

While in Korea, Wilder helped to capture 19 North Korean prisoners on April 18, 1953. Three months after this event, he returned to the United States and received a permanent promotion to field sergeant, a rank Major Acuff had temporarily bestowed on him in Korea. Wilder was discharged from the U.S. Army in December of 1953. He also won a bronze star for his role in capturing the Korean soldiers but kept the honor a secret until he began his 1969 campaign for the Virginia state legislature.

Enters the Law Profession

After his stint in the army, Wilder returned to his parents' Church Hill home still uncertain about his future. He spent six months working sporadically as a waiter, eventually becoming a mail carrier. His next position, a technician in the state's medical examiner's office, allowed him to make use of his chemistry degree. In 1956, he finally realized that the career he desired was in law and entered Howard University's Law School. The state of Virginia strongly discouraged blacks from attending the University of Virginia's School of Law, although a black student had been admitted there in 1950. Rather than integrate its law school, the state preferred to give black law students scholarships to go elsewhere.

While at Howard, Wilder met Howard undergraduate Eunice Montgomery, an economics major from Philadelphia. The couple wed on October 11, 1958. Their first child, Lynn Diana, was born May 19, 1959, the same month Wilder earned his law degree from Howard and Eunice Wilder her bachelor's degree in economics. After graduating from Howard, Douglas and Eunice Wilder returned to the Wilder home. Wilder went to work as a law clerk for William A. Smith, a Newport News, Virginia, lawyer who specialized in personal injury cases, and commuted to Richmond on weekends to visit his wife—who worked in a Richmond bank—and their infant daughter. After four months of this arrangement, Wilder returned to Richmond to study for the Virginia bar examination. Wilder passed and set up a law office close to his parents' home in office space above Ike's Shrimp House. Wilder won his first case and his legal practice began to thrive. By 1962, Wilder was clearly beginning to realize the ''American dream.'' That year the Wilders bought their first house, Eunice Wilder gave birth to a son, Lawrence Douglas Jr., on February 17, 1962, and Wilder was now an attorney with his father's firm. Their third child, Loren Deane, was born November 5, 1963.

Political Aspirations and Success

As Wilder's reputation as a trial lawyer grew, so did his ambition. In 1969 he made a successful bid for the Virginia State Senate, the first African American elected to this office in Virginia. During his 16 years as a state senator, Wilder proved himself a force to be reckoned with. Less than a month into his first term as senator, Wilder upset many of his colleagues when he introduced a bill to repeal the state's official song, ''Carry Me Back to Old Virginni,'' which includes the line ''that's where this old darkie's heart am long to go.'' Twenty–seven years later, the Virginia Senate finally decided that Wilder had a point and retired the song. As Margaret Edds observed:

> Throughout the 1970s Wilder pursued a liberal, civil rights–oriented legislative agenda. He pushed for fair housing laws and a holiday honoring Martin Luther King Jr. He backed proposals to strip the sales tax from food and nonprescription drugs. . . He opposed the death penalty and fought tough crime legislation including bills creating a sentence of life in prison without parole and prescribing a separate offense for the use of a gun in committing a felony.

In the midst of his political triumphs, Eunice Wilder filed for divorce in 1975. The court documents from the divorce proceedings were sealed. In 1979, a year after the divorce became final, Eunice Wilder filed a suit asking for half of the property Wilder, by now a wealthy man, had amassed during their marriage. She lost the suit and received only $52,000. Wilder continued to support the children, who lived with their mother.

Aside from these personal difficulties, Wilder continued to enjoy political success throughout the 1970s and 1980s, although many of his critics claimed that he sacrificed the concerns of African Americans for the sake of his own aspirations. While his reasons for becoming more moderate on subjects such as the death penalty, underage abortions, and parole remain open to debate, by the time he became the state's lieutenant governor, Wilder's platform was most assuredly that of a moderate Democrat, not that of a liberal. By his own admission, Wilder had never been a black activist or a civil rights leader, though he often used his political clout to fight discrimination and to promote the careers of African American political allies. Describing his relationship with Jesse Jackson, to whom he is sometimes unfavorably compared, Wilder observed in Baker's biography of him, ''Jesse

Jackson understands me and I understand him. He runs to strike the conscience of the country; I am running to be elected.'' When Wilder announced his decision to run for the governor's seat in 1989, Jackson supported his candidacy and praised him for his courage.

First Elected Black Governor

During his four–year term as governor of the state of Virginia that began in 1990, Wilder placed his name on the list of contenders for the 1992 Democratic presidential nomination. He eventually withdrew from the race, stating that the campaign was keeping him from devoting his full attention to his gubernatorial duties. While in office, among other programs, he trimmed the state's budget, eliminated the $2.2 billion deficit, and stressed the need for civil rights legislation. After completing his term as governor— Virginia does not allow its governor to serve consecutive terms—he remained a major figure in Virginia politics, in part because of what has become known as the Robb–Wilder feud. In 1994 Wilder declared himself an independent candidate for the U.S. Senate seat held by Charles Robb. Also vying for this seat were Republican Oliver North and Marshall Coleman, who, like Wilder, was running as an independent candidate. Democratic solidarity led Wilder to set aside his considerable differences with Robb. He withdrew from the race and openly supported Robb. Since 1995 Wilder has hosted *The Doug Wilder Show,* which can be heard Monday evenings from 8:00 to 10:00 on WRVA–AM, ''Richmond's News and Information Station.'' In *Jet* magazine, Wilder called the show, ''My way of continuing in public service.''

Each time Wilder has thrown his hat into the political ring and declared himself a candidate for office, his campaigns have served as instruments for measuring the effects race and racism have on American politics. On the one hand, Wilder seems to be an African American willing to play the race card while simultaneously denying that he is doing so and a team player who sometimes prefers to wear a maverick's stripes rather than conform to others' game plans. On the other hand, he is a consummate politician wise in the ways of the political arena dominated by white people, a man who knows that his personal political victories herald a brighter future for all African Americans. In 1998 he was named president of his alma mater, Virginia Union University, but he declined the offer shortly before he was to take office.

Current address: ''Doug Wilder Show,'' WRVA-AM, 200 N. 22nd St., Richmond, VA 23223-7020.

REFERENCES

Baker, Donald. *Wilder: Hold Fast to Dreams, a Biography of L. Douglas Wilder.* Washington, DC: Seven Locks Press, 1989.

Edds, Margaret. *Claiming the Dream: The Victorious Campaign of Douglas Wilder of Virginia.* Chapel Hill, NC: Algonquin Books, 1990.

Jones, David R. *Racism As a Factor in the 1989 Gubernatorial Election of Doug Wilder.* Lewiston, NY : Edwin Mellen Press, 1991.

Salzman, Jack, David Lionel Smith, and Cornel West, eds. *Encyclopedia of African American Culture and History.* New York: Macmillan Library Reference USA/Simon and Schuster Macmillan, 1996.

''Wilder Hosts New Radio Talk Show in Virginia.'' *Jet* 28 (January 30, 1995): 25.

''Wilder Library Rich Part of VUU Founder's Day.'' *Richmond Times Dispatch,* February 15, 1997.

Yancey, Dwayne. *When Hell Froze Over: The Untold Story of Doug Wilder: A Black Politician's Rise to Power in the South.* Roanoke, VA: Taylor Publishing Company, 1988.

Candis LaPrade

J. Ernest Wilkins
(1894–1959)
Government official, lawyer

As assistant secretary of labor in charge of international affairs, J. Ernest Wilkins was the first African American to hold that position and the second black official to hold a sub–cabinet post. He was the ranking black in the nation's capitol during the Dwight D. Eisenhower administration and became internationally known for his position.

Jesse Ernest Wilkins was the son of a Baptist minister, Henry Byrd Wilkins, and Susie Olivia Douthit Wilkins. He was born on February 1, 1894, in Farmington, Missouri. After attending a Farmington primary school he entered Lincoln Institute (later Lincoln University) in Jefferson City, Missouri, where he took preparatory work. Wilkins then enrolled in the University of Illinois, Urbana, and won election to Phi Beta Kappa. Wilkins specialized in mathematics and wrote a thesis on algebraic numbers theory. In 1918 he graduated with a B.A. degree and special honors. In the fall of 1918 he enlisted in the U.S. armed forces and was sent to France as a supply sergeant in the 809th infantry.

Wilkins returned to Chicago after the war and worked his way through the University of Chicago law school. He was awarded an LL.B. degree in 1921 and was admitted to the Illinois bar in that same year. He entered private law practice in Chicago and acquitted himself well as an attorney and civic leader. He was elected president of the Bar Association of Cook County for the 1941–42 term.

President Dwight D. Eisenhower appointed Wilkins, a Republican, as vice–chair of the newly established President's Committee on Government Contracts. Vice–president Richard M. Nixon chaired the panel that had been set up by executive order to enforce federal policy prohibiting discrimination due to race, creed, or national origin in employment or promotion of individuals who worked in establishments involved in government business. Wilkins's work on the committee was so impressive that Nixon suggested to Eisenhower that the Chicago lawyer deserved a higher position in the administration.

Named Assistant Secretary of Labor

On March 12, 1954, Wilkins, who had been nominated for the post on March 4, was confirmed by the Senate as assistant secretary of labor, whose chief concern would be with foreign affairs for the Department of Labor. Wilkins held the first such appointment for an African American since William Henry Lewis became assistant attorney general in 1911. Wilkins became the nation's first black assistant secretary of labor and the first black leader of a U.S. delegation to International Labor Organization meetings in Europe and Cuba. Appointed under the William Howard Taft administration, Lewis was the first black to hold a sub–cabinet post. The nation would not have a black U.S. Secretary of Labor until May of 1997, when President Bill Clinton's nominee, Alexis Herman, was sworn into office.

The build–up of Wilkins later became a nightmare for those who made administrative policy. Some sources suggest that racism lurked in the shadow of Wilkins's career and fate. Although Washington officials claimed that he had done a tremendous job and learned his work rapidly, those in labor circles questioned his qualifications for the position. Notwithstanding the fact that Wilkins was acclaimed for his speeches before worldwide labor leaders, developed a labor program in Africa, and set up labor exchange programs, he was still a black man at risk.

Wilkins endeared himself to his own staff, however, and did much to help black people. He made sure that, for the first time, black secretaries accompanied Labor Department delegations overseas. He appointed top race aides in his section and protested all–white sections in the department.

Wilkins was said to be an uncompromising crusader who believed in charting his own course. Some thought he may also have been too honest to realize what his role was as a diplomat. For example, at the 1957 labor delegation meeting in Switzerland, a Russian speaker attacked America for spawning segregationists such as Mississippi Senator James Eastland. Rather than silencing the speaker, according to Simeon Booker, Wilkins said, "He's telling the truth, isn't he?"

By the fall of 1957, the Labor Department Secretary James P. Mitchell claimed dissatisfaction with the way Wilkins handled labor leaders in 79 countries and believed he had made a mistake in appointing Wilkins. After that, the move was on to force his resignation or to appoint him to another position. Then Mitchell persuaded the White House to appoint Wilkins to the newly–created Civil Rights Commission. He became the commission's only black member.

After it was clear that Wilkins no longer had the president's support, Wilkins became a dejected and wounded man. Although the president announced at a White House press conference in mid–August of 1958 that Wilkins had considered resigning, by the first week of November the news was that he was leaving for personal reasons. As he left office, he refused to be honored at a testimonial dinner. Although in failing health then, Wilkins still refused to quit public life. Instead, as a member of the Civil Rights Commission, he appointed Howard Law School dean George Johnson as legal director of the commission, and put a black representative on its publicity staff. Wilkins and the commission attended a hearing in Montgomery, Alabama, early in November of 1958. Due to segregated housing in Montgomery, they had to stay at nearby Maxwell Air Force Base. In the commission's probe of Alabama vote denial cases for 45 black residents, Wilkins, a sharp, soft–spoken, quiet crusader, exploded before judges and witnesses in the federal courthouse.

Wilkins was a member of such professional associations as the National Bar Association and the American Judicature Society. In the civic field, he was a member (1942–52) and treasurer (from 1952) of the board of trustees of Provident Hospital in Chicago. He was a director of the Hyde Park–Kentwood Community Conference. He belonged to several social organizations, including Sigma Pi Phi (the Boule), Kappa Alpha Psi Fraternity, the Masons, and was a Knight of Pythias. Among his awards was an honorary degree from Lincoln University in Missouri in 1941. In 1954 the National Association of Colored Women gave him the award of merit for pioneer work to advance the black race.

Prominent in the Methodist church, from 1942 to 1948 Wilkins was a member of the commission on world service and finance and was a member of its executive committee from 1944 to 1948. He served on the church's judicial council (the church's supreme court) beginning 1948 and was elected council secretary in 1953.

Wilkins rejected alcohol, cigarettes, and foul language and made it clear that he was devoted to carrying out his duties in the government. Simeon Booker described Wilkins as "soft–voiced gentle 'prince of a man,'" and a "pacesetter for a brilliant family." He is said to have had an even temper and a natural modesty. Wilkins had been dubbed "The Puritan of Mahogany Row" and was widely admired as a headlined race figure in the federal government. Some called him ultra–conservative. Booker also said that Wilkins deserved a rightful and lasting place in civil rights.

On November 23, 1922, Wilkins married Lucile Beatrice Robinson. They had three sons: Julian B., who joined his father in his Chicago law practice; Jesse Ernest Wilkins, Jr., who became an industrial physicist; and John R., who was a lawyer with the Department of Justice.

Wilkins suffered a heart attack in his office in May of 1958, brought on, according to some sources, by efforts to ease or force him from office. Later that year he suffered a fall in Flint, Michigan, and broke a leg. He had attended a second Civil Rights Commission hearing in Montgomery in January of 1959. Ten days later, on January 19, he suffered a fatal heart attack at his Washington, D.C., home. He lay in state at Foundry Methodist Church in downtown Washington, the first time a black had been so honored; his funeral was held in

Chicago. Labor secretary James P. Mitchell said in the *New York Times* at his death: ''He was an admirer and able public servant . . . [who] advanced the welfare not only of our country's minority citizens, but that of all our citizens.''

REFERENCES

Booker, Simeon. ''The Last Days of J. Ernest Wilkins.'' *Ebony* 15 (March 1960): 141–46.

Christian, Walter, ed. *Negroes in Public Affairs and Government.* Yonkers, NY: Educational Heritage, 1966.

Current Biography Yearbook. New York: H. W. Wilson, 1954, 1959.

''J. Ernest Wilkins, U.S. Aide, 64, Dies.'' *New York Times,* January 20, 1959.

Smith, Jessie Carney, ed. *Black Firsts.* Detroit: Gale Research, 1994.

Jessie Carney Smith

Roy Wilkins

Roy Wilkins
(1901–1981)
Civil rights leader, journalist, organization executive

During his 22 years as executive director of the NAACP, Roy Wilkins devoted tireless effort to improving the economic, political and social status of blacks. He played a vital role in passage of the landmark civil rights legislation of the 1950s and 1960s, including the Civil Rights Acts of 1957, 1960, and 1964, the Voting Rights Act of 1965, and the Civil Rights Act of 1968 with its fair housing provision. These civil rights gains have benefitted all Americans but particularly blacks.

Wilkins was born on August 30, 1901, in St Louis, to William D. and Mayfield Edmondson Wilkins. The previous year his parents had relocated from Holly Springs, Mississippi. Although his father was a college graduate and a minister, the only work he could find was tending a brick kiln. Wilkins's mother died of tuberculosis when the boy was four. In his book, *Standing Fast,* written in collaboration with Tom Matthews, a *Newsweek* senior editor, Wilkins revealed that his mother, knowing she was terminally ill, had written to her sister in St. Paul, Minnesota, asking her to rear her children. His father, fulfilling her last request, sent Roy and his younger brother and sister to live with the designated aunt and uncle, the Samuel Williamses. They lived in a low–income, integrated neighborhood but stressed to the children the value of an education and moral principles. Wilkins attended the integrated Mechanic Arts High School and became editor of the school newspaper.

After graduating from high school in 1919, Wilkins attended the University of Minnesota, majoring in sociology and minoring in journalism. As a student, he earned money to pay for his education by working as a porter, redcap, dishwasher, caddy, dining car waiter, and packinghouse laborer. Despite his class work and many jobs, he was able to serve as night editor of the campus newspaper, the *Minnesota Daily,* and editor of a black weekly newspaper, the *St. Paul Appeal.* At the same time, he actively participated in the local branch of the NAACP, thus beginning a lifetime struggle for social justice.

Taking on Jim Crow

While Wilkins was studying at the university, there was a brutal lynching of a black man in Duluth, Minnesota. The episode had a profound effect on the direction of Wilkins's life. His moral outrage and sense of disgust prompted him to enter an oratorical contest at the university. His entry entitled ''Democracy or Democracy?'' was a strong antilynching speech. It took first prize.

Upon completing his A.B. degree at the University of Minnesota in 1923, Wilkins accepted a job as a staff writer for the *Kansas City Call,* a black weekly newspaper, of which he later became managing editor. It was in Kansas City that Wilkins witnessed widespread segregation for the first time. Quoted in the *New York Times* of September 1981, he said

''Kansas City ate my heart out. It wasn't any one melodramatic thing. It was a slow accumulation of humiliations and grievances. I was constantly exposed to Jim Crow [legally enforced segregation of the races] in the schools, movies, downtown hotels and restaurants.'' To counter this oppressive atmosphere, Wilkins used the *Kansas City Call* to persuade blacks to vote against any politicians supportive of Jim Crow policies. In addition, he personally became active in the Kansas City chapter of the NAACP, where he was elected secretary. While in Kansas, he married Amende Ann Bandeau, an assistant commissioner of the New York City Department of Welfare in 1929. The marriage was childless.

Exposes Exploitation

Wilkins's relentless campaign against the reelection of Henry Allen, a militant racist, to the U.S. Senate in 1930, brought him to the attention of the national leaders of the NAACP. His dogged determination encouraged Walter White, executive secretary of the NAACP, to hire Wilkins in 1931 as assistant executive secretary. A year later, Wilkins and journalist George Schuller investigated charges of discriminatory pay practices, along with the maltreatment and despicable working conditions of black laborers on the flood control projects on the Mississippi Delta. According to Wilkins, who posed as a day laborer in order to collect data, blacks who worked to rebuild the levees on the river were paid ten cents an hour. He documented his findings in a widely publicized 1932 report entitled ''Mississippi Slave Labor.'' His exposé was instrumental in helping the NAACP force a congressional investigation which led to improved wages and working conditions for blacks in the levee labor camps.

Continuing his struggle for social justice in 1934, Wilkins was arrested in Washington, D.C. (Wilkins was also arrested in 1962 in Jackson, Mississippi, for protesting against segregation.) His ''crime'' was participating in a demonstration against U.S. Attorney General Homer Cummings, who held a national conference on crime without including lynching as an agenda item. That same year, when W. E. B. Du Bois (sociologist, black protest leader) resigned as editor of the NAACP's *Crisis* magazine, Wilkins replaced him, serving in that position until 1949. In addition to his duties as editor, he traveled and wrote many pamphlets and magazine articles pertaining to racial issues. He also wrote one of the chapters in the book, *What the Negro Wants,* published by the University of North Carolina Press. He served as a consultant to the U.S. War Department in 1941 to advise on the training and use of black troops, and along with White and Du Bois, was a consultant to the U.S. Department of State in San Francisco during the founding conference of the United Nations in 1945.

Heads NAACP

When White took a leave of absence in 1949, Wilkins served as acting executive secretary. Simultaneously, he chaired the National Emergency Civil Rights Mobilization gathering in Washington in 1950, called to press for executive and legislative action to end job discrimination and guarantee the civil rights of blacks in all areas of American society. When White returned in 1950, the NAACP had been reorganized and Wilkins was appointed internal administrator. Following the death of White in 1955, Wilkins was approved unanimously by the board of directors as executive secretary of the country's oldest and largest civil rights organization. In 1964, his title was officially changed to executive director.

Under Wilkins's leadership the NAACP continued to work for school desegregation through the courts, desegregation of the armed forces, mobilization of a nationwide voter registration drive for blacks, and pressuring presidents to implement civil rights legislation. Much of the civil rights legislation of the 1950s and 1960s was steered through Congress by Wilkins and Clarence Mitchell, the NAACP's Washington lobbyist. While there were those who believed that Wilkins's leadership inaugurated a more militant approach by the organization, since he was one of the chief architects and leaders of the 1963 March on Washington for jobs and freedom, the association continued its traditional tactics of lawsuits, lobbying, and publicity. Many activists thought the association was out of step with the philosophy of the direct action tactics of the time, saying it was too conservative. However, the NAACP lawyers defended the more radical protestors when they were arrested and financially assisted them.

Staying the Course

Wilkins rejected the rhetoric of the young activists such as Malcolm X, Stokley Carmichael, and Eldridge Cleaver. He believed, as did Mitchell, that social justice must be achieved through constitutional means and racial integration. He also emphasized that for any blacks, revolutionary fantasies of separation were genocidal. In the context of this statement, he said in the May 1969 *Crisis,* ''For a minority, violence, whose hand maidens are death and destruction, is only a reprieve on the way to suicide.'' Wilkins added that ''violence as a weapon, as a technique, as a major instrument of social change, was not the weapon of success.'' He continued to focus on the goals of voter registration and voting, improvements in welfare, health services, and the educational system.

By the early 1970s, partly due to failing health, Wilkins had been challenged from within the NAACP to relinquish his position. He refused, insisting that he had the physical and mental stamina to lead the association. He continued as executive director until his retirement in 1977. The NAACP board of directors elected Benjamin L. Hooks to succeed him.

At his final appearance as executive director, Wilkins told his audience to ''work harder to secure our rights to equal education, decent housing, jobs, and equal protection of the law.''

Following his retirement, Wilkins's health continued to decline. On September 8, 1981, Wilkins died at the New York University Medical Center of heart failure and kidney complications at the age of 80.

Wilkins received the NAACP's Spingarn Medal in 1964, and the presidential Medal of Freedom in 1969. The Saint Paul Civic Center Auditorium was renamed the Roy Wilkins Auditorium in 1984, the University of Minnesota established the Roy Wilkins Center for Human Relations and Social Justice at the Hubert Humphrey Institute of Public Affairs, and endowed a chair in his name in 1992. In addition, a Roy Wilkins Memorial was erected between the State Capitol and the St. Paul Cathedral.

Wilkins, the last of the civil rights giants of the 1950s and 1960s, contributed much to correcting injustices through his civil and human rights activities.

REFERENCES

Booker, Simeon. "Nation Mourns Death of NAACP Pioneer Roy Wilkins, 80." *Jet* 61 (1 October 1981): 6–8.

———. "Roy Wilkins Showered with Affection as He Leaves Top NAACP Post." *Jet* 57 (14 July 1977): 10.

Contemporary Black Biography. Vol. 4. Detroit: Gale Research, 1993.

"Roy Wilkins: A Cool, Solid and Respected Leader." *New York Times,* September 9, 1981.

"Roy Wilkins: A Ten Year Record of Leadership, 1955 to 1965." Crisis 72 (April 1965): 236.

"Roy Wilkins, 50–Year Veteran of Civil Rights Fight, Is Dead at 80." *New York Times,* September 9, 1981.

"Roy Wilkins New NAACP Head." *Crisis* 62 (May 1955): 273.

Sanders, Charles L. "A Frank Interview with Roy Wilkins." *Ebony* 29 (April 1974): 35–42.

"Tribute to Roy Wilkins." *Crisis* 8 (June/July 1977): 203–204.

Who's Who in America. 41st ed. Chicago: Marquis Who's Who, 1980.

"Wilkins Calls Little Rock Integration Top Achievement." *Ebony* 20 (May 1965): 134–38.

Wilkins, Roy, with Tom Matthews. *Standing Fast: The Autobiography of Roy Wilkins.* New York: Viking Press, 1982.

———. "Violence is not the Answer." *Crisis* 76 (May 1969): 201, 205, 223.

Williams, Michael W., ed. *The African American Encyclopedia.* North Bellmore, NY: Marshall Cavendish, 1993.

COLLECTIONS

The principal location of Roy Wilkins's papers is the Library of Congress, Washington, D.C.

Patricia A. Pearson

Williams, Egbert Austin.
See Williams, Bert.

Avon Nyanza Williams Jr. (1921–1994)

Attorney, civil rights leader, politician

Throughout most of his career, Avon N. Williams Jr. was an ardent, controversial, and feared leader of the African American community in Tennessee and one of its most dominant and articulate spokespersons. An attorney, civil rights leader, and Tennessee State Senator for more than 20 years, he used his powerful voice to fight for equality and justice. Whether litigating discrimination lawsuits for the impoverished, seeking state funding for Meharry Medical College and Tennessee State University, or struggling to desegregate the public schools, Williams exhibited the same fiery fervor.

Avon Nyanza Williams Jr. was born on December 22, 1921, in Knoxville, Tennessee, the fourth of five children of Avon and Carrie Belle Williams. He received his primary and secondary education in the public schools of Knoxville and graduated with an A.B. degree from Johnson C. Smith University in Charlotte, North Carolina, in 1940. After completing his undergraduate work, Williams entered Boston University's School of Law. But, before he could complete law school, his studies were interrupted by the United States's entry into World War II. He joined the army and when his tour of duty ended, Williams returned to Boston University's law school in 1946. A year later, he earned the LL.B. degree in 1947 and the LL.M. degree in 1948. In 1948 Williams was admitted to the bar in the states of Massachusetts and Tennessee. He interned with Z. Alexander Looby, who was nationally known and considered the dean of black attorneys in Nashville. In 1949 Williams set up his own law practice in Knoxville, where he remained until 1953.

From the time Williams entered the practice of law in Knoxville, he took on civil right cases. He had been in practice less than a year when he filed suit for four African American students applying to the University of Tennessee graduate school. When the case of *Gray v. the University of Tennessee* reached the U.S. Supreme Court, the university capitulated and admitted the young men. In 1950, Williams, along with attorneys Looby and Carl Cowan of Knoxville, filed the Anderson County School desegregation case, which resulted in the U.S. Supreme Court–ordered desegregation of Tennessee public high schools.

Williams returned to Nashville in 1953 and went into general practice of law in association with Z. Alexander Looby, where he remained for 16 years. In 1953 he was admitted to practice in the U.S. Court of Appeals for the Sixth Circuit Court, and in 1946 he was admitted to practice in the U.S. Court of Military Appeals. That same year, he married Joan Marie Bontemps, the daughter of Arna and Alberta Johnson Bontemps. Joan's father, a prolific writer of articles, short stories, and novels, was among African America's leading poets during the Harlem Renaissance. Joan and Avon

Williams had two children, Avon Nyanza III and Wendy Janette.

The U.S. Supreme Court nullified the doctrine of ''separate but equal'' in the 1954 *Brown v. Board of Education of Topeka, Kansas* case. In 1955, on behalf of his son Robert and others, A. Z. Kelly initiated a class–action suit against the Nashville Board of Education. Looby and Williams, in consultation with the NAACP, Legal Defense and Education Fund, and Thurgood Marshall—Williams's cousin—represented the plaintiffs. Although filed in 1955, the suit was not decided until 1971, when U. S. District Court Judge L. Clure Morton ordered a massive cross–town busing plan to desegregate the public schools of Nashville. Ten years later, because of a new plan drawn up by the Metropolitan Board of Education, Williams filed an appeal that ended in a modification handed down by the Sixth U.S. Court of Appeals.

Williams's interest in politics began in 1962, when he facilitated the founding of two political organizations: the Davidson County Independent Political Council, for which he served as president from 1962 through 1966, and the Tennessee Voters Council, for which he served as general chairman from 1966 to 1985. In 1963 he was admitted to practice in the U.S. Supreme Court.

During the turbulent decades of the 1950s and 1960s, Williams involved himself, without remuneration, in more than 24 major civil rights suits. In addition to the numerous cases in which he defended students and other persons arrested in demonstrations for civil rights, these cases involved such issues as school desegregation, teacher discharge, public accommodations, employment and housing discrimination, and police brutality.

Never one to back down, Williams and Looby were held in contempt of court in 1964, after an unyielding debate with Judge Andrew J. Doyle during the hearing of a civil rights case. Doyle fined the two attorneys. They refused to pay the fines and were sentenced to the workhouse. Nashville Mayor Beverly Briley arranged to have their fines paid, and the two were freed. Again, in 1971 Williams was found in contempt of court by Criminal Court Judge Raymond Leathers, when he strongly objected to a prospective juror not being impaneled. Sentenced to two days in jail and fined ten dollars, Williams chose incarceration.

Elected to State Senate

After qualifying for the senatorial race in late May, Williams was announced as a candidate for the state Senate on June 15, 1968. In his first bid for public office, Williams ran for Davidson County's newly created 19th Senatorial District. Williams's opponent for the senatorial race was Dorothy L. Brown, a state representative from Davidson County's 5th District. Brown was the first African American woman to win a seat in the Tennessee General Assembly and the first African American woman to practice surgery in the South. Williams won the Democratic Primary and the general election, making him the second African American elected to a seat in the Tennessee Senate. He was preceded in the Tennessee Senate by Attorney James O. Patterson Jr., a Memphis Democrat and former state representative, who was elected in 1966. Williams served in the state Senate from 1969 to 1991. He also left the law office of Z. Alexander Looby in 1969 and established his own law practice in Nashville.

Williams entered office with the same determination to redress the inequities perpetrated upon African Americans and those of the underclass that energized him in the courtroom. He helped pass bills requiring schools to include African American studies and introduced the bill to establish the Tennessee Housing Development Agency.

In 1972 Williams became the attorney of record in the *Geier v. Tennessee* case, which resulted in the University of Tennessee in Nashville merging with Tennessee State University, also in Nashville, in July of 1979. In this way, the state finally dismantled its dual system of higher education.

Because of his proactive stance and unbridled passion on the stage of the African American modern Civil Rights Movement, Williams, like his former law associate, Looby, was the target of many death threats and other acts of intimidation and violence by conservative whites. For example, in 1972 a cross was burned on his front lawn.

Williams, who forthrightly asserted his opinions, often ran afoul of his senatorial associates. Speaking in 1973 at a legislative retreat, and quoted in his untitled autobiographical manuscript, he declared, ''white women accomplish anything they want in this world through the bedroom . . . all the injustice and inequity that goes on in this country lies at the feet of white women.'' This allegation infuriated State Senator James H. Roberson Jr., of the 18th Senatorial District. ''A shame and an outrage,'' Roberson said in the *Nashville Tennessean* for February 16, 1986. '' [It was] ill–timed and in very bad taste.'' Roberson had Williams's remarks transcribed, copied, and disseminated to every senate member. Although Williams's commentary caused quit a stir among the General Assembly's senators, nothing ever developed. Williams's litigious and manner continued to typify his approach to civil rights issues.

Beginning in 1985, there was speculation among some quarters that Williams would not seek reelection to his senate seat due to a motor neuron disease, Pseudo Bular Palsy, which affected Williams's speech and his ability to walk. He was restricted to a wheelchair and needed a translator. To counteract these physical problems, Williams's interpreter accompanied him in senate committee hearings, on the senate floor, and to meetings with others who could not understand the senator's slurred speech. On May 20, 1986, Williams announced he was going to seek reelection. He won handily.

When Williams first entered the Tennessee law–making body, because of his caustic personality, many doubted his effectiveness. Williams proved his detractors wrong. Indeed, Williams served his constituency well. Between 1972 and 1986 he successfully introduced bills that allocated more than $15 million for health, treatment, research, and many other programs at Meharry Medical College. Williams was the primary sponsor of bills that provided state dollars for facilities at the historically neglected Tennessee State University, including a $9 million health and physical education center, a $3.5 million engineering building, a $2.4 million renovation for the biology building, and $1.9 million for overall maintenance. In addition to serving his immediate constituency, Williams sponsored a bill that became law, establishing elementary school guidance counselors statewide, as well as a "character education bill," the purpose of which was the instruction of elementary students in personal conduct and motivation to acquire the necessary academic skills and tools for learning. He also sponsored a bill that became the Civil Rights Act of 1978, which was the state's first to prohibit discrimination on the basis of race, religion, sex, or national origin.

Williams was a member of the American, Tennessee, Nashville, and Napier–Looby Bar Associations; the American Judicature Society; and the Davidson County Trial Lawyers Association. Holding the rank of lieutenant colonel in the U.S. Army reserve, where he served as judge advocate general, Williams also served on the boards of a number of community and civic organizations, including Davidson County Citizens for Tennessee Valley Authority, the Davidson County Anti–Tuberculosis Association, and the Southern Regional Council. He was a member of the executive committee of the NAACP; an elder and trustee of St. Andrews Presbyterian Church; and a member of the Appeals and Review Committee of Meharry Medical College.

On September 26, 1986, the State Board of Regents and the Tennessee General Assembly honored Williams by naming Tennessee State University's downtown campus the Avon N. Williams Jr. Campus. On December 12, 1991, the Nashville Bar Association awarded Williams its highest honor, the John C. Tune Public Service Award, in recognition of his outstanding work in both professional and community affairs. Said Williams of the honor bestowed upon him in a statement read by his son and published in the December 13, 1991, *Nashville Tennessean,* "Thirty–nine years ago, my law partner, the late Z. Alexander Looby, and I were denied membership in the Nashville Bar Association because we were black. Now you have blacks on your board of directors and present me this . . . award. I am truly grateful."

In addition to being an active attorney and a public servant, Williams also wrote numerous articles and case studies, including "Negro Subculture, the White Man's Problem," in *New South* (1961); "Race Relations A Community Problem," in *Negro Digest* (1962); "Does a Child Have a Right Not to be Brainwashed by Adults?" in *Peabody Journal of Education* (1973); and "Nashville's Greatest Challenge," in *Nashville* magazine (1975).

Williams was the recipient of numerous awards and citations, some of which are: Outstanding Citizen of the Year, Omega Psi Phi Fraternity, 1963; Outstanding Service in Civil Rights from the Nashville Branch of the NAACP, 1967; Award for Meritorious Service from the General Alumni Association, Johnson C. Smith University, 1967; citation by Capitol Hill Press Corps as "one of the most effective Senators," 1973; Award for Dedicated Religious Service from Saint Andrew's Presbyterian Church, 1976; Recognition Award for Services to Community and to Tennessee State University from Tennessee State University Women's Association, 1976; Legislator of the Year from the Black Caucus of the Tennessee General Assembly, 1978; Martin Luther King Jr. Award from the Interdenominational Ministers Fellowship of Nashville, 1982; Award of Excellence from the Black Caucus of the Tennessee General Assembly, 1984; and a plaque for Legal Work for Civil Rights from the NAACP, 1989.

On May 24, 1990, Williams announced that he would not seek reelection to the state senate. On November 6, 1990, Williams was succeeded by Metro Nashville Councilwoman Thelma Harper, who became the state's first African American woman senator.

On August 29, 1994, after being hospitalized for two weeks at Meharry's Hubbard Hospital, the life of Avon Nyanza Williams Jr. came to an end. He is survived by his wife, Joan B. Williams; son, Avon N. Williams III; daughter, Wendy J. Williams; and mother–in–law, Alberta Bontemps. Quoted in the *Nashville Tennessean* for August 30, 1994, Benjamin Hooks, former executive director of the NAACP, summed up Williams's importance when he said, "He was a truly outstanding person dedicated to the advancement of civil rights . . . he fought to the end." On September 2, 1994, hundreds of lawyers, senators, political leaders, and friends gathered in the Senate Chamber for services in memory of Williams. Later, in a separate service on the same day, William was eulogized at St. Andrews Presbyterian Church and his ashes were interred in Greenwood Cemetery's Taylor Circle.

REFERENCES

Cornwell, Ilene J. *Biographical Directory of the Tennessee General Assembly.* Vol. 5. Nashville: Tennessee Historical Commission, 1990.

———. *Biographical Directory of the Tennessee General Assembly.* Vol. 6. Nashville: Tennessee Historical Commission, 1991.

Doyle, Don H. *Nashville Since the 1920s.* Knoxville: University of Tennessee Press, 1985.

Lovett, Bobby L., and Linda T. Wynn. *Profiles of African Americans in Tennessee.* Nashville: Local Conference on Afro–American Culture and History, 1996.

Nashville Banner, November 3, 1979; December 24, 1984; May 22, 1986; March 19, 1990; August 30, 1994.

Nashville Tennessean, June 16, 1968; November 19, 1984; December 24, 1984; April 17, 1986; May 21, 1986; July 3, 1986; July 16, 1986; July 28, 1986; September 27, 1986; May 25, 1990; December 13, 1991; September 3, 1994.

Tennessee Blue Book, 1969–1970; 1973–1974; 1974–1975; 1985–1986. Nashville: Office of the Secretary of State.

Williams, Avon N. Williams, Jr. Interview with Linda T. Wynn, November and December, 1984.

———. Untitled autobiographical manuscript in the possession of Avon N. Williams III.

COLLECTIONS

The papers and memorabilia of Avon N. Williams Jr. are housed in Special Collections of the Brown–Daniel Library at Tennessee State University. The papers include legal documents from his tenure as state senator. There are also photographs, personal items, and the desk from his Legislative Plaza office.

Linda T. Wynn

Bert Williams
(1873–1922)
Entertainer

Bert Williams was a blackface comedian who established an impressive number of firsts. He was the first black to become a star comedian on Broadway. He starred in 1902 in the first black musical comedy—*In Dahomey*—to open on Broadway. He was the first black featured in a Broadway revue: he first appeared in the *Ziegfeld Follies of 1911* and continued to appear in *Follies* until 1919. Before becoming a solo performer, he won acclaim for his work with George Walker. The pair became stars as an act, and together they were the first black stars to record in 1901. In 1910 he seems to have been the first black star to appear in a motion picture. Williams took the stereotypical comic role imposed upon him by his society and infused it with humanity to become one of the most popular and beloved comedians of his time, and possibly one of the greatest of all time.

Williams explained his aims in an 1916 interview cited by Smith:

> I try to portray the shiftless darky to the fullest extent, his fun, his philosophy. Show this shiftless darky a book and he won't know what it is about. He can't read or write, but ask him a question and he'll answer it with a philosophy that has something in it. I have studied him; his joys and sorrows... He is not me... If I were free to do as I would like, I would give both sides of the shiftless darky, the pathos as well as the fun.

Egbert Austin Williams was born in Nassau, the Bahamas, on November 12, 1874, the son of Frederick and Julia Monceur Williams. He was light–skinned, listed on his birth certificate as ''mixed race.'' All accounts of his family and his early show business career depend heavily on Bert Williams's own testimony and are subject to caution, especially since he was a very private man. We are not even sure if he had siblings. The outlines of his early career are firm, while precise chronology and details vary from source to source.

At the time of Williams's birth his father was a waiter in a tourist hotel. The family moved briefly to New York in 1876 but did not permanently settle in the United States until about 1885, when they moved first to Florida and then to Riverside, California.

Bert Williams said that he graduated from high school in 1893, and had ambitions to attend Stanford University to become an engineer. While the exact extent of his education is not clear, in later years he was an avid reader and built an extensive personal library. What is clear is that he worked in hotels, holding one job as a singing waiter and exploring the possibilities of show business. Among his early jobs was an appearance as a Polynesian entertainer. In 1893 he joined *Martin and Selig's Minstrel Show.* There he was joined by George Walker, with whom he formed an act. The pair based themselves in San Francisco and worked in second–string establishments. By 1895 they were publishing songs, and in that year they headed East, looking for a way to break into big–time show business.

Some time during this move, apparently in Cripple Creek, Colorado, a mob decided that the pair's clothing was too fine for African Americans and forced Williams and Walker to disrobe and put on burlap. The team arrived in Chicago in rags. They were still scrabbling for work and seeking ways to make their act more effective. Williams began to wear blackface makeup–which he had not done since a disastrous minstrel show debut when his blacking ran in streaks due to his nervous perspiration–and emerged as the comedian of the team.

Breaks into Vaudeville

After going to New York where they appeared in a series of short–lived plays as a featured attraction, Williams and Walker found work at Koster and Bial's vaudeville house in November of 1896. In the second week of January they added two women and a performance of the cakewalk to the act and began to build their popularity as vaudeville performers into stardom. One of them, Aida Reed Overton, became George Walker's wife and a star performer in her own right. The act's first appearance abroad was not a success. When it followed the Monte Carlo Ballet in a London music hall performance, it flopped. However, Williams and Walker were American vaudeville stars by the time they met Will Marion Cook in 1898.

Cook produced with Paul Laurence Dunbar, the poet, a show called *Clorindy, or the Origin of the Cakewalk,* which ran during the summer of 1898. Cook and Dunbar wished to use Williams and Walker in the shows, but they were unavailable. The show also featured Lottie Thompson, who became Williams's wife. Cook and Dunbar then collaborated on *Senegambian Carnival* (1898), the first touring show built around the talents of Williams and Walker. This was followed in December by *A Lucky Coon.* Williams and Walker collaborated with Jesse Shipp on their next show, *The Policy Players.* These three plays were modest successes, but Williams and Walker had a big hit in 1900 with the next show, *Sons of Ham,* which ran for two seasons.

Bert Williams (right) with George Walker, 1901.

By November of 1901 Lottie Thompson was using the name Lottie Williams. No record of her divorce from Sam Thompson or of his death or of a wedding between Thompson and Williams has yet been found. Lottie Williams adored her husband; she was very solicitous of him and also domineering. There were no children from the union.

Cook produced the next Williams and Walker show *In Dahomey* (1902), basing his work on a book by James Rosamond Johnson, James Weldon Johnson, and Bob Cole. In February of 1802, the show opened at a Broadway theater, becoming the first full–length show written and performed by blacks to do so. The New York success led to a London booking, during which an abbreviated performance was presented before King Edward VII at a command performance at Buckingham Palace on June 23, 1903, another first for a black show. After the performances in England, the American tour consolidated Williams's star status.

After a quarrel with their current managers and a subsequent lawsuit which revealed that Williams and Walker earned $40,000 for one season, the team began to prepare their next show, Abyssinia, which opened in February of 1806. It featured Williams's song *Nobody,* which became so identified with the comedian that he had to repeat it at every performance he gave for the rest of his life. Relations between Williams and Walker were becoming cool. They had never really been close friends. In the early years they appeared offstage together constantly to build public awareness of their act. With success, differences in temperament meant that the two were together only to work.

With a new manager, the next Walker and Williams vehicle was *Bandanna Land,* which was a big hit in 1908. Lottie Williams gave her last performances in this show in late spring and made an announcement of her retirement from show business for health reasons in December. This was the year that Williams joined a group of leading black performers to found a social and benevolent club, The Frogs.

Becomes Solo Star

It was during the run of *Bandanna Land* that George Walker began to suffer from the symptoms of syphilis. In February of 1809 he had to stop performing. His departure meant that Williams was forced to take charge of the business arrangements which had been handled by Walker. In May of

1809 Williams gave his first solo vaudeville performance in Boston. When the new show, *Mr. Lode of Koal,* opened in 1909, Aida Overton Walker also left. Williams found managing a company a very difficult chore for which he was temperamentally unsuited. In spite of good reviews, the musical closed in early March of 1810 with a loss. Williams went on to perform successfully at major vaudeville theaters despite the attempts of a group of white performers called the White Rats to force the management to deny him star billing. Florenz Ziegfeld had already begun in April to approach him about performing in the *Follies* that winter. Williams signed a three–year contract but won the right to perform for Ziegfeld only after another lawsuit.

Ziegfeld had to face a revolt by some of his white performers but held fast, saying he could replace everybody in the show except Williams, who was unique. In June of 1910 Williams became the first black to perform regularly in a Broadway revue. He got very good reviews although the top new performer was Fanny Brice. He may also have appeared in his first film *The Pullman Porter,* made by black filmmaker William Foster—no print survives and even the date is contested. In September Booker T. Washington published a magazine article in which he praised Williams highly. Williams himself published an article on blacks in the theater in the December 1910 *Green Book Magazine.* George Walker died on January 6, 1911, at the age of 38. Aida Overton Walker died three years later.

Williams was a big hit in the 1911 and 1912 *Follies,* and renewed his contract with Ziegfeld for three more years. Williams cut more records in January of 1813; over the years he had considerable success as a recording star. In May he announced that he would not be in the 1913 *Follies.* It has been suggested that this decision was connected with the death of his sister–in–law in Chicago leaving three daughters who came to live with the Williamses in Harlem. Williams worked that season in vaudeville. In 1914 he did two more short films, and then appeared in the *Follies. Darktown Jubilee,* one of the films, may be the first with an all–black cast. Williams is supposed to have played without blackface and wearing a top hat and fancy suit. This elicited hostile reaction from whites in a mixed audience in Brooklyn, and the film was never widely distributed. The only surviving films featuring Williams are *Fish* and *A Natural Born Gambler,* both from 1916.

Williams had always been a very private and reserved man, and he now appeared to be increasingly unhappy and suffering from bouts of depression. Even though he refused to perform in the South, he faced much discrimination on the *Follies* tours and found good material hard to come by; nonetheless, he appeared in the 1916 and 1917 versions. In the January 1918 *American Magazine* Williams published an autobiographical essay in which he discussed his experiences with segregation and his art. He was at the same time becoming more outspoken about the conditions he faced as a black performer. Smith quoted an interview he gave to the *New York Age* in May of 1818 in which he asked:

> Why is it a colored passenger can sleep over or under a white passenger on a Pullman and no color question is raised, but just as soon as a citizen of color applies at a hotel for a room where he would be separated by wall and doors, objection is made to his presence?

That same year Williams made his most famous statement on race in an article published in the *American Magazine*:

> People sometimes ask me if I would give anything to be white. I answer, in the words of the song, ''No''. . . I have never been able to discover that there was anything disgraceful in being a colored man. But I have often found it inconvenient—in America.

On June 14, 1918, Williams became a naturalized citizen. While not appearing in that year's *Follies,* he did perform in a lesser Ziegfeld show, the *Ziegfeld Midnite Frolic,* and also in vaudeville. In 1919 he returned to the *Follies* for the last time. That summer Equity organized a strike that dimmed the house—typically Williams was never asked to join Equity—and he found out about it only when he arrived dressed and made up for his appearance to find the auditorium empty.

In 1920 Williams appeared in *Broadway Brevities of 1920,* a vehicle designed for him and Eddie Cantor. Cantor had been a Equity strike leader and was out of Ziegfeld's good graces. Williams desired to explore new possibilities. The success of Charles Gilpin in the leading role in *The Emperor Jones* inspired Williams with the desire to undertake a serious part. He tried without success to find backing for a production of a play—it could have been *Taboo* by white Mary Hoyt Wilborg, a play finally produced in April of 1822, shortly after his death.

A new line of theater did not open up for Williams. Following the success of *Shuffle Along* in June of 1821, which reopened the Broadway stage to black musicals, Williams worked hard on a all–black show called *Under the Bamboo Tree.* The show was not an immediate success, losing money about half of the time, and money problems arose between Williams and the producers. In addition, his health was visibly breaking down—he was suffering from heart and circulatory problems which eventually contributed to his death.

Williams had to stop after ten minutes during a performance in Detroit on February 27, 1922. He died of pneumonia in his New York home on March 4, 1922. Public funeral services were held at St. Phillips Episcopal Church—there were three in all, including two Masonic services, held at the Masonic Temple. Williams was buried in New York's Woodlawn cemetery.

Bert Williams was a great comedian. His voice was not good, but he knew how to win an audience in a half–singing, half–speaking presentation. His seemingly awkward dancing was a deliberate contrast to the stylish movements of his partner George Walker. In addition to having a superb timing in his verbal material, Williams was a master of pantomime—

one of his most famous bits involved acting out all the players in a poker game. He was the first black superstar.

REFERENCES

Charters, Ann. *Nobody.* New York: Macmillan, 1970.
Logan, Rayford W., and Michael R. Winston, eds. *Dictionary of American Negro Biography.* New York: Norton, 1982.
Rowland, Mabel, ed. *Bert Williams: Son of Laughter.* New York: The English Crafters, 1923.
Smith, Eric Ledell. *Bert Williams.* Jefferson, NC: MacFarland and Co., 1992.
Watkins, Mel. *On the Real Side.* New York: Simon and Schuster: 1994.

Robert L. Johns

Daniel Hale Williams
(1856–1931)
Physician, educator, hospital founder and administrator

Daniel Hale Williams

Daniel Hale Williams became nationally and internationally known for his pioneering contributions to the field of medicine. In 1893 in Chicago, he performed the first open heart surgery and then went on to complete other history–making operations. He founded the first black–owned hospital, Provident Hospital in Chicago. In the field of medical education, he developed training and internship sites for African American doctors and nurses and became a medical lecturer. In medical organizations, he was an officer in the charter group of the National Medical Association. He also contributed to the medical field by publishing articles.

Williams was born January 18, 1856, to Daniel Williams Jr. and Sarah Price Williams, in Hollidaysburg, Pennsylvania; he was the youngest of five children. His siblings included: Ann Effine, Henry Price, Sarah C., and Ida. His parents were of mixed ancestry. When young Williams was 11–years old, his father died. His mother withdrew him from school and apprenticed him to a Baltimore shoemaker. She left her daughters with relatives, or in school, and moved to Rockford, Illinois. His mother deserted Williams again after he had visited her in Rockford, leaving him to make his own way by working in barbershops, on lake boats, and wherever else he could find employment.

Williams was driven to achieve. He began his education in Hollidaysburg, then studied in Maryland at the Freedmen's Bureau's Stanton School, and later in Janesville, Wisconsin, at Jefferson High School and the Classical Academy. It was in Wisconsin, while working as a barber, that he developed a passion for reading. Williams also played bass fiddle in a musical group operated Harry Anderson, his friend and owner of the barbershop where he worked. After finishing the academy, he read law but he was unimpressed with law as a career. He began working as an apprentice to Henry Palmer, a physician, where he learned the art of medicine from textbooks, and observing Palmer's practice. Palmer accepted two other apprentices and ran an all–night clinic. In 1880, Williams and the two apprentices, Pember and Mills, left Palmer and headed for Chicago Medical School.

Mrs. John Jones, the widow of a friend of Williams's father's friend, befriended him and gave him a place to stay in her home. Williams struggled financially to stay in school. He had to rely heavily on his friend from Wisconsin, Harry Anderson, to send money periodically to meet his school expenses. He passed his first year of study. After a bout with small pox, he had to return to Janesville to recuperate, and passed up a summer job in Springfield, Illinois.

Williams returned to Chicago Medical School. Joseph Laster, who concentrated in anesthesia, enabled the students at the medical school to see for the first time a complete operation with the use of ether.

Williams continued to struggle with finances through his years in medical school and accepted aid wherever he could. At one time he had a job with Mrs. Jones taking care of her horse and buggy in exchange for his board. Anderson, who invested in traveling shows, remained his constant supporter when he could afford to. In time, however, Anderson's funds became scarce as well. In 1883, Williams, Pember, and Mills completed their training together at Chicago Medical School.

Begins Medical Career

Williams established his practice in Chicago at 3034 South Michigan, and, as it grew he began paying back the money owed to Anderson. Denied admission to practice in hospitals because of his race, Williams was forced to perform operations in homes. His practice flourished as Williams became popular. He attended All Souls Unitarian Church and joined the Hamilton Club, a Republican organization.

Williams hoped to establish a hospital where African American nurses could be trained and practice, African American doctors could intern and practice, and African American patients could receive good medical care. Others recognized a need for an interracial hospital where white and African American doctors could administer the sick. At that time no hospital training program in Chicago would accept African Americans. Williams went to various organizations and churches on the west and south sides to sell the idea of such a hospital. As a result of his efforts, in 1891 Provident Hospital and Training School Association opened as the first African American hospital in the United States. Funds were raised through all kinds of efforts such as bake and ice cream sales, and individuals furnished the hospital with items from their homes.

Williams became known affectionately as "Dr. Dan" for his concern and desire to improve the health of people. When Frederick Douglass, Williams's mother's cousin, was in Chicago as Haitian Commissioner to the World's Fair in 1893, he spoke at the South Side's Bethel Church, escorted by Fannie Barrier Williams and Ida Wells Barnett, during a drive to support Provident Hospital. Douglass contributed his lecture proceeds to the struggling hospital.

In July of 1893 at Provident Hospital, Williams performed the first successful open heart surgery. James Cornish was stabbed in the chest during a fight, and Williams stopped the bleeding. However, Cornish became ill during the evening, and Williams had to operate on his chest, closing the blood vessel and pericardium tissue near the heart. Cornish lived for more than 20 years after the surgery. The story of the successful operation was published in the *Chicago Daily Inter–Ocean* for July 22, 1893, and Williams achieved an international reputation. He performed other successful heart operations; one patient who was wounded in the early 1900s survived for 50 years after the operation.

In February of 1894, President Grover Cleveland appointed Williams chief surgeon at Freedmen's Hospital in Washington, DC, replacing Charles B. Purvis, son of abolitionist Robert Purvis. Williams welcomed the challenge. After taking the oath of office, he returned to Chicago to wind up his affairs. While on a weekend quail shooting excursion in Illinois, he was accidentally shot in the right foot. The injury delayed his move to Washington until mid–May. After a relapse and suffering from infection, Williams returned to Chicago for a slow healing process in the Emergency Hospital on the North Side. It was mid–September before he was able to return to Freedmen's. During his illness, however, his adversary, George Cleveland Hall, whose earlier appointment to the staff of Provident Hospital Williams protested, seized the opportunity of Williams's illness to attack him. He wrote a letter to the *Colored American* in Washington, DC, claiming that Williams would never join the Freedmen's Hospital because of his illness. The *Washington Star* took up the false claim as well. In effect, noted African American physicians, Purvis and Furman L. Shadd, did not welcome Williams's appointment.

Williams concentrated on his new assignment. To improve the delivery of health services at Freedmen's, then located near 6th and Bryant Streets beyond the District of Columbia's boundary, Williams organized the 200–bed hospital into departments: medical, surgical, gynecological, obstetrical, dermatological, genitourinary, and throat and chest. Internships and ambulance services were provided, and the nurses' training program was enhanced. He welcomed black and white doctors. A rigorous taskmaster, he insisted that all of the health care professionals function in an orderly and proper manner. He maintained, for example, that a person's limbs should be saved whenever possible. Helen Buckler quoted him in *Daniel Hale Williams* as saying, "we must have continuity of the parts." He used this phrase so often that his students began calling him "Mr. Continuity–of–the–Parts." In spite of the success of the program, Williams resigned from Freedmen's on February 5, 1898, citing his disgust with the politics of running the institution. Freedmen's was owned by the federal government, and many of the hospital's federally–mandated operations and procedures proved to be more than Williams could tolerate. Controversy surrounded him during his administration of Freedmen's; after he left, he was accused of malfeasance but later vindicated.

Williams returned to Provident Hospital and became active again in Chicago and other communities. He returned to his old office and remained on Provident's board of trustees. Earlier in 1896 a new Provident Hospital facility had been erected, and although Williams was again its chief surgeon, there was friction between him and colleagues. George Cleveland Hall had also joined Provident's board in Williams's absence.

In June of 1898, Williams was selected to examine recruits for the 8th Illinois Regiment, formerly known as the 9th Battalion. It was the first black regiment with a full staff of black officers and now expanded for service in the Spanish–American War. He also provided free medical service to the Old Folks Home, newly founded, on West Garfield Avenue.

After successful tenures at Provident and Freedmen's hospitals, Williams assisted in the founding of 40 other hospitals. He stressed the need for hospitals and training programs for blacks, urging blacks to protest the deplorable conditions of black health care and training, and to provide institutions and programs for themselves.

Becomes Charter Member of Medical Associations

Williams was a leader in the advancements of African Americans in the medical profession. He determined that African Americans in the health fields should lead the way in improving health conditions for African American citizens. In 1895 in Atlanta, Williams became co–founder of the National Medical Association, an organization of African American physicians. He served as vice–president after declining the position as president. At the association's national meetings, he demonstrated surgical procedures. Also in 1895, he formed in Chicago the Medico–Chirurgical Society, an interracial group of doctors. The American College of Surgeons was formed in 1913, and Williams became the only black charter member of that society.

Through his writings, Williams shared his professional knowledge with the medical community. These included: "Several Cases of Inflammation starting in the Caecum and Vermiform Appendix" (*American Journal of Obstetrics*); "Stab Wound of the Heart and Pericardium, Suture of the Pericardium. Recovery. Patient Alive Three Years Afterward" (*New York Medical Record*); and the "Need of Hospitals and Training Schools for Colored People in the South" (*National Hospital Record*).

Williams shared his knowledge with medical schools and hospitals, serving as clinical professor and member of the visiting staff. He was involved in the training of medical students and practicing physicians at Municipal Hospital in St. Louis, Meharry Medical College in Nashville (without compensation), and St. Luke's Hospital in Chicago, where he was associate attending surgeon. Williams served the Protestant Orphan Asylum, South Side Dispensary, and, in 1889, was appointed to the Illinois State Board of Health. He delivered papers at medical conferences, among them the Gynecological Society, and the Chicago Medical Society. Despite his devotion to the health care of blacks, some blacks called him disloyal to the race and accused him of preferring the company of white and fair–skinned blacks.

A handsome, fair–skinned, red–haired man, Williams married Alice D. Johnson of Washington, DC, in 1898. Their only child died in childbirth in 1899, which caused both parents tremendous grief. Alice, a victim of Parkinson's disease, spent most of her four years with her husband in their home in Idlewild, Michigan. She was confined to a wheelchair and died in 1924.

Before his death, Williams sent his medical books to Henry Minton, as the beginning of a library at Mercy Hospital. He also provided cash sums to medical schools at Howard and Meharry. The largest gift went to the NAACP. He had a series of strokes over several years that left him an invalid and mentally impaired. Williams died on August 4, 1931, in his Idlewild home. Funeral services were held in St. Anselm's Roman Catholic Church. He was buried in a corner of Chicago's Graceland Cemetery, separated from his wife, and without a grave marker.

Williams made a strong impact on the advancement of medicine, as well as on the improvement of health care and training for African Americans. His contributions to modern day surgery are a part of medical history. Through the establishment of a hospital primarily for African Americans, devoted to the sick and training of nurses and interns, he provided a model for other African American health care professionals.

REFERENCES

Buckler, Helen. *Daniel Hale Williams, Negro Surgeon.* New York: Pitman Publishing Co., 1954.

Hine, Darlene Clark. *Speak Against the Truth.* New York: Carlson Publishers, 1995.

Logan, Rayford W., and Michael R. Winston, eds. *Dictionary of American Negro Biography.* New York: Norton, 1982.

Who's Who in Colored America. Vol. 1. New York: Who's Who in America Corp., 1927.

COLLECTIONS

The papers of Daniel Hale Williams are in the Moorland–Spingarn Research Center, Howard University, Washington, DC, and the National Archives.

Barbara Williams Jenkins and Jessie Carney Smith

Edward Christopher Williams

(1871–1929)

Librarian, educator, writer

In the annals of American librarianship, Edward Christopher Williams—librarian, teacher, and writer—is considered the first professionally trained black librarian. Were it not for his untimely death he would have received the first Ph.D. degree in librarianship.

Williams was born February 11, 1871, in Cleveland, Ohio. He was the only son of Daniel P. Williams, a distinguished African American, and Mary Kilkary Williams of Irish descent. Williams attended Cleveland public schools, and in 1892 received his B.A. degree from Adelbert College, the male undergraduate division of Western Reserve University, Cleveland. He was elected to Phi Beta Kappa honorary scholastic fraternity in his junior year and was valedictorian of his graduation class.

Williams began his library career in 1892 as first assistant librarian of Adelbert College, and he was the librarian of the Hatch Library of Western Reserve from 1894 to 1898. In 1898 Williams was appointed the university librarian of the college; he held this position for one year. Williams stayed at the university until 1900.

The university was in the midst of organizing a library school, and during its development, Williams taught a course in national bibliography to a few seniors. He came to be known as an intelligent and stimulating teacher who offered instruction in bibliography and reference work. The new library school opened in 1904 and Williams joined the new library school faculty teaching courses in Public Documents, and The Criticism and Selection of Books. On leave–of–absence in the 1899–1900 school year, he studied at the New York State Library School in Albany, completing nearly all of the two–year master's degree program in one year.

Williams returned to teaching at Western Reserve. His scholarship in history, literature, and language drew the respect of his students who spoke admiringly of him as a superior teacher. He spent a great deal of his time in collection–building at Western Reserve and fixed the foundation for the present excellence of the library resources.

Williams was a founding charter member of the Ohio Library Association and served as secretary of the association in 1904 and chairman of its college section. Each year he lectured at the Ohio Institute of Library Workers which were held during the Ohio Library Association's annual meetings. He chaired the constitutional committee of the OLA. He was also an active member of the American Library Association, and in May of 1928 he addressed a session of ALA's College and Reference section about "Library Needs of Negro Institutions."

After 15 years at Western Reserve, Williams left for Washington, D.C., to become principal of the M Street School (later renamed Dunbar High School), where he remained until June of 1916. The school had a reputation for educating an extremely large number of gifted students who went on to achieve greater eminence after pursuing work at elite colleges. More than any principal in the school's record, Williams fostered an environment for rich and varied scholarship.

Williams assumed the positions of professor of bibliography, director of the library training class, and librarian of Howard University in 1916. In the next several years he developed library training courses, extended library resources, and enlarged the library staff.

In 1921 Williams was selected as the head of the Romance Languages Department and taught courses in Italian, French, and German. He served on many campus committees and supported activities in dramatics. He was associate faculty editor of the *Howard University Record* to which he contributed articles. He also addressed civic, literary, and professional groups in the community. He served on the staff of the 135th Street Branch of the New York Public Library during his summer vacations, where he devoted three summers to organizing the Arthur A. Schomburg collection of Negroana for the New York Public Library.

Williams was an accomplished and gifted writer as well; had he lived, some sources speculate that he might have become a creative writer of note. The Howard University Players performed his classical dramas. Williams authored *The Exile,* an Italian classical two–act drama, and two other dramas: *The Sherriff's Children,* an adaptation of his father–in–law's short story, and *The Chasm,* in collaboration with the noted dramatist Willis Richardson. His series on Washington black society's foibles, "Letters of Davy Carr: A True Story of Colored Vanity Fair," was published as a series from January of 1925 to June of 1926 in the *Messenger* magazine. Williams also published poems and short stories anonymously and, according to Dorothy B. Porter in *Phylon,* he probably used the pseudonym of Bertuccio Dantino.

Through a Rosenwald Fellowship in the 1929–30 school year, Williams studied for a Ph.D. degree at Columbia University's School of Library Service. While on leave from Howard University in December of 1929, Williams became ill in New York City and died on December 24 in Freedmen's Hospital, Washington, D.C. He was survived by his wife Ethel Chesnutt Williams, a daughter of the well–known writer Charles Waddell Chesnutt; a son Charles; and a granddaughter Patricia Ann Williams. The funeral rites were held on December 27 in the Andrew Rankin Memorial Chapel on the Howard University campus. Mordecai Wyatt Johnson, president of Howard conducted the services. He was buried in Lincoln Cemetery, Suitland, Maryland.

The April 1930 issue of *Crisis,* the official organ of the NAACP, summarized the work of the noted scholar: "Edward Williams was more than a scientific librarian. . . . He died a comparatively young man in a career but half–finished, and left the memory of a scientist, a writer, and a loyal and genial friend."

REFERENCES

Josey, E. J. "Edward Christopher Williams, Librarian's Librarian." *Journal of Library History* 4 (April 1969): 106–122.

———, and Ann A. Shockley, eds. *Handbook of Black Librarianship.* Littleton, CO: Libraries Unlimited, 1977.

Logan, Rayford W. and Michael R. Winston, eds. *Dictionary of American Negro Biography.* New York: Norton, 1982.

Porter, Dorothy B. "Phylon Profile XIV: Edward Christopher Williams." *Phylon* 8 (Fourth Quarter, 1947): 315–21.

"Williams." *Crisis* 37 (April 1930): 138.

Casper L. Jordan

George Washington Williams (1849–1891)

Historian, minister, journalist

In a short life, George Washington Williams, a gifted but restless man, displayed a multitude of talents. He was a soldier during and after the Civil War. Twice he pastored leading Baptist churches. He was the first African American to write a column for a white newspaper and twice tried to establish his own paper. He was a lawyer as well. Williams was an indefatigable political worker and an outstanding orator who was the first African American elected to the Ohio legislature. He was principally remembered as the writer of the first coherent and documented history of African American history.

Williams was born on October 16, 1849, in Bedford, Pennsylvania, to Thomas Williams and Ellen Rouse Williams. He was their second child and first son. His sister, Margaret, was born in 1846, his brother, John, in 1852, his brother, Thomas, in 1855, and his brother, Harry, in 1860. Williams's father came from Virginia. He was of mixed parentage and was reputed to be the son of a well–off planter. His father worked as a day laborer. Williams's mother may have been a sister of Bedford's only African American barber. She, too, was of mixed parentage. The most reliable description of their son as an adult said he was five–feet seven–inches tall with blue eyes, dark hair, and a light complexion.

By the time young Williams was a year old, his father had moved his family to Johnstown, Pennsylvania, where he became a boatman and fell into trouble. His mother took the children to Newcastle, Pennsylvania, to live with her mother. Williams's father reformed his ways and moved to Newcastle, where he became a barber and minister.

The children received little education. Williams became a wayward teenager and was placed in a house of refuge, where he began to acquire an interest in religion which dwindled after his release. In the summer of 1864, he went to another town, changed his name, lied about his age, and joined the army. Williams saw active duty during the final stages of the fighting in Virginia, including the capture of Petersburg on April 2, 1865. His unit was then transferred to Texas.

Williams either deserted or was mustered out and he crossed the Rio Grande to join the Mexican republican army fighting the troops supporting Emperor Maximilian. He returned home to Pennsylvania in the spring of 1867. On August 29, 1867, he enlisted in an African American cavalry unit of the regular army and was sent first to Fort Riley, Kansas, and then to Fort Arbuckle, in what was then known as Indian Territory. On the morning of May 19, 1868, Williams was shot through the lung in an incident which was not in the line of duty nor was it considered to have involved misconduct on his part. He was discharged from the army on September 4, 1868.

The 18–year–old Williams had now sobered up considerably. In St. Louis he joined a Baptist church. In 1869 he was licensed to preach by a church in Hannibal, Missouri. He was living in Quincy, Illinois, when he wrote a long autobiographical letter to O. O. Howard seeking admission to the newly founded Howard University. (This letter, now in the Moorland–Spingarn Research Center at Howard University, was the primary source of information on his early life.) Williams's admission to Howard was approved but he did not study at there, choosing instead to attend the Baptist–related

George Washington Williams

Wayland Seminary, in Washington, D.C. On September 9, 1870, he was admitted to the Newton Theological Institution, a Baptist seminary near Boston.

Since Williams's academic preparation was severely limited, his authoritative biographer, John Hope Franklin, called him semi–literate at best. Williams was placed in the two–year general English course, which he successfully completed. In 1872 Williams entered the three–year theological program, which he completed in only two years and graduated on June 10, 1874. He became an ordained minister the next day. His four years of study had transformed him into an educated man who wrote and carried himself well. By the time of his graduation, he had married and found a pulpit.

During his time at the Newton seminary, Williams made contact with the Boston African American community. He also traveled widely. It seems likely that he met Sarah A. Sterrett of Chicago, a seamstress and hairdresser, in a visit to that city in 1873. They were married in Chicago on June 2, 1874. They had one child, George, who was born in 1875. Although the marriage began well, husband and wife were later estranged, and they did not live together after 1884. Williams had acquired a reputation of being a negligent father and husband by the time he unsuccessfully sought a divorce in the summer of 1886.

Holds Boston Pulpit

In Boston, Leonard Grimes, pastor of the Twelfth Baptist Church, had died suddenly in March of 1873. In August of that year, Williams was named acting pastor, a position which became permanent the following year. He was installed on June 28. He spent the summer producing *History of the Twelfth Baptist Church,* his first historical work. Part of the spur to produce the book was the hope to secure funds for a sorely needed expansion of the church building. Williams was making a success of his pastorate and seemed destined to lead the church for an number of years. During the summer of 1875, however, it became known that he was leaving Boston to establish a newspaper in Washington, D.C.

There was a great need for a national African American newspaper. The successor to the *National Era,* which was founded in January of 1870 by John Sella Martin with the support of Frederick Douglass, had expired in September of 1874. Throughout the summer and fall of 1875, Williams traveled and sought support for his venture. A swing through Louisiana and Mississippi made him acutely aware of the perilous state of African American citizens, as force was bringing a violent end to Reconstruction. William's *Commoner* began publication on September 4, 1875, and reached eight issues before it ended on December 18. Williams then worked for two months at the Post Office before he was called to the Union Baptist Church in Cincinnati on February 10, 1876.

Union Baptist was the oldest and most prestigious African American Baptist church in Cincinnati. Things began well. On October 23, 1876, the *Cincinnati Daily Express* did a feature article on him, for which Williams must have supplied biographical information. He took the occasion to improve his impressive achievements by claiming, for example, that he was a war correspondent—while an officer in the army—and a graduate of Harvard University. From December 3, 1876, to November 24, 1878, Williams wrote a column for the *Cincinnati Commercial Appeal* under the name Aristides, making him the first African American columnist on a white paper. He also became very active in politics.

In 1876 Williams supported the election of Hayes to the presidency and was adamant about seeking office after the election. Since the Republicans in the 1877 state elections faced almost sure defeat, the party was willing to nominate him for a seat in the legislature. He lost, although he campaigned vigorously for the whole Republican ticket. On December 1, 1877, he resigned his pastorate, apparently with no recriminations from the church. Williams began to study law in the offices of prominent lawyer and politician Alphonso Taft. He also tried his hand at editing another newspaper, although none of the 18 issues of the *Southwestern Review* survive. He became secretary to the Cincinnati Southern Railway, a local project, and, in September of 1878, found work in the Revenue Service. After considerable maneuvering, Williams was again nominated for the legislature, in the elections of 1879. This time he won.

When he took office on January 5, 1880, he became the first African American to sit in the Ohio legislature. In Columbus he was an active and energetic representative. He also served as secretary to Cincinnati millionaire Charles Fleischman, a fellow representative. Fleischman lived in the Cincinnati suburb of Avondale, which housed an African American cemetery. Williams imprudently championed a bill which would have the effect of eventually closing the cemetery as a nuisance. The uproar in the African American community effectively ended his legislative career. In the meantime, Williams had become active in veteran's affairs. He served as judge's advocate with the rank of colonel in the Ohio Grand Army of the Republic from 1881 until 1882.

Writes Black History

Williams's service in the legislature gave him the chance to seriously work on his major historical epic, *History of the Negro Race from 1619 to 1880* (volume I, December 1882; volume II, spring of 1883). Williams did much research for this first professional history of African Americans. Two years was too short a period for him to fully assimilate the materials he had collected. Still, this pioneering work won many favorable reviews. Williams produced another extensive historical work, *History of the Negro Troops in the War of the Rebellion,* which appeared in 1887, the same time that Joseph T. Wilson covered the same subject in *The Black Phalanx.* A projected history of Reconstruction was announced but never appeared.

While Williams's histories sold well, they did not bring him great sums of money. They did lend support a sideline occupation, however. Williams was able to earn some money in the following years as a lecturer. From 1888 to 1889, he was client of a professional lecture bureau. His one attempt at fiction, *The Autocracy of Love,* remained incomplete after the *Indianapolis World* published eight installments from January to June of 1888.

In 1883 Williams moved back to Boston, where he became a member of the Massachusetts Bar. Williams told the Massachusetts Supreme Judicial Court that he had passed the Ohio Bar in 1879 although he passed it only in June 1881 after two failures. He became counsel to the Cape Cod Canal Company.

In the summer of 1884, Williams traveled in Europe using a letter of introduction from the State Department procured for him by Blanche K. Bruce. Complaints reached the State Department about Williams borrowing and not repaying money. Despite the documents in his file, outgoing president Chester A. Arthur appointed him United States Minister to Haiti on March 2, 1885, shortly before leaving office. The Senate confirmed the appointment the same evening. The new Democratic administration, which had taken over the State Department just two hours after Williams's commission was issued, refused to give Williams permission to take up the post. Eventually, on January 3, 1888, he lost his suit for any salary connected with the post.

On May 17, 1887, the State University of Louisville, Kentucky, an African American Baptist school headed by William J. Simmons, conferred an honorary doctor of laws degree on Williams. Williams traveled to Europe in 1888 to attend the Centenary Conference of Protestant Missions held in London and to do research. By this time his life was in considerable disarray and he suffered from bouts of illness. As he unsuccessfully sought the diplomatic appointment to Haiti again in 1889—when Benjamin Harrison was inaugurated president—he was the subject of attacks in the African American press and few African Americans rallied to his defense. Even T. Thomas Fortune, editor of the *New York Age* and a long–time supporter, broke with him. From September 28 to December 9, 1889, he was again in Europe where he attended an antislavery conference in Brussels and earned some money by writing articles for William McClure, head of the Associated Literary Press, which syndicated material to the press.

By this time, he was planning a trip to Africa with the primary aim of investigating Belgian King Leopold's activities in the Congo territories, which were personally under royal control. He interviewed Leopold in November. His African trip was subsidized by railroad magnate Collis P. Huntington.

On January 30, 1890, after returning briefly to the United States, Williams set sail from Liverpool for the Congo. Soon after his arrival, he evaluated the situation in a very unfavorable light. In spite of his precarious finances and health, he undertook extensive travel in the interior of the territory. On July 18 at Stanley Falls, the farthest point he reached, Williams wrote *Open Letter . . . to Leopold, King of the Belgians,* a courageous and vigorous denunciation of Leopold's colonial policy which aroused a vigorous debate once it became public. Following his stay in the Congo, Williams toured Angola and other parts of Africa for the remainder of the year. He reached Cairo in January of 1891. He was seriously ill, in Cairo, but recovered enough to return, to England, where he planned to write extensively, on his African experiences.

During his return to England in May of 1891, he met Alice Fryer, who was returning from India. By the time they reached England, they were engaged to be married. His health was rapidly declining. Fryer accompanied him to Blackpool, where he died on August 2, 1891, at the age of 41, from a combination of tuberculosis and pleurisy. He was buried in Blackpool's Layton Cemetery. His grave was marked by a stone placed by Franklin, his biographer. The stone was inscribed "George Washington Williams, Afro–American Historian, 1849–1891."

Williams was well–nigh forgotten after his death, and his life was largely unknown until the research of Franklin. For those who knew of him, he has, for the most part, remained the author of *The History of the Negro Race.* He was a man of considerable interest and did much in his short, restless life.

REFERENCES

Franklin, John Hope. *George Washington Williams.* Chicago: University of Chicago Press, 1985.

Robert L. Johns

John A. Williams
(1925–)
Author, educator, journalist

John A. Williams said in *Interviews with Black Writers,* "[W]hat I try to do with novels is to deal in forms that are not standard, to improvise as jazz musicians do with their music, so that a standard theme comes out looking brand new. This is all I try to do with a novel, and, like those musicians, I am trying to do things with form that are not always immediately perceptible to most people." Using these word improvisations, he produced over 20 books. These combined politics, history, biography, and commentary in various ways. In his writing, as he reminded us in *Interviews,* "[T]he individual black must not only struggle with his own past but [also] with his race's." Williams was described as one of the most underrated writers of his day. He was not daunted by public opinion, but driven by his artistic genius. Thus, his works at times are the subject of controversy. H. Bruce Franklin, professor at Rutgers University, reminded us in *Jet* that, "[B]ecause John A. Williams is such an original, prolific and increasingly innovative writer, the literary world has yet to find a category into which he can be neatly fitted."

John Alfred Williams was born December 5, 1925, on his grandfather's farm near Jackson, Mississippi, where his parents had travelled for his birth. His parents—John Henry, a laborer, and Ora Mae, a domestic—soon returned to Syracuse, New York, where Williams was reared and attended school.

Williams was one of four children growing up in a household rife with tension because of economic problems and friction between parents. This ultimately led to divorce. In an attempt to help the family, Williams went to work, eventually quit high school, and joined the Navy in 1943. After his stint of duty, he returned to Syracuse and graduated from Central High School.

Following graduation, Williams enrolled briefly in Morris Brown College in Atlanta, Georgia, before matriculating at Syracuse University. In 1947, during his college years, he married Carolyn Clopton; they later divorced. There were two children born to this marriage: Gregory D. and Dennis A. Williams received his A.B. degree in English and Journalism in 1950 and completed a year of graduate study at Syracuse. In 1965, he married Lorrain Isaac; they have one son, Adam J.

Following school, Williams embarked on a variety of jobs, because he could not find employment in journalism. Jobs held by Williams included one in the county welfare department and one in public relations as an officer for Doug Johnson and Associates. In 1953 he moved to California for a brief period, where he worked in Hollywood as a staff member for radio and television programs at the Consolidated Broadcasting Company (CBS). He returned to New York in 1955 and became the publicity director for Comet Press, an experience which he fictionalized as Rocket Press in *The*

Angry Ones, his first novel. Following the Comet Press experience, he became the editor and publisher of the *Negro Market Newsletter,* the contributor of articles to many newspapers, and later an assistant to the publisher at Abelard–Schuman. He spent a year in Europe as a correspondent for *Ebony* and *Jet* magazines. In 1959 Williams worked for WOV Radio in New York City and he later wrote and produced programs for WNET television.

In the 1960s Williams traveled throughout Europe and Africa contributing work to a number of magazines, including *Holiday* and *Newsweek*; in 1964–65 he was African correspondent for *Newsweek. Holiday* magazine commissioned him in 1963 to take an automobile trip across the United States and gauge the country's racial attitudes. In addition, he has lectured or taught at the City College of the City University of New York; College of the Virgin Islands; University of California, Santa Barbara; LaGuardia Community College in New York; the University of Hawaii; Boston University; and Rutgers University in New Jersey, where he was Paul Robeson Professor of English in 1996. In 1968 he was interviewer for *Newsfront* on National Educational Television.

A Writer of Fiction

In 1960, at the age of 35, Williams began his publishing career with *The Angry Ones,* later republished under its original title, *One for New York.* It presented many of the themes that continued to develop in his writing: relationship, structure, and transcendence of history; guilt; black and Jewish relationships; and the military. Additionally, there is the use of biography, personal experiences, and impending death as a part of his narrative device. According to James L. de Jongh, "Williams's . . . novels [prior to 1985] are grouped in three phases: an initial cautious optimism about the black struggle is followed by a darker vision of racial apocalypse and by a subsequent consciousness of an emerging black unity." This first phase included *The Angry Ones* which presented an artist working at a publishing house. The artist sees his work place as like the larger society which attempts to eradicate his creativity and his humanity.

The second book, *Night Song* (1961), was reputed to include elements of Charlie Parker's life with its emphasis on jazz and the dying musician, Richie Stokes. In 1962 this novel won for Williams the Prix de Rome—a cash award and a year's residency in the American Academy in Rome, from the American Academy of Arts and Letters. However, after an interview with the director of the academy in Rome, the award was rescinded. Following this there was a great deal of discussion, and Williams was offered a $2,000 consolation prize, which he refused. Williams attributed the Academy's actions to the fact that he was to marry a white woman and to rumors regarding his personal life and character: that events in *Night Song* were reflected in his life. The third book in this first phase, *Sissie* (1965), published in England as *Journey Out of Anger,* was praised for its use of folk elements. It presented the black family and explored the relationship between mother (Sissie) and children.

The second phase of Williams's career, the manipulation of the black man by white society, began with *The Man Who Cried I Am* (1967), which is the story of Max Reddick, an African American journalist living abroad who is dying of colon cancer and reflecting on his career and his rivalry with Harry Ames, an older writer. Reddick discovers a conspiracy drawn up by the government to eradicate African Americans, the King Alfred Plan. The main characters were loosely modeled on Richard Wright and Chester Himes; many other characters in the work were based on real–life personages. This work brought him international recognition. The conspiracy in his next book, *Sons of Darkness, Sons of Light: A Novel of Some Probability* (1969), was set in 1973 and illustrated the despair about the race situation; it tells what happened when an Irish American policeman killed a black teenager.

The third novel in the group is *Captain Blackman* (1972). Through flashbacks, Captain Abraham Blackman, a soldier wounded in Vietnam, experiences moments in Black military history and shows what an integral force black soldiers have been. The historical point is that black men fought and died in every war in which America was involved. Overall, these three books show ways in which the black man was used, abused, and eliminated.

The third group of three novels is seen by James L. de Jongh in *Afro–American Fiction Writers After 1955* as "distinguished by a consciousness of growing black unity and emerging group values which offer a foundation for future progress." *Mothersill and the Foxes* (1975) focused on Odell Mothersill who reviews the road travelled to his successful life and his relationship with women; in so doing, he comes to see the relationship between love and sex. Following this came *The Junior Bachelor Society* (1976) which presented a picture of the black middle class, when nine boyhood friends come together to celebrate the 70th birthday of their high school coach and to catch up on what they have been doing. With the exception of one, all are fairly successful when they reunite. The novel was well received and was made into a television miniseries, *The Sophisticated Gents,* in 1981. *Click Song* (1982) completed the phase and was called his very best by Williams, himself. It takes place immediately after World War II. According to *Current Biography,* the hero, a black man named Cato Douglass, "is hampered in his effort to build a literary reputation by racism on the part of the publishers."

Two other novels written by Williams are *The Berhanma Account* (1985), called by Williams a pop novel, and *Jacob's Ladder* (1987). *Jacob's Ladder* portrayed a Third World country trying to wrest itself from Western domination and the tensions (West versus Africa) faced by an African American military officer sent to its aid.

Writes Nonfiction

Williams also produced several works of nonfiction. Among them are *Africa: Her History, Lands and People* (1963) which pointed out the ancient heritage of black people; *The Protectors: The Heroic Story of the Narcotics, Agents, Citizens and Officials in Their Unending, Unsung Battles*

Against Organized Crime in America and Abroad (1964) by J. Angelinger, former U.S. Commissioner of Narcotics, with J. Dennis Gregory (a pseudonym constructed by Williams using the initial of his first name and the first names of his two oldest sons); *This is My Country Too* (1965), which contains material garnered from his trek across America commissioned by *Holiday* magazine, and *Minorities in the City* (1975). The latter two books presented his views on the black experience in America. Additionally, he wrote several portraits of famous men: *The Most Native of Sons* (1970), a biography of Richard Wright; *The King God Didn't Save* (1970), a highly controversial depiction of Martin Luther King Jr., which condemned him for not seeing the way in which black leaders were manipulated by white power; and *If I Stop I'll Die: The Comedy and Tragedy of Richard Pryor* (1991), in which Williams and his son, Dennis, a former *Newsweek* editor, collaborated on a depiction of the life and career of this highly regarded comedian.

Williams edited the following publications: *The Angry Black* (1962), an anthology later titled and reissued as *Beyond the Angry Black* (1966); with Charles Harris, *Amistad I* (1970) and *Amistad II* (1971); *Yardbird No.1*; and *The McGraw–Hill Introduction to Literature.* He wrote material for National Educational Television—*The History of the Negro People: Omwale—The Child Returns Home* (1965) which was filmed in Nigeria and *The Creative Person: Henry Roth* (1966), filmed in Spain. In 1967 he wrote a screenplay entitled *Sweet Love, Bitter.* The play *Last Flight from Ambo Ber* was first produced in Boston in 1981 and published in 1984. He has contributed numerous stories and articles to magazines and newspapers such as *Negro Digest, Yardbird,* and *New York.* In 1973, his *Flashbacks: A Twenty Year Diary of Article Writing* was published.

Williams's awards include those granted by the National Endowment for the Arts, Before Columbus Foundation, Rutgers University, Syracuse University, New Jersey State Council on the Arts, and the National Institute of Arts and Letters. He was granted honors and awards from universities and organizations including an LL.D. from Southeastern Massachusetts University.

Williams's work continues to explore what it means to be black in America, conspiracy theories, relationships, and the vital contributions of African Americans to America. His work represents both fiction and nonfiction, conventional and diverse in style, and has represented an awareness and knowledge of African American history.

Current address: 693 Forest Avenue, Teaneck, NJ 07666.

REFERENCES

Black Writers. Detroit: Gale Research, 1989.

Cash, Earl. *John A. Williams: The Evolution of a Black Writer.* New York: Third World Press, 1974.

Current Biography Yearbook. New York: H. W. Wilson, 1994.

de Jongh, James L. "John A. Williams." In *Afro–American Fiction Writers After 1955.* Edited by Trudier Harris and Thadious M. Davis. Detroit: Gale Research, 1984.

"John A. Williams Named Paul Robeson Professor at Rutgers University." *Jet* 78 (16 April 1990): 38.

O'Brien, John, ed. *Interviews with Black Writers.* New York: Liveright, 1973.

COLLECTIONS

The John Williams archives are located at the University of Rochester in New York.

Helen R. Houston

Paul R. Williams

(1894–1980)

Architect, entrepreneur

One of the country's first black architects and a leading architect in the West, for six decades Paul R. Williams designed and co–designed more than 3,000 private residences, ranging from modest to lavish, and a variety of commercial and public buildings. Although most of his work was done in California, he designed projects elsewhere in the United States and its possessions, and in Colombia, France, and other foreign countries. His impressive array of "firsts" also included becoming the first black member of the American Institute of Architects (Southern California Chapter), and first black Fellow of the American Institute of Architects (AIA).

Paul Revere Williams was born in Los Angeles on February 18, 1894, the son of Chester Stanley Williams (1863–1896) and Lila Wright Williams (1864–1898). The family had moved from Memphis, Tennessee, to Los Angeles in the early 1890s. To provide for his family, Chester Williams established a small fruit business in the old town plaza. Orphaned by the age of four, Paul Williams and his older brother, Chester Jr., were brought up in separate homes; Paul was raised by the Clarkson family and later the Burnetts. At an early age he began to spend long hours drawing everything in sight and whatever came to mind. A local builder saw Williams's drawings and encouraged him to become an architect. Williams entered Polytechnic High School in Los Angeles; while there he determined that he would become an architect. He graduated in 1912.

Although he grew up in a racially mixed neighborhood, Williams was introduced to racial prejudice while he was in high school, when he was refused a job because of his race. Commenting on the experience in *Current Biography* for 1941, he said: "I passed through successive stages of bewilderment, inarticulate resentment and, finally, reconciliation to the status of my race. Eventually . . . as I grew older and thought more clearly, I found in my condition an incentive to personal accomplishment, an inspiring challenge. Without

Paul R. Williams

having the wish to 'show them,' I developed a fierce desire to 'show myself.''' One of his instructors added fuel to the racial fire by asking Williams, ''Who ever heard of a Negro architect[?]'' He determined that he would not be defeated in his goals and that he owed it to himself and his race to accept the challenge he set for himself.

To improve his drawing skills, Williams attended the Los Angeles School of Art and from about 1913 through 1916 took evening classes at the Los Angeles component of the Beaux Arts Institute of Design, where he won the Beaux Arts Medal. Williams paid his way through school by assisting a number of local architects.

After graduating from the Beaux Arts Institute, Williams identified all of the architects in the city, and visited each of them until he found one who would hire a black draftsman. At some time between 1913 and 1914 he found work in an unidentified architectural office but he never discussed his experience there in his writings. Between 1914 and 1916 he worked with the planner and landscape architect Wilbur D. Cook, whose firm was successful in planning private estates, public parks, and new cities. About this time Williams enrolled in the engineering school at the University of Southern California—one of eight students in the program—where he remained until about 1919, although he never graduated. Since his experience with Cook came in planning and landscape architecture, he submitted drawings to a Pasadena city planning competition, Four Corners, and won the first prize of $200. In 1915 he also won first honorable mention in architecture at the Chicago Emancipation Celebration. From about 1916 to 1919 he worked with Reginald D. Johnson, an important local residential architect who specialized in the design of fine homes. By this time he also had designed some fraternity and sorority houses at the University of Southern California. While working with Johnson, Williams entered the 1919 Hollow Tile House Competition sponsored by a local brick company and won first prize, with a design for a one–story $5,000 house. In 1919 Williams joined the larger commercially–oriented firm of John C. Austin, where he remained until 1921, gaining experience on such large–scale projects as the Shrine Civic Auditorium and the First Methodist Church, and gaining exposure to designs from Beaux arts classicism to Hispanic and Moorish architecture.

Williams became a registered architect in 1915, was licensed to practice in California in June 1921, and opened his own architectural firm, Paul R. Williams and Associates, in the offices of the Stock Exchange Building, in 1922. Racial prejudice followed him. Williams met potential clients who entered his office ready for business, but when they learned that he was black they tried to withdraw gracefully by saying that they were just ''shopping around.'' He also learned to draw upside–down and right–side–up, to entice prospective clients who sat opposite him. He won commissions for projects by working twice as hard as his competitors.

On one major construction job that cost $100,000, Williams beat out two white competitors by working all night to complete his drawings—his competitors had set their design time at two to three weeks. Impressed as well with Williams's design of a small French cottage for an elderly woman, automobile magnate E. L. Cord asked Williams to proceed, and he won the contract to design Cord's 32–room mansion with an 18–car garage in Beverly Hills.

Williams's architectural business flourished. Most of his clients in the 1930s were upper middle class and wealthy whites. He also built nonresidential projects in the black community of Los Angeles, including a few public schools, Second Baptist Church (the second black church in Los Angeles), and the 28th Street Young Men's Christian Association (YMCA). He adorned the facade of the ''Y'' with portraits of Booker T. Washington and Frederick Douglass. Unlike some of his fellow architects, Williams's business was not deterred by the Great Depression. By the end of the 1930s and through World War II Williams and other architects of that period were involved in constructing public housing projects. After the war he built a substantial house for himself and his family. Generally, however, his clients during the post–war years were upper middle class and wealthy whites in Los Angeles and throughout the United States, Mexico, the Caribbean, and Latin America. By 1950 he had as many as 50 draftsmen and other personnel on staff, and during his lifetime he designed over three thousand residences and buildings.

In addition to his office on Wiltshire Boulevard in Los Angeles, he had offices in Washington, D.C. and in Bogota, Columbia. When planning private houses, Williams studied the economic problems, tastes, and habits of the client. He took a major interest in designing homes for the small builder and believed skillful planning was necessary to reduce the floor space—a primary measure of building costs. He eliminated unnecessary partitions and incorporated a variety of options to reduce cost.

Williams also advocated cooperative remodeling for entire neighborhoods, enabling a whole block of homeowners to come together with an architect and plan a mass face–lifting. He wrote in *Many Shades of Black,* "In each home that I design, regardless of size or price, I try to include an unusual conversation piece, which might be a specially planned kitchen with a glass wall overlooking an outdoor patio or garden, or a kitchen located at the front of the house convenient to the front door where the housewife would have a view of the passing street parade as she prepared dinner."

A firm believer in affordable housing, Williams created the Pueblo del Rio housing project on a tight budget. He also developed a large, low–income project for the impoverished Watts area of Los Angeles.

Builds Stately Mansions

Williams's work took him as far as France, South America, Hawaii, Liberia, and the West Indies, where he built numerous homes as well as large hotels. Most of Williams's work, however, was done in California. In time, Williams was in such demand that he had to turn down 25 percent of the offers he had for contracts. He became best known for his work with celebrities and for the design of posh hotels and other well–known structures. The homes he designed reflected his ability to work in traditional, revival, or modern style. He incorporated in his designs features of the English Tudor, Georgian, French Norman, Spanish Colonial, Italianate, and Regency periods. He gave particular attention to the effects of lighting on the interior and to details on doors, windows, and stairs. Some of his homes of the Prohibition era included wine cellars hidden behind sliding walls and panels. His works included houses for such Hollywood legends as Bud Abbott, Richard Arlen, Lucille Ball and Desi Arnaz, Lon Chaney, Zsa Zsa Gabor, Betty Grable, Bert Lahr, William "Bojangles" Robinson, Tyrone Power, Barbara Stanwyck, Danny Thomas, and William Paley.

Williams also designed a bachelor home atop a hill in Hollywood for Frank Sinatra, creating a functional, low–slung modern place with a big, expansive look. This was another example of the homes that Williams built to fit individual needs. The Sinatra house contained many features unique for that time, among them electronically–controlled draperies. Williams and one of his daughters, Karen, an interior designer, worked as a team on the home. The house was a showplace that received widespread attention and established Williams as master builder of small homes.

Williams was an architect for the U.S. Navy during World War II and among his military projects was the design of the U.S. Naval Station at Long Beach. Also during the war years he was involved with the War Finance Program of the U.S. Treasury Department. He designed two public projects, the first the Langston Terrace, the first federally–funded housing project, with Hilyard Robinson in Washington, D.C., and the second, a War Housing project at Fort Huachua, Arizona, in 1942. Commercial and public buildings that Williams designed included the Saks 5th Avenue Beverly Hills store, the Music Corporation of America building in Beverly Hills, the Palm Springs Tennis Club, the Beverly Wilshire Hotel, additions and alterations to the Ambassador Hotel, and ten branches of the Bank of America. He also built a number of restaurants, including Perino's and Chasen's.

Beyond California Williams was a licensed architect in the District of Columbia and in a number of states, including Tennessee. His expression of his love for children was manifest in his design of the main building of St. Jude Hospital in Memphis, Tennessee, which he created without charge; the building was dedicated to Williams posthumously.

Williams helped design a number of public buildings including the Los Angeles International Airport, the Los Angeles County Court House, the Federal Customs Building in Los Angeles, and the United Nations Building in Paris. He was associate architect on many government jobs in Washington, D.C. He saw the importance of the historical black colleges and shared his talents with them: in Nashville at Fisk University as consulting architect for a women's residence hall and in a joint venture at nearby Meharry Medical College (1962), and in the District of Columbia at Howard University in a joint venture in a men's residence hall (1939), a joint venture in the dental school building (1948), and as co–designer with Hilyard Robinson of the new engineering and architecture building.

Williams's views on housing are illustrated in two pattern books with drawings and plans: *The Small Homes of Tomorrow* (1945), which addresses the housing problem and calls for ingenious planning and total use of floor space, and *New Homes for Today* (1946). He also wrote the article "I Am a Negro" for the July 1937 issue of *American Magazine.* In the March 1994 issue of *Ebony,* Karima A. Hayes republished from that article Williams's views on his progress as a black man: "I survived a few financial hardships which might have been avoided had my face been White. But I do not regret those difficulties, for I think that I am a far better craftsman today than I would have been had my course been free."

Among his numerous memberships were the board of directors of the YMCA, the Los Angeles Urban League, the West Side Improvement Association and the NAACP. He was a member of the AIA, which he joined after only one year of private practice to become its first African American member. In 1957 he became a fellow of the AIA, the first African American to hold this honor. Other memberships included the City Planning Commission, Unity Finance Company, Los Angeles Art Commission, Board of Trustees of Howard University, Board of Trustees of Meharry Medical College, and California Redevelopment Commission and State Housing Commission. In 1929 President Calvin Coolidge appointed him to the National Monuments Committee, and in 1953 President Eisenhower appointed him to the Advisory Committee on Government Housing Policies and Programs. Among his community activities he served as director of such organizations as Big Brothers of Los Angeles, the Red Cross, the Southern California Heart Association, the Southwest March of Dimes Foundation, Traveler's Aid Society of the Los Angeles Area, and United Service Organizations.

In the political arena Williams was a two–time delegate to the National Republican Convention, in 1952 and in 1960. He was also occupation director for ''WIN with the Nixon–Lodge Program,'' and he was a member of the Republican Community Service Center. Williams was a 33rd Degree Mason and a member of the Omega Psi Phi Fraternity, Sigma Pi Phi (the Boulé), and the Pacific Town Club.

Williams received numerous honors from various institutions, organizations, and governments, among them honorary degrees from Lincoln University in Missouri (1941), Howard University (presented to him by President Harry Truman, 1952), Tuskegee Institute (now Tuskegee University, 1956), and Atlanta University (now Clark Atlanta, 1964). The NAACP recognized Williams's work by awarding him the Spingarn Medal in 1953. Quoted in *Crisis* magazine, in his acceptance speech Williams urged African Americans to increase their ''home ownership and standard of citizenship'' and to be a part of the progress of America. He also received the AIA gold medal for ''excellence of design'' for the Music Corporation of America building in Beverly Hills, and in 1955 the Los Angeles Chamber of Commerce Award for Creative Planning. In 1966 he was awarded the University of Southern California Alumni Merit Award.

Known by his friends as ''PR,'' Williams was light–skinned and sometimes mistaken for white. He was a courtly man, one of self–confidence, dignity, and congeniality, always impeccable in dress and manners. He remained calm, poised, never raised his voice, and kept a twinkle in his eye. Although his clients were black as well as white, he maintained strong ties to his black heritage. Williams was a strong family man who separated work from family, and although he often took his work home, he would sketch or read only after his family had gone to bed. He loved back–yard barbecuing for family and friends and enjoyed family drives through the city. Williams also loved parties but rarely socialized with his clients. His favorite sport throughout life was tennis. Toys and gadgets fascinated him as did the simple pleasure of enjoying a hot dog, hamburger, or popcorn from a beach or street stand.

After a career that spanned six decades, Williams retired from architectural practice in 1973. He died in Los Angeles on January 23, 1980, of complications from diabetes. He was survived by his wife, Della Mae Givens, whom he married on June 27, 1917, and two daughters, Marilyn Hudson and Norma Harvey. His granddaughter Karen E. Hudson, has preserved her grandfather's legacy in *Paul R. Williams, Architect: A Legacy of Style,* and *The Will and the Way.* In the first book Hudson called Williams him ''a man with a vision whose love of beauty brought joy to all. . . . [He was] a gentleman with a dream.'' Faced with racism throughout his life, he found refuge in his work and his family. His rich legacy is reflected in the architectural vision he had and that he expressed in the range of structures that he designed.

REFERENCES

Cederholm, Theresa D. *Afro–American Artists.* Boston: Trustees of the Boston Public Library, 1973.

Contemporary Black Biography. Vol. 9. Detroit: Gale Research, 1994.

Current Biography Yearbook. New York: H. W. Wilson, 1941.

Duncan, Ray. ''Paul Williams Tells: How to Build a Home for $5,000.'' *Ebony* 4 (March 1949): 42–48.

''Forty–fourth Annual NAACP Conference.'' *Crisis* 60 (August–September 1953): 422–25.

Hudson, Karen E. *Paul R. Williams, Architect: A Legacy of Style.* New York, Rizzoli, 1993.

Obituary. *Current Biography.* New York: H. W. Wilson, 1980.

''Paul R. Williams: The Rich Legacy of a Black Architect.'' *Ebony* 49 (March 1994): 57–60, 100–102.

Who's Who in America, 1976–77. Chicago: Marquis, 1976.

Wormley, Stanton L., and Lewis H. Fenderson, eds. *Many Shades of Black.* New York: Morrow, 1969.

COLLECTIONS

Paul R. Williams's autobiographical notes, designs, unpublished speeches, and other writings are in the Paul R. Williams Collection in the possession of Karen E. Hudson.

Jessie Carney Smith

August Wilson

(1945–)

Playwright, poet

Prolific playwright August Wilson is a modern–day *griot,* who has eloquently and consistently chronicled black American life. His critically acclaimed dramas, *Ma Rainey's Black Bottom, Fences, Joe Turner's Come and Gone, The Piano Lesson, Two Trains Running,* and *Seven Guitars,* have been performed at regional theaters across the United States as well as on Broadway. They also have been published, transporting audiences and readers on odysseys of black American life through Wilson's focus on identity, culture, and history. Wilson is the first black American to have two plays running simultaneously on Broadway and is one of seven American playwrights to win two Pulitzer Prizes.

August Wilson was born Frederick August Kittel on April 27, 1945, in Pittsburgh, Pennsylvania. Earlier, his maternal grandmother exhibited great strength and determination when she walked from North Carolina to Pennsylvania

August Wilson

in search of a better life. Wilson's mother, Daisy, inherited her mother's strength and determination, qualities she needed to raise six children in a Bedford Avenue two–room apartment behind a grocery store in Pittsburgh's Hill District—a poor neighborhood inhabited by black Americans, Italians, and Jews. Daisy supported her family as a cleaning lady. Her husband, Frederick Kittel, a German immigrant and baker, seldom spent time with his family. Decades later, in the 1970s, August—Daisy and Frederick's fourth child and eldest son—adopted his mother's maiden name, Wilson, and dropped his paternal surname.

During Wilson's teen years, his mother married David Bedford, and the Bedford family moved from the Hill to a predominantly white suburban neighborhood, Hazelwood, in the late 1950s. There, they encountered racial hostility; bricks were thrown through a window at their new home, and when Wilson transferred to Gladstone High School, he was subjected to additional racial incidents. His white schoolmates frequently left notes on his desk advising, ''Nigger go home.'' Yet an even greater insult to Wilson was the inability of a teacher to fathom that a black student could create a well–written term paper. After reading Wilson's paper centered on Napoleon, the instructor accused him of plagiarism. The racial animosity exhibited at Gladstone led Wilson, at age 15, to drop out of school.

Although Wilson's formal education ended abruptly, he continued to learn through disciplined self–study at the Carnegie Library. Wilson, who learned to read at age four and began reading black writers at age 12, spent the remainder of his teen years educating himself by reading black works in the public library. Reading works by Ralph Ellison, Richard Wright, Langston Hughes, Arna Bontemps, and other black writers, as noted by *Contemporary Black Biography,* Wilson was caught up in the power of words.

Wilson's fascination with the power of words generated tension at home. During his teens, Wilson was determined to become a writer and worked at a series of odd jobs. His mother, who wanted Wilson to pursue a career as an attorney, disapproved and forced him to leave the family residence. He enlisted in the U.S. Army in 1963 only to be discharged in 1964.

Begins Writing Career

On April 1, 1965, a few weeks shy of his twentieth birthday, Wilson invested in his writing career by purchasing his first typewriter. During the fall of 1965, Wilson moved to a rooming house in his native city. Reflecting on that period in his youth, Wilson described himself in the preface to *Three Plays* as ''a twenty–year–old poet wrestling with the world and his place in it, having discovered the joy and terror of remaking the world in his own image through the act of writing.'' He supported himself by working at a series of low–paying jobs—as dishwasher, short–order cook, porter, stock boy, gardener, and mail room clerk—for approximately the next 12 or 13 years. During his leisure time, Wilson frequently sat in a restaurant and created poems on paper bags. His initial writing efforts were poetic, and although he did not gain fame as a poet, his poems were published in the late 1960s and early 1970s in several periodicals such as *Negro Digest*—which later became *Black World*—as well as *Black Lines* and in at least one anthology published in the early 1970s, *The Poetry of Black Americans: Anthology of the Twentieth Century,* edited by Arnold Adoff. Among the poems published during this period were ''For Malcolm X and Others,'' ''Morning Song,'' ''Muhammad Ali,'' ''Theme One: The Variations,'' and ''Bessie.''

In the fall of 1965, Wilson played Bessie Smith's record ''Nobody in Town Can Bake a Sweet Jellyroll Like Mine.'' Wilson acknowledged in his preface to *Three Plays* that hearing Smith's voice led to an awakening; he realized he was a representative and carrier of black American culture. After listening to Smith's voice, Wilson assumed the responsibility passed on from his black American ancestors; hearing the blues motivated, challenged, and empowered the young poet to document black American culture and history in his writings.

During the remainder of the 1960s, Wilson continued to write and was instrumental in founding two organizations that promoted black American writing: the Center Avenue Poets Theatre Workshop, formed in 1965, and Black Horizons, formed in 1968. Wilson cofounded Black Horizons with his friend, Rob Penny, a playwright and teacher, in an effort to politicize black Americans and to increase their race consciousness. Wilson's earliest plays were written for Black Horizons, including: *Recycle,* written in 1973 and produced at a Pittsburgh community theater; *The Homecoming,* about blues singer and guitarist Blind Lemon Jefferson, written in 1976 but not produced until 1989; and *The Coldest Day of the Year,* a drama focusing on relationships between black American men and women that was written in 1977 but unproduced until 1989.

In 1969 Wilson married Brenda Burton, a member of the Nation of Islam. One year later, their daughter, Sakina, was born. The Wilsons divorced in 1972.

In 1978 Wilson traveled to St. Paul, Minnesota, to visit his friend Claude Purdy who had worked in theater while in Pittsburgh before becoming the director of St. Paul's Penumbra Theatre. Wilson decided to move to St. Paul and was employed as a scriptwriter for the Science Museum of Minnesota. On the museum's behalf, Wilson wrote several brief scripts, including *An Evening with Margaret Mead, How Coyote Got His Special Power and Used it to Help the People,* and *Eskimo Song Duel.* His employment at the museum was an early milestone in his literary career; for the first time, Wilson was being paid to write.

In his spare time, Wilson continued to create plays. According to *Contemporary Black Biography,* in 1979 "in ten days of writing while sitting in a fish-and-chips restaurant," he wrote *Jitney!,* a drama about Pittsburgh's black jitney drivers set in 1971. *Jitney!* was accepted by the Minneapolis Playwrights Center in 1980; the theater group named Wilson an associate playwright, and awarded him a $200 monthly fellowship. In 1982 *Jitney!* was produced at Pittsburgh's Allegheny Repertory Theatre. *Jitney!* was followed by Wilson's *Fullerton Street,* written in 1980 and set in the 1940s. His next play, *Black Bart and the Sacred Hills,* is a musical satire written in 1977, produced in 1981, and is based on a series of poems about a legendary outlaw of the Wild West. Wilson quit his job as the museum's scriptwriter in order to devote more time to creating his own plays. He was encouraged in this endeavor by his second wife, Judy Oliver, a white social worker he married in 1981.

Debuts on Broadway

In 1980 Rob Penny encouraged Wilson to apply to the National Playwrights Conference at the O'Neill Theatre Center in Connecticut where each summer 15 playwrights are selected to participate from the approximately 1,500 who apply. The O'Neill rejected five Wilson scripts before accepting *Ma Rainey's Black Bottom* for a workshop in 1982—the same year Wilson wrote the play. The National Playwrights Conference director, Lloyd Richards, who is also director of the Yale Repertory Theatre and dean of the Yale School of Drama, staged a production of *Ma Rainey's Black Bottom* at the Yale Repertory Theatre in April, 1984. The play marked the beginning of Wilson's association with Richards. Wilson stated in the preface to *Three Plays* that Richards is "my guide, my mentor, and my provocateur" and added that "From the O'Neill to Yale to Broadway, each step, in each guise, his hand has been firmly on the tiller as we charted the waters from draft to draft and brought the plays safely to shore without compromise." *Ma Rainey's Black Bottom* is the first of six Wilson plays that Richards, at Yale and on Broadway, has directed.

Ma Rainey's Black Bottom opened, after a brief stint at the University of Pennsylvania's Annenberg Center, on October 11, 1984, at Broadway's Cort Theater. Set in Chicago in 1927, the play focuses on white record companies' exploitation of black musicians. According to *Masterpieces of African-American Literature,* this relationship mirrors the position of black people in the society at large—a society dominated by white racism." *Ma Rainey's Black Bottom,* which brought Wilson national attention, was a popular and critical success. It closed in June 1985, after 275 performances, received several Tony nominations, and won the New York Drama Critics Circle Award.

Wilson plans to create a play for each decade of the twentieth century, each focusing on a major black American issue. *Ma Rainey's Black Bottom* is the first play of this ten-drama cycle. Although Wilson's earlier plays are set in various decades, the cycle begins with *Ma Rainey's Black Bottom,* his 1920s play while his next drama, *Fences,* is Wilson's 1950s drama.

Wins First Pulitzer

Fences, written in 1983, was staged at the O'Neill in 1983, produced at the Yale Repertory Theatre in April 1985, and opened on Broadway at the 46th Street Theatre on March 26, 1987. The play depicts 1950s' black family's personal and economic problems. *Fences* was a commercial and critical success. It grossed $11 million in one year, breaking the record for nonmusical plays. *Fences* solidified Wilson's reputation as a major playwright. The *Chicago Tribune* named Wilson as Artist of the Year. *Fences* won the New York Drama Critics Circle Award for Best Play, four Tony Awards (Best Play: Wilson; Best Director: Richards; Best Actor: James Earl Jones; and Best Featured Actress: Mary Alice), and the Pulitzer Prize for Drama.

While *Fences* was still on Broadway, Wilson's *Joe Turner's Come and Gone* opened at the Ethel Barrymore Theatre earning Wilson the honor of being the first black American with two concurrent plays on Broadway. Written in 1984 and prior to its Broadway debut, *Joe Turner's Come and Gone* was staged at the O'Neill, produced at the Yale Repertory Theatre in 1986, and at Washington's Arena Stage in 1988. Wilson, who cited artist Romare Bearden as a major influence on his work because he views Bearden's paintings as as expressive and varied as the blues, was inspired by Bearden's "Millhand Lunch Bucket" as he created *Joe Turner's Come and Gone.* The play, set in Pittsburgh in 1911, focuses on slavery's lingering effects, blacks fleeing from the agrarian South to the urban North in the earlier years of the century, and black Americans' search for identity. *Joe Turner's Come and Gone,* Wilson's drama of the second decade, received Tony nominations, the New York Drama Critics Circle Award, and the Drama Desk Award.

Romare Bearden's painting *The Piano Lesson* inspired Wilson to create a play with the same title. *The Piano Lesson,* written in 1986, was staged at the O'Neill in 1987, produced at the Yale Repertory Theatre in 1988, and opened April 16, 1990, at Broadway's Walter Kerr Theatre. Set in 1937 Pittsburgh, *The Piano Lesson* examines family conflict over an heirloom built by a slave ancestor. According to the *Encyclopedia of African–American Culture and History,* ''This play perhaps best expresses Wilson's view of black history as something to be neither sold nor denied, but employed to create an ongoing, nurturing, cultural identity.'' *The Piano Lesson,* Wilson's drama of the 1930s, won the New York Drama Critics Circle Award, the Tony for Best Play, the Drama Desk Award, the American Theatre Critics Outstanding Play Award, and the Pulitzer Prize for Drama. Thus, Wilson is one of seven American playwrights to win two Pulitzers.

Wilson's next play, *Two Trains Running,* was written in 1989, produced at the Yale Repertory Theatre in 1990, and it opened on Broadway at the Walter Kerr Theatre in 1992. *Two Trains Running,* Wilson's drama of the 1960s, is centered on a group of friends in Pittsburgh who are caught up in the chaos generated by the Vietnam War and racial unrest. Nominated for a Tony, *TTR* received the New York Drama Critics Award and American Theatre Critics Association Award.

Wilson's drama of the 1940s, *Seven Guitars,* set in Pittsburgh, opened at the Walter Kerr Theatre on Broadway on March 28, 1996. *Seven Guitars* focuses on Floyd ''Schoolboy'' Barton's friends who gather after his death and the sense of hope for black American empowerment and self–reliance. It received the New York Drama Critics Circle Award for Best New Play.

Additional honors have been bestowed upon Wilson. He is the recipient of Bush, McKnight, Rockefeller, and Guggenheim Foundation fellowships in playwrighting. An alumnus of New Dramatists, Wilson was elected to the American Academy of Arts and Sciences and inducted into the American Academy of Arts and Letters.

Wilson lives in Seattle, Washington, with his third wife, Constanza Romero. Romero is a costume designer, and her credits include *Seven Guitars.*

August Wilson, former poet turned preeminent playwright, eloquently and diligently provides a panoramic vision of his people to regional theaters, Broadway, and the world as he remains steadfast in his quest to dramatically document twentieth century black American life decade by decade.

Current address: 600 First Avenue, Suite 301, Seattle, Washington 98104.

REFERENCES

Andrews, William L., Frances Smith Foster, and Trudier Harris, eds. *The Oxford Companion to African American Literature.* New York: Oxford University Press, 1997.

Contemporary Black Biography. Vol. 7. Detroit: Gale Research, 1994.

Current Biography Yearbook. New York: H. W. Wilson, 1987.

Salzman, Jack, David Lionel Smith, and Cornel West, eds. *Encyclopedia of African–American Culture and History.* New York: Macmillan Library Reference USA/Simon and Schuster Macmillan, 1996.

Shannon, Sandra G. ''August Wilson Explains His Dramatic Vision: An Interview.'' In *The Dramatic Vision of August Wilson.* Washington: Howard University Press, 1995.

Wilson, August. *Three Plays.* Pittsburgh: University of Pittsburgh Press, 1991.

COLLECTIONS

The Yale School of Drama Library contains information and clippings about Wilson's plays performed at the Yale Repertory Theatre and elsewhere.

Linda M. Carter

William J. Wilson

(b. 1810s?)

Journalist, writer, educator, school administrator, activist, banker

An important black figure of the nineteenth century, William J. Wilson used the press, the pen, black rights organizations, and the classroom to fight for racial uplift. He was a contributor to the early black press, such as *Frederick Douglass' Paper.* He was also a pioneer educator in Brooklyn as well as in the schools founded by the American Missionary Association (AMA) in Washington, D.C.

William J. Wilson was born and raised in Washington, D.C. (Some sources say that he was born a slave on a Southern plantation.) Except that he married a woman Mary A. and had a daughter, Annie M., nothing more is known thus far about his early background or his family life. In 1837 he was already a shoemaker in New York, and operated his business in a basement at 15 Ann Street. He manufactured fine boots and shoes that he sold at reasonable rates, either on terms or for cash.

In the 1840s and 1850s, perhaps earlier, Wilson was a teacher and principal of ''colored'' public schools in Brooklyn. The early schools in Brooklyn were in the charge of churches; later, when the city took them over, Wilson was among the earliest recorded black male teachers. Wilson struggled hard to keep his school filled with black children, as did his successors. When writing about his departure from the school system in a letter dated June 6, 1864, to an unnamed correspondent of the American Missionary Association (probably S. S. Jocelyn), Wilson cited a difference with the Brooklyn Board of Education: "The truth is, my course was too Anti Slavery for some of the gentlemen to longer remain & so I resigned."

At this same time Wilson became active in a number of local black rights organizations. He helped establish the New York Society for the Promotion of Education among Colored Children as well as the Committee of Thirteen—an organization to assist fugitive slaves. Fellow black abolitionist leaders George T. Downing, Thomas Downing, and James McCune Smith were also members of the committee. Considering the race problems of that period, in the 1850s blacks began to discuss the need to bear arms. Wilson supported the idea, and when a group of blacks in New York City met at the Shiloh Presbyterian Church in April of 1851, they urged young men in New York, Williamsburg, and Brooklyn to organize military companies.

Wilson was a delegate to the National Council of the Colored People in New York held at Shiloh Church in New York City from May 8 to 10, 1855. Those present included James McCune Smith, George T. Downing, Charles L. Remond, Frederick Douglass, William C. Nell, John Mercer Langston, and J. W. C. Pennington. He favored the group's plan to establish an industrial college to educate black youth and help them rise above menial employment and become prosperous tradesmen. Speaking in support of the plan, according to Blassingame's *The Frederick Douglass Papers,* volume 3, Wilson said: "Such a school . . . would be a nucleus around which colored children could gather and be indoctrinated with such a spirit of enterprise as they never before felt, and as would enable them to achieve independence." At the convention Wilson, along with William C. Nell and Stephen Smith, was appointed to the National Council of the Colored People's three–member committee on finance. Wilson was also asked to report on black benevolent societies, including the Odd Fellows and Masons, and to give statistics on the number of members and the monies they spent on their activities.

Using the name Ethiop, Wilson regularly wrote free articles for Frederick Douglass's newspaper, editorials for Thomas Hamilton's *The Weekly Anglo–African* (published from 1859 to 1863), and poems and satirical works for Hamilton's *The Anglo–African Magazine* (published monthly from 1859 to 1860). James McCune Smith, another forceful writer of the time, edited both the weekly and monthly journals. Wilson is known best through the views expressed in his writings.

When Frederick Douglass and Samuel Ringgold Ward, both fugitive slaves, held a debate in New York City on May 11, 1849, to argue whether or not the Constitution was a proslavery document, Wilson wrote the fullest eyewitness account. Published as "A Leaf from My Scrapbook," the article appeared in a number of sources, including *Autographs for Freedom.* Wilson recognized the talent of the two eminent men. Although he saw power in Douglass that was rarely found in other men, he considered Ward as his equal. Wilson found Douglass to be a lecturer and Ward a debater. Douglass dealt in generalities, while Ward reduced everything to a point. In the end Wilson found that both men had powerful minds and were well qualified for the debate. Some writers conclude that Wilson's essay gave Ward the edge.

In the 1850s Wilson advocated strongly for his race. According to *They Who Would Be Free,* on April 22, 1852, he addressed his comments in the *Frederick Douglass' Paper* to white antislavery colleagues, saying that they must "toe the mark." He condemned them for lecturing "colored people to merely be good and honest and not to think too highly of themselves, and hence get out of their place." He knew no abolitionist who would "admit him, nor his son, nor his son's son to [his] counting–room, nor [his] work–bench nor to any other respectable station in [his] gift." By 1853 Wilson still commented on the facelessness of black America. Writing in *Frederick Douglass' Paper* on March 11 that year, as quoted in *They Who Would Be Free,* Wilson said: "At present, what we find around us, either in art or literature, is made so to press upon us, that we depreciate, we despise, we almost hate ourselves, and all that favors us. We may well scoff at black skins and wooly heads, since every model set before us for admiration, has pallid face and laxen head, or emanations thereof." He advocated the promotion of black history to stimulate racial pride. In the 1860s he continued to speak out on race issues, and again he called for blacks to bear arms.

Wilson wrote a lengthy, sharp commentary on the morality of white people published in the February 1860 issue of *The Anglo–African Magazine* called "What Shall We Do with the White People?" and excerpted in Dorothy Sterling's *Speak Out in Thunder Tones.* In the essay he comments on the early white settlers' injustices toward the native peoples, the internal slave trade later on, and whites' violation of their own government that recognized that "all men are created free and equal." Wilson called for peace in this country, hoping that one day whites "will make a way for a milder and more genial race."

Described by William Wells Brown in *The Black Man* as writer of "some of the raciest and most amusing essays to be found in the public journals" at the time, Wilson also wrote of historical scenes and characters. He made an imaginary visit to the "Afric–American Picture Gallery," writing of poet Phyllis Wheatley as if her picture actually hung in a gallery and adding his own poems in the essay. He praised her work as poet at the age of 14, her book of poems published at age 19, and questioned "what one of America's paler daughters" had achieved at so early an age.

Joins AMA Schools

Wilson wrote to S. S. Jocelyn of the American Missionary Association on April 28, 1864, asking to become head of the Camp Barker AMA school for black children located near the corner of 12th and R streets in Washington, D.C. By June 6, 1864, his letter to an unnamed correspondent indicates that he had been hired by the AMA in one of its schools for $50 a month, obviously as its head. At Wilson's request, Mary his wife, who had been hired in another school for $20 month, was assigned to his school, and by mid–July of 1864, his daughter Annie was assigned there as well. An ungraded school, Camp Barker became the largest of the AMA schools in Washington, D.C., with 225 or more children. As he had done in Brooklyn, Wilson was determined to hire black teachers to teach black children in the AMA schools. Until then, the teachers had been white. Wilson wrote to AMA official George Whipple on April 30, 1864—in a letter located in the Amistad Research Center—''We the colored people must be taught to do our own work, being ably assisted only by the dominant class.''

Wilson's work with the AMA schools remained a struggle. The schools needed supplies and books, and faculty salaries were generally late arriving. Frequently Wilson asked for a salary increase. In the fall of 1864, he wrote to Whipple again and sent a copy of his May letter addressed to the Pennsylvania Freeman's Relief Association, where he had applied for the position of superintendent of a portion of the ''colored'' schools in Washington, D.C. This would, of course, aid his low salary. By March of 1865 he was still teaching at Camp Barker as well as serving as superintendent of two evening schools. He also worked for the Army Pay Department.

Since Camp Barker School was in serious disrepair, it appears to have been closed. By October 25, 1865, Wilson was in charge of the Third Street School and had over 200 ''scholars,'' as the students were called then. In time the school was renamed Douglass School.

In July of 1865 Wilson was appointed head cashier of the Freedman's Savings Bank, Washington branch. He worked at the bank in the evenings, usually leaving his school assignment intact. On December 23, 1865, however, he wrote to Whipple on bank stationery admitting that he had been absent from the school for eight days while engaged in bank business. Apparently he received a ''Report of Dissatisfaction'' and had to deal with a strained relationship at the school. When or how he left teaching is unclear.

Wilson's work at the bank continued. Although he was instrumental in bringing numerous depositors to the bank and advised them well in financial matters, he was unable to balance his books. In 1873 the bank demoted him to traveling agent.

After the U.S. Congress passed a bill in February of 1865 ending slavery, which later became the Thirteenth Amendment, President Abraham Lincoln called for a commemoration of the historic measure. Henry Highland Garnet was asked to give a memorial sermon in the House chamber during a special Sunday morning service on February 14. Wilson attended and recorded the event. During the Reconstruction period, Wilson was a delegate to the Colored National Labor Union Convention of 1869. He also was a proponent of the Freedman's Homestead Company. On March 15, 1869, he was elected to the Howard University Board of Trustees and served on its executive committee from 1872 until 1874. From 1869 to 1870 Wilson was a lecturer in the university's commercial department. He was elected secretary of the board pro tempore on June 16, 1875, and his board tenure ended in 1879. Beyond that date, sources give no further information on Wilson.

Wilson was also a public speaker. In *The Rising Son,* William Wells Brown said Wilson was ''pleasing in style, with the manners of a gentleman.'' He was known as a deep thinker and a fine conversationalist as well. According to Brown, Wilson, of unmixed race, was a small man with a profile ''more striking than his front face.'' His wit transcended his smiling countenance.

Dorothy Sterling called Wilson ''one of the ablest writers of the black abolitionist movement'' and one who has been ''overlooked by literary historians.'' He has been overlooked as a pioneer teacher and administrator as well.

REFERENCES

Blassingame, John W., ed. *The Frederick Douglass Papers.* Series 1, Vols. 2–3. New Haven: Yale University Press, 1982, 1985.

Brown, William Wells. *The Black Man, His Antecedents, His Genius, and His Achievements.* 4th ed. Boston: Robert F. Wallcut, 1865.

———. *The Rising Son.* Boston: A. G. Brown and Co., 1876.

DeBoer, Clara Merritt. *His Truth is Marching On: African Americans Who Taught the Freedmen for the American Missionary Association 1861–1877.* New York: Garland Publishing, 1995.

Griffiths, Julia, ed. *Autographs for Freedom.* Auburn, NY: Alden, Beardsley and Co., 1854.

Logan, Rayford W. *Howard University: The First Hundred Years 1867–1967.* New York: New York University Press under the auspices of Howard University, 1969.

Pease, Jane H., and William H. Pease. *They Who Would Be Free.* New York: Atheneum, 1974.

Quarles, Benjamin. *Black Abolitionists.* New York: Oxford University Press, 1969.

Schor, Joel. *Henry Highland Garnet.* Westport, CT: Greenwood Press, 1977.

Sterling, Dorothy, ed. *Speak Out in Thunder Tones.* Garden City, NY: Doubleday, 1973.

Wheeler, B[enjamin] F. *The Varick Family.* Mobile, AL: The Author, c.1907.

COLLECTIONS

The American Missionary Association Archives, Amistad Research Center, and Tulane University, contain letters from

William J. Wilson to various correspondents, including M. E. Strieby, S. S. Jocelyn, and George Whipple, the principal's monthly report from Camp Barker and Douglass schools, and other items.

Jessie Carney Smith

Hale A. Woodruff

(1900–1980)

Painter, printmaker, muralist, educator

Internationally renowned Hale Woodruff was one of the key New Negro artists who became one of the most significant African American college art teachers, influencing hundreds of students at Atlanta and New York universities. Master of many styles, Woodruff initially worked in a provincial, academic manner, then in cubist, regional, social realist, and abstract modes, depicting African American and African subjects and motifs. His media included oils, woodblock prints, and murals.

Hale Aspacio Woodruff was born August 26, 1900, in Cairo, Illinois, the only child of Augusta Bell and George Woodruff, who died soon after his son's birth. Woodruff and his mother then moved to East Nashville, Tennessee, where she earned a living as a domestic servant. In 1934 Woodruff an attractive, slim, copper–colored man married Theresa Ada Baker, a teacher from Topeka, Kansas. The two would have a son, Roy, in 1935. Woodruff died in New York on September 26, 1980.

As a child, Woodruff copied engravings by Gustave Doré in the family Bible and worked in Holt's Cafe. There were no art courses in Nashville's public schools, but Woodruff frequently copied Greek and Roman statues from his ancient history textbooks. He continued to develop his drawings skills as a cartoonist for his high school newspaper, *The Pearl High Voice.*

Early Work in Indianapolis

After graduation from high school in 1918, Woodruff left Nashville with his best friend, George Gore, to find summer work in Indianapolis. He continued for two years as a menial laborer at the Claypool Hotel, the Indianapolis Athletic Club, and the Stegemeier Restaurant, living at the YMCA.

In the fall of 1920 Woodruff entered the Herron Art School, where he studied oil and watercolor landscape painting with William Forsyth (1854–1935). Because most of his landscapes were of imaginary sites, Woodruff labeled himself "ultra–impressionistic" and "Romantic." His treatment of the human figure, however, was conservative. One of his first portraits, *William Pickens, Sr.,* 1921, depicts the bust of a solemn, bespectacled man in a dark suit and tie against a plain background.

In the early 1920s Woodruff drew political cartoons for the local African American newspaper, *The Indianapolis Ledger.* Many of his sketches depicted police brutality, lynching, and segregation in education and housing. Since Woodruff's slight income was not enough to meet tuition expenses, he had to withdraw permanently by 1923. Hoping for improved wages, Woodruff moved further north to Chicago. He briefly studied part–time at the Art Institute, then believed he could do as well on his own. Finding living conditions no better in Chicago, Woodruff soon returned to Indianapolis.

Sharing evening studio expenses with artists Wilbert Holloway (who was the only other African American student in the class of about 40 students at Herron) and John Wesley Hardrick over the years, Woodruff painted independently and had a solo exhibition at the Pettis Galleries in Indianapolis in 1923. He also displayed his work in group exhibitions at the YMCA, the Annual Indiana Artists Exhibitions (1923, 1924), and the Herron Art Museum (1923, 1924, 1926).

In 1925 Woodruff submitted five paintings under the pseudonym Icabod Crane to the Amy Spingarn Competition at the NAACP's *Crisis* magazine. One of his landscapes won ten dollars for third prize in the illustration category. These paintings so impressed W. E. B. Du Bois that he not only requested that Woodruff submit cover designs for *Crisis* from time to time, but he also hung them in his office.

From 1925 to 1926, Woodruff significantly aided the development of the Senate Avenue YMCA as its membership secretary. During that year, he was responsible for the largest membership for a black YMCA in the country. The institution became one of the country's outstanding black branches and a cultural hub. The YMCA's Sunday afternoon "Monster Meetings" drew poets, artists, and musicians, such as writer Countee Cullen and painter William Edouard Scott, both of whom befriended Woodruff and urged him to study abroad. The head of the YMCA, Fayburn E. DeFrantz, invited leading scholars to lecture there. DeFrantz took a special interest in Woodruff and introduced him to some of the speakers, such as John Hope, president of Morehouse College, and Colonel Joseph H. Ward, director of the veterans' hospital at Tuskegee, both of whom purchased Woodruff's work. Hope was so impressed with Woodruff's work that he suggested that the young artist consider a position as art instructor at Morehouse within a few years.

In the spring of 1926 Woodruff traveled with DeFrantz to Topeka, Kansas, where they stayed at the Baker home. There, Woodruff met Theresa Ada Baker, a student at Washburn College. The two would court, largely by mail, for the next eight years until they married in 1934.

In 1926 Woodruff won two major awards, one of which was second prize for drawing in the *Crisis* contest. More significantly, after Woodruff submitted four landscapes and a figurative work to the Harmon Foundation, he achieved national acclaim by winning the Bronze Award for *Two Old Women.*

Woodruff planned to use the $100 award to help finance a two–year trip to Europe, where he would study landscape painting in France, Italy, and Spain. Many people helped Woodruff raise additional funds. For example, Walter White, assistant executive secretary of the NAACP in New York, solicited the white banker and fine arts patron, Otto H. Kahn to contribute $250 for each of the two years. Members of the all–white Florentine Club of Franklin, Indiana, performed a play in his honor to raise money for his trip and presented him with $200.

Among Woodruff's patrons in Indianapolis was Hermann Lieber, the owner of an art and photography supply shop, who offered to sell at least one of Woodruff's paintings a month. He had first befriended Woodruff when the artist brought some of his work to the little Pettis gallery on the second floor of the shop. Lieber gave Woodruff one of the earliest books solely devoted to African art, Carl Einstein's *Afrikanische Plastik.* Woodruff could not read the German text, but, according to Bearden and Henderson in *A History of African–American Artists,* he was profoundly moved by the photographs of African sculpture. He explained:

> You can't imagine the effect that book had on me. Part of the effect was due to the fact that as a black artist I felt very much alone there in Indianapolis. I had heard of [early African American acclaimed painter Henry O.] Tanner, but I had never heard of the significance of the impact of African art. Yet here it was! And all written up in German, a language I didn't understand! Yet published with beautiful photographs and treated with great seriousness and respect! Plainly sculptures of black people, my people, they were considered very beautiful by these German art experts! The whole idea that this could be so was like an explosion. It was a real turning point for me. I was just astonished at this enormous discovery.

The gift initiated Woodruff's lifelong interest in African art.

The Education of a Modernist: 1927–1931

On September 3, 1927, Woodruff left for Paris. Upon his arrival, he found the city beautiful and inspiring and was grateful for painter Palmer Hayden's help in getting settled. He attended two small schools, the Académies Scandinave and Moderne, and wrote about tourist attractions for the *Indianapolis Star.* His first article, "The Gardens of Luxembourg," unillustrated and written in a rather dry, reportorial manner, was not published until January 6, 1928. The others would appear over the next 14 months as bimonthly features illustrated by the artist's pen and ink drawings. Topics included Versailles, Meudon, the bookstalls of the Seine, Notre Dame, the Tuileries gardens, Montparnasse, and the current arts scene. Woodruff was intrigued and overwhelmed by all of the new developments in art. In his article in the *Indianapolis Star* for March 18, 1928, "Local Negro Artist Finds Painters Hard to Classify," he declared, "If one should attempt to keep pace with all of the different movements that are now evident in Paris, there would be little time for anything else."

Disappointed with his French instructors, Woodruff's true artistic education abroad took place in the museums, galleries, and annual exhibitions. He frequented the Louvre, the Salon des Indépendants, the Jeu de Paume (where he admired Cézanne's work), and the Musée de l'Homme. Howard University professor of philosophy Alain Locke encouraged Woodruff's interest in African art. In 1928 they went to a flea market where Woodruff bought a Bembe male figure and a Yoruba Shango staff. Later he declared in a letter to Edwin Coates dated August 16, 1973, in the Archives of American Art, "Cézanne was my (European) image." He recalled, "I went back again and again and, between the Cézannes and the African work, I was off and winging."

In the spring of 1928 Woodruff traveled to Henry O. Tanner's home in Étaples and spent several hours discussing art with the master, who encouraged him to work on the human figure. In the following months, Woodruff made a number of trips to the Luxembourg Museum to study Tanner's masterpiece, *The Resurrection of Lazarus,* 1896. While Woodruff never painted religious imagery, he admired Tanner's draftsmanship, use of color, and his international reputation. That summer, Woodruff painted along the English Channel and the Eure River. These picturesque watercolors, while vivid and well designed, are less experimental than his oil paintings and more like nineteenth–century illustrations.

By fall Woodruff was at the end of his resources, unable to get a job since he was not a French citizen. He could neither pay rent nor eat for several days because his housemates had left the area. His health suffered to such an extent that at times he could not paint and was forced to borrow money from friends.

In February of 1929, Woodruff checked his mail in Paris and found four of his works were exhibited by the Harmon Foundation. *Medieval Chartre* was reproduced in the catalogue, and it and *Normandy Landscape* had been sold for a total of $135.00. However, the Harmon judges had made their decision before his paintings had arrived, which meant that he was ineligible for any of the awards.

In 1929 Woodruff continued to produce tourist scenes, but he also produced at least three works depicting black people. He explained in his October 12, 1929, letter to George Edmund Haynes in the Harmon Foundation papers, "I did this because I thought it would add more weight and significance to my submission [to the Harmon Foundation]." *Washer Women* and *Old Woman Peeling Apples* were included in the 1930 exhibition, along with *The Banjo Player,* which won honorable mention.

In the spring of 1930, Woodruff had small exhibitions in Paris at the Galerie Jeune Peinture and the Galerie Paquereau, but apparently sold nothing. His health worsened, and he needed a less expensive place to stay. In the summer of 1930, Woodruff moved to an artists' colony called Cagnes–sur–Mer. There he obtained a position as a road laborer by passing himself off as a North African. The job paid his living expenses for several months and allowed him to rent a studio in expressionist painter Chaim Soutine's old atelier.

Among Woodruff's acquaintances in the south of France were the artist Victor Thal, Nigel and Suzanne Newton (of the Winsor and Newton family, internationally known color–makers in England), Joycean scholar Abraham Lincoln Gillespie, actresses Gwen and Eva La Gallienne, dancers Raymond and Isadora Duncan, and composer George Antheil. Woodruff also met Jean Renoir, son of the great painter. The American painter, poet, musician, and nightclub owner (of the Jockey Club in Paris) Hilaire Hiler, became a good friend. The two traveled throughout Provence.

Invigorated by the hot and beautiful climate, Woodruff worked feverishly, ten to 12 hours a day. One of his oils, *Provençal Landscape,* 1930, depicts the countryside with its steep hills, dense foliage, terraced fields, and white–washed, red–roofed homes. Only a sliver of silvery sky appears above this compact scene which echoes Cézanne's treatments of the Mt. St. Victoire in its geometric reduction of forms. Woodruff's style had definitely evolved from the type of illustrations he had produced in Paris; now drawing and painting were one. Later Woodruff explained his technique in an interview with Esther G. Robick by quoting Cézanne, "When I draw I paint and when I paint I draw." This process was also apparent in *The Card Players,* 1930, Woodruff's most daring and "moderne" French work. Woodruff's depiction of two figures playing cards in a cafe offers a unique interpretation of a subject explored by Cézanne in five canvases from 1890 to 1892. No doubt Woodruff had seen the last of these, of two men rather than the original five, in the Louvre. In this work and the others, Cézanne used reverse perspective, a technique borrowed from Japanese woodcuts. Woodruff pushed the perspective further, in the manner of Picasso's cubism.

When Woodruff's new work was shown at the Harmon Foundation in early 1931, it elicited positive responses from white collectors and writers, such as Edward Alden Jewell, *New York Times* critic, who saw a distinct French influence in Woodruff's work. Locke and White also admired the change, but Du Bois did not care for the modern look.

During Woodruff's last year in France, he studied fourteenth– and fifteenth–century media and methods of painting and began to work in gouache on wood. In his letter to Alain Locke dated March 24, 1932, and located on the Moorland–Spingarn Research Center, he said he believed these pieces were "without doubt the most promising things I've done. . . . I was really on the road to true accomplishment." In April of 1931 Woodruff also produced his first mural for two weeks' board at a café. Finally realizing he could no longer support himself in France, the painter accepted Atlanta University president John Hope's offer to teach in Georgia.

Teaching in Atlanta

Woodruff had an enormous impact on Atlanta University. He founded the art department, broke the color bar at the High Museum by bringing students there to view the collections, secured a Carnegie Corporation gift of 5,000 art history slides, brought in traveling exhibitions of American art, recruited sculptor Nancy Elizabeth Prophet for the faculty, and organized a series of annual exhibitions that began in 1942. The shows offered African Americans exhibition opportunities and purchase prizes. By the time they ended in 1970, the university had acquired 350 works of art.

Woodruff's semi–cubist style altered drastically as he began to depict American southern landscapes in regionalist and expressionist modes. Woodblock prints such as *Returning Home* (1935) and *By Parties Unknown* (1938) documented his outrage against African American ramshackle housing and lynching. Woodruff's pupils (including Wilmer Jennings, Frederick Flemister, Eugene Grigsby, and Hayward Oubré) worked in a similar mode and were dubbed the "Atlanta School" because of their African American subjects in the city. *Time* magazine for September 21, 1942, mocked Woodruff's self–described "Painter's Guild" as "Outhouse Art" because some students included privies in their Georgia landscapes.

After studying Mexican art and working gratis for muralist Diego Rivera in Mexico City in the summer of 1934, Woodruff produced two murals as part of the Works Progress Administration, one for the Atlanta School of Social Work. This piece had two panels, *Shantytown* and *Mudhill.* Murals which followed included *The Founding of Talladega College* (1938–1939) and the *Amistad Murals,* 1839 (1939) at Talladega College in Alabama, *Settlement and Development* (1850–1949) [of California by African Americans] for the Golden State Mutual Life Insurance Company in Los Angeles (1949), and *The Art of the Negro* in the Trevor Arnett Library at Atlanta University (1950–1951).

Going Abstract in New York

In 1943 Woodruff received a Rosenwald Foundation Fellowship which allowed him to study and paint in New York for two years. In 1946 New York University hired Woodruff as associate professor of art, a position he would hold until 1967. Two years prior to retirement as professor emeritus, students elected him "Great Teacher."

By 1955 Woodruff's style was almost virtually abstract, incorporating elements from African motifs and forms. Stylized Dogon granary doors with symbols of Ashanti gold weights, for instance, appeared in his *Celestial Gate* series of the 1960s, and Woodruff drew many torsos derived from sculptures of Shango, the Yoruba thunder god. Yet he also continued to paint landscapes in brilliant colors, and such representative works as a series of children playing. Woodruff shared his theories on art and the civil rights struggle with fellow painters Romare Bearden and Norman Lewis as the founding members of Spiral, a weekly discussion group begun in 1962. Bearden and Henderson quoted a statement he made in the 1970s: ''any black artist who claims he is creating art must begin with some black image . . . [it] can be the environment, it can be the look on a man's face. It can be anything. . . . But if it's worth its while, it's also got to be universal in its broader impact and its presence.''

Truly one of the first African American modernists, Woodruff's impact and presence continue to be felt in his many and varied paintings, prints, and murals, as well as in the profound influence he had on several generations of students throughout the United States.

REFERENCES

Bearden, Romare and Harry Henderson. *A History of African–American Artists from 1792 to the Present.* New York: Pantheon Books, 1993.

''Black Beaux Arts.'' *Time* 40 (21 September 1942): 74.

Campbell, Mary Schmidt. *Hale Woodruff: 50 Years of His Art.* New York: The Studio Museum in Harlem, April 29–June 24, 1979.

Crawford, Doris. Hale Aspacio Woodruff. M.A. thesis, Howard University, 1972.

Leininger–Miller, Theresa. African–American Artists in Paris, 1922–1934. Ph.D. dissertation, Yale University, 1995.

Murray, Al. Audio interview with Hale Woodruff, November 18, 1968. Transcript. Archives of American Art, Washington, DC.

Perisho, Sally. *Woodruff, Hardrick and Scott.* Indianapolis: Indianapolis Museum of Art, February 1, 1977–March 16, 1977.

Robick, Esther G. Audio interview with Hale Woodruff, November 10, 1970. Transcript. Archives of American Art, Washington, DC.

Stoelting, Winifred. Hale Woodruff, Artist and Teacher: Through the Atlanta Years. Ph.D. dissertation, Emory University, 1978.

Wilson, Judith. *Selected Essays: Art and Artists from the Harlem Renaissance to the 1980's.* Atlanta, GA: National Black Arts Festival, 1988.

Woodruff, Hale. ''My Meeting with Henry O. Tanner.'' *Crisis* 77 (January, 1970): 7–12.

Articles by Woodruff in the *Indianapolis Star,* January 6, 27, 1928; February 5, 1928; March 18, 1928; April 22, 1928; May 27, 1928; June 10, 1928; July 8, 1928; October 7, 1928; November 4, 1928; February 17, 1929.

COLLECTIONS

Woodruff's works are in the collections of the Metropolitan Museum of Art, the Detroit Institute of Arts, the Studio Museum in Harlem, the Newark Museum, Yale University, and many black colleges and universities. His papers and correspondence are in the Archives of American Art; Harmon Foundation Papers; W. E. B. Du Bois Papers, Library of Congress; Countee Cullen Papers, Amistad Center; Rosenwald Archives, Fisk University; and Alain Locke Papers in the Moorland–Spingarn Research Center, Howard University.

Theresa Leininger–Miller

Granville T. Woods
(1856–1910)
Inventor, entrepreneur

Granville T. Woods, often called the ''Black Edison,'' was an inventor who collected more than 60 patents in his lifetime. These inventions were vital to the development and improvement of electrical and mechanical equipment, the transmission of messages by electricity, and several other devices ranging from an incubator for young chickens to motor vehicles at amusement parks. His works continue to have a significant impact on the world.

Woods was born free in Columbus, Ohio, on April 23, 1856, to Martha and Tailer Woods. Although his formal education only lasted until he was ten years old, Woods continued to educate himself by spending a great deal of time in public libraries studying and reading about electricity. He also borrowed many books on this subject from neighbors and employers.

Woods started working when he was ten. He held an apprenticeship in a machine shop as a machinist and also learned the blacksmith trade. This work experience was the catalyst for many of his later inventions. He supplemented on–the–job experiences with reading and studying electronics. Woods moved to Springfield, Illinois in 1876 and worked in a rolling mill. Then he worked in a New York City machine shop and in the evenings he studied mechanical engineering at a local college. On February 6, 1878, Woods was hired as an engineer on a British steamer called the *Ironside* which took him on a long tour abroad. He worked on the steamer for two years and traveled a great deal. In 1882 Woods was hired as a fireman on the Danville and Southern Railroad and later moved up to become engineer.

Woods lived in Cincinnati from 1884 to 1890. There he opened his own electrical shop in 1884 with his brother, Lyates. The shop, Woods Electric Company, was one of the earliest companies of its kind to be owned and managed by African Americans. Some of the products manufactured at their company included telephone, telegraph, and electrical equipment. Because of his interest in steam engines and thermal power, Woods received his first patent for a steam boiler furnace on January 3, 1884. His invention provided a more efficient manner of combustion.

Granville T. Woods

Woods received another patent on December 2 that year for inventing the telephone transmitter. This invention made it possible for telephone messages to be transmitted through electricity. According to *The Black Book,* Woods included the following specifications describing his product, the Telephone System and Apparatus, to the U.S. Patent Office:

> My invention relates to a method of and apparatus for the transmission of articulate speech and other sounds through the medium of electricity, its object being to obtain an increased force of transmission of the impulses controlling the action of the diaphragm at the receiving end; also, to obviate the disturbing effects now attributed to induction from neighboring lines.

The induction telegraph system, called the Synchronous Multiplex Railway Telegraph, patented in 1887, was the most advanced of Woods's many inventions. The *Negro Almanac* notes that this instrument was designed ''for the purpose of adverting accidents by keeping each train informed of the whereabouts of the one immediately ahead or following it, in communicating with stations from moving trains, and in promoting general social and commercial intercourse.'' Prior to this invention, trains were unable to communicate; thus, Woods's invention greatly improved the safety of railway travel and transportation.

After the invention, Thomas Edison challenged Woods's product in two court cases. Each time Woods was able to prove that he was the inventor. The U.S. Patent also recognized that the induction telegraph was Woods's invention and he marketed his product through his own company. His company remained in operation until 1893. He continued his inventions but moved to New York City in 1890.

The dispute with Edison over the invention brought widespread publicity to Woods and his work. In 1888 the *American Catholic Tribune* hailed Woods as ''the greatest electrician in the world.'' Some historians noted that his inventions surpassed those of Thomas Edison and Alexander Graham Bell, and were astonished by his expertise and skills in electricity and mathematics. With his skills, Woods patented nearly fifty inventions pertaining to electric railways which ultimately had a significant impact on railway transportation. It was these inventions that brought him the most recognition.

Although Woods gained notoriety for his electric railway patents, he also received patents for other inventions. He made one of the early types of incubators used for hatching eggs. Other inventions included a relay instrument (1887), an electromechanical brake (1887), a tunnel construction for electric railways (1898), an automatic safety cut–out for electric circuits (1889), and an apparatus for use with motor vehicles at amusement areas (1889). His last patent, for a vehicle controlling apparatus, was on September 24, 1907.

Although Woods was very talented and his inventions greatly contributed to society, he faced the ugly effects of racism. Often when he and his company tried to market their products to larger companies, they received small profits. When Woods sold his patents to other companies; the companies received all the profits and recognition, leaving the inventor with nothing. Woods, like other black inventors of this era, was able to make the products but remained basically unable to function as a businessman. Woods sold several of his patents to Thomas Edison's General Electric Company, Westinghouse Electric Company, and American Bell Telephone Company and assigned a number of patents to other companies.

Apparently Woods never married. Following a stroke on January 28, he died on January 30, 1910, in Harlem Hospital in New York City. He was buried on February 3 in St. Michael's Cemetery in Astoria, Queens, New York. Patents for over sixty of his inventions were recorded with the United States Patent Office. In 1969 a school, Elementary Public School No. 335, in Brooklyn, New York, was named in his honor. On October 11, 1974, The governor of Ohio, John J. Gilligan, issued a proclamation to officially recognize Woods's accomplishements. Woods was a man of greatness whose intelligence, perseverance, and diligent work led him to significant and lasting contributions in the field of electricity.

REFERENCES

Brown, Mitchell. ''Granville T. Woods: Inventor.'' http://www.lib.lsu.edu/lib/chem/display/woods.html (last modified February 24, 1998), accessed 1997.

Christopher, Michael C. ''Granville T. Woods: The Plight of a Black Inventor.'' *Journal of Black Studies* 11 (March 1989): 269–76.

Haber, Louis. *Black Pioneers of Science and Inventions.* New York: Harcourt, Brace, and World, 1970.
Harris, Middleton, with the assistance of Morris Levitt, Roger Furman, and Ernest Smith. *The Black Book.* New York: Random House, 1974.
Logan, Rayford W., and Michael R. Winston, eds. *Dictionary of American Negro Biography.* New York: Norton, 1982.
Low, W. Augustus, and Virgil A. Clift, eds. *Encyclopedia of Black America.* New York: McGraw–Hill, 1981.
Ploski, Harry A., and Roscoe A. Brown. *Negro Almanac.* New York: Bellwether Publishing Co., 1967.
Simmons, William J. *Men of Mark.* Cleveland: Geo. M. Rewell, 1887.

Theodosia T. Shields

Tiger Woods
(1975–)
Professional golfer

Tiger Woods

Golf sensation Tiger Woods won the prestigious sixty–first Masters golf tournament in Augusta, Georgia, on Sunday, April 13, 1997, and at age 21 became the youngest winner and the first black to claim a major professional golf championship. His lead was the greatest winning margin in a major event since 1962. Already a champion, Woods had won three consecutive U.S. Golf Association (USGA) junior title championships, three consecutive U.S. Amateur championships, the 1996 Las Vegas Invitational, the Walt Disney World/Oldsmobile Classic, the 1997 Mercedes Championship, and a host of other competitions.

Eldrick ''Tiger'' Woods was born in a Long Beach, California, hospital on December 20, 1975. His father Earl Woods, a mixture of African American, Chinese, and Cherokee, was at one time a catcher for Kansas State University and the first black to play baseball in the Big Seven Conference (now the Big Eight). He was also a Green Beret who served two tours of duty for the U.S. Army in Vietnam. His son was nicknamed Tiger in memory of Earl Woods's Vietnamese combat friend, Nguyen Phong. Earlier Earl Woods had been a U.S. Army public information officer stationed in Brooklyn, and had two sons and a daughter from a previous marriage. Tiger Woods's mother, Kultida ''Tida'' Punsawad Woods met Earl Woods while she was a secretary in the U.S. Army office in Bangkok. They married in 1969. A Buddhist from Thailand, her parents separated when she was five; she then grew up in a boarding school. Earl and Tida Woods, who lacked security in their own childhoods, feel a special need to be totally committed to their son and so shower him with love.

After the war, Earl and Tida Woods moved to Brooklyn where Earl was stationed at Fort Hamilton. He first played golf when he was 42, at an army base in Fort Dix, New Jersey, and was hooked on golf since then. After Earl Woods retired from military service in 1974 with the rank of colonel, he and his wife moved to Orange County, California, where Woods worked for the McDonnell Douglas rocket program. Before young Tiger could walk, his father took him to the garage of their Cypress, California, home, strapped him in a high chair to restrain him, then practiced his golf shots. Tiger Woods hit his first golf ball at age two. When he was three, he won a Pitch, Putt and Drive competition against 10– and 11–year–olds; then news spread about his golf swing. A sportscaster from Los Angeles wrote a feature story on the young golfer. After the producers of the *Mike Douglas Show* saw the story, they put young Tiger Woods on the air where he played with Bob Hope. The show, *That's Incredible,* followed by putting him on with Fran Tarkenton. Quoted in *Tiger Woods,* he said, ''When I get big I'm going to beat Jack Nicklaus and Tom Watson.'' After *That's Incredible* was aired, his schoolmates in kindergarten, where he was the only black, began to ask for his autograph, but Woods, who could not yet write in script, responded by printing his name.

Wins Amateur Championships

During his early life, Tiger Woods ''hung out'' with his father at golf tournaments, where he mixed and played with golfers from five to 30 years older than he. At an early age Woods's good hand–eye coordination was noticed; by the time he was five or six, he is said to have demonstrated remarkable precision in golf. He did well in other sports, but preferred golf. Although at times his parents tried to restrain him from playing so much golf, it was Tiger Woods himself who wanted to play regularly and to enter every tournament he could find. His parents stressed schoolwork and said that was the primary issue.

Woods, whose career is managed by the International Management Group (IMG), shot five under par at Presidio Hills to win the Junior World Championship in the ten and under division when he was eight years old. By age ten, he had won two Junior World ten–and–under championships in San Diego. In August of 1989, he was 13 and about to enter the eighth grade; he played his first national tournament, the 21st Insurance Golf Classic at the Texarkana Country Club. Although he lost the match, he drew heavy applause from the audience. In the summer of 1989 he won his fourth Optimist Junior World title and by age 14 he had won the Optimist Junior World for a record fifth time.

On July 28, 1991, Woods won his first national title, the U.S. Junior Amateur Championship. He was 15–years old, the youngest winner in the Junior Amateur in golf, and the third black to win a USGA title. He won the title again in 1992 at the championship in Milton, Massachusetts, and his third consecutive amateur championship in 1993 at the Waverly Golf Course and Country Club in Portland, Oregon, becoming the first person ever to win the title three times consecutively.

After finishing middle school in Anaheim California, Woods entered Western High School. At Western, Woods was an honor student as well as an athlete, and won the Dial Award as the top high school male athlete in the country. During his high school years, he won a number of other championships, including the CIF–SCGA High School Invitational Championship, the Southern California Junior Championship, the Ping Phoenix Junior, the Los Angeles City Junior, the Optimist International Junior World (for the sixth time), and others.

Woods had become interested in Stanford University after watching ice skater Debi Thomas perform in the Olympics and wanted to study there for a degree in accounting. His interest in the University of Nevada$_L$as Vegas, known for athletics, was so intense that he became physically ill as he tried to make a choice between the two schools. He preferred Stanford for its academics and announced his decision on November 10, 1993, at the Western High School gymnasium. In the spring of 1994, his final semester of high school, Woods had a hectic schedule: a host of golf tournaments from Orlando to New York to Chicago. On December 30, 1993, his eighteenth birthday, Tiger Woods and his father plotted a game plan to prepare the young golfer for the U.S. Amateur Championship at the Sawgrass–TPC in Florida, with a view toward the majors. He also won three U.S. Amateur championships. His win in August of 1994, which he did with a dramatic comeback, made him the youngest player ever to win the Amateur. His 1994 win of the U.S. Amateur Championship was a benchmark for Tiger Woods; he appeared for the first time before a national audience on television.

His hometown, Cypress, gave Tiger Woods the key to the city before he left for Palo Alto. He was recognized wherever he went, and, hoping to camouflage himself, began

Tiger Woods gets excited about his play, 1998.

wearing dark glasses. He turned down offers to appear on the *Tonight Show* and *Late Night with David Letterman.* He entered Stanford in the fall of 1994 where he took a rather light academic load. When he fell behind in calculus, he dropped the course and abstained from watching television. On December 2, 1994, while returning to his dormitory one night, Woods was mugged by a knife–wielding assailant who demanded his wallet; when he learned that there was no wallet he took the Buddha that Woods's mother had given him. The attacker struck Woods in the jaw with the knife handle, knocking him to the ground.

Woods played college golf while at Stanford and was a member of Stanford's NCAA defending championship team. He won the 1996 NCAA, shooting 69–67–69–80, and the U.S. Amateur that year to become one of only two golfers to win both titles in the same year. After his freshman year, he returned to Cypress with a summer schedule that included play in his first U.S. Open and his first British Open. He would return for a play in the Western Open and make his debut in the Scottish Open. Woods's success and popularity caused speculation that he would leave college and turn professional. In Tim Rosaforte's biography of Woods, Woods denied the successive rumors, stating that he would not turn pro until graduation in 1998 ''unless something exciting happens.'' Sometime later Woods said on *The Tonight Show with Jay Leno* that a viable offer that outweighed both Stanford and amateur golf would persuade him to turn pro. About this time IMG was house hunting for Woods in Orlando. On August 28, 1996, Woods turned professional, leaving Stanford after two years of study.

The Race Issue

Tida Woods believes her son is "the Universal Child." She told *Sports Illustrated* for December 23, 1996, "Tiger has Thai. African, Chinese, American Indian and European blood. He can hold everyone together." While Tiger Woods has a multiracial background, he acknowledges that, in the United States, even the smallest amount of black blood means that he is black. He told Oprah Winfrey that he came up with the name "Cablinasian" to describe his mixed heritage. In school he was asked to identify his racial background; he said in the interview that he checked African American and Asian. "Those are the two I was raised under and the only two I know," he added. As a three–year–old, he and his father were forbidden on the golf courses, including the Navy Gold Course in Cypress. Racism was demonstrated in the integrated neighborhood where the Woods family lived. Their home was pelted with limes and BB gunfire. Since he was five years old, he has known the racism that goes with being black. On his first day of kindergarten, when he was five years old, a gang of older children tied him to a tree, threw rocks at him, and called him monkey and nigger. He kept the experience to himself for several days trying to sort out the meaning of it all.

Woods's climb up the professional ladder was quick. He had nine tournament appearances. Participating in the Los Angeles Open in March of 1992, he was also the youngest person ever to play in a Professional Golf Association event. By the time he won the 1997 Mercedes Championship in Carlsbad, California, he had earned his first million dollars faster than any other golfer in history. Woods's professional golfing lessons began with Rudy Doran when he was four and continued until he was ten. Then John Anselmo taught him and, along with Butch Harmon, continues as his teacher.

After turning professional, Woods immediately won two PGA Tour events in seven attempts,he first in Las Vegas and the second at Disney World. Crowds turn out to witness his golfing techniques. Tiger Woods's first win for 1997 was the Mercedes Championship. He won $216,000 as first place prize, pushing him past the $1 million mark. In nine tournament appearances, he had become the fastest golfer to reach that level. Since turning pro, he has made endorsements totaling $100 million. In November of 1996, he made a commercial for Titleist, a leading golf–equipment manufacturer, for more than $20 million over a five–year period. Predictions are that he will win another $40 million from five–year endorsements he has signed with Nike, the makers of athletic wear. In May of 1997 Woods added to his wealth again when he signed a five–year contract for reportedly $40 million to become a spokesman for American Express. Of this amount, some sources report that American Express donated $1 million to Woods's foundation to benefit junior golf for minorities. American Express executive Kenneth Chenault told the *New York Times* for May 20, 1997, "In Tiger Woods, we have a representative who has captured the imagination of many different kinds of people." He added that "discipline, hard work, and preparation" characterize woods, and those "are the pillars of our business." In March of 1998, Woods became the eighth permanent spokesperson for Wheaties, the cereal popularly known as the "breakfast of champions." Wheaties featured him on three different box covers.

Wins the Masters

When he was 19–years old, in April of 1995, Tiger Woods first competed in the Masters tournament, at Augusta, Georgia. Although he lost the match, he made history by becoming the first black amateur to compete in the Masters. He made history again on April 13, 1997, when he overpowered the course and the field with a record four–round score of 18–under–par 270 and a 12–stroke margin over the runner–up and became the youngest man and the first man of color to win the sixty–first Masters tournament. When he won the Masters he and his father had a long, emotional embrace that was one of the most revealing moments in golf history and came to be known as "The Hug." Quoted in the *New York Times* for April 30, 1997, President Clinton called the image that was shown around the country "the best shot of the day." Woods then slipped on his green jacket, a Masters tradition, accepted his prize of $486,000 and the rite of passage into the elite status that the championship brought. Although he failed to follow by winning the U.S. Open, in June he was able to move Greg Norman from the number one spot in the world golf rankings. Woods had difficulty winning games after the Masters, but he made a great comeback in January of 1998, overcoming an eight–stroke deficit to win the Johnnie Walker Classic in Phuket, Thailand.

Quoted in *USA Today* for April 14, 1997, Woods praised black pioneers Charlie Sifford, Lee Elder, and Ted Rhodes, saying: "these are the guys who paved the way. . . . Coming up 18, I said a little prayer of thanks to those guys. Those guys are the ones who did it." Quoted in the same source, Elder said he was proud. "We have a black champion. That's going to have major significance. It will open the door for more blacks to become members here. It will get more minority kids involved in golf." Quoted in the *New York Times* for April 14, 1997, the 74–year old Charlie Sifford, still active in senior PGA Tour matches, called Wood's win "a wonderful thing for golf,never mind the racial thing. . . . This is the kid who's doing what wanted to do, but never had the chance to do." Golf legendary Jack Nicklaus, who first played with Woods in 1996, was not surprised at the victory.

Woods's performance and appearance at the Masters led to record–breaking audiences on the court and before television sets. The overnight television ratings set a record for Saturday viewing. Woods had raised golf's level as a sport and increased its lure. His success continued when he won the 1997 GTE Byron Nelson Classic played in Irving, Texas, in May.

In 1992 Woods was named *Golf World's* Man of the Year. He was honored at the Fred Haskins Award dinner which cited America's outstanding college golfer of 1996. In December of 1996 *Sports Illustrated* named Woods Sportsman of the Year and published his photograph on the cover of the December 23 issue as well as carrying a lengthy article on Woods and his family. He was named 1997 PGA Tour Player of the Year while in January of 1998 the Associated Press named him Male Athlete of the Year. He has appeared on the cover of numerous magazines such as *Jet* (April 26, 1997) and for *Sports Illustrated* again (April 21, 1997). *Time* for April 21, 1997, named Woods, along with other notables, one of ''The Most Influential People in America. Results of the latest *Wall Street Journal*/NBC popularity poll, cited in *Jet* magazine for May 19, 1997, show that Americans gave Woods a 76 percent positive rating, placing him higher than Michael Jordan, but lower than Colin Powell. The three men were then rated America's most popular Americans.

According to the *Sports Illustrated* article, Tida Woods believes that the her son's life is a ''directed scenario,'' having been persuaded by monks from a Buddhist temple in Los Angeles and another in Bangkok that Tiger has ''wondrous powers.'' She was told that, ''If he becomes a politician, he will be either a president or a prime minister. If he enters the military, he will be a general.'' Tiger Woods likes Buddhism; in the same issue of *Sports Illustrated* he said that Buddhism is ''a whole way of being and living.'' Each year on his birthday he visits a Buddhist temple with his mother and makes gifts of rice, sugar, and salt to the monks. His Thai grandfather's gift to him of a mother–of–pearl Buddha watches over him in bed, and he wears a gold Buddha on a chain around his neck. Buddhism is ''based on discipline and respect and personal responsibility.... I believe in Buddhism. Not every aspect, but most of it,'' he continued.

Woods admits that he is a ''fast food freak'' who often forgets to ask others if he may bring food for them when he goes to the fast food restaurants. During his stay in Augusta for the 1997 Masters, he ate burgers and fries. He loves riding roller coasters, spinning out golf carts, winning at card games, and telling dirty jokes. Although his father introduced him to jazz music when he was a newborn, he prefers rap music. According to *Sports Illustrated* for December 23, 1996, his favorite expression is ''I knew that.'' Now that he has become an international sports figure, Woods told Oprah Winfrey that his loss of privacy has been the most difficult thing to accept.

The six–feet two–inch tall golfer has broad shoulders, powerful thighs, and a 28–inch waist, and weighs 150 pounds. He rotates his torso and hips more quickly than any golfer that his swing coach Rick Smith has ever seen. In addition to golf, Woods likes basketball and fishing. According to *Sports Illustrated* for December 23, 1996, Earl Woods believes his son is the chosen one to change the world. Tiger Woods has stamina, an excellent memory, and a powerful and creative mind.

Tiger Woods draws a crowd and creates excitement on the golf course. Many who come to see him previously displayed no interest in the sport, and many of his followers are young children and minority groups. This may well be what inspired Woods and his father to establish a Tiger Woods Foundation to provide golf scholarships for inner–city youngsters across the country, set up golf clinics and coaches, and provide the youngsters access to golf courses. Woods plans to complete his Stanford degree by enrolling in correspondence courses. He told Oprah Winfrey that he is a firm believer in education and wants to return to school because of the value of education instilled in him by his parents. He regularly wears red when playing golf on Sundays, in part because of his mother's astrology belief that he is ''going for the kill.''

Quoted in *Training a Tiger,* Woods remembers the strength, support, and guidance that he received from his parents from the beginning: ''Their teachings assist me in almost every decision I make. They are my foundation.'' Tiger Woods is an artist who transcends golf and continues to overwhelm audiences and other golfers with his winning record and magical golfing technique. Tiger Woods currently lives in Orlando, Florida. He has a will to win, and he does. Woods suffered a long victory drought in the United States. In May of 1998, however, he won the BellSouth Classic in Duluth, Georgia; it was his seventh win in 37 PGA Tour events since becoming a professional.

Current address: International Management Group, Attn. Tiger Woods, One Erieview Plaza, Suite 1300, Cleveland, OH 44114.

REFERENCES

Anderson, Dave. ''Sports of the Times.'' *New York Times,* April 14, 1997.

Blauvelt, Harry. ''Tiger Leaps Into Master's History.'' *USA Today,* April 14, 1997.

Diaz, Jaime. ''The Big Bang.'' *Sports Illustrated* 85 (23 December 1996): 54–55.

Dorman, Larry. ''Tiger Woods Adds Chapter to His Legend.'' *New York Times,* October 21, 1996.

———. ''Earl Woods: Tiger's Dad Has It All Under Control.'' *New York Times,* April 30, 1997.

———. ''Lee Elder Was There to Celebrate.'' *New York Times,* April 14, 1997.

———. ''Woods Tears Up Augusta and Tears Down Barriers.'' *New York Times,* April 14, 1997.

''From Eight Back, Tiger Wins.'' *Nashville Tennessean,* January 26, 1998.

''Mercedes Champion.'' *Jet* 91 (27 January 1997): 51.

''Powell, Woods, Jordan Most Popular Americans.'' *Jet* 91 (19 May 1997): 5.

Reilly, Rick. ''Stroke of Genius.'' *Sports Illustrated* 86 (21 April 1997): 30–49.

———. ''Top Cast.'' *Sports Illustrated* 85 (28 October 1996): 48–50.

Rosaforte, Tim. *Tiger Woods: The Making of a Champion.* New York: St. Martin's Press, 1997.

''Tiger Woods Makes History at The Masters.'' *Jet* 91 (28 April 1997): 52–59.

Smith, Gary. ''The Chosen One.'' *Sports Illustrated* 85 (23 December 1996): 28–53.

''Tiger Woods Signs Pact with American Express.'' *New York Times,* May 20, 1997.

''Time's 25 Most Influential Americans.'' *Time* 149 (21 April 1997): 40–66. Woods, Bob. ''The Natural.'' *Profiles: The Magazine of Continental Airlines* 8 (April 1995): 30–34.

Woods, Earl, with Pete McDaniel. *Training a Tiger.* New York: HarperCollins, 1997.

"Woods Ends Slide with BellSouth Victory." *USA Today*, May 1, 1998.

Woods, Tiger. Interview with Oprah Winfrey. *Oprah Winfrey Show*, April 24, 1997.

Woods, Tiger. (Website) http://www.tigerwoods.com (accessed March 1998).

Jessie Carney Smith

Carter G. Woodson

(1875–1950)

Historian, writer, publisher, organization cofounder

Carter G. Woodson

Carter Godwin Woodson, called "The Father of Black History," worked tirelessly to incorporate African American history into the schools at a time when American society deliberately denied African Americans their rights. From Woodson's desire to learn came a desire to educate others about the misrepresented African American history. First as a teacher, and later as a publisher and founder of scholarly journals and societies, Woodson taught African Americans to be proud of their heritage while simultaneously proving to whites that black history was just as noteworthy as white history. He willingly offered all of his time, talent, and money to demonstrate to the world that African American history and culture offered an engrossing study for any who cared to pursue it.

Woodson, the son of former slaves, Ann Eliza and James Henry Woodson, was born in 1875, just ten years after the close of the Civil War in New Canton, Virginia. The war had left the South in a state of near–chaos and resistance to the improved legal status of former slaves was fierce. At the time of Woodson's birth, Social Darwinism proclaimed that of all the races of the world, blacks were least capable of intellectual prowess. Even in schools and colleges for the emancipated slaves, racist philosophies so hampered African American students that most—consciously or unconsciously—admired European culture and civilization and despised their own African past. In the same way that the institution of slavery had held blacks captive, racial discrimination took hold of African American history, either by denying it a place in the schoolrooms or by using it as a justification for racial subjugation.

Freed slaves like Woodson's parents had to find some way to provide for their needs. Most received little help in finding employment or establishing their households. Woodson was one of nine children, two of whom died in infancy. He worked hard, long hours as a sharecropper along with the other Woodsons. Because of the rigors of farming, the local school opened only four months out of the year. When it was open, Woodson and his siblings attended as often as possible. Woodson had an intense hunger for more education, a desire which had its seed in the stories of slavery shared by the adults around him. His father often asked him to read aloud, particularly newspapers. In this way young Woodson learned about various places and events on the international scene.

Woodson had a greater opportunity to learn about black history when his family traveled to West Virginia where Carter Woodson worked in the mines. While working there, he often had the opportunity to go to a black–owned establishment where the laborers could eat and relax. The owner, Oliver Jones, was a black Civil War veteran who had a keen interest in the history of blacks in America. Jones owned a few books about black life, and the miners who frequented his shop subscribed to newspapers owned by blacks and whites. Woodson used his leisure time to read the history texts and regularly read to the group of black laborers from a wide variety of newspapers. The knowledge he gained through these exercises partially slaked his thirst for education but he was not yet satisfied. He also listened to accounts from these men about their lives in antebellum days.

Only after his family settled into a new home in Huntington, West Virginia, and Woodson had earned enough to support his needs, did he go to school full–time. He enrolled in Frederick Douglass High School in Huntington, just a few months before his twentieth birthday. An exceptional student, Woodson graduated in less than two years. He continued his education from 1896 to 1898 at an integrated institution in Kentucky, Berea College. Returning to West Virginia, Woodson got a job teaching in Fayette County where he performed all of the duties necessitated by a one-room school house including lighting the stove in the morning and cleaning up in the evening. He subsequently returned to his alma mater, Douglass High School, where he became principal. Hunger for education drew him back to Berea for more training and eventually to the University of Chicago after a Kentucky law closed Berea's doors to black students. With the aid of the courses he took in Chicago, he finally earned his bachelor of literature degree from Berea in 1903 when the school reopened to black students.

During the year he studied at the University of Chicago, Woodson applied for a teaching position in the Philippines and earned a position with the United States Bureau of Insular Affairs as a general superintendent of education. The prospect of traveling to see the world that he had read about in newspapers thrilled Woodson. He went by train to California and by ship to Hong Kong and finally Manila. At first Woodson could not communicate effectively with his students at the school in San Isidro. To improve his skills, he started studying English and French by taking University of Chicago correspondence courses and was soon fluent in both languages. Woodson taught English, health, and agriculture in the Philippines until 1907 when physical problems prompted him to return to the United States.

After recovering, Woodson decided to travel to other parts of Asia and into Europe and North Africa. He studied for a semester at the Sorbonne and improved his French-speaking skills, visited numerous libraries and museums, and learned much more about the peoples and cultures of the world. He also learned the rudiments of locating primary source materials for research and methods of integrating these materials into his writing. Far from satisfying Woodson's desire to learn, his travels only enhanced his thirst for education.

Woodson decided to return to the University of Chicago to work on a graduate degree. University officials did not accept all of his courses from Berea so Woodson had to take some undergraduate courses. Undaunted, he worked on another bachelor's degree and his master's simultaneously. History was his major and his thesis discussed French diplomatic relations with Germany in the eighteenth century. After much hard work Woodson received a bachelor of arts degree in 1907 and a master's degree in history, romance languages, and literature in 1908 from the University of Chicago. He then enrolled in Harvard University and completed his coursework by 1909.

Upon receiving a scholarship to pursue his dissertation research, Woodson sought a teaching position in Washington, D.C., where he could use the vast resources of the Library of Congress to prepare his dissertation on the secession of Virginia. Although he taught at several district schools, his longest tenure—1911 to 1917—was at the M Street High School where he taught French, Spanish, English, and American history.

During his time at M Street, Woodson passed his doctoral examinations, completed a dissertation on "The Disruption in Virginia," and earned a doctorate in history from Harvard University in 1912. His was an arduous journey fraught with difficulties and prejudice, but Woodson remained undaunted by the obstacles he faced. The other Woodson children and some of their near-relatives became teachers, doctors, businessmen, and professionals in other fields, but only Woodson would command prominence as a black intellectual. He was the first person of slave ancestry—and the second black—in United States history to receive a doctor of philosophy degree, preceded only by the eminent scholar W. E. B. Du Bois, whose parents were free persons of color.

Woodson unsuccessfully attempted to enlist the support of his Harvard professors to procure a publisher for his dissertation. Still resolute in his desire to become a published historian, Woodson submitted another book, *The Education of the Negro Prior to 1861,* to G. P. Putnam's Sons which they published in 1915. Black suffragist and civil rights advocate Mary Church Terrell reviewed the book in the *Journal of Negro History,* noting that she found it hard to imagine any phase of black history "more thrilling than an account of the desperate and prolonged struggle . . . for the mental and spiritual enlightenment of the slave." Terrell, expressing nothing but admiration for Woodson's first book, commented upon its thorough documentation and called it a "work of profound historical research."

Helps Establish Black History Association

Even with these great accomplishments under his belt, Woodson did not really find his life's work until he, along with several other men, founded the Association for the Study of Negro Life and History in 1915. From that point until he died in 1950 he spent almost every hour of each day in an effort to see that all persons–black and white, rich and poor–could have the opportunity to learn about African American history. Finding little time for family or friends, Woodson never married or had children. The association and its work became his obsession, and he jealously guarded it from outside control. His experience taught him that whites doubted the value of African American history, and that blacks were so afflicted by the specter of racial inferiority and the humiliation of slavery that they did not seek to know more about their past. Woodson decided that he would use his historical training to demonstrate to the world that blacks had an interesting and admirable history.

In 1916, the year after the establishment of the association Woodson started the *Journal of Negro History,* a vehicle through which scholars could disseminate their scholarship in the area of black history and culture. The first issue included an article by Woodson entitled "The Negroes of Cincinnati Prior to the Civil War," another by Tuskegee sociologist and fellow ASALH founder Monroe N. Work called "The Passing Tradition of African Civilization" and two others by A. O. Stafford and W. B. Hartgrove. Mary Church Terrell, teacher and writer Jessie R. Fauset, and historian Walter Dyson contributed book reviews in the first issue. Years later, black theologian Benjamin E. Mays commented upon the journal's contribution in the first 65 years of its existence. In "I Knew Carter G. Woodson," he stated that the journal had documented black life so well that "no term paper, no thesis, no monograph, and no book dealing with the Negro can be written'' without consulting its pages.

With the incorporation of the association and the launching of the journal, Woodson had found his niche. Even though the association had a small office and a secretary, Woodson still needed further employment in order to survive. He became the principal of Armstrong Manual Training School in the District of Columbia from 1918 to 1919 but left that position to work at Howard University where he served as dean of the School of Liberal Arts, head of the graduate faculty, and professor of history. Although Woodson worked full–time, he continued his tireless research and writing. In 1918 the association published Woodson's study, *A Century of Negro Migration.*

At Howard, Woodson had charge of five graduate students. Four of them did not survive the rigors of his program but one, Arnett J. Lindsay, was able to successfully complete it. Lindsay later wrote that Woodson warned his five students that they had to maintain at least a B average in order to remain in the program, stressed the seriousness of graduate study, and urged the students to develop a broad concept of history considering the contributions of blacks to American history as ''constructive parts of a whole, not as solitary fragments.'' Lindsay said that Woodson ''added romance and spice to our study of American history.'' Woodson instructed Lindsay, the lone survivor of the program, to spend at least six hours each day at the Library of Congress in order to write his thesis and complete his program by May 1. Lindsay met his deadline and submitted ''The Diplomatic Relations between the United States and Great Britain Bearing on the Return of Fugitive Slaves, 1776–1828,'' in May of 1920. Woodson published it, in part, in the October 1929 issue of the *Journal of Negro History.*

Because of disputes with the University president, J. Stanley Durkee, Woodson stayed at Howard only from 1919 to 1920 and then became dean at West Virginia Collegiate Institute from 1920–22. After his second stint as a dean, Woodson worked full–time as the director of the Association for the Study of Negro Life and History. In addition to issuing a variety of publications, Woodson regularly spoke at churches, schools, civic associations, and scholarly meetings including the association's annual conferences. Woodson also frequently did research at the Library of Congress where he was pleased to discover the reading rooms were not segregated. J. Franklin Jameson, who served as the chief of the library's Manuscript Division from 1928 to 1937, aided Woodson in his research and his efforts to identify funding for the association.

Largely because of the library's open access to researchers regardless of race, Woodson decided to donate a 5,000–item collection of black history materials to the Manuscript Division. He sent the collection in several installments. The 1929 *Report of the Librarian of Congress* noted that the first group of documents received dated from 1804 to 1927 and included letters, bills of sale of slaves, certificates of freedom and manumission, diaries, and manuscript books. The report noted that ''an item of especial interest is a bill of sale, dated April 19, 1809, of a slave conveyed by Thomas Jefferson to James Madison.'' Association members held annual meetings to present research papers on various subjects relating to black history and culture. Woodson published information about the proceedings of the conferences and some complete papers in the *Journal of Negro History.* Woodson's interests also included the black nationalist movement led by Marcus Garvey, and by the early 1920s he regularly wrote articles for Garvey's newspaper, the *Negro World.* Woodson also developed several other important means of popularizing black history materials including the establishment of the Associated Publishers in 1921. This press published a number of volumes by Woodson and other scholars relating to black history and culture. For example, he published his study *The History of the Negro Church* in 1921, *The Negro in Our History* in 1922, and *The Mind of the Negro As Reflected in Letters Written During the Crisis, 1800–1860* in 1926.

Begins Negro History Week

Because Woodson wanted to reach young people, teachers, and laymen, he developed the idea of having one week each year when churches, schools, and other organizations would hold a special commemoration of people and events of historical significance.

Negro History Week began in February 1926 between the birthdays of Booker T. Washington, Abraham Lincoln, and Frederick Douglass. The association published history kits with materials to be used for exhibits, lectures, skits, and curriculum development.

Woodson often printed the contents of his press's books in the *Journal of Negro History* near the time that they were issued in book form. For example, the three articles in the Associated Publishers' eighth book, *The Negro As a Businessman* (1929) also appeared in volume fourteen of the journal in 1929. This study, comprised of a collection of three essays by Woodson and two other authors—John Henry Harmon Jr. and Arnett Grant Lindsay—is significant because it was published the year of the stock market crash heralding the onslaught of the Great Depression. Because of racism and the complexities of the economic market, black businesses in the post–Civil War era rarely lasted for more than a generation even during times when the economy flourished. In hard times, then, it is not difficult to believe that many of the businesses discussed in the text did not survive. However, this work attempts to explore some of the reasons why these enterprises were unsuccessful.

Woodson's most popular work, however, is the *Mis–Education of the Negro.* Originally issued by Associated Publishers in 1933, this book condemns any educational institution for blacks that fails to make the education relevant to the needs of the students. He argues that education that venerates European and white American culture, while condemning Africa and belittling the contributions of blacks to the development of American life, undermines the whole purpose of academic training and produces a sense of inferiority among the students.

Although Woodson's scholarly works and the articles in the journal addressed scholars, Woodson felt that the association needed a periodical aimed at elementary and secondary school teachers. To this aim he began publishing the *Negro History Bulletin* in 1937. He believed that children who learned about the accomplishments of their African American forebears would grow into productive, emotionally balanced adults.

Because of Woodson's indefatigable efforts, his ideas slowly caught on and by the bicentennial year, 1976, Negro History Week became Black History Month with a celebration of the achievements of African Americans extended to encompass the entire month of February. The name of Woodson's organization changed to the Association for the Study of Afro–American Life and History.

The fact that the nation now commemorates Black History Month proves that Woodson's mission was successful and his sacrifices beneficial. Today, African American history programs are celebrated not just in February but throughout the year because of the work of pioneers like Woodson.

Woodson died in Washington, D.C., on April 3, 1950. A contemporary black artist, Charles Alston, commented in an illustration for *Owl,* located in the National Archives, that Woodson, "through his scholarly writings, is responsible more than any other single person for familiarizing the American public with the contribution of the Negro to world history." Quoted by Jacqueline Goggin in *Carter G. Woodson,* W. E. B. Du Bois remarked that Woodson "kept to one great goal, worked at it stubbornly and with unwavering application, and died knowing that he accomplished much if not all that he planned."

REFERENCES

Goggin, Jacqueline. *Carter G. Woodson: A Life in Black History.* Baton Rouge, Louisiana State University Press, 1993.

Greene, Lorenzo J. *Working with Carter G. Woodson, The Father of Black History: A Diary, 1928–1930.* Baton Rouge: Louisiana State University Press, 1989.

Lindsay, Arnett G. "Dr. Woodson as a Teacher." *Negro History Bulletin* 13 (May 1950): 183, 191.

Mays, Benjamin. "I Knew Carter G. Woodson." *Journal of Negro History* 44 (1959): 21.

Meier, August, and Elliott Rudwick. *Black History and the Historical Profession 1915–1980.* Chicago: University of Illinois Press, 1986.

Reviews of Books. *Journal of Negro History* 1 (1916): 96.

Romero, Patricia W. "Carter G. Woodson: A Biography." Ph.D. diss., Ohio State University, 1971.

Scally, Sister Marie Anthony. *Carter G. Woodson: A Bio–Bibliography.* Westport, Conn.: Greenwood Press, 1985.

———. *Walking Proud: The Story of Dr. Carter Godwin Woodson.* Washington, D.C.: Associated Publishers, 1987.

Winston, Michael R. Winston. *Howard University Department of History, 1913–1973.* Washington, D.C: Howard U. Press, 1973.

COLLECTIONS

Information on Carter G. Woodson may be found in the Bureau of Insular Affairs Records and the Office of War Information Records, National Archives and Records Administration, Washington, D.C. His papers are in the Library of Congress, Manuscript Division, Washington, D.C.

Debra Newman Ham

John Wesley Work III
(1901–1967)
Composer, music educator, scholar

John W. Work III devoted an active lifetime to service in several fields as a composer, choral director, teacher, and scholar, ever in search of the roots of African American folk songs. In particular, documenting the jubilee song or spiritual was central to his efforts. He spent many hours and days listening to countless church choirs and other groups performing sacred songs in this tradition, carefully noting new or variant performing styles. His search took him to many of the churches near his home in Nashville, as well as to festivals, "shape–note" singing conventions, and other important performances, some a day's journey away. The fruits of his research informed his notations, harmonizations, and arrangements of these sacred songs and flavored his compositions with a deep resonance of black history. His extensive correspondence, documented in his collection at Fisk, showed him in constant contact with the acknowledged leaders in his field, black and white alike, music educators, composers, scholars, conductors, graduates of Fisk University, and educational administrators.

As a music educator, Work's focus was ever on the student. He was a demanding taskmaster, spending many hours on careful class preparation, quizzing, testing, and engaging his students in active dialogue during music theory classes. He was their champion, writing many letters of support for them, urging their acceptance as festival performers, as prospective teachers, and as candidates for special awards. He called for performance excellence, and his students eagerly responded, as is attested by the many splendid reviews his choral groups earned. His choral compositions and arrangements were carefully crafted to serve a teaching function, by being performed by choirs at choral festivals, included in music collections for school use, and in the repertoires of school choruses.

John Wesley Work III was born on June 15, 1901, in Tullahoma, Tennessee, the eldest of seven children of John Wesley Work Jr. and Agnes Haynes Work. His grandfather, John Wesley Work, born a slave about 1830, relocated to Nashville following the Civil War, and became a church choir

John Wesley Work III

director. His father was a Fisk graduate who taught history and Latin at the school, later serving as chairman of both departments. Disappointed with administrative policies, he resigned to accept the presidency of Roger Williams University, also in Nashville.

Work III was enrolled in kindergarten at the Daniel Hand Training School at Fisk and completed his primary and secondary education at the Fisk school. His musical education began at home where he participated in musical activities from his early youth. Starting piano study at the age of 12, he began composing while in high school, and his musical study continued through college. He earned his B.A. degree from Fisk in 1923. While there, he met his future wife, Edith McFall, of Charleston, South Carolina.

Following graduation he continued his study in music at the Institute of Musical Art in New York City. Work's study program for the M.A. degree included courses in education and music as well as private voice study under Gardner Lamson of Columbia University. Work's father died in September of 1925, whereupon he had to assume responsibility for the family including his mother, two sisters, and youngest brother. His mother, very active in music and training singers at Fisk, assuming the directorship of the Jubilee Singers succeeding her husband. Work at this time returned to his graduate studies in New York. When his mother died in 1927, he was urged to return to Fisk, taking her place on the faculty.

Work was appointed director of Jubilee Music for the 1927–28 school year. His duties included directing the Mozart Choral Society in performance of spirituals. The organization (now the Fisk University Choir) is Tennessee's oldest chartered choral organization.

Work also organized the Men's Glee Club, directing them in concerts and on tour during the next several years. Their programs were varied, including works by Rachmaninoff and Coleridge–Taylor, sacred and secular compositions, and Work's own arrangements of jubilee songs. As a performing aggregate, they gained national recognition under Work's directorship for the next four years. An excellent review by George Pullen Jackson, noted authority on the spiritual song, in the *Nashville Banner* referred to their performance as imparting "new life, new soul, when these men sang."

During this same period, Work renewed his acquaintance with his former classmate, Edith McFall, and they were married in 1928. He was a devoted family man, and he and his new wife assumed parental responsibility and support for his brother and sisters until their maturity. They had two sons, John Wesley Work IV and Frederick Taylor Work. His academic activities were fruitful as well; the choral performances were well received and his reviews were excellent. He was showing progress as a composer and arranger, capturing especially effectively the spirit expressed in the words and choral passages of the jubilee songs, and encouraging his singers to transmit the sentiments and emotions of the text to their audience.

Studies Black Songs and Spirituals

Work's progress towards his master's degree progressed well during the intervening summers in New York, and he finished his academic study program in 1930. His master's thesis, entitled "Folk Songs of the American Negro" was also completed and he received his M.A. degree from Columbia University in 1930. The thesis study was later enlarged, some 230 jubilee songs and folk song arrangements by Work were included, and the work, entitled *American Negro Songs and Spirituals,* was published in 1940. This volume has since taken on considerable stature, accepted by scholars, composers, arrangers, and choral conductors alike as the standard collection of jubilee songs and spirituals and required for study and performance reference in choral libraries. In addition to the published music, the textual commentary on African American secular and sacred song, including blues, worksongs and spirituals, is highly valuable to folk song scholars.

In addition to his teaching responsibilities, Work was active during the years 1927–30 as a vocal recitalist on many occasions, in Nashville and in the region. A lyric baritone, his recitals featured standard classical repertoire: songs by Caldara, Lotti, Rachmaninoff, and Schubert, as well as jubilee song arrangements. In addition, he fulfilled several engagements as an oratorio soloist in Theodore Dubois's *Seven Last Words of Christ* and similar compositions.

Feeling the need for additional study in music, Work applied for a fellowship from the Julius Rosenwald Foundation for study at Yale University. He was awarded the fellowship, and took a sabbatical leave for study during 1931–

32; the fellowship was renewed for an additional year, 1932–33. He was able thereby to complete his studies in theory, composition and instrumentation, earning the Yale bachelor of music degree in 1933. During these years also, he increased his output as a composer as well as infusing his choral arrangements with renewed vigor.

Work returned to Fisk in 1933, with his faculty responsibilities centering on teaching theory, music education, and composition. He was to spend the next 33 years at Fisk, until his retirement in 1966. He and Alan Lomax of the Archive of Folksong conducted research through field recording trips for the Library of Congress. The recordings made available from these trips were issued originally by the Library of Congress. Some have recently been reissued on CD by Rounder Records; for example, *Negro Blues and Hollers* (Rounder #1501, issued in 1997), originally recorded in 1941–42.

Work was appointed director of the Fisk Jubilee Singers in 1947, and reorganized the group as a student ensemble. Their performing responsibilities gradually increased under his leadership for the next ten years, and their maturity as an ensemble reached a climax with their successful European tour in 1956–57. This period of leadership under Work represented the continuation of a proud tradition, establishing a history of more than 100 years within his family in the service of the spiritual or jubilee song, including two major publications, *The Folk Songs of the American Negro* (by his father), and *American Negro Songs and Spirituals,* and close association with several generations of Fisk Jubilee Singers.

Composes and Publishes

During the years following his return to Fisk, Work's output as a composer increased, and his compositions were well received. From about 1930 until 1965 he composed and published about 115 works. The years 1946–56 were particularly active, with some 50 compositions added to his published catalogue. Work's compositions are in a variety of media, for orchestra, instrumental combinations, voice, and chorus. He arranged and published more than 70 spirituals and jubilee songs, many of which have become standard performance repertoire. As characterized by his biographer, William B. Garcia, the choral works emphasize a smooth, diatonic, tonal style. The spiritual arrangements stress their folk heritage, and are varied in texture and dynamics. Technical factors aside, however, his compositions derive inspiration also from the various facets of his career.

Work was inspired by the theme of a Longfellow text, for example, and set it to a cantata entitled ''The Singers,'' first performed by the Fisk Choir in May of 1941. The work subsequently was awarded first prize by the Fellowship of American Composers in 1946 and performed at their Detroit convention in that year. Concerning this composition as well as Work's personal heritage in music, Andrew A. Allison, chairman of Fisk's 75th anniversary celebration in 1941, wrote to Work that the performance at that occasion ''lifted me, because I not only had in mind appreciation of you as an individual, but also all that had been poured in during the past through your mother and father and grandparents to make this work possible.''

In 1945 Work traveled to Haiti under the auspices of the Foundation of Inter-American Education to review the country's educational program and advise the government. Work, of course, concentrated on helping to develop an effective music education program. During the course of his study and research he was able to make many recommendations, and visit a number of areas to hear traditional music, including music for *Vodun* (voodoo) ceremonies. Upon his return he completed a composition for string orchestra drawn thematically from these experiences; he entitled it ''Yenvalou.'' The piece enjoyed a good reception, including a performance on May 24, 1959, with Richard Bales directing the National Gallery Orchestra in Washington, D.C.

G. Wallace Woodworth, Harvard professor of choral music and a member of the Fisk board of trustees for 25 years, commissioned a setting by Work of ''My Lord, What a Morning,'' for choir, to be performed at the First International University Choral Festival. The work was completed and first performed at the festival in Boston's Philharmonic Hall in September of 1965, and then repeated at the United Nations. Approximately 850 singers in choirs from more than nine countries participated in the concert.

Work's activities in music education included appearances as a guest conductor at regional meetings and festivals. He was guest conductor of the Kentucky All State Chorus in April of 1948, as well as choral groups at the Middle Tennessee Teachers Association meetings in 1948 and 1950, and for a 1,000-voice choir at the High School Music Festival at Morgan State University in Baltimore in April of 1954.

Work was appointed chairman of Fisk's music department in 1951, succeeding John Ohl. He was the first African American to hold this position (C. Warner Lawson, his former teacher and colleague, served as acting chairman in 1933–34). The Fisk music department continued to grow and prosper under Work, as did his stature as a composer, clinician, and authority on the jubilee song, with numerous lectures and publications to his credit.

Work had an overriding interest in the folk song itself. African American songs, in his view, represented a ''total mirror'' of life in the period up to and including Reconstruction. One can see this broad view in his article in the *Journal of American Folklore,* entitled ''Changing Patterns in Negro Folk Songs.'' The article, written in 1940, principally concerns sacred music performance practices, drawing on his extensive research in oral traditions gleaned while attending a broad variety of congregational and choral performances throughout the geographic area near Fisk.

Work was particularly intrigued by the styles heard at the Zema Hill Primitive Baptist Tabernacle in Nashville. Hill explained to Work that the newer styles of rhythmic piano accompaniment to the newer gospel songs then in favor among the youth helped the church greatly in bringing young members to into the congregation and the choir—a most prophetic observation. At Hill's funeral in February of 1970, a very large congregation was present, including several choirs; one could hear the newer gospel music as well as the old–style hymns. The older church members still remembered Professor Work of Fisk University.

Another indication of his breadth of interest is the series of articles he wrote for the *Harvard Dictionary of Music* (second edition), on "Blues," "Bop," "Jazz," and "Negro Music." The articles contain incisive, scholarly observations on these topics. The articles were written when he was not in good health in the period shortly before his death, but he was insistent that they be finished and submitted for publication in this prestigious music reference source. In addition Work delivered two papers on Negro folk music to the first Race Relations Institute, held at Fisk in 1944 and sponsored by the university's founding organization, the American Missionary Association.

Directs the Fisk Jubilee Singers

Work's activities as a teacher and composer continued during this period. It seems that each aspect of his contribution to Fisk and his students influenced another one. Central, of course, was his commitment to the jubilee song. His role as director of the Fisk Jubilee Singers was always demanding, and their performances were uniformly well received. The Fisk Jubilee Singers' European tour in 1956 was greatly successful and the reviews uniformly excellent. The tour took a toll on Work's health, however, and he felt it necessary to resign as director of the Jubilee Singers in May of 1957, and as chairman of the music department in July.

Work reduced his teaching load somewhat, but remained active as a teacher, composer, and scholar until his retirement. The faculty and students of Fisk, appreciative of his devotion to them, presented two concerts of his music in his honor, on June 1, 1963, and June 20, 1966. He was also awarded an honorary doctor of music degree.

Work died of heart failure on May 17, 1967. Of his contribution to Fisk and his students, Oscar Henry, one of his students and chairman of the voice faculty at Eastern Michigan University, asserted in the journal BANC in 1973 that "most of all, Dr. Work believed in young people, and he sought to encourage them to seek and be happy with nothing but the best in music scholarship and performance."

REFERENCES

Apel, Willi, ed. *Harvard Dictionary of Music.* 2nd ed. Cambridge: Harvard University Press, 1969.

Fisk University Library. Special Collections, Fiskiana File, Men's Glee Club File.

Garcia, William B. "The Life and Choral Music of John W. Work (1901–1967)." Ph.D. dissertation, University of Iowa, 1973.

Henry, Oscar. "John Wesley Work and His Music." *BANC* 3 (December 1973): 1–8.

Hitchcock, H. Wiley, ed. *New Grove Dictionary of American Music.* New York: Macmillan, 1986.

"John W. Work Collection." *BANC* 3 (December 1973). Fisk University Library, Special Collections.

Lovell, John. *Black Song; The Forge and the Flame.* New York: Paragon House, 1986.

Mitchell, Reavis. "Elder Zema W. Hill." *Leaders of Afro–American Nashville.* Nashville: Conference on Afro–American Culture and History, 1990.

Roach, Hildred. *Black American Music.* Boston: Crescendo Publishing Co, 1973; 2nd ed., Malabar, FL: Krieger Publishing Co., 1992.

Southern, Eileen. *Biographical Dictionary of Afro–American and African Musicians.* Westport, CT: Greenwood Press, 1982.

———. *The Music of Black Americans.* 3rd ed. New York: Norton, 1997.

White, Evelyn D. *Choral Music by Afro–American Composers.* Metuchen, NJ: Scarecrow Press, 1981.

Work, John W. II. *Folk Songs of the American Negro.* Nashville: Fisk University Press, 1915.

Work, John W. III. *American Negro Songs and Spirituals.* New York, Bonanza Press, 1940.

———. "Changing Patterns in Negro Folk Songs." *Journal of American Folklore* 62 (April–June, 1949): 136–44.

———. "Plantation Meistersingers." *Musical Quarterly* 27 (January, 1941): 97–106.

COLLECTIONS

The papers of John W. Work III, including some of his field recordings, are in the Special Collections of Fisk University Library.

Darius L. Thieme

Monroe Nathan Work

(1866–1945)

Sociologist, editor, bibliographer

Educated in the world–renowned sociology department of the University of Chicago, Monroe Nathan Work became the nation's foremost collector and disseminator of social science data pertaining to American blacks. In his capacity as director of Tuskegee Institute's Department of Records and Research, he assembled vast quantities of articles and statistical reports in order to respond to inquiries from around the world. He thus provided supporting documentation for the speeches of Tuskegee's illustrious leader, Booker T. Washington, and created the foundation for broader scholarly applications. Work issued nine editions of the *Negro Year Book: An Annual Encyclopedia of the Negro* (published between 1912 and 1937); he established the Tuskegee Lynching Record (1914–1954), an authoritative source; and he published *A Bibliography of the Negro in Africa and America* (1928) which contained 15,000 entries and served for more than 40 years as the principal source for scholarship on the black experience.

Monroe Nathan Work was born in Iredell County, North Carolina, on August 15, 1866. His parents, former slaves Eliza Hobbs and Alexander Work, reared six girls and five boys. Photographs reveal that Monroe Work grew to be a man of average height and slender frame who wore glasses and, as he aged, gained little weight. The quiet, genteel spirit observed by contemporaries did not indicate timidity but rather a natural reserve. On December 27, 1904, Work married Florence Evelyn Hendrickson of Savannah, Georgia, initiating a lifelong companionship and research collaboration. Although Monroe and Florence Work lost their children in childbirth or infancy, their home was frequently enlivened by the presence of Florence's nieces and nephews. Work died of natural causes on May 2, 1945, and is buried in the Tuskegee Cemetery; Florence survived him by nearly a decade.

Learning and Labor Before Sociology

By 1876 the Work family had joined the "exodusters," black migrants to Kansas in search of economic opportunity. The family settled in Ashton, about ten miles west of Arkansas City, and acquired 160 acres on which to raise corn, oats, and wheat. At Ashton, Monroe Work was first exposed to elementary education in a rural setting in a small building that served the multiple purposes of church, community center, and schoolhouse. According to Jessie P. Guzman in the *Journal of Negro History,* early on, he displayed an interest in "books and not in farming." He dutifully remained on the land until his mother died and his father had moved to live with a married child.

In 1889 at age 23, Work resumed his quest for formal learning, at the same time expressing concern that he might be too old and that opportunities had passed him by. He supported himself with odd jobs while enrolled in the high school in Arkansas City. He grew discouraged and turned for advice to the local superintendent, David Ross Boyd, who later became president of the University of Oklahoma. Boyd counseled Work to remain in school and continue his education. His relationship with Boyd provided the context for a turning point in his life; he had made an irrevocable commitment that education would be his aim regardless of any external factor. Among personal attributes beginning to emerge were a willingness to assume responsibility, patience, persistence amidst troublesome circumstances, and an understanding that stability was essential to productivity and success. Work ranked third in his graduating class and earned Boyd's praise as the best mathematician in the school's history. According to Guzman, Boyd described Work as "able" and "trustworthy," and as possessed of "an untiring spirit in the effort to procure an education."

Since further study would require financial support, Work secured a teaching position in a private school in Creek and Cherokee territory. For one term of employment Guzman said he was paid only "room and board and malaria." Work

Monroe Nathan Work

considered the ministry and in the fall of 1892 won ordination to preach in the African Methodist Episcopal Church. He obtained a pastorate in Wellington, Kansas, but stayed for only a short time; his scholarly rhetorical style seemed ill–suited for a frontier congregation. He returned to the soil in 1894 when the government opened Cherokee lands. Staking a claim to 80 acres near Perry, Oklahoma, Work raised flax and wheat and delivered cattle to meat packers in Chicago. He finally realized his dream for further learning in 1895 when he sold his land and enrolled in Chicago Theological Seminary.

The Calls of Reform and Research

In moving to Chicago, Work entered academic life, and he never turned back. He sought an advanced degree to qualify for a ministerial position appropriate to his intellectual style. His future did not begin to take shape, however, until he studied Christian sociology under Graham Taylor, founder of a major settlement house. Taylor urged students to examine the role of the church in addressing the urban social problems engendered by the Industrial Revolution, and he influenced Work to consider sociological research as essential in dealing with racial problems. Work's mathematical skills made sociology an attractive option, and he was soon captivated by the possibility of pursuing racial studies in a context that fruitfully integrated intellectual interests with efforts to ameliorate the ills of society. He enjoyed success immediately. For Taylor's course, he wrote "Crime Among the Negroes of Chicago: A Social Study," which appeared in the *American Journal of Sociology.* Published by the University of Chicago, this bimonthly served until the 1920s as the only scholarly journal in the field, and Work had become its first black contributor. Although Work had enrolled in seminary to prepare for the Christian ministry, he discovered his true calling in sociology.

In 1898 Work enrolled in the Department of Sociology at the University of Chicago. This move proceeded naturally since Work's mentor from seminary lectured in the department. While Work was deeply influenced by Chicago's Social Gospel advocates, he was also much attracted to another aspect of sociology learned principally from William I. Thomas. The latter modeled for Work the role of the detached, scientific, and unemotional scholar who favored concrete, objective studies of human behavior over impulses to reform society. Work identified with the methods of Thomas's research but also with its subjects. Thomas studied the values and assumptions inherent in a "group mind," especially that ideas, interests, sentiments, and beliefs emerged from historical and geographical foundations rather than biological classification. Even within a spirit of disinterested inquiry, Work came to believe that racial progress could be promoted when the factual results of valid research became an essential tool of policymakers.

Two speeches illustrate Work's training at Chicago and identify subjects that he found irresistible. In "The Importance of Sociology to the Negro," he asserted that no people had suffered more than Negroes due to lack of knowledge of themselves, and therefore it became imperative that he devote his life to the gathering of information concerning his race. In "The Importance of Exact Race Knowledge," cited by the author in *Libraries and Culture,* he claimed that blacks and whites both remained ignorant of the black experience, that sociology was designed to determine the truth about that experience, and that verifiable facts would become the "strongest agencies for bringing about satisfactory racial adjustment." Work earned the bachelor of philosophy degree in 1902 and the master of arts in sociology and psychology in 1903. He had absorbed and would come to embody throughout his career two of sociology's strongest early impulses to reform society and to examine it in such a way that the results of objective research would serve the reform effort.

Between Du Bois and Washington

Work joined a group of blacks among the nation's first sociologists. Among those who had been attracted to this emerging discipline for its potential in addressing racial issues were W. E. B. Du Bois, who had been educated as a historian at Harvard. Du Bois had moved to Atlanta to edit the Atlanta University Publications, a series of lengthy scientific studies that Ernest Kaiser said in the introduction were the first designed to "make factual, empirical evidence the center of sociological work on the Negro." Work and Du Bois had coauthored a study of black churches in Illinois, and the possibility of future collaboration likely influenced Work's decision to move to Georgia State Industrial College in Savannah, where in 1903 Work had been appointed to teach literature and education. Work was especially attracted to the local community since blacks constituted nearly 52 percent of Savannah's population of 54,244. An absence of municipal codes enforcing segregation, combined with the existence of viable black educational and economic institutions, made Savannah both a potential laboratory for research and a site for social activism.

Work participated briefly in community and political affairs. He launched the Savannah Men's Sunday Club which hosted national speakers, lobbied for better funding for black education, supported programs for infant and child care, and raised money for a hospital addition. He also joined Du Bois in the Niagara Movement, designed to offer an alternative to Booker T. Washington's leadership as a spokesman for black America. Work attended the 1905 conference at Niagara Falls as secretary of the Committee on Crime, Rescue, and Reform and as a member of the Committee on Interstate Conditions and Needs. As racial tension heightened, Work felt the need to concentrate his own energies in the academic arena. He would, however, never denounce direct public action as a strategy for racial progress. In 1908 Booker T. Washington, feeling keenly the need for better social science documentation, recruited Work to the faculty of Tuskegee Institute.

Work held a strategic position between the two giants of early twentieth–century black leadership, W. E. B. Du Bois and Booker T. Washington. Du Bois was the nation's leading black intellectual as an activist and editor of *Crisis,* the journal of the NAACP, and he experimented with a range of responses to racial oppression including historical and sociological scholarship, Pan–Africanism, and Marxism. He promoted the concept of the "Talented Tenth," saying that blacks should create a liberally educated, culturally advantaged middle class that would lead the race to new levels of opportunity and prosperity. Washington, on the other hand, was a brilliant politician who accommodated the white power structure of government, the press, and northern philanthropy. He established a nationwide system of political patronage and sought power for his people through adjustment and compromise. He promoted training in the industrial arts and in the techniques of farming and managing small businesses.

While their ultimate goals were the same, Du Bois and Washington differed as to method. Should blacks make immediate demands for constitutionally–guaranteed rights and human dignity or should they simply take advantage of the limited possibilities open to them? Work had been most closely allied with Du Bois during the latter's sociological research at Atlanta University and opposition to Washington's monopoly on the attentions of the dominant culture, but Work also had the capacity and the rare opportunity to appreciate both Du Bois and Washington. So now he traveled to the Black Belt region of Alabama and joined Washington at Tuskegee. There Work documented Washington's publications and speeches and developed comprehensive records on the institute's students and alumni in order to demonstrate their economic and cultural value to local communities and to the nation. But Work conceived of a much larger role for himself than had the powerful black leader who had recruited him. He envisioned a systematic gathering of data about blacks in Africa and America, their historical and anthropological origins, and their current status and conditions. Work did not conduct regular classes at Tuskegee but rather directed the activities of the Department of Records and Research. The death of Washington in 1915 and his succession by Robert Russa Moton resulted in stronger administrative support and the transformation of Work's unit into a research center. Writing in *Libraries and Culture,* Sybil E. Moses noted Moton's claim that Tuskegee was "looked upon as the center of the Negro life" and that the Institute provided "more information regarding the Negro in the course of a year than all other agencies combined."

Work's major achievements became possible in light of Tuskegee's international reputation. The nature of Washington's leadership and the visibility of the institute made it a natural information bureau. Requests arrived from all parts of the globe. If information was available in a magazine, Work's assistants had been clipping the article and sending it. Work revised this practice by writing a letter and keeping the article. In this way he began compiling reference information that over the years exceeded 350,000 books and other items, filling scores of filing cabinets with articles, pamphlets, reports from government agencies and private boards, surveys, statistical studies, and clippings from more than 130 newspapers. Work and his colleagues provided data about black agriculture, business and industry, crime, education, health, history, literature, migration, music, prohibition, and taxation. They routinely supplied information to foreign governments, research scholars, the press, and private organizations such as the Commission on Interracial Cooperation, the YMCA International Committee, and the Federal Council of Churches.

With his vast and growing collection as a solid foundation, Work set the standard for reference book publishing pertaining to blacks. In 1912 he issued the first *Negro Year Book* on key events of the previous year with information on association activity, civil status, crime, economics, education, the fine arts, health, the military, politics, population, publishing, race, and religion. The *Negro Year Book* attracted favorable reviews from the *American Sociological Review,* the *Journal of Applied Sociology,* the *Journal of Negro History, Rural Sociology,* the *Social Service Review,* and other scholarly periodicals. The *Year Book* also drew criticism from the *Crisis* for giving inadequate credit to the NAACP for its work on race–related issues including opposition to lynching and segregation.

The lynching statistics that Work compiled fueled controversy in the 1920s when it appeared possible that the Dyer anti–lynching bill might be passed. The NAACP compiled its own data developed from on– site investigations; James Weldon Johnson criticized Work for excluding victims of riots. Work offered to collaborate with the NAACP in coordinating data but later came to regard the organization as more interested in propaganda than in facts, and negotiations were broken off. While the NAACP regarded Work's statistics as too conservative, those same statistics achieved great credibility among white newspapers. In the single year of 1932, for example, Work's lynching reports were discussed in more than 200 editorials.

Work regarded his monumental bibliography as his most important achievement. The need for such a source was most compelling in the 1920s, when blacks were regrouping and creating a new sense of identity with a fresh outpouring of literature, history, music, and art. Bibliographic entries in the *Year Book* had grown from 408 in 1912 to 1,927 in 1922. By 1925 Work and his staff had accumulated more than 30,000 entries and were arranging 10,000 of them into a classified scheme. Meanwhile his department and his compilation–in–progress had attracted philanthropic attention. Grants from the Carnegie Corporation and the Laura Spelman Rockefeller Memorial strengthened the department's ability to collect and organize materials while the Phelps–Stokes Fund more directly influenced the bibliography. The fund supported a tour of European libraries for Monroe and Florence Work to further develop the African section of the bibliography and to make the final publication more multilingual and international.

The *Bibliography of the Negro in Africa and America* was published in 1928 by the H. W. Wilson Company. Fifteen thousand entries were arranged into 74 chapters with sections on Africa, on America, and on contemporary conditions in the West Indies and Latin America. Readers making the most effective use of the bibliography would need some knowledge of English and Latin plus six European languages. Reviewers were impressed with the magnitude of the project and the accuracy of the entries, and they freely used terms like "scholarly" and "authoritative." The bibliography served as the principal bibliographical source until at least the 1960s, when the G. K. Hall Company began publishing book catalogs of special collections of African Americana.

Although Work retired from regular departmental responsibilities in 1938, he continued collecting bibliographic citations. A true visionary, he planned a gargantuan project tentatively entitled, "Bibliography of European Colonization and the Resulting Contacts of Peoples, Races, and Cultures." This effort would consume much of the final years of his life and, though it never came to fruition, resulted in the amassing of some 75,000 entries.

Yet reference and bibliographic publishing had not become Work's only concerns. Throughout his career his stature as a scholar led him to engage in biracial activities for groups such as the Commission on Interracial Cooperation, the Social Science Research Council, and the Southern Sociological Society. He was accepted and respected among predominantly white associations devoted to history, sociology, and political and social science. He launched National Negro Health Week, which featured consciousness–raising programs in homes, schools, and public buildings, and he was appointed the only black statistician for the National Tuberculosis Association. He won a gold medal from the Harmon Foundation of New York for his educational publicity and scholarly research, a citation for public service from the

Alumni Association of the University of Chicago, and an honorary doctorate from Howard University. Although he promoted his faith in the gospel of facts in more than 70 scholarly articles and 150 speeches, he had served his race and nation most admirably by publishing reference books; of these, his *Bibliography of the Negro in Africa and America* stands as his greatest achievement.

REFERENCES

Guzman, Jessie P. "Monroe Nathan Work and His Contributions." *Journal of Negro History* 34 (October 1949): 428–61.

Kaiser, Ernest. Introduction to *Atlanta University Publications,* Nos. 1, 2, 4, 8, 9, 11, 13–18. Edited by W. E. B. Du Bois. Reprint, New York: Arno Press, 1968.

Kellner, Bruce, ed. *The Harlem Renaissance: A Historical Dictionary for the Era.* Westport, CT: Greenwood Press, 1984.

Logan, Rayford W., and Michael R. Winston, eds. *Dictionary of American Negro Biography.* New York: Norton, 1982.

McMurry, Linda O. *Recorder of the Black Experience: A Biography of Monroe Nathan Work.* Baton Rouge, LA: Louisiana State University Press, 1985.

Moses, Sibyl E. "The Influence of Philanthropic Agencies on the Development of Monroe Nathan Work's Bibliography of the Negro in Africa and America." *Libraries and Culture* 31 (Spring 1996): 326– 41.

Salzman, Jack, David Lionel Smith, and Cornel West, eds. *Encyclopedia of African–American Culture and History.* New York: Macmillan Library Reference USA/Simon and Schuster Macmillan, 1996.

Tucker, John Mark. "'You Can't Argue with Facts': Monroe Nathan Work as Information Officer, Editor, and Bibliographer." *Libraries and Culture* 26 (Winter 1991): 151–68.

Work, Monroe Nathan. "Crime Among the Negroes of Chicago: A Social Study." *American Journal of Sociology* 6 (September 1900): 204–23.

Work, Monroe Nathan. *Bibliography of the Negro in Africa and America.* New York: H. W. Wilson, 1928.

COLLECTIONS

Materials about Monroe Nathan Work are housed in the University Archives, Tuskegee University.

John Mark Tucker

Wright, Isaac.

See Coker, Daniel.

Louis Tompkins Wright (1891–1952)

Physician, civil rights activist

Louis Tompkins Wright was a pioneering physician, researcher, and hospital administrator whose commitment to racial equality led him to the chairmanship of the NAACP's board of directors. He was born in LaGrange, Georgia, on July 23, 1891, to Ceah Ketcham Wright (d. 1895) and Lulu Tompkins Wright and was the younger of their two sons. Ceah Wright graduated from Meharry Medical School in 1881 but practiced medicine only briefly before entering the clergy. He died when Wright was four years old.

In 1899, Wright's mother married William Fletcher Penn (b. 1870), a native of Amherst County, Virginia, and younger bother of I. Garland Penn, a noted educator, editor, and longtime secretary of the Methodist Episcopal Church's Board for Negro Education. Penn graduated from Yale University's School of Medicine in 1897 and was one of its first black graduates. He moved to Atlanta that same year to establish his practice.

Louis Tompkins Wright received all his early education in schools operated by the Methodist–connected Clark University, where his mother taught. In 1907, the year he finished high school, he experienced a profound brush with racism when he had to prepare to defend the family home during the Atlanta race riot. He received his bachelor's degree from Clark University in 1911.

Inspired by his family's example, Wright decided to pursue his amibition to become a medical researcher and applied to Harvard Medical School. After performing well on a chemistry examination, he was admitted in 1911. He graduated cum laude, fourth in his class, in 1915; but because of his race, he had to march last in the graduation procession. Outraged, he attended the ceremony only to avoid disappointing his family. During his medical training he had initially been told he would not be allowed to attend deliveries at Boston Lying–In Hospital, a decision that was reversed when he challenged it. Discrimination continued when he sought an internship, and he finally interned at Freedmen's Hospital in Washington, D.C. Wright had already published a paper in the *Boston Medical and Surgical Journal* on work he had done as a medical student. At Freedmen's he produced a study on the Schick diphtheria test in blacks, the first publication based on work done at that hospital.

Establishes Medical Practice

Wright returned to Atlanta in 1916 to establish a private practice. After the United Stated entered World War I, he became a first lieutenant in the Army Medical Corps. He suffered the effects of a gas attack during front line service in France, won a Purple Heart, and was discharged as a captain in 1918. He rose to the rank of lieutenant colonel in the

Louis Tompkins Wright

Medical Reserve Corps. He had to resign from the corps, reluctantly, because of his health when World War II broke out.

Wright spent only one more year practicing medicine in Atlanta, but during that time he helped organize the city's first chapter of the NAACP. He became chapter president with Walter White as secretary, initiating a long relationship which culminated in Wright's service as chairman of the board of directors of the NAACP (1935–1952), where White served as executive secretary.

On May 18, 1918, Wright married Corrine Cooke of New York City and established an active practice there the following year. Convinced that ''separate but equal'' meant in practice separate and unequal, he devoted his energies to combating discrimination and de facto segregation in medicine. In 1919, Wright and a few other doctors were appointed adjunct visiting surgeons and physicians at Harlem Hospital, where he worked in the women's medical outpatient department. Wright became a member of the permanent staff the following year, but he was not appointed to the outpatient surgical service until 1925. Wright used the hospital administration experience he had acquired in the army to work toward improving the quality of care available to the growing black population of Harlem and increasing the number of blacks on the hospital staff.

Change at Harlem Hospital involved a reorganization of the city hospitals which was not complete until 1929. Wright was involved in a selection process which led to the dismissal of 23 white doctors and the hiring of 19 black doctors; but he was resented by some black doctors who believed he favored the black graduates of white medical schools over doctors produced by black medical schools.

Montague Cobb traced the hostility Wright inspired in physicians of both races to Wright's strict professional standards and goals. Wright, he wrote, ''was as intolerant of mediocrity and the appearance of privilege seeking in Negroes as of aggressive presumption and patronizing condescension in whites. With his hospital staff he was a strict disciplinarian and permitted no excuses for slipshod work.''

Wright also made his mark in other areas of medicine. In 1928 he became the first black police surgeon in New York City through a competitive civil service examination. In 1934 he became the first black member of the American College of Surgeons since Daniel Hale Williams, who had been a founding member in 1913. In 1930 Wright withdrew from the black North Harlem Medical Society to form the Manhattan Medical Society, an integrated and more militant group; later, in 1937, he founded the Harlem Surgical Society. The Manhattan Medical Society spearheaded opposition in 1930–31 to the Rosenwald Fund's plan to construct an all–black hospital in New York and in 1932 to the federal government's plan to construct a second black veterans hospital in the North. (In the South, Tuskegee was already the site of a segregated veterans hospital.) In 1946 Wright fought unsuccessfully against the transfer to a new governing board of a small hospital which had fallen into financial straits as its neighborhood became all–black and thus was threatened with becoming a de facto segregated public hospital.

Guides the NAACP

In 1935 Wright became chairman of the board of directors of the NAACP, a position he held until his death. This election gave effective control of the organization to Walter White, since the two men were close friends. Wright had once saved White's life by carrying him in his arms to Harlem Hospital and performing surgery on him, and the two men were strongly united in their opposition to any form of segregation. Significant decisions for the organization were made by a small group at White's apartment the day before the board's monthly meetings.

In 1939 Wright contracted pulmonary tuberculosis and spent the next three years in bed at Biggs Memorial Hospital in Ithaca, New York. The following year the NAACP awarded him the Spingarn Medal. He was still in the hospital but on the road to recovery when he was offered a position as director of the Department of Surgery at Harlem Hospital, a post he took up in 1943 along with a strict health regimen which he maintained for the rest of his life. In 1948 he became president of the hospital's Medical Board, thus becoming the first black to head a large public hospital with an integrated staff. On April 30, 1952, the hospital's library was named in his honor. Eleanor Roosevelt praised him before a thousand guests at a dinner honoring the occasion.

Wright died at home on October 8, 1952, from a heart attack. He was survived by his wife; three granddaughters; his half–sister Jessie Penn West, who had married Harold D.

West, the first black president of Meharry Medical College; and two daughters, who also had become physicians. Jane Cooke Wright succeeded her father as head of the Harlem Hospital Cancer Research Foundation, and Barbara Penn Wright married Samuel R. Pierce Jr., a lawyer who was secretary of HUD from 1981 to 1988. Funeral services were held at St. Philip's Church on October 11.

In his career, Wright published 89 papers with 51 coauthors, including a chapter on head injuries in a standard textbook on skull fractures, a first for a black physician. The early articles covered a wide range of subjects, but later ones focused on specific areas. Wright published extensively on trauma (14 papers) and on a venereal disease, lymphogranuloma venereum (15 papers). In 1948 he led the integrated team which first used the antibiotic chlortetracycline in humans (30 papers, with 8 on oxytetracycline). In that year Wright also established the Harlem Hospital Cancer Research Foundation, of which he became director. He also published 15 papers on chemotherapy. Other highlights of his medical career include work on the intradermal method of small–pox vaccination (1918) and appliances for neck fractures (1936) and thigh and shin fractures (1948).

The open expression of outrage against racial injustice was a constant in Wright's life. As a student at Harvard Medical School, he had missed three weeks of class to join protests organized by William Monroe Trotter against the Boston screening of *Birth of A Nation.* When Wright arrived in New York City in 1919, Harlem Hospital's entire staff and personnel was white in an area which was rapidly becoming black, but by the time he died he had become head of the hospital. By precept and example, Wright pursued a practice of medicine where ability, not race, was the basis of achievement.

Roy Wilkins, Walter White's successor as executive secretary of the NAACP, paid tribute to Wright in a speech at Harlem Hospital on March 6, 1963. Wilkins praised Wright's fighting spirit by saying, "There was never any doubt about where he stood. His language was plain, usually Anglo–Saxon, and the time for action was now." He also summed up Wright's achievement:

> So Louis Wright not only taught excellence. He demanded excellence and he would have no truck with "getting by."
>
> In the remaining campaigns for civil rights and for full citizenship Louis Wright has left us, it seems to me, a priceless legacy.
>
> He wanted what was his by right as a human being and by right of his ability in his chosen field. He had a sense of personal outrage and we, too, must have a sense of personal outrage over injustice, over inequality, over less than the best.

REFERENCES

Cobb, W. Montague. "Louis Tompkins Wright, 1891–1952." *Negro History Bulletin* 16 (May 1953): 170, 178–80.

Contemporary Black Biography. Vol 4. Detroit: Gale Research, 1993.

"Dr. Wright Honored." *Crisis* 59 (June–July 1952): 376–77.

Logan, Rayford W., and Michael R. Winston, eds. *Dictionary of American Negro Biography.* New York: Norton 1982.

"Medical Family." *Ebony* 6 (January 1951): 71–74.

"Miracle Drug." *Ebony* 4 (June 1949): 13–17.

"NAACP Mourns Dr. Louis T. Wright." *Crisis* 59 (November 1952): 548–50.

Ovington, Mary White. *Portraits in Color.* New York: Viking, 1927.

Smith, Jessie Carney, ed. *Notable Black American Women.* Detroit: Gale Research, 1992.

Wilkins, Roy. "Louis T. Wright: Fighter for Equality and Excellence." *Crisis* 70 (May 1963): 261–69.

Who's Who among African Americans, 1996–97. 9th ed. Detroit: Gale Research, 1996.

Who's Who in Colored America. 7th ed. Yonkers–on–Hudson, NY: Christian E. Burckel, 1950.

Robert L. Johns

Richard Wright
(1906–1960)
Novelist, poet, dramatist, screenwriter

Richard Wright is one of the most important writers of the twentieth century. During his remarkable literary career Wright worked as a dramatist, essayist, novelist, short story writer, screenwriter, autobiographer, and poet. Wright wrote about the experiences of African Americans in a hostile and racist society.

Born on September 4, 1908, in a sharecropper's cabin on a plantation in Roxie, near Natchez, Mississippi, Richard Nathaniel Wright was the first–born son of Nathan Wright, a sharecropper, and Ella Wilson Wright, a school teacher. Two years later, the Wrights had another child, Leon Alan Wright, born on September 24, 1910.

Life in the racially segregated "Jim Crow" South greatly influenced Wright's literary works. Poverty forced Ella Wright and her two sons to move in 1911 from the farm to Natchez, Mississippi, to live with her family. Nathan Wright eventually abandoned farming to become an itinerant worker. He later joined his family in Natchez where he found work in a sawmill. In his efforts to improve the family's economic status, Wright moved his family by steamboat from Natchez, Mississippi, to Memphis, Tennessee, in 1913.

By 1914 Wright's father had deserted his family for another woman. With Richard's mother working only at low–paying, menial jobs, Wright and his brother were frequently left without food. Because of their destitute condition, Wright's mother often sent Richard to his father's job or home to beg

Richard Wright

for money. Wright wrote in *Black Boy*: "As the days slid past the image of father became associated with my pangs of hunger, and whenever I felt hunger I thought of him with a deep biological bitterness." Because of this Wright remained estranged from his father into his adulthood.

Wright's mother became ill in 1915. She was unable to care for her sons and they were sent to the Settlement House, a Methodist orphanage. By the summer of 1916, when his mother recovered from her illness, she took her sons to stay with her parents in Jackson, Mississippi. In that same year, Ella Wright and her sons moved again to Elaine, Arkansas, to live with her sister and her husband, Silas Hopkins. Wright became very fond of his uncle and spent a considerable amount of time with him. However, his first encounter with racial violence occurred when he was about nine years old. A group of white men murdered his uncle in order to seize his valuable property. Fearful for their own lives, the Wrights and the widowed aunt fled to West Helena, Arkansas.

This murder was one of the events that would change his life forever. Eventually the Wrights returned to Mississippi for several months in 1917 but went back to West Helena by the winter of 1918. Wright's mother became ill once again and the brothers were separated. Wright wanted to be near his mother so he reluctantly chose to live with his Aunt Jody and Uncle Clark in Greenwood, Mississippi.

Wright's education was disrupted by his family's frequent moves. His mother's illnesses made regular attendance at school nearly impossible. However, Wright entered school in 1915 at Howe Institute in Memphis, Tennessee. He enrolled and remained for a year in 1920 at the Seventh Day Adventist school in Jackson, Mississippi.

In September of 1921 when he entered a fifth grade class at Jim Hill Public School in Jackson, Mississippi, Wright's keen intelligence allowed him to be promoted to the sixth grade within two weeks of his enrollment. During this time Wright showed an interest in writing. In addition to school, Wright found part–time employment that assisted the family's financial situation. As a newspaper delivery boy Wright had the opportunity to read material that was forbidden at home.

After numerous part–time jobs and further interruptions in his education, he entered the eight grade at Smith Robertson Junior High in 1923 where his excellent grades earned him a position as a part–time supervisor of the class. When he entered the ninth grade at Smith Robertson, the community noticed his talent as a writer when his first story, "The Voodoo of Hell's Half Acre," was published in the *Southern Register,* a black newspaper in Jackson, Mississippi. On May 29, 1925, Wright graduated as valedictorian of his ninth grade class. The next fall he entered the newly founded Lanier High School but he stopped attending after a few weeks in order to earn money for his family.

Writing Career Begins to Flourish

By November of 1925, Wright left Jackson and returned to Memphis where he found work as a dishwasher and delivery boy for the Merry Optical Company. Wright's mother and brother joined him in Memphis. Wright continued his passion for learning by reading magazines and literary works of H. L. Mencken, Fedor Dostoevski, Sinclair Lewis, Sherwood Anderson, and Theodore Dreiser. He forged a note to present to the librarian at the "whites only" public library to gain access to such works. Wright was strongly influenced by the works of Mencken, whose writings awakened him to the possibility of social protest.

Wright and his family left Memphis and moved to Chicago in 1927. Chicago for Wright was an interesting and stimulating city that was not as racially oppressive as the South, although this urban center had other problems. After a series of menial jobs as dishwasher, porter, insurance salesman, and substitute postal clerk, the Depression forced him into unemployment and government relief.

In 1931 Wright published a short story "Superstition" in *Abbott's Monthly Magazine*—a black periodical. Although Wright was unemployed he continued to read, write, and study other writers. During the 1930s he became acquainted with Communist activities in the African American community. He was particularly interested in the views of Communist organizers and orators who were affiliated with the League of Struggle for Negro Rights. By 1932 Wright began attending meetings of the Chicago John Reed Club—a communist literary organization whose purpose was to use art to achieve revolutionary results. Wright's talents won him easy acceptance in the left–wing literary circle of the John Reed Club. Wright began to read and study the organ of the

International League or Revolutionary Writers, *New Masses* and *International Literature.*

Elected executive secretary of the Chicago John Reed Club, which was predominantly white, Wright organized a lecture series that allowed him to interact with a variety of intellectuals. He published several revolutionary poems in magazines such as *Left Front, The Anvil, International Literature,* and *New Masses.* By 1934, the communist party decided to disband the John Reed Clubs.

In 1935 Wright was hired by the Federal Writer's Project, which was a division of the Works Progress Administration, to assist with the research on the history of Illinois and blacks in Chicago. Wright continued to publish poetry in small journals. Wright traveled to New York in 1935 to attend the American Writer's Congress, where he spoke on ''The Isolation of the Negro Writer.'' He also published a poem about lynching in *Partisan Review* during the same year, and he wrote an article for *New Masses* in 1935 entitled ''Joe Louis Uncovers Dynamite.'' By 1936 Wright published ''Transcontinental,'' a six–page radical poem that was published in *International Literature.*

Wright transferred to the Federal Theatre Project, where he served in the capacity of adviser and press agent for the Negro Federal Theatre of Chicago. He also became involved in the dramatic productions of this group and finished two one–act plays based on a portion of his unpublished novel. Wright joined the new South Side Writers' Group and took an active role in this organization, which included members such as Arna Bontemps, Frank Marshall Davis, Theodore Ward, Fenton Johnson, Horace Cayton, and Margaret Walker.

By 1936 Wright took a major role in organizing the Communist party–sponsored National Negro Congress, and reporting on it for *New Masses.* His short story ''Big Boy Leaves Home'' appeared in the Federal Writers Project anthology, *The New Caravan,* (1936) where it attracted mainstream critical attention.

In 1937 Wright turned down a permanent position with the postal service and moved to New York City to pursue his writing career. After residing briefly in Greenwich Village he moved to Harlem, where he became the Harlem editor of the *Daily Worker.* He also helped to launch the magazine *New Challenge,* which he said in *Black Boy* was ''designed to present black life in relationship to the struggle against war and Fascism.'' Wright published ''The Ethics of Living Jim Crow'' in *American Stuff: WPA Writers' Anthology* (1937).

Wright's influential essay *''Blueprint for Negro Writing''* appeared in the first and only issue of *New Challenge* in 1937 and presented Marxist criticism of earlier black literature. During this time he developed a friendship with the young and upcoming writer Ralph Ellison. His short story ''Fire and Cloud'' (1938) won first prize of $500 in *Story Magazine's* writers' contest. After being hired by the New York Federal Writers' Project, Wright had the opportunity to write the Harlem section for *New York Panorama* and ''The Harlems'' section for *The New York City Guide* (1938).

In 1938 Wright hired a literary agent, Paul Reynolds Jr., who assisted him with the publication of *Uncle Tom's Children: Four Novellas* with Harper and Brothers. *Uncle Tom's Children* was published in March of 1940 to wide acclaim. As a result Wright was awarded a Guggenheim Fellowship of $2,500 in March of 1939. This award allowed him to continue his writing and resign from the Federal Writers' Project.

Native Son

Wright met Ellen Poplar, daughter of Polish Jewish immigrants and a Communist party organizer, in Brooklyn and they developed a friendship. Wright considered marrying Poplar but instead he began dating Dhima Rose Meadman, a dance teacher of Russian–Jewish ancestry. He married Meadman in August of 1939 at the Episcopal Church with Ralph Ellison as his best man. It was not a successful match. By 1941 Wright began divorce proceedings. Shortly after his divorce, he married Ellen Poplar on March 12, 1941. This marriage produced two daughters. Julia Wright was born April 14, 1942 and Rachel Wright was born on January 17, 1949.

Wright's story, *''Bright and Morning Star''* (1938) appeared in *New Masses* and *Best American Short Stories.* He soon joined the *New Masses* editorial board and began work on a new novel. About this time he wrote Margaret Walker, also an African American writer, to send him newspaper clippings relating to the Robert Nixon case in Chicago. By October, he finished the first draft of his novel relating to the case, *Native Son.* By June he had completed the second draft of *Native Son.*

Native Son, published by Harper and Brothers Publishers in March of 1940, became the main selection Book–of–the–Month Club. Less than six weeks after its publication, *Native Son* had sold a quarter of a million hardcover copies, and it was on the best seller list for 12 to 15 weeks. Moreover, every major newspaper and periodical in the country reviewed *Native Son.* According to some critics, *Native Son* was a powerful, intense, and stirring novel.

Wright traveled to Mexico with his family in 1940. During this time his wife's demands and his work put a strain on their marriage. He left Mexico alone in June and traveled throughout the South. There he visited his father, who was poor and working as a farm laborer. Although Wright tried to reconcile his differences with him, they still remained distant. Wright also traveled to Chapel Hill, North Carolina, to begin talks with Paul Green about the stage adaptation of *Native Son.* He later became unhappy with Green's work. Consequently, Wright and John Houseman revised it with Orson Welles as director. *Native Son* opened on June 15, 1940, at the St. James Theater and ran until March 24, 1941.

When he left the South, Wright traveled to Chicago to conduct research for a new book on African American life. His story ''Almos' a Man'' appeared in the *O. Henry Award Prize Stories of 1940.*

The period of the 1940s was an extremely busy and critical time for Wright. He was involved in many activities including travel abroad, debates, lecturing, and writing. His writings continued his previous themes of racism, oppression, poverty, migration, bondage, and nationalism. *Uncle Tom's Children* was reissued with two additional essays: ''Bright and Morning Star'' and ''The Ethics of Living Jim Crow.'' Wright expressed opposition to World War II first by signing an antiwar appeal by the League of American Writers, and second by publishing ''Not My People's War.'' Both items appeared in *New Masses* in 1941. However, following the Japanese attack on Pearl Harbor, Wright signed a petition, which appeared in *New Masses,* supporting America's entry into the war. Wright avoided the draft because he was his family's sole support.

In January of 1941 the NAACP awarded Wright the Spingarn Medal, given annually to an African American who has made the most notable achievement during the preceding year. In his acceptance speech he criticized the Roosevelt administration's racial policies.

Black Boy

Wright's creativity also led him to become involved in music. His ''Note on Jim Crow Blues'' prefaced blues singer Josh White's *Southern Exposure* album. Paul Robeson, accompanied by the Count Basie orchestra, recorded Wright's blues song, ''King Joe,'' in 1941. Wright's work *Twelve Million Black Voices: A Folk History of the Negro in the United States* was published in October of 1941. He continued to publish articles in magazines including ''The Man Who Lived Underground'' in *Accent* (1942) and ''What You Don't Know Won't Hurt You'' in *Harper's Magazine.*

Wright traveled to Fisk University in April of 1943 with Horace Cayton and delivered a talk on his experiences with racism. Because of the strong audience reaction that he received, he began to write the novel, *American Hunger,* in December of 1943. The Book–of–the–Month Club informed Harper that it only wanted the first section of *American Hunger,* which described Wright's southern experiences. Wright agreed to this demand and titled the new volume *Black Boy.* The second section was published posthumously in 1977 as *American Hunger.* Harper published *Black Boy: A Record of Childhood and Youth* in March of 1945 to favorable reviews. This novel remained on the best seller list form April 29 until June 6.

In 1942 he parted ways with the Communists because of his disillusionment with the party. Wright aired his split with the Communist Party in his essay, ''I Tried To Be a Communist,'' which appeared in the *Atlantic Monthly* (1944), causing *New Masses* and *Daily Worker* to denounce and disown Wright. Wright continued some leftist activities, developing friendships with C. L. R. James, a Trinidad historian and Trotskyite, and his wife Constance Webb.

Continuing his amazing level of productivity, Wright completed in 1944 ''Melody Limited,'' a story about a group of black singers during Reconstruction. The Wrights moved to Greenwich Village in 1945. To circumvent racial discrimination they used their lawyer as the middle man to purchase a house. As young writers emerged, Wright befriended many, including James Baldwin, whom he assisted in winning the Eugene F. Saxton Foundation fellowship in 1945.

When Wright met Jean–Paul Sartre in New York, Sartre extended an invitation to him to visit France. On May 1, Wright left New York for Paris, where Gertrude Stein welcomed him. He assisted Leopold Sedar Senghor, Aime Cesaire, Alioune Diop, and others in the Negritude movement by establishing the magazine *Presence Africaine.* He left Paris in December of 1946 and returned to New York.

Becomes an Expatriate

During his time in France, Wright decided to move his family to Europe permanently. They arrived in Paris in August of 1947. The French translation of *Native Son* came out in the fall. Wright deepened his interest in existentialism by reading Edmund Husserl and Martin Heidegger and hanging out with Jean–Paul Sartre and Simone de Beauvoir. Camus's *The Stranger* strongly impressed Wright, and he begun working on an existentialist novel, which became *The Outsider.*

On March 30, 1951, the film version of *Native Son,* filmed in Argentina, opened in Buenos Aires, where it was titled *Sangre Negra.* Wright's acting in this version was considered awkward by American critics, yet praised by the Milan (Italy) press. In February of 1952, Wright traveled to England, where he completed a full version of *The Outsider.* It was published by Harper and Brothers in March. Despite initially selling well the novel's momentum did not last because of mixed critical reviews.

Wright continued his quest to write and publish. His next book required him to collect materials on Africa. Wright traveled during the summer of 1953 to the British colony of the Gold Coast (which became Ghana following its independence in 1957). During the trip he met with pro–independence leaders, as well as with ethnic group rulers. His travels throughout the continent allowed him to visit slave–trade fortresses and dungeons. On September 22, 1954, Wright's book about Africa, *Black Power: A Record of Reactions in a Land of Pathos,* appeared to mixed reviews in America but enthusiasm in France. Avon published the paperback *Savage Holiday,* Wright's novel about a white psychopathic murderer. A hardback edition was published by Banner Books, the University Press of Mississippi, in 1994.

Wright returned to Paris in December of 1956, where he started working on a novel set in Mississippi. In February of 1957, *Pagan Spain* appeared although it failed to sell well, despite favorable reviews. Doubleday published a collection of Wright's lectures entitled *White man, Listen!* in 1957, based on interviews of African American servicemen during World War II.

In 1958, Wright finished *The Long Dream,* his novel about Mississippi, and he began to work on its sequel, *Island of Hallucination,* which was set in France. When *The Long Dream* was published by Doubleday in October of 1958 it received poor and even hostile reviews. Wright contemplated moving to England during this time; however, his mother, who was still in the United States, became seriously ill . On January 14, 1959, Wright's mother died.

Wright's ''Big Black Good Man'' was included in *Best American Stories of 1958.* The stage adaptation of *The Long Dream* opened of Broadway, February 17, 1960, to poor reviews and closed within a week. The French translation of *The Long Dream* did better that its English version, but it did not sell well enough to satisfy Wright. He began a new novel, *A Father's Law,* during the summer of 1960, but when he returned to Paris in September, he became ill with amoebic dysentery. On November 26, 1960, he received Langston Hughes at his home, but later in the day he checked into the Eugene Gibez Clinic for diagnostic examinations. Two days later, at 11 p.m. on November 28, Wright died. The cause of death was listed as heart attack. On the third of December, Wright's body was cremated along with a copy of *Black Boy.* His ashes remain at the Père Lachaise cemetery.

Richard Wright was one of the literary giants of the twentieth century. His books and articles have been translated into numerous languages throughout he world. He exposed oppression and racial discrimination to the world, and his autobiographical works revealed his experiences as an African American male growing up in the ''Jim Crow'' South. His works are classic pieces that are used in classrooms throughout the United States.

REFERENCES

Black Literature Criticism. Vol. 3. Detroit: Gale Research, 1992.

Fabre, Michel. *TheUnfinished Quest of Richard Wright.* 2nd ed. Urbana: University of Illinois Press, 1993.

Gayle, Addison. *Richard Wright: Ordeal of a Native Son.* Garden City, NY: Anchor Press, 1980.

Hakutani, Yoshinobu. *Critical Essays on Richard Wright.* Boston: G. K. Hall, 1982.

Kinnamon, Keneth, and Michel Fabre. *Conversations with Richard Wright.* Jackson: University Press of Mississippi, 1993.

Logan, Rayford W., and Michael R. Winston, eds. *Dictionary ofAmerican Negro Biography.* New York: Norton, 1982.

Obituary. *New York Times,* November 30, 1960.

Reilly, John M., ed. *Richard Wright: The Critical Reception.* New York: Burt Franklin and Company, 1978.

Walker, Margaret. *Richard Wright: Daemonic Genius.* New York: Warner Books, 1988.

Webb, Constance. *Richard Wright: A Biography.* New York: G. P. Putnam's Sons, 1968.

Wright, Richard. *American Hunger.* New York: Harper and Row, 1983.

———. *Black Boy: A Record of Childhood and Youth.* New York: Harper and Brothers, 1945.

———. *Rite of Passage.* New York: Harper Collins, 1994.

COLLECTIONS

Richard Wright's papers are located in the Richard Wright Archive in the Beinecke Rare Book and Manuscript Library at Yale University. Rare magazines and newspapers that contain some of Wright's writings are housed in the Schomburg Collection of the New York Public Library, the American Library in Paris, and Howard University Libraries. Several letters of Wright are located at Kent State University and one of the manuscripts of *Black Power* is at Northwestern University.

Vivian Njeri Fisher

Stephen J. Wright
(1910–1996)
College president, organization official

Stephen Wright spent a lifetime broadening and enriching educational opportunities for African Americans. He fought to dismantle racial barriers in other areas as well, such as at testing centers in southern colleges, and his support of the student sit–ins in Nashville helped to improve race relations in that city and beyond. He led the United Negro College Fund in increasing its annual fund raising campaign and in providing budgetary assistance to member schools. A highly respected educator, his service was sought out by numerous organizations as well as presidents of the United States.

One of four children, Stephen Junius Wright was born September 8, 1910, in the small town of Dillon, South Carolina, to Rachel Eaton Wright and Stephen Junius Wright, Sr. His father, a physician, practiced medicine in Dillon until he died. Then only five years old, Stephen Wright, Jr. and the other three children moved to Williamsboro, in Vance County, North Carolina, to live with their maternal grandparents on a farm while their mother went North in search of work.

Wright attended four elementary schools in Vance County, including a one–room school and a one–teacher school built by the Rosenwald Foundation. When he was 15 he went to Hampton Institute Academy in Virginia to study. Since he wanted to become a physician, he prepared himself for medical school by majoring in science while he was in college. By the time he received his undergraduate degree from Hampton Institute—now University—in 1934, the nation was in the midst of the Great Depression and medical school was beyond his reach. He told Louise Davis for the *Nashville Tennessean Magazine,* ''I didn't have any medical school money. It had been awfully rough going all the way. But I never did pay a cent of tuition. I won scholarships all the way, for all three degrees.''

Wright had to fit in graduate study while he worked. In 1939 he received his master of arts degree in education from

Stephen J. Wright

Howard University in Washington, D.C. He also did graduate study at Columbia University and at City College of New York. With a General Education Board Fellowship, he studied at New York University, graduating with a Ph.D. in 1943.

Begins Career of Education

To support himself while he finished his education, Wright initially took the best job he could find, as science teacher (he also taught civics and world history), director of the glee club, and coach at Kennard High School in Centreville, Maryland, where he was paid $75 a month. Three years later he moved into administrative work in Upper Marlboro, Maryland, where he was principal of Douglass High School and was paid $50 more each month. He was fired for fighting to equalize salaries between white and black teachers. From 1939 to 1941 he was assistant professor of education and director of student teaching at North Carolina College (now North Carolina Central University), an historically black college in Durham. In 1943–44 Wright was professor of education and acting dean of men at the college. In September 1944 he returned to his alma mater, Hampton Institute, as professor of education and director of the division of education. In 1945, with the rank of professor, he was named dean of the faculty.

Wright left Hampton in 1953 to become president of Bluefield State College in Bluefield, West Virginia, where he remained until 1957. Ironically, the chief speaker for his inauguration at Bluefield was Charles Spurgeon Johnson, the man whom he would succeed in 1957 as the seventh president and the second black president of Fisk University in Nashville, Tennessee.

When he went to Fisk, Wright took with him experiences well suited to the temper of the times. The period of the 1950s and 1960s ushered in the desegregation era for colleges and schools and the removal of many racial barriers throughout society. At Bluefield Wright saw peaceful integration on campus, as white students came there for a special course not offered at their colleges. As well, whenever he could, he took advantage of his connections with educational groups to hammer away for integration and helped to sway the U.S. Supreme Court in its desegregation decision regarding the public schools.

At Fisk, Wright gave his inaugural address on the topic ''Fisk University and the Vision of Greatness,'' and voiced optimism about the role of the school in higher education. He also predicted that the years ahead would be turbulent. He saw a role for the students, the faculty, the alumni, the Board of Trustees, and himself, as president, in moving from vision to reality. Since he was a strong advocate of the liberal arts college and Fisk was such an institution, he could work in total commitment to a liberal education. To strengthen Fisk, he erected two new residence halls, refurbished historic Jubilee Hall (another residence facility), began a new library building, strengthened the faculty, established a writer–in–residence program, and established a sizeable Centennial Campaign fund. He worked beyond the institution for black causes as well. He convinced black colleges to raise their academic standards by requiring the Scholastic Aptitude Test as part of admission policies. He led a movement to desegregate testing centers at southern colleges, and when colleges refused to provide testing sites for black students, he persuaded the U.S. Department of Defense to open military bases as testing centers.

Wright believed in maintaining a racially integrated teaching faculty. While Bluefield had no white faculty during Wright's tenure, he had studied at Hampton when the faculty was nearly all white. He commented that Fisk had had the advantage of always having a biracial faculty. ''It is part of a youngster's education to find out what white people are really like,'' he said in the *Nashville Tennessean Magazine.* As well, when black students studied under white teachers, they sometimes had their first opportunity to learn that ''not all white people are mean,'' he continued.

Supports Student Sit–ins

Wright's ability to handle student demonstrations was put to test, on February 25, 1960, when students from local black colleges began the sit–in movement in Nashville. Since the movement's leaders and a number of the demonstrators were from Fisk, Wright had an intense interest in their civil rights activities. As the movement gained momentum and students were continuously arrested, Nashville mayor Ben West appointed a biracial committee to act as mediator between the students and Nashville business leaders in order to bring peaceful solutions to the problems. Wright and Tennessee State University (then Tennessee Agricultural and

Industrial State College) president Walter S. Davis were the only two blacks on the seven–member committee. Not only did Wright work through the committee to resolve the difficulties, he made it known to the students that he supported the cause and that, as long as the students were dignified and poised in their demonstrations, the university would support their efforts and would not expel them. In a statement issued to the local press on February 28, 1960, and quoted in the April 30, 1960, *Nashville Tennessean,* Wright said:

> As president of Fisk, I approve the ends our students are seeking by these demonstrations. From all I have been able to learn they have broken no law by the means they have employed, and they have not only conducted themselves peaceably, but with poise and dignity. These are fine young citizens who in their post–college years will make significant contributions to the nation.

Wright also spoke out publicly in favor of the demonstrations. Quoted in the *Nashville Banner* on April 20, 1960, he stated in an address before the Panel of Americans luncheon in New York, "In the long history of the Negro's struggle for equal access to the great democratic promise of America, nothing. . .has done more in recent years to arouse public sympathy and concern than the student demonstrations in the South." Students of that era were not "the silent generation," he said, and predicted that their efforts "will advance the cause of equality in America." He was praised for his bold public statements and emerged from the sit–in period with new stature.

Wright's feelings about the demonstrations and civil unrest were deeply entrenched; in his view, the civil unrest had ushered in a new black in the South. On August 26, 1961, Wright reflected on the student demonstrations and told the National Conference for Interracial Justice:

> Whether the demonstration is a lunch "sit–in," a theatre line "stand–in," a pool "wade–in," or a "Freedom Rider," the activity involved essentially one or more students exercising some right or privilege which he, in the South, is denied either by law or by custom solely because of his race.

Wright's travels throughout the South kept him alert to the civil rights struggle. He told the *Richmond (Virginia) Times–Dispatch* that, after Martin Luther King's assassination and the 1964 Civil Rights Act outlawing discrimination in employment, public accommodations, and voting, "President Lyndon B. Johnson called a whole bunch of us to be his monitors. He gave us a telephone number to call if we found anything seriously jeopardizing that law." As the South changed its behavior, he never had to dial that number.

In 1963, Wright turned down President John F. Kennedy's offer to serve as U.S. ambassador to Libya. Since the appointment was to be immediate, Wright believed that the programs he had underway at Fisk would suffer if the presidency suddenly changed. He left Fisk, however, in 1966 and became the first full–time president of the United Negro College Fund in New York, where he helped raise money for the 30 member institutions. He left UNCF in 1969 and from then until he retired in 1976, Wright was in turn a trustee, consultant, vice–president, acting president, and senior advisor at the College Board.

Wright's concern for the education of black people never wavered and in 1995 he was still a strong advocate of higher education as well. He told the *Newport–News/Hampton Daily Press* in 1985 that "black colleges and universities must change with the times to survive new obstacles." They compete with white institutions for black students and must respond to changes in the higher education environment if they are to survive. Where affirmative action was concerned, he told *Black Issues in Higher Education,* "New devices, new policies, new strategies are going to have to be developed to assure the necessary flow of young Black men and women into higher education." Wright understood that some young blacks lack perspective on the importance of the court's decision on affirmative action, and further explained:

> Young blacks don't understand because they haven't been told, in language that they need to understand, the point from which their parents, their forebears, had to come. . .the distance they have come and what has been involved in making that distance possible. We have a heavy obligation. . .to provide our young people with a history of the struggle, what the odds were, and how tall the mountains were in the perspective of that time.

Extracurricular Activities

Wright's professional public service affiliations included 39 boards, councils, and agencies in the field of education. Among these were the Association of Colleges and Secondary Schools for Negroes and the American Association of Higher Education, both of which he served as president; he was also executive vice–president of the Virginia Air and Space Museum, and served on the board of directors of several organizations such as the New World Foundation, the Educational Policies Commission, the Institute of International Education, and the Association of American Colleges. Over the years he was an expert witness for the U.S. Justice Department in a number of cases involving equality of educational opportunity, including *Brown v. Board of Education.*

In addition to being an articulate and dynamic public speaker, Wright wrote widely on the subject of education and contributed to a number of scholarly publications, including *Educational Abstracts,* the *Journal of Educational Sociology,* the *Journal of Negro Education,Quarterly Review of Higher Education Among Negroes,* and the *Harvard Educational Review.*

Wright's awards and honors were numerous. While at Fisk President Lyndon B. Johnson appointed Wright to serve as a special U.S. Ambassador to the inauguration of President William V. C. Tubman of Liberia. He was named Outstanding Alumnus of the Year by Hampton, Howard, and New York Universities. The Grand Lodge of the Elks and Frontiers

International named him Educator of the Year. He also received the Brotherhood Citation from the National Conference of Christians and Jews, the National Leadership Award in Higher Education from the National Association of Equal Opportunity in Education, and the UNCF Frederick D. Patterson Award for distinguished service to black students at historically black colleges. Fifteen colleges and universities, including the University of Notre Dame, New York University, and the College of William and Mary awarded Wright honorary degrees.

In private life, Wright collected classical records and enjoyed hunting, and fishing. He kept a Doberman Pincher named Rusty, who was very popular on campus at Bluefield State and at Fisk. Wright returned to Hampton, Virginia, in his retirement years and retained a voracious appetite for knowledge and sustained his scholarship by reading widely until several months before he died.

On Tuesday, April 16, 1996, Wright died at Johns Hopkins Medical Center in Baltimore. He was 85 years old. He was survived by his wife, Rosalind, whom he married in 1938. There were no children. He was buried in Franklinton, North Carolina, the hometown of his wife.

Reflecting on Wright's life, Robert M. Thomas Jr. wrote in the *New York Times* that, ''In a career that could stand as a road map of black educational progress in the 20th century, Wright did more than show the way. He also blazed the trail for generations of black students who no longer regard a college education as a rarity but as an integral part of their culture.''

REFERENCES

''Black Colleges Facing Changes.'' *Newport News/Hampton Daily Press,* March 11, 1985.

''A Celebration of the Life of Dr. Stephen J. Wright, Jr.'' Hampton University Chapel, Hampton, Virginia. April 22, 1996.

Davis, Louise. ''A Decisive Man for Fisk.'' *Nashville Tennessean Magazine,* July 14, 1957: 8–16.

''Educator Wright Has 'Done It All.''' *Richmond (Virginia) Times–Dispatch,* October 19, 1986.

''Elder Educator: Dr. Stephen J. Wright Reflects on Education Today and His Many Years on the Firing Line.'' *Black Issues in Higher Education,* November 30, 1995.

''Fisk Board Backs Sit–ins.'' *Nashville Tennessean,* April 30, 1960.

''Fisk President Says Sit–Ins Arouse Sympathy.'' *Nashville Banner,* April 20, 1960.

''Fisk President Turns Down Libyan Ambassadorship.'' *Baltimore Afro–American,* February 9, 1963.

''Fisk Seizes a Fresh Opportunity.'' Reprinted from the Nashville Tennessean, n.d. Biography File, Fisk University Library.

''Partial Integration Urged.'' *Nashville Tennessean,* April 6, 1960.

''Stephen Wright, College Educator, is Dead at 85.'' *New York Times,* April 19, 1996.

''Stephen Wright Former Fisk President, Dies.'' *Nashville Tennessean,* April 20, 1996.

Vita. Copy provided to the author by Rosalind Wright.

Who's Who among African Americans, 1996–97. 9th ed. Detroit: Gale Research, 1996.

Wright, Rosalind. Telephone interviews with Jessie Carney Smith, August 8, 1996 and August 19, 1996.

Wright, Stephen J. ''Fisk University and the Vision of Greatness.'' Speech at his inauguration as seventh president of Fisk University, April 26, 1958. Biography File, Special Collections, Fisk University Library.

———. ''The New Negro of the South.'' Speech delivered at the meeting of the National Catholic Conference for Interracial Justice, Detroit, Michigan, August 26, 1961. Biography File, Special Collections, Fisk University Library.

COLLECTIONS

The papers of Stephen J. Wright from his years as Fisk University president as well as information on the student sit–ins in Nashville are in Special Collections, Fisk University Library. His personal papers are to be preserved in the library at Hampton University.

Jessie Carney Smith

Malcolm X
(1925–1965)
Human rights activist, lecturer, organizer

Malcolm X was a central figure in the African American fight for social justice in the 1950s and 1960s. As a minister of the militant Nation of Islam, he urged blacks to defend themselves ''by any means necessary,'' advocating a position of violence that many whites found disturbing. The controversial leader inspired both devotion and hatred with his aggressive stance on civil rights issues, and was known for the power of his speeches. He embraced and rejected ideologies as he pursued with enthusiasm and charisma, powerful intellectual and spiritual journeys that for many African Americans represented their own struggle with confronting the racist systems of America.

Malcolm Little

Malcolm Little was born May 19, 1925, to Earl and M. Louise Norton Little in Omaha, Nebraska. His father was a Baptist preacher and local president of Marcus Garvey's Universal Negro Improvement Association, and his mother was a native of Grenada. As a Garveyite, Reverend Little and his family were often harassed by white terrorist groups and eventually their house was burned down. The family moved to Lansing, Michigan, in 1929, where Reverend Little continued to offer inspiring sermons to his congregations while beating his wife and children at home. In 1931 Reverend Little was found dead near a streetcar line. Although authorities termed it a suicide, others suspected that Malcolm's father was killed by the Ku Klux Klan or a similar group and placed on the streetcar line to make it look like an accident. By the age of six, Malcolm Little's life had been besieged by violence and tragedy.

Unable to bear the tragic loss of her husband and what seemed like harassment from the state welfare representatives, Louise Little was deemed psychologically unstable and eventually institutionalized. Her seven children were separated and placed into foster homes by the caseworker. Malcolm spent time with several foster families over the next few years, but even though he became an excellent student, he continually fought racist perceptions of African Americans. Young Malcolm informed his white teacher at Mason Junior High School that he wanted to be a lawyer and, according to Deidre Mullane in *Crossing the Danger Water,* was told that a lawyer was not a ''realistic goal for a nigger.''

Recognizing that these racist attitudes hindered his personal ambition, Malcolm left school after completing the eighth grade. With little opportunity in Lansing for a young African American man, Malcolm left at the age of seventeen and moved to Boston to live with his half–sister, Ella.

The next four years of Malcolm Little's life were spent enjoying the best and the worst that Detroit, Boston, and New York could offer. While working on a railroad with a run between Boston and New York, he frequented Harlem and was exposed to black performers such as Billie Holiday, Duke Ellington, and Lionel Hampton. Malcolm Little soon became involved in a variety of activities, both legal and illegal, including waiting tables, shining shoes, gambling, hustling, selling bootleg liquor, and dealing drugs. In 1946, at the age of 21,''Detroit Red,'' as Malcolm Little was called on the street, was sentenced to ten years in prison on burglary charges.

While in prison Malcolm Little's attitude earned him the nickname ''Satan'' because of his anti–Christian attitudes. After being introduced to the Nation of Islam by his brother Wilfred who had converted the year before, Malcolm Little converted to the teachings of Elijah Muhammad, the leader of the Nation of Islam. The group believed in African American superiority and a theory that a white scientist was responsible for the degradation of blacks. This faith resolved many issues in Malcolm Little's life for, according to *Contemporary Black Biography,* it confronted ''his treatment and his family's at the hands of whites, the lack of opportunity he endured as a young black man, and the psychological damage of systematic and black racism–that is the damage of self–hatred.'' In prison Malcolm Little grew intellectually as he read works by W. E. B. Du Bois, Mahatma Gandhi, Will Durant, Kant, Nietzsche, and numerous others. He challenged his own thinking as he debated with other inmates about the teachings of Elijah Muhammad.

After being paroled in 1952, Malcolm Little went to live with Wilfred, his older brother in the Detroit suburb of Inkster. Within a month Malcolm Little met Elijah Muhammad in Chicago while visiting the headquarters of the Nation of Islam. Shortly after this meeting Malcolm Little was given the ''X'' to replace the slave name of Little. The ''X'' represents the African origins that he would never know. Malcolm X was later invited to Chicago to study Islam and began a long–standing relationship with the Nation of Islam. In his ministry, Malcolm X was second only to Elijah Muhammad himself.

The Man and His Ministry—Malcolm X

Malcolm X began his activism, at the age of 27, as national minister, speechwriter, inspired speaker, and philosopher in the Nation of Islam in 1952. He later went on to

Malcolm X

become the founder of the newspaper *Muhammad Speaks.* The first temple Malcolm X opened, in Boston, was a great success, as was the new temple he opened in Philadelphia in 1954. As Malcolm X became more visible to both white and black America, his Muslim views were often reported by the media, shaking the racist complacency of America's social system of inequality. In *The Autobiography of Malcolm X,* he called the white man a "devil" and said that blacks had to fight back and seize their rights "by any means necessary." In his book he also promoted the idea that "The American black man should be focusing his every effort toward building his own businesses and decent homes for himself. We have never initiated any violence against anyone, but we do believe that when violence is practiced against us we should be able to defend ourselves. We don't believe in turning the other cheek."

Such statements by Malcolm X which openly rejected the ideologies and racist attitudes of white America caused him to be known as a "messenger of hate" in the white media. Malcolm X preached that since whites would never cede power, separation of the races was the only way for blacks to obtain justice and the full power of their identity. Other prominent African American leaders saw integration, Christianity, and nonviolence as the means of obtaining justice for black people, and rejected the philosophy of the Nation of Islam.

Malcolm X openly criticized many of the conservative African American leaders such as Martin Luther King Jr., and in his autobiography referred to the March on Washington in 1963 as the "Farce on Washington." He saw such activities as a means to pacify the growing anger of African Americans. According to a February 1998 issue of *Emerge* magazine, King in turn described Malcolm X as "clearly a product of the hate and violence invested in the Negro's blighted existence in this nation. He like so many of our number, was a victim of the despair inevitably deriving from the conditions of oppression, poverty and injustice which engulf the masses of our race." Although Malcolm X and King met only briefly over the years, each came to realize that the differences between them were slight when compared to their common goal of racial pride, strong community–based institutions, and the goal of achieving equal rights within the American political system. According to the same *Emerge* article, Federal Bureau of Investigation director J. Edgar Hoover, who was among white leaders seeking to exploit any differences of ideologies of social change, "saw Malcolm and Martin as among the potential messiahs who might have been able, in the words of his infamous 1968 memorandum expanding the Bureau's Counterintelligence Program, to 'unify, and electrify' the militant Black movement."

Malcolm X and Family

During his years of ministry, Malcolm X met in New York at the Brooklyn State Hospital of Nursing a young nursing student who later became his wife. Born Betty Dean Sanders on May 28, 1936, Hajj Bahiyah Betty Shabazz was the adopted daughter of Lorenzo Don and Helen Malloy, a middle–class family on the east side of Detroit. Betty Shabazz attended Tuskegee Institute in Alabama and later moved to New York where she met Malcolm X, then the charismatic and militant leader of the Nation of Islam's Temple No. 7 in Harlem. They were married in 1958 when she was 23 and he was 32. After about a year of marriage, Malcolm X and Betty Shabazz had their first daughter, Attallah, who was followed by daughters Qubilah, Ilyasah, Gamilah, and the twins Malikah and Malaak, born after their father's death. In accordance with strict Muslim laws, Malcolm X rejected alcohol, drugs, and tobacco, and followed a very disciplined life with his family. Betty Shabazz stayed close to home as Malcolm X continued to carry the message of Muhammad around the country. Betty Shabazz was an important part of Malcolm X's focus and strength. In a letter written in 1964 to Alex Haley, his biographer, Malcolm wrote, "Without her [Betty's] high morale I could never take my place in history."

Racist to Humanist: El–Hajj Malik El–Shabazz

As Malcolm X's family grew, his relationship with Elijah Muhammad and the Nation of Islam weakened as he began to question the integrity of the group. The exclusionary nature of the Nation of Islam—which did not give aid to African Americans outside the faith—bothered him. He was likewise troubled by the ideological link between the separationist stance of the Nation of Islam and the segregationist beliefs of the white supremacists. In January of 1961 Muhammad sent Malcolm X to Atlanta, Georgia, to meet with officials of the Ku Klux Klan to get support for a separate state. Malcolm X's experiences over the years led him to believe that there needed to be a group which embraced all black men and was political and morally credible.

Just as Malcolm X entertained misgivings about the Nation of Islam, leaders within the organization were experiencing problems with their young minister. Malcolm X's media attention and overall successes created jealousy within the group. Relationships were further aggravated when Malcolm X made the controversial statement to the media regarding the assassination of President John F. Kennedy that it was a case of "chickens coming home to roost." White media such as *Rolling Stone* magazine accused Malcolm X of saying the president deserved to be assassinated, and Malcolm X was "silenced" for 90 days by Muhammad. To add to the growing rift, Malcolm X discovered that his esteemed Elijah Muhammad was guilty of adultery. This hypocrisy appalled him as Muhammad had been Malcolm X's idol as well as judge and jury for the Nation of Islam.

At the age of 39 Malcolm X set out to manifest his own vision of equality and rights for African Americans. In March of 1964 he quit the Nation of Islam after almost 12 years of service to form his own group, Muslim Mosque, Inc. He also founded the Organization of Afro–American Unity in June of 1964 which he wrote in his autobiography was to "embrace all faiths of black men." To create a strong religious foundation to his new organization and to show his continued dedication to Islam, Malcolm X decided to make a pilgrimage to Mecca in the spring of 1964. During his travels, which extended to the Middle East and the African countries of Egypt, Lebanon, Nigeria, and Ghana, Malcolm X, discovered a global sympathy for the plight of the African American. He saw the problem of the American black as not just a problem of civil rights, but as one of human rights. He recognized during his travels and interaction with Muslims of all races that the racist teachings of Elijah Muhammad were inconsistent with the word of Allah. Malcolm X decided at this point to convert to orthodox Islam and change his name to El–Hajj Malik El–Shabazz before returning to the United States. With Malcolm X's break with the Nation of Islam, his humanistic rhetoric, and his call to African Americans to demand their rights of the United Nations made him the target of both Elijah Muhammad's Nation of Islam and the U.S. government.

Final Days

Once back home Malcolm X disclosed to a bevy of reporters who flocked to report his changed philosophy, that America's injustices were known all over the world, and that true Islam saw the indictment of all whites or all blacks as wrong. Malcolm X worked to place branches of his new organization in Africa, Europe, and throughout the United States. He also sought to form alliances with grass–roots organizations as well as repair rifts made between various civil rights leaders. At one point on March 26, 1964, Malcolm X orchestrated a surprise meeting with Martin Luther King Jr. on the steps of the U.S. Capitol after King emerged from a news conference. Although nothing came of this brief encounter with King, Malcolm X continued to meet with other groups such as the Student Nonviolent Coordinating Committee (SNCC) along with its chairman, John Lewis; Mississippi organizer Fannie Lou Hamer; and civil rights icon Rosa Parks. Malcolm X's efforts were in many ways thwarted by his prior militant image, but he continued to move forward.

After continual death threats and harassment by governmental and nongovernmental factions, Malcolm X began to grow weary. In December of 1964 a three–part series denouncing him was printed in the Muslim paper *Muhammad Speaks.* It was written by a fellow minister, Louis X, later to be known as Louis Farrakhan. According to Arthur J. Magida in *Prophet of Rage,* Louis X fanned the flames of hatred by saying that Malcolm X had "made the foolish and ignorant mistake . . . [of saying] his best friends were among such non–

believing people as Hindus . . ., Jews, Christians, Catholics, and even 'Uncle Toms.' No Muslim is a Muslim who accepts such people as his brothers. Such a man as Malcolm is worthy of death. . .''

On February 14, 1965, shortly after 2:00 a.m. Malcolm X's house in Queens, New York, was firebombed. His family all escaped unharmed but the house was not insured against fire. Malcolm X later told Alex Haley that he would die by violence and would not see his autobiography published. The following Sunday, February 21, 1965, in the Audubon Ballroom on West 166th Street in New York City, Malcolm X was set to give a speech to some of his followers. *Prophet of Rage* reported that he was introduced as ''a man who would give his life for you.'' As Malcolm X—El–Hajj Malik El–Shabazz—rose to speak, three men stood up and fired sixteen shots at him. About ninety minutes later, he died at Columbia Presbyterian Hospital. Malcolm X was murdered in the presence of his wife, Betty, who was pregnant with twins, his four daughters all under the age of seven, and numerous followers and friends. The three men were arrested and identified as members of the Nation of Islam.

The funeral for Malcolm X was on a Saturday morning, February 27, 1965, at the Faith's Temple of God and Christ on Amsterdam Avenue and 150th Street in Harlem. According to *Crossing the Danger Water,* Elijah Muhammad said of him that, ''Malcolm died according to his preaching.'' Twenty–two thousand people viewed his body which was laid out in the traditional Muslim burial shroud. Martin Luther King Jr. said in a telegram to Betty Shabazz that, ''While we did not always see eye to eye on methods to solve the race problem, I always had a deep affection for Malcolm and felt that he had a great ability to put his finger on the existence and root of the problem.'' The eulogy was give by actor Ossie Davis who in his final words challenged the perceptions of Malcolm X as ''demon, monster, subverter, and an enemy of the black man—did he ever do a mean thing. . . . Was he associated with violence or any public disturbance?'' Ossie Davis went on to confirm that ''Malcolm was our manhood, our living black manhood. And in honoring him, we honor the best in ourselves.''

REFERENCES

Carson, Claybourne. ''A 'Common solution:' Were Martin and Malcolm Compatible.'' *Emerge* 9 (February 1998): 44–52.

Coleman, Trevor W. ''A Mother's Struggle: Betty Shabazz's Private Moments.'' *Emerge* 8 (September 1997): 44–58.

Contemporary Black Biography. Vol. 1. Detroit: Gale Research, 1992.

Edwards, Audrey. ''The Fire This Time.'' *Essence* 28 (October 1997): 74–75, 155–156.

Hine, Darlene Clark, Elsa Barkley Brown, and Rosalyn Terborg–Penn, eds. *Black Women in America.* Vol. 2. Bloomington: Indiana University Press, 1993.

Magida, Arthur J. *Prophet of Rage.* New York: Basic Books, 1996.

Mullane, Deidre. *Crossing the Danger Water: Three Hundred years of African–American Writing.* New York: Doubleday, 1993.

Salley, Columbus. *The Black 100.* Secaucus, NJ: Citadel Press, 1993.

X, Malcolm. *By Any Means Necessary.* New York: Pathfinder Press, 1992.

X, Malcolm. *Malcolm X Speaks.* New York: Pathfinders Press, 1992.

———, with Alex Haley. *The Autobiography of Malcolm X.* New York: Ballantine Books 1964.

Leañtin LaVerne Bracks

Andrew Young

(1932–)

Clergyman, civil rights activist, politician, diplomat

In 1976 Andrew Young was called America's most powerful black man, having become the first black man since Reconstruction elected to Congress from the South (Barbara Jordan was the first black woman in 1972). A public servant in numerous ways, Young has ministered to the spiritual needs of black Americans, and served as Martin Luther King Jr.'s trusted aid, as ambassador to the United Nations, and twice as mayor of Atlanta. He helped create a new South with his unwavering commitment to freedom and justice for all.

Andrew Jackson Young Jr., popularly known as Andy Young, was born March 12, 1932, in New Orleans, Louisiana. His father was a dentist, trained at Howard University, and his mother, Daisy Fuller Young, was a teacher. She taught young Andy to read and write before he entered school. Young began the third grade at Valena C. Jones Public School.

Young graduated from Gilbert Academy, a private high school, when he was 15, and in the fall of 1947 he enrolled at Dillard University in New Orleans. The next fall he transferred to Howard University in Washington, D.C. Majoring in biology, Young prepared to follow in his father's footsteps and become a dentist. He pledged his father's fraternity, Alpha Phi Alpha. David Dinkins, a marine veteran a year older than Young, was the pledgemaster. Dinkins would later become mayor of New York City. Young made the swim team and ran track. All seemed to be going as planned until his senior year. Young was greatly influenced by Howard's first black president, Mordecai Wyatt Johnson, who preached Mahatma Gandhi's idea of passive resistance. He also became acquainted with a young minister on his way to Africa to become a missionary, John Heinrich. Young recalled in his autobiography, *A Way Out of No Way,* that the young white man was willing to travel to Africa in order to help others. "No one at the schools I had attended ever suggested that I try to help black folk. Howard University's emphasis, and the mission of most black colleges in those days, was to better yourself and advance the race through your own achievements."

Young received his bachelor of science degree in biology from Howard University in 1951, but the 19-year old would not be attending dental school. He had decided to enter the ministry. Young traveled to Connecticut where he enrolled in the Hartford Theological Seminary. After studying the teachings of Mahatma Gandhi, Young was convinced that

Andrew Young

he could change the injustice in America without violence. In 1955 he graduated with a bachelor of divinity degree and was ordained a minister in the United Church of Christ.

Young spent the summer following his first year in seminary in Alabama. He had planned to go to New York to work at a settlement house, so that he could run with the Pioneer Track Club of Harlem. Instead, he was asked to take an internship at a small Congregational church in Marion as temporary pastor until a permanent minister could be found.

Young arrived in town on a Saturday afternoon. He went to the home of Norman and Idella Childs, members of the church who welcomed him and provided his meals. Their youngest daughter, Jean, was a college student at Manchester College in Indiana. When Young arrived, Jean Childs was still away at school. Before meeting her, Young discovered that she was a serious student of the Bible and also a good swimmer.

Chance of a Lifetime

Young, who had been upset about not being able to run with the track club, suddenly began to wonder if God had plans for him that were better than his own. When he met Jean

Childs he knew the answer. Describing his future wife, Young said in his autobiography, ''I had known many beautiful women, but with Jean, the beauty was not external. It was her spirit, her dedication, and her purpose to serve others which made her the 'one in a million, chance of a lifetime.''' They married on June 7, 1954.

Writing in his autobiography, Young said, ''Jean and I . . . have always felt that our union was made in heaven. We both decided that God's plan for us was greater and better than we could make for ourselves.''

Wanting to do missionary work in Africa, Young asked permission to establish a mission in rural Angola upon his graduation from Hartford Seminary in 1955. His request was denied because the church would not send single people. Jean Childs Young had applied from Indiana and Young from Connecticut. By the time it was clear they were a couple, the Youngs had returned South where he became pastor of a small church in Georgia from 1955 to 1957.

In the South, the Youngs hoped to work for the liberation of black people. Jean Young and Coretta Scott King had grown up in the same town; this led to Young's introduction to Martin Luther King Jr. In 1957, however, almost as soon as they began to make headway in the South, the sign came for them to move again. Young was offered a job as associate director of the department of youth works for the National Council of Churches of Christ in America, an opportunity too good to refuse. The couple moved to New York City and Young took over the Council's athletic and media programs. Jean Young enrolled in graduate school.

Young felt that his sojourn in the North prepared him to return to the South. He recalls being deeply moved by the student effort at the Nashville sit–in, which he watched on television from his living room in Queens, New York, during the summer of 1960. Young says in his autobiography that as he and his wife watched they ''could literally feel God calling [them] back to the South.'' At the time Jean Young was pregnant with their third child and completing a master's degree in education at Queens College. The decision to leave a secure position and return to the South with a young and growing family was not easy.

In 1961, however, the United Church of Christ started a voter education program in the South. Young was selected as the Field Foundation's new supervisor to work with Septima Clark's citizenship schools. By the fall of that year, the family had moved back to Georgia and purchased a small home in southwest Atlanta. Young worked with Clark and Dorothy Cotton touring the South, recruiting workers and voters. One of their first recruits was Fannie Lou Hamer. It was at this point that Young joined the Southern Christian Leadership Conference (SCLC).

In the Valley of the Shadow of Death

Young marched in the front line of Martin Luther King Jr.'s protests and demonstrations, directed the massive campaign against segregation in Birmingham, and was in charge of the May 3, 1963, demonstration when police commissioner ''Bull'' Connor unleashed attack dogs and high pressure fire hoses to stop the peaceful marchers. On the night of Medgar Evers's assassination on June 12, 1963, Young and two other civil rights workers drove into Mississippi to rescue Fannie Lou Hamer and two others from jail. The South was becoming increasingly dangerous. Young recalled that he and other workers talked about death as inevitable, but they believed they would be fortunate if they were able to die for their cause. Over the next five years Young became an expert in nonviolent resistance tactics. In 1964, Young helped draft the Civil Rights Act and the Voting Rights Act of 1965.

When Martin Luther King Jr. was assassinated in April 1968, Young heard the shots and mistook them for fire crackers or a car backfiring until he saw his leader and friend fall. Then he knew what he had felt all along was true. He wrote in his autobiography, ''God had changed the world through the shedding of innocent blood.'' He thought:

> It often takes the courageous death of an innocent human being doing the right thing in the right place, at the right time, to mobilize the ''coalition of conscience'' that changes the world and takes human history to higher levels. Death is an inevitable part of life to be embraced rather than feared.

Following King's death, Ralph David Abernathy took over the leadership of SCLC and Young became his executive vice president. Together they planned the Poor People's Campaign, a protest designed to force attention on racism in America and to show that racism had impoverished thousands of people. The campaign climaxed in a second March on Washington to pressure Congress to enact anti–poverty legislation. By 1969, SCLC had lost much of the support that surged forth following King's death. Young outlined its new course, stressing voter registration and political action.

Runs for Political Office

Young resigned from SCLC in 1970 to run for the United States House of Representatives. He organized a biracial campaign but lost to the conservative Republican Fetcher Thompson, who told voters that if Young won it would lead to the end of western civilization. Two years later Young ran again. This time the Fifth District, which had been predominantly white in the previous election, had been reapportioned to reflect the changing demography. Still, the district was 62 percent white. Young won with 53 percent of the vote. He was the first black from Georgia to serve in the U.S. House since the Reconstruction period. He returned to Congress in 1974 with 72 percent of the votes and again in 1976 with an 80 percent victory.

During his freshman year in Congress, Young established himself as a hard–working representative sensitive to the needs of his constituents. He served on the House Banking and Currency Committee and also made frequent weekend visits to his district. He believed he needed to keep in touch with the people who sent him to Washington. Young was always an advocate for the poor. He voted to increase the minimum wage and to extend it to domestic workers, to broaden the food stamp program, to establish federal day care programs, to expand the Medicaid program to include coverage for abortions, and to create federally–funded public service jobs for the unemployed. Young also voted for the creation of a consumer protection agency and introduced a bill outlining a comprehensive national health care plan.

Young met Jimmy Carter when Carter was running for governor of Georgia. Carter was impressed with Young and actively sought his support. Young, on the other hand, had his doubts about Carter but was aware of Carter's great empathy for black people and the nation's poor. While Young wanted a more liberal Democrat, he supported Carter. What made Carter less than perfect were his comments about whites having the right to resist "black intrusion" and "alien groups" and the need to preserve "ethnic purity" of their neighborhoods. To Carter's credit, when Young pointed to the "loaded and Hitlerian connotations" of Carter's statement, Carter issued an apology.

Young gave the seconding speech for Carter's nomination at the Democratic Convention in New York City in July 1976. Then he went to work to garner the black vote for Carter. In the end, he was the only person to whom Jimmy Carter felt he owed a political debt. Young had mobilized a massive door–to–door voter registration in the inner cities. When Carter became president, he nominated Young as ambassador to the United Nations. Young was unanimously confirmed on January 25, 1977.

Works for Human Rights

Young saw the world from the perspective of his experience. His friendship with students from all over the world at Hartford Seminary and from his association in the World Council of Churches rendered the world not an alien place but one where people faced the same problems of human survival and development. When Young became U.S. ambassador to the United Nations, he was surprised to find himself labeled a radical by the New York media simply because he was the most outspoken proponent for human rights in the Carter Administration.

Both Young and his wife had a long–standing interest in Angola. People were shocked when one ambassador said that the presence of Cuban troops brought a certain stability and order to Angola. Until Young's tenure, the U.N. ambassador had acted as a spokesperson for the State Department. Clearly Young had no intention of doing likewise. He told *New York Times* reporter Joseph Lelyveld:

> There is a sense in which the United States Ambassador speaks to the United States, as well as for the United States. I have always seen my role as a thermostat, rather than a thermometer. I have always had people advise me on what to say, but never on what not to say.

While his statements on apartheid in South Africa and his attacks on human rights violations and racism in the United States often angered conservative Americans who called for his resignation, Young kept President Carter's support. Carter understood that possibly for the first time since Ralph Bunche, an American official was credible in the Third World.

All were not pleased when Young left Congress for the U.N. According to the *New York Times Magazine,* veteran civil rights colleague Hosea Williams called Young's appointment a "political kidnapping [engineered] by Atlanta's white power structure to retake political control of Atlanta." Members of the Congressional Black Caucus also expressed disappointment. They felt he would have been more useful in Congress. Quoted in the same source, from the beginning Young made it clear that he would not be "'the White House nigger' in the Carter Administration." He never was.

When it became a choice between what was correct and what was morally right, Young always chose the latter. As U.N. ambassador this choice led to his undoing. In August 1979, Young met with Zehdi Labib Terzi, the U.N. observer for the Palestine Liberation Organization (PLO). The State Department expressly forbade official contact with the PLO. When news of the meeting became public, Young was forced to resign. He expressed no regrets.

After leaving the U.N., Young, his wife, and youngest child and only son, Andrew III (Bo), returned to Atlanta. Andrea, the oldest daughter, graduated from Georgetown Law School and came to Atlanta to study for the Georgia Bar. Paula Jean entered Duke University, and Lisa was completing her final year in the School of Engineering at Howard University. Young recalled in his autobiography, "Our family hardly missed a step due to my resignation."

Called to Serve Again

On returning to Atlanta, Young established his own consulting firm, Young Ideas, with the intention of living life as a private citizen. In 1981, Coretta Scott King and other black Atlantans urged Young to run for mayor. Maynard Jackson, two–term mayor of Atlanta, could not run for a third term. During Jackson's tenure as mayor the city had moved toward racial polarization. State and federal aid was drying up, whites were fleeing to the suburbs, and nationwide white backlash sent Ronald Reagan to the White House. In Young's opinion, Jackson had been a good mayor. In fact, he had made so many necessary changes, Young stated in his autobiography, "that there was the same backlash emerging locally that helped elect Reagan nationally." Thinking that he could mend some of the strained relationships, Young agreed to run.

Some critics doubted Young's ability to do the job as mayor. They thought he was a weak administrator. Young soon silenced the critics. By 1984, there was so much new business in Atlanta it experienced a major growth spurt. The crime rate dropped dramatically and the city became the first choice of executives looking to locate a business. In 1985, Young won reelection with a wide margin of victory.

In his second term as mayor, Young got the idea from Horace Sibley and Billy Payne, successful Atlanta attorneys, for Atlanta to host the 1996 Olympics. He recalls that most of his staff laughed at the idea. Young bought the idea at once and was off and running with it. With Billy Payne in charge, Young believed the Olympics would come to Atlanta. Although competing with 14 other cities hoping to host the 1996 Olympics, in 1990 Atlanta was the site chosen. Young credits the many people who were involved who sacrificed time and money to develop the idea. Others credit Young, his vision of Atlanta as an international city, and his friends on the International Olympic Committee from the 73 nations and countries where he had visited as U.N ambassador.

In 1990, Young decided to run for governor of Georgia. Apparently he felt compelled to run but at the same time was tired of politics, for he had said if he did not win, he would be "free" to pursue other things. Young's record as mayor—Atlanta's economic boom, the Olympics—made him a viable candidate. However, the conundrum of race entered the picture, and excuses were made. Since the crime rate had risen again, Young was blamed. Black voters were again apathetic, and some were angered by Young's effort to win white votes, taking black votes for granted. Many blacks especially resented Young's campaign in Marietta in the "redneck bar" that played racist songs on its jukebox. In the end, low black voter turnout and Young's failure to win the white vote caused him to lose the primary election to lieutenant governor Zell Miller.

When Young lost the Democratic primary for governor, he saw it as a major setback but said in his autobiography, "I have never been so totally dominated by politics that I could not readily adjust to alternatives." Little did he know that the next phase of his life would be the most trying, and most extreme test of his faith.

On July 26, 1991, following a three–week business trip he and his wife took to Zimbabwe, and a weekend in the Bahamas with their children, sons–in–law, and grandchildren, Young and his wife returned to Atlanta. After they returned, Jean Young became ill and was rushed to Crawford Long's emergency room. Shortly thereafter Young was told that his wife of thirty–seven years had cancer of the colon that had metastasized to her liver.

The week that Young's wife came home from surgery, his son, Bo—in his first week as a freshman at Howard University—was stopped by police a block from campus and beaten in full view of witnesses, for no apparent reason. An investigation later cleared the Washington, D.C. police from any wrongdoing. Although these were trying times for Young, he never lost faith. Jean Childs Young died September 16, 1994.

A deeply spiritual person, Young believes that at each stage of his life, God has provided for all of his needs. Young was co–chair for the Atlanta Olympics Committee, and is chairman of the Metro Atlanta Chamber of Commerce and vice chairman of Law Companies Group, a consulting firm. In April 1996, Young married Carolyn McClain, a longtime family friend, in Cape Town, South Africa.

Young received the Pax–Christ Award from St. John's University in 1970, the Spingarn Medal from the NAACP in 1978, and the Presidential Medal of Freedom from President Jimmy Carter in 1980. Andrew Young, a veteran of the Civil Rights Movement, a politician with integrity, and a spiritual leader, has earned his place in American history as an elder statesman.

Current address: c/o Thomas Nelson, Inc., 501 Nelson Place, Nashville, TN 37214.

REFERENCES

Bims, Hamilton. "A Southern Activist Goes to the House." *Ebony* 28 (February 1973): 83–90.

Branch, Taylor. *Parting the Waters: America in the King Years.* New York: Simon and Schuster, 1988.

Cheers, Michael. "Andrew Young Weds Carolyn McClain in Cape Town, S. Africa." *Jet* 89 (April 15, 1996): 12–14.

Clement, Lee, ed. *Andrew Young at the United Nations.* Salisbury, NC: Documentary Pub., 1978.

Contemporary Black Biography. Vol. 3. Detroit: Gale Research, 1993.

Current Biography Yearbook. New York: H. W. Wilson, 1977.

Gardner, Carl. *Andrew Young: A Biography.* New York: Drake, 1978.

Lelyveld, Joseph. "Our New Voice at the U.N." *The New York Times Magazine* (February 6, 1977): 6–8.

Young, Andrew. *A Way Out of No Way.* Nashville: Thomas Nelson, 1994.

Nagueyalti Warren

Charles Young
(1864–1922)
Military officer, cartographer, congressman, educator

The third African American to graduate from the U.S. Military Academy at West Point, Charles Young overcame racial prejudice to become a lieutenant colonel in the U.S. Army and for many years the Army's highest ranking black officer. He served as an officer in the Spanish–American War as well as various parts of the United States, the Philippines, Haiti, and Mexico and on special assignments in Liberia. Young revised maps and drew new ones of uncharted areas in the Dominican Republic and Liberia.

Born in a long cabin in Mayslick, Kentucky, on March 12, 1865, Charles Young was the son of former slaves. His father may have been a private in the Union Army. When Charles was nine years old, the family moved a short distance away, to Ripley, Ohio, where he attended public schools and in 1880 graduated from the Colored High School. A studious young man with a continuing ambition for learning, he was allowed to use the personal library of a local resident, Percival Parks, with whom he often discussed current events and miscellaneous subjects. Young had a talent for foreign lan-

Charles Young

guages and music and was a high school teacher for several years while he prepared to enroll in a Jesuit college.

In 1884 Young successfully completed the competitive examination for admittance to the U.S. Military Academy at West Point. Young's West Point experience was trying and unpleasant. Although the academy already had graduated two blacks—Henry O. Flipper in 1877 and John H. Alexander in 1887—the white cadets resented Young's presence and ostracized him because of his race. During his first year no one spoke to him or took notice of him except to haze him. They attempted to force his resignation. He graduated on August 31, 1889, however, and two months later was commissioned a second lieutenant in the Tenth Cavalry. After Young's graduation, nearly half a century would pass before another black, Benjamin O. Davis Jr., would complete the program.

Young was stationed at Fort Robinson, Nebraska, in September of 1889 and served there until September of 1890. He was transferred to Fort Du Chesne, Utah, for four years, serving in the Thirty–fifth Infantry, then the Ninth Cavalry. After a military department was established at Wilberforce University in Ohio, Young was appointed professor of tactics and military science there. He also taught French and mathematics. He remained at Wilberforce from 1894 to 1898, and was promoted to first lieutenant.

Serves in Spanish–American War

The Spanish–American War began in 1898. Young requested that the War Department reassign him to his regiment when it was activated. He received a wartime rank of major and was put in charge of the all–black Ninth Ohio Volunteer Infantry serving in Virginia, Pennsylvania, and South Carolina from May 14, 1898, until the regiment was mustered out on January 18, 1899. He rejoined the Ninth Cavalry at Fort Du Chesne. He was promoted to captain in the regular army on February 2, 1901, and was sent to the Philippines in April where he commanded troops in the jungles and earned the nickname ''Follow Me.''

Young returned to the United States in October of 1902 and went to California where, until late 1903, he was acting superintendent of Sequoia and General Grant National Parks. The next year he became commander of troops at the Presidio of San Francisco. He joined this country's first black military attaché in Port–au–Prince, Haiti, in 1904. As part of his assignment, he rode horseback through the Dominican Republic, revising maps, and drawing new ones of many uncharted portions of the island. In 1925 the army destroyed many of the maps and reports that he prepared and sent back to the Army War College.

In April of 1907 Young was detached from Haiti and returned to the United States. He was assigned to the Second Division Intelligence of the War Department's general staff in Washington, D.C., from May of 1907 until June of 1908. He sailed for Camp McGrath in the Philippines in August of 1908, where he was a commander. He returned to the United States in June of 1909, where until December of 1911 he commanded the Second Squadron located at Fort D. A. Russell (later called Fort Francis E. Warren) in Wyoming.

At the urging of his friend, Booker T. Washington, Young accepted an assignment as military attaché in Liberia and left for that country in March of 1912. He traveled throughout Liberia and again engaged in cartography. He was promoted again, this time to major, on August 28, 1912. That December he was ambushed by a Gola tribesman while rescuing a fellow American officer and received a bullet wound in his right arm. The next year blackwater fever weakened him for a considerable time, and he took a leave of absence. He was called home in 1915, under the State Department's ''Manchu Law'' which permitted army officers to serve no more than three years abroad except on troop duty. In Mexico from February of 1910 to March of 1917, Young again was commander of a cavalry squadron. On June 1, 1916, he was promoted to lieutenant colonel. This promotion made him the highest ranking black officer in the U.S. Army.

The United States entered World War I in April of 1917. Considering his successful experiences and promotions in rank, Young expected that he would be given a suitable assignment in France. On June 22, 1917, after he took a physical examination, he was said to have a physical disability and was suddenly retired from the military. Although sources questioned the results reported, claiming that the race issue had surfaced in his case, Nancy Gordon Heine wrote in *Dictionary of American Negro Biography* that Young, in fact, suffered from an advanced case of nephritis, which was the cause of his death nearly five years later. In an unsuccessful protest and to demonstrate his fitness, Young rode horseback from Ohio to Washington. After Young was retired, the army board recommended him for an advanced rank promotion to full colonel. He was recalled to duty when the war was nearly over and assigned to the Ohio National Guard at Camp Grant, Illinois.

Young returned to Monrovia, Liberia, for the last time, in 1919, as military attaché to the U.S. embassy. In early 1922 he took an expedition to Nigeria and on January 8 died in Grey's Hospital in Lagos. Although he was buried in Lagos with full military honors by British troops, his widow's request to have his remains returned home was honored. English law, however, prohibited the removal of his body within a year of burial. The body was exhumed and began its journey home in February of 1923, without dignity on a tramp steamer. The Colonel Charles Young Post 398 of the American Legion in New York held services in his honor on May 27, 1923, at the City College of New York. Among the speakers were W. E. B. Du Bois, Joel E. Spingarn, and Franklin D. Roosevelt, then assistant secretary of the U.S. Navy.

Young's body was shipped to Washington, D.C., where a military cortege escorted it to Arlington National Cemetery in Virginia. He was reinterred on June 1, 1923. The District's black schools closed that day to honor the fallen soldier. Funeral participants also included representatives of the U.S. Army, the Grand Army of the Republic, United Spanish–American War Veterans, unaffiliated veterans of World War I, and prominent white and black citizens. In addition to his widow, Ada Mills Young of Xenia, Ohio, whom he married on February 18, 1904, Young was survived by two children Charles Noel (b. 1906) and Marie Aurelia (b. 1909).

In addition to his talent as military leader and cartographer, Young was a writer. In 1912 he wrote the work *Military Morale of Nations and Races* while he was on tour in Haiti. He also wrote a drama based on the life of Toussaint L'Ouverture, the black hero credited for Haiti's freedom, as well as an English–French–Creole dictionary. On February 22, 1916, Young became the second winner of the NAACP's Spingarn medal.

Quoted in *Dictionary of American Negro Biography,* a Haitian newspaper called Young "a handsome Black with distinguished bearing and charming manners." His career was followed intensely by blacks, who held him in high esteem. Although he was recognized publicly as a soldier, he had many other notable qualities: he spoke several languages and had a keen interest in music and poetry. He aimed for excellence and was never satisfied with mediocrity. He was also conscious of his blackness and proud of his race. While at Wilberforce he aided a number of promising young blacks both spiritually and financially. Those closest to him knew him for his laughter, joy of living, patience, forgiving attitude, and eagerness to show sympathy to those in distress.

In honor of the brave, loyal, and patriotic soldier who overcame racial prejudices to become a distinguished military servant, on May of 1974, the Department of the Interior declared his home a National Historical Landmark. The Charles Young House is located on Columbus Pike between Clitton and Stevenson Roads in Wilberforce, Ohio.

REFERENCES

Brawley, Benjamin. *Negro Builders and Heroes.* Chapel Hill: University of North Carolina Press, 1937.

Cantor, George. *Historic Landmarks of Black America.* Detroit: Gale Research, 1991.

Logan, Rayford W., and Michael R. Winston, eds. *Dictionary of American Negro Biography.* New York: Norton, 1982.

Smith, Gene. "A Fighting Man." *American Legacy* 4 (Spring 1998): 12, 14.

Spivey, Mary Elizabeth. "Colonel Charles Young." *Negro History Bulletin* 5 (May 1942): 185–86.

COLLECTIONS

The National Archives contains extensive references to Young's work in Haiti and Liberia. His records once housed in the Personnel Archives in St. Louis were burned on July 12, 1973. The text of his multilingual dictionary is in the library of the Army War College, Carlisle, Pennsylvania.

Jessie Carney Smith

Coleman A. Young
(1918–1997)
Mayor, state senator, civil rights activist

Coleman A. Young was a man of vision who kept his mind firmly on one goal: full and equal rights for all the citizens of this country. Oftentimes aggressive, salty, and abrasive in speech, he remained true always to his Detroit inner–city background. Proud of his family roots and heritage, he sought advancement for his people. An activist in the strongest and best sense of the word, he chose means to suit the task wherever his occupation found him. "Whatever works best" might be a good phrase to use in characterizing his approach.

Coleman Alexander Young was born in Tuscaloosa, Alabama, on May 24, 1918, the son of Coleman and Ida Reese Young. His father, a World War I veteran, went to Huntsville in about 1921 to study tailoring at Alabama Agricultural and Mechanical College, utilizing his veteran's benefits. He then moved to Detroit, following the urban migration pattern of seeking better employment opportunities. Some of young Coleman's earliest memories, reflected in his autobiography, are of Ku Klux Klan activities in Tuscaloosa, and then in Huntsville.

In 1923 Coleman Young's family moved into the Detroit section called "Black Bottom," so named for the good, rich

Coleman A. Young

soil farmed by Detroit's early settlers. His early education was in the Detroit public schools, followed by St. Mary's Catholic School, where he was enrolled upon his parents' conversion to Catholicism. His parents valued education. His mother was a teacher, his father an avid reader who kept himself closely informed on politics and current events. It is little surprising then, that young Coleman excelled in school. Ironically, his academic acumen led to some direct encounters with discrimination. One of the earliest was with scouting. He joined the Boy Scout troop attached to St. Mary's School, applied himself, and advanced through all the ranks to patrol leader, senior patrol leader, and finally to junior assistant scoutmaster, the highest scout rank within a troop. At this point, the troop was dissolved, apparently to foreclose the possibility of a black youth becoming the leader.

Upon his eighth grade graduation from St. Mary's, he had finished among the top ten students in Detroit's parochial schools, entitling him to a scholarship to one of the city's Catholic high schools. His application was refused. Then, that summer, a graduation party was scheduled for Boblo, an amusement park on an island in the Detroit River. In boarding the boat for the outing, one of the guides removed his cap, examined his hair, and told him the park did not admit black children. This event changed his life, and remained with him until his later years.

Following his graduation from St. Mary's, he attended Eastern High School. Once again he excelled in his studies, graduating second in his class. Finding the doors to a promised scholarship closed to him, he decided to go to work, and enrolled in an electrician's apprentice program at the Ford plant. He did very well, and completed the program with high scores. The apprentice job, however, went to the other student in the program, a white whose father was a plant foreman. Young was assigned to the assembly line. He came under suspicion at the plant because of his union organizing sympathies. Harry Bennett, Ford's security chief, had a staff of strong–armed men in the plant whose job it was to suppress pro–union activities. One of these men confronted Young, and a fight broke out. Young won the skirmish but was fired for fighting.

Develops Activist's Outlook

Young found jobs as a cook, in a dry cleaning firm, and as a post office clerk, meanwhile acquiring more street acumen, an activist outlook, and more radical ideals. He also began working with the National Negro Congress (NNC), a church–supported organization espousing the rights of working people. His mentors were his politically astute father; the Reverend Charles Hill, president of the Michigan branch of NNC and pastor of the Hartford Avenue Baptist Church; John Conyers Sr., father of the current Congressman; Charles Diggs, a prominent funeral home director and an early organizer for the Detroit Democratic Party; and Haywood Maben, a self–proclaimed dialectic Marxist, as well as the regular visitors to Maben's barber shop.

The shop hosted frequent meetings where politics and social issues were the topics of discussion. Jobs, neighborhood issues, trade unionism, equal opportunity, and similar issues were raised. There was sympathy expressed for radical points of view. Local meetings at churches at other venues sometimes featured speakers with known Communist connections, and Detroit activists attended meetings in other cities and read literature distributed by the Communist Party. Unionism and the rights of the worker were central issues of the times. These connections would later be explored by committees of the U.S. Senate and House of Representatives. Coleman Young's education was proceeding at full speed.

Young's work with NNC expanded, and he took on the role of secretary of the Detroit chapter. The organization began agitating for equal housing opportunity, and stayed closely in touch with union organizing activities at the Ford plant. The unionists received support from Hill, who opened his church to union organizing meetings. After a long struggle that reached a head in 1941 with picketing and a memorable battle at the plant between the unionists and security men, several more minor confrontations occurred before a vote on organizing the plant was held. Young participated in the struggle, and reported that public sympathy shifted to the unionists; the union won the vote. A very liberal contract was negotiated between Ford and the United Auto Workers.

The NNC next became highly active in the battle for desegregation in housing. Young and the NNC led the battle to open the Sojourner Truth housing development to blacks. Community organizations arose in heated dispute on both sides, and a riot was barely avoided. Eventually the project was opened to black residents under the protection of troops and police. Meanwhile, Coleman Young was fired from his post office job, ostensibly for failing a test, but more probably for being a union organizer. At this time also, the Japanese bombed Pearl Harbor, the United States formally entered World War II, the draft was initiated, and Young and his brother, George, were drafted into the army in February of 1942.

Much of army life at this time was segregated, particularly in the South. As he moved through a variety of army posts, Young fought segregation in the military service with a consuming passion. Initially assigned to the infantry at Fort McClellan, Alabama, he qualified for Officer Candidate School upon completion of his basic training. He graduated from OCS at Fort Benning, Georgia, and was commissioned a second lieutenant in the U.S. Army. He was sent to Fort Breckenridge, Kentucky, where a black unit, the 92nd Infantry Division, was being assembled. After training, they were sent to Fort Huachuca, Arizona, for further training and to prepare for overseas assignment.

Fights Racism in the Military

For black officers, there were constant indignities. They were often denied access to Bachelor Officers' Quarters and Officers' Clubs, and also the respect of command. For the ordinary soldier, the situation was often worse. Discrimination and mistreatment were present, and the bases were often situated near towns where racial bigotry was rife.

Discontent reached the crisis stage at Fort Huachuca. The company commander became concerned, lectured his officers, and sent for the army's only black general, Benjamin O. Davis Sr., to address the troops. Davis stressed patriotism, and the "good soldier" tradition. Young, however, arranged a greeting for him by a group of fellow officers displaying handkerchiefs on their heads (the Uncle Tom symbol), and General Davis left the base. Fortunately, Young's tour of duty with the infantry soon ended. He heard of the formation of the new air force training school for bombardiers and pilots at Tuskegee Institute, Alabama, and was able to apply for a transfer to the air force.

Young's progress through several air force bases was eventful as he kept on fighting for equality of treatment and an end to racial discrimination in military service. At Tuskegee he proceeded smoothly through flight school, up to the point of his final flight test. There his examiner failed him, apparently on orders from the Federal Bureau of Investigation (FBI); he learned this later from a Detroit friend who had served with him and worked in a base administrative office. Young next was sent to bombardier school in Tyndal Field, Florida, from there to Midland Field, Texas, Godman Field, Kentucky, and Freeman Field, Indiana. At most of these installations the air force followed segregationist policies and discrimination was present in facilities, promotion and living conditions. Black Officers' Clubs were set up in separate locations, separate quarters were provided, and other indignities perpetrated.

Young and his fellow officers constantly used a variety of means to combat the offenses, culminating in the occupation of the Officers' Club at Freeman Field, with 69 officers wilfully disobeying an order to leave. Eventually more than 100 officers were moved to fenced–in quarters at nearby Godman Field and imprisoned there while the case was investigated. After a full scale review, they were exonerated and the base commander relieved of command. During most of these defiant encounters Young used his friends, the black press, and various couriers including war hero and later general Daniel "Chappie" James and others to see that letters were delivered and the conditions they were protesting were fully publicized in the media, with communications going to all of the appropriate levels in government. Following the end of the war in August of 1945, War Department Memorandum No. 450–50 was issued early in 1946, officially eliminating racial discrimination in the U.S. armed forces.

Meanwhile, Young heard that Col. Benjamin O. Davis Jr. was to be their commander. He found an escape route, applied, and was granted one final transfer, to celestial navigation school at Selman Field, Louisiana. In a final incident before his discharge, he and some friends decided to crash the V–J victory celebration at the segregated Officers' Club on base. The next day, those in command realized the situation: the black officers had entered the club without authorization, and could be charged. A Mississippi colonel came up with a face–saving compromise. He offered the "offending" officers a choice between reenlistment and honorable discharge. Young chose the latter and left the service at Maxwell Field, Alabama, on December 23, 1945.

Young returned immediately to Detroit and civilian life. His progression from union activism to politics was steady. Having been introduced at a Congress of Industrial Organizations (CIO) organizational banquet in 1944, while briefly at home on a pass, he naturally sought involvement again. He resumed work at the post office for a short time and began working with the United Public Workers union. His organizational and tactical skills were put to good use right away in helping the Garbage Workers Union gain a new contract.

Young sought to establish a black presence on the Wayne County CIO board, and succeeded in amending the constitution to make this possible. After some negotiations, Young was elected to the board as director of organization. However, his cards were unfortunately trumped at the next union organizing convention, where Walter Reuther and his associates used their strength to overwhelm their opposition, displaced the board, and captured all of the executive positions in the union. Reuther, who feared the radicals and Communist sympathizers within the labor movement in Michigan, purged this element.

Young, meanwhile, chose to support the Progressive Party under Henry Wallace in the election campaign of 1948, with attendant campaign marches, concerts, and speeches featuring actor, singer and activist Paul Robeson among others. Despite the party's poor showing in the election, Young and his Wayne County colleagues continued their support. They were outspoken in their support of the "Foley Square Eleven," so named after the arrest in New York City of a group of avowed Communists and sympathizers, charged with violating the Smith Act of 1940 by allegedly advocating the overthrow of the U.S. government.

Unionist and pro–labor sentiments were strong among Detroiters. There were frequent meetings, rallies, and lectures featuring Robeson, folksinger Pete Seeger, Benjamin Davis (the leftist, not the general) and scholar W. E. B. Du Bois. These activities, of course, were monitored by the FBI and by Young's opponents in the CIO, and reported to the Congressional committees investigating the Communist movement. Nevertheless, Young and his friends pushed on, feeling that the central issues remained equal opportunity and the rights of the working man. In 1951 a movement coalesced in a charter meeting in Cincinnati, establishing the National Negro Labor Council (NNLC). William Hood of UAW Local 600 was elected president and Coleman Young executive secretary, with the council headquarters in Detroit. The NNLC became very active in union and political affairs.

Young was asked to testify before the House Un–American Activities Committee in 1952. He was not a weak witness, however. He refused to answer some questions, accused the committee of a witch hunt, corrected the counsel's pronunciation of "Negro," and accused one committee member of "Un–American activities," because he represented a constituency that was 75 percent black and many could not vote. The following year the NNLC was placed on the attorney general's list of subversive organizations. Knowing that the members would all be listed as subversives, Young protested but eventually decided that rather than register and turn over the membership list, it was better to disband the organization. He did so in 1956.

Enters Political Arena

In the meantime, Young's friends, including those at the barber shop, urged him to seek political office. He ran unsuccessfully for the city council in 1959, and for state representative in 1959, served as a delegate to the Constitutional Convention in 1961–62, and was elected to two terms in the State Senate (1964–73). Elected Democratic minority floor leader, he proceeded to introduce and was instrumental in passing Michigan's open housing law. His success in the Senate prompted his entry into the campaign for mayor of Detroit. His first victory in November of 1973 was hard fought and very close, with the vote divided sharply along racial lines—Young received over 90 percent of the black vote. He and Tom Bradley of Los Angeles were the first black men elected as mayors of major U.S. cities. Young was elected to four more terms, serving for 20 years before retiring in 1993. An indication of his political style and leadership posture is exemplified by the legend on a small name plate on his desk, "M.F.I.C."

Among Young's major accomplishments as mayor was the revitalizing and renovation of downtown Detroit as a commercial, industrial, and entertainment center with substantial contributions from Detroit's corporate community. Another was his extended efforts over several years to build better police–community relations in the aftermath of the 1967 Detroit riot. This involved working for integration and equal employment opportunity on the force, frequent meetings with the community, and aggressive oversight of police practices. The better climate thus established was almost shattered with the police murder of Malice Green, an inner city resident, in 1992. Young helped avoid a riot by taking an active role in the situation and moving the prosecution of the case aggressively forward. Another major accomplishment was his campaign to pass the 1981 tax referendum, which resulted in addressing a serious city budget shortfall. He marshalled community support and brought civil–rights icon Rosa Parks to speak at a rally in this successful effort.

Young was president of the U.S. Conference of Mayors, member of the Democratic Conference of Mayors, vice–chairman of the National Democratic Party (1977–71), chairman of the 1980 Democratic Convention platform committee, and a member of the national advisory committee to the White House Conference on Aging, 1981. He was awarded the NAACP's Spingarn Medal in 1981 and the 1982 Adam Clayton Powell Award for outstanding political leadership from the Congressional Black Caucus.

In retirement, Young was a professor of urban affairs at Wayne State University, a remarkable turnaround for one who had been unable to use a college scholarship. He was married and divorced twice and had one son, Joel Loving (age 15 in 1997), by his companion, Annivory Calvert. Young's health began to fail due to heart trouble and chronic emphysema. He was treated and hospitalized several times for heart and respiratory problems, and died on November 29, 1997, of respiratory failure, ending a lifetime of activism and in support of African American people.

REFERENCES

"Coleman Young, 79, Former Mayor of Detroit." *New York Times,* November 30, 1997.

Contemporary Black Biography. Vol. 1. Detroit: Gale Research, 1992.

Current Biography Yearbook. New York: H. W. Wilson, 1997.

Decker, Brett M. "The Man Who Drove Detroit Down." *Human Events* 53 (12 December 1997): 5.

"Former Detroit Mayor dies." *Nashville Tennessean,* November 30, 1997.

Hirsch, Arnold R. "Academia Ain't Ready for Reform." *Journal of Urban History* 18 (November 1991): 98–107.

"A Job Fit for Heroes." *The Economist* 328 (28 August 1993): 25–27.

"Newspoints; Words in the News." *Black Enterprise* 24 (February 1994): 32.

Poinsett, Alex. "Motor City Makes a Comeback." *Ebony* 33 (April 1978): 29–40.

Rich, Wilbur C. *Coleman Young and Detroit Politics: From Social Activist to Power Broker.* Detroit: Wayne State University Press, 1989.

Smith, Jessie Carney, ed. *Black Firsts.* Detroit: Gale Research, 1994.
''Young No Longer.'' *The Economist* 327 (26 June 1993): 27.
Young, Carlito H. ''Constant Struggle: Coleman Young's Perspective on American Society and Detroit Politics.'' *The Black Scholar* 27 (June 1997): 31–41.
Young, Coleman, and Lonnie Wheeler. *Hard Stuff; The Autobiography of Coleman Young.* New York: Viking Penguin, 1994.
Who's Who among African Americans, 1998–99. 10th ed. Detroit: Gale Research, 1997.
Who's Who in America, 48th ed. New Providence, NJ: Marquis, 1993.

Darius L. Thieme

Whitney M. Young Jr.

(1921–1971)

Social worker, civil rights leader

Whitney M. Young Jr.

Whitney Moore Young Jr., a social worker by profession, served as the head of the National Urban League during the most turbulent years in civil rights history. Young propelled the Urban League, a conservative organization, to the forefront of the civil rights movement through his aggressive programs for equal opportunity in education, employment, and housing for black Americans. He sought a ''domestic Marshall Plan'' to remedy the economic and educational problems that plagued African Americans.

Born at Lincoln Institute, a private high school for blacks in Lincoln Ridge, Kentucky, on July 31, 1921, Young was destined to become a household name in American civil rights history. His father, Whitney Moore Young Sr., was the first black principal of the small private high school for blacks in the rural central Kentucky community. His mother, Laura Ray Young, was the first black postmaster in Kentucky and the second black postmaster in the United States. Young and his siblings, Arnita and Eleanor, all obtained their college degrees from Kentucky State College (now University) and each became prominent in their respective fields of study.

Young married Campbellsville, Kentucky, native Margaret Buckner, whom he met while in college and they had two daughters, Marcia Elaine and Lauren Lee. Young's wife would go on to write several children's books on civil rights and history.

Young grew up during the Jim Crow era but remained in a sheltered and isolated black environment during most of his formative years. While his father was principal of Lincoln Institute, from 1936 to 1966, the family resided on the school campus. Lincoln Institute had both white and black teachers on the faculty, a combination which provided examples of racial understanding and cooperation for Lincoln students and the Young children.

The senior Young taught his son, who was called ''Junior,'' the importance of ambition, high moral and religious standards, and racial tolerance. The father also emphasized education and convinced the youngster that he could accomplish anything. Young Sr. always presented a calm, controlled manner, never displaying a temper or raising his voice to his children. Young's mother served as a strong role model for the young man through her benevolent acts. She was known for helping orphans and caring for the elderly and sick. It was not unusual for her to feed vagabonds who were traveling by train or to take clothing and packages of food to people in the rural areas near the campus or to house orphans at Lincoln so they could acquire an education. She would also send small amounts of money inside cards to ill persons and others. From his mother Young learned skills in human relations, compassion, and caring—skills that would serve him throughout his professional care. As children, Young and his sisters engaged in various activities on the Lincoln campus including movies and ball games. The family took advantage of the freedom of the isolated rural environment by planting gardens, playing cards and croquet, and engaging in other family activities. Like other black educated people, Young and his sisters participated in activities with other black families who were middle class. They went on family outings and visited friends in Lexington, Louisville, Chicago, Indianapolis, and other areas. Young sometimes spent the summer out of town with friends and family. This nurturing environment instilled in him a strong sense of self–confidence.

After completing his high school curriculum with valedictory honors, Young enrolled in Kentucky State College in Frankfort. On campus he gained a reputation for being an efficient organizer and was affectionately called "Hitler" by classmates. After graduating from college in 1941, Young planned to become a doctor because of the freedom the profession offered him politically and economically. He felt that doctors, unlike other black professionals, could speak their minds and not fear white politicians.

To earn money for medical school, Young initially coached and taught school at Rosenwald High School in Madisonville, Kentucky, for a year. His plans changed, however, after he enlisted in the army in May 1943. Still hoping to become a doctor after his military service, he signed up for the Army Specialized Training Program and was sent to the Massachusetts Institute of Technology for a short period before receiving an assignment with an engineer combat unit in Virginia. As an educated black man, he was promoted to first sergeant after only two weeks in the field. Most of his responsibility involved administrative duties, but he soon became the liaison between the white officers and the black recruits. The white officers used Young as a negotiator with the troops, who often challenged their officer's authority once they were in Europe. His army experiences revealed many differences between him and the other black recruits, and perhaps for the first time he understood the exact state of most of black America, economically, morally, culturally, and in other ways. This experience changed Young's career goals, and he decided to move into the field of race relations.

Becomes Activist

While on a five–day military leave, Young and Margaret Buckner were married on January 2, 1944. After military service, Young applied for admission to the University of Kentucky for graduate study, but because Kentucky law did not allow blacks to attend the university's graduate programs, both Young and his wife pursued masters degrees at the University of Minnesota. As a graduate student, he joined the Congress of Racial Equality and protested in student demonstrations and sit–ins in Minneapolis. These protests resulted in the integration of restaurants and lunch counters near the school.

While he pursed his degree, Young's first field placement was with the Hennepin County Welfare Board in Minneapolis, in an area with a large underprivileged black clientele. He requested that he also receive some white clients so he could see both sides of the problems. Young was assigned to work in the Minneapolis Urban League for his second year of field placement. His masters degree, received in 1947, was in the field of social work. After finishing the program, Young began his career as the industrial relations secretary of the St. Paul Urban League. He was appointed to head the Omaha Urban League office in 1950. His work with the Omaha black community showed his acceptance of different tactics for accomplishing social change in America. In Omaha other groups, including the DePorres Club, were engaged in boycotts, picket lines, and other types of direct action against racial injustice. Although these activities were too radical for the Urban League to support, Young formed close relationships with these groups. He also worked with them and city officials to settle disputes.

Kentuckian Rufus E. Clement, who was president of Atlanta University, went to Omaha in 1953 to invite Young to head his School of Social Work. The Civil Rights Movement was gaining momentum in the South and Young wanted to be involved to a greater extent, so he agreed to the proposition. Under Young's direction, the school became one of the top social work schools in the South. Young expanded the school's curriculum, provided additional training and professional development opportunities for his faculty, doubled the school's budget, and increased the number of full time faculty.

In the Atlanta community, Young continued to be involved in the Civil Rights Movement by serving as co–chair of the Atlanta Council on Human Relations. In this leadership role, he led the fight for the integration of the public libraries in Atlanta. He was also one of the founders of Atlanta's Committee for Cooperative Action (ACCA), which was comprised of both professional and business persons who worked for civil rights initiatives. *A Second Look: The Negro Citizen in Atlanta* was the major publication produced by the ACCA and it was coauthored by Young. *A Second Look,* published in 1958, documented the inequities in health services, education, and social services in Atlanta at the time.

Becomes National Urban League Head

In 1960 Young interrupted his tenure at Atlanta University to continue his studies through a Rockefeller grant at Harvard University. The next year he became the executive director of the National Urban League, one of the two oldest black civil rights organizations. Young, who was adept at human relations, focused his energies on corporate America to win support for black causes and black employment. It was not unusual for him to receive promises of thousands of jobs for blacks as well as financial support for Urban League programs from white corporate leaders after a meeting with them. He was an outstanding salesperson for the Urban League. Young implemented several new programs, including the National Skills Bank, On–the–Job Training with the Department of Labor, the Secretarial Training Project, and the Broadcast Skills Bank. During the ten years that Young headed the Urban League, his efforts brought financial stability while increasing the budget from $270,000 to $3 million. He also expanded the number of branches from 62 to 98, and increased the staff from 300 to more than 1,200.

In 1964 Young published *To Be Equal,* which included a full discussion of the plea for a domestic Marshall Plan, which would increase educational and economic opportunities for African Americans. President Lyndon Johnson incorporated parts of Young's plan in his War on Poverty program.

Although the Urban League was traditionally a conservative organization, under Young's administration it began to take on a more activist stance within the Civil Rights Movement. The league remained one of the most conservative groups working for civil rights, but Young's aggressive leadership expanded its programs and increased funding. Young, a skilled negotiator, served black interests on a national and international scale. He interacted with the presidential administrations of John F. Kennedy, Lyndon B. Johnson, and Richard M. Nixon, corporate moguls, and local black groups. He was one of the sponsors of the March on Washington for Jobs and Freedom in 1963, and he organized the Community Action Assembly to fight poverty in black neighborhoods in 1964. In 1968 Young introduced the "New Trust" program of the Urban League. The program's goals were to attack the problems of the ghettos, including poor housing, inadequate health care, and limited educational opportunities.

Other blacks criticized him for his moderation, but understanding the aversion that some whites felt toward the militant black movement, he took advantage of his own polite demeanor. To the white leadership Young represented a more respectable and acceptable black leader for them to negotiate with, and they did not view him as a threat. Young, who had a highly developed gift for understanding and relating to people of all backgrounds, effectively served as an outspoken leader for the league, providing a somewhat more aggressive approach than leaders in the past.

Non–NUL Endeavors

Young was less visible than the majority of black leaders in the civil rights movement era who offered a different idealogy and approach. He emphasized the racial uplift perspective as a member of the black middle class. His family upbringing had included many black role models who had stressed that it was the responsibility of the more fortunate and more educated blacks to help others who were from less economically–sound backgrounds. In a National Urban League press release issued July 11, 1966, Young stated:

> What we will continue to do . . . is expand and develop positive programs of action which bring jobs to the unemployed, housing to the dispossessed, education to the deprived, and necessary voter education to the disenfranchised. In the final analysis, these are the things . . . which bring power to both black and white citizens, and dignity and pride to all.

Young possessed excellent writing skills. He wrote a weekly syndicated newspaper column, published many articles in professional journals, and published the text of many of his addresses in these journals. In 1969, Young published his second book, *Beyond Racism: Building an Open Society,* which received the Christopher book award in 1970.

Young was involved in many community groups and projects. He had become a member of Alpha Phi Alpha Fraternity while in college and continued to be a active member of this black service fraternity throughout his life. Other involvements included the NAACP, Greater Atlanta Council on Human Relations, and the Atlanta Committee for Cooperative Action.

During his career, Young served in many professional capacities, including vice–president and president of the National Association of Social Workers. He was a member of the Advisory Board of the New York School of Social Work, a consultant to the U.S. Public Health Organization, and president of the National Conference on Social Welfare. He served on seven presidential commissions during the eight years of the Kennedy and Johnson administrations. More concerned about helping his people than about personal economic gain, Young turned down offers of corporate and cabinet positions.

Young received the Florina Lasker Award in 1959 for outstanding achievement in the field of social work. The University of Minnesota named Young the recipient of the 1960 Outstanding Alumni Award, and in 1961 North Carolina Agricultural and Technical College, as it was then known, gave Young an honorary doctorate. In 1969 Young was awarded the nation's highest civilian honor, the Medal of Freedom.

While swimming in Lagos, Nigeria, Young had a heart attack and died March 10, 1971. A memorial service held in New York was attended by such dignitaries as Roy Wilkins, Vernon Jordan Jr., James L. Buckley, Edward Kennedy, Nelson Rockefeller, John Lindsay, and John Mitchell. The service was followed by a procession down Broadway and through Harlem, where thousands of mourners lined the streets to pay their last respects to the controversial leader. Young's body was later flown to Louisville, Kentucky, for a second memorial service followed by a funeral procession of three hundred cars. The cortege passed the Lincoln Institute campus, then on through the Frankfort campus of Kentucky State University before ending in Lexington. Despite some conflict between President Nixon and Young's widow, Margaret Young finally agreed to permit Nixon to deliver the eulogy.

Whitney M. Young Jr. became nationally known for his work as the head of the National Urban League. Throughout the United States many facilities bear his name as a lasting tribute to his work. In his home state of Kentucky, an elementary school in Louisville is named for him as well as two educational programs. One program, the Whitney M. Young, Jr. College of Leadership Studies at Kentucky State University, his alma mater, is an honors program which strives to develop leadership abilities in its students through a comprehensive liberal studies curriculum. The other program, administered by Young's sister Eleanor Young Love through the Lincoln Institute, provides educational enrichment programs and funds college scholarships for talented, underprivileged high school students. The state of Kentucky has recognized the Lincoln Institute birth site of Whitney M. Young Jr. with an historic marker.

Young always wore a lapel pin that bore the algabraic symbol for ''equal.'' This easily sums up Young's philosophy. Quoted in *Kentucky's Black Heritage,* he once said, ''we must learn to live together as brothers or we will all surely die together as fools.''

REFERENCES

Contemporary Black Biography. Vol. 3. Detroit: Gale Research, 1993.

Dunnigan, Alice A. *Fascinating Story of Black Kentuckians: Their Heritage and Tradition.* Washington, DC: Associated Publishers, 1982.

Kentucky's Black Heritage. Frankfort: Kentucky Commission on Human Rights, 1971.

Outstanding Alumni: Centennial Booklet. Frankfort: Kentucky State University, 1986.

Weiss, Nancy J. *Whitney M. Young, Jr., and the Struggle for Civil Rights.* Princeton, NJ: Princeton University Press, 1989.

COLLECTIONS

The collection of Whitney M. Young Jr. is housed at Columbia University. The collection of his father, Whitney M. Young Sr., which contains personal material on them both, is found in the archives of the Paul G. Blazer Library at Kentucky State University.

Karen Cotton McDaniel

Geographic Index

ALABAMA

Anniston

Dawson, William Levi 272
Satcher, David 1044

Birmingham

Gaston, Arthur G. 445
Jones, Prophet 654
Lowery, Joseph E. 742

Brewton

Harvey, William R. 516

Demopolis

Gaston, Arthur G. 445

Evergreen

Henry, Warren E. 539

Fairfield

Mays, Willie 784

Florence

DePriest, Oscar S. 294
Handy, W. C. 508
Rapier, James T. 994

Gadsden

Dykes, De Witt S., Sr. 352

Huntsville

Lowery, Joseph E. 742

Lafayette

Louis, Joe 740

Lowndes County

Denby, Charles 291
Edwards, Nelson J. 361

Mobile

Aaron, Hank 1
Europe, James Reese 382
Paige, ''Satchel'' 901

Montgomery

Cole, Nat ''King'' 215
Denby, Charles 291
Julian, Percy L. 672
King, Martin Luther, Jr. 686
Nixon, E. D., Sr. 878

Oakville

Owens, Jesse 893

Saffold

Gibson, Benjamin F. 452

Talladega

Pickens, William 931

Troy

Lewis, John R. 718

Tuscaloosa

Young, Coleman A. 1285

Tuskegee

Carver, George Washington 177
Davis, Benjamin O., Jr. 255
Davis, Benjamin O., Sr. 259
Dawson, William Levi 272
Harvey, William R. 516
Moton, Robert Russa 847
Patterson, Frederick D. 914
Scott, Emmett Jay 1051
Washington, Booker T. 1181
Work, Monroe Nathan 1262

ARIZONA

Phoenix

Cleaver, Eldridge 203
Riles, Wilson C. 1011

Tucson

Kay, Ulysses S. 679

ARKANSAS

Arkansas City

Johnson, John H. 630

Fordyce

Cone, James H. 223

Little Rock

Gibbs, Mifflin Wistar 450

Jones, Scipio Africanus 660
Lewis, David Levering 713
Madhubuti, Haki 750
Massie, Samuel Proctor, Jr. 775
Still, William Grant 1082

Osceola

Whitman, Albery 1213

Pine Bluff

Foster, Henry W., Jr. 414
Haynes, George Edmund 528

Tulip

Jones, Scipio Africanus 660

Wabbaseka

Cleaver, Eldridge 203

West Helena

Warfield, William 1179

CALIFORNIA

White, Charles .1204

Beverly Hills

Abdul-Jabbar, Kareem 6

Cypress

Woods, Tiger 1252

Hollywood

Jones, Quincy 656
Poitier, Sidney .944

Long Beach

Woods, Tiger 1252

Los Angeles

Abdul-Jabbar, Kareem 6
Ailey, Alvin 8
Armstrong, Henry 26
Barnes, Steven 55
Belafonte, Harry .68
Bradley, Thomas 104
Bunche, Ralph J. 152
Chamberlain, Wilt 184
Charles, Ray 186
Cleaver, Eldridge 203
Cleveland, James 211
Cochran, Johnnie 212
Cole, Nat "King" 215
Freeman, Morgan 431
Gordy, Berry 468
Gumbel, Bryant .492
Hampton, Lionel 506
Hawkins, Augustus F. 522
Jones, James Earl 648
Lewis, Henry 716
Little Richard 724
Majors, Monroe A. 753
Mason, Charles Harrison 770
Mosley, Walter 839
Moss, Carlton 841
Muse, Clarence 864
Riles, Wilson C. 1011
Robinson, Bill "Bojangles" 1016
Robinson, Sugar Ray 1027
Seymour, William Joseph 1056
Still, William Grant 1082
Thurman, Wallace 1118
Washington, Denzel 1186
Williams, Paul R. 1238

Oakland

Binga, Jesse 75
Dellums, Ronald V. 289
Maynard, Robert C. 778
Newton, Huey P. 874
Russell, Bill 1035

Pasadena

Barthé, Richmond 60

Riverside

Little Richard 724

Sacramento

Riles, Wilson C. 1011

San Fernando Valley

Jackson, Michael 605

San Francisco

Brown, Grafton Tyler 124
Brown, Willie L., Jr. 141
Glover, Danny 464
Johnson, Sargent 642
Leidesdorff, William A. 711
Mays, Willie 784
Thurman, Howard 1114
Van Peebles, Melvin 1152

San Jose

Ribbs, Willy T. 1008

San Pablo

Bristow, Lonnie R. 118

Santa Monica

Chamberlain, Wilt 184

Davis, Miles 262
Santa Ynez Valley
Jackson, Michael 605
Sherman Oaks
Johnson, Rafer 638
Woodland Hills
Campanella, Roy 166

COLORADO
James, Daniel "Chappie," Jr. 610

CONNECTICUT
Bridgeport
Latimer, Lewis Howard 698
Hartford
Hammon, Jupiter 504
Pennington, James W. C. 923
New Haven
Bouchet, Edward A. 97
Pennington, James W. C. 923
Powell, Adam Clayton, Jr. 954
Norwich
Ruggles, David 1034
West Hartford
Haynes, Lemuel 532

DELAWARE
New Castle
Petersen, Frank, Jr. 930
Sussex
Jones, Absalom 644
Sussex County
Cornish, Samuel 229
Wilmington
Redding, J. Saunders 1000

DISTRICT OF COLUMBIA
Alexander, Clifford L., Jr. 15
Branson, Herman R. 110
Brawley, Benjamin G. 112
Brimmer, Andrew F. 116
Brooke, Edward W. 121
Brown, Ron 131
Brown, Tony 136
Burgess, John M. 156
Caliver, Ambrose 160
Cardozo, Francis L. 171
Coleman, William T., Jr. 217
Crockett, George W., Jr. 236
Crummell, Alexander 238
Darlington, Roy Clifford 251
Davis, Allison 252
Davis, Benjamin O., Jr. 255
Davis, Benjamin O., Sr. 259
Dodson, Howard, Jr. 312
Dodson, Owen 315
Douglass, Frederick 326
Drew, Charles R. 331
Driskell, David C. 333
Eckstine, Billy 357
Elder, Lee 362
Ellington, Duke 364
Europe, James Reese 382
Fauntroy, Walter E. 396
Fisher, Rudolph 400
Forman, James 406
Franklin, John Hope 421
Frazier, E. Franklin 428
Grimké, Archibald Henry 487
Grimké, Francis J. 490
Hastie, William Henry 519
Henry, Warren E. 539
Henson, Matthew A. 541
Holder, Eric H., Jr. 556
Holly, James T. 560
Houston, Charles Hamilton 575
Jackson, Jesse L. 598
Johnson, Mordecai W. 635
Johnson, Robert L. 640
Jordan, Vernon 667
Julian, Percy L. 672
Just, Ernest Everett 675
Langston, John Mercer 693
Locke, Alain Leroy 728
Logan, Rayford W. 732
Long, Richard A. 734
Marino, Eugene Antonio 756
Maynard, Robert C. 778
Miller, Kelly 815
Mitchell, Clarence M., Jr. 822
Molineaux, Tom 826
Morton, "Jelly Roll" 834

Murray, Daniel 860
Murray, Peter Marshall 862
Napier, James C. 868
Patterson, Frederick D. 914
Pierce, Samuel R., Jr. 936
Poston, Ted 949
Powell, Colin 958
Raspberry, William J. 996
Richardson, Willis 1010
Robinson, Bill ''Bojangles'' 1016
Robinson, Randall 1025
Rowan, Carl 1031
Scott, Emmett Jay 1051
Shaw, Bernard 1059
Slaughter, Henry Proctor 1067
Sullivan, Louis 1092
Thomas, Clarence 1108
Toomer, Jean 1125
Tyler, Ralph 1142
Vann, Robert L. 1149
Vashon, George Boyer 1157
Washington, Walter E. 1191
Weaver, Robert C. 1195
Wesley, Charles H. 1200
Wideman, John Edgar 1214
Wilkins, J. Ernest 1220
Williams, Daniel Hale 1230
Williams, Edward Christopher 1232
Wilson, William J. 1244
Woodson, Carter G. 1256

FLORIDA

Cape Canaveral

McNair, Ronald E. 798

Crescent City

Randolph, A. Philip 983

Daytona Beach

Thurman, Howard 1114

Jacksonville

Charles, Ray 186
Crockett, George W., Jr. 236
Fortune, T. Thomas 411
Johnson, J. Rosamond 621
Johnson, James Weldon 626
Randolph, A. Philip 983

Marianna

Fortune, T. Thomas 411

Miami

Plinton, James O., Jr. 943
Poitier, Sidney 944
Powell, Adam Clayton, Jr. 954

Orlando

Woods, Tiger 1252

Pensacola

James, Daniel ''Chappie,'' Jr. 610

Sanford

Barnett, Claude A. 58

Tallahassee

Gray, William H., III 478

GEORGIA

Craft, William 234

Albany

Charles, Ray 186
Davis, Sammy, Jr. 266
Dawson, William L. 269
Imes, Elmer S. 589

Atlanta

Aaron, Hank 1
Bond, Horace Mann 88
Bond, Julian 91
Braithwaite, William Stanley 108
Brawley, Benjamin G. 112
Brazeal, Brailsford R. 113
Clement, Rufus E. 208
Davis, Benjamin Jefferson 253
Dodson, Howard, Jr. 312
Dorsey, Thomas Andrew 319
Du Bois, W. E. B. 336
Flipper, Henry O. 403
Frazier, E. Franklin 428
Gibson, Truman K., Jr. 456
Herndon, Alonzo F. 544
Hill, Jesse, Jr. 549
Hope, John 568
Jackson, Maynard H. 602
Jordan, Vernon 667
King, Martin Luther, Jr. 686
Lee, Spike 705
Lewis, John R. 718
Logan, Rayford W. 732

Long, Richard A. 734
Lowery, Joseph E. 742
Marino, Eugene Antonio 756
Massey, Walter E. 773
Mays, Benjamin E. 780
Mays, Willie 784
McMillan, Elridge W. 797
Metcalfe, Ralph H. 803
Penn, I. Garland 921
Proctor, Henry Hugh 968
Sullivan, Louis 1092
Turner, Henry McNeal 1133
Walker, Leroy T. 1166
White, Walter 1209
Whitman, Albery 1213
Wright, Louis Tompkins 1266
Young, Andrew 1280
Young, Whitney M., Jr. 1289

Augusta

Brown, James 125
Hope, John 568
Tobias, Channing H. 1122

Barnesville

McMillan, Elridge W. 797

Cairo

Robinson, Jackie 1022

Cogdell

Davis, Ossie 264

Columbus

Bullard, Eugene 148

Covington

Pace, Harry H. 897

Curryville

Hayes, Roland 526

Cuthbert

Henderson, Fletcher 537

Dawson

Davis, Benjamin Jefferson 253
Washington, Walter E. 1191

Dublin

Brazeal, Brailsford R. 113

Frederick (on St. Simon Island)

Abbott, Robert Sengstacke 3

Jonesboro

Herndon, Alonzo F. 544

La Grange

Wright, Louis Tompkins 1266

Macon

Healy, James Augustine 533
Little Richard 724
Pinchback, P. B. S. 938
Turner, Henry McNeal 1133

Pin Point

Thomas, Clarence 1108

Sandersville

Muhammad, Elijah 853

Savannah

Abbott, Robert Sengstacke 3
Bryan, Andrew 146
Josey, E. J. 670
Thomas, Clarence 1108
Turner, Henry McNeal 1133
Work, Monroe Nathan 1262

Thomasville

Flipper, Henry O. 403

ILLINOIS

Alton

Davis, Miles 262

Cairo

Ingram, Rex 591
Woodruff, Hale A. 1247

Centralia

Burris, Roland 158

Chicago

Abbott, Robert Sengstacke 3
Armstrong, Louis "Satchmo" 29
Barnett, Claude A. 58
Binga, Jesse 75
Burris, Roland 158
Calloway, Cab 162
Campbell, E. Simms 169
Cayton, Horace R. 182
Cleveland, James 211
Cole, Nat "King" 215
Davis, Allison 252
Dawson, William L. 269
DePriest, Oscar S. 294
Dorsey, Thomas Andrew 319
Du Sable, Jean Baptiste Pointe 349
Farrakhan, Louis 393

Forman, James .406
Foster, Rube 417
Franklin, John Hope 421
Fuller, S. B. 433
Gibson, Truman K., Jr. 456
Greener, Richard T. 483
Gregory, Dick 484
Gumbel, Bryant .492
Hall, George Cleveland 499
Hampton, Lionel 506
Harrison, Richard B. 513
Jackson, Jesse L. 598
Jarrett, Vernon D. 612
Jefferson, Blind Lemon 614
Johnson, Charles S. 616
Johnson, Jack 624
Johnson, John H. 630
Jones, Quincy 656
Jordan, Michael .664
Julian, Percy L. 672
Lawless, T. K. .700
Lynch, John Roy 748
Madhubuti, Haki 750
Metcalfe, Ralph H. 803
Micheaux, Oscar 810
Mollison, Irvin C. 828
Morton, ''Jelly Roll'' 834
Motley, Archibald J., Jr. 843
Motley, Willard .845
Muddy Waters 850
Muhammad, Elijah 853
Oliver, Joseph ''King'' 883
Overton, Anthony 890
Pace, Harry H. .897
Parker, Charlie ''Yardbird'' 904
Ransom, Reverdy C. 990
Shaw, Bernard .1059
Taylor, Marshall W. ''Major'' 1103
Van Peebles, Melvin 1152
Warfield, William 1179
Washington, Harold 1189
White, Charles .1204
Wilkins, J. Ernest 1220
Williams, Daniel Hale 1230

East St. Louis
Davis, Miles 262

Metropolis
Micheaux, Oscar 810

Urbana
Warfield, William 1179
Wedgeworth, Robert, Jr. 1198

INDIANA

Gary
Jackson, Michael 605

Greencastle
Julian, Percy L. 672

Indianapolis
Shirley, George I. 1061
Taylor, Marshall W. ''Major'' 1103

Terre Haute
Meyzeek, Albert E. 806

IOWA

Centerville
Estes, Simon 381

Des Moines
McCree, Wade H., Jr. 789

KANSAS

Bruce, Blanche Kelso 143

Ashton
Work, Monroe Nathan 1262

Fort Scott
Parks, Gordon 907

Kansas City
Parker, Charlie ''Yardbird'' 904

Topeka
Douglas, Aaron 322
Petersen, Frank, Jr. 930

KENTUCKY

Brandenburg
Steward, William Henry 1078

Cane Springs
Simmons, William J. 1066

Crescent Hills
Marrs, Elijah P. 757

Danville
Whitman, Albery 1213

Fayette County
Murphy, Isaac 858
Frankfort
Anderson, Charles W., Jr. 24
Steward, William Henry 1078
Underwood, Edward Ellsworth 1145
Hart County
Whitman, Albery 1213
Hopkinsville
Poston, Ted 949
Lexington
Brown, William Wells 138
Murphy, Isaac 858
Parrish, Charles H., Sr. 911
Lincoln Institute
Young, Whitney M., Jr. 1289
Louisville
Ali, Muhammad 17
Anderson, Charles W., Jr. 24
Blue, Thomas Fountain 84
Clement, George Clinton 207
Clement, Rufus E. 208
Cullen, Countee 243
Hampton, Lionel 506
Meyzeek, Albert E. 806
Parrish, Charles H., Sr. 911
Simmons, William J. 1066
Slaughter, Henry Proctor 1067
Steward, William Henry 1078
Wesley, Charles H. 1200
Mayslick
Young, Charles 1283
Owensboro
Sleet, Moneta J., Jr. 1069
Paris
Morgan, Garrett A. 829

LOUISIANA

Alexandria
Bontemps, Arna W. 93
Riles, Wilson C. 1011
Baton Rouge
Gray, William H., III 478
Burnside
Ward, Douglas Turner 1176
Centerville
Seymour, William Joseph 1056
Houma
Murray, Peter Marshall 862
Lafayette
Francis, Norman C. 420
Lake Charles
Perry, Harold R. 927
Monroe
Fuller, S. B. 433
Newton, Huey P. 874
Overton, Anthony 890
Russell, Bill 1035
New Orleans
Armstrong, Louis "Satchmo" 29
Chester, Thomas Morris 197
Elliott, Robert Brown 367
Francis, Norman C. 420
Gumbel, Bryant 492
Lafon, Thomy 692
Lawless, T. K. 700
Marsalis, Wynton 758
Martin, John Sella 767
Morial, Ernest 831
Morton, "Jelly Roll" 834
Motley, Archibald J., Jr. 843
Murray, Peter Marshall 862
Oliver, Joseph "King" 883
Perry, Harold R. 927
Pinchback, P. B. S. 938
Quarles, Benjamin A. 979
Young, Andrew 1280
Newellton
Brimmer, Andrew F. 116
Shreveport
Cochran, Johnnie 212
Hawkins, Augustus F. 522
Sterling
Perkins, Edward J. 925
Thibodaux
Lawless, T. K. 700
Trout
Jacob, John E. 608
Vidalia
Lynch, John Roy 748

MAINE

Portland

Healy, James Augustine 533

MARYLAND

Pennington, James W. C. 923

Ward, Samuel Ringgold 1177

Annapolis

Massie, Samuel Proctor, Jr. 775

Baltimore

Banneker, Benjamin 49

Blake, Eubie 77

Coker, Daniel 214

Frazier, E. Franklin 428

Hooks, Benjamin L. 565

Johnson, Joshua 634

Lewis, Reginald F. 720

Long, Richard A. 734

Mfume, Kweisi 808

Marshall, Thurgood 762

Mitchell, Clarence M., Jr. 822

Mitchell, Parren J. 824

Murray, Daniel 860

Muse, Clarence 864

Myers, Isaac 865

Quarles, Benjamin A. 979

Robinson, Frank 1020

Wright, Stephen J. 1272

Berlin

Tindley, Charles Albert 1121

Charles County

Henson, Matthew A. 541

Frederick

Coker, Daniel 214

Frederick Town

Coppin, Levi Jenkins 227

Georgetown

Molineaux, Tom 826

Hyattsville

Driskell, David C. 333

Kent County

Garnet, Henry Highland 437

Rockville

Divine, M. J. "Father" 307

Tacoma Park

Brown, Sterling A. 133

Tuckahoe

Douglass, Frederick 326

Turners Station

Mfume, Kweisi 808

MASSACHUSETTS

Amherst

Wideman, John Edgar 1214

Andover

Poor, Salem 947

Boston

Attucks, Crispus 40

Bell, Derrick A., Jr. 71

Braithwaite, William Stanley 108

Brooke, Edward W. 121

Brown, William Wells 138

Craft, William 234

Farrakhan, Louis 393

Gates, Henry Louis, Jr. 448

Grimké, Archibald Henry 487

Hall, Prince 502

Healy, James Augustine 533

Johnson, Sargent 642

Latimer, Lewis Howard 698

Lucas, Sam 746

Nell, William C. 871

Poussaint, Alvin F. 951

Quarles, Benjamin A. 979

Ransom, Reverdy C. 990

Russell, Bill 1035

Sullivan, Louis 1092

Trotter, Monroe 1130

Walker, David 1165

Chelsea

Brown, William Wells 138

Latimer, Lewis Howard 698

Cuttyhunk Island

Cuffe, Paul 241

Dartmouth

Cuffe, Paul 241

Framingham

Attucks, Crispus 40

Great Barrington

Du Bois, W. E. B. 336

Hyde Park

Trotter, Monroe 1130

Lenox
Van DerZee, James 1147
Lynn
Matzeliger, Jan E. 776
Middle Granville
Haynes, Lemuel 532
New Bedford
Carney, William H. 176
Salem
Remond, Charles Lenox 1003
South Reading (now Wakefield)
Remond, Charles Lenox 1003
Vineyard Haven
Burgess, John M. 156
Worcester
Taylor, Marshall W. ''Major'' 1103

MICHIGAN

Ann Arbor
Hayden, Robert E. 523
Shirley, George I. 1061
Berrien Springs
Ali, Muhammad 17
Detroit
Binga, Jesse 75
Brown, Tony 136
Bunche, Ralph J. 152
Conyers, John, Jr. 225
Crockett, George W., Jr. 236
Denby, Charles 291
Diggs, Charles C., Jr. 301
Duncanson, Robert S. 347
Edwards, Nelson J. 361
Gibson, Benjamin F. 452
Gordy, Berry 468
Hayden, Robert E. 523
Jones, Prophet 654
Louis, Joe 740
McCoy, Elijah 787
McCree, Wade H., Jr. 789
Robinson, Sugar Ray 1027
Shirley, George I. 1061
Young, Coleman A. 1285
Dublin
Jones, James Earl 648
East Lansing
Brimmer, Andrew F. 116
Grand Rapids
Burgess, John M. 156
Gibson, Benjamin F. 452
Lansing
Gibson, Benjamin F. 452
Ypsilanti
Hall, George Cleveland 499
McCoy, Elijah 787

MINNESOTA

Hallock
Jones, Frederick McKinley 647
Minneapolis
Parks, Gordon 907
Rowan, Carl 1031
St. Paul
Brown, Grafton Tyler 124
Mitchell, Clarence M., Jr. 822
Page, Alan Cedric 899

MISSISSIPPI

Church, Robert Reed, Sr. 200
Aberdeen
Revels, Hiram Rhoades 1005
Arkabutla
Jones, James Earl 648
Bay St. Louis
Barthé, Richmond 60
Perry, Harold R. 927
Biloxi
Marino, Eugene Antonio 756
Brook
O'Neal, Frederick D. 885
Clarksdale
Muddy Waters 850
Cleveland
Moses, Bob 837
Columbus
Armstrong, Henry 26
Decatur
Evers, Medgar 386
Fayette
Evers, Medgar 386

Hattisburg
Massey, Walter E. 773
Hickory
Johnson, Robert L. 640
Holly Springs
Revels, Hiram Rhoades 1005
Indianola
King, B. B. 683
Jackson
Espy, Mike 378
Evers, Medgar .386
Jones, Laurence Clifton 652
Meredith, James H. 801
Williams, John A. 1236
Kilmichael
King, B. B. 683
Kosciusko
Meredith, James H. 801
Macomb
Thomas, Jesse O. 1113
Natchez
Lynch, John Roy 748
Noxubee County
Boyd, Richard Henry 99
Okolona
Raspberry, William J. 996
Rolling Fork
Muddy Waters 850
Roxie
Wright, Richard 1268
Sledge
Pride, Charley 966
Vicksburg
Mollison, Irvin C. 828
Woodville
Still, William Grant 1082
Yazoo City
Espy, Mike 378

MISSOURI

Diamond Grove
Carver, George Washington 177
Farmington
Wilkins, J. Ernest 1220
Jefferson City
Himes, Chester .553
Joplin
Hughes, Langston 580
Kansas City
Overton, Anthony 890
Paige, ''Satchel'' 901
Parker, Charlie ''Yardbird'' 904
Wilkins, Roy 1222
St. Joseph
Jones, Laurence Clifton 652
St. Louis
Armstrong, Henry 26
Ashe, Arthur 36
Campbell, E. Simms 169
Gregory, Dick 484
Hill, Jesse, Jr. 549
Jacob, John E. 608
Joplin, Scott 661
O'Neal, Frederick D. 885
Scott, Dred 1049
Wilkins, Roy 1222
Sedalia
Joplin, Scott 661

MONTANA

Missoula
Pride, Charley 966

NEBRASKA

Omaha
X, Malcolm 1276

NEVADA

Las Vegas
Louis, Joe 740

NEW JERSEY

Estes, Simon 381
Atlantic City
Lawrence, Jacob 702
Bordentown
Granger, Lester B. 472
Burlington County
Still, William 1080
Greenwich
Ward, Samuel Ringgold 1177

Hackensack
Morrow, E. Frederic 833
Newark
Baraka, Amiri 52
Leevy, Carroll M. 709
Moss, Carlton 841
Patterson
Pippin, Horace 941
Princeton
Robeson, Paul 1013
Red Bank
Fortune, T. Thomas 411
Short Hills
Leevy, Carroll M. 709
Somerville
Robeson, Paul 1013
Teaneck
Kay, Ulysses S. 679
Trenton
Dinkins, David N. 304
Higginbotham, A. Leon, Jr. 548
Westfield
Plinton, James O., Jr. 943

NEW YORK

Duncanson, Robert S. 347
Albany
Josey, E. J. 670
Auburn
Holland, Jerome "Brud" 558
Baldwin
Sleet, Moneta J., Jr. 1069
Binghamton
Mitchell, Loften 823
Brooklyn
Dodson, Owen 315
Graves, Earl G. 475
Hunton, William Alphaeus 584
Jordan, Michael 664
Lee, Spike 705
Maynard, Robert C. 778
Murphy, Eddie 856
Proctor, Henry Hugh 968
Robinson, Jackie 1022
Thomas, Franklin A. 1112
Wilson, William J. 1244
Geneseo
Kelley, William Melvin 681
Glen Cove
Pierce, Samuel R., Jr. 936
Goshen
Pippin, Horace 941
Hempstead
Chenault, Kenneth I. 191
Erving, Julius 375
Ithaca
Haley, Alex 496
Jamaica, L.I.
Mitchell, Loften 823
Mt. Vernon
Haynes, George Edmund 528
Washington, Denzel 1186
New York
Abdul-Jabbar, Kareem 6
Ailey, Alvin 8
Aldridge, Ira 12
Alexander, Clifford L., Jr. 15
Armstrong, Louis "Satchmo" 29
Ashe, Arthur 36
Baldwin, James 46
Baraka, Amiri 52
Barthé, Richmond 60
Bearden, Romare 64
Belafonte, Harry 68
Bell, Derrick A., Jr. 71
Blake, Eubie 77
Bledsoe, Jules 79
Bontemps, Arna W. 93
Bradley, Ed 102
Braithwaite, William Stanley 108
Bristow, Lonnie R. 118
Brown, James 125
Brown, Ron 131
Brown, Tony 136
Bullard, Eugene 148
Bullins, Ed 150
Bunche, Ralph J. 152
Calloway, Cab 162
Campbell, E. Simms 169
Carmichael, Stokely 173
Chamberlain, Wilt 184
Chenault, Kenneth I. 191

Coltrane, John 220
Cone, James H. 223
Cosby, Bill 230
Crummell, Alexander 238
Cullen, Countee .243
Davis, Miles 262
Davis, Ossie 264
Davis, Sammy, Jr. 266
Day, William Howard 276
DeCarava, Roy .280
Delany, Hubert T. 281
Delany, Samuel R. 286
Dinkins, David N. 304
Dixon, Dean 310
Dodson, Howard, Jr. 312
Douglas, Aaron .322
Du Bois, W. E. B. 336
Dudley, Edward R. 341
Eckstine, Billy 357
Ellison, Ralph 369
Europe, James Reese 382
Farrakhan, Louis 393
Fisher, Rudolph .400
Fraunces, Samuel 427
Freeman, Morgan 431
Garvey, Marcus .441
Gilpin, Charles S. 460
Goode, Mal 466
Granger, Lester B. 472
Graves, Earl G. .475
Greaves, William ''Bill'' G. 481
Gumbel, Bryant .492
Handy, W. C. 508
Harrington, Oliver W. 511
Harrison, Richard B. 513
Hayes, Roland 526
Haynes, George Edmund 528
Henderson, Fletcher 537
Henson, Matthew A. 541
Hewlett, James .546
Holder, Eric H., Jr. 556
Holstein, Caspar A. 563
Hooks, Benjamin L. 565
Hughes, Langston 580
Imes, Elmer S. 589
Ingram, Rex 591
Jack, Hulan 594
Jackman, Harold 596
Johnson, Charles S. 616
Johnson, J. Rosamond 621
Johnson, James Weldon 626
Jones, Eugene Kinckle 645
Jones, James Earl 648
Jones, Quincy 656
Jordan, Vernon 667
Kelley, William Melvin 681
Latimer, Lewis Howard 698
Lawrence, Jacob 702
Leidesdorff, William A. 711
Lewis, Henry 716
Lewis, Reginald F. 720
Locke, Alain Leroy 728
Marsalis, Wynton 758
Marshall, Thurgood 762
McKay, Claude 791
McKissick, Floyd 795
Mitchell, Arthur 819
Mitchell, Loften 823
Mollison, Irvin C. 828
Morrow, E. Frederic 833
Morton, ''Jelly Roll'' 834
Moses, Bob 837
Mosley, Walter 839
Moss, Carlton 841
Motley, Willard 845
Murray, Peter Marshall 862
Muse, Clarence 864
Oliver, Joseph ''King'' 883
O'Neal, Frederick D. 885
Ottley, Roi 888
Parker, Charlie ''Yardbird'' 904
Parks, Gordon 907
Patterson, Frederick D. 914
Pennington, James W. C. 923
Pierce, Samuel R., Jr. 936
Poitier, Sidney 944
Poston, Ted 949
Poussaint, Alvin F. 951
Powell, Adam Clayton, Jr. 954
Powell, Colin 958
Proctor, Samuel D. 971
Randolph, A. Philip 983

Rangel, Charles B. 987
Reason, Charles Lewis 998
Reid, Ira De A. 1002
Robeson, Paul 1013
Rogers, J. A. 1029
Ruggles, David 1034
Russworm, John Brown 1038
Rustin, Bayard 1039
Schomburg, Arthur Alfonso 1046
Shirley, George I. 1061
Sleet, Moneta J., Jr. 1069
Smith, James McCune 1073
Still, William Grant 1082
Sullivan, Leon H. 1089
Sutton, Percy E. 1094
Thomas, Franklin A. 1112
Thomas, Jesse O. 1113
Thurman, Wallace 1118
Tobias, Channing H. 1122
Toomer, Jean 1125
Van DerZee, James 1147
Varick, James 1155
Vincent, U. Conrad 1163
Walker, Leroy T. 1166
Waller, Fats 1171
Walrond, Eric 1173
Ward, Douglas Turner 1176
Ward, Samuel Ringgold 1177
Washington, Walter E. 1191
Weaver, Robert C. 1195
West, Cornel 1202
White, Charles 1204
White, Clarence Cameron 1206
White, Walter 1209
Wilkins, Roy 1222
Williams, Bert 1227
Williams, Edward Christopher 1232
Williams, John A. 1236
Wilson, William J. 1244
Woodruff, Hale A. 1247
Woods, Granville T. 1250
Wright, Louis Tompkins 1266
X, Malcolm 1276
Young, Andrew 1280
Young, Whitney M., Jr. 1289

Newburgh
Varick, James 1155
Oyster Bay
Hammon, Jupiter 504
Rochester
Calloway, Cab 162
Dett, R. Nathaniel 297
Douglass, Frederick 326
Warfield, William 1179
Roosevelt
Erving, Julius 375
Syracuse
Vashon, George Boyer 1157
Westchester County
Harrington, Oliver W. 511
White Plains
Calloway, Cab 162

NORTH CAROLINA

Ahoskie
Vann, Robert L. 1149
Asheville
McKissick, Floyd 795
Caswell County
Day, Thomas 275
Charlotte
Bearden, Romare 64
Martin, John Sella 767
Micheaux, Oscar 810
Sifford, Charlie 1063
Columbus
Mitchell, Loften 823
Columbus County
Spaulding, Charles C. 1075
Durham
Brewer, J. Mason 114
Franklin, John Hope 421
Massie, Samuel Proctor, Jr. 775
McKissick, Floyd 795
Spaulding, Charles C. 1075
Walker, Leroy T. 1166
Eatonton
Driskell, David C. 333
Elizabeth City
Price, J. C. 963

Fayetteville
Chesnutt, Charles Waddell 193
Hosier, "Black Harry" 573
Revels, Hiram Rhoades 1005
Granville County
Chavis, John 190
Greensboro
Dett, R. Nathaniel 297
Harrison, Richard B. 513
Proctor, Samuel D. 971
Hamlet
Coltrane, John 220
High Point
Coltrane, John 220
Iredell County
Work, Monroe Nathan 1262
Milton
Day, Thomas 275
Mocksville
Clement, George Clinton 207
New Bern
Price, J. C. 963
Near Burlington
Drew, Charles R. 331
Northampton County
Horton, George Moses 571
Raleigh
Delany, Hubert T. 281
Vincent, U. Conrad 1163
Salisbury
Clement, George Clinton 207
Clement, Rufus E. 208
Price, J. C. 963
Soul City
McKissick, Floyd 795
Wilmington
Jordan, Michael 664
Richardson, Willis 1010
Walker, David 1165

OHIO

Canton
Page, Alan Cedric 899
Chillicothe
Trotter, Monroe 1130
Cincinnati
Duncanson, Robert S. 347
Hubbard, William DeHart 579
Jones, Frederick McKinley 647
Morgan, Garrett A. 829
Seymour, William Joseph 1056
Woods, Granville T. 1250
Cleveland
Chesnutt, Charles Waddell 193
Davis, Benjamin O., Jr. 255
Davis, Benjamin O., Sr. 259
Day, William Howard 276
Hubbard, William DeHart 579
Hughes, Langston 580
Morgan, Garrett A. 829
Owens, Jesse 893
Paige, "Satchel" 901
Stokes, Carl B. 1086
Walker, Moses Fleetwood 1168
Williams, Edward Christopher 1232
Columbus
Gibson, Truman K., Jr. 456
Tyler, Ralph 1142
Woods, Granville T. 1250
Dayton
Dunbar, Paul Laurence 344
Emerson
Underwood, Edward Ellsworth 1145
Flushing
Ransom, Reverdy C. 990
Gallipolis
Bell, James Madison 73
Lincoln Heights
Burgess, John M. 156
Massilon
Darlington, Roy Clifford 251
Mt. Pleasant
Underwood, Edward Ellsworth 1145
Walker, Moses Fleetwood 1168
Oberlin
Langston, John Mercer 693
Steubenville
Walker, Moses Fleetwood 1168
Toledo
Bell, James Madison 73
Meyzeek, Albert E. 806

Walker, Moses Fleetwood 1168

Washington

Lucas, Sam 746

Wilberforce

Arnett, Benjamin W. 34

Branson, Herman R. 110

Davis, Benjamin O., Sr. 259

Delany, Martin R. 282

Payne, Daniel A. 917

Ransom, Reverdy C. 990

Wesley, Charles H. 1200

Young, Charles 1283

OKLAHOMA

Oklahoma City

Ellison, Ralph 369

Rentiesville

Franklin, John Hope 421

Tulsa

West, Cornel 1202

PENNSYLVANIA

Bedford

Williams, George Washington 1233

Brownsville

Arnett, Benjamin W. 34

Bryn Mawr

Reid, Ira De A. 1002

Carlisle

Vashon, George Boyer 1157

Harrisburg

Brown, Grafton Tyler 124

Chester, Thomas Morris 197

Day, William Howard 276

Temple, Edward S. 1105

Hazelwood

Wilson, August 1241

Hollidaysburg

Williams, Daniel Hale 1230

Homestead

Goode, Mal 466

Lincoln Institute

Branson, Herman R. 110

Norristown

Blockson, Charles L. 82

Philadelphia

Allen, Richard 21

Blockson, Charles L. 82

Bluford, Guy 86

Bouchet, Edward A. 97

Bradley, Ed 102

Brimmer, Andrew F. 116

Brown, Morris 129

Bullins, Ed 150

Campanella, Roy 166

Chamberlain, Wilt 184

Coleman, William T., Jr. 217

Coltrane, John 220

Coppin, Levi Jenkins 227

Cornish, Samuel 229

Cosby, Bill 230

Divine, M. J. "Father" 307

Erving, Julius 375

Forten, James 408

Gibbs, Mifflin Wistar 450

Gillespie, Dizzy 458

Gloucester, John 462

Gray, William H., III 478

Greener, Richard T. 483

Hastie, William Henry 519

Higginbotham, A. Leon, Jr. 548

Horton, George Moses 571

Hosier, "Black Harry" 573

Johnson, Frank 619

Jones, Absalom 644

Lawrence, Jacob 702

Locke, Alain Leroy 728

Long, Richard A. 734

Nix, Robert N. C., Sr. 876

Purvis, Robert 976

Reason, Charles Lewis 998

Still, William 1080

Sullivan, Leon H. 1089

Tanner, Benjamin Tucker 1098

Tindley, Charles Albert 1121

Watts, André 1193

Pittsburgh

Bell, Derrick A., Jr. 71

Eckstine, Billy 357

Goode, Mal 466

Josey, E. J. 670

Pratt, Awadagin .961
Tanner, Benjamin Tucker 1098
Tanner, Henry Ossawa 1099
Vann, Robert L. 1149
Vashon, George Boyer 1157
Wideman, John Edgar 1214
Wilson, August 1241
West Chester
Dodson, Howard, Jr. 312
Pippin, Horace 941
Rustin, Bayard .1039

RHODE ISLAND
Newport
Gardner, Newport 436
Remond, Charles Lenox 1003

SOUTH CAROLINA
Anderson County
Pickens, William 931
Barnwell
Brown, James 125
Beaufort
Smalls, Robert .1071
Charleston
Brown, Morris 129
Cardozo, Francis L. 171
Grimké, Archibald Henry 487
Grimké, Francis J. 490
Just, Ernest Everett 675
Payne, Daniel A. 917
Smalls, Robert .1071
Simmons, William J. 1066
Sullivan, Leon H. 1089
Vesey, Denmark 1158
Walker, David .1165
Cheraw
Gillespie, Dizzy .458
Columbia
Brawley, Benjamin G. 112
Elliott, Robert Brown 367
Leevy, Carroll M. 709
Dillon
Wright, Stephen J. 1272
Goose Creek
Bryan, Andrew 146
Greenville
Jackson, Jesse L. 598
Lake City
McNair, Ronald E. 798
Newberry Court House
Turner, Henry McNeal 1133
Ninety-Six
Mays, Benjamin E. 780
Orangeburg
Nix, Robert N. C., Sr. 876
Stateburg
Ellison, William 373
Winnsboro
Miller, Kelly 815

TENNESSEE
Brown, Sterling A. 133
Bartlett
Mason, Charles Harrison 770
Chattanooga
Hayes, Roland 526
Clarksville
White, Clarence Cameron 1206
Clifton
Proctor, Henry Hugh 968
Fayetteville
Proctor, Henry Hugh 968
Knoxville
Dykes, De Witt S., Sr. 352
Hastie, William Henry 519
Williams, Avon Nyanza, Jr. 1224
Memphis
Church, Robert Reed, Sr. 200
Freeman, Morgan 431
Handy, W. C. 508
Hooks, Benjamin L. 565
Imes, Elmer S. 589
King, B. B. 683
Mason, Charles Harrison 770
Paige, "Satchel" 901
Pride, Charley 966
Nashville
Bailey, DeFord 43
Bond, Horace Mann 88
Bond, Julian 91
Bontemps, Arna W. 93

Boyd, Richard Henry 99
Caliver, Ambrose 160
Douglas, Aaron 322
Driskell, David C. 333
Edmondson, William 359
Foster, Henry W., Jr. 414
Frazier, E. Franklin 428
Harvey, William R. 516
Hayden, Robert E. 523
Haynes, George Edmund 528
Holland, Jerome ''Brud'' 558
Hope, John 568
Imes, Elmer S. 589
Johnson, Charles S. 616
Johnson, James Weldon 626
Looby, Z. Alexander 737
Massie, Samuel Proctor, Jr. 775
Napier, James C. 868
Temple, Edward S. 1105
Williams, Avon Nyanza, Jr. 1224
Work, John Wesley, III 1259
Wright, Stephen J. 1272

Newport

Dykes, De Witt S., Sr. 352

Paris

Johnson, Mordecai W. 635

Ravenscroft

Rowan, Carl 1031

Saulsbury

Jarrett, Vernon D. 612

Smith County

Bailey, DeFord 43

Tullahoma

Work, John Wesley, III 1259

TEXAS

Boyd, Richard Henry 99

Austin

Brewer, J. Mason 114
Pickett, Bill 935

Beaumont

Robinson, Frank 1020

Calvert

Bradley, Thomas 104
Foster, Rube 417

Dallas

Elder, Lee 362
Jackson, Maynard H. 602
Jefferson, Blind Lemon 614
Johnson, Rafer 638
Majors, Monroe A. 753
Pride, Charley 966

Ennis

Wedgeworth, Robert, Jr. 1198

Freestone County

Jefferson, Blind Lemon 614

Ft. Worth

Brewer, J. Mason 114

Galveston

Cuney, Norris Wright 246
Johnson, Jack 624

Goliad

Brewer, J. Mason 114

Hillsboro

Johnson, Rafer 638

Houston

Cuney, Norris Wright 246
Foreman, George 404
Scott, Emmett Jay 1051

Marshall

Farmer, James L., Jr. 389

Mineola

Brown, Willie L., Jr. 141

Navasota

Ailey, Alvin 8

Rogersville

Ailey, Alvin 8

San Antonio

Sutton, Percy E. 1094

Taylor

Pickett, Bill 935

Texarkana

Joplin, Scott 661

Tyler

Pickett, Bill 935

Waco

Bledsoe, Jules 79
Majors, Monroe A. 753
Miller, Dorie 814

Waller County

Cuney, Norris Wright 246

UTAH

Salt Lake City

Thurman, Wallace 1118

VIRGINIA

Chavis, John 190
Liele, George 723
Marrs, Elijah P. 757

Alexandria

Johnson, Sargent 642

Amelia County

Moton, Robert Russa 847

Bristol

Johnson, Charles S. 616

Charles City County

Cary, Lott 180

Clifton Forge

Reid, Ira De A. 1002

Danville

Scott, Wendell 1054

Fairfax

Gray, William H., III 478

Farmville

Blue, Thomas Fountain 84
Bruce, Blanche Kelso 143

Hale's Ford

Washington, Booker T. 1181

Halifax County

Day, Thomas 275

Hampton

Dett, R. Nathaniel 297
Harvey, William R. 516
Holland, Jerome "Brud" 558
Moton, Robert Russa 847

Henrico County

Prosser, Gabriel 973

Jerusalem

Turner, Nat 1137

Louisa County

Langston, John Mercer 693

Lynchburg

Penn, I. Garland 921

New Canton

Woodson, Carter G. 1256

New Glasgow

Penn, I. Garland 921

Newport News

Granger, Lester B. 472

Norfolk

Carney, William H. 176
Hunton, William Alphaeus 584
Josey, E. J. 670
Proctor, Samuel D. 971

Pocahontas

Branson, Herman R. 110

Richmond

Ashe, Arthur 36
Gilpin, Charles S. 460
Gravely, Samuel L., Jr. 473
Jones, Eugene Kinckle 645
Langston, John Mercer 693
Logan, Rayford W. 732
Proctor, Samuel D. 971
Prosser, Gabriel 973
Robinson, Bill "Bojangles" 1016
Robinson, Randall 1025
Wilder, L. Douglas 1217

Roanoke

Dudley, Edward R. 341

Saltville

Caliver, Ambrose 160

South Boston

Dudley, Edward R. 341

Southampton County

Scott, Dred 1049
Turner, Nat 1137

Tidewater

Turner, Nat 1137

White Plains

Goode, Mal 466

Williamsburg

Smith, James McCune 1073

WASHINGTON

Bremerton

Miller, Dorie 814

Seattle

Cayton, Horace R. 182
Charles, Ray 186
Haley, Alex 496
Lawrence, Jacob 702
Wilson, August 1241

Vancouver
Barnes, Steven 55

WEST VIRGINIA
Charles Town
Delany, Martin R. 282
Charleston
Brown, Tony 136
Johnson, Mordecai W. 635
Sullivan, Leon H. 1089
Huntington
Woodson, Carter G. 1256
Keyser
Gates, Henry Louis, Jr. 448
Malden
Washington, Booker T. 1181

AFRICA
Gardner, Newport 436

THE BAHAMAS
Nassau
Williams, Bert 1227

CANADA
Duncanson, Robert S. 347
Chatham, Ontario
Bell, James Madison 73
Day, William Howard 276
Delany, Martin R. 282
Hunton, William Alphaeus 584
Colchester, Ontario
McCoy, Elijah 787
Drummondville, Ontario
Dett, R. Nathaniel 297
London, Ontario
Harrison, Richard B. 513
Ottawa, Ontario
Hunton, William Alphaeus 584
Toronto, Ontario
Meyzeek, Albert E. 806
Victoria, British Columbia
Brown, Grafton Tyler 124
Gibbs, Mifflin Wistar 450

ENGLAND
Blackpool
Williams, George Washington 1233
London
Aldridge, Ira 12
Garvey, Marcus 441
Jackman, Harold 596

FRANCE
Paris
Baldwin, James 46
Bullard, Eugene 148
Tanner, Henry Ossawa 1099
Woodruff, Hale A. 1247
Wright, Richard 1268

GERMANY
East Berlin
Harrington, Oliver W. 511

GHANA
Du Bois, W. E. B. 336

GUYANA
Georgetown
Walrond, Eric 1173

HAITI
Du Sable, Jean Baptiste Pointe 349
Holly, James T. 560

IRELAND
Molineaux, Tom 826

JAMAICA
Liele, George 723
Kingston
Plinton, James O., Jr. 943
Negril
Rogers, J. A. 1029
Port Antonio
Russworm, John Brown 1038
St. Ann's Bay
Garvey, Marcus 441
Sunny Ville
McKay, Claude 791

LIBERIA
Cary, Lott 180
Perkins, Edward J. 925
Monrovia
Coker, Daniel 214
Craft, William 234
Crummell, Alexander 238
Garnet, Henry Highland 437
Russworm, John Brown 1038

PUERTO RICO
San Juan
Schomburg, Arthur Alfonso 1046

SPAIN
Himes, Chester .553

SURINAME
Paramaribo
Matzeliger, Jan E. 776

TRINIDAD AND TOBAGO
Port-of-Spain
Carmichael, Stokely 173

VIRGIN ISLANDS
Hastie, William Henry 519

ST. CROIX
Holstein, Caspar A. 563
Leidesdorff, William A. 711

WEST INDIES
Fraunces, Samuel 427
Antigua and Barbuda
Looby, Z. Alexander 737
Martinique
Johnson, Frank 619
St. Lucia
Jack, Hulan 594

Occupation Index

Abolitionist

Bell, James Madison 73
Brown, William Wells 138
Coker, Daniel 214
Craft, William 234
Day, William Howard 276
Delany, Martin R. 282
Douglass, Frederick 326
Forten, James 408
Garnet, Henry Highland 437
Gibbs, Mifflin Wistar 450
Hall, Prince 502
Martin, John Sella 767
Nell, William C. 871
Pennington, James W. C. 923
Purvis, Robert 976
Reason, Charles Lewis 998
Remond, Charles Lenox 1003
Ruggles, David 1034
Russworm, John Brown 1038
Smith, James McCune 1073
Still, William 1080
Walker, David 1165
Ward, Samuel Ringgold 1177

Activist

Ali, Muhammad 17
Ashe, Arthur 36
Baraka, Amiri 52
Belafonte, Harry 68
Brown, Tony 136
Clement, George Clinton 207
Davis, Benjamin Jefferson 253
Denby, Charles 291
Garvey, Marcus 441
Gregory, Dick 484
Grimké, Francis J. 490
Holly, James T. 560
Jackson, Jesse L. 598
Johnson, Charles S. 616
Josey, E. J. 670
Meredith, James H. 801
Meyzeek, Albert E. 806
Mitchell, Parren J. 824
Powell, Adam Clayton, Jr. 954
Ransom, Reverdy C. 990
Robeson, Paul 1013
Robinson, Randall 1025
Sullivan, Leon H. 1089
Trotter, Monroe 1130
Vann, Robert L. 1149
Williams, Avon Nyanza, Jr. 1224
Young, Coleman A. 1285

Activist—Black Panther Party

Cleaver, Eldridge 203
Newton, Huey P. 874

Activist—Congress of Racial Equality (CORE)

Farmer, James L., Jr. 389
McKissick, Floyd 795
Rustin, Bayard 1039

Activist—Nation of Islam

Farrakhan, Louis 393
Muhammad, Elijah 853
X, Malcolm 1276

Activist—National Association for the Advancement of Colored People (NAACP)

Bell, Derrick A., Jr. 71
Bond, Julian 91
Du Bois, W. E. B. 336
Evers, Medgar 386
Grimké, Archibald Henry 487

Hastie, William Henry 519
Johnson, James Weldon 626
Jones, Scipio Africanus 660
Jordan, Vernon 667
Looby, Z. Alexander 737
Mfume, Kweisi 808
Mitchell, Clarence M., Jr. 822
Nixon, E. D., Sr. 878
Parrish, Charles H., Sr. 911
Pickens, William 931
Steward, William Henry 1078
Underwood, Edward Ellsworth 1145
White, Walter 1209
Wright, Louis Tompkins 1266

Activist—National Urban League
Jordan, Vernon 667
Young, Whitney M., Jr. 1289

Activist—Southern Christian Leadership Conference (SCLC)
Fauntroy, Walter E. 396
King, Martin Luther, Jr. 686
Lowery, Joseph E. 742
Rustin, Bayard 1039
Young, Andrew 1280

Activist—Student Nonviolent Coordinating Committee(SNCC)
Bond, Julian 91
Forman, James 406
Lewis, John R. 718
Moses, Bob 837

Actor
Aldridge, Ira 12
Cosby, Bill 230
Davis, Ossie 264
Davis, Sammy, Jr. 266
Freeman, Morgan 431
Gilpin, Charles S. 460
Glover, Danny 464
Harrison, Richard B. 513
Hewlett, James 546
Ingram, Rex 591
Jones, James Earl 648
Lee, Spike 705
Lucas, Sam 746
Moss, Carlton 841
Murphy, Eddie 856
Muse, Clarence 864
O'Neal, Frederick D. 885
Poitier, Sidney 944
Robeson, Paul 1013
Van Peebles, Melvin 1152
Warfield, William 1179
Washington, Denzel 1186
Williams, Bert 1227

Architect
Dykes, De Witt S., Sr. 352
Williams, Paul R. 1238

Artist—Cartoonist
Campbell, E. Simms 169
Harrington, Oliver W. 511

Artist—Collagist
Bearden, Romare 64

Artist—Illustrator
Douglas, Aaron 322

Artist—Muralist
Douglas, Aaron 322

Artist—Painter
Brown, Grafton Tyler 124
Driskell, David C. 333
Duncanson, Robert S. 347
Johnson, Joshua 634
Lawrence, Jacob 702
Motley, Archibald J., Jr. 843
Pippin, Horace 941
Tanner, Henry Ossawa 1099
White, Charles 1204
Woodruff, Hale A. 1247

Artist—Sculptor
Barthé, Richmond 60
Edmondson, William 359
Johnson, Sargent 642

Astronaut
Bluford, Guy 86
McNair, Ronald E. 798

Athlete—Auto/Bicycle Racing
Ribbs, Willy T. 1008
Scott, Wendell 1054
Taylor, Marshall W. "Major" 1103

Athlete—Baseball
Aaron, Hank 1
Campanella, Roy 166
Foster, Rube 417
Mays, Willie 784
Paige, "Satchel" 901
Pride, Charley 966
Robinson, Frank 1020
Robinson, Jackie 1022
Walker, Moses Fleetwood 1168

Athlete—Basketball
Abdul-Jabbar, Kareem 6
Chamberlain, Wilt 184
Erving, Julius 375
Jordan, Michael 664
Russell, Bill 1035

Athlete—Boxing
Ali, Muhammad 17
Armstrong, Henry 26
Bullard, Eugene 148
Foreman, George 404
Johnson, Jack 624
Louis, Joe 740
Molineaux, Tom 826
Robinson, Sugar Ray 1027

Athlete—Golf
Elder, Lee 362
Sifford, Charlie 1063
Woods, Tiger 1252

Athlete—Horse Racing
Murphy, Isaac 858

Athlete—Olympics
Hubbard, William DeHart 579
Johnson, Rafer 638
Metcalfe, Ralph H. 803
Owens, Jesse 893
Walker, Leroy T. 1166

Athlete—Rodeo
Pickett, Bill 935

Athlete—Tennis
Ashe, Arthur 36

Author. *See* **Writer.**

Banker
Binga, Jesse 75
Church, Robert Reed, Sr. 200
Gaston, Arthur G. 445
Overton, Anthony 890

Baseball Player. *See* **Athlete—Baseball.**

Basketball Player. *See* **Athlete—Basketball.**

Bibliophile
Arnett, Benjamin W. 34
Blockson, Charles L. 82
Brawley, Benjamin G. 112
Jackman, Harold 596
Murray, Daniel 860
Schomburg, Arthur Alfonso 1046
Slaughter, Henry Proctor 1067

Boxer. *See* **Athlete—Boxing.**

Boxing Promoter
Gibson, Truman K., Jr. 456

Businessman (*see also* **Banker** *or* **Publisher**)
Binga, Jesse 75
Brimmer, Andrew F. 116
Chenault, Kenneth I. 191
Cuffe, Paul 241
Day, Thomas 275
Du Sable, Jean Baptiste Pointe 349
Ellison, William 373
Erving, Julius 375
Forten, James 408

Fraunces, Samuel 427
Fuller, S. B. 433
Garvey, Marcus 441
Gaston, Arthur G. 445
Gordy, Berry 468
Graves, Earl G. .475
Herndon, Alonzo F. 544
Hill, Jesse, Jr. 549
Holland, Jerome "Brud" 558
Holstein, Caspar A. 563
Johnson, Robert L. 640
Jones, Quincy 656
Lafon, Thomy 692
Leidesdorff, William A. 711
Lewis, Reginald F. 720
McKissick, Floyd 795
Morgan, Garrett A. 829
Myers, Isaac 865
Overton, Anthony 890
Pace, Harry H. 897
Plinton, James O., Jr. 943
Spaulding, Charles C. 1075
Sullivan, Leon H. 1089
Sutton, Percy E. .1094

Coach

Metcalfe, Ralph H. 803
Robinson, Frank 1020
Russell, Bill 1035
Temple, Edward S. 1105
Walker, Leroy T. 1166

College President

Bond, Horace Mann 88
Branson, Herman R. 110
Clement, Rufus E. 208
Francis, Norman C. 420
Harvey, William R. 516
Holland, Jerome "Brud" 558
Hope, John 568
Johnson, Charles S. 616
Johnson, Mordecai W. 635
Massey, Walter E. 773
Massie, Samuel Proctor, Jr. 775
Mays, Benjamin E. 780
Patterson, Frederick D. 914
Payne, Daniel A. 917
Price, J. C. 963
Proctor, Samuel D. 971
Revels, Hiram Rhoades 1005
Satcher, David 1044
Simmons, William J. 1066
Washington, Booker T. 1181
Wesley, Charles H. 1200
Wright, Stephen J. 1272

Colonizationist

Cary, Lott 180
Coker, Daniel 214
Crummell, Alexander 238
Cuffe, Paul 241
Russworm, John Brown 1038
Turner, Henry McNeal 1133

Comedian

Cosby, Bill 230
Gregory, Dick 484
Murphy, Eddie 856
Williams, Bert 1227

Composer, Songwriter, Arranger

Bailey, DeFord 43
Blake, Eubie 77
Bledsoe, Jules 79
Brown, James 125
Calloway, Cab 162
Charles, Ray 186
Cleveland, James 211
Cole, Nat "King" 215
Coltrane, John 220
Davis, Miles 262
Dawson, William Levi 272
Dett, R. Nathaniel 297
Dorsey, Thomas Andrew 319
Ellington, Duke 364
Gardner, Newport 436
Gillespie, Dizzy 458
Hampton, Lionel 506
Handy, W. C. 508
Jackson, Michael 605
Jefferson, Blind Lemon 614
Johnson, Frank 619

Johnson, J. Rosamond 621
Johnson, James Weldon 626
Jones, Quincy 656
Joplin, Scott 661
Kay, Ulysses S. 679
Marsalis, Wynton 758
Morton, ''Jelly Roll'' 834
Parks, Gordon 907
Still, William Grant 1082
Tindley, Charles Albert 1121
Van Peebles, Melvin 1152
Waller, Fats 1171
White, Clarence Cameron 1206
Work, John Wesley, III 1259

Conductor
Dixon, Dean 310
Lewis, Henry 716

Critic
Baraka, Amiri 52
Bontemps, Arna W. 93
Braithwaite, William Stanley 108
Brown, Sterling A. 133
Delany, Samuel R. 286
Gates, Henry Louis, Jr. 448
Hall, George Cleveland 499
Johnson, James Weldon 626
Maynard, Robert C. 778
Moss, Carlton 841
Redding, J. Saunders 1000
Wideman, John Edgar 1214

Dancer
Ailey, Alvin 8
Davis, Sammy, Jr. 266
Jackson, Michael 605
Mitchell, Arthur 819
Robinson, Bill ''Bojangles'' 1016

Diplomat
Ali, Muhammad 17
Bunche, Ralph J. 152
Douglass, Frederick 326
Dudley, Edward R. 341
Holland, Jerome ''Brud'' 558
Johnson, James Weldon 626
Langston, John Mercer 693
Perkins, Edward J. 925
Young, Andrew 1280

Doctor. *See* **Medical/Health Care Professional.**

Dramatist. *See* **Writer—Playwriting, Screenwriting.**

Economist
Brimmer, Andrew F. 116
Brazeal, Brailsford R. 113

Editor
Brown, Sterling A. 133
Coppin, Levi Jenkins 227
Cornish, Samuel 229
Day, William Howard 276
Delany, Martin R. 282
Denby, Charles 291
Douglass, Frederick 326
Du Bois, W. E. B. 336
Elliott, Robert Brown 367
Grimké, Archibald Henry 487
Hayden, Robert E. 523
Hughes, Langston 580
Jackman, Harold 596
Johnson, James Weldon 626
Majors, Monroe A. 753
Maynard, Robert C. 778
McKay, Claude 791
Pinchback, P. B. S. 938
Ruggles, David 1034
Russworm, John Brown 1038
Scott, Emmett Jay 1051
Simmons, William J. 1066
Steward, William Henry 1078
Tanner, Benjamin Tucker 1098
Trotter, Monroe 1130
Tyler, Ralph 1142
Underwood, Edward Ellsworth 1145
Vann, Robert L. 1149
Work, Monroe Nathan 1262

Educator (*see also* **College President**)

Bell, Derrick A., Jr. 71
Blake, Eubie 77
Bontemps, Arna W. 93
Bouchet, Edward A. 97
Brawley, Benjamin G. 112
Brazeal, Brailsford R. 113
Brewer, J. Mason .114
Brimmer, Andrew F. 116
Brown, Sterling A. 133
Bruce, Blanche Kelso 143
Bullins, Ed 150
Caliver, Ambrose 160
Cardozo, Francis L. 171
Chavis, John 190
Clement, Rufus E. 208
Cone, James H. 223
Craft, William 234
Darlington, Roy Clifford 251
Davis, Allison 252
Davis, Benjamin O., Sr. 259
Day, William Howard 276
DeCarava, Roy 280
Delany, Samuel R. 286
Dett, R. Nathaniel 297
Dinkins, David N. 304
Dodson, Howard, Jr. 312
Dodson, Owen 315
Douglas, Aaron 322
Drew, Charles R. .331
Driskell, David C. 333
Du Bois, W. E. B. 336
Farmer, James L., Jr. 389
Foster, Henry W., Jr. 414
Franklin, John Hope 421
Frazier, E. Franklin 428
Gardner, Newport 436
Gates, Henry Louis, Jr. 448
Gibbs, Mifflin Wistar 450
Greener, Richard T. 483
Harrison, Richard B. 513
Hastie, William Henry 519
Hayden, Robert E. 523
Hayes, Roland 526
Haynes, George Edmund 528
Henry, Warren E. .539
Higginbotham, A. Leon, Jr. 548
Houston, Charles Hamilton 575
Imes, Elmer S. 589
Jackman, Harold 596
Johnson, James Weldon 626
Jones, Laurence Clifton 652
Julian, Percy L. 672
Just, Ernest Everett 675
Kay, Ulysses S. 679
Langston, John Mercer 693
Lawrence, Jacob 702
Leevy, Carroll M. 709
Lewis, David Levering 713
Locke, Alain Leroy 728
Logan, Rayford W. 732
Long, Richard A. 734
Looby, Z. Alexander 737
Madhubuti, Haki 750
Marrs, Elijah P. 757
McCree, Wade H., Jr. 789
McMillan, Elridge W. 797
Meyzeek, Albert E. 806
Miller, Kelly 815
Mitchell, Arthur 819
Mitchell, Parren J. 824
Moses, Bob 837
Moss, Carlton 841
Moton, Robert Russa 847
Parrish, Charles H., Sr. 911
Penn, I. Garland 921
Pickens, William 931
Poussaint, Alvin F. 951
Quarles, Benjamin A. 979
Raspberry, William J. 996
Reason, Charles Lewis 998
Redding, J. Saunders 1000
Reid, Ira De A. 1002
Richardson, Willis 1010
Riles, Wilson C. 1011
Scott, Emmett Jay 1051
Shirley, George I. 1061
Sullivan, Louis 1092
Temple, Edward S. 1105
Thomas, Jesse O. 1113
Turner, Henry McNeal 1133
Vashon, George Boyer 1157

Walker, Leroy T. 1166
Warfield, William 1179
Wedgeworth, Robert, Jr. 1198
West, Cornel 1202
Wideman, John Edgar 1214
Williams, Daniel Hale 1230
Williams, Edward Christopher 1232
Williams, John A. 1236
Wilson, William J. 1244
Woodruff, Hale A. 1247
Work, John Wesley, III 1259
Young, Charles 1283

Explorer

Delany, Martin R. 282
Du Sable, Jean Baptiste Pointe 349
Henson, Matthew A. 541

Farmer

Craft, William 234
Ellison, William 373
Rapier, James T. 994

Filmmaker

Brown, Tony 136
Greaves, William ''Bill'' G. 481
Lee, Spike 705
Micheaux, Oscar 810
Moss, Carlton 841
Parks, Gordon 907
Van Peebles, Melvin 1152

Folklorist

Brewer, J. Mason 114

Golfer. *See* **Athlete—Golf.**

Government Official (elected)

Anderson, Charles W., Jr. 24
Arnett, Benjamin W. 34
Bond, Julian 91
Bradley, Thomas 104
Brooke, Edward W. 121
Brown, Willie L., Jr. 141
Bruce, Blanche Kelso 143
Burris, Roland 158
Cardozo, Francis L. 171
Conyers, John, Jr. 225
Crockett, George W., Jr. 236
Cuney, Norris Wright 246
Davis, Benjamin Jefferson 253
Dawson, William L. 269
Dellums, Ronald V. 289
DePriest, Oscar S. 294
Diggs, Charles C., Jr. 301
Dinkins, David N. 304
Elliott, Robert Brown 367
Espy, Mike 378
Fauntroy, Walter E. 396
Gibbs, Mifflin Wistar 450
Gray, William H., III 478
Hawkins, Augustus F. 522
Holder, Eric H., Jr. 556
Jack, Hulan 594
Langston, John Mercer 693
Lewis, John R. 718
Looby, Z. Alexander 737
Lynch, John Roy 748
Metcalfe, Ralph H. 803
Mfume, Kweisi 808
Mitchell, Parren J. 824
Morial, Ernest 831
Napier, James C. 868
Nix, Robert N. C., Sr. 876
Pinchback, P. B. S. 938
Powell, Adam Clayton, Jr. 954
Rangel, Charles B. 987
Rapier, James T. 994
Revels, Hiram Rhoades 1005
Smalls, Robert 1071
Stokes, Carl B. 1086
Underwood, Edward Ellsworth 1145
Washington, Harold 1189
Washington, Walter E. 1191
Wilder, L. Douglas 1217
Williams, Avon Nyanza, Jr. 1224
Williams, George Washington 1233
Young, Andrew 1280
Young, Coleman A. 1285

Government Official (non-elected)

Alexander, Clifford L., Jr. 15
Brown, Ron 131

Bunche, Ralph J. 152
Caliver, Ambrose 160
Chester, Thomas Morris 197
Coleman, William T., Jr. 217
Cuney, Norris Wright 246
Espy, Mike 378
Gibbs, Mifflin Wistar 450
Greener, Richard T. 483
Grimké, Archibald Henry 487
Hastie, William Henry 519
Hubbard, William DeHart 579
Jackson, Jesse L. 598
Jones, Eugene Kinckle 645
Marshall, Thurgood 762
McCree, Wade H., Jr. 789
Morrow, E. Frederic 833
Pickens, William 931
Pierce, Samuel R., Jr. 936
Rapier, James T. 994
Rowan, Carl 1031
Satcher, David 1044
Sullivan, Louis 1092
Tyler, Ralph 1142
Underwood, Edward Ellsworth 1145
Vann, Robert L. 1149
Washington, Walter E. 1191
Weaver, Robert C. 1195
Wilkins, J. Ernest 1220
Young, Andrew 1280

Health Care Professional. *See* **Medical/ Health CareProfessional.**

Humanitarian, Philanthropist

Alexander, Clifford L., Jr. 15
Belafonte, Harry 68
Binga, Jesse 75
Cosby, Bill 230
Davis, Sammy, Jr. 266
Douglass, Frederick 326
Herndon, Alonzo F. 544
Jackson, Michael 605
Jones, Quincy 656
Lafon, Thomy 692
Lawless, T. K. 700
Leevy, Carroll M. 709
Lewis, Reginald F. 720
Page, Alan Cedric 899
Robinson, Sugar Ray 1027
Thomas, Franklin A. 1112
Washington, Denzel 1186

Inventor. *See* **Scientist, Inventor.**

Insurrectionist

Prosser, Gabriel 973
Turner, Nat 1137
Vesey, Denmark 1158

Journalist—Broadcast

Bradley, Ed 102
Brown, Tony 136
Goode, Mal 466
Gumbel, Bryant 492
Jarrett, Vernon D. 612
Raspberry, William J. 996
Shaw, Bernard 1059

Journalist—Print

Abbott, Robert Sengstacke 3
Barnett, Claude A. 58
Chester, Thomas Morris 197
Fortune, T. Thomas 411
Grimké, Archibald Henry 487
Hughes, Langston 580
Jarrett, Vernon D. 612
Majors, Monroe A. 753
Maynard, Robert C. 778
Miller, Kelly 815
Ottley, Roi 888
Poston, Ted 949
Raspberry, William J. 996
Rogers, J. A. 1029
Rowan, Carl 1031
Russworm, John Brown 1038
Simmons, William J. 1066
Smith, James McCune 1073
Tanner, Benjamin Tucker 1098
Thurman, Wallace 1118
Tyler, Ralph 1142
Vann, Robert L. 1149
Walrond, Eric 1173

Ward, Samuel Ringgold 1177
Wilkins, Roy 1222
Williams, George Washington 1233
Williams, John A. 1236
Wilson, William J. 1244

Judge

Crockett, George W., Jr. 236
Dudley, Edward R. 341
Gibson, Benjamin F. 452
Holder, Eric H., Jr. 556
Marshall, Thurgood 762
McCree, Wade H., Jr. 789
Mollison, Irvin C. 828
Page, Alan Cedric 899
Thomas, Clarence 1108

Labor Leader, Labor Official

Edwards, Nelson J. 361
Nixon, E. D., Sr. 878
Weaver, Robert C. 1195

Lawyer

Alexander, Clifford L., Jr. 15
Anderson, Charles W., Jr. 24
Bell, Derrick A., Jr. 71
Brooke, Edward W. 121
Brown, Ron 131
Burris, Roland 158
Chenault, Kenneth I. 191
Chesnutt, Charles Waddell 193
Chester, Thomas Morris 197
Cochran, Johnnie 212
Coleman, William T., Jr. 217
Conyers, John, Jr. 225
Crockett, George W., Jr. 236
Delany, Hubert T. 281
Dinkins, David N. 304
Dudley, Edward R. 341
Elliott, Robert Brown 367
Francis, Norman C. 420
Gibbs, Mifflin Wistar 450
Gibson, Benjamin F. 452
Gibson, Truman K., Jr. 456
Greener, Richard T. 483
Grimké, Archibald Henry 487
Hastie, William Henry 519
Higginbotham, A. Leon, Jr. 548
Holder, Eric H., Jr. 556
Hooks, Benjamin L. 565
Houston, Charles Hamilton 575
Jackson, Maynard H. 602
Johnson, James Weldon 626
Jones, Scipio Africanus 660
Jordan, Vernon .667
Langston, John Mercer 693
Lynch, John Roy .748
Marshall, Thurgood 762
McCree, Wade H., Jr. 789
McKissick, Floyd 795
Mollison, Irvin C. 828
Morrow, E. Frederic 833
Napier, James C. 868
Nix, Robert N. C., Sr. 876
Pace, Harry H. 897
Page, Alan Cedric 899
Pierce, Samuel R., Jr. 936
Rangel, Charles B. 987
Robinson, Randall 1025
Thomas, Clarence 1108
Thomas, Franklin A. 1112
Vann, Robert L. .1149
Vashon, George Boyer 1157
Washington, Harold 1189
Washington, Walter E. 1191
Wilder, L. Douglas 1217
Wilkins, J. Ernest 1220
Williams, Avon Nyanza, Jr. 1224

Lecturer, Orator

Bell, James Madison 73
Brown, William Wells 138
Bruce, Blanche Kelso 143
Day, William Howard 276
Delany, Samuel R. 286
Dodson, Howard, Jr. 312
Douglass, Frederick 326
Franklin, John Hope 421
Harrison, Richard B. 513
Hughes, Langston 580
Hunton, William Alphaeus 584
Jackson, Jesse L. 598

Langston, John Mercer 693
Mays, Benjamin E. 780
Pickens, William .931
Price, J. C. 963
Proctor, Henry Hugh 968
Proctor, Samuel D. 971
Raspberry, William J. 996
Sutton, Percy E. 1094
X, Malcolm 1276

Librarian, Curator

Blockson, Charles L. 82
Blue, Thomas Fountain 84
Dodson, Howard, Jr. 312
Josey, E. J. 670
Murray, Daniel 860
Schomburg, Arthur Alfonso 1046
Wedgeworth, Robert, Jr. 1198
Williams, Edward Christopher 1232

Medical/Health Care Professional

Bristow, Lonnie R. 118
Darlington, Roy Clifford 251
Delany, Martin R. 282
Drew, Charles R. 331
Fisher, Rudolph .400
Foster, Henry W., Jr. 414
Hall, George Cleveland 499
Lawless, T. K. 700
Leevy, Carroll M. 709
Majors, Monroe A. 753
Murray, Peter Marshall 862
Patterson, Frederick D. 914
Poussaint, Alvin F. 951
Ruggles, David .1034
Satcher, David .1044
Smith, James McCune 1073
Sullivan, Louis .1092
Underwood, Edward Ellsworth 1145
Vincent, U. Conrad 1163
Williams, Daniel Hale 1230
Wright, Louis Tompkins 1266

Military Figure

Attucks, Crispus 40
Brooke, Edward W. 121
Carney, William H. 176
Cuffe, Paul 241
Davis, Benjamin O., Jr. 255
Davis, Benjamin O., Sr. 259
Delany, Martin R. 282
Flipper, Henry O. 403
Gravely, Samuel L., Jr. 473
Henson, Matthew A. 541
James, Daniel "Chappie," Jr. 610
Miller, Dorie 814
Petersen, Frank, Jr. 930
Poor, Salem 947
Powell, Colin 958
Smalls, Robert 1071
Young, Charles 1283

Musician

Armstrong, Louis "Satchmo" 29
Bailey, DeFord 43
Blake, Eubie 77
Brown, James 125
Charles, Ray 186
Cleveland, James 211
Cole, Nat "King" 215
Coltrane, John 220
Davis, Miles 262
Davis, Sammy, Jr. 266
Dorsey, Thomas Andrew 319
Ellington, Duke 364
Europe, James Reese 382
Gillespie, Dizzy 458
Hampton, Lionel 506
Handy, W. C. 508
Henderson, Fletcher 537
Hewlett, James 546
Jefferson, Blind Lemon 614
Jones, Quincy 656
King, B. B. 683
Marsalis, Wynton 758
Morton, "Jelly Roll" 834
Muddy Waters 850
Oliver, Joseph "King" 883
Parker, Charlie "Yardbird" 904
Pratt, Awadagin 961
Waller, Fats 1171
Watts, André 1193

White, Clarence Cameron 1206

Olympic Figure. *See* **Athlete—Olympics.**

Orator. *See* **Lecturer, Orator.**

Organization and Foundation Official
Blue, Thomas Fountain 84
Bond, Julian 91
Bristow, Lonnie R. 118
Carmichael, Stokely 173
Driskell, David C. 333
Foster, Rube 417
Garvey, Marcus 441
Granger, Lester B. 472
Hall, Prince 502
Haynes, George Edmund 528
Hooks, Benjamin L. 565
Hunton, William Alphaeus 584
Jackson, Jesse L. 598
Jacob, John E. 608
Lowery, Joseph E. 742
Marshall, Thurgood 762
Martin, John Sella 767
McMillan, Elridge W. 797
Mfume, Kweisi 808
Myers, Isaac 865
Newton, Huey P. 874
Nixon, E. D., Sr. 878
O'Neal, Frederick D. 885
Patterson, Frederick D. 914
Randolph, A. Philip 983
Slaughter, Henry Proctor 1067
Thomas, Franklin A. 1112
Tobias, Channing H. 1122
Washington, Booker T. 1181
Wedgeworth, Robert, Jr. 1198
White, Walter 1209
Wilkins, Roy 1222
Woodson, Carter G. 1256
Wright, Stephen J. 1272

Painter. *See* **Artist—Painter.**

Pan Africanist
Carmichael, Stokely 173
Du Bois, W. E. B. 336
Garvey, Marcus 441

Philosopher
Locke, Alain Leroy 728

Photographer
DeCarava, Roy 280
Sleet, Moneta J., Jr. 1069
Parks, Gordon 907
Van DerZee, James 1147

Physician. *See* **Medical/Health Care Professional.**

Pilot
Bullard, Eugene 148
Plinton, James O., Jr. 943

Playwright. *See* **Writer—Playwriting, Screenwriting.**

Poet. *See* **Writer—Poetry**

Politician. *See* **Government official (elected).**

Printer
Day, William Howard 276
Elliott, Robert Brown 367
Fortune, T. Thomas 411
Garvey, Marcus 441
Woodruff, Hale A. 1247

Publisher
Baraka, Amiri 52
Barnett, Claude A. 58
Boyd, Richard Henry 99
Braithwaite, William Stanley 108
Graves, Earl G. 475
Handy, W. C. 508
Johnson, John H. 630
Madhubuti, Haki 750
Maynard, Robert C. 778
Slaughter, Henry Proctor 1067
Steward, William Henry 1078
Trotter, Monroe 1130
Woodson, Carter G. 1256

Radio Personality
Brown, Tony 136
Jarrett, Vernon D. 612
Wilder, L. Douglas 1217

Religious Figure
Allen, Richard 21
Armstrong, Henry 26
Arnett, Benjamin W. 34
Bouchet, Edward A. 97
Boyd, Richard Henry 99
Brown, Morris 129
Bryan, Andrew 146
Burgess, John M. 156
Cardozo, Francis L. 171
Cary, Lott 180
Chavis, John 190
Clement, George Clinton 207
Clement, Rufus E. 208
Cleveland, James 211
Coker, Daniel 214
Cone, James H. 223
Coppin, Levi Jenkins 227
Cornish, Samuel 229
Crummell, Alexander 238
Day, William Howard 276
Divine, M. J. "Father" 307
Dykes, De Witt S., Sr. 352
Farrakhan, Louis 393
Fauntroy, Walter E. 396
Foreman, George 404
Gardner, Newport 436
Garnet, Henry Highland 437
Gloucester, John 462
Gray, William H., III 478
Grimké, Francis J. 490
Haynes, Lemuel 532
Healy, James Augustine 533
Holly, James T. 560
Hooks, Benjamin L. 565
Hosier, "Black Harry" 573
Jackson, Jesse L. 598
Johnson, Mordecai W. 635
Jones, Absalom 644
Jones, Prophet 654
King, Martin Luther, Jr. 686
Liele, George 723
Lowery, Joseph E. 742
Marino, Eugene Antonio 756
Marrs, Elijah P. 757
Martin, John Sella 767
Mason, Charles Harrison 770
Mays, Benjamin E. 780
Muhammad, Elijah 853
Parrish, Charles H., Sr. 911
Payne, Daniel A. 917
Penn, I. Garland 921
Pennington, James W. C. 923
Perry, Harold R. 927
Powell, Adam Clayton, Jr. 954
Price, J. C. 963
Proctor, Henry Hugh 968
Proctor, Samuel D. 971
Ransom, Reverdy C. 990
Revels, Hiram Rhoades 1005
Seymour, William Joseph 1056
Simmons, William J. 1066
Steward, William Henry 1078
Tanner, Benjamin Tucker 1098
Thurman, Howard 1114
Tindley, Charles Albert 1121
Tobias, Channing H. 1122
Turner, Henry McNeal 1133
Underwood, Edward Ellsworth 1145
Varick, James 1155
Ward, Samuel Ringgold 1177
Wesley, Charles H. 1200
Whitman, Albery 1213
Williams, George Washington 1233
Young, Andrew 1280

Researcher
Carver, George Washington 177
Cayton, Horace R. 182
Haley, Alex 496
Rowan, Carl 1031
Satcher, David 1044
Work, Monroe Nathan 1262

Scholar
Bunche, Ralph J. 152
Driskell, David C. 333

Du Bois, W. E. B. 336
Gates, Henry Louis, Jr. 448
Haynes, George Edmund 528
Henry, Warren E. 539
Imes, Elmer S. 589
Locke, Alain Leroy 728
Mays, Benjamin E. 780
Mollison, Irvin C. 828
Quarles, Benjamin A. 979
Redding, J. Saunders 1000
Rowan, Carl 1031
Weaver, Robert C. 1195
West, Cornel 1202
Work, John Wesley, III 1259

Scientist, Inventor
Banneker, Benjamin 49
Bluford, Guy 86
Branson, Herman R. 110
Carver, George Washington 177
Drew, Charles R. 331
Flipper, Henry O. 403
Henry, Warren E. 539
Imes, Elmer S. 589
Jones, Frederick McKinley 647
Julian, Percy L. 672
Just, Ernest Everett 675
Latimer, Lewis Howard 698
Massey, Walter E. 773
Massie, Samuel Proctor, Jr. 775
Matzeliger, Jan E. 776
McCoy, Elijah 787
McNair, Ronald E. 798
Morgan, Garrett A. 829
Reid, Ira De A. 1002
Walker, Moses Fleetwood 1168
Woods, Granville T. 1250

Sculptor. *See* **Artist—Sculptor.**

Singer
Bledsoe, Jules 79
Brown, James 125
Calloway, Cab 162
Charles, Ray 186
Cole, Nat ''King'' 215
Davis, Sammy, Jr. 266
Eckstine, Billy 357
Estes, Simon 381
Hayes, Roland 526
Jackson, Michael 605
Jefferson, Blind Lemon 614
King, B. B. 683
Little Richard 724
Muddy Waters 850
Pride, Charley 966
Robeson, Paul 1013
Shirley, George I. 1061
Waller, Fats 1171
Warfield, William 1179

Slave
Attucks, Crispus 40
Brown, William Wells 138
Ellison, William 373
Horton, George Moses 571
Hosier, ''Black Harry'' 573
Prosser, Gabriel 973
Scott, Dred 1049
Turner, Nat 1137
Vesey, Denmark 1158

Sports Figure. *See* **Athlete.**

Television Executive
Brown, Tony 136
Johnson, Robert L. 640
Sutton, Percy E. 1094

Tennis Player. *See* **Athlete—Tennis.**

Theater Director, Founder
Bullins, Ed 150
Dodson, Owen 315
Ward, Douglas Turner 1176

Track and Field Athlete. *See* **Athlete—Olympics.**

Writer—Fiction
Baldwin, James 46
Barnes, Steven 55
Bontemps, Arna W. 93

Brewer, J. Mason 114
Brown, William Wells 138
Chesnutt, Charles Waddell 193
Cullen, Countee 243
Delany, Samuel R. 286
Dodson, Owen 315
Dunbar, Paul Laurence 344
Ellison, Ralph 369
Fisher, Rudolph 400
Haley, Alex 496
Himes, Chester 553
Hughes, Langston 580
Kelley, William Melvin 681
McKay, Claude 791
Micheaux, Oscar 810
Mitchell, Loften 823
Mosley, Walter 839
Motley, Willard 845
Ottley, Roi 888
Parks, Gordon 907
Thurman, Wallace 1118
Toomer, Jean 1125
Walrond, Eric 1173
Wideman, John Edgar 1214
Williams, John A. 1236
Wright, Richard 1268

Writer—Non-fiction

Arnett, Benjamin W. 34
Baldwin, James 46
Bell, Derrick A., Jr. 71
Blockson, Charles L. 82
Bontemps, Arna W. 93
Brawley, Benjamin G. 112
Brewer, J. Mason 114
Brown, William Wells 138
Caliver, Ambrose 160
Cayton, Horace R. 182
Cleaver, Eldridge 203
Cullen, Countee 243
Darlington, Roy Clifford 251
Driskell, David C. 333
Du Bois, W. E. B. 336
Franklin, John Hope 421
Frazier, E. Franklin 428
Gates, Henry Louis, Jr. 448
Haley, Alex 496
Higginbotham, A. Leon, Jr. 548
Johnson, James Weldon 626
Lewis, David Levering 713
Locke, Alain Leroy 728
Logan, Rayford W. 732
Long, Richard A. 734
Madhubuti, Haki 750
Miller, Kelly 815
Mitchell, Loften 823
Ottley, Roi 888
Parks, Gordon 907
Quarles, Benjamin A. 979
Redding, J. Saunders 1000
Rogers, J. A. 1029
Rowan, Carl 1031
Still, William 1080
Walker, David 1165
Washington, Booker T. 1181
West, Cornel 1202
Williams, George Washington 1233

Writer—Playwriting, Screenwriting

Baldwin, James 46
Baraka, Amiri 52
Barnes, Steven 55
Bullins, Ed 150
Cullen, Countee 243
Davis, Ossie 264
Dodson, Owen 315
Hughes, Langston 580
Jackman, Harold 596
Lee, Spike 705
Micheaux, Oscar 810
Mitchell, Loften 823
O'Neal, Frederick D. 885
Richardson, Willis 1010
Thurman, Wallace 1118
Van Peebles, Melvin 1152
Ward, Douglas Turner 1176
Wilson, August 1241
Wright, Richard 1268

Writer—Poetry

Baraka, Amiri 52
Bell, James Madison 73

Braithwaite, William Stanley 108
Brewer, J. Mason 114
Brown, Sterling A. 133
Cullen, Countee 243
Dodson, Owen 315
Dunbar, Paul Laurence 344
Fortune, T. Thomas 411
Hammon, Jupiter 504
Hayden, Robert E. 523
Horton, George Moses 571
Hughes, Langston 580
Johnson, James Weldon 626
Madhubuti, Haki 750
McKay, Claude 791
Whitman, Albery 1213
Wilson, August 1241
Wright, Richard 1268

Subject Index

Personal names, place names, events, institutions, and other subject areas or key words contained in *Notable Black American Men* are listed in this index with corresponding page numbers indicating text references. Page numbers are also given in **bold** type for each of the volume's main entries.

9th Battalion 1231
9th Cavalry 1284
9th Ohio Volunteer Infantry 1284
10th Cavalry Regiment 260, 403
12th U.S. Colored Artillery 758
15th Infantry Regiment 385, 942
48 Hrs 857
54th Massachusetts Regiment 329, 1005
55th Massachusetts Regiment 176, 198
60 Minutes 102-03
92nd Infantry Division 261, 1287
99th Pursuit Squadron 257, 943, 1095
"The 306 Group" 703
332nd Fighter Group 257
369th Colored Infantry Regiment 385, 942

A. Philip Randolph Institute 1042
A. W. Best School of Art 642
Aaron Douglas Gallery 334
Aaron, Hank 1
Abarca, Lydia 821
Abbey Alrich Rockefeller Collection of Folk Art 360
Abbott, Bud 1240
Abbott, Robert Sengstacke 3, 499
Abbott's Monthly Magazine 1269
ABC News 467, 1060
ABC Records 188
Abdul-Jabbar, Kareem 6, 376
Abernathy, Ralph 397, 600, 745, 880, 1090, 1281
Abraham Lincoln 461
Abyssinian Baptist Church 954-55
Abyssinian Housing Development Program 973
Académie Julien 1101
Academy Award 1186
Academy of Design 169
ACTION program 720
Actors' Workshop 1176
Adderley, Cannonball 221
"An Address to the Negroes in the State of New York" 505
Adelbert College 1232
Adventures of Huckleberry Finn 593
Aeolian Opera Company 81
Africa and America: Essays in Afro-American Culture 735
Africa: Her History, Lands and People 1237
African Aid Society 235, 278
African American Athletic Association 40
African Benevolent Society 436
African Church. *See* St. Thomas Episcopal Church.
African Civilization Society 440, 767, 999
African Communities Imperial League 394
African Development Foundation 479
African Education Society 1157
African Grove Theater 546
African Growth and Opportunities Act 989
African Methodist Bethel Society 214
African Methodist Episcopal (AME) Church 917-20
  and Allen, Richard 21
  and Arnett, Benjamin W. 34
  and Brown, Morris 129
  and Coker, Daniel 214
  and Ransom, Reverdy C. 990
  and Revels, Hiram Rhoades 1005
  and Tanner, Benjamin Ossawa 1098
  and Turner, Henry McNeal 1134
  and Varick, James 1156
African Methodist Episcopal (AME) Zion Church 207, 277, 1155
African Theatre 12
African Union Society 436
Afro-Academic, Cultural, Technological and Scientific Olympics 613
Afro-American Historical and Cultural Museum (Philadelphia) 84
The Afro-American Press and Its Editors 921
Afro-American Symphony 1084
Age 412
Agricultural and Technical College of North Carolina 972
Aida 81, 381

Ailey, Alvin 8, 365, 820
"Ain't Misbehavin'" 1171-72
ALA. *See* American Library Association.
ALA Yearbook 1199
Alabama Agricultural and Mechanical College 743
Alabama Christian Movement for Human Rights 689
Alabama State University, E. D. Nixon Collection 882
Albany Movement 397
Albion Cycle Club 1104
Alcindor, Lew. *See* Abdul-Jabbar, Kareem.
Alcorn Agricultural and Mechanical College 386, 1158
Alcorn, James Lusk 145
Alcorn University (Alcorn State University) 1007
Aldridge, Ira 12
Aldridge Players 886-87
Ales, Barney 470
Alexander, Clifford L., Jr. 15
Algebra Project 838
Ali, Muhammad 17, 405, 1037
All God's Chillun Got Wings 1014
Allen, Debbie 315
Allen, Richard 21, 990
  Bethel Church and 409
  Brown, Morris, succeeded by 129
  Coker, Daniel, and 214
  Cuffe, Paul, support of 243
  Jones, Absalom, and 644-45
Allen, Sarah 24
Along This Way 629
Alpha Omega Alpha Fraternity 415
Alpha Phi Alpha Fraternity 121, 269, 355, 645, 733, 832, 834, 892, 1200-01, 1291
Alston v. Board of Education 577
Alvin Ailey Dance Theatre 8, 10
AMA. *See* American Medical Association.
AMA. *See* American Missionary Association.
AME Church Review 993, 1099
American and Foreign Anti-Slavery Society 230, 439, 1074
American Anti-Slavery Society
  and Brown, William Wells 139
  and Cornish, Samuel 230
  and Forten, James 410
  and Langston, John Mercer 696
  and Nell, William C. 873
  and Purvis, Robert 977-78
  and Remond, Charles Lenox 1003-05
  and Still, William 1081
  and Ward, Samuel Ringgold 1178-79
  Pittsburgh 1157
American Artists School 703
American Baptist 1067, 1078, 1080
American Baptist Theological Seminary 102, 718
American Black Achievement Award 633
American College of Surgeons 1267
American Colonization Society 24, 243, 410, 975, 999, 1039, 1135
American Committee on Africa 1042
American Conservatory of Music 273
American Conservatory Theater 1187
American Derby 858
American Express 191
American Federation of Labor 985
American Folklore Society 115
American Giants 417-19
American Golf Classic 363
American Library Association 85, 670-71, 1198, 1199
American Library Association, Black Caucus 670-71
American Medical Association 118-20, 863
American Missionary Association 172, 230, 768, 924, 969, 1244-45
American Moral Reform Society 410
American National Baptist Convention 1067, 1079
American Negro Academy 489-90, 1048, 1068
American Negro Dance Company 820
American Negro Exposition 95
American Negro League 1
American Negro Songs and Spirituals 1260
American Negro Theatre 481, 886-87
American Opera Society 1207
American Pacifist Movement 1039
American Press Association 315
American Racing Cyclists Union 1104
American Red Cross 331-32
American Revolution 409, 428, 532, 947-48
American Ryder Cup team 363
American School of the Air 274
American Society of Composers, Authors, and Publishers (ASCAP) 45
American Society of Internal Medicine 119
American Theatre Wing 649
American University 93, 1191
American Youth Orchestra 311
America's Black Forum 93
Amherst College 253, 331
Amistad Murals 1249

Amistad Research Center 173, 832, 971
AMNEWS 1096
Anderson, Charles W., Jr. 24
Anderson, Marian 282, 1181
Angelic Choir 211
The Anglo-African Magazine 1245
The Angry Ones 1237
Anheuser-Busch Companies 608-09
Anita Bush Stock Company 461
Anna Lucasta 265, 267, 887
Anthology of Magazine Verse 109
Anthony, Susan B. 328
Anti-Apartheid Acts 479
Anti-Separate Coach Movement 758, 913, 1080, 1145
Anti-Slavery Movement 1178
Apollo Theater 127, 841
Arafat, Yasir 398
Archives of American Art, Hale A. Woodruff Papers 1250
Argonne National Laboratory 773
Arizona Fall League 1021
Arizona State College 1011
Arkansas Agricultural, Mechanical, and Normal College 775
Armstrong, Henry 26
Armstrong, Lil 31
Armstrong, Louis "Satchmo" 29, 164, 537, 883-84
Arnett, Benjamin W. 34, 991-92
Art Institute of Chicago 60, 169, 844, 1101, 1205, 1247
The Art of the Negro 1249
Art Students League 61, 65, 169, 1205
Artesian Productions 842
Arthur Ashe Stadium 40
Arthur, Chester A. 1235
Arthur Schomburg Collection 646
Arvey, Verna 1085
Asbury, Francis 214, 573-74
ASCAP. *See* American Society of Composers, Authors, and Publishers (ASCAP).
Ascending Poems 736
Ashe, Arthur 36, 494
Ashe-Bollettieri Cities program 40
Assemblies of God 1056
Associated Negro Press 58-59, 1151
Associated Publishers 1258
Association for the Study of Afro-American Life and History 1200, 1259
Association for the Study of Negro Life and History 501, 1257-58
Association of Colleges and Secondary Schools 529
Atlanta Baptist College. *See* Morehouse College.
Atlanta Braves 1-2
"Atlanta Compromise" speech 922, 1051, 1184
Atlanta Life Insurance Company 550
Atlanta Music Festival Association 970
Atlanta Mutual Insurance Association 545
Atlanta Olympics Committee 1167, 1283
Atlanta Riot 970
Atlanta Symphony 1195
Atlanta University. *See also* Clark Atlanta University. 90
  Atlanta University Publications 339
  Bond, Horace Mann, and 89
  Countee Cullen-Harold Jackman Memorial Collection 597
  Department of Sociology 339
  Flipper, Henry O., and 403
  Hale A. Woodruff art 1249
  Johnson, James Weldon, and 627
  Pace, Harry H., and 897
  president of 209, 568
  School of Social Work 429, 1113
  White, Walter, and 1210
Atlanta University Center 92, 209
  Henry P. Slaughter Collection 1069
  Rufus Clement Papers 211
  W. E. B. Du Bois Collection 341
Atlanta's Committee for Cooperative Action 1290
Attucks, Crispus 40, 873
Augusta National Golf Club 1065
Auld, Thomas 327
The Autobiography of an Ex-Colored Man 629
Autobiography of Malcolm X 496-97
Avery College 440, 1098, 1157
Avery Home for Working Girls 970
Avery Institute 171-72
Azusa Street Mission 771, 1057-58

Babel-17 287-88
Back on the Block 659
Bailey, DeFord 43
Bailey, Pearl 165
Baker, Ella 688-89
Baker, George. *See* Divine, M. J. "Father."
Bakke v. the University of California at Davis 790
Balanchine, George 819-20
Baldwin, James 46, 1271

Baldwin, Maria 1131
Ball, J. P. 348
A Ballad of Remembrance 525
Baltimore Afro-American 822, 1001, 1032
Baltimore Elite Giants 166
Baltimore Orioles 1021
Banana Bottom 794
The Banjo Player 1248
Bank of America 834
Bankhead-Jones Farm Tenancy Act 618
Banneker, Benjamin 49
Baptist Herald 1079
Baptist Women's Educational Convention of Kentucky 1067
Baraka, Amiri 52, 151, 315
Barclay Disques (Paris) 658
Barnes Foundation 324-25
Barnes, Steven 55
Barnett, Claude A. 58
Barnett, Ross R. 802
Barrow, Joseph Louis. *See* Louis, Joe.
Barthé, Richmond 60, 844
Baseball Hall of Fame 2, 166, 168, 420
Basilio, Carmen 1029
Basketball Hall of Fame 8, 186, 378
Bates College 315, 782
Bates, Daisy 415
"Baxter's Procrustes" 196
Bayreuth Wagner Festival 381
Beale Street Historic District 202
A Bear for the F.B.I. 1153
Bearden, Romare 64, 335, 1244
Beatrice International 720, 722
Beaux Arts Institute of Design 1239
Belafonte, Harry 68, 945-46
Belafonte, Shari 69
Bell, Alexander Graham 699
Bell, Derrick A., Jr. 71
Bell, James Madison 73
Bell, Philip A. 230
Bell, Tommy 1028
Bellevue Hospital 1163
Benedict College 1166
Bennett, Batteau 1161
Bennett College 300-01
Bennett, Ned 1160-61
Bennett, Rolla 1160-61
Bennett Women's Choir 300
Benny Goodman Quartet 507
Berea College 1256
Berkeley City Council 289
Berkelman, Robert 316
Berklee School of Music 657
Berkshire Music Center 759
Berlin Philharmonic 1194
Bernadotte, Folke 155
Berry, Chu 165
BET (Black Entertainment Television) 640
BET Movies/STARZ!3 641
Bethune, Mary McLeod 326, 1114, 1196
Bethune-Cookman College 922
Beverly Wilshire Hotel 1240
Beyond the Angry Black 1238
Bibb, Henry 284
Bibliography of the Negro in Africa and America 1265
The Bill Cosby Show 232
Billiken Club 846
Binga, Jesse 75, 892
"Birdland" 906
Birmingham Black Barons 785, 902, 967
Birmingham demonstrations 397
The Birth of a Band 658
The Birth of a Nation 812, 1132
The Birth of a Race 1053
"Birth of the Blues" 268
Birth of the Cool 263
Bishop College 80
Bitches Brew 263
Black Abolitionists 980
Black Arts movement 150
Black Athletes Hall of Fame 168
Black Bart and the Sacred Hills 1243
Black Bourgeoise 430
Black Boy 1271
Black, Brown and Beige 365
Black Cabinet 521, 618, 645-46
Black Child Care 952
Black College Act 479
"Black College Day" 137
Black Convention Movement 1034
Black Drama 824
"Black Eagle" 610
Black Enterprise 475-76
Black Genealogy 83
Black Gospel, White Church 158
"Black Harry." *See* Hosier, "Black Harry."
Black History Month 1259
Black History Museum (Hempstead) 1070
Black Horizons 1242
Black House 151
Black Journal. See also *Tony Brown's Journal.* 136, 481-82
Black Laws (Ohio) 278
Black Magic 54
Black Manhattan 629

Black Manifesto 408
Black Man's March to the Library 803
Black Muslims. *See* Nation of Islam.
Black Odyssey: The Story of the Negro in America 890
Black Panther movement 175
Black Panther Party 151, 173, 203-06, 408, 874
Black Periodical Literature Project 449
Black Power 175
Black Power movement 224
"Black Sam." *See* Fraunces, Samuel.
Black Star Line 442-43
Black Swan 897-98
Black Thunder 95
Black Workers and the New Unions 183
Black World 633
Blackbirds 81
Blackbirds of 1928 1018
Blackboard Jungle 946
The Blacker the Berry the Sweeter the Juice 1120
"Black-Red Conference" 293
The Blacks 649
Blackthink 896
Blake, Eubie 77, 385
Blakely, Art 759
Bledsoe, Jules 79
Blockson, Charles L. 82
Blood on the Fields 761
"Blue Moon" 358
Blue Note Club 460
Blue Steel 1084
Blue, Thomas Fountain 84
Bluefield State College 1273
The Blues Brothers 165
Blues Foundation's Hall of Fame 852
Bluford, Guy 86
Blyden, Edward W. 240
Body Heat 658
Bojangles. *See* Robinson, Bill "Bojangles."
Bond, Horace Mann 88, 91
Bond, Julian 89, **91**
Bontemps, Arna W. 93, 246, 597, 1119, 1130, 1270
The Book of American Negro Poetry 629
Book of Elizabethan Verse 109
Book of Life 752
Booker T. Washington Insurance Company 446-47
The Books of American Negro Spirituals 629
Boone, Pat 206
"Bootsie" 511
Born Black 909
Boston Celtics 1035-36
Boston Literary and Historical Society 1131
"The Boston Riot" 1132
Boston Suffrage League 1132
Boston University 166, 353, 407, 687, 972, 1114
  Howard Thurman Papers 1118
  Loften Mitchell Papers 824
  Marsh Chapel 1117
  School of Law 122, 1224
  School of Medicine 1092
  William Monroe Trotter Papers 1133
Boston Victoria Concert Orchestra 1207
Boston Vigilance Committee 873
Bouchet, Edward A. 97
Boulanger, Nadia 299
Bowdoin College 191, 833, 1038
Boyd, Henry Allen 101
Boyd, Richard Henry 99
Boyer International Laboratories 433
Bradley, Ed 102
Bradley, Thomas 104, 1288
Braithwaite, William Stanley 108
Brandeis, Louis D. 637
Branson, Herman R. 110
Branton, Wiley A. 414, 668
Brawley, Benjamin G. 112, 569
Brazeal, Brailsford R. 113
Brazilian Ballet Company 820
Breadloaf Writers Conference 287
Brer Soul 1153
Brewer, J. Mason 114
Brice, Carol 1208
Brice, Fanny 1229
Bridges, Todd 213
Brimmer, Andrew F. 116
Bristow, Lonnie R. 118
Broadcast Music Industry 680
Broadside Press 135
Broadway Brevities of 1920 1229
Broken Strings 865
Brooke, Edward W. 121
Brooklyn College 305, 424, 1095
Brooklyn Dodgers 166-67, 1023-24
Brooks, Gwendolyn 1069
Brotherhood of Sleeping Car Porters 113-14, 983, 985-86
Brothers and Keepers 1216
Broughton, Virginia Walker 101
Brown Buddies 1017
Brown, Dorothy L. 1225
Brown, Elaine 205

Brown Fellowship Society 1159
Brown, Grafton Tyler 124
Brown, James 125
Brown, Jim 213
Brown, John 140, 278, 284, 329, 976-77
Brown, Morris 129, 919
Brown, Ron 131, 988
Brown, Sterling A. 133, 154
Brown, Tony 136
Brown University 400, 402, 1000
Brown v. Board of Education 89, 765, 1209, 1212
Brown, William Wells 138, 235, 328
Brown, Willie L., Jr. 141
Brownies Book 339
Bruce, Blanche Kelso 143, 201
Bruce, John Edward (Bruce Grit) 411-12
Bruce, Josephine Beall 146
Bryan, Andrew 146
Bubbling Brown Sugar 824
Buckingham Palace 1228
Buffalo Soldiers 403
Bullard, Eugene 148
Bullins, Ed 150
Bunche, Ralph J. 121, **152,** 1024
Burgess, John M. 156
Burleigh, Harry T. 299, 383
Burns, Isaac. *See* Murphy, Isaac.
Burrill, Mary 1010
Burris, Roland 158
Burrows, Daniel 305
Bush, George 517, 926, 1093, 1110
But We Had Each Other 614
Butcher, Margaret Just 732
By Parties Unknown 1249
Byrd Amendment 303
Byrd, Bobby 127

"Cabin in the Cotton" paintings 942
Cable, George Washington 196
Cady, Elizabeth Stanton 328
Cain, Richard Harvey 367
California Angels 1021
California Historical Society, William Leidesdorff Papers 713
California School of Fine Arts 642
California State Assembly 142
California State Department of Education 1012
Caliver, Ambrose 160
Calloway, Blanche 162-63
Calloway, Cab 162, 169
Calloway, Chris 165
Cambridge University 424
Camille Olivia Hanks Cosby Academic Center 233
Campaign to End Slums 690
Campanella, Roy 166
Campbell, E. Simms 164, **169**
Campbell, Lucy 321
Campus Unrest Commission 258
Cane 1125, 1127-29
Cantor, Eddie 1229
Caravans 211
The Card Players 1249
Cardozo, Francis L. 171, 368
Carey, Archibald J. 992
Carey, Lott. *See* Cary, Lott.
Carlos, John 7, 405
Carmichael, Stokely 173, 398, 796
Carnegie Hall 365, 381, 384, 1194
Carney, William H. 176
Carter, Benny 538
Carter, Jimmy 398, 421, 1282
Carver Democratic Club 305, 341
Carver, George Washington 177, 291, 915
Cary, Lott 180
Case Western Reserve University 1045
Cast the First Stone 554
Cat Ballou 217
Catholic University of America 333
Catlett, Elizabeth 1205
The Cavalcade of the American Negro 95
Cayton, Horace R. 182, 1270
CBS news 1060
CBS Reports 103
CBS Sunday Night News 104
CBS television 274
Celestial Gate series 1249
Center Avenue Poets Theatre Workshop 1242
Centers for Disease Control 416, 1044-45
Central College 999, 1157
Central High School (Little Rock) 415
Central State University 110, 1200-01
A Century of Negro Migration 1258
Century of Negro Progress Exposition 365
Cézanne, Paul 335
Challenge 597
The Challenge of Change: Crisis in Our Two-Party System 123
Challenger 798-800
Chamberlain, Wilt 184
Championship Auto Racing 1009
Charles, Ray 186, 657-58
Charleston Independent 285

Charlie Parker's Reboppers 263
Chattanooga Black Lookouts 902
Chavis, John 190
Cheekwood Fine Arts Center 360
Cheeseborough, Chandra 1107
Chenault, Kenneth I. 191
Chesnutt, Charles Waddell 193
Chester, Thomas Morris 197
Cheyney State College 103
Cheyney State Teachers College 98, 1040
Chicago Bears 899
Chicago Bee 892
Chicago Bulls 664-666
Chicago City Council 804
Chicago Daily News 1032
Chicago Defender 3-4, 846
Chicago Historical Society 845
Chicago Medical School 1230
Chicago Music Publishing Company 320
Chicago Negro Chamber of Commerce 435
Chicago No-Jury Society of Artists 844
Chicago Public Library, Vivian Harsh Collection 184
Chicago School of Composition and Arrangement 320
Chicago settlement 351
Chicago Sun-Times 613
Chicago Theological Seminary 1263
Chicago Tribune 613, 889
Chicago Union Giants 418
Chicago-Kent College of Law 269
Child, Lydia Maria 1035
Chip Woman's Fortune 1010
Chirac, Jacques 205
A Choice of Weapons 909
Choreographer's Workshop 819
Choynoski, Joe 624
Christian Methodist Episcopal Church 1122
Christian Recorder 283, 1099, 1134-35
Church for the Fellowship of All Peoples 1117
Church of God in Christ 770-71
Church of Simon of Cyrene 993
Church of the Messiah 239
Church of the Universal Triumph the Dominion of God 655
Church, Robert Reed, Sr. 200
Church, Roberta 201
Church (Terrell), Mary 991
Cincinnati Art Museum 348
Cincinnati Commercial Appeal 1235
Cincinnati Reds 1020-21
Cinema Supplies 647
Cinque, Joseph 976
Citizens Saving and Trust Company Bank 102, 869
City College of New York 95, 119, 281, 287, 823, 955, 958, 1174
City Hotel 712
Civil Rights Act of 1957 822, 956
Civil Rights Act of 1964 397, 690, 822, 956, 1281
Civil Rights Act of 1968 1222
Civil Rights Acts 1222
Civil Rights Bill 368
Civil Rights Commission 1221
  and Denby, Charles 292-93
  and Forman, James 406
  and Lewis, John R. 719
  and Moses, Bob 838
  and Poussaint, Alvin F. 952
  and Randolph, A. Philip 986
  and Rustin, Bayard 1042
  and Sleet, Moneta J., Jr. 1069-70
  and Stokes, Carl B. 1087
  and Thomas, Clarence 1110
  and Williams, Avon Nyanza, Jr. 1225
  and Young, Whitney M., Jr. 1290
Civil War 176, 198, 696, 1006, 1071-72, 1233
Civilian Conservation Corps 296
Claflin University 4
Clara Elizabeth Jackson Carter Foundation 335
Clark Atlanta University. *See also* Atlanta University. 246, 319, 352, 429, 1266
Clark Center for the Performing Arts 10
Clark College 797
Clark, Septima 1281
Clarkson, Thomas 409
Classical Jazz Festival 760
Clay, Cassius. *See* Ali, Muhammad.
Cleaver, Eldridge 151, **203,** 875
Cleaver, Kathleen Neal 204
Clef Club 382-85
Clement, Emma Clarissa 208
Clement, George Clinton 207, 208
Clement, Rufus E. 207, **208,** 1290
Clemorgan, Jacques 349-50
Cleveland Advocate 1144
Cleveland Association of Colored Men 830
Cleveland Call 830
Cleveland Indians 903, 1020-21
Cleveland, James 211, 322
Cleveland Marshall School of Law 1086
Cleveland Now! 1088

Clinton, Bill 117, 132, 220, 335, 380, 414, 416, 421, 667, 669, 839, 926, 1088, 1221
Clinton, Hillary Rodham 335
Club Rivoli 967
CNN 1060
Coalition of Black Elected Democrats 305
Cochran, Johnnie 212
Coke, Thomas 574
Coker, Daniel 214
Colbert, Virgis 609
The Coldest Day of the Year 1243
Cole, Bob 383, 621-22
Cole, Cozy 165
Cole, Nat "King" 215
Coleman Hawkins' band 263
Coleman, William T., Jr. 217
Coleridge-Taylor, Samuel 346, 1083, 1207
Colgate University 955, 1118
The Collapse of Cotton Tenancy 618
College Endowment Funding Plan 917
Colonel Charles Young Post 398 (American Legion) 1285
The Colonel's Dream 195-96
The Color Purple 465, 659
Colored American 229-30, 1074
Colored Business Men's Association of Baltimore 866
Colored City Hospital (Waco) 755
Colored Convention movement 977
Colored Educational Convention 912
Colored Intercollegiate Athletic Association 209
Colored M. E. Church of Baltimore 214
Colored Men's Convention 248
Colored Methodist Episcopal Church 1122
Colored National Labor Union 768, 866, 1246
The Colored Patriots of the American Revolution 872-73
Colored People's Convention 198, 367
Colored Press Association 1067
Colson, Charles 206
Coltrane, John 220, 281, 905
Columbia University
  Baraka, Amiri, and 53
  Bontemps, Arna W., and 95
  Brazeal, Brailsford R., and 113
  Caliver, Ambrose, and 160
  College of Physicians and Surgeons 400
  Department of History 714
  Douglas, Aaron, and 325
  Drew, Charles R., and 332
  Jackman, Harold, and 596
  Johnson, James Weldon, and 628
  Josey, E. J., and 670
  Kay, Ulysses S., and 680
  Poussaint, Alvin F., and 951
  Powell, Adam Clayton, Jr., and 955
  Redding, J. Saunders, and 1000
  Reid, Ira De A., and 1003
  School of Law 737, 802, 1095, 1112
  School of Library Service 1198, 1233
  School of Modern Photography 1069
  Sullivan, Leon H., and 1090
  Teachers College 310, 797
  Thomas, Franklin A., and 1112
  Walker, Leroy T., and 1166
Columbus Dispatch 1142
Commission on Civil Rights 956
Commission on Interracial Cooperation 848
Committee of Thirteen 924, 1245
Committee of Twelve 195
Committee on Appeal for Human Rights 92
Commoner 1235
Communist Party 253, 255
Community Action Assembly 1291
The Competitor 1150
Comprehensive Anti-Apartheid Act 1026
Concerned Citizens for Police Reform 805
The Condition, Elevation, Emigration and Destiny of the Colored People of the United States, Politically Considered 284
Cone, James H. 223
Conference of Church Workers among Colored People 157
Confessions of Nat Turner 1141
The Congregational Worker 971
Congress of Racial Equality (CORE) 599
  and Farmer, James L., Jr. 389-91
  and King, Martin Luther, Jr. 689
  and Lewis, John R. 719
  and McKissick, Floyd 795-96
  and Rustin, Bayard 1039, 1041
  and Young, Whitney M., Jr. 1290
Congressional Black Caucus
  and Dellums, Ronald V. 290
  and Diggs, Charles C., Jr. 301-02
  and Fauntroy, Walter E. 399
  and Gray, William H., III 479
  and Mfume, Kweisi 809
  and Mitchell, Parren J. 825
  and Nix, Robert N. C., Sr. 878
  and Rangel, Charles B. 989
  and Thomas, Clarence 1110
  and Young, Andrew 1282
The Conjure Woman 195-96

Connie's Hot Chocolates 164
Connor, "Bull" 689, 1281
The Conquest 811
The Cosby Show 232, 268, 335, 953
Consolidated Lasting Machine Company 777
Constab Ballads 792
Constitutional Convention of 1868 368
Contender 949
Continental Army 948
Contribution of the Negro to American Democracy 1205
Convention of Colored Citizens 139
Conyers, John, Jr. 225
Cook (Parrish), Mary V. 1067
Cook, Will Marion 1206
Cookman Institute 983
Coolidge, Calvin 849
Cooper, George C. 1017
Cooper Union School of Art 280
Coordinating Council of Community Organizations 599
Copacabana (New York City) 69
Coppin, Fannie Jackson 227
Coppin, Levi Jenkins 227
Coppin State College 166
Corcoran Gallery of Art 336, 348
Cornell University 408, 645, 915, 936, 952
Cornish, Samuel 229, 999, 1034
Cosby, Bill 230, 377, 946, 1009
Cosby, Bill and Camille 335
Cosby Collection of Fine Art 336
Cosmopolitan Opera Company 81
"Cottage for Sale" 358
Cotton Blossom Singers 653
Cotton Club 164, 365, 1014, 1019
The Cotton Club 165
Cotton Comes to Harlem 265
Cotton States and International Exposition 965, 1184
Council for the Economic Development of Black Americans 137
Council on African Affairs 1015
Council on Minority Planning and Strategy 392
Councill, William H. 993
Countee Cullen Library 324-25
Covent Garden Theatre (London) 14
Cox, Hannibal 257
Craft, Ellen 234-36
Craft, William 234
Crane College 163
Crawford, Hank 189
Cremona Trio 125
Cribb, Tom 827
Crisis magazine
Amy Spingarn Competition 1247
contributions of Douglas, Aaron 324
contributions of Walrond, Eric 1174
editor of 339, 817, 1223
financial difficulties 1211
Richardson, Willis, and 1010-11
Crockett, George W., Jr. 236
Cromwell, John W. 1048
Cronkite, Walter 1059
Crosby, Bing 1084
Crozer Theological Seminary 687, 972
Crummell, Alexander 238, 345, 437, 1074, 1178
Cry Freedom 1188
Cry, the Beloved Country 946
Crystal Palace 545
Cuban Giants 418
Cuban X-Giants 418
Cuffe, Paul 241, 409-10
Cullen, Countee 94, **243,** 596, 1175, 1211, 1247
Cullen, Frederick Asbury 244
Cuney, Norris Wright 246, 412, 1051
Currier, Theodore S. 423

Daily American 627
Daily Worker 1270
Daley, Richard J. 270
Daley, William 805
Dallas Symphony 1195
Dance Theater of Harlem 819, 821
Danforth, John C. 1109
Danville Fairgrounds Speedway 1054
Daphne Hiding from Apollo 335
Dark, Alvin 786
Dark Laughter 511
Darlington, Roy Clifford 251
Dartmouth College 675
Daughters of the American Revolution 282
Davidson County Independent Political Council 1225
Davis, Allison 252
Davis, Benjamin Jefferson 253
Davis, Benjamin Jefferson, Sr. 897, 970
Davis, Benjamin O., Jr. 255
Davis, Benjamin O., Sr. 255, **259,** 1287
Davis, Miles 221-22, **262,** 357, 905
Davis, Ossie 264, 1279
Davis, Sammy, Jr. 266
Davis Walker's Appeal 1165
Dawson, William L. 269, 296, 322-23

Dawson, William Levi 272
Day of Absence 1176
Day, Thomas 275
Day, William Howard 276, 873
Dayton Herald 345
Dayton Tattler 345
Dean Dixon Symphony 310
Dean, Dizzy 902
DeCarava, Roy 280
Declaration of Rights of the Negro Peoples of the World 443
Dee, Ruby 265
De La Beckwith, Byron, Jr. 387
Delaney, Beauford 47
Delany, Annie Elizabeth "Bessie" 281
Delany, Hubert T. 281
Delany, Martin R. 197-98, **282,** 328, 440, 872
Delany, Samuel R. 286
Delany, Sarah Louise "Sadie" 281
De Large, Robert C. 367
De Lavallade, Carmen 9, 820
De Lavallade-Ailey Dance Theater 10
Delaware State College 559
"De Lawd" character 591-92
Dellums, Ronald V. 289
Democratic National Committee 132, 159, 271, 305
Democratic National Convention 92, 1282
  1940 993
  1948 270
  1956 302, 877
  1992 306
Denby, Charles 291
DePauw University 667, 672
DePriest, Jessie Williams 296
DePriest, Oscar S. 256, 270, **294**
D'Estaing, Valéry Giscard 205
Detroit College of Law 302
Detroit Courier 136
Detroit Grand Prix 1009
Detroit Institute of Arts 348, 1250
Detroit Public Library 789, 1070
The Dett Collection of Negro Spirituals 300
Dett, R. Nathaniel 297, 1207
Deutsche Oper (Berlin) 1062
Devil in a Blue Dress 839
De Witt S. Dykes & Associates, Architects 354
Dexter Avenue Baptist Church 687-88
Dhalgren 288
A Dialogue Between a Virginian and an African Minister 214
Dickinson University 864
A Different Drummer 682
Diggs, Charles C., Jr. 237, **301**
Diggs, Charles C., Sr. 301
Dillard University 89, 110, 862
Dinkins, David N. 304, 988, 1095, 1280
"Dipper Mouth Blues" 884
Discovery orbiter 87
District Cablevision Incorporated 640
District of Columbia Self-Government and Governmental Reorganization Act 303
District of Columbia Voting Rights Amendment 399
Divine, M. J. "Father" 307, 317, 656, 950
Divine, Mother 308-09
The Dixie Duo 78
Dixon, Dean 310
Do the Right Thing 707
Dodson, Howard, Jr. 312
Dodson, Owen 315
Domestic Life and Accident Insurance Company 807
"Don't Be a Weary, Traveler" 299
Dorsey, Thomas Andrew 319
The Doug Wilder Show 1220
Douglas, Aaron 95, **322**
Douglas murals 325
Douglass, Anna Murray 327
Douglass, Frederick 326
  American Anti-Slavery Society, speaking for 1003-04
  Chester, Thomas Morris, and 198, 199
  Garnet, Henry Highland, opposition to 439-40
  Nell, William C., work with 872-73
  New Era 769
  North Star 283
  Noted Negro Women, contribution to 754
  Radical Political Abolitionists 1074
  Ruggles, David, aid from 1034
  Ward, Samuel Ringgold, debate with 1245
Douglass, Joseph 382
Douglass Monthly 329
Douglass National Bank 890, 892
Downing, George 999
Drake, St. Clair 182
"Dream Team" (Olympic Basketball) 665
Drew, Charles R. 331
Drew Theological Seminary 1122
Driskell, David C. 333, 842
Driving Miss Daisy 432
A Drop of Patience 682
Du Bois, Shirley Graham 317

Du Bois, W. E. B. 336
Atlanta University 569-70
Bond, Horace Mann, and 89
Crisis 324, 489, 817, 1010, 1211
Cullen, Countee, and 243
Garvey, Marcus, opposition to 444
Globe 412
Moon Illustrated Weekly 897
Niagara Movement 934, 1132
Proctor, Henry Hugh, and 970
Ransom, Reverdy C., and 992
Rogers, J. A., praise of 1030
Woodruff, Hale A., and 1247
Work, Monroe Nathan, and 1264
Du Bois, Yolande 245
Dudley, Edward R. 341
Dudley, Joe L. 435
Duke University 191, 276, 365, 424
Dunayevskaya, Raya 291, 293
Dunbar, Alice Moore 345
Dunbar, Paul Laurence 109, **344,** 514, 755, 933, 992
Duncanson, Robert S. 347
Dunfords Travels Everywheres 683
Dunham, Katherine 1084
Duquesne University 72
Durocher, Leo 786
Du Sable, Jean Baptiste Pointe 349
Du Sable Museum of African-American History 351
Dutchman 54
Dwight, Edward, Jr. 87
Dyer Anti-Lynching Bill 628
Dykes, De Witt S., Sr. 352
Dykes Masonry Company 354
Dynamite Voices: Black Poets of the 1960s 751

Eakins, Thomas 1100
East Vine Avenue Methodist Church 353
Eastern Airlines 944
Eastman Kodak Company 908
Eastman School of Music 273, 300, 679, 1084, 1179
"Easy Rawlins" novels 839
Ebenezer Baptist Church 686
Ebony 630, 632-33
Ebony Cosmetics 630
Ebony Fashion Fair 630
Ebony Music Awards 633
Ebony Reflections 809
Eckstein Norton Institute 911-12
Eckstine, Billy 217, **357,** 1064
Edison Electric Light Company 699
Edison Research Laboratories 179
Edison, Thomas 1251
Edmondson, William 359
The Education of the Negro Prior to 1861 1257
Edwards, Nelson J. 361
The Einstein Intersection 288
Eisenhower, Dwight D. 833, 956, 1065
Elder, Lee 362, 1065
Elders, Jocelyn 416
Electric Company 232, 432
Elijah McCoy Manufacturing Company 788
Ellington, Duke 164, **364**
Elliott, Robert Brown 367
Ellison, Ralph 369, 1270
Ellison, William 373
"The Emancipation of Negro Music" 299
Emancipation Proclamation 279, 329, 977, 1134
Emancipator 1034
"Embraceable You" 216
Emerge 641
Emmalyn II Enterprises 266
The Emperor Jones 81, 265, 460-61
Epiphany Episcopal College 756
Episcopal Church, Diocese of Massachusetts 157
Episcopal Theological Seminary 157
"Epistles on the Education of the Ministry" 919
Equal Employment Opportunities Commission 16
Erving, Julius 375
Esmeralda School of Painting 1205
Espy, Mike 378
Essence 910
Estes, Simon 381
Ethiopian Art Players 1010
Eugene Bullard Day 150
Europe, James Reese 382
The Everlasting Stain 818
Evers, Charles 476
Evers, Medgar 386, 801
Evers, Myrlie 387
Every Ready Gospel Singers 126
Excello Manufacturing Company 1105
Executive Order 9981 258, 986
The Exile 813, 1233
The "Extinguisher" Extinguished 1034
Eyes on the Prize 93

Face to Face with Vernon Jarrett 613
Facets 680

Faggs, Mae 1106
Fair Deal 127
Fair Housing Act 822
Famous Flames 126
Fard, W. D. 394, 853-54
Farmer, James L., Jr. 389, 485, 1041
Farmer's and Mechanics Bank 1076
Farrakhan, Louis 393, 855, 1278
Farrow, Lucy 1056
Fashion Fair Cosmetics 633
Fat Albert and the Cosby Kids 232
Father Divine. *See* Divine, M. J. "Father."
Fatheralong; A Meditation on Fathers and Sons 1216, 1217
Fats Waller's Rhythm 1173
Fauntroy, Walter E. 396
Fauset, Jessie 94, 1174
Fayetteville State University 194
Federal Aviation Administration 258
Federal Bureau of Investigation (FBI) 70
Federal Government Service in the South for Negroes 179
Federal Reserve System 116-17
Federal Theatre Project 402, 864, 887, 1270
Feeder Program 1091
Fellowship of Reconciliation (FOR) 390, 1041
Female Anti-Slavery Society of Salem 1004
Fences 1241, 1243
Fifteenth Amendment 329
Fire! 325, 1118-20
First African Baptist Church 146, 148
First African Presbyterian Church 463
First Annual Convention of the People of Color 230
First Artists Corporation 946
First Congregational Church 969-70
The First One Hundred Years 845
Fisher, Rudolph 400
Fisher, Willie Mae 321
Fisk University
  Art Department 325, 334
  Carl Van Vechten Gallery 326
  Douglas, Aaron, art at 325
  Du Bois, W. E. B., and 337
  Early Entrants Program 714
  faculty at 160, 183, 423, 430, 524, 530, 616
  Film Program 842
  Fisk Herald 338
  Fisk Jubilee Singers 202, 1200, 1261-62
  Fisk University Choir 1260
  Graduate School 775
  Imes, Elmer S., and 589
  James Carroll Napier Papers 871
  Lewis, John R., and 718
  McCree, Wade H., Jr., and 789
  president of 1273
  Proctor, Henry Hugh, and 969
  Sargent Johnson Collection 643
Fisk University Library 95
  Aaron Douglas Collection 326
  Ambrose Caliver Collection 162
  Charles W. Chesnutt Papers 197
  Elmer Imes Papers 591
  John Mercer Langston Papers 698
  John W. Work Papers 1262
  Scott Joplin Collection 664
  Stephen J. Wright Papers 1275
  Thomas Elsa Jones Papers 162
  W. E. B. Du Bois Collection 341
  William L. Dawson Papers 272
  Z. Alexander Looby Papers 740
Flavio 910
Flipper, Henry O. 403, 1284
Floyd McKissick Enterprises 796
Foley, Red 322
Follies 1229
Football Hall of Fame 900
For Blacks Only 613
For Love of Imabelle 555
Ford Foundation 1112, 1177
Fordham University 756, 1187
Foreman, George 404
Forman, James 92, 174, **406**
Fort Huachuca Museum, Henry O. Flipper Collection 404
Fort Valley State College 90-91
Fort Worth Yellow Jackets 417
Forten, James 242-43, **408,** 976
Fortune, T. Thomas 411
Foster, Henry W., Jr. 414
Foster, Rube 417
The Founding of Talladega College 1249
Fourie, Bernardus G. 399
Francis, Norman C. 420
Frank, Waldo 1127
Frankfurter, Felix 218
Franklin, Aretha 211
Franklin, C. L. 211
Franklin, John Hope 421
Fraunces, Samuel 427
Frazier, E. Franklin 154, **428**
Frazier, Joe 405
Frederick Douglass' Paper. See also *North Star.* 328, 1244

Frederick Douglass 681
Free African Society 22, 644
Free and Easy 658
Free Democratic Party 695
Free Soil Party 277, 1005
Free South Africa Movement 1026
Freedmen's Bureau 285, 696, 1157
Freedmen's Bureau schools 279
Freedmen's Hospital 332, 499, 1231
Freedmen's Savings and Trust Bank 145, 329, 1246
Freedom Association 873
Freedom Bank 1024
Freedom National Bank 937
Freedom Rides 174, 391, 397, 689, 718-19, 1041
Freedom's Journal 229, 230, 1038-39, 1165
Freeman. See *New York Age.*
Freeman, Morgan 431
Freemen's Employment Agency 1082
From Slavery to Freedom 425
From Superman to Man 1029
Fugitive Slave Act of 1793 410
Fugitive Slave Act of 1850 234, 284, 873, 1005, 1081
Fuller Guaranty Corporation 434
Fuller Products Company 433-35
Fuller, S. B. 433
Fuller-Philco Home Appliance Center 434
Fund for an Open Society 392
Fundamentals in the Education of Negroes 161
Funky Beat 1153
The Future of the American Negro 413

G. A. Morgan Hair Refining Company 829
G. A. Morgan Safety System 830
Gabor, Zsa Zsa 1240
Gabriel. *See* Prosser, Gabriel.
Gabriel Insurrection 975
Gallery of Modern Art (New York) 326
Gammon Theological Seminary 353
Gandhi, Mahatma 1116
Gardner, Newport 436
Garner v. Louisiana 765
Garnet Equal Rights League 198
Garnet, Henry Highland 198, 238, 328, **437,** 562, 873, 977, 999, 1074, 1178, 1246
Garrett Biblical Institute 209, 223
Garrison, Snapper 859
Garrison, William Lloyd 230, 284, 327, 439, 872-73, 1035, 1166
Garvey, Marcus 394, 413, **441,** 793, 984, 989, 1048, 1151, 1174, 1258
Garveyism 898
Gaston, Arthur G. 445
Gates, Henry Louis, Jr. 71, **448**
Geier v. Tennessee 1225
Gell, Monday 1160, 1162
General Association of Baptists 1080
General Vigilance Committee 999, 1081
George Foreman Youth and Community Center 405
George R. Smith College 662
George Shearing Quintet 358
George Washington Carver Art School 280
George Washington Carver Research Foundation 179
George Washington University 930, 959
Georgia Democratic Party Forum 93
Georgia Legislative Black Caucus 91
Georgia State Senate 91, 93
Georgia Tom and Tampa Red 321
Get on the Bus 707
GGG Studio 1147
Ghosts of Mississippi 803
Gibbs (Hunt), Ida 991
Gibbs (Marshall), Harriet 1207
Gibbs, Mifflin Wistar 450
Gibson, Benjamin F. 452
Gibson, Truman K., Jr. 456, 841
Gillespie, Dizzy 165, 221-22, 263, 357, **458,** 905
Gillespie's Big Band and Sextet 222
Gilpin, Charles S. 460, 824, 864
Girl 6 707
Giuliani, Rudolph 306
Glamour 909
Glaser, Joe 32
Glasgow Emancipation Society 1073
Glasgow University 1073
Globe 412
Glory 433, 1188
Gloucester, John 230, **462**
Glover, Danny 464
God Sends Sunday 95-96
Goddard College 839
God's Stepchildren 813
God's Trombones: Seven Negro Sermons in Verse 629
The Golden Boy 268
Golden State Mutual Life Insurance Company (Los Angeles) 1249
Gone Are the Days 265
Gone Fishin' 840

"A Good Man is Hard to Find" 898
Goode, Mal 466
Goode (Robeson), Eslanda "Essie" Cardozo 1013
Goodman, Benny 538
"The Goophered Grapevine" 195
Gordon Parks Academy 911
Gordy, Berry 468, 605
Gordy-De Passe Productions 472
Gosnell, Harold 182
Gospel All Stars 211
Gospel Chimes 211
Gospel Choral Union of Chicago 322
Gospel Music Workshop of America 212
Gospelaires 211
Got to Be There 606
Goteborg Symphony Orchestra 311
Government Printing Office 1067
Grace, "Sweet Daddy" 656
Graham, Billy 206
Grainger, Percy 299
Grand National (NASCAR) 1054-55
Grand Ole Opry 43, 45, 966, 968
Grand Order of True Reformers 1076
"Grandfather's Clock (Was Too Tall for the Shelf)" 747
Granger, Lester B. 472
Gravely, Samuel L., Jr. 473
Graves, Earl G. 475, 609
Gray, Frizzell. *See* Mfume, Kweisi.
Gray v. the University of Tennessee 1224
Gray, William H., III 478
Graziana, Rocky 1028
Greased Lightning 1055
Great Depression 296, 554, 630, 836, 846, 853
Great Migration 792
Great Performers Series 1194
The Great White Hope 650
Greater New York Coordinating Committee for Employment 955
Greaves, William "Bill" G. 481
Green Pastures 61, 513, 591-92
Greener, Richard T. 483, 699
Greenfield, Elizabeth Taylor 898
Greensboro Open 1065
Gregory, Dick 484
Grier, Rosey 82
Griffith, D. W. 842
Grimké, Angelina 345
Grimké, Archibald Henry 487
Grimké, Charlotte Forten 491
Grimké, Francis J. 487, **490**
Grimké, Sarah 488
Growing Up in the Black Belt 617
GTE Byron Nelson Classic 1254
Guarantee Photos 1147
The Guardian 1130-32
A Guest of Honor 663
Gula Matari 658
Gumbel, Bryant 492
Gurdjieff, George 1128

Hackley, E. Azalea 298-99
Haitian Revolution 1159
Hale, Daniel 201
Haley, Alex 496
Half-Century 891-92
Hall, George Cleveland 499, 1231
Hall, Prince 502
Hamer, Fannie Lou 1278
Hamilton College 837
Hammarskjold, Dag 155
Hammon, Jupiter 504
Hampton Institute (Hampton University) 4, 85, 299, 326, 516-17, 847, 849, 1183, 1272
- Camera Club 346
- Choir 299
- Hampton Quartet 299
- Hampton Women's Chorus 299
- Musical Arts Society 299
- R. Nathaniel Dett Papers 301
- Robert R. Moton Papers 850

Hampton, Lionel 506, 657
Hampton, Wade 285
The Handy Brothers Music Company 898
Handy, W. C. 202, 320, **508,** 836, 898, 1083
Hansberry v. Lee 828
Happy Ending 1176
Hare, Maud Cuney 248
Harlem Academy 95
Harlem Art Workshop 702
The Harlem Book of the Dead 317, 1148
Harlem Commission 430
Harlem Community Art Center 280
"The Harlem Dancer" 794
Harlem Experimental Theatre Company 597
Harlem Federal Theatre 841
Harlem Globetrotters 163, 165, 185
Harlem Hospital 862, 1267-68
Harlem Orchestra 1147
Harlem Renaissance 164, 596-97, 1118
- Johnson, Charles S. 617
- Literature 93, 288, 400, 791, 793-94, 1119, 1173-74

Locke, Alain Leroy 728
Music 1083
The New Negro 1211
Painting 843
Poetry 134, 243-45
Schomburg, Arthur Alfonso 1048
Sculpture 642
Theater/Drama 1010
Visual Art 314, 322, 324-25
Harlem Shadows 793
Harlem Suitcase Theater 582
Harleston, Edwin A. 325
Harmer, Fannie Lou 1281
Harmon Foundation 112, 531, 642-43, 1248, 1250
Harper's Ferry raid 976
Harrington, Oliver W. 511
Harrison, Benjamin 382
Harrison, Richard B. 513, 592
Harsh, Vivian 1190
Hart, Charles 623
Hartford School of Music 1207
Hartford Stage Company 1177
Hartford Theological Seminary 1280
Harth, Mingo 1161
Harvard University
Alexander, Clifford L., Jr., and 15
Bunche, Ralph J., and 154
Chemistry Department 673
Cullen, Countee, and 245
Davis, Allison, and 252
Divinity School 636
Du Bois, W. E. B., and 338
first black graduate of 483
first black Phi Beta Kappa 1130
Franklin, John Hope, and 423
Hiram Revels Papers 1008
Paul Laurence Dunbar Papers 347
Law School 71, 191, 218, 254, 721, 789, 1025
Medical School 284, 1266
Philosophy Department 728-29
School of Business Administration 117
West, Cornel, and 1203
Harvey, William R. 516
Hastie, William Henry 154, 456, **519,** 1212
Having Our Say 281
Hawkins, Augustus F. 522
Hawkins, Coleman 538
Hawkins Fair Employment Practices Act 522
Hayden, Robert E. 523
Hayes, Roland 299, **526,** 1181
Haynes, Elizabeth Ross 531
Haynes, George Edmund 528, 586
Haynes, Lemuel 532
Healy, James Augustine 533
Healy, Patrick 533, 535
Hearts in Dixie 864
The Heir of Slaves 932, 934
Hello, Dolly! 165, 432
Henderson, Fletcher 537, 898
Henderson, George W. 98, 969
Henry Armstrong Youth Foundation 28
Henry Street Settlement 700
Henry, Warren E. 539
Henson, Matthew A. 541
Hepster's Dictionary 165
Herman, Alexis 1221
Herndon, Alonzo F. 544
Herndon, Angelo 254
Herndon, Norris 551
Herron Art School 1247
Hertford College 728
Hessischer Rundfunk Orchestra 311
Hewlett, James 546
Hidden Heritage, 1750-1950 335
Higginbotham, A. Leon, Jr. 548
High Museum 1249
High-Brown Products 891
High-Risk Young People's Program 416
Hill, Anita 1111
Hill, Jesse, Jr. 549
Himes, Chester 553
Hindemith, Paul 679
Hirshhorn Museum and Sculpture Garden 360
History of the African Methodist Episcopal Church 920
The History of the Negro Church 1258
History of the Negro Race from 1619 to 1880 1235
History of the Negro Troops in the War of the Rebellion 1235
History of the Twelfth Baptist Church 1235
Hocutt, Thomas R. 520
Hogan, Ernest 383
Holder, Eric H., Jr. 556
Holder, Geoffrey 820
Holiday, Billie 281
Holland, Jerome "Brud" 558
Holly, James T. 284, **560**
Holmes, Hamilton 668
Holstein, Caspar A. 563
Holt, Nora 1207
Home: Social Essays 54
Home to Harlem 794
The Homecoming 1242

"Honeysuckle Rose" 1171-72
Hood, James Walker 964
Hooks, Benjamin L. 565
Hooks, Robert 1176
Hoover, Herbert 273
Hoover, J. Edgar 690
Hope, John 568, 897
Horne, Lena 104, 165, 246, 265, 1019
Horne, Marilyn 716
Horner Institute of Fine Arts 272-73
Horton, George Moses 571
Horton, Lester 9
Hosier, "Black Harry" 573
Hot Five 31
Hotel Messenger. See *Messenger.*
House Armed Services Committee 290
The House Behind the Cedars 196
House Committee on the District of Columbia 290
House Judiciary Committee 225
House Military Installations and Facilities Subcommittee 290
The House of Falling Leaves 109
House Un-American Activities Committee 1024
House Ways and Means Committee 989
Houser, George 1041
Housing and Community Development Act 380
Houston, Charles Hamilton 519, **575,** 637, 763-64, 1212
Houston, Whitney 1188
Howard, Theodore 387
Howard Thurman Educational Trust Fund 1118
Howard University
  Baraka, Amiri, and 52
  Brown, Sterling A., and 133
  Carmichael, Stokely, and 174
  chaplain of 157
  collections in 113, 326, 336
  College of Arts and Sciences 676, 815
  College of Liberal Arts 112
  College of Pharmacy and Pharmacal Sciences 251
  Davis, Benjamin O., Sr., and 259
  Davis, Ossie, and 264
  Dental School 341
  Department of Art 334
  Department of Chemistry 673
  Department of Physics 110, 540
  Department of Sociology 430
  Dinkins, David N., and 304
  Eckstine, Billy, and 357
  Espy, Mike, and 379
  Evening School 1157
  Fortune, T. Thomas, and 411
  Frazier, E. Franklin, and 428
  Howard University Players 1010
  Law School 25, 121, 158, 575, 637, 667, 697, 763, 868, 1068, 1219
  Locke, Alain Leroy, and 729
  Logan, Rayford W., and 732
  Looby, Z. Alexander, and 737
  Medical School 332, 400, 862
  president of 636, 782
  Public Policy Training Institute 392
  Rankin Chapel 1116
  School of Communications 137
  School of Music 670
  School of Religion 389
  Simmons, William J., and 1066
  Washington, Walter E., and 1191
  Wright, Stephen J., and 1273
  Young, Andrew, and 1280
Howe Institute 636, 1269
Howells, William Dean 196
Hubbard Hospital 415, 1045
Hubbard, William DeHart 579
Huey P. Newton Foundation 875
Hughes, Langston 94-95, 280, 325, 370, **580,** 865, 934, 984, 1048, 1083, 1085, 1175
Hull House 846
Humphrey-Hawkins Full Employment Bill 523
Hunter, Charlayne 668
Huntington Library, William Leidesdorff Collection 713
Hunton, William Alphaeus 584, 1123
Hurok, Sol 81
Hurston, Zora Neale 887, 934
Huston-Tillotson College 115

"I Have a Dream" speech 690
I Have Changed 896
I Spy 232
"I Surrender Dear" 358
Ickes, Harold 520
If He Hollers, Let Him Go 554
"If I Were a Negro" 632
Illinois State House of Representatives 1190
Imes, Elmer S. 589
In a Silent Way 263
In Dahomey 1227-28
In Friendship (organization) 1042

In the Bottoms 299
In the Matter of Color 548
Independent Black Singers 1062
Independent Political Council 984
Indiana Central College (University of Indianapolis) 997
Indianapolis 500 1008-09
Indianapolis Freeman 755
Indianapolis Ledger 1247
Indianapolis Recorder 997
Indignant Heart 291
Ingersoll, Edwin D. 584
Ingram, Rex 591
Inner City Broadcasting Corporation 1096
Institute for Colored Youth 98, 728, 998-99
Institute of Medicine, National Academy of Sciences 417
Institute of Musical Art 1260
Institutional Church and Settlement House 992
Interdenominational Ministers Alliance 397
International Boxing Hall of Fame 29
International Duke Ellington Conferences 366
International Foundation for Education and Self-Help 1092
International Jazz Festival (Paris) 906
International Labor Defense 254
International League 1169
International Migration Society 1136
International Motorsports Association 1009
International Sweethearts of Rhythm 654
International Union 361
International Volleyball Association 186
Interracial Committee of Atlanta 970
Interstate United Newspaper Company 1151
Invisible Man 369, 371
Iowa State College of Agricultural and Mechanical Arts 178
Iowa State University 652, 775, 914-15
Isaacs, W. D. 321

Jack, Gullah 1160
Jack, Hulan 594
Jackman, Harold 245, **596**
Jackson Five 471, 605-06
Jackson, Jesse L. 305, 395, **598,** 722, 989, 1090, 1096
Jackson, Joe 605-06
Jackson, LaToya 607
Jackson, Mahalia 211, 322
Jackson, Maynard H. 192, **602,** 1282
Jackson, Michael 213, 471, **605,** 659
Jackson State College 801
Jacob, John E. 608
Jacob's Ladder 1237
James Brown and the Famous Flames 126
James, C. L. R. 291, 1271
James Cleveland Singers 212
James, Daniel "Chappie," Jr. 610, 930, 943, 1287
James Van DerZee Institute 1148
Jamison, Judith 11, 1208
Jarrett, Vernon D. 612
Jarrett's Journal 613
Jefferson, Blind Lemon 614
"Jelly Roll Blues" 834-35
Jesup Wagon 179
Jet 633, 1069
Jimmy Johnson Big Band 221
Jitney! 1243
Joachim, Joseph 1206
Job Corps Center 404
Jobete Company 470
Joe Turner's Come and Gone 1243
John Brown 704
John F. Kennedy Club 1096
John Reed Club 1269
John Street Methodist Church 1155
John W. Coltrane Cultural Society 221
John Wanamaker Orchestra 1147
John Wesley Methodist Episcopal Church 1121
Johnnie Walker Classic 1254
Johns Hopkins University 809, 816
Johnson C. Smith University 341, 1224
Johnson, Charles S. 94-95, 324, 326, **616,** 1002, 1048, 1273
Johnson, Earvin "Magic" 475
Johnson, Fenton 1270
Johnson, Frank 619
Johnson, Hall 1181
Johnson, Hallie Tanner 1098
Johnson, J. Rosamond 383, **621,** 627, 629
Johnson, Jack 360, 418, **624**
Johnson, James P. 1172
Johnson, James Weldon 325, 621-22, **626,** 889, 934, 1048, 1127, 1210
Johnson, John H. 630
Johnson, Joshua 634
Johnson, Lyndon B. 16, 116, 128, 271, 391, 397, 690, 765, 822, 1290
Johnson, Mordecai W. 154, 296, **635,** 677, 817, 1052, 1280
Johnson Publishing Company 630, 633-34, 1069
Johnson, Rafer 638

Johnson, Robert L. 640
Johnson, Sargent 642
Johnson State College 839
Johnson, Virginia 821
"Johnson's Celebrated Cotillion Band" 620
Joint Chiefs of Staff 960
Jones, Absalom 242, 409, **644**
Jones, Brutus 325
Jones, Charles Price 771
Jones, Eugene Kinckle 645, 1114, 1149
Jones, Frederick McKinley 647
Jones, Grace Allen 653
Jones, J. Raymond 305
Jones, James Earl 648
Jones, James Francis Marion. *See* Jones, Prophet.
Jones, Jois Mailou 334
Jones, K. C. 1036
Jones, Laurence Clifton 652
Jones, LeRoi. *See* Baraka, Amiri.
Jones, Prophet 654
Jones, Quincy 189, 606-07, **656**
Jones, Scipio Africanus 660
Joplin, Scott 661
Jordan, Michael 664
Jordan, Vernon 398, 608, **667**
Josey, E. J. 670
Journal of Negro History 1200, 1257
Journal on Health Care for the Poor and Underserved 1045
Joy Street Baptist 767
Juilliard School of Music 263, 310, 381, 759
Julian Laboratories 674
Julian, Percy L. 154, **672**
Julius Rosenwald Fund 89
Jungle Fever 707
The Junior Bachelor Society 1237
Junior Olympic Games 895
Just, Ernest Everett 675
Juvenile Anti-Slavery Society 1157

Kamoinge Workshop 281
Kansas City Call 1222
Kansas City Monarchs 903, 1023
Kappa Alpha Psi Fraternity 208, 227, 237, 415, 807, 926, 998, 1078, 1221
Karamu House 195
Kay, Ulysses S. 679
Keller, Louise 321
Kelley, William Melvin 681
Kellogg, William Pitt 199
Kelly, Edward J. 270
Kelly Miller's Monographic Magazine 818
Kelly, Sharon Pratt 399
Kennedy Center for the Performing Arts 11
Kennedy, Edward 132
Kennedy, John F. 270, 855, 1032, 1278
Kennedy, Robert F. 475, 639
Kent College of Law (Chicago-Kent) 4
Kentucky Derby 858
Kentucky Home Society for Colored Children 912
Kentucky Legislature 24-25
Kentucky Negro Education Association 807
Kentucky Normal and Theological Institute 758, 912
Kentucky State College 24, 1069, 1290
A Key to Uncle Tom's Cabin 83
Kid Ory's Band 883
Kind of Blue 263
King 266, 714
King, B. B. 683
King Cole Trio 216
King, Coretta Scott 687, 1069, 1281
King, Don 1009
King Features Syndicate 171
The King God Didn't Save 1238
King, Lonnie 92
King, Martin Luther, Jr. 686
  assassination of 1060
  at Morehouse College 783
  Birmingham Jail 70, 447
  Bond, Julian, and 92
  Bristow, Lonnie R., and 119
  Cone, James H., and 224
  Denby, Charles, and 293
  Evers, Medgar, and 387
  Farmer, James L., Jr., and 391
  Fauntroy, Walter E., and 396-97
  Jackson, Jesse, and 600
  Lowery, Joseph E., and 743-44
  Nixon, E. D., Sr., and 880-81
  Prayer Pilgrimage 986
  Robinson, Jackie, and 1024
  Rustin, Bayard, and 1042
  Selective Patronage Program 1090
  Sleet, Moneta J., Jr., photographs by 1070
  X, Malcolm, opinion of 1279
  Young, Andrew, and 1280-81
King Oliver's Creole Jazz Band 31, 883-84
King Records 126-27
King, Riley. *See* King, B. B.
King, Rodney 107, 306
King-Drew Sickle Cell Center 1045
Knock on Any Door 845-47
Knox College 1006

Knoxville College 160, 612, 743
Koch, Edward 305
Kongi's Harvest 1177
Ku Klux Klan 1278
Kunta Kinte 496-97

La Guiablesse 1084
La Motta, Jake 1028
La Scala (Milan) 1062
Lady Sings the Blues 471
Lafayette Flying Corps 149
Lafayette Players 812, 841, 864
Lafayette Theater 402, 841
Lafon, Thomy 692
LaGuardia, Fiorello 1090
A Land Beyond the River 823
Lane Theological Seminary 34
Langston, John Mercer 411, 568, **693**
LaRouche, Lyndon 595
Larsen, Nella 590
Las Dos Antillas (The Two Islands) 1047
Latimer Lamp 699
Latimer, Lewis Howard 698
Lautier, Louis Howard 1151
Lawless, T. K. 700
Lawrence, Jacob 702
Lawrence, Robert, Jr. 87
Le Gallienne Collection 113
League for Industrial Democracy 390
League of American Wheelmen 1104
The Learning Tree 909
The Learning Tree (film) 907, 910
Lee, Canada 341
Lee, Don L. *See* Madhubuti, Haki.
Lee, Spike 705, 1188
Leevy, Carroll M. 709
Legal Defense and Education Fund. *See* NAACP; Legal Defense and Education Fund.
Leidesdorff, William A. 711
Leile, George. *See* Liele, George.
Leland Giants 418
Lennon-Seney United Methodist Church 353, 355
"Letter from Birmingham Jail" 690
Levine, Jack 334
Levison, Stanley 1042
Lewis, David Levering 713
Lewis, Edmonia 696
Lewis, Henry 716
Lewis, John R. 93, 174, 391, **718,** 1278
Lewis, Oliver 858
Lewis, Reginald F. 720
Lewis, William Henry 1221
Lexington Kentucky Standard 1068
Liberator 284, 327, 792, 872-73
Liberia College 240
Liberia Herald 1039
Liberty 889
Liberty Bank and Trust 421
Liberty Party 277, 439, 1178
Library of Congress 191, 860, 1261
- A. Philip Randolph Personal Files 986
- Booker T. Washington Papers 1186
- Brotherhood of Sleeping Car Porters Collection 986
- Carter G. Woodson Papers 1259
- Daniel A. Murray Papers 861
- Francis L. Cardozo Papers 173
- Frederick Douglass Papers 330
- Hiram Revels Papers 1008
- Irvin C. Mollison Papers 829
- Mary Church Terrell Papers 203
- Ralph Ellison Papers 373
- Roy Wilkins Papers 1224

Lie, Trygve 155
Liele, George 146, **723**
Life 907, 909-10
The Life and Times of Frederick Douglass 330
"Lift Every Voice and Sing" 622, 626
Lilies of the Field 944, 946
Lincoln, Abraham 199, 285, 329
Lincoln Center for the Performing Arts 11
Lincoln Hospital 1077
Lincoln Institute (Kentucky) 88
Lincoln League 201
Lincoln University (Pennsylvania) 88, 90-91, 763, 822, 876, 943, 964, 1000
The Lion and the Archer 525
"Listen to the Lambs" 299
Little, Malcolm. *See* X, Malcolm.
Little Richard 126, **724**
Little Richard and the Tempo Toppers 725
Live from Lincoln Center 1195
Living Legacy Award 1148
Livingstone College 115, 207, 209, 964, 1068
Llewellyn, J. Bruce 377
Locke, Alain Leroy 94, 154, 243, 245, 264, 324, **728,** 1010, 1048, 1211
Lockheed Missile and Space Company 540
Logan, Rayford W. 732
Loguen, Jermain 328
Lomax, Alan 834
London School of Economics 714
London Symphony Orchestra 1194

Lone Star State Medical, Dental and Pharmaceutical Society 754
The Lonely Crusade 554
Long, Richard A. 734
A Long Way from Normal 962
Looby, Z. Alexander 737, 1224-25
Looking Backward at Us 997
Los Angeles Chamber Orchestra 716
Los Angeles City College 56, 151
Los Angeles City Council 105
Los Angeles Dodgers 1021
Los Angeles Lakers 8, 186
Los Angeles Open 1065
Los Angeles Philharmonic 716
Los Angeles School of Art 1239
Los Angeles the Cornerstone Institutional Baptist Church 212
Lott Carey Baptist Foreign Mission Convention 180, 182
Lou Rawls Parade of Stars 268
Louis, Joe 362, 456, 626, **740,** 1064
Louis, Marva 909
Louisiana Court of Appeal 832
Louisiana State University Law School 831
Louisville Municipal College 208-09
Louisville Urban League 807
Lowery, Joseph E. 742
Lowndes County Christian Movement for Human Rights 293
Loyola University Law School 212, 420
Lucas, Sam 746
A Lucky Coon 1227
Lynch, John Roy 748, 1007
Lynchburg Baptist University 911-12
Lynchburg Laborer 921
Lyrics of Life and Love 108

M Street High School 816, 1010, 1233, 1257
Ma Rainey's Black Bottom 1243
Mabley, Moms 864
Madhubuti, Haki 750
Magill Medical College 332
Magnolia Suite 299
Mahogany 471
Major Taylor Manufacturing Company 1105
Majors, Monroe A. 753
Makeba, Miriam 175
Malcolm X 707, 1188
Malcolm X. *See* X, Malcolm.
Malone, Annie Turnbo 886
Man and Superman 1187
The Man Who Cried I Am 1237
Mandela, Nelson 399, 1026
Manhattan Medical Society 1267
Mannes, David 384
Manning, Madeline 1106
"Maple Leaf Rag" 661, 663
Mapp, Grace A. 999
March Against Fear 802
March on Washington
  1942 985-86
  1963 391, 397, 1039, 1041-42, 1291
  DeCarava, Roy, photographs by 281
  Second 1281
  Sleet, Moneta J., Jr., photographs by 1069
  X, Malcolm, criticism of 1277
Marigold Gardens Theater 1018
Marino, Eugene Antonio 756
Markings 680
Marquette University 803
The Marrow of Tradition 194-96
Marrs, Elijah P. 757
Marsalis, Wynton 758
Marshall, Thurgood 205, 218, 342, 425, 521, 577, 738, **762,** 1110, 1212, 1225
Martin and Selig's Minstrel Show 1227
Martin, Dean 267
Martin, John Sella 767, 999
Martin Luther King Jr. Club 1096
Martin, Roberta 211
Martin, Sallie 322
Marxist-Humanist News and Letters Committees 291
Marycoo, Occramer. *See* Gardner, Newport.
Maryland Colonization Society 215
Mason, Charles Harrison 770
Mason, Charlotte 581
Masons 502
Massachusetts Anti-Slavery Society 139, 327, 1004
Massachusetts General Colored Association 871, 1165
Massachusetts Institute of Technology 799
Massey, Walter E. 773
Massie, Samuel Proctor, Jr. 775
Master Harold . . . and the Boys 465
Masters Tournament 362-63
Matzeliger, Jan E. 776
Maxim electric lamp 699
Maxim, Joe 1028
Maxwell Air Force Base, Daniel "Chappie" James Collection 612
Maynard, Robert C. 778
Maynor, Dorothy 300
Mays, Benjamin E. 415, **780,** 1045, 1116
Mays, Willie 784

McAuliffe, Christa 87
McCall Pattern Company 720, 722
McCoy, Elijah 787
McCoy system 788
McCree, Wade H., Jr. 789
McFerrin, Robert 1181
McKay, Claude 109, **791,** 1048, 1127
McKinley, William 249
McKissick, Floyd 391, **795**
McLaughlin v. Florida 218
McMillan, Elridge W. 797
McNair, Ronald E. 87, **798**
McQueen, Steve 946
McSwain v. Board of Anderson County, Tennessee 738
Meany, George 986
Medal of Merit Award for Civilians 456
Medico-Chirurgical Society 1232
Medieval Chartre 1248
Meharry Medical College 415, 753, 1045
"Memphis Blues" 509
Memphis Red Sox 967
Memphis Riots 200
Memphis Students 383
Men of Mark 1067
Mencken, H. L. 1269
Mending Socks 844
Mercury Records 127, 658
Meredith Institute 803
Meredith, James H. 796, **801**
Meredith Publishing 803
Merrick, John 1075
Merritt Community College 874
Messenger 984-85
Messiah 1180
Metcalfe, Ralph H. 271, **803**
Methodist Episcopal Church 921-22
Metro Arts Commission Gallery 360
Metropolitan Cable Club 641
Metropolitan Museum of Art 1070, 1148, 1250
Metropolitan Opera 382, 717, 1061
Meyzeek, Albert E. 806, 1079
Mfume, Kweisi 808
Michael Jordan Foundation 666
Micheaux Film and Book Company 811
Micheaux Film Corporation 813
Micheaux, Oscar 810, 1014
Michigan Central Railroad 787
Michigan-Lowndes County Christian Movement for Human Rights 292
"Middle Passage" 525
Middlebury College 131
The Mighty Gents 432
The Migration of the Negro 703
Mike Douglas Show 1252
Milady, Samuel. *See* Lucas, Sam.
Miller, Dorie 814
Miller, Kelly 815, 1048
Million Man March 73, 396
Milwaukee Bucks 8
Mimo Professional Club 1019
Ministers' Union of Washington, D.C. 240
Minneapolis Millers 785
Minneapolis Tribune 1032
Minnesota Vikings 899
Minority Business Enterprise Legal Defense and Education Fund 825
Mis-Education of the Negro 1258
Missionary Record 367
Mississippi Freedom Democratic Party (MFDP) 92, 838
Mississippi Freedom Summer 719
Mississippi Improvement Association for Students 802
Mississippi Project 237
Missoula Timberjacks 967
Missouri ex rel Gaines v. Canada 577
Mr. Wonderful 268
Mitchell, Abbie 383
Mitchell, Arthur 271, 297, **819**
Mitchell, Clarence M., Jr. 822, 825, 1223
Mitchell, Loften 823
Mitchell, Parren J. 809, 823, **824**
Mitterand, François 205
Mo' Better Blues 707, 1188
Mobile Black Bears 1
Model Inner City Community Organization 397
Molineaux, Tom 826
Mollison, Irvin C. 828
Monk, Thelonious 221-22
Montgomery Bus Boycott 688, 743, 880, 882, 950, 1039, 1042
Montgomery Improvement Association 743, 880, 1042
Montgomery Voter's League 879
Montgomery Welfare League 879
Moon Illustrated Weekly 897
Moon on a Rainbow Shaw 649
The Moorland Foundation 817
Moorland, Jesse E. 586, 817
Moorland-Spingarn Research Center 113
  Alain Locke Papers 732
  Benjamin E. Mays Papers 784
  Daniel Hale Williams Papers 1232

E. Fraklin Frazier Papers 431
Ernest E. Just Papers 678
Frederick Douglass Papers 331
Henry McNeal Turner Papers 1137
Howard University 319
Mary Church Terrell Papers 203
Mordecai Johnson Papers 638
P. B. S. Pinchback Collection 941
Peter Marshall Murray Papers 863
R. Nathaniel Dett Collection 301
Rapier Family Papers 996
Rayford W. Logan Papers 734
Robeson Family Archives 1016
Morand, Paul 325
Morehouse College
Bond, Julian, and 91
Brawley, Benjamin G., and 112
Bristow, Lonnie R., and 119
Crockett, George W., Jr., and 236
Davis, Benjamin Jefferson, and 253
Dean of Men 113
Foster, Henry W., Jr., and 415
Hope, John, and 568
Jackson, Maynard H. 603
King, Martin Luther, Jr., and 687
Lee, Spike, and 706
McKissick, Floyd, and 795
president of 569, 773, 780
Reid, Ira De A., and 1002
Satcher, David, and 1044
School of Medicine 1093
Sullivan, Louis, and 1092
Thurman, Howard, and 1115
Morgan, Garrett A. 829
Morgan Skirt Factory 829
Morgan State College 825, 841
Morgan State University 809, 826, 934, 984, 1054
Morganfield, McKinley. *See* Muddy Waters.
Morial, Ernest 831
Morning Star Baptist Church 28
Morrill Acts 870
Morris, Samuel 308
Morristown College 352
Morrow, E. Frederic 833
Morton, "Jelly Roll" 834
Moses, Bob 837
Mosley, Walter 839
Moss, Carlton 841
Mossell, Gertrude Bustill 412
The Most Native of Sons 1238
Mother Bethel Church 130
Motley, Archibald J., Jr. 843, 845
Motley, Constance Baker 801
Motley, Willard 845
Moton, Jennie Dee Booth 848
Moton, Robert Russa 847, 914-15, 1265
Motown 470-72, 606
Mott, Lucretia 1004
Moveable School 915
Moynihan, Daniel Patrick 206
Muddy Waters 850
Mudhill 1249
Muhammad, Elijah 394-95, **853,** 1276, 1278-79
Muhammad Speaks 1277-78
Muhammad, Wallace D. 395
Murphy, Eddie 856
Murphy, Isaac 858
Murray, Daniel 860
Murray, Peter Marshall 862
Murray v. University of Maryland 577
Muse, Clarence 864
Museum of Modern Art 359
Music Settlement School 384-85
Muslim Mosque, Inc. 1278
Muste, A. J. 390, 1041
My Bondage and My Freedom 329
Myers, George A. 1142
Myers, Isaac 865
Myrdal, Gunnar 155
The Mystery 283

NAACP 93, 339, 387
Board of Directors 1123
Chief Executive Officer 810
Cleveland Association of Colored Men 830
Du Bois, W. E. B., and 339
founding of 931, 934
Frankfort Branch 1145
Garvey, Marcus, and 444
Grimké, Archibald Henry, and 489-90
Hooks, Benjamin L., and 565-67
Jackson State College demonstrations 802
Johnson, James Weldon, and 626, 628
Jones, Scipio Africanus, and 660-61
Kansas City chapter 1223
King, Martin Luther, Jr., and 689
Legal Defense and Education Fund 72, 192, 575-77, 1225
Marshall, Thurgood, and 762, 764
McKissick, Floyd, and 795
Mitchell, Clarence M., Jr., and 822
Morrow, E. Frederic, and 833
New Orleans Chapter 832
Niagara Movement 1132

Vann, Robert L., and 1151
White, Walter, and 1209-12
Wilkins, Roy, and 1222-23
Wright, Louis Tompkins, and 1266-67
Napier, James C. 201, **868**
Napier, Nettie Langston 869
Narrative of the Life of Frederick Douglass 328
NASCAR 1054-56
Nash, Diane 391
The Nashville Globe 102
Nashville Negro Board of Trade 870
Nathan, Syd 126
Nation of Islam 393-95, 854-56, 1278-79
National Academy of Design 1101
The National Advisory Committee on the Education of Negroes 161
National Aeronautics and Space Administration (NASA) 87, 799
National Afro-American Council 412
National Afro-American League 412
National Archives 162
National Association for the Advancement of Colored People. *See* NAACP.
National Association of Colored Professional Base Ball Clubs 419
National Association of Colored Women 412
National Association of Negro Musicians 299, 1207
National Baptist Convention 99-103, 689
National Baptist Convention of America, Unincorporated 101-02
National Baptist Convention of the United States, Inc. 101-02, 322
National Baptist Publishing Board 99, 101-02
National Bar Association 1151
National Basketball Association 6, 186, 375, 377, 664-65
National Black Economic Development Conference 408
National Black Political Convention 398
National Board of Commissioners of the Colored People of Canada 278
National Board of Medical Examiners 417
National Boxing Enterprises 457
National Business League, Nashville Chapter 102
National Capital Housing Authority 1191
National Collegiate Athletic Association (NCAA) 1035
National Colored Soldiers Comfort Committee 1143
National Conference of Black Churchmen 224
National Conference of Catholic Bishops 756
National Convention of Colored Citizens 1004
National Convention of Colored Men 198, 912, 1158
National Convention of Gospel Choirs and Choruses 321-22
National Council of Negro Women 233
National Council of People 278
National Council of the Colored People in New York 1245
National Cycling Association 1104
National Emigration Convention 284
National Endowment for the Humanities 313
National Equal Rights League 1132
National Federation of Afro-American Women 412
National Football League (NFL) 899
National Insurance Association 1078
National Interscholastic Championship Track Meet 894
National League of Cities 1087
National Medical Association 119, 499, 862-63
National Missionary Baptist Convention of America 102
National Moral Reform Society 919
National Museum of American History 366
National Negro Business League 501, 848, 869, 1143
National Negro Congress 985, 1286
National Negro Convention 24, 277-78, 923-24
National Negro Finance Corporation 849
National Negro Health Week 1265
National Negro Insurance Association 899
National Negro Labor Council 1288
National Negro Labor Union 995
National Negro Open 1064
National Negro Opera Company 1208
National Negro Press Association 315
National Negro Suffrage League 1132
National Negro Symphony Orchestra 384
National Publicity Bureau 1150
National Rainbow Coalition 601
National Reform Convention of the Colored Inhabitants of the United States 1035
National Rodeo Cowboy Hall of Fame 936
National Safety Hood 829
National Science Foundation (NSF) 774
National Security Council 960

National Skills Bank 1290
National Survey of Higher Education of Negroes 161
National Survey of Vocation and Guidance of Negroes 161
National Symphony Orchestra 1194
National Urban League
and Granger, Lester B. 472-73
and Haynes, George Edmund 529-30
and Jacob, John E. 608
and Johnson, Charles S. 616
and Jones, Eugene Kinckle 645-46
and Jordan, Vernon 668
and Reid, Ira De A. 1002
and Thomas, Jesse O. 1113
and Young, Whitney M., Jr. 1289-90
National Voter Registration Act 408
National War College 930, 959
Native Son 1270
A Natural Born Gambler 1229
Nazarene Congregational Church 971
NBA. *See* National Basketball Association.
NBC Sports 493
NBC Symphony 311
Negro Actor's Guild 888
Negro Airmen International 944
Negro American Labor Council 986
Negro American League 903, 967, 1023
The Negro and His Music 731
The Negro as a Businessman 1258
The Negro at the North Pole 543
Negro Book Collectors Exchange 1068
The Negro Caravan 135
The Negro Church in America 431
Negro Congress 1270
Negro Digest 632-33
Negro Ensemble Company 1176-77
Negro Experimental Theatre Company 596
The Negro Family in the United States 430
Negro Federal Theatre 1270
Negro Folk Symphony 273-74
Negro History Bulletin 1259
Negro History Week 1258
The Negro in American Culture 732
The Negro in Business 413
The Negro in Our History 1258
The Negro in the Making of America 979-80
The Negro in the United States 430
The Negro in Virginia 135
Negro League (baseball) 901-03
Negro Library Conference (1930) 85
Negro Market Newsletter 1237
Negro Migration during the War 1053
Negro National Anthem 626
Negro National Congress 1286
Negro National Labor Union 285
Negro National League (baseball) 166, 417, 419, 902
Negro Players 461
Negro Quarterly 371
Negro Seaman's Act 1162
Negro Society for Historical Research 1048
The Negro Soldier 841-42
Negro Southern League 902
"The Negro Speaks of Rivers" 580
Negro Spiritual 274
Negro Theatre Ensemble 1187
Negro Women's Convention 412
A Negro Work Song 274
Negro World 413, 1174, 1258
Negro Year Book 1262, 1265
The Negro's Church 782
Nell, William C. 871
Nelson, Willie 968
Netherlands Institute for the History of Art 334
New Bethel Baptist Church 211, 399
New Black Theater Movement 151
New Challenge 1270
New Demeter Street Presbyterian Church 230
New England Conservatory 621
New England Suffrage League 1132
New Era 769, 1158
New Homes for Today 1240
New Jersey Nets 377
New Jersey Symphony Orchestra 716-17
New Masses 1270
New National Era 329
The New Negro 325, 730, 934, 1175, 1211
A New Negro for a New Century 413
New Negro Movement. *See* Harlem Renaissance.
New Orleans Louisianian 940
New Orleans University 862
New Thought Movement 307
New World A-Coming 890
New York African Free Schools 230
New York Age 337, 412-13, 628, 778
New York Amsterdam News 413, 950, 1096
New York Amsterdam Star-News 889
New York Anti-Slavery Society 230, 1178
New York Chamber Orchestra 310
New York City Ballet 820
New York City Draft Riots 440
New York City Federal Writers' Project 371, 889

New York City Opera Company 1180
New York City Temperance Society 1034
New York Committee of Vigilance 327, 924, 1034
New York Giants 785
New York Legal Rights Association 925
New York Mets 787
New York Philharmonic 311, 1194
New York Post 950
New York Public Library 413, 591, 1048, 1070
New York School for Social Work 1113
New York Shakespeare Festival Theater 650
New York State Assembly 305, 341, 988, 1096
New York State University at Albany 670
New York Sun 412
New York University
  Bearden, Romare, and 64
  Blake, Eubie, and 79
  College of Medicine 119
  Cullen, Countee, and 244
  Jackman, Harold, and 596
  Law School 73, 282, 737, 937
  Poston, Ted, and 949
  School of Commerce 987
  Sleet, Moneta J., Jr., and 1069
  Tisch School of the Arts 706
  Walker, Leroy T., and 1166
  Wright, Stephen J., and 1273
Newark Agreement 711
Newark (baseball team) 1169
Newman, Paul 946
Newport Jazz Festival 852
News and Letters 291-93
Newton, Huey P. 151, 175, 205, **874**
Newton Theological Institution 1234
Niagara Falls Public Library, R. Nathaniel Dett Collection 301
Niagara Movement 339, 412, 546, 569, 934, 993, 1132, 1264
Nicklaus, Jack 363
Nigger Heaven 1119
''Niggerhead Laster'' 777
Night Song 1237
Niven, Larry 56
Nix, Robert N. C., Sr. 479, **876**
Nix, W. M. 320
Nixon Administration 17
Nixon, E. D., Sr. 878
Nixon, Richard M. 123, 421
No Day of Triumph 1001
No Way Out 945
Nobel Peace Prize 155, 690, 1042
Nobody 1228
Noland, Ken 334
Norfolk Journal and Guide 413
Normal and Theological School (Louisville) 1067
Normandy Landscape 1248
North American Convention 284
North Carolina Agricultural and Technical State University 276, 599, 799
North Carolina Central University 603, 1167
North Carolina College 775, 796
North Carolina Division of Archives and History 276
North Carolina Museum of History 276
North Carolina Mutual and Provident Association 1075
North Carolina Mutual Life Insurance Company 1075, 1077-78
North Pole Expedition 541-43
North Star. See also *Frederick Douglass' Paper*. 284, 328, 872
Northeastern Life Insurance Company 898
Northern Arizona University 1012
Northwestern League 1168
Northwestern University 209, 223, 612, 701, 1190
Norton, Eleanor Holmes 399
Notable Negro Women 753
The Notorious Eleanor Lee 813
Numero, Joseph 647-48

Oak and Ivy 345
Oakland Tribune 778-79
Oakwood Junior College 95, 726
Oasis Club (Los Angeles) 358
Oberlin College 74, 277, 298, 695, 828, 868, 991, 1032, 1157, 1168
  Conservatory of Music 1083, 1206
  R. Nathaniel Dett Papers 301
  Theology Department 695
Odd Fellows Journal 1068
Of Black America 232
Of New Horizons 679
Off the Wall 606, 659
Ohio General Assembly 1087
Ohio Historical Society, Paul Laurence Dunbar Papers 347
Ohio Library Association 1233
Ohio State Journal 1143
Ohio State University 251, 894-95
Ohio Wesleyan University 1152
''Ol' Man River'' 1014-15

Olatunji, Michael 221-22
The Old Man's Boy 461
Old Woman Peeling Apples 1248
Oliver, Joseph "King" 31, 320, **883**
Olson, Carl "Bobo" 1028
Olympics 1107
 1924, Summer 579
 1932, Summer 804
 1936, Summer 894-95
 1956, Summer 1035
 1960, Summer 18, 639
 1968, Summer 7, 405
 1976, Summer 1167
 1984, Summer 665
 1996, Summer 1070, 1166, 1282
 U.S. boycott 20
Omega Psi Phi Fraternity 158, 676, 739, 1114, 1167, 1198, 1241
One for New York 1237
O'Neal, Frederick D. 885
One-Cent Savings Bank. *See* Citizens Saving and Trust Company Bank.
O'Neill, Eugene 461
Operation Breadbasket 600, 745, 1090
Operation PUSH (People United to Save Humanity) 159, 600, 602
Operation Safe Harbor 960
Opportunities Industrialization Center 1091
Opportunity 245, 324, 616, 646, 1002, 1113, 1174
Orlando Magic 375, 378
Ornstein School of Music 221
The Ossie Davis and Ruby Dee Hour 266
Othello 1014-15
Ottley, Roi 888
Ouanga 1206-07
Our World 633, 1069
Out of the House of Bondage 818
Overton, Anthony 890
Overton Great Bee Victory Douglass Syndicate 892
Overton Hygienic Products Company 890-92
Overton (Walker), Aida Reed 1227
Overton's Great Northern Realty Company 892
Owen, Chandler 984-85
Owens, Buck 968
Owens, Jesse 804, **893**
Oxford University 1215

Pace and Handy Music Publishers 509, 537, 898, 1083
Pace, Harry H. 509, 631, **897**
Pace Phonograph Company 1084
Pacific Apostolic Faith Mission 1058
Pacific Union College 94
Page, Alan Cedric 899
Page Education Foundation 899-900
Paige, "Satchel" 901
Paine College 743, 1122
Palm Springs Tennis Club 1240
Palmerstown 498
Pan African Conference 338
Pan African Congress 339-40, 733
Pan African Movement 175
Pan African-USA track meet 1167
Pan-American Games 639, 1107
Panther 1154
"Papa's Got a Brand New Bag" 127
Paradise Publishing Company 1122
Paramount Records 320
Paramount Theater 358
Parchman Penitentiary 174
Paris Exposition, "Negro Literature" presentation 861
Park, Robert E. 182, 616, 1185
Parker, Charlie "Yardbird" 221, 262-63, **904**
Parker, George 412
Parks, Gordon 174, **907**
Parks, Rosa 880, 1042, 1069, 1278, 1288
Parrish, Charles H., Sr. 911, 1067, 1079-80
Parrish, Mary Virginia Cook 913
Patterson, Frederick D. 914
Paul R. Williams and Associates 1239
Paul, Thomas 1165
Paul Whiteman Orchestra 1084
Paul, William 1161
Pauling, Linus 111
The Pawnbroker 658
Payne, Benny 165
Payne, Daniel A. 917, 990-92
Payne, John 239
PBS Riverwalk series 1181
Peabody Conservatory of Music 961, 1194
Peace and Freedom Party 205
Peace Corps 313, 972
Peace Mission 307, 309
Pearl Harbor 814-15
Peary, Robert 542
Peete, Calvin 1065
Pekin Stock Company 461
Pemberton, James 242
Pembroke, Jim. *See* Pennington, James W. C.
Penn, Anna Belle Rhodes 921

Penn, I. Garland 921, 1266
Penniman, Richard Wayne. *See* Little Richard.
Pennington, James W. C. 923
Pennsylvania Abolition Society 84, 198
Pennsylvania Academy of the Fine Arts 1101
Pennsylvania Anti-Slavery Society 1082
Pennsylvania Colonization Society 197
Pennsylvania Society for Promoting the Abolition of Slavery 977
Pennsylvania State University 82, 86
Pennsylvania Supreme Court 199
Pentagon 959
People Organized to Work for Economic Rebirth 396
People's Committee 955
People's Convention 368
People's Voice 955
Pepperdine University 56
Perkins, Edward J. 925
Perry, Harold R. 927
Persian Gulf War 958, 1060
Petersen, Frank, Jr. 930
PGA Tour 362-63, 1064-65
Phelps Stokes Fund 914, 916-17, 1123
Phi Beta Kappa 98, 154, 210, 237, 244, 298, 400, 675, 710, 714, 728, 732, 828, 931, 933, 936, 1000, 1003, 1013, 1094, 1131, 1201, 1220, 1232
Philadelphia 76ers 186, 377
Philadelphia Academy of Music 1193
Philadelphia Academy of the Fine Arts 1099
Philadelphia Citizens Committee Against Juvenile Delinquency and Its Causes 1090
Philadelphia Female Anti-Slavery Society 410
Philadelphia Fire 1216-17
Philadelphia Giants 418
The Philadelphia Negro 338
Philadelphia Orchestra 273, 312, 1194-95
Philadelphia Phillies 903
Philadelphia Press 198
Philadelphia Vigilant Society 410
Philadelphia Warriors 185
Philander Smith College 223
Philanthropic Society 283
Phillips, Wendell 328
Philosophy and Opinions of Marcus Garvey 444
Philosophy and Revolution 293
A Photographer's Gallery 281
Phylon 209, 340, 597, 1003
The Piano Lesson 1241, 1244
Pickens, Harriet 934
Pickens, William 931
Pickett, Bill 935
Pierce, Samuel R., Jr. 936
Pinchback, P. B. S. 145, 198, 201, **938,** 1125
Piney Woods Country Life School 652
Pinktoes 556
Pinky 842, 887
Pinson, Vada 1020
Pippin, Horace 941
Pittsburgh Courier 467, 950, 1029, 1149-52
Pittsburgh Crawfords 902
Places in the Heart 465
Pledger, William A. 412
Plessy v. Ferguson 577, 869
Plinton, James O., Jr. 943
Poems of a Slave 572
Poitier, Sidney 265, **944**
The Political Destiny of the Colored Race on the American Continent 284
"The Political Plight of the Negro" 818
Poole, Elijah. *See* Muhammad, Elijah.
Poor People's Campaign 398, 690, 1281
Poor, Salem 947
Populist Party 249
Porgy 864
Porgy and Bess 165, 267, 382, 1179-80
Porter, James A. 334
Porter (Wesley), Dorothy B. 1201
Portrait of Daniel Coker 635
Poston, Ted 949
Poussaint, Alvin F. 232, **951**
Powell, Adam Clayton, Jr. 226, 802, 863, **954,** 972, 988, 1089
Powell, Adam Clayton, Sr. 954
Powell, Colin 958
Poyas, Peter 1160-61
Pozo, Chano 459
Prairie View Agricultural and Mechanical College 914
Pratt, Awadagin 961
"Precious Lord, Take My Hand" 319, 321
Preface to a Twenty-Volume Suicide Note 53
Presence Africaine 1271
Presidential Medal of Freedom 218, 220, 366, 373, 392, 421, 548-49, 896, 917, 960, 1291
Presidential Medal of Honor 156
Presley, Elvis 322
Presley, Lisa Marie 607
The Pretender 649
Price, J. C. 963

Price, Leontyne 1180
Pride, Charley 966
The Primitive 555
Prince Hall Masons 504
Princeton University 190, 1203
Proctor, Henry Hugh 968, 1209
Proctor, Samuel D. 971
Professional Golf Association. *See also* PGA Tour. 1063-65
Progress Garment Manufacturing Enterprises 1091
Progress Haddington Shopping Plaza 1091
Progress Plaza 1091
Progressive Democratic Association 879
Project Alert 608
Project for Literacy Education 161
Prophet, Nancy Elizabeth 1249
Prosser, Gabriel 973
Provençal Landscape 1249
Provident Hospital 499-500, 1231
Provincial Freeman 1081, 1179
Public Eye 494
Public Policy Training Institute 392
Pulitzer Prize 498, 613, 715, 761, 780, 996, 998, 1069, 1241, 1243-44
Pullman Company 985
Purlie 265
Purvis, Harriet Forten 977
Purvis, Robert 976
PUSH EXCEL 601

QDE (Quincy Jones-David Salzman Entertainment) 659
Quarles, Benjamin A. 979
Queen 498
Quinn, Paul 130, 919
Qwest Records 659

R. J. Reynolds Tobacco Company 1094
Race Adjustment 818
Race Matters 1204
Race Statesmanship Series 818
Radical Club of New Orleans 692
Radical Political Abolitionists 1074
Raeletts 188
"Ragtime Dance" 663
Railway Labor Act 985
Rainey, Joseph H. 367
Rainey, Ma 320
A Raisin in the Sun 265, 945-46
Raising Black Children 952
Randolph, A. Philip 490, **983,** 1124
  March on Washington 391, 1041-42
  Nixon, E. D., Sr., and 879, 881
  Sullivan, Leon H., and 1090
Rangel, Charles B. 957, **987,** 1096
Ransier, Alonzo J. 367
Ransom, Reverdy C. 990
Rapier, James T. 295, **994**
Rashad, Phylicia 232
Raspberry, William J. 996
"Rat Pack" 268
The Raya Dunayevskaya Collection 291
Razaf, Andy 79
Reader's Digest 1032
Reagan, Ronald 399, 421, 926, 1110, 1282
Reason, Charles Lewis 998, 1178
Rebecca 1158
Reconstruction Era 994, 1072
Recycle 1242
The Red Moon 383
Redding, J. Saunders 1000
Redman, Don 537-38
Regional Council of Negro Leadership 387
Reid, Ira De A. 1002
Reiss, Winold 324
Remond, Charles Lenox 198, **1003**
Republican National Convention
  1864 1072
  1868 939-40
  1876 758
  1880 145, 369
  1884 248, 749
  1896 1142-43
  1900 202
  1908 295-96
Requiem for a Heavyweight 281
Reserve Officers Training Corps 1052
Returning Home 1249
Reuther, Walter 292
Revelations 8, 10
Revels, Hiram Rhoades 182, **1005**
Rhodes Scholar 728
Rhodes, Ted 362, 1064
Ribbs, Willy T. 1008
Richard, Little. *See* Little Richard.
Richardson, Elliot 218
Richardson, Willis 1010, 1233
Richmond African Baptist Missionary Society 181
Richmond, Bill 826
Richmond Theological Seminary 85
Rickey, Branch 166, 1023
The Rights of All. See *Freedom's Journal.*
Riles, Wilson C. 1011
The River Niger 1177

Rivera, Diego 1249
"Riverside Blues" 320
Riverside Church 408
Roach, Max 905
Robert S. Abbott Publishing Company 4
Robert W. Kelley, et al. v. Board of Education 738
Robert Wood Johnson Foundation 416
Roberta Martin Singers 211
Robeson, Eslanda Goode 173
Robeson, Paul 280, 339, 400, 812, **1013,** 1040, 1211
Robinson, Bill "Bojangles" 32, **1016,** 1240
Robinson, Frank 1020
Robinson, Hilyard 1240
Robinson, Jackie 168, 903, **1022,** 1064
Robinson, Luther. *See* Robinson, Bill "Bojangles."
Robinson, Randall 1025
Robinson, Smokey 470
Robinson, Sugar Ray 1027
Rochester National Black Convention 873
Rochester Theological Seminary 636, 1116
Rock 'n' Roll Hall of Fame 852
Roger Williams University 102, 636, 758, 1260
Rogers, J. A. 1029, 1151
Rollins, Frances 285
Roosevelt, Eleanor 311, 360, 1267
Roosevelt, Franklin D. 161, 236, 273, 879, 993, 1124, 1196
Roosevelt, Theodore 489
Roosevelt University 407, 1190
Roots 496
Rose McClendon Players 264, 823
Rosenwald, Julius 636, 676
Ross, Diana 471, 606
Rostenkowski, Dan 557
Rowan, Carl 1031
The Rowan Report 1033
Rowfant Club 196
Roy Wilkins Center for Human Relations and Social Justice 1224
Royal Gardens Cafe 883
Royal Opera 1062
Ruby, George T. 247
Rudolph, Wilma 1106, 1187
Ruffin, George L. 201
Ruggles, David 230, 327, **1034**
Russell, Bill 1020, **1035**
Russell, Kurt 1020
Russell, Tom 1160
Russworm, John Brown 230, **1038**
Rust College 921
Rustin, Bayard 391, 688, 744, 881, 985-86, **1039**
Rutgers University 52, 1013, 1198

Sacramento Kings 1037
Sager Gear Company 1104
St. Augustine Seminary 927
St. Bonaventure College 889
St. Elsewhere 1187
St. John's University, School of Law 132, 341, 889, 987
St. Joseph's Major Seminary 756
St. Jude Hospital 1240
St. Louis Blues 217, 509, 1083
St. Louis Browns 903
St. Louis Negro Businessman's League 886
St. Marks Playhouse 1177
St. Mary's Seminary (Techny, IL) 927
St. Paul Appeal 1222
St. Paul Normal and Industrial School 357
St. Peter's AMEZ Church 964
St. Thomas Episcopal Church 22, 409, 644
Salem, Peter 948
Sammy and His Friends 268
The Sammy Davis Jr. Show 268
San Diego Conquistadors 186
San Diego Open 1064
San Francisco Giants 786, 1021
San Francisco Law School 874
San Francisco Museum of Art 361
San Francisco Opera 381
San Francisco State College 9, 141, 151, 289
San Jose City College 1008
Sanchez, Sonia 151
Sanhedrin 818
Saperstein, Abe 163, 185
Satcher, David 416, **1044**
Satchmo. *See* Armstrong, Louis "Satchmo."
Saturday Night Live 856
Savoy Ballroom 164
Savoy Records 211
Say Hey 786
Schmeling, Max 740-41
Schomburg, Arthur Alfonso 314, **1046**
Schomburg Center for Research in Black Culture 312, 314, 325-26, 1048, 1096
  Arthur A. Schomburg Collection 1049
  Clarence Cameron White Collection 1208
  Claude McKay Papers 794
  Hiram Rhoades Revels Papers 1008
  Langston Hughes Papers 584

Loften Mitchell Papers 824
Paul Laurence Dunbar Papers 347
Ralph Bunche Papers 156
Sargent Johnson Collection 644
William A. Hunton Papers 588
William Pickens Papers 935
Schomburg Library of Nineteenth-Century Black Women Writers 449
School Daze 707
School of American Ballet 819
Schuyler, George 984, 1151
Scoop 511
Scott, Dred 1049
Scott, Emmett Jay 1051, 1143, 1150, 1185
Scott v. Sanford 977, 1049-50
Scott, Wendell 1054
Scott, Willard 493
Scott, William Edouard 1247
Scottsboro Boys 246
Seale, Bobby 151, 204, 874
Search for Education, Elevation, and Knowledge 1096
Seattle Supersonics 1037
Second African Presbyterian Church 464
Secretary of Commerce 131-32
Secretary of Health and Human Services 1094
Secretary of the Army 15
Secretary of Transportation 219
Seeger, Pete 287
Seeking to Be a Christian in Race Relations 783
Selective Patronage Program 1090
Selma to Montgomery March 426, 1069
Senegambian Carnival 1227
Sengstacke, John H. H. 6
Sent for You Yesterday 1216
Settlement and Development 1249
Seven Guitars 1244
Seven Traceries 1085
Seymour, William Joseph 307, 771, **1056**
Shabazz, Betty 1095, 1278-79
Shades of Freedom 549
Shadow of the Plantation 617
Shantytown 1249
Sharp, Granville 409
Sharp Street Church 214
Shaw, Bernard 1059
Shaw, Robert Gould 176
Shaw University 112, 357, 963, 979, 1163
Shelby County Public Library, Sarah Roberta Church Papers 203
Shepard, James 315, 1076
She's Gotta Have It 706
Shiloh Church (New York City) 440
Shine, Ted 315
Shirley, George I. 1061
The Shoo-Fly Regiment 383, 622
Shook, Karel 819-20
A Short Overture 679
Shorter College 223, 660
Show Girl 365
Showboat 79, 81, 1014-15, 1180
Shuffle Along 77
Shuttleworth, Fred 689
Siefert, Charles 703
Sifford, Charlie 363, **1063**
Sigma Pi Phi (the Boulé) Fraternity 158
The Signifying Monkey 450
Simmons University 757-58, 912-13
Simmons, William J. 912, **1066**
"Simple" character 582-83
Simpson College 178
Simpson, O. J. 213
Sinatra, Frank 267, 1240
Sissie 1237
Sissle, Noble 78, 385
Sit-in Movement 689, 1273
Skowhegan School of Painting and Sculpture 333
Slaughter, Henry Proctor 1067
The Slave 54
Sleet, Moneta J., Jr. 633, **1069**
The Slender Thread 658
The Small Homes of Tomorrow 1240
Smalls, Robert 367-68, **1071**
Smart Set 383
Smith, Amanda Berry 770
Smith, Gerrit 1074
Smith, James Howard Lorenzo 321
Smith, James McCune 999, **1073**
Smith, Tommie 7, 405
Smith, Walter. *See* Robinson, Sugar Ray.
Smithsonian Institution, Frederick D. Patterson Papers 917
SNCC. *See* Student Nonviolent Coordinating Committee (SNCC).
Socialist Party 984
Socialist Workers Party 291
Society for the Promotion of Education among Colored Children 924, 999, 1245
Society of the Divine Word 927
A Soldier's Story 1187-88
Songs of Jamaica 792
Sonnemann, Nell 334
Sons of Darkness, Sons of Light 1237

Sons of Ham 1227
The Sophisticated Gents 1237
Sorbonne 65
Soul City 796
Soul Echoes Publishing Company 1122
Soul on Ice 203-04
The Souls of Black Folk 338
Sousa, John Philip 382
South African PGA Open 363
South Carolina Leader. See *Missionary Record.*
South Side Writers' Group 1270
Southern Baptist Convention 101-02
Southern California Community Choir 212
Southern Christian Leadership Conference (SCLC)
  and Bond, Julian 92
  and Evers, Medgar 387
  and Fauntroy, Joseph E. 398
  and Fauntroy, Walter E. 397
  and Jackson, Jesse 600
  and King, Martin Luther, Jr. 688-90
  and Lowery, Joseph E. 744-45
  and Moses, Bob 837
  and Rustin, Bayard 1039, 1042
  and Young, Andrew 1281
Southern Coordinating Committee to End the War in Vietnam 719
Southern Education Foundation 797
Southern Illinois University 158
Southern Negro Leaders Conference 744
Southern Regional Council 210
Southern Regional Education Board 915
Southern States Negro Convention 995
Southwestern University (Los Angeles) 105
Soyinka, Wole 1177
Spacelab mission 87
Spanish-American War 260, 586, 1231, 1283
Spaulding, Charles C. 1075
Spike/DDB 708
Spike's Joint 708
Spingarn, Joel E. 934, 1211
Spiral (artists group) 66, 1250
"Stand By Me" 1122
Standard Oil Company 909
Stanton, Lucy 278
Star of Zion 208
State Colored Men's Convention 868
State Convention of Blacks 1074
State University. *See* Simmons University.
State University of New York at Binghamton, Loften Mitchell Papers 824
Steele v. Louisville and Nashville 577
Steichen, Edward 280
Steward, William Henry 1078
Still, William 1080
Still, William Grant 510, 582, 898, **1082**
Stoessel, Albert 310
Stokes, Carl B. 258, **1086**
Stokes, Louis 1087
Stokowski, Leopold 273
Stormy Weather 1019
Storrs School 969
The Story of a Three-Day Pass 1153
The Story of My Life and Work 1185
Stowe, Harriet Beecher 83
Straker, Daniel Augustus 368
Stranger and Alone 1001
Street Literacy Clinic and the Magic of Learning 1096
Street Smart 432
Streisand, Barbara 946
Struggle--History of the American People 704
Stryker, Roy Emerson 909
Student Nonviolent Coordinating Committee (SNCC)
  and Bond, Julian 91-92
  and Carmichael, Stokely 173
  and Farmer, James L., Jr. 390
  and King, Martin Luther, Jr. 689
  and Lewis, John R. 406, 408, 718-19
  and Moses, Bob 837
Studio Museum in Harlem 1070, 1250
Succeeding Against the Odds 630
Sullivan, Leon H. 1089
Sullivan, Louis 1092
Sullivan Principles 1091
Sumner, Charles 198
Sumner, William Graham 529
Sun Shipbuilding and Dry Dock 1053
Supreme Life and Casualty Company of Ohio 456
Supreme Life Insurance Company 897-98
The Supremes 471
Sutton, Percy E. 305, **1094**
The Sweet Flypaper of Life 280
Sweet Love, Bitter 1238
Sweet Sweetback's Baadasssss Song 1154
Sweet Swing Blues on the Road 761
Sydney Symphony Orchestra 311
Synchronous Multiplex Railway Telegraph 1251
Syncopation 844
Syracuse University 1236
The System of Dante's Hell 54

''Talented Tenth'' 729, 1264
Talladega College 334-35, 824, 933, 1249
Tallchief, Maria 820
Tamla Records 470
Tammany Hall 594
Tan Confessions 633
Tanglewood Music Center 1061
Tanner, Benjamin Tucker 1098, 1099
Tanner, Henry Ossawa 1098, **1099**
Tappan, Lewis 1074
Tatum, Art 905
Taylor, Marshall W. ''Major'' 1103
Teague, Colin 181
Team Work 261, 841-42
Telephone System and Apparatus 1251
Temple, Edward S. 1105
Temple, Shirley 1019
Temple University 83, 231, 734
Tempo Club 382, 384-85
Ten Nights in a Barroom 462
Tennessee Agricultural and Industrial State College 949
Tennessee Centennial Exposition 869
Tennessee Senate 1225
Tennessee State Agricultural and Industrial College 1106
Tennessee State Museum 360
Tennessee State University 1031, 1107
  Avon N. Williams Papers 1227
  Edward S. Temple Papers 1108
  Tigerbelles track team 1106
Tennessee Voters Council 1225
Terre Haute School Board 806
Terrell, Mary Church 201
Terrell, Robert 201
Terry, Clark 262
Texarkana Minstrels 662
Texas Freeman 1051
Texas Institute of Letters 115
Texas Negro Baptist Association 100
Texas State University for Negroes (Texas Southern University) 342
TFF Study Group 1112
Thant, U 155
Theater Set 680
Theatre Royal (Stockholm) 14
Think Black 751
Think of One 760
Third World Press 751-52
This is How I Feel about Jazz 658
This is My Country Too 1238
Thomas, Clarence 1108
Thomas, Danny 1240
Thomas, Franklin A. 1112
Thomas, Jesse O. 1113
Thomson, Virgil 311
Thousand Points of Light 416
''The Thrill is Gone'' 685
Thriller 606, 659
Thurman, Howard 40, 390, **1114**
Thurman, Sue Bailey 1117
Thurman, Wallace 1118
Tiger Woods Foundation 1255
Till, Emmett 302
Tillotson College and Normal School 753
Tindley, Charles Albert 1121
Tindley Temple 1121
To Bird with Love 460
To Diz with Love 460
To Make a Poet Black 1001
To Sir, With Love 946
Tobias, Channing H. 1122
Toccoa Band 126
Today show 493
Tolan, Eddie 804
Tolson, Melvin 389
The Tonight Show 232, 268
Tony Brown's Journal. See also *Black Journal.* 136-37
Toomer, Jean 938, 941, **1125**
Tougaloo College 336
Tourgee, Albion 196
''Toward a Black Theater'' 841
Trans World Airlines 943
TransAfrica 1026-27
TransAfrica Forum 1026
Treemonisha 663-64
Tribe of Shabazz 394
Triennial Symposium of African Art 736
A Trip to Coontown 747
Tropic Death 1173, 1175
Trotter, Monroe 489, 993, **1130,** 1268
The True American 1153
True Democrat 278
Truman, Harry S 342, 456, 521, 577, 829, 986, 1015, 1124, 1209
Truth, Sojourner 1035
Tubb, Ernest 968
Tubman, Harriet 328
Tubman, William V. S. 342
Tunstall v. Brotherhood of Locomotive Firemen and Enginemen 577
Ture, Kwame. *See* Carmichael, Stokely.
Turead, A. P. 831
Turner, Henry McNeal 225, 977, 990, 992, **1133**

Turner, Nat 1137
Turpin, Randy 1028
Tuskegee Airmen 87, 255-57, 610, 916, 931, 943, 1095
Tuskegee Army Air Base 256
Tuskegee Institute 58
  Booker T. Washington Papers 1186
  Caliver, Ambrose, and 160
  Department of Records and Research 1262
  Ellison, Ralph, and 370
  faculty at 272, 428
  founding of 1183
  hospital for black soldiers 849
  John A. Andrew Memorial Hospital 415
  president of 849, 914-15
  Robert R. Moton Papers 850
  School of Veterinary Medicine 915
  Scott, Emmett Jay, and 1051-52
  Tuskegee Choir 272-73
  Tuskegee Singers 273
  Washington, Booker T., and 1184
  William Levi Dawson Papers 275
Tuskegee Lynching Record 1262
Tuskegee Machine 1185
Tuskegee "Red-Tails." *See* Tuskegee Airmen.
"Tutti Frutti" 726
Twenty Years of Poem, Moods, and Meditation 28
"The Two Real Coons" 461
Two Trains Running 1241, 1244
Tyler, Ralph 1142, 1150
Tyson, Cicely 264

"Under the Bamboo Tree" 622, 628, 1229
Underground Railroad 1080-81
  Buffalo (NY) Station and Brown, William Wells 139
  General Vigilance Committee, aid from 999
  Gibbs, Mifflin Wistar, and 450
  Pennington, James W. C., and 924
  Rochester (NY) Station and Douglass, Frederick 328
  study of 83-84
The Underground Railroad 84
Underwood, Edward Ellsworth 1079-80, **1145**
Unemployment and Poverty Action Committee 408
Union Institute 408
Union Missionary Society 230
Union of Black Episcopalians 157
Union Theological Seminary 955, 1090
United Auto Workers 291-92
United Golf Association 362, 1064
United Nations 155, 302, 406, 1223, 1282
United Negro Bus Strike Committee 955
United Negro College Fund (UNCF/The College Fund) 268, 480, 607, 914, 916, 1272, 1274
United Negro Improvement Association 1148
United Service Organization (USO) 210
United States Thermo Control Company 648
Unity School of Christianity 307
Universal Military Training Act 271
Universal Negro Improvement Association 394, 441, 985, 1151, 1174, 1276
University of Arizona 679
University of Arkansas 415, 1086
University of Berlin 338
University of California, Berkeley 246, 289, 313, 713
University of California, Hastings College of Law 141
University of California, Los Angeles 7, 9, 37, 56, 94, 105, 154, 156, 212, 639, 952, 1023
University of California, Santa Cruz 875
University of Chicago 110
  Chicago Theological Seminary 599
  English Department 95
  faculty at 252, 424
  Irvin C. Mollison Papers 829
  School of Education 89
  School of Law 828, 1220
  School of Religion 782
  School of Sociology 182-83, 613, 616, 1262, 1264
  Woodson, Carter G., and 1257
  Zoology program 676
University of Cincinnati 110
University of Copenhagen 429
University of Hamburg 158
University of Houston 87
University of Illinois 599, 640, 961, 1220
University of Illinois, Champaign 1198
University of Illinois, Chicago 1060
University of Indiana 115
University of Iowa 381, 750
University of Kansas 184, 323
University of Kansas City 612, 891
University of Louisville, Charles H. Parrish Papers 913
University of Maryland 764, 822, 825, 925

University of Massachusetts 233, 341, 376, 839
University of Memphis, Robert R. Church Family Papers 203
University of Michigan 157, 524, 589, 649, 889, 894
Baseball team 1168
Medical School 709
University of Minnesota 900, 1032, 1222, 1290
Channing H. Tobias Papers 1125
Law School 1086
William A. Hunton Papers 588
University of Mississippi 801-02
University of Nebraska 323
University of Newark 943
University of North Carolina at Chapel Hill 191, 572, 665
University of Notre Dame 899
University of Paris 701
University of Pennsylvania 218, 734, 876, 972, 1163, 1215
University of Pittsburgh 72, 110, 732, 1002
University of Poitiers (Paris) 734
University of Rochester, John Williams Archives 1238
University of San Francisco 1035-36
University of Santa Clara 379
University of South Carolina 483
University of Southern California 407, 716, 804, 926, 1118, 1239
University of Utah 1118
University of Vienna 673
University of Virginia 93
University of Washington 116, 182
University of Wisconsin 160
University of Wisconsin-Madison 979, 1127
University Radio Singers 322
Up from Slavery 1185
Upholsterer's International Union of North America 390
Upsetters 726
U.S. Air Force 87, 255
U.S. Amateur Golf Championship 1253
U.S. Army 958-59, 1061
U.S. Army Air Corps, Central Instruction School 943
U.S. Colored Troops 1072, 1134
U.S. Commission on Civil Rights 822
U.S. Congress 805
U.S. Court of Appeals 762, 764-65, 789, 1224
U.S. Court of Military Appeals 1224
U.S. Department of Agriculture 380
U.S. Department of Health and Human Services 1092
U.S. Department of Housing and Urban Development 937-38
U.S. Department of Justice 72, 1151
U.S. Department of Labor 236
U.S. Department of Transportation 258
U.S. District Court, Eastern Division of Michigan 789
U.S. House of Representatives
Crockett, George W., Jr. 236
Dawson, William L. 271
Mfume, Kweisi 808-09
Mitchell, Parren J. 824
Nix, Robert N. C., Sr. 876-77
Powell, Adam Clayton, Jr. 956
Rangel, Charles B. 987-88
Smalls, Robert 1072
Young, Andrew 1281
U.S. Naval Academy 775
U.S. Naval Research Laboratory 540
U.S. Naval Station (Long Beach) 1240
U.S. Navy 474, 814, 930, 1072
U.S. Office of Education 161
U.S. Olympic Committee 1166-67
U.S. Open (tennis) 37
U.S. Senate 123, 145, 1005, 1007
U.S. space program 798
U.S. Supreme Court 254, 762, 765, 828, 936, 1108, 1111
U.S. Surgeon General 1045
U.S.S. Arizona 814
U.S.S. Liscome Bay 815

Van DerZee, James 317, **1147**
Vann, Robert L. 1149
Van Peebles, Mario 1152, 1154
Van Peebles, Melvin 1152
Van Vechten, Carl 95, 400, 597, 1119, 1211
Varick, James 1155
Vashon, George Boyer 1157
Vashon, John B. 283
Vaughan, Sarah 357
Vee Jay Records 470
Vereen, Ben 821
Vesey, Denmark 130, **1158**
Victory Life Insurance Company 890, 892
Vigilance Committee of Philadelphia 977
Villanova University 313
Vincent, U. Conrad 1163
Vincent's Sanatorium 1163

Virginia Collegiate and Industrial Institute 922
Virginia Normal and Collegiate Institute 697
Virginia Squires 377
Virginia State College 721, 972
Virginia State Senate 1219
Virginia State University 110
Virginia Union University 80, 396, 616, 645, 972, 1025, 1090, 1149, 1218
Vocational and Educational Guidance of Negroes 161
Vogue 909
Voice of the Fugitive 561, 1081
Voice of the People 1137
Voices in the Mirror 907, 910
Voices of Tabernacle Choir 211
Voorhees, Don 1084
Voorhees Normal and Industrial Institute 1113
Voter Education Program 689, 720
Voting Rights Act of 1965 719
  and Fauntroy, Walter E. 397
  and Mitchell, Clarence M., Jr. 822
  and Nix, Robert N. C., Sr. 877
  drafting of 1281
  implementation of 668
  passing of 1222
V.S.O.P. quartet 759

W. D. Cook Gospel Choir 321
Wabash College 1198
Wake Forest University Library, J. C. Price Papers 966
Walcott, Louis Eugene. *See* Farrakhan, Louis.
Walk Don't Run 658
Walker, David 1165
Walker, George 461, 1227
Walker, Leroy T. 1166
Walker, Madame C. J. 984
Walker, Margaret 1270
Walker, Moses Fleetwood 1168
Walker, Wyatt T. 396-97
Walking in Space 658
Waller, Fats 1171
Walrond, Eric 94, **1173**
Wanamaker, Rodman 383
War on Poverty 1290
Ward, Douglas Turner 1176
Ward, Samuel Ringgold 328, 1245, **1177**
Ward, Theodore 1270
Warfield, William 1179
Warner Brothers 232
Warren Commission 219
Washburn College 891
Washburn University 930
Washer Women 1248
Washington Academy 190
Washington Bar Association 576
Washington, Booker T. 1181
  Atlanta Compromise Speech 922, 970
  Carver, George Washington, and 178
  Church, Robert Reed, Sr., and 201
  Dawson, William Levi, and 272
  Dodson, Owen, and 315
  Du Bois, W. E. B., and 338-39
  Fortune, T. Thomas, and 412-13
  Garvey, Marcus, and 442
  Grimké, Archibald Henry, and 489
  Grimké, Francis J., and 492
  Hope, John, opposition from 569
  Napier, James C., and 869
  Price, J. C., and 965
  Proctor, Henry Hugh, and 970
  Ransom, Reverdy C., opposition from 992
  Scott, Emmett Jay, and 1051
  Trotter, Monroe, differences with 1131
  Tuskegee Institute 699, 1113, 1262, 1264
  Tyler, Ralph, and 1143
  William Pickens, and 933
Washington Cathedral 157
Washington, Denzel 1186
Washington, George 427, 948
Washington, Harold 1189
Washington, Joseph 224
Washington, Margaret Murray 869, 1184
Washington Post 778-79
Washington Sun 413
Washington University 773
Washington, Walter E. 1191
Washington's Policy 817
Waters, Ethel 537-38
Waters, Muddy. *See* Muddy Waters.
Watson, Ella 909
Watts, André 1193
Watts riot 116, 998
Way Down South 864-65
Wayland Baptist Academy 616
Wayland Seminary 1234
Wayne College of Mortuary Science 302
Wayne County Circuit Court 789
Wayne State University 136, 226, 1061
We Are the World 607, 659
We Walk the Way of the New World 751
Weaver, Robert C. 154, 822, **1195**
Wedgeworth, Robert, Jr. 1198

Weekly Anglo-African 1073, 1075, 1245
Weinberger, Caspar 960
Weld, Angelina Grimké 488
"We'll Understand It Better By and By" 1122
Welles, Orson 341
Wells Barnett, Ida B. 330, 412
Wells, Mary 470
Wesley, Charles H. 1200
Wesley, John 1056
Wesley Union Christian Association 279
West Chester Court House 942
West Chester State College 313
West, Cornel 1202
West Point (U.S. Military Academy) 256, 403, 1283
West Virginia State College 1086, 1089
Western Reserve Historical Society Library 197, 831
Western Reserve University 255, 1086, 1145
Western Theological Seminary 1098
Western University of Pennsylvania 1150
Weston Electric Light Company 699
Wexler Film Productions 842
"What Shall We Do with the White People?" 1245
What the Negro Thinks 849
"What to the Slave is the Fourth of July?" 328
The Whispering Syncopators 320
White, Bukka (Booker T.) 684
White, Charles 280, **1204**
White Citizen's Council 434
White, Clarence Cameron 1206
White, George L. 296
White House Conference on Civil Rights 719
White House Initiative on Race and Reconciliation 426
White, Josh 1040
White Rose Mission 412
White, Walter 1209
- Du Bois, W. E. B., and 339-40
- Nixon, E. D., Sr., and 879
- Pickens, William, and 934
- Schomburg, Arthur Alfonso, and 1048
- Tobias, Channing H., and 1124
- Vann, Robert L., and 1151
- Wilkins, Roy, and 1223
- Woodruff, Hale A., and 1248
- Wright, Louis Tompkins, and 1267

Whiteman, Paul 1084
Whitman, Albery 1213
Whitman Sisters 1213
Whitney M. Young Jr. College of Leadership Studies 1291
Wideman, John Edgar 1214
The Wife of His Youth and Other Stories of the Color Line 196
Wilberforce University 24, 34, 285, 868, 919, 991, 1040, 1083, 1200-01
Wilder, L. Douglas 192, **1217**
Wiley College 115, 389, 1051
Wiley Memorial Methodist Church 353
Wiley Wilson Sanitarium 862
Wilkins, J. Ernest 1220
Wilkins, Roy 273, 391, 565, 632, 879, 986, 1211-12, **1222,** 1268
Will Mastin Trio 267
Willard Robison's Deep River Hour 1084
William Greaves Productions 481
Williams and Walker 1227-28
Williams, Avon Nyanza, Jr. 738, **1224**
Williams, Bert 383, 461, 824, **1227**
Williams College 133, 252, 732
Williams, Daniel Hale 499-500, **1230**
Williams, Edward Christopher 1232
Williams, Egbert Austin. *See* Williams, Bert.
Williams, George Washington 1233
Williams, Hosea 745
Williams, John A. 1236
Williams, Nat D. 684
Williams, Paul R. 1238
Williamson, Sonny, II 684
Williston, J. P. 277
Wilmore, Gayraud 224
Wilson, August 1241
Wilson Riles and Associates 1013
Wilson, William J. 1244
Wilson, Woodrow 489, 870
WIND (radio station) 1060
Winkfield, Jimmy 858
Winston Cup (NASCAR) 1054-55
Winston-Salem Teacher's College 393
With Ossie and Ruby 266
Within Our Gates 812
The Wiz 606, 659
Woman's Rights Convention 328
Wonder, Stevie 471
Woodruff, Hale A. 1247
Woods Electric Company 1250
Woods, Granville T. 1250
Woods, Ione E. 1067
Woods, Tiger 1252
Woodson, Carter G. 1030, 1048, 1200, **1256**
Worcester Art School 642
The Word on the Brazos 115

Words in the Mourning Time 525
Work, John Wesley, III 326, **1259**
Work, Monroe Nathan 1262
"Worker's Journal" 293
Works Progress Administration 65, 135, 845, 950, 1205
  Easel Project 703
  Federal Arts Project 65, 360, 643
  Federal Theatre Project 341
  Federal Writers' Project 135, 524, 1162, 1270
  Illinois Writer's Project 95
  National Recreation Association 1208
World Anti-Slavery Convention 924, 1004
World Community of Al-Islam 395
World Community of Islam in the West 855
World Series 785-86, 1021, 1024
World War I 942, 1142, 1150, 1284
World War II 582, 814, 841, 903, 1095, 1212, 1287
World's Columbian Exposition 1101
Wright, Isaac. *See* Coker, Daniel.
Wright, Louis Tompkins 862, 1210, 1212, **1266**
Wright, Richard 95, 183, 370, 512, **1268**
Wright, Stephen J. 1272
Wright, Theodore Sedgewick 438
Wright-Patterson Air Force Base 87
WSM radio 44

X, Malcolm 1276
  attorney of 1095
  Autobiography of Malcolm X 496-97
  Nation of Islam 394, 854-55
  Robinson, Jackie, differences with 1024
Xavier University 420, 831

Yale University
  Claude McKay Papers 794
  Divinity School 396, 969
  Duke Ellington Collection 367
  Elmer Imes Papers 591
  first black graduate of 97
  Gates, Henry Louis, Jr., and 449
  James Weldon Johnson Collection 246, 319, 630
  Jean Toomer Collection 1130
  Langston Hughes Papers 584
  Law School 15, 1109
  Pickens, William, and 933
  Repertory Theatre 1243
  Richard Wright Papers 1272
  Ruby Dee and Ossie Davis Collection of Black Film 266
  School of Fine Arts 316
  Wallace Thurman Papers 1121
  Walter White Papers 1212
  Wesley, Charles H., and 1200
  Woodruff artwork 1250
  Work, John Wesley, III, and 1260
Yeah, Inc. 1153
Yeargan, Max 1163
YMCA 584-87, 1122-23
Yorty, Sam 105
Young, Andrew 397-98, **1280**
Young, Charles 1283
Young, Coleman A. 237, **1285**
Young, Faron 968
Young, Fay 5
Young, Jean Childs 1281
Young Men's Convention 999
Young, Whitney M., Jr. 1289
Ypsilanti Historical Museum, Elijah McCoy Collection 789
YSB (*Young Sisters and Brothers*) 641

Ziegfeld, Florenz 1229
Ziegfeld Follies of 1911 1227
Zion Baptist Church 1089-90
Zion Gardens 1091
Zion Investment Associates 1091
Zion Standard and Weekly Review 279
Zion Wesley Institute 964